The **Rough Gu**

USA

written and researched by
Samantha Cook, Greg Ward, and Tim Perry

with additional contributions from
**Nicky Agate, Glenda C. Booth, Jeff Becan,
Colleen Corcoran, JD Dickey, Mark Ellwood,
Adrien Glover, Adam Gold, Melissa Marshall,
Luke O'Brien, Todd Obolsky, Marissa Pareles,
Sophie Pragnell, Ross Velton, and Paul Whitfield**

**ROUGH
GUIDES**

NEW YORK • LONDON • DELHI
www.roughguides.com

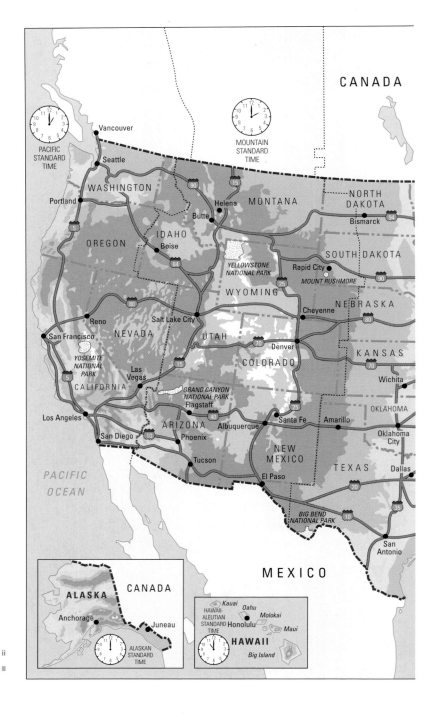

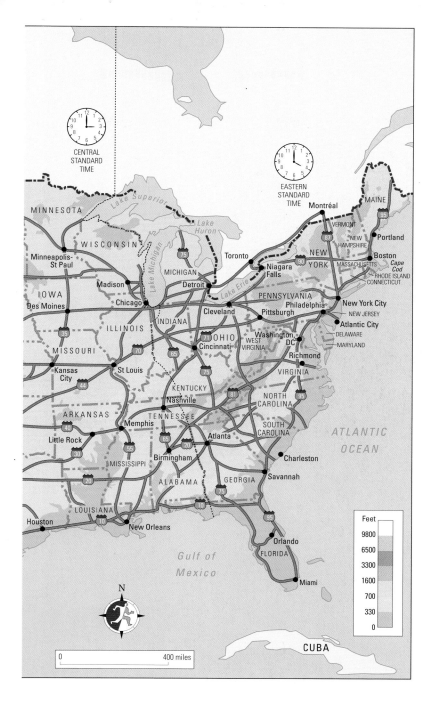

Introduction to the

USA

For five centuries, travelers have brought their hopes and dreams to America. For the earliest pioneers, it was a virgin wilderness ready to be shaped into a "New World," a potential paradise wasted on its native peoples. Millions of immigrants followed, to share in the building of the new nation and to better their lives, far from the hidebound societies of Europe and Asia. Eventually, slaves, who had been shipped over from Africa and the Caribbean, joined them as free citizens. As the United States expanded to fill the continent, something genuinely new was created: a vast

country that took pride in defining itself in the eyes of the world.

Every traveler in the United States – be they foreigners on a coast-to-coast road trip or locals exploring their extraordinarily diverse land – has some idea of what to expect. American culture has become so thoroughly shared throughout the globe that one of the principal joys of getting to know the country is the repeated, delicious shock of the familiar. Yellow taxis on busy city streets; roadside mailboxes straight out of *Peanuts* cartoons; wooden porches overlooking the cottonfields; tumbleweed skittering across the desert; endless highways dotted with pick-up trucks and chrome-plated diners; the first sight of the Grand Canyon or the Manhattan skyline.

In this book, we've picked out the highlights across the entire USA, from Maine to Hawaii, and Alaska to Florida. We've divided the country region by region and state by state, and covered every area of every state. As well as the big cities and national parks, we've explored the highways and byways, singling out detours worth making, and places to avoid. For every area covered, we've done more than simply provide up-to-date practicalities: we've delved into the history and provided background on the people who have

Fact file

- The US government is divided into three branches: the executive, headed by the president; the legislative, which consists of the Senate and the House of Representatives; and the judicial, with the Supreme Court as its highest office.

- Despite New York's status as the cultural and economic center of the US, the federal capital is in Washington, DC, which doesn't even rank among the top twenty cities in terms of population (though officially, it is a "district," rather than a city).

- The population of the US (some 281 million) owns 200 million cars and trucks (roughly 1 vehicle for every 1.4 people), with more than 5.7 million miles of paved highway on which to drive them.

- With an area of 9.6 million square kilometers, the US is the third-largest country in the world (ranking behind Russia and Canada).

- The US is the only country that contains all six major climate zones: tropical humid, dry, mild mid-latitude, severe mid-latitude, polar, and highland.

- With its Aleutian Islands crossing the Greenwich Meridian, Alaska is technically home to both the easternmost and westernmost points in the US. Alaska also has the highest point in the US, Mount McKinley (20,320ft), and is the largest state by area (Rhode Island being the smallest).

made America what it is. Our hope is to inform and entertain travelers, and to point in unexpected directions as well as to the obvious landmarks, no matter whether you've lived here all your life or are seeing it all for the first time.

Where to go

Traveling in the United States is extremely easy; in a country where everyone seems to be forever on the move, there's rarely any problem finding a room for the night, and you can almost invariably depend on being able to eat well and inexpensively. The development of transportation has played a major role in the growth of the nation; the railroad opened the way for transcontinental migrations, while most of the great cities have been shaped by the automobile. Your experience of the country will be very much flavored by how you choose to get around.

By far the best way to explore the country is to **drive your own vehicle**: it takes a long time before the sheer pleasure of cruising down the

The great outdoors

The horizon-spanning wildernesses of North America are magnificently uplifting. Any coast-to-coast drive is liable to leave you feeling dwarfed by the sheer scale of the continent, whether your route takes you across the sweeping deserts of the Southwest or the forbidding mountains to the north. East of the Mississippi River, the vistas of Virginia's Blue Ridge Parkway and Tennessee's Great Smoky Mountains seem far removed from all civilization, while to the west stretch the snowy summits of Wyoming and Montana, the vast canyonlands of Utah, and the mighty redwood forests of California. State and national parks (see p.50 for a rundown) provide the best opportunities to see wildlife, from the alligators of the Everglades to the wolves and bears of Yellowstone, and to escape your car by hiking out along the trails.

highway, with the radio blaring blues or country music, the signs to Chicago, Memphis, or Monument Valley flashing past, begins to pall. Car rental is a bargain, every main road is lined with budget motels charging around $40 per night for a good room, and the price of gasoline remains relatively low.

We also give detailed **public transportation** options throughout; you can pretty much get to wherever you choose by a nationwide network of air, bus, and rail. However, if you do travel this way, there's a real temptation to see America as a succession of big **cities**. True enough, **New York** and **Los Angeles** have an exhilarating dynamism and excitement, and among their worthy rivals are **New Orleans**, the wonderfully decadent home of jazz, **Chicago**, a showcase of modern architecture, and **San Francisco**, on its beautiful Pacific bay. Few other cities – with the possible, and idiosyncratic, exception of **Las Vegas**, shimmering in the desert – can quite match this level of interest, however, and following a heavily urban itinerary will cut you off from the astonishing **landscapes** that make the USA truly distinctive. Especially in the vast open spaces of the West, the scenery is often breathtaking. The glacial splendor of **Yosemite**, the thermal wonderland of **Yellowstone**, the awe-

vii

some red-rock **canyons** of Arizona and Utah, and the spectacular **Rocky Mountains** are among many of the treasures preserved and protected in the excellent national park system. Once you reach such wilderness, the potential for **hiking** and **camping** is magnificent – but it's usually essential to have a car to get near these spots.

Above all, travelers can enjoy the sheer thrill of experiencing American popular culture in the places where it began. Rock 'n' roll place-names spring to life; panoramas etched on our consciousness from a century of movies spread across the horizon; and road trips taken by your favorite literary characters are still there to be traveled.

For **music** fans, the chance to hear country music in Nashville or

> **Road trips taken by your favorite literary characters are still there to be traveled**

rhythm and blues in New Orleans, to shake it in a Mississippi jook-joint, or to visit Elvis's grave in Memphis, verges on a religious experience; readers brought up on the **books** of Mark Twain can ride a sternwheeler on the Mississippi; while **moviegoers** can live out their Wild West fantasies in the rugged Utah deserts.

The United States is all too often dismissed, even by its own inhabitants, as a land almost devoid of **history**. Though mainstream America tends to trace its roots back to the Pilgrims and Puritans of New England, the rest of the continent has a longer history, stretching back way beyond the French culture of Louisiana and the Spanish presence in California to the majestic cliff

Music

Music is the lifeblood of the USA, with every mile along the highways seeming to evoke a favorite song or performer. Devotees flock to the cities that gave birth to jazz, blues, country, soul, and rap. Those worthy of special pilgrimages include the party town of New Orleans, which boasts an unrivaled jazz and R&B scene; Nashville, with its honky-tonks and rhinestone glitter; and of course Memphis, the home of Sun and Stax

record labels as well as the ultimate rock 'n' roll shrine, Graceland. Out in the country too, there's plenty of excitement. Explore rural Appalachia and you may find ensembles of backwoods fiddlers; Louisiana's sleepy bayous are enlivened by foot-stomping Cajun and zydeco sounds; and the jook-joints of Mississippi Delta hamlets enrapture blues purists. Indie rockers can head for Los Angeles and New York, while college towns like Austin, Texas, and Athens, Georgia, are the places to catch rising stars. And don't forget Las Vegas, where every act arrives in the end (and Tom Jones seldom leaves).

palaces built by the Ancestral Puebloans in the Southwest a thousand years ago. There are also any number of fascinating strands to America's post-revolutionary history: relics of the Gold Rush in California, of the Civil Rights years in the South, or of the Civil War anywhere east of the Mississippi.

Though we've had to structure this book regionally, the most invigorating expeditions are those that take in more than one area. You do not, however, have to cross the entire continent from shore to shore in order to appreciate its amazing diversity, or to be impressed by the way in which such an extraordinary range of topography and people has been melded into one nation. It would take a long time to see the whole country, and the more time you spend on the road simply getting from place to place – no matter how enjoyable in itself that can be – the less time you'll have to savor the small-town pleasures and back-roads oddities that may well provide your strongest memories. It doesn't take long to realize that there is no such thing as a typical American person, any more than there is a typical American landscape, but there can be few places where strangers can feel so confident of a warm reception.

When to go

All US cities are pretty much year-round destinations (though Fairbanks, Alaska, in winter and Houston, Texas, in summer can be said to be less than ideal), national parks and mountain ranges sometimes less so.

The US **climate** is characterized by wide variations, not just from

region to region and season to season, but also day to day and even hour to hour. Even setting aside far-flung Alaska and Hawaii, the main body of the US is subject to dramatically shifting weather patterns, most notably produced by westerly winds sweeping across the continent from the Pacific.

In general, temperatures tend to rise the further south you go, and to fall the higher you climb, while the climate along either coast is, on the whole, milder and more uniform than inland.

The Wild West

Nowhere in the US is imbued with myth and history quite like the Wild West, much of which remains unchanged since the days of pioneers, prospectors, and, of course, "cowboys and Indians." In Lincoln, New Mexico, you can trace the footsteps of Billy the Kid; in Tombstone, Arizona, you can relive the gunfight at the OK Corral; and at Little Bighorn, Montana, you can climb the windswept hillside where General Custer made his "Last Stand." Colorado and California still abound with ghost towns abandoned when the gold and silver mines played out, while the great cattle drives are commemorated in Dodge City, Kansas, and Fort Worth, Texas. Above all, many Native Americans continue to inhabit their ancestral lands, especially in the Southwest, where the Hopi and the Ácomans survive in remote mesa-top villages, the Navajo ride through Monument Valley, and the Havasupai still farm alongside magical waterfalls deep in the Grand Canyon.

The **Northeast**, from Maine down to Washington, DC, experiences relatively low precipitation as a rule, but temperatures can range from bitterly cold in winter to uncomfortably hot (made worse by humidity) in the short summer. Farther south, summers get warmer and longer. **Florida**'s air temperatures are not necessarily dramatically high in summer, being kept down by the proximity of the sea both east and west; in the winter, the state is warm and sunny enough to attract visitors from all over the country.

The **Great Plains**, which for climatic purposes can be said to extend from the Appalachians to the Rockies, are alternately exposed to icy Arctic winds streaming down from Canada and humid tropical airflows from the Caribbean and the Gulf of Mexico. Winters in the north, around the Great Lakes and Chicago, can be abjectly cold, with driving winds and freezing rain. It can freeze or even snow in winter as far south as the Gulf of Mexico, though spring and fall get progressively longer and milder farther south through the Plains. Summer is much the wettest season in the South as a whole, the time when thunderstorms are most likely to strike. One or two hurricanes each year rage across Florida and/or the Southeast, from obscure origins in the Gulf of Mexico on the way to extinction out in

See overleaf for corresponding climate chart

Food

There's far more to American food than hot dogs and burgers (though to be sure, either can be had almost anywhere, done up in hundreds of different ways). In a place with a dozen types of sandwich (among them subs, cheesesteaks, muffalettas, and po-boys), the sheer variety of culinary experiences is overwhelming. One of the great pleasures of any road trip is discovering quirky diners dishing up delicious home-cooked food – fiery chili, Cajun jambalaya, creamy clam chowder, hulking barbecue ribs, and huge Southern feasts of fried chicken and catfish – while the major cities leave you spoiled for choice for world-class restaurants. Each region has its specialties, which we've detailed in relevant sections of the Guide. For more on food and drink, see p.48.

the Atlantic. Tornadoes (or "twisters") are usually a much more local phenomenon, tending to cut a narrow swath of destruction in the wake of violent spring or summer thunderstorms. Average rainfall dwindles to lower and lower levels the further west you head across the Plains.

Temperatures in the **Rockies** correlate closely with altitude; beyond the mountains in the south lie the extensive arid and inhospitable deserts of the **Southwest**. Much of this area is within the rain shadow of the California ranges. In cities such as Las Vegas and Phoenix, the mercury regularly soars above 100°F, though the atmosphere is not usually humid enough to be as enervating as that might sound.

West of the barrier of the Cascade Mountains, the fertile **Pacific Northwest** is the only region of the country where winter is the wettest season, and throughout the year the European-style climate is wet, mild, and seldom hot. **California** weather more or less lives up to the popular idyllic image, though the climate is markedly hotter and drier in the south than in the north, where there's enough snow to make the mountains a major skiing destination. San Francisco is kept milder and colder than the surrounding district by the propensity of the Bay Area to attract sea fog, while the Los Angeles basin is prone to filling up with smog, as fog and pollution become trapped beneath a layer of warm air.

Average temperature (°F) and rainfall

To convert °F to °C, subtract 32 and multiply by 5/9

	Jan	Feb	Mar	Apr	May	June	July	Aug	Sept	Oct	Nov	Dec
Anchorage												
av. max temp	19	27	33	44	54	62	65	64	57	43	30	20
av. min temp	5	9	13	27	36	44	49	47	39	29	15	6
days of rain	7	6	5	4	5	6	10	15	14	12	7	6
Boston												
av. max temp	36	37	43	54	66	75	80	78	71	62	49	40
av. min temp	20	21	28	39	49	58	63	62	55	46	35	25
days of rain	12	10	12	11	11	10	10	10	9	9	10	11
Chicago												
av. max temp	32	34	43	55	65	75	81	79	73	61	47	36
av. min temp	18	20	29	40	50	60	66	65	58	47	34	23
days of rain	11	10	12	11	12	11	9	9	9	9	10	11
Honolulu												
av. max temp	76	76	77	78	80	81	82	83	83	82	80	78
av. min temp	69	67	67	68	70	72	73	74	74	72	70	69
days of rain	14	11	13	12	11	12	14	13	13	13	13	15
Las Vegas												
av. max temp	60	67	72	81	89	99	103	102	95	84	71	61
av. min temp	29	34	39	45	52	61	68	66	57	47	36	30
days of rain	2	2	2	1	1	1	2	2	1	1	1	2
Los Angeles												
av. max temp	65	66	67	70	72	76	81	82	81	76	73	67
av. min temp	46	47	48	50	53	56	60	60	58	54	50	47
days of rain	6	6	6	4	2	1	0	0	1	2	3	6
Miami												
av. max temp	74	75	78	80	84	86	88	88	87	83	78	76
av. min temp	61	61	64	67	71	74	76	76	75	72	66	62
days of rain	9	6	7	7	12	13	15	15	18	16	10	7
New Orleans												
av. max temp	62	65	71	77	83	88	90	90	86	79	70	64
av. min temp	47	50	55	61	68	74	76	76	73	64	55	48
days of rain	10	12	9	7	8	13	15	14	10	7	7	10
New York City												
av. max temp	37	38	45	57	68	77	82	80	79	69	51	41
av. min temp	24	24	30	42	53	60	66	66	60	49	37	29
days of rain	12	10	12	11	11	10	12	10	9	9	9	10
San Francisco												
av. max temp	55	59	61	62	63	66	65	65	69	68	63	57
av. min temp	45	47	48	49	51	52	53	53	55	54	51	47
days of rain	11	11	10	6	4	2	0	0	2	4	7	10
Seattle												
av. max temp	45	48	52	58	64	69	72	73	67	59	51	47
av. min temp	36	37	39	43	47	52	54	55	52	47	41	38
days of rain	18	16	16	13	12	9	4	5	8	13	17	19
Washington, DC												
av. max temp	42	44	53	64	75	83	87	84	78	67	55	45
av. min temp	27	28	35	44	54	63	68	66	58	48	38	29
days of rain	11	10	12	11	12	11	11	11	8	8	9	10

37

things not to miss

It's not possible to see everything that the USA has to offer in one trip – and we don't suggest you try. What follows is a selective and subjective taste of the country's highlights: stimulating cities, memorable celebrations, dramatic drives, magnificent parks, and stunning natural phenomena. They're arranged in five color-coded categories to help you find the very best things to see, do, and experience. All highlights have a page reference to take you straight into the Guide, where you can find out more.

01 **Yosemite Valley, CA** Page **1170** • Enclosed by near-vertical, mile-high cliffs, and laced with hiking trails and climbing routes, the dramatic geology of Yosemite Valley is at the heart of California's best-loved park.

02 Ancestral Puebloan sites

Page **979** • Scattered through desert landscapes like Arizona's magnificent Canyon de Chelly, the dwellings of the Ancestral Puebloans afford glimpses of an ancient and mysterious world.

04 Big Bend National Park, TX

Page **799** • Forcing the Rio Grande – and the Mexican frontier – to take a very big bend indeed, Texas's remote Chisos Mountains form a vast, barely charted enclave that bursts into color each spring.

03 Driving Highway 1

Page **1155** • The rugged Big Sur coastline, pounded by Pacific waves, makes an exhilarating route between San Francisco and LA.

xiv

05 Chicago's modern architecture, IL

Page **357** • The history of modern architecture is writ large on Chicago's dramatic skyline, where the world's first skyscrapers now stand in the shadow of sleek corporate monoliths.

06 **Miami's Art Deco, FL** Page **642** • This flamboyant city is justly famed for the colorful pastel architecture of its restored South Beach district.

07 **Saguaro cactus** Page **1006** • The astonishing saguaro, which can reach fifty feet tall, grow as many as forty arms, and live for two centuries, is emblematic of the desert Southwest.

08 **The Mall, Washington, DC** Page **426** • From the Lincoln Memorial to the US Capitol by way of the towering Washington Monument – the capital's Mall is an awesome showcase of American culture and history.

09 Graceland, Memphis, TN Page **587** • Pilgrims from all over the world pay homage to the King by visiting his grave, his pink Cadillac, and the legendary Jungle Room at his surprisingly small Memphis home.

10 Sweet Auburn, Atlanta, GA Page **550** • This historic black district, just a stone's throw from downtown's ultra-modern skyscrapers, holds the birthplace of Dr Martin Luther King Jr, among other spots commemorating its native son.

11 Baseball Page **370** • America's summer pastime is a treat to watch wherever you are, but at Chicago's ivy-clad Wrigley Field, where the score and the pitchers' numbers are still changed by hand, it's simply irresistible.

12 Glacier National Park, MT Page **950** • Pressing hard against the Canadian border, Montana's loveliest park holds not only fifty glaciers, but also two thousand lakes, a thousand miles of rivers, and the exhilarating Going-to-the-Sun road.

13 The Strip, Las Vegas, NV

Page **1068** • With its erupting volcanoes, pirate battles, Eiffel Tower, and Egyptian pyramid, the legendary Strip will blow your mind as well as your wallet.

14

Swamps

Page **694** & **743** • From the steamy Everglades of Florida to the ghostly bayous of Louisiana's Cajun country, America's swamplands harbor some pretty ornery critters.

15 Yellowstone National Park, WY

Page **927** • The national park that started it all has it all, from steaming fluorescent hot springs and spouting geysers to sheer canyons and meadows filled with wildflowers and assorted grazing beasts.

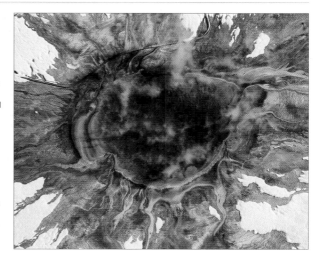

16 **New York City** Page **67** • With world-class museums, restaurants, nightlife, and shops aplenty, the Big Apple truly desreves the whole chapter we devote to it.

17

Savannah, GA Page **560** • Mint juleps on wide verandas, horsedrawn carriages on cobbled streets, and lush foliage draped with Spanish moss; this historic cotton port remains the South's loveliest town.

18 **Walt Disney World, Orlando, FL** Page **677** • Though each of Orlando's theme parks strives to outdo the rest, Walt Disney World remains the one to beat.

19 **Philly cheese-steak, PA** Page **169** • Born in Philadelphia's South Side, the cheesesteak is a sloppy feast that inspires passionate partisanship on behalf of many Philadelphians.

20 **Mount St Helens, WA** Page **1262** • A breathtaking example of volcanic devastation, wrought by a powerful eruption in 1980.

21 **Cheyenne Frontier Days, WY** Page **917** • Relive the Old West with some cowboys and cowgirls at the world's most prestigious outdoor rodeo.

22
Austin nightlife, TX Page **777**
• Laid-back, progressive, and home to an eclectic live-music scene – Austin is like nowhere else in the state.

23 **Aurora borealis, AK** Page **1336** • Winter visitors to Alaska just might see the skies ablaze with the shimmering veils of the Northern Lights.

24
Balti-more crabs, MD Page **487** •
Delicious, fresh steamed crabs are the pride of this characterful port city.

25 Skiing in the Rocky Mountains
Pages **877** • The site for some of the best skiing anywhere, from glitzy resorts to atmospheric mining towns.

26 Country Music Hall of Fame, Nashville, TN
Page **593** • Everything you ever wanted to know about country music, enshrined and explained in loving detail.

27 Hawaii's volcanoes
Page **1359** • Hawaii's Big Island grows bigger by the minute, as the world's most active volcano pours molten lava into the ocean.

28 New England in the fall
Page **201** • Fall in the Northeast is a breathtaking spectacle, the copious foliage presenting an ever-changing palette of color and light.

29
Kentucky Derby, KY
Page **574** •
Thousands gather in Louisville for a two-week binge of beer guzzling, wild partying – and even a bit of thoroughbred racing.

30
Mardi Gras, New Orleans, LA Page **732** • Crazy, colorful, debauched, and historic – this is the carnival to end them all.

31
Niagara Falls, NY Page **156** • The sheer power of Niagara Falls is even more overwhelming when seen from below, aboard the *Maid of the Mist*.

32 Monticello, VA Page **465** • A squirrel's hop from the Blue Ridge Mountains, this elegant plantation was the home and final resting place of Thomas Jefferson, author of the Constitution and third US president.

33 San Francisco, CA Page **1172** • This enchanting, fog-bound city by the bay is still bohemian and individualistic at heart.

34 Pike Place Market, Seattle, WA Page **1236** • Piled high with salmon, lobster, clams, and crab, the oldest public market in the nation is also home to some great seafood restaurants.

35
Mount Rushmore, SD Page **864** •
Preserved in the sternest granite, these four larger-than-life presidents now preside forever above the Black Hills of South Dakota.

36
Stern-wheeler rides Pages **581**, **710**, & **824** •
Just as they did in Mark Twain's day, steam-driven sternwheelers still ply the Mississippi from great old river towns like New Orleans, St Louis, and Memphis.

xxiv

37 Hitting the open road • There's no better way to experience the staggering diversity of places and peoples in this vast country.

Contents

Using this Rough Guide

We've tried to make this Rough Guide a good read and easy to use. The book is divided into five main sections, and you should be able to find whatever you want in one of them.

Color section

The front color section offers a quick tour of the USA. The **introduction** aims to give you a feel for the place, with suggestions on where to go. We also tell you what the weather is like and include a basic country fact file. Next, our authors round up their favorite aspects of the USA in the **things not to miss** section – whether it's great food, amazing sights, or a special activity. Right after this comes a full **contents** list.

Basics

The Basics section covers all the **pre-departure information** to help you plan your trip. This is where to find out which airlines fly to your destination, what paperwork you'll need, what to do about money and insurance, about Internet access, food, security, public transportation, car rental – in fact just about every piece of **general practical information** you might need.

Guide

This is the heart of the Rough Guide, divided into user-friendly chapters, each of which covers a specific region.

Every chapter starts with a list of **highlights** and an **introduction** that helps you to decide where to go, depending on your time and budget. Likewise, introductions to the various towns and smaller regions within each chapter should help you plan your itinerary. We start most town accounts with information on arrival and accommodation, followed by a tour of the sights, and, finally, reviews of places to eat and drink, plus nightlife details.

Contexts

Read Contexts to get a deeper understanding of what makes the USA tick. There's a **history** section, which covers prehistoric times to the present day, as well as reviews of the best **books** and **movies** concerning, or set in, America.

Index and small print

Apart from a **full index**, which includes maps as well as places and people, this section contains publishing information, credits, and acknowledgments, and also has our **contact details**, in case you want to send in updates, corrections, or suggestions for improving the Guide.

Map and chapter list

AL - ALABAMA
AR - ARKANSAS
CT - CONNECTICUT
DE - DELAWARE
FL - FLORIDA
IL - ILLINOIS

IN - INDIANA
LA - LOUISIANA
MA - MASSACHUSETTS
MD - MARYLAND
ME - MAINE
MI - MICHIGAN

MN - MINNESOTA
MS - MISSISSIPPI
NC - NORTH CAROLINA
NH - NEW HAMPSHIRE
NJ - NEW JERSEY
PA - PENNSYLVANIA

RI - RHODE ISLAND
SC - SOUTH CAROLINA
VA - VIRGINIA
VT - VERMONT
WI - WISCONSIN
WV - WEST VIRGINIA

Contents

Color section

Basics

Guide

Contexts

Index + small print

Basics

Basics

Getting there

The USA is so vast that you'll have no end to the options of places to start and finish your travels. Clearly part of the battle is deciding which area to explore and then locating its hub, whether you're hitting the swamps of Florida, the frozen tundra of Alaska, the summer heat of Southern cities, or the splendor of the Rockies and Southwest.

While flights to popular holiday destinations such as Florida tend to cost the same whenever you go, other airfares can vary depending on the season. If you're heading to the States from abroad, note that, in general, **high season** is July to September, and then around Easter and Christmas. Fares drop during the **shoulder seasons** – April to June, and October. You'll get the best prices during the **low season**, November to March (excluding Easter, Christmas, and the New Year, when prices are hiked up and seats are at a premium). Certain destinations might actually be less costly and less crowded during high season: southern Florida and New Orleans, for example, are both extremely hot – almost swampy – between May and September, which counts as off-season. The extra you might spend on a summer flight can be more than compensated for by low prices once you're on the ground – as long as you can handle the heat. Watch for slack-season bargains and check the exact dates of the seasons with your tour operator or airline. You might be able to save a lot by shifting your departure date by a week – or even a day. **Taxes** vary almost monthly, but creep relentlessly upward. Flying on weekends ordinarily adds a substantial amount to the round-trip fare; prices quoted below assume midweek travel.

You may cut costs by using a **specialist flight agent** – either a consolidator, who buys blocks of tickets from the airlines and sells them at a discount, or a **discount agent**, who deals with discounted flights and may also offer special student and youth fares and other services, including insurance, rail passes, car rental, and tours. Some agents specialize in **charter flights**, which may be cheaper than scheduled flights, though departure dates are fixed and withdrawal penalties are high. For some of the more popular destinations, it may sometimes be cheaper to pick up a bargain **package deal** from one of the tour operators listed below and then find your own accommodation when you get there; however, you won't find such deals often.

If the USA is only one stop on a longer journey, you might consider buying a **round-the-world ticket**. Some travel agents can sell you an "off-the-shelf" RTW ticket that will have you touching down in about half a dozen cities (New York, Miami, and Los Angeles are on many itineraries). Others will assemble one for you, tailored to your needs but apt to be more expensive. Figure on Aus$2300/£800 for an RTW ticket including the US.

Booking flights online

Many airlines and discount travel websites offer you the opportunity to book your tickets online, cutting out the costs of agents and middlemen. Good deals can often be found through discount or auction sites, as well as through the airlines' own websites. Always check with a local or student travel agent too, as sometimes they will offer surprisingly attractive alternatives.

Online booking agents and general travel sites

ⓦ **www.cheapflights.com** Flight deals and travel agents, plus links to other travel sites. UK only.
ⓦ **www.cheaptickets.com** Discount flight specialists.
ⓦ **www.expedia.com** Discount airfares, all-airline search engine, and daily deals (US only; for the UK ⓦ www.expedia.co.uk; for Canada ⓦ www.expedia.ca).

Ⓦ **www.flyaow.com** Online air travel info and reservations site.

Ⓦ **www.gaytravel.com** Gay online travel agent, concentrating mostly on accommodation.

Ⓦ **www.hotwire.com** Bookings from the US only. Last-minute savings of up to forty percent on regular published fares. Travelers must be at least 18 and there are no refunds, transfers, or changes allowed. Log-in required.

Ⓦ **www.lastminute.com** Offers good last-minute holiday package and flight-only deals. UK only.

Ⓦ **www.priceline.com** Name-your-own-price website that has deals at around forty percent off standard fares. You cannot specify flight times (although you do specify dates) and the tickets are nonrefundable, nontransferable, and nonchangeable.

Ⓦ **www.skyauction.com** Bookings from the US only. Auctions tickets and travel packages using a "second bid" scheme. The best strategy is to bid the maximum you're willing to pay, because if you win you'll pay just enough to beat the runner-up, regardless of your maximum bid.

Ⓦ **www.smilinjack.com/airlines.htm** Lists an up-to-date compilation of airline Web addresses.

Ⓦ **travel.yahoo.com** Incorporates a lot of Rough Guides material in its coverage of destination countries and cities across the world, with information about places to eat, sleep, and so on.

Ⓦ **www.travelocity.com** Destination guides, hot Web fares, and best deals for car rental, accommodation, and lodging, as well as fares. Provides access to the travel agent system SABRE, the most comprehensive central reservations system in the US (for UK Ⓦ www.travelocity.co.uk; for Canada Ⓦ www.travelocity.ca).

Ⓦ **www.travelshop.com.au** Australian website offering discounted flights, packages, insurance, and online bookings.

From the UK and Ireland

More than twenty US cities are accessible by nonstop flights from the UK. At these gateway cities, airport hubs for US air carriers, you can connect with extensive networks of domestic flights on into the rest of the country. Direct services (which may land once or twice on the way, but are called direct if they keep the same flight number throughout their journey) fly from Britain to nearly every other major US city.

Nonstop flights to **Los Angeles** from London take eleven or twelve hours; the London–**Miami** flight takes eight hours; while flying time to **New York** is seven or so hours. Following winds ensure that return flights are always an hour or two shorter than outward journeys. One-stop direct flights to destinations beyond the East Coast add time to the journey, but can work out cheaper than nonstop flights. They can even save you time, because customs and immigration are cleared on first touchdown into the US rather than the final destination, which may be a busy international gateway.

Only two airlines run nonstop scheduled services to the US **from Ireland**. From both Dublin and Shannon airports, Aer Lingus flies to New York (six or seven hours), Chicago (eight hours), Boston (nine hours), and Los Angeles (eleven hours), while Delta flies to New York and Atlanta (both eight and a half hours). Both can arrange onward flights to any American destination, and may have good-value special deals. Otherwise, the cheapest flights – if you're under 26 or a student – are available from USIT. Ordinary advance purchase – sometimes known as **Apex** – fares may be only marginally higher. These can come with a variety of restrictions, including having to travel at a certain time of day or on certain days of the week, or having to stay for a fixed length of time (usually including a Saturday night); tickets must be booked between 7 and 21 days in advance. Fares operate on a sliding scale, usually based on how far ahead you book.

Fares

Britain remains one of the best places in Europe to obtain flight bargains, though fares vary widely according to season, availability, and the current level of inter-airline competition. The chart above and to the right will give you a broad idea of typical rates offered by the operators listed opposite and on p.12.

The comments that follow serve only as a general guide. The lowest-priced tickets usually must be booked in advance and may carry restrictions, with heavy penalties for changes. The travel ads in the weekend papers and the holiday pages of ITV's *Teletext* give an idea of what's available; in London, scour *Time Out* and the *Evening Standard*. A good local travel agent will give you cost-saving advice as well as competitive quotes. Giveaway magazines aimed at young travelers, such as *TNT*, are also useful resources.

Sample air fares from Britain and Ireland

The prices given below (in £ sterling) are a general indication of the (minimum) transatlantic airfares obtainable from specialist companies for return (round-trip) flights, including tax. Each airline decides the exact dates of its own seasons.

LOW: Nov–March (excluding Christmas and Easter). HIGH: Easter, July–Sept, Christmas

	LOW	HIGH		LOW	HIGH
London to	return	return	**Manchester to**		
Boston	200	470	Chicago	280	470
Chicago	250	500	Los Angeles	345	530
Denver	265	630	New York	250	445
Houston	290	590			
Los Angeles	240	560	**Dublin to**		
Miami	240	550	Boston	285	300
New York	190	450	Chicago	315	400
San Francisco	230	610	Los Angeles	425	630
Seattle	300	680	New York	285	300
Washington	200	490			

For an overview of the various offers, and unofficially discounted tickets, go straight to an agent specializing in low-cost flights. Especially if you're under 26 or a student, they may be able to knock up to thirty percent off the regular fares. In low or shoulder season, you should be able to find a return flight to East Coast destinations such as New York for around £200, or to California for more like £250, while high-season rates tend to be £100–400 more expensive. A Visit USA Airpass (VUSA) can be a good idea if you want to see a lot of the country. These are available only to non-US residents, and must be bought before reaching the US (see box, p.33).

With an open-jaw ticket you can fly into one city and out of another; fares are calculated by halving the return fares to each destination and adding the two figures together. Remember to check whether there is a high drop-off fee for returning a rental car in a different state from the one where you picked it up (see p.35).

Nonstop flights

From London
(Heathrow, Gatwick, or Stansted)

Atlanta British Airways, Delta, United
Baltimore British Airways
Boston American Airlines, British Airways, Delta, United, Virgin Atlantic

Chicago Air India, American Airlines, British Airways, United, Thai Airways, Virgin Atlantic
Cincinnati Delta
Dallas/Fort Worth American Airlines, British Airways
Detroit Northwest, British Airways
Houston British Airways, Continental
Las Vegas Virgin Atlantic
Los Angeles Air New Zealand, American Airlines, British Airways, Continental, United, Virgin Atlantic
Miami American Airlines, British Airways, Virgin Atlantic
Minneapolis Northwest
New York Air India, American Airlines, British Airways, Continental, Kuwait Airways, United, Thai Airways, Virgin Atlantic
Orlando British Airways, Continental, Virgin Atlantic
Philadelphia British Airways, US Airways
Phoenix British Airways
Pittsburgh US Airways
Raleigh/Durham American Airlines
St Louis TWA
San Diego British Airways
San Francisco British Airways, Continental, United, Virgin Atlantic
Seattle British Airways
Washington DC British Airways, Continental, United, Virgin Atlantic

From Birmingham

New York Continental

From Manchester

Atlanta Delta
Chicago American Airlines, BMI (seasonal)

New York British Airways, Continental, Delta, Pakistan International
Orlando Virgin Atlantic
Philadelphia US Airways, BMI (seasonal)
Washington DC BMI

From Glasgow

New York British Airways, Continental, American Airlines (summer only)

From Dublin/Shannon

Atlanta Aer Lingus, Delta
Boston Aer Lingus
Chicago Aer Lingus
Los Angeles Aer Lingus, American Airlines
New York Aer Lingus

Airlines

Aer Lingus Republic of Ireland ☎0645/737 747, ⓦwww.aerlingus.ie
Air India UK ☎020/8560 9996, ⓦwww.airindia.com
Air New Zealand UK ☎020/8741 2299, ⓦwww.airnz.co.uk
American Airlines UK ☎0345/789 789, ⓦwww.americanairlines.co.uk
British Airways UK ☎0345/222 111, Republic of Ireland ☎01/222 2345, ⓦwww.britishairways.com
BMI in UK ☎0870/607 0555, ⓦwww.flybmi.com
Continental UK ☎0800/776 464, ⓦwww.continental.com/uk, Republic of Ireland ☎01/814 5311, ⓦwww.continental.com/ie
Delta UK ☎0800/414 767, Republic of Ireland ☎1800/768 080, ⓦwww.delta.com
Kuwait Airways UK ☎020/7412 0006, ⓦwww.kuwait-airways.com
Northwest UK ☎0990/561 000, ⓦwww.klm.com/uk_en/index.jsp
Pakistan International UK ☎020/8741 8066, ⓦwww.piac.com.pk
Thai Airways UK ☎0870/606 0911, ⓦwww.thaiair.com
TWA UK ☎0345/333 333, ⓦwww.twa.com
United UK ☎0845/844 4777, Republic of Ireland ☎1800/535 5300, ⓦwww.unitedairlines.co.uk
US Airways UK ☎0845/600 3300, ⓦwww.usairways.co.uk
Virgin Atlantic UK ☎01293/747 747, Republic of Ireland ☎01/873 3388, ⓦwww.virgin-atlantic.com

Flight agents

Apex Travel Dublin ☎01/241 8000, ⓦwww.apextravel.ie
Bridge The World London ☎0870/443 2399, ⓦwww.bridgetheworld.com
CIE Tours International Dublin ☎01/703 1888, ⓦwww.cietours.ie
Co-op Travel Care Belfast ☎028/9047 1717
Flightbookers London ☎020/7757 2444, Dublin ☎01/241 5689, ⓦwww.ebookers.com
Joe Walsh Tours Dublin ☎01/676 0991, ⓦwww.joewalshtours.ie
Premier Travel Derry ☎028/7126 3333, ⓦwww.premiertravel.uk.com
STA Travel UK nationwide ☎0870/160 0599, ⓦwww.statravel.co.uk

Belfast	☎028/9024 1469
Bristol	☎0870/167 6777
Cambridge	☎01223/366 966
Edinburgh	☎0131/226 7747
Glasgow	☎0141/338 6000
Leeds	☎0870/168 6878
Manchester	☎0161/834 0668
Oxford	☎0870/163 6873

Student & Group Travel Dublin ☎01/677 7834. Student groups only, to New York and Boston.
Trailfinders London ☎020/7628 7628, ⓦwww.trailfinders.com

Belfast	☎02890/271 888
Birmingham	☎0121/236 1234
Bristol	☎0117/929 9000
Dublin	☎01/677 7888
Glasgow	☎0141/353 2224
Manchester	☎0161/839 6969

The Travel Bag London ☎0870/890 1456, ⓦwww.travelbag.co.uk
Twohigs Dublin ☎01/670 9750
USIT Now Belfast ☎028/9032 4073, ⓦwww.usitnow.ie

Cork	☎021/427 0900
Derry	☎028/7137 1888
Dublin	☎08/1820 0020

Tour operators

Airtours UK ☎0870/238 7788, ⓦwww.airtours.co.uk
American Holidays Belfast ☎028/9023 8762, Dublin ☎01/673 3840, ⓦwww.american-holidays.com
Bon Voyage Southampton ☎0800/316 3012, ⓦwww.bon-voyage.co.uk
British Airways Holidays worldwide ☎0870/242 4245, ⓦwww.baholidays.co.uk

Florida & Fly Drives UK general ☎0870/442 3800, UK US city-specific ☎0870/242 4243
Explore Worldwide Aldershot ☎01252/760 000, ⓦwww.explore.co.uk
Greyhound International East Grinstead ☎01342/317 317, ⓦwww.greyhound.com
North America Travel Service Leeds ☎0113/246 1466, ⓦwww.northamericatravelservice.co.uk
Trans Atlantic Vacations Horley ☎01293/789 400
Thomas Cook London ☎0870/566 6222, ⓦwww.thomascook.co.uk
TrekAmerica Banbury ☎01295/256 777, ⓦwww.trekamerica.co.uk
Unijet Haywards Heath ☎0870/600 8009, ⓦwww.unijet.com
United Vacations UK ☎0870/606 2222, ⓦwww.unitedvacations.co.uk
Virgin Holidays Crawley ☎0870/220 2788, ⓦwww.virginholidays.co.uk

Packages

Packages – fly-drive, flight accommodation deals, and guided tours (or a combination of all three) – can work out cheaper than arranging the same trip yourself, especially for a short-term stay. High-street travel agents have plenty of brochures and information.

Flight and accommodation deals

There are countless **flight and accommodation packages** to all the major American cities. Although you can often do things cheaper independently, these allow you to leave the organizational hassles to someone else. Drawbacks include the loss of flexibility and the fact that you'll probably be made to stay in hotels in the mid-range to expensive bracket, even though less expensive accommodation is almost always readily available.

A typical example might be a return flight plus middle-range Midtown hotel accommodation for three nights in New York City, starting at around £480 per person in low season and more like £740 at peak periods. Virgin Holidays is among the least expensive of the many possibilities (see "Tour operators," opposite). Pre-booked accommodation schemes, where you buy vouchers for use in a specific group of hotels, are not normally good value.

Fly-drive deals

Fly-drive deals, which give cut-rate (sometimes free) car rental when a traveler buys a transatlantic ticket from an airline or tour operator, are always cheaper than renting on the spot, and give great value if you intend to do a lot of driving. On the other hand, you'll probably have to pay more for the flight than if you booked it through a discount agent. Competition between airlines and tour operators means that it's well worth phoning to check on current special promotions.

Getaway (☎020/797 3007) arranges fly-drive deals with various carriers. Holiday America (☎01424/224 400, ⓦwww.holiday-america.net) offers excellent deals for not much more than an ordinary Apex fare (see p.10). Several of the companies listed opposite offer similar, and sometimes cheaper, packages. A good travel agent will put one together for you. There will often be little to choose between prices; the most important determining factors are the current strength of the dollar against the pound, and your destination in the US. **Florida** and **California** usually offer the lowest rates, ridiculously cheap in off-peak times (and all year in Florida), starting at around £17 per week for a small family sedan or £120 for a seven-seat passenger van (Northwest Flydrive). Watch out for hidden extras, such as taxes, drop-off charges, and insurance; all are detailed on p.35 onward.

Several of the operators listed opposite go one stage further and book accommodation for self-drive tours. Bon Voyage, for example, arranges tailor-made packages in the Southwest, with two weeks in Arizona, including the flight to Phoenix and standard hotels, costing around £1200 per person.

Touring and adventure packages

A simple and exciting way to see a chunk of America's great outdoors, without being hassled by too many practical considerations, is to take a specialist **touring and adventure package**, which includes transportation, accommodation, food, and a guide. Some of the more adventurous, such as AmeriCan Adventures and TrekAmerica, carry small groups around on minibuses and use a combination of budget hotels (or hostels, in the case of AmeriCan) and camping (all equipment, except sleeping bags, is provided). Most concentrate on the West – ranging from Arizona to Alaska, and lasting from seven days to five weeks; cross-country treks and Eastern adventures that take in New York or Florida are also available. Typical rates for a two-week trip – excluding transatlantic flights – range from £519 in low season up to £699 in midsummer. Trips to Alaska cost a good bit more. For another touring and adventure package option, see the box on Green Tortoise, p.34.

From Australia and New Zealand

Other than seasonal bargains and all-in packages that may be on offer from time to time, the best deals from Australasia are available from the travel agents listed opposite. Various add-on fares and air passes valid in the continental US are available with your main ticket, allowing you to fly to destinations across the States. These must be bought before you go, though.

Fares

Whatever kind of ticket you're after, your first call should be to one of the **travel agents** listed opposite, who can fill you in on all the latest fares and any special offers. The **most expensive** time to fly is during the northern summer (mid-May to end Aug) and over the Christmas period (Dec to mid-Jan); shoulder seasons cover March to mid-May and September, while the rest of the year is **low season**. The exact dates vary slightly between the airlines, so it's worth shopping around, especially if you have the flexibility to change your departure date by a day or two. Los Angeles is the main US gateway airport for flights **from Australia**: excluding tax, the regular Air New Zealand, Qantas, and United flights cost around Aus$1500 from the eastern states in low season, rising to Aus$2000 from Western Australia; flying during peak season will add at least another Aus$500. Through-flights to New York start at Aus$2150, tax excluded, with Qantas or

United from Sydney, Brisbane, or Cairns, although sometimes you can get a Aus$99 add-on to your cheaper LA fare. Expect to pay upwards of Aus$2100, excluding tax, from Perth to New York on Qantas.

From **New Zealand**, low-season fares from Auckland or Christchurch start at around NZ$1950 to LA or San Francisco, NZ$2500 to New York. Add another NZ$150–300 for Wellington departures.

Airlines

Air Canada Australia ☎02/9232 5222, New Zealand ☎09/377 8833, ⓦwww.aircanada.ca
Air New Zealand Sydney ☎13 24 76, Auckland ☎09/357 3000 or 0800/737 000, ⓦwww.airnz.co.nz
America West Airlines Sydney ☎1300/364 757, ⓦwww.americawest.com
American Airlines Sydney ☎1300/650 747, Auckland ☎09/309 0735 or 0800/887 997, ⓦwww.aa.com
British Airways Sydney ☎1300/767 177, Auckland ☎09/356 8690, ⓦwww.british-airways.com
Continental Airlines Sydney ☎02/9244 2242, New Zealand ☎09/308 3350, ⓦwww.flycontinental.com
Delta Airlines Sydney ☎02/9251 3211, Auckland ☎09/379 3370 or 0800/440 876, ⓦwww.delta-air.com
Japan Airlines Sydney ☎02/9272 1111, Auckland ☎09/379 9906, ⓦwww.japanair.com
KLM/Northwest Sydney ☎1300/303 747, Auckland ☎09/309 1782, ⓦwww.klm.com
Korean Air Sydney ☎02/9262 2009, Auckland ☎09/307 3687
Malaysia Airlines Sydney ☎02/9364 3500, Auckland ☎09/373 2741 or 0800/657 472, ⓦwww.malaysiaair.com
Qantas Sydney ☎13 13 13, Auckland ☎09/357 8900 or 0800/808 767, ⓦwww.qantas.com.au
Singapore Airlines Sydney ☎02/9350 0100, Auckland ☎09/303 2129 or 0800/808 909, ⓦwww.singaporeair.com
South African Airways Sydney ☎02/9286 8960, Auckland ☎09/379 3708, ⓦwww.saa-usa.com
United Airlines Sydney ☎02/9292 4111, Auckland ☎09/379 3800, ⓦwww.unitedairlines.com.au
Virgin Atlantic Airways Sydney ☎02/9244 2747, New Zealand ☎09/308 3377, ⓦwww.virgin-atlantic.com

Air passes and RTW tickets

Unless you're combining your US trip with jaunts to Europe and/or Asia, US **air passes** (see p.33) and add-on fares generally offer greater savings and more flexibility than round-the-world (RTW) tickets. However, there are endless possibilities for **RTW routings**; for example, prices for Sydney to Tahiti to Los Angeles, traveling overland to New York, then continuing to Frankfurt and Bangkok on the way back to Sydney, start at Aus$2700 on the "Star Alliance" (ⓦ www.star-alliance.com), which includes Air New Zealand, Lufthansa, United Airlines, Thai, Varig, SAS, and Air Canada. The "Star Alliance" works on a mileage basis and is a flat rate year-round. If you're departing in low season, cheaper still is the "One World" (ⓦ www.oneworld.com) fare offered by Qantas and British Airways, in conjunction with American Airlines, Canadian Airlines, and Cathay Pacific, which covers four continents from Aus$2599. Kiwi travelers could start in Auckland and take in Sydney, Harare, Nairobi, London, New York, LA, and Brisbane for around NZ$3250. Agents such as STA (see opposite) specialize in putting together RTW airfares using various airlines, and can help you plan your trip.

Packages and tours

There are many variations on **package deals** available to Australasian travelers, from fly-drive deals to fully escorted bus tours, skiing packages, and camping treks, which can often work out cheaper than making the same arrangements yourself. Some of the no-frills **fly-drive packages**, for example, can cost less than a flight alone, and you'll often get extras, such as stopovers in Hawaii or Tahiti, or passes to Disneyland, thrown in. Creative Holidays (see opposite) tours start at about Aus$1900 for seven days, including all accommodation, but excluding flights.

Small-group **hotel and camping tours** can get you further off the beaten track. TrekAmerica offers several itineraries ranging from one to nine weeks. Its seven-day "Western Wonder" tour starts and ends in LA, taking in Death Valley, Las Vegas, and the Grand Canyon, and costs from around Aus$1100/NZ$1200, not including flights. The

25-day "Coast to Coast" trip, which crosses the continent from Miami to San Francisco, or vice versa, starts at Aus$2100/NZ$2400 (again, airfares are extra).

Flight agents and tour operators

Anywhere Travel Sydney ☏ 02/9663 0411, ⓦ www.anywheretravel.com.au
Budget Travel Auckland ☏ 09/366 0061 or 0800/808 040, ⓦ www.budgettravel.com /zealand.htm
Destinations Unlimited Auckland ☏ 09/4141 685, ⓦ www.holiday.co.nz
Flight Centres Sydney ☏ 13/3133 350, Auckland ☏ 09/358 4310, ⓦ www.flightcentre.com.au
STA Travel Australia ☏ 13 17 76 or 1300/733 035 for fastfare telesales, ⓦ www.statravel .com.au; Auckland ☏ 0508/782 872, ⓦ www .statravel.co.nz. Many branches scattered around both countries; call for nearest branch.
Student Uni Travel Sydney ☏ 02/9232 8444, ⓦ www.sut.com.au. Branches also in Brisbane, Cairns, Darwin, Melbourne, and Perth.
Trailfinders Sydney ☏ 02/9247 7666, ⓦ www.trailfinders.com.au
Usit Beyond Auckland ☏ 09/379 4224 or 0800/874 823, ⓦ www.usitbeyond.co.nz. Branches also in Christchurch, Dunedin, Palmerston North, Hamilton, and Wellington.

Specialist agents and operators

Adventure Specialists 1/69 Liverpool St, Sydney ☏ 02/9261 2927. Overland and adventure tour agent.
Adventure World Sydney ☏ 02/8913 0755, ⓦ www.adventureworld.com.au; also a branch in Perth. In Auckland ☏ 09/524 5118, ⓦ www.adventureworld.co.nz. Agents for a vast array of international adventure travel companies that operate trips to every continent.
Canada and America Travel Specialists Sydney ☏ 02/9922 4600, ⓦ www.canada-americatravel.com.au. Wholesalers of Greyhound Ameripasses (see p.32), plus flights and accommodation.
Creative Holidays Sydney ☏ 02/9386 2111, ⓦ www.creativeholidays.com.au. Packages to New York, San Francisco, LA (eg, Disneyland), and Hawaii.
Sydney International Travel Centre ☏ 02/9250 9320, ⓦ www.sydneytravel.com.au. US flights, accommodation, city stays, and car rental.
Wiltrans 10/189 Kent St, Sydney ☏ 02/9255 0899. Luxury cruise and tour specialist; Australian representative for Maupintour.

Entry requirements for foreign visitors

For trips to the US of less than ninety days, citizens of Britain, Ireland, Australia, and New Zealand, as well as most European countries, need only to have a full, machine-readable passport; visas are not required. However, every person traveling into the country – infants and children included – must have their own individual passport. If you can't meet these requirements, you'll be required to obtain a non-immigrant tourist visa. For more information, or to apply, visit ⓦ www.travel.state.gov/vwp.

If you do have your own machine-readable passport, and don't plan to stay for more than three months, all you need to do is fill out a **visa waiver form**, which will be distributed during your incoming flight. This form, which requires details of where you'll be staying your first night in the States, as well as the date you intend to leave the country, will be processed at your initial point of arrival on American soil. You should also be able to prove that you have enough money to support yourself while in the US. Keep in mind that if you admit to being HIV-positive, or having AIDS or TB, you may experience difficulties. After your visa waiver form is processed, part of it will be attached to your passport, where it must remain until you leave. The same form also covers entry across the land borders with Canada and Mexico.

If you are not a citizen of a visa waiver scheme country, you should contact your local US embassy or consulate for details of current entry requirements. For advice on working or studying in the US, see p.18.

Customs

All passengers arriving in the US must present a completed **customs declaration form** (also handed out on incoming planes). Customs officers check whether you're carrying any fresh foods and ask if you've visited a farm in the last month: if you have, you could well lose your shoes. As well as foods and anything agricultural, it's prohibited to carry into the country any articles from such places as North Korea, Cambodia, Iraq, Libya, or Cuba; obscene publications; lottery tickets; chocolate liqueurs; or pre-Columbian artifacts. Anyone caught bringing drugs into the country will not only face prosecution but be entered in the records as an undesirable and probably denied entry for all time. The duty-free allowance if you're over 17 is 200 cigarettes and 100 cigars (*not* Cuban); if you're over 21, you'll be allowed the smokes as well as a liter of spirits.

US embassies and consulates

In Australia

Embassy 21 Moonah Place, Canberra, ACT 2600 ☎02/6214 5600, ⓦusembassy-australia .state.gov

---

Canadian visitors

Canadian citizens do not necessarily need even a passport for a short excursion to the US (though you do need official photographic ID). If you're setting off on a longer trip, you should carry a passport, and if you plan to stay for more than ninety days you need a visa, too.

Bear in mind that if you cross into the States in your car, trunks and passenger compartments are subject to spot searches by US Customs personnel, and that since September 11th, security has been greatly increased. Remember, too, that Canadians are legally barred from seeking gainful employment in the US.

Consulates Melbourne: 553 St Kilda Rd, VIC 3004
℡03/9526 5900, ⓦmelbourne.usconsulate.gov
/melbourne/index.html
Sydney: 19–29 Martin Place, NSW 2000
℡02/9373 9200, ⓦsydney.usconsulate.gov
/sydney/index.html
Perth: 16 St George's Terrace, 13th floor, WA 6000
℡08/9202 1224,
ⓦperth.usconsulate.gov/perth/index.html
Visa hotline ℡1902/941 641 (premium-rated,
Aus$1.05 per minute) or 1800/687 844 (live
operators; total cost of Aus$11)

In Canada

Embassy 490 Sussex Drive, Ottawa, ON K1N 1G8
℡613/238-5335, ⓦwww.usembassycanada.gov
Consulates Calgary: 615 Macleod Trail SE, 10th
floor, AB T2G 4T8 ℡403/266-8962
Halifax: Wharf Tower II, 1969 Upper Water St, suite
904, NS B3J 3R7 ℡902/429-2480
Montreal: 1155 St Alexandre St, PQ H3B 1Z1
℡514/398-9695
Québec City: 2 Place Terrasse Dufferin, PQ G1R
4T9 ℡418/692-2095
Toronto: 360 University Ave, ON M5G 1S4
℡416/595-1700, ⓦwww.usconsulatetoronto.ca
Vancouver: 1095 W Pender St, 21st floor, BC V6E
2M6 ℡604/685-4311

In Ireland

Embassy 42 Elgin Rd, Ballsbridge, Dublin 4
℡01/668 8777, ⓦwww.usembassy.ie

In New Zealand

Embassy 29 Fitzherbert Terrace, Thorndon,
Wellington ℡04/462 2000, ⓦusembassy.org.nz
Consulate 3rd floor, Citibank Building, 23
Customs St, Auckland ℡09/303 2724
Address for visa applications: Non-Immigrant
Visas, Private Bag 92022, Auckland

In the UK

Embassy London: 24 Grosvenor Square, W1A 1AE
℡020/7499 9000, visa hotline ℡0906/820 0290
Consulates Edinburgh: 3 Regent Terrace, EH7
5BW ℡0131/556 8315
Belfast: Queens House, 14 Queen St, BT1 6EQ
℡028/9032 8239

Foreign embassies and consulates in the US

Australia

Embassy 1601 Massachusetts Ave NW,
Washington DC 20036 ℡202/797-3000,
ⓦwww.austemb.org

Canada

Embassy 501 Pennsylvania Ave NW, Washington
DC 20001 ℡202/682-1740,
ⓦwww.canadianembassy.org
Consulates Boston: Three Copley Place, suite
400, MA 02216 ℡617/262-3760
Chicago: Two Prudential Plaza, 180 N Stetson Ave,
suite 2400, IL 60601 ℡312/616-1860
Los Angeles: 550 S Hope St, 9th floor, CA
90071–2627 ℡213/346-2700
New York: 1251 Avenue of the Americas, NY
10020–1175 ℡212/596-1793
San Francisco: 555 Montgomery St, suite 1288, CA
94111 ℡415/834-3180

Ireland

Embassy 2234 Massachusetts Ave NW,
Washington DC 20008 ℡202/462-3939,
ⓦwww.irelandemb.org

New Zealand

Embassy 37 Observatory Circle NW, Washington
DC 20008 ℡202/328-4800, ⓦwww.nzemb.org

UK

Embassy 3100 Massachusetts Ave NW,
Washington DC 20008 ℡202/588-6500,
ⓦwww.britainusa.com/consular/embassy
Consulates Atlanta: Georgia Pacific Centre, suite
3400, 133 Peachtree St NE, GA 30303 ℡404/954-
7700, ⓦwww.britainusa.com/atlanta
Boston: One Memorial Drive, suite 1500,
Cambridge, MA 02142 ℡617/245-4500,
ⓦwww.britainusa.com/boston
Chicago: 13th floor, The Wrigley Building, 400 N
Michigan Ave, IL 60611 ℡312/970-3800,
ⓦwww.britainusa.com/chicago
Denver: Suite 1030, World Trade Center, 1675
Broadway, CO 80202 ℡303/592-5200,
ⓦwww.britainusa.com/denver
Los Angeles: 11766 Wilshire Blvd, suite 400, CA
90025 ℡310/481-0031, ⓦwww.britainusa.com/la

Miami: Brickell Bay Office Tower, 1001 Brickell Bay Drive, suite 2800, FL 33131 ☎305/374-1522, Ⓦwww.britainusa.com/miami
New York: 845 Third Ave, NY 10022 ☎212/745-0200, Ⓦwww.britainusa.com/ny
San Francisco: 1 Sansome St, suite 850, CA 94104 ☎415/617-1300, Ⓦwww.britainusa.com/sf
Seattle: 900 Fourth Ave, suite 3001, WA 98164 ☎206/622-9255, Ⓦwww.britainusa.com/seattle
Houston: Wells Fargo Plaza 1000 Louisiana, suite 1900, TX 77002 ☎713/659-6270, Ⓦwww.britainusa.com/houston

Extensions

The date stamped on your passport is the latest you're legally allowed to stay. Leaving a few days later may not matter, especially if you're heading home and are not planning on returning to the US any time soon. **Staying over** more than a week or so, however, can result in a protracted, rather unpleasant interrogation from officials, which may cause you to miss your flight. Overstaying may also cause you to be turned away the next time you try to enter the US.

To get an **extension** before your time is up, apply at the nearest US Bureau of Citizenship and Immigration Services (BCIS) office. Addresses for these can be found in the Federal Government Offices listings in local telephone directories, or on Ⓦwww.bcis.gov. When you go to the bureau, they will assume that you're working illegally, and it's up to you to convince them otherwise. Do this by providing evidence of ample finances, and, if you can, bring along an upstanding American citizen to vouch for you. You'll also have to explain why you didn't plan for the extra time initially.

Work and study

Only the US Bureau of Citizenship and Immigration Services can grant permission to **work** in the country. Contact your local embassy or consulate for advice on current regulations and BCIS addresses; however, unless you have relatives (parents or children over 21) or a prospective employer to sponsor you, your chances are at best slim.

Illegal work is not as easy to find as it once was, now that the government imposes fines of up to $10,000 for companies caught employing anyone without the legal right to work in the US. Even in the traditionally more casual establishments, like restaurants and bars, things have really tightened up. If you do find work, it's likely to be of the less visible, poorly paid kind – like as a dishwasher.

Students have the best chance to prolong their stay in the US. One way is to get onto an **Exchange Visitor Program**; participants get a J-1 visa that entitles them to accept paid summer employment and apply for a Social Security number (required for any employment in the US). However, most of these visas are issued for jobs in American summer camps, which aren't everybody's idea of a good time; they fly you over, and after a summer's work you end up with around $500 and a month to six weeks in which to blow it. If you live in Britain and are interested, contact BUNAC (☎020/7251 3472, Ⓦwww.bunac.com/uk) or Camp America (☎020/7581 7373, Ⓦwww.campamerica.co.uk). If you want to **study** at an American university, apply to that institution directly; once accepted, you're more or less entitled to unlimited visas so long as you remain enrolled in full-time education.

Applicants for **au pair visas** must prove that they have at least 200 hours' experience with infants, 24 hours' instruction in child development, and 8 hours' child-safety training. Prospective employers must provide a written description of the job they expect their au pair to perform, so there is protection on both sides. The American Institute for Foreign Study runs a program called Au Pair in America (☎207/581-7322, Ⓦwww.aifs.com/aupair/), open to men and women aged 18 to 26. There is a placement fee of $75, a $100 contribution toward insurance, and a good-faith deposit of $400; the combined amount covers the interviewing and selection process, a visa, and a flight to the US. On-the-job payment is about US$139 per week, more if you have a childcare qualification or more than two years' experience; if you last the whole year you get your good-faith deposit back in dollars.

Insurance, health, and personal safety

Insurance

Though not compulsory, **travel insurance** is essential for foreign travelers, as the US has no national healthcare system. You can lose an arm and a leg (so to speak) having even minor medical treatment. Before purchasing a new policy, however, it's worth checking whether you are already covered; this is recommended for US residents as well. Some all-risks home insurance policies, for example, may cover your possessions against loss or theft when overseas, and many private medical plans include cover when abroad. **In Canada**, provincial health plans usually provide partial coverage for medical mishaps in another country, while holders of official **student/teacher/youth cards** in Canada and the US (visit ⓦwww.istc.org) are entitled to meager accident coverage and hospital in-patient benefits. Students will often find that their student health coverage extends during vacations and for one term beyond the date of last enrollment. Some bank and credit cards include certain levels of medical or other insurance, and you may automatically get travel insurance if you use a major credit card to pay for your trip.

After exhausting the possibilities above, you might want to contact a **specialist travel insurance company**, or consider the **travel insurance deal** offered by Rough Guides (see box, below). A typical travel insurance policy usually provides cover for the loss of baggage, tickets, and – up to a certain limit – cash or checks, as well as cancellation or curtailment of your journey. Most of them exclude so-called **dangerous sports** unless an extra premium is paid: in the US this can mean scuba-diving, whitewater rafting, windsurfing, and hiking (trekking), though probably not kayaking or jeep safaris. Many policies can be chopped and changed to exclude coverage you don't need – for example, sickness and accident benefits can often be excluded or included at will. If you do take medical coverage, ascertain whether benefits will be paid as treatment proceeds or only after you return home, and whether there is a 24hr **medical emergency number**. When securing baggage cover, make sure that the per-article limit will cover your most valuable possession. If you need to make a claim, keep receipts for medicines and medical treatment; in the event you have anything stolen, you must obtain an official statement from the police.

Health advice

If you have a serious **accident** while in the US, emergency medical services will get to

---

Rough Guides travel insurance

Rough Guides Ltd offers a low-cost **travel insurance policy**, especially customized for our statistically low-risk readers by a leading British broker, provided by the American International Group (AIG) and registered with the British regulatory body, GISC (the General Insurance Standards Council).

There are five main Rough Guides insurance plans: **No Frills** for the bare minimum for secure travel; **Essential**, which provides decent all-round cover; **Premier** for comprehensive cover with a wide range of benefits; **Extended Stay** for cover lasting four months to a year; and **Annual Multi-trip**, a cost-effective way of getting Premier cover if you travel more than once a year. Premier, Annual Multi-Trip, and Extended Stay policies can be supplemented by a **"Hazardous Pursuits Extension"** if you plan to indulge in sports considered dangerous, such as scuba-diving or trekking. For a **policy quote**, call the Rough Guide Insurance Line: toll-free in the UK ☏0800/015 0906 or ☏+44 1392 314 665 from elsewhere. Alternatively, get an online quote at ⓦwww.roughguides.com/insurance.

you quickly and charge you later. For emergencies or ambulances, dial ☎911, the nationwide emergency number.

Should you need to see a doctor, consult the *Yellow Pages* telephone directory under "Clinics" or "Physicians and Surgeons." The basic consultation fee is $50–100, payable in advance. Medications aren't cheap either – keep all your receipts for later claims on your insurance policy.

Foreign visitors should bear in mind that many pills available over the counter at home – most codeine-based painkillers, for example – require a **prescription** in the US. Local brand names can be confusing; ask for advice at the **pharmacy** in any drugstore.

In general, **inoculations** aren't required for entry to the US.

Crime and personal safety

No one could pretend that America is trouble-free, although away from the urban centers **crime** is often remarkably low-key. Even the lawless reputations of Miami, Detroit, or Los Angeles are far in excess of the truth, and most parts of these cities, by day at least, are safe; at night, though, some areas are completely off-limits. All the major tourist areas and the main nightlife zones in cities are invariably brightly lit and well policed. By planning carefully and taking good care of your possessions, you should, generally speaking, have few real problems.

Mugging and theft

The biggest fear for most travelers is **mugging**, though it's nothing to get overly paranoid about. It's impossible to give hard and fast rules about what to do if confronted by a mugger. Whether to run, scream, or fight depends on the situation – but most locals would just hand over their money.

Of course, the best thing is simply to avoid being mugged. Remember a few basic rules: don't flash money around; don't peer at your map (or this book) at every street corner, thereby announcing that you're a lost stranger; if drunk, take a taxi to your hotel; avoid dark streets; and in the wee hours stick to the street-side edge of the sidewalk,

so you can run into the street to attract attention. If you must ask for directions, choose your target carefully. Consider carrying a wad of cash, perhaps $50, separate from the bulk of your holdings, so that if you do get confronted, you can hand over something of value without losing everything.

If the worst happens and your assailant is toting a gun or (more likely) a knife, try to stay calm: remember that he (for this is generally a male pursuit) is probably scared, too. Keep still, make no sudden movements – and hand over your money. When he's gone, find a phone and dial ☎911, or hail a cab and ask the driver to take you to the nearest police station. Once arrived, report the theft and get a reference number on the report to claim insurance and travelers check refunds. If you're in a big city, call the local Travelers Aid (their numbers are listed in the telephone directory) for sympathy and practical advice. For specific advice for **women** in the case of mugging or attack, see p.43.

Hotel-room burglary is another potential problem. Always store valuables in the hotel safe when you go out, and, when inside, keep your door locked and don't open it to anyone who causes you to be suspicious. If they claim to be hotel staff and you don't believe them, call reception to check.

Obviously, losing your travel documents – and especially your passport – is a traveler's nightmare. If you are unlucky in this respect, go to the nearest consulate and get a **temporary passport** (little more than a sheet of paper saying you've reported the loss) which will suffice to get you out of America and back home.

Useful phone numbers to report stolen checks and cards

American Express checks ☎1-800/221-7282, cards ☎1-888/412–6945,
Ⓦ www.travel.americanexpress.com
Citibank ☎1-800/645-6556,
Ⓦ www.citibank.com
Diners Club ☎1-800/234-6377,
Ⓦ www.dinersclub.com
MasterCard ☎1-636/722-7111 or ☎1-800/MC-ASSIST, Ⓦ www.mastercard.com
Thomas Cook/MasterCard ☎1-800/233-7373,
Ⓦ www.us.thomascook.com
Visa checks ☎1-800/227-6811, cards ☎1-800/847-2113, Ⓦ www.usa.visa.com

Car crime

Crimes committed against tourists driving **rented cars** aren't as common as they once were, but it still pays to be cautious. In major urban areas, any car you rent should have nothing on it – such as a particular license plate – that makes it easy to spot as a rental car. When driving, under no circumstances should you stop in any unlit or seemingly deserted urban area – and especially not if someone is waving you down and suggesting that there is something wrong with your car. Similarly, if you are accidentally rammed by the driver behind you, do not stop immediately, but proceed on to the nearest well-lit, busy area and call ☏911 for assistance. Keep your doors locked and windows never more than slightly open. Do not open your door or window if someone approaches your car on the pretext of asking for directions. Hide any valuables out of sight, preferably locked in the trunk or in the glove compartment.

Costs and money

This book contains detailed price information for lodging and eating throughout the US. Accommodation rates are coded according to the system explained in the box on p.45, which excludes any local taxes that may apply, while restaurant prices include food only and not drinks or tip. For museums and similar attractions, the entrance fees quoted are for adults, unless stated otherwise; if we do not list a discount for senior citizens or children, inquire if discounts are available. Costs may change during the life of this edition.

Costs

Traveling in the States can seem quite the deal or very expensive, depending in part on prices you're used to and where you're headed. New York prices, for example, are well above those in rural America. New England, Hawaii, and Alaska are among other areas that can be quite pricey.

Accommodation is likely to be your biggest single expense. Typical motel rooms in rural areas cost a few dollars either side of $40 per night, while hotel and motel rates in cities tend to start at around $60. Hostels offering dorm beds – usually for $10 to $20 – are reasonably common, but don't save all that much money for two or more people traveling together. Camping, of course, is cheap, ranging from free to perhaps $20 per night, but is rarely practical in or around the big cities.

Visa Travel Money

Visa Travel Money is a **disposable debit card** pre-paid with dedicated travel funds that you can access from more than 810,000 Visa ATMs in more than 150 countries with a PIN that you select. When your funds are depleted, simply throw the card away. Because you can buy up to nine cards to access the same funds – useful for couples/families traveling together – it's recommended that you buy at least one extra as a backup, in case your first is lost or stolen. You can call a 24hr Visa global customer assistance services center from any of the 150 countries toll-free: ☏1-800/847-2399 for lost or stolen cards; visit also ⓦwww.visa.com. In the UK and the US, Travelex (ⓦwww.travelex.com) sells the card.

Money: a note for foreign travelers

US currency comes in $1 **bills** and coins, bills of $5, $10, $20, $50, and $100, plus various larger (and rarely seen) denominations. Confusingly, all are the same size and same green color (except for the new $20, which has peach and blue accents), making it necessary to check each bill carefully. The dollar is made up of 100 cents, in **coins** of 1 cent (usually called a **penny**), 5 cents (a **nickel**), 10 cents (a **dime**), and 25 cents (a **quarter**). Fifty-cent and $1 coins are less frequently seen, though not entirely uncommon. Change – especially quarters – is needed for buses, vending machines, and telephones, so always carry a few.

Generally speaking, one pound sterling will buy $1.60, one Canadian dollar is worth around 75¢, one Australian dollar equals about 68¢, and one New Zealand dollar is equivalent to about 59¢. At time of publication, the euro was strong, equalling around $1.15.

As for **food**, $20 a day is enough to get an adequate life-support diet, consisting of perhaps one full meal in a local diner, supplemented by a stash of groceries. For a daily total of around $35–40, you can probably eat all of your meals out (though not at the finest restaurants). Expect to pay more in hip or swanky neighborhoods and big cities. Beyond this, everything hinges on how much sightseeing, taxi-taking, drinking, and socializing you do. Much of any of these – especially in a major city – and you're likely to be spending at least $60 a day, if not more. If you're visiting a significant number of national parks and monuments, buy a National Parks or Golden Eagle pass (see p.51); the $50 or $65 fee covers all passengers in your vehicle.

Renting a car, at around $150 per week, is a far more efficient way to explore the country than public transportation, and, for a group of two or more, it's no more expensive, either. Having your own vehicle also enables you to stay in budget motels along the interstates instead of expensive city-center hotels. (Keep in mind, though, that for those under 25 years of age, there are often supplements of $20 a day tacked onto car rental fees.)

In almost every state, **sales tax**, at rates varying up to ten percent, is added to virtually everything you buy in shops, but it isn't part of the marked price (for more details, see p.61).

Taking, changing, and accessing money

Expect to pay most of your major expenses by **credit or debit card**; hotels and car rental agencies usually require a credit card imprint as security, even if you intend to settle the bill in cash, and you'll be at a serious disadvantage if you don't have one. Visa, MasterCard, Diners Club, American Express, and Discover are the most widely accepted.

You'll also need to carry a certain amount of **cash**. If you have a MasterCard or Visa, or a cash-dispensing card linked to an international network such as Cirrus, Plus, Maestro, or Visa Debit – check with your home bank before you set off – you can not only withdraw cash from appropriate **automatic teller machines** (**ATMs**) but often use your debit card for purchases, as you would at home. For both American and foreign visitors, US dollar **travelers checks** are a better way to carry money than ordinary bills; they offer the great security of knowing that lost or stolen checks will be replaced. Checks such as American Express, Visa, and Thomas Cook are universally accepted as cash in shops, restaurants, and gas stations, and change from your transactions will be rendered in hard currency. Be sure to have plenty of $10 and $20 denominations, and don't be put off by "no checks" signs, which refer only to personal checks, which American businesses don't like one bit. Foreign travelers should not bring travelers checks issued in their own currencies; it can be hard to find a bank prepared to change them, and no other business is likely to accept them.

Emergencies

Having **money wired** from home using one of the companies listed in this section is never convenient or cheap, and should be considered a last resort. It's also possible to have money wired directly from a bank in your home country to a bank in the US, although this is somewhat less reliable because it involves two separate institutions. If you go this route, your home bank will need the address of the branch bank where you want to pick up the money and the address and telex number of the head office, which will act as the clearinghouse. Money wired this way normally takes two working days to arrive, and costs around the equivalent of $40 per transaction. Assuming you know someone prepared to send you money in a crisis, the quickest way is to have them take the cash to the nearest **Moneygram** (℡ 1-800/666-3947, ⓦ www .moneygram.com) office and have it instantaneously wired to the branch nearest you. In the US, this process should take no longer than ten minutes. They charge

according to the amount sent (ranging from $12 to wire $100, to $70 for $1000). The fees differ slightly if the money is being sent from outside the US (from the UK, for example, it costs $20 to wire $100, and $50 to wire $1000). **Thomas Cook** (℡ 1-800/287-7362, ⓦ www.thomascook.us) and **Western Union** (US ℡ 1-800/325-6000, UK ℡ 0800/833 833) offer a similar service, at slightly higher rates. If credit cards are involved, the latter charges an extra $10.

If you have a few days' leeway, it's cheaper to have someone mail you a postal **money order**, which is exchangeable at any post office (see p.25). The equivalent for foreign travelers is the international money order, for which you need to allow up to seven days in the mail. An ordinary (personal) check sent from overseas takes two to three weeks to clear.

Telephones, mail, email, and time zones

In general, keeping in touch with folks back home while traveling around the US is easy; you'll find a pay phone on the corner of every other block, and Internet cafés, especially in the big cities, are widespread. The exception would be in very rural areas where you may find it slightly frustrating getting to the nearest public phone – which may be many miles away. US telephones are run by a large number of local companies, the main ones being AT&T, Sprint, and Verizon.

Public telephones usually work, and in cities can be found everywhere – on street corners, in train and bus stations, hotel lobbies, bars, and restaurants. They take 25¢, 10¢, and 5¢ coins. The cost of a **local call** (ie, intracity) from a public phone is usually 50¢, sometimes 25¢ – when necessary, a voice comes on the line telling you to pay more.

Some numbers covered by the same area code are considered so far apart that calls between them count as **non-local** (zone calls). These cost much more and sometimes require you to dial 1 before the seven-digit number. Pricier still are **long-distance calls** (to a different area code, again with the 1 in front), for which you'll need plenty of

change. Non-local calls and long-distance calls are much less expensive if made between 6pm and 8am (the cheapest rates are 11pm–8am) and calls from **private phones** are always much cheaper than those from public phones. Detailed rates are listed at the front of the telephone directory (the *White Pages*, a copious source of information on many matters).

Making telephone calls **from hotel rooms** is usually more expensive than from a payphone, though some budget hotels offer free local calls – ask when you check in. An increasing number of phones accept both debit and credit cards, while anyone who holds a credit card issued by an American bank can obtain an **AT&T calling card**

Note that in the US, many businesses will use **"name" numbers** in an attempt to make their phone number easy to remember. For example, the number for the Arkansas Department of Parks & Tourism is 1-800/NATURAL (the corresponding number is the much less catchy 1-800/628-8725). This can be confusing to foreigners, but all US phones have letters as well as numbers printed on the dial – simply press those that correspond with the word.

International calls

International calls can be dialed direct from private or (more expensively) public phones. Most expensive of all is dialing direct from your hotel room, which often gets billed at the highest rate and then has a surcharge of up to forty percent slapped on top – so avoid doing this if at all possible. You can get assistance from the operator (☎0), who may also interrupt every three minutes asking for more money. The lowest **rates** for international calls to Europe are between 6pm and 7am, when the rate is about $5 for the first three minutes.

One of the most convenient ways of phoning home from abroad is via a **telephone charge card**. Using access codes for the particular country you are in, as well as a PIN number, you can make calls from most hotel, public, and private phones that will be charged to your own account. While rates are always cheaper from a residential phone at off-peak rates, that's normally not an option when you're traveling. If you do use a calling card in conjunction with a residential phone – when you're staying as a guest, for instance – you will be paying the calling card

company's rates, which will usually be more expensive than the local operator's. You may be able to use it to minimize hotel phone surcharges, but don't depend on it. Really, the benefit of calling cards is mainly one of **convenience**, as rates aren't necessarily cheaper than calling from a public phone while abroad and can't compete with discounted off-peak times many local phone companies offer. But because most major charge cards are free to obtain, it's certainly worth getting one at least for emergencies. If you like to chat on the phone for a long time, consider the **area-specific calling cards** on sale at delis and corner stores in most major urban areas. They come in denominations of $5, $10, and $20 and allow bargain overseas rates – calls to the UK work out around 3¢/minute from a private phone, slightly more from a pay phone.

In the **UK and Ireland**, British Telecom (☎0800/345 144, ⓦwww.payphones.bt.com/2001/phone_cards/chargecard/charge card.html) will issue free to all BT customers the BT Charge Card, which can be used in 116 countries. AT&T (dial ☎0800/890 011, then 888/641-6123 when you hear the AT&T prompt to be transferred to the Florida Call Center, free 24hr) has the Global Calling Card. NTL (☎0500/100 505) issues its own Global Calling Card, which can be used in more than sixty countries abroad, though the fees cannot be charged to a normal phone bill.

To call **Australia and New Zealand** from overseas, telephone charge cards such as Telstra Telecard or Optus Calling Card in Australia, and Telecom NZ's Calling Card can be used. Fees are charged back to a domestic account or credit card. Apply to Telstra (☎1800/038 000, ⓦwww.telstra.com.au), Optus (☎1300/300 990, ⓦwww.optus.com.au), or Telecom NZ (☎123 or ☎0800/800 070, ⓦwww.telecom.co.nz).

Toll-free numbers and area codes

Many government agencies, car rental firms, hotels, and so on have **toll-free numbers**, which usually have the prefix 1-800 (or, increasingly, 1-888 or 1-877). From within the US, you can dial any number that starts with those digits free of charge.

To make international calls from the US, dial ☎011 followed by the country code:
Australia 61
New Zealand 64
Republic of Ireland 353
UK and Northern Ireland 44
For codes not listed here, dial ☎0 for the operator or check the front of the local *White Pages*.

Mobile phones

If you're coming to the US **from overseas**, and want to use your **mobile** in America, you should ask your service provider if your phone will work abroad; and, if so, what the call charges will be. Unless you have an expensive tri-band phone, which will automatically switch to the US frequency, it is unlikely that a mobile bought for use outside the US will work inside the US. If you find out your phone won't work in the States, and shudder to think about being without a mobile, you might consider renting a phone or buying a cheap prepaid card phone for the duration of your stay in the USA.

US residents setting out on a cross-country trip should make sure that their mobile phone will work – and if additional charges will be imposed – when using the phone outside of its "home" area code. Travelers **from Canada** will have no problems using their phones, though they may have to pay roaming charges, depending on their plan and network.

Phone numbers with the prefix 1-900 are pay-per-call lines, generally quite expensive and almost always involving either sports or phone sex.

The US currently has about one hundred **area codes** – three-digit numbers that must precede the seven-figure number if you're calling from abroad or from a region with a different code. It can get confusing, especially as certain cities have several different area codes within their boundaries; for clarity, in this book, we've included the local area codes in all telephone numbers.

Mail

Post offices are usually open Monday to Friday from 9am until 5pm, and Saturday from 9am to noon, and there are blue mail boxes on many street corners. At time of publication, **mail within the US** cost 37¢ for a letter weighing up to an ounce. **Air mail** between the US and Europe may take a week. Postcards and aerograms to Europe are 70¢, while letters weighing up to an ounce (roughly four thin sheets) are 80¢. In the US, the last line of the address includes the city or town and an abbreviation denoting the state (California is "CA" and Texas is "TX," for example, though you can spell it in full if you're unsure; each abbreviation appears with the State Tourist Office addresses given in the box on pp.28–29). The last line also includes a five-digit number – the **zip code** – denoting the local post office. (The additional four digits that you will sometimes see appended to zip codes are not essential.) Letters that don't carry the

zip code may get lost or at least delayed, so be sure to include it; telephone directories carry a list for their service area. Alternatively, look on the US Postal Service website: ⓦ www.usps.com. Some addresses will contain what's called a **PO Box** number. This is used for mail only, and is not the actual address of a business or organization. If a place has both a PO Box number and a street address, know that the PO Box is for mail, and the street address for visiting.

Letters can be sent c/o **General Delivery** (what's known elsewhere as poste restante) to the relevant city's post office. They *must* include the zip code and will be held for only thirty days before being returned to sender – so make sure there's a return address on the envelope. If you're receiving mail at someone else's address, it should include "c/o" and the regular occupant's name; otherwise it, too, is likely to be returned.

Rules on sending **parcels** are very rigid: packages must be in special containers bought from post offices and sealed according to their instructions, which are given at the start of the *Yellow Pages*. To send anything out of the country, you'll need a green **customs declaration form**, available from a post office.

Email

One way to keep in touch while traveling is to sign up for a free Internet **email address** that can be accessed from anywhere. Yahoo! Mail or Hotmail, two of the largest providers, are accessible through

www.yahoo.com and www.hotmail
.com. Once you've set up an account, use
one of these sites to pick up and send mail
from any Internet café or hotel with Internet
access.

A useful website – www.kropla.com –
has information on how to plug in a laptop
when abroad, as well as phone country
codes around the world and details on electrical systems in different countries. For a
database of 8000 Internet cafés and public
Internet access points worldwide, go to
www.cybercaptive.com.

Time zones

The continental US spreads over four different **time zones**, plus one each for Alaska
and Hawaii; these are shown on the color
map at the front of this book. The Eastern
zone is five hours behind Greenwich Mean
Time (GMT), so 2pm London time is 10am in
New York City. The Central zone, starting
approximately on a line down from Chicago
and spreading west to Texas and across the
Great Plains, is an hour behind the East
(10am in New York is 9am in Dallas). The
Mountain zone, which covers the Rocky
Mountains and most of the Southwest, is
two hours behind the East Coast (10am in
New York is 8am in Denver). The Pacific
zone includes the three coastal states and
Nevada, and is three hours behind New York
(10am in the Big Apple is 7am in Los
Angeles). Lastly, most of Alaska (except for
the St Lawrence Islands, which are with
Hawaii; see below) is nine hours behind
GMT (noon in Alaska is 4pm in New York, or
9pm in London), while Hawaii is ten hours
behind GMT (noon in Honolulu is 5pm in
New York, or 10pm in London).

Information and maps

Each state has its own tourist office, as listed in the box on pp.28–29. These
offer prospective visitors a colossal range of free maps, leaflets, and
brochures. You can either contact them before you set off, or, as you travel
around the country, look for the state-run Welcome Centers, usually along main
highways close to the state borders. In heavily visited states, these often have
piles of discount coupons for cut-price accommodation and food. In addition,
visitor centers in most towns and cities – often known as the "Convention and
Visitors Bureau," or CVB, and listed throughout this book – provide details on
the area.

Maps

The free **road maps** distributed by each
state through its tourist offices and
Welcome Centers are usually fine for general driving and route planning. For something more detailed – say, for hiking purposes – camping shops generally have a
good selection, and park ranger stations in
national parks, state parks, and wilderness
areas all sell good-quality local hiking maps
for $1–3.

Rand McNally produces maps for each
state, bound together in the *Rand McNally*
Road Atlas, and runs 24 US stores
(call ☎1-800/333-0136 ext 2111, or visit
www.randmcnally.com for their locations
or maps by mail). Britain's best source for
maps is Stanfords, at 12–14 Long Acre,
London WC2E 9LP (☎020/7836 1321,
www.stanfords.co.uk); it also has a mail-
order service.

The **American Automobile Association**,
or AAA ("Triple A"; ☎1-877/244-9790,
www.aaa.com), based at 4100 E
Arkansas Drive, Denver, CO 80222, provides
free maps and assistance to its members,

and to British members of the AA and RAC. Call the main number to get the location of a branch near you; bring your membership card, or at least a copy of your membership number.

Map outlets

In the USA and Canada

Book Passage 51 Tamal Vista Blvd, Corte Madera, CA 94925 ☎415/927-0960, ⓦwww.bookpassage.com

Distant Lands 56 S Raymond Ave, Pasadena, CA 91105 ☎1-800/310-3220, ⓦwww.distantlands.com

Elliot Bay Book Company 101 S Main St, Seattle, WA 98104 ☎206/624-6600 or 1-800/962-5311, ⓦwww.elliotbaybook.com

Forsyth Travel Library 226 Westchester Ave, White Plains, NY 10604 ☎1-800/367-7984, ⓦwww.forsyth.com

Globe Corner Bookstore 28 Church St, Cambridge, MA 02138 ☎617/497-6277, ⓦwww.globecorner.com

Map Link 30 S La Patera Lane, unit 5, Santa Barbara, CA 93117 ☎805/692-6777, ⓦwww.maplink.com

Rand McNally 444 N Michigan Ave, Chicago, IL 60611 ☎312/321-1751; 150 E 52nd St, New York, NY 10022 ☎212/758-7488; 595 Market St, San Francisco, CA 94105 ☎415/777-3131; other stores across the US – call ☎1-800/333-0136 ext 2111 or visit ⓦwww.randmcnally.com for the nearest store.

Travel Books & Language Center 4437 Wisconsin Ave, Washington, DC 20016 ☎1-800/220-2665

The Travel Bug Bookstore 3065 W Broadway, Vancouver, BC V6K 2G29 ☎604/737-1122, ⓦwww.swifty.com/tbug

World of Maps 1235 Wellington St, Ottawa, ON K1Y 3A3 ☎613/724-6776, ⓦwww.worldofmaps.com

In the UK and Ireland

Blackwell's Map and Travel Shop 53 Broad St, Oxford OX1 3BQ ☎01865/792 792, ⓦwww.bookshop.blackwell.co.uk

Easons Bookshop 40 O'Connell St, Dublin 1 ☎01/873 3811, ⓦwww.eason.ie

Heffers Map and Travel 20 Trinity St, Cambridge CB2 1TJ ☎01223/568 568, ⓦwww.heffers.co.uk

James Thin Melven's Bookshop 29 Union St, Inverness IV1 1QA ☎01463/233 500, ⓦwww.jthin.co.uk

John Smith and Sons 127 Market St, St Andrews, Fife KY16 9PE ☎01334/475 122, ⓦwww.johnsmith.co.uk

The Map Shop 30a Belvoir St, Leicester LE1 6QH ☎0116/247 1400, ⓦwww.mapshopleicester.co.uk

National Map Centre 22-24 Caxton St, London SW1H 0QU ☎020/7222 2466, ⓦwww.mapsnmc.co.uk

Newcastle Map Centre 55 Grey St, Newcastle upon Tyne NE1 6EF ☎0191/261 5622

Ordnance Survey of Northern Ireland Colby House, Stranmillis Court, Belfast BT9 5BJ ☎028/9066 1244, ⓦwww.ordsvy.gov.uk/getamap

Ordnance Survey Service Phoenix Park, Dublin 8 ☎01/820 5300

Stanfords 12–14 Long Acre, London WC2E 9LP ☎020/7836 1321, ⓦwww.stanfords.co.uk. Other branches within British Airways offices at 156 Regent St, London W1R 5TA ☎020/7434 4744 and 29 Corn St, Bristol BS1 1HT ☎0117/929 9966.

The Travel Bookshop 13-15 Blenheim Crescent, London W11 2EE ☎020/7229 5260, ⓦwww.thetravelbookshop.co.uk

In Australia and New Zealand

The Map Shop 6 Peel St, Adelaide, South Australia 5000 ☎08/8231 2033, ⓦwww.mapshop.net.au

Mapland 372 Little Bourke St, Melbourne, Victoria 3000 ☎03/9670 4383, ⓦwww.mapland.com.au

Mapworld 173 Gloucester St, Christchurch ☎03/374 5399, ⓦwww.mapworld.co.nz

Specialty Maps 46 Albert St, Auckland ☎09/307 2217

Alabama Alabama Bureau of Tourism & Travel, PO Box 4927, Montgomery, AL 36103-4927 ☎334/242-4169 or 1-800/ALABAMA, ⓦwww.touralabama.org

Alaska Alaska Travel Industry Association, 2600 Cordova St, suite 201, Anchorage, AK 99503 ☎907/929-284, ⓦwww.travelalaska.com

Arizona Arizona Office of Tourism, 1110 W Washington St, suite 155, Phoenix, AZ 85007 ☎1-866/275-5816, ⓦwww.arizonaguide.com

Arkansas Arkansas Dept of Parks & Tourism, One Capitol Mall, Little Rock, AR 72201 ☎501/682-7777 or 1-800/NATURAL, ⓦwww.arkansas.com

California California Division of Tourism, PO Box 1499, Sacramento, CA 95812 ☎916/856-5200 or 1-800/GO-CALIF, ⓦwww.gocalif.com

Colorado Colorado Tourism Office, 1625 Broadway, suite 1700, Denver, CO 80202 ☎303/892-3885 or 1-800/265-6723, ⓦwww.colorado.com

Connecticut Connecticut Tourism Division, 505 Hudson St, Hartford, CT 06106 ☎860/270-8081 or 1-800/282-6863, ⓦwww.ctbound.org

Delaware Delaware State Tourism Office, 99 Kings Hwy, Dover, DE 19901 ☎302/739-4271 or 1-866/284-7483, ⓦwww.visitdelaware.net

Florida Visit Florida, 661 E Jefferson St, Tallahassee, FL 32399 ☎850/488-5607 or 1-888/735-2872, ⓦwww.flausa.com

Georgia Georgia Dept of Industry, Trade & Tourism, 285 Peachtree Center Ave, suite 1000, Atlanta, GA 30303 ☎404/656-3590 or 1-800/847-4842, ⓦwww.georgia.org

Hawaii Hawaii Visitors Bureau, 2270 Kalakaua Ave, suite 801, Honolulu, HI 96815 ☎808/923-1811 or 1-800/464-2924, ⓦwww.gohawaii.com

Idaho Idaho Travel Council, 700 W State St, Boise, ID 83720 ☎208/334-2470 or 1-800/842-5858, ⓦwww.visitid.org

Illinois Illinois Bureau of Tourism, 100 W Randolph St, suite 3-400, Chicago, IL 60601 ☎312/814-4732 or 1-800/226-6632, ⓦwww.enjoyillinois.com

Indiana Indiana Dept of Tourism, 1 N Capitol Ave, suite 700, Indianapolis, IN 46204-2288 ☎317/232-8860 or 1-888/365-6946, ⓦwww.indianatourism.com

Iowa Iowa Division of Tourism, 200 E Grand Ave, Des Moines, IA 50309 ☎515/242-4705 or 1-888/472-6035, ⓦwww.traveliowa.com

Kansas Kansas Travel & Tourism Division, 700 SW Harrison St, suite 1300, Topeka, KS 66603 ☎785/296-2009 or 1-800/252-6727, ⓦwww.travelks.com

Kentucky Kentucky Dept of Travel, 500 Mero St, suite 2200, Frankfort, KY 40601 ☎502/564-4930 or 1-800/225-8747, ⓦwww.kentuckytourism.com

Louisiana Louisiana Office of Tourism, PO Box 94291, Baton Rouge, LA 70804-9291 ☎225/342-8100 or 1-888/225-4003, ⓦwww.louisianatravel.com

Maine Maine Office of Tourism, 59 State House Station, Augusta, ME 04333-0059, ☎1-888/624-6345, ⓦwww.visitmaine.com

Maryland Maryland Office of Tourism, 217 E Redwood St, 9th floor, Baltimore, MD 21202 ☎1-800/634-7386, ⓦwww.mdisfun.org

Massachusetts Massachusetts Division of Tourism, 10 Park Plaza, suite 4510, Boston, MA 02116 ☎617/973-8500 or 1-800/227-6277, ⓦwww.massvacation.com

Michigan Travel Michigan, PO Box 26128, Lansing, MI 48909 ☎517/373-0670 or 1-888/784-7328, ⓦtravel.michigan.org

Minnesota Minnesota Office of Tourism, 100 Metro Square, 121 7th Place E, St Paul, MN 55101 ☎651/296-5029 or 1-800/657-3700, ⓦwww.exploreminnesota.com

Mississippi Mississippi Division of Tourism, PO Box 849, Jackson, MS 39205-0849 ☎601/359-3297 or 1-866/733-6477, ⓦwww.visitmississippi.org

Missouri Missouri Division of Tourism, PO Box 1055, Jefferson City, MO 65102 ☎573/751-4133 or 1-800/810-5500, ⓦwww.missouritourism.org

Montana Travel Montana, 301 South Park, PO Box 200533, Helena, MT 59620 ☎406/841-2870 or 1-800/847-4868, ⓦwww.visitmt.org

Nebraska Nebraska Travel & Tourism, PO Box 98907, Lincoln, NE 68509 ☎402/471-3796 or 1-877/NEBRASKA, ⓦwww.visitnebraska.org

Nevada Nevada Commission on Tourism, 401 N Carson St, Carson City, NV 89701 ☎775/687-4322 or 1-800/638-2328, ⒲www.travelnevada.com

New Hampshire New Hampshire Office of Travel, 172 Pembroke Rd, Concord, NH 03302 ☎603/271-2655 or 1-800/386-4664, ⒲www.visitnh.gov

New Jersey New Jersey Division of Travel & Tourism, PO Box 820, Trenton, NJ 08625-0820 ☎609/777-0885 or 1-800/847-4865, ⒲www.state.nj.us/travel

New Mexico New Mexico Dept of Tourism, 491 Old Santa Fe Trail, PO Box 20002, Santa Fe, NM 87501 ☎505/827-7400 or 1-800/733-6396, ⒲www.newmexico.org

New York City New York City CVB, 810 7th Ave, New York, NY 10019 ☎212/484-1222, ⒲www.nycvisit.com

New York State Empire State Plaza, main concourse, room 10, Albany, NY 12220 ☎518/474-4116 or 1-800/225-5697, ⒲www.iloveny.com/main.asp

North Carolina North Carolina Travel & Tourism, 301 N Wilmington St, Raleigh, NC 27601-2825 ☎919/733-8372 or 1-800/847-4862, ⒲www.visitnc.com

North Dakota North Dakota Tourism Division, Century Center, 1600 E Century Ave, suite 2, Bismarck, ND 58503 ☎701/328-2525 or 1-800/435-5663, ⒲www.ndtourism.com

Ohio Ohio Office of Travel & Tourism, PO Box 1001, Columbus, OH 43266 ☎614/466-8844 or 1-800/282-5393, ⒲www.ohiotourism.com

Oklahoma Oklahoma Travel & Tourism Division, PO Box 52002, Oklahoma City, OK 73102 ☎405/521-2406 or 1-800/652-6552, ⒲www.travelok.com

Oregon Oregon Tourism Commission, 775 Summer St NE, Salem, OR 97310 ☎503/986-0000 or 1-800/547-7842, ⒲www.traveloregon.com

Pennsylvania Pennsylvania Bureau of Travel, room 404, Forum Building, Harrisburg, PA 17120 ☎717/787-5453 or 1-800/847-4872, ⒲www.experiencepa.com

Rhode Island Rhode Island Tourism Division, One W Exchange St, Providence, RI 02903 ☎401/222-2601 or 1-800/556-

2484, ⒲www.visitrhodeisland.com

South Carolina South Carolina Parks, Recreation, and Tourism, Dept of International Marketing, 1205 Pendleton St, Columbia, SC 29201 ☎803/734-1700 or 1-800/346-3634, ⒲www.discoversouthcarolina.com

South Dakota South Dakota Dept of Tourism, c/o 500 E Capitol Ave, Pierre, SD 57501 ☎605/773-3301 or 1-800/732-5682, ⒲www.travelsd.com

Tennessee Tennessee Dept of Tourism, Rachel Jackson Building, 320 6th Ave, 5th floor, Nashville, TN 37243 ☎615/741-2159 or 1-800/462-8366, ⒲www.tnvacation.com

Texas Texas Dept of Commerce, Tourism Division, PO Box 141009, Austin, TX 78714-1009 ☎512/462-9191 or 1-800/888-8839, ⒲www.traveltex.com

Utah Utah Travel Council, Council Hall, Capitol Hill, Salt Lake City, UT 84114 ☎801/538-1030 or 1-800/200-1160, ⒲www.utah.com

Vermont Vermont Dept of Tourism and Marketing, 6 Baldwin St, drawer 33, Montpelier, VT 05633 ☎802/828-3676 or 1-800/837-6668, ⒲www.travel-vermont.com

Virginia Virginia Tourism Corp, 901 E Bird St, Richmond, VA 23219 ☎804/786-4484 or 1-800/847-4882, ⒲www.virginia.org

Washington DC Washington DC Visitor Information, 1212 New York Ave NW, suite 200, Washington, DC 20005 ☎202/789-7000 or 1-800/422-8644, ⒲www.washington.org

Washington Washington State Tourism, PO Box 42500, Olympia, WA 98504 ☎360/725-5052 or 1-800/544-1800, ⒲www.tourism.wa.gov

West Virginia West Virginia Division of Tourism, 90 MacCorkle Ave SW, Charleston, WV 25303 ☎304/558-2200 or 1-800/225-5982, ⒲www.callwva.com

Wisconsin Wisconsin Dept of Tourism, 201 W Washington Ave, PO Box 7976, Madison, WI 53707 ☎608/266-2161 or 1-800/432-8747, ⒲www.travelwisconsin.com

Wyoming Wyoming Division of Tourism, I-25 at College Drive, Cheyenne, WY 82002 ☎307/777-7777 or 1-800/225-5996, ⒲www.wyomingtourism.org

Getting around

Distances in the US are so great that it's essential to think carefully in advance about how you plan to get from place to place. Your choice of transportation will have a crucial impact on your trip. Amtrak provides a skeletal but often scenic rail service, and there are usually good bus links between the major cities – though Greyhound, the mainstay of the US bus network, has cut back on routes as of late. But even in rural areas, by adroit advance planning, you can usually reach the main points of interest without too much trouble by using local buses and charter services.

That said, travel is almost always easier if you have a **car**. Also, many worthwhile and memorable US destinations are far removed from cities: even if a bus or train can take you to the general vicinity of one of the great national parks, for example, it can be nearly impossible to explore the area without a vehicle. For that matter, the cities themselves can be so vast, and so heavily car-oriented, that the lack of a car can seriously impair your enjoyment.

By train

Traveling by **rail** is rarely the fastest way to get from point A to point B, though if you have the time it can be a pleasant and relaxing experience. As you will see from our map, opposite, the Amtrak system isn't at all comprehensive – such popular destinations as Nashville and Santa Fe, and even some entire states, are left out altogether. What's more, the cross-country routes tend to be served by one or at most two trains per day, so in large areas of the nation the only train of the day passes through at three or four in the morning. That said, the train is by far the most comfortable way to travel, and especially on long-distance rides it can be a great way to meet people. A number of local train services connect stops on the Amtrak lines with towns and cities not on the main grid. Amtrak also runs the coordinated Thruway **bus service** that connects some cities that their trains don't reach. However, this network is not comprehensive, either.

For any one specific journey, the train can be more **expensive** than taking a Greyhound bus, or even a plane – the standard rail fare from New York to Los Angeles, for example, is around $150 one-way – though special deals, especially in the off-peak seasons (Sept–May), bring the cost of a coast-to-coast round-trip down to well around $250. In addition to these, Amtrak's All Aboard America fares, allowing three stopovers en route, are available by region (Florida, for some reason, is excluded). Foreign travelers can benefit from the passes detailed in the box on p.32.

Always **reserve as far in advance** as possible; all passengers must have seats, and some trains, especially between major East Coast cities, are booked solid. Sleeping compartments (which are around $300 per night, including three full meals, for one or two people) and the plush Metroliner carriages cost extra. However, even standard Amtrak carriages are surprisingly spacious, and there are additional dining cars and lounge cars (with full bars and sometimes glass-domed 360° viewing compartments).

Beautiful East Coast Amtrak trips include the Hudson River Valley north of New York City (on several routes); along the Potomac River at Harpers Ferry, West Virginia (on the *Capitol Limited* out of Washington, DC); and the New River Gorge (on the *Cardinal*). In the West, the *California Zephyr*, which runs between Chicago and San Francisco, follows a stunning route west of Denver over the Rockies, rivaled a day later by the towering Sierra Nevada. Last but not least, the *Coast Starlight* gives unsurpassed views of the California coast on its journey between San Luis Obispo and Santa Barbara. Verify when you book your journey that the train passes through the scenic splendor during daylight hours.

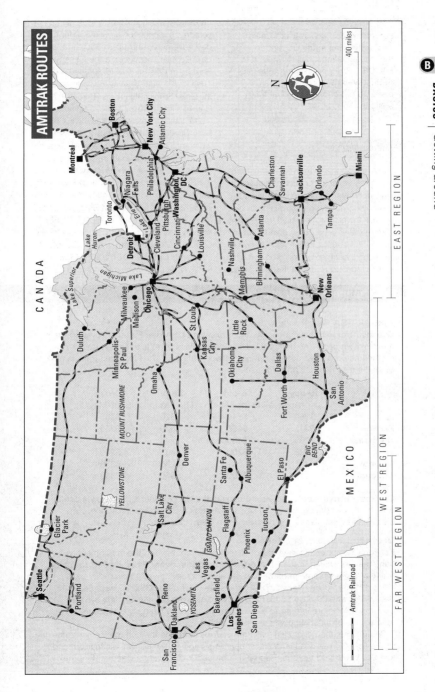

AMTRAK ROUTES

CANADA

MEXICO

—— Amtrak Railroad

0   400 miles

N

EAST REGION

WEST REGION

FAR WEST REGION

For information on **Amtrak fares and schedules** in the US, and to make reservations, call toll-free ☎1-800/USA-RAIL, or check out the Amtrak **website**, ⓦwww.amtrak.com. Do not phone individual train stations.

Historic railroads

While Amtrak has a monopoly on long-distance rail travel, a number of **historic** or **scenic railways**, some steam-powered or running along narrow-gauge mining tracks, bring back the glory days of train travel. Many are purely tourist attractions, doing a full circuit through beautiful countryside in two or three hours, though some can drop you off in otherwise hard-to-reach wilderness areas.

Fares vary widely according to the length of your trip, but count on around $30 for a half-day adventure, and up to $60 for a whole day. Popular lines include the Cass Scenic Railroad in West Virginia (☎304/456-4300 or 1-800/2255 982, ⓦwww.cassrailroad.com); the Great Smoky Mountains Railroad in North Carolina (☎1-800/872-4681, ⓦwww.gsmr.com); the Cumbres and Toltec line in Chama, New Mexico (☎1-888/286-2737, ⓦwww.cumbrestoltec.com); the Durango & Silverton Narrow Gauge Railroad in Colorado (☎1-800/872–4607, ⓦwww.durangotrain.com); the Big Trees and Roaring Camp Railroad in Santa Cruz (☎831/335-4484, ⓦwww.roaringcampprr.com) and the Fort Bragg-Willits line (☎707/964-6371 or 1-800/777-5865, ⓦwww.skunktrain.com), both in California; and the Mount Hood Railroad, outside Portland, Oregon (☎541/386-3556 or 1-800/872 4611, ⓦwww.mthoodrr.com).

Pre-trip planning for overseas travelers

Amtrak USA Rail Passes
Overseas travelers have a choice of the following **USA Rail Passes**, covering the areas shown on the map on p.31. The Coastal Pass permits unlimited train travel on the East and West coasts, but not between the two. The Northeast Pass is also available as a five-day offer, for $149.

	15-day (June–Aug)	15-day (Sept–May)	30-day (June–Aug)	30-day (Sept–May)
East	$260	$210	$320	$265
Far West	$245	$190	$320	$250
Northeast	$205	$185	$240	$225
West	$325	$200	$405	$270
Coastal	–	–	$285	$235
National	$440	$295	$550	$385

On production of a passport issued outside the US or Canada, the passes can be bought at Amtrak stations in the US. The Amtrak website, ⓦwww.amtrak.com, also lists several places you can buy them internationally.

Greyhound Discovery Passes
Foreign visitors, especially those inclined to venture beyond the major meccas, can – before leaving home – buy a **Greyhound Discovery Pass**. It offers unlimited travel within a set time period. Most travel agents sell them. A seven-day pass costs $219; a 10-day pass $279; 15 days $349; 21 days $399; 30 days $459; 45 days $519; and 60 days $649. Passes combining the US and Canada are also available – for more info go to ⓦwww.greyhound.com. No daily extensions are available. International agents are listed below.

On first use, the ticket clerk will date your pass (this is the commencement date of the ticket). Your destination is written on a page that the driver will tear out and keep as you board the bus. Repeat this procedure for every subsequent journey.

By bus

If you're traveling on your own and making a lot of stops, **buses**, by far the cheapest way to get around, make a lot of sense. The main long-distance operator, **Greyhound** (☎1-800/229-9424, ⓦwww.greyhound.com) links all major cities and many towns. Out in the country, buses are fairly scarce, sometimes appearing only once a day; here, you'll need to plot your route with care. However, along the main highways, buses run around the clock to a fairly full timetable, stopping only for meal breaks (almost always fast-food dives) and driver changeovers. Greyhound buses are slightly less uncomfortable than you might expect.

To avoid possible hassle, lone **female travelers** in particular should take care to sit as near to the driver as possible, and to arrive during daylight hours – many bus stations are in fairly dodgy areas. It used to be that any sizable community would have a Greyhound station; now, in some places, the post office or a gas station doubles as the bus stop and ticket office, and in many others bus service has been canceled altogether. **Reservations**, either in person at the station or via the toll-free number, are not essential, but recommended – if a bus is full, and you don't have a reservation, you may be forced to wait until the next one, sometimes overnight or longer.

Fares on shorter journeys average out at about 12¢ a mile, but discounts are common on longer hauls (for example, it could cost you $126 to get a round-trip ticket from Los Angeles to San Francisco, but for $250 you could get all the way to New York and back). For long-trip travel though, considering thewide routes, but this is not distributed to travelers. To plan your route, pick up the free route-by-route timetables from larger bus stations.

Where to buy Amtrak and Greyhound passes abroad

STA Travel UK ☎0870/160 0599, ⓦwww.statravel.co.uk; Australia ☎1300/360 960, ⓦwww.statravel.com.au; New Zealand ☎0800/874 773, ⓦwww.statravel.co.nz

Trailfinders UK ☎020/7628 7628, ⓦwww.trailfinders.com; Republic of Ireland ☎01/677 7888, ⓦwww.trailfinders.ie; Australia ☎02/9247 6556, ⓦwww.trailfinders.com.au

USIT UK ☎0870/240 1010, ⓦwww.usitcampus.co.uk; Republic of Ireland ☎01/602 1600, ⓦwww.usitnow.ie; Australia ☎02/9232 8444, ⓦwww.usitbeyond.com.au; New Zealand ☎09/379 4224, ⓦwww.usitbeyond.co.nz

Walshes World Australia ☎02/9232 7499 or 1800/227 122; New Zealand ☎09/379 3708

Air passes

The main American airlines (and British Airways, in conjunction with various carriers) offer **air passes** for visitors who plan to fly a lot within the US. These must be bought in advance. In the UK, they are usually sold with the proviso that you cross the Atlantic with the same airline or group of airlines (such as Star Alliance). All the deals involve the purchase of between three and ten coupons; the North America Airpass offered by United, Mexicana, and Air Canada, for instance, can charge as little as $130 per pass, depending on the number of coupons bought and the season. Each coupon is valid for a flight of any duration in the 48 contiguous US states – you purchase additional coupons for flights to Alaska and Hawaii at varying rates. American Airlines, Northwest, and Continental offer comparable itineraries. The situation is similar for Australasian visitors.

Other plans entitle foreign travelers to **discounts** on regular US domestic fares, again with the proviso that you buy the ticket before you leave home. However you do it, flying within the US is only a wise choice for travel in regions where fares are low anyway; flights within Florida, for example, are very expensive.

time expended (around 65 hours coast-to-coast, if you eat and sleep on the bus), riding the bus is not necessarily a much better deal than flying, unless you plan to do a lot of stops using a **Discovery Pass** (see p.32).

By plane

Don't be misled by movie scenes in which characters stroll into large airports and casually buy cross-country tickets. That kind of plane travel is outrageously expensive – $1000 for a one-way flight is not unheard of. However, with planning, air travel can work out to be quite reasonable; indeed, it can cost less than the train – especially if you take into account how much you save not paying for food and drink while on the move – and only a little more than the bus. Flying can also make sense for relatively short local hops, turning a full day's cross-desert $25 bus journey, for example, into a quick and scenic $50 flight of under an hour. We mention such options wherever appropriate throughout this guide.

Most airlines offer comparable **Apex** (see p.10) fares, but any good travel agent, especially student- and youth-oriented ones like Council Travel and STA, can usually get you a much **better deal**. Phone the airlines or visit their websites to find out routes and schedules, then buy your ticket using the Fare Assurance Program, which processes all the ticket options to find the cheapest fare, taking into account the requirements of individual travelers. One agent using the service is Travel Avenue (℡1-800/333-3335, ⓦwww .travelavenue.com). Few standby fares are available, and the best discounts are usually offered on tickets booked and paid for at least two weeks in advance. These are almost always nonrefundable and hard to change.

Toll-free airline numbers and websites in the US

Aer Lingus ℡1-800/232-6537, ⓦwww.aerlingus.ie
Air Canada ℡1-888/247-2262, ⓦwww.aircanada.ca
Air France ℡1-800/237-2747, ⓦwww.airfrance.com
Alaska Airlines ℡1-800/426-0333, ⓦwww.alaskaair.com
Alitalia ℡1-800/223-5730, ⓦwww.alitaliausa.com
America West ℡1-800/235-9292, ⓦwww.americawest.com
American Airlines ℡1-800/433-7300, ⓦwww.aa.com
American Trans Air ℡1-800/435-9282, ⓦwww.ata.com
British Airways ℡1-800/247-9297, ⓦwww.british-airways.com
Cathay Pacific ℡1-800/233-2742, ⓦwww.cathay-usa.com
Continental Airlines international ℡1-800/231-0856, domestic ℡1-800/523-3723, ⓦwww.continental.com
Delta Airlines international ℡1-800/241-4141, domestic ℡1-800/221-1212, ⓦwww.delta.com
Hawaiian Airlines ℡1-800/367-5320, ⓦwww.hawaiianair.com
Iberia ℡1-800/772-4642, ⓦwww.iberia.com
Icelandair ℡1-800/223-5500, ⓦwww .icelandair.com
orthwest Airlines international ℡1-800/447-4747, domestic ℡1-800/225-2525, ⓦwww.nwa.com
Qantas ℡1-800/227-4500, ⓦwww.qantas.com
SAS ℡1-800/221-2350, ⓦwww.scandinavian.net

Green Tortoise

One alternative to Long-Distance Bus Hell is the fun, countercultural **Green Tortoise**, whose buses, complete with foam cushions, bunks, fridges, and rock music, ply the major cities of the West Coast, running between Los Angeles, San Francisco, and Seattle. In summer, they also cross the country to New York and Boston, trips that amount to mini-tours of the nation, taking twelve to fourteen days ($499–539, not including food) and allowing plenty of stops for hiking, river-rafting, and hot springs. Other Green Tortoise excursions go to the major national parks (in 16 days for $659), south to Mexico ($399–599 for between nine and 17 days), and north to Alaska ($1699 for 28 days, including airfare from Alaska, or $699 for 14 days, excluding flight). Green Tortoise's main office is at 494 Broadway, San Francisco, CA 94133 (℡415/956-7500 or 1-800/867-8647, ⓦwww.greentortoise.com).

Japan Airlines ☏1-800/525-3663,
ⓦwww.japanair.com
JetBlue ☏1-800/538-2583, ⓦwww.jetblue.com
KLM ☏1-800/374-7747, ⓦwww.klm.com
Lufthansa ☏1-800/645-3880,
ⓦwww.lufthansa.com
NSouthwest ☏1-800/435-9792,
ⓦwww.southwest.com
Swissair ☏1-800/221-4750,
ⓦwww.swissair.com
TWA international ☏1-800/892-4141, domestic
☏1-800/221-2000, ⓦwww.twa.com
United Airlines international ☏1-800/538-2929,
domestic ☏1-800/241-6522, ⓦwww.ual.com
US Airways international ☏1-800/622-1015,
domestic ☏1-800/428-4322,
ⓦwww.usairways.com
Virgin Atlantic ☏1-800/862-8621,
ⓦwww.virgin-atlantic.com

By car

For many people, the concept of cruising
down the highway, preferably in an open-top
convertible with the radio blasting, is one of
the main reasons to set out on a tour of the
US. The romantic images of countless road
movies, from *Bonnie and Clyde* to *Thelma
and Louise*, are not far from the truth, though
you don't have to embark on a wild spree of
drink, drugs, crime, and murder to enjoy
driving across America. Apart from anything else, a car makes it possible to choose
your own itinerary and to explore the wide-
open landscapes that may well provide your
most enduring memories of the country.

Driving in the cities, on the other hand, is
not exactly fun, but places tend to be so
large that a car is by far the most convenient
way to negotiate your way around, especially
as public transportation may be spotty outside the major cities. Many cities, especially
in the West, have grown up and assumed
their present shapes since cars were
invented. As such, they sprawl for so many
miles in all directions – Los Angeles and
Houston are classic examples – that your
hotel may be fifteen or twenty miles from the
sights you came to see, or perhaps simply
on the other side of a freeway that can't be
crossed on foot. Only in a few cities, more
often in the East, are the main attractions
and facilities concentrated within walking
distance of each other. Even in smaller
towns the motels may be six miles or more

out along the interstate, and the restaurants
in a brand-new shopping mall on the far side
of town.

Drivers wishing to **rent cars** are supposed
to have held their licenses for at least one year
(though this is rarely checked); people under
25 years old may encounter problems, and
will probably get stuck with a higher than normal insurance premium, plus a daily supplement of around $20. **Car rental companies**
(listed overleaf) will also expect you to have a
credit card; if you don't have one, they may let
you leave a hefty deposit (at least $200, cash),
but don't count on it. The likeliest tactic for
getting a good deal is to phone the major
firms' toll-free numbers and ask for their best
rates – most will try to beat the offers of their
competitors, so it's worth haggling.

In general, the **lowest rates** are available
at the airport branches – $150 a week for a
compact is a fairly standard budget rate,
Keep in mind that rates are always more
expensive in the Northeast. Always be sure
to get free unlimited mileage. Leaving the car
in a different city from the one in which you
rent it is likely to incur a **drop-off charge** –
as much as $200 or more (though these
rules vary greatly depending on the rental
company). Also, don't automatically go for
the cheapest rate, as there's a big difference
in the quality of cars from company to company; industry leaders like Alamo, Hertz, and
Avis tend to have newer, lower-mileage cars,
often with air-conditioning and stereo CD
players as standard equipment – no small
consideration on a 2000-mile desert drive.

Alternatively, various **local companies** rent
out new and not so new vehicles. They are
certainly cheaper than the big chains if you
just want to spin around a city for a day, but
free mileage is not included, so they work
out far more costly for long-distance travel.
Look for them in the *Yellow Pages* of the
telephone directory.

When you rent a car, read the small print
carefully for details on **Collision Damage
Waiver (CDW)**, sometimes called Liability
Damage Waiver (LDW), usually included in
the price if you pre-pay outside the US, but

Specific information on public transportation and car rental for **travelers
with disabilities** can be found on p.40.

Car rental companies

	US	UK
Alamo	☎1-800/462-5266 ⓦwww.alamo.com	☎0870/400 4562 ⓦwww.alamo.co.uk
Avis	☎1-800/230-4898 ⓦwww.avis.com	☎0870/606 0100
Budget	☎1-800/527-0700 ⓦwww.budgetrentacar.com	☎01442/276 266
Dollar	☎1-800/800-3665 ⓦwww.dollar.com	☎0800/085 5478 ⓦwww.dollar.co.uk
Enterprise	☎1-800/325-8007 ⓦwww.enterprise.com	☎0870/350 3000
Hertz	☎1-800/654-3001 ⓦwww.hertz.com	☎0870/844 8844
Holiday Autos	☎1-800/422 7737 ⓦwww.holidayautos.com	☎0990/300 400 ⓦwww.holidayautos.co.uk
National	☎1-800/227-7368 ⓦwww.nationalcar.com	☎0870/536 5365 ⓦwww.nationalcar.co.uk
Rent-a-Wreck	☎1-800/944-7501 ⓦwww.rent-a-wreck.com	
Thrifty	☎1-800/847-4389 ⓦwww.thrifty.com	☎01494/751 4600 ⓦwww.thrifty.co.uk,

well worth considering if it isn't. This form of insurance specifically covers the car that you are driving yourself – you are in any case insured for damage to other vehicles. At $10–15 a day, it can add substantially to the total cost, but without it you're liable for every scratch to the car – even those that aren't your fault. Some credit card companies offer automatic CDW coverage to Americans and Canadians using their card; read the fine print beforehand in any case.

Increasing numbers of states (New York, for one) are requiring that this insurance be included in the weekly rental rate and are regulating the amounts charged to cut down on rental-car company profiteering. Companies may also check up on the driving records of would-be renters and refuse to rent to high-risk drivers.

Another policy that rental companies try to get you to accept (and they've trained their staff to drive fear deep into your soul about this one) is **liability cover** if you cause injury to others while in a rental car. This usually costs around the same as CDW, and when both these are taken together, with taxes, it can double the cost of the rental. It's worth reading the small print of your holiday insurance to see if you are covered: the American Express annual Premier Plus policy, available only to UK residents, includes up to $50,000 CDW coverage and $1 million top-up liability (☎0800/028 7574); the policy pays for itself in two weeks.

In case you **break down** in a rented car, call the emergency number pinned to the dashboard. Otherwise, sit tight and wait for the highway patrol or state police, who cruise by regularly. Raising your car hood is a call for assistance, although **women traveling alone** should be wary of doing this. Another tip, for women especially, is to rent a

Ireland	Australia	New Zealand
☏ 01/428 1111 ⓦ www.avis.ie	☏ 13 63 33	☏ 0800/655 111
☏ 01/878 7814 ⓦ www.budget.com.au	☏ 1300/362 848 ⓦ www.budget.co.nz	☏ 0800/652 227
☏ 1850/206 088 ⓦ www.irishcarrentals.com		
☏ 0870/350 3000		
☏ 01/813 3416 ⓦ www.hertz.ie	☏ 1800/550 067	☏ 0800/655 955
☏ 01/454 9090	☏ 0800/144 040 ⓦ www.holidayautos.com.au	☏ 0800/144 040 ⓦ www.holidayautos.co.nz
☏ 028/9045 0904	☏ 13 10 45 ⓦ www.nationalcar.com.au	☏ 0800/800 115 ⓦ www.nationalcar.co.nz
☏ 1800/515 800 ⓦ www.thrifty.ie	☏ 1300/367 227 ⓦ www.thrifty.com.au	☏ 0800/737 070 ⓦ www.thrifty.co.nz

mobile telephone from the car rental agency – you often have to pay only a nominal amount until you actually use it; in larger cities, they increasingly come built into the car. Having a phone can be reassuring at least, and a potential lifesaver should something go wrong (see p.21).

Driveaways

One variation on renting is a **driveaway**: you drive a car from one place to another for the owner, paying only for the gas you use. The same rules as for renting apply, but look the car over before you take it; you'll be charged for any repair costs in addition to a large fuel bill if it's a big gas-guzzler. Some driveaway companies want a personal reference from someone either in the town you're leaving or in the car's eventual destination. Get in touch in advance, to spare yourself a week's wait for

a car to turn up. The most common routes are between the coasts, but there's a fair chance of finding something that needs transporting to where you want to go. You needn't drive flat out, although three to four hundred miles a day – around six hours – is expected. Look under Automobile Transporters in the *Yellow Pages* and phone around for current offers, or try one of the sixty branches of Auto Driveaway, 310 S Michigan Ave, Chicago, IL 60604 (☏ 312/939-3600 or ☏ 1-800/346-2277, ⓦ www.autodriveaway.com).

Renting an RV

Recreational vehicles (**RVs**) – those juggernauts that rumble down the highway, often complete with multiple bedrooms, bathrooms, and kitchens – can be rented from around $900 per week for a basic camper on the back of a pickup truck. Though good for groups or

Driving for foreigners

Fly-drive deals are good value if you want to **rent** a car (see p.13), though you can save up to sixty percent simply by booking in advance with a major firm. If you choose not to pay until you arrive, be sure you take a written confirmation of the price with you. Remember that it's safer not to drive just after a long transatlantic flight – and that most standard rental cars have **automatic transmissions**.

UK, Irish, Australian, and NZ nationals can drive in the US on a **full driving license** (International Driving Permits are not always regarded as sufficient). If you want to book an **RV** (see overleaf), it's easier and cheaper to do this from abroad. Most travel agents who specialize in the US can arrange RV rental, and usually do it cheaper if you book a flight through them as well. A price of US$650 for a five-berth van for two weeks is fairly typical.

families traveling together, these can be unwieldy on the road. Also, rental outlets are not so common. On top of the rental fees, take into account the cost of **gas** (some RVs get twelve miles to the gallon or less) and any **drop-off charges**, in case you plan a one-way trip across the country. It is rarely legal simply to pull off in an RV and spend the night at the roadside: you are expected to stay in designated RV parks that cost up to $20 per night. The Recreational Vehicle Dealers Association, 3930 University Drive, Fairfax, VA 22030 (☎703/591-7130, ⊛www.rvda.org), publishes a newsletter and a directory of rental firms.

By bike

In general, **cycling** is a cheap and healthy way to get around all the big cities, an increasing number of which have cycle lanes and local buses equipped to carry bikes (strapped to the outside). In country areas, roads are usually well maintained and have wide shoulders. For a $15 fee, Greyhound will take bikes (so long as they're in a box or other carrying case not exceeding 8" by 32" by 60"). For a $5 fee, Amtrak will transport your bike, though they ask you to reserve in advance and have your bike in a container; bicycles may only travel as checked luggage. A number of companies organize multiday cycle tours, with camping or

stays in country inns; we've mentioned local firms where appropriate. The biggest nationwide organization is the not-for-profit Adventure Cycling Association (formerly Bikecentennial), 150 E Pine St, PO Box 8308, Missoula, MT 59807 (☎406/721-1776 or 1-800/755-2453, ⊛www.adv-cycling.org), which was founded in 1974 to promote transcontinental cycle trips. It publishes maps ($11 each, or $8 for members) of several 400-mile routes, detailing campgrounds, motels, restaurants, bike shops, and sites of interest. Many individual states issue their own **cycling guides**; contact the tourist offices listed on pp.28–29. Backroads Bicycle Tours, 801 Cedar St, Berkeley, CA 94710-1800 (☎510/527-1555 or 1-800/462-2848, ⊛www.backroads.com), and the HI-AYH hosteling group (see p.46) also arrange group tours.

For more casual riding, bikes can be **rented** for $15–30 per day, or at discounted weekly rates, from outlets that are usually found close to beaches, university campuses, and good cycling areas. Rates in heavily visited areas can be much higher. Local visitor centers should have details. Before setting out on a **long-distance cycling trip**, you'll need a good-quality, multispeed bike, panniers, tools and spares, maps, padded shorts, and a helmet (legally required in some states and localities). Plan a route that avoids interstate highways (on which cycling is unpleasant and usually illegal). Of **problems** you'll encounter, the main one is traffic – RVs driven by buffoons who can't judge their width, and huge eighteen-wheelers (or in the western states, logging trucks) that scream past and create intense backdrafts capable of pulling you out into the middle of the road.

The usual advice given to **hitchhikers** is that they should use their common sense; but common sense should tell anyone that hitchhiking in the United States is a **bad idea**. We do not recommend it under any circumstances.

Driving Distances in Miles

The distances shown on this chart represent the total mileages between selected cities and national parks in the US and Canada. They are calculated according to the shortest available route by road, and are thus higher than figures obtained by drawing a straight line on a map.

	Albuquerque	Atlanta	Boston	Chicago	Dallas	Denver	Grand Canyon NP	Great Smoky Mtns NP	Las Vegas	Los Angeles	Memphis	Miami	Nashville	New Orleans	New York	Orlando	St Louis	Salt Lake City	San Francisco	Seattle	Washington DC	Yellowstone NP	Yosemite NP	Montréal	Toronto	Vancouver
Albuquerque NM																										
Atlanta GA	1404																									
Boston MA	2220	1108																								
Chicago IL	1312	708	994																							
Dallas TX	644	822	1753	921																						
Denver CO	437	1430	1998	1021	784																					
Grand Canyon NP AZ	407	1818	2627	1732	1051	708																				
Great Smoky Mtns NP	1457	177	917	585	905	1385	1831																			
Las Vegas NV	586	1979	2752	1780	1230	758	283	2036																		
Los Angeles CA	811	2191	3017	2048	1399	1031	555	2254	272																	
Memphis TN	1010	382	1341	537	454	1043	1416	450	1603	1807																
Miami FL	1970	663	1520	1397	1343	2107	2499	614	2570	2716	997															
Nashville TN	1225	246	1092	466	659	1184	1610	221	1811	2011	209	910														
New Orleans LA	1157	480	1507	919	517	1277	1548	622	1732	1858	414	860	532													
New York NY	1997	854	208	809	1559	1794	2401	706	2572	2794	1102	1334	900	1335												
Orlando FL	1741	426	1301	1147	1098	1879	2271	614	2350	2429	776	229	688	648	1092											
St Louis MO	1042	565	1207	289	655	863	1449	522	1620	1836	283	1226	321	698	976	1004										
Salt Lake City UT	604	1934	2376	1417	1257	534	365	1910	419	570	1703	2566	1551	1775	2189	2337	1362									
San Francisco CA	1109	2483	3128	2173	1752	1255	954	2592	570	387	2116	3093	2011	2278	2930	2871	2118	752								
Seattle WA	1453	2625	3016	2052	2131	1341	1213	2630	1180	1134	2317	3303	2325	2590	2841	3088	2135	848	810							
Washington DC	1849	618	448	709	1307	1616	2304	469	2420	2646	854	1057	659	1099	237	856	862	2048	2843	2721						
Yellowstone NP WY	973	1944	2382	1388	1343	563	755	1907	809	1081	1604	2568	1712	1840	2213	2432	1385	390	1027	827	2081					
Yosemite NP CA	971	2375	2961	2021	1634	1000	641	2384	358	348	1946	2928	2184	2096	2777	2708	1863	558	182	928	2616	1003				
Montréal Canada	2131	1199	310	847	1770	1824	2542	1035	2583	2855	1315	1649	1112	1651	382	1462	1101	2225	2959	2714	607	2009	2644			
Toronto Canada	1787	1011	609	515	1435	1492	2198	807	2251	2523	956	1494	776	1307	516	1346	749	1910	2823	2564	571	2303	2938	344		
Vancouver Canada	1590	2756	3155	2176	2234	1484	1357	2774	1322	1278	2461	3447	2566	2734	2943	3232	2191	990	954	144	2887	971	1072	3014	2820	

Travelers with disabilities

By international standards, the US is exceptionally accommodating for travelers with mobility problems or other physical disabilities. All public buildings, including hotels and restaurants, must be wheelchair accessible and provide suitable toilet facilities. Almost all street corners have dropped curbs. Most public transportation systems have such facilities as subways with elevators and buses that "kneel" to let people board.

Most states provide **information** for disabled travelers – contact the tourism departments listed in the box on pp.28–29. SATH, the Society for Accessible Travel and Hospitality, 347 Fifth Ave, #610, New York, NY 10016 (☎212/447-7284, ⒲www.sath.org), is a not-for-profit travel-industry group of travel agents, tour operators, hotel and airline management, and people with disabilities. They pass on any inquiry to the appropriate member; you should allow plenty of time for a response. Mobility International USA, PO Box 10767, Eugene, OR 97440 (☎541/343-1284, ⒲www.miusa.org), offers travel tips to members ($35 a year) and operates exchange programs for disabled people. They also serve as a national information center on disability.

Disabled Outdoors is a quarterly magazine specializing in facilities for disabled travelers who wish to explore the great outdoors; its friendly office (see "Tour Operators," opposite) serves as a clearinghouse for all related information. Other useful publications include *Travel for the Disabled* ($20), *Wheelchair Vagabond* ($15), *Directory of Accessible Van Rentals* ($10), and *Directory for Travel Agencies for the Disabled* ($20), all produced by Twin Peaks Press and available from ⒲www.amazon.com or ⒲www.bookfinder.com.

The **Golden Access Passport**, issued without charge to permanently disabled or blind US citizens, gives free lifetime admission to all national parks. It can only be obtained in person at a federal area where an entrance fee is charged; you'll have to show proof of permanent disability, or that you are eligible for receiving benefits under federal law.

Getting around

Most **airlines**, transatlantic and within the US, do what they can to ease your journey, and will usually let attendants of more seriously disabled people accompany them at no extra charge. The Americans with Disabilities Act (1990) obliges all air carriers to make the majority of their services accessible to travelers with disabilities.

Almost every Amtrak **train** includes one or more coaches with accommodation for handicapped passengers. Guide dogs travel free and may accompany blind, deaf, or disabled passengers. Be sure to give 24 hours' notice. Hearing-impaired passengers can get information on ☎1-800/523-6590 (though it can take a while to get through; the service is poorly staffed).

Greyhound, however, is not recommended. **Buses** are not equipped with lifts for wheelchairs, though staff will assist with boarding (intercity carriers are required by law to do this), and the "Helping Hand" policy offers two-for-the-price-of-one tickets to passengers unable to travel alone (carry a doctor's certificate). The American Public Transportation Association, 1666 K St NW, suite 1100, Washington, DC 20006 (☎202/496-4800, ⒲www.apta.com), provides information about the accessibility of public transportation in cities.

The American Automobile Association (☎1-877/244-9790, ⒲www.aaa.com) produces the *Handicapped Driver's Mobility Guide* for disabled drivers. The larger car-rental companies provide cars with hand controls at no extra charge, though only on their full-sized (ie, most expensive) models; reserve well in advance.

Tour operators

A few **tour operators** cater to disabled travelers or arrange disabled group tours. Directions Unlimited, 720 N Bedford Rd, Bedford Hills, NY 10507 (☎914/241-1700 or 1-800/533-5343) and Wheels Up! (☎1-888/389-4335, ⓦwww.wheelsup.com) provide discounted airfares and tour and cruise prices for disabled travelers, as well as a free monthly newsletter.

Senior travelers

For many senior citizens, retirement brings the opportunity to explore the world in a style and at a pace that is the envy of younger travelers. As well as the obvious advantages of being free to travel during the quieter, more congenial, and less expensive seasons, as well as for longer periods, anyone over age 62 (with appropriate ID) can enjoy a vast range of discounts. Both Amtrak and Greyhound, for example, offer (smallish) percentage reductions on fares to older passengers.

In addition, any US citizen or permanent resident 62 or over is entitled to free admission for life to all national parks, monuments and historic sites, using a **Golden Age Passport**, issued for a one-time fee of $10 at any such site. This free admission applies to all accompanying travelers in the same vehicle – a welcome encouragement to families to travel together – and also gives a fifty percent reduction on park user fees (such as camping charges). For more information on national parks passes, see p.51.

AARP (formerly the American Association of Retired Persons), 601 E St NW, Washington, DC 20049 (☎202/434-2277 or 1-800/424-3410, ⓦwww.aarp.org), membership in which is open to US residents 50 or over for an annual $12.50 fee, organizes group travel for seniors and can provide discounts on accommodation and vehicle rental. **Elderhostel**, 75 Federal St, Boston, MA 02110 (☎1-877/426-8056, ⓦwww.elderhostel.org), runs an extensive network of educational and activity programs for people over 60 throughout the US, at prices broadly in line with those of commercial tours. Similar is **Saga Holidays**, 222 Berkeley St, Boston, MA 02116 (☎1-800/343-0273, ⓦwww.sagaholidays.com). Less educational group tours are available from **Vantage Travel** (☎1-800/322-6677, ⓦwww.vantagetravel.com).

Traveling with children

Traveling with kids in the United States is relatively problem-free. Children are readily accepted – indeed welcomed – in public places across the country. Hotels and motels are quite accustomed to them, most state and national parks organize children's activities, every town or city has clean and safe playgrounds – and, of course, Disneyland in California and Disney World in Florida provide the ultimate in kids' entertainment.

Restaurants encourage parents to bring in their offspring. All the national chains provide highchairs and a special kids' menu, packed with huge, excellent-value (if not necessarily healthful) meals – cheeseburger and fries for 99¢, and so on. Virtually all museums and tourist attractions offer **reduced rates** for kids. Most large cities have natural history museums or aquariums, and quite a few also have hands-on children's museums.

State tourist offices can provide specific **information** (see the box on pp.28–29). **Guidebooks** for parents traveling with children include the *Unofficial Guide to California with Kids* ($18) and *New York City with Kids* ($16), both in the Frommer's Family Guides list, and Vicki Lansky's helpful *Trouble-Free Travel with Children* ($9), available from Publishers Group West, ⓦ www.amazon .com, and most good bookstores. Each of the John Muir Publications' *Kidding Around* series covers the history and sights of a major US city in a family-friendly way.

Getting around

Children under two years old fly free on domestic routes and for ten percent of the adult fare on international **flights** – though that doesn't mean they get a seat, let alone frequent-flier miles. Kids aged between two and twelve years old are usually entitled to **half-price tickets**.

Traveling **by bus** may be the cheapest way to go, but it's also the most uncomfortable for kids. Under-twos travel (on your lap) for free. Children under twelve are charged half the standard fare.

Even if you discount the romance of the railroad, taking the **train** is by far the best option for long journeys – not only does everyone get to enjoy the scenery, but you can get up and walk around. Most cross-country trains have sleeping compartments, which may be quite expensive, but are likely to be seen by the kids as a great adventure. Children's **discounts** are much the same as for bus or plane travel.

All that said, most families choose to travel **by car**. If you hope to enjoy a driving vacation with your kids, make plans. Don't set unrealistic targets; pack sensible snacks and drinks; stop every couple of hours; arrive at your destination before sunset; and avoid traveling through big cities during rush hour. Car rental companies usually provide **kids' car seats** – which are required by law for children under the age of four – for about $4 or $5 a day. You would, however, be advised to check, or bring your own; they are not always available.

Recreational vehicles (**RVs**) are a good option for families, combining the convenience of kitchens and bedrooms with the freedom of the road (see "Getting around," p.37).

Resources

Rascals in Paradise, One Daniel Burnham Court, suite 105-C, San Francisco, CA 94109 (☎415/921-7000, ⓦ www.rascalsin-paradise.com), can arrange scheduled and customized itineraries built around activities for kids in the US and abroad, ranging from hiking and horseriding to mountain biking and watersports. **Travel with Your Children**, 40 Fifth Ave, New York, NY 10011 (☎212/477-5524 or 1-888/822-4388), publishes a newsletter, *Family Travel Times* (ⓦ www.familytraveltimes.com), as well as books on travel with children, including *Great Adventure Vacations with Your Kids*.

Women travelers

A woman traveling alone in America is not usually made to feel conspicuous, or liable to attract unwelcome attention. Cities can feel a lot safer than you might expect from recurrent media images of demented urban jungles, simply because there are so many people around. Like anywhere, though, particular care must be taken at night: walking through unlit, empty streets is never a good idea, and, if there's no bus service, take a taxi. Women who look confident are less likely to encounter trouble; those who stand around looking lost and a bit scared are prime targets.

In the major **urban centers**, if you stick to the better parts of town, going into bars and clubs alone should pose few problems: there's generally a pretty healthy attitude toward women who do so, and your privacy will be respected. Lesbian bars are usually a trouble-free and welcoming alternative.

However, **small towns** may lack the same liberal or indifferent attitude toward lone women travelers. People seem to jump immediately to the conclusion that your car has broken down, or that you've suffered some strange misfortune; you may get fed up with well-meant offers of help. If your vehicle does break down on heavily traveled roads, wait in the car for a police or highway patrol car to arrive. You should also rent a **mobile phone** with your car, for a small charge – a potential lifesaver.

Women – even more so than for men – should **never hitchhike** in the US. It's just asking for trouble. Similarly, you should never pick up anyone who's trying to hitchhike. If someone is waving you down on the road, ostensibly to get help with a broken-down vehicle, just drive on by – the highway patrol will be along soon enough to see what the trouble is.

Avoid traveling at night by **public transportation** – deserted bus stations, if not actually threatening, will do little to make you feel secure. Where possible, team up with a fellow traveler (there really is safety in numbers). On Greyhound buses, sit near the driver. Should disaster strike, all major towns have some kind of rape counseling service;

if not, the local sheriff's office will arrange for you to get help and counseling, and, if necessary, get you home.

The **National Organization for Women** (ⓦ www.now.org) is a leader in seeking to advance issues of importance to women. NOW branches, listed in local phone directories, can provide information on rape crisis centers, counseling services, feminist bookstores, and lesbian bars.

Resources and specialists

Call of the Wild 2519 Cedar St, Berkeley, CA 94708 ☏ 510/849-9292 or 1-888/378-1978, ⓦ www.callwild.com. This established outfitter offers hiking adventures for women of all ages and abilities. Trips include visits to Native American ruins, backpacking in California national parks, cross-country skiing, yoga, and jaunts to Hawaii.
Outward Bound 100 Mystery Point Rd, Garrison, NY 10524 ☏ 1-888/882-6863 or 914/424-4000, ⓦ www.outwardbound.com. Year-round programs include canoeing, sledding, and desert and canyon hiking. No previous experience is required.
Prairie Women Adventures and Retreats RR1, Box 32, Matfield Green, KS 66862 ☏ 620/753-3416, ⓦ www.vacationranches.com/homestead /women.htm. This 5000-acre cattle ranch is owned by women. Guests can work alongside ranch hands, with free time to hike, bike, and ride horses.
Womanship 137 Conduit St, Annapolis, MD 21401 ☏ 410/267-6661 or 1-800/342-9295, ⓦ www.womanship.com. Live-aboard, learn-to-sail cruises for women of all ages. Destinations include Chesapeake Bay, Florida, the Pacific Northwest, and Mystic, Connecticut.

Gay and lesbian travelers

The gay scene in America is huge, albeit heavily concentrated in the major cities. San Francisco, where between a quarter and a third of the voting population is reckoned to be gay or lesbian, is arguably the world's premier gay city. New York runs a close second, and up and down both coasts gay men and women enjoy the kind of visibility and influence those in other places can only dream about. Gay officeholders and police officers are no longer a novelty. Resources, facilities, and organizations are endless.

In the heartland, however, life can look more like the Fifties – away from large cities, homosexuals are still oppressed and commonly reviled. Gay travelers need to watch their step to avoid hassles and possible aggression.

Virtually every major city has a predominantly gay area – Chelsea and Christopher Street in New York City, Los Angeles' West Hollywood, San Francisco's Castro district, Houston's Montrose, Seattle's Capitol Hill, and so on. Things change quickly in the gay and lesbian (and emerging bisexual) scene, but we've tried to give an overview of local resources, bars, and clubs in each large urban area.

National **publications** are available from any good bookstore. Bob Damron, PO Box 422458, San Francisco, CA 94142 (☎415/255-0404 or 1-800/462-6654, ⓦwww.damron.com) produces the best. These include the *Men's Travel Guide*, a pocket-sized yearbook listing hotels, bars, clubs, and resources for gay men ($19); the

Women's Traveler, which provides similar listings for lesbians ($17); the *Damron City Guide*, which details lodging and entertainment in major cities ($22); and *Damron Accommodations*, which lists 1000 accommodations for gays and lesbians worldwide ($20). On the website, you can buy any of these books for twenty percent off.

Gayellow Pages, PO Box 533, Village Station, New York, NY 10014 (☎212/674-0120, ⓦwww.gayellowpages.com) publishes a useful **directory** of businesses in the US and Canada ($16), plus regional directories for New England, New York, and the South. *The Advocate*, Liberation Publications, PO Box 4371, Los Angeles, CA 90078 ($3; ⓦwww.advocate.com) is a bimonthly national gay news magazine, with features, general info, and classified ads. Finally, the **International Gay & Lesbian Travel Association**, 4331 N Federal Hwy #304, Fort Lauderdale, FL 33308 (☎1-954/776-2626, ⓦwww.iglta.org), is a comprehensive, invaluable source for gay and lesbian travelers.

Accommodation

Accommodation costs form a significant proportion of the expenses for any traveler exploring the US – in part, because the standards of comfort and service are usually fairly high.

If you're on your own, it's possible to pare down what you pay by sleeping in dormitory-

style **hostels**, where a bed usually costs between $10–20 a night. However, with basic

Accommodation price codes

Throughout this book, **accommodation prices** have been graded with the symbols below, according to the cost of the least expensive double room throughout most of the year.

However, except at interstate budget motels, there's rarely such a thing as a set rate for a room. A basic motel in a seaside or mountain resort may double its prices according to the season, while a big-city hotel that charges $200 per room during the week will often slash its rate on the weekend. Because the high and low seasons for tourists vary widely across the country, astute planning can save a lot of money. Watch out also for local events – Mardi Gras in New Orleans, Spring Break in Myrtle Beach, college football games – which can raise rates far above normal.

Only where we explicitly say so do these room rates include local **taxes**.

❶ up to $35
❷ $35–50
❸ $50–75
❹ $75–100
❺ $100–130
❻ $130–160
❼ $160–200
❽ $200–250
❾ $250+

room prices away from the major cities starting at around $40 per night, groups of two or more will find it little more expensive to stay in the far more abundant **motels and hotels**. Many hotels will set up a third single bed for around $15 on top of the regular price, reducing costs for three people sharing. On the other hand, the lone traveler has a hard time of it: "singles" are usually double rooms at an only slightly reduced rate.

Wherever you stay, you'll be expected to **pay in advance**, at least for the first night and perhaps for further nights, too. Most places ask for a credit card imprint when you arrive, but they'll also accept cash or US dollar travelers checks. **Reservations** – essential in busy areas in summer – are held only until 5 or 6pm, unless you've warned the hotel you'll be arriving late.

Hotels and motels

Drivers approaching any significant town encounter endless lines of motels along the highway, and the choice along major cross-country routes is phenomenal. **Hotels** and **motels** are essentially the same thing, although motels tend to be found beside the main roads away from city centers – and thus are much more accessible to drivers. The budget ones are pretty basic affairs, but in general there's a uniform standard of comfort everywhere – each room comes with a double bed (often two), a TV and phone, and an attached bathroom – and you don't

get a much better deal by paying, say, $60 instead of $40. Over $60, the room and its fittings simply get bigger and more luxurious, and there'll probably be a swimming pool, free for guests (in states with warmer weather, this is often included in even the cheaper motels).

The cheapest properties tend to be family-run, independent motels, but there's a lot to be said for paying a few dollars more to stay in motels belonging to the **national chains**. After a few days on the road, if you find that a particular chain consistently suits your requirements, you can use its central reservation number, listed overleaf, to book ahead, and possibly obtain discounts as a regular guest.

During **off-peak periods**, many motels and hotels struggle to fill their rooms, and it's worth **bargaining** to get a few dollars off the asking price. Staying in the same place for more than one night will bring further reductions. Also, look for **discount coupons**, especially in the free magazines distributed by local visitor centers and interstate Welcome Centers. These can offer amazing value – $20 for a double room in a comfortable mid-range chain – but read the small print, as rates sometimes turn out to be a per-person charge for two people sharing and are often limited to midweek.

Few budget hotels or motels bother to compete with the ubiquitous diners by offering **breakfast**, although many provide free self-service coffee, sticky buns, and sometimes fruit or cereal – ubiquitously referred to as "continental breakfast."

Staying in a **bed-and-breakfast** has become an ever more popular option, often as a luxurious alternative to conventional hotels. Some B&Bs consist of no more than a couple of furnished rooms in someone's home, and even the larger establishments tend to have fewer than ten rooms, without TV or phone, but often laden with pot pourri, chintzy cushions, and an almost over-contrived homey atmosphere.

The price you pay for a B&B – which varies from around $50 to $200 for a double room – always includes a huge and wholesome breakfast (sometimes a buffet on a side-board, but more often a full-blown cooked meal). The crucial determining factor is whether each room has an en suite bathroom; most B&Bs feel obliged to pro-vide private bath facilities, although that can damage the authenticity of a fine old house. Prices in those that do tend to start at more like $60 or $70. At the top end of the spec-trum, the distinction between a hotel and a "bed-and-breakfast inn" may amount to no more than that the B&B is owned by a pri-vate individual rather than a chain.

In many areas, B&Bs have united to form central **booking agencies**, making it much easier to find a room at short notice; we've given contact information for these where appropriate.

National accommodation chains

Best Western ☎1-800/780-7234,
ⓦwww.bestwestern.com. ❸–❻
Baymont Inns & Suites ☎1-866/999-1111,
ⓦwww.baymontinns.com. ❸
Comfort Inns ☎1-877/424-6423,
ⓦwww.comfortinns.com. ❸–❺
Courtyard by Marriott ☎1-800/321-2211,
ⓦwww.courtyard.com. ❺–❻
Days Inn ☎1-800/329-7466,
ⓦwww.daysinn.com. ❹–❺
Econolodge ☎1-877/424-6423,
ⓦwww.econolodge.com. ❷–❹
Embassy Suites Hotels ☎1-800/362-2779,
ⓦwww.embassysuites.com. ❻
Fairfield Inns ☎1-800/228-2800,
ⓦwww.fairfieldinn.com. ❹–❺
Hallmark Inns ☎1-888/448-4449,
ⓦwww.hallmarkinns.com. ❷–❸

Hampton Inns ☎1-800/426-7866,
ⓦwww.hamptoninn.com. ❹–❺
Hilton Hotels ☎1-800/774-1500,
ⓦwww.hilton.com. ❺ and up
Holiday Inns ☎1-800/465-4329,
ⓦwww.holiday-inn.com. ❺ and up
Howard Johnson ☎1-800/446-4656,
ⓦwww.hojo.com. ❷–❹
La Quinta Inns ☎1-866/725-1661,
ⓦwww.laquinta.com. ❹
Marriott Hotels ☎1-888/236-2427,
ⓦwww.marriott.com. ❻ and up
Motel 6 ☎1-800/466-8356,
ⓦwww.motel6.com. ❷
Ramada Inns ☎1-800/272-6232,
ⓦwww.ramada.com. ❹ and up
Red Carpet Inns ☎1-800/251-1962,
ⓦwww.reservahost.com. ❷
Red Roof Inns ☎1-800/843-7663,
ⓦwww.redroof.com. ❸
Renaissance Hotels ☎1-888/236-2427,
ⓦwww.renaissancehotels.com. ❺ and up
Rodeway Inns ☎1-800/228-2000,
ⓦwww.rodeway.com. ❸
Sheraton ☎1-888/625-5144,
ⓦwww.sheraton.com. ❺ and up
Select Inns ☎1-800/641-1000,
ⓦwww.selectinn.com. ❷
Sleep Inns ☎1-800/753-3746,
ⓦwww.sleepinn.com. ❸

Youth hostels and Ys

Although **hostel-type accommodation** is not as plentiful in the US as it is in Europe, provision for backpackers and low-budget travelers is on the rise. Unless you're travel-ing alone, most hostels work out little cheaper than motels; stay in them only if you prefer their youthful ambiance and sociability. Many are not accessible on public trans-portation, or convenient for sightseeing in the towns and cities, let alone in rural areas.

The official **HI-AYH** (Hostelling International-American Youth Hostels; ☎1-800/909-4776) network has more than 150 hostels in major cities and rural locations throughout the US. Urban hostels tend to have 24hr access, while rural ones may have a curfew and limit-ed daytime hours. Annual membership is cur-rently $28 and rates range from $12 to $29 for HI members; nonmembers generally pay an additional $3 per night. Check the HI-AYH website (ⓦwww.hiayh.org) for comprehensive listings.

For advice on **camping**, see the "National parks and outdoor activities" section on p.50.

A growing number of **independent hostels**, some of which fail to meet HI's fairly rigid criteria, choose not to be tied down by HI regulations. Many are no more than converted motels, where the "dorms" consist of a couple of bunk beds in a musty room, which is also let out as a private room on request. Others may be purpose-built rural properties, or at least converted and modernized to a high standard. The **American Association of Independent Hostels** (AAIH) is a loose affiliation of independent hostels.

In addition, **YMCA/YWCA** hostels (known as "Ys"), provide mixed-sex or, in a few cases, women-only accommodation, at prices ranging from around $12 for a dormitory bed to $70 for a single or double room. Ys offering accommodation (and not all do; many are basically just health clubs) are often in older buildings in less than ideal neighborhoods, but facilities can include a gym, a swimming pool, and an inexpensive cafeteria.

Especially in high season, **reserve ahead**; call or email the relevant hostel to learn how to go about this. Some hostels will allow you to use a sleeping bag, though, officially, HI affiliates should insist on a sheet sleeping bag. The **maximum stay** is often restricted to three days, though this rule is often ignored if there's space. Few hostels provide meals, but most have cooking facilities.

Note that youth hostels are often shoestring organizations, prone to changing address or closing down altogether. Similarly, new ones appear each year; check the notice boards of other hostels for news. The *Hostel Handbook for the USA and Canada*, published each May, lists four hundred hostels and is available for $5 from Jim Williams, *Sugar Hill House International House Hostel*, 722 St Nicholas Ave, New York, NY 10031 (☏212/926-7030, ⓦwww.hostelhandbook.com). *Hostelling North America*, the HI guide to hostels in the USA and Canada, is available free to members and any overnight guest at HI-AYH hostels, or for $3 direct from the HI national office, 8401 Colesville Rd, suite 600, Silver Spring, MD 20910 (☏202/495-1240, ⓦwww.hiayh .org).

B

BASICS | Accommodation

Hosteling organizations abroad

Overseas travelers will find a comprehensive list of hostels in the *International Youth Hostel Handbook*, available from the following hosteling organizations. These organizations all sell **hosteling memberships** as well, which are accepted at affliated hostels around the world.

In the UK and Ireland

An Óige (Irish Youth Hostel Association) 61 Mountjoy St, Dublin 61 ☏01/830 4555, ⓦwww .irelandyha.org. Annual membership €25, or €10.50 for under-18s.

Hostelling International Northern Ireland 22 Donegall Rd, Belfast BT12 5JN ☏02890/324 733, ⓦwww .hini.org.uk. Annual membership £13, or £6 for under-18s.

Scottish Youth Hostels Association 7 Glebe Crescent, Stirling FK8 2JA ☏01786/891 400, ⓦwww.syha.org .uk. Annual membership £6, or £2.50 for under-18s.

YHA England & Wales Trevelyan House, Dimple Rd, Matlock ☏01629/592 700, ⓦwww.yha.org .uk. Annual membership £13.50, or £6.75 for under-18s.

In Australia and New Zealand

YHA Australia PO Box 314, Camperdown 1450, NSW ☏02/9565 1699, ⓦwww.yha.com .au. Annual membership Aus$52, or Aus$16 for under-18s.

YHA New Zealand Moorhouse City, level 1, 166 Moorhouse Ave, Christchurch ☏03/379 9970, ⓦwww .stayyha.com. Annual membership NZ$40, NZ$30 if you're renewing, or free for under-18s.

Food and drink

"Fast food" may be America's most enduring contribution to the modern culinary world, but the sheer variety – and, for the most part, quality – of the foods available are really quite astonishing. In the cities, you can pretty much eat whatever you want, whenever you want. And along all the highways and on every main street, restaurants, fast-food places and coffeeshops try to outdo one another with flashing neon signs as well as bargains and special offers.

Whatever you eat and wherever you eat, service is usually enthusiastic – thanks in large part to the institution of **tipping**. Waiters depend on tips for the bulk of their earnings; fifteen to twenty percent is the standard rate, and a bare minimum in major cities.

Regional specialties

While the predictable enormous steaks, burgers, and piles of ribs or half a chicken, served up with salads, cooked vegetables, and bread, are found everywhere, it's more rewarding to explore the diverse **regional and ethnic cuisines** around the country. Beef is especially prominent in the Midwest and Texas, while fish and seafood dominate the menus in Florida, Louisiana, around Chesapeake Bay in Maryland, and in the Pacific Northwest. Shellfish, such as the highly rated Dungeness crab – smoother and creamier than the average crab – and the Chesapeake's unique soft-shell crab, highly spiced and eaten whole, is popular too. Maine lobsters and steamers (clams), eaten alone or mixed up in a chowder, are a great reason to visit New England.

Cajun food, which originated in the bayous of Louisiana as a way to use up leftovers, is centered on red beans and rice, enlivened with unusual seafood like crawfish and catfish, and always highly spiced. The oft-misunderstood distinction between Cajun and Creole cooking is explained in our "Louisiana" chapter, on p.724.

Southern cooking – sometimes known as "soul food" – is not always easy to find outside the South, but is worth seeking out. You may not fancy grits (ground white corn served hot, mixed with butter) for breakfast, but full meals can be delicious, and incredibly filling. Vegetables such as collard greens, black-eyed peas, fried eggplant, and okra (a principal ingredient of the Cajun gumbo) are added to staples such as fried chicken, roast beef, and hogjaw – meat from the mouth of a pig. Chitterlings (or chitlins) are a delicacy prepared from the innards of a pig. Meat dishes are usually accompanied by cornbread to soak up the thick gravy poured over everything; while with fried fish, you'll often get hush puppies – fried corn balls with tiny bits of chopped onion. **Barbecue** – smoked meats, usually pork or beef, served with a wide variety of tangy, spicy sauces – is also very popular in the South, where a mouth-watering plate, with sides, can be had for usually less than $10. (Generally, the more ramshackle the restaurant, the better the food.) There's also great barbecue outside of the South, particularly in Texas, Kansas City, and Chicago.

California cuisine is geared toward health and aesthetics. It's basically a development of French nouvelle cuisine, utilizing the wide mix of fresh, locally available ingredients. Vegetables are harvested before maturity and steamed to preserve both vitamins and flavor. Seafood comes from oyster farms and the catches of small-time anglers, and what little meat there is tends to be from animals reared on organic farms. The result is small but beautifully presented portions and high prices: not unusually $50 a head (or much more) for a full dinner with wine.

A spin-off from California cuisine is the so-called **New New Mexican** or **Santa Fe–style** food, again emphasizing ultrafresh and unusual ingredients, and spiced with chilis to reflect the Spanish and Mexican heritage of the Southwest desert region.

Although technically ethnic, **Mexican food** is so common it often seems like an indigenous cuisine, especially in southern California. In the States, though, Mexican food is different from that found south of the border, making more use of fresh meats and vegetables. The essentials, however, are the same: lots of rice and pinto beans, often served refried (boiled, mashed, and fried), with variations on the tortilla, a thin corn-dough or flour pancake that can be wrapped around food and eaten by hand (a burrito); folded, fried, and filled (a taco); rolled, filled, and baked in sauce (an enchilada); or fried flat and topped with a stack of filling (a tostada). Meals are usually served with complimentary tortilla chips and a hot salsa dip. The chile relleno is a good vegetarian option – a green pepper stuffed with cheese, dipped in egg batter, and fried.

In Texas, **Tex-Mex** is a somewhat less spicy local version of Mexican food, whose distinguishing dish is beef and bean chili con carne. Day or night, this is the cheapest type of food to eat: even a full dinner with a few drinks will rarely be more than $10 anywhere except in the most upmarket establishment.

Other **local variations** in cuisine are endless. Many farming and ranching regions – Nevada in particular – have a surprising number of **Basque** restaurants; the **Amish** communities of Pennsylvania have their own traditions; and **Portuguese** restaurants, dating from whaling days, can be found along the New England coast. **Chinese** food is everywhere and can often be as cheap as Mexican; **Japanese**, found on the coasts and in all big cities, is rather more expensive and fashionable. **Italian** food is popular, and specialist Italian regional cooking can often

be found too. **French** cuisine is usually pricey, and rarely found outside the larger cities. **Thai**, **Korean**, **Indian**, and **Indonesian** is similarly city-based, though cheaper.

Drinking

Across the country, **bars** and **cocktail lounges** are often long, dimly lit counters with a few customers perched on stools before a bartender-cum-guru, and tables and booths for those who don't want to join in the drunken bar-side debates. New York, Baltimore, Chicago, New Orleans, and San Francisco are the consummate boozing towns, but almost anywhere you shouldn't have to search very hard for a comfortable place to drink. Keep in mind that to **buy and consume alcohol** in the US, you need to be 21, and could well be asked for ID even if you look much older.

"**Blue laws**" – laws that restrict when, where, and under what conditions alcohol can be purchased – are a source of annoyance. The most common of these, held by many states, prohibits the sale of alcohol on Sundays; on the extreme end of the scale, some counties (known as "dry") don't allow any alcohol, ever. The famous whiskey and bourbon **distilleries** of Tennessee and Kentucky, including Jack Daniels (see p.597), can be visited – though maddeningly, several are in dry counties, so they don't offer samples. A few states – Vermont, Oklahoma, and Utah (which, being predominantly Mormon, has the most byzantine rules) – restrict the alcohol content in beer to just 3.2 percent, almost half the usual strength. Rest assured, though, that in a few of the **more liberal** parts of the country

---

Coping as a vegetarian

In the big cities at least, being a **vegetarian** in the United States presents few problems. Most towns of any size boast at least one wholefood or vegetarian café. However, don't be too surprised in rural areas if you find yourself restricted to a diet of eggs, cheese sandwiches (you might have to ask them to leave the ham out), salads, and pizza. In the Southeast, most soul-food cafés offer great-value vegetable plates (four different vegetables, including potatoes) for around $5, but these are often also cooked with pork fat. Similarly, baked beans, and the nutritious-sounding red beans and rice, usually contain bits of diced pork. Of the major fast-food chains, the Mexican-ish *Taco Bell*, selling good meatless tostadas and burritos, or the cheap but filling sandwiches at *Subway*, are your best bet.

(New York City, for one), alcohol can be bought and drunk any time between 6am and 4am, seven days a week. Last but not least, New Orleans is a law unto itself, with certain bars open 24 hours, and a far from rigid policy on ID.

The most popular American **beers** are fizzy, light national brands like Budweiser, Miller, and Coors, but there is no lack of alternatives. On the East Coast look for Boston-based Samuel Adams or Philadelphia's Yuengling, made by the oldest brewery in the country. The Texan brand Lone Star has its dedicated followers, as do Pete's Wicked Ales in Minnesota. In California, the full-bodied, San Francisco-brewed Anchor Steam beer is available all over, while the rarer Red Sail Ale is among the finest brews in the country. New Orleans-based Abita does a few unique, well-loved beers (Purple Haze and Turbo Dog), as does the New Belgium Brewing Company, in Fort Collins, Colorado (Fat Tire is especially good). Keep an eye out in local stores rather than supermarkets for bottled specialty beers.

Microbreweries and **brewpubs**, in which you can drink excellent beers brewed on the premises, pretty much originated in the West but can now be found in virtually every sizable US city and college town. Almost all serve a wide range of good-value, hearty food to help soak up the drink.

California and, to a lesser extent, Oregon, Washington, and a few other states (see below), are famous for their **wines**. In California, it's the Napa and Sonoma valleys that boast the finest grapes, and beefy reds such as Merlot, Pinot Noir, and Cabernet Sauvignon, as well as crisp or buttery whites such as Chardonnay and Sauvignon Blanc all do very well up here. Some quaffable but not horridly expensive brands include Frog's Leap, Beaulieu, Bontera, and Terre Rouge for reds; Andrew Murray, Ridge, and Bighorn for whites. In Oregon, seek out Cristom and Foris for reds, Adelsheim and WillaKenzie for whites. In Washington, reds from Chatter Creek and Barnard Griffin are good, or whites from Chateau Ste Michelle and Paul Thomas. Throughout this book, you'll find details of **tours** and **tastings** for visitors, for example in California (p.1218), Ohio (p.320), and even Hawaii (p.1366).

National parks and outdoor activities

The US is blessed with fabulous backcountry and wilderness areas, coated by dense forests, cut by deep canyons, and capped by great mountains. Even the heavily populated East Coast has its share of open space, notably along the Appalachian Trail, which winds from Mount Katahdin in Maine to the southern Appalachians in Georgia – some two thousand miles of untrammeled forest. In order to experience the full breathtaking sweep of America's wide-open stretches, however, head west to the Rockies, to the red-rock deserts of the Southwest, or right across the continent to the amazing wild spaces of the West Coast. In some areas, the shoreline can be disappointingly hard to access, with a high proportion under private ownership.

National parks and monuments

The **National Park Service** administers both national parks and national monuments. The park service is sadly underfunded, and in style and design most of its visitor centers and other facilities still date conspicuously from the 1950s. Nonetheless, its rangers do a superb job of providing information and advice to visitors, maintaining trails, and organizing such activities as free guided hikes and campfire talks.

In principle, a **national park** preserves an area of outstanding natural beauty, encompassing a wide range of terrain and the very best examples of particular landforms and wildlife. Yellowstone has boiling geysers and herds of elk and bison. Yosemite offers towering granite walls and cascading waterfalls. The awesome and colorful Grand Canyon is so deep that you can barely see the river that carved it. A **national monument** is usually much smaller, focusing perhaps on just one archeological site or geological phenomenon, such as Devil's Tower in Wyoming. Altogether, there are more than 375 units of the national park system, including national seashores, lakeshores, battlefields, and other historic sites.

National parks tend to be perfect places to **hike** – almost all have extensive trail networks – but they're all far too large for most people to tour on foot. (Yellowstone, for example, is bigger than the states of Delaware and Rhode Island combined.) Even in those rare cases where you can use public transportation to reach a park, you'll almost certainly need some sort of vehicle to explore it once you're there. The Alaskan parks are mostly howling wilderness, with virtually no roads or facilities for tourists – you're on your own.

Most parks and monuments charge **admission fees** ranging from $4 to $20, which cover a vehicle and all its occupants. For $50, they also sell the **National Parks pass**, which gives a named driver, and all passengers in the same vehicle, a year's unlimited access to (almost) every national park and monument. The more deluxe **Golden Eagle pass** ($65) allows access to absolutely all parks. Separate passes are available for disabled travelers and senior citizens – see p.40 and p.41, respectively.

While hotel-style **lodges** are found only in some major parks, every park or monument tends to have at least one well-organized **campground** for visitors. Often, a cluster of motels can be found not far outside the park boundaries. With appropriate free permits – subject to some restrictions in popular parks – backpackers can also usually camp in the **backcountry** (a general term for areas inaccessible by road).

For up-to-the-minute **information** on the **national park system**, access the official Park Service website at ⓦ www.nationalparks.org. It features full details of the main attractions of the national parks, plus opening hours, the best times to visit, admission fees, hiking trails, and visitor facilities.

Other public lands

National parks and monuments are often surrounded by tracts of **national forest**, also federally administered, but much less protected. These too usually hold appealing rural campgrounds – but, in the words of the slogan, each is a "Land Of Many Uses," and usually allows logging and other land-based industry (thankfully, more often ski resorts than strip mines).

Other government departments administer a whole range of wildlife refuges, national scenic rivers, recreation areas, and the like. The **Bureau of Land Management** (BLM) has the largest land holdings of all, most of it open rangeland, such as in Nevada and Utah, but also including some enticingly out-of-the-way reaches. Environmentalist groups engage in endless running battles with developers, ranchers, and the extracting industries over uses – or alleged misuses – of the federal lands.

State parks and **state monuments**, administered by individual states, preserve sites of more limited, local significance. Many are explicitly designed for recreational use, and thus hold better campgrounds than their federal equivalents.

Camping and backpacking

The ideal way to see the great outdoors – especially if you're on a low budget – is to tour by car, and **camp** at night in state and federal campgrounds, which tend to be far more peaceful and scenic than their commercially run equivalents. Typical public campgrounds range in price from free (usually when there's no water available, which may be seasonal) to around $8 per night. Fees at the commercial campgrounds –

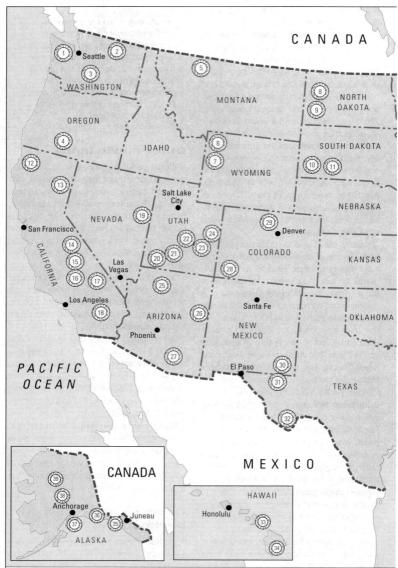

1. Olympic, WA → p.1256
2. North Cascades, WA → p.1259
3. Mount Rainier, WA → p.1261
4. Crater Lake, OR → p.1289
5. Glacier, MT → p.950
6. Yellowstone, WY → p.927
7. Grand Teton, WY → p.934
8. T. Roosevelt (north), ND → p.873

9. T. Roosevelt (south), ND → p.872
10. Wind Cave, SD → p.867
11. Badlands, SD → p.858
12. Redwood, CA → p.1223
13. Lassen Volcanic, CA → p.1225
14. Yosemite, CA → p.1169
15. Kings Canyon, CA → p.1167
16. Sequoia, CA → p.1167

17. Death Valley, CA → p.1144
18. Joshua Tree, CA → p.1142
19. Great Basin, NV → p.1080
20. Zion, UT → p.1042
21. Bryce Canyon, UT → p.1047
22. Capitol Reef, UT → p.1050
23. Canyonlands, UT → p.1051
24. Arches, UT → p.1054

US NATIONAL PARKS
for a detailed description of each park
see the page indicated

NEW
HAMPSHIRE   MAINE
VERMONT

MINNESOTA

Lake Superior

(40)   (41)

WISCONSIN

Lake Huron

MICHIGAN

Lake Michigan

Detroit

Lake Erie

MASSACHOSETTS   Boston

NEW YORK

RHODE IS.
CONNECTICUT

IOWA

Chicago

INDIANA   OHIO

PENNSYLVANIA   New York City

NEW JERSEY

DELAWARE
MARYLAND

ILLINOIS

Washington, DC

St Louis

KENTUCKY

WEST
VIRGINIA   (45)   VIRGINIA

MISSOURI

(43)

Nashville   (44)

NORTH
CAROLINA

TENNESSEE

ARKANSAS   Memphis

SOUTH
CAROLINA

(46) Little
Rock

Atlanta

MISSISSIPPI   ALABAMA   GEORGIA

ATLANTIC
OCEAN

LOUISIANA

Houston   New Orleans

FLORIDA

Gulf of Mexico

Miami

(47)

N

CUBA

0   200 miles

abundant near major towns, many of them resembling open-air hotels, complete with shops and restaurants – are more like $15–22. There may be plenty of campgrounds, but there are also plenty of people who want to use them: if you're camping in high season, either **reserve in advance** or avoid the most popular areas.

Backcountry camping in the national parks is usually free, by permit only. Before you set off on anything more than a half-day hike, and whenever you're headed for anywhere at all isolated, be sure to inform a ranger of your plans, and ask about weather conditions and specific local tips. Carry sufficient food and drink to cover emergencies, as well as all the necessary equipment and maps. Check that fires are permitted before you start one; even if they are, try to use a camp stove in preference to local materials – in some places firewood is scarce, although you may be allowed to use deadwood. In wilderness areas, try to camp on previously used sites. Where there are no toilets, bury human waste at least six inches into the ground and a hundred feet from the nearest water supply and campground. Burn what trash you can, and take the rest away.

Backpackers should **never drink from rivers and streams**, however clear and inviting they may look; you never know what acts people – or animals – have performed further upstream. **Giardia** – a water-borne bacteria that causes an intestinal disease characterized by chronic diarrhea, abdominal cramps, fatigue, and weight loss – is a serious problem. Water that doesn't come from a tap should be boiled for at least five minutes, or cleansed with an iodine-based purifier (such as Portable Aqua) or a Giardia-rated filter, available from any camping or sports store.

Hiking at lower elevations should present few problems, though the swarms of **mosquitoes** that you may encounter near water can drive you crazy; Avon Skin-so-soft, or anything containing DEET, are fairly reliable repellents. **Ticks** – tiny beetles that plunge their heads into your skin and swell up – are another hazard. They sometimes leave their heads inside, causing blood clots or infections, so get advice from a park ranger if you've been bitten. One species of tick causes **Lyme Disease**, a serious condition that can even affect the brain. Nightly inspections of your skin are strongly recommended.

Beware, too, of **poison oak**, an allergenic shrub that grows all over the western states, usually among oak trees. Its leaves come in groups of three (the middle one on a short stem) and are distinguished by prominent veins and shiny surfaces. If you come into contact with it, wash your skin (with soap and cold water) and clothes as soon as possible – and don't scratch. In serious cases, hospital emergency rooms can give antihistamine or adrenaline shots. A comparable curse is **poison ivy**, similar in appearance, found throughout the country. For both plants, remember the sage advice, "Leaves of three, let it be."

Mountain hikes

When hiking at **higher elevations**, for instance in the 14,000ft peaks of the Rockies, or in California's Sierra Nevada (and certainly in Alaska), you should take special care. Late snows are common, and in spring there's a real danger of avalanches, not to mention meltwaters that make otherwise simple stream crossings hazardous. Weather conditions can also change abruptly. **Altitude sickness**, brought on by lower levels of oxygen in the air, can affect even the fittest of athletes: you should take it easy for your first few days above seven thousand feet. Drink lots of water, avoid alcohol, eat plenty of carbohydrates, and protect yourself from the increased power of the sun.

Desert hikes

If you intend to hike in the **desert**, tell someone where you are going, and write down all pertinent information, including your expected time of return. Carry an extra two days' food and water and never go anywhere without a map. Cover most of your ground in early morning: the midday heat is too debilitating. Don't even think about hiking when the mercury tops 90°F (the temperature in California's Death Valley, for example, has reached 136°F). If you get lost, find some shade and wait. As long as you've registered, the rangers will eventually come looking for you.

At any time of year, you'll stay cooler during the day if you wear full-length sleeves and trousers. Shorts and short sleeves will expose you to far too much sun – something you won't be aware of until it's too late. A wide-brimmed hat and good sunglasses will spare you the blinding headaches that can result from the desert light. You may also have to contend with **flash floods**, which can appear from nowhere: a distant cloud can turn a dry wash into a raging river. Never camp in a dry wash, and don't attempt to cross flooded areas until the water has receded.

It's essential to carry – and drink – **large quantities of water** in the desert. An eight-hour hike in typical summer temperatures above 100°F would require you to drink a phenomenal thirty pints of water. Loss of appetite and thirst are early symptoms of **heat exhaustion**, so it's possible to become seriously dehydrated without feeling thirsty. Watch out for signs of dizziness or nausea; if you feel weak and stop sweating, it's time to get to the doctor. Is water available on your trail? Rangers keep abreast of the latest conditions. Carry at least a quart per person even if it is.

When **driving** in the desert, carry two gallons of water per person in the car, and take along an emergency pack with flares, a first-aid kit and snakebite kit, matches, and a compass. A shovel, tire pump, and extra gas are always a good idea. If the engine overheats, don't turn it off; instead, try to cool it quickly by turning the front end of the car towards the wind. Carefully pour some water on the front of the radiator, and turn the air conditioning off and the heat up full blast. In an emergency, never panic and leave the car: you'll be harder to find wandering around alone.

Adventure travel

The opportunities for **adventure travel** in the US are all but endless, from whitewater rafting down the Colorado River, to mountain biking in the volcanic Cascades, canoeing down the headwaters of the Mississippi River, horseback riding in Big Bend on the Rio Grande in Texas, and Big Wall rock-climbing on the sheer granite monoliths of Yosemite Valley.

While an exhaustive listing of the possibilities could fill another volume of this book, certain places have an especially high concentration of adventure opportunities, such as Moab, Utah (p.1057), or New Hampshire's White Mountains (p.268). Throughout the book we recommend guides, outfitters, and local adventure-tour operators.

Wildlife

Watch out for bears, deer, moose, mountain lions, and rattlesnakes in the backcountry, and consider the effect your presence can have on their environment.

Other than in a national park, you're highly unlikely to encounter a **bear**. Even there, it's rare to stumble across one in the wilderness. If you do, don't run, just back away slowly. As friendly as they may appear, they are *wild* animals. Most fundamentally, they will be after your food, which should be stored in airtight containers when camping. Ideally, hang both food and garbage from a high branch (too weak to support the weight of a bear) some distance from your camp. Never attempt to feed bears (frequently they'll beg, but once fed will become aggressive in their demands for more), and never get between a mother and her young. Young animals are cute; irate mothers are not.

Snakes and creepy-crawlies

Though the deserts in particular are home to a wide assortment of **poisonous creatures**, these are rarely aggressive towards humans. To avoid trouble, observe obvious precautions. Don't attempt to handle wildlife; keep your eyes open as you walk, and watch where you put your hands when scrambling over obstacles; shake out shoes, clothing, and bedding before use; and back off if you do spot a creature, giving it room to escape.

If you are **bitten** or **stung**, current medical thinking rejects the concept of cutting yourself open and attempting to suck out the venom. Whether snake, scorpion, or spider is responsible, apply a cold compress to the wound, constrict the area with a tourniquet to prevent the spread of venom, drink lots of water, and bring your temperature down by resting in a shady area. Stay as calm as possible and seek **medical help** immediately.

Sports

Besides being good fun, catching a baseball game at Chicago's Wrigley Field on a summer afternoon, or joining in with the screaming throngs at a Ravens football game in Baltimore, can give visitors an unforgettable insight into a town and its people. Professional teams almost always put on the most spectacular shows, but big games between college rivals, minor league baseball games, and even Friday night high-school football games provide an easy and enjoyable way to get on intimate terms with a place.

Baseball, because the major league teams play so many games – 162 in total, usually five or so a week throughout the summer – is probably the easiest sport to catch when traveling. The ballparks – such as Wrigley Field, Boston's Fenway Park, LA's glamorous Dodger Stadium, or Baltimore's evocative Camden Yards – are great places to spend time. It's also among the cheapest sports to watch (from around $10 a seat), and tickets are usually easy to come by.

Pro football is quite the opposite. Tickets are exorbitantly expensive and almost impossible to obtain (if the team is any good), and most games are played in anonymous municipal bunkers; you'll do better stopping in a bar to watch it on TV. (American football is not the game called football in other countries.)

College football is a whole lot better and more exciting, with chanting crowds, cheerleaders, and cheaper tickets. Although New Year's Day games such as the Rose Bowl or the Orange Bowl are all but impossible to see live, big games like Nebraska vs Oklahoma, Michigan vs Ohio State, or Notre Dame vs anybody are not to be missed if you're anywhere nearby.

Basketball also brings out intense emotions. The interminable – though invariably exciting – pro playoffs run well into June. The men's month-long college tournament, called "March Madness," is acclaimed by many as the nation's most exciting sports extravaganza.

Hockey, long the preserve of Canada and cities in the far north of the US, is now penetrating the rest of the country. Tickets, particularly for successful teams, are hard to get.

The **Kentucky Derby**, held in Louisville on the first Saturday in May (see p.574), is the biggest event on the **horse-racing** calendar. Also in May, the NASCAR Indianapolis 500, the largest **motor-racing** event in the world, fills that city with visitors throughout the month, with practice sessions and carnival events building up to the big race.

We've listed the major league teams for the three major sports (baseball, football, and basketball) on pp.57–58; local tourist offices can also help with schedules and ticket information.

Skiing

Skiing is the biggest mass-market participant sport, and downhill **resorts** can be found all over the US. The Eastern resorts of Vermont and New York State, however, pale by comparison with those of the Rockies, such as Vail and Aspen in Colorado, and the Sierra Nevadas in California. Expect to pay $20–50 per day (depending on the quality and popularity of the resort) for lift tickets, plus another $20 or so per day to rent equipment.

A cheaper option is **cross-country skiing**, or ski touring. Backcountry ski lodges dot mountainous areas along both coasts and in the Rockies. They offer a range of rustic accommodation, equipment rental, and lessons, from as little as $10 a day for skis, boots, and poles, up to about $150 for an all-inclusive weekend tour.

Baseball teams

Major League Baseball team **websites** follow the pattern of: cityname.teamname.mlb.com (except where the team is associated with a state, as with the Florida Marlins; in these instances, the website is formed as follows: statename.teamname.mlb.com). The website for the Anaheim Angels is ⓦangels.mlb.com; the Tampa Bay Devil Rays ⓦdevilrays.mlb .com; and so on.

Major League Baseball ☏212/931-7800, ⓦmlb.com
Anaheim Angels ☏1-888/796-4256
Arizona Diamondbacks ☏602/514-8400
Atlanta Braves ☏404/522-7630
Baltimore Orioles ☏410/685-9800
Boston Red Sox ☏1-877/REDSOX9
Chicago Cubs ☏1-866/652-2877
Chicago White Sox ☏312/674-1000
Cincinnati Reds ☏513/765-7400
Cleveland Indians ☏216/420-HITS
Colorado Rockies ☏1-800/388-7625
Detroit Tigers ☏313/471-2255
Florida Marlins ☏305/626-7400
Houston Astros ☏1-877/927-8767
Kansas City Royals ☏816/504-4040 or 1-800/676-9257
Los Angeles Dodgers ☏323/224-1HIT
Milwaukee Brewers ☏414/902-4400 or 1-800/933-7890
Minnesota Twins ☏612/33-TWINS or 1-800/33-TWINS
New York Mets ☏718/507-TIXX
New York Yankees ☏718/293-6000
Oakland Athletics ☏510/762-BALL or 1-800/225-2277
Philadelphia Phillies ☏215/463-1000
Pittsburgh Pirates ☏412/323-5000
St Louis Cardinals ☏314/421-3060
San Diego Padres ☏1-877/374-2784
San Francisco Giants ☏510/762-BALL
Seattle Mariners ☏206/346-4000
Tampa Bay Devil Rays ☏727/898-RAYS
Texas Rangers ☏1-888/283-2254

Basketball teams

But for a few exceptions (which are picked out in the listings below), NBA team **websites** follow the pattern: www.nba.com /teamname/. The website for the Atlanta Hawks is ⓦwww.nba.com/hawks/; the Minnesota Timberwolves ⓦwww.nba.com /timberwolves/; and so on.

National Basketball Association (NBA) ☏212/407-8000, ⓦwww.nba.com
Atlanta Hawks ☏404/827-3865
Boston Celtics ☏617/523-3030
Charlotte Bobcats ☏704/357-0252
Chicago Bulls ☏312/455-4000

Cleveland Cavaliers ☏216/420-2287 or 1-800/332-2287
Dallas Mavericks ☏214/747-MAVS
Denver Nuggets ☏303/405-8555
Detroit Pistons ☏248/377-0100
Golden State Warriors ☏510/986-2200 or 1-888/479-4667
Houston Rockets ☏1-866/4HOU-TIX
Indiana Pacers ☏317/239-5151
Los Angeles Clippers ☏310/426-6001
Los Angeles Lakers ☏213/480-3232
Memphis Grizzlies ☏901/888-4667
Miami Heat ☏786/777-HOOP
Milwaukee Bucks ☏414/227-0500
Minnesota Timberwolves ☏612/673-1600
New Jersey Nets ☏1-800/4NBA-TIX
New Orleans Hornets ☏1-866/444-HOOP or 504/525-HOOP
New York Knicks ☏1-800/4NBA-TIX
Orlando Magic ☏407/89-MAGIC
Philadelphia 76ers ☏215/339-7676, ⓦwww.nba.com/sixers/
Phoenix Suns ☏1-800/4NBA-TIX
Portland Trailblazers ☏1-800/4NBA-TIX, ⓦwww.nba.com/blazers/
Sacramento Kings ☏916/649-TIXS or 209/551-TIXS
San Antonio Spurs ☏1-800/4NBA-TIX
Seattle Supersonics ☏206/281-5800, ⓦwww.nba.com/sonics/
Utah Jazz ☏801/325-2500
Washington Wizards ☏301/773-2255

Football teams

National Football League (NFL) ☏212/450-2000, ⓦwww.nfl.com
Arizona Cardinals ☏602/379-0101, ⓦwww.azcardinals.com
Atlanta Falcons ☏404/249-6400 or 1-800/326-4000, ⓦwww.atlantafalcons.com
Baltimore Ravens ☏410/481-7328 or 1-800/551-7238, ⓦwww.baltimoreravens.com
Buffalo Bills ☏1-877/BB-TICKS, ⓦwww.buffalobills.com
Carolina Panthers ☏704/552-6500, ⓦwww.panthers.com
Chicago Bears ☏847/295-6600, ⓦwww.chicagobears.com
Cincinnati Bengals ☏513/621-8383, ⓦwww.bengals.com
Cleveland Browns ☏216/241-5555, ⓦwww.clevelandbrowns.com
Dallas Cowboys ☏972/785-4800, ⓦwww.dallascowboys.com
Denver Broncos ☏303/830-TIXS, ⓦwww.denverbroncos.com

Detroit Lions ☎313/262-2003 or 1-800/616-7627, ⓦwww.detroitlions.com
Green Bay Packers ☎920/496-5719, ⓦwww.packers.com
Indianapolis Colts ☎317/239-5151, ⓦwww.colts.com
Jacksonville Jaguars ☎904/633-6000, ⓦwww.jaguars.com
Kansas City Chiefs ☎816/931-3330 or 1-800/676-5488, ⓦwww.kcchiefs.com
Miami Dolphins ☎305/573-TEAM, ⓦwww.miamidolphins.com
Minnesota Vikings ☎612/338-4537, ⓦwww.vikings.com
New England Patriots ☎617/931-2222, ⓦwww.patriots.com
New Orleans Saints ☎504/733-0255, ⓦwww.neworleanssaints.com
New York Giants ☎201/935-8222, ⓦwww.giants.com

New York Jets ☎516/560-8100, ⓦwww.newyorkjets.com
Oakland Raiders ☎510/569-2121 or 1-888/447-2433, ⓦwww.raiders.com
Philadelphia Eagles ☎215/463-5500, ⓦwww.philadelphiaeagles.com
Pittsburgh Steelers ☎412/323-1200, ⓦwww.steelers.com
St Louis Rams ☎314/425-8830, ⓦwww.stlouisrams.com
San Diego Chargers ☎619/220-TIXS, ⓦwww.chargers.com
San Francisco 49ers ☎408/562-4949, ⓦwww.sf49ers.com
Seattle Seahawks ☎206/622-4295, ⓦwww.seahawks.com
Tennessee Titans ☎1-888/313-8326, ⓦwww.titansonline.com
Washington Redskins ☎301/276-6800, ⓦwww.redskins.com

Festivals and public holidays

Someone, somewhere, is always celebrating something in the US – although, apart from national holidays, few festivities are shared throughout the country. Instead, there is a diverse multitude of engaging local events: arts-and-crafts shows, county fairs, ethnic celebrations, music festivals, rodeos, sandcastle-building competitions, chili cook-offs, and countless others.

Listed opposite are some of the best local festivals covered in this book. The tourist offices for each state (see pp.28–29) can provide you with full lists. Or simply phone the visitor center in a particular region and ask what's coming up. Certain festivities, such as **Mardi Gras** in New Orleans, are well worth planning your vacation around; obviously other people will have the same idea, and visiting during these times requires an extra amount of advance effort.

Public holidays

The biggest and most all-American of the **national festivals and holidays** is **Independence Day**. On the Fourth of July, the entire country takes time out as people picnic, drink, salute the flag, and watch or participate in firework displays, marches, beauty pageants, eating contests, and more, all in commemoration of the signing of the Declaration of Independence in 1776.

Halloween (October 31) lacks any such patriotic overtones, and is not a public holiday, despite being one of the most popular yearly flings. Traditionally, masked kids ran around the streets banging on doors and demanding "trick or treat," returning home piled high with candy and apples. These days that sort of activity is mostly confined to rural and suburban areas, though, and in some bigger cities Halloween has evolved into a massive gay-oriented celebration. In LA's West Hollywood, New York's Greenwich Village, New Orleans' French Quarter, and San Francisco's Castro district, the

Jan 1 New Year's Day
Third Mon in Jan Martin Luther King Jr's Birthday
Third Mon in Feb Presidents' Day
Last Mon in May Memorial Day
July 4 Independence Day
First Mon in Sept Labor Day
Second Mon in Oct Columbus Day
Nov 11 Veterans' Day
Fourth Thurs in Nov Thanksgiving Day
December 25 Christmas Day

night is marked by mass cross-dressing, huge block parties, and wee-hours partying.

More sedate is **Thanksgiving Day**, on the fourth Thursday in November. Relatives return to the familial nest to share a meal together (traditionally, roast turkey and stuffing, cranberry sauce, and all manner of delicious pies) and give thanks – hence the holiday's name – for family and friends. Ostensibly, the holiday recalls the first harvest of the Pilgrims in Massachusetts. In fact, Thanksgiving was a national holiday before anyone thought to make that connection.

Goverment offices (including post offices) and banks will almost surely be closed on the national **public holidays** listed in the box above. As for shops and grocery stores, a good number of these remain open on holidays, except for New Year's Day, Thanksgiving, and Christmas, when pretty much everything is closed. Many states also have their own holidays, and in some places, Good Friday is a half-day holiday. The traditional summer season for tourism runs from Memorial Day to Labor Day; some tourist attractions are open only during that period.

Annual festivals and events

For further details of the selected **festivals and events** listed below, including more precise dates, see the relevant page of the *Guide*, or contact the local authorities direct. The state tourist boards listed in the box on pp.28–29 can provide more complete calendars for each area.

January

Elko, NV Cowboy Poetry Gathering, p.1081

St Paul, MN Winter Carnival, p.401

February

Daytona Beach, FL Daytona 500 stock-car race, p.667
Fort Worden, WA Hot Jazz Festival, p.1253

March

Austin, TX South by Southwest Music and Media Conference, p.778
Butte, MT St Patrick's Day, p.945
Fairbanks, AK Ice Festival, p.1333
Los Angeles, CA Academy Awards (the "Oscars"), p.1118
New Orleans, LA Mardi Gras, p.732; also elsewhere in Louisiana, p.738

April

Boston, MA Patriot's Day Marathon, p.221
Lafayette, LA Festival International de Louisiane, p.738
New Orleans, LA French Quarter Festival, and Jazz and Heritage Festival (into May), p.733
Santuario de Chimayó, NM Easter Pilgrimage, p.982

May

Black Mountain, NC Folk Festival, p.532
Breaux Bridge, LA Crawfish Festival, p.738
Charleston, WV Vandalia Festival of Appalachian Culture, p.479
Flagstaff, AZ Zuni Crafts Show, p.1019
Indianapolis, IN Indianapolis 500 sports-car race, p.354
Louisville, KY Kentucky Derby (horse race), p.574
Memphis, TN Memphis in May International Festival, p.589
San Antonio, TX Tejano Conjunto Festival, p.772

June

Fort Worth,TX Chisholm Trail Round-up, p.792
Hardin, MT Little Bighorn Days, p.941
Nashville, TN CMA Music Festival, p.597
Telluride, CO Bluegrass Festival, p.911

July

Blowing Rock, NC Highland Games, p.531
Cheyenne, WY Cheyenne Frontier Days, p.917
Elko, NV National Basque Festival, p.1081
Fairbanks, AK Eskimo/Indian Olympics, p.1333

Flagstaff, AZ Hopi Crafts Show, p.1019;
Navajo Crafts Show (into Aug), p.1019
Fort Totten, ND Powwow and rodeo, p.870
Milwaukee, WI Great Circus Parade, p.384
Minneapolis, MN Aquatennial, p.399
St Paul, MN Taste of Minnesota, p.401
Talkeetna, AK Moose Dropping Festival, p.1329
Traverse City, MI Cherry Festival, p.343

August

Asheville, NC Mountain Dance and Folk Festival,
p.532
Elkins, WV Augusta Festival of Appalachian
Culture, p.476
Gallup, NM Inter-tribal Indian Ceremonial, p.995
Memphis, TN anniversary of Elvis's death, p.589
Newport, RI folk and jazz festivals, p.252
San Antonio, TX Texas Folklife Festival, p.772
Santa Fe, NM Indian Market, p.975
Sturgis, SD Motorcycle Rally and Races, p.862

September

Fort Worth, TX Pioneer Days, p.792
Greenville, MS Delta Blues Festival, p.615
Lafayette, LA Festivals Acadiens, p.738
Lubbock, TX Panhandle South Plains Fair, p.796
Monterey, CA Monterey Jazz Festival, p.1161
New York, NY Festa di San Gennaro, p.84
Opelousas, LA Zydeco Festival, p.738
Pendleton, OR Pendleton Round-up, p.1292
Santa Fe, NM Fiestas de Santa Fe, p.975
Savannah, GA Jazz Festival, p.565
Claremore, OK Chile Cookoff and Bluegrass
Festival, p.813

October

Albuquerque, NM Hot-air Balloon Rally, p.989
Charleston, SC Moja Arts Festival, p.543
Custer State Park, SD Round-up of bison, p.867
Helena, AR King Biscuit Blues Festival, p.625
Opelousas, LA Louisiana Yambilee p.738
Tombstone, AZ Helldorado Days, p.1009

Directory

Addresses Generally speaking, roads in built-up areas of the US are laid out on a grid system, creating "blocks" of buildings. The first one or two digits of a specific address refer to the block, which will be numbered in sequence from a central point, usually Downtown; for example, 620 S Cedar Avenue will be six blocks south of Downtown. It is crucial, therefore, to take note of components such as "NW" or "SE" in addresses; 3620 SW Washington Boulevard will be a very long way indeed from 3620 NE Washington Boulevard.

Airport tax This is invariably included in the price of your ticket.

Cigarettes and smoking The country that first gave tobacco to the world is now probably the most concerned about its detrimental effects on health. Restaurants are usually divided into nonsmoking and smoking sections – California and New York City have banned smoking altogether in restaurants and bars – and smoking is forbidden on public transportation and flights.

Dates In the American style, the date 1/8/04 means not 1 August but January 8.

Electricity 110V AC. All plugs are two-pronged and rather insubstantial. Some travel plug adapters don't fit American sockets.

Floors The first floor in the US is what would be the ground floor in Britain; the second floor would be the first floor, and so on.

ID Should be carried at all times. Two pieces should suffice, one of which should have a photo: a passport and credit card(s) are your best bets. Not having your license with you while driving is an arrestable offense.

Measurements and sizes US measurements are in inches, feet, yards, and miles; weights are in ounces, pounds, and tons. American pints and gallons are about four-fifths of Imperial ones. Clothing sizes are four figures less what they would be in the UK – a British or Australian women's size 12 is a US size 8 – while British shoe sizes are one half-size below American ones for women, and one size below for men.

Tax A sales tax is added to virtually everything you buy in a shop, but isn't included in the marked price. The actual rate varies from place to place: in New York and parts of California, it's above eight percent, while some states – Alaska, Delaware, Montana, and Oregon – have no sales tax at all. A hotel tax will add five to fifteen percent to most bills. You also often must pay a tax on top of the cost of a car rental if you pick up the vehicle at an airport.

Temperatures Always given in Fahrenheit.

Time zones See p.26.

Tipping Expected for all bar and restaurant service, at a rate of fifteen to twenty percent on the bill (unless the service is utterly abominable). About the same amount should be added to taxi fares. A hotel porter who has lugged your suitcases up several flights of stairs should get $3 to $5.

Videos The standard format used for video cassettes in the US is different from that used in the United Kingdom, Ireland, Australia, New Zealand, and elsewhere. This means that prerecorded videotapes bought in the US will not be compatible with a video player bought in another country. However, blank tapes in the US can be used with cameras bought elsewhere, as the camera will format the tape to record and play in the correct standard.

B

BASICS | Directory

Guide

Guide

New York City

CHAPTER 1 **Highlights**

✳ **Ellis Island** Once the first stop for millions of prospective immigrants from all over the world. **See p.77**

✳ **The Brooklyn Bridge** Take a stroll across this much-loved bridge for spectacular views of the skyline. **See p.83**

✳ **Grand Central Station tours** Admire the magnificent Beaux Arts building and savor the seafood in its subterranean *Oyster Bar*. **See p.92**

✳ **Central Park** A massive, gorgeous greenspace, filled with countless bucolic amusements; it's

been called "the lungs of the city." **See p.96**

✳ **The Metropolitan Museum** The museum's mammoth collection could keep you busy for days. **See p.97**

✳ **Coney Island** The world's tallest Ferris wheel is among the landmark attractions at this beachside amusement park. **See p.106**

✳ **A baseball game at Yankee Stadium** Between April and October, it would be a shame not to take in a Bronx Bombers ballgame. **See p.125**

New York City

The most beguiling city in the world, **New York City** is an adrenaline-charged, history-laden place that holds immense romantic appeal for visitors. Whether gazing at the flickering lights of the Midtown sky-scrapers as you speed across the Queensboro Bridge, experiencing the 4am half-life in the Village, or just wasting the day away in Central Park, you really would have to be made of stone not to be moved by it all. There's no place quite like it.

New York City comprises the central island of **Manhattan** and the four outer boroughs – **Brooklyn**, **Queens**, the **Bronx**, and **Staten Island**. Manhattan, to many, *is* New York; certainly, this is where you're likely to spend most of your time, and to stay. The island is broadly divided into three areas: **Downtown** (below 14th St), **Midtown** (from 14th St to Central Park/59th St), and **Uptown** (north of 59th St). Though you could spend weeks here and still barely scratch the surface, there are some key attractions and pleasures that you won't want to miss. These include the different **ethnic neighborhoods**, like Chinatown, and the more artsy concentrations of SoHo, TriBeCa, and the East and West villages. Of course, there is the celebrated **architecture** of Midtown and the Financial District, as well as many fabulous **museums** – not just the Metropolitan and MoMA, but countless other smaller collections that afford weeks of happy wandering. In between sights, you can **eat** just about anything, at any time, cooked in any style; you can **drink** in any kind of com-pany; and enjoy any number of obscure **movies**. The more established arts – **dance**, **theater**, and **music** – are superbly presented. For the avid consumer, the choice of **shops** is vast, almost numbingly exhaustive, in this heartland of the great capitalist dream.

Manhattan is a hard act to follow, and the four **outer boroughs**, essentially residential in character, inevitably pale in comparison. However, all hold treas-ures that are worth seeking out. **Brooklyn Heights** is one of the city's most beautiful neighborhoods; **Long Island City** and **Astoria**, both in Queens, hold many innovative museums; and a visit to the **Bronx Zoo** is sure to be rewarding. Last but not least, a trip on the **Staten Island Ferry** is not to be missed; a sea-sprayed, refreshing good time, it provides excellent views of the city.

Some history
The first European to see Manhattan Island, then inhabited by the Algonquin Indians, was the Italian navigator Verrazano, in 1524. Dutch colonists estab-lished the settlement of **New Amsterdam** exactly one hundred years later. The first governor, Peter Minuit, was the man who "bought" the whole island

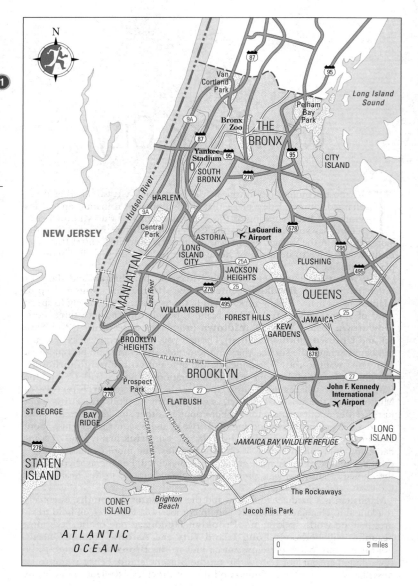

for a handful of trinkets. Considering that the Indians he actually paid were not locals, but only passing through, it might be said that they received a fine deal, too. A strong defensive wall – today's Wall Street follows its course – surrounded the colony. By the time the British laid claim to the area in 1664, the heavy-handed rule of governor **Peter Stuyvesant** had so alienated its inhabitants that the Dutch handed over control without a fight.

Renamed New York, the city prospered and grew, its population reaching 33,000 by the time of the American Revolution. The opening of the Erie Canal in 1825 facilitated trade farther inland, spurring the city to become the economic powerhouse of the nation, the base later in the century of **financiers** such as Cornelius Vanderbilt and Pierpont Morgan. The **Statue of Liberty** arrived in 1886, a symbol of the city's role as the gateway for generations of immigrants, and the early twentieth century saw the sudden proliferation of Manhattan's extraordinary **skyscrapers**, which cast New York as the city of the future in the eyes of an astonished world.

Almost a century later, the events of **September 11th, 2001**, which destroyed the World Trade Center, shook New York to its core. Several years on, the site of the attacks at Ground Zero has been cleared, and plans are under way to commemorate those who were killed, as well as erect a new jewel in the city's skyline – the **Freedom Tower** (see box, p.80).

Arrival, information, and city transportation

New York City is served by three major **airports**: most international flights use **John F. Kennedy**, or **JFK**, in Queens, though some Virgin, British Airways, and Continental flights land at **Newark**, in New Jersey. Most domestic arrivals touch down at **LaGuardia**, also in Queens, or at Newark, which has easier access to Lower Manhattan.

From JFK, New York Airport Service buses run to the Port Authority Bus Terminal, Grand Central Station, Penn Station, and major Midtown hotels in Manhattan (every 15–20min 6am–midnight; trip time 45min–1hr; $13 one-way, students $6). Another option is the bus/subway link, which costs just the $2 subway fare: take the free shuttle bus (labeled "Long-term parking") to the Howard Beach station on the #A subway line, then the 90min subway ride to central Manhattan.

From Newark, Olympia Airport Express buses take up to forty minutes to get to Manhattan, where they stop at Grand Central, Penn Station, Port Authority, and multiple locations in Lower Manhattan (every 20–30min 4am–midnight; $12 one-way, $19 roundtrip). Alternatively, you can use the **AirTrain** service, which runs for free between all Newark terminals, parking lots, and the Newark Airport Rail Link station, where you can connect with NJ Transit or Amtrak trains into New York Penn Station. It usually takes about 20min, and costs $11.55 one-way (every 20–30min 6am–midnight).

From LaGuardia, New York Airport Service buses take 45 minutes to get to Grand Central and Port Authority (every 15–30min 7am–midnight; $10 one-way, $17 roundtrip, students one-way $6). Alternatively, for $2, you can take the #M60 bus to 125th Street in Manhattan, where you can transfer (for another $2) to multiple Downtown-bound subway lines.

Taxis are pricey from the airports; expect to pay $18–24 from LaGuardia, a flat rate of $35 from JFK, and $35–55 from Newark (airport taxis at Newark will tell you their flat fares to different parts of Manhattan before you leave). You should only use official yellow taxis.

Minibus shuttle services are a decent mid-priced option if you don't mind multiple stops along the way and a very early start. Super Shuttle minivans run 24hr and arrange pick-ups three hours before domestic departures and five hours before international ones (☎1-800/BLUE-VAN or 212/BLUE-VAN). One-way fares to the airport run $20, more for a ride from the airport into the city ($30–35). Be forewarned that, if your van has many pick-ups, the time spent picking up riders is not always equal to the money saved. For **general information** on getting to and from the airports, call the Port Authority ground transportation and parking hotline at ☎1-800/AIR-RIDE.

Greyhound buses pull in at the Port Authority Bus Terminal, 42nd Street and Eighth Avenue. **Amtrak** trains come in to Penn Station, at Seventh Avenue and 33rd Street. From either Port Authority or Penn Station, multiple subway lines will take you where you want to go from there.

If **arriving by car**, you have multiple options: Rte-495 transects Midtown Manhattan from New Jersey through the Lincoln Tunnel and from the east through the Queens-Midtown Tunnel. From the southwest, I-95 (the New Jersey Turnpike) and I-78 serve Canal and Spring streets (near SoHo and TriBeCa) via the Holland Tunnel. From the north, I-87 (New York State Thruway) and I-95 serve Manhattan's loop roads. Be prepared for **delays** at tunnels and bridges; most charge tolls. Also, when **parking** your car in Manhattan, try for a garage as near to the rivers as possible to avoid high fees.

Information

The best place for information is the **New York Convention and Visitors' Bureau**, 810 Seventh Ave at 53rd Street (Mon–Fri 8.30am–6pm, Sat & Sun 9am–5pm; ☎212/484-1222, ⓦwww.nycvisit.com). It has leaflets on what's going on in the arts, bus and subway maps, and information on accommodations – though they can't actually book anything for you. You can also find lots of listings at ⓦnewyork.citysearch.com. For trendier offerings, go to ⓦwww.dailycandy.com. Free city maps are available at the tourist cubicle in Grand Central.

The **James A. Farley Post Office**, Manhattan's main branch, is at 421 Eighth Ave, between West 31st and 33rd streets (Mon–Sat 24hr for all services except registered mail; zip code 10001).

City transportation

Few cities equal New York for sheer street-level stimulation, and **walking** is the most exciting way to explore. However, it's also exhausting, so at some point you'll need to use some form of **public transportation**. Citywide sub-

---

City streets and orientation

The first part of Manhattan to be settled was what is now Downtown; this is why the streets here have names (as opposed to numbers) and are somewhat randomly arranged. A map (see p.79) is key for getting around Lower Manhattan effectively. Oftentimes you will hear of places referred to as being either on the **West Side** or the **East Side**; what this means, simply, is whether the place in question lies west or east of **Fifth Avenue**, the greatest of the main avenues, which begins Downtown at the arch in Washington Square Park and runs north to cut along the east side of Central Park. On the East Side above Houston Street (pronounced "Howstun"), and on the West Side above 14th, the streets follow a sensible **grid pattern**, progressing northward one by one. When looking for a specific **address**, keep in mind that on streets, house numbers increase as you walk away from Fifth in either direction; on avenues, house numbers increase as you move north.

way and bus system **maps** – the subway map is especially invaluable – are available from all subway station booths, the Convention and Visitors' Bureau (see above), and the concourse office at Grand Central.

The subway

The fastest way to get from point A to point B in Manhattan and the boroughs is the **subway**, open 24hr a day. Intimidating at first glance, the subway system is actually quite user-friendly. A number or letter identifies each train and route, and most routes run uptown or downtown, rather than crosstown. Every trip, whether on the **express** lines, which stop only at major stations, or the **locals**, which stop at all stations, costs $2. The old-fashioned subway token is no longer accepted; now all riders must use a **MetroCard**, available at station booths or credit/debit/ATM card-capable vending machines. MetroCards can be purchased in any amount from $4 to $80; a $20 purchase allows 12 rides for the cost of 10. Unlimited rides are available with a 24hr "Fun Pass" ($7), a 7-day pass ($21), and a 30-day pass ($70).

Once you get past the turnstile, forget everything you've seen in the movies. New York City subways are generally **quite safe**, in part because they are almost always crowded, even at night. The key to being safe is to use common sense. Always use the more crowded center subway cars late at night, and, while you're waiting, keep to where the booth attendants can see you. Once inside the subway system, you can ride around for as long as you like, as long as you don't pass back out through the turnstiles; if you do that, you'll have to swipe your card again to get back in.

Buses

New York's **bus system** is clean, efficient, and fairly frequent. Its one disadvantage is that it can be extremely slow – in peak hours almost down to walking pace – but it can be your best bet for traveling crosstown. Buses leave their route terminal points at five- to ten-minute intervals, and stop every two or three blocks. The fare is payable on entry with a MetroCard (the same one used for the subway); you can **transfer** for free from subway to bus, or from bus to bus (though not from bus to subway), within two hours of swiping your MetroCard. Keep in mind, though, that transfers can only be used to continue on in your original direction, not for return trips on the same bus line.

Taxis

Taxis are reasonably priced – and they're everywhere. Although the rudimentary English of many drivers is notorious, they can normally get you where you want to go. Knowing the exact address and its cross street is helpful. You should only use official yellow taxis.

Guided tours

Countless businesses and individuals compete to help you make sense of the city, offering all manner of **guided tours**. One of the more original – and least expensive – ways to get oriented is with Big Apple Greeter, 1 Centre St, suite 2035 (T 212/669-8159, W www.bigapplegreeter.org). This not-for-profit group matches you with a local volunteer and points you to places that interest you. It's free, so get in touch well ahead of time.

New York City Vacation Packages (T 1-888/692-8701, W www.nycvp.com) can book rooms at some of the city's finest hotels, land tickets to sold-out Broadway shows, and organize a walking tour of Ground Zero or Chinatown for you; just pick from an à la carte menu of offerings. Package

CityPass

For significant **discounts** at six of the city's major tourist and cultural attractions – the American Museum of Natural History, the Guggenheim Museum, the Museum of Modern Art, the *Intrepid* Sea-Air-Space Museum, the Circle Line Harbor Cruise, and the Empire State Building – you can purchase a **CityPass** ($45; ☏707/256-0490, ⓦwww.citypass.com). Valid for nine days, it allows you to skip most lines and save (up to $46, if you visit all six sights). CityPasses are sold at each of the six attractions to which the pass provides admission.

prices vary widely, so call or email ⓔinfo@nycvp.com for information.

Gray Line, the biggest operator of guided **bus tours** in the city, is based in Midtown Manhattan at Eighth Avenue between 47th and 48th streets (☏1-800/669-0051, ⓦwww.grayline.com); they also have an office at the Port Authority Bus Terminal. Half-day double-decker bus tours, taking in the main sights of Manhattan, go for around $35, while a full day costs $79–89; these are bookable through any travel agent, or directly at the bus stops. If you're not happy with your tour guide (quality can vary widely), you can hop off the bus and wait another 15 minutes for the next bus and guide.

A good way to see the city skyline is with the **Circle Line Ferry**, which sails around Manhattan in three hours from Pier 83 at the west end of 42nd Street (at 12th Ave), with a commentary and on-board bar (March–Dec with varying regularity; $21 for 2hr tour, $26 for 3hr; ☏212/563-3200, ⓦwww .circleline.com). They also operate more exhilarating tours on "The Beast," a speedboat (May–Oct; $15 adults, $10 children for 30min ride). Alternatively, the **Staten Island Ferry** provides a beautiful panorama of the Downtown skyline for free (see p.109 for more).

For a bird's-eye view, Liberty Helicopter Tours, at the west end of 30th Street near the Jacob Javits Convention Center (☏212/967-4550, ⓦwww.liberty helicopters.com), offers **helicopter flights** from around $56 for 7 minutes to $162 for 17 minutes per person.

Walking tours

Adventure on a Shoestring ☏212/265-2663. This 40-year-old tour company offers such wonderfully off-beat options as "Marilyn Monroe's Manhattan," the "When Irish Eyes Were Smiling" tour of Hell's Kitchen, and "Greenwich Village Ghosts Galore." Tours ($5) run 90 minutes, and are offered on weekends, rain or shine, throughout the year.

Big Onion Walking Tours ☏212/439-1090, ⓦwww.bigonion.com. The Onion guides peel off the many layers of the city's history (all guides hold advanced degrees in American history). Tours run from $12; call or visit the website for schedules and meeting places. Expect to add $4 if the tour includes "noshing stops."

Harlem Heritage Tours 230 W 116th St, suite 5C ☏212/280-7888, ⓦwww .harlemheritage.com. Cultural walking tours of Harlem, general and specific (such as Harlem jazz clubs), are led middays and evenings seven days a week for $10–100 (most tours average $25); reservations are recommended and can be booked online.

Municipal Arts Society 457 Madison Ave ☏212/935-3960 or 212/439-1049, ⓦwww.mas.org. Architectural, public art, historic preservation, and cultural tours. Weekday walking tours $15–20; free Wednesday lunchtime tours of Grand Central Station begin at 12.30pm from the main information booth; Saturday walking and bus tours may require reservations.

Accommodation

Prices for **accommodation** in New York are well above the norm for the US as a whole. Most hotels charge more than $100 a night (although exceptions and decent double rooms from $75 a night do exist). Most of New York's **hotels** are in Midtown Manhattan – a good enough location, though you may well want to travel downtown for less expensive (and usually better) food and nightlife. **Booking ahead** is strongly advised; at certain times of the year – Christmas and early summer particularly – everything is likely to be full. Phone the hotels directly, or at no extra charge contact a booking service, such as Meegan's (☎718/995-9292 or 1-800/441-1115), CRS (☎407/740-6442 or 1-800/555-7555), The Room Exchange (Mon–Fri only ☎212/760-1000), or Express Reservations (Mon–Fri only ☎1-800/356-1123). Rates are often reduced on weekends, so it's always worth asking.

Apartment stays and **bed-and-breakfasts** are an attractive alternative. Staying in a New Yorker's spare room or subletting an apartment is an increasingly popular (and somewhat less expensive) option. Reservations are normally arranged through an agency such as those listed above. Rates run about $80–100 for a double, or $100 and up a night for a studio apartment. Book well in advance.

Hostels offer still more savings, and run the gamut in terms of quality, safety, and amenities for backpackers and budget travelers. It pays to do research ahead of time so as to ensure satisfaction upon arrival; most of the city's best cheap sleeps have websites. Average hostel rates range from $30–60.

Hotels

60 Thompson 60 Thompson St, between Spring and Broome ☎212/431-0400, ⓦwww .60thompson.com. Designed by Thomas O'Brien's Aero Studio, this boutique property oozes sophistication and tempts guests with countless amenities, including gourmet minibars, DVD players, and a summertime rooftop lounge overlooking the SoHo skyline. All this fabulousness comes at a price, though. ❾

Algonquin 59 W 44th St, between 5th and 6th aves ☎212/840-6800, ⓦwww.algonquinhotel .com. At New York's classic literary hangout, you'll find a resident cat named Matilde, cabaret performances, and suites with silly names. The decor remains little changed, though the bedrooms have been refurbished to good effect, and the lobby recently received a mini-facelift. Ask about summer and weekend specials. ❼–❾

Amsterdam Inn 340 Amsterdam Ave, at 76th St ☎212/579-7500 or 1-800/373-1116, ⓦwww.nyinns.com. This hotel is within easy walking distance of Central Park, Lincoln Center, and the American Museum of Natural History. Rooms are basic but clean, with TVs, phones, and maid service. The staff is friendly and there's a 24hr concierge. ❹–❻

The Chelsea Hotel 222 W 23rd St, between 7th and 8th aves ☎212/243-3700, ⓦwww .hotelchelsea.com. One of New York's most noted landmarks, this aging neo-Gothic building boasts a fabulous past (see p.89). Ask for a renovated room, with wood floors, log-burning fireplaces, and plenty of space for a few extra friends. Studio room with kitchenette ❼, suite ❾

Dylan 52 E 41st St, between Park and Madison ☎212/338-0500 or 1-866/55-DYLAN, ⓦwww.dylanhotel.com. The hardwood floors, warm light, and vaguely lemony-tasting air in the lobby are indicative of the whole experience at *Dylan* – classy and clever. If you can afford it, book the Alchemy Suite, a one-of-a-kind Gothic bedchamber with a vaulted ceiling and unusual stained glass windows. ❽–❾

Edison 228 W 47th St, between Broadway and 8th Ave ☎212/840-5000, ⓦwww.edisonhotelnyc .com. The most striking thing about the funky 1000-room *Edison*, a good value for Midtown, is its beautifully restored Art Deco lobby. The rooms, though not fancy, have been recently renovated. ❼

Gramercy Park 2 Lexington Ave, at E 21st St ☎212/475-4320, ⓦwww.grammercyparkhotel .com. In a lovely location, this hotel is pleasant enough, with a mixture of newly renovated (75 percent) and tatty rooms. Be sure to ask for one of the new rooms. Guests get a key to the adjacent private park (see p.88). **7**

Hudson 356 W 58th St, between 8th and 9th aves ☏ 212/554-6000 or 1-800 444-4786, ⊛ www.ian-schragerhotels.com. The latest Schrager addition to NYC, this overly designed hotel features a space-age cocktail lounge, library, cavernous "cafeteria," and miniscule rooms, which are significantly cheaper during the week. **7**

Larchmont 27 W 11th St, between 5th and 6th aves ☏ 212/989-9333, ⊛ www.larchmont-hotel.com. This budget hotel, on a tree-lined street in Greenwich Village, has small but nice, clean rooms. Terrific location. Singles **3**, doubles **5**; slightly more expensive on weekends.

Lucerne 201 W 79th St, at Amsterdam ☏ 212/875-1000 or 1-800/492-8122, ⊛ www.newyorkhotel.com. This beautifully restored 1904 brownstone, with its extravagantly Baroque red terracotta entrance, charming rooms, and friendly, helpful staff, is just a block from the Natural History Museum and close to the liveliest stretch of the Columbus Avenue scene. **8**, with summer rates at **7**

Mercer 147 Mercer St, at Prince ☏ 212/966-6060, ⊛ www.mercerhotel.com. Housed in a land-mark Romanesque Revival building, this hot SoHo hotel has been the choice of celebs such as Leonardo DiCaprio since 1998. Some loft-like guest rooms also have massive baths with 90 square feet for splashing around, and the *Mercer Kitchen* restaurant garners rave reviews. **9**

Milburn 242 W 76th St, between Broadway and West End ☏ 212/362-1006, ⊛ www.milburnhotel .com. This welcoming and well-situated hotel, great for families, has recently been renovated in gracious style. Doubles **5**; large two-room suites, with kitchenettes **8**

Paramount 235 W 46th St, between Broadway and 8th Ave ☏ 212/764-5500, ⊛ www.ianschragerhotels .com. A former budget hotel renovated a decade or so ago by Ian Schrager (co-founder of *Studio 54*), the *Paramount* offers chic but closet-size rooms. It also boasts a trendy (and sometimes raucous) bar. **8**, with summer specials at **7**

Pickwick Arms 230 E 51st St, between 2nd and 3rd aves ☏ 212/355-0300, ⊛ www.pick-wickarms.com. This thoroughly pleasant budget hotel is one of the best deals in Midtown. All 370 rooms are air-conditioned, with cable TV, direct-dial phones, and room service. The open-air roof deck has stunning views, and there are two restaurants (one French, one Mediterranean) downstairs. A single room with shared bath is $79. **4**

Roger Smith 501 Lexington Ave, at E 47th St ☏ 212/755-1400, ⊛ www.rogersmith.com. One of

the best Midtown hotels. Plusses include individu-ally decorated rooms, a great restaurant, helpful service, and artwork on display in public spaces. Breakfast is included. **8**, summer at **7**

Royalton 44 W 44th St, between 5th and 6th aves ☏ 212/869-4400, ⊛ www.ianschragerhotels.com. Attempting to capture the market for the arbiters of style, the Philippe Starck–designed *Royalton* has tony, nautical-themed rooms that are comfort-able and quiet, affording a welcome escape from the bustle of Midtown. The bathrooms in the lobby are not to be missed, either. **9**

Seventeen 225 E 17th St, between 2nd and 3rd aves ☏ 212/475-2845, ⊛ www.hotel17ny.com. Recently remodeled, *Seventeen*'s rooms feature AC, cable TV, and phones, though they still have shared baths. It's clean, friendly, and nicely situat-ed on a pleasant tree-lined street minutes from Union Square and the East Village. Check out the excellent weekly rates. Nightly rates **3**–**4**

SoHo Grand 310 W Broadway, at Grand ☏ 212/965-3000, ⊛ www.sohogrand.com. In a great location at the edge of SoHo, this hotel draws guests of the model/media-star/actor vari-ety. Its appeal includes small but stylish rooms, a good bar, restaurant, and fitness center. Call for info about its sister property, the *Tribeca Grand*. **9**

Stanford 43 W 32nd St, between Broadway and 5th Ave ☏ 212/563-1500 or 1-800/365-1114, ⊛ www.hotelstanford.com. In this clean, moder-ately priced hotel on the block known as Little Korea, rooms are a tad small, but attractive and very quiet. Free continental breakfast, valet laun-dry, and an efficient, friendly staff. **4**

W 541 Lexington Ave, between 49th and 50th sts ☏ 212/755-1200, ⊛ www.whotels.com; Downtown location at 201 Park Ave S at 17th St ☏ 212/253-9119. These two branches of the stylish luxury hotel chain offer top-to-bottom comfort, priding themselves on the wired in-room services, sleek neutral tones, and trendy public spaces, such as the *Whisky Blue Bar* in the Midtown location, or celebrity chef Todd English's *Olives* restaurant in the Downtown one. **9**

Wales 1295 Madison Ave, between 92nd and 93rd sts ☏ 212/876-6000, ⊛ www.waleshotel .com. Just steps from NYC's "Museum Mile" (see p.96), this Carnegie Hill hotel has hosted guests for over a century. Rooms are attractive with antique details, thoughtful in-room amenities, and some views of Central Park. There's also a rooftop terrace, fitness studio, famous *Sarabeth's Café*, and live harp music during breakfast. **7**–**8**

Washington Square 103 Waverly Place, at Washington Square Park ⓣ212/777-9515, ⓦ www.washingtonsquarehotel.com. The ideal location in the heart of Greenwich Village is a stone's throw from the NYU campus. Don't be deceived by the posh-looking lobby – the rooms are surprisingly shabby for the price, but serviceable. Continental breakfast is included. ❻–❼

Wyndham 42 W 58th St, between 5th and 6th aves ⓣ212/753-3500 or 1-800/257-1111. This worn-around-the-edges Midtown standby can't be beat for its location, price, and spacious guest-rooms, many of which include kitchenettes. Staff is very friendly, too. A great choice for families. ❻–❼

Bed-and-breakfasts

Affordable New York City 21 E 10th St ⓣ212/533-4001, ⓦ www.affordablenyc.com. Detailed descriptions are provided for this estab-lished network of 120 properties (B&Bs and apart-ments) around the city. B&B accommodations from $85 (shared bath) and $100 (private bath), unhost-ed studios $135–160 and one-bedrooms $175–225. Cash or travelers checks only; three-night minimum. Very customer-oriented and per-sonable. ❻–❾

Bed and Breakfast Network of New York 130 Barrow St ⓣ212/645-8134 or 1-800/ 900-8134, ⓦ www.bedandbreakfastnetny.com. Call at least a month in advance, and ask about weekly and monthly specials. Hosted doubles ❺–❻; unhost-ed accommodation ❻–❾

CitySonnet.com ⓣ212/614-3034, ⓦ www.citysonnet.com. This small, personalized, artist-run B&B/short-term apartment agency offers accommodations all over the city, but specializes in Greenwich Village. Singles start at $85, doubles are $100–155, and unhosted studio flats start at $120. ❹–❺

Colby International 139 Round Hey, Liverpool L28 1RG, England UK ⓣ0151/220 5848, ⓦ www.colbyinternational.com. Guaranteed B&B accommodations can be arranged from the UK. Book at least a fortnight ahead in high season for these excellent-value double apartments (❹) and studios (❹–❾).

Urban Ventures 38 W 32nd St, suite 1412 ⓣ212/594-5650, ⓔreservations@gamutnyc.com. Book up until the last minute for nightly, weekly, or monthly rentals; there's a minimum stay of only two nights. Budget doubles from $75 (❹), "com-fort range" rooms from $149 (❻), unhosted apartments ❾

Hostels

Chelsea International Hostel 251 W 20th St, between 7th and 8th aves ⓣ212/647-0010, ⓦ www.chelseahostel.com. In the heart of Chelsea, this is a smart Downtown choice: beds are $27 a night, with 4 or 6 sharing the clean, rudimentary rooms. Private double rooms are $65 a night. Guests must leave a $10 key deposit. No curfew; passport required. ❸

Gershwin 7 E 27th St, between 5th and Madison aves ⓣ212/545-8000, ⓕ684-5546, ⓦ www.gershwinhotel.com. This hostel/hotel geared toward young travelers offers Pop Art decor and dormitories with 2, 6, or 10 beds per room (from $33 a night) and private rooms from $99. Reservations recommended for both room types. ❷

Hostelling International-New York 891 Amsterdam Ave, at W 103rd St ⓣ212/932-2300, ⓦ www.hinewyork.org. Dorm beds cost $32 (in 10-bed rooms) to $38 (in 4-bed rooms); members pay a few dollars less per night. The massive facilities – 624 beds in all – include a restaurant, library, travel shop, TV room, laundry, and kitchen. Reserve well in advance – this hostel is very pop-ular. ❶–❷

Jazz on the Park 36 W 106th St, at Central Park West ⓣ212/932-1600, ⓦ www.jazzonthepark .com. This groovy bunkhouse boasts a TV/games room, the *Java Joint Café*, and lots of activities, including live jazz on weekends. Rooms sleep between 2 and 14 people, are clean, bright, and air-conditioned, and range from $26 to $90 per night. Reserve at least one week in advance. ❶–❹

West Side YMCA 5 W 63rd St, at Central Park West ⓣ212/441-8800, ⓦ www.ymcanyc.org. The "Y," just steps from Central Park, houses two floors of recently renovated rooms, an inexpensive restaurant, swimming pool, gym, and laundry. All rooms are air-conditioned. Singles $65, doubles $115 with private bath. ❸–❺

Whitehouse Hotel of New York 340 Bowery ⓣ212/477-5623, ⓦ www.whitehousehotelofny .com. This is the only hostel in the city that offers single and double rooms at dorm rates. Unbeatable prices combined with an ideal Downtown location, and amenities such as AC, ATMs, cable TV, and linens, make this hostel an excellent pick. Private singles start at $26, private doubles at $50. ❶–❸

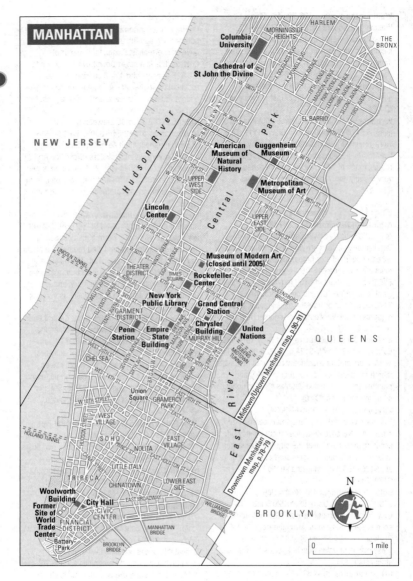

Downtown Manhattan

DOWNTOWN MANHATTAN – the patchwork of neighborhoods below 14th Street – runs the gamut from high finance and cutting-edge cool to Old World charm and bewitching urban decay; it's truly one of the most vibrant, exciting parts of the city. Downtown's interest actually begins below Manhattan's southern tip in New York Harbor, which holds the compulsory attractions of the **Statue of Liberty** and **Ellis Island**. The southernmost neighborhood on the mainland is the **Financial District**, with Wall Street at its center, flanked by Battery Park and the South Street Seaport; less than a half-mile north, the buildings of the **Civic Center** transition into the jangling street life of **Chinatown**, which is fast encroaching upon the once-authentic, now-touristy **Little Italy**. East of Chinatown and Little Italy, the **Lower East Side** marks the traditional point of entry into the city for many different immigrant groups. For most of the twentieth century, the neighborhood was predominantly Jewish; now it's a mix of Dominicans and young artistic types – and very trendy to boot, with chic bars and restaurants opening up weekly.

West of Chinatown and Little Italy, respectively, the one-time industrial areas of **TriBeCa** and **SoHo** are now expensive residential (and, in the case of SoHo, shopping) districts, ostensibly home to Manhattan's film and art scenes, but with few sights to reflect either fact. The smallish area known as **NoLita** takes in numerous boutiques and hip restaurants in its few well-manicured blocks. North of Houston Street, the activity picks up even more in the **West Village** and **East Village**, two former bohemian enclaves that are now more traditional than their residents would like to think. Still, both are good fun, the former for its charming backstreets and brownstones, the latter for its energetic nightlife.

It's hard to talk for too long about Lower Manhattan without mentioning the terrorist attack on the World Trade Center on **September 11th, 2001**, which killed more than three thousand people and destroyed the Twin Towers, long-time symbol of the Financial District. A pilgrimage to **Ground Zero**, as the former site of the towers has come to be called, is for many an integral part of a visit to New York.

The Statue of Liberty and Ellis Island

Standing tall and proud in the middle of New York Harbor, the **Statue of Liberty** has for more than a century served as a symbol of the American Dream. Depicting Liberty throwing off her shackles and holding a beacon to light the world, the monument was the creation of the French sculptor Frédéric Auguste Bartholdi, crafted a hundred years after the American Revolution, in recognition of fraternity between the French and American people. The statue, which consists of thin copper sheets bolted together and supported by an iron framework designed by Gustave Eiffel, of Eiffel Tower fame, was built in Paris between 1874 and 1884. Bartholdi enlarged his original terracotta model to its present size through four successive versions; one of these now stands beside the Seine in Paris. The one here was formally dedicated by President Grover Cleveland on October 28, 1886. Due to security restrictions, you can no longer enter the monument; however, the Statue's home, **Liberty Island**, remains open if you want a close-up look at Lady Liberty.

Just across the water, **Ellis Island** was the first stop for more than twelve million prospective immigrants. Originally called Gibbet Island by the English (who used it for punishing unfortunate pirates), it became an immigration station in 1892, mainly to handle the massive influx from southern and eastern Europe. It remained open until 1954, when it was left to fall into atmospheric ruin.

The immigrants who arrived at Ellis Island were all steerage-class passengers; richer voyagers were processed at their leisure on-board ship. Most families

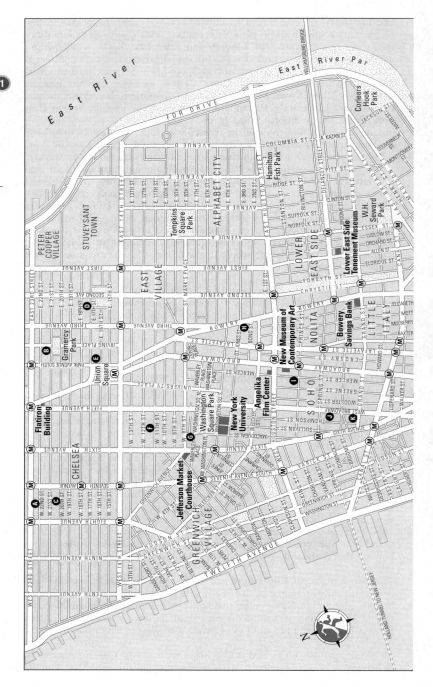

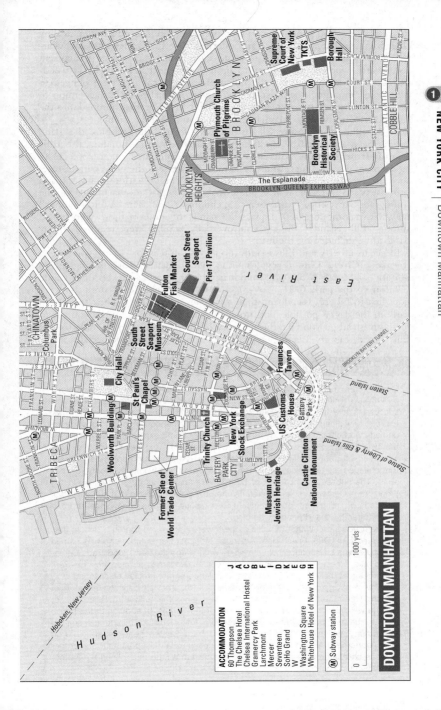

DOWNTOWN MANHATTAN

Supreme Court of New York

TKTS

Borough Hall

Plymouth Church of Pilgrims

BROOKLYN

Brooklyn Historical Society

The Esplanade
BROOKLYN-QUEENS EXPRESSWAY

BROOKLYN HEIGHTS

COBBLE HILL

East River

South Street Seaport

Pier 17 Pavilion

Fulton Fish Market

South Street Seaport Museum

CHINATOWN

Columbus Park

Fraunces Tavern

City Hall

St Paul's Chapel

US Customs House

Battery Park

Staten Island

Woolworth Building

Trinity Church

New York Stock Exchange

TRIBECA

Former Site of World Trade Center

BATTERY PARK CITY

Museum of Jewish Heritage

Castle Clinton National Monument

Statue of Liberty & Ellis Island

BROOKLYN BATTERY TUNNEL

Hoboken, New Jersey

Hudson River

1000 yds

ACCOMMODATION
60 Thompson .... J
The Chelsea Hotel .... A
Chelsea International Hostel .. C
Gramercy Park .... B
Larchmont .... F
Mercer I
Seventeen .... D
SoHo Grand .... K
W .... E
Washington Square .... G
Whitehouse Hotel of New York H

Ⓜ Subway station

79

arrived hungry and penniless; con men preyed on them from all sides, stealing their baggage as it was checked and offering rip-off exchange rates for whatever money they had managed to bring. Each family was split up – men sent to one area, women and children to another – while a series of checks weeded out the undesirables and the infirm. Steamship carriers were obliged to return any immigrants not accepted to their original port, but according to official records only two percent were rejected. Many of those jumped into the sea and tried to swim to Manhattan rather than face going home.

By the time of its closure, Ellis Island was a formidable complex, the island having been expanded by landfill. In the turreted central building, the **Ellis Island Immigration Museum** (daily 9am–5pm; free; ℡212/363-3200, ⓦ www.nps.gov/stli) successfully recaptures the spirit of the place with features such as "Treasures from Home," a collection of family heirlooms, photos, and other artifacts, as well as live, somewhat hit-or-miss re-enactments of the immigrant experience (April–Sept; $5, children $2.50). The "Wall of Honor" (ⓦ www.wallofhonor.com) displays the names of some of those who passed through Ellis Island – though controversially, families were required to pay $100 to be included on the list.

To get to Liberty and Ellis islands (no admission fees for either), you'll need to take a **Circle Line ferry** from the pier in Battery Park (sailings every 30min, daily 9.30am–3.30pm; roundtrip $10, children $4; tickets from Castle Clinton, in the park; ℡212/269-5755, ⓦ www.circlelineferry.com); the ferry goes first to Liberty Island, and then continues on to Ellis. It's best to leave as early in the day as possible, both to avoid long lines and to insure you get to see both islands; if you take the last ferry of the day, you won't be able to visit Ellis Island. Liberty Island needs a good couple of hours, especially if the

The World Trade Center

Completed in 1973, the Twin Towers of the **World Trade Center** were an integral part of New York's legendary skyline, and a symbol of the city's social and economic success. While the WTC's claim to be the world's tallest building was quickly usurped by Chicago's Sears Tower (and later on by other buildings), and despite the damage wrought in February of 1993 by a terrorist bomb explosion which killed six, the Twin Towers were, as of 2001, very successful, having become both a busy workspace and a much-loved tourist destination. However, on September 11th, all that changed, as two hijacked planes crashed into the towers just twenty minutes apart. The subsequent collapse of both towers (as well as other buildings in the World Trade Center complex) served as a terrible wake-up call, and took the lives of hundreds of firefighters, police officers, and rescue workers, among the approximately three thousand people who died.

Several years on, all that remains of the towers is the deep "bathtub" where they once stood. In 2003, Polish-born American architect Daniel Libeskind was named the winner of a competition held to decide what shape the new World Trade Center would take. Libeskind's visionary design includes two large public spaces: the Park of Heroes and the Wedge of Light, which will incorporate precise engineering worthy of ancient Egypt. Each year, on September 11th, precisely between the hours of 8.46am, when the first plane hit, and 10.30am, when the second tower collapsed, the sun will shine without shadow in honor of the victims. In addition to the public spaces, the new building itself – the Freedom Tower – will culminate in a soaring 1776ft spire, which will make the new World Trade Center the tallest structure on earth. Underneath it all, Libeskind is leaving space for a museum about September 11th, as well as an official memorial, whose design will be determined by another international competition.

weather's nice and there aren't too many people; Ellis Island, too, demands at least two hours for the Museum of Immigration. If you just want the views and some time out on the water, take the free, fun **Staten Island Ferry** into the harbor; see p.109 for full details.

The Financial District

The **Financial District** has been synonymous with the Manhattan of popular imagination for some time, its tall buildings and powerful skyline symbols of economic strength and financial wheeling and dealing. Though New York City had an active securities market by 1790, the **New York Stock Exchange** wasn't officially organized until 1817, when 28 stockbrokers adopted their own constitution and established membership rules. It's been one of the world's great financial centers ever since, having most recently weathered the fallout from the World Trade Center attacks. Besides visiting a temporary viewing platform where you can glimpse the first phase of the new construction at Ground Zero (see box, opposite), there is plenty more to see and do here – it remains the city's most historic district, with many winding streets, old churches, and fine twentieth-century architecture.

Wall Street and around

When the Dutch arrived in New York and settled at the site of the future Financial District, they built a wooden wall at the edge of their small settlement to protect themselves from pro-British settlers to the north. Hence, the narrow canyon of **Wall Street** gained its name. Today, behind the Neoclassical mask of the **New York Stock Exchange**, at Broad and Wall streets, the purse strings of the world are pulled. Due to security concerns, however, the public can no longer observe the frenzied trading on the floor of the exchange.

The **Federal Hall National Memorial**, at 26 Wall St, looks a little foolish surrounded by skyscrapers. The building was once the Customs House, but the exhibit inside (Mon–Fri 9am–5pm; free; ☎212/825-6888, ⓦ www.nps.gov /feha) relates to the headier days of 1789, when George Washington was sworn in as president from a balcony on this site. Washington's statue stands, very properly, on the steps outside the gently domed hall. At Wall Street's western end, on Broadway between Rector and Church streets, **Trinity Church** (guided tours daily at 2pm; free) is an ironic onlooker to the street's dealings, a knobbly neo-Gothic structure erected in 1846, and the city's tallest building for fifty years thence. The place has much the air of an English church, especially in its sheltered graveyard, which is the resting place of early luminaries including the first Secretary of the Treasury (and the man on the ten-dollar bill) Alexander Hamilton, who was killed in a duel by then-Vice President Aaron Burr.

Just down from Trinity Church, Broadway comes to a gentle end at **Bowling Green Park**, an oval of turf used for the game (of bowling) by eighteenth-century colonial Brits, on a lease of "one peppercorn per year." Earlier still, the green was the site of one of Manhattan's more memorable business deals: Peter Minuit, first director general of the Dutch colony of New Amsterdam, bought the whole island from the Indians for a handful of baubles worth sixty guilders (about $25). At the green today, office workers picnic in the shadow of Cass Gilbert's 1907 **US Customs House**, a monument to New York's once-booming maritime economy. Four statues at the front (sculpted by Daniel Chester French, who also created the Lincoln Memorial in Washington, DC) represent the African, Asian, European, and North American continents, while the twelve statues near the top personify the world's great past and present commercial centers – Genoa and Phonecia among them. The building's Corinthian columns each feature the head of Mercury, the god of commerce.

The Customs House contains the superb **Smithsonian National Museum of the American Indian** (daily 10am–5pm, Thurs until 8pm; free; ℡212/514-3700, Ⓦwww.si.edu/nmai), a fascinating assembly of artifacts from almost every tribe native to the Americas. The curators give a creative presentation of their material, which includes large wood and stone carvings from the Pacific Northwest; elegant featherwork from Amazonia; a large array of masks; Aztec mosaics; Mayan textiles; seven-foot house posts shaped like animals; a handful of scalps; and a tribe's worth of elaborately beaded moccasins.

Battery Park and around

Across State Street from the Customs House, Downtown Manhattan lets out its breath in **Battery Park**, where the nineteenth-century Castle Clinton (daily 8.30am–5pm) once protected the southern tip of Manhattan and now sells ferry tickets to the Statue of Liberty and Ellis Island (see p.77). The newly spruced-up park stretches for blocks up the West Side and is dotted with piers, cool corners, and some inventive landscaping. Not far from where the World Trade Center stood is one of the city's first (and few official, so far) memorials to the victims of September 11th; its focal point is the cracked 15-foot steel-and-bronze spherical sculpture, designed by Fritz Koenig, that once stood in the World Trade Center Plaza.

Further toward the tip of the island, in the adjacent Robert F. Wagner Park, the **Museum of Jewish Heritage**, 36 Battery Place (April–Sept Sun–Tues & Thurs 10am–5.45pm, Wed 10am–8pm, Fri 10am–5pm; Oct–March same hours, except the museum closes at 3pm on Fri; $7; ℡212/509-6130, Ⓦwww.mjhnyc.org), is essentially a memorial of the Holocaust, and has three floors of exhibits on twentieth-century Jewish history. The moving and informative collection features practical accoutrements of everyday Eastern European Jewish life, prison garb survivors wore in Nazi concentration camps, photographs, personal belongings, and multimedia presentations.

South Street Seaport and the Brooklyn Bridge

North up Water Street from Battery Park stands the partly reconstructed **Fraunces Tavern**, at Pearl and Broad streets (Tues, Wed & Fri 10am–5pm, Thurs 10am–7pm, Sat 11am–5pm; $3; ℡212/425-1778, Ⓦwww.frauncestav-ernmuseum.org). Here, on December 4, 1783, with the British conclusively beaten, a weeping George Washington took leave of his assembled officers, intent on returning to rural life in Virginia. The second floor recreates the site's history with a series of illustrated panels; the restaurant is still in business, and even serves decent tavern fare.

Further up Water Street, at the eastern end of Fulton Street, is the renovated **South Street Historic District**, formerly New York's bustling sail-ship port. Trade eventually moved elsewhere, and the blocks of warehouses and ship's chandlers were left to rot until they were renovated in the 1970s. Regular guided tours of the area run from the **South Street Seaport Museum**, 207 Front St (April–Sept Wed–Mon 10am–6pm; Oct–March 10am–5pm; $5; ℡212/748-8600, Ⓦwww.southstseaport.org), and feature refitted ships and chubby tugboats (the largest US collection of sailing vessels by tonnage), plus a handful of maritime art and trade exhibits. The museum also offers daytime, sunset, and nighttime **cruises** around New York Harbor on the *Pioneer*, an 1895 schooner that accommodates up to forty people (May–Sept; $25, $20 for students and seniors, $15 for children under 12; reservations on ☎212/363-5481); it's a good alternative to the crowded and noisy Circle Line cruises.

Opening onto South Street just around the corner from the museum, **Fulton Fish Market** is also worth a look. The tatty building wears its eighty years as the city's wholesale outlet with no pretensions. Visit while you still can (the market has, for some time, been on the verge of moving to a somewhat unsavory location in the Bronx), preferably around 6am, when buyers' trucks park up beneath the highway to collect the catches – invigorating stuff. Tours ($12; ☎212/748-8786) can be arranged through the Seaport Museum for the first and third Wednesdays of the month. The adjacent **Pier 17 Pavilion**, an overdeveloped complex of restaurants and shops, sticks out like a sore thumb.

From just about anywhere in the seaport you can see the much-loved **Brooklyn Bridge**. Now just one of several spans across the East River, it was in its day a technological quantum leap. At the time of its opening in 1883, it was the first bridge to use steel cables, and it towered majestically over the low brick structures below it. For its first twenty years in use, it was the world's largest suspension bridge. The impressive structure didn't go up easily, though: John Augustus Roebling, its architect and engineer, crushed his foot taking measurements for the piers and died of gangrene three weeks later. His son Washington took over, only to be crippled by the bends from working in an insecure underwater caisson; he then directed the work from his sick bed. Twenty workers died during the construction, and, a week after the opening day in 1883, twelve people were crushed to death in a panicked rush on the bridge's footpath. Despite this gory history, the beauty of the bridge itself and the spectacular views of Manhattan it offers make a walk across its wooden planks an essential part of any New York trip. Watch out, however, for rollerbladers and cyclists going at a clip.

West from the foot of the Brooklyn Bridge, at the corner of Vesey Street and Broadway, the defiantly antique **St Paul's Chapel** seems decidedly out of place in this downtown temple to modernity. The oldest church in Manhattan dates from 1766 – eighty years earlier than Trinity Church and almost prehistoric by New York standards.

City Hall Park and the Civic Center

Immediately north of St Paul's Chapel, Broadway and Park Row form the apex of **City Hall Park**, a recently restored, brightly flowered triangle now worthy of its handsome setting. Cass Gilbert's 1913 **Woolworth Building**, at 233 Broadway, between Barclay Street and Park Place, is a venerable onlooker. For many, this is New York's definitive skyscraper, its soaring lines fringed with Gothic decoration. Frank Woolworth made his fortune from "five and dime" stores and, true to his philosophy, he paid cash for his skyscraper. The whimsical reliefs at each corner of the lobby show him doing just that, counting out the money in nickels and dimes. Facing him in caricature are the architect (medievally clutching a model of his building), the renting agent, and the builder. Within, vaulted ceilings ooze honey-gold mosaics, and even the mailboxes are magnificent.

At the top of the park, marking the beginning of the **Civic Center**, with its incoherent jumble of municipal offices and courts, stands **City Hall**, which was completed in 1812. After New York saluted the hero aviator Charles A. Lindbergh in 1927, City Hall became the traditional finishing point for Broadway ticker-tape parades given for astronauts, returned hostages, and sports champions. Inside, it's an elegant meeting of arrogance and authority, with the sweeping spiral staircase delivering you to the precise geometry of the Governor's Room and the self-important rooms that formerly contained the Board of Estimates Chamber.

Chinatown, Little Italy, and NoLita

A short stroll northeast from the Civic Center leads into **Chinatown**, Manhattan's most thriving ethnic neighborhood, which over recent years has extended north across Canal Street into Little Italy and east into the Lower East Side. With more than 150,000 residents (125,000 of them Chinese), seven Chinese newspapers, about 150 restaurants and more than 300 garment factories, it is a model for poor neighborhoods; it has the lowest crime rate, highest employment, and least juvenile delinquency of any city district. There aren't many sights; rather, the appeal of the neighborhood lies simply in its unbridled energy, in the hordes of people coursing the sidewalk all day long – and, of course, for its excellent **Chinese food** (see p.110 for some restaurant suggestions).

By the mid-nineteenth century, the Chinese began to arrive in New York. Most had previously worked out West, building railroads and digging gold mines, and few intended to stay here. Mostly, their idea was simply to make a nest egg and retire with their families (99 percent of the workers were men) back in China. Some did go back, but on the whole they stayed, and Chinatown took shape as a permanent settlement. Today, **Mott Street** is the most vibrant thoroughfare, and the streets around – Canal, Pell, Bayard, Doyers, and the Bowery – host a positive glut of restaurants, tea and rice shops, grocers, and vendors selling everything from jewelry to toy robots.

On the north side of Canal Street, **Little Italy** is light years away from the solid ethnic enclave of old. Originally settled by the huge nineteenth-century influx of Italian immigrants, the neighborhood has far fewer Italians living here now. Families were driven away by the high rents or the encroaching expanse of Chinatown. The restaurants (of which there are plenty) tend to have high prices and a touristy feel. However, some original bakeries and *salumerias* (specialty food stores) do survive, and you can still indulge yourself with a good cappuccino and a tasty pastry. During September's ten-day **Festa di San Gennaro**, a wild and raucous party held in honor of the patron saint of Naples, Italians from all over the city converge on **Mulberry Street**, transforming Little Italy's main strip with food outlets and street stalls.

North of Little Italy, the trendy enclave of **NoLita** runs from Houston to Grand Street between Bowery and Lafayette. Originally an authentic Italian neighborhood, NoLita now brims with hipsters and fashionistas who take advantage of the many chic boutiques and restaurants that have popped up.

SoHo and TriBeCa

Since the early 1980s, **SoHo**, the grid of streets that runs South of Houston Street, has been all about fashion chic, urbane shopping, and cosmopolitan art galleries. However, for the first half of the twentieth century, this area was a wasteland of manufacturers and warehouses. But as rising rents drove artists out of Greenwich Village in the 1940s and 1950s, SoHo suddenly became "in." Its commercial spaces were ideal for large, low-rent lofts, art studios, and galleries. In the 1960s, largely due to the effort of artists living illegally in these lofts (as well as for the area's magnificent **cast-iron architecture**; see box below), SoHo was declared an historic district. Following this, yuppification – albeit an ultra-trendy strain of it – set in, bringing the fashionable boutiques, hip restaurants, and tourist crowds that are SoHo's signature today.

SoHo's cast-iron architecture

The technique of **cast-iron architecture** originated as a way of assembling buildings quickly and inexpensively, with iron beams rather than heavy walls carrying the weight of the floors. The result was the removal of supporting walls, greater space for windows, and, most noticeably, decorative facades. Almost any style or whim could be cast in iron and pinned to a building, and architects indulged themselves in Baroque balustrades, forests of Renaissance column, and all the effusion of the French Second Empire to glorify SoHo's sweatshops. Have a look at **72–76 Greene Street**, a neat extravagance whose Corinthian portico stretches the whole five stories, all in painted metal, and at the strongly composed elaborations of its sister building at nos. 28–30. At the northeast corner of Broome Street and Broadway the magnificent **Haughwout Building** is perhaps the ultimate in the genre, with rhythmically repeated motifs of colonnaded arches framed behind taller columns in a thin sliver of a Venetian palace.

Apart from consumer culture, there's also the **New Museum of Contemporary Art**, 583 Broadway between Houston and Prince (Tues–Sun noon–6pm, Thurs until 8pm; $6, students and seniors $3, under-18s free, Thurs 6–8pm free; ☎212/219-1222, Ⓦ www.newmuseum.org), which has earned a reputation as one of the most exciting, cutting-edge arts institutions in town. Primarily dedicated to showing emerging artists, expect any and all manner of media at its exhibitions.

TriBeCa, the *Tri*angle *Be*low *Ca*nal Street, has caught some of the fallout of SoHo's artists (the rest went to Williamsburg, in Brooklyn, and to Chelsea), and has rapidly changed from a wholesale garment district to a very upscale community. Less a triangle than a crumpled rectangle – the area is bounded by Canal and Chambers streets, Broadway, and the Hudson River – TriBeCa contains spacious industrial buildings that house the apartments of a new gentry, including Nathan Lane and Robert De Niro (whose film production company, TriBeCa Film Center, and restaurant, *TriBeCa Grill*, are at 375 Greenwich St). There's not much to see here, but a weekend walk around this serene neighborhood is a pleasant affair.

Greenwich Village

For many visitors, **Greenwich Village** (or simply "the Village") is the most-loved neighborhood in New York, despite having lost any radical edge long ago. Its bohemian image endures well enough if you don't live in the city, and it still sports many attractions that brought people here in the first place: a busy streetlife that stays up later than many other parts of the city; more restaurants per head than anywhere else; and bars cluttering every corner.

Greenwich Village grew up as a rural retreat from the early and frenetic nucleus of New York City. During the yellow fever epidemic of 1822 it became a refuge from the infected streets Downtown. Refined Federal and Greek Revival townhouses lured some of the city's highest society names, and later, at the start of World War I, the Village proved fertile ground for struggling artists and intellectuals, who were attracted to the area's cheap rents and growing community of free-thinking residents. During Prohibition (1920–1933), speakeasies were more prolific and accessible here than anywhere else in the city, and the rebellious fervor that permeated the Village then extended beyond the Twenties and Thirties. It was here that progressive New Yorkers gave birth to countless small magazines, unorthodox "happenings," and bacchanalian parties that were promoted as "pagan romps," while the neighborhood's off-Broadway theatres, cafés, and literary and folk clubs came to define Village life.

The natural heart of the Village, **Washington Square Park**, is not exactly elegant, though it does retain its northern edging of redbrick row houses – the "solid, honorable dwellings" of Henry James's eponymous novel – and Stanford White's imposing **Triumphal Arch**, built in 1892 to commemorate the centenary of George Washington's inauguration. The park is also the heart of the truly urban campus of New York University. As soon as the weather gets warm, the park becomes a sports field, performance space, chess tournament, protest site, and social club, feverish with life as street entertainers strum, skateboards flip, and the pulsing bass of hip-hop resounds through the whispered offers of the few surviving dope peddlers (who are just as likely to be undercover cops as dealers).

From the bottom of the park, follow **MacDougal Street** south and you hit **Bleecker Street** – the Village's main drag, packed with shops, bars, people, and restaurants. This junction is also the area's best-known meeting place, a vibrant corner whose European-style sidewalk cafés have been turned from the literary hangouts of Modernist times to often overpriced tourist draws – though they're still fun for a spot of people-watching.

Right onto Bleecker, then right again (north) on Sixth Avenue, walk until you see the unmistakable clock tower of the nineteenth-century **Jefferson Market Courthouse**, voted, in 1885, the fifth most beautiful building in America. This imposing High Victorian–style edifice first served as an indoor market, but later went on to be a firehouse, a jail, and finally a women's detention center before enjoying its current incarnation as a public library.

West of here, in the brownstone-lined side streets off Seventh Avenue, such as Bedford and Grove, you'll glimpse one of the city's most desirable living areas. Nearby, **Christopher Street** joins Seventh at **Sheridan Square**, home of the *Stonewall Inn's* gay bar where, in 1969, a police raid precipitated a siege that lasted the best part of an hour. If not a victory for gay rights, it was the first time that gay men had stood up to the police en masse, and as such represents a turning point in the struggle for equal rights, remembered by the **Annual Lesbian, Gay, Bisexual, and Transgender March** (often just referred to as the **Gay Pride March**). Typically held on the last Sunday in June, the parade, which is arguably the city's most exciting, and certainly its most colorful, begins at Fifth Avenue and 52nd Street, and ends among the snarl of streets around Sheridan Square.

The East Village

The **East Village** differs quite a bit from its western counterpart. Once, like the adjacent Lower East Side, the East Village was a refuge for immigrants and solidly working-class people. Home to New York's nonconformist intelligentsia in the early twentieth century, it later became the haunt of **the Beats** – Kerouac, Burroughs, Ginsberg, et al – who would get together at Ginsberg's house on East Seventh Street for declamatory poetry readings. Later, Andy Warhol debuted the Velvet Underground here; the *Fillmore East* hosted almost every band under the sun; and Richard Hell, Patti Smith, and The Ramones invented punk rock at a hole-in-the-wall club called **CBGB** (see review, p.120).

Much of the East Village has changed since the economic boom of the mid-1980s and the 1990s, not least of which has been escalating rents and gentrification, stripping it of its former status as a hotbed of dissidence and creativity. Nevertheless, the area's main drag, the vaudevillian **St Mark's Place** (Eighth Street), is still one of downtown's more vibrant strips, even if the thrift shops, panhandlers, and political hustlers have given way to more sanitized forms of rebellion and a cluster of chain sandwich and coffeeshops.

Astor Place, at the western end of St Mark's Place, was one of the city's most desirable neighborhoods in the 1830s. The now-undistinguished Lafayette Street was home to such wealthy names as John Jacob Astor, one of New York's most hideously greedy tycoons. The antique Astor Place **subway station**, bang in the middle of the junction, discreetly remembers the man on its platforms, where colored reliefs of beavers recall Astor's first big killings – in the fur trade.

A stone's throw from the subway, **Cooper Square** is dominated by the seven-story brownstone mass of **Cooper Union**, erected in 1859 by the industrialist Peter Cooper as a college for the poor, and now a prestigious art and architecture school. Early in 1860, Abraham Lincoln wowed top New Yorkers here with his "might makes right" speech, in which he boldly criticized the pro-slavery South and helped propel himself to the Republican nomination for president.

Further east, **Alphabet City** (avenues A, B, C, and D), a former Slavic enclave – and erstwhile turf of drug dealers and gangs – has gentrified at an alarming rate. Along Avenue A, you'll pass a number of worthwhile fashion and design shops, as well as sushi bars, cafés, and record stores. **Tompkins Square Park**, between avenues A and B, and Seventh and Tenth streets, is the area's center, and the streets that frame it continue the restaurant and bar theme. Further west, Avenue D is an edgy affair you'll have little need to see.

The Lower East Side

Below the eastern stretch of Houston Street, the **Lower East Side** began life toward the end of the nineteenth century as an insular slum for more than half a million Jewish immigrants. Since then it has changed considerably, with many Dominican and Chinese inhabitants, being followed by a recent influx of well-off students, artists, designers, and the like. It's all made the neighborhood quite cool, and the hotbed for trendy shops, bars, and restaurants; **Clinton Street** is the epicenter.

You can still **buy** just about anything cut-price in the Lower East Side, especially on Sunday mornings, when **Orchard Street** is filled with stalls and stores selling hats, clothes, and designer labels at hefty discounts. Next to this melee is the excellent **Lower East Side Tenement Museum**, 90 Orchard St between Broome and Delancey (Mon–Wed & Fri 11am–5.30pm, Thurs 11am–7pm, Sat & Sun 11am–6pm; $10; ☎212/431-0233, ⓦwww.tenement.org), which offers the lowdown on the neighborhood's immigrant past. The museum gives tours through an 1863 tenement building, whose restored rooms re-create the poverty that many area residents withstood while trying to build a new life in America. This is one of New York City's most interesting museums.

On the western edge of the Lower East Side, **The Bowery** runs up as far as Cooper Square on the edge of the East Village. This wide thoroughfare has gone through many changes during its long history: it took its name from *bouwerij*, the Dutch word for farm, when it was the city's main agricultural supplier; later, in the closing decades of the nineteenth century, it was lined with music halls, theaters, hotels, and restaurants, drawing people from all parts of Manhattan. The only city thoroughfare never to have been graced by a church, it is still – in some sections – a skid row; see, for instance, the Bowery Mission at no. 227. However, such days are surely limited, as the demand for apartments grows and the tide of gentrification continues to sweep through the Lower East Side. The one – bizarre – focus is the **Bowery Savings Bank** (now the restaurant-club *Capitale*) at Grand Street. Designed by Stanford White in 1894, its splendid architecture makes the surrounding debris even more depressing (much as its sister bank does on 42nd Street; see p.92).

Midtown Manhattan

MIDTOWN MANHATTAN encompasses everything from the East River to the Hudson between 14th Street and 59th Street, the southern border of Central Park. New York's most glamorous (and most expensive) stretch, **Fifth Avenue** cuts through Midtown's heart, with the neon theater strip of **Broadway** running just to the west for much of the way. The character of Midtown is very different depending on which side of Fifth you find yourself. On the avenue itself and to the east are corporate businesses and prestigious skyscrapers – including the Empire State, Chrysler, and Seagram buildings – as well as Grand Central Station and the UN. Here you'll also find the residential neighborhoods of **Murray Hill** and elegant **Gramercy Park**. Just below Gramercy's eponymous park, busy **Union Square** is always great for interesting people-watching. Meanwhile, west of Fifth, **Chelsea** is home to many quality art galleries, and bordered by the **Garment District**, where apparel-shop employees still roll racks of clothing through the streets. Around 42nd Street, the **Theater District** heralds a cleaned-up, frenetic area of entertainment that culminates at **Times Square**. West of Broadway in the 40s and low 50s, colorful **Hell's Kitchen** is now more or less wholly gentrified.

Union Square and Gramercy Park

Downtown Manhattan ends at 14th Street, which slices across from the housing projects of the East Side through rows of cut-price shops to the meatpacking warehouses on the Hudson. In the middle is **Union Square**, its shallow steps enticing passers-by to sit and watch the skateboarders and buskers, or to stroll the cool, tree-shaded paths and lawns. On any Monday, Wednesday, Friday, or Saturday, you'll find a terrific farmer's market at the paved north and west edges of the square. The stretch of **Broadway** north of here, once known as Ladies' Mile for its fancy stores and boutiques, has been reinvented as an urban mall, with large chain stores on every block in the 20s. The interesting architecture includes sculptured facades, massive windows, and curvy lintels.

East from here, between 20th and 21st streets, where Lexington Avenue becomes Irving Place, Manhattan's clutter suddenly breaks into the ordered open space of **Gramercy Park**. This former swamp, reclaimed in 1831, is one of the city's best parks, its center tidily planted and, most noticeably, completely empty for much of the day – principally because the only people who can gain access are those rich enough to live here and possess keys to the gate. (There is, however, another way: guests at the *Gramercy Park Hotel* are allowed into the park; see p.74.)

Broadway and Fifth Avenue meet at 23rd Street at **Madison Square**, by day a maelstrom of cars and cabs, but with a serene, well-manicured **park** to take the edge off. Most notable among the elegant structures nearby, the **Flatiron Building**, 175 Fifth Ave, between 22nd and 23rd streets, rises cheekily on a triangular plot of land on the square's southern side; its twenty stories dwarfed nearby structures when it was built in 1902. The building's uncommonly thin, tapered shape creates unusual wind currents at ground level – so much so, that years ago police officers prevented men from gathering to watch the wind raise the skirts of women passing on 23rd Street. Just north from here, the new **Museum of Sex**, 233 Fifth Ave at 27th St (Sun–Fri 11am–6.30pm, Sat 11am–8pm; $14.50; ☎212/689-6337 or 1-866/667-3984, ⓦwww.museumof-sex.com), offers other titillating views of the city through a scholarly lens.

Chelsea and the Garment District

Home to a thriving **gay community**, as well as many good **art galleries** (check out West 24th, between Tenth and Eleventh aves), the heart of **Chelsea** lies west of Broadway between 14th and 23rd streets. The neighborhood took shape in 1830 when its owner, Charles Clarke Moore, laid out his land for sale in broad lots. It failed to achieve the desirability he sought, taking until recent decades for real estate to get hot here. Now, though, up and down Eighth Avenue, you'll see all manner of trendy bars and restaurants mingled in with bodegas, frequented by the neighborhood's mixed clientele.

During the nineteenth century, Chelsea was a focus of New York's theater district. Nothing remains of that now, but the hotel that put up all the actors, writers, and attendant entourages – the **Chelsea Hotel** – remains a New York landmark, with a down-at-the-heel Edwardian grandeur all its own (for a review, see p.73). Mark Twain and Tennessee Williams lived here, Brendan Behan and Dylan Thomas staggered in and out during their New York visits, and in 1951, Jack Kerouac, armed with a customized typewriter (and a lot of Benzedrine), typed the first draft of *On the Road* nonstop onto a 120ft-long roll of paper. In the 1960s Andy Warhol and his doomed protege Edie Sedgwick holed up here and made the film *Chelsea Girls* in (sort of) homage to the place. In October 1978 Sid Vicious stabbed Nancy Spungen to death in their suite, a few months before his own life ended with an overdose of heroin. The hotel also inspired Joni Mitchell to write *Chelsea Morning*.

The **Garment District**, a loosely defined patch north of Chelsea between 34th and 42nd streets and Sixth and Eighth avenues, produces three-fourths of all the women's and children's clothes in America. You'd never guess it, though; the outlets are strictly wholesale, with no need to woo customers. Retail stores, abound, however: **Macy's**, the famed old department store with two million square feet of floor space and $5 million in sales a day, is on **Herald Square** at 34th Street and Seventh Avenue.

The district's dominant landmark is the **Penn Station** and **Madison Square Garden** complex, a combined box and drum structure that swallows up millions of commuters in its train station below and accommodates the Knicks and Liberty basketball – and Rangers hockey – teams up top. The original Penn Station, demolished to make way for this structure, is now hailed as a lost masterpiece, which reworked the ideas of the Roman baths of Caracalla to awesome effect: "Through it one entered the city like a god . . . One scuttles in now like a rat," mourned one observer. Immediately behind Penn Station, the same architects – McKim, Mead, and White – were responsible for the **General Post Office**. The old joke is that it had to be this big to fit in the sonorous inscription above the columns: "Neither snow nor rain nor heat nor gloom of night stays these couriers from the swift completion of their appointed rounds."

The Empire State Building

Up Fifth, overshadowing the shops of lower Fifth Avenue, is the **Empire State Building**, 34th Street and Fifth Avenue (daily 9.30am–midnight, last trip up at 11.30pm; $11, bring photo ID; ☎212/736-3100, ⓦwww.esbnyc.com), which

Ⓐ, Ⓑ, The Cloisters, Columbia University, ▲ Cathedral of St John the Divine & Studio Museum in Harlem, ▲ Museum of the City of New York & El Barrio, ▲ Cooper Hewitt Museum

Roosevelt Island

QUEENSBORO BRIDGE

Carl Schurz Park

Gracie Mansion

EAST END AVENUE

FDR DRIVE

John Jay Park

YORK AVENUE

Roosevelt Island Tram

U P P E R   E A S T   S I D E

FIRST AVENUE

SECOND AVENUE

Bloomingdale's

Guggenheim Museum

Metropolitan Museum of Art

THIRD AVENUE

Whitney Museum

Seventh Regiment Armory

PARK AVENUE

The Frick Collection

Temple Emanu-El

MADISON AVENUE

Plaza Hotel

FIFTH AVENUE

The Reservoir

TRANSVERSE ROAD NO. 3

The Great Lawn

Turtle Pond

Loeb Boathouse

Delacorte Theater

TRANSVERSE ROAD NO. 2

New-York Historical Society

The Ramble

Rowboat Lake

Bow Bridge

C e n t r a l   P a r k

Sheep Meadow

Zoo

Skating Rink

CENTRAL PARK SOUTH

CENTRAL PARK WEST

Strawberry Fields

EIGHTH AVENUE

COLUMBUS CIRCLE

American Museum of Natural History

W. 87TH ST.
W. 86TH ST.
W. 85TH ST.
W. 84TH ST.
W. 83RD ST.
W. 82ND ST.
W. 81ST ST.
W. 80TH ST.
W. 79TH ST.
W. 78TH ST.
W. 77TH ST.
W. 76TH ST.
W. 75TH ST.
W. 74TH ST.
W. 73RD ST.
W. 72ND ST.
W. 71ST ST.
W. 70TH ST.
W. 69TH ST.
W. 68TH ST.
W. 67TH ST.
W. 66TH ST.
W. 65TH ST.
W. 64TH ST.
W. 61ST ST.
W. 60TH ST.
W. 59TH ST.

E. 88TH ST.
E. 87TH ST.
E. 86TH ST.
E. 85TH ST.
E. 84TH ST.
E. 83RD ST.
E. 82ND ST.
E. 81ST ST.
E. 80TH ST.
E. 79TH ST.
E. 78TH ST.
E. 77TH ST.
E. 76TH ST.
E. 75TH ST.
E. 74TH ST.
E. 73RD ST.
E. 72ND ST.
E. 71ST ST.
E. 70TH ST.
E. 69TH ST.
E. 68TH ST.
E. 67TH ST.
E. 66TH ST.
E. 65TH ST.
E. 64TH ST.
E. 63RD ST.
E. 62ND ST.
E. 61ST ST.
E. 60TH ST.
E. 59TH ST.

AMSTERDAM AVENUE

BROADWAY

COLUMBUS AVE.

The Dakota Building

U P P E R   W E S T   S I D E

Lincoln Center

TENTH AVENUE

ELEVENTH AVENUE

FREEDOM PLACE

HENRY HUDSON PARKWAY

ACCOMMODATION

Algonquin	O
Amsterdam Inn	F
Dylan	Q
Edison	M
Gershwin	S
Hostelling International– New York	B
Hudson	H
Jazz on the Park	A
Lucerne	D
Milburn	E
Paramount	N
Pickwick Arms	J
Roger Smith	P
Royalton Hotel	L
Stanford	R
W	K
Wales	C
West Side YMCA	G
Wyndham	I

Ⓓ Ⓔ Ⓕ Ⓖ

East River

QUEENS MIDTOWN TUNNEL

FDR DRIVE

N

M Subway stations

0   800 yds

▶ Flatiron Building

MIDTOWN/UPTOWN MANHATTAN

Circle Line Ferry

LINCOLN TUNNEL TO NEW JERSEY

Dewitt Clinton Park

Jacob Javits Convention Center

HELL'S KITCHEN

THEATER DISTRICT

TIMES SQUARE

BROADWAY

GARMENT DISTRICT

Port Authority Bus Terminal

Chelsea Park

General Post Office

Madison Square Garden

Penn Station

Macy's

Carnegie Hall

Museum of Modern Art (closed until 2005)

Museum of TV & Radio

Radio City Music Hall

St Patrick's Cathedral

Rockefeller Center

Trump Tower

Citicorp Center

Seagram Building

GE Building

Waldorf Astoria Hotel

Met Life Building (Pan Am)

Chrysler Building

Grand Central Terminal

New York Public Library

Bryant Park

MURRAY HILL

Pierpont Morgan Library (Closed until 2006)

Empire State Building

Museum of Sex

Madison Square Park

United Nations

H
I
J
K
L
M
O
P
Q
R
S

i

FIRST AVENUE
SECOND AVENUE
THIRD AVENUE
LEXINGTON AVENUE
MADISON AVENUE
FIFTH AVENUE
SIXTH AVENUE
BROADWAY
SEVENTH AVENUE
EIGHTH AVENUE
NINTH AVENUE
TENTH AVENUE
ELEVENTH AVENUE
TWELFTH AVENUE

E 57TH ST
E 56TH ST
E 55TH ST
E 54TH ST
E 53RD ST
E 52ND ST
E 51ST ST
E 50TH ST
E 49TH ST
E 48TH ST
E 47TH ST
E 46TH ST
E 45TH ST
E 44TH ST
E 43RD ST
E 42ND ST
E 40TH ST
E 38TH ST
E 37TH ST
E 36TH ST
E 35TH ST
E 34TH ST
E 33RD ST
E 32ND ST
E 31ST ST
E 30TH ST
E 29TH ST
E 28TH ST
E 27TH ST
E 26TH ST
E 25TH ST
E 24TH ST

W 57TH ST
W 56TH ST
W 55TH ST
W 54TH ST
W 53RD ST
W 52ND ST
W 51ST ST
W 50TH ST
W 49TH ST
W 48TH ST
W 47TH ST
W 46TH ST
W 45TH ST
W 43RD ST
W 42ND ST
W 40TH ST
W 38TH ST
W 37TH ST
W 36TH ST
W 35TH ST
W 34TH ST
W 33RD ST
W 32ND ST
W 31ST ST
W 30TH ST
W 29TH ST
W 28TH ST
W 27TH ST
W 26TH ST
W 25TH ST

has been a muscular 102-story symbol of New York since being completed in 1931. After the terrorist attacks of September 11th, it became, as it once was, the city's tallest building. Inside, its basement is an underground marbled shopping precinct, finished everywhere with delicate Art Deco touches. An elevator takes you to the 86th floor, which was the summit of the building before the radio and TV mast was added. The views from the outside walkways here are as stunning as you'd expect: Manhattan, as well as the outer boroughs and New Jersey beyond, spreads on all sides. For the best views, you should try to time your visit so that you'll reach the top at sunset. (Be advised that during peak season, wait times to ascend are often upwards of an hour.)

East of the Empire State Building, the residential district of **Murray Hill** was once dominated by the crusty old financier J.P. Morgan and his son, J.P. Jr; the latter's brownstone, at 37th Street and Madison Avenue, is now headquarters of the American Lutheran Church. The home of the elder Morgan, once adjacent to his son's, was razed to make way for the **Pierpont Morgan Library**. Apart from the library, which is closed until 2006 for expansion renovations, there's not much to see around here.

Forty-second Street

On the corner of **42nd Street** and Fifth Avenue stands the Beaux Arts **New York Public Library** (Tues & Wed 11am–7pm, Thurs–Sat 10am–6pm; ☎212/930-0830, ⓦwww.nypl.org). Leon Trotsky worked occasionally in the large coffered Reading Room at the back of the building during his brief sojourn in New York, just prior to the 1917 Russian Revolution. He was introduced to the place by his Bolshevik comrade Nikolai Bukharin, who was bowled over by a library one could visit so late in the evening. The opening times are less impressive now, but the library still boasts one of the five largest collections of books in the world. It's worth going inside just to appreciate its reverent, church-like atmosphere.

East on 42nd Street at Park Avenue looms the huge bulk of **Grand Central Terminal**, built around a basic iron frame but clothed with a Beaux Arts skin. The structure's immense size is now dwarfed by the Met Life building behind it. Regardless, the main station's **concourse** is a sight to behold – 470ft long and 150ft high, it boasts a barrel-vaulted ceiling speckled like a Baroque church with a painted representation of the winter night sky. The 2500 stars are shown back to front – "as God would have seen them," the painter is reputed to have explained.

You can explore Grand Central on your own, or you can take the Municipal Arts Society's excellent **free tour**. For the best view of the concourse – as well as the flow of commuters and commerce – climb up to the catwalks that span the sixty-foot-high windows on the Vanderbilt Avenue side. After that, seek out the station's more esoteric reaches, including the *Oyster Bar* – one of the city's most highly regarded seafood restaurants, deep in the terminal's bowels and jam-packed every lunchtime. Near the restaurant, testing an acoustical fluke, two visitors can stand on opposite sides of any of the vaulted spaces and hold a conversation just by whispering. Nearby, there's a lower concourse brimming with take-out options for a quick bite.

Across the street from Grand Central, the former **Bowery Savings Bank** (now *Cipriani 42nd Street*) echoes the train station's grandeur, extravagantly lauding the virtues of sound investment and savings. Built in the style of a Roman basilica, it has a floor paved with mosaics, columns (each fashioned from a different kind of marble), and bronze bas-reliefs on the elevator doors. The more famous **Chrysler Building**, at 405 Lexington Ave, also dates from a time (1930) when architects carried off prestige with grace and style. For a short while, this was the world's tallest building; today, it's one of Manhattan's best-loved structures. The car-motif friezes, jutting gargoyles, and arched stainless-steel pinnacle give the solemn Midtown skyline a welcome touch of whimsy. Chrysler moved out some time ago, and for a while the building was left to degenerate by a company that didn't fully appreciate its spirited silliness. Thankfully, the new owner has pledged to keep it lovingly intact. The lobby, once a car showroom, with its opulently inlaid elevators, walls covered in African marble, and murals depicting airplanes, machines, and the brawny builders who worked on the tower, is for the moment all you can see of the building.

At the eastern end of 42nd Street, the **United Nations** complex comprises the glass-curtained **Secretariat**, the curving sweep of the **General Assembly**, and, connecting them, the low-rising **Conference Wing**. Guided **tours** (daily every 20–30min, weekdays 9.30am–4.45pm, weekends 10am–4.30pm; tours last 45min–1hr, and leave from the General Assembly lobby; $10, bring ID; ☎212/963-8687, ⓦwww.un.org/MoreInfo/pubsvs.html) take in the UN conference chambers and its constituent parts. For those interested in global goings-on, the United Nations is a must-visit. Even more revealing than the stately chambers are its thoughtful exhibition spaces and artful country gifts on view, including a painting by Picasso. Note that tours may vary depending on official room usage.

Times Square and the Theater District

Forty-second Street meets Broadway at the southern margin of **Times Square**, center of the **Theater District** and a top tourist attraction. Here, countless monolithic advertisements for Coke, Budweiser, NBC, and the like jostle brightly for attention from the crowds of gawking visitors. It wasn't always this way: traditionally a melting pot of debauchery, depravity, and fun, Times Square was cleaned up in the 1990s and turned into a largely sanitized universe of popular consumption, with refurbished theaters and blinking signage, an homage to days gone by. It's hard not to get swept up in the thronging excitement of it all, even if it is highly manufactured.

North of Times Square along Seventh Avenue, **Carnegie Hall**, an overblown, warehouse-like venue for opera and concerts at 154 W 57th St, is the thing to see. Tchaikovsky conducted the program on opening night and Mahler, Rachmaninov, Toscanini, Frank Sinatra, and Judy Garland have played here. Carnegie Hall has dropped in status since Lincoln Center opened (see p.101 & the box on p.119), but the superb acoustics still ensure full houses most of the year (Sept–June only; tours available Mon, Tues, Thurs, & Fri at 11.30am, 2pm, & 3pm; $6; general info ☎212/903-9600, tours ☎212/903-9765, tickets ☎212/247-7800, ⓦwww.carnegiehall.org).

East of Seventh Avenue, **Sixth Avenue** is properly named "the Avenue of the Americas," though no New Yorker ever calls it this and the only manifestation is the flags of Central and South American countries still flying on some blocks. If nothing else, Sixth's distinction is its width, a result of the Elevated Railway that once ran along here, now replaced by the Sixth Avenue subway underground. In its day the Sixth Avenue "El" marked the borderline between respectability to the east and vice to the west, and the avenue still separates the glamorous strips of Fifth, Madison, and Park avenues from the less salubrious western districts.

At 1260 Sixth Ave, at 50th Street, **Radio City Music Hall** (1hr tours Mon–Sat 10am–8pm, Sun 11am–8pm; $17, seniors $14, students $14; general info ☎212/307-7171, tour info ☎212/247-4777, Ⓦ www.radiocity.com) is the last word in 1930s luxury. The staircase is regally resplendent, with the world's largest chandeliers, and the huge auditorium looks like an extravagant scalloped shell; the original murals from the men's restrooms are now in the Museum of Modern Art.

Fifth Avenue and east

Fifth Avenue has been a great stretch for as long as New York has been a great city, and its very name evokes wealth and opulence. All who consider themselves suave and cosmopolitan end up here, and the stores showcase New York's most conspicuous consumerism. That the shopping is beyond the means of most people needn't put you off, for Fifth Avenue has some of the city's best architecture, too; the boutiques and stores are just the icing on the cake.

At the heart of the glamour is **Rockefeller Center**, built between 1932 and 1940 by John D. Rockefeller Jr, son of the oil magnate. One of the finest pieces of urban planning anywhere, the Center balances office space with cafés, a theater, underground concourses, and rooftop gardens that work together with a rare intelligence and grace. The **GE Building** here rises 850ft, its monumental lines matching the scale of Manhattan itself, though softened by symmetrical setbacks to prevent an overpowering expanse of wall. At its foot, the **Lower Plaza** holds a sunken restaurant in summer, linked visually to the downward flow of the building by Paul Manship's sparkling *Prometheus*; in winter, the plaza becomes a small **ice rink**, allowing skaters to show off their skills to passers-by. Inside, the Center is no less impressive. In the GE lobby, José Maria Sert's murals, *American Progress* and *Time*, are a little faded but eagerly in tune with the Thirties Deco ambiance – presumably more so than the original paintings by Diego Rivera, removed by John D.'s son Nelson when the artist refused to scrap a panel glorifying Lenin. A leaflet available from the lobby desk details a **self-guided tour** of the Center. Among the GE Building's many offices are the **NBC Studios** (1hr behind-the-scenes tours leave every 30 minutes Mon–Fri, and every 15 minutes on weekends; Mon–Fri 8.30am–5.30pm, Sat & Sun 9.30am–4.30pm; reservations at the NBC Experience Store Tour Desk; $17.75, children $15.25; ☎212/664-7174). If you're a TV fan, pick up a free ticket for a **show recording** from the mezzanine lobby or out on the street. Keep in mind that the most popular tickets evaporate before 9am. The newer glass-enclosed **Today Show** studio is at the southwest corner of the plaza at 49th Street, surrounded in the early morning by avid fans waiting to get on TV by way of the cameras that obligingly pan the crowds from time to time. Adjacent is the old Associated Press building, recognizable by the unusual Stalinesque frieze by Japanese-American artist Isamu Noguchi.

Almost opposite Rockefeller Center, on 50th Street and Fifth Avenue, **St Patrick's Cathedral**, designed by James Renwick and completed in 1888, seems the result of a painstaking academic tour of the Gothic cathedrals of Europe – perfect in detail, but lifeless in spirit, with a sterility made all the more striking by the glass-black **Olympic Tower** next door, an exclusive apartment block where Jackie Kennedy Onassis once lived. Between Fifth and Sixth avenues at 25 W 52nd St, the **Museum of Television and Radio** (Tues–Sun noon–6pm, Thurs noon–8pm; $10; ☎212/621-6800, Ⓦ www.mtr.org) holds an excellent archive of American TV and radio broadcasts. The museum's computerized reference system allows you to search for programs, then watch them on one of 96 video consoles.

Continuing north, the **Trump Tower** at 57th Street is the last word in Fifth Avenue extravagance, with an outrageously over-the-top atrium filled with designer stores. Perfumed air, polished marble paneling, and a five-story waterfall are calculated to knock you senseless with expensive yet somewhat garish taste. But the building is clever: a neat little outdoor garden is squeezed high in a corner, and each of the 230 apartments above the atrium gets views in three directions.

East of Fifth, **Madison Avenue** makes for pleasant strolling, and is filled with expensive galleries, haute couture shops, and elegantly dressed Eastsiders. The next avenue east, **Park Avenue**, was said in 1929 to be the place "where wealth is so swollen that it almost bursts." Things haven't changed much: corporate headquarters and four-star hotels jostle in triumphal procession, led by the massive New York Central Building (now the **Helmsley Building**) that literally sits above Park Avenue at 46th Street and boasts a lewdly excessive Rococo lobby. In its day this formed a skillful punctuation mark to the avenue, but its thunder was stolen in 1963 by the **Met Life Building**, 200 Park Ave at 45th Street, which looms behind it.

Wherever you placed it, the solid mass of the **Waldorf Astoria Hotel**, on Park between 49th and 50th streets, would hold its own, a resplendent statement of Art Deco elegance. Crouched behind it is **St Bartholomew's Church**, a low-slung Byzantine hybrid that adds immeasurably to the street and gives the lumbering skyscrapers a much-needed sense of scale. The spiky-topped **General Electric Building** behind seems like a wild extension of the church, its slender shaft rising to a meshed crown of abstract sparks and lightning bolts that symbolizes the radio waves used by its original owner, RCA. The lobby (entrance at 570 Lexington) is yet another Deco delight.

Among all this, it's difficult at first to see the originality of the **Seagram Building**, at 375 Park Ave, between 52nd and 53rd streets. Designed by Mies van der Rohe (with Philip Johnson) and built in 1958, this was the seminal curtain-wall skyscraper, the floors supported internally, allowing a skin of smoky glass and whisky-bronze metal (Seagram's is known for distilled liquors), now weathered to a dull black. Every interior detail – from the fixtures to the lettering on the mailboxes – was specially designed. It was the supreme example of Modernist reason, and its opening was met by a wave of approval. The plaza, an open forecourt designed to set the building apart from its neighbors, was such a success as a public space that the city revised the zoning laws to encourage other high-rise builders to supply plazas. Alas, you see the result in the windswept, sterile places all over the city.

A block east, the chisel-topped **Citicorp Center**, on Lexington Avenue between 53rd and 54th streets, finished in 1979, is one of Manhattan's most conspicuous landmarks. The slanted roof was designed to house solar panels to

MoMA on the Move

While its main location at 11 W 53rd St undergoes expansion and its most comprehensive reconfiguration yet, the **Museum of Modern Art** (MoMA) is temporarily housed in a facility in Queens (MoMAQNS, 45-20 33rd St at Queens Blvd, ☏212/708-9400, ⓦ www.moma.org), where selections from its permanent collection of late nineteenth- and twentieth-century art, covering every medium – illustration, design, photography, painting, sculpture, and film – are on view, along with new curated exhibitions designed and mounted expressly for the museum's temporary space. The original location is expected to re-open in the winter of 2004–2005; check the website for updates.

provide power for the building. However, the idea was ahead of the technology, and Citicorp had to content itself with adopting the distinctive building-top as a corporate logo.

① Uptown Manhattan

UPTOWN MANHATTAN begins above 59th Street, where the businesslike bustle of Midtown gives way to the comfortable domesticity of the Upper East and West sides. In between, people come to **Central Park**, the city's giant back garden, to play, jog, and escape Midtown's crowds in a particularly intelligent piece of urban landscaping.

The **Upper East Side** is at its most opulent in the several blocks just east of Central Park, and at its most distinguished in the Metropolitan and other great museums of "Museum Mile," from 82nd to 104th streets along Fifth Avenue. The predominantly residential **Upper West Side** is somewhat less refined, though its Lincoln Center hosts New York's most prestigious arts performances, and there are certainly plenty of expensive townhouses and apartment buildings. The northern reaches embrace the monolithic Cathedral of St John the Divine and Columbia University. North and east from here, **Harlem**, the cultural capital of black America, is experiencing a new renaissance. Still farther north, in the Washington Heights area, you'll find one of the city's most intriguing museums, the medieval arts collection of The Cloisters.

Central Park

"All radiant in the magic atmosphere of art and taste." So enthused *Harper's* magazine upon the opening of **Central Park** in 1876, and, to this day, few New Yorkers could imagine life without it. Set just about smack in the middle of Manhattan, extending from 59th to 110th streets, it provides residents (and street-weary tourists) with a much-needed refuge from the harshness of big-city life. Whether you're into jogging, baseball, boating, botany, or just plain strolling, or even if you rarely go near the place, there's no question that Central Park makes New York a better place to live.

The poet and newspaper editor William Cullen Bryant had the idea for an open public space in 1844, and spent seven years trying to persuade City Hall to carry it out. Eventually, 840 desolate and swampy acres north of the city limits, then occupied by a shantytown of squatters, were set aside. The two architects commissioned to design the landscape, **Frederick Law Olmsted** and **Calvert Vaux**, planned to create a rural paradise, a complete illusion of the countryside in the heart of Manhattan – even then growing at a fantastic rate. At its opening, Central Park was declared a "people's park" – though most of the impoverished masses it was allegedly built to serve had neither the time nor the means of transportation to come up from their Downtown slums and enjoy it. But as New York grew and workers' leisure time increased, people started to flood in, and the park began to live up to its mission, sometimes in ways that might have scandalized its original builders. Today, although the skyline has changed greatly, and some of the open space has been turned into asphalted playgrounds, the sense of captured nature that they intended largely survives. For general park **information**, call ☎212/310-6600, or visit ⓦ www.centralparknyc.org; for special events information, call ☎1-888/NYPARKS.

One of the best ways to explore the park is to rent a **bicycle** from either the Loeb Boathouse (between 74th and 75th streets, roughly $9–15 an hour) or

Metro Bicycles (Lexington at 88th St; $7 per hour; ☎212/427-4450); other-wise, it's easy to get around **on foot**, along the many paths that crisscross the park. There's little chance of getting lost, but to know exactly where you are, find the nearest lamppost: the first two figures signify the number of the near-est street. After dark, however, you'd be well advised not to enter on foot. If you want to see the buildings illuminated from the park at night, one option is to fork out for a **carriage ride**; the best place to pick up a hack is along Central Park South, between Fifth and Sixth avenues. It's not cheap, though: a twenty-minute trot costs approximately $35, excluding tip.

Most places of interest in the park lie in its southern reaches. Near **Grand Army Plaza**, the main entrance at Fifth Avenue and 59th Street, is the **Central Park Zoo**, which tries to keep caging to a minimum and the ani-mals as close to the viewer as possible (April–Oct Mon–Fri 10am–5pm, Sat & Sun 10am–5.30pm; Nov–March daily 10am–4.30pm; $6, ages 3–12 $1, under 3 free; ☎212/439-6500). Beyond here, the **Dairy**, once a ranch building intended to provide milk for nursing mothers, now houses a **visitor's center** (Tues–Sun 10am–5pm; ☎212/794-6564), which distributes free leaflets and maps, sells books, and puts on exhibitions. Also, weekend **walking tours** often leave from here; call for times.

Nearby, the **Wollman Rink** (63rd St at mid-park) is a lovely place to skate in winter, or to practice your in-line skating skills in the warmer months. From the rink, you may wish to swing west past the restored **Sheep Meadow**, a dust bowl in the 1970s, now emerald green. Then, head north up the formal Mall to the terrace, with the sculptured birds and animals of **Bethesda Fountain** below, on the shore of the **Rowboat Lake**. To your left (west) is **Strawberry Fields**, a tranquil, shady spot dedicated to John Lennon by his widow, Yoko Ono, and the **Imagine mosaic** – both are near where he was killed in 1980; see p.101 for more. On the eastern bank of the lake, you can rent a **rowboat** from the Loeb Boathouse (March–Oct daily 10am–6pm, weather permitting; $10 for the first hour, and $2.50 per 15min after; $30 refundable cash deposit required; ☎212/517-2233) or cross the water by the elegant cast-iron **Bow Bridge**.

Beyond the bridge, delve into the wild woods of **The Ramble** along a maze of paths and bridges; this area is best avoided at night. At 81st Street, near the West Side, stands the mock citadel of **Belvedere Castle**, another visitor cen-ter that has nature exhibits and boasts great views of the park from its terraces. Next to the castle is the **Delacorte Theater**, home to the thoroughly enjoy-able **Shakespeare in the Park** performances in the summer (tickets are free, though they go very quickly; visit ⓦwww.publictheater.org for details), and the immense **Great Lawn**, the preferred sprawling ground for many sun-lov-ing New Yorkers. Near the north end of the park is the beautifully terraced and landscaped **Conservatory Garden**, at 103rd Street off Fifth Avenue, encom-passing three distinct garden styles: English, Italian, and French.

The Metropolitan Museum of Art

One of the world's great art museums, the **Metropolitan Museum of Art** (usually referred to as just "the Met") juts into the park at Fifth Avenue and 82nd Street (Tues–Thurs & Sun 9.30am–5.30pm, Fri & Sat 9.30am–9pm; sug-gested donation $12, seniors and students $7; includes same-day admission to The Cloisters, see p.105; ☎212/535-7710, ⓦwww.metmuseum.org). Its all-embracing collection amounts to more than two million works of art, spanning America and Europe as well as China, Africa, the Far East, and the classical and

Islamic worlds. You could spend weeks here and not see everything. The choice of works that follows – among the Met's greatest hits – is inevitably selective in the extreme.

If you can make just one visit, head for the **European Painting** galleries. Of the early (fifteenth- and sixteenth-century) **Flemish and Dutch paintings**, the best are by Jan van Eyck, who is generally credited with having started the tradition of North European realism, and Rogier van der Weyden, whose *Christ Appearing to His Mother* is one of his most beautiful works. Later canvases include Bruegel's *Harvesters*, part of the series of six paintings that included his familiar Christmas-card *Hunters in the Snow*. To the left from here are the **Spanish paintings**, including the very different landscape of El Greco's extraordinary *View of Toledo* and Velázquez's *Portrait of Juan de Pareja*. When this somber portrait was first exhibited in 1650, one critic remarked of it, "All the rest are art, this alone is truth."

The **Italian Renaissance** is less spectacularly represented here but a worthy selection includes an early *Madonna and Child Enthroned with Saints* by Raphael, a late Botticelli, and Filippo Lippi's *Madonna and Child Enthroned with Two Angels*. The culmination of the European Galleries is the **Dutch paintings** section, dominated by the major works of Rembrandt, Vermeer, and Hals. Vermeer, genius of the domestic interior, is represented by five works, most haunting of which is the *Portrait of a Young Woman*, and there are some fine portraits by Rembrandt – a beautiful painting of his common-law wife, Hendrike Stoffjels, painted three years before her early death, and a superb *Self-portrait* from 1660, the year he was declared bankrupt.

The **nineteenth-century galleries** house a startling array of **Impressionist** and **Post-Impressionist art**, beginning with Manet, the movement's most influential precursor, and his striking *Young Lady in 1866*. The prolific Monet is widely represented, including three superb works – *Rouen Cathedral*, *The Houses of Parliament (Effect of Fog)*, and *The Doge's Palace Seen from San Giorgio Maggiore* – in which you can detect the beginnings of his final phase of near-Abstract Impressionism. Nearby is Courbet's erotic *Woman with a Parrot* (which inspired Manet's similar work), along with a casting of Degas' *Little Dancer*, complete with real tutu, bodice, and shoes. The Post-Impressionists Paul Gauguin and Toulouse-Lautrec follow, and there are also major works by Van Gogh (including *Irises* and *Self Portrait with Straw Hat*), Pissarro, and Seurat (*Circus Sideshow*).

Housed over two floors in the Lila Acheson Wallace Wing, the Met's compact **twentieth-century collection** features paintings such as Picasso's *Portrait of Gertrude Stein* and *The Blind Man's Meal*, alongside works by Klee, Hopper, Matisse, Braque, and Klimt. Postwar pieces include Pollock's masterly *Autumn Rhythm (Number 30)*, Thomas Hart Benton's rural idyll *July Hay*, Charles DeMuth's *The Figure 5 in Gold*, and Warhol's *Last Self Portrait*, as well as works by Max Beckmann, Lichtenstein, Rothko, Johns, and de Kooning.

The **American Wing**, in the northwest corner of the Met, is virtually a museum in its own right, with 25 furnished historical rooms, starting with the Early Colonial period and the Hart Room of around 1674, and ending with Frank Lloyd Wright's Room from the Little House, Minneapolis, originally windowed on all four sides, demonstrating Wright's emphasis on minimal interior–exterior division. The **American paintings** include the nineteenth-century canvases of William Sidney Mount, who depicted genre scenes on his native Long Island, and the landscape artists of the Hudson Valley School, Thomas Cole and his pupil Frederick Church. Winslow Homer gets a gallery to himself, while later rooms bring the Met's American art into the twentieth

sumptuous life enjoyed by New York's big industrialists. The collection includes paintings by Reynolds, Hogarth, Gainsborough (*St James's Park*), and Bellini, whose *St Francis* suggests his vision of Christ by means of pervading light, a bent tree, and an enraptured stare. Above the fireplace, El Greco's *St Jerome* reproachfully surveys the riches all around, looking out to the South Hall, where one of Boucher's intimate depictions of his wife hangs near an early Vermeer, *Officer and Laughing Girl*. In the opposite direction are the library's British works, most notably one of Constable's *Salisbury Cathedral* series, and the North Hall, which holds an engaging and sensitive portrait of the Comtesse de Haussonville by Ingres. But the West Gallery holds Frick's greatest prizes: two Turners, views of Cologne and Dieppe; van Dyck's informal portraits of Frans Snyders and his wife; and a set of piercing self-portraits by Rembrandt, along with his enigmatic *Polish Rider*. A tiny room on the other side of the West Gallery houses an exquisite set of Limoges enamels and a collection of small-scale paintings that includes a *Virgin and Child* by Jan van Eyck.

Just a few blocks north, over on Madison Avenue at 75th Street, the **Whitney Museum of American Art** (Tues–Thurs, Sat & Sun 11am–6pm, Fri 1–9pm; $10; ⊕212/570-3676, ⓦwww.whitney.org) boasts a pre-eminent collection of twentieth-century American art and a superb exhibition locale. Every other year the museum mounts the Whitney Biennial show of contemporary American art – an event that has become a lightning rod for critical abuse since the 1995 show, when a giant mound of cooking fat presented as sculpture set right-wing aesthetes into a frenzy. When that's not on, check out the somewhat arbitrary Highlights of the Permanent Collection, arranged both by chronology and theme. Enjoy the prominent Abstract Expressionists collection, with great works by high priests Pollock and De Kooning, leading on to Rothko and the Color Field painters and the later Pop Art works of Warhol, Johns, and Oldenburg. The museum is especially strong on Hopper, O'Keeffe, and Calder, with galleries concentrating on each.

A ten-minute walk north from the Whitney, the **Guggenheim Museum**, Fifth Avenue at 89th Street (Sat–Wed 10am–5.45pm, Fri 10am–8pm, closed Thurs; $15, seniors & students $10, Fri 6–8pm pay what you wish; ⊕212/423-3500, ⓦwww.guggenheim.org), is better known for the building than its collection. Designed by Frank Lloyd Wright, this unique structure caused a storm of controversy when it was unveiled in 1959. Its centripetal spiral ramp, which wends you continuously all the way to its top floor (affording a vertiginous view of the lobby at the center), is still thought by some to favor Wright's talents over those of the exhibited artists. More outrage accompanied recent construction of a tower extension – though visitors will have difficulty understanding the fuss; it melds seamlessly with the ramp, and its galleries allow a much greater part of the museum's collection to be on rotational display. One of the newer additions is the Mapplethorpe Gallery, which houses some of the museum's odder pieces, including Louise Bourgeois' wood-chip sculpture *Femme Volage*, as well as several Calder mobiles. Much of the building is still given over to temporary exhibitions, but the permanent collection includes work by Chagall, Léger, the major Cubists and, most completely, Kandinsky. Additionally, there are some late nineteenth-century paintings, not least the exquisite Degas' *Dancers*, Modigliani's *Jeanne Héburene with Yellow Sweater*, and some sensitive early Picassos.

Two blocks up, at Fifth Avenue and 91st Street, lies the Smithsonian-run **Cooper Hewitt National Design Museum** (Tues–Thurs 10am–5pm, Fri 10am–9pm, Sat 10am–6pm, Sun noon–6pm; $8; ⊕212/849-8400, ⓦwww.ndm.si.edu). This wonderful institution is the only museum in the US devoted exclusively to historic and contemporary design. Founded in 1897, it's housed in the magnificent mansion once owned by Andrew Carnegie and functions as a research center as well as museum. If you're a history buff, the **Museum of the City of New York**, Fifth Avenue at 103rd Street (Wed–Sun 10am–5pm, groups only Tues; suggested donation $7; Ⓣ212/534-1672, Ⓦwww.mcny.org), might also grab your interest, with an informative rundown on the history of the city from Dutch times to the present day.

At the far eastern end of 88th Street, overlooking the East River, **Gracie Mansion** was built in 1799 on the site of a Revolutionary fort as a country manor house; it is one of the best-preserved colonial buildings in the city. Roughly contemporary with the Morris–Jumel Mansion (see p.104), Gracie Mansion has been the official residence of the mayor of New York City since 1942, when Fiorello LaGuardia, "man of the people" that he was, reluctantly set up house – though "mansion" is a bit overblown for what's a rather cramped clapboard cottage.

The Upper West Side

North of 59th Street, Manhattan's West Side becomes less commercial, fading north of Lincoln Center into a residential area of mixed charms. This is the **Upper West Side**, now one of the city's more desirable addresses, though in truth an area long favored by artists and intellectuals. Streets have been rechristened in honor of erstwhile residents like Isaac Bashevis Singer and Edgar Allan Poe. However, gentrification during the 1990s saw it become a bit yuppified and noticeably less funky than it once was.

Broadway shears north from Columbus Circle to the **Lincoln Center for the Performing Arts**, a marble assembly of buildings put up in the early 1960s on the site of some of the city's worst slums. Home to the Metropolitan Opera, the New York Philharmonic, and to a host of other smaller companies (see p.119), the center is worth seeing even if you don't catch a performance (tours daily 10am–4.30pm, leaving from the main concourse under the Center; $12.50; call Ⓣ212/875-5350 to reserve). At the center of the complex, the **Metropolitan Opera House** is an impressive marble and glass building, with murals by Marc Chagall behind each of its high front windows. On the left, the first of the Chagall murals, *Le Triomphe de la Musique* is cast with a variety of well-known performers, landmarks snipped from the New York skyline, and a portrait of Sir Rudolph Bing, the man who ran the opera for more than three decades, garbed as a gypsy. The other mural, *Les Sources de la Musique*, is reminiscent of Chagall's renowned set for the Metropolitan production of *The Magic Flute*: the god of music strums a lyre while a Tree of Life, Verdi, and Wagner all float down the Hudson River.

The most famous of the monumental apartment buildings of **Central Park West** is the **Dakota**, a grandiose Renaissance-style mansion on 72nd Street, built in the late nineteenth century to persuade wealthy New Yorkers that life in an apartment could be just as luxurious as in a private house. Over the years, big-time tenants have included Lauren Bacall and Leonard Bernstein, and in the late 1960s the building was used as the setting for Roman Polanski's film *Rosemary's Baby*. Now, though, most people know it as the former home of **John Lennon** – and (still) of his wife Yoko Ono, who owns a number of the apartments. Outside the *Dakota*, on the night of December 8, 1980, Lennon was murdered – shot to death by a man who professed to be one of his greatest admirers (see p.97 to read about the nearby Lennon memorial in Central Park).

North up Central Park West, at 77th Street, the often-overlooked **New York Historical Society** (Tues–Sun 10am–6pm; suggested donation $8, students $5, children under 12 free; ☎212/873-3400, ⓦwww.nyhistory.org) is more a museum of American than of New York history. Its collection includes paintings by James Audubon, the Harlem naturalist who specialized in lovingly detailed watercolors of birds; a broad sweep of nineteenth-century American portraiture (including the picture of Alexander Hamilton that found its way onto the $10 bill); Hudson River School landscapes (among them Thomas Cole's fantastically pompous *Course of Empire* series); and a glittering display of Tiffany glass, providing an excellent all-around view of Louis Tiffany's attempts "to provide good art for American homes."

Up the street looms the **American Museum of Natural History**, Central Park West at 79th Street (daily 10am–5.45pm; suggested donation $12, students $9, children $7; IMAX films, Hayden Planetarium & special exhibits extra; for tickets call ☎212/769-5200; for general info call ☎212/769-5100 or visit ⓦwww.amnh.org). This, the largest such museum in the world, is a strange architectural melange of heavy Neoclassical and rustic Romanesque styles covering four city blocks. Restored in the mid-1990s, the museum boasts superb nature dioramas and anthropological collections, interactive and multimedia displays, lively signage, and an awesome assemblage of bones, fossils, and models.

Top attractions range from the **Dinosaur Halls** to the **Hall of Biodiversity**, which focuses on both the ecological and evolutionary aspects of nature. Other delights include the massive totems in the **Hall of African Peoples**, the taxidermic marvels in **North American Mammals** (including a vividly staged bull moose fight), and the two thousand gems in the **Hall of Meteorites**, among them a dazzling two-ton hunk of raw copper. The **Hall of Ocean Life** features a replica of, among other aquatic beings, a blue whale, thought to be the largest animal ever to grace planet Earth, and whose weight equals that of 24 elephants, or 400,000 pounds.

The **Rose Center for Earth and Space**, comprising the **Hall of the Universe** and the **Hayden Planetarium** (contained in a huge central sphere), opened in 2000. The center boasts all the latest technology and a truly innovative design, with open construction, spiral ramps, and dramatic glass walls on three sides of the facility. One exhibit, "The Scales of the Universe," depicts the relative size of things, from galaxies, stars, and planets down through cells and atoms, each in comparison to the central sphere. It's simply presented and effective, yet the concepts still manage to boggle the mind. The Planetarium screens a visually impressive 40-minute 3D film "Passport to the Universe," in addition to the ponderous film entitled "The Search for Life: Are We Alone?" (both are screened throughout the day; $22, students $16.50, $13 children). For a head-trip of a different sort, check out SonicVision (Fri & Sat 7.30, 8.30, 9.30 & 10.30pm; $15), a "digitally animated alternative music show," which features groovy overhead graphics and songs by bands such as Radiohead and Coldplay mixed by spinmaster Moby. Additionally, on the first Friday of every month, the Rose Center for Earth and Space brings in esteemed jazz musicians for "Starry Nights," complete with drinks and tapas; admission is included in the cost of your museum ticket.

After Central Park West, the Upper West Side's second-best address is **Riverside Drive**, which weaves its way from 72nd Street up the western edge of Manhattan, flanked by palatial townhouses put up in the early twentieth century and by **Riverside Park**, landscaped in 1873 by Frederick Law Olmsted, of Central Park fame. Riverside Drive makes the most pleasant route up to prestigious **Columbia University**, whose campus fills seven blocks between 114th and 121st streets and Amsterdam Avenue and Morningside Drive. The campus plazas were designed by McKim, Mead & White in grand Beaux Arts style. Regular guided **tours** start from the information office at 116th Street and Broadway.

At Amsterdam Avenue and 112th Street, one of New York's tourist gems, the **Cathedral Church of St John the Divine** rises up with a solid kind of majesty. A curious mix of Romanesque and Gothic styles, the church was begun in 1892, though building stopped with the outbreak of war in 1939 and only sporadically resumed in the early 1990s; today, it's still barely two-thirds finished. On completion (which is unlikely before 2050), it will be the largest cathedral structure in the world, its floor space – 600ft long, and 320ft wide at the transepts – big enough to swallow both the cathedrals of Notre Dame and Chartres whole.

Harlem

Home to a culturally and historically – if not economically – rich **black** community, **Harlem** is still a focus of black activism and culture, and well worth seeing. Up until recently, because of a near-total lack of support from federal and municipal funds, Harlem formed a self-reliant and inward-looking community. For many downtown Manhattanites, white and black, 125th Street was a physical and mental border not willingly crossed. Today, the fruits of a cooperative effort involving businesses, residents, and City Hall are manifest in new housing, retail, and community projects, and much has been made of former president Bill Clinton's new offices here as well. But while brownstones triple in value and Harlem's physical proximity to the Upper West Side is touted, poverty and unemployment are still evident in large patches. Though it's unlikely you'll be hassled in daytime, 125th Street, 145th Street, Convent Avenue, and Malcolm X Boulevard (formerly Lenox Avenue) are the safest areas; at night, stick to the clubs.

Harlem's sights are very spread out; it's not a bad idea to get acquainted with the area via a **guided tour** (see p.73), and follow that up with further trips. Harlem's working center is 125th Street between Broadway and Fifth Avenue, a flattened expanse spiked with the occasional skyscraper. At 253 W 125th is the famous **Apollo Theatre** – not much to look at from the outside, but for many years the center of black entertainment in the Northeast. Almost all the great figures of jazz and the blues played here – James Brown recorded his seminal *Live at the Apollo* album here in 1962 – though a larger attraction today is the Wednesday Amateur Night, open to all; call ☏212/531-5300 for information. At 144 W 125th is the **Studio Museum in Harlem** (Wed–Fri & Sun noon–6pm, Sat 10am–6pm; $7, free on the first Sat of every month; ☏212/864-4500, ⓦ www.studiomuseum.org), a small but vibrant collection of African and African-American art from all eras.

Close by, **Adam Clayton Powell Jr Boulevard** pushes north, a broad and busy thoroughfare named after the 1930s minister who helped force the white-owned stores of Harlem to employ the blacks on whom their economic survival depended. Powell became the first African-American on the city council, then New York's first black representative in the US House. In 1967, amid rumors of the misuse of public funds, his House colleagues excluded him from Congress by majority vote. However, this failed to diminish his standing in Harlem, where voters twice re-elected him before his death in 1972.

One avenue block east, the **Schomburg Center for Research in Black Culture**, 515 Malcolm X Blvd at 135th Street (Mon–Wed noon–8pm, Thurs & Fri noon–6pm; free; ☏212/491-2200, ⓦ www.nypl.org/research/sc), has displays on black history, and literally millions of artifacts, manuscripts, artwork, and photographs in its archives. Meanwhile, just north, at 132 W 138th St, Powell preached at the **Abyssinian Baptist Church**. The church is also famed for its revival-style Sunday morning services and a gospel choir of gut-busting vivacity. Cross over west to 138th Street between Powell and Eighth, and you're in what many consider the finest, most articulate block of rowhouses in Manhattan – **Strivers' Row** – commissioned during the 1890s housing boom and taking in designs by three sets of architects. Within the burgeoning black community at the turn of the last century this came to be the desirable place for ambitious professionals to reside – hence its nickname.

From Park Avenue to the East River, Spanish Harlem, or **El Barrio**, dips down as far as East 96th Street to collide head-on with the affluence of the Upper East Side. The center of a large Puerto Rican community, El Barrio is quite different from Harlem in look and feel. The area was originally a working-class Italian neighborhood (a small pocket of Italian families survives around 116th St and First Ave) and the quality of the architecture here is nowhere as good as that immediately to the west. The result is a shabbier and more intimidating atmosphere. Cultural roots are in evidence, however, at **La Marqueta**, on Park Avenue between 111th and 116th streets, a five-block street market of tropical produce, sinister-looking meats, and much shouting, and the **Museo del Barrio,** 1230 Fifth Avenue at 104th Street (Wed–Sun 11am–5pm; suggested donation $6; ☎212/831-7272, ⊛www.elmuseo.org), which showcases Latin American and Caribbean art and culture, and features summertime concerts.

Washington Heights and the Cloisters

North of Harlem, starting from West 145th Street or so, is the neighborhood of **Washington Heights**, an area that evolved from poor farmland to highly sought-after real estate in the early part of the twentieth century; the wealthiest New Yorkers competed for estate plots with views of the Hudson River. In 1965, Washington Heights grabbed the world's attention when black activist **Malcolm X** was assassinated in the Audubon Ballroom here. Today, the area is home to the largest Dominican population in the US, as well as one of New York City's most dangerous and crime-ridden neighborhoods. And while its points of interest are safely accessed during the daylight hours, it's advisable to stay clear of Washington Heights after dark.

At Broadway and West 155th Street, **Audubon Terrace** is a complex of nineteenth-century Beaux Arts buildings that house an odd array of museums. The adjacent **Hispanic Museum** (Tues–Sat 10am–4.30pm, Sun 1–4pm; free; ☎212/690-0743) holds one of the largest collections of Hispanic art outside Spain. The three thousand paintings include works by Goya, El Greco, and Velázquez, and more than six thousand decorative works of art.

Another uptown surprise, on 160th Street between Amsterdam and Edgecombe avenues, is the **Morris–Jumel Mansion**, the oldest house in Manhattan (Wed–Sun 10am–4pm; $3; ☎212/923-8008). The house, with its proud Georgian outlines, faced by a later Federal portico, was built as a rural retreat in 1765 by Colonel Roger Morris, and served briefly as George Washington's headquarters, before it fell to the British. Later, wine merchant Stephen Jumel bought the mansion and refurbished it for his wife Eliza, formerly a prostitute and his mistress. When Jumel died in 1832, Eliza married ex-vice president Aaron Burr, twenty years her senior. The marriage lasted six months before old Burr took off, to die on the day of their divorce. Eliza battled on to the age of 91, and on the top floor of the house you'll find her obituary, a magnificently fictionalized account of a "scandalous" life.

From most western stretches of Washington Heights you get a glimpse of the **George Washington Bridge**, a dazzling concoction of metalwork and graceful lines that links Manhattan to New Jersey. Even better views are available from **the Cloisters** in Fort Tryon Park. This reconstructed monastic complex houses the pick of the Metropolitan Museum's (see p.97) medieval collection (take subway #A to 190th St–Ft Washington Ave; Tues–Sun 9.30am–5.15pm, closes 4.45pm Nov–Feb; suggested donation $12, students $7, includes admission to Metropolitan Museum on same day; ☏212/923-3700, ⓦ www.metmuseum.org). The collection is the handiwork of collectors George Barnard and John D. Rockefeller, who spent the early twentieth century shipping over all they could buy of medieval Europe. Among its larger artifacts are a monumental Romanesque Hall made up of French remnants and a frescoed Spanish Fuentiduena Chapel, both thirteenth-century. At the center of the museum is the Cuxa cloister from a twelfth-century Benedictine monastery in the French Pyrenees; its capitals are brilliant works of art, carved with weird, self-devouring grotesque creatures. The Early Gothic Hall houses smaller sculptures, among them a memorably tender *Virgin and Child*, carved in England in the fourteenth century. Tapestries include the spectacular *Unicorn Tapestries*. Campin's *Merode Altarpiece*, housed in its own antechamber, depicts the Annunciation in a typical Flemish interior of the day, while through the windows, life goes on in a fifteenth-century market square. The amazing downstairs Treasury houses the *Belles Heures de Jean, Duc de Berry* – perhaps the greatest of all medieval "Books of Hours," executed by the Limburg Brothers with dazzling genre miniatures of seasonal life – and the twelfth-century altar cross from Bury St Edmunds in England, a mass of tiny expressive characters from biblical stories.

The outer boroughs

Many visitors to New York don't stray off Manhattan. But if you're staying a while, choose to investigate the **outer boroughs** and you'll be well rewarded. **Brooklyn** is certainly worth a trip, primarily for the salubrious neighborhood of Brooklyn Heights just across the East River, bucolic Prospect Park and the Brooklyn Botanical Garden, and the Brooklyn Museum. For inveterate nostalgics, Coney Island and its Russian neighbor, Brighton Beach, lie at the far end of the subway line. Few indeed make it to **Queens**, though the borough holds the bustling Greek community of Astoria and the Museum of the Moving Image. **Staten Island** has a couple of unusual museums, and the ferry ride out is fun in and of itself. The **Bronx**, renowned for the desolate and bleak environs of its southern reaches, which are in fact slowly improving, has the city's largest zoo and another glorious botanical garden.

Brooklyn

If it were still a separate city, **Brooklyn** would be the fourth largest in the US – but until as recently as the early 1800s it was no more than a group of autonomous towns and villages distinct from the already thriving Manhattan. Robert Fulton's steamship service across the water first changed the shape of Brooklyn, starting with the establishment of a leafy retreat at Brooklyn Heights. What really transformed things, though, was the opening of the Brooklyn Bridge on May 24, 1883. Thereafter, development spread deeper inland, as housing was needed to service a more commercialized Manhattan. By 1900, Brooklyn was fully established as part of the newly incorporated New York City, and its fate as Manhattan's perennial kid brother was sealed.

Brooklyn Heights (#2, #3, #4, #5, #M, #N, #R, or #W to Court St–Borough Hall, or simply walk from Manhattan over the Brooklyn Bridge) one of New York City's most beautiful neighborhoods, has little in common with the rest of the borough. The peaceful, tree-lined enclave was settled by financiers from Wall Street and remains exclusive. Such noted literary figures as Truman Capote, Tennessee Williams, and Norman Mailer lived here. Although there isn't much to see as you wander its perfectly preserved terraces and breathe in the air of civilized calm, students of urban architecture can have a field day. Begin your tour at the **Esplanade** – more commonly known as the **Promenade** – with its fine Manhattan views across the water. **Pierrepoint** and **Montague** streets, the Heights' main arteries, are studded with delightful brownstones, restaurants, bars, and shops.

Farther into Brooklyn, Flatbush Avenue leads to **Grand Army Plaza** (#2 or #3 train to the eponymous subway station), a grandiose junction laid out by Calvert Vaux late in the nineteenth century as a dramatic approach to their new Prospect Park just beyond. The triumphal **Soldiers and Sailors' Memorial Arch** was added thirty years later, topped with a fiery sculpture of Victory – Frederick William MacMonnies' rider, chariot, four horses, and two heralds – in tribute to the Union triumph in the Civil War.

The enormous swath of green that rolls forth from behind the arch is **Prospect Park**. Landscaped in the early 1890s, the park remains remarkably bucolic, providing an ideal place for exercise, picnics, and family gatherings. During the day it's perfectly safe – though in light of several after-hours attacks in recent years, it's best to stay clear of the park at night. The adjacent **Brooklyn Botanic Garden** (April–Sept Tues–Fri 8am–6pm, Sat & Sun 10am–6pm; Oct–March Tues–Fri 8am–4.30pm, Sat & Sun 10am–4.30pm; $5, students $3, free Tues & Sat before noon; ☎718/623-7200, Ⓦwww.bbg.org), one of the city's most enticing park and garden spaces, is smaller and more immediately likeable than its more celebrated cousin in the Bronx (see p.109).

Though doomed to stand perpetually in the shadow of the Met, the **Brooklyn Museum of Art**, 200 Eastern Parkway (#2 or #3 train to Eastern Parkway; Wed–Fri 10am–5pm, Sat & Sun 11am–6pm, first Sat of every month 11am–11pm; $6, students $3; ☎718/638-5000, Ⓦwww.brooklynart.org), is a major museum and a good reason to forsake Manhattan for an afternoon. Highlights include the ethnographic department on the ground floor, the arts and applied arts from Oceania and the Americas and the classical and Egyptian antiquities on the second floor, and the evocative American period rooms on the fourth floor. Look in on the top-story American and European Painting and Sculpture Galleries, where the eighteenth-century portraits include one of George Washington by Gilbert Stuart. Pastoral canvases by William Sidney Mount, alongside the heavily romantic Hudson River School and paintings by Eastman Johnson (such as the curious *Not at Home*) and John Singer Sargent lead up to twentieth-century work by Charles Sheeler and Georgia O'Keeffe. European artists on display include Degas, Cézanne, Toulouse-Lautrec, Monet, Dufy, and Rodin.

Generations of working-class New Yorkers came to relax at one of Brooklyn's farthest points, **Coney Island** (Ⓦwww.coneyislandusa.com), reachable from Manhattan on the #Q, #W, #F, or #N subway lines; allow 45min to 1hr for the ride. At its height, 100,000 people came here daily; now, however, it's one of the city's poorest districts, and the Astroland amusement park is peeling and run-down. The boardwalk, though, has undergone extensive and successful renovation of late, and, if you like down-at-the-heel seaside resorts, there's no better place on earth on a summer weekend. An undeniable highlight is the nearly eighty-year-old wooden roller coaster, the **Cyclone** – it's way more thrilling than many modern rides. The beach, a broad swath of golden sand, is beautiful, although it is often crowded on hot days and the water might be less than clean. In late June, catch the **Mermaid Parade**, one of the country's oddest and glitziest small-town fancy dress parades, which culminates here. Meanwhile, the **New York Aquarium** on the boardwalk opened in 1896 and is still going strong, displaying fish and invertebrates from the world over in its darkened halls, along with frequent open-air shows of marine mammals (Mon–Fri 10am–5pm, Sat, Sun & holidays 10am–5.30pm; $11, students $7; ☎718/265-3474, ⓦwww.nyaquarium.com).

Farther east along the boardwalk, **Brighton Beach**, or "Little Odessa," is home to the country's largest community of Russian émigrés – around 20,000, who arrived in the 1970s – and a long-established and now largely elderly Jewish population who, much to the surprise of visiting Russians, still live as if they were in a 1970s Soviet republic. Livelier than Coney Island, it's also more prosperous, especially along its main drag, **Brighton Beach Avenue**, which runs underneath the #Q subway line in a hodgepodge of food shops and appetizing restaurants. In the evening, the restaurants really heat up, becoming a near-parody of a rowdy Russian night out, with loud live music, much glass-clinking, and the frenzied knocking back of vodka. It's definitely worth a visit.

Queens

Queens, named after the wife of Charles II of England, was one of the rare places where postwar immigrants could buy their own homes and establish their own communities. **Astoria**, for example, holds the world's largest concentration of Greeks outside Greece. It also has a long **filmmaking** tradition: Paramount had its studios here until the company was lured away by Hollywood's reliable weather. The area was then left empty and disused by all except the US Army, until Hollywood's stranglehold on the industry finally weakened. The new studios here – not open to the public – now rank as the country's fourth largest, and are set for a major expansion. The **American Museum of the Moving Image**, in the old Paramount complex at 35th Avenue at 36th Street (#R or #V train to Steinway; Wed–Fri 11am–5pm, Sat & Sun 11am–6pm, Fri open until 7.30 for screenings; $10; ☎718/784-0077, ⓦwww.ammi.org), is devoted to the history of film, video, and TV. In addition to viewing posters and kitsch movie souvenirs from the 1930s and 1940s you can listen in on directors explaining sequences from famous movies; watch fun short films made up of well-known clips; add your own sound effects to movies; and see some original sets and costumes. A wonderful, mock-Egyptian pastiche of a 1920s movie theater shows kids' movies and TV classics.

Until early 2005, Queens is also the temporary home of the **Museum of Modern Art**, while the original museum is being reconstructed on 53rd Street in Manhattan (see box, p.95). Along with the permanent collection, most of which has been moved to **MoMAQNS**, 45-20 33rd St at Queens Blvd (#7 subway to the 33rd Street stop; Mon, Thurs, Sat & Sun 10am–5pm, Fri 10am–7.45pm; $12, seniors and students $8.50, pay-what-you-wish Fri 4–7.45pm; ☎212/708-9400, ⓦwww.moma.org). Despite its logistical hurdles, the museum fits smartly in its temporary home, a well-organized prefab-style warehouse space. In addition to some of its greatest sculpture and paintings hits from the permanent collection (Braque, Brancusi, Matisse), there are, during any given month, a generous handful of curated exhibitions that range from video installations to pencil drawings.

Now affiliated with MoMA, **P.S. 1 Contemporary Art Center**, 22-25 Jackson Ave at 46th St (Thurs–Mon noon–6pm; $5; ☎718/784-2084, Ⓦwww.ps1.org), is one of the oldest and biggest organizations in the US devoted exclusively to contemporary art and showing leading emerging artists. Founded in 1971, the public school-turned-funky exhibition space also hosts lively evening club events.

The **Isamu Noguchi Garden Museum**, 36-01 43rd Ave at 36th St, on the 2nd floor (Mon, Thurs & Fri 10am–5pm, Sat & Sun 11am–6pm; suggested donation $5; ☎718/204-7088, Ⓦwww.noguchi.org), has also moved to a temporary 6000-square-foot home and is a short walk away from MoMAQNS. The museum administrators have done a wonderful job of paring down the permanent collection of this prolific and dynamic Japanese-American artist's works. Noguchi's "organic" sculptures, drawings, modern dance costumes, and well-known Akari Light Sculptures are all on display. The main museum and its Zen-like garden, at 32-37 Vernon Blvd at Broadway on the East River, is slated to re-open in late 2004; call or visit the website for updates. Just upstairs from the current location of the Noguchi Museum, the **Museum for African Art** (Mon, Thurs & Fri 10am–5pm, Sat & Sun 11am–5pm; $6; ☎718/784-7700, Ⓦwww.africanart.org) is a marvelous institution exclusively devoted to historical and contemporary African art.

Lastly, where Broadway and Vernon Boulevard intersect on the shores of the East River, **Socrates Sculpture Park** (daily 10am–sunset; free; ☎718/956-1819, Ⓦwww.socratessculpturepark.org) has been transformed from an illegal dumpsite into one of the city's most distinctive places to view and experience art, namely large-scale sculptures.

The Bronx

The city's northernmost borough, **The Bronx** was for a long time believed to be its toughest and most crime-ridden district, and presented as such in films like *Fort Apache* and *The Bronx*, as well as books like *Bonfire of the Vanities*, even after urban renewal was under way. In fact, it's not much different from the other outer boroughs, though geographically it has more in common with Westchester County to the north than it does with the island regions of New York City: steep hills, deep valleys, and rocky outcroppings to the west, and marshy flatlands along Long Island Sound to the east. Settled in the seventeenth century by the Swede Jonas Bronk, it became, like Brooklyn, part of New York proper around the end of the nineteenth century, and soon became one of the most sought-after residential areas of the city. Its main thoroughfare, **Grand Concourse**, became lined with luxurious Art Deco apartment houses; many, though greatly run-down, still stand.

The **Bronx Zoo** (Mon–Fri 10am–5pm, Sat & Sun 10am–5.30pm; $11, kids $8, free every Wed; ☎718/367-1010, Ⓦwww.wcs.org) is accessible either by its main gate on Fordham Road or by a second entrance on Bronx Park South. The latter is the entrance to use if you come directly here by subway (#2 or the #5 to E Tremont Ave). With over 4000 animals, it's the largest urban zoo in the US, and is better than most; it was one of the first institutions of its kind to realize that animals both looked and felt better out in the open. The "Wild Asia" exhibit is an almost forty-acre wilderness through which tigers, elephants, and deer roam relatively free, visible from a monorail (May–Oct; $3). Look in also on the "World of Darkness," which holds nocturnal species, the "Himalayan Highlands," with endangered species such as the red panda and snow leopard, and the new "Tiger Mountain" exhibit, which allows visitors the opportunity to get up close and personal with six Siberian tigers.

Across the road from the zoo's main entrance is the back turnstile of the **New York Botanical Gardens** (April–Oct Tues–Sun 10am–6pm, Nov–March 10am–5pm; $6, free Wed & Sat 10am–noon; ☎718/817-8700, Ⓦwww.nybg.org), which in parts is as wild as anything you're likely to see upstate.

Staten Island

Until 1964, **Staten Island** was isolated from the rest of the city – getting here meant a ferry trip or a long ride through New Jersey, and commuting into Manhattan was a bit of a haul. The opening of the Verrazano Narrows Bridge changed things: upwardly mobile Brooklynites found inexpensive property on the island and swarmed over the bridge to buy their parcel of suburbia. Today, Staten Island has swollen to accommodate dense residential neighborhoods amid the rambling greenery and endless backwaters of neat homes. Residents pining for a lost sense of isolation have voted to begin the long process of divorcing their borough from New York City altogether (though that seems unlikely to happen any time soon).

Without a car, the best way to reach the fifth borough is via the **Staten Island Ferry** (☎718/815-BOAT, Ⓦwww.siferry.com), which sails from Battery Park around the clock, with departures every 15–20min during rush hours (between 7–9am and 5–7pm), every 30min midday and evenings, and once an hour late at night; on weekend, service is less frequent. Truly New York's best bargain, the ferry gives great wide-angled views of Lower Manhattan and the Statue of Liberty absolutely free.

Once you get to the island, the ferry terminal in which you arrive quickly dispels any romance – though it's easy to escape to the adjoining bus station and catch the #S74 bus to the **Jacques Marchais Center of Tibetan Art**, 338 Lighthouse Ave (Wed–Sun 1–5pm; $5; ☎718/987-3500, Ⓦwww.tibetan-museum.com). Jacques Marchais was the alias of Jacqueline Kleber, a New York art dealer who reckoned she'd get on better with a French name. In the 1920s and 1930s, she assembled the largest collection of Tibetan art in the Western world and housed it in a hillside "Buddhist temple." The exhibition is small enough to be accessible, with magnificent bronze Bodhisattvas, fearsome deities in union with each other, musical instruments, costumes, and decorations from Tibet. During the first or second week of October the museum hosts a harvest festival, where Tibetan monks in maroon robes perform the traditional ceremonies, and Tibetan food and crafts are sold.

From Richmond Road, one of Staten Island's main drags, it's just a short walk to **Historic Richmond Town** (June–Aug Wed–Sat 10am–5pm, Sun 1–5pm; Sept–May Wed–Sun 1–5pm; $4; ☎718/351-1611, Ⓦwww.historicrichmond-town.org), where a dozen or so old buildings have been transplanted from their original sites in other areas of Staten Island and grafted onto the village of Richmond, which dates from 1695–1880. Half-hourly **tours** negotiate the best of these – including the oldest elementary school in the country, a picture-book general store, and the atmospheric Guyon-Lake-Tysen House of 1740. It's all carried off to picturesque effect in rustic surroundings, a mere twelve miles from Downtown Manhattan.

Eating

There isn't anything you can't eat in New York. The city has innumerable restaurants, and many New Yorkers not only eat out often, but take their food incredibly seriously, obsessed with new cuisines, new dishes, and new restaurants. Certain areas are pockets of ethnic restaurants – **Chinatown** (including Malaysian, Thai, and Vietnamese) below Canal Street; **Little Italy** just to the north; and **Indian Row**, on Sixth Street between First and Second avenues – but you can generally find whatever you want, wherever (and whenever) you want. The **outer boroughs** of Brooklyn, the Bronx, and Queens all have excellent dining opportunities worth seeking out, in neighbourhoods such as Jackson Heights, Astoria, Williamsburg, and Park Slope.

Downtown Manhattan (below 14th St)

Blue Hill 75 Washington Place, between 6th Ave and Washington Square Park ☏ 212/539-1776. Tucked into a brownstone just steps from the park, this restaurant has earned countless accolades in recent years for its superb seasonal menu of American dishes served with flair.

Café de Bruxelles 118 Greenwich Ave, at W 13th St ☏ 212/206-1830. Taste the city's most delicious frites (served with homemade mayo) and mussels at this Belgian family-run restaurant. Its zinc bar is the oldest around, and there's a nice selection of Belgian beers, too.

Café Le Figaro 184 Bleecker St, at MacDougal ☏ 212/677-1100. Discover the ersatz Left Bank at its finest at this 1950s Beat hangout. On the menu: good people-watching and first-rate burgers and soups.

Cendrillon 45 Mercer St, between Broome and Grand ☏ 212/343-9012. This fine pan-Asian restaurant serves consistently exceptional food, not to mention creative cocktails. The prices are decent, and the desserts will make you swoon.

Corner Bistro 331 W 4th St, at Jane ☏ 212/242-9502. This down-home tavern serves some of the best burgers and fries in town. An excellent place to unwind and refuel in a friendly neighborhood atmosphere, it's also a longstanding literary haunt; can get quite crowded.

Ear Inn 326 Spring St, between Washington and Greenwich ☏ 212/226-9060. This cozy pub serves basic, reasonably priced American food (the cowboy chili and the burgers are excellent) and has a good mix of beers on tap. It claims to be the second-oldest bar in the city (after *McSorley's*; see p.114). It may also be one of the best.

Florent 69 Gansevoort St, between Washington and Greenwich ☏ 212/989-5779. In the heart of the Meatpacking District, see and be seen at this almost-always-open, fashionable eatery, serving great moderate-to-pricey French bistro fare.

Grange Hall 50 Commerce St, at Barrow ☏ 212/924-5246. Hiding on a dead-end picturesque street, and inspired by community suppers in Maine, this feel-good restaurant features healthful, seasonal dishes at reasonable prices. It's popular, so make a reservation.

'ino 21 Bedford St, between Downing St and 6th Ave ☏ 212/989-5769. Duck in here for a satisfying snack; choose from a list of *bruschette*, *tramezzine* (a hearty cousin of the tea sandwich), and Italian wines.

Joe's Shanghai 9 Pell St, between Bowery and Mott ☏ 212/233-8888. Probably Chinatown's most famous restaurant, this place is always packed, for good reason. Try the soup dumplings and the seafood main courses at its communal tables, or visit its newer, less crowded sister, *Joe's Ginger*, at 113 Mott St, between Hester and Canal.

Katz's Delicatessen 205 E Houston St, at Ludlow ☏ 212/254-2246. Venerable Lower East Side Jewish deli serving archetypal overstuffed pastrami and corned-beef sandwiches. Best known as the site of the orgasm scene in *When Harry Met Sally*.

Lavagna 545 E 5th St, between aves A and B ☏ 212/979-1005. This red-hued hideaway seduces East Villagers with potato cheese gratin, pasta with sausage, and succulent pork dishes. The prices are relatively reasonable, to boot.

Lombardi's 32 Spring St, between Mott and Mulberry ☏ 212/941-7994. The oldest pizzeria in Manhattan serves some of the best pie in town, including an amazing clam pizza; no slices, though. Ask for roasted garlic on the side.

Mary's Fish Camp 64 Charles St, at W 4th St ☏ 646/486-2185. Lobster rolls, bouillabaisse, and seasonal veggies adorn the menu at this intimate West Village spot, where you can almost smell the salt air. Go early, as the reservation line lasts into the night.

Moustache 90 Bedford St, between Grove and Barrow ☏ 212/229-2220; also 265 E 10th St, between 1st Ave and Ave A ☏ 212/228-2022. A small, cheap Middle Eastern spot with a "pitza" specialty (pizzas of pita bread and eclectic toppings); also great hummus, chickpea and spinach salad, and bargain lamb chops.

Otto Enoteca and Pizzeria 1 5th Ave, at Washington Square N ☏ 212/995-9559. The newest (and cheapest) addition to Italian chef Mario Battali's restaurant empire is a popular pizza and antipasti joint with a superb wine list and a beautiful crowd. The acoustics aren't great, but the atmosphere is festive and you can't beat the *lardo* (bacon) and *vongole* (clam) pizza.

Paradou 8 Little W 12th St, between Greenwich and Washington ☎ 212/463-8345. Sure to transport you to Provence, this underrated French bistro is a far better (and more authentic) option than overexposed *Pastis* around the corner. Great wines by the glass.

Pearl Oyster Bar 18 Cornelia St, between Bleecker and W 4th sts ☎ 212/691-8211. With only 25 seats, you may have to fight for a table here, but it's worth it for the thoughtfully executed seafood dishes and primo lobster rolls.

Podunk Café 231 E 5th St, between 2nd Ave and Cooper Square ☎ 212/677-7722. The desserts at this homey bakery/café are unbeatable; the chewy, delicious coconut bars can't miss.

Prune 54 E 1st St, between 1st and 2nd aves ☎ 212/677-6221. Adventurous and full of surprises, this East Village Mediterranean restaurant boasts dishes such as sweetbreads wrapped in bacon, seared sea bass with Berber spices, and buttermilk ice cream with pistachio puff pastry. It's cramped, but this makes for a festive atmosphere.

Raoul's 180 Prince St, between Sullivan and Thompson ☎ 212/966-3518. This sexy French bistro is comfortable, authentic, and entertaining for its people-watching into the night. A beloved New York standby, if at a price.

Sammy's Roumanian Steakhouse 157 Chrystie St at Delancy ☎ 212/673-0330. This basement Jewish steakhouse gives diners more than they bargained for: schmaltzy songs, delicious-but-heartburn-inducing food (topped off by homemade rugelach and egg creams for dessert), and chilled vodka in blocks of ice. Keep track of your tab, if you can.

Veselka 144 2nd Ave, at 9th St ☎ 212/228-9682. The terrific grilled kielbasa, vegetarian stuffed cabbage, and Ukrainian pierogi at Eastern European *Veselka* are all great for sopping up alcohol and killing hunger pangs at 4am.

Wallse 344 W 11th St, at Washington ☎ 212/352-2300. New-fangled (and lighter) Austrian fare takes center stage here. Chef Kurt Gutenbrunner has crafted a unique menu that abounds with surprises – the light-as-air schnitzel, frothy riesling sauces, and strudels are good enough to make an Austrian grandma sing with pride. The dining room resonates sophistication, and the wine list tempts with some hard-to-find Austrian vintages.

Xunta 174 1st Ave, between 10th and 11th sts ☎ 212/614-0620. This East Village gem buzzes with hordes of young faces perched on rum barrels, downing pitchers of sangría and choosing

from the dizzying tapas menu – try the mussels in fresh tomato sauce, or shrimp with garlic. You can eat (and drink) very well for around $20.

Midtown Manhattan (14th St to 59th St)

Artisanal 2 Park Ave, at 32nd St ☎ 212/725-8585. Cheese is the name of the game here – there's a cave with 700 varieties. If you don't want the full experience, grab a small table at the bar and try the *gougere* (gruyere puffs) with one of the excellent wines on offer.

Carmine's 200 W 44th St, between Broadway and 8th Ave ☎ 212/221-3800; also 2450 Broadway, between W 90th and W 91st sts ☎ 212/362-2200. Mountainous portions of tasty homestyle Southern Italian food are made to share at this large, loud favorite. Be prepared to wait; only parties of six or more can make reservations after 6pm.

City Bakery 3 W 18th St, between 5th and 6th aves ☎ 212/366-1414. A smart stop for a satisfying lunch or a sweet-tooth craving. The vast array of pastries is head-and-shoulders above most in the city.

Eisenberg's Sandwich Shop 174 5th Ave, between 22nd and 23rd sts ☎ 212/675-5096. A colorful luncheonette, this slice-of-NY-life spot serves great tuna sandwiches, matzo ball soup, and old-fashioned fountain sodas.

Empire Diner 210 10th Ave, at 22nd St ☎ 212/243-2736. Spangled in silver, this all-night diner charms with its festive vibe and good, moderately priced food.

Emporio Brasil 15 W 46th St, between 5th and 6th aves ☎ 212/764-4646. Check out the great Brazilian food and atmosphere at *Emporio Brasil*, with reasonable prices for Midtown. On Saturday afternoon, from noon to 5pm only, try Brazil's national dish, the tasty *feijoada* (a stew of meaty pork and black beans, with rice).

F&B 269 W 23rd St, between 7th and 8th aves ☎ 646/486-4441. Terrific European-style street food (namely hot dogs) at digestable prices. Other items include salmon dogs, bratwursts, and mouth-watering Swedish meatballs; there's also a selection of vegetarian offerings.

Gramercy Tavern 42 E 20th St, between Broadway and Park ☎ 212/477-0777. By many accounts, NYC's best and most-beloved restaurant; its neo-Colonial decor, exquisite New American cuisine, and perfect service make for a memorable meal. The lively front room is a great place to drop in for a drink, or a more casual (and cheaper) meal.

Guastavino's 409 E 59th St, between 1st and York aves ☎ 212/980-2455. This magnificent, soaring space underneath the Queensboro Bridge is a hot spot for beautiful people who come to drink *flirtinis* and choose from a dizzying array of seafood dishes. Book upstairs for a quieter – and super expensive – meal.

Hallo Berlin 402 W 51st St, between 9th and 10th aves ☏212/541-6248. All manner of tasty wursts, served by an owner who once sold them from a pushcart and now vends in this pleasant bench-and-table beer-garden setting.

Joe Allen's 326 W 46th St, between 8th and 9th aves ☏212/581-6464. The tried-and-true formula of checkered tablecloths, old-fashioned barroom feel, and reliable American food at moderate prices works excellently at this popular pre-theater spot. Make a reservation, unless you plan to arrive after 8pm.

Oyster Bar lower level, Grand Central Station ☏212/490-6650. This wonderfully atmospheric old place, down in the vaulted dungeons of Grand Central, draws Midtown office workers for lunch, who come to choose from a staggering menu featuring daily catches – she-crab bisque, steamed Maine lobster, and sweet Kumamoto oysters. Prices are moderate to expensive; you can eat more cheaply at the bar.

Rosa Mexicano 1063 1st Ave, at 58th St ☏212/753-7407; also 61 Columbus Ave, at 62nd St ☏212/977-7700. Festive decor, authentic dishes such as *bisteca al hongos* (beef with creamy mushroom sauce) and pomegranate margaritas make this the best Mexican restaurant in NYC. Not surprisingly, it's pricey.

Sugiyama 251 W 55th St, between Broadway and 8th Ave ☏212/956-0670. You may want to take out a loan before dining at this superb Japanese restaurant, where you're guaranteed an exquisite experience, from its enchanting *kaiseki* (chef's choice) dinners (vegetarian or non-) to its royal service.

Vatan 409 3rd Ave, at 29th St ☏212/689-5666. Nab a table here for a vegetarian Indian feast amid garish decor.

Uptown Manhattan (60th St and above)

Amy Ruth's 113 W 116th St, between Lenox and 7th aves ☏212/280-8779. The honey-dipped fried chicken is reason enough to travel to this casual, family restaurant in Harlem. The place gets especially busy after church on Sundays.

Barking Dog Luncheonette 1678 3rd Ave, at E 94th St ☏212/831-1800; also 1453 York Ave, at 77th St ☏212/861-3600. This diner-like place offers outstanding, cheap American food (like mashed potatoes and gravy). Very kid-friendly.

Big Nick's Burger Joint 2175 Broadway, between 76th and 77th sts ☏212/362-9238. This welcoming greasy spoon with gargantuan portions is heaven for hungry diners, be it after-hours or early in the morning.

Boat House in Central Park (enter from 72nd St), at Central Park Drive N ☏212/517-2233. The New American cuisine here is fine – but it's the picturesque setting that makes the pumped-up prices worth every penny, especially at sunset. If you don't feel like splurging, go for a drink at the water's edge.

El Pollo 1746 1st Ave, between E 90th and E 91st sts ☏212/996-7810. Come here for a tasty and cheap meal of Peruvian-style rotisserie chicken, dusted with spices and cooked over a spit. Bring your own wine.

Fujiyama Mama 467 Columbus Ave, between W 82nd and W 83rd sts ☏212/769-1144. The West Side's best – and most boisterous – sushi bar comes with high-tech decor and loud music.

Gabriela's 685 Amsterdam Ave, at 93rd St ☏212/961-0574; also 311 Amsterdam, at 73rd St ☏212/875-8532. Count on good, inexpensive, authentic Mexican – not just your usual enchiladas and burritos, but also a wide array of regional chicken and seafood dishes in a large, crowded room. Noisy, lively, and thoroughly enjoyable. Expect to wait.

Gray's Papaya 2090 Broadway, at 72nd St ☏212/799-0243. Open 24/7, this insanely popular hot-dog joint is an NYC institution, now famous for its "Recession Special": 2 dogs and a drink for $2.45. Call for several other locations around the city.

Heidelburg 1648 2nd Ave, between E 85th and 86th sts ☏212/628-2332. At one of the last Yorkville German joints, the food is the real deal, with excellent liver dumpling soup, Bauernfruestuck omelettes and pancakes (both sweet and potato). Have a huge, boot-shaped glass of Weissbeer with anything.

Jean Georges in the *Trump International Hotel*, 1 Central Park West, between 60th and 61st sts ☏212/299-3900. This contemporary French restaurant drips with elegance; its celebrity chef, Jean Georges Vongerichten, has been known to make such inventive dishes as asparagus with frothy truffle vinaigrette, or dill-stuffed shrimp with baked lemon. The staff here is polished, and its prices steep. If you aren't up for the full-blown gastronomic experience, try the prix fixe lunch menu ($20) in the more casual Nougatine Room.

La Caridad 78 2199 Broadway, at W 78th St ☏212/874-2780. This neighborhood institution doles out plentiful and inexpensive Cuban-Chinese food (the Cuban is better, though). Bring your own beer and expect to wait.

Mughlai 320 Columbus Ave, at 75th St ☏ 212/724-6363. This upscale Indian spot is surprisingly affordable. Entrees, which include batter-light samosas and comforting curries, run $11–16.

Ouest 2315 Broadway, between 83rd and 84th sts ☏ 212/580-8700. This New American restaurant has earned a loyal following for its celeb spottings and exceptional gourmet comfort food, such as bacon-wrapped meatloaf with wild mushroom gravy. There's a $26 three-course pre-theater menu served Mon–Fri 5–6.30pm.

Sarabeth's 423 Amsterdam Ave, between 80th and 81st sts ☏ 212/496-6280; also in the *Hotel Wales*, 1295 Madison Ave, between 92nd and 93rd sts ☏ 212/410-7335. Best for brunch, this country-style restaurant serves delectable baked goods and impressive omelettes – a fact reflected by the long lines outside.

Serendipity 3 225 E 60th St, between 2nd and 3rd aves ☏ 212/838-3531. The long-established eatery/ice cream parlor serves out-of-this-world frozen hot chocolate; the wealth of ice cream offerings are a real treat, too.

Terrace in the Sky 400 W 119th St, between Amsterdam Ave and Morningside Drive ☏ 212/666-9490. Enjoy harp music, marvelous Mediterranean fare, and great views of Morningside Heights in this romantic Uptown spot.

Vinnie's Pizza 285 Amsterdam Ave, at W 73rd St ☏ 212/874-4382. For those who prefer their pizza thick, doughy, loaded with cheese, and cheap, this Upper West Side place is for you. You can sit, or order a slice to go.

The outer boroughs

360 360 Van Brunt St, at Wolcott St, Red Hook, Brooklyn ☏ 718/246-0360. Seasonal ingredients, bohemian ambiance, and a passionate chef make this hands-on French restaurant worth the adventure of finding it. The menu here changes every day, but there's always a fine selection of unusual wines.

Diner 85 Broadway, at Berry St, Williamsburg, Brooklyn ☏ 718/486-3077. A fave with artists and hipsters, this groovy eatery (in a Pullman diner car) serves tasty American bistro grub (hangar steaks, roasted chicken, fantastic fries) at good prices. Stays open late, with an occasional DJ spinning tunes.

Elias Corner 24-02 31st St, at 24th Ave, Astoria, Queens ☏ 718/932-1510. Pay close attention to the seafood on display as you enter, for this Astoria institution doesn't have menus and the staff is not always forthcoming. Serves some of the best and freshest fish; try the marinated grilled octopus.

Grocery 195 Smith St, Carroll Gardens, Brooklyn ☏ 718/596-3335. Smith Street is at the epicenter of a massive upswing in Brooklyn dining, and this tiny entry, featuring a seasonal menu full of unique, New American dishes, is the best of the bunch. Entrees $20 and up; call well in advance for reservations.

Jackson Diner 37-47 74th St, between 37th and Roosevelt aves, Jackson Heights, Queens ☏ 718/672-1232. Come here hungry and stuff yourself silly with amazingly light and reasonably priced Indian fare. The samosas and mango lassis are not to be missed.

Peter Luger's Steak House 178 Broadway, at Driggs Ave, Williamsburg, Brooklyn ☏ 718/387-7400. Catering to carnivores since 1873, *Peter Luger's* may just be the city's finest steakhouse. The service is surly and the decor plain, but the porterhouse steak – the only cut served – is divine. Cash only, and very expensive; expect to pay at least $60 a head.

Planet Thailand 133 N 7th St, between Bedford Ave and Berry St, Williamsburg, Brooklyn ☏ 718/599-5758. This funky, massive restaurant serves Thai and Japanese food at attractive prices. The food is dependable, the sake flowing, and there's a DJ to ensure the party flows into the night.

Primorski 282 Brighton Beach Ave, between 2nd and 3rd sts, Brighton Beach, Brooklyn ☏ 718/891-3111. Perhaps the best of Brighton Beach's Russian hangouts, with a huge menu of authentic Russian dishes, including blintzes and stuffed cabbage, at absurdly cheap prices. Live music in the evening.

Drinking

New York's best **bars** are in **Downtown Manhattan** – the West and East villages, SoHo, and the Lower East Side. The **Midtown** places tend to be geared to an after-hours office crowd and (with a few exceptions) are pricey and rather dull. **Uptown**, the Upper West Side at least, between 60th and 85th streets along Amsterdam and Columbus avenues, has several good places to drink. Most of the bars listed below serve food of some kind and have happy hours sometime between 4pm and 8pm during the week. See also the bars listed in "Gay New York," p.122.

Downtown Manhattan (to 14th St)

Barramundi 147 Ludlow St, between Stanton and Rivington ☎212/529-6900. The magical, fairy-lit garden makes this bar a blessed sanctuary from the painfully hip Lower East Side.

Blind Tiger Ale House 518 Hudson St, at W 10th St ☎212/675-3848. You could easily leave here with things looking a bit foggy, after taking on 24 beers on tap, an eclectic bottled selection, and assorted liquors. Free hot dogs during Monday-evening happy hour.

Chumley's 86 Bedford St, between Grove and Barrow ☎212/675-4449. As much fun to find (there's no sign) as it is to drink in, this atmospheric former speakeasy has a great selection of beers and good American pub food.

Decibel 240 E 9th St, between 2nd and 3rd aves ☎212/979-2733. A rocking atmosphere (with good tunes) envelops this beautifully decorated underground sake bar. The inevitable wait for a wooden table is worth it.

Double Happiness 173 Mott St, between Broome and Grand ☎212/941-1282. Low ceilings, dark lighting, nooks, crannies, and the superlative green-tea martinis make this Asian-themed bar a decadently seductive place to be.

Drinkland 339 E 10th St, between ave A and B ☎212/228-2435. Dizzying psychedelic decor fused with DJs spinning big-beat and trip-hop – plus strong mixed drinks – have turned this place into a favorite among East Villagers. Closed Mon. Cash only.

Grassroots Tavern 20 St Mark's Place, between 2nd and 3rd aves ☎212/475-9443. This roomy, wooden, and wonderful underground den has Brooklyn beers for $3, an extended happy hour, and at least three animals roaming around at any hour of the day or night.

Hogs & Heifers 859 Washington St, at W 13th St ☎212/929-0655. It's honky-tonk cheesy but fun; this raucous Meatpacking District watering hole has inspired thousands of women to dance on the bar, as well as donate their bras to the growing collection that adorns the joint.

McSorley's Old Ale House 15 E 7th St, between 2nd and 3rd aves, ☎212/472-9148. Yes, it's touristy and often full of local frat boys, but you'll be drinking in history at this landmark bar that served its first beer in 1854.

Other Room 143 Perry St, between Washington and Greenwich ☎212/645-9758. The cozy-cool atmosphere, excellent drink menu, and "way-West" location of this wine and beer bar has guaranteed it a special place in locals' hearts.

Rhône 63 Gansevoort St, between Washington and Greenwich ☎212/367-8440. As the name implies, this large, well-designed, sexy lounge serves red and white wines from the Rhone Valley. It's a little too popular for its own good, though, as the place can get very crowded on weekend nights.

St Dymphna's 118 St Marks Place, between 1st Ave and Ave A ☎212/254-6636. With a tempting pub menu and some of the city's best Guinness, *Dymphna's* is great place to warm up on a cold winter's night.

Temple Bar 332 Lafayette St, between Bleecker and Houston sts ☎212/925-4242. One the most discreet and romantic spots for a drink Downtown, this sumptuous, dark lounge evokes the 1940s and is ideal for a tryst. They take their martinis very seriously here.

West West Side Highway, at W 11th St ☎212/242-4375. Design-forward cement floors, Moderne furniture, and exceptional bartenders make this monochromatic bar/cocktail lounge a happening place to watch the sun set over the Hudson River.

White Horse Tavern 567 Hudson St, at W 11th St ☎212/989-3956. At this convivial, inexpensive, old-time Village institution, Dylan Thomas drank up before his last trip to the hospital.

Midtown Manhattan (14th St to 59th St)

21 Club 21 W 52nd St, between 5th and 6th aves ☎212/582-7200. Simply one of New York's most enduring institutions, this is where the Old Boys meet, surrounded by dark wood paneling and sublime service. There's a dress code, so wear a jacket and tie.

Bar and Books, Beekman 889 1st Ave, at 50th St ☎212/980-9314. One of the few spots you can still drink and smoke in the city (thanks to its cigar status), this upper-crust bar attracts all types, including a healthy contingent of Wall Streeters. Call for other locations.

Campbell Apartment southwest balcony, Grand Central Terminal ☎212/953-0409. Once the home of businessman John W. Campbell, who oversaw the construction of Grand Central, this majestic space – built to look like a thirteenth-century Florentine palace – was sealed up for years. Now, it's one of New York's most distinctive bars. Go early and don't wear sneakers; you won't be allowed in if you do.

Enoteca I Trulli 124 E 27th St, between Lexington and Park ℡212/481-7372. Just adjacent to a lovely Italian restaurant by the same name, this wine bar serves a jaw-dropping selection from Italy only, available by the glass, flight, or bottle. Servers are happy to give you a wine lesson as they pour. Ask for bread with ricotta spread or a plate of Italian cheeses to accompany your tipple.

Lever House 390 Park Ave, at 53rd St ℡212/888-2700. NYC's newest power-drink scene is also a 1950s landmark, in a building that revolutionized skyscraper design. The new interior strikes a balance between retro and futuristic; it's worth a look and a cocktail, or two.

McHale's 750 8th Ave, at 46th St ℡212/997-8885. This good, old-fashioned bar offers a respite from the full-throttle consumerism of Times Square. A regular menu of bar food (burgers, fries, nachos, wings) comes at affordable prices, as well.

Old Town Bar & Restaurant 45 E 18th St, between Broadway and Park ℡212/529-6732. This atmospheric old-world bar is popular with publishing types, models, and photogs in the Flatiron district. Has a good pub menu, too.

Park 118 10th Ave, between 17th and 18th sts ℡212/352-3313. It's easy to get lost in this vast warren of rooms filled with fireplaces, geodes, and even a Canadian redwood. The large garden is a treat, and the place is filled on weekend nights with only the most beautiful people.

Pen-Top Bar & Terrace in the *Peninsula Hotel*, 700 5th Ave, at 55th St ℡212/903-3097. High above the city, this rooftop bar delivers stunning views of the skyline (on a clear day) and a good selection of beefy drinks.

Pete's Tavern 129 E 18th St, at Irving Place ℡212/473-7676. This former speakeasy, which opened in 1864, has hosted such illustrious patrons as John F. Kennedy Jr and O. Henry, who allegedly wrote "Gift of the Magi" in his regular booth here. A fun and oft-raucous spot to grab a pint near Gramercy Park.

Uptown Manhattan (60th St and above)

Abbey Pub 237 W 105th St, between Broadway and Amsterdam ℡212/222-8713. Half a century old, the *Abbey* still brings in locals and students for learned conversations in wooden booths and cheap beer.

Dead Poet 450 Amsterdam Ave, between 81st and 82nd sts ℡212/595-5670. You'll be waxing poetical and then dropping down dead if you stay

for the duration of this sweet little bar's happy hour: it lasts from 4 to 8pm and offers draft beer at $3 a pint. The backroom has armchairs, books, and a pool table.

Dublin House Tap Room 225 W 79th St, between Broadway and Amsterdam ℡212/874-9528. This lively Upper West Side Irish pub, pouring a very nice Black & Tan, is dominated at night by the young, inebriated, and rowdy.

Metropolitan Museum of Art 1000 5th Ave at 82nd St ℡212/535-7710. It's hard to imagine a more romantic spot to sip a glass of wine, whether on the Cantor Roof Garden (open only in warm weather), enjoying one of the best views in the city, or on the Great Hall Balcony listening to live chamber music (year-round Fri and Sat 5–8.30pm).

Prohibition 503 Columbus Ave, between 84th and 85th sts ℡212/579-3100. A pool table, live jazz, and outdoor tables combine to make *Prohibition* one of the liveliest singles scenes on the Upper West Side.

Ruby's Tap House 1754 2nd Ave, between 91st and 92nd sts ℡212/987-8179. At this raucous, popular joint, they've got pool, darts, and a whopping 26 beers on draft.

Subway Inn 143 E 60th St, at Lexington ℡212/223-8929. This downscale neighborhood dive bar, across from Bloomingdale's, is great for a late-afternoon beer.

The outer boroughs

Bohemian Hall and Beer Garden 29-19 24th Ave, between 29th and 30th sts, Astoria, Queens ℡718/721-4226. This old Czech bar is the real deal, catering to old-timers and serving a good selection of pilsners, as well as hard-to-find brews. In back, there's a very large beer garden, complete with picnic tables, trees, burgers and sausages, and a bandshell for polka groups.

Boogaloo Bar 168 Marcy Ave, between S 5th and Broadway, Williamsburg, Brooklyn ℡718/599-8900. This funkadelic lounge serves as a meeting-ground for experimental artists, DJs, and thirsty patrons, who can choose, among other drinks, from a selection of over 30 rums from around the world.

Galapagos 70 N 6th St, between Wythe and Kent aves, Williamsburg, Brooklyn ℡718/782-5188, ⓦwww.galapagosartspace.com. Gorgeous design – this converted factory features placid pools of water and elegant candelabras – as well as excellent avant-garde movies on Sunday nights. Live music, literary readings, or some oddball event most other nights of the week.

Pete's Candy Store 709 Lorimer, between Frost

and Richardson, Williamsburg, Brooklyn ☎718/302-3770, ⊛www.petescandystore.com. This terrific little spot to tipple was once a real candy store. There's free live music every night, poetry on Mondays, Scrabble and Bingo nights, and even an organized "Stitch and Bitch" knitting group.

Tupelo 34-18 34th Ave, at 35th St, Astoria, Queens ☎718/707-9588. Take your pick of beers and enjoy the music upstairs (DJ, Eighties, or live local bands) at this trendy Astoria meeting place.

Nightlife and entertainment

You'll never be at a loss for something fun or culturally enriching to do while in New York. The **live music** scene, in particular, well reflects New York's diversity: on any night of the week, you can hear pretty much any type of music your heart could desire, from thumping hip-hop to pogoing punk, and, of course, plenty of jazz. There are also quite a few **dance clubs**, where you can move to hard-hitting drum'n'bass or cheesy tunes from the 1970s and 80s.

Home to Broadway and 42nd Street (as well as off-Broadway and the Fringe Festival), New York is also one of the world's great **theater** centers, with productions that range from lavish, over-the-top musicals to experimental productions in converted garages. **Classical music**, **opera**, and **dance** are all very well-represented, too, at venues such as the dignified Lincoln Center and the more funky Brooklyn Academy of Music. As for **film**, you couldn't hope for better pickings: the city has several large indie theaters, numerous revival and art-house cinemas, and countless Hollywood-blockbuster multiplexes. Last but not least, NYC has many excellent **comedy** clubs, as well as a healthy **spoken-word** and **poetry slam** scene.

For **listings** of what's on during any particular week, check out *Time Out New York* ($3; available from newsstands citywide) or *The Village Voice* (free; available in newspaper boxes and many other spots around town).

Clubs and live music

New York has plenty of great **live music venues**, from storied *CBGB*, where the Ramones got their start, and the cutting-edge *Knitting Factory*, to *S.O.B.'s* and *Joe's Pub*, which cater to world music and more eclectic fare. Numerous **jazz clubs**, ranging in quality from passable to sublime, keep the black-clad, turtleneck-wearing set happy. **Cover charges** at any of these smaller places will run you from $8 to $25 or so. There are also many larger music venues, which attract touring bands from around the world; here, a ticket can cost anywhere from $25 to $100. If the show's not sold out, tickets are usually available from the door. For advance tickets, turn up to the venue's box office, or visit **Ticketmaster** or **Ticketweb** (see box below).

As for **club life** in the city, it's a very amorphous creature. Parties change at a rapid pace, so be sure to check the listings in *The Village Voice* or *Time Out New York* before you make any plans. Musically, drum 'n' bass, electronica, 1980s

---

Ticketmaster and Ticketweb

Two of the most useful ticket-selling companies in New York are **Ticketmaster** (☎212/307-4100 or 1-800/755-4000 outside NY, ⊛www.ticketmaster.com), which sells tickets to higher-profile concerts and cultural events, and **Ticketweb** (⊛www.ticketweb.com), which mostly deals in smaller to mid-sized music venues and museums. Contact information for other, more specialized ticket agencies is listed, where appropriate, in the text below.

△ The Empire State Building

nostalgia, and house hold sway at the moment, though Latin freestyle, dance-hall reggae, funk, and hip-hop all get their due. Nothing gets going much before midnight, so there's no point turning up earlier (unless to avoid cover charges, which are sometimes waived before 10 or 11pm). During the week is the best time to go out – **prices** are cheaper, crowds are smaller, and service is better. All venues tend to be strict about **ID**. **Cover charges** range from $15 to $50, though most average out at around $20. Oftentimes, you can check out a club's website and get on the **guestlist**, which will bring you reduced or free admission.

Theater

Even if you're not normally a **theater** buff, going to see a play or a musical while in New York is virtually de rigueur. The various theater venues are referred to as **Broadway**, **Off-Broadway**, or **Off-Off Broadway**, representing a descending order of ticket price, production polish, elegance, and comfort. Broadway offerings consist primarily of large-scale musicals, comedies, and dramas with big-name actors, while Off-Broadway theaters tend to combine high production qualities with a greater willingness to experiment. Off-Off Broadway is the fringe – drama on a shoestring, perhaps with sensitive or uncommercial subjects. As for **location**, most Broadway theaters are just east or west of Broadway, between 40th and 52nd streets; the rest are sprinkled throughout Manhattan, with a concentration in the East and West villages, Union Square, Chelsea, and the 40s and 50s west of the Theater District. Specific Broadway **listings** appear in the free, widely available *Official Broadway Theater Guide*; for other productions, check out *Time Out New York* or *The Village Voice*.

On Broadway, **ticket prices** run $50–100; Off-Broadway, expect to pay $25–50; Off-Off will run you around $15. The prices of Broadway and Off-Broadway shows can be cut considerably if you can wait in line on the day of the performance at the red-and-white **TKTS** booth in Times Square (Mon–Sat 3–8pm, Sun 11am–7pm, also Wed & Sat 10am–2pm for 2pm matinees). The booth has tickets for many Broadway and Off-Broadway shows, at 25- to 50-percent off (plus a $3 per ticket service charge), payable in **cash or travelers checks only**. Keep in mind that you may have to wait in line for a couple of hours, and that the show you want to see may be sold out by the time you get to the front of the line.

If you're prepared to pay **full price**, you can go directly to the theater box office, or use **Tele-charge** (℡212/239-6200 or 1-800/432-7250 outside NY, Ⓦwww.telecharge.com) or **Ticketmaster**. For these ticket agencies, you will need a credit card and should expect to pay a $3–9 surcharge per ticket. Make sure to ask the operator to explain where your seats will be – if you are unhappy with the seating arrangements, now's the only time to say something. For Off-Broadway shows, **Tickets Central** (℡212/279-4200, Ⓦwww.tickets-central.com) sells tickets to many of these from noon to 8pm daily. For Off-Off Broadway productions, check out **SmartTix** (℡212/868-4444, Ⓦwww.smarttix.com) or **TheaterMania** (Ⓦwww.theatermania.com, ℡212/352-0255).

Classical music, opera, and dance

New Yorkers take **classical music** seriously. Long queues form for anything popular, many concerts sell out, and on summer evenings a quarter of a million people may turn up in Central Park for free performances by the **New**

York Philharmonic. Besides **Lincoln Center** (see box, below), the most important venue is **Carnegie Hall**, 154 W 57th St, at Seventh Ave (☎212/247-7800, Ⓦ www.carnegiehall.org), where the greatest names from all schools of music have performed. The acoustics are superb, and a recent renovation has amended years of structural neglect, restoring the place to its former glory.

The 120-year-old **Metropolitan Opera**, in Lincoln Center, is New York City's premier venue for opera. The soaring theatre has pitch-perfect acoustics and regularly draws big crowds who come to hear sopranos, baritones, and tenors from around the world sing some of the greatest operatic works ever to have been scored. The nosebleed seats are surprisingly reasonable. Contact Met Ticket Service at ☎212/362-6000 for information. The **New York State Theater**, also in Lincoln Center, hosts performances, too; while it may not draw top names, it is a fine place to see opera. Tickets are often half of what they are at the Met; see the box below for contact information.

When it comes to **dance,** Lincoln Center once again serves as a showcase, though a number of other venues regularly host events. The **Brooklyn Academy of Music** (or **BAM**), at 30 Lafayette St in Brooklyn, between Ashland Place and Street Felix Street (☎718/636-4100, Ⓦ www.bam.org), is America's oldest performing arts academy and one of the most daring producers in New York – definitely worth crossing the river for. Meanwhile, back in Manhattan, six dance troupes are in residence at the **City Center**, 131 W 55th St, between sixth and seventh avenues (☎212/581-1212, Ⓦ www.citycenter.org), including America's two undisputed choreographic giants, the Merce Cunningham Dance Company and the Paul Taylor Dance Company. In spring, City Center

---

Lincoln Center for the Performing Arts

Lincoln Center, located on Broadway between W 62nd and W 66th streets (☎212/875-5456, Ⓦ www.lincolncenter.org), is New York's powerhouse of performing art. Each major venue is in active use through the year, and there are some twenty venues in all. Listed below are four of the most renowned; all are located in Lincoln Center Plaza.

Alice Tully Hall ☎212/875-5050. This smaller venue is used by chamber orchestras, string quartets, and instrumentalists. Tickets run $20–115, and are available from Centercharge (☎212/721-6500).

Avery Fisher Hall ☎212/875-5656. The permanent base of the New York Philharmonic is also a temporary home for visiting orchestras and soloists. Ticket prices are similar to those at Alice Tully Hall, and are available online at Ⓦ www.newyorkphilharmonic.org, or in person at the box office (Mon–Sat 10am–6pm, Sun noon–6pm).

Metropolitan Opera House ☎212/362-6000, Ⓦ www.metopera.org. Holds the Metropolitan Opera Company from Sept to April, as well as the American Ballet Theater from May to June. Tickets are outrageously expensive and difficult to get, though 175 standing-room tickets ($12–16) go on sale every Saturday morning at 10am (the line has been known to form at dawn).

New York State Theater ☎212/870-5570. During six months of the year, this theater is home to the New York City Ballet, considered by many to be the greatest dance company in existence. This accessible venue is also where the New York City Opera plays David to the Met's Goliath. Seats go for less than half the Met's prices, and standing-room tickets are available if a performance sells out. Tickets must be purchased through the company's website (Ⓦ www .nycballet.com), or through Ticketmaster.

also hosts the **American Ballet Theater**. For small and mid-sized companies, the most important space in Manhattan is the **Joyce Theater**, 175 8th Ave, at 19th St (☎212/242-0800, 🌐www.joyce.org). The Joyce hosts companies from around the world, and also has a small Downtown satellite – Joyce SoHo – at 155 Mercer St, between Houston and Prince (☎212/431-9233).

Rock and pop venues

Arlene's Grocery 95 Stanton St, between Ludlow and Orchard ☎212/358-1633, 🌐www.arlene-grocery.com. This intimate, erstwhile bodega hosts free gigs by local indie talent during the week. Monday is "Punk/Heavy Metal Karaoke" night, where you can wail along (with a live band, no less) to your favorite Stooges and Led Zeppelin songs.

The Bowery Ballroom 6 Delancey St, at Bowery ☎212/533-2111, 🌐www.boweryballroom.com. A minimum of attitude, great sound, and even better sightlines make this a local favorite to see well-known indie-rock bands. Shows $12–25. Pay in cash at the *Mercury Lounge* box office (see below), at the door, or by credit card through Ticketweb.

CBGB and OMFUG 315 Bowery, at Bleecker ☎212/982-4052, 🌐www.cbgb.com. This legendary punk/art noise bastion has seen far better days. Run-of-the-mill rock bands crowd today's bills, with often five or six acts playing a night starting at 7 or 8pm. Cover's $10, on average.

Irving Plaza 17 Irving Place, between E 15th and E 16th sts ☎212/777-6800, 🌐www.irvingplaza.com. Once home to Off-Broadway musicals, this venue now hosts an impressive array of rock, electronic music, and techno acts – a good place to see popular bands in a manageable setting. $15–30.

The Mercury Lounge 217 E Houston St, between Ludlow and Essex ☎212/260-4700, 🌐www.mercuryloungenyc.com. The dark, medium-sized, innocuous space showcases a mix of local, national, and international pop and rock acts. It's owned by the same crew as *Bowery Ballroom*, which usually gets the better-known bands. Around $8–15. Purchase tickets in cash at the box office, at the door, or via Ticketweb.

Northsix 66 N 6th St, Williamsburg ☎718/599-5103, 🌐www.northsix.com. In the heart of hipster Williamsburg, this unassuming Brooklyn rock club has become one of the number one places to play – outside of Manhattan – for touring indie acts.

Eclectic venues

Fez under the *Time Café*, 380 Lafayette St, at Great Jones ☎212/533-7000, 🌐www.feznyc.com. The mirrored bar and sparkling gold stage curtain suggest a disco fantasy; the eclectic performances (everything from cabaret to acoustic singer-songwriters) are high-caliber. $10–15 average, sometimes as high as $25.

Groove 125 MacDougal St, at W 3rd St ☎212/254-9393, 🌐www.clubgroove.com. This hopping Downtown joint features rhythm & blues and soul music; it's one of the best bargains around. Happy hour from 6–9pm. Music starts at 9.30pm. No cover.

Joe's Pub at the Public Theater, 425 Lafayette St, between Astor Place and E 4th St ☎212/539-8770, 🌐www.publictheater.org. The word "pub" is a misnomer for this swanky nightspot, which features a vast array of musical, cabaret, and dramatic performances. Star spottings abound. Shows nightly at 7 or 7.30pm, 9.30pm, and 11pm. Covers range from $7 to $50 depending on the performer.

Knitting Factory 74 Leonard St, between Church and Broadway ☎212/219-3006, 🌐www.knittingfactory.com. At this intimate Downtown space, you can hear all kinds of aural experimentation, from art-rock and avant-garde jazz to electronica and indie-rock. Highly recommended. Cover prices vary wildly, so call ahead.

S.O.B.'s 204 Varick St, at W Houston ☎212/243-4940. Short for "Sounds of Brazil," this lively club/restaurant, with regular Caribbean, salsa, and world music acts, puts on two performances a night. Admission is $10–20 for standing room with a $10–15 minimum cover at tables. No cover, however for those with dinner reservations. Be sure to check out Samba Saturday, the venue's hottest night.

Tonic 107 Norfolk St, between Rivington and Delancey ☎212/358-7503, 🌐www.tonicnyc.com. This hip Lower East Side home to "avant-garde, creative & experimental music" flourishes on two levels, with no cover charge to the lower lounge. Occasional movies and Klezmer-accompanied brunch on Sundays. Cover $8–12.

Jazz venues

Arthur's Tavern 57 Grove St, between Bleecker and 7th Ave ☎212/675-6879, 🌐www.arthurstavernnyc.com. This low-key 50-year-old club is housed in a landmark building and features the Grove Street Stompers, who've been playing every Monday for the past 40 years. Jazz 7–9.30pm, blues and funk 10pm–3.30am. No cover. One-drink minimum.

Birdland 315 W 44th St, between 8th and 9th aves ☎212/581-3080, 🌐www.birdlandjazz.com.

Celebrated alto saxophonist Charlie "Bird" Parker has served as the inspiration for this important jazz venue for 50 years. Sets are at 9pm & 11pm nightly. Cover $20–40, with a $10 food and drink minimum.

Lenox Lounge 288 Lenox Ave, at 125th St ☎212/427-0253, ⓦwww.lenoxlounge.com. Entertaining Harlem since the 1930s, this historic jazz lounge has an over-the-top Art Deco interior (check out the Zebra Room). Three sets nightly at 9pm, 10.45pm & 12.30am. Cover $15, with a one-drink minimum.

Smoke 2751 Broadway, at 106th St ☎212/864-6662, ⓦwww.smokejazz.com. This Upper West Side joint is a real neighborhood treat. Sets start at 9pm, 11pm & 12.30am; there's a retro happy hour with $4 cocktails and $2 beers, Mon–Sat 5–8pm. Cover $16–25 Fri & Sat.

Village Vanguard 178 7th Ave S, between W 11th and Perry sts ☎212/255-4037, ⓦwww.villagevanguard.com. This jazz landmark still lays on a regular diet of big names. Cover is $15–20, with a $10 drink minimum. Cash only.

Zinc Bar 90 W Houston, at La Guardia Place ☎212/477-8337, ⓦwww.zincbar.com. This great jazz venue, with strong drinks and loyal regulars, hosts new talent, as well as established greats such as Max Roach and Grant Green. The Ron Affit Trio plays four sets on Mondays, and throughout the week there's a mélange of Brazilian and African jazz. Cover is $5 with a one- or two-drink minimum.

Larger music venues

Beacon Theater 2124 Broadway, at W 74th St ☎212/496-7070. This beautiful restored theater caters to a more mature rock crowd, hosting everything from Tori Amos to Radiohead. Tickets are $25–100, and are sold through Ticketmaster.

Madison Square Garden W 31st–33rd sts, between 7th and 8th aves ☎212/465-6741, ⓦwww.madisonsquaregarden.com. New York's principal large stage plays host to big rock acts. However, it's not the most atmospheric place to see a band, with seating for yourself and 20,000 of your closest friends. Tickets are sold through Ticketmaster.

Radio City Music Hall 1260 6th Ave, at 50th St ☎212/247-4777, ⓦwww.radiocity.com. Although not as prestigious a venue as it once was, the building is a star in its own right. Here, you can see everyone from rock stars to the famous high-kicking Rockettes. Tickets are sold at the box office or through Ticketmaster.

Roseland Ballroom 239 W 52nd St, between Broadway and 8th Ave ☎212/247-0200,

ⓦwww.roselandballroom.com. This venue has retained the grand ballroom feel of its heyday; good place to catch big names before they hit the arena/stadium circuit. The box office only sells tickets the day of the show, otherwise tickets can be purchased through Ticketmaster.

Clubs and discos

Avalon 37 W 20th St, at 6th Ave ☎212/807-7780. Formerly the infamously wild *Limelight*, this is one of the most dramatic party spaces in New York, housed in a vast church designed by Trinity Church–builder Richard Upjohn. Cover $25.

Plaid 76 E 13th St, between Broadway and 4th Ave ☎212/388-1062. With a new, colorful face-lift and a chill vibe, this club (formerly known as *Spa*) still manages to lure young lovelies. It hosts hip DJs and some wild performances. $20 cover.

Filter 14 432 W 14th St, between 9th and 10th aves ☎212/366-5680. This not-quite-finished (ever) space was once home to *Mother*, and almost to Armani – hence the perpetual unfinishedness. The Friday-night deep house parties here are superb, with talented guests such as David Morales spinning top-quality tunes. Nightly 10pm–4am. No dress code.

Frying Pan Pier 63, Chelsea Piers, at 23rd St ☎212/989-6363. This old lightship is one of the coolest club venues in the city. With great views, consistently rockin' parties, and a relaxed door policy. $12.

Pyramid Club 101 Ave A, between 6th and 7th sts ☎212/228-4888. This small, colorful club has been an East Village standby for years. Wednesdays feature an open-mic music competition, and Thursdays are New Wave – but it's the insanely popular 1984 Dance Party on Fridays that's not to be missed. $8 on Friday; otherwise, cover averages $5.

Suede 161 W 23rd St, between 6th and 7th aves ☎212/633-6113. This cool, neutral-toned nightclub is a magnet for hipsters and celebs. Its small dance floor and delicious people-watching make for a good time. Cover $20.

Film

American Museum of the Moving Image 35th Ave, at 36th St, Queens ☎718/784-0077, ⓦammi.org. Shows an array of avant-garde films.

Angelika Film Center 18 W Houston St, at Mercer ☎212/995-2000, ⓦwww.angelikafilmcenter.com. The latest indie offerings, as well as European art-house movies.

Anthology Film Archives 32-34 2nd Ave, at Bond ☎212/505-5181, ⓦwww.anthologyfilmarchives.org. Expect any and every kind of indie film here, from animated shorts to riveting documentaries.

Film Forum 209 W Houston St, between Varick and 6th Ave ☎212/727-8110, ⊛www.filmforum .com. Shows the best in independent film and documentary, as well as themed revivals.

Landmark's Sunshine Cinema 143 E Houston St, between Forsyth and Eldridge sts ☎212/358-7709. This former synagogue and vaudeville theater is now one of the plushest indie art-house movie theaters in town.

Museum of Modern Art at the Gramercy Theater, 127 E 23rd St, at Lexington ☎212/777-4900, ⊛www.moma.org. A vast collection of well-chosen films, from Hollywood screwball comedies to hand-painted Super 8, entry to which is free with museum admission (see p.107). This location will be open until the newly renovated MoMA opens in 2005.

Poetry slams and literary readings

Bowery Poetry Club 308 Bowery, at Bleecker ☎212/614-0505, ⊛www.bowerypoetry.com. Terrifically welcoming joint featuring the Urbana Poetry Slam every Thursday night at 7pm ($5). This event is dedicated to showcasing the city's most innovative voices in poetry.

NuYorican Poet's Café 236 E 3rd St, between aves B and C ☎212/505–8183, ⊛www .nuyorican.org. The godfather of all slam venues

often features stars of the poetry world who pop in unannounced. SlamOpen on Wednesdays (except the first Wed of every month) and the Friday Night Slam both cost $5 and come highly recommended.

Poetry Project at St Mark's Church, 131 E 10th St, at 2nd Ave ☎212/674-0910, ⊛www.poet-ryproject.com. The late Allen Ginsberg, a *Poetry Project* protege, said, "The poetry project burns like red hot coal in New York's snow." Make of that what you will, the twice-weekly reading series (Mon and Wed at 8pm) features some truly, ahem, hot stuff. Closed July & Aug.

Comedy clubs

Caroline's 1626 Broadway, between W 49th and 50th sts ☎212/757-4100, ⊛www.carolines.com. This glitzy room books some of the best acts in town. $12–22 cover, with a two-drink minimum; more expensive on weekends.

Chicago City Limits 1105 1st Ave, at 61st St ☎212/888-5233, ⊛www.chicagocitylimits.com. New York's oldest improv theater puts on one show nightly and attracts decent national talent. Closed Tues. Admission is $20, $8 on Sun.

Comic Strip Live 1568 2nd Ave, between E 81st and E 82nd sts ☎212/861-9386, ⊛www.comicstriplive.com. This famed showcase draws stand-up comics going for the big time. Three shows Fri & Sat. Cover $12–17, with $12 drink minimum.

Gay New York

There are few places in America where **gay culture** thrives as it does in New York. **Chelsea** (centered on Eighth Ave between 14th and 23rd streets) and the **East Village** have replaced the **West Village** as the hubs of gay New York, although a strong presence still lingers around Christopher Street. The other haven is Brooklyn's **Park Slope**, though perhaps more for women than for men. Up-to-the-minute news can be found in *HomoXtra* (*HX*) or *Blade*, provocative weekly free-listings magazines.

Resources

Bluestockings 172 Allen St, between Stanton and Rivington ☎212/777-6028. Collectively run feminist bookstore on the Lower East Side. Daily 1–10pm.

Creative Visions 548 Hudson St, between Perry and Charles ☎212/645-7573 or 1-800/997-9899, ⊛www.creativevisions.citysearch.com. Well-stocked gay bookstore.

Gay Men's Health Crisis (GMHC) 119 W 24th St, between 6th and 7th aves ☎212/807-6655 or 1-800/AIDS-NYC, ⊛www.gmhc.org. Despite the

name, this organization – the oldest and largest not-for-profit AIDS organization in the world – provides information and referrals to everyone, no matter their gender or sexual orientation.

Gayellow Pages ⊛www.gayellowpages.com. Available for $12 from the bookstores listed above and below, this is a good all-in-one resource; New York is in the East & South edition.

The Lesbian, Gay, Bisexual & Transgender Community Center 208 W 13th St, at 7th Ave ☎212/620-7310, ⊛www.gaycenter.org. The LGBT Community Center, which houses countless organizations (including ACT UP, the Center for Mental Health and Social Services, and even the Metro Gay Wrestling Alliance), also sponsors workshops, dances, movie nights, guest speakers, youth services, programs for parents and kids, an archive and library, the annual Center Garden Party, and lots more.

The Oscar Wilde Memorial Bookshop 15 Christopher St, between 6th and 7th sts ⓣ212/255-8097, ⓦ www.oscarwildebooks.com. The first gay bookstore in the US. Unbeatable.

Bars and clubs

Barracuda 275 W 22nd St, between 8th and 9th aves ⓣ212/645-8613. A favorite spot in New York's gay scene, though as un-sceney as you'll find in Chelsea. Check out the two-for-one happy hour 4–9pm during the week, crazy drag shows, and the sweet hideaway lounge out back.

The Cock 188 Ave A, at 12th St ⓣ212/777-6254. Unashamed of its theme, but without the overblown muscles and the tiny white tee. With amateur "talent" contests and strip karaoke, it's dirty, sleazy – and a whole lot of fun.

Cubby Hole 281 W 12th St, at W 4th St ⓣ212/243-9041. This pocket-sized lesbian bar is warm and welcoming, with a busy festive atmosphere and unpretentious clientele.

Duplex 61 Christopher St, at 7th Ave ⓣ212/255-5438. This Village cabaret is popular with a gay crowd but entertaining for all, and features occasional bitchy barb routines from Joan Rivers, among others. Two-drink minimum. Cover $5–15.

Ginger's 363 5th Ave, between 5th and 6th sts,

Park Slope, Brooklyn ⓣ718-788-0924. This new addition to Park Slope's sapphic scene is dark, moody, and has a great happy hour from 5 to 8pm.

Hell 59 Gansevoort St, between Greenwich and Washington ⓣ212/727-1666. Upscale, male-dominated lounge in the Meatpacking District.

Henrietta Hudson 438 Hudson St, at Morton ⓣ212/924-3347. This lesbian hangout serves food and gets fairly brimming at night. The lounge, pool, and dancing areas are all separated, and guys are welcome, too.

Julius 159 W 10th St, at Waverly Place ⓣ212/929-9672. As the oldest gay bar in the city, dating from much harder times, this quaint, wooden affair deserves at least one drink.

Meow Mix 269 E Houston St, at Suffolk ⓣ212/254-0688, ⓦ www.meowmixchix.com. Lipstick lesbians, leather ladies, and all types in between dance at this temple to *les femmes*. Cover free–$5.

Rubyfruit Bar & Grill 531 Hudson St, between Charles and W 10th ⓣ212/929-3343. A cozy, friendly place for grown-up dykes, *Rubyfruit* is all about couches, cheap drinks, and good company.

Stonewall 53 Christopher St, between Waverly Place and 7th Ave ⓣ212/463-0950. The site of the seminal 1969 riot is mostly refurbished and flies the pride flag like they own it – which, one supposes, they do.

Wonder Bar 505 E 6th St, between aves A and B ⓣ212/777-9105. Cramped, festive, and lesbian-friendly, this is an unpretentious find for the thinking boy.

Shopping

When it comes to consumerism, New York leaves all other cities behind. You can **shop** for every possible taste, preference, creed, or quirk, in any combination (and often at any time of day or night). Shopping can be extraordinarily cheap, like in the markets of the **East and West villages**, but move further uptown and it can also be phenomenally expensive. **Midtown Manhattan** is mainstream territory, with the department stores, big-name clothes designers, and branches of the larger chains. Downtown plays host to a wide variety of more offbeat stores – **SoHo** is perhaps the most popular shopping neighborhood in these parts, and generally the most expensive, although with some affordable alternatives for the young and trendy. The **Upper East Side** is uncompromisingly upmarket, while the funkier **Upper West Side** has an array of off-the-wall stores to compare with anything SoHo or the Village can offer.

Department stores

Barney's 660 Madison Ave, at 61st St ⓣ212/826-8900, ⓦ www.barneys.com. The

hippest and most fashion-forward of the big NYC department stores. Check the website for dates of its famous semi-annual warehouse sales, where couture bargains (and catfights) abound.

Bergdorf Goodman 754 5th Ave, at 58th St ☎212/753-7300, ⊛www.bergdorfgoodman.com. Housed in what used to be a Vanderbilt mansion, this venerable department store caters to the city's wealthiest clientele. Even if you can't afford to shop, it's still fun to browse and dream.

Bloomingdale's 1000 3rd Ave, between 59th and 60th sts ☎212/705-2000, ⊛www.blooming-dales.com. Perhaps Manhattan's most famous department store, Bloomingdale's is packed with designer clothiers, perfume concessions, and the like.

Henri Bendel 712 5th Ave, at 55th St ☎212/247-1100, ⊛www.henribendel.com. One of the best stores in town for cosmetics and designer labels. There's a superb salon, and its public powder room is worth a peek.

Macy's 151 W 34th St, at Broadway ☎212/695-4400, ⊛www.macys.com. The world's largest department store embraces two buildings, two million square feet of floor space, and ten floors (housing, unfortunately, fairly mediocre wares, except for the excellent Cellar housewares department downstairs).

Saks Fifth Avenue 611 5th Ave, at W 50th St ☎212/753-4000, ⊛www.saks5thavenue.com. Although Saks remains virtually synonymous with style and quality, it has also updated itself to carry the merchandise of all the big designers.

Bookstores

Asian American Writers' Workshop suite 10A, 16 W 32nd St, at 5th Ave ☎212/494-0061, ⊛www.aaww.org. In addition to its list of classes, speakers, and readings, the adjacent bookstore carries the nation's largest selection of literary works by Asian-American authors, both established and on-the-rise.

Barnes & Noble ⊛www.bn.com. The main location is at 105 5th Ave, at 18th St (☎212/807-0099), with twelve others scattered around the city. These megasized bookstores offer generous selection, late hours, comfortable chairs, and coffee bars.

Biography Bookshop 400 Bleecker St, at W 11th St ☎212/807-8655. The city's most comprehensive collection of biographies and autobiographies.

Complete Traveler 199 Madison Ave, at W 35th St ☎212/685-9007. Manhattan's premier travel bookshop, well stocked with both secondhand and new titles.

Drama Book Shop 250 W 40th St, between 7th and 8th aves ☎1-800/322-0595. The best theater and film bookstore around, with more than 50,000 titles and a very knowledgeable staff.

Housing Works Used Books Café 126 Crosby St, between Houston and Prince ☎212/334-3324. Very cheap books, comfy and spacious. Proceeds benefit AIDS charity.

Partners & Crime 44 Greenwich Ave, at Charles ☎212/243-0440, ⊛www.crimepays.com. Superb, informed shop with 4000 mystery titles, with a generous selection of hardboiled and British titles. Author signings, a lending library, authoritative staff recommendations, and radio play re-enactments the first Sat of every month ($5) make it a find for devout mystery fans.

St Mark's Bookshop 31 3rd Ave, between 8th and 9th sts ☎212/260-7853. Wonderfully eclectic selection of new titles from mainstream to alternative. Open late.

Strand Bookstore 828 Broadway, at 12th St ☎212/473-1452, ⊛www.strandbooks.com. With about eight miles of books and a stock of 2.5 million+, this is the largest book operation in the city. Recent review copies and new books show up at half price; older books are from 50¢ up.

Universal News & Café 484 Broadway, between Broome and Grand ☎212/965-9042; also 2873 Broadway, at 72nd St ☎212/875-8824; and 105 W 42nd St, between 6th Ave and Broadway ☎212/398-0558. By far the city's best selection of magazines and periodicals, including plenty of foreign publications.

Record stores

Breakbeat Science 181 Orchard St, between Houston and Stanton ☎212/995-2592. The first drum'n'bass-only store to open in the US is still going strong. Closed Fri and Sat.

Etherea 66 Ave A, between 4th and 5th sts ☎212/358-1126. Specializing in indie rock and electronica, both domestic and import, CD and vinyl, this is one of the best shops in the city. Good used selection.

Footlight Records 113 E 12th St, between 3rd and 4th aves ☎212/533-1572. *The* place for showtunes, soundtracks, and jazz.

Generation Records 210 Thompson St, between Bleecker and W 3rd sts ☎212/254-1100. The focus here is on hardcore, metal, and punk, with some indie thrown in. New CDs and vinyl are upstairs, while the used records are downstairs.

Kim's 6 St Mark's Place, between 2nd and 3rd aves ☎212/598-9985; also 144 Bleecker, at La Guardia Place ☎212/260-1010; 85 Ave A, between 5th and 6th sts ☎212/529-3410; 2906 Broadway, at 114th St ☎212/864-5321. Extensive selection of new and used indie obscurities on CD and vinyl, some real cheap. Esoteric videos upstairs. Be warned: a serious attitude

Sports in New York

Seeing either of New York's two **baseball** teams involves a trip across the East River to the outer boroughs. The **Yankees** play in the Bronx, at **Yankee Stadium**, 161st St and River Ave (☎718/293-6000, ⓦ www.yankees.com). Get there on the #C, #D, or #4 subway lines direct to the 161st Street station. The **Mets** are based in Queens, at **Shea Stadium**, 123-01 Roosevelt Ave, at 126th St (☎718/507-METS, ⓦ www.mets.com). Take the #7 train to the Willets Point/Shea Stadium station. Tickets are priced between $8 and $55, depending on the team (Yankee tickets are generally more expensive) and where you sit. For an unbelievably raucous New York experience, show up on game day for bleacher seats at Yankee Stadium: the hooligan regulars and the bouncers who keep an eye on them are often more fun to watch than the game.

New York's football teams – the **Jets** and the **Giants** – play at the **New Jersey Meadowlands Sports Complex**, East Rutherford, New Jersey (☎201/935-3900, ⓦ www.meadowlands.com). Buses from the Port Authority Bus Terminal, 42nd Street, at 8th Ave (☎212/564-8484, ⓦ www.meadowlands.com) serve the stadium. Call ahead before you head out there, though; tickets are hard to come by, and range from $100 to $550.

Basketball's two New York pro teams are the NBA's **Knicks** (ⓦ www.nba .com/knicks) and the WNBA's **Liberty** (ⓦ www.wnba.com/liberty). Both play at **Madison Square Garden**, W 33rd St, at 7th Ave (☎212/465-6741, ⓦ www.thegarden.com), which is served by the #1, #2, #3, #A, #C, and #E trains. Tickets for the Knicks are very expensive, and, due to impossibly high demand, available in only limited numbers, if at all. The women's games are fairly exciting and cheaper at $8–58. Another area team, the **New Jersey Nets**, play in an arena at the Meadowlands Complex (see above); tickets range from $25 to $75, and are relatively easy to procure. New York's hockey team, the **Rangers** (ⓦ www.newyorkrangers.com), also plays at Madison Square Garden; tickets range from $20 to $90.

problem comes with the job description here.
Other Music 15 E 4th St, between Broadway and Lafayette ☎212/477-8150. This excellent small shop has perhaps the most engaging and curious indie-rock and avant-garde collection in the city. Records here are divided into categories like "In," "Out," and "Then." Definitely worth a visit. Great used selection.
Vinyl Mania 60 Carmine St, between Bedford St and 7th Ave ☎212/924-7223. First port of call for DJs seeking the newest, rarest releases and imports.

Food

Chelsea Market 75 9th Ave, between 15th and 16th sts. A wonderful array of food shops line this former Nabisco factory warehouse's ground floor; go for pad Thai, panini, chewy breads, sinful brownies, kitchenware, or simply to browse.
Citarella 2135 Broadway, at 75th St ☎212/874-0383; also 1313 3rd Ave, at 75th St ☎212/874-0383; 1250 6th Ave, at 49th St ☎212/874-0383 (take-out prepared foods only); 424 6th Ave, at 9th St ☎212/874-0383; and 461 W 125th St, between Amsterdam and Morningside aves, Harlem ☎212/874-0383. Originally a neighborhood fish

shop in Harlem's Sugar Hill, this gourmet store still prides itself on its fine products from the sea, and everything else under the sun.
Murray's Cheese Shop 257 Bleecker St, at Cornelia ☎212/243-3289 or 1-888/692-4339. The city's number-one stop for cheese lovers; go to learn about the cheese-making process, sample the wares, or pick up a pungent sandwich.
Russ & Daughters 179 E Houston St, between Allen and Orchard ☎212/475-4880. This small family-run shop has been serving fine Jewish edibles such as smoked whitefish, chopped liver, and herring soaked in schmaltz since 1914. A must-visit.
Union Square Green Market in Union Square, at 16th St. A bit of country in the city, this delightful open-air market (open Mon, Wed, Fri & Sat) offers local seasonal produce and natural goods sold by regional farmers and purveyors. You'll find hand-carded wools, wildflowers, and infused honeys, too.
Zabar's 2245 Broadway, at 80th St ☎212/787-2000. Beloved family store offers a quintessential taste of New York: bagels, lox, all manner of schmears, not to mention a dizzying selection of gourmet goods at reasonable prices. Fine kitchenware is sold upstairs.

The Mid-Atlantic

AL - ALABAMA	IN - INDIANA	MN - MINNESOTA	RI - RHODE ISLAND
AR - ARKANSAS	LA - LOUISIANA	MS - MISSISSIPPI	SC - SOUTH CAROLINA
CT - CONNECTICUT	MA - MASSACHUSETTS	NC - NORTH CAROLINA	VA - VIRGINIA
DE - DELAWARE	MD - MARYLAND	NH - NEW HAMPSHIRE	VT - VERMONT
FL - FLORIDA	ME - MAINE	NJ - NEW JERSEY	WI - WISCONSIN
IL - ILLINOIS	MI - MICHIGAN	PA - PENNSYLVANIA	WV - WEST VIRGINIA

CHAPTER 2 # Highlights

✳ **Fire Island, Long Island, NY** A great weekend get-away from NYC, with fewer tourists and better beaches than the swanky Hamptons. **See p.133**

✳ **The Adirondacks, NY** A vast and rugged alpine wilderness offering superb hiking, skiing, fishing, and mountain-climbing opportunities. **See p.145**

✳ **Ithaca, NY** New York State's answer to San Francisco, built on a steep hill and complete with a solar-powered library, its own legal tender, more restaurants per capita than New York City, waterfalls, gorges, and local vineyards. **See p.149**

✳ **Niagara Falls, NY** Take the memorable *Maid of the Mist* boat trip, or visit the Cave of the Winds and stand close enough to feel the spray from these majestic falls. **See p.156**

✳ **Art and architecture, Pittsburgh, PA** The Warhol Museum, Cathedral of Learning, and two outlying Frank Lloyd Wright houses lend a surprising cultural flair to the so-called Steel City. **See p.179**

✳ **The boardwalk, Atlantic City, NJ** Tacky and trashy, the boardwalk is the heart and soul of this seaside gambling resort town. **See p.194**

The Mid-Atlantic

The three **MID-ATLANTIC** states – **New York**, **Pennsylvania**, and **New Jersey** – stand at the heart of the most populated and industrialized corner of the US. Although dominated in the popular imagination by casinos, the gray smokestacks of New Jersey, and the coalfields and steel factories of Pennsylvania (most of which no longer exist), these states actually encompass expanses of virtual wilderness, as well as beaches, mountains, islands, lakes, forests, rolling green countryside, and many worthwhile small cities and towns.

European settlement here was characterized by considerable shifts and turns: the **Dutch**, who arrived in the 1620s, were methodically squeezed out by the **English**, who in turn fought off the **French** challenge to secure control of the region by the mid-eighteenth century. The Native American population, including the **Iroquois Confederacy** and Lenni Lenape Indians, had sided with the French against the English, and were soon confined to reservations or pushed north into Canada. At first, the economy depended on the fur trade, though by the 1730s English **Quakers**, along with **Amish** and **Mennonites** from Germany, plus a few Presbyterian **Irish**, had made farming a significant force, their holdings extending to the western limits of Pennsylvania and New York.

All three states were important during the **Revolution**: over half the battles were fought here, including major American victories at **Trenton** and **Princeton**, in New Jersey. Upstate New York was geographically crucial, as the British forces knew that control of the Hudson River would effectively divide New England from the other colonies; and the long winter spent by the ragtag Continental Army at **Valley Forge** outside Philadelphia turned it into a well-organized force.

After the Revolution, industry became the region's prime economic force, with **mill towns** springing up along the numerous rivers. By the mid-1850s the large **coalfields** of northeast Pennsylvania were powering the smoky steel mills of Pittsburgh, and the discovery of high-grade **crude oil** in 1859 marked the beginning of the automobile age. Though still significant, especially in the regions near New York City, heavy industry has now by and large been replaced by tourism as the economic engine.

Although many travelers to the East Coast may not consider venturing much further than New York City itself (covered in Chapter 1 of the *Guide*), the region is much more than just an overspill of the Big Apple. Each region has a distinct identity. Just thirty minutes outside of Manhattan, **Long Island** offers both the crashing surf of the Atlantic Ocean and the cool calm of the Long Island Sound. **Upstate New York** is for outdoors enthusiasts: the wooded

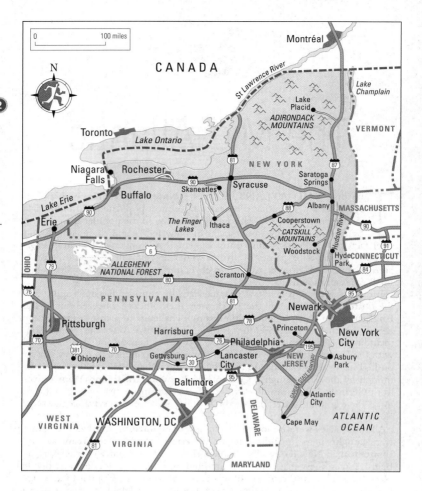

Catskill Mountains line the Hudson River (which Henry James claimed was "in the geography of the ideal"), the imposing **Adirondack Mountains** spread over a quarter of the state, and the **Finger Lakes** region offers a cultured and pastoral break from the industrial and post-industrial Erie Canal cities along I-90. In the northwest corner of the state, on the Canadian border, are the awesome **Niagara Falls** and artsy post-industrial **Buffalo**. **Pennsylvania** is best known for the fertile **Pennsylvania Dutch** country and the two great cities of **Philadelphia** and **Pittsburgh**. **New Jersey**, often pictured as one big industrial carbuncle, offers shameless tourist pleasures along the shore – day-trippers in the millions flock each year to the boardwalk and casinos of **Atlantic City**.

The entire region is well covered by **public transportation**, with New York's JFK and New Jersey's Newark airports acting as major international gateways, and New York's LaGuardia Airport serving domestic flights. In

Pennsylvania, both Philadelphia and Pittsburgh have reasonably busy airports. Amtrak **trains** run routes up and down the Northeast Corridor through New York, New Jersey, and Pennsylvania, while the New Jersey Transit rail and bus network serves all of New Jersey, extending from Atlantic City west to Philadelphia and north to Manhattan. Metro-North and the Long Island Rail Road connect New York City to Long Island and points north. Greyhound **buses** follow the major interstates, with a few subsidiary lines running to more out-of-the-way places.

New York State

However much exists to attract visitors, the vast state of **NEW YORK** stands inevitably in the shadow of America's most celebrated city. The words "New York" bring to mind soaring skyscrapers and congested streets, not the 50,000 square miles of rolling dairy farmland, Colonial villages, workaday towns, lakes, waterfalls, and towering mountains that spread north and west from New York City and constitute **upstate New York**. Just an hour's drive north of Manhattan, the valley of the **Hudson River**, with the moody **Catskill Mountains** rising stealthily from the west bank, offers a respite from the intensity of the city. Much wilder and more rugged are the peaks of the vast **Adirondack Mountains** further north – far beyond the scope of a casual excursion, but holding some of eastern America's most enticing scenery. To the west, the slender Finger Lakes and endless miles of dairy farms and vineyards occupy the central portion of the state. Of the larger cities, only **Buffalo** holds much of interest, but some of the smaller towns, like Ivy-League **Ithaca**, can be quite captivating, while the venerable spa town of **Saratoga Springs** attracts thousands of gamblers during the August horse-racing season.

In the seventeenth and eighteenth centuries, as nation-molding political and military battles were taking place, semi-feudal **Dutch landowning dynasties** such as the Van Rensselaers held sway upstate. Their control over tens of thousands of tenant farmers was barely affected by the transfer of colonial power from Holland to Britain, or even by American independence. Only with the completion of the **Erie Canal** in 1825, linking New York City with the Great Lakes, did the interior start to open up; improved opportunities for trade enabled canal-side cities like **Rochester**, **Syracuse**, and especially **Buffalo** to undergo massive expansion. On the other hand, this industrial and agricultural growth in the hinterland served, inevitably, to increase the financial standing of the Wall Street capitalists. The story of the past century and a half has been one of New York City's political and economic domination of New York State, though Governor George Pataki's popularity and a growing prison economy have buoyed upstate politicians, if not fully redressed the imbalance.

Getting around New York State
From New York City, the **Long Island Railroad** (leaving from Penn Station)

and **Metro North** (leaving from Grand Central Station) shuttle commuters to and from the suburbs of Long Island and Westchester, Putnam, and Dutchess counties, respectively. For journeys further north, Greyhound and Adirondack Trailways **buses** run to all the major towns, while Amtrak operates a **train** service along a beautiful route through the Hudson Valley to the state capital, Albany; from there, trains continue north to Montréal, via the Adirondacks, and west along the Erie Canal to Buffalo and Niagara Falls.

Car rental in and around New York City is expensive; lower rates can be found by taking public transportation away from the metropolitan area. Be aware as well that the New York State Thruway (I-87) is a toll road, around $15 end-to-end. **Cycling** is best enjoyed as a means of exploring areas such as the Finger Lakes or Catskills.

Long Island

Just east of New York City, **Long Island** unfurls for 125 miles of lush farmland and broad sandy beaches, and is perhaps best explored as an excursion of a few days from the metropolis. Its western end abuts the urban boroughs of Brooklyn and Queens, and for a while continues as a suburban sprawl of shopping malls and fast-food outlets; but further east, the settlements begin to thin out and the countryside can get surprisingly remote. The **north** and **south shores** differ greatly – the former more immediately beautiful, its cliffs topped with luxurious mansions and estates, while the South Shore is fringed by almost continuous sand, interspersed with holiday resorts such as **Jones Beach** and **Fire Island**. At its far end, Long Island splits in two, the **North Fork** retaining a marked rural aspect while the **South Fork**, much of which is known as **the Hamptons**, sets itself apart as an enclave of New York's richest and most famous.

The quickest way to reach Long Island is via the reliable if rather worn **Long Island Railroad** from Penn Station (☎718/217-LIRR in NYC, ☎718/558-3022 from elsewhere, ⓦwww.mta.nyc.ny.us/lirr), which runs ten routes to over a hundred destinations on Long Island. You can also arrive via **ferry** from New England: Cross Sound Ferry makes the trip from New London, CT to Orient Point, Long Island (see p.256; ☎860/443-5281 in New England, ☎631/323-2525 on Long Island, ⓦwww.longislandferry.com). Numerous **bus services** (operated by the usual major companies, as well as Hampton Jitney; ☎1-800/936-0440, ⓦwww.hamptonjitney.com) cover most destinations. **Parking permits** for most of Long Island's beaches are issued only to local residents, so on the whole it works out to be less expensive to head to the beach on public transport. If you are **driving** to Long Island, you'll take the Brooklyn–Queens Expressway (the BQE) to I-495 East.

There's plenty of **accommodation**, listed in the text below; A Reasonable Alternative (117 Spring St, Port Jefferson, NY 11777; ☎631/928-4034, ⓦwww.areasonablealternative.com) offers a good range of B&B lodging throughout Long Island.

The South Shore and Fire Island

Long Island's **South Shore** merges gently with the wild Atlantic, with shallow, creamy sand beaches and rolling dunes – two of the most popular options are Long Beach and **Jones Beach**, which together run along fifty miles of seashore. These get less crowded the further east you go; once you get as far as

Gilgo or **Oak Beach**, or cross the water to **Robert Moses State Park**, on the western tip of Fire Island, you can find solitude. **Long Beach** has a die-hard surfer contingent, while just east, **Ocean Parkway** leads along the narrow offshore strand from Jones Beach to **Captree**, a good base for fishing expeditions organized by the Captree Boatman's Association (☎631/669-6484, ⓦ www.captreefleet.com), before crossing back to **Bay Shore**, a dull town that serves as a **ferry terminal** for Fire Island. This way you bypass the sprawling mess of **Amityville**, famous for its "horror" of thirty years ago. The house on the hill, in which a mysterious supernatural force is said to have victimized the occupants, still stands as a private residence.

Fire Island

Fire Island, a slim spit of land parallel to the South Shore, is in many ways a microcosm of New York City. On summer weekends, half of Manhattan seems to be holed up in its tiny settlements. Though the population is definitely mixed, certain parts of the island are primarily known as **gay** resorts: lesbians, young partyers, and a few older men make for **Cherry Grove**, and wealthier gay men for **The Pines**, where the social scene revolves around private house parties as opposed to bars. **Ocean Beach** has also a lively (straight) nightlife; and **Point O'Woods** is the most exclusive of the lot. A mixed crowd hangs out in the **Sunken Forest** (aka Sailor's Haven), so called because it's the only part of the island that lies below sea level – and the pressure, barometric and otherwise, is less intense.

The **season** is as rigidly defined as the neighborhoods. From Memorial Day onwards, Fire Island hums with activity and is swamped with crowds – though it's always possible to escape for gorgeous wild walks along the sand (there is a national seashore here, with a beautiful restored lighthouse). After Labor Day, the weather may still be very warm, but the throngs diminish dramatically.

Most **ferries** dock at Ocean Beach, where trippers pile up groceries on trolleys (cars are forbidden) and set off for their vacation pads. Ferry schedules are subject to change; Fire Island Ferries (30–45min; $6.50 one way; ☎631/665-3600, ⓦ www.fireislandferries.com) run from Bay Shore, the Sayville Ferry Service (25–45min; $6 one way; ☎631/589-0810, ⓦ www.sayvilleferry.com) from Sayville, and the Davis Park Ferries (25–35min; $5.50 one way; ☎631/475-1665, ⓦ www.pagelinx.com/dpferry) from Patchogue.

All **accommodation** should be booked well in advance; options include the hopping *Grove Hotel*, Bayview Walk and Holly Walk, Cherry Grove (☎631/597-6600, ⓦ www.grovehotel.com; ❹); *Cleggs Hotel*, 478 Bayberry Walk, Ocean Beach (open May–Oct only; ☎631/583-5399, ⓦ www.cleggshotel.com; ❺), which, along with regular rooms, offers garden apartments with full kitchens and baths; and the *Fire Island Hotel & Resort*, at 25 Cayuga Walk, in nearby Ocean Bay Park (☎631/583-8000, ⓦ www.fireislandhotel.com; ❻–❾), which used to be a Coast Guard station. If you'd like to splash out on a **meal**, try nearby *Matthew's*, 935 Bay Walk (☎631/583-8016), for its terrific fish specials for around $28. At weekends, the *Ice Palace*, at the *Grove Hotel* (☎631/597-6600), and *Flynn's*, at 1 Cayuga St in Ocean Beach (☎631/583-5000), are good for riotous boozing and dancing. Pick up the *Fire Island News* (ⓦ www.fireislandnews.com) or the gay and lesbian *Fire Island Q News* (ⓦ www.fireislandqnews.com) at a newsstand to find out what's happening while you're here.

The North Shore and North Fork

Along the rugged **North Shore**, Long Island drops to the sea in a series of bluffs, coves, and wooded headlands. The expressway beyond Queens leads straight onto the **Gold Coast**, where **Great Neck** was F. Scott Fitzgerald's West Egg in *The Great Gatsby*, home of Gatsby himself. Some of this real estate is so expensive that only the richest of the rich can afford to live here. The motley French Norman–style buildings at Falaise in **Sands Point**, on the sharp tip of the next peninsula, were once owned by the Guggenheims; they now house a self-celebratory **museum** (May–Oct Wed–Sun tours hourly noon–3pm; $6; ☎516/571-7900). The 209 acres of unkempt parkland offer great views over what Fitzgerald called "the most domesticated body of salt water in the Western hemisphere, the great barnyard of Long Island Sound." In Old Westbury, at 71 Old Westbury Rd, **Old Westbury Gardens** is a classier attraction: a Georgian mansion with beautiful, well-tended gardens and some pleasant works of art, including a few Gainsboroughs (April–Oct daily except Tues 10am–5pm, Nov Sun 10am–5pm; $10; ☎516/333-0048).

Sagamore Hill, on the coast road in Oyster Bay, twelve miles north of Old Westbury, is the heavily touristed former country retreat where **Teddy Roosevelt** lived for thirty-odd years (May–Sept daily 10am–4pm, closed Mon & Tues rest of year; tours only, first-come first-served; $5; ☎516/922-4788, Ⓦwww.nps.gov/sahi). Its 23 rooms are adorned everywhere with the great man's trophies, sprouting horns from walls or grinning toothily up from the firesides. Within the site, near the parking lot, the **Old Orchard Museum** (May–Sept 9am–5pm, closed Mon & Tues rest of year; free) recounts Teddy's political and personal life – but the real reason to come is to stroll the gorgeous grounds, open daily dawn to dusk at no charge, where green lawns drop to Oyster Bay and the sea. It's a very pleasant trip altogether, with helpful and knowledgeable tour guides (often Roosevelt descendants) taking you around on 45-minute tours.

Nearby **COLD SPRING HARBOR** grew up as a whaling port, and retains some of its looks. A fully equipped whaleboat and a 400-piece assembly of scrimshaw work help its **Whaling Museum** (Tues–Sun 11am–5pm; $3; ☎631/367-3418, Ⓦwww.cshwhalingmuseum.org) to recapture that era. The **Vanderbilt Museum and Planetarium** just outside Centerport (May–Sept Tues–Sat 10am–5pm, Sun noon–5pm, rest of year Tues–Sun noon–5pm; $7 planetarium, $3 mansion tour; ☎631/854-5555) displays the dubious taste typical of Vanderbilt residences. In the style of a Baroque Spanish palace, it's heavily ornate both outside and in, with marble-encased galleries, swirling staircases, and gaudy fireplaces.

On the less touristed **North Fork** – once an independent colony – the scenery is typical of the wild Atlantic coast. In **GREENPORT**, its most picturesque town, a clutter of narrow streets and alleys leads down to a harbor pierced by the masts of visiting yachts, where there's a small **maritime museum** nearby (May–Oct Wed–Mon 10am–5pm; $2; ☎631/477-2100). Plentiful **accommodation** includes Victorian B&Bs like the ten-room *Bartlett House Inn*, 503 Front St (☎631/477-0371, Ⓦwww.greenport.com/bartlett; ❺), and the waterfront *Watson's by the Bay*, 104 Bay Ave (May–Sept; no children; ☎631/477-0426, Ⓦwww.greenport.com/watsons; ❺). Regular **ferries** connect with Shelter Island and the South Fork every 15 to 30 minutes (pedestrians $1 each way, cars $9.75 round-trip; Ⓦwww.northferry.com); others cross to New London, CT, described on p.132.

△ Independence Hall, Philadelphia, Pennsylvania

The South Fork

The US holds few wealthier quarters than the small towns of Long Island's **South Fork**, where huge mansions lurk among the trees or stand boldly on the flats behind the dunes. Nowhere is consumption as deliberately conspicuous as in **the Hamptons** – among the oldest communities in the state, settled by restless New Englanders in the mid-1650s, but relatively isolated until the rich began to turn up in their motor cars. The current generation of high-rollers clog the roads in Range Rovers and Mercedes, and the sidewalks in slow, sauntering processions; pretty as the Hamptons are, avoid them if you are at all antisocial. Nightlife venues are expensive and notoriously changeable; pick up *Dan's Papers* (ⓦwww.danspapers.com) or the *East Hampton Star* (ⓦwww.easthamptonstar.com) to find out what's happening.

Southampton

Long association with the smart set has left **SOUTHAMPTON** unashamedly upper class. Its streets are lined with galleries and clothing and jewelry stores, but the nearby beaches are superb. The **visitor center** at 76 Main St (Mon–Fri 10am–4pm, Sat & Sun 11am–4pm; ☎631/283-0402, ⓦwww.southamptonchamber.com) has lists of **B&Bs** like the charming, slightly out-of-the-way *Mainstay*, 579 Hill St (☎631/283-4375, ⓦwww.themainstay.com; ❻). You can get marvelous fresh seafood in a number of **restaurants**, notably *Barrister's*, at 36 Main St (☎631/283-6206), and the venerable brewpub-restaurant *Southampton Publick House*, at 40 Bowden Square (☎631/283-2800). Relatively casual **nightspots** like *Southampton Tavern* on Tuckahoe Lane nestle down the road from impossibly upscale clubs, like *Jet East* on North Sea Road, where super-rich regulars shell out hundreds of dollars to reserve Saturday-night tables.

Sag Harbor

Historic **SAG HARBOR**, in its heyday a harbor second only to that of New York, was designated first Port of Entry to the New Country by George Washington; the **Old Custom House** (May–June & Sept–Oct Sat & Sun 10am–5pm; July–Aug daily 10am–5pm; $3; ☎631/692-4664) dates from this era. The **Whaling Museum** on Main Street (May–Oct Mon–Sat 10am–5pm, Sun 1–5pm; Oct–Dec Sat & Sun noon–4pm; $3; ☎631/725-0770, ⓦwww.sagharborwhalingmuseum.org) commemorates the town's brief whaling days with guns and scrimshaw. Nearby, the **First Presbyterian "Old Whalers" Church** is crenellated with jutting rows of whale-blubber spades, and beautiful memorials in **Oakland Cemetery** commemorate deceased young whalers.

In summer, the windmill where John Steinbeck once lived serves as a **visitor center** (June–Sept daily 10am–5pm, Fri & Sat until 8pm; rest of year Sat & Sun only 10am–5pm; ☎631/725-0011, ⓦwww.sagharborchamber.com). You can get a nice **room** at the *Baron's Cove Inn*, at 31 W Water St (☎631/725-2100, ⓦwww.baronscove.com; ❹–❼), but at the well-heeled *American Hotel* on Main Street (☎631/725-3535, ⓦwww.theamericanhotel.com; ❼) you can also get a splendid French meal and a good cigar from the hotel's humidor. There are several good, less expensive **restaurants** along Main Street, such as the superb sushi bar *Sen* at no. 23 (☎631/725-1774).

East Hampton and Amagansett

EAST HAMPTON is the trendiest of the Hamptons, filled with the mansions of celebrities like Renee Zellweger, Jerry Seinfeld, and Steven Spielberg

– as well as obnoxiously chic shops and restaurants. However, if you're here, it's worth driving or biking around **Further Lane**, **Lily Pond**, and some of the other exclusive neighborhoods to catch sight of the spectacular (and just plain beautiful) homes. **Amagansett** is a village within East Hampton, and, though crowded in the summer, tends to be more down-to-earth than the rest of town. Note the old shingle homes along quiet leafy side streets and enjoy the lively weekend scene (and fresh muffins) at *Farmer's Market*, on Main Street. Don't miss the partying at *Stephen Talkhouse*, 161 Main St, a terrific **bar** and music joint that draws well-known folk, jazz, and rock performers year-round (T631/267-3117, W www.stephentalkhouse.com).

Montauk

Blustery, wind-battered **MONTAUK**, beyond Amagansett on the farthest tip of Long Island, never quite made it as a resort; plans to develop it were shattered by the Wall Street Crash of 1929. The town isn't chic or quaint – but real people actually live here, and it provides access to the rocky wilds of **Montauk Point**, whose rare beauty figures in all the tourist brochures. A **lighthouse** – New York State's oldest, dating from 1796 – forms an almost symbolic finale to this stretch of the American coast.

Motels in the town center offer reasonably priced rooms (a rarity in the eastern end of Long Island); for something fancier, try *Gurney's Inn* on Old Montauk Highway (T631/668-2345; ❽–❾). The ultimate Montauk **dining** experience is *The Lobster Roll*, on Montauk Hwy/Rte-27 (technically in Amagansett; T631/267-3740), which serves excellent fresh fish, including the eponymous delectation. Other good options include the moderately priced *Shagwong* on Main Street (T631/668-3050) and the delicious sushi at *West Lake Clam & Chowder House*: from the tables here, you can watch the fishermen bring home their catch and have it delivered to you via the kitchen in minutes.

The Hudson Valley and the Catskills

You only need to travel a few miles north of Manhattan before the Hudson River Valley takes on a Rhine-like charm, with prodigious historic homes, such as those of the Roosevelt, Vanderbilt, and van Cortland families, rising from its steep and thickly wooded banks. A little further on come the forests of the **Catskill Mountains**, whose brilliant fall colors rival anything to be seen in New England. Few of the cities along the Hudson, including the large but lackluster state capital of **Albany**, hold much to attract the visitor, though many of the small towns are worth checking out, such as regional historic and culinary mecca **Hyde Park**.

The lower Hudson Valley

A mere 25 miles north of central New York City, the leafy town of **TARRYTOWN** and village of **IRVINGTON** were the original setting for Washington Irving's tales of *Rip Van Winkle* and *The Legend of Sleepy Hollow*. In 1835 the author rebuilt a farm cottage on West Sunnyside Lane (off Broadway/US-9), now nestled between the town and the village. He named the house **Sunnyside**: "a little old-fashioned stone mansion, all made up of gable ends, and as full of angles and corners as an old cocked hat." Tours squeeze through its cozy rooms, and are enjoyable even if you've never read a word of Irving (March–Dec Wed–Mon 10am–4pm; $8; ☎914/591-8763).

It's also worth looking around the spikily crenellated **Lyndhurst Castle** on Broadway, as dapper a piece of nineteenth-century Gothic Revivalism as you're likely to find, with grounds to match (April–Oct Tues–Sun 10am–5pm; Nov–March Sat & Sun 10am–4pm; $4 grounds, $10 tour; ☎914/631-4481, Ⓦwww.lyndhurst.org). Also of interest here is **Kykuit** (pronounced "Kigh-cut"), the old Rockefeller Estate. The mansion is filled with modern artwork (particularly sculpture) and the collection in the gardens and grounds is just as impressive, with works by Picasso, Calder, Noguchi, Henry Moore, and many others – although the pretentious guided tour detracts somewhat from the masterpieces (late April to early Nov daily 9am–3pm; $20; tours first-come first-served; ☎914/631-9491, Ⓦwww.hudsonvalley.org/web/kyku-main .html).

The charming Main Streets of Irvington and Tarrytown have a range of good **food** options, from cheap, delicious *Irvington Pizza*, 106 Main St (☎914/591-7050), to upscale Italian, Spanish, and American restaurants. Irvington's brand-new **Hudson Park** makes for a scenic riverside picnic or after-dinner stroll.

About ten miles north of Tarrytown along US-9, the town of **OSSINING** holds two impressive mid-Victorian creations: one is a huge bridge carrying the **Old Croton Aqueduct**, New York City's first water supply; the other, just south of town, is **Sing Sing Prison**, which for over 150 years has been the place where New York City criminals get sent "up the river." Slightly north in **CROTON-ON-HUDSON** is **Croton Point Park**, a 508-acre peninsula that hosts major summer festivals and, occasionally, the sloop *Clearwater* (for docking and sailing times and venues consult ☎845/454-7673, Ⓦwww .clearwater.org).

The west bank and Catskill Mountains

Rising above the west bank of the Hudson River, the magnificent crests of the **Catskills**, cloaked with maple and beech that turn orange, ochre, and gold each fall, have a rich and absorbing beauty. This dislocated branch of the Appalachians is inspiring country, filled with amenities – campgrounds, hiking, fishing, and, especially, skiing. To enjoy it to the fullest, venture onto the trails; the mountains are so tightly packed that good roadside overlooks are rare.

West Point

The first real place of interest on the west bank of the Hudson, sixty miles out of New York City, is the United States Military Academy at **WEST POINT**, which Congress established in 1802 after realizing that the ragged troops who had won the Revolutionary War had been knocked into shape almost exclusively by European officers. Homegrown skills had to be cultivated in case foreign help wasn't so readily forthcoming again. Since then, West Point has provided the military training for US Army generals Grant, Lee, MacArthur, Eisenhower, Patton, and Schwarzkopf, to name but a famous few. Today, four-thousand-odd candidates on a tough four-year course fill the smart showpiece campus, which protectively overlooks the Hudson from a wide, strategic bluff. What draws most people are the patriotic parade-ground drills, at their most frequent during spring and late summer/early fall; West Point's **visitor center** (daily 9am–4.45pm; ☎845/938-2638, Ⓦwww.usma.edu) can provide a full schedule as well as tours. The free **West Point Museum** (daily 10.30am–4.15pm) shows trophies of war, including pistols that belonged to George Washington, Napoleon Bonaparte, and Adolf Hitler and, disturbingly, the pin from the Nagasaki atomic bomb.

Kingston

Of the various towns on the fringes of the mountains, **KINGSTON** is one of the most pleasant and convenient places to stop. An agreeable mix of well-preserved old houses and neat little businesses lines Green and Crown streets at the center of town, much of which dates from the late eighteenth century, when Kingston played a vital political and military role in the fight for American independence.

Kingston is very easy to reach – it's just off I-87 (exit 19), and Adirondack Trailways buses heading north from New York City stop ten minutes' walk from the center. The town's two **visitor centers**, on Clinton Avenue (℡845/331-9506, ⓦwww.ci.kingston.ny.us) and "Lower" Broadway (℡845/331-7517), have leaflets for suggested walking tours around the historic sights. If you want to **stay**, the large *Holiday Inn*, 503 Washington Ave (℡845/338-0400, ⓦwww.holidayinnkingston.com; ❹), is probably the best value, complete with sauna, pool, and games area, though its rates rise on summer weekends. The *Market Basket Deli*, 308 Wall St (℡845/338-2755), serves fresh breads and bagels. Further **food and drink** options can be found across the river in Hyde Park and Rhinebeck (see pp.141 and 142).

Woodstock

West from Kingston, Hwy-28 meanders into the Catskills, looping past the lovely Ashokan Reservoir where Hwy-375 branches off to **WOODSTOCK**. The village, carved out of the lush deciduous woodlands and cut by fast-rushing creeks, was not actually the venue of the famed **psychedelic picnic** of August 1969. That was some sixty miles southwest in Bethel, where a monument at Herd and West Shore roads marks the site on the farm owned by Max Yasgur where the first festival was held. However, Woodstock has enjoyed a bohemian reputation since the foundation in 1902 of the **Byrdcliffe Arts Colony** (which runs summer residency courses; ℡845/679-2079, ⓦwww.woodstockguild.org), and during the 1960s it was a favorite stomping ground for the likes of Dylan, Hendrix, and Van Morrison.

Woodstock still bears signs of its **hippie** past: shops sell crystals and tie-dyed T-shirts, and there's even the odd commune out in the woods. That said, in the cafés you're just as likely to bump into a successful Manhattanite who owns a second home here as you would a long-haired beatnik-type. Woodstock's galleries and craft shops command a regional reputation and the village is also a hub for the performing arts: the **Maverick Concert** series (late June–Aug; $20 per concert/$5 students; ℡845/679-8217, ⓦwww.maverickconcerts.org) has played host to some of the world's finest chamber musicians since 1916. Just west of Woodstock, in the small town of Mount Tremper, the **Kaatskill Kaleidoscope** (Sun–Thurs 10am–5pm, Fri & Sat 10am–7pm; $8; ℡1-888/303-3936) claims to be the world's largest, created by a local hippie artist and now knee-deep in psychedelic souvenirs and T-shirts. The kaleidoscope, in reality a 60ft-high converted grain silo, plays ten-minute sound and light shows throughout the day, and makes a tacky but entertaining roadside stop.

Woodstock is a great base for exploring the Catskills, and the best option for **accommodation** is the cozy *Twin Gables Guest House*, in the center of the village at 73 Tinker St (℡845/679-9479, ⓦwww.twingableswoodstockny .com; ❹). If this is full, as is often the case, try the *Woodstock Lodge* on Country Club Lane (℡1-800/383-5567, ⓦwww.woodstocklodge.com; ❹–❺). Alternatively, there are chain motels like *Howard Johnson*, 2764 Hwy-32 (℡845/246-9511; ❸), ten miles northeast in Saugerties. Between Saugerties and Woodstock are the *Rip Van Winkle* **campgrounds** (May–Oct; $23.50 per tentsite; ☎845/246-8334), which have full facilities for both tents and RVs. The best **places to eat** are a little way out of the village: the menu at the *New World Home Cooking Company*, 1411 Rte-12 (April–Oct; ☎845/246-0900), has Caribbean and Creole-influenced dishes for about $16, while two miles west of Woodstock, on Hwy-212 in tiny **Bearsville**, the *Bear Café* (☎845/679-5555) serves French bistro food unparalleled in these parts – with prices to match.

Several daily **buses** take two and a half hours to reach Woodstock from New York City's Port Authority Bus Terminal (Adirondack Trailways; ☎1-800/858-8555, ⓦescapemaker.com/adirondacktrailways). Sturdy **bikes** can be rented from Overlook Mountain Bikes, 93 Tinker St (Wed–Sat, Mon 10am–6pm, Sun 11am–6pm; ☎845/679-2122, ⓦwww.overlookmountainbikes.com). For more **information**, visit the Chamber of Commerce booth on Rock City Road, just off the village green (11am–6pm Thurs–Mon, closed for lunch; ☎845/679-6234, ⓦwww.woodstockchamber.com).

On through Catskill Park

As you continue along Hwy-28, the picturesque hamlet of **PHOENICIA**, in a hollow to the right of the road, is an ideal resting place and a great base for hiking trails in the area. You can catch the circular **Catskill Mountain Railroad** (late May–Aug Sat, Sun & holidays 11am–5pm; Sept–Oct Sat, Sun & holidays noon–4pm; $8 round-trip; ☎845/688-7400, ⓦwww.catskillmtrailroad.com) through scenic Esopus Creek. The *Phoenicia Hotel*, on Main Street (☎845/688-7500, ⓦwww.phoeniciahotel.com; ❷), is a basic and inexpensive place to stay. Next door is the *American Café* (☎845/688-2900), which serves great burgers plus a tasty selection of Mexican fare; the *Phoenicia Diner* is another good option on Hwy-28 (☎845/688-9957).

A few miles further west, Hwy-49A affords a good vista of the rambling Catskills from the parking lot of the Belleayre ski resort. The *Belleayre Hostel*, Main Street, Pine Hill (☎845/254-4200, ⓦwww.belleayre-hostel.com; ❷–❹), has newly renovated private rooms and log cabins, as well as some rather inferior dorms with beds for $20. Other accommodation includes the large, budget Victorian-style *Colonial Inn* (☎845/254-5577, ⓦwww.colonialinn.com; ❹) and the nicer six-room *Birchcreek Inn* (☎845/254-5222; ❹), in a wooded setting out on Hwy-28.

The return route to I-90, along Hwy-23A, includes a breathtaking view of the dramatic **gorge** between the villages of Hunter and Catskill, along with the area's premier **ski runs** on Hunter Mountain (☎518/263-4223, ⓦwww.huntermtn.com). The resort's Skyride chair lifts also operate after the snow has melted (late June–Oct Sat & Sun 10am–5pm; $6). Accommodation rates rise significantly during the ski season: *Scribner Hollow Lodge*, half a mile from the mountain on Hwy-23A (☎518/263-4211, ⓦwww.scribnerhollow.com; ❺), boasts 38 deluxe rooms, a fine-dining restaurant with great views, and a multi-pool swimming grotto. Rooms in the hamlet of Catskill, such as in the *Red Ranch Motel* on Hwy-32 (☎518/678-3380 or 1-800/962-4560; ❷), are much more basic, but more affordable.

The east bank

Interest on the east bank of the Hudson River starts in little **BEACON**, some 75 miles north of Manhattan, at the excellent **Dia:Beacon**, 3 Beekman St (mid-April to mid-Oct Thurs–Mon 11am–6pm; mid-Oct to mid-April Fri–Mon 11am–4pm; ☎845/440-0100, ⓦwww.diabeacon.org; $10). The contemporary art museum, a project of New York City's Dia Art Foundation, showcases large, primarily abstract exhibits by single artists, in a converted steel, concrete, and glass factory.

Hyde Park and around

HYDE PARK, set on a peaceful plateau on the east bank of the Hudson just north of Beacon, is worth a stop for the homes of **Franklin D.** and **Eleanor Roosevelt**. Well-signposted off US-9 at 519 Albany Post Rd, the house where the "New Deal" president was born and spent much of his adult life is preserved here along with a library and a good **museum** (daily 9am–5pm, grounds 7am–sunset; no charge for the grounds; museum and first-come first-served guided house tour $14; ☏845/229-9115, ⓦ www.nps.gov/hofr). The museum contains extensive photos and artifacts, including the intriguing specially adapted car FDR drove after being struck down by polio in 1921, and the letter from Einstein that led to the development of the atomic bomb. A combination pass to Hyde Park, Val-Kill, and the Vanderbilt estate (see below) is available for $22.

FDR lies buried in the Rose Garden, beside his wife (and distant cousin) Eleanor, a gifted and influential Democratic politician without whose help his career might well not have survived his long bouts of illness. Unlike other First Ladies, who had mainly served as hostesses at society functions, Eleanor Roosevelt played a prominent role in the New Deal programs and in promoting women's and working people's rights. After FDR's death in 1945, Eleanor moved to **Val-Kill** (May–Oct daily 9am–5pm; Nov–April Thurs–Mon 9am–5pm; grounds daily until sunset; tours $8, grounds no charge; ☏845/229-9115, ⓦwww.nps.gov/elro), the nearby cottage retreat that she had shared for many years with the labor activist couple Marion Dickerman and Nancy Cook. Here, she carried on her work as chair of the United Nations Human Rights Commission, receiving dignitaries such as Tito, Nehru, Khrushchev, and John F. Kennedy, until her death in 1962.

A three-mile-long clifftop **path** along the Hudson from the Roosevelt complex winds up at the Beaux Arts **Vanderbilt Mansion** (daily 9am–5pm; $8). This virtual palace is, believe it or not, the smallest of the family's residences, built for Frederick, a grandson of railroad baron Cornelius. The furnishings are quite garish, but the formal gardens are very pretty and offer a fine view of the Hudson River. The grounds are open year-round from 7am to dusk, at no charge.

Apart from these historic homes, Hyde Park has one other huge tourist draw: the excellent restaurants and fascinating campus of the **Culinary Institute of America** (lunch and dinner Mon–Sat; reservations on ☏845/471-6608), the most prestigious cooking school in the country, which stands along US-9, south of Hyde Park at 1946 Campus Drive. The outstanding restaurants here – ranging from the casual, affordable *Apple Bakery Café* and the healthy, Asian-inflected *St Andrew's Café* to the Italian dinners, fine wine, and elevated atmosphere of *Caterina de Medici* and the four-star *American Bounty* and *Escoffier* restaurants – have trained some of America's best chefs. Frequent dining events, "boot camps," and classes are held for food and wine enthusiasts (schedules vary; ☏845-452-2230 or 1-800/888-7850, ⓦwww.ciachef.edu); biweekly campus **tours** (Mon 10am and 4pm, Thurs 4pm; $5) require reservations.

Rhinebeck and Olana

Beyond Hyde Park, US-9 cuts slightly inland from the Hudson, passing through a number of sleepy towns on its way north toward Albany.

RHINEBECK, six miles north of Hyde Park, is the first and most worthwhile of these, holding a number of good restaurants as well as **America's oldest hotel**. The lovely, white Colonial *Beekman Arms* on Rte-9 has been hosting and feeding travelers in its warm, wood-paneled rooms since 1766 (☎845/876-7077, ⓦwww.beekmanarms.com; ❺).

Two good places to **eat** are the *Calico Restaurant & Patisserie*, 6382 Mill St (☎845/876-2749; lunch and dinner only, closed Mon & Tues), which has a menu featuring strong Northern Italian and regional French influences, as well as tasty breakfast pastries, and the all-American *Foster's Coachhouse Tavern*, 6411 Montgomery St (☎845/876-8052). Nearby is the pricier but very authentic French *Le Petit Bistro*, at 8 E Market St (☎845/876-7400; closed Tues & Wed). Rhinebeck is also home to the New Agey **Omega Institute for Holistic Studies**, which runs a spa and a wide range of health and wellness workshops at a large campus east of town on Lake Drive; call for details of current programs (☎1-800/944-1001, ⓦwww.eomega.org).

The other good stop on the east bank of the Hudson is **Olana**, the hilltop home of **Frederic Church** (1826–1900), one of the foremost artists of the Hudson River School. High above a bend in the river, across the bridge from the town of Catskill, the quirky but very attractive house rises in an odd blend of Persian and Moorish motifs. Obligatory (and very popular) guided **tours** (April–May & Oct Wed–Sun 10am–5pm; June–Sept Wed–Sun 10am–6pm; Nov Wed–Sun 10am–4pm; $3; last tour one hour before closing; for reservations call ☎518/828-0135, ⓦwww.olana.org) take in the bric-a-brac clogged rooms, as well as a number of Church's picturesque paintings. The grounds are also open daily from 8am until sunset.

Albany

Founded by Dutch fur-trappers in the early seventeenth century, **ALBANY** made its money by controlling trade along the Erie Canal, and its reputation by being capital of the state. It's not an unpleasant town, just rather boring, with its contemporary character almost exclusively shaped by political and bureaucratic affairs – though there are a few livelier areas on the fringes.

A good place to start a tour is the **Quackenbush House**, the city's oldest building, built along the river in 1736 and now serving as part of the **Albany Urban Culture Park**. The modern **visitor center**, next door at Broadway and Clinton (Mon–Fri 9am–4pm, Sat & Sun 10am–4pm; ☎518/434-0405, ⓦwww.albany.org), has free maps and occasionally leads guided **tours** of the downtown area, where there are a number of Revolutionary-era homes. The visitor center also has engaging displays tracing Albany's history, with a special emphasis on the impact of the Erie Canal, and maps detailing driving tours of the surrounding area, taking in a still-functioning set of locks from the original canal, along with the impressive industrial legacy of **Troy**, across the Hudson via I-787 N.

Uphill from the waterfront, carved out from the heart of the city in the Sixties and Seventies as part of a controversial urban renewal project, Nelson A. Rockefeller's **Empire State Plaza** replaced 98 acres of nineteenth-century buildings (and displaced hundreds of Albanian families) with a complex that includes a subterranean retail arcade lined with impressive modern art. The view from the **Corning Tower**'s 42nd-floor observation deck (daily 10am–2.30pm; free) looks out far across the state, beyond the twisting Hudson River to the Adirondack foothills, the Catskills, and the Berkshires in Massachusetts. It also peers down on the neighboring Performing Arts Center, known locally as "**The Egg**" (☎518/473-3997,

@www.albany.edu/pac) – which adds the only curves to the Plaza's harsh angularity.

The **New York State Museum** (daily 9.30am–5pm; free; T518/474-5877), one level down at the south end of the plaza, reveals everything you could want to know about New York State in imaginative, if static, tableaux. The excellent section on New York City history is better than anything like it in Manhattan itself, with exhibits on immigration and skyscraper construction, storefronts and trolley cars, and the original set of *Sesame Street*.

The most engaging part of Albany is the few blocks west of the plaza, stretching between Washington and Madison avenues to the open green spaces of **Washington Park**, laid out by Frederick Law Olmsted, the father of American landscape architecture. The recently renovated **Albany Institute of History and Art**, 125 Washington Ave (Wed–Sat 10am–5pm, Sun noon–5pm; $7; T518/463-4478, @www.albanyinstitute.org), has a good range of Hudson River School paintings, and the neighborhood is full of the same sort of nineteenth-century brick-built homes Rockefeller had pulled down to build his Empire State Plaza.

Practicalities

Arrive by Greyhound or Adirondack Trailways (T1-800/858-8555, @www.escapemaker.com/adirondacktrailways) and it's a short, hilly walk to the heart of downtown; come in via Amtrak and you face a two-mile bus ride across the river in Rensselaer. If you intend to **stay** the night, bear in mind that downtown lodging is not particularly cheap. Suburban chain motels start at $50 a night, while downtown options amount to the *Ramada Inn*, 300 Broadway (T518/434-4111; ❹), the more comfortable *Albany Crowne Plaza*, at State and Lodge streets (T518/462-6611; ❻), and the exceptionally nice *Mansion Hill Inn*, 115 Philip St (T518/465-2038, @www.mansionhill.com; ❻), a B&B in a restored home just down the hill from the state governor's mansion; it also has a fine restaurant.

Other good **places to eat** are located on or near **Lark Street**, a few blocks west of the plaza; this is also the center of much nightlife activity and home to the local gay scene. *Justin's*, at no. 301 (T518/436-7008), and *Café Hollywood*, at no. 275 (T518/472-9043), serve good, progressive American food at moderate prices, while the welcoming *Mamoun's*, 206 Washington Ave (T518/434-3901), has great inexpensive lamb, chicken, and vegetarian dishes. The *Lionheart Blues Café*, 256 Lark St (T518/436-9530), puts on **live music** most nights. A bit farther east, the crowded *Big House Brewing Company*, 90 N Pearl St (T518/445-2739), serves up live acoustic tunes and its own brews, while nearby *Jillian's*, 59 N Pearl St (T518/432-1997), has dancing, plus liquid and electronic entertainment. The college town of **Troy**, across the river, also has a number of lively spots.

North through the Adirondacks

Mountaineers, skiers, and dedicated hikers form the majority of visitors to the vast northern region between Albany and the Canadian border. Outdoor pursuits are certainly the main attractions in the rugged wilderness of the **Adirondack Mountains**, though a few small resorts, especially the former Winter Olympic venue of **Lake Placid**, offer creature comforts in addition to breathtaking scenery; and the elegant spa town of **Saratoga Springs** nestles invitingly in the delicate countryside of the southern foothills.

Saratoga Springs

Saratoga was fast, man, it was real fast. It was up all night long.

Hattie Gray, founder of *Hattie's*

For well over a century, **SARATOGA SPRINGS**, just 42 miles north of Albany on I-87, was very much the place to be seen for the Northeast's richest and most glittering names. At first, the town's curative waters were the main attraction; then John Morrisey, an Irish boxer, transformed things by opening a **racetrack** and **casino** here during the 1860s. At one time, the Morgans, Vanderbilts, and Whitneys all had houses in the town, and Diamond Jim Brady, the flashiest among the 1920s nouveau riche, was one of its most ostentatious visitors. During the August horse-racing season, Saratoga Springs retains the feel of an exclusive vintage resort – but for the rest of the summer it is accessible, affordable, and fun.

Broadway, the main axis, takes in just about every aspect of the modern town, from lurid motel signs to the Gothic and Renaissance residential palaces on the northern tip of downtown; most of Saratoga Springs' many good bars are here or in the few blocks just east. The carefully cultivated **Congress Park**, off South Broadway, laid out for the original spa-goers, remains a shady retreat from town-center traffic. Three of the original mineral springs still flow up to the surface here, funneled out into drinking fountains (the water is tepid and salty, but some people swear by it). Also here is the original **casino**, which when built formed part of a whole city block; it now houses a small historical **museum** (end May to Labor Day daily 10am–4pm; Labor Day–April Wed–Sat 10am–4pm; Sun 1–4pm, closed Jan; $4; ☎518/584-6920). The **racetrack** (season runs late July through August, post time 1pm; grandstand $3; ☎518/584-6200, ⓦwww.nyracing .com/saratoga) still functions in a rather grand, old-fashioned manner, though there is no longer a strict dress code (beyond shirt and shoes) for the grandstand or the clubhouse (no shorts or tank tops). There's no such pretension at the **harness track**, aka the Equine Sports Center, on nearby Crescent Avenue (evening races several times a week May–Nov; $2; ☎518/584-2110). If you can't get to either, visit the array of paintings, trophies, and audiovisual displays at the **National Museum of Racing and Thoroughbred Hall of Fame**, on Union Avenue at Ludlow Street (Mon–Sat 10am–4.30pm, Sun noon–4.30pm, during race meet open daily 9am–5pm; $7; ☎518/584-0400, ⓦwww.racingmuseum.org).

On the southern edge of town, green **Saratoga Spa State Park** (daily 8am–dusk; $6 per car; ☎518/584-2535) presents opportunities to swim in great old Victorian pools, picnic, hike, or even "take the waters," ie, take a hot bath of the tingly, naturally carbonated stuff and receive a variety of spa treatments. Try the historic Lincoln Mineral Baths, just past the park entrance at 65 S Broadway (10am–4pm: July & Aug daily; June & Sept Wed–Mon; Oct–May Wed–Sun; $18 for 20min bath and 20min wrap-and-nap in a warm sheet; reservations 2–3 weeks in advance in summer; ☎518/583-2880). The **Saratoga Performing Arts Center** (June to early Sept, box office opens early May; ☎518/587-3330, ⓦwww.spac.org) – or SPAC – was built during the 1960s in a successful attempt to revive the town's fortunes. As well as being home to the New York City Ballet in July, and the Philadelphia Orchestra in August, it also hosts Freihofer's (formerly Newport) Jazz Festival and promotes other high-quality festivals.

Practicalities

Central Saratoga Springs is easily explored on foot. **Accommodation** is only a problem during August's race season, or if there's a big gig on at SPAC, when prices can more than double. One good central motel is the *Turf and Spa*, 140 Broadway (April–Nov; ☎518/584-2550 or 1-800/972-1229, ⓦwww .saratogaturfandspa.com; ❸). Both the lavishly restored landmark *Adelphi Hotel*, 365 Broadway (May–Oct; ☎518/587-4688, ⓦwww.adelphihotel.com; ❻), and the grand *Gideon Putnam Hotel*, located right in Saratoga Spa State Park (☎518/584-3000, ⓦwww.gideonputnam.com; ❼–❾), have more character. The **Chamber of Commerce**, 28 Clinton St (☎518/584-3255, ⓦwww .saratoga.org), has full lists of accommodations.

Eating is also easy. One longtime favorite is the soul food at *Hattie's*, 45 Phila St (☎518/584-4790), where huge entrees cost under $15; another good bet is *Wheat Fields*, 440 Broadway (☎518/587-0588, ⓦwww.wheatfields.com), with good salads and pasta served on an outdoor patio. *Beverly's*, 47 Phila St (☎518/583-2755), serves great but pricey breakfasts. There's usually good Irish **music** at the *Parting Glass Pub*, 40 Lake Ave (☎518/583-1916). *Nine Maple Avenue*, logically enough at 9 Maple Ave (☎518/583-2582), offers live jazz and blues until the early hours, while folksy *Caffé Lena*, 47 Phila St (Thurs–Sun; ☎518/583-0022, ⓦwww.caffelena.com) – where Don McLean first inflicted "American Pie" on the world – still pulls in the crowds.

The Adirondacks

The **Adirondacks**, which cover an area larger than Connecticut and Rhode Island combined, are said by locals to be named after an Iroquois insult for enemies they'd driven into the forests and left to become "bark eaters." Until recent decades the area has been almost the exclusive preserve of loggers, fur trappers, and a few select New York millionaires who really knew how to get away from it all (E.L. Doctorow's novels *Loon Lake* and *Billy Bathgate* both describe the bucolic retreats of Manhattan mobsters). For sheer grandeur, the region is hard to beat: 46 peaks reach to over 4000ft; in summer the purple-green mountains span far into the distance in shaggy tiers, in fall the trees form a russet-red kaleidoscope.

Though Adirondack Trailways buses serve the area, you'll find it hard-going without a **car**. General **information** and some special deals can be had from the Adirondack Region tourist office (☎1-800/487-6867, ⓦwww.adirondacks .org). The Adirondack Mountain Club (ADK), 814 Goggins Road, Lake George (☎518/668-4447, ⓦwww.adk.org), or the Adirondack Park **Visitor Interpretive Centers**, in Paul Smiths, north of Saranac Lake (daily 9am–5pm; ☎518/327-3000, ⓦwww.northnet.org/adirondackvic), and in Newcomb on Hwy-28 N, right in the heart of the park (☎518/582-2000), can provide details on hiking and camping.

Lake George

Though the undulating scenery around **LAKE GEORGE**, 25 miles up I-87 from Saratoga Springs, is undeniably some of the most gorgeous in the region, the village itself is overrun with cheap souvenir shops catering to the thousands of tourists who come here in search of a quick taste of the Adirondacks. The numerous sightseeing cruises, fun parks, factory outlet stores, and other diversions now on offer, here and in neighboring Glens Falls, obscure the natural splendor, as well as the region's considerable history. James Fenimore Cooper's *Last of the Mohicans* was based on the Battle of **Fort William Henry**, which was fought here between the British and the French in 1757; the replica fort

(May–Oct daily 9am–6pm; $12), along the lakeshore on Canada Street in the center of town, does little to evoke the era.

Blue Mountain Lake

While Lake George and the eastern fringes of the Adirondacks in general hold little to compete with the interior, an hour's drive northwest along Hwy-28 takes you past the headwaters of the Hudson River to the tiny resort of **BLUE MOUNTAIN LAKE**. A handful of **motels** and lakeside **cabins** provide accommodation, and you can swim at the pretty little **beach** that fronts the village center.

Sagamore Great Camp, about fifteen miles west, in the woods above Raquette Lake, is the only one of the many "Great Camps" that wealthy Easterners constructed in the Adirondacks around the end of the nineteenth century that is open to the public. Not to be confused with the four-star *Sagamore Resort* on an island in Lake George, Sagamore Great Camp was a summer home of the **Vanderbilts**, basically a huge and luxurious log cabin in which they entertained illustrious guests – including Hoagy Carmichael, who supposedly wrote the song "Stardust" while driving the four-mile dirt road that leads up to the house. The still-intact house and grounds are now used as a conference and educational center, and for cross-country skiing in winter; call for details of summer art and photography **classes**, or to reserve a place on a guided two-hour **tour** (May–June Sat & Sun 1.30pm; July–Aug daily 10am & 1.30pm; Sept–Oct Mon–Fri 1.30pm, Sat & Sun 10am; $10; ☎315/354-5311, Ⓦwww.sagamore.org). Alternatively, if you'd like to get closer to the other, still-private Great Camps, you can take a short tour of the area by plane, which gives good views of several; it also gives a clear idea of how uninhabited the region really is. In Inlet, near Raquette Lake, try Bird's Seaplane Service (9am–5pm; $25 per person, $50 minimum; ☎315/357-3631) or Payne's (same prices; ☎315/357-3971).

Just north of Blue Mountain Lake on Hwy-30, the otherwise rather bland twenty-building **Adirondack Museum** (late May to mid-Oct daily 10am–5pm; $14; Ⓦwww.adirondackmuseum.org) is perhaps most memorable for its grand views out over the lake and surrounding mountains.

Lake Placid

The winter sports center of **LAKE PLACID**, twice the proud host of the Winter Olympics, lies thirty miles west of I-87 on Hwy-73. In winter there's thrilling alpine skiing at imposing Whiteface Mountain and all manner of Nordic disciplines at Mount Van Hoevenberg; in summer you can watch luge athletes practice on refrigerated runs, freestyle skiers somersaulting off dry slopes into swimming pools, and top amateur ice hockey games. The mountain slopes also provide challenging terrain for hikers and cyclists; good **mountain bikes**, maps of local trails, and **guided tours** are available from High Peaks Cyclery, 331 Main St (☎518/523-3764). The **Lake Placid Summer Passport** package (June–Oct; $19; ☎518/523-1655, Ⓦwww.orda.org) takes you by chair lift to the top of the 393ft ski jump and eight miles up the sheer Whiteface Mountain toll road and back again. At **Mount Van Hoevenberg**, you can do a blood-curdling bobsled run ($30) or bike the extensive trail network ($18 bike rental; $5 trail fee; for information on both, call Olympic Sports Center on ☎518/523-4436).

The town itself is set on two lakes: **Mirror Lake**, which you can sail on in summer and skate on in winter, and larger **Lake Placid**, just to the west, on which you can take a narrated **cruise** in summer ($7.50; ☎518/523-9704).

Other attractions include the **Olympic Center** on Main Street (self-guided audio tour including museum $5; ☎518/523-1655), which houses four ice rinks and the informative **1932 and 1980 Lake Placid Winter Olympic Museum** ($4).

Outside the village on Hwy-73, the **John Brown Farm State Historic Site** was where the famous abolitionist brought his family in 1849 to aid a small colony of black farmers and where he conceived his ill-fated raid on Harper's Ferry in an attempt to end slavery. The house is less interesting than his story (see p.472; late May to late Oct Wed–Mon 10am–5pm; $2; ☎518/523-3900).

Practicalities

Lake Placid's **information center** is in the Olympic Center, at 216 Main St (☎518/523-2445 or 1-800/44-PLACID, ⓦwww.lakeplacid.com). **Accommodation** in town ranges from the somewhat economical to the opulent. The casually elegant *Mirror Lake Inn Resort & Spa*, 5 Mirror Lake Drive (☎518/523-2544, ⓦwww.mirrorlakeinn.com; ❺–❾), has over 120 rooms, the best of them palatial, but feels as cozy as a small B&B. Facilities include pool, sauna, health club, skating rink, private beach, and a top-notch but reasonably priced restaurant. *Edelweiss Motel*, on the east side of town at 14 Hwy-86, has clean if somewhat dated rooms (☎518/523-3821; ❸). The *Keene Valley Hostel*, in nearby Keene Valley (☎518/576-2030; dorm beds $18; ❷–❸), is a great base to be within walking distance of all the best hiking trails. Free **Internet** access is available for 15 minutes at a time at the information center.

It's possible to **eat** well, with a view, for relatively little. *Leslie's* is a much-loved local bakery at 99 Main St (☎518/523-4279), while nearby *Nicola's Over Main* (☎518/523-4430) does Greek and Italian dinners, including good wood-fired pizza. With its British chef, Asian-Southwestern fusion meals, and vaguely Alaskan and Caribbean decor, the affordable *Caribbean Cowboy*, at 89 Saranac Ave (☎518/523-3836), manages to transcend confusion and serve up some of the best food and atmosphere in Lake Placid. The waterfront *Cottage Café*, 5 Mirror Lake Drive (☎518/523-9845), is a café/pub serving snacks and unusual specials such as chilled strawberry soup; it's also the town's top apres-ski spot. The central *Hilton* is the main place for **live music**.

Saranac Lake

SARANAC LAKE, ten miles northwest of Lake Placid, is a smaller, more laid-back community. The tranquil lakeshore is lined with lovely gingerbread cottages, most of them built during the late 1800s, when this was a popular middle-class retreat and spa. **Robert Louis Stevenson** spent the winter of 1888 in a small cottage on the east side of town at 44 Stevenson Lane; it's now preserved as a **museum** (July–Sept Tues–Sun 9.30am–noon & 1pm–4.30pm; rest of year by appointment; ☎518/891-1462). Saranac Lake is still a rather quiet year-round resort, but it makes a great alternative base to Lake Placid: it's close to all facilities, plenty scenic, and offers better-value **accommodation**. Among the many motels on Lake Flower Avenue, *Sara-Placid Motor Inn*, no. 120 (☎518/891-2729 or 1-800/794-2729, ⓦwww.sara-placid.com; ❸), has rooms and suites to suit most budgets, as well as friendly management. Surprisingly good, if not fully authentic Mexican **food** can be had at the boisterous *Casa del Sol*, 154 Lake Flower Ave (☎518/891-0977); the *Hotel Saranac*, 101 Main St (☎518/891-2200; ❹), has a friendly **bar** downtown.

The Thousand Islands

Beyond the Adirondacks, on the broad St Lawrence River (which forms the border with Canada), there are 1800 barely populated hunks of earth known as the **Thousand Islands**. The reason they share their name with a salad dressing is because one c.1900 visitor, George Boldt, president of New York's *Waldorf-Astoria* hotel, is said to have asked the steward on his yacht to concoct something different for a special luncheon. The resultant orange goo is now famous the world over.

For **information** about the area, contact the Thousand Islands International Tourism Council (℡1-800/847-5263, Ⓦwww.visit1000islands.com). From both Alexandria Bay and the smaller fishing port of Clayton, **boat excursions** set out to explore the waterway; the tiny craft are all but swamped by the huge passing cargo ships, larger than many of the islands. For departure times, contact Uncle Sam Boat Tours (May–Oct daily; prices vary; ℡315/686-3511 or 1-800/ALEXBAY, Ⓦusboattours.com).

The Finger Lakes

At the heart of the state, southwest of Syracuse on the far side of the Catskills from New York City, are the eleven **Finger Lakes**, narrow channels gouged out by glaciers that have left tell-tale signs in the form of drumlins, steep gorges, and a number of waterfalls. With the exception of progressive, well-to-do **Ithaca** and tiny **Skaneateles**, few towns compete with the lakeshore scenery. That said, the area as a whole is a relaxing place to spend some time, particularly if you enjoy sampling **wine**: the Finger Lakes region – and much of upstate New York – produces a number of good vintages.

Skaneateles and Seneca Falls

SKANEATELES (pronounced "Skinny-Atlas"), crouching at the neck of Skaneateles Lake, is perhaps the prettiest Finger Lakes town. It's also the best place to go swimming in the region: just a block from the town center, and lined by huge resort homes, the appealing bay sports a **beach** and the Skaneateles Marina, where you can rent watersports equipment (℡315/685-5095) and take boat trips, from Mid-Lakes Navigation ($8 for 1hr; ℡315/685-8500). **Accommodation** is sparse; the handful of motels includes the *Colonial Motel*, one mile west on Hwy-20 (℡315/685-5751, Ⓦwww.skaneateles.com /colonialmotel; ❸), and, overlooking the lake, the *Sherwood Inn* (℡315/685-3405, Ⓦwww.thesherwoodinn.com; ❹), which is not as expensive as it looks, and also has a good dining room and tavern, which serve traditional meat, fish, and pasta dishes. Cheaper but still scrumptious meals can be had at the ever-popular *Doug's Fish Fry*, 7 Jordan St (℡315/685-3288).

At **SENECA FALLS**, just west of the northern tip of Cayuga Lake, Elizabeth Cady Stanton and a few colleagues planned and held the first Women's Rights Convention in 1848 – 72 years before the 19th amendment gave all women in the US the right to vote. On the site of the **Wesleyan Chapel**, 136 Fall St, where the first campaign meeting was held, is the terrific **Women's Rights National Historical Park** (daily 9am–5pm; $3; ℡315/568-2141, Ⓦwww.nps.gov/wori), which sets the early and contemporary women's movements in their historical contexts, with a strong emphasis on the connections between the African-American and women's-rights movements. The center, featuring exhibits and a neat little gift and book shop, also offers a **walking tour** that takes in the small museum at the Cady Stanton house and passes the (privately owned) former home of **Amelia Bloomer**, whose crusade to urge women out of their cumbersome undergarments won her a place in the dictionary. A block east of the visitor center, at 76 Fall St, the **National Women's Hall of Fame** (May–Sept Mon–Sat 10am–4pm, Sun noon–4pm; Oct–Dec & Feb–April Wed–Sat 10am–4pm; $3; ☎315/568-8060, ⓦ www.greatwomen.org), where about two hundred women, including Emily Dickinson and Sojourner Truth, have been honored for their efforts in fields such as humanitarianism, sports, and the arts, makes an interesting stop.

The town itself is a blend of old mills and homes of various architectural styles, tucked away among the mature trees. If you want to stop over, the best **place to stay** is the *Guion House B&B*, at 32 Cayuga St (☎315/568-8129, ⓦ www.flare.net/guionhouse; ❸). There are several reasonable **cafés** along Fall Street. Hwy-89, between Seneca Falls and Ithaca, has been dubbed the **Cayuga Wine Trail**, with dozens of small wineries operating along the west shore of the largest of the Finger Lakes.

Ithaca

Cayuga Lake comes to a halt at its southern end at picturesque **ITHACA**, piled like a diminutive San Francisco above the lakeshore and culminating in the towers, sweeping lawns, and shaded parks of Ivy-League **Cornell University**. Information is available at the helpful **visitor center** at 904 East Shore Drive, off Hwy-34 N (Mon–Fri 9am–5pm, Sat 10am–5pm, Sun 10am–4pm, some extended hours in summer; ☎607/272-1313 or 1-800/28-ITHACA, ⓦ www.visitithaca .com). On campus, which is cut by striking gorges, creeks, and lakes, the sleek, I.M. Pei–designed **Herbert F. Johnson Museum of Art** (Tues–Sun 10am–5pm; free; ☎607/255-6464, ⓦ www.museum.cornell.edu), across the street from the gorge-straddling **suspension bridge**, merits a visit more for its fifth-floor view of the town and lake than for the (on the whole) unspectacular collection of Asian and contemporary art. Adjacent to campus lie the **Cornell Plantations** (daily: dawn to dusk; free; ☎607/255-2400, ⓦ www.plantations.cornell.edu), the extensive botanical gardens and arboretum run by the university.

The pick of the countless **waterfalls** within a few miles of town are the slender **Taughannock Falls**, which are taller than Niagara at a height of 215ft and lie ten miles north of town just off Hwy-89, with a swimming beach close at hand. **Buttermilk Falls State Park**, two miles south of town on Rte-13, is a delightful spot, and the dangerous-looking Lucifer Falls, at lush **Robert H. Treman State Park**, three miles further south, should not be missed. Parking is $7 for the day, which covers all three parks. Cayuga Lake provides excellent **boating** and **windsurfing** opportunities; boards and boats can be rented from several places, including Cayuga Boat Rentals (☎607/277-5072 or 607/227-4095), next to the Visitors Bureau.

Practicalities

Greyhound and other **buses** operate out of the terminal at W State and N Fulton. Free **Internet** access is available at the huge, partially solar-powered library on Cayuga Avenue next to the Ithaca Commons.

Accommodation is, on the whole, reasonably priced. Try the *Elmshade Guest House*, 402 S Albany St (☎607/273-1707; ❷), or the *Best Western University Inn*, 1020 Ellis Hollow Rd, on the east edge of campus (☎800/528-1234, ⓦ www.bestwestern.com; ❹); its rooms are larger and probably worth the extra expense. *Breathe the Dream* (☎607/533-4804, ⓦ www.lakefrontinn.com), a luxurious B&B in a gorgeous lakeview setting north of town, is a great option if you don't mind the quirky pricing, which depends on availability, the season, and "how good your heart is." The *Statler Hotel*, on East Avenue within the campus proper (T 1-800/541-2501, W www.statlerhotel.cornell.edu; ❺), is the teaching hotel of the Cornell School of Hotel Administration and makes a pleasant option, particularly out of term.

Ithaca boasts two **dining** and **entertainment** zones. **Downtown**, centered around the vehicle-free Commons, is the larger and better of the two. It features the top-rated vegetarian **restaurant** of cookbook fame, *Moosewood*, in DeWitt Mall, which is on the corner of Cayuga and Seneca streets (T 607/273-9610, W www.moosewoodrestaurant.com), as well as the *Café DeWitt* (T 607/273-3473), also in the mall, which offers healthy and filling salads at lunchtime. A block away, *Just a Taste*, 116 N Aurora St (T 607/277-9463), is a lively wine and tapas bar, while *Simeon's on the Commons*, 224 E State St (T 607/272-2212), does gourmet sandwiches. Slightly out of downtown, *Maxie's*, 635 W State St (T 607/272-4136), serves up superlative blackened catfish, and has a raw oyster bar and happy-hour jazz. Numerous cheap student-oriented places to eat line the streets of **Collegetown**: check out *The Nines*, which serves up the best deep-dish pizza around and has live music, on 311 College Ave (T 607/272-1888). *Common Ground* (T 607/273-1505) is a gay-friendly **bar** down Route 96B with Ping-Pong, billiards, and a gorgeous patio.

The Kitchen Theatre produces new and avant-garde **plays** in its intimate auditorium (T 607/272-0403, W www.kitchentheatre.com); for news of the lively **music** scene, pick up the free *Ithaca Times*.

Corning

Forty miles southwest of Ithaca, world-famous **Steuben glass** has been manufactured in the otherwise undistinguished town of **CORNING** since Frederick Carder started making his characteristic Art Nouveau pieces in 1903. The excellent **Museum of Glass** in the Corning Glass Center traces the history of glass from ancient heads and amulets to modern sculptures and paperweights, and allows you to watch glassmaking in action (daily: July & Aug 9am–8pm; Sept–June 9am–5pm; $12; July & Aug children under 18 free; T 607/937-5371 or 1-800/732-6845, W www.cmog.org).

The **Rockwell Museum of Western Art**, ten minutes' stroll away at 111 Cedar St and Denison Pkwy (July & Aug Mon–Sat 9am–8pm, Sun 11am–8pm; rest of year Mon–Sat 9am–5pm, Sun 11am–5pm; $6.50, combined pass with Museum of Glass $18; T 607/937-5386, W www.stny.com/rockwellmuseum), has more than two thousand pieces of Steuben glass, plus antique toys and a strong, historically informed collection of Western American art – and is not to be confused with the Norman Rockwell Museum in Stockbridge, Massachusetts (see p.241). For further information on these attractions and for help in finding accommodation, contact the **visitors bureau** at 5 W Market St (T 607/936-6544 or 1-866/946-3386, W corningsteuben.com).

Toward Niagara Falls: the Erie Canal towns

The fertile farming country stretching from Albany at the head of the Hudson to Buffalo on Lake Erie, along the route of the **Erie Canal**, comprises the agricultural heartland of New York State. The eastern parts – also known as **Central Leatherstocking**, after the protective leggings worn by the area's first settlers – are well off the conventional tourist trails. Unless you want to check out one of the specialist sports museums or visit the lovely village of **Cooperstown**, this is not a high-priority destination.

With the captivating exceptions of **Niagara Falls**, one of the continent's biggest crowd-pullers, and the emerging tourist destination of **Buffalo**, there's little to see in the northwest reaches of New York State. Standing out from the mostly flat farmland, the industrial giants of **Rochester** and **Syracuse** each possess a couple of worthy attractions and restaurants, but are best approached as bases for seeing the surrounding area.

Cooperstown

Seventy miles west of Albany, sitting gracefully on the wooded banks of tranquil Otsego Lake, is pleasant **COOPERSTOWN**, christened "Glimmerglass" by novelist James Fenimore Cooper, son of the town's founder. The birth of baseball, said to have originated here on Doubleday Field, is commemorated by the inspired and spacious **National Baseball Hall of Fame**, on Main Street (daily: May–Aug 9am–9pm; Oct–April 9am–5pm; $9.50; ☏607/547-7200, Ⓦwww.baseballhalloffame.org). Everything is displayed in such an attention-grabbing manner that even if you know nothing about the game it's difficult to remain uninterested. Babe Ruth gets a whole display to himself, while more of the greats are shown in action in photographs and videos. The delightful **Fenimore Art Museum**, just north of town on Lake Road/Rte-80 (April–May & Oct–Dec Tues–Sun 10am–4pm; June–July daily 10am–5pm; $9; ☏607/547-1400 or 1-888/547-1450, Ⓦwww.fenimoreartmuseum.org), has innovative special exhibits and a fine collection of folk and North American Indian art, as well as a good café and gift shops. In summer, Cooperstown hosts **classical concerts** and the **Glimmerglass Opera** at Alice Busch Opera Theater, north on Hwy-80 by the lake (☏607/547-5704, Ⓦwww.glimmerglass.org).

The local chamber of commerce runs a helpful little **visitor center** at 31 Chestnut St (daily 9am–7pm in summer, call for winter hours; ☏607/547-9983, Ⓦwww.cooperstownchamber.org); the website is an excellent way to arrange accommodation. If you're here May through October, leave the car at one of the free parking lots on the edge of town and take the trolley around the various sights (trolley runs 8am–9pm: end June through Labor Day daily, Memorial Day to end June and Labor Day through Oct weekends only; $2 all-day pass). **Accommodation** in the town itself is expensive, but there's a cluster of clean motels right on pretty Otsego Lake, a few miles north on Rte-80; the *Lake 'N Pines* (☏607/547-2790 or 1-800/615-5253, Ⓦwww.cooperstown.net/lake-n-pines; ❸; closed Nov–March) offers superb value. North along Rte-80, the gorgeous lakeside *Blue Mingo Inn* (☏607/547-9414, Ⓦwww.bluemingoinn.com; ❻) maintains one of the area's best and most creative **restaurants**, the *Blue Mingo Grill* (☏607/547-7496), where fusion and New American dishes change nightly. *Clete Boyer's*, three miles south on Hwy-28 (☏607/544-1112), serves gimmicky but tasty American food. For a bite in town away from the crowds, try the *Cooperstown Diner*, 136 1/2 Main St (☏607/547-9201), open until 2pm for breakfast and burgers.

Syracuse

A lively but largely unattractive modern city, busy **SYRACUSE** made its name first for the production of salt and, more importantly, for its central position on the Erie Canal. There's little to see, though the presence of Syracuse University gives downtown an active and youthful feel. The redevelopment of **Armory Square**, around Franklin and Fayette streets, as an area of specialty shops, galleries, and cafés has also added some character to the city center.

The **Erie Canal Museum** (Tues–Sat 10am–5pm, Sun 10am–3pm; donation; ☎315/471-0593, ⓦwww.eriecanalmuseum.org), housed in one of the few surviving canal-era buildings, an 1850s weighing station at 318 E Erie Blvd, tells the story of the long battle between politicians and taxpayers before work on the canal began in 1810. The waterway was designed to link the Great Lakes with New York City via the Hudson, thereby cutting hefty transportation costs – which it did by an average of ninety percent. At first, however, not everyone was in favor; critics labeled the proposed canal a "big ditch" in which "would be buried the treasure of the state." The project eventually took fifteen years and more than one thousand lives, and went three million dollars over budget, but it spawned America's first generation of engineers, and, after it opened in 1825, prosperous towns quickly sprung up alongside the canal. Erie Boulevard itself was created by filling in the old canal bed, and the industrial surroundings do little to evoke the era (though the reconstructed **canal boat** inside the museum is definitely worth a look).

Excellent **rooms** can be found in the lakeside *Ancestors Inn*, just outside of town in Liverpool (☎315/461-1226, ⓦwww.ancestorsinn.com; ❹). The fairly central *HI-Downing International Hostel*, 535 Oak St (☎315/472-5788; ❶), has $14–17 dorm beds. For **food**, *Movino*, 214 Walton St (☎315/472-0844), has great, inexpensive pizza, while *Pastabilities*, 311 S Franklin St (☎315/474-1153), is delicious and popular. Student numbers ensure a lively **music** scene; consult the resourceful and free *Syracuse New Times* (ⓦnewtimes.rway.com). Good hangouts include the loud, bluesy *Dinosaur BBQ*, 246 W Willow St (☎315/476-1662, ⓦwww.dinosaurbarbque.com). The city's small **visitor center** is in the Erie Canal Museum (☎315/470-1800 or 1-800/234-4SYR, ⓦchamber.cny.com).

Rochester

In contrast to its sprawling suburbs, downtown **ROCHESTER** is a salubrious place, with its central office-block area bordered by well-heeled mansions on spacious boulevards. High-tech companies such as Bausch & Lomb, Xerox, and Kodak have created a thriving local economy throughout the years, which has recently been affected by national and regional economic downturn. Kodak's (and its founder, George Eastman's) legacies throughout the metropolitan area include Kodak Park, the Eastman Theater, and above all the **International Museum of Photography** at George Eastman House, two miles from downtown at 900 East Ave (Tues, Wed, Fri & Sat 10am–5pm, Thurs 10am–8pm, Sun 1–5pm; $8; ☎585/271-3361, ⓦwww.eastman.org). In the modern annex at the rear, a first-rate exhibition of photographic history ranges from high-quality Civil War prints to modern experimental works. There's also a space which houses temporary exhibitions, as well as an arthouse cinema. The house itself, fussily restored to its early twentieth-century glory, is mildly interesting; upstairs there's the fun, hands-on Discovery Room, plus an informative exhibition on Eastman. Fittingly, given Eastman's passion for horticulture, the gardens have been superbly maintained and are worth a visit in themselves.

An obsessive collector of anything and everything, local bigwig Margaret Woodbury Strong (1897–1969) bequeathed her estate to the city as the **Strong Museum** on Manhattan Square (Mon–Thurs 10am–5pm, Fri

10am–8pm, Sat 10am–5pm, Sun noon–5pm; $7; ☎585/263-2700, ⓦwww.strongmuseum.org). Half devoted to a history of the American family, and half obsessed with a history of American children's pop culture, it features interactive kid-oriented exhibits such as a history of *Sesame Street*. Pop culture addicts will enjoy its kitsch sensibility, which includes a fully working 1920s carousel and a 1950s diner shipped here wholesale from its original site in Pennsylvania. The theme of celebrating former Rochester residents continues at the **Susan B. Anthony House** at 17 Madison St, where this renowned suffragist lived from 1866 to 1906 (June–Aug Tues–Sun 10am–5pm; rest of year Wed–Sun 11am–4pm; $6; ☎585/235-6124, ⓦwww.susanbanthonyhouse.org).

Practicalities

Greyhound drops off at Broad and Chestnut streets downtown. The Amtrak station, 320 Central Ave, is on the north side beyond the I-490 inner loop road; it's served by Regional Transit Service (RTS) public **buses** (☎585/288-1700, ⓦwww.rgrta.com). Rochester's **visitor center** is at 45 East Ave between Chestnut and Main (Mon–Fri 8.30am–5pm, Sat 9am–5pm, Sun 10am–3pm; closes on Sat in winter at 4pm; ☎1-800/677-7282, ⓦwww.visitrochester .com). **Accommodation** is somewhat expensive. Downtown choices include the excellent *428 Mt Vernon B&B* (☎716/271-0792, ⓦwww.428mtvernon .com; ⑤), at the entrance to lush Highland Park, with private baths in all rooms. Among budget options in the south of the city is the *Red Roof Inn*, 4820 W Henrietta Rd, off I-90 exit 46 (☎585/359-1100; ②).

Popular **places to eat** downtown include *Aladdin's Natural Eatery*, 646 Monroe Ave (☎585/442-5000), serving inexpensive Middle Eastern food, the pub-style *Old Toad*, 277 Alexander St (☎585/232-2626), where British staff serve beer and cheap meals, and the restored Art Deco *Highland Park Diner*, 960 S Clinton Ave (☎585/461-5040). *Jine's Restaurant*, 658 Park Ave, is good value for breakfast (☎585/461-1280), and if you want to sample a "Garbage Plate" – the local delicacy comprising a platter of just about anything that can be successfully deep-fried – head over to *Nick Tahou Hots* at 320 W Main St (☎585/436-0184).

Out from Rochester

The **Lake Ontario State Parkway** is a quiet, scenic way of driving to Niagara Falls from Rochester, taking about an hour longer than the standard route along I-90 via Buffalo. The parkway starts eight miles from downtown at the end of Lake Avenue, near the popular **Ontario Beach Park**. This short golden strand of shore, rimmed by exclusive holiday homes, is a real poseur's paradise; you may well feel self-conscious if your shades don't match up to the ubiquitous, locally manufactured Ray-Bans.

If big crowds and the churning noise of speedboats are not your thing, head twenty miles along the parkway to the more secluded **Hamlin Beach State Park** ($7 per car). The parkway passes through few towns, and the best place to stop for refreshments is the small and attractive Point Breeze harbor, ten miles on from Hamlin.

Buffalo

As I-90 sweeps down into the state's second largest city, **BUFFALO**, downtown looms up in a cluster of Art Deco spires and glass-box skyscrapers – Manhattan in miniature on Lake Erie. The city's early twentieth-century prosperity, which busted while many other American cities were booming, and thus exempted Buffalo's historic buildings from destruction and replacement, is reflected in such architecturally significant structures as the towering 1928 **City Hall** (the tallest in the country, and with a free observation deck on the top floor); the deep red terracotta relief of Louis Sullivan's **Guaranty Building** on Church Street; major buildings by H.H. Richardson and Eliel Saarinen; and several houses (and even a gas station-in-progress) designed by Frank Lloyd Wright. The massive abandoned **grain elevators**, which rise proudly along the Erie waterfront like wonders of the industrial world, provide an interesting architectural counterpoint, testifying to the city's history as a center of production and American working-class life. Because of its proximity to the Canadian border, Buffalo also has numerous Underground Railroad sites.

That Buffalo's wealthy merchants were a cultured lot is also apparent in the excellent **Albright-Knox Art Gallery**, 1285 Elmwood Ave (Tues–Sat 11am–5pm, Sun noon–5pm; $6 adults, $12 for a family of four; ☎716/882-8700, ⓦwww.albrightknox.org), two miles north of downtown amid the green spaces of the Frederick Law Olmsted–designed **Delaware Park**. Not a gallery at all, but a museum with one of the top modern collections in the world, it's especially strong on recent American and European art: the Color Field painters, Abstract Expressionism, Pop, Op and Kinetic Art, with Pollock, Rothko, Warhol, and Rauschenberg among the names. Other highlights are thirty large paintings by Clyfford Still, a Surrealism collection (which includes Dalí), and a fine selection of pieces by earlier artists such as Matisse, Picasso, and Monet. There's also a tasty, chic restaurant open daily for lunch (Tues–Sat 11.30am–3pm, Sun 11am–3pm).

The area around Delaware Park is Buffalo's choicest neighborhood; it features several homes designed by **Frank Lloyd Wright**, most notably the Darwin D. Martin House Complex ($10; tours only, reservations required; ☎716/947-9217, ⓦwww.darwinmartinhouse.org). Between here and downtown is **Allentown**, a National Historic District and Buffalo's most bohemian quarter. Its leafy streets are lined with lovely Victorian homes and numerous good cafés, bars, restaurants – as well as most of Buffalo's gay and lesbian venues. Allen Street between Main and Elmwood Avenue holds some of the best examples of nineteenth-century architecture; some of the area around Theatre Place downtown is also good. On the border of Allentown, the slightly more upscale **Elmwood Avenue** nonetheless has great food and shopping at prices that will seem low to many out-of-towners.

As a traditionally blue-collar city, Buffalo loves its professional **sports** teams: football's Bills (☎1-877/BB-TICKS), ice hockey's Sabres (☎1-888/GO-SABRES), and minor-league baseball's Bisons (☎1-888/223-6000), who, as the top farm team for the Cleveland Indians, attract over a million fans per season to downtown's modern and very pleasant ballpark.

West of Buffalo, the **Lake Erie shoreline** is lined by numerous beaches where **windsurfers** skim across the water and do flips in the waves, while the Miss Buffalo boat tours ($12 and up; ☎716/856-6696, ⓦwww.missbuffalo.com), which leave from 79 Marine Drive next to the Naval and Servicemen's Park, provide a good view of the city skyline. Minutes from the grain elevators, the 264-acre **Tifft Nature Preserve** holds a fresh marsh, untamed urban wildlife, and five miles of trails. To the south, in the town of Orchard Park, the friendly, engaging **Pedaling History Bicycle Museum** (Mon–Sat 11am–5pm, Sun 1.30–5pm; $6; ☎716/662-3853, ⓦwww.pedalinghistory.com) holds over four hundred antique bikes and tens of thousands of pieces of cycling memorabilia.

Arrival and information

Greyhound, Metro Bus, and Metro Rail, the city's new tramway (both Metros ☏716/855-7211, Ⓦwww.nfta.com/metro), all operate from the downtown depot at Ellicott and Church streets. Several routes go to **Niagara Falls** (see overleaf). Amtrak **trains** stop some six blocks away, at Exchange Street, as well as in the eastern suburb of Depew, eight miles from town but close to the **airport** (☏716/630-6020, Ⓦwww.nfta.com/airport). There's a helpful **visitor center** at 617 Main St (☏716/852-0511 or 1-800/BUFFALO, Ⓦwww.visit-buffaloniagara.com), which suggests numerous themed driving tours and has plenty of other information.

Accommodation

Beau Fleuve 242 Linwood Ave ☏716/882-6116 or 1-800/278-0245, Ⓦwww.beaufleuve.com. Extremely comfortable, well-appointed B&B with great breakfasts. ❹

Hampton Inn & Suites 220 Delaware Ave ☏716/855-2223, Ⓦwww.hamptoninnbuffalo.com. A safe bet in the heart of the nightlife district downtown, with free breakfasts. ❹

HI-Buffalo Hostel 667 Main St ☏716/852-5222, Ⓦwww.hostelbuffalo.com. Very central hostel with beds for $19. Nothing special, but the cheapest option by far. ❶

The Mansion at Delaware 414 Delaware Ave ☏716/886-3300, Ⓦwww.mansionondelaware .com. Centrally located luxury inn. ❻–❼

Roycroft Inn 40 S Grove St, East Aurora ☏716/652-5222 or 1-877/652-5552, Ⓦwww.roycroftinn.com. Immaculately refurbished inn located a half-hour drive east of Buffalo, formerly the centerpiece of the Roycroft Arts and Crafts Community. The on-site restaurant serves tasty meals. ❺

Eating, drinking, and nightlife

The heart of Buffalo's downtown centers on Chippewa and Main; plenty of restaurants are within easy reach and there's ample parking. For a quick snack, the cheap food stalls and tiny Polish cafés of ancient **Broadway Market**, 999 Broadway, are well worth perusing. The main **nightlife** drag, along Chippewa from Delaware Avenue to Main Street, has plenty of sports bars and nightclubs. The majority of theaters and venues that house the city's burgeoning **arts scene** are handily grouped nearby along Main between Chippewa and Tupper streets. For further information, pick up the free weeklies *Blue Dog Press* or *Art Voice* (Ⓦwww.artvoice.com), or the gay and lesbian *Outcome* (Ⓦwww.outcomebuffalo.com).

Anchor Bar 1047 Main St ☏716/886-8920, Ⓦwww.anchorbar.com. The city's specialty of buffalo (spicy chicken) wings with blue cheese and celery dressing is said to have been invented here.

Calumet Arts Café 56 W Chippewa St ☏716/855-2220. A good late-night bar and restaurant, with jazz, blues, folk, and world music.

Colter Bay 561 Delaware Ave, Allentown ☏716/882-1330. Western-themed restaurant with great, inexpensive lunches for a variety of tastes.

India Gate 1116 Elmwood Ave ☏716/886-4000. Good, inexpensive Indian restaurant with generous lunch buffet.

Nietzsche's 248 Allen St ☏716/886-8539, Ⓦwww .nietzsches.com. Bar with friendly staff and cheap drinks, hosting a wide variety of live acts seven days a week; there's room for dancing in the back.

Osake 235 Delaware Ave ☏716/842-6261. This casual café serves cheap sushi and noodles; not a place to linger, but good value.

Spot Coffee 227 Delaware Ave ☏716/856-BREW; 765 Elmwood Ave ☏716/332-LATTE, Ⓦwww .spotcoffee.com. Lively, happening neighborhood institution serving basic food and good drinks. The location on Elmwood is connected to New World Records, one of the best music stores in Buffalo.

Niagara Falls

Every second, almost three quarters of a million gallons of water explode over the knife-edge **NIAGARA FALLS**, right on the border with Canada some twenty miles north of Buffalo on I-190. This awesome spectacle is made even more impressive by the variety of methods laid on to help you get closer to it: boats, catwalks, observation towers, and helicopters all push as near to the curtains of gushing water as they dare. At night, the falls are lit up, and the colored waters tumble dramatically into blackness, while in winter the whole scene changes as the falls freeze to form gigantic razor-tipped icicles.

Some visitors will, no doubt, find the whole experience a bit too gimmicky; no commercial opening has been left unexploited, and now corporate big-hitters like the *Hard Rock Café* have joined in the action, pushing the place closer to an aquatic Vegas (there's now a casino on each side). Don't expect too much from the touristy small city of **Niagara Falls** or the more developed tinseltown of **Niagara Falls, Ontario**. Once you've seen the falls, from as many different angles as you can manage, and traced the **Niagara Gorge**, you'll have a better time heading back to Buffalo. Unless, that is, bargain hunting is your thing: one of the biggest **factory outlet malls** in the country, Prime Outlets, is just east of the city, and seems these days to be almost as big a draw as the falls.

Arrival, information, and getting around

Amtrak **trains**, en route between New York City and Toronto, stop a long two miles from downtown at 27th Street and Lockwood Road. **Buses** stop downtown at 4th and Niagara streets, a little over half a mile from the falls. Arriving **by car**, follow the signs to the main parking lot, which is right next to the falls and costs $5 – watch out for the unofficial rangers who'll steer you into privately owned, high-priced lots just outside the park. **Information** is available at the Buffalo Niagara CVB (☎716/852-0511 or 1-800/BUFFALO, ⓦwww.visitbuffaloniagara.com) and from the Niagara Falls State Park Visitors Center (☎716/278-1796) near the falls. To send the obligatory postcards, visit the **post office** at 615 Main St (Mon–Fri 8.30am–5pm, Sat 8.30am–2pm; ☎716/285-7561). As for **getting around**, local Metro Transit System **buses** ($1.50 base fare, plus 25¢/zone; ☎716/285-9319, ⓦwww.nfta.com) run to all areas of the city and to Buffalo (see p.153).

Accommodation

Places to stay in central Niagara can be quite expensive if you don't plan ahead or shop around – though US-62, east of I-190, is lined with dozens of inexpensive motels. Many of these are pretty tacky, targeting the thousands of honeymoon couples who come here every year (despite Oscar Wilde's assertion that the falls "must be one of the earliest if not keenest disappointments of American married life"). Buffalo makes a much better base. The closest place to **camp** is seven miles from downtown at *Niagara Falls Campground & Lodging*, 2405 Niagara Falls Blvd in Wheatfield (☎716/731-3434); campsites are $20 a night for two people.

Budget Inn 492 Main St ☎716/285-8366. No-frills downtown motel, closed in the off-season. ❸
HI-Niagara Falls 1101 Ferry Ave ☎716/282-3700. Friendly, well-run hostel with dorm beds for $14–17. Preference is given to HI members and reservations are necessary in summer. ❶
Park Place B&B 740 Park Place ☎716/282-4626, ⓦwww.parkplacebb.com. Comfortable home near downtown, with full breakfast and afternoon pastries. ❸–❹

Red Coach Inn 2 Buffalo Ave ☎716/282-1459, ⓦwww.redcoach.com. Popular, well-appointed B&B with views of the falls. ❹
Travelodge Fallsview 201 Rainbow Blvd ☎716/285-9321 or 1-800/876-3297, ⓦwww.niagarafallstravelodge.com. Landmark hotel with grand lobby but rather plain rooms. The rates fluctuate, dropping dramatically in the off-season. ❷–❺

The Falls

Niagara Falls comprises three distinct cataracts. The tallest are the **American** and **Bridal Veil falls** on the American side, separated by tiny Luna Island and plunging over jagged rocks in a 180ft drop; the broad **Horseshoe Falls** which curve their way over to Canada are probably the most impressive. Together, they date back a mere twelve thousand years, when the retreat of melting glaciers allowed water trapped in Lake Erie to gush north to Lake Ontario. Back then the falls were seven miles downriver, but constant erosion has cut them back to their present site.

Getting around Niagara Falls State Park is easy, thanks to the convenient but tacky **Niagara Scenic Trolley** ($5) which connects all parking lots and the major sightseeing points. The best views on the American side are from the **Observation Tower** (daily 10am–5pm; 50¢), and from the area at its base where the water rushes past. In the middle of the river, Terrapin Point on **Goat Island** has similar views of Horseshoe Falls. Near here, the nineteenth-century tightrope-walker Blondin crossed the Niagara repeatedly, and even carried passengers across on his back. Other suicidal fools over the years have taken the plunge in barrels – or less (see box, below). The reason such craziness has long been banned becomes self-evident when you approach the towering cascade on the not-to-be-missed **Maid of the Mist** boat trip, which leaves from the foot of the observation tower (April–Oct daily 9.15am–7.30pm every 15 mins; $10.50, children $6.25; T716/284-4233, Wwww.maidofthemist.com). Another excellent way to see the falls is the **Cave of the Winds** tour (mid-May to late Oct daily 8am–10pm; $8; T716/278-1730), which leads from Goat Island by elevator down to the base of the falls. Bringing you to within almost touching distance of the water, the tour can provide a magical night-time view, as it runs well into the evening. A **MasterPass** for these and other attractions costs $27.50 for adults, or $19.25 for children; it can be purchased at the Niagara Falls State Park Visitor Center.

Rainbow **helicopter** tours (T716/284-2800) are a more expensive proposition, at $60 per person for a ten-minute ride. To check the view out from Niagara, Ontario, it's a twenty-minute walk across the **Rainbow Bridge** to the Canadian side (50¢ to Canada, free to US; bring ID and check with the US immigration officials before heading across), where you get an arguably better view, bigger crowds, and even more tawdry commercialism. Driving across is inadvisable: the toll for a car is just $2.50, but parking on the other side can cost more than $15.

As you look on in awe, reflect that you're seeing only about half the volume of water – the rest is diverted to hydroelectric power stations. The full story of this engineering feat is related at the free **Niagara Power Project Visitors Center** in nearby Lewiston (daily 9am–5pm; free; T716/286-6661 or 1-866/NYPA-FUN, Wwww.nypa.gov/vc/nvcdir.htm). With your own transportation it's also possible to trace the inhospitable Niagara Gorge two miles along the dramatic Robert Moses Parkway to the **Whirlpool Rapids**, a violent maelstrom swollen by broken trees and other flotsam, and to hike down

---

Maniacs and miracles

Fifteen people have taken the plunge over Niagara's 170-foot **Horseshoe Falls** – and, remarkably, ten of them survived the fall. The first daredevil was 63-year-old Annie Taylor in 1901, who rode in a wooden barrel and suffered only minor bruises from her journey. Since then, thrillseekers have followed her lead, using everything from giant rubber balls to water tanks as craft. The last successful navigation of the falls was in 2003, by a man who claimed he was trying to commit suicide; after surviving the plunge, the man decided life was worth living. Those less lucky include Red Hill, killed in 1945 while using a vessel he called "The Thing," built of little more than inner tubes and netting. Other deaths have been equally pointless: from a would-be stuntman in a kayak, who refused a helmet for fear it would obscure his face on film, to a jet-skier whose parachute, improperly packed, failed to open when he overshot the falls.

The most miraculous survival story, though, is that of Roger Woodward, a seven-year-old on a boat trip with his teenage sister in the upper Niagara River in the summer of 1960. When the boat developed motor trouble and capsized, they were thrown into the river. His sister was plucked from the water, but Roger and the captain, James Honeycutt, went over the falls wearing nothing but swimsuits and life preservers. Honeycutt was killed, but the boy surfaced near a tour boat at the base of the falls, bruised and concussed but alive, making him the only person ever to survive an unprotected trip over the falls.

into striking **Whirlpool State Park**. Ten miles east of Niagara Falls, the town of **Lockport** takes its name from the series of locks that raise and lower boats some 65ft at the western end of the Erie Canal. You can see the impressive flight of locks from the Pine Street Bridge, or up close on canal **boat tours** (May–Oct daily at 12.30pm & 3pm, also 10am on Sat; June–Aug additional daily tours at 10am & 7pm; $12.50; ☎716/693-3260, ⓦwww .llecc.com).

Eating and drinking

Though most of the **eating options** in Niagara Falls are fast-food joints of indifferent quality, there are a few decent local bars and restaurants – with some better places over in Canada.

Atrium in the *Ramada Inn*, 219 4th St ☎716/282-1734. Affordable American standards and pasta.

The Bakery and Ports of Call Restaurant 3004 Niagara St ☎716/282-9498. A bit out-of-the-way, but offering a wide variety of European dishes for $10–20. The bar makes a good spot for a quiet drink.

Como Restaurant 2200 Pine Ave ☎716/285-9341. A good, posh option with huge portions of Italian cuisine and a reasonably priced deli.

Hard Rock Café 333 Prospect St ☎716/282-

0007. Although a bit cliched and expensive, this branch of the rock-homage American-food chain restaurant has a lively, dependable bar.

Provenzo's 1300 Buffalo Ave ☎716/278-1264. Italian restaurant serving popular seafood and veal dishes, as well as meat, chicken, and pasta.

Riverside Inn 115 S Water St, Lewiston ☎716/754-8206. Waterfront property built in 1871, ten minutes' drive north of the falls, with an extensive wine list and a menu of steak and fish entrees that approaches fine dining.

Pennsylvania

PENNSYLVANIA, which but for a small stretch on Lake Erie is the only landlocked state in the Northeast, was explored by the Dutch in the early 1600s, settled by the Swedes forty years later, and claimed by the British in 1664. Charles II of England, who owed a debt to the Penn family, rid himself of the potentially troublesome young **William Penn**, an enthusiastic advocate of religious freedom, by granting him land in the colony in 1682. Penn Jr. immediately established a "holy experiment" of "brotherly love" and tolerance, naming the state for his father and setting a good example by signing a peaceful cohabitation treaty with the Native Americans. Most of the early agricultural settlers were religious refugees, Quakers like Penn himself and Mennonites from Germany and Switzerland, to be joined by Irish Catholics during the potato famines of the nineteenth century.

"The Keystone State" was crucial in the development of the United States. Politicians and thinkers like **Benjamin Franklin** congregated in Philadelphia – home of both the Declaration of Independence and the Constitution – and were prominent in articulating the ideas behind the Revolution. Later, the battle in Gettysburg, in south Pennsylvania – best remembered for Abraham Lincoln's immortal **Gettysburg Address** – marked a turning point in the Civil War. Pennsylvania was also vital industrially: Pittsburgh, in the west, was the world's leading steel producer in the nineteenth century, and nearly all the nation's anthracite coal is still mined here.

The two great urban centers of **Philadelphia** and **Pittsburgh**, both lively and vibrant tourist destinations, are at opposite ends of the state. The three hundred miles between them, though predominantly agricultural, are topographically diverse. There are over one hundred state parks, with green rolling countryside in the east, brooding forests in the west, and in the northeast, the rivers, lakes, and valleys of the **Poconos**. **Lancaster County**, home to traditional Amish farmers, and the **Gettysburg** battlefield both heave with busloads of day-trippers, while the Hershey chocolate factory, minutes away from **Harrisburg**, the capital, draws thousands of cocoa-loving visitors each year.

Getting around Pennsylvania

If you organize your trip carefully, **public transporation** is adequate to navigate Pennsylvania – although it's best to have a **car**. Both I-76 (the Pennsylvania Turnpike) and I-80 sweep all the way across to Ohio, nearly five hundred miles east to west. US-30 (the Lincoln Highway) also runs east–west between Philadelphia and Pittsburgh, past Lancaster City, York, and Gettysburg. The prettiest north–south route is US-15, from Maryland to New York State, which follows the Susquehanna River for about fifty miles. **Amtrak** crosses daily from Philadelphia to Pittsburgh, stopping at Lancaster City, Harrisburg, and other smaller towns. **Greyhound** covers all the major cities and some small towns not served by rail.

Philadelphia

The original capital of the nation, **PHILADELPHIA** was laid out by William Penn Jr. in 1682, on a grid system that was to provide the pattern for most American cities. It was envisaged as a "greene countrie towne," and today, for all its historical and cultural significance, it still manages to retain a certain quaintness. Just a few blocks away from the noise, crowds, heat, and dust of downtown, shady cobbled alleys stand lined with red-brick colonial houses, while the peace and quiet of huge Fairmount Park make it easy to forget you're in a major metropolis.

Settled by **Quakers**, Philadelphia prospered swiftly on the back of trade and commerce, and by the 1750s had become the second largest city in the British Empire. Economic power fueled strong revolutionary feeling, and the city was the capital during the **War of Independence** (except for nine months under British occupation in 1777–1778) and the US capital until 1800, while Washington, DC, was being built. The **Declaration of Independence** was written, signed, and first publicly read here in 1776, as was the **US Constitution** ten years later. Philadelphia was also a hotbed of new ideas in the arts and sciences, as epitomized by the scientist, philosopher, statesman, inventor, and printer **Benjamin Franklin**.

Philadelphia, which translated from Greek means "City of Brotherly Love," is in fact one of the most **ethnically mixed** US cities, with substantial communities of Italians, Irish, Eastern Europeans, and Asians living side-by-side among the large **African–American** population. Many of the city's black residents are descendants of the migrants who flocked here after the Civil War when, like Chicago, Philadelphia was seen as a place of tolerance and liberalism. More recently, it voted in the nation's first black mayor, and erected the country's best museum of African-American history and culture. Philly also retains its Quaker heritage, with large "meetings" or congregations of **The Society of Friends**.

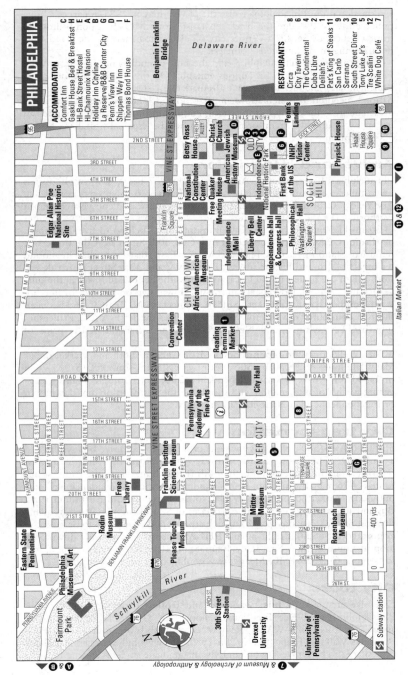

PHILADELPHIA

ACCOMMODATION

Comfort Inn	C
Gaskill House Bed & Breakfast	H
HI-Bank Street Hostel	E
HI-Chamounix Mansion	A
Holiday Inn Cityline	B
La Reserve/B&B Center City	G
Penn's View Inn	D
Shippen Way Inn	I
Thomas Bond House	F

RESTAURANTS

Circa	8
City Tavern	6
The Continental	4
Cuba Libre	2
Delilah's	1
Pat's King of Steaks	11
San Carlo	9
Serrano	3
South Street Diner	10
Tony Luke Jr's	5
Tre Scalini	12
White Dog Café	7

Delaware River

Benjamin Franklin Bridge

Betsy Ross House

Christ Church

American Jewish History Museum

National Constitution Center

Free Quaker Meeting House

Independence Mall

Liberty Bell Center

First Bank of the US

Independence National Historic Park

Independence Hall & Congress Hall

Philosophical Hall

Washington Square

Penn's Landing

INHP Visitor Center

Physick House

Head House Square

SOCIETY HILL

African American Museum

CHINATOWN

Convention Center

Reading Terminal Market

City Hall

Pennsylvania Academy of the Fine Arts

Mütter Museum

Rittenhouse Square

Franklin Institute Science Museum

Free Library

Please Touch Museum

Rodin Museum

Eastern State Penitentiary

Philadelphia Museum of Art

Fairmount Park

Edgar Allan Poe National Historic Site

Franklin Square

CENTER CITY

Rosenbach Museum

Schuylkill River

30th Street Station

Drexel University

University of Pennsylvania

Italian Market

Subway station

0   400 yds

Museum of Archaeology & Anthropology

161

On the downside, Philadelphia is also the place where in 1985, as part of a huge police effort to dislodge the black separatist group MOVE, a bomb dropped from a helicopter set fire to entire city blocks, killing men, women, and children, leaving many hundreds homeless.

Once known as "Filthydelphia," and the butt of endless derision from W.C. Fields in the 1930s (as in his famous epitaph: "On the whole, I'd rather be in Philadelphia"), the city underwent a remarkable resurgence preparing for the nation's bicentennial celebrations in 1976. Philadelphia's strength today is its great energy – fueled by history, strong cultural institutions, and grounded in its many staunchly traditional neighborhoods, especially Italian **South Philadelphia**.

Arrival and information

Philadelphia's **International Airport** (☎215/937-6800, ⓦwww.phl.org) is seven miles southwest of the city off I-95. **Taxis** into town cost around $20 (try Yellow Cab; ☎215/829-4222), and the South East Pennsylvania Transit Authority (**SEPTA**) runs trains from the airport every thirty minutes (4.30am–11.30pm; $5.50; see "City transportation," below) to five downtown destinations: Eastwick Station, University City, 30th Street near the university, Suburban Station near City Hall, and Market East, adjacent to the Greyhound terminal at 11th and Filbert streets. The very grand 30th Street **Amtrak** station, one of the busiest in the US, is just across the Schuylkill River in the university area (Amtrak passengers can transfer downtown on SEPTA for free; ask when you purchase your ticket). SEPTA connects to **NJ Transit**, and between the two commuter rail systems you can travel to the Jersey shore, Princeton, suburban Pennsylvania, and New York City for a fraction of the price of Amtrak.

The excellent new **Independence Visitor Center**, at 6th and Market streets (daily: late June–Aug 8.30am–5pm; rest of year 8.30am–7pm; ☎215/965-7676 or 1-800/537-7676; ⓦwww.independencevisitorcenter.com), contains a staggering wealth of information, and should be the first stop on any downtown or Independence Hall National Park itinerary.

City transportation

SEPTA (☎215/580-7800, ⓦwww.septa.org) runs an extensive **bus** system and a **subway**. The most useful subway lines cross the city east–west (Market–Frankford line) and north–south (Broad Street line); the handiest bus route is **#76**, which runs from Penn's Landing and the Independence Hall area out along Market Street past City Hall to the museums and Fairmount Park. Bus and subway services require exact fares of $2 (tokens, purchased in quantity, cost only $1.30); **day passes**, which are also good for a ride to or from the airport, go for $5.50. Bright purple **PHLASH** buses run a handy downtown loop in summer (June–Sept daily 10am–8pm; $1, exact change required, free for seniors; ☎215/4-PHLASH, ⓦwww.gophila.com/phlash/body.htm).

City tours

Extensive architectural **bus**, **walking**, and **trolley tours** are run by Walk Philadelphia (April–Dec Tues–Sun; walking tour $10, trolley and bus tours about $25; ☎215/625-WALK, ⓦwww.centercityphila.org/tours), while Poor Richard's Walking Tours (☎215/206-1682, ⓦwww.phillywalks.com; call for prices) are run by University of Pennsylvania graduate students and are for serious history buffs. Philadelphia Neighborhood Tours leads three-hour excursions through the city's ethnic neighborhoods (May–July, Sept & Oct Sat 10am; $32, or $27 for students and seniors; ℡215/599-2295), and the Mural Arts Program conducts two-hour trolley tours of the city's extensive neighborhood murals (May–Oct Sat 11am; $18, or $15 for students and seniors; ℡215/685-0754). Centipede Tours offers candlelight walks through the hidden gardens and courtyards of Society Hill, complete with a costumed guide; the tours leave from the Welcome Park at 2nd and Walnut (May–Oct Sat 6.30pm; $5; ℡215/735-3123), and Ghosts of Philadelphia leads morbid historical tours every evening from next to Independence Hall (April–Nov, call for times, reservations required; $12, or $6 for children; ℡215/413-1997, ⓦwww.ghosttour.com/Philadelphia.htm).

Accommodation

Philadelphia's luxury downtown **hotels** are prohibitively expensive, though at weekends there's a chance of getting a reduced rate. The visitor center is a great resource for accommodation discounts. **B&Bs** are a good option, but often need to be arranged in advance. La Reserve/B&B Center City (see below) can arrange rooms throughout the metropolitan area for between $50 and $100 per night.

Comfort Inn 100 N Christopher Columbus Blvd ℡215/627-7900, ⓦwww.comfortinn.com. High-rise hotel in a good location near Penn's Landing; rates include continental breakfast. Reserve online for cheaper rates. ❹

Gaskill House Bed & Breakfast 312 Gaskill St ℡215/413-0669, ⓦwww.gaskillhouse.com. Luxury three-room B&B with full kitchen, run by Guy Davis and his whippet dog Zephyr. Reservations required; discounts available for frequent and business travelers. ❺

HI-Bank Street Hostel 32 S Bank St ℡215/922-0222, ⓦwww.bankstreethostel.com. Friendly hostel wedged between Independence Hall National Park and Old City, with bunk beds for $18 (members; $21 for nonmembers), plus free tea and coffee. Cash and travelers checks only. Closed 10am–4.30pm; curfew 12.30am weekdays, 1am Fri & Sat. ❶

HI-Chamounix Mansion Philadelphia W Fairmount Park ℡215/878-3676 or 1-800/379-0017, ⓦwww.philahostel.org. Quaker country estate in a gorgeous park setting, but a bit of a trek from downtown (take bus #38 from Market St to Ford and Cranston and then walk for a mile). Midnight curfew, closed 11am–4.30pm and mid-Dec to mid-Jan; beds $15 members, $18 non-members, or $7.50 for children. ❶

Holiday Inn Cityline 4100 Presidential Blvd at City Ave ℡215/477-0200 or 1-800/642-8982. Comfortable hotel with bar, restaurant, and indoor pool in exclusive Main Line district, 10 miles from downtown. ❸–❹

La Reserve/B&B Center City 1804 Pine St ℡215/735-1137 or 215/735-0582, ⓦwww .centercitybed.com. Lovely rooms and excellent if not overly filling breakfast. The welcoming owner dispenses loads of information. ❺

Penn's View Hotel Front & Market sts ℡215/922-7600, ⓦwww.pennsviewhotel.com. Exceptional service and clean, comfortable rooms in Old City, with a very fine wine bar next to the lobby. Continental breakfast included, parking $16 per day. ❼–❽

Shippen Way Inn 418 Bainbridge St ℡215/627-7266. Newly renovated, family-run B&B with nine cozy rooms, a block from South St. ❹

Thomas Bond House 129 S 2nd St ℡1-800/845-BOND. Twelve-room restored 1769 B&B near Independence Hall National Park, slightly marred by an ugly parking lot at the rear. ❹–❺

The City

Philadelphia stretches for about two miles from the Schuylkill (pronounced "school-kill") River on the west to the Delaware River on the east; the urban area extends for many miles to the north and south, but everything you're likely to want to see is right in the central swath. The city's central districts are compact, walkable, and readily accessible from each other; Penn's sensibly planned grid system makes for easy sightseeing.

Independence Hall National Park

Any tour of Philadelphia should start with **Independence National Historic Park**, or **INHP** (☎215/597-8974 or ☎215/965-2305, ⊛www.nps .gov/inde), "America's most historic square mile." Though the park covers a mere four blocks just west of the Delaware River, between Walnut and Arch streets, it can take more than a day to explore in full. The solid redbrick buildings here, not all of which are open to the public, epitomize the Georgian (and after the Revolution, Federalist) obsession with balance and symmetry.

All INHP sites (unless otherwise specified) are open 365 days a year and admission is free; hours are usually 9am to 5pm, sometimes longer in summer. Free **tours** set off from the rear of the east wing of Independence Hall, the single most important site – call to check schedules. Throughout the day, costumed actors perform patchy but informative skits in various locations across the site – pick up a copy of the *Historic Philadelphia Gazette* pamphlet for listings.

It's best to reach **Independence Hall** early, to avoid the hordes of tourists and school parties. In peak season, free tickets must be obtained at the Independence Visitor Center. Built in 1732 as the Pennsylvania State House, this was where the Declaration of Independence was prepared, signed, and, after the pealing of the Liberty Bell, given its first public reading on July 8, 1776. Today, in the room in which Jefferson et al drafted and signed the United States Constitution, you can see George Washington's high-backed chair with the half-sun on the back – Franklin, in optimistic spirit, called it "the rising sun."

The **Liberty Bell** itself hung in Independence Hall from 1753, ringing to herald vital announcements such as victories and defeats in the Revolutionary War. Stories as to how it received its famous crack vary; one tells that it occurred while tolling the funeral of Supreme Court Chief Justice John Curtis Marshall in 1835. Whatever the truth, it rang publicly for the very last time on George Washington's birthday in 1846. Later in the century, the bell's inscription from Leviticus, advocating liberty "throughout all the land unto all the inhabitants," made it an anti-slavery symbol for the New England abolitionists – the first to call it the Liberty Bell. After the Civil War, the silent bell was adopted as a symbol of reconciliation and embarked on a national rail tour. The well-traveled and somewhat lumpen icon now rests in a shrine-like space in the new multimedia **Liberty Bell Center** in INHP.

Next door to Independence Hall, on 6th and Chestnut streets, **Congress Hall**, built in 1787 as Philadelphia County Courthouse, is where members of the new United States Congress first took their places, and where all the patterns for today's US government were established. The **First Bank of the United States**, at 3rd and Chestnut streets, was established in 1797 to formalize the new union's currency – a vital task given that even Rhode Island, the smallest state, had, at the time, three different types of currency in use.

In 1774, delegates of the first Continental Congress – predecessor of the US Congress – chose defiantly to meet at **Carpenter's Hall**, 320 Chestnut St, rather than the more commodious State House, to air their grievances against the English king. Today the building exhibits early tools and furniture (Tues–Sun 10am–4pm). Directly north, **Franklin Court**, 313 Market St, is a tribute, on the site of his home, to Benjamin Franklin. The house no longer stands, but steel frames outline the original structure. An underground museum has dial-a-quote recordings of his pithy sayings and the musings of his contemporaries, as well as a working printshop. The **B Free Franklin Post Office**, 316 Market St, sells stamps and includes a small postal museum.

Other buildings in the park include the original **Free Quaker Meeting House**, two blocks north of Market at 5th and Arch, built in 1783 by the small group of Quakers who actually fought in the Revolutionary War. There's also the **Philosophical Hall**, 104 S 5th St, still used today by the nation's first philosophical debating society (which was founded by Franklin). Although most of the building is closed to the public, exhibitions such as "Stuffing Birds, Pressing Plants, Shaping Knowledge: Natural History in North America 1730–1860" (March–Sept Wed–Sun 10am–4pm; rest of year Thurs–Sun 10am–4pm; free) provide insights into the history of American science. The must-see new **National Constitution Center**, 525 Arch St (daily 9.30am–5.30pm; $6; ☎1-866/917-1787 or ☎215/409-6600, ⓦwww.constitutioncenter.org), a modern, interactive, and provocative museum dedicated to the nation's best-known document, offers a wealth of information and a number of understated but delicious jabs at the current presidential administration.

Old City

INHP runs north into **Old City**, Philadelphia's earliest commercial area, above Market Street near the riverfront. Washington, Franklin, and Betsy Ross all worshiped at **Christ Church**, on 2nd Street just north of Market. Dating from 1727, it is surrounded by the gravestones of signatories to the Declaration of Independence (call for tour schedules; donation; ☎215/922-1695, ⓦwww.christchurchphila.org). The church's official burial ground, two blocks west at 5th and Arch, includes **Benjamin Franklin's grave**. At 239 Arch St, the **Betsy Ross House** (April–Oct daily 10am–5pm; Nov–March Tues–Sun 10am–5pm; donation; ☎215/686-1252, ⓦwww.betsyrosshouse.org), by means of unimpressive wax dummies, salutes the woman credited with making the first American flag. The story is probably apocryphal, as it wasn't until the centennial celebrations in 1876 that a man claiming to be Ross's grandson came forward to stake his grandmother's claim. Even if she did live at 239 Arch St, the building that currently holds that address was not her home; the streets have been extensively renamed and renumbered since the Revolution. Inside the house, there's a gift shop and shady **garden**, an oasis away from the busy streets outside.

The claim of **Elfreth's Alley** – a pretty little cobbled way off 2nd Street between Arch and Race streets – to be the "oldest street in the United States" is somewhat dubious, though it has been in continuous residential use since 1727; its thirty houses, notable for their wrought-iron gates, water pumps, wooden shutters, and attic rooms, date from the eighteenth century. At no. 126 is the **Mantua Maker's Museum** (March–Oct Mon–Sat 10am–5pm, Sun noon–5pm; Nov–Feb Thurs–Sat 10am–5pm, Sun noon–5pm; $2; ☎215/574-0560), where furniture was made for Philadelphia's elite in the eighteenth century.

The area north of Market Street also holds two excellent museums: the **National Museum of American Jewish History**, 55 N 5th St (Mon–Thurs 10am–5pm, Fri 10am–3pm, Sun noon–5pm; free; ☎215/923-3811, ⓦwww.nmajh.org), which is dedicated to the experiences of Jews in the States and includes a synagogue and a Statue of Religious Liberty; and the emotive and politically informed **African American Museum in Philadelphia**, 7th and Arch streets (Tues–Sat 10am–5pm, Sun noon–5pm; $6; ☎215/574-0380, ⓦaampmuseum.org). The latter tells the stories of the thousands of blacks who migrated north to Philadelphia after Reconstruction (see p.1386) and in the early twentieth century. As well as lectures, films, and concerts, there are photos, personal memorabilia, poems by black poet Langston Hughes, and a piped-in Billie Holiday soundtrack. The **Edgar Allan Poe National Historic Site**, 532 N 7th St, just north of Spring Garden Street (Wed–Sun 9am–5pm; free;

T 215/597-8780, W www.nps.gov/edal), is the only one of Poe's five Philadelphia residences that survives; it's also where he wrote "The Black Cat" in 1843. The stripped-down walls and bare wooden floors do little to evoke Poe's presence; however, if you're a true Poe fanatic, the staff in the small **museum** adjacent to the house can answer almost any Poe-related question. If you're keen on literary pilgrimages, you might also want to visit the grave of another key figure of American letters, **Walt Whitman**; he's buried in the Harleigh Cemetery, on Haddon Avenue across the river in Camden, New Jersey (see below for ferry information). The Old City is also home to a number of **art galleries**, clustered around N 2nd and 3rd streets (information and gallery map at W www.oldcity.org), and to September's annual Philadelphia Fringe Festival, a popular experimental theater series (T 215/413-9006, W www .pafringe.org).

Penn's Landing

Just east of Old City along the Delaware River, where William Penn stepped off in 1682, spreads the huge and heavily industrialized port of Philadelphia. Along the port's southern reaches, on the river side of the I-95 freeway, the old docklands have been renovated as part of the **Penn's Landing** development, which includes the **Independence Seaport Museum** (daily 10am–5pm; $8, free Sun 10am–noon; T 215/925-5439, W seaport .philly.com) and a variety of historical **ships**, including the flagship USS *Olympia* and the World War II submarine *Becuna* (both daily 10am–5pm; $8), and the three-masted Portuguese Tall Ship *Gazela*, built in 1883 (open irregularly for admission, though always for the annual Halloween "Haunted Ship" event; donation requested; W www.gazela.org). All along the riverfront promenade are food stalls, landscaped pools, and fountains, and regular outdoor concerts and festivals are held here. A **ferry** crosses the Delaware (Riverlink Ferry; $6 round trip; T 215/925-LINK, W www.riverlinkferry .org) to the down-at-heel town of **Camden**, where the main attraction is the **New Jersey State Aquarium** (mid-April to mid-Sept daily 9.30am–5.30pm; mid-Sept to mid-April Mon–Fri 9.30am–4.30pm, Sat & Sun 10am–5pm; $14; T 856/365-3300, W www.njaquarium.org) – good for kids but otherwise eminently missable. A $21.50 River Pass covers the museum, ships, aquarium, and a round-trip on the ferry.

Society Hill

Society Hill, an elegant residential area west of the Delaware and directly south of INHP, spreads between Walnut and Lombard streets. Though it is indeed Philadelphia's high society that lives here now, the area was named for its first inhabitants, the Free Society of Traders – a rather more fun-loving bunch than the strict Quakers who lived to the north. After falling into disrepair, the Hill itself was flattened in the early 1970s to provide a building site for I.M. Pei's twin skyscrapers, Society Hill Towers. Luckily, the rest of the neighborhood has been restored to form one of the city's most picturesque districts: cobbled gas-lit streets are lined with immaculately kept Colonial, Federal, and Georgian homes, often featuring the state's namesake keystones on their window frames, and markers everywhere point out the area's rich history. One of the few buildings open to the public is the **Physick House**, 321 S 4th St, home to Dr Philip Syng Physick, "the Father of American Surgery," and filled with eighteenth- and nineteenth-century decorative arts (June–Aug Thurs–Sat noon–4pm; Sept–May Thurs–Sat 11am–2pm; $4; T 215/925-2251, W www .philalandmarks.org).

Center City

Center City, Philadelphia's main business and commercial area, stretches from 8th Street west to the Schuylkill River, dominated by the endearing Baroque wedding cake of **City Hall** and its 37ft bronze statue of Penn. Before ascending thirty stories to the observation deck at Penn's feet, check out the quirky sculptures and carvings around the building, including the cats and mice at the south entrance.

A couple of blocks north at Broad and Cherry streets, the **Pennsylvania Academy of the Fine Arts** (Tues–Sat 10am–5pm, Sun 11am–5pm; $5; ☎215/972-7600, ⊛www.pafa.org), housed in an elaborate, multicolored Victorian pile, exhibits three hundred years of American art, including works by Mary Cassatt, Thomas Eakins, and Winslow Homer.

Beginning at 8th Street, **Chinatown**, marked by the gorgeous 40ft Friendship Gate at 10th and Arch, has some of the best inexpensive food in the city. A block over on 12th Street is the century-old **Reading Terminal Market** (☎215/922-2317, ⊛www.readingterminalmarket.org), where many Amish farmers come to the city to sell their produce. It's always good for a lively time and makes a great lunch spot. Next door, the decade-old Convention Center helped usher in flashy hotels, coffeehouses, and restaurants, to replace the previously derelict shops and offices.

Rittenhouse Square

Grassy **Rittenhouse Square**, one of Penn's original city squares, is in a very fashionable part of town. On one side it borders chic Walnut Street, on the other a residential area of solid brownstones with beautifully carved doors and windows. The redbrick 1860 **Rosenbach Museum**, 2010 Delancey Place, holds over thirty thousand rare books, as well as James Joyce's original hand-scrawled manuscripts of *Ulysses* (Tues, Thurs, Fri–Sun 10am–5pm, Wed 10am–8pm; $8, including tour; ☎215/732-1600, ⊛www.rosenbach.org). On summer evenings there are free outdoor jazz and R&B concerts in the square.

Three blocks northwest from the square, the **Mütter Museum**, 19 S 22nd St in the College of Physicians (between Chestnut and Market; daily 10am–5pm; $9; ☎215/563-3737, ⊛www.collphyphil.org/musadm.htm), is not for the squeamish. Filled with weird pathological and medical oddities – including sickeningly lifelike wax models of tumors and skin infections, alongside closets full of skeletons, syphilitic skulls, pickled internal organs, and the death cast of a pair of Siamese twins – it's unique to say the least.

Museum Row

The mile-long Benjamin Franklin Parkway, known as Museum Row – or, less convincingly, as "America's Champs-Elysees" – sweeps northwest from City Hall to the colossal Museum of Art in **Fairmount Park**, an area of countryside annexed by the city in the nineteenth century. Spanning nine hundred scenic acres on both sides of the Schuylkill River, this is one of the world's largest landscaped city parks, with jogging, biking, and hiking trails, early American homes, an all-wars memorial to the state's black soldiers, and a zoo – the country's first – at 3400 W Girard Ave (Feb–Nov 9.30am–5pm, Dec–Jan 9.30am–4pm; $15 in season, $10 out of season; ☎215/243-1100, ⊛www.phillyzoo.org). In the late 1960s, local residents **Muhammad Ali** and **Joe Frazier** all but brought the city to a standstill with the announcement one afternoon that they were heading to Fairmount for an informal slug-out.

Sylvester Stallone later immortalized the steps of the **Philadelphia Museum of Art**, 26th St and Franklin Pkwy (Tues, Thurs, Sat & Sun 10am–5pm, Wed

& Fri 10am–8.45pm, second-floor galleries closed except to tours after 5pm; $10, Sun pay what you wish; ☎215/763-8100, Ⓦwww.philamuseum.org), by running up them in the film *Rocky*, but he missed out on a real treat inside: one of the finest collections in the US, with a twelfth-century French cloister, Renaissance art, a complete **Robert Adam** interior from a 1765 house in London's Berkeley Square, Rubens tapestries, Pennsylvania Dutch crafts and **Shaker furniture**, a strong **Impressionist** collection, and the world's most extensive collection of the works of **Marcel Duchamp**. Exhibits are displayed in an easy-to-follow chronological order. On Wednesday and Friday nights, there are excellent programs of live jazz and classical music along with film showings and artistic debate – all included in the admission price.

A few blocks away, at Franklin Parkway and 22nd Street, the exquisite **Rodin Museum** (Tues–Sun 10am–5pm; $3 suggested donation; ☎215/763-8100, Ⓦwww.rodinmuseum.org), marble-walled and set in a shady garden with a green pool, holds the largest collection of Rodin's Impressionistic sculptures and casts outside of Paris, including *The Burghers of Calais*, *The Thinker*, and *The Gates of Hell*. Among the rare books at the **Free Library of Philadelphia**, 19th and Vine streets (Mon–Thurs 9am–9pm, Fri 9am–6pm, Sat 9am–5pm, tours at 11am; free; ☎215/686-5322, Ⓦwww.library.phila.gov), are cuneiform tablets from 3000 BC, medieval manuscripts, first editions of Dickens and Poe, and such intriguing titles as the 1807 *Inquiry into the Conduct of the Princess of Wales*.

Over the road, in the vast **Franklin Institute Science Museum**, N 20th St and Benjamin Franklin Pkwy (Sat–Thurs 9.30am–5pm, Fri 9am–9pm; $12.75; ☎215/448-1200, Ⓦsln.fi.edu), are a **Planetarium**, the **Tuttleman IMAX Theater** ($8), and the **Mandell Futures Center**. A combination ticket ($16.75) covers admission to all three. Continuing the educational theme, the nearby **Academy of Natural Sciences** exhibits dinosaurs, mummies, and gems (Mon–Fri 10am–4.30pm, Sat, Sun & holidays 10am–5pm; $9; ☎215-299-1000, Ⓦwww.acnatsci.org), while the **Please Touch Museum**, 210 N 21st St (daily: July–Aug 9am–5pm rest of year 9am–4.30pm; $9; ☎215/963-0667, Ⓦwww.pleasetouchmuseum.org), is a hands-on adventureland aimed at youngsters.

Eastern State Penitentiary

One of Philadelphia's most significant historic sites stands, all but forgotten, just a short walk from the Fairmount Park museums. The **Eastern State Penitentiary**, whose gloomy Gothic fortifications fill an entire block of the residential neighborhood along Fairmount Ave at 22nd St, embodies an almost complete history of attitudes toward crime and punishment in the US. Since it opened in 1829, the Quaker-inspired prison's radical efforts to rehabilitate inmates via isolation, rather than use physical abuse and capital punishment, attracted curious social commentators from around the world; when Charles Dickens came to America in 1842, he wanted to see two things, this prison and Niagara Falls. Though it underwent substantial changes in its 140-year history, and has slowly decayed since its final closure in 1970, the bulk of the Panopticon-style radial prison survives, and preservationists have recently completed a major restoration program. **Guided tours** leave on the hour (April–Nov Wed–Sun 10am–5pm; May–June & Oct–Nov Sat & Sun 10am–5pm, last entry 4pm; $9, or $7 for students and seniors, and $4 for children; ☎215/236-3300, Ⓦwww.easternstate.org) and point out the prison's many novel architectural features, as well as its old synagogue, the cell where Al Capone cooled his heels, and the block where Tina Turner filmed a music video.

West Philadelphia

Across the Schuylkill River, **West Philadelphia** is home to the Ivy-League **University of Pennsylvania**, where Franklin established the country's first medical school. The compact but extremely pleasant campus blends into fairly gritty urban areas, but has some great museums: the small **Institute of Contemporary Art**, 118 S 36th St (Wed–Fri noon–8pm, Sat & Sun 11am–5pm; $3, free Sundays; ☎215/898-5911, ⓦwww.icaphila.org), which displays cutting-edge traveling exhibitions in an airy space, complete with a very comfortable bean-bag chair lobby, and the intriguing **Arthur Ross Gallery**, 220 S 34th St (Tues–Fri 10am–5pm, Sat & Sun noon–5pm; free; ☎215/898-2083, ⓦwww.upenn.edu/ARG), which features changing exhibits, particularly of international and innovative work, many of which have a strong emphasis on the use of color. The superlative **Museum of Archeology and Anthropology**, 33rd and Spruce streets (year-round Tues–Sat 10am–4.30pm; Sept–May also Sun 1–5pm; $5, free Sundays; ☎215/898-4000, ⓦwww.museum.upenn.edu), is the university's top draw. Regarded by experts as one of the world's finest science museums, its exhibits span all the continents and their major epochs – from Nigerian Benin bronzes to Chinese crystal balls. Most astonishing is the priceless twelve-ton granite Sphinx of Rameses II, c.1293–1185 BC, in the Lower Egyptian Gallery. The Meso-American and Greco-Roman Galleries also hold plenty of highlights.

South Philadelphia

Staunchly blue-collar **South Philadelphia**, center of Philadelphia's black community since the Civil War, is also home to many of the city's Italians; opera singer **Mario Lanza** (who has his own museum at 712 Montrose St) and pop stars Fabian and Chubby Checker grew up here. It's also where to come for an authentic – and very messy – **Philly cheesesteak** (see "Eating," below), and to rummage through the wonderful **Italian Market** (another *Rocky* location) which runs along 9th Street south from Christian Street. One of the last surviving urban markets in the US, the wooden market stalls that have stood here for generations are packed to overflowing with bric-a-brac, produce, secondhand Levis, live seafood, and, most famously, mozzarella.

South Street, the original boundary of the city, is now Philadelphia's main **nightlife** district, with dozens of cafés, bars, restaurants, and nightclubs lined up along the few blocks west from Front Street. During the day you can wander amongst the many good book, record, and clothing **shops** (the Book Trader, 501 South St, is open daily until midnight). At night, it makes a lively, if highly commercial, evening out – and is perhaps best avoided on summer weekends when the throngs of visitors can be especially overwhelming.

Eating

Eating out in Philadelphia is a real treat: the ubiquitous street stands sell **soft pretzels** with mustard for 40¢, Chinatown and the Italian Market are good for ethnic food, and Reading Terminal Market makes a bargain lunch stop in Center City. South Street has plenty of good, if well-touristed, eateries, while pricier, trendier restaurants cluster along S 2nd Street in the Old City. The South Philly **cheesesteak**, a sandwich of wafer-thin roast beef topped with melted cheese (or, if you're going to be truly authentic, Cheez Whiz), varies from place to place around town; some of the best are to be found around 9th and Passyunk in South Philadelphia (see *Pat's*, below). Bear in mind that a cheesesteak is hot, while a **hoagie** (complete with lettuce and tomato) is not.

Circa 1518 Walnut St ☎215/545-6800. Stylish Center City restaurant decked out in marble, mirrors, and chandeliers, offering reasonably priced meat and seafood dinners with innovative twists. Great happy hours on Thurs & Fri; techno music later at night.

City Tavern 138 S 2nd St ☎215/413-1443, ⓦwww.citytavern.com. Reconstructed 1773 tavern in INHP, familiar to the city's founders, and called by John Adams "the most genteel tavern in America." Chef Walter Staib cooks and costumed staff serve "olde style" food (pasties, turkey rarebit) to a harpsichord accompaniment – entrees start around $18. Lunch is less expensive.

The Continental 138 Market St ☎215/923-6069. Trendy Asian-inflected diner and martini bar, with chic indoor decor and a nondescript facade.

Cuba Libre 10 S 2nd St ☎215/627-0666. Decidedly average Cuban fare, redeemed by decor strongly resembling the set of the film *Original Sin* and decked liberally with real palm trees, and a small bar offering good cocktails and excellent *mojitos*.

Delilah's Reading Terminal Market, 12th and Spruce sts ☎215/574-0929. Superb, extremely cheap soul food with scatty service. Oprah Winfrey nominated their mac and cheese as the best in the nation.

Pat's King of Steaks 1237 E Passyunk Ave ☎215/468-1546, ⓦwww.patskingofsteaks.com.

At this delightfully decrepit, outdoor-seating-only cheesesteak joint, take care to order correctly (there's a sign to help "rookies") or prepare yourself to be sent to the back of the line. The cheesesteaks here are the real deal. Open 24hr, 361 days a year.

San Carlo 214 South Street ☎215/592-9777. Excellent fresh pasta dishes, nice atmosphere, and attentive – if pushy – service at reasonable prices.

Serrano 20 S 2nd St ☎215/928-0770. Intimate Old City café serving creative international fusion cooking, with good fresh seafood. Try the appetizer tasting menu. Diners get preferential seating at the *Tin Angel* folk club upstairs (see below).

Sonoma 4411 Main St, Manayunk ☎215/483-9400. Pleasant, reasonably priced California-style Italian restaurant.

South Street Diner 140 South St ☎215/627-5258. Huge menu with Greek and Italian specialties from $6.95. Open daily 7am–3am.

Tony Luke Jr's 118 S 18th St ☎215/568-4630. Excellent steak sandwiches and hoagies.

Tre Scalini 1533 S 11th St ☎215/551-3870. A taste of traditional South Philly Italian, with reasonably priced dishes and a low-key atmosphere.

White Dog Café 3420 Sansom St ☎215/386-9224, ⓦwww.whitedog.com. Delicious, creative food in three Victorian brownstones near the universities. Artsy, student crowd; lunch entrees $7–12; happy hour Sun–Thurs 10pm–midnight.

Drinking

The most popular place for bar-hopping is **South Street**, although **2nd Street** in the Old City is rapidly becoming the area for the trendiest bars. Local brews are popular and inexpensive; try Yuengling lager, bottled by "America's Oldest Brewery." Philly's growing number of **cafés** are spread around the city; South Street, 2nd Street, and Center City have the densest concentrations.

Dirty Frank's 347 S 13th St ☎215/732-5010. Popular with a very mixed crowd, this Philly institution touts itself as "one of the few places in the world where you can drink a $2.25 pint of Yuengling underneath oil paintings by nationally recognized artists."

The Khyber 56 S 2nd St ☎215/238-5888, ⓦwww.thekhyber.com. Philly's most convivial bar, with a huge range of beers; it's also a reliable place to hear local bands (see "Nightlife and entertainment," below).

Last Drop Coffeehouse 1300 Pine St ☎215/893-9262. Trendy café serving Philly's best espresso. Moderately reliable Internet access and lots of flyers.

The Mean Bean Co. 1112 Locust St ☎215/925-2010. Coffeeshop serving a mixed gay and straight crowd, with outdoor seating next to the lovely Sartain St private community garden.

Society Hill 301 Chestnut St ☎215/925-1919. Swanky bar a stone's throw from the *Bank Street Hostel*. Live jazz piano music Tuesday evenings.

Sugar Mom's Church Street Lounge 225 Church St ☎215/925-8219. Popular basement bar where the jukebox ranges from Tony Bennett to Sonic Youth, with a dozen international beers on tap.

Tangier Café 1801 Lombard St ☎215/732-5006. Cozy, attractive local bar with inexpensive bottles of Yuengling, friendly bar staff, and a low-key atmosphere.

Woody's Bar and Restaurant 202 S 13th St ☎215/545-1893. Large, friendly downtown beer bar popular with Philly's gay community.

Nightlife and entertainment

Few reminders are left of the 1970s "Philly Sound"; stars like Patti LaBelle, the O'Jays, and Harold "If You Don't Love Me By Now" Melvin and the Blue Notes have waned, though their legacy is readily apparent in the soulful lyrics of contemporary artists like rapper Eve. It's also a decent place to see rock bands: most of the names that play New York come down here and tickets are half the price or even less. The world-famous **Philadelphia Orchestra** performs at the grand new Kimmel Center for the Performing Arts (℡215/893-1999, ⓦwww.kimmelcenter.org). Philadelphia's other great strength is its **theater** scene, where small venues abound. Check the **listings** in the free *City Paper* or *Philadelphia Weekly* newspapers, or visit the Theatre Alliance website at ⓦwww.theatrealliance.org, which also features the StageTix discount ticket program. Discount offers to various events are also available on the GoPhila website at ⓦwww.gophila.com/events.

The Khyber 56 S 2nd St ℡215/238-5888, ⓦwww.thekhyber.com. Small rock venue with a gargoyle-lined bar, bluesy jukebox, and casual young clientele. Cover around $7–8 when bands are on.

Painted Bride Art Center 230 Vine St ℡215/925-9914, ⓦwww.paintedbride.org. Art gallery with live jazz, dance, and theater performances after dark.

Silk City Lounge 5th and Spring Garden sts ℡215/592-8838, ⓦwww.silkcitylounge.com. Very mixed musical bag – funk, hip-hop, acid jazz, indie, dance, and soul – in an ultratrendy but unflashy club. Local bands play on weekends.

Theater of Living Arts 334 South St ℡215/922-1011, ⓦwww.theateroflivingarts.net. Converted movie palace that's the best place to catch rock bands.

Tin Angel 20 S 2nd St ℡215/928-0770, ⓦwww.tinangel.com. Intimate upstairs bar and coffeehouse, featuring top local and nationally known folk and acoustic acts.

Trocadero 1003 Arch St ℡215/922-LIVE, ⓦwww.thetroc.com. Trendy downtown music venue, sometimes featuring big-name alternative bands. Cover varies, and ID is essential.

Warmdaddy's 4 S Front St ℡215/627-2500, ⓦwww.warmdaddys.com. Restaurant and bar with live blues nightly, frequent special events, and a buzzing atmosphere; something of a Penn's Landing institution.

Zanzibar Blue 200 S Broad St in the *Bellevue Hotel* ℡215/732-4500, ⓦwww.zanzibarblue.com. Classy restaurant and club with contemporary New York–style jazz nightly, often by famous names; expect a hefty cover charge and two-drink minimum.

Central Pennsylvania

Central Pennsylvania, cut north to south by the broad **Susquehanna River**, has no major cities – though the state capital, **Harrisburg**, is an excellent base from which to explore sights that include the **Hershey** chocolate empire and the rolling Amish farmlands of **Lancaster County** to the east, and the Civil War site of **Gettysburg** on the state's southern border. To the north, the mighty forests of the "Grand Canyon of Pennsylvania," around **Williamsport**, reveal the legacy of its great nineteenth-century lumber wealth in mansion-lined streets. **Johnstown**, beyond the dramatic Allegheny Mountains in the west, and **Scranton** are industrial towns with little of interest for the casual visitor.

Lancaster County – Pennsylvania Dutch Country

Lancaster County, fifty miles west of Philadelphia, stretches for about 45 miles from Churchtown in the east to the Susquehanna River in the west.

Although tiny, uncosmopolitan Lancaster City, ten miles east of the river, was US capital for a day in September 1777, the region is famed more for its preponderance of agricultural religious communities, known collectively as the **Pennsylvania Dutch** (who have no connection to the Netherlands; the name is a mistaken derivation of Deutsch, or German).

An extremely touristy place even before it was brought to international fame by the movie *Witness*, Lancaster County has maintained its natural beauty in the face of encroaching commercialization. It is a region of gentle countryside and fertile farmlands, mule-drawn ploughs, tiny roadside bakeries crammed with jams and pies, Amish children wending on old-fashioned scooters to and from their one-room schoolhouses, and flower-filled, immaculate farmhouses. However, attempting to live a simple life away from the pressures of the outside world has proved too much for many Pennsylvania Dutch. A few (mainly Mennonites) have succumbed to commercial need by offering rides in their buggies and meals in their homes. Members of the stricter orders in particular have moved away from the ceaseless intrusions of privacy – as well as soaring land prices – to less touristed Ohio, Indiana, Minnesota, and Iowa. Be prepared for a strong smell of horses and cows in much of the county; remember also that as Sunday is a day of rest for the Amish, many attractions, restaurants, and other amenities will be closed.

Arrival and information

The Pennsylvania Turnpike sweeps across the north of the region, but most activity is concentrated further south near US-30, which runs east–west. **Amtrak** arrives at the train station at 53 McGovern Ave, Lancaster, as do buses from Capital Trailways (☎717/397-4861) and Greyhound. The bustling **Pennsylvania Dutch Convention and Visitors Bureau**, just off US-30 at 501 Greenfield Rd (daily 8.30am–5pm, longer hours in summer; ☎717/299-8901 or 1-800/PADUTCH, ⊛www.padutchcountry.com), does an excellent job of providing orientation and advice on accommodation. Visitors keen to learn about Pennsylvania Dutch culture should head to the excellent **People's Place**, Main Street, Intercourse, eleven miles east of Lancaster City, which has a well-stocked bookstore, an informative if sentimental slide show, an Amish museum, showings of *Hazel's People*, a fictional film about a non-Mennonite

The Pennsylvania Dutch

The people now known as the Pennsylvania Dutch originated as **Anabaptists** in sixteenth-century Switzerland, under the leadership of Menno Simons. His unorthodox advocacy of adult baptism and literal interpretation of the Bible led to the order's persecution; they were invited by William Penn to settle in Lancaster County in the 1720s. Today the twenty or so orders of Pennsylvania Dutch include the "plain" Old Order **Amish** (a strict order that originally broke away from Simons in 1693) and freer-living **Mennonites**, as well as the "fancy" **Lutheran** groups (distinguished by the colorful circular "hex" signs on their barns). Living by an unwritten set of rules called Amish Ordnung, the Amish are the strictest and best-known: the men with their wide-brimmed straw hats and beards (but no "military" mustaches), the women in bonnets, plain dresses (with no fripperies like buttons), and aprons. Shunning electricity and any exposure to the corrupting influence of the outside world, the Amish power their farms with generators, and travel (at roughly ten miles per hour) in handmade horse-drawn buggies. For all their insularity, the Amish are very friendly and helpful; resist the temptation to photograph them, however, as the making of "graven images" offends their beliefs.

encountering the Mennonite community, plus displays of quilts and artwork (late May–Aug Mon–Sat 9.30am–7pm; rest of year Mon–Sat 9.30am–5pm; $8 film and exhibit; ☎717/768-7171, ⓦwww.thepeoplesplace.com). The **Mennonite Information Center**, off US-30 at 2209 Millstream Rd, organizes lodging with Mennonite families. Call at least two hours ahead for a guide to take you on a two-hour, $28 tour in your car (April–Oct Mon–Sat 8am–5pm; Nov–March Mon–Sat 8.30am–4.30pm; ☎717/299-0954, ⓦwww .mennoniteinfoctr.com).

Getting around and tours

Winding country lanes weave through Pennsylvania Dutch Country, passing small villages with eccentric-sounding names such as **Intercourse** (source of many droll postcards, but supposedly named for its location on the junction of two main roads). Although a **car** will get you to the quieter back roads that the tour buses miss, it's more fun to **ride a bike**. Only then can you feel the benefits of all that fresh air – and it shows more consideration for the horse-drawn buggies with which you share the road. For self-guided **bike tours**, contact Dreamride in Lancaster City (☎717/397-2503).

The Amish Experience, on US-30 at Plain & Fancy Farm (☎717/768-3600, ⓦwww.amishexperience.com), runs two-hour farmlands **tours** (Mon–Sat 10.30am & 2pm, Sun 11.30am only) for $21, though some accommodations (see the *Village Inn*, below) offer a similar service for free. Ed's Buggy Rides on US-896, north of Strasburg, offers lolloping three-mile countryside excursions for $8 (☎717/687-0360).

Accommodation

Accommodation options in Pennsylvania Dutch Country range from reasonably priced **hotels** and **B&Bs** (consult ⓦwww.authenticbandb.com for a list of local establishments) in and around Lancaster City, through **farm vacations** (ask at the Pennsylvania Dutch Visitors Bureau; see "Arrival and information," above) to **campgrounds**. *White Oak Campgrounds*, 372 White Oak Rd, Quarryville, four miles north of Strasburg (reservations recommended; $20 for tent for two; ☎717/687-6207), overlooks the heart of the Dutch farmlands and hosts a county auction on Saturdays.

Cameron Estate Inn & Restaurant 1855 Mansion Lane, Mount Joy ☎717/492-0111, ⓦwww.cameronestateinn.com. Out-of-the-way gay-friendly inn on fifteen acres with sparkling, comfortable rooms (one with Jacuzzi), free full breakfast, restaurant, and reasonable prices. ❹
Countryside Motel 134 Hartman Bridge Rd ☎717/687-8431. Clean and simple place six miles east of Lancaster City on Hwy-896. ❸
Historic Strasburg Inn Rte-896, Strasburg ☎717/687-7691 or 1-800/872-0201, ⓦwww.historicstrasburginn.com. One hundred luxury rooms tucked away in sixty rolling acres of land. ❹–❻

O'Flaherty's Dingeldein House 1105 E King St, Lancaster City ☎717/293-1723 or 1-800/779-7765, ⓦwww.dingeldeinhouse.com. Friendly seven-room B&B. Rates include a large country breakfast. ❸
Village Inn 2695 Old Philadelphia Pike, Bird-in-Hand ☎1-800/665-8780, ⓦwww.bird-in-hand .com/villageinn. Excellent old inn with modern amenities, large breakfast, deck, lawn, and back pasture. Price includes 2hr tour of Amish Country and use of the adjacent motel's pool. Book ahead. ❹

Touring Pennsylvania Dutch Country

Though useful for a general overview and historical insight, the attractions that interpret Amish culture tend toward overkill. It's far more satisfying just to explore the countryside for yourself. Here, among the streams with their covered bridges and fields striped with corn, alfalfa, and tobacco, the reality hits you – these aren't actors re-creating an ancient lifestyle, but real people, part of a living, working community. There's no guarantee as to what you'll see: on Sunday, for example, there are no quilt sales or bake shops, and the farmers don't work the fields, but there may well be a large gathering of buggies outside one of the farms, indicating an Amish church service (in High German) or a "visiting day," when families gather socially. Church services and visiting days take place on alternating Sundays; visits sometimes occur during the week as well.

Among the widely spread formal attractions, the **Ephrata Cloister**, 632 W Main St, Ephrata (on US-272 and 322), re-creates the eighteenth-century settlement of German Protestant celibates that acted, amongst other things, as an early publishing and printing center (Mon–Sat 9am–5pm, Sun noon–5pm, closed Mon in Jan & Feb; $7; ☎717/733-6600). Further south, about three miles northeast of Lancaster City, the **Landis Valley Museum**, 2451 Kissell Hill Rd (Tues–Sat 9am–5pm, Sun noon–5pm; $9; ☎717/569-0401, ⓦwww.landisvalleymuseum .org), is a living history museum of rural life, with demonstrations of local crafts.

In Lancaster City itself, a stolid redbrick town with tree-lined avenues, the **Heritage Center Museum**, in Penn Square (mid-April through Dec Tues–Sat 10am–5pm; free; ☎717/299-6440, ⓦwww.lancasterheritage.com), exhibits Lancaster master crafts, including wagons and rifles, ancient Amish calligraphy known as fraktur, clocks, wooden toys, weathervanes, and quilts. At **Strasburg**, a mixture of tourist kitsch and historical authenticity southeast of Lancaster City on US-896, the **Strasburg Railroad** gives 45-minute round-trip rides in original steam trains through patchwork farmland to Paradise (daily, hours vary, call for updated schedule; $9.25, or $4.75 for children; ☎717/687-7522, ⓦwww.strasburgrailroad.com). Disappointingly, **Paradise** holds no heavenly delights, but there are some good views on the way (if little that couldn't be seen by bike or car), and the train makes regular picnic stops. The oldest building in the county, the **Hans Herr House**, 1849 Hans Herr Drive, five miles south of downtown Lancaster City off US-222 (April–Nov Mon–Sat 9am–4pm; $4; ☎717/464-4438, ⓦwww.hansherr.org), is a 1719 Mennonite church with a pretty garden and orchard, a medieval German facade, and exhibits on early farm life.

Eating, drinking, and entertainment

Lancaster County **food** is delicious, Germanic, and served in vast quantities. There are no Amish-owned restaurants, but Amish roadside stalls sell fresh homemade root beer, jams, pickles, breads, and pies. The huge "all-you-care-to-eat" **tourist restaurants** on US-30 and US-340 may look off-putting, all pseudo-rusticism with costumed waitresses, but most serve good meals, for around $13.50, "family-style" – you share long tables and mountains of fried chicken, sauerkraut, noodles, pickles, cottage cheese and apple butter, corn, hickory-smoked ham, schnitz und knepp (apple, ham, and dumpling stew), shoo-fly pie and the like with crowds of other out-of-towners. None stays open later than 8pm. A few other restaurants, particularly **diners** in busy areas, are open later at night. Rural Lancaster County is, unsurprisingly, not known for its nightlife – though there are a couple of very friendly **bars** in downtown Lancaster City worth checking out. The Fulton Opera House, 12 N Prince St (☎717/394-7133, ⓦwww.fultontheatre.org), is a plush red-and-gold restored Victorian **theater**, hosting dance, plays, and special events.

Central Market Penn Square, Lancaster City. Covered market selling fresh local farm produce and lunch to loyal Lancastrians and tourists alike.

Tues, Fri & Sat 6am–4.30pm.
Good 'n' Plenty East Brook Rd, US-896, Smoketown ☎717/394-7111. Not Amish-owned,

though Amish women cook and serve food in this, the best of the family-style restaurants. Open early Feb to mid-Dec Mon–Sat 11.30am–8pm.
Lancaster Brewing Co. 302 N Plum St, Lancaster City ☎717/391-MALT, ⓦwww .lancasterbrewing.com. Brewpub serving good bar food and five different microbrews. Tours given Fri & Sat by appointment. Open daily.
Lancaster Dispensing Co. 33-35 N Market St, Lancaster City ☎717/299-4602, ⓦwww .dispensingco.com. Downtown Lancaster's trendiest, friendliest bar, with live weekend jazz and

blues, plus overstuffed sandwiches for around $6.
Lapp's 2270 Lincoln Hwy E ☎717/394-1606. A solid diner with the family atmosphere and ample Germanic food typical of Lancaster County, open seven days a week.
Molly's Pub 253 E Chestnut St, Lancaster City ☎717/396-0225. Neighborhood bar with lively atmosphere and good burgers. Closed Sun.
Plain and Fancy 3121 Old Philadelphia Pike (Rte-340), Bird-in-Hand ☎717/768-4400. Standard family-style restaurant, the only one in the area that's open on Sundays.

Harrisburg and Hershey

HARRISBURG, Pennsylvania's capital, lies on the Susquehanna River thirty or so miles northwest of Lancaster City. It's a surprisingly attractive small city, its lush waterfront lined with shuttered colonial buildings, and is well-complemented by its kitschy Chocolatetown neighbor **Hershey**. Harrisburg is also known as the site of the **Three Mile Island** nuclear facility, which suffered a famous meltdown in the 1970s and stands along the river on the east side of town.

The ornate, attractive Italian Renaissance **capitol** at Third and State streets has a dome modeled after St Peter's in Rome (tours Mon–Fri 8.30am–4pm; Sat, Sun & holidays at 9am, 11am, 1pm & 3pm; free; ☎1-800/TOUR-N-PA). The complex includes the archeological and military artifacts, decorative arts, tools and machinery exhibited in the four-floor **State Museum of Pennsylvania**, a cylindrical building that holds a planetarium, at Third and North (Tues–Sat 9am–5pm, Sun noon–5pm; free; ☎717/787-4980, ⓦwww.statemuseumpa.org). But undoubtedly the real attraction here is the excellent **National Civil War Museum**, at Lincoln Circle off Market Street (Mon–Sat 9am–5pm, Sun 10am–5pm; $7; ☎717/260-1861 or 1-866/258-4729, ⓦwww.nationalcivilwarmuseum.org). Almost 730,000 Americans were killed in the Civil War – more than in all other conflicts since the Revolution combined – and the museum offers an intelligent analysis of the reasons for, and results of, the war. Especially evocative are the fictionalized monologues, playing on video screens in every gallery, which focus on the human cost of the conflict. There's also a good terrace café with great views across the city.

One of the best ways to spend a Harrisburg afternoon is to stroll along the gorgeous east bank of the Susquehanna, then cross the river along the Walnut Street footbridge and walk through **City Island**, a waterfront development with vast facilities, including a kite-flying area, a tourist railroad, a family-filled concrete beach (somewhat reminiscent of a public pool), and paddlewheeler rides (May–Aug, groups Sept–Oct; rides $5; ☎717/234-6500).

HERSHEY, ten miles east, was built in 1903 by candy magnate Milton S. Hershey for his chocolate factory – so it has streets named Chocolate and Cocoa avenues and streetlamps in the shape of Hershey's Chocolate Kisses. **Hershey's Chocolate World** (Mon–Sat 9am–5pm, Sun 11am–5pm; longer hours in summer; ☎717/534-4900, ⓦwww.hersheyschocolateworld.com) offers a free mini-train ride through a romanticized simulated chocolate factory and a 3-D chocolate musical ($5). Those not content with the free sample given out at the end of the ride can gorge themselves in the vast gift and souvenir shops and cafés.

Hersheypark, which began in 1907 as a picnic ground for Hershey factory workers, is now a huge, if poorly organized, **amusement park**, with roller coasters and sundry other rides (mid-May to Sept, hours vary; $36; ☎717/534-3090 or 1-800/HERSHEY). The adjacent **Hershey Museum** (June–Aug daily 10am–6pm; Sept–May daily 10am–5pm; $6.50; ☎717/534-3439, ⓦwww.hersheymuseum.org) has exhibits on the Pennsylvania Dutch and tells the Milton S. Hershey story.

Thirty-five miles south of Hershey, via Harrisburg, the blue-collar town of **York** is home to the final-assembly plant of motorcycle legend **Harley-Davidson**. The company has a visitor center with exhibitions and runs free factory tours (Mon–Fri 10am–4pm, tour center also Sat 9am–noon; ☎1-877/883-1450); closed-toed shoes are required.

Practicalities

Amtrak **trains** share the central station at Fourth and Chestnut streets with Greyhound, whose **buses** also stop in Hershey at 337 W Chocolate St. Harrisburg's **visitor center** (☎717/231-7788, ⓦwww.visithhc.com) is not open to walk-ins, but can be contacted for good local and regional information.

In leafy Camp Hill, just across the river from Harrisburg, the *Radisson Penn Harris* (☎717/763-7117, ⓦwww.radisson.com; ❹) has good-value rooms in relaxing surroundings. Options in Hershey include the standard *Spinners Inn*, 845 E Chocolate Ave (☎717/533-9157, ⓦwww.spinnersinn.com; ❸), which has a very good restaurant, and the standard *Chocolatetown Motel*, a mile further on at no. 1806 (☎717/533-2330, ⓦwww.chocolatetownmotel.com; ❸; closed Jan & Feb). Upscale lodging is available at the palatial *Hotel Hershey*, Hotel Road (☎717/533-2171; ❽–❾), complete with an onsite spa offering chocolate-based beauty treatments (which strangely lack any sense of fun). Weekend spa appointments must be made far in advance.

Budget **restaurants** line Second Street in downtown Harrisburg, the best being *Fisaga's*, at Locust and N Second streets (☎717/441-1556), which serves good basic sandwiches and pasta. *Scott's*, 212 Locust St (☎717/234-7599), is a popular bar and grill, with live music some nights.

Gettysburg

The small town of **GETTYSBURG**, thirty miles south of Harrisburg near the Maryland border, gained tragic notoriety in July 1863 for the cataclysmic **Civil War** battle in which fifty thousand men died. There were more casualties during these three days than in any American battle before or since – a full third of those who fought were killed or wounded – and entire regiments were wiped out when the tide finally turned against the South.

Four months later, on November 19, Abraham Lincoln delivered his **Gettysburg Address** at the dedication of the National Cemetery. His two-minute speech, in memory of all the soldiers who died, is acknowledged as one of the most powerful orations in American history. Lincoln himself was convinced that it was a "flat failure," and prefaced his remarks with the words "the world will little note nor long remember what we say here . . ."; on the contrary, you'll be muttering it in your sleep by the time you leave.

Gettysburg, by far the most baldly commercialized of all the Civil War sites, is overwhelmingly geared toward **tourism**, relentlessly replaying the most minute details of the battle. Fortunately, it is perfectly feasible to avoid the crowds and commercial overkill and explore for yourself the rolling hills of the battlefield (now a national park) and the tidy town streets with their shuttered historic houses.

Information and getting around

Gettysburg Travel Council, 31 Carlisle St (daily 8am–5.30pm; ☏717/334-6274, Ⓦwww.gettysburg.com), is housed next door to the tiny historic train depot where Lincoln disembarked in November 1863 and should be the first stop on any visit. Though the town is compact and easy to walk around, there is no public transportation, and a car helps when touring the huge battlefield. Two-hour **Battlefield Bus Tours**, running through the town and making numerous stops, depart from 778 Baltimore St (8 tours daily; $18 for open-air bus tour, or $22 for tour with AC; ☏717/334-6296).

Accommodation

There is plenty of lodging in and around Gettysburg, including many **B&Bs**. The most central place to **camp** is at *Artillery Ridge Resort*, 610 Taneytown Rd (☏717/334-1288; $20.35 for basic, no-electricty site for two; open April–Oct only).

Baladerry Inn 40 Hospital Rd ☏717/337-1342, Ⓦwww.baladerryinn.com. Historic hospital turned B&B, with nine en suite rooms. ❺
Doubleday Inn 104 Doubleday Ave ☏717/334-9119, Ⓦwww.doubledayinn.com. A memorabilia-packed luxury B&B, the only one within the battle-field itself. ❹–❺
Gettysburg Travelodge 613 Baltimore St ☏717/334-9281. Standard motel between down-town and the battlefield. ❹

HI-Ironmaster's Mansion 1212 Pine Grove Rd, Gardners ☏717/486-7575, Ⓦwww.hi-dvc.org/hostels/ironmaster. Out-of-the-way hostel located on the Appalachian Trail in Pine Grove Furnace State Park. Busiest during ski season. Beds $14 members, or $17 nonmembers.
Historic Farnsworth House Inn 401 Baltimore St ☏717/334-8838, Ⓦwww.farnsworthhousedin-ing.com. An 1810 townhouse, used as Union HQ in the war and still riddled with bullet holes. Includes 11 rooms, a bookstore, and a theater. ❺

The Town

For a sense of Gettysburg's history, you should check out just a couple of the numerous museums in town, and follow the Travel Council's fourteen-block downtown walking tour. The **National Civil War Wax Museum**, 297 Steinwehr Ave (Jan & Feb Sat, Sun & holidays; March–Dec daily; $5.50; ☏717/334-6245), uses dreadful dummies in its displays on the lead-up to the Civil War, the Underground Railroad for escaped slaves, abolitionist John Brown, and the famous Southern belle spies Rose Greenhow and Belle Boyd. Across the National Cemetery in the battlefield, there are yet more mannequins in the **Hall of Presidents and First Ladies**, 504 Baltimore St (daily: June–Aug 9am–9pm; Sept 9am–7pm; Oct, Nov & March–May 9am–5pm; $6; ☏717/334-5717), complete with pearls of presidential wisdom and stirring patriotic music.

Next to the Gettysburg Tour Center, on Baltimore Street, the **Jennie Wade House** (same hours and price as Hall of Presidents; ☏717/334-4100) is the former home of the only civilian to die in the battle; Wade was killed by a stray bullet as she made bread for the Union troops in her sister's kitchen. Today, the residence looks more or less as it did on July 3, 1863, with bullet holes in the front door and on the bedpost, an artillery shell hole ripped through the wall adjoining the neighboring house, and a macabre model of Jennie's corpse lying under a sheet in the cellar.

To the west of the park, President Eisenhower, who retired to Gettysburg, is commemorated at the **Eisenhower National Historic Site**, where his Georgian-style mansion holds an array of memorabilia. The site is accessible only on shuttle-bus tours from the National Park Visitor Center, a mile south of Gettysburg in Taneytown (daily 9am–4pm; $5.25; ☏717/338-9114, Ⓦwww.nps.gov/eise).

The battleground

It takes most of a day to see the 3500-acre **Gettysburg National Military Park**, which surrounds the town (daily 6am–10pm; free; ⓦ www.nps .gov/gett). The **visitor center** on Taneytown Road (daily: summer 8am–6pm, rest of year 8am–5pm; ☎717/334-1124) doubles as the best **museum**, with guns, uniforms, surgical and musical instruments, tents and flags, as well as touching photos of the 1938 Joint Soldiers Reunion. A thirty-minute, painstakingly thorough **electric map show** ($3) plots the intricacies of the battle; at the visitor center, you can pick up details of a self-guided **driving route**, or a **guide** will join you in your car for a personalized two-hour tour ($40). The guides are available on a first-come, first-served basis, and the visitor center does not accept reservations – so it's best to arrive just before it opens at 8am to secure a guide for the same day.

Directly opposite the visitor center, the **Gettysburg National Cemetery** contains thousands of graves arranged in a semicircle around the Soldiers' National Monument, on the site where Lincoln gave the Gettysburg Address. Most stirring of all are the hundreds of small marble gravestones marked only with numbers. A short walk away, the **Cyclorama Center** holds a 356ft circular painting of **Pickett's Charge**, the suicidal Confederate thrust across open wheatfields in broad daylight; it is accompanied by a recitation of the Gettysburg Address (daily 9am–5pm; $3). The earliest existing draft of the Address (not, as commonly believed, scrawled on the back of an envelope) sits in a hallowed cabinet in a dark room on the lower story. The battlegrounds themselves, golden fields reminiscent of an English country landscape, are peaceful now except for their names: **Valley of Death**, **Bloody Run**, **Cemetery Hill**. Uncanny statues of key figures stand at appropriate points, while heavy stone monuments honor different regiments.

Eating and entertainment

Evenings in Gettysburg tend to be quiet; the tour buses have gone home and many people choose to drink in their hotel bars. However, there are some good **restaurants**, many in historically important buildings.

Blue Parrot Bistro 35 Chambersburg St ☎717/337-3739. Pasta and steaks with a good choice of sauces. Like most restaurants in town, things wind down soon after 8.30pm.
Dobbin House Tavern 89 Steinwehr Ave ☎717/334-2100. The oldest house in the city, dating from 1776 and once a hideout for former slaves on the Underground Railroad. Lunch from $8–18; candlelit dinners are more expensive. Food veers among Pennsylvania Dutch, early American, and (almost) contemporary.
Gettysbrew Restaurant & Brewery 248 Hunterstown Rd ☎717/337-1001, ⓦ www.gettys-brew.com. Also a pub and historic site. Brews five beers, plus its own root beer and soda.

Western Pennsylvania

Western Pennsylvania, a key point for frontier trade and an important thoroughfare to the West, was the focus of the fighting between the English and the French in the seven-year French and Indian War for Colonial and maritime power (1756–1763). This region grew to industrial prominence in the nineteenth century, with the exploitation of its coal resources gathering pace after the Civil War, and the opening of the world's first oil well at Titusville (now Drake Well Memorial Park) in northwestern Pennsylvania in 1859.

Today, tourism in western Pennsylvania is concentrated around the surprisingly appealing city of **Pittsburgh**. To the south of the city, the **Laurel Highlands** features Frank Lloyd Wright's not-to-be-missed architectural masterpiece, **Fallingwater**, as well as nearby **Ohiopyle State Park** and the **Youghiogheny River**, which offer plenty of outdoor activities. In the overwhelming rural northwest corner of the state, another great wilderness area to explore is the lush **Allegheny National Forest**, which begins twenty miles north of I-80. The region's only major conurbation, **Erie**, is located on the eponymous great lake. **Presque Isle State Park** is also worth a visit for its sandy lake beaches and wooded hiking trails.

Pittsburgh

The vibrant ten-block district known as the Golden Triangle, at the heart of downtown **PITTSBURGH**, stands at the confluence of the Monongahela, Allegheny, and Ohio rivers; this area was once bitterly fought over as the gateway to the West. The French built Fort Duquesne on the site in 1754, only for it to be destroyed four years later by the British, who replaced it with **Fort Pitt**. Industry began with the development of iron foundries in the early 1800s, and by the time of the Civil War, Pittsburgh was producing half of the iron and one third of the glass in the US. Soon after, the city became the world's leading producer of steel, thanks to the vigorous expansion programs of **Andrew Carnegie**, who by 1870 was the richest man in the world. Present-day Pittsburgh is dotted with his cultural bequests, along with those of other wealthy forefathers, including the Mellon bankers, the Frick coal merchants, and the Heinz food producers.

Still inaccurately saddled with a Victorian reputation for dirt and pollution, the city experienced a transformation after the 1950s. A face-lift involved large-scale demolition of abandoned steel mills, which freed up much of the downtown waterfront. That said, all-out sanitization has been kept in check by the student population, the small-town feel of the older ethnic neighborhoods to the north and south, and the effects of economic downturn. Pittsburgh today is one of America's most attractive and most liveable cities; coal fumes no longer fill the air, and sleek architecture and green parks supplant smokestacks and slums. Since the mid-1990s, and the opening of the popular **Andy Warhol Museum**, Pittsburgh has established itself as a destination to be reckoned with.

Each of Pittsburgh's close-knit neighborhoods – the **South Side** and **Mount Washington**, across the Monongahela River from the **Golden Triangle**, the **North Side** across the Allegheny River, and **Oakland**, the university area in the east – attests in its own way to the city's history and its resurgence. Easily accessible from each other, these neighborhoods retain individual identities while remaining part of a proud whole.

Arrival, information, and getting around

Greyhound pulls in at Eleventh Street and Liberty Avenue downtown, across from Amtrak. From the modern, efficient **Pittsburgh International Airport**, fifteen miles west (☎412/472-3525, ⓦwww.pitairport.com), several shuttle services run to Pittsburgh. Almost as quick, more frequent, and significantly cheaper, the excellent West Busway #28 runs roughly every 20mins between the airport and twelve Pittsburgh stops, including downtown, Oakland, and the universities (daily 5am–midnight; $1.95).

Pittsburgh's main **visitor center** is downtown on Liberty Avenue, adjacent to the Gateway Center (Mon–Fri 9am–5pm, Sat & Sun 9am–3pm,

closed on Sun in Jan & Feb; ☎412/281-7711 or 1-800/366-0093, Ⓦwww
.visitpittsburgh.com), with subsidiary branches at the airport, in the Strip
District, and at the Senator John Heinz Pittsburgh Regional History Center.
The main **post office** is at Seventh and Grant (Mon–Fri 7am–6pm, Sat
8am–2.30pm).

Though Pittsburgh is a city of distinct districts, **transportation** between
them is simple. **Buses** through town (free–$2.75), the Monongahela and
Duquesne Heights trolley inclines ($1.75), and a small "T" **subway** system
(free downtown; further out the fare runs up to $3.25 at rush hour) are all
excellent transportation options; **PAT**, the area transit authority (☎412/442-
2000, Ⓦwww.portauthority.org), has a downtown service center at 534
Smithfield St (Mon & Thurs 7.30am–6pm, Tues & Wed 7.30am–5pm, Fri
7am–4.30pm), where you can pick up timetables. Twenty-five to fifty-cent
transfers, which must be bought simultaneously with your fare if needed, allow
you to connect with any of the system's vehicles within three hours. For **taxis**,
call Yellow Cab (☎412/665-8100).

Accommodation

Pittsburgh's **hotels** and few **B&Bs** are generally pricey, although weekend
packages at luxury downtown hotels can bring rates down to below $100.
Oakland has a couple of reasonably priced business hotels, while the only real
budget place is the affiliated **youth hostel** on the South Side. You can check
out all of the Pittsburgh area's B&Bs at Ⓦwww.pittsburghbnb.com.

Appletree Bed & Breakfast 703 S Negley Ave
☎412/661-0631, Ⓦwww.theinnsonnegley.com
/appletree.html. Friendly, upmarket establishment
with 16 rooms and suites, several with Jacuzzi, in
Shadyside. ❼

Best Western University Center 3401 Blvd of the
Allies ☎412/683-6100 or 1-800/245-4444,
Ⓦwww.bestwestern-pittsburgh.com. Standard motel
rooms, but one of the best deals in Oakland. ❺

Hampton Inn University Center 3315 Hamlet St
☎412/681-1000 or 1-800/426-7866,
Ⓦwww.hamptoninn.com. Welcoming branch of
chain in Oakland offering a generous self-service
continental breakfast bar, plus free shuttle to
downtown and surrounding areas. ❻

HI-Pittsburgh 830 E Warrington Ave ☎412/431-
1267, Ⓦtrfn.clpgh.org/ayh. Housed in a former
bank (which is still intact), this 50-bed hostel

(dorm beds $19–22) is located on the South Side
in Allentown, a 15–20min walk from Station Sq/E
Carson St. Check-in 8–10am and 5pm–midnight.
❶

The Priory–A City Inn 614 Pressley St
☎412/231-3338, Ⓦwww.thepriory.com. Restored
1880s inn, originally built to house traveling
Benedictine monks; now, it's the North Side's
nicest B&B. Room rates include continental breakfast, evening wine, weekday limo service, and use
of fitness room. ❺

Ramada Plaza Suites One Bigelow Square
☎412/281-5800, 1-800/225-5858, Ⓦwww.plaza-
suites.com. Convenient downtown suites with
kitchens. ❹–❺

The Westin 1000 Penn Ave ☎412/281-3700 or
1-800/937-8461, Ⓦwww.westin.com. Flashy
downtown tower with pool and gym. ❼

Downtown: the Golden Triangle

The *New York Times* once described Pittsburgh as "the only city with an
entrance" – and, true enough, the view of the **Golden Triangle** skyline on
emerging from the tunnel on the Fort Pitt Bridge is undeniably breathtaking.
Surrounded by water and fronted with a huge fountain, Pittsburgh's downtown
pays tribute to both its coal-grimed past and sunny future. In the core of the
original city, the Triangle's imaginative contemporary architecture stands next
to Gothic churches and redbrick warehouses. Philip Johnson's magnificent
postmodern concoction, the black-glass Gothic **PPG Place** complex, looms
incongruously over the old **Market Square**, lined with historic restaurants
and shops and a venue for free live lunchtime entertainment most weekdays.
History is also apparent on the faded buildings along Liberty Avenue, with

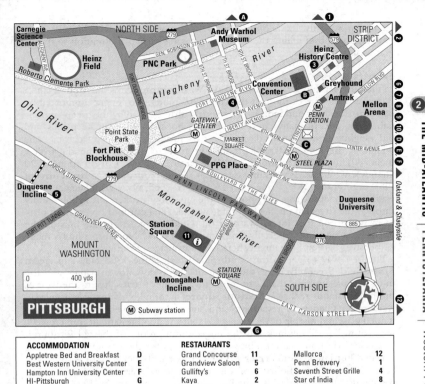

ACCOMMODATION

Appletree Bed and Breakfast	**D**
Best Western University Center	**E**
Hampton Inn University Center	**F**
HI-Pittsburgh	**G**
The Priory – A City Inn	**A**
Ramada Plaza Suites	**C**
The Westin	**B**

RESTAURANTS

Grand Concourse	**11**	Mallorca	**12**
Grandview Saloon	**5**	Penn Brewery	**1**
Gullifty's	**6**	Seventh Street Grille	**4**
Kaya	**2**	Star of India	**8**
Kim's Coffee Shop	**10**	Valhalla	**3**
La Feria	**7**	Yumwok/Lulu's Noodles	**9**

1940s and 1950s fronts left in place during successive face-lifts. At the flat end of the triangle, the spaceship-like dome of **Mellon Arena** looms above the transport stations – it hosts large concerts and exhibitions, and is home to the **Pittsburgh Penguins** ice hockey team (for tickets, call ☎412/642-7367, or visit ⓦwww.pittsburghpenguins.com).

Point State Park, at the peak of the Triangle, is where it all began. The site of five different forts during the French and Indian War, it still contains the 1764 **Fort Pitt Blockhouse**, the city's oldest structure, a lookout of sandstone and rough brick. The park itself is now a popular gathering area, with a 150ft fountain with a pool, as well as great views of port activity and across to the colorful old buildings on verdant Mount Washington. It's a great place to view sunsets and an excellent venue for the city's outdoor festivals.

Northeast of downtown, along Penn Avenue, the characterful **Strip District** has a bustling early-morning market with wholesale outlets and fresh produce stalls, popular with bargain hunters and good for cheap breakfasts; it's also a good place to head to at night. Down by the river is an entertainment complex, with restaurants, bars, a marina, and a floating boardwalk. The seven-floor **Senator John Heinz Pittsburgh Regional History Center**, at 1212

Smallman St (daily 10am–5pm; $6; ☏412/454-6000, ⓦwww.pghhistory.org), does a good job of telling the city's story, paying particular attention to immigrants of various eras.

South Side

In the nineteenth century, 400ft **Mount Washington**, across the Monongahela River, was the site of most of the city's coal mines. No longer dominated by belching steel mills and industry, the **South Side**, banked by the green "mountain," is an area of many churches, colorful houses nestled on steep hills, and old neighborhoods. These days, only two survive of the twelve cable cars which, at the height of steel production, used to carry coal up the trolley inclines. The 1877 **Duquesne Incline**, from 1197 W Carson St to 1220 Grandview Ave, is a working cable-car station containing a **museum** of Pittsburgh history ($1.75 one-way; ☏412/381-1665, ⓦwww.incline.cc) in the waiting room at the top: old photos of the city show workers struggling blindly through the streets in pitch-black midday smog. The outdoor observation platform is a prime spot for **views** over the Golden Triangle to the hills on the horizon, which are especially awesome after dark. Not surprisingly, many (expensive) bars and restaurants here take advantage of the vista.

The best way to get to the South Side is across the 1883 blue-and-cream **Smithfield Street Bridge**, the oldest of fifteen downtown bridges and the most unusual-looking, thanks to its elliptical "fisheye" truss. Just to the west of the bridge stands redbrick **Station Square**, a complex of renovated railroad warehouses filled with restaurants and shops. Its showpiece is the beautiful stained glass and marble of the *Grand Concourse* seafood restaurant (for a review, see "Eating," p.185), which fills the huge waiting room of the old Pittsburgh and Lake Erie train station. This is also the jetty for the enjoyable hour-long narrated Just Ducky Tours **river cruises** (daily April–Oct 10.30am–6pm; Nov Sat & Sun only, same hours; $15, children $12; tours every 90mins on summer weekends, less frequently during shoulder seasons; ☏412/402-3825, ⓦwww.justduckytours.com).

Along the banks of the Monongahela, **East Carson Street** is the main drag of the lively mixed residential and commercial South Side, where a longstanding community of Polish and Ukrainian steelworkers has gradually absorbed an offbeat mix of artsy residents, along with the attendant cafés, bars, and bookstores. Onion-domed churches stand alongside thrift stores and galleries, and the narrow backstreets are lined by brick rowhouses. This is also Pittsburgh's most extensive and varied **nightlife** center (see "Nightlife and entertainment," p.186).

North Side

The star attraction on the **North Side**, annexed by Pittsburgh only in 1907, is undoubtedly the **Andy Warhol Museum**, 117 Sandusky St, just over the Seventh Street Bridge from downtown (Tues–Thurs, Sat & Sun 10am–5pm, Fri 10am–10pm; $8, Fri 5–10pm $3; ☏412/237-8300, ⓦwww.warhol.org). The museum documents the life and work of Pittsburgh's most celebrated son over eight floors of a spacious Victorian warehouse; it claims to be the largest museum in the world devoted to a single artist.

Born in Pittsburgh in 1928, **Andy Warhol** (born Andrew Warhola, the youngest son of working-class Carpatho-Rusyn, or Eastern Slovakian, immigrants) moved to New York City at the age of 21, after graduating from Carnegie-Mellon University. By the end of the 1950s, he was one of the most successful commercial artists in the nation, before turning his attention to fine and pop art. During the early 1960s he started shooting 16mm films – *Empire*, *Chelsea Girls*, and *Lonesome Cowboys* – and developed the "Exploding Plastic Inevitable" multimedia show, featuring erotic dancers and music by The Velvet Underground, whom he managed. After founding *Interview* magazine in 1969, Warhol became transfixed with the rich and famous and, up until his death in 1987, was perhaps best known for his celebrity portraits and his appearances at society events.

Although the majority of Warhol's most famous pieces are in the hands of private collectors, the museum boasts an impressive and ever-changing selection of exhibits, with over five hundred items on display at any one time, including pop art (Campbell's soup cans) and portraiture (Elvis, Marilyn Monroe, Jackie Kennedy). It pays equal attention to archival material, and chronological **self-guided tours** give a good idea of Warhol's artistic development and his eventful lifestyle. At any given time, two or three non-Warhol exhibits show work related in some way to Warhol themes. A **cinema** shows two films or videos daily, both usually Warhol productions. There's an excellent, informative Archives Study Department and a popular **Weekend Factory** (Sat & Sun noon–4pm; free with admission), where Warhol's techniques are explained and visitors can have a go themselves. During "**Good Fridays**" (Fri 5–10pm; $3), there is a cash bar, and the lobby buzzes with live bands or other performance arts. The museum also has a well-stocked gift shop and a café.

Elsewhere on the North Side, revitalization centers around the intriguingly named **Mexican War Streets**, on the northern edge of Allegheny Commons. In this unevenly restored, tree-lined area of nineteenth-century gray-brick and limestone terraces, old families, descendants of German and Scandinavian immigrants, live in an uneasy truce alongside young professionals. The excellent and highly unusual **Mattress Factory**, 500 Sampsonia Way (Tues–Fri 10am–5pm, Sat 10am–7pm, Sun 1–5pm, closed Aug; $8, kids free, free for all on Thurs; ☎412/231-3169, ⓦwww.mattress.org/home.html), has contemporary installations by top mixed-media artists, and is a must on any visit to the city. The **National Aviary**, Allegheny Commons West (daily 9am–5pm; $5; ☎412/323-7235, ⓦwww.aviary.org), is a huge indoor bird sanctuary with over two hundred species, including foul-mouthed parrots, in free flight under a showpiece 30-foot glass dome. Nearby, **The Children's Museum of Pittsburgh**, 10 Children's Way, Allegheny Square (Mon–Sat 10am–5pm, Sun noon–5pm; $5, kids $4.50, Thurs $3.50 for all; ☎412/322-5058, ⓦwww.pittsburghkids.org), offers a plethora of games, events, and special exhibitions.

Heading northwest along the river, the huge, state-of-the-art **Carnegie Science Center**, 1 Allegheny Ave (Sun–Thurs 10am–5pm, Fri & Sat 10am–7pm; $14, kids $10; ☎412/237-3400, ⓦwww.carnegiesciencecenter .org), is also predominantly aimed at children, with, among other exhibits, an interactive engineering playspace and a miniature railroad. The center contains an impressive OMNIMAX theater and a planetarium ($8 for one show, $12 for two); combination tickets are available ($18 for exhibits and one theater or planetarium ticket). Outside, the **USS Requin**, a 1945 submarine, bobs on the shores of the Allegheny River (daily 10am–4.30pm; free with Science Center admission); the kid-friendly tour focuses on submarine engineering, but also explores day-to-day life underwater.

Next door from the Science Center, **Heinz Field**, one of two new sports venues that opened in 2001 to replace the shared Three Rivers Stadium, is home to football's **Pittsburgh Steelers** (call ☎412/432-7800 for tickets or tours). The other, further along the river toward the Seventh Street Bridge, is **PNC Park**, the home of the **Pittsburgh Pirates** baseball team. Beautifully constructed so that from most seats you get a sweeping view of the Allegheny and downtown, it's a real treat to watch a game here on a balmy summer night (call ☎1-800/289-2827 for tickets).

Oakland and the East Side

Oakland, Pittsburgh's university area, is dotted with the mansions of wealthy industrialists, as well as university-related sights, concentrated around the campuses of **Carnegie-Mellon University**, the **University of Pittsburgh** (always known as "Pitt"), and several other colleges. At Fifth Ave and Bigelow Blvd, the 42-story, 2529-window Gothic Revival **Cathedral of Learning** is a university building with a difference: over twenty classrooms are furnished with antiques and specially crafted items donated by the city's different ethnic groups, from Lithuanian to Chinese to Irish. These rooms have been used by students since the 1930s, and all are open to the public except the exotic Syria-Lebanon room and the Early American room, complete with trap door and secret passage; these are shown only on ninety-minute **guided tours** (Mon–Fri 9am–2.30pm, Sat 9.30am–2.30pm, Sun 11am–2.30pm; $3; ☎412-624-6000). Alternatively, you can do your own tape-recorded tour on weekends (also $3) or follow the useful booklet ($1.25). On the grounds behind the Cathedral of Learning is the French Gothic **Heinz Memorial Chapel** (Mon–Fri 9am–5pm, Sun 1–5pm; free), notable for its long, narrow, stained-glass windows depicting political, literary, and religious figures.

Across from the cathedral at 4400 Forbes Ave, the **Carnegie** cultural complex holds two great museums – the **Museum of Natural History**, famed for its extensive dinosaur relics and sparkling gems, and the **Museum of Art**, with Impressionist, Post-Impressionist and American regional art, as well as an excellent modern collection (both museums Tues–Sat 10am–5pm, Sun noon–5pm, summer Mon 10am–5pm; $8, or $5 for students, seniors, and children; ☎412/622-3131, Ⓦwww.carnegiemuseums.org). Nearby, Schenley Park includes the colorful flower gardens of **Phipps Conservatory** (Tues–Sun 9am–5pm, Fri 9am–9pm; $6, students $4; Ⓦwww.phipps.conservatory.org) and wild wooded areas beyond.

If you're coming to the East Side from downtown, be sure to avoid the area along Center Avenue known as **The Hill District**; this is one of Pittsburgh's toughest districts, especially after dark. Many cab drivers avoid the area, but as it neighbors the college precincts, tourists can easily stumble into it. An alternative route from downtown is along Liberty Avenue via the predominantly Italian neighborhood of **Bloomfield**, a busy area of shops, restaurants, and quaint rowhouses.

The stretch of Fifth Avenue from around the Cathedral of Learning up to Shadyside is lined with important and architecturally beautiful academic buildings, places of worship, and early private mansions. The imposing **Soldiers and Sailors Memorial**, 4141 Fifth Ave (Tues–Sun 10am–4pm; $2 tours), also serves as a museum, and is filled with military paraphernalia and historic exhibits. Further on, opposite the exquisite external mural of the Byzantine Catholic **Church of the Holy Spirit**, is the humble broadcasting complex of **WQED**, notable for being the first publicly-funded TV station when it opened in April 1954 and home to the long-running kids' show *Mr Rogers' Neighborhood*.

Shadyside, on the eastern fringes of Oakland, is an upmarket, trendy neighborhood containing the particularly chic commercial section of Walnut Street. There are several art galleries here, and the **Pittsburgh Center for the Arts**, at 6300 Fifth Ave in Mellon Park, showcases innovative Pittsburgh art in various media (Mon–Sat 10am–5.30pm, Sun noon–5pm; $6; ☎412/361-0873, Ⓦwww.pittsburgharts.org). A short way to the south, **Squirrel Hill** is another lively area, housing a mixture of students and the city's largest Jewish community, with a fine selection of shops and restaurants lining Murray and Forbes avenues.

Further east, the small **Frick Art Museum**, in the **Frick Art and Historical Center**, 7227 Reynolds St (Tues–Sat 10am–5pm, Sun noon–6pm; free; ☏412/371-0600, Ⓦwww.frickart.com), shows Italian, Flemish, and French art from the fifteenth to the nineteenth centuries; its collection of decorative arts includes two of Marie Antoinette's chairs. The **Clayton mansion**, at the center of the Frick complex, is furnished exactly as it was when industrial magnate Henry Clay Frick lived there. Obligatory **guided tours** ($10) walk you around the house, pointing out the various late-Victorian decorative touches, as well as the bed where Frick recovered after being stabbed by an anarchist during the bitter Homestead Steel Strike. Frick and most of his family are buried, under tons of protective concrete and steel, just south of the family home, on the highest hill in **Homewood Cemetery**, which also holds the tombs of H.J. Heinz (of the ketchup and baked beans fortune) and sundry Mellons. Three miles north, bordering the Allegheny River, the green expanse of **Highland Park** contains the nicely landscaped and enjoyable **Pittsburgh Zoo and PPG Aquarium** (summer daily 10am–6pm, rest of year 9am–5pm; April–Nov $8, Dec–March $6; ☏412/665-3640, Ⓦzoo.pgh.pa.us), which has the distinction of owning a Komodo dragon and, in recent years, having bred at least two baby elephants.

Eating

Eating in downtown Pittsburgh can prove expensive, and the area is rather deserted at night. There's a growing range of places in the adjacent **Strip District** and good neighborhood Mediterranean and Eastern European restaurants along and around **East Carson Street** on the South Side. **Station Square** and **Mount Washington** cater to a more upmarket crowd, while **Oakland** is, as you might expect, home to an array of cheap student hangouts clustered around S Craig Street – look out for the ultra-cheap mobile ethnic food vans at lunchtime. A little further east, **Shadyside** and **Squirrel Hill** have a number of good mid-priced places.

Grand Concourse 1 Station Square ☏412/261-1717, Ⓦwww.muer.com/grandcon.html. Pricey, plush seafood restaurant in a gorgeous setting inside the Station Square complex.
Grandview Saloon 1212 Grandview Ave ☏412/431-1400. Relaxed Mount Washington restaurant, usually packed with a young crowd enjoying huge plates of pasta. Arrive early for a deck table with a view.
Gullifty's 1922 Murray Ave ☏412/521-8222. Squirrel Hill establishment serving fine pasta, meat dishes, and sumptuous sweets. Look out for the twice-yearly Garlic Festival (usually held in April and October).
Kaya 2000 Smallman St ☏412/261-6565. Stylish Caribbean restaurant in the Strip District with a varied vegetarian selection, as well as a huge range of beers, rums, and other spirits.
Kim's Coffee Shop 5447 Penn Ave ☏412/362-7019. Friendly, cozy, and very cheap Vietnamese joint also serving some Chinese and Thai – the spicy, cold beef Siamese is a treat. Licensed to sell liquor, but you can BYOB too. Closed Mon.
La Feria 5527 Walnut St ☏412/682-4501. Colorful upstairs Peruvian shop-cum-restaurant offering a limited but tasty selection of inexpensive specials from the Andes. BYOB.
Mallorca 2228 E Carson St ☏412/488-1818. In a smart setting on the South Side, this restaurant serves excellent paella and Mediterranean dishes, as well as fine sangría. Try the delicious goat in red-wine sauce for $20.
Penn Brewery 800 Vinial St ☏412/237-9402, Ⓦwww.pennbrew.com. On the North Side, this is Pittsburgh's longest-established brewpub, serving up decent German food and festivities.
Seventh Street Grille 130 7th St, Century Building ☏412/338-0303. Excellent Californian- and Italian-influenced menus strong on pasta and seafood. Very popular despite being a little pricey.
Star of India 412 S Craig St ☏412/681-5700. Indian restaurant in Oakland offering tasty North Indian cooking. Wash down the great $7 lunch buffet with a smooth, creamy *lassi* (yogurt drink).

Valhalla 1150 Smallman St ☎ 412/434-1440. At the start of the Strip, close to Greyhound, this trendy microbrewery with cool decor serves a range of New American specialties like mango salmon, as well as its own beer.

Yumwok/Lulu's Noodles 400 S Craig St ☎ 412/687-7777. Combined establishment serving filling noodles and good standard pan-Asian cuisine at bargain prices. Justifiably popular with students. BYOB.

Nightlife and entertainment

Pittsburgh's **nightlife** offers rich pickings in everything from the classics to jazz and alternative rock. The nationally regarded City Theatre, 57 S 13th St (☎ 412/431-4400, ⓦ www.citytheatrecompany.org), puts on groundbreaking productions in a converted South Side church. The widely traveled **Pittsburgh Symphony Orchestra** plays at the Heinz Hall, 600 Penn Ave (☎ 412/392-4900, ⓦ www.pittsburghsymphony.org), and the city's ballet, dance, and opera companies perform at the downtown **Benedum Center for the Performing Arts**, 719 Liberty Ave (☎ 412/456-6666, ⓦ www .pgharts.org/venues/benedum.cfm). *City Paper*, a free weekly newspaper published on Wednesdays (ⓦ www.pittsburghcitypaper.ws), has extensive **listings**.

31st St Pub 3101 Penn Ave ☎ 412/391-8334, ⓦ www.31stpub.com. It won't win any prizes for decor, but this place draws a crowd to hear up-and-coming local indie and hardcore bands, plus the odd underground celebrity act from out of town.

Club Café 56–58 S 12th St ☎ 412/431-4950, ⓦ www.clubcafelive.com. Laid-back South Side club with regular live music, including rock, folk, and salsa.

Club Laga 3609 Forbes Ave ☎ 412/682-2050, ⓦ www.clublaga.com. Large, loud student disco that also hosts live rock bands of some standing.

Dee's 1314 E Carson St ☎ 412/431-5400. This South Side institution has a great jukebox, pool, darts, and a lively crowd.

M (Metropol) 1600 Smallman St ☎ 412/261-2232. Huge, popular Strip District dance club (mainly techno and industrial) that also promotes some live rock. Right next door to *Rosebud* (see below).

Nick's Fat City 1601–1605 E Carson St ☎ 412/481-6880, ⓦ www.nicksfatcity.com. Popular, gay-friendly South Side pool bar with (usually) good live rock bands. Karaoke some nights.Closed Sun & Mon.

Rosebud 1600 Smallman St ☎ 412/261-2232, ⓦ www.rosebudstage.com. Generally considered Pittsburgh's best music venue, this atmospheric bar/restaurant features acoustic, rockabilly, and indie acts.

The Sharp Edge 302 S St Clair ☎ 412/661-3537, ⓦ www.sharpedgebeer.com Friendly beer emporium on the edge of Shadyside, with good food and hundreds of imported and American beers, including cask ales. The jukebox plays rock tunes and there's sports on TV.

Smokin' Joe's 2001 E Carson St ☎ 412/431-6757. One of the South Side's most convivial bars, with a vast range of beers on tap and over 200 bottled brands.

Around Pittsburgh: Fallingwater and Ohiopyle

Just over an hour southeast of Pittsburgh, the **Laurel Highlands** takes in seventy miles of rolling hills and valleys. The main reasons to come this way down Hwy-381 are to see one of Frank Lloyd Wright's most unique creations and to take advantage of some prime outdoor opportunities around the small town of Ohiopyle.

You do not need to be an architecture buff to appreciate Wright's **Fallingwater** (mid–March to late Nov Tues–Sun 10am–4pm; Dec & early March Sat & Sun 10am–3pm; closed Jan & Feb; $12, weekends $15; ☎ 724/329-8501, ⓦ www.paconserve.org/fallingwaterhome.htm), which was built in the late 1930s for the Kaufmann family, owners of Pittsburgh's premier department store. Signposted off Hwy-381, some twenty miles south of I-70, it is set on Bear Run Creek in the midst of the gorgeous deciduous forest that constitutes the 5000-acre Bear Run Nature Reserve. It is the only one of

Wright's buildings to be on display exactly as it was designed, and for good reason – it's built right into a set of cliffside waterfalls. Wright used a cantilever system to make the multi-tiered structure "cascade down the hill like the water down the falls"; the house's almost precarious position is truly stunning, and it is remarkable how well its predominantly rectangular shapes blend in with nature's less uniform lines. The slow, well-presented hour-long tour, free with admission (more extensive and expensive tours are available), takes visitors up through the different levels of the building, allowing plenty of time to admire the setting from the various terraces as well as the beauty of the interior design. Among the house's pioneering features is a lack of load-bearing walls, which gives an extra sense of space, and natural skylights. When Edgar Kaufmann Jr entrusted the house to the Western Pennsylvania Conservancy in 1963, he donated all the furnishings and artwork with it. Objects on display include some fine East Asian sculpture of buddhas and Indian deities. Tours begin and end a few hundred yards from the house in the wooden reception pavilion, where there is a café and shop. Allow one to two hours for a visit to the site.

Ohiopyle and around

Five miles south of Fallingwater, tiny **OHIOPYLE** is the most convenient base from which to enjoy the wilds of **Ohiopyle State Park** or activities like whitewater rafting on the **Youghiogheny River**. The park fans out around the town and river, offering a maze of trails for hiking or biking, and natural delights such as **Cucumber Falls** and the unique habitat of the **Ferncliff Peninsula**, known for its wildflowers. At the built-up end of a massive steel and wooden footbridge high above the river, a small **visitor center** dispenses local information (daily 10am–4.30pm; ☎724/329-8591). Just beyond it the *Ohiopyle House Café*, 144 Grant St (☎724/329-1122), serves up tasty dishes like lobster ravioli and caramel pudding, while a couple of seasonal canteens and a general store sell basic snacks and provisions. The *Yough Plaza Motel* on Sherman Street (☎1-800/992-7238; ❹) has reasonable standard units and efficiency apartments; even better for budget travelers is camping or renting a cabin in the park itself (☎1-888/727-2757). For **rafting**, White Water Adventurers at 6 Negley St (☎1-800/WWA-RAFT, ⓦwww.wwaraft.com) is one of several outfits that rent equipment and give instruction.

Three miles southwest of Ohiopyle, there is another Frank Lloyd Wright house, **Kentuck Knob** (daily 10am–4pm; Tues–Fri $10, Sat–Mon $15; ☎724/329-1901, ⓦwww.kentuckknob.com), also known as the I.N. Hagan House. A hexagonal structure of fieldstone and cypress, it sits on a hilltop, giving wonderful views of the surrounding countryside. Further down the Youghiogheny, in the village of Confluence, the cozy *River's Edge Café* (☎814/395-5059) serves good meat and pasta dishes at moderate prices, right on the banks of the river.

Allegheny National Forest

Occupying over half a million acres and a sizeable portion of four counties, the pristine **Allegheny National Forest** (☎814/723-5150, ⓦwww.fs.fed .us/r9/Allegheny) affords a bounty of opportunities for engaging in outdoor pursuits like hiking, fishing, snowmobiling, and, best of all, admiring the **fall foliage**, which rivals any in New England.

In the north, there are several points of interest within easy access of Hwy-6, the major route through the forest. Entering the region from the east, on the highway, it is worth a stop to admire the **Kinzua Viaduct** railroad bridge, the highest and longest in the world when constructed in 1882, which is accessible by foot and allows tremendous views of the creek below. It is possible to ride over the bridge on the **Knox Kane Kinzua Railroad**, whose office in Marienville to the southwest (☎814/927-6621, ⓦwww.knoxkanerr.com) can provide fare and schedule information.

The dominant feature of the forest's northern section is the huge **Kinzua Reservoir**, created by a dam at the southern end. Swimming is possible at **Kinzua** and **Kiasutha beaches** or you can enjoy a picnic at **Rimrock Overlook** or at **Willow Bay** in the very north. The summer-only Kinzua Point Information Center on Hwy-59 (☎814/726-1291) has details on trails and private campgrounds, or you can make **camping** reservations directly for any of the forest's 715 state-run sites on ☎1-877/444-6777. Campground fees range from about $17 to $34 a night.

Erie

The focal point of Pennsylvania's forty-mile slice of Lake Erie waterfront is the pleasant city of **ERIE** itself. It bears no resemblance to the major urban centers of Pittsburgh or Philadelphia, being entirely low-rise and extremely leafy; indeed you hardly realize you are downtown until you find yourself in the shady park-like town square, on 6th Street between the main thoroughfares of Peach and State streets. There are several places of cultural interest in the city, all within walking distance of the square, including the Neoclassical **Court House** and several **museums** devoted to history, art, and science. Better than these, the **Erie Maritime Museum** at 150 E Front St in the Bayfront Historical District (Mon–Sat 9am–5pm, Sun noon–5pm; $6; ☎814/452-2744, ⓦwww.brignia-gara.org/museum.htm) has a fascinating display on the geological and ecological development of the Great Lakes and also focuses on warships of different periods; the elegant **US Brig Niagara**, usually moored outside, is part of the museum.

Undoubtedly, Erie's main attraction is the elongated comma-shaped peninsula of **Presque Isle State Park**, which bends east from its narrow neck three miles west of downtown until it almost touches the city's northernmost tip. The park is maintained as a nature preserve and has wide sandy **beaches** good for swimming, backed by thick woods offering a series of trails. Rangers at the Park Office (daily 8am–4pm; ☎814/833-7424, ⓦwww.presqueisle.org) provide general information and a map, but the main visitors center is the **Stull Interpretive Center and Nature Shop** (spring & fall 10am–4pm; summer 10am–5pm; ☎814/833-0351). Those without a vehicle can hop on the Presque Isle Aquabus (Mon noon–6pm, Tues–Sun 10am–6pm; $3 one-way, $5 round-trip; ☎814/881-2502 or 814/899-9059), which leaves on the hour from Dobbins Landing on the Erie Bayfront.

Practicalities

Erie has frequent Greyhound **bus** connections to Pittsburgh, Cleveland, and Buffalo; the station is at 5759 Peach St (☎814/864-5949), some three miles out of downtown, and is served by local bus #9 to Mill Creek Mall. The **CVB**, downtown at 208 E Bayfront Drive (Mon–Fri 9am–5pm; ☎814/454-7191 or 1-800/524-ERIE, ⓦwww.TourErie.com), is the place to go for information.

Accommodation is often twice as expensive in the summer as in the off-season. The centrally located *Holiday Inn Erie-Downtown*, 18 W 18th St (☎814/456-2961 or 1-800/832-9101, ⓦwww.holiday-inn.com; ❸), provides the usual amenities, but the elegant *Boothby Inn B&B*, at 311 W 6th St (☎814/456-1888 or 1-866/BOOTHBY, ⓦwww.theboothbyinn.com; ❺), makes for a far more pleasant stay. Numerous decent **motels** also line Peninsula Drive. The well-sited *Sara Coyne Campground*, 50 Peninsula Drive (☎814/833-

4560), is just before the entrance to Presque Isle. Nearby at 35 Peninsula Drive, the friendly *Joe Root's Grill* (℡814/836-7668) serves up hearty portions of seafood, steaks, and pasta; downtown, try the *Marketplace Grill*, 319 State St (℡814/455-7272), for steaks and a filling pizza-and-pasta lunchtime buffet, or the cheap *Chinese Happy Garden*, 418 State St (℡814/452-4488).

New Jersey

The skinny coastal state of **NEW JERSEY** has been at the heart of US history since the Revolution, when a battle was fought at **Princeton**, and George Washington spent two bleak winters at **Morristown**. As the Civil War came, the state's commitment to an industrial future ensured that, despite its border location along the Mason–Dixon Line, it fought with the Union.

That commitment to industry has doomed New Jersey in modern times. Most travelers only see "the Garden State" (so called for the rich market garden territory at the state's heart) from the stupendously ugly New Jersey Turnpike toll road which, heavy with truck traffic, cuts through a landscape of gray smokestacks and industrial estates. Even the songs of **Bruce Springsteen**, Asbury Park's golden boy, paint his home state as a gritty urban wasteland of empty lots, gray highways, lost dreams, and blue-collar heartache. The majority of the refineries and factories hug only a mere fifteen-mile-wide swath along the turnpike, but bleak cities like **Newark**, home to the major airport, and **Trenton**, the capital, do little to improve the look of the place. Suffice it to say, the state suffers from a major image problem.

But there is more to New Jersey than factories and pollution. Alongside its revolutionary history, Thomas Paine and Walt Whitman both wrote nostalgically of the happy years they spent here; while the northwest corner near the Delaware Water Gap is traced with picturesque lakes, streams, and woodlands. Best of all, the Atlantic shore offers many bustling resorts, from the compelling tattered glitz of **Atlantic City** to the Old World charm of **Cape May**.

Getting around New Jersey

With a **car**, New Jersey is easily accessible from New York City, via I-95, while the New Jersey Turnpike (a $6.45 toll end-to-end) sweeps from the northeast down to Philadelphia. The Garden State Parkway runs parallel to the Atlantic from New York to Cape May (with a 25–35¢ toll every twenty miles), and gives easy access to the shoreline resorts.

Newark Liberty International Airport (℡973/961-6000, ⓦwww.newarkairport.com) is served by all the major international carriers and popular for its convenient access to Manhattan (a 15–30min bus ride away on Olympia Airport Express; $12; ℡908/354-3330 or 1-877/894-9155, ⓦwww.olympiabus.com; or a 20min train ride via AirTrain and New Jersey Transit; $11.55; ℡1-800/AIR-RIDE, ⓦwww.airtrainnewark.com) rather than for being in New Jersey.

PATH trains connect northern New Jersey to New York City (℡1-800/234-7284, ⓦwww.panynj.gov/path), while New Jersey Transit

(☏ 973/762-5100 or 1-800/772-2222, ⓦ www.njtransit.com) provides good, inexpensive train and bus service from New Jersey hubs to Philadelphia, New York, and the coast. Numerous **Amtrak** trains pass through Newark, Princeton, and Trenton, en route between Philadelphia, New York, and Washington, DC. Greyhound covers most of the state, while New Jersey's south coast is connected to Delaware by the Cape May–Lewes **ferry** (in Cape May ☏ 609/889-7200, in Lewes ☏ 302/644-6030, ⓦ www.capemaylewesferry.com).

Inland New Jersey

Visitors most often travel from New York to northern New Jersey for the great **shopping**: from huge malls and designer outlet stores to ethnic emporiums like Mitsuwa Marketplace, the Japanese shopping center in Edgewater (☏ 201/941-9113, ⓦ www.mitsuwa.com), both prices and taxes are lower than across the Hudson River. The well-off towns along the river also contain some fine Italian and Asian restaurants. Traveling west on the interstates from the shore or from New York City, however, visitors see the New Jersey of popular imagination: heavily industrialized, a cultural desert, peppered with run-down cities like Trenton and Paterson. Newark, the state's largest city, is perhaps the nation's drabbest, redeemed only by its marvelously efficient airport, new performing arts center, and views over the Hudson to the Statue of Liberty (which is, incidentally, in New Jersey waters). The one place that holds interest in inland New Jersey is **Princeton**, an Ivy-League town that makes a pretty afternoon stopoff.

Princeton

Self-satisfied **PRINCETON**, on US-206 eleven miles north of Trenton, is home to **Princeton University** – the nation's fourth oldest, which broke away from the overly religious Yale in 1756. It began its days inauspiciously as Stony Brook in the late 1600s and then in 1724 became known as Princes Town, a coach stop between New York and Philadelphia. In January 1777, a week after Washington's triumph against the British at Trenton, the **Battle of Princeton** occurred southwest of town. This victory, a turning point in the Revolutionary effort, bolstered the morale of Washington's troops before their long winter encampment at Morristown to the north. After the war, in 1783, the **Continental Congress**, fearful of potential attack from incensed unpaid veterans in Philadelphia, met here for four months; the leafy, well-kept town was then left in peace to follow its academic pursuits. Graduates of the university include actor James Stewart, Jazz-Age writer F. Scott Fitzgerald, actress Brooke Shields, and presidents Wilson and Madison. Today, there is little to do in this self-important place other than tour the university and see the historic sites.

Arrival, information, and getting around

A shuttle **bus**, the Princeton Airporter, makes the run from Newark airport to town (daily every hour 7.15am–8.15pm; 1hr 30mins trip; $23; ☏ 609/587-6600, ⓦ www.goairporter.com). On their New York–Philadelphia runs, Amtrak and NJ Transit stop at Princeton Junction, three miles south of Princeton. From there, you can take a SEPTA shuttle (☏ 215/580-7800, ⓦ www.septa.com) to Princeton's train terminal, on-campus at University Place, a block north of Alexander Road. You must buy a ticket for the shuttle ahead of time, preferably as a connecting ticket from your point of origin.

Suburban Transit **buses** from New York's Port Authority bus station (℡1-800/222-0492, Ⓦwww.suburbantransit.com) stop every thirty minutes from 6am to 11pm at Palmer Square.

Information is available from the Frist Campus Center at the university (℡609/258-1766, Ⓦwww.princeton.edu/frist) or from the **Chamber of Commerce** at 216 Rockingham Row (Mon–Fri 8.30am–5pm; ℡609/520-1776, Ⓦwww.princetonchamber.org). The **Historical Society museum**, 158 Nassau St (Tues–Sun noon–4pm; ℡609/921-6748, Ⓦwww.princetonhistory .org), organizes **walking tours** through town (Sun 2pm; $6) and also provides **maps** so you can do it yourself. Central Princeton is easily **navigable on foot**, but weather extremes in the winter and summer, as well as the distance of accommodation options from downtown, may make you glad to have a **car**.

The Town and the university

Mercer Street, the long road that sweeps southwest past the university campus to Nassau Street, is lined with elegant Colonial houses, graced with shutters, columns, and wrought-iron fences. The **Princeton Battlefield State Park**, a mile and a half out, includes the **Thomas Clarke House**, 500 Mercer St, a Quaker farmhouse that served as a hospital during the battle. The simple house at 112 Mercer, back toward town, is where **Albert Einstein** lived while teaching at the Institute of Advanced Study (unfortunately, the house is not open to the public).

Princeton University's tranquil and shaded campus is a beautiful place for a stroll. Just inside the main gates on Nassau Street, **Nassau Hall**, a vault-like historic building containing numerous portraits of famous graduates and one of King George II, was, when constructed in 1756, the largest stone building in the nation; its 26-inch-thick walls (now patterned with plaques and patches of ivy placed by graduating classes) withstood American and British fire during the Revolution. It was also the seat of government during Princeton's brief spell as national capital. The 1925 **chapel**, based on one at Kings College, Cambridge University, in England, has stained-glass windows showing scenes from works by Dante, Shakespeare, and Milton, as well as the Bible. Across campus, the **Prospect Gardens**, a flowerbed in the shape of the university emblem, are a blaze of orange in summer. There are student-led **tours** that take you around to all of these sights, though they're somewhat complacent, and on summer afternoons they can be painfully crowded. That said, they are free; tours leave from the Frist Campus Center, which faces Washington Road (Mon–Sat 10am, 11am, 1.30pm & 3.30pm, Sun 1.30pm & 3.30pm; ℡609/258-1766).

In the middle of the campus, fronted by the Picasso sculpture *Head of a Woman*, the **University Art Museum**, not included on the standard tours, is well worth a look for its collection from the Renaissance to the present, including works by Modigliani, Van Gogh, and Warhol, as well as Asian and pre-Columbian art (Tues–Sat 10am–5pm, Sun 1–5pm; free; ℡609/258-3788, Ⓦwww.princetonartmuseum.org).

Accommodation, eating, and drinking

The only **hotel** in the center of Princeton is the ersatz-Colonial *Nassau Inn* on Palmer Square (℡609/921-7500 or 1-800/8-NASSAU, Ⓦwww.nassauinn .com; ❾). Budget **motels** can be found along US-1 and in the suburb of **Lawrenceville** a few miles south of town; there's the functional *Red Roof Inn*, 3203 US-1 (℡609/896-3388, Ⓦwww.redroof.com; ❸), and the more comfortable *McIntosh Inn*, by the Quaker Bridge Mall on US-1 (℡609/896-3700, Ⓦwww.mcintoshinn.com/view-princeton.asp; ❹).

Despite its affluence, Princeton is by no means the culinary capital of New Jersey. There's cheap diner-type **food** along Witherspoon Street; *Teresa's*, 19–23 Palmer Square E (☎609/921-1974), serves creative, good-value Italian food; and *Mediterra*, at 29 Hulfish St (☎609/252-9680), is an upscale Mediterranean restaurant with a welcoming atmosphere and well-prepared food. **Nightlife** is limited, especially out of term time, but the *Triumph Brewery*, 138 Triumph St (☎609/942-7855), has good, home-brewed beers, and is popular with a mixed crowd; meanwhile, the old *Tap Room* bar, downstairs at the *Nassau Inn*, is usually full of ancient revelers drinking, reminiscing, and enjoying live jazz.

The New Jersey shore

New Jersey's Atlantic coast, a 130-mile stretch of almost uninterrupted **resorts** – some rowdy, some run-down, some undeveloped and peaceful – has long been reliant on farming and tourism. No profitable ports were established, nor did short-lived attempts at whaling come to anything. In the late 1980s, the whole coastline suffered severe and well-publicized pollution from ocean dumping. But today, the beaches, if occasionally somewhat crowded, are safe and clean: sandy, broad, and lined by characteristic wooden **boardwalks**, some of which, in an attempt to maintain their condition, charge admission during the summer. The rowdy, sleazy glitz of **Atlantic City** is perhaps the shore's best known attraction, though there are also quieter resorts like **Spring Lake** and Victorian **Cape May**.

Spring Lake and Asbury Park

SPRING LAKE, about twenty miles down the Jersey coast, is one of the smallest, most uncommercial communities on the shore, a gentle respite on the road south to Atlantic City. Tourism in this elegant Victorian resort evolved slowly, without the booms, crises, resurgences, and depressions of other seaside towns – partly due to the strict zoning laws prohibiting new building. You can walk the undeveloped two-mile **boardwalk** and watch the crashing ocean from battered gazebos, swim and bask on the white beaches (in summer, compulsory beach tags, badges that provide admission to the beach, cost a fee), or sit in the shade by the town's namesake, **Spring Lake** itself. Wooden footbridges, swans and geese, and the grand St Catharine Roman Catholic Church on the banks of the lake give it the feel of a country village. What little activity there is centers on the upmarket shops of Third Avenue.

Bruce Springsteen fans can use the town as a base for visiting nearby **ASBURY PARK**, a decaying old seaside town where The Boss lived for many years and played his first gigs. Almost nothing remains of the carousels and seaside arcades that Springsteen wrote about on early albums such as his debut, *Greetings from Asbury Park*; the sole survivor is Madam Marie's now-defunct fortune-telling salon, which still stands amid the rubble and half-completed condominium developments that line the boardwalk. The **Stone Pony**, 913 Ocean Ave (☎732/502-0600, ⓦwww.stoneponyonline.com), where Springsteen played dozens of times in the mid-1970s and to which he has returned intermittently over the years, is the one obligatory stop for devotees.

Practicalities

Spring Lake is accessible by US-34 from the New Jersey Turnpike, and served by New Jersey Transit from New York. The Chamber of Commerce (☎732/449-0577, ⓦwww.springlake.org) keeps erratic hours but the Spring

Lake Hotel and B&B Association (☎732/449-6685) can help find lodging, especially on summer weekends. There are no cheap **motels**, and **B&Bs** can be expensive. The *Chateau Inn*, 500 Warren Ave (☎732/974-2000 or 1-877/974-LAKE, ⊛www.chateauinn.com; ❹–❼), is slightly less expensive than average. Adjacent to Asbury Park, in the much more attractive Victorian resort of **Ocean Grove**, friendly *Lillagaard B&B*, 5 Abbot Ave (☎732/988-1216, ⊛www.lillagaard.com; ❹), is right on the beach. Most of Spring Lake's **restaurants** are in the elegant Victorian hotels along the seafront, and can be pricey. The **North Pavilion** on the boardwalk sells cheap breakfasts and snacks, but there are no fast-food stands along the walk itself. *Who's On Third*, 1300 Third Ave (☎732/449-4233), is a no-nonsense café serving breakfast and lunch. For a blowout, *The Sandpiper*, 7 Atlantic Ave (BYOB; ☎732/449-4700), serves superb fresh fish and seafood in elegant, candlelit surroundings.

Atlantic City

What they wanted was Monte Carlo. They didn't want Las Vegas.
What they got was Las Vegas. We always knew that they would get Las Vegas.

Stuart Mendelson, *Philadelphia Journal*

ATLANTIC CITY, on Absecon Island just off the midpoint of the Jersey shoreline, has been a tourist magnet since 1854, when Philadelphia speculators created it as a rail terminal resort. In 1909, at the peak of the seaside town's popularity, Baedeker wrote "there is something colossal about its vulgarity" – a glitzy, slightly monstrous quality which it sustains today. The real-life model for the modern version of the board game **Monopoly**, it has an impressive popular history, boasting the nation's first **boardwalk** (1870), the world's first **Ferris wheel** (1892), the first color **postcards** (1893), and the first **Miss America Beauty Pageant** (cunningly devised in 1921 to extend the tourist season, and still held here every year). During Prohibition and the Depression, Atlantic City was a center for rum-running, packed with speakeasies and illegal gambling dens. Thereafter, in the face of increasing competition from Florida, it slipped into a steep decline, until desperate city officials decided in 1976 to open up the decrepit resort to legal **gambling**.

Arrival, information, and getting around

Traveling to Atlantic City by bus can be a real deal: **casino-sponsored buses** (⊛www.atlanticcitynj.com/businfo1.asp) from New York, Philadelphia, and other points along the coast give away vouchers exchangeable for cash and free meals. The **bus terminal** at Atlantic and Michigan is served by NJ Transit and Greyhound. NJ Transit trains stop at the **train station** next to the Convention Center, at 1 Miss America Way, and are connected by free shuttle service to all casinos.

Atlantic City International Airport in Pomona (☎609/645-7895, ⊛www.acairport.com) has direct flights to Philadelphia, as well as some flights further afield; from the airport, cabs cost $27 to downtown. For maps and information, head for the Atlantic City Convention & Visitors Authority's helpful **boardwalk information center** outside of Boardwalk Hall (daily 9.30am–5.30pm, summer Fri–Sun 9.30am–8pm; ☎609/449-7130 or 1-888/AC-VISIT, ⊛www.atlanticcitynj.com).

Atlantic City is easy to **walk** around, though it's unwise to stray further from the five-mile boardwalk along the ocean than the parallel Pacific, Atlantic, and Arctic avenues, as other parts of the city can be dangerous at night. Ventnor and Margate, to the south on Absecon Island, are served by **buses** along Atlantic

Avenue. Pale blue Jitneys ($1.50, exact change; ☎609/344-8642, Ⓦwww
.visitac.com/jitney) offer a 24-hour minibus service the length of Pacific
Avenue. Along the boardwalk, various **bike rental** stands and rickshaw-like
rolling chairs (☎609/347-7148) provide alternative means of transportation.

Accommodation

Atlantic City is not Vegas – there's no chance of getting a $40 room at one of
the casinos. The already high **accommodation** rates rise on weekends and in
summer, though rates plunge off-season; if you book ahead and business is slow,
many places will offer discounted **package deals**, with $200 suites going for
under half-price. Otherwise, room prices at the casinos are astronomical, though
reasonably priced **motels** line Pacific and Atlantic avenues behind the boardwalk, and things are cheaper in quiet Ocean City, a family resort to the south.

Bally's Atlantic City Park Place and Boardwalk
☎609/340-2000, Ⓦwww.parkplace.com/ballys
/atlanticcity. The closest Atlantic City gets to the
way-out theme casinos of Vegas. The *Bally's*
megalopolis, with full-service spa and more than
20 restaurants, now encompasses *Claridge's*,
Caesar's, and *Hilton* casino hotels, each with its
own feel but all more or less under one roof. ❼
Econo Lodge Boardwalk 117 S Kentucky Ave
☎609/344-9093, Ⓦwww.choicehotels.com.
Standard chain motel next to the boardwalk and
the *Sands Casino*. ❸
The Irish Pub Inn 164 St James Place
☎609/344-9063, Ⓦwww.theirishpub.com/irish-
pubinn2.htm. Basic, cheap rooms above one of the
town's best bars (for review, see "Entertainment
and nightlife," below). ❶–❷

Quality Inn Beach Block 119 S South Carolina
Ave ☎609/345-7070, Ⓦwww.choicehotels.com.
Chain motel housed in a converted school. The
lobby and shared areas are rather shabby, but the
clean, newly refurbished rooms make up for it.
Prices double on weekends. ❸
Resorts Atlantic City Casino Hotel 1133
Boardwalk ☎1-800/336-6378, Ⓦwww.resort-
sac.com. The most pleasant of the huge casino
hotels, with pool and spa. ❺–❻
Rodeway Inn 124 S North Carolina Ave ☎609/345-
0155, Ⓦwww.choicehotels.com. Clean, basic, reasonably priced rooms close to the boardwalk. ❷
Surfside Resort Hotel 18 S Mount Vernon Ave
☎609/347-SURF, Ⓦwww.surfsideresorthotel.com.
A gay-friendly hotel with standard rooms and a
lively club attached. ❸

The Town

Arriving by train, you'll be confronted by the monstrous **Convention
Center**, which houses a massive food court and standard mall shops along with
its meeting spaces and countless hotel rooms. Most of the hopeful new arrivals,
however, head straight for the casinos, with an ample overspill flooding the
boardwalk and beach. Beyond the boardwalk there is little to see in Atlantic
City, although a quick walk around the eerily quiet slums of the South Inlet
district makes a chilling contrast to the manic jollity a mere block away. This is
not an area in which to linger for any length of time, or indeed at all at night
– the **danger** for tourists is very real, though crime has decreased over the past
few years.

Atlantic City's wooden **boardwalk** was originally built as a temporary walkway, raised above the beach so that vacationers could take a seaside stroll without treading sand into the grand hotels. Alongside the brash 99¢ shops and
exotically named palm-readers, a few beautiful Victorian buildings that survived the wrecking ball invoke past elegance, despite the fact that many now
house fast-food joints. Early in the morning, when the breezes from the ocean
are at their most pleasant, the boardwalk is peaceful, peopled only by keen
cyclists and a few lost souls down on their luck.

The **Central Pier** offers all the fun of a fair, with rides, games, and old-
fashioned "guess your weight" challenges. A few blocks south, another pier has
been remodeled into an ocean-liner-shaped shopping center. The small and
faded **Atlantic City Arts Center** (☎609/347-5837, Ⓦwww.aclink

The casinos of Atlantic City

Each of Atlantic City's dozen **casinos**, which also act as luxury hotels, conference centers, and concert halls, has a slightly different image, though you might not guess it among the apparent uniformity of vast, richly ornamented halls, slot machines, relentless flashing lights and incessant noise, chandeliers, mirrors, and a disorienting absence of clocks or windows.

The most outwardly ostentatious (and "The Donald" wouldn't have it any other way) is Donald Trump's **Taj Mahal**. Occupying nearly twenty acres and over forty stories high, dotted with glittering minarets and onion domes, this gigantic but oddly anticlimactic piece of Far Eastern kitsch stands opposite the arcade-packed Steel Pier at the north end of the boardwalk. It is one of the largest gambling casinos on earth, precariously tottering on the edge of bankruptcy.

Bally's charmingly garish Wild West Casino is much more outlandish and fun, and also offers complete access to the games and memberships of Roman-themed **Caesar's**, smaller, "friendly" **Claridge's**, and the **Hilton**. **Sands**, next door at South Indiana Ave, is a noisy and popular venue with a vaguely circus-related theme. **Resorts**, on the northern end of the boardwalk, is grand without being flashy.

All casinos are **open 24 hours** a day, including holidays, and have a strict minimum **age requirement**, so be prepared to show ID that proves you're 21.

.org/acartcenter), on the Garden Pier at the quiet northern end of the boardwalk, has a free collection of seaside memorabilia, postcards, photos, and a special exhibit on Miss America, as well as traveling art shows. A block off the boardwalk, where Pacific and Rhode Island avenues meet, and at the heart of some of the city's worst deprivation, stands the **Absecon Lighthouse**. Active until 1933, it's recently been fully restored and offers a terrific view from its 167ft tower (July–Aug daily 10am–5pm; rest of year Thurs–Mon 11am–4pm; $5; Ⓦ www.abseconlighthouse.org).

Atlantic City's **beach** is free, family-filled, and surprisingly clean, considering its proximity to the boardwalk. Beaches at well-to-do **Ventnor**, a Jitney ride away, are quieter, while three miles south of Atlantic City, New Jersey's beautiful people pose on the beaches of **Margate** (both beaches charge a nominal fee), watched over by Lucy the Margate Elephant at 9200 Atlantic Ave. A 65ft wood-and-tin Victorian oddity, Lucy was built as a seaside attraction in 1881 and used variously as a tavern and a hotel. Today, her huge belly is filled with a **museum** of Atlantic City memorabilia, as well as photos and artifacts from her own history (April & May and Sept & Oct Sat & Sun 10am–5pm; June–Aug Mon–Sat 10am–8pm, Sun 10am–5pm; $4; Ⓣ 609/823-6473, Ⓦ www.lucytheelephant.org).

Eating

One effect of Atlantic City's rabid commercialization is an abundance of **fast food**. The boardwalk is lined with pizza, burger, and sandwich joints, while the diners on Atlantic and Pacific avenues serve soul food and cheap breakfasts. All the large casinos boast several restaurants, ranging in price and menu but all of average quality, as well as all-you-care-to-eat **buffets** – most cost around $14 for lunch, and a little more for dinner. Some of the casinos offer half-price buffets to "members" or "VIPs" – all you have to do to join is fill out a form and give some proof of address. If money's running low after too many days in the casino, there are bargain buffets on the boardwalk for less than $5 – but inevitably, you get what you pay for.

Hunan Chinese Restaurant 2323 Atlantic Ave ℡609/348-5946. Reasonably priced Chinese food two blocks from the boardwalk. Combination plates run $6–11.

Los Amigos 1926 Atlantic Ave ℡609/344-2293. Great for cheap, late-night food, this pleasant but average Mexican restaurant and bar across from the bus station is open until 3am Friday and Saturday.

Pappa T's Pizza 445 Boardwalk ℡609/348-

5030. One of the better cheap boardwalk joints, with pizza and breakfast from $3.50.

Planet Hollywood at *Caesar's*, 2100 Pacific Ave on the boardwalk ℡609/347-STAR. Decent burgers and salads at hyped-up prices in a hyped-up atmosphere.

White House Sub Shop 2301 Arctic Ave ℡609/345-1564. This bright and super-efficient Atlantic City institution is where the submarine sandwich was born; definitely worth a visit.

Entertainment and nightlife

Atlantic City sells itself as the fun nighttime city; but the **nightlife** centers on the casinos and boardwalk amusements. Once you get bored with slot machines there is little else to do. Big-name entertainers perform regularly at the casinos, with tickets in the $30 range – the free weekly *Whoot* (Ⓦ www.whootnews.com) has listings. The Comedy Stop **comedy club** at the Tropicana (℡1-800/THE-TROP, Ⓦ www.tropicana.net/comedystop) has nightly shows (twice nightly Fri & Sat; $19 Fri, $22 Sat). For cheaper informal fun, try the friendly, dark-paneled *Irish Pub*, 164 St James Place (℡609/344-9063, Ⓦ www.theirishpub.com), which serves extremely cheap food and often has live Irish music. *Studio Six*, 12 S Mt Vernon Ave (℡609/344-2222, Ⓦ www.studiosix.com) is a gay club with cheap drinks and frequent go-go dancing.

Cape May

CAPE MAY was founded in 1620 by the Dutch Captain Mey, on the small hook at the very southern tip of the Jersey coast, jutting out into the Atlantic and washed by the Delaware Bay on the west. After being briefly settled by New England whalers in the late 1600s, it turned in the eighteenth century to more profitable farming and, soon after, to tourism. In 1745 the first advertisement for Cape May's restorative air and fine accommodation appeared in the Philadelphia press, heralding a period of great prosperity, when Southern plantation owners, desiring cool sea breezes without having to venture into Yankee land, flocked to the fashionable boarding houses of this genteel "resort of Presidents."

The Victorian era was Cape May's finest; nearly all its gingerbread architecture dates from a mass rebuilding after a severe fire in 1878. However, the increase in car travel after World War I meant that vacationers could go further, more quickly and more cheaply, and the little town found itself something of an anachronism, while the gaudier charms of Atlantic City became the brightest stars on the Jersey coast. During the 1950s, Cape May began to dust off its most valuable commodity: its history. Today, the whole town is a National Historic Landmark, with over six hundred **Victorian buildings**, tree-lined streets and beautifully kept **gardens**, and a lucrative B&B industry. It teeters dangerously on self-parody at times, thanks to its glut of cutesy olde shoppes, but if you avoid the main drags and wander through the backstreets, you'll enjoy the historical authenticity. The town also boasts good **beaches**.

Arrival, information, and getting around

New Jersey Transit runs an express **bus** to Cape May from Philadelphia and the south Jersey coast, as well as services from New York and Atlantic City. **Ferries** connect the town to Lewes, Delaware (see p.503; $6–8 per person, $20–25 per car; schedules on ℡1-800/64-FERRY, Ⓦ www.capemaylewesferry.com). Maps and **information** are available from the **Welcome Center** at 405

Lafayette St (daily approx 8.30am–4.30pm; ⓣ609/884-9562, ⓦwww
.capemaynj.com), which can also help with finding accommodation.

Though Cape May itself is best enjoyed on foot, to venture out a bit further
rent a **bike** from the Village Bike Shop near the bus terminal, at 609 Lafayette
(summer 8am–6pm, call for off-season hours; $5 per hour, $12 per day;
ⓣ609/884-8500). The Cape May Whale Watcher, at Second Avenue and Wilson
Drive (ⓣ609/884-5445 or 1-800/786-5445, ⓦwww.capemaywhalewatcher
.com), offers three trips (both daily March to Dec) around Cape May Point: two
dolphin-watches (2hrs; 10am & 6.30pm; $20) and a **whale-watching voy-
age** (3hrs; 1pm; $28).

Accommodation

Most of Cape May's pastel Victorian homes seem to be pricey **B&Bs** or **guesthouses**, and the resort is so popular that choice plummets on summer weekends. During July and August even old motor inns can command over $100 a
night; June and September rates are often around half that. Standard **hotels**
front the ocean on Beach Drive, and you can **camp** at *Seashore Campsites*, 720
Seashore Rd (basic campsite $33, with electric and water $36, with full hook-
up $40; reservations recommended July & Aug; ⓣ609/884-4010 or 1-
800/313-CAMP, ⓦwww.seashorecampsites.com).

Abigail Adams Bed and Breakfast 12 Jackson St
ⓣ609/884-1371 or ⓣ1-888/827-4354, ⓦwww
.abigailadamsinn.com. High-quality lodging 100ft
from the beach. Rates include afternoon tea. ⑤–⑥

Inn of Cape May 7 Ocean St ⓣ1-800/582-5933,
ⓦwww.innofcapemay.com. This once-fashionable
Victorian shorefront hotel now has a small adjoining modern motel wing. The cheapest rooms are
those with shared baths in the main building. Open
daily April–Oct, weekends only late Oct–Dec.
④–⑦

Manor House 612 Hughes St ⓣ609/884-4710,
ⓦwww.manorhouse.net. Great breakfasts and a
relaxing porch in the heart of the historic district. ⑤

Queen Victoria 102 Ocean St ⓣ609/884-8702,
ⓦwww.queenvictoria.com. Twenty-one rooms in
four buildings, including a cottage and a carriage
house. Rates include bicycle loans, beach chairs,
breakfast (in bed if desired), and afternoon tea.
⑤–⑦

Sea Breeze Motel 204 Pittsburgh Ave
ⓣ609/884-3352, ⓦwww.seabreezemotel.com.
No-nonsense budget motel in a residential street a
couple of blocks from the beach, a mile from
downtown. ③

Summer Cottage Inn 613 Columbia Ave
ⓣ609/884-4948, ⓦwww.summercottageinn.com.
1867 inn with verandas and cupola. ⑤–⑦

The Town and the beaches

Cape May's brightly colored houses were built by nouveau riche Victorians with
a healthy disrespect for subtlety. Cluttered with cupolas, gazebos, balconies, and
"widow's walks," the houses follow no architectural rules except excess. They
were known as "patternbook homes," with designs and features chosen from cat-
alogs and thrown together in accordance with the owner's taste. The Victorian
obsession with the Near East is everywhere: Moorish arches and onion domes
sit comfortably next to gingerbread- and Queen Anne–style turrets.

The **Emlen Physick House**, 1048 Washington St (call for hours; $8;
ⓣ609/884-5404), now a part of the Mid-Atlantic Center for the Arts, was
built by the popular Philadelphia architect Frank Furness. It has been restored
to its 1879 glory, with whimsical "upside-down" chimneys, a mock Tudor half-
timbered facade, and much original furniture.

West of town, where the Delaware Bay and the ocean meet, the 1859 **Cape
May Lighthouse**, visible from 25 miles out at sea, offers great views from a
gallery below the lantern (199 steps up) and a small exhibit on its history at
ground level (daily April–Nov, winter weekends, call for hours; $5; ⓣ609/884-
8656). Three miles north of town on US-9, **Historic Cold Spring Village**,

Wildwood

The traditionally blue-collar resort of nearby **Wildwood**, on a barrier island east off Rte-47, offers a counterpoint to the old-world fakery (pretty though it may be) of Cape May. Its 1950s architecture, left lovingly intact, includes dozens of gaudy and fun-looking hotels with names like *Pink Orchid*, *Waikiki*, and *The Shalimar*, all still featuring plastic palm trees, kidney-shaped swimming pools, and plenty of aqua, orange, and pink paint. To best appreciate the town's brash charm, take a stroll along the boardwalk, and stop along the wide, throbbing, free beaches.

720 Rte-9 (late May through mid-June & Sept Sat & Sun 10am–4.30pm; June–Aug Tues–Sun 10am–4.30pm; $7; ☎609/898-2300, ⊛www.hcsv.org), depicts a typical nineteenth-century south Jersey farming community. Restored buildings from the region house a jail, school, inn, and shops, and there are various craft shows and special events.

Cape May's excellent **beaches** literally sparkle with quartz pebbles. Beach tags ($4 per day, $11 per week, $13 for a seasonal pass purchased before Memorial Day) must be worn from 10am until 6pm in the summer, and are available at the beach, from official vendors, and from **City Hall**, 643 Washington St (☎609/884-9525, ⊛www.capemaycity.com).

Eating

Cape May lacks the usual boardwalk snack bars, but it has plenty of cheap **lunch** places. **Dinner**, however, is far more expensive. Cape May's liquor laws are stringent, which means that many restaurants are BYO – call to check.

Bellevue Tavern 7 S Main St ☎609/463-1738. Functional c.1900 bar serving crab cakes and inexpensive hot sandwiches; dinners of steak, veal, and seafood average $18.

Gecko's Carpenter's Lane ☎609/898-7750. A good lunch stop with a tasty Southwestern menu and great desserts. Patio seating available.

The Lemon Tree 101 Liberty Way ☎609/884-2704. A good antidote to the coffeeshops along the street; the cheesesteaks at this cheap, cheerful deli are Philly-quality.

Louie's Pizza 7 Gurney St ☎609/884-0305. Opposite the beach, fresh pizza from $12.75, or $2.25 per slice.

Mad Batter 19 Jackson St ☎609/884-5970. Splash out on meat and fresh fish dishes, served by candlelight in the garden. Lunch is $7–15, dinner $14–30.

Nightlife and entertainment

Cape May is a friendly and laid-back place to be after dark; the day-trippers have gone home and the **bars** and **music venues** are enjoyed by locals and tourists alike. If you're after something a bit more lively, head a few miles north to the raucous nightclubs of **Wildwood**. Again, remember that you may have to travel a little farther than you expect to find a drink.

Cabana's 429 Beach Ave ☎609/884-4800. Two-level bar which often hosts live music downstairs; upstairs is a low-key cocktail lounge.

Carney's 401 Beach Ave ☎609/884-4424. Spacious and relaxed Irish bar, with raucous live music.

Ugly Mug Washington St Mall and Decatur St ☎609/884-3459. This friendly bar is a local favorite, and serves chowder, sandwiches, and seafood.

New England

AL - ALABAMA	IN - INDIANA	MN - MINNESOTA	RI - RHODE ISLAND
AR - ARKANSAS	LA - LOUISIANA	MS - MISSISSIPPI	SC - SOUTH CAROLINA
CT - CONNECTICUT	MA - MASSACHUSETTS	NC - NORTH CAROLINA	VA - VIRGINIA
DE - DELAWARE	MD - MARYLAND	NH - NEW HAMPSHIRE	VT - VERMONT
FL - FLORIDA	ME - MAINE	NJ - NEW JERSEY	WI - WISCONSIN
IL - ILLINOIS	MI - MICHIGAN	PA - PENNSYLVANIA	WV - WEST VIRGINIA

CHAPTER 3 **Highlights**

✳ **Boston, MA**
Revolutionary history
come to life around
every charming corner,
in one of America's most
storied, walkable cities.
See p.205

✳ **Provincetown, MA** Wild
beaches, lovely flower-
filled streets, and an
alternative vibe on the
outer reaches of Cape
Cod. See p.230

✳ **Historic "summer cot-
tages," Newport, RI**
Conspicuous consump-
tion gone crazy in this
yachtie WASP resort.
See p.249

✳ **Grand resort hotels,
NH** At the opulent hotels
of *Mount Washington*

and *Balsams* you'll
understand why vaca-
tioning in the White
Mountains was once the
preserve of the
extremely well off. See
p.269

✳ **Montpelier, VT** Relaxed,
friendly, and relatively
tourist-free, pretty
Montpelier is bounded
by rivers and a forest of
tall trees. See p.278

✳ **Acadia National Park,
ME** Remote mountains
and lakes, stunning
beaches, and the
chance to catch the sun-
rise before anyone else
in the US. See p.295

New England

The six **NEW ENGLAND** states of **Massachusetts**, **Rhode Island**, **Connecticut**, **New Hampshire**, **Vermont**, and **Maine** like to view themselves as the repository of all that is intrinsically American. In this version of history, the tangled streets of old Boston, the farms of Connecticut, and the village greens of Vermont are the cradle of the nation. Certainly, nostalgia is at the root of the region's tourist trade. While the real business of making a living happens in cities for the most part well off the tourist trail, innumerable small towns have been dolled-up to recapture a past that is at best wishful, and at times purely fictional. Picturesque though they may be, with white-spired churches beside immaculate rolling greens, they're not always authentic: there's little to distinguish a clapboard house built last year from another, two hundred years old, which has just had its annual coat of white paint.

The genteel seaside towns of modern Cape Cod and Rhode Island are a far cry from the first European settlements in New England. While the Pilgrims congregated in neat, pristine communities, later arrivals, with so much land to choose from, felt no need to reconstruct the compact little villages they had left behind in Europe. Instead, they fanned out across the Native American fields, or straggled their farmhouses in endless strips along the newly built roadways (thus establishing a more genuinely American style of development). As the European foothold on the continent became more certain, the coastline came increasingly to be viewed as prime real estate, to be lined with grand patrician homes, from the Vanderbilt mansions of Newport to the presidential compounds of the Bush and Kennedy families.

The Ivy League colleges – Harvard, Yale, Brown, Dartmouth, et al – still embody New England's strong sense of its own superiority, though in fact the region's traditional role as home to the WASP elite is due more to the vagaries of history and ideology than to economic or cultural realities. Its thin soil and harsh climate made it difficult for the first pioneers to sustain an agricultural way of life, while the industrial prosperity of the nineteenth and early twentieth centuries is now for the most part a distant memory. Despite recent diversification, and the development of some high-tech industries, New England has pockets, mostly in rural Vermont and New Hampshire, that are as poor as any in the US.

New England can be a rather pricey place to visit, especially in late September and October, when visitors flock to see the magnificent **fall foliage**. Its tourist facilities are aimed at weekenders from the big cities as much as outsiders; places like **Cape Cod** and the **Berkshires** make convenient short breaks for locals. **Connecticut** and **Rhode Island** in particular

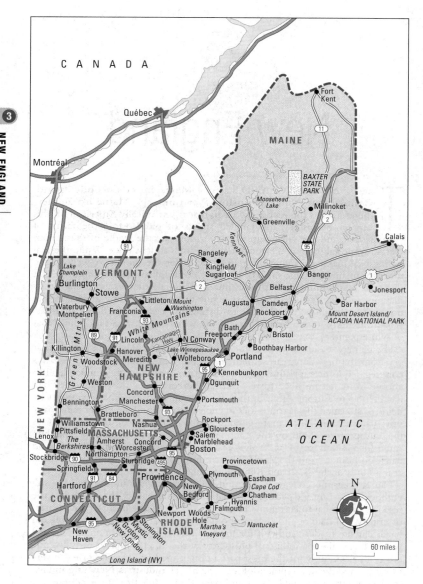

clearly form part of the great East Coast megalopolis, which stretches from Washington to Boston. **Boston** itself, however, is a vibrant and stimulating city, while further up the coast the towns finally thin out and the scenery gets appealing (as does the **seafood**). Inland, too, the lakes and mountains of **New Hampshire** and particularly **Maine** offer rural wildernesses to rival any in the nation. **Vermont** is slightly less diverse, but its country roads offer pleasant wandering through tiny villages and serene forests.

Some history

The Algonquin, **Native Americans** who first inhabited the northeast shore-line, lived by farming and fishing along the coast in summer, retreating with their animals to the relative warmth of the inland valleys in winter. Though the natives did not always live in harmony with each other, they did manage to repel the first European invaders, earning themselves five hundred years' grace, some time around 1000 AD, by forcing the Viking Leif Eriksson to abandon the settlement of **Vinland the Good** – which may have been anywhere between Newfoundland and Massachusetts.

Six years after Columbus's first voyage, John Cabot nosed by in 1498, in search of the Northwest Passage. Over the next century, European fisher-men began to return each year, though it was not until the early 1600s that the French and English attempted to found permanent colonies, in what is now Maine. The name – New England – was given in 1614 by surveyor-cum-explorer John Smith, who particularly appreciated the plentiful lob-sters.

This was not promising land: as a character in Robert Lowell's *Endecott and the Red Cross* put it, "I'm not a birdwatcher or an Indian . . . I don't see the point of this outpost of England." Without precious metals to be mined, or the potential to grow lucrative crops, the first major impetus for emigration was **religion**. Refugees from intolerance – notably the Puritans, beginning with the **Pilgrims** in 1620 – made the arduous voyage to search for the freedom to build their own communities. The Pilgrims only survived at first thanks to the Indians: they were aided by a certain Squanto, who had been kidnapped, sold as a slave in Spain, and returned home via England. In thanks, the Pilgrims forced the natives from the terraces they had farmed for generations, dismiss-ing as inappropriate their solution to the problems of survival in such terrain: "Their land is spacious and void, and there are few and do but run over the grass . . . They are not industrious, neither have art, science, skill or faculty to use either the land or the commodities of it."

The possibility of a serious Native American threat was eliminated in **King Philip's War** of 1675–1676, in which a leader of the Narragansett Indians (known as Philip) persuaded feuding groups to bury their differences in one last, and ultimately hopeless, stand against the settlers. By then, though, white colonization had gathered an unstoppable momentum. The **Salem witch tri-als** of 1692 provided a salutary lesson on the potential dangers of fanaticism, and as immigration became less English-based, with influxes of Huguenots after 1680 and Irish in 1708, Puritan domination decreased and a definite class structure began to emerge.

While the strand of history that began with the Pilgrims is just one among many in the colonization of America – the Spanish were in Santa Fe before the Pilgrims ever left England – the metropolis of **Boston** deserves to be cele-brated as the place where the great project of **American independence** first captured the popular imagination. This leading port of colonial America was always the likeliest focus of resentment against the latest impositions of the British government, and was ready to take up the challenge thrown down by British Prime Minister Townshend in 1767: "I dare tax America." So many of the seminal moments of the **Revolutionary War** took place here: the Boston Massacre of 1770, the Boston Tea Party of 1773, and the first shots in nearby Lexington and Concord in 1775.

Once nationhood was secured by the signing of the **Declaration of**

Independence on July 4, 1776, New England's prosperity was ironically hit hard by the loss of trade with England, and Boston was slowly eclipsed by Philadelphia, New York, and the new capital, Washington. The **Triangular Trade** in slaves, sugar, and rum provided one substitute source of income, the brief heyday of **whaling** another. New England was also momentarily at the forefront of the **Industrial Revolution**, when water-powered mills created a booming textile industry, most of which quickly moved south where wages were scandalously cheaper. The attempt to farm the north, however, foundered: careless techniques served to exhaust the land, and as the vast spaces of the western US opened to settlement, many of the inland towns fell silent.

Massachusetts

To the first colonists of the **Massachusetts Bay Company**, their arrival near the site of modern Salem in 1629 marked a crucial moment in history. **Puritans** who had decided to leave England before it was engulfed by civil war saw their purpose, in the words of Governor John Winthrop, as the establishment of a utopian "**City upon a hill.**" Their new colony of **MASSACHUSETTS** was to be a beacon to the rest of humanity, an exemplar of sober government along sound spiritual principles. Not all those who followed, however, shared the same motivation; the story is often told of the preacher who told his congregation that they had come to New England to build a new kingdom of God, only to be challenged by a vociferous parishioner who said he had come to fish.

In their own terms, the Puritans were not successful: as waves of immigration brought all kinds of dissenters and free-thinkers from Europe, society in New England inevitably became secular. However, their **influence** remained. A clarity of thought and forcefulness of purpose can be traced from the foundation of Harvard College in 1636, through the intellectual impetus behind the Revolution and the crusade against slavery, to the nineteenth-century achievements of **writers** such as Melville, Emerson, Hawthorne, and Thoreau.

Other traditions, too, have helped shape the state – poor migrants from **Ireland** and **Italy**, freed and escaped **slaves** from the Southern states, **Portuguese** seamen – even if they have not always been welcome. The anti-immigrant "Know-Nothing" party of the 1850s acquired considerable public support; in 1927, the Italian anarchists **Sacco and Vanzetti** came up against conservative old Massachusetts, and were framed and executed on murder charges. As recently as the 1970s, Boston experienced African-American racial conflicts that matched the bitterness of those erupting throughout the nation. This has been somewhat healed of late, as have any economic doldrums that plagued the city for the latter half of the twentieth century, and a new sense of confidence – so emblematic of Boston's storied past – has taken hold.

Boston is East Coast America at its best, and spending a few days there is strongly recommended. It's a place that isn't content to rest on its laurels – the history is visible, but there's a great deal of modern life and energy besides, thanks in part to the presence of **Cambridge**, the home of Harvard University, just across the river. Several further historic towns are within easy reach – **Salem** to the north, **Concord** and **Lexington** just inland, and **Plymouth** to the south. **Provincetown**, a three-hour ferry ride across the bay at the tip of Cape Cod, is great fun to visit, and the rest of the Cape offers historic towns and lovely beaches – with the requisite huge crowds. Except for a handful of college towns such as **Amherst**, **inland Massachusetts** is much quieter; its settlements are naturally concentrated where the land is fertile, such as along the Connecticut River Valley and in the **Berkshires** to the west.

Getting around Massachusetts

Massachusetts is an easy state to tour on **public transportation**: planes, trains, and buses all radiate out from Boston; connections to **Cape Cod** in particular are legion. The **Amtrak** line that connects Boston with New York, Philadelphia, and Washington is the best regional **train** service in the nation, while the *Vermonter* gives access via Springfield to Montréal, Toronto, and Chicago. The recently introduced *Downeaster* service – linking Boston to Portland, in Maine – follows a scenic route along the New England coast. **Buses** from Boston are also plentiful. The main east–west artery across the state is I-90; the major north–south route is I-91, which runs along the Connecticut River Valley.

Boston

Although the metropolitan area of **BOSTON** has long since expanded to fill the shoreline of **Massachusetts Bay**, and stretches for miles inland as well, the seventeenth-century port at its heart is still discernible. Forget the neat grids of modern urban America; the twisting streets clustered around **Boston Common** are a reminder of how the nation started out, and the city is enjoyably human in scale.

Boston was, until 1755, the biggest city in America; as the one most directly affected by the latest whims of the British Crown, it was the natural birthplace for the opposition that culminated in the **Revolutionary War**. Numerous evocative sites from that era are preserved along the **Freedom Trail** through downtown. Since then, however, Boston has in effect turned its back on the sea. As the third busiest port in the British Empire (after London and Bristol), it stood on a narrow peninsula. What is now Washington Street provided the only access by land, and when the British set off to Lexington in 1775 they embarked in ships from the Common itself. During the nineteenth century, the Charles River marshlands were filled in to create the posh Back Bay residential area. Central Boston is now slightly set back from the water, separated by the hideous John Fitzgerald Expressway that carries I-93 across downtown. The city has been working on routing the traffic underground and disposing of this eyesore – a project a decade in the making, known as "the **Big Dig**." Although this gargantuan task was once hoped to be finished by 2002, today many locals say that they will consider themselves lucky if it's completed within their lifetimes.

There is a certain truth in the charge leveled by other Americans that Boston likes to live in the past; echoes of the "Brahmins" of a century ago can be heard in the upper-class drawl of the posher districts. But this is by no means just a city of WASPs: the Irish who began to arrive in large numbers after the Great Famine had produced their first mayor as early as 1885, and the president of

ACCOMMODATION
82 Chandler Street — H
Back Bay Summer Hostel — O
Beantown Hostel — B
Best Western –
Inn at Longwood Medical — Q
Boston Park Plaza — D
Charles Street Inn — C
Copley Square Hotel — I
Eliot Hotel — L
Harborside Inn — A
HI-Boston — M
Howard Johnson Lodge — P
Lenox Hotel — J
Newbury Guest House — K
The Tremont Boston — E
YMCA Central Branch — N
YWCA — F&G

Logan Airport

Bunker Hill

CHARLESTOWN

PROSPECT
MT VERNON
CHESTNUT
WINTHROP ST
PARK ST
HIGH STREET
SOLEY ST
MONUMENT AVE
PLEASANT ST
TREMONT STREET

Constitution Inn

USS Constitution

CHARLESTOWN BRIDGE

Museum of Science

Charles River Dam

LAND BOULEVARD
FIRST STREET

FleetCenter & North Station

Copp's Hill Burying Ground

Old North Church

NORTH END

SALEM ST
SNOW HILL ST
HULL ST
UNITY ST
CHARTER STREET
COMMERCIAL STREET
HANOVER STREET
PRINCE ST
HANOVER STREET
ENDICOTT ST
N WASHINGTON ST
MARGIN ST
THACHER ST
PORTLAND ST
FRIEND ST
CANAL ST
HAVERHILL ST
MERRIMAC STREET
NEW CHARDON ST
LOMASNEY WAY
NASHUA ST
BLOSSOM ST
MCLEAN ST

Paul Revere House

New England Holocaust Memorial

TED WILLIAMS TUNNEL
SUMNER TUNNEL

COMMERCIAL ST
ATLANTIC AVENUE

Long Wharf

New England Aquarium

Rowes Wharf

Columbus Park

Quincy Market

Faneuil Hall

Old State House

Government Center

Old City Hall

Old Court House

King's Chapel Burying Ground

State House

BEACON HILL

Boston Common

Abiel Smith School

Smith Court & African Meeting House

Hayden House

CAMBRIDGE STREET
BOWDOIN ST
TEMPLE ST
HANCOCK ST
SOMERSET ST
DERNE ST
MYRTLE ST
REVERE ST
PHILLIPS ST
PINCKNEY ST
MT VERNON ST
CHESTNUT ST
BEACON STREET
CHARLES STREET
CEDAR LANE WAY
W CEDAR ST
ANDERSON ST
GARDEN ST
GROVE ST
IRVING ST
S RUSSELL ST
JOY ST
WALNUT ST
SPRUCE ST
BRANCH ST
ACORN ST

Old South Meeting House

Omni Parker House

Old Granary Burying Ground

Park Street Church

PARK ST
TREMONT STREET
WASHINGTON STREET
WINTER ST
BROMFIELD ST
SCHOOL ST
BOYLSTON ST
WEST ST
AVERY ST
CHAUNCY ST
HARRISON AVENUE
KINGSTON ST
BEDFORD ST
LINCOLN ST
SOUTH ST
ESSEX ST

STATE ST
CONGRESS STREET
FRANKLIN ST
FEDERAL ST
DEVONSHIRE STREET
ARCH ST
SUMMER ST
HIGH ST
PEARL ST
OLIVER ST
BROAD ST
PURCHASE STREET
ATLANTIC AVENUE
MATHEWS ST
MILK ST
WATER ST
INDIA ST
BATTERYMARCH ST

Children's Museum

Boston Tea Party Ship & Museum

South Station

SOUTH BOSTON

MIDWAY ST
A STREET
MELCHER ST
NECCO CT
NECCO ST
SUMMER STREET
CONGRESS STREET
WORMWOOD ST
WARRENTON ST
BINFORD ST
SOBIN PARK ST

TUNNEL

TED WILLIAMS TUNNEL

N

0   400 yds

1 2 3 4 5 6 7 8 9 10 11 12 13 14 15 16

A

B

C

BOSTON

RESTAURANTS & BARS

Big Fish Seafood	15
Restaurant	10
The Black Rose	17
Bull and Finch Pub	11
Commonwealth Brewery	
Company	22
Crossroads Irish Pub	4
Daily Catch	21
Division Sixteen	8
Durgin Park	1
Gabriele's	2
Giacomo's	12
JJ Foley's	9
Kingfish Hall	18
Legal Sea Foods	3
Mamma Maria	13
Mike's Pastries	23
News	24
Other Side Cosmic Café	14
Pad Thai Café	7
Panificio Bakery	16
Rabia's	
Sevens Ale House	20
Steve's Greek-American	6
Cuisine	19
Trattoria Il Panino	
Tremont 647	

Charles River

Cambridge

the whole country within a hundred years. The liberal tradition that spawned the Kennedys remains alive, fed in part by the presence in the city of more than one hundred universities and colleges, the most famous of which – **Harvard University** – is actually in the city of Cambridge, just across the Charles River.

The slump of the Depression seemed to linger in Boston for years – even in the 1950s, the population was actually dwindling – but these days the place definitely has a rejuvenated feel to it. **Quincy Market** has served as a blueprint for urban redevelopment worldwide, and with its busy street life, imaginative museums and galleries, fine architecture, and palpable history, Boston is the one destination in New England there's no excuse for missing.

Arrival and information

Boston may not be the "hub of the universe," as Oliver Wendell Holmes once said, but it is the center of New England's transportation networks. An increasing number of direct flights from Europe means that it provides many visitors with their first taste of America, while efficient rail and bus services from New York, Montréal, and further afield make this an obvious starting point, wherever you're heading in New England.

By air

Logan Airport (☎617/561-1800 or 1-800/23-LOGAN), constantly busy with both international and domestic services, is a mere three miles from downtown Boston, on an artificial peninsula jutting into Boston Harbor. A **taxi** into town costs $15–20, plus an extra $4.50 in fees and tolls; the trip should take twenty minutes, but most traffic passes through the Sumner or Callahan tunnels, which can get very congested. The construction of the Ted Williams Tunnel has alleviated the problem somewhat. Between 5.30am and 1am, free **shuttle buses** run every few minutes from all airport terminals to the airport **subway** station on the MBTA Blue line (see "City transportation and tours," opposite), from where it's an easy ten-minute ride to the city center.

By train

Amtrak (☎1-800/USA-RAIL, ⓦwww.amtrak.com) trains along the Northeast Corridor from Providence, Washington, DC, and New York, and from Chicago and Canada via Springfield, as well as the summer-only Cape Cod specials, arrive a short walk from downtown Boston near the waterfront at **South Station**, Summer Street and Atlantic Avenue. The renovated station houses information booths, newsstands, restaurants, and a fantastic old clock, though no currency exchange. The Red subway line inside the station can whisk you to the center of town or out to Cambridge. Some Amtrak services also make an extra stop at **Back Bay Station**, 145 Dartmouth St, on the Orange subway line near Copley Square. **North Station** is used only by MBTA commuter trains.

By bus

Several **bus** companies provide direct links between Boston and the rest of New England. Vermont Transit (☎1-800/451-3292, ⓦwww.vermonttransit .com) covers western Massachusetts, New Hampshire's White Mountains, Vermont, and Montréal; while Concord Trailways (☎1-800/639-3317, ⓦwww.concordtrailways.com) runs to southern New Hampshire and up the Maine coast. Heading south, Bonanza Bus Lines (☎1-888/751-8800, ⓦwww.bonanzabus.com) connects Providence and Newport, Cape Cod, and

New York City; and Peter Pan Bus Lines (☎1-800/237-8747, ⓦwww.peter-panbus.com) services New York and western Massachusetts. Greyhound (☎1-800/231-2222, ⓦwww.greyhound.com), with its many connections, offers nationwide service. Plymouth and Brockton Bus Co. (☎508/746-0378, ⓦwww.p-b.com), serving Hyannis, has buses that leave from Logan Airport; all other buses leave from South Station (see "By train," above).

Information

The most convenient place to get advice and maps is the **Visitor Information Center** (Mon–Sat 8.30am–5pm, Sun 9am–5pm; ☎617/536-4100 or 1-800/888-5515, ⓦwww.bostonusa.com) above the Park Street subway stop on the Tremont Street side of Boston Common. There are also information kiosks in **Quincy Market**, the **John Hancock Tower** at Copley Square in Back Bay, and in the **Prudential Center**, also in Back Bay. For advance information, the **Boston By Phone** service (☎1-888/SEE-BOSTON) allows visitors anywhere in North America to connect directly with a wide range of hotels and services. The city's main **post office** is at McCormack Station, Post Office Square (Mon–Fri 8am–5pm; ☎617/720-4754).

City transportation and tours

Much of the pleasure of visiting Boston comes from being in a city that was built long before cars were invented. Walking around town can be a joy; conversely, driving is an absolute nightmare. The freeways won't take you where you want to go, the one-way traffic systems can have you circling for hours, and if you ever do arrive, parking lots are thin on the ground and very expensive. There's no point renting a car in Boston until the day you leave, especially since the city's public transportation is so good and the local drivers so bad.

The Massachusetts Bay Transportation Authority (MBTA, known as the "T") is responsible for Boston's **subway** system and **trolleys**. The subway, which opened in 1897, is the oldest in the US; its first station, **Park Street**, remains its center (any train marked "inbound" is headed here), and is the place to pick up all schedules and information. Four lines – Red, Green, Blue, and Orange – operate daily from 5am until 1am, although certain routes begin to shut down earlier. Away from downtown, the trains emerge from tunnels to run along the city's major arteries. Though maps are posted at each station, it's a good idea to pick up the widely available Rapid Transit maps for reference. Trains are fast and safe; only some parts of the Orange line might be said to be unsafe after dark.

Within the city, the standard fare is $1, paid with tokens inserted into turnstiles, but on incoming aboveground routes you have to pay extra, up to $2.75 (conversely, some outbound aboveground routes are free). You can buy eleven tokens for the price of ten, and a **Boston Visitor Pass** covers all subway and local bus journeys at a cost of $6 for a day, $11 for three days, or $22 for a week. For MBTA **information** call ☎617/222-3200 or 1-800/392-6100, or visit ⓦwww.mbta.com.

The normal fare on MBTA's **local buses** is 75¢, but longer distances, such as out to Salem or Marblehead, cost up to $2.75. MBTA also runs **commuter rail lines**, extending as far as Salem, Ipswich, and Concord; these are based at the unlovely **North Station** (☎617/222-3200) on Causeway Street, under the FleetCenter.

In and around Boston are some eighty miles of **bike trails**, making it an excellent city to explore on two wheels. Bicycles can be rented from Back Bay Bikes & Boards, 333 Newbury St (☎617/247-2336), from mid-March through mid-October, and from Boston Bike Tours and Rentals, near the Visitor Information Center on Boston Common (☎617/308-5902). Rentals are around $15 for two hours, or $20–25 per day.

City tours

It's easy enough to get to know Boston by following the **Freedom Trail** on foot (see p.212). If you prefer to be guided, though, narrated trips run throughout the day aboard the hundred-minute Old Town Trolley Tours (☎617/269-7010; $25, kids aged 4–12 $7) or the similarly priced Discover Boston Trolley Tours (☎617/268-1861, ⓦwww.discoverbostontours.com), which specializes in narrated audio tours in multiple languages. But nothing is as popular (or as novel) as a Boston Duck Tour (adults $23, kids 4–11 $14; ☎617/723-DUCK, ⓦwww.bostonducktours.com), a very entertaining romp by land and by sea aboard a real WWII amphibious landing vehicle. Same-day tickets are sold inside the Prudential Center daily, April through November. Boston By Foot, 77 N Washington St (☎617/367-2345), conducts ninety-minute walking tours for $9. Also useful are the **bus excursions** further afield to Lexington, Concord, Salem, and Plymouth with Brush Hill Tours/Gray Line (☎617/720-6342, ⓦwww.brushhilltours.com or www.grayline.com). Boston Bike Tours (☎617/308-5902, ⓦwww.bostonbiketours.com), on Boston Common, can take you around for a couple of gentle hours by bike. A two-hour tour costs $20, or only $15 if you have your own bike; either way, a helmet, map, and water are included.

Accommodation

Good-quality inexpensive **accommodation** is hard to find in Boston – any hotel room within walking distance of downtown for under $120 has to be considered a bargain. Citywide Reservation Services (☎617/267-7424 or 1-800/468-3593, ⓦwww.cityres.com) can often get discounts of ten percent or more at hotels, inns, or guesthouses, though a more enjoyable and affordable way of staying in the Boston area is to use a **B&B agency**. The excellent B&B Agency of Boston, 47 Commercial Wharf (☎617/720-3540 or 1-800/248-9262; in the UK ☎0800/895 128, ⓦwww.bbonline.com/ma/bnbagency /bnb.html), offers hundreds of properties across the city for $80–120 a night. Host Homes of Boston (☎617/244-1308 or 1-800/600-1308, ⓦwww .hosthomesofboston.com) and Boston Reservations (☎617/332-4199, ⓦwww.bostonreservations.com) both provide a similar service.

Hotels, motels, and B&Bs

82 Chandler Street 82 Chandler St ☎617/482-0408. One of Boston's best in-town B&Bs, this refreshingly restored 1863 brownstone is on one of the most up-and-coming streets of the South End. Good breakfasts are served communally on the sun-splashed top floor, where you'll find the best room in the house. ❺–❻

A Cambridge House 2218 Massachusetts Ave, Cambridge ☎617/491-6300 or 1-800/232-9989, ⓦwww.acambridgehouse.com. Classy, restored B&B near Porter Square, a 30min walk from Harvard Square. Tasty breakfasts, served on the patio in summer, and early-evening nibbles and wine. ❻

Best Western – Inn at Longwood Medical 342 Longwood Ave ☎617/731-4700 or 1-800/528-1234. Above-average motel rooms near Longwood T station and within walking distance of Fenway Park. ❻

Boston Park Plaza 64 Arlington St ☎617/426-2000 or 1-800/225-2008. Spacious, high-ceilinged rooms in Bill Clinton's favorite grand old Boston hotel, in the Back Bay. The presence of the swank *Whiskey Park* bar and several airline offices in the hotel ensure that it's always a hub of activity. ❻–❽

Charles Street Inn 94 Charles St ☎617/314-8900, ⓦwww.charlesstreetinn.com. Pampered luxury in the heart of Beacon Hill, with nine rooms, each named after a famous local figure (Ralph Waldo Emerson, Henry James, and the like). ❾

Copley Square Hotel 47 Huntington Ave ☎617/536-9000 or 1-800/225-7062. Situated on the eastern fringe of Copley Square, this quiet hotel is also home to the *Café Budapest*, widely considered the most romantic restaurant in Boston. ❽–❾

Eliot Hotel 370 Commonwealth Ave at Massachusetts Ave ☎617/267-1607 or 1-800/443-5468, ⓦ www.eliothotel.com. West Back Bay's answer to the *Ritz*, at the busy crossroads of Boston's upscale student enclave. Rooms have luxurious Italian marble bathrooms and private pantries. Nice breakfasts, too, and possibly the best (if not the most expensive) restaurant in Boston, *Clio*. ❾

Harborside Inn 185 State St ☎617/723-7500, ⓦ www.hagopianhotels.com. Luxurious hotel with a Victorian accent in a renovated mercantile warehouse, across from Quincy Market and the Custom House. Rates drop some $30 a night Dec–March. ❻–❼

Howard Johnson Lodge 1271 Boylston St ☎617/267-8300 or 1-800/654-2000. Reasonably priced motel rooms next to Fenway Park. The free parking's a plus. ❺

Kendall Hotel 350 Main St, Cambridge ☎617/577-1300, ⓦ www.kendallhotel.com. Newly renovated 1895 Victorian firehouse in Kendall Square is now a boutique hotel with 65 rooms. High-speed Internet access included in all rooms. ❻–❼

Lenox Hotel 710 Boylston St ☎617/536-5300 or 1-800/471-1422, ⓦ www.lenoxhotel.com. Lovingly maintained, medium-sized hotel in Back Bay, where the 200-plus rooms are graced with brass chandeliers, dark wood furniture, and marble bathrooms. ❾

Newbury Guest House 261 Newbury St ☎617/437-7666 or 1-800/383-1550, ⓦ www.hagopianhotels.com. Well-located, big, 32-room Victorian brownstone house, with rates at the lower end of Boston's price range. $10 parking and free continental breakfast are also available. Rates go down substantially Dec–Feb. ❺–❻

The Tremont Boston 275 Tremont St ☎617/426-1400 or 1-800/331-9998, ⓦ www.wyndham.com. Well-restored, 322-room Art Deco hotel, in the Theater District two blocks from the Common. ❺–❾

Hostels

Back Bay Summer Hostel 575 Commonwealth Ave ☎617/267-8599, or 617/531-0459 in the off-season, ⓦ www.bostonhostel.org. A well-located Boston University dorm operates as a hostel in the summer months. Dorm beds $33–39. ❶–❷

Beantown Hostel 222 Friend St ☎617/723-0800. Dorm beds for $25 next door to and above the *Irish Embassy* pub (232 Friend St), about 5 minutes' walk north of Faneuil Hall. Free admission to pub gigs on most nights, and free barbecues Tues and Sun. ❶

Constitution Inn (formerly the Charlestown YMCA) 150 2nd Ave, Charleston Navy Yard ☎617/241-8400. Rooms near the USS *Constitution*, popular with military personnel, with private bath and TV for $99 a night. Guests enjoy free use of the excellent gym. ❹

HI-Boston 12 Hemenway St ☎617/536-9455, ⓦ www.bostonhostel.org. In the Fenway area (Hynes Convention Center T station), close to the hip end of Newbury St and the Lansdowne St clubs, this is the best hostel in town, with Internet access and a Council Travel office on the ground floor (as well as no curfew). Dorm beds are $33–39 a night. In summer, book ahead, or check in at 8am, to be sure of a place. ❶–❷

YMCA Central Branch 316 Huntington Ave ☎617/536-7800. Best budget rooms in Back Bay, next to Northeastern T station. Rates – around $45 for one person, or $65 for two – include breakfast. Co-ed June–Sept, otherwise men-only. ❷–❸

YWCA 40 Berkeley St ☎617/375-2524, ⓦ www.ywcaboston.org. Women-only singles ($65), doubles ($100), and triples ($120) in a convenient South End location, near Arlington and Back Bay T stations. There's another YWCA building nearby at 140 Clarendon St and rooms can be arranged there, as well. Non-YWCA members pay $2 for temporary membership. Nightly and weekly rates. ❸–❺

The City

Boston has grown up around **Boston Common**, which was set aside as public land in 1634. The obvious first stop on any tour of the city, it is also one of the gems in the string of nine parks (six of which were designed by Frederick Law Olmsted, America's foremost landscape architect) known as Boston's **Emerald Necklace**. Another is the lovely **Public Garden**, across Charles Street from the Common, where the two-ton swan boats ($2.50), which paddle across the main pond, are a less-than-natural, though whimsical, focal point.

The visitor center, which marks the start of the **Freedom Trail**, is near the tapering north end of the Common. As you stand here, facing up Tremont Street with the State House away to your left, the main shopping district, **Quincy Market**, and the **waterfront** are slightly ahead and down to the right. The modern concrete wasteland of **Government Center** is straight up Tremont Street, with the **North End** beyond – first Irish, then Jewish, and now very definitely Italian. A short way behind you on the left rises **Beacon Hill**, every bit as elegant as when Henry James called Mount Vernon Street "the most prestigious address in America" (and far removed from its eighteenth-century nickname of "Mount Whoredom"). Heading away from the center down Tremont Street brings you to **Chinatown** and the **Theater District**, while grand boulevards such as Commonwealth Avenue lead west from the Public Garden into the **Back Bay**, where Harvard Bridge runs across the Charles River into **Cambridge**.

The Freedom Trail

Probably the best way to orient yourself in downtown Boston – and to appreciate the city's role in American history – is to walk some or all of the **Freedom Trail**. You can pick up or leave this easy self-guided route anywhere – a line of red bricks marking the trail is embedded in the pavement – but technically it begins on Boston Common at the **Visitor Information Center**.

From here, head for the golden dome of the **Massachusetts State House** (free tours Mon–Sat 10am–3.30pm), which was completed in 1798 to a design by Charles Bulfinch. It remains the seat of Massachusetts' government; its most famous feature, the wooden Sacred Cod, symbolizing the wealth Boston accrued from its fisheries, hangs in front of the Speaker, and faces in different directions according to which party is in office.

Though **Park Street Church** (July & Aug Tues–Sat 9.30am–3.30pm; rest of year by appointment; free) is by no means "the most interesting mass of bricks and mortar in America," as Henry James once claimed, its ornate white steeple is undeniably impressive. This was where the orator William Lloyd Garrison launched his campaign to free the slaves on July 4, 1829. Just around the corner, the 1600 graves of the **Old Granary Burying Ground** (daily 9am–5pm; free) include those of Paul Revere, Samuel Adams, and John Hancock, as well as the so-called Mother Goose, a Bostonian named Elizabeth Vergoose (or Vertigoose), said to have collected nursery rhymes for her grandchildren. Meanwhile, **King's Chapel Burying Ground** (daily 9.30am–5pm; free) contains Boston's earliest colonists and the first governor, John Winthrop. A statue of Benjamin Franklin marks the site of **Boston Latin School**, America's first public school, attended by Franklin and Samuel Adams. Guests at the nearby **Omni Parker House Hotel** (not officially on the Trail) have included Charles Dickens, John F. Kennedy, Malcolm X, and Ho Chi Minh.

Next come the Trail's two most striking and significant buildings. At the **Old South Meeting House** (daily: April–Oct 9.30am–5pm; Nov–March 10am–4pm; $5), the largest building in Colonial Boston and an old Puritan house of worship, Samuel Adams addressed the patriots about to carry out the Boston Tea Party on December 16, 1773. This was no raucous and unruly mob: they were solemn men, well aware of the likely impact of their actions. The elegant **Old State House**, built in 1712 and still proud, although dwarfed by surrounding skyscrapers, was the seat of Colonial government. From its balcony the Declaration of Independence was read on July 18, 1776; exactly two hundred years later Queen Elizabeth II appeared on that same balcony. Inside is a **museum** of Boston history (daily 9am–5pm; $5). Outside, a plain ring of cobblestones set on a traffic island at the intersection of Devonshire and State streets marks the site of the **Boston Massacre** on March 5, 1770, when British soldiers fired on a crowd that was pelting them with stone-filled snowballs, and killed five, including Crispus Attucks, an ex-slave.

Modern visitors gravitate to **Quincy Market** and **Faneuil Hall** (rhymes with "Daniel"; daily 9am–5pm; free) for the lively shops, restaurants, and take-away food stalls that made this a pioneer example of successful urban renewal (by the developer who went on to transform London's Covent Garden). Faneuil Hall was, however, once known as the "Cradle of Liberty," a meeting place for Revolutionaries and, later, abolitionists. Nearby on Union Street, step off the Freedom Trail to visit **The New England Holocaust Memorial**, six tall hollow glass pillars built to resemble smokestacks and etched with quotes and facts about the Holocaust, with an unusual degree of attention to its non-Jewish victims.

Passing under the six-lane John Fitzgerald Expressway and into the North End, you reach **Paul Revere House**, Boston's last surviving seventeenth-century house (daily: mid-April–Oct 9.30am–5.15pm; Nov–mid-April 9.30am–4.15pm; closed Mon Jan–March; $3), built after the Great Fire of 1676, and home to Paul Revere – patriot, silversmith, Freemason, and father of sixteen children – from 1770 until 1800. When Revere embarked upon his famous **ride** of April 18, 1775, to warn Lexington of imminent British attack, two lanterns were hung from the belfry of **Old North Church**, 193 Salem St (daily: June–Oct 9am–6pm; Nov–May 9am–5pm), to alert Charlestown in case he got caught. A little further up, from **Copp's Hill Burial Ground** (daily 9am–5pm; free), you can see across the harbor to Charlestown; as indeed could the British, who planted their artillery near for the Battle of Bunker Hill.

In theory, the Freedom Trail now crosses the Charlestown Bridge, but that's a long walk over. Its final two sites are better reached by the frequent **ferries** from Long Wharf to Charlestown Navy Yard (Mon–Fri every 15–30mins 6.30am–8pm, Sat & Sun every 30mins 10am–6pm; $1.25 each way). First is the

The Black Heritage Trail

Massachusetts was the first state to declare slavery illegal, in 1783 – partly as a result of black participation in the Revolutionary War – and a large community of free blacks and escaped slaves swiftly grew in the North End and on Beacon Hill. Ironically, very few blacks now live on Beacon Hill, but the **Black Heritage Trail** through the area celebrates important sites in local black history (the various visitor centers provide maps).

Pick up the Trail either at 46 Joy St, where the **Abiel Smith School** contains a **Museum of Afro-American History** (summer daily 10am–4pm; rest of year Mon–Sat 10am–4pm; free), which illustrates the national civil rights campaign as well as local history, or at the **African Meeting House** at 8 Smith Court (off Joy St), for displays and talks from well-informed rangers. Built in 1806 as the first African-American church in the United States, this became known as "Black Faneuil Hall" during the abolitionist campaign; Frederick Douglass issued his call here for all blacks to take up arms in the Civil War. Among those who responded were the volunteers of the **Massachusetts 54th Regiment**, commemorated by a monument at the edge of Boston Common, opposite the State House, which depicts their farewell march down Beacon Street. Robert Lowell won a Pulitzer Prize for his poem, "For the Union Dead," about this monument, and the regiment's tragic end at Fort Wagner was depicted in the movie *Glory*.

From the monument, the Trail then winds around Beacon Hill, passing schools, other institutions, and residences ranging from the small, cream clapboard houses of Smith Court to the imposing **Lewis and Harriet Hayden House** at 66 Phillips St, once a stop on the famous "Underground Railroad," sheltering runaway slaves from pursuing bounty-hunters.

USS Constitution, also known as "Old Ironsides," the oldest commissioned warship afloat in the world. Launched in Boston in 1797, it played a significant role in the War of 1812. Every July 4 it is ceremonially turned around – sailed out into the bay and its cannon fired – mainly to equalize the weathering on its two sides. Unless it's closed due to ongoing rehabilitation work, free tours of the ship are led by costumed guides (daily 9.30am–3.50pm; ⓦ www.usscon-stitution.navy.mil). You can also visit the **USS Constitution Museum** (daily: summer 9am–6pm; rest of year 10am–5pm; free), which brings to life the war-ship's 200-year history with a collection of 3000 artifacts, as well as a number of interactive exhibits, including simulated sailing exercises and the firing of a replica cannon. Above the museum, the **Bunker Hill Monument** sits on Breed's Hill, the actual site of the battle fought on June 17, 1775, which, although won by the British, did much to convince them that they could not hope to triumph in the end. A spiral staircase of almost three hundred steps leads to the top; a small **museum** (daily 9am–4.30pm; free) at the base has dated but informative exhibits on the battle.

The waterfront

It comes as a disappointment to realize that you can't walk along Boston's **waterfront** for any distance, broken up as it is by over a dozen heavily devel-oped wharfs jutting into the harbor. However, if you head straight for the sea from Quincy Market, **Columbus Park**, next to the ugly *Marriott Long Wharf Hotel*, makes a nice place to sit. Faneuil Hall originally stood at the head of **Long Wharf**, which stuck out nearly two thousand feet into the harbor, and was the site of the final British evacuation on March 17, 1776. Later, a thousand-foot expanse of the waterfront was filled in, and the **Custom House Tower** erected to mark the end of the wharf, though it too now finds itself inland, as a further thousand feet of new land has been added.

Out on the water, **Boston Harbor Cruises** (inner and outer harbor $17, inner harbor only $8; ☎617/227-4321 or 1-877/733-9425, ⓦ www.boston-harborcruises.com) from Long Wharf are not all that exciting. The port is nowhere near as busy as when fishing boats lined the quays three or four deep on all sides. Instead you pass vast rows of freshly imported Japanese cars on the quayside, and get a close-up view of the airport. You can get off one cruise in Charlestown, to see the USS *Constitution*, and catch the next one back for no extra charge.

Close by on Central Wharf, the **New England Aquarium** (July & Aug Mon, Tues & Fri 9am–6pm, Wed & Thurs 9am–8pm, Sat & Sun 9am–7pm; Sept–June Mon–Fri 9am–5pm, Sat & Sun 9am–6pm; $15.50) has an outdoor pool of basking sea otters. Inside, the colossal Giant Ocean Tank, a four-story glass cylinder, holds sharks, giant turtles, and tropical marine life (with an unsettling emphasis on how "delicious" certain species are). Scuba divers hand-feed the fish five times a day, and sea lion shows are held in a floating amphithe-ater alongside.

If you follow the shoreline past **Rowes Wharf**, a short distance before South Station the **Congress Street Bridge** leads off to the left across the Fort Point Channel. Moored to the bridge is the **Boston Tea Party Ship and Museum** (ⓦ www.bostonteapartyship.com). Although damaged by fire in 2001 and closed until further notice, this site still manages to draw quite a crowd. Nevertheless, this is not the original *Beaver*, one of the three ships stormed by patriots in 1773, but a replica, *Beaver II*, sailed here from Denmark in 1973. Neither is it the original mooring, which was on the now-demolished Griffin's Wharf; instead it's the site of the house where the conspirators prepared their assault.

On the far side of the bridge, a forty-foot **milk bottle**, which serves as an ice-cream parlor and sandwich bar, marks the **Children's Museum**, 300 Congress St (Mon–Thurs, Sat & Sun 10am–5pm, Fri 10am–9pm; $8, Fri 5–9pm $1). The five floors of educational exhibits are designed to entice kids into learning by doing, with plenty of buttons to push, strings to pull, and tunnels to crawl through, as well as costumes, water toys, and climbing structures.

The Museum of Science

At the northern end of the waterfront, clear across the Boston peninsula from the Children's Museum, the **Museum of Science** (summer daily 9am–7pm; rest of year Mon–Thurs, Sat & Sun 9am–5pm, Fri 9am–9pm; $13; Science Park T) has several floors of hands-on exhibits illustrating basic principles of natural and physical science. An impressive OMNIMAX cinema takes up the full height of one end of the building, and the Hayden Planetarium pays its way with Pink Floyd laser-light shows and the like ($8.50; call ☎617/723-2500 for showtimes).

Back Bay and beyond

From 1857 onwards, the spacious boulevards and grand houses of **Back Bay** were built as each portion of the tidal flats of the Charles River was filled in. Thus a walk through the area from east to west provides an object lesson in Victorian architecture. One of the most architecturally significant – if not the prettiest – of its buildings is the Romanesque **Trinity Church**, on Clarendon Street (Mon–Sat 9am–5pm, Sun 1–5.30pm; $4). Towering over the church is Boston's signature skyscraper, the **John Hancock Tower**, an elegant wedge designed by I.M. Pei. Construction defects caused the Hancock Tower to shed three thousand panes of glass during its first year; the cost of insuring a neighboring hotel against damage was so prohibitive that it was cheaper for the developers to buy it outright. **Copley Square** nearby is an upmarket shopping mall with several good snack bars and restaurants.

The **Christian Science Center** at Huntington and Massachusetts avenues is the "Mother Church" of the First Church of Christ, Scientist, and the home of the *Christian Science Monitor* newspaper; Nelson Mandela made a point of paying a personal visit in 1990 to thank the paper for its support of his release from prison. The complex houses the **Mapparium** (Tues–Fri 10am–9pm, Sat 10am–6pm, Sun 11am–5pm; free), an impressive glass globe of the world, through which you can walk on a footbridge. Part of its interest is that it was built in 1932, and thus shows national boundaries as they were then.

Further south, beyond the boundaries of Back Bay and a long enough walk to warrant taking the Green subway line rather than walking (take the train marked "E"), is the **Museum of Fine Arts** at 465 Huntington Ave (Mon & Tues 10am–4.45pm, Wed–Fri 10am–9.45pm, Sat & Sun 10am–4.45pm; $15, which includes a free repeat visit within 30 days, under-17s free; ☎617/267-9300, ⓦwww.mfa.org). From its magnificent collections of Asian and ancient Egyptian art onwards, the MFA (as it's known) holds sufficient marvels to detain you all day. High points include Edward Hopper's tranquil, hopeful *Room in Brooklyn* (American Modern room); Andrew Wyeth's *Corner of the Woods* (William Coolidge room); Degas' *The Little Dancer*; Gauguin's *Where do we come from, What are we, Where are we going?* (both Impressionists room); and Millet's *The Sower* (English and French room). Don't miss the **American Decorative Arts**, either: a gloriously nostalgic jamboree of coffee urns, speak-your-weight machines, and reconstructed living rooms. The I.M. Pei–designed West Wing holds special exhibits and the contemporary art collection.

A smaller-scale and rather more idiosyncratic collection of fine arts can be found at the **Isabella Stewart Gardner Museum**, down the road at 280 The Fenway (Tues–Sun 11am–5pm; $10, weekends $11; ℡617/278-5166, ⓦwww.gardnermuseum.org). Styled after a fifteenth-century Venetian villa, the Gardner has a stunning central courtyard, and is crammed with a hodge-podge of works collected by the eponymous eccentric Boston socialite. Some of the most interesting pieces are unlabeled, such as the tapestry of a lion, a sea lion, and an elephant above the door of the Italian room, or the sculpted pigeon on the nearby windowsill. Relaxing weekend music concerts are held Saturday and Sunday at 1.30pm and cost an additional $10.

Cambridge ⓣ

The excursion across the Charles River to **Cambridge** merits at least half a day, starting with a fifteen-minute ride on the Red T line from Park Street to **Harvard Square**. This is not so much a square as a number of interlocking streets, filled with small shopping malls and bookstores, at the point where Massachusetts Avenue runs into JFK and Brattle streets. It's an exceptionally lively area, filled with students from nearby Harvard University and MIT; the café terrace at *Au Bon Pain* makes for enjoyable people-watching, and in the summer, street musicians are a common sight. The **Cambridge Visitor Information Booth** here (Mon–Sat 9am–5pm; ℡617/497-1630) sporadically organizes walking tours in summer, and sells local maps and guides. More thorough information is available from the **Harvard Events & Information Center**, Holyoke Center, 1350 Massachusetts Ave (Mon–Sat 9am–5pm; ℡617/495-1573, ⓦwww.hno.harvard.edu), which also arranges student-led tours.

Feel free to wander into **Harvard Yard** and around the core of the university, founded in 1636; its enormous Widener Library (named for a victim of the *Titanic*) boasts a Gutenberg Bible and a first folio of Shakespeare. Five minutes' walk west along Brattle Street is the imposing yellow-fronted mansion at no. 105, known as the **Longfellow House**, after the author of *Hiawatha*, who lived here until 1882. A century earlier it was briefly the headquarters of General George Washington. The site has been undergoing extensive renovation: call ℡617/876-4491 or visit ⓦwww.nps.gov/long to check hours and admission fee. Dexter Pratt, immortalized in Longfellow's "Under the spreading chestnut tree, the village smithy stands," lived at 56 Brattle St, now a popular bakery and café.

Cambridge has several first-class art museums on offer, along with more specialized science museums, with a few engaging exhibits of note. The **Harvard University Art Museums** (Mon–Sat 10am–5pm, Sun 1–5pm; $6.50, free on Sat before noon; ℡617/495-9400) encompass over 150,000 works of art across three museums. Highlights of Harvard's substantial collection of Western art are showcased in the **Fogg Art Museum**, 32 Quincy St, while the **Busch-Reisinger Museum** on the second floor has a small but excellent selection focusing on German Expressionists and the work of the Bauhaus. Just steps away at 485 Broadway, the **Arthur M. Sackler Museum** is devoted to classical, Asian, and Islamic art. The **Harvard Museum of Natural History**, 26 Oxford St (daily 9am–5pm; $7.50), operates three museums devoted to botany, zoology, and minerals and geology, respectively.

Also on the Harvard campus, the **Carpenter Center for the Visual Arts**, 34 Quincy St, houses a more or less impressive student art gallery, as well as the **Harvard Film Archive**, which screens a diverse selection of foreign and independent films, seven nights a week ($7 general public, $5 for students; ℡617/495-4700, ⓦwww.harvardfilmarchive.org).

A couple of miles southeast of Harvard Square is the **Massachusetts Institute of Technology** (MIT), whose **List Visual Arts Center**, 20 Ames St (Tues–Thurs, Sat & Sun noon–6pm, Fri noon–8pm; ☎617/253-4680), exhibits contemporary art in all media, including photography and video, and often has accompanying lectures.

Lexington and Concord

On the night of April 18, 1775, **Paul Revere** rode down what is now Massachusetts Avenue from Boston, racing through Cambridge and Arlington on his way to warn the American patriots gathered at **Lexington** of an impending British attack. Close behind him was a force of more than four hundred British soldiers, intent on seizing the supplies that they knew the "rebels" had hoarded at **Concord** further north.

Although much of Revere's route has been turned into major freeways, the various settings of the first military confrontation of the Revolutionary War – "the shot heard 'round the world" – remain much as they were then. The triangular **Town Common** at Lexington was where the British encountered the opposition. Captain John Parker ordered his 77 American "**Minutemen**" to "stand your ground. Don't fire unless fired upon, but if they mean to have a war let it begin here." No one knows who fired the first shot, but the Minuteman Statue commemorates the eight Americans who died during the battle. Guides in period costume lead tours of the **Buckman Tavern**, where the Minutemen waited for the British to arrive; the **Hancock-Clarke House**, a quarter of a mile north, where Samuel Adams and John Hancock were awakened by Paul Revere, is now a museum; and one mile east of the Town Common, the **Munroe Tavern** was occupied by the British as a makeshift hospital and headquarters (all three Mon–Sat 10.30am–4.30pm, Sun 1pm–5pm; $5 each, $12 to visit all).

By the time the British soldiers marched on Concord, on the morning after the encounter in Lexington, the surrounding countryside was up in arms, and the Revolutionary War was in full swing. In running battles in the town itself, and along the still-evocative **Battle Road** leading back toward Boston, 73 British soldiers and 49 colonials were killed over the next two days. The relevant sites now form the **Minuteman National Historic Park**, with visitor centers at the scenic North Bridge, 174 Liberty St, in Concord, and at Battle Road in Lexington. Paul Revere's ride and the Battle of Lexington are re-enacted annually on Patriot's Day, a city holiday on the third Monday in April (also the day of the Boston Marathon; see "Sports," p.221).

South of Concord, **Walden Pond** was where Henry David Thoreau conducted the experiment in solitude and self-sufficiency described in his 1854 book *Walden*. "I did not feel crowded or confined in the least," he wrote of life in his simple log cabin. The site where it stood is now marked with stones, and at dawn you can still watch the pond "throwing off its nightly clothing of mist." Thoreau is interred, along with Ralph Waldo Emerson, Nathaniel Hawthorne, and Louisa May Alcott, atop a hill in **Sleepy Hollow Cemetery**, just east of the center of Concord.

As well as guided bus tours from Boston (see p.210), **buses** (25min) run to Lexington from Alewife Station, at the northern end of the Red T line, and **trains** to Concord run from North Station (40min; $4 one way).

Eating

There is far more to eating in Boston than its nickname "Beantown" might suggest. Above all, there's the **seafood**, especially lobsters, scrod (a generic term for young, white-fleshed fish), clams (served steamed and dipped in butter, or as creamy chowder), and oysters (some of the world's best come fresh daily from Wellfleet and other Cape Cod spots). You could base a day's tour of the different neighborhoods around the foods on offer: breakfast in the cafés of **Beacon Hill**; lunch in the food plazas of **Quincy Market** or **The Garage** on JFK Street in Cambridge, or dim sum in **Chinatown**; for dinner, a budget **Indian** restaurant in Cambridge, an **Italian** place around Hanover Street in the North End, or expensive seafood overlooking the Harbor.

The central aisle of **Quincy Market**, lined with restaurants and brasseries, is superb for all kinds of take-out, including fresh clams and lobster, ethnic dishes, fruit cocktails, and cookies (all over the city, you'll find marvelous chocolate and ice cream), which you can buy from different vendors and eat in the central seating area.

Chinatown, where restaurants stay open until 2 or 3am, is the best place for **late-night eating**.

Boston

Big Fish Seafood Restaurant 18–20 Tyler St ☏617/423-3288. Restaurant in the heart of Chinatown offering a vast array of traditional Chinese dishes (not limited to big fish).

Daily Catch 323 Hanover St ☏617/523-8567 and 261 Northern Ave ☏617/338-3093. Sicilian-style seafood restaurant, noted for its many styles of calamari. Expect to pay from $10 to $40 for an entree.

Division Sixteen 955 Boylston St ☏617/353-0870. While the food is good and the wine list inspired, the real draw is the atmosphere, a converted police stable with a decidedly 1920s feel, in which locals sip martinis and any number of frozen concoctions.

Durgin Park 340 N Market St, Faneuil Hall ☏617/227-2038. Crowded, hurried, and proud of its surly service, but a Boston institution for its chunky prime rib and seafood specialties – not to mention the baked beans. Tables are shared, and no reservations are taken. Entrees start from $7.

Gabriele's 1 1st Ave, Charlestown Navy Yard ☏617/242-4040. Excellent upscale Italian restaurant, with a terrace for outdoor dining.

Giacomo's 355 Hanover St ☏617/523-9026. Fresh, flavorful food, with an emphasis on seafood and pasta specialties – the pumpkin tortellini in a sage butter sauce is a North End classic. Note the restaurant doesn't take reservations or credit cards.

Kingfish Hall 188 S Market Bldg ☏617/523-8862. Well-regarded, stylish seafood house worth the splurge ($20 to $30 an entree).

Legal Sea Foods at the *Park Plaza Hotel*, 26 Park Square ☏617/426-4444. Citywide chain deservedly renowned for its top-quality seafood, especially their excellent oysters.

Mamma Maria 3 North Square ☏617/523-0077. Widely acknowledged as the best of the North End's traditional Italian restaurants, noted for seafood dishes and fresh breads. Expensive and also popular for special occasions.

Mike's Pastries 300 Hanover St ☏617/742-3050. Considered by many – including a regular customer by the name of Bill Clinton – to be the best pastry shop in the North End.

News 150 Kneeland St ☏617/426-6397. Upscale restaurant by day, trendy dance club by night. Menu includes a vast array of appetizers, salads, pasta, and seafood dishes at surprisingly reasonable prices. Mind the dress code (no hats).

Other Side Cosmic Café 407 Newbury St ☏617/536-9477. Popular, trendy café with great salads, sandwiches, beer, wine, coffee, and tea. Across from Virgin Records and the Mass Turnpike. Open late.

Pad Thai Café 1116 Boylston St ☏617/247-3399. Fresh Thai soups, salads, and curries, with highly recommended house specials, all in the $5–10 range. Popular with students, the place gets crowded fast.

Panificio Bakery 144 Charles St ☏617/227-4340. Consistently rated the best bakery in Boston; try to make time for their brunch, served weekends from 10am–4.30pm.

Rabia's 73 Salem St ☏617/227-6637. The best thing about this small restaurant is its Express Lunch special, from noon to 2pm, when you can pay under $7 for a heaping plate of Italian left-overs.

Steve's Greek–American Cuisine 316 Newbury St ☏617/267-1817. One of Boston's classic cheap eats, with heavenly Greek food and divine grilled-chicken sandwiches.

Trattoria Il Panino 11 Parmenter St ☏617/720-1336. An old North End standby popular with locals. The great Amalfi-coast chicken and pasta dishes are complemented by a good wine list and friendly service.

Tremont 647 647 Tremont St ☎617/266-4600. Part of the burgeoning South End dining scene, with big portions of New American food, much of it grilled, as well as superb desserts and a good selection of wines.

Cambridge

Bombay Club 57 JFK St, second floor, Harvard Square ☎617/661-8100. One of the very best of Cambridge's many Indian restaurants, with a good-value lunch buffet.

Boston Sail Loft 1 Memorial Drive, Kendall Square ☎617/227-7280. Fine array of inexpensive seafood near MIT.

Dalí 415 Washington St, Somerville ☎617/661-3254. Excellent tapas and Spanish entrees amid decor nearly as surreal as its namesake. Often crowded, the lively sangría bar makes the long waits tolerable.

East Coast Grill 1271 Cambridge St, Inman Square ☎617/491-6568. Fairly pricey, but tasty Southern-style food – BBQ and the like – in a good restaurant area.

Elephant Walk 2067 Massachusetts Ave, Porter Square ☎617/492-6900 and 900 Beacon St, Boston ☎617/247-1500. Their French fare is very good, but the adventurous Cambodian side of the menu steals the show: try the excellent *poulet dhomei* – chicken with basil, bamboo shoots, and pineapple.

John Harvard's Brew House 33 Dunster St, Harvard Square ☎617/868-3585. Cozy brewpub, serving a good menu with exciting little twists on American grill standards. $30 should suffice for a big meal with a couple of drinks.

Mr Bartley's Gourmet Burgers 1246 Massachusetts Ave, Harvard Square ☎617/354-6559. Delicious, shamelessly unhealthy burgers and other diner fare served in an Americana-festooned atmosphere.

Redbone's 55 Chester St, Somerville ☎617/628-2200. Excellent, inexpensive ribs, chicken, and cat-fish with a big range of vegetable side dishes. Just off Davis Square, two T stops from Harvard Square.

Rhythm & Spice 315 Massachusetts Ave, Central Square ☎617/497-0977. Lively restaurant with a young clientele not far from MIT, serving good-value Caribbean food.

Bars, clubs, and live music

Boston has a lively **nightlife** scene that offers the best of both old and new, from tried-and-true neighborhood taverns to young, trendy lounges. The **live music** circuit in Boston and Cambridge is dominated by the very best local and touring indie bands. The free weekly *Boston Phoenix* (ⓦ www.thephoenix.com) is the best source of up-to-date **listings**. Key nightlife zones include **Lansdowne Street**, an entire block of nightclubs next to Fenway Park; **Boylston Place**, on the south side of Boston Common; and Cambridge's **Central Square** district. Note that most establishments are unusually officious in demanding **ID**.

Boston

Avalon 15 Lansdowne St ☎617/262-2424, ⓦ www.avalonboston.com. An anchor on the Lansdowne Street club scene, *Avalon* is a local favorite for late-night dancing, with different themes on different nights (Saturday is techno night) and a live concert venue. Dress tends to be casual.

The Black Rose 160 State St ☎617/742-2286. Large Irish pub beside Faneuil Hall, with traditional music every night and Guinness galore.

Bull and Finch Pub 84 Beacon St, Beacon Hill ☎617/227-9605. As the original setting of TV's *Cheers*, the *Bull and Finch* is totally touristy, though at least it's central and lively.

Chaps 100 Warrenton St, off Stuart St ☎617/695-9500. Glitzy gay club filled with lots of decked-out young men.

Commonwealth Brewery Company 138 Portland St ☎617/523-8383. Brewpub right by the FleetCenter, near North Station, serving good pub food and its own ales.

Crossroads Irish Pub 495 Beacon St ☎617/262-737. Popular with locals and college students, this friendly neighborhood bar claims to be the oldest pub in the Back Bay. Great weekly specials include free wings on Tuesdays and Thursdays.

JJ Foley's 21 Kingston St ☎617/338-7713. A blue-collar Irish bar in the heart of downtown, with decent food, sports on TV, and a great jukebox. Has been around since 1909.

Sevens Ale House 77 Charles St, Beacon Hill ☎617/523-9074. This unpolished gem of a neighborhood pub provides local flavor in the midst of upscale Beacon Hill; much more authentic than the *Bull and Finch*.

Cambridge

The Cellar 991 Massachusetts Ave ☎617/876-2580. An eclectic mix of students and locals gather in this laid-back niche between Harvard and Central squares. Two stories, two bars, and some live entertainment on weekends.

Club Passim 47 Palmer St, Harvard Square ☎617/492-5300. A four-decades-old, intimate "coffeehouse" that has been a noted folk/blues venue since Joan Baez performed here as an unknown 17-year-old.

House of Blues 96 Winthrop St, Harvard Square ☎617/491-2583. The original, surprisingly small branch of this popular chain of live-music venues features high-quality blues nightly. There's also a decent Cajun-themed restaurant and a heaving bar.

Man Ray 21 Brookline Ave, Central Square ☎617/864-0400. Nightly themes draw very different crowds to Cambridge's most popular dance club. Wednesday is gothic/industrial, Thursday and Saturday (when the club is known as *Campus*) draw a lively gay crowd, and Friday is reserved for the fetish/bondage scene.

Middle East 472/480 Massachusetts Ave, Central Square ☎617/492-9181. Cambridge's best alternative music venue, with three stages and a good, inexpensive Arabic restaurant. Cover is usually $3–10 in the main rooms, with free music in the restaurant – acts that have played here gratis include Morphine, Buffalo Tom, and Tracy Bonham.

Phoenix Landing 512 Massachusetts Ave, Central Square ☎617/576-6260. Affable neighborhood bar and restaurant, featuring soccer beamed in from Europe and a down-to-earth mix of music on the weekends.

Plough & Stars 912 Massachusetts Ave, between Harvard and Central squares ☎617/441-3455. Time-worn Irish pub with music most nights. Cover free or up to $8.

Ryles Jazz Club 212 Hampshire St ☎617/876-9330. Eclectic jazz and world music club charging $10–20 cover.

T.T. the Bear's Place 10 Brookline St, Central Square ☎617/492-BEAR, ⓦwww.ttthebears.com. Highly esteemed, intimate venue, showcasing cutting-edge live music seven nights a week.

Western Front 343 Western Ave, Central Square ☎617/492-7772. This former jazz and blues club is now dedicated to reggae, with live music Friday and Saturday nights, and Jamaican food Thursday through Saturday.

Performing arts

Mainstream Boston's pride and joy, the **Boston Symphony Orchestra** is based at Symphony Hall, 301 Massachusetts Ave (☎617/266-1200, ⓦwww.bso.org), which Stravinsky called the best auditorium in the world. The orchestra's winter season is supplemented by the **Boston Pops** concerts in May, June, and on July 4.

The city's **theater** scene divides into the safe productions of the Theater District (often Broadway cast-offs) and more experimental companies in Cambridge. The **BosTix** ticket kiosks (☎617/482-BTIX, ⓦwww.arts-boston.org/bostix.cfm) at Faneuil Hall and in Copley Square sell tickets for all major events – as well as tours, T passes, and so on – with some half-price same-day tickets. They're open Tuesday through Saturday 10am to 6pm and Sunday 11am to 4pm; the Copley Square location is also open on Monday 10am to 6pm.

Sports

The Red Sox play **baseball** at Fenway Park (Kenmore subway stop on the Green T line; tickets $18–55; information ☎617/267-8661, tickets ☎617/267-1700, ⓦwww.redsox.mlb.com). The whole stadium, squeezed in 1912 into the odd-shaped plot that was all its builders could buy, is painted green, including the 37-foot wall in the left field known as the "**Green Monster**".

Basketball's Celtics and **hockey's** Bruins both play at the FleetCenter, 150 Causeway St near North Station; Celts tickets will run you $10–150, Bruins tickets $19–99 (box office open daily 11am–7pm; call Ticketmaster for tickets by phone ☎617/931-2000, ⓦwww.fleetcenter.com).

The 26.2-mile **Boston Marathon**, first run in 1897, is now held on Patriot's Day, the third week in April, and finishes on Boylston Street at Copley Square (☎617/236-1652, ⓦwww.bostonmarathon.org).

The north shore

As you head northward out of Boston, you pass through a succession of rich little ports that have been all but swallowed up by the suburbs. The most obvious day-trip from Boston is the half-hour ride out to **Salem** and neighboring

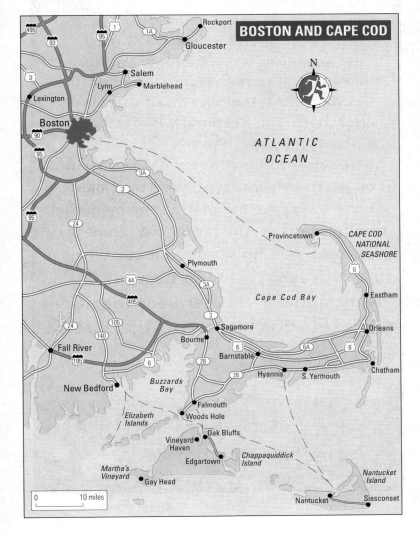

BOSTON AND CAPE COD

THE SALEM WITCH TRIALS TERCENTENARY MEMORIAL

The memorial is surrounded on three sides by a granite wall. Inscribed on the threshold are the victims' protests of innocence. This testimony is interrupted mid-sentence by the wall, symbolizing society's indifference to oppression. Locust trees represent the stark injustice of the trials. At the rear of the memorial, tombstones in the adjacent cemetery represent all who stood in mute witness to this tragedy. Stone benches within the memorial perimeter bear the names and execution dates of the victims.

△ The Salem Witch Trials Memorial, Massachusetts

Marblehead. If you have the time, the atmospheric old fishing ports of **Gloucester** and **Rockport**, further out on Cape Ann, are worth a look. They have strong artistic and literary connections – T.S. Eliot used to come here for his family vacations, and "The Dry Salvages" of the third of his *Four Quartets* are a group of offshore rocks – and are the best places on the East Coast for **whale-watching** trips. Cape Ann Whale Watch (☎978/283-5110 or 1-800/877-5110, ⓦwww.seethewhales.com) offers three- to four-hour trips for $30 between April and October.

Salem

Ironically, **SALEM** is remembered less as the site where the colony of Massachusetts was first established, with the most elevated of intentions, than as the place where just sixty years later Puritan self-righteousness reached its apogee in the horrific **witch trials** of 1692. While the town itself was to prosper as a port – as evidenced by its fine old buildings – the witch scare did much to discredit the idea that the New World conducted its affairs on a different moral plane than the Old. Nineteen Salem women were hanged as witches (and one man, Giles Corry, was pressed to death with a boulder), thanks to a group of impressionable teenage girls who reported as truth a garbled mixture of fireside tales told by a West Indian slave, Tituba, and half-digested scare stories published by Cotton Mather, a pillar of the Puritan community.

That this unpleasant history is now the basis of a child-oriented tourist industry – all black hats and broomsticks – makes Salem an unsettling place. The **Salem Witch Museum** in Washington Square (daily: July & Aug 10am–7pm; rest of year 10am–5pm; $6.50) draws parallels with modern racism and political persecution, but is at heart a rather tacky show of illuminated dioramas and prerecorded commentary. Innumerable other witch-related attractions in town are best ignored.

Salem's later seafaring years are remembered in the **Peabody Essex Museum** in East India Square (daily 10am–5pm, Thurs 10am–7pm; $12), which since 1799 has assembled a remarkable collection of objects brought home by voyaging New Englanders. As well as extensive Japanese and Asian displays, it has one of only three existing breadfruit-wood idols of the Hawaiian god Ku, and details about the town's ships themselves.

Little of Salem's original waterfront remains, though the long **Derby Wharf** is still standing, together with the imposing **Custom House** at its head, where Nathaniel Hawthorne once worked. The **House of Seven Gables** at 54 Turner St, the star of Hawthorne's eponymous novel, is a rambling old mansion beside the sea (summer daily 10am–7pm; rest of year 10am–5pm; $10). Hour-long guided tours of the complex also take in the author's birthplace, moved here from its original site on Union Street.

Practicalities

Regular MBTA **buses** run to Salem from Boston's Haymarket (weekdays hourly; $2.75 each way) and Wonderland stations (weekends every half-hour; same price). Frequent **trains** also leave from North Station (weekdays 2–3 an hour, weekends hourly; $2.50 each way). For **accommodation**, the best-value motel rooms are at the *Clipper Ship Inn*, 40 Bridge St (☎978/745-8022; ❸), though the *Salem Inn*, 7 Summer St (☎978/741-0680 or 1-800/446-2995, ⓦwww.saleminnma.com; ❺), a 39-room trio of Federal-style homes, is classier. *Nick's Firehouse Coffee Shoppe*, 30 Church St (☎978/745-9432), is the best deal in town for breakfast or lunch, where a meal can still be had for under $5. *Lyceum Bar & Grill*, 43 Church St (☎978/745-7665), is more elegant and expensive, with alternating menus emphasizing global cuisine made with fresh local ingredients.

Marblehead

When Salem's witch-related attractions grow tiresome, head five miles south and east along the bay to **MARBLEHEAD**, a lovely waterfront village whose historic homes date back as far as the mid-1700s, and which is known as the birthplace of the US Navy – George Washington's first five vessels were built here. Free walking-tour **maps** are available from the information booth in the center (June–Oct; ☎781/639-8469, ⓦwww.marbleheadchamber.org), while 250-year-old **Fort Sewall**, jutting into the harbor, gives pretty views. The *Seagull Inn*, 106 Harbor Ave (☎781/631-1893, ⓦwww.seagullinn.com; ❻), has comfortable B&B **rooms** overlooking the water, and the *Marblehead Inn*, 264 Pleasant St (☎781/639-9999 or 1-800/399-5843, ⓦwww.marbleheadinn .com; ❺), offers renovated two-room suites, some with a fireplace. *Flynnie's*, 28 Atlantic Ave (☎781/639-2100), serves fresh, inexpensive **seafood**, as does its outpost at Devereux Beach (May–Oct only).

The south shore

Heading south, it can take a while to get clear of Boston, especially on summer weekends, when the traffic down to Cape Cod can be horrendous. Two historic towns, one north and one west of the Cape, are worth exploring: **Plymouth** and **New Bedford**.

Plymouth

"America's Hometown," little **PLYMOUTH**, on the south shore of Massachusetts Bay, forty miles south of Boston, is given over to commemorating, in various degrees of taste, the landing of the 102 **Pilgrims** in December of 1620. By the sea, a solemn pseudo-Greek temple encloses the nondescript **Plymouth Rock**, where the Pilgrims are said to have first touched land. However, as the Pilgrims had already spent two months on Cape Cod before settling at Plymouth, and there are no historic references to the rock until one hundred years after their arrival, it is of symbolic importance only.

Two worthier memorials make no claim to authenticity, but meticulously reproduce the experience of the Pilgrims. Both the replica of the **Mayflower** in town (the *Mayflower II*), and **Plimoth Plantation** three miles south, are staffed by costumed "interpreters," each of whom acts out the part of a specific Pilgrim, Indian, or sailor (both attractions April–Nov daily 9am–5pm; *Mayflower II* alone $8, Plantation alone $20, together $22; ☎508/746-1622, ⓦwww.plimoth.org). The charade visitors are obliged to perform – pretending to have stepped back into the seventeenth century – can be a little tiresome, but ultimately the sheer depth of detail in both endeavors makes them fascinating. At the Plantation, everything you see in the Pilgrim Village of 1627, and the Wampanoag Indian Settlement, has been created using traditional techniques.

Another reasonably interesting way to pass some time is to sample the free tastings of **cranberry wines** offered by the Plymouth Bay Winery, 114 Water St (☎508/746-2100 or 1-877/683-5463), across from Plymouth Harbor.

Practicalities

Plymouth's **Visitor Information Center** is located on the waterfront at no. 130 (☎508/747-7525 or 1-800/USA-1620, ⓦwww.visit-plymouth.com). Plymouth & Brockton provides a regular **bus** service to and from Boston ($9 one way, $17 round-trip; ☎508/746-0378, ⓦwww.p-b.com). There are also express ferries from Plymouth to Provincetown (June–Sept daily 10am; $30; ☎508/747-2400 or 1-800/242-2469, ⓦwww.provincetownferry.com). Standard **motels** include the *Blue Spruce Motel*, 710 State Rd (☎508/224-3990 or 1-800/370-7080, ⓦwww.bluespruce-motel.com; ❸), and the *Best Western Cold Spring*, 188 Court St (open April–Dec only; ☎508/746-2222 or 1-800/678-8667; ❹). The *Governor Bradford Motor Inn*, 98 Water St (☎508/746-6200 or 1-800/332-1620, ⓦwww.governorbradford.com; ❹), overlooking the harbor, has slightly better facilities, including a heated outdoor pool. As for **eating**, *Cabby Shack* (☎508/746-5354) and *East Bay Grill* (☎508/746-9751) are good, reasonably priced seafood places; the *Lobster Hut* (☎508/746-2270) serves a cheaper, greasier variety of fish and seafood; and *Al's Restaurant* ☎508/746-3383) specializes in pizza. All four establishments are on the waterfront.

New Bedford

The famous old whaling port of **NEW BEDFORD**, 45 miles due south of Boston, is still home to one of the nation's most prosperous fishing fleets: every year, they haul in the largest catch on the East Coast. Ongoing development and a waterfront highway have obscured some of New Bedford's past, but on County Street the fine old houses still stand, of which Herman Melville commented:

New Bedford is a queer place. Had it not been for us whalemen, that tract of land would this day perhaps have been in as howling condition as the coast of Labrador . . . all these brave houses and flowery gardens came up from the Atlantic, Pacific and Indian oceans. One and all, they were harpooned and dragged hither from the bottom of the sea.

The roster of the whaling ship *Acushnet*, in the **New Bedford Whaling Museum** at 18 Johnny Cake Hill (daily 9am–5pm, Thurs until 9pm; $8), shows Melville as one of the crew. Other evocative displays include a half-size replica of a whaling vessel. Immediately opposite the museum stands the **Seamen's Bethel**; it really does have the ship-shaped pulpit described in *Moby Dick*, but this one was rebuilt after a fire in 1866.

The town's **visitor centers**, at 47 N Second St (☎508/991-6200) and at Pier 3 (☎508/979-1745), can book **accommodation**. One good choice is *The Orchard Street Manor*, 139 Orchard St (☎508/984-3475; ❻–❼), an atmospheric B&B built in 1845. A favorite local place to **eat** is the Portuguese *Antonio's*, 267 Coggeshall St (☎508/990-3636), where long lines often form outside the door. For fine dining, *Candleworks*, 72 N Water St (☎508/997-1294), is a highly regarded Italian restaurant that's housed in an 1810 whale-oil candle factory.

For information on **ferries to Martha's Vineyard**, see the box on p.234.

Cape Cod and the islands

Here a man may stand, and put all America behind him.

Henry David Thoreau

These days, the trouble with standing on **Cape Cod** is that "all America" tends to be a lot closer behind you than you might prefer. The Cape's main haunts are packed in the summer, its roads circled by a grim procession of crawling vehicles, searching in vain for some unspoiled bit of beach or undiscovered old town. Unless you have your own, preferably very secluded, place to stay, it's barely worth turning up on weekends, especially between June and August, and putting yourself through the hassle of trying to find what little available (and premium-priced) accommodation there is. However, the place is undeniably beautiful; if you find yourself in the region midweek in May or September – when hotel prices are much lower, the crowds have thinned, and the weather usually very pleasant – the Cape is certainly worth a visit.

Cape Cod was named by Bartholomew Gosnold in 1602, on account of the prodigious quantities of cod caught by his crew off Provincetown. Less than twenty years later the Pilgrims landed nearby; in the few months before moving on to Plymouth, they began the process, continued by generations of Europeans, of stripping the interior of the Cape bare of its original covering of thick woods. Today, much of the land on the Cape, from its salt marshes to its ever-eroding dunes, is considered a fragile and endangered ecosystem – though this designation hasn't especially dampened the persistence of developers.

If you imagine the Cape as an arm, its **upper** section, the thirty-mile eastward stretch closest to mainland Massachusetts, would be represented by the biceps. Much of the worst beachfront development lies along the southern shore, and Hwy-28, running from Falmouth via Hyannis to Chatham, gets especially clogged. Only once you get beyond the "elbow" and head north to the **Outer Cape** or, anatomically speaking, the forearm, past the spectacular dunes of **Cape Cod National Seashore**, do you get a feeling for why the Cape still has a reputation as a seaside wilderness. **Provincetown**, right at the end, is the one town on the Cape that can be unreservedly recommended.

The islands of **Martha's Vineyard** and **Nantucket**, off the Cape to the south, are largely dependent on summer tourism for their livelihood. At the same time, they remain highly committed to preserving their unique heritage and natural environment. A trip out to Nantucket in particular still evokes haunting memories of its proud seafaring days. The off-season has a charm all its own, when you can sink into the rhythms of life on the islands without the distraction of hordes of day-trippers.

Getting to the Cape

It was the Pilgrims who first suggested the construction of a canal between Cape Cod Bay and Buzzards Bay, so that coastal shipping could avoid the dangers of the open ocean. When the waterway was finally completed at the start of the twentieth century, it left the Cape Cod peninsula as an island. Now all traffic to the Cape bottlenecks at two enormous bridges across the canal – Bourne on Hwy-28 and Sagamore on Hwy-6 – and you may regret trying to **drive** there on a summer Friday (or back on a Sunday). Each bridge has an **information office** for the Cape (daily 9am–7pm) on its mainland side.

One way to dodge the traffic is to **fly**. US Airways affiliate Colgan Air (☎1-800/428-4322, ⓦwww.colganair.com) serves Hyannis, Martha's Vineyard, and Nantucket from Washington, DC, New York City, Boston, and points further north, such as Augusta, Maine. Cape Air (☎1-800/352-0714, ⓦwww.flycapeair.com) flies several times daily from Boston, New Bedford, and Providence, Rhode Island, to Hyannis, Provincetown, and the islands. Bonanza **buses** run regularly from New York City and Boston (☎617/345-0539 or 1-800/556-3815, ⓦwww.bonanzabus.com), and the Plymouth & Brockton (☎508/746-0378, ⓦwww.p-b.com) runs daily to Hyannis and Provincetown from Boston, Plymouth, New York City, and Rhode Island. **Ferries** from Boston (see p.230) take 90 minutes to cross to Provincetown; for boats to the various islands, see the box on p.234.

The Upper Cape

The **Upper Cape**, just across the bridges, was the first part of the peninsula to attract visitors in any numbers – and it sometimes shows. Upon approaching the various communities of the south coast, you might easily be taken aback by the degree of commercialization that surrounds them. But just beyond the thickets of malls, motels, and fast-food joints there remains a measure of quaintness in some of the small coastal towns, each arranged around a prim central green and decorated with old-fashioned Main Streets and waterfront seafood joints.

Falmouth and Woods Hole

One obvious base for catching a **ferry** to the islands is **FALMOUTH**, where central motels include the comfortable *Shoreway Acres Inn*, 59 Shore St (☎508/540-3000 or 1-800/352-7100, ⓦwww.shorewayacresinn.com; ❺), with indoor and outdoor pools, and the harborfront *Best Western Marina Tradewinds*, at 26 Robbins Rd (☎508/548-4300 or 1-800/341-5700, ⓦwww .vacationinnproperties.com; ❺). The *Sippewissett Campground & Cabins*, a couple of miles out at 836 Palmer Ave (☎508/548-2542, ⓦwww.sippewissett.com; peak season $23, plus $8 each additional camper; off-season $19, plus $5 each additional camper; ❶), offers a free shuttle service to the ferries and beaches.

   Restaurants abound in Falmouth, though with the possible exception of *Betsy's Diner*, 457 Main St (☎508/540-0060), built in the Fifties and serving no-nonsense food from that era, the best meals are to be found in the assorted moderately priced seafood places along the waterfront at **WOODS HOLE**, four miles southwest. The *Fishmonger's Café*, 56 Water St (☎508/548-9148), is a natural-foods restaurant that serves eggs, granola, and the like at breakfast, with seafood specials at lunch and dinner. As for sights, the **Woods Hole Oceanographic Institution's exhibit center**, at 15 School St, near Little Harbor (May–Oct Mon–Sat 10am–4.30pm, Sun noon–4.30pm; Nov, Dec, March & April Tues–Fri 10am–4.30pm, Sun noon–4.30; free), focuses on the Institution's underwater research, including their sensational finding of the *Titanic* in 1986. Ocean Quest, a private nonprofit, runs ninety-minute research-based **ocean cruises** in summer (reservations recommended; $20; ☎1-800/37-OCEAN, ⓦwww.oceanquestonline.org).

Hyannis

It stands to reason that **HYANNIS** – the largest port on the Cape, and its main commercial hub – would be a little less charming than Falmouth and Woods Hole. Nevertheless, it still clings to the glamour it earned when the **Kennedy compound** at Hyannis Port placed it at the center of world affairs. Hence the existence of the **John F. Kennedy Museum**, 397 Main St (Mon–Sat 9am–5pm, Sun 12–5pm; $5), which shows photographs, newsclippings, and film footage of the days JFK spent on the Cape. The Kennedys are still here, though their property can only be glimpsed, at a considerable distance, from the sea: Hy-Line Cruises, Ocean Street Dock ($12; ☎508/778-2600, ⓦwww.hy-linecruises.com), runs one-hour harbor cruises that peek in at the compound.

   There are many **hotels** to choose from in Hyannis, though most of them are pretty generic. A good **B&B** in Hyannis Port – actually, the only one – is the *Simmons Homestead Inn*, 288 Scudder Ave (☎508/778-4999 or 1-800/637-1649, ⓦwww.simmonshomesteadinn.com; ❻). On Main Street, *The Egg & I*, at no. 521 (☎508/771-1596), does a decent breakfast, while *Alberto's*, no. 360 (☎508/778-1770), offers good but pricey Italian meals. *Perry's*, at 546 Main (☎508/775-9711), is a great deli with three-decker clubs and other "stacked" sandwiches; they also serve breakfast.

The Mid-Cape

The middle stretch of Cape Cod holds some of its prettiest, most unspoiled places. Time-worn old fishing communities like Wellfleet and Chatham, along with dozens of carefully maintained, mildly touristy hamlets along the many winding roads, are what most people hope to find when they come to the Cape. Cutting across the middle, the **Cape Cod Rail Trail** follows a paved-over railroad track from Dennis to Eastham, through forests and cranberry bogs – the saturated bodies of peat in which the fruit is cultivated. It makes a good **cycling** trip; bikes can be rented in all the main towns.

One desirable destination is the whitewashed old town of **CHATHAM**, tucked away in a protected harbor between Nantucket Sound and the open Atlantic Ocean. Hang out at the **Fish Pier** on Shore Road and wait for the fleet to come in during the mid-afternoon, or head a mile south on Hwy-28 to **Chatham Light**, one of many lighthouses built to protect mariners from the treacherous shoals. Tour **maps** are available from the booth at 533 Main St. The *Impudent Oyster*, 15 Chatham Bars Ave, just off Main Street (℡508/945-3545), serves excellent **seafood**; reservations are recommended. If you're going to **stay** in Chatham, pricey inns abound; one reasonable option is the charming *Chatham Seafarer*, at Rte-28 and Ridgevale Road (℡508/432-1739, ⓦwww.seafarerofchatham.com; ❻).

One of the nicest **places to stay** on the whole East Coast is the romantic *Whalewalk Inn*, at 220 Bridge Rd in the town of **EASTHAM** (℡508/255-0617 or 1-800/440-1281, ⓦwww.whalewalkinn.com; ❼). Rates for the secluded B&B rooms and a converted barn and carriage house include free use of bicycles to ride the many nearby trails. Out on Queen Anne Road, a five-minute walk from Eastham's downtown, the *Queen Anne Inn*, no. 70 (℡508/945-0394 or 1-800/545-INNS, ⓦwww.queenanneinn.com; ❻), and the *Bow Roof House*, no. 59 (℡508/945-1346; ❹), are two B&Bs where all rooms have private baths. The nearest **hostel**, with beds from $20 to $27, is the *HI-Mid Cape*, between Chatham and Provincetown at 75 Goody Halet Drive (℡508/255-2785; ❶; open May–Sept).

As for **places to eat** in Eastham, *Arnold's Lobster and Clam Bar*, 3580 Rte-6 (℡508/255-2575), is a popular restaurant and beer garden, offering good seafood and award-winning onion rings. For something a bit more unusual, the *Old Jailhouse Tavern*, 28 West Rd (℡508/255-5245), is an imposing nineteenth-century jail that serves traditional New England cuisine.

Cape Cod National Seashore

After the bustle of Cape Cod's towns, the **Cape Cod National Seashore** really does come as a proverbial breath of fresh air. These protected lands, spared by President Kennedy from the rampant development further south, take up virtually the entire Atlantic side of the Cape, from Chatham north to Provincetown. Most of the way you can park by the road, sometimes for a fee, and strike off across the dunes to windswept, seemingly endless beaches – though in places parking is limited to local residents. A program of grass-planting helps to hold the whole place together: three feet of the sands south of the National Seashore are washed away each year, much of it carried here by the ocean.

It was on these shifting sands that the **Pilgrims** made their first home. They obtained their water from Pilgrim Spring, near Truro, and at Corn Hill Beach they uncovered the freshly buried cache of Indian corn that kept them alive. After a couple of months, which they survived with the help of the

△ Vermont Pumpkins

Wampanoag Indians, they moved on to Plymouth. (The reconstructed Indian village at Plimoth Plantation is based on one found at Eastham; see p.228.)

Displays and movies at the main **Salt Pond Visitor Center**, on US-6 just north of Eastham (daily 9am–5pm; ☎508/255-3421), trace the geology and history of the Cape. A road and a hiking/cycling trail head east to the sands of **Coast Guard Beach** and **Nauset Light Beach**, both of which offer excellent swimming. Another fine beach is the **Head of the Meadow**, halfway between Truro and Provincetown on the northeast shore. The *HI-Truro* **hostel**, on North Pamet Road in Truro (☎508/349-3889, ⓦwww.capecodhostels .org; ❶; mid-June to early Sept), has beds from $20 to $27 in a former Coast Guard station, offering spectacular views of the seashore and the dunes.

Provincetown

The compact fishing village of **PROVINCETOWN** (or, as it's popularly known, "P-Town") is right on the knuckle of what would be Cape Cod's clenched fist. It's a gorgeous place, with silvery clapboard houses, with gloriously unruly gardens, lining the town's tiny winding streets. Self-professed bohemians and artists have long flocked here for the dazzling light and vast beaches; in 1914 Eugene O'Neill established the Provincetown Playhouse in a small hut. The town has also become renowned, since the Beatnik 1950s, as a **gay** center, and today its population of five thousand rises tenfold in the summer. Commercialism, though rampant, tends to be countercultural: gay, environmentalist, and feminist gift shops join arty galleries, restaurants, and bars on the aptly named **Commercial Street**. Meanwhile, Provincetown also retains a firm grip on its past. Strict zoning ensures that there are few new buildings in town, and there is barely a sign of ugly development. Albeit crowded and raucous from July through September, P-Town remains a place where history, natural beauty, and, above all, difference, are respected and celebrated.

Arrival and information

Provincetown lies 120 miles from Boston by land, but less than fifty miles by sea, nestled in the second largest natural harbor in the world (after Le Havre, in France). By far the nicest way to arrive is on the **ferry**. Boston Harbor Cruises (daily May to mid-June, additional departures on weekends in early June through early Oct; $35 one way, $55 round trip; ☎617/227-4321 or 1-877/733-9425, ⓦwww.bostonharborcruises.com) leave Long Wharf Ferry Terminal in Boston at 9am, arriving at MacMillan Wharf in Provincetown ninety minutes later; ferries return at 4pm. A cheaper option are the Plymouth & Brockton **buses**, which run to Provincetown twice a day ($23 one way from Boston; $9 one way from Hyannis; ☎508/746-0378, ⓦwww.p-b.com).

The tiny **visitor center**, in the Chamber of Commerce at the end of the wharf, 307 Commercial St (summer daily 9am–5pm; rest of year Mon–Sat 9.30am–4.30pm; ☎508/487-3424, ⓦwww.ptownchamber.com), has a wealth of information on area attractions, distributes discount coupons for whale-watching cruises, and also sells **ferry tickets**.

It couldn't be easier to **walk** around tiny P-Town, though many visitors prefer to **cycle** the narrow streets, hills, and the undulating Province Lands Bike Trail, a difficult six-mile route with great vistas. One good bike-rental outlet in town is Arnold's, 329 Commercial St (☎508/487-0844); they charge about $20 a day.

For those without transportation, **tours** to the more isolated dunes and moors include ones led by Provincetown Trolley, Inc., from the town hall on Commercial Street (daily every half-hour from 10am–4pm, or until 7pm in season; $9; ☎508/487-9483, ⓦwww.provincetowntrolley.com), and Art's Sand

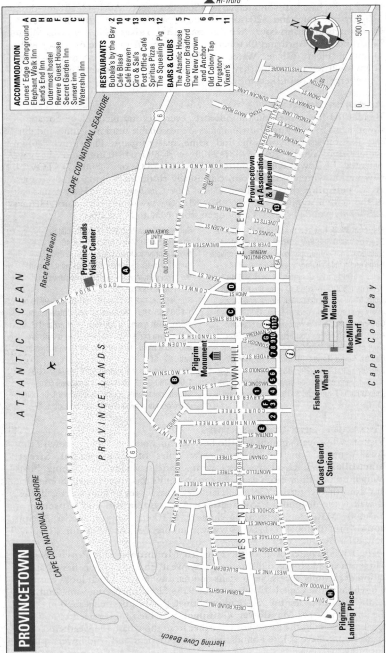

PROVINCETOWN

ATLANTIC OCEAN

CAPE COD NATIONAL SEASHORE

Race Point Beach

✈

Province Lands Visitor Center

PROVINCE LANDS

Pilgrim Monument

TOWN HILL

WEST END

EAST END

Herring Cove Beach

Provincetown Art Association & Museum

Fishermen's Wharf

Whydah Museum

MacMillan Wharf

Coast Guard Station

Pilgrims' Landing Place

Cape Cod Bay

▲ *HI-Truro*

▼ *Long Point Beach*

ACCOMMODATION
Dunes' Edge Campground	A
Elephant Walk Inn	D
Land's End Inn	H
Outermost hostel	B
Revere Guest House	F
Secret Garden Inn	G
Sunset inn	C
Watership Inn	E

RESTAURANTS
Bubala's by the Bay	2
Café Blasé	10
Café Heaven	4
Ciro & Sal's	13
Post Office Café	8
Spiritus Pizza	3
The Squealing Pig	12

BARS & CLUBS
The Atantic House	5
Governor Bradford	7
The New Crown and Anchor	6
Old Colony Tap	9
Purgatory	1
Vixen's	11

N

0   500 yds

Dune Tours, based at Commercial and Standish streets (April–Oct 10am–dusk; $15 daytime tour and $20 sunset tour; ☎508/487-1950 ☎800/894-1951, Ⓦwww.artsdunetours.com). **Whale-watching cruises** leave from MacMillan Wharf between April and October 31; one of the main cruise operators is the Dolphin Fleet Whale Watch (☎508/349-1900 or 1-800/826-9300, Ⓦwww.whalewatch.com); they have a ticket office within the Chamber of Commerce and sell tickets for about $22.

Accommodation

Besides the few motels on the outskirts, every second picturesque cottage in town seems to be a **guesthouse**. Prices are reasonable until mid-June, and during the off-season you can find some real bargains. The Provincetown Reservation System (☎508/487-2400 or 1-800/648-0364) and the gay-oriented In Town Reservations (☎508/487-1883 or 1-800/67P-TOWN, Ⓦwww.intownreservations.com) can usually rustle up lodging at busy times. As for **camping**, the welcoming *Dunes' Edge Campground*, on Hwy-6 just east of the central stoplights (☎508/487-9815, Ⓦwww.dunes-edge.com), charges $25 for its wooded sites; it's only open from May to September.

Elephant Walk Inn 156 Bradford St ☎508/487-2543 or 1-800/889-WALK, Ⓦwww.elephant-walkinn.com. Central, spacious rooms with private baths and a video library. Free parking. ④–⑤

Land's End Inn 22 Commercial St ☎508/487-0706 or 1-800/276-7088, Ⓦwww.landsendinn .com. Meticulously decorated rooms and suites, many with sweeping ocean views. ④–⑤

Outermost Hostel 28 Winslow St ☎508/487-4378. Very basic five-dorm cabins with $19-a-night beds. Open May–Oct.

Revere Guest House 14 Court St ☎508/487-2292 or 1-800/487-2292. B&B with relaxing garden patio and continental breakfast. Rooms with shared baths for around $115 a night in summer. ④–⑤

Secret Garden Inn 300a Commercial St ☎508/487-9027 or 1-866/786-9646, Ⓦwww.provincetown.com/secretgardeninn. Homey five-room guesthouse in a quiet lane off the town center, with sundeck, sea views, and fresh baked goods. ④

Sunset Inn 142 Bradford St ☎508/487-9810 or 1-800/965-1801, Ⓦwww.sunsetinnptown.com. Clean, quiet rooms in a house full of art and close to the town center. Rooms with shared bath are $20–30 a night cheaper than those with private bath. ④–⑤

Watership Inn 7 Winthrop St ☎508/487-0094 or 1-800/330-9413, Ⓦwww.watershipinn.com. Fifteen rooms with private bath in an 1820s home; rates include a good continental breakfast. ④

The town and the beaches

Visitors who head straight for the beaches miss out on Provincetown's tiny core, centered on the three narrow miles of **Commercial Street**. **MacMillan Wharf**, always busy with charters, yachts, and fishing boats (which unload their catch each afternoon), splits the town in half. Somewhat out from the center, on Commercial Street, are scores of quaint art galleries, as well as the delightful **Provincetown Art Association and Museum**, at no. 460 (May–Oct daily noon–5pm & 8–10pm; Nov–April Sat & Sun noon–4pm; ☎508/487-1750, Ⓦwww.paam.org; $3), which features displays by local artists.

The 252ft granite tower of the **Pilgrim Monument and Provincetown Museum** on High Pole Hill, in the pretty **West End** of P-Town, has an observation deck (only accessible by stairs and narrow ramps) which looks out over the whole of the Cape (daily: April–Nov 9am–5pm; July & Aug 9am–7pm; $7). At the bottom of the hill, on Bradford Street, there's a bas-relief monument to the Pilgrims' 1620 **Mayflower Compact**, in which they agreed to unite as one body to build the first colony. Further from the wharf, the weathered clapboard houses have colored blinds, white picket fences, and wildflowers spilling out of every crevice.

A little way beyond the town's narrow strip of sand, undeveloped **beaches** are marked only by dunes and a few shabby beach huts. You can swim in the clear water from the uneven rocks of the two-mile breakwater, where the sea bed crunches with soft-shell clams, or head through scented wild roses and beach plums to find blissful isolation on undeveloped beaches nearby. West of town, **Herring Cove Beach**, easily reached by bike or through the dunes, is more crowded, but never unbearably so. In the wild **Province Lands**, at the Cape's northern tip, vast sweeping moors and bushy dunes are buffeted by a deadly sea, site of three thousand known shipwrecks. The **visitor center** (May–Oct daily 9am–5pm; ☎508/487-1256), in the middle of the dunes on Race Point Road, has an observation deck from which you might spot a whale.

Eating

Food in Provincetown can be expensive: the snack bars around MacMillan Wharf are generally extortionate, and eating in one of the – undeniably good – *nouvelle cuisine* restaurants can cost you more than $10 for a simple salad and a coffee. Portuguese bakeries, relics of early settlement, and bland family restaurants abound on Commercial Street.

Bubala's by the Bay 183 Commercial St ☎508/487-0773. Breakfast, lunch, or dinner on the water in a local and fun hangout serving all kinds of sandwiches, seafood, and breakfast items.

Café Blasé 328 Commercial St ☎508/487-9465. Popular café with outdoor seating. Very reasonable prices for diverse fare, including ostrich and bison burgers.

Café Heaven 199 Commercial St ☎508/487-9639. Artsy restaurant serving a variety of Thai and Asian dishes for around $15.

Ciro & Sal's 4 Kiley Court ☎508/487-6444. Tasty, traditional Italian cooking, though quite expensive.

Reservations are recommended.

Post Office Café 303 Commercial St ☎508/487-3892. Small, gay-run restaurant serving healthy lunches and dinners for $10–20. Gay/feminist cabaret performed nightly.

Spiritus Pizza 190 Commercial St ☎508/487-2808. Combination pizza place and coffee bar with a hipster scene that intensifies as the night marches on.

The Squealing Pig 335 Commercial St ☎508/487-5804. Excellent pub (with a classic name) right in the middle of town, featuring live music some nights.

Nightlife and entertainment

Each weekend, boatloads of revelers from the mainland seek out P-Town's notoriously wild **nightlife**. From house-music raves to drag cabarets, from torch singing to R&B, the variety is huge.

The Atlantic House 6 Masonic Place, behind Commercial St ☎508/487-3821. The "A-House" – a dark drinking hole favored by Tennessee Williams and Eugene O'Neill – is now a trendy gay music club and bar.

Governor Bradford 312 Commercial St ☎508/487-2781. Popular mixed two-level bar, with nightly drag shows on the upper level, and live jazz, reggae, and R&B on the lower.

The New Crown and Anchor 247 Commercial St ☎508/487-1430. Noisy pub with nightly drag cabaret and a mostly gay crowd.

Old Colony Tap 323 Commercial St ☎508/487-2361. This tattered and torn drinking hole, catering to salty dogs for more than fifty years, is about as authentic as they come. Considered by many to be the last predominantly straight bar in Provincetown.

Purgatory 9–11 Carver St ☎508/487-3490. Within the *Gifford House Inn*, a lively dance club and video bar celebrating a leather and Levi's fetish.

Vixen's 336 Commercial St ☎508/487-6424. High-energy, primarily lesbian club, though welcoming to all.

Martha's Vineyard

The island of **MARTHA'S VINEYARD**, just seven miles south of Cape Cod and twenty-four miles long by ten wide, may or may not have been named by the seventeenth-century seafarer Bartholomew Gosnold after his daughter, Martha (some old maps call it *Martin's* Vineyard). The "Vineyard" part, however, was for its "incredible store of vines"; considerably more fertile than bleak little Nantucket, it has never been quite so dependent on the sea to make a living. Now more than ever, though, **tourism** is at the root of the island's economy, boosted by the gaggle of celebrities, not least the Clintons, who show up year after year. The popularity of the island with the rich, famous, and/or well-connected has driven up housing prices and lowered availability to extremes. The many second-homeowners who spend the summer here get a better deal than mere day-trippers, though – some of the best beaches are off-limits to nonresidents.

Ferries to the island arrive either at **Oak Bluffs**, where genteel Victorian terraced cottages look down on the harbor, and a colorful century-old fairground carousel sits near the jetty, or at the more upmarket **Vineyard Haven**. **Edgartown**, over to the east, is the oldest settlement on the island, and has been extravagantly dolled-up for visitors (you may recognize it as the location

Ferries to Martha's Vineyard and Nantucket

Unless otherwise specified, all the ferries below run several times daily in midsummer (mid-June to mid-Sept). Most have fewer services from May to mid-June, and between mid-September and October. There is at least a skeleton service to each island, though not on all routes, all year round. To discourage clogging of the roads, round-trip costs for cars are exceptionally high in the peak season (mid-May to mid-Sept), while costs for bikes are just $5 each way.

To Martha's Vineyard
Falmouth to Oak Bluffs: pedestrians only; $10 round trip; the *Island Queen* ferry ☏508/548-4800, ⓦwww.islandqueen.com.
Falmouth to Edgartown: pedestrians only; $24 round trip; Falmouth Ferry Service ☏508/548-9400, ⓦwww.falmouthferry.com.
Woods Hole to Vineyard Haven and Oak Bluffs: pedestrians $11 round trip; May–Oct vehicles $110 round trip; off-season vehicles $68 round trip; Steamship Authority ☏508/477-8600, ⓦwww.islandferry.com.
Hyannis to Oak Bluffs: pedestrians only; $27 round trip; early May through late Sept only; Hy-Line ☏508/778-2600 in Hyannis, ☏508/693-0112 on Martha's Vineyard, ⓦwww.hy-linecruises.com.
New Bedford to Oak Bluffs: pedestrians only; $20 round trip; Steamship Authority ☏508/477-8600, ⓦwww.islandferry.com.
Montauk, Long Island, to Oak Bluffs: pedestrians only; summer Sundays only; $80 round trip; Viking Ferry ☏631/668-5700, ⓦwww.vikingfleet.com.

To Nantucket
From Hyannis: pedestrians $26 round trip (2hr journey); pedestrians $52 round trip (1hr journey); May–Oct vehicles $165 one way; off-season vehicles $105 one way; Steamship Authority ☏508/477-8600 for auto reservations, ☏508/771-4000 on the mainland, ☏508/228-0262 on Nantucket. Also Hy-Line Cruises, pedestrians only; 2hr journey $27 round trip; 1hr journey $58 round trip; ☏508/778-2600 in Hyannis, ☏508/228-3949 on Nantucket, ⓦwww.hy-linecruises.com.
From Harwich Port: pedestrians only; $46 round trip; late May through early Oct only; Freedom Cruise Line ☏508/432-8999, ⓦwww.nantucketislandferry.com.

In summer, the Hy-Line ferry company also runs a **connecting service** between Oak Bluffs, Martha's Vineyard, and Nantucket (three departures daily; pedestrians only; $27 round trip; ☏508/693-0112). The trip takes about two hours.

for the *Jaws* films). A little ferry shuttles back and forth from Edgartown to adjacent **Chappaquiddick Island** (the bridge that Senator Ted Kennedy made infamous is on the far side).

The three principal island communities are connected by a regular bus service and offer full facilities and shops of every kind. They're quite mellow places to pass a summer's day, but a little exploring can yield some pleasant surprises, such as quiet beaches and bird-filled lagoons. Bringing a car over is expensive and pointless, as the island is jam-packed with cars throughout the summer and you can easily get around by **bike**; rent one at the rental places lined up by the ferry landing. The best bike ride is along the State Beach Park between Oak Bluffs and Edgartown, with the dunes to one side and marshy Sengekontacket Pond to the other; purpose-built cycle routes continue to the youth hostel at West Tisbury (see below).

Trips around the west side of the island are decidedly bucolic, with nary a peep of the water beyond the rolling hills and private estates; however, you do eventually come to the **lighthouse** at **Gay Head Cliffs**, where the multicolored clay was once the main source of paint for the island's houses – now, anyone caught removing any clay faces a sizeable fine. The cliffs are not vast, and they're crumbling away so fast that it's not safe to get too close to them. From Gay Head public beach below, however, you can get some great views of this spectacular mass.

Accommodation

If accommodation is booked up, as is very likely, the main **Chamber of Commerce** office at Beach Road in Vineyard Haven (℡ 508/693-0085, ⓦ www.mvy.com) may be able to help. There is a **campground** in Vineyard Haven at 569 Edgartown Rd (℡ 508/693-3772, ⓦ www.campmvfc.com); tentsites cost $38 per day for two people and include water and electricity hookups.

Attleboro House 42 Lake Ave, Oak Bluffs ℡ 508/693-4346. Charming, old-fashioned guesthouse on a distinguished harbor-view terrace. No private bathrooms. ❹

Colonial Inn 38 N Water St, Edgartown ℡ 508/627-4711 or 1-800/627-4701, ⓦ www.colonialinnmvy.com. Extremely central white clapboard inn, part of a largish mall, with clean, airy rooms in view of the water. Some off-season bargains (❺) can be found, but midsummer rates are high. ❼

HI-Martha's Vineyard Edgartown–West Tisbury Rd 525 ℡ 508/693-2665, ⓦ www.capecodhostels.org. In an appealing setting at the forest's edge and away from town, near the island's main bike path. Shuttle buses run to here from the ferry terminal. Open April to mid-November. Dorm beds $20–27 a night.

Nashua House B&B across from the Post Office, 30 Kennebec Ave, Oak Bluffs ℡ 508/693-0043, ⓦ www.nashuahouse.com. Small, sunny, Victorian-style rooms with shared baths and ocean views, in the heart of Oak Bluffs. ❸–❺

Shiretown Inn 44 N Water St, Edgartown ℡ 508/627-3353 or 1-800/541-0090, ⓦ www.shiretowninn.com. A variety of B&B rooms done up in different styles, including some very costly – but fancy – ones, right in the center of town. ❻

Tuscany Inn 22 N Water St, Edgartown ℡ 508/627-5999 or 1-800/638-9027, ⓦ www.tuscanyinn.com. Savor an unexpected slice of Italy in the center of Edgartown. The owner has given her inn Tuscan touches, from the garden to the cooking classes that are taught on-site in the off-season. ❻

Wesley Hotel 70 Lake Ave, Oak Bluffs ℡ 508/693-6611, ⓦ www.wesleyhotel.com. Large but characterful hotel near the ferries, with a great wraparound deck and pretty views. Most rooms are $110+, with prices rising dramatically in summer. All have private bath. ❺

Eating and drinking

It's not at all hard to find something to **eat** on Martha's Vineyard. The ports in particular have rows of places to tempt tourists just off the ferries. Only in Edgartown and Oak Bluffs can you order alcohol with meals, but you can bring your own elsewhere. Many **pubs**, too, serve inexpensive food, though the people partaking of it often look like they're on a break from a Ralph Lauren photo shoot.

The Black Dog Bakery 11 Water St, Vineyard Haven ☎508/693-4786. Skip the overrated *Black Dog Tavern* next door and stock up on delicious muffins and breads for the ferry ride back.

Giordano's 107 Circuit Ave, Oak Bluffs ☎508/693-0184. Crowded and reasonably priced Italian place, often closed out of season.

Lambert's Cove 90 Manaquayak Rd, off Lambert's Cove Rd, West Tisbury ☎508/693-2298. The restaurant at *Lambert's Cove Country Inn* is a gem, set in over seven acres of lawn and serving vegetables grown on the property; try the delectable soups. Reservations suggested.

Louis' 350 State Rd, Vineyard Haven ☎508/693-

3255. Lively, well-priced Italian place that also serves clams, located right near the ferry dock.

The Newes from America attached to the *Kelley House Inn*, 23 Kelley St, Edgartown ☎508/627-4397. Drink 500 beers in this atmospheric pub (not necessarily all in the same night) and they'll name a stool after you.

The Wharf Lower Main St, Edgartown ☎508/627-9966. On the east side of town, this is one of the better-priced seafood joints on the island; features home-brewed ales, too.

Zapotec 10 Kennebec Ave, Oak Bluffs ☎508/693-6800. Exciting seafood variations based on Mexican cuisine.

Nantucket

The thirty-mile, two-hour sea crossing to **NANTUCKET** may not be an oceangoing odyssey, but it does set the "Little Grey Lady" apart from her larger, shore-hugging sister, Martha. Halfway here from Hyannis, neither mainland nor island is in sight, and once you've landed you can avert your eyes from the smart-money double-deck cruisers with names like *Pier Pressure* and *Loan Star* and let the place remind you that it hasn't always been a rich folk's playground. Indeed, despite the formidable prowess of its seamen (see box, opposite), survival for early settlers on the island's scrubby soil was always a struggle.

The tiny cobbled carriageways of **Nantucket Town** itself, once one of the largest cities in Massachusetts, were frozen in time by economic decline 150 years ago. Today, this area of delightful old restored houses – the town has more buildings on the National Register of Historic Places than Boston – is very much the center of activity. From the moment you get off the ferry you're besieged by bike rental places and tour companies. **Straight Wharf** leads directly onto **Main Street** with its shops and restaurants; the **information office** – which has a daily list of accommodation vacancies, but doesn't make reservations – is nearby at 25 Federal St (☎508/228-0925). The **Chamber of Commerce**, 48 Main St (☎508/228-1700, ⊛www.nantucketchamber.org), carries the best range of island information.

Unfortunately, the two main sights in town – the excellent **Whaling Museum**, on Broad Street, at the head of Steamboat Wharf, and the **Peter Foulger Museum**, next door – are closed for renovations until 2005. In the meantime, the **Nantucket Historical Association** (☎508/228-1894, ⊛www.nha.org) gives highly acclaimed lectures at the **Quaker Meeting House**, 10 Pine St, on the history of whaling and the tragedy of the Nantucket whaleship *Essex* – the true story that inspired Herman Melville to write *Moby Dick*. A $15 "History Pass," available from the Museum Shop, 11 Broad St, includes admission to the Quaker Meeting House as well as a number of other historical sites, including the **Oldest House**, built in 1686, the **Old Gaol**, and the **Old Mill**. The pass also includes guided walking tours that cover the history of the town itself.

After a stroll around Nantucket Town, it's customary to cycle the seven flat miles east to the village of **Siaconset** (always abbreviated to 'Sconset), where the venerable cottages stand literally encrusted with salt, and then to meander back across the heaths and moorland. **Bikes** can be rented from Young's Bicycle Shop, 6 Broad St (around $20 for a full day; ☏508/228–1151). If you don't fancy cycling, **buses** also link Nantucket Town and 'Sconset: NRTA (☏508/228–7025) runs shuttles from late May through early October and charges $2 each way.

The whalers of Nantucket

Scores of anonymous Captains have sailed out of Nantucket, that were as great, and greater than your Cook . . . for in their succorless empty-handedness, they, in the heathenish sharked waters, and by the beaches of unrecorded, javelin islands, battled with virgin wonders and terrors that Cook with all his marines and muskets would not have willingly dared.

from *Moby Dick*, by Herman Melville

In 1659, a sober group of twenty-seven Quaker and Presbyterian families arrived on Nantucket and set about imposing order on the haphazard business of **whaling**. Whales had always beached themselves on the treacherous sandy shoals all around – up to a dozen might be washed ashore in a major storm – and the local **Indians** had become skilled in hunting them in nearby waters. At first, the white settlers treated the island itself as their vessel, erecting tall masts from which a permanent watch was kept for passing whales. As the years went by, they stopped waiting at home, and sent large ships out into the ocean to pursue their prey. The Wampanoag Indians played an integral part in the process: the actual kill was effected by two rowboats working in tandem, and at least five of each thirteen-man crew, usually including the crucial **harpooneer**, would be Indian. The common occurrence when an injured whale would speed away, dragging a boat helter-skelter behind it for endless terrifying hours, was known as a "**Nantucket Sleighride**."

The early chronicler Crèvecoeur provides an extensive account of Nantucket as it was in 1782 in his *Letters from an American Farmer*. Although perturbed by the islanders' universal habit of taking a dose of opium every morning, he held them up as a model of diligence and good self-government. Whaling was a disciplined profession, unmarred by the stereotyped debauchery of sailors elsewhere, and to feed themselves and equip their ships the islanders kept up a shrewd and extensive trade with the mainland. At that time, there were already more than a hundred ships. The whalers were not paid; instead each had a share (a "lay") of the final proceeds of the voyage. Crèvecoeur was impressed by the Nantucketers' ambition: "Would you believe that they have already gone to the Falkland Islands and I have heard several of them talk of going to the South Sea."

They did indeed reach the Pacific – see p.1363 in Chapter 16, "Hawaii," for an account of their experiences there. The great days of Nantucket were immortalized by Herman Melville:

And thus have these naked Nantucketers, these sea hermits, issuing from their ant-hill in the sea, overrun and conquered the watery world like so many Alexanders . . . two thirds of this terra-queous globe are the Nantucketer's. For the sea is his; he owns it, as Emperors own empires.

In fact *Moby Dick* is a valediction; by the time it was published in 1851, Nantucket's fortunes had gone into an abrupt decline. Soon after a devastating fire in 1846, reports of the Californian Gold Rush lured young men westwards; the discovery of underground oil in Pennsylvania came as the final blow. A magazine article of 1873 reported, "Let no traveler visit Nantucket with the expectation of witnessing the marks of a flourishing trade . . . of the great fleet of ships which dotted every sea, scarcely a vestige remains."

Accommodation

But for the youth hostel, accommodation on Nantucket is somewhat expensive; the going rate in B&Bs and guesthouses starts at $85 a night.

Cliff Lodge 9 Cliff Rd ☏ 508/228-9480, ⓦ www.clifflodgenantucket.com. An eighteenth-century hilltop B&B with a rooftop deck, twelve sunlit rooms, and homemade muffins in the morning. Lower-priced singles are available in the off-season. ❻

Hawthorn House 2 Chestnut St ☏ 508/228-1468, ⓦ www.hawthorn-house.com. Central, well-appointed guesthouse with ten antique rooms. Rates include vouchers for breakfast in town. ❻

HI-Nantucket Star of the Sea Surfside ☏ 508/228-0433, ⓦ www.capecodhostels.org. Dorm beds ($20–27 a night) at Surfside Beach, just over three miles south of town. Lockout 10am–4pm. Open April–Oct only.

Jared Coffin House 29 Broad St ☏ 508/228-2400 or 1-800/248-2405, ⓦ www.jaredcoffin-house.com. In four adjacent buildings in the town center, sixty rooms, all with period furniture. There's also a superb restaurant and likeable bar onsite. ❻

Le Languedoc 24 Broad St ☏ 508/228-4298, ⓦ www.lelanguedoc.com. Comfortable, well-regarded inn and restaurant with decent rates. Ten cozy rooms, plus annex. ❹–❺

The Nesbitt Inn 21 Broad St ☏ 508/228-0156. The central location and affordable rooms, most with original furniture, compensate for the shared baths in this Victorian inn, built in 1872. ❹

Eating and drinking

Crèvecoeur (see box, overleaf) reported that on Nantucket, "music, singing, and dancing are holden in equal detestation." **Seafood** fortunately is not; the only trouble is that Nantucket's restaurants, good as they may be, tend to be exceptionally expensive, easily costing $30–40 for an entree.

Arno's Main Street Grill 41 Main St ☏ 508/228-7001. Good-value snacks and lunches served in generous portions. The grill is usually saddled with pancakes, bacon, and burgers, but *Arno's* excels at inventive seafood dishes and quesadillas, too. Breakfast served until 2pm, lunch until 4pm.

The Brotherhood of Thieves 23 Broad St (no phone). A lively old whaling bar serving up thick burgers and chowder. Cash only.

Henry's 2 Broad St ☏ 508/228-0123. Family-owned sandwich shop in operation for more than thirty years. Excellent value, sweet homemade bread, and possibly the best lobster rolls on the island.

Rose and Crown 23 S Water St ☏ 508/228-2595. Seafood saloon with live music, DJs, karaoke nights, and comedy. Cover charges vary, but are generally inexpensive.

Seagrille 45 Sparks Ave ☏ 508/325-5700. One of the best places in Nantucket for seafood, with a good wine list, and not too badly priced.

Topper's 120 Wauwinet Rd ☏ 508/228-8768. Pricey but outstanding New American cuisine in this quiet, upscale flagship restaurant at the *Wauwinet* hotel and resort, a few miles outside Nantucket Town.

Central and western Massachusetts

The 150 miles of Massachusetts that stretch inland to the west of Boston have always been obliged to play second fiddle to the state capital. Just ten years after the Revolutionary War, the farmers who struggled to make a living from this indifferent soil rose in Shay's Rebellion to prevent creditors from the east from seizing their property to help recover the war debt; their pitchforks were no match for the guns of the new nation.

These days, the citizens of the west are eager to promote themselves as cultural rivals of the big city, with the **Berkshires** hosting the celebrated **Tanglewood** summer music festival and boasting museum-filled towns such as **North Adams** and **Williamstown** – both in the far northwest corner of the state, at the end of the incredibly scenic **Mohawk Trail**. **Amherst** and **Northampton** are stimulating college towns in the verdant **Pioneer Valley**, with all the cafés, restaurants, and bookstores you could want. The industrial city of **Worcester** has a good art museum, while culture of a more popular variety is on offer at the Basketball Hall of Fame in **Springfield**.

Worcester

Forty miles west of Boston on I-90, **WORCESTER** is Massachusetts' second largest city, and the only major industrial city in the US not beside a sea, lake, or river. Birthplace of American icons such as the Valentine's Day Card and the yellow Smiley Face, Worcester should not take up too much of your time. The highlight is the **Worcester Art Museum**, 55 Salisbury St (Wed, Fri & Sun 11am–5pm, Thurs 11am–8pm, Sat 10am–5pm; $8, or free Saturday from 10am–noon; ☎508/799-4406, ⓦwww.worcesterart.org), with its vast collection of paintings, mosaics, photographs, and a Romanesque chapter house from the twelfth century. Also worth a visit are the **Higgins Armory Museum**, at 100 Barber Ave (Tues–Sat 10am–4pm, Sun noon–4pm; $7.75; ☎508/853-6015, ⓦwww.higgins.org), which houses weapons and armor from all over the world, and the **American Antiquarian Society**, 185 Salisbury St (Mon, Tues, Thurs & Fri 9am–5pm, Wed 10am–8pm, tours Wed 2pm; free; ☎508/755-5221, ⓦwww.americanantiquarian.org), which holds copies of two-thirds of all the material published in America before 1821 – more even than the Library of Congress.

Among local **accommodation**, the central *Hampton Inn*, 110 Summer St (☎508/757-0400 or 1-800/426-7866, ⓦwww.hamptoninnworcester.com; ❺), has comfortable rooms. *The Sole Proprietor*, 118 Highland St (☎508/798-3474, ⓦwww.thesole.com), is a reliable fish **restaurant**. For a good selection of other eateries, head to Shrewsbury Street. About twenty miles west of Worcester, but worth a detour, is the *Salem Cross Inn*, off Rte-9 in West Brookfield (☎508/867-8337, ⓦwww.salemcrossinn.com), a rambling restaurant in a restored 1705 farmhouse that serves consistently high-quality Yankee cooking.

Springfield

SPRINGFIELD, at the point where I-90 crosses I-91 – in an extremely confusing way – ninety miles from Boston at the southern border of the Pioneer Valley, has an odd assortment of claims to fame, including being the home of the Springfield rifle and the late children's author Dr Seuss. However, visitors are drawn to this unwieldy and unattractive city, split by the wide Connecticut

---

Old Sturbridge Village

Halfway between Worcester and Springfield on US-20, near the junction of I-90 and I-84, the restored and reconstructed **Old Sturbridge Village** (daily: winter 9.30am–4pm; rest of year 9.30am–5pm; $20; ☎508/347-3362 or 1-800/SEE-1830, ⓦwww.osv.org), made up of preserved buildings brought from all over the region, gives a somewhat idealized but engaging portrait of a small New England town of the 1830s. Costumed interpreters act out roles – working in blacksmiths' shops, planting and harvesting vegetables, tending cows, and the like – but they pull it off in an unusually convincing manner. The 200-acre site itself, with mature trees, ponds, and dirt footpaths, is very pretty, and worth a half-day visit. The nearby *Old Sturbridge Village Lodges*, 371 Main St (☎508/347-3327; ❹), owned by the museum, is a reasonable **place to stay** – ten of the more atmospheric rooms are in an eighteenth-century mansion, and there is access to an outdoor heated pool.

River, by the 1890s invention of Dr James Naismith – the sport of **basketball**. Naismith designed the game as a way of providing exercise for athletes at the YMCA, and its popularity spread with amazing speed. First opened in 1959, the **Basketball Hall of Fame** at 1150 W Columbus Ave, next to the river just south of Memorial Bridge (Sun–Thurs 10am–6pm, Fri & Sat 10am–8pm; $15; ☎413/781-6500 or 1-877/4HOOPLA, ⓦwww.hoophall.com), was revamped and enlarged in 2002, and includes movies, videos, memorabilia, and interactive gadgets which allow you to test your own skills.

Springfield's Amtrak **train** station is very central, at 66 Lyman St (☎413/785-4230). Peter Pan Trailways (☎413/781-2900 or 1-800/237-8747, ⓦwww.peterpanbus.com) provides daily **bus** services to and from Boston and New York City, the Pioneer Valley, and the Berkshires from the nearby bus station at 1776 Main St (☎413/781-3320). The **Convention & Visitors Bureau** is downtown at 1441 Main St (Mon–Fri 9am–5pm; ☎413/787-1548 or 1-800/723-1548, ⓦwww.valleyvisitor.com). Downtown **lodging** includes the expensive *Sheraton Springfield*, 1 Monarch Place (☎413/781-1010; ❻), and the much cheaper *Cityspace YMCA*, 275 Chestnut St (☎413/739-6951 ext 130; ❸). A number of budget motels can be found over the river in West Springfield. Tiny Fort Street has been home to the *Fort/Student Prince Restaurant* (☎413/734-7475) for over sixty years – a local favorite serving Wiener schnitzel, goulash, and sauerbraten.

Amherst and Northhampton

North of Springfield, the Pioneer Valley is a verdant corridor created by the Connecticut River, home to the college towns of **AMHERST** and **NORTHAMPTON**, both good places to kick back for a few days, hang out in cafés, and browse bookstores in one of New England's most liberal and progressive areas (*Newsweek* has dubbed Northampton the "lesbian capital of the Northeast").

Amtrak **trains** stop in Amherst at 13 Railroad St, while you can catch Peter Pan Trailways **buses** at 1 Roundhouse Plaza in Northampton (☎413/586-1030) and 79 S Pleasant St in Amherst (☎413/256-0431). Good **accommodation** is available at Northampton's historic *Hotel Northampton*, 36 King St (☎413/584-3100 or 1-800/547-3529, ⓦwww.hotelnorthampton.com; ❼), or the *Lord Jeffery Inn* at 30 Boltwood Ave in Amherst (☎413/253-2576 or 1-800/742-0358, ⓦwww.lordjefferyinn.com; ❹), a quintessentially New England inn. Among the numerous places to **eat**, *Paul and Elizabeth's*, 150 Main St, Northampton (☎413/584-4832), has good vegetarian choices, while *Amherst Chinese Food*, 62 Main St, Amherst (☎413/253-7835), serves healthy Oriental specialties.

The Berkshires

The swath of hills and forests where Massachusetts borders New York, known as the **Berkshires**, are a cross between the English Lake District and the grand seafront resort of Newport, Rhode Island (see p.247). Especially in the area nearest the Massachusetts Turnpike (I-90), the green hillsides are dotted with ostentatious Victorian mansions, while the towns are chic, arty – if not snooty – summer tourist magnets.

The Mohawk Trail: North Adams and Williamstown

In the northwest corner of the region, the **Mohawk Trail** passes through **NORTH ADAMS** and **WILLIAMSTOWN**, following the very scenic route the Native Americans used to travel between the valleys of the Connecticut and Hudson rivers. North Adams is home to the **Massachusetts Museum of Contemporary Art** (MASS MoCA), 87 Marshall St (daily: June–Oct 10am–6pm; Nov–May Wed–Mon 11am–5pm; $9 June–Oct, $7 Nov–May, free tours Sat & Sun noon & 3pm, more during summer; ☎413/662-2111, ⓦwww.massmoca.org), which is poised to become one of the country's leading centers for visual, performing, and media arts. Williamstown has two worthy art museums: the highlight of the **Sterling and Francine Clark Art Institute**, 225 South St (Tues–Sun 10am–5pm, July–Aug daily 10am–5pm; $10 June–Oct, rest of year free; ☎413/458-2303, ⓦwww.clarkart.edu), is the thirty-strong collection of Renoir paintings, while the **Williams College Museum of Art**, 15 Lawrence Hall Drive (Tues–Sat 10am–5pm, Sun 1–5pm; free; ☎413/597-2429, ⓦwww.wcma.org), has good exhibits of ancient Middle Eastern and modern American art.

Stockbridge

STOCKBRIDGE, just south of I-90 fifty miles west of Springfield, started out as "Indian Town," because the Nipmuck Indians had several villages in the area. The Reverend John Sergeant built the simple wooden **Mission House**, now located on Main Street, in 1739 in an attempt to live in close proximity with the local Native Americans and convert them to Christianity by sheer force of example. His success barely lasted beyond his own death; later settlers were far less keen on having the natives around.

That Stockbridge today looks like the archetypal New England small town – most of all when there's snow on the ground – is due largely to the artist **Norman Rockwell**, who lived here for 25 years until his death in 1978. Many of his *Saturday Evening Post* covers, whose sentimentality was made palatable by his sharp wit, featured the town; a collection of covers can be seen at the **museum** on Hwy-183 (daily: May–Oct 10am–5pm; Nov–April Mon–Fri 10am–4pm, Sat & Sun 10am–5pm; $12; ☎413/298-4100 ext 220, ⓦwww.nrm.org). Some of the tour guides modeled for Rockwell as children and recall that for every few minutes they managed to hold still he'd slip them a coin from his large pile of nickels.

Magnificent houses in the hills around Stockbridge include **Chesterwood**, half a mile south of the Norman Rockwell Museum at 4 Williamsville Rd (May–Oct daily 10am–5pm; $10, grounds only $5; ☎413/298-3579, ⓦwww.chesterwood.org), the luxurious home and studio of Daniel Chester French, sculptor of the Lincoln Memorial, and **Naumkeag**, on Prospect Hill Road (late May to mid-Oct daily 10am–5pm; $10, gardens only $8; ☎413/298-3239), which belonged to Joseph Choate, US ambassador to Queen Victoria. Stockbridge was also the setting for Arlo Guthrie's song, and movie, *Alice's Restaurant*.

Lenox and around

Roughly five miles north of Stockbridge on US-7, well-heeled tourists flock to **LENOX** each year for the summer season of the Boston Symphony Orchestra at **Tanglewood**, 297 West St (for ticket info, call ☎413/637-1666 or visit ⓦwww.bso.org). Open-air orchestral concerts are held on weekends from July to late August, with chamber music and recitals given on other days; covered seats are pricey and often hard to get, but you can sit and picnic on the lush lawns for an admission fee of around $15. Some midweek rehearsals are also open to the public, and there's a **jazz** festival on Labor Day weekend (the first weekend of September).

Further north on US-7, **Arrowhead** (late May–Oct daily 9.30am–5pm; $8; ☎413/442-1793, ⓦwww.mobydick.org), near Pittsfield, was Herman Melville's home while he wrote *Moby Dick*; declining sales of his books eventually forced him to sell his house and move to New York. The **Hancock Shaker Village**, five miles west of Pittsfield (daily: April–Nov 9.30am–5pm; rest of year 10am–4pm; summer and fall $15, rest of year $12; ☎413/443-0188, ⓦwww.hancockshakervillage.org), was a going concern from 1783 to 1960. Its legacy includes the large dwelling-place, in which almost one hundred people slept and ate, and a round stone barn for their cattle. A more important, and much less commercialized, Shaker village, **Mount Lebanon**, is another five miles west on US-20, just over the New York State border; much has been dismantled and moved to museums, but a visit still gives a sense of the Shaker way of life ($6; ☎518/794-9500).

Berkshires practicalities

Try to visit the excellent **Berkshire Visitors Bureau**, at the Berkshire Common Plaza in Pittsfield (Mon–Fri 8.30am–5pm; ☎413/443-9186 or 1-800/237-5747, ⓦwww.berkshires.org), the best source for information on the Berkshires. Much of the **accommodation** is concentrated in Lenox and neighboring Lee, about five miles southeast; when the Tanglewood concerts are on, prices naturally go through the roof, and a last-minute vacancy is almost impossible to find. One of the more reasonably priced (provided you stay in off-season) and atmospheric places is the *Historic Merrell Inn*, 1565 Pleasant St/Rte-102, South Lee (☎413/243-1794 or 1-800/243-1794, ⓦwww.merrell-inn.com; ❹), an old stagecoach inn. Also good value if you visit during spring is *The Village Inn*, in Lenox at 16 Church St (☎413/637-0020 or 1-800/253-0917, ⓦwww.villageinn-lenox.com; ❹). At the other end of the scale, stay in total luxury at *Blantyre*, Blantyre Road, Lenox (closed winter; ☎413/637-3556, ⓦwww.blantyre.com; ❾). Williamstown has several mid-priced motels, as well as stately accommodation – like *The Williams Inn* on Main Street (☎413/458-9371 or 1-800/828-0133, ⓦwww.williamsinn.com; ❻). The *Red Lion Inn* is one of the grander edifices on Main Street in Stockbridge (☎413/298-5545, ⓦwww.redlioninn.com; ❹), and the **restaurant** has big portions of reliable Yankee fare, from prime rib to sole *meunière*. Other worthwhile places to **eat** include the cheap and cheerful *Joe's Diner*, 85 Center St, at Main (☎413/243-9756), or, for urban chic that wouldn't be out of place in New York City, *Eleven*, in building 11 at the MASS MoCA, North Adams (☎413/662-2004).

Rhode Island

A mere 48 miles long by 37 miles wide, **RHODE ISLAND** is the smallest state in the Union, and tends to be overlooked as a destination, even if it is home to more than twenty percent of the nation's historical landmarks. It was established by Roger Williams in 1636 as a "lively experiment" in religious freedom. He had been expelled from Puritan Salem for his radical ideas (including the notion that Indians should be paid for their land and that there should be a complete separation of church from state), and the Massachusetts Puritans liked to call the state he settled in "**Rogues Island**."

Despite its size, Rhode Island has over four hundred miles of coastline, hacked out of the Narragansett Bay; it is, in fact, made up of over thirty tiny islands, including Hope and Despair. The "**Ocean State**" developed through sea trade, whaling, and smuggling. Partly due to this commercial interest, Rhode Islanders, resenting the stringent economic pressures placed on them from England, were in the front rank of the Revolutionary groundswell. However, no Revolutionary battles were fought on Rhode Island soil, and the state, apprehensive at the prospect of yielding power to the newly-formed Federal government, turned out to be the last state to ratify the Constitution. Between the Revolution and the Civil War, Rhode Island shifted from a maritime economy to lead the **Industrial Revolution**, with Samuel Slater's creation of the nation's first water-powered **textile mill** in Pawtucket, just outside Providence.

Today, although still heavily industrialized, the state's principal destinations are its two original ports: well-heeled **Newport**, yachting capital of the world, with its good beaches and outrageously extravagant mansions, and the Colonial college town of **Providence**.

Getting around Rhode Island

Rhode Island is tiny enough to make **getting around** ridiculously easy. Major interstate I-95 runs through **Providence** on its way from Massachusetts to Connecticut. The more scenic US-1 follows the coast of Narragansett Bay into Connecticut. **Newport** is accessible from Hwy-138, which connects the small islands in Narragansett Bay to the mainland. **Public transportation** is good: local buses connect Providence and Newport, and Amtrak stops regularly in Providence. **Ferries** link Providence and Newport.

Providence

Splayed across seven hills on the Providence and Seekonk rivers, **PROVIDENCE** was Rhode Island's first settlement, founded "in commemoration of God's providence" on land given to Roger Williams by the Narragansett Indians (his insistence that Indians should be paid for their land being waived in his own case). Now New England's third largest city, it has been the **state capital** since 1901, and flourished as one of the most important ports of call in the notorious "triangle trade," where New England rum was exchanged for African slaves, who were then sold for West Indian molasses. Since Slater's invention of the water-powered textile mill, port trade and industry have been the mainstays of Providence's economy. Today, Ivy League **Brown University** and the **Rhode Island School of Design** (RISD, or "Rizdee") give the place a certain cultural verve (although this admittedly doesn't stray far beyond the immediate environs of College Hill, on the east bank of the river), and the many original Colonial homes on **Benefit Street** emphasize a historical importance almost absent from the somewhat drab downtown across the river. Ethnic diversity is provided by **Little Italy** on Federal Hill, west of the river, and by fairly voluble Greek and Portuguese – and especially Cape Verdean – communities.

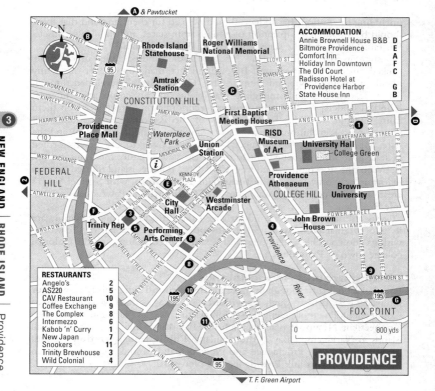

ACCOMMODATION
Annie Brownell House B&B   D
Biltmore Providence   E
Comfort Inn   A
Holiday Inn Downtown   F
The Old Court   C
Radisson Hotel at
    Providence Harbor   G
State House Inn   B

RESTAURANTS
Angelo's   2
AS220   5
CAV Restaurant   10
Coffee Exchange   9
The Complex   8
Intermezzo   6
Kabob 'n' Curry   1
New Japan   7
Snookers   11
Trinity Brewhouse   3
Wild Colonial   4

PROVIDENCE

0   800 yds

T. F. Green Airport

Arrival, information, and getting around

T.F. Green Airport is in Warwick, nine miles south of Providence. The **Amtrak station** (daily 5am–10.30pm; ☏401/351-8983) is at 100 Gaspee St, in a domed building a short walk southeast of the capitol. Greyhound and Bonanza **buses** (☏401/751-8800 or 1-888/751-8800) stop downtown at Kennedy Plaza.

The **Convention and Visitors Bureau**, 1 W Exchange St (Mon–Fri 10am–5pm; ☏401/274-1636 or 1-800/233-1636, ⓦwww.goprovidence .com), provides maps and brochures, while the **Rhode Island Historical Society** at 110 Benevolent St (Mon–Fri 9am–5pm; ☏401/831-7440, ⓦwww.rihs.org), conducts several themed tours of the city's historic areas (Tues–Sat in summer; $10). There's another **information center** in the Roger Williams National Memorial Park, 282 N Main St (daily 9am–4.30pm; ☏401/521-7266).

Sightseeing around Providence is best done **on foot**, though there is **bus transportation** within the city (as well as around the state), provided by RIPTA ($1.25; ☏401/781-9400, ⓦwww.ripta.com). Most local and long-distance buses leave from Kennedy Plaza, where schedules are available from an information booth (Mon–Fri 8am–5pm, Sat 8am–4pm). RIPTA also runs a daily **ferry service** between Providence and Newport (through New England Fast Ferry; May–Oct; $12 round trip; ⓦwww.nefastferry.com).

Accommodation

Downtown Providence has few budget rooms, but **B&B**s are a viable option – Citywide Reservation Services (☎1-888/248-9121) can help you find a place. Motorists can take advantage of the mid-priced **motels** along I-95, or north in Pawtucket, and south near the airport at Warwick.

Annie Brownell House B&B 400 Angell St ☎401/454-2934. Spacious 1899 Colonial Revival house has bright, airy rooms, each with bath. Within walking distance of Brown and RISD. ❻

Biltmore Providence 9 Kennedy Plaza ☎401/421-0700 or 1-800/294-7709, ⓦwww.providencebiltmore.com. Around since 1922, the *grand dame* of the city's hotels is centrally located, with gorgeously appointed rooms (think plush chairs and original artwork), excellent service, and good views. ❼

Comfort Inn 2 George St, Pawtucket ☎401/723-6700 and 1940 Post Rd, Warwick ☎401/732-0470. Decent rooms near exit 27 off I-95 and Slater Mill, or by the airport. ❺

Holiday Inn Downtown 21 Atwells Ave ☎401/831-3900. Next to the Civic Center, this chain hotel makes a good base from which to explore Little Italy. ❻

The Old Court 144 Benefit St ☎401/751-2002, ⓦwww.oldcourt.com. Luxury ten-room Victorian B&B in an old rectory. ❼

Radisson Hotel at Providence Harbor 220 India Point ☎401/272-5577 or 1-800/528-9931. Standard chain hotel with all the usual modern conveniences, plus a good restaurant on-site. ❼

State House Inn 43 Jewett St ☎401/351-6111, ⓦwww.providence-inn.com. Pleasant, central B&B rooms, in a restored old home near the capitol building. ❻

The City

Providence's main attractions focus around three of its seven hills. Downtown, which centers on Kennedy Plaza, is situated just below **Constitution Hill**. **City Hall**, at the western end of the plaza, is mainly notable for the star-spangled midnight-blue ceiling in the Alderman's Chamber. Though no longer used as a train terminal, the nearby 1898 Beaux Arts **Union Station** is a fine example of the historic restoration at which the city excels. South of the plaza, the 1828 **Westminster Arcade**, the oldest enclosed shopping mall in the nation, features small specialty shops and a food court in a small, bright, sky-lit hall.

The **Roger Williams National Memorial**, at N Main and Smith streets, includes part of city-founder Williams' original settlement (daily: 9am–4.30pm; free), while at the top of Constitution Hill, the white-marble **Rhode Island Statehouse** boasts a huge unsupported dome, the fourth-largest in the world. The dome is topped with a statue called *Independent Man*, an 11-foot-tall bronze figure created by George Brewster as a symbol of freedom and independence. A handsome full-length portrait of George Washington painted by Gilbert Stuart adorns the Reception Room (Mon–Fri 8.30am–4.30pm; free guided tours daily at 9am, 10am, and 11am by appointment; ☎401/222-2357).

College Hill and Federal Hill

Laid-back **College Hill**, eastward across the river, is an attractive district of Colonial buildings and museums. Part of Williams' holy experiment was the establishment of the Baptist Church in 1638. The white clapboard **First Baptist Meeting House**, at the foot of the hill at 75 N Main St, dates from 1775, and is remarkable for its very tall steeple. This street leads into **South Main Street**, once bustling with waterfront activity, now a small stretch of upmarket restaurants, potpourri stores, and pottery shops. **Benefit Street**, a block up the hill, is Providence's "**mile of history**," lined with the ice-cream-colored former clapboard homes of merchants and sea captains. Now beautifully restored, the street was once just a dirt path leading to graveyards until it was improved in the nineteenth century for the "benefit of the people of Providence" – hence its name. The elegant **John Brown House**, 52 Power St, at Benefit St (Jan–March Fri & Sat 10am–5pm & Sun noon–4pm; April–Dec Tues–Sat 10am–5pm, Sun noon–4pm; $7), was home to the patriot and entrepreneur who made his fortune trading in slaves and with China. The first house built on the hill (nicely conspicuous from the river), it retains its original furnishings and holds displays on the formidable Brown family and the city itself.

Ivy League **Brown University** sets the tone for this three-centuries-old district with its relaxed, intellectual feel; for free tours, contact the admissions office, 45 Prospect St (call ahead for tour schedule, ☎401/863-2378). At the eastern edge of College Hill, **Wickenden Street** buzzes with an assortment of bookstores, cafés, and antique and thrift stores.

The small but excellent collection of the **RISD Museum of Art**, 224 Benefit St, is worthy of its status as one of the best art-school museums in the country, and includes ancient and Oriental works, Impressionist and Post-Impressionist American art, and one of Rodin's statues of Balzac (Tues–Sun 10am–5pm; $6; ☎401/454-6500). Also on the RISD campus, the **Woods-Gerry Gallery**, 62 Prospect St (Mon–Sat 10am–4pm, Sun 2–5pm; free; ☎401/454-6141), exhibits innovative student art in a solid redbrick mansion set in a tree-shaded garden with heavy stone benches.

Across the road, the Greek Revival **Providence Athenaeum**, 251 Benefit St (Mon–Thurs 9am–7pm, Fri & Sat 9am–5pm, Sun 1–5pm, closed Sat afternoon and Sun in summer; free), is where Edgar Allan Poe unsuccessfully wooed fellow poet Sarah Whitman. Today the library holds original Audubon prints and rare books, and the place feels more like a living room, with its piano and hand-painted chairs in the cozy reading rooms.

Federal Hill, west of downtown, is Providence's **Little Italy**, entered through a large arch topped by a bronze pinecone at Atwells Avenue. Long a powerful Mafia stronghold, this area is one of the friendliest and safest in the city – alive with cafés, delis, bakeries, and bars, and with a large Italianate fountain in the Piazza de Pasquale.

Slater Mill Historic Site

A ten-minute drive north of Providence, Pawtucket is home to the **Slater Mill Historic Site**, on Roosevelt Ave, exit 28 off I-95 (May–Sept Tues–Sun 10am–5pm; $8; ☎401/725-8638, ⓦwww.slatermill.org), which illustrates the move to the industrial age led by Samuel Slater, who secretly imported the technology from England in 1793. The site features the landmark **Old Slater Mill**, which today contains a spinning frame and mule, as well as some rare textile machines that date from 1838, all for transforming raw cotton to yarn. Also found here is the 1810 **Wilkinson Mill**, where a machine shop, complete with belt-driven machine tools, still operates, and the **Sylvanus Brown House**, a worker's home with replica early-1800s furnishings, and interpreters performing (and explaining) their nineteenth-century chores.

Eating

Popular with students, **Thayer Street** is lined with inexpensive lunch places, almost all of which remain open until late. **Wickenden Street** is more alternative, and more expensive. The family-run Italian restaurants on Federal Hill serve good food at reasonable prices, and the **downtown** area is your best bet for a quick breakfast or lunch.

Angelo's 141 Atwells Ave ☎401/621-8171. Family-style restaurant offering inexpensive Italian standards.

CAV Restaurant, Antiques and Gifts 14 Imperial Place ☎401/751-9164. A hip, mid-priced Mediterranean restaurant with live entertainment after 9.30pm Thurs–Mon.

Coffee Exchange 207 Wickenden St ☎401/273-1198. This trendy coffee bar is a popular meeting place for arty intellectuals. Deck chairs and barrels act as sidewalk seating and tables.

Intermezzo 220 Weybosset St ☎401/331-5100. Conveniently located next to the Providence Performing Arts Center (see "Nightlife and entertainment," below) this cozy New York-style bistro restaurant with Rhode Island prices is a great place for a pre- or post-theater meal.

Kabob 'n' Curry 261 Thayer St ☎401/273-8844. On trendy Thayer Street, above-average Indian meals for less-than-average prices.

New Japan 145 Washington St ☎401/351-0300. Reasonably priced Japanese place, with sashimi six days a week and sushi on Sunday.

Nightlife and entertainment

As Providence's **nightlife** is largely student-oriented, things get quiet during the vacations, though Thayer Street is always lively. For **film**, the Avon Rep Cinema at 250 Thayer (☎401/421-3315) shows good independent and art flicks, and the Cable Car Cinema at 204 S Main St (☎401/272-3970) has comfy sofas instead of seats. The **Providence Performing Arts Center**, downtown at 220 Weybosset St (☎401/421-2787, ⓦwww.ppacri.org), hosts musicals and the occasional concert in a grand old Art Deco movie house. In the warmer months, **WaterFire** (several times a month, May–Oct; ⓦwww.waterfire.org) enthralls visitors and locals alike with over eighty small bonfires set in the center of the Providence River starting at Waterplace Park, tended by gondoliers and accompanied by rousing music. Complete entertainment **listings** can be found in the free weekly *Providence Phoenix* and the *Providence Journal*'s Thursday edition.

AS220 115 Empire St ☎401/831-9327. Unabashedly artsy café/bar hangout for locals and students. Also a music venue featuring everything from mellow jazz to performance art. Gallery on second floor. Cover $2–5.

The Complex 180 Pine St ☎401/751-4263. Four dance clubs on one site, with every type of music imaginable. Cover $5–7.

Snookers 145 Clifford St ☎401/351-7665. Lively pool hall with a variety of table games. Its green

room features alternative DJs and is one of the city's most sociable spots. No cover.

Trinity Brewhouse 186 Fountain St ☎401/453-2337. Hang out here after a Providence Bruins (minor league hockey) or Friars (college basketball) game to drink microbrews either in celebration or despair. There's a full menu as well.

Wild Colonial 250 S Water St ☎401/621-5644. This is the place for a bit of British air, with pub food, English ales, and darts.

Newport

Thirty miles south of Providence, **NEWPORT** stands at the southern tip of the largest island in Narragansett Bay, **Aquidneck Island**. It was established as a colony by William Coddington of Providence in 1639. Due to its excellent harbor, it grew rapidly as a port for the "triangle trade" (see p.243) and as a privateering center. Religious tolerance led to an influx of Jews, Quakers, and Baptists, who formed lucrative international trade links – though this great prosperity was severely knocked back by the British occupation of 1776–1779, when half the population fled and much of the town was burned down. Fortunately, enough of its original eighteenth-century homes have survived to rival Boston's collection.

In the 1850s, Newport became fashionable again, as a resort for wealthy

Southern merchants, and very soon nouveau riche industrialists such as the Astors, Belmonts, and Vanderbilts were building "summer cottages" – better described as mansions – along the rocky coastline. The obscene ostentation of this era (now known by Mark Twain's disparaging phrase as the Gilded Age) shocked Massachusetts' old wealth to the core.

The Great Depression killed off the decadence, but Newport kept going as a naval town until the 1970s. Today, the town feeds off tourism: much of it caters to the tennis and yachting set, but there are as many people looking at – and envying – the wealth as enjoying it. Though sanitized by the ugly new **America's Cup Avenue**, which replaced the sea-salt rawness of the waterfront with bars and boutiques, the rough old port still rears its boozy head, with beer and R&B clubs as evident as cocktails and cruises, making it an essential stop, especially during the summer **festival season**.

Arrival and information

There are actually three towns on Aquidneck Island: **Portsmouth** is at the northern edge, with the appropriately named **Middletown**, then **Newport**, below it. The mainland (and I-95) is connected to the island by US-138, which passes over the **Jamestown Bridge** to Conanincut Island, and from there by the **Newport** (or **Claiborne Pell**) **Bridge** ($2 toll each way). Bonanza **buses** (☎401/846-1820) pull into town at the Gateway Center, which is also the least expensive place in town to park a car. Adjacent to the Gateway Center is the large **visitor center**, at 23 America's Cup Ave (daily 9am–5pm; ☎401/845-9123 or 1-800/976-5122, ⓦwww.gonewport.com), which can provide maps and advice.

Newport itself, spanning only ten miles, is easy to **walk** around. Thames (pronounced "Thaymz") Street is the main road, with Bellevue Avenue, or Mansion Row, parallel to the east. RIPTA **buses** ($1.25; ☎401/781-9400, ⓦwww.ripta.com) leave from Gateway Center, and run regularly through town and to the beaches. Also based at the Center are free **shuttle buses** (summer only, daily 10am–7pm) which connect the main sights and shopping areas. Rented **bikes**, good for getting to the quieter beaches, cost $5 per hour (or $25 a day) at Ten Speed Spokes, 18 Elm St, next to the visitor center (Mon–Sat 9.30am–5.30pm, summer also Sun noon–5pm; ☎401/847-5609).

The Newport Historical Society, at 82 Touro St (☎401/846-0813), organizes **walking tours** through Colonial Newport at 10am on Thursdays, Fridays, and Saturdays in summer (from $8; information at (☎401/841-8770), while Viking Tours runs **bus** and **harbor excursions** from Gateway Center ($10–42; includes admission to one or more mansions; ☎401/847-6921). Easily the best and most relaxing way of getting a good look at the mansions and the town is a **schooner cruise** on the beautiful *Madeleine* (☎401/847-0298, ⓦwww.cruisenewport.com). The ship leaves several times daily from Bannister's Wharf, off America's Cup Avenue. The $25 price for a ninety-minute tour (or $30 for the sunset tour, which includes complimentary champagne, beer, or soda) is ultimately a better value than the cheaper motorboat tours.

Accommodation

Though there are plenty of reasonably priced **guesthouses** in Newport, it's still a good idea to make reservations in advance, especially on summer weekends, when prices jump. The visitor center (see above) has free phone links to inns and motels in all price ranges. **B&Bs** are by far the most prevalent form of lodging. Two established agencies are Bed and Breakfast of Rhode Island (☎401/849-

1298 or 1-800/828-0000), which can find rooms from around $75 in the off-season, and Bed & Breakfast of Newport (☎401/846-5408 or 1-800/800-8765), which specializes in smaller B&Bs you might otherwise find difficult to locate.

Admiral Fitzroy Inn 398 Thames St ☎401/848-8000 or 1-866/848-8780, ⓦwww.admiralfitzroy.com. Cheerfully decorated B&B in the heart of town, with a roof deck overlooking the harbor and excellent breakfasts. ❻

Attwater Villa 22 Liberty St ☎401/846-7444. Fifteen comfortably appointed rooms, with black-and-white tiled baths, in a cheerfully restored one-time "house of the evening." ❺

Cliffside Inn 2 Seaview Ave ☎401/847-1811 or 1-800/845-1811, ⓦwww.cliffsideinn.com. Gorgeous and romantic Victorian manor house, one minute from the Cliff Walk and First Beach. ❼

Howard Johnson Inn 351 W Main Rd, Middletown ☎401/849-2000 or 1-800/446-4656, ⓦwww.hojo.com. Just two miles from downtown Newport, this chain offers the best hotel value in the area. Rates heavily reduced outside of July and August. ❹

The Melville House 39 Clarke St ☎401/847-0640, ⓦwww.melvillehouse.com. Located two blocks from the harbor, in Newport's Hill District, a quiet, Colonial-style B&B serving delicious breakfasts. Within walking distance of all the sights. ❻

The Willows Romantic Inn 8–10 Willow St ☎401/846-5486, ⓦwww.thewillowsofnewport.com. A dreamy inn popular with newlyweds and couples celebrating anniversaries, complete with canopy beds and frilly bedspreads, and an outdoor garden that frequently receives awards. Breakfast is served in bed by staff in black-tie. ❽

The Town

Newport's main draw is its magnificent **mansions**. Strolling around the predominantly Colonial **downtown** is pleasant enough, too, though the ever-growing profusion of souvenir shops is somewhat off-putting. When you tire of the opulence and the kitsch, head down to the shoreline, to enjoy Newport's attractive **beaches**.

The mansions

The phrase "**conspicuous consumption**" was coined by sociologist Thorstein Veblen, who visited Newport c.1900 and witnessed the desperate need of new, entrepreneurial **millionaires** to flaunt their wealth. More than just a summer resort, Newport became an arena in which families competed to outdo each other – though the "season" of wild and decadent parties lasted only a few weeks, and many of the ten-million-dollar mansions lay empty for months at a time. It's difficult to grasp the sheer wealth involved by merely gawking at the mansions' facades, but after being herded in and rushed through more than a couple, the opulence rapidly begins to pall. Choose one or two, at the most, to see.

The most important mansions stand on Bellevue Avenue. **Marble House** is the most over-the-top example of Gilded Age excess, with a golden ballroom and a Chinese teahouse on the grounds. Both this and **Rosecliff**, with its colorful rose garden and heart-shaped staircase, were used as sets during the filming of *The Great Gatsby*. **Kingscote** is a quirky Gothic Revival cottage with a lovely interior, while the biggest and best of the lot, Cornelius Vanderbilt's **The Breakers**, on Ochre Point Avenue, just off Bellevue, is a sumptuous Italian Renaissance palace overlooking the ocean. All four mansions are run by the **Preservation Society of Newport County**, 424 Bellevue Ave (☎401/847-1000, ⓦwww.newportmansions.org), whose combination tickets slightly help to beat the hefty individual admission prices (April–Oct daily 10am–5pm, *Breakers* opens at 9am; rest of year schedules vary; *Breakers* costs $15, all others $10; any five Society properties $31).

Independent from the Preservation Society mansions, the Astors' **Beechwood**, 580 Bellevue Ave (mid-May to Oct daily 9am–4pm; Nov &

Dec, call for hours; Feb to mid-May Fri, Sat & Sun 9am–4pm; $15; ☎401/846-3772), is an entertaining antidote to the drier historical drills given on other tours. Costumed actors welcome visitors as house guests who have arrived for a party held by Mrs Astor, the self-proclaimed queen of American society (she devised the notion of the **Four Hundred**, an elite group of individuals whose lineage had to go back at least three generations). Anecdotes, bitchy asides, and a constant stream of activity – as well as strawberry tea in the servants' kitchen – make it all great fun.

One way to see the Bellevue Avenue mansions on the cheap is to peer in the back gardens from the **Cliff Walk**, which begins on Memorial Boulevard where it meets First Beach. This three-and-a-half-mile oceanside path alternates from jasmine and wild roses to unappealing concrete underpasses through perilous rocks. For those with a car, Ocean Drive continues from Bellevue Avenue where the Cliff Walk ends, following the coast westwards; after it joins Ridge Road, you'll pass **Hammersmith Farm**, John and Jackie Kennedy's 28-room shingled summer home (though the farm is now a private residence and closed to the public). The First Couple's wedding reception was held on the beautiful grounds.

Downtown Newport

Newport's Colonial, political, and business center, **Washington Square**, lies just south of the Gateway Center, beginning where Thames Street meets the Brick Market. The 1762 market, off **Long Wharf** (the most important of Newport's Colonial wharves), has been reconstructed to house galleries and pricey gift shops. Across the square stands the **Old Colony House**, one of Rhode Island's few pre-Revolutionary brick buildings, and seat of government from 1739 to 1900 (July–Sept Thurs–Sat 10am–4pm; ☎401/846-0813). Admission is $4, but a combination ticket of $6 allows entry to the Great Friends Meeting House as well (see below). To the north, the **Easton's Point** district, between Washington Street by the water and Spring Street to the east, is lined with the eighteenth-century homes of ships' captains. Only the 1748 **Hunter House**, at 54 Washington St, and run by the Preservation Society of Newport County, is open to the public (May–Oct daily 10am–5pm; $10).

The oldest religious building in town is the shabby 1699 **Great Friends Meeting House**, at Marlborough and Farewell streets, restored to its nineteenth-century appearance and completely free of adornment (tours by appointment; $4; ☎401/846-0813). The Quakers, like other religious sects, received a warm welcome in Rhode Island. Indeed, the state's penchant for religious tolerance is echoed by the presence of the elegant Georgian **Touro Synagogue**, 85 Touro St (tours given May, June, Sept & Oct: Mon–Fri 1–3pm, Sun 11am–3pm; July & Aug Sun–Fri 10am–5pm; last tour 30mins before closing; free; ☎401/847-4794, ⓦwww.tourosynagogue.org). Built in 1763, this oldest Jewish house of Jewish worship in America was modeled on Sephardic Jewish temples in Portugal and Holland. In 1790, Newport's Jewish community wrote to George Washington expressing their hopes for his new government; you can see his enthusiastic reply advocating religious liberty exhibited here.

Down the hill, the **Museum of Newport History**, 127 Thames St (April–Oct Mon & Wed–Sat 10am–5pm, Sun 1–5pm; Nov–March Fri–Sat 10am–4pm, Sun 1–4pm; $5), may be small, but it has a superb understanding of the evolution of not just Newport but the whole of maritime New England, displayed through photographs, artifacts, and a huge computer database. The price of the **walking tours** organized by the Newport Historical Society (see p.248) include admission to the museum. The Society's offices at 82 Touro St also have changing exhibits on Newport's past (Tues–Fri 9.30am–4.30pm, Sat 9.30am–noon; free).

Washington himself worshiped at the 1726 **Trinity Church** on Queen Anne Square, a Colonial structure based on the Old North Church in Boston and the designs of Sir Christopher Wren (daily: June–Sept 10am–4pm; free). A few blocks south, **St Mary's Church**, Spring St and Memorial Blvd, is the oldest Catholic Church in Rhode Island, and the place where Jackie Bouvier married John Kennedy (Mon, Tues, Thurs & Fri 7.30am–1pm, Wed 7.30–11am; free).

Apart from the mansions, Bellevue Avenue also has two museums of note. The **Newport Art Museum**, at no. 76, is housed in the 1864 mock-medieval Griswold House, and exhibits New England art from the last two centuries (June to mid-Oct Mon–Sat 10am–5pm, Sun noon–5pm; closes at 4pm rest of year; $6; ☏401/848-8200). At no. 194, the grand **Newport Casino** was an early country club, which held the first national tennis championship in 1881. It is now the **International Tennis Hall of Fame**, and still keeps its grass courts open to the public. The museum includes exhibits on tennis fashion – or what has passed for it – and trophies (daily 9.30am–5pm; $8; ☏401/849-3990 or 1-800/457-1144).

The beaches

The indubitable attraction of Newport's shoreline, with its many coves and gently sloping sands, is slightly marred by the fact that many of the beaches are strictly private. Of those that are public, **Gooseberry Beach**, on the southern edge of the island, is surrounded by grand houses, while the town beach, **First** (or Newport, or Easton's) **Beach**, is at the east end of Memorial Boulevard; **Second** and **Third** beaches are further along the same route toward Middletown. The visitor center (see p.248) provides a **guide** to all of these (most of which have parking fees of $8–15 per car).

Eating

Many of Newport's **restaurants** are smug and overpriced, and visitors on a tight budget may have to make do with snacks. However, there are some gems, even along touristy Thames Street. The **seafood** here is well worth the blowout if you have the extra cash.

Asterix & Obelisk 599 Thames St ☏401/841-8833. Happening, moderately priced eatery in a former garage, with abstract paintings on the walls and Oriental rugs on an orange cement floor. The eclectic menu (entrees $18–32) is mainly American with a touch of Asian.

The Black Pearl Bannisters Wharf ☏401/846-5264. A Newport institution famous for its chunky clam chowder; repair to the Commodore Room for more formal dining.

Brick Alley Pub & Restaurant 140 Thames St ☏401/849-6334. Attracts a good mix of locals and tourists for the rather uninspired menu of cheap to moderately-priced lunches and dinners.

Ocean Coffee Roasters 22 Washington Square ☏401/846-6060. Hip, upbeat café serving flavored coffees and teas to aspiring artists and poets. For a mere $6, you can have crepes in the morning, or a lunchtime sandwich with an international edge. Holds occasional poetry readings and art exhibitions.

Salvation Café 140 Broadway ☏401/847-2620. Healthy, mainly vegetarian food, with an Asian focus.

Smokehouse Cafe America's Cup Ave ☏401/848-9800. The *Smokehouse* – an oddity in Newport's world of seafood – has great barbeque and a lively crowd.

Via Via 372 Thames St ☏401/848-0880. Specialty oven-fired pizza – shrimp pesto or chicken and goat's cheese, for example – that can also be delivered until 2am.

West Deck Waites Wharf ☏401/847-3610. Inexpensive, family-style clam chowder, lobster, and grilled sandwiches, with outdoor seating.

White Horse Tavern 26 Marlborough St ☎ 401/849-3600. Intensely atmospheric restaurant (the building dates from 1687) serving solid American fare, such as New York sirloin, sauteed lobster, and rack of lamb. More affordably priced at lunchtime.

Festivals and nightlife

There is always something afoot in Newport, which is famed for its duo of music festivals: the **Folk Festival** in late July or August, followed by the **JVC Jazz Festival** in mid-August. Both are held in Fort Adams State Park (information at ☎ 401/847-3700). The lesser-known but arguably more memorable **Newport Music Festival**, with a focus on classical music, unfolds in the mansions during July (☎ 401/846-1133, ⓦ www.newportmusic.org), while the **Irish Waterfront Festival**, held on Labor Day weekend with music, folk art, and stepdancing, is great fun (☎ 401/646-1600, ⓦ www.newportfestivals.com).

Otherwise, there is plenty of shamelessly unrefined **nightlife**. Noisy bars abound near the waterfront, and among the **live music venues** in town, two of the best are the *Red Parrot*, 348 Thames St (☎ 401/847-3140), for live jazz and world music nightly, and the *Wharf Deli & Pub*, 37 Bowen's Wharf (☎ 401/846-9233), which puts on R&B and jazz. At the safari-themed *Rhino Bar & Grille*, 337 Thames St (☎ 401/846-0707), original live bands (in the bar) and the best area DJs playing dance, hip-hop, and techno (in the Mamba Room) keep things hopping.

Connecticut

CONNECTICUT was named *Quinnehtukqut* by the Native Americans for the "great tidal river" that splits it in two before spilling out into the Long Island Sound and washing the old whaling ports of the coast. This small and densely populated state is a sort of conservative, high-rent suburb of New York City, enabling commuters to earn Big Apple salaries while avoiding some New York state and city taxes. Its first white settlers arrived in the 1630s: refugees from Massachusetts seeking liberty, good farmland, and trading opportunities. Connecticut soon became a center for "**Yankee ingenuity**," prospering through the invention and marketing (often by notorious and not always honorable Yankee peddlers) of many a useful little household object. Although hit very badly by English raids in the Revolutionary War, its role in providing the war effort with crucial supplies made it known as "**the provisions state**." After the war, the original charter of Connecticut's first colonists was used as a model for the American Constitution, which gave rise to another nickname: "**the Constitution state**."

Connecticut continued to prosper during the eighteenth and nineteenth centuries, with steady industrialization and lucrative whaling along the southeastern coast. Today, much of the old industry, especially in the north, has withered away, leaving areas of green countryside untroubled by noisy interstates, many verdant forests, and the idyllic rural villages that typify New England's PR image – but also unemployment and poverty in its larger cities. In particular, **New Haven**, home to Yale University, has addressed (and significantly eased) distinctly urban problems like drugs, homelessness, and crime, which belie New England's myth of rural tranquility. The linchpins of Connecticut's economy – insurance companies, medical research, and military bases – hardly make for pleasing aesthetics, as demonstrated by the rather dull capital city, **Hartford**; and even the historic and otherwise attractive coastline is marred by some unfortunate stretches of sprawling gray concrete.

Getting around Connecticut

Except for a few isolated areas in the north, Connecticut is well-connected with major **roads**: I-95 is the main interstate, running from New York to Rhode Island along the shore of the Long Island Sound. I-91 travels north from I-95 at New Haven, weaving its way along the Connecticut River to Vermont. It's a shame to miss out on the quiet countryside scenery along the side roads, so it's worth getting off the interstates if you have the time.

Greyhound, Bonanza (☎1-800/556-3815, ⓦwww.bonanzabus.com), and Peter Pan Trailways (☎1-800/343-9999, ⓦwww.peterpanbus.com) all run **buses** to most of the main towns. Connecticut Transit buses (☎860/525-9181 or 1-888/BUS-RIDE) serve the inland area around Hartford. Metro North (☎1-800/638-7646) **trains** carry passengers between New Haven and New York City, with connecting services to numerous other towns; Amtrak's line runs between New York City and Boston, with various stops along the shore and a connection to Hartford.

Southeastern Connecticut

The much-visited **southeastern coast** of Connecticut spans 25 miles from Stonington in the east to Niantic in the west, bisected by the Thames (pronounced "Thaymz") River. Each of the handful of tiny, picturesque Colonial communities and old whaling villages along the Long Island Sound is a mere stone's throw from the next. No longer are they the iniquitous and rumbustious ports that so inspired Melville, but they're still keen to preserve a sense of their history. The restored nineteenth-century **Mystic Seaport** justifies at least a day's visit, while nearby are the less lovely US Naval Submarine Base at **Groton** and the pretty fishing harbor of **Stonington Borough**.

Mystic

As purists will tell you, the town of **MYSTIC**, right on I-95, does not in fact exist; it is an area governed partly by Groton and partly by Stonington. Nonetheless, the old whaling port and shipbuilding center does have a small, well-kept, and somewhat touristy **downtown**, lined with typical New England–quaint clapboard galleries and antique shops. The old bridge across the bustling **Mystic River** that divides the town down the middle still opens hourly, and self-guided walking tours take in the many old houses built by well-off sea captains. The **Olde Mistick Village**, at the intersection of I-95 and US-27, is a pleasant enough outdoor mall, with over sixty upmarket shops in Colonial-style buildings. For a scenic walk or bike ride away from the tourists, take the four-mile River Road, winding along the western bank of the river, which is protected from cars and development; the road passes by Downes Marsh, a sanctuary for osprey.

What brings the tourists to Mystic is the impeccably reconstructed seventeen-acre waterfront village of **Mystic Seaport** at the mouth of the river, where more than sixty weathered buildings house old-style workshops, an apothecary, stores, and a printing press (daily: April–Oct 9am–5pm; rest of year 10am–4pm; $17, children $9; ℡1-888/9SEAPORT, Ⓦwww.visitmysticseaport.com). Its **Stillman Building** exhibits exquisitely carved scrimshaw and a vast amount of products made from whales' wax-like spermaceti; it also shows film of a bloody whale capture. There are demonstrations of shanty-singing, fish-splitting, and sail-setting, among other salty pastimes, as well as storytelling and theater. Meanwhile, in the **shipyard**, you can watch the building, restoration, and maintenance of wooden ships. The *pièce de résistance* is the restored *Charles W. Morgan*, a three-masted wooden Yankee **whaling ship** built in 1841. The last of its kind, the *Morgan* is a remnant of an age of exploration and arrogant expansion remembered now with a mixture of nostalgia and shame. Done up ready to embark on a hypothetical two-year voyage, the ship is filled with whaling memorabilia; below deck, accessible by perilously narrow stairs, the blubber room is crowded with huge iron try-pots for melting down the stinking blubber.

Over six thousand weird and wonderful sea creatures glug about the **Mystic Aquarium**, at exit 90 off I-95. Hourly shows at the Marine Theater (daily: March–Nov 9am–6pm; rest of year 10am–5pm; $16) showcase African penguins, seals, sea lions, and a beluga whale; the explanations of the various creatures' behavior make this a step up from standard aquarium fare. For those interested in the history of underwater exploration, there's the high-tech "Challenge of the Deep" exhibit, hosted by Dr Robert D. Ballard, of the team that found the *Titanic*.

Practicalities

Mystic has an **information office** in the Olde Mistick Village shopping mall (Mon–Sat 9.30am–6.30pm, Sun 10am–6pm; ℡860/536-1641 or 1-800/863-6569, Ⓦwww.mysticmore.com). The office lists current rates and books **accommodation**; places to stay in town are at a premium in July and August. Options include the *Comfort Inn* (℡860/572-8531 or 1-800/228-5150; ❹), *Days Inn* (℡860/572-0574 or 1-800/572-3993; ❺), and the *Best Western Sovereign Hotel* (℡860/536-4281 or 1-800/528-1234; ❹); all of these are on Whitehall Avenue (just off exit 90 on I-95), and all are handy for the Seaport. Also on Whitehall Avenue, the *Whitehall Mansion*, at no. 42 (℡860/572-7280; ❻), is a painstakingly restored 1771 mansion with five guest rooms, each furnished with antiques and queen-sized canopy beds. The *Inn at Mystic*, a Colonial Revival mansion hidden away at the junction of routes 1 and 27 (℡860/536-9604 or 1-800/237-2415, Ⓦwww.innatmystic.com; ❻), also makes for a memorable stay. The *Seaport* **campground** is on US-184 in Old Mystic, three miles from the Seaport, but is only open April to mid-November (℡860/536-4044, Ⓦwww.seaportcampground.com; $33 per night for up to two adults and two children, $26 per night April to mid-May & mid-Sept to mid-Nov).

Without a doubt the best-known **restaurant** is *Mystic Pizza*, at 56 W Main St (℡860/536-3700), a small, family-run pizza place that continues to serve huge, inexpensive, and fresh "pies," unruffled by its movie-title status. The *Sea View Snack Bar*, on Hwy-27 between the visitor center and downtown (℡860/572-0096), serves seafood and sandwiches in a covered picnic area overlooking the Mystic River; *The Green Marble*, 8 Steamboat Wharf (℡860/572-0012), roasts its own coffee; and *Kitchen Little*, 81 1/2 Greenmanville Ave (℡860/536-2122), serves a mean breakfast along the riverfront.

Ten minutes' drive south, in the small fishing port of **NOANK**, the casual *Abbott's Lobster in the Rough*, 117 Pearl St (May–Aug daily noon–9pm; Sept to mid–Oct Fri–Sun noon–7pm; ℡860/536-7719), serves superb fresh steamed lobster and seafood at outdoor picnic tables. A giant New England dinner for four costs $28 per person, a lobster plate around $16; bring your own alcohol.

Stonington Borough

STONINGTON BOROUGH, five miles east of Mystic, is geographically a district within the town of Stonington, though it has its own government. It's an overwhelmingly pretty old fishing village, originally Portuguese but now very New England, characterized by appealing whitewashed cottages (which were once factory houses), white picket fences, and colorful flower gardens. Stonington Borough's main street, **Water Street**, is chock-a-block with antique shops and upmarket thrift stores, crowded with well-heeled bargain-hunters on the weekend.

The **Lighthouse Museum**, 7 Water St, dates from 1823, and is full of local memorabilia, maps, and drawings; fresh flowers everywhere add a nice touch. You can climb the stone steps and iron staircase to the top for views over the water and Connecticut's neighboring states (May–Oct daily 10am–5pm; $4; ☎860/535-1440). The waterfront itself is a great place to pass a few sunny hours, peaceful and quiet with a few bobbing fishing boats and clean water for swimming.

The most central **place to stay**, though not cheap, is *The Inn at Stonington*, 60 Water St (☎860/535-2000, ⓦwww.innatstonington.com; ❼), where sunny harbor- and bay-views are available from the cozy rooms with large baths and some modern amenities. Authentic New England clam chowder, and full meals, can be had at *Noah's*, 113 Water St (☎860/535-3925), an old Portuguese **restaurant** with a friendly, trendy atmosphere and delicious home-baked cakes. Two seafood restaurants – *Water Street Café*, 142 Water St (☎860/535-2122), and *Skipper's Dock*, 66 Water St (☎860/535-0111) – are worth a visit; the former is elegant, the latter less expensive and rowdier, with an open deck sporting fabulous views of the ocean.

Groton

Seven miles west of Mystic Seaport, **GROTON** is a suitably unpleasant name for the hometown of the hideous **US Naval Submarine Base**, headquarters for the North Atlantic fleet. The **USS Nautilus**, the country's first nuclear-powered submarine, was built in Groton. In 1958, four years after it was launched, it became the first vessel to sail under the polar icecap. It's now moored on the Thames, and self-guided tours allow access to its terrifyingly claustrophobic corridors, one-person-wide in many places. The sub looks pretty much as it did in the 1950s, complete with pin-ups of Marilyn Monroe. The **Submarine Force Museum** next door has exhibits on the history of submersibles from the minuscule *American Turtle*, built in 1775, to the frighteningly powerful *Trident* (hours vary; free; ☎860/694-3174 or 1-800/343-0079, ⓦwww.ussnautilus.org).

New London

NEW LONDON, opposite Groton on the west side of the Thames, is the closest thing southeastern Connecticut has to a city, although it spreads over only six square miles. Originally settled in 1646, New London was a wealthy whaling port in the nineteenth century. Today, it's home to the **US Coast Guard Academy**, off I-95 at 15 Mohegan Ave, where visitors can wander around a museum of Coast Guard history and visit the training ship USS *Eagle* when it's in port (Mon–Fri 9am–5pm, Sat 10am–5pm, Sun noon–5pm; free; ☎860/444-8511). Overlooking the academy is the **Lyman Allyn Art Museum**, part of Connecticut College at 625 Williams St (Tues–Sat 10am–5pm, Sun 1–5pm; $5; ☎860/443-2545); it specializes in American Impressionist works and local decorative arts.

A self-guided walking tour of downtown (using maps available from the Southeastern Connecticut CVB at 470 Bank St ☎860/444-2206) passes along prosperous Huntington Street, where four adjacent Greek Revival mansions are known as **Whale Oil Row**. For swimming and sunbathing, **Ocean Beach Park**, at 1225 Ocean Ave, has a sugar-sand beach and huge saltwater pool, as well as a wooden boardwalk (summer daily 9am–midnight; $8–12 per carload, or $4 for pedestrians).

New London was the birthplace of boozy playwright **Eugene O'Neill**. His childhood home, the **Monte Cristo Cottage**, 325 Pequot Ave (call for hours at ☎860/443-0051; $5), is open for tours, complete with juicy details of his trauma-ridden early life – though they may already be familiar to you from his autobiographical play *Long Day's Journey into Night*. The writer's influence is further felt at the O'Neill Memorial Theater Center, 305 Great Neck Rd (exit 82 off I-95) in nearby **WATERFORD**, an acclaimed testing ground for playwrights and actors where audiences can watch new, often experimental, shows in rehearsal (performances held sporadically May–Aug; ☎860/443-5378, ⓦwww.theoneill.org).

Groton and New London practicalities

You can arrive in New London by **ferry** from Orient Point on Long Island (see p.132; via Cross Sound Ferry, 2 Ferry St, ☎860/443-5281 in New England, ☎631/323-2525 on Long Island, ⓦwww.longislandferry.com). Reservations are strongly recommended. Greyhound serves New London, which is also the center of the far from comprehensive local **bus** system run by Southeast Area Transit ($1.10; ☎860/886-2631).

In New London, at the corner of Golden Street and Eugene O'Neill Drive, the **Trolley Info Station** has brochures and a helpful staff (summer daily 10am–4pm; mid-April to May and Sept to mid-Oct Fri–Sun 10am–4pm; ☎860/444-7264). The **Southeastern Connecticut Chamber of Commerce** has offices at 105 Huntington St, New London (Mon–Fri 8am–5pm; ☎860/443-8332, ⓦwww.chamberect.com), which can provide details on restaurants and local events. New London has reasonably priced

---

Native American casinos

Connecticut has become home to two major Native American casinos, over objections from environmentalists, anti-gambling agencies, and residents. The massive **Foxwoods Casino and Resort**, Rte-2, Ledyard (☎1-800/752-9244, ⓦwww.fox-woods.com), rises dramatically above the virgin pine forests north of New London and draws millions of visitors annually. Built by the Mashantucket-Pequot Indians, the casino's visitors have three huge hotels to accommodate them, as well as all manner of slots, gaming tables, and bingo. Just a few miles away, the **Mohegan Sun Casino**, Rte-2A, Uncasville (☎1-888/226-7771, ⓦwww.mohegansun.com), opened its doors in 1996, as Foxwood's much smaller and quieter competitor. But after a $1 billion expansion effort, the Mohegan Sun, with its traditional Indian reverence for nature readily apparent in the planetarium ceiling and the crystal mountain installed on one of the casino walls, is more of a draw. That said, both casinos have plenty of restaurants and shops to pull even more of your cash away.

motels along I-95, including the *Holiday Inn*, I-95 and Frontage Rd (☎860/442-0631 or 1-800/HOLIDAY, ⓦwww.holiday-inn.com; ❺), and the *Red Roof Inn*, 707 Colman St (☎860/444-0001 or 1-800/RED-ROOF, ⓦwww.redroof.com; ❸). In Groton there are plenty of budget motels off I-95 exit 86, including a *Super 8* (☎860/448-2818 or 1-800/800-8000; ❸).

New London has a few good **restaurants** worth stopping into, including *Timothy's*, 181 Bank St (☎860/443-8411), for Continental cuisine overlooking Long Island Sound, or, on the cheaper side, the *Recovery Room*, 445 Ocean Ave (☎860/443-2619), an award-winning pizzeria. Over the water in Groton, *G. Williker's*, 156 King's Highway (☎860/445-8043), has an enormous menu of steaks, seafood, and sandwiches.

Hartford

The unattractive modern capital of Connecticut, **HARTFORD**, right in the middle of the state on the Connecticut River, is also the insurance center of the United States. Its central gold-domed **state capitol**, sitting on a hill in Bushnell Park, houses a small museum of Connecticut history; free hourly tours of the capitol are available during the week from 9.15am until 1.15pm (July and Aug until 2.15pm; April–Oct, also Sat 10.15am–2.15pm). Marginally more thrilling is the antique merry-go-round in the park, which gives jangling rides for 50¢. Housed in the Connecticut State Library, across the street at 231 Capitol Ave, the **Museum of Connecticut History** (Mon–Fri 9am–4pm, Sat 9am–3pm; free; ☎860/757-6534) holds Colt rifles and revolvers, and the desk at which Abraham Lincoln signed the Emancipation Proclamation.

Hartford's pride and joy is the Greek Revival **Wadsworth Atheneum**, at 600 Main St (Tues–Fri 11am–5pm, Sat & Sun 10am–5pm; $9, free before noon on Sat; ☎860/278-2670). As the nation's oldest continuously operating public art museum, it holds some 45,000 pieces, among which are many fine and decorative arts. Residing here are Old Masters including Rubens' *The Return of the Holy Family from Egypt* and, in the French Impressionists collection, Renoir's *Monet Painting in His Garden at Argenteuil*. Lectures and films are put on at the Atheneum Theater, and there's an excellent café, too.

About a mile west of downtown Hartford on Hwy-4, a hilltop community known as Nook Farm was home in the 1880s to next-door neighbors **Mark Twain** and **Harriet Beecher Stowe**. Their Victorian homes, furnished much as they were then, are both open for tours. Twain lived at 351 Farmington Ave from 1874 until 1891, writing many of his classic works, including *Huckleberry Finn*. He spent a fair portion of his publishing royalties building and redecorating this outrageously ornate home, with its unusual black-and-orange brickwork and luxurious Tiffany stained-glass interior (daily Mon–Sat 9.30am–4pm, Sun noon–4pm, closed Tues Jan–April and Nov; $9; ☎860/247-0998 ext 26).

At 77 Forest St, the much less flamboyant home of Harriet Beecher Stowe reflects her Southern sensibility (Tues–Sat 9.30am–4pm, Sun noon–4.30pm; June to mid-Oct & Dec also open Mon 9.30am–4pm; $6.50; ☎860/522-9258). An ardent abolitionist, Stowe was the author of *Uncle Tom's Cabin*, one of the most important American literary works of the nineteenth century. She also found time to write about housekeeping ideals in the book she penned with her sister, *The American Woman's Home*. Inside her house you can see Stowe's writing table and some of her paintings.

Practicalities

Hartford, which lies at the junction of I-91 and I-84, is easily accessible by car. Greyhound, Peter Pan, and Bonanza **buses**, and Amtrak **trains**, all pull into Union Station, near the north side of Bushnell Park. For **information**, visit Hartford's **Convention & Visitors Bureau**, downtown at Civic Center Plaza (Mon–Fri 9am–5pm; ☎860/728-6789 or 1-800/446-7811, ⓦwww.enjoy-hartford.com), or pick up a copy of the free local weekly, *The Hartford Advocate*.

There are budget **motels** along I-91, including the *Super 8* (☎860/246-8888 or 1-800/800-8000, ⓦwww.super8motel.com; ❸) and the *Red Roof Inn* (☎860/724-0222 or 1-800/843-7663; ❸), both of which are off exit 33. **Hotels** in Hartford itself cater mainly to business visitors and are correspondingly pricey, though they are more reasonable on the weekends – try the central *Crowne Plaza Downtown*, 50 Morgan St (☎860/549-2400; ❺). The *YMCA*, 160 Jewell St (☎860/246-9622, ⓦwww.ghymca.org), often has rooms with shared bath for $20 and with private bath for $25. The HI-affiliated *Mark Twain Hostel*, 131 Tremont St (☎860/523-7255), charges $21. A popular **restaurant** is *Black Eyed Sally's*, 350 Asylum St (☎860/278-7427), which serves hearty Cajun cooking with great selections of Cajun beer, plus live blues Wednesday through Saturday. Despite its name, *No Fish Today*, 80 Pratt St (☎860/244-2100), serves moderately-priced Italian-style seafood in a relaxed downtown location. For tasty, inexpensive home-cooking, check out *Timothy's*, 243 Zion St (☎860/728-9822), a popular hangout with local artists and musicians, feasting on classic American dishes; bring your own booze.

New Haven

I-91 leads south from Hartford to **NEW HAVEN**, on a large natural harbor at the mouth of the Quinnipiac River. Founded in 1638 by a group of wealthy Puritans from London, New Haven developed a solid economy based on shipping and, later, industry. In 1716 it became the seat of **Yale University**, the third oldest college in the States – but it was hardware, firearms, gas, and other types of manufacturing in the nineteenth century that really brought the city into its own. New Haven churned out Winchester rifles, musical instruments, tools, carriages, and corsets, and **Eli Whitney**, inventor of the revolutionary cotton gin, discovered in his workshop here a method of mass production that eliminated expensive skilled labor. Little manufacturing remains in New Haven, and the city has struggled for decades to revitalize and redevelop.

The resultant friction between the town's two sides (tension-ridden urbanity and Ivy League idyll) once made New Haven a somewhat uneasy place; however, town-versus-gown conflicts have been minimized over the past decade. New Haven is certainly less WASPish and smug than many other Ivy League towns, and its ethnic diversity, alongside the undeniable vitality provided by the much-maligned Yalies, make it a stimulating place to spend some time.

Arrival, information, and getting around

New Haven lies where interstates I-91 and I-95 fork, and is on the main **train** line between Washington and Boston; services also run to Canada and New York. The Amtrak terminal is in the colossal and nicely renovated **Union Station**, on Union Avenue six blocks southeast of the Yale campus downtown. To or from New York, the Metro-North Commuter Railroad (☎1-800/638-

7646) is a better deal than Amtrak. Greyhound, Bonanza, and Peter Pan **buses** from Boston arrive at 45 George St (℡203/772-2470). On arrival, it's advisable to catch a cab to your hotel, as the bus and train terminals are in potentially dodgy areas. One reputable firm is Metro Taxi (℡203/777-7777).

The **Greater New Haven CVB** is at 59 Elm St (Mon–Fri 8.30am–5pm; ℡203/777-8550 or 1-800/332-STAY, ⓦwww.newhavencvb.org). **Public transportation** to areas outside downtown is provided by Connecticut Transit, 470 James St ($1; ℡203/624-0151, ⓦwww.cttransit.com), though service is poor after 6pm or so. An **information booth** at 200 Orange St, two blocks east of the Green (the town's park), has bus schedules and route maps for the free downtown trolley.

Accommodation

For a college town, New Haven has surprisingly few **hotels**. The few that there are downtown, although slightly overpriced, are worth it for their convenient location and safety. **B&Bs** from around $70 can be arranged in advance through Nutmeg Bed and Breakfast (℡860/236-6698 or 1-800/727-7592, ⓦwww.bnb-link.com). Because of the shortage of rooms, be sure to make reservations in advance if you're going to be visiting during graduation, in late May, or October's Parents' Weekend.

Best Western Executive–West Haven 490 Saw Mill Rd, West Haven ℡203/933-0344, ⓦwww.bestwestern.com /executivehotelwesthaven. Standard rooms not far from downtown (take exit 42 off I-95). Features indoor pool and fitness center. ❹

Colony Inn 1157 Chapel St ℡203/776-1234, ⓦwww.colonyatyale.com. Downtown luxury hotel furnished in Colonial style, with modern amenities. ❺

Holiday Inn 30 Whalley Ave ℡203/777-6221 or 1-800/HOLIDAY, ⓦwww.holiday-inn.com /newhavenct. Generic rooms in a dependable chain hotel. ❹

Hotel Duncan 1151 Chapel St ℡203/787-1273. Comfortable rooms in an old-fashioned hotel, a few steps away from Yale, with singles available for around $45. ❹

New Haven Hotel 229 George St ℡203/498-3100, ⓦwww.newhavenhotel.com. Small quiet hotel with nice standard rooms and a health club with pool. ❺

The City

Thanks in part to some sensitive restoration, New Haven's **downtown**, centering on the **Green**, remains both attractive and walkable, despite a succession of remarkably ugly buildings built during the 1950s that rather blighted New Haven. This area, laid out in 1638, was the site of the city's original settlement; around the Green are three churches, a grand library, and a number of stately government buildings. The park itself is now home to a handful of homeless residents, and borders the student-filled district centered around College and Chapel streets. The surrounding five blocks are a genuinely lively place in which to hang out, filled with bookstores, cafés, clubs, and hip clothing stores; the **Neon Garage**, an art exhibit in a real parking lot on Crown Street, is especially notable for its glass and neon sculptures. There are some very rough pockets, but in general New Haven is reasonably safe to wander around, even at night, and especially during term time.

New Haven's prime attraction, **Yale University**, stands proudly right in the center of things. You can wander at will, though free, hour-long, student-led **tours** set off daily from the Yale Visitor Information Center at 149 Elm St, across from the north side of the Green (Mon–Fri 9am–4pm, Sat & Sun 10am–4pm; tours Mon–Fri 10.30am & 2pm, Sat & Sun 1.30pm; ℡203/432-2300); the Information Center also supplies maps for self-guided tours. The tours will have you trooping to and fro quite a bit, starting with the beautiful old spires and ivy-strewn cobbled courtyards of the old campus (mostly built in the 1930s, but painstakingly distressed to look suitably ancient). For student and visitor alike, foremost among campus buildings is the remarkable **Sterling Memorial Library**, 120 High St (Mon–Fri 8.30am–5pm, Sat 10am–5pm, Sun 1–5pm, closed Sun in summer; free). Designed by alum James Gamble in modern Gothic style with fifteen buttresses, it has the symbolic appearance – inside and out – of a cathedral, albeit one to the power of knowledge and the written word. Inside, leaded-glass windows illustrate the history of the Library, Yale, New Haven, and the history of books and printing; the would-be altar is the Circulation Desk, crowned with a fifteenth-century Italian-style mural. Also impressive, the **Beinecke Rare Books Library**, 121 Wall St, is where venerable manuscripts and delicate hand-printed books are viewed with the aid of natural light seeping through the translucent marble walls (Mon–Fri 8.30am–5pm, Sat 10am–5pm, closed Sat in Aug; free). Other buildings of interest include the modernist, Louis Kahn–designed **Center for British Art**, 1080 Chapel St, where British paintings range from Elizabethan portraits to modern works by Peter Blake and Francis Bacon (Tues–Sat 10am–5pm, Sun noon–5pm; free; ☎203/432-2800). The impressive **Yale University Art Gallery**, just across the road at 1111 Chapel St (Tues–Sat 10am–5pm, Sun 1–6pm; closed mid-July to Aug; free; ☎203/432-0600), is the nation's oldest university art collection, and holds American decorative arts, regional design and furniture, and African and pre-Columbian works. Among major European paintings is Van Gogh's famous *Night Café*, said by the artist to be "one of the ugliest pictures I have done." A quirky **Collection of Musical Instruments** is at 15 Hillhouse Ave (limited hours, phone ahead ☎203/432-0822), and the **Peabody Museum of Natural History**, 170 Whitney Ave (Mon–Sat 10am–5pm, Sun noon–5pm; $5; ☎203/432-5050), is a solid nineteenth-century collection of fossils, skeletons, and gems.

Another source of New Haven affection and pride is its close-knit **Italian District**, based since 1900 among the well-kept brownstones and colorful window boxes of **Wooster Street** (just beyond Crown Street southeast of the Green). This was where the city's original Italian immigrants settled when they came to work on the railroad. There's little to see here, but there are some incredibly popular restaurants, and it's well worth stopping by when there's a festival on.

Eating

You can't leave New Haven without trying the local **pizza** (known here as tomato pies). The *New York Times* discovered New Haven's pizzas several years ago, and since then queues have been forming down the street at all the family pizza restaurants in Wooster Square. There are also plenty of reasonably priced and innovative restaurants around the Green, on College and Chapel streets.

Atticus Bookstore Café 1082 Chapel St ☎203/776-4040. Salads, soups, sandwiches, brioches, and good coffee, in a relaxed bookstore open until midnight.

Claire's Corner Copia 1000 Chapel St ☎203/562-3888. Eclectic Mexican and Middle Eastern food, including vegetarian dishes, at moderate prices.

Frank Pepe's Pizzeria 157 Wooster St ☎203/865-5762. Most popular of the Wooster Street restaurants; plain, functional, and friendly, with huge "combination pies" baked in coal-fired ovens. Cash only.

Ibiza 39 High St ☎203/865-1933. A bright, mural-filled place with diverse tapas, meals, and wines from Spain.

Louis' Lunch 263 Crown St ☎203/562-5507. Small, dark, and ancient burger house that claims to have served the first hamburger in the US, and presents the meat between two slices of toast. Highly popular, but worth the inevitable wait. Closed Sun and Mon.

Roomba 1044 Chapel St, Sherman's Alley ☎ 203/562-7666. Innovative Nuevo Latino cuisine in a stylish room. Trendy and loud.

Willoughby's Coffee & Tea 1006 Chapel St ☎ 203/789-8400. Self-consciously trendy gourmet coffee bar frequented by hip intellectual types and fashionable locals. Superb coffee from $1, sticky cakes for slightly more. Three other locations around New Haven.

Yankee Doodle 260 Elm St ☎ 203/865-1074. Yalies' favorite coffee shop, with original Fifties fittings and shop sign, serving greasy-spoon favorites such as burgers and cherry Cokes.

Performing arts and nightlife

New Haven has an undeniably rich **cultural scene**, and is especially strong on **theater**. The Yale Rep Company, 1120 Chapel St (☎ 203/432-1234), which boasts among its eminent past members Jodie Foster and Meryl Streep, turns out consistently good shows during the school year. The Long Wharf Theater, 222 Sargent Drive, just off I-95 (☎ 203/787-4282), has a nationwide reputation for quality performances, as does the refurbished Schubert Performing Arts Center, 247 College St (☎ 203/562-5666).

There are several good **bars** and **clubs**, concentrated on College and Chapel streets. The free biweekly paper *Hip*, available from the clothes shops along Chapel Street, has information on happenings in and around New Haven, while the *New Haven Advocate*, a free news and arts weekly, has more comprehensive listings.

Bar 254 Crown St ☎ 203/495-8924. Plain name, outrageous place – this is where the New Haven gay community lets its collective hair down on Tuesday nights.

Café Nine 250 State St ☎ 203/789-8281. Decades-old intimate, divey club with live jazz Wed through Sun nights and open blues jams on a regular basis.

Gotham Citi 130 Crown St ☎ 203/498-2484. Large, steamy club where revelers head for a late night of drinking, dancing, and simply looking good. Gay nights on Mon and Sat.

The Playwright 144 Temple St ☎ 203/752-0450. Five bars, ranging from rowdy pub to dance club, inside a church bought in Ireland, dismantled, and reassembled here. An unusual must-stop.

Toad's Place 300 York St ☎ 203/624-8623. Mid-sized nationally renowned live music venue, where the likes of Springsteen and the Stones used to "pop in" occasionally to play impromptu gigs. Tickets $10–25.

New Hampshire

Long after sailors, fishermen, and agricultural colonists had domesticated the entire coastline of New England, the harsh, glacier-scarred interior of **NEW HAMPSHIRE**, with its dense forests and forbidding mountains, remained the exclusive preserve of the Algonquin Indians. Only the few miles of seashore held sizeable seventeenth-century communities of European settlers, such as the one at **Portsmouth**.

Even when the Indians were finally driven back, following the defeat of their French allies in Canada, the settlers could make little agricultural impact on the rocky terrain of this "granite state." Towns such as Nashua, Manchester, and Concord grew up in the fertile **Merrimack Valley**, but not until the Industrial Revolution made possible the development of water-powered **textile mills** did the economy take off. For a while, ruthless **timber** companies looked set to strip all northern New Hampshire bare, but they were brought under control when the state recognized that the pristine landscape of the **White Mountains** might turn out to be its greatest asset. Large-scale **tourism** began towards the end of last century; at one time fifty trains daily brought travelers up to Mount Washington.

Ever since becoming the first American state to declare independence, in January 1776, New Hampshire has been proud to go its own idiosyncratic way. The absence of a sales tax, or even a personal income tax, is seen as a fulfillment of the state motto, "Live Free or Die." Alternative sources of revenue include state-owned liquor stores, set up after Prohibition and enthusiastically promoted: they even have them in freeway rest areas. The state has long gained inordinate political clout as the venue of the first **primary election** of each presidential campaign, with its villages well used to playing host to would-be world leaders.

One less ideological aspect of New Hampshire's individualism is the emphasis on a healthy outdoor lifestyle. Hiking, climbing, cycling, and **skiing** are enjoyed both by energetic locals and by the many visitors who drive up from Boston and New York. The major destinations are **Lake Winnipesaukee**, and **Conway**, **Lincoln**, and **Franconia** in the mountains further north. Some of these have grown rather too large and commercial for their own good, but if you steer clear of the paying "attractions," the lakes, islands, and snowcapped peaks themselves remain spectacular. To see the bucolic rural scenery more usually associated with New England, take a detour off the main roads up the Merrimack Valley – to **Canterbury Shaker Village** near Concord, for example.

Getting around New Hampshire

Three **Interstate highways** run through New Hampshire: I-89 connects the state capital, Concord, with Vermont; I-95 runs along the short stretch of New Hampshire coastline that separates Massachusetts and Maine; and I-93 is the main north–south road, giving southern New England access to the White Mountains. In the mountains themselves, the 35-mile Kancamagus Highway between Lincoln and Conway is the most traveled of a number of **scenic routes** found across the state.

Concord Trailways (☎1-800/639-3317, ⓦwww.concordtrailways.com), C&J Trailways (☎603/430-1100 or 1-800/258-7111, ⓦwww.cjtrailways.com), and Vermont Transit Lines (☎1-800/552-8737, ⓦwww.vermonttransit.com) all go from Boston to several towns in the southern part of New Hampshire. Only a few services (mainly on Concord Trailways) continue north to the Lakes Region and one or two places in the White Mountains. **Train** services are limited to Amtrak's *Downeaster*, which links Boston to Portland, Maine, stopping in New Hampshire at the sleepy towns of Exeter, Durham, and Dover.

The coast

Of all the US states with ocean access, New Hampshire has the shortest coastline – just eighteen miles. Driving north from Boston along either I-95 or the quieter Rte-1, you enter New Hampshire after roughly forty miles, to be confronted almost immediately by the nuclear power plant at **Seabrook Station**, which opened in 1990 after years of determined opposition, not least from neighboring Massachusetts.

HAMPTON BEACH, a little further on, is a traditional family-oriented, if somewhat tacky, seaside resort (its free information line has the optimistic number ☎1-800/GET-A-TAN). The usual assortment of motels and fast-food places lines the approaches to the boardwalk and crowded beaches, but in a place this close to Boston, summer **accommodation** rates can be high. The *Breakers by the Sea Motel*, 409 Ocean Blvd (☎603/926-7702, ⓦwww.breakers-bythesea.com; ❷), is one of the least expensive options, offering roomy one- or two-bedroom apartments along with normal rooms.

Portsmouth

New Hampshire's oldest community, **PORTSMOUTH**, might look like a major city on the map, but once there, you'll find a small-town accessibility blended with the enthusiasm of a rejuvenated city. This character places it well above some of the more tourist-focused communities along the coast. Its position at the mouth of the Piscataqua River has always made it an important port – it was the state capital until 1808 – but it has barely grown, and the spire of **North Church** in the central **Market Square** remains the highest building you'll see in town.

Of a striking selection of grand **Colonial homes**, the 1761 gambrel-roofed, boxy, yellow **John Paul Jones House**, 43 Middle St, at State (mid-May to mid-Oct Thurs–Tues 11am–5pm; $5; ☎603/436-8420), is the most distinctive. In **Prescott Park** along the waterfront, the **Sheafe Warehouse Museum** (summer only; free; ☎603/431-8748) has a fascinating collection of mostly nautical paraphernalia.

Indeed Portsmouth's fortunes have long rested with its **naval shipyard**, visible across the bay (in Kittery, Maine; see p.284). Founded in 1800 by John Paul Jones as the US government's first shipyard, it has remained active ever since – it launched 31 submarines in 1944 alone, and built its first Polaris **nuclear submarine** in 1961.

Strawbery Banke

The lack of any great pressure on space has made it possible to preserve ten acres of Portsmouth's original site as **Strawbery Banke**, 64 Marcy St (May–Oct Mon–Sat 10am–5pm, Sun noon–5pm; Nov–April Thurs–Sat 10am–2pm, Sun noon–2pm; $12, tickets good for two consecutive days; ☎603/433-1100, ⓦwww.strawberybanke.org). The area serves as a living museum full of buildings from Portsmouth's past, most of which you can explore either on a guided tour or on your own (several of the houses have well-informed attendants). The area now taken up by the museum began life as the home of wealthy shipbuilders, and was successively the lair of privateers and a red-light district before turning into respectable – and, in the 1950s, ultimately decaying – suburbia. It was then decided to re-create its former appearance, mainly by clearing away the newer buildings.

Each building is shown in its most interesting former incarnation, whether that be 1695 or 1955; in the **Drisco House**, the first you come to, each individual room dates from a different era. The 1766 **Pitt Tavern** holds most historic significance, having served as a meeting place during the Revolution for patriots and loyalists (it still functions as a masonic lodge, one of the four oldest in the US – which explains why you can't go upstairs). Other restricted areas can be explained by the one or two people who still live in houses on the museum site, tucked away on the upper floors. Officially an educational institution, Strawberry Banke offers year-round lectures and courses on such subjects as traditional crafts. Some of these can be viewed in the **Dinsmore Shop**, where an infinitely patient cooper manufactures barrels with the tools and methods of 1800, as well as the **Mills Zoldak pottery shop**, which produces attractive low-priced ceramics (and can be visited without paying the Strawbery Banke admission).

Practicalities

Vermont Transit Lines **buses** (☎1-800/552-8737) stop in Market Square, en route between Boston and Portland, Maine. You can pick up **information** from the **visitor center** at 500 Market St, about a 10-minute walk from Market Square (Mon–Fri 8.30am–5pm; June–Sept also Sat & Sun 10am–5pm; ☎603/436-1118, ⓦwww.portsmouthchamber.org), or, during summer only, from the kiosk in Market Square (daily 9am–5pm). Portsmouth Harbor Cruises (☎603/436-8084 or 1-800/776-0915, ⓦwww.portsmouthharbor.com) is one of several operators offering **boat trips**, from $14.

Accommodation in the town center is restricted to expensive places such as the grand *Sise Inn*, 40 Court St (☎603/433-1200 or 1-877/747-3466, ⓦwww.siseinn.com; ❺), a nicely preserved Queen Anne–style house with large rooms; the peaceful, rambling seven-room *Inn at Strawbery Banke*, 314 Court St (☎603/436-7242 or 1-800/428-3933, ⓦwww.innatstrawberybanke.com; ❺); and the waterfront *Bow Street Inn*, 121 Bow St (☎603/431-7760, ⓦwww.bowstreetinn.com; ❺). Cheaper motels near the traffic circle where I-95 and Rte-1 bypass include the good-value *Port Inn*, Rte-1 Bypass South (☎603/436-4378 or 1-800/282-PORT, ⓦwww.theportinn.com; ❸).

Portsmouth likes to bill itself, with some justification, as the "food capital of New England." Of the in-town **restaurants**, *The Stockpot*, 53 Bow St (☎603/431-1851), has hearty, reasonably priced American food, along with great river views and an outdoor seating area; *Anthony Alberto's*, 59 Penhallow St (☎603/436-4000), is a gourmet Italian restaurant with an excellent wine list; and funky *Friendly Toast*, 121 Congress St (☎603/430-2154), makes for an inexpensive breakfast and lunch spot, with generous portions. At night, the *Portsmouth Brewery*, 56 Market St (☎603/431-1115), is raucous with occasional live music, while *The Press Room*, 77 Daniel St (☎603/431-5186), has jazz, blues, folk, and bluegrass performances.

Odiorne Point State Park

The one brief patch of semi-wilderness along the New Hampshire coast is, ironically, where the first white settlers landed in 1623. Some of the scattered ruins in the marshy duneland of **Odiorne Point State Park** ($3; ☎603/436-7406) date from those early days; others, far more modern, were World War II defenses. The two park entrances are on Hwy-1A near **Rye**, four miles southeast of Portsmouth. The offshore **Isles of Shoals**, a supposed haunt of Blackbeard the pirate, can be visited by taking a boat trip from Portsmouth Harbor ($19; ☎603/431-5500 or 1-800/441-4620, ⓦwww.islesofshoals.com).

The Merrimack Valley

The financial and political heartland of New Hampshire is the **Merrimack Valley**, which – first by water and now by road – has always been the main thoroughfare north to the White Mountains and Québec. None of its towns is of any great interest to tourists, though all are pleasant enough, and equipped with relatively inexpensive motels.

The southernmost (and New Hampshire's second-biggest) town on the river, **NASHUA**, was rated by *Money* magazine less than a decade ago as the number one place to live in America, a somewhat surprising choice given its suburban sprawl dominated by strip malls and car dealerships. **MANCHESTER**, like its namesake in England, was a major nineteenth-century cotton producer. Although its massive Amoskeag Mills closed in the 1930s, it remains the largest city in the state, and is now notable mainly for the paintings in the **Currier Museum of Art**, 201 Myrtle Way (Mon, Wed, Fri, Sun 11am–5pm, Thurs 11am–8pm, Sat 10am–5pm; $5; ☎603/669-6144, ⓦwww.currier.org), New Hampshire's best fine-arts museum. The focal point of **CONCORD** is the gold dome of the State House on Main Street (Mon–Fri 8am–4.30pm; ☎603/271-2154), the seat of New Hampshire's state legislature – the largest in the country, with some 400 members. Local schoolteacher Christa McAuliffe, a victim of the *Challenger* shuttle tragedy, is commemorated by a planetarium, at 3 Institute Drive, off I-93, exit 15E (Mon–Sat 10am–5pm, Sun noon–5pm; $8; ☎603/271-7827, ⓦwww.starhop.com).

About twenty miles north of Concord, off I-95, exit 18, 288 Shaker Rd, **Canterbury Shaker Village** (daily: May–Oct 10am–5pm; Nov, Dec & April weekends 10am–4pm; $12; ☎603/783-9511, ⓦwww.shakers.org) was the sixth Shaker community to be founded by Ann Lee (in 1774), and was 300-strong by 1860. Three different thirty-minute tours show Shaker crafts and techniques – such as furniture-making – and the attached *Creamery* restaurant serves delicious and imaginative Shaker-inspired food. South of Concord, outside Derry just off Rte-28 (take exit 4 from I-93), the **Robert Frost Farm** (mid-June to early Sept Mon–Sat 10am–5pm, Sun noon–5pm; mid-May through mid-June Sat & Sun 10am–5pm; $3; ☎603/432-3091) has been evocatively restored to its condition when New England's poet laureate lived here from 1900 to 1911. Displays in the barn highlight his work, and a half-mile "poetry nature trail" leads past the sites that inspired many of his best-known poems.

The Lakes Region

Of the literally hundreds of lakes created by snowmelt flowing south from the White Mountains and occupying the state's central corridor, the biggest by far is **Lake Winnipesaukee**, which forms the center of the vacation-oriented Lakes Region. Long segments of its 300-mile shoreline, especially in the east, consist of thick forests sweeping down to waters dotted with little islands, which are disturbed only by pleasure craft. The most sophisticated of the towns along the shoreline is **Wolfeboro**; the most fun to visit has to be **Weirs Beach**.

Ideally, you would bring your own small boat here and get thoroughly lost in the maze of small channels and islets. Failing that, the **cruise ship** *Mount Washington*, a 230-foot monster of a boat, departs from the dock in the center of Weirs Beach several times a day to sail to Wolfeboro, on the western side of the lake (mid-May to late Oct; $19, 2 1/2 hours; ☎603/366-5531 or 1-888/843-6686, ⓦwww.cruisenh.com). The ship also sets sail for dinner and dance cruises several times per week (from $32). Other day-cruises are available on the smaller *MV Doris E* ($10, 1 hour) and the US mail boat, *MV Sophie C* ($16, 2 hours), which gives you a better opportunity to see some of the lake's many islands close-up as the boat delivers the mail.

Wolfeboro

Because Governor Wentworth of New Hampshire built his summer home nearby in 1768, tiny **WOLFEBORO** claims to be "the oldest summer resort in America." Sandwiched between lakes Winnipesaukee and Wentworth, it has little to show for that history, but it's a relaxing place to spend a few hours, especially along the short but bustling main street, next to the quay where the *Mount Washington* (see above) comes in.

For **accommodation**, the 1812 *Wolfeboro Inn*, 90 N Main St (℡603/569-3016 or 1-800/451-2389, ⓦwww.wolfeboroinn.com; ④), stands in a dignified waterfront position just a few yards from the town proper. The *Tuc' Me Inn B&B*, 118 N Main St (℡603/569-5702, ⓦwww.tucmeinn.com; ④), is a homey place with tastefully furnished rooms, close to both the town and lake. *Wolfeboro Campground* is on Haines Hill Road (℡603/569-9881; $16), and is open mid-May to mid-October. For **food**, *Wolfe's Tavern*, at the *Wolfeboro Inn*, serves good-value steaks, seafood, burgers, and sandwiches, as does *Garwoods*, 6 N Main St (℡603/569-7788), with its dining room overlooking the bay. *Lydia's Café*, 33 N Main St (℡603/569-3991), is an excellent, veggie-oriented place for breakfast, lunch, or smoothies.

The eastern shore of Lake Winnipesaukee makes for great walking. One fascinating stopoff, a few miles north of Wolfeboro on Hwy-109, is the curious **Libby Museum** (June to mid-Sept Tues–Sat 10am–4pm, Sun noon–4pm; $2; ℡603/569-1035), where dentist Henry Forset Libby's obsession with evolution is illustrated by various ineptly stuffed animals (one can only hope that he was a better dentist than he was a taxidermist) and the skeletons of bears, orangutans, and humans. There's also a mastodon's tooth, a "Niddy-Noddy" spinning device, and a fingernail supposedly pulled out by its Chinese owner to demonstrate his new Christian faith. The front steps of the museum command a superb view over the lake.

Weirs Beach, Laconia, and Loudon

The short boardwalk at **WEIRS BEACH**, the very essence of seaside tackiness (even if it is fifty miles inland), is in summer the social center of the Lakes Region. Its little wooden jetty throngs with vacationers, the amusement arcades jingle with cash, and there's even a neat little crescent of sandy beach, suitable for family swimming. The better of its two competing **water parks** is Surf Coaster (daily: late June to early Sept 10am–6pm; $25) on Hwy-11B just south of town, which offers dramatic rides and a powerful wave machine.

Nearby **LACONIA**, though it's the most populated town in the Lakes Region, isn't really worth a visit except to stop at the White Mountain National Forest Headquarters at 719 Main St (Mon–Fri 8am–4.30pm; ℡603/528-8721, ⓦwww.fs.fed.us/r9/white), which has helpful maps and camping info.

Around the third weekend in June, at least twenty thousand **bikers** cruise up for a gigantic motorcycle race and rally in **LOUDON**, about eight miles south of Laconia on Hwy-106. The New Hampshire International Raceway here (℡603/783-4931, ⓦwww.nhis.com) also hosts NASCAR on a regular basis. Even at quieter times, room rates in Laconia are high; the best choice is the *Landmark Inn of the Lakes Region*, 480 Main St, Laconia (℡603/524-8000; ③), though other motel options are abundant along Rte-3 between Weirs Beach and Meredith (see below). The heartiest place to eat is *Water Street Café*, 141 Water St, Laconia (℡603/524-4144), which serves healthy helpings of old-fashioned food for breakfast, lunch, and dinner. The nearest **campground** is the *Gunstock*, just past Gilford on Rte-11A (☎603/293-4341 or 1-800/486-7862, ⓦwww.gunstock.com; $25 a night for up to two adults and three children).

Meredith

Four miles north of Weirs Beach, **MEREDITH**, the last of Lake Winnipesaukee's resorts, enjoys a peaceful location and has an upscale character, making it the best place to stay on the lake's western shore. The *Inns at Mill Falls*, which is actually three separate hotels (☎603/279-7006 or 1-800/622-6455, ⓦwww.millfalls.com; ❺), are the best choice for **accommodation**. Of the three, choose from the *Inn at Mill Falls* and the *Chase House at Mill Falls*, both on the hill overlooking the lake, or the *Inn at Bay Point*, directly on the water with some balconied rooms offering unrivalled lake views. *Mame's*, 8 Plymouth St (☎603/279-4631), serves gargantuan seafood, chicken, and steak **dinners** in an old village home; there's also a pub which can get busy at weekends. A nice diversion here is the **Winnipesaukee Railroad** (late May to early June & early Sept to mid-Oct weekends; daily mid-June to early Sep; $9 for 1hr, $10 for 2hrs; ☎603/279-5253, ⓦwww.hoborr.com), which operates scenic trips along the lakeshore between Meredith and Weirs Beach.

North to the mountains

Hwy-25 northeast from Meredith leads to Conway in the White Mountains; US-3 northwest, on the other hand, keeps you in the Lakes Region a little longer, leading past **Squam Lake**, where portions of the movie *On Golden Pond* were filmed. Educational tours of the **Squam Lake Natural Science Center** at **Holderness** (daily: May–Oct 9.30am–4.30pm; $11; ☎603/968-7194, ⓦwww.nhnature.org) lead through a largely natural landscape, in which animals such as deer, bobcat, otters, bears, and foxes are kept (mostly short-term) in enclosures. Squam Lake Tours (May–Oct, three tours daily; $15; ☎603/968-7577, ⓦwww.squamlaketours.com) offers two-hour boat tours of the lake, where the focus is on observing endangered loons.

The White Mountains

Thanks to their accessibility from both Montréal to the north and Boston to the south, the **White Mountains** have become a year-round tourist destination, popular with summer hikers on the Appalachian Trail and winter skiers on the slopes alike. Commercialized they may be, with considerable tourist development flanking the main highways, but the great granite massifs retain much of their majesty and power. **Mount Washington**, the highest peak in the Northeast, can claim some of the most severe weather in the world, and conditions are harsh enough for the timberline to be at four thousand feet (as compared to the norm in the Rockies of ten thousand).

Just a few high passes – here called "**notches**," discovered only after infinite pains by the early pioneers – pierce the range, and the roads through these gaps, such as the **Kancamagus Highway** between Lincoln and Conway, make for an enjoyable driving tour (compulsory **parking permits** are $3 for 1 day, or $5 for 7 consecutive days). However, you won't really have made the most of the White Mountains unless you also set off, on foot or on skis, across the long expanses of thick evergreen forest that separate them, with snowcapped peaks poking out in

> ## Hiking, skiing, and cycling in the White Mountains
>
> **Hiking** in the White Mountains is coordinated by the **Appalachian Mountain Club** (AMC), whose chain of information centers, hostels, and huts along the Appalachian Trail, traversing the region from northeast to southwest, is detailed below. Call ☏603/466-2725 for trail and weather information, and pick up a copy of the *AMC White Mountain Guide* ($23) before you attempt any serious expedition.
>
> Downhill and cross-country **skiers** can choose from several resorts that double up as summertime activity centers. Both the Waterville Valley Resort (☏603/236-8311 or 1-800-468-2553, ⒲www.waterville.com) and Loon Mountain (☏603/745-8111 or 1-800/229-LOON, ⒲www.loonmtn.com), both just east of I-93, are good for downhill, while Jackson (☏603/383-9355, ⒲www.jacksonxc.org), about fifteen miles north of Conway on Rte-19, has some of the finest cross-country skiing trails in the Northeast. General information on the skiing centers is available from Ski NH, PO Box 10, North Woodstock, NH 03262; ☏603/745-9396 or 1-800/88SKI-NH, ⒲www.skinh.com.
>
> Though obviously the hills can make for strenuous **biking**, there are easier ways of enjoying the White Mountains from the saddle, such as taking lifts up the slopes (at the resorts mentioned above) and riding back down. In summer, many of the cross-country skiing trails are taken over by bikers, and provide relatively flat, scenic terrain. Bikes can be rented from North Country Adventures on the Kancamagus Highway in Lincoln (☏603/745-8600, ⒲www.e-northcountryadventures.com), and from Joe Jones on Main Street in North Conway (☏603/356-9411, ⒲www.joejonessports.com).

all directions. The best sources of **information** in the region are the White Mountains Visitor Center, at I-93 exit 32 in North Woodstock (daily 9am–5pm; ☏603/745-8720 or 1-800/FIND-MTS, ⒲www.visitwhitemountains.com) and the Appalachian Mountain Club's info center at Pinkham Notch, Rte-16 (daily 6.30am–10pm; ☏603/466-2721, ⒲www.outdoors.org).

White Mountains accommodation

Thanks to the influx of young hikers and skiers to the White Mountains, there's a relative abundance of **budget** accommodation in the area. From the hostel-esque lodges at Crawford and Pinkham notches, to reasonably priced inns and B&Bs – where bargaining at quiet times occasionally pays off – there's sure to be an option to suit every traveler. Keep in mind, too, that rates vary dramatically between seasons – the most expensive times being winter, summer, and from late September to late October, for the fall foliage – and even from weekday to weekend.

Along the Appalachian Trail itself, there are eight **Appalachian Mountain Club huts**, which can only be reached on foot. In summer, each hut provides meals and bedding for between forty and ninety people. Prices range from $20 to $72 a night, according to the amount of privacy, luxury, and food you're after (and depending on whether or not you're an AMC member; individual membership is $36; see the website, ⒲www.outdoors.org, for details). **Reservations** are strongly recommended (call ☏603/466-2727, or visit the website, above), and you'll be expected to pay in full when you book the accommodation.

Campers can pitch their tents anywhere below the treeline and away from the roads in the White Mountains National Forest, provided they show consideration for the environment. There are also numerous official campgrounds ($14–16 per night), particularly along the Kancamagus Highway.

The AMC runs a **shuttle van service** for hikers between major trailheads and the lodges from June to mid-October ($11).

AMC lodges

Highland Lodge US-302, Crawford Notch
☎603/466-2727, ⓦwww.outdoors.org. Opened in late 2003, this innovatively designed and environmentally friendly building offers beds in a shared room for $54–66 or double rooms for $79–96. Open year-round.

Joe Dodge Lodge Hwy-16, Pinkham Notch
☎603/466-2727, ⓦwww.outdoors.org. Filled with hikers, this second AMC lodge-cum-hostel has bunks for $35–37 or double rooms for $70–74. Located near the base of the Mount Washington Auto Road. The visitor information center is open daily 6.30am–10pm. Open year-round.

Motels, hotels, and B&Bs

Adair Country Inn 80 Guider Lane, Bethlehem
☎603/444-2600 or 1-888/444-2600,
ⓦwww.adairinn.com. Deluxe antique-furnished rooms, with sweeping views of the landscaped grounds, and an impeccable staff, all reflected in the steep prices. ➐

Balsams Dixville Notch ☎603/255-3400, 1-800/255-0800 in NH, or 1-800/255-0600 outside NH, ⓦwww.thebalsams.com. Like the *Mount Washington* (see below), another of the last grand White Mountains resort hotels. Rates include all meals and use of facilities. ➏

Boulder Motor Court junction of routes 3 and 302, Twin Mountain ☎603/846-5437 or 1-866/846-5437, ⓦwww.bouldermotorcourt.com. One- and two-bedroom cottages with kitchens, fireplaces, and other amenities. Snowmobile tours and rentals also available. ➌

Eagle Mountain House 2 Carter Notch Rd, Jackson ☎603/383-9111 or 1-800/966-5779, ⓦwww.eaglemt.com. Highly atmospheric inn with a roaring fireplace in the lobby and a wraparound porch filled with rocking chairs, far above the bustle of North Conway. Has its own nine-hole golf course. ➍

The Forest Inn Rte-16A, Intervale ☎603/356-9772 or 1-877/854-6535, ⓦwww.forest-inn.com. Welcoming B&B between North Conway and Jackson, where many of the rooms include a fireplace. Organizes inn-to-inn cross-country skiing and biking holidays in conjunction with other B&Bs in the region. ➍

Franconia Inn Easton Valley Rd/Hwy-116, Franconia ☎603/823-5542 or 1-800/473-5299, ⓦwww.franconiainn.com. Comfortable 32-room inn two miles south of town, with great views. Makes for a good cross-country ski base. ➍

Hillwinds Lodge Dow Ave/Hwy-18, Franconia ☎603/823-5551 or 1-800/473-5299, ⓦwww.franconiainn.com/hillwinds.html. Standard, well-priced rooms, plus a sauna and outdoor pool. ➋

Indian Head Resort US-3, Lincoln ☎1-800/343-8000, ⓦwww.indianheadresort.com. An unpretentious resort motel with plenty of facilities and outdoor activities. Climb the motel's 100-foot observation tower for fine views of the surrounding hills. ➌

Mount Washington Hotel Rte-302, Bretton Woods ☎603/278-1000 or 1-800/258-0330, ⓦwww.mtwashington.com. Beautiful hotel dating from 1902, with a quarter-mile terrace, stellar views, indoor pool, and complete range of activities, including golf, horseback riding, and skiing. Also runs the less-fancy *Bretton Arms*, on the same property, which is much cheaper (➎), though rooms are still spacious. ➑

Thayer's Inn 111 Main St, Littleton ☎603/444-6469 or 1-800/634-8179, ⓦwww.thayersinn.com. Creaky but comfortable and classy old inn near the Vermont border, which has hosted such notables as Ulysses S. Grant and Richard Nixon. ➌

Franconia Notch

I-93, speeding up towards Canada, and the more leisurely US-3 merge briefly about ten miles beyond **Lincoln** to pass through **Franconia Notch State Park**. From a roadside pullout you used to be able to look back and upwards to the **Old Man of the Mountain**, a natural rock formation resembling an old man's profile. It became New Hampshire's ubiquitous state symbol, appearing on road signs, license plates, state quarters, and the like. However, in May 2003, this fragile formation, already held together with cables and epoxy, came tumbling down in high winds and heavy rain. The governor immediately declared that the face should be "revitalized," a decision no doubt influenced by the millions of tourists who have passed through Franconia Notch to see it.

Franconia Notch itself is a slender valley crammed between two great walls of stone. From the park **visitor center** (May to late Oct daily 9am–5pm;

☎603/745-8391), you can, for $8, walk along a two-mile boardwalk-cum-nature trail to the **Flume** and look down at the Pemigewasset River as it rages through the narrow, rock-filled gorge. Alternatively, take a $10 **cable-car** ride up the sheer granite face of **Cannon Mountain** (mid-May to mid-Oct daily 9am–5pm; ☎603/823-8800, Ⓦwww.cannonmt.com), or hike the various, well-marked trails up to panoramic views for free.

Further on, one mile south of the friendly village of **FRANCONIA**, the **Frost Place** on Ridge Road (June Sat & Sun 1–5pm; July to mid-Oct Wed–Mon 1–5pm; $3; ☎603/823-5510, Ⓦwww.frostplace.com) is a former home of poet Robert Frost, memorable largely for an inspiring panorama of unspoiled mountains. Each summer the poet-in-residence will often give poetry readings during visiting hours; however, Frost's farm outside Concord (see p.265) makes for a better destination to get a sense of the poet's life and works.

Bretton Woods

The ease with which US-302 now crosses the middle of the mountains belies the effort that went into cutting a road through **Crawford Notch**, halfway between Franconia and Conway. Just north, the magnificent **Mount Washington Hotel** (see overleaf) stands in splendid isolation in the wide mountain valley of **BRETTON WOODS**. The hotel's glistening white facade, capped by red cupolas and framed by the western slopes of Mount Washington rising behind, has barely changed since the place opened in 1902. In its heyday, a stream of horse-drawn carriages brought families (and their servants) up from the train station, deliberately located at a distance to enhance the sense of grandeur. Displays in the grand lobby commemorate the Bretton Woods Conference of 1944, which laid the groundwork for the postwar financial structure of the capitalist world, by setting the gold standard at $35 an ounce (it's now about $360) and creating the International Monetary Fund and the World Bank.

Restoration has ensured that the hotel remains marvelously evocative, with its quarter-mile terrace and white wicker furniture; the place is worth checking out even if you're not staying here. The hotel is not the one featured in the movie *The Shining*, though it's said to have inspired the story. Weekend golfing and tennis packages are available, and there's skiing in winter.

Mount Washington

The 6288ft **Mount Washington** was named for George Washington *before* he became president – but over the years, other mountains in this "Presidential Range" have taken the names of Madison, Jefferson, and even Eisenhower. (Mount Nancy was called that long before the Reagans were in the White House; and Mount Deception just happens to be close by.)

From the top of Mount Washington you can, on a clear day, see all the way to the Atlantic and into Canada – but the real interest in making the ascent lies in the extraordinary severity of the weather up here, which results from the summit lying right in the path of the principal storm tracks and air-mass routes affecting the northeastern US. The wind here exceeds hurricane strength on more than a hundred days of the year, and in 1934 it reached the highest speed ever recorded anywhere in the world – 231mph. At the top, you'll see the remarkable spectacle of buildings actually held down with great chains; many have been blown away over the years, including the old observatory, said to be the strongest wooden building ever constructed. There's now a **viewing platform**, with a weatherproof **museum** ($2) and **café** just below. Among the roll call of the 124 victims to have died on the mountain are two who attempted to slide down on "improvised boards." Be sure to check the **weather conditions** before attempting any ascent, and be aware that a fine day can turn bad very quickly in these parts.

On the way to the top, you pass through four distinct climatic zones, starting with century-old fir and ash trees so stunted as to be below waist-height and ending with Arctic tundra. The drive up the **Mount Washington Auto Road** (early May to late Oct, weather permitting, at least 8am–4pm; call ☏603/466-3988 to check weather conditions, ⓦ www.mtwashingtonautoroad.com) isn't as hair-raising as you might expect, though the hairpin bends and lack of guardrails certainly keep you alert. There is an $18 **toll** for private cars and driver (plus $7 for each additional adult and $4 for kids), which comes with an audio tape or CD detailing the road's history. Specially adapted minibuses, called "stages," after the horse-drawn carriages that first used the road, give **narrated tours** (daily 8.30am–5pm; $24). Driving takes thirty or forty minutes under sane conditions, though rally-drivers have done it in less than ten. The record for the annual **running** race each June – heading up the mountain – now stands at an incredible 58 minutes 20 seconds.

Last but far from least, you can also ride to the top on the coal-fired steam train of the **Mount Washington Cog Railway**, which noisily climbs the exposed western flank of the mountain, ascending gradients of up to 38 degrees on a track completed in 1869. It's truly a unique experience, inching up the steep wooden trestles while avoiding descending showers of coal smut. The three-hour round trip costs $49, and trains leave hourly (daily, weather permitting: mid-June to late Oct, call for other dates and times; ☏603/278-5404 or 1-800/922-8825, ⓦ www.thecog.com) from a station off Rte-302 six miles northeast of Bretton Woods. Reservations are recommended.

North Conway

A few miles south of Mount Washington, heading past Glen, US-302 and Hwy-16, as they approach **NORTH CONWAY**, run through a hodgepodge of shopping malls, fast-food joints, and theme parks such as Heritage New Hampshire and Story Land. The strip between North Conway and **Conway** proper offers all sorts of outlet stores (including a branch of Maine's L.L. Bean – see p.289) for discount shopping. The towns are not terribly interesting, though there are plenty of secluded lodging options in the foothills to either side, as well as bars and restaurants in the malls. There's also the useful **White Mountain National Forest Saco Ranger Station**, 33 Kancamagus Hwy near Rte-16 in Conway (daily 8am–5.30pm; ☏603/447-5448), which sells maps and books and provides a ton of resources for travel planning. It also handles backcountry cabin rentals and sells parking permits ($3 for one day, $5 for seven consecutive days), which are mandatory within the White Mountains region. If you're traveling through here in high season, be warned that, due to congested roads, it can take over half an hour to drive five miles.

The Kancamagus Highway

The **Kancamagus Highway** (Hwy-112) connecting Conway and Lincoln is the least busy road through the mountains, and makes for a very pleasant 34-mile drive. Several campgrounds are situated in the woods to either side, and various walking trails are signposted. The half-mile hike to **Sabbaday Falls**, off to the south roughly halfway along the highway, leads up a narrow rocky cleft in the forest to a succession of idyllic waterfalls.

White Mountains eating and drinking

Family **restaurants** and fast-food joints line the main drags of major centers such as North Woodstock and North Conway. The best places are in less conspicuous areas and worth rooting out. Some of the hotels and B&Bs recommended on p.269 also serve food.

1785 Inn & Restaurant 3582 Hwy-16, just north of North Conway ☎ 603/356-9025 or 1-800/421-1785. Original appetizers, gourmet meals such as boned rabbit in a cream sherry sauce, and fine wines, with prices to match – entrees are $15–30.
Flying Moose Café 2 W Main St, Littleton ☎ 603/444-2661. Intimate bistro serving a mix of classic cuisines with contemporary flair, such as braised lamb shank over polenta.
Polly's Pancake Parlor I-93 exit 38, Rte-117, Sugar Hill ☎ 603/823-5575. Yes, it's in the middle of nowhere, but it's a scenic nowhere and well worth the trip if you love pancakes.

Red Parka Pub US-302, Glen ☎ 603/383-4344. Evening-only steakhouse with bar until 12.30am. Live rock music on weekends, and open-mic night Mondays.
Thompson House Eatery Rte-16A, Jackson ☎ 603/383-9341. Huge portions of very reasonably priced American comfort food, plus homemade root beer.
Truant's Taverne 96 Main St, North Woodstock ☎ 603/745-2239. Cozy, affordable restaurant, serving well-cooked American grill fare for under $15 a plate.

West to Vermont

Much of the western side of New Hampshire, as you approach the Connecticut River that forms the entire border with Vermont, amounts to a less-developed – and therefore less touristy – version of the Lakes Region (see p.265). For a tranquil day or two, the area around **Lake Sunapee**, the northern tip of which just brushes I-89, can be very appealing. Good bets for local inns include *The Back Side Inn*, behind Mount Sunapee at 1171 Brook Rd in Goshen (☎ 603/863-5161, ⓦ www.bsideinn.com; ❹), a former farm and now family-run Victorian with ten simple but comfortable rooms and a sumptuous breakfast buffet; and, overlooking the lake, the *Inn at Sunapee*, 125 Burkehaven Hill Rd (☎ 603/763-4444 or 1-800/327-2466, ⓦ www.innatsunapee.com; ❺), a converted 1875 farmhouse with sixteen rooms decorated with a mixture of period items and Asian antiques.

Hanover

HANOVER, near Lebanon and just across from Vermont, is home to the venerable and elegant **Dartmouth College**, founded in this remote spot in the eighteenth century "for the instruction of the Youth of Indian tribes . . . and others." The main attraction here is the small **Hood Museum of Art** on the college green (Tues & Thurs–Sat 10am–5pm, Wed 10am–9pm, Sun noon–5pm; free; ☎ 603/646-2808, ⓦ www.dartmouth.edu/~hood), which has works by Picasso and Monet alongside Assyrian bas-reliefs. In the adjacent cultural complex, the Dartmouth Film Society screens international art-house films and classic movies year-round ($7).

Hanover itself is enjoyable to wander around, with lively places to **eat and drink**, such as *Murphy's on the Green*, 11 S Main St (☎ 603/643-4075), the best place for a beer and some healthy food, and the always-busy *Lou's Restaurant & Bakery*, 30 S Main St (☎ 603/643-3321), good for breakfast. The finest **accommodation** is at the expensive and luxurious *Hanover Inn*, overlooking Dartmouth Green from the corner of Main and Wheelock streets (☎ 603/643-4300 or

1-800/443-7024, ⓦ www.hanoverinn.com; ❾). The *Chieftain Motor Inn*, at 84 Lyme Rd, which is also known as Rte-10 N (☎603/643-2550, ⓦ www.chieftaininn.com; ❺), represents the best budget option you'll find in this generally expensive area.

Nearby, one secluded and memorable place to stay is *Moose Mountain Lodge* (☎603/643-3529, ⓦ www.moosemountainlodge.com; ❼, with at least a 2-night stay required; closed mid–Oct to late Dec), a steep climb up in the hills above **Etna**, overlooking Vermont. All year it feels blissfully remote from the world below, but it really comes into its own for **cross-country skiing** in winter. The friendly owners, who love the country life, charge $90 per day per person, which includes a hearty breakfast, lunch, and dinner.

Vermont

VERMONT comes closer than any other New England state to realizing the quintessential image of small-town Yankee America, with its white churches and red barns, covered bridges and clapboard houses, snowy woods and maple syrup. No city in Vermont manages a population of more than forty thousand (only **Burlington** comes close) and the chief tourist attraction is Ben & Jerry's ice-cream factory in Waterbury. Though rural, the landscape is not all that agricultural, as much is covered by mountainous forests (the state's name comes from the French "*vert mont*," or green mountain). The people who choose to live here are a mix of hippies and diehard conservatives working together to preserve their environment and lamenting the arrival of yet more ski resorts. One striking feature of Vermont is the absence of billboards – though the cutesy "country stores" which seem to grace every other crossroads can become tedious.

This was the last area of New England to be settled, early in the eighteenth century, with French explorers working their way down from Canada, and American colonists beginning to spread north. Even as that rivalry died down, another developed between settlers from New Hampshire and those from New York. The wealthy New York merchants who built fine homes along the Connecticut River Valley thought of themselves as the "River Gods," but the hardy settlers of the lakes and mountains to the west had little time for their patrician ways. Their leader, the now-legendary **Ethan Allen**, formed his **Green Mountain Boys** in 1770, proclaiming that "the gods of the hills are not the gods of the valley." During the Revolutionary War, this all-but-autonomous force captured Fort Ticonderoga from the British and helped to win the decisive Battle of Bennington. By 1777, Vermont was an independent republic, with the first constitution in the world explicitly forbidding slavery and granting universal (male) suffrage, but once its boundaries with New York were agreed upon, it joined the Union in 1791. A more recent example of Vermont's progressive attitude occurred in 1999, when Governor Howard Dean signed the **civil union** bill into law, making Vermont the first state in the US to sanction same-sex marriage. Curiously, the two seminal figures of the **Mormon** religion were both born in Vermont – Joseph Smith in 1805, and his lieutenant and successor Brigham Young in 1801.

With the occasional exception, such as the extraordinary assortment of Americana at the **Shelburne Museum** near Burlington, there are few specific goals for tourists. Visitors come in great numbers during two well-defined seasons: to see the **fall foliage** in the first two weeks of October, and to **ski** in the depths of winter, when the resorts of **Killington**, and **Stowe** further north (home of *The Sound of Music*'s Trapp family), spring into life. For the rest of the year, you might just as well explore any of the state's minor roads that take your fancy, confident that some picturesque village will be around the next corner.

Getting around Vermont

Vermont's main north–south road is I-91, which runs from the Québec border to Massachusetts, hugging the edge of New Hampshire for most of the way. I-89 traverses the center of the state, passing Montpelier and Burlington on its way from New Hampshire to Canada. Greyhound-affiliated Vermont Transit Lines **buses** (☎802/864-6811, 1-800/642-3133 in Vermont, or 1-800/451-3292 elsewhere in New England, ⓦwww.vermonttransit.com) connect Montréal with Boston and New York, passing through towns such as Burlington, Montpelier, Rutland, White River Junction, and Brattleboro. Other services traverse the Green Mountains, including stops at Killington and Woodstock. Towns in the northern part of the state near the Québec border are also on the bus route. Amtrak's *Vermonter* **train** (☎1-800/872-7245), which runs between Washington, DC, and St Albans, stops at Brattleboro, White River Junction, Montpelier, Waterbury, and Burlington. The main **airport** is in Burlington.

Lake Champlain Ferries (☎802/864-9804, ⓦwww.ferries.com) carries cars across Lake Champlain between Vermont and New York (for more details, see p.280). Bike Vermont (☎802/457-3553 or 1-800/252-2226, ⓦwww.bikevt.com) and Adventure Guides of Vermont (☎802/425-6211 or 1-800/747-5905, ⓦwww.adventureguidesvt.com) organize **cycling tours**, including itineraries that take you from one rural inn to another.

Southern Vermont

Of the two low-key towns at either end of Vermont's southern corridor – a mere forty miles from east to west, and linked by Hwy-9 – **Brattleboro** has the atmosphere of a college town (but no college), while **Bennington** has the college (but not the atmosphere). The birthplace of Mormon prophet Brigham Young is marked by a monument at **Whitingham**, halfway between the two towns.

Brattleboro

If **BRATTLEBORO**, in the southeastern corner of the state, is your first taste of Vermont, it may come as a surprise. Not the quaint, 1950s-throwback village you might expect, its style owes more to the central and northern Massachusetts college towns, with numerous little stores catering to the youthful and vaguely "alternative" population that has moved into the surrounding hills over the past few decades. The town's one unlikely claim to fame is that this was where **Rudyard Kipling** wrote his two *Jungle Books*.

Trains follow the river into town and stop behind the Old Union Railroad Station, which, as the **Brattleboro Museum & Art Center** (mid-May to Dec Tues–Sun noon–6pm; $3; ☎802/257-0124, ⓦwww.brattleboromuseum.org), now displays locally made Estey organs, one of the most popular reed organs ever produced, and exhibits by local painters, sculptors, photographers, and the like. **Buses** pick up and drop off at the junction of US-5 (Putney Road) and I-91, a couple of miles north. The most popular place to **stay** is in one of the restored rooms at the Art Deco *Latchis Hotel*, 50 Main St (☎802/254-6300, ⓦwww.brattleboro.com/latchis; ❸); it also has a good **restaurant**, *Lucca's Bistro* (☎802/254-4747; closed Mon & Tues), which serves Tuscan-inspired cuisine. They've also got quality beer and dancing in the **bar** upstairs. The nearby *Common Ground*, at 25 Elliot St (☎802/257-0855), is a long-established worker-owned vegetarian **restaurant**, with a hippie-friendly atmosphere and **live music**. Homemade baked goods and specialty coffee make *Mocha Joe's*, 82 Main St (☎802/257-7794), a good place for a morning snack or an evening dessert.

Bennington

In the past two hundred years, little has happened in **BENNINGTON** to match the excitement of the days when Ethan Allen's Green Mountain Boys – known as the "Bennington Mob" – were based here. A 306ft hilltop obelisk (mid-April to late Oct daily 9am–5pm; $1.50) commemorates the **Battle of Bennington** of 1777, in which the Boys were a crucial factor in defeating the British under General Burgoyne (though the battle itself was fought just across the border in New York).

About a mile north of the sleepy intersection at the town center, three **covered bridges** span the Walloomsac River. Hikers set out from the southern end of the Long Trail (see below) roughly five miles east. The *Paradise Motor Inn* at no.141 (☎802/442-8351, ⓦwww.theparadisemotorinn.com; ❸) is one of a few downtown **motels** located on W Main Street. Ten miles east of town on Rte-9, by the Prospect Ski Mountain, is the *HI-Greenwood Lodge* **hostel** (open mid-May to late Oct; ☎802/442-2547, ⓦwww.campvermont.com/greenwood), which has beds for $17. As for food, students from the small and exclusive arts-oriented Bennington College crowd into the *Blue Benn* **diner** at 102 Hunt St (☎802/442-5140).

The Green Mountains

The **Green Mountains**, which form the backbone of Vermont, are not as harsh as New Hampshire's White Mountains – though the forests for which they are named are invariably buried in snow for most of the winter, and the higher roads are liable to be blocked for long periods. Here and there, denuded patches mark where trees have been shaved away to create ski-runs, but for the most part, the usually peaceful **Hwy-100** running up from the south offers unspoiled mountain views to either side.

In summer, hikers take up the challenge of the **Long Trail** along the central ridge, 265 miles from the Massachusetts border to Québec. This trail predates the Appalachian Trail, which now joins its southern portion, and is looked after by the **Green Mountain Club** (☎802/244-7037, ⓦwww.greenmountainclub.org), whose *Long Trail Guide* ($19) is invaluable.

Hwy-100 Scenic Drive: Weston

One of the prettiest villages along Hwy-100 is **WESTON**, which spreads out beside a little river and centers on a perfect green, where a somber stone slab commemorates the seventeen local soldiers who were killed on the same day during the Civil War, in Virginia at Alexandria. Nearby, the **Farrar-Mansur House** (July & Aug Wed, Sat & Sun 2–5pm; early Sept to late Oct Sat & Sun 2–5pm; $2 donation; ☎802/824-5294) is a 1795 house and tavern, which re-creates early settler life with collections of clocks, dolls, guns, and weaving equipment; while the **Weston Playhouse** is a typical little Vermont theater, putting on light summer and fall performances (Tues–Sun; $27–36; ☎802/824-5288, ⓦwww.westplay.com).

Stores selling antiques, toys, and fudge are scattered up and down Weston's main street. The **Vermont Country Store**, south of the green, is larger than it looks from its modest facade. For all its seeming quaintness, this Vermont institution, known as the "Purveyors of the Practical and Hard-to-Find," is part of a chain of superstores that has a successful mail-order business. Opposite, the **Weston Village Store** leans more on the side of kitsch, but is still a fun place to browse all kinds of books, chairs, gardening tools, and kitchen implements.

Weston's best **accommodation** is the lovely *Inn at Weston*, Hwy-100, near the village green (☎802/824-6789, ⓦwww.innweston.com; ❼), whose homey rooms are complemented by an excellent restaurant and a cozy pub. A decent alternative is the family-run *Colonial House Inn & Motel* (☎802/824-6286 or 1-800/639-5033, ⓦwww.cohoinn.com; ❸), two miles south of Weston on Hwy-100. A small but magnificent soda fountain dominates the 1885 mahogany bar of the lunch-only *Bryant House* **restaurant**, next door to the Vermont Country Store (closed Sun; ☎802/824-6287); the menu includes such country goodies as "johnny cakes" of cornbread with molasses.

Killington

The ski resort of **KILLINGTON** (☎802/422-6200 or 1-800/621-6867, ⓦwww.killington.com), in the center of the Green Mountains halfway between Woodstock to the east and Rutland to the west, has grown out of nothing since 1958. Despite a miniscule permanent population (around fifty), it's estimated that in season there are enough beds within twenty miles to accommodate some ten thousand people each night. The resort sprawls over seven mountains (Pico Mountain is the best for skiers of mid-range ability), and is notorious for its rowdy nightlife (for 24-hour taped skiing information, call ☎802/422-3261).

In winter, the Killington Access Road up from US-4 is humming with crowded **bars and restaurants**: *Mother Shapiro's* (☎802/422-9933) is good for American comfort food, while the *Pickle Barrel* (☎802/422-3035) is a rowdy bar that gets particularly crazy on weekends. Most of these places close in summer, though during the warm months you can still take the **gondola** ($9 one way, $13 round trip) up to the observation deck and cafeteria on the bleak summit. Hiking routes that meet here include the Long and Appalachian trails. The *Cortina Inn & Resort* (☎802/773-3333 or 1-800/451-6108, ⓦwww.cortinainn.com; ❺) is one of several **inns** on Hwy-4 offering reduced summer rates; the *Inn at Long Trail*, Sherburne Pass (☎802/775-7181 or 1-800/325-2540, ⓦwww.innatlongtrail.com; ❹), is perfectly located for hikers on the Long Trail (see overleaf).

Woodstock

Since its settlement in the 1760s, **WOODSTOCK**, a few miles west of the Connecticut River up US-4, has been one of Vermont's more refined centers and a beautiful place to spend time. Its distinguished houses cluster around an oval green, now largely taken over by antiques stores and tearooms. It should most certainly not be confused with Woodstock, New York, of music festival fame.

Woodstock's main paying attraction is the **Billings Farm and Museum**, Rte-12, at River Rd (May–Oct daily 10am–5pm; Dec Sat & Sun 10am–3pm; $9; ☎802/457-4663, ⓦwww.billingsfarm.org): part modern dairy farm, part museum of farm life, it puts on demonstrations of antiquated skills and shows an excellent biographical film of the farm's various owners. The surrounding **hiking trails** are also great for a leisurely stroll.

An **information booth** on the green (June–Oct 9.30am–5.30pm; ☎802/457-1042) can help find **accommodation**. Options include the well-refurbished *Shire Motel*, 46 Pleasant St (☎802/457-2211, ⓦwww.shiremotel .com; ❹), the upscale *Woodstock Inn and Resort*, 14 The Green (☎802/457-1100 or 1-800/448-7900, ⓦwww.woodstockinn.com; ❻), and the cozy *Applebutter Inn*, four miles east of town on Hwy-4, in Taftsville (☎802/457-4158, ⓦwww.applebutterinn.com; ❹). The nearest **hostel** is over twenty miles south in Ludlow: beds at the *Trojan Horse Hostel*, 44 Andover St (☎802/228-5244 or 1-800/547-7475), cost $18 in summer and $20 in winter. Of the several places to **eat** in Woodstock, *Bentley's*, 3 Elm St (☎802/457-3232), has a range of microbrews and upscale versions of traditional bistro food, while *The Prince and the Pauper*, 24 Elm St (☎802/457-1818), serves more expensive continental cuisine in a casual setting. *Pane Salute*, 61 Central St (☎802/457-4882), has the area's best cappuccino and pastries.

Quechee

In recent years, the grand houses on the hills around **QUECHEE**, six miles east of Woodstock, have been joined by a proliferation of new condos and second homes. It's all reasonably well landscaped, but a shame nonetheless, and adds nothing to the environs of **Quechee Gorge State Park**, which was created in time to spare the splendors of the **Quechee Gorge**. A delicate bridge spans the 165ft chasm of the Ottauquechee River, and hiking trails lead down to the park through the fir trees. You can **camp** here at one of Vermont's many state-run campgrounds ($14–21 per night; two-night minimum stay; ☎802/295-2990 or 1-888/409-7579). If you'd rather not rough it, the *Quality Inn*, on Hwy-4 between the gorge and the tourist shops of the Quechee Gorge Village (☎802/295-7600 or 1-800/732-4376, ⓦwww.qualityinnquechee .com; ❹), offers the best-value **accommodation**.

A waterfall on the river turns the turbines of the **Simon Pearce Glass Mill** (daily 9am–9pm), housed in a former woolen mill along Main Street in Quechee. Here, you can watch bowls and pots being made, and then eat from them at the on-site **restaurant**, which serves, among other dishes, shepherd's pie and beef-and-Guinness stew for around $15; reservations recommended (☎802/295-1470).

White River Junction

Probably the most exciting thing ever to happen in **WHITE RIVER JUNCTION** was the first use of laughing gas as an anesthetic, in 1844. The town has little to offer on its own, but it's an invaluable transportation hub: Amtrak trains stop right by North Main Street, and buses run east from here into New Hampshire – **Hanover** (see p.272) is just across the river – and throughout Vermont.

A good old-fashioned railroad **hotel** – the *Hotel Coolidge*, at 39 S Main St (☎802/295-3118 or 1-800/622-1124, Ⓦwww.hotelcoolidge.com; ❸) – still survives in the town center, and has added an HI-affiliated hostel wing with kitchen space and dorm beds ($19 for HI-members, $29 for others). In the same building, the *Gandy Dancer Café* serves good soups and sandwiches at bargain rates.

Montpelier and Barre

Fifty miles north up I-89, **MONTPELIER** is the smallest state capital in the nation, with fewer than ten thousand inhabitants. Surrounded by leafy gardens, the golden domed **capitol** is well worth a free tour for its marble-floored and mural-lined hallways. Copious information on accommodation, here and throughout the state, is available from the **Vermont Division of Travel and Tourism**, 134 State St (Mon–Fri 8am–6pm, Sat & Sun 10am–6pm; ☎802/828-5981). Good **B&B rooms** can be had at the central yet quiet *Betsy's Bed & Breakfast*, 74 E State St (☎802/229-0466, Ⓦwww.betsysbnb.com; ❸). For more luxurious digs, try the *Capitol Plaza Hotel*, 100 State St (☎802/223-5252, Ⓦwww.capitolplaza.com; ❺). There's also the three-bed HI-affiliated *Capitol Home Hostel*, out on RD1 (phone for directions; ☎802/223-2104), with beds at $14 for members, and $17 for nonmembers.

For **food**, students from the local New England Culinary Institute run both the *Main St Grill & Bar* at 118 Main St (☎802/223-3188) and the more upmarket *Chef's Table*, at the same address (☎802/229-9202), each one serving excellent, inexpensive, experimental dishes from all over the world. *Coffee Corner*, on Main Street, at State (☎802/229-9060), has been serving dirt-cheap diner food for over sixty years, and the *Mountain Café*, 7 Langdon St (☎802/223-0888; closed Mon), dishes up wholesome and largely organic breakfasts and lunches.

The immigrant stoneworkers of the adjacent town of **BARRE** (pronounced "berry") were famed for their union militancy at the start of the twentieth century. Their most enduring legacy is the elaborate gravestones they carved for their own graves, found in **Hope Cemetery** on Hwy-14 (though the Scots among them did also erect a rather incongruous statue of Robert Burns downtown). Southeast of town, you can watch workers cut huge blocks out of the earth at the world's biggest granite quarry, the **Rock of Ages** (May–Oct Mon–Sat 8.30am–5pm, Sun noon–5pm; free; guided tours June to mid-Oct Mon–Fri 9.15am–3pm; $4; ☎802/476-3119, Ⓦwww.rockofages.com). The *Hollow Inn & Motel* at 278 S Main St (☎802/479-9313 or 1-800/998-9444, Ⓦwww.hollowinn.com; ❹) has rooms with TV, VCR, and mini-kitchens. It also has a fitness center and provides complimentary continental breakfast. For other **meals**, *Del's*, 248 N Main St (☎802/476-6684), serves affordable pasta and pizzas.

Waterbury

Few people paid much attention to **WATERBURY** before 1978; even then, the opening of a homemade ice-cream stand run by a pair of hippies on the forecourt of a gas station excited little interest. However, **Ben & Jerry's Ice Cream Factory**, one mile north of I-89 on Rte-100 in the center of Waterbury, on the way up to Stowe, has grown so huge, so fast, that it is now the number-one tourist destination in Vermont. Half-hour tours (daily: July & Aug 9am–8pm; Sept & Oct 9am–6pm; Nov–May 10am–5pm; June 9am–5pm; $3; ☎802/882-1240 or 1-866/BJ-TOURS, Ⓦwww.benjerry.com) include a short film, a view of the workforce from an observation platform, and a free mini-scoop of the stuff that made it all possible – you can buy more at the overpriced gift shop and ice-cream stall outside. The omnipresent black-and-white cow logo, and the sanctimonious reminders to recycle, eat organic, and buy milk from farming co-ops can get to be a bit much; if the summer crowds seem intolerable, bear in mind there are better things to do in Burlington and Stowe.

Stowe

At the foot of Vermont's highest mountain, the 4393ft **Mount Mansfield**, lies the popular summer- and wintertime resort of **STOWE**. There is still a beautiful nineteenth-century village at the town's heart – with a white-spired meeting house and a pretty green to stroll around – though a century's worth of catering to large crowds of skiers and outdoor enthusiasts has rather swamped the approach road to the main ski area (Mountain Road) with equipment stores, resort spas, and sprawling condo complexes. Nevertheless, Stowe's setting remains spectacular.

Stowe's **visitor center** is on Main Street, at Mountain Road (Mon–Sat 9am–8pm, Sun 9am–5pm; ☎802/253-7321 or 1-877/GO-STOWE), and can provide information on skiing conditions and finding accommodation in the resort. **Bikes** can be rented from the Mountain Sports & Bike Shop, 580 Mountain Rd (☎802/253-7919, ⓦwww.mountainsportsvt.com); an excellent biking trail climbs the mountain. The **Vermont Ski Museum**, 1 S Main St (Mon, Wed & Sun noon–6pm; Thurs, Fri & Sat noon–8pm; $3 donation; ☎802/253-9911, ⓦwww.vermontskimuseum.org), is worth a look for its skiing memorabilia.

Hwy-108 – **Mountain Road** – leads close to the mountain through the dramatic **Smugglers' Notch**. The resort here (☎802/644-8851 or 1-800/451-8752, ⓦwww.smuggs.com) is a less crowded, more family-orientated alternative to Stowe. Weather permitting, you can get to the top of Mount Mansfield either by driving four and a half miles up the **Toll Road**, which itself starts seven miles up Mountain Road (mid-May to mid-Oct daily 9am–4pm; $16 per car plus $4 per person over six passengers), or by taking the **gondola** (mid-June to mid-Oct daily 10am–5pm; $12; ☎802/253-3000 or 1-800/253-4754, ⓦwww.stowe.com) up to the *Cliff House Restaurant*, and hiking for another half-hour from there. There's also a skate park ($15 a day) that offers rollerblading lessons and rentals, plus a 2300-foot-long luge-type ride known as the Alpine Slide ($11 a ride). What really made Stowe's name as a **cross-country ski resort** was its connection to the **Trapp family**, of *The Sound of Music* fame. After fleeing Austria during World War II, they established the *Trapp Family Lodge* at 700 Trapp Hill Rd (☎802/253-8511 or 1-800/826-7000, ⓦwww.trappfamily.com; ❼). The original lodge, where Maria von Trapp held her singing camps, has burned down, and she herself died in 1987, but an equally luxurious building has taken its place: its *Austrian Tea Room* serves incredibly heavy Germanic cakes and pastries. Good hiking and cross-country ski trails lead out from the lodge.

Practicalities

The best of the plentiful **accommodation** (save the lodge above) includes the streamside *Inn at Turner Mill*, 56 Turner Mill Lane (☎802/253-2062 or 1-800/992-0016, ⓦwww.turnermill.com; ❹); the sumptuous *Stoweflake Mountain Resort & Spa*, 1746 Mountain Rd (☎802/253-7355 or 1-800/253-2232, ⓦwww.stoweflake.com; ❻); and the central 1833 *Green Mountain Inn*, 18

Main St (℡802/253-7301 or 1-800/253-7302, ⓦwww.greenmountaininn
.com; ➎). Cheaper rooms are available at the *Riverside Inn*, 1965 Mountain
View Rd (℡802/253-4217 or 1-800/966-4217, ⓦwww.rivinn.com; ➋). The
Gold Brook **campground** is two miles south on Hwy-100 (℡802/253-7683;
$20 per site).

There are plenty of places to **eat** in and around Stowe. On Mountain Road,
next to the cinema, *McCarthy's* (℡802/253-8626) is best for breakfast; the *Shed
Restaurant & Brew Pub*, at no. 1859 (℡802/253-4364), has moderately-priced
American food and good beer; and the always-crowded *Pie in the Sky*, at no.
492 (℡802/253-5100), serves relatively inexpensive pizza and pasta dishes. A
more upscale option is the *Blue Moon Café*, 35 School St (℡802/253-7006),
which offers an innovative menu including Vermont rabbit and venison, as well
as a quality wine list.

Lake Champlain

The 150-mile-long **Lake Champlain**, which forms the boundary between
Vermont and New York State, and just nudges its way into Canada in the
north, never exceeds twelve miles in width. Across the water from the flatlands
of the Champlain Valley, the imposing Adirondacks are always visible, looming
in the west. The first non-native to see the lake, Samuel de Champlain, in 1609,
who named it after himself, was also the first to claim that it held a sinuous
Loch Ness–type monster, which is referred to affectionately in the region as
"Champ."

The heart and soul of the valley is the French-influenced city of **Burlington**,
whose longstanding trade connections with Montréal has filled it with elegant
nineteenth-century architecture. Within just a few miles of the center, US-2
leads north onto the supremely rural **Champlain Islands**, covered in meadows and orchards.

Vermont is one of the few states with designated **Underwater Historic
Preserves** (details at ℡802/828-3226), where divers can see shipwrecks on
the lake floor. Several of these underwater "state parks" are close to Burlington,
and the best place to learn more about them is at the **Lake Champlain
Maritime Museum** in Basin Harbor, six miles east of Vergennes (daily: May
to mid-Oct 10am–5pm; $10; ℡802/475-2022, ⓦwww.lcmm.org). The
museum is on the grounds of the *Basin Harbor Club* (℡802/475-2311 or 1-
800/622-4000, ⓦwww.basinharbor.com; ➎), an oddly part down-home family resort, part well-heeled country club with golf course, where males over
twelve must wear a jacket and tie around the resort after 6pm during summer.

Lake Champlain Ferries (℡802/864-9804, ⓦwww.ferries.com) crosses
the lake from Vermont to New York from **Burlington** (to Port Kent; 9–13 ferries a day; $13.75); **Charlotte** (to Essex; 4–7 ferries a day; $7.75); and **Grand
Isle** (to Plattsburgh; 20–22 ferries a day; $7.75). All these rates are one way for
a car and driver; additional passengers, cyclists, and walk-ons pay $3.75–4.75.

Burlington

Lakeside **BURLINGTON**, Vermont's largest "city," with a population nudg-
ing forty thousand, is one of the most enjoyable towns in New England, a hip,
relaxed fusion of Montréal, eighty miles to the north, and Boston, over two
hundred miles southeast. In fact, from its earliest days, Burlington looked as
much to Canada as to the south. Shipping connections with the St Lawrence

River were far easier than the land routes across the mountains, and the harbor became a major supply center. The city's founders included Ethan Allen and family – far from being some impoverished Robin Hood figure (see overleaf), Ethan was a wealthy landowner, and his brother Ira set up the University of Vermont.

Burlington today, as the home of the University of Vermont, is the definitive youthful, outward-looking college town. It's one of the few American cities to offer something approaching a café culture, with a downtown you can stroll around on foot, especially around the **Church Street Marketplace**, and plenty of open-air terraces. Politically, too, it's unusual: Bernard Saunders, the former "socialist" mayor of Burlington, was in 1990 elected to the House of Representatives from Vermont – the first political independent to go to Congress in forty years.

Arrival, information, and getting around

Vermont Transit **buses** stop in downtown Burlington, four blocks south of Main Street at 345 Pine St. The Amtrak **train** station is an inconvenient five miles northeast, in the small community of Essex Junction (connecting buses run every half-hour; $1). The **airport**, Vermont's largest, is a few miles east of town along US-2.

Information and help with accommodation is available from the **Lake Champlain Regional Chamber of Commerce**, 60 Main St (year-round Mon–Fri 8am–5pm, late May to late Sept also Sat 10am–6pm and Sun 9am–5pm; ℡802/863-3489 or 1-877/686-5253, ⓦwww.vermont.org), or the kiosk on Church Street.

The local CCTA **bus** company (℡802/864-2282, ⓦwww.cctaride.org) runs a free shuttle (roughly every 15 mins, Mon–Fri 6.15am–7.15pm; extended hours during summer) connecting the university campus, downtown, and the waterfront. Lake Champlain Ferries (see opposite) leave from the jetty at the end of King Street; Lake Champlain Shoreline Cruises ($10 narrated tour; $26 lobster dinner cruise; ℡802/862-8300, ⓦwww.soea.com) departs from the Burlington Boathouse at the end of College Street. Skirack, 85 Main St (℡802/658-3313), rents **bikes**.

Accommodation

Burlington has no shortage of moderately priced accommodation, especially along Shelburne Road between Burlington and Shelburne, while for **camping** the lakeside *North Beach Campground* (℡802/862-0942 or 1-800/571-1198; $21–29) is less than two miles north on Institute Road.

Burlington Redstone B&B 497 S Willard St ℡802/862-0508, ⓦwww.burlingtonredstone.com. A few blocks south of the town center, this B&B is in a gorgeous home with lake and mountain views. ❺

Colonial Motor Inn 462 Shelburne Rd ℡802/862-5754. Sixties-era decor lends a campy touch to this clean motel with pool and cable TV. ❸

Ho-Hum Motel 1660 Williston Rd ℡802/863-4551 or 1-800/228-7031. Simple, reasonably priced motel, three miles east of downtown on US-2, near the airport. ❸

Inn at Essex 70 Essex Way, Essex Junction ℡802/878-1100 or 1-800/727-4295,

ⓦwww.innatessex.com. Classy establishment with a good restaurant, near the Amtrak station about eight miles from the town center. ❼

Mid-Town Motel 230 Main St ℡802/862-9686, ⓔmid-town@juno.com. Spartan, inexpensive quarters in the heart of downtown. No phones in the rooms. ❸

Mrs Farrell's Home Hostel (HI/AYH) 27 Arlington Court ℡802/865-3730. Six dorm beds three miles from the center. $15 members, $18 nonmembers; 10pm curfew; closed Nov–April. ❶

Sunset House B&B 78 Main St ℡802/864-3790, ⓦwww.sunsethousebb.com. Centrally located, homely B&B with shared bathrooms. ❹

The City

Your natural inclination on setting out to explore Burlington might be to head for the **waterfront**. In fact, this is a surprisingly undeveloped area, though Battery Park at its northern end makes a good place to watch the sun go down over the Adirondacks – especially when there's a band playing, as there often is at weekends.

A better target is the pedestrianized **Church Street Marketplace**, a few blocks back, which holds Burlington's finest old buildings and its modern cafés and boutiques. The **Robert Hull Fleming Museum**, on Colchester Avenue (May to early Sept Tues–Fri noon–4pm, Sat & Sun 1–5pm; early Sept to April Tues–Fri 9am–4pm, Sat & Sun 1–5pm; $3; ℡802/656-0750, Ⓦwww.fleming-museum.org), has an interesting collection of art and artifacts from all over the world, including pre-Columbian pieces, while north on Rte-127, the **Ethan Allen Homestead** (June–Oct Mon–Sat 10am–5pm, Sun 1–5pm; $5; ℡802/865-4556) offers a multifaceted look at the life and times of Vermont's controversial founding father.

The Shelburne Museum

It takes a whole day, if not more, to appreciate fully the remarkable fifty-acre collection of unalloyed **Americana** gathered at the **Shelburne Museum**, on US-7 in Shelburne, three miles south of Burlington (daily: May–Oct 10am–5pm; $17.50, valid for two successive days; ℡802/985-3346, Ⓦwww.shelburnemuseum.org). Created in 1947 by heiress Electra Webb, the museum is built around her parents' French Impressionist paintings, including works by Degas and Monet, displayed in a meticulous reconstruction of their New York City apartment. However, Electra's own interests ranged far wider, and she put together what is probably the nation's finest celebration of its own inventions outside of the Smithsonian.

More than thirty buildings, some original and some constructed specially for the museum, focus on aspects of everyday American life over the past two centuries; most are staffed by well-informed attendants. The village includes a general store, complete with painted "cigar store Indians" and an apothecary, a Shaker shed, a railroad station, and even an enormous **steam paddlewheeler** from Lake Champlain, the SS *Ticonderoga*, with its own rock-surrounded lighthouse.

Eating, drinking, and entertainment

During term time, the presence of ten thousand students ensures that Burlington has ample choice of inexpensive and good restaurants, as well as some pretty raucous nightspots. Note that this is one of the most vehement **anti-smoking** towns in the East, and smoking is banned in most restaurants and some bars.

Bourbon Street Grill 211 College St ℡802/865-2800. Crowded and dimly lit place, with Cajun specials from $8.

Club Metronome 188 Main St ℡802/865-4563. Very hip club with some live acts, but mainly house and techno music.

Daily Planet 15 Center St, behind Church Street Marketplace ℡802/862-9647. Innovative menu combining Asian and Mediterranean cooking with old-fashioned American comfort food.

Five Spice Café 175 Church St ℡802/864-4045. Excellent southeast Asian food, including a dim sum Sunday brunch and vegetarian dishes.

Muddy Waters 184 Main St ℡802/658-0466. Eclectic interior and colorful clientele distinguish this popular coffeehouse. The caffeine beverages pack quite a punch.

NECI Commons 25 Church St ℡802/862-6324. The Burlington outpost of the New England Culinary Institute offers wonderful food such as halibut in plum-wine broth, vegan risotto, and "uncommon meatloaf"; attentive service, too. Cakes and sandwiches available at the on-site deli.

Pauline's Café & Restaurant 1834 Shelburne Rd, South Burlington ☎802/862-1081. Inventive American cuisine with a continental flavor. Light meals in a casual setting downstairs, more formality and higher prices upstairs.

Red Onion Café 140 Church St ☎802/865-2563. Inviting bakery with outdoor seating and the best sandwich shop around. Some good vegetarian options.

Shanty on the Shore 181 Battery St ☎802/864-0238. Truly fresh seafood in a laid-back setting, with views of Lake Champlain.

Smokejack's 156 Church St ☎802/658-1119. Creative meat and seafood dishes smoked over an oak-wood grill, served with punchy Bloody Marys and custom martinis.

Vermont Pub and Brewery 144 College St ☎802/865-0500. Roomy, convivial brewpub with a good menu of burgers, sandwiches, and other American-style food and occasional live music.

Maine

As big as the other five New England states combined, **MAINE** barely has the population of tiny Rhode Island. In theory, therefore, there's plenty of room for its massive summer influx of visitors; in reality, the majority of these make for the southern stretches of the extravagantly corrugated **coast**. You only really begin to appreciate the size and space of the state further north, or **inland**, where vast tracts of mountainous forest are dotted with lakes, and barely pierced by roads – more like the Alaskan interior than the RV-cluttered roads of the Vermont and New Hampshire mountains, and ideal territory for hiking and canoeing (and moose-spotting).

Although Maine is in many ways inhospitable – the **Algonquin** called it "Land of the Frozen Ground" – it has been in contact with Europe ever since the arrival of the **Vikings**, around 1000 AD. For the navigator Giovanni da Verrazano, in 1524, the "crudity and evil manners" of the Indians made this the "Land of Bad People," but before long European fishermen were setting up camps each summer to dry their catch. Francis Bacon in turn said that the English were "worse than the very Savages, impudently lying with their Women, teaching their men to drink drunke, and . . . to fall together by the eares."

North America's first agricultural **colonies** were in Maine: de Champlain's **French** Protestants near Mount Desert Island in 1604, and an **English** group that survived one winter at the mouth of the Kennebec three years later. In the face of the unwillingness of subsequent English settlers to let them farm in peace, the local Indians formed a long-term alliance with the French, and until as late as 1700 regularly drove out streams of impoverished English refugees. However, by 1764, the official census could claim that even Maine's black population was more numerous than its Native Americans.

Originally part of Massachusetts, Maine became a separate entity only in 1820, when the Missouri Compromise made Maine a free, and Missouri a slave, state. In the nineteenth century, its people had a reputation for conservatism and resistance to immigration, manifested in anti-Irish riots. The state's **economy** has always been heavily based on the sea, although long expeditions are now rare, and many of those who fish also farm. Recently they have been selling their catch direct to Russian factory ships anchored just offshore. Lobster fishing in particular has defied gloomy predictions, and has even boomed again, as evidenced by the many thriving **lobster pounds**.

Maine's climate is famously harsh. In winter, most of Maine is under ice; summer is short and usually heralded in early June by an infestation of tiny black flies. **Fall colors** begin to spread from the north in late September – when, unlike elsewhere in New England, off-season prices apply – but temperatures drop sharply, becoming quite frosty by mid-October.

Getting around Maine

The vast majority of visitors to Maine **drive**. The most enjoyable route to follow is US-1, which runs within a few miles of the coast all the way to Canada, with innumerable turnoffs to hidden seaside villages. If you're in a hurry, I-95, initially the (tolled) Maine Turnpike, offers speedy access to Portland and beyond. In the **interior**, the roads are quiet and the views spectacular; many belong to the lumber companies, who keep careful track of who you are and where you're going (and charge you for the privilege). At any time of the year, bad weather can render these roads suddenly impassable; be sure to check before setting off (Nov–April call ☎207/287-3427, or visit ⓦwww.state.me.us/mdot).

Public transportation falls a long way short of meeting travelers' needs. The seven daily Greyhound buses – from Boston to Portland, five of which continue on to Bangor – link the main towns of the southern coast, as does Concord Trailways (☎1-800/639-3317, ⓦwww.concordtrailways.com), but that's about all there is. Amtrak has few services save for the *Downeaster*, which leaves from Boston's North Station and terminates in Portland; it's a great value at $20 each way.

The Maine coast

Considering that the state has a **coastline** of three thousand miles, finding access to the sea in Maine can be a frustrating business. The oceanfront is monopolized by an endless succession of private homes and vacation residences – most famously that of former president Bush at Kennebunkport. In fact, only two percent of the shore is publicly owned – and not all of that is beach. Rather than long walks on coastal footpaths, travelers can expect attractive if rather commercial harbor villages, linked mostly by roads set well back from the water and packed with diners, motels, and factory outlets.

The liveliest destinations are **Portland** and **Bar Harbor** (at the edge of **Acadia National Park**); there's a wide choice of smaller seaside towns, such as **Belfast** and **Wiscasset**, if you're looking for a more peaceful base. **Beaches** are more common (and the sea warmer) further south, for example at **Ogunquit**.

The best way to see the coast itself is by **boat**: ferries and excursions operate from even the smallest harbors, with major routes including the ferries to **Canada** from Portland and Bar Harbor, and the shorter trips to **Monhegan** and **Vinalhaven** islands from Boothbay Harbor and Rockland, respectively.

South of Portland

I-95 crosses from Portsmouth, New Hampshire (see p.263), into an area of Maine so dense with little communities that Mark Twain alleged one couldn't "throw a brick without danger of disabling a postmaster." Three miles over the Maine border, at the intersection with US-1, an **information center** at **Kittery** provides copious details on the whole state (daily: July–Aug 7am–9pm; rest of year 9am–5pm; ☎207/439-1319).

If you want to avoid the tolls on the interstate and follow more scenic US-1 instead, you'll soon find yourself in **YORK**, which was in 1639 the first English city to be chartered in North America. Its seventeenth-century **Old Gaol** ("Old Jail") now serves as a museum, commemorating its own past and that of the local Native Americans.

Ogunquit

The three-mile spit of sand that shields **OGUNQUIT** from the open ocean is Maine's finest **beach**, a long stretch of sand and calm surf that is ideal for long walks. Thankfully, though, the town remains small enough to be a pleasant resort. The summer season at the **Ogunquit Playhouse** (☎207/646-5511) usually attracts a few big-name performers. Worth stopping into, if even just for a look, is the **Harbor Candy Shop**, at 26 Main St (☎207/646-8078), an old-style artisan candy shop piled with incredible confectionaries. Bread & Roses Bakery (☎207/646-4227), next door, is just as tempting.

Among dozens of **inns**, many of which close for the winter, are the *Betty Doon Motor Hotel*, 5 Beach St (☎207/646-2469, ⓦwww.bettydoon.com; ❸; be sure to ask for the penthouse, a three-room suite with full kitchen, roof deck, and room to sleep six; ❺), and *The Aspinquid*, 57 Beach St (☎207/646-7072, ⓦwww.aspinquid.com; ❺), which has ocean-view rooms. The nearest campground, *Pinederosa*, is north of town at 128 North Village Rd (May–Sept; ☎207/646-2492, ⓦwww.pinederosa.com; $20 for two adults); it operates a free shuttle to Ogunquit Beach in July and August. The misnamed Marginal Way, a clifftop path, leads from central Ogunquit to **Perkins Cove** a mile south, where well-priced **seafront restaurants** include *Barnacle Billy's* (☎207/646-5575), which serves seafood and American entrees.

Kennebunkport

Before its worldwide exposure as the home of George Bush's "summer White House," **KENNEBUNKPORT** was perfectly happy as a self-contained and exclusive residential district. If anything, locals seem to feel that George lowered the tone of the place by becoming president. However, Kennebunkport is not actually all that different from anywhere else along the coast – which is presumably what's really bothering the locals. The best place to hang out (and eat seafood) is *Alisson's*, at 8 Dock Square (☎207/967-4841), where dinner is served until 10pm and the bar stays open until 1am. There's no great point paying in-town hotel rates when there are so many motels along the highways.

Forty miles north of Kennebunkport, on the outskirts of South Portland, is the **Cape Elizabeth lighthouse**, commissioned by George Washington in 1791 and familiar from postcards and posters. Just below the light, the *Lobster Shack* (☎207/799-1677) is great for fresh **seafood**.

Portland

The largest city in Maine, **PORTLAND** was founded in 1632 in a superb position on the Casco Bay Peninsula, and quickly prospered, building ships and exporting the great inland pines for use as masts. A long line of wooden **wharves** stretched along the seafront, with the merchants' houses on the hillside above.

From its earliest days, Portland was a cosmopolitan city, with a large free black population that traditionally worked as longshoremen; great bitterness arose when Irish immigrants began to muscle in on the scene in the 1830s. When the **railroads** came, the Canada Trunk Line had its terminus right on Portland's quayside, bringing the produce of Canada and the Great Plains one hundred miles closer to Europe than it would have been at any other major US port. Some of the wharves are now taken up by new condo developments, though **Custom House Wharf** remains much as it must have looked when Anthony Trollope passed through in 1861 and said, "I doubt whether I ever saw a town with more evident signs of prosperity." Most of what he saw of the town was destroyed by an accidental **fire** in 1866 (Indians in 1675, and the British in 1775, had previously burned Portland deliberately).

Grand Trunk Station was torn down in 1966, and downtown Portland appeared to be in terminal decline – until, that is, a group of committed residents undertook the energetic redevelopment of the area now known as **Old Port Exchange**. Their success has revitalized the city, keeping it at the heart of Maine life – though you shouldn't expect a hive of energy. Portland is simply a quite pleasant, sophisticated, and in places very attractive town, where one can experience the benefits of a large city at a lesser cost and without the hassle.

Arrival, information, and getting around

Both I-95 and US-1 skirt the promontory of Portland, within a few miles of the city center. **Portland International Jetport** is next to I-95, and connected with downtown by regular city buses. Congress Street is the main central thoroughfare, while Fore Street runs along the harbor just to the south. Concord Trailways (☎1-800/639-3317, ⓦwww.concordtrailways .com) and Greyhound are the principal **bus** operators along the coast, with frequent service to Boston, as well as north to Bangor (and, in summer, Bar Harbor). Vermont Transit Lines (☎207/772-6587 or 1-800/552-8737, ⓦwww.vermonttransit.com) runs to Montréal, New Hampshire, and Vermont, as well as destinations within Maine; the station is at 950 Congress St, on the eastern edge of downtown.

The **visitor center** is at 305 Commercial St (mid-May to mid-Oct Mon–Fri 8am–6pm, Sat & Sun 10am–6pm; rest of year Mon–Fri 8am–5pm, Sat & Sun 10am–3pm; ☎207/772-5800, ⓦwww.visitportland.com).

Though served by public **buses** ($1), downtown Portland is compact enough to stroll or bike around; Cyclemania, at 59 Federal St (☎207/774-2933), rents **bicycles** for $15 a day. You can also take a **trolley tour** of the city with Mainely Tours, 3 Moulton St ($14; ☎207/774-0808), or Olde Port Trolley Fleet, Long Wharf, at Commercial St ($9–12; ☎207/772-0429); both companies offer a combination ticket of a trolley tour with a **cruise** of Casco Bay.

Between mid-May and late October, the Prince of Fundy Company's *Scotia Prince* **ferry** leaves Portland for **Yarmouth** in Nova Scotia at 8pm each evening, returning the next day. The trip takes eleven hours each way. High-season fare is $160 per person round-trip, and there are various discount and excursion fares – it's not an option to ferry your car as well due to the exorbitant price. You can get details by calling ☎207/775-5616 or 1-800/845-4073, or by visiting ⓦwww.scotiaprince.com.

Accommodation

Finding a room in Portland is no great problem, though you can expect to pay more to stay in town than in the **budget motels** around exit 8 off I-95. The closest **campground** is *Wassamki Springs*, off Hwy-114 (May to mid-Oct only; ☎207/839-4276).

Best Western Merry Manor Inn 700 Main St, South Portland ☎207/774-6151 or 1-800/528-1234, ⓦwww.bestwestern.com/merrymanorinn. Clean and comfortable, with a pool and on-site restaurant, four miles from the Old Port district. ❹

The Danforth 163 Danforth St ☎207/879-8755 or 1-800/991-6557, ⓦwww.danforthmaine.com.

Twelve rooms, ten with private baths and working fireplaces, in an 1820s Federal-style home near the Old Port. Full breakfast served. ⑥

Eastland Park 157 High St ☎ 207/775-5411 or 1-888/671-8008, ⓦ www.eastlandparkhotel.com. A central luxury hotel that recently spent $4 million on a massive refurbishment; the fine-dining restaurant and ornate lobby are jewels in the crown, but the well-appointed rooms are worth every penny as well. ⑥

Embassy Suites 1050 Westbrook St ☎ 207/775-2200 or 1-800/EMBASSY, ⓦ www.embassysuites .com. Spacious suites for the price of a hotel room, overlooking Portland's tiny Jetport (with a free link to and from). Rates include full breakfast

and afternoon cocktails. ⑥

Inn at St John 939 Congress St ☎ 207/773-6481 or 1-800/636-9127, ⓦ www.innatstjohn .com. Century-old hotel convenient to downtown, with comfortable, though small, rooms and narrow hallways. No elevator. Free airport pick-up and continental breakfast. ⑥

Pomegranate Inn 49 Neal St ☎ 207/772-1006 or 1-800/356-0408, ⓦ www.pomegranateinn.com. Romantic B&B with eight rooms – some with fireplaces – and a quiet garden. ⑤

YMCA 70 Forest Ave ☎ 207/874-1105. Often full, this men-only hostel accommodation is north of Congress St near Deering Oaks Park. $107 per week for dorms; no single-night options.

The City

Thanks to the several fires, not all that much of old Portland survives, though various grand mansions can be seen along Congress and Danforth streets. The **Wadsworth-Longfellow House/Maine Historical Society**, at 485–489 Congress St (May–Oct & Dec Mon–Sat 10am–4pm, Sun noon–4pm; Nov Sat only, 10am–4pm; $7 includes museum, below; 45min tours on the hour), was Portland's first brick house when built in 1785 by Peleg Wadsworth. However, the house owes its fame primarily to Wadsworth's grandson, the poet Henry Wadsworth Longfellow, who spent his boyhood here. The Historical Society Museum (Mon–Sat 10am–5pm, Sun noon–5pm; $4; ☎ 207/879-0427) has changing displays of state history and art.

The **Portland Museum of Art** at 7 Congress Square is a much more modern affair, built in 1988 by the I.M. Pei partnership (Tues–Thurs, Sat & Sun 10am–5pm, Fri 10am–9pm; June to mid-Oct Mon 10am–5pm; $8, free Friday 5–9pm; ☎ 207/775-6148, ⓦ www.portlandmuseum.org). All parts of the museum give superb views over the bay. In fact, at times the collection seems subordinate to the design, which does not allow much room for extensive displays. The lower stories usually hold temporary exhibitions – though there's a lovely open-air garden café as well – while the works upstairs include a lively and flirtatious set of 1880s Winslow Homer engravings, some Andrew Wyeths, and an array of early nineteenth-century European ceramics commemorating heroes of the American Revolution.

For relaxed wandering, the restored **Old Port Exchange** near the quayside, between Exchange and Pearl streets, can be quite entertaining, with all sorts of redbrick antiquarian shops, specialist book and music stores (particularly on Exchange Street), and other esoterica. Several companies operate **boat trips** from the nearby wharves: the *Palawan*, a vintage 58ft ocean racer, sails around the harbor and Casco Bay islands and lighthouses from DiMillo's Long Wharf, off Commercial Street (2hr trip; $20; ☎ 207/773-2163), while Bay View Cruises, 184 Commercial St, offers **seal-watching** tours (daily May–Oct; $12; ☎ 207/761-0496). Casco Bay Lines runs a twice-daily mail boat all year, and additional cruises in summer, to six of the innumerable **Calendar Islands** in Casco Bay, from its terminal at 56 Commercial St, at Franklin ($10–16; ☎ 207/774-7871, ⓦ www.cascobaylines.com). **Long**, **Peaks**, and **Cliff islands** all have accommodation or camping facilities. If you follow Portland's waterfront to the end of the peninsula, you'll come to the **Eastern Promenade**, a remarkably peaceful two-mile harbor trail that connects to East End Beach, below the headland. Above the promenade, at the top of Munjoy

Hill, at 138 Congress St, is the eight-sided, shingled 1807 **Portland Observatory** (June to mid–Oct daily 10am–5pm; $4; ☎207/774-5561), which affords an exhilarating view of the bay.

Eating

Not only is Portland rich in affordable **restaurants**, but most of its entertainment venues and bars, listed separately under "Nightlife and entertainment," below, serve food as well. The bountiful **Farmer's Market**, in Monument Square (open Wed, May–Nov) offers the perfect opportunity to sample local produce and culture.

Benkay 2 India St ☎207/773-5555. Great sushi and other Japanese dishes keep this place packed for lunch and dinner.

Boone's 6 Custom House Wharf ☎207/774-5725. Traditional waterfront restaurant in old wharf buildings, overlooking the fishing docks. Serves good lobster and grilled seafood in general.

Federal Spice 225 Federal St ☎207/774-6404. Eclectic fare influenced by South American, Southeast Asian, and Caribbean cuisine, all very hot and spicy.

Flatbread Company 72 Commercial St ☎207/772-8777. A popular spot (located right next to the ferry terminal) specializing in tasty

wood-fired pizzas, with homemade tomato sauce and all-natural ingredients.

Old Port Tavern 11 Moulton St ☎207/774-0444. Old-style tavern with good food and an Old World atmosphere.

Silly's 40 Washington Ave ☎207/772-0360. Burgers, pies, and particularly fine milkshakes in a space adorned with wacky Americana. Closed Mon.

Village Café 112 Newbury St ☎207/772-5320. No-nonsense, well-priced family dining, with well-cooked steak and seafood plus several Italian dishes on the menu.

Nightlife and entertainment

There are several options for the **performing arts** in chamber music, opera, dance, and touring theater, some as part of PCA Great Performances held at City Hall's Merrill Auditorium (tickets ☎207/842-0800, ⓦwww.pcagreatper-formances.org); larger productions are put on by the Portland Stage Company at the Portland Performing Arts Center, 25A Forest Ave (☎207/774-0465). Maine Arts, Inc. (☎207/772-9102, ⓦwww.mainearts.org) and Portland Parks and Recreation (☎207/874-8793, ⓦwww.ci.portland.me.us) both sponsor free outdoor noontime and evening **jazz** and **blues concerts** at various locations throughout the city during the summer. Maine's biggest gigs take place each summer roughly ten miles south of Portland at **Old Orchard Beach**. The free *Portland Phoenix* has weekly **listings** of local events.

Brian Boru Public House 57 Center St ☎207/780-1506. Traditional Irish pub serving Guinness, with a big, if typical, menu and plenty of benches.

Great Lost Bear 540 Forest Ave ☎207/772-0300. Fifteen state microbrews flow from 53 taps. Also serves good-value burgers, as well as spicy chicken wings and the like.

Gritty McDuff's 396 Fore St ☎207/772-2739. Portland's first brewpub, serving food and their own Portland Head Pale Ale and Black Fly Stout at long wooden benches. There's sometimes folk music, and the friendly (if a little self-consciously British) atmosphere gets rowdy on Saturday night.

Three Dollar Dewey's 241 Commercial St ☎207/772-3310. Raucous beer hall, with a wide selection of draft beers and good food.

North from Portland: the mid-coast

The coastal towns immediately north of Portland are no less commercialized than those to the south; **Freeport**, for example, is one long shopping mall (albeit a good one). However, soon after **Brunswick**, I-95 veers inland toward Augusta, and US-1 is left to run on alone parallel to the ocean. From here, things become much less frenetic, and prices a whole lot lower; even on the main road you'll find pleasant communities such as **Bath** and **Belfast**, while the many headlands can be even more peaceful.

Freeport

Much of the current prosperity of **FREEPORT**, fifteen miles north of Portland, rests on the invention by Leon L. Bean, in 1912, of a particularly ugly rubber-soled fishing boot. That original boot is still selling, and **L.L. Bean** has grown into a successful mail-order business with an enormous clothing store on Main Street that never closes. Originally, this was so pre-dawn hunting expeditions could stock up; all the relevant equipment is available for rent or sale, and the store runs regular workshops to teach back-country lore. However, with the outdoor look in vogue, L.L. Bean is now more of a fashion emporium. Freeport has expanded to welcome its 2.5 million annual customers a year with a mile-long strip of top-name **factory outlets** along US-1, most of which do give genuine reductions on usual shop prices.

Freeport is not an ideal place to stay – everything falls quiet once the shoppers have gone home – but if you need **accommodation**, the *Harraseeket Inn* at 162 Main St (☎207/865-9377 or 1-800/342-6423, ⓦwww.harraseeketinn.com; ❻) is a wonderful clapboard B&B inn with some eighty rooms. The *Freeport Inn & Café*, 31 Hwy-1 S (☎207/865-3106 or 1-800/998-2583, ⓦwww.freeportinn .com; ❹), provides good-value rooms and no-frills food.

For a complete change of pace, head a mile south of Freeport to the sea, where the *Harraseeket Lunch & Lobster Co* (☎207/865-3535), extending on its wooden jetty into the peaceful bay, makes a great outdoor lunch spot. The very green promontory visible just across the water is **Wolfe's Neck Woods State Park**. In summer, for $1.50, you can follow hiking and nature trails along the unspoiled fringes of the headland (daily 9am–6pm; ☎207/865-4465).

Brunswick

Only a few miles north from Freeport is **BRUNSWICK**, home since 1794 to the private Bowdoin College, which lists President Franklin Pierce and author Nathaniel Hawthorne among its alumni. Free tours of the college (Mon–Sat; call ☎207/725-3100 for schedule) take in the intriguing **Peary-MacMillan Arctic Museum** (Tues–Sat 10am–5pm, Sun 2–5pm; free; ☎207/725-3416). Experts generally agree that former student Admiral Robert Peary was the first man to reach the North Pole in 1909 (decades earlier, others claimed the title, and some researchers first believed Peary was up to sixty miles off). The admiral's assembled equipment and notebooks are a powerful testament to arctic exploration, and to his own perseverance.

It was while her husband Calvin was teaching here in the early 1850s that Harriet Beecher Stowe wrote *Uncle Tom's Cabin*, a book whose portrait of slavery had such an impact that Lincoln is said to have greeted her with the words "so this is the little lady that made this big war." The rambling old **Harriet Beecher Stowe House** at 63 Federal St, which used to be an inn, is now privately owned, but you can stay at the friendly *Traveler's Inn*, 130 Pleasant St/US-1 (☎207/729-3364 or 1-800/457-3364; ❸). The *Great Impasta* at 42 Maine St (☎207/729-5858) serves excellent, well-priced Italian **food**; the *Broadway Deli*, 142 Maine St (closed Tuesdays in winter; ☎207/729-7781), does great breakfasts; and *Bohemian*, 111 Maine St (☎207/725-9095), is a pleasant sidewalk **café** with good coffee.

The ideal time to visit Brunswick is Labor Day Weekend (first weekend in Sept), when the town hosts its **Bluegrass Festival** (☎207/725-6009) a little further on at Thomas Point Beach, reached by following Hwy-24 from Cook's Corner. The festival, among the best of its kind, attracts some of the biggest bluegrass names from the US and abroad. On the same road, **Orrs Island** has a well-equipped oceanfront **campground** (☎207/833-5595; $21 per day for two adults).

Bath

Eight miles on, the small town of **BATH** has an exceptionally long history of **shipbuilding**: the first vessel to be constructed and launched here was the *Virginia* in 1607, by Sir George Popham's short-lived colony. **Bath Iron Works**, founded in 1833, attracted job-seeking Irishmen in such numbers as to provoke a mob of anti-immigrant "**Know-Nothings**" to burn down the local Catholic church in July 1854. The works continue to produce ships – during World War II, more destroyers were built here than in all Japan – and only admit visitors for special occasions such as ceremonial launchings. However, at the **Maine Maritime Museum**, 243 Washington St, next to the Iron Works two miles south of the town center (daily 9.30am–5pm; $9.50; ☎207/443-1316), you can tour a functioning shipyard where apprentices learn to build wooden schooners using traditional techniques.

As you head up the coast, **accommodation** starts to be better value. The *Inn at Bath*, 969 Washington St (☎207/443-4294 or 1-800/423-0964, ⓦwww .innatbath.com; ❻), is a wonderful B&B with beautiful gardens and all the amenities. For a more rural experience, try the *Fairhaven Inn* on North Bath Road (☎207/443-4391 or 1-888/443-4391; ❹), which has shared and private bathrooms, serves a fine full breakfast, and offers hiking and cross-country skiing in season.

Places to eat include *Kristina's*, 160 Centre St (☎207/442-8577), specializing in inventive American dishes, as well as great breads and desserts; and *Beale Street Barbecue & Grill*, at 215 Water St (☎207/442-9514), offering slow-smoked chicken, pulled pork, and ribs, to stay or to go. Be warned, however, that everything in Bath closes very early in the evenings.

Boothbay Harbor

BOOTHBAY HARBOR, at the southern tip of Hwy-27, twelve miles south from US-1, is one of Maine's most crowded resorts. The town lays on boat trips of all kinds, including daily whale-watching excursions courtesy of Boothbay Whale Watch ($28, children $15; ☎207/633-3500 or 1-888/WHALE-ME) that leave from Pier 6. There's no reason to stay overnight here, but if you do pass by, the *Lobstermen's Co-op* at 99 Atlantic Ave (☎207/633-4900), a working lobster pound, dishes up ultrafresh lobsters at low prices, as well as a range of sandwiches. *Fisherman's Wharf Inn* at Pier 6, 22 Commercial St, serves good seafood in a more formal setting, and also has waterfront rooms (☎207/633-5090 or 1-800/628-6872, ⓦwww.fishermanswharfinn.com; ❻). *Moody's Diner*, back on Hwy-1 E, in Waldoboro (☎207/832-7785), is a longstanding haunt of police and truckers; the place just oozes nostalgia.

Rockland and Monhegan Island

ROCKLAND, where US-1 reaches Penobscot Bay, is the world's largest distributor of **lobsters**, and holds the annual Maine Lobster Festival the first weekend of August (for more info call ☎1-800/LOB-CLAW, ⓦwww .mainelobsterfestival.com). The town's cultural centerpiece is the outstanding **Farnsworth Museum**, 352 Main St (June to mid-Oct daily 9am–5pm; rest of year Tues–Sat 10am–5pm, Sun 1–5pm; $9; ☎207/596-6457, ⓦwww .farnsworthmuseum.org). The impressive collection spans two centuries of

American art, much of it Maine-related, and spreads over several buildings, including the **Wyeth Center**, a beautiful gallery space in a converted old church that holds two floors' worth of works by Jamie, Andrew, and N.C. Wyeth.

For **dining**, one of the best of the town's traditional lobster pounds is *Miller's* (T207/594-7406), on the shore of Wheeler's Bay in an isolated cove at Spruce Head on Hwy-73, open from 10am until 7pm in season, for succulent lobsters and steamers. The *Brown Bag* bakery, 606 Main St (T207/596-6372), has low-fat breads and lunches. The best food in town can be had at funky and perennially crowded *Café Miranda*, tucked away at 15 Oak St, just off Main Street (T207/594-2034), with an array of moderately priced international entrees. The *White Gates*, four miles north on US-1 (T207/594-4625; ❸), is the cleanest budget **motel** in the area.

South of Rockland, the pretty **St George Peninsula**, in particular the village of Tenants Harbor, inspired writer Sarah Orne Jewett's classic Maine novel *Country of the Pointed Firs*. At the tip of the peninsula, boats leave from the hamlet of Port Clyde for tiny **Monhegan Island**, eleven miles off the coast and with a year-round population of less than a hundred. The island makes a great day-trip away from the tourist bustle of the mainland; you can get there via the *Laura B* (May–Oct daily; Nov–April Mon, Wed & Fri; three sailings a day in summer, fewer at other times; $27 round trip; T207/372-8848, Wwww.monheganboat .com).

On this rocky outcrop, **lobsters** are the main business, though the stunning cliffs and isolated coves have long attracted artists, as well – including Edward Hopper. Fifteen miles of hiking trails twist through the wilderness and past a magnificent 1824 lighthouse. **Accommodation** – such as the *Island Inn* (T207/596-0371, Wwww.islandinnmonhegan.com; ❻; May to mid-Oct) – is generally pricey; you may want to try the simple comfort of *The Monhegan House* (T207/594-7983 or 1-800/599-7983, Wwww.monheganhouse.com; ❹; May–Oct).

Camden and Rockport

The adjacent communities of **CAMDEN** and **ROCKPORT** split into two separate towns in 1891, in a dispute over who should pay for a new bridge over the Goose River between them. Rockport was at that time a major lime producer, but a fire at the kilns in 1907 not only put an end to that business but also destroyed the ice-houses that were the town's other main source of income. Now it's a quiet working port, among the prettiest on the Maine coast, home to numerous lobster boats, pleasure cruisers, and little else; clearly, Camden has won the competition for tourists. The one essential stop in the area is **Camden Hills State Park**, two miles north of Camden ($2), where you can hike or drive up to a tower that affords one of the best views of the Maine coastline; on a clear day it's possible to see as far as Acadia National Park.

Camden and Rockport specialize in organizing sailing expeditions of up to six days in the large schooners known as **windjammers**. Expeditions sail from late May into mid-October. Vessels include the *Appledore* (T207/236-8353), which does two-hour cruises for $20 from Camden. Contact the Maine Windjammer Association (T207/807-9463) for information and schedules for longer three- to six-day trips out of the area. Maine Sport Outfitters in Rockport (T1-800/722-0826, Wwww.mainesport.com) rents **kayaks** and **bikes**. Camden's **information** office is at the Public Landing (T207/236-4404 or 1-800/223-5459, Wwww.visitcamden.com).

The classy **place to stay** in town is the *Whitehall Inn*, 400 yards north of the center at 52 High St (☎207/236-3391 or 1-800/789-6565, Ⓦwww.whitehall-inn.com; ❼), which provides great evening meals with their lodging. *Castleview by the Sea*, 59 High St (☎1-800/272-8439, Ⓦwww.castleviewinn.com; ❼), is the only oceanside B&B in town, with the attendant views as well as great breakfasts. The nearby *Maine Stay*, 22 High St (☎207/236-9636; ❻), is a cozy 1813 white-clapboard inn, and the *Snow Hill Lodge*, north on Hwy-1 near Lincolnville Beach (☎207/236-3452 or 1-800/476-4775; ❸), ranks as a good budget option.

Among busy **eating** and **drinking** spots in Camden are *Quarterdeck*, 21 Bay View St (☎207/236-3272), good for chops and steaks, and the nearby *Waterfront*, 40 Bay View St (☎207/236-3747), for seafood served in a casual setting and a great harbor location. *Gilbert's Publick House* on Sharp's Wharf (☎207/236-4320) has pool tables and microbrews on tap, while the *Sea Dog Brewing Company*, 43 Mechanic St (☎207/236-6863), is the town's popular brewpub.

Belfast

Homey **BELFAST** feels like the most lived-in and liveable of the towns along the Maine coast. Here, eighteen miles from Camden, the shipbuilding boom is long since over (and the chicken-processing plant that regularly turned the bay blood-red has also gone), and the town has declared the waterfront a historic district, sparing it from over-commercialization and condo development. As you stroll around, look out for the old-fashioned Greyhound and Western Union office (complete with jukebox) and any number of whitewashed Greek Revival houses. Belfast was a lively center in the 1960s, a fact still reflected in its stores, community theater groups, and festivals. Unfortunately, except for its several eating establishments and one cinema, most businesses close early in the evening.

The convivial **information office**, at the foot of Main Street by the bay (☎207/338-5900, Ⓦwww.belfastmaine.org), is next to the old **railroad station** used by the Belfast and Moosehead Lake Railroad (☎207/948-5500 or 1-800/392-5500, Ⓦwww.belfastrailroad.com). Their excursions ($20) take place in reconditioned Pullman cars run from here up the lush banks of the Passagassawakeag River, along tracks laid in 1870 to connect logging operations with the sea – though whatever impression you might get from their advertisements, the trains are pulled by diesel, not steam. En route to the villages of Brooks and Burnham Junction, you pass through thick forests, at their most colorful in the fall. The same company offers **cruises** on an old-style paddleboat in Penobscot Bay (combination rail-cruise ticket available).

For **accommodation**, try the *Alden House*, 63 Church St (☎207/338-2151 or 1-877/337-8151, Ⓦwww.thealdenhouse.com; ❺), a beautiful 1840 Greek Revival house run as a B&B, or the *Londonderry Inn*, 133 Belmont Ave (☎207/338-2763 or 1-877/529-9566, Ⓦwww.londonderry-inn.com; ❺), an old farmhouse that serves huge breakfasts. Along Hwy-1 across the Passagassawakeag River in East Belfast are several inexpensive motels, including the *Gull*, 196 Searsport Ave (☎207/338-4030; ❹), and the *Seascape Motel*, 202 Searsport Ave (☎207/338-2130; ❹). There's an oceanfront **campground**, *Searsport Shores Camping Resort*, at 209 W Main St, in Searsport (☎207/548-6059; $27–32 per tentsite).

As for **eating**, *Weathervane Seafood*, right beside the rail terminal (☎207/338-1774), has tables outside on the wooden jetty, where you can chow down on your freshly-caught dinner; across the bay, *Young's Lobster Pound* (☎207/338-

1160) serves $11 fresh-boiled lobster dinners, among the best in the state, along with sunset views. Historic *Darby's Restaurant*, at 105 High St (☎207/338-2339), serves tasty, inventive lunches and dinners to a congenial mix of locals and visitors, while the *Gothic*, 4 Main St (☎207/338-9901), is a cozy little spot for **coffee**, ice cream, and pastries.

Mount Desert Island

Considering that five million visitors come to **MOUNT DESERT ISLAND** each year; that it contains most of New England's only national park; and that it boasts not only a genuine fjord but also the highest headland on the entire Atlantic coast north of Rio de Janeiro, it is an astonishingly small place, measuring just sixteen miles by thirteen. It is, of course, simply one among innumerable rugged granite islands along the Maine coast; the reason to come here is that it is the most accessible, linked to the mainland by bridge since 1836, and has the best facilities.

The island was named *Monts Deserts* (bare mountains) by Samuel de Champlain in 1604 and fought over by the French and English for the rest of the century. Although all existing settlements date from long after the final defeat of the French, the name remains, still pronounced in French (more like *dessert*, actually).

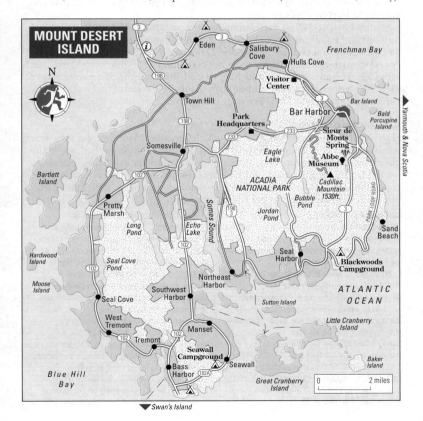

The social center, **Bar Harbor**, has accommodation and restaurants to suit all pocketbooks, while you'll find lower-key communities all over the island. **Acadia National Park**, which covers much of the island, offers active travelers with plenty of outdoor opportunities, including camping, cycling, canoeing, kayaking, and bird-watching.

Getting there and getting around

If you're **driving**, Mount Desert is easy enough to get to, traveling along Hwy-3 off US-1. In high summer, though, roads on the island get congested – the horse-drawn tours don't help – and the 55 miles from Belfast seem much longer.

Public transportation to Mount Desert is minimal. Greyhound buses run to Bar Harbor from Bangor (see p.299) from mid-June through August. Concord Trailways has a seasonal shuttle between Bar Harbor and the Bangor airport, with connecting service to Boston's Logan airport – reservations are required (☎207/942-8686 or 1-888/741-8686, ⓦwww.concordtrailways.com/bar_harbor.htm). West Coastal Connections (☎207/546-2823 or 1-800/596-2823) goes as far as Ellsworth and Bar Harbor, as does Downeast Transportation (Mon, Wed & Fri; ☎207/667-5796), which also runs buses across the island from Bar Harbor to Southwest Harbor (Mon & Thurs) and Northeast Harbor (Tues & Wed).

Nearby Hancock City/Bar Harbor Airport (☎207/667-7432) has a limited service run by Colgan Air (☎1-800/272-5488); Bangor International Airport, 45 miles away, is served by Northwest, Delta, and Continental. The *Cat* **high-speed catamaran** takes under three hours to link Bar Harbor with Yarmouth, Nova Scotia (July–Sept $55; mid-May to mid-June and the first two weeks of Oct $45; ferries leave Bar Harbor daily 8am). For reservations, contact Bay Ferries (☎1-888/249-7245, ⓦwww.catferry.com).

Accommodation

Hwy-3 into and out of Bar Harbor (which becomes Main Street on the way south) is lined with budget **motels**, which do little to improve the look of the place but satisfy an enormous demand for accommodation. Many places are open May to October only, and rates increase drastically in July and August; anywhere offering sea views will cost a whole lot more, as well. The quieter places on the island tend to get booked up early.

Bar Harbor Inn Newport Drive, Bar Harbor ☎207/288-3351 or 1-800/248-3351, ⓦwww.barharborinn.com. Bar none, the nicest place to stay, with spacious rooms looking out over the bay from the heart of town. ➏

Cadillac Motor Inn 336 Main St, Bar Harbor ☎207/288-3831 or 1-888/207-2593, ⓦwww.cadillacmotorinn.com. A quiet inn surrounded by woods near the center of town. Offers standard motel-type rooms and larger apartments with fireplaces and big kitchens. ➍

Emery's Cottages on the Shore Sand Point Rd, five miles north of Bar Harbor ☎207/288-3432 or 1-888/240-3432, ⓦwww.emeryscottages.com. Sweet little cottages with kitchenettes on a private pebble beach just off Hwy-3. Weekly stays in high season cost $500 and up. ➍

HI-Bar Harbor 321 Main St, Bar Harbor ☎207/288-5587. Newly relocated, this hostel is scheduled to reopen in May of 2004. One private room with bath (➍), and dorm beds $16–25. ➊

Maine Street Motel 315 Main St, Bar Harbor ☎207/288-3188 or 1-800/333-3188, ⓦwww.mainestreetmotel.com. Simple motel with clean, good-sized rooms in a convenient location. Children under 15 stay free. ➎

Moorings Inn Shore Rd, Southwest Harbor ☎207/244-5523 or 1-800/596-5523, ⓦwww.mooringsinn.com. Lovely 200-year-old inn, two miles east of Southwest Harbor, with a private beach and boats for rent next door. ➎

YWCA 36 Mount Desert St, Bar Harbor ☎207/288-5008. Very central, women-only accommodation, open sporadically May through September – call ahead. Beds in shared rooms start at $30.

Bar Harbor

The town of **BAR HARBOR** began life as an exclusive resort, summer home to the Vanderbilts and the Astors; the great fire of October 1947 that destroyed their opulent "cottages" ended all that. It's now firmly geared towards tourists, though it's by no means downmarket. There's not all that much to do in town, even in high summer. However, the ambiance is sufficient enough that it takes a while to realize that once you've strolled around the village green, and walked past the headland of the *Bar Harbor Inn* for views of the ocean and Frenchman Bay, you've seen most of what the town has to offer.

Bar Harbor's main **tourist information** office is at the ferry terminal (☎207/288-5103). In summer, there's another in the basement of the Municipal Building on Cottage Street. Both offices offer many free and comprehensive maps of the area. In high season, up to twenty-one different **sea trips** set off each day, ranging from deep-sea fishing to cocktail cruises. Among the most popular are the *Friendship V* and *Acadian* **whale-watching** expeditions, departing from Harbor Place, next to the Town Pier (June–Oct at least twice daily; ☎207/288-2386, ⊚www.whalesrus.com), and the two-hour cruises on the impressive **four-masted schooner** *Margaret Todd* from the *Bar Harbor Inn* (daily June–Oct; $29.50; ☎207/288-4585, ⊚www.downeastwindjammer.com).

In its heydey, one of the town sights was the "Indian village," a summer encampment where Native Americans came to sell goods to tourists; it was cleared away in the 1930s to make room for a new ballpark. Now the only signs of the island's first inhabitants are the artifacts at the **Robert Abbe Museum**, which were found at Fernald Point near Southwest Harbor and attributed to a nomadic people who made birch-bark canoes. What became of these people is summed up by a classic understatement on a map contrasting the tribal areas of 1600 with the modern reservations: "The native population did not view territorial boundaries as we do today." The museum is a couple of miles south of Bar Harbor – not a particularly pleasant walk – at Sieur de Monts Spring, just off the Park Loop Road (daily: June & Sept to mid-Oct 10am–4pm; July & Aug 9am–5pm; $2). A new branch of the Abbe is located downtown at 26 Mount Desert St (June to mid-Oct Sun–Wed 10am–5pm, Thurs–Sat 10am–9pm; mid-Oct to May Thurs–Sun 10am–5pm; $4.50; ☎207/288-3519).

Acadia National Park

Not all of **ACADIA NATIONAL PARK** is on Mount Desert Island – there are sections on the Isle au Haut to the west, reached by ferry from Stonington, and on the Schoodic Peninsula to the east – but there's all you could want here in terms of mountains and lakes for secluded rambling, and **wildlife** such as seals, beavers, puffins, and bald eagles. The two main geographical features are the narrow fjord of **Somes Sound**, which almost splits the island in two, and **Cadillac Mountain**, only 1530ft high, but offering tremendous ocean views. The summit, the first place in the United States to see the sun rise each morning, can be reached either by a moderately strenuous climb – more than you'd want to do before breakfast – or by a very leisurely drive, winding up a low-gradient road.

Open all year, the park has the Hulls Cove **visitor center** near the entrance to the Loop Road north of Bar Harbor (mid-April to Oct daily 8am–4.30pm, open until 6pm July & Aug; ☎207/288-3338), and its headquarters at Eagle Lake (daily 8am–4.30pm; same number as above). The entrance fee is $10 per vehicle or $5 per motorcycle or bike, and is good for seven days. There are two official **campgrounds**: *Blackwoods*, five miles south of Bar Harbor, off Rte-3 (reserve through the National Park Service at ☎1–800/365-2267 or Ⓦreservations.nps.gov; $20 per tentsite), and *Seawall* on Hwy–102A, four miles south of Southwest Harbor (☎207/244-3600; tentsites $14–20). Both are in woods, near the ocean, and have full facilities in summer; only *Blackwoods* is open in winter, with minimal facilities.

Once here, the free Island Explorer (Ⓦwww.exploreacadia.com) **shuttle buses** travel through Acadia to Bar Harbor, and even out to the airport. However, the most enjoyable way to explore is to ride a rented **bicycle** around the fifty miles of gravel-surfaced "**carriage roads**," built by John D. Rockefeller to protest the 1917 vote allowing "infernal combustion engines" onto the island. Three Bar Harbor companies rent mountain bikes between 8am and 6pm, at less than $20 a day: Bar Harbor Bicycle Shop, at 141 Cottage St, on the edge of town (☎207/288-3886), Acadia Bike & Canoe, across from the post office at 48 Cottage St (☎207/288-9605 or 1-800/526-8615), and Southwest Cycle, on Main Street, in Southwest Harbor (☎207/244-5856). All outlets provide excellent **maps**. Be sure to carry water, as there are very few refreshment stops inside the park. You can take a 4hr guided **kayak tour** ($45) from mid-May to mid-October with National Park Sea Kayak Tours, 39 Cottage St (☎1-800/347-0940, Ⓦwww.acadiakayak.com). Another popular tour operator, Coastal Kayaking Tours (Ⓦwww.acadiafun.com), has the same location and phone numbers as Acadia Bike.

The one and only sizeable beach, five miles south of Bar Harbor, is a stunner: called simply **Sand Beach**, it's a gorgeous strand bounded by twin headlands, with restrooms, a parking lot, and a few short hiking trails. The water, sadly, is usually arctic.

Eating, drinking, and nightlife

Mount Desert's most memorable **eating** experiences are to be found in the many **lobster pounds** all over the island. For nightlife (such as it is), Bar Harbor is where the people are. Cottage Street is a much more promising area to look for food and evening atmosphere than the surprisingly subdued waterfront. The Art Deco Criterion cinema at 35 Cottage St (☎207/288-3441), which shows current favorites, looks exactly as it did when built in 1932.

The Alternative Market 16 Mount Desert St, Bar Harbor ☎207/288-8225. Bag lunches, big sandwiches, soups, smoothies, and fresh-squeezed juices.
Beal's Lobster Pier Clark Point Rd, Southwest Harbor ☎207/244-3202. Fresh seafood for under $10, on a rickety wooden pier crammed full of lobsters. Closed Nov–April.
Eat a Pita 326 Main St, Southwest Harbor ☎207/244-4344. A great casual, cozy, and affordable spot for delicious, healthy gourmet food (pasta, salads, pita sandwiches, seafood), candlelit tables, and friendly service. Lunch and dinner served. Credit cards not accepted.
Galyn's 17 Main St, Bar Harbor ☎207/288-9706. Delicious fish and prime rib in an unpretentious setting.
Gringo's 30 Rodick St, Bar Harbor ☎207/288-BEAN. A fun, cheap place to get burritos and smoothies.

Jordan Pond House Park Loop Rd ☎207/276-3316. Worthy concession restaurant in the heart of Acadia National Park. Serves light meals, ice cream, and popovers (light, puffy egg muffins). Afternoon tea served in the beautiful lakeside garden.
Lompoc Café & Brewpub 36 Rodick St, Bar Harbor ☎207/288-9392. A healthy Middle Eastern menu for $14–20, with local Thunder Hole Ale and other Atlantic Brewing Company beers on draft. Live music every night. Open 11.30am–1am.
Morning Glory Bakery 39 Rodick St, Bar Harbor ☎207/288-3041. Fresh-baked breads, coffee, and pastries served from a purple-trimmed cottage.
Rupununi 119 Main St, Bar Harbor ☎207/288-2886. Late-night pub grub – the burgers are best; the bar stays open until 1am.
Seafood Ketch McMullen Ave, Bass Harbor ☎207/244-7463. Great, super-fresh fish and seafood, with views over Bass Harbor. Reservations recommended.

Thirsty Whale 40 Cottage St, Bar Harbor ☎207/288-9335. As rowdy as Bar Harbor gets, with live music every night of the week in season; good pub grub, too.
West Street Café 76 West St, Bar Harbor ☎207/288-5242. Family restaurant with basic

seafood at very reasonable prices.
XYZ Restaurant & Gallery across from Manset Town Dock, Shore Rd, Manset ☎207/244-5221. Ocean views from every table, seafood from $7, and Mexican specialties. Open mid-May to mid-Oct.

Downeast Maine: the coast to Canada

Looking at a map of the United States, you'd never dream that Canada stretches for five hundred miles beyond Maine to the east. In fact, few travelers venture far beyond Acadia National Park, which is one reason why what's known as **Downeast Maine** remains so little touched by change. Another reason is that this is bleak and windswept country, where high cliffs are battered by harsh seas. In summer, though, the weather is no worse than in the rest of Maine, and the coastal drive can be exhilarating. At those points where the road runs next to the sea, the overwhelming power of the ocean is undeniable, sweeping in as it does to create the highest tides in the nation.

A short way northeast of Acadia, a loop road leads from US-1 to the rocky outcrop of **Schoodic Point**, which offers good bird-watching, great views, and a splendid sense of solitude. Tourism is not big business in these parts, but each village has one or two B&Bs and well-priced restaurants. **Machias**, almost 40 miles further once you rejoin US-1 at Gouldsboro, is quite picturesque, with a little waterfall right in the middle of town. The town was the unlikely scene of the first naval battle of the Revolutionary War, in 1775: the townsfolk commandeered the British schooner *Margaretta* and proceeded to terrorize all passing British shipping, an attack they planned in the still-standing gambrel-roofed **Burnham Tavern** on Rte-192, just off US-1 (mid-June to early Sept Mon–Fri 9am–5pm; $2.50; ☎207/255-4432). For good-value **meals**, there's *Helen's Restaurant*, 28 E Main St/Rte-1 (☎207/255-8423), a diner-type place that's part of the *Machias Motor Inn* (☎207/255-4861; ❸), which in turn has sun decks and superb views. Perhaps the best place to eat in town is the *Artist's Café*, 3 Hill St (☎207/255-8900), with its moderately priced and frequently changing menu; chicken parmesan and lobster linguini are typical offerings.

West Quoddy Head and around

Continuing east, and abandoning US-1 after 17 miles to continue on Hwy-189 for 15 miles, you come to the prominently striped **lighthouse** at **West Quoddy Head**, the easternmost point of the US, where an international bridge crosses to Campobello Island in Canada. The nearby settlement of **Bailey's Mistake** is named for a sea captain who beached his lumber vessel in thick fog in 1830, and chose to settle here with his crew, building homes with their erstwhile cargo, rather than face the wrath of the ship's owners back in Boston. Just beyond the turnoff for Quoddy Head, tiny **Lubec** was once home to more than twenty sardine-packing plants. Though only one remains (McCurdy's Fish Company on Water Street), it's enough to evoke visions of more prosperous times. Lubec is the gateway to **Campobello Island**, in New Brunswick, Canada, where President Franklin D. Roosevelt summered from 1909 to 1921, and returned to sporadically during his time in office. His barn-like house (mid-May to mid-Oct daily 9am–5pm; free) is now open to the public, and it's furnished just as the Roosevelts left it. The rest of **Roosevelt Campobello International Park** (daily sunrise–sunset; free; ❿ www.fdr.net), located on Canadian soil but established jointly with the United States, is good for a couple of hours of wandering – the coastal trails and the drive out to **Liberty Point** are worth the effort.

The border between the United States and Canada weaves through the center of Passamaquoddy Bay; the towns to either side get on so well that they refused to fight against each other in the War of 1812, and promote themselves jointly to tourists as the **Quoddy Loop** (Ⓦwww.quoddyloop.com). It's perfectly feasible to take a "two-nation vacation," but each passage through customs and immigration between **Calais** (pronounced "callous") in the States (fifty miles north of Lubec) and **St Stephen** in Canada does take a little while – and be aware, also, that the towns are in different time zones. In Calais, the *Wickachee*, on Main Street (Ⓣ207/454-3400), serves big plates of seafood and steak. *Heslin's Motel and Dining Room*, on US-1 (Ⓣ207/454-3762; May–Oct), has cabins (❸), cottages (❺), and motel rooms (❹); their menu features fish chowders, steaks, and home-baked bread.

Inland and western Maine

The vast expanses of the **Maine interior**, stretching up into the cold far north, consist mostly of evergreen forests of pine, spruce, and fir, interspersed with the white birches and maples responsible for the spectacular fall colors. Only in the remote north is much of it genuine wilderness, however; elsewhere, what you see is more likely to be woodlands cultivated by the timber companies.

Distances here are large. Once you get away from the two largest cities nearer the sea – **Augusta**, the state capital, and **Bangor** – it's roughly two hundred miles by road to the northern border at **Fort Kent**, while to drive between the two most likely inland bases, **Greenville** and **Rangeley** (where exiled psychologist Wilhelm Reich lived and is buried), takes three hours or more. Driving (there's no public transportation) through this mountainous scenery can be a great pleasure, but you do need to know where you're going. There are few places to stay, and beyond Bangor many roads are tolled access routes belonging to the lumber companies: gravel-surfaced, vulnerable to bad weather, and in any case often not heading anywhere in particular.

If you have the time, this is great territory in which to **hike** – the **Appalachian Trail** starts its 2000-mile course down to Georgia at the top of Mount Katahdin – or **raft** on the **Allagash Wilderness Waterway**. Especially around **Baxter State Park**, the forests are home to deer, beaver, a few bears, some recently introduced caribou – and plenty of **moose**. These endearingly gawky creatures (they look like badly drawn horses, and are virtually blind), tend to be seen at early morning or dusk; you may spot them feeding in shallow water. They do, however, cause major havoc on the roads, particularly at night, and each year significant numbers of drivers (and moose) are killed in collisions.

Augusta

The capital of Maine since 1832, **AUGUSTA** is much quieter and less visited now than it was a hundred years ago. The lumber industry here really took off after the technique of making paper from wood was rediscovered in 1844. Augusta also had a lucrative sideline: each winter, hundreds of thousands of tons of **ice**, cut from the Kennebec River, were shipped out, as far south as the Caribbean, in a trade now all but forgotten by history. There are informative displays on Maine's landscape and industrial past at the lively **Maine State**

Museum, a short way south of the capitol on State Street (Tues–Fri 9am–5pm, Sat 10am–4pm; $2; ☎207/287-2301).

If you plan to stay in Augusta, the best-value **accommodation** is the *Best Inn*, at 65 Whitten Rd, at the Maine Turnpike's Augusta–Winthrop exit (☎207/622-3776 or 1-800/237-8466, ⓦwww.bestinnmaine.com; ❹). For **food**, the lobster rolls at *Burnsie's Homestyle Sandwiches*, on Hichborn St, next to the capitol (☎207/622-6425), are favorites with the politicians, while *Curly's*, 750 Main St (☎207/933-2745), does good, moderately priced seafood.

Bangor

In its prime, **BANGOR**, 120 miles northeast of Portland, was the undisputed "Lumber Capital of the World." Every winter its raucous population of "River Tigers" went upstream to brand the felled logs, which they then maneuvered down the Penobscot as the thaw came in April, reaching Bangor in time to carouse the summer away in the grog shops. Bangor exported ice to the West Indies – and got rum in return. Those days were coming to an end when, in October 1882, Oscar Wilde addressed a large crowd at the new Opera House and spoke diplomatically of "such advancement . . . in so small a city."

Bangor today is not a place to spend much time, although its plentiful motels and the big Bangor Mall on Hogan Road north of town make it a good last stop before the interior. Its twin claims to fame are that it's the unlikely home of **Stephen King**, the horror fiction writer (Bett's Bookstore at 584 Hammond St ☎207/947-7052 stocks King limited editions and collectibles), and that it possesses what, at 31ft, may well be the largest statue of **Paul Bunyan** in the world – though it is easy to miss on the way into town.

From mid-May until the end of July there's **harness racing** at Bass Park on Main Street (☎207/947-6744), just behind the Bunyan statue; admission is $1, but the potential to lose your money gambling is unlimited. The same venue hosts the **Bangor State Fair**, in the last week of July and the first in August. A few miles north of Bangor, the Maine Center for the Arts (☎207/581-1755, ⓦwww.mainecenterforthearts.org), at the University of Maine in **Orono**, runs a series of big-name concerts each summer. Orono is named after the revered eighteenth-century Penobscot Native American Chief Joseph Orono, whom, it's rumoured, assisted George Washington during Revolutionary times.

Practicalities

Bangor is the last sizeable town along I-95, before the interstate finally veers from the coast and heads north up the Penobscot towards Canada. It's also the end of the line for Greyhound, whose three daily services from Boston and Portland terminate at 158 Main St (☎207/945-3000).

Accommodation possibilities include the *Main Street Inn*, opposite Paul Bunyan at 480 Main St (☎207/942-5282; ❸), the *Charles Inn*, right downtown at 20 Broad St on West Market Square (☎207/982-2820; ❺), and the *Holiday Inn* at 500 Main St (☎207/947-8651 or 1-800/799-8651; ❹). For the best breakfasts in Bangor, try *Bagel Central*, 33 Central St (☎207/947-1654), the state's only kosher deli, or load up on subs and salads at *Sweet's Market*, 26 Main St (☎207/947-5217). Other options include a handful of Indian and Pakistani places, and the massive Mexican *Pepino's* at 570 Stillwater Ave (☎207/947-1233). The *Whig and Courier*, 18 Broad St (☎207/947-4095), is a straightahead pub, with burgers, cheesesteaks, and a wide variety of beers on tap. Across the street, the *New Moon Café*, 21 Main St (☎207/990-2233), is a favorite hangout for Bangor's hip younger set, with snacks, coffee and espresso, and live music.

Baxter State Park and the far north

Driving through northern Maine can feel as though you're trespassing on the private fiefdoms of the logging companies; only **BAXTER STATE PARK** is public land. However, you're pretty much free to hike, camp, and explore anywhere you like, so long as you let people know what you're doing. The scenery is more or less the same everywhere – although to experience what Thoreau described in his book *Maine Woods*, you'll need to leave your car at some point and set off into the backwoods.

Five miles north of Brownsville Junction on Hwy-11, an inconspicuous left turn leads to the 1843 **Katahdin Iron Works** at Silver Lake (☎207/965-8135). It's remarkable how little remains of what one hundred years ago was a thriving industrial community: one solitary brick oven and the tower of the blast furnace, stark and forlorn at the end of a few miles of gravel track. In good summer weather it's possible to continue along the track across the hills to Greenville.

Further north (about 70 miles from Bangor), **MILLINOCKET** is a genuine company town, built on a wilderness site by the Great Northern Paper Company in 1899–1900. The town grew "like magic," and thus came to be known as the "magic city of the North." Ever since, the company has produced massive quantities of newsprint; in 1990, it was taken over by the Georgia Pacific Corporation.

Next to **Millinocket Lake**, ten miles northwest, the splendidly ramshackle old *Big Moose Inn* (☎207/723-8391, ⓦwww.bigmoosecabins.com; ❷) makes a great place to stay, with cabins and an inn, and a wide range of activities available. There's also an adjacent campground ($10 per person). A more standard place to stay is the clean *Katahdin Inn*, 740 Central St/Hwy-11 (☎207/723-4555 or 1-877/902-4555, ⓦwww.katahdininn.com; ❹), which provides a free continental breakfast. Unicorn Expeditions (☎1-800/UNICORN) conducts day **rafting** and **canoeing** expeditions, as well as "**moose safaris**" and snowmobile vacations and rentals, according to the season

Approaching the southern end of **Baxter State Park** itself, on a clear day the 5268ft peak of **Mount Katahdin** (or, "greatest mountain," in the language of the local Penobscot tribe) is visible from afar. All 200,000 acres of the enormous park was the single-handed creation of former Maine governor Percival P. Baxter, who, having failed to persuade the state to buy Katahdin and the land around it, bought all 200,000 acres, bit by bit, between the 1930s and 1960s and deeded it to the state on condition that it remain "forever wild."

The area's **chamber of commerce** resides in Millinocket at 1029 Central St (☎207/723-4443, ⓦwww.katahdinmaine.com); the **Baxter State Park Authority** is at 64 Balsam Drive (☎207/723-9616).

North to Canada

The northernmost tip of Maine is taken up by Aroostook County, which covers an area larger than several individual states. Although its main activity is the large-scale cultivation of potatoes, it is also the location of the **Allagash Wilderness Waterway**; this is where most of the **whitewater rafting** companies in this area actually carry out their expeditions.

Britain and the United States all but went to war over Aroostook in 1839; at **Fort Kent**, the northern terminus of US-1 (which runs all the way from Key West, Florida; see p.655), the main sight is the solid cedar **Fort Kent Blockhouse**, built to defend American integrity and looking like a pioneer throwback. *Doris' Café*, at Fort Kent Mills on Hwy-161, just off Hwy-11 toward Eagle Lake (☎207/834-6262), serves big breakfasts.

Greenville

GREENVILLE, at the southern end of Moosehead Lake, is another nine-teenth-century lumber town that now makes its living primarily from tourism. It's not exceptionally pretty or very large, but it is well positioned for exploring the Maine woods. In town, the main attraction is the restored **steamboat** *Katahdin*, which tours the lake (cruises Tues–Thurs, Sat & Sun July–Aug; Sat & Sun only in Sept; $21–37; ☎207/695-2716). Next to the dock resides the (nonprofit) Moosehead Marine Museum, which restored the boat.

The **Chamber of Commerce** on Main Street, near the T-junction at the lake (summer daily 10am–5pm; rest of year Thurs–Tues 10am–4pm; ☎207/695-2702, ⓦwww.mooseheadarea.com), has details on **accommodation**, including the *Kineo View Motor Lodge* (☎207/695-4470 or 1-800/659-VIEW, ⓦwww.kineoview.com; ❸), overlooking the lake from deep in the woods on the hill three miles above town; the *Chalet Moosehead*, Birch St (☎207/695-2950 or 1-800/290-3645, ⓦwww.mooseheadlodging.com; ❹), the only motel right on the lake; and the antiques-filled *Greenville Inn* on Norris Street (☎207/695-2206 or 1-888/695-6000, ⓦwww.greenvilleinn .com; ❼). Among local **rafting** companies, which charge $85–135 for a day in the water, is Wilderness Expeditions (☎1-800/825-WILD), associated with the *Birches Resort* in North Rockwood (☎207/534-2242), where you can stay in a lodge room (❸), a cabin (❻), or a yurt (❷).

Greenville is also the place people come hoping to see the **wild moose** (indigenous to the area) which the town has been quick to exploit; there is nary a business around here that doesn't somehow incorporate the animal into its name. For several weeks in June, there's even an annual celebration, creatively named MooseMainea (call ☎207/695-2702 for more information). The town is also the largest **seaplane** base in New England; contact Currier's Flying Service (☎207/695-2778) or Folsom's (☎207/695-2821).

Rangeley

RANGELEY is only just in Maine, a little way east of New Hampshire and an even shorter distance south of the border with Québec. Furthermore, as the café/bar *Doc Grant's* on Main Street (☎207/864-3449) makes a great show of telling you, it's equidistant (at 3107.5 miles) from the North Pole and the Equator. That doesn't mean it's on the main road to anywhere, although if you're avoiding the coast altogether you can get here direct from the northern side of the White Mountains (see p.267). Rangeley has always been a resort, served in 1900 by two train lines and several steamships (though now you have to get here on your own), with the main attraction then being the fishing in the spectacularly named Mooselookmeguntic Lake.

This small and very cozy one-street town, nestling amid a complex system of lakes and waterways, serves as a base for summer explorations, and in winter as the nearest town to the **ski** area at **Saddleback Mountain**. Rangeley also has one unlikely tourist attraction, about halfway along the north side of Rangeley Lake, a mile up a side track off Rte-16. The remote **Wilhelm Reich Museum** at **Orgonon** (July & Aug Wed–Sun 1–5pm; Sept Sun 1–5pm; $5; ☎207/864-3443) is where Wilhelm Reich eventually made his American home after fleeing Germany in 1933. An associate of Freud in Vienna, who wrote the acclaimed *Mass Psychology of Fascism*, Reich is best remembered for developing the orgone energy accumulator, which he claimed could create rain and dissipate nuclear radiation. Skeptical authorities focused on the rather unspecific way in which it was said to collect and harness human sexual energy. He is buried here, amid the neat lawns and darting hummingbirds, and his house remains a center for the study of his work.

Practicalities

The *Rangeley Inn* on Main Street (℡207/864-3341 or 1-800/MOMENTS, Ⓦwww.rangeleyinn.com; ❺) stands between Rangeley Lake and the smaller bird sanctuary of Haley Pond, so you can stay right in town and have a room that backs onto a scene of utter tranquility; there's also a gorgeous old wooden dining room. *North Country Inn B&B*, also on Main Street (℡207/864-2440 or 1-800/295-4968; ❺), is a good second choice. For **food**, try the *Red Onion*, 77 Main St (℡207/864-5022), which offers steaks, pizza, and some vegetarian options in a casual, friendly setting.

Twenty miles north of Rangeley, the peaceful *Grant's Kennebago Camps* beside Kennebago Lake (℡207/864-3608) arranges fishing, canoeing, and windsurfing, with accommodation in comfortable cabins, including all meals, costing around $135 per person per day; there are slightly lower weekly rates. A more accessible campground is *Cathedral Pines* ($15–20 per site; ℡207/246-3491), just north of **Stratton** on Eustis Road. At its entrance stands a memorial to Benedict Arnold's expedition to Québec in 1775, which passed this way, and to Colonel Timothy Bigelow, who climbed what is now Mount Bigelow in a "vain endeavor to see the city of Québec." Both lodgings are open mid-May through mid-October.

Rangeley Lakes' **Chamber of Commerce**, down by Lakeside Park (℡207/864-5364 or 1-800/MT-LAKES, Ⓦwww.rangeleymaine.com), has details of various activities, including snowmobiling and dawn moose-watching **canoeing** expeditions. One really fun thing to do is to take a **seaplane** trip with the Mountain Air Service (℡207/864-5307) – a fifteen-minute tour, flying low over vast forests and tiny lakes, costs only $25 per person. Boat cruises are also available, and various outfits along Main Street rent out canoes and mountain bikes.

Sugarloaf USA and Kingfield

The road east of Rangeley cuts through prime moose-watching territory – locals call Hwy-16 East "Moose Alley." After about fifty miles, in the Carrabassett Valley, looms the huge mountain of the **Sugarloaf USA** ski resort (℡1-800/THE-LOAF, Ⓦwww.sugarloaf.com). A brilliant place for skiers of all abilities, this condo-studded center would be a more popular destination if it wasn't for the fact that the nearest airport is a two-hour drive away in Portland. In summer, one of the most likely places to spot a gangly **moose** is behind the check-in building on the resort's approach road. Other summer activities include guided **mountain-bike tours** with the Sugarloaf Outdoor Center (℡207/237-6830) through their extensive trail system.

The best base for Sugarloaf is fifteen miles south in the tiny town of **KINGFIELD**. The gorgeous *Inn on Winter's Hill*, 33 Winter Hill St (℡207/265-5421 or 1-800/233-WNTR, Ⓦwww.wintershill.com; ❺), is a lovingly restored Georgian Revival house with big rooms, an outdoor pool, hot tub, a tennis court, and the excellent, though expensive, *Julia's* dining room (winter only). Down on the main street, the big white *Herbert Grand Hotel* (℡207/265-2000, Ⓦwww.herbertgrandhotel.com; ❹) has less attractive but functional rooms. For **food**, *Longfellows Restaurant*, on Main Street (℡207/265-4394), serves pasta, sandwiches, and chicken for $10–16; *Anni's Café*, next to the gas station, is an inexpensive place to get take-out Italian.

Kingfield was the birthplace of twins Francis and Freelan Stanley, who invented, among other things, a steam-powered car and the dry plate photographic process (which they sold to Kodak, amassing a fortune). The **Stanley Museum**, on School Street (May–Oct Tues–Sun 1–4pm; Nov–April Tues–Fri 1–4pm; $4; ☎207/265-2729), celebrates their story. Part of the main room is given over to their sister, Chansonetta, a remarkable photographer whose studies of c.1900 rural and urban workers have been widely published.

The Great Lakes

AL - ALABAMA	IN - INDIANA	MN - MINNESOTA	RI - RHODE ISLAND
AR - ARKANSAS	LA - LOUISIANA	MS - MISSISSIPPI	SC - SOUTH CAROLINA
CT - CONNECTICUT	MA - MASSACHUSETTS	NC - NORTH CAROLINA	VA - VIRGINIA
DE - DELAWARE	MD - MARYLAND	NH - NEW HAMPSHIRE	VT - VERMONT
FL - FLORIDA	ME - MAINE	NJ - NEW JERSEY	WI - WISCONSIN
IL - ILLINOIS	MI - MICHIGAN	PA - PENNSYLVANIA	WV - WEST VIRGINIA

CHAPTER 4 # Highlights

* **Rock and Roll Hall of Fame and Museum, Cleveland, OH** From rockabilly to Motown to punk – it's all here inside this striking museum. **See p.313**

* **The Henry Ford Museum, Detroit, MI** Home to such oddities as the car JFK was riding in when he was shot. **See p.336**

* **Ann Arbor, MI** A plethora of bookshops, sidewalk cafés, and cultural activities make this the quintessential college town. **See p.339**

* **Chicago architecture, IL** Superb examples of modern architecture make up the city's distinctive skyline. **See p.362**

* **Wrigley Field, Chicago, IL** Soak in the Old-World ambiance of this ivy-covered ballpark, with a cold beer and a hot dog. **See p.370**

* **The Mall of America, Bloomington, MN** The mall you'll never have to leave: hundreds of stores and an amusement park, plus bars and nightclubs. **See p.401**

* **Boundary Waters Canoe Area Wilderness, MN** Canoe, hike, or just marvel at more than one million acres of lakes, rivers, and forest. **See p.407**

The Great Lakes

Swept by tumultuous storms and traversed by fleets of oceangoing tankers, the interconnected **Great Lakes** form the largest body of fresh water in the world; Lake Superior alone is more than three hundred miles from east to west. Left untouched, the shores of these inland seas can rival any coastline: Superior and the northern reaches of Lake Michigan offer stunning rocky peninsulas, craggy cliffs, tree-covered islands, mammoth dunes, and deserted beaches. However, for lengthy stretches along Lake Erie, and the bottom lips of lakes Michigan and Huron, sluggish waters lap against large cities and the unused wharves of decaying ports.

To varying degrees, all the states that line the American side of the lakes – **Ohio**, **Michigan**, **Indiana**, **Illinois**, **Wisconsin**, and **Minnesota** – share this mixture of natural beauty and aging industry. Cities such as **Chicago** and **Detroit**, with all their good and bad points – Chicago in particular, with its magnificent architecture, museums, music, and restaurants, is an unmissable destination – should not be seen as characterizing the entire region. Within the first hundred miles or so of the lakeshores, especially in Wisconsin and Minnesota, tens of thousands of smaller lakes and tumbling streams are scattered through a luxuriant rural wilderness; beyond that, you are soon in the heart of the **Corn Belt**, where you can drive for hours and encounter nothing more than a succession of crossroads communities, grain silos, and giant barns. Garrison Keillor's wry stories about the fictional backwater town of Lake Wobegon (where "all the women are strong and all the men are beautiful"), set in Minnesota, carry more than a ring of truth.

Some history

The first foreigner to reach the Great Lakes, the French explorer Champlain, found the region in 1603 inhabited mostly by tribes of Huron, Iroquois, and Algonquin. France soon established a network of military forts, Jesuit missions, and fur-trading posts here, which entailed treating the native people as allies rather than subjects. Territorial disputes with their colonial rivals, however, culminated in the **French and Indian War** with Britain from 1754 to 1761. The victorious British felt under no constraints to deal equitably with the Native Americans, and things grew worse with large-scale American settlement after independence. The **Black Hawk War** of 1832 put a bloody end to traditional Native American life.

Settlers from the east were followed to Wisconsin and Minnesota by waves of **Scandinavians** and **Germans**, while the lower halves of Illinois and Indiana attracted **Southerners**, who attempted to maintain slavery here and resisted Union conscription during the Civil War. These areas often still have more in common with neighboring Kentucky and Tennessee than with the industrial cities of their own states.

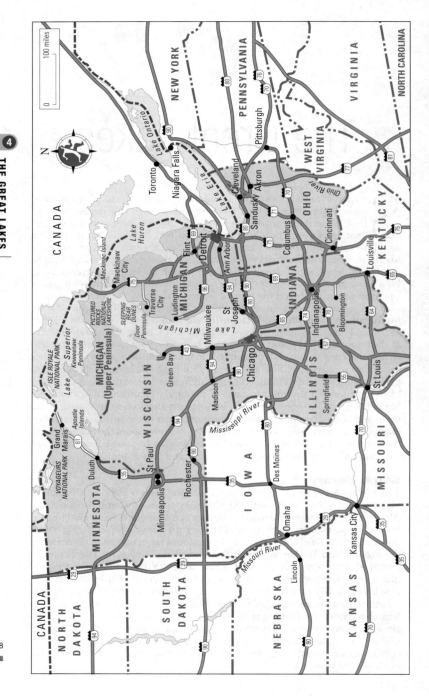

Great Lakes' climate

During the summer, breezes coming off the Great Lakes keep the **temperature** down to a comfortable average of 70°F, though heat waves can push temperatures over 100°F. Even in spring and fall, **freezing** occurs in the northern reaches of the region, where winter readings of -50°F are not uncommon, and parts of the lakes are frozen solid.

The impetus given to **industry** by the Civil War was encouraged by abundant supplies of ores and fuel, as well as efficient transportation by water and rail. As lakeshore cities like Chicago, Detroit, and Cleveland grew, their populations swelled with hundreds of thousands of poor **blacks** who migrated from the Deep South in search of jobs. Many of these migrants worked in munitions during the two world wars. But a lack of planning, inadequate housing, and mass layoffs at times of low demand bred conditions that led to the riots of the late 1960s and current inner-city deprivation. Depression in the 1970s ravaged the economy – especially the **automobile** industry, on which so much else depended – and brought to the area the unwanted title of "**Rust Belt**." Since then, urban centers have battled back, with **Cleveland**, Ohio, perhaps the most dramatic example of a turnaround in fortunes.

Ohio

OHIO, the easternmost of the Great Lakes states, lies to the south of shallow Lake Erie. This is one of the nation's most industrialized regions, but the industry is largely concentrated in the east, near the Ohio River; to the south the landscape becomes less populated and more forested. Ohio also has the world's largest **Amish** population. They farm in the northeast and west into mid-Indiana, and are much less of a tourist attraction than the highly publicized Pennsylvania Dutch (see p.171).

Enigmatic traces of Ohio's earliest inhabitants can be seen at the **Great Serpent Mound**, a grassy state park sixty miles east of Cincinnati, where a cleared hilltop high above a river was reshaped to look like a giant snake swallowing an egg, possibly by the Adena Indians around 800 BC. When the French claimed the area in 1699, it was inhabited by the **Iroquois**, in whose language Ohio means "something great." In the eighteenth century, the territory's prime position between Lake Erie and the Ohio River made it the subject of fierce contention between the French and British. Once the British had acquired control of most French land east of the Mississippi, settlers from New England began to establish communities along both the Ohio River and the Iroquois War Trail paths on the shores of the lake.

During the Civil War, Ohio was at the forefront of the struggle, producing two great Union generals, **Ulysses Grant** and **William Tecumseh Sherman**, and sending more than twice its quota of volunteers to fight for the North. Its progress thereafter has followed the classic "Rust Belt" pattern: rapid industrialization, aided by its natural resources and crucial location, which during the 1970s foundered alarmingly and has only recently begun to revitalize.

Although the state is dominated by its triumvirate of "C" towns (**Cleveland**, **Columbus**, and **Cincinnati**), its most visited destinations are the **Lake Erie Islands**, which have benefited from the recent cleanup of the polluted lake and now attract thousands of partying mainlanders. Cincinnati and Cleveland, the latter hit especially hard by the recession, have both undergone major face-lifts and are surprisingly attractive, as is the comparatively unassuming state capital of Columbus.

Getting around Ohio

Amtrak **trains** between New York or Washington and Chicago stop at either Cincinnati or Cleveland and Toledo. Ohio is well served by Greyhound **buses**, and there are major **airports** at Cleveland and Cincinnati. I-71 is the major interstate linking Cincinnati, Columbus, and Cleveland, while I-70 bisects the state from west to east, passing through Columbus as well. A 325-mile **biking trail**, following former railroad and canal routes, is also under development; when finished, it will link the three "C" cities.

Cleveland and around

Today, the great industrial port of **CLEVELAND** – for so long the butt of jokes after the heavily polluted Cuyahoga River caught fire in the early 1970s – is no longer the "Mistake on the Lake." Although the path back from acute recession (another 1970s legacy) is by no means complete on a citywide basis, the downtown area is now a hub of energy. Cleveland boasts a sensitive and fond restoration of the Lake Erie/Cuyahoga River waterfront, a superb constellation of museums, glittering city-center malls, and new downtown super-stadiums. Add to that the recent arrival of several major corporate headquarters and classy hotels – and, of course, the **Rock and Roll Hall of Fame** – and there's an unmistakable buzz about the place.

Founded in 1796, Cleveland profited greatly, thirty years later, from the opening of the **Ohio Canal** between the Ohio River and Lake Erie. During the city's heyday, which began with the Civil War and lasted until the 1920s, its vast iron and coal supplies made it one of the most important **steel** and **shipbuilding centers** in the world. **John D. Rockefeller** made his billions here, as did the many others whose now-decrepit old mansions line "Millionaires' Row." This has become a no-go area, along with several other bleak and faceless danger spots. Despite the investment of billions of dollars, the scars of deprivation are still visible if you wander too far off the tourist path.

South and west of the city are several spots of interest, including the quaint lakeshore community of **Vermilion**, the tiny liberal college sanctuary of **Oberlin**, and the charming hamlet of **Peninsula**.

Arrival, information, and getting around

Cleveland Hopkins International Airport is ten miles southwest of downtown. The twenty-minute **taxi** ride into town costs around $20, but the Regional Transit Authority (RTA; ☎216/621-9500, ⓦ www.gcrta.org) **train** is only $1.50 and takes just ten minutes longer. Greyhound arrives at 1465 Chester Ave, at the back of Playhouse Square, while the Amtrak station is on the lakefront at 200 Cleveland Memorial Shoreway NE.

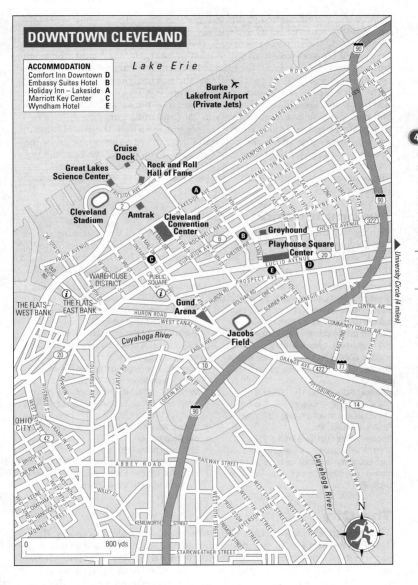

DOWNTOWN CLEVELAND

ACCOMMODATION
Comfort Inn Downtown **D**
Embassy Suites Hotel **B**
Holiday Inn – Lakeside **A**
Marriott Key Center **C**
Wyndham Hotel **E**

Lake Erie

Burke Lakefront Airport (Private Jets)

Cruise Dock

Great Lakes Science Center

Rock and Roll Hall of Fame

Cleveland Stadium

Amtrak

Cleveland Convention Center

Greyhound

Playhouse Square Center

WAREHOUSE DISTRICT

PUBLIC SQUARE

THE FLATS WEST BANK

THE FLATS EAST BANK

Gund Arena

Jacobs Field

Cuyahoga River

OHIO CITY

ABBEY ROAD

RAILWAY STREET

Cuyahoga River

KENILWORTH STREET

STARKWEATHER STREET

0 | 800 yds

N

Maps and **information** can be had in advance from the Cleveland **CVB** (Mon–Fri 9am–9pm; ☎1-800/321-1004, ⓦwww.travelcleveland.com). The handiest **visitor centers** are in the lobby of the Terminal Tower in Public Square (Mon–Fri 10am–8pm, Sun noon–6pm; ☎216/621-7981) and on the east bank of the Flats next to *Hooter's* (summer daily 11am–7pm; ☎216/621-2218).

Cleveland is concentrated in different pockets and, as the potentially dangerous areas are scattered pretty wide (it is not safe, for example, to stray into the streets around the three-block-deep Cleveland Clinic, very close to the much-frequented University Circle), you're safest in a **car**. The RTA runs an efficient **bus** service ($1.25 or $1.50 for express services; 50¢ within downtown) and a small train line ($1.50), known locally as "the Rapids," until about 12.30am. A **light rail** system – the Waterfront Line – connects Terminal Tower, the Flats, the Rock and Roll Hall of Fame, and other downtown sights; it costs $1.50 and runs every fifteen minutes between 7am and midnight.

    City tours, run by Trolley Tours of Cleveland, leave from the Powerhouse on the west bank of the Flats and cover all of the major sights. These are somewhat of a walk, especially University Circle, so if you don't have a car, the trolley is a good option (May–Oct daily; Nov–April Fri & Sat; $10 for 1hr, $15 for 2hr, reservations required; ☎216/771-4484 or 1-800/848-0173, ⓦwww.lollytrolley.com).

Accommodation

Travelers without cars in Cleveland are largely limited to the somewhat expensive downtown **hotels**. Most now offer packages that include admission to the Rock and Roll Hall of Fame or other attractions. **B&Bs** can be arranged through Private Lodgings, Box 18590, Cleveland, OH 44118 (☎216/321-3213).

Baymont Inn 4222 W 150th St ☎216/251-8500, ⓦwww.baymontinns.com. Standard motel rooms; easy downtown access via train and only two miles to the airport. ④

Comfort Inn Downtown 1800 Euclid Ave ☎216/861-0001, ⓦwww.comfortinn.com. The standard *Comfort Inn* rooms are on the edge of downtown, a little far to walk to bars and restaurants. ⑤

Embassy Suites Hotel 1701 E 12th St ☎216/523-8000, ⓦwww.es-cleveland.com. These spacious downtown rooms are near Playhouse Square. ⑦

Glidden House 1901 Ford Drive ☎216/231-8900, ⓦwww.gliddenhouse.com. Your bed and large continental breakfast are in a huge Gothic mansion with 60 rooms; very handy for University Circle. ⑦

Holiday Inn – Lakeside 1111 Lakeside Ave ☎216/241-5100, ⓦwww.holiday-inn.com. This functional, unexciting downtown hotel is near the Rock and Roll Hall of Fame. ⑥

Marriott Key Center 127 Public Square ☎216/696-9200, ⓦwww.marriotthotels.com. Probably the best value of the downtown upscale hotels, the *Marriott* is clean, bright, and close to the action. ⑥

Omni International Hotel 2065 E 96th St ☎216/707-4300, 1-800/THE OMNI, ⓦwww.omni-hotels.com. This luxury hotel in University Circle is handy for Little Italy and Coventry Village. Rooms are over $200 during the week – ask about weekend discounts. ⑦

Wyndham Hotel 1260 Euclid Ave ☎216/615-7500, ⓦwww.wyndham.com/hotels/CLEPS/main.wnt. The best luxury option in the downtown theater district, Playhouse Square. ⑥

The City

The main streets in Cleveland lead to the stately nineteenth-century Beaux Arts **Public Square**, at the very center of downtown, and dominated in its southwestern corner by the landmark **Terminal Tower**. **Ontario Street**, which runs north–south through the Square, divides the city into east and west. Cleveland's most interesting areas are at two opposite ends of the spectrum: the industrial romance of the **Flats** in the northwest, and the cultural institutions of **University Circle**, east of the river.

Downtown and around

Downtown Cleveland is once again a bustling place, and its recent redevelopment has seen the emergence of several distinct subsections. In its traditional

The Rock and Roll Hall of Fame

Cleveland, not the most obvious candidate, convincingly won a hotly contested bid to host the **Rock and Roll Hall of Fame** largely because **Alan Freed**, a local disc jockey, popularized the phrase "rock and roll" here back in 1951. Since then, Cleveland has hardly produced a roll call of rock icons – Joe Walsh, Pere Ubu, and Nine Inch Nails are about the biggest names – but the city embraced the idea of the museum with enthusiasm. Few can now argue that it was not the correct choice. However, cynics are quick to snipe that Cleveland won out over Memphis, New York, and other cities with a richer musical heritage because, quite simply, it bagged up the most cash – a financial package that some put as high as $65 million.

The idea for a definitive rock museum was first floated in 1983, with the establishment of the **Rock Hall of Fame Foundation** to honor all those who have made "an exceptional contribution to modern music." The inductees are selected annually by an international panel of rock "experts," but only those performers who have released a record 25 years prior to their nomination are eligible.

The museum's octogenarian architect – **I.M. Pei** – wanted the building "to echo the energy of rock and roll." One of Pei's trademark tinted-glass pyramids (a smaller version of the one he did at the Louvre), this white concrete, steel, and glass structure strikes a bold pose on the shore of Lake Erie. A tall main tower supports sweeping geometric extensions and dramatic cantilevered offshoots in cylindrical, triangular, and rectangular shapes, all fronted by the pyramid (or tent, as Pei likes to call it), which looks spectacular when lit up at night. The base of the pyramid extends into an impressive entrance plaza shaped like a turntable, complete with a stylus arm attachment.

The museum is much more than an array of mementos and artifacts. Right from the start, with the excellent twelve-minute films *Mystery Train* and *Kick Out the Jams*, the emphasis is on the contextualization of rock. The exhibits chart the art form's evolution and progress, acknowledging influences ranging from the blues singers of the Delta to the hillbilly wailers of the Appalachians. Look for "The Beat Goes On" display – a bank of interactive computers that reveals the inspirational earlier artists who shaped the sound of a series of contemporary bands.

Elsewhere in the subterranean main exhibition hall, there's an in-depth look at seven crucial rock genres through the cities that spawned them: rockabilly (Memphis), R&B (New Orleans), Motown (Detroit), psychedelia (San Francisco), punk (London and New York), hip-hop (New York), and grunge (Seattle). Much space is taken up by exhibits on what the museum sees as key artists of all time, including Elvis Presley, the Beatles (featuring a collection of John Lennon's possessions donated by Yoko Ono), U2, Jimi Hendrix, George Clinton, and the Rolling Stones.

Above ground, Pei's airy structure feels like a modern art gallery. Several East German Trabant cars, which U2 used during its Zooropa tour, are suspended from the ceiling, while a fifteen-foot hot dog flown by Phish during their 1994 tour, as well as photographic portraits by Annie Leibovitz et al, adorn the area by the stairwells.

On the top floor is the **Hall of Fame** itself. Compared with the racket elsewhere, this is a darkened, self-consciously reverential space. The images of the hundred-plus inductees are flicked up on tiny screens, beside which are their autographs etched on glass.

The museum is at North Coast Harbor (daily 10am–5.30pm, Wed also until 9pm; summer Sat until 9pm; $18; reservations ✆216/781-ROCK or 1-800/493-ROLL). It gets particularly crowded at weekends: if that's the only time you can make it, you'll need to make reservations in advance and be given a time to turn up. However, because it takes a good half-day to see just a decent proportion of the exhibits, it's much better to go on a weekday morning, when you can take full advantage of the interactive displays. Plan a visit to coincide with the extensive series of seminars and workshops that feature Hall of Fame inductees and leading rock writers. Check out details of these events on the Rock Hall's website (Ⓦ www.rockhall.com).

heart, among the banks and corporate headquarters, stand a couple of glamorous shopping malls. One, the **Avenue at Tower City**, is located in the Terminal Tower. Another, the **Arcade**, is a skylit hall built in 1890. Twelve blocks away, at 1501 Euclid Ave, the **Playhouse Square Center** (℡216/241-6000, ⓦwww .playhousesquare.com) is an impressive complex of four renovated old theaters; the small Ohio Theater, with its gorgeous starlit-sky lobby ceiling, is worth a look.

Just to the southwest, in what were once mostly vacant lots, is the **Gateway District**. New restaurants and bars surround **Jacobs Field** stadium, home of the Indians baseball team (℡216/420-4200, ⓦwww.indians.com), and the equally modern multipurpose **Gund Arena** (℡216/420-2000, ⓦwww .gundarena.com), which hosts the Cavaliers basketball team, along with major sporting and entertainment events.

West of the Gund is the **riverfront**, where one of the nation's busiest waterways shares space with excellent bars, clubs, and restaurants, all strung out along a boardwalk. On both banks of the Cuyahoga River, the **Flats**, long known for its nightlife, has an atmospheric industrial setting. Magnificent grimy old buildings, warehouses, and slag heaps, set among fourteen **bridges**, appear powerful and romantic rather than depressing, a proud testimony to Cleveland's manufacturing history.

A short but steep walk uphill from the Flats leads to the **Warehouse District**, a nicely developing stretch of nineteenth-century commercial buildings between West Third and West Tenth streets, given over to shops, galleries, cafés, and trendy new restaurants. North of here, on the other side of the busy Cleveland Memorial Shoreway (Hwy-2), the waters of Lake Erie lap gently into **North Coast Harbor**, a showpiece of Midwest regeneration. To see the city from the water, try a two-hour cruise on the *Goodtime III* ($12.50; ℡216/861-5110) from the dock at East Ninth Street Pier, just beyond the I.M. Pei–designed **Rock and Roll Hall of Fame** (see box, p.313). Next door to the Rock Hall – as Clevelanders refer to it – is the giant **Great Lakes Science Center** (daily 9.30am–5.30pm; $7.75, $11 OMNIMAX combo ticket; ℡216/694-2000, ⓦwww.greatscience.com), whose white paneling and glass frontage perfectly complement its neighbor. There are no standout displays, though the cumulative effect of the 350 interactive exhibits (many on meteorological and aquatic themes) makes this a very enjoyable place to spend a few hours. Across the road, the futuristic, 72,000-seat **Cleveland Stadium** is the home of the Browns pro football team (℡440/891-5000, ⓦwww.clevelandbrowns.com).

To the west of the river, **Ohio City** is one of Cleveland's more hip neighborhoods, with junk stores, Victorian clapboard houses, and the busy **West Side Market** at Lorain Ave and West 25th St (Mon & Wed 7am–4pm, Fri & Sat 7am–6pm), selling all manner of ethnic foods. It's easily spotted by its redbrick Victorian clock tower.

Out from downtown

Five miles east of downtown, **University Circle** is a cluster of more than seventy cultural and medical institutions, and is also home to several major performing arts companies (see p.316) as well as Frank Gehry's twisted-steel School of Management building at Case Western University. The eclectic **Museum of Art**, fronted by a lagoon at 11150 East Blvd (Tues, Thurs, Sat & Sun 10am–5pm, Wed & Fri 10am–9pm; free; ℡216/421-7340, ⓦwww.clevelandart.org), has a collection that ranges from Renaissance armor to African art, with a good café. Also notable is the **Museum of Natural History**, Wade Oval (Mon–Sat 10am–5pm, Sun noon–5pm; summer Tues–Thurs until 7pm;

Sept–May Wed until 10pm; $7, planetarium $3; ☎ 1-800/317-9155, ⓦ www.cmnh.org), with exhibits on dinosaurs and Native American culture. The **Cleveland Botanical Garden**, 11030 East Blvd (daily 10am–5pm; $7; 1-888/853-7091, ⓦ www.cbgarden.org), has a greenhouse which features a cloud forest, a desert ecosystem, free-roaming chameleons and butterflies, a waterfall, and a treetop walkway. Meanwhile, dotted along East and Martin Luther King Jr boulevards in Rockefeller Park, twenty-four small landscaped cultural **gardens** are dedicated to and tended by Cleveland's diverse ethnic groups, including Croatians, Estonians, and Finns. Adjacent to University Circle, **Murray Hill** is Cleveland's Little Italy; beyond this attractive area of brick streets, small delis, and galleries is the trendy neighborhood of **Coventry Village**.

Five miles southwest of downtown via I-71 (exit at W 25th or Fulton Rd), the **Cleveland Metroparks Zoo**, 3900 Wildlife Way (summer Mon–Fri 9am–5pm, Sat & Sun 9am–7pm; rest of year daily 10am–5pm; rainforest also open Wed until 8pm; $9; ☎ 216/661-6500, ⓦ www.clemetzoo.com), features a "Wolf Wilderness," while the spectacular 164-acre rainforest building is populated by some seven thousand plants and 118 species of animals, including orangutans, American crocodiles, and Madagascan hissing cockroaches. During summer, the RTA runs special **buses** from downtown to the zoo.

Eating

At first sight, corporate chains seem to dominate Cleveland – especially in the Flats – but the city has many culinary delights, many of them ethnic. The **West Side Market** in Ohio City is one of the best places for cheap and unusual picnic food, and there are some excellent (if pricey) fine-dining restaurants downtown. Little Italy and Coventry Village are worth exploring for authentic Italian food and coffee bars, respectively. The *Arabica* chain also serves up good-quality espresso at several locations around the city; there's one in University Circle at 11300 Juniper Rd (☎ 216/791-0300).

Cleveland Chophouse and Brewery 824 W St Clair ☎ 216/623-0909. Try the mashed potatoes at this spacious, casual brewery and steakhouse – they're fantastic.

Flat Iron Café 1114 Center St ☎ 216/696-6968. Landmark Irish-American tavern on the east (downtown) bank of the Flats, serving up good sandwiches, salads, and desserts, plus a smooth pint of Guinness.

Hornblower's Barge & Grille 1151 N Marginal Rd ☎ 216/363-1151. Good-value pasta, sandwiches, and seafood are offered in a fine location overlooking Lake Erie, just a short stroll from the Rock Hall.

Mama Santa 12305 Mayfield Rd ☎ 216/231-9567. In Little Italy, unpretentious and inexpensive Southern Italian home-cooking.

Nate's Deli & Restaurant 1923 W 25th St ☎ 216/696-7529. This Middle Eastern café serves great gyros and plenty of vegetarian dishes. The *hummus*, in particular, has quite a reputation. Open only during the day.

Que Tal? 1803 Coventry Rd ☎ 216/932-9800. The best place to grab some quick Mexican food in Coventry Village.

Ruthie & Moe's Diner 4002 Prospect Ave ☎ 216/881-6637. This friendly, traditional diner is well worth the 5min drive from downtown for its breakfasts, lunches, and huge desserts.

Tommy's 1824 Coventry Rd ☎ 216/321-7757. Great-value food, much of it Middle Eastern vegetarian, is dished up in a trendy, bright setting in lively Coventry Village. Try the famous shakes and check out the adjoining used-book store.

Watermark Restaurant 1250 Old River Rd ☎ 216/241-1600. *Watermark* offers an excellent, extensive seafood menu, in classy Flats digs overlooking the river.

Nightlife and entertainment

The **Flats** area boasts the greatest conglomeration of drinking, live music, and dancing venues, although they tend to be cheesier than their counterparts in the **Warehouse District** and the more bohemian **Ohio City** across the river. Five miles east, both **University Circle** and youthful **Coventry Village** have good bars, though the Circle contains no-go zones you shouldn't wander into. Cleveland's **rave** scene remains strong and mostly underground; if you're interested, look for flyers at Record Revolution 1832 Coventry Rd (☏216/321-7661).

For more refined entertainment, the **Cleveland Opera** (☏216/575-0903, Ⓦwww.clevelandopera.org) and **Ballet** (☏216/861-5545) perform in **Playhouse Square Center** (☏216/241-6000), which also hosts drama. The well-respected **Cleveland Orchestra** (☏216/231-1111) is based in University Circle at Severance Hall, 11001 Euclid Ave, close to the leading regional theater of the **Cleveland Play House** (☏216/795-7000). For **listings** information, try one of Cleveland's two free weeklies: the well-written *Free Times* covers all of the arts, while *Scene* concentrates mostly on music.

Club Isabella 2025 University Hospitals Drive, University Circle ☏216/229-1177. This popular, reasonably priced Italian restaurant also features live jazz Wednesday through Saturday.

Great Lakes Brewing Co. 2516 Market St, Ohio City ☏216/771-4404. At this famous old joint, Cleveland's best brewpub, the huge mahogany bar still bears the bullet holes made during a 1920s shootout involving lawman Elliot Ness.

Grog Shop 2785 Euclid Heights Blvd, Cleveland Heights ☏216/321-5588. Near Coventry Village, the *Grog Shop* is a fun, sweaty collegiate punk and alternative venue.

Harbor Inn 1219 Main Ave ☏216/241-3232. A great old-fashioned bar amid the hyped chain outfits of the Flats, one with 180 beers, a few video games, and lots of character.

Mercury Lounge 1392 W 6th St ☏216/566-8840. In the Warehouse District, this hip martini lounge tends to attract Cleveland's fashionable set.

Around Cleveland

Less than an hour outside the city are several small towns and sights well worth exploring. **VERMILION**, beyond the western suburbs of Cleveland, is also known as Harbor Town, for its attractive lakeside area, which has thrived since 1837. Today it's a quaint old hamlet lined with clapboard houses, cedar trees, and tidy gardens. Old-style galleries and shops hug the small downtown, a stone's throw from the boat rides, seafood restaurants, and fishing boats on the dockside. The **Inland Seas Maritime Museum**, 480 Main St (daily 10am–5pm; $6; ☏1-800/893-1485, Ⓦwww.islandseas.org), does a worthy job of exploring shipping on the Great Lakes, spanning from the late seventeenth century to the wreckage of the *Edmund Fitzgerald* freighter almost 300 years later. Vermilion's **Chamber of Commerce** is at 5495 Liberty Ave (summer Mon–Fri 10am–4pm; rest of year Mon–Fri 10am–3pm, closed Wed; ☏440/967-4477, Ⓦwww.vermilionohio.com). The best place to **stay** in town is the comfortable *Motel Plaza*, 4645 Liberty Ave (☏440/967-3191; ❸).

Some twenty miles southeast of Vermilion, the famously liberal college town of **OBERLIN** clusters around the green acres of Tappan Square. Founded in 1834, **Oberlin College**, on the square's north and east sides, was America's first co-ed university, and one of the first to enroll black students. From the start, it played a pivotal role in facilitating the movement of black slaves from the Deep South to Canada via the Underground Railroad. A **sculpture** of railroad tracks emerging from the earth, opposite the Conservatory of Music on South Professor Street, is one of several such commemorative sights detailed in a fascinating **walking tour** leaflet available from the **Chamber of Commerce**, inside the *Oberlin Inn* at 7 N Main St, suite 117 (Mon–Thurs 10am–3pm, Fri 9am–noon; ☏440/774-6262, Ⓦwww.oberlin.org). Also of interest is the **Allen Memorial Art Museum**, 87 N Main St (Tues–Sat 10am–5pm, Sun 1–5pm;

free; Ⓦwww.oberlin.edu/allenart). Recognized as one of the best college art museums in the US, it holds more than 14,000 objects, from ancient African icons to Japanese scroll paintings, plus a fine array of contemporary art. As for **accommodation**, try the pleasant *Oberlin Inn*, 7 N Main St (Ⓣ440/775-1111, Ⓦwww.oberlininn.com; ❻), or the *Ivy Tree Inn & Garden*, 195 S Professor St (Ⓣ440/774-4510; ❹), which offers a well-tended garden in a comfortable B&B atmosphere. Oberlin also boasts half a dozen hip coffeehouses and bars.

Twenty miles south of Cleveland off US-77, the village of **PENINSULA** is nestled in the heart of the **Cuyahoga Valley National Recreation Area**, where the Ohio & Erie Canal Towpath's hiking and biking trail follows the meandering Cuyahoga River for twenty miles. You can **rent a bike** in town at Century Cycles, 1621 Main St ($6 per hour; Ⓣ330/657-2209). A few miles south of town off Riverview Road, the sprawling **Hale Farm and Village** (summer Tues–Sat 11am–5pm, Sun noon–5pm; $12; Ⓣ1-877/HALEFARM, Ⓦwww.wrhs.org) brings to life the fictional 1848 Ohio township of Wheatfield, complete with good-natured role-playing townsfolk and artisans who demonstrate skills like brick-making and glass-blowing. The best place to stay in the area is *HI-Stanford House*, 6093 Stanford Rd (Ⓣ330/467-8711; ❶), a hostel in a lovely old farmhouse where a bed costs $15 per night.

A few miles farther south in **AKRON** (home of the Goodyear Tire and Rubber Co.), visitors can tour Goodyear co-founder F.A. Seiberling's palatial **Stan Hywet Hall and Gardens**, 714 N Portage Path (Feb–March Tues–Sat 10am–4pm, Sun 1–4pm; April–Dec daily 10am–4.30pm; $10, gardens only $5; Ⓣ330/836-5533), a magnificent 65-room Tudor Revival country house finished in 1915, with secret passageways, hand-carved wood paneling, and an indoor swimming pool.

Sixty miles south of Akron, the world's largest Amish community resides in **HOLMES COUNTY**, a meandering section of hills, farms, and backroads. **Berlin** is the commercial center of Amish country, a somewhat saccharine arts-and-crafts center. A good dose of Amish simplicity is better found in the surrounding countryside: at **Yoder's Amish Home**, between the towns of Walnut Creek and Trail on Rte-515 (April–Oct Mon–Sat 10am–5pm; $7; Ⓣ330/893-2541), visitors can tour two Amish homes and a barn, and ride in a horse-drawn carriage.

The Lake Erie Islands

The **LAKE ERIE ISLANDS** – **Kelleys Island** and the three **Bass Islands** further north – were early stepping stones for the **Iroquois** on the route to what is now Ontario. French attempts to claim the islands in the 1640s met with considerable hostility, and they were left more or less in peace until 1813, when in the **Battle of Lake Erie**, fought off South Bass Island, the Americans established their control over the Great Lakes by destroying the entire English fleet.

The islands first tasted prosperity in the 1860s, when a boom in **wine production** meant that nearly every available acre was planted with grapes. Tourism arrived almost simultaneously, as steamboats brought wealthy visitors to spend their summers here in grand hotels. However, the economy was hit hard by Prohibition and the emergence of the California wineries, as well as by the advent of the automobile. In the 1970s, Lake Erie's appalling pollution was the final straw for many inhabitants, who undertook a huge cleanup of the lake and islands. Their plan has worked; today the islands are heavily visited, especially in summer, with fishing, swimming, and partying the main attractions. Various mainland towns off of Rte-2, such as **Sandusky** and **Port Clinton**, act primarily as jump-off points for the islands.

The mainland

The large coal-shipping port of **SANDUSKY**, fifty miles west of Cleveland on US-2, is probably the most visited of the lakeshore towns, thanks to **Cedar Point Amusement Park**, five miles southeast of town (May–Oct daily 9am–10pm; $44, after 5pm $24; ☏419/627-2350, ⊛www.cedarpoint.com). The largest ride park in the nation – and considered by many to be the best in the world – Cedar Point boasts no less than sixteen roller coasters. The neighboring **Soak City** water park (June–Aug daily 10am–9pm; $24, after 5pm $15) provides a good way to cool off, with eighteen acres of water slides and a wave pool. Otherwise, Sandusky is a nice enough town in a pleasant farmland setting, but there's not much to it apart from its pretty downtown square.

The smaller resort town of **PORT CLINTON**, twelve miles west across the Sandusky Bay Bridge, is another departure point for the islands. Its pleasant lakefront is dotted with decent cafés and jet-ski rental outlets. Try not to leave the area without exploring the rest of the peninsula, which has some glorious views, particularly around little **Marblehead**, fourteen miles east of Port Clinton.

Eight miles south of Sandusky, tiny **MILAN** (pronounced "MY-lan") boasts a pleasant, leafy village square and many well-preserved Greek Revival–style homes. Its most famous building is the two-story brick **Thomas Edison Birthplace**, 9 Edison Drive (summer Tues–Sat 10am–5pm, Sun 1–5pm; April & May, Sept & Oct Tues–Sun 1–5pm; Nov–March Wed–Sun 1–4pm; $5; ☏419/499-2135), with guided tours and an adjacent museum dedicated to the inventor of the light bulb.

Practicalities

Amtrak **trains** pass through Sandusky once daily en route between Chicago and Boston or New York, via Cleveland. The station, at North Depot and Hayes avenues, is in a dodgy area, and is unstaffed. Greyhound **buses** stop way out at 6513 Milan Rd. Sandusky's **visitor center** is at 4424 Milan Rd, suite A (summer Mon–Thurs 8am–8pm, Fri 8am–9pm, Sat 9am–9pm, Sun 10am–4pm; rest of year Mon–Fri 8.30am–5.30pm; ☏419/625-2984 or 1-800/255-ERIE, ⊛www.sanduskycounty.org).

Accommodation in Sandusky can be quite expensive in high season – it's not unheard-of for a standard motel room to cost $200-plus on peak weekends. Along the main drag of Cleveland Road (US-6), the *Best Western Cedar Point*, no. 1530 (☏419/625-9234; ❺), has a pool. **Camping** is available at the *Bayshore Estates*, 2311 Cleveland Rd (☏419/625-7906 or ☏1-800/962-3786; $12), and at the *Milan Travel Park*, just off US-80 at 11404 US-250 N (☏419/499-4627; $20), which has laundry facilities, free showers, and a pool. In **Milan**, the *Colonial Inn South*, 11211 US-250 (☏419/499-3403 or 1-800/886-9010; ❹), is a nice family-owned motel, while **Port Clinton** has the *Sunnyside Tower*, 3612 NW Catawba Rd (☏419/797-9315, ⊛www.sunnysidetower.com ❺), a Victorian-style B&B half a mile from the Miller Boat Line dock (see box, opposite). For a good **meal** and **live music** in fun surroundings (there's an on-site waterfall), head for *Margaritaville* in Sandusky, at the junction of highways 6 and 2 (☏419/627-8903).

Getting to the Islands

Ferries to **Kelleys Island** are operated by Neuman Boats, and leave from the foot of Frances Street in **Marblehead** every hour from dawn until dusk, or more frequently on weekends and during peak times (March–Dec; $10 roundtrip, bikes $3 extra; ☏419/798-5800 or 1-800/876-1907, ⓦwww.neumanferry.com). Kelleys Island Ferry Boat Lines (☏419/798-9763, ⓦwww.kelleysislandferry.com) offers year-round service from Main Street in Marblehead for the same prices. From Jackson Street Pier, the *Island Rocket* (☏419/627-1500 or 1-800/854-8121, ⓦwww.islandrocket .com), a powerful boat, whisks through the water to Kelleys for $12 one way.

You can also take the *Island Rocket* from **Sandusky** to **South Bass Island** for a one-way fare of $14. A better value is the *Island Rocket* same-day "island hopper" ticket, which allows you to visit both islands for $32 (☏1-800/854-8121, ⓦwww.islandrocket.com).

From **Port Clinton**, the *Jet Express* (April–Nov; $12 one way; ☏1-800/2451-JET, ⓦwww.jet-express.com) takes a mere 22 minutes to reach **South Bass Island**, and runs until 11.30pm in the summer.

From **Catawba Point**, at the end of US-53 N, ferries by Miller Boat Line (March–Nov daily 7am–7.30pm; $5 one-way; ☏419/285-2421, ⓦwww.millerferry .com) run hourly to Lime Kiln Dock, on South Bass Island's southern tip. **Cruises**, run by Goodtime from Sandusky's Jackson Street Pier (☏419/625-9692, ⓦwww.goodtimeboat.com), depart daily at 9.30am and stop at both Kelleys Island and South Bass Island, for a roundtrip fare of $22.

Flights to both Kelleys Island and South Bass Island leave daily from Sandusky and Port Clinton and cost about $66 roundtrip. Contact Griffing Airlines (☏419/626-5161).

Kelleys Island

About nine miles north of Sandusky, **KELLEYS ISLAND** lies in the western basin of Lake Erie. Seven miles across at its widest, it's the largest American island on the lake, but it's also one of the most peaceful and picturesque, home to just 175 permanent residents. The whole island – green, sleepy, and with few buildings less than a century old – is a National Historic District. Its seventy-plus archeological sites include **Inscription Rock**, a limestone slab carved with 400-old pictographs; you can find it east of the dock on the southern shore. The **Glacial Grooves State Memorial**, on the west shore, is a 400-foot trough of solid limestone, scoured with deep ridges by the glacier that carved out the Great Lakes.

Settled in the 1830s, Kelleys was initially a working island, its economy based on lumber, then wine, and later limestone quarrying. All but the last have collapsed, though a steady **tourist industry** has developed. Today, hundreds of Clevelanders come here on weekends to swim from the sandy public beach on the north shore, bird-watch with the island's active Audubon Society, and hike through some dramatic abandoned quarries, which now sprout cedars.

Practicalities

The Kelleys Island **Chamber of Commerce** is on Division Street, straight up from the *Island Rocket* dock (summer daily 10am–5pm; ☏419/746-2360, ⓦwww.kelleysislandchamber.com). Getting around the island is easy; cars are heavily discouraged, and most people, when not strolling, use **bikes** ($2 per hour/$8 per day) or **golf carts** ($12 per hour/$65 per day), available from First Place Rentals, at the top of the Neuman ferry dock (☏419/746-2741). One comfortable **accommodation** option is *The Inn on Kelleys Island*, 317 W

Lakeshore Drive (☎1-866/878-2135, ⓦwww.aves.net/the-inn; ❹), a restored nineteenth-century Victorian home with a great lake view and a private beach; the Chamber of Commerce can provide you with details of other places to stay. You can **camp** for $15 at the first-come, first-served state park on the north bay near the beach. The jovial *Village Pump*, 103 W Lakeshore Drive (☎419/746-2281), serves good homestyle **food and drink** until 2am, while the menu at the *Kelleys Island Brewery*, 504 W Lakeshore Drive (☎419/746-2314), includes several choices for vegetarians.

South Bass Island

SOUTH BASS ISLAND is the largest and southernmost of the Bass Island chain, three miles from the mainland northwest of Kelleys Island; the islands are named for the excellent bass fishing in the surrounding waters. Also referred to as **Put-in-Bay** (the name of its one and only village), this is the most visited of the American Lake Erie Islands, with its permanent population of 450 swelling to ten times that in summer.

Just a year after its first white settlers arrived, British troops invaded the island during the War of 1812. The Battle of Lake Erie (1813), which took place on the island's southeastern edge, is commemorated by **Perry's Victory and International Peace Memorial**, set in a 25-acre park where the island dramatically nips in at the waist. You can see the battle site, ten miles away, from an observation deck near the top of the 352ft stone Doric column (May–Oct daily 10am–7pm; $3).

After the war, with the lake safe from Canadian invasion, South Bass Island grew both as a port (transporting cedar to the mainland for the construction of steamboats) and as a tourist destination. In fact, during the 1890s its *Victory Hotel* was one of the largest hotels in the world. Wine was also big business, though only one of its twenty-six vineyards survived Prohibition (by producing grape juice): the **Heineman Winery**, 900 Catawba Ave. Winery tours (May–Sept daily 11am–5pm; $5; ☎419/285-2811) include a glass of wine or grape juice.

All this history is well documented at the **Lake Erie Islands Historical Society**, 441 Catawba Ave (summer daily 10am–6pm; $1; ☎419/285-2804), which features dozens of model ships, exhibits on the shipping and fishing industries, and memorabilia of life on the islands.

Despite the colorful past, and the island's undeniable beauty, visitors today may well be struck most by the hordes of boozers staggering between bars whose repertoire extends little beyond Jimmy Buffet songs.

Practicalities

Put-in-Bay's **visitor center** is downtown in Harbor Square, just next to the northern dock (summer daily 9am–6pm; rest of year call for hours; ☎419/285-2832, ⓦwww.put-in-bay.com). To get around, as on Kelleys Island, most people rent either **golf carts** from Baycarts Rental, Harbor Square ($10–20 per hour; ☎419/285-5785), or **bikes** from Island Bike Rental, at both docks ($9 per day; ☎419/285-2016). A **shuttle bus** ($1) runs between the northern dock, the winery, and the state park. A narrated jump-on/jump-off **tram tour** ($8) sets off from the dock every thirty minutes. The local **taxi** will take you anywhere on the island for $3 per person (8am–3am; ☎419/285-2311).

Hotel rooms are heavily booked on weekends and during the summer, and **B&Bs** often require a two-night minimum stay on weekends. The *Stagger Inn B&B*, 182 Concord Ave (☎419/285-2521, ⓦwww.staggerinn.put-in-bay.com;

❹), and the *Commodore Motel*, 272 Delaware Ave (☎419/285-3101; ❹), which has a pool, offer some of the most competitive rates. You can **camp** for $12 in the state park (you must arrive by 9am) or at the *Fox's Den Campground* on the southern shore ($25 for one or two; ☎419/285-5001).

Food on the island is expensive everywhere. The grill meals and seafood sandwiches at *The Boardwalk* (summer only; ☎419/285-3695, ⓦwww.theboardwalk.com) are no exception, but this is the only downtown restaurant directly on the water. Just across the street, *Frosty's* (☎419/285-3278) does good pizza. Put-in-Bay's wild **nightlife** – it really does get raucous here – pulls in revelers from the other islands and the mainland. Numerous **live music** venues include the *Beer Barrel Saloon* (☎419/285-BEER, ⓦwww.beerbarrelpib.com) – said to have the longest uninterrupted bar in the world, complete with 160 bar stools – and the appropriately named *Round House* (☎419/285-4595, ⓦwww.theroundhousebar.com).

Columbus

COLUMBUS – Ohio's largest city, state capital, and home to the massive Ohio State University – is a likeable place to visit. Its position in the rural heart of the state also makes it the only center of culture for a good three-hour drive in any direction.

Ohio became a state in 1803, and after trying Zanesville and Chillicothe, legislators designated this former patch of rolling farmland on the high east bank of the Scioto River its capital in 1812. The fledgling city was built from scratch, and its considered town planning is evident today in broad thoroughfares and green spaces. Statuary forms another part of the cityscape, with monuments seemingly erected on any spare scrap of land, many of them of its namesake, **Christopher Columbus**; there's even a replica of his ship, the *Santa Maria*, docked downtown on the Scioto River.

Though Columbus has more people, it always seems to lag behind Cincinnati or Cleveland in terms of public recognition. As such, the place is best enjoyed for what it is – a lively college city with a smattering of good **museums**, some gorgeous Germanic **architecture**, and a particularly vibrant **nightlife**, including Ohio's most active **gay scene**. The spacious, orderly, and easygoing **downtown** area holds several attractions, as well as the giant Columbus City Center mall. The main entertainment districts – the bohemian **Short North** and the more mainstream **Brewery District** – are on the north and south fringes of the city, respectively.

Arrival, information, and getting around

Port Columbus International Airport is seven miles northeast of downtown. **Taxis** into the center cost around $16–18, while a cheaper alternative is the Capital City Flyer bus, run by the Central Ohio Transit Authority (COTA; $5; ☎614/228-1776, ⓦwww.cota.com). **Greyhound** stops at 111 East Town and Third streets, but Amtrak bypasses it altogether. The main **visitor center** is at 90 N High St (Mon–Fri 9am–5.30pm; ☎614/221-CITY or 1-800/345-4FUN, ⓦwww.surpriseitscolumbus.com or www.columbuscvb.org), with another branch on the second level of the Columbus City Center mall, just south of the Ohio Statehouse at High and Rich streets (Mon–Sat 11am–6pm, Sun noon–6pm). COTA also runs a good central **bus service** connecting downtown with German Village, the Short North, and North Campus; a day pass costs $2.50.

Accommodation

Compared with other cities in the region, Columbus offers a good choice of mid-range places to **stay** that are well-placed to let you discover the city by day and night. Downtown rates are good while even more savings can be made by staying in the German Village/Brewery District locales.

Best Western Clarmont 650 S High St ☎614/228-6511. A 2min walk from the Brewery District and German Village, this chain motel is a little run-down but good value nonetheless. ➍

German Village Inn 920 S High St ☎614/443-6506. This family-run motel, on the south edge of the German Village/Brewery District, is similar to the *Clarmont*, above. ➍

Harrison House B&B 313 W 5th Ave ☎614/421-2202 or 1-800/827-4203, ⓦwww.columbus-bed-breakfast.com. This welcoming big home is in Victorian Village, an up-and-coming district close to the Short North. ➎

Holiday Inn City Center 175 E Town St ☎614/221-3281, ⓦwww.holiday-inn.com. This reliable motel with a pool and bar is within easy walking distance of the main museums, German Village, and the Statehouse. ➏

The Westin Columbus 310 S High St ☎614/228-3800. Columbus's grand downtown Victorian hotel. ➐

Downtown

As good a place as any to start a walking tour of downtown is the **Ohio Statehouse**, pleasantly set in ten acres of park at the intersection of Broad and High streets, the two main downtown arteries (Mon–Fri 7am–7pm, Sat & Sun 11am–4pm; tours Mon–Fri 9.30am–3pm, Sat & Sun 11.15am–3pm; free; ☎1-888/644-6123). Highlights of the free guided tours in this 1839 Greek Revival structure – one of the very few state capitols without a dome – are the ornate Senate and House chambers.

From here, most places of interest lie a few blocks east and west along Broad Street. The **Center of Science and Industry**, or **COSI**, is housed in a streamlined structure across the river at 333 W Broad St (Mon–Sat 10am–5pm, Sun noon–6pm; adults $12, kids $7; ☎614/228-COSI or 1-877/257-COSI, ⓦwww.cosi.org), and boasts more than 300,000 square feet of exhibit space, most of it geared toward children. A mile east of COSI, the **Wendy's Original Restaurant**, 257 E Broad St (Mon–Fri 10am–8pm, Sat 10am–7pm, Sun 11am–6pm), pays homage to Dave Thomas's enduringly down-home national burger chain, started here in 1969. There's the usual menu, plus pictures of famous patrons, glass cases full of "Wendy" dolls, the original homemade dress Thomas's daughter Wendy wore when she posed for the logo that's still used today, and other memorabilia.

Three blocks east, a giant Henry Moore sculpture stands at the entrance to the inviting **Columbus Museum of Art**, 480 E Broad St (Tues, Wed, Fri–Sun 10am–5.30pm, Thurs 10am–8.30pm, closed Mon; $6, free Thurs; ☎614/221-6801, ⓦwww.columbusmuseum.org). Indoors, this airy space holds particularly good collections of Western and modernist art, including a dramatic mixed-media piece by Anselm Kiefer just by the entrance. The museum also hosts touring exhibits, and has a renowned photography gallery and a pleasant sculpture garden.

South of the museum, at the corner of Washington Ave and East Town St, the **Topiary Garden**, in Old Deaf School Park (open daylight hours; free), provides a quirky photo opportunity. In the center of this verdant little park, a group of locals have re-created in topiary Georges Seurat's famous post-Impressionist work, *Sunday Afternoon on the Island of La Grande Jatte*. Believed to be the only painting reinterpreted in evergreen shrubbery, it features fifty pruned humans, three dogs, a monkey, a cat, and eight leafy boats floating in a pond.

German Village and Brewery District

Just six blocks south of the Statehouse, I-70 separates downtown from the delightful **German Village** neighborhood. During the mid-nineteenth century, thousands of German immigrants settled in this part of Columbus, building neat redbrick homes, the most lavish of which surround the 23-acre **Schiller Park**. Their descendants, however, started leaving the area during World War I, and with Prohibition and World War II further depleting their numbers, few were left by the 1950s. The area, then known as the Old South End, soon became run-down, and by the 1960s the big corporations were eyeing it for office developments, until a group of local preservationists, determined to save these gorgeous homes from the wrecker's ball, decided to designate the area as the German Village. They formed a preservation society, drew up a list of renovation guidelines for residents, and won a place on the National Register of Historic Places.

Today the eighteen-block village is the biggest privately funded body on that register, a professional residential district with a sizeable gay community. The best way to explore its brick-paved streets, corner bars, old-style restaurants, Lutheran churches, and grand homes is to stop in at the **German Village Meeting Haus**, 588 S 3rd St (April–Sept Mon–Fri 9am–4pm, Sat 10am–2pm; rest of year closed Sun; ☎614/221-8888, ⓦwww.germanvillage.com), where popular walking tours run by the German Village Society start with a twelve-minute video presentation. The Society also oversees the immensely popular **Haus und Garten Tour** on the last Sunday in June, and the **Oktoberfest** celebrations in early September. The Village caters especially well to book-lovers; the **Book Loft**, 631 S 3rd St (daily 10am–11pm), crams its books, many of them discounted, into thirty-two rooms of a former residence.

Just across High Street (US-23) are the warehouses of the **Brewery District**, where, until Prohibition, the German immigrants brewed beer by traditional methods. Many of the original buildings still stand, but today the beer is produced by a handful of microbreweries such as **Columbus Brewing Co.**, 525 Short St, which sometimes sets up free tours of its operation (by appointment only; ☎614/224-3626). This area is also the focus of Columbus's more mainstream **nightlife**, home to several restaurants, theme pubs, music venues, and, inevitably, brewpubs.

North of downtown

Across Nationwide Boulevard at the top end of downtown is the **Short North**, a former red-light district that's now Columbus's most vibrant enclave. Standing on either side of High Street – the main north–south thoroughfare – two landmark buildings mark the transition into the area. To the left is the restored Victorian warehouse of **North Market** (see "Eating," overleaf), while to the right is the strikingly deconstructivist **Greater Columbus Convention Center**, a massive pile of angled blocks designed by Peter Eisenman and completed in 1993.

A few blocks further north across I-670 is the start of the trail of galleries, bars, and restaurants that makes the area so popular with locals. The first Saturday of each month sees the **Gallery Hop**, when all the local art dealers throw open their doors – complementing the artworks with wine, snacks, and occasional performance pieces – and the socializing goes on well into the evening (ⓦwww.theshortnorth.com).

Businesses become a little more low-rent for a mile before High Street cuts through the **university campus** and suddenly sprouts cheap eating places and funky shopping emporia. For bargain vinyl, head to Used Kids Records, 1980 N High St. On the other side of the road, the **Wexner Center for the Arts**, North High St at 15th Ave (Mon 10am–4pm, Tues–Sat 10am–6pm; ☎614/292-3535, Ⓦwww.wexarts.org), is another Eisenman construction, even more extreme than the Convention Center; it's home to cutting-edge contemporary art exhibitions, movies, mixed-media performances, a café, and a bookstore.

Eating

The Short North and German Village neighborhoods are crammed with places to **eat**, be they bottom-dollar snack bars or stylish and adventurous bistros. For a wide range of ethnic and organic snacks during the day, try the **North Market**, downtown at 59 Spruce St (Tues–Fri 9am–7pm, Sat 8am–5pm, Sun noon–5pm; ☎614/463-9664), which also sells fresh produce.

Barcelona 263 E Whittier St, German Village ☎614/444-1130. Noted for its *tapas* and desserts, this stylishly decorated local favorite also does tasty Mediterranean entrees.

Cap City Fine Diner 1299 Olentangy River Rd ☎614/291-3663. A self-proclaimed "upscale diner," this big, lively joint, just off downtown, serves up comfort food (meatloaf) with new twists (chili-onion rings and buttermilk mashed potatoes). Huge portions, especially the desserts; lunch entrees around $8, dinner $14.

Cup O' Joe Coffee & Dessert House 627 S 3rd St, German Village ☎614/221-1JOE. One of

Columbus's best-loved coffeehouses, it offers great desserts, coffees, and comfy sofas.

Katzinger's 475 S 3rd St, German Village ☎614/228-3354. A mesmerizing range of sandwiches, Jewish munchies, and cheesecakes, though prices are high for a deli.

Schmidt's Restaurant und Sausage Haus 240 E Kossuth St, German Village ☎614/444-6808. This Columbus landmark (since 1886) serves schnitzel and strudel in a former slaughterhouse.

Tapatio 491 N Park St, Short North ☎614/221-1085. Inventive Caribbean and South American food, with a great patio.

Nightlife

Not long ago, Columbus was being tipped as "the next Seattle"; while that didn't happen, this youthful university town has a rich source of local **bands**, from country revivalists to experimental alternative acts. In addition to the German Village, the **gay scene** is concentrated in the Short North on and around North High Street, with a few additional bars and clubs downtown – the biweekly *OUTlook* has complete listings. On most summer Friday evenings there are **free concerts** in downtown Bicentennial Park on the Scioto River. The *Other Paper* and *Columbus Alive* provide free details of what's happening around town.

Dick's Den 2417 N High St ☎614/268-9573. This campus dive bar has good jazz on the weekends.

Little Brother's 1100 N High St, Short North ☎614/421-2025, Ⓦwww.littlebrothers.com. Underground sounds, from alternative rock to swing and spoken-word.

Ludlow's 485 S Front St, Brewery District ☎614/224-1212. Pick of the more mainstream Brewery District venues, with live bands Thurs–Sat.

Oldfield's On High 2590 N High St ☎614/784-0477, Ⓦwww.oldfieldsonhigh.com. Predominantly collegiate campus bar with eclectic live music tastes.

Short North Tavern 674 N High St, Short North ☎614/221-2432. The oldest bar in the neighborhood, with live bands playing on the weekend.

Union Station Video Café 630 N High St, Short North ☎614/228-3740. Popular gay video bar with a decent selection of appetizers and sandwiches, plus a pool table and Internet access.

Cincinnati

CINCINNATI, just across the Ohio River from Kentucky and roughly three hundred miles from both Detroit and Chicago, is a dynamic commercial metropolis with a definite European flavor and a sense of the South. Its tidy center, rich in architecture and culture, lies within a few minutes' easy walk of the arty **Mount Adams** district, the attractive **riverfront**, and the lively **Over-the-Rhine** area, in the north end of downtown.

The city was founded in 1788 at the point where a Native American trading route crossed the river. Its name comes from a group of Revolutionary War admirers of the Roman general Cincinnatus, who saved Rome in 458 BC and then returned to his small farm and refused to accept any reward or glory. Cincinnati quickly became an important supply point for pioneers heading west on flatboats and rafts, and its population skyrocketed with the establishment of a major steamboat **riverport** in 1811. Tens of thousands of **German** immigrants poured in during the 1830s.

Loyalties were split by the **Civil War**. At first, merchants were perturbed by the loss of important markets; then they began to pick up lucrative government contracts, and the city decided that its future lay with the Union. In the prosperous postwar decade, Cincinnati acquired Fountain Square, the prodigious Music and Exhibition Hall, a zoo, art museum, public library, and the country's first professional baseball team. **Sport** remains a great source of pride: downtown gift shops are decked out in the orange and black of the **Bengals** football team and the red and white of baseball's **Reds**.

Arrival, information, and getting around

Cincinnati–Northern Kentucky International Airport is twelve miles south of downtown, in Covington, Kentucky. **Taxis** to the city center (☎859/586-5236) cost $24. The **Greyhound** station is on the eastern fringe of the city center, just off Broadway, at 1005 Gilbert Ave. Amtrak **trains** arrive a mile northwest of downtown at the Union Terminal museum complex, which is on the daytime citywide Metro **bus** network (50¢; ☎513/621-4455).

Cincinnati's main **visitor center** is at 300 W 6th St (Mon–Fri 9am–5pm; ☎513/621-2142 or 1-800/CINCY-USA; ⓦwww.cincyusa.com); there's another – and perhaps more accessible – visitor center in Fountain Square (Mon–Sat 10am–5pm, Sun noon–5pm), as well as information booths around Fountain Square and at 605 Philadelphia St in Covington (daily 10am–6pm; ☎859/655-4159).

Downtown Cincy (as the city is affectionately known) is easily walkable. The best way to move between there and the sights across the river in Covington and Newport, KY, is via the South Bank Shuttle Tank **shuttle bus**, which picks up at Fountain Square in front of the *Westin* – and costs only 25¢. Outlying areas and attractions can be accessed by car or by Metro buses (☎513/621-4455).

Accommodation

Although Cincinnati's quality **hotels** are reasonable by big-city standards, budget travelers may have problems finding affordable downtown rooms. Uptown **motels** – about two miles north – are much cheaper, but you'll need a car to get around safely at night.

Budget Host Inn 3356 Central Parkway ☎513/ 559-1600, ⓦwww.budgethost.com. Just about the cheapest place in uptown Cincinnati, though doubles vary greatly in price. Three miles from downtown. ❸

Gateway B&B 326 E 6th St, Newport, KY
☎859/581-6447. Comfortable, affordable Victorian
place, five minutes from downtown Cincy and
Covington, KY. **⑤**
Holiday Inn Downtown 800 W 8th St
☎513/241-8660, ⓦwww.holiday-inn.com. Fairly
priced downtown rooms. **⑤**
Marriott at River Center 10 W River Center Blvd,
Covington, KY ☎859/261-2900 or 1-800/228-
9290, ⓦwww.marriotthotels.com. This luxury hotel
on the river has spacious rooms and great service,

and an on-site pool and spa. **⑥–⑧**
Vernon Manor Hotel 400 Oak St ☎513/281-
3300, ⓦwww.vernonmanor.com. 1924 landmark
that features huge suite rooms in an old-style
hotel. Though a good location for the university
and zoo, don't walk around at night. **⑦**
Westin Hotel 21 E 5th St ☎513/621-7700,
ⓦwww.westin.com. Another top luxury option
right downtown. **⑦–⑧**

Downtown

Downtown Cincinnati rolls back from the Ohio River to fill a flat basin area
ringed by a disarray of steep hills. During the city's emergent industrial years,
the filth, disease, crime, and general commotion of the so-called Sausage and
Rat rows led the middle classes to abandon downtown en masse. Nowadays,
however, attractive stores, street vendors, restaurants, cafés, open spaces, and gardens occupy the area. The city's rich blend of architecture is best appreciated
on the **walking tour** detailed in an excellent free booklet from the visitor
centers. Over, among, and even right through the hotel plazas, office lobbies,
and retail areas, the **Skywalk** network of air-conditioned passages and flyovers
spans sixteen city blocks.

At the geographic center of downtown, the **Genius of the Waters** in
Fountain Square sprays a cascade of hundreds of jets, meant to symbolize the
city's trading links. Surrounded by a tree-dotted plaza and all but enclosed by
soaring facades of glass and steel, the area is a popular lunch spot and venue for
daytime concerts. Looming above at Fifth and Vine streets, the 48-story Art
Deco **Carew Tower** has a viewing gallery on its top floor that gives a wonderful panorama of the tight bends of the Ohio River and the surrounding
hillsides (Mon–Thurs 9.30am–5.30pm, Fri & Sat 9.30am–5pm, Sun
11am–5pm; $2).

Just east of Fountain Square are the Art Deco headquarters of the detergents
and personal hygiene giant **Procter & Gamble**. The company was formed in
1837 by candlemaker William Procter and soapmaker James Gamble, to exploit
the copious supply of animal fat from the slaughterhouses of "**Porkopolis**," as
Cincinnati was then known. A shady style of management has spawned tales of
dubious religious and political links; the corporate logo even had to be
changed to counter accusations that it was a satanic symbol. By sponsoring
radio's "Puddle Family" in 1932, the company created the world's first **soap
opera**.

Nearby, the left-field multimedia modern art exhibitions at the superb
Contemporary Arts Center, in the Mercantile Center at 44 E Sixth St (Sun,
Tues & Fri 11am–6pm, Mon 11am–9pm, Sat noon–6pm; $6.50; ☎513/721-
0390, ⓦwww.spiral.org), lead to continual run-ins with Cincy's more conservative citizens. By contrast, the **Taft Museum**, just east of downtown in an
immaculate 1820 Federal-style mansion at 316 Pike St (Mon–Sat 10am–5pm,
Sun 1–5pm; $4; ☎513/241-0343, ⓦwww.taftmuseum.org), contains a price-
less collection of works by Rembrandt, Goya, Turner, and Gainsborough, plus
some staggering Ming porcelain and French enamels. The statue of a weary
Abraham Lincoln in **Lytle Park**, in front of the museum, was criticized as
unpatriotic when unveiled in 1917; it's now seen as a great example of sculptural realism.

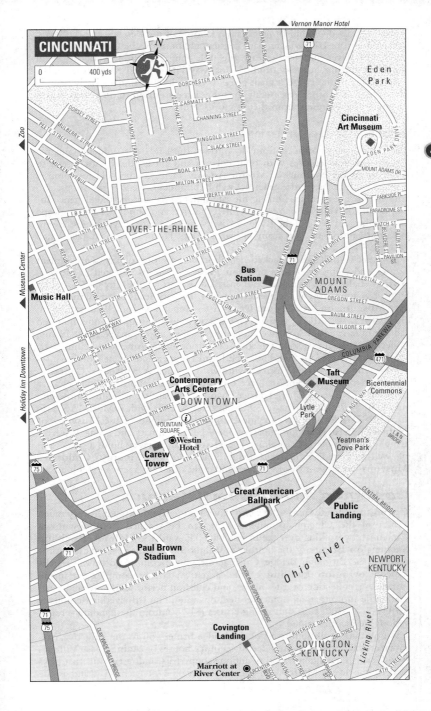

CINCINNATI

0   400 yds

N

Vernon Manor Hotel

Zoo

Museum Center

Holiday Inn Downtown

DORSEY STREET

MULBERRY STREET

PEETE STREET

McMICKEN AVENUE

REPUBLIC STREET

CLAY STREET

VINE STREET

RACE STREET

ELM STREET

COURT STREET

PLUM STREET

CENTRAL AVENUE

ALVIN STREET

SYCAMORE TERRACE

JOSEPHINE STREET

BURNET AVENUE

RYAN AVENUE

DORCHESTER AVENUE

CARMATT ST

CHANNING STREET

RINGGOLD STREET

SLACK STREET

PEUBLO

BOAL STREET

MILTON STREET

LIBERTY HILL

HIGHLAND AVENUE

READING ROAD

71

Eden
Park

GILBERT AVENUE

Cincinnati
Art Museum

EDEN PARK DRIVE

MOUNT ADAMS DR.

PARKSIDE PL.

PARADROME ST.

HATCH ST.

ELSINORE AVENUE

IDA STREET

VAN METER STREET

BELCREST ST.

FULLER ST.

ST. GREGORY ST.

PAVILION
ST.

LIBERTY STREET

LIBERTY STREET

OVER-THE-RHINE

15TH STREET

14TH STREET

13TH STREET

12TH STREET

READING ROAD

Bus
Station

GILBERT AVENUE

71

MONASTERY STREET

MARCHAM DRIVE

CELESTIAL ST.

MOUNT
ADAMS

OREGON STREET

BAUM STREET

KILGORE ST.

Music Hall

CENTRAL PARKWAY

12TH STREET

BOWEN STREET

MAIN STREET

WALNUT STREET

SYCAMORE STREET

BROADWAY

9TH STREET

GARFIELD
PLACE

7TH STREET

Contemporary
Arts Center

DOWNTOWN

6TH STREET

i

5TH STREET

FOUNTAIN
SQUARE

Westin
Hotel

Carew
Tower

4TH STREET

COURT STREET

EGGLESTON AVENUE

COURT STREET

8TH STREET

READING ROAD

Taft
Museum

Lytle
Park

COLUMBIA PARKWAY

471

Bicentennial
Commons

PETE ROSE WAY

L & N
BRIDGE

Yeatman's
Cove Park

3RD STREET

71

Great American
Ballpark

STADIUM DRIVE

Public
Landing

CENTRAL BRIDGE

75

71

Paul Brown
Stadium

PETE ROSE WAY

MEHRING WAY

ROEBLING SUSPENSION BRIDGE

Ohio River

NEWPORT,
KENTUCKY

71

75

CLAY WADE BAILEY BRIDGE

Covington
Landing

RIVERSIDE DRIVE

2ND STREET

COVINGTON,
KENTUCKY

ROEBLING SUSPENSION BRIDGE

RIVERCENTER BLVD

SCOTT STREET

GREENUP STREET

COURT AVENUE

GARRARD ST.

4TH STREET

Licking River

Marriott at
River Center

South across I-71, Paul Brown Stadium, home of the Bengals, and the Reds' Great American Ballpark are giant cement additions on the Cincinnati side of the Ohio River. Just to the east, the mile-long **riverside walk** begins at **Public Landing**, at the bottom of Broadway. The cobbled wharf here, on the original site of the city, is a great place to take a look at immaculately painted showboats and other river craft. Nearby, **Bicentennial Commons** was a 200th-birthday present from the city to itself in 1988.

North of downtown

Just over a mile northeast from downtown, the land rises suddenly and the streets – narrow courses with tight corners and abrupt dead ends – start to conform to the contours of **Mount Adams**. Here, century-old townhouses coexist with avant-garde galleries, stylish boutiques, trendy gift shops, and international restaurants. During the late nineteenth century, the elegant dining rooms of Mount Adams entertained the rich and famous eager to escape the squalor and noise of the Basin. Today its lively bars attract yuppies, students, hedonists, and iconoclasts from all over the city. From downtown, take a taxi or the #49 bus.

Adjacent to this tightly packed neighborhood are the rolling lawns, verdant copses, and scenic overlooks of **Eden Park**, its features reflected in the new **Mirror Lake**, a man-made pool installed as part of the city's Millennium Project. A loop road at the western end of the park leads to the **Cincinnati Art Museum**, on Art Museum Drive (Tues–Sun 11am–5pm, Wed until 9pm; free; ☎513/721-ARTS; ⓦwww.cincinnatiartmuseum.org). Its one hundred labyrinthine galleries span five thousand years, taking in an excellent Islamic collection as well as a solid selection of European and American paintings by the likes of Matisse, Monet, Picasso, Edward Hopper, and Grant Wood.

Meanwhile, northwest from downtown, Cincinnati's **Museum Center** is housed in the magnificent Art Deco **Union Terminal**, approached via a stately driveway off Ezzard Charles Drive (Mon–Sat 10am–5pm, Sun 11am–6pm; museums $6.75 each, any two $9.75, all three $12.75, with OMNIMAX $15; ☎513/287-7000, ⓦwww.cincymuseum.org). Highlights of the **Museum of Natural History** are dioramas of Ice Age Cincinnati and "The Cavern," which houses a living bat colony. The **Historical Society** holds a succession of well-presented, short-term exhibitions, and the **Cinergy Children's Museum** has a two-story treehouse and eight other interactive exhibit areas.

Covington and Newport, Kentucky

Covington, directly across the Ohio River on the Kentucky side, is very much a part of the Cincinnati hinterland. It can be reached from downtown Cincinnati by walking over the bright-blue 355-yard 1867 **John A. Roebling Suspension Bridge**, at the bottom of Walnut Street, which served as a prototype for the Brooklyn Bridge. Once across, you're confronted by the much-hyped **Covington Landing** – "the largest waterfront complex on inland waters" – a collection of cafés, shops, and clubs on permanently moored boats that's little more than an upmarket mall on water. The BB riverboat company (☎859/261-8500) runs sightseeing cruises ($12.50) from the Landing – reservations are recommended.

Ten minutes' walk southwest of the bridge brings you to the attractive, narrow, tree-lined streets and nineteenth-century houses of **MainStrasse Village**. It's a Germanic neighborhood of antique shops, bars, and restaurants that plays host to the lively **Maifest** on the third weekend of each May, and is the centerpiece of the citywide **Oktoberfest** on the weekend after Labor Day. At 6th and Philadelphia streets, 21 mechanical figures accompanied by glockenspiel music toll the hour on the German Gothic **Carroll Chimes Bell Tower**. Just beyond Covington at I-75 exit 186 is the **Oldenberg Brewery**, crammed with boozing memorabilia; tours of the microbrewery and its museum cost $3 (daily 10am–5pm).

Across the Licking River from Covington, the subdued town of **Newport** has gotten a lot livelier since the opening of a large shopping complex and the impressive **Newport Aquarium**, One Aquarium Way (daily: summer 10am–7pm; rest of year 10am–6pm; ☎859/491-FINS or 1-800/406-FISH, ⓦ www.newportaquarium.com). Clear underwater tunnels and see-through floors allow visitors to literally be surrounded by sharks and snapping gators.

Eating

Cincinnati boasts enough excellent home-grown gourmet and continental **restaurants** to ensure that national chains have a low profile in the city. It's also famous for fast-food **Cincinnati chili**, a combination of spaghetti noodles, meat, cheese, onions, and kidney beans, with chains such as *Skyline Chili*, open from breakfast to midnight at more than forty locations, including Vine and 7th streets downtown.

Aralia 815 Elm St ☎513/723-1217. Excellent Sri Lankan curries in a handy downtown location.
Courtyard Café 1211 Main St, Over-the-Rhine ☎513/723-1119. Good grill food, burgers, and desserts, at value-for-money prices.
Dee Felice 529 Main St, Covington, KY ☎859/261-2365. This small and atmospheric restaurant/jazz venue specializes in Cajun cuisine, with lots of fresh seafood dishes.
Longworth's 1108 St Gregory St, Mount Adams ☎513/651-2253. Good hamburgers, sandwiches, salads, and pizzas at attractive prices in a delightful garden setting. Food is served all day until midnight, with music until 2.30am.
Mullane's Parkside Café 723 Race St

☎513/381-1331. This friendly joint, bedecked with local art, has an excellent choice of vegetarian options.
Rookwood Pottery 1077 Celestial St, Mount Adams ☎513/721-5456. Steaks and sandwiches are served inside the former kilns of Cincinnati's celebrated pottery.
Scalea's Ristorante 320 Greenup St, Covington, KY ☎859/491-3334. An atmospheric and inventive Italian eatery, with entrees at $12–25; the restaurant's attached deli/market offers cheaper options.
Tucker's 1637 Vine St ☎513/721-7123; also 18 E 13th St, Over-the-Rhine ☎513/241-3354. Get a perfect start on your day with traditional and gourmet breakfasts in a 1950s setting.

Nightlife and entertainment

After dark, the hottest area with the widest appeal is the **Over-the-Rhine** district, which fans out from Main Street around 12th and 14th streets, and buzzes every night – though be careful where you park or walk, as it backs onto some dodgy areas. The bars, restaurants, and cafés of scenic **Mount Adams** offer a good choice of music, food, and atmosphere, especially on warm summer nights, when the narrow streets are full of revelers. The studenty **Corryville** neighborhood, a five-minute drive northwest from downtown, has a lively undergraduate edge, while **Covington Landing**, Kentucky, is busy but bland. A proliferation of **brewpubs** has sprung up all over town in the past few years, always dependable for a good drink in friendly surroundings. Entertainment **listings** for the whole city can be found in the free *Cincinnati CityBeat*.

For more cultured entertainment, **Music Hall**, 1243 Elm St (☎513/744-3344, ⓦ www.cincinnatiarts.org), an 1870s conglomeration of spires, arched windows, and cornices, is said to have near-perfect acoustics. Home to Cincinnati's Opera and Symphony Orchestra, it also hosts the May Festival of choral music. The **Cincinnati Playhouse in the Park**, in Eden Park (☎513/421-3888, ⓦwww.cincyplay.com), puts on drama, musicals, and comedies, with performances throughout the year.

Arnold's 210 E 8th St ☎513/421-6234. A fun and funky downtown spot, it's a favorite with jazz fans, though it also puts on roots and acoustic acts. Good restaurant upstairs.

Blind Lemon 936 Hatch St, Mount Adams ☎513/241-3885. Beyond the intimate, low-ceilinged bar, you'll find a relaxed patio crowd. Music (mostly acoustic) nightly at 9.30.

Bogart's 2621 Vine St, Corryville ☎513/281-8400, ⓦwww.bogarts.com. Established indie acts play this mid-sized venue directly opposite *Sudsy Malone's* (see opposite).

The Pavilion 949 Pavilion St, Mount Adams ☎513/744-9200. From its terraced outdoor deck, you'll have great views of the city and the Ohio River.

Rhythm & Blues Café 1142 Main St, Over-the-Rhine ☎513/684-0080. Good food and great atmosphere. Live rock, blues, and various genres Wed through Sat nights.

Sudsy Malone's Rock & Roll Laundry & Bar 2626 Vine St, Corryville ☎513/751-2300, ⓦwww.sudsys.com. You can drink beer, catch a live indie act, and wash your clothes all at the same time in this fun Corryville landmark. Daily 7am–2am.

Warehouse 1313 Vine St, Over-the-Rhine ☎513/241-6696, ⓦwww.warehousecincinnati .com. A popular dance club, *Warehouse* plays alternative and industrial sounds midweek and the latest house on the weekends.

Michigan

Mention **MICHIGAN** and most people think of cars, heavy industry, and inner-city Detroit. Midwesterners prefer to focus on the state's magnificent scenery. The beaches, dunes, and cliffs along the 3200-mile shoreline of its two vividly contrasting **peninsulas** – bordering four of the five Great Lakes – rival many an oceanfront state.

The mitten-shaped **Lower Peninsula** is dominated from its southeastern corner by the industrial giant of **Detroit**, surrounded by satellite cities heavily devoted to the automotive industry. In the west, the scenic 350-mile Lake Michigan shoreline drive passes through likeable little ports before reaching the stunning **Sleeping Bear Dunes** and resort towns such as **Traverse City**, in the peninsula's balmy northwest corner. The desolate, dramatic, and thinly populated **Upper Peninsula**, reaching out from Wisconsin like a claw to separate lakes Superior and Michigan, is a far cry indeed from the cosmopolitan south.

In the mid-seventeenth century, **French explorers** forged a successful trading relationship with the Chippewa, Ontario, and other Native American tribes. The **British**, who acquired control after 1763, were far more brutal. Governor Henry Hamilton, the "Hair Buyer of Detroit," advocated taking scalps rather than prisoners. Ever since, Michigan's economy has developed in waves, the eighteenth-century fur, timber, and copper booms culminating in the state establishing itself at the forefront of the nation's manufacturing capacity, thanks to its abundant raw materials, good transportation links, and the genius of innovators such as **Henry Ford**. Despite the slumps of the Seventies and Eighties, **automobile production** remains the major source of Michigan income – though tourism is now a four-season money-spinner, too.

Getting around Michigan

Greyhound **buses** run regularly throughout Michigan's south, but services elsewhere are less frequent, and those few buses that serve the remote Upper Peninsula travel through at night. Amtrak **trains** between New York and Chicago stop at Detroit, Dearborn, and Ann Arbor. Michigan's principal **airport** is just outside Detroit. **Cycling** is both feasible and rewarding, particularly with the abundance of bike paths in and around Traverse City; Michigan Bicycle Touring in Kingsley (☎616/463-5885, ⓦwww.bikembt.com) organizes tours and can help with routes.

Detroit

DETROIT, the birthplace of the mass-production **car industry** and the **Motown** sound, has long had an image problem. The city boasts a billion-dollar downtown development, ultramodern motor-manufacturing plants, some excellent museums, and one of the nation's biggest art galleries – but since the 1960s, media attention has dwelt instead on its huge tracts of urban wasteland, where for block after block there's nothing but the occasional heavily fortified loan shop or grocery store. Although cities like Atlanta, Newark, and Washington, DC post much worse crime statistics, the press seems intent on painting Detroit as some kind of war zone.

Such views incur the wrath of many Detroiters, who claim that the press has magnified the city's problems. Though that assertion certainly carries weight, Detroit – which has lost nearly half its citizens, almost a million people, in forty years – has unarguably suffered. However, following the resurgence of Cleveland, Pittsburgh, and other Rust Belt cities, Detroit, under the leadership of **Mayor Dennis Archer**, is showing signs of turning the corner. Two sports stadiums and three big-time casinos have recently opened, and plans are afoot to enhance the waterfront and build two thousand new hotel rooms downtown. The overall goal is to beautify and edify the city by the time the Super Bowl comes to town in 2006. And, while these developments won't wipe out the city's problems in one fell swoop, they're an exciting start.

Founded in 1701 by **Antoine de Mothe Cadillac**, as a trading post for the French to do business with the Chippewa, Detroit was no more than a medium-sized port two hundred years later. Then **Henry Ford**, **Ransom Eli Olds**, the **Chevrolets**, and the **Dodge** brothers began to build their automobile empires. Thanks to the introduction of the mass assembly line, Detroit sped into high gear in the 1920s, expanding into the countryside and booming like a mining town – fast, compulsive, and indifferent to the needs of its population. The auto barons sponsored the construction of segregated neighborhoods and unceremoniously dispensed with workers during times of low demand. Such policies created huge ghettos, and the city came to a boil in July 1967 in the bloodiest **riot** in the USA for fifty years. More than forty people died and 1300 buildings were destroyed. Nothing was solved, and little even improved. The **inner city** was left to fend for itself, while the all-important motor industry was rocked by the oil crises and Japanese competition.

Today, though heavily scarred and bruised, Detroit is not the apocalyptic mess some would have it. New businesses and theaters are opening downtown, and suburban residents have started to return to the city's festivals, theaters, clubs, and restaurants. As for orientation, it makes sense to think of Detroit as a region rather than a concentrated city – and, so long as you plan your time and don't mind driving, it holds plenty to see and do. For the moment, **downtown** is not so much the heart of the giant as just another segment. Other interesting segments include the huge **Cultural Center**, freewheeling **Royal Oak**, posh **Birmingham**, the Ford-town of **Dearborn**, nearby **Windsor, Ontario**, and the college town of **Ann Arbor**, a short drive west.

Arrival, information, and getting around

Flights come into **Detroit Metropolitan Wayne County Airport** in Romulus, eighteen miles southwest of downtown and a hefty $30-plus taxi ride, though Metropolitan (☎734/727-1740) runs a shuttle for $22.

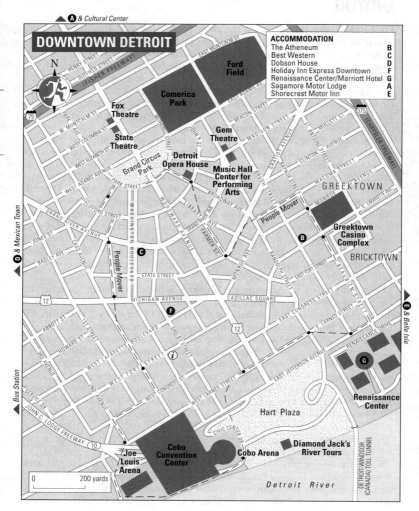

DOWNTOWN DETROIT

ACCOMMODATION
The Atheneum — B
Best Western — C
Dobson House — D
Holiday Inn Express Downtown — F
Renaissance Center/Marriott Hotel — G
Sagamore Motor Lodge — A
Shorecrest Motor Inn — E

The main **Greyhound** (1001 Howard Ave) and **Amtrak** (2601 Rose St) terminals are in areas where it's inadvisable to walk around at night. Amtrak also stops ten miles out at 16121 Michigan Ave, Dearborn, near the Henry Ford Museum and several mid-range motels, and at unstaffed suburban stations at Birmingham, Pontiac, and Royal Oak.

Detroit's main **visitor center** is downtown at 211 W Fort St, on the tenth floor (Mon–Fri 9am–5pm; ☎313/202-1800 or 1-800/DETROIT, Ⓦwww.visitdetroit.com). An information booth is at the entrance to the Henry Ford Greenfield Village (May–Sept daily 9am–5pm; ☎313/271-1620). The main **post office** is at 1401 W Fort St, at Eighth St (Mon–Fri 8.30am–5pm, Sat 8am–noon; zip code 48200).

Downtown, the People Mover elevated **railway** loops around thirteen art-adorned stations (Mon–Thurs 7am–11pm, Fri 7am–midnight, Sat 9am–midnight, Sun noon–8pm; 50¢). Otherwise, public transportation is inadequate. DOT **buses** (☎313/933-1300) run a patchy inner-city service for $1.25 per ride, while the slightly better SMART buses ($1.50; ☎313/962-5515) serve suburbia. Transportation in the Motor City is geared firmly towards the **car**; driving is not too much of a challenge, but you do need to know where you're headed. During the day, April through August, the Attractions Shuttle **minibuses** (☎313/259-8726) run between the major sights, with unlimited stops for $4.

Accommodation

Downtown Detroit caters well for expense-account travelers – its top-range hotels are as secure as any city's – but if your budget is restricted it's harder to find lodging that is both cheap and safe at night. A fifteen-percent tax comes tacked onto room bills.

The Atheneum 1000 Brush St ☎313/962-2323 or 1-800/772-2323, Ⓦwww.atheneumsuites.com. At this swish all-suite hotel in Greektown, some units fetch more than $300 a night; others are a third of that price. ❼

Detroit Marriott Renaissance Center Renaissance Center ☎313/568-8000 or 1-800/228-9290, Ⓦwww.mariotthotels.com. A fun place to stay, it towers over the city by the river – ask for a room on the upper floors. ❻

Dobson House 1439 Bagley Ave ☎313/965-1887. Near the former Tiger Stadium, a functional Victorian B&B that includes continental breakfast in its rates. ❺

Fairfield Inn – Auburn Hills 1294 Opdyke Rd ☎248/373-2228. On the north edge of town, this clean motel is close to the Pontiac Silverdome. ❹

Fairfield Inn – Metro Airport 31119 Flynn Drive, Romulus ☎734/728-2322. The pick of the budget motels near the airport. ❹

HI-Country Grandma's Home Hostel 22330 Bell Rd, New Boston ☎734/753-4901. This friendly home hostel on the outskirts of Dearborn is halfway between Detroit and Ann Arbor. Beds are $11 for HI-AYH members, $14 for others. ❶

Holiday Inn Express 34952 Woodward Ave, Birmingham ☎248/646-7300. Recently renovated, this *Holiday Inn* is reasonably well-placed for Birmingham and Royal Oak restaurants and bars. ❼

Holiday Inn Express Downtown 1020 Washington Blvd ☎313/887-7000. This mid-range hotel offers a pool, athletic room, and complimentary continental breakfast. ❹

Hotel St Regis 3071 W Grand Blvd ☎313/873-3000. This nice old hotel is about four miles from downtown. Other than the Motown Museum, there's little to see in the immediate area, though it is well-placed for those with a car. Weekend rates see a price drop of around $35. ❻

Hyatt Regency Dearborn Fairlane Town Center, Dearborn ☎313/593-1234 or 1-800/233-1234. A candy-brown colossus, it has every imaginable amenity. Though not cheap, it does have special deals. ❼

Red Roof Inn 24130 Michigan Ave, Dearborn ☎313/278-9732 or 1-800/843-7663. Clean budget lodgings near the Henry Ford Museum. ❹

Royal Oak Travel Lodge 30776 N Woodward Ave

248/549-1600. A recently renovated motel close to a trendy Royal Oak. To get here, follow Woodward Ave away from the river (north) for 8 miles. ❸

Shorecrest Motor Inn 1316 E Jefferson Ave ☎313/568-3000 or 1-800/992-9616. A friendly, family-run place in lively Rivertown, just off downtown, this place has clean, good-value rooms. ❹

Downtown

Futuristic glass-box office buildings and a tastefully revamped park overlook the deodorant-green **Detroit River**, but for the most part downtown seems rather empty – even in the middle of the day, its streets are quiet and uncrowded. One reason is that most offices and stores are squeezed into the six gleaming towers of the **Renaissance Center**, a virtual city within a city. Zooming up 73 stories from the riverbank, the towers offer a great view of the metropolis from an observation deck ($5). This giant business, convention, and retail center, known locally as the RenCen, was one of many complexes developed by **Detroit Renaissance** (a joint public/private sector project) to rejuvenate downtown in the aftermath of the 1967 riot. Seen by some as the savior of the city, the consortium is viewed less favorably by those who were compelled to sell their small businesses and homes to make way for its mammoth projects. Nevertheless, it's an attractive public space: a soaring glass atrium known as the "Winter Garden" has recently opened on the river side, while future plans to rescue the east riverfront from industrial use include a public park and boardwalk to Belle Isle (see below).

Rare greenspace is found among the fountains and sculptures of **Hart Plaza**, which rolls down to the river in the shade of the RenCen. The plaza hosts free lunchtime concerts and lively weekend ethnic festivals all summer long. The US leg of the annual **Ford–Detroit International Jazz Festival**, the largest free jazz festival in the world, takes place here in early September. Across the plaza from the RenCen is the Cobo Convention Center; next to this is **Joe Louis Arena** (☎313/983-6859), home of Detroit's beloved Red Wings hockey team.

Ten blocks north of the RenCen up Woodward Avenue is the **Theater District**, downtown's prime nightlife spot. Highlights are the magnificently restored Siamese-Byzantine **Fox Theatre**, 2211 Woodward Ave (☎313/983-6611, ⓦwww.olympiaentertainment.com), a huge old movie palace that is the city's top concert, drama, and film venue, and the grand Italian Renaissance **State Theatre** next door (☎313/961-5450). This area is at the center of the city's massive **Columbia Street** redevelopment project, home to the new baseball and football stadiums (see "Sports," p.339), as well as microbreweries, coffeehouses, and the inevitable themed restaurants, including a *Hard Rock Café*.

Three miles east of the RenCen, **Belle Isle Park** is an inner-city island retreat with twenty miles of walkways, sports facilities, a marina, and free attractions including an aquarium, a Great Lakes Museum, and elaborate gardens. It is quiet during the week but can attract crowds on the weekend. Belle Isle Park is also home to the annual **Detroit Grand Prix** Indy car race. To see the island, use Diamond Jack's River Tours (June–Sept; $12; ☎313/843-7676, ⓦwww.diamondjack.com), which depart from Hart Plaza downtown, last two hours, and loop round Belle Isle, or just take DOT bus #25 and transfer at MacArthur Bridge to the #12.

The Detroit Cultural Center

Three miles northwest of downtown, next to Wayne State University, the top-class museums of the **Detroit Cultural Center** are clustered within easy walking distance of one another; you can easily spend a whole day here.

One of America's most prestigious art museums, the colossal **Detroit Institute of Arts**, 5200 Woodward Ave (Wed & Thurs 10am–4pm, Fri 10am–9pm, Sat & Sun 10am–5pm; $4; ☎313/833-7900, ⓦwww.dia.org), traces the history of civilization through one hundred galleries, most notably Chinese, Persian, Egyptian, Greek, Roman, Dutch, and American collections – not to mention the largest Italian collection outside of Italy. The museum has masterpieces such as a Van Gogh self-portrait and Joos Van Cleeve's *Adoration of the Magi*, as well as Diego Rivera's enormous, show-stealing, 1933 *Detroit Industry* mural. Guided **tours** (no additional charge) take place at 1pm, with an extra tour on Sunday at 2.30pm.

The impressive Charles H. Wright **Museum of African American History**, 315 E Warren St (Tues–Sat 9.30am–5pm, Sun 1–5pm; $5; ☎313/494-5800, ⓦwww.maah-detroit.org), is the largest African-American museum in the world. Its massive core exhibit covers 600 years of history in eight distinct segments, starting with a chilling sculpture of a slave boat, before moving through the Civil War, the Depression, and the work of Dr Martin Luther King Jr and Malcolm X, before settling on contemporary African-American society. Every Friday night at 6pm, at the museum's 300-seat **General Motors Theater**, "Friday Night Fever" is a weekly performance series that celebrates the talents of African-Americans, in everything from film and theater to dance and music. **Tickets** usually run $20–25, and can be obtained in advance or at the door.

Also in the Cultural Center, the **Detroit Historical Museum**, 5401 Woodward Ave (Tues–Fri 9.30am–5pm, Sat 10am–5pm, Sun 11am–5pm; $5; ☎313/833-1805, ⓦwww.detroithistorical.org), interprets the city's past through its "**Streets of Old Detroit**" display of reconstructed shops dating from the 1840s to the 1900s. The most interesting exhibit, not surprisingly, examines the automobile, with an automated display of the "body drop" process on an assembly line, in which a car's frame is lowered onto its chassis.

The Motown Museum

Unlike cities such as Memphis, Nashville, and New Orleans, Detroit is devoid of the bars, clubs, and homes of its musical heroes. The golden age of Motown was very much confined to a specific time and a place, and, disappointingly, only at the **Motown Museum**, 2648 W Grand Blvd (Tues–Sat 10am–6pm; $8; ☎313/875-2264, ⓦwww.motownmuseum.com), can Tamla fans pay homage to one of the world's most celebrated record labels. The museum, run independently as a not-for-profit organization, is housed in the small white-and-blue clapboard house that served as Motown's recording studio from 1959 to 1972. On the ground floor, Studio A remains just as it was left: battered instruments stand piled up against the nicotine-stained acoustic wall-tiles, and a well-scuffed Steinway piano all but fills the room. Upstairs are the former living quarters of label founder **Berry Gordy**, while in the adjoining house (once Motown's publishing office), record sleeves, gold and platinum discs, and other memorabilia are displayed. The enthusiastic and knowledgeable staff will quite happily give one person the full **tour**. Each October, Motown legends contribute to the museum's upkeep by performing at the annual 2648 Grand.

The Motown sound

The legend that is Tamla Motown started in 1959 when Ford worker and part-time songwriter **Berry Gordy Jr** borrowed $800 to set up a studio. From his first hit onward – the prophetic "Money (That's What I Want)" – he set out to create a crossover style, targeting his records at white and black consumers alike.

Early Motown hits were pure **formula**. Gordy softened the blue notes of most contemporary black music in favor of a more danceable, poppy beat, with **gospel**-influenced singing and clapping. Prime examples of the early approach featured all-female groups like the **Marvelettes** ("Needle in a Haystack"), the **Supremes** ("Baby Love"), and **Martha Reeves and the Vandellas** ("Nowhere to Run"), as well as the all-male **Miracles** ("Tracks of My Tears"), featuring the sophisticated love lyrics of lead singer **Smokey Robinson**. Gordy's "Quality Control Department" scrutinized every beat, playing all recordings through speakers modeled on cheap transistor radios before the final mix.

The Motown organization was an intense, close-knit community: **Marvin Gaye** married Gordy's sister, while "Little" **Stevie Wonder** was the baby of the family. The label did, however, move with the times, utilizing such innovations as the wah-wah pedal and synthesizer. By the late 1960s its output had acquired a harder sound, crowned by the acid soul productions of Norman Whitfield with the versatile **Temptations**. In 1968 the organization outgrew its premises on Grand Avenue; four years later it abandoned Detroit altogether for LA, to be closer to Hollywood. Befitting the MOR tastes of the 1970s, the top sellers now were the high-society soul of **Diana Ross** and the ballads of the **Commodores**. White artists began to appear on the label: Tom Jones is said to have turned down a contract, though R. Dean Taylor ("Indiana Wants Me") and the less successful Kiki Dee accepted.

The 1970s saw many top artists, dissatisfied with Gordy's constant intervention, leave the label. The crack songwriting team of Holland-Dozier-Holland, responsible for most of the **Four Tops'** hits, stayed in Detroit to produce the seminal **Chairmen of the Board** ("Gimme Just A Little More Time"), along with **Aretha Franklin** and **Jackie Wilson**. Today, Motown is owned by the giant **PolyGram** corporation. Artists on the label include Boyz II Men, Queen Latifah, and, to this day, Stevie Wonder.

The Henry Ford Museum, Greenfield Village, and the Automotive Hall of Fame

The enormous **Henry Ford Museum**, ten miles from downtown at 20900 Oakwood Blvd, Dearborn (Mon–Sat 9am–5pm, Sun noon–5pm; $14, or $24 with Greenfield Village, see opposite; ☎313/271-1620 or 1-800/835-5237, Ⓦwww.hfmgv.org; accessible on SMART bus routes #200 and #250), pays fulsome tribute to its founder, an inveterate collector of Americana, as a brilliant industrialist and do-gooder. The former is certainly true. The hero of the "second industrial revolution" and inventor of the assembly line didn't succeed by being a philanthropist. His Service Department of 3500 private policemen prompted the *New York Times* in 1928 to call him "an industrialist fascist – the Mussolini of Detroit." To Ford, unions were "the worst things that ever struck the earth," though he was forced to let the United Auto Workers (UAW) into his factories in 1943, after only 34 out of 78,000 workers voted against joining a union. Ford also bowed to the economic necessity of employing blacks, though he banned them from the model communities he built for his white workers. Instead, the company constructed a separate town, which he sardonically named Inkster.

In addition to the massive "**The Automobile in American Life**" exhibit ranging from early Ford models and postal carriages to NASCAR vehicles and electric cars, the twelve-acre museum amounts to a giant curiosity shop, holding several planes and trains, rows and rows of domestic inventions, and cabinets full of schoolchild collectibles like dime novels, comics, and baseball cards. Real oddities include the chair Lincoln was sitting in and the car Kennedy was riding in when each was shot, and even a test tube holding Edison's last breath. One pertinent item not on view is the Iron Cross that Hitler presented to Ford (a notorious anti-Semite) in 1938. Slated to begin in spring 2004, the **Ford Rouge Factory Tour** will guide visitors through the car manufacturing process at a historic Ford plant, using multiple-screen films, interactive displays, and demonstrations.

Down the street from the main museum complex, **Greenfield Village** is a collection of homes owned by famous Americans, relocated from across the country to this site by Ford (same hours as Ford Museum; $18, or $24 with Ford Museum; same contact info). Among the 240 buildings, you'll find Ford's own birthplace, the Wright Brothers' cycle shop, Edison's laboratory, and Firestone's farm. Costumed hosts demonstrate everything from weaving to puncture-repairing.

Directly next door to the Ford sprawl, the **Automotive Hall of Fame**, 21400 Oakwood Blvd (summer daily 10am–5pm; rest of year closed Mon; $6; ☎313/240-4000, ⊛www.automotivehalloffame.org), is more interesting than it might at first sound. In paying homage to the innovators and inventors of the global (not just the Detroit) auto industry, the interactive exhibits lets visitors see how they would have handled problems encountered by Buick, Honda, and the like. It's not just for mechanical types, either – there's a chance to pit your wits against the dealmakers who set up General Motors.

Windsor, Ontario

The riverside cafés of the easygoing Canadian city of **WINDSOR**, due south of Detroit across the Detroit River, offer pleasant views of their larger neighbor's skyline. Like Detroit, Windsor's main industry is auto manufacturing, but it's much smaller and more relaxed, and makes a good place simply to hang out. However, two downtown **casinos** have added significant traffic to the streets. For those not hooked on slots and blackjack, the most interesting attraction is booze oriented: the **Hiram Walker plant**, where Canadian Club whiskey is distilled, stands just a short stroll from downtown at Riverside and Walker (free tours and samplings daily 11am–6pm; ☎519/561-5499).

Transit Windsor **buses** (☎519/944-4111) connect the downtowns of Detroit and Windsor for $2.35 each way. Bring proper identification for customs and immigration officials. To **drive**, take the Windsor Tunnel or the less claustrophobic Ambassador Bridge ($2.25 toll). Windsor has two **visitor centers**, one across the Ambassador Bridge at 1235 Huron Church Rd, and one at 110 Park St E in the city center (both open daily 8.30am–5pm; ☎519/973-1338 or 1-800/265-3633).

Eating

Detroit's **ethnic** restaurants dish up the best (and least expensive) food in the city. **Greektown**, basically one block of Monroe Avenue between Beaubien and St Antoine streets, is crammed with authentic Greek places; it also contains Trappers Alley, a small mall brimming with good stalls and shops. Less commercial, but offering just as high a standard, are the bakeries, bars, and cantinas of **Mexican Town**, five minutes from downtown. **Royal Oak**, ten miles north, has a wide range of vaguely alternative wholefood places, along with bars, record stores, and bookstores; it's the liveliest suburban hangout in this sprawling metropolis.

Atwater Block Brewery 237 Joseph Campau St ☎ 313/393-2073. This spacious Rivertown brew-pub serves up excellent beer-battered fish, mushrooms, mussels, wings, and whatever else the chefs can think of.

Fishbone's Rhythm Kitchen Café 400 Monroe Ave, Greektown ☎ 313/965-4600. Noisy, fun, and often-packed authentic New Orleans Cajun joint with whiskey ribs, crawfish, gumbo, and lots more.

Intermezzo 1435 Randolph St ☎ 313/961-0707. The cigar-and-martini set hangs out at this modern downtown Italian place. Good food.

La-Shish 12918 Michigan Ave, Dearborn ☎ 313/584-4477. This is one in a local chain of Lebanese restaurants serving traditional Middle Eastern *tabbouleh*, falafel, kebabs and shawarma.

New Hellas Café 583 Monroe St, Greektown ☎ 313/961-5544. Known as "The One on the Corner in Greektown," this popular hangout serves *saganaki* (flaming cheese), moussaka, and lamb tips, all at reasonable prices.

Original Pancake House 33703 Woodward Ave, Birmingham ☎ 248/642-5775. This top breakfast spot offers a huge variety of superb crêpes, waffles, omelets, and pancakes.

Pronto! 608 S Washington, Royal Oak ☎ 248/544-0123. Big salads and a huge selection of sandwiches are the specialties in this soothing pastel space.

Rattlesnake Club 300 River Place, Rivertown ☎ 313/567-4400. Owned by creative Detroit master chef Jimmy Schmidt, the *Rattlesnake Club* has a setting to match the exquisite food. Dinner will set you back $30–50 per main course; lunch costs a lot less. Closed Sun.

Woodbridge Tavern 289 St Aubin St, Rivertown ☎ 313/259-0578. Excellent burgers and sandwiches, amid 1920s decor, and with a great outdoor terrace and live rock music Thurs–Sun.

Xochimilco 3409 Bagley Ave ☎ 313/843-0179. The cornerstone restaurant of Detroit's authentic Mexican Town, *Xochimilco* delivers on huge portions, great service, and superb value. Open till 2am. If it's full, try *El Zocala* across the street.

Nightlife

There's lots to do at night in Detroit – the city where the **techno** beat originated and is still going strong – though if you're unfamiliar with the layout it's best to travel by **taxi**. In the past few years young whites from the suburbs have started to come back downtown for nights out, particularly to the bars and clubs of the **Theater District**, while the **Rivertown** area is renowned for its chic bistros and funky jazz and blues bars, tucked in among rambling warehouses. The suburbs of upmarket **Birmingham** and youthful **Royal Oak** are good places to hang out, while there are a couple of fun establishments in the blue-collar neighborhood of **Hamtramck**. Way up on the northern fringe, once-deserted **Pontiac** now has a range of well-attended rock venues, dance clubs, and lounges. Canadian **Windsor** also has some good nightlife, with an age limit of 19 as opposed to Michigan's 21. For event **listings** in Detroit, Ann Arbor, and Windsor, pick up the free weekly *Metro Times*.

Gusoline Alley 309 S Center St, Royal Oak ☎ 248/545-2235. Cramped and dark with a loaded jukebox, this is a legend among Detroit bars. Go early for a seat; the wildly mixed crowd is a people-watcher's dream.

Magic Bag 22920 Woodward Ave, Ferndale ☎ 248/544-3030, ⓦ www.themagicbag.com. About two miles south of Royal Oak, this popular club boasts a huge range of beers, top blues artists, and regular roots acts.

Magic Stick 4120 Woodward Ave ☎ 313/833-9700, ⓦ www.majesticdetroit.com/stick.asp. This great venue incorporates billiards, bands, and, of course, alcoholic beverages. It's next to the Majestic Theater, a venue for big rock shows and huge techno nights.

Moto 3515 Caniff St, Hamtramck ☎ 313/369-0090. *The* place to see, be seen, and dance to techno and funk. Also books occasional live acts.

Rhinocero 265 Riopelle St, Rivertown ☎ 313/292-9230. Poppy jazz hangout – a tight squeeze but fun.

Saint Andrew's Hall/Shelter 431 E Congress St ☎ 313/961-MELT. This cramped downtown club promotes top bands on the alternative circuit. It only holds 800 people, so get a ticket in advance. Downstairs is the *Shelter* club, with lesser-known touring bands followed by dance music.

Tonic 29 S Saginaw St, Pontiac ☎ 248/334-7411, ⓦ www.tonicdetroit.com. Open Thursday through Sunday until 2am, *Tonic* bills itself as the premiere concert after-party: three levels of dancing and all the DJ vibe you can handle.

The performing arts

Most of Detroit's major arts venues are handily grouped together in the north-west section of downtown. A sweeping staircase and giant chandeliers are part of the splendor at the **Detroit Opera House**, 1526 Broadway (☎313/237-SING, ⓦwww.detroitoperahouse.com). Close by, the **Music Hall Center for Performing Arts**, 350 Madison Ave (☎313/963-2366, ⓦwww.musichall.org), is the primary venue for **dance** in the city; it also hosts rock concerts, youth theater, and Broadway shows. In the Theater District, the gorgeous **Fox Theatre**, 2211 Woodward Ave (☎313/983-6611, ⓦwww.olympiaentertain-ment.com), is the biggest draw, hosting big Broadway shows, while the cozy 450-seater **Gem Theatre**, 333 Madison Ave (☎313/963-9800, ⓦwww.gemtheatre.com), and the **Masonic Temple Theatre**, nearby at 500 Temple St (☎313/832-2232, ⓦwww.themasonic.com), a hall with near-perfect acoustics, are also worth a visit. A little further on toward the Cultural Center, the **Detroit Symphony Orchestra** performs at **Orchestra Hall**, 3711 Woodward Ave (☎313/576-5100, ⓦwww.detroitsymphony.com).

Sports

Detroit is one of the few cities with franchises competing at the professional level in all four major team sports. **Hockey**'s Red Wings are arguably the town favorites, and tickets are hard to get; they play downtown at the Joe Louis Arena (☎313/983-6859, ⓦwww.detroitredwings.com). **Baseball**'s Tigers (☎313/962-4000, ⓦdetroit.tigers.mlb.com) call the snazzy Comerica Park, or COPA, home, while Ford Field, where the Lions play **football** (☎313/262-2003, ⓦwww.detroitlions.com), will be the site of Super Bowl 40 in 2006. Lastly, twenty-five miles north of town, the Pistons (☎248/377-0100, ⓦwww.nba.com/pistons) play **basketball** in the Palace of Auburn Hills.

Around Detroit: Ann Arbor

Although its population just tops 114,000, **ANN ARBOR**, 45 minutes' drive west of Detroit along I-94, offers a greater choice of restaurants, live music venues, and cultural activities than most towns ten times its size. The **University of Michigan** has shaped the economy and character of the town ever since it was moved here from Detroit in 1837, providing the city with a very conspicuous radical edge.

The best thing to do in Ann Arbor is to stroll around downtown and the campus, which meet at South State and Liberty streets. Downtown's twelve blocks of brightly painted shops and sidewalk cafés offer all you would expect from a college town, with forty bookshops and more than a dozen record stores. Don't miss the huge flagship store of Border's Books at 612 E Liberty St, or the extensive vinyl and CD selection at Encore Recordings, 417 E Liberty St.

Though the huge university campus doesn't look particularly appealing, it does emanate a sense of excitement, especially around the central meeting place of the **Diag** (or Diagonal Walkway). Worth a look are the **Museum of Natural History**, 1109 Geddes Ave (Mon–Sat 9am–5pm, Sun noon–5pm; $2; ☎734/764-0478), packed with huge dinosaur skeletons, rare Native American artifacts, and a planetarium, and the small but eclectic **Museum of Art**, 525 S State St (Tues–Sat 10am–5pm, Thurs until 9pm, Sun noon–5pm; free).

Practicalities

Frequent **Greyhound** services from Detroit stop at 116 W Huron St; **Amtrak** is on the north edge of downtown at 325 Depot St; and the **visitor center** is at 120 W Huron St (Mon–Fri 9am–5pm; ☎734/995-7281 or 1-800/888-9487, ⓦ www.annarbor.org).

The *Lamp Post Inn*, 2424 E Stadium Blvd (☎734/971-8000, ⓦ www.lamppostinn.com; ❸), is a good-value motel about a mile from campus, though the choice place to stay is the *Campus Inn*, right downtown at 615 E Huron St (☎734/769-2200 or 1-800/666-8693, ⓦ www.campusinn.com; ❼). A good **B&B** is the unusual *Artful Lodger*, on the edge of campus at 1547 Washtenaw Ave (☎734/769-0653, ⓦ www.artlodger.com; ❹), decorated with art, theater, and music memorabilia. The modern downtown *YMCA*, 350 S Fifth Ave (☎734/663-0536; ❷), is open to both sexes.

Restaurants worth trying include the good-value Indian *Raja Rani*, 400 S Division St (☎734/995-1545), and the vegetarian *Seva*, 314 E Liberty Ave (☎734/662-1111). *Jerusalem Garden*, 307 S Fifth Ave (☎734/995-5060), serves the best falafel in town, while *Zingerman's*, 422 Detroit St (☎734/663-DELI), is an excellent (if expensive) deli. A pair of popular **brewpubs** – the *Arbor Brewing Co*, 114 E Washington St (☎734/213-1393), and the *Grizzly Peak Brewing Co*, 120 W Washington St (☎734/741-7325) – are within a couple of blocks of each other.

Ann Arbor's **live music** scene has enjoyed a nationwide reputation ever since the Stooges, MC5, and Bob Seger made their names here. Unlike many college towns, the place doesn't go to sleep during the summer, either. For news of gigs, grab a copy of *Current*, a free monthly. Likely venues include the jazzy *Bird of Paradise*, 312 S Main St (☎734/662-8310, ⓦ www.thebirdofparadise.com), and the oft-crowded *Del Rio*, 122 W Washington Ave (☎734/761-2530), which serves good Mexican food and hosts free Sunday jazz sessions. The *Blind Pig*, 208 S First St (☎734/996-8555, ⓦ www.blindpigmusic.com), is the best place to watch live rock, alternative, and blues, while *The Ark*, 316 S Main St (☎734/761-1451, ⓦ www.a2ark.org), is an important venue for folk, acoustic, and roots music. From time to time there are also live bands at the beautiful Art Deco Michigan Theater, 603 E Liberty St (☎734/668-8480, ⓦ www.michtheater.org), otherwise a great place to watch movies on the cheap.

Festivals are also a key part of Ann Arbor life. In June, the orchestral Summer Festival kicks off activities with music and film; July sees the hectic Street Art Fair with hundreds of stalls; and early September brings the recently revived Ann Arbor Blues and Jazz Festival.

The rest of the Lower Peninsula

Between Ann Arbor and the Lake Michigan coast, a little over 150 miles west along I-94, there's not a whole lot worth stopping for, though Kellogg's **Cereal City USA**, 171 W Michigan Ave, in Battle Creek (summer Mon–Fri 9.30am–5pm, Sat 9.30am–6pm, Sun 11am–5pm; call for winter hours; $8; ☎616/962-6230, ⓦ www.kelloggscerealcity.org), is a fun diversion that traces the history of cereal – and, of course, magnate Kellogg's impact on it. Once you reach Lake Michigan, quaint **St Joseph** is just the first of many small ports along the lake's 350-mile eastern shoreline.

North from St Joseph along Hwy-31, the northwest reaches of the lower peninsula attract sportspeople and tourists from all over the Midwest. Here, out on the unspoiled **Leelanau Peninsula** you'll find the beautiful **Sleeping Bear Dunes**, as well as the charming towns of **Charlevoix** and **Petoskey**; all three are within striking distance of larger **Traverse City**. At the northern tip of the lower peninsula, revitalized **Mackinaw City** is the departure point for the state's major tour-bus attraction, Old-World **Mackinac Island**.

Along Lake Michigan

Less than thirty miles north of Indiana, **ST JOSEPH** lies just north of "Harbor Country" – a string of small towns offering good swimming, boating, and fishing opportunities. St Joseph's neat, ice cream parlor-riddled downtown perches on a high bluff, from which steep steps lead down to sandy Silver Beach and two lighthouses atop two piers. You can watch the yachts go by while eating great **food** such as nachos, steak salad, and pasta at *Clementine's Too*, 1235 Broad St (☎269/983-0990), or gumbo, ostrich burgers, and "mile high" sandwiches at a sidewalk table at *Schu's*, 501 Pleasant St (☎269/983-7248). **Places to stay** include the classy lakeside *Boulevard Suite Hotel*, 521 Lake Blvd (☎269/983-6600; ❻), where all the rooms are suites, and the good-value *Econolodge*, two miles from downtown at 2723 Niles Ave (☎269/983-6321; ❷). For general information on the area, stop in at the **visitor center**, just off I-94 exit 29 (summer Mon–Sat 8.30am–5pm; rest of year closed Sat; ☎269/925-6301).

Fifty miles north, **HOLLAND** was settled in 1847 by Dutch religious dissidents. Today's residents lose no opportunity to let visitors know of their roots: tens of thousands of tulips brighten the town in early summer, while the Netherlands museum, a Dutch village, a clog factory, and the inevitable windmill all attract tourist dollars. Twenty miles farther up the shoreline, **GRAND HAVEN** boasts one of the largest and most appealing sandy beaches on the Great Lakes, best seen on a leisurely stroll along the one-and-a-half-mile boardwalk (for the most part a concrete path). At the top of Dewey Hill stands a huge, electronically controlled musical fountain which operates during the summer.

Just under one hundred miles farther north, a string of pleasant small villages starts with **LUDINGTON**, where a long stretch of public beach precedes **Ludington State Park**, eight miles north on Hwy-116, which offers great hiking and sightseeing amid sweeping sand dunes and virgin pine forests; admission is $4 per car. **Camping** in some beautiful sites costs $16 a night, though sites for the summer tend to fill up a year in advance (☎800/447-2757). The **visitor center** is on the east side of town at 5827 US-10 (Mon–Fri 8am–5pm; ☎231/845-0324 or 1-800/542-4600). From downtown, the **Lake Michigan Car Ferry** departs for Manitowoc, Wisconsin ($40 per adult, $47 per car, not including driver; ☎231/845-5555 or 1-800/841-4243, ⓦwww.ssbadger.com) – a comparative bargain when you weigh up the cost of braving the cross-Chicago traffic. The best place to **stay overnight** is *Snyder's Shoreline Inn*, 903 W Ludington Ave (☎231/845-1261 or 1-800/843-2177, ⓦwww.snydersshoreinn.com; ❹), the only downtown property with uninterrupted views of the lakeshore. *House of Flavors*, 402 W Ludington Ave (☎231/845-5785), is a chrome-heavy diner with breakfasts, burgers, and a huge range of ice cream. *The Old Hamlin Restaurant*, 122 W Ludington Ave (☎231/843-4251), serves breakfast, lunch, and dinner, featuring steaks, seafood, and especially good Greek dishes.

Surrounded by forest, **MANISTEE**, 32 miles north, boasts an attractive Victorian downtown and a mile-long **boardwalk** that runs alongside the Manistee River onto Lake Michigan. One of several pretty lakeside areas is **Douglas Park** – with a good sandy beach, small marina, and picnic area – next to the *Lake Shore Motel*, 669 First St (☎231/723-2667; ❺). To stay downtown, try the *Maples B&B*, 435 Fifth St (☎231/723-2904; ❸). The **Chamber of Commerce** is at 11 Cypress St (Mon–Fri 9am–5pm; ☎231/723-2575).

Thirty miles north, tiny **FRANKFORT** nestles under bluffs overlooking Lake Michigan. With a grassy park and a small beach at either end of its main street, the town not only makes a charming stop for lunch or a picnic, but also provides cheaper **accommodation** than the Leelanau Peninsula settlements just to the north. The *Harbor Lights Motel and Condos*, 15 Second St (☎231/352-9614; ❹), stands right on the beach, while the *Still Grinning Inn*, 670 Crystal Ave (☎231/352-7669; ❷), is a great-value B&B. Along the main drag, the *Frankfort Deli*, 327 Main St (☎231/352-3354), has good sandwiches; directly across the street, the *Coho Café* (☎231/352-6053) serves up well-priced contemporary American cuisine. A few doors down, the **visitor center** is at 400 Main St (Mon–Fri 9am–noon & 1–5pm; ☎231/352-7251).

The Leelanau Peninsula

The southwestern edge of the heavily wooded **Leelanau Peninsula** is occupied by the **Sleeping Bear Dunes National Lakeshore**, a constantly re-sculpted area of towering dunes and precipitous 400ft drops; admission is $7 per car. The area was named by the Chippewa, who saw the mist-shrouded North and South Manitou islands as the graves of two drowned bear cubs, and the massive mainland dune, covered with dark trees, as their grieving mother. Fierce winds off Lake Michigan cause the dunes to edge inland, burying trees that reappear years later stripped of foliage, while the continual attack of high water undercuts the massive sand banks, occasionally sending massive chunks into the lake. Stunning overlooks can be had along the hilly, nine-mile loop of the **Pierce Stocking Scenic Drive**, off Hwy-109. You can also clamber up the strenuous but enjoyable **Dune Climb**, four miles farther north on Hwy-109 (best done barefoot, as shoes soon fill with sand).

The **visitor center**, at the junction of highways 22 and 109 (daily: summer 9am–6pm; rest of year 9am–4pm; ☎231/326-5134, ⓦwww.leelanau.com), provides details on trails, campgrounds, and beaches. Nearby, the village of **GLEN ARBOR**, dotted with some interesting galleries, is the closest community to the dunes. Decent places to **eat** here include *Le Bear*, 5707 Lake St (☎231/334-4640), where affordable lunches and costly seafood dinners are served on a waterfront deck, and *Art's Tavern*, 6487 Western Ave (☎231/334-3754), a pleasant tavern delivering great hamburgers and inexpensive fried fish.

Fifteen miles north, **LELAND** makes a great base to visit the dunes. Its harbor, crammed with expensive launches, holds a quaint collection of well-weathered sheds, known as **Fishtown**, where the day's catch was once hauled in for gutting and smoking; most are now touristy knick-knack shops. *The Cove*, 111 River St (☎231/256-9834), serves up tasty Great Lakes fish dishes and a superb Key Lime Pie. **Ferries** from Leland ($22 roundtrip; ☎231/256-9061) go to the uninhabited North and South Manitou islands.

At the tip of the peninsula, **NORTHPORT** is another relaxing fishing village with a disproportionate number of art galleries. Eleven miles south on the peninsula's east coast, **SUTTONS BAY** may not be as pretty, but its main artery, St Joseph Avenue, has some of the area's best places to eat. *Hatties*, no. 111 (☎231/271-6222), serves fine meals like chicken with cherry sauce and Thai scallops; *Café Bliss*, no. 420 (☎231/271-5000), specializes in vegetarian and Native American cuisine, with entrees around $12; while the *Hose House Deli*, in a restored 1913 fire station at no. 303 (☎231/271-6303), serves large sandwiches and coffee.

Nowhere on the peninsula is **accommodation** inexpensive. The best option is the *Leelanau Country Inn*, midway between Glen Arbor and Leland at 149

East Harbor Hwy, Maple City (☎231/228-5060, ⓦwww.leelanaucoun-tryinn.com; ❸), a good-value Victorian B&B with large breakfasts.

Traverse City

Smooth beaches and striking bay views help make lively **TRAVERSE CITY**, roughly 20 miles south of Suttons Bay, the favorite in-state resort for Michigan natives. A town of 15,000 year-round residents, it was saved from the stagnation that overtook many communities when their lumber mills closed down, because the stripped fields proved to be ideal for fruit-growing. Today, the area's claim to be "**Cherry Capital of the World**" is no idle boast. Thousands of acres of cherry orchards envelop the town, their wispy, pink blossoms bringing a delicate beauty each May. At the **National Cherry Festival**, held during the first full week in July, visitors can watch parades, fireworks, and concerts, while sampling every imaginable cherry product. Coca-Cola chose the event to launch its cherry-flavor soda in the 1980s.

Traverse City's neat **downtown** rests along the bottom of the west arm of **Grand Traverse Bay**, below the Old Mission Peninsula. This slender seventeen-mile strip of land, which divides the bay into two inlets, makes for a pleasant short driving tour. Narrow roads slice through miles of cherry orchards and vineyards, with tremendous simultaneous views of the bay on either side. Five sandy public beaches and a small harbor can be found around the town itself. Various companies offer boat, windsurfer, jet-ski, and mountain bike rental (the surrounding countryside is excellent for cycling). There are 36 **golf courses** in the immediate area, as well – some of them among the most beautiful in the country.

Practicalities

Greyhound stops near downtown at 3233 Cass Rd. The **visitor center**, downtown at 101 Grandview Parkway (summer Mon–Fri 9am–7pm, Sat 9am–6pm, Sun noon–4pm; rest of year Mon–Sat 9am–5pm; ☎231/947-1120 or 1-800/TRAVERS, ⓦwww.tcvisitors.com), can help with finding **accommodation**, though there's a dearth of inexpensive central lodging in summer. The attractive little *Bay Shore Resort*, near downtown at 833 E Front St (☎231/935-4400; ❻), has a private beach and nice rooms. The remodeled and very central *Park Place Hotel*, 300 E State St (☎231/946-5000 or 1-800/748-0133, ⓦwww.park-place-hotel.com; ❻), is reliable, as are the well-maintained *Days Inn & Suites*, 420 Munson Ave (☎231/941-0208; ❺), and the basic but clean *Sierra Motel*, 230 Munson Ave (☎231/946-7720; ❹), both a couple of miles southeast. There's **camping** at Traverse City State Park, just outside town at 1132 US-31 N (☎231/922-5270; $20/night).

Affordable **places to eat** in Traverse City are easy to find. Big breakfasts with home-baked bread are served at *Mabel's*, 472 Munson Ave (☎231/947-0252), while *Mode's Bum Steer*, 125 E State St (☎231/947-9832), is a ribs joint. The best bet for a meal, though, particularly in the evening, is to drive north onto the Old Mission Peninsula where the *Boathouse*, 14039 Peninsula Drive (☎231/223-4030), dishes up fresh seafood, pasta, and vegetarian food right by the lake. Farther up, on the peninsula's central spine road, the popular *Old Mission Tavern*, 17015 Center Rd (☎231/223-7280), has classic European dishes and lots of local art. The *U & I Lounge*, 214 E Front St, is the best **bar** in town; it also serves up great gyros, burgers, and salads. *Union Street Station*, 117 S Union St (☎231/941-1930), has pool tables and **live music** of all sorts most nights.

North to Mackinaw City

On its way north from Traverse City, scenic Hwy-31 skims along Lake Michigan through **Charlevoix** and other pretty lakeside towns. The northern tip of the peninsula is occupied by **Mackinaw City**, where ferries take excursionists to much-hyped **Mackinac Island** – billboards advertise its attractions for fifty miles before you arrive.

Charlevoix, Petoskey, and Harbor Springs

CHARLEVOIX boasts a positively idyllic setting, fronting onto three separate lakes: Michigan, Charlevoix, and the beautiful, bowl-shaped Round Lake. Petunia-lined **Bridge Street**, the two-block downtown, looks over a picturesque, almost landlocked harbor on Round Lake, hemmed in on the other sides by terraced ridges. Though an undeniably beautiful place, in recent years the town has become a bit too fancy. That said, it does have two sandy beaches (on the Michigan shoreline) that are great places to watch the sunset; and from 103 Bridge Park Drive, the Beaver Island Boat Company runs **ferries** to **Beaver Island**, the most remote inhabited island in the Great Lakes (April–Dec; $34 roundtrip; 2hr trip; ☎231/547-2311 or 1-888/446-4095, ⓦwww.bibco.com).

Charlevoix's helpful **visitor center** is at 408 E Bridge St (☎231/547-2101 or 1-800/367-8557, ⓦwww.charlevoix.org). Lakeside **hotels**, such as the turreted *Weathervane Terrace*, 111 Pine River Lane (☎231/547-9955, ⓦwww.weathervane-chx.com; ❼), may charge more than $300 a night on peak weekends. The *Charleboyne Motel*, one mile north of town at US-31 and Boyne City Road (☎231/547-9340; ❸), is small, basic, and clean. One of the best-value **B&Bs**, the *MacDougall House*, 109 Petoskey Ave (☎231/547-5788, ⓦwww.michiganbandb.com; ❹), has private bathrooms and huge breakfasts. As for **food**, *Whitney's Oyster Bar*, 305 Bridge St (☎231/547-0818), serves fresh seafood and snacks until 2am, with lots of beers and seating.

In bigger and busier **PETOSKEY**, high above Lake Michigan sixteen miles north along US-31, grand Victorian houses encircle the downtown's nicely restored **Gaslight District**. Ernest Hemingway spent many of his teenage summers here – his novel *The Torrents of Spring* alludes to several local landmarks. The town's **visitor center** is at 401 E Mitchell St (Mon–Fri 8am–5pm, Sat 10am–3pm, Sun noon–4pm; ☎1-800/845-2828, ⓦwww.petoskey.com). For a **place to stay**, try the *Serenity B&B*, 504 Rush St (☎231/347-1338 or 1-877/347-6171, ⓦwww.serenitybb.com; ❻), a big Victorian house serving superb full breakfasts, or the venerable *Stafford's Perry Hotel*, centrally located at Bay and Lewis streets (☎231/347-4000 or 1-800/737-1899, ⓦwww.staffords.com; ❺); its *Noggin Room Pub* has good snacks and pizza. Other options for something to eat include one of Hemingway's favorite hangouts, *Jesperson's*, 312 Howard St (☎231/347-3601), which still does great pies and sandwiches, and the popular *Mitchell Street Pub*, 426 E Mitchell St (☎231/347-1801), which has decent snacks.

Twelve miles up Hwy-119, **HARBOR SPRINGS** is a favorite with the Midwestern elite. The charming Main Street and small shaded beach of this "Cornbelt Riviera" resort are certainly captivating. The comfy *Harbor Springs Cottage Inn*, at Bay and Zoll streets (☎231/526-5431; ❺), has the only reasonably affordable rooms in town.

From Harbor Springs, the "**Tunnel of Trees**" scenic drive follows a section of Hwy-119 to Mackinaw City. Along this narrow winding road, occasional breaks in the overhanging trees afford views of Lake Michigan and Beaver Island.

Mackinaw City

Forty miles northeast of Petoskey, **MACKINAW CITY** has long enjoyed a steady tourist trade as the major embarkation point for Mackinac Island. The town was once little more than a bland colony of cheap motels and fudge shops looking for business from those who couldn't get a place to stay on the island. Now, though, the streets have been landscaped with trees that are lit up at night, while visitors flock to **Mackinaw Crossings** on South Huron Street. This mall-cum-entertainment zone has given the town a lift, offering vacationers several dozen niche retail stores, a food court, a multiscreen cinema, and an amphitheater that hosts nightly live acts and a laser show at 10pm during the summer.

The **visitor center** is located at 10300 S US-23 (summer Mon–Fri 8am–6pm, Sat 9am–1pm; rest of year Mon–Fri 8am–5pm; ☎231/436-5991 or 1-800/666-0160). Several mid-priced **motels** have been built alongside the shore, among them the *Ramada Limited Waterfront*, 723 S Huron St (☎231/436-5055; ❺), and the *Best Western Dockside Waterfront* (☎231/436-5001; ❺–❽). A much better rate is available a couple of blocks north at 111 Langlade St, where the *Welcome Inn* (☎231/436-5525; ❸) offers simple, clean rooms. A good **meal** can be had outdoors at the *Depo*, 250 S Huron St (☎231/436-7060), a refurbished train station in the Courtyards of Mackinaw City mall complex. Enjoy the tasty grill food and seafood dips with a good view of the free evening concerts and laser light shows in the adjacent amphitheater.

To reach Mackinac Island, contact Arnold Transit (June–Sept, call for schedule; $16.50 for pedestrians, $6.50 for bikes; ☎906/847-3351 or 1-800/542-8528, ⓦwww.arnoldline.com) or Shepler's Ferry (June–Sept, call for schedule; $16.50 for pedestrians, $6.50 for bikes; ☎231/436-5023 or 1-800/828-6157, ⓦwww.sheplersferry.com); both companies offer **high-speed catamaran crossings** from the Ferry Terminal in Mackinaw City, and do not require reservations.

Mackinac Island

Viewed from an approaching boat, the tree-blanketed rocky limestone outcrop of **MACKINAC ISLAND** (pronounced "Mackinaw"), suddenly thrusting out from the swirling waters, is an unforgettable sight. As you near the harbor, large Victorian houses come into view, dappling the hillsides with white and pastel. The most conspicuous is the imposing, $250-a-night *Grand Hotel* (☎906/847-3331 or 1-800/33-GRAND, ⓦwww.grandhotel.com; ❾), where just to enter the foyer costs $5. On disembarking, you'll see rows of horses and buggies (all motorized transportation is banned from the island, except for emergency vehicles) and inhale the omnipresent smell of fresh manure. Also ubiquitous on the island is **fudge**, relentlessly marketed as a Mackinac "delicacy."

Mackinac's crowded **Main Street** and contrived nostalgia can get irritating, but the island is still worth visiting, not least for the ferry ride over and the chance to cycle along the hilly back roads. Underneath the tourist trimmings is a rich history. French priests established a mission to the Huron Indians here during the winter of 1670–1671. The French built a fort here in 1715, but within fifty years had lost control of the island to the British. Since independence, Mackinac has been a base for John Jacob Astor's American Fur Company, a fishing port, and a jail for Confederate officers during the Civil War. The government acknowledged the island's beauty by designating it as the country's second national park, two years after Yellowstone in 1875, though management was handed over to the state of Michigan twenty years later. To get a feel for the history, hike or cycle up to the whitewashed stone **Fort Mackinac**, a US

Army outpost until 1890. Its ramparts afford a great view of the village and lake below, though admission is a steep $8 (May to mid-Oct 9.30am–6.30pm).

On Main Street, an **information kiosk** (daily 9am–5pm; ☎906/847-3783) provides full details of accommodation, horseback rides, and bike rental. The average **room** on Mackinac costs more than $130 per night; the least costly hotel is *Murray's* (☎906/847-3360 or 1-800/462-2546; ❺), which serves a large continental breakfast buffet. Unpretentious **B&Bs** such as the *Bogan Lane Inn* (☎906/847-3439; ❸) and the secluded *Small Point* (☎906/847-3758; ❹) are more affordable. *Haan's 1830 Inn* (☎906/847-6244; ❻) is a big Greek Revival home close by the harbor. **Places to eat** on Main Street include *The Pilot House Pub* (☎906/847-0270) in the *Lakeview Hotel*, which has American fare and live entertainment nightly, and *Patrick Sinclair's* (☎906/847-6454), an Irish pub serving sandwiches, seafood, and salads, as well as corned beef.

The Upper Peninsula

From the map, it would seem logical for Michigan's **Upper Peninsula**, separated from the rest of the state by the **Mackinac Straits**, to be part of Wisconsin. However, when Michigan entered the Union in 1837 (eleven years before Wisconsin), its legislators, keen to tap the peninsula's huge mineral wealth, incorporated it into their new state.

Before then the UP, as it's commonly known, figured prominently in French plans to create an empire in North America. Father Jacques Marquette and other missionaries made peace with the native people and established settlements, including the port of Sault Ste Marie in 1688. The French hoped to press further south, but before they could get much past Detroit, the British inflicted a severe military defeat in 1763.

Vast, lonesome, and wild, the Upper Peninsula is full of stunning landmarks, exemplified by the **Pictured Rocks National Lakeshore**. Most of the eastern section is marked by low-lying, sometimes swampy land between softly undulating limestone hills. It has been said that there are only two seasons in the UP – winter and the Fourth of July; the record-breaking winter of 1997 saw 272 inches of snow. The northwest corner is the most desolate, especially the rough and broken **Keewanaw Peninsula** and **Isle Royale National Park**, fifty miles offshore. The UP's only real city is **Marquette**, a college town with a quiet buzz – a good base from which to explore the peninsula's rugged terrain. Until 1957 you could get to the UP from lower Michigan only by ferry. Today, the five-mile **Mackinac Bridge** ($2.50 toll), lit up beautifully at night, stretches elegantly across the bottleneck Straits of Mackinac.

Sault Ste Marie

Perched at the northeast corner of the UP, **SAULT STE MARIE** (pronounced "Soo Saint Marie" and known locally as "The Soo") stands across St Mary's Rapids from the Canadian town bearing the same name. It's one of the oldest settlements in the US – not that you'd guess that from its bedraggled, 1950s-looking downtown and the industrial sprawl of the waterfront. The Soo owes most of its trade and industry to the St Mary's Locks, the only water connection between Superior and the other Great Lakes, built in 1855 and later expanded to handle oceangoing vessels. Four giant reservoirs raise upbound boats 21 feet to the level of Lake Superior. To see this impressive operation, which accounts for more tonnage than the Suez and Panama canals combined, take one of the **Soo Locks boat tours** ($18; ☏906/632-6301 or 1-800/432-6301, Ⓦwww.soolocks.com) from Dock #1 or Dock #2 on East Portage Avenue, or watch for free from the **visitor center** on the upper grounds of the St Mary's Falls canal (April–Nov daily 7am–11pm; ☏906/632-2394).

Despite efforts to increase its tourist trade, the Soo is not a place where you'd want to spend much time. The *Crestview Thrifty Inn*, 1200 Ashmun St (☏906/635-5213; ❹), has clean, comfortable rooms, while the *Bambi Motel*, further along at no. 1801 (☏906/632-7881; ❸), sports one of the most garish signs you'll ever lay eyes on. *Antler's*, 804 E Portage Ave (☏906/632-3571), looks like a dive bar but is in fact a historic Prohibition-era **pub**, where you can also get decent steaks and fish.

Paradise

Native Americans who lived in the area sixty miles west and north of the Soo called it *Tahquamenon* ("Marsh of the Blueberries"). Now it's called **PARADISE**, and in summer this elongated lakeside village can live up to its name, cut as it is out of thick, dark green forests and surrounded by small, reed-cluttered ultramarine lakes. Life is slow and easy here, but the choppy waters of Superior deny absolute calm to the beach. In winter, temperatures drop to -40°F and snowmobiles are the usual mode of transportation. Ten miles west on Hwy-123, one of the most popular spots on the UP for hiking, boating, and camping is the gorgeous **Tahquamenon Falls State Park** ($3 per car; ☏906/492-3415), made famous in Longfellow's epic "The Song of Hiawatha," where "by the rushing Tahquamenon" Hiawatha built his canoe. The waters, dyed a translucent brown by tannic acid, spill over two sets of cataracts.

Whitefish Road winds eleven miles north of town to where shingly **Whitefish Point** nudges into the harsh waters of Lake Superior. Raging northwesterly winds, which build up over almost four hundred miles of open lake funneling into this narrower section, have contributed to more than five hundred shipwrecks along the eighty-mile stretch of lakeshore westward to Munising. The story of these wrecks is told at the **Great Lakes Shipwreck Historical Museum**, located at the dead end of Whitefish Point Road (mid-May to mid-Oct daily 10am–6pm; $8.50; ☏906/635-1742, Ⓦwww.shipwreckmuseum.com), with the help of subtle lighting and atmospheric background music. It's not all ancient history, either; on November 10, 1975, the cargo ship *Edmund Fitzgerald* foundered in 96mph gusts, losing all of its 29-person crew.

Curley's Motel & Cabins on M-123 in Paradise (☏906/492-3445; ❸) is your best bet for **accommodation**: six-person cabins cost under $100, and there's a nice beach on-site. A clean, inexpensive option is the *Vagabond Motel* across the street (☏906/492-3477; ❷). The *Yukon Inn* next door (☏906/492-3264) is not an inn, but rather a **restaurant** and **bar** with stuffed trophy animals for decor, and serving burgers and sandwiches; DJs spin on Saturday nights.

Pictured Rocks National Lakeshore

The 42 miles between the attractive fishing villages of Grand Marais and Munising form the **Pictured Rocks National Lakeshore**, a splendid array of multicolored cliffs, rolling dunes, and secluded sandy beaches. Rain, wind, ice, and sun have carved and gouged arches, columns, and caves into the face of the lakeshore, all stained different hues. Hiking trails run along the clifftops, and the partially unpaved Hwy-58 takes you close to the water, but the best way to see the cliffs is by **boat**. Pictured Rocks Cruises offers a three-hour narrated **tour** that leaves from the City Pier in Munising (July & Aug 5–7 trips daily; June, Sept & early Oct 2 trips daily; $22; ☎906/387-2379, ⊛www .shipwrecktours.com). Less than a mile farther along the lake, at 1204 Commercial St, Shipwreck Tours gives two-hour narrated cruises in a glass-bottomed boat, with surprisingly clear views of three shipwrecks – one intact (June to early Oct 2–3 trips daily; $23; ☎906/387-4477). Those in a hurry can get a glimpse of the cliffs by visiting the **Miners Castle Overlook**, just east of Munising, or **Munising Falls**, one of a half-dozen nearby waterfalls, near the village's well-signposted **visitor center** (Mon–Fri 9am–5pm; ☎906/387-2138, ⊛www.picturedrocks.com). In Munising, *Scotty's Motel*, 415 Cedar St (☎906/387-2449; ❸), and the *Munising Motel*, 332 E Onota St (☎906/387-3187; ❹), are fairly comfortable places to stay. At 101 E Munising Ave, *The Navigator* (☎906/387-1555 or 1-866/387-2399, ⊛www.the-navigator.net) is the only **restaurant** in Munising with a view of Lake Superior, and serves breakfast any time along with steaks, seafood, pizza, and burgers.

Marquette

Forty miles west of Munising is the unofficial capital of the UP, the low-key college town of **MARQUETTE**, also the center of the area's massive ore industry. The helpful **state welcome center**, just south of town at 2201 US-41 S (daily: summer 9am–6pm; rest of year 9am–5pm; ☎906/249-9066, ⊛www.marquettecountry.org), has vouchers for local hotel discounts and lots of information about Marquette's sights. Premier among them is rugged **Presque Isle Park**, north of town on Lakeshore Boulevard, almost completely surrounded by Lake Superior and with stunning views of the lake. Back in town, at East Ridge St and Lakeshore, the **Marquette Maritime Museum** (late May–Sept daily 10am–5pm; $3; ☎906/226-2006) has exhibits on the fishing and freighting industries, as well as a video about the fabled Superior wrecking of the *Edmund Fitzgerald* (see overleaf). The area's most curious sight is the **Superior Dome**, on Northern Michigan University's campus at 1401 Presque Isle Ave, the largest wooden dome in the world.

Ten miles west of Marquette on Hwy-41 in Ishpeming, the birthplace of ski-jumping, is the **National Ski Hall of Fame** (Mon–Sat 10am–5pm; free; ☎906/485-6323, ⊛www.skihall.com). Housed in a cone-shaped building with a ski jump running down the roof, this low-tech museum chronicles the history of skiing via photos and artifacts from the 10th Mountain Division (a World War II US combat unit that travelled on skis), the first chairlift from Sun Valley, Idaho, and lots of ski-jumping memorabilia.

Accommodation in Marquette is abundant and inexpensive. Cheap motels cluster west of town on US-41, but there are better, equally affordable options downtown. The *Village Inn*, 1301 N Third St (☎906/226-9400 or 1-800/800-8909; ❸–❹), offers high-quality, good-value rooms (some with a kitchen), but by far the nicest place to stay is the grand *Landmark Inn*, 230 N Front St (☎906/228-2580; ❺–❻), which has rooms overlooking the lake. You can **camp** at the *Tourist Park Campground* on Sugarloaf Avenue (☎906/228-0465; $10). *JJ's Shamrock*, downtown at 113 S Front St (☎906/226-6734), serves basic bar **food** along with occasional live music. For a more formal dining experience, locals favor the *Northwoods Supper Club*, just west of town off US-41 (☎906/228-4343), with a meat-and-potatoes menu in a rustic setting. One popular watering hole is *Remie's Bar*, 111 Third St (☎906/226-9133), with a rowdy local crowd and live music on Wednesdays.

The Keweenaw Peninsula

Beyond Marquette, along US-41, the landscape becomes progressively more rough-hewn, culminating in the **Keweenaw Peninsula**, which juts like a dorsal fin eighty miles out into Lake Superior. Encircled by a dramatic shoreline and enriched by crags and precipices, it's a great place for a short driving tour, with roads winding through forests, past old copper workings, and up and down steep hills.

Halfway up the peninsula, in the small college town of **HOUGHTON** on Portage Lake, the *College Motel*, next to the Michigan Tech campus at 1308 College Ave (☎906/482-2202; ❷), is good value. The luxury option is the 100-year-old *Charleston House Inn B&B*, downtown by the water at 918 College Ave (☎906/482-7790, ⓦwww.charlestonhouseinn.com; ❼). The *Suomi Home Bakery and Restaurant*, at 54 N Huron St (☎906/482-3220), serves cheap pasties and Finnish food. At the northern tip of Kewanaw, best reached along Hwy-26 (Brockway Mountain Drive) from Eagle River, handsome little **COPPER HARBOR** was once so rich in minerals that early miners could pick up chunks of pure copper from the lakeshore; today you can tour the **Delaware Mine**, ten miles west on US-41 (daily: summer 10am–6pm; Sept & Oct 10am–5pm; ☎906/289-4688, ⓦwww.copperharbor .org). Inexpensive **accommodation** is available at the *Norland Motel* (☎906/289-4815; ❷), two miles east of the mine on US-41, next to Fort Wilkins State Park.

Isle Royale National Park

Much closer to Canada than the US, the 45-mile sliver of **Isle Royale National Park**, fifty miles out in Lake Superior, is in a double sense as far as you can get in Michigan from Detroit. All cars are banned and, instead of freeways, 166 miles of hiking trails lead past windswept trees, swampy lakes, and grazing moose. Aside from other outdoors types, the only traces of human life you're likely to see are ancient mineworks (thought to be two millennia old), shacks left behind by commercial fishermen in the 1940s, and a few lighthouses and park buildings. Hiking, canoeing, fishing, and scuba-diving among shipwrecks are the principal leisure activities.

The park is open from mid-May until the end of September. **Camping** is free, though you should visit the **park headquarters** at 800 E Lakeshore Drive in Houghton (Mon–Fri 8am–4.30pm; ☎906/482-0984, ⓦwww.nps.gov/isro) before you leave the mainland, for advice on water purity, mosquitoes, and temperatures that can drop well below freezing even in summer. Aside from camping, you can stay in a self-catering cottage or a more expensive lodge room (including all meals) at the *Rock Harbor Lodge* (mailing address: 800 E Lakeshore Drive, Houghton, MI 49931; ☎906/337-4993, Oct–April ☎270/773-2191, ⓦwww.isleroyaleresort.com; ❻). The lodge rents canoes and motorboats for $22 and $48 per day, respectively, and offers cruises for $11.

Ferries to Isle Royale leave from Copper Harbor ($40 one way; ☎906/289-4437), Houghton ($47 one way; ☎906/482-0984), and Grand Portage, Minnesota ($32–52 one way; ☎715/392-2100). If there are enough in your party, it may be just as economical to charter a **plane** from the Isle Royale Seaplane Service in Houghton (☎906/482-8850).

Indiana

Thanks to an early nineteenth-century influx of northward migrants, much of **INDIANA** still retains vestiges of the easygoing South. Among these early settlers was the family of Abraham Lincoln, who set up home near the present village of Santa Claus in 1816 and stayed for fourteen years before moving to Illinois. Unlike the abolitionist Lincolns, many brought slaves to this new territory; Indiana allowed a system of "voluntary servitude" to operate until 1843. At the outbreak of the Civil War, thousands of ex-Southerners rioted against the draft, in part out of concern that Indiana was every bit as subservient to the Northeast as Deep South slaves were to their masters. However, since the 1870s, industrialization has integrated Indiana into the regional economy. The sports-happy state is at the forefront of the nation in automobile racing and high school basketball.

Despite some beautiful dunes and beaches, the most lasting memories provided by Indiana's fifty-mile **lakeshore** (by far the shortest of the Great Lake states) are of the grimy steel mills and poverty-stricken neighborhoods of towns like Gary and East Chicago. In northern Indiana, the area in and around Elkhart and Goshen contains one of the nation's largest **Amish settlements**. The central plains are characterized by small market towns, except for the sprawling capital, **Indianapolis**, which has brightened up its downtown to the point that it's not a bad stopover. Hilly southern Indiana, at its most appealing in the fall, is a welcome contrast to the central cornbelt, boasting several quaint towns such as Nashville, while thriving Columbus exhibits a great array of contemporary architecture for such a small city.

As to why residents of the state are called "**Hoosiers**," dozens of explanations have been offered; the most believable is that its use spread from the days of the Ohio Falls Canal construction in the 1820s, when a contractor, Samuel Hoosier, gave employment preference to those living on the Indiana side of the Ohio River.

Getting around Indiana

Nine interstates – five of them slicing through Indianapolis – provide boring but fast ways of traversing Indiana. Greyhound runs frequent services, particularly on I-65 between Chicago and Louisville, and I-70 between the Eastern US and St Louis. **Indianapolis**, **Michigan City**, and **South Bend** are the major stops on the three different Amtrak routes that cut through the state. Flights from most Midwestern and Eastern cities land at **Indianapolis International Airport**.

Northern Indiana

Lying just off I-80/90, halfway along the northern fringe of Indiana, **SOUTH BEND** briefly rivaled Detroit as the country's leading car manufacturer during the early 1920s, when now-defunct Studebaker was going strong. These days it's better known for the **University of Notre Dame**, the most famous Roman Catholic college in the US and home of the Fighting Irish team that once dominated college football. Free tours of the campus (☎574/631-5726, ⓦwww.nd.edu) take in the gold-domed Administration Building and sights such as a replica of the grotto at Lourdes in France. For something more active, head to the **East Race Waterway**, 126 N Niles Ave (Sat noon–5pm, Sun 1–5pm; ☎574/235-9401), where you can **kayak** or **raft** the first artificial whitewater course in North America. For $2, you can navigate the one-third-mile course that runs, believe it or not, through downtown South Bend. Afterward, head to the *Emporium Restaurant* at 121 S Niles Ave (☎574/234-9000), by the Jefferson Street bridge, for delicious prime rib and seafood. Budget **motels** are grouped along US-31 N. For something cozier, try the *Cushing Manor Inn B&B*, 508 W Washington St (☎574/288-1990 or 1-877/288-1990, ⓦwww.cushingmanorinn.com; ❺), which offers gourmet breakfasts.

Forty miles west, smaller **MICHIGAN CITY** marks the start of the twenty-mile **Indiana Dunes National Lakeshore**, intended to prevent further encroachment on the state's shoreline. There's not much to the "city" itself but it is the handiest place to stay near the lake. The basic *Knights Inn* motel, 201 W Kieffer Rd (☎219/874-9500, ⓦwww.knightsinn.com; ❸), offers the best value. Just west of town, the impressive **Mount Baldy** is, in fact, a giant sand dune, while twelve miles farther along, good swimming beaches and hiking trails through woods and marshes can be found at **Indiana Dunes State Park**.

Indianapolis

INDIANAPOLIS began life in 1821, when a tract of barely inhabited marshes was designated the state capital. Its location in the middle of Indiana's rich farmland bore terrific commercial advantages, but the absence of a navigable river prohibited the transportation of bulky materials such as coal and iron to sustain heavy industry. Though home to more than sixty car manufacturers by 1910, the city never seriously threatened Detroit's supremacy. Nevertheless, it has become one of the biggest cities in the world not accessible by water, attracting food, paper, and pharmaceutical industries, including the giant Eli Lilly Corporation.

Today the city has shaken off such nicknames as Naptown, India–no–place, and Brickhouse in the Cornfield in favor of its chosen designation as the country's unofficial amateur sports capital – "amateur" events like the Pan-American Games and national Olympic trials being worth big money these days. (Major league pro teams include the basketball Pacers and the football Colts.) In recent years, it has constructed several world-class sports arenas – including the retro-styled **Conseco Fieldhouse** downtown – along with new hotels, a gaggle of top-class museums, and a zoo – and its old downtown landmarks have become cultural, shopping, and dining complexes. No longer is it (quite) true that nothing happens here except for the glamorous **Indianapolis 500 car race** each May – "the most televised annual event in the world" (see box, p.354).

Arrival and information

Indianapolis International Airport is twelve miles west of downtown, on the #8 IndyGo bus route ($1; ☎317/635-3344). A **taxi** into the center costs around $27; try Yellow Cabs (☎317/487-7777). Greyhound **buses** pull in at 127 N Capitol Ave (☎1-800/231-2222), just off Monument Circle, while Amtrak **trains** arrive at 350 S Illinois St (☎317/267-3071), next to the fairly central Union Station complex. The **visitor center** is at 201 S Capitol St

(Mon–Fri 10am–5.30pm, Sat 10am–5pm, Sun noon–5pm; ☏ 317/237-5200 or 1-800/824-INDY, Ⓦ www.indy.org), beside the RCA Dome.

Accommodation

Indianapolis has plenty of quality **places to stay**, but few real budget downtown options, and prices can double during the race months of May, August, and September.

Canterbury Hotel 123 S Illinois St ☏ 317/634-3000 or 1-800/538-8186. The gracious landmark hotel in the heart of downtown was built in 1928, and includes continental breakfast. ❼

Crowne Plaza Union Station 123 W Louisiana St ☏ 317/631-2221. Regular hotel rooms plus suites in converted railway carriages. ❻

Days Inn Downtown 401 E Washington St ☏ 317/637-6464 or 1-800/329-7466. This reliable chain offers centrally located lodgings. ❹

Hampton Inn Downtown 105 S Meridian St ☏ 317/261-1200 or 1-800/HAMPTON. Clean motel, next to Circle Centre, with a fitness room and coin-operated laundry. ❺

Renaissance Tower Historic Inn 230 E 9th St ☏ 317/261-1652. The rooms here are occasionally very inexpensive, but at all times come complete with four-poster bed, toaster, coffeemaker, and popcorn popper. Just off central downtown. ❺

The Villa Inn 1456 N Delaware St ☏ 317/916-8500, Ⓦ www.thevillainn.com. Two miles north of downtown, and somewhere between a hotel and a B&B. Spa services and a restaurant are also available. ❽

Downtown

Though spacious and unhurried, downtown Indianapolis lacked a nerve center until the opening of the relatively tasteful **Circle Centre** shopping and entertainment complex in 1995. That year also saw the completion of the spectacular **Indianapolis Artsgarden**, an eight-story glass rotunda illuminated with fairy lights and suspended over the busy Washington and Illinois intersection. A performance and exhibition space, it also acts as a walkway to Circle Centre and several downtown hotels. One block north, streets radiate from **Monument Circle**, the starting point for a lengthy series of memorials and plazas dedicated to war veterans. Though many climb the 330 steps to the top of the renovated 284ft **Soldiers and Sailors Monument** (daily 10am–7pm; free) – there are often queues for the tiny elevator – the view of the city from here is unspectacular.

Five blocks east of here, the serene tree-shaded **Lockerbie Square Historic District**, starting at New York and East streets, is a small enclave of picturesque residences that were once home to nineteenth-century artisans and business leaders. Small wood-frame cottages line the cobblestone streets, many of them painted in bright pinks, blues, and yellows, and fronted by ornately carved porches.

Several blocks west of Monument Circle, the **Indiana State Museum**, 650 W Washington St (Mon–Sat 9am–5pm, Sun noon–5pm; $7; ☏ 317/232-1637, Ⓦ www.indianamuseum.org), gives a useful insight into the state's history through exhibits on everything from geology to sport. The nearby **Eiteljorg Museum of American Indians and Western Art**, on the western edge of downtown (June–Aug Mon–Sat 10am–5pm, Sun noon–5pm; rest of year closed Mon; tours at 1pm; $7; ☏ 317/636-9378, Ⓦ www.eiteljorg.org), is housed in a building constructed of stone, wood, and adobe at 500 W Washington St. Harrison Eiteljorg, an industrialist who went West in the 1940s to speculate in minerals, fell so deeply in love with the art of the region that he brought as much of it back with him as possible. On display are works by Frederic Remington, Charles M. Russell, and Georgia O'Keeffe, tribal artifacts from all over North America, as well as a 38ft Haida totem pole on the grounds. There are also frequent displays of beading and basket-weaving, superb touring exhibits, and a gorgeous gift shop. The Eiteljorg stands amid the rolling greenery of **White River State Park**, which is also home to the sizeable **Indianapolis Zoo** and the lush **White River Gardens** (Mon–Fri 9am–4pm, Sat & Sun 9am–5pm; $12.50; ☎317/630-2001, ⓦwww.indyzoo.com). In the park's southeast corner stands the superb new **Victory Field**, home of the Indianapolis Indians (☎317/269-3545), the farm team for baseball's Cincinnati Reds.

Out from downtown

Although the bodies of former president Benjamin Harrison and Hoosier poet James Whitcomb Riley lie in the enormous **Crown Hill Cemetery**, at 38th Street and Michigan Road, the most visited grave belongs to 1930s bank robber **John Dillinger**, supposedly buried at Section 44 Lot 94 (though some researchers allege that another man was killed in his place). Designated Public Enemy Number One, he completed thirteen bank raids – killing four policemen, three FBI agents, one sheriff, and an undetermined number of innocent bystanders – in a single-year career. Something of a folk hero, he escaped from jail twice, but was eventually ambushed by the FBI outside a Chicago theater in 1934 (see p.370).

Opposite the cemetery at 1200 W 38th St, more than 150 lush wooded acres accommodate the capacious **Indianapolis Museum of Art** (Tues, Wed, Fri & Sat 10am–5pm, Thurs 10am–8.30pm, Sun noon–5pm; free; ☎317/923-1331, ⓦwww.ima-art.org). The main building is surrounded by a lake, botanical garden, sculpture courtyard, and a concert terrace. Inside, the exceptional displays include the largest collection of Turner paintings outside of Britain and an array of paintings and prints from Gauguin's Pont Aven school, as well as an extensive collection of masks, figures, jewelry, and household items from northern Africa.

The city's most offbeat museum, the **Indiana Medical History Museum**, three miles west of downtown at 3045 W Vermont St (Thurs–Sat 10am–4pm, or by appointment; $5; ☎317/635-7329, ⓦwww.imhm.org), is housed in the old Pathology Building of what was once a huge psychiatric hospital. The guides give a fascinating account of medical practices in the late nineteenth century, pointing out the cabinets of preserved brains and similarly gruesome exhibits.

The **Children's Museum of Indianapolis**, 3000 N Meridian St, four miles north of downtown off of I-65 (summer daily 10am–5pm; rest of year closed Mon; $9.50, children $4; ☎317/334-3322, ⓦwww.childrensmuseum.org), is arguably the best of its kind in the country and one of the largest in the world. An excellent exhibit on African-American storytelling highlights the importance of oral tradition, while those less educationally minded can dig for dinosaur fossils or view Kermit the Frog and two hundred other puppets in a gallery devoted to them.

Eating

Circle Centre, the swish mall at Illinois and Washington, houses dozens of **places to eat**, but most of these are chains. You'd do better to stick to the more established restaurants downtown or head up to **Broad Ripple Village** (bus #17) at College Avenue and 62nd Street, which is packed with bars and cafés (along with galleries and shops). At lunchtime, **City Market**, 222 E Market St, is a maze of lunch counters and tables where you can feast cheaply on all sorts of international food amid a cacophonous din.

The Indianapolis 500

Seven miles northwest of downtown, the **Indianapolis Motor Speedway** stages only two events each year; but one does happen to be the legendary **Indianapolis 500** (the other is the prestigious NASCAR Brickyard 400 in August).

Held on the last Sunday in May, the Indy 500 is preceded by two weeks of qualification runs that whittle the hopeful entrants down to a final field of 33 drivers, one of whom will scoop the million-dollar first prize. The two-and-a-half-mile circuit was built as a test track for the city's motor manufacturers. The first 500-mile race held in 1911 – won in a time of 6hr 42min, at an average speed of 74.6mph – was a huge success, vindicating the organizers' belief that the distance was the optimum length for spectators' enjoyment. Cars now hit 225mph, though the official times of the winners are reduced by delays caused by accidents. The automotive technology is marvelous, but the true legends in the eyes of their fans are such championship drivers as A.J. Foyt, Mario Andretti, and members of the Unser dynasty.

The big race crowns one of the nation's largest festivals, attended by up to 450,000. At first, the city's conservative hierarchy saw it as an infringement on the traditional observance of Memorial Day weekend. However, it brings so much money into the city, with thousands of "Indy" racing fanatics staying for up to two weeks, that it is now exploited to the full, with civic events such as the crowning of the Speedway Queen, a Mayor's Ball, and a street parade. Seats for the race usually sell out well in advance, but you may gain admittance to the infield, where the giddy and boozy atmosphere makes up for the poor view.

Adjoining the track, the impressive display of race-car history at the **Indianapolis Motor Speedway Hall of Fame Museum**, 4790 W 16th St (daily 9am–5pm; $3; ☎317/492-6784, ⓦwww.indy500.com), provides a good background to the hysteria. For an extra two dollars, a rickety old bus saunters around the super-smooth asphalt track (only a small patch of the original bricks remains), ringed by huge banked grandstands. The circuit also holds four of the eighteen holes of the unique **Brickyard Crossing golf course** (☎317/484-6572, ⓦwww.brickyardcrossing.com), home to the annual Senior PGA Tournament; greens fees are $90.

Bazbeaux 334 Massachusetts Ave, downtown ☎317/636-7662 and 811 E Westfield Blvd, Broad Ripple Village ☎317/255-5711. The best (thin-crust) pizzas in town, with a range of exotic toppings.

Elbow Room 605 N Pennsylvania St ☎317/635-3354. This pub serves specialty sandwiches and lots of import beers.

India Garden 830 Broad Ripple Ave ☎317/253-6060. The curries are a highlight, along with the good-value lunchtime buffet.

Rathskeller Restaurant 401 E Michigan St ☎317/636-0396. Continental dishes, including lots of German specialties, served in the beer-hall style basement of the historic Atheneum building.

Ruthellen's 825 N Pennsylvania St ☎317/631-RUTH. Upscale dining in a wildly baroque but nonetheless cozy atmosphere, with a piano bar featured on Friday and Saturday nights. Closed Mon. Must be 21 and over.

St Elmo Steak House 127 S Illinois St ☎317/635-0636. One of the most famous steak restaurants in the meat-mad Midwest, if rather pompous and expensive ($40–50 per person), but good nonetheless.

Shapiro's 808 S Meridian St ☎317/631-4041. Landmark deli just a few blocks off downtown, where you can fill up on lox, tongue, and other specialties in an old-style cafeteria atmosphere. Leave room for the huge desserts.

Nightlife and entertainment

The emerging **nightlife** area in downtown is Massachusetts Avenue, where along with some good bars and restaurants, the 3000-seat **Murat Centre**, a former Masonic shrine at 502 N New Jersey St (☎317/231-0000), hosts headliners and Broadway musicals. Otherwise, head north to chic **Broad Ripple**

Village. Check the free weekly *NUVO* for full details of gigs and events.

On the **performing arts** scene, the 1927 Spanish Baroque Indiana Repertory Theatre, 140 W Washington St (℡317/635-5252), puts on dramatic productions between October and May, while the Indianapolis Symphony Orchestra has weekly concerts at the equally elaborate 1916 Hilbert Circle Theatre, 45 Monument Circle (℡317/639-4300).

Broad Ripple Brew Pub 840 E 65th St ℡317/253-2739. Atmospheric brewpub located six miles north of downtown Indianapolis.

Chatterbox 435 Massachusetts Ave ℡317/636-0584. Lively local bar, hosting live jazz nightly. Closed Sun.

Madame Walker Theatre Center 617 Indiana Ave ℡317/236-2099. Black cultural and heritage center putting on *Jazz on the Avenue* every Friday, plus regular dance events, plays, and concerts.

Slippery Noodle 372 S Meridian St ℡317/631-6968. Indiana's oldest bar, established in 1850, is next to Union Station. Cheap beer Monday and Tuesday, and live blues every night.

Vogue 6259 N College Ave ℡317/259-7029. Popular Broad Ripple rock and indie venue with retro club nights.

Out from Indianapolis: Bloomington

BLOOMINGTON, by far the liveliest small city in Indiana, is 45 miles southwest of Indianapolis on Hwy-37. It owes its vibrancy to the main campus of Indiana University, east of downtown. The I.M. Pei–designed **Indiana University Art Museum** on East Seventh Street (Wed–Sat 10am–5pm, Sun noon–5pm; free) holds a fine international collection of painting and sculpture. Across the street from the pastoral campus, law student Hoagy Carmichael composed *Stardust* on the piano of a popular hangout. The architecturally rich downtown also features a host of good shops.

Practicalities

Greyhound, 409 S Walnut St (℡812/332-1522), runs **bus** service to Indianapolis. Bloomington's friendly **visitor center** can be found at 2855 N Walnut St (Mon–Fri 8.30am–5pm, Sat 9am–4pm; ℡812/334-8900, Ⓦwww.visitbloomington.com).

If you need **to stay**, try *Motel 6 – Bloomington University*, 1800 N Walnut St (℡812/332-0820; ❷), the best budget accommodation in central Bloomington, or, for a bit more luxury, the cozy and central Victorian *Grant Street Inn*, 310 N Grant St (℡812/334-2353, Ⓦwww.grantstreetinn.com; ❻). The Indiana Memorial Union on Seventh and Park (℡812/856-6381), a good source of campus information, also offers a range of cheap places to **eat**. Student bars and cafés are strung out along Kirkwood Avenue, including the vegetarian *Laughing Planet*, at no. 322 E Kirkwood (℡812/323-2233). Among the wide range of ethnic restaurants in town are the Japanese/Indian/Tibetan *Snow Lion*, 113 S Grant Ave (℡812/336-0835), and the *Siam House*, 430 E Fourth St (℡812/331-1233), which serves delicious Thai cuisine. The *Runcible Spoon*, 412 E Sixth St (℡812/334-3997), is a favorite local place for breakfast, coffee, and dessert, while the *Brewpub at Lennie's*, 1795 E Tenth St (℡812/323-2112), is the best place in town for microbrewed ales.

Illinois

Nearly everything in the agricultural powerhouse state of **ILLINOIS** revolves around **Chicago**, the largest and most exciting of the Great Lakes cities. At the state's northeastern corner, on the shores of **Lake Michigan**, Chicago has a skyline to rival any city's, a gamut of top-rated museums, restaurants, and cafés, and innumerable bars and nightclubs that pay homage to the town's strong jazz and blues heritage. Seventy-five percent of the state's twelve-million-strong population live within commuting distance of the Windy City's energetic center, which controls the bulk of the state economy – the third-largest crops producer in the US. Outside of Chicago, the sole exception to the endless flat prairies is far to the south, where the forested **Shawnee Hills** rise between the Mississippi and Ohio rivers. The contrast between Illinois' quiet rural hinterlands and its buzzing urban center could hardly be greater. Still, the state does hold a few places to head for – though apart from a couple of mildly exciting college towns, most are of historic rather than current interest.

Illinois was first explored and settled by the French, though in 1763 the territory was sold to the English. Granted statehood in 1818, Illinois remained a distant frontier until the mid-1830s, when, after a series of uprisings, the native **Sauk** were subjugated; only then did settlers began to arrive in sizeable numbers. Among these were the first followers of Joseph Smith, founder of the Mormon Church, who established a large colony along the Mississippi at Nauvoo. The **Mormons** met with suspicion and persecution and, after Smith was murdered by a lynch mob in 1844, fled west to Utah. Other early immigrants included the young **Abraham Lincoln**, who practiced law from 1837 onward in **Springfield**, state capital and home to a wide range of Lincolniana, including his restored home, his law offices, and various other period buildings and artifacts, as well as his monumental tomb. Indeed, Illinois' self-proclaimed nickname – emblazoned on its car license plates – is "Land of Lincoln."

Getting around Illinois

Because Chicago is the site of **O'Hare Airport** (the world's busiest), as well as the hub of the national Amtrak **train** network, you're likely to at least to pass through it. If you plan to spend time in the rest of Illinois, Amtrak, numerous commuter railroads, and, to a lesser extent, Greyhound, make getting around on public transportation feasible. **Cycling** is also generally easy on these endless flat plains. Half a dozen **interstates** fan out across the country from Chicago. The famous Chicago-to-LA Route 66 has been defunct since the 1960s, though I-55 southwest to St Louis, followed by I-44 and I-40, follow its general route.

Chicago

CHICAGO is in many ways the nation's last great city. Sarah Bernhardt called it "the pulse of America" and, though long eclipsed by Los Angeles as the nation's second most populous city after New York, Chicago really does have it all, with less of the hassle and infrastructural problems of its coastal rivals.

Founded in the early 1800s, Chicago grew up with the country, serving as the main connection between the established East Coast cities and the wide-open Wild West frontier. This position on the sharp edge between civilization and wilderness made the city into a crucible of innovation. Many aspects of modern life, from skyscrapers to suburbia, had their start, and perhaps their finest expression, here on the shores of Lake Michigan.

Despite burning to the ground in the legendary fire of 1871, Chicago boomed thereafter, doubling in population every decade and reaching two million people around 1900, swollen by **Irish** and **Eastern European** immigrants (Chicago still has the largest Polish population in the world outside Warsaw). In the early years of the twentieth century, it cemented its reputation as a place of apparently limitless opportunity, with jobs aplenty for those willing to work. The attraction was strongest among **blacks** from the Deep South: from 1900 to 1920, African-Americans poured into the city, with more than 75,000 arriving during the war years of 1916–1918 alone.

Long hours, poor pay, and squalid working conditions were the catalysts that made Chicago the cradle of American **trade unions**. By around 1900 most workers were organized under the American Federation of Labor, and the 1894 Pullman strike saw black and white workers unite for almost the first time in the US. As hostilities intensified, the city's workers became the driving force behind the left-wing "Wobblies." Chicago has also long been an important center for black organization – both the Reverend Jesse Jackson's **Operation PUSH** (People United to Save Humanity) and the more militant **Nation of Islam**, founded by Elijah Mohammed in the 1940s, have their national headquarters on the city's South Side.

During the Roaring Twenties, Chicago's self-image as a no-holds-barred free market was pushed to the limit by a new breed of entrepreneur. Criminal syndicates, ruthlessly and brazenly run by the likes of **gangsters** like Al Capone and Bugsy Moran, took advantage of Prohibition to sell bootleg alcohol. Shootouts in the street between sharp-suited, Tommy-gun-wielding mobsters were not as common as legend would have it, but the backroom dealing and iron-handed control they pioneered was later perfected by politicians such as former mayor **Richard Daley** – father of the present mayor – who ran Chicago single-handedly from the 1950s until his death in 1976. His brutal handling of antiwar demonstrators at the **1968 Democratic convention** remains notorious. These days, the tourist authorities play down the mobster era; few traces of the hoodlum years exist, and those that do owe more to Hollywood than contemporary Chicago.

Today, Chicago's towering **skyline** – the city has one of the world's best collections of **modern architecture**, from Frank Lloyd Wright houses to the 110-story **Sears Tower** – dominates the pancake-flat prairies for hundreds of miles around. Chicago's status as the cultural and financial heart of middle America is beyond question. **The Loop** downtown holds the head offices of many major US companies and some of the nation's most important **commodity markets**, which together handle the buying and selling of one-third of the world's agricultural and industrial products.

For visitors, Chicago offers the **Art Institute of Chicago** and a wide range of excellent **museums**, along with restaurants, sports, and highbrow cultural activities. However, its strongest suit is **live music**, with a phenomenal array of **jazz** and **blues** clubs packed into the back rooms of its amiable bars and cafés. The **rock** scene is also one of the healthiest in the country, with a prolific number of bands having come out of the city in the 1990s, including Smashing Pumpkins and Wilco. And almost everything is noticeably less expensive than in other US cities – **eating out**, for example, costs much less than in New York or LA, but is every bit as good. Though locals might deny it, the city has a surprisingly low-key and generally welcoming population – Chicagoans on the whole are proud of their city and usually keen to point out its best features. Two great ways to get a real feel for the city are to head out to ivy-covered **Wrigley Field** on a sunny summer afternoon to catch baseball's Cubs in action, or take a cruise boat under the bridges of the Chicago River at sunset.

Arrival, information, and getting around

Chicago's **O'Hare International Airport** (Ⓦwww.ohare.com), the national headquarters for United, American, and several other airlines, is seventeen miles northwest of downtown Chicago. It is connected to the city center by 24hr CTA (Blue Line) **trains** from the station under Terminal 4, which take

O'Hare Airport (3 miles)

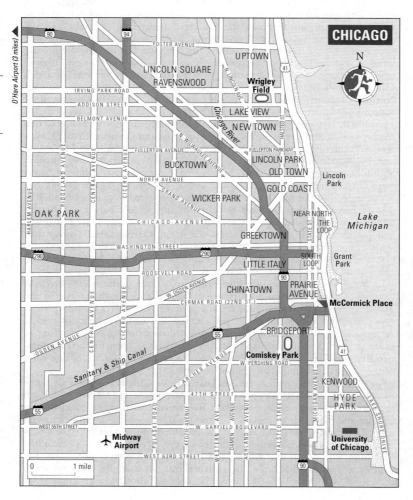

CHICAGO

N

FOSTER AVENUE

UPTOWN

LINCOLN SQUARE
RAVENSWOOD

Wrigley
Field

IRVING PARK ROAD

ADDISON STREET

BELMONT AVENUE

LAKE VIEW

NEW TOWN

Chicago River

FULLERTON AVENUE

FULLERTON PARKWAY

BUCKTOWN

LINCOLN PARK

OLD TOWN

Lincoln
Park

NORTH AVENUE

GRAND AVENUE

WICKER PARK

GOLD COAST

OAK PARK

CHICAGO AVENUE

NEAR NORTH

THE
LOOP

Lake
Michigan

GREEKTOWN

WASHINGTON STREET

LITTLE ITALY

SOUTH
LOOP

Grant
Park

ROOSEVELT ROAD

CHINATOWN

PRAIRIE
AVENUE

McCormick Place

CERMAK ROAD (22ND ST.)

W. OGDEN AVENUE

OGDEN AVENUE

Sanitary & Ship Canal

BRIDGEPORT

Comiskey Park

W. PERSHING ROAD

S. ARCHER AVENUE

KENWOOD

47TH STREET

HYDE
PARK

WEST 55TH STREET

W. GARFIELD BOULEVARD

LAKE SHORE DRIVE

Midway
Airport

University
of Chicago

WEST 63RD STREET

0   1 mile

around forty minutes and cost $1.50 (see "City transportation," below). **Midway Airport**, smaller than O'Hare but used by an increasing number of domestic airlines, is eleven miles southwest of downtown; take one of CTA's Midway (Orange Line) trains, which take thirty minutes, or the #99M Midway Express bus (weekday rush hours only). **Taxis** into town from O'Hare cost around $25–30 (there's also a ride-share program with a flat rate of $15), and take thirty minutes to an hour. From Midway the fare is about $25 (shared rides are $10) and the journey time is twenty to forty minutes. Another option is Continental Air Transport's **express bus and van service** between the airports and downtown hotels ($20 from O'Hare, $15 from Midway; ☎312/454-7799, ⓦ www.airportexpress.com).

Chicago is the hub of the nationwide **Amtrak** rail system, and almost every cross-country route passes through **Union Station**, west of the Loop at Canal and Adam streets. Greyhound and a number of regional bus companies pull into the large 24hr **bus station** at 630 W Harrison St, three blocks southwest of Union Station.

Arriving in Chicago **by car**, racing towards the gleaming glass towers of the Loop, can be memorable. Bear in mind, though, that traffic on the expressways to and from downtown can be bumper-to-bumper during rush hours. **Parking** can also be a problem. Meters are expensive (25¢ for 15min) and usually have a 2hr limit. Check street signs for additional restrictions, which are rigidly enforced – violations may result in your car being towed and impounded. Perhaps the best place to leave a car in the downtown area is in the garage under Grant Park, at Columbus Street and Monroe Drive, close to the east side of the Art Institute ($13 for 24hr; ☎312/742-7644).

Information

Pick up information and maps from the **Chicago Office of Tourism**, in the lobby of the Chicago Cultural Center, 77 E Randolph St (Mon–Thurs 10am–7pm, Fri 10am–6pm, Sat 10am–5pm, Sun 11am–5pm; ☎1-800/877-CHICAGO, ⓦ www.ci.chi.il.us/AboutTown.html). There are also **information centers** in the Historic Water Tower, 800 N Michigan Ave on the Magnificent Mile (daily 7.30am–7pm) and in the Illinois Market Place Visitor Information Center at Navy Pier, 700 E Grand Ave (Mon–Thurs & Sun 10am–8pm, Fri & Sat 10am–10pm).

Chicago's main **post office**, the largest in the world, is at 433 W Harrison St (Mon–Sat 8am–5pm; ☎1-800/275-8777; zip code 85907). In downtown, there's a branch at 211 S Clark St (Mon–Fri 7am–7pm).

City transportation

Getting around Chicago is simple and quick, thanks to buses and the "El," a system of elevated trains operated 24 hours a day by the Chicago Transit Authority (CTA; ☎312/836-7000, ⓦ www.transitchicago.com). Pick up a CTA System

---

CityPass

For significant **discounts** at six of the city's major tourist and cultural attractions – the Hancock Observatory, the Art Institute of Chicago, the Field Museum, Shedd Aquarium, Adler Planetarium & Astronomy Museum, and the Museum of Science and Industry – you can purchase a **CityPass** ($49; ☎208/787-4300, ⓦ www.city-pass.com). Valid for nine days, it allows you to skip most lines and save (up to $43, if you visit all six sights). CityPasses are sold at each of the six attractions to which the pass provides admission, or from the website.

Guided tours

Various sightseeing companies run **guided bus tours** of the city center. Hour-long tours by Chicago Trolley (daily 9.30am–5pm; $20 for one day, $25 for two days, hop on and off; ℡773/648-5000, 🅦www.chicagotrolley.com), often voted "best tour in Chicago" by locals, begins at the Sears Tower. Otherwise, Chicago Motor Coach ($10; ℡312/666-1000) runs double-decker buses that pick up at the Sears Tower, the Art Institute, and Navy Pier.

The **Chicago Architecture Foundation**, in the Santa Fe Building at 224 S Michigan Ave (℡312/922-3432, 🅦www.architecture.org), runs a number of highly recommended tours throughout the city. Among these are two information-packed walking tours of the Loop, giving a friendly in-depth introduction to Chicago's buildings and history ($10 for one 2hr tour, $15 for both). The Foundation also offers walking tours of Frank Lloyd Wright's buildings in Oak Park, Historic Pullman, and other neighborhoods, as well as bus tours of the Loop and Near North ($15; 2hr), and Hyde Park and Frank Lloyd Wright's Robie House ($25; 3hr 30min). Perhaps the most popular of all are the excellent ninety-minute Chicago Architecture by Boat tours, which leave from Michigan Avenue and Lower Wacker Drive (May–Oct Mon–Sat 3 departures, Sun 2 trips; $21). **Other sightseeing boat tours** include those offered along the river by Mercury ($14; ℡312/332-1368, 🅦www.cruisechicago.com) and Wendella ($16; ℡312/245-0162; 🅦www.wendellaboats.com) during the summer season; and Spirit of Chicago Harbor Cruises ($17; ℡312/836-7888), who sail year-round from Navy Pier. Shoreline Sightseeing Tours ($17 for architectural cruises, $10 for lake cruises; ℡312/222-9328, 🅦www.shorelinesightseeing.com) is another good option; their architectural river cruises provide a somewhat different look at the architecture of Chiago.

Map, available at most subway stations and visitor centers, or from the CTA office on the seventh floor of the Merchandise Mart, 300 N Wells St, just north of the Chicago River. **Buses** run every five to fifteen minutes during rush hours and every eight to twenty minutes at most other times. **Rapid transit trains** run every five to fifteen minutes during the day and every fifteen to sixty minutes all night. Lines are color-coded and denoted by route rather than destination. The Howard–Dan Ryan is the Red Line; Lake–Englewood–Jackson Park is the Green Line; the O'Hare–Congress–Douglas is the Blue Line; the Ravenswood is the Brown Line (whose trains circle the Loop, giving the area its name); the Evanston Express is the Purple Line; the Midway–Loop is the Orange Line; and the Skokie Swift is the Yellow Line. The **Metra Commuter Trains** run from various points downtown to and from the suburbs and outlying areas, including Oak Park and Hyde Park. One ride costs $1.95.

The CTA no longer accepts tokens; instead, riders purchase a **transit card** (available in all El stations) and add value to it. One ride costs $1.50; another ride within two hours costs just 30¢. If you plan to be on the move, passes good for one ($5), two ($9), three ($12), or five ($18) days of unlimited rides might be a good idea. They're available at O'Hare and Midway airports and at Union Station. Passes can be used for both the El and for buses.

Chicago's **taxis**, despite a recent increase in fares, are more reasonable than those of many other major US cities. Charges are $1.50 at the drop of the flag, $1.20 per mile, and 50¢ for each additional passenger. Cabs can be hailed anytime in the Loop and other central neighborhoods; otherwise call Yellow (℡312/829-4222) or Checker taxis (℡312/243-2537).

A **River Bus** (April–Oct; $2; ℡312/337-1446) operates on the river during rush hour in summer, running from the Michigan Avenue Bridge to Union

Station in eight minutes. Free **trolleys** run during the summer from 10am–6pm from the Loop to Navy Pier, the Magnificent Mile, and the Museum Campus.

Accommodation

Most central **accommodation** is oriented towards business and convention trade rather than tourism, but there are still plenty of moderately priced rooms. A number of clean (if unexciting) prewar hotels in and around the Loop offer reasonable rates, especially on weekends, and motorists can pick from scores of motels along the interstates. Even top-class downtown hotels are, comparatively, not that expensive. Under the Chicago's Got It program, hotels in all price ranges offer discounts of fifteen to forty percent on Thursday to Sunday nights, when the business types have gone home, so you can often get a room in a really plush place for around $100. If you're stuck, Hot Rooms is a reservation service offering hotel rooms at discount rates (☎773/468-7666 or 1-800/468-3500). While they're not as prominent as elsewhere, **bed-and-breakfast** rooms are available from $75 per night through Chicago B&B, PO Box 14088, IL 85914 (☎312/951-0085). Just under fifteen-percent room tax is added to all bills.

Allegro 179 W Randolph St ☎312/236-0123, ⓦwww.allegrochicago.com. With a colorful, updated Art Deco design, this boutique hotel is sure to delight. Luxury amenities throughout. ❽

Arlington House International Hostel 616 W Arlington Place ☎773/929-5380 or 1-800/467-8355, ⓦwww.arlingtonhouse.com. Easygoing hostel close to loads of good bars and Wrigley Field, with both segregated and mixed dorms. Members pay $19.50, others $3 extra. Open 24hr. ❶

Best Western Grant Park 1100 S Michigan Ave ☎312/922-2900 or 1-800/528-1234, ⓦwww.bestwestern.com. A large hotel with outdoor pool, it's handy for Grant Park and lakeside attractions. Good value if a little far south. ❻

Cass 640 N Wabash Ave ☎312/787-4030, ⓦwww.casshotel.com. This clean, basic hotel is the best value in the Near North area. ❹

Chicago International Hostel 6318 N Winthrop Ave ☎773/262-1011, ⓦwww.chicagointernationalhostel.com. A big hostel, open 24hr, 365 days a year, it's a short walk from the Loyola El station. Dorm beds cost $17. ❶

Days Inn Lincoln Park North 644 W Diversey Parkway at Clark ☎773/525-7010, ⓦwww.lpdaysinn.com. This good, friendly motel is popular with visiting musicians and a convenient base for North Side nightlife. Free continental breakfast. ❺

The Drake 140 E Walton Place ☎312/787-2200 or 1-800/553-7256, ⓦwww.thedrakehotel.com. Chicago's society hotel, just off the Magnificent Mile, has been modernized without sacrificing its sedate charms. Its well-appointed rooms feature high-speed Internet access and Jacuzzis. You can always just pop in for a drink at the elegant *Palm Court Lounge*. ❽–❾

Hampton Suites Hotel 33 W Illinois Ave ☎312/832-0330, ⓦwww.hamptoninn.com. Clean motel in a good River North location, just four blocks east of the Magnificent Mile. ❼

HoJo Inn 720 N LaSalle St ☎312/664-8100 or 1-800/446-4656, ⓦwww.hojo.com. Standard *HoJo* rooms in a good Near North location. ❺

Hotel 71 71 E Wacker Drive ☎312/346-7100, ⓦwww.hotel71.com. In a magnificent setting by the Michigan Avenue Bridge, an extra $10 gets a river view. Big weekend discounts. ❼

House of Two Urns 1239 N Greenview Ave, Wicker Park ☎773/235-1408 or 1-877/TWO-URNS, ⓦwww.twourns.com. This rambling, artist-owned B&B, three blocks from the El and close to Wicker Park, is filled with contemporary art. ❹

The Inn at Lincoln Park 601 W Diversey Parkway ☎773/348-2810 or 1-800/228-5150, ⓦwww.innlp.com. Medium-sized motel, with free continental breakfast, in the accommodation-starved Lincoln Park district. ❻

J. Ira & Nicki Harris Hostel at HI-Chicago 24 E Congress St ☎312/360-0300, ⓦwww.hichicago.org. Huge, centrally located hostel, with clean and spacious dorms (beds cost $30); good for easy downtown access. A friendly staff organizes weekly outings for the masses of students and international travelers who frequent this hostel. ❶

Lenox Suites Hotel 231 N Rush St ☎312/337-1000, ⓦwww.lenoxsuites.com. Just a few blocks north of the river, a great all-suite hotel. ❼

Monaco 225 N Wabash Ave ☎ 312/960-8500 or 1-800/397-7661, ⓦ www.monaco-chicago.com. A stylish and luxurious French Deco hotel with a 24hr fitness room. ❽

Red Roof Inn 162 E Ontario St ☎ 312/787-3580 or 1-800/733-7663, ⓦ www.redroof.com. A few yards off the Magnificent Mile, this clean, no-frills option is in the center of the shopping action. ❺

Windy City Urban Inn 607 W Deming Place ☎ 773/248-7091 or 1-877/897-7091, ⓦ www .windycityinn.com. In the Lincoln Park neighborhood, a luxurious B&B on a quiet street of grand old homes. ❻

Wooded Isle Suites 5750 S Stony Island Ave, Hyde Park ☎ 773/288-6305 or 1-800/288-6305, ⓦ www.woodedisle.com. A short-term apartment complex, near the University of Chicago, where studio and one-bedroom apartments are equipped with full kitchens. Guests staying for more than one week can receive reduced nightly rates. ❻

The City

Chicago is an easy city to negotiate: streets form a grid and numbering is consistent, beginning at State and Madison streets. State Street – "that great street" in Sinatra's song – is at zero east and west and Madison at zero north and south. **Lake Michigan**, which provides Chicago with some of its most attractive open space (twenty miles of lakeshore lie within the city limits), serves as a clear point of reference for getting your bearings – the lake is always to the east of the urban grid. **Michigan Avenue** is the city's main thoroughfare, running between the lakeside museums and parklands, the densely packed skyscrapers of downtown, and the diverse low-rise neighborhoods that spread to the north, south, and west. It's here that you might experience the full force of "The Hawk," the nickname given to the strong wind that blows off the lake. The nickname "**Windy City**" was coined by a New York newspaper editor describing the boastful claims of the city's promoters when pitching for the World's Columbian exhibition of 1893. The **Chicago River**, which cuts through the heart of downtown Chicago to Lake Michigan, separates the business district from the shopping and entertainment areas of the North Side. The latter include the upscale **Near North** and **Gold Coast** neighborhoods; the artists' lofts and galleries of **River North**; the modestly charming area of **Old Town**; the young professional enclaves of **Lincoln Park**, **Wrigleyville**, and **Lakeview**, as well as hip **Wicker Park**.

In contrast to the wealth and prosperity of the North Side, the deprived **South Side** is more like New York's South Bronx: a huge and, in places, desperately poor expanse with a justifiably dangerous reputation. But while large areas are definitely unsafe after dark and dodgy even at midday, a few corners of the South Side are well worth visiting – particularly the Gothic campus of the **University of Chicago** and neighboring **Hyde Park**, site of the **Museum of Science and Industry**, one of the largest and most popular museums in the US. Other than **Oak Park** to the west, which holds the childhood home of **Ernest Hemingway** and more than a dozen well-maintained examples of the influential architecture of **Frank Lloyd Wright**, suburban Chicago has little to offer.

Downtown Chicago: The Loop

Downtown Chicago puts on what is perhaps the finest display of **modern architecture** in the world, from the prototype skyscrapers of the 1890s to Mies van der Rohe's "less is more" modernist masterpieces, and the second tallest building in the world, the quarter-mile-high **Sears Tower**. Just about all these edifices are workplaces of one kind or another; the whole place is bustling during the day and virtually empty at night.

The compact heart of Chicago is known as **the Loop**, because it's circled by the elevated tracks of the CTA "El" trains. For a first impression of downtown,

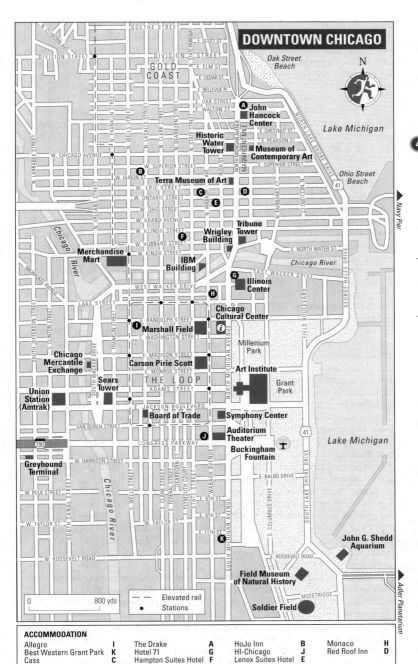

DOWNTOWN CHICAGO

N

Oak Street
Beach

Lake Michigan

Ohio Street
Beach

41

GOLD
COAST

DIVISION STREET

GOETHE STREET

E. SCOTT ST

DIVISION STREET

E. ELM ST.

E. CEDAR ST.

E. BELLEVUE PL.

E. OAK STREET

E. WALTON ST.

John
Hancock
Center

E. CHESTNUT ST.

E. PEARSON ST.

Historic
Water
Tower

Museum of
Contemporary Art

E. SUPERIOR STREET

W. SUPERIOR STREET

Terra Museum of Art

W. HURON ST.

W. ERIE STREET

W. ONTARIO STREET

W. OHIO STREET

W. GRAND AVENUE

W. ILLINOIS STREET

Wrigley
Building

Tribune
Tower

W. HUBBARD STREET

W. KINZIE STREET

IBM
Building

Merchandise
Mart

E. NORTH WATER ST.

Chicago River

Chicago River

EAST WACKER DRIVE

Illinois
Center

WEST WACKER DRIVE

LAKE STREET

E. RANDOLPH STREET

Chicago
Cultural Center

Marshall Field

E. WASHINGTON STREET

E. MADISON STREET

Carson Pirie Scott

E. MONROE STREET

THE LOOP

E. ADAMS STREET

Chicago
Mercantile
Exchange

Sears
Tower

Union
Station
(Amtrak)

E. JACKSON BOULEVARD

Board of Trade

VAN BUREN STREET

CONGRESS PARKWAY

290

Greyhound
Terminal

W. HARRISON STREET

Chicago River

W. POLK STREET

W. TAYLOR STREET

W. TAYLOR ST.

W. ROOSEVELT ROAD

Millenium
Park

Art Institute

Grant
Park

Symphony Center

Auditorium
Theater

Buckingham
Fountain

E. BALBO DRIVE

Lake Michigan

41

E. 8TH ST.

E. 9TH ST.

E. 11TH ST.

E. ROOSEVELT ROAD

John G. Shedd
Aquarium

Field Museum
of Natural History

MCFETRIDGE

Soldier Field

▶ Navy Pier

▶ Adler Planetarium

| 0 | 800 yds | – – Elevated rail |
| | | ● Stations |

ACCOMMODATION

Allegro	**I**	The Drake	**A**	HoJo Inn	**B**	Monaco	**H**
Best Western Grant Park	**K**	Hotel 71	**G**	HI-Chicago	**J**	Red Roof Inn	**D**
Cass	**C**	Hampton Suites Hotel	**F**	Lenox Suites Hotel	**E**		

start your explorations by seeing the energy, drive, and greed exposed in the trading pits of the various **commodity marketplaces**. Half the world's wheat and corn (and pork-belly futures) are bought and sold amid the cacophonic roar of the **Chicago Board of Trade**, housed in a gorgeous Art Deco tower, appropriately topped by a 30ft stainless steel statue of Ceres, the Roman goddess of grain. From the entrance at 141 W Jackson St, where it intersects with LaSalle Street, take the elevator to the fifth-floor visitor gallery (Mon–Fri 8am–1.15pm; free), where displays trace the evolution of the various frantic shouts and signals by which trade is actually carried out. A similarly energetic ballet goes on from the early hours within Chicago's stock options exchange, the largest in the US. At the **Chicago Mercantile Exchange**, three blocks away at 30 S Wacker Drive (Mon–Fri 7.30am–3.15pm; free), precious metals, currencies, and commodities are bought and sold to the tune of some $50 billion a day. The **best time to visit** the exchanges is just before the close of trade, when the pressure is at its peak and tempers are most frayed.

A couple of other buildings in the immediate vicinity are worth nosing around during business hours. Half a block from the Board of Trade, **The Rookery**, 209 S LaSalle St, built in 1886 by Burnham and Root, is one of the city's most celebrated and photographed edifices. Its forbidding Moorish Gothic exterior gives way to a wonderfully airy lobby, decked out with cool Italian marble and gold leaf during a major 1905 remodeling by Frank Lloyd Wright; the spiral cantilever staircase rising from the second floor must be seen to be appreciated. A couple of doors down toward the Board of Trade, check out the **Continental Illinois Bank** lobby, with its 28 Ionic marble columns and intricate murals.

Looking up at the proud facade of the **Reliance Building**, 32 N State St, you'd be forgiven for thinking it dates from the Art Deco Thirties, but it was in fact completed way back in 1895 by Daniel Burnham, who did much to shape the face of Chicago. His **Fisher Building**, with its tongue-in-cheek, aquatic-inspired ornamental terracotta, stands at 343 S Dearborn St. A block farther south, the 1890 **Manhattan Building** was the world's first tall all-steel-frame building, and is generally acknowledged as the progenitor of the modern curtain-walled skyscraper. Now converted into luxury apartments, it preserves some noteworthy exterior ornament.

The Loop holds some of Chicago's grandest c.1900 **department stores**. The best looking of these, the 1899 **Carson Pirie Scott** store, at 1 S State St (Mon–Sat 9.45am–8pm, Sun 11am–6pm ☎312/641-7000, Ⓦwww.carsons .com), boasts a magnificent ironwork facade that blends botanic and geometric forms in an intuitive version of Art Moderne. Its architect, Louis Sullivan, was also responsible for the gorgeous spherical bronze clocks suspended from the corners of the **Marshall Field's** department store (Mon–Thurs 9am–8pm, Fri & Sat 9am–9pm, Sun 11am–6pm; ☎312/781-1000), two blocks north at State and Washington streets. The comparatively bland exterior of Marshall Field's oldest and grandest branch masks one of the world's great stores, with seven floors of merchandise.

A resurrected stretch of the riverfront walk follows the west bank of the river, with open-air cafés and gardens. Farther south, and back on the Loop side at South Wacker Drive and Adams Street, is the 1468ft **Sears Tower**, the tallest building in the world until 1997, when Malaysia's Petronas Towers nudged it from the top by the length of an antenna. Various companies occupy the tower (Sears has moved to the suburbs), and it's so huge that it has more than one hundred elevators. Two ascend, in little more than a minute, from the ground-level shopping mall to the 103rd-floor **Skydeck Observatory** (daily:

May–Sept 10am–10pm, Oct–April 10am–8pm; $10), for breathtaking views that on a clear day take in four states – Illinois, Michigan, Wisconsin, and Indiana. Look east for the distinctive triangular **Metropolitan Detention Center**, where prisoners exercise on the grassy roof beneath wire netting to ensure they don't get whisked away by helicopter.

The Chicago River

The Loop is usually said to end at the "El" tracks, but the blocks beyond this core, to either side of the Chicago River, hold plenty of interest. Broad, double-decked **Wacker Drive**, parallel to the water, was designed as a sophisticated promenade, lined by benches and obelisk-shaped lanterns, by Daniel Burnham in 1909. Though never completed, and despite the almost constant intrusion of construction works, it makes for a nice extended walk. The river itself had its direction reversed c.1900, in an engineering project more extensive than the digging of the Panama Canal. As a result, rather than letting its sewage and industrial waste flow east into Lake Michigan, Chicago now sends it all south into the Corn Belt.

A **boat tour** from beneath the Michigan Avenue Bridge gives magnificent views of downtown and a good insight into the city's history (see the "Guided tours" box, p.360). However, half an hour's walk, especially at lunchtime when the office workers are out in force, will do the trick nearly as well. Burnham's promenade runs along both sides of the river, crossing back and forth over the twenty-odd drawbridges that open and close to let barges and the occasional sailboat pass. The **State Street Bridge** is a superb vantage point. On the south bank, at 35 E Wacker Drive, the elegant Beaux Arts **Jewelers Building** was built in 1926 and is capped on the seventeenth floor by a domed rotunda that once housed Al Capone's favorite speakeasy. Across the river stands what's commonly considered Ludwig Mies van der Rohe's masterpiece – the 1971 **IBM Building**, 330 N Wabash Ave. The gentle play of light and shadow across the detailed bronze and smoked-glass facade has been the model for countless other less considered copies worldwide. The building is so huge that it acts as a funnel for winter winds off Lake Michigan, and heavy ropes sometimes must be tied across the broad plaza at its base to protect people from getting blown away.

Perhaps Chicago's most successful and acclaimed building of recent years stands four blocks west at **333 W Wacker Drive**. Towering over a broad bend in the river, and bowed to follow its curve, the green glass facade reflects the almost fluorescent green of the river (recently upgraded from "toxic" to merely "polluted"). On the lower floors, a more classically detailed stone base actively addresses its stalwart elder neighbors.

South Michigan Avenue and the Art Institute of Chicago

Many of Chicago's major cultural attractions are gathered on the eastern edge of the Loop, along Michigan Avenue between the city's commercial core and the shores of Lake Michigan. On the lake side of South Michigan Avenue, at the east end of Adams Street, the **Art Institute of Chicago** (Mon–Fri 10.30am–4.30pm, Tues until 8pm, Sat 10am–5pm, Sun noon–5pm; suggested donation $10, free Tues; ☎312/443-3600, ⊛www.artic.edu) has an excellent collection of Impressionist and Post-Impressionist paintings, Asian art (particularly Japanese prints), photography, and architectural drawings. The Neoclassical facade of the main entrance does its best to look dignified, but the numerous added-on wings can make it hard to find your way around inside.

Most visitors head straight upstairs to the Impressionist works, which include a wall full of Monet's *Haystacks* captured in various lights, next to Seurat's immediately familiar pointillist *Sunday Afternoon on La Grande Jatte*. A handful of Post-Impressionist masterpieces by Van Gogh, Gauguin, and Matisse are arrayed nearby. Beyond here, a tortured, tuxedoed self-portrait by **Max Beckmann** – his last Berlin painting before fleeing the Nazis – welcomes you into a crowded gallery of early twentieth-century American and European works, in which moody portraits by Balthus and Picasso, and Surrealist landscapes by Max Ernst and Yves Tanguy, hang side by side with Edward Hopper's lonely *Nighthawks* and Georgia O'Keeffe's disquieting *Black Cross, New Mexico*.

Also look for the pitchfork-holding farmer of Grant Woods' oft-parodied *American Gothic* – a picture he painted as a student at the Art Institute school, and sold to the museum for $300 in 1930 – and for the delightful seventh-century Indonesian-sculptured stone monkeys in the Southeast Asia collections displayed around the McKinlock Court Garden, which in summer is employed as an **open-air café**. Also here, in the east end of the complex, is the immaculately reconstructed Art Moderne trading room of the Chicago Stock Exchange, designed by Louis Sullivan in 1893 and moved here in the 1970s.

A few blocks north from the Art Institute, the **Chicago Cultural Center** takes up most of the splendid old Public Library building at 78 E Washington St, and offers a range of free activities. As well as the city's main **visitor center**, it features various galleries (including some great photos of Chicago's most famous landmarks), major touring exhibits, and free lunchtime and evening recitals, readings, and concerts (Mon–Wed 10am–7pm, Thurs 10am–9pm, Fri 10am–6pm, Sun 11am–5pm; ☏312/346-3278). The highlight is the **Museum of Broadcast Communications** (Mon–Sat 10am–4.30pm, Sun noon–5pm; free; Ⓦwww.mbcnet.org), where you can watch old advertisements, newsreels, and sporting moments.

In 1900 this lakefront strip around the Art Institute on South Michigan Avenue was the city's prime entertainment district. Today, many of that era's grand structures preserve a sense of its unabashed artistic aspirations. The world-renowned **Chicago Symphony Orchestra**, now run by Daniel Barenboim after many successful years under the baton of Sir Georg Solti, performs to sell-out crowds at the **Symphony Center**, 220 S Michigan Ave (☏312/294-3030, Ⓦwww.cso.org). Down the street, the **Fine Arts Building** at no. 410 once held the offices of *Wizard of Oz* author L. Frank Baum, as well as the drafting studio of the young Frank Lloyd Wright. At no. 430, the stately 1889 **Auditorium Theater** (☏312/922-2110, Ⓦwww.auditoriumtheatre.org) was built by a group of Chicago's civic leaders in a bid to compete with the more established Eastern cities. It incorporates lavish use of gold, mosaics, and murals, and boasts an acoustically perfect theater.

Farther south on Michigan stand two of Chicago's most famous old **hotels**, including the recently renovated *Hilton*, the world's largest when it opened in 1927, and the more affordable and atmospheric *Blackstone*, currently undergoing renovation and transformation into a luxury condominium development. South of here, the neighborhood gets a bit dodgy; apart from the Prairie Avenue Historic District described on p.372, there's little of interest before the Hyde Park district three miles south. However, R&B fans may like to know that the southwest corner of Michigan Avenue and 21st Street held the studios and offices of **Chess Records**, immortalized in the early Rolling Stones song "2120 S Michigan Avenue." Plans to turn this hallowed building into a museum and resource center for local musicians have so far failed to get beyond the argument stage.

Grant Park

East of the Art Institute toward Lake Michigan, **Grant Park** provides a welcome, but not entirely complete, break from the downtown urban grid – wide strips of high-speed road and railroad slice through it, so casual rambling can be frustrating. The northern half of the park centers on the immense **Buckingham Fountain**, which features daily light and water shows from dusk to 11pm. The whole two-hundred-acre swath is sprinkled with sculptures and monuments, from a moping Columbus to a proud Plains Indian on horseback. Nearly every weekend in summer sees a musical festival (be it gospel, blues, country, jazz, or classical) held in the area around the Petrillo Music Shell, located just behind the Art Institute. In early July, the **Taste of Chicago** festival (Ⓦ www.tasteofchicago.com) attracts more than two million people to a week-long feeding frenzy, garnished with concerts and other live entertainment. North of the fountain, the 24-acre, Frank Gehry–designed **Millennium Park** will have gardens, outdoor performance space, a skating rink, and a music pavilion; completion is scheduled for the summer of 2004.

The major attractions are gathered in the landscaped southern half of Grant Park, known as **Museum Campus**. The extensive and engaging **Field Museum of Natural History**, 1200 S Lake Shore Drive, at Roosevelt Road (daily 9am–5pm; $8, free Wed; Ⓦ www.fieldmuseum.org), is ten minutes' walk south of the Art Institute, in a huge, marble-clad, Daniel Burnham–designed Greek temple. "Natural history" here includes anything non-white and non-European: the collection ranges from Egyptian tombs – the entire burial chamber of the son of a Fifth Dynasty pharaoh was brought here in 1908 – to the man-eating lions of Tsavo. Folklorists in an earthen lodge in the Native American section tell myths and legends, intended for young kids but not overly sentimental or simple-minded. Also kid-oriented is "Underground Adventure," a simulated environment that "shrinks" you to 1/100th your size, giving you an entirely new perspective on the soil.

Just across busy Lake Shore Drive, on the shores of Lake Michigan, the **Shedd Aquarium** (summer daily 9am–6pm; rest of year Mon–Fri 9am–5pm, Sat & Sun 9am–6pm; $8 aquarium only, $17 wild reef and aquarium, $17 Oceanarium and aquarium, $21 for all exhibits; ☏ 312/939-2438, Ⓦ www.sheddaquarium.org) proclaims itself the largest indoor aquarium in the world. The 1930s structure is rather old-fashioned, but the lighthearted and often tongue-in-cheek displays – some use *Far Side* cartoons – are informative and entertaining. The central exhibit, a 90,000-gallon re-creation of a coral reef, complete with sharks (who get fed at 11am and 2pm daily), turtles, and thousands of tropical fish, is surrounded by more than a hundred lesser tanks. Highlights include the new wild reef exhibit, which features floor-to-ceiling living reefs, tropical fish, sharks, and rays. The **Oceanarium** provides an enormous contrast, with its modern lake-view home for marine mammals such as Pacific dolphins and beluga whales. Designed to replicate a rocky Alaskan coastline, it's a carefully disguised amphitheater for demonstrations of the animals' "natural behavior," such as jumping out of the water and fetching plastic rings. Performances are four times daily; at other times, watch from underwater galleries as the animals cruise around the tank, and listen to the clicks, beeps, and whistles they use to communicate with each other. Get to the Shedd early to beat the long lines and school groups.

In summer, Shoreline Marine Sightseeing ($9; ☏ 312/222-9328, Ⓦ www.shorelinesightseeing.com) runs hour-long **cruises** along the lakeshore from a jetty just north of the aquarium. At the tip of the Museum Campus peninsula, the **Adler Planetarium** (summer Sat–Wed 9am–6pm, Thurs & Fri

9am–9pm; rest of year Mon–Fri 9.30am–4.30pm, Sat & Sun 9am–4.30pm; $13–18, determined by exhibits entered, free Tues; ☎312/922-STAR, ⓦwww.adlerplanetarium.org) has an interactive 360-degree movie theater, and offers one of the best views of the city skyline.

The Near North Side

Chicago's **Near North Side**, where you're likely to spend much of your time, has few big-name attractions, but it's great for simply wandering around, chancing upon odd **shops**, neighborhood bars, and historic sites in a generally low-rise tangle containing some of the city's most characteristic corners.

When the Michigan Avenue Bridge was built over the Chicago River in 1920, the warehouse district along its north bank quickly changed into one of the city's most upmarket quarters, now known as the **Magnificent Mile**, famed for its fashionable shops and department stores. Throughout the Roaring Twenties one glitzy tower after another was thrown up along Michigan Avenue. To the north, the opulent **Drake Hotel** rose off Lincoln Park. To the south, the white terracotta, wedding-cake colossus of the **Wrigley Building** was put up just over the river at no. 400; it's spectacularly lit up at night. Built by the Chicago-based chewing-gum magnate, it was eclipsed almost immediately by the "Mag Mile's" most famous structure, the **Tribune Tower**. Still housing the editorial offices of Chicago's morning newspaper, as well as, on the ground floor, the studios of its main AM radio station, WGN (you can peer in from the street and watch the DJs in action), the tower was completed in 1925. Its flying buttresses and Gothic detailing turn their back on the then-prevalent Moderne style. Look closely at its lower floors and you'll see pieces of historic buildings – like the Parthenon and the Great Pyramid – pilfered from around the world by *Tribune* staffers and embedded here.

While the Tribune Tower anchors its southern end, the Mag Mile's northern reaches are dominated by the cross-braced steel **John Hancock Center** at 875 N Michigan Ave. Though it's about 325 feet shorter than the Sears Tower, the 360-degree panorama on a clear day from its 94th-floor **Skydeck Observatory** (daily 9am–11pm; $9) is unforgettable. If you prefer quality over quantity, the Hancock Observatory is a better, less trafficked experience than the Sears.

Back at ground level, you're right at the heart of Chicago's prime **shopping district**, where Neiman-Marcus and Tiffany & Co. rub shoulders with Benetton and Nike Town. Some front onto Michigan Avenue, but most of the shops are enclosed within multistory complexes, or "vertical shopping malls." The oldest of these – and still the best – is **Water Tower Place**, 835 N Michigan Ave, with more than a hundred stores on seven floors, plus a bustling food court. The **900 N Michigan Avenue** mall offers a less-cramped space and more upscale shops, anchored by Bloomingdale's and including Gucci and Aquascutum.

Across from Water Tower Place, at the very center of this consumer paradise, stands the **Historic Water Tower** – a whimsically Gothic stone castle, topped by a 100ft tower, that was built in 1869 and is one of the very few structures to have survived the 1871 fire. The **Museum of Contemporary Art**, one block east of the Water Tower at 220 E Chicago Ave (Tues 10am–8pm, Wed–Sun 10am–5pm; $10; ⓦwww.mcachicago.org), is a spare space with photography, video, and installation works, as well as a permanent collection featuring pieces by Calder, Nauman, Warhol, and others. At the rear is a sculpture garden and patio where a café serves good bistro food.

Away from the Magnificent Mile, the area along the river between Michigan Avenue and the lake is at the center of a massive redevelopment project, at least partially attributed to the success of the renovated **Navy Pier**, at East Illinois Street (Ⓦ www.navypier.com). After undergoing a facelift in 1995, the pier has become the city's premier tourist destination, attracting more than eight million visitors annually to its shops, chain restaurants, IMAX theater, and fifteen-story Ferris wheel. Home to the **Chicago Children's Museum**, with its three floors of imaginative interactive exhibits (Thurs–Sun 10am–5pm; $6.50, free Thurs 5–8pm; Ⓣ 312/527-1000, Ⓦ www.chichildrensmuseum.org), the pier is also a venue for concerts and weekend festivals in summer, and an embarkation point for several boat tours, including those run by Shoreline Sightseeing (year-round, weather permitting; $9; 30min; Ⓣ 312/222-9328, Ⓦ www.shorelinesightseeing.com).

The more heavily industrial area west of Michigan Avenue is also experiencing a revival, though on a smaller scale and with a different character. In the rechristened **River North**, many old brick warehouses and factory premises have been converted to house avant-garde art galleries, restaurants, and nightclubs. Huron and Superior streets, around their intersections with Wells Street, hold the most concentrated collection. Before you begin gallery-hopping, pick up a copy of the free *Chicago Gallery News* from city information centers, museums, hotels, or galleries.

The Gold Coast and Old Town

As its name suggests, the **Gold Coast**, stretching north from the Magnificent Mile along the lakeshore, is one of Chicago's wealthiest and most desirable neighborhoods. This residential district is primarily notable for Chicago's most central (and style-conscious) beach. The broad strand of **Oak Street Beach** is accessible via a walkway under Lake Shore Drive, across from the *Drake Hotel*. After dark, the summertime crowds are apt to be found in the myriad bars of Rush and Division streets. The more northerly reaches of the Gold Coast, approaching Lincoln Park, are also its most exclusive, nowhere more so than the stretch of Astor Street running south from the park. **Old Town**, west of LaSalle Street to either side of North Avenue, has a much more lived-in look than does the dandified Gold Coast. Originally a German immigrant community based around the 1873 **St Michael's Church**, the neighborhood today boasts a broad ethnic and cultural mix. While its many century-old rowhouses and workers' cottages are now prime real estate, its then-shabby housing stock and derelict factories once attracted a variety of creative types. **Wells Street**, the main drag, emerged in the late 1960s as a mini-Haight-Ashbury. Although almost all signs of that era have vanished (or, as in the case of the folk club *Earl of Old Town*, moved uptown), at least one survivor, the *Second City* comedy club (see p.380), is still going strong. The rest of the neighborhood is packed with some of the city's best bars, galleries, and barbecue joints, and makes for a diverting afternoon's wander. Especially noteworthy is the House of Glunz, 1206 N Wells St, a wine shop dating to 1888.

Lincoln Park and Wrigleyville

In summer, Chicago's largest greenspace, **Lincoln Park**, gives a much-needed respite from the gridded pavements of the rest of the city. Unlike Grant Park to the south, Lincoln Park is packed with leafy nooks and crannies, monuments and sculptures, and has a couple of friendly, family-oriented **beaches**, at the eastern ends of North and Fullerton avenues. Near the small **zoo** at the heart of the park (grounds daily 9am–6pm, buildings 10am–5pm; free), you can rent paddleboats or bikes. If the weather's bad, head for sauna-level conditions at the **conservatory**, 2400 N Stockton Drive (daily 9am–5pm; free), or bone up on Chicago's captivating past at the **Chicago Historical Society Museum**, at the south end of the park at 1601 N Clark St (Mon–Sat 9.30am–4.30pm, Sun noon–5pm; $5, free on Mon; ☎312/642-4600, ⊕www.chicagohistory.org). The museum is home to 700 hours of sound recordings from *The Studs Terkel Show*, whose eponymous host was a former landmark Chicago radio personality and one of the nation's finest practitioners of oral history. The museum also has a nice, skylit café.

The Lincoln Park neighborhood, inland from the lake between North Avenue and Diversey Parkway, centers on **Lincoln Avenue** and **Clark Street**, which run diagonally from near the Historical Society Museum; **Halsted Street**, with its blues bars and nightclubs, runs north–south through the neighborhood's heart. Any of these main roads merits an extended stroll, with forays into the many book and record stores, while smaller and quieter tree-lined side streets show off why Lincoln Park is such a popular place to live. Look for the **Biograph Theatre** movie house, 2433 N Lincoln Ave, where **John Dillinger** was ambushed and killed by the FBI in 1934, thanks to a tip from his companion, the legendary Lady in Red.

Chicago spreads north from Lincoln Park for block after low-rise block of houses and shops, many of which date from the late 1800s, when thousands of German immigrants settled in what was then the separate enclave of Lakeview. This area is now dubbed **Wrigleyville** in honor of **Wrigley Field**, 1060 W Addison St at N Clark Street, the ivy-covered 1920s stadium of baseball's much-loved Cubs, and one of the best places to get a real feel for the game – the club is so traditional that it fought the installation of floodlights (for night games) until 1988. Even if you know nothing about the rules, there are few more pleasant and relaxing ways to spend an afternoon than drinking beer, eating hot dogs, and watching a ballgame in the sunshine, among the Cubs' faithful. See "Sports," p.380, for ticket information. **Field tours** run from May through September on select days every half-hour from 10am to 4pm. For details on the schedule, and to reserve tickets, call ☎1-800/THE-CUBS.

Wicker Park and Bucktown

Three miles northwest of the Loop, radiating out from the intersection of Milwaukee, North, and Damen avenues, **Wicker Park/Bucktown** is Chicago's newest neighborhood. Once a Polish and German community referred to as the "Polish Gold Coast," it is now a trendy, upscale enclave of shopping, clubbing, and Victorian mansions. Stylish health-food cafés, galleries, tattoo parlors, smoky clubs, boutiques, and alternative bookstores follow Damen Street north to Bucktown. The boundary between the two areas is vague if nonexistent, and the neighborhoods diverse enough to satisfy any taste.

The West Side and Oak Park

West of the Chicago River, Chicago's **West Side** was where the **Great Fire of 1871** started – supposedly when Mrs O'Leary's cow kicked over a lantern. The flames spread quickly east to engulf the entire central city, which was built of wood and fed the fire for three full days. Appropriately enough, the O'Leary cottage is now the site of the Chicago Fire Department training academy. The West Side also saw 1886's **Haymarket Riots**, when striking workers assembled at the old city market at Desplaines and Randolph streets; after a peaceful demonstration, as police began to break up the crowd, a bomb exploded, killing an officer. Six more policemen and four workers died in the resulting panic. Four labor leaders were later found guilty of murder and hanged, despite the fact that none of them had been present at the event.

Though the West Side has little to see compared with the rest of the city, it does provide a good look at its day-to-day realities, having served as the port of entry for Chicago's myriad ethnic groups, now congregated in its distinct neighborhoods. **Milwaukee Avenue**, which stretches under the "El" tracks diagonally from the Loop out towards O'Hare Airport, has long been home to a sizeable Eastern European community, mainly Poles – over a million altogether, including some 60,000 who came to Chicago during the martial-law era of the 1980s. For an introduction, stop by the **Polish Museum of America**, 984 N Milwaukee Ave (daily 11am–4pm, closed Thurs; free; Ⓦwww.prcua.org/pma), or the **Ukrainian National Museum**, 721 N Oakley (Thurs–Sun 11am–4pm and by appointment; free; Ⓦwww.ukrntlmuseum.org). **Greektown**, the few blocks of Halsted Street north of the I-290 freeway, and **Little Italy**, along Taylor Street west of Halsted, are both just a short walk from the University of Illinois subway station, on the CTA Congress line. Four blocks southeast of Little Italy is Maxwell Street, site of the historic **Maxwell Street Market**, dating to 1871. Although the city banned the market for various reasons in 1994, a new Maxwell Street Market was born on Canal Street and Roosevelt Road about half a mile east of the old market. It's still a lively place to visit on Sundays, when blues bands entertain on street corners and kielbasa replaces bagels among the stallholders.

Ten miles west of the Loop, the affluent and attractive c.1900 suburb of **Oak Park** has been preserved as a National Historic District, thanks in part to its early influence on two very different but very American figures, **Ernest Hemingway** and **Frank Lloyd Wright**. Oak Park is easily accessible by public transportation: just take the Green Line west to the Harlem Avenue stop. The area's **visitor center**, just over two blocks east of the station at 158 N Forest Ave (daily: summer 10am–5pm; rest of year 10am–4pm; ☎708/524-7800 or 1-888/OAK-PARK, Ⓦwww.visitoakpark.com), has an excellent architectural **walking tour map**, as well as guidebooks and free brochures.

Hemingway was born and raised in Oak Park, editing his high school newspaper and living a normal middle-class life. Both his birthplace (at 339 N Oak Park Ave) and his boyhood home (600 N Kenilworth Ave) bear commemorative plaques, and there's an engaging collection of memorabilia at the **Oak Park and River Forest Historical Society**, a block south of the subway station at 217 Home Ave (Thurs–Sun 1–4pm; $4, Thurs free).

In 1889, a decade before Hemingway's birth, an ambitious young architect named Frank Lloyd Wright arrived in Oak Park, which he used for the next twenty years as a testing ground for his innovative design theories. Most of the 25 buildings he put up here are in keeping with conventional Victorian design, and few are open to the public; fortunately, however, his most interesting and groundbreaking edifices are maintained as monuments. His ideal of an "organic architecture," in which all aspects of the design derive from a single unifying concept – quite at odds with the fussy "gingerbread" style popular at the time – is exemplified by the **Unity Temple** at 875 Lake St (summer Mon–Fri 10am–5pm; rest of year Mon–Fri 1–4pm, $4; ☎708/383-8873). Though the simplicity of this angular, reinforced-concrete structure was largely dictated by economics, its unembellished surfaces contribute to a masterful manipulation of space, especially in the skylit interior, where the subtle interplay of overlapping planes creates a dynamic spatial flow. Though little noticed in the US, Unity Temple was very influential in Europe as a precursor of modern architecture.

Wright built his small, brown-shingled **home and studio**, nearby at 951 Chicago Ave, on the corner of Forest Ave, at age 22 in 1889, and remodeled it repeatedly thereafter. It shows all his hallmarks: large fireplaces to symbolize the heart of the home and family; free-flowing, open-plan rooms; and the visual linking of interior and exterior spaces. The furniture of the kitchen and dining rooms is Wright's own design; he added a two-story studio in 1898, with a mezzanine drafting area suspended by chains from the roof beams. In 1909 Wright abandoned Oak Park and his family for new pastures; he was eventually to design such landmarks as New York's Guggenheim Museum (see p.100). You can see the house itself on a 45min guided tour (Mon–Fri 11am, 1pm & 3pm, Sat & Sun every 20min 11am–3.30pm; $9). Lengthier, self-guided walking tours ($9, including use of a Walkman) take in the dozen other Wright-designed houses within a two-block radius. Booking the walking and house tours at the same time will save you $2.

Chinatown

Close by the gentrified blocks of the South Loop neighborhoods, **Chinatown** – estimated population nine thousand within a narrow ten-block radius – looks much as it did in the mid-1900s. A colorful tile-covered gate at Wentworth and Cermak marks the edge of the district. Once through here you could just as well be in downtown Hong Kong – indeed, some older residents speak no English and rarely pass through the gate to the outer world. More than forty **restaurants** (the best of them listed on p.375) serve Mandarin, Szechuan, Shanghai, and Cantonese cuisine; it's a good place to eat and to poke around the little groceries filled with spices, teas, herbs, and vegetables.

The South Side

The **South Side** of Chicago has always had a raw deal, cursed with the presence of bad-neighbor heavy industries like the sprawling **Chicago Stockyards**, the slaughterhouses and meatpackers that Upton Sinclair exposed in his 1906 novel *The Jungle*, and whose stink covered most of the South Side until the 1950s. Even today, the overriding impression is one of misery and downtrodden poverty, with block after block of deprived and dangerous neighborhoods. That said, there are exceptions: not just the **Prairie Avenue** and **Hyde Park** districts described below, but also the buzzing **Chinatown** around Wentworth Avenue and 22nd Street; the artsy, predominantly Mexican **Pilsen** district, a few blocks north and west; and the largely Irish, blue-collar **Bridgeport**, formerly known by the evocative name "Hardscrabble," around Halsted and 37th – Mayor Daley's old fiefdom, the home of Comiskey Park and baseball's White Sox (see p.380). Mayor Daley has been busy tearing down his father's South Side housing projects, which have played no small role in hiking the murder rate in Chicago to the nation's highest. They are being replaced by mixed-income developments in what has become the largest demolition of public housing in the nation's history. To reach the South Side, double-decker Illinois Central commuter trains run beside the lake to Prairie Avenue (a block from the 18th St station) and Hyde Park (near the 59th St station). CTA bus #1 follows Michigan Avenue to the same places, while bus #8 runs every fifteen minutes south through Pilsen to Bridgeport.

Two blocks east of Michigan Avenue, a mile from the Loop and only a quarter of a mile from the lake, **Prairie Avenue** started life as an exclusive suburb. Though just ten minutes' walk south from Grant Park and the Field Museum, it's best reached by taxi, bus, or train; the route is confusing and the streets are just not safe. As the one part of Chicago to remain unscathed in the Great Fire of 1871, this area had a brief moment of glory as the city's finest address. However, by 1900 the railroads had cut it off from Lake Michigan, and the expansion of the stockyards had encouraged the wealthy to flee back to their traditional North Side haunts.

One of the few structures to have survived the intervening years is the Romanesque 1887 **Glessner House**, Chicago's only surviving H.H. Richardson–designed house, standing sentry on the southwest corner of Prairie Avenue and 18th Street. Behind the forbidding stone facade, the house opens onto a garden court, its interior filled with Arts and Crafts furniture, and swathed in William Morris fabrics and wall coverings. The place is maintained by the Chicago Architecture Foundation, which gives guided tours (Wed–Sun noon–3pm; $9, or $14 joint admission with Clarke House, see below; ☎312/326-1480). A block away, at 1827 S Indiana Ave, stands Chicago's oldest building, the **Clarke House** (same info as Glessner House), a plain white 1836 Greek Revival pioneer home that spent many years as a community center before being gussied up as a minor museum of interior decor. Much more interesting, and proof of the wealth once concentrated here, is the lavish Gothic **Presbyterian Church**, a block away at 1936 S Michigan Ave, with its Burne-Jones and Tiffany stained-glass windows.

Six miles south of the Prairie Avenue district, **Hyde Park** is an island of middle-class prosperity surrounded by urban poverty, and the most attractive and sophisticated South Side Chicago neighborhood. It's also one of the more racially integrated areas of the city, and among its more erudite: the **University of Chicago**, endowed by Rockefeller in 1892 and now among the top institutions in the US, has encouraged a college-town atmosphere, with bookshops and numerous cafés surrounding its compact campus, especially along East 57th Street. On the campus itself, two buildings are well worth searching out: the massive Gothic pile of the **Rockefeller Memorial Chapel**, 59th Street and Woodlawn Avenue (daily 9am–4pm; free), and the Prairie-style, Frank Lloyd Wright–designed **Robie House**, two blocks north at 5757 S Woodlawn Ave (tours Mon–Fri 11am, 1pm & 3pm, Sat & Sun every 15min 11am–3.30pm; $9; ⓦwww.wrightplus.org). If you'd like to take a tour of the campus, these start from the admissions office at 1116 E 59th St (Mon–Fri 10.30am and 1.30pm, winter 10.30am only; free).

From the University of Chicago campus, **Woodlawn Avenue** runs north past one of the South Side's most popular taverns, *Jimmy's Woodlawn Tap*, at 1172 E 55th St (☎773/643-5516), before turning a whole lot grander. Besides its enormous mansions, Woodlawn Avenue illustrates the social and racial mix for which Hyde Park is renowned. Within two blocks of each other are the Midwest's largest Jewish temple, the ornate **Isaiah Israel** at 1100 E Hyde Park Blvd, and the home of **Minister Louis Farrakhan** at 4955 S Woodlawn Ave, leader of the Nation of Islam, which was started here on the South Side in the 1940s by the late Elijah Muhammad. In between the two, at 4944 S Woodlawn Ave, stands the huge brick manor where boxer **Muhammad Ali** lived for many years.

Just west of the university, on the eastern edge of lush Washington Park, the **DuSable Museum of African American History**, 740 E 56th Place (Mon–Sat 10am–5pm, Sun noon–5pm; $3; ⓦwww.dusablemuseum.org), takes a look at the experience of African-Americans from slavery to the present day; it's the oldest institution of its kind in the country. Named for Jean DuSable, the Haitian-born Francophone who was Chicago's first permanent settler, the museum focuses on the works of WPA-sponsored artists of the 1930s and on the civil rights movement of the 1960s.

Washington Park wraps around the south side of the University of Chicago campus to join the long green strip of the **Midway** – one of the few reminders that in the late nineteenth century Chicago was the site of the **World's Columbian Exposition**. Attracting some thirty million spectators in the summer of 1893 (at the time, 45 percent of the US population), the Midway was then filled with full-sized model villages from around the globe, including an Irish market town and a mock-up of Cairo, complete with belly dancers. These days it's used mainly by joggers and students tossing Frisbees.

A short stroll east, in Jackson Park, the cavernous **Museum of Science and Industry**, 57th Street at Lake Shore Drive (summer Mon–Fri 9.30am–5.30pm; rest of year Mon–Fri 9.30am–4pm, Sat & Sun 9.30am–5.30pm; $9, free on Thurs; ☎773/684-1414, ⊛www.msichicago.org), was Chicago's single most popular tourist destination (and ranked second in the US) until it started charging admission in 1991. Besides interactive computer displays, the best of which explores the inner workings of the brain and heart, exhibits include a captured German U-boat, a trip down a replica coal mine, the Apollo 8 command module, and a simulated space-shuttle journey. It's fun for kids, but adults may not feel like staying very long. The complex also hosts a giant OMNI-MAX movie dome; admission is $6 extra.

East of the museum, **Promontory Point** juts into Lake Michigan, giving great views of the Chicago skyline, including a close-up look at Mies van der Rohe's first highrise, the Promontory Apartments at 5530 S Lake Shore Drive.

Eating

Chicago's cosmopolitan make-up is reflected in its plethora of ethnic restaurants. **Italian** food, ranging from hearty **deep-dish pizza** (developed in 1953 at *Pizzeria Uno*; see p.376) to delicately crafted creations presented at stylish trattorias, continues to dominate a very dynamic scene. In recent years there's been a surge of popularity for **New American** cuisine. **Thai** restaurants still thrive, as do ones with a broad **Mediterranean** slant, many of which serve *tapas*; and there are still plenty of opportunities to sample more longstanding Chicago cuisines – Eastern European, German, Mexican, Chinese, Indian, even Burmese and Ethiopian. Of course, a number of establishments serve old-fashioned **barbecue ribs**, a legacy of Chicago's days as the nation's meatpacker. And no visit is complete without sampling a messy Italian beef sandwich, or a Chicago-style hot dog, laden with tomatoes, onions, hot peppers, and a pickle.

The largest concentration of restaurants is found north and west of the **Loop**. To the west, **Greektown**, around Halsted Street at Jackson Boulevard, and **Little Italy**, on and around Taylor Street, are worth a look. The **Near North** and **River North** areas harbor a good number of upscale places. **Chinatown**, though not pretty, is a predictably good neighborhood for Cantonese and Szechuan food. Many bars and cafés listed in the "Drinking" section below also serve **snacks** and **light meals**, and dozens of places in the Loop offer great breakfast and lunch specials.

Downtown

The Berghoff 17 W Adams St ☎312/427-3170. The beautifully preserved Chicago landmark, dating from 1893, offers plentiful Germanic specialties plus dishes and corned beef and cabbage. Try the draft or root beer. A bargain.

Billy Goat Tavern 430 N Michigan Ave, lower level ☎312/222-1525. This legendary journalists' haunt opens early and closes late, serving the "cheezborgers" made famous by John Belushi's comedy skit. Very reasonable.

Everest One Financial Place, 440 S LaSalle St ☎312/663-8920. Take in the stunning vista from the 40th floor and tuck into chef Jean Joho's wild mushroom consommé and roasted Maine lobster. Very expensive. Closed Sun & Mon.

Italian Village 71 W Monroe St ☎312/332-7005. Three Italian establishments flourish under one roof.

The *Village* has traditional Italian-American food and a world-class wine cellar; the basement *La Cantina* serves chicken Vesuvio, a Chicago creation, among its reasonably priced dishes; and the expensive *Vivere* (☎312/332-4040) has an adventurous menu, a mesmerizing wine list, and a large pre-theater crowd (meaning it's best to arrive after 8pm).

Lou Mitchell's 565 W Jackson Ave ☎312/939-3111. Near Union Station, *Lou's* has been around since 1923, serving terrific omelets, waffles, and hash browns all day long. Try the pecan-laden cookies.

Marché 833 W Randolph St ☎312/226-8399. Creative French cuisine is served in an eclectic atmosphere in the Market District. Entrees $17–35.

Prairie 500 S Dearborn St, in the *Hyatt* ☎312/663-1143. Modeled on a Frank Lloyd Wright interior, this place uses only fresh Midwestern ingredients in dishes such as sirloin of buffalo and brandied loaf of duck.

Printers Row 550 S Dearborn St ☎312/461-0780. Seafood and game are highlights among the captivating New American concoctions devised by owner/chef Michael Foley.

Russian Tea Time 77 E Adams St ☎312/360-0000. This Midwestern nod to New York's *Russian Tea Room* (now closed) offers a sampling of authentic fare from the former Soviet empire. Pricey.

Sorriso 321 N Clark St ☎312/644-0283. The alfresco dining comes with a spectacular view of the Loop riverfront and skyline. The menu features Italian and American dishes including *scungilli* (conch) salad.

Trattoria No. 10 10 N Dearborn St ☎312/984-1718. This charming surprise, in a series of underground rooms, serves up delicious ravioli, grilled sea scallops, and risotto.

Greektown and Little Italy

Costa's 340 S Halsted St ☎312/263-9700. Try the stuffed grilled *calamari* or the cheese-stuffed peppers at this casual, reasonably priced Greek place.

Gennaro's 1352 W Taylor St ☎312/243-1035. The speakeasy atmosphere is enhanced by the locked front door, opened only after you're checked out through the peephole. Fine *gnocchi*.

Greek Islands 200 S Halsted St ☎312/782-9855. A large place, it has several rustic "taverna" nooks. The grilled sea bass and red snapper are fresh and flavorful.

Mia Francesca 1400 W Taylor St ☎312/829-2828. The most subdued of the Francesca restau-

rant family (see overleaf). That said, it offers some of the best Italian in the city, period. Don't be surprised to find a crowd here all day.

Parthenon 314 S Halsted St ☎312/726-2407. One of the oldest places in Greektown: *saganaki* (fried cheese doused with Metaxa brandy and ignited) was invented here.

Pegasus 130 S Halsted St ☎312/226-3377. True hospitality and evocative wall murals add to the appeal of this popular establishment. Stuffed squid and *pastitsio* (macaroni, meat, and cheese casserole) are recommended. During the summer the rooftop garden has a superb view of the Loop skyline.

Santorini 800 W Adams St ☎312/829-8820. The decor re-creates a Greek island village, and the food is beguiling, too; grilled octopus and lamb *exohiko* (wrapped in filo pastry and fried) are highlights.

Tufano's Vernon Park Tap 1073 W Vernon Park Place, near the United Center ☎312/733-3393. A neighborhood landmark for more than 70 years, with chalkboard specials, good service, and moderate prices. The antipasto and homemade ravioli are standouts.

Tuscany 1014 W Taylor St ☎312/829-1990. The creative menu here includes wood-roasted chicken and terrific risotto. Service is very attentive, and there's a huge, bustling bar.

Chinatown

Emperor's Choice 2238 S Wentworth Ave ☎312/225-8800. This attractive storefront serves delicious egg rolls and seafood dishes. Try steamed clams, poached shrimp, or the lobster.

Seven Treasures 2312 S Wentworth Ave ☎312/225-2668. Cantonese and some spicier Szechuan dishes concentrate on soups, dumplings, and noodles. Reasonable prices.

Sixty-Five 2414 S Wentworth Ave ☎312/225-7060. Two-story Cantonese restaurant that emphasizes exceptional seafood. Try the family-style meals.

Near North Side and River North

Big Bowl Asian Kitchen 60 E Ohio St ☎312/951-1888. Diner with an Asian accent. Filling soups and pot stickers make this an inexpensive option near the Magnificent Mile.

Café Iberico 739 N LaSalle Blvd ☎312/573-1510. At this authentic and reasonably priced *tapas* bar, you can share plates of eggplant stuffed with goat's cheese or grilled octopus on potatoes.

Eli's The Place For Steak 215 E Chicago Ave ☎312/642-1393. This glitzy room is perfect for celebrity-spotting and for great steaks, seafood, and other nicely rendered dishes – and a famous cheesecake.

Frontera Grill & Topolobampo 445 N Clark St ☎312/661-1434. Wildly imaginative Mexican food: *Frontera Grill* is crowded and boisterous; *Topolobampo* is more refined and pricier. The front door and bar are shared between the two.

Gino's East 633 N Wells St ☎312/943-1124. A Chicago tradition: huge deep-dish pizzas (no need for appetizers here) and graffiti-covered walls. Expect to wait.

Nacional 27 325 W Huron St ☎312/664-2727. This popular Latin place serves food from a variety of Central American cuisines, with salsa dancing on weekends.

Pizzeria Uno 29 E Ohio St ☎312/321-1000. The place that put Chicago deep-dish pizza on the map.

Portillo's 100 W Ontario St ☎312/587-8930. This local chain serves good Chicago hot dogs and the best Italian beef sandwich in the city.

Scoozi! 410 W Huron St ☎312/943-5900. At this ebullient mixture of nostalgic (there's an accordion player) and trendy (it's a place to be seen), the emphasis is on Northern Italian cuisine, with splendid pizza and risotto.

Shaw's Crab House 21 E Hubbard St ☎312/527-2722. This large 1930s Key West–style dining room is crowded at lunch and after work; its consistently high-quality fare includes baked crab cakes, Dungeness crab in garlic butter, seafood gumbo, and popcorn shrimp. Not cheap.

Star of Siam 11 E Illinois St ☎312/670-0100. Terrific Thai food served in a spacious, inviting setting. The *tom yum* soup, pad Thai, and curries are top-notch.

Old Town

Café Ba-Ba-Reeba! 2024 N Halsted St ☎773/935-5000. One of the city's Spanish hot spots, it delivers with a good variety of hot and cold *tapas*, filling paella, and, of course, sangría.

Flat Top Grill 319 W North Ave ☎312/787-7676. Create-your-own stir-fry with a wide variety of meats, vegetables, and mild-to-spicy sauces.

Old Jerusalem 1411 N Wells St ☎312/944-0459. This old-time favorite serves reasonable Middle Eastern dishes; the falafel is great. Bring your own beer or wine.

Topo Gigio 1516 N Wells St ☎312/266-9355. The well-prepared Italian cuisine is served by the very friendly staff in a peaceful garden amid the Old Town bustle. The homemade tiramisu is fabulous.

Twin Anchors 1655 N Sedgwick St ☎312/266-1616. You'll wait for a seat in this neighborhood

spot, famed for its BBQ ribs, but the interesting clientele and 1950s-style bar make it worth it.

Lincoln Park and around

Ann Sather 929 W Belmont Ave ☎773/348-2378; also four other locations around town. This Chicago institution serves Swedish-inspired breakfast, brunch, and dinner.

Charlie Trotter's 816 W Armitage Ave ☎773/248-6228. Prepare for a superb, and appropriately pricey, experience. Chef Trotter is a true artist, and his daring creations, such as caviar-stuffed quail eggs or Maine salmon with blood sausage, are constantly evolving.

Chicago Diner 3411 N Halsted St ☎773/935-6696. This vegetarian restaurant incorporates international influences in its expansive menu. Soup, salads, tempe burgers, and the macrobiotic plate are popular. All dishes can be made vegan.

Little Bucharest 3001 N Ashland Ave ☎773/929-8640. A Romanian inn that serves huge stews, roasts, and pork loin. Rich desserts come with a complimentary *slivovitz* (plum brandy).

Mia Francesca 3311 N Clark St ☎773/281-3310. Huge servings of pasta and tasty pizzas (try the *quattro formaggi*) ensure that this cozy Italian place is always packed.

RJ Grunts 2056 Lincoln Park W ☎773/929-5363. Check out the great burgers and a top-notch salad bar – purported to be the nation's first – in a casual neighborhood atmosphere.

Wishbone 1001 W Washington Blvd ☎312/850-2663; also 1800 W Grand Ave ☎312/829-3597. The rich, down-home Southern cooking comes in large portions at reasonable prices. The yardbird chicken (served with a red-pepper sauce), baked ham, and sweet-potato pie are wonderful.

Yoshi's Café 3257 N Halsted St ☎773/248-6160. An East–West fusion with a French accent, *Yoshi's* does especially well with tuna or fluke (sea urchin). More Asian is the three-course *kaiseki* menu of tiny dishes. Very expensive.

Wicker Park

Café Absinthe 1954 W North Ave ☎773/278-4488. Fine French dining in a romantic, casual setting. One of the city's best restaurants.

Irazu 1865 N Milwaukee Ave ☎773/252-5687. Wonderful Costa Rican diner, serving great burritos, plus a small selection of authentic main courses.

Smoke Daddy 1804 W Division St ☎773/772-6656. Arguably Chicago's best BBQ, with jazz and blues nightly. Also offers vegetarian options.

Soul Kitchen 1576 N Milwaukee Ave ☎773/342-9742. An energetic and youthful joint that focuses on American Southern regional cuisine. Its motto is, appropriately, "loud food, spicy music."

The South Side: Hyde Park

Dixie Kitchen 5225 S Harper, Harper Court ☏773/363-4943. Great soul food here includes pulled-pork sandwiches, breaded oysters with chili sauce, and desserts like peach cobbler and pecan pie.

Medici on 57th 1327 E 57th St ☏773/667-7394. At this quintessential collegiate hangout next to the University of Chicago, the chummy crowd chows down on burgers, pizza, salads, and ice cream.

Mellow Yellow 1508 E 53rd St ☏773/667-2000. A soul food emphasis is evident in the catfish, steaks, seafood, and rotisserie chicken served at this casual, popular place – they do crêpes and quiche, too.

Valois Cafeteria 1518 E 53rd St ☏773/667-0647. An inexpensive menu featuring baked chicken, barbecue ribs, and pork sandwiches. Don't skip the freshly baked biscuits.

Drinking

If not quite as wild as in the bootlegging days of speakeasies and Prohibition, Chicago remains a consummate boozer's town, and is one of the best US cities for **bars**, catering to just about every group and interest, with many open until 3, 4, or even 5am. At "**sports bars**" – Chicago has more of them than anywhere else – banks of TV screens broadcast Cubs, Sox, Bears, Bulls, and Blackhawks games. These are great places for beer-drinking and male bonding, but not for thoughtful conversation. Although far from picturesque, the cement strip that is **Division Street**, in the two blocks west of State Street, has become one of the hippest night spots, with a handful of joints tucked away on side streets off the main drag. **Wicker Park** is the trendiest hangout zone, while Halsted Street between Belmont and Addison is known as **Boystown** for its gay bars and clubs.

The hundred-plus **cafés and coffeehouses** across the city may not have taken the place of the traditional taverns, but they're a growing alternative.

Saloons, pubs, and bars

Bar Louie 226 W Chicago Ave ☏312/337-3313. Friendly, casual place in River North, with tables out front and cheap bar food. Open until 4am.

Berghoff's 17 W Adams St ☏312/427-3170. This former men-only stand-up bar in a showcase c.1900 tavern next to *The Berghoff* restaurant is crowded and congenial at lunchtime and after work.

Cavanaugh's 53 W Jackson St ☏312/939-3125. Visit this Loop favorite in the historic Monadnock Building for an after-work drink. Experience the warm interior with antique woodwork, Harp on draft, and a full menu.

Delilah's 2771 N Lincoln Ave ☏773/472-2771. At this dimly lit bar (playing underground records – from rock to alt-country – at night), choose from a great selection of beers (150) and whiskeys.

Goose Island Brewing Co. 1800 N Clybourn Ave ☏312/915-0071. Forty ales and lagers, including the popular Honker's Ale, are brewed on the premises at this lively Lincoln Park haunt.

Green Door Tavern 678 N Orleans St ☏312/664-5496. In an unlikely spot near the galleries of River North, this historic place is chock-full of Chicago memorabilia: some pure kitsch, others genuine antiques. Drink at the long bar or settle into a cozy back room to sample home-style cooking.

John Barleycorn 658 W Belden Ave ☏773/348-8899. A dimly lit Lincoln Park pub dating to 1890. This former speakeasy and John Dillinger haunt has retained many of its original fixtures. The lovely garden is open in summer.

O'Neil's 152 E Ontario St ☏312/787-5269. This dark little Near North space is popular with media types and serves good burgers. Its ace card is the patio out back.

Old Town Ale House 219 W North Ave ☏312/944-7020. An eclectic crowd of scruffy regulars and yuppies mingle in this convivial haunt, complete with a pinball machine and a library of paperbacks.

Rainbo Club 1150 N Damen Ave ☏773/489-5999. Busy Wicker Park bar and hangout for indie-rock types.

The Red Lion Pub 2446 N Lincoln Ave ☏773/348-2695. British ales and ciders, fish and chips, and shepherd's pie enhance an authentic pub atmosphere.

Resis' Beerstube 2034 W Irving Park Rd ☏773/472-1749. An old-time German tavern, featuring good imported draft and bottled beers, platters of wurst, and a delightful shaded beer garden.

Sports bars

ESPNZone 43 E Ohio St ☎312/644-3776. Part futuristic game parlor, part megalithic sports bar/restaurant, the *Zone* offers so-so food and service is sluggish, but sports fans still pack it up.

Harry Caray's 33 W Kinzie St ☎312/828-0966. In an old River North brick warehouse, this great sports bar/Italian restaurant was founded by the well-loved former Cubs radio and TV announcer Caray. The huge bar, packed with beer drinkers until the early hours, has floor-to-ceiling Cubs memorabilia.

Murphy's Bleachers 3655 N Sheffield Ave ☎773/281-5356. The bar to be at before, during, and after Cubs games. It doesn't get much more Chicago than this.

Slugger's 3540 N Clark St ☎773/248-0055. At probably the only bar in the world with its own indoor batting cage, this raucous beer joint fairly rattles and hums during Cubs, Bears, and Bulls games. Beer is ridiculously inexpensive during happy hour.

Gay and lesbian bars

Big Chicks 5024 N Sheridan Rd, Andersonville

☎773/728-5511. A friendly place for a mixed crowd, with a no-charge jukebox and free barbecues out back on summer Sundays.

The Closet 3325 N Broadway ☎773/477-8533. A tiny, cramped but congenial lesbian bar, it attracts gay men as well.

Gentry 440 N State St ☎773/836-0933. Cabaret and piano bar popular with corporate types after work.

Sidetrack 3349 N Halsted St ☎773/477-9189. One of the most popular bars along Halsted's gay strip in Lakeview.

Cafés

The Bourgeois Pig 738 W Fullerton Ave ☎773/883-5282. Inventive sandwiches in a laid-back student atmosphere, plus over 100 varieties of tea.

Kopi, A Traveler's Café 5317 N Clark St, Andersonville ☎773/989-5674. A bit of a trek from downtown will bring you to a really splendid combo coffee- and tea-house, Indonesian art gallery, boutique, and bookstore stocked with travel guides and literature. Occasional live music and prose/poetry readings.

Nightlife and entertainment

From its earliest frontier days, Chicago has had some of the best **nightlife** in the US. "Sweet Home Chicago," birthplace of Muddy Waters' **urban blues**, as well as R&B's Chess Records, is still going strong, inspiring the energetic dance beat of 1980s **house music** as well as the groundbreaking **jazz** of the Art Ensemble of Chicago. **Nightclubs** aplenty are all over town, especially along Halsted Street, Lincoln Avenue, and Clark Street on the North Side. **Uptown**, at the intersection of North Broadway and Lawrence, is a bit down-at-the-heel, but has half a dozen good venues. The best **gay clubs** congregate in the Lincoln Park area. Highbrow pursuits are also well provided for: Chicago's **classical music**, **dance**, and **theater** are world-class.

For **what's-on information**, Chicagoans pick up the excellent free newspaper *The Reader* (copies come out Thursday afternoon). The weekly *New City* and the gay and lesbian *Windy City Times* are good sources as well. Full listings also appear in the Friday issues of the *Chicago Sun-Times* and the *Chicago Tribune*, while *Chicago* magazine has useful arts and restaurant listings. The Gramaphone Ltd record store at 2663 N Clark St (☎773/472-3683) is the best place for details of **dance** nights.

Blues

B.L.U.E.S. 2519 N Halsted St ☎773/528-1012, ⓦwww.chicagobluesbar.com. Opened in the 1970s, B.L.U.E.S. is still going strong, though a little over-touristed. The tiny stage has been graced by all the greats.

Buddy Guy's Legends 754 S Wabash Ave ☎312/427-0333, ⓦwww.buddyguys.com. South Loop club owned by veteran bluesman Buddy Guy, with great acoustics and atmosphere, aims to

present the very best local and national acts. Not as touristy as other downtown blues clubs.

Kingston Mines 2548 N Halsted St ☎773/477-4646. Top-notch local and national acts on two stages play to an up-for-it, partying crowd.

Rosa's Lounge 3420 W Armitage Ave ☎773/342-0452, ⓦwww.rosaslounge.com. Run by Mama Rosa and her son and dedicated to the blues greats, this is undoubtedly the friendliest blues joint around. For real aficionados.

Jazz

Andy's 11 E Hubbard St ☎312/642-6805. Very popular with the after-work crowd; informal with moderate prices.

The Cotton Club 1710 S Michigan Ave ☎312/341-9787. A sophisticated live-music venue and disco, *The Cotton Club* attracts a well-dressed, mellow crowd.

Green Dolphin Street 2200 N Ashland Ave ☎773/395-0066, ⓦ www.jazzitup.com. This swanky, pricey restaurant and jazz club offers a solid line-up of regular performers.

The Green Mill 4802 N Broadway ☎773/878-5552. *The Green Mill* had a checkered past during Prohibition, and is in the tough Uptown neighborhood, but it's one of the best – and most beautiful – rooms for local and national talent.

Joe Segal's Jazz Showcase 59 W Grand Ave ☎312/670-2473, ⓦ www.jazz-showcase.com. A classy, dressy room hosts premier jazz by top names.

Rock

Cubby Bear 1059 W Addison St ☎773/327-1662, ⓦ www.cubbybear.com. A sports bar during the day – right next to Wrigley Field – this place transforms itself after dark into one of the city's most boisterous and eclectic live venues. Popular with aging dinosaurs more than new bands, but still fun.

Double Door 1572 N Milwaukee Ave ☎773/489-3160, ⓦ www.doubledoor.com. This former biker bar, now a hip music venue, anchors the scene in the Wicker Park/Bucktown neighborhood. There's live music almost every night, and Sundays usually feature Liquid Soul, the acid jazz legends of Chicago.

Elbo 2871 N Lincoln Ave ☎773/549-5549, ⓦ www.elboroomchicago.com. Emerging bands with styles that range from indie and pop to funk and ska.

Empty Bottle 1035 N Western Ave ☎773/276-3600, ⓦ www.emptybottle.com. Experimental jazz, alternative rock, hip-hop, house, dub, and progressive country, among other styles.

House of Blues 329 N Dearborn St ☎312/527-2583, ⓦ www.hob.com. Despite its name, this Near North venue puts on all kinds of music.

Metro 3730 N Clark St ☎773/549-0203, ⓦ www.metrochicago.com. Arguably the top spot in the city, this club, in an old cinema building, regularly hosts young English bands trying to break the States, plus DJ mixes.

Folk, country, and world music

Baby Doll Polka Club 6102 S Central Ave ☎773/582-9706. For 40 years, this Southwest Side club has been full of locals doing the polka, two-step, and the occasional tango.

Fitzgerald's 6615 W Roosevelt, Berwyn ☎708/788-2118. In the western suburb of Berwyn, an excellent venue for alt-country, Americana, Cajun, and zydeco.

Old Town School of Folk Music 909 W Armitage Ave ☎773/728-6000, ⓦ www.oldtownschool.org; also 4544 N Lincoln Ave, at W Montrose Ave. Established in 1959, this place presents about 80 concerts a year, including just about every type of folk.

Schuba's 3159 N Southport Ave at Belmont Ave ☎773/525-2508. Some of the best alt-country and roots revival bands play this likeable bar on weekends.

Dance

Circus 901 W Weed St ☎312/266-1200. This celebrity hangout features cartoonish, technicolor decor and a live trapeze act.

Crobar 1543 N Kingsbury St ☎312/266-1900, ⓦ www.crobarnightclub.com. Exclusive, hyper-trendy warehouse club near the river, spinning the newest techno and house. Sunday is gay night.

Excalibur 632 N Dearborn St ☎312/266-1944. City institution blasting out rock, R&B, and Motown on several floors.

Iggy's 700 N Milwaukee Ave ☎312/829-4449. *Iggy's* gets lively at about 3am on the weekend. The red-velvet interior looks like a bordello, and there's a cute patio.

Red Dog 1958 W North Ave ☎773/278-1009. This small Wicker Park club, or "funk parlor" as they like to call it, plays house, soul, and funk. The entrance is in the alley.

Smart Bar 3730 N Clark St, underneath the *Metro* (see opposite) ☎773/549-0203, ⓦ www.smartbarchicago.com. Great techno and house on the weekend in post-industrial Wrigleyville surroundings. Weekdays see a mix of punk, goth, and Eighties. The whole complex is open late – until 5am Fri and Sat.

Voyeur 151 W Ohio St ☎312/832-1717. For club-goers who take their people-watching seriously, this popular space offers two-way mirrors, fish-eye lenses, and closed-circuit TV cameras trained on the stainless-steel dance floor.

Theater and comedy

While it was once every Chicago actor and playwright's ambition to end up in New York, many are now quite content to remain here. The city supports numerous **theater** companies, many of them – notably Steppenwolf, John Malkovich's former company, at 1650 N Halsted St (☎312/335-1888, ⓦwww.steppenwolf.org) – with reputations as good as any in the US. Renowned Chicago theaters include the Court Theater, 5535 S Ellis St (☎773/753-4472, ⓦwww.courttheater.org), and the Goodman Theater, 200 S Columbus Ave (☎312/443-3800, ⓦwww.goodman-theatre.org). **Comedy**, too, is particularly vibrant; Chicago's improvisational scene is considered the best in the nation, with the troupe at **Second City**, 1231 N Wells St (☎312/337-3992, ⓦwww.secondcity.com), especially heralded.

Classical music, opera, and dance

Under Daniel Barenboim, who is committed to including more contemporary music in its repertoire, the profile of the world-famous **Chicago Symphony Orchestra** – based at the Orchestra Hall, 220 S Michigan Ave (☎312/435-8122 or 312/435-8172, ⓦwww.chicagosymphony.org) – looks like it's being raised yet higher. The 186-member **Symphony Chorus** performs both classical and contemporary choral works with the CSO, specifically in summer at the open-air **Ravinia Festival**, 25 miles north of downtown Chicago (ⓦwww.ravinia.org). The **Lyric Opera of Chicago**, 20 N Wacker Drive (☎312/332-2244, ⓦwww.lyricopera.org), now under the directorship of William Mason, performs in the beautiful Civic Opera House; its season is from mid-September to early February, and most performances end up being sold out. The **Joffrey Ballet** is the city's prime classically oriented dance company, based at 70 E Lake St (☎312/739-0120, ⓦwww.joffrey.com); **Hubbard Street Dance Chicago**, 1147 W Jackson Blvd (☎312/850-9744, ⓦwww.hubbardstreetdance.com), is more contemporary but equally talented.

Sports

Staunchly blue-collar Chicago must be among the best US cities for watching **sports**, as Chicagoans are, for better or worse, loyally supportive of their teams. The city's most successful outfit in recent memory was the Michael Jordan–led **Bulls** basketball team, winner of six NBA championships in the 1990s (☎312/559-1212, ⓦwww.nba.com/bulls). Now, though, with the Jordan era long gone, Bulls fans have little to cheer about. The team plays in the ultra-modern United Center, 1901 W Madison St, as do hockey's **Blackhawks** (same phone, ⓦwww.chicagoblackhawks.com). The **Bears** football team (☎847/615-2327, ⓦwww.chicagobears.com) can be seen at the 66,000-capacity Soldier's Field, 425 E McFetridge Drive, at the south end of Grant Park. As for baseball, neither Chicago team – the Cubs or the White Sox – has won a World Series since 1917. The **White Sox** (☎312/831-1SOX, ⓦchicago.whitesox.mlb.com) play at the modern Comiskey Park, on the South Side at 333 W 35th St, while the **Cubs** (☎312/831-CUBS, ⓦchicago.cubs.mlb.com) call grand old Wrigley Field home. For **tickets**, call the teams directly, or visit their websites.

Central Illinois

Interstates 55 and 57 slice south through the Corn Belt of **central Illinois** from Chicago. Parallel to I-55, the legendary **Route 66** began its run here, cutting through the state before running all the way to the Pacific Coast – you might try to catch a glimpse of it, as some old-time diners and other Americana still stand. One worthwhile stop, reachable by either interstate, is the state capital, **Springfield**, which interestingly commemorates US president and former resident **Abraham Lincoln**. Otherwise, if you're on your way south, the college towns of **Bloomington–Normal** and **Champaign–Urbana** are the only good urban stops, while if you're heading west from Chicago it's well worth pausing at the delightful old river town of **Galena**.

Springfield

The Illinois state capital, **SPRINGFIELD**, spreads out from a neat, leafy downtown grid, 200 miles south of Chicago. Abraham Lincoln honed his legal and political skills here, and tourists flock to his old homes, haunts, and final resting place. What they find is neither tacky nor pompous. The sites portray the life of the sixteenth president of the USA and, as well, the uncertainty and turmoil of a nation on the brink of civil war.

Twenty miles northwest of Springfield on Hwy-97, **Lincoln's New Salem State Historic Site** marks where the future president first came to live in this area, from 1831 to 1837. In this backwoods clearing he clerked in a store, volunteered for the Black Hawk War, served as postmaster, and failed in business before taking up legal studies and moving to Springfield to pursue his political career. Today the authentically re-created village features simple homes, workshops, a store, and a tavern. Meanwhile, the **visitor center** hosts a worthwhile exhibit on pioneer lifestyles (March–Oct Wed–Sun 9am–5pm; Nov–Feb Wed–Sun 8am–4pm; ☏217/632-4000, ⓦwww.lincolnsnewsalem .com). On summer weekends, "Theatre in the Park" presents *Abraham!*, a musical that dramatizes Lincoln's New Salem years in an outdoor ampitheater ($9; ☏217/632-5440 or 1-800/710-9290).

For a narrarated tour of the only house Lincoln ever owned, and which he shared with his wife Mary from 1844 to 1861, pick up tickets at the **Lincoln Home Visitor Center**, at Eighth and Jackson streets. Though tours are free (daily 8.30am–5pm; ☏217/492-4241), you might have to wait. Various displays and a brief film at the visitor center are good ways to pass the time.

In the restored Greek Revival **Old State Capitol**, three blocks away from the Lincoln Home Visitor Center at Sixth and Adams (March–Oct Tues–Sat 9am–5pm; Nov–Feb Tues–Sat 9am–4pm; free; ☏217/785-7960), Lincoln attended at least 240 Supreme Court hearings, and proclaimed in 1858, "A house divided against itself cannot stand. I believe this government cannot endure permanently, half slave and half free." Objects, busts, and papers relating to Lincoln and the Democrat Stephen A. Douglas, whom he debated in the 1858 US Senate election (Douglas won that election) and whom he defeated in the 1860 presidential race, can be found throughout the building. At the tastefully renovated **Lincoln Depot** on Tenth and Monroe streets (April–Aug daily 10am–4pm; free), the newly elected president said goodbye to Springfield in February 1861 and boarded a train for his inauguration in Washington, DC (a video illustrates the twelve-day journey). The next time he returned was in his funeral train. **Lincoln's Tomb**, a 117ft-tall obelisk, stands in beautiful Oak Ridge Cemetery on the north side of town. The vault, adorned with busts and statuettes, is open to the public (daily: March–Oct 9am–5pm; Nov–Feb 9am–4pm; free). Inside are inscribed the words, "Now he belongs to the ages."

At the current **Illinois State Capitol**, in majestic limestone at Second Street and Capitol Avenue, tour highlights include the chambers of the state Senate and House of Representatives, in striking red and blue, respectively (tours Mon–Fri 8am–4pm, Sat & Sun 9am–3pm; free; ☏217/782-2099). The **Illinois State Museum**, on Spring and Edwards streets, is crammed with natural history and Native American and contemporary art exhibits, along with the interactive "**At Home in the Heartland**" display, which traces Illinois family life from 1700 to 1970 (Mon–Sat 8.30am–5pm, Sun noon–5pm; free). Completed in 1904, the **Dana-Thomas House**, 301 E Lawrence Ave (tours Wed–Sun 9am–4pm; $3; ☎217/782-6776), survives as the best-preserved and most completely furnished example of **Frank Lloyd Wright**'s early Prairie house, with more than four hundred pieces of glasswork, original art, and light fixtures. Just north of town, at 2075 Peoria Rd, Bill Shea proudly displays 50 years' worth of road signs, gas pumps, and Route 66 memorabilia at **Shea's Gas Station Museum** (Tues–Fri 7am–4pm, Sat 7am–noon; free).

Practicalities

Amtrak **trains** from Chicago and St Louis roll in at Third and Washington streets downtown, at manageable times. Greyhound drops off two miles east of downtown at 2351 S Dirksen Parkway. The **Convention and Visitors Bureau**, 109 N Seventh St (Mon–Fri 8am–5pm; ☎217/789-2360 or 1-800/545-7300), has brochures and maps.

The best selection of inexpensive **accommodation**, including a *Days Inn* (☎217/529-0171; ❸), lies off I-55 at the Dirksen Parkway exit. Downtown accommodation is reasonably priced – even the swanky politicians' hotels offer affordable deals on the weekend. Central options include the *Best Western Clearlake Plaza*, next to the capitol and Amtrak at 3440 E Clearlake Ave (☎217/523-5661 or 1-800/528-1234, ⓦwww.bestwestern.com; ❹), and the *Mansion View Inn & Suites*, 529 S Fourth St (☎217/544-7411 or 1-800/WESTERN, ⓦwww.mansionview.com; ❹). *The Inn at 835*, 835 S Second Ave (☎217/523-4466, ⓦwww.innat835.com; ❺), is a charming twelve-room **B&B** converted from a 1909 downtown apartment block.

Springfield's cafés seem to have exclusive rights to a phenomenon known as the **Horseshoe** – ostensibly a sandwich, but fried, covered in melted cheese, and very tasty. *Norb Andy's*, 518 E Capitol Ave (☎217/523-7777), musters up the best Horseshoes around. The *Cozy Dog Drive-In*, 2935 S Sixth St (☎217/525-1992), claims to be the birthplace of the **Cozy Dog** (also known as the corn dog), a deep-fried, batter-drenched hot dog on a stick. At the other end of the health spectrum, *Augie's Front Burner*, 2 W Old State Capitol Plaza (☎217/544-6979), serves up good California-style and vegetarian meals, while *Sebastian's Hideout*, 221 S Fifth St (☎217/789-8988), has a wide-ranging Mediterranean menu with good couscous dishes and occasional jazz or blues.

Galena

The neat little town of **GALENA**, a few miles short of both Iowa and Wisconsin in the far northwest corner of Illinois, has changed little since its nineteenth-century heyday. Thanks to its sheltered location just a few miles up the Galena River, it was a major port of call for Mississippi River steamboats. These days, the only traffic it gets are the day-trippers who come to admire the gentle crescent of Main Street, tucked in behind an immaculate grassy levee. Its impeccable redbrick facades and graceful skyline of spires and crosses place it among the most attractive river towns in the US. With the aid of the free *Galenian* guide from the visitor center (see opposite), you can spend an enjoyable few hours on a walking tour of the various historic sites along both Main and Bench streets (the latter is squeezed onto a steep bluff above Main).

Galena boasts of having contributed nine generals to the Union army during the Civil War, the most significant of whom was **Ulysses S. Grant**. Grant moved to the town in 1860, working as a clerk in a leather store owned by his father and operated by his two brothers. Some contemporary accounts speak of him as the town lush, the kind of person decent folk crossed the street to avoid. However, his West Point education encouraged the townspeople to appoint him as colonel when they raised the 21st Illinois regiment on the outbreak of war. When he came home, in August 1865, it was as overall commander of the victorious Union army.

The grateful citizens of Galena presented Grant with a **house**, a couple of blocks up Bouthillier Street on the far side of the river (daily 9am–5pm; suggested donation $2; ☎815/777-3310). It's not a grand place by any means, but it was in the plainly furnished downstairs drawing room that Grant received the news of his election as president in 1868. Although he went on to serve two terms, he is commonly agreed to have been a better general than president. His administrations were plagued by scandal, and he lost all his own money through unwise investments. The family fortunes were restored just before his death in 1885, when Mark Twain first persuaded him to write, and then published, Grant's best-selling *Memoirs*.

Practicalities

The 1857 Railroad Museum, across the river from the town proper at 101 Bouthillier St, serves as the local **visitor center** (Mon–Thurs 9am–5pm, Fri & Sat 9am–7pm, Sun 10am–5pm; ☎815/777-4390). Greyhound **buses** stop at the R and L Gas Mart on the east edge of town on US Rte-20. The plush *DeSoto House Hotel*, 230 S Main St (☎815/777-0090 or 1-800/343-6562, ⓦwww.desotohouse.com; ❼), was Grant's campaign headquarters in 1868. Its grand *Generals' Restaurant* serves steak and seafood dinners. If your budget won't stretch that far, the *Triangle Motel*, at highways 20 and 84 (☎1-877/GALENA9 or 815/777-2897; ❸), makes a good-value alternative. As for inexpensive spots to **eat**, *Boone's Place*, 305 S Main St (☎815/777-4488), is a reliable espresso and sandwich bar.

Wisconsin

As many cows as humans call **WISCONSIN** home. About four million of each eat to their hearts' content in this rich, rolling farmland, which has a higher proportion of overweight people than any other state. However, America's self-proclaimed "Dairyland" is more than just one giant pasture. Beyond the massive red barns and silvery silos lie endless pine forests, some 15,000 sky-blue lakes, postcard-pretty valleys, and dramatic bluffs. The state, whose Ojibway name means "gathering of the waters," is bordered by Lake Michigan to the east, Lake Superior in the north and, to the west, the Mississippi and St Croix rivers. Only the southern boundary, with Illinois, is dry.

The **history** of Wisconsin exemplifies the standard formula for westward expansion. Seventeenth-century French and British explorers began by trading with the Native Americans and soon ousted them from their land. The European settlers who followed – predominantly Germans, Scandinavians, and Poles – tended to be liberal and progressive; such major national social programs as labor laws for women and children, assistance for the elderly and the disabled, and unemployment compensation were rooted here. On the downside, Senator Joseph McCarthy, the infamous 1950s witch-hunter, was born in Grand Chute, former headquarters of the right-wing John Birch Society.

Wisconsin today is best known for its liquids. The **milk** from all those cattle yields cheeses of all kinds, while the **beer**, as the song says, is what made **Milwaukee** famous. Sparkling Madison apart, Wisconsin's other cities – **La Crosse**, **Green Bay**, **Oshkosh** – can veer toward the dull side, but they're also clean, safe, and amiable, while the smaller towns can be distinctive and charming.

Getting around Wisconsin

You'll be hard put to explore Wisconsin's remote north, or key locales like the Door County peninsula, without a vehicle. Public transportation is better in the south. Milwaukee and, to a lesser extent, Madison are hubs for Greyhound and Amtrak. Five **trains** daily connect Milwaukee and Chicago, a ninety-minute journey, while one crosses the state in the south en route for Seattle, via Columbus (near Madison), Portage, Wisconsin Dells, Tomah, and La Crosse.

Milwaukee

Bustling **MILWAUKEE**, the "Deutsch Athens" of southeastern Wisconsin, is a combination of the down-home and the sophisticated, known for its lakeside and ethnic **festivals** and huge **breweries**. Visually it's a mix of elegant Teutonic architecture, rambling Victorian warehouses, and tasteful waterfront developments. Its prime position on the shores of Lake Michigan, at the confluence of three rivers, made it a meeting place for Native American groups long before white settlers moved in, while the opulent mansions lining the lake commemorate the industrialists who helped make this Wisconsin's economic and manufacturing capital. By 1850, less than two decades old and with a population of twenty thousand, Milwaukee already had a dozen breweries and 225 saloons. The contemporary estimate of six thousand bars – one per hundred residents – is not necessarily apocryphal.

Arrival, information, and getting around

Milwaukee is well served by air, rail, and bus. Its **airport**, eight miles south of downtown at 5300 S Howell Ave, is connected with the city center by bus #80 ($1.35), and by limousine service ($9). A taxi will set you back about $17. Amtrak is at 433 W St Paul Ave, while Greyhound and Wisconsin Coach (☏414/272-2156), serving southeastern Wisconsin, operate out of the same terminal at 606 N James Lovell Drive. Badger Bus (☏414/276-7490, ⓦwww.badgerbus.com), across the street at no. 635, runs an express service to Madison (six daily; $22 roundtrip). Take care in and around the stations at night, which can be dodgy.

Milwaukee's **Convention and Visitors Bureau** is at 400 W Wisconsin Ave (summer Mon–Fri 8am–5pm, Sat 9am–2pm, Sun 11am–3pm; rest of year Mon–Fri 8am–5pm; ☏414/273-7222 or 1-800/554-1448, ⓦwww.milwaukee.org), and has details on such **festivals** as the eleven-day Summerfest (late June to early July), also known as "The Big Gig," Great Circus Parade (usually mid-July), and the Wisconsin State Fair (early Aug). The main **post office** is at 345 W St Paul Ave (Mon–Fri 7.30am–8pm; ☏1-800/275-8777; zip code 53203).

Getting around Milwaukee is easy and inexpensive via the county's extensive **transportation system** (flat fare $1.35; 24hr info ☎414/344-6711). The Milwaukee Loop is a special trolley service connecting eighteen stops in the city center (Wed–Sat 10am–10pm, Sun till 6pm; $1 to hop on and off all day).

Accommodation

Lodgings in Milwaukee run the gamut from low-budget to upmarket chains to luxury hotels. Alternatively, Cedarburg is a tranquil, picture-postcard-like village twenty miles north; the *Washington House* (☎414/375-3550, Ⓦwww.washingtonhouseinn.com; ❹) and *Stagecoach* (☎414/375-0208 or 1-888/375-0208, Ⓦwww.stagecoach-inn-wi.com; ❹) inns here are charming.

The Astor 924 E Juneau Ave ☎414/271-4220 or 1-800/558-0200, in Wisconsin ☎1-800/242-0355, Ⓦwww.theastorhotel.com. This classy, historic 1920s hotel offers free continental breakfast and health club passes. Extended stays are available. ❺

Brumber Mansion 3046 W Wisconsin Ave ☎414/342-9767 or 866/793-3676. Fabulously decorated, enormous B&B with an in-house theater, just minutes from downtown. ❹

Crane House B&B 346 E Wilson St ☎414/483-1512. Handsome B&B in the self-contained suburb of Bay View. Excellent breakfasts. ❹

HI–Milwaukee Summer Hostel 1530 W Wisconsin Ave ☎414/288-3232, Ⓦwww.hostellingwisconsin.org. A hostel in Marquette University, with common rooms, kitchens, laundry, and Internet access. Dorm beds cost $17. Open June–Aug; office hours 8–11am and 5–10pm. ❶

Park East Hotel 916 E State St ☎414/276-8800 or 1-800/328-PARK, Ⓦwww.parkeasthotel.com. Clean, very comfortable rooms in a nice part of downtown. Good value compared with the city's bigger hotels. ❺

Red Barn Hostel 6750 W Loomis Rd ☎414/529-3299. Hostel thirteen miles southwest of town, via Hwy-894 or buses #10 and #35 (best avoided at night), with check-in 5–10pm and access to the 76-mile Long Leaf hiking and biking trail. It is located in the lower level of a 1923 barn with separate dorms for men and women, and one room that can accommodate a family. Dorm beds cost $14. Open May–Oct only. ❶

The City

Downtown Milwaukee, split north to south by the Milwaukee River, is only a mile long and a few blocks wide. Handsome old buildings and gleaming, modern steel-and-glass structures are comfortably corralled together on three sides by spaghetti-like strands of freeway, with Lake Michigan forming the fourth boundary. To bolster the allure of downtown, the city has successfully poured millions into its **Riverwalk** development along the Milwaukee River, now something of a nightlife center and the site of many public entertainment events. East of the river on the lakefront, the **Milwaukee Art Museum**, 700 N Art Museum Drive (daily 10am–5pm, Thurs 10am–8pm; $8; ☎414/224-3200, Ⓦwww.mam.org), contains works by European masters and twentieth-century Americans. One wing – with stunning views of the lake – is devoted to a comprehensive collection of Post-Impressionist paintings. Architect Santiago Calatrava's spectacular expansion is an attraction in itself, the white wings of the building flapping up and down several times each day to reduce heat gain and glare. The **Museum Center** complex, downtown at 800 W Wells St, is a three-attraction entity (combination ticket $10.50). At the **Milwaukee Public Museum** (daily 9am–5pm; $7; ☎414/278-2702, Ⓦwww.mpm.edu), the intertwined histories and mysteries of the earth, nature, and humankind are imaginatively presented through dioramas such as "The Streets of Old Milwaukee" and a battle of the dinosaurs. Next, **Discovery World – The James Lovell Museum of Science, Economics, and Technology** (daily 9am–5pm; $6; ☎414/765-9966, Ⓦwww.discoveryworld.org), features popular hands-on exhibits and laser light shows. Lastly, the **Humphrey IMAX Dome Theater** has a giant, wraparound screen (Mon–Wed 11.30am–4.30pm, Thurs & Fri 11.30am–8.30pm, Sat 10.30am–8.30pm, Sun 10.30am–5.30pm; shows on the half-hour; weekday matinees $5.25, evenings $7; ☎414/319-4629, ⓦwww.mpm.edu/imax).

North of Discovery World, the 37-room **Pabst Mansion**, at 2000 W Wisconsin Ave (Feb–Oct Mon–Sat 10am–3.30pm, Sun noon–3.30pm; Nov–Jan Mon–Sat 10am–4pm, Sun noon–4pm; $7), was completed in 1893 as the castle of a local beer baron and is a knockout example of ornate Flemish Renaissance architecture, featuring exquisite wood-, glass-, and ironwork. Although the Pabst Brewery here has shut down, the **Miller Brewing Company**, five miles west of downtown at 4251 W State St, still offers free behind-the-scenes tours (Mon–Sat, usually 10am–4pm but times change frequently; ☎414/931-2467 or 1-800/944-LITE; bus #71), culminating in generous samples for over-21s. The more primitive microbrewery **Sprecher**, seven miles north of downtown, just off of I-43 at 701 W Glendale Ave (Sat 1pm, 2pm & 3pm; also Mon–Fri 4pm in June, July, Aug & holiday weeks; rest of year Sat 1pm, 2pm & 3pm, Fri 4pm; reservations necessary; $3; ☎414/964-2739), serves samples straight out of the barrel. Schlitz, the "beer that made Milwaukee famous," was bought out by Stroh's in the late 1980s and is now produced in Detroit.

Twelve miles west of downtown in Wanwatosa, the blue-domed, neo-Byzantine **Annunciation Greek Orthodox Church** stands like a mushroom crossed with a spaceship at 9400 W Congress St. Completed in 1961, it was one of the last major works by native Wisconsin architect Frank Lloyd Wright. The interior is a jaw-dropping blend of the streamlined and the ornate. Unfortunately, tours have been phased out and visits discouraged. About the only way to see inside is to attend the Sunday service (9am summer, 9.30am rest of year; bus #57).

You can also take one-hour tours of the engine plant responsible for Milwaukee's other legendary brand name, **Harley-Davidson**, located in Wanwatosa in a rough area of town on 11700 W Capitol Drive at Hwy-45. It's really for Harley devotees; bikes aren't assembled here and if you don't know your shovelheads from your knuckleheads you might feel out of place (free tours June–Aug Mon–Fri 9.30am, 11am & 1pm; Sept–Dec Mon, Wed & Fri same times; ☎414/535-3666). For those more interested in Harley chic, there's ample opportunity to purchase all kinds of merchandise throughout Milwaukee. Milwaukee Iron Motorcycle Tours (☎262/482-1525) provides safe, friendly chauffeured tours aboard Harleys at reasonable rates and tailored to clients' needs.

Eating

The Germans who first settled in Milwaukee determined its **eating** style – heavy on bratwurst, rye bread, and beer. Subsequent immigrants threw the collective kitchen wide open, making for a culinary cornucopia. With Lake Michigan lapping the city's feet, freshwater fish can hardly be overlooked, especially on a Friday night when fish boils (see p.390) break out all over the place. Wherever you go, portions tend to be big.

J Pandl's Whitefish Bay Inn 1319 E Henry Clay St ☎414/964-3800. The suburban landmark is famous for reasonably priced grilled whitefish, colossal oven-baked pancakes, and its stein collection.

The King & I 823 N 2nd St ☎414/276-4181. Good medium-priced Thai food option in downtown Milwaukee.

Milwaukee Ale House 233 N Water St ☎414/226-BEER. Milwaukee's sole all-grain, old-style

brewpub serves filling food and its own beer.
Mimma's Café 1307 E Brady St ☎414/264-6640. This unmissable Italian restaurant is classy yet casual, with imaginative, mouthwatering cuisine and an extensive wine list.

Old Town Serbian Gourmet House 522 W Lincoln Ave ☎414/672-0206. Tasty Serbian food on the Pole-dominated south side. Try a *burek*, a tasty meat- or spinach-filled pie the size of a Frisbee. Live music Fri–Sun.

Nightlife and entertainment

The concept of neighborhoods is vital to Milwaukee's nightlife. **Brady Street** in the near northeast, a counterculture haven in the 1960s, is now filled with Italian restaurants and bars. **Walker's Point**, on the edge of downtown, has all sorts of gay and straight watering holes, while the Polish locals can be found farther south. Downtown gets busy on the weekend, especially either side of the river on **Water** and **Old World Third** streets between Juneau and State.

With more live theater than Chicago, high culture in downtown Milwaukee revolves around the **Marcus Center for the Performing Arts**, 929 N Water St (☎414/273-7206 or 1-888/612-3500, ⊛www.marcuscenter.org), and the plush, historic **Pabst Theater**, 144 E Wells St (☎414/286-3663). Nearby, the **Milwaukee Repertory Theater**, 108 E Wells St (☎414/224-9490, ⊛www.milwaukeerep.com), has a reputation for risk-taking productions, as does the arty, eclectic **Theatre X** (☎414/278-0555), in the Broadway Theater Center in the Third Ward, a restored warehouse district on the edge of downtown. The Center, located at 158 N Broadway, is also home to the adventurous Skylight Opera (☎414/291-7800, ⊛www.skylightopera.com) and **Milwaukee Chamber Theatre** (☎414/276-8842, ⊛www.chamber-theatre .com), where the focus is split between classical and contemporary plays.

Café Vecchio 1137 N Old World Third St ☎414/273-5700. Upscale European-style coffee/wine bar featuring a one-hundred-plus wine list, espresso drinks, and twenty different martinis.
John Hawk's Pub 100 E Wisconsin Ave ☎414/272-3199. Riverside British-style establishment downtown serving food all day. Hosts jazz on Fri and Sat.
Safe House 779 N Front St ☎414/271-2007, ⊛www.safe-house.com. This unique, tongue-in-cheek nightclub seems to come straight out of a spy film. Open from 11am, it also serves light

meals. Hint: Enter through the "International Exports Ltd." office.
Up and Under Pub 1216 E Brady St ☎414/276-2677, ⊛www.upandunderpub.com. Milwaukee's top blues bar.
Velvet Room 730 N Old World Third St ☎414/319-1190. Premier cocktail lounge with a fun, plush setting, billiards, and "New American" menu.
Von Trier 2235 N Farwell Ave ☎414/272-1775. Black Forest decor and lots of imported beers – the Weise is a house specialty.

Wisconsin's eastern shores

North of Milwaukee, **eastern Wisconsin** is a melange of the industrial and the maritime, with a nod to agriculture, shaped by its proximity to **Lake Michigan** and the smaller **Lake Winnebago**. Of its towns, Appleton was the birthplace of escapologist Harry Houdini, **Green Bay** is home to the legendary Packers, and **Oshkosh** is a household name for its overalls and baby clothes, but it's all best seen as a prelude to the most romanticized part of the state, **Door County**.

Green Bay

Few cities are as closely associated with a sports team as **GREEN BAY** is with the football Packers: 108 miles north of Milwaukee, it's the smallest city in the

US to have a major-league professional sports franchise and the only one to own a team. **The Green Bay Packer Hall of Fame**, 1265 Lombardi Ave (daily: June–Aug 9am–6pm; rest of year 10am–5pm; $8; ☏920/499-4281), celebrates the dynastic years of the 1960s when the Pack won Superbowls I and II, as well as more recent stars such as Antonio Freeman and Brett Favre. Stuffed with hands-on displays, movie theaters, and memorabilia, the museum offers more than enough to satisfy any football fan. The Hall of Fame is located in a new atrium inside the Packers' **Lambeau Field** stadium, which you can also tour (summer daily 9.30am–3.30pm; $7.50, or $10 combination ticket with Hall of Fame; ⓦwww.packerhalloffame.com).

Also in this busy but not particularly attractive port, the **National Railroad Museum**, 2285 S Broadway (Mon–Sat 9am–5pm, Sun 11am–5pm; $7 in summer including train ride, $6 in winter; ☏920/437-7623, ⓦwww.nationalrrmuseum.org), gives pride of place to the 1.1 million-ton 1941 *Union Pacific Big Boy* locomotive, one of many such trains that served Green Bay's still-enormous freight depot. West on Hwy-172, opposite the airport, stands Wisconsin's biggest casino – **Oneida Bingo & Casino**. Tribal history, and the way in which profits from blackjack, video poker, and bingo have improved education and social and health facilities, are examined at the **Oneida Nation Museum**, seven miles west of Hwy-41 as it runs south from downtown (summer Tues–Sat 9am–5pm; rest of year closed Sat; $2; ☏920/869-2768, ⓦwww.oneidanation.org).

The city's **visitor center** (☏920/494-9507 or 1-888/867-3342, ⓦwww.greenbay.com) sits in the shadow of the football stadium, off Lombardi Avenue. Nearby, the *Best Western Midway Hotel*, 780 Packer Drive (☏920/499-3161 or 1-800/528-1234, ⓦwww.bestwestern.com; ❹), has standard rooms, an indoor pool, and fitness facilities. *Titletown Brewing Company*, 200 Dousman St (☏920/437-2337), has a great setting for drinks in a former railroad depot downtown, while *Brett Favre's Steakhouse*, 1004 Brett Favre Pass (☏920/499-MVP4), is an upscale family restaurant/sports bar serving Southern cuisine.

Door County

From Sturgeon Bay, 140 miles north of Milwaukee, **Door County** sticks into Lake Michigan like a gradually tapering candle for 42 miles. With thirteen lighthouses and a dozen fishing villages, its coastline smacks more of New England than the Midwest. The name derives from "Porte des Morts" or "**Door of the Dead**," French for the treacherous eight-mile strait that severs Washington Island at its tip. Despite drawing a million-plus warm-weather tourists, the peninsula (actually an island split off from Wisconsin by a canal) is not an oversized theme park. Prices can get a little steep, but you get what you pay for – a small sliver of America devoid, for the most part, of crude billboards, sloppy diners, bland chain motels, and tacky amusements. Activities include browsing around galleries and attending arts festivals, as well as hiking, fishing, and boating. Renting a **bicycle** gives you the chance to follow an excellent **cycle trail**; try Fish Creek's Nor Door Cyclery (☏920/868-2275, ⓦwww.nordoorsports.com), on Hwy-42 just north of the entrance to Peninsula State Park (see opposite), which has the best models. Winter is considerably quieter, with ice fishing, cross-country skiing, and snowmobiling being the predominant outdoor activities.

Pick up road and trail maps at the **visitor center** on Hwy-42/57 upon entering Sturgeon Bay (summer Mon–Fri 8.30am–8pm; rest of year Mon–Fri 8.30am–8pm; ☏920/743-4456 or 1-800/52-RELAX, ⓦwww.doorcounty .com), where you can also phone local lodgings for free.

Exploring Door County

Door County's only sizeable town, **Sturgeon Bay** is a pleasant enough ship-building community, if not exactly abundant in small-town splendor. Ten miles north on Hwy-57 is the rolling **Whitefish Dunes State Park**, with its wispy sand dunes and popular mile-long beach (daily; $7 per car). A short trail beginning at the park's Nature Center leads to the spectacular rocky **Cave Point County Park** (free), studded with wind- and wave-sculptured caves that are particularly dramatic in winter. In general beaches are better this side of the peninsula; Jacksonport's (free) **Lakeside Park** ranks as the best of the lot. You can also swim in several placid inland lakes.

Over on the western side, biking and hiking trails traverse the thickly forested hills of **Peninsula State Park** (situated between tiny Fish Creek and elegant Mennonite **Ephraim**, with its resplendent white-clapboard architecture). An observation tower and lighthouse stand on the park's extensive shoreline. Peninsula Park is one of the most popular parks in Wisconsin and summer camping reservations usually book up in January. Just outside it on Hwy-42, the anachronistic Skyway Drive-In movie theater (☎920/854-9938) offers a couple of hours' diversion on a warm night. Northeast of Ellison Bay near the peninsula's tip, **Newport State Park** is one of Wisconsin's least visited parks, with hiking, mountain biking, cross-country skiing, and backpack camping opportunities.

Washington Island, off the peninsula's northern tip, offers a different cultural perspective. During Prohibition, the Icelandic community here convinced authorities that (40 percent alcohol) bitters were an ancient cure for rheumatism and dyspepsia. Cases of the stuff were shipped in, and the habit stuck; drop into the historic *Nelsen's Hall Bitters Pub and Restaurant* (☎920/847-2496), about two miles from the Detroit Harbor dock, and you're likely to find old-timers drinking bitters by the pint. **Motel rooms** are available on Washington, but there's no such luxury on the primitive neighboring 950-acre Rock Island. Once the private estate of a millionaire, it's dotted with stark, stone buildings; no cars are allowed, so see them by foot or bike.

The islands are served by the Washington Island Ferry from Northport at the tip of the peninsula (daily; $8 roundtrip, cars $18, bikes $3; ☎920/847-2546 or 1-800/223-2094, ⓦwww.wisferry.com) and the Rock Island Ferry out of Jackson Harbor (May–Aug daily; $8 roundtrip; ☎414/847-2546).

Accommodation

Door County has a full range of **accommodation**, including some overpriced resorts. Prices given are for shoulder seasons (the best time to come); expect to pay up to 25 percent extra at the grander hotels in July and August, and a small weekend premium. Camping is idyllic. State park sites cost $10–15 (plus $9.50 reservation fee and $7 daily admission, annual $25; ☎1-888/947-2757). Recommended private campgrounds include *Path of Pines*, County Road F off Hwy-42, near Fish Creek (mid-May to mid-Oct; $20–36; ☎920/868-3332 or 1-800/868-7802).

Century Farm Motel 10068 Hwy-57 ☎920/854-4069. Basic cottages (sleeping up to six people) are set in farmland halfway between Sister Bay and Ephraim, with rates among the lowest on the peninsula. ❸

Chal-A-Motel 3910 Hwy-42, 57 Sturgeon Bay ☎920/743-6788. This offbeat, clean, year-round budget motel has a huge collection of dolls, toys, and old autos that you can see for $1 ($2 for nonguests). ❸

Liberty Park Lodge and Shore Cottages Hwy-42 N, Sister Bay ☎920/854-2025. Spotless complex with a lakeside porch and sandy beach. Good value. ❸

Peninsula Park-View Resort City Rd A and Hwy-42 ☎920/854-2633, ⓦwww.peninsulaparkview .com. This cordial motel is conveniently situated on the edge of Fish Creek at the quiet end of Peninsula

State Park. Offers rooms as well as suites and cottages. Guests also have free use of bikes. ❸

Waterbury Inn 10321 Water St, Ephraim ☎920/854-2821 or 1-800/720-1624, ⓦwww .waterburyinn.com. This luxury property has one- and two-bedroom suites with fully equipped kitchens. ❺

White Gull Inn 4225 Main St, Fish Creek ☎920/868-3517, ⓦwww.whitegullinn.com. This elegant old inn, next to delightful Sunset Park, is the county's crown jewel, has a good restaurant on site (breakfast not included), and a fish boil (see below) every night in summer. ❻

Eating

One reward of a midsummer visit to Door County is the chance to sample the cherry in all its guises. Another traditional treat is the **fish boil**, a delicious outdoor ritual involving whitefish steaks, potatoes, and onions cooked in a cauldron over a wood fire. Rounded off with coleslaw and cherry pie, it's widely available for between $10 and $16.

Al Johnson's Swedish Restaurant Hwy-42, Sister Bay ☎920/854-2626. Pancakes, meatballs, and other fine Scandinavian dishes are featured at this local spot where goats are tethered atop the sod roof.

Bayside Tavern Main St, Fish Creek ☎920/868-3441. A convivial pub serves a celebrated chili, burgers, and a mean Friday-night perch-fry.

Dal Santo's 341 N 3rd Ave, Sturgeon Bay ☎920/743-6100. Pizza, pasta, and bar snacks are served in an old railroad depot with a good microbrewery. The cherry ale is surprisingly palatable and refreshing.

Square Rigger Lodge and Galley 6332 Hwy-57, Jacksonport ☎920/823-2408. This cocktail lounge and restaurant, on a private sandy beach, serves one of the county's best fish boils.

Wilson's 9990 Water St, Ephraim ☎920/854-2041. Burgers, sandwiches, and (along with the Door County Ice Cream Factory in Sister Bay) the top ice cream on the peninsula.

Upstate Wisconsin

Sparsely settled **northern Wisconsin** has no large cities (and few small ones), and no interstates. It's a lake-studded wilderness, covered by enormous tracts of forest. Canoe its rivers, fish for record-breakers, or ski or snowmobile cross-country trails without having to fight for space. **Bayfield** and the **Apostle Islands** in the northwest are the obvious destinations, but Hayward, southeast of Superior, is home to the amazing **National Freshwater Fishing Hall of Fame** (mid-April to Nov daily 10am–5pm; closed on weekends after Nov 1; $5), where you're invited to "Walk through the biggest fish in the world!" – a four-story, five-hundred-ton, fiberglass monster.

The Apostle Islands

All but one of the 22 islands scattered off **Bayfield Peninsula** in Lake Superior are part of the **Apostle Islands National Lakeshore** – a prized preserve for outdoors enthusiasts seeking to recharge depleted spiritual batteries.

The jumping-off point for the islands, **BAYFIELD**, once a lumbering and fishing village, is now a pleasant soft-sell tourist trap. Its sumptuous *Old Rittenhouse Inn*, 301 Rittenhouse Ave (☎715/779-5111 or 1-800/779-2129, ⓦwww.rittenhouseinn.com; ❻), offers gourmet meals and well-appointed **rooms**. *Tree Top House*, 225 N Fourth St (☎715/779-3293; ❷), has clean, simple doubles, while *Island View Place*, Hwy 13, Box 46 (☎715/779-5307 or 1-800/484-8189, ⓦwww.island-view.com; ❹), a half-mile outside of town, is one of many waterside condominiums with nightly and weekly accommodation. Lodges and cottages are the centerpiece for the thirty gorgeous lakeside acres of *Rocky Run* (☎715/373-2551; ❺), a resort outside **Washburn** eleven miles south. Bayfield's **visitor center** is at 42 S Broad St (☎715/779-3335 or 1-800/447-4094).

Campers heading for the islands require permits ($15, $30 for eight people or more) from the visitor center at 410 Washington Ave (summer daily; weekdays in winter; ☎715/779-3397). Getting around the islands is straightforward: Apostle Island Cruise Service boats ($24.95; ☎715/779-3925, ⓦwww.apostleisland.com) wend their way past all of the islands, and will set down and pick up campers.

Madeline Island

By the fifteenth century **Madeline Island** was known to the Ojibway as Moningwunakauning – home of the golden-shafted woodpecker. Frenchman Michel Cadotte founded a fur-trading post there for the British in 1793, and subsequently married Equaysayway, daughter of a tribal leader, who took the name the island bears today. Madeline is now the only commercially developed Apostle island, but it remains pretty low-key. Cadotte is buried in an overgrown cemetery in its sole town, **LA POINTE**.

La Pointe is accessible in summer via the twenty-minute ride on the Madeline Island Ferry Line from Bayfield (every 30min in peak season; cars $9.25, passengers $4, bikes $1.75; ☎715/747-2051, ⓦwww.madferry.com). Its 180 year-round residents maintain an interesting little **historical museum** (May–Oct daily 10am–6pm; $5), and assorted sandy beaches, wide bays, scenic points, and forests can also be explored along 45 miles of sometimes rough road in the area; rent **bikes** near the dock for $22 per day. The Ferry Line conducts two-hour bus tours of the island (mid-June to Sept 10.30am and 1.30pm; $9).

The **visitor center** on Main Street (☎715/747-2801 or 1-888/ISLE-FUN, ⓦwww.madelineisland.com) can offer advice on **places to stay**; the *Madeline Island Motel* (☎715/747-3000; ❸) and *The Island Inn* (☎715/747-2000; ❹), both near the ferry dock, are probably the best value. A wooden footbridge from La Pointe across the lagoon leads to **Big Bay State Park** ($11–14; no reservations), where the campgrounds share a splendid mile-long beach. Camping sites, on top of a bluff and close to caves in the park (☎1-888/947-2757, ⓦwww.wiparks.net), cost $10–14 plus a $9.50 reservation fee, and include park admission. **Eating options** include the pub in *The Inn on Madeline Island* resort (☎715/747-6315 or 1-800/822-6315, ⓦwww.madisland.com) where homes, cottages, and condominiums can also be rented along a private beach. Homestyle meals in a casual harborside setting can be found at *The Beach Club* (☎1-800/822-6315).

Southern Wisconsin

Assorted highways and back roads lace up **southern Wisconsin**, passing over rolling hills and deep dales. The main urban center of Wisconsin's most populated region is the immensely likeable lakeside college town of **Madison**, which doubles as the state capital. Cozy Madison-area communities like New Glarus or Mount Horeb, and historic settlements like Little Norway, attest to a mixed European heritage. Further north, Wisconsin Dells has a picturesque setting, but may appeal only to those who revel in tacky attractions and Americana. Undulating down the state's western border, alongside the Mississippi River, the scenic highway designated as **The Great River Road** runs from near Canada to the Gulf of Mexico.

Madison

The history books record that **MADISON**, just over an hour west of Milwaukee, was little more than a wooded, mosquito-infested swamp when it was selected to be the political nucleus of the Wisconsin Territory in 1836. Today this stimulating, youthful metropolis is one of the most beautifully set cities in the US, with a handful of diverting museums.

Downtown is neatly laid out on an isthmus between lakes Mendota and Monona, with the sumptuous white granite **State Capitol** sitting benignly on a hill at its center, surrounded by shady trees, lawns, and park benches. The state capitol square here is the site of a fun **farmers' market** (May–Oct Sat 6am–2pm), where you can browse the local produce, and arts and crafts. **Madison Civic Center**, close by at 211 State St, houses a professional repertory theater (box office ☎608/266-9055) and **art museum** (Tues–Thurs 11am–5pm, Fri 11am–9pm, Sat 10am–9pm, Sun 1–5pm; free; ☎608/257-0158, Ⓦ www.madisonartcenter.org), and also presents concerts and touring shows. Frank Lloyd Wright designed the **Unitarian Meeting House**, 900 University Bay Drive, in the late 1940s. Its sweeping, dramatically curved ceiling and triangle motif are definitely worth a look (May–Oct Tues–Fri 10am–4pm, Sat 9am–noon; $3). The lakeside **Monona Terrace Community and Convention Center**, 1 John Nolen Drive, is a more recently realized example of Wright's grand vision (daily tours 11am & 1pm; $3). Surprisingly intimate and full of architectural detail, the Center, with its curves, arches, and domes, echoes the State Capitol building just a few blocks away.

If the capitol is the city's governmental heart, the 46,000-student **University of Wisconsin** is its spirited, liberal-thinking head, now mellowed since its protest heyday in the late 1960s. The **Memorial Union**, 800 Langdon St (☎608/262-1583), holds a cafeteria and pub, the *Rathskeller*, with tables strewn beneath huge, vaulted ceilings and live music most nights. Out back, the spacious **UW Terrace** offers beautiful sunset views over Lake Mendota. Capitol and campus are arterially connected by State Street, eight tree-lined, pedestrianized blocks of restaurants, cafés, bars, and funky stores.

Practicalities

Greyhound **buses** run regularly to Milwaukee, Green Bay, and beyond, while Badger Coaches make six trips daily to Milwaukee ($22 roundtrip; ☎608/255-6771, Ⓦ www.badgerbus.com). Both operate out of the terminal at 2 S Bedford St. Van Galder buses depart from the Memorial Union to Chicago's O'Hare Airport (10 daily; $21; ☎608/752-5407 or 1-800/747-0994, Ⓦ www.vangalderbus.com). The **visitor center** is at 615 E Washington Ave (Mon–Fri 8am–4.30pm; ☎608/256-8348 or 1-800/373-MDSN, Ⓦ www.visitmadison.com).

Accommodation can be had all over the city, though the budget chains lie to the east, off I-90/94. *Collins House*, 704 E Gorham St (☎608/255-4230, Ⓦ www.collinshouse.com; ⑤), is a beautiful B&B a few blocks from the capitol with free parking on site. The upscale *Madison Concourse Hotel*, 1 W Dayton St (☎608/257-6000 or 1-800/356-8293, Ⓦ www.concoursehotel.com; ⑤), is even closer and offers spacious, well-appointed rooms. *Canterbury Inn*, 315 W Gorham St (☎608/258-8899 or 1-800/838-3850, Ⓦ www.madisoncanterbury.com; ⑦), has six splendid Chaucer-inspired rooms above a welcoming bookstore-cum-coffeehouse. There's also a *Hostelling International* hostel at 141 S Butler St (☎608/441-0144, Ⓦ www.hiayh.org; ①) with 28 beds and four private rooms, and all the usual amenities: kitchen, laundry, Internet access, storage, and lockers.

State Street is a veritable smorgasbord of **food** and **drink**, ranging from the vegetarian and vegan fare at the tiny Nepalese *Himal Chuli* at no. 318 (☎608/251-9225) and its sister restaurant, *Chautara*, at no. 334 (☎608/251-

3626), to the kosher-style food and rich ice cream at veteran *Ella's Deli* at 2902
E Washington (☎608/241-5291). *Deb & Lola's* at no. 227 (☎608/255-0820)
serves fresh, eclectic Southwestern-influenced cuisine. The *Essen Haus*, 514 E
Wilson St (☎608/255-4674), is a raucous *biergarten* with a phenomenal selection of beers. *Dotty Dumpling's Dowry*, 116 N Fairchild St (☎608/255-3175),
is a local landmark thanks to its great burgers and kooky nostalgic decor.

There's plenty of **entertainment**, often free, on campus (call the events line
☎608/265-3000). The soulful neighborhood *Crystal Corner*, 1302 Williamson
St (☎608/256-2953), puts on blues acts, while *O'Cayz Corral*, 504 E Wilson
St (☎608/256-1348), spans heavy metal, folk, and acoustic. *The Cardinal*, 418
E Wilson St (☎608/251-0080), with its handsome 1908 decor, is one of the
best dance club-cum-bars. For details of what's on, check the free weekly
Isthmus, which carries full listings.

Baraboo

Between 1884 and 1912, the **Ringling Brothers' Circus** kept winter quarters
in **BARABOO**, thirty miles northwest of Madison. The **Circus World
Museum**, 426 Water St, successfully recaptures the pre-TV glory days of big-top
history, via an enormous collection of memorabilia and daily performances
including an old-time circus show that is both tawdry (elephants with bows on
their tails do leg kicks to "*New York, New York*") and irresistible (mid-July and Aug
daily 9am–9pm, with shows at 11am, 3pm & 7.30pm; May to early July daily
9am–6pm, same schedule, without 7.30pm show; Sept–April Mon–Sat
9am–5pm, Sun 11am–5pm museum only, no shows; $5–15, varies with season;
Ⓦwww.circusworldmuseum.com). Every summer, usually in the first half of July,
75 meticulously restored circus wagons set out on a four-day rail journey through
small-town Wisconsin and Illinois, culminating in a horse-drawn parade through
downtown Milwaukee – an unbeatable extravaganza of Americana. Built in 1915
and modeled after the grand opera house at Versailles, the **Al Ringling Theatre**
(summer tours, noon Thurs–Sun; $3; ☎608/356-8864, Ⓦwww.alringling.com) in
the town center is one of America's prettiest small playhouses.

Baraboo itself is calmer, quieter, and more affordable than nearby Wisconsin
Dells. The elegant *Victorian Gollmar Guest House B&B*, 422 Third St (☎608/356-
9432, Ⓦwww.gollmar.com; ❹), plays up the fact that it was once home to a circus family. More basic **rooms** are available at the *Spinning Wheel Motel*, 809
Eighth St (☎608/356-3933; ❷). *Kristina's Family Restaurant* at 506 W Pine near
Hwy-12 (☎608/355-9213), serves low-cost **meals**. Baraboo's **visitor center** is
at the intersection of highways 12, 33, and 136 (Mon–Fri 9am–7pm, Sat
9am–3pm; ☎608/356-8333 or 1-800/227-2266, Ⓦwww.baraboo.com).

Spring Green

During his seventy-year career, Wisconsin-born architect and social philosopher **Frank Lloyd Wright** designed such monumental structures as New
York's spiraling Guggenheim Museum and Tokyo's earthquake-proof *Imperial
Hotel*. Three miles south of **SPRING GREEN**, itself forty miles west of
Madison on Hwy-14, stand more intimate examples of his work: Wright's
magnificent former residence, **Taliesin**, and his **Hillside Home School**. The
streamlined geometry and functional grandeur of the latter, opened in 1932,
exemplify Wright's break from the boxy, fusty Victorian style (May–Oct daily,
tours on the hour 10am–4pm; $16). His studio is imposing, and there's also a
theater space on the estate. Extensive and varied tours are also available of the
house (daily 10am–4pm; reservations recommended; $40) and grounds

(May–Oct daily at 10.45am & 1.45pm; $15). These and other, pricier, tours leave from the **Frank Lloyd Wright Visitor Center** (℡608/588-7900, ⓦwww.taliesinpreservation.org), which was designed by Wright in 1953 as a restaurant; it now features displays, a café, and a bookstore. Among numerous other Wright-influenced buildings in Spring Green are the bank, pharmacy, and the lounge of the *Post House*, 127 E Jefferson St (℡608/588-2595), a mid-priced restaurant downtown.

From 1944 onward, Alex Jordan built the **House on the Rock**, six miles south of Taliesin on Hwy-23, on and out of a natural, 60ft, chimney-like rock – for no discernible reason. He certainly never lived in it, nor did he intend it to become Wisconsin's number one tourist attraction (mid-March to Oct daily 9am–dusk; Nov & Dec tour daily 10am–6pm; $19.50, or $12.50 Nov & Dec; ℡888/935-3960, ⓦwww.thehouseontherock.com). Only the first section of this multilevel series of furnished nooks and chambers bears any resemblance to a house of any kind. With its low ceilings, indirect lighting, indoor pools, waterfalls, trees, and pervasive shag carpeting, the style brings to mind Frank Lloyd Wright meets *The Flintstones*. The rest of the house is a logic-free labyrinth, containing Jordan's astounding collection of collections (antiques, nickelodeons and pneumatic music machines, miniature circuses, dolls and dolls' houses, maritime memorabilia, armor and firearms, ad infinitum), with little to indicate what is genuine or imitation, and no clue as to what it all means. The net effect is overwhelming and disorienting, alternately great fun and ghastly. Highlights include the **Infinity Room**, comprising three thousand small glass panels tapering to a point and cantilevered several hundred feet above the Wyoming Valley. A complex of other attractions has been added to the fifty-acre grounds, including the utterly dazzling **World's Largest Carousel** (with 269 fabulous figures and some 20,000 lights), a circus building, a giant dolls' house, and an old-style shopping street.

Practicalities

Spring Green is a pretty **place to stay**, but prices can be high in summer. *Round Barn Lodge*, Hwy-14 (℡608/588-2568, ⓦwww.roundbarn.com; ❹), has a pool, sauna, and restaurant on a former dairy farm. *The Usonian Inn*, Hwy-14/Hwy-23 (℡608/588-2323 or 1-877/USONIAN, ⓦwww.usonianinn .com; ❸), offers alternative, Taliesin-style lodgings. Locals hang out at *The Shed* (℡608/588-9049), an easygoing diner and bar on Lexington Street downtown. The **American Players Theatre** (℡608/588-2361, ⓦwww.american-players.org) performs Shakespeare and other classics in a wooded amphitheater each evening from mid-June to October. For information, stop by the Winsted Shop on Hwy-23 or call ℡608/588-7544.

Minnesota

Though **MINNESOTA** is more than a thousand miles from either coast, it's virtually a seaboard state, thanks to **Lake Superior**, connected to the Atlantic via the St Lawrence Seaway. The glaciers that, millions of years ago, flattened all but its southeast corner also gouged out more than 15,000 **lakes**, and major **rivers** run along the eastern and western borders. Ninety-five percent of the population lives within ten minutes of a body of water, and the very name Minnesota is a Sioux word meaning "land of sky-tinted water."

French explorers in the sixteenth century encountered prairies to the south and, in the north, dense forests whose abundant waterways were an ideal breeding ground for beavers and muskrats. **Fur trading**, **fishing**, and **lumbering** flourished, and the Ojibway and Sioux were eased out by waves of French, British, and American immigrants. Admitted to the Union in 1858, the new state of Minnesota was at first settled by Germans and Scandinavians, who farmed in the west and south. Other ethnic groups followed, many drawn by the massive **iron ore** deposits of north central Minnesota, which are expected to hold out for two more centuries.

Minnesota still thrives on its natural resources and on a progressive social outlook typified by such Democratic heavyweights as Hubert Humphrey, Walter Mondale, and Eugene McCarthy. More recently, former governor (and one-time professional wrestler) **Jesse Ventura**, garnered attention nationally and beyond for his unconventional and outspoken approach to politics.

More than half of Minnesota's hardy inhabitants, who endure some of the fiercest winters in the nation, live in the southeast, around the so-called Twin Cities of **Minneapolis** and **St Paul**. These attractive and basically friendly rivals together rank as the Midwest's great civic double act for their combined cultural, recreational, and business opportunities. Smaller cities include the northern shipping port of **Duluth**, the gateway to the Scenic Hwy-61 lakeshore drive, and **Rochester**, near pretty river towns like Red Wing and Winona. The tranquil waters of **Voyageurs National Park** lie halfway along the state's boundary with Canada.

In recent years, the state has earned a reputation as the "Hollywood of the North," thanks to its increased use as an affordable, talent-rich filmmaking locale. Internationally acclaimed fraternal filmmakers Joel and Ethan Coen, responsible for the Oscar-winning, Minnesota-set *Fargo*, were raised in the Twin Cities' suburb of St Louis Park.

Getting around Minnesota

Minneapolis/St Paul **airport**, home base for Northwest Airlines, handles routes to Europe as well as domestic flights. Amtrak **trains** cross the state once a day east and west from Chicago and Seattle, with stops in Winona, Red Wing, St Paul, St Cloud, Staples, and Detroit Lakes. Greyhound, founded upstate in Hibbing although no longer based there, is the largest of the several **bus** companies plying Minnesota's roads. Seven buses per day make the nine-hour journey to Chicago from the Twin Cities. Duluth, St Louis, and Kansas City are also served several times daily from the state's major metropolises.

Minneapolis and St Paul

Commonly known as the **Twin Cities**, **MINNEAPOLIS** (a hybrid Sioux/Greek word meaning "water city") and **ST PAUL** are competitive yet complementary. Fraternally rather than identically twinned, they may be even better places to live than they are to visit, thanks to their good looks, cleanliness, cultural activity, social awareness, and relatively low crime rates. About thirty of *Fortune Magazine*'s 500 top corporations are based here; many extend substantial financial support to local arts, community projects, and sports. Life for a majority of Twin City residents seems so vibrantly wholesome that the most significant threat would appear to be their own creeping complacency.

St Paul has been called "the last city of the East," making Minneapolis across the curving Mississippi "the first city of the West." Only a twenty-minute expressway ride separates their respective downtowns, but each has its own character, style, and strengths. **St Paul**, the state capital – originally called Pig's Eye, after a scurrilous French-Canadian fur trader who sold whisky at a Mississippi River landing in the 1840s – is the staid, slightly older sibling, careful to preserve its buildings and traditions. Its residents are mainly German, Irish, and Catholic. The compact but stately downtown is built, like Rome, on seven hills: the **Capitol** and the **Cathedral** occupy one each, both august monuments that keep the city mindful of its responsibilities.

Minneapolis, founded on money generated by the Mississippi's hundreds of flour and saw mills, is livelier, artier, and more modern, with skyscraping, up-to-date architecture and an upbeat and even brash attitude that never quite jeopardizes its essential affability. The mostly Slavonic, Nordic, and Lutheran residents are spread over wider ground than in St Paul, and dozens of lakes and parks underscore the city's appeal. The home-grown superstar **Prince** and the recording company Flyte Tyme cast a global spotlight on the local music scene.

Arrival, information, and getting around

Twin Cities International Airport lies about ten miles south of either city in suburban Bloomington. Airport Express (℡612/827-7777 or 1-800/333-1532) shuttles travelers between the airport and major hotels for around $10, and some lodgings lay on their own transportation. **Taxis** to Minneapolis will set you back close to $25, and to St Paul $15. Bus #7 goes to Minneapolis, #54 to St Paul (6am–midnight: $1–1.50). Amtrak is midway between the cities at 730 Transfer Rd, off University Avenue. The Greyhound terminals, both in convenient downtown locations, are at 950 Hawthorne St (℡612/371-3325) in Minneapolis and the less-used 166 W University Ave location (℡651/222-0507) in St Paul. Metropolitan Council Transit Operations **buses** (℡612/349-7000 or 612/373-3333) make both cities relatively easy to explore without a car. Money-saving multiple-ride tickets can be bought at the Metro Transit Store at 719 Marquette Ave in Minneapolis or numerous locations in either city. Old-style **trolleys** run through both downtowns; St Paul's is a bargain 50¢ per ride, but in Minneapolis it costs $10 for a two-hour pass or $15 all day.

In Minneapolis, the **visitor center** is at 4000 Multifoods Tower, 33 S Sixth St (Mon–Fri 8am–5pm; ℡612/661-4700 or 1-800/445-7412), with an additional location on the second level of the City Center shopping complex, Seventh Street and Nicollet Mall (℡612/335-5827). In St Paul, it's at 102 Norwest Center, 55 E Fifth St (℡612/297-6985 or 1-800/627-6101, ⓦwww.stpaulcvb.org). The main Minneapolis **post office** is on First Street and Marquette Avenue (zip code 55401), St Paul's at 180 E Kellogg Blvd (zip code 55101). The state-run website (ⓦwww.minneapolis.org) has loads of practical travel information, as does the Minnesota Historical Society site (ⓦwww.mnhs.org).

Accommodation

You're likely to pay more for lodgings downtown than in the suburbs, where dozens of cheap **motels** line I-494 near the airport, though some of the pricier central hotels offer reduced rates and special package deals on weekends. The pretty riverside community of **Stillwater**, 25 miles from St Paul via I-35 N and Hwy-36 E, has many grand old B&Bs and motels – (⊤612/439-7700 for information). For **bed–and–breakfast** options in the Twin Cities, consult Ⓦ www.bedandbreakfast.com, as many B&Bs do not have their own websites.

Minneapolis

Christopher Inn 201 Mill St, Excelsior ⊤952/474-6816. This year-round suburban B&B on Lake Minnetonka offers good discounts off-season and midweek. ❺

Evelo's B&B 2301 Bryant Ave S ⊤612/374-9656. Three comfortable rooms in a well-preserved Victorian home near bus lines, lakes, and downtown. Nonsmokers preferred. Also known as *The Bell House*. ❸

Hotel Amsterdam 828 Hennepin Ave ⊤612/288-0459 or 1-800/649-9500. Friendly, low-cost gay/lesbian-owned hotel above a noise-controlled saloon bar/disco downtown. ❷

Le Blanc House 302 University Ave NE ⊤612/379-2570, Ⓦ www.leblanchouse.com. Gourmet breakfasts and fine rooms in a fancy Victorian home just minutes from downtown. ❺

Minneapolis Hilton and Towers 1001 Marquette Ave ⊤612/376-1000, Ⓦ www.theunionstation .com/minhilton. The classiest downtown lodgings feature a great gym and pool. Weekend rates are around $100 a night. ❻

Minneapolis International House 2400 Stevens Ave ⊤612/522-5000, Ⓦ www.minneapolishostel .com. This conveniently situated independent hostel has $29 private rooms and $19 dorm beds. ❶–❷

Nicollet Island Inn 95 Merriam St ⊤612/331-1800, Ⓦ www.nicolletislandinn.com. Pricey, mid-river establishment with the edge on other downtown hotels because of its delightful location and excellent restaurant. ❻

St Paul

Chatsworth B&B 984 Ashland Ave ⊤651/227-4288, Ⓦ www.chatsworth-bb.com. A beautiful 1902 home now run as a welcoming B&B. ❹

The Covington Inn Pier 1, Harriet Island ⊤651/292-1411. A compact, one-of-a-kind B&B occupies a converted towboat facing downtown. ❻

Embassy Suites 175 E 10th St ⊤651/224-5400 or 1-800/EMBASSY, Ⓦ www.embassy-suites.com. The tropical atrium is the outstanding feature of this comfortable chain hotel on the edge of downtown. ❻

The Garden Gate B&B 925 Goodrich Ave ⊤651/227-8430, Ⓦ www.gardengatebandb .com. Large Victorian home with four simple rooms in St Paul's Crocus Hill neighborhood. ❹

Holiday Inn Express 1010 Bandana Blvd W ⊤651/647-1637 or 1-800/HOLIDAY. This is a unique lodging in a former railroad car repair shop attached to a mall complex. Indoor pool and sauna. ❺

The Saint Paul Hotel 350 Market St ⊤651/292-9292 or 1-800/292-9292, Ⓦ www.stpaulhotel .com. This grand 1910 establishment is rated Minnesota's top hotel. Rooms tend to be smaller than those of other luxury hotels, but the staff and atmosphere make up for it. The *St Paul Grill*, in the hotel, provides some of the city's finest dining, while the classy bar has tons of great scotches and cognacs. ❻

Exploring Minneapolis

Downtown Minneapolis is laid out on a simple grid. The riverfront, dubbed the **Mississippi Mile**, continues to be developed as a place for strolling, dining, and entertainment. Each city has its own landing site for narrated summertime **paddleboat** cruises (summer noon and 2pm; $12; ⊤651/227-1100, Ⓦ www.riverrides.com). The vast Third Avenue Bridge makes an ideal vantage point for viewing **St Anthony Falls**, a controlled torrent in a wide stretch of the river. The missionary Father Hennepin discovered the falls in 1680, but it wasn't until the early nineteenth century that the first permanent settlement of present-day Minneapolis was begun nearby.

Downtown's major stores line up along the pedestrianized **Nicollet Mall**. **Hennepin Avenue**, the other main drag, is a block west. It has been revitalized as an entertainment district in recent years thanks, in part, to the beautifully restored **Orpheum** and **State theaters**, twin hosts to top-quality Broadway shows and concerts. The **IDS Center**, on the Mall, is the tallest building in either city; its indoor glass atrium – the Crystal Court – is

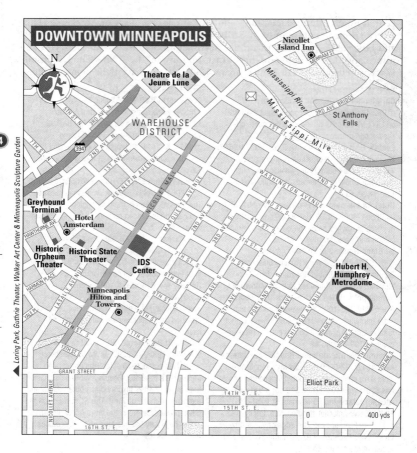

essentially modern Minneapolis's town square. Citizens escape weather extremes via a skyway system of climate-controlled glass walkways connecting more than forty buildings. Culturally, Minneapolis would be poorer without the **Walker Art Center**, Vineland Place (Tues, Wed, Fri & Sat 10am–5pm, Thurs 10am–9pm, Sun 11am–5pm; $6, free Thurs and 1st Sat of month; ☎612/375-7622, ⓦwww.walkerart.org), on the edge of downtown. This multipurpose contemporary art and performance space balances its permanent collection of sculpture and paintings (such as German Expressionist Franz Marc's *Blue Horses*) with exciting temporary exhibitions. Slated for completion in 2005 are new galleries, a multidisciplinary performance space, and several rooftop terraces. The eleven-acre outdoor **Sculpture Garden** is a work of collective genius featuring pieces by Calder, Louise Bourgeois, and Frank Gehry. Its most striking piece is the gigantic, whimsical *Spoonbridge and Cherry* (not exactly a bridge, more like a fountain) by Claes Oldenburg and Coosje van Bruggen. One mile from downtown, at 2400 Third Ave S (bus #9), the huge **Minneapolis Institute of Arts** has a thoroughly comprehensive collection of art from 2000 BC to the present (Tues, Wed, Fri & Sat 10am–5pm, Thurs

10am–9pm, Sun noon–5pm; free; ☎612/870-3131, ⒲www.artsmia.org). Antiques, crafts, and artifacts fill the exquisite 1908 mansion setting of the nearby **American Swedish Institute**, 2600 Park Ave S (Tues, Thurs, Fri & Sat noon–4pm, Wed noon–8pm, Sun 1–5pm; $5; ☎612/625-9494, ⒲www.americanswedishinstitute.org). In stark contrast, changing exhibitions and the University of Minnesota's permanent art collection share space in the controversial **Frederick R. Weisman Museum**, on campus at 333 E River Rd (Tues, Wed & Fri 10am–5pm, Thurs 10am–8pm, Sat & Sun 11am–5pm; free; ⒲www.weismanfoundation.org). Architect Frank O. Gehry's airy structure, with its boldly irregular stainless-steel west facade overlooking the Mississippi, is the most startling love-it-or-hate-it design in the cities.

Arctic winters apart, hordes of Minneapolitans flock to the shores of lakes **Calhoun** and **Harriet** and also **Lake of the Isles**, all in residential areas within two miles south of downtown. The **Hubert H. Humphrey Metrodome**, 900 S Fifth St (☎612/332-0386), squats on the eastern edge of downtown like a giant white pincushion; the dome is home to the state's pro baseball and football teams, the Twins and the Vikings. Each July the **Minneapolis Aquatennial** celebrates the lifestyle fostered by the lakes with two huge downtown parades and water-based events such as milk-carton boat races. Illuminated floats with storybook themes dominate the evening **Holidazzle** parades, on Nicollet Mall in the run-up to Christmas. **Minnehaha Falls**, south of downtown on bus #7, was featured in Longfellow's 1855 poem "*Song of Hiawatha*" without his ever having laid eyes on it. The adjacent park is a favorite spot for hikes and picnics.

Exploring St Paul

St Paul, Minnesota's capital city, reached along I-94 (and served by buses #16A, #21A, or downtown express route #94BCD), has more expensive old homes and civic monuments than Minneapolis. Here, too, downtown buildings are linked via skyways. Call in at the jazzy Art Deco lobby of the **City Hall and Courthouse**, Fourth and Wabasha streets, to see Swedish sculptor Carl Milles' revolving 36ft *Vision of Peace*, carved in the 1930s from white Mexican onyx. The castle-like **Landmark Center**, a couple of blocks away at Fifth and Market streets, and the glittering **Ordway Music Theatre** both overlook Rice Park, probably the prettiest little square in either city. A sculpture garden with characters from Charles Schulz's "Peanuts" comic strip, the artist himself a St. Paul native, has been added to **Schulz Park** next to the Landmark Center. A few blocks east, **Town Square Park** is a lush, multilevel indoor garden in a shopping complex at Minnesota and Sixth streets. The gorgeous granite and limestone **Minnesota History Center**, 345 W Kellogg Blvd (Mon–Sat 10am–5pm, Thurs until 8pm, Sun noon–5pm; rest of year closed Mon; free; ☎888/727-8386, ⒲www.mnhs.org), with its extensive research facilities and some inventive exhibits for the more casual visitor, is the best place to grasp the state's story. An immense steel iguana is the doorkeeper at the exciting hands-on **Science Museum of Minnesota**, 120 W Kellogg Blvd (Mon–Wed 9.30am–5pm, Thurs–Sat 9.30am–9pm, Sun 10.30am–5.30pm; $10; ☎651/221-9444, ⒲www.smm.org), which also has a domed Omnitheater (entry included in ticket) where you can see giant-screen films. Or check out the **Minnesota Children's Museum**, 10 W Seventh St (summer daily 9am–5pm, Thurs till 8pm; rest of year closed Mon; $7.95; ☎651/225-6000, ⒲www.mcm.org), where even big kids will be diverted by the five interactive galleries.

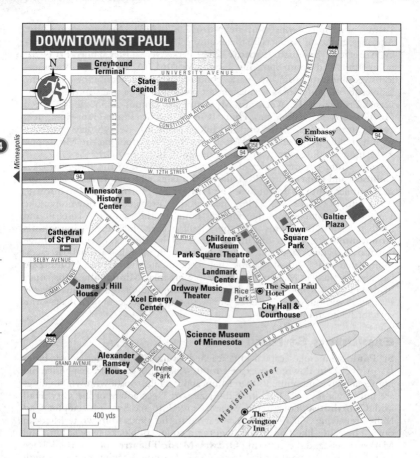

DOWNTOWN ST PAUL

N

Greyhound Terminal

State Capitol

UNIVERSITY AVENUE

AURORA

RICE STREET

CONSTITUTION AVENUE

COLUMBUS AVENUE

Embassy Suites

35E

94

94

W 12TH STREET

12TH STREET

Minnesota History Center

KELLOGG BOULEVARD

W 11TH ST

W 10TH ST

EXCHANGE ST

CEDAR STREET

MINNESOTA STREET

ROBERT STREET

JACKSON STREET

SIBLEY STREET

Cathedral of St Paul

SELBY AVENUE

W 9TH ST

Children's Museum

Park Square Theatre

WABASHA ST

Town Square Park

Galtier Plaza

7TH PLACE

7TH STREET

James J. Hill House

SUMMIT AVENUE

Landmark Center

Ordway Music Theater

W 5TH ST

Rice Park

MARKET ST

The Saint Paul Hotel

KELLOGG BOULEVARD

Xcel Energy Center

W 3RD ST

City Hall & Courthouse

35E

WALNUT ST

Science Museum of Minnesota

SHEPARD ROAD

Alexander Ramsey House

GRAND AVENUE

S EXCHANGE ST

CHESTNUT ST

Irvine Park

Mississippi River

WABASHA STREET

0   400 yds

The Covington Inn

A well-preserved five-mile Victorian boulevard, Summit Avenue, leads away from downtown. **F. Scott Fitzgerald**, who was born close by, finished his first success, *This Side of Paradise*, in 1918 while living in a modest row house at no. 599. He disparaged the avenue as a "museum of American architectural failures." Look for the coffin atop no. 465, once the home of an undertaker, and visit the **James J. Hill House** at no. 240, a railroad baron's sumptuous mansion from around 1891 (tours every half-hour Wed–Sat 10am–3.30pm; $6; reservations recommended; ☎651/297-2555). Minnesota's first territorial governor **Alexander Ramsey**'s house, nearby at 265 S Exchange St, in the fashionable Irvine Park district, remains a showcase of Victorian high style (tours on the hour Fri & Sat 10am–3pm; $6; ☎651/296-8760).

The costumed staff does a fine job of interpreting Minnesota's frontier past at **Fort Snelling** (May–Oct Mon–Sat 10am–5pm, Sun noon–5pm; $6; ☎612/726-1171), near the airport off highways 5 and 55. Built between 1819 and 1825 on a strategic bluff at the confluence of the Mississippi and Minnesota rivers, this was Minnesota's first permanent structure – a successful attempt by the US government to establish an official presence in the wilderness that had recently been won from Great Britain. Another good bet is the venerable and picturesque **Como Park Zoo and Conservatory**, reached by taking I-94 to the Lexington Avenue exit, then continuing north on Lexington for about three miles (daily: summer 10am–6pm; rest of year 10am–4pm; free; ☎631/487-8200). Farther afield, in suburban Apple Valley, off Hwy-775 (take bus #77Z from the Mall of America), is the spacious, highly regarded **Minnesota Zoo** (May–Sept Mon–Sat 9am–6pm, Sun 9am–8pm; Oct–April daily 9am–4pm; $11, $3 parking fee; ☎951/431-9500, ⓦwww.mnzoo.org), where the animals reside in reconstructions of their natural habitats. The Komodo dragon exhibit, Imation IMAX Theater, and Discovery Bay aquatic center, in particular, are outstanding.

Annual celebrations in St Paul include a beanfeast called **Taste of Minnesota** (tons of food, live entertainment, rides, and fireworks) running from late June to July 4 on Harriet Island and the nation's largest **State Fair** (end of Aug to early Sept). The **Winter Carnival** (late Jan to early Feb) is a frosty gala designed to make the most of the season with ice and snow sculpturing, hot-air ballooning, team sports, parades, and more. Perhaps, though, the longest-running celebration here is **Hockey Season** – in the months outside summer. The Twin Cities finally have a pro hockey squad again – the Minnesota Wild – and the Xcel Energy Center, 317 Washington St (☎651/222-9543, ⓦwww.wild.com), is testament to the sport's importance round these parts.

The Mall of America

Shopping addicts make the pilgrimage to the **Mall of America** from all over the Midwest – and far beyond, including parties from as far away as Japan. Opened in 1992, this mind-boggling 4.2-million-square-foot, four-story monument to squeaky-clean consumerism has fast become the country's most-visited destination, tallying 42 million visits in a recent year. The futuristic superstructure contains twice as much steel as the Eiffel Tower, and there's enough room to play a week's NFL games side by side. It incorporates more than five hundred stores, with a seven-acre theme park – the pay-per-ride Camp Snoopy. Featured rides include **UnderWater Adventures** ($14), with 1.2 million gallons of water and amazing Gulf of Mexico and Caribbean aquariums; and **NASCAR Silicon Motor Speedway** ($9), which offers simulated stock-car racing. There's also a comedy club, several dance and music bars, a multiscreen cinema, a bowling alley, and a vast array of eateries. *Café Odyssey*, the latest in "diner-tainment," serves international foods in global and mythological settings. The science and educational store **Brainstorms**, the custom-made **Basic Brown Bear Factory** (where you can custom-design a cuddly ursine companion), **Lake Wobegon USA** (an eclectic gift store inspired by folksy Minnesota humorist Garrison Keillor's fictional community), and the hands-on demonstrations at **Oshman's Super Sports USA** are the highlights of a tour. Evidence of the Mall's all-under-one-roof convenience is provided by the **Chapel of Love** retail store, where more than 1500 couples have legitimately tied the knot. The mall is open Monday through Friday 10am–9.30pm, Saturday 9.30am–9.30pm, and Sunday 11am–7pm (☎952/883-8800, ⓦwww .mallofamerica.com).

The Mall is twenty minutes south of the cities on I-494 at 24th Avenue, Bloomington. Take bus #54M from St Paul's West Sixth Street (between Jackson and Kellogg) or #80AB, #5E, #7DEF, or #19EFG from various loca-

△ The Mall of America, Bloomington, Minnesota

tions in downtown Minneapolis. For the #80 bus, head to Nicollet Mall between Third and Twelfth streets, from where they run every twenty minutes. All buses and taxis drop off at the Transit station on the lower level of the East parking ramp. Buses also run between the mall and the airport every thirty minutes. Taxis between the mall and the cities range from $20–25. Some high-end hotels run shuttles to and from the mall. Check with them directly, as their service changes often.

Eating

Preconceptions of Midwestern blandness are swiftly put to rest by an almost bewildering array of **restaurants** in the Twin Cities. In **Minneapolis**, head for the downtown warehouse district, the southerly Nicollet neighborhood, the funky Uptown, and Lyn–Lake areas, or the university's Dinkytown. In **St Paul**, try Galtier Plaza downtown, the Asian restaurants on University Avenue, or the horde of ethnic options all along Grand Avenue. Of the **local chains**, *Lotus* serves budget Vietnamese meals, *LeeAnn Chin* has adequate Chinese cuisine, while *Keys* offers great breakfasts and fresh lunches. Be sure to sample **wild rice**, a Minnesota specialty.

Minneapolis

Broder's Cucina Italiana 2308 W 50th St ☎612/925-3113. Terrific deli offering eat-in or take-out, with a full-service restaurant across the street.

Buca di Beppo 1204 Harmon Place ☎612/288-0138. This irresistibly festive Italian restaurant dishes out massive portions. There's another branch in St Paul.

Café Brenda 300 1st Ave N ☎612/342-9230. Excellent, moderately priced *nouvelle* vegetarian cuisine in the downtown warehouse district.

Café Havana 1119 N Washington Ave ☎612/338-8484. This Cuban addition to the trendy warehouse district offers classy decor, music, and excellent – though pricey – food.

Chez Bananas 129 N 4th St ☎612/340-0032. Order spicy, Caribbean-influenced food, and play with the toys provided at the tables while you wait.

Emily's Lebanese Deli 641 University Ave NE ☎612/379-4069. Friendly, low-cost local place for Lebanese staples.

Goodfellows 40 S 7th St ☎612/332-4800. Award-winning and expensive American cuisine served in a posh setting.

Modern Café 337 13th Ave NE ☎612/378-9882. Eclectic, cheap, and flavorsome food in a former neighborhood diner gone hip.

Monte Carlo 219 N 3rd Ave ☎612/333-5900. Locals swear by this century-old steak-house. Expect to pay close to $20 for an entree.

Palomino 825 Hennepin Ave ☎612/339-3800. This stylish, popular downtown bistro specializes in Mediterranean fare.

Pizza Luce 119 N 4th St ☎612/333-7359. The decor is no-frills, the staff hip, and the pizza excellent.

Peter's Grill 114 S 8th St ☎612/333-1981. This downtown lunch/early dinner institution is old-style, uncomplicated, and quintessentially American. Past diners have included President Clinton.

Sawatdee 607 Washington Ave S ☎612/373-0840. The delicious Thai food is always well pre-pared, with main courses ranging from $8 to $15. There are several branches in the Twin Cities.

St Paul

Mickey's Dining Car 36 W 7th St ☎651/698-0259. Landmark 24hr diner in a 1930s dining car.

Moscow on the Hill 371 Selby Ave ☎651/291-1236. Exquisite Russo-European food served up in a modest ambiance.

St Paul Grill 350 Market St ☎651/292-9292. Traditional American fare in a classic downtown hotel.

Taste of Scandinavia 75 W 5th St ☎651/222-1100. Delicious, authentic Scandinavian lunches and daytime snacks served cafeteria-style in Landmark Center – the most central of the chain's three locations.

Trattoria DaVinci 400 Sibley St ☎651/222-4050. Exceptional Northern Italian cuisine served in an Italian Renaissance–inspired setting.

W.A. Frost Selby and Western aves ☎651/224-5715. This former pharmacy and F. Scott Fitzgerald hangout has been converted into a plush restaurant with garden patio. The menu spans Mediterranean, Asian, and Middle Eastern cuisines, and the wine cellar stocks some 3000 bottles.

Entertainment and nightlife

The Greater Twin Cities have been dubbed a "cultural Eden on the prairie," where 2.5 million people support upwards of one hundred **theater** companies, more than forty **dance** troupes, twenty **classical music** ensembles, and more than a hundred art galleries. Sir Tyrone Guthrie began the theatrical boom back in 1963, enrolling large-scale local assistance to establish the classical repertory company named for him. The Guthrie Theater is at 725 Vineland Place, in Minneapolis (☎612/377-2224 or 1–877/44STAGE, ⓦwww .guthrietheater.org). The cities now have more theaters per capita than anywhere in the US apart from New York City.

Unusually, **nightlife** in Minneapolis (and, to a lesser extent, St Paul) hasn't been siphoned off by suburbia – one hundred thousand students ensure a vibrant club scene. Before the Seattle music explosion in the 1990s, Minneapolis natives Bob Mould and Paul Westerberg pioneered the grunge sound with their seminal bands **Hüsker Dü** and **The Replacements**. The city still churns out great guitar bands like **Soul Asylum**, while erstwhile **Prince Rogers Nelson** continues to noodle in his multimedia Paisley Park studio in suburban Chanhassen. For complete entertainment **information and listings**, check out the ubiquitous free weekly *City Pages*. *Lavender* and *focusPOINT* provide a similar service from a lesbian and gay perspective.

Minneapolis and St Paul theaters

Bryant-Lake Bowl Theatre 810 W Lake St, Minneapolis ☎612/825-3737, ⓦwww.bryantlake-bowl.com. Theatre performances, bowling alley, café, and bar all under one funky roof.

Chanhassen Dinner Theater 521 W 78th St, Chanhassen ☎952/934-1525 or 1-800/362-3515. Mainstream musicals, popular comedies, and drama on four stages, plus meals. Thirty minutes from downtown.

Dudley Riggs' Theatres 1430 Washington Ave S, Minneapolis ☎612/332-6620. The oldest of the local satirical comedy troupes.

Fitzgerald Theater 10 E Exchange St, St Paul ☎651/290-1221, ⓦwww.fitzgeraldtheater.org. Best known as the venue for Garrison Keillor's weekly *A Prairie Home Companion* performance, it also hosts other concerts and lectures.

Great American History Theater 30 E 10th St, St Paul ☎612/292-4323. Original plays deal with events and personalities from the region's past.

Jungle Theater 2951 Lindell Ave S, Minneapolis ☎612/822-7063, ⓦwww.jungletheater.com. Theater/cabaret putting on an eclectic mix of classic and contemporary plays.

Park Square 408 St Peter St, St Paul ☎651/291-7005, ⓦwww.parksquaretheater.org. The venue for well-executed classic and contemporary plays.

Penumbra 270 N Kent St, St Paul ☎651/224-3180, ⓦwww.penumbratheatre.org. African-American theater company focusing on works by African-American playwrights.

Red Eye Collaboration 15 W 14th St, Minneapolis ☎612/870-0309. Arts center dedicated to experimental theater, as well as dance, film, and music. s

Theatre de la Jeune Lune 1st St and 1st Ave, Minneapolis ☎612/332-3986, ⓦwww.jeunelune.org. A unique ensemble of Parisians and Minneapolitans offer dynamic, highly physical productions based on commedia dell'arte, vaudeville, and the like.

Minneapolis bars and clubs

Figlio Calhoun Square, 3001 Hennepin Ave ☎612/822-1688. Top late-night dining and people-watching venue, with a menu featuring Italian staples.

Fine Line 318 1st Ave ☎612/338-8100. Sleek, small, and musically eclectic downtown club.

First Avenue and 7th St Entry 701 1st Ave ☎612/338-8388 or 332-1775, ⓦwww.first-avenue.com. The landmark rock venue where Prince's *Purple Rain* was shot still packs them in with top bands and dance music.

Gay 90s 408 Hennepin Ave S ☎612/333-7755. This sprawling, predominantly gay club has two dance floors, a piano lounge, dining, and polished weekend drag shows.

Ground Zero 15 NE 4th St ☎612/378-5115. The mixed clientele come here for the great space, varied themes, Gothic influences, and occasional fetish nights.

Kieran's Irish Pub 330 2nd Ave S ☎612/339-4499. A downtown pub with a friendly atmosphere built round good food, drink, music, and poetry readings.

Loon Café 500 1st Ave N ☎612/332-8342. Try the chili at this noisy, likeable sports bar, which offers great food.

Loring Café Bar & Playhouse 1624 Harmon Place ☎612/338-6258 or 332-1617. Beautiful people with attitude drink, dine, or drift upstairs to the dance/theater Playhouse.

New French Café & Bar 128 N 4th St ☎612/338-3790. Cozy warehouse district mainstay with French and Mediterranean food.

Nye's Polonaise Room 112 E Hennepin Ave ☎612/379-2021. Experience old-time atmosphere at the piano and polka bars, and in the Polish-American restaurant.

Quest 110 N 5th St ☎612/338-3383, ⓦwww.thequestclub.com. State-of-the-art dance club, with live acts. Dress flash.

St Paul bars and clubs

The Dakota Bar and Grill 1021 Bandana Blvd ☎651/642-1442, ⓦwww.dakotacooks.com. Gourmet Midwestern food and great local and national jazz acts in a converted shopping mall location.

Gallivan's 354 Wabasha St ☎651/227-6688. This downtown white-collar pub, one of St Paul's oldest bars, has a comfortable neighborhood feel.

McGovern's 225 W 7th St ☎651/224-5821. A quintessential Irish pub where you're likely to strike up some decent conversation.

O'Gara's Bar and Grill 164 N Snelling Ave ☎651/644-3333, ⓦwww.ogaras.com. Dimly lit bar/restaurant with its own handcrafted beers. Draws a mixed clientele and hosts live bands in the adjoining *Garage*.

Tom Reid's Hockey City Pub 258 W 7th St ☎651/292-9916. This pre- and post-game hangout is where locals gather to honor the state's favorite sport.

Town House 1415 University Ave ☎651/646-7087. Gay/lesbian bar with dance, drag, and C&W nights, plus a piano lounge.

Northern Minnesota

Minnesota's substantial **northern** half, covered with forested lakes, remains much as it was when the Europeans first traded with the Indians. The northeast – **the Arrowhead**, poking into Lake Superior – holds the greatest charm: most visitors choose secluded outdoor vacations centered on fishing, canoeing, and snowmobiling, but there's infinite potential for driving tours in a wilderness comparable to the Alaskan interior.

The Arrowhead is anchored by busy **Duluth**. From here, **Scenic Hwy-61** skirts the clifftops around Lake Superior, passing waterfalls, state parks, and neat little towns on the way northeast to the Canadian border. Sleepy **Grand Marais** is poised at the edge of the wild **Boundary Waters Canoe Area Wilderness** and the **Gunflint Trail**, while inland, the **Iron Range** makes a scenic route north to the idyllic **Voyageurs National Park**. To the southwest, in **Itasca State Park**, the Mississippi River begins its great roll down to the Gulf of Mexico; you can cross the headwaters on stepping-stones. Everywhere you'll find campgrounds and mom-and-pop lakeside **resorts**, havens of homey simplicity dedicated to soothing urban-ravaged souls.

Duluth

DULUTH, at the western extremity of Lake Superior, 150 miles north of Minneapolis and St Paul, forms a long crescent at the base of the Arrowhead. Named for a seventeenth-century French officer, Daniel Greysolon, Sieur du Lhut, the town cascades down from the granite bluffs surrounding **Skyline Drive** (an exhilarating thirty-mile route) to a busy **harbor**, shared with Superior, Wisconsin. Together these "twin ports" constitute the largest inland harbor in the US. Originally the main cargo was fur; now it ships grain, lumber, and ore to the Atlantic via the St Lawrence Seaway.

In the 1980s, Duluth had a face-lift and began to encourage tourism. The main drawback is that it's **cold** here. The seaway is frozen through the winter, and even spring and fall evenings can be chilly. Temperatures are always significantly cooler near the lake – as fate would have it, the location of nearly all the attractions and activities.

From the Convention and Visitors Bureau (see below), a short walk down Lake Avenue leads to the free **Marine Museum** (June to early Sept daily 10am–9pm; rest of year times vary; ☎218/727-2497, ⓦwww.lsmma.com) in Canal Park, a vantage point for watching big boats from around the world pass under the delightfully archaic Aerial Lift Bridge. Originating at Canal Park, Duluth's **Lakewalk** is the free way to take in the view, though in summer you can also take 2hr **harbor cruises** ($9.75; ☎218/722-6218, ⓦwww.vistafleet.com). Also worthwhile is a visit to the stately lakeside Jacobean Revival mansion **Glensheen**, 3300 London Rd (May–Oct daily 9.30am–4pm; Nov–April Fri–Sun 11am–2pm; $10; reservations required on ☎218/726-8910 or 1-888/454-GLEN). The vast interior features finely crafted original furnishings, and the grounds are immaculate.

Rail excursions along the Superior shoreline to the busy harbor community **Two Harbors** run from **The Depot** complex at 506 W Michigan St (mid-May to mid-Oct; $9.50 for 90min, $18 for 6hr; ☎218/722-1273 or 1-800/423-1273, ⓦwww.lsrm.org). The Depot (summer 9.30am–6pm; winter 10am–5pm; $8.50) also houses the Lake Superior Railroad Museum, a children's museum, cultural heritage center, and art museum; at night, it's home to performing arts companies. From the parking lot at Grand Avenue and 71st Avenue W, across from the zoo, the historic **Lake Superior and Mississippi Railroad** takes a 90min journey along the scenic St Louis River (mid-June to early Oct Sat & Sun 10.30am & 1.30pm; $7; ☎218/624-7549, ⓦwww.lsmrr .org). Duluth's Spirit Mountain **ski area** (☎1-800/642-6377, ⓦwww.spiritmt .com) boasts the best downhill runs in the Midwest.

Practicalities

Greyhound **buses** pull into town four miles south of town just off I-35 at 4426 Grand Ave. The **Convention and Visitors Bureau** is at 100 Lake Place Drive (☎218/722-4011 or 1-800/4-DULUTH, ⓦwww.visitduluth.com). For a **place to stay**, the *Charles Weiss Inn*, 1615 E Superior St (☎218/724-7016 or 1-800/525-5243; ❺), is a nice Victorian-styled **B&B**, while better **motels** include the *Best Western Edgewater East*, 2400 London Rd (☎218/728-3601 or 1-800/777-7925; ❹), which has a good pool, and the central *Canal Park Inn*, 250 Canal Park Drive (☎218/727-8821 or 1-800/777-8560; ❹). Keep in mind that accommodation rates and availability fluctuate in summer. *Indian Point* **campground**, west off Hwy-23 at 75th Street and Grand Avenue (☎218/624-5637; ❶), has summer bayside tent sites for $15; full hook-ups are also available.

The Italian-American **food** at *Grandma's Saloon And Deli*, in view of the bridge at 522 Lake Ave S (☎218/727-4192), is not for dieters. *Grandma's Sports Garden*, across a parking lot at no. 425 (☎218/722-4724), is similarly convivial, dishing up tasty food when not functioning as either dance floor or (bizarrely) a basketball court. Best of all are the revolving *Top of the Harbor*, serving American cuisine atop the *Radisson Hotel* at 505 W Superior St (☎218/727-8981), and the lovely *Bennett's on the Lake*, 600 E Superior St (☎218/722-2829), where you can dine on steaks and seafood with a superb view of the lake.

North from Duluth: Highway 61

Memorialized on vinyl by Minnesota native Bob Dylan, stunning **Scenic**

Highway 61 follows Lake Superior for 150 miles northeast from Duluth to the US/Canadian border, its precipitous cliffs interspersed with pretty little ports and picture-postcard picnic sites.

At **Gooseberry River State Park**, forty miles along from Duluth, the river splashes over volcanic rock through waterfalls and cascades to its outlet in Lake Superior. Like all but one of the seven other state parks along Hwy-61, it provides access to the rugged three-hundred-mile **Superior Hiking Trail**, divided into easily manageable segments for day-trekkers. To camp at any of the state parks, reserve at ☎218/834-2700 or 1-800/246-CAMP.

Just beyond **Cascade River State Park**, the road dips into the somnolent little port of **GRAND MARAIS**, where a walk around the photogenic Circular Harbor will soon cure car-stiff legs. The **visitor center**, 13 N Broadway (☎218/387-2524 or 1-888/922-5000, Ⓦ www.grandmarais.com), has lists of **outfitters** for those going into the Boundary Waters Canoe Area Wilderness (see below). An inexpensive **room** option is the ultra-clean *Sandgren Motel* on Hwy-61 (☎218/387-2975 or 1-800/796-2975; ❸), while *Naniboujou Lodge*, fifteen miles further east (☎218/387-2688, Ⓦ www.naniboujou.com; ❺), is a bit pricier, but worth dropping by just to see the restaurant's eye-popping Cree Indian designs. For the best view and hospitality there's *Jägerhaus*, a German-style B&B just north of Grand Marais on Country Road 14 (☎218/387-1476 or 1-877/387-1476, Ⓦ www.jagerhaus.com; ❺); the Superior Hiking Trail runs through the inn's driveway. Fifty-eight miles inland from Grand Marais, the *Spirit of the Land Island Hostel*, on an island in Seagull Lake (☎218/388-2241 or 1-800/454-2922; ❶), has bunks for $17–19 ($2 extra for nonmembers). For herring and imported beer, or just a well-priced **snack**, head for *Sven & Ole's Pizza*, 9 W Wisconsin St, in Grand Marais (☎218/387-1713).

The town of **GRAND PORTAGE**, just below the Canadian border, is at the lake end of the historic 8.5-mile portage route – so vital to the nineteenth-century fur trade – now preserved in the form of Grand Portage National Monument, where a clutch of fur-trade era buildings has been superbly reconstructed (summer daily 9am–5pm; ☎218/387-2788). In town, residents of the Grand Portage Indian Reservation operate a **casino**. In summer, ferries run daily to remote **Isle Royale National Park** (see p.349).

The Boundary Waters Canoe Area Wilderness and the Gunflint Trail

The huge **Boundary Waters Canoe Area Wilderness**, west of Grand Marais, is one of the most heavily used wilderness areas in the country. It is also accessible from Tofte, Cook, and especially from easygoing **Ely**, home of the intriguing **International Wolf Center** (May–Oct daily 9am–5pm; Nov–April Fri–Sun 10am–5pm; $5.50). During a "wind throw" in 1999, 90mph winds blew down over 30 million trees, damaging campsites, portages, and trails. For the next several years, some travel routes and entry points may be closed during prescribed burns of the fallen trees. Otherwise, the wilderness is a paradise for canoeing, backpacking, and fishing. Overland trails, or "portages," link more than a thousand lakes; in winter you can ski and dogsled cross-country. The unpaved sixty-mile **Gunflint Trail** from Grand Marais cuts the wilderness in two; otherwise there are no roads in this outback, let alone electricity or telephones. Most lakes remain motor-free, and stringent rules limit entry to the wilderness: in summer you need a date-specific **permit** that local outfitters can issue. For the following year, permit applications may be submitted by website, fax, or mail beginning November 1; in January, they are processed by lottery. Phone reservations are accepted beginning February 1 ($12 reservation fee and a $20 deposit; ☎218/365-7561 or 1-800/745-3399, ℉218/884-9951, ⓦwww.bwcaw.org). For those who don't want to rough it, several rustic lodges lie strung out along the trail; the **Gunflint Trail Association** (☎218/387-2870 or 1-800/338-6932, ⓦwww.gunflint-trail.com) can offer good advice.

The Iron Range

In the **Iron Range**, a few miles west of Ely, which is itself about one hundred miles west of Grand Marais, a number of fabulously rich mines continue to function more than a century after their construction. If you're interested in surveying old workings, it's possible to descend 2300ft at the **Soudan Underground Mine State Park** on Hwy-169 (summer daily 10am–4pm; $6, plus $4 vehicle fee).

Seventy miles southwest on Hwy-169 in **Chisholm**, the **Ironworld USA** cultural theme park (June 11 to Sept 12 9.30am–5pm; $7) turns ecological disaster into tourist spectacle, inviting you on a trolley ride to see "the scenic wonder of an open-pit mine." Further opportunities to view such wonders (this time for free) occur during the ten-minute drive to **Hibbing** – a plain little community, of interest mainly as the birthplace of Bob Dylan (born Robert Zimmerman) in 1941. Oddly enough, the museum in City Hall has no exhibits on him.

Extensive strip-mining in the city has created both the largest man-made pit and the largest slag heap in the world. Hibbing was also the home of America's biggest bus company. With the help of model buses and old advertisements the **Greyhound Origin Center**, 1201 Greyhound Blvd (mid-May to end Sept Mon–Sat 9am–5pm; $3), looks back to its roots transporting local miners to and from the pits. The Hull–Rust Mahoning Mine, once the world's largest open-pit iron ore mine, can be toured or viewed from an overlook just past the Center (mid-April to end Sept daily 9am–7pm; free).

Voyageurs National Park

Set along the border lakes between Minnesota and Canada, **VOYAGEURS NATIONAL PARK** is like no other in the US national park system. To see it properly, or indeed to grasp its immense beauty at all, you need to leave your car behind and venture into the wild by boat. Once out on the lakes, you're in a great, silent world. Kingfishers, osprey, and eagles swoop down for their share of the abundant walleye; moose and bear stalk the banks; and sunrises and sunsets inspire poets and photographers.

The park's name comes from the intrepid eighteenth-century French-Canadian trappers, who needed almost a year to get their pelts back to Montréal in primitive birchbark canoes. They paddled for sixteen hours a day, fighting off attacks from Native Americans – and each other. Their "customary waterway" became so established that the treaty of 1783 ending the American Revolution specified it as the international border.

You can't do Voyageurs justice on a day-trip, though daily cruises from the **Rainy Lake visitor center** (early May to late Sept; from $35 for a range of special tours; ⓦwww.nps.gov/voya/vvcenter/rlvc.htm) do at least allow a peek at the lake country. If you're here for a few days, rent a **boat** (reckon on $40 a day) and camp out. It's easy to get lost in this maze of islands and rocky outcrops, and unseen sandbanks lurk beneath the surface. If you're at all unsure, hire a guide from one of the resorts for the first day (around $200 per 8hr day).

During **freeze-up** – usually from December until March – the park takes on a whole new aura, as a prime destination for skiers and snowmobilers (rentals from $120 per day).

The only sizeable nearby community is **International Falls**, at the end of US-53. The name might make it sound attractive, but really it's a messy array of motels, duty-free shops, fast-food joints, and lumber yards; the falls, never more than glorified rapids anyway, were dammed in 1906.

Practicalities

Most travelers access Voyageurs from Hwy-53, which runs northwest from Duluth. After just over one hundred miles, at Orr, Hwy-53 intersects with Rte-23, which runs northeast toward **Crane Lake**, at the eastern end of the park. About 28 and 31 miles past Hwy-53's junction with Rte-23, highways 129 and 122 lead, respectively, to the **visitor centers** at **Ash River** (May–Sept daily 9am–5pm; ☎218/374-3221) and **Kabetogama Lake** (same hours; ☎218/875-2111). Another prime visitor center is at **Rainy Lake**, at the westernmost entrance, 36 miles farther on via International Falls (May–Sept daily 9am–5pm; rest of year times vary; ☎218/286-5258).

Once inside the park, you need to take a few **precautions**. Check (natural) mercury levels in fish before eating them, don't pick wild rice (only Native Americans may do this), be wary of Lyme Disease (a tick-induced gastric illness), boil drinking water, and watch out for bears. Discuss such matters along with customs procedures in case you plan to paddle into Canadian waters, with a ranger before venturing out.

The definitive way to experience the park is to **camp** on one of its many scattered islands, most plentiful around Crane Lake (if you don't have your own boat, cruise operators can drop you off and pick you up at a later date). There are also first-come, first-served state-owned campgrounds on the mainland at Ash River and Woodenfrog, near Kabetogama. However, most visitors stay in one of more than sixty **resorts**. Basically family-run cottages, these usually cater for weekly stays, with all meals, though you can rent rooms nightly. Most popular are those around Kabetogama, such as *Watson's Harmony Beach* (☎218/875-2811, ⓦwww.fishandgame.com/harmonybeach; ❸), a great place for picking up tips on the park; *Arrowhead Lodge* (☎218/875-2141, ⓦwww.arrowheadlodgeresort.com; ❸), well-known for its restaurant; and the basic, cheap, and cheerful *Driftwood Lodge* (☎218/875-3841, ⓦwww.driftwoodlodgeresort.com; ❶). You can make reservations through the Kabetogama Lake Association (☎1-800/524-9085, ⓦwww.kabetogama.com). Resort associations for Crane Lake (☎218/993-2346), Ash River (☎1-800/950-2061), and Rainy Lake/International Falls (☎218/283-9400) can also fix you up with lodgings, including houseboats (usually $1000 and up per week).

Southern Minnesota

Southern Minnesota is split between high plains, timbered ravines, and slow-flowing Mississippi tributaries in the east, and the drier, flatter prairie and checkerboard farmland of the west. In the scenic **southeast**, spared a grinding-down by the last glacial advance, attractive small towns sit along the Mississippi, or on bluffs above it, in the ninety-mile **Hiawatha Valley**. Mississippi shipping helped sustain easygoing communities like Winona, Red Wing, Lake City (where water skiing was invented in about 1922), and Wabasha, all of which share well-preserved old homes and hotels. **Rochester** occupies the rolling farmland to the west.

The agricultural and college center of Northfield, off I-35 thirty miles south of the Twin Cities, annually commemorates the Jesse James gang's foiled attempt to rob the town bank in September 1876. Harmony, almost in Iowa and near Minnesota's largest **Amish colony**; Lanesboro, with a storybook setting on the hillsides of the Root River; and Mantorville have all kept at least one foot in the nineteenth century. Further west, New Prague and New Ulm were prime targets for the beleaguered Sioux during a six-week war with the US government in 1862.

Rochester

The metropolis of **ROCHESTER**, a white-collar community in a rural setting about eighty miles southeast of Minneapolis and St Paul, was settled in the 1850s by migrants from Rochester, New York, as a humble crossroads campground for wagon trains. After a tornado devastated the town in 1883, Dr William Worral Mayo established the huge **Mayo Clinic**, 200 First St SW (℡507/284-2511, ⓦwww.mayohealth.org). Free tours serve as ninety-minute promotions for "the first and largest private group medical practice in the world" (Mon–Fri 10am; art tour Tues–Thurs 1.30pm). You can also tour the sprawling family home, **Mayowood**, 3720 Mayowood Rd southwest of Hwy-52 (May to mid-June Sat & Sun at 1pm, 2pm & 3pm, plus Sat at 11am; mid-June to Oct Tues, Thurs, Sat & Sun same hours; $10; ℡507/282-9447).

Jefferson Union Bus Depot, 405 SW First Ave (℡507/289-4037), is the hub for **bus services**. Rochester Express (℡507/282-8673 or 1-800/479-7824) and Rochester Direct (℡507/280-9270 or 1-800/280-9270) make between eight and eleven van runs daily to the Minneapolis–St Paul International Airport or the Mall of America for $19 one way, $36 roundtrip. Rochester's **visitor center** is at 150 S Broadway (℡507/288-4331 or 1-800/634-8277, ⓦwww.rochestermn.com).

Rochester is rife with chain and budget **accommodation**, especially within the five-block radius of downtown, including the *Kahler Hotel*, 20 SW Second Ave (℡507/282-2581 or 1-800/533-1655, ⓦwww.kahler.com /kahlergrand; ❹). *The Broadstreet Café and Bar*, 300 NW First Ave (℡507/281-2451), a bistro in a renovated warehouse, serves excellent **meals**; there's also live music in the cozy *Redwood Room* downstairs.

Pipestone National Monument

The town of **PIPESTONE**, eight miles east of the South Dakota border, is named for a soft red clay, within the local quartzite, that was used for centuries by Great Plains Indians to make ceremonial calumets, or peace pipes. The quarry site, a gathering place for Native American tribes, is now the **Pipestone National Monument** (daily 8am–5pm, longer on summer weekends; $2). A self-guided **trail** winds from the visitor center through stands of trees, past rock formations and exposed quarry pits and over a creek, complete with picturesque falls.

Pipestone's small **historic district** includes a sleepy county museum and a building with several amusing sandstone gargoyles. Pick up a walking-tour brochure from the town's **visitor center** (℡507/825-3316 or 1-800/336-6125), near the junction of highways 75 and 23. You can **sleep and eat** at the grand old *Calumet Inn*, 104 W Main St (℡507/825-5871 or 1-800/535-7610,

Ⓦwww.calumetinn.com; ❹), though the *Arrow Motel*, Hwy-75 N, is less expensive and adequate (Ⓣ507/825-3331 or 1-888/825-9599; ❷). Each late July to early August the town puts on the nine-day "Song of Hiawatha" **Indian pageant** in an outdoor amphitheater.

From a distance the red rocks at **Blue Mounds State Park**, sloping into a long cliff a few miles north of the junction of I-90 and US-75 at Luverne, create a great hump that appeared blue at sunset to approaching pioneers. Twice a year, at the equinoxes, the sun lines up with a curious 1250ft row of rocks, aligned on an east–west axis. There are seasonal **campgrounds** (Ⓣ1-800/246-CAMP) and a permanent small herd of buffalo in the park. Call the same number for camping in picturesque **Split Rock Creek State Park**, only seven miles south of Pipestone and the site of a dam dating from 1935.

The Capital Region

CANADA

WASHINGTON · MONTANA · NORTH DAKOTA · MN · MI · ME · VT · NH
OREGON · (14) · (11) · SOUTH DAKOTA · WI · (4) · MI · NEW YORK · (3) · MA
IDAHO · WYOMING · · · · (2) · RI
NEVADA · · NEBRASKA · IOWA · · OHIO · PA · CT
· UTAH · COLORADO · (10) · IL · IN · · · NJ
(13) · · · KANSAS · · WV · (5) · VA · DE
CALIFORNIA · (12) · · MISSOURI · KENTUCKY · · MD
· · NEW MEXICO · OKLAHOMA · · TENNESSEE · NC
PACIFIC OCEAN · ARIZONA · · AR · · SC · ATLANTIC OCEAN
· · · MS · AL · (6) · GEORGIA
· MEXICO · (9) · (8) · · N
(15) · HAWAII · TEXAS · LA · Gulf of Mexico · (7) · FL
ALASKA · (16)

AL - ALABAMA	IN - INDIANA	MN - MINNESOTA	RI - RHODE ISLAND
AR - ARKANSAS	LA - LOUISIANA	MS - MISSISSIPPI	SC - SOUTH CAROLINA
CT - CONNECTICUT	MA - MASSACHUSETTS	NC - NORTH CAROLINA	VA - VIRGINIA
DE - DELAWARE	MD - MARYLAND	NH - NEW HAMPSHIRE	VT - VERMONT
FL - FLORIDA	ME - MAINE	NJ - NEW JERSEY	WI - WISCONSIN
IL - ILLINOIS	MI - MICHIGAN	PA - PENNSYLVANIA	WV - WEST VIRGINIA

CHAPTER 5

Highlights

* **Adams–Morgan and Georgetown, Washington, DC** The best neighborhoods in which to discover that DC isn't all monuments, memorials, and museums. See p.442

* **National Air and Space Museum, Washington, DC** Soaring planes and real-life spacecraft make this the most popular of DC's Smithsonian Institution museums. See p.430

* **Colonial Williamsburg, VA** As good an insight as you could hope for into pre-Independence British America, apothecaries and all. See p.456

* **Charlottesville, VA** See Thomas Jefferson's architectural imprint and then head off into the Blue Ridge Mountains on gorgeous Skyline Drive. See p.464

* **Seneca Rocks, WV** These 1000ft limestone cliffs are just one of the highlights of the pristine Monongahela National Forest. See p.475

* **Cape Henlopen State Park, DE** With rolling sand dunes backed by pine forest, the park makes a fine base to enjoy the coast away from the more frenetic resorts. See p.503

The Capital Region

The city of **Washington, DC**, and the four states of **Virginia**, **West Virginia**, **Maryland**, and **Delaware** – collectively known as the **CAPITAL REGION** – constitute a cross-section of the nation. Since the days of the first American colonies, US history has been shaped here, from agitation toward independence to the battles of the Revolutionary and Civil wars. Now, the contrasts and incongruities of contemporary America are shown in high relief: the corridors of power in Washington are literally a stone's throw away from dire inner-city poverty while, nearby, dozens of time-worn farming and fishing towns seem straight out of some Norman Rockwell idyll.

Early in the seventeenth century, the first British settlements began to take root along the rich estuary of the **Chesapeake Bay**; the colonists hoped for gold, but found their fortunes growing tobacco. Virginia, the first settlement, was the largest and most populous; it originally included most of what are now Kentucky, Tennessee, and Ohio, and as late as the 1790s had double the population of any other state. Fully half of these people were **slaves**, brought from Africa to do the backbreaking work of harvesting the tobacco. Despite its central position on the East Coast, the whole region lies below the Mason-Dixon Line – the symbolic border between North and South, drawn up in 1763 as the boundary between slave and free states – and until the Civil War one of the country's busiest slave markets was just two blocks from the White House.

Besides generating the bulk of Colonial wealth, the region also produced many of early America's great leaders, from firebrand politicians like **Patrick Henry** ("Give me Liberty or Give me Death") to patrician intellectuals such as **Thomas Jefferson**. Another Virginian, **George Washington**, led the Continental Army against the British in the Revolutionary War and served as the first president, while **James Madison** was the primary author of the Constitution.

For all its Colonial importance, by the mid-nineteenth century the region had lost power and status to the industrial and mercantile centers of Philadelphia and New York. Tensions between North and South finally erupted into the **Civil War**, of which traces are still visible everywhere. The hundred miles between the capital of the Union – Washington, DC – and that of the Confederacy – Richmond, Virginia – were a constant and bloody battleground for four long years. This sense of a nation divided against itself is especially acute at the grand manor of **Robert E. Lee**, the Confederacy's military leader: high on a hill overlooking the heart of Washington, DC, its grounds are now filled with the war dead of the Arlington National Cemetery.

Washington, DC, itself, with its magnificent monumental architecture, is an

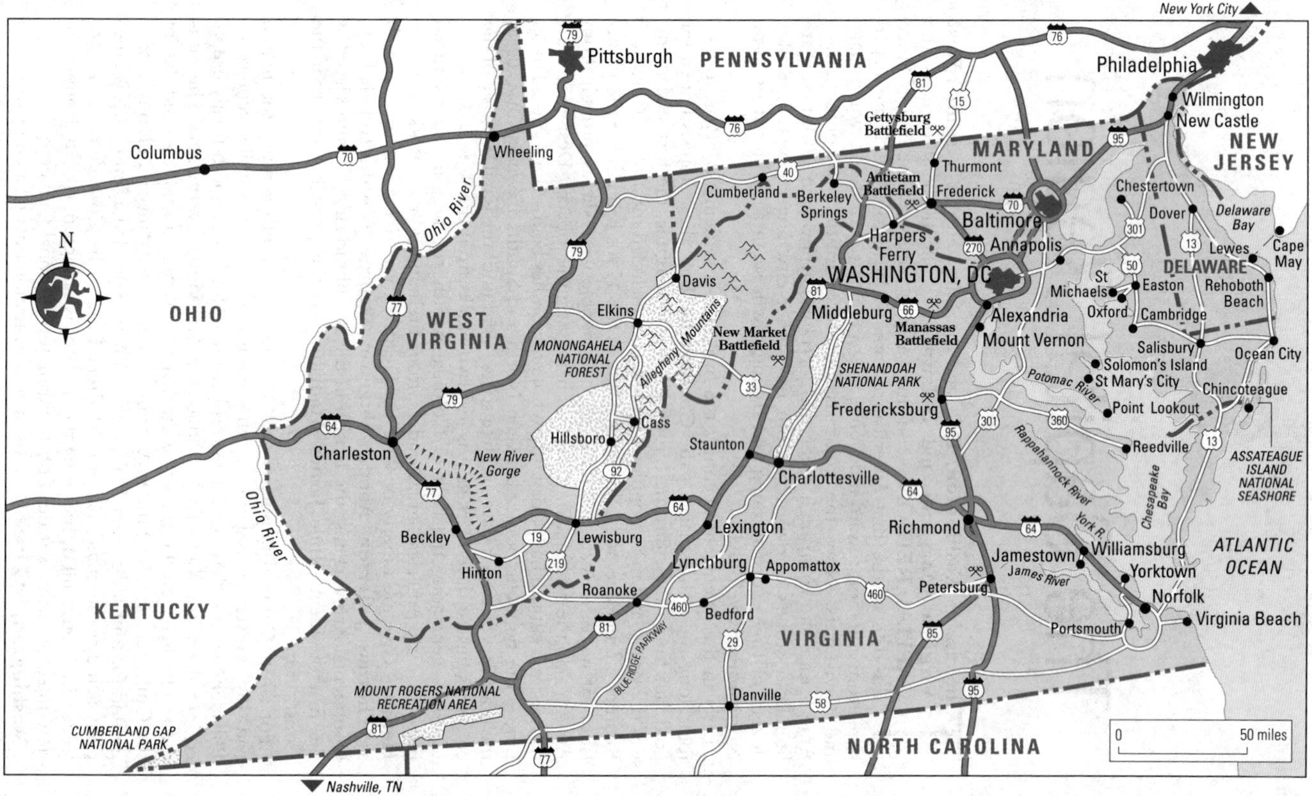
New York City
Philadelphia
Wilmington
New Castle
NEW JERSEY
Pittsburgh
PENNSYLVANIA
Gettysburg Battlefield
MARYLAND
Thurmont
Columbus
Wheeling
Cumberland
Berkeley Springs
Antietam Battlefield
Frederick
Baltimore
Chestertown
Dover
Delaware Bay
Lewes
Cape May
DELAWARE
Ohio River
Harpers Ferry
Annapolis
WASHINGTON, DC
St Michaels
Easton
Rehoboth Beach
Oxford
Cambridge
Davis
Elkins
Allegheny Mountains
New Market Battlefield
Middleburg
Manassas Battlefield
Alexandria
Mount Vernon
Salisbury
Ocean City
OHIO
WEST VIRGINIA
MONONGAHELA NATIONAL FOREST
SHENANDOAH NATIONAL PARK
Solomon's Island
St Mary's City
Potomac River
Chincoteague
Fredericksburg
Point Lookout
Cass
Hillsboro
Staunton
Charleston
New River Gorge
Charlottesville
Rappahannock River
Reedville
ASSATEAGUE ISLAND NATIONAL SEASHORE
Chesapeake Bay
York R.
Beckley
Lewisburg
Lexington
Richmond
Williamsburg
ATLANTIC OCEAN
Hinton
Lynchburg
Appomattox
Jamestown
James River
Yorktown
Roanoke
Petersburg
Norfolk
KENTUCKY
Bedford
Virginia Beach
Portsmouth
BLUE RIDGE PARKWAY
VIRGINIA
MOUNT ROGERS NATIONAL RECREATION AREA
Danville
CUMBERLAND GAP NATIONAL PARK
NORTH CAROLINA
0
50 miles
Nashville, TN
N
79
76
81
15
95
70
40
13
301
270
50
77
66
33
360
64
92
19
219
460
29
85
58

essential stop on any tour of the region. **Virginia**, to the south, holds literally hundreds of historic sites, from the homes of early politicians to the Colonial capital of **Williamsburg**, as well as the narrow forested heights of **Shenandoah National Park**, along the crest of the Blue Ridge Mountains. Much greater expanses of wilderness, crashing white-water rivers, and innumerable backwoods villages await you in less-visited **West Virginia**.

Most tourists come to **Maryland** for the maritime traditions of Chesapeake Bay – though many of its quaint old villages have been gentrified by weekend pleasure-boaters. **Baltimore** is full of character and enjoyably unpretentious (and has a phenomenal concentration of bars), while **Annapolis**, the pleasant state capital, is linked by bridge and ferry to the Eastern Shore, where **Assateague Island** remains an Atlantic paradise. **New Castle**, across the border in **Delaware**, is a perfectly preserved Colonial-era town; nearby are some of the East Coast's best and least crowded beaches.

Washington, DC

That the marshy swamp where **WASHINGTON, DC**, now stands was chosen as the site of the **capital** of the newly independent United States of America says a lot about then-prevalent attitudes toward government. Washington, District of Columbia (the boundaries of the two are identical) – also known as "**DC**" and "**The District**" – can be unbearably hot and humid in summer, and bitterly cold in winter. Such an unpleasant climate, it was hoped, would discourage elected leaders from making government a full-time job. This disdain for politics is still apparent: DC is run as a virtual colony of Congress, where residents have only non-voting representation and couldn't vote in presidential elections until the 23rd Amendment was passed in 1961.

Besides the federal government, DC's other big industry is **tourism**, with the city attracting almost twenty million visitors each year. Conveniently, most arrive in midsummer, when the lawmakers have gone home, so overcrowding is rarely a problem. The nation's showcase puts on quite a display for its guests, and admission to virtually all major attractions is free. The most famous sites are concentrated along the central **Mall**, including the White House, individual memorials to four of the greatest presidents, and the superb museums of the Smithsonian Institution. Downtown, however (broadly speaking the area immediately north of the Mall, between the White House and the Capitol), can seem very empty, even intimidating, at night, and you're more likely to spend your evenings in the hotels and restaurants of the city's more vibrant neighborhoods, such as historic **Georgetown**, arty **Dupont Circle**, and the funkier **Adams–Morgan** district.

Some history

The decision to establish the national capital at this spot had much to do with the fact that it lies midway between the rural South and the northern cities of Boston, New York, and Philadelphia (the last, the previous capital, was thought too exciting for a seat of government). It was also accessible from the sea, via the

WASHINGTON, DC

0 500 yds

Ⓜ Metro station

N

KALORAMA RD
ADAMS-MORGAN
COLUMBIA RD
CALIFORNIA STREET
FLORIDA AVENUE

Montrose Park

R STREET
SHERIDAN CIRCLE
S STREET
NEW HAMPSHIRE AVENUE
19TH STREET
18TH STREET
17TH STREET
16TH STREET

Q STREET
DUPONT CIRCLE
SCOTT CIRCLE

GEORGETOWN

P STREET
29
NEW DOWNTOWN
O STREET

N STREET
M STREET

PROSPECT ST
FARRAGUT NORTH
MCPHERSON SQUARE

WHITEHURST FREEWAY
WASHINGTON CIRCLE
K STREET
FARRAGUT WEST
I STREET

Francis Scott Key Memorial Bridge
PENNSYLVANIA AVENUE
VIRGINIA AVENUE
FOGGY BOTTOM-GWU Ⓜ
I STREET
H STREET
The White House

George Washington University
FOGGY BOTTOM
G STREET
F STREET

Potomac River
Theodore Roosevelt Island
Little River
ROCK CREEK AND POTOMAC PKWY

Kennedy Center
E STREET

Ⓜ ROSSLYN
Department of State
C STREET
The Ellipse

Theodore Roosevelt Bridge
CONSTITUTION AVENUE

Arlington National Cemetery
ARLINGTON CEMETERY Ⓜ

Vietnam Veterans Memorial
Constitution Gardens
Washington Monument

Arlington Memorial Bridge
Lincoln Memorial
Korean War Veterans Memorial
Holocaust Museum

INDEPENDENCE AVENUE

FDR Memorial
Bureau of Engraving & Printing

West Potomac Park
Tidal Basin
14th St Bridge

George Mason (14th St) Memorial Bridge

Arlington National Cemetery

ACCOMMODATION

Adams Inn	E
Allen Lee Hotel	T
Brickskeller Inn	K
Bull Moose B&B	W
Carlyle Suites	G
Embassy Inn	I
Four Seasons	O
Harrington Hotel	V
Hay-Adams Hotel	S
HI-Washington DC	R
Kalorama Guest House	B
Monticello	P
Omni Shoreham	A
Simpkins' B&B	J
State Plaza	U
Swiss Inn	Q
Tabard Inn	M
Topaz	N
Washington International Student Center	D
Washington Terrace Hotel	L
The William Lewis House	H
Windsor Inn	F
Woodley Park Guest House	C

Pentagon
Ⓜ PENTAGON
SHIRLEY HIGHWAY
JEFFERSON DAVIS HWY
COLUMBIA PIKE
395

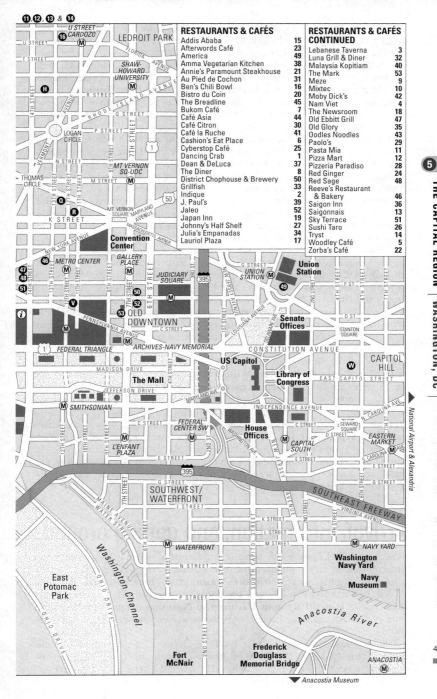

RESTAURANTS & CAFÉS

Addis Ababa	15
Afterwords Café	23
America	49
Amma Vegetarian Kitchen	38
Annie's Paramount Steakhouse	21
Au Pied de Cochon	31
Ben's Chili Bowl	16
Bistro du Coin	20
The Breadline	45
Bukom Café	7
Café Asia	44
Café Citron	30
Café la Ruche	41
Cashion's Eat Place	6
Cyberstop Café	25
Dancing Crab	1
Dean & DeLuca	37
The Diner	8
District Chophouse & Brewery	50
Grillfish	33
Indique	2
J. Paul's	39
Jaleo	52
Japan Inn	19
Johnny's Half Shelf	27
Julia's Empanadas	34
Lauriol Plaza	17

RESTAURANTS & CAFÉS CONTINUED

Lebanese Taverna	3
Luna Grill & Diner	32
Malaysia Kopitiam	40
The Mark	53
Meze	9
Mixtec	10
Moby Dick's	42
Nam Viet	4
The Newsroom	18
Old Ebbitt Grill	47
Old Glory	35
Oodles Noodles	43
Paolo's	29
Pasta Mia	11
Pizza Mart	12
Pizzeria Paradiso	28
Red Ginger	24
Red Sage	48
Reeve's Restaurant & Bakery	46
Saigon Inn	36
Saigonnais	13
Sky Terrace	51
Sushi Taro	26
Tryst	14
Woodley Café	5
Zorba's Café	22

National Airport & Alexandria

Anacostia Museum

Potomac River – a bit too easily so, as demonstrated by the burning and ransacking of the city by the British during the War of 1812. Best of all, the land was cheap – the state of Maryland ceded sovereignty to the federal government, which had to pay only for the individual sites it chose for its buildings. Though the baroque plan of the city was laid out in 1791 – by a Frenchman, **Pierre L'Enfant**, assisted by the black American scientist **Benjamin Banneker** – few buildings were put up, apart from the actual houses of government, until near the end of the century. Charles Dickens, visiting in 1842, found "spacious avenues that begin in nothing and lead nowhere."

After the Civil War, thousands of Southern **blacks** arrived in search of a sanctuary from racial oppression; to some extent, they found one. Segregation was banned in public places, and **Howard University**, the only US institution of higher learning that enrolled black people, was set up in 1867. By the 1870s African-Americans made up more than a third of the 150,000 population, but economic resources were soon stretched to the breaking point. As poverty and squalor worsened, official **segregation** was reintroduced in 1920. Blacks were banned from government buildings – including, in an ironic twist, the Lincoln Memorial – and the jobs they had come to find.

After World War II, the city's economy and population boomed. Although segregation of public facilities was declared illegal in the 1950s, civil rights protests divided the city during the following decade – culminating in the destructive downtown riots of 1968. The city's problems have changed little since: DC has one of the country's highest murder rates, as well as appalling levels of unemployment, illiteracy, and drug abuse. After years of mismanagement by city leaders, a control board appointed by Congress took charge of the city's finances in 1995, in an attempt to turn around the massive budget deficit (which was due in part to a middle-class flight to the suburbs). The city rebounded under the board, which by virtue of its success put itself out of a job in 2001. Power was restored to the mayor, **Anthony Williams**, and the city council. The city's rising fortunes can be seen in lower crime rates, newly paved roads, and a revitalized downtown, where restaurants, cultural happenings, and sports events have begun to attract visitors to areas once overrun by drug dealers.

However, just as things seemed to be getting back on track, terror struck the capital on **September 11, 2001**, when terrorists hijacked a United Airlines jet and crashed it into the Pentagon, killing nearly 200 people, including those on the plane. Security throughout the capital was tightened in the aftermath of the attack and has remained so; it's a good idea to call ahead to individual attractions for the latest details.

Arrival, information, and getting around

Washington, DC, is served by three major **airports**, two on the outskirts and one right in the city center. **Dulles International Airport**, 26 miles west in northern Virginia, and **Baltimore-Washington International Airport** (BWI), halfway between DC and Baltimore, get the majority of the international traffic. **Ronald Reagan Washington National Airport** and its major state-of-the-art terminal, along the Potomac River just west of the Mall, is mostly used by domestic flights.

Taking a **taxi** downtown from BWI or Dulles costs around $50, while SuperShuttle (℡1-800/BLUE-VAN, Ⓦwww.supershuttle.com) offers **door-to-door** service from Dulles (45min; $21) and BWI (1hr; $30). Cheaper are the express **buses** that run every half-hour from both airports to nearby Metro subway stations. From Dulles, take the Washington Flyer Coach Service (☎1-888/WASH-FLY, ⓦwww.washfly.com) to the West Falls Church Metro station (25min; $8). From BWI, take the BWI Express Bus (☎202/637-7000) to Greenbelt Metro station (30min; $2.50). BWI also provides a free shuttle to frequent Amtrak and MARC trains bound for Union Station (30min; $6/$9). National Airport conveniently has its own subway stop and is just a short ride from the city center. A taxi downtown from National costs around $15.

By **train** – from Philadelphia, New York, and Boston – you arrive amid the gleaming malls of bustling **Union Station**, 50 Massachusetts Ave NE, three blocks north of the US Capitol and with a connecting Metro station. Greyhound and other **buses** stop at a modern terminal at 1005 First St NE, in a fairly dodgy part of the city, ten blocks from downtown; take a cab, especially at night, at least as far as Union Station Metro (around $6). **Driving** into DC is a sure way to experience some of the worst traffic on the East Coast – the main I-95 and I-495 freeways circle Washington on the **Beltway** and are jammed eighteen hours a day.

Once in the city, stop at the **DC Chamber of Commerce Visitor Center**, Ronald Reagan Building, 1300 Pennsylvania Ave NW (spring and summer Mon–Fri 8.30am–5.30pm, Sat 9am–4pm; fall and winter Mon–Fri 9am–4.30pm; ☎202/328-4748, ⓦwww.dcvisit.com), which can help with maps, tours, bookings, and citywide information. Look for visitor information desks at the airports and Union Station, too. The **White House Visitor Information Center**, 1450 Pennsylvania Ave NW (daily 7.30am–4pm; ☎202/208-1631), supplies free maps and handy guides to museums and attractions; the most useful is the free *Washington DC Visitors Guide*.

The main **post office** is across from Union Station on Massachusetts Avenue and Capitol Street NE (Mon–Fri 7am–midnight, Sat & Sun 7am–8pm; ☎202/523-2368; zip code 20013).

City transportation

Getting around DC is easy. Most places downtown, including the Mall museums, the major monuments, and the White House, are within walking distance of each other, and an excellent **public transportation** system reaches outlying sights and neighborhoods. The clean, efficient, and still-growing **Metro subway** (☎202/637-7000, ⓦwww.wmata.com) is the envy of other cities; one-way fares start at $1.20, with a slight rush-hour surcharge from 5.30 to 9.30am and from 3 to 7pm. The Metrorail One Day Pass costs $6 and is valid weekdays from 9.30am to closing and weekends from 7am to closing (trains run Mon–Thurs 5.30am–midnight, Fri 5.30am–3am, Sat 7am–3am & Sun 7am–midnight). The standard fare on the more extensive **bus** network is also $1.20. **Taxis** are a good-value alternative, with most cross-town fares ranging from $5 to 15. (Surcharges kick in during peak hours and for each additional passenger.) There are taxi stands at major hotels and transportation terminals (like Union Station), or call Yellow Cab (☎202/544-1212) or Diamond Cab (☎202/387-6200).

Tours

During the day, open-sided **Tourmobiles** (daily 9.30am–4.30pm; ☎202/554-5100, ⓦwww.tourmobile.com) connect the major museums and sites, allowing you to stop for as long as you choose at over twenty different locations. A $20 one-day ticket covers Downtown DC and Arlington Cemetery and allows unlimited free re-boarding; tickets for the seasonal three-hour "twilight tour," which departs from Union Station at 7pm, also cost $20. Tourmobile sells a two-day pass for $30. All tickets can be bought from kiosks at Union Station and Arlington Cemetery or the bus itself.

If you want to **cycle** or **cruise** along the Potomac River or the historic C&O Canal, both Thompson's Boat Center, 2900 Virginia Ave NW at Rock Creek Parkway (daily 8am–6pm; ☎202/333-9543), near the Watergate complex, and Fletcher's Boat House, 4940 Canal Rd NW, two miles farther up the canal towpath (daily 9am–7pm; ☎202/244-0461), rent touring bikes, rowboats, and canoes (bikes $12–25 a day; boats $20–30 a day). You could also get to know the city on a three-hour cycling trip with Bike the Sites Inc ($40 per person including bike and helmet; ☎202/842-BIKE, ⓦwww.bikethesites.com), or call Better Bikes (daily 24hr; ☎202/293-2080), which will deliver rental bikes anywhere in DC ($38–48 a day). In addition, mule-drawn **canal boats**, staffed by costumed National Park Service guides, follow the old C&O Canal from the Georgetown Visitor's Center (1057 Thomas Jefferson St; ☎202/653-5190) on an hour-long narrated cruise (April–Oct; $8). The city's best **walking tours** are led by Anthony S. Pitch ($15; ☎301/294-9514, ⓦwww.dcsightseeing.com), who ambles around Washington neighborhoods on Sunday mornings beginning at 11am.

In general, it's worth calling ahead to major sites for any changes to tour procedures due to heightened **security concerns**.

Accommodation

Most DC **hotels** cater to business travelers and political lobbyists, and during the week are quite expensive. At weekends, however, and throughout July and August, when Congress is in recess, many cut their rates by up to fifty percent – it's always worth asking about special rates. For a list of vacancies, call Washington DC Accommodations (☎202/289-2220 or 1-800/554-2220, ⓦwww.wdcahotels.com), which provides a general hotel reservation and travel planning service.

Similarly, a number of **B&B** agencies offer comfortable doubles starting from around $55–65: try Capitol Reservations (☎202/452-1270 or 1-800/847-4832, ⓦwww.capitolreservations.com) or Bed & Breakfast Ltd (☎413/582-9888 or 1-877/893-3233, ⓦwww.bedandbreakfastdc.com). There's no good **camping** anywhere near DC but, besides the **youth hostel**, the Catholic University (☎202/319-5200, ⓦconferences.cua.edu), Georgetown University (☎202/687-3001, ⓦhousing.georgetown.edu), and George Washington University (☎202/496-6305, ⓦgwired.gwu.edu/cllc/housing) offer **budget rooms** (starting at $25) in summer; these must be arranged well in advance and may have lengthy minimum-stay requirements.

DC in summer is hot and humid, and **air-conditioning** is essential for a good night's rest.

Adams Inn 1744 Lanier Place NW ☎202/745-3600 or 1-800/578-6807, ⓦwww.adamsinn.com. Clean, simply furnished B&B rooms, with and without bath, spread across three adjoining Victorian townhouses on a quiet Woodley Park street. Near the zoo. ❹

Allen Lee Hotel 2224 F St NW ☎202/331-1224 or 1-800/462-0186, ⓦwww.allenleehotel.com. Slightly faded, musty rooms come with clunky air-conditioning, but the hotel is handy and cheap, three blocks from Foggy Bottom–GWU Metro. Worth the extra $10 or so for a private bath. ❸–❹

Brickskeller Inn 1523 22nd St NW ☎202/293-1885, ⓦwww.thebrickskeller.org. Simple rooms, some with private baths, above a raucous late-opening bar near Dupont Circle. ❹

Bull Moose B&B 101 5th St NE ☎202/547-1050 or 1-800/261-2768, ⓦwww.bullmoose-b-and-b.com. This ten-room turreted brick Victorian evokes themes from the life and times of legendary US president and Bull Moose Party founder Teddy Roosevelt. Extras include free continental breakfast, evening sherry, Internet access, and use

5

of a kitchen. Close to Union Station and Capitol South Metro. ❺–❼

Carlyle Suites 1731 New Hampshire Ave NW ☎202/234-3200 or 1-866/468-3532. Art Deco beauty in a surprisingly tranquil street near Dupont Circle. Comfortable self-catering suites with dining areas and small kitchens. Other pluses are a café, parking, and laundry. ❼

Embassy Inn 1627 16th St NW ☎202/234-7800 or 1-800/423-9111. Welcoming inn on a residential side street in Dupont Circle East offering good-value rooms (with attractive weekend rates), free continental breakfast, and an early-evening sherry to speed you on your way. ❹–❺

Four Seasons 2800 Pennsylvania Ave NW ☎202/342-0444 or 1-800/332-3442, ⓦwww .fourseasons.com. DC's most luxurious hotel, a sympathetic modern redbrick at the eastern end of Georgetown, is stuffed with leisure facilities. ❾

Harrington Hotel 436 11th St NW ☎202/628-8140 or 1-800/424-8532, ⓦwww.hotel-harrington.com. Popular with groups, this large, old-fashioned hotel has a great location, between the Capitol and the White House, off Pennsylvania Ave. Mention *Rough Guides* and get ten percent off. ❺

Hay-Adams Hotel 800 16th St NW ☎202/638-6600 or 1-800/424-5054, ⓦwww.hayadams.com. Historic (and very expensive) townhouse hotel overlooking the White House. ❾

HI-Washington DC 1009 11th St NW ☎202/737-2333, ⓦwww.hiwashingtondc.org. Huge (270 beds), clean, and very central hostel four blocks north of Metro Center, with Internet access and no curfew. It may accept members only in busy summer months. Reservations recommended. ❶

Kalorama Guest House 1854 Mintwood Place NW ☎202/667-6369 and 2700 Cathedral Ave NW ☎202/328-0860. Cozy, nicely furnished rooms (no TVs though) in several restored Victorian townhouses at two locations. Rates include breakfast, coffee, and an evening sherry. ❸–❺

Monticello 1075 Thomas Jefferson St NW ☎202/337-0900, ⓦwww.hotelmonticello.com. All-suite hotel nicely located off M Street near the canal towpath in Georgetown. Rates include complimentary breakfast and access to the business center. Ask for discounts on weekends. ❼–❾

Omni Shoreham 2500 Calvert St NW ☎202/234-0700 or 1/800/843-6664, ⓦwww.omnihotels .com. Plush Washington institution, near Woodley Park Metro, that's bursting with history.

State Plaza 2117 E St NW ☎202/861-8200 or 1-800/424-2859, ⓦwww.stateplaza.com, Check out the excellent weekend rates for these spacious suites with fully equipped kitchens, close to Foggy Bottom Metro. ❺–❻

Swiss Inn 1204 Massachusetts Ave NW ☎202/371-1816 or 1-800/955-7947, ⓦwww.theswissinn.com. Friendly townhouse accommodation, four blocks from Metro Center, offering eight air-conditioned rooms with kitchenettes, TV, and bath, plus multilingual hosts, and parking (free at weekends) outside. Reserve well in advance; prices don't get much better downtown. ❸–❹

Tabard Inn 1739 N St NW ☎202/785-1277, ⓦwww.tabardinn.com. Very pleasant small hotel with individually decorated, antique-stocked rooms and a good restaurant, just two blocks from Dupont Circle Metro. Rates, for doubles with shared bath, include breakfast and a pass to the fully equipped YMCA gym nearby. ❺–❻

Topaz 1733 N St NW ☎202/393-3000, ⓦwww.topazhotel.com. A contemporary boutique hotel, a short hop from the Dupont scene, with 99 funky rooms, several of which are outfitted for exercise or yoga. ❻–❽

Washington International Student Center 2451 18th St NW ☎202/667-7681 or 1-800/567-4150. Backpacker accommodation in plain dorms in the heart of Adams–Morgan, with Internet access, lockers, and free pickup from bus and train stations (advance reservation required). Coffee-and-toast breakfast included. A few private rooms also available. ❹

Washington Terrace Hotel 1515 Rhode Island Ave NW ☎202/232-7000 or 1-866/984-6835, ⓦwww.washingtonterracehotel.com. Stylish hotel near the White House, with comfortable suites, great outdoor dining, and an on-site gym. High-speed Internet access available in some rooms. Close to Dupont Circle Metro. ❻–❽

The William Lewis House 1309 R St NW ☎202/462-7574 or 1-800/465-7574, ⓦwww.wlewishous.com. A pair of elegantly decorated townhouses are home to this gay B&B near Logan Circle, with ten antique-filled rooms, all with shared bath, plus a porch and Jacuzzi out back. Reserve in advance. ❹

Windsor Inn 1842 16th St NW ☎202/667-0300 or 1-800/423-9111. Under the same management as the *Embassy Inn*, the *Windsor* is a few blocks farther north, its rooms a shade larger. Includes free continental breakfast and evening sherry with snacks. ❹–❺

Woodley Park Guest House 2647 Woodley Rd NW ☎202/667-0218 or 1-866/667-0218, ⓦwoodleyparkguesthouse.com. Sixteen cozy rooms (the cheapest share facilities) that come with free continental breakfast and cheap parking, too. Close to the zoo, the Metro, and plenty of restaurants. ❹–❺

The City

Because the city was built from scratch, Washington's regular **town plan** is easy to grasp. Centered on Capitol Hill and its governmental monoliths, the District is divided into four **quadrants** – northeast, northwest, southeast, and southwest. Dozens of broad **avenues**, all named after states, run diagonally across a standard grid of **streets**, meeting up at monumental traffic circles like Dupont Circle. North–south streets are numbered, east–west ones are lettered. J Street was intentionally skipped to avoid confusion with I Street, which is often written Eye Street. You won't find X, Y, or Z streets on a map either.

Be sure to note the relevant two-letter code in any **address** (NW, NE, SW, SE), which shows its quadrant; 1600 Pennsylvania Ave NW is a *long* way from 1600 Pennsylvania Ave SE.

Until you get your bearings, stick to the established tourist trail; almost all the most famous sights are on **Capitol Hill** or in the comparatively affluent northwest quarter. To the west of the Capitol, the broad, green **Mall** holds monuments to presidents Washington, Jefferson, Lincoln, and Franklin D. Roosevelt, as well as the **White House**, official home of the current president. Also here are the bulk of the city's many marvelous museums, including the peerless collections of the **Smithsonian Institution**.

However, there is more to Washington than an endless succession of museums and monuments, and it's well worth your time to seek out the many attractive **neighborhoods**. Despite its reputation, most of the city is in surprisingly good shape, with row after row of nineteenth-century brick-fronted houses set along leafy boulevards. Between the Mall and the main spine of **Pennsylvania Avenue** – the route connecting Capitol Hill to the White House – the Neoclassical buildings of the **Federal Triangle** offer a sobering contrast to the rest of the city's neighborhoods. North and east of here, what's known as **Old Downtown** has been revitalized after years of neglect, and now features new plazas, galleries, and restaurants alongside traditional attractions like the FBI Building, Old Post Office, and the theater where Abraham Lincoln was shot. The area around the **MCI Center**, particularly along Seventh Street NW, is fast developing as an entertainment and nightlife scene, with a good selection of bars and restaurants. The oldest area, **Georgetown**, where popular bars and restaurants now line M Street and Wisconsin Avenue above the **Potomac River**, actually precedes the establishment of the District. Georgetown is a fifteen-minute walk from the Foggy Bottom–GWU Metro, but its Federal-era and Victorian townhouses and the towpath along the **C&O Canal** make it a fine target for a day's poking about. Other neighborhoods to check out – especially for eating and drinking – are **Dupont Circle** at Massachusetts, Connecticut, and New Hampshire avenues, which pulls in a dynamic mix of urban professionals of all stripes, and the gentrifying Latin immigrant community of **Adams–Morgan**, a favored destination of the weekend party crowd that's a short walk from Dupont Circle up 18th Street at Columbia Road.

Most DC visitors also take the short Metro ride to **Arlington** in Virginia to see the National Cemetery (burial place of President John F. Kennedy) and the Pentagon.

Capitol Hill

Though there's more than one hill in Washington, DC, when people talk about what's happening on "**The Hill**" they mean **Capitol Hill** – a shallow knoll topped by the giant white dome of the US Capitol building and rising at the very center of the city. When Washington, DC, was first laid out, Capitol Hill was intended to be both the symbolic and real seat of the federal government. Home of both the legislature – **Congress** – and the judiciary – the **Supreme Court** – this is still the place where the law of the land is made and refined; it also holds the newly refurbished **Library of Congress**.

US Capitol

Visible from all over the city, the **US Capitol**, located at the east end of the Mall between Constitution and Independence avenues (Mon–Sat 9am–4.30pm; free; tour information ☎202/225-6827, general information ☎202/224-3121, ⓦwww.aoc.gov), provides an opportunity to appreciate the immense power wielded by the nation's elected officials. The grand halls and public spaces are packed with monuments and statues of deceased political leaders, while the current crop of legislators can be seen arguing over the finer points of law and policy in committee rooms and the ornate main chambers.

George Washingon, in Masonic garb, laid the cornerstone in 1793, and the Capitol was repeatedly expanded over the ensuing years. Nine presidents – most recently LBJ (Nixon declined in advance) – have lain in state in the impressive **Rotunda**, which, capped by a dome 180ft high and 96ft across, links the two halves of the Capitol – the **Senate** in the north wing, the **House of Representatives** in the south. When the "Tholos" lantern above the dome is lit, Congress is in session.

Tight security means that walk-up access to the Capitol is limited to **guided tours** that leave every thirty minutes (9am–3.30pm; 35min; free). The tour meanders through several historical rooms, including the National Statuary Hall and the Capitol crypt. Since advance tickets are unavailable, arrive early at the Capitol Guide Service kiosk (near 1st St SW and Independence Ave) during spring and summer months. Tickets are distributed – only one per person – starting at 9am, and lines can form as early as 7am. US citizens who want to see the legislative chambers must arrange "VIP tours" through their representatives. Visitors from other countries should bring a passport or photo ID and first go to the South Visitor Receiving Facility, where they can obtain international passes. A new Capitol Visitor's Center is slated to open in December 2005. Armed Forces' **bands** perform four nights a week (June–Aug 8pm; free) on the West Terrace of the Capitol, a tradition dating back to the Civil War. The National Symphony Orchestra follows suit on the west lawn on Memorial Day, July 4, and Labor Day.

Library of Congress

With 75 million books and manuscripts, and countless microfilm rolls and photographs kept on more than five hundred miles of shelving, the **Library of Congress** is the largest library in the world. Housed across from the Capitol in the Jefferson, Madison, and John Adams buildings between 1st and 3rd streets SE and E Capitol and C streets SE (Mon–Sat 10am–5.30pm; free; ☎202/707-8000, ⓦwww.loc.gov), the library was set up to serve members of Congress in 1800. The entire collection was lost when the British used its books as kindling to torch the Capitol in 1814, an act that prompted Thomas Jefferson to sell the nation his six-thousand-volume personal collection as a replacement. In 1870, the library became the national copyright repository, and in time it outgrew its original home. The exuberantly eclectic **Thomas Jefferson Building** opened in 1897, complete with a domed octagonal **Reading Room**, and hundreds of mosaics, murals, and sculptures in its stunning Great Hall. The **American Treasures** exhibit, on the second floor, contains a vast array of original documents, including the typescript for Dr Martin Luther King Jr's "I Have a Dream" speech and architect Maya Lin's drawing of the Vietnam Veterans Memorial. You'll also find presidential ice cream recipes, antique baseball cards, and some of "Jelly Roll" Morton's earliest compositions. Rotating exhibits of especially significant documents – those associated with Washington, Lincoln, and Jefferson, among others – are shown in an environmentally controlled cabinet. Free **tours** – the only way to see the Jefferson Building – depart Monday to Saturday at 10.30am, 11.30am, 1.30pm, and 2.30pm (with an additional tour at 3.30pm on weekdays), but are subject to change.

Supreme Court

The **Supreme Court**, across from the US Capitol at First Street NE and Maryland Avenue NE (Mon–Fri 9am–4.30pm; free; ☎202/479-3211, Ⓦ www.supremecourtus.gov), is the nation's final arbiter of what is and isn't legal. The federal judiciary dates to 1787, but the court didn't receive its own building until 1935, when Cass Gilbert – architect of New York's Woolworth Building – designed this Corinthian masterpiece. The grand interior spaces, especially the marble and damask drapes of the courtroom itself – where guides give lectures (hourly Mon–Fri 9.30am–3.30pm; free) when the court is not in session – make it worth climbing the gleaming white steps and going inside. Sessions run from October to June (Mon–Wed) and the cases to be heard are listed in the day's *Washington Post*. Sessions begin at 10am and typically last one hour per case. Arrive early to get a seat, or join the separate line if you're happy to settle for a three-minute stroll through the standing gallery.

The Mall

One of the main features of L'Enfant's grand plan for Washington was a large central parkland. Today the two-mile-long **Mall** stretches west from the Capitol to the Potomac River. It wasn't always such a carefully manicured park, however: when the Capitol was built, it looked out across a muddy, bug-infested swamp and, by the 1870s, the south side was lined by meat-markets and warehouses and crisscrossed by railroad tracks. For a time a stark reminder of L'Enfant's unfulfilled dream, the Washington Monument stood unfinished for more than twenty years due to lack of funds, an ugly stone stump cut off halfway. The Mall has since become DC's most popular green space, used for summer softball games and Fourth of July concerts. Yet its central role in a planned capital city also places it at the very heart of the country's political and social life. When there's a protest gesture to be made, the Mall is the place to make it, whether it's a demonstration by the Million Men marchers of black America, a mass prayer meeting of the Promise Keepers, or the unveiling of the commemorative AIDS Memorial Quilt. In addition to numerous museums, it boasts a quartet of presidential monuments, along with the White House and the powerful Vietnam and Korean war veterans memorials.

Washington Monument

The Mall's most prominent feature, the **Washington Monument**, is an unadorned marble obelisk built in memory of George Washington. At 555ft, it's the tallest all-masonry structure in the world, towering over the city from its hilltop perch at 15th Street NW and Constitution Avenue (daily 9am–5pm; free; ☎202/426-6841, Ⓦ www.nps.gov/wamo). Work started on the monument in 1848, but various internal arguments, and later the Civil War, so disrupted construction that it wasn't completed until 1884. When the US Government took over the project in 1876, marble from a slightly different source was used; the transition line where work resumed at the 152ft level is readily apparent. To visit the monument pick up a free ticket from the 15th Street kiosk (8am–4:30pm, just south of Constitution Ave on Madison Drive), which allows you to turn up at a fixed time later in the day. The kiosk is first-come, first-served; tickets run out early during the peak season. You can also book a ticket in advance with the National Park Service ($2; ☎1-800/967-2283, ⓦreservations.nps.gov). The elevator to the observation deck takes seventy seconds and deposits you at the 500ft level to enjoy the monument's panoramic 360° views of the city. The Park Service plans to build a security wall around the monument grounds and will close the building to the public for five months beginning in the fall of 2004. Call ahead for details.

The White House

For nearly two hundred years, the **White House** has been the residence and office of the President of the United States. Standing at the edge of the Mall, due north from the Washington Monument at America's most famous address, 1600 Pennsylvania Ave NW, this grand, Neoclassical edifice was completed in 1800 by Irish immigrant James Hoban, who modeled it on the Georgian manors of Dublin. Each of its presidential occupants has made his mark: Thomas Jefferson added the first toilets, just before the British burned the place down in the War of 1812. It was quickly rebuilt and then expanded, often in such a hurry that the whole building was on the verge of collapse. Harry Truman had to move out for four years from 1948 while the structure was stabilized: all the rooms were dismantled and a modern steel frame was inserted. Truman also added the balcony to the familiar south-side portico.

Though many visitors are surprised by how small and homey it is, security at the White House is every bit as tight as you'd imagine. Protesters are still allowed to set up camp opposite the main entrance, but the stretch of Pennsylvania Avenue immediately outside was closed to traffic in 1995, shortly after the bombing of a federal building in Oklahoma City. Since 2001, White House **tours** (free; ☎202/456-7041, ⓦwww.whitehouse.gov) have been suspended indefinitely, with exceptions made for school groups and members of the military. US citizens may still reserve tickets for a guided tour by contacting their Member of Congress, although this must be done well in advance. In the past, tours consisted of a lot of waiting around followed by a quick shuffle through the basement and the ground-floor reception rooms, before peeping in at a succession of plush, railed-off rooms filled with portraits of ex-presidents. Tickets for the tour would often be gone by 8:30am during the spring and summer, sometimes as early as 6:30am. Expect a similar experience if the White House re-opens to the public in the near future.

If you're interested in the history of the place and its occupants, walk a few blocks southeast to the **Visitor Center** at 1450 Pennsylvania Ave (daily 7.30am–4pm; ☎202/208-1631). It's filled with photos and film footage of First Families and their distinguished guests – including a portly President Hoover playing "Hooverball" with a group of lumbering judges, and the Wright Brothers showing off their latest airplane – and the inaugural portraits, in which a series of drawn and exhausted presidents hand over power to their beaming successors.

Lincoln Memorial

Modeled after the Parthenon, the **Lincoln Memorial**, with its Doric columns and long reflecting pool, anchors the west end of the Mall in West Potomac Park (daily 24hr, staffed 8am–midnight; free; ⓦwww.nps.gov/linc). The memorial is a fitting tribute to the man who put down the southern rebellion during the Civil War, preserving the Union and ending slavery in the US.

During the Civil Rights March on Washington in 1963, Dr King delivered his epic "I Have a Dream" speech here. Ironically, when this monument to the Great Emancipator was dedicated in 1922, the crowds were segregated by color. Even black leader Dr Robert Moton, the main speaker at the ceremony, was forced to watch from a roped-off area to the side.

Inside the monument, an enormous craggy likeness of Lincoln sits firmly grasping the arms of his throne-like chair, apparently deep in thought. Inscriptions of his two most celebrated speeches – the Gettysburg Address and the Second Inaugural Address – are carved on the south and north walls.

Vietnam Veterans Memorial

A wedge of black granite, slashing into the green lawn of the Mall at Constitution Avenue and 21st Street NW, the **Vietnam Veterans Memorial** (daily 24hr, staffed 8am–midnight; free; Ⓦwww.nps.gov/vive) serves as a somber and powerful reminder of the nearly 60,000 US soldiers who died in Vietnam. The pathway that slopes down from the grass forms a gash in the earth, its increasing depth symbolizing the increasing involvement of US forces in the war. Alongside, the polished surface is carved with the names of every soldier who died, in chronological order from 1959 to 1975.

The memorial was designed by Maya Ying Lin, a 21-year-old architecture student. When it was first erected in 1982, there was some outcry from veterans' groups about its antiwar connotations. In 1984, to achieve a balance, a more traditional statue of three heroic soldiers was placed nearby, under a floodlit American flag. More lobbying led to the establishment in 1993 of the **Vietnam Women's Memorial**, which stands in a grove of trees at the east end of the main site; it honors the 11,000 American women who served in the conflict.

Korean War Veterans Memorial

The **Korean War Veterans Memorial**, dedicated in 1995 in West Potomac Park (south of Reflecting Pool off Daniel French Drive SW; daily 24hr, staffed 8am–midnight; free; Ⓦwww.nps.gov/kwvm), incorporates a dramatic Field of Remembrance in which nineteen life-sized combat troops sculpted from stainless steel advance across an open field toward the Stars and Stripes. Between 1950 and 1953, almost 55,000 Americans were killed in Korea (with 8000 more missing in action and more than 103,000 wounded). It's an affecting memorial to an often-forgotten conflict, featuring the names of 22 other countries that contributed humanitarian or military aid, and a plaque at the flagstand that proclaims: "Our nation honors her sons and daughters who answered the call to defend a country they never knew and a people they never met."

Jefferson Memorial

Completed in 1943 and modeled on his country home, Monticello (see p.465), the **Jefferson Memorial**, located in West Potomac Park near 14th Street SW and Ohio Drive (daily 24hr, staffed 8am–midnight; free; Ⓦwww.nps.gov/thje), consists of a shallow dome hovering over a bronze statue of Thomas Jefferson, the author of the Declaration of Independence and the third US president. The interior walls, encircled by an Ionic colonnade, are carved with Jefferson's words, and an inscription around the frieze reads: "I have sworn upon the altar of God eternal hostility against every form of tyranny over the mind of man."

In front of the building, the picturesque **Tidal Basin** stretches almost to the Lincoln Memorial and helps prevent the western end of the Mall from being inundated by Potomac floods. The reflections off the Tidal Basin are especially pretty in spring when the rows of **Japanese cherry trees** come out in full bloom (usually early April). Rent a pedal boat from the Tidal Basin Boat House (March–Sept Mon–Sun 10am–6pm; $8–16/hr; ℡202/479-2426) for a spectacular view of the memorial from atop the water.

FDR Memorial

The **FDR Memorial** was opened alongside the Tidal Basin in West Potomac Park in 1997 (West Basin Drive SW and Ohio Drive; daily 24hr, staffed 8am–midnight; free; Ⓦwww.nps.gov/fdrm/home.htm). Its four outdoor "gallery" rooms highlight President Franklin Delano Roosevelt's achievements during twelve years in office. Bronze sculptures of FDR and his wife, Eleanor, along with waterfalls and remembrance pools, offset inscriptions from the president's best-known speeches. In a belated nod to the fact that FDR was crippled by polio (a fact kept from the American people throughout his presidency), a statue of the former president in a wheelchair was installed after the memorial's dedication.

The Smithsonian Institution

The cream of Washington, DC's remarkable panoply of historical artifacts and fine art works comes under the general auspices of the **Smithsonian Institution**, which holds the US national collections of everything under the sun. Endowed by an Englishman – James Smithson, illegitimate son of the first Duke of Northumberland, who never even visited the US – the Smithsonian was established in 1846 "for the increase and diffusion of Knowledge." This broad brief is reflected in its impressive range of research centers and museums. Ten line up along the Mall, four more are just north, and the zoo is a few miles north beyond Rock Creek.

The original home of the Smithsonian, the 1855 Norman-style Smithsonian Institution Building, known as **The Castle**, stands on the Mall halfway between the Capitol and the Washington Monument. It was at first devoted to scientific research but, as the Smithsonian became more of a museum, the sheer accumulation of items necessitated the construction of the various other buildings along the Mall. The old Castle is now the Smithsonian headquarters and main **visitor center**, 1000 Jefferson Drive SW (daily 9am–5.30pm; ℡202/357-2700), with the latest details on all the galleries available from the high-tech information desk. The ornate tomb of James Smithson (after death, he finally made it to the US) is in an alcove just off the Mall entrance, and the lovely flower-filled Enid A. Haupt Garden (daily: summer 7am–9.15pm; winter 7am–5.45pm) fronts the Castle on the south side. You can still get a feel for the days when the Smithsonian was known as "the nation's attic" by visiting the adjacent **Arts and Industries Building**, DC's first "National Museum," which once displayed the hundreds of objects sent here for safekeeping after

Smithsonian details

All the Smithsonian museums and galleries are **open** daily all year (except December 25) from 10am until 5.30pm. To cope with the summer crowds, however, several museums – depending on annual budgets – usually extend hours from 10am until 7.30 or 8pm from June to September. **Admission** to all the museums is free. For **details** on current exhibitions, hours, and events, or a copy of the *Smithsonian Access* brochure for disabled visitors, call the visitor center at ℡202/357-2700 or visit the Smithsonian's website at Ⓦwww.si.edu.

the 1876 Centennial Exhibition in Philadelphia. Although some of the Victoriana remains on display, the building's main focus now is temporary exhibitions often from sources outside the Smithsonian collection. The displays rotate every few months and cover a broad range of artistic, historical, and scientific subjects.

National Air and Space Museum

The **National Air and Space Museum**, situated on the south side of the Mall between Fourth and Seventh streets SW (daily 10am–5.30pm; free; tour info ☏202/357-1400, ⓦwww.nasm.si.edu) is by far DC's most popular attraction, drawing nearly ten million people every year. Most of them may seem to be here on the day you come, but the hangar-like building can accommodate everyone without feeling crowded, and you can always see the hundreds of historic aircraft close up. Hanging from the rafters in the main entrance gallery, the **"Milestones of Flight"** include the hand-made plane in which the **Wright Brothers** made the first powered flight in 1903; **Charles Lindbergh**'s *Spirit of St Louis*, which he flew solo across the Atlantic in 1927; the claustrophobic *Mercury* capsule in which **John Glenn** orbited the earth in 1962; and the ultra-light *Voyager*, which flew around the world nonstop in 1986.

Most of the museum is taken up with exploring the space race from both American and Soviet perspectives, using models and actual spacecraft to show the development from Werner von Braun's V1 rockets up to a gawky-looking lunar module. **"Apollo to the Moon"** is one of the most fascinating galleries, centering on the Apollo 11 (1969) and 17 (1972) missions, the first and last, respectively. Check out Neil Armstrong's and Buzz Aldrin's spacesuits, navigation aids, space food, clothes, and charts, and the astronaut's survival kit (complete with shark repellent). Further galleries include **"Rocketry and Space Flight,"** a history of rocket propulsion dating from the twelfth century; **"Looking at Earth,"** where the aerial photographs include Boston snapped from a balloon in 1860 and German castles recorded by camera-toting pigeons; and **"The Great War in the Air,"** bursting with dogfighting biplanes.

The museum also shows a rotating program of super-large-screen **IMAX** movies ($7.50, advance purchase $2 extra; ☏202/663-IMAX or ⓦwww.si.edu/imax), all of which have some connection with flying. Pizza and burgers at the *Wright Place* **restaurant** enable star-struck families to stay in the building all day. The culinary specialty of the museum, however, is the crunchy freeze-dried ice cream developed for Apollo astronauts and sold in the gift shop.

National Museum of Natural History

At Tenth Street NW and Constitution Avenue, the imposing three-story entrance rotunda of the **National Museum of Natural History** (daily: 10am–5.30pm; summer 10am–7.30pm; free; ☏202/357-2700, ⓦwww.mnh.si.edu) feels like the busiest and most boisterous crossroads in all of DC, with troops of screeching school kids endlessly chasing each other around a colossal African elephant. Hundreds of other stuffed animals, tracing evolution from fossilized four-billion-year-old plankton to dinosaurs' eggs and beyond, are on display all over the place – pick up floor plans and guides from the information desk at the elephant's feet.

Naturally enough, the **"Dinosaurs"** section is the most popular part of the museum, with hulking skeletons reassembled in imaginative poses and accompanied by informative text, written with a light touch and accessible to children.

"**Exploring Marine Ecosystems**" uses videos, aquariums, and the odd furry seal to illustrate life on the "Rocky Shore of Maine" and a "Coral Reef from the Caribbean." Nearby you can admire a rare specimen of the giant squid; scientists don't know quite where it lives, but reckon it grows to fifty feet in length.

Upstairs are hundreds of creepy-crawly critters – lizards, snakes, tarantulas, and the like – as well as an **Insect Zoo**, filled with all types of bugs, which you can play with should you so desire. The museum also boasts a truly exceptional array of gemstones, including the legendary 45-carat **Hope Diamond** that once belonged to Marie Antoinette, on display in a new **Gem and Mineral Hall**, which features natural and reconstructed environments, interactive exhibits, and hands-on specimens.

As at the Air and Space Museum, you'll also find a rotating selection of **IMAX** movies ($7.50, advance purchase $2 extra; ☎202/663-IMAX, ⓦwww.si.edu/imax). As you'd expect, the films shown here portray more earth-bound themes, the massive screens plunging you far beneath the oceans or whisking you away to the Galapagos.

National Museum of American History

If you like kitsch, you won't want to miss the bizarre melange of cultural artifacts at the **National Museum of American History**, located at 14th Street NW and Constitution Avenue (daily 10am–5.30pm; free; ☎202/357-2700, ⓦamericanhistory.si.edu). Judy Garland's ruby slippers from *The Wizard of Oz*, Muhammad Ali's boxing gloves, and TV puppet star Howdy Doody are set among didactic displays tracing the country's development. It's not so much a center for scholarly study as a sanctuary for vanishing Americana, incorporating Model T Fords, old post offices, and even a restored, c.1900 ice-cream parlor, which still serves up sundaes.

As you enter from the Mall, directly onto the second floor, head for the west wing and the battered red, white, and blue flag that inspired the US national anthem – the **Star-Spangled Banner** itself, which survived the British bombardment of Baltimore harbor during the War of 1812. The flag has been undergoing a lengthy conservation treatment in a climate-controlled lab, a project slated for completion in 2004 (after which the flag will remain in the lab until a permanent home has been chosen). In the meantime, visitors can watch white-coated technicians at work through a glass wall.

The worthier exhibits are also on this floor: "**Field to Factory**," an examination of the mass movement of African-Americans from Southern farms to the wartime industries of northern cities. A Woolworth lunch counter from Greensboro, North Carolina, evokes the historic sit-in of 1960. "**American Encounters**" focuses on New Mexico, looking at how contact between Native Americans and Europeans has affected – and continues to change – communities such as the Pueblo Indians of Santa Clara and the Hispanic Chimayo. On the first floor, the "**Information Age**" gallery traces communications from Morse's first telegraph to modern information technology. Separate galleries display in glorious profusion the artifacts and machines that have shaped modern America – from light bulbs and motorbikes to trains and atomic clocks. The top floor holds political memorabilia (much of it more than a century old), coin collections, old musical instruments, and a history of the famous military academy at West Point. Two final outstanding exhibits inject a serious tone. "**Personal Legacy: the Healing of a Nation**" brings together some of the 25,000 items left by relatives at the Vietnam Memorial in DC. "**A More Perfect Union**" deals candidly with the shameful internment of Japanese-American citizens during World War II.

Hirshhorn Museum

Housed in the most clearly modern building on the Mall – a windowless cylinder balanced on fourteen-foot stilts above a concrete plaza, looking like a spaceship poised for takeoff – the **Hirshhorn Museum and Sculpture Garden** holds an extensive collection of late nineteenth- and twentieth-century art (daily 10am–5.30pm, in summer Thurs 10am–8pm; free; ☎202/633-4674, ⓦhirshhorn.si.edu). From the main entrance on Independence Avenue, escalators climb to the upper-floor galleries, where major works by Picasso, de Kooning, Mondrian, Pollock, Matisse, and other notables are on display. The gallery downstairs hosts touring exhibitions, and critically acclaimed films are shown in the evenings.

A stimulating collection of modern **sculpture** is displayed in an open-air garden across Jefferson Drive, on the Mall side of the museum. Alongside assorted Moores, Rodins, Smiths, and Malliols are two expressive abstract figures by Marino Marini, and a stalwart *Yucatán Woman* by Mexican sculptor Francisco Zuniga. The landscaped garden, sunk below ground level, perhaps to spare members of Congress from having to look at modern art, is also a nice place for a picnic lunch.

National Museum of African Art

Built in 1987 on the south side of the Mall, the curved and domed **National Museum of African Art** at 950 Independence Ave SW (daily 10am–5.30pm; free; ☎202/357-4600, ⓦwww.nmafa.si.edu), holds more than six thousand sculptures and artifacts, both spiritual and functional, from the numerous tribal cultures of sub-Saharan Africa. The permanent collection ranges from Nigerian carved-ivory cult figures to Zairean mother-and-child fertility fetishes and puppet heads from eastern Mali. Look out for an extraordinary seventeenth-century bronze from the Lower Niger, consisting of a vase swarmed over by eight bizarre chameleons, all cast in one piece. While the museum celebrates the **"Art of the Personal Object,"** highlighting the grace of everyday objects such as combs and pipes, much of its sculpture is highly abstract, and its influence on the Cubists is obvious. About half the space is devoted to changing exhibitions on specific regions, and the gift shop sells woven and dyed fabrics and clothes, as well as books and postcards.

Arthur M. Sackler Gallery

The angular and pyramidal counterpart of the African Art museum is the **Arthur M. Sackler Gallery** at 1050 Independence Ave SW (daily 10am–5.30pm; free; ☎202/633-4880, ⓦwww.asia.si.edu), filled with art works and devotional objects from Asia and the Middle East. Most of the exhibitions are temporary, and occasionally draw from other museums' collections, so it's not possible to predict what will be on display at any one time. However, exhibitions might take in Sackler's noted collection of translucent jade dragons and intricate, three-thousand-year-old bronzes from China; stone deities from India and Tibet; and lushly illustrated early Islamic texts from Iran, gorgeously colored in gilt, silver, and crushed stone pigments. Inexpensive posters and prints are sold in the gift shop. Underground galleries – featuring temporary exhibitions – connect the Sackler to the Freer Gallery and the African Art museum.

Freer Gallery of Art

From the day it opened in 1923, the **Freer Gallery** – on Jefferson Drive at 12th Street NW – has been one of the more unusual Smithsonian museums (daily 10am–5.30pm; free; ☎202/633-4880, ⓦwww.asia.si.edu). Put together and paid for by railroad millionaire Charles Freer, it contains more than one thousand prints, drawings, and paintings by London-based American artist **James McNeil Whistler** – the largest collection of his works anywhere. The collection also includes Chinese jades and bronzes, Byzantine illuminated manuscripts, Buddhist wall sculptures, and pieces of Persian metalwork, all of which were collected by Freer under Whistler's tutelage. Among other works are pieces by Whistler's contemporaries Winslow Homer, Albert Pinkham Ryder, and John Singer Sargent.

In addition to his portraits and landscapes, Whistler is also represented by the magnificent **Peacock Room**, which started life as a simple painting commissioned by Frederick Leyland for his mantelpiece. The eccentric artist, however, decided to cover the ceiling with imitation gold leaf and paint the entire room with blue and gold peacocks and feather patterns. Leyland was outraged but left the room untouched; after his death, Freer bought it and shipped it over from London (he also kept live peacocks in the museum's central courtyard).

National Museum of the American Indian

Scheduled to open in September 2004 on the Mall's last available spot at Fourth Street and Independence Avenue SW, the **National Museum of the American Indian** will be dedicated to preserving and understanding Native American history and culture (call for hours; free; ☎202/357-2700, ⓦwww.nmai.si.edu). Built from sandy-colored limestone, the curvilinear structure is designed to reflect the importance of nature in the Native American world – only natural materials were used in its construction and the grounds have been planted with indigenous species to re-create DC's original habitat. Inside, permanent exhibitions will showcase the massive collection of Native American art and artifacts gathered by wealthy New Yorker George

---

Smithsonian American Art Museum and the National Portrait Gallery

Two important cogs in the Smithsonian system are closed for renovation until July 4, 2006. Separated from the main Mall galleries, the **Smithsonian American Art Museum**, Eighth and G streets NW (☎202/275-1500, ⓦamericanart.si.edu), may not get the traffic of the other museums, but it's perhaps the most worthwhile of all, and in the past has mounted thought-provoking shows. Opened in 1829, the museum was known as the National Gallery of Art before Andrew Mellon usurped that name. The collection includes Revolutionary portraits and dramatic American landscapes, as well as almost five hundred paintings by George Catlin, who spent six years on the Great Plains. More recent pieces have been displayed on the top floor in the vaulted and colonnaded **Lincoln Gallery**, which was the 1865 venue for President Lincoln's second inaugural ball and remains one of DC's most celebrated interior spaces. The **Renwick Gallery**, a separate location on Pennsylvania Avenue and 17th Street NW, will host exhibitions from the collection until renovations are complete on the Greek Revival–style **Old Patent Office**, which has been home to both the American Art Museum and the National Portrait Gallery since 1968.

The **National Portrait Gallery** at Eighth and F streets NW (☎202/275-1738, ⓦwww.npg.si.edu) holds pretty much what you'd expect: paintings, sculptures, and photographs of famous and not-so-famous people, from Pocahontas to Mark Twain, and includes Gilbert Stuart's famous "Lansdowne" portrait of George Washington, as well as portraits and sculptures of every president. There's also the odd masterpiece on show – like Edgar Degas' severe portrait of his friend, Impressionist Mary Cassatt.

Gustav Heye around the beginning of the twentieth century, with over 800,000 items representing hundreds of tribes throughout the Western Hemisphere.

The National Zoo

Few people realize that the **National Zoo** – in the north of town at 3001 Connecticut Ave NW, and a short walk from the Metro – forms part of the Smithsonian ensemble (buildings open daily April–Oct 10am–6pm; rest of year 10am–4.30pm; grounds open daily April–Oct 6am–8pm; rest of year 6am–6pm; free; ☎202/673-4717, ⓦwww.nationalzoo.si.edu). It sprawls down the steep slopes of the gorge cut by Rock Creek, with trails through lush vegetation and simulations of the home environments of more than 2700 animals. Among the zoo's star attractions are the **pandas** Mei Xiang and Tian Tian, who arrived from the People's Republic of China in December 2000. The pair fills the absence left by the passing of Ling Ling and Hsing Hsing, the famous bears presented by Beijing during Richard Nixon's 1972 visit. The best time to catch the duo is first thing in the morning, when the lines are shorter and the animals tend to be most active. In addition to the expected menagerie of giraffes and elephants, birds and bees, and lions and tigers, the zoo boasts an unusual feature in its **Think Tank**, where orangutans assemble, commuting to and from their enclosures daily by means of overhead cables across public areas of the zoo.

Other museums and attractions

While you could easily spend a week wandering around the Smithsonian, the national collections are by no means the only worthwhile museums in DC – or, for that matter, along the Mall. The large **National Gallery of Art**, at the foot of the US Capitol, is the best art museum in the city, and one of the top ten in the world. In addition to more quality art galleries, you can tour various **federal buildings** – to watch the FBI track down criminals, or count brand-new dollar bills as they roll off the presses – or honor the nation's dead, including the Kennedys, at **Arlington National Cemetery**.

National Gallery of Art

Though the visually stunning **National Gallery of Art**, located on Constitution Avenue between Third and Ninth streets NW (Mon–Sat 10am–5pm, Sun 11am–6pm; free; ☎202/737-4215, ⓦwww.nga.gov), is not in fact a government institution, it fully deserves its name. It owes its prominence to the efforts of the industrialist **Andrew Mellon**, who bought the building and donated most of the paintings. Many were purchased from the cash-poor post-revolutionary government of the USSR, where they had previously hung in the Hermitage in St Petersburg. Mellon's family has continued as benefactors, raising countless millions to build I.M. Pei's modernistic East Building in 1978.

The original Neoclassical gallery, designed by John Russell Pope and opened in 1941, is now called the **West Building** and holds the bulk of the permanent collection. If you only have limited time, latch onto one of the informative daily **free tours** – ask for a schedule at the information desk. To find a particular work, visit the interactive **Micro Gallery** in the West Building (main floor, Mall entrance). Touch-screen computers here enable you to learn more about your favorite artists and easily locate paintings throughout the expansive building.

From the domed central rotunda, where you can pick up a floor plan and gallery guide, a vaulted corridor runs the length of the building. Galleries to the west on the main floor display major works by Renaissance masters, arranged by nationality: half a dozen Rembrandts fill the **Dutch** gallery, Van Eyck and Rubens dominate the **Flemish**, and El Greco and Velázquez face off in the **Spanish**, near eight progressively darker Goyas. There's also the only Leonardo in the Americas, the 1474 *Ginevra de' Benci*, painted in oil on wood, plus works by Botticelli, Crivelli, and Raphael – including the latter's celebrated *Alba Madonna* (1510), one of Mellon's purchases from the Hermitage. The other half of the West Building holds an exceptional collection of nineteenth-century **French** paintings – Gauguin from Pont-Aven to Tahiti, a couple of Van Goghs, some Monet studies of Rouen Cathedral and water lilies, Cézanne still lifes, and the like. At either end of the building, the skylit, fountain-filled **Garden Courts** make an ideal place to rest weary feet, while Salvador Dalí's *The Last Supper* overlooks the escalators down to the café.

The triangular **East Building** houses **twentieth-century** paintings and sculpture. As in the Guggenheim in New York, the attention-grabbing spatial choreography of the architecture all but overpowers the works of art. You emerge from under the oppressively low entrance into a central atrium, from where an escalator, literally carved out of a 40ft granite wall, climbs to the main galleries – which, squeezed into the corners, can seem like an afterthought. Exhibitions change and go on tour throughout the year, so the bulk of the permanent collection is rarely on display. Nonetheless, you may catch Picasso's haunting *Family of Saltimbanques* and the very blue *The Tragedy*, as well as Giacometti bronzes and paintings, plenty of Alexander Calder pieces (whose huge red-and-black mobile is usually in place), early Mirós, some Warhol soup cans, and Chuck Close's *Fanny* – a finger painting *par excellence*. The underground concourse that links the two buildings contains a good bookstore, an espresso bar, and a large cafeteria – topped by pyramidal skylights and bordered by a glassed-in waterfall. Every Friday during the summer, an outdoor sculpture garden features live jazz, while in winter, it transforms into a popular skating rink.

National Archives

On display at the **National Archives**, at 700 Pennsylvania Ave NW (daily: April to Memorial Day 10am–7pm; Memorial Day to Labor Day 10am–9pm; rest of year 10am–5.30pm; free; ℡1-866/272-6272, ⓦwww.archives.gov), are the three short texts upon which the United States is founded: the **Declaration of Independence**, the **Constitution**, and the **Bill of Rights**. These three original sheets of parchment, drafted respectively in 1776, 1787, and 1789, are secured in bomb-proof argon-filled glass and titanium containers, which slide into a vault in case of fire or other threat. You can usually look at them as long as you like, but if there's a crowd you have to shuffle on past. The impressive Neoclassical Greek edifice – designed by John Russell Pope – also displays a 1297 revised copy of the **Magna Carta**, which established in Britain such basic concepts as trial by jury and equality before the law. Temporary exhibitions often include fascinating documents such as the Louisiana Purchase, the Marshall Plan, Nixon's resignation letter, the Emancipation Proclamation, and the Japanese surrender from World War II. As the official repository of all US national records – census data, treaties, passport applications – the Archives also attracts thousands of visitors who come here each year in search of their roots. A 294-seat **theater** for documentary film screenings is set to open in 2004.

Federal Bureau of Investigation

A fortress-like modern building on Pennsylvania Avenue, between Ninth and Tenth streets, holds the headquarters of the FBI – the **Federal Bureau of**

Investigation, the nation's elite law-enforcement organization (Mon–Fri 9am–4pm; free; ☎202/324-3000, ⓦwww.fbi.gov). Set up in 1908, the FBI came into its own chasing bootleggers and bank robbers like Al Capone and Machine Gun Kelly during the 1920s and 1930s. Due to building renovation, **tours** have been suspended until late 2004 (call ☎202/324-3447 to check if they've resumed), but normally hordes of visitors queue outside to get a look at displays on the infamous gangsters and dangerous subversives from whom the Feds shield the American people (they kept extensive files on Dr Martin Luther King Jr). Ideology aside (the FBI still struggles to emerge from the shadow of its long-time iron-fisted director, J. Edgar Hoover), future tours promise to be more interactive, familiarizing visitors with criminal investigative techniques and the Bureau's counter-terrorist activities. The real draw, however, will likely remain the climactic display of sharpshooting and firepower: agents blasting away at cut-out targets with a battery of small arms and automatic weapons.

International Spy Museum

The **International Spy Museum**, 800 F St NW (daily: April–Oct 10am–8pm; rest of year 10am–6pm; $13; ☎202/393-7798, ⓦwww.spymuseum .org), celebrates espionage in all forms – from feudal Japan's silent and deadly ninjas, surveillance pigeons armed with cameras from World War I, all the way up to infamous modern-day CIA moles like Aldrich Ames. Although the museum offers up little in-depth information in its exhibits on spy training, code-breaking, and the Cold War, it is loaded with gadgets and tongue-in-cheek displays to keep visitors entertained. There's a replica of James Bond's Aston Martin that rattles to life with machine-gun headlamps, and even a radio transmitter disguised as a dog turd. Rather disturbing, however, are the wartime cartoons put out by Walt Disney to encourage government employees to keep quiet in public, lest enemy spies be lurking.

Ford's Theatre National Historic Site

Ford's Theatre National Historic Site, 511 Tenth St NW (daily 9am–5pm, closed during rehearsals and matinees; free; ☎202/426-6924, ⓦwww .nps.gov/foth), is a beautiful restoration of the nineteenth-century playhouse, which continues to stage regular productions of contemporary and period drama (see p.000). However, because of its role in one of the greatest national tragedies, it lives a double life as a tourist attraction in its own right. It was here, on April 14, 1865, a mere five days after the end of the Civil War, that **Abraham Lincoln** was shot by the actor and Southern sympathizer John Wilkes Booth during a performance of *Our American Cousin*.

Entertaining talks (hourly 9.15am–4.15pm; free) set the scene in the theater itself, after which you can file up to the circle for a view of the presidential box where it all happened, and then go down to the basement **Lincoln Museum**. Macabre relics here include the clothes that Lincoln was wearing, Booth's .44 single-shot Derringer pistol, and the assassin's diary, in which he wrote: "I hoped for no gain. I knew no private wrong. I struck for my country and that alone." The mortally wounded president was carried across the street to the **Petersen House**, where he died the next morning. That, too, is open to the public (daily 9am–5pm), who troop through its gloomy parlor rooms to see a replica of Lincoln's death bed.

Old Post Office

Built in 1899, the fanciful Romanesque **Old Post Office**, just across from the FBI at 1100 Pennsylvania Ave, is one of the most recognizable of downtown's monuments (Mon–Sat 10am–7pm, Sun noon–6pm; free; ☏202/289-4224, ⊛oldpostofficedc.com). Its glorious galleried interior is now known as the Pavilion, in which guise it supports dozens of shops, stalls, and a food court. The more clued-up visitors make a beeline here, rather than to the Washington Monument, for their first aerial view of the city from the **clock tower** (summer Mon–Sat 9am–7.45pm, Sun 10am–5.45pm; rest of year Mon–Sat 9am–4.45pm, Sun 10am–5.45pm; free; ☏202/606-8691). It stands 270ft above Pennsylvania Avenue, and the glass elevator ride allows you to see the iron, glass, and wood interior in all its fine glory.

Corcoran Gallery of Art

The **Corcoran Gallery of Art**, just down the street from the White House at 17th St NW and New York Ave, is one of the oldest and most respected art museums in the US (Mon, Wed & Fri–Sun 10am–5pm, Thurs 10am–9pm, closed Tues; $5, free on Mon and after 5pm on Thurs; ☏202/639-1700, ⊛www .corcoran.org). It's also one of the nicest to visit in DC, with good guided tours (Wed–Mon noon), an excellent gallery shop, and a café that features rousing gospel Sunday brunches ($24 for brunch and museum admission). Especially strong on American art – from frontier landscapes by Albert Bierstadt, to portraiture by Mary Cassatt and Thomas Eakins, and modern works by Calder, Warhol, and Rothko – it also includes a sampling of Dutch masters, medieval tapestries, and French Impressionists. In the **Salon Doré** (Gilded Room), an eighteenth-century Parisian interior has been re-created to stunning effect, with floor-to-ceiling hand-carved paneling, gold-leaf decor, and ceiling murals.

US Holocaust Memorial Museum

Nothing in DC is more disturbing than the large and generously laid-out **US Holocaust Memorial Museum**, 100 Raoul Wallenburg Place SW (daily 10am–5.30pm, extended hours 10am–8pm on Tues and Thurs in spring and summer; free; ☏202/488-0400, ⊛www.ushmm.org). Commemorating the persecution and murder of six million Jews by the Nazis, it places Hitler in historical perspective while personalizing the suffering of the individual victims.

In addition to case after case of newspapers and newsreels documenting Nazi activities from the early 1930s through the "Final Solution," reconstructions and, in many cases, actual relics of Warsaw Ghetto streets, railroad cattle-cars, and concentration-camp barracks fill the top floors. The sheer numbers of people killed is chillingly evoked throughout, first by a whole room filled with shoes stolen from deportees, later by a crisp glass wall etched with the names of the hundreds of Eastern European Jewish communities wiped off the map.

Tickets for specific entry times are available free of charge from 10am each day – with a limit of four per person – at the 14th Street entrance. You can also reserve in advance through Tickets.com (☏1-800/400-9373; fee charged). If you arrive without a ticket any later than mid-morning, you're unlikely to get into the permanent exhibition, but a certain number of temporary displays are usually open to all visitors.

The Bureau of Engraving and Printing

The **Bureau of Engraving and Printing** – one block south of the Mall at 14th and C streets SW – is no ordinary printing plant (Mon–Fri 9am–2pm, extended summer hours 5–7pm, closed Christmas to New Year's Day; free; ☏202/847-3188, ⊛www.moneyfactory.com). Every day, the presses here crank out at least $38 million in currency. Bills print in 32-note sheets before being checked for defects and cut down to size by powerful machines. In their never-ending battle against counterfeiters, the government money-makers have devised numerous security measures, the latest of which is the addition of color to the venerable greenback. A short film explains the basics of intaglio printing, and visitors can watch it all happen from a glassed-in upstairs gallery. From March to September, arrive early to pick up a timed ticket; tickets are not needed the rest of the year.

Phillips Collection

One of the country's best assemblages of modern paintings is kept at the **Phillips Collection**, 1600 21st St and Q St NW (Tues–Sat 10am–5pm, Thurs until 8.30pm, Sun noon–7pm except in summer noon–5pm; prices vary depending on exhibition, usually $8–12; ☎202/387-2151, ⊛www.phillipscollection.org). Unfortunately, many of the European masterpieces, including the prized *Luncheon of the Boat Party* by Renoir, are away on tour until January 2005, while the Phillips is renovated and expanded. Works by Cézanne, O'Keeffe, Kandinsky, Diebenkorn, Klee, Mondrian, and others remain on display in the Phillips family's ornate 1890s mansion, while a special exhibition rotates every three months. The permanent exhibition is free during the week; on weekends, it is bundled with special exhibition tickets available at the door or from Ticketmaster (☎202/432-SEAT, ⊛www.ticketmaster.com). Popular free concerts take place in the oak-paneled Music Room on Sundays (Sept–May 5pm); free gallery tours on Wednesdays and Saturdays at 2pm; on Thursdays, the Artful Evenings program ($8) has gallery talks at 6 and 7pm.

National Museum of Women in the Arts

Housed in a converted Masonic Temple at 1250 New York Ave NW, the **National Museum of Women in the Arts**, which opened in 1987, is the country's only museum dedicated to women artists (Mon–Sat 10am–5pm, Sun noon–5pm; $5; ☎202/783-5000, ⊛www.nmwa.org). It includes hundreds of works by "unknown" painters – a policy inspired by the fact that, as recently as the 1960s, not one female artist was mentioned in the leading American art history textbook. It also features sculptures by Barbara Hepworth and Camille Claudel (Rodin's assistant and mistress) and paintings by Frida Khalo (the only ones in DC), Helen Frankenthaler, Georgia O'Keeffe, Mary Cassatt, and Elaine de Kooning, and has one of the city's better museum cafés.

Washington National Cathedral

The twin towers of **Washington National Cathedral** – the world's sixth largest cathedral – are visible long before you reach the heights of Mount St Alban where the church sits (Mon–Fri 10am–5.30pm, Sat 10am–4.30pm, Sun 8am–6.30pm, open until 8pm on weekdays May–Aug; suggested donation $3; ☎202/537-6200, ⊛www.cathedral.org).

Built from Indiana limestone and modeled entirely in the medieval English Gothic style, the Protestant cathedral took 83 years to build and measures more than a tenth of a mile from the west end of the nave to the high altar at the opposite end. Among other things, you'll find the sarcophagus of **Woodrow Wilson**, the only president to be buried in the District, and the **Space Window**, whose stained glass incorporating a sliver of moon rock commemorates the flight of Apollo 11. From the south porch (near the Washington statue), an elevator ascends to the **Pilgrim Observation Gallery**, which affords stupendous city views from the highest point in DC.

For a floor plan and information, descend to the crypt floor, where there's an **information desk** and gift shop. **Guided tours** are available on request at the west entrance (Mon–Sat 10am–3.15pm, Sun 12.30–2.30pm; suggested donation $3); just ask one of the purple-hatted docents.

To get there, hop on any of several **buses** from Dupont (N2, N3, N4, or N6) or take buses 30, #32, #34, or #36 from Pennsylvania Avenue (Downtown) or Wisconsin Avenue (Georgetown).

Arlington National Cemetery

The vast sea of identical white headstones on the hillsides of **Arlington National Cemetery** in Virginia (daily: April–Sept 8am–7pm; rest of year 8am–5pm; free; ☎703/607-8000, ⓦwww.arlingtoncemetery.org) stands in poignant contrast to the grand monuments of the capital across the river. The country's most honored final resting place was first used during the Civil War, when the grand mansion at the top of the hill, and all the surrounding land, belonged to Confederate leader **Robert E. Lee**. Nearly 300,000 US war dead lie here. Soldiers who died in world wars I and II, Korea, and Vietnam are buried in the **Tomb of the Unknowns**, where visitors can watch a solemn Changing of the Guard ceremony every thirty minutes (every hour Oct through March). An eternal flame marks the grave of **President John F. Kennedy**, near his brother Robert and next to his wife, Jacqueline Kennedy Onassis, while the gravesite of Pierre L'Enfant offers a superb view over the Mall and the District that he designed. The recent **Women in Military Service Memorial**, by the main gate, is one of several memorials to celebrated personnel and the country's first national monument to American servicewomen.

Unless you have strong legs and lots of time, the best way to see the vast cemetery is by Tourmobile (see p.421), which leaves from the visitor center at the entrance. You can also walk here from the Lincoln Memorial across the Arlington Bridge.

The Pentagon

Wedged between the Potomac and I-395 in Virginia, the **Pentagon** (Mon–Fri 9.30am–5pm; free; ☎703/697-1776, ⓦwww.defenselink) is the headquarters of the US military establishment and one of the world's largest chunks of architecture: though it's only five stories tall, the total floor area – 6.5 million square feet – is three times that of the Empire State Building. Each of the five sides is more than 900ft long, and the combined length of all the internal corridors exceeds seventeen miles. These and other useless factoids are about all you get from visiting the behemoth building, apart from the opportunity to see at first-hand the people responsible for thwarting the country's adversaries. In the one novel departure from the norm, the service-personnel guides who accompany you walk backward the entire time to ensure that foreign agents posing as gawking tourists don't slip off into the restrooms.

Ninety-minute **guided tours** used to leave every thirty minutes from the small waiting area inside the entrance. Nowadays, you should call ahead to check on the status of tourist visits. Tours were suspended indefinitely after September 11, 2001, when terrorists crashed a hijacked airplane into the Pentagon, killing nearly two hundred people and destroying a sizeable section of the building.

The Newseum

The **Newseum** is temporarily closed while it relocates from Arlington to Washington, DC, and is scheduled to re-open at Pennsylvania Avenue and Sixth Street (☎703/284-3544, ⓦwww.newseum.org) in 2006. The museum's mission is to provide an interactive look at the history, theory, and practice of journalism. Visitors will be greeted by a daily dose of news from the front pages of papers around the world, and various "icons" of freedom will be on display, among them a South African ballot box, a toppled statue of Lenin, and the largest section of the Berlin Wall outside of Berlin. Also here is the world's first **Journalists Memorial**, a 24-foot-high spiraling glass prism, etched with the names of the more than 1400 journalists killed while reporting.

Eating

Just as the faces in government change with every election, so too do **restaurants**, which come and go more quickly in Washington, DC, than just about anywhere else in the US. Within this constant flux a few long-standing favorites endure. Certain neighborhoods – Connecticut Avenue around **Dupont Circle**, 18th Street and Columbia Road in **Adams–Morgan**, M Street in **Georgetown**, and downtown's **Seventh Street** and **Chinatown** – always seem to hold a good range of dining options. There are handy **food courts** in Union Station and at the Old Post Office and National Place, the last two both on Pennsylvania Avenue. A few citywide chains, like *Teaism*, *Firehook*, and the *Chesapeake Bagel Bakery*, offer good coffee and quick snacks; otherwise, the cafés in the main museums are good for downtown lunch breaks.

Downtown

America Union Station, 50 Massachusetts Ave NE ☎ 202/682-9555. The huge, reasonably priced menu has been culled from all over the US. Choose between the double-decker restaurant inside and the concourse seating outside.

The Breadline 1751 Pennsylvania Ave NW ☎ 202/822-8900. DC's best sandwiches are made with DC's best bread. Mon–Fri 7am–6pm.

Café Asia 1720 I St NW ☎ 202/659-2696. Situated in an old townhouse, the café serves exellent-value dishes such as *sashimi*, Thai noodles, and lemongrass-grilled chicken. Sushi happy hour Mon–Sat 5.30–7.30pm.

District Chophouse & Brewery 509 7th St NW ☎ 202/347-3434. This classy swing-era joint delivers great music, a grillhouse menu, and good house beers on tap.

Grillfish 1200 New Hampshire Ave NW ☎ 202/331-7310. One of the best finds in DC offers casual dining, perfectly cooked fish and seafood, and excellent desserts.

Jaleo 480 7th St NW ☎ 202/628-7949. Call in early for a glass of wine and nibbles, because the notoriously long waits at this fashionable, upscale tapas bar can spoil an otherwise perfect evening.

Julia's Empanadas 1221 Connecticut Ave NW ☎ 202/861-8828. Tasty South American turnovers of beef, chicken, and veggies will fill the stomach without emptying the wallet.

Malaysia Kopitiam 1827 M St NW ☎ 202/833-6232. A no-frills basement eatery, where the extensive selection of Malay, Chinese, and Indian fare is a first-class ticket to Southeast Asia.

The Mark 401 7th St NW ☎ 202/783-3133. This chic and expensive spot features seasonal menus of New American cuisine and a select choice of wines by the glass.

Old Ebbitt Grill 675 15th St NW ☎ 202/347-4801. At this very plush, old-style Downtown tavern, check out the immaculate mahogany bar, gilt mirrors, and stylish clientele. Serves everything from burgers to oysters.

Oodles Noodles 1120 19th St NW ☎ 202/293-3138. A lunch-crowd favorite offering flavorful, hearty bowls of noodles on the cheap. Open Sun after 12pm.

Red Sage 605 14th St NW ☎ 202/638-4444. This renowned and expensive Southwestern restaurant drips with Santa Fe chic, but you can also eat for less at the funky *Chili Bar*. Reservations essential.

Reeve's Restaurant and Bakery 1306 G St NW ☎ 202/628-6350. A classic daytime diner turns out big fried breakfasts, crisp-coated chicken at lunchtime, and strawberry pies. Mon–Sat 7am–6pm.

Sky Terrace *Washington Hotel*, 515 15th St NW ☎ 202/638-5900. From its hilltop perch above the White House, this restaurant has magnificent views that more than make up for the unremarkable food. May–Oct only.

Dupont Circle

Afterwords Café 1517 Connecticut Ave NW ☎202/387-1462. In the back of Kramerbooks (hence the punny name), the café serves imaginative meals and a fine Sunday brunch. Open late every night and all night Fri & Sat, with live music Wed–Sat.

Annie's Paramount Steakhouse 1609 17th St NW ☎202/232-0395. This easy-going steakhouse, an institution in the Dupont gay scene, is open all night Fri & Sat, when midnight brunch is served.

Bistro du Coin 1738 Connecticut Ave NW ☎202/234-6969. Visit a rare treat in DC – a classic bistro with a superb bar, boisterous atmosphere, and genuine French food. Closed Mon.

Café Citron 1343 Connecticut Ave NW ☎202/530-8844. Bright restaurant serving tasty Caribbean-influenced Latin food – try the *ceviche* or fill up on one of their popular *fajitas*. Stick around for a smooth late-night scene at the bar.

Cyberstop Café 1513 17th St NW ☎202/234-2470. One of DC's few cybercafés, this laid-back neighborhood coffee shop serves good coffee, cakes, and bagels, with seating inside the arty townhouse or out on the sidewalk.

Johnny's Half Shelf 2002 P St NW ☎202/296-2021. Retro 1920s decor and a swank marble bar sit well with this bistro's down-to-earth menu, which features local seafood specialties. Open Mon–Sat for lunch and dinner, Sun 5pm for dinner only.

Lauriol Plaza 1801 18th St NW ☎202/387-0035. Lines form early at this packed, family-run Mexican–Spanish restaurant, which is renowned for its excellent food.

Luna Grill & Diner 1301 Connecticut Ave NW ☎202/835-2280. A quirky, comfy diner with wholesome blue-plate specials, "green plate" (vegetarian) dishes, and organic coffees and teas. Also makes an excellent weekend brunch spot.

The Newsroom 1803 Connecticut Ave NW ☎202/332-1489. The newsstand offers a wide selection of hipster magazines, British and French imports, and hard-to-find newspapers, plus Internet access, coffee, and snacks.

Pizzeria Paradiso 2029 P St NW ☎202/223-1245. Arguably DC's best pizzeria, with thunderingly good food, affordable house wine, and a charming atmosphere – though you can expect to wait in line.

Sushi Taro 1503 17th St NW ☎202/462-8999. The steady stream of Japanese suits seeking a taste of home testifies that this is indeed one of DC's best Japanese restaurants. Dinner only on Sat.

Zorba's Café 1612 20th St NW ☎202/387-8555. A self-serve café where you'll find filling Greek combo platters, kebabs, and pita-bread sandwiches. The sidewalk seating is hard to get in summer.

Adams–Morgan

Addis Ababa 2106 18 St NW ☎202/232-6092. Tasty vegetables and thick stews with traditional *injera* flatbread are the highlights at this inexpensive and authentic Ethiopian restaurant.

Ben's Chili Bowl 1213 U St NW ☎202/667-0909. Outside of Adams–Morgan, but well worth the hike for legendary chili dogs, milk shakes, and cheese fries at a DC landmark.

Bukom Café 2442 18th St NW ☎202/265-4600. Delicious West African dishes – such as *obe ila*, a soup with okra and smoked fish, and *nkatikwan*, chicken with peanuts (figure $10) – which you can wash down with African beer and music.

Cashion's Eat Place 1819 Columbia Rd NW ☎202/797-1819. A chef's restaurant, *Cashion's* serves fabulous – and expensive – New American cuisine. Book ahead or sip a proper cocktail at the very chic bar while you wait. Closed Mon. Dinner and Sunday brunch only.

The Diner 2453 18th St NW ☎202/232-8800. It's more stylish café than down-at-the-heels diner, but with greasy classics adorning the eggs-and-sandwich-rich menu, classic coffee counter, and 24hr service, it's a winner. Late-night lines form on the weekends.

Meze 2437 18th St NW ☎202/797-0017. A wide array of delicious Turkish *mezze* (the Middle East's answer to *tapas*) is served up hot or cold in a fashionable setting.

Mixtec 1792 Columbia Rd NW ☎202/332-1011. The great-tasting, low-priced Mexican food includes superb tacos and tortillas, plus spit-roasted chicken, mussels steamed with chilis, and a soothing *menudo* (an aromatic soup).

Pasta Mia 1790 Columbia Rd NW ☎202/328-9114. Expect long lines at this no-frills, family-run pasteria, which piles on the pasta at prices so low it's worth the wait. Mon–Sat 6.30–10pm.

Pizza Mart 2445 18th St NW ☎202/234-9700. The elephantine slices at this hole-in-the-wall pizzeria are a club-hopper's late-night salvation. Open until 4am.

Saigonnais 2307 18th St NW ☎202/232-5300. The gourmet-quality Vietnamese food includes such specialties as whole steamed fish and an amazing fish soup. The food is worth the slightly higher prices.

Tryst 2459 18th St NW ☎202/232-5500. Hipster hangout that serves coffee and tasty baked goods to sofa-dwelling clientele before transforming into a bar at night.

Georgetown

Amma Vegetarian Kitchen 3291 M St NW ℡202/625-6625. A scrumptious haven for strict vegetarians, this South Indian joint specializes in *dosa* – lentil and rice flour wraps – but also has very good curries and yummy breads.

Au Pied de Cochon 1335 Wisconsin Ave NW ℡202/337-6400. This casual, enjoyable 24hr bistro is great for breakfasts and early-bird dinners (around $10).

Café la Ruche 1039 31st St NW ℡202/965-2684. Seek out this relaxing, inexpensive bistro away from M Street's maddening crowds, with patio seating ideal for dining alone or in twos. Count on the onion soup, quiches, and croques or drop by for a pastry and an espresso. Open until 10pm (weekends until midnight).

Dean & Deluca 3276 M St NW ℡202/342-2500. The conservatory-style café and attached deli-market are in one of Georgetown's handsomest redbrick buildings. Open until 8pm (weekends 9pm).

J Paul's 3218 M St NW ℡202/333-3450. The best of Georgetown's saloons is not cheap, but worth it for the famous crab cakes and house-brewed Amber Ale.

Japan Inn 1715 Wisconsin Ave NW ℡202/337-3400. Choose between a private room with *tatami* mats or upstairs seating where cooks slice and dice at your table. The menu has many traditional dishes rarely seen outside of Japan, like raw quail's egg over taro root and seaweed-wrapped *onigiri* rice balls with salted plums.

Moby Dick's 1070 31 St NW ℡202/333-4400. Just steps from the canal, this cramped kitchen does great Persian food – tender kebabs, *lavash* bread, rice, and yogurt – all for under $10.

Old Glory 3139 M St NW ℡202/337-3406. At this rollicking barbecue spot, hickory smoke rises in earnest from the kitchen. Choose from six different sauces to add tang to your meal.

Paolo's 1303 Wisconsin Ave NW ℡202/333-7353. Designer Italian dining – gourmet pizzas and even better pasta – is your reward. Compete for the few sidewalk tables.

Saigon Inn 2928 M St NW ℡202/337-5588. Bargain lunch deals during the week pull in the crowds – though the Vietnamese food is a bit too Westernized to be authentic.

Red Ginger 1564 Wisconsin Ave NW ℡202/965-7009. This colorful Caribbean bistro brings a splash of the islands to Georgetown, with plenty of rum for everyone. Dinner only.

Upper Northwest

Dancing Crab 4611 Wisconsin Ave NW ℡202/244-1482. Noisy, messy, and fun, this crab house serves up piles of the area's best softshells.

Indique 3512 Connecticut Ave NW ℡202/244-6600. Recipes from all over India come together with a modern twist at this stylish and affordable restaurant. Don't miss the tasty *samosa* appetizer.

Lebanese Taverna 2641 Connecticut Ave NW ℡202/265-8681. Delicious Middle Eastern joint with soothingly dark, authentic decor inside and ample sidewalk tables under shady umbrellas outside.

Nam Viet 3419 Connecticut Ave NW ℡202/237-1015. You really can't go wrong at this no-frills Vietnamese spot: excellent food, heaping portions, extensive menu, and exceptionally low prices.

Woodley Café 2619 Connecticut Ave NW ℡202/332-5773. This roomy neighborhood café/bar attracts a mellow crowd. Breakfast and Sunday brunch are good, and there's a full menu for lunch and dinner.

Entertainment and nightlife

DC's **bar** and **nightlife** scene is less developed than those in more settled cities. Peak times for drinking tend to be the rush hours, and comparatively few people who work in the District during the week venture back into town at the weekend. However, things are slowly improving, and in the well-worn haunts of collegiate **Georgetown**, yuppified **Dupont Circle**, and boisterous **Adams–Morgan**, you should be able to pass a pleasant evening or two. For clubs, expect to pay a cover of $5 to $15 (highest at weekends); ticket prices for most gigs run $5 to $20. Check the free weekly *CityPaper* for up-to-date **listings** of music, theater, and other events in the area – as well as good alternative features and reporting. The *Washington Blade* and *Metro Weekly* focus on **gay** and **lesbian** life, which is at its most outgoing in Dupont Circle.

Apex 1415 22nd St NW ☏ 202/296-0505. The popular gay dance club, at its best on Friday and Saturday nights, draws a party crowd.

Bedrock Billiards 1841 Columbia Rd NW ☏ 202/667-7665. A comfortable, lively subterranean setting, top bartenders, and loyal clientele set this funky pool hall apart from Adams–Morgan's more frenzied club scene.

The Black Cat 1811 14th St NW ☏ 202/667-7960. Showcases new bands and veteran alternative acts. The separate bar has no cover charge.

Blue Room 2321 18th St NW ☏ 202/332-0800. Classier than the typical Adams–Morgan fare, this swank venue boasts a bar worthy of Bogart's elbows. Closed Mon.

Blues Alley 1073 Wisconsin Ave NW (rear) ☏ 202/337-4141, ⊛ www.bluesalley.com. The small, celebrated Georgetown jazz bar, in business for more than thirty years, attracts top names. Reserve in advance.

The Brickskeller 1523 22nd St NW ☏ 202/293-1885. Brick-lined basement saloon serves "the world's largest selection of beer" – more than 800 different types.

Chi-Cha Lounge 1624 U St NW ☏ 202/234-8400. This upscale candlelit lounge oozes atmosphere, with live Latin music and regulars toking on fruit-cured tobacco from Middle Eastern–style hookahs.

Dream 1350 Okie St NE ☏ 202/636-9030. Mobs of Washingtonians from all walks of life flock to this massive four-story club to dance to hip-hop, techno, pop, and Latin – each floor plays a different style. Take a cab home at night. Cover $10.

The Dubliner 520 N Capitol St NW, in the *Phoenix Park Hotel* ☏ 202/737-3773. At this bare-bones Irish bar, go for the Guinness on draft, live music, and boisterous conversation.

Eighteenth Street Lounge 1212 18th St ☏ 202/466-3922. An ultra-hip club housed discreetly in Teddy Roosevelt's former mansion, where the beats – mostly acid jazz, dub, and trip-hop – are always smooth. Dress the part.

ESPN Zone 555 12th St NW ☏ 202/783-3776. The sports empire's DC branch has hundreds of TVs – even above the urinals – all tuned into the games of the moment.

Fox and Hounds 1537 17th St NW ☏ 202/232-6307. Smack in the middle of the 17th Street scene, this easygoing bar draws a diverse crowd, all there to enjoy the very stiff and very cheap rail drinks. Hit the patio in the summer.

Hawk and Dove 329 Pennsylvania Ave SE ☏ 202/543-3300. The famous old pub rolls on with a battered bar and a young, loud crowd.

Habana Village 1834 Columbia Rd NW ☏ 202/462-6310. The intoxicating Latin dance joint is infused with the eclectic spirit of the Adams–Morgan of old.

Lucky Bar 1221 Connecticut Ave NW ☏ 202/331-3733. This everybody-knows-your-name kind of place has plenty of room and booths at the back to hang out in and shoot pool, plus $2 beers on Thursday and international soccer on TV.

Madam's Organ 2461 18th St NW ☏ 202/667-5370. A refreshingly attitude-free Adams–Morgan standby that mixes eccentric characters, loud music, and cheap beer.

McFadden's Saloon 2401 Pennsylvania Ave NW ☏ 202/223-2338. This big two-story bar attracts a younger crowd from nearby George Washington University with 25¢ wings and $5 pitchers of beer during the week. Weekends can get wild, especially on nights when nurses and flight attendants drink free.

Mie N Yu 3125 M St NW ☏ 202/333-6122. With house DJs and a menu of clever cocktails, this swish Asian/Middle Eastern restaurant and bar draws an urbane crowd eager for a respite from Georgetown's collegiate scene.

Mr Smith's 3104 M St NW ☏ 202/333-3104. This brick-walled saloon bar on the Georgetown drag serves up decent burgers and beer, and has live piano music and sing-along every night.

Nanny O'Brien's 3319 Connecticut Ave NW ☏ 202/686-9189. An authentic Irish pub, *Nanny's* is a dark and cozy nook with live music several nights a week.

Nation 1015 Half St SE ☏ 202/554-1500. This mid-sized warehouse concert venue doubles as a dance club featuring international guest DJs. Thursdays attract a Goth crowd, the 18-and-over raves at *Code* on Fridays, and Saturday's *Velvet Nation* is a favorite on the gay scene. Take a cab home as the neighborhood is not the place to linger.

9:30 Club 815 V St NW ☏ 202/265-0930. Top musicians love to play at this spacious yet intimate club, deservedly famous as DC's best venue for live acts, from indie rock and pop to reggae and rap.

Red 1802 Jefferson Place NW ☏ 202/466-3475. Hipsters show up well past midnight at this underground hideout to dance to deep-house beats, often until dawn. Closed Mon–Wed.

Rumba Café 2443 18th St NW ☏ 202/588-5501. Great Latin bands tuck into a tight space to set the atmosphere at this funky bar/restaurant.

Sequoia 3000 K St NW ☏ 202/944-4200. This popular restaurant/bar at the eastern end of Washington Harbor provides outdoor terrace seating overlooking the river.

The Tombs 1226 36th St NW ☎202/337-6668. Basement Georgetown haunt for burgers and beers.

Velvet Lounge 915 U St NW ☎202/462-3213. Schmooze and booze in a relaxed bar, with laid-back live music five nights a week (small cover).

Performing arts

With five different theater spaces, the **Kennedy Center**, 2700 F St NW (☎202/467-4600, ⓦwww.kennedy-center.org), next to the Watergate complex, hosts most of the capital's highbrow cultural events (including Washington Opera and Washington Ballet Company performances). It also presents nightly **film** screenings organized by the American Film Institute (☎202/785-4600; $8.50). The highly regarded, often pioneering **Arena Stage**, 1101 Sixth St SW at Maine Avenue (☎202/488-3300, ⓦwww .arenastage.org), puts on contemporary **theater** and performance pieces at its three-stage complex, while the historic **Ford's Theatre**, 511 Tenth St NW (☎202/347-4833, ⓦwww.fordstheatre.org), has a family-friendly program of mainstream musicals and dramas, frequently historical in nature. The celebrated **Shakespeare Theatre**, 450 Seventh St NW (☎202/547-1122, ⓦwww.shakespearedc.org), stages five productions a year, plus a free summer performance in Rock Creek Park.

The experimental **Woolly Mammoth Theatre** stages productions in the Kennedy Center but will move to a new home on Seventh and D streets NW in the fall of 2004 (☎202/289-2443, ⓦwww.woollymammoth.net). The **Source Theatre Company**, 1835 14th St NW (☎202/462-1073), rounds out DC's alternative theater scene.

Twenty minutes out of the city, **Wolf Trap Farm Park**, 1551 Trap Rd, Vienna, VA (☎703/255-1900, ⓦwww.wolf-trap.org), is the country's first national park for the performing arts, and presents concerts, opera, ballet, and dance at the outdoor Filene Center or the indoor Barns. There's a Metro shuttle bus service from West Falls Church station for most performances (every 20 min; $4). For **tickets** call ☎703/218-6500 or go online at ⓦtickets .com. You can also buy tickets in person at the Wolf Trap box office (☎703/255-1868).

Spectator sports

Tickets to the Washington Redskins **football** games at FedEx Field, just inside the Capital Beltway in Landover, Maryland (☎301/276-6050, ⓦwww.red-skins.com), are sold on a season-ticket basis only.

You'll have better luck catching the DC United **soccer** team at RFK Stadium, 2400 E Capitol St SE (☎703/478-6600, ⓦwww.dcunited.com; metro Stadium-Armory). The huge downtown **MCI Center** (☎202/628-3200, ⓦwww.mcicenter.com; next to Gallery Place–Chinatown Metro) hosts home games of the pro **basketball** Washington Wizards (ⓦwww.nba.com/wizards) and Mystics (ⓦwww.wnba.com/mystics), as well as the pro **hockey** Washington Capitals (ⓦwww.washingtoncaps.com). The prospects for the woebegone Wizards look murky after Michael Jordan's return to the court in 2001 and subsequent firing two years later. The Caps have serious star power in their line-up with Czech phenom and perennial all-star Jaromir Jagr "lighting the lamp" for them on a regular basis.

Virginia

Traveling through **VIRGINIA**, the oldest, largest, and wealthiest of the American colonies and the single most powerful influence on the early United States, is a nonstop history lesson. Pretty and rural it may be, but it's the past that predominates: wherever you go you're pointed towards this or that painstakingly restored two-hundred-year-old building, where something or other happened a long time ago. The more you know about it all, the more rewarding Virginia is to visit, but the historical plaques get a bit ridiculous after a while, marking every spot where George Washington slept, Thomas Jefferson thought, or Robert E. Lee tied his horse to a tree.

Virginia's recorded history began at **Jamestown**, just off the Chesapeake Bay, with the establishment in 1607 of the first successful British colony in North America. Though the first colonists hoped to find gold, it was **tobacco** that made their fortunes. The native strain – used for hundreds of years by Virginia's indigenous population, of whom almost no trace remains – was too strongly flavored for European tastes. When a smoother, more palatable variety of tobacco was introduced in 1615 by John Rolfe – the same man whose shipwreck on Bermuda inspired Shakespeare's *The Tempest* – tobacco quickly became the colony's major cash crop. Before long, vast plantations, owned by a very few aristocratic families, sprang up along the many broad rivers that flow into the Chesapeake Bay. To grow and harvest tobacco required both an immense amount of land – so the Native Americans had to go – and intensive labor that led to the plantation owners bringing in **slaves** from Africa. By the end of the seventeenth century, enslaved African-Americans accounted for nearly half of the colony's 75,000 people; a hundred years later, they numbered over 300,000. Virginians had an enormous impact on the foundation of the nascent United States: George Mason, Thomas Jefferson, and James Madison wrote the Declaration of Independence and the Constitution, and four of the first five US presidents were from Virginia. However, by the mid-1800s the state was in decline, its once fertile fields depleted by overuse and its agrarian economy increasingly eclipsed by the urban and industrialized North.

As the confrontation between North and South over slavery and related economic and political issues grew more divisive, Virginia was caught in the middle. Though this slaveholding state initially voted against secession from the Union, it joined the Confederacy when the **Civil War** broke out, providing its capital, Richmond, and its military leader, Robert E. Lee, who had previously turned down an offer to lead the Union army. Four long years later, Virginia was ravaged, its towns and cities wrecked, its farmlands ruined, and most of its youth dead. It has never regained its early prosperity, or its prominence in national affairs.

Richmond itself was largely destroyed in the war; today it's a small city, with some good museums, and is the best starting point for seeing Virginia. The bulk of the **Colonial** sites are concentrated just to the east, in what is known as the **Historic Triangle**. Here the remains of **Jamestown**, the original colony, **Williamsburg**, the restored Colonial capital, and **Yorktown**, site of the final battle of the Revolutionary War, lie within half an hour's drive of each other.

Another historic center, Thomas Jefferson's **Charlottesville**, sits at the foot of the gorgeous **Blue Ridge Mountains**, an hour west of Richmond. An attractive small college town in its own right, it's also within easy reach of the natural splendors of **Shenandoah National Park** and the little towns of the western valleys. **Northern Virginia**, often visited as a day-trip from Washington, DC, features several posh suburbs and a number of restored historic homes, the closest Colonial architecture to the capital being in **Alexandria**, and **Manassas**, the scene of two important Civil War battles.

Getting around Virginia

Virginia is an easy place to explore. Two north–south Amtrak routes from Washington, DC, cross the state, one through Charlottesville towards Atlanta and the other through Fredericksburg and Richmond on the way to Florida; in addition, daily connections run east from Richmond to the Historic Triangle, and west from Charlottesville towards Chicago. Greyhound **buses** reach dozens of smaller towns. **Drivers** heading south can take the stunning Blue Ridge Parkway along the Appalachians. If you've got the time, there's ample opportunity for **cycling**, whether on quiet country roads or up in the mountains, and **hiking** or **walking** are also worth thinking about.

Northern Virginia

Northern Virginia, almost all of which lies within commuting distance of Washington, DC, holds some extremely exclusive suburbs, including McLean and the rest of Fairfax County, which are home to a high proportion of US senators. In contrast, **Alexandria**, nestled on the Potomac just beyond the limits of the nation's capital, seems at least two centuries removed from the modern political whirl. Further afield, this Anglophile heartland of Virginia's landed gentry – often called "Hunt Country" for their love of horses and fancy-dress blood sports – holds well-preserved eighteenth- and nineteenth-century stately homes, cottages, churches, barns, and taverns tucked away along the quiet back roads. It's all very popular with tourists, nowhere more so than **Mount Vernon**, the longtime home of George Washington, while **Manassas** to the west was the site of the bloody battles of Bull Run.

Alexandria

The sheer amount of well-preserved eighteenth- and nineteenth-century architecture in Old Town Alexandria, which extends a good half-mile west of the Potomac and several blocks north and south of it, makes **ALEXANDRIA** a must, especially for those who are staying in Washington, DC, but do not have time to venture very far into Virginia. Originally an important Colonial trading post and a busy port named after the pioneer John Alexander, the town was actually ceded to the newly created nation's capital in 1801 until it was returned to Virginia in 1847. When the Civil War broke out, it was occupied by Union forces and was the only place in the South to remain so for the duration of the war, which must have been a sore point for Robert E. Lee, whose boyhood home was here. In earlier days, George Washington had also maintained close ties with Alexandria, owning property here and attending gatherings at the famous **Gadsby's Tavern**, 134 N Royal St, now a restaurant and a museum (April–Oct Tues–Sat 10am–5pm, Sun and Mon 1–5pm; Nov–March Wed–Sat 11am–4pm, Sun 1–4pm; $4). Among other meticulously restored buildings open to the public are **Carlyle House**, 121 N Fairfax St (Tues–Sat 10am–5pm, Sun noon–4:30pm; $4), a 1752 manor house that was home to five royal governors, and **Lee-Fendall House**, 614 Oronoco St (Tues–Sat 10am–3pm, Sun noon–3pm; $4), which belonged to a local family that lived here for over a century and contains many of their possessions. Down on the waterfront, a former munitions factory houses the **Torpedo Factory Art Center**, 105 N Union St (Tues–Fri 10am–3pm, Sat 10am–5pm, Sun 1–5pm; free), where you can watch artists at work in over 160 studios and browse several galleries. In the same building, the **Alexandria Archaeology Museum** (Tues–Fri 10am–3pm, Sat 10am–5pm, Sun 1–5pm; free; ☏703/838-4399, ⓦ www.alexandria.org) displays various aspects of the town's history and prehistory. The Georgian **Christ Church** at 118 N Washington St was built in 1773 and often counted George Washington among its worshippers (pew no. 60).

Next to the Amtrak and subway King Street Station stands the obelisk of the **George Washington National Masonic Memorial** (daily 9am–5pm, except New Year's Day, Thanksgiving, and Christmas; free), which is visible for miles around.

Practicalities

Alexandria has the distinct advantage of being on the Washington **Metro** line, making it easy to reach from the city. For that reason, few tourists choose to stay here; should you decide to, however, central motels include *Embassy Suites*, 1900 Diagonal Rd (☏703/684-5900; ➒), *Hampton Inn*, 1616 King St (☏703/299-9900 or 1-800/HAMPTON, ⓦ www.hamptoninn.com; ➏), both near the King Street Metro station, and the *Holiday Inn*, just across from the town square, at 480 King St (☏703/549-6080, ⓦ www.holiday-inn.com; ➑).

The friendly **visitor center** is located in the town's oldest house at 221 King St (☏703/838-4200, ⓦ www.FunSide.com), and can provide the usual tourist information as well as details on walking tours. There's a great range of **places to eat**. Try the tasty, local seafood at the *Fish Market*, 105 King St (☏703/836-5376), or the New Orleans–style Creole fare at *Two-Nineteen*, 219 King St (☏703/549-1141). *Gadsby's Tavern* (see opposite) is also the place to sample eighteenth-century cuisine like peanut soup, Sally Lunn bread, black-eyed pea succotash, ducklings, and Virginia ham.

Mount Vernon – George Washington's home

Set on a bluff overlooking the broad Potomac River, eight miles south of Alexandria, **Mount Vernon** (daily: April–Aug 8am–5pm; March, Sept & Oct 9am–5pm; Nov–Feb 9am–4pm; $11) is among the most attractive historic houses in the US. The country estate of **George Washington**, with its five hundred acres of landscaped and planted grounds, has been restored to the year 1799, the last year of Washington's life. Just fifteen miles from downtown DC, it's close enough to be reached as a day-trip on the city's Tourmobiles ($25; see p.421), or by the Fairfax Connector 101 bus from Huntington Metro station. Besides illuminating the life and times of the leader of the revolutionary armies and the first US president, Mount Vernon also provides an eye-opening look into the lifestyle of the Colonial gentlemen who founded the United States of America.

A small museum and outbuildings give an overview of life at Mount Vernon; in the house itself, the furnishings and decoration reflect Washington's preference for plain living, but few items – a reading chair with built-in fan, and a key to the destroyed Bastille, presented by Thomas Paine on behalf of Lafayette – give much of a sense of his character. The four-poster bed upon which he died stands in an upstairs bedroom; he and his wife Martha are buried in a simple tomb on the south side of the house.

Gunston Hall – George Mason's home

Gunston Hall, the 1755 Georgian brick home of Washington's contemporary **George Mason**, stands just around a bend in the river, a twenty-minute drive south along Hwy-1, at the east end of Hwy-242 near Lorton (daily 9.30am–5pm; $8; ☎703/550-9220). It was Mason's revolutionary idea "that all men are by nature equally free and independent and have certain inherent rights," which Jefferson incorporated into the Declaration of Independence. Mason was later one of the main framers of the US Constitution, which he subsequently refused to support because it neither included a Bill of Rights nor abolished slavery. Unlike Washington and Jefferson, Mason eschewed public power, preferring to stay here with his family – which is understandable once you've seen the place. One of the most impressive works of architecture in Virginia, much of it was designed and constructed by William Buckland; the masterful interiors, particularly in the stately drawing room, feature exquisite carved ornamentation (a fireplace mantel in the Chinoiserie style is particularly distinctive). The house fronts onto a large formal garden, beyond which lie extensive grounds surrounded by a riverfront state park and wildlife refuge.

Manassas Battlefield National Park

Manassas Battlefield National Park extends over grassy hills at the western fringes of the Washington, DC, suburban belt, just off I-66. Such is the power of these brooding hillsides that you don't have to know the details of what happened here to get a sense of the site's historical importance. Soon after the first shots were fired at Fort Sumter, the first major land battle of the Civil War – known as the **Battle of Bull Run** – was fought here on the morning of July 21, 1861. Expecting an easy victory, some 25,000 Union troops attacked a Confederate detachment that controlled a vital railroad link to the Shenandoah Valley. The rebels proved powerful opponents, their strength in battle earning their commander, General Thomas Jackson, the famous nickname "Stonewall." He and General Lee also masterminded a second Confederate victory here in late August 1862.

Displays in the small **visitor center** at the entrance (daily 8.30am–5pm; June–Aug Sat & Sun until 6pm; park admission $2) describe how the first battle took shape, and detail other aspects of the war.

Richmond and the tidewater

At the very heart of Virginia, **Richmond** and the **Chesapeake Bay tidewater** are, in many ways, where the US was born. Not only does this fairly compact area hold some of the most important surviving Colonial-era sites, it is also where the strength of the nation was tested by the Civil War. The greatest interest is to be found in the compact **Historic Triangle**, east of Richmond, and in **Fredericksburg**, to the north, around which several crucial battles were waged.

Richmond and around

Founded in 1737 at the furthest navigable point on the James River, **RICHMOND** remained a small outpost until just before the end of the Colonial era, when independence-minded Virginians, realizing that their capital at Williamsburg was open to British attack, shifted it fifty miles further inland. The move to Richmond failed to offer much protection – the city was raided many times and twice put to the torch, once by troops under the command of Benedict Arnold.

Richmond subsequently flourished, its population reaching 100,000 by the time of the Civil War. When war broke out it was named the **capital of the Confederacy**, despite the fact that Virginia had voted two-to-one against secession from the Union just a month before. The massive **Tredegar Iron Works**, now a dedicated visitor-center-cum-museum, became the main engine of the Confederate war machine. For four years the city was the focus of Southern defenses and Union attacks, but despite an almost constant state of siege – General McClellan came within six miles as early as 1862, and General Grant steamrolled remorselessly towards it through the last months of the war – it held on until the very end. It was less than a week after the fall of Richmond, on April 3, 1865, that General Lee surrendered to General Grant at Appomattox, a hundred miles west.

After the war, Richmond was devastated. Much of its downtown was burned, allegedly by fleeing Confederates who wanted to keep its stores of weapons and its warehouses full of tobacco out of the victors' hands. Rebuilding, however, was quick, and the city's economy has remained among the strongest in the South. Today's Richmond has an extensive inventory of architecturally significant older buildings alongside its modern office towers. **Tobacco** is still a major industry – machine-rolled cigarettes were invented here in the 1870s, and Marlboro-maker **Phillip Morris** runs a huge manufacturing plant just south of downtown. Richmond is also a leading **banking** center.

Arrival, information, and getting around

Two hours by car from Washington, DC, via I-95, which cuts through the east side of downtown, Richmond is also served by Amtrak, which pulls into 7519 Staples Mill Rd, five miles northwest of downtown (a new downtown train station is slated to open in 2004 or 2005). Greyhound, which stops just off I-64 at 2910 N Blvd, is also a good way from the center of town. The **airport**, ten miles east of downtown, is served by major carriers and has a small **visitor center** (Mon–Fri 9am–5pm; ☎804/236-3260) in the arrivals terminal.

Another small visitor center is located in the bell tower on the state capitol grounds (Mon–Fri 10am–4pm; ☎804/786-4484); the main **visitor center** (daily: June–Aug 9am–7pm; Sept–May 9am–5pm; ☎804/783-7450 or 804/888-RICHMOND), which provides discounts for some of the area's hotels and advises on tours, joined the **CVB** head office at 403 N 3rd St (☎804/782-2777 or 1-888/RICHMOND, ⓦwww.richmondva.org).

Much of Richmond is compact enough to walk around, but to get to outlying places (like the stations or the Museum of Fine Arts) you might want to take a GRTC **bus** (zone system, most fares $1.25; ☎804/358-GRTC). More convenient for museum-hopping is the weekend-only **Cultural Connection bus** (June to mid-Sept Sat 10am–5.30pm, Sun noon–5.30pm; $1; ☎804/783-7499), whose three separate routes link all major sites.

Accommodation

Finding well-priced **accommodation** in Richmond isn't difficult, with plenty of anonymous downtown hotels catering to the business and government trade. If you prefer to get a feel for the old city, stay the night in a **B&B** in one of the historic quarters.

The Berkeley 1200 E Cary St ☎804/780-1300 or 1-888/780-4422, ⓦwww.berkeleyhotel.com. Elegant small hotel on historic Shockoe Slip. **❻**
The Jefferson 101 W Franklin St ☎804/788-8000 or 1-800/424-8014, ⓦwww.jefferson-hotel.com. Beautifully maintained, five-star grand hotel,

with fabulous marble-columned lobby. **❼**
The John Marshall Hotel 101 N Fifth St ☎804/783-1929, ⓦwww.thejohnmarshall.com. Landmark hotel in a central downtown location, with refurbished rooms and complimentary breakfast. **❹**

Linden Row Inn 100 E Franklin St ☎804/783-7000 or 1-800/348-7424, ⓦ www.lindenrowinn.com. A magnificent row of redbrick Georgian terrace houses, now a comfortable modern hotel with antique furnishings. ➍

Midtown Inn and Conference Center 3200 W Broad St ☎804/359-4061 or 1-800/866-0553, ⓦ www.briggshospitality/midtown.html. Good location, near the Fan District and Fine Arts Museum; has the usual hotel chain amenities. ➌

Downtown Richmond

Richmond's **downtown** centers on a few blocks rising up from the James River to either side of Broad Street. Modern office towers front onto a riverside park, while up the hill in the **Court End District**, dozens of well-preserved antebellum homes provide a suitable backdrop for some important museums and historic sites.

The **Virginia State Capitol** (Mon–Fri 9am–5pm, Sat 10am–4pm, Sun 1–4pm, last tour 4.15pm; free), which has been in use since 1788 as the seat of the state (and, during the Civil War, Confederate) government, is the focal point of the city, visible from all over Richmond and offering a sweeping view from its columned portico. Thomas Jefferson had a hand in the design, based on his favorite building, the Roman Maison Carré in Nîmes, France. The domed central rotunda, which is not visible from outside, holds the only marble statue of George Washington modeled from life, and busts of Jefferson and the seven other Virginia-born US presidents line the walls. Likenesses of famous Virginians, including a solemn bronze Robert E. Lee, fill the adjacent **Old House Chamber**, where Aaron Burr was tried and acquitted of treason in 1807.

Just two blocks north of the capitol, the **Museum of the Confederacy**, 1201 E Clay St (Mon–Sat 10am–5pm, Sun noon–5pm; $7), covers the history of the Civil War through weapons, uniforms, and the like. Personal effects of Confederate leaders include J.E.B. Stuart's plumed hat, the tools used to amputate Stonewall Jackson's arms at Chancellorsville (he died), and Robert E. Lee's revolver and the pen he used to sign the surrender. Next door, the so-called **White House of the Confederacy** (same hours; $7), a Neoclassical mansion where Jefferson Davis lived as Confederate president, has been restored to its 1860s appearance. Tours of the house itself are reverential, but offer a useful perspective on the man himself. A $10 combination ticket allows access to both the house and museum.

Two blocks to the west, the 1812 **Wickham House** now forms part of the excellent **Valentine Richmond History Center** at 1015 E Clay St (Mon–Sat 10am–5pm, Sun noon–5pm; $7). This Neoclassical monolith houses a small local history museum, focusing on the experience of working-class and black Americans, as well as an extensive array of furniture and pre–Civil War clothing such as whalebone corsets and other *Gone With the Wind*–era apparel.

West of the Convention Center on Sixth Street is a neighborhood of early nineteenth-century houses, many fronted by ornate wrought-iron balconies similar to those in New Orleans' French Quarter. Known as **Jackson Ward**, and filling a dozen blocks around First and Clay streets, this has been the center of Richmond's African-American community since well before the Civil War, when Richmond had the largest free black population in the US. As well as covering local history, the **Maggie L. Walker House**, 110 E Leigh St (Mon–Sat 9am–5pm; free; ☎804/771-2017, ⓦ www.nps.gov/mawa), traces the working life of the physically disabled black Richmond woman who, during the 1920s, was the first woman in the US to found and run a bank, now the Consolidated Bank and Trust. Nearby, the **Black History Museum** at 00 Clay

St (Tues–Sat 10am–5pm, Sun 11am–5pm; $4) contains displays on Richmond's role as a center of Southern black society, and includes a well-presented gallery of artifacts of the Civil Rights movement.

A refreshing example of recent urban revitalization is the landscaping of a 1.25-mile stretch of waterfront into **Canal Walk**, which runs between downtown and Shockoe Bottom. For an interesting (and free) insight into the Confederate period, you can start or end your stroll at the **Richmond Civil War Visitor Center**, 490 Tredegar St (☎804-771-2145, ⓦwww.nps .gov/rich), at the refurbished Tredegar Iron Works, down by the river below Fourth Street. More of a museum in reality, it has a regular slide show about Civil War history and three floors of exhibits, including moving personal accounts of the war from ordinary soldiers.

Shockoe Bottom, the Poe Museum, and Church Hill

A short walk southeast from the Court End District, a very different neighborhood allows a glimpse of another side of the Richmond story. Split down the middle by the raised I-95 freeway, the increasingly gentrified (and regularly flooded) riverfront warehouse district of **Shockoe Bottom** still holds a few palpable reminders of Richmond's industrial past among the restaurants and nightclubs on its cobblestone streets. From **Shockoe Slip**, a prettified old wharf area rebuilt in the 1890s after being destroyed in the Civil War, Cary Street runs east along the waterfront, lined by a wall of brick warehouses known as **Tobacco Row**.

Nearby, Richmond's oldest building, an appropriately gloomy 250-year-old stone house at 1914 E Main St, serves as the **Edgar Allan Poe Museum** (Tues–Sat 10am–5pm, Mon & Sun 11am–5pm; ☎804/648-5523; $6). Poe spent much of his youth in Richmond and considered it his home town; he wrote the *Narrative of Arthur Gordon Pym* while working on the Richmond-based magazine *Southern Literary Messenger*. The museum displays Poe memorabilia plus a model of Richmond as it was in his day.

Church Hill, a few blocks northeast, is one of Richmond's oldest surviving residential districts, its decorative eighteenth-century houses, adorned with cast-iron porches and rambling magnolia-filled front gardens, looking out over the James River. Capping the hill at the heart of the neighborhood, **St John's Church** at 2401 E Broad St (Mon–Sat 10am–4pm, Sun 1–4pm, last tour 3.30pm; $5), which dates back to 1741, is best known as the place where, during a 1775 debate on whether the Virginia colony should raise a militia against the British, **Patrick Henry** made the impassioned plea: "Is life so dear, or peace so sweet, to be purchased at the price of chains of slavery? I know not what course others may take, but as for me, give me liberty or give me death." His speech is re-enacted by an actor every Sunday between Memorial and Labor days at 2pm, after the religious services.

The Fan District and Carytown

An interesting Richmond neighborhood, surrounding the campus of Virginia Commonwealth University, is the **Fan District**, so named because its tree-lined avenues fan out at oblique angles. The district spreads west from the downtown area, beyond Belvidere Street (US-1), and its centerpiece, **Monument Avenue**, is lined with garish mansions from the turn of the twentieth century. Richmond's most imposing boulevard was laid out by unabashed city planners from 1889 onwards to commemorate key figures of the Confederacy. Four successive grand intersections hold statues of J.E.B. Stuart, Robert E. Lee, Stonewall Jackson, and Jefferson Davis. In recent times, many of the city's black population expressed dissatisfaction with this choice of heroes, and in 1996 a statue of the late tennis champion **Arthur Ashe** was duly erected. A native of Richmond, Ashe felt obliged to leave the city in 1961 because its tennis courts were segregated. The statue shows Ashe's dedication to education as well as the game of tennis – he's encircled by children and holds books and tennis racquet aloft.

South of Monument Avenue, at 2800 Grove Ave, stands the **Virginia Museum of Fine Arts** (Wed & Fri–Sun 11am–5pm, Thurs until 8pm; $5 donation). An extensive collection of Impressionist and Post-Impressionist paintings is displayed alongside American paintings ranging from George Catlin's romantic images of Plains Indians to the Pop Art creations of Roy Lichtenstein and Claes Oldenburg in the vast West Wing. Other galleries contain such diverse items as Frank Lloyd Wright furniture, Lalique jewelry, and Hindu and Buddhist sculpture from the Himalayas; but perhaps the most popular part of the museum is a world-class array of over three hundred Carl Fabergé works, including four of his trademark jewel-encrusted Easter eggs crafted in the 1890s for the Russian tsars.

Just beyond the Fan District, **Carytown** is a thriving nine-block area of trendy shops offering Asian art, tarot readings, and holistic medicines alongside restaurants on Cary Street, adding a definite flavor of Eastern and New Age sensibilities to the capital of the Old South.

Eating

Richmond has a good choice of **eating** options at both ends of the price spectrum, with barbecue being a specialty.

Acacia 3325 W Cary St ☎804/354-6060. Quality regional cuisine with alfresco dining at this highly-rated Carytown bistro, with a good range of meats in barbecue and other flavorful sauces. Closed Sun & Mon.

Awful Arthur's Seafood Company 101 N 18th St ☎804/643-1700. Shockoe Bottom hangout catering to all budgets, with raw oysters, clams, shrimp, and crabs, and steak for those not wanting seafood.

Millie's Diner 2603 E Main St ☎804/643-5512. Refurbished diner, complete with mini-jukeboxes on each table, a bit out of downtown beyond Shockoe Bottom. The changing menu includes fairly expensive but delicious meals.

Peking Pavilion 1302 E Cary St ☎804/649-8888. Very good, inexpensive (especially at lunchtime) Chinese restaurant in Shockoe Slip serving Szechuan and Mandarin specialties. There's also a branch at 5710 Grove Ave in the West End.

Penny Lane 207 N 7th St ☎804/780-1682. British-style establishment with a full menu of grilled food and other pub grub, plus a full range of English and other beers, and soccer on TV.

Strawberry Street Café 421 N Strawberry St ☎804/353-6860. Casual and comfortable Fan District neighborhood café offering mainly quiches, pasta, and salads.

Third Street Diner 218 E Main St ☎804/788-4750. Relaxed 24hr diner with particularly good breakfasts and Greek dishes. Draws a stylish student crowd, especially at night when it's also a bar.

The Tobacco Company 1201 E Cary St ☎804/782-9431. Inventive New American food in a stunningly restored three-story tobacco warehouse, complete with antique elevator. There's also a cocktail bar with nightly live entertainment in the leafy ground-floor atrium.

Drinking and nightlife

Richmond's main **drinking** and **nightlife** spots are concentrated around the riverside **Shockoe Slip** and **Shockoe Bottom** areas, just east of downtown, where you'll find the likes of the *Richbrau Brewery*, 1214 E Cary St (☎804/644-3018), a watering hole that's especially lively at weekends, and the *Have a Nice Day Café*, 18th and Main streets (☎804/771-1700), a cheesy but fun retro-1970s café and nightclub. In the **Fan District**, try *Cabo's Corner Bistro*, 2053 W Broad St (☎804/355-1144), which has creative steak, seafood, and pasta dishes, and nightly live jazz; *Buddy's Place*, 325 N Robinson St (☎804/355-3701), for standard American fare; or the *Border Chophouse and Bar*, 1501 W Main St (☎804/355-2907), where the specialties are beef, veal, and lamb dishes.

A good bet for live **theater** is the Barksdale Theatre, 1601 Willow Lawn Drive (☎804/282-2620, ⓦwww.barksdalerichmond.org). For details on music and events, check the listings in the free *Style Weekly* newspaper or ⓦwww.arts.Richmond.com.

Fredericksburg

Only a mile off the I-95 highway, about halfway to Richmond from Washington, DC, and easy to reach on Amtrak or Greyhound, **FREDER-ICKSBURG** is one of Virginia's prettiest historic towns, with elegant down-town streets backed by residential avenues lined with white picket fences. In Colonial days, this was an important inland port, where tobacco and other plantation products were loaded onto boats that sailed down the Rappahanock River. Dozens of eighteenth- and nineteenth-century buildings along the waterfront now hold antique stores and secondhand bookshops.

In the 1816 town hall, the **Fredericksburg Area Museum**, 907 Princess Anne St (March–Nov Mon–Sat 10am–5pm, Sun 1–5pm; Dec–Feb Mon–Sat 10am–4pm, Sun 1–4pm; $5), has a broad range of displays tracing local history, from Native American settlements to the present day. The **Rising Sun Tavern**, at 1304 Caroline St, was built as a home in 1760 by George Washington's brother, Charles. As an inn, it became a key meeting place for patriots and a hotbed of sedition. It is now a small **museum** (March–Nov Mon–Sat 9am–5pm, Sun 11am–5pm; Dec–Feb Mon–Sat 10am–4pm, Sun noon–4pm; $5), where costumed guides take visitors around a collection of pub games and ancient pewterware. Guides are also on hand to explain eighteenth-century medicine (and show you live leeches) at **Hugh Mercer's Apothecary Shop**, 1020 Caroline St (March–Nov Mon–Sat 9am–5pm; Dec–Feb Mon–Sat 10am–4pm, Sunday noon–4pm).

Fredericksburg's strategic location made it vital during the **Civil War**, and the land around the town was heavily fought over. More than 100,000 men lost their lives in the major battles of Fredericksburg, Chancellorsville, Spotsylvania, and countless other bloody skirmishes. Indeed Stonewall Jackson himself was mistakenly killed by his own troops at Chancellorsville in May 1863. The **Fredericksburg and Spotsylvania National Battlefield Park**, south of town (visitor center open daily: summer 8.30am–6.30pm; rest of year 9am–5pm; $4 for a weekly pass; ☎540/373-6122 or 1-800/654-4118), has informative exhibits and can provide self-guided tour information. Other major battlefields in the area are **Wilderness** and **Chancellorsville**, west of town.

Practicalities

Fredericksburg's **visitor center** at 706 Caroline St (daily: summer 9am–7pm; rest of year 9am–5pm; ☎540/373-1776 or 1-800/678-4748, ⓦwww.freder-icksburgvirginia.net) can provide maps of walking tours and details about dis-counted tickets to the area's attractions.

Fredericksburg's many old-fashioned **B&Bs** include the eighteenth-century *Kenmore Inn*, 1200 Princess Anne St (restaurant closed Mon; ☎540/371-7622, ⓦwww.kenmoreinn.com; ❹), which has antique-furnished rooms and a cozy pub in the basement that serves traditional fish and ham dishes, occasionally accompanied by live jazz; and the *Richard Johnston Inn*, 711 Caroline St (☎540/899-7606 or 877-557-0770; ❹), an elegant, eighteenth-century B&B

near the visitor center. A pleasant motel to try is the *Fredericksburg Colonial Inn*, 1707 Princess Anne St (☎540/371-5666, ⓦwww.fci1.com; ❸).

Thanks to a lot of weekend activity, the town has several good places to **eat** and **drink**. The closest contemporary equivalent to the bawdy *Rising Sun* is probably *Sammy T's*, 801 Caroline St (☎540/371-2008), a popular bar and diner with substantial sandwiches and a huge range of bottled beers. *Smythe's Cottage* at 303 Fauquier St (☎540/373-1645) serves up tasty Southern cooking in an early nineteenth-century cottage. For a cappuccino and chocolates, head diagonally across from the visitor center to *Java Connection*, at 615 Caroline St (☎540/371-4435), while if it's ice cream you crave, try *Carl's*, a tiny 1950s-era drive-up ice cream restaurant north of town at 2200 Princess Anne St.

The Historic Triangle: Jamestown, Williamsburg, and Yorktown

The **Historic Triangle**, on the thin peninsula that stretches east of Richmond between the James and York rivers, holds by far the richest concentration of Colonial-era sites in the US. **Jamestown**, founded in 1607, was Virginia's first settlement; **Williamsburg** is an animated resurrection of the Colonial capital; and it was at **Yorktown** that American independence from the English crown was finally secured. All three sites are within an hour or so by car from Richmond.

Although I-64 is the quickest way to cover the fifty miles from Richmond to Williamsburg, a far more pleasing drive along US-5 rolls through **plantation** country, where many eighteenth-century mansions, with lovely grounds, are open to the public. Once you're in the Historic Triangle area, the best way to get around is along the wooded **Colonial Parkway**, which winds west to Jamestown and east to Yorktown, twenty miles end-to-end. Most of the area's numerous tourist facilities – this is the most visited destination in the state – are to be found around Williamsburg. We've listed a few suggestions under "Historic Triangle practicalities," on p.458.

Jamestown National Historic Site

The first successful English colony in the New World, **JAMESTOWN** was established as a commercial venture, sponsored by King James I but paid for and owned by the **Virginia Company**. On May 13, 1607, the colonists, thirty adventure-minded male aristocrats and seventy-five indentured servants,

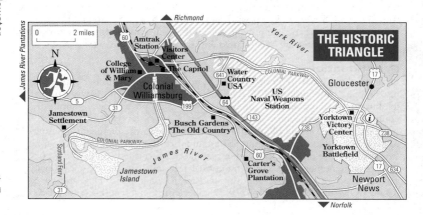

arrived at the mouth of the Chesapeake Bay after four months at sea, and within two weeks had established a fortified settlement on a low-lying island forty miles up the James River.

Despite the fact that Jamestown was intended to be self-supporting, not one member of the party had any experience with farming or fishing – their leader, **John Smith**, wrote in 1608 that "though there be Fish in the Sea, and Foules in the ayre, and Beasts in the woods, their bounds are so large, they are so wilde, and we so weake and ignorant, we cannot much trouble them." The Virginia Company continued to send new recruits, but the loss of life was extreme: of more than seven thousand settlers who came to Jamestown in its first decade, six thousand perished within a year of arriving.

What saved Jamestown, besides the provisions brought by new settlers, was **tobacco**: by 1619 the colony was shipping some twenty tons a year back to England. As it expanded, the colony began to encroach upon the **Powhatan**, an Algonquin-speaking people who controlled most of tidewater Virginia and who until then had been fairly peaceable. In 1622 and again in 1644 provocations caused the Powhatan to attack the colonists, killing around five hundred settlers each time. The most serious damage to Jamestown, however, was caused by the colonists themselves, when they burned the fort to the ground in 1675 in protest at the lack of protection offered them by the Crown. Rather than rebuild the tiny island outpost, by the end of the 1600s they had shifted the capital and most of the commercial activity inland to Williamsburg, and Jamestown slowly disappeared.

To visit Jamestown, you'll want to visit both the original site and the re-created site by taking the scenic Colonial Parkway or highways 5 and 31 from Williamsburg. The one bit of seventeenth-century Jamestown to survive, protected within the **Jamestown National Historic Site** on Jamestown Island, is the 50ft tower of the first brick church, built in 1639 – the rest was destroyed by fire in 1698. Around it are sundry foundations, as well as some memorial shrines and monuments, and current archaeology digs.

At the **visitor center** at the end of the Colonial Parkway (daily: June–Aug 8.30am–5.30pm; Sept–May 8:30am–4:30pm; $6 per car, or $9 if combined with the Yorktown battlefield, see p.458; ☎757/229-1733), artists' drawings and audiovisual exhibits endeavor to conjure up the past, and from here a footpath leads down to the river, where the remains of the original fortress, now underwater, are vaguely visible.

Jamestown Settlement

Next to the authentic site of Jamestown, the state of Virginia has re-created the **Jamestown Settlement** (daily 9am–5pm; $11.25, or $16.75 with Yorktown Victory Center, see p.458), a complex of museums and full-sized replicas that elucidate the details of what went on here. A short film dramatizes Jamestown's early days, and displays look at Europe's need for colonies, documenting the economic and social conditions, in England especially, which led to the founding of Jamestown.

Behind the museum, two groups of reconstructed buildings are staffed by interpretive guides in period costume. In the **Powhatan Village**, people wearing buckskins practice weaving, pottery, and other Native American crafts, while in the larger replica of **James Fort**, some fifteen thatched, wattle-and-daub buildings – all built with period tools – include a blacksmith's, a storehouse, and a church. Full-sized replicas of the three **ships** that carried the first settlers here – the *Godspeed* (which retraced the route from England in 1985), the *Susan Constant*, and the *Discovery* – are moored on the James River.

Williamsburg

A year after mosquito-plagued Jamestown burned down, the Colonial capital was moved inland to a small village known as the Middle Plantation, soon rechristened **WILLIAMSBURG** in honor of King William III. To reflect the increasing wealth of the colony, a grand city was laid out, centering on a mile-long, hundred-foot-wide avenue. Buildings were constructed, beginning with the **capitol** in 1704 and culminating in the opulent **Governor's Palace** in 1720. By the mid-1700s, tobacco-rich Virginia was the most prosperous of the American colonies, and Williamsburg was its largest city – though with some two thousand residents, not on the scale of Philadelphia, New York, or Boston. Williamsburg remained the seat of Colonial government, and emerged as one of the leading centers of **revolutionary thought**: at the College of William and Mary, George Wythe, Thomas Jefferson, James Monroe, and George Mason argued the finer points of law and democracy, while in the capitol, and in the many raucous taverns that surrounded it, firebrand politicians like Patrick Henry held forth on the iniquities of colonialism and organized the first resistance to British rule. When the Revolutionary War broke out, the government moved to the more secure Richmond, and Williamsburg slowly faded from view.

Fortunately, many of the Colonial structures survived intact until the 1920s, when oil baron **John D. Rockefeller** answered the pleas of a local priest, W.A.R. Goodwin, to support Williamsburg's restoration. Over the ensuing years, Rockefeller, with Goodwin acting as his agent, spent some $90 million buying and restoring the surviving structures to their original condition, in many cases building replicas from scratch. In 1934, **Colonial Williamsburg** opened as the first historic "theme park" in the US, with costumed guides as interpreters. While you have to buy a ticket to look inside most of the buildings (see box, opposite), the entire historic area, which includes many fine gardens, is open all the time, and you can wander freely down the cobblestone streets and across the lush green commons. Cars are banned, and Williamsburg as a whole is a remarkably pleasant – if sometimes crowded – place.

Most of the **modern town** of Williamsburg lies to the west of the historical area and includes some fairly attractive architecture that is over a century old itself. It is dominated by the William and Mary College campus, whose students and staff comprise the majority of customers for the modest selection of shops and restaurants, and inhabit the leafy residential streets further west. East of Colonial Williamsburg holds little more than functional motels and drab commercial outlets.

Colonial Williamsburg

Crowds flock to **Colonial Williamsburg** in high summer, and tickets are expensive, but a visit really is educational. The meticulously restored buildings and the interpretive activities and craftspeople – encompassing over eighteen Colonial trades, from apothecary to wig-maker – are both entertaining and true to life. As Rockefeller's influence has waned (his idea of restoration was that everything should be made to look new), Williamsburg has tried to come to grips with the less savory realities of Colonial life. Thus people previously referred to as servants are now acknowledged to have been slaves – fully half of Williamsburg's population was African-American – and their lives and conditions are covered. On another level, houses and outbuildings formerly repainted every year are now left to age naturally, and once-manicured lawns are now allowed to become a bit overgrown.

From the **Wren Building** on the William and Mary campus, built in 1716 at the west end of Williamsburg and now separated from the historic area by a mock-Colonial shopping center, **Duke of Gloucester Street** runs east through the historic area to the capitol (see below). The first of its eighteenth-century buildings, a hundred yards along, is the Episcopalian **Bruton Parish Church** where Goodwin preached (Mon–Sat 9am–5pm, Sun noon–5pm; donation). It was built in 1715, at a time when all white Virginians were required by law to attend services at least once a month. Behind it, the broad **Palace Green** spreads north to the Governor's Palace (see below). West of the church, the **courthouse** – built in 1770 and still in use when Rockefeller bought it – and the octagonal **Powder Magazine** face each other in the midst of the Market Square. Further along, **Chowning's Tavern**, a reconstruction of an alehouse that stood here in 1766, is one of four functioning pubs in the district. As a law student, Thomas Jefferson rented a room in the (no longer used) **Market Square Tavern** across the street.

Various other buildings along Duke of Gloucester Street house blacksmiths' shops, printers, and milliners, open only to Colonial Williamsburg ticket-holders. At the east end of the street, a fife-and-drum corps assembles in front of the capitol before the nightly march through town.

The real architectural highlight is the **capitol**, a monumental edifice at the east end of Duke of Gloucester Street. The current building, a 1945 reconstruction of the 1705 original, has an open-air ground-floor **arcade** linking two keyhole-shaped wings. One wing housed the elected, legislative body of the Colonial government, the **House of Burgesses**, while the other held the chambers of the **General Court** – where alleged felons, including thirteen of Blackbeard's pirates, were tried, architecturally hinting at an early example of the American notion of the balance of powers in government. The eleven justices of the General Court, all of whom were appointed by the king, served as a second legislative body, much as the US House and Senate work today; if the two became deadlocked, they'd meet jointly in a conference chamber bridging the two wings.

A number of fully stocked gift shops along Duke of Gloucester Street have been done up as eighteenth-century apothecaries, cobblers, and silversmiths. The **Raleigh Tavern** here was where the independence-minded Colonial government reconvened after being dissolved by the loyalist governors in 1769 and again in 1774; the original tavern burned down in 1859. Considering that most Virginians of the time, even well-to-do landowners, lived in one- or two-room log cabins, the imposing two-story **Governor's Palace** at the north end of the Palace Green, with its grand ballroom and opulent furnishings, must have served as a telling declaration of the power vested within.

Tickets for Colonial Williamsburg

To set foot inside any of the buildings that have been restored or rebuilt as part of Colonial Williamsburg, you need to buy a ticket, either from the main **visitor center** (daily 8.30am–9pm; ☏1-800/HISTORY, ⊛www.colonialwilliamsburg.com), north of the center off the Colonial Parkway, or from a smaller office at the west end of Duke of Gloucester Street. There are two types of **tickets**, both of which include an introductory guided tour and unlimited free parking at the visitor center. The basic **Day Pass** ($39, 6–17 yrs $19.50), valid for one day only, gets you into everything including Carter's Grove Plantation, six miles east on Rte-60; the better-value **Freedom Pass** ($49, 6–17 yrs $24.50) gives you unlimited access to everything in Colonial Williamsburg for an entire year – you can upgrade it by paying the difference if you're so impressed the first day that you decide to stick around. There are additional charges, however, for the various special programs and events offered by Colonial Williamsburg, such as staged trials in the courthouse, evening dances, and candlelit walking tours.

The smaller of the two conventional museums in Williamsburg, the **Abby Aldrich Rockefeller Folk Art Center** (daily 11am–6pm), on the south side of town, has an intriguing collection of household implements, children's toys, and general bric-a-brac, as well as art by primitive or natural artists. The other, the **DeWitt Wallace Decorative Arts Museum**, features clothing, fine furniture, porcelain, and portraits, and offers "Meet the Curator" tours and visits to conservation labs. The entrance is through the reconstructed facade of the **Public Hospital**, two blocks south of Bruton Parish Church. The first asylum in North America, the hospital has reconstructions of the compartments in which patients were kept and compelling exhibits with recorded conversations tracing the evolution of the treatment of mental illness in the US.

Yorktown battlefield

YORKTOWN, along the York River on the north side of the peninsula, gave its name to the decisive final battle of the **Revolutionary War**. The smallest and least visited of the Historic Triangle sites, Yorktown was little more than farmland when, on October 18, 1781, overwhelmed and besieged British (and German) troops under the command of Charles, Lord Cornwallis surrendered to the joint American and French forces commanded by George Washington. At the heart of the battlefield, a **visitor center** (daily 9am–5pm; $5 per car, or $9 combined with Jamestown National Historic Site, see p.455) has informative interpretive displays, racks of military artifacts, and a short audiovisual presentation on the war. The **Siege Line Overlook** on the roof gives good views of strategic points, while maps and an audio tour ($3) are available if you want to explore in greater detail.

The **Moore House**, where the British surrender was agreed, survived later Civil War battles (and eventual use as a barn) before John D. Rockefeller had it restored; it stands along the York River, a mile east of the visitor center.

Yorktown Victory Center

Though Yorktown survived the battle more or less unscathed – the fighting took place on open fields to the east, and in the waters of the Chesapeake Bay – much of the town was destroyed by fire in 1814, and very little of substance survives from Colonial days. Many of the surviving homes are privately owned, and not open to visitors. To make up for this, as at Jamestown, the state of Virginia and the National Park Service have constructed a mini-theme park – this time a re-created Continental Army encampment – as part of the **Yorktown Victory Center** (daily 9am–5pm; $8.25, or $16.75 with Jamestown Settlement, see p.455), west of the battlefield on US-17. The museum covers both sides, British and American, and events leading up to the Revolution. Two outdoor museums portray life on a middle-class farm and in a Revolutionary War encampment.

Historic Triangle practicalities

Of the three main sites, only Williamsburg is easily reached without a car. Amtrak **trains** and Greyhound **buses** stop at the **Transportation Center** at 408 N Boundary St, two blocks from the Governor's Palace. An airport **shuttle** from Norfolk Airport runs to Williamsburg for $50 (℡757/857-3991). Once there, the Colonial Parkway makes an excellent, scenic cycling route to Jamestown or Yorktown, but there's no other transportation available; rent a **bike** for $15 a day from Bikes Unlimited at 759 Scotland St in Williamsburg (℡757/229-4620). In Colonial Williamsburg, ticket-holders can use the hop-on, hop-off **shuttle buses** (8:50am–10pm) that leave from the visitor center every ten minutes or so and stop at convenient points in the historic area.

Considering the wealth of historic structures here, it's surprising how few hotels or B&Bs there are with any character. All central **accommodation** is handled by Colonial Williamsburg (℡1-800/HISTORY), which ranges from motel to four-star luxury, and they even offer rooms in some of the restored eighteenth-century homes and inns within the historic area – for which you must reserve well in advance. Good-value packages are available – with meals, two nights' lodging, and admission – from around $175 per person. Otherwise places to stay around the Historic Triangle are generally bland and rarely cheap; to make your search easier, the Williamsburg Hotel/Motel Association (℡757/220-3330 or 1-800/446-9244) can find you a bed at no extra charge. West of the center, US-60 is lined with endless motels, and there are also several lower-end options just a few blocks east of the capitol, including the *Bassett Motel*, 800 York St (℡757/229-5175; ❷), and the *Quarterpath Inn*, 620 York St (℡1-800/446-9222, ⓦwww.quarterpathinn.com; ❹). For a change of pace, the *Duke of York Motel*, 508 E Water St in Yorktown (℡757/898-3232; ❸), has reasonable beachfront doubles along the York River. Finally, there are several **campgrounds** along US-5 and US-60 west of Williamsburg that charge around $20 per tent.

The various old-style **restaurants** and taverns along Duke of Gloucester Street in Colonial Williamsburg feature good (though overpriced) pub food and can be fun; all except *Chowning's Tavern* must be reserved in advance (℡1-800/HISTORY). West of the historic area, in the **Merchants Square** shopping mall, the excellent *Trellis Café* (℡757/229-8610) serves international food in an up-market setting. There is also a clutch of restaurants near the William and Mary campus, including the *Green Leafe Café*, 765 Scotland St (℡757/220-3405), offering a solid dose of hearty fare and good beers. Ten-minutes' drive west of Colonial Williamsburg, the *Seafare*, 1632 Richmond Rd (℡757/229-0099), has good fresh seafood.

The Atlantic coast

One of the busiest of the east coast ports, **Norfolk** sits midway along the coast at the point where the Chesapeake Bay empties into the Atlantic Ocean. Virginia's only heavily industrial center, it is not a particularly pretty place, but it does have a rich maritime and naval heritage, as well as the Chrysler Museum, one of the nation's best art galleries. Fifteen miles east of Norfolk, along the open Atlantic, **Virginia Beach** draws summer sun-seekers to the state's busiest seashore.

The rest of Virginia's Atlantic coast is on its isolated and sparsely populated **Eastern Shore**, where the attractive little island town of **Chincoteague** serves as the headquarters of a wildlife refuge that straddles the Maryland border and forms part of the Assateague Island National Seashore.

Norfolk

A strategic location at the broad mouth of the Chesapeake Bay and an extensive deep-water harbor made Colonial **NORFOLK** the main American trading port, and in the mid-eighteenth century it was the largest city in Virginia. After being burned by the British in 1775, and suffering naval bombardments during the Civil War, Norfolk never regained much character, and despite recent efforts to redevelop its waterfront, the modern city is little more than a supply depot for the vast naval shipyards. Along with Hampton and Newport News on the north side of the James River, Norfolk is home to the largest naval base outside Russia, and carriers, cruisers, and all manner of gray-steel behemoths steam past incessantly,

The Town

The downtown waterfront features Norfolk's premier attraction, **Nauticus: The National Maritime Center** (June–Aug daily 10am–6pm; rest of year Tues–Sat 10am–5pm, Sun noon–5pm; $9.95; ☎757/664-1000, ⓦwww.nauticus.org), housed in a formidable replica battleship. Besides interactive oceanography exhibits, among them a shark petting lagoon, and giant-screen films, the Nauticus has informative displays on naval history and technology. The **Hampton Roads Naval Museum** (same hours; free) on the second floor documents the growth of naval operations in the area. The adjacent pier is frequented by colossal US (usually the USS *Wisconsin*) and foreign ships, which can be toured if they're docked for any length of time (call ☎757/664-1000 or 1-800/664-1080 for information). The small Elizabeth River **ferry** (June–Aug Mon–Fri 7am–midnight, Sat & Sun 10am–midnight; rest of year, call for schedule); $1; ☎757/222-6100) shuttles from nearby Waterside Park across the harbor to the historic **Portsmouth** neighborhood, where brick-lined streets are flanked by eighteenth- and nineteenth-century houses.

Two blocks from the harbor, the **Douglas MacArthur Memorial** on Bank Street (Mon–Sat 10am–5pm, Sun 11am–5pm; free) houses the mortal remains and personal effects of the flamboyant US general. The leader of the Allied armies in the Pacific during World War II, who as head of the occupying armies wrote the constitution of Japan, MacArthur was relieved of his command during the Korean War, apparently because of his alarming desire to bomb China.

An extraordinary array of oriental antiquities is displayed in the intimate Tudor-style former home now known as the **Hermitage Foundation Museum**, by the Lafayette River at 7637 N Shore Rd (Mon–Sat 10am–5pm, Sun 1–5pm; $5, guided tours only). Among the featured items are Persian rugs, medieval tapestries, rare ancient Chinese ceremonial vessels, and Roman glass.

The **Chrysler Museum**, half a mile north of the downtown waterfront on Olney Road and Mowbray Arch (Wed 10am–9pm, Thurs–Sat 10am–5pm, Sun 1–5pm; $7, free on Wed; ☎757/664-6200, ⓦwww.chrysler.org), holds the eclectic collection of car magnate Walter Chrysler Jr. It includes a little bit of everything, from ancient Greek statuary to French Impressionist paintings, Franz Klein abstractions, and Mayan funerary objects, as well as a world-class collection of Tiffany and Lalique glassware.

Practicalities

Airport Shuttle (☎757/857-3001) services connect downtown Norfolk with **Norfolk International Airport** ($19), five miles northeast. Amtrak **bus** connections from Newport News stop at the *Radisson Hotel*, 700 Monticello Ave, and Greyhound stops opposite at no. 701. Norfolk's downtown **visitor center** is in the Nauticus Center on the waterfront (daily 10am–5pm; ☎757/664-1000 or 1-800/664-1080, ⓦwww.norfolkcvb.com); drivers can go to a convenient visitor center with easy parking at exit 273 off I-64, at Fourth View Street (daily 9am–5pm; ☎757/441-1852 or 1-800/368-3097). Free **NET buses** provide transportation to major sites (Mon–Fri 6:30am–11pm; ☎757/664-6222, ⓦwww.norfolk.gov/Visitors/net.asp).

With far more accommodation options available nearby in Virginia Beach (see p.462), there should be no need to resort to the standard hotel and motel chains available in Norfolk that are the most affordable options in the city. You can **eat** fish specialties and continental cuisine at the somewhat pricey *Voila*, 509 Botetourt St (☎757/640-0343), or try the eclectic Cajun-Asian blend at *The 219*, 219 Granby St (☎757/627-2896). For a taste of Americana, stop by *Doumar's*, a 1950s-era drive-in restaurant at 616 Monticello Ave (☎757/627-4163), where white-hatted waitstaff bring the food wrapped in wax paper to your car. **Waterside Park**, downtown at the mouth of the Elizabeth River, has something of a party atmosphere during summer weekends with live music, cheap beer, and heaps of atmosphere. Also downtown, the ornate Art Nouveau Wells Theater (☎757/627-6988) puts on **plays** and small concerts.

Virginia Beach

In both character and geography, **VIRGINIA BEACH** is about halfway between Maryland's frenzied Ocean City and North Carolina's untamed Outer Banks. Virginia's only real summer resort has grown to become the largest city in the state, but takes care to pitch itself as a family destination; among steps to deter the Spring Break crowd, Virginia Beach – home to evangelist/politician Pat Robertson's Regent College – has enacted anti-cruising laws that make it illegal to drive past the same spot twice within three hours. That said, the oceanfront vicinity can be a monument to tackiness, and there are many testosterone-filled surfer bars. Fortunately, a multi-million-dollar program to widen the beach keeps it from getting too sardine-like and the overall lazy atmosphere actually leads some to stay longer than planned.

The City

The city's focus is its long, straight sandy **beach**, which is lined with all the usual hotels and motels, and backed by a boardwalk strip of bars, restaurants, and nightclubs. The forty-block downtown area is too spread out to walk the length of, but you should find all you need within a smaller radius, as it's fairly homogenous. During the day, the main activities are sunbathing and playing in the waves; in fact, Virginia Beach is one of the main East Coast **surfing centers**, hosting the summer-long Billabong competitions. You can rent surf, skim, and boogie boards from Wave Riding Vehicles, at 19th Street and Cypress Avenue (☎757/422-8823). Away from the sands, most of the action is along Atlantic Avenue, the main beachfront drag.

High-tech interactive exhibits and an IMAX theater are featured at the **Virginia Marine Science Museum**, 717 General Booth Blvd (daily: mid-June to early Sept 9am–7pm; rest of year 9am–5pm; $11, or $16 with IMAX show; ☎757/425-FISH, ⓦwww.vmsm.com), which explores all things aquatic, from submarines to seabirds, and has a short, pleasant nature trail through a salt marsh linking its two main buildings. The museum also organizes regular **dolphin-watching** expeditions in summer ($12; ☎757/437-BOAT), for which you should reserve a day in advance.

The eccentric but interesting **A.R.E. Center** at the headquarters of the Association for Research and Enlightenment, at 67th Street and Atlantic Avenue (Mon–Sat 9am–8pm, Sun noon–8pm; free; ☎757/428-3588), focuses on Edgar Cayce (1877–1945), a pioneer in various forms of ESP, known as "the sleeping prophet" because of his alleged ability, while in a trance, to diagnose and heal the ailments of individuals anywhere in the world. Visitors can use an enormous metaphysical library, or join "testings" of group ESP (daily June–Aug at 2pm; free).

Once the people-watching on the city beach starts to pall, head a few miles up or down the coast to find some beautiful and much more peaceful stretches of golden sand. To the south lie the four-mile-long **Back Bay National**

Wildlife Refuge (daily dawn to dusk; $5 per car, hikers and cyclists $2; ☎757/721-2412, ⊛backbay.fws.gov), where you can walk or fish but not officially swim or sunbathe, and False Cape State Park, a mile-wide barrier spit. Closer to Virginia Beach to the north, the thick woodlands of **First Landing State Park** was the site where the first English settlers touched land in 1607 before moving on to Jamestown; it is now popular with weekend boaters and cyclists, and has a beach on the Chesapeake Bay. Several adventure organizations such as Sandbridge Eco Sports, 577 Sandbridge Rd (☎757/721-6210 or 1-800/695-4212, ⊛www.sandbridgeecosports.com), run **kayaking** and **dolphin-watching** expeditions in the area.

Practicalities

Greyhound stops at 1017 Laskin Rd, off 31st Street, while the Amtrak bus connection from Newport News arrives at 19th Street and Pacific Avenue. The **visitor center** at 2100 Park Ave (daily 9am–5pm; ☎757/437-4919 or 1-800/822-3224, ⊛www.VBFUN.com) is at the east end of I-264, half a mile west of the beach at 21st Street. Beach **trolleys** called The Wave (daily 8am–2am; $1; ☎757/252-6100, ⊛www.hrtransit.org) are the easiest way to get around; there are three different routes covering the city, the most useful being up and down Atlantic Avenue.

Virginia Beach has one great boon for **budget travelers** – just a block from the beach, there are dorm beds from $20 (IYHF members $17) and bargain B&B singles and doubles at *HI-Angie's Guest Cottage Hostel*, 302 24th St (☎757/428-4690, ⊛www.angiescottage.com; ❶–❸). Typical rates at the seafront hotels tend to approach $150 in summer, with cheaper options at the appealingly old-style *Thunderbird Motor Lodge*, on the oceanfront at 35th Street and Atlantic Avenue (☎757/428-3024 or 1-800/633-6669, ⊛www.va-beach .com/thunderbird.com; ❸), which also has a nice café; the adjacent *Budget Lodge*, 34th and Oceanfront (☎757/428-4413 or 1-800/446-8388; ❷); and the smallish *Sea Side* at 27th and Atlantic (☎757/428-9341 or 1-800/348-7263; ❷), which makes a nice break from the surrounding highrises. For details of the lovely oceanside **campground** at First Landing State Park on the Chesapeake Bay, call ☎757/412-2300 or 1-800/933-7275, or visit ⊛www .dcr.state.va.us/parks/1stland.htm.

The town also offers some great **restaurants** and a frenetic **nightlife**. *Capt. John's Crabhouse*, 33rd and Atlantic (☎757/425-3719), has fine seafood and an evening buffet, while *Mahi Mah's*, by the ocean at 7th and Atlantic (☎757/437-8030), offers a creative menu of sushi, sashimi, and other seafood, plus a wide selection of beers. *Baja Cantina*, 206 23rd St (☎757/437-2920), is a friendly bar serving tasty Mexican food to a decent rock soundtrack. For details of **live music events**, check the listings newspaper, *Port Folio*. Good possibilities include the *Abbey Road Pub* at 203 22nd St (☎757/425-6330), a lively bar with over a hundred different beers and live Rock 'n' Roll. Hostelers congregate most nights at the *Jewish Mother*, 3108 Pacific Ave (☎757/422-5430), a daytime deli and late-night beer bar with free live music.

The Eastern Shore

Virginia's longest and least visited stretch of Atlantic coastline, the **Eastern Shore**, lies separated from the rest of the state on the far side of the Chesapeake Bay. Only the southernmost segment of what's known as the Delmarva peninsula (see p.494) belongs to Virginia, by which point it has narrowed to become a flat spit of sand protected by a fringe of low-lying islands.

US-13, which runs straight down the center of the peninsula and provides a handy short cut from Philadelphia or points north, crosses seventeen miles of open sea at the mouth of the Chesapeake Bay via the **Chesapeake Bay Bridge–Tunnel** ($10 per car one way; $14 roundtrip). For most of its length, the roadway runs just a few yards above the water, bringing you almost eye-to-eye with passing ships; it twice burrows beneath the surface between artificial islands, before reaching its southern extremity halfway between Norfolk and Virginia Beach. To either side of US-13, little villages and fishing harbors such as Nassawadox, Assawoman, and Accomac are tucked away on rambling back roads.

Chincoteague

Much the most appealing destination on the Eastern Shore, **CHIN-COTEAGUE** occupies a beautiful barrier island just south of the Maryland border. Although it's little more than a village, its two principal streets hold a fair assortment of motels and restaurants, and it makes an appropriately relaxed base for exploring **Assateague Island National Seashore**. The northern half of Assateague, which holds several popular hiking trails, can only be reached from Maryland (see p.479); the southern half, just a mile onwards from Chincoteague, is taken up by the **Chincoteague National Wildlife Refuge**, notable for its seabirds and wild ponies. Call in at the **visitor center** (daily 9am–5pm; $5 per car; ☎757/336-6122, ⓦchinco.fws.gov) for a schedule of ranger-guided wildlife safaris ($10), or if you just want a day at the beach, drive straight past to **Tom's Cove**. Families fill the area nearest the parking lot, but set off walking north and you may end up with several miles of sand to yourself. If you're in Chincoteague on the last Wednesday and Thursday of July, don't miss the annual **Pony Penning Carnival**, when the wild ponies that roam Assateague Island to the north are herded together and directed on a swim through the channel to Chincoteague Memorial Park to be sold by auction to help the local community. It can be a crowded event, but the sight of dozens of ponies swimming in convoy in such pristine surroundings is unforgettable.

Central **accommodation** options in Chincoteague include the grand *Island Manor House*, 4160 Main St (☎757/336-5436; ❺), an antique-furnished B&B, and the large but peaceful *Mariner Motel*, 6273 Maddox Blvd (☎757/336-6565; ❸), on the main road to Assateague. Next door, at no. 6251, is *Steamers* (☎757/336-5478), a brightly lit **restaurant** serving all-you-care-to-eat spiced crab and/or shrimp meals for around $20. Located in the small waterfront plaza, *Landmark Crab House*, 6172 N Main St (☎757/336-5552), also serves tasty seafood and is open from April to November.

Charlottesville and the Shenandoah Valley

The densely forested 4000ft peaks of the **Blue Ridge Mountains** form a definite barrier between the history-rich worlds of tidewater Virginia to the east and the rougher river-and-valley country to the west. In between the two, at the geographical center of the state, sits the friendly, manageably small college town of **Charlottesville**, which holds two great monuments to the mind of **Thomas Jefferson**. South of Charlottesville, the village of **Appomattox** is the site where papers were signed to officially end the Civil War, and is now preserved as an engaging national historic site. To the west, the northern Blue Ridge Mountains, crowned by the dense forests of **Shenandoah National Park**, run south to Tennessee, culminating in 5729ft Mount Rogers. There's a slower pace in the lush Shenandoah Valley, on the far side of the mountains, once a vital battleground during the Civil War.

I-81, the main highway through the Shenandoah Valley, is joined in the north by I-66 from Washington, DC, and in the middle by I-64 from Richmond through Charlottesville. Numerous scenic routes are slower but more worthwhile, such as **Skyline Drive** and the **Blue Ridge Parkway**, which both weave along the four-hundred-mile-long mountain crest. You'll need a car to get the most out of the region, though cycling is a good option along the many back roads and, for hikers, the **Appalachian Trail** runs right down the middle. There are plenty of roadside motels, so you needn't be too concerned about advance planning – in fact, it's a great place for aimless exploration.

Charlottesville

If you only have a couple of days to see Virginia, **CHARLOTTESVILLE**, seventy miles west of Richmond, should be near the top of your itinerary. Abounding in history and holding some of the finest examples of early American architecture, it is at once small enough to feel comfortable in and large enough to have good restaurants and nightspots. Its compact, low-rise center is crisscrossed by magnolia-shaded streets, and makes a fine area to amble around, particularly in the six pedestrianized blocks of **Main Street**, site of the nightly town promenade. However pleasant the town, the compelling attraction is the legacy of Thomas Jefferson, whose home and final resting place, **Monticello**, stands atop a hill just east of town, overlooking the beautifully landscaped Neoclassical campus of the University of Virginia.

The University of Virginia

Though he wrote the Declaration of Independence and served as the third US president, Thomas Jefferson took more pride in having established the **University of Virginia** than in any of his other achievements, and after a visit you may well understand why. In 1976 the university was officially designated the greatest piece of architecture in the US; it also reveals the ideology of its patron, who, besides designing every building down to the most minute detail, also planned the curriculum and selected the faculty. Uniquely for universities of the time, which functioned primarily as seminaries, the University of Virginia was not rooted in religious training, but emphasized instead a broadly based liberal arts education, not surprising as Jefferson had been one of the prime proponents of the separation of church and state.

The highlight and architectural focus of the campus is the redbrick, white-domed **Rotunda** (℡ 434/982-3200), which was modeled on the Pantheon and completed in 1821 to house the library and classrooms. A basement gallery tells the story of the university, while upstairs three elliptical classrooms are linked by a richly decorated central hall. A staircase winds up to the **Dome Room**, where Corinthian columns rise to an ocular skylight. From the Rotunda, where 45-minute guided tours of the campus begin (daily 10am–4pm, except mid-Dec to Jan; free), twin colonnades stretch along either side of a lushly landscaped quadrangle, linking together a string of single-story student apartments and taller pavilions in which professors live and hold tutorials. While the overall feel is harmonious, each individual block is unique, the differing facades and rooflines designed to show off the various orders and styles of Neoclassical architecture.

Parallel to the quadrangle buildings, two further rows of dormitory buildings, the East and West ranges, front on to serpentine walled gardens. **Edgar Allan Poe** stayed in one of these dorms while studying at the University of Virginia in 1826, but was forced to drop out after his stepfather cut off his allowance, apparently because Edgar had lost all of his money gambling. His room – Number 13, of course – in the West Range is now restored to how it would have looked during his occupancy.

Monticello – Thomas Jefferson's home

One of America's most familiar buildings – it graces the back of the nickel coin – **Monticello**, three miles southeast of Charlottesville on Hwy-53, was the home of Thomas Jefferson for most of his life. A visit provides a distinctive insight into the most intriguing of America's founding fathers. Surrounded by acres of beautifully landscaped hilltop grounds, which once comprised an enormous plantation, with fine views out over the Virginia countryside, Monticello is a handsome house. The symmetrical brick facade, centered upon a white Doric portico, belies the quirky irregularities of the interior – furnished as it was when Jefferson lived, and died, here.

To see Monticello you have to join one of the **guided tours** (daily: March–Oct 8am–5pm; rest of year 9am–4.30pm; $13; ☎434/984-9822, Ⓦwww.Monticello.org) that leave continuously from the parking lot at the bottom of the hill. There's often a line, especially at weekends, so try to get there as early as possible in the morning. From the outside, Monticello looks like an elegant, Palladian-style country home, but as soon as you enter the domed entrance hall, with its funhouse mirror and displays of fossilized bones and elk antlers (from Lewis and Clark's epic 1804 journey across North America, which Jefferson sponsored as president), you begin to get a sense that Jefferson was a somewhat more interesting character than the sober statesman portrayed by most histories. His love of gadgets and clever contraptions, which fill the house, marked him as a multi-talented man: examples of these include the elaborate dual-pen device he used to make automatic copies of all his letters, and the weather vane over the front porch, which is connected to a dial so he could see which way the wind was blowing without having to step outside. Even Jefferson's **private chambers**, also viewable on the tour, are rather interesting: he slept in a tiny alcove that linked his dressing room and his study, and would get up on the right side of the bed if he wanted to make some late-night notes, or on the left if he wanted to get dressed. The upstairs rooms, where Jefferson's daughter lived, however, are not open to the public.

On the grounds around the house you get a feeling for how Monticello, a five-thousand-acre plantation, really functioned. Extensive flower and vegetable gardens spread to the south and west, and a dank passage runs under the house from the kitchen and beer cellar (Jefferson was a keen home-brewer) to the remains of Mulberry Row, Monticello's **slave quarters**. Despite calling slavery an "abominable crime," Jefferson owned almost two hundred slaves and recent research indicates that he may have also sired a child with one of them. At the south end of Mulberry Row, a grove of ancient hardwood trees surrounds Jefferson's grave, which is marked by a simple stone obelisk; beyond this, a footpath winds back down to the bottom of the hill.

Charlottesville practicalities

Amtrak trains from DC stop in Charlottesville at 810 W Main St, and Greyhound pulls in a few blocks away at 310 W Main St. Once you arrive, you can get to everything on foot, including the downtown **visitor center**, 108

△ Inside Monticello, Thomas Jefferson's home in Virginia

2nd St SE (Mon–Sat 10am–5pm, Sun 11am–3pm; ☎434/977-6100 or 1-877/386-1102, ⓦwww.charlottesvilletourism.org). Another visitor center (daily: March–Oct 9am–5.30pm; Nov–April 9am–5pm; ☎434/977-1783), well-signposted on Hwy-20 just south of I-64, houses a superb free exhibit of four hundred items called "Thomas Jefferson at Monticello," and is an excellent starting point for a trip to Monticello.

For its size, Charlottesville has quite a good range of **accommodation**. The usual motels line Emmet Street (US-29) at the west end of town, with one of the least expensive being the *Budget Inn*, at no. 140 (☎434/293-5141 or 1-800/293-5144, ⓦwww.budgetinn-charlottesville.com; ❸). *Hampton Inn & Suites* (☎434/923-8600 or 1-800/426-7866, ⓦwww.hampton-inn.com; ❹) offers standard rooms right near the university at 900 W Main St. Good-value **B&B rooms** are available at the two beautifully restored houses of the *200 South Street Inn*, 200 South St (☎434/979-0200, ⓦwww.southstreetinn.com; ❺), and also at the *Inn at Court Square*, 410 E Jefferson St (☎434/295-2800; ❺). You can also arrange a stay in a B&B through Guesthouses (☎434/979-7264).

The best **eating** and **drinking** is to be had near the university and on the downtown mall. In between the two, *Southern Culture*, 633 W Main St (☎434/979-1990), is an inexpensive local favorite, with a slightly retro-1950s feel and fabulous tuna steak. *Metropolitan*, 214 W Water St ☎434/977-1043), is a suitably pricey downtown restaurant, but the fresh fish is worth every dollar. Just north of the downtown mall at Fifth and Market streets, *Tastings* (☎434/293-3663) offers grilled meats and a grand selection of wines, including many from the vineyards surrounding Charlottesville, while Virginia's best selection of beers, plus a range of light meals, can be sampled a block further north at the *Court Square Tavern*, 500 E Jefferson St (☎434/296-6111). The *C&O Restaurant*, 515 E Water St (☎434/971-7044), housed in an old railroad engineers' diner, offers bistro-style food in its humming bar and more upscale French *nouvelle cuisine* in the upstairs dining room.

Being a college town, Charlottesville isn't short of **nightlife**, whether at bars like the *Outback Lounge*, 110 N Fourth St (☎434/979-7211), or in its two main nightclubs, *Max's*, 120 S 11th St (☎434/295-6299), and *Starr Hill*, 709 W Main St (☎434/977-0017), which hosts live bands.

Appomattox

Settled amid the pleasant, roaming hills of central Virginia, some sixty miles south of Charlottesville on US-460 and Hwy-24, **APPOMATTOX** marks the spot where Robert E. Lee and Ulysses S. Grant met on April 9, 1865, to signify the end of the Civil War. After four years of enormous bloodshed on both sides, the Confederacy bowed out with a mere whimper. Grant's Union troops had cut off a nearby railroad line upon which Lee's final battalion depended for vital supplies, and the half-starved Confederate army had no choice but to submit. Final papers were signed in a private home near the Appomattox Court House. This event, a defining moment in American history, is remembered in the **Appomattox Court House National Historical Park** (daily 8.30am–5pm; $4), a place refreshingly free of the usual tourist baggage that accompanies most similarly important sites in the state. The tiny village has been handsomely restored, though the home and courthouse, now containing a museum, are reconstructions of the originals.

Getting to Appomattox requires a car, and the nearest accommodation is available in the newer city of the same name, a few miles west. Here, the cozy

Longacre B&B, 107 South Church St (☎434/352-9251 or 1-800/758-7730, ⓦwww.longacreva.com; ⑤), is nestled among century-old boxwoods and includes a lap pool.

Shenandoah National Park

SHENANDOAH NATIONAL PARK, which contains seemingly endless acres of dark forests, deep rocky ravines, and surging waterfalls, has one of the most unusual histories of any US national park. Far from being untouched for the past three hundred years, this "natural" landscape was created when hundreds of small family farms and homesteads were bought up by the state and federal governments during the Depression, and the land was left to revert to its natural state.

Shenandoah, meaning "river of high mountains," has one of the most scenic byways in the US, the **Skyline Drive**, a thin ribbon of pavement curving along the crest of the Blue Ridge Mountains. It starts just off I-66 near the town of **Front Royal**, 75 miles west of DC, and winds south through the park, giving great views over the surrounding area.

Admission to the park is $10 for cars and $5 for pedestrians, cyclists, and motorcyclists; permits are good for six days. The views are especially fine, and the crowds especially large, in the fall, but at any time of year you can get the best of what the park has to offer by following one of the many **hiking trails** that split off from the ridge. One favorite leaves from the parking area of Big Meadows Lodge, in the southern half of the park, and winds along to tumbling **Dark Hollow Falls**; another trail, leaving Skyline Drive at mile marker 45, climbs up a fairly treacherous incline to the top of **Old Rag Mountain** for 360° views out over the whole of Virginia and the Allegheny Mountains in the west. More ambitious hikers, or those who want to spend the night out in the backcountry, head for the **Appalachian Trail**; details on any of these hikes, and free overnight camping permits, can be picked up at one of the three **visitor centers** (mid-April to late Nov; call for hours; ☎540/999-3500, ⓦwww.nps.gov/shen): Dickey Ridge at mile 4.6; Harry F. Byrd Visitor Center at milepost 51; Loft Mountain at mile 79.5.

Two rustic **lodges** and a clutch of **cabins**, near the center of the park, offer beds and food; reservations are handled by ARAMARK Services (☎540/743-5108 or 1-800/999-4714, ⓦwww.visitshenandoah.com). The northernmost of these, the 1894 *Skyland Lodge*, has cabins (❸) and modern hotel rooms (⑤), as well as a large restaurant with panoramic views; *Big Meadows Lodge*, near the visitor center at milepost 51, has similar facilities (❸); while *Lewis Mountain Cabins*, at milepost 57.5 on the Parkway, offers cozy, family-style accommodation (❸). There are also five campgrounds in the park, charging $16 to $19 per night; reserve online or by calling 1-800/365-CAMP.

The Shenandoah Valley

The small, characterful towns of the **SHENANDOAH VALLEY**, down below Skyline Drive, are as rich in human history as any in Virginia. Many were left in ruins after the war, but have since been restored to their original antebellum condition, and numerous memorials, monuments, and cemeteries line the back roads, surrounded by spacious horse farms and apple orchards.

Given its strategic importance and fertile soil, the Shenandoah Valley was inevitably one of the most fought-over battlegrounds in the Civil War, changing hands over seventy times at a cost of some 100,000 dead or maimed. The whole bloody story is told in evocative detail in the small but outstanding

museum (daily 9am–5pm; $8) at the **New Market Battlefield**, just off I-81, thirty miles south of the I-66 junction. This was the scene of the legendary 1864 confrontation that involved a company of 14-year-old cadets from the Virginia Military Institute.

Besides its Civil War history, the northern Shenandoah Valley also holds half a dozen of Virginia's many underground **limestone caverns**, all of which are privately owned and cost $10–15 to enter. You'll no doubt see billboards advertising each one as the best, though that title really belongs to the largest, **Luray Caverns**, twelve miles east of New Market off Hwy-211 (mid-March to mid-June 9am–6pm; mid-June to Labor Day 9am–7pm; Labor Day to Oct 31 9am–6pm; Nov 1 to mid-March 9am–4pm; $17), a subterranean wonderland featuring an underground "organ" with stalagmites as "pipes," which you can see on the daily one-hour guided tours. Your ticket also gives access to the adjacent **Historic Car and Carriage** exhibit (daily 9am until 1hr after the caverns close), a collection of vintage automobiles starring an 1892 Benz.

Further south, off Hwy-250 northwest of the town of **STAUNTON**, the **Museum of Frontier American Culture** (daily 9am–5pm; $8) brings to light how the various immigrants who settled here melded their traditions to develop a joint American culture. Most of the exhibits are about farming techniques and other somewhat mundane activities, but it's all engagingly presented and well worth a look. Close by, just off Hwy-660 near Stuarts Draft, the lovely *Shenandoah Acres Resort* (⊤540/337-1911 or 1-800/654-1714, ⓦ www.shenacres.com; ➍) offers large cabins and motel units, as well as camping facilities ($22 per tent) and an artificial lake for swimming.

Lexington

Though it's one of the region's smaller towns, **LEXINGTON**, in the heart of the Shenandoah Valley, easily has the most to offer visitors. From horse-drawn carriages parading along its quiet, brick-lined streets, to the fine rolling countryside all around – displayed to great effect in the movie *Sommersby* – Lexington makes a great place to sit back, stroll, or delve deeply into Civil War and assorted military memorabilia at its small museums and memorials.

One of the most engaging of these, the **Lee Chapel** (April–Oct Mon–Sat 9am–5pm, Sun 1–5pm; Nov–March Mon–Sat 9am–4pm, Sun 1–4pm; free), is on the imposing colonnaded campus of **Washington and Lee University**, a short walk north of the town center. A commodious and somber building, the chapel is named in honor of Confederate General Robert E. Lee, who taught here after the Civil War. Behind the pulpit is a marble statue of Lee in repose, surrounded by an array of authentic battle flags; along with many members of his family, Lee is interred downstairs in the chapel crypt, and his horse Traveler is buried just outside.

On the austere campus of the **Virginia Military Institute**, just east of the Lee Chapel, the **VMI Museum** (daily 9am–5pm; free) tells the story of the state-supported military academy (male-only until 1997), founded in 1836. VMI has the dubious claim to fame of being the only university in US history to have sent its entire student body into battle. If possible, time your visit to coincide with the 4pm Friday full-dress parade held on the parade ground. Starting in the winter of 2004, the museum will close for two years, but will continue to show exhibits at the nearby Marshall Museum. At the opposite end of the parade ground, the **George C. Marshall Museum** (daily 9am–5pm; $3; ⊤540/463-7103, ⓦ www.marshallfoundation.org) documents the life of World War II US general and later secretary of state George C. Marshall, whose plan for the reconstruction of Europe after World War II earned him the Nobel Peace Prize in 1953.

In the town center, the **Stonewall Jackson House**, 8 E Washington St (Mon–Sat 9am–5pm; $5), is where the noted Confederate general and Virginia Military Institute philosophy professor lived for fifteen years before his death at the battle of Chancellorsville. His Spartan brick townhouse is furnished as it was in the years before the war. Jackson is buried, along with hundreds of his fellow soldiers, in the **Stonewall Jackson Memorial Cemetery** off South Main Street. This is now the prime destination for twilight **ghost tours** (May–Oct only; nightly at 8.30pm; $8), leaving from the town's visitor center at 106 E Washington St, which are amusing if you're traveling with kids.

Twenty miles south of Lexington on US-11 is the spectacular **Natural Bridge** (daily 8am until dark; $10), where meandering Cedar Creek has gradually carved away at the softer limestone to form a 215ft archway that has dazzled several distinguished visitors over the years: George Washington allegedly carved his initials into the rock (though it takes a keen eye to see them), and Thomas Jefferson was so impressed that he bought the site to preserve it and owned it for fifty years. It's worth the hefty admission price, but don't expect it to be "one of the Seven Natural Wonders of the World" as its publicists suggest. The Natural Bridge **Caverns** are also on-site ($8), but save your money for the more spectacular Luray Caverns, further north (see overleaf). Another option is the $18 combination ticket, which gets you into the caverns, the Bridge, and the cheesy **Wax Museum** that's also here.

Even if you're not thrilled by war stories and natural bridges, Lexington still makes a good stop, as it has dozens of fine old homes to see; pick up a walking tour map from the friendly **visitor center** at 102 E Washington St (daily: June–Aug 8.30am–6pm; Sept–May 9am–5pm; ℡540/463-3777 or 1-877/543-9822, ⓦwww.lexingtonvirginia.com). For **food**, the *Southern Inn Restaurant*, right in the center at 37 S Main St (℡540/463-3612) offers good old Southern cooking such as a scrumptious meatloaf; it's attached to a bar that churns out **live music** Friday and Saturday nights. If your taste tends towards tofu, you may prefer the *Blue Heron Café*, 4 E Washington St (℡540/463-2800), one block from the visitor center, which serves vegetarian dishes daily. In addition to the usual motels along the highways, the comfy German- and French-speaking *Asherowe B&B*, 314 S Jefferson St (℡540/463-4219; ❸), is located six blocks southwest of the visitor center. There are several **campgrounds** nearby as well, including one along Rte-11, south of town near Natural Bridge (℡540/291-2727, ⓦwww.campnbr.com); ask at the visitor center for further details.

The Blue Ridge Parkway

Once out of Shenandoah National Park, Skyline Drive becomes the **Blue Ridge Parkway**, which winds southwest along the crest of the Appalachians at an average elevation of three thousand feet. It's a beautiful drive, though **I-81**, sweeping along the flank of the mountains, is a more efficient way of getting from Virginia to North Carolina and on to the Great Smokies, a route covered in detail on p.529. From June to November, the *Rocky Knob Cabins* (℡540/593-3503; ❸), at milepost 174 on the Parkway itself, offers a memorable night's stay in the idyllic Meadows of Dan.

Of the nearby towns, **ROANOKE**, sandwiched between I-81 and the Parkway, is the largest community in western Virginia. Beyond its drab modern approaches, the town has a few attractions that make for a pleasant stopoff, particularly the historic farmers' market (Mon–Sat) and the modern Center In The Square mall. The latter contains the engaging **Roanoke Valley History**

Museum (Tues–Fri 10am–4pm, Sat 10am–5pm, Sun 1–5pm; $2; ☎540/342-5770, ⓦwww.history-musuem.org), which documents settlement of the region by the Scottish, Welsh, and Germans. There's also the **Virginia Museum of Transportation**, 303 Norfolk Ave (Mon–Fri 11am–4pm, Sat 10am–5pm, Sun 1–5pm; $6), home to the largest collection of diesel locomotives in the South and offering some insight into Roanoke's railroad foundations. The helpful **visitor center**, 114 Market St (daily 9am–5pm; ☎540/345-8622 or 1-800/635-5535, ⓦwww.visitroanokeva.com), can provide information and walking tour maps. For sweeping views of the valley, make the fifteen-minute drive from the farmers' market up Mill Mountain to the site of the **Roanoke Star**, an 89-foot illuminated star built in 1949. (Ask at the visitor center for directions.)

If you find the need **to stay**, the *Jefferson Lodge* at 616 S Jefferson St (☎540/342-2951; ❷) is basic but very centrally located, while the least expensive of the interstate motels is the *Rodeway Inn*, 526 Orange Ave NE, at exit 4E off I-581 (☎540/981-9341 or 1-800/228-2000; ❸). Campbell Avenue downtown sports a number of appealing **restaurants**, including *Awful Arthur's Seafood Co*, 108 Campbell Ave (☎540/344-2997), a good lunch or dinner spot with tasty specials; *Italiano*, at 125 Campbell Ave (☎540/981-0280), featuring standard Italian fare; and the *Tavern on the Market*, at 32 Market Square (☎540/343-2957), which serves up typical pub fare and a range of beers.

History buffs surfeited on the Civil War might want to call in to the town of **BEDFORD**, about twenty miles east of Roanoke and not far from the Parkway. An unprepossessing place in itself, this small community of 3200 lost twenty-one men (out of thirty-five) at Omaha Beach during the Allied invasion of Normandy on June 6, 1944, the highest per capita loss of anywhere in the US. Thus, Bedford was chosen as the site for the **National D-Day Memorial** ($5; ☎540/586-DDAY or 1-800/351-DDAY, ⓦwww.D-Day.org), which opened on the anniversary of the event in 2001. Situated on a landscaped hilltop, the monuments, statues, and structures depicting the beach landing culminate in the 44ft arch of Victory Plaza. It is signposted just off US-460, on the southwest side of town.

West Virginia

The people of **WEST VIRGINIA** are only half joking when they call their state the Ireland of the US. Generally poor and almost entirely rural, it shares a similar history of exploitation by outside powers, with **timber** and **coal-mining** companies taking advantage of the rich natural resources while giving little in return. But, quite apart from the almost Third World deprivation that endures in some areas, West Virginia is also, in places at least, incredibly beautiful, and can boast the longest white-water rivers and most extensive wilderness areas in the eastern US. The extreme topography, which has historically isolated its inhabitants, now makes the state a popular destination for hikers and outdoors enthusiasts, and the moonshiners of old have been replaced by ski instructors and mountain-bike guides. Pioneer settlers started to cross the mountains of western Virginia in significant numbers during the middle of the seventeenth century. Farming small plots of land with their own labor, they came to have ever less in common with the slave-holding plantation owners of old Virginia, and when the Civil War broke out, the area declined to secede from the Union. The Supreme Court never ruled whether West Virginia was legally entitled to declare itself a state, and Virginia itself has still not officially recognized the split. West Virginia has, however, developed a political and economic identity of its own. Around 1900, when railroads from the East Coast first reached into the mountainous interior, timber companies clear-cut stand after stand of forest, setting up a succession of mill towns, each dismantled in its turn when they moved on somewhere new. **Cass**, now preserved within the Allegheny National Forest, is one of the few that was left intact. Later on, coal-mining conglomerates, especially in the south, perfected the "company town" approach, wherein workers were paid a little bit less each month than the amount they owed for their company-provided food and lodging. Coal companies still exert immense power in West Virginia, but the real key to the state's future prosperity is tourism, which in places now accounts for over half its income.

The state's most popular destination, the restored 1850s town of **Harpers Ferry**, is barely in West Virginia at all, standing just across the broad rivers that form its Maryland and Virginia borders. To the west, the **Allegheny Mountains** stretch for over 150 miles, with more than a million acres of hardwood forest that rival New England for brilliant autumnal color. West Virginia's oldest town, **Lewisburg**, sits just off I-64 at the mountains' southern foot, while the capital, **Charleston**, lies in the comparatively flat Ohio River Valley of the west.

Getting around West Virginia

With its many mountains and rivers making straight, flat roads virtually nonexistent, **getting around** West Virginia is as much a part of its attraction as is any specific destination – a bike and a stout pair of legs, or a motorcycle, would be ideal, but a car is pretty necessary if you really want to see the state. Greyhound is basically useless here, and Amtrak, apart from serving Harpers Ferry from Washington, DC, has only one – albeit spectacular – route, running through the New River Gorge to the capital, Charleston. To really see the state, plan on driving narrow, serpentine roads endlessly up and down, and allow yourself lots of time.

Harpers Ferry

HARPERS FERRY is a ruggedly sited eighteenth-century town restored as a national historic park. Clinging to steep hillsides above the rocky confluence of the Potomac and Shenandoah rivers, many of the town's forty-odd brick and stone buildings date from the days when George Washington set up the country's first **national munitions factory** here to arm the young Republic. During the mid-1800s Harpers Ferry was a thriving industrial complex, home to some five thousand workers and linked to the capital by the B&O Railroad and the Chesapeake & Ohio Canal. After suffering the ravages of the Civil War and a series of torrential floods, however, it was all but abandoned, the empty shells of its homes and factories slowly becoming overgrown by the dense forest that covers the surrounding hills. Almost all of Harpers Ferry has since been reconstructed as an outdoor museum combining historical importance and natural beauty.

However pretty Harpers Ferry may be – and in the fall, when the leaves blaze with color, it's hard to imagine a more picture-perfect setting – it's best known for its place in US history. The 1859 raid on its huge US arsenal by anti-slavery revolutionary **John Brown** rocked the already fragmenting nation, and was the clearest foreshadowing of the Civil War, which broke out just eighteen months later. In the hope of fomenting a widespread slave revolt, Brown and twenty-one other abolitionists, including two of his sons and five black men, seized the munitions factory and its large store of weapons on the night of October 16. They held out for two days before US troops, under the command of Robert E. Lee, stormed the buildings, killing many of the raiders and capturing Brown. He was taken to nearby Charles Town, put on trial just nine days later, and convicted of treason; by the time he was hanged on December 2, he was far from alone in regarding himself as a martyr to the abolitionist cause.

As one of only two places operated by the US government, with the capacity to manufacture munitions, Harpers Ferry was a major prize in the Civil War, and it never got back on its feet after the resultant devastation. The arsenal buildings were burned in 1861 to keep the weapons out of Confederate hands, while in 1862 Stonewall Jackson captured the town along with 12,500 Union soldiers. Enough of the original buildings and cobbled streets survive, however, to give a good sense of how things used to be, and the restoration project has re-created the town without making it feel like a theme park.

The Town

Almost everyone who comes to Harpers Ferry drives. Parking is virtually banned in the old town area; shuttle buses run from the large **visitor center** on US-340 (visitor center and attractions open daily 8am–5pm; buses run 8am–5.45pm, 6.45pm in summer; ☏304/535-6298, ⓦwww.nps.gov/hafe) – where you pay the $4-per-person or $6-per-car entry fee – to the old town, dropping off conveniently at the end of gas-lit Shenandoah Street in the heart of the restored area. There's an information desk on Shenandoah Street, next to the shuttle drop-off station, with maps and helpful park staffers. Across the street, displays in the **Master Armorer's House** will teach you about gun-making; adjacent buildings include a restored blacksmith's shop, a general store, and a tavern.

John Brown's **fort** – actually the firehouse, where he and his raiders were captured – originally stood directly across from the tavern, but was rebuilt a block away, near the point where the rivers meet. It's no more than an empty shell, however, and if you want to get the full story of the raid you'd do better to spend half an hour in the **John Brown Museum** opposite. Here, as throughout Harpers Ferry, debate continues to rage over Brown's sanity or sanctity; many regard him as a borderline psychotic. A monument on Potomac Street, erected by the Daughters of the Confederacy, salutes the attack's first victim, a free black railroad baggage-master named Hayward Shepherd, as epitomizing the "character and faithfulness of thousands of negroes" in the old South; across from it stands another monument honoring Brown's "heroism" on the wall of the engine house.

Other museums, housing exhibits on the Civil War and local black history, line both sides of **High Street** as it climbs away from the river. At one point, a set of stone steps ascends between them through the residential area, to the 1782 **Harper House**, the oldest house in town and preserved as a typical worker's rooming house of the period.

A footpath continues uphill, past overgrown churchyards hemmed in by dry-stone walls, to **Jefferson Rock**, a huge gray boulder affording a great view over the two rivers; Thomas Jefferson said the vista was worth a voyage across the Atlantic. For a longer hike, several trails lead onwards into the surrounding forest: the **Appalachian Trail** continues from Jefferson Rock across the

Shenandoah River into the Blue Ridge Mountains of Virginia, while the **Maryland Heights Trail** makes a four-mile roundtrip around the headlands across the Potomac River. You can also float down the river in a **raft** or inner-tube provided by one of the many outfitters along the rivers east and south of town.

Practicalities

Harpers Ferry makes a popular excursion from Washington, DC, and is served by several trains daily on the Maryland Rail Commuter network (☎1-800/325-7245), and by one daily Amtrak service, which arrives at 6.30pm, en route to Chicago. Greyhound, however, comes no closer than Frederick, Maryland (see p.489).

If you want to **spend the night**, the century-old *Hilltop House Hotel and Restaurant* on Ridge Street (☎304/535-2132 or 1-800/338-8319, ⓦwww.hilltophousehotel.com; ❸) may be showing its age, but still has reasonable prices and good views, while appealing **B&Bs** are sprinkled throughout the surrounding region, among them *Harpers Ferry Guest House*, 800 Washington St (☎304/535-6955, ⓦwww.harpersferry-wv.com; ❹); nearby budget motels include the *Comfort Inn* on US-340 (☎304/535-6391 or 1-800/228-5150; ❸). The *Harpers Ferry Hostel*, seven miles east at 19123 Sandy Hook Rd in Knoxville, MD (☎301/834-7652, ⓦwww.harpersferryhostel.org; closed Nov 15 to March 15; ❶), has dorm beds from $15, and its own campground; there's plenty more **camping** available along the Potomac River in the C&O Canal Historic Park. The park's **visitor center** has further details, as does the **Jefferson County tourist bureau** (☎304/535-2627 or 1-800/848-TOUR), across US-340.

As for **eating** in Harpers Ferry, there is a range of choices within a four-block area. The *Mountain House Café* on High Street (☎304/535-2339) and the *Coffee Mill* on Potomac Street (☎307/535-1257) are good and relatively inexpensive.

Around Harpers Ferry

Among small towns worth seeing nearby is **CHARLES TOWN**, four miles south of Harpers Ferry on US-340, where John Brown was tried and hanged; the **Jefferson County Museum** at Washington and Samuel streets (Mon, Wed & Fri 9am–5pm, Tues & Thurs 11am–7pm, Sat 9am–1pm; free) tells the story of his trial, conviction, and execution, and remembers his last words: "I, John Brown, am now quite certain that the crimes of this guilty land will never be purged away but with blood." **SHEPHERDSTOWN**, a cozy village along the Potomac ten miles to the north, is prettier and better for wandering, with quaint old shops and cafés looking across the river to Maryland's infamous **Antietam Battlefield** (see p.490).

Further afield, and of more salubrious interest, is the old spa town of **BERKELEY SPRINGS**, now preserved as a state historic park thirty miles west of Harpers Ferry on Hwy-9, seven miles south of I-70. Berkeley Springs was a favorite summer retreat of the Colonial elite – George Washington and Lord Fairfax were among the regulars who came here to take the waters – and assorted massage and steam bath treatments are still available at its many health spas. You can take a soak in the old **Roman Bath House** (call ☎304/258-2711; reservations strongly recommended), in active use since 1815 and now run by the state; the spring's waters are 74°F year-round but heated to 102°F for bathers. The town's **central square** is leafy and green, with footpaths fanning out in all directions, one climbing the hill up to the fortress-like mid-Victorian **Berkeley Castle**. Among the **B&Bs** in Berkeley Springs are the *Highlawn Inn*, 304 Market St (☎304/258-5700 or 1-888/290-4163, ⓦwww.highlawninn.com; ❹), and the *Manor Inn*, 415 Fairfax St (☎304/258-1552, ⓦwww.bathmanorinn.com; ❹). The *Best Western*, one mile south of town on Hwy-522, offers a full complimentary Sunday breakfast (☎304/258-9400 or 1-800/937-8376; ❹).

The Allegheny Mountains

Considering that it's the most extensive wilderness area near the East Coast, within just a few hours' drive of a dozen big cities, surprisingly few people have heard about, much less bothered to visit, the backcountry reaches of the **Allegheny Mountains**, West Virginia's segment of the Appalachian chain. The entire 140-mile crest is protected as part of the **Monongahela National Forest**, within which numerous state parks contain the most spectacular sights. There are no cities and few towns, public transportation is nonexistent, and not much goes on after dark – the area is so rural that whole counties do without a single traffic light – but if you like to backpack, ski, cycle, climb, canoe, or just wander around the great outdoors, the Alleghenies are well worth a visit. For maps and more detailed information, contact the state tourist office (see p.29) or the Monongahela National Forest Supervisor, 200 Sycamore St, Elkins, WV 26241 (Mon–Fri 8am–4.45pm; ☎304/636-1800).

Blackwater Falls, the Canaan Valley, and Seneca Rocks

Some of the most beautiful stretches of the Monongahela National Forest are in the central northern part of the state, where the thundering torrents of the **Blackwater Falls** pour over a 60ft limestone cliff before crashing down through a steeply walled canyon. South from here spreads the dense maple, oak, walnut, and birch forest of broad **Canaan Valley**, while to the east rise the barren sub-arctic highlands of the **Dolly Sods Wilderness**, the whole area crisscrossed by hiking, cycling, and skiing trails.

Rising up at the south end of the Canaan Valley, the state's highest point, 4861ft Spruce Knob, stands out over the headwaters of the Potomac River – you can actually drive all the way to the summit. Even more impressive views can be had from the top of **Seneca Rocks**, some twenty miles to the northeast, whose 1000ft limestone cliffs present what is widely considered the most challenging rock-climb on the East Coast. If you want to take the easy way up, a good trail leads in around the back of the North Peak, and takes well under an hour to the top. The helpful **Discovery Center** at the junction of US-33 and Hwy-28, at the base of Seneca Rocks (summer daily 8am–4.30pm; rest of year Sat & Sun only 10am–4pm; ☎304/567-2827, ⓦwww.fs.fed.us/r9/mnf), has details of outdoor recreation opportunities in the entire region. *Yokum's* (☎304/567-2351 or 1-800/772-8342, ⓦwww.yokum.com), near the base of Seneca Rocks, takes care of all your vital needs, with a cheap **motel** (❷), self-service **cabins** (❹), and a pretty riverside **campground** (from $5), plus a country store and down-home **restaurant** that serves tasty, good-value meals.

The old logging town of **DAVIS** (population 800), just east of US-219 at the north end of the Canaan Valley, makes another convenient base, with a couple of **places to stay**: the *Alpine Lodge* (☎304/259-5245; ❸) has standard motel rooms, and the *Bright Morning Inn* (☎304/259-5119, ⓦwww.brightmorninginn.com; ❸) on William Avenue doubles as the town **café**. *Muttley's* next door (☎304/259-4858) serves great-value steaks. Among local **outdoor guides and**

outfitters, Blackwater Outdoor Adventures, nearly twenty miles away on Rte-72 at St George (℡304/478-3775, ⓦ www.raftboc.com), runs rafting, caving, and canoeing trips, and also rents out bikes. Timberline Resort (℡304/866-4801 or 1-800/SNOWING, ⓦ www.timberlineresort.com) operates one of the state's largest downhill ski areas several miles southeast of town. For more information on the region, contact the **visitor center** on Main Street (daily 9am–5pm; ℡304/259-5315 or 1-800/782-2775, ⓦ www.canaanvalley.org).

Elkins and the Augusta Festival

ELKINS, the biggest town in northern West Virginia, lying just west of the Canaan Valley, is one of the best places for visitors to experience the vibrant folk traditions of the West Virginia mountains. The **Augusta Heritage Center**, located on the campus of Davis and Elkins College at 100 Campus Drive (℡304/637-1209), works to keep Appalachian cultural traditions alive in music, arts, and crafts. Concerts and events are held throughout the summer, and there are celebrations of dulcimer-playing in April and fiddle music in October, but its major annual showcase is mid-August's **Augusta Festival**. This offers public workshops in such diverse down-home pursuits as banjo-playing, blacksmithing, quilt-making, and folk dancing, and after dark, performers get together for a nightly hoedown, featuring storytellers and bluegrass bands, among other things.

Elkins' main **visitor center** is in the center of town at 315 Railroad Ave (Mon–Fri 8.30am–5.00pm; ℡304/636-2717 or 1-800/422-3304, ⓦ www.randolphcountywv.com) and can provide full details on local **accommodation**, including several B&Bs, while the *Super 8*, at the intersection of US-219 and US-250 (℡304/636-6500 or 1-800/800-8000, ⓦ www.super8 .com; ❸), has inexpensive, clean motel rooms. The *Kissel Stop Café*, 23 Third St, one block from the visitor center (℡304/636-8810), serves tasty sandwiches and coffee amid railroad-car decor.

Pocahontas County

The southern half of the Monongahela National Forest is contained within hilly **Pocahontas County**, known as "the birthplace of rivers" because it holds the headwaters of the Greenbrier, Cheat, Gauley, and other great West Virginia rivers. Like most of the Alleghenies, it's a mountainous, fairly inaccessible region – two roads, US-219 and Hwy-92, wind north-to-south, with a handful of minor roads twisting between them – offering outstanding outdoor recreation as well as endless scenic vistas.

Besides gorgeous scenery, Pocahontas County is also home to the state-run **Cass Scenic Railroad**, a restored, steam-powered logging railroad built in 1902. Running on regular-gauge tracks, the chugging Shay locomotive carries visitors up to the top of 4842ft Bald Knob on a converted logging train (schedule varies; ℡304/456-4300 or 1-800/CALL-WVA, ⓦ www.cassrailroad.com), starting at the old lumber-mill village of **CASS**, five miles west of Hwy-28 near the town of **Greenbank**. Cass was built by the local logging company that provided subsidized housing for its workers, thereby ensuring their faithful economic dependence; it has been preserved in its entirety as a historic park. You can wander around the logging-railroad town or even **stay the night** in one of thirteen rail-employees' cottages built in 1902 and converted into self-service accommodation (℡1-800/CALL-WVA; ❸–❹), which have room for up to ten people. A short way west of Cass, *Whittaker Campground* (℡304/456-3218; $20) offers basic camping facilities in a fine hillside setting.

Just outside of Greenbank, it's impossible to miss the gigantic white dish of the **Green Bank Telescope** and its smaller cousins, standing out against the mountain ridges. At sixteen million tons, the national radio astronomical telescope is the largest steerable object on the planet. The site, chosen because of the state's minimal radio interference, is open to the public, who can view exhibits and join free hourly tours on a shuttle bus, following an introductory presentation (daily: May–Oct 9am–6pm; Nov–May Wed–Sun 9am–4pm; ☎304/456-4008; ⓦwww.gb.nrao.edu). Four miles north on Hwy-28 in Boyer, *Ryder's* restaurant (☎304/456-4308) dishes up good home-style cooking at bargain prices.

A rigorous five-mile walk downhill from Cass leads along the tracks to the start of the bicycle-friendly **Greenbrier River Trail**, which follows the river and the railroad for 75 miles, coming out near Lewisburg (see below). You can also rent a **mountain bike** from Elk River Touring Center (☎304/572-3771 or 1-866/572-3771, ⓦwww.ertc.com), fifteen miles north of **Marlinton**, the county seat, off US-219 in the hamlet of **Slatyfork**, and set off into the mountains. The company runs a shuttle service to the trailheads and organizes backcountry cycling trips and ski tours in winter, as well as an inn, comfortable cabins, and a good-value restaurant. The Pocahontas County **visitor center** in Marlinton (☎304/799-4636 or 1-800/336-7009) provides maps of the local area.

Another spot well worth visiting is **Cranberry Glades Botanical Area**, off Hwy-39/55, five miles west of the junction with the exquisite Highland Scenic Highway (Rte-150). A half-mile boardwalk is set out around a rare patch of peat bog swamp; it's fun trying to identify the minute carnivorous plants that hide among the mosses and other flora. Leaflets and further information can be obtained from the Cranberry Mountain Nature Center (daily April–Nov 9am–5pm; ☎304/653-4826) at the junction itself.

Another attraction in this part of the Alleghenies is the birthplace of **Pearl S. Buck**, author of *The Good Earth* and one of only two American women – the other being Toni Morrison – to win the Nobel Prize for Literature. Her "home" at **HILLSBORO**, on US-219 halfway between Marlinton and Lewisburg (May–Nov 9am–4.30pm; $6; ☎304/653-4430), is actually her grandparents' house and contains family memorabilia.

Lewisburg and the Greenbrier Resort

Located just off I-64 on the southern edge of the Monongahela National Forest, **LEWISBURG** is the archetypal West Virginia town, its few square blocks of old buildings surrounded by rich pastureland, with good roads allowing quick access to the wilder mountain reaches. Originally a frontier outpost during the Indian Wars of the 1770s, Lewisburg was greatly prized during the Civil War for its location at the head of the Greenbrier Valley, but nowadays its attractions are those of a classic American small town, where everyone seems to know everyone else, and where the houses and shops have remained in the same family for generations. In mid-August each year, Lewisburg plays host to the **West Virginia State Fair** (call ☎304/645-1090 for exact dates).

Washington Street, the four-block business district, is lined on both sides by brick-faced early nineteenth-century houses, and makes for pleasant wandering; no. 106 has been a two-chair barbershop for over a hundred years. A block away, in a small park at 200 N Jefferson St, stands the oldest surviving structure in Lewisburg, a rough-hewn limestone shed built in 1770 to protect a freshwater spring that is still flowing today.

The **visitor center**, 111 N Jefferson St (Mon–Fri 9am–5pm, Sat 10am–4pm; ☎304/645-1000 or 1-800/833-2068, ⓦwww.greenbrierwv.com), hands out walking tour maps of the town and can suggest driving tours around

Greenbrier Valley. It can also put you in touch with various cozy **hotels**, such as the *General Lewis Inn*, 301 E Washington St (☏304/645-2600 or 1-800/628-4454, Ⓦwww.generallewisinn.com; ❹), which also has a fine, moderately priced **restaurant**.

Just east of Lewisburg, outside the faded spa of **WHITE SULPHUR SPRINGS**, two dozen US presidents have escaped the pressures of politics at *The Greenbrier*, 300 W Main St (☏304/536-1110 or 1-800/624-6070, Ⓦwww.greenbrier.com; ❾). The grandest and plushest hotel in West Virginia, it is five-star all the way, from the pillared entrance hall to the 6500 acres of lush grounds and golf courses. The hotel's four restaurants are all open to the public and require reservations.

The New River Gorge

One of West Virginia's most spectacular river canyons, the **New River Gorge**, lies just thirty miles west of Lewisburg along I-64. Stretching for over fifty miles, and now protected as a national park, the thousand-foot cleft was carved through the limestone mountains by the New River – despite its name, one of the oldest rivers in North America. Apart from one daily train (see below), there's no easy access to most of the gorge – to see it, you have to get out on the water, with the help of any of over fifty professional rafting companies. Visitor centers located near the most impressive spots give details of recreational opportunities. The **Canyon Rim visitor center** (daily 9am–5pm; ☏304/574-2115), seven miles north of Oak Hill on Hwy-19, is the only visitor center open year-round and sits alongside the New River Gorge Bridge, which rises nine hundred feet above the river. The other visitor centers are in Grandview, Thurmond, and Sandstone.

Fortunately for car-less travelers, Amtrak **trains** from Washington, DC, pass right through the gorge on one of the most stunning railway journeys in the East. Though the ride itself is memorable enough, for a close-up look you can get off at the southern end of the gorge at the former railroad town of **HINTON**. The train's only stop, it's a fascinating, if somewhat dilapidated remnant of the glory days of the railroads around the turn of the twentieth century. An almost perfectly preserved purpose-built company town – the National Park Service intends someday to restore it as a living museum – it is beautifully sited, with brick-lined streets angling up from the water, lined by dozens of grand civic buildings as well as row after row of slowly decaying workers' houses. A walking tour map of Hinton is available from the **Chamber of Commerce**, 206 Temple St (Mon–Fri 10am–4pm; ☏304/466-5420).

Although the town has definitely seen better days, Hinton still makes a workable base for visitors to the gorge. There are some decent budget **motels**, including the *Coast-to-Coast* (☏304/466-2040; ❷) and the *Sandman* (☏304/466-1700; ❷), and a couple of riverfront taverns. Local **river-rafting** outfits include New River Whitewater Tours (☏304/466-2288 or 1-800/292-0880, Ⓦwww.newriverscenic.com) and Cantrell Canoes (☏304/466-0595 or 1-800/470-RAFT), both charging from $49 per person (with occasional specials) for trips through the gorge. All of these facilities are to be found on Hwy-20, just south of town.

Charleston

CHARLESTON, West Virginia's state capital and largest city, on the Kanawha River, isn't a place many people set out to visit, mainly because there's not very much to see or do; the riverfront **state capitol** (Mon–Fri 7am–7pm, Sat

9am–7pm, Sun noon–7pm), designed by Lincoln Memorial architect Cass Gilbert and completed in 1932, is pleasant enough, with a small monument to African-American activist Booker T. Washington on its grounds. The **West Virginia Cultural Center** (Mon–Thurs 9am–8pm, Fri & Sat 9am–6pm, Sun noon–6pm; free; ☎304/558-0162, ⊛www.wvculture.org), in the same compound as the capitol, acts as the state museum and has extensive displays on coal mining, geology, forestry, wars, and the state's history. The main live showcase of traditional West Virginian culture takes place here during the annual **Vandalia Festival**, Appalachia's largest celebration of folk arts and crafts, held on Memorial Day weekend and featuring lively bluegrass music and tall-tale-telling contests. The annual **Regatta** on Labor Day weekend is one of the city's other big events.

There are three hundred **rooms** at the very central *Elk River Town Center Inn*, 2 Kanawha Blvd E (☎304/343-4521; ❸), which also has a sauna and swimming pool; other motels abound along the interstates. *General Seafood*, on the river behind the Riverwalk shopping center, offers a switch from down-home cooking (Tues–Fri 11am–2pm and 4–10pm; ☎304/744-8331). Capitol Street downtown boasts a string of eateries such as the *Mykonos Café* at no. 218 (☎304/347-9220), which has good Greek lunch specials. On the western edge of downtown, almost alongside I-64 between Lee and Quarrier streets, the gleaming **Charleston Civic Center** mall is the liveliest area to while away a couple of hours.

Maryland

Founded as the sole Catholic colony in strongly Protestant America, and isolated as the northernmost slave state, **MARYLAND** has always been unusual. Within its small, irregularly shaped area, its attractions range from the frantic, boardwalk beaches of **Ocean City** to the sleepy fishing villages of the **Chesapeake Bay**, and the bustling urban center of **Baltimore** to peaceful Appalachian hill country. Once one of the world's most productive fishing areas, the Chesapeake Bay is slowly recovering from near annihilation due to pollution and overfishing. Its abundant oyster stocks are a thing of the past, but legendary **blue crabs** and sweet rockfish are available. The Bay now supports a diverse, decentralized economy, buoyed by the hundreds of weekend boaters who cruise from one to another of its Colonial-era towns.

Maryland's heritage isn't quite as obvious as Virginia's, with nowhere near as many historical sites, but it boasts plenty of firsts for the United States, including the first Catholic cathedral, gas–lit street, and telegraph line between Baltimore and Washington, DC. Kent Island on Maryland's **Eastern Shore** was the third permanent English settlement (behind Jamestown and Plymouth Rock), founded in 1631. And during the War of 1812, the British forces attempted a last-ditch effort to wrest back the colonies, in which they burned down much of Washington, DC, and moved on to the shipyards of Baltimore. In a valiant battle, they were staved off at **Fort McHenry**; the fort's resistance inspired an onlooker, Francis Scott Key, to write the words to the United States' national anthem, **The Star-Spangled Banner**.

Maryland's largest city is the busy port of **Baltimore**, a quirky and engaging metropolis with a revitalized urban waterfront, thriving cultural scene, and eclectic neighborhoods that characterize its diverse residents. **Western Maryland** stretches over a hundred miles to the Appalachian foothills, its rolling farmlands notable chiefly for the Civil War battlefield at **Antietam**. Just twenty miles south of Baltimore, along the Chesapeake Bay, picturesque **Annapolis** has served as Maryland's capital since 1694. Some of the state's most worthwhile destinations, from the pretty fishing and yachting town of **St Michaels** to the untouched wilderness of **Assateague Island**, are across the Chesapeake Bay on the Eastern Shore, connected to the rest of the state by the US-50 bridge but otherwise still a world apart – except for the sprawling resort of Ocean City.

Getting around Maryland

The best way to get around Maryland is by **boat**, sailing around the gorgeous Chesapeake Bay. **Cycling** is also a good option, especially on the Eastern Shore, where the roads are wide-shouldered and little traveled, and wind through cornfields from one Colonial-era hamlet to another – the state tourist office (see p.28) puts out an excellent free map of the safest and most scenic routes. Baltimore is on the main Amtrak line between New York, Philadelphia, and Washington, DC, and is linked by regular buses with Annapolis.

Baltimore

I would never want to live anywhere but Baltimore. You can look far and wide, but you'll never discover a stranger city with such extreme style. It's as if every eccentric in the South decided to move north, ran out of gas in Baltimore, and decided to stay.

John Waters, *Shock Value*

BALTIMORE is among the more enjoyable stops on the East Coast, and its closely knit neighborhoods and historic quarters provide an engaging backdrop to many diverse attractions, especially those along its celebrated **waterfront**, like the Inner Harbor's National Aquarium and the Pier 6 Concert Pavilion and Power Plant entertainment complex. The city also boasts top-rated **museums**, including the Walters Art Museum and the child-oriented Port Discovery, which cover everything from fine arts to black history to urban archeology. That Baltimore has been home to such diverse figures as writers Edgar Allan Poe and Anne Tyler, and civil rights activists Frederick Douglass and Thurgood Marshall goes some way towards explaining its sometimes bizarrely varied character, but it's still hard to pin down exactly what makes it such an engaging city to visit.

Arrival, information, and getting around

Baltimore-Washington International Airport (BWI), ten miles south of the city center and twenty-five miles northeast of DC, is one of the busier East Coast hubs. The cheapest and best way to get into the city is on the MTA **light rail** system, which takes around 25 minutes (☎410/539-5000 or 1-800/RIDE-MTA, ⓦ www.mtamaryland.com); see p.482 for more details. **Shuttle vans** into Baltimore, including Airport Shuttle ($10–18; ☎410/821-5387 or 1-877/VANFORU) and Let's Go Transportation (☎410/977-1855,

BALTIMORE

ACCOMMODATION

Admiral Fell Inn	E
Celie's Waterfront B&B	F
Days Inn Inner Harbor	D
The Inn at Government House	A
Mount Vernon Hotel	B
Radisson Plaza Lord Baltimore	C

STATE CENTER

CHASE STREET

EAGER STREET

READ STREET

Mount Vernon

MADISON STREET

Washington Monument

Maryland Historical Society

Peabody Conservatory of Music

Mother Seton House

CENTRE STREET

Walters Art Museum

FRANKLIN STREET

MULBERRY STREET

Lexington Market

LEXINGTON MARKET

Greyhound Bus Station

SARATOGA ST

Westminster Church & Edgar Allan Poe Grave

FAYETTE STREET

LEXINGTON STREET

City Hall

BALTIMORE STREET

CHARLES CENTER

SHOT TOWER

REDWOOD STREET

WATER STREET

Port Discovery

Flag House

LOMBARD STREET

World Trade Center

CAMDEN STREET

PRATT STREET

Harborplace

Baltimore Maritime Museum

Oriole Park at Camden Yards

CONWAY STREET

USS Constellation

National Aquarium

Inner Harbor

Pier 6 Concert Pavilion

M&T Stadium

Maryland Science Center

FEDERAL HILL DISTRICT

American Visionary Art Museum

Federal Hill Park

CROSS STREET

Cross Street Market

RESTAURANTS

Donna's Coffee Bar	3
Five Seasons	5
Helmand	1
Thairish	2
Women's Industrial Exchange Restaurant	4

Ⓜ Metro station

0   400 yds

N

THE CAPITAL REGION | MARYLAND

5

▲ Great Blacks in Wax Museum (3/4 mile)

▲ Little Italy & Fells Point, Canton

▲ Water Taxi to Fell's Point

◄ B&O Railroad Museum (1/2 mile) & Babe Ruth Birthplace

481

Ⓦ www.letsgotransportation.com), take around twenty minutes to reach downtown. **Taxis** cost around $30. **MARC** commuter trains ($3.25 one way, $6 roundtrip; ☎410/539-5000 or 1-800/325-RAIL), operating weekdays from DC, stop at the airport before continuing on to the restored **Pennsylvania Station** (commonly known as Penn Station), half a mile north of downtown at 1525 N Charles St, which is also the arrival point of Amtrak **trains** (☎1-800/USA-RAIL) from all destinations. Greyhound **buses** stop on the west side of downtown at 210 W Fayette St, but be careful in this area at night since it borders on the rougher part of the city.

Pick up free maps and the seasonal *Quick Guide* at the **Baltimore Area Convention and Visitors Association**, on Light Street, in front of the Maryland Science Center (☎410/837-7024 or 1-877/BALTIMORE, Ⓦ www.baltimore.org), or from its booths at the airport and train station.

City transportation

Because the city is compact – most things of interest are within a mile or two of the center – you can cover a lot of territory on foot. A **water taxi** nips between the Inner Harbor and more than forty area attractions, including the National Aquarium, Fell's Point, the Civil War Museum, and the Canton area (Nov–March Mon–Sun 11am–6pm; April Mon–Thurs & Sun 10am–8pm, Fri & Sat 10am–midnight; May 1 to Sept 1 Mon–Thurs 10am–11pm, Fri & Sat 10am–midnight, Sun 10am–9pm; Sept 2 to Oct 31 Mon–Thurs & Sun 10am–8pm, Fri & Sat 10am–midnight; all-day pass $6; ☎410/563-3901 or 1-800/658-8947, Ⓦ www.thewatertaxi.com). Red **jitneys** run to Fort McHenry National Monument, birthplace of the "Star Spangled Banner," every fifteen to eighteen minutes in season. Several other operators run **harbor cruises** from the Inner Harbor, including Seaport Taxi (☎410/675-2900) and Harbor Cruises (☎410/727-3113). The city-operated **MTA** bus, subway, and lightrail system ($1.35, day pass $3; ☎410/539-5000, Ⓦ www.mtamaryland.com) covers many locations, including the airport, and runs from 6am until 11pm (Sat 7am–11pm, Sun 11am–7pm). On buses, have exact change ready. **Taxi** companies include Yellow Cab (☎410/685-1212) and Royal Cab (☎410/327-0330).

Accommodation

Baltimore has few budget options, but the usual chain **hotels** provide moderately priced accommodation downtown. A more pleasant alternative – and certainly worth the price if bar-hopping is on your agenda – are the **B&Bs** clustered around the historic waterfront area of Fell's Point. A central reservation office (☎410/263-2553 or 1-877/BALTIMORE) can help. Room discounts may be found by phoning the Baltimore Hotel Hotline ☎1-800/964-6835 (or visit Ⓦ www.hotels.com).

Admiral Fell Inn 888 S Broadway ☎410/522-7377 or 1-800/292-4667, Ⓦ www.harbormagic.com. Nicely restored historic hotel in the heart of Fell's Point. Breakfast included. Valet parking $15 per night. ❻–❽

Celie's Waterfront B&B 1714 Thames St ☎410/522-2323 or 1-800/432-0184, Ⓦ www.Baltimore-Bed-Breakfast.com. Seven exquisite rooms, some with private balcony, and a rooftop deck with superb views of Fell's Point harbor. ❺

Days Inn Inner Harbor 100 Hopkins Place ☎410/576-1000 or 1-800/DAYSINN, Ⓦ www.daysinnerharbor.com. Standard hotel chain with cheaper rates than the rest, centrally located within walking distance to most sights, including the Inner Harbor. ❺

The Inn at Government House 1125 N Calvert St ☎410/539-0566, Ⓦ www.baltimorecity.gov. Elaborate Victorian mansion with antique-filled rooms, breakfast and parking included. Substantially cheaper Oct–May. ❹–❺

Mount Vernon Hotel 24 W Franklin St
ⓣ410/727-2000 or 1-800/245-5256,
ⓦwww.bichotels.com. Formerly a youth hostel,
this large hotel has comfortable rooms and a central location. Reserve ahead in summer. ❹

Radisson Plaza Lord Baltimore 20 W Baltimore
St ⓣ410/539-8400, ⓦwww.radisson.com. Plush
downtown hotel, two blocks from the Inner Harbor.
❻

Downtown Baltimore

When the whole of **downtown Baltimore** burned to the ground in 1904,
everything from the waterfront to the Mount Vernon area was destroyed,
except for the domed 1867 **City Hall** at 100 N Holliday St. Though it wasn't
a place to spend much time a few years ago, many sections of Baltimore have
undergone a dramatic face-lift, especially in the **Inner Harbor**. Injected with
new restaurants and bars, this area – originally a tourist magnet for shopping –
now makes for a pleasant stroll along the brick-lined waterfront and features
attractions like the National Aquarium, Science Center, and Baltimore-built
Navy frigate USS *Constellation*. It's also within walking distance of the two
sports stadiums, which makes it a convenient spot for baseball and football
fans to meet for a pre-game meal or post-game drink.

The main cluster of businesses, restaurants, and cafés is found west of the central **Charles Street**, in Baltimore's original shopping district, now coming
back after falling into decline. One Baltimore landmark here, dating from 1782,
is a must: the oldest and loudest of the city's covered markets, **Lexington
Market**, has some 140 food stalls, including *Faidley's*, the best (and cheapest)
of many outlets serving oysters, clams, crabs, and other Chesapeake Bay produce. Safely busy during the day, the surrounding streets can become threatening after dark, when the area is best avoided.

Three blocks up, at 600 N Paca St, the **Mother Seton House** (Sat & Sun
1–4pm; free; ⓣ410/523-3443) is a small, late eighteenth-century brick house,
now a museum dedicated to **Elizabeth Seton**, the first American woman to
achieve sainthood, who founded the Daughters of Charity Catholic order
here.

Just south of the market, **Westminster Church** was built in 1852 on top of
the main Baltimore cemetery, and many ornate tombs are now located in dark
catacombs underneath. Among the prominent citizens buried here is **Edgar
Allan Poe**, who lived in Baltimore for three years in the 1830s, marrying his
13-year-old cousin and beginning a career in journalism before moving on to
Richmond, Virginia. In 1849, while passing through Baltimore, Poe was found
incoherent near a polling place and died soon afterwards. In 1875 his remains
were moved from a pauper's grave and entombed within the stone memorial
that stands along Green Street on the north side of the church.

A particularly fun place to visit is the narrow brick rowhouse where baseball
great **Babe Ruth** was born in 1895, at 216 Emory St (daily: April–Oct
10am–5pm; Nov–March 10am–4pm; $6; ⓣ410/727-1539, ⓦwww
.BabeRuthMuseum.com). Chock-full of photographs, film clips, and baseball
memorabilia, it not only traces the life and achievements of the much-loved
home-run hitter, but also serves as an enjoyable introduction to the game and
its personalities.

Appropriately enough, **Oriole Park at Camden Yards**, the beautiful baseball stadium of the Baltimore Orioles, is just two blocks west, on the site of the
old railroad terminal at Camden Yards (for tickets to a game, phone
Ticketmaster ⓣ410/481-7328). Guided tours of the ballpark cost $5
(April–Sept Mon–Sat 11am, noon, 1pm & 2pm, Sun 12:30pm, 1pm, 2pm &

3pm; ☎410/547-6234, ⓦwww.TheOrioles.com), leave from the ticket office at Eutaw and Camden streets; tickets can only be purchased in person. The centenary of the Babe's birth was marked by the unveiling of a bronze statue in 1995; try to spot the mistake, which was immediately picked up on by hardcore baseball buffs.

Just next door, looking very much like an alien ship that just landed, is the 68,400-seat **M&T Stadium** – home to the **Baltimore Ravens** football team and opened in 1998. Fans were amply rewarded by the team's unexpected Super Bowl victory in 2001. Tickets can be purchased through Ticketmaster (☎410/481-7328), and tours are offered daily (☎410/261-RAVE, ⓦwww.baltimoreravens.com).

The Inner Harbor and the National Aquarium

Sooner or later, if you're in Baltimore you're bound to be drawn to the **Inner Harbor**, a success story of urban revitalization. The rotting wharves and derelict warehouses that stood here through the 1970s have been replaced by the sparkling steel-and-glass **Harborplace** shopping mall, crammed with thriving restaurants like the *Cheesecake Factory*, *Wayne's Barbecue*, and seafood specialist *Phillips*, as well as sports memorabilia and bric-a-brac shops that swarm day and night with tourists and locals. It is quite an enjoyable place, with the waterfront promenade enlivened by busking guitar-players and the occasional magician. Sweeping views of the entire city and beyond can be admired from the Top of the World observation deck of Baltimore's own **World Trade Center** on the north pier (Oct–April Wed–Sun 10am–6pm; May–Sept 10am–9pm; $4; ☎410/836-VIEW). Nothing in the Inner Harbor dates from before its rebuilding, but to lend an air of authenticity, remnants from the city's proud maritime past have been assembled here, including the graceful **USS Constellation** (daily Oct 15 to April 30 10am–4pm; $6.50; ☎410/539-1797), the only Civil War vessel still afloat and the last all-sail warship built by the US Navy. Another collection of ships – a Coast Guard cutter that survived Pearl Harbor, a Chesapeake Bay lightship, and a World War II submarine – and a charming lighthouse make up the **Baltimore Maritime Museum** (Mon–Thurs 10am–5.30pm, Fri–Sun 10am–6pm; Jan–March Fri–Sun; $6.00; ☎410/396-3453, ⓦwww.baltomaritimemuseum.org) on the next pier.

In the southwest corner of the harbor at 601 Light St, the sparkling glass, steel, and concrete **Maryland Science Center** (Tues–Fri 10am–5pm, Sat & Sun 10am–6pm; $12, IMAX show $7.50, combination ticket $15.50; ☎410/685-5225, ⓦwww.mdsci.org) is especially fun for kids; it features imaginative and interactive displays on themes ranging from dinosaurs to space travel. Keep in mind that frequent special exhibits can extend visiting hours, as well as raise prices.

The National Aquarium

Far and away the biggest tourist attraction in Baltimore, the **National Aquarium** is certainly well worth visiting, so long as you avoid the weekend throngs (July & Aug Sun–Thurs 9am–6pm, Fri 9am–8pm; Nov–Feb 10am–5pm, Fri 10am–8pm; Sept–Oct & March–June Sat–Thurs 9am–5pm, Fri 9am–8pm; always open for two hours after last admission; $17.50, $5 after 5pm on Fridays; ☎410/576-3800, ⓦwww.aqua.org). The main exhibition building, a rather gray, 1970s concrete space with a confusing jumble of escalators and ramps, rises in levels from a tank full of bat rays past a simulated South Pacific reef up to the rooftop rainforest garden. From here, another ramp winds down past the **Open Ocean Exhibit**, which features a number of slow-moving sharks and dolphins.

While the displays in the main building are generally educational, if not all that innovative or thought-provoking, the separate **Marine Mammal Pavilion**, at the end of an adjacent pier, is a lot more entertaining: this is where the aquarium's trained **dolphins** and beluga **whales** are put through their paces. Dolphin shows are scheduled throughout the day, with the best views to be had from either end of the pavilion where transparent acrylic panels allow you to watch the animals above and below the water as they run the gamut of tail-walking, breaching, and spitting water into the audience.

Mount Vernon

Baltimore's most elegant quarter is just north of downtown on the shallow rise known as **Mount Vernon**, where a couple of good museums sit amid rows of eighteenth-century brick townhouses. The neighborhood, which is good for strolling, takes its name from the home of George Washington, whose likeness tops the 165ft marble column of the central **Washington Monument**, located in a small leafy park next to the spire of the sham-Gothic Mount Vernon Methodist Church at Charles Street and Monument Place. You can climb the monument for a great view over the city, but it opens only on random days.

Across the street, the solemn stone facade of the **Peabody Conservatory of Music** hides one of the city's best interior spaces: the beautiful, skylit atrium of the **Peabody Library** (Mon–Fri 9am–3pm; free; ☎410/659-8179). Closed for remodeling until May 2004, the library features five tiers of intricate wrought-iron balconies rising above ground-floor displays of sixteenth-century books, including a wonderful illustrated 1555 edition of Boccaccio's *Decameron*, and a 1493 printing of the *Nuremburg Chronicles*.

Two blocks west, the **Maryland Historical Society** museum (Tues–Fri 10am–5pm, Sat 9am–5pm, Sun 11am–5pm $4; ☎410/685-3750, ⊛www .mdhs.org) has a fairly tame collection of portraits of Maryland society and documents tracing local history, though its antique-filled chambers give a strong sense of the maritime wealth created here through nineteenth-century trade. Other items of interest include nifty models of Chesapeake Bay boats, vintage Baltimore hair dryers, and the original manuscript of the lyrics to "The Star-Spangled Banner."

Walters Art Museum

Perhaps Baltimore's classiest museum, the **Walters Art Museum** at 600 N Charles St, a block south of the Washington Monument, provides a comprehensive survey of art from ancient statuary to French Impressionist painting (Tues–Sun 10am–5pm, first Thurs of every month until 8pm; $8, free Sat 10am–1pm and first Thurs of the month; ☎410/547-9000, ⊛www.thewalters.org). Entry includes a free **audio tour**, except when museum entry is free, when it costs $3. The main building's core is a large sculpture court, modeled on an Italian Renaissance palazzo, beyond which modern galleries show off Greek and Roman antiquities, medieval illuminated manuscripts, Islamic ceramics, and some very fine Byzantine silver. The top floor has pre-Columbian stone carvings in a grand hall filled with late nineteenth-century paintings, including Manet's beer-drinking *At the Café*.

Almost everything on display was bought by William Walters, one of the first US collectors of **Chinese** and **Southeast Asian** art. The adjacent restored **Hackerman House** holds some especially beautiful pieces, including a roomful of Chinese jade figurines, a Ming dynasty handscroll, some lovely Japanese prints, and a pair of polychrome-and-gilt temple doors carved to look like peacock feathers. The seventh-century lacquered wood statue here of a svelte Buddha is perhaps the oldest such image in the world.

The Flag House and 1812 Museum, and Little Italy

A quarter of a mile east of downtown and the Inner Harbor, across the busy Falls Expressway, is the intriguing **Flag House and 1812 Museum**, 844 E Pratt St (Tues–Sat 10am–4pm; last tour at 3.30pm; $5; ☎410/837-1793). It was here, in 1813, that Mary Pickersgill sewed the 30ft-by-45ft US flag whose presence at the harbor fort attack inspired Francis Scott Key to write "The Star-Spangled Banner." The actual banner is now in the Museum of American History in Washington, DC (see p.431), but the house is full of other such patriotic tributes.

The densely tangled streets of **Little Italy**, still a strongly Italian neighborhood, spread to the south and east of downtown. Besides dozens of restaurants and cafés (many of them very good), the area holds plenty of Baltimore's trademark stone-fronted rowhouses, almost all with highly polished marble steps. As a sort of traditional local substitute for air-conditioning, in the heat of summer residents move their furniture outdoors, thereby turning each street into an extended living room.

Fell's Point and Canton

Beyond Little Italy stands Baltimore's oldest, liveliest, and funkiest quarter, **Fell's Point**. Projecting into the main harbor, its deepwater frontage made it the heart of the city's extensive shipbuilding industry; the shipyards are long gone, but many old bars and earthy pubs have hung on to form one of the best nightlife districts in the country. The Fell's Point **visitor center** at 808 S Ann St, provides good walking maps (daily noon–4pm; ☎410/675-6750), and offers daily tours of the 1765 **Robert Long House**, the oldest surviving urban residence in Baltimore ($3). The **Pink Flamingos** junk shop, actually named Edith's Shopping Bag and owned and run by Edith Massey – inspiration for many of John Waters' offbeat films – was at 728 S Broadway, a block from the water; it's now a novelty store specializing in John Waters memorabilia. The NBC cop drama *Homicide* also called this area home for a while, using the abandoned police station and local coffee shops as a backdrop.

Canton is also an area awakening to new businesses, restaurants, and nightlife, and rivals Fell's Point and Federal Hill for top billing in nightly entertainment. Heading east from Fell's Point, you'll see the first wave of trendy restaurants and bookstore cafés along Boston Street, but the main concentration of bars and eateries surround the square between the two branches of O'Donnell Street.

Other Baltimore attractions

The city's newest – and perhaps most intriguing – museum, designated by the US Congress as "America's official national museum, repository, and education center for the best in original, self-taught artistry," is the **American Visionary Art Museum**, 800 Key Hwy (Tues–Sun 10am–6pm; $9; ☎410/244-1900, Ⓦ www.avam.org), which holds a diverse array of art handcrafted from, among other things, everyday objects such as glass, porcelain, sand, stone, toothpicks, metal, and wood. There's also a good organic café on site.

The **B&O Railroad Museum**, housed in an 1830 passenger station at 901 W Pratt St, just under a mile west of the Inner Harbor (daily 10am–5pm;

$6.50; ☎410/752-2490, Ⓦwww.borail.org), commemorates the first large-scale railroad in the US, which was founded in 1827. Now undergoing repairs, the attraction will reopen in the fall of 2004 with displays of dozens of ornate carriages, including some wacky parasol-covered early models, and row upon row of locomotives, from steam engines to sleek 1940s diesels.

Perhaps Baltimore's most unusual museum is about a mile northeast of the center, in an old fire station off Broadway at 1601 E North Ave. The **Great Blacks in Wax Museum** (mid-Jan to mid-Oct Tues–Sat 9am–6pm, Sun noon–6pm; mid-Oct to mid-Jan Tues–Sat 9am–5pm, Sun noon–5pm; $6; ☎410/563-3404, Ⓦwww.greatblacksinwax.org) uses wax models to illustrate black history, from Egyptian pharaohs and early Muslims through to Dr Martin Luther King Jr, Marcus Garvey, and Malcolm X. The models are posed in prop-filled dioramas – Rosa Parks being dragged off a Montgomery bus, for example, stands across from a pair of Jim Crow–era drinking fountains, with a spotless enamel one labeled "Whites Only" and a rusty spigot for "Colored People." Upstairs, figures in the Maryland Room include Baltimore-born rag-time piano-player and composer Eubie Blake, and blues legend Billie Holiday, who was born and raised on Dallas Street just around the corner.

Further out on the north side, two miles from downtown at the top of Charles Street, is the **Baltimore Museum of Art**, 10 Art Museum Drive (Wed–Fri 11am–5pm, Sat & Sun 11am–6pm; $7, free on first Thurs of the month; ☎410/396-7100, Ⓦwww.artbma.org). As well as great Italian and Dutch works by Botticelli, Raphael, Rembrandt, and Van Dyck, an overview of contemporary art spotlights Gilbert and George's *Hellish* self-portrait. One gallery in the West Wing is devoted to Warhol, while the American Wing holds furniture and decorative arts, as well as paintings. The highlight is the Cone Collection of works by Delacroix, Degas, Cézanne, and Picasso, as well as over a hundred drawings and paintings by Matisse.

A short walk south of the Inner Harbor, gradual revitalization is making the **Federal Hill District** a great place to escape from the crowds. Stop by the **visitor center** on Main Street (☎410/727-4500) for walking tour maps and information. Lined with interesting shops, restaurants, and galleries, its main thoroughfare, Light Street, leads to the indoor **Cross Street Market**, which opened in 1875 and, though smaller than its downtown counterpart, is more welcoming. Its two blocks of open-air markets boast some excellent delis, seafood bars, and fruit stalls. **Federal Hill Park** in the northeast is a quiet pub-lic space with fine views over the harbor and the downtown cityscape. In the summer months, it's a popular spot for sunset canoodling.

As part of the city's regeneration, the decrepit fish market across from the Harbor was relaunched as the gleaming **Port Discovery**, 35 Market Place (Oct–May Tues–Fri 9.30am–4.30pm, Sat 10am–5pm, Sun noon–5pm; Sept Fri 9.30am–4.30pm, Sat 10am–5pm, Sun noon–5pm; June–Sept Mon–Sat 10am–5pm, Sun noon–5pm; ☎410/727-8120, Ⓦwww.portdiscovery.org), a children's museum packed to the ceiling with hands-on exhibits and – sur-prisingly – fun for visitors of all ages. You can even treat yourself to a bird's-eye view from the **HiFlyer**, a tethered helium balloon fifty feet above the muse-um (Fri & Sat 11:30am–10pm, Sun noon–5pm; $12, $15 after 8pm; ☎410/949-2359).

Eating

Baltimore is affectionately known as **Crab City**, and locals will argue to their graves that Maryland produces the best **steamed crabs** this side of heaven.

The city has dozens of reasonably priced fresh **seafood** places, as well as the usual range of diners and more than a dozen good family-run restaurants side by side in Little Italy, just east of the Inner Harbor. Canton holds a wider selection, ranging from Irish to Mexican, while Fell's Point boasts numerous vegetarian and waterfront restaurants, and even high tea at *Bertha's* pub (see below). The Colonnade Market, in the Light Street Pavilion of **Harborplace Mall**, holds a wide selection of fast-food outlets, including several Phillips counters offering steamed clams, soft-shell crab sandwiches, and so on. In general, the city's restaurants tend to be unpretentious, family oriented, and reasonably priced.

Babalu Grill 332 Market Place ☎410/234-9898. A popular restaurant serving well-priced traditional Cuban and Nuevo Latino cuisine in a lively setting.

Bertha's 734 S Broadway ☎410/327-5795. Casual and inexpensive yet stylish seafood restaurant, tucked away behind a tiny Fell's Point bar, and known for its delicious mussels.

Crabby Dick's 606 S Broadway ☎410/327-7900. Lively seafood restaurant-cum-sports bar offering lots of crab and shellfish specials, plus pasta, sandwiches, and barbecue dishes.

Da Mimmo 217 S High St ☎410/727-6876. Intimate, romantic Little Italy café, with a wide-ranging menu, live piano music, and even a complimentary limo service from any downtown location. Main dishes $10–15.

Donna's Coffee Bar 2 W Madison St at Charles St ☎410/385-0180. Espressos, pastries, and light, savory dishes in elegant Mount Vernon, with sidewalk seating.

Five Seasons 322 N Charles St ☎410/625-9787. Ethiopian restaurant serving a variety of meat dishes including goat in rich Berbere sauces.

Helmand 806 N Charles St ☎410/752-0311. Inexpensive but chic dinner-only Afghan restaurant in Mount Vernon, with plenty of lamb dishes, as well as *aushak* (leek-filled vegetarian ravioli) and the delicious *kaddo borawni* (a fried-pumpkin appetizer).

Obrycki's 1727 E Pratt St ☎410/732-6399. Baltimore's best and longest established seafood restaurant, offering delicious fresh crabs at premium prices. Closed in winter.

Rick's Café Americain 2903 O'Donnell St ☎410/675-1880. Snazzy eatery with *Casablanca* theme in Canton, featuring a good range of burgers, sandwiches, and main courses; the wine list is quite pricey, though.

Thairish 804 N Charles St ☎410/752.5857. Tiny, basic, and very cheap Mount Vernon spot with a limited but tasty range of authentic Thai favorites.

Woman's Industrial Exchange Restaurant 333 N Charles St ☎410/685-4388. Excellent-value 1940s café with full breakfasts for under $3, huge plates of chicken gumbo for $5, and delicious crabcakes.

Drinking and nightlife

Baltimore's waterfront **Fell's Point** neighborhood may well have the densest assembly of drinking places in the US. One bar after another lines up along Broadway and the many smaller side streets; almost all feature some sort of entertainment, usually live bands, and on summer nights the sidewalks are packed solid with revelers. The **Power Plant Live!** complex, next to the Inner Harbor at 34 Market Place (☎410-727-LIVE), offers a wide selection of dining and entertainment choices that open onto an outdoor plaza. Those tired of long waiting lines are now heading to the up-and-coming areas of **Canton** and **Federal Hill**, which offer plenty of venues – and more space – for the thirsty. Meanwhile, the city's highbrow culture is concentrated northwest of the center, in the Mount Royal Avenue area, which is home to both the **Meyerhoff Symphony Hall**, 1212 Cathedral St (☎410/783-8000, Ⓦwww.baltimoresymphony.com), and the **Lyric Opera House**, 110 W Mount Royal Ave (☎410/727-6000, Ⓦwww.baltimoreopera.com). For a full rundown of what's on, pick up a copy of the excellent free *City Paper*, available at newsstands and book and record stores all over town, or check out Ⓦwww.Baltimore.org.

The 13th Floor *Belvedere Hotel*, 1 E Chase St ☏ 410/347-0888. A plush Mount Vernon cocktail lounge with a small dance floor and expansive views of the city.

Bohagers 701 S Eden St ☏ 410/563-7220. Raucous dance club, with live bands several times a week and crab cakes every night.

Cat's Eye Pub 1730 Thames St ☏ 410/276-9085. Cozy, crowded bar, offering a good range of beers and live music nightly.

The Funk Fox 10 E Cross St ☏ 410/625-2000. Just west of Inner Harbor, this Federal Hill joint puts on live bands every night except Monday, with the emphasis on indie rock and reggae.

Looney's Pub 2900 O'Donnell St ☏ 410/675-9235. This animated hangout, serving up a variety of snacks and beers, is one of Canton's most popular watering holes.

Max's on Broadway 735 S Broadway ☏ 410/675-6297. Huge corner venue with a very long bar, pool tables, and a multitude of beer taps. Upstairs, there's a more refined atmosphere in the leather-upholstered cigar lounge.

Mount Royal Tavern 1204 W Mount Royal Ave ☏ 410/669-6686. Welcoming bar, popular with art students as well as nightcapping musicians.

Wharf Rat Bar 801 S Ann St ☏ 410/276-9034. This friendly bar, well stocked with English ales, packs in a trendy and discerning crowd.

Western Maryland

Stretched between West Virginia and the razor-straight Pennsylvania border, **western Maryland** ranges for some two hundred miles east to west, but is in places well under five miles north to south. In general, the further west you go the more hilly and rural the feel, somewhat similar to Maryland's Appalachian neighbors.

Though the countryside is very pretty and great for hiking and camping, specific points of interest are few. Apart from the Civil War battlefield at **Antietam**, west of the only sizeable town, **Frederick**, the best reason to come to this part of the state is to cycle or hike the footpath of the restored old **Chesapeake and Ohio Canal**, which winds along the Maryland side of the Potomac River from Washington, DC, for over 180 miles to **Cumberland** in the western mountains. Even further west is the state's largest freshwater lake, **Deep Creek Lake**, popular with watersports enthusiasts. It also has more than 70,000 acres of public parks and forests surrounding it, some of which makes smooth cross-country skiing during the winter.

Frederick and around

One of the first towns settled in northwestern Maryland, **FREDERICK**, at the junction of I-70 and I-270 an hour west of Baltimore, was laid out in 1745 by German farmers lured from Pennsylvania by the promise of cheap fertile land. It grew to become a main stopover on the route west to the Ohio Valley, and the bulk of today's tidy town survives from the early 1800s. A **visitor center** at 19 E Church St (daily 9am–5pm; ☏ 301/228-2888 or 1-800/999-3613) has walking tour maps of the town pointing out such places as the **Schifferstadt House**, just off US-15 (Wed–Fri 10am–4pm, Sat & Sun noon–4pm; $3; ☏ 301/668-6088), a stonewalled farmhouse built in 1753 and largely unaltered since.

According to a romantic poem, 95-year-old Barbara Fritchie defiantly waved the US flag while Confederate soldiers marched past her home, the tiny **Barbara Fritchie House** at 154 W Patrick St in downtown (April–Sept Mon & Thurs–Sat 10am–4pm, Sun 1–4pm; $2; ☏ 301/698-8992). When Winston Churchill passed through, he stopped at the house and recited the poem from memory. At publication time, the house was closed due to water damage; call for the latest details. A short walk east from here, the **National Museum of Civil War Medicine** at 48 E Patrick St (Mon–Sat 10am–5pm, Sun 11am–5pm; $6.50; ☎ 301/695-1864, ⓦ www.CivilWarMed.org) offers intriguing walk-in exhibits on mid-nineteenth-century military medicine, including amputation tools and battlefield triage. Besides being a nice detour off the highway, Frederick is also a good base for exploring places such as **Antietam** (see below) and **Harpers Ferry** in West Virginia (see p.472).

Camp David, the mountain retreat used by US presidents since FDR, where Jimmy Carter brought Menachem Begin and Anwar Sadat together in 1978 to sign the historic Camp David accords between Israel and Egypt, is hidden away in the mountains north of Frederick. Nearby **Cunningham Falls State Park** (8am–sunset) and the **Catoctin Mountain Park** (open dawn to dusk; free) both hold seemingly endless hardwood forests – great for fall color – in the midst of which are numerous preserved remnants of early homesteads. Pick up details on hiking and camping at the main **visitor center**, off Hwy-77 two miles west of US-15 (Mon–Thurs 10am–4pm, Fri 10am–5pm, Sat & Sun 8.30pm–5pm; ☎ 301/663-9388).

There are **motels** along both I-70 and US-15, and in town the *Tyler Spite House*, 112 W Church St (☎ 301/831-4455, ⓦ www.tylerspitehouse.com; ❻), is a pleasant **B&B** in an elegant 1814 mansion. For a bite to **eat**, try the soups and steaks at the *Brown Pelican*, 5 E Church St, or the burgers and steamed crabs at *Cactus Flats*, three miles north off US-15.

Antietam National Battlefield

The site of the single bloodiest battle in the Civil War, **Antietam National Battlefield** spreads over unaltered farmlands outside the whitewashed and balconied village of **Sharpsburg**, fifteen miles west of Frederick. Here, on the morning of September 17, 1862, forty thousand troops faced a Union army twice that number in an effort to consolidate rebel gains after their victory at the Battle of 2nd Manassas. Hours later, some 25,000 men from both sides lay dead or dying. The fiercest fighting, and the worst bloodshed, occurred in cornfields to the north; Union general Joseph Hooker recorded: "In the time that I am writing, every stalk of corn in the northern and greater part of the field was cut as closely as could have been done with a knife, and the slain lay in rows precisely as they had stood in their ranks a few moments before."

The battle continued throughout the day without a clear result. It may not have been decisive, but the Confederates' lack of success lost them the support of their erstwhile ally Great Britain, while the Union performance encouraged Lincoln to issue the Emancipation Proclamation. Pick up a brochure and driving tour map of the park at the **visitor center**, a mile north of Sharpsburg off Hwy-65 (daily: summer 9am–5pm; winter 8:30am–5pm; ☎ 301/432-5124, ⓦ www.nps.gov/anti), where you also pay the $3 park entry fee. Numerous plaques and memorials have been constructed around the fields, but otherwise the site, with its various farm buildings and country churches, is unchanged, and the entire park serves as a mute but evocative memorial to the conflict. Special events are always held around the battle's anniversary.

Cumberland and the C&O Canal

The only large town in the far west of Maryland, **CUMBERLAND** started life as a coal-mining center in the late 1700s. Often confused with Daniel Boone's Cumberland Gap in southwest Virginia, this Cumberland was also an important trans-Appalachian crossing, but its main place in history is as the terminus of the never-completed **C&O (Chesapeake and Ohio) Canal**, an impressive engineering feat begun in 1813 but not completed until 1850, by which time the railroads had already made it obsolete.

The **visitor center** in the **Western Maryland Station Center**, at 13 Canal St (daily 9am–5pm; ☎301/777-5138, ⓦwww.mdmountainside.com), can provide information on hiking, cycling, canoeing, and camping in the area. In summer, the historic trains of the **Western Maryland Scenic Railroad** leave from here to make the three-hour trip to Frostburg through the surrounding mountains (May–Sept Thurs–Sun 11:30am; Oct daily 11:30am; Nov to Dec 14 Sat & Sun 11.30am; $19; ☎301/759-4400 or 1-800/872-4650, ⓦwww.wmsr.com). The only other sight of note in town is the tiny black and white log cabin where George Washington served his first commission in the 1750s, which stands directly opposite the station on the other side of the canal.

About thirty miles east of Cumberland, I-68 slices straight through a 1600-foot wedge of sedimentary rock, exposing a dramatic "Smiley Face" rock formation called a syncline that can be viewed from a platform at the excellent **Sideling Hill Exhibit Center** (daily 9am–5pm; ☎301/842-2155), where there's a special **geologic exhibit** and stunning views all around.

Annapolis and southern Maryland

While Baltimore has grown into the state's largest and busiest city, **Annapolis**, Maryland's Colonial and current capital, has changed little in size and outward appearance. Before the US broke free from English rule, this was considered to be one of the most genteel and attractive Colonial centers, and though its time-worn streets are now often crowded, Annapolis is still among the more engaging small US cities. Its once-vital Chesapeake Bay **waterfront** now has little of the feel of Colonial maritime life, but the real attractions of Annapolis, amid its narrow streets, include fine homes, the Beaux Arts campus of the US Naval Academy, and the beautiful state capitol. If you like the look of Annapolis, and want to get a better feel for the Chesapeake Bay region away from the crowds, head south to places like **St Mary's City** – the first capital of Maryland, completely reconstructed in the 1960s – or **Solomons Island**, one of many small Chesapeake Bay towns that seem not to have changed for decades.

Annapolis

At the center of **ANNAPOLIS**, overlooking the town's dense web of streets, the **Maryland State House** (daily 9am–5pm, tours at 11am & 3pm; free) was completed in 1779 and soon after served as an early capitol of the US. It remains the oldest state house still in use. The **Old Senate Chamber**, off the grand entrance hall, is where the Treaty of Paris was ratified in 1784, officially ending the Revolutionary War. A statue of George Washington stands here on the spot where he resigned his commission as head of the Continental Army, and exhibits document the role Annapolis played in the life of the young republic. Free guided tours are given twice a day, or you can wander around on your own, perhaps stopping by to listen to the proceedings of Maryland's current legislators, who meet from January to April in the more modern wing to the north of the old building. Also on the grounds of the State House is the cottage-sized **Old Treasury Building**, built in 1735 to hold Colonial Maryland's currency reserves.

Many grand late eighteenth-century brick homes line the streets of Annapolis, but for substance and grace none surpasses the **Hammond-Harwood House**, two blocks west of the State House at 19 Maryland Ave, off

King George Street (Jan–March & Nov–Dec open most Fridays, Saturdays & Sundays; April–Oct Wed–Sun noon–5pm; tours 40min; $6; ☎410/263-4683, Ⓦwww.hammondharwoodhouse.org). The warm redbrick Palladian villa, which consists of two symmetrical wings connected by a central hall, was built in 1774 to the designs of William Buckland and is most notable for its beautifully carved decorative woodwork, especially evident in the intricate front doorway.

Another historic Annapolis mansion nearby, the 1765 **William Paca House**, 186 Prince George St (Mon–Sat 10am–5pm, Sun noon–5pm; $8 including tour), was a downmarket rooming house until it was restored to its period appearance in time for the 1976 Bicentennial; the interior is decorated in warm rich colors and ornate furniture, while the splendid formal garden, which you can peer into from King George Street, is being constantly landscaped and boasts an impressive viewing pavilion.

Besides such elite manors, dozens of eighteenth-century clapboard cottages and commercial structures fill the narrow streets that run down to the waterfront. Of those that have escaped the gentrification, the **Waterfront Warehouse**, 4 Pinkney St, is a Colonial tobacco warehouse that now sets out to explain the handling and storage of the valuable leaves.

For a unique insight into Maryland's history, stop by the **Banneker-Douglass Museum**, at 84 Franklin St, a few blocks northeast of the state house (Tues–Fri 10am–3pm, Sat noon–4pm; free; ☎410/216-6180 or 1-866/521-6173, Ⓦwww.marylandhistoricaltrust.net/bdm.html), home of the state's largest holding of African-American art and artifacts, photography, documents, and books.

The waterfront and US Naval Academy

Although few Colonial sites survive along the modern **Chesapeake Bay waterfront**, the rebuilt 1850s dockside city **Market House** – an early nineteenth-century replacement of a Colonial warehouse used by the revolutionary army – gives a hint of the port's former maritime strength. The rest of the waterfront, locally known as "city dock," is pleasant enough for an afternoon's wandering, especially on summer weekends when the harbor and bay are full of clanging halyards and billowing sails. In amongst the boat-supply shops and harborside bars, the gray stone walls of the **US Naval Academy** (daily: March–Dec 9am–5pm; Jan–Feb 9am–4pm; free; ☎410/263-6933, Ⓦwww.usna.edu) seem designed to exacerbate the sensory deprivation endured by the over four thousand crew-cut young men and handful of women (all of whom line up in formation outside **King Hall**, the dining commons, every day at noon) who spend four strictly disciplined years here before embarking on careers as naval officers. The moment of transition, at the end of each summer's graduation ceremony, is marked by the traditional "Hat Toss." A small museum on the campus holds models of various British and US warships and other naval memorabilia. Superb guided tours of the Academy leave twice a day from the **Armel-Leftwich Visitor Center** (same hours as the Academy) in Halsey Field House, through Gate 1 at the end of King George Street, and include the elaborate crypt and marble sarcophagus of Scottish naval hero, John Paul Jones.

Practicalities

Compared to the rest of Maryland, Annapolis is easy to reach, on Greyhound and a rail-bus combination – Amtrak and Maryland's MARC trains connect by Sky Blue Bus from Baltimore-Washington International Airport;

☎1-800/RIDE-MTA). By road, it's only about half an hour from Washington (via US-50) or Baltimore (via I-97), though parking is difficult. Central, historic Annapolis is very walkable, and the city's **visitor center**, 26 West St (daily 9am–5pm; ☎410/280-0445, ⓦwww.visit-annapolis.org), can provide free maps and practical information about walking tours, and minibus and water tours. If you'd rather see the city on your own, consider picking up one of the *Historic Annapolis* audiocassette tours, narrated by newsman Walter Cronkite, from the Historic Annapolis Foundation Museum Store at 77 Main St. Other options include a one-hour minibus tour that leaves from the visitor center ($14), and water tours.

Finding a **place to stay** is not usually a problem, though prices are fairly steep. There's a free accommodations bureau (☎1-800/715-1000), or you can choose from **B&Bs** like the central and characterful *Scot-Laur Inn*, 165 Main St (☎410/268-5665; ❹), the pricier *Prince George Inn*, 232 Prince George St (☎410/263-6418; ❺), or the attractive *Flag House Inn*, 26 Randall St (☎410/280-2721 or 1-800/437-4825, ⓦwww.flaghouseinn.com; ❹). You'll also find dozens of motels along US-50 on the west side of town.

Restaurants and **bars** are both plentiful and good. Worthwhile options include the no-frills *Chick and Ruth's Delly*, 165 Main St (☎410/269-6737), which offers big breakfasts and has a booth on permanent reserve for Maryland's governor; the ritzier *Harry Browne's*, 66 State Circle (☎410/263-4332), popular with politicos and expense-account lobbyists; and the waterfront *Middleton Tavern Oyster Bar & Restaurant*, 2 Market Space (☎410/263-3323), one of the city's oldest buildings and a great place to dine on fish and chips while people-watching from the sunny porch. There's also the *Market House* on the waterfront, which contains a good range of cheap snack bars, a raw bar, and shared outside seating; many places here serve crab dishes, a staple of the Chesapeake Bay. After dark, the *King of France Tavern*, in the historic *Maryland Inn*, 16 Church Circle (☎410/263-2641), puts on live jazz.

Southern Maryland

The little-visited back roads of **southern Maryland** resemble in many ways the agricultural Deep South. All along both main routes, US-301 from Baltimore and Hwy-2 from Annapolis, fields of corn and tobacco, dotted with aging wooden barns, fill the arable lands in scattered parcels, and narrow, tree-lined country lanes branch off suddenly to rivers or coves of the broad Chesapeake Bay.

Solomons Island

Towns in southern Maryland are few and far between, but a couple are worth seeking out. The old shipbuilding community of **SOLOMONS ISLAND**, sixty miles south of Annapolis via Hwy-2, is not actually an island but a narrow two-mile peninsula between the Patuxent River and Back Creek Bay. The best reason to stop here is the **Calvert Marine Museum**, on Hwy-2 at the north end of town (daily 10am–5pm; $5; ⓦwww.calvertmarinemuseum.com), which focuses specifically on the Patuxent River and on the unique estuarine ecosystem of the Chesapeake Bay tidal areas. The museum's two protected marshland wildlife areas, one saltwater and one freshwater, can be explored on raised walkways, while inside the main building, exhibits follow the development of local boat-building and commercial fishing, and dozens of historic boats are on show. In summer, an old oyster bay-boat, the *William B. Tennison*, leaves from the museum dock on hour-long **cruises** (May–Oct Wed–Sun

2pm; $6) around the bay. The waterfront is dotted with cozy **B&Bs**, among them the *Locust Inn* (☎410/326-9817; ❸), and fresh seafood **restaurants**, including the *Lighthouse Inn* (☎410/326-2444) on the bay side, and *Solomon's Pier* (☎410/326-2424) across the road, both of which have tasty food and sunny outdoor decks.

St Mary's City and Point Lookout State Park

The reconstructed village of **ST MARY'S CITY** is worth a look, both for its lovely location and attention to detail in all the buildings and archeological sites. Set on a broad Potomac cove near the southern tip of the Maryland peninsula, twenty miles south of Solomons Island, St Mary's City is a small-scale but accurate reconstruction of Maryland's first Colonial capital, established here in 1634 before being moved to Annapolis sixty years later. The entire complex, including a working tobacco plantation and a replica of the tiny *Maryland Dove* (a replica of a square-rigged ship that transported the settlers' provisions to the site in 1634 from England) is run as a sort of Colonial theme park, complete with costumed guides who are approachable and knowledgeable (March–June and Sept–Nov Tues–Sat 10am–5pm; July–Sept Wed–Sun 10am–5pm; $7.50; ⓦwww.stmaryscity.org). Its main feature is a reconstruction of the long-vanished **State House**, where in 1689 Protestant rebels seized control of what had been a Catholic-run colony; unfortunately it's all a bit too manicured to provide much of a sense of history.

South from St Mary's City is **Point Lookout State Park** (open 24hr; $3; ☎301/872-5688) at the very tip of the southern Maryland peninsula. During the Civil War, the area was a **prisoner-of-war camp** for rebel forces captured at the Battle of Gettysburg. In just over a year, from March 1864 to June 1865, more than four thousand died due to the appalling conditions, including some seven hundred Union guards. Most of the Confederate soldiers were buried in a mass grave, now marked by a granite obelisk; the actual camp – where the ramparts have been rebuilt and now includes a small and somewhat gruesome museum – was a mile south. The point in the park where the Potomac flows into the Chesapeake is a good place to watch the sun rise or set.

The Eastern Shore

Maryland's compelling **Eastern Shore** occupies over half of the broad Delmarva (*De*laware, *Mar*yland, *V*irginia) peninsula that protects the Chesapeake from the open Atlantic. Its miles of back roads are perfectly suited to aimless exploration and sudden discovery of such sights as the odd wooden farmhouse or tobacco barn marooned in the middle of a field, or an old sailboat tied up at an apparently decrepit dock that springs to life when the fishing craft return. The US-50 bridge, built across the Chesapeake Bay in the early 1960s, may have made the Eastern Shore more accessible, but the area off the main roads still has a sleepy air. Branching off from US-50 as the highway races down to the beach resort of **Ocean City**, quiet country lanes lead to two-hundred-year-old waterfront towns like **Chestertown**, **St Michaels**, and **Oxford**.

Chestertown and Rock Hall

A stopping place for travelers since Colonial days, when it was a prime Chesapeake port, **CHESTERTOWN** stretches west along High Street from the Chester River. It is surprisingly intact, with its fine old riverfront homes, a courthouse square lined with ornate wooden cottages, and a generally languorous feel that makes it a popular weekend escape from Baltimore or DC. The only house regularly open to the public is the eighteenth-century **Geddes-Piper House**, 101 Church Alley (May–Oct Sat & Sun 1–4pm; tours available Nov–April with two days' notice; $3; ☎410/778-3499, ⓦwww.hskcmd.com), which has a good collection of kitchen tools and eighteenth-century furnishings. Many of the old houses, like the *Widow's Walk Inn*, 402 High St (☎410/778-6455 or 1-888/778-6455, ⓦwww.chestertown.com/widow; ❹), have been converted into **B&Bs**, while others now house top-notch **restaurants** like the *Feast of Reason*, 203 High St (☎410/778-3828; closed Sun), and the *Imperial Hotel* (☎410/778-5000) across the street, with its swanky dining room. The **visitor center**, 122 North Cross St (spring & summer Mon–Fri 9am–5pm, Sat & Sun 10am–4pm; fall and winter Mon–Fri 9am–4pm, Sat & Sun10am–2pm; ☎410/778-9737, ⓦwww.kentcounty.com), has information about walking and cycling tours.

To the west of town, fifteen miles of country lanes lead down to the wharves and dockside restaurants of **ROCK HALL**, an old fishing port where you can watch the day's catch being unloaded while chewing on crab legs at the bare-bones *Waterman's Crabhouse* (☎410/639-2261) on the main pier.

St Michaels

A contender for prettiest harbor on the Chesapeake Bay, **ST MICHAELS**, twelve miles west of US-50 on Hwy-33, is also one of its oldest ports. Founded during the mid-1600s, it grew into one of Colonial America's prime ship-building centers, and its fast sloops and shallow-draft "bugeyes" evaded British blockades during the Revolutionary War. St Michaels languished while Baltimore blossomed, but since the early 1960s it has been revitalized, its old buildings now gentrified into art galleries, boutiques, and cozy B&Bs.

Some corners of the town survive intact, however; among them the old town green, **St Mary's Square**, a block off the main Talbot Street on Mulberry Street. To get a clear sense of the history of Chesapeake Bay, head north along the docks to the extensive and modern **Chesapeake Bay Maritime Museum** (daily March–May & Oct 9am–5pm; June–Sept 9am–6pm; Nov–Feb 9am–4pm; $9.00; ☎410/745-2916, ⓦwww.cbmm.org). The complex focuses on the restored **Hooper Strait Lighthouse** (which you can tour), at the foot of which float several Chesapeake Bay sailboats, designed to make the most of the bay's shallow waters. Nearby, other boats include a Native American dugout canoe, while in the museum workshop skilled artisans and legions of volunteers restore and maintain historic boats using painstaking traditional techniques. If you want to get out on the bay, Patriot Cruises (☎410/745-3100) run one-hour **excursions** for $10.50, while other companies operate shorter (and cheaper) trips.

Among St Michaels' revered seafood **restaurants**, the *Crab Claw* (March to early Dec; ☎410/745-2900, ⓦwww.thecrabclaw.com) occupies a prime chunk of the waterfront alongside the Maritime Museum and boasts an extensive menu. Though many of its customers turn up for the beer and the views, the real reason to come is for their all-you-care-to-eat **steamed crabs**. On weekends especially, the rest of the town's wharves and docks are filled with boaters who flock to restaurants-cum-bars such as the *Town Dock* (☎410/745-5577 or 1-800/884-0103, ⓦwww.town-dock.com) and *St Michaels Crab House* (☎410/745-3737, ⓦwww.stmichaelscrabhouse.com), both at the end of Mulberry Street. As a result, **B&Bs** such as the period-furnished *Hambleton Inn*,

202 Cherry St (☎410/745-3350 or 1-866/745-3350, Ⓦwww.hambletoninn .com; ❺), and the *Kemp House Inn*, 412 S Talbot St (☎410/745-2243, Ⓦwww.kemphouseinn.com; ❹), charge much higher rates on weekends and tend to be fully booked; for slightly cheaper rooms your choice is restricted to the *St Michaels Motor Inn* (☎410/745-3333 or 1-800/528-1234, Ⓦwww .bestwestern.com; ❹), a branch of the *Best Western* chain at 1228 S Talbot St, on the rather featureless main road into town.

Tilghman Island

If you want to see the real, down-home, workaday Chesapeake, **TILGHMAN ISLAND**, west of St Michaels across the Knapps Narrows drawbridge (which rules over vehicle traffic and opens for every single boat coming through), was once home to most of the Chesapeake's skipjack fleet. Partly in response to the continued depletion of oyster stocks, the government has made it illegal to harvest oysters except from small, graceful, and hopelessly outmoded sailing boats called **skipjacks**, of which just a handful are still in use. Most are moored at **Dogwood Harbor**, on the east side of the island; during the fall and winter harvest, they unload at the Harrison Oyster Packing Company, at the foot of the bridge. You can buy oysters fresh off the boat here, or sample them and other local delicacies at two very good restaurants on either side of the bridge: the *Bay Hundred* (☎410/886-2126) and the more upscale *Bridge Restaurant* (☎410/886-2330, Ⓦwww.bridge-restaurant.com). Many locals and visiting weekend fishermen head straight for *Harrison's Chesapeake House Restaurant* (☎410/886-2121, Ⓦwww.chesapeakehouse.com), two miles south of town, for a traditional Eastern Shore dinner stacked with corn on the cob and fresh fried chicken. You can also hook up with fishing excursions at the restaurant (☎410/886-2121, Ⓦwww.chesapeakehouse.com).

Oxford

Just west of US-50, or seven miles south of St Michaels via country lanes and a ferry, the leafy waterfront hamlet of **OXFORD** seems to have slumbered peacefully since Colonial days. Along with Annapolis, Oxford was one of the two ports of entry for all of Colonial Maryland, a role remembered by the reconstructed one-room **Customs House** (Fri–Sun 2–5pm), next to the ferry landing on the north side of town. After Independence, Oxford was all but forgotten; its full-time population is under a thousand and there's hardly any tourist trade. Wandering the quiet streets, however, or lolling on the lawns of the long riverfront promenade can be quite relaxing and enjoyable. A trip across the Tred Avon River on the small **ferry**, which has been in continuous operation since 1836, makes for a nice excursion en route to or from St Michaels (every 20min; June 1 to Labor Day daily 7am–9pm, except Sat & Sun 9am–9pm; Labor Day to June 1 daily 7am–sunset, except Sat & Sun 9am–sunset; Dec 1 to March 1 closed; $6 per car and driver, $1.25 per passenger; journey 10min; ☎410/745-9023, Ⓦwww.oxfordferry.com).

Schooner's Landing (☎410/226-0160) is a friendly, inexpensive seafood **restaurant** with a large deck right on the main harbor, at the end of Tilghman Street; at the *Pier Street Marina & Restaurant* (☎410/226-5171), further south, you can sample fresh crabs, crabcakes, crab soup, and crab balls in a spectacular waterfront setting. The *Robert Morris Inn*, in operation since 1710 on Morris Street at The Strand (☎410/226-5111, Ⓦwww.robertmorrisinn.com; ❺), is named for the Oxford man who personally financed the Continental Army during the Revolutionary War. Its restaurant serves author James Michener's favorite crabcakes. In the larger town of **EASTON** on US-50, the *Bishop's*

House B&B, 214 Goldsborough St (☎410/820-7290 or 1-800/223-7290, ⓦwww.bishopshouse.com; ❺), offers a comfortable alternative to the highway motels.

Ocean City

With more than ten miles of broad Atlantic beach, a boisterous boardwalk, amusement park, and hundreds of thousands of visitors every summer weekend, **OCEAN CITY** is Maryland's number one warm-weather resort. No matter how you get here – up or down the coastal highway or across the Eastern Shore via US-50 – its tower-block hotels, commercialism extraordinaire, and massive overcrowding could come as a shock; it is so overgrown, in fact, that its northern reaches now encroach into Delaware. If you're after a quiet weekend by the sea, avoid it like the plague and take extra care to avoid college vacation season in the spring.

Ocean City is, at least, easy to reach: Carolina Trailways **buses** from DC end up in the southern end of town at Second Street and Philadelphia Avenue (☎410/289-9307). The Beach Express (☎1-866/628-7433, ⓦwww.beach-express.com) runs **shuttles** to and from the Baltimore, Washington, DC, and Philadelphia airports.

The city has two helpful **visitor centers**. The first is the Chamber of Commerce center, on US-50 as you approach the city (daily 9am–5pm; ☎1-888/626-3386, ⓦwww.oceancity.org), while the second is at 4001 Coastal Hwy (daily 9am–5pm; ☎410/289-2800 or 1-800/626-2326, ⓦwww.ococean.com); both have the usual brochures and can help with accommodation.

Places to **stay** are plentiful except on summer weekends, and off-season rates are at least half prime-time ones. For lodging information, call ☎1-800/638-2106 or check out ⓦwww.ococean.com, which has links to hotels. The lone **hostel**, *Summer Place*, at 100 Somerset St (April–Oct; ☎410/289-0350; ❷), is open only to international students staying several months, and doesn't accept reservations. **Motels** in the same area include the *Oceanic* on the tip of the peninsula at the south end of Baltimore Street (☎410/289-6494; ❸). The bright and breezy *Nassau Motel*, further up at 60th Street and Oceanfront (☎410/524-6451, ⓦwww.ocnassaumotel.com; ❹), has reasonable rates. Other alternatives range from the faded seaside grandeur of the *Commander Hotel*, on the boardwalk at 14th Street (☎410/289-6166 or 1-888/289-6166, ⓦwww.commanderhotel.com; ❺). The closest campsite to the beach is at *Ocean City Travel Park*, on the bayside at 105 70th St (☎410/524-7601, ⓦwww.occamping.com). The visitor center has a camping guide.

Dominated by the boardwalk fast-food joints and the national franchises along the Coastal Highway, Ocean City has few good **eating** options. The *Angler Restaurant*, on the bay at Talbot Street (☎410/289-7424), has fresh seafood, as well as beers and tropical cocktails. **Nightspots** include the frenetic *Big Kahuna Surf Club*, 18th and Coastal Highway (☎410/289-6331), and *Shenanigan's*, 4th and Boardwalk (☎410/289-7181), which has a full menu and live music until 2am. Pick up the free *Ocean City Today* or *The Beachcomber* to find out what's on.

Assateague Island National Seashore

If you find yourself in the Ocean City area in the peak of summer and want to escape the crowds, head nine miles down the coast to **Assateague Island National Seashore** – a 37-mile stretch of entirely undeveloped beach and marshland stretching into Virginia. Until 1933, Assateague Island was attached to Ocean City; then a hurricane drove a wedge between them, and it became a separate barrier island, which is progressively being pushed by the elements back towards the mainland. Another storm in 1962 led to the abandonment of construction plans, under which nine thousand residential lots had been set aside, and instead the island was designated a national seashore.

Assateague's main **visitor center** (daily 9am–5pm; ☎410/641-1441, ⓦwww.nps.gov/asis) is eight miles from Ocean City, just before the humpback bridge across to the island ($5 park entry per car, valid one week). If you plan to do any walking, pick up the $2.25 booklet detailing the park's three main trails. Of these, the Life of the Marsh Trail guides you along half a mile of boardwalks through low-lying leeward wetlands, while Life of the Dunes, over the thick white sands just back from the beach, is a little longer, and harder going. Most visitors, however, come strictly for the beaches themselves, which feel a world away from Ocean City. Seashore **camping facilities** on Assateague Island are available year-round (☎410/641-3030 or 1-888/432-2267; $10–14 per site), but if you want a bit more comfort, the best **lodging** is to be found near the southern half of the island, across the Virginia border in **Chincoteague** (see p.463).

Delaware

DELAWARE has some beautiful spots – including some of the mid-Atlantic's best beaches – and some historic areas, but its tourist boards have a challenge. Most of the images potential visitors have of the state are negative: Delaware is known for the massive chemical plants of the **DuPont** Corporation and for **Dover Air Force Base**, as well as for tolerating shady business practices – half of America's largest companies have their official bases in this tiny state, thanks to its permissive tax, banking, and incorporation laws. The upside of this is that state museums are free and there's no sales tax, which certainly makes shoppers happy.

To downplay the state's dubious contemporary image, Delaware's promoters emphasize its past – for example, as the first ex-colony to ratify the Constitution, it claims the title of **America's First State**. Dutch whalers established a settlement at the mouth of the Delaware Bay in 1631, and soon afterwards the Swedes built a larger colony at present-day **Wilmington**. The two groups fought amongst themselves until the British took over in 1664. Delaware was part of neighboring Pennsylvania – Philadelphia is only ten miles north of the present, arching state border – until separating itself off in 1776.

Much of Delaware's fortunes (and misfortunes) since then can be traced directly to the **du Pont family**, who, fleeing the wrath of revolutionary France, set up a gunpowder mill that became the main supplier of conventional explosives to the US government. After World War I, the du Ponts went public and made millions in the stock-market frenzies of the Roaring Twenties, since which time the company has diversified, its labs inventing such modern essentials as nylon and cellophane.

The du Ponts built huge mansions for themselves in the **Brandywine Valley** north of Wilmington, near the perfectly preserved old Colonial capital, **New**

Castle, on the Delaware Bay just five miles south of I-95. Further south, **Dover**, the capital, may not detain you long, but beyond it, the small and amiable resorts of **Lewes** and **Rehoboth Beach** mark the northern extent of over twenty miles of rather unspoiled Atlantic beaches.

Getting around Delaware

Apart from Wilmington, which is on the main East Coast **train** and **bus** lines, Delaware is hard to get around without a car. Greyhound services are limited to a summer-only route from DC to **Rehoboth**, and local public transportation is nonexistent.

I-95 and the New Jersey Turnpike converge at Wilmington, from where US-13 runs south through the state. More often called the **Du Pont Highway**, it was paid for and constructed by the industrialists so that they could ride in comfort between their Wilmington mansions and Dover. A direct car **ferry** connects Cape May, the southern tip of New Jersey, and Lewes, at the mouth of the Delaware Bay (see p.503).

Wilmington and around

WILMINGTON may not be the most compelling place in America, but this medium-sized city can make for a refreshing break from the interstates and the tourist trail: not only does it boast the excellent Delaware Art Museum and some pretty waterside parks, but the surrounding Brandywine Valley holds the manor homes and gardens (and factories) of the du Ponts, all open to the public and providing an inside look at the First State's First Family and America's de facto aristocracy.

If you arrive in Wilmington by train, on the Amtrak line between New York and Washington, you'll pull in to the quirky 1907 terracotta station on the somewhat dangerous and run-down south side of the city. From here, the two main streets, Market and King, run north for about a mile to the Brandywine River. Their partly pedestrianized lengths hold a standard array of stores and other small businesses, as well as a handful of restored eighteenth-century rowhouses clustered around the Georgian **Delaware History Museum**, at 504 Market St (Mon–Fri noon–4pm, Sat 10am–4pm), and the **Delaware Historical Society**, at 512 Market St (March–Dec Mon–Fri noon–4pm, Sat 10am–4pm; $4; ☎302/656-0637, ⓦwww.hsd.org), both small museums of local history. The faceless gray monoliths that tower over the cityscape house the headquarters of hundreds of national companies.

A short walk north of the downtown commercial district, at the top end of Market Street, **Brandywine Park** comes as a welcome relief from the concrete pavement, with its grassy knolls lining both banks of the Brandywine River. In the residential districts to the north are some of the city's oldest and most elegant houses, many dating from the Revolutionary War, when Wilmington's flour mills fed the American forces. The nearby **Delaware Art Museum**, 800 S Madison St (Tues–Fri 10am–4pm, Sat 10am–5pm, Sun 1–5pm; $7, free on Sat 10am–1pm; ☎302/571-9590, ⓦwww.delart.org), has a good range of works by American painters like Thomas Eakins, Winslow Homer, and Edward Hopper, as well as a comprehensive collection of English Pre-Raphaelite paintings and drawings.

Most of Wilmington's surprising number of important Colonial sites are hidden away amid the decrepit and heavily industrialized waterfront to the east of downtown. A poorly signposted "Historic Wilmington" loop stops first at the foot of Seventh Street, where a small monument marks the site of Delaware's first European colony, **Fort Christina**, set up by Swedish settlers in 1638.

Nearby, at 606 Church St, the **Hendrickson House Museum and Old Swedes Church** (Wed–Sat 10am–4pm; free) is one of the oldest houses of worship in the US, built in 1690 and still retaining its impressive black-walnut pulpit.

The downtown **CVB**, 100 W 10th St (Mon–Fri 9am–5pm; ☎302/652-4088 or 1-800/489-6664, ⓦwww.VisitWilmingtonDe.com), has walking and driving tour maps, and practical information. A DART **trolley** runs around downtown for 25¢ (☎302/652-3278). Few people choose to spend a night in Wilmington, but if you do, the standard **hotel** and **motel** chains exist, or you can shell out $250 a night at the splendidly ornate *Hotel du Pont*, 100 W 11th St (☎302/594-3100 or 1-800/441-9019, ⓦwww.hoteldupont.com; ❾). For **eating**, the excellent *Waterworks Café*, 16th and French streets in Brandywine Park (☎302/652-6022), is classy (and pricey), or you can scout around the happening Trolley Square area northwest of downtown, where *Kelly's Logan House*, 1701 Delaware Ave (☎302/652-9493), serves tasty burgers and other pub fare in a pleasant garden setting. There's also a range of medium-priced eateries on Market Street.

The du Pont mansions

Various generations of the du Pont family built opulent homes in the rural Brandywine Valley twenty minutes northwest of Wilmington. To learn how their fortune was made, stop first at the **Hagley Museum**, off Hwy-141 just north of Wilmington (mid-March to Dec daily 9.30am–4.30pm; Jan to mid-March Sat & Sun 9.30am–4.30pm; $11; ☎302/658-2400, ⓦwww.hagley.org). Although Pierre du Pont, the patriarch, was minister of finance to Louis XVI, the museum begins later with the founding in 1802 of a small water-powered gunpowder mill along the banks of the Brandywine River. Mirroring the development of nineteenth-century American industry, the complex grew over the next hundred years to include ever-larger steam-powered and eventually electrically powered factories – almost all of which are still in working order.

The enormous dusty pink **Nemours Mansion**, just a mile up the road, gives an idea of the wealth and power the family garnered (May–Oct Tues–Sat 9am–3pm, Sun 11am–3pm; tours every two hours; $12; ☎302/651-6912 or 1-800/651-6912, ⓦwww.Nemours.org). Built by Alfred du Pont in 1910 and named for the family's ancestral home in France, it is surrounded by a three-hundred-acre, Versailles-style formal garden. Inside the mansion, you'll find plenty of lavish rooms along with a 1910 fitness room, bowling alley, ice-making room, and a collection of shiny, early twentieth-century automobiles. Two miles northwest, off Hwy-52, the one-time du Pont family estate of **Winterthur** (Tues–Sun 10am–5pm; $20, gardens only $15; ☎302/888-4600 or 1-800/488-3883, ⓦwww.winterthur.org) has evolved into the country's finest museum of early American decorative arts. Since 1927, when Henry du Pont took over the twelve-room cottage to house himself and his antique furniture, Winterthur has grown into a vast private museum, each of its two hundred rooms showcasing a particular decorative style. Ranging from the simplicity of a Shaker cottage to a beautiful three-story elliptical staircase taken from a North Carolina plantation home, the various pieces of furniture, textiles, silverwork, and paintings – all made in America between 1640 and 1860 – form a rich catalog of the diversity of American applied arts.

New Castle

Delaware's well-preserved first capital, **NEW CASTLE**, fronts the broad Delaware River, just six miles south of Wilmington via Hwy-141. Founded in the 1650s by the Dutch – who were intent on expanding from their colony at New Amsterdam – and taken over by the British in 1664, New Castle was the main stopping point between Baltimore and Philadelphia. William Penn first set foot in the New World here in October 1682. Largely bypassed when railroads and highways replaced the riverboats, it has managed to survive intact, its quiet cobbled streets and immaculate eighteenth-century brick houses shaded by ancient hardwood trees.

The heart of New Castle is the tree-filled **town green** that spreads east from the shops of Delaware Street. Laid out in 1655 by Peter Stuyvesant, and ringed by a cracked red-brick sidewalk, it is dominated by the stalwart tower of the **Immanuel Episcopal Church**, built in 1703 and bordered by tidy rows of two-hundred-year-old gravestones. The church's modern, pristine white interior was reconstructed after a disastrous fire in the 1980s. On the west edge of the green, the **Old Court House** (Tues–Sat 10am–3.30pm, Sun 1.30–4.30pm; free) was built in 1732 and served as the first state capitol. Its dainty cupola was the centerpoint from which surveyors determined the state's curved northern border, drawn up when Delaware seceded from Pennsylvania in 1776.

Fine Colonial houses fill the few blocks around the town green. The largest, and only one regularly open to the public, is the **George Read II House** (Tues–Sat 10am–4pm, Sun noon–4pm; $5; ☎ 302/322-8411, Ⓦ www.hsd.org), two blocks south along the river at 42 The Strand. Built between 1797 and 1804 for a signatory of the Declaration of Independence, the original house burned down in 1824. The sumptuously detailed rebuilt version holds marble fireplaces, brightly painted walls, elaborately carved woodwork, and some of the finest plasterwork ornamentation of the Federal period. The spacious gardens behind the building were laid out in 1847 to the picturesque designs of Andrew Jackson Downing. The large houses across the street, backing onto the Delaware River, also date from the early nineteenth century. A large riverfront park spreads south from the foot of Delaware Street, with rolling lawns and sheltered benches – its pride and joy a tiny white-clapboard ticket office that dates from the opening of the town's first railroad in 1832 and stands next to a small piece of track.

Practicalities

Many visitors are content to see New Castle, just off the interstate, as a daytrip from Washington, DC, or Philadelphia, but there's enough here to merit a longer visit. For further information, or to pick up the self-guided **walking tour** map, drop by the **visitor center** at 211 Delaware St, in the Old Court House (Tues–Sat 10am–3.30pm, Sun 1.30–4.30pm; ☎ 302/323-4453), or call the **Historic New Castle Visitor's Bureau** at ☎ 1-800/758-1550. Comfortable **B&Bs** include the *William Penn Guest House*, 206 Delaware St (☎ 302/328-7736; ❸), and the *Terry House*, 130 Delaware St (☎ 302/322-2505, Ⓦ www.terryhouse.com; ❹), both nineteenth-century townhouses in the center of town. There's good beer and pub grub, including crabs and clams, at the popular *Jessop's Tavern*, 114 Delaware St (☎ 302/322-6111), while more refined taste buds will enjoy the French-influenced seafood dishes at the grand *Arsenal at Old New Castle*, next to the Episcopal Church on Market Street (☎ 302/328-1290).

Dover

DOVER, the capital of Delaware, struggles to attract visitors as they bypass the city en route to the beach resorts of Rehoboth and Maryland's Ocean City.

Located in the mostly agricultural center of the state, just west of US-13, Dover is basically a very small town, with a low-rise business district hemmed in by blocks of suburban houses. South of **Lockerman Street**, the main route through town, government buildings center on the 1792 **Old State House**, its old judicial and legislative chambers now restored as a museum (Tues–Sat 10am–4.30pm, Sun 1.30–4.30pm; free) and furnished with early American antiques. To the west, around the oval **town green**, lawyers and insurance brokers have taken over historic buildings such as the former Golden Fleece Tavern, where Delaware's early legislators agreed to ratify the Constitution.

In the same building as the friendly **visitor center** (Mon–Sat 8.30am–4.30pm, Sun 1.30–4.30pm; ☎302/739-4266), at the corner of Duke of York and Federal streets next to the Old State House, the impressive **Biggs Museum of American Art** (Wed–Sat 10am–4pm, Sun 1.30–4.30pm; free; ☎302/674-2111, ⓦwww.biggsmuseum.org) has historical and decorative art displays, as well as American paintings, furniture, and silver. The **Delaware State Museums** (Tues–Sat 10am–3.30pm; free; ⓦwww.destatemuseums .org/default.shtml) includes a quaint trio located a short walk west of the green; the **Archaeology Museum** traces the area's history from 12,000 years back, and the **Museum of Small Town Life** features an early 1900s pharmacy and print shop – but not to be missed is the **Johnson Victrola Museum**, which houses a large collection of phonographs, dedicated to the memory of Dover-born engineer Eldridge Reeves Johnson, who helped to invent the **Victrola**. The layout is like a 1920s music store: dozens of "talking machines," from early wind-ups to prototype jukeboxes, play period recordings, and comical photographs document early, pre-electric recording techniques – entire orchestras crowd together around huge megaphones. Pride of place goes to a painting of a dog, Nipper, listening to a Victrola, an image made familiar as "His Master's Voice." In 1929 Johnson sold the rights to his machine, and to his trademark dog, to RCA for $29 million.

A few miles outside town, Dover Air Force Base also serves as the US military mortuary, perhaps most familiar from the televised arrivals of overseas casualties. At the **Air Mobility Command Museum** on-site (entrance at Hwy-9 and US-13; Tues–Sat 9am–4pm; free; ☎302/677-5938, ⓦwww.amc-museum.org), visitors have a chance to enter a 247-foot-long C-5 Galaxy cargo plane and also learn about bombers, helicopters, and flight training from exhibits and knowledgeable guides.

Every Tuesday and Friday for over fifty years, **Spence's Bazaar**, two blocks south on Queen Street at New Burton Road, has hosted a free-for-all **flea market**. All of Dover turns out for this, including dozens of local **Amish**, who ride here in their old horse-drawn buggies to sell homegrown fruits and vegetables. Though it's not as well known as the Amish community of Pennsylvania's Lancaster County (see p.171), the area around Dover has nearly as large an Amish population, concentrated in the farmlands to the west of town; happily for them, their presence has yet to become a tourist attraction.

Many chain **motels** line US-13, such as the *Comfort Inn* (☎302/674-3300; ❸), two blocks south of Lockerman Street, near the **Dover Downs International Speedway** (☎302/674-4600), the lively scene of harness and NASCAR racing. As for **eating**, most of Dover's restaurants are concentrated on Lockerman and State streets in the town center, just north of the green. *W.T. Smithers* at 140 State St (☎302/674-8875) offers reasonably priced steaks and seafood, while *C'Moore's*, 24 Lockerman St (☎302/674-8875), is a fine spot to fill up on home-style dinners and sandwiches.

The Delaware coast

The thirty-mile-long Delaware coast is one of the little-known jewels of the East Coast. Its only really built-up resort, which is packed solid in summer, is the traditional seaside town of **Rehoboth Beach**. The historic fishing community of **Lewes** is also attractive, but what really sets the area apart is the ease with which you can find long stretches of sand to yourself. For every developed stretch, about ten times more has been preserved as open space, most extensively at **Delaware Seashore State Park**, which stretches south from Rehoboth to the Maryland border.

Lewes

Whether you come down Hwy-1, or cruise across on the ferry from Cape May, New Jersey, **LEWES** makes a good introduction to the Delaware coast. Its natural harbor at the mouth of Delaware Bay has attracted seafarers ever since a Dutch whaling company set up a small colony here in 1631. Lewes's current role as a summer resort hasn't obscured its substantial history (including its ill-fated start as a Dutch settlement), outlined in the mock-Dutch **Zwaanendael Museum**, in the heart of town on Savannah Road at Kings Highway (Tues–Sat 10am–4.30pm, Sun 1.30–4.30pm; free). The **CVB** next door (June–Sept Mon–Fri 10am–4pm, Sat & Sun 10am–2pm; Oct–May Mon–Fri 1–4pm; ☏302/645-8073 or 1-877/465-3937, ⊛www.leweschamber .com), housed inside a gambrel-roofed 1730s farmhouse, has walking tour maps of the town, which point out the handful of eighteenth-century houses and outbuildings collected from around the area to form the **Lewes Historical Complex** (mid-June to early Sept Mon–Fri 10am–4pm, Sat 10am–1pm; $6; ☏302/645-7670) on Third and Ship Carpenter streets three blocks north. Along the canal, keep an eye out for the **Overfalls Lightship**, which lit the entrance to Delaware Bay until 1961, and, lined up along the top of **Memorial Park,** the array of cannons, one said to be from an old pirate ship. You can walk almost everywhere in town, or **rent a bike** from Lewes Cycle Sports, 514 Savannah Rd (☏302/645-4544).

Though Lewes can justly boast of being "the First Town in the First State," most people come here for its beach rather than its history. There's an extensive strand along the usually calm Delaware Bay at the foot of the town, while three-thousand-acre **Cape Henlopen State Park** (☏302/645-8983), where the bay meets the open ocean just a mile east of the town center, offers the chance to camp beside the biggest sand dunes north of Cape Hatteras. For a nice day out, or a possible next leg of your journey, take the seventy-minute **ferry trip** across the Delaware Bay from beside the state park to the pleasant Victorian beach resort of **CAPE MAY**, New Jersey (6–15 services daily all year; starting times vary by day and season; $25 per car, $8 per person, April–Oct; $20/$6 Nov–March; ☏302/645-6030 or 1-800/64-FERRY; see also p.196).

Except on peak summer weekends, Lewes is quiet enough that you should have no trouble finding a **motel** room along Savannah Road, such as *Vesuvio's* (☏302/645-2224; ❹), just before the drawbridge, or *The Captain's Quarters* (☏302/645-7924, ⊛www.captainsquartersmotel.com; ❹) on the far side. Most of the **restaurants**, not surprisingly, feature seafood, including the *Lighthouse* (☏302/645-6271) by the bridge, where you get a free sunset cruise if you dine between 4 and 6pm in the summer, or you can opt for the more formal Italian dining at *La Rosa Negra* at 1201-F Savannah Road (☏302/645-1980).

Rehoboth Beach

A nonstop parade of motels and shopping malls along the six miles of Hwy-1 links Lewes with **REHOBOTH BEACH**, Delaware's largest and liveliest beach resort, which merges into **Dewey Beach** at its southern end. Crowded all summer, but nearly empty the rest of the year, Rehoboth – which started life as a Methodist revival camp, and attracts so many escapees from DC that it's known as the Nation's Summer Capital – is more family oriented than other beach towns in the state, lacking the nightlife of Ocean City but making up for it with miles of clean and uncrowded sands.

Rehoboth has less of a history than Lewes, though its wooden **boardwalk** is one of the last ones left on the East Coast. It stretches along the Atlantic to either side of Rehoboth Avenue – always "**The Avenue**" – which acts as the main drag, its four short blocks clogged with souvenir-shoppers browsing though the usual array of T-shirts and seaside kitsch. Most of the **restaurants** and **nightspots** are concentrated here, with *Thrashers French Fries* stands (fresh-cut Idaho potatoes with salt and vinegar) and burger bars mixed in with the mock-Caribbean beach-shack decor of the *Back Porch Café*, 59 Rehoboth Ave (T 302/227-3674), and the bright *Iguana Grill*, which has Southwest cuisine, a block north at 52 Baltimore Ave (T 302/227-5957). The *Dogfish Head*, 320 Rehoboth Ave (T 302/226-2739), serves moderately priced, wood-grilled seafood and steaks, and has an upstairs bar that hosts live music on Friday and Saturday nights.

If shopping is your passion, Rehoboth has the largest concentration of **outlet stores** in the Delmarva area, with more than 140 brand-name shops like Nike, L.L. Bean, Donna Karan, Gap, and Coach, where, as in all of Delaware, you can shop tax-free. You can't miss the blatant consumerism along Rte-1 – just follow the tide of cars inching towards the latest bargains.

Apart from the peak times of July and August, it shouldn't be too difficult to find a bed in one of Rehoboth's many **motels**: two good options just off the boardwalk are the *Sandcastle*, 123 Second St (T 302/227-0400 or 1-800/372-2112, W www.thesandcastlemotel.com; ❹), and the *Admiral*, a block south at 2 Baltimore Ave (T 302/227-2130 or 1-888/882-4188; ❸). The *Crosswinds Motel*, three blocks from the boardwalk, at 312 Rehoboth Ave (T 302/227-7997 or 1-888/581-WIND, W www.beach-net.com/crosswindsmotel) offers rooms with refrigerators. Beachside **B&Bs** are a nice alternative; try the upmarket *Corner Cupboard Inn*, 50 Park Ave (T 302/227-8553, W www.corner-cupboardinn.com; ❼), just four blocks from the beach and with its own pleasant restaurant, or the *Rehoboth Guest House*, 40 Maryland Ave (T 302/227-4117 or 1-800/564-0493, W www.rehobothguesthouse.com; ❺), which has outdoor cedar showers and a tree-shaded backyard. Rates at all of the above can soar well above $100 on summer weekends. For more information, contact the **Chamber of Commerce**, 501 Rehoboth Ave (T 302/227-2233 or 1-800/441-1329, W www.beach-fun.com).

South of Rehoboth, **Delaware Seashore State Park** (T 302/227-2800, W www.destateparks.com) stretches for miles along a thin, sandy peninsula, split by Hwy-1 and bounded on the east by the Atlantic and on the west by various freshwater marshlands. There's little here apart from beachfront parking areas ($5) and the park's campground (T 302/539-7202 or 1-877/98PARKS; $26) until you approach the Maryland border, where the concrete tower blocks of **Bethany Beach** do little to prepare you for the Costa del Sol–like concentrations of hotels and condos in Ocean City, ten miles further along (see p.497).

The South

CANADA

WASHINGTON

MONTANA

NORTH DAKOTA

MN

ME

VT NH

OREGON

14

11

IDAHO

WYOMING

SOUTH DAKOTA

WI

MI

NEW YORK

MA

RI

CT

NEVADA

UTAH

NEBRASKA

IOWA

4

MI

PA

2

1

13

COLORADO

KANSAS

10

IL

IN

OHIO

WV

5

NJ

DE

CALIFORNIA

12

ARIZONA

NEW MEXICO

OKLAHOMA

MISSOURI

KENTUCKY

VA

MD

PACIFIC OCEAN

AR

TENNESSEE

NC

ATLANTIC OCEAN

AL

6

SC

9

TEXAS

MS

GEORGIA

MEXICO

8

LA

Gulf of Mexico

7

FL

N

15

HAWAII

ALASKA

16

AL - ALABAMA	IN - INDIANA	MN - MINNESOTA	RI - RHODE ISLAND
AR - ARKANSAS	LA - LOUISIANA	MS - MISSISSIPPI	SC - SOUTH CAROLINA
CT - CONNECTICUT	MA - MASSACHUSETTS	NC - NORTH CAROLINA	VA - VIRGINIA
DE - DELAWARE	MD - MARYLAND	NH - NEW HAMPSHIRE	VT - VERMONT
FL - FLORIDA	ME - MAINE	NJ - NEW JERSEY	WI - WISCONSIN
IL - ILLINOIS	MI - MICHIGAN	PA - PENNSYLVANIA	WV - WEST VIRGINIA

CHAPTER 6

Highlights

* **Blue Ridge Parkway, NC** A tortuous but exhilarating wilderness highway that makes a destination in itself. See p.529

* **Martin Luther King Birth Home, Atlanta, GA** Engaging tours take you around King's childhood home, in the South's most dynamic city. See p.551

* **Savannah, GA** With its romantic overgrown garden squares and busy waterfront, this gorgeous, atmospheric town is a dream to walk around. See p.560

* **Memphis, TN** Especially exciting for music fans, who could spend days checking out Beale Street, Sun Studio, the Stax Museum, Al Green's church, and, of course, Graceland. See p.579

* **Country Music Hall of Fame, Nashville, TN** Both a fascinating interactive museum and a treasure trove of memorabilia, including Elvis's gold Cadillac. See p.593

* **The Mississippi Delta, MS** The birthplace of the blues holds an irresistible appeal, with Clarksdale as the obvious first port of call. See p.614

The South

M ark Twain put it best, as early as 1882: "In the South, the [Civil] war is what AD is elsewhere; they date everything from it." Several generations later, the legacies of slavery and "The War Between the States" remain evident throughout the southern states of **North Carolina**, **South Carolina**, **Georgia**, **Kentucky**, **Tennessee**, **Alabama**, **Mississippi**, and **Arkansas**. It's impossible to travel through the region without experiencing constant jolting reminders of the two epic historical clashes that have shaped its destiny: the **Civil War**, and the **civil rights** movement of the 1950s and 1960s.

Although enough white Southerners continue to identify with the Confederate past to make it debatable whether a "New South" has truly come into being, the last few decades have unquestionably seen considerable change. The inspirational campaigns that finally secured black participation in Southern elections have not only resulted in the advent of black political leaders – even Selma, Alabama, now has a black mayor – but also in the emergence of liberal white counterparts such as Jimmy Carter and Bill Clinton. High-tech industries have moved in, luring considerable inward migration – one in five residents were now born elsewhere – while urban centers such as **Atlanta**, the birthplace of Dr Martin Luther King Jr and venue for the 1996 Olympics, are booming.

That said, it's misleading in any case to generalize too much about "the South." Even during the Civil War there were substantial pockets of pro-Union support, particularly in the mountains, while during the long century of segregation that followed, certain states, such as Mississippi and Alabama, were far more brutally oppressive than others. These days, inequities within the South, between for example the industrialized "Sun Belt" centers of North Carolina and northern Alabama and the much poorer rural backwaters of southern Georgia, Mississippi, or Tennessee, are just as significant as those between the South and the rest of the nation, and are no longer so clearly demarcated along racial lines.

For many travelers, the most exciting aspect of a visit to the South has to be its **music**. Fans flock to the homelands of Elvis Presley, Hank Williams, Robert Johnson, Dolly Parton, and Otis Redding, heading to the country and blues meccas of **Nashville** and **Memphis**, or seeking out backwoods barn dances in Appalachia or blues jook joints in the Mississippi Delta or South Carolina. The Southern experience is also reflected in a rich regional **literature**, its communities and people documented by the likes of William Faulkner, Carson McCullers, Eudora Welty, Margaret Mitchell, and Harper Lee.

Other major destinations for visitors include the elegant coastal cities of **Charleston** and **Savannah**, frenzied beach resorts such as **Myrtle Beach**, college towns like **Athens** and **Chapel Hill**, and the historic Mississippi River

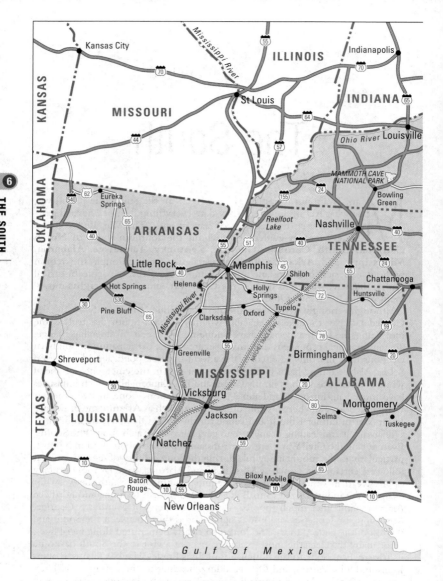

ports of **Natchez** and **Vicksburg**. Away from the urban areas, much Southern scenery consists of fertile but sun-baked farmlands, the undulating hillsides dotted with wooden shacks and rust-red barns, and broken by occasional forests. Highlights include the misty Appalachian **mountains** of Kentucky, Tennessee, and North Carolina; the subtropical **beaches** and tranquil **barrier islands** along the Atlantic and Gulf coasts; and the river road through the tiny settlements of the flat Mississippi Delta.

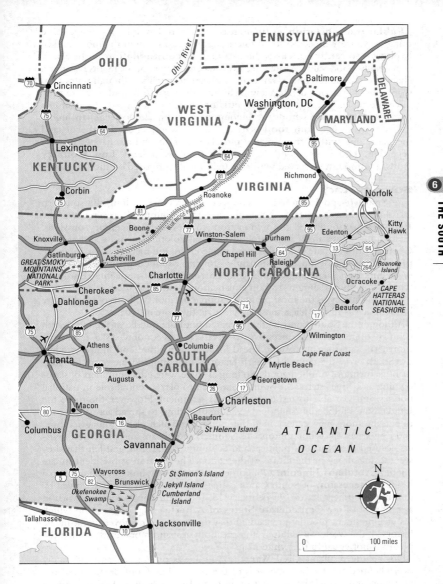

Unless your primary goal is the coastline, where the beaches offer a less expensive alternative to neighboring Florida, it's better to avoid visiting during midsummer. During July and August, the daily high **temperature** is mostly a very humid 90°F, and while almost every public building is air-conditioned, the heat can be debilitating. May and June are more bearable, and tend to see a lot of local festivals, while the fall colors in the mountains – just as beautiful and a lot less expensive and congested than New England – are at their headiest during October.

Public transportation in rural areas is poor. In any case, it's best to take things at your own pace – you'll find things to see and do in the most unlikely places – so **renting a car** is the best idea. **Accommodation** in the South is generally good value. Motels are everywhere, while abundant B&Bs offer a chance to sample the much-vaunted Southern hospitality – though unless you share a broadly Confederate view of history, they can also tend to be socially uncomfortable. The region's varied **cuisine**, much of it dished out at simple roadside shacks, ranges from the ubiquitous grits (maize porridge) to highly calorific, irresistible **soul food** – fried chicken, wood-smoked barbecue, and the like, along with turnip greens, spinach, macaroni, and all manner of tasty vegetables. Fish is also good, from catfish to the wonderful **Low Country Boils** – seafood stews served with rice, traditionally prepared on the sea islands.

Some history

The **Spanish** and **French** both constructed settlements along the southern coastline of North America during the sixteenth century. However, it was the **British** who dominated the region from the seventeenth century onwards, establishing increasingly successful agricultural colonies in the Carolinas and Georgia. Both climate and soil favored staple crops, and massive labor-intensive **plantations** sprang up, predominantly growing **tobacco** prior to independence, and then increasingly shifting to **cotton**. No self-respecting European would cross the Atlantic to toil on a plantation, though, so the big landowners turned to **slavery** as the most profitable source of labor. Millions of blacks were brought across from Africa, most arriving via the port of Charleston.

Although the South consistently prospered until the middle of the nineteenth century, there was little incentive to diversify its economy. As a result, the Northern states began to surge ahead in both agriculture and industry; while the South grew the crops, Northern factories monopolized the more lucrative manufacturing of finished goods. So long as there were equal numbers of slave-owning and "free" states, the South continued to play a central role in national politics, and was able to resist **abolitionist** sentiment. However, the more the United States fulfilled its supposed "Manifest Destiny" to spread across the continent, the more new states joined the Union for which plantation agriculture, and thus slavery, was not appropriate. Southern politicians and plantation owners accused the North of political and economic aggression, and felt that they were losing all say in the future of the nation. The election as president in late 1860 of **Abraham Lincoln**, a longtime critic of slavery, brought the crisis to a head. The **secession** of South Carolina that December was swiftly followed by ten more Southern states. On February 18, 1861, Jefferson Davis was sworn in as president of the **Confederate States of America** – an occasion on which his vice president proudly proclaimed that this was the first government in the history of the world "based upon this great physical and moral truth . . . that the Negro is not equal to the white man."

During the resultant **Civil War**, the South was outgunned and ultimately overwhelmed by the vast resources of the North. The Confederates fired the first shots and scored the first victory in April 1861, when the Union garrison at Fort Sumter (outside Charleston, South Carolina) surrendered. The Union was on the military defensive until mid-1862, when its navy blockaded the coast of Georgia and the Carolinas and occupied several key ports. Then Union forces in the west, under generals Grant and Sherman, swept through Tennessee, and by the end of 1863 the North had taken Vicksburg, the final Confederate-held port on the Mississippi, as well as the strategic mountain-locked town of Chattanooga on the Tennessee–Georgia border. Grant proceeded north to Virginia, while Sherman captured the transportation nexus of Atlanta and began a bloody and ruthless march to the coast, burning everything in his path. With 258,000 men dead (a quarter of the South's adult white male population), the Confederacy's defeat was total, and General Robert E. Lee **surrendered** on April 9, 1865, at Appomattox in Virginia.

The war left the South in chaos. Along with the devastating death toll, two-thirds of Southern wealth had been destroyed. From controlling thirty percent of the nation's assets in 1860, the South was down to twelve percent in 1870, while the spur the war gave to industrialization meant that the North was booming. For a brief period of **Reconstruction**, the South was occupied by Union troops. Newly freed Southern blacks were able to vote, and black representatives were elected to both state and federal office. However, unrepentant former Confederates, spurred in part by allegations of profiteering by incoming Northern Republican "carpetbaggers," thwarted any potential for change, and by the end of the century the Southern states were firmly back under white Democratic control. "**Jim Crow**" segregation laws were imposed, backed by the terror of the **Ku Klux Klan**, and poll taxes, literacy tests, and property qualifications disenfranchised virtually all blacks. Many found themselves little better off as **sharecroppers** – in which virtually all they could earn from raising crops went to pay their landlords – than they had been as slaves, and there were mass migrations to cities like Memphis and Atlanta, as well as to the North.

Not until the landmark 1954 Supreme Court ruling in *Brown* v. *Topeka Board of Education* outlawed segregation in schools was there any sign that the federal authorities in Washington might concern themselves with inequities in the South. Even then, individual Southern states proved extremely reluctant to effect the required changes. In the face of massive, institutionalized white resistance, non-violent black protestors coalesced to form the **civil rights movement**, and broke down segregation through their own mass action. After tackling such issues as public transportation, as in the Montgomery bus boycott and the Freedom Rides, and segregated dining facilities, as in the Greensboro lunch-counter sit-in, the campaign culminated in finally restoring full black voter registration. One obvious itinerary for modern travelers is to trace the footsteps of **Dr Martin Luther King Jr**, from his birthplace in Atlanta, through his church in Montgomery, to the site of his assassination in Memphis.

The dispossession of the **Native Americans** is often the forgotten chapter of Southern history. Colonial powers at best tolerated the Indians, for the most

Kudzu

The southern states are badly afflicted by **kudzu**, a leafy climbing vine introduced from Japan in 1876 for decoration and shade. Its use was encouraged by the federal government from the 1930s to stop soil erosion. Unbelievably, it can grow as much as a foot a day in hot weather, and eventually kills trees by cutting off the sunlight. So far, it has covered at least two million acres of forest. In places it's amazing, totally carpeting whole stands of trees, as well as telephone poles and wires. South Carolina folk poet James Dickey's poem "Kudzu" portrays it as a mysterious, evil invader from the east:

**In Georgia, the legend says
that you must close your windows
at night to keep it out of the house
the glass is tinged with green, even so . . .**

part peaceful agrarian tribes, and used them as allies in their imperialist wars with each other. However, after the Revolution, pressure from plantation owners and small farmers led to the forced removal in the 1830s of the "five civilized tribes" – the Cherokee, Creek, Choctaw, Chickasaw, and Seminole – to malarial Oklahoma. Today only a few thousand Native Americans live in the South.

North Carolina

NORTH CAROLINA, though the most industrialized of the Southern states, remains relatively rural and poor, with just six million people spread over an area larger than England. The state suffered heavily during the **Civil War**, and **Reconstruction** brought mixed fortunes: although poverty and hostility were still endemic, the Democrats, once they regained control in 1870, were effective in stamping out the Ku Klux Klan. Since then, there have been parallel traditions of radical black, and white racist, activity. **Greensboro**, for example, where **Jesse Jackson** served his political apprenticeship, was the site of the 1960 lunch-counter sit-in by black students, and also of the Greensboro Massacre of 1979, when Klansmen – active again, as in the rest of the South, since the 1910s – killed five people at a Communist Workers Party demonstration.

Geographically, North Carolina breaks down into three distinct areas – running from east to west, the coast, the Piedmont, and the mountains – which helps make it one of the more interesting states to tour around. For visitors, the **coast** is the most promising area, with good beaches, beautiful landscapes, and a fascinating history. The inner coast consists largely of the less developed **Albemarle Peninsula**, with colonial **Edenton** nearby. The central **Piedmont** is dominated by manufacturing cities, and by the academic institutions of the prestigious "Research Triangle": **Raleigh**, the state capital, is home to North Carolina State University; Durham has Duke; and the University of North Carolina is in trendy **Chapel Hill**. **Winston–Salem** combines tobacco culture and Moravian heritage, while **Charlotte**, which bills itself as the next boom city of the South, is distinguished by little but its downtown skyscrapers. In the **mountains**, one of the most stunning stretches of Appalachia, the only towns of any size, **Boone**, and especially **Asheville**, are nice places to stop along the spectacular **Blue Ridge Parkway**; **Great Smoky Mountains National Park** overlaps the border with Tennessee.

Getting around North Carolina

North Carolina's major **airports** are at Charlotte, an arrival point for transatlantic flights, Raleigh-Durham, and Wilmington, all of which will connect you with several major US cities. A tiny airport at Manteo in the Outer Banks (℡ 252/473-2227) runs charter flights to the barrier islands, but driving is easier. Charlotte, Raleigh, Durham, and Greensboro (with an express bus link to Winston-Salem) are served by **Amtrak**, but unfortunately there is no coastal route. Plenty of **buses** run within the Piedmont; schedules are much less frequent in the mountains and along the coast, both of which are best explored by car. The state also has a good network of **cycling** routes along quiet country roads; for information, contact the Department of Transportation (☎919/733-2804).

The North Carolina coast

The **North Carolina coast**, which ranges through salt marshes, beaches, barrier islands, and estuaries, holds most of the state's more interesting **historic sites**. The continent's earliest English colonists vanished inexplicably from **Roanoke Island** in 1590; just over three centuries later, the Wright brothers achieved the first powered flight a few miles up the road, at **Kill Devil Hills**. The **Outer Banks**, the long reef of barrier islands that stretch down from Virginia, are in parts tacky and elsewhere beautifully unspoiled.

Edenton and the Albemarle

The huge **Albemarle Peninsula** remains largely unexploited. Local towns try to make much of their **Colonial history** – this was the first area in North Carolina to have permanent European settlements, around the end of the seventeenth century – but often there's not a lot left to see. It's not an uninteresting region, however, if you like to travel off the beaten path, its sleepy old towns and remote plantations set in wide swathes of rural farmland and endless marshes, that eventually give way altogether to water in a ragged pattern of sounds and lakes.

Edenton

EDENTON, set along a beautiful, placid Albemarle Sound waterfront, was established as North Carolina's first state capital in 1722. A major center of unrest in the American Revolution, it remained a prosperous port until the early nineteenth century, when it began to fade. Nowadays, if you like peace and quiet, it makes a nice little base for explorations of the coast, with some good B&Bs and restaurants, and a nostalgic small-town ambiance.

The town's main road, **Broad Street**, is interesting in an offbeat way, with its Victorian facades, old-fashioned stores, and three-screen vintage Liberty Theater. The Historic Edenton **Visitor Center**, 108 N Broad (April–Oct Mon–Sat 9am–5pm, Sun 1–5pm; Nov–March Tues–Sat 10am–4pm, Sun 1–4pm; ☎252/482-2637), runs **trolley tours** (Tues–Sat 10am, 11am, 3pm & 4pm; no 4pm tours Nov–March; $7) that take in all the major sites, including a fine collection of Colonial and pre–Civil War houses (there's also a free, self-guided walking tour).

The visitor center provides an **African-American history** walking tour map as well; among other important figures, Edenton was home to the remarkable **Harriet Jacobs**, a runaway slave who hid for seven years in her grandmother's attic. In 1842, she finally escaped to the North, and was eventually reunited in Boston with the two children she had had by a white man in Edenton. She wrote this amazing story as *Incidents in the Life of a Slave Girl*, one of the most famous published slave narratives of the nineteenth century. None of the buildings mentioned in the book are still standing, but the walking and trolley tours give you an idea of where places were.

Luxurious **B&Bs** include the peaceful *Trestle House Inn*, set in seven acres overlooking a nature refuge on a lake; it's five miles south of town, off Hwy-32,

at 632 Soundside Rd (☎252/482-2282, Ⓦwww.edenton.com/trestlehouse;❹).
A few minutes' walk from the waterfront, the friendly *Governor Eden Inn*, 304 N
Broad St (☎252/482-2072, Ⓦwww.governoredeninn.com;❹), offers appealing
rooms and a huge veranda. Edenton has a gratifying number of good places to
eat. *Chero's*, 112 W Water St (☎252/482-5525), is a funky, colorful place serving delicious Mediterranean and regional food, while the fishy *Waterman's Grill*,
427 S Broad St (☎252/482-7733), gets packed with convivial locals at dinner-
time. For Carolina pit-cooked barbecue, try *Lane's Family BBQ*, 421 E Church
St (☎252/482-4008). The *Acoustic Café*, 302 S Broad St (☎252/482-7465), has
coffee, pastries, and live music on Friday evenings.

Exploring the Albemarle

Albemarle **plantation life** is brought alive in the informed, illuminating tours
of **Hope**, the home of David Stone, a state governor and US senator of the
Revolutionary and Federal periods. It's a remote place, set in the sleepy fields
of the rural heartland; you'll find it off Hwy-308, a few miles west of **Windsor**,
which is about 25 miles southwest of Edenton (tours: April–Oct Mon–Sat
10am–5pm, Sun 2–5pm; Nov–March 10am–5pm, Sun 2–5pm; $6.50). The
main house at Hope, dating from 1803, was built to an English template, and
is now filled with hand-carved wooden furniture. Admission also includes
entrance to the 1763 **King-Bazemore House**, a simple planter's home.

At Creswell, 25 miles southeast of Edenton on US-64, a vivid picture of slave
life is given by **Somerset Place State Historic Site** (April–Oct Mon–Sat
9am–5pm, Sun 1–5pm; Nov–March Tues–Sat 10am–4pm, Sun 1–4pm; free).
The small museum here tells the history of the plantation, from its origins in
the 1780s to its growth, by 1860, into a 2000-acre enterprise, and its demise
after the Civil War. Old photos, documents, and a timeline detail the steady
accumulation of more than 300 enslaved Africans and the work they did. On
the grounds – a sweeping vista of lowland fields and huge oaks, dissolving into
marshland beyond – you can walk through reconstructions of the plantation
hospital and two typical slave houses.

There's a **campground** at neighboring **Pettigrew State Park** (☎252/797-
4475; $12; first-come, first-served), an area of mighty trees ranged around a
shallow rainwater-fed lake, ideal for fishing. Even if you don't stay, you should
visit the tiny **museum** at water's edge, where the interesting display on local
Native Americans includes two 4000-year-old dugout canoes that were raised
from the lake.

The southern shore of the Albemarle Peninsula holds less to see, though the
marshy countryside and tree-lined roads make for a pleasant drive. **Lake
Mattamuskeet Wildlife Refuge** (☎252/926-4021) is an amazing sight in
winter, when thousands of swans migrate here from Canada. The refuge's
entrance is on Hwy-94, about a mile north of its intersection with US-264.
South of Mattamuskeet, you can catch a **ferry** from **Swan Quarter** to
Ocracoke on the Outer Banks (see p.518).

The Outer Banks

The **OUTER BANKS** are a string of skinny barrier islands, the remnants of
ancient sand dunes, that stretch about 180 miles from the Virginia border to
Cape Lookout, near Beaufort. This is a great region to meander, with some
wonderful wild beaches sprinkled with wispy sea oats, otherworldly marshes,
and attractive small towns not totally given over to commercialization. Note
that when Outer Banks hotels describe themselves as "**waterfront**," it simply

means they are on the coastal side of the road, not that they necessarily have ocean views. There is **no public transportation** on the Outer Banks, apart from the ferries between islands and to the mainland.

If you come in on the main road from the north, US-158, stop at the well-stocked Cape Hatteras National Park Service **visitor center** (daily 9am–5pm; ☎252/261-4644) as you cross the low bridge from the mainland. South along US-158 and the parallel shoreline Beach Road, the coastal towns of **Kitty Hawk**, **Kill Devil Hills**, and **Nags Head** are strung out without a break, and the fine warm-water **beaches** are lined with motels, restaurants, and huge vacation "cottages." Arriving from the west on Hwy-64, you'll come to another very useful **visitor center** (daily 9am–5.30pm; ☎252/473-2138) on **Roanoke Island**. The island, site of the first English settlement in the US, has obvious historical interest; its village, **Manteo**, is perhaps the nicest on the Outer Banks.

Kill Devil Hills and Nags Head

The main feature of the **Wright Brothers National Memorial** (daily: summer 9am–6pm; rest of year 9am–5pm; $3; ☎252/441-7430), just off the main road at **KILL DEVIL HILLS**, is the Wright Brothers Monument, a 60ft granite fin atop a 90ft dune (which is in fact *the* Kill Devil Hill). The memorial commemorates the plucky Orville Wright's **first powered flight**, on December 17, 1903. (Most histories say the flight took place at **Kitty Hawk**, a town eight miles north, but that was just the name of the nearest post office.) A boulder next to the memorial's **visitor center** marks where Orville's first aircraft hit the ground, and successive numbered markers show the distance of each of his three subsequent flights. A **museum** in the visitor center records the brothers' various experiments. After several years of trials with kites and gliders, visiting the Outer Banks for a few weeks at a time and living in makeshift shacks on the beach, Orville and Wilbur finally launched their powered plane on a cold December morning, shaking hands before the takeoff. As one of the locals acting as ground crew remarked, "We couldn't help notice how they held on to each other's hand, sort o' like folks parting who weren't sure they'd ever see one another again." The phlegmatic Orville recorded the historic moment of take-off in his diary: "The machine lifted from the truck . . . I found control of the front rudder quite difficult . . . the machine would rise suddenly to about 10 feet and then as suddenly, on turning the rudder, dart for the ground . . . time about twelve seconds."

A few miles south in **NAGS HEAD**, at Mile 12 on Hwy-158, **Jockey's Ridge State Park** (☎252/441-7132) boasts the largest sand dunes on the east coast. The park has trails and summer nature programs, and instructors from Kitty Hawk Kites (☎252/441-4124, ⊛www.kittyhawk.com) will teach you the basics of **hang-gliding** (around $90). It's a beautiful place to be at sunset.

Motels line the beaches north of Oregon Inlet, which separates Bodie Island and Cape Hatteras National Seashore. The *First Colony Inn*, a luxurious **B&B** at 6720 S Virginia Dare Trail, Nags Head (☎252/441-2343 or 1-800/368-9390, ⊛www.firstcolonyinn.com; ❺–❽), is housed in a 1930s beach hotel, with wonderful verandas and a pool. In Kitty Hawk, there's a nice **hostel**, *Outerbanks International*, 1004 W Kitty Hawk Rd (☎252/261-2294, ⊛www.outer-bankshostel.com; ❶–❷), in a 1919 schoolhouse set in ten acres at the edge of a forest. Dorm beds cost $16–19 per night, camping is from $15, and there are some private rooms with shared bath. No alcohol is allowed. The standard of **food** around these parts varies considerably, but *Etheridge's*, at Mile 9.5 in Kill Devil Hills (☎252/441-2645), is a local favorite for wonderfully fresh seafood.

In Nags Head, *Tortuga's Lie*, at Mile 11 on Beach Road (☎ 252/441-7299), is a funky place for creative shellfish, Tex-Mex, and Asian-influenced dishes.

Roanoke Island and Manteo

ROANOKE ISLAND, which lies between the mainland and Bodie Island, is accessible from both by bridges. This was the **first English settlement** in North America, founded in 1585, and makes much of its semi-mythical status as Sir Walter Raleigh's so-called "Lost Colony" (see box, below).

Nothing authentic survives of the Roanoke settlement, though **Fort Raleigh National Historic Site**, three miles north of Manteo off US-64, contains a tiny conjectural reconstruction of the colonists' earthwork fort, set

Roanoke – The Lost Colony

According to popular myth, the first English attempt to settle in North America – Sir Walter Raleigh's colony at **Roanoke** – remains an unsolved mystery, in which the "Lost Colony" disappeared without trace.

Sir Walter himself never visited North America. The original patent to establish a colony was granted by Queen Elizabeth I to his half-brother, Sir Humphrey Gilbert, but Gilbert died following an abortive landfall in Newfoundland in 1583. Raleigh assumed responsibility, and directed subsequent explorations further south. A 1584 expedition pinpointed Roanoke Island, behind the Outer Banks of North Carolina and thus hidden from the view of the Spanish, who were by now jealously patrolling the Atlantic seaboard from their bases in Florida. The English named the region **Virginia**, in honour of the Virgin Queen.

A party led by Ralph Lane in 1585 was far more interested in searching for gold than in the hard graft of agriculture; their hopes of finding a fortune were quickly dashed, however, and they sailed home with Sir Francis Drake the following year. In 1587, 117 more colonists set off, intending to farm a more fertile site beside Chesapeake Bay; but, fearing Spanish attack, the ships that carried them dumped them at Roanoke once again. Their leader, **John White**, who went home to fetch supplies a month later, was stranded in England when war broke out with Spain, and the Spanish Armada set sail. When he finally managed to persuade a reluctant sea captain to carry him back to Roanoke in 1590, he found the island abandoned. Even so, he was reassured by the absence of the agreed-upon distress signal, a carved Maltese cross, while the word **"Croatoan"** inscribed on a tree seemed a clear message that the colonists had moved south to the eponymous island. However, fearful of both the Spanish and of the approaching hurricane season, White's ships refused to take him any further.

There the story usually ends, with the colonists never seen again. In fact, during the next decade, several reports reached the subsequent, more durable colony of **Jamestown** (in what's now Virginia), of English settlers being dispersed as slaves among the Native American tribes of North Carolina. Rather than admit their inability to rescue their fellow countrymen, and thus expose a vulnerability that might deter prospective settlers or investors, the Jamestown colonists seem simply to have written their predecessors out of history.

In a little-known footnote, Roanoke Island gained and lost another colony during the **Civil War**. After it was captured by Union forces in February 1862, so many freed and runaway slaves made their way there through Confederate lines that the federal government formally declared it to be a **"Freedmen's Colony."** Around four thousand blacks were living on Roanoke by the end of the war, and many of the men served in the Union army. During Reconstruction, the government returned all land to its former owners, and the colony was disbanded. Still, Roanoke retains a substantial black population to this day.

in a wooded glade with a canopy of Spanish moss (daily: June–Aug 9am–6pm; Sept–May 9am–5pm; free; ☎252/473-5772). A museum covers the history of the expeditions and local Indian interaction with colonists, and an outdoor amphitheater on the ocean hosts performances of *The Lost Colony*, an undeniably impressive drama, staged here since 1937 (June–Aug Mon–Sat 8.30pm; $16–20; ☎1-800/488-5012, ⊛www.thelostcolony.org). Outside, a simple monument commemorates the Underground Railroad and the **Freedmen's Colony** that formed here during the Civil War. Adjacent to the fort, the **Elizabethan Gardens** are elegantly landscaped with walkways, statues, and subtropical blooms (daily; times vary with season; $5; ☎252/473-3234).

Just across from the waterfront at **Manteo**, the **Roanoke Island Festival Park** has a slew of lively historical attractions that, if seen in full, take several hours (daily: April, May & mid-Aug through Oct 10am–6pm; June through mid-Aug 10am–7pm; Nov–Dec & mid-Feb through early April 10am–5pm; $8 tickets valid for 2 consecutive days; ☎252/475-1500). Highlights include the **adventure museum**, an interactive trot through the history of the Outer Banks, the **settlement site**, a living museum peopled with "Elizabethan" soldiers and craftsmen, and the *Elizabeth II*, a reconstruction of a sixteenth-century English ship. Wherever you go, you won't escape the attentions of the wandering costumed docents, ever keen to engage hapless visitors in Elizabethan-style chat.

If you're after fine **dining** on the Outer Banks, Manteo is the place. *Clara's Seafood Grill* (☎252/473-1727), right on the waterfront, offers tasty and creative shellfish dishes, with nice views, while the *Full Moon Café*, across from the waterfront at the corner of Sir Walter Raleigh and Queen Elizabeth streets (☎252/473-MOON), is more casual, serving chowder, gourmet sandwiches, quiche, and coffee. Manteo also has a good range of places to **stay**. *The Outdoors Inn*, 406 Uppowoc St (☎252/473-1356, ⊛www.theoutdoorsinn .com; ❸), has two simple, stylish **B&B** rooms in a lovely, airy home; the owners offer a range of dive trips, kayaking, and fishing charters. The *Island Guesthouse*, on Hwy-64 (☎252/473-2434, ⊛www.theislandmotel.com; ❸), is more of a **motel**, with fully equipped rooms and a sociable atmosphere.

Cape Hatteras National Seashore

CAPE HATTERAS NATIONAL SEASHORE stretches south from South Nags Head on Bodie Island onto **Hatteras** and **Ocracoke** islands, with forty miles of wonderful unspoiled beaches on its seaward side. Most tourists just drive straight through on Hwy-12, and even in high season you can pull off the road and walk across the dunes to deserted beaches. The salt marshes on the western side are also beautiful, and at the northern end of Hatteras Island the **Pea Island National Wildlife Refuge** (☎252/473-1131) offers guided canoe tours, trails, and observation platforms from which you can see a wide variety of birdlife.

Nearly a thousand ships have been wrecked along this treacherous stretch of coast since the sixteenth century. At the south end of Hatteras Island, not far from the early nineteenth-century black-and-white-striped **Cape Hatteras Lighthouse**, a **visitor center** (daily: summer 9am–6pm; rest of year 9am–5pm) has exhibits on the island's maritime history. The 208ft lighthouse itself, which you can climb (March–Oct; $4), was moved 2900ft inland from its original location to protect it from encroaching Atlantic waters. Further south, at the village of **Frisco**, the **Native American Museum** is a loving collection of arts and crafts from around the US, including a drum from a Hopi *kiva*, or prayer chamber. The museum also offers several acres of forested **nature** trails (Tues–Sun 11am–5pm, Mon by appointment; $2; ☎252/995-4440).

In **Hatteras**, next to the Ocracoke ferry landing, the **Graveyard of the Atlantic Museum** (Tues–Fri 10am–4pm, Sat 11am–2pm; free) tells the stories of the explorers, pirates, and Civil War blockade-runners who perished along this wild stretch of coast, with lots of models, photos, and artifacts retrieved from Outer Banks shipwrecks.

Various **motels**, food shops, and **restaurants** are scattered through the fly-blown settlements along Hwy-12. The *Cape Hatteras Motel* in Buxton, a mile from the lighthouse (℡252/995-5611, ⓦwww.capehatterasmotel.com; ❹–❼), has comfy oceanfront rooms, a pool, and a relaxed, friendly atmosphere. A good place for breakfast and seafood is *Diamond Shoals*, also in Buxton on Hwy-12 (℡252/995-5217), while on the waterfront at Hatteras, *Austin Creek Grill* serves stylish salads, shellfish, and pasta nightly (℡252/986-1511). **Camping** is best at one of the first-come, first-served National Park Service campgrounds at Oregon Inlet on Bodie Island; at Cape Point near Buxton; or at Frisco (all campgrounds ℡252/473-2111, ⓦwww.nps.gov/caha; $18 per night; summer only except Oregon Inlet, open April–Dec).

Ocracoke Island

Peaceful, undeveloped **OCRACOKE ISLAND** is forty minutes by free ferry from Hatteras (see box, below) – and is even more beautiful. This 16-mile ribbon of land is bisected by Hwy-12, and it's perfectly possible to pull over anywhere and enjoy a deserted patch of beach. Despite the crowds of tourists in the tiny village of **Ocracoke** itself, at its southern tip, the island somehow seems to have hung on to its easy-going atmosphere. There's nothing in particular to see, except perhaps the harbor and squat lighthouse (you can't go in), and a tiny British World War II naval cemetery. It's nicer instead just to catch some rays, take a stroll, or enjoy a cycle ride; a number of places, including hotels, **rent bikes**.

Hotels and **B&Bs** in Ocracoke village get full in summer, and are fairly expensive; as elsewhere on the Outer Banks, rates drop come September. The

---

Ocracoke ferries

In summer, free **ferries** run **between Hatteras and Ocracoke**. The crossing takes forty minutes, although you may have to wait if you have a car – there's room for only 30 cars, and it's loaded on a first-come, first-served basis.

Hatteras–Ocracoke May 1–Oct 31 hourly 5–7am; every 30min 7.30am–7pm; hourly 8pm–midnight. Nov 1–April 30 hourly 5am–midnight.

Ocracoke–Hatteras May 1–Oct 31 hourly 5–8am; every 30min 8.30am–7pm; hourly 8pm–midnight. Nov 1–April 30 hourly 5am–midnight.

Ferries **from Ocracoke** also head south down the coast to **Cedar Island** on the mainland (2hr 15min; $1 pedestrian, $3 bike, $10 motorbike, $15 car) and to **Swan Quarter** on the Albemarle Peninsula (2hr 30min; same fares). Both require **reservations** in summer, preferably a day or two in advance (Ocracoke ℡1-800/345-1665, Cedar Island ℡1-800/856-0343, Swan Quarter ℡1-800/773-1094); at short notice you should be able to get the day you want, if not the time.

Between Ocracoke and Cedar Island summer nine departures 7am–8.30pm; spring & fall six departures 7am–8.30pm; winter four departures 7am–4pm.

Ocracoke–Swan Quarter May 20–Sept 1 6.30am, 12.30pm, 4pm; no 4pm sailing rest of year.

Swan Quarter–Ocracoke May 20–Sept 1 7am, 9.30am, 4pm; no 7am sailing rest of year.

For **further information** call ℡1-800/BY-FERRY.

Anchorage Inn, on Hwy-12 (☎252/928-1101, ⓦwww.theanchorageinn.com; ❺), is comfortable, with sea views, a pool, and complimentary continental breakfast. Or you could sleep in one of the unusual "crow's-nest" rooms in the 1901 *Island Inn and Dining Room*, on Hwy-12 (☎1-877/456-3466, ⓦwww.ocracokeislandinn.com; ❺), whose **restaurant** is renowned for its crabcakes (☎252/928-7821). Other, less expensive restaurants include the *Back Porch*, on Back Road (☎252/928-6401), which serves great fish, and the lively *Howard's Pub & Raw Bar*, a mile north of the village on Hwy-12 (☎252/928-4441), which offers more than two hundred beers, plus a full menu until 2am. It's one of the few places on the island that's open all year. The fairly isolated Park Service **campground** tends to be the first of the Outer Banks sites to fill up; unlike the others, it accepts reservations from June to August (☎1-800/365-2267; $18 per night; open May–Dec).

Cape Lookout National Seashore

The mainland between Cedar Island and Beaufort (see below) is a rural backwater, sparsely settled and hardly touched by tourists. The most likely reason to pass through is to get to the all-but-deserted **CAPE LOOKOUT NATIONAL SEASHORE**, a narrow ribbon of sand stretching south of Ocracoke Island along three undeveloped Outer Banks, with no roads or habitation. The seashore is only accessible by **ferry** (mid-March to early Dec) or private boat, and its few visitors share a total of around 56 miles of beach along all three islands, with the marshes on the landward side supporting rich and unusual plant- and birdlife that have adapted to the harsh, salty conditions. The **visitor center** is at the eastern end of the low-key mainland settlement of **Harker's Island** (daily 8.30am–4.30pm; ☎252/728-2250), thirty miles south of the Cedar Island ferry terminal.

At the northern tip of the first island, **North Core Banks**, across from Ocracoke, stand the pretty, but eerie, ruins of the abandoned village of **Portsmouth**, whose last two residents left in 1971. Ferries arrive in Portsmouth from Ocracoke (around $15 roundtrip; call Rudy Austin on ☎252/928-4361). The ferry from **Atlantic**, south of Cedar Island on the mainland ($14 roundtrip; call Morris Marina on ☎252/225-4261), lands at **Long Point**, seventeen miles south of Portsmouth, which you can only reach on foot. **Cabins** on the island are operated by Morris Marina ($100 per night for up to six people); otherwise there's only primitive **camping**.

South Core Banks is served by private ferry from **Davis**, south of Atlantic on the mainland ($13 roundtrip; call Alger Willis on ☎252/729-2791). Here, too, the ferry company manages more than twenty **cabins**, all with showers (❸–❻). **Camping** is as primitive as on the north island, but the ferry operator can pick up food for you on the mainland and bring it across. Three passenger ferries run to the southern tip of the south island from Beaufort (see overleaf) and from Harker's Island, to within two or three miles of **Cape Lookout** itself and its lighthouse.

To get to the peaceful **Shackleford Banks**, inhabited by wild mustangs since the early 1500s, when they are thought to have swum ashore from shipwrecks, you can catch ferries from Beaufort and Morehead City (see below).

Beaufort

BEAUFORT, about 150 miles southeast of Raleigh, is probably the nicest of North Carolina's coastal towns. A good base for visiting the nearby beaches, it's also a relaxing place in its own right, with an attractive waterfront that's particularly lively at night. The **Maritime Museum**, 315 Front St, has good displays on local ecology and shipping history (Mon–Fri 9am–5pm, Sat 10am–5pm, Sun 1–5pm; free; ☎252/728-7317), while across the road you can watch boats being made at the **Watercraft Center**, a working boatyard (Wed–Fri 9am–5pm, Sat 10am–5pm, Sun 1–5pm; free).

North Carolina's third-oldest town, Beaufort also has an appealing twelve-block **historical district**, centering on Turner Street, off the waterfront. Here you'll find handsome old houses, an apothecary, and the city jail; the town **welcome center**, 130 Turner St (daily: March–Nov 9.30am–5pm; Dec–Feb 10am–4pm; ☎252/728-5225, ⓦwww.historicbeaufort.com), offers a number of tours and self-guided walking tour brochures.

Ferries to **Shackleford Banks** (see overleaf) are run by Island Ferry Adventures (mid-March to mid-Nov; $28 roundtrip for two adults minimum; ☎252/342-7555), Mystery Tours (from $12; ☎252/728-2527), and Outer Banks Ferry Service (☎252/728-4129), all on the waterfront. You can also get there from **Morehead City**, a couple of miles down the coast (call Anderson Maritime ☎252/728-3988 or Waterfront Ferry Service ☎252/726-7678). Beaufort Inlet Watersports, next to the Outer Banks Ferry Service at 328 Front St (☎252/728-7607), offers **parasailing** for around $50 single, $90 tandem.

Among the many historic **B&Bs** in the shady residential streets off Turner, *Langdon House*, 135 Craven St (☎252/728-5499, ⓦwww.langdonhouse.com; ⑤), is friendly and relaxed; the *Cedars Inn*, 305 Front St (☎252/728-7036, ⓦwww.cedarsinn.com; ⑥), is rather plush. The *Inlet Inn*, on the waterfront at 601 Front St (☎252/728-3600 or 1-800/554-5466, ⓦwww.inlet-inn.com; ⑤), has huge hotel rooms and serves continental breakfast in your room. Morehead City and the Bogue Banks boast plenty of **motels**.

As for **eating and nightlife**, Beaufort's waterfront is vibrant at night, milling with yachties and vacationers drinking, listening to live music at the *Dock House Bar*, and simply strolling. There are a number of decent bar/restaurants on the wooden **boardwalk** right on the water, with other good options a block or so inland. For exquisite – if pricey – New American cuisine, head for the stylish *Front Street Grill*, Front St, at Stillwater (☎252/728-4956), which is cheaper at lunchtime. The *Beaufort Grocery Co*, 117 Queen St (closed Tues; ☎252/728-3899), prides itself on inventive dishes made from superbly fresh ingredients, while the buzzy, hip *Aqua*, 114 Middle Lane (☎252/728-7777), offers Carolina-style tapas and big desserts.

The beaches

South of Beaufort, the **beaches** along the twenty-mile offshore **Bogue Banks** are always pretty crowded, especially Atlantic Beach at the east end, with Emerald Isle, to the west, marginally less so. On **Bear Island** to the south – reached from **Swansboro** by boat taxi or ferry (April–Oct, hours vary; $2; ☎910/326-4881) – the stunning **Hammocks Beach State Park** has high sand dunes, a wooded shore, and perfect beaches. If you want to **camp** ($8), you need to register at the small park center (daily: Sept–May 8am–5pm; June–Aug 8am–6pm; ☎910/326-4881). No camping is permitted in turtle season (March and April), when **loggerhead sea turtles** come ashore to lay their eggs.

On the far side of the massive Camp Lejeune US Marine base – home to around 40,000 Marines – **Topsail Island**, yet another sand bar of resorts (accessible via Hwy-172 on the mainland), is considerably less built up than the Bogue Banks, presumably because its beaches aren't quite as good. Both **Surf City** and **Topsail** were once slightly run-down family resorts, but have improved nicely. Public beach access points are signposted from the main road, but you can get down from lots of other places.

△ Where Robert Johnson sold his soul to the Devil

Wilmington

Though it's the largest town on North Carolina's coast, **WILMINGTON**, set back along the **Cape Fear River**, fifty miles short of the state's southern border, has a welcoming, laid-back feel. During the Civil War, it was briefly the Confederacy's most important harbor, exporting cotton all over the world. "**Blockade-runners**" would attempt to outrun the Union navy, racing into the safety of Fort Fisher's guns some twenty miles to the south of town; "Rebel Rose" Greenhow, glamorous Confederate spy, drowned here during a run in 1864. Dozens of blacks were murdered in Wilmington by white mobs in the **Race Riot** of 1898 – a backlash to the election of a "Fusionist" (Republican-Populist-black) governor two years earlier.

Today, Wilmington is attractive, friendly, and buzzy. Its notoriety as a popular **movie location** has earned it the nickname "Hollywood East," or even "Wilmywood", and the influx of creative types has led to a certain gentrification that feels very different from the rest of the coast. That's not to call it ersatz – its lively cobbled waterfront and historic district, starting on the south side of Market Street and stretching east along Third Street, feel genuinely lived in.

At 814 Market St, the **Cape Fear Museum** (summer Mon–Sat 9am–5pm, Sun 1–5pm; rest of year closed Mon; $5) gives a lively account of local history, while the **Louise Wells Cameron Art Museum**, 3201 S 17th St (Tues–Sat 10am–5pm, Sun 10.30am–4pm; $5), features American paintings, North Carolina art, and works by the Impressionist Mary Cassatt and African-American painter Minnie Evans. Architecture fans should head for the **Bellamy Mansion Museum of History and Design Arts**, 503 Market St (Tues–Sat 10am–5pm, Sun 1–5pm; $6); in an ornate antebellum mansion built by slaves and freedmen, exhibits concentrate on restoration, preservation, and local design. The extravagant houses, ornate **City Hall**, and lovely old **Thalian Hall** demonstrate Wilmington's former wealth, but it's the cobbled streets of the weathered, boardwalked **waterfront**, dotted with cafés and restaurants, that really appeal. **Chandler's Wharf**, an upmarket mall in a restored warehouse, is typical of the area's revitalization, while the **Cotton Exchange**, 321 N Front St, sells crafts and food in a group of buildings that once housed a grain mill, warehouse, and cotton business. At the foot of Market Street, at the small **Riverfront Park**, you can pick up **harbor tours** or a **river taxi** to the battleship USS *North Carolina*, which participated in every naval offensive in the Pacific during World War II.

To get a sense of how Wilmywood works, take a tour of **EUE/Screen Gems Studios**, 1223 N 23rd St, the site of productions as diverse as David Lynch's *Blue Velvet* and hit TV teen-drama *Dawson's Creek* (Memorial Day–Labor Day Sat & Sun noon & 2pm; ☎910/343-3433, ⓦwww .screengemsstudios.com).

Twenty miles south of Wilmington on Hwy-421, near Kure Beach, **Fort Fisher State Historic Site** commands a spectacular rocky position overlooking both the sea and the mouth of the Cape Fear River. This used to be the largest earthen fort in the South, and you can walk a trail around the remains; a small **museum** focuses on its days as a Confederate stronghold, with relics from sunken blockade-runners and various weaponry (April–Oct Mon–Sat 9am–5pm, Sun 1–5pm; Nov–March Tues–Sat 10am–4pm; free). Nearby, the **Fort Fisher Aquarium** recreates local river, swamp, and ocean habitats (Mon–Sat 9am–5pm; $6). You can catch a **ferry** from Fort Fisher to the little mainland town of **Southport** (roughly every 45min; call to check exact schedule; $5 per vehicle; 30min trip; ☎1-800/368-8969).

Practicalities

The **bus station** is at 201 Harnett St, a mile north of downtown off Third Street. Wilmington's **visitor center**, 24 N Third St (Mon–Fri 8.30am–5pm, Sat 9am–4pm, Sun 1–4pm; ☎1-800/222-4757, ⓦwww.cape-fear.nc.us), has maps and walking tours, including a good African-American site map and a *Dawson's Creek* FAQ sheet. The funniest, most informative overviews of the city are given by Adventure Walking Tours, which leave from the flagpole at Market and Water streets (April–Oct 10am & 2pm; $10; ☎910/763-1785). There's also a brochure-packed **information kiosk** (April–Oct daily 9.30am–4.30pm) at the bottom of Market Street.

Wilmington has some lovely **B&Bs**: the movie stars stay at the atmospheric *Graystone Inn*, on Third and Dock (☎910/763-2000, ⓦwww.graystoneinn.com; ❼); the *Inn on Orange*, 410 Orange St (☎910/815-0035, ⓦww.innonorange.com; ❹), which has spacious rooms, a pool, and a garden, makes a nice alternative. At the non-smoking *Best Western Coastline Inn*, on the riverfront at 503 Nutt St (☎910/763-2800, ⓦwww.coastlineinn.com; ❹), rates include breakfast served in your room. You could also head a dozen miles east to **Wrightsville Beach**, where among the string of weatherworn condos and pricey resort hotels, the *Silver Gull*, 20 E Salisbury St (☎910/256-3728, ⓦwww.beachonline.com; ❺), offers comfortable motel rooms next to the fishing pier.

Downtown has its share of stylish, swanky **restaurants**, but you can eat very well for little, too. For a quick meal try the *Dock Street Oyster Bar*, 12 Dock St (☎910/762-2827), a funky little place serving cheap raw oysters and seafood. Around the corner, at 5 Water St, in an old riverfront warehouse, *Water Street* (☎910/343-0042) is a popular, pubby place with outdoor seating and live music on the weekends. The food – crab cakes, salads, pasta – is good. If you're really hungry, *Taste of Country*, at Front and Ann streets (☎910/343-9888), serves a delicious buffet of fried chicken, barbecue, chitlins, and the like. Wilmington has a thriving **nightlife** as well; for **listings**, pick up a copy of the free weekly *Encore*. The hip *Paleo Sun Atomic Bar*, 35 N Front St (☎910/762-7600), has regular live music, while the *Barbary Coast*, 116 Front St (☎910/762-8996), is a dingy hole-in-the-wall that has gained some cachet from being Mickey Rourke's favorite bar in town. Built in 1858, Thalian Hall, 310 Chestnut St (☎1-800/523-2820, ⓦwww.thalianhall.com), hosts dance, music, theater, and movies.

The North Carolina Piedmont

North Carolina's **PIEDMONT** is a fairly industrialized area of textile and tobacco towns, mostly in decline. Even close to the towns, though, it can still be very rural; little has changed here since the 1950s. The main area of interest is the **Research Triangle** trio of neighboring college towns: **Raleigh**, the state capital; relaxed **Durham**, with its strong black community; and countercultural **Chapel Hill**. **Winston–Salem**, famous for its tobacco industry, boasts the excellent Old Salem village, while **Charlotte**'s international airport is the point of arrival for many European visitors.

Raleigh

RALEIGH, founded in 1792 as North Carolina's capital, stands on I-40 at the very heart of the state. The town focuses around the central, pedestrianized **Capitol Square**. The **Capitol** itself is worth a look, if only to see the copy of

Canova's statue of George Washington in Roman garb (Mon–Fri 8am–5pm, Sat 10am–4pm, Sun 1–4pm; free). Just steps away, the **North Carolina Museum of History**, 5 E Edenton St (Tues–Sat 9am–5pm, Sun noon–5pm; free; ☎919/715-0200), is impressively far-reaching, a chronological trot through the state's history from the viewpoint of its people, with particularly strong sections on women. Opposite is the **North Carolina Museum of Natural Sciences**, 11 W Jones St (Mon–Sat 9am–5pm, Sun noon–5pm; free), which looks at local geology, as well as animal and plant life, going all the way back to the dinosaur age.

South of the capitol, the four-block **City Market**, a lamplit, cobbled enclave at the intersection of Blount and Martin streets, holds a number of good shops and restaurants. Check out the local artists and sculptors at work in **Artspace**, 201 E Davie St (Tues–Sat 10am–6pm), which also hosts free lectures, movies, and poetry readings. Seventeenth US President **Andrew Johnson** was born in a tiny hut just north of where the capitol now stands; his birthplace has since been moved to **Mordecai Historic Park**, north of town at the corner of Wake Forest Rd and Mimosa St (Tues–Sat 10am–4pm; 1hr tours begin on the hour, with last tour at 3pm; $6). Other historic buildings in the park include the antebellum **Mordecai House**, built by a wealthy plantation-owner and continuously inhabited by the same family for two centuries.

A little way out to the northwest via I-40, the impressive **North Carolina Museum of Art**, 2110 Blue Ridge Rd (Wed–Sat 9am–5pm, Sun 10am–5pm; tours daily 1.30pm; free except for special exhibitions), has an eclectic display of works from the ancient world, Africa, Europe, and the US, along with a great restaurant (see below).

Practicalities

Raleigh-Durham **airport** (ⓦwww.rdu.com) is off I-40, fifteen minutes northwest of town. The **taxi** ride into town costs around $30, while a circuitous **shuttle service** will set you back $25. Amtrak drops you off at 320 W Cabarrus St, while the Greyhound station is in a seedy part of downtown at 321 W Jones St. The **visitor center**, 301 N Blount St (Mon–Fri 8am–5pm, Sat 10am–4pm, Sun 1–4pm; ☎919/733-3456, ⓦwww.raleighcvb.org), has the usual racks of leaflets.

If you want to **stay**, avoid the more anonymous downtown hotels and instead head out to Hillsborough Street, near North Carolina State University, where the *Velvet Cloak Inn* at no. 1505 offers comfortable rooms, free coffee, tea, and cookies, and an indoor pool (☎919/828-0333, ⓦwww.velvetcloakinn.com; ❹–❺). For **food**, *Big Ed's*, in the City Market at 220 Wolfe St (closed Sun; ☎919/836-9909), serves fabulous Southern breakfasts, while *Cup a Joe*, near the university at 3100 Hillsborough (☎919/876-4588), is a bohemian coffee bar that attracts a mixed crowd. The huge *42nd St Oyster Bar*, downtown at 508 Jones St (☎919/831-2811), is a popular spot for fresh fish and seafood, and the art museum boasts the contemporary *Blue Ridge Restaurant* (Wed–Sat lunch, Sun brunch; ☎919/833-3548).

Hillsborough Street, lined with bars and restaurants, is the epicenter of Raleigh's student **nightlife**. *The Brewery*, at no. 3009 (☎919/834-7018), hosts the best regional rock and alternative bands. Away from Hillsborough, *Berkeley Café*, 217 W Martin (☎919/821-0777), specializes in roots, alt-country, and rock, while *Kings*, 424 S McDowell St (☎919/831-1005), is a laid-back place for anything from drum 'n' bass to New Romantic nights, with retro video games, free food, and go-go girls to boot. Pick up the free *Spectator* for nightlife **listings**.

Durham

Twenty miles northwest of Raleigh, **DURHAM** found itself at the center of the nation's tobacco industry after farmer Washington Duke came home from the Civil War with the idea of producing cigarettes – by 1890 he and his three sons had formed the **America Tobacco Company**, one of the nation's most powerful businesses. The **Duke Homestead Historical Site**, north of I-85 at 2828 Duke Homestead Rd (Tues–Sat 10am–4pm; free), is an absorbing living museum covering the social history of tobacco farming, with demonstrations of early farming techniques and tobacco-rolling.

In 1924, the Duke family's $40 million endowment to the previously small-scale Trinity College enabled it to expand into a world-respected medical research facility, swiftly changing its name to **Duke University**. On campus, the **Museum of Art** on Campus Drive (Tues, Thurs & Fri 10am–5pm, Wed 10am–9pm, Sat 11am–2pm, Sun 2–5pm; free; ☏919/684-5135) has good African, pre-Columbian, medieval, and Asian collections; it is moving to new premises in 2004, so call ahead to check where it's currently located. The Gothic west campus centers on the soaring cathedral-style **chapel** (☏919/681-1704), which boasts one of the most powerful Flentrop organs in the world, with more than 5000 pipes. Also on campus, the terraces and bowers of the beautifully landscaped **Sarah P. Duke Gardens** (daily 8am–dusk; free) are a blaze of fragrance and color surrounded by pine forest, especially in May.

Durham takes pride in its vibrant **black heritage**. Seven miles north of town, in rural Treyburn Park, the fascinating **Historic Stagville** (Mon–Fri 9am–4pm; free; ☏919/620-0120) illustrates North Carolina plantation life, in particular the slave experience, from the early 1800s to Reconstruction. Around eighty to a hundred enslaved Africans worked on the Stagville plantation; on the grounds you can see the small two-story houses they lived in, four families (one per room) per dwelling, as well as the plantation owners' house and a colossal barn built by skilled slave carpenters. For a very good **African-American heritage map**, head to the visitor center (see below).

Downtown Durham has little of interest, though **Brightleaf Square**, an upbeat shopping area of restored tobacco warehouses at Gregson and Main streets, is a nice enough place to take a stroll, browsing its galleries, bookstores, and specialty stores. It's also the best area if you're after something to eat (see below).

For a different kind of shopping experience, drive out to **Patterson's Mill Country Store**, at 5109 Farrington Rd, between Hwy-54 and Old Chapel Hill Road (closed Mon). At the end of a rutted country lane, it looks like something straight out of *The Waltons*, selling everything from old signs and used books to crafts, candy, soap, and spices. A back room is stuffed with vials and potions, and upstairs there's a bewildering panoply of tobacco memorabilia.

Practicalities

Greyhound **buses** stop at 820 W Morgan St. Pick up maps and local information from the Durham **visitor center**, 101 E Morgan St (Mon–Fri 8.30am–5pm, Sat 10am–2pm; ☏919/687-0288, ⓦwww.durham-nc.com). The comfortable *Brownestone Inn*, 2424 Erwin Rd (☏919/286-7761; ❸), is a large **hotel** a mile from Duke University. There's a pool and sauna, and free shuttles transport you anywhere within a five-mile radius.

For **food**, try the places around Brightleaf Square: *Fowler's*, 112 S Duke St (☏919/683-2555), serves organic gourmet sandwiches and coffee, while

Anotherthyme, 109 N Gregson St (☎919/682-5225), specializes in creative pasta and seafood. Durham has historically been at the center of the North Carolina Piedmont **blues** scene, with musicians such as Reverend Gary Davis playing for tips in the 1920s at Raleigh's tobacco markets. Today, the **Bull Durham Blues Festival**, held over a weekend in early September, attracts local, regional, and national stars (Ⓦwww.hayti.org/blues).

Chapel Hill

The hip, villagey atmosphere of **CHAPEL HILL**, on the southwest outskirts of Durham, has benefited from the rise to national prominence of such local bands as Superchunk and Archers of Loaf, and musicians such as Ben Folds and Ryan Adams. It's also the hometown of James "Carolina on My Mind" Taylor. About fifty percent of the 45,000 population are students, and its position as a bastion of white liberalism in a poor rural state brings the town its detractors. That said, it's a pleasant enough place to hang out for a while, joining the hordes of students in the laid-back bars and coffeehouses along **Franklin Street**, which fringes the north side of campus. Franklin continues west into the adjacent city of **Carrboro**, where it becomes **Main Street**; bars and restaurants here have a slightly hipper, post-collegiate edge.

The **University of North Carolina**, dating from 1789, was the nation's first state university and holds some fine eighteenth-century buildings. The earliest of these is **Old East**, its original brick painted a fashionable tan in the 1840s. Evidence of the university's wealth can be seen at the splendid **Morehead Planetarium** on E Franklin St (Sun–Wed 12.30–5pm, Thurs–Sat 10am–5pm & 6.30–9.30pm; mid-June to mid-Aug same hours, except open 10am Tues & Wed; call for star show schedule; star shows $4.75, movies $3, star show/movie combo $6; ☎919/549-6863), which served as an early NASA training center, and at the **Ackland Art Museum**, South Columbia and Franklin streets (Wed–Sat 10am–5pm, Sun 1–5pm; free), which is particularly strong on Asian art and antiquities. The UNC **visitor center** (Mon–Fri 9am–5pm), in the west lobby of the Planetarium, lends out Walkmans and self-guided walking tour maps of the campus. Allow thirty to forty-five minutes.

Practicalities

Greyhound **buses** stop downtown at 138 E Franklin St, in front of the *Carolina Coffee Shop*. The Chapel Hill/Orange County **visitors bureau** is at 501 W Franklin (Mon–Fri 8.30am–5pm, Sat 10am–2pm; ☎1-888/968-2060, Ⓦwww.chocvb.org). Chapel Hill has few places to **stay**; one of the most popular spots is the swanky 1920s *Carolina Inn*, on campus at 211 Pittsboro St (☎919/933-2001, Ⓦwww.doubletreehotels.com; ❼). Five miles northeast of town, *The Sheraton*, 1 Europa Drive (☎919/968-4900; ❺), has stylish, very comfortable rooms; the nearby *Hampton Inn*, 1740 Hwy-15/501 (☎919/968-3000; ❹), is cheaper, but you get what you pay for.

Chapel Hill abounds in great **restaurants**. The minimalist *Lantern*, 423 W Franklin St, dishes up fabulous pan-Asian food until late (closed Sun; ☎919/969-8846), and has an atmospheric bar. At 610 Franklin, *Crooks Corner* (☎919/929-7643) offers a daily changing menu of delicious, stylish Southern cooking. *Elmo's Diner*, in the Carr Mill Mall in Carrboro, 200 N Greensboro St (☎919/929-2909), does great breakfasts, tasty veggie choices, and daily specials. Nearby, the community-owned *Weaver Street Market*, 101 E Weaver St (☎919/929-0010), serves healthy, homemade European veggie food that you can eat in a nice garden.

For **nightlife**, stay on Franklin and Main streets. *Orange County Social Club*, 108 E Main St, Carrboro (℡919/933-0669), is a stylish, laid-back **bar** with vintage decor, a pool table, a great jukebox, and a garden (you'll need to get someone at the bar to sign you in, which is no problem). Most **music** venues have an eclectic booking policy: *Local 506*, 506 W Franklin St (℡919/942-5506, ⓦwww.local506.com), features wild bands, open-mic hip-hop, and the annual Sleazefest in August, while over in Carrboro, the friendly *Cat's Cradle*, 300 E Main St (℡919/967-9053, ⓦcatscradle.com), books the best bands on the national touring circuit. Check **listings** in the free *Independent Weekly*.

Winston-Salem

Though synonymous with the brand names of its cigarettes, **WINSTON-SALEM**, around 80 miles west of Chapel Hill, instead owes its spot on the tourist itinerary to the delightful **Old Salem**, a well-preserved twenty-block area that honors the heritage of the city's first Moravian settlers. Escaping religious persecution in what are now the Czech and Slovak republics, the first Moravians settled in this rolling area of the Piedmont in the mid-seventeenth century. They soon established trading links with the frontier settlers and founded the town of Salem on a communal basis – they permitted only those of the same religious faith to live here. The demand for their crafts helped establish the adjacent community of Winston, which, accruing tremendous wealth from tobacco, soon outgrew the older community. The two merged in 1913 to form Winston-Salem.

Today visitors can tour ten of Old Salem's **restored buildings** (Mon–Sat 8.30am–4.30pm, Sun 12.30–4.30pm; $20, or $23 for two days) and, with the help of costumed guides, learn about the skills, trades, and customs of the Moravians. Start at the **visitor center** on Academy and Old Salem Rd (Mon–Sat 8.30am–5.30pm, Sun 12.30–5.30pm) and, if time is tight, prioritize the **St Philips Moravian Church**, an African-American church originally built in 1823, and the **Single Brothers House**, built in 1771, where unmarried men would sleep, worship, and make items such as silverware, hats, and paper. Admission includes entrance to the **Museum of Early Southern Decorative Arts** (Mon–Sat 9.30am–5pm, Sun 1.30–5pm; last tour at 3.30pm), the **Children's Museum**, geared toward under-9s (Tues–Fri 9am–5pm, Sun & Mon 1–5pm; $5 if not part of Old Salem ticket), and the striking **Toy Museum** (Mon–Sat 9am–5pm, Sun 1–5pm), which has thousands of antique toys dating from 225AD. There's a **tavern** at 736 S Main (℡336/748-8585), where beers and large lunches and dinners are served, and a **bakery** at 525 S Main that produces great cookies.

Three miles northwest of downtown, the **Reynolda House Museum of American Art**, 2250 Reynolda Rd (Tues–Sat 9.30am–4.30pm, Sun 1.30–4.30pm; $6), throws together pieces by all the top American artists from the eighteenth century to the present day, in what was the home of tobacco baron Richard Joshua Reynolds. The mansion, designed by Charles Barton Keen, is set in lush, landscaped gardens, with a number of its surrounding buildings converted into fancy stores and restaurants known collectively as **Reynolda Village**. Nearby, the occasionally controversial **Southeastern Center for Contemporary Art** (SECCA), 750 Marguerite Drive (Tues–Sat 10am–5pm, Sun 2–5pm; $5), gets all the area's major shows. At Winston-Salem State University, the renowned **Diggs Gallery**, 601 Martin Luther King Blvd (Tues–Sat 11am–5pm; free), focuses on African-American art.

Practicalities

Greyhound **buses** stop at 250 Greyhound Court, on the east side of town by Hwy-52. Amtrak has bus connections to the *Best Western Salem Inn* (see below) from the nearest **train station**, which is in Greensboro, 28 miles away. A few blocks away from Old Salem, on the outskirts of downtown, Winston-Salem's **visitor center** is at 200 Brookstown Ave (☎336/728-4200, ⊛www.visitwinstonsalem.com). Next door, the *Brookstown Inn* (☎336/725-1120 or 1-800/845-4262, ⊛www.brookstowninn.com; ❻), is a lovely small **hotel** in a former textile mill. The *Best Western Salem Inn*, 127 S Cherry St (☎1-800/533-8760, ⊛www.saleminn.com; ❹), offers clean motel rooms and a good complimentary breakfast.

Eating options aren't that exciting, though the *Twin City Diner*, 1425 W First St (☎336/724-4203), does tasty sandwiches and grills; *Bistro 420*, 420 W 4th St (☎336/721-1336), serves good Southern cuisine. Touring roots, rock, and reggae **bands** play the atmospheric *Ziggy's*, 433 Baity St (☎336/748-0810), out by Wake Forest University campus.

Charlotte

CHARLOTTE, at the junction of I-77 and I-85 near the South Carolina border, can genuinely claim to have made it: today, it's a banking and transportation center that has become the largest city in the state, "boosted," in much the same way as Atlanta, by ambitious business and city leaders. Though they like to project the image of a sophisticated, fast-lane cultural metropolis, its center is in fact somewhat soulless, though many nearby neighborhoods are more appealing. Served by direct British Airways flights from London, however, it does make one of the best and most manageable arrival points in the region.

Although most restaurants and stores are tucked away inside the city's skyscrapers, **Tryon Street** is the busiest thoroughfare in downtown Charlotte, an unlovely mass of tall buildings and concrete known as "uptown." At the intersection of Tryon and Trade streets is **Independence Square**, where giant modern statues depict transportation, commerce, industry, and the future. A few blocks away, the excellent **Museum of the New South**, 200 E 7th St (Tues–Sat 10am–5pm, Sun noon–5pm; $6), looks at the growth of the region from Reconstruction onwards. Interesting vignettes include those on musical history, with the spotlight falling on local names such as gospel legends the Golden Gate Quartet. **Discovery Place**, 301 N Tryon St, is a kids-oriented science museum with an indoor rainforest, an OMNIMAX theater, and a planetarium (June–Sept Mon–Sat 10am–6pm, Sun 12.30–6pm; Sept–June Mon–Fri 9am–5pm, Sat 10am–6pm, Sun 12.30–5pm; $7.50, OMNIMAX $7.50, combo ticket $13). The **Mint Museum of Craft and Design**, 220 N Tryon St, is worth a stop for its eclectic collection of metal, glass, wood, fiber, and ceramic works (Tues–Sat 10am–5pm, Sun noon–5pm; $6). Admission includes same-day entrance to the **Mint Museum of Art**, three miles southeast at 2730 Randolph Rd (Tues 10am–10pm, Wed–Sat 10am–5pm, Sun noon–5pm), which has a good array of Indian, pre-Columbian, and African art, plus a noted collection of pottery and porcelain.

Practicalities

Charlotte/Douglas International Airport, seven miles west of town on Old Dowd Road or I-85, is served by the #5 **bus** ($1.45), which runs hourly from the Charlotte Transportation Center, uptown on Brevard Street, between Fourth and Fifth streets, to the airport; **taxis** cost about $15 and **shuttle buses** $8. Greyhound stops centrally at 601 W Trade St, while Amtrak trains pull in at 1914 N Tryon St. The huge **visitor center** is at 330 S Tryon St (Mon–Fri 8.30am–5pm, Sat 9am–3pm; ☎704/331-2700 or 1-800/231-4636, ⓦwww .charlottecvb.org).

Most of Charlotte's **hotels** are aimed at the conference trade, though the 1929 *Dunhill Hotel*, 237 N Tryon St (☎704/332-4141, ⓦwww.dunhillhotel .com; ❻), possesses an Old World elegance. The *Days Inn*, 601 N Tryon St (☎704/333-4733; ❸), is a cheap central option. As for **restaurants**, trendy *Providence Café*, 110 Perrin Place (☎704/376-2008), offers vegetarian and New American cuisine; good alternatives include the French bistro *Bijoux*, 201 N Tryon St (☎704/377-0900), and the *Southend Brewery & Smokehouse*, 2100 South Blvd (☎704/358-4677), for ribs and wood-fired pizza, with **live music** at weekends. **Nightlife** is concentrated between the easily walkable grid of Tryon, College, Seventh, and Fifth streets, and in the South End, southwest of uptown. Check **listings** in the free weekly *Creative Loafing*.

The North Carolina mountains

The best way to see the **mountains** of North Carolina is from the pristine **Blue Ridge Parkway**, which runs across the northwest of the state from Virginia (see p.470) to the **Great Smoky Mountains National Park**. It's a delight to drive; the vast panoramic expanses of forested hillside, with barely a settlement in sight, may astonish travelers fresh from the crowded centers of the east coast. This predominantly poor region has been a breeding ground since the early twentieth century for **bluegrass music**, which you will still find, along with traditional **clogging**, performed regularly throughout the region; tiny towns like laid-back **Asheville** are good places to see the edgier "new-grass."

The North Carolina High Country Host, 1700 Blowing Rock Rd, in Boone (see p.530; ☎1-800/438-7500, ⓦwww.mountainsofnc.com), is a helpful **visitor center** that services most of the mountain area.

The Blue Ridge Parkway

The peak tourist season for the **BLUE RIDGE PARKWAY** is October, when the leaves of the deciduous trees which cover the landscape turn from bright yellow and gold through browns to vivid red. Year-round, however, this

---

Mountain activities

Organized **outdoor pursuits** available along the Blue Ridge Parkway include excellent **whitewater rafting** and **canoeing**, most of it on the Nolichucky River near the Tennessee border, south of Johnson City, Tennessee, but also on the Watauga River and Wilson Creek. Companies running trips include Nantahala Outdoor Center (☎1-800/232-7238, ⓦwww.noc.com) and High Mountain Expeditions (☎1-800/262-9036, ⓦwww.highmountainexpeditions.com), who also offer biking, hiking, and caving trips. Expect to pay around $70 for a full day of rafting.

Winter sees **skiing** at a number of slopes and resorts, particularly around **Banner Elk**, twelve miles southwest of Boone (see p.530). Resort accommodation is expensive, ski passes less so. Appalachian Ski Mountain (☎1-800/322-2373, ⓦwww.app-skimtn.com) is near Blowing Rock, and Ski Beech (☎1-800/438-2093, ⓦwww.skibeech.com), the highest ski area in the east, is at Beech Mountain. You can pick up full listings at visitor centers, or check ⓦwww.skithehighcountry.com.

magnificent, twisting mountain road – largely built in the 1930s by President Roosevelt's Civilian Conservation Corps volunteers – is a worthwhile vacation destination in itself, peppered with state-run campgrounds, short hiking trails, and dramatic overlooks. When planning your itinerary, note that though the Parkway is closed to commercial vehicles, and only particularly crowded near one or two hyped beauty spots, the constant curves make it difficult to average anything approaching the 45mph speed limit.

Boone

BOONE is the most obvious northern base for exploring the mountains; the town itself holds little of interest, though as home to the Appalachian State University it does have a certain verve. On campus, just off US-321, the small **Appalachian Cultural Museum** (Tues–Sat 10am–5pm, Sun 1–5pm; $4, free Tues) gives a good overview of the area, concentrating on mountain pastimes like music, storytelling, stock-car racing, and making moonshine whiskey. Nearby, corny family entertainments dot US-321, while pretty backroads hold offbeat settlements such as **Valle Crucis**, off US-194, where the 1883 Mast General Store (summer Mon–Sat 7am–6.30pm, Sun noon–5pm; winter hours vary; ☎828/262-0000) is well worth a look for its cast-iron cookware, fresh coffee beans, rustic furniture, outdoor gear, and fat barrels overflowing with candies.

Boone's **visitor center** is downtown at 208 Howard St (☎828/262-3516 or 1-888/251-9867, ⓦwww.visitboonenc.com). For clean **hotel** rooms, head for the *High Country Inn*, 1785 Hwy-105 (☎828/264-1000 or 1-800/334-5605, ⓦwww.highcountryinn.com; ❸), which also has a decent café and bar; good **B&Bs** include the *Lovill House Inn*, set in eleven wooded acres at 404 Old Bristol Rd (☎828/264-4206 or 1-800/849-9466, ⓦwww.lovillhouseinn.com; ❺), and, in Valle Crucis, the amusingly named *Cat Pause Inn*, 2044 Broadstone Rd (☎828/963-7297, ⓦwww.catpauseinn.com; ❹). Most of the best places to **eat** and **drink** are along King Street; the *Caribbean Café*, no. 489 (☎828/265-2233), serves award-winning spicy food, with some great veggie choices, while *Angelica's*, no. 506 (☎828/265-0809), is exclusively vegetarian, with a juice bar. The gourmet pizzas, pasta, and Mexican food at the *Red Onion Café*, 227 Harden St (☎828/264-5470), are local favorites.

South along the Parkway

Eight miles south of Boone, **BLOWING ROCK** is a pleasant, if touristy, resort just south of the Blue Ridge Parkway. The "Blowing Rock" itself, a high cliff from which light objects thrown over the side will simply blow back up, is nowhere near as impressive as photos suggest. At the nearby **Parkway Craft Center**, milepost 294 on the Parkway (March 15–Nov 30, hours vary; ☎828/295-7938), you can buy traditional folk crafts and watch them being made. The three-mile steam-driven **Tweetsie Railroad**, which is now the center of a family theme park on Hwy-321, is all that remains of a train line that used to run across the mountains to Johnson City, Tennessee (summer daily 9am–6pm; late Aug–Nov Fri–Sun 9am–6pm; $24, children $18).

Blowing Rock's **visitor center** (Mon–Sat 9am–5pm; ☎828/295-7851) is on Park Avenue. On Main Street you'll find **hotels** such as the *Boxwood Lodge* at no. 637 (☎828/295-9984, ⓦwww.boxwoodlodge.com; ❹). At *Woodland's* (☎828/295-3651), on the Hwy-321 bypass, the pork **barbecue** is excellent; it's also a good spot to drink beer, as is the comfy back porch of *The Canyons*, Hwy-321 (☎828/295-7661), which dishes up contemporary Southwestern and regional cuisine.

The Canyons has a fine view of the privately owned **Grandfather Mountain** (5964ft), fifteen miles south of Blowing Rock, with access near milepost 304 (daily: spring & fall 8am–6pm; summer 8am–7pm; winter 8am–5pm; $12). The price may be high, but the owners make a genuine attempt to protect this unique environment, and the view from the top – especially on the "mile-high swinging bridge" between the peaks – is superb, as are some of the trails. Bears, otters, and other animals, including golden and bald eagles that were wounded by gunshot in their western homelands, are held in habitat-like settings. During the **Highland Games** and "Gathering of the Clans" held here in the second full week in July, distantly Scottish Americans (take a look at the local phone book and see just how many names begin with "Mc") dress up in kilts, toss cabers, and tootle away on bagpipes.

Of various short and easy **trails** off the Parkway hereabouts, the one leading half a mile or so up to **Rough Ridge**, near milepost 301, is especially picturesque at dusk. Rough Ridge is one of several access points to the 13.5-mile **Tanawha Trail**, which runs along the ridge above the Parkway from Beacon Heights to Julian Price Park, looking out over the lush, dense forests to the east. If you plan a longer backpacking trip, equip yourself with a large-scale visitor center map; though the actual walking is not that difficult, it's easy to get lost in the woods.

Another good hike heads through the **Linville Gorge Wilderness**, near milepost 316 a couple of miles outside Linville Falls village. The high and spectacular **Linville Falls** themselves are at one end of the wilderness where the gorge begins. Breathtaking views from either side of the gorge look down 2000ft to the **Linville River** below, which has perfect, long, deep swimming pools. Be warned that ascents are steep, and some of the fainter paths are near-jungle. You can also climb **Hawksbill** or **Table Rock** mountains from the nearest unsurfaced forest road, which leaves Hwy-181 south of the village of Jonas Ridge (signposted "Gingercake Acres," with a small, low sign to Table Rock). The unremarkable but amiable villages of **Linville** and **Linville Falls** have the usual **motels** and restaurants; Linville Falls also has a **campground** (☎828/765-2681, ⓦwww.linvillefalls.com; $23 per night), and *Spears Restaurant*, Hwy-221 (☎828/765-0026), is worth a detour for its hickory-smoked pork barbecue. Alternatively, travel south along the Parkway to milepost 328.3 and stock up on apple cider, homemade honey, and fudge at the **Orchard at Altapass** (June–Oct daily; ☎828/765-9531, ⓦwww.altapassorchard.com), which also hosts storytelling, hayrides, and live mountain music on weekend afternoons.

The views from the Parkway in the **Mount Mitchell State Park** (☎828/675-4611) area, south toward Asheville, are tremendous. Sadly, however, this is largely because the trees around the summit of Mount Mitchell – the highest point in the eastern US, at 6684ft – have been ravaged by acid rain from coal-burning industries in the Chattanooga Basin to the west, and the large barren patches leave the horizon clear.

Asheville and Black Mountain

Encircled by a ring of interstates, and skirted to the east and south by the Parkway, arty **ASHEVILLE**, roughly 100 miles southwest of Boone, retains an appealing 1920s downtown core. With a strong student community from UNC, it's also become something of an alternative center, studded with funky coffee bars, galleries, vintage shops, and bohemian bookstores. Vibrant yet laid-back, it's a nice place to walk around, with a number of handsome **Art Deco** buildings; pick up a walking tour from the visitor center (see overleaf).

Woolworth Walk, 25 Haywood St, is a typically quirky space, exhibiting more than 100 local artists in a vintage Woolworth store, while Malaprop's Bookstore, 55 Haywood, has a wonderful selection of titles. Two miles south on Biltmore Avenue, the **Biltmore Estate** is the largest private mansion in the US, with 250 rooms (daily: April–Dec 8.30am–5pm; Jan–March 9am–5pm; $36). Built in the late nineteenth century by George Vanderbilt and loosely modeled on a Loire chateau, it's a wild piece of nouveau riche folly, from the Victorian chic of the indoor palm court to the gardens designed by Frederic Law Olmsted, he of New York's Central Park. You could spend a whole day here, taking a self-guided or guided tour, checking out the tastings at the winery, renting a raft or bike to explore the 250 acres of grounds, eating at the four restaurants, and maybe even staying at the 213-room "inn" (☎828-225-1600; ⑧).

Asheville's **Greyhound/Trailways** terminal is inconveniently located at 2 Tunnel Rd, two miles out of downtown; take bus #13 or #4 stopping at the Innsbruck Mall. There's a good little **visitor center** downtown at 151 Haywood St (Mon–Fri 8.30am–5.30pm, Sat & Sun 9am–5pm; ☎828/258-6111 or 1-800/257-1300, ⓦwww.ashevillechamber.org). Central **motels** include the *Days Inn*, 120 Patton Ave (☎828/254-9661; ❸); for a bit of pampering, head for the luxurious *Cedar Crest* **B&B**, set in four acres three blocks from the Biltmore Estate, at 674 Biltmore Ave (☎1-800/252-0310, ⓦwww.cedarcrestvictorianinn.com; ❼). The nearest **campground** is *Bear Creek RV Park*, 81 S Bear Creek Rd, off I-40 to the west (☎828/253-0798, ⓦwww.ashevillebearcreek.com; around $26 per night).

Asheville has by far the best **places to eat** in the region, with lots of ethnic and organic food. The fabulous *Laughing Seed Café*, 40 Wall St (☎828/252-3445; closed Tues), dishes up really good vegetarian cuisine from around the world, while tiny *Salsas*, 6 Patton Ave (☎828/252-9805), offers Mexican and Caribbean dishes. *Beanstreets Coffee*, 3 Broadway (☎828/255-8180), is a friendly place to hang out, with good java, pies, and breakfasts, and live music on Friday evenings. There's a lively **nightlife** scene, too; *Jack of the Wood*, an enjoyable bar at 95 Patton Ave (under the *Laughing Seed*; ☎828/252-5445), and the *Grey Eagle*, 188 Clingman Ave (☎828/232-5800), both feature regular live bluegrass, folk, and newgrass. For funk, world, jazz, and R&B, head to *Orange Peel*, 101 Biltmore Ave (☎828/225-5851), or *Tressa's*, 28 Broadway (☎828/254-7072), a stylish club in one of the town's fine restored buildings. In summer, you can sit outdoors and listen to traditional mountain music at "Shindig on the Green" (Sat nights on the city council plaza) or enjoy big concerts – past names have included Isaac Hayes and Alison Krauss – at the Biltmore.

Among the area's numerous local summer music and craft **festivals**, August's **Mountain Dance and Folk Festival** (ⓦwww.folkheritage.org) features bluegrass, newgrass, string bands, and traditional clogging, while the hugely enjoyable **Leaf Festival** (ⓦwww.theleaf.com), a folk music and arts and crafts gathering held in mid-May and October in **BLACK MOUNTAIN**, fourteen miles east on I-40, showcases Appalachian and world folk music, usually attracting major European and African musicians. There's little to do in Black Mountain otherwise, though the clear fresh air, pretty views, and relaxed pace make a visit worthwhile. The *Monte Vista*, at 308 W State St (☎828/669-2119, ⓦwww.montevistahotel.com; ❹), is a small, comfy, nicely old-fashioned **hotel**; *Dripolator*, nearby at 221 W State St, serves fantastic coffee, smoothies, and desserts. For nightlife, the *Town Pump Tavern*, 135 Cherry St (☎828/669-4808), has live bluegrass and roots music five nights a week.

Twenty-five miles southeast of the Parkway on US-64/74A, the natural granite tower of **Chimney Rock** sticks out from the almost-sheer side of Hickory Nut Gorge (daily: summer 8.30am–5.30pm; rest of year 8.30am–4.30pm; park stays open 90min past last ticket sale; $14; ☏828/625-9611 or 1-800/277-9611). After taking the elevator twenty-six stories up through the body of the mountain, you can walk along protected walkways along the impressive cliffs. Many of the climactic moments of *The Last of the Mohicans* were filmed here; you may recognize the mighty **Hickory Nut Falls**, which tumble 400ft from the western end of the gorge.

Great Smoky Mountains National Park

West of Asheville, **GREAT SMOKY MOUNTAINS NATIONAL PARK** is the most visited national park in the US. It straddles the border with Tennessee, and is covered in more detail – with a map – in our Tennessee section on p.600. In summer and fall, the North Carolina approaches to the park are every bit as clogged with traffic as those in Tennessee, and all accommodation can be booked up weeks in advance.

The largest of the possible bases for touring the park is **CHEROKEE**, where a few Cherokee managed to hang on when the tribe was "removed" along the Trail of Tears to Oklahoma in 1838 (see p.603). Now known as the "Eastern Band of the Cherokee Nation," they have a small reservation on the edge of the park, which derives its main income from tourism. As a result, Cherokee itself, nicely set in the cleft of a valley, has its fair share of fast-food restaurants, cornily named motels, moccasin retailers, and themed attractions (including **Santa's Land** – star attraction, the Rudicoaster) – along with, of course, the requisite casino.

Away from the kitsch and cliché, however, the impressive **Museum of the Cherokee Indian**, Hwy-441 at Drama Rd (mid-June to Aug Mon–Sat 9am–8pm, Sun 9am–5pm; Sept to mid-June daily 9am–5pm; $8, or $17 combo with Oconaluftee, see below), has good archeological and interactive displays on Cherokee arts and history – including Sequoyah's invention of a syllabary in 1821, to preserve the oral Cherokee culture in writing. Qualla Arts and Crafts, across the street, is a Cherokee-owned co-operative selling high-quality traditional **crafts** (daily: June–Aug 8am–8pm; Sept & Oct 8am–6pm; Nov–May 8am–4.30pm; ☏828/497-3103). Nearby, the **Oconaluftee Indian Village** (mid-May to late Oct daily 9am–5.30pm; $13, or $17 combo with the museum, see above) is a reconstruction of a mid-eighteenth-century Cherokee village. Amid the log cabins, you can see demonstrations of weaving and basketmaking, as well as crafts and skills that have long since died out, such as dugout canoe construction and blowpipe hunting. During summer (mid-June to late Aug Mon–Sat), at the Mountainside Theater on Hwy-441, an outdoor drama, *Unto these Hills*, re-enacts the Cherokee plight from Hernando De Soto's arrival to the Trail of Tears ($14–16; ☏828/497-2111, ⓦwww.untothesehills.com).

The friendly **visitor center** (daily: Nov to late Aug 8am–9pm; late Aug–Oct 8am–5pm; ☏828/497-9195 or 1-800/438-1601, ⓦwww.cherokee-nc.com), in the center of town on Hwy-441 by the river, has lots of informaton on the National Park and the Parkway. Though the motels in town are fine – try the central *Cherokee Plaza* (☏828/497-2301 or 1-800/535-4798; ❸–❹), which overlooks the river – you might just as well stay in Maggie Valley (see below). You'll do fine for **eating** if you like fast food and buffets – note also that as a reservation town, Cherokee is entirely dry.

The **Oconaluftee visitor center**, the headquarters of the North Carolina side of the park, is two miles north of Cherokee on US-441 (daily: summer 8am–7pm; fall & spring 8am–6pm; winter 9am–5pm; ☎828/497-1904). It has good displays on Appalachian farming life, and a re-created pioneer village.

Fifteen miles east, the small community of **MAGGIE VALLEY** boasts a string of motels with peaceful views over the valleys – one of the cheapest, the *Riverlet*, on US-19 (☎828/926-1900; ❸), overlooks two streams. It's all rather tranquil here, with trout farms, wooden shacks, the occasional boiled peanut and honey stand, and clear, fresh air. Tourism focuses on hillbilly culture, with lots of hoedowns and the like; the nearby **Ghost Town in the Sky** is an extraordinary piece of kitsch, with a chairlift that sweeps you up to a hokey Wild West–style theme park complete with gunfights, cancan girls, and Indian dancers (summer daily; fall Sat & Sun only; $23, children $14). During the last fortnight in July, Maggie Valley hosts North Carolina's **International Folk Festival** (Ⓦwww.folkmoot.com).

Southwestern North Carolina

The area west of Asheville, and south of the national park, holds a number of dramatic **waterfalls. Looking Glass Falls**, about twelve miles south of the Parkway on US-276, is in a particularly beautiful section of the **Pisgah National Forest**. The falls drop 85 feet, with a great (albeit very cold) swimming hole at the bottom. **Connestee Falls**, a few miles south on US-276 toward Brevard, is a double waterfall and even higher. Unbridled optimists can pay to pan for **gemstones**, such as rubies, at outwashes of the numerous gem mines near the 250ft **Cullasaja Falls**, further west on US-64.

The far west corner of the state is famous for its superb **whitewater**. Plenty of companies offer canoeing and rafting on the **Nantahala River**, which is ideal for first-timers and families, as well as on a number of neighboring rivers that provide a full-on white-knuckle experience. Raft expeditions can cost anything from $25–70, depending on the level of difficulty and length of the trip; one company, Nantahala Outdoor Center, in Bryson City (☎1-800/232-7238, Ⓦwww.noc.com), also runs a **hostel** (❶). USA Raft is similar, offering a variety of family and adventure trips on the Nantahala, Pigeon, and Nolichucky rivers (☎1-800/USA-RAFT, Ⓦwww.usaraft.com/cat).

West of the Nantahala, off US-129 almost in Tennessee, **Joyce Kilmer National Forest** is worth a detour, being one of the last remaining stands of unlogged virgin forest in the southeastern US, including some enormous hardwood trees.

South Carolina

The relatively small state of **SOUTH CAROLINA** remains, with Mississippi, one of the poorest and most rural in the US; there are no cities to speak of, and though the pockets of prime real estate along its coast have been developed into exclusive golf courses and tennis clubs, these are self-contained enclaves that make little impression on the rest of the state. **Politics** in South Carolina, the first state to secede from the Union in 1860, have traditionally been conservative. Reconstruction was mired in terrible Klan violence, while demagogues openly espoused lynching and enforced "Jim Crow" laws with frightening zeal. Today, the state contains two of the country's most right-wing minor universities – football-fixated Clemson, and Christian Bob Jones University in Greenville, a training-ground for the fundamentalist right.

For travelers, however, the state has a lot to offer. Its main fascination lies in the subtropical coastline, also called the **Low Country**, and its **sea islands**. Great beaches, swampy marshes, and lush palmetto groves preserve traces of a virtually independent black culture (featuring the unique patois, "Gullah"), dating back to when enslaved Africans escaped here from the mainland plantations. There are no interstates along the coast, so journeys take longer than you might expect, and the pace of life definitely feels slower. Beyond the grand old peninsular port of **Charleston** – arguably the most elegant town in the US, with its pastel-colored old buildings, appealing waterfront, and magnificent, tree-lined avenues – restored plantations stretch as far north as **Georgetown**, en route toward the poseur's paradise of **Myrtle Beach**. Inland, the rolling Piedmont and flat coastal plain hold little to see.

Getting around South Carolina

Charleston has South Carolina's biggest **airport**, with flights to and from major towns on the east coast. Three Amtrak routes cut through the state, stopping at Greenville and Clemson in the west, Columbia and other towns in the center, and Charleston on the coast. **Buses** run along I-85 between Charlotte, North Carolina, and Atlanta, while a less regular service operates along the coast, stopping at Myrtle Beach and Charleston.

Myrtle Beach and the north coast

MYRTLE BEACH is a brazen splurge of seaside fun, an unmitigated stretch of commercial development twenty miles down the coast from the North Carolina border, at the center of the sixty-mile "Grand Strand." Predominantly a family resort, it's packed fit to burst during mid-term vacations with leering, jeering students drinking and partying themselves into a frenzy. Fans of crazy golf, water parks, factory outlet malls, funfairs, and parasailing will be in heaven, and the **beach** itself isn't at all bad. The widest stretch is at North Myrtle Beach, a chain of small communities among which Ocean Boulevard is the center.

South of Myrtle Beach lies **Murells Inlet**, a fishing port with lots of good seafood restaurants, and **Pawleys Island**, a secluded resort once favored by plantation owners and today retaining a far slower pace than its neighbors. Between the two on Hwy-17 is the beautifully landscaped **Brookgreen Gardens** (daily: summer 9.30am–9.30pm; rest of the year 9.30am–5pm; $8.50; ☎1-800/849-1931), a former rice and indigo plantation with an outdoor display of American figurative sculpture, and the setting for many of Julia Peterkin's novels of Gullah life. There's also a wildlife sanctuary, where you can often see alligator and deer.

Practicalities

US- or Hwy-17 (also called Kings Highway) is Myrtle Beach's main traffic thoroughfare; the parallel Ocean Boulevard is lined with hotels and motels.

Greyhound **buses** from Charleston and Wilmington come in at 511 7th Ave N. Minimal transportation in the beach areas is provided by Coastal Rapid Public Transit buses (☎843/626-9138); Great American Trolley runs a route along Ocean Boulevard from 29th Ave S to Broadway at the beach (March–Oct; ☎843/236-0337). The main **visitor center** at 1200 Oak St (☎1-800/356-3016, Ⓦwww.myrtlebeachinfo.com) provides bus timetables, events listings, and stacks of hotel brochures.

During the summer, **accommodation** rates increase dramatically; it may be cheaper to stay in **Conway**, about eleven miles to the west of US-501, where there's another visitor center at 2090 Hwy-501 E. In Myrtle Beach, the vast *Compass Cove Resort*, 2311 S Ocean Blvd (☎1-800/331-0934, Ⓦwww .compasscove.com; ❺), features six turquoise pools, plus ocean views from the more expensive tower rooms; *Serendipity Inn*, near the sea at 407 71st Ave N (☎843/449-5268, Ⓦwww.serendipityinn.com; ❸–❹), is an old motel that's been converted into a B&B, with a pretty courtyard and a nice breakfast buffet. There's also a **hostel**, the *Oceanview Retreat*, at 307 1st Ave, six blocks from the bus station and "170 steps from the beach" (☎843/626-7069, Ⓦwww .oceanviewretreat.org; ❶). A number of commercial **campgrounds** lie along Kings Highway in North Myrtle Beach; *Barefoot Camping Resort*, 4825 US-17 (☎843/272-1790; $18–42 per site, depending on location and season), is just one of them.

If you crave surf'n'turf, burgers, or diner food, you'll have no problem finding somewhere to **eat**. Creative seafood (along with gourmet breakfasts, innovative lunch specials, and sea views) can be had at the classy *Sea Captain's House*, 3002 N Ocean Blvd (☎843/448-8082), or at a number of similar establishments in Murrells Inlet; for a Mediterranean-influenced meal in a funky, colorful atmosphere, stop by the *Collector's Café*, 7726 N Kings Hwy (☎843/449-9370).

As for **nightlife**, there are scores of themed bars and music venues competing for the tourist dollar. There's a *House of Blues* at Barefoot Landing, 4640 Hwy-17 (☎843/913-3740), which attracts top national bands. More kitschy are the glut of **country music variety shows**; the longest-running is the *Carolina Opry*, Hwy-17 N (☎843/913-4000, Ⓦwww.thecarolinaopry.com), where powerful singers belt out corny, family-oriented rock'n'roll, country, and bluegrass, with a couple of hymns thrown in for good measure. Next door at the Dolly Parton–owned *Dixie Stampede* (☎1-800/433-4401, Ⓦwww.dixiestampede.com) you can see a patriotic, surreal take on the Civil War with some impressive horsemanship, all while chowing down on a huge dinner without the aid of utensils.

South to Charleston: Georgetown and the plantations

The peaceful waterfront of **GEORGETOWN** – the first town in forty miles beyond Myrtle Beach that's anything more than a beach resort – makes a refreshing contrast, even with the views of the monstrous paper works on the opposite bank. It's hard to imagine today, but in the eighteenth century Georgetown was the center of a thriving network of Low Country rice plantations; by the 1840s the surrounding area produced nearly half the rice grown in the United States.

Though Georgetown's main street has a time-warped, late-1950s feel, the town's 32-block **historic district** features many fine eighteenth-century and antebellum houses; the **visitor center**, 1001 Front St (☎1-800/777-7705, Ⓦwww.georgetownchamber.com), has self-guided walking tours. The **Rice**

Museum, in the Clock Tower at 633 Front St (Mon–Sat 10am–4.30pm; $5), tells the story of the Low Country's long history of rice cultivation, and its dependence upon a constant supply of enslaved Africans brought over from the Windward coast for their rice expertise.

If you want to **stay** in sleepy Georgetown, the *Carolinian Inn*, 706 Church St (☎843/546-5191, ⊛www.choicehotels.com; ❸), is a good bet, and has a pool. To **eat**, you needn't stray from its restaurant, *Hook, Line, and Sinker*, which serves tasty crabcakes, fish stews, and Low Country Boils; *Rice Paddy*, 819 Front St (☎843/546-2021), and *River Room*, 801 Front St (☎843/527-4110), are fancier seafood places with waterfront views. For light lunches and pastries, head for *Kudzu Bakery*, 120 King St (☎843/546-1847).

Hopsewee Plantation, the grand 1740 mansion home of Thomas Lynch, a signatory of the Declaration of Independence, is set in Spanish-moss-draped grounds, twelve miles south of Georgetown on US-17 (March–Oct Mon–Fri 9.30am–4.30pm; Nov–Feb Thurs & Fri 9.30am–4.30pm; $8). In additon to the main house, you can also see two slave cabins, inhabited by slaves and their descendants until the 1940s. Wooded trails lead through pretty grounds, but clouds of ferocious mosquitoes drift up from the river, so think twice before wandering around in summer.

Hampton Plantation State Historic Site, further south, two miles off US-17 on Hwy-857, is probably closer to the look of a typical plantation. The grounds (9am–6pm; free) are attractive, but the house (summer daily 11am–4pm; rest of year Thurs–Mon 11am–4pm; $2) is most impressive, a huge eighteenth-century Neoclassical monolith built by Huguenots; while its exterior has been restored, the inside is relatively bare. The plantation itself is isolated in the heart of the dense **Francis Marion National Forest**. This heavily African-American area is particularly known for its sweetgrass basket-weaving, a craft that originated with the slaves in West Africa, using tight bundles of grasses to make intricate baskets and pots. Despite the enormously time-consuming work and the cost of materials, the baskets you see being made at roadside stalls here cost at most $25.

Further south, beyond the forest and a few miles north of Charleston on US-17, is the much-publicized **Boone Hall Plantation** (April–Sept Mon–Sat 8.30am–6.30pm, Sun 1–5pm; Sept–March Mon–Fri 9am–5pm, Sun 1–4pm; $12.50). Though the plantation dates from the late seventeenth century, the house is a twentieth-century reconstruction; tours are conducted by hapless young women in Southern Belle costumes who rather overplay the connections with *Gone With the Wind*. The grounds are more interesting, with a long, tree-lined drive and a slave street, this time of small mid-eighteenth-century brick cabins that housed the more "privileged" slaves – domestic servants and skilled artisans.

Charleston

CHARLESTON, one of the finest-looking towns in the US, today spreads far beyond its original confines on the tip of a peninsula at the confluence of the Ashley and Cooper rivers, roughly one hundred miles south of Myrtle Beach and north of Savannah, Georgia. It's a compelling place to visit, its **historic district** lined with tall, narrow houses of peeling, multicolored stucco, adorned with wooden shutters and wide porches (known here as piazzas). The Caribbean feel is augmented by palm trees and the dreamy, tropical climate, while the town's pretty hidden gardens, leafy patios, and ironwork balconies evoke the romance of New Orleans.

Founded in 1670 by a group of English aristocrats as a money-making venture, Charles Towne swiftly boomed as a **port** serving the rice and cotton plantations. It became the region's dominant town, a commercial and cultural center which right from the start had a mixed population, with immigrants including French, Germans, Jews, Italians, and Irish, as well as the English majority. One-third of all the nation's **enslaved Africans** came through Charleston, sold at the market on the riverfront and bringing with them their ironworking, building, and farming skills. The town had a sizeable **free black** community too, and its then unusually urban density allowed an anonymity and racial openness that, although still dominated by slavery, went a lot further than in the rest of the South. Nevertheless there was still slave unrest, culminating in the abortive Veysey revolt of 1823, after which the city built the Citadel armory and later the military university to control future uprisings.

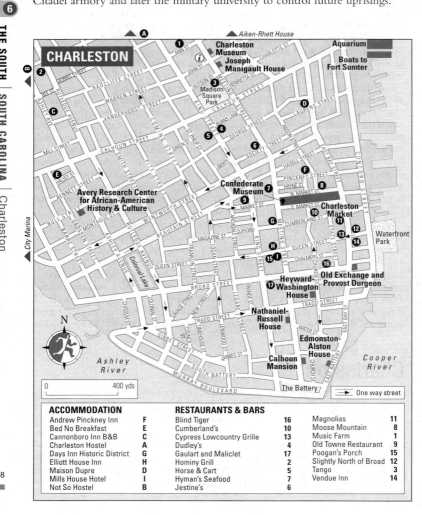

ACCOMMODATION		**RESTAURANTS & BARS**			
Andrew Pinckney Inn	F	Blind Tiger	16	Magnolias	11
Bed No Breakfast	E	Cumberland's	10	Moose Mountain	8
Cannonboro Inn B&B	C	Cypress Lowcountry Grille	13	Music Farm	1
Charleston Hostel	A	Dudley's	4	Old Towne Restaurant	9
Days Inn Historic District	G	Gaulart and Maliclet	17	Poogan's Porch	15
Elliott House Inn	H	Hominy Grill	2	Slightly North of Broad	12
Maison Dupre	D	Horse & Cart	5	Tango	3
Mills House Hotel	I	Hyman's Seafood	7	Vendue Inn	14
Not So Hostel	B	Jestine's	6		

The **Civil War** started on Charleston's very doorstep, at **Fort Sumter** in the harbor, and the city was practically ruined by it. Fire swept through, destroying large chunks, in 1861, and Union bombardment was relentless; it was eventually taken by Union forces in February 1865. The decline of the plantation economy and slump in cotton prices led to an economic crash after the war, made worse by a catastrophic earthquake in 1886. As the upcountry industrialized, capital steadily deserted the city, and it only really recovered when World War II restored its importance as a port and naval base. Since then, a steady program of preservation and restoration has made **tourism** Charleston's main focus, based primarily on its rich Colonial history. Downtown, especially, there's a rather genteel air about the place, and prices tend to be high, whether you're looking for a room, a quick lunch, or a beer. Despite the gentrification, however, Charleston has kept its atmosphere, while maintaining all the energy and life of a real, working town. The traditions of the sea islands are a tangible presence here, too: "basket ladies" weave their sweetgrass baskets all around the market and near the post office, and many people – black and white – speak the distinctive **Gullah** dialect.

Arrival and information

Charleston International Airport is about twelve miles north of downtown, off I-526; the airport **shuttle** (☎843/767-7113) costs $12, while a **taxi** ride with Yellow Cabs (☎843/577-6565) costs around $23. Both Amtrak – 4565 Gaynor Ave, eight miles north of downtown – and Greyhound – at 3610 Dorchester Rd, out near I-26 – are in inconvenient and potentially dangerous locations. Local **public transportation** isn't bad: CARTA buses ($1.25 exact change; Ⓦwww.ridecarta.com) cover most areas, including the Amtrak (though you should take a cab at night) and Greyhound stations, as well as

---

Guided tours

Charleston is ideal for **walking tours**; the visitor center has details on scores of them. For a lively, informed overview, set off from the circular fountain in Waterfront Park with **Tour Charleston LLC** (April–Oct 10am & 5pm; Nov–March 10am & 4pm; $15; ☎843/723-1670). The same company offers popular **pirate tours** (10am & 4pm; $14) and **ghost tours** (5pm, 6pm, 7.30pm, 9pm & 9.30pm; $15). The **Civil War Walking Tour** sets out from the *Mills House Hotel*, 115 Meeting St (March–Dec daily 9am; $17; private tours available all year; ☎843/722-7033). **Architectural Walking Tours of Charleston** run two 2hr tours – the morning tour covering the eighteenth century, the afternoon tour the nineteenth (Mon & Wed–Sat 10am & 2pm; $15; ☎1-800/931-7761); both leave from the *Meeting Street Inn*, 173 Meeting St. In fall, the **Preservation Society**, 147 King St (☎1-800/968-8175), organizes candlelit tours of the Historic District, visiting a few private old homes (Sept & Oct Thurs–Sat 7–10pm; $35; Ⓦwww.preservationsociety.org).

There are two good **black history tours**. **Al Miller**'s van tours include material on slave uprisings, the Civil War, and the lives of the freed slaves; they leave from the visitor center (1hr/2hr; $10/15; ☎843/762-0051). **Gullah Tours**, which depart from Gallery Chuma, 43 John St, diagonally across from the visitor center, include folktales told in Gullah and a meeting with renowned local ironworker Philip Simmons (Mon–Fri 11am & 1pm, Sat 11am, 1pm & 3pm; ☎843/763-7551).

Horse and carriage rides provide a lively and leisurely overview of the town, especially lovely in the cool of the early evening. Try **Olde Town Carriage Co**, which leaves regularly between 9am and 5pm from 20 Anston St (1hr; $15, children $8; with harbor tour, 1hr 45min, $26, children $13; ☎843/722-1315).

nearby beaches (see p.544). The Downtown Area Shuttles (DASH; $1.25 exact change) comprise four useful trolley routes, three of which stop at the visitor center. You can buy **passes** that cover both buses and trolleys (day pass $4, 3-day pass $9, 10-ride pass $10). Charleston's huge, well-equipped **visitor center**, 375 Meeting St (daily: March–Oct 8.30am–5.30pm; Nov–Feb 8.30am–5pm; ℡843/853-8000, ⓦwww.charlestoncvb.com), has discount coupons, leaflets, maps, and bus passes; they also show a short film about Charleston's history ($2). The **post office** is at 83 Broad St.

Accommodation

Though Charleston accommodation is pricey, it's worth budgeting to stay within walking distance of downtown. As well as hotels, a lot of grand Historic District houses serve as **B&Bs**, with prices starting at around $80 a night; agencies include Historic Charleston B&B, 60 Broad St (℡843/722-6606, ⓦwww.historiccharlestonbedandbreakfast.com). There are also two good **hostels** not too far from downtown. Further out, the usual **motels** cluster around US-17 in West Ashley and Mount Pleasant, and along I-26 in North Charleston.

Andrew Pinckney Inn 40 Pinckney St ℡843/937-8800 or 1-800/505-8983, ⓦwww.andrewpinckneyinn.com. Stylish, Caribbean-style rooms in this boutique inn located beside Charleston's historic market. Continental breakfast served on the rooftop terrace overlooking the city. **④–⑤**

Bed no Breakfast 16 Halsey St, Cannonboro ℡843/723-4450. Two simple rooms, shared bath, and, obviously, no breakfast, in a comfy family home with a little courtyard. No credit cards. **③–④**

Cannonboro Inn B&B 184 Ashley Ave, Cannonboro ℡843/723-8572, ⓦwww.charleston-sc-inns.com. Fine, columned house with attractive patio and garden. Very comfortable nonsmoking rooms, delicious breakfasts, and free use of bicycles. **⑥–⑥**

Charleston Hostel 194 St Philip St ℡843/478-1446, ⓦwww.charlestonhostel.com. Newer, and slightly nearer downtown than *Not So* (see below), but a little less spacious. Free Internet access, free laundry, and Sunday barbecues on the porch. Dorms $19 per night, $15 for three or more nights, $85 per week; one private room. **①–②**

Days Inn Historic District 155 Meeting St ℡843/722-8411 or 1-800/329-7466, ⓦwww.daysinn.com. Standard rooms with attractive wrought-iron balconies; one of the least expensive downtown options, near the market. **④–⑦**

Elliott House Inn 78 Queen St ℡843/723-1855 or 1-800/729-1855, ⓦwww.elliotthouseinn.com. Atmospheric accommodation in an old Charleston building. Free wine and afternoon tea served in a pretty courtyard, which also has a Jacuzzi. Free bicycle use and a good continental breakfast. **⑤–⑦**

Maison Dupre 317 E Bay St ℡843/723-8691, ⓦwww.maisondupre.com. Beautiful inn in a crumbling 1804 European-style building. An idyllic garden holds fountains and a wishing well. Offers complimentary high teas and good continental breakfast. **⑦–⑧**

Mills House Hotel 115 Meeting St ℡843/577-2400 or 1-800/874-9600, ⓦwww.millshouse.com. One of central Charleston's better large hotels, with elegantly furnished rooms. The nice bar features occasional live music. **⑤–⑦**

Not So Hostel 156 Spring St, Cannonboro ℡843/722-8383, ⓦwwww.notsohostel.com. Appealing hostel in a double-porched 1850 house. Rates include Internet access, bike rental, and breakfast, with a free shuttle from the airport, bus, and train stations. Regular live music on a small stage in the back yard. Dorms $19 per night, $15 for three or more nights, $85 per week. There are two private rooms (six more to come) and you can also camp in their yard. **①–②**

The City

Charleston's **historic district** is fairly self-contained, a predominantly residential area of leaning lines, weathered colors, and exquisite hidden courtyards, bounded by Calhoun Street to the north and East Bay Street by the river. The further south of Broad you head, the posher, prettier, and more residential the streets become. The district is best taken in by strolling at your own pace – though that pace can get pretty slow in high summer, when the heat is intense. Attractive spots to pause in the shade include the swinging benches at **Waterfront Park**, a beautifully landscaped piazza with fountains and board-walks leading out over the river, and **White Point Gardens**, by the Battery on the tip of the peninsula, where the flower-filled lawns have good views across the water and a breeze even in the sweltering summer.

Most of the city's fine **houses** are private, and can only be admired from the outside; some, however, are available for **tours**. The late nineteenth-century **Calhoun Mansion**, 16 Meeting St, is fabulously over-the-top, with its ornate plaster and woodwork, hand-painted porcelain ballroom chandeliers, and simi-lar extravagances (Wed–Sun 10am–4pm, closed Jan; $15). Nearby, the stately antebellum **Edmonston–Alston House** overlooks the harbor at 21 E Battery St (Tues–Sat 10.30am–4.30pm, Sun & Mon 1.30–4.30pm; $8); this was one of the first houses built on the Battery, in 1825, and retains its furniture from 1838. The Neoclassical **Nathaniel-Russell House**, 51 Meeting St (Mon–Sat 10am–5pm, Sun 2–5pm; $7), is noted for its daring flying staircase, which soars unsupported for three floors. Tremendously elegant both inside and out, its piazza-free design also sets it apart from the other mansions. The Charleston Museum's $18 combination ticket (see below) gets you into the 1803 **Joseph Manigault House**, a lovely Neoclassical structure built by descendents of Huguenot settlers, opposite the museum, and the 1772 **Heyward-Washington House**, 87 Church St, built by Thomas Heyward, a rice baron and signatory of the Declaration of Independence. (George Washington stayed here for a month in 1791, thus the name). Admission to each separately is $8 (Mon–Sat 10am–5pm, Sun 1–5pm). North of downtown at the antebellum **Aiken-Rhett House**, 48 Elizabeth St, the work-yard and slave quarters are intact, while the mansion itself retains its original decor and furnishings (Mon–Sat 10am–5pm, Sun 2–5pm; $7).

Built in 1771 as the Customs House and used as a prison during the Revolutionary War, the **Old Exchange and Provost Dungeon**, 122 E Bay St (daily 9am–5pm; $7), is a hugely significant Colonial structure. Today the upper floors are given over to learned exhibits detailing the history of the building and the city; the tone changes in the dank dungeon down below, where groups of spotlit animatronic dummies recount tales of revolutionaries, gentlemen pirates, and all manner of derring-do.

Charleston's **market area** runs from Meeting Street to East Bay Street, focusing on a long, narrow line of enclosed, low-roofed, nineteenth-century sheds, but also spilling out onto the surrounding streets. Undeniably touristy, packed with hard-headed "basket ladies," this is one of the liveliest spots in town, selling junk, spices, tacky T-shirts, jewelry, and rugs. With downtown Charleston's heavy emphasis on its Colonial history, it's easy to overlook just how central the city was to the Civil War; a visit to the **Confederate Museum**, on the market's upper level (Oct–March Tues–Sat 11am–3.30pm; April–Sept Tues–Sat 11am–4.30pm; $6) tips the balance by showing just how close to home the "Lost Cause" still feels to many old Charlestonians. A shrine to the Rebel forces, the museum's one room is packed with everything from battleship splinters to blood-stained ladies' gloves, mess tins, canteens, and tat-tered flags.

Far more satisfying, the huge **Charleston Museum**, opposite the visitor center at 360 Meeting St (Mon–Sat 9am–5pm, Sun 1–5pm; $9, $14 with the Joseph Manigault House or the Heyward-Washington House, $18 with both), is the nation's oldest, dating from 1773 (although the original building no longer stands). It's filled with a wealth of city memorabilia, with videos on subjects from rice-growing to the Huguenots, and strong sections on Native Americans, architecture, and the devastation of the Civil War. One room holds exhibits from its early collections, where pickled snakes once shared space with Egyptian mummies and casts from the British Museum in London. The "head of a New Zealand chief" and a "fine electrical machine," however, were destroyed in a fire of 1778. A good source for black history is the **Avery Research Center for African-American History and Culture**, 125 Bull St (tours Mon–Fri 2–4pm, Sun noon–5pm; donation), based in what was once a prestigious African-American private school. Centering on an archive of personal papers, photographs, oral histories, and art, the center also shows periodic films, lectures, and exhibitions.

At the end of Calhoun Street, overlooking the harbor, you'll find Charleston's hugely popular **Aquarium** (mid-Aug to end March Mon–Sat 9am–5pm, Sun noon–5pm; April to mid-Aug Mon–Sat 9am–6pm, Sun noon–6pm, last ticket sold 1hr before closing; $14, plus Fort Sumter (see below) $23, plus IMAX $20, plus Fort Sumter and IMAX $29). It's a well-designed space, with a 40ft-deep tank at the core and open, eye-level exhibits recreating North Carolina's various watery habitats – including the Piedmont, swamps, salt marshes, and ocean – and their indigenous aquatic plant and animal life. As well as thousands of sea creatures you'll also find gators, snakes, and turtles, soaring birds, and frolicking otters. The porch-like terrace, with giant rocking chairs, is a nice place to catch the river breezes; watch out for schools of dolphins playing in the water below.

Fort Sumter National Monument

The first shots of the Civil War were fired on April 12, 1861, at **Fort Sumter**, a redoubtable federal garrison that entirely occupied a small artificial island at the entrance to Charleston Harbor. After secession, the federal government had to decide whether to reprovision its forts in the south. When a relief expedition was sent to Fort Sumter, Confederate General Pierre Beauregard demanded its surrender. In one of the ironies that so characterized the war, Beauregard, who personally coordinated the bombardment, had attended artillery classes taught by the fort's commander, Major Robert Anderson, at West Point. After a relentless barrage, the garrison gave in the next day.

Fort Sumter can be seen today on regular **boat tours** that leave from alongside the Aquarium at the eastern end of Calhoun Street (summer daily 9.30am, noon & 2.30pm, less frequently in winter; $12; for combined tickets with the aquarium, see above; ℡843/722-2628, ⓦwww.nps.gov). It takes 35 minutes for boats to reach the island, with great views of Charleston along the way. Only one of the fort's original three stories is left standing, thanks not to the assault that started the war, but to its subsequent siege and bombardment by Union troops, who finally recaptured it on Good Friday 1865, the very day Lincoln was assassinated. A small on-site **museum** holds the flags that flew over the fort, while a more comprehensive one back at the Fort Sumter visitor center on the mainland recounts the history not only of the fort but also of Charleston, and the build-up to the conflict (daily 8.30am–5pm; free).

Eating

Historic Charleston's elegant ambiance lends itself very well to classy **New Southern cooking** served up in a variety of innovative, upbeat restaurants – prices tend to be high, but it's worth splashing out on a rather special meal. There are also plenty of ethnic restaurants, and cappuccino bars and cafés line Market and King streets.

Cypress Lowcountry Grille 167 E Bay St
☏ 843/727-0111. Exquisite Southern/Pan-Asian
fusion food – raw and baked oysters, grouper with
okra and herb broth, tuna sashimi – in a fashionable, soaring space. The wine list is exemplary,
too. If you're going to splurge, let this be the place.
Gaulart and Maliclet aka *Fast and French*, 98
Broad St ☏ 843/577-9797. Intimate French bistro,
popular with locals. Check out the fondue nights
on Thursdays.
Hominy Grill 202 Rutledge Ave ☏ 843/937-0930.
This simple, stylish neighborhood restaurant is a
favorite for fabulous gourmet Low Country cooking
– try the amazing brunches.
Hyman's Seafood 213–215 Meeting St
☏ 843/723-6000. Sprawling, family-owned restaurant serving great seafood – try the she-crab
soup, oysters, or flounder – in a convivial, casual
setting; the fried green tomatoes are great, too.
Deli take-out available.
Jestine's 251 Meeting St ☏ 843/722-7224.
Authentic black Low Country cooking, with superb
fried chicken and meat-and-three-veggie deals.

Magnolias 185 E Bay St ☏ 843/577-7771.
Nouvelle Southern cuisine – shrimp with grits and
such – in a buzzy monochrome setting with a circular bar.
Moose Mountain 50 N Market St ☏ 843/853-
0008. Spacious marketside espresso bar serving
coffees, smoothies, and healthy breakfasts, with
salads, sandwiches, and soups for lunch.
Old Towne Restaurant 229 King St ☏ 843/723-
8170. Tasty grilled seafood, chicken, and steaks at
this great-value Greek restaurant.
Poogan's Porch 72 Queen St ☏ 843/577-2337.
Delicious local food in a big, old Charleston house,
including Low Country Boils, crabcakes, and catfish. Very popular for Sunday brunch. Dine on the
porch or on the shady patio.
Slightly North of Broad 192 E Bay St
☏ 843/723-3424. Another *nouvelle* Southern
restaurant – scallops with smoked sausage, blue
crab salad, and the like. It's lively at lunchtime
(Mon–Fri only), when they offer an inexpensive
prix-fixe menu.

Nightlife and entertainment

Charleston has lots of **music venues**, **clubs**, and **bars**. For listings, see the free
weekly *City Paper*. Ask at the visitor center about the city's many **festivals**:
chief among them, the **Spoleto Festival** (☏ 843/722-2764, ⓦ www.spole-
tousa.org), an international arts extravaganza inspired by its Italian namesake,
runs for seventeen days in May/June, alongside its funkier sibling, **Piccolo
Spoleto** (☏ 843/724-7305, ⓦ www.piccolospoleto.com). October's **Moja
Arts Festival** (ⓦ www.mojafestival.com) celebrates African-American and
Caribbean theater, dance, and film.

Blind Tiger 38 Broad St ☏ 843/577-0088. Local
bar with hidden entrance, busy deck, and regular
live music.
Cumberland's 20 Cumberland St ☏ 843/577-
9469, ⓦ www.cumberlands.net. Friendly venue for
indie, blues, bluegrass, rock, reggae, and folk.
Dudley's 346 King St ☏ 843/723-2784. Cosy,
friendly gay bar; it bills itself a private club, but
visitors need only call to make a reservation, then
pay the $1 cover.
Horse & Cart 347 King St ☏ 843/722-0797.
Friendly, bohemian neighborhood café serving

cheap food and more than 100 beers. Live performances (including drumming, folk, and poetry
jams) every night.
Music Farm 32 Ann St ☏ 843/853-FARM,
ⓦ www.musicfarm.com. The best place in
Charleston to see regional and national touring
bands.
Tango 39 Hutson St ☏ 843/577-2822. Popular
multilevel dance club, open Thurs through Sat.
Vendue Inn 23 Vendue Range ☏ 843/723-0485.
Elegant rooftop bar and restaurant with great
views over the city.

Around Charleston

The **river road**, Hwy-61, leads **west** from Charleston along the Ashley River,
past a series of magnificent **plantations**. Many can be visited, although in best
Southern tradition, house tours tend to dwell on the furniture and dining
habits of the slave masters rather than provide much sense of social history.
Drayton Hall, closest to Charleston at 3380 Ashley River Rd (daily:
March–Oct 10am–4pm; Nov–Feb 10am–3pm; $12), is a particularly elegant

Georgian mansion, looking much as it did in the mid-eighteenth century, with its handcarved wood and plasterwork; there is little furniture on show, and house tours concentrate on the fine architecture. At 11.15am and 2.15pm, however, special talks, backed up by photographs and artifacts, emphasize the role of **African-Americans** in the Low Country, tracing the story of slavery and emancipation and how it related to Drayton Hall.

The nearby **Magnolia Plantation and Gardens**, ten miles from downtown Charleston, is most notable for its stunning ornamental gardens, particularly in spring when the azaleas are blooming (March–Oct daily 8am–dusk; last tickets sold 5.30pm; Nov–Feb hours vary; $13, ticket valid for 6 days; ☏ 1-800/367-3517). The admission price gives you access to the gardens, which include a tropical greenhouse, a petting zoo, a maze, and a wildlife observation tower, but you have to pay extra for **house tours** (daily 9.30am–4.30pm; $7). You don't have to pay the general admission charge to explore the **Audubon Swamp Garden** ($5), a preserved swamp complete with alligators and lush flowers. If you've paid general admission you can also take a "nature train" tour of the grounds, or a "nature boat" tour of the swamp; both cost $7 and last 45min.

Across the Ashley River, on Hwy-171, west of the Ashley River Bridge three miles northwest of Charleston, **Charles Towne Landing** is a 663-acre state park, located on the site where in 1670 the English colonists established the first permanent settlement in the Carolinas (daily: summer 8.30am–6pm; rest of year 8.30am–5pm; $5; shuttle buses $1). As well as the landing site itself, you can see a living history settlement, a replica of a seventeenth-century merchant ship, and a zoo, home to species the colonists would have encountered when they landed here – pumas, bison, alligators, black bears, and wolves. There are also seven miles of hiking and biking trails; you can rent bikes for $3.

East of Charleston, **beaches** such as **Isle of Palms** and **Sullivan's Island** are heavily used by locals at weekends. The further you get from town, the more likely you are to find a stretch to yourself. It's possible to get to Isle of Palms and Sullivan's Island using CARTA bus route #8 (Ⓦ www.ridecarta .com). If you want to stay, there are plenty of motels and **eating** places. On Isle of Palms, head for the *Sea Biscuit Café*, 21 J.C. Long Blvd (☏ 843/886-4079), which does great Southern breakfasts, and *Windjammer*, 1000 Ocean Blvd (☏ 843/886-8596), a late bar with live music at weekends. On Sullivan's Island, *Bert's*, 2209 Middle St (☏ 843/883-4924), is a friendly little bar and grill.

The sea islands

South of Charleston toward Savannah, the coastline dissolves into small, marshy islands. **Edisto Island**, south of US-17 on Hwy-174, is typical: huge live oaks festooned with great drapes of Spanish moss line the roads, beside bright green marshes with rich birdlife, and fine beaches on the seaward side. If you want to stay, there are no budget motels, but the **campground** at **Edisto Beach State Park** (☏ 843/869-2156) is near a great beach lined with palmetto trees and other semitropical plants. They have a few air-conditioned cabins which get reserved months in advance, and are rented by the week-only in summer (❸).

The largest town in the area, **BEAUFORT** (pronounced "Byoofert"), is a little twee, though its old district is lovely – offset somewhat by racial tensions and the baleful proximity of the Parris Island US Marine Base, notorious for the brutality of its training regime. Think *The Big Chill* meets Kubrick's *Full Metal Jacket*; both movies are set here. The Greyhound **bus** station is two miles north of town on US-21. The **visitor center** at 1106 Carteret St (☎843/524-3163, ⓦ www.beaufortsc.org) has details of tours around the historic district and discount coupons for the **motels** out on US-21. In town, the *Best Western Sea Island Inn*, near the water at 1015 Bay St (☎843/522-2090, ⓦ www.sea-island-inn; ❺), has nice rooms with an old-fashioned feel. For a luxurious **B&B**, head for the *Beaufort Inn*, 809 Port Republic St (☎843/521-9000, ⓦ www.beaufortinn.com; ❻), which also has a superb Low Country/New American **restaurant**. Breakfast is best (try the corned-beef hash) at *Blackstone's*, 205 Scott St (☎843/524-4330); if you're after coffee and a light meal (and a good read), there's *Firehouse Books and Espresso*, 706 Craven St (☎843/522-2665). *Ollie's by the Bay*, 822 Bay St (☎843/524-2500), has river views and great oysters. In spring and fall, Beaufort's waterfront stages a series of live gospel, jazz, and bluegrass **concerts**; check with the visitor center for schedules.

St Helena Island and Hunting Island Beach

Across the bridge to the southeast of Beaufort, **ST HELENA ISLAND**, dotted with small shrimp- and oyster-fishing communities, is among the least spoiled of the eastern sea islands. The further south you go the more gorgeous the **landscape** gets: amazing Spanish moss hangs from ancient oaks, while enormous, wide views stretch out across bright marshes. Occasionally you see what looks like a fleet of ships in the middle of a field, only to realize that in fact the boats are anchored in a small salt creek, hidden by bright green marsh reeds.

This is an area of strong **black communities**, descended from slaves, who were given parcels of land when they were freed by the Union army in February 1865; they speak a dialect known as Gullah, an Afro-English patois with many West African words. The **Gullah Institute**, in the **Penn Center Historic District** off US-21 (☎843/838-2432), houses the **school** started for freed slaves by Charlotte Forten, a black Massachusetts teacher, who remarked, "I have never seen children so eager to learn . . . the majority learn with wonderful rapidity. Many of the grown people are desirous of learning to read. It is wonderful how a people who have been so long crushed to the earth . . . can have so great a desire for knowledge, and such a capability for attaining it." The school was an important retreat for civil rights leaders in the 1960s, used by Dr Martin Luther King Jr's SCLC and others. Set back from the road is a **museum** containing fascinating old pictures of black fishermen and farmers, plus weathered tools, shrimp nets, and rattlesnake skins (Mon–Sat 11am–4pm; donation). Nearby, off US-21 and nestled among the thick Spanish moss, the ruined black **Chapel of Ease**, with seashell-adorned interior walls, was built in 1742.

There are some great **places to eat** around here. *Ultimate Eating*, 859 Sea Island Parkway (☎843/838-1314), serves nourishing Low Country and Gullah-style dishes, while at 1929 Sea Island Parkway, before the bridge across to Hunting Island, the tiny *Shrimp Shack* (March–Dec Mon–Sat from 11am; ☎843/838-2962), is a wonderful fresh **seafood** joint. Don't miss the fat, juicy shrimp burgers.

St Helena's main **beach**, at **Hunting Island State Park** on the east shore (daily dawn–dusk; $4), can get crowded, but it's simply ravishing: soft white sand, wide and gently shelving, scattered with shards of pearly shells and fringed with a mature maritime forest of palmettos, palm trees, and sea oats.

The water is incredibly warm. Pelicans come here to feed, particularly in the early morning, and the shrimp fleet sails past soon after; it's also a turtle-nesting site. You can **stay** near the beach in weather-beaten cabins backing onto a glassy lagoon full of jumping fat fish, although you need to stay at least a week in summer, and reserve about a year in advance (☎843/838-2011; ⊙). There's also the larger Hunting Island **campground**: head first to the **park office**, next to a sluggish, alligator-filled pool (Mon–Fri 9am–5pm, Sat & Sun 11am–5pm).

Georgia

Away from the bright lights of its capital Atlanta, **GEORGIA**, the largest of the Southern states, is overwhelmingly rural. Its highly indented coastline holds some beaches and towns, but mostly the state is composed of slow, easygoing settlements, where the best – and sometimes the only – way to enjoy your time is to sip iced tea and have a chat on the porch.

Settlement in Georgia, the thirteenth British colony (named after King George II), started in 1733 at **Savannah**, intended as a haven of Christian principles for poor Britons, with both alcohol and slavery banned. However, under pressure from planters, **slavery** was introduced in 1752, and by the time of the **Civil War** almost half the population were black slaves. Little fighting took place on Georgian soil until Sherman's troops marched in from Tennessee, burned Atlanta to the ground, and, in the infamous "March to the Sea," laid waste to all property on the way to the coast. The economy did successfully re-establish itself after the war, though, attracting substantial investment in the latter years of the nineteenth century.

Today, bustling **Atlanta** stands as the unofficial capital of the South. The city where **Dr Martin Luther King Jr** was born, preached, and is buried bears little relation to *Gone With the Wind* stereotypes, and its forward-looking energy is upheld as a role model for other cities with large black populations. Atlanta's main rival as a tourist destination is the **Georgia coast**, stretching south from beautiful old **Savannah** via the **sea islands** to the semitropical **Okefenokee Swamp**, inland near Florida. In the **northeast**, the **Appalachian foothills** are particularly fetching in fall, while the college town of **Athens** has a reputation for producing offbeat rock groups such as R.E.M. and the B-52's.

Getting around Georgia

Georgia's main points of interest are easily accessible, but local transportation is poor. Amtrak **trains** from Washington, DC, to New Orleans and Florida call at Atlanta and Savannah, respectively. **Bus** services in most areas are patchy and infrequent, though Atlanta has regular connections to the major cities, and several daily buses along the coast call at Savannah. Atlanta has the world's largest passenger **airport**, and Savannah has a reasonable service – but airfares between the two are high.

Atlanta

ATLANTA is a relatively young city. It only came into being in 1837, when an almost random dot on the map was named "Terminus" during plans for railroad construction. The Chattahoochee River here is not navigable, and the land poor for agriculture, but after the railroads arrived, the re-named Atlanta proved to be a crucial transportation center in the Civil War. Its new accessibility made it a good site for the huge Confederacy munitions industry – and, consequently, a major target for the Union army. In 1864 Sherman's army **burned** the city, an act immortalized in *Gone With the Wind*. Recovery after the war took just a few years: Atlanta was the archetype of the aggressive, urban, industrial "New South," championed by "**boosters**" – newspaper owners, bankers, politicians, and city leaders. Industrial giants who based themselves here included **Coca-Cola**, source of a string of philanthropic gifts to the city. Heavy **black** immigration increased its already considerable African-American population and led to the establishment of the thriving community, centered around **Auburn Avenue**, that was to produce **Martin Luther King Jr**.

Today's Atlanta is at first glance a typical large American city. The flip side of the fact that there was no great reason to put a city here is that neither are there any obvious geographical reasons to prevent it from **growing** indefinitely. Its population has reached 3.5 million, and urban sprawl is such a problem that each citizen is obliged to travel an average of 34 miles per day by car – the highest figure in the country. Cut off from each other by roaring freeways, bright lights, and an enclave mentality, its neighborhoods tend to have distinct racial identities – broadly speaking, "white flight" was to the northern suburbs, while the southern districts are predominantly black. That said, the city is undeniably progressive, with little interest in lamenting a lost Southern past. Since electing the nation's first black mayor, the late Maynard Jackson, in 1974, it has remained the most conspicuously **black-run** city in the US.

Arrival and information

The colossal **Hartsfield International Airport** (☎404/530-6600), the busiest passenger airport in the US, is ten miles south of downtown Atlanta, just inside I-285 ("the perimeter"). It marks the southern terminus of the south line of the **subway** (see below), a 15min ride from downtown, and is also served by Atlanta Airport Shuttle **buses** (daily 7am–11pm; $15 to downtown; ☎404/524-3400 or 1-800/842-2770) and Checker Cab **taxis** (☎404/351-8255; $18 to downtown).

Atlanta's **Amtrak** station, 1688 Peachtree St, is at the north end of Midtown, just under a mile north of the nearest subway station, Arts Center; catch a cab or bus #23 to connect. Greyhound **buses** arrive south of downtown at 232 Forsyth St, near the Garnett Street subway station.

Atlanta's principal **visitor center** is downtown at Pryor and Atlanta streets (Mon–Sat 10am–6pm, Sun noon–6pm; ☎404/523-2311, ⊛www.atlanta.net). The adjoining **AtlanTIX** (Tues 11am–3pm, Wed–Sat 11am–6pm, Sun noon–3pm; ☎678/318-1400, ⊛www.atlantaperforms.com) sells tickets for local events and performances, with half-price discounts available every day. Other **visitor centers** are located in the North Terminal at the **airport** (Mon–Fri 9am–9pm, Sat 9am–6pm, Sun noon–6pm) and in the Lenox Square mall in **Buckhead** (Mon–Sat 11am–5pm, Sun noon–6pm).

The city's safe, efficient **subway** system consists of two distinct lines, one east–west and one north–south; they intersect downtown at Five Points

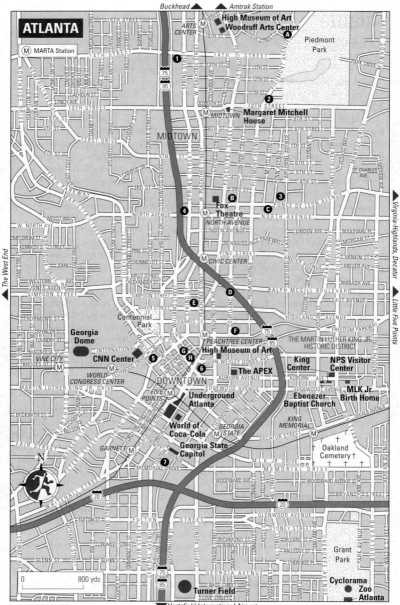

ATLANTA

Ⓜ MARTA Station

Buckhead ▲ ▲ *Amtrak Station*

High Museum of Art
Woodruff Arts Center

Piedmont Park

ARTS CENTER

Ⓐ

❶

❷ Margaret Mitchell House

MIDTOWN

Virginia-Highlands, Decatur

Fox Theatre

Ⓑ

❸

Ⓒ

❹ NORTH AVENUE

The West End

Little Five Points

CIVIC CENTER

Ⓓ

Ⓔ

Centennial Park

Ⓕ

THE MARTIN LUTHER KING JR. HISTORIC DISTRICT

Georgia Dome

CNN Center

❺

PEACHTREE CENTER

Ⓖ High Museum of Art

Ⓗ

❻ ■ The APEX

King Center

NPS Visitor Center

WORLD CONGRESS CENTER

DOWNTOWN

FIVE POINTS

Underground Atlanta

Ebenezer Baptist Church

MLK Jr. Birth Home

World of Coca-Cola

GEORGIA STATE

Georgia State Capitol

GARNETT

❼

KING MEMORIAL

Oakland Cemetery †

N

Grant Park

Cyclorama
Zoo Atlanta

0 ———— 800 yds

Turner Field

▼ *Hartsfield International Airport*

ACCOMMODATION				RESTAURANTS			
Ansley Inn	A	Quality Hotel	H	Flying Biscuit	2	Tamarind	1
Atlanta International Hostel	C	Sheraton	F	Mary Mac's Tearoom	3	Thelma's Kitchen	5
Days Inn	E	Super 8	G	Mumbo Jumbo	6	The Varsity	4
Georgian Terrace Hotel	B	Travelodge	D	Sylvia's	7		

(daily 5am–1am; daily pass $3.50, Fri–Sun pass $9, weekly pass $13). The system is run by the Metropolitan Area Rapid Transit Authority (MARTA; ☏ 404/848-5501, ⓦ www.itsmarta.com), which also operates a wide network of **buses**.

The Atlanta Preservation Center runs a varied program of ninety-minute **walking tours** of different Atlanta neighborhoods, including Sweet Auburn (with emphasis on the churches), the West End, and an architectural tour of downtown (March–Nov only, daily except Tues; $10; ☏ 404/876-2041).

Accommodation

The most economical **accommodation** options in **downtown** Atlanta are the chain hotels. So many conventioneers come to town that even these aren't particularly inexpensive, though weekend rates can be better. **Midtown** is generally cheaper, and puts you nearer the nightlife, while **Buckhead** boasts some of the swankiest hotels in the country. If you're driving into Georgia, you can save a good deal of money by picking up **discount coupons** from state visitor centers. The B&B Atlanta agency can reserve **B&B** rooms (☏ 404/875-0525 or 1-800/967-3224, ⓦ www.bedandbreakfastatlanta.com).

Ansley Inn 253 15th St ☏ 404/872-9000 or 1-800/446-5416, ⓦ www.ansleyinn.com. Lovely, friendly Midtown B&B, near Ansley Park, whose 22 rooms have stripped-wood floors, antique furnishings, wet bars, and whirlpool tubs. ❶

Atlanta International Hostel 223 Ponce de Leon Ave ☏ 404/875-9449 or 1-800/473-9449, ⓦ www.hostel-atlanta.com. Around a hundred $19 beds in male, female, and mixed dorms, in a central Midtown location close to the North Ave MARTA station. Has a pool table, kitchen, and laundry room. ❶

Days Inn – Atlanta Downtown 300 Spring St NW ☏ 404/523-1144, ⓦ www.daysinn.com. Reliable chain hotel in the heart of downtown, with restaurant and outdoor pool. ❸

Georgian Terrace Hotel 659 Peachtree St NE ☏ 404/897-1991 or 1-800/651-2316, ⓦ www.thegeorgianterracehotel.com. Stylish century-old hotel in prime Midtown location across from the Fox Theatre. Very classy rooms and suites – some bedrooms are round, offering great views – plus fine restaurants and a rooftop pool. ❻

Quality Hotel 89 Luckie St ☏ 404/524-7991 or 1-800/228-5151. Very hospitable, central downtown hotel with views of the Atlanta skyline. Rates include continental breakfast. ❸

Ritz-Carlton Buckhead 3434 Peachtree Rd NE ☏ 404/237-2700, ⓦ www.ritzcarlton.com. Exquisite, elegant hotel, one of the finest in the Ritz-Carlton group, with one of Atlanta's best haute cuisine restaurants. ❼

Sheraton Atlanta Hotel 165 Courtland St NE ☏ 404/659-6500 or 1-800/833-8624, ⓦ www.sheratonatlantahotel.com. Luxury downtown hotel with wonderful indoor pool surrounded by foliage, plus its own mini-shopping mall. ❻

Super 8 111 Cone St ☏ 404/524-7000 or 1-800/800-8000, ⓦ www.super8atlanta.com. Very atypical *Super 8*, housed in a converted downtown hotel and offering bargain rates for a great spot near Peachtree Plaza, CNN, and Underground Atlanta. ❹

Travelodge Downtown 311 Courtland St NE ☏ 404/659-4545 or 1-800/578-7878, ⓦ www.travelodge.com. Small, central motel, offering standard rooms on the east side of downtown, plus a pool. ❺

The City

Atlanta's layout is confusing, with its roads following old Native American trails rather than a logical grid. An absurd one hundred streets are named "Peachtree"; be sure to note whether you're looking for Avenue, Road, Boulevard, and so forth. The most important of the Peachtrees, **Peachtree Street**, cuts a long north–south swath through the city. Sights are scattered, but relatively easy to reach on public transportation. Most individual neighborhoods, including **downtown**, the Martin Luther King Jr Historic District (ranged along **Auburn Avenue**), and trendy **Little Five Points** and **Virginia-Highland**, are easy to explore on foot.

Downtown Atlanta

Downtown Atlanta, still centering on the railroad terminus for which the city was founded, is for the most part overshadowed by the usual anonymous big-city skyscrapers, but here and there urban spaces open up where tourists can congregate. Prime among these, and the only place open after dark, is **Underground Atlanta** (or "the Underground"), where an open piazza buzzing with street performers provides access to a four-block subterranean maze of shops, stalls, restaurants, and bars. This was the original heart of the city, effectively buried during the late nineteenth century by the construction of railroad viaducts. The underground labyrinth of cobbled gas-lit streets has in the last twenty years been restored to its original appearance and dotted with historical markers. As a revitalized showpiece, though, it has in all truth passed its prime and begun to deteriorate.

The eastern side of the piazza is dominated by the super-glossy **World of Coca-Cola** pavilion (June–Aug Mon–Sat 9am–6pm, Sun 11am–6pm; Sept–May Mon–Sat 9am–5pm, Sun noon–6pm; $6; ☏404/676-5151, Ⓦwww.woccatlanta.com). This three-story spin through Coca-Cola's history, from its origins in the non-air-conditioned nineteenth-century Hotlanta, through the evolution of the famed contour bottle to "the Real Thing," is surprisingly fun. On the third floor you can quench your thirst with Coke products from all over the world, such as Stoney Ginger Beer from South Africa or Japan's Vegita Beta.

A quarter-mile northwest of Underground Atlanta, several downtown blocks were razed prior to the 1996 Olympics to make way for the open space of **Centennial Park**. Intended as a focus for public festivities during the Games, it was immediately forced into temporary closure by the pipe-bombing that killed two revelers. Since the Olympics, the park has been re-landscaped, and is usually filled with kids in summer playing in the 25 water jets of the **Fountain of Rings**.

Across from the park's southwest corner, the **CNN Center** is the headquarters of Atlanta's very own world-spanning TV station, now the largest news broadcaster in the world. Unlike the Coke pavilion, this is a working facility – adrenalin-fueled, forty-minute **guided tours** (daily 9am–5pm, every 15min; $8) rush past frazzled producers and toothy anchorpersons – but you can videotape yourself reading the (real) news of the day ($15 in the gift shop). If you're desperate to appear on TV, time your visit to coincide with the 3pm filming of *TalkBack Live*, when you may get to join the audience.

Sweet Auburn

A mere half-mile east of downtown, **Auburn Avenue** stands as a monument to Atlanta's black history. During its heyday in the 1920s, "**Sweet Auburn**" was a prosperous, progressive area of black-owned businesses and jazz clubs, but it went into a decline with the Depression, from which, despite repeated attempts at revitalization, it has never truly recovered.

Nonetheless, several blocks have been designated as the **Martin Luther King Jr National Historic Site**, in honor of Auburn's most cherished native son. Despite the lack of official promotion by the city, this short stretch of road is the most visited attraction in the entire state of Georgia, and it's a moving experience to watch the crowds of schoolkids listening patiently to the guided tours and waiting in turn to take photographs. Head first for the Park Service's purpose-built **visitor center**, 450 Auburn Ave (daily: summer 9am–6pm; winter 9am–5pm; ☏404/331-5190, Ⓦwww.nps.gov/malu), where the "Courage To Lead" exhibition covers King's life and campaigns. If you're looking for an account of the civil rights years, the museum at Memphis is much more comprehensive (see p.584), but this provides a powerful potted summary, with alternative simplified captions for children. It ends with the mule-drawn wagon that was used in King's funeral procession in Atlanta on April 9, 1968.

As soon as you arrive at the visitor center, register for a free half-hour tour of King's **Birth Home**, a short walk east at 501 Auburn (same hours as visitor center). The lively, anecdotal tours start from Fire Station no. 6, nearby at 39 Boulevard; as only fifteen people can visit at a time, and school groups often visit en masse, you may have to settle instead for a "virtual tour," utilizing the computers at the visitor center. The home itself is a 14-room Queen Anne–style shotgun house, restored to its prosperous 1930s appearance, and now looking smarter than its neighbors. Home to Martin until he was 12, it remained in his family until 1971.

Across from the visitor center, the **King Center**, at 449 Auburn, is privately run by King's family (same hours). Chiefly an educational and research facility, it also features displays of treasured artifacts such as King's Bibles and traveling case, as well as separate rooms devoted to Mahatma Gandhi and Rosa Parks. King's mortal remains, guarded by an eternal flame, are held in a plain marble **tomb**, inscribed with the words "Free at last, free at last, thank God Almighty I'm free at last," which stands in the shallow, five-tiered Reflecting Pool outside.

Dr Martin Luther King Jr (1929–1968)

Martin Luther King Jr was born in Atlanta at 501 Auburn Avenue on January 15, 1929. The house was then home to his parents and his grandparents; both his maternal grandfather, Rev A.D. Williams, and his father, Martin Luther King Sr, served as pastor of the nearby **Ebenezer Baptist Church**. Young Martin was ordained at 19 and became co-pastor at Ebenezer with his father, but continued his studies at Crozer Theological Seminary in Pennsylvania, where he was profoundly influenced by the ideas of Mahatma Gandhi, and at Boston University.

Returning to the South, King became pastor of Dexter Avenue Baptist Church in **Montgomery**, Alabama, in 1954, where his leadership during the bus boycott a year later (see p.610) brought him to national prominence. A visit to India in 1957 further cemented his belief in non-violent resistance as the means by which racial segregation could be eradicated. He returned to Atlanta in 1960, becoming co-pastor at Ebenezer once more, but also taking on the presidency of the **Southern Christian Leadership Conference**. As such, he became the figurehead for the **civil rights** struggle, planning strategy for future campaigns, flying into each new trouble spot, and commenting to the news media on every latest development. His apotheosis in that role came in August 1963, when he addressed the **March on Washington** with his famous "I Have a Dream" speech. He was awarded the Nobel Peace Prize in 1964.

Despite King's passionate espousal of non-violence, J. Edgar Hoover's **FBI** branded him "the most dangerous and effective Negro leader in the country," and persistently attempted to discredit him over his personal life. King himself became more overtly politicized in his final years. Challenged by the stridency of Malcolm X and the radicalism of urban black youth, he came to see the deprivation and poverty of the cities of the North as affecting black and white alike, and only solvable by tackling "the triple evils of racism, extreme materialism, and militarism." In the South, he had always been able to appeal to the federal government as an (albeit often reluctant) ally; now, having declared his opposition to the war in **Vietnam**, he faced a sterner and lonelier struggle. In any event, his **Poor People's Campaign** had barely got off the ground before King was assassinated in Memphis on April 4, 1968.

Next door, the **Ebenezer Baptist Church**, where King's funeral took place – and where his mother was assassinated while playing the organ in 1974 – has been converted into another museum (Mon–Sat 9am–5pm, Sun 1–5pm), staffed by volunteers eager to share their memories. It's now only used for special occasions, while its congregation has decamped to a much larger church alongside the visitor center.

Midtown

Midtown stretches from Ponce de Leon Avenue, lined with funky restaurants, to 26th Street. In recent years, it has become dominated by massive cutting-edge skyscrapers – look out for the spiky, futuristic **One Atlantic Center**, at 15th and Peachtree streets, designed by Philip Johnson and John Burgee. The wildly flamboyant Art Deco **Fox Theatre**, 660 Peachtree St, at Ponce de Leon (☎404/881-2100, Ⓦwww.foxtheatre.org), with its strong Moorish theme, should also not be missed. Unless you buy a ticket for one of its fairly mainstream theatrical shows, the only way to see the theater is on an organized tour (Mon, Wed & Thurs 10am, Sat 10am & 11am; $10; call to confirm ☎404/688-3353).

Three blocks north of the theater, the only ordinary brick home left on Peachtree Street, at no. 990, has survived because of its status as the **Margaret Mitchell House** (daily 9.30am–5pm; $12; ☎404/249-7015, Ⓦwww.gwtw .org). Mitchell and her husband were living in the small basement apartment she called "the dump" during the ten years she took to write the best-selling novel of all time, *Gone With the Wind*. Published in 1936, it took just six weeks to sell enough copies to form a tower fifty times higher than the Empire State Building; the 1939 movie version scaled further peaks of popularity. Guided tours and various exhibits tell the whole fascinating story. After a compulsory hard-sell interval in the gift store, you can then see more memorabilia in the separate but linked **movie museum** (same hours and ticket).

A little further up Peachtree, at no. 1280, the huge **Woodruff Arts Center**, designed by Richard Meier, holds Atlanta's **High Museum of Art** (Tues–Sat 10am–5pm, Sun noon–5pm; $8, free Thurs after 1pm; ☎404/773-4444, Ⓦwww.high.org). As well as excellent contemporary and non-Western exhibitions – particularly strong on African art – the museum has a good gift shop, and a peaceful little espresso bar in the airy atrium.

Buckhead

North of Midtown, the affluent, predominantly white suburb of **Buckhead** is a trendy area of glitzy, youthful malls and swanky hotels. Within the space of two and a half blocks of Peachtree at Paces Ferry Road, celebrity residents such as (occasionally) Elton John can enjoy over a hundred top-quality restaurants. For those who have the money to enjoy it, this is the city's premier **nightlife** and **shopping** district, even if it's short on must-see attractions.

Tucked away a short distance west of central Buckhead, the permanent exhibits at the superb **Atlanta History Center**, 130 W Paces Ferry Rd (Mon–Sat 10am–5.30pm, Sun noon–5.30pm; $12; ☎404/814-4000, Ⓦwww.atlantahistorycentre.com), focus on two main aspects. One section covers Atlanta history in exhaustive detail, with fascinating old photos and movie footage; black and women's history is well-represented, though there's very little on Dr King. Several other rooms display a remarkable collection of Civil War artifacts; even if the military minutiae don't captivate you, the human stories surely will, and the whole combines to provide a clear year-by-year history of the war, albeit with a definite leaning towards the Confederate cause. You can also tour two houses in the extensive grounds: the ponderous 1920s mock-classical **Swan House**, a mansion, and the antebellum **Tullie Smith Farm** and garden.

The West End

The **West End**, Atlanta's oldest quarter, is a slightly shabby but slowly reviving district southwest of downtown. Historically a black residential area, it remains so today: a buzzy, more upbeat counterpoint to Sweet Auburn. Here, you'll find Georgia's only museum dedicated to African-American and Haitian art, the **Hammonds House**, 503 Peeples St (Tues–Fri 10am–6pm, Sat & Sun 1–5pm; $2; Ⓦ www.hammondshouse.org), as well as the 1910 Beaux Arts **Herndon Home**, 587 University Place (Tues–Sat 10am–4pm; $5; Ⓦ www.herndon-home.org), which was designed and lived in by Alonzo Herndon, a former slave who became a barber, founded the Atlanta Life Insurance Company (from 1920 to 1980 the nation's largest black-owned business), and went on to become the city's first black millionaire.

You can also visit the **Wren's Nest**, at 1050 R.D. Abernathy Blvd, the former home of Joel Chandler Harris, the (white) author of *Br'er Rabbit* (Tues–Sat 10am–2pm; $7). The house has been open to visitors since soon after Harris died in 1908, and remains much as he left it, complete with a stuffed owl given to him by President Theodore Roosevelt. A short film explains that he first heard the Uncle Remus stories from slaves, when he trained as a printer on a plantation newspaper. Occasional storytelling sessions take place in the peaceful, untamed garden.

Grant Park

A mile southeast of downtown, **Grant Park** – named for a Confederate defender of Atlanta, not the victorious Union general – is home to two neighboring attractions. A purpose-built theater houses the **Cyclorama**, a huge circular painting depicting the Civil War Battle of Atlanta, executed by a group of German and Polish artists in 1885–86. Cycloramas used to travel around the country as entertainment in the days before movies; you sit inside the circle of the painting while the whole auditorium slowly rotates. It makes an especially impressive spectacle because, in part to mask deterioration of the canvas, a 3D diorama has been constructed in front that makes it hard to see where the painting ends and the mannequins begin. An accompanying **museum** treats the war from the viewpoint of the average soldier, interspersing distressing statistics with photos and memorabilia (daily: summer 9.20am–5.30pm; rest of year 9.20am–4.30pm; $6).

The adjacent **Zoo Atlanta** features a pair of giant pandas from Chengdu, 23 gorillas, and several orangutans, plus re-creations of African rainforests and other habitats (daily: summer 9am–6.30pm; rest of year 9.30am–5.30pm; $16.50; Ⓦ www.zooatlanta.org).

Little Five Points to Emory University

Northeast of Auburn Avenue, around Euclid and Moreland avenues, the youthful **Little Five Points** district is the center of Atlanta's alternative community, a tangle of thrift stores, secondhand record stores, funky restaurants, body-piercing and branding parlors, bars, and clubs. By way of contrast, just a few blocks north at 1 Copenhill Ave, on the hill where Sherman is said to have watched Atlanta burn, the **Jimmy Carter Presidential Library and**

Museum is devoted to the peanut farmer who rose to become Georgia state governor and the 39th president of the USA. In addition to viewing film footage and a reconstruction of his Oval Office, you can read 12-year-old Jimmy's school essay on health, in which he earnestly urges his readers to keep their teeth clean (Mon–Sat 9am–4.45pm, Sun noon–4.45pm; $5; Ⓦwww.jimmycarterlibrary.org).

Northeast of here, beyond the yuppie **Virginia–Highland** restaurant district, the trek to **Emory University**'s campus is rewarded by the stylish, airy **Michael C. Carlos Museum**, 571 S Kilgo St (Tues, Wed, Fri & Sat 10am–5pm, Thurs 10am–9pm, Sun noon–5pm; $5 donation; Ⓣ404/727-4282, Ⓦcarlos.emory .edu), which has a huge collection of fine art and antiquities from all six inhabited continents. Sub-Saharan African art is unusually well-represented, including Nigerian headcrests woven with snake-like tendrils; among the extraordinary pre-Columbian collection, note the Andean *Human as a Peanut*.

Stone Mountain

Half an hour's drive east of Atlanta's city center, **Stone Mountain State Park** is arrayed around the base of what's said to be the world's largest natural granite dome, a full five miles in circumference. One face of this outcrop holds a massive **bas-relief sculpture**, measuring 90ft by 190ft, and depicting Confederates Jefferson Davis, Robert E. Lee, and Stonewall Jackson. Started in 1924 by Gutzon Borglum, who went on to carve Mount Rushmore in South Dakota (see p.864), the sculpture was not completed until 1970. For most visitors, however, the carving is just one feature of what's become an all-around family destination. You can see it if you simply pay the $7 per vehicle fee to drive into the park, but paying an additional, steep fee of $23 per adult or $17 per child aged 3–11 (reduced to $12 for everyone after 4pm) entitles you to a host of other attractions and activities. These include a 30min **train ride** around the mountain; **paddlewheel** and **pedal-boat** rides on the nearby lake; two **mini-golf** courses; and the Crossroads **theme park**, which features a "4D" movie theater and various hokey countrified stalls and diners. It's also possible to **hike** up the mountain on a 45min trail, or ride a skylift to the top. The park itself is open daily 6am to midnight, with the major paying attractions 10am to 8pm in spring and summer, 10am to 5pm in fall and winter. Contact Ⓣ770/498-5690 or Ⓦwww.stonemountainpark.com for full details.

Eating

Atlanta has scores of good **restaurants** to suit all budgets. Most of the downtown options close down fairly early and are quite upmarket, while Buckhead is even glitzier. Southern **soul food** is best around Auburn Avenue, and **vegetarians** can get plenty of choice in Little Five Points and Virginia–Highland.

Atlanta Fish Market 265 Pharr Rd NE Ⓣ404/262-3165. Buckhead's top seafood specialist, at the sign of the giant fish, with ultra-fresh oysters and crabs; dinner can get expensive, but lunch (daily except Sun) is great value.
Buckhead Diner 3073 Piedmont Rd, at E Paces Ferry Ⓣ404/262-3336. Glitzy postmodern diner, always packed with locals enjoying Southern food with a (frequently Asian) twist, like crab egg rolls, stuffed grits, or veal and wild mushroom meatloaf. No reservations taken, so expect a wait.

Café Sunflower 2140 Peachtree Rd Ⓣ404/352-8859. Friendly, classy, good-value vegetarian restaurant on the southern fringes of Buckhead. Tasty stir-fried tofu and pad Thai noodles, several "mock chicken" dishes, delicious steamed dumplings, and amazing dairy-free desserts. Closed Sun.
DeKalb Farmers' Market 3000 E Ponce de Leon Ave Ⓣ404/377-6400. This enormous indoor market, 20 minutes' drive east of downtown towards Stone Mountain, is the perfect spot for a take-out

lunch. Stalls sell goat stew, tofu stir-fry, and glazed duck; other goodies include fresh farm-fattened catfish and pretty blue crabs, as well as aromatic coffees from around the world.

Doc Chey's Noodle House 1424 N Highland Ave ℡404/888-0777. Plain but friendly Virginia-Highland noodle joint, serving bargain-priced Asian food that also includes rice and soup dishes. There's also a spacious patio.

Fat Matt's Rib Shack 1811 Piedmont Ave ℡404/607-1622. Atlanta's best barbecue, halfway between Midtown and Buckhead, plus live blues at 8pm nightly. It makes little difference if you choose a plateful of juicy pork or chicken, or a "sandwich" (a slab of ribs piled on a slab of bread) – everything here is delicious.

Flying Biscuit 1001 Piedmont Ave ℡404/874-8887. Jazzed-up café/diner at lively Midtown intersection, renowned locally for its healthy/organic breakfasts in particular, but also serving medium-priced New American lunches and dinners, all with a Southern twist. Also in a smaller location near Little Five Points, at 1655 McLendon Ave NE (℡404/687-8888).

Harvest 853 N Highland Ave NE ℡404/876-8244. Appealing, flavorful "inspired regional cuisine," such as cornbread-crusted chicken or cane sugar pork loin, served for lunch and dinner in a bright, characterful frame house in the heart of Virginia-Highland.

Mary Mac's Tearoom 224 Ponce de Leon Ave ℡404/876-1800. Cute little Midtown restaurant, straight out of the 1940s, famous for its cheap traditional Southern cuisine. Mon–Sat 11am–8.30pm, Sun 11am–3pm.

Mumbo Jumbo 89 Park Place NE ℡404/523-0330. Very chic downtown restaurant at Woodruff Park, offering Tuscan/American cuisine, with an open kitchen and a bar full of posers. Dinner nightly, lunch weekdays only.

Nava 3060 Peachtree Rd NW ℡404/240-1984. Spicy, imaginative modern Southwestern food, plus mighty margaritas, in glitzy Buckhead surroundings, with a great outdoor terrace. Dinner nightly, lunch weekdays only.

Roy's Buckhead 3475 Piedmont Rd NE ℡404/231-3232. Very fancy outlet, just west of central Buckhead, for Roy Yamaguchi's delicious "Hawaiian Fusion Cuisine." Dinner entrees like the fabulous misoyaki butterfish or grilled filet mignon cost around $25, though lunch works out cheaper. Dinner nightly, lunch weekdays only.

Sylvia's 241 Central SW ℡404/529-9692. This classy downtown affiliate of the legendary Harlem restaurant is a must if you're in the mood for soul food. Live jazz Fri & Sat, gospel brunch Sun.

Tamarind 80 14th St NW ℡404/873-4888. Stylish Midtown Thai place with a great selection of flavorful dishes. Dinner nightly, lunch weekdays only.

Thelma's Kitchen 768 Marietta St NW ℡404/688-5855. Inexpensive downtown soul-food institution; try the salmon and grits for breakfast, and, of course, fried chicken for lunch. Mon–Fri 7.30am–4.30pm, Sat 8am–3pm.

The Varsity 61 North Ave NW ℡404/881-1706. Vast, packed Midtown fast-food drive-in diner: a true Fifties throwback, with chili dogs at $1.50. Open until at least 11.30pm nightly.

Nightlife

Atlanta is a place where you can have a very good time; budget for blowing some money hopping between its bars and clubs. The main concentrations are in the overlapping yuppie **Virginia-Highland** and punky **Little Five Points**, and the more upmarket **Midtown**, the center of Atlanta's thriving **gay and lesbian** scene. **Buckhead** can be a lot of fun if you've got bags of cash. Major venues for touring acts include the *Tabernacle* at Centennial Park, 152 Luckie St (℡404/659-2022), and the *Variety Playhouse*, 1099 Euclid Ave, in Little Five Points (℡404/659-2022, ⓦwww.variety-playhouse.com). Up-to-the-minute listings can be found in the free weekly *Creative Loafing* (ⓦwww.creativeloafing.com).

Blind Willie's 828 N Highland Ave NE ℡404/873-2583. The best blues venue in town, with appearances by major artists, this Virginia-Highland hangout is also a lively bar. Daily 8pm–late.

Eddie's Attic 515B N McDonough St, Decatur ℡404/377-4976, ⓦwww.eddiesattic.com. Nightly acoustic music, from traditional fiddlers to contemporary singer-songwriters, plus occasional stand-up comedy.

Euclid Avenue Yacht Club 1136 Euclid Ave NE ℡404/688-2582. Classic neighborhood bar in Little Five Points, which also dishes up fine pork barbecue and Brunswick stew.

Manuel's Tavern 602 N Highland Ave NE ℡404/525-3447. Relaxed, studenty neighborhood bar-cum-restaurant near the Carter Center. Wooden benches, ceiling fans, and portraits of Jack Kennedy – plus the occasional presence of Jimmy himself.

Masquerade 695 North Ave NE ☎404/577-8178, Ⓦwww.masq.com. Groovy grunge/punk hangout in a converted Midtown mall, split into rooms done up as Heaven, Hell, and Purgatory, with a big outdoor auditorium. Live bands Wed–Sun.

Star Community Bar 437 Moreland Ave NE ☎404/681-9018. Enjoyable Little Five Points watering hole, in a former bank bursting with Elvis memorabilia, and offering live music Wed–Sat. Cover charge. Closed Sun.

North from Atlanta: the mountains

Some spectacular **Appalachian mountain scenery** – at its best in October, when the leaves turn a brilliant red and gold – lies just a short drive from Atlanta. A drive through the mountains on the secondary roads takes you through endless hairpins and narrow passes; Hwy-348 ascends a particularly impressive pass at the White County line, crossed at the top by the **Appalachian Trail**. Of the various towns and villages, **Dahlonega** makes the best base; most of the rest – like **Helen**, 35 miles northeast, now a pseudo-Bavarian village – are either kitsch or downright dull. The region does, however, abound in delightful **state parks**, several of which offer both camping and hotel-style lodges.

Dahlonega

The attractive small town of **DAHLONEGA**, in the Appalachian foothills fifty miles northeast of Atlanta on US-19, owes its origins to the first-ever **Gold Rush** in the US. Benjamin Parks discovered gold at Auraria, six miles south, in 1828; Dahlonega was established five years later, to serve as the seat of Lumpkin County. Within another five years, enough gold had been unearthed for Dahlonega to acquire its own outpost of the US Mint, which, by the time production was terminated by the Civil War, had produced over $6 million of gold coin. The whole saga is recounted by videos and displays in the **Gold Museum**, housed in the handsome former courthouse on the main square (Mon–Sat 9am–5pm, Sun 10am–5pm; $3; ☎706/864-2257). You can also pan for gold at various small mines in the area, although you're unlikely to make your fortune. In the third week of June, the town hosts one of Appalachia's biggest annual **bluegrass** festivals, while October sees the **Gold Rush Days**, a real downhome hoedown, with food, crafts, clogging, and music.

Dahlonega's **visitor center** is across from the courthouse (daily 9am–5.30pm; ☎706/864-3711 or 1-800/231-5543, Ⓦwww.dahlonega.org). The *Smith House*, just down from the square at 84 S Chestatee St (☎706/867-7000 or 1-800/852-9577, Ⓦwww.smithhouse.com), is a classic Southern **restaurant**, serving superb all-you-care-to-eat meals at low prices, and also offering comfortable double **rooms** (❹).

Amicalola Falls State Park

Twenty miles west of Dahlonega on Hwy-52, **Amicalola Falls State Park** (daily 7am–10pm; $2 per vehicle; ☎706/265-4703) focuses on a dramatic multi-tiered waterfall that cascades down a steep wooded hillside. Having driven to the overlook at the top, continue for another half-mile to reach the park's modern **lodge** (☎706/265-8888 or 1-800/573-9656, Ⓦwww.amicalolafalls.com; ❹), which holds comfortable double rooms and a restaurant with panoramic views. For even more seclusion, hike for five miles from here toward the start of the **Appalachian Trail**, to reach the irresistible *Len Foote Hike Inn* (☎770/389-7275 or 1-800/864-7275, ⓦwww.hike-inn.com; ➏), accessible only on foot, which offers basic rooms, with two bunk beds in each, and serves breakfast and dinner family-style, included in the overnight rates. You can also **camp** ($15) or stay in individual guest cabins (➍) closer to the park entrance.

Athens

The small and very likeable city of **ATHENS**, almost seventy miles northeast of Atlanta, is home to the 30,000-plus students of the University of Georgia, and has a liberal feel – and city government – that's unusual for the South. Its compact downtown area north of the campus is alive with book and record stores, clubs, bars, restaurants, and cafés; **Broad Street** in particular is lined with sidewalk tables.

Although Athens may hold little in terms of conventional tourist attractions, it has become internationally famed as the home of rock groups such as R.E.M., Widespread Panic, and the B-52's. R.E.M. started out playing at the *40 Watt Club*, originally housed at 171 College Ave, but repeatedly relocated until it found its sixth, and largest, premises in 1990 at 285 W Washington St (☎706/549-7871, ⓦwww.40watt.com), where it continues to host an eclectic program of gigs. The biggest music names tend to appear at the *Georgia Theatre*, 215 N Lumpkin St (☎706/353-3405, ⓦwww.georgiatheatre.com), a converted movie theater that still shows films on quiet nights, while up-and-coming bands can be heard at the *Caledonia Lounge*, 256 W Clayton St (☎706/549-5577, ⓦwww.caledonialounge.com). The free weekly *Flagpole* (ⓦwww.flagpole.com) carries full **music listings**.

Practicalities

From Atlanta, Greyhound arrives at 220 W Broad St; the Athens Transit System operates **buses** around town (every 30min; 75¢ flat fare). The **visitor center** is situated in the city's oldest surviving home, the 1820 Church-Waddel-Brumby House, a couple of blocks north of campus at 280 E Dougherty St (Mon–Sat 10am–6pm, Sun noon–6pm; ☎706/353-1820, ⓦwww.visitathensga.com). They can provide an excellent self-guided **walking tour** on local music history, while a good 90min bus tour of historic Athens leaves daily at 2pm ($10; ☎706/208-8687).

Lodging can be a problem during graduation or when there's a big football game. Otherwise, choices include the good-value, business-oriented *Courtyard by Marriott*, 166 Finley St (☎706/369-7000 or 1-800/321-2211, ⓦwww.courtyard.com/ahncy; ➍); the trusty *Holiday Inn Downtown*, 197 E Broad St (☎706/549-4433 or 1-800/862-8436, ⓦwww.hi-athens.com; ➍); or the seven-room *Magnolia Terrace* B&B, 277 Hill St (☎706/548-3860, ⓦwww.bbonline.com/ga/magnoliaterrace; ➍).

As for **food**, R.E.M. devotees will want to head straight for the original home of their **Automatic for the People** album title – *Weaver D's* soul-food café, a short walk east of downtown at 1016 E Broad St (☎706/353-7797), which serves delicious fried chicken and vegetables. The *Grit*, similarly close to downtown on the northwest side, at 199 Prince Ave (☎706/543-6592), offers tasty, inexpensive vegetarian dishes, while the central *Five Star Day Café*, 229 E Broad St (☎706/543-8552), is a funky little place with a cheap but wide-ranging menu. Athens has a thriving **bar** scene, although Georgia's blue laws require drinks-only bars to close on Sundays.

Central Georgia

South of Atlanta, the broad expanse of **central Georgia** is famous more for its people than for places to see. **Otis Redding**, **James Brown**, **Little Richard**, and the **Allman Brothers** were all born here or grew up in the area, while former president **Jimmy Carter** came from little Plains, roughly 120 miles due south of the capital.

Few of the small towns hold much interest, though vegetable fanatics may enjoy tiny **Juliette**, twenty miles north of Macon, where the *Whistle Stop Café* dishes up the fried green tomatoes of book and movie fame (℡478/992-8886; Tues & Sun 11am–4pm, Wed–Sat 11am–7pm), and **Vidalia** further east, the "Sweet Onion Capital of the World." The largest communities are Columbus, a dull army center, and likeable **Macon**.

Macon

MACON, eighty miles southeast of Atlanta on I-75, where I-16 branches off to the coast, makes an attractive stop en route to Savannah, especially when its 280,000 **cherry trees** erupt with frothy blossoms (celebrated by a festival in the third week of March). As the highest navigable point on the **Ocmulgee River**, Macon was laid out in 1823 and became a major cotton port. Although downtown is no longer the commercial center it once was, particularly since the Colonial Mall Macon appeared near the intersection of the two freeways, signs of urban renewal are everywhere.

Macon was home to **Little Richard**, **Otis Redding**, and the **Allman Brothers**, while **James Brown** recorded his first smash, the epoch-making "Please Please Please," in an unlikely looking mansion at 830 Mulberry St. Otis is commemorated by a bronze statue next to the frankly unremarkable Otis Redding Memorial Bridge, just east of downtown, while his daughter Karla still runs an upscale shoe store downtown. Duane Allman and Berry Oakley, killed here in motorcycle smashes in 1971 and 1972, respectively, are buried in **Rose Hill Cemetery** on Riverside Drive, the inspiration for several of the band's songs. That heritage is celebrated in the exuberant **Georgia Music Hall of Fame**, next door to the visitor center (see below) at Martin Luther King Jr Blvd and Walnut St (Mon–Sat 9am–5pm, Sun 1–5pm; $8; ℡478/750-8555, ⓦwww.gamusichall.com). A huge roster of Georgian musicians are recalled via themed interactive displays that include a gospel chapel, a rock'n'roll soda shop, and a country café. As well as admiring Redding's trademark black sweater and the B-52s' wigs, you can watch footage of Ray Charles singing "Georgia on My Mind" to the state legislature, inspect a photo of James Brown confiding to the pope that he feels like a sex machine, and listen to 75 years' worth of jukebox recordings.

Ocmulgee National Monument

Between 900 and 1100 AD, people of the Mississippian culture, the predominant Native American group in the South at this time, migrated from the Mississippi Valley to a spot a couple of miles east of modern downtown Macon, where they leveled the site overlooking the Ocmulgee River that is now **Ocmulgee National Monument** (daily 9am–5pm; free; ⓦwww.nps.gov /ocmu). Their settlement of thatched huts has vanished, though two grassy mounds, each thought to have been topped by a temple, still rise prominently from the plateau. Near the visitor center, which holds artifacts from excavations in the area, you can enter the underground chamber of a ceremonial

△ Mississippi Delta cotton fields

earthlodge. Modern wooden supports now hold up the roof, replacing the original timbers whose fiery destruction baked the clay floor, thereby preserving a ring of individually molded seats, and a striking bird-shaped altar or dais. Native American performers and crafts workers come to the monument in late September each year for the annual **Ocmulgee Indian Celebration**.

Practicalities

Macon's **visitor center**, in the imposing Terminal Station at the foot of Cherry Street (Mon–Sat 9am–5.30pm; ☎478/743-3401 or 1-800/768-3401, ⓦ www.maconga.org), is also the base for guided **trolley tours** and visits to the major attractions ($14).

Greyhound pulls into town at 65 Spring St, where Little Richard is said to have written "Tutti Frutti" while washing dishes. The best **accommodation** is downtown: for old-fashioned southern hospitality, head for the grand *1842 Inn*, 353 College St (☎478/741-1842, ⓦ www.the1842inn.com; ❼), which offers a full Southern breakfast in its lovely courtyard. Otherwise, *Scottish Inns*, 1044 Riverside Drive (☎478/746-3561; ❷), is the best budget option.

As for **food**, the atmospheric, wood-paneled *Len Berg's*, 240 Old Post Office Alley, off Walnut St (☎478/742-9255), has been serving downhome Southern lunches at bargain prices for almost a century. *Bert's*, downtown at 442 Cherry St (☎478/742-9100; closed Sun), is a nice little place where the food ranges from cheap Greek feta burgers at lunch to pricey wasabi tuna at dinner. For a true Southern **barbecue** experience, drive 45min north of town on US-23 to *Fresh Air Barbecue*, near Jackson (☎478/775-3182); it's a roadside shack serving pork that's been hickory-smoked for 24 hours, along with succulent Brunswick stew and crisp coleslaw.

Popular places to hear **live music** in Macon include *River Front Bluez*, 550 Riverside Drive (☎478/741-9970; Wed–Sun), and the jazz-oriented *Trio Lounge*, 430 Cherry St (☎478/743-8746; Wed–Sat).

Savannah

American towns don't come much more beautiful than **SAVANNAH**, seventeen miles up the Savannah River from the ocean, on the border with South Carolina. The ravishing **historic district**, ranged around Spanish-moss-swathed garden squares, formed the core of the original city, and today boasts examples of just about every architectural style of the eighteenth and nineteenth centuries. The atmospheric cobbled **waterfront** on the Savannah River, key to the postwar economy, is edged by towering old cotton warehouses.

Savannah was founded in 1733 by James Oglethorpe as the first settlement of the new British colony of Georgia. His intention was to establish a haven for debtors, with no Catholics, lawyers, or hard liquor – and, above all, no slaves. However, with the arrival of North Carolinian settlers in the 1750s, plantation agriculture, based on slave labor, thrived. The town became a major export center, at the end of important railroad lines by which **cotton** was funneled from far away in the South. General Sherman arrived here in December 1864 at the end of his "March to the Sea"; he offered the town to Abraham Lincoln as a Christmas gift, but at Lincoln's urging left it intact and set to work apportioning land to freed slaves. This was the first recognition of the need for "reconstruction," though such concrete economic provision for slaves was rarely to occur again.

After the Civil War, the plantations floundered; cotton prices slumped, and Savannah went into decline. There was little industry beyond the port, and as that fell into disuse and decay, so too did Savannah's graceful townhouses and tree-lined boulevards. Not until the 1960s did local citizens start to organize what has been, on the whole, the successful restoration of their town – recently, and tentatively, extended to the predominantly black **Victorian District**, southeast of the Historic District. In the last decade, the private **Savannah College of Art and Design** (SCAD) has injected Savannah with even more vitality, attracting a population of lively young artists and regenerating downtown even further by buying up a number of wonderful old buildings.

Savannah acquired notoriety in the mid-1990s thanks to its starring role in John Berendt's best-selling *Midnight in the Garden of Good and Evil*; both book

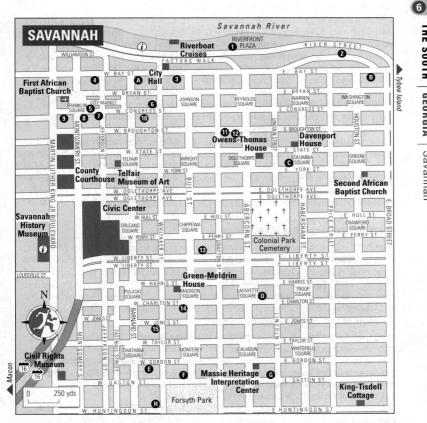

ACCOMMODATION				RESTAURANTS & BARS					
17 Hundred 90	C	Hamilton-Turner		45 Bistro	12	Huey's	1	Mrs Wilkes'	
Bed and Breakfast		Inn	D	Bistro Savannah	7	Lady and Sons	6	Boarding House	15
Inn	E	Magnolia Place	H	Club One	4	Mercury		Nita's Place	11
Days Inn	A	The Mulberry	B	Gallery Espresso	13	Lounge	10	Rail Pub	9
The Gastonian	G	Savannah Hostel		Garibaldi	8	Moon River		Savannah Blues	5
The Granite Steps	F	& Pension	I	Gryphon	14	Brewing Co.	3	Shrimp Factory	2

and movie detailed a delicious brew of cross-dressing, voodoo, and murder. For a sense of what goes on behind closed doors in the city, it's an unbeatable read, and locals still delight in making dark hints as to how much they knew, or even did, themselves. If you want to look behind the closed doors for yourself, however, few locations in "The Book" – as it's universally known – are open to the public, and none is likely to satisfy your curiosity.

Arrival, information, and getting around

Savannah's **airport** is eight miles west of the city; from there, a taxi to downtown costs around $24. The **bus station** is on the western edge of downtown at 610 W Oglethorpe Ave, while the **train station** is about three miles southwest, at 2611 Seaboard Coastline Drive. The latter isn't served by buses; a taxi from the station to downtown usually costs about $10.

The historic district is best explored on foot, but if you want to get further out, Chatham Area Transit (CAT; ⓦwww.catchacat.org) operates a reasonable **bus** network (75¢) and a free **trolley** service that runs between downtown, the visitor center, the waterfront, and the City Market. Route maps are available from the **visitor center**, 301 Martin Luther King Jr Blvd (Mon–Fri 8.30am–5pm, Sat & Sun 9am–5pm; ☏912/944-0455, ⓦwww.savannahvisit .com), along with direct phones to various hotels and tour companies. The center also sells $8 passes that entitle visitors to unlimited **parking** at certain city meters and garages for two days. There's another small tourist information office at River Street on the waterfront (daily 10am–10pm).

The main visitor center can provide details of countless **walking tours**, and serves as the starting point for several different **trolley tours**, costing from around $19. The best **black heritage tours** are run by the Civil Rights Museum (see p.564). For $19 or so, you can join leisurely **horse–and– carriage tours**; they set off from the City Market every 20 to 30min. **Riverboat cruises** start from behind City Hall (from $15; ☏912/232-6404).

Accommodation

Ideally, if you're staying in Savannah you're staying in the **Historic District**, which is packed with gorgeous **B&Bs** (and a few nice hotels). For those on a tight budget there's a **hostel**, with the usual chain **motels** near the Greyhound station and further out on Ogeechee Road (US-17). The nearest **campground** is six miles southeast, at Skidaway Island State Park (from $20; ☏1-800/864-7275), a barrier or "sea" island that features an interesting combination of salt- and freshwater habitats.

17 Hundred 90 307 E President St ☏912/236-7122, ⓦwww.17hundred90.com. The oldest inn in town, said to be haunted, with an atmospheric bar and elegant restaurant. Rooms are small, but many come with original brick fireplaces. ❺

Bed and Breakfast Inn 117 W Gordon St ☏1-888/238-0518, ⓦwww.savannahbnb.com. Great-value B&B, in two 1853 townhouses overlooking shady Chatham Square – reservations are essential. ❹

Days Inn 201 W Bay St ☏912/236-4440, ⓦwww.daysinn.com. Though it lacks the character of the B&Bs, this is an affordable, central choice. ❹

Hamilton-Turner Inn 330 Abercorn St ☏912/233-1833 or 1-888/448-8849, ⓦwww.hamilton-turnerinn.com. Charming 1873 French Second Empire–style B&B on Lafayette Square; it was also once owned by "Mandy" from "The Book." ❼

Magnolia Place 503 Whitaker St ☏912/236-7674 or 1-800/238-7674, ⓦwww .magnoliaplaceinn.com. Exquisite B&B in a fine old building overlooking leafy Forsyth Park; friendly staff, huge rooms, afternoon teas, and gourmet breakfasts served in the pretty patio, on the vast porch, or in the comfortable lounge. ❼

The Mulberry 601 E Bay St ☎912/238-1200, ⓦwww.savannahhotel.com. Friendly *Holiday Inn*–owned hotel with a B&B feel (free iced tea and cookies in the lounge). Rooftop Jacuzzi, pool, courtyard, and luxurious riverview rooms. ❼

Savannah Hostel and Pension 304 E Hall St ☎912/236-7744. Hostel in a historic Victorian District building. Dorm beds $21 (March–Oct only) and several basic private rooms. Call ahead in winter. ❶–❷

The Town

Savannah's **historic district** is flanked by the river, Martin Luther King Jr Boulevard to the west, and, to the east, Broad Street, the old commercial main street, now a series of boarded-up stores and offices. Broughton Street has since become the main thoroughfare of downtown Savannah. You can get an overview at the **Savannah History Museum**, behind the visitor center in the restored Railroad Station at 303 Martin Luther King Jr Blvd (Mon–Fri 8.30am–5pm, Sat & Sun 9am–5pm; $4), where an informative jaunt through Native American culture, colonial development, the river, and the Civil War is let down slightly by a slide show that is less a history lesson than a hard-sell promotion of Savannah's considerable charms.

The best way to get a feel for the place is simply to wander the "tabby" streets – made from a kind of primitive concrete mashed up with oyster shells – lined with shuttered Federal, Regency, and antebellum houses adorned with intricate iron balconies, and intriguing details such as false "earthquake decorations." These sturdy iron rods embedded in the walls served no purpose, but were placed there simply to keep up with elegant South Carolina neighbor Charleston in architectural cachet. The lush subtropical **greenery** is as stunning as the buildings, creeping its way through the ornate railings, cracking open the sidewalk, casting cool shadows, and filling the air with its warm, sensual scent. More than twenty shady residential **garden squares**, ablaze with Spanish-moss-tangled dogwood trees, azaleas, and creamy magnolias, offer peaceful respite from the blistering summer heat. Each one has its own personality and its own monument in the center. Forrest Gump told his life story from a bench in **Chippewa Square**, but eager movie-buffs will find instead an imposing statue of James Oglethorpe, and no such bench.

In between strolling and sitting, most visitors take in one or two of Savannah's old **mansions**, such as English architect William Jay's Regency-style **Owens-Thomas House**, 124 Abercorn St (tours Mon noon–5pm, Tues–Sat 10am–5pm, Sun 2–5pm; $8) – Jay was just 24 when he designed this extraordinarily elegant place. The first restoration project of the Historic Savannah Foundation, the Georgian **Davenport House**, nearby at 324 E State St (Mon–Sat 10am–4pm, Sun 1–4pm; $5), boasts a wonderful elliptical staircase and delicate plasterwork. The **Green–Meldrim House**, on Madison Square (Tues, Thurs & Fri 10am–4pm, Sat 10am–1pm; $5), is a splendid Gothic Revival mansion which General Sherman used as his headquarters. Its dramatic ironwork is a rare example of pre–Civil War craftsmanship; most iron in Savannah was melted down during the Civil War, and many of the balconies and railings you see today are later copies.

At the southern edge of the Historic District, on Calhoun Square, the **Massie Heritage Interpretation Center**, 207 E Gordon St (Mon–Fri 9am–4pm; $3), is housed in Savannah's first public elementary school. Today, it's a simple, effective museum, illuminating Savannah's architecture with displays on its city plan, its neighborhoods and growth, and tracing influences from as far away as London and Egypt. Another of Jay's Regency mansions, the **Telfair Museum of Art**, 121 Barnard St (Mon noon–5pm, Tues–Sat 10am–5pm, Sun 1–5pm; $8), also has the distinction of being the oldest art museum in the South.

Though the city squares may be redolent of the Old South, Savannah's **waterfront**, at the foot of a steep little bluff below Bay Street, and reached by assorted stone staircases and atmospheric alleyways, resembles more an eighteenth-century European port. The main thoroughfare, **River Street**, is cobbled with the ballast carried by long-vanished sailing ships, while its tall brick cotton warehouses are said to be haunted by the ghosts of the slave stevedores. It's now a touristy com mercial district, lined with seafood restaurants and salty bars that heave with partying crowds on Saturday nights. Looking out over the water from the paved **Riverfront Plaza**, across the way, you can appreciate just how busy the port still is.

As the one-time point of entry for many of Georgia's slaves, Savannah plays a significant role in **black history**. Two blocks south of the visitor center, at 460 Martin Luther King Jr Blvd, the uncompromising **Civil Rights Museum** (Mon–Sat 9am–5pm; $4) is a must-see. With a sustained program of mass meetings, lunch-counter sit-ins, dangerous "wade-ins" at whites-only Tybee Island beaches, and a fifteen-month boycott of local department store Levy's – the longest-running store boycott in the history of the movement – Savannah was very active in the campaigns of the 1960s; by 1964, Dr King called it "the most integrated city south of the Mason-Dixon Line." Artifacts in this small but fascinating place include an original burnt cross and a Klan robe; visitors should decide for themselves whether to follow the signs on the separate "Colored" and "White" restrooms.

The museum also operates excellent **African-American history tours**, which leave from the visitor center (Mon–Sat 10am & 2pm; $17; book by calling ☎912/234-8900). Tours usually take in the **Second African Baptist Church**, 123 Houston St, where in December 1864, Sherman read the Emancipation Proclamation and issued the famous **Field Order #15**, which granted each freed slave forty acres and a mule. In the Historic District at 23 Montgomery St, the 1775 **First African Baptist Church** is the oldest black church in North America, built by slaves (Mon–Fri 10am–3.30pm). Note the tribal carvings on the sides of the pews upstairs, and, downstairs, the diamond shapes made by holes in the floor – ventilation holes for slaves hiding in the 4ft subterranean crawl spaces while waiting to escape to safe havens via the Underground Railroad.

Southeast of downtown, the predominantly black **Victorian District** is being slowly restored, and has a couple of good, if underfunded, museums. The nerve center of the restoration process is the **King-Tisdell Cottage**, 514 E Huntingdon St, owned by a middle-class black family at the turn of the nineteenth/twentieth century (Tues–Sat noon–4.30pm; $4). In addition to a fine collection of Gullah baskets and African woodcarving, it illustrates the history of slaves and free blacks before the Civil War, and of the freed slaves after. The airy **Beach Institute**, 502 E Harris St (Tues–Sat noon–5pm; $4), Georgia's first school for freed slaves, today houses an African-American art gallery with a permanent display of extraordinary woodcarvings by folk artist Ulysses Davis.

A ten-minute drive east from Savannah will take you to the lovely **Bonaventure Cemetery**, swathed in trees and sloping down to the Wilmington River. The final resting place of local luminaries such as Johnny Mercer and Conrad Aiken, it's also a major sight in *Midnight in the Garden*, in which it's written about to great effect. Sylvia Shaw Judson's *Bird Girl* statue, which graces the book's cover and used to be situated here, has since been moved to the Telfair Museum of Art (see p.563).

Eating

Savannah has lots of **restaurants**. With a couple of exceptions, most places on the **waterfront** are eminently avoidable. Far better to head for the **City Market** – four blocks of restored grain warehouses just a few blocks back from the river – which is downtown's prime restaurant and nightlife district.

45 Bistro in the *Marshall House Hotel*, 123 E Broughton St ☎912/234-3111. Delicate, adventurous food – quail and sausage fritters, sea scallop lasagna, seared ahi tuna – in a pretty, lamplit internal brick courtyard. Prices are reasonable for this level of quality and atmosphere.

Bistro Savannah 309 W Congress St ☎912/233-6266. A City Market favorite, with lovely decor – cherry-red walls, fairy lights – and a sophisticated menu of seafood and organic specials. Try the succulent grilled flounder. Dinner only, nightly.

Gallery Espresso 6 E Liberty St ☎912/233-5348. Artsy coffee bar with nice cakes, crumpets, and muffins, along with the best coffee in town (try the Iced Thai) and wine. Open late.

Garibaldi 315 W Congress St ☎912/232-7118. This atmospheric City Market restaurant, all gold mirrors and pressed-tin ceiling, serves great Northern Italian dishes, nouvelle cuisine, and seafood.

Gryphon Bull and Charlton sts ☎912/525-5880. There's an atmospheric mix of art students, lecturers, and ladies-that-lunch in this sweet tearoom, housed in an old pharmacy with its original counter, tiled floor, and mirrors. Hundreds of special teas, genteel gourmet lunches, and mouthwatering cakes.

Huey's 115 E River St ☎912/234-7385. Touristy waterfront restaurant serving authentic Cajun/Creole food; go straight for the Oysters Rockefeller. Live music wafts in from the adjoining bar, and there's a nice jazz brunch at weekends.

Lady and Sons 102 W Congress St ☎912/233-2600. Hugely popular Southern restaurant with a gut-busting buffet of fried chicken, Low Country Boil, macaroni, fried green tomatoes, and the like.

Mrs Wilkes' Boarding House 107 W Jones St ☎912/232-5997. This local institution offers a real Southern experience, serving all-you-care-to-eat breakfasts and lunches only. Everyone sits around large tables, helping themselves to delicious mounds of fried chicken, sweet potatoes, spinach, beans, and spaghetti. There's no sign outside; get there early and join the line. No credit cards.

Nita's Place 129 E Broughton St ☎912/238-8233. Friendly, no-nonsense little soul-food restaurant, serving good-value all-you-care-to-eat crab cakes, fried chicken, and so on. Lunch only.

Shrimp Factory 313 E River St ☎912/236-4229. It may look tacky, but the shrimp dishes are great; try Shrimp Stuffed Savannah, packed with deviled crab, chicken, baked rice, and lemon butter.

Entertainment and nightlife

Savannah's **nightlife** is laid-back and enjoyable, though many places are unusually strict about requiring ID. Everything is fairly close together, ranged between the City Market and the river, and almost uniquely in the US (New Orleans is another exception) you can drink **alcohol** on the streets in open cups. For **listings**, pick up the free weekly *Connect* newspaper.

Savannah has the largest Irish population per capita in the US, and **St Patrick's Day** (March 17) is a big deal. Nowadays nearly a million revelers descend on the town to guzzle green beer, green grits, and copious amounts of Guinness; many of the 130,000 permanent residents choose this weekend to leave town. Far less frenetic is the annual **jazz festival**, held in Forsyth Park in late September. For information on this or other jazz events and venues, contact the Coastal Jazz Association (☎912/232-2222, ⊛www.coastaljazz .com).

Club One 1 Jefferson St ☎912/232-0200. Decadent gay club, where drag acts occasionally include Lady Chablis, from "The Book"; everyone is welcome.

Mercury Lounge 125 W Congress St ☎912/447-6952. Super-hip lounge, with kooky decor, regular swing music, and live jazz.

Moon River Brewing Co. 21 W Bay St ☎912/447-0943. Popular brewpub near the waterfront.

Rail Pub 405 W Congress St ☎912/238-1311. Near the City Market, this lively, endearingly shabby multilevel bar is frequented by an interesting local crowd.

Savannah Blues 206 W Julian St ☎912/447-5044. Steamy City Market club that features live blues and drink specials. Mon–Sat from 10pm.

Out from Savannah

Tybee Island, eighteen miles east of the city on US-80, has Savannah's best – and not too overdeveloped – **beach**, as well as a 154ft **lighthouse** dating from 1736, with a small museum (summer daily except Tues 9am–5.30pm; $5). Abundant **accommodation** options include the oceanfront *DeSoto Beach Hotel*, 212 Butler Ave (☎912/786-4542, ⓦwww.desotobeachhotel.com; ❺). For great **Low Country food**, head for *The Crab Shack*, 40 Estill Hammock Rd, Chimney Creek (☎912/786-9857), where you can dine on delicious fresh crabs and shrimp in a shabby old shack by the creek – if you can find it, that is: take a right turn off the main road to the beach, about two miles before you reach the lighthouse turnoff.

    Fort Pulaski National Monument, off US-80 E en route to Tybee Island (daily: May–Sept 9am–7pm; rest of year 9am–5pm; $3), is the most interesting of several local forts. An impressive Confederate stronghold, set on its own idyllic (if rather buggy) little island and ringed by a moat inhabited by the occasional alligator, it was nevertheless taken by Union troops, the first masonry fortress to be pierced by rifled cannon fire.

    Ten miles south of Savannah, at 7601 Skidaway Rd, you come to **Wormsloe State Historic Site** (Tues–Sat 9am–5pm, Sun 2–5pm; $3). In the eighteenth century this was an important defensive plantation; the atmospheric tabby ruins of the fortified house of British settler Noble Jones are now overgrown with palms and lush forest. Inside the house, a museum covers the early settlement of Savannah, with archeological finds and demonstrations of the skills and crafts of the first settlers.

    Much of the Georgia coast is taken up by a string of **National Wildlife Refuges**, on the small marshy islands that make up the **barrier island chain**. It's well worth detouring or backtracking along the quiet side roads to cross to **Blackbeard Island**, **Wolf Island**, **Pinckney**, or **Wassaw**, where tranquil swamps are filled with nesting birds and offer great fishing.

Brunswick and the southern coast

BRUNSWICK, the one sizeable settlement south of Savannah, is a hop-off point for the offshore **sea islands**. The town in itself is not very exciting, although the shrimp docks can be quite interesting when the catch is brought in. In the unlikely event you'll need to stay in town, the **visitor center**, 4 Glynn Ave (daily 8.30am–5pm; ☎912/265-0620 or 1-800/933-2627, ⓦwww.bgivb.com), has lists of budget **motels** and central **B&Bs**. A more unusual alternative is the wonderful *Hostel in the Forest*, a couple of miles west of I-95 exit 6, reached via an inconspicuous muddy driveway on the south side of US-82 (☎912/264-9738, no reservations; ❶). For $15 per person you'll get either a dorm bed in a geodesic dome or a private room (with electricity!) in one of nine treehouses. The price includes a communal dinner, and all guests are expected to perform a small chore. Otherwise, the best **food** nearby is at the superlative *Georgia Pig*, in an unlikely setting next to a gas station at exit 6 on I-95 (☎912/264-6664), where luscious smoky barbecue comes with the local Brunswick stew, coleslaw, honey-flavored baked beans, and fragrant sauce.

The sea islands

Several of Georgia's **sea islands**, like those of South Carolina, were divided among freed slaves after the Civil War. However, these islands remained poor agricultural communities, and little now remains from those years for an outsider to see. Today they make handy alternatives to Florida as seashore breaks for tired inlanders.

Jekyll Island

The **southern islands** are the most developed, thanks largely to **Jekyll Island**, which was originally bought in 1887 for use as an exclusive "club" by a group of millionaires including the Rockefellers, the Pulitzers, the Macys, and the Vanderbilts. Their opulent residences are still standing, though in perpetual need of refurbishment. A small **Welcome Center** stands on the causeway (daily 9am–5pm; ☎912/635-3636, ⓦwww.jekyllisland.com), though the **Jekyll Island Museum Center** (daily 9am–5pm) gives a more useful overview of the island's history, and runs hourly guided tours of the mansions for $10. To reach the Museum Center, turn left after paying the $3 island toll, then head along Riverview Drive onto Stable Road. The "historic district" here centers on the rambling old original club building, which, as the *Jekyll Island Club Hotel*, now offers elegant and surprisingly affordable (☎912/635-2600, ⓦwww.jekyllclub .com; ❺). Other **accommodation** options are strung along Beachview Drive next to the ocean: the *Georgia Coast Inn*, at no. 150 (☎912/635-2111 or 1-800/835-2110, ⓦwww.georgiacoastinn.com; ❹), has ocean views and a big Georgia-shaped pool. There's a **campground** a little further north (☎912/635-3021; $19), near the nesting sites of loggerhead turtles.

St Simon's Island and Cumberland Island

Most of **St Simon's Island**, reached across a green marsh inhabited by wading birds (35¢ toll), is still an evocative landscape of marshes, palms, and live oaks covered with Spanish moss. The tiny village is pleasantly quiet, little more than a handful of T-shirt shops and cafés. Although the beach by the village is nice and firm for strolling, fierce currents render **swimming** unsafe: head instead for the east side of the island, where the flat, fine sand stretches out for miles. Southeast Adventures, 313 Mallory St (☎912/638-6732, ⓦwww.southeastadventure.com), rents out **kayaks** and runs bird- and dolphin-watching tours. **Fort Frederica National Monument**, seven miles north of the causeway (daily 8.30am–5pm; $5 per vehicle), was built by General Oglethorpe in 1736 as the largest British fort in North America; it's now an atmospheric ruin.

As well as **resorts** like the lovely *Sea Palms*, 5445 Frederica Rd (☎912/638-3351 or 1-800/841-6268, ⓦwww.seapalms.com; ❹), whose atmospheric rooms overlook the marshes, **accommodation** options include *Saint Simon's Inn*, 609 Beachview Drive, a block from the beach near the village (☎912/638-1101, ⓦwww.stsimonsinn.com; ❹). By far the best place to **eat** is *Frannie's Place Restaurant*, 318 Mallery St (☎912/638-1001), famed for its Brunswick stew; try also the specialty sandwiches, crabcakes, and to-die-for desserts.

To the south, **Cumberland Island** is a stunning wildlife refuge of marshes, beaches, and semitropical forest roamed by wild horses, with the odd deserted planter's mansion. You can get there by ferry from the village of St Mary's, back on the mainland near the Florida border (March–Nov daily 9am & 11.45am; Dec–Feb Thurs–Mon 9am & 11.45am; 45min; $12).

Okefenokee Swamp

The dense semitropical **Okefenokee Swamp** stretches over thirty miles down to Florida from a point roughly thirty miles southwest of Brunswick. Tucked away among its astonishing profusion of luxuriant plants and trees are something like 20,000 alligators and over thirty species of snakes, as well as bears and pumas. You can only get in at the **Okefenokee Swamp Park**, a private charity-owned concession at the northeast tip, on Hwy-177 off US-23/1 (daily 9am–5.30pm; ☎912/283-0583, ⓦwww.okeswamp.com). Admission is $12, which enables you to see a serpentarium, a good interpretive center on wildlife, an observation tower, and reconstructed pioneer buildings; you can pay $4–18 extra for intriguing **boat tours** through the swamp of 30 to 90 minutes (be sure to slick yourself with bug repellent).

For nearby accommodation, unlovely **Waycross**, ten miles north, holds bargain **motels** such as the *Pinecrest*, 1761 Memorial Drive (☎912/283-3580; ❶).

Kentucky

Two hundred years after it was wrested from the Native Americans, **KENTUCKY** still hasn't quite decided whether it belongs in the North or the South. Both of the rival presidents during the Civil War, Abraham Lincoln and Jefferson Davis, were born here, and divisions were acute between slave-owning farmers and the merchants who depended on trade with the nearby cities of the industrial North. While the state remained officially neutral, seventy thousand Kentuckians joined the Union army and forty thousand the Confederates. After the war, Kentucky sided with the South in its hostility to Reconstruction, and since then it has remained solidly Democrat.

Kentucky's rugged beauty is at its most appealing in the mountainous **east** and the small historic towns of the **Bluegrass Downs**, with visits enlivened by the varied attractions of bourbon whiskey, thoroughbred horses, and bluegrass music. **Louisville**, home of the **Kentucky Derby**, is a busy manufacturing and arts center; the more reserved **Lexington**, eighty miles east, is a major horse-breeding market.

Getting around Kentucky

Kentucky's limited **public transportation** can be a real headache. There's full Greyhound service along the interstates south of Louisville and Lexington, but a lot of ground is left uncovered. Amtrak doesn't operate here at all. **Cycling** is a pleasant and manageable option; if you're **driving**, be sure to keep small change for the tolls on the state highways.

Lexington, Bluegrass, and eastern Kentucky

The fertile **Bluegrass Downs**, just eighty miles across, form the base of America's thoroughbred racing industry, with **Lexington** quietly prospering at its heart. The name comes from the unique steel-blue sheen of the buds in the meadows, only visible in early morning during April and May. Kentucky's first white pioneers, who trekked in the 1770s through the 150 miles of wilderness now called the **Daniel Boone National Forest**, were amazed to find this "Eden" deserted while the Indians lived in much less attractive terrain. Archeologists have now discovered that the area's twelfth-century inhabitants were plagued by fatal bone diseases, due to mineral deficiencies in the soil.

The area around Lexington holds some of the oldest towns west of the Alleghenies. However, amid the fine scenery of the **Natural Bridge** and **Cumberland Gap** districts, eastern Kentucky suffers from acute rural poverty.

Lexington

The productivity of the bluegrass fields has kept **LEXINGTON**'s economy ticking over since 1775, though the lack of a navigable river has always made its traders vulnerable to competition from Louisville. Eighty miles east of Louisville and ninety south of Cincinnati, Ohio, the city still retains a large number of fine antebellum houses. However, its current affluence dates from after World War I, when smoking caught on internationally and Lexington emerged as the world's largest burley **tobacco** market. Despite a population exceeding 200,000, Lexington maintains a quasi-rustic atmosphere; its most conspicuous activity is the **horse** trade, with an estimated 450 farms in the vicinity.

Arrival and information

Lexington's **airport** is six miles west of town on US-60 W, near Keeneland racetrack (handy for the jets of the horse-breeders). **Greyhound** drops off about a mile from downtown at 477 New Circle Rd – in front of Wal-Mart, across the street from the bus station (take bus #3 to get downtown). Lex–Tran (☎859/253-4636) operates a good service from downtown to the university and suburbs, but you'll need a **car** to reach the horse-related attractions. The **visitor center** is at 301 E Vine St (Mon–Fri 8.30am–5pm, Sat 10am–5pm, Sun May–Aug noon–5pm; ☎859/233-7299 or 1-800/845-3959, ⓦwww.vis-itlex.com). Check the free *ACE Weekly* for local **listings** and events.

Accommodation

Lexington has very little accommodation to offer downtown, though budget **motels** can be found around the exits from I-75. If you're stuck, the visitor center (see above) can help find rooms. The best **campground** (☎859/233-4303, ⒻF859/255-2690) is at the Horse Park (tentsites $13).

Comfort Suites South 5527 Athens-Boonesboro Rd, I-70 exit 104 ☎859/263-0777 or 1-800/228-5150. Spacious, good-value chain motel six miles southeast of the city center. ❷

Holiday Inn North 1950 Newtown Pike ☎859/233-0512, ⓦwww.hilexingtonnorth.com. Vast and very upscale affiliate of the *Holiday Inn* chain northeast of downtown, complete with a covered "Holidome" holding a swimming pool, sports hall, and gym. ❺

Homewood B&B 5301 Bethel Rd ☎859/255-2814. An appealing rural retreat, offering two comfortable guest suites on a 21-acre horse farm. ❺

La Quinta 1919 Stanton Way, junction of I-64 & I-75, exit 115 ☎859/231-7551 or 1-800/531-5900. Handily placed motel with comfortable rooms and free continental breakfast. ❸

University of Kentucky 700 Woodland Ave ☎859/257-3721. The university sets aside a few fully equipped rooms for short stays all year, with plenty more available during summer. ❶

Downtown Lexington

The plush hotels, glass office blocks, skywalks, and shopping malls of Lexington's city center, set in a dip on the Bluegrass Downs, crowd in on fountain-filled **Triangle Park**. Despite its age, the city has few buildings of architectural interest; the early merchants threw up mostly functional structures, preferring to get on with making money. The ivy-covered redbrick buildings of small 1780 **Transylvania University** (the name means "across the woods," an appropriate description of Kentucky at the time) are behind the Courthouse at N Broadway and Third St. On the other side of downtown, the **University of Kentucky Art Museum**, in the Singletary Center for the Arts, at Rose St and Euclid Ave (Tues–Thurs, Sat & Sun noon–5pm; Fri noon–8pm; free) displays contemporary American art and Native American artifacts. The best photo opportunity comes in the form of **Thoroughbred Park**, at Main St and Midland Ave, where an impressive life-sized bronze sculpture depicts a horse race in progress.

Lexington's horses

Along **Paris** and **Ironworks pikes**, northeast of Lexington in an idyllic Kentuckian landscape, sleek thoroughbred horses cavort in bluegrass meadows. Some farms are still staked out by miles of immaculate white-plank fences, though most now use the cheaper but much less attractive black creosote to protect the wood. To the west, you can watch the horses' early-morning workouts at **Keeneland racetrack** (April–Oct daily dawn–10am; free; ☎859/254-3412 or 1-800/456-3412), and then eat a super-cheap breakfast at the adjacent *Keeneland Kitchen*. Tasteful dark-green grandstands emphasize the crisp white rails around the one-mile oval track. Until recently, there was no public-address system, which made for a unique atmosphere, with thousands of puzzled voices trying to work out which horse was which, breaking into cheers as they hurtled into the final furlong; even today, coverage remains muted (racing for 3 weeks in April, Wed–Sun 7.30pm, and 3 weeks in Oct, Wed–Sun 1pm; call for reserved tickets; $3.50–25; ☎859/288-4299).

Tours of horse farms used to be very popular, but some owners have become reluctant to let the public get too close to the shy creatures. The easiest way to be sure of seeing at least one farm is to take a guided bus tour out of Lexington; **Blue Grass Tours** (March–Oct daily 9am; Nov–Feb by appointment; $25; ☎859/252-5744 or 1-800/755-6956, ⓦwww.bluegrasstours.com) offer a three-hour, fifty-mile itinerary that includes a stop at a private farm, plus a visit to Keeneland or Red Mile racetrack. Alternatively, a handful of farms welcome individual visitors, special events permitting; most are free, but you should tip the groom. **Calumet Farm**, off Versailles Rd, has bred a record nine Kentucky Derby winners (March–Sept Mon–Fri 10am; free; ☎859/231-8272). **Three Chimneys** on Old Frankfort Pike, about fifteen minutes west of downtown, offers tours by appointment only, (☎859/873-7053 ⓦwww.threechimneys.com). The **Thoroughbred Center**, 3380 Paris Pike (April–Oct Mon–Fri 9am, 10.30am & 1pm, Sat 9am & 10.30am; Nov–March Mon–Fri 10.30am; $10; ☎859/293-1853, ⓦwww.thethoroughbredcenter.com), allows you to watch trainers at work.

The enjoyable **Kentucky Horse Park** is a little further along at 4089 Ironworks Parkway (mid-March to Oct daily 9am–5pm; Nov to mid-March Wed–Sun 9am–5pm; $9–20; ☎859/233-4303, ⓦwww.kyhorsepark.com). Its **International Museum of the Horse** traces the use of horses throughout history, from Roman chariot races through cavalry regiments, commercial haulage, and modern sports. The 1032-acre park features real live horses of over thirty different breeds, a working farm, and guided **horseback rides** ($14 extra). In nearby Georgetown, at Whispering Woods, experienced equestrians can ride unsupervised, while novices can ride with a guide ($20 for 1hr, up to $60 per day; ☎502/570-9663, ⓦwww.whisperingwoodstrails.com).

Eating, drinking, and nightlife

Lexington's large student population means it has several lively, youth-oriented **eating places**, besides the steakhouses catering for the horse crowd and conventioneers. Fast-food cafés, open until early evening, fill the third floor of central **Festival Market**, at Main St and Broadway; the streets around the back hold a few lively bars, which flourish despite the Baptist-inspired 1am curfew on drinking places.

Alfalfa Restaurant 557 S Limestone St ☎859/253-0014. Hippyish café near the University of Kentucky. A wide range of inexpensive international food, with vegetarian dishes. Live music some evenings, plus temporary art exhibits.

Atomic Café 265 N Limestone St ☎859/254-1969. Fun Caribbean ambiance, with good spicy food and potent cocktails. Live reggae Thurs–Sat.

Common Grounds 343 High St ☎859/233-9761. Popular downtown coffeehouse, open until at least midnight daily with live music at weekends. A great rendezvous for coffee, sandwiches, and simple snacks.

Ed and Fred's Desert Moon 148 Grand Blvd ☎859/231-1161. Wacky decor, good Southwestern food and pizza. Closed Mon.

Good Foods Coop 455-D Southland Drive ☎859/278-1813. Healthy deli, open daily for coffee, sandwiches, and self-serve hot and cold specials.

Kentucky Theatre 214 E Main St ☎859/231-6997. Evocatively restored 1920s movie palace showing offbeat and art-house films, as well as being a great venue for rock, blues, and jazz concerts. Serves alcohol and decent snacks.

Ramsey's Diner 496 E High St ☎859/259-2708. Very popular and atmospheric diner, with four other outlets in town, all serving tasty sandwiches, burgers, and meals for $4–8. Open until 1am.

Bluegrass country

Other than the horse farms directly to the north, most places of interest near Lexington lie southwards, including the fine old towns of **Danville** and **Harrodsburg**, and the restored **Shaker Village** at Pleasant Hill. After about forty miles, the meadows give way to the striking **Knobs** – random lumpy outcrops, shrouded in trees and wispy low-hanging clouds, that are the eroded remnants of the Pennyrile Plateau.

The Shaker Village at Pleasant Hill

The utopian settlement of **PLEASANT HILL**, hidden among the bluegrass hillocks near Harrodsburg, 25 miles southwest of Lexington, was established by **Shaker missionaries** from New England around 1805. Within twenty years, five hundred villagers here were producing seeds, tools, and cloth, for sale as far away as New Orleans. During the Civil War, the pacifist Shakers were obliged to billet Union and Confederate troops alike. Numbers thereafter declined until the last member died in 1923, but a non-profit organization has returned the village to its nineteenth-century appearance.

The Shaker values of absolute celibacy, hygiene, simplicity, and communal ownership have left their mark on the thirty-four gray and pastel-colored dwellings, which women and men entered via different doors. Visitors can watch demonstrations of broom-making, weaving, quilting, and other traditional handicrafts (April–Oct daily 10am–5pm; Nov–March reduced hours and a lesser program of events; $12), and also take excursions on the sternwheeler *Dixie Belle* (late April to Oct daily noon, 2pm & 4pm; $16 including admission). An on-site **inn** offers good-value rooms, and also houses a superb **restaurant** specializing in boiled ham, lemon pie, and other Kentucky favorites (☎859/734-5411 or 1-800/734-5611, Ⓦwww.shakervillageky.org; ❹); reserve well in advance to either eat or sleep.

Berea

Thirty miles south of Lexington, just off I-75 in the foothills where Bluegrass Country meets Appalachia, the unique **Berea College** gives its 1500 mainly local students free tuition in return for work in any of 120 crafts, ranging from needlework to wrought ironwork. Founded in 1855 by abolitionists as a vocational college for the young people of East Kentucky – both white and black, making it for forty years the only integrated college in the South – it was briefly shut down four years later by mobs opposed to the board's support for John Brown's raid at Harpers Ferry (see p.472).

The college's reputation has attracted many private art and craft galleries to little **BEREA**. For details on all, a chance to buy representative local crafts, and general local information, visit the **Kentucky Artisan Center** at exit 77 off I-75 (daily 8am–8pm; ☎859/985-5548, ⓦwww.kentuckyartisancenter.ky .gov). Free tours of both the campus and assorted student craft workshops leave from the sumptuous *Boone Tavern Hotel*, a student-run inn and restaurant at Main and Prospect streets (☎859/985-3700 or 1-800/366-9358; ❹).The hotel has a **dining room** open to nonresidents, and staying here includes free admission to the college fitness center. If you're on a tight **budget**, *Mario's Pizza*, 636 Chestnut St (☎859/986-2331), is a good option.

Daniel Boone National Forest

Almost the entire eastern length of Kentucky is taken up by the steep slopes, narrow valleys, and sandstone cliffs of the unspoiled **DANIEL BOONE NATIONAL FOREST**. Few Americans can have been so mythologized as **Daniel Boone**, who first explored the region in 1767, and thus ranks as one of Kentucky's earliest fur-trapping pioneers. Perhaps the most famous legend tells of the time he was captured by Shawnee Indians and initiated as "Sheltowee," or Big Turtle. Learning of their plans to attack pioneer communities, Big Turtle escaped just in time to warn the citizens of his own settlement at **Boonesborough**, southeast of Lexington. But all did not end happily. Boone failed to legalize his land claims, and lost practically all the Kentucky land he had claimed for himself and his sponsors. The resultant animosity forced the aging frontiersman to press further west to Missouri in 1798, where he died in 1820 at the age of 86.

Natural Bridge and around

The geological extravaganza of the **Red River Gorge**, sixty miles east of Lexington via the Mountain Parkway, is best seen by taking a thirty-mile loop drive from the **Natural Bridge State Resort Park** on Hwy-77, near the village of Slade. Natural Bridge itself is a large sandstone arch surrounded by steep hollows and exposed clifflines; for the best panoramic view, continue to the solid span of **Sky Bridge**, which stretches along the top of a thin ridge. As well as hiking trails, canoeing, fishing, rock-climbing, and camping, there's cottage **accommodation** at the secluded *Hemlock Lodge* (☎606/663-2214 or 1-800/325-1710; ❹), where weekends are usually reserved a year in advance.

Toward the southeast

In 1940, "Colonel" Harlan Sanders opened a small clapboard diner, the *Sanders Café*, alongside his motel and gas station in tiny **Corbin**, ninety miles south of Lexington on I-75. His **Kentucky Fried Chicken** empire has since spread to over sixty countries. The original 100-seat restaurant, near the junction of US-25 E and US-25 W, has been restored with 1940s decor and an immense amount of memorabilia (daily 10am–10pm; ☎606/528-2163).The food served is usual KFC, but it's an atmospheric little spot – and no, they'd don't tell you what's in the secret recipe. Incidentally, the bespectacled Sanders (1890–1980) was not a soldier, but a member of the Honorable Order of Kentucky Colonels.

On the tristate border of Kentucky, Tennessee, and Virginia, the **Cumberland Gap National Historic Park** is one of the most visited parts of the area. A natural passageway used by migrating deer and bison, the area served as a gateway to the West for Boone and other pioneers. **Pinnacle Overlook**, a 1000ft lookout over the three states, is near the **visitor center**, on US-25 E in Middlesboro (daily: summer 8am–6pm; rest of year 9am–5pm; ☎606/248-2817, ⓦwww.nps.gov/cuga).

Louisville, central, and western Kentucky

In such a heavily rural state, the manufacturing giant of **Louisville** stands out, with its lively cultural and racial mix. Only occasionally does it bother with the laid-back Southern image other parts of the state are so keen to promote. In the **southern** hinterland, numerous small towns retain their tree-shaded squares and nineteenth-century townhouses – and their strict Baptist beliefs – while the endless caverns of **Mammoth Cave National Park** attract spelunkers and hikers in the thousands. The **west**, where the Ohio River meets the Mississippi, is flat, heavily forested, and generally less attractive.

Louisville

LOUISVILLE, just south of Indiana across the Ohio River, is firmly embedded in the American national consciousness for its multimillion-dollar **Kentucky Derby**. Each year, the horse race attracts over half a million fans to this cosmopolitan and well-diversified industrial city, which still bears the traces of the early French settlers who came upriver from New Orleans. Louisville also produces a third of the country's **bourbon**.

The city's history revolves around a perennial rivalry with Cincinnati, a mere one hundred miles upstream. Thus despite being pro-Union during the Civil War, it promoted itself thereafter – erecting Confederate statues and so on – as *the* place for Southern business to invest, as opposed to Midwestern Yankee cities like Cincinnati. Today, besides a lively arts scene and lots of citywide festivals, Louisville boasts an unrivaled network of public parks, many designed by Frederick Law Olmsted. One native son who took advantage of the recreation facilities was three-time world heavyweight boxing champion **Muhammad Ali**, who used to do his early-morning training in the scenic environs of Chickasaw Park.

Arrival and information

Most major US airlines fly into **Louisville International Airport** (☎502/368-6524), five miles south of downtown on I-65; take bus #2 or pay an $18 cab fare to get into the city center. **Greyhound** terminates at fairly central 720 W Muhammad Ali Blvd. Free downtown **trolleys** run from 7.30am to 6pm. The **visitor center** is in the Convention Center at Third and Market streets (Mon–Fri 8.30am–5pm, Sat 9am–4pm, Sun 11am–4pm; ☎502/582-3732 or 1-888/568-4784, ⓦwww.gotolouisville.com). For news of upcoming events, pick up a copy of the free **listings** magazine *LEO* (*Louisville Eccentric Observer*).

Accommodation

Most of the year, Louisville's **accommodation** is plentiful and reasonably priced, though of course it's solidly booked up for the Derby. You can **camp** just over the river in Indiana at the central *KOA*, 900 Marriott Drive, Clarksville, IN (☎812/282-4474).

Central Park B&B 1353 S Fourth St ☎502/638-1505 or 1-877/922-1505, ⊛www.centralpark-bandb.com. Opulent seven-room Victorian B&B in the heart of the Historic District. ❹

The Columbine B&B 1707 S Third St ☎502/635-5000 or 1-800/635-5010, ⊛www.thecolumbine.com. Six-room B&B, all with private baths, in a colonnaded mansion close to the university. Great garden and gourmet breakfasts. ❺

Doubletree Club Louisville Downtown 101 E Jefferson St ☎502/585-2200, ⊛www.doubletree.com. Comfortable rooms come with compli-

mentary breakfast and access to an indoor pool and fitness center. ❺

Galt House 140 Fourth St ☎502/589-5200 or 1-800/626-1814, ⊛www.galthouse.com. This massive, 25-story hotel on the Ohio riverfront has an unmistakable Kentucky feel, with grand ballrooms, sweeping staircases, and avenue-like corridors. ❺–❻

Super 8 Motel 927 S Second St ☎502/584-8888 or 1-800/800-8000, ⊛www.super8.com. Downtown chain motel offering a fitness room and continental breakfast, plus free local shuttle. ❸

Central Louisville

Downtown Louisville rolls gently down toward Main Street, then abruptly lunges to the river. **Riverfront Plaza**, between Fifth and Sixth streets, is a prime observation point for the natural **Falls of the Ohio**. Two sternwheelers, the *Belle of Louisville* and the *Spirit of Jefferson*, cruise from the wharf at Fourth St and River Rd in the summer (Tues & Thurs noon & 7pm; Wed, Fri & Sat noon, Sun 1pm; $12; ☎502/574-2355 or ⊛www.belleoflouisville.org).

Even non-baseball fans will likely be impressed by the **Louisville Slugger Museum**, at 800 W Main St (Mon–Sat 9am–5pm; Sun April–Nov noon–5pm; $6; ☎502/588-7228, ⊛www.sluggermuseum.com). Frequent **tours** start with a short, emotive movie featuring prominent shots of Louisville Slugger bats being used to good effect, before visiting displays honoring key players, a batting cage, and a lucid explanation of how wooden bats are made. All visitors receive a souvenir miniature bat.

The Kentucky Derby

The **Kentucky Derby** is one of the world's premier horse races; it's also, as Hunter S. Thompson put it, "decadent and depraved." Derby Day itself is the first Saturday in May, at the end of the two-week **Kentucky Derby Festival**. Since 1875, the leading lights of Southern society have gathered at **Churchill Downs**, three miles south of downtown, for an orgy of betting, haute cuisine, and mint juleps in the plush grandstand, while tens of thousands of the beer-guzzling proletariat cram into the infield. Apart from the $40 infield tickets available on the day – offering virtually no chance of a decent view – all seats are sold out months in advance. The actual race, traditionally preceded by a mass drunken rendition of "My Old Kentucky Home," is run over a distance of one and a quarter miles, lasts barely two minutes, and offers close to a million dollars in prize money. Churchill Downs also hosts thoroughbred races from May to July, and from October to November ($2; ☎502/636-4400 or 1-800/283-3729).

The excellent hands-on **Kentucky Derby Museum** (mid-March to Nov Mon–Sat 7am–5pm, Sun noon–5pm; Dec to mid-March Mon–Sat 9am–5pm, Sun noon–5pm; $8; ☎502/637-7097, ⊛www.derbymuseum.org), next to Churchill Downs at 704 Central Ave, will appeal to horse-racing enthusiasts and neophytes alike. Admission includes a tour of Churchill Downs, and a magnificent audiovisual display that captures the Derby Day atmosphere on a 360° screen.

The **Speed Art Museum**, at 2035 S Third St on the University of Louisville campus (Tues, Wed & Fri 10.30am–4pm, Thurs 10.30am–8pm, Sat 10.30am–5pm, Sun noon–5pm; free; ☎502/634-2700, ⓦwww.speedmuseum.org) hosts traveling exhibits and has a small, but interesting, permanent collection of art and sculpture from medieval to modern times, featuring works by Rembrandt, Monet, Rodin, and Henry Moore.

Eating

Louisville's **restaurants** cater for all tastes, though downtown prices are fairly high.

Brasserie Dietrich's 2862 Frankfort Ave ☎502/897-6076. Atmospheric converted movie house in the Crescent Hill district, serving inventive seafood and meat dishes from a wood-burning grill.

Bristol Bar & Grille 1321 Bardstown Rd ☎502/456-1702. A perennial Louisville favorite, offering good bistro-style salads and entrees, as well as great desserts. Two other locations at 300 N Hurstbourne Parkway and 614 W Main St.

Heine Brothers Coffee 1295 Bardstown Rd ☎502/456-5108. Friendly espresso bar, attached to Carmichael's, a good independent bookstore.

Jicama Grill 1538 Bardstown Rd ☎502/454-4383. Stylish Latin American grill in the busy Deer Park district. Six different *ceviches* for around $6 each, Brazilian *feijoada* stew or steak for well under $20. Closed Sun.

Ramsi's Café on the World 1293 Bardstown Rd ☎502/451-0700. Atmospheric café open nightly until late and offering eclectic and very tasty selections from around the world. A downtown branch, at 215 S Fifth St, opens for weekday lunches only, served cafeteria-style.

Rudyard Kipling 422 W Oak St ☎502/636-1311. The decor has a hint of *The Jungle Book*, but the food is local with a few Indian dishes thrown in. Live music, usually acoustic, most nights. Closed Sun.

Vietnam Kitchen 5339 S Mitscher Ave ☎502/363-5154. A small, basic eatery, fifteen minutes' drive out of downtown in the South End, where the city's Asian chefs eat on their days off. The menu is huge. Closed Wed.

Nightlife and entertainment

Fronted by several outlandish sculptures, the **Kentucky Center for the Arts**, 501 W Main, between Fifth and Sixth avenues (☎502/562-0100 or 1-800/775-7777), is Louisville's main venue for high culture. Meanwhile, the **Actors' Theatre of Louisville**, 316 W Main St (☎502/584-1205 or 1-800/428-5849), has a national reputation for its new productions. As for **drinking** and **live music**, the two-mile strip around Bardstown Road and Baxter Avenue (take bus #17) is punctuated by fun bars and restaurants; the best **gay** clubs are on the eastern edge of downtown.

Connections 130 S Floyd St ☎502/585-5752. The pick of Louisville's gay scene. At weekends, this giant club, complete with terrace garden, holds over 2000.

Molly Malone's 933 Baxter Ave ☎502/473-1222. Enjoyable Irish pub and restaurant, with live music on the weekends.

Phoenix Hill Tavern 644 Baxter Ave ☎502/589-4957, ⓦwww.phoenixhill.com. Big bar with four

separate areas; occasionally hosts national touring acts.

Stevie Ray's 230 E Main St ☎502/582-9945, ⓦwww.stevieraysbluesbar.com. As the name suggests, a loud, rocking blues bar.

Twice Told Performance Café 3507 W Hwy-146 ☎502/222-4506. Cozy singer-songwriter venue that often gets noted names and surprise appearances.

Out from Louisville

South from Louisville to Tennessee, **central Kentucky** offers great scope for a one- or two-day driving tour. There's small-town charm and well-aged bourbon in **Bardstown** and Abraham Lincoln's birthplace of **Hodgenville**, while the top natural attraction is the amazing **Mammoth Cave National Park**, the largest underground cave system in the world.

Kentucky's **western** stretches don't compare with the rugged east for scenic beauty; all the significant lakes here were created by damming rivers, and much of the land is scarred by strip mines, oilfields, and commercial forests. There's little of real interest except for the **Land Between the Lakes** recreation area, squeezed between Kentucky and Barkley lakes, and overlapping the Tennessee border.

Fort Knox

Legendary **FORT KNOX** straddles 100,000 acres on either side of US-31 W, thirty miles southwest of Louisville. The bomb-proof **Bullion Depository**, on Gold Vault Road, surrounded by security fences, machine-gun turrets, patrol guards, and huge floodlights, stores nine million pounds of the federal gold reserve behind doors weighing twenty tons apiece. No visits are allowed at the depository; you can only stop by the road for a maximum of five minutes.

Bardstown and the bourbon distilleries

Forty miles south of Louisville on US-31 E, attractive **BARDSTOWN** is the place to get acquainted with Kentucky **bourbon whiskey**, created in earliest pioneer days, so the story goes, when Elijah Craig, a Baptist minister, added corn to the usual rye and barley. Named for Bourbon County near Lexington, Kentucky's whiskey soon gained a national reputation, thanks to crisp limestone water and the skills of small-scale distillers. Under federal law, corn must make up at least 51 percent of all solid ingredients, and the drink must mature for two years in new oak barrels with charred interiors.

Get into the spirit at Bardstown's free **Oscar Getz Museum of Whiskey History**, 114 N Fifth St (May–Sept Mon–Sat 9am–5pm, Sun 1–5pm; rest of year Mon–Sat 10am–4pm, Sun 1–4pm). Fourteen miles west at **Clermont**, you can stop at the **Jim Beam American Outpost** (Mon–Sat 9am–4.30pm, Sun 1–4pm; free), which has an informative museum, a film on the whiskey-making process, an outdoor moonshine still and barrel-making museum, and a Beam family home. **Maker's Mark Distillery**, twenty miles south of Bardstown near **Loretto**, is an out-of-the-way collection of beautifully restored black, red, and gray plankhouses, in which whiskey is still made manually (Mon–Sat 10.30am–3.30pm, Sun 1.30–3.30pm; free; ☎502/865-2099). However, don't expect a sample at either distillery; like most of rural Kentucky, the area is **dry**.

Abraham Lincoln's birthplace

On February 12, 1809, **Abraham Lincoln**, the sixteenth president of the US, was born in a one-room log cabin in the frontier wilds, son of a wandering farmer and, if some accounts are to be believed, an illiterate and illegitimate mother. Three miles south of Hodgenville, on US-31 E, the **National Historic Site** (summer daily 8am–6.45pm; rest of year daily 8am–4.45pm; free; ☎270/358-3137, ⊛www.nps.gov/abli) has a symbolic cabin of his birth, enclosed in a granite and marble Memorial Building with 56 steps, one for each year of Lincoln's life. The family moved ten miles northeast in 1811 to the **Knob Creek** area, where Lincoln's earliest memory was of slaves being forcefully driven along the road. Here you can visit another re-creation of his boyhood home (daily April–Oct varying hours; $1). Knob Creek, which the Lincolns left in 1816 for Indiana, doesn't overplay the presidential connection, and its down-home cafés make it a good place to stop.

Mammoth Cave National Park

The three hundred and fifty miles of labyrinthine passages (with an average of five new miles discovered each year) and domed caverns of **MAMMOTH CAVE NATIONAL PARK** lie halfway between Louisville and Bowling Green, ten miles off I-65. Its amazing geological formations, carved by acidic water trickling through limestone, include a bewildering display of stalagmites and stalactites, a huge cascade of flowstone known as **Frozen Niagara**, and **Echo River**, 365ft below ground, populated by a unique species of colorless and sightless fish. Among traces of human occupation are Native American artifacts, a former saltpeter mine, and the remains of an experimental tuberculosis hospital, built in 1843 in the belief that the cool atmosphere of the cave would help clear patients' lungs. It's possible to take a limited-access self-guided tour, but by far the best way to appreciate the caves is by joining one of the lengthy daily program of **ranger-guided tours**, which range in length from two to six hours, and cater for most tastes and abilities, including the physically challenged ($5–45). Tickets are available from the **visitor center** (summer daily 7.30am–7.30pm; fall daily 8am–6pm; rest of year Mon–Fri 9am–5pm, Sat & Sun 8am–5pm; ☎270/758-2328 or ⓦwww.mammothcave .com for info; ☎1-800/967-2283 or ⓦreservations.nps.gov for tour reservations). Make reservations in advance, especially in summer. Also keep in mind that the temperature in the caves is a constant 54°F, so take a sweater or jacket.

The park's attractions are by no means all subterranean. You can explore the scenic **Green River**, as it cuts through densely forested hillsides and jagged limestone cliffs, by following hiking trails, or renting a canoe from Green River Canoeing (☎270/597-2031 or 1-800/651-9909). **Camping** is free in the backcountry; however, a permit must be picked up first at the visitor center; the *Mammoth Cave Hotel* (☎270/758-2225, ⓦwww.mammothcavehotel.com) has cottages and motel **rooms** (both ❷).

The privately owned caves all around, many of which ruin the sights with garish light shows, and the "attractions" in nearby Cave City and Park City, are best ignored.

Bowling Green and around

BOWLING GREEN, thirty miles southwest of Mammoth Cave and just sixty miles northeast of Nashville, Tennessee, is a busy little town that offers a treat for **sports car** enthusiasts. One-hour tours of the **General Motors Corvette Assembly Plant**, on Louisville Road, off I-65, take a step-by-step look at the manufacture of one of the great symbols of the American Dream (Mon–Fri at 9am & 1pm; closed Dec & first half of July; ☎502/745-8419; free; reservations advisable). For real Corvette junkies, there's also the **National Corvette Museum**, south of the plant at 350 Corvette Drive (daily 8am–5pm; $8; ⓦwww.corvettemuseum.com).

By way of contrast, a former **Shaker settlement**, with furniture displays and crafts for sale, is located in **South Union**, 11 miles west of Bowling Green off US-68/80 (March, Apri, Nov & Dec Mon–Sat 9am–4pm, Sun 1–4pm; May–Oct Mon–Sat 9am–5pm, Sun 1–5pm; $5; ☎1-800/811-8379, ⓦwww.logantele.com/shakmus). A mile or two away on Hwy-73, the 1869 *Shaker Tavern* has reopened as a comfortable **B&B** (☎270/542-6801 or 1-800/929-8701; ❹); guests can also sample traditional Kentucky recipes such as chess pie.

Tennessee

Stretching almost five hundred miles from east to west, **TENNESSEE** is less open to easy generalization than most Southern states. The history and traditional culture of the Smoky Mountains are a far cry indeed from the blues-soaked, cotton-picking culture of the Mississippi valley, while the more prosperous central region between the two, focused on state capital Nashville, is different once again. Nonetheless Tennessee remains as integral to the South as it has ever since the Civil War, from its music and cuisine to its political conservatism.

Only one sizeable settlement has found a foothold above the marshlands that line the Mississippi, but it's the state's greatest attraction for visitors – the exhilarating port of **Memphis**. Tennessee's largest city is a magnet for music fans, as the birthplace of urban **blues** and long-time home of **Elvis**. The fine plantation homes and tidy old towns of **middle Tennessee**'s rolling farmland reflect the comfortable lifestyle of its pioneers; smack at the heart of this is **Nashville**, still synonymous with **country music**. The mountainous **east** shares its top attraction with North Carolina – the peaks, streams, and meadows of **Great Smoky Mountains National Park**.

Some history

Tennessee's first white settlers, most of them British Protestants, arrived across the mountains in the 1770s to settle in the hills and hollows of the Appalachians. Initially relations with the **Cherokee** were good. However, demand for land increased, and confrontations throughout the state culminated in 1838 with the forced removal of the Indians on the "Trail of Tears." One of the main congressional opponents of this process was **Davy Crockett**, familiar from legend as the heavy-drinking hunter in a coonskin cap. When the **Civil War** came, the plantation owners of the west manuvered Tennessee into the Confederacy, against the wishes of the non-slaveholding smallhold farmers in the east. The last state to secede became the primary battlefield in the west, the site of 424 battles and skirmishes.

Despite economic development to rival any in the country, soil erosion and farm mechanization led to a mass migration to the cities in the years before World War I. The fundamentalist beliefs of these transplanted hill-dwellers (whose folk and fiddle music served to spark Nashville's country scene) influenced a **prohibition** movement that kept all of Tennessee bone-dry until 1939, and still sees a majority of counties forbidding the sale of alcohol. The New Deal of the 1930s brought significant changes. In particular, the **Tennessee Valley Authority**, created in 1933, harnessed the flood-prone **Tennessee River**, providing much-needed jobs and cheap power, and ignited the transition from an agricultural to an industrial economy.

Getting around Tennessee

For such a popular tourist destination, Tennessee has disappointing **transportation** connections. **Amtrak** only calls at Memphis, and while Greyhound provides a reasonable service to major towns and cities, traveling **by bus** through the small towns in the east is very difficult. The **airports** at Memphis and Nashville have extensive connections throughout the US, though fares between the two are high. If you harbor fantasies of traveling by **boat** along the Mississippi, note that only luxury craft make the trip these days, at prohibitive prices (see p.585).

Memphis

Perched above the Mississippi River, **MEMPHIS** ranks as perhaps the single most exciting destination in the South. Visitors flock to celebrate the city that gave the world **blues**, **soul**, and **rock 'n' roll**, as well as to chow down in the unrivaled barbecue capital of the nation. Memphis is both deeply atmospheric – with its somewhat faded downtown streets dotted with characterful stores

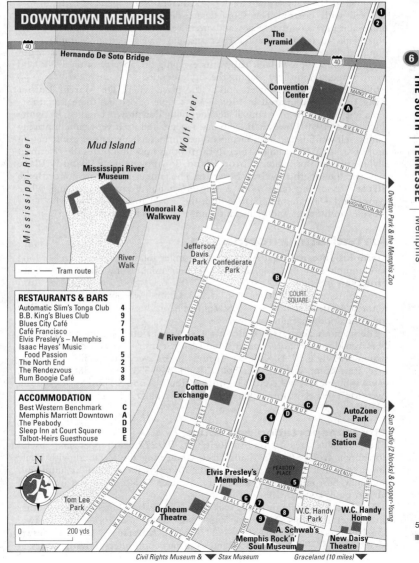

DOWNTOWN MEMPHIS

The Pyramid

Hernando De Soto Bridge

Convention Center

MARKET AVE

EXCHANGE AVENUE

A

POPLAR AVENUE

Wolf River

Mud Island

WASHINGTON AVE

Mississippi River Museum

WATER STREET

PROMENADE STREET

FRONT STREET

ADAMS AVENUE

Monorail & Walkway

Mississippi River

River Walk

Jefferson Davis Park

Confederate Park

JEFFERSON AVENUE

B

MAIN STREET MALL

2ND STREET

3RD STREET

COURT SQUARE

COURT AVENUE

— – – Tram route

RIVERSIDE DRIVE

CENTER LANE

MADISON AVENUE

Riverboats

MONROE AVENUE

RESTAURANTS & BARS
Automatic Slim's Tonga Club	4
B.B. King's Blues Club	9
Blues City Café	7
Café Francisco	1
Elvis Presley's – Memphis	6
Isaac Hayes' Music Food Passion	5
The North End	2
The Rendezvous	3
Rum Boogie Café	8

3

Cotton Exchange

UNION AVENUE

C

AutoZone Park

4 D

ACCOMMODATION
Best Western Benchmark	C
Memphis Marriott Downtown	A
The Peabody	D
Sleep Inn at Court Square	B
Talbot-Heirs Guesthouse	E

FRONT STREET

GAYOSO AVENUE

E

Bus Station

GAYOSO AVENUE

4TH STREET

N

RIVERSIDE DRIVE

Tom Lee Park

PEABODY PLACE

Elvis Presley's Memphis

McCALL AVENUE

5

BEALE STREET

6
7

Orpheum Theatre

8 W.C. Handy Park

W.C. Handy Home

9

MAIN STREET

2ND STREET

A. Schwab's

Memphis Rock 'n' Soul Museum

New Daisy Theatre

0 —— 200 yds

WAGNER PLACE

LINDEN AVENUE

Civil Rights Museum & ▼ Stax Museum

Graceland (10 miles) ▼

▶ Overton Park & the Memphis Zoo

▶ Sun Studio (2 blocks) & Cooper-Young

and diners, and the sun setting nightly across the broad Mississippi – and invigorating, with a cluster of superb **museums** to complement its frequent **festivals** and action-packed **nightlife**. If it's the **Elvis** connection that draws you here, you surely won't leave disappointed – let alone empty-handed – but even the King represents just one small part of the rich musical heritage of the home of Sun and Stax.

Culturally and geographically, Memphis has always had more in common with the Delta of Mississippi and Arkansas than with the rest of Tennessee. Founded in 1819 and named for Egypt's ancient Nile capital, its fortunes rose and fell with **cotton**. The Confederate defeat that ended slavery briefly plunged it into economic chaos, and severe yellow-fever epidemics didn't help, but thanks to its potential for river and rail transportation Memphis soon bounced back. The nation's second largest inland port became a major stopping-off point for **black migrants** escaping the poverty of the Delta, and many stayed, significantly shaping the city's identity.

Memphis reached its lowest ebb as the place where **Dr Martin Luther King Jr** was **assassinated** in 1968. For a couple of decades thereafter, it tottered on the brink of terminal decline, with downtown blighted by white flight. Since 1990, however, the city has regenerated itself yet again, displaying a new self-confidence by pouring money into such expensive construction projects as the 321ft stainless steel **Pyramid** that now dominates the riverfront skyline; the transformation of **Mud Island**; downtown's huge **Peabody Place** mall; and the superb new **Stax Museum**. The famous **blues** corridor of **Beale Street** is booming once more, a little ersatz but always entertaining, while **Graceland** – a refreshing change from the usual "gracious southern home" – provides an intimate and exuberant glimpse of the city's most famous son.

Arrival and information

Memphis International Airport is ten miles south of downtown – a long and complicated bus trip, but just fifteen minutes by the Yellow Cabs **limo/van** service ($12; ☏901/577-7700 or 1-800/796-7750) or **taxi** ($15–25). Greyhound **buses** stop at 203 Union Ave downtown, while the restored **Amtrak** station at 545 S Main St is on the southern edge of downtown, in a not especially safe area.

The spacious **Tennessee Welcome Center**, just off I-40 downtown at 119 N Riverside and Adams – facing Mud Island at river level, and complete with statues of Elvis and B.B. King – is open 24 hours every day (staffed daily: summer 9am–6pm; winter 9am–5pm; ☏901/543-5333 or 1-888/633-9099, ⓦwww.memphistravel.com). The **post office** is at 555 S Third St, at Calhoun Ave (Mon–Fri 8.30am–5.30pm, Sat 10am–2pm; ☏901/521-2245; zip code 38101).

City transportation and tours

The Memphis Area Transit Authority (☏901/274-6282) operates a useful downtown **trolley** along Main Street, connecting the Pyramid with Beale Street, the Civil Rights Museum, and the Amtrak station (Mon–Sat until after midnight, Sun until 6pm; 60¢ flat fare, day pass $2.50). Slow and infrequent MATA buses cover the rest of the city.

Horse-drawn **carriage tours** start from *The Peabody* hotel and seven other downtown locations (Mon–Fri 5pm–1am, Sat & Sun 1pm–1am; for two, $35/half-hour or $60/hr; ☏901/527-7542). **American Dream Safari** (☏901/527-8870, ⓦwww.americandreamsafari.com) offers **driving tours** in a 1955 Cadillac that range from the Sunday gospel service at Al Green's church ($75; see p.583) up to week-long blues pilgrimages into the Delta. **Sternwheelers** offer two-hour sightseeing trips of the mighty Mississippi for $14.50, leaving Riverside Drive at Monroe Ave (April–Oct at least one daily at 2.30pm, with greater frequency in summer and also regular musical dinner cruises; March & Nov Fri & Sat 2.30pm; ☏901/527-5694, Ⓦwww.memphisqueen.com).

Accommodation

Downtown Memphis has a reasonable mixture of grand hotels and inexpensive **places to stay**, though most budget motels are concentrated along Elvis Presley Boulevard to the south. The visitor center (see above) gives good advice, and is particularly helpful at busy times, such as the anniversary of Elvis's death in mid-August, and the month-long Memphis in May festival. The closest **campground** to Graceland is right across the street, at the *Memphis–Graceland RV Park*, 3691 Elvis Presley Blvd (☏901/396-7125 or 1-866/571-9236).

Best Western Benchmark 164 Union Ave ☏901/527-4100 or 1-800/380-3236, Ⓦwww.bestwestern.com. Chain option in prime downtown location immediately north of *The Peabody* hotel (see below); good value, though somewhat worse for wear. ❸

Elvis Presley's Heartbreak Hotel 3677 Elvis Presley Blvd ☏901/332-1000 or 1-877/777-0606, Ⓦwww.heartbreakhotel.net. Themed hotel across from Graceland, where every room has a fridge and microwave, plus 24hr Elvis videos. Several suites are gloriously lavish. There's also a (small) heart-shaped pool, the *Jungle Room* lounge sells burgers and peanut butter sandwiches, and they offer package deals that include the other Elvis attractions. ❹

Memphis Hostel/Days Inn Riverbluff 340 W Illinois St ☏901/948-9005 or 1-800/329-7466. Some rooms are kitted out as co-ed dorms, with beds costing $15. The standard private rooms are also good value, but the neighborhood, beside the river several blocks south of downtown, near the (US-55) Memphis–Arkansas Bridge, is not safe for walking. ❶–❸

Memphis Marriott Downtown 250 N Main St ☏901/527-7300 or 1-888/557-8740,

Ⓦwww.marriott.com/memdt. Good-quality large hotel with pool and health club, opposite the Convention Center, with views of the river and Pyramid. ❻

The Peabody 149 Union Ave ☏901/529-4000 or 1-800/732-2639, Ⓦwww.peabodymemphis.com. Opulent downtown landmark hotel, right near Beale Street. Don't miss the legendary mascot ducks, who waddle from the elevator (to the strains of the "King Cotton March") promptly at 11am; they spend the day in the lobby fountain, and return to their penthouse at 5pm. Standard guestrooms are overpriced, but if you can afford the luxury ones it's a great place to stay. ❽

Sleep Inn at Court Square 40 N Front St ☏901/522-9700 or 1-800/424-6423, Ⓦwww.sleepinn.com. Friendly, good-value motel in the heart of downtown, facing the river near Mud Island and backing right onto Main Street; rates include a small breakfast. ❹

Talbot-Heirs Guesthouse 99 S Second St ☏901/527-9772 or 1-800/955-3956, Ⓦwww.talbothouse.com. Upscale B&B-cum-guesthouse, very close to Beale Street, where each of the nine themed suites has a kitchen, CD player, and Internet access. ❺

The City

Downtown Memphis still retains a healthy ensemble of fine buildings from the cotton era, best admired either along the riverfront or from the trolley route down **Main Street**. Today these edifices are more likely to have been converted into expensive apartments than to house thriving businesses, but at least the city streets are once more busy with pedestrians. While atmospheric, however, the central blocks hold few significant tourist attractions. Instead, visitors tend to head southwards, beyond the large new **Peabody Place** mall – which has unarguably succeeded in luring locals back downtown, even if it could really be anywhere in the US – to the music mecca of **Beale Street**, with the **Civil Rights** and **Rock'n'Soul** museums just beyond that, and **Sun Studio** not far east. Elsewhere, **Mud Island** on the river itself merits half a day, as does the **Stax** museum, while **Graceland**, ten miles out, should on no account be missed.

Beale Street

Beale Street began life as one of Memphis's most exclusive enclaves; its elite residents were driven out by yellow fever epidemics, to be replaced by a diverse mix of blacks, whites, Greeks, Jews, Chinese, and Italians. But it was **black culture** that gave the street its fame. Beale Street was where black roustabouts, deckhands, and travelers passing through Memphis immediately headed; rural blacks came for the bustling Saturday market; and, in the Jim Crow era, Beale served as the center for black businesses, financiers, and professionals.

As the black Main Street of the mid-South, Beale in its Twenties' heyday was jammed with vaudeville theaters, concert halls, bars, and jook joints (mostly white-owned). Along with the frivolity came a reputation for heavy gambling, voodoo, murder, and prostitution. One appalled evangelist proclaimed that "if whiskey ran ankle deep in Memphis . . . you could not get drunker quicker than you can on Beale Street now."

Although Beale still drew huge crowds in the Forties, the drift to the suburbs and, ironically, the success of the **civil rights** years in opening the rest of Memphis to black businesses, almost killed it off. The **bulldozers** of the late Sixties spared only the Orpheum Theatre and a few commercial buildings between Second and Fourth streets.

Beale Street has now been restored as a **Historic District**, no longer geographically separated from downtown now that the Peabody Place mall has bridged the former gap. Its shops, clubs, and cafés are bedecked with Twenties-style facades and signs, while a Walk of Fame with brass musical notes embedded into the sidewalk honors musical greats such as B.B. King and Howlin' Wolf. Tourist money has led to extensive development, but with the exception of a few out-and-out souvenir shops, most of the new businesses remain in tune with the past, and for blues fans in particular its music venues showcase top regional talent. At Beale's western end, the former home of **Lansky's**, tailors to the Memphis stars, at no. 126, was remodeled in 1997 to become *Elvis Presley's – Memphis* (see p.589), which now rivals *B.B. King's* opposite as the street's busiest nightspot.

A short way east of *B.B. King's*, **A. Schwab's Dry Goods Store**, at no. 163 (closed Sun), looks much as it must have done when it opened in 1876, with an incredible array of such voodoo paraphernalia, familiar from the blues, as Mojo Hands and High John the Conqueror lucky roots in fragrant oil, as well as 99¢ neckties and Sunday School badges. Next door, the free **Memphis Police Museum**, open around the clock, holds an assortment of old photos, newspapers, and crime-fighting accoutrements – great fun at night after club-hopping.

A block off Beale to the south, the **Memphis Rock'n'Soul Museum**, on the second floor of the Gibson Guitar Plant, 145 Lt George W. Lee Ave (Mon–Sun 10am–6pm; ⓦ www.memphisrocknsoul.org; $8.50), is run in collaboration with the Smithsonian Institution. Designed to present the story of Memphis music in the context of such issues as migration, racism, civil rights, and youth culture, it's a fascinating exhibition, though you may find yourself racing past the rather academic introductory section in order to reach the holy relics on display, which range from Elvis's stage gear and one of B.B. King's

"Lucille" guitars to Al Green's Bible. After you're done with the museum, you can check out the **Gibson Guitar Plant** itself, which offers guided **tours** on which visitors can watch the manufacture of six-string and bass guitars ($10, ages 12 and over only; call ☏901/543-0800 for times and reservations).

The sound of Memphis

Since the start of the twentieth century, Memphis has been a meeting place for black musicians from the Delta and beyond. During the Twenties, the city's downtown bars, clubs, and street corners were alive with the sound of the blues. **Jug bands**, in which singers were given a bass accompaniment by a musician blowing across the neck of a jug, were a specialty. Several songs by **Gus Cannon's Jug Stompers** – such as "Walk Right In" – became hits for white artists during the folk revival of the Sixties. **Bukka White**, **Memphis Slim**, and guitarist **Memphis Minnie** appeared at nightspots like *Mitchell's Hotel* and *Pee Wee's Saloon*, all long since defunct. After World War II, young musicians and radio DJs such as **Bobby Bland** and **B.B. King** experimented by blending the traditional blues sound with jazz, adding electrical amplification to create **rhythm'n'blues**.

White promoter Sam Phillips started **Sun Records** in 1953, employing Ike Turner as a scout to comb the Beale Street clubs for new talent. Among those whom Turner helped introduce to vinyl were his own girlfriend, Annie Mae Bullock (later **Tina Turner**), **Howlin' Wolf**, and **Little Junior Parker**, whose "Mystery Train" was Sun's first great recording. Later in the same year Sun was founded, the 18-year-old **Elvis Presley** hired the studio to record "My Happiness," supposedly as a gift for his mother, and something prompted Phillips' assistant Marion Keisker to file away his details. The next summer, Phillips called Elvis back to the studio to cut "That's All Right," and thereby set out towards proving his much-quoted conviction that "If I could find a white man who had the Negro sound and the Negro feel, I could make a billion dollars." Phillips swiftly dropped his black artists, and signed other white **rockabilly** singers like **Carl Perkins** and **Jerry Lee Lewis** to record classics such as "Blue Suede Shoes" and "Great Balls of Fire." Elvis – who in the words of Carl Perkins had the advantage that he "didn't look like Mr. Ed, like a lot of the rest of us" – was soon sold on to RCA (for just $35,000), and didn't record in Memphis again until 1969, when, at Chips Moman's American Studios, he produced the best material of his later career, including "Suspicious Minds."

In the Sixties and early Seventies, Memphis's **Stax Records** provided a rootsy alternative to the poppier sounds of Motown. This hard-edged **southern soul** was created by a multiracial mix of musicians, with **Steve Cropper**'s fluid guitar complementing the blaring **Memphis Horns**. The label's first real success was "Green Onions," by studio band **Booker T. and the MGs**; further hits followed from **Otis Redding** ("Try A Little Tenderness"), **Wilson Pickett** ("Midnight Hour"), **Sam and Dave** ("Soul Man"), and **Isaac Hayes** ("Theme from Shaft"). The label eventually foundered in acrimony; the last straw for many of its veteran soulmen was the signing of the British child star Lena Zavaroni for a six-figure sum.

Memphis has been renowned for its **gospel** music since the Thirties, when Rev. Herbert Brewster wrote **Mahalia Jackson**'s "Move On Up a Little Higher." Following a religious revelation, the consummate soul stylist **Al Green**, who achieved chart success for **Hi Records** with hits like "Let's Stay Together" and "Tired of Being Alone," has preached since the early 1980s at his own Full Gospel Tabernacle, at 787 Hale Rd in the leafy suburb of Whitehaven. Visitors are welcome at the 11am Sunday services; to get there, continue a mile south of Graceland, then turn west (phone ahead to make sure the Reverend is in town; ☏901/396-9192, ⓦwww.algreen.com). While they're very much church services rather than concerts, Green remains a charismatic performer, and he does sing, backed by an absolutely smoking four-piece soul band.

Back on Beale and further east, the tiny former home of **W.C. Handy** stands at no. 352, having been moved here from 659 Janette St in 1983 (summer Tues–Sat 10am–5pm; winter Tues–Sat 11am–4pm; $2; ☎901/527–3427). In 1910, Handy was the first man to publish blues tunes (often blues in name only; see p.616). His "Memphis Blues" – originally called "Mr. Crump" – was the theme song for the 1909 mayoral election of Edward H. Crump, whose crooked political machine was to run the city until the early Fifties.

Sun Studio

After Graceland, Memphis's principal shrine to the memory of Elvis has to be **Sun Studio**, where he made his earliest recordings. It's located ten minutes' walk east of Beale Street at 706 Union Ave – though if you have the option, it makes more sense to drive. Sun Records moved out in 1959, but even when the building briefly became a scuba-diving store – not surprisingly, a commercial failure – all its soundproofing remained in place, making possible its restoration as a functioning studio in 1987. Every hour on the half-hour, twenty-minute tours (10am–6pm daily; $9.50; ☎901/521-0664, ⓦwww.sunstudio.com), lead past the display cases upstairs, one of which holds Elvis's actual high school diploma, and down into the single-room studio itself. Measuring just eighteen feet by thirty feet, the room focuses around Elvis's original mic stand, where you can pose for photos while the guide plays tapes of legendary recording sessions.

The National Civil Rights Museum

The **National Civil Rights Museum**, which provides the most rewarding and comprehensive history of the tumultuous struggle for civil rights to be had anywhere in the South, is located a few blocks south of Beale Street at 450 Mulberry St (June–Aug daily except Tues 9am–6pm; March–May & Sept–Jan Mon & Wed–Sat 9am–5pm, Sun 1–5pm; Feb Mon–Sat 9am–5pm, Sun 1–5pm; ⓦwww.civilrightsmuseum.org; $10). It's built around the shell of the former *Lorraine Motel*, where **Dr Martin Luther King Jr** was assassinated by James Earl Ray on April 4, 1968. Dr King was killed by a single bullet as he stood on the balcony, the evening before he was due to lead a march in Memphis in support of a strike by black sanitation workers.

The *Lorraine* itself was one of the few places where blacks and whites could meet in Memphis during the segregation era; thus black singer Eddie Floyd and white guitarist Steve Cropper wrote soul classics such as "Knock on Wood" there, and Dr King was a regular guest. The outer facade of the motel is still all too recognizable from images of King's death, but once inside visitors are faced with a succession of galleries that recount the major milestones of the movement, from A. Philip Randolph of the Brotherhood of Sleeping Car Porters, who originally called for a march on Washington in 1941, through to the Nation of Islam and the Black Panthers. Dioramas and reconstructions include a Montgomery bus, on which sitting on the front seat triggers a recorded message instructing you to move to the back, and a scene from the sanitation workers' dispute. However, by far the most affecting moment comes when you reach King's actual room, still laid out as he left it, and see the spot where his life was cut short.

A new wing of the museum, across from the motel, completes the story by incorporating the rooming house from which the fatal shot was fired. The bedroom rented that same day by James Earl Ray, and the sordid little bathroom that served as his sniper's nest, can both be inspected behind glass, with the death site clearly visible beyond. King's own family remain highly sceptical as to whether Ray acted alone, and very detailed panels lay out all sorts of conspiracy theories.

The Stax Museum of American Soul Music

The latest symbol of Memphis's revitalization arrived in 2003, in the resurrection of one of the city's most famous addresses, 926 E McLemore Avenue. In 1960, this spot, two bleak miles southeast of downtown, was occupied by the Capitol Theater, the central landmark of a neighbourhood where blacks had just started to outnumber whites. The theater then became the headquarters of the **Stax** record label, where over the next fifteen years artists such as Otis Redding, Isaac Hayes, Albert King, and the Staples Singers cut fifteen US number-one singles, and achieved 237 entries in the top 100. By 1990, however, with Stax long since defunct (see p.583), this was no more than a derelict lot.

Now Stax has resurfaced, the whole complex reconstructed larger than ever as the **Stax Museum of American Soul Music**, also known, thanks to the sign on the theater marquee, as **Soulsville** (March–Oct Mon–Sat 9am–4pm, Sun 1–4pm; Nov–Feb Mon–Sat 10am–4pm, Sun 1–4pm; Ⓦwww.soulsvilleusa.com; $9). Visits start with an honest film history of the label, incorporating both the triumphs and the tensions that arose from its all-but-unique status as a joint black-white enterprise in the segregated South. The first exhibit beyond, designed to emphasize the gospel roots of soul music, is an entire Episcopal Church, transported here from Duncan,

The Big Muddy

I do not know much about gods; but I think that the river
Is a strong brown god – sullen, untamed and intractable.

St Louis–born T.S. Eliot, *The Four Quartets*

North America's principal waterway, the **Mississippi** – the name comes from the Algonquin words for "big" and "river" – starts just ninety miles south of the Canadian border at Lake Itasca, Minnesota, and winds its way nearly 2400 miles to the Gulf of Mexico, taking in over one hundred tributaries en route and draining all or part of thirty-one US states and two Canadian provinces.

The **"Big Muddy"** – it carries 2lb of dirt for every 1000lb of water – is one of the busiest commercial rivers in the world, and one of the least conventional. Instead of widening toward its mouth, like most rivers, the Mississippi grows narrower and deeper. Its **delta**, near Memphis, more than three hundred miles upstream from the river's mouth, is not a delta at all, but an alluvial flood plain. Furthermore, its estuary deposits, which extend the land six miles out to sea every century, are paltry compared to other rivers; gulf currents disperse the sediment before it has time to settle.

The Mississippi is also, in the words of Mark Twain, who spent four years as a riverboat pilot, "the **crookedest** river in the world." As it weaves and curls its way extravagantly along its channel, it continually cuts through narrow necks of land to shape and reshape oxbow lakes, meander scars, cutoffs, and marshy backwaters. A bar could operate one day in Arkansas and then find itself in dry Tennessee the next, thanks to an overnight cutoff.

A more serious manifestation of the Mississippi's power is its propensity to **flood**. Although the river builds its own levees, artificial embankments have, since as early as 1717, helped to safeguard crops and homes. After the disastrous floods of 1927, the federal government installed a wide range of flood-protection measures; virtually the entire riverfront from Cape Girardeau, Missouri, to the sea is now walled in, and it's even possible to drive along the top of the larger levees.

While it's no longer feasible to sail Twain's route for yourself, **riverboat excursions** operate in most sizeable river towns. Longer cruises, between St Louis and New Orleans – or even further afield – on the luxurious *Delta Queen*, *American Queen*, and *Mississippi Queen* **paddlewheelers**, are expensive; contact the Delta Queen Steamboat Company (℡1-800/543-1949, Ⓦwww.deltaqueen.com).

Mississippi. Then follows a glorious celebration of soul history, by no means restricted to Stax, and abounding in video footage and recordings, as well as showpiece artifacts like Isaac Hayes' peacock-blue Cadillac, on which even the windscreen wipers are gold-plated. The actual studio has been re-created in loving detail – Elvis did use it, to record "Promised Land," while the Beatles wanted to – and features the original two-track tape recorder used by Otis Redding to record "Mr Pitiful" and "Respect," as well as Al Jackson's drum kit. A map of the immediate neighborhood, still in truth rundown, shows what an amazing assembly of talent lived nearby; Aretha Franklin was born at 406 Lucy Ave, while other local luminaries included Booker T, David Porter, and Memphis Slim.

The riverfront

The northern boundary of downtown Memphis is marked by the surreal 32-story, 321ft **Pyramid**, two-thirds the size of Egypt's Great Pyramid. Completed in 1991, it was intended as a symbolic link with the Nile Delta. Each summer, it plays host to a different internationally-themed exhibition in the so-called Wonders series, including "Florence and the Italian Renaissance" in 2004 and "Queen Victoria" in 2005 (for information and prices contact ☏901/312-9161, ⓦwww.wonders.org). Meanwhile, throughout the year, its 22,500-seat **theater** puts on Memphis's biggest concerts and ball games.

From Riverside Drive, **monorail trains** and a walkway reach **Mud Island** (June–Aug daily 10am–8pm; April, May, Sept & Oct daily except Mon 10am–5pm; park access free, monorail $2 or included in museum admission, museum $8; ⓦwww.mudisland.com) across Wolf Channel, which formed in 1910 when the river began depositing silt alongside a stationary boat. Highlights of the **Mississippi River Museum** here, an enjoyable and ingenious romp through the history of the river, include a full-sized reconstructed steam packet squeezed into the core of the building, a morbidly fascinating "Theater of Disasters," and the tales of little-known characters such as keelboatman Mike Fink, who in 1830 styled himself "half horse, half alligator"; there's also an overview of Memphis music. You can also visit the original **Memphis Belle**, a World War II B17 bomber, nearby. Cool your feet afterwards by strolling the half-mile **River Walk** to the southern tip of the island. This scale model of the Mississippi, complete with town grids, ends in the "Gulf of Mexico," where you can rent paddle boats at $1 per person to explore an enclosed basin. From the pavilion nearby, it's also possible to rent canoes and kayaks, or take an airboat ride, out on the real Mississippi (☏901/576-7241).

Back on the mainland from Mud Island, the small, tree-shaded **Jefferson Davis** and **Confederate parks** by the river are popular lunchtime meeting places. When the Union took Memphis during the Civil War, thousands of dismayed residents watched from these sites as seven out of eight Confederate gunboats were sunk.

South from Confederate Park down Front Street, the imposing buildings of **Cotton Row** might have seen busier days, but this is still the largest spot cotton market (meaning actual cotton is sold here, for cash) in the world. At the south end of downtown, **Tom Lee Park**, the venue for major outdoor events such as the Memphis in May festival, commemorates a black boatman who rescued 32 people from a sinking boat in 1925 – despite the fact that he couldn't swim. Plans are afoot to build a new landing area at the river end of Beale Street, which will become the base for river cruises.

Graceland attractions

Graceland is ten miles from downtown Memphis, at 3734 Elvis Presley Blvd, on bus route #13 from Third and Union streets. The ticket office is open April–Oct Mon–Sat 9am–5pm, Sun 9am–4pm; Nov–March Mon & Wed–Sun 10am–4pm. The last house tour starts at the ticket office's closing time, while the other attractions remain open for roughly two more hours.

A combined "Platinum" **ticket** to all attractions (allow three hours) is $25.25; house tours only, $16.25 (closed Tues Nov–Feb); automobile museum $7.25; airplanes $6.25; "Sincerely Elvis" $5.25; parking fee $2. **Reservations** are recommended, especially in August (℡901/332-1000 or 1-877/777-0606, ⊛www.elvis.com).

Graceland

In itself, Elvis Presley's **Graceland** was a surprisingly modest home for the world's most successful entertainer. It's certainly not the "mansion" you may have imagined, and while Elvis was clearly a man who indulged his tastes to the fullest, there's none of the pomposity that characterizes so many other showpiece Southern residences. Visits, run under the auspices of his widow Priscilla and daughter Lisa Marie, are affectionate celebrations of the man; never exactly tongue-in-cheek, but not cloyingly reverential either.

Elvis was just 22 when he paid $100,000 for Graceland in 1957. It was then considered one of the most desirable properties in Memphis, though now the neighborhood is distinctly less exclusive, its main thoroughfare – **Elvis Presley Boulevard** – lined with motels, fast-food joints, and surprisingly few Elvis-related souvenir shops. Tours start opposite the house in **Graceland Plaza**; excited visitors, kitted out with audio "wands", are ferried across the road in minibuses, which depart every few minutes and sweep through the musical gate in the "**Wall of Love**," scrawled with tens of thousands of messages from fans.

Though the audio tours, peppered with spoken memories from Lisa Marie and rousing choruses from the King, allow you to spend as long as you wish, it's not easy to get an accurate sense of the house's size and layout, as the upstairs rooms are out of bounds to visitors. The interior is a frozen tribute to the taste of the Seventies; choice moments include the Hawaiian-themed **Jungle Room**, with its waterfall and green shag-carpeted ceiling, where he recorded "Moody Blue" and other gems from his latter years, and the navy-and-lemon **TV Room**, mirrored and fitted with three screens that now display 1970s talk shows. By way of contrast, a former garage holds the original, much plainer leather furniture Elvis installed when he first moved in. In the separate **Trophy Room**, you parade past Elvis's platinum, gold, and silver records, stage costumes, outfits from many of his 31 films, and his extensive gun collection; the tour of the interior ends with the racquetball court where he played on the morning he died. Elvis (Jan 8, 1935 to Aug 16, 1977), his mother Gladys, his father Vernon, and his grandmother lie buried beside the swimming pool in the **Meditation Garden** outside, their graves strewn with flowers and soft toys sent daily from fans. Elvis's body was moved here two months after his death, when the security problems inherent in keeping it in the local cemetery became obvious.

The Plaza itself, resounding with nonstop Elvis hits and lined with gift shops, holds several enjoyable related attractions: don't miss the wittily edited free film *Walk a Mile in My Shoes*, the "**Sincerely Elvis**" collection of personal belongings – which features a TV punctured by a bullet fired by Elvis himself (he also shot his fridge, his stereo, and even Lisa Marie's slide), as well as the King's Hai

Karate and Brut aftershave – and Elvis's personal **airplanes**, including the *Lisa Marie*, customized with 24-carat gold washroom and a blue suede bathroom. End your tour with a sit-down in the **Elvis Presley Automobile Museum**, which, quite apart from a Harley-Davidson golf cart and powder-pink Cadillac, has a reconstructed drive-in showing clips from his movies. A couple of Elvis-themed diners – the barbecue at the *Cadillac Grill* is the best option – make it easy to stay all day.

Midtown and East Memphis

A mile east of downtown, the **Memphis Pink Palace Museum and Planetarium** at 3050 Central Ave (Mon–Thurs 9am–4pm, Fri & Sat 9am–9pm, Sun noon–6pm; $8) centers on the pink marble mansion of Clarence Saunders, who founded America's first chain of self-service **supermarkets**, Piggly-Wiggly, in 1916. Saunders went bankrupt in 1923, and never actually lived here; instead the building has acquired several new wings in the process of becoming an all-embracing museum of Memphis history, holding all kinds of stuffed animals and oddities, including a miniature circus, an IMAX cinema, and the **Sharpe Planetarium**, as well as a walk-through model of the first Piggly-Wiggly store, complete with 2¢ packets of Kellogg's Cornflakes and 8¢ cans of Campbell's Soup.

The centerpiece of the mile-long, heavily wooded expanse of **Overton Park**, three miles east of downtown (#50 bus) on Poplar Ave, is the **Memphis Zoo** (daily: March–Oct 9am–6pm; Nov–Feb 9am–5pm; $10), entered between two dramatic Egyptian-styled towers. If the usual array of gorillas, orangutans, and giraffes doesn't satisfy you, you can pay $3 extra to visit with a pair of giant pandas. The park also holds the wide-ranging **Memphis Brooks Museum of Art** (Tues–Fri 10am–4pm, Sat 10am–5pm, Sun 11.30am–5pm; $6; first Wed of the month free, except June–Aug; ⓦwww.brooksmuseum.org); **Overton Square**, the city's top suburban entertainment, dining, and shopping district, is within walking distance.

South of Overton Square, the tiny, hip **Cooper-Young** intersection is as yet little more than a handful of shops, with coffee bars interspersed with vintage stores where the city's punks and hippies burrow through secondhand psychedelic threads, and richer arty types muse over retro knickknacks. It's a lively place, quite different from downtown, where you're likely to stumble across poetry readings and yard sales, art exhibits and antique auctions.

Eating

Memphians are fond of their food, proclaiming their city to be the **pork barbecue** capital of the world, with over one hundred specialty restaurants. There's also a good selection of reasonably priced soul-food cafés, and a couple of cool *nouvelle* Southern places. **Downtown** has a good selection – note that several of the Beale Street clubs reviewed under "Nightlife" below also serve food. For a bit of variety, head out to **Overton Square** or **Cooper-Young** in Midtown.

Arcade 540 S Main St ☏ 901/526–5757. Said to be Memphis's oldest restaurant, this landmark diner in the burgeoning South Main District, a short walk south of the Civil Rights Museum, was featured in Jim Jarmusch's movie *Mystery Train*. It serves up large Southern breakfasts, and pizzas later in the day.

Automatic Slim's Tonga Club 83 S Second St ☏ 901/525-7948. Trendy Southwestern/Caribbean restaurant and nightspot, complete with tumbleweed and excellent if pricey food, with most entrees at over $20. Closed Sun.

Café Francisco 400 N Main St ☏ 901/578-8002. Large, funky deli-style café-cum-antique store (with Internet access), especially good for coffee and breakfasts, on the trolley route a block from the Pyramid.

Café Ole 959 S Cooper Ave ☎901/274-1504. Very popular Mexican restaurant in Cooper-Young, with good fajitas and veggie specialties such as spinach-and-mushroom quesadillas.

Ellen's Soul Food 601 S Parkway E ☎901/942-4888. Soul food to die for, south of downtown; fried chicken, barbecue, and an irresistible array of vegetables.

Interstate Bar-B-Que 2265 S Third St ☎901/775-2304. Legendary barbecue restaurant, south of downtown on the way to the Delta. Closed Sun.

Isaac Hayes' Music Food Passion 150 Peabody Place ☎901/529-9222, ⓦwww.isaachayesclub .com. Upscale soul-food restaurant that brings black locals flocking to the otherwise bland Peabody Place mall. The barbecued ribs and chicken reflect Hayes' incarnation as *South Park*'s "Chef" – individual entrees are well under $20, while a Hot Buttered Soul platter for 4–5 costs

$53. A $10 cover charge for entertainment – a funky-smooth soul band plays a couple of sets nightly – makes this a pricey, special-occasion venue.

Java Cabana 2170 Young Ave ☎901/272-7210. Cool alternative coffeehouse in the Cooper-Young district, featuring poetry readings and live music. Closed Mon.

Otherlands 641 S Cooper Ave ☎901/278-4994. Funky Midtown coffee bar that's good for lattes and bagels but poor for actual meals. Has its own gift shop, colorful "naïve" artworks, and a laid-back crowd. Open until 7pm weekdays, 8pm weekends.

The Rendezvous General Washburn Alley, 52 S Second St ☎901/523-2746. Downtown Memphis's top-rated pork barbecue joint is a colossal and very crowded institution, though you could walk past without noticing it. Good-value meat feasts in a hectic atmosphere. Open Tues–Sat.

Tsunami 928 S Cooper Ave ☎901/274-2556. Seafood restaurant in the Cooper-Young district with delicious pan-Asian dishes on the menu.

Nightlife and entertainment

Live music is at its best in Memphis during the city's many **festivals**, such as the month-long **Memphis in May** (which also features the World Championship Barbecue Cooking Contest) and August's **Elvis Tribute Week**. However, while it would be easy to look down on **Beale Street** as sanitized and inauthentic, its close-packed assortment of blues and soul clubs have plenty to offer fans all year round. The whole enclave is successful both architecturally and atmospherically, and tightly patrolled to ensure visitor safety, but buskers are sanctioned – keep an ear open for the raw electric blues of the "Wolfman." On Friday nights, a $10 wristband offers admission to all the major clubs.

The best sources of **listings** are the free weekly *Memphis Flyer*, and *Kreature Comforts*, a guide to the city produced by the hip folks at Shangri-La Records, 1916 Madison Ave ($3; ☎901/274-1916, ⓦwww.shangri.com).

B.B. King's Blues Club 143 Beale St ☎901/524-5464. Despite accusations from purists of having "sold out," this remains Beale's most popular club. Spacious and atmospheric, with barbecue ribs, catfish, and beer, and nightly blues enjoyed by a wildly enthusiastic crowd who make good use of the dance floor. B.B. himself makes an appearance or two per year.

Blues City Café 138 Beale St ☎901/526-1724. City branch of Mississippi soul-food specialist *Doe's Eat Place* (see p.615), open daily 11am–4am. Live music nightly until late, in a down-home atmosphere where you can join musicians from nearby clubs for well-priced ribs, catfish, tamales, and gumbo.

Elvis Presley's – Memphis 126 Beale St ☎901/527-6900, ⓦwww.epmemphis.com. Lansky's, the tailors where Elvis bought his

sharpest suits, has been transformed into a restaurant and bar with a heavily Elvis-themed menu – an $8 hunka hunka burnin' burger, for example. Lots of memorabilia, including the very pool table on which Elvis played against the Beatles in 1964, a nice outdoor patio upstairs, and live bands nightly.

HiTone Café 1913 Poplar Ave ☎901/278-8663, ⓦwww.hitonememphis.com. From Memphis garage bands via jazz and comedy to Elvis impersonators, this eclectic Midtown club is always worth checking out.

New Daisy Theatre 330 Beale St ☎901/525-8979, ⓦwww.newdaisy.com. Restored movie theater at the east end of Beale that puts on two or three grungy punk or metal bands most nights, but also makes a great venue for the occasional big-name artist.

The North End 346 N Main St ☎ 901/526-0319. Friendly bar-cum-restaurant in the Pinch District opposite the Pyramid, specializing in substantial, if not all that exciting, wild-rice dishes, plus a killer hot-fudge pie, and putting on live jazz, folk, or soul on weekends. Open until 3am nightly.

Rum Boogie Café 182 Beale St ☎ 901/528-0150. Live blues nightly until midnight in the main room, while the smaller and more intimate *Blues Hall*, adjoining, is a mocked-up jook joint that regularly hosts the frenetic punkabilly band Turbo 350.

W.C. Handy Performing Arts Park Third Ave and Rufus Thomas Blvd ☎ 901/526-0110. Outdoor amphitheater just off Beale, featuring live music – most nights for free.

Wild Bill's 1580 Vollintine Ave ☎ 901/726-5473. Genuine neighborhood jook joint three miles northeast of downtown in North Memphis, where visitors are welcome to join locals at the long tables to enjoy laid-back live blues, especially on Wed & Sat.

Shiloh National Military Park

Approximately 110 miles east of Memphis and twelve south of Savannah, Tennessee, via US-64 and Hwy-22, **Shiloh National Military Park** (daily 8am–5pm; $5 per vehicle; ☎ 731/689-5696, ⓦ www.nps.gov/shil) commemorates one of the most crucial battles of the Civil War. After victories at Fort Henry and Fort Donelson, General Grant's confident Union forces were all but defeated at Shiloh by a surprise early-morning Confederate attack on April 6, 1862. A stubborn rump of resistance held on until around 5pm, and the Confederates elected to finish the task off the next morning rather than launching a twilight assault. However, Grant's decimated regiments were bolstered by the overnight arrival of reinforcements, and instead it was their dawn initiative that forced the tired and demoralized Confederates to retreat.

Shiloh was the first encounter on a scale that became common as the war continued, putting an abrupt end to the romantic innocence of many a raw volunteer soldier. Over 20,000 men in all were killed. Even the war-toughened General Sherman spoke of "piles of dead soldiers' mangled bodies . . . without heads and legs . . . the scenes on this field would have cured anyone of war."

The **visitor center** displays artifacts recovered from the battlefield and shows a twenty-minute film. A self-guided ten-mile driving tour takes in the **National Cemetery**, whose moss-covered walls contain thousands of unidentified graves.

Nashville

Set amid the gentle hills and fertile farmlands of central Tennessee, **NASHVILLE** attracts six million visitors each year. The great majority – devoted fans and the just plain curious alike – come to immerse themselves in **country music**, whether at mainstream showcases like the **Country Music Hall of Fame** and the **Grand Ole Opry**, or in the smaller clubs and honky-tonks found not only downtown but also in Nashville's many disparate neighborhoods.

However, there's still a real city amid all the rhinestone glitter and showbiz razzmatazz. Nashville has been the leading settlement in middle Tennessee since **Fort Nashborough** was established in 1779. State capital since 1843, it is now the **financial** and **insurance** center of the mid-South, as well as a fast-growing **manufacturing** base. Giant Nissan and Saturn motor plants have been attracted to its immediate hinterland, and rapid growth since

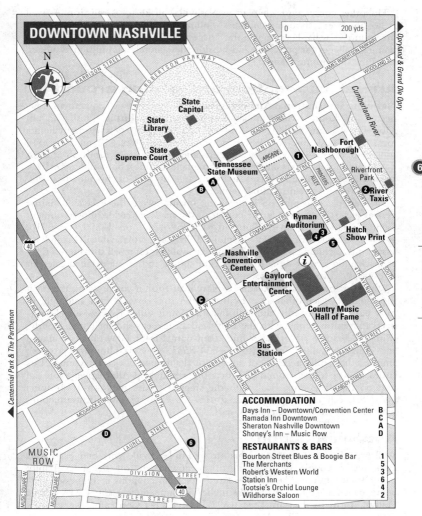

DOWNTOWN NASHVILLE

0   200 yds

N

State Capitol

State Library

State Supreme Court

Tennessee State Museum

Fort Nashborough

Riverfront Park

River Taxis

Ryman Auditorium

Hatch Show Print

Nashville Convention Center

Gaylord Entertainment Center

Country Music Hall of Fame

Bus Station

MUSIC ROW

Centennial Park & The Parthenon

Opryland & Grand Ole Opry

Cumberland River

ACCOMMODATION

Days Inn – Downtown/Convention Center	B
Ramada Inn Downtown	C
Sheraton Nashville Downtown	A
Shoney's Inn – Music Row	D

RESTAURANTS & BARS

Bourbon Street Blues & Boogie Bar	1
The Merchants	5
Robert's Western World	3
Station Inn	6
Tootsie's Orchid Lounge	4
Wildhorse Saloon	2

World War II has transformed a once-compact city into a sprawling conurbation stretching out in all directions along the undulating roads, here known as **pikes**.

For all its blue-collar "Nash-Vegas" image, Nashville has maintained a strong reputation for **learning** since planter times, and is home to sixteen higher education establishments, including Vanderbilt University and the renowned black colleges of Fisk University and Meharry Medical School. The city has long billed itself as the "Athens of the South," and even boasts a replica of the Parthenon to bolster this claim. It has also attracted teams from the NFL (the Tennessee Titans) and NHL (the Nashville Predators).

The other conspicuous element in Nashville's make-up is **religion**. As well as holding over a thousand churches – more per capita than anywhere else in the country – it has been tagged the "Protestant Vatican" for its proliferation of training colleges for preachers and missionaries, church administrative offices, and Bible-publishing plants.

Arrival, information, and getting around

Nashville International Airport is eight miles southeast of downtown, connected by hourly Metropolitan Transit Authority **buses** (until 5.33pm Mon–Fri, 4.13pm Sat & Sun; $1.45; ☎615/862-5950, ⓦwww.nashvillemta.org). The Gray Line shuttle (every 15min 6am–11pm; $12 one way, $18 roundtrip; ☎615/883-5555, ⓦwww.graylinenashville.com) drops off at most downtown hotels. **Taxis** are probably the quickest option but will set you back around $25. Greyhound **buses** arrive in a seedy part of downtown at 200 Eighth Ave S; there's no Amtrak service.

The best place to pick up information on the city is the excellent **visitor center** at 501 Broadway, at the corner of the massive Gaylord Entertainment Center (daily 8.30am–5.30pm; ☎615/259-4747 or 1-800/657-6910, ⓦwww.nashvillecvb.com). The helpful staff here can provide details on all local attractions, including a detailed downtown walking tour; sell discounted tickets packaging two or more local sights or shows; and post a detailed calendar of each day's live music and events.

While downtown can be readily explored **on foot**, if you're without a car it is possible to reach other areas by **bus**. MTA runs services until midnight to most parts of the county, although the #34 Music Valley Express, which connects the visitor center with the Opryland area, keeps shorter hours (hourly; Mon–Fri 10am–8.30pm, Sat & Sun 10am-6pm; $1.45). Gray Line (see above) and Johnny Walker Tours (☎615/834-8585, ⓦwww.johnnywalkertours), among others, offer a variety of both cultural and specialist country music **bus tours**; expect to pay around $30 for a three-hour trip. Alternatively, you can hop on the "Big Pink Bus" with the singing guides of Nash-Trash Tours (Wed–Sat; call for schedule; $25; ☎615/226-7300, ⓦwww.nashtrash.com), who dish the dirt on the country stars.

Accommodation

Well-priced **rooms** are not too hard to find in Nashville, with budget **motels** gathering a couple of miles north of downtown, off the I-65 Trinity Lane/Brick Church Pike exit (be sure to pick up coupons in Tennessee welcome centers). Rates are usually higher in June during the CMA Music Festival (formerly Fan Fair; see p.597). The CVB's **Central Reservations Center** (☎1-800/657-6910) offers discounted rates on most city hotels. There's RV and tent **camping** at *Opryland KOA*, 2626 Music Valley Drive (☎615/889-0282 or 1-800/562-7789, ⓦwww.koa.com), set in 27 attractive acres and with free live music shows in the summer.

Cat's Pajamas B&B 818 Woodland St ☎615/650-4553, ⓦwww.bbonline.com/tn/catspajamas. Friendly, simple three-room B&B, owned by musicians and a short walk east of downtown. Only one room has an en suite bathroom. **❹**

Days Inn – Coliseum 211 N First St ☎615/254-1551 or 1-800/251-3038, ⓦwww.daysinn.com. Inexpensive hotel close to downtown, with a good view of the city skyline. **❸**

Days Inn – Downtown/Convention Center 711 Union St ☎615/242-4311 or 1-800/627-3297, ⓦwww.daysinn. Excellent central downtown location, facing the capitol and offering good weekend rates. **❸**

Gaylord Opryland Resort 2800 Opryland Drive ☎615/889-1000 or 1-877/456-6779, ⓦwww

.gaylordhotels.com. Unbelievably vast and expensive 3000-room place – included here not because it's recommended, but simply because it's used by so many tour groups – laid out around lavish gardens and glass-roofed courtyards, permeated with syrupy music. It takes an age simply to get to or from your room, let alone drive the nine miles downtown. Suites can cost as much as $3500. **❼**

Ramada Inn Downtown 920 Broadway ☎615/244-0150 or 1-800/272-6232, ⓦwww .ramadainn.com. Reasonably priced downtown convention hotel, with pool and free breakfast buffet. **❺**

Sheraton Nashville Downtown 623 Union St ☎615/259-2000 or 1-800/447-9825, ⓦwww.sheratonnashville.net. Downtown high-rise in easy walking distance of the central attractions, offering very comfortable rooms, many with fine city views, plus good dining and amenities. **❻**

Shoney's Inn – Music Row 1501 Demonbreun St ☎615/255-9977 or 1-800/522-4667, ⓦwww.shoneysinn. Good-value accommodation complete with complimentary continental breakfast. **❹**

The City

Other than the venerable structures you'd expect in a state capital, such as the Capitol building itself, and various imposing courthouses and banks, the major landmarks of **downtown Nashville** are the unmissable new **Country Music Hall of Fame** at Fifth and Demonbreun streets, and the gigantic **Gaylord Entertainment Center** sports and entertainment complex (formerly the Nashville Arena) at Fifth Avenue and Broadway.

Further afield, **Music Row**, which centers on Demonbreun Street a mile southwest of downtown, used to be a major tourist destination, but since the Country Music Hall of Fame relocated downtown almost all its other tacky "museums" and souvenir stores have closed down. It remains the heart of Nashville's recording industry, with companies like Warner Bros., Mercury, and Sony operating out of plush office blocks, but otherwise there's no reason for tourists to visit.

The other main concentration of attractions is nine miles northeast of downtown in the **Opryland** area and in nearby **Music Valley**, which as well as playing host to the live *Grand Ole Opry* radio show holds several old-fashioned country music-related sights, including wax and car museums, mini-golf courses, and the like. The Opryland theme park that used to stand here has been replaced by the giant, upscale **Opry Mills** shopping mall.

The Country Music Hall of Fame

Nashville's premier visitor attraction is the superb **Country Music Hall of Fame**, 222 Fifth Ave S (daily 10am–6pm; $16, or 2-day pass $25; ☎615/416-2096, ⓦwww.countrymusichalloffame.com). The building itself is an architectural tour de force, laden with musical symbolism – the whole thing is in the shape of a bass clef; the central tower is topped by representations of a 12-inch LP, a 7-inch single, and a CD; a Cadillac fin pokes from one corner; and so on – but what really makes it special are the exhibits inside. These strike a clever balance between the music itself and the memorabilia that goes with it. Alongside stage costumes and paraphernalia from countless stars, including Elvis's gold Cadillac, you get a fascinatingly detailed history of all aspects of the genre from its earliest roots, with films and recordings constantly playing. Separate sound-proof booths are devoted to such milestone waxings as Ferlin Husky's 1956 "Gone," hailed as the first instance of the "Nashville Sound," while younger stars reminisce on video about the older generations. Songwriters and musicians give regular live demonstrations of their skills, and you can also use touch-screen technology to "interview" the likes of Dolly Parton. The **Hall of Fame** itself, right at the end, is somewhat anticlimactic, simply consisting of a circular chamber filled with plaques. In the main foyer,

THE SOUTH | **TENNESSEE** | Nashville

6

Nashville Country: The Grand Ole Opry

Country music is generally reckoned to have resulted from the interaction of British and Irish folk music, as brought by Tennessee's first Anglo settlers, with other ethnic musics, including the spirituals and gospel hymns sung by African-American slaves and their descendants. It first acquired its current form during the 1920s, with the arrival in **Nashville** of thousands of migrants fleeing rural poverty. As radios and record players became widely available, the **recording industry** took off, and Nashville became the obvious base for the musicians of the mid-South.

Local radio station **WSM** – "We Shield Millions," the slogan of its insurance-company sponsor – first broadcast on October 5, 1925, and swiftly established itself as a champion of the country sound. Two years later, at the start of his *Barn Dance* show, disc jockey George D. Hay announced "for the past hour we have been listening to music taken largely from Grand Opera, but from now on we will present **The Grand Ole Opry**." This piece of slang became the name of America's longest-running radio show, still broadcast live out to millions two to three nights every week on WSM-AM (650).

Swiftly outgrowing the WSM studios, the show moved in 1943 to a former tabernacle – the **Ryman Auditorium**. There it acquired a make-or-break reputation; up-and-coming singers could only claim to have made it if they had gone down well at the Opry. Among thousands of hopefuls who tried to get on the show were Elvis Presley, advised by an Opry official in 1954 to stick to truck-driving. The first appearance of **Hank Williams**, in 1949, commanded an unequaled six encores. Four years later, the Opry audience responded to his drink- and drug-induced death by singing his song "I Saw the Light."

The decade of prosperity after World War II witnessed country's first commercial boom. Recording studios, publishing companies, and artists' agencies proliferated in Nashville, and the major labels recognized that a large slice of the (white) record-buying public wanted something less edgy than rockabilly. The easy-listening **Nashville Sound** they came up with, pioneered by Patsy Cline and Jim Reeves, perpetuated by the likes of Barbara Mandrell and Kenny Rogers, and rendered even further twang-free by Shania Twain and Garth Brooks, remains the clean-cut face of country, even if the music has always retained its earthier side.

While the **clubs** and **bars** listed on p.597 can usually offer a livelier look at the contemporary scene, for a quick, enjoyable fix of what Nashville is all about, you can't beat an evening at the Grand Ole Opry. Since 1974, the Opry has been ensconced nine miles northeast of downtown, in a 4424-seat theater at what's now the Opry Mills mall. Around seventy artists rank as "members," including old-timers like Charlie Louvin and Porter Wagoner, perennial superstars like Dolly Parton and Loretta Lynn, and more recent chart-toppers such as Garth Brooks and Alison Krauss. Each show features at least a dozen acts, including guests as well as members, and there's usually a heavier concentration at the older end of the spectrum, as rising stars tend to be out on the road. However, for many younger performers, appearing at the Opry remains the greatest of honors – the stage incorporates a small piece of the original Ryman Auditorium stage – so the tradition is no danger of dying out.

the *SoBro Grill* sells good **food** – salads, sandwiches, and barbecue – and there's also a decent book and CD store.

For $10 extra, according to a changing daily schedule, the Hall of Fame also offers short **bus tours** that provide the only way to visit RCA's legendary **Studio B** on Music Row. Between 1957 and 1977, forty gold records were cut here, starting with Don Gibson's "Oh Lonesome Me" and including Dolly Parton's "Jolene," but it's probably most famous for a thirteen-year run of Elvis hits (invariably recorded at night) like "Are You Lonesome Tonight?" and "It's Now or Never." Recently restored and re-wired, it's once again open for business, but only the most dedicated of fans are likely to find walking through the bare rooms worth the time and money.

Downtown Nashville

Most of **downtown Nashville** looks much like any other regional business center, dominated by office blocks and parking lots, though it's well worth strolling along both **Broadway** and **Second Avenue** to enjoy their atmospheric assortment of honky-tonks, bars, restaurants, and gift stores. In business since 1879, **Hatch Show Print**, at 316 Broadway (Mon–Fri 9am–5pm, Sat 10am–5pm; ☎615/256-2805), prints and sells evocative posters from the early days of country and rock 'n' roll, using the original blocks, and continues to produce new work. At the foot of Broadway, **Riverfront Park** is a thin stretch of grass and terracing dipping down to the **Cumberland River**. Immediately north, set above the river on a promontory, a replica of the wooden **Fort Nashborough** (Tues–Sun 9am–5pm; free) serves as a monument to the city's founders of 1779.

The original home of the Grand Ole Opry, the **Ryman Auditorium**, at 116 Fifth Ave, can be seen on self-guided tours (daily 9am–4pm; $8; ☎615/889-3060, ⓦwww.ryman.com). Its wooden church pews, and display cases filled with flowered frocks and bootlace ties belonging to the stars, evoke the heyday of traditional country, and it still presents live evening performances by big-name bands.

A few blocks north, the worthy **Tennessee State Museum**, 505 Deaderick St (Tues–Sat 10am–4pm, Sun 1–4pm; free; ⓦwww.tnmuseum.org), is strongest on the Civil War, highlighting the hardships suffered by the ill-clad, ill-fed soldiers on both sides, of whom 23,000 out of 77,000 died at Shiloh alone. Other displays in this huge space focus on frontier life and on black Tennesseans, looking at slavery, Reconstruction, the founding of the Ku Klux Klan, and the civil rights movement.

Marking downtown's northern boundary, at Sixth and Charlotte avenues, the resplendent **Tennessee State Capitol** (Mon–Fri 9am–4pm; free), modeled on an Ionic temple, looks out across the city from its hilltop perch. Early in the twentieth century, this area was yet another "Hell's Half Acre," notorious for its drinking holes, gambling clubs, sex shows, and dope dens; it's considerably tamer now, housing hotels and offices.

West of Downtown

In 1897, Tennessee celebrated its Centennial Exposition in **Centennial Park**, two miles southwest of downtown at West End and 25th avenues. Nashville honored its nickname as the "Athens of the South" by constructing a full-sized wood-and-plaster replica of the **Parthenon**. That proved so popular that it was replaced by a permanent structure in 1931, an impressive edifice that's now home to Nashville's premier **art museum** (Tues–Sat 9am–4.30pm; April–Sept also Sun 12.30–4.30; $3.50). The lower level contains American paintings, including Sanford R. Gifford's luminous 1871 *Autumn in the Catskills*, as well as displays on the construction and restoration of the original Greek Parthenon. The upper hall is dominated by a freshly gilded 42ft replica of Phidias's statue of the goddess Athena – said to be the largest indoor statue in the western world – surrounded by reproductions of the Elgin Marbles.

Just across West End Avenue from Centennial Park, weather-beaten Gothic structures sit alongside more modern utilitarian buildings on the campus of the prestigious, and highly conservative, **Vanderbilt University**. South of there, 21st Avenue S runs through the heart of **Hillsboro Village**, perhaps Nashville's most characterful residential neighborhood, abounding in cafés, restaurants, and book and antique stores.

Half a mile northeast of Centennial Park, **Fisk University** is one of the nation's oldest black colleges, and produced several of the student leaders who pioneered the sit-in movement and integrated downtown Nashville at the start of the civil rights era. The excellent **Van Vechten Gallery**, on campus at Jackson St and D.B. Todd Blvd (Tues–Fri 10am–5pm, Sat & Sun 1–5pm; closed Sun in summer; donation), holds works by Picasso, Cézanne, Renoir, and Georgia O'Keeffe; it also has changing exhibits on African-American themes.

Eating

Nashville has its share of awful chain restaurants, but it also offers many down-home Southern joints, as well as upmarket places well suited for expense-account dining. Many live music venues (see below) also serve food. If you have a car, be sure to get out to *The Loveless Café*, quite simply one of the best **country restaurants** in the South.

Brown's Diner 2102 Blair Blvd ☎615/269-5509. A classic diner where the cheeseburgers are to die for. Order one with everything on it – a perfect hangover cure.

Cock o' the Walk 2624 Music Valley Drive ☎615/889-1930. Fantastic catfish served in cheery riverboat-themed environs. Open for dinner daily, Sun lunch only.

Jimmy Kelly's 217 Louise Ave ☎615/329-4349. Nashville's favorite steakhouse for seventy years, just off West End Ave near Vanderbilt. Open for dinner only Mon–Sat.

The Loveless Café 8400 Hwy-100, 20 miles south of town ☎615/646-9700. Friendly motel café famed for its superb country food. Breakfasts are best: hunks of salty ham with gravy, eggs, toast, and fluffy biscuits slicked with succulent homemade jams.

The Merchants 401 Broadway ☎615/254-1892. This historic and very central downtown building

houses two reliably good dining rooms; the casual grill downstairs, which is ideal for a tasty lunch, and the more formal restaurant upstairs, serving classic American favorites.

Nashville Deli 1918 Broadway ☎615/329-6674. Great breakfasts, huge sandwiches, and wicked shakes until midnight on Fri and Sat in this student-friendly haunt.

Pancake Pantry 1796 21st Ave ☎615/383-9333. One of Nashville's most popular breakfast spots – expect to wait for a table. Close to Vanderbilt University and Music Row, in the like-able Hillsboro Village district. Open daily 6am–4pm.

Sunset Grill 2001 Belcourt Ave ☎615/386-3663. Stylish restaurant in Hillsboro Village, serving upmarket food such as fresh fish in smoky sauces. The terrace is great for people-watching. Lunch Tues–Fri only, dinner until late nightly, costing around $30 per head.

Nightlife and entertainment

The two most obvious ways to experience **live country music** in Nashville are either to take a walk past the cluster of **honky-tonks** that line Broadway between Second and Fourth avenues – they're all pretty down-to-earth, hard-drinking places, though out-of-towners nonetheless make up a large proportion of the clientele – or to buy a ticket for a rather more genteel show at the **Grand Ole Opry**, a fair drive out from downtown (see box, p.594). If you're in town for a few nights, however, it's worth making the effort to catch up-and-coming or more specialized acts at places like the *Bluebird Café* and the *Station Inn*; also look out too for special events at the **Ryman Auditorium** (see p.594).

For **listings** of upcoming gigs and events, check the free weeklies *Nashville Scene* or *The Rage*, Thursday's *Nashville Banner*, or Friday and Saturday's *Tennessean*. Every Thursday evening in summer, the **Dancin' in the District** event at Nashville Coliseum Field, just across the river from downtown, features big-name stars (ranging from George Clinton to Hootie and the Blowfish) for a token cover charge. In mid-June, the **CMA Music Festival** (formerly known as the **Fan Fair**) is a week-long series of concerts and opportunities to meet the stars (T 1-800/262-3378, W www.cmafest.com).

Nashville's prime venue for theater, dance, and classical music is the **Tennessee Performing Arts Center**, at 505 Deaderick St (T 615/782-4000, W www.tpac.org), which holds four separate stages. From June to August, its **symphony orchestra** also puts on concerts in **Centennial Park**.

Bluebird Café 4104 Hillsboro Rd T 615/383-1461, W www.bluebirdcafe.com. Intimate café, six miles west of downtown, that's *the* place to see the latest honky-tonk and country artists. Early evening entertainment – often open-mic sessions for aspiring songwriters, from 6.30pm – is free, but a cover of $8–15 is charged for the second show. Reservations recommended.

Bourbon Street Blues & Boogie Bar 220 Printers Alley T 615/242-5837, W www .bourbonstreetblues.com. Consistently good blues, live every night, in the otherwise awful downtown Printers Alley.

Ernest Tubb's Record Store Midnight Jamboree Texas Troubadour Theatre, 2414 Music Valley Drive T 615/885-0028. A live radio show, recorded every Sat from midnight to 1am, in a purpose-built theater adjoining the Music Valley branch of *Tubb's* (there's another one on Broadway), and featuring genuinely promising newcomers as well as major Opry stars.

Exit/In 2208 Elliston Place T 615/321-3340. Dependable venue for rock, reggae, and country, with the occasional big name, not to mention beer and pizza. Open nightly; $5–20 cover after 9pm.

Robert's Western World 416 Broadway T 615/244-9552. Some of the best country music on Broadway, plus rockabilly and Western swing, in a honky-tonk that doubles up as a cowboy boots store.

Station Inn 402 12th Ave T 615/255-3307, W www.stationinn.com. Very popular bluegrass and acoustic venue, near Music Row, with a strict no-smoking policy. Shows at 9pm nightly.

Tootsie's Orchid Lounge 422 Broadway T 615/726-0463. Venerable downtown honky-tonk, with a raucous atmosphere and good, gutsy live performers.

Wildhorse Saloon 120 Second Ave T 615/902-8200. Busy downtown dance hall/restaurant with big-screen transmission of TNT (The Nashville Network) and CMT (Country Music Television), both of which film here occasionally.

South from Nashville

Southeast of Nashville, nineteenth-century plantation homes line US-31 between suburban Brentwood and historic **Franklin**, eighteen miles out. One of the bloodiest battles of the Civil War was fought here on November 30, 1864, when 8500 men fell in less than an hour. Twenty-two thousand Confederates forced a Union retreat to Nashville, but incurred such heavy casualties as to shatter their Army of Tennessee beyond further use. Among strategic buildings open to visitors is **Carnton Plantation**, a former Confederate hospital where bloodstains are still visible on the floor, a mile southeast of town on Hwy-431 (Mon–Sat 9am–5pm, Sun 1–5pm; $8; T 615/794-0903, W www.carnton.org). Franklin's entire fifteen-block center, now filled with antique and specialty shops, is listed in the National Register of Historic Places. Country stars who favor the area include Billy Ray Cyrus, who owns a 400-acre ranch here.

Jack Daniel's at Lynchburg

The change-resistant village of **LYNCHBURG**, seventy miles southeast of Nashville, is home to **Jack Daniel's Distillery** (daily 9am–4.30pm; free). Founded in 1866, this is the oldest registered distillery in the country (hence the famous "No. 1" appellation). Entertaining seventy-minute **tours** lead through every step of the sour-mash whiskey-making process; ironically, you can't actually sample the stuff, as this is a dry county (though you can purchase special-edition bottles, every day but Sunday).

Lynchburg itself is a pretty hamlet, laid out around a neat town square with a redbrick courthouse and a number of old-fashioned stores. One enjoyable throwback is *Miss Mary Bobo's Boarding House*, which serves enormous **Southern dinners** (fried chicken, turnip greens, country ham, and the like) at group tables in a lovely 1805 home (reservations essential; ☎615/759-7394).

Eastern Tennessee

Until the creation of the Tennessee Valley Authority, the opening of **Great Smoky Mountains National Park**, and the construction of the interstate highways, life had remained all but unchanged in the remote hills and valleys of **eastern Tennessee** since the arrival of the earliest pioneers. Now visitors flock here for the endless expanses of natural beauty; and as a result, especially in the fall, the Smokies can get very clogged with traffic. Most communities in the area are small, and either over-touristed or just bland. Of the two main cities – modern **Knoxville** and picturesque **Chattanooga**, both of which have benefitted from considerable industrial growth thanks to cheap TVA power – only Chattanooga holds much appeal for tourists.

Smoky Mountain gateway towns

Most visitors who approach the Smokies from the north or west leave I-40 twenty miles east of Knoxville, or 200 miles east of Nashville, and sweep south on **Hwy-66** and **US-441** through the 25-mile procession of heavily commercialized "**gateway towns**" that leads to the national park. This is Tennessee's most conspicuously touristed area, its endless motels, sprawling campgrounds, chain diners, country music theaters, and expensive novelty "attractions" consistently geared towards vacationing families. The odd motel might enjoy an appealing rural setting, but if you're on a road trip it makes more sense to think of the various communities as cheapish overnight stops – though **accommodation** prices fluctuate seasonally, from $20 up to $80, and also rise significantly on weekends – than as stimulating destinations in their own right.

Sevierville

SEVIERVILLE, eight miles south of the I-40, is still just about recognizable as a small market town, though it now feels pretty much swamped by the mass of chain motels that line the highway through. A statue of native daughter **Dolly Parton** stands on the lawn outside the courthouse. Local **information** can be had from the **visitor center** just off I-40 (daily 9am–5.30pm). Inexpensive **motels** include a *Super 8*, 1410 Winfield Dunn Parkway (☎865/429-0887 or 1-800/800-8000; ❷), while the three-room **B&B** *Calico Inn*, 757 Ranch Way (☎865/428-3833 or 1-800/235-1054; ❺), does great breakfasts. The best spot for **lunch** in the town center is *Virgil's*, 109 Bruce St (☎865/453-2782), a 1950s diner serving up big plates of burgers and home-cooking.

Pigeon Forge

The dry town of **PIGEON FORGE** is theoretically five miles south of Sevierville, though in fact there's barely a break in the relentless strip of discount outlets, diners, and motels between the two. With fifty or so themed **attractions**, ranging from Dollywood (see opposite) to the *Black Bear Jamboree Dinner and Show*, there's ostensibly lots to do here – though most everything is

Dolly Parton's Dollywood

Born in 1946, one of twelve children, **Dolly Parton** lived in several modest homes around Pigeon Forge, the most isolated of them two miles from the nearest neighbor and over four miles from the mailbox. As a child she sang every week on local radio, before leaving for Nashville on the day she finished at Sevier County High School. Her first success, duetting with Porter Wagoner, came to an acrimonious end in the early Seventies, but she scored a major country hit in 1976 with "Jolene." She then crossed over to a poppier sound, and into Hollywood films like *9 to 5* and *The Best Little Whorehouse in Texas*. Her songs have been acclaimed for their readiness to address issues like rural poverty, and a refusal to tag along with the Nashville stereotype of subservient females.

Dollywood, Dolly Parton's "homespun fun" theme park at 700 Dollywood Lane in Pigeon Forge (April–Dec; call or visit the website for schedule; April–Oct $40, children ages 4–11 $30; Nov & Dec $35, children $18; ℡865/428-9488, Ⓦwww.dollywood.com), blends ersatz mountain heritage with the glamour of its celebrity shareholder. One section showcases Appalachian **crafts**, making everything from lye soap to horse-drawn carriages; a museum looks at Dolly herself in entertaining detail; and music shows are constantly on the go. The thrill rides, however, are mostly unspectacular (the **Tennessee Tornado** roller coaster being the exception), and the whole place can get insufferably precious.

There's an adjoining water park, **Dolly's Splash Country** (late May to mid-Sept; call for schedule; $30, children $25; combo tickets valid in either park for 3 days within a week $62, children $47; same phone, Ⓦwww.dollyssplashcountry.com).

appealing only on a kitschy level. Pigeon Forge's brand-new **welcome center** will open in summer of 2004 at 1950 Parkway (℡865/453-8574 or 1-800/251-9100, Ⓦwww.mypigeonforge.com). Reasonable **motels** include the *Parkview*, 2806 Parkway (℡865/453-5051 or 1-800/239-9116; ❸; April to mid-Dec), and the comfortable, friendly *Shular Inn*, 2708 Parkway (℡865/453-2700 or 1-866/657-2739; ❸), both of which have pools. The *Smoky Mountain Pancake House*, 4160 Parkway (℡865/453-6746), is good for **breakfast**.

Gatlinburg

If you can't bring yourself to stop in Pigeon Forge, you'll likely end up in **GATLINBURG**, another five miles south on US-441. It's a marginally more attractive place, squeezed amid the foothills of the Smokies, where the odd genuine relic of its Germanic heritage still shows through. As well as being a little more upmarket, it's also "wet," so its restaurants serve alcohol. While there is at least a town center to stroll through, it's once again bursting with overpriced, gimmicky tourist attractions, including **Christus Gardens**, with its dioramas of the life of Christ, and a mini-golf course that "transports you back to Gatlinburg's historic past, while challenging your putting skills." It also offers a couple of chair lifts up the surrounding peaks, one of which leads to the year-round Ober Gatlinburg **ski resort** and **amusement park**.

Gatlinburg's central Parkway holds three separate **visitor centers** (℡1-800/568-4748, Ⓦwww.gatlinburg.com). **Accommodation** options here are relatively high-priced (this being the closest town to the park), but the *Sidney James Mountain Lodge*, slightly up from the mayhem at 610 Historic Nature Trail (℡865/436-7851 or 1-800/362-9394, Ⓦwww.sidneyjames.com; ❸), offers large comfortable rooms and two pools, while the more luxurious *Bon Air Lodge*, 950 Parkway (℡865/436-4857 or 1-800/848-4857, Ⓦwww.smoky-mountainresorts.com; ❹), is also good value. East of town, *Bell's Wa-Floy Retreat* at 3610 E Parkway (℡865/436-5575; ❶) is a Christian **youth hostel** with beds for $15 (two-night minimum stay) and a pool. Central **eating** options include *Linebergers*, 903 Parkway (☎865/436-9284), which serves decent seafood, and *Panera*, a chain bakery-café at 815 Parkway (☎865/430-7388).

Townsend

A much less frenetic approach to the Smokies, if you're driving in from the east, is to follow the pretty Foothills Parkway through woods and across misty mountains, and then take US-321 for the final seven miles to **TOWNSEND**, twelve miles west of Pigeon Forge. There's no town to speak of, just a peaceful strip where the motels are laid-back and the air is clear. The peaceful *Highland Manor*, 7766 E Lamar Alexander Parkway (☎865/448-2211 or 1-800/213-9462, ⓦwww.highlandmanor.com; ❷–❹), is a friendly place with great views, while the rustic *Wonderland Lodge*, closer to Pigeon Forge at 3889 Wonderland Way (☎865/428-0779 or 1-877/428-0779, ⓦwww.smoky.net /wonderland.com; ❸), is even more idyllic. The *Hearth and Kettle*, opposite the *Highland Manor* at 7767 E Lamar Alexander Parkway (☎865/448-6059), dishes up fresh trout and crispy fried chicken in a country-store atmosphere.

Great Smoky Mountains National Park

The northern boundary of **GREAT SMOKY MOUNTAINS NATION-AL PARK**, which stretches for seventy miles along the Tennessee–North Carolina border (see also p.533), lies just two miles south of Gatlinburg on US-441. Don't expect immediate tranquility, however: the roads, particularly in the fall, can be lined almost bumper-to-bumper with cars, and if you're not staying in Gatlinburg it's best to use the well-marked bypass rather than drive through the town.

Located within a day's drive of the major urban centers of the East Coast and the Great Lakes – and of two-thirds of the entire US population – the Smokies attract over ten million visitors per year, more than twice as many as any other national park. These heavily contorted peaks are named for the **bluish haze** that hangs over them, made up of moisture and hydrocarbons released by the lush vegetation (a mature tree emits up to 900 gallons on a summer day). Since

the Sixties, however, **air pollution** has been adding sulphates to the filmy smoke, and has cut back visibility by thirty percent. More than 120 tree species and over 1400 flowering plants clothe the mountains and meadows in color from early spring to late fall. Sixteen peaks rise above 6000ft, their steep elevation accounting for dramatic changes in climate.

While between late March and mid-May is a great time to visit for the delicate spring flowers, the **busiest periods** in the park are midsummer (from mid-June to mid-August), and, especially, October, when the hills are shrouded in a magnificent canopy of glaring reds, subtle yellows, and faded browns. During June and July, rhododendrons blaze fiercely in the sometimes stifling summer heat.

Just inside the park on US-441, **Sugarlands Visitor Center** (daily: summer 8am–7pm; fall and spring 8am–6pm; winter 8am–5pm; ☎865/436-1200, ⓦwww.nps.gov/grsm) is a useful source of leaflets covering hiking trails, driving tours, forests, and wildlife, and can provide details on each day's program of ranger-led tours and activities. Many visitors however do no more than follow US-441, here known as the Newfound Gap Road, all the way through to North Carolina. From the gap itself, ten miles along on the state line, a spur road to the right winds for seven more miles up to **Clingman's Dome**, at 6643ft the highest point not only in the park but in all of Tennessee. A surreal concrete spiral walkway on top affords a panoramic, though hazy, view of the mountains, rather spoiled by the fact that virtually all the mature balsam firs in the area have been killed off by insect infestation.

If you want to spend longer exploring within the park, the main focus of visitor activity is in the **Cades Cove** area, which can be reached either by branching west at Sugarlands along the scenic **Little River Road**, or directly from Townsend via **Rich Mountain Road** (closed in winter). The eleven-mile driving loop here, always jam-packed with cars in summer and fall, passes deserted barns, homesteads, mills, and churches that stand as a reminder of the farmers who carved out a living from this wilderness, before they were forced to move out when national-park status was conferred in 1934. Halfway along, there's another **visitor center** (mid-April to Oct 9am–7pm; call ☎865/436-1200 for winter hours). This whole loop is reserved for **cyclists** on Saturday and Wednesday mornings in summer, from dawn until 10am; bikes can be rented at the *Cades Cove Campground*.

The best way of all to escape the crowds is to sample the eight hundred miles of **hiking** trails. On the **Appalachian Trail**, however, you can now only camp in designated areas, caged in behind iron bars to keep out the bears.

Chattanooga

Few cities can be so identified with a single song as **CHATTANOOGA**, in the southeast corner of Tennessee. Though visitors expecting Tex Beneke's and

---

Camping in the Smokies

Hikers intending to stay out overnight must obtain free **backcountry permits**, available from visitor centers (except in Cades Cove) and ranger stations. The park also has ten developed **campgrounds**, of which only one, *Smokemont*, remains open year-round. Most of the rest are open mid-March through October, the three most popular of which – *Cades Cove*, *Elkmont*, and *Smokemont* – are always fully booked in advance. If you want a space in the summer or fall, you should make **reservations** on ☎1-800/365-2267 or at ⓦreservations.nps.gov.

Glenn Miller's "Chattanooga Choo-Choo" may be disappointed that it's no longer served by Amtrak, the town continues to celebrate its railroad history, and has plenty more to offer besides – not least its beautiful location on a deep bend in the **Tennessee River**, walled in by forested plateaus on three sides. This setting led John Ross, of Scottish and Cherokee ancestry, to found a trading post on the spot in 1815, and its strategic importance made it a great prize during the Civil War. Victory here in 1863 helped establish the reputation of General Grant as the man who might win the war for the Union.

The Town

The centerpiece of Chattanooga's twenty miles of reclaimed riverfront is **Ross's Landing** (the town's original name), a park at the bottom of Broad Street. Here the splendid five-story **Tennessee Aquarium** traces the aquatic life of the Mississippi from its Tennessee tributaries to the Gulf of Mexico, and also shows giant IMAX movies (daily 10am–6pm; longer hours in summer; $14, IMAX $7.75, combined ticket $18; ☎ 423/265-0695 or 1-800/262-0695, Ⓦ www.tnaqua.org). Different **cruises** available on the *Southern Belle* **riverboat** (☎ 423/266-4488, Ⓦ www.chattanoogariverboat.com), from the foot of nearby Chestnut Street, include the daunting experience of bobbing around in the bottom of a huge lock on Chickamauga Lake. Prices start from $12 for a ninety-minute daytime sightseeing tour.

A few blocks from the river, the **Chattanooga Regional History Museum**, 400 Chestnut St (Mon–Fri 10am–4.30pm, Sat & Sun 11am–4.30pm; $4), takes a look at the area's rich history, with displays on the steel, soft-drink bottling, and power industries, as well as the Cherokee Indians. A short walk further along are the grand century-old buildings of the lively **business district**, such as the eye-catching Tivoli Theatre at 709 Broad St.

The further Chattanooga sprawls back from the river, the more run-down it becomes. Still, it's well worth heading the two miles up to the **Choo-Choo complex**, where the 1909 Beaux Arts–style Southern Railroad Terminal, 1400 Market St, is now a *Holiday Inn* – the *Chattanooga Choo-Choo Hotel*. The impressive high-domed waiting room serves as the lobby, leading through to the former platform area, where restored carriages act as hotel suites. Gift shops and cafés share space with a steam engine similar to the original Choo-Choo (the name given by the local paper to the first passenger train to come in from Cincinnati in 1880). You're free to roam around; admission to the world's largest model railway display, on site, is $3.

The authentic **steam trains** of the **Tennessee Valley Railroad** offer stunning six-mile rides, crossing the river, running through deep tunnels, and turning round on a giant turntable (April–Oct daily; Nov Sat & Sun only; $12; ☎ 423/894-8028, Ⓦ www.tvrail.com). The two main stations, restored to their 1930s look, are at 2200 N Chamberlain Ave in east Chattanooga and 4119 Cromwell Rd (I-75 exit 4 to Hwy-153); some routes pick up at the *Choo-Choo Hotel*.

Lookout Mountain

The name Chattanooga comes from a Creek word meaning "rock rising to a point"; the rock in question, the 2215ft **Lookout Mountain**, looms six miles south of downtown. To reach the top, either drive the whole way along a complicated, poorly signposted road, or catch the world's steepest **incline railway**, which grinds its tentative way up through a narrow gash in the lush forest from 3917 St Elmo Ave, near the foot of the mountain (on bus route #15), tackling nerve-racking gradients of up to 72.7 percent (daily: summer 8.30am–8.50pm; rest of year 9am–5.50pm; 3 trips per hour; $10; ☎ 423/821-4224). Once there, a steep five-minute walk through **Point Park** brings you to **Point Lookout**, the northern promontory of the mountain, which commands a not-to-be-missed view of the city and the meandering Tennessee River below. This forms part of the **Chickamauga and Chattanooga National Military Park**, covering several sites around the city and in nearby Chickamauga, Georgia, that witnessed fierce Civil War fighting in 1863. The battle here that November, in which Confederate forces that had been laying seige to Chattanooga were finally forced to withdraw, was also known as the "Battle Above the Clouds"; thick mantles of fog often obscure the city below to this day. Among the many memorials in Point Park is the only **statue** in the country to show Union and Confederate soldiers shaking hands.

Practicalities

Greyhound connections with Nashville, Knoxville, and Atlanta arrive on Broad Street downtown. The **visitor center**, adjacent to the Aquarium (daily 8.30am–5.30pm; ☎423/756-8687 or 1-800/322-3344, ⓦwww.chattanooga-fun.com), provides the usual range of help, along with a useful guide for travelers with disabilities. Countless inexpensive **motels** line the interstates, such as the *Super 8*, at 1410 Mack Smith Rd off I-75 S, exit 1 (☎423/892-3888 or 1-800/800-8000, ⓦwww.super8.com; ❷), but the *Choo-Choo* is far more atmospheric, if you can get a room on the train (☎423/266-5000 or 1-800/872-2529, ⓦwww.choochoo.com; ❺). There's **camping** at *Raccoon Mountain Campground*, 319 West Hills Drive (☎423/821-9403, ⓦwww.raccoonmountain.com; cabins ❶–❷, tentsites $13).

The Cherokee and the Trail of Tears

During the eighteenth and early nineteenth centuries, the **Cherokee** were the most powerful Indian tribe in the tri-state region of Tennessee, Georgia, and North Carolina. They forged close links with white pioneers, adopting white methods in schooling and agriculture, intermarrying, and even owning African slaves. The only Native Americans to develop their own written alphabet, they had a regular newspaper, *The Cherokee Phoenix*. They even supplied soldiers for Andrew Jackson's US forces against the Creek Indians and the British in 1814, hoping to buy influence with the federal government.

Thirteen years later, against a background of aggressive territorial claims by settlers, the Cherokee produced a written constitution modeled on that of the US, stating their intention to continue to be a self-governing nation. John Ross, founder of Ross's Landing, and at most one-eighth Cherokee, was elected as their first Principal Chief in 1828 in an effort to appease and negotiate with national and state governments over their lands. However, as white encroachment increased, their former ally Jackson, now US president, was pressured by the Georgians into "offering" the Cherokee western lands in exchange for those east of the Mississippi. Although the tribal leadership refused, a minority faction accepted, giving the government the opportunity they required. The Cherokee were ordered to leave within two years, and 14,000 were forcefully removed to Oklahoma in 1838 along the horrific **Trail of Tears**: four thousand died of disease and exposure on the way. In the meantime, their land was sold by lottery, and Ross's Landing was renamed Chattanooga. Descendants of the one thousand Cherokee who managed to avoid removal by escaping into the mountains now occupy a small reservation in North Carolina (see p.533).

The **Red Clay State Historic Park**, twenty miles east of Chattanooga off Hwy-317, recounts the old Cherokee way of life, with replica houses, tools, and household implements. Its balsamic Sacred Council Spring was once a meeting place for Cherokee elders.

The obvious place to **eat** in Chattanooga is the *Choo-Choo* complex, where the enclosed *Gardens Restaurant* serves standard meals for around $10; the more romantic *Silver Diner* serves steaks and seafood in a railroad car behind, and there's also an *Espresso Café* (all three ☎423/266-5000). For inventive Southern cooking in a stylish atmosphere, try the *Southside Grill*, 1400 Cowart St (☎423/266-9211). The *Big River Grille & Brewing Works*, 222 Broad St (☎423/267-2739), is a cavernous brewpub and restaurant near the Aquarium.

Alabama

Just 250 miles from north to south, **ALABAMA** ranges from the fast-flowing rivers, waterfalls, and lakes of the **Appalachian foothills** to the subtropical bayous and white beaches of the **Gulf Coast**. Most of its industry is concentrated in the **north**, around rejuvenated **Birmingham** and **Huntsville**, first home of the nation's space program. The sun-scorched farmlands of middle Alabama envelop sober **Montgomery**, the state capital. Away from the French-influenced coastal strip around the pretty little town of **Mobile**, fundamentalist Protestant attitudes have traditionally backed a succession of right-wing demagogues, such as **George Wallace**, the four-time state governor who received ten million votes in the 1968 presidential election, and, more recently, Alabama Chief Justice **Roy Moore**. In 2003, Moore was dismissed from his post after failing to obey a federal court order to remove a monument of the Ten Commandments that he had placed in the rotunda of Alabama's state judicial building in Montgomery.

While times have ostensibly moved on since the epic **civil rights** struggles in Montgomery, Birmingham, and **Selma** – monuments and civic literature celebrate the achievements of the campaigners, and even Wallace renounced his racist views, courting, and winning, black votes in his successful campaign for governor in 1982 – a quick visit to most of Alabama's urban centers demonstrates that the state still has a long way to go.

Getting around Alabama

Public transportation is relatively good in Alabama. Daily Amtrak **trains** from New York and Atlanta to New Orleans stop at Anniston, Birmingham, and Tuscaloosa, while the line from Jacksonville to New Orleans passes through Mobile; Amtrak **buses** connect Birmingham and Mobile by way of Montgomery, while Greyhound serves the major towns and cities.

Northern Alabama

Northern Alabama, on the trailing edges of the Appalachians, is brightened up by the mountain lakes, rivers, and canyons of the **Tennessee River Valley**. The area's first white settlers were small farmers who had little in common with the big plantation owners further south, and attempted to dissociate from the Confederacy during the Civil War. Substantial postwar mineral finds led to an industrial boom that peaked in the early Thirties.

Huntsville

Many Southern cities aspire to blend the old with the new; few achieve it as dramatically as **HUNTSVILLE**, a hundred miles south of Nashville, just inside the Alabama border. Its sleepy center still recalls the days when it was dominated by cotton merchants and railroad owners, a history absorbingly recounted in the **Huntsville Depot Museum**, 310 Church St N (Sat 9am–4pm, June–Aug until 5pm; closed Jan & Feb). Nearby, **Alabama Constitution Village**, 109 Gates Ave (same hours as Depot Museum), recalls earlier history, with actors dressed in period clothing going about their olde-worlde business in eight reconstructed Federal-style buildings. When Huntsville was founded, in 1808, it was called Twickenham – anti-British sentiment in the run-up to the 1812 War dictated that it should be renamed for its first settler, a Virginian named John Hunt. From Constitution Village you can take free guided walking tours of the **Twickenham Historic District** (May–July Sat 10am), a neighborhood of early nineteenth-century brick homes. Nearby, in Courthouse Square, Harrison Hardware (Mon–Fri 10am–4pm, Sat 10am–2pm) is an atmospheric old store unchanged since 1879.

Time was when Huntsville was content to be the "Watercress Capital of the World"; the great leap forward came after World War II, when the army consolidated its **rocket and missile research** efforts in the city. Spearheading the project were **Dr Wernher von Braun** and 118 other German scientists, who came to Huntsville after a token period of rehabilitation. Von Braun's contribution of the V-2 ballistic missile to the Nazi war effort is ignored by the city, which prefers to laud his later Space Age achievements, such as **Explorer I**, the nation's first satellite, and the mighty **Saturn V** rocket.

The giant **US Space and Rocket Center**, five miles west of downtown on Hwy-20, off I-65 (daily: summer 9am–6pm; rest of year 9am–5pm; $12, $17 with IMAX), contains a mind-boggling array of technological exhibits, hands-on displays, and weightlessness simulators, as well as a giant IMAX cinema. Outdoors, in the surreal Rocket and Space Shuttle parks, rockets protrude skywards in the blazing Alabama sunshine; the four-story *Saturn V* is laid on its side to emphasize its immensity.

Practicalities

Huntsville's **visitor center** is at 700 Monroe St (Mon–Sat 9am–5pm; ☎256/551-2230, ⓦ www.huntsville.org). Chain **motels** on the outskirts include a *Best Value Inn*, near the Space Center at 2201 N Memorial Parkway (☎256/536-7441; ❷). As for **restaurants**, *Ol' Heidelberg*, 6125 University Drive NW (☎256/922-0556), offers German specialties including sauerkraut and Wiener schnitzel. *Eunice's Country Kitchen*, on the western fringes of downtown at 1006 Andrew Jackson Way (☎256/534-9550; closed Tues), is an inexpensive rendezvous for home-cooked Southern breakfasts.

Birmingham

The rapid transformation of farmland into the city of **BIRMINGHAM** began in 1870, when two railroad routes met in the Jones Valley, a hundred miles south of Huntsville. What attracted speculators was not the scenery, but what lay under it – a mixture of iron ore, limestone, and coal, perfect for the manufacture of iron and steel. The expansion of heavy industry was finally brought to an abrupt halt by the Depression, and today iron and steel production accounts for only a few thousand jobs. New service and medical industries have helped transform this once smog-filled metropolis into a prosperous and thriving city.

Civil rights in Birmingham

In the first half of 1963, civil rights leaders chose Birmingham as the target of "Project C" (for confrontation), aiming to force businesses to integrate lunch counters and employ more blacks. Despite threats from Police Chief **"Bull" Connor** that there would be "blood running down the streets of Birmingham," the pickets, sit-ins, and marches went forward, resulting in mass arrests. Over 2000 protesters flooded the jails; one was Dr Martin Luther King Jr, who wrote his *Letter from a Birmingham Jail* after being branded as an extremist by local white clergymen. Connor's use of high-pressure hoses, cattleprods, and dogs against demonstrators acted as a potent catalyst of support. Pictures of snarling German shepherds sinking their teeth into the flesh of schoolkids were transmitted around the world, and led to an agreement between civil rights leaders and businesses in June 1963. Success in Birmingham sparked demonstrations in 186 other cities, which culminated in the 1964 **Civil Rights Act** prohibiting racial segregation.

The headquarters for the campaign, the **16th Street Baptist Church**, on the corner of Sixth Avenue, was the site of a sickening Klan bombing on September 15, 1963, which killed four young black girls attending a Bible class. In 2000, two of the three murderers were finally jailed. The church's basement contains a small shrine dedicated to the murdered girls, and displays a number of related artworks. Across the road, prettily landscaped **Kelly Ingram Park**, the site of many huge rallies during the Sixties (and now home to some of the city's dispossessed) has a Freedom Walk, lined with several impressive sculptures that memorialize the city's turbulent history of race relations.

Nearby, the admirable **Civil Rights Institute**, 520 16th St (Tues–Sat 10am–5pm, Sun 1–5pm; $8), is an affecting attempt to interpret the factors that led to such violence and racial hatred in the US. Exhibits re-create life in a segregated city, complete with a burned-out bus and heart-rending videos of bus boycotts and the March on Washington.

Being known as the "Pittsburgh of the South" might seem faint praise enough; however, during the civil rights era Birmingham also earned the label of the "Johannesburg of America" for the brutality and intolerance of its police force. An intense **civil rights campaign** in 1963 was the turning point, setting Birmingham on the road to smoother race relations. After 1979, under five-term black mayor Richard Arrington, the city slowly but surely turned itself around, and the 1990s in particular saw a growing self-confidence in Birmingham's potential to be the "next Atlanta." Nonetheless, even a short stroll around downtown leaves the impression that a lot remains to be done.

Arrival and information

Birmingham Airport is just four miles from downtown; call Yellow Cabs ($12) on ☎205/252-1131. The Greyhound station is at 19th Street N, between Sixth and Seventh avenues – a rough area – while **Amtrak** pulls in downtown at 1819 Morris Ave. **Public transportation** is poor, and most of the attractions are well spread out, so you'll need a **car** to see the city properly. The main **visitor center** can be found just off I-20/59 at 2200 Ninth Ave N (Mon–Fri 8.30am–5pm; ☎205/458-8000 or 1-800/458-8085, ⒲www.sweetbirmingham.com). Birmingham has two free **listings** magazines: *The Birmingham Weekly* and the bi-weekly *Black and White*.

Accommodation

Although the downtown **hotels** are pricier than the chain motels near the highway, many of them offer advantageous weekend rates. The nearest place to

camp is the *Birmingham South KOA*, eight miles south in Pelham, off I-65 S (☎205/664-8832; from $23 a night).

Crowne Plaza Inn Redmont 2101 5th Ave N ☎205/324-2101, ⓦwww.crowneplaza.com/cpbh-mdowntown. Modernized, handsome historic hotel, a few blocks northeast of Amtrak. ❻–❼
Pickwick Hotel 1023 S 20th St ☎205/933-9555 or 1-800/255-7304, ⓦwww.pickwickhotel.com. Charming hotel within walking distance of Five

Points South, with all the amenities. Complimentary continental breakfast and free airport shuttle. ❺
Tutwiler Hotel 2021 Park Place ☎205/322-2100, ⓦwww.wyndham.com/hotels/BHMTW/main.wnt. Luxurious restored 1920s hotel near the Civil Rights Institute. ❺

The City
Downtown Birmingham extends north from the railroad tracks at Morris Avenue to Tenth Avenue N; it's bounded to the east and west by 25th and 15th streets. The landscaped greenery and early skyscrapers of **20th Street** are not enough to save these one-hundred-plus blocks from anonymity, with shopping now firmly anchored in the malls and suburbs. The main interest is the powerful **Civil Rights Institute** and the **16th St Baptist Church** (see box, opposite). Call in too at the lovely old **Carver Theatre for the Performing Arts**, 1631 Fourth Ave N, where the **Alabama Jazz Hall of Fame** (Tues–Sat 10am–5pm, Sun 1–5pm; free) is a fond memorial to great jazz artists with Alabama links, from boogie-woogie maestro Clarence "Pinetop" Smith, via Erskine Hawkins (he of "Tuxedo Junction"), to jazzy space cadet Sun Ra.

Much livelier than downtown is the **Five Points South** district, a mile or so south of the tracks, on 20th St and 11th St S; thanks to the proximity of the university, the narrow streets and alleys are packed with bars and restaurants, and busy with revelers – mostly students – every weekend.

Northwest of downtown, the concrete colossus of the Birmingham-Jefferson Civic Center, 22nd St and Tenth Ave N, contains the **Alabama Sports Hall of Fame** (Mon–Sat 9am–5pm, Sun 1–5pm; $5), a tribute to sporting greats such as 1936 Olympic hero **Jesse Owens**, **Le Roy "Satchel" Paige** – legendary Negro League pitcher – and boxer **Joe Louis**. There's even a space for George Wallace, on the excuse that he was state amateur boxing champion. Weave your way past the monotonous white-walled legal buildings to the nearby **Museum of Art**, 2000 Eighth Ave N (Tues–Sat 10am–5pm, Sun noon–5pm; free), which is strong on Oriental pieces, American landscapes, and, oddly enough, Wedgwood pottery.

East of downtown, at First Ave N and 32nd St, stand the massive sheds and tall chimney stacks of **Sloss Furnaces** (Tues–Sat 10am–4pm, Sun noon–4pm; free; guided tours Sat & Sun 1pm, 2pm & 3pm), which produced pig iron to feed the city's mills and foundries from 1882 until 1971. Self-guided **tours** through the boilers, stoves, and casting areas vividly portray the harsh working conditions endured by the ex-slaves, prisoners, and unskilled immigrants who labored here. Imagining the searing heat and cramped space, the heavy loads and putrid gaseous emissions, it's easy to appreciate why one former Sloss worker claimed "if mules had to do this work they would have banned it."

Eating and drinking
Birmingham has some fantastic **barbecue** joints; for something a little more upmarket, the best bet is to ignore downtown in favor of **Five Points South**.

Bottega 2240 Highland Ave S ☎205/933-2001. Elegant 1920s clothing store that now houses one of Five Points South's classiest restaurants, serving luscious, garlic-rich Mediterranean cui-

sine; prices are slightly lower in the adjoining café.
Dreamland Barbecue 1427 14th Ave S ☎205/933-2133. Superlative barbecue in a

huge, cheery space. Place your order for a big plate of ribs with white sliced bread and sauce and watch as they cook it up right before your eyes.

The Mill 1035 20th St S ☎205/939-3001. Bakery, brewery, and general snackery, with outdoor patio, in Five Points South. Ideal for morning coffees and inexpensive lunches.

West of Birmingham

Just west of Birmingham's city limits, I-20/59 passes **Bessemer**, a likeable small town named in 1887 after Sir Henry Bessemer, the English engineer who perfected the steel-making process. The **Hall of History Museum** here, in the 1916 Southern Railroad depot at 1905 Alabama Ave (Tues–Sat 10am–4pm; free), displays Native American artifacts alongside exhibits from the industrial pioneer years. *Bob Sykes*, 1724 Ninth Ave (☎205/426-1400), is a mouthwatering **barbecue** joint in town.

Tuscaloosa, home of the lively main campus of the University of Alabama, but little else of interest, lies 32 miles southwest of Bessemer. If you're hungry, combine eating with a view of the **Black Warrior River** at *Cypress Inn*, 501 Rice Mine Rd N (☎205/345-6963), which specializes in reasonably priced seafood and catfish. If you're not in the mood for fancy, *Dreamland Barbecue*, on Jug Factory Road, just off Hwy-82, south of Hwy-11 (☎205/758-8135), dishes up luscious, sweet pork ribs with wonderful BBQ sauce.

Sixteen miles south of Tuscaloosa on US-69, the **Moundville Archeological Park** (8am–8pm) preserves 28 earthen mounds, carpeted in lush grass, with the largest (60ft) supporting a rebuilt Native American temple. An estimated three thousand people lived here on the banks of the Black Warrior River during the twelfth century; the on-site museum (daily 9am–5pm; $4) exhibits items found in burial grounds, including jewelry, ceremonial vessels, and a few skeletons.

South central Alabama

Southern Alabama – memorably depicted in Harper Lee's child's-eye view of racial conflict, *To Kill a Mockingbird* – still consists mostly of small, sleepy, God-fearing rural communities. Only state capital **Montgomery**, with a population of just over 200,000, achieves metropolitan status. It lies in the heart of the **Black Belt**, originally named for the rich loamy soil, but these days more usually taken to refer to the region's ethnic make-up. Cotton was the major earner here until the boll weevil infestation of 1915. Now it has been supplanted (officially) by soybeans, corn, and peanuts – though surveys suggest that the leading cash crop is, in fact, marijuana.

Montgomery

MONTGOMERY's Black Belt position, 90 miles south of Birmingham and 160 west of Atlanta, made it a natural political center for the plantation elite, leading to its adoption as state capital in 1846 and temporary capital of the Confederacy fifteen years later. Despite its administrative importance, and its preponderance of stately monumental buildings **downtown**, Montgomery is strangely quiet, largely because many businesses have relocated to the suburbs. Most neighborhoods are either exclusively white or totally black; integration sadly does not appear to be on the social agenda in the city that saw the first successful mass civil rights activity in 1955–56.

Arrival, information, and accommodation

Dannelly Field Airport is fifteen miles from downtown on US-80; the Greyhound station is much more conveniently located at 210 S Court St. The **visitor center**, in the old train station at 300 Water St (Mon–Sat 8am–5pm, Sun noon–4pm; ☎334/262-0013, ⊕www.visiting montgomery.com), has the usual brochures and maps. As for accommodation, there are a couple of homey **B&Bs** in town, plus the usual **motels** alongside the highways.

Capitol Inn 205 N Goldthwaite St ☎334/265-3844. Old-fashioned motel perched on a small hill fifteen minutes' walk from downtown; it's a somewhat bleak location at night. **❷**

Lattice Inn 1414 S Hull St ☎334/832-9931 or 1-800/525-0652, ⊕www.latticeinn.com. Lovingly restored 1906 house offering four B&B rooms and a pool; it's a mile or so southeast of downtown in the neighborhood of Cloverdale. **❹**

Red Bluff Cottage 551 Clay St ☎334/264-0056, ⊕www.redbluffcottage.com. Friendly B&B near the capitol, with comfortable rooms, a big porch, and good food. **❹**

The City

Although 1993 saw Alabama's state flag finally replace the Confederate flag over the white-domed Greek Revival **State Capitol** at the top of Dexter Avenue, downtown Montgomery still bears reminders of its white-supremacist past. You can tour the capitol itself (Mon–Fri 9am–5pm, Sat 9am–4pm; free), where a bronze star marks the spot where Jefferson Davis was sworn in as president of the Confederacy on February 18, 1861 (see p.1385) – a hundred years later Governor George Wallace stood on these steps and proclaimed "Segregation forever!" Davis's temporary home, the **First White House of the Confederacy**, 644 Washington Ave (Mon–Fri 8am–4.30pm; free), is crammed with sentimental Confederate oddments. As "attractions," these sit uneasily with **Dr Martin Luther King's church**, the **Civil Rights Memorial**, and the **Rosa Parks Museum** (see box, overleaf), an uncomfortable tension which permeates the city itself.

On a different note, Montgomery was jammed with mourners in 1954 for the funeral of 29-year-old country star **Hank Williams**, who died of a heart attack on his way to a concert on New Year's Eve 1953. An Alabama native from Butler County, Williams was as famous for his drink- and drug-sustained lifestyle as he was for writing honky-tonk classics like "Your Cheating Heart" and "I'm So Lonesome I Could Cry." His hit single at the time of his death was called "I'll Never Get Out of This World Alive." The **Hank Williams Memorial**, a large white-marble headstone complete with song lyrics and an image of the singer, dominates the Oakwood Cemetery Annex, 1304 Upper Wetumpka Rd, near downtown; Hank's statue stands at Lister Hill Plaza on N Perry Street. There's also the **Hank Williams Museum**, at 118 Commerce St (Mon–Sat 9am–5pm, Sun 1–4pm; $7), complete with the 1952 Cadillac in which he made his final journey.

Situated off Woodmere Boulevard, ten miles southeast of the city, the stunningly landscaped **Blount Cultural Park** gives credence to Montgomery's claim to be a regional center for the arts. It's home to the acclaimed **Alabama Shakespeare Festival** (Nov–June; ☎334/271-5353 or 1-800/841-4273, ⊕www.asf.net) and the slick **Montgomery Museum of Fine Arts** (Tues–Sat 10am–5pm, Sun noon–5pm; free), which spans more than two hundred years of American art and has an impressive selection of masters including Dürer, Rembrandt, and Picasso. There's a nice café, too, overlooking the lake.

Eating and drinking

Downtown Montgomery isn't bad when it comes to eating, with some especially good soul food. A few minutes' drive southeast, suburban **Cloverdale**

Civil rights in Montgomery

During the Fifties, Montgomery's **bus system** was a miniature model of segregated society – as was the norm in the South. The regulation ordering blacks to give up seats to whites came under repeated attack from black organizations, culminating in the call by the Women's Political Council for a mass boycott after seamstress **Rosa Parks** was arrested on December 1, 1955, for refusing to give up her seat, stating wearily that she was simply too tired. Black workers were asked to walk to work, while black-owned taxis carried those who lived further away for the same 10¢ fare as buses. The protest attracted over ninety-percent support, and the Montgomery Improvement Association (MIA), set up to coordinate activities, elected the 26-year-old pastor **Dr Martin Luther King Jr** as its chief spokesperson. Meanwhile, the laid-off white bus drivers were employed as temporary police officials. Despite personal hardships, bombings, and jailings, the boycott continued for eleven months, until in November 1956 the US Supreme Court declared segregation on public transportation to be illegal.

King remained pastor at the small brick **Dexter Avenue King Memorial Baptist Church**, in the shadow of the capitol at 454 Dexter Ave (call for tours a week in advance; Mon–Thurs 10am & 2pm, Fri 10am, Sat 10.30am, 11.15am, noon & 12.45pm; $2), until his move back to his hometown of Atlanta in 1960. A mural along a basement wall chronicles his life, while the upstairs sanctuary, left much as it was during his ministry, contains his former pulpit.

One block away at the corner of Washington Avenue and Hull Street, in front of the Southern Poverty Law Center (which specializes in helping victims of racial attacks), the deeply moving **Civil Rights Memorial**, designed by Maya Lin, consists of a cone-shaped black granite table. It's inscribed with a circular timeline of events structured around the deaths of forty martyrs murdered by white supremacists and police; the circle ends with the assassination of Dr King. You can run your hands through the cool water that pumps slowly and evenly across it, softly touching the names while being confronted with your reflection. The wall behind, also running with water, is engraved with the quotation employed so often by Dr King: "(We will not be satisfied) until justice rolls down like waters and righteousness like a mighty stream." An armed security guard stands nearby.

A few blocks west of the memorial, the **Rosa Parks Museum**, 252 Montgomery St (Mon–Fri 9am–5pm, Sat 9am–3pm; $5.50), commemorates "the mother of the civil rights movement." Exhibits cover her life, the bus boycott, and other major civil rights figures.

offers a selection of fancier restaurants. With its bars and jazz clubs, Cloverdale is also the place to head for **nightlife**; downtown, things get quiet at night.

Farmers' Market Café 315 N McDonough St ☏334/262-9163. Montgomery's best spot for Southern-style breakfasts, just off downtown, next to the busy marketplace. Mon–Fri 5.30am–2pm.
Jubilee Seafood Co. 1057 Woodley Rd, Cloverdale ☏334/262-6224. Tiny fish restaurant that serves an extensive and creative menu. Dinner only; closed Sun & Mon.
Lek's Railroad Thai 300b Water St ☏334/269-0708. Next to the visitor center, this elegant down-town oddity serves tasty pad Thai, sushi, noodles, and soups, along with lots of good veggie options.
Martha's Place 458 Sayre St ☏334/263-9135. Superb downtown Southern food, from collard greens to fried chicken. Lunch only; closed Sat.
Vintage Year 405 Cloverdale Rd, Cloverdale ☏334/264-8463. One of Alabama's best restaurants, with *haute nouvelle* Southern cuisine in a bistro setting. Dinner only, reservations recommended; closed Sun & Mon.

Selma

The tidy market town of **SELMA**, fifty miles west of Montgomery, became in the early Sixties the focal point of the national civil rights campaign. Black demonstrations, meetings, and attempts to register to vote were repeatedly met by police violence, before the murder of a black protester by a state trooper prompted the decision to organize the historic **march from Selma to Montgomery**. On "Bloody Sunday," March 7, 1965, six hundred unarmed marchers set off across the steep incline of the imposing, narrow **Edmund Pettus Bridge**. As they went over the apex of the bridge, a line of state troopers fired tear gas without warning, lashing out at the panic-stricken demonstrators with nightsticks and cattleprods. This violent confrontation, broadcast all over the world, is credited with having directly influenced the passage of the **Voting Rights Act** the following year. The full, devastating story is told in the **National Voting Rights Museum**, beside the bridge at 1012 Water Ave (Mon–Fri 9am–5pm, Sat 10am–3pm; $4), which is packed with personal testimony. Outside the 1965 movement headquarters at the **Brown Chapel AME Church**, 410 Martin Luther King St, a bust of Dr King forms part of a monument to the struggle that also includes explanatory plaques along the street.

Lined with independently owned stores and cafés, **Broad Street** is the town's busy main thoroughfare, running into the wide riverfront **Water Avenue**, with its frontier-style storefronts, seed warehouses, and garages. Just a few blocks away stand the beautiful homes of Selma's **historic district**.

Practicalities

Selma's privately owned **visitor welcome center** is at 2207 Broad St, north of town at the junction with Hwy-22 (daily 8am–8pm; ☎334/875-7485). Downtown is very short of inexpensive **places to stay**; if the historic *St James Hotel*, close to the Pettus Bridge at 1200 Water Ave (☎334/872-3234; ❺), is beyond your budget, head for the *Holiday Inn*, three miles west on US-80 at 1806 W Highland Ave (☎334/872-0461; ❸). Among several soul-food **restaurants** is the *Downtowner*, 1114 Selma Ave (☎334/872-5933) – service can be surly, but the food is great. *Major Grumbles*, near the *St James* at 1 Grumbles Alley (☎334/872-2006), is an upmarket riverside **pub** serving burgers, salads, and hot sandwiches; you may be put off by the disturbing "Indian giant" skeleton draped in a Confederate flag.

Alabama's Gulf Coast

Alabama's narrow share of the **Gulf coastline** is blessed with an abundance of fine white sand beaches, lapped by clear blue waters. The coast veers sharply inward to the port city of **Mobile**, featuring hundreds of antebellum buildings in a tree-shaded center. Away from the water's edge, agriculture, dominated by pecans, peaches, and watermelons, flourishes on the gently sloping coastal plain.

Mobile

The busy port and paper-manufacturing city of **MOBILE** (pronounced "Mobeel") traces its origins back to a French community founded in 1702 by Jean-Baptiste Le Moyne, Sieur de Bienville, who went on to establish the cities of Biloxi and New Orleans. These early white settlers brought with them **Mardi Gras**, which has been celebrated in Mobile continuously since 1704, several years before New Orleans was even dreamed of. With its early eighteenth-century Spanish and Colonial-style buildings, parallels with New Orleans are everywhere you look, from the wrought-iron balconies to street names like Conti and Bienville and gumbo specials in the restaurants, but there the comparisons end. It's a pretty place – especially in **spring**, when virtually every street is transformed by the delicate colors of azaleas, camellias, and dogwoods – but there's little actually to do, and though they generally liven up on weekends, Mobile's downtown **bars** and **restaurants** can be decidedly sleepy during the week.

Mobile survived the torches of the Union army during the Civil War, and possesses enough antebellum buildings to designate four sizeable areas as historic districts. The obvious place to start exploring is **Fort Conde**, 150 S Royal St (daily 8am–5pm; free), a reconstruction of the city's 1724 French fort, built to mark the nation's bicentennial in 1976. Dioramas in the low-ceilinged rooms cover local history; don't miss the atmospheric old photos of carnival, the old city, and local African-American figures. Nearby, you can tour the World War II battleship **USS Alabama** (daily: April–Sept 8am–6pm; Oct–March 8am–4pm; $10, parking $2). Fanning out north of the fort, the **Church Street Historic District** holds fifty-nine, mostly pre–Civil War buildings. Don't miss the terrific **Museum of Mobile**, in the airy old City Hall at 111 S Royal St (Mon–Sat 9am–5pm, Sun 1–5pm; $5), which tells the story of the town from its earliest days.

Practicalities

Downtown Mobile is somewhat under the shadow of I-10 as it sweeps to meet I-65 a few miles west. The **Amtrak** and **Greyhound** stations are centrally located, at nos. 11 and 2545 Government St, respectively. Mobile's resourceful **visitor center**, in Fort Conde (see above), can help with accommodation (daily 8am–5pm; ℡251/434-7304, ⓦwww.mobile.org). Cheap **motels** cluster around exit 3 of I-65; it's nicer, however, to stay downtown. Set in an 1862 twin townhouse, the atmospheric *Malaga Inn*, 359 Church St (℡251/438-4701, ⓦwww.malagainn.com; ❹), has huge rooms, a pretty courtyard, and free continental breakfast. Another historic **hotel**, the *Admiral Semmes*, 251 Government St (℡251/432-8000, ⓦwww.radisson.com /mobileal; ❺), is a Radisson-owned property with all the usual amenities.

Unsurprisingly, Mobile abounds in **places to eat fish**: the 1938 *Wintzels' Oyster House*, 605 Dauphin St (℡251/432-4605), serves good-value seafood platters and fresh oysters. If you want views of the water, take Hwy-98 across the bridge and beyond the USS *Alabama*; the *Original Oyster House*, on the bay (℡251/626-2188), is a lively family restaurant dishing up fresh seafood – try the fried blue-crab claws.

Nightlife in downtown Mobile is concentrated along a few lively blocks of Dauphin Street. *The Bicycle Shop*, at no. 661, is a popular, laid-back **pub** with an extensive drink selection; at *Grand Central*, no. 256, an array of eclectic bands play for no cover; while *Soul Kitchen*, no. 455, hosts good jazz, blues, and reggae on the weekends. *Lagniappe* is the free weekly **listings** paper.

Around the bay area

Twenty miles south of Mobile, off I-10, the 65 acres of landscaped color that make up **Bellingrath Gardens** – once the home of a Coca-Cola magnate – include a quarter of a million azaleas (daily 8am–5pm; $7.50, $13.50 with house tour). Fifteen miles further south on Hwy-193 are the quiet beaches and undisturbed pine forest of sunny **Dauphin Island**, which has a **campground** (℡251/861-2742).

The Mobile Bay Ferry links Dauphin with the larger **Pleasure Island**, five miles away (roundtrip $5 pedestrians, cars $25; ℡251/540-7787). The real gem here, and indeed on the entire Alabama Gulf Coast, lies twenty miles east, in the form of **Gulf Shores**, a stunning **beach** where ultramarine waters sweep gently over blinding snow-white sands, just beyond the junction of Hwy-59 and Hwy-180. Although it never gets overcrowded, the beach is particularly busy on Sundays, when young people from all over "LA" – as Lower Alabama is known locally – choose the resort over those of the more expensive Florida Panhandle. A smattering of lively cafés specialize in freshly caught **shrimp**; the lurid *Pink Pony Pub* (℡251/948-6371) features regular **live music**.

   Accommodation tends to be pricey, and often booked up at summer weekends, though the *Holiday Inn White Sands Resort*, 365 E Beach Blvd (℡251/948-6191; ❹), is good value and has its own stretch of sand. Three miles further east, the state-owned *Gulf State Park Resort* (℡1-800-544-4853) has cabins (❸–❹), motel rooms (❸), and a campground (from $15). The Gulf Coast **visitor center**, 3150 Gulf Shores Parkway/Hwy-59 (℡251/968-7511 or 1-800/745-SAND, ⓦwww.gulfshores.com), provides comprehensive information.

Mississippi

Before the Civil War, when cotton was king and slavery remained unchallenged, **MISSISSIPPI** was the fifth wealthiest state in the nation. Since the war, however, it has consistently been the poorest, its dependence on cotton a handicap that leaves it victim to the vagaries of the commodities market.

   From Reconstruction onwards, Mississippi was also infamous for being the strongest bastion of segregation in the South. It witnessed some of the most notorious incidents of the **civil rights** era, from the lynching of Chicago teenager Emmett Till in 1955 to the murder of three activists during the "Freedom Summer" of 1964. Not until the early Seventies did the church bombings and murders come to an end, and, even today, no one could claim that **racial tension** has ceased to exist.

   To some extent, the **economy** has regenerated since gambling was legalized in the early 1990s; the giant casinos of Tunica and Biloxi may be lumbering eyesores, but they draw considerable revenue across the state line from Tennessee and Alabama. Nevertheless, many visitors still report being shocked both by encounters with the truly scandalous **poverty** that still lurks down many a rural backroad, and by lingering traces of racism.

   Mississippi's major city is its capital, **Jackson**, while historic river towns like **Vicksburg** and **Natchez** provide good reasons to stray off the interstates. Gulf Coast resorts such as **Biloxi** welcome family vacationers, literary **Oxford** attracts with a learned ambiance, and **blues** fans will need no encouragement to go exploring sleepy **Delta settlements** such as Alligator or Yazoo City.

Getting around Mississippi

Although **Greyhound** serves most of Mississippi, including the Delta, only along the coastal stretch are services at all frequent. Jackson has the only **airport** of any size, while Amtrak **trains** from New Orleans head north to Memphis by way of Jackson and Greenwood; northeast to Atlanta, passing through a succession of unexciting small towns; and along the coast to Florida, stopping at Biloxi. Trips on the Mississippi itself are run on expensive luxury **cruisers** (see p.585).

The Delta

> That Delta. Five thousand square miles, without any hill save the bumps of dirt the
> Indians made to stand on when the River overflowed.
>
> William Faulkner, *Sanctuary*

"That Delta" is not in fact a delta at all; technically it's an alluvial flood plain, a couple hundred miles short of the mouth of the Mississippi. The name stems from its resemblance to the fertile delta of the Nile (which also began at a city named **Memphis**); the extravagant meanderings of the river on its way down to **Vicksburg** deposit enough rich topsoil to make this one of the world's finest cotton-producing regions.

The Delta is a land of scorching sun, parched earth, flooding creeks, and thickets of bone-dry evergreens, best seen at dawn or dusk, when the glassy-smooth waters of the Mississippi reflect the sun and the foliage along the banks. Just containing the sheer volume of water is a never-ending battle, with giant levees in place to protect the farmland. Though the main thoroughfare south is the legendary **Hwy-61**, exploring is best done on the back roads, which are characterized by huge, silent, empty views, interrupted only by road-side shacks, tiny churches, and the sound of the blues.

Clarksdale

CLARKSDALE, the first significant town south of Memphis, has an unquestionable right to consider itself the home of the blues. Its quite phenomenal roll call of former residents – stretching from Muddy Waters, John Lee Hooker, Howlin' Wolf, and Robert Johnson up to Ike Turner and Sam Cooke – is celebrated in the **Delta Blues Museum**, housed at 1 Blues Alley (Mon–Sat 9am–5pm; $6; ☎662/627-6820, ⓦwww.deltabluesmuseum.org). The center-piece among the photos, instruments, personal possessions, videos, and recordings is the "Muddywood" guitar, created by ZZ Top using wood from Waters' old cabin; the cabin itself has been re-assembled nearby.

Long a rundown rural community, Clarksdale has been boosted by an influx of money and visitors triggered by the large complex of **casinos** a dozen miles north at **Tunica**. Attempts to revitalize, and build on the town's blues heritage, currently focus on the **Blues Alley** district, a general name for the area around the restored passenger depot of the Illinois Central Railroad, through which many black Mississippians, including Muddy, started their migration to the cities of the north. Each year, around the second weekend in August, the town holds the **Sunflower River Blues and Gospel Festival** (free; ☎1-800/626-3764, ⓦwww.clarksdale-ms.com).

Practicalities

The most unusual and characterful **accommodation** near Clarksdale is at **Hopson Plantation**, two miles south of town on US-49. The old sharecroppers' cabins still look much as they did when this was a working cotton plantation, though several have been converted, with the addition of air-conditioning and kitchen facilities, to serve as the *Shack Up Inn* (☎662/624-8329, ⓦwww.shackupinn.com; ❸), where B&B stands for "bed and beer." There's sometimes **live blues** at the adjoining *Commissary* (☎662/624-5756). Another option is the very basic *Riverside Hotel*, 615 Sunflower Ave (☎662/624-9163; ❷), which used to be a hospital, famous as the site of **Bessie Smith**'s death in 1937 after a car crash. If you do spend the night, be sure to talk to "Rat," the son of the original owner, and learn the "true history of the blues."

As for **eating**, *Abe's*, 616 S State St (☎662/624-9947), is a good central barbecue joint, while *Sarah's Kitchen*, 208 Sunflower Ave (☎662/627-3239), serves decent soul food and occasionally puts on live blues. The more upscale *Madidi*, 164 Delta Ave (☎662/627-7770; closed Sun & Mon), which offers a classy French take on Southern cuisine, is owned by a consortium that includes Morgan Freeman; the group also operates the *Ground Zero Juke Joint*, nearby at no. 387 (☎662/621-9009), which books top local musicians on weekends. Otherwise, catching a live blues show takes a bit of luck; ask at the Delta Blues Museum about upcoming events at more authentic venues like the *Red Top Lounge* (aka *Smitty's*), 377 Yazoo Ave (☎662/627-1525), or *Red's*, 395 Sunflower Ave (☎662/627-3166).

Delta towns

Seventy miles south of Clarksdale, **GREENVILLE** is the largest town on the Delta. Still an important riverport, it hosts the **Mississippi Delta Blues Festival** (☎1-888/812-5837, ⓦwww.deltablues.org) every year on the third weekend of September. Tree-lined avenues lead from the characterless outskirts of town into the business district, beyond which pallid warehouses stand in the shadow of a huge levee. One good, safe **accommodation** option near the river is the *Greenville Inn*, 211 Walnut St (☎662/332-6900; ❸). For a **meal**, stop by *Doe's Eat Place*, 502 Nelson St (☎662/334-3315), which serves arguably the best down-home cooking in the entire Delta.

LELAND, seven miles east of Greenville off US-82, is where Mississippi native **Jim Henson** created Kermit the Frog from his mother's old coat, and named him after his childhood playmate, Kermit Scott, now a professor of philosophy. A small exhibit, located on the banks of Deer Creek, at the intersection of Hwy-82 and Hwy-61 (Mon–Sat 10am–4pm; free), is well worth a stop, with displays following Henson's life, Muppet memorabilia, and videos showing much of his work, including his early efforts. At Broad and Fourth streets, the friendly little **Highway 61 Blues Museum** (Mon–Sat 10am–5pm, Sun 1–5pm; $5) recounts the stories of local artists such as Little Milton and Johnny and Edgar Winter (whose father was mayor of Leland during the 1930s).

Sixteen miles further east on US-82, **INDIANOLA** is the home of the largest catfish-processing company in the world; they're called Delta. **B.B. King**, who was born here, plays an open-air hometown show once a year under the auspices of *Club Ebony*, 404 Hannah Ave (☎662/887-9915).

Forty miles east of Indianola on US-82, **GREENWOOD**, a sleepy town of 20,000 people, is the country's second largest cotton exchange after Memphis. The nineteenth-century offices of downtown's Cotton Row overlook the shady Yazoo River, and graceful mansions line pretty Grand Boulevard. The **Cottonlandia Museum** (Mon–Fri 9am–5pm, Sat & Sun 2–5pm; $4), about two miles west of the town center on the US-82 W bypass, is a rag-tag collection of old hardware, Native American beads, stuffed birds, intriguing artwork, and oddly long wooden benches polished by the tongues of mules. Greenwood has recently begun to play up its connection to Robert Johnson (he died here), though the **Cotton Capital Blues Festival** in October remains the city's current contribution to the Delta Blues music legacy.

Of the many **motels** along US-49 and US-82, the *Travel Inn* at 623 US-82 W (☎662/453-8810; ❷) is basic, clean, and good value, with an outdoor pool. By far the best **food** in Greenwood is the Italian/Cajun cuisine at *Lusco's*, on the wrong side of the railway tracks at 722 Carrolton Ave (☎662/453-5365). Each table in this eccentric old place is hidden away in a small booth, veiled

The Delta blues

As recently as 1900, much of the **Mississippi Delta** remained an impenetrable wilderness of cypress and gum trees, roamed by panthers and bears and plagued with mosquitoes. Bit by bit, land was cleared for cotton plantations – but, though the soil was fertile, white laborers could not be enticed to work in this godforsaken backcountry. After emancipation, the economy came to depend on black **sharecroppers**, who would work a portion of the land on a white-owned plantation in return for a share (often pitifully small) of the eventual crop. As a rule, this lifestyle ensured long periods of poverty and debt interspersed with occasional windfalls; but in the Delta the returns tended to be greater than elsewhere, and blacks moved here from all over Mississippi.

In 1903, W.C. Handy, often credited as "the Father of the Blues," but at that time the leader of a vaudeville orchestra, found himself waiting for a train in Tutwiler, fifteen miles southeast of Clarksdale. At some point in the night, a ragged black man carrying a guitar sat down next to him and began to play what Handy called "the weirdest music I had ever heard." Using a pocketknife pressed against the guitar strings to accentuate his mournful vocal style, the man sang that he was "Goin' where the Southern cross the Dog."

This was the **Delta blues**, characterized by the interplay between words and music, with the guitar aiming to parallel and complement the singing rather than simply provide a backing. Though a local, place-specific music – the "Southern" and the "Dog" were railroads that crossed a short way south at Moorhead – it did not simply spring up from the ground, but combined traditional African instrumental and vocal techniques with slave "field hollers," as well as the reels and jigs then at the basis of popular entertainment.

The blues started out as young people's music; the old folks liked the banjo, fife, and drum, but the younger generation were crazy for the wild showmanship of bluesmen such as **Charley Patton**. Born in April 1891, Patton was the classic itinerant bluesman, moving from plantation to plantation and wife to wife, and playing Saturday-night dances with a repertoire that extended from rollicking dance pieces to documentary songs such as "High Water Everywhere," about the bursting of the Mississippi levees in April 1927. Another seminal artist, the enigmatic **Robert Johnson**, was rumored to have sold his soul to the Devil in return for a few brief years of writing songs such as "Love in Vain" and "Stop Breakin' Down." His "Crossroads Blues" spoke of being stranded at night in the chilling emptiness of the Delta; themes carried to metaphysical extremes in "Hellhound on My Trail" and "Me and the Devil Blues" – "you may bury my body down by the highwayside / So my old evil spirit can catch a Greyhound bus and ride."

Both Patton and Johnson died in the 1930s. However, within a few years the Delta blues had been carried north to **Chicago** by men such as **Muddy Waters** and **Howlin' Wolf**. Their electrified urban blues was the most immediate ancestor of rock 'n' roll.

In addition to towns such as Clarksdale (see p.614) and Helena, Arkansas (p.625), blues enthusiasts may want to search out the following rural sites:

Stovall Plantation Stovall Road, 7 miles northwest of Clarksdale. Where tractor-driver Muddy Waters was first recorded; a few cabins remain standing, though Muddy's own is now in the museum at Clarksdale.

Sonny Boy Williamson II's Grave Outside Tutwiler, 13 miles southeast of Clarksdale.

Parchman Farm Junction US-49 W and Hwy-32. Mississippi State Penitentiary, immortalized by former prisoner Bukka White.

Dockery Plantation On Hwy-8, between Cleveland and Ruleville. One of Patton's few long-term bases, also home to Howlin' Wolf and Roebuck "Pops" Staples.

Charley Patton's Grave New Jerusalem Church, Holly Ridge, off US-82, 6 miles west of Indianola.

Robert Johnson's Grave Payne Chapel in Quito, off Hwy-7, roughly 6 miles southwest of Greenwood, where he was poisoned.

by chintz curtains – an arrangement dating from the days of Prohibition, when *Lusco's* was the renowned haunt of cotton barons who came here to drink moonshine.

Northeastern Mississippi

Cutting its way south through Mississippi, I-55 acts as an approximate boundary between the Delta and the luscious green forests of the **northeast**. Of the area's small market towns, the most appealing are the old-style shopping center of **Columbus**, and **Holly Springs**, whose oak-lined streets hide one of the most extraordinary attractions in the state. The only other places of major interest in the region are genteel **Oxford** and tidy blue-collar **Tupelo**, birthplace of **Elvis Presley** and **John Lee Hooker**.

Holly Springs

Centered on a neat courthouse square, **HOLLY SPRINGS** is a time-warped little town that's said to have changed hands 62 times during the Civil War; the minutiae of its otherwise uneventful history fill three splendidly eclectic floors in the local **museum**, at 220 E College Ave (Mon–Fri 10am–5pm, Sat 10am–2pm; $3). However, were it not for **Graceland Too**, 200 E Gholson Ave (open 24hr year-round; $5), Holly Springs would today be of little note. The home of Paul McLeod and, at times, his son Elvis Aaron Presley McLeod, this shrine to the King is a quite remarkable labor of love. Walls, ceiling, and stairwells are crammed with memorabilia from the kitsch to the priceless, and, just as in Graceland, the upper floor is blocked off – the stairs lined with glassy-eyed mannequins kitted out in Elvis and Priscilla outfits. Mr McLeod insists that this is above all an archive and research center; as well as collecting records, cuttings, and books, he works around the clock to monitor and log every reference to Elvis transmitted on TV and radio. **Tours** last up to three hours, depending on the mood of your host and how busy he is compiling Elvis info, but are sure to include the chance to buy an infinitesimal snip of rug from Graceland's Jungle Room.

There's no reason to spend a night in Holly Springs, but it's well worth pausing for a **meal** here. Housed in a former "blind tiger" (brothel) beside the railroad tracks east of town, *Phillips Grocery*, 541 E Van Dorn Ave (☎662/252-4671), is a ramshackle old grocery store that serves sublime fresh-ground hamburgers and Southern vegetables.

Oxford

Twelve thousand residents and eleven thousand students enable **OXFORD**, an enclave of wealth in a predominantly poor region, to blend rural charm with a busy nightlife. Its central square is archetypal smalltown America, but the leafy streets have a vaguely European air – the town named itself after the English city as part of its campaign to persuade the **University of Mississippi**, known as Ole Miss, to locate its main campus here.

It's an undeniably pretty, appealing place today, but in September 1962, this was the site of one of the most bitter displays of racial hatred seen in Mississippi. After eighteen months of legal and political wrangling, federal authorities ruled that **James Meredith** should be allowed to enroll as the first black student at Ole Miss. The news that Meredith had been sneaked into college by federal troops sparked a riot that left three dead and 160 injured. Despite constant threats, Meredith graduated the following year, wearing a "NEVER" badge (the segregationist slogan of Governor Ross Barnett) upside down. A memorial commemorating his achievement was finally unveiled in September 2002, on the fortieth anniversary of his admission. Also on campus, the **Blues Archive** (Mon–Fri 9am–5pm; free; ☎662/915-7408) holds thousands of recordings and B.B. King's personal memorabilia, while the **Center for the Study of Southern Culture** looks at Southern folkways (Mon–Fri 8am–5pm; free; ☎662/232-5593).

From Ole Miss, a ten-minute walk through lush Bailey Woods leads to secluded **Rowan Oak**, the former home of novelist **William Faulkner**, preserved as it was on the day he died in July 1962 (Tues–Sat 10am–noon & 2–4pm, Sun 2–4pm; free). The fictional Deep South town of Jefferson in Yoknapatawpha County, where the Nobel Prize–winner set his major works, was based heavily on Oxford and its environs. Each year, during the last week in July, the University holds a Faulkner and Yoknapatawpha Conference.

In town, a walk around the **square** brings you to Neilson's, a delightfully old-fashioned department store (the oldest in the South, in fact), little changed since 1897. You can pick up a piece of quirky Mississippi folk art at one of the offbeat gift shops here, or join the students sipping lattes and reading on the balcony of the exemplary Square Books, at Van Buren and Lamar streets.

Practicalities

Oxford's **visitor center** (Mon–Fri 9am–5pm, Sat 10am–4pm, Sun 1–4pm; ☎662/234-4680 or 1-800/758-9177), next to Neilson's in the town square, hands out good walking tour leaflets. **Accommodation** options include the *Downtown Inn*, 400 N Lamar St (☎662/234-3031; ❹), and the comfortable B&B *Oliver-Britt House*, 512 Van Buren Ave (☎662/234-8043; ❸). On the town square, you can **eat** homestyle meals at the *Ajax Diner* (☎662/232-8880; closed Sun), or more sophisticated Southern cuisine at *City Grocery* (☎662/232-8080; closed Sun). The *Bottletree Bakery*, 923 Van Buren Ave (☎662/236-5000), is a friendly café with soups and sandwiches.

Tupelo

On January 8, 1935, **Elvis Presley** and his twin brother Jesse were born in **TUPELO**, an industrial town in northeastern Mississippi. Jesse died at birth, while Elvis grew up to be a truck driver. Their parents, Gladys and Vernon Presley, who lived in poor, white East Tupelo, found it hard to make ends meet. Such was the financial strain of rearing the young Elvis that his sharecropper father was reduced to forgery in a desperate attempt to raise cash, and was jailed for three years. Their home was repossessed, and the family moved to Memphis in 1948.

The Tupelo **CVB**, 399 E Main St (Mon–Fri 8am–5pm; ☎662/841-6521 or 1-800/533-0611, ⓦwww.tupelo.net), has details of a four-mile driving tour that takes in Elvis's first school and the shop where he bought his first guitar. The town doesn't go in for overkill, however; Main Street is a long, placid stretch of nondescript buildings, with nary a gift shop to be seen. The actual **Elvis Presley Birthplace**, 306 Elvis Presley Drive (May–Sept Mon–Sat 9am–5.30pm, Sun 1–5pm; Oct–April Mon–Sat 9am–5pm, Sun 1–5pm; $2), is tiny. A two-room shotgun house, built for $150 in 1934, it's been furnished to look as it did when Elvis was born, with the judicious addition of a large can of lard in the kitchen and a love-seat swinging from the porch. The separate

museum alongside (same hours; $5) is filled with memorabilia collected by a family friend of the Presleys, Janelle McComb, and includes her photos of, poems about, and shrines to the King, as well as selling everything from match-books to Elvis pendulum clocks. Nearby, a modern **meditation chapel** was built with donations from fans (but, oddly, the pews and altar remain roped off to visitors).

Among local **motels**, there's a central *Comfort Inn*, 1190 Gloster St (☎662/842-5100, ⓦwww.comfortinn.com; ❸), and other chain accommodations close by. Main Attraction, 214 W Main St (☎662/842-9617), is a vintage clothing store with eccentric accessories that also holds a coffee bar, while there's more substantial Italian and Greek **food** at *Vanelli's*, 1302 N Gloster St (☎662/844-4410).

South central Mississippi

South of the Delta, the rich woodlands and meadows of **central Mississippi** are heralded by steep loess bluffs, home to engaging historic towns such as **Vicksburg** and **Natchez**. Driving around the area is a real pleasure, especially along the unspoiled **Natchez Trace Parkway** – devoid of trucks, buildings, and neon signs – which runs through Jackson and on up to Tupelo.

Jackson

JACKSON, set two hundred miles from both Memphis and New Orleans, has been Mississippi's state capital since 1821. Only in the twentieth century, how-ever, did it become the largest conurbation in the state, flourishing as a center for health and technological industries.

The **Old Capitol Museum of Mississippi History** (Mon–Fri 8am–5pm, Sat 9.30am–4.30pm, Sun 12.30–4.30pm; free), charts the state's unenviable saga, with excellent displays on civil rights and slavery; note the chilling notices for slave auctions. The "new" **Mississippi State Capitol**, 400 High St (Mon–Fri 8am–5pm; free), built in 1903 as a Beaux Arts–style showpiece, is much more ornate. In true rebel fashion, the gilt eagle on the roof looks away from Washington.

A block west at 528 Bloom St, the unmissable **Smith–Robertson Museum and Cultural Center** (Mon–Fri 9am–5pm, Sat 10am–1pm, Sun 2–5pm; $1), housed in what was Jackson's first public school for blacks (open from 1894–1971), tells the story of black Mississippians since the French first imported slaves in 1719. Subjects covered include "folk architecture" – black homesteads built in the same period as the grand antebellum homes so beloved of the tourist boards, but left to decay – and patterns of migration after the Civil War. Photos and personal testimony show how Mississippians survived the onslaught of Jim Crow laws through their institutions of school, church, and family.

Practicalities

Greyhound **buses** currently arrive at 201 S Jefferson St, though they are due to share the **Amtrak** station at 300 W Capitol St when renovations are completed. The main **visitor center** is at 921 N President St (Mon–Fri 8.30am–5pm; ☎601/960-1891 or 1-800/354-7695, ⓦwww.visitjackson.com).

Central **rooms** can be had close to the State Capitol at the flamboyant *Sun'n'Sand Motel*, a glorious 1950s relic at 401 N Lamar St (☎601/354-2501;

②), or a few blocks west at the *Holiday Inn Express*, 310 Greymont Ave (☏601/948-4466 or 1-800/945-7667; ④). Downtown Jackson more or less closes down at 6pm, with the exception of *Hal & Mal's Restaurant & Brewery*, 200 S Commerce St (☏601/948-0888; closed Sun), which specializes in New Orleans cuisine and puts on **live bands** throughout the week.

Vicksburg

Forty-four miles west of Jackson, the historic port of **VICKSBURG** straddles a high bluff on a bend in the Mississippi. During the Civil War, the town's domination of the river halted Union shipping, and led Abraham Lincoln to call Vicksburg the "key to the Confederacy." It was a crucial target for General Grant, who eventually landed south of the city in the spring of 1863, circled inland, and attacked from the east. After a 47-day siege, the outnumbered Confederates surrendered on the Fourth of July – a holiday Vicksburg declined to celebrate for the next hundred years – and Lincoln was able to rejoice that "the Father of Waters again goes unvexed to the sea."

Entered via Clay Street (US-80) just northeast of town, **Vicksburg National Military Park** preserves the main Civil War battlefield (daily: summer 8am–7pm; rest of the year 8am–5pm; $5 per vehicle; ☏601/636-0583, ⓦwww.nps.gov/vick). A sixteen-mile loop drive through the rippling green hillsides traces every contour of the Union and Confederate trenches, punctuated by statues, refurbished cannon, and over 1600 state-by-state monuments. Also at the site are the substantial remains of the squat black ironclad **USS Cairo**, which was sunk without casualties by a "torpedo," as mines were then known, in 1862, and salvaged a century later. It now stands protected by a giant canopy, with a museum alongside of artifacts retrieved from the waters. Nearby, in the **Vicksburg National Cemetery**, 13,000 of the 17,000 Union graves are simply marked "Unknown."

As the Mississippi has changed course since the 1860s, it's now the slender, canalized Yazoo River rather than the broad Mississippi that flows alongside the battlefield and most of downtown Vicksburg. The core of the city has changed little, however, despite the arrival of four permanently moored **casinos**. It's a bare but attractive place of precipitous streets, steep terraces, and wooded ravines, where the entire downtown area is progressively being restored to its original late-Victorian appearance. Most of its finest buildings were destroyed during the siege, so the place is largely characterized by middle-class homes, not sumptuous mansions.

The fascinating **Old Court House Museum**, 1008 Cherry St (summer Mon–Sat 8.30am–5pm, Sun 1.30–5pm; rest of year same hours, but closes at 4.30pm; $3), covers the Civil War era in great depth, even selling genuine minié balls (bullets) for $2. The museum also holds displays on Vicksburg's first settlement, Nogales, which was founded in 1796, as well as the post-war years. One room is devoted to Confederate president Jefferson Davis, who started his career here with a speech from the balcony in 1843; the victorious Ulysses Grant returned to Vicksburg as president in 1869, and addressed thousands of ex-slaves from that same balcony. A small museum at the **Biedenharn Candy Company**, 1107 Washington St (Mon–Sat 9am–5pm, Sun 1.30-4.30pm; $2.25), marks the spot where Coca-Cola was first bottled, with vivid displays on how it all came about.

Practicalities

Vicksburg has two major **visitor centers**, both just off I-20: the Mississippi Welcome Center, at exit 1A beside the river (daily 8am–6pm), and the town's own tourist information center near exit 4, opposite the battlefield entrance on Clay Street (daily: summer 8am–5.30pm; winter 8am–5pm; ☏601/636-9421 or 1-800/221-3536, ⓦwww.vicksburgcvb.org).

The military park is the prime area for **motels**, such as the spartan *Hillcrest*, 4503 Hwy-80 E (☏601/638-1491; ❶), which has a pool, and the comfortable *Battlefield Inn*, at 4137 I-20 Frontage Rd (☏601/638-5811 or 1-800/359-9363; ❸), which includes use of the pool, two free cocktails, and a free breakfast buffet. Among appealing central **B&Bs** are *Anchuca*, housed in the town's first colonnaded mansion, at 1010 First East St (☏601/661-0111 or 1-888/686-0111, ⓦwww.anchucamansion.com; ❺), which has seven guestrooms, including a gorgeous suite extending through the former slave quarters, as well as a pool and fine breakfasts; and the 1868 Victorian-Italianate *Annabelle*, 501 Speed St (☏601/638-2000 or 1-800/791-2000, ⓦwww.annabellebnb.com; ❹). You can **camp** at the *Magnolia RV Park*, 211 Miller St (☏601/631-0388; $18 per tentsite).

When it's time to **eat**, tuck into superb all-you-care-to-eat "round table" lunches of fried chicken and other Southern delicacies at *Walnut Hills*, 1214 Adams St at Clay (☏601/638-4910; closed Sat), or else stop by the *Baldwin House*, a converted townhouse at 1022 Crawford St (☏601/638-8130), which serves light lunches (Tues–Sun), espresso, and more formal dinners (Wed–Sat). At *The Biscuit Company*, 1100 Washington St (☏601/631-0099), you can eat pizza or po'boys, drink till late, and hear **live jazz** or **blues** most weekends.

Natchez

Sixty miles south of Vicksburg, the river town of **NATCHEZ** is the oldest permanent settlement on the Mississippi River. By the time it first flew the Stars and Stripes in 1798, it had already been home to the Natchez people (see below) and their predecessors, as well as French, British, and Spanish colonists. Unlike its great rival, Vicksburg, Natchez was spared significant damage during the Civil War, ensuring that its abundant Greek Revival antebellum mansions remained intact, complete with meticulously maintained gardens. Interspersed among them are countless simpler but similarly attractive white clapboard homes, set along broad leafy avenues of majestic oaks, making Natchez one of the prettiest towns in the entire South. **Horse and carriage** tours (see p.622) explore the downtown area, while fourteen individual mansions stay open all year round, among them the elaborate, octagonal **Longwood**, 140 Lower Woodville Rd (daily 9am–4.30pm; $6), with its huge dome, snow-white arches and columns, and the palatial **Stanton Hall**, 401 High St (daily 9am–4.30pm; $6). All these and more can be seen on tours that set off from 200 State St during the twice-yearly **Natchez Pilgrimage** (mid-March to mid-April & 2 weeks in mid-Oct; $26; ⓦwww.natchezpilgrimage.com). At the Presbyterian Stratton Chapel, 405 State St, a fascinating collection of **photographs** gives an idea of life in Natchez spanning from the Civil War era to World War II (Mon–Sat 10am–5pm; donation $3).

While Natchez proper perches well above the river, a small stretch of riverfront at the foot of the bluff constitutes **Natchez Under-the-Hill**. Once known as the "Sodom of the Mississippi," it now houses a handful of bars and restaurants, plus the 24-hour *Isle of Capri* riverboat **casino**, a cacophony of slot machines and craps tables. Each year, on the third weekend in April, the **Natchez Bluff Blues Fest** (☏601/442-2988, ⓦwww.natchezbluffbluesfest .com), a "city-wide house party" held in some fifteen different venues, celebrates an eclectic mix of regional blues styles.

Natchez takes its name from the **Natchez Indians**, regarded as one of the most significant flowerings of the widespread Mississippian culture. They survived here in strength until 1729, when they rose en masse against French plans to replace one of their villages with a tobacco plantation. Joined by African slaves, they killed 250 colonists before the French and their Choctaw allies crushed the rebellion. The former Natchez spiritual center known as the **Grand Village**, home to a leader revered as the "Great Sun," can now be explored at 400 Jefferson Davis Blvd (Mon–Sat 9am–5pm, Sun 1.30–5pm; free). It's an atmospheric place, holding an informative visitor center and some reconstructed dwellings, as well as a large park-like area with an imposing ceremonial mound at either end. Another Natchez site, the much larger **Emerald Mound**, stands just off the Natchez Trace northeast of town (free 24hr access).

Natchez's rich **African-American** heritage – Richard Wright, the author of *Native Son*, was born nearby and lived in the town as a small boy – is chronicled in an excellent 26-page free booklet, available from the visitor center.

Practicalities

Natchez's vast **Visitor Reception Center** occupies a panoramic location overlooking the river at 640 S Canal St, alongside the Mississippi River bridge (March–Oct Mon–Sat 8.30am–6pm, Sun 9am–4pm; rest of year same hours, but closing Mon–Sat 5pm; ☎601/446-6345 or 1-800/647-6724, ⓦwww.natchez.ms.us). It's the starting point for all kinds of **trolley** and **bus tours** of town, and sells tickets for the **carriage tours** ($10; 45min) that leave from Canal and State streets, slightly closer to downtown.

As for **accommodation**, the *Ramada Inn*, across from the visitor center at 130 John R. Junkin Drive (☎601/446-6311 or 1-800/256-6311, ⓦwww.ramada .com; ❹), enjoys much the same magnificent views, while the *Natchez Eola*, 110 N Pearl St (☎601/445-6000 or 1-866/445-3652, ⓦwww.natchezeola.com; ❺), is a venerable downtown hotel of considerable charm. The *Mark Twain Guesthouse*, 33 Silver St (☎601/446-8023; ❸), is an atmospheric option down by the river; its three simple rooms share a bathroom. For a quintessential Natchez experience, consider staying in a more upmarket **B&B**, such as the opulent *Burn*, 712 N Union St (☎601/442-1344 or 1-800/654-8859, ⓦwww.theburnbnb .com; ❻), which has a beautiful pool.

For **food**, *Cock of the Walk*, on the bluff at 200 N Broadway (☎601/446-8920), serves irresistibly tasty catfish, while *Fat Mama's Tamales*, 500 S Canal St (☎601/442-4548), has Mexican and Cajun cuisine, and is renowned for its "knock-you-naked" margaritas. The *Marketplace Café*, 613 Main St (☎601/304-9399; closed Mon), occupies most of a large open-sided market building downtown, selling good, inexpensive breakfasts and lunches. *Biscuits and Blues*, 315 Main St (☎601/446-9922), combines burgers and barbecue with **live blues** on weekends.

Mississippi's Gulf Coast

Mississippi's hundred-mile strip of **coast** is utterly unlike the rest of the state, culturally as well as physically – a strong Mediterranean (Catholic) heritage is conspicuous amid the subtropical beauty. Some of the towns are scarred by hurricanes, but the **beaches** are often superb. Along the **Gulf Islands National Seashore**, four beautiful barrier islands boast brilliant white sand

and clear blue waters, while the 26-mile artificial **Harrison County Beach** runs parallel with the busy coast road from **Biloxi**, the major resort town.

Biloxi

Neon-lit **BILOXI** is not the prettiest resort in the world. However, it's less expensive than Florida, it's near New Orleans, and it has sufficient diversity to satisfy local beach poseurs, senior citizens, and families alike. Topping it all off, the seafront is lined with permanently moored **casinos**, several of which have spawned large hotels on dry land – but really, it's probably not a place you'll feel the need to linger in for long.

Old Biloxi, starting at the far end of Lameuse Boulevard, consists of narrow streets of stuccoed buildings, in a tree-shaded tranquility that seems miles from the roar of US-90. Across the highway, shrimp and oyster fleets unload their catch at the **Small Crafts Harbor**. You can rent boats to visit windblown **Deer Island**, half a mile offshore, or just to go fishing (70min shrimping tours; $12; ☎228/385-1182). A mile west, a glut of the usual shops selling T-shirts, seashells, trinkets, and other ephemera marks the approach to the most popular stretch of **Harrison County Beach**, in front of the *Broadwater Resort East*.

Five miles west of Main Street, the compact white raised cottage of **Beauvoir** (March–Oct 9am–5pm; Nov–Feb 9am–4pm; $7.50; Ⓦ www.beauvoir.org), set in beautiful wooded grounds across from the ocean, was the final home of Confederate president Jefferson Davis, who lived here until his death in 1889. Though not sponsored by the federal government, a **presidential library** has been opened here in honor of the man; it includes an interesting museum chronicling his life. The area's role as a shrine for unrepentant Confederates is typified by the grandiose title of the Civil War museum – "Experiment in Nationalism" – and a bookstore that's bursting with back issues of *Southern Partisan*, a magazine featuring such editorials as "Why the South Was Right."

West Ship Island

Hailed by *USA Today* as one of the nation's top ten beaches, the barrier island of **West Ship** was only created in 1969, when the 200mph winds and 30ft tide of Hurricane Camille ripped Ship Island in half. It's basically a giant sandbank, dotted with inland ponds (home to a family of alligators), marshlands, sand dunes, and warm tidal pools. Everywhere you go, you come across delicate sea oats; even touching them incurs a heavy **fine**, as their elaborate root structure is all that holds the island together.

The small, idyllic **beach** boasts fine white sand, free showers, and a reasonable café, though umbrella and deckchair rental is expensive. Alongside, the "D"-shaped **Fort Massachusetts** was built in 1859 and captured by the Union navy early in the Civil War. Free tours give a wonderful panoramic view from its grass-topped roof.

West Ship is the only barrier island served by regular **ferry**, at **Gulfport Yacht Harbor**, at the intersection of US-90 and US-49 (mid-May to Aug Mon–Fri 9am, noon & 3.30pm, Sat & Sun Fri 9am, 10.30am, noon, 2.30pm & 3.30pm; March to mid-May, Sept & Oct Mon–Fri 9am, Sat & Sun 9am & noon; $18; ☎228/864-1014 or 1-866/466-7386, Ⓦ www.msshipisland.com).

Practicalities

Biloxi's **visitor center** is at 710 Beach Blvd, at Main St (☎228/374-3105 or 1-800/245-6943, Ⓦ www.gulfcoast.org). Greyhound **buses** from New Orleans and Mobile come in at 166 Main St, not far from the tiny **Amtrak** station, which is served by New Orleans–Miami trains. Beachcomber **trolleys** run hourly along the coast to the unspectacular business center of Gulfport (all-day passes $4; ☎228/896-8080).

The casinos tend to offer comfortable **rooms** for rates that differ little from those in the many smaller motels along the seafront: contact the *Imperial Palace*, 850 Bay View Ave (☎228/436-3000 or 1-888/946-2847, ⓦwww.ipbiloxi .com; ❸), or the *Grand Casino*, 265 Beach Blvd (☎228/436-2946 or 1-800/354-2450, ⓦwww.grandbiloxi.com; ❹), for current deals. Otherwise, the most convenient area to stay is near the **Loop**, the central spot where I-10 curves out over the ocean before joining US-90, Beach Boulevard. Options along Beach Boulevard include the *Sun Tan Motel* at no. 780 (☎228/432-8641; ❸), and the *Gulf Beach Resort* at no. 2428 (☎228/385-5555 or 1-800/323-9164, ⓦwww.gulfbeachresort.com; ❹).You can **camp** at the *Southern Comfort Camping Resort*, 1766 Beach Blvd (☎228/432-1700); tentsites start from $13.

McElroy's Harbor House, 695 Beach Blvd (☎228/435-5001), is a cheery place for good **seafood**. At the homey *Ole Biloxi Schooner*, 159 E Howard Ave (☎228/374-8071; closed Sun), you can get great lunch specials and drink a local specialty, Barq's Root Beer, from the original long-necked bottles. There's excellent upscale dining at the 1737 *Mary Mahoney's Old French House*, 116 Rue Magnolia (☎228/374-0163; closed Sun).

Arkansas

Historically, **ARKANSAS** belongs very much to the American South. It sided firmly with the Confederacy in the Civil War, and its capital, Little Rock, was in 1957 one of the most notorious flashpoints in the struggle for civil rights. Geographically, however, it marks the beginning of the Great Plains. Unlike the other Southern states on the east side of the Mississippi River, Arkansas remained very sparsely populated until almost a century ago. Westward expansion was blocked by the existence of the Indian Territory in what's now Oklahoma, and not until the railroads opened up the forested interior during the 1880s did settlers stray in any numbers from their small riverside villages. Only once the Depression and mechanization had forced thousands of farmers to leave their fields did Arkansas begin to develop any significant industrial base. In 1992, local boy Bill Clinton's accession to the presidency catapulted Arkansas into national prominence. Four towns lay claim to him: Hope, his birthplace; Hot Springs, his "home town"; Fayetteville, where he and Hillary married; and, of course, Little Rock. Of the four, only sleepy **Little Rock** and the nearby spa resort of **Hot Springs** are really worth a trip, whatever the tourist brochures may say.

Though Arkansas encompasses the **Mississippi Delta** in the east, oil-rich timber lands in the south, and the sweeping **Ouachita** ("Wash-ih-taw") **Mountains** in the west, the cragged and charismatic **Ozark Mountains** in the north are its most scenic asset, where the main attractions for tourists are the uncrowded parks and unspoiled rivers. Incidentally, "Arkansas" is a distorted version of the name of a small Indian tribe; the state legislature declared once and for all in 1881 that the correct pronunciation is "Arkansaw."

Getting around Arkansas

It's extremely difficult to venture beyond Little Rock and Hot Springs using **public transportation**. Greyhound runs intermittent services, while Amtrak cuts diagonally east–west through the state, calling at Little Rock, which also holds the only sizeable **airport**. To see the Ozarks you'll need a **car**.

Eastern Arkansas

What's surprising about the eastern Arkansas deltalands is that they are far from totally flat: **Crowley's Ridge**, a narrow arc of windblown loess hills, breaks up the uniform smoothness, stretching 150 miles from southern Missouri to the atmospheric river town of **Helena**. Despite scenic rivers and sleepy bayous, the pine-clad woodlands of the Gulf Coastal Plain in southern Arkansas are of little real interest.

Helena

The small Mississippi port of **HELENA**, roughly sixty miles south of Memphis, was once the shipping point for Arkansas's cotton crop, when Mark Twain described it as occupying "one of the prettiest situations on the river." A small **historic district** bordered by Holly, College, and Perry streets reflects that brief period of prosperity, before the arrival of the railroad left most of the river towns obsolete; today Helena's central core is little more than the slightly run-down **Cherry Street** on the levee.

That said, it's not an unappealing place, with some very good reasons to visit. Musicians among its large black population have ensured that the town is an important stop for **Delta blues** enthusiasts. Radio station KFFA (1360 AM), with living legend "Sunshine" Sonny Payne, a DJ who started out in 1941, still hosts the legendary **King Biscuit Time Show** (Mon–Fri 12.15–12.45pm), which has been broadcast more than 14,000 times, from the foyer of the **Delta Cultural Center Visitor Center**, 141 Cherry St (☎870/338-4350, ⓦ www.kingbiscuittime.com); visitors are welcome.

Helena was for many years the home of harmonica great **Sonny Boy Williamson II** ("Rice" Miller), and featured in intimate detail in many of his (usually extemporized) recordings. He used to advertise Sonny Boy's Biscuit Meal on the radio show, which continues to maintain the illusion that he is present in the studio. You can buy – and hear – a great assortment of blues records at **Bubba Sullivan's Blues Corner**, nearby in the small mall at 105 Cherry St (☎870/338-3501); Bubba himself is a mine of friendly information on local gigs and music events. Each fall, on the weekend before Columbus Day, the city holds the free **King Biscuit Blues Festival** (ⓦ www.kingbiscuitfest.org), which attracts big-name blues, acoustic, and gospel performers.

At the south end of Cherry Street, the excellent **Delta Cultural Center**, 95 Missouri St (Tues–Sat 10am–5pm; free), is a must-see; it covers, among other things, the first settlers of this soggy frontier, contemporary racism, and, of course, the region's musical heritage. From here you can walk along the levee to **River Park**, which has fabulous views of the Mississippi. For some unexpected historic artifacts, stop by the **Phillips County Museum**, next to the Phillips County Public Library at 623 Pecan St (Tues–Sat 10am–4pm; free). Here, besides paintings, period clothing, and Native American arrowheads, you'll find letters written by General Lafayette, Charles Lindbergh, and Robert E. Lee, as well as Samuel Clemens (Mark Twain).

Practicalities

The best of the few **places to stay**, the 1904 *Edwardian Inn*, 317 Briscoe St, on the main highway into town north of the Mississippi Bridge (ⓣ870/338-9155, ⓦ www.edwardianinn.com; ❹), is an opulent **B&B** with large oak-paneled rooms, slightly marred by views from the front over a chemical plant on the river. For **food**, *Bullock's Café*, on the corner of Missouri and Frank Frost streets, dishes up traditional Southern cuisine; *Cherry Street Deli*, 420 Cherry St (ⓣ870/817-7706), is good for soup and sandwiches.

Central and western Arkansas

Little Rock sits right in the middle of the state, just fifty miles west of the quirky spa town of **Hot Springs**, which marks the eastern gateway to the remote **Ouachita Mountains**. The rippling farmland of the **Arkansas River Valley** is sandwiched by the Ouachita crests on the south side and the craggy ridges of the Ozarks to the north. Mining and logging communities dot the east–west roads, and former frontier towns like **Fort Smith** and **Van Buren** retain their Old West flavor. Fayetteville and Hope are both in west Arkansas; there's nothing to see in either.

Little Rock

The geographical, political, and financial center of Arkansas, **LITTLE ROCK** is at the meeting point of the state's two major regions, the northwestern hills and the eastern Delta. The town today has a relaxed, open feel, a far cry from the dramatic events of 1957 (see box, opposite). In the rapidly expanding **River Market District**, 500 President Clinton Ave, the **Museum of Discovery**, geared largely toward kids (Mon–Sat 10am–5pm, Sun 1–5pm; $6.35), is a welcome addition. This area contains the majority of Little Rock's activity, with a splash of restaurants and bars, and a farmers' market on the river. Behind the museum is **Riverfront Park**, a thin strip of greenery and fountains that runs for several blocks – here, a commemorative sign marks the "little rock" for which the city is named (it's not particularly striking, but then the name probably gives that away).

The **Historic Arkansas Museum**, 200 E Third St (Mon–Sat 9am–5pm, Sun 1–5pm; $2), is a living museum of frontier life, incorporating original buildings peopled by well-meaning actors garbed in gaiters and jerkins; the Hinderliter Grog Shop, Little Rock's oldest standing building, dates from around 1827. A **gallery** displays locally made crafts from the last two centuries, temporary historical exhibits, and contemporary Arkansas art.

In MacArthur Park, the **Arkansas Museum of Art** (Tues–Sat 10am–5pm, Sun 11am–5pm; free) features work by local and international artists, with a collection of drawings dating from the Renaissance to the present. Also in the park, the **Macarthur Museum of Arkansas Military History** (Tues–Sat 10am–4pm, Sun 1–4pm; free) exhibits a variety of hardware from the territorial period onward.

Surrounded by smooth lawns and shaded by evergreens, the **Old State House Museum**, in the old capitol building at 300 W Markham St, backs onto the Arkansas River. The displays – everything from Civil War battle flags to African-American quilts – do an admirable job of covering Arkansas history, with strong sections on women, and, naturally, political history. Don't miss the two senate chambers, restored to their original grandeur (Mon–Sat 9am–5pm,

Crisis at Central High

In 1957, Little Rock unexpectedly became the battleground in the first major conflict between state and federal government over **race relations**. At the time, the city was generally viewed as progressive by Southern standards. All parks, libraries, and buses were integrated, a relatively high thirty percent of blacks were on the electoral register, and there were black police officers. However, when the Little Rock School Board announced its decision to phase in **desegregation** gradually – the Supreme Court having declared segregation of schools to be unconstitutional – James Johnson, a candidate for state governor, started a campaign opposed to interracial education. Johnson's rhetoric began to win him support, and the incumbent governor, **Orval Faubus**, who had previously shown no interest in the issue, jumped on the bandwagon himself.

The first nine black students were due to enter **Central High School** that September. The day before school opened, Faubus, "in the interest of safety," reversed his decision to let blacks enroll, only to be overruled by the federal court. He ordered state troopers to keep out the black students anyway; soldiers with bayonets forced Elizabeth Eckford, one of the nine, away from the school entrance into a seething crowd, from which she had to jump on a bus to escape. As legal battles raged during the day, at night blacks were subject to violent attacks by white gangs. Three weeks later, President Eisenhower somewhat reluctantly brought in the 101st Airborne Division, and, amid violent demonstrations, the nine were at last able to enter the school. Throughout the year, they experienced immense intimidation; when one retaliated, she was expelled. The graduation of James Green, the oldest, at the end of the year, seemed to put an end to the affair, but Faubus, up for re-election, renewed his political posturing by closing down all public schools in the city for the 1958–59 academic year – and thereby increased his majority.

The school itself is an enormous brown, crescent-shaped structure, more like a fortress, at 1500 S Park Ave, about a mile from the capitol. Across the street, the **Central High Visitor Center** (Mon–Sat 10am–4pm, Sun 1–4pm; free), in a restored former Mobil gas station, has an interesting exhibit titled "All the World Is Watching Us: Little Rock and the 1957 Crisis."

Sun 1–5pm; free). This was where Clinton announced his bid for the presidency on October 3, 1991, and made his acceptance speech thirteen months later – and then again in 1996, when he became the first Democrat since Franklin Delano Roosevelt to be elected for a second term. There's a special exhibit in the museum on his path to the presidency.

Practicalities

Greyhound arrives at 118 E Washington Ave in North Little Rock, across the river. **Amtrak** enjoys a more central location at Markham and Victory streets. The **visitor center** is at Markham and Broadway (Mon–Fri 8.30am–4.30pm; ☎501/376-4781 or 1-800/844-4781, ⓦwww.littlerock.com).

Finding a **room** downtown should be no problem. The best inexpensive option is just outside downtown at the *Masters Inn*, 707 I-30 (☎1-800/633-3434, ⓦwww.mastersinn.com; ❸), while the *Rosemont B&B*, 515 W 15th St (☎501/374-7456, ⓦwww.rosemontoflittlerock.com; ❹–❺), is conveniently situated in the downtown historic district. The grand 1876 *Capital Hotel*, 111 W Markham (☎501/374-7474 or 1-800/766-7666, ⓦwww.thecapitalhotel .com; ❼), is a long-time haunt of political wheelers and dealers. Even if you can't afford to stay, take a look at its elaborate cast-iron facade and have a drink in the swanky bar.

As for **eating** and **nightlife**, *Vino's*, 923 W Seventh St (☎501/375-8468), is an unpretentious, friendly brewpub serving great ales and good pizza; a popular spot for office lunches, after dark it takes on a more alternative edge, with live punk music. *Juanita's Cantina*, 1300 S Main St (℡501/372-1228), an atmospheric and imaginative Mexican place, also hosts excellent live bands, with a blues jam on Monday. *Doe's Eat Place*, 1023 W Markham St (℡501/376-1195), a branch of the Greenville, Mississippi, restaurant, serves excellent steak and tamales in unpretentious surroundings; it's a longtime favorite of former president Clinton.

Hot Springs

Fifty miles southwest of Little Rock, the low-key, somewhat surreal spa town of **HOT SPRINGS** nestles in the heavily forested Zig Zag Mountains on the eastern flank of the Ouachitas. Its **thermal waters** have attracted visitors since Native Americans used the area as a neutral zone to settle disputes. Early settlers fashioned a crude resort out of the wilderness, and after the railroads arrived in 1875 it became a European-style spa, its hot waters said to cure rheumatism, arthritis, kidney disease, and liver problems. The resort reached its heyday during the Twenties and Thirties, when the mayor reputedly ran a gambling syndicate worth $30 million per annum, and players included Al Capone and Bugsy Siegel. However, Hot Springs' popularity waned when new cures appeared during the Fifties, and all but one of the bathhouses closed down. There was a surge of interest in the place after Clinton's election – he lived here between 1953 and 1964 – and today it makes an odd, charmingly old-fashioned place to visit.

Downtown Hot Springs is crammed into a looping wooded valley, barely wide enough to accommodate the main thoroughfare of Central Avenue. Eight magnificent buildings here, behind a lush display of magnolia trees, elms, and hedgerows, make up the splendid **Bathhouse Row**. Between 1915 and 1962, the grandest of them all was the **Fordyce Bathhouse**, at the 300 block of Central, which reopened in 1989 as the **visitor center** for **Hot Springs National Park** – the only national park to fall within city limits. Apart from the Buckstaff (see below), this is the only bathhouse you can actually enter, and it's worth a trip: the interior, restored to its former magnificence, is an atmospheric mixture of the elegant and the obsolete. The heavy use of veined Italian marble, mosaic-tile floors, and stained glass lend it a decadent feel, while the gruesome hydrotherapy and electrotherapy equipment, including an electric shock massager, seem impossibly brutish (daily 9am–5pm; free; ℡501/624-3383).

It's still possible to take a "**bath**" – an hour-long process involving brisk rubdowns, hot packs, steam baths, and a needle shower – on Bathhouse Row. The only establishment still open for business is the 1912 **Buckstaff**, where a thermal mineral bath costs $15, a massage $18 (March–Nov Mon–Sat 7–11.45am & 1.30–3pm; Dec–Feb Mon–Fri 7–11.45am & 1.30–3pm, Sat 7–11.45am; ℡501/623-2308). This is good fun, but Aveda it's not; swathed in cotton sheets, you are marched by no-nonsense guides from bath to shower to massage table in a municipal, rather prosaic, atmosphere. Full bathing facilities are also available at several hotels. Hot Springs' water lacks the strong sulfuric taste often associated with thermal springs; to "quaff the elixir," as they used to say, fill up a bottle at any of the drinking fountains on and near Central Avenue. Most of them pump out warm water – if you prefer it cold, head for the Happy Hollow Spring on Fountain Street.

To the rear of the Fordyce, two small **springs** have been left open for viewing. The **Grand Promenade** from here is a half-mile brick walkway overlooking downtown. Trails of various lengths and severity lead up the steep slopes of **Hot Springs Mountain**. To reach the summit, take a short drive or any of several different trails, including a testing two-and-a-half-mile hike through dense woods of oak, hickory, and short-leafed pine. The observation decks of the 216ft **Mountain Tower** at the top (daily: summer 9am–9pm; spring and fall 9am–6pm; winter 9am–5pm; $6) offer superb views of the town, the Ouachitas, and surrounding lakes.

Quite apart from its waters, Hot Springs boasts some wonderfully weird Americana. The **Josephine Tussaud Wax Museum**, 250 Central Ave (daily 9am–7pm; $7), presents a sequence of atrocious dummies, all of them terrifying; the **IQ Zoo**, 201 Central Ave (daily 10.30am–2.30pm; $5), is far livelier, a cavalcade of disco-dancing chickens, piano-playing rabbits, and some seriously grumpy raccoons.

Practicalities

Most places of interest are within easy distance of the town's central hotels. Though rates can rise by up to 25 percent in the long high season (Feb–Nov), luxury **accommodation** is surprisingly inexpensive. Dominating the town center, the vast, elegant *Arlington Resort/Spa*, at 239 Central Ave (☎501/623-7771, Ⓦwww.arlingtonhotel.com; ❹; bath and whirlpool $23, massage $30), is a wonderful 1920s structure – Al Capone rented the entire fourth floor when he stayed in town, and President Clinton attended his junior and senior proms in the ballroom. Nearby, the *Downtowner*, 135 Central Ave (☎501/624-5521 or 1-800/251-1962, Ⓦwww.angelfire.com/ar/downtownerhs; ❸; bath and whirlpool $16.50, massage $18.50), is another timewarped old hotel, far less fancy. A number of mom-and-pop places nearby offer varying standards; the *Happy Hollow*, 231 Fountain St (☎501/321-2230; ❷), isn't bad. The nearest place to **camp** is *Gulpha Gorge Campground* in the national park, two miles northeast on Hwy-70 B, off Hwy-70 E (☎501/624-3383; $10 per night).

Hidden among the usual family **restaurants** along Central Avenue, the faded *Venetian*, in the *Arlington*, presents Hot Springs' version of haute cuisine in a somewhat eccentric atmosphere; nearby, the *Downtowner*'s *Jennigan's* (☎501/623-3909) offers a solid soul-food buffet for $6. *McClard's Bar-B-Q*, three miles south of downtown at 505 Albert Pike (☎501/624-9586; closed Sun & Mon), is not to be missed, its pork ribs, slaw, beans, and hot tamales all prepared by hand – apparently Bill and Hillary stopped by here on their wedding day.

As you might expect, Hot Springs' **nightlife** is marvelously cheesy, ranging from variety shows and jamborees to *The Witness*, an outdoor musical of Christ's life as sung by the Apostle Peter; it's held six miles from downtown on 1960 Millcreek Rd (June–Oct Fri & Sat 8pm; $10; ☎501/623-9781). Those with more secular tastes might prefer the *Theater of Magic*, 817 Central Ave (summer Tues–Sat 8pm; $12; ☎501/623-6200), starring "Master of Illusion" Maxwell Blade. On a different note, there's a prestigious **documentary film festival** held each October (Ⓦwww.docufilminst.org).

Western Arkansas

West of Hot Springs, US-270 cuts through the **Ouachita Mountains**, unique to the continent in that they run east–west rather than north–south. On its way to Oklahoma, the road passes over uneven crests separated by wide valleys speckled with tiny communities, so isolated that, in the Thirties, hill-dwellers supposedly spoke a form of Elizabethan English. Separating the Ouachitas from the northerly Ozarks, the **Arkansas River Valley**, a natural east–west path for bison, was used for centuries by Native Americans and white hunters before steamboats arrived in the 1820s.

Fort Smith

Now an industrial city of roughly 70,000 people, **FORT SMITH**, on the Oklahoma border, maintains a pronounced Western feel. Until Isaac C. Parker – the "Hanging Judge" – took over in 1875, this was a rowdy pioneer town uncomfortably close to Indian Territory, a sanctuary for robbers and bandits. Parker sent out two hundred marshals to round up the fugitives; in 21 years he sentenced 160 to death and saw 79 go to the gallows.

On Rogers Avenue, **Fort Smith National Historic Site** (daily 9am–5pm; $3) features remains of the original fort, Parker's courtroom, the dingy basement jail, and a set of gallows. The **Museum of History**, no. 320 (summer Tues–Sat 10am–5pm, Sun 1–5pm; winter Tues–Sat 10am–5pm; $5), tells the story of the town, and serves old-fashioned ice cream in its 1920s soda fountain. **Old Main Street** in **Van Buren**, on the opposite bank of the Arkansas River, is a stretch of more than seventy restored buildings that has been used in numerous Westerns.

Fort Smith's **visitor center**, Miss Laura's, 2 North B St (Mon–Sat 9am–4pm, Sun 1–4.30pm; ☎1-800/637-1477), is housed in a restored former brothel. **Lodgings** include the central *Holiday Inn*, 700 Rogers Ave (☎501/783-1000, ⓦwww.holiday-inn.com/ftsmithar; ❹–❺). For good-value, tasty home-cooked Italian **food**, try *Taliano's*, 201 N 14th St (☎501/785-2292).

The Ozark Mountains

Although the highest peak fails to top 2000 feet, the **Ozark Mountains**, which extend beyond northern Arkansas into southern Missouri, are characterized by severe steep ridges and jagged spurs. Hair-raising roads weave their way over the precipitous hills, past rugged lakeshores and pristine rivers. When ambitious speculators poured into Arkansas in the 1830s, those who missed the best land etched out remote hill farms that were no better than what they'd left behind in Kentucky or Tennessee. They remained utterly isolated until the last few decades; the Ozarks have now become the fastest-growing rural section of the US, a major tourist and retirement destination. Much-needed cash has flooded in, bringing with it the cafés and souvenir shops that have converted centers such as **Harrison** into cookie-cutter American towns.

The word "Ozark" is everywhere, used to entice tourists into music shows or gift emporia, which owe more to Nashville and Branson, Missouri, than to these mountains. With all the hype, it's getting increasingly difficult to tell the genuine article from imitations – which is a good reason for visiting the **state park** at **Mountain View**, a serious attempt to preserve traditional Ozark skills and music. The most-visited town in the region, **Eureka Springs**, just inside the Missouri border, is a pretty mountainside Victorian spa town, though not one where you should expect to learn much about Ozark life.

Mountain View

Roughly sixty miles north of Little Rock, the state-run **Ozark Folk Center**, two miles north of the town of **MOUNTAIN VIEW** on Hwy-14, is a very good living history museum that attempts to show how life used to be in these remote hills, not reached by paved roads until the Fifties. Homestead skills are displayed in reconstructed log cabins, and folk musicians and storytellers perform throughout the park. Special events, including regular Ozark and roots music **concerts**, are held most evenings (mid-April to early Nov, varying hours; concerts $9, craft displays $9, combination ticket $15.50; ☎870/269-3851, ⊛www.ozarkfolkcenter.com).You can even **stay** at the *Dry Creek Lodge* (☎1-800/264-3655; ❸) on the grounds.

Mountain View's **visitor center**,107 N Peabody Ave (April–Nov Mon–Fri 9am–5pm, Sat 10am–4pm, Sun 12.30–3pm; Dec–March Mon–Fri 8.30am–4.30pm; ☎870/269-8068, ⊛www.mtnviewcc.org), can help with **accommodation** elsewhere in town. The friendly *Inn at Mountain View*, 307 W Washington St (☎870/269-4200 or 1-800/535-1301, ⊛www.innatmountainview.com; ❹), is a pretty B&B owned by folk musicians; they serve a full country breakfast. Good **restaurants** include the Folk Center's *Iron Skillet Restaurant* (☎870/269-3139) and *Tommy's Famous…*, an award-winning pizzeria and rib joint at 205 Carpenter St, four blocks west of the town square (☎870/269-FAST). For entertainment, even in winter, it's hard to beat the friendly **jam sessions** in the square, or on the porch of Mountain View Music Store, on the square at 123 W Washington St; it's a great shop, selling instruments, CDs, and books (☎870/269-9044). There are also a number of **festivals**. Two of the most popular are the venerable **Spring Folk Festival** (music, crafts, food stalls, parades), held during the third weekend in April, and the **Bean Festival** (beans, cornbread, music, outhouse races), held on the last Saturday in October; reserve a room well in advance during these times.

The **Buffalo River** – a prime destination for white-water canoeing – flows across the state north of Mountain View. **Buffalo Camping and Canoeing** (☎870/439-2888, ⊛gilbertstore.com) rents canoes and equipment, and runs a free shuttle bus to the river, which is at its most spectacular around **Pruitt Landing**, thirteen miles south of the small settlement of Harrison. They also offer a few **cabins** for four people (❹).

Eureka Springs

Picturesque **EUREKA SPRINGS**, set on steep mountain slopes in Arkansas's northwestern corner, began life a century ago as a health center. As that role diminished, its striking location turned it into a regular tourist destination, given a kitsch edge by its specialty in weddings and honeymoons. It's an enjoyable place to stroll around, filled with tasteful Victorian buildings, and you can ride on the **Eureka Springs and North Arkansas Railway** through wooded Ozark valleys. Rolling stock includes a magnificent "cabbage-head" wood-burning locomotive; trips depart on the hour from the depot at 299 N Main St (mid-April to Oct Mon–Sat 10am–4pm; $9).

Three miles east of town on US-62 E, an incredible religious complex includes the seven-story **Christ of the Ozarks** – a surreal statue of Jesus with a 60ft arm span – a **Bible Museum**, and a **Sacred Arts Center**. Elna M. Smith, whose foundation runs the whole show, was so worried that the holy sites of the Middle East would be destroyed by war that she decided to build replicas in the Ozarks, safe from Arab attacks. Minibuses whisk visitors through the two-and-a-half hour **New Holy Land Tour** past scaled-down versions of the Sea of Galilee, the River Jordan, and Golgotha. The complex is open from the last Friday in April to the last Saturday in October (Mon, Tues & Thurs–Sat 9am–3.30pm, Wed 9am–11.45am; $15). In the evenings, the **Great Passion Play** re-enacts Christ's last days on earth with a cast of 250, including live animals, in a 4100-seat amphitheater (same months; nightly except Sun and Wed 8.30pm, after August 7.30pm; $23.25; ☎1-800/882-7529, ⓦwww.greatpassionplay.com).

Practicalities

In town, US-62 becomes Van Buren. **Accommodation** rates vary seasonally, but you can usually find inexpensive lodging just over a mile from downtown on US-62 E. More central is the *Best Western Eureka Inn* (☎479/253-9551, ⓦwww.eurekabw.com; ❹), at the junction of US-62 and S Main Street. The local **visitor center** is at 137 W Van Buren (daily 9am–5pm; ☎479/253-8737, ⓦwww.eurekasprings.com).

For **food**, *Sparky's Road House Café*, 41 Van Buren (☎479/253-6001), is an atmospheric pub with an inexpensive menu and a great beer selection. Just off the well-worn tourist paths, *Chelsea's Corner*, 10 Mountain St, off Spring St (☎479/253-6723), has **live music** most evenings. Eureka Springs also holds a good **folk festival** in October (☎479/253-7788).

Florida

CHAPTER 7

Highlights

✱ **Ocean Drive, Miami**
South Beach's finest Art Deco showpiece, buzzing with cosmopolitan cafés, flashy vintage cars, and wannabe models. **See p.642**

✱ **Little Havana, Miami**
Lunch on Cuban specialties and sip *café con leche* in this Hispanic enclave. **See p.646**

✱ **Mangrove Mama's, Sugarloaf Key**
Quintessential Florida Keys food joint, serving super-fresh conch fritters and Key Lime Pie. **See p.655**

✱ **Key West** This funky, anything-goes town feels like it's at the end of the world. **See p.655**

✱ **St Augustine** Sixteenth-century Spanish town packed with historic interest and a handful of lovely beaches. **See p.668**

✱ **Walt Disney World, Orlando** Pure entertainment, planned down to the last detail. Simply irresistible. **See p.677**

✱ **Everglades National Park** Bike or hike through the vast sawgrass plains of the legendary Everglades, or canoe through alligator-filled mangrove swamps. **See p.694**

7

Florida

B rochure images of tanning tourists and Mickey Mouse give an inaccurate and incomplete picture of **FLORIDA**. Although the aptly nicknamed "Sunshine State" is indeed devoted to the tourist trade, it's also among the least-understood parts of the US. Away from its over-exposed resorts lie forests and rivers, deserted strands filled with wildlife, vibrant cities, and primeval swamps. Contrary to the popular retirement-community image, new Floridians tend to be a younger, more energetic breed, while Spanish-speaking enclaves provide close ties to Latin America and the Caribbean.

By far, the essential stop is cosmopolitan, half-Latin **Miami**. A simple journey south from here brings you to the **Florida Keys**, a hundred-mile string of islands known for sports fishing, coral-reef diving, and the sultry town of **Key West**, legendary for its sunsets and anything-goes attitude. Back on the mainland, west from Miami stretch the easily accessible **Everglades**, a swampy sawgrass plain filled with camera-friendly (but otherwise unfriendly) alligators.

Much of Florida's **east coast** is disappointingly urbanized, albeit with miles of unbroken beaches rolling alongside. The residential stranglehold is loosened further north, where **Kennedy Space Center** launches NASA shuttles, and where communities such as **Daytona Beach** have become subservient to the local sands. Farther along, historical **St Augustine** stands as the longest continuously occupied European settlement in the US.

In **central Florida** the terrain turns green, though it's no rural idyll, thanks in most part to **Orlando** and **Walt Disney World**, which sprawls out across the countryside. From here it's just a skip north to the towns and beaches of the **Gulf Coast**, and somewhat further to the forests of the **Panhandle**, Florida's link with the Deep South.

Weather-wise, warm sunshine and blue skies are almost always the norm. The state does, however, split into two **climatic zones**: subtropical in the south and warm temperate in the north. Orlando and points south have a mild season from October to April, with warm temperatures and low humidity. Down here, this is the **peak tourist season**, when prices are at their highest. Conversely, the southern summer (May to September) brings high humidity and afternoon storms; the rewards for braving the mugginess are lower prices and fewer tourists.

North of Orlando, winter is the off-peak period, even though daytime temperatures are (generally – snow has been known to fall on the Panhandle) comfortably warm. During the northern Florida summer, the crowds arrive, and the days and nights are hot and sticky. Keep in mind that June to November is **hurricane season**, and the possibility of big storms is very much a reality.

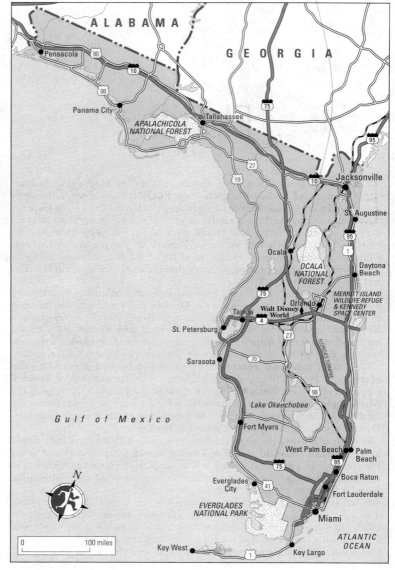

Some history

The **first European sighting** of Florida, just six years after Christopher Columbus reached the New World, is believed to have been made by John and Sebastian Cabot in 1498, when they spotted what is now Cape Florida, on Key Biscayne in Miami. Nothing much came of the sighting, though, as the Cabots did not take formal possession of the land. At the time, the area's 100,000 inhabitants formed several distinct **tribes**: the Timucua across northern

Florida, the Calusa around the southwest and Lake Okeechobee, the Apalachee in the Panhandle, and the Tequesta along the southeast coast.

In 1513, a Spaniard, **Juan Ponce de León**, sighted land during *Pascua Florida*, Spain's Easter celebration; he named what he saw *La Florida*, or "Land of Flowers." Eight years later he returned with a mandate from the Spanish king to conquer and colonize the territory; this was the first of several Spanish incursions prompted by rumors of gold hidden in the north of the region. When it became clear that Florida did not harbor stunning riches, interest waned – but the arrival of French Huguenots in 1562 forced the Spanish into a more determined effort at settlement.

Three years later, the conquistador Pedro Menéndez de Avilés, sent to the continent by empire-minded King Philip II of Spain, founded **St Augustine** – site of the longest continuous European habitation in North America. In 1586, St Augustine was razed by a British naval bombardment led by Francis Drake. The ensuing bloody confrontation for control of North America was eventually settled when the British captured the crucial Spanish possession of Havana, Cuba; Spain willingly parted with Florida to get it back. By this time, indigenous Floridians had been largely wiped out by disease. The area's Native American population now largely comprised disparate tribes that had arrived from the west, collectively known as the **Seminoles**, who were generally left undisturbed in the inland areas.

Following American independence, the US began to think in terms of controlling Florida. As a result, in 1814, the US general (and future president) Andrew Jackson – on the pretext of subduing the Seminole, but with the actual intention of taking the region – marched south from Tennessee, killing hundreds of Indians and triggering the **First Seminole War**. Following the war, in 1819, Spain **ceded Florida** to the US, in return for American assumption of $5 million of Spanish debt. Not long after, Jackson was sworn in as Florida's first American governor, and Tallahassee was selected as the new administrative center.

Eleven years later, the **Act of Indian Removal** decreed that all Native Americans in the eastern US should be transferred to reservations in the Midwest. Most Seminole were determined to stay and, as a result, the **Second Seminole War** broke out, with the Indians steadily driven south, away from the fertile lands of central Florida and into the Everglades, where they eventually agreed to remain. Florida became the **27th state** on March 3, 1845, coinciding with the prosperity brought by the railroads. As a member of the Confederacy during the **Civil War**, Florida's primary contribution was the provision of food – a foretaste of its postwar economic role after being readmitted to the Union.

At the beginning of the twentieth century, the country's newspapers extolled the curative virtues of Florida's climate, and northern speculators began to invest in the state. These early efforts to promote Florida as a **tourist destination** brought in the wintering rich: Henry Flagler opened luxury resorts on the northeast coast and extended his Florida East Coast Railroad south, giving birth to communities such as Palm Beach. Meanwhile, Henry Plant connected his own railroad to Tampa, turning it into a thriving port city. Florida's climate enabled citrus fruits to be grown during the winter and sold to the cooler north. The state became a major beef producer, as well. After World War I, it seemed that everyone in America wanted a piece of Florida, and chartered trains brought in thousands of eager buyers. But most deals were on paper only, and in 1926 the banks began to default. The **Wall Street Crash** then made paupers of the millionaires whose investments had helped shape the state.

What saved Florida was **World War II**. During the war, thousands of troops arrived to guard the coastline, providing them with a taste of Florida that would entice many to return. Furthermore, in the mid-Sixties, the state government bent over backwards to help the Disney Corporation turn a sizable slice of central Florida into **Walt Disney World**, the biggest theme park ever. Its enormous commercial success helped solidify Florida's place in the international tourist market: directly or indirectly, tourism now makes up 20 percent of the total state economy.

Behind the optimistic facade, however, lie many **problems**. There's a broadening gap between the relative liberalism of the big cities and the archconservatism of the northern Bible Belt: while Miami promotes its multicultural make-up, the Ku Klux Klan holds picnics in the Panhandle. Gun laws remain notoriously lax, and the multimillion-dollar **drug trade** shows few signs of abating – at least a quarter of the cocaine entering the US is said to arrive via Florida. **Racial issues** continue, too, with tension on several fronts: between Anglo-Americans and nouveau riche Cubans, between blacks and whites, blacks and Hispanics, and between police and the inner-city poor. Increased protection of the state's **natural resources** has been a more positive feature of the last decade and impressive amounts of land are under state control – overall, wildlife is less threatened now than at any time since white settlers first arrived.

Getting around Florida

Surprisingly compact, Florida is **fairly easy to navigate** if you have a car: crossing between the east and west coasts takes just a couple of hours, and determined drivers can make one of the longest trips – between the western extremity of the Panhandle and Miami – in a full day's drive. Getting around by **public transportation**, on the other hand, requires adroit advance planning. Greyhound **buses** link all major towns and cities, but many rural areas and some of the most enjoyable sections of the coasts are not covered. That said, Florida's **railroads** were built to service boomtowns in the 1920s, and consequently some rural nooks are well-linked by rail. Although inadvisable in the cities, **cycling** is a great way to see large parts of Florida – miles of cycle paths follow the coasts, and long-distance bike trails cross the state's interior.

Miami

Far and away the most exciting city in Florida, **MIAMI** is a stunning and often intoxicatingly beautiful place. Awash with sunlight-intensified natural colors, there are moments – when the neon-flashed South Beach strip glows in the warm night and the palm trees sway in the breeze – when a better-looking city is hard to imagine. Away from the beaches and the tourists, the gleaming skyscrapers of downtown herald Miami's proud status as the site of many international banks' Latin American headquarters. Even so, it's the people, not the climate, the landscape, or the cash, that makes Miami so noteworthy. Half of the two-million-strong population is Hispanic, the vast majority of which are **Cuban**. Spanish is the predominant language almost everywhere – in many places it's the only language you'll hear – and news from Havana, Caracas, or Managua frequently gets more attention than the latest word from Washington.

Just a hundred years ago Miami was a swampy outpost of mosquito-tormented settlers. The arrival of Henry Flagler's railroad in 1896 gave the city its first fixed land-link with the rest of the continent, and cleared the way for the Twenties property boom. In the Fifties, after WWII, Miami Beach became a celebrity-filled resort area, just as thousands of Cubans fleeing the regime of Fidel Castro began arriving here as well. The Sixties and Seventies brought decline, and Miami's dangerous reputation in the Eighties was at least partly deserved. As the cop show *Miami Vice* so glamorously underlined, drug smuggling was (and, albeit in a more underground way, still is) endemic; what's more, in 1980 the city had the highest murder rate in America.

Since then, much has changed, for two very different reasons. First, the gentrification of South Beach helped make tourism the lifeblood of the local economy again in the early Nineties. Second, the city's determined wooing of Latin America brought rapid investment, both domestic and international: many US corporations run their South American operations from Miami, and certain neighborhoods, such as Key Biscayne, are now home to thriving communities of expat Peruvians, Colombians, and Venezuelans.

Arrival and information

Miami International Airport (☎305/876-7000, ⓦwww.miami-airport .com) is six miles west of the city. A cab from the airport costs $18–41, depending on your destination. You can opt for one of the 24-hour SuperShuttle minivans, which will deliver you to any address in Miami for $9–15 (☎305/871-2000, ⓦwww.supershuttle.com). Via **public transportation**, take the #7 Metrobus to downtown, a trip of 30 minutes or so ($1.25, exact fare required; every 40min Mon–Fri 5.30am–8.30pm, Sat & Sun 7am–7pm), or the J Metrobus ($1.25 plus a 25¢ surcharge to South Beach; every 30min daily 5.30am–11.30pm) to Miami Beach farther on. Late at night, the Airport Owl shuttle runs in a loop through South Beach, downtown and back to the airport ($1.25; once hourly, 11.50pm–5.50am). **Greyhound's** Miami West station, 4111 NW 27th St is in an inconvenient location; instead, try and get off at the downtown terminal, 100 W 6th St (☎305/374-6180 or 1-800/231-2222, ⓦwww.greyhound.com). The **Amtrak** station, at 8303 NW 37th Ave, is seven miles northwest of the city center; to get from the station to downtown, Coconut Grove, or Coral Gables, take the L Metrobus to the nearest Metrorail station (see below), a ride of around eight blocks; Metrorail then can connect you with the central and southern districts.

There's no official **tourist information** booth downtown: the two best-equipped sources are both in South Beach. These are the **Miami Beach Chamber of Commerce**, 1920 Meridian Ave (Mon–Fri 9am–6pm, Sat & Sun 10am–4pm; ☎305/672-1270, ⓦwww.miamibeachchamber.com), which is packed with leaflets and staffed by helpful locals, and the **Art Deco Welcome Center**, 1001 Ocean Drive (daily 10.30am–7pm; ☎305/672-2014, ⓦwww.mdpl.org), which has details on walking tours and events.

City transportation and tours

Downtown and South Beach, the two main tourist areas, are eminently walkable – and, indeed, are best enjoyed **on foot**. However, if you want to see more of the city, **driving** is the most practical option. An integrated **public transport network** run by Metro-Dade Transit (℡305/770-3131, ⓦwww.co.miami-dade.fl.us/transit) covers Miami, making the city easy – if time-consuming – to get around, at least by day (nighttime services are more skeletal). **Metrorail** trains (5am–midnight) run along a single line between the northern suburbs and South Miami; useful stops are Government Center (for downtown), Coconut Grove, and Douglas Road or University (for Coral Gables). Single-journey **fares** are $1.25. Downtown Miami is also ringed by the **Metromover** (5.30am–midnight; free), a monorail that doesn't cover much ground but gives a great bird's-eye view. **Metrobuses** (24hr) cover the entire city, but services dwindle at night; the flat-rate single-journey fare is $1.25, with a 25¢ surcharge for transfers. **Route maps** and **timetables** for all Metro-Dade Transit services can be had at Government Center Station, or at the Metrorail station at NW 1st Avenue and 1st Street.

Taxis are abundant in Miami; either hail one on the street or call Central Cab (℡305/532-5555) or Metro Taxi (℡305/888-8888). If you want to rent a **bike**, you can do so from one of the many outlets around town, such as the Miami Beach Cycle Center, 601 5th St ($5/hr or $20/day; ℡305/674-0150).

For an informed stroll, take one of **Dr Paul George's Walking Tours** from the Historical Museum of South Florida (call for schedule; no tours July & Aug; $15 and up; ℡305/375-1621, ⓦwww.historical-museum.org). Or, try the various excellent **Art Deco walking tours** of South Beach (Thurs 6.30pm & Sat 10.30am; $15), which begin at the Art Deco Welcome Center on Ocean Drive (see p.639). The latter organization also offers a self-guided audio walking tour of the district (available daily 10.30am–7pm; 90min; $10).

Accommodation

Accommodation is rarely a problem in Miami – though you should expect rates to skyrocket on weekends and holidays in the winter. Otherwise, there are rooms to suit every taste and budget, with the majority of travelers opting for any one of the numerous Art Deco **South Beach** hotels. Though it can be great fun to stay in one of these photo-ready masterpieces, Deco hotels were built in a different era, and, as such, rooms can be tiny. Elsewhere, **Coral Gables** and **Coconut Grove**, though somewhat out-of-the-way, both have an appealing option or two; **Downtown** is filled with chain hotels. Prices are steepest during the main tourist season, from December through April, though bargains can be found year-round in several well-run **hostels** on Miami Beach.

Albion Hotel 1650 James Ave, South Beach ℡1-877/RUBELLS or 305/913-1000, ⓦwww.rubellhotels.com. A sensitive conversion of a classic Nautical Deco building, this is one of the best-value hotels on the beach. Rooms are hip but simple; the raised pool – with portholes cut into its sides – is also a big draw. ❻

Brigham Gardens Guesthouse 1411 Collins Ave, South Beach ℡305/531-1331, ⓦwww.brigham-gardens.com. The large rooms here all have either basic or fully equipped kitchens; a tropical garden patio and friendly atmosphere help make this one of the most pleasant places to stay in South Beach. ❸

Clay Hotel and Hosteling International 1438 Washington Ave, South Beach ℡305/534-2988 or 1-800/379-2529, ⓦwww.clayhotel.com. This beautiful converted monastery serves as the city's best budget hotel and youth hostel. Dorm beds are $16 for IYH members, $18 for nonmembers.

Gables Inn 730 S Dixie Hwy, Coral Gables ℡305/661-7999, ✉thegablesinn@aol.com. Basic but clean, this Mediterranean Revival–style inn is Coral Gables' answer to a motel – meaning it's fancier than most. ❸

Hampton Inn 2800 SW 28th St, Coconut Grove ℡305/448-2800, ⓦwww.hamptoninns-florida.com. Basic but bright accommodation, geared to the business traveler – though the free local calls, free breakfast, and onsite coin laundry are attractive for budget travelers, too. **4**

Miami River Inn 118 SW South River Drive, Little Havana ℡ 305/325-0045, ⓦ www.miamiriverinn .com. Most of the buildings that comprise this inn date to 1908, providing comfortable accommodations clustered together around a tree-shaded pool. Not in the best neighborhood, so stay here only if you have access to a car. **3**

Ninth Street Hostel 236 9th St, South Beach ℡ 305/534-0268, ⓦ www.sobehostel.com. Friendly, centrally located hostel with beds in four-person dorms starting at $13 ($15 for non-IYHA members), as well as private singles and doubles (from $36). **1**

Park Central 640 Ocean Drive, South Beach ℡ 305/538-1611, ⓦ www.theparkcentral.com. The Colonial safari style of the wicker-crammed rooms is a little outdated (this was one of the first hotels to be renovated in the late 1980s) but the reasonable prices more than make up. **5**

Pelican 826 Ocean Drive, South Beach ℡ 305/673-3373 or 1-800/7-PELICAN, ⓦ www.pelicanhotel.com. Each room at this campy, quirky hotel is individually themed and named – try the lush red bordello known as the "Best Little Whorehouse" or the dentists' office-themed "With Drill." **6**

The Shore Club 1901 Collins Ave, South Beach ℡ 305/895-3100, ⓦ www.shoreclub.com. White-hot, supercool hotel on the beach, with minimalist, brightly colored rooms and several swanky bar/restaurants, like the poolside *Sky Bar* (see review p.651). **8**

Townhouse 150 20th St, South Beach ℡ 305/534-3800 or 1-877/534-3800, ⓦ www.townhousehotel.com. Small but stylish rooms, great staff, free breakfast, and squishy rooftop waterbeds – all at a fraction of most boutique hotel prices. Highly recommended. **4**

The Whitelaw 808 Collins Ave, South Beach ℡ 305/398-7000, ⓦ www.whitelawhotel.com. Apart from its sleek, all-white rooms, this boutique hotel offers great freebies, from complimentary airport pick-up to lavish breakfasts and a complimentary happy hour every evening in the lobby. **5**

The City

Each of Miami's **districts** has a character very much its own. Separated from the mainland by Biscayne Bay, the most popular is **Miami Beach**, especially the world-famous **South Beach** portion. This is where many of the city's famed Art Deco buildings can be found, all pastels, neon, and wavy lines. Though touted as a chic gathering-place for globe-trotting fashionistas, South Beach is not as exclusive as you might expect, especially on weekend afternoons, when families and out-of-towners join in the fun along Ocean Drive right with the washboard stomachs and bulging pecs.

Back on the mainland, **downtown** has a few good museums, but is most appealing for its throbbing Latin American vibe. To the north are two areas that have only recently started attracting visitors: the chichi **Design District** and the earthy, Caribbean enclave known as **Little Haiti**. Meanwhile, west of downtown, there's nowhere better for a Cuban lunch than **Little Havana**. Immediately south, the spacious boulevards and neighborhood entrances of **Coral Gables** are as impressive now as they were in the 1920s, when the district set new standards in town planning. Independently minded, but equally wealthy, **Coconut Grove** is also worth a look, thanks to its walkable center and a couple of Miami's most popular attractions. Lastly, sun-worshippers should make time for **Key Biscayne**, a smart, secluded island community with some beautiful beaches, an easy five miles off the mainland by causeway.

Miami Beach

A long slender arm of land between Biscayne Bay and the Atlantic Ocean, **MIAMI BEACH**, three miles off the mainland, has been a headline-grabbing resort town for almost a hundred years, from its first heyday in the Art

Deco–dominated 1920s, through a slick-as-Vegas era in the 1950s, to the hip hedonism of today. Until the 1910s – when its Quaker owner, John Collins, formed an unlikely partnership with a flashy entrepreneur, Carl Fisher – it was nothing more than an ailing fruit farm. With Fisher's money, Biscayne Bay was dredged, and the muck raised from its murky bed was used as landfill to transform this wildly vegetated barrier island into a carefully sculptured landscape of palm trees, hotels, and tennis courts. After a hurricane in 1926 devastated Miami (and especially the beach), damaged buildings were replaced by grander structures in the new Art Deco style, and Miami Beach as we know it appeared. Since then, its history has been checkered: by the 1980s, crack dens and retirement homes were equally commonplace in South Beach, but the 1990s saw a renaissance spearheaded by a few savvy hoteliers and Miami's gay community. It's still a popular resort with the tanned and toned, though the gay pioneers have now largely decamped to quieter quarters up the coast in Fort Lauderdale.

South Beach

Occupying the southernmost three miles of Miami Beach is gorgeous **SOUTH BEACH**, with its hundreds of dazzling pastel-colored 1920s and 1930s buildings. By day, the sun blares down on sizzling bodies on the sand – though it's worth braving an early morning wake-up call to catch the dawn glow, which bathes the Deco hotels in pure, crystalline white light. By night, the ten blocks of Ocean Drive become one of the liveliest stretches in Miami, as terrace cafés spill across the specially widened sidewalk, crowds of tourists and locals saunter by the beach, and Jazz Age neon illuminates the starry sky.

Loosely bordered north/south by 5th and 23rd streets, and west/east by Euclid Avenue and the ocean, the area referred to as the **Deco District** actually incorporates a variety of styles: take one of the excellent walking or cycling tours from the **Miami Design Preservation League Welcome Center** (see p.639) to learn the difference between Streamline, Moderne, and Florida Deco, not to mention Mediterranean Revival.

The most famous buildings lie along **Ocean Drive**, where revamped hotels make much of their design heritage. There's one private residence amid the hotels: **Casa Casuarina**, at the corner of 10th Street, the former home of the late fashion designer Gianni Versace.

If the tourist hordes get to be too much, head a block west to **Collins Avenue**, lined with more Deco hotels and fashion chains, or on to **Washington Avenue**, which tends more toward funky thrift stores and cool coffee bars. At 1001 Washington Ave, the imaginative **Wolfsonian–FIU** (Tues, Wed, Fri & Sat 11am–6pm, Thurs 11am–9pm, Sun noon–5pm; $5; ☎305/531-1001, ⓦ www.wolfsonian.fiu.edu) houses an eclectic collection of decorative arts from the late nineteenth century to 1945. The displays of old books, photos, paintings, posters, and all manner of domestic objects are impressive, if a bit muddled.

Throughout Miami Beach's history, one group that has kept a constant presence is its sizable Jewish population, which includes many Holocaust survivors and their families. This contingent is the reason for the **Holocaust Memorial**, near the north tip of South Beach, at 1933–1945 Meridian Ave (daily 9am–9pm; $2 donation for brochure; ☎305/538-1663, ⓦ www .holocaustmmb.org). A complex, uncompromising reminder to their experience, the monument looks from a distance like a giant, defiant hand punching into the sky. However, as you get closer, you begin to make out the mass of wailing people scrabbling up the wrist. Following the wall of

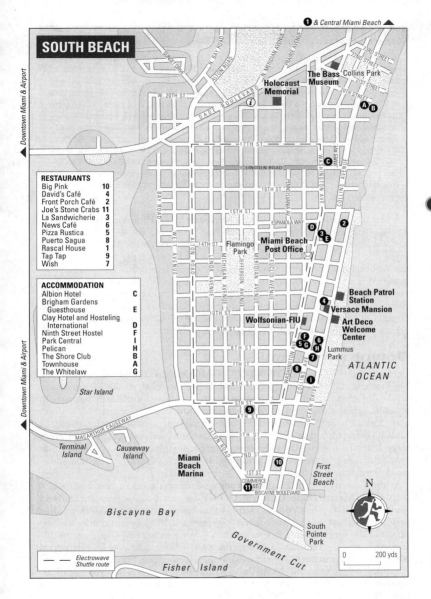

SOUTH BEACH

The Bass Museum

Holocaust Memorial

Collins Park

ⓘ

❶ ❷

Ⓖ

LINCOLN ROAD

RESTAURANTS

Big Pink	10
David's Café	4
Front Porch Café	2
Joe's Stone Crabs	11
La Sandwicherie	3
News Café	6
Pizza Rustica	5
Puerto Sagua	8
Rascal House	1
Tap Tap	9
Wish	7

ACCOMMODATION

Albion Hotel	C
Brigham Gardens Guesthouse	E
Clay Hotel and Hosteling International	D
Ninth Street Hostel	F
Park Central	I
Pelican	H
The Shore Club	B
Townhouse	A
The Whitelaw	G

ESPANOLA WAY

Flamingo Park

Miami Beach Post Office

Ⓓ ❸ Ⓔ ❷

Beach Patrol Station

Versace Mansion

Wolfsonian-FIU

Art Deco Welcome Center

❹

Ⓕ ❻ Ⓖ Ⓗ

❺

Lummus Park

ⓘ ❼

ATLANTIC OCEAN

❽

Star Island

MACARTHUR CAUSEWAY

Terminal Island

Causeway Island

Miami Beach Marina

❾

❿

First Street Beach

N

Biscayne Bay

⓫

BISCAYNE BOULEVARD

South Pointe Park

0   200 yds

— — Electrowave Shuttle route

Government Cut

Fisher Island

Downtown Miami & Airport ▲

7

FLORIDA | Miami

names, inscribed with a relentless list of Holocaust victims, brings you to the foot of the sculpture, hidden from the road, where distressing statues portray more writhing, emaciated human figures. The heart-wrenching ensemble is underscored by the accompanying quote from Anne Frank: "Ideals, dreams, and cherished hopes rise within us only to meet the horrible truth and be shattered."

Miami beaches

If you took away the Art Deco, the beautiful people, and the glittering nightlife, you'd still be left with the simple truth that Miami Beach has a fabulous **choice of beaches**. With twelve miles of calm waters, clean sands, swaying palms, and candy-colored lifeguard towers, you can't go wrong picking a spot. The young and the beautiful soak up the rays between 5th and 21st streets, a convenient hop from the juice bars and cafés on Ocean Drive. From 6th to 14th streets, **Lummus Park** – much of whose sand was shipped in from the Bahamas – is the heart of the South Beach scene; there's an unofficial gay section roughly around 12th Street. North of 21st, things are more family-oriented, with a **boardwalk** running between the shore and the hotels up to 46th. To the south, **First Street Beach** and **South Pointe** are favored by Cuban families, and are especially convivial at weekends. For good **swimming**, head up to 85th, a quiet stretch that's usually patrolled by lifeguards.

A few blocks northeast is the **Bass Museum**, 2121 Park Ave (Tues, Wed, Fri & Sat 10am–5pm, Thurs 10am–9pm, Sun 11–5pm; $6; ☎ 305/673-7530, ⓦ www.bassmuseum.org). The only fine art museum on the beach, the Bass is housed in a 1930 building designed by Russell Pancoast, the architect son-in-law of beach pioneer John Collins. After years of delays, the museum's much-heralded expansion by Japanese architect Arata Isozaki has finally been completed; the white box he grafted onto the original building along Park Avenue has tripled its exhibition space. The museum's permanent collection consists of fine, if largely unremarkable, European paintings, although its temporary exhibitions are often lively and worth visiting.

Downtown Miami

Back on the mainland, **DOWNTOWN MIAMI** divides into distinct halves: big business and big buildings line Brickell Avenue south of the Miami River, while the commercial bazaar around Flagler Street to the north hums with jewelers, fabric stores, and cheap electronics outlets. Latin culture is comfortably dominant here – from office workers grabbing a midmorning *cafecito*, or Cuban coffee, from tiny streetside cafés, to the bilingual signage in almost every store. If at first it seems overwhelming, persevere: downtown is compact, holds two of Miami's best museums, and provides the clearest sense of Cuba's continuing influence on the city.

At the western end of **Flagler Street**, downtown's loudest, brightest, busiest strip, is the **Metro-Dade Cultural Center**, an ambitious attempt by architect Philip Johnson to create a postmodern Mediterranean-style piazza. Art shows, historical collections, and a library frame the courtyard, but Johnson overlooked the power of the south Florida sun: rather than pausing to rest and chat, most people scamper across the open space toward the nearest shade. The center's **Historical Museum of Southern Florida** (Mon–Sat 10am–5pm, Sun noon–5pm, 3rd Thursday of each month 10am–9pm; $5; ☎ 305/375-1492, ⓦ www.historical-museum.org) provides a comprehensive look into the region's history, with an especially strong section on refugees and immigration since 1960.

On the east side of the plaza, the **Miami Art Museum** (Tues–Fri 10am–5pm, Sat & Sun 12–5pm; $5, Sundays free; ☎ 305/375-1700, ⓦ www.miamiartmuseum.org) houses a strong collection of post-1940 art, and showcases outstanding international traveling exhibits. The museum is planning to relocate to a waterfront space known as Museum Park Miami late in 2004 (call or check ⓦ www.sciencecenteroftheamericas.org).

The eastern edge of downtown is bounded by Biscayne Boulevard, near which is the **Bayside Marketplace**, a large pink shopping mall enlivened by street entertainers and food stands. Across the boulevard, the **Freedom Tower** (☎305/592-7768, ⓦwww.canf.org), built in 1925 and modeled on a Spanish belltower, earned its name by housing the Cuban Refugee Center in the 1960s. Now owned by the Cuban-American National Foundation, the tower is undergoing extensive renovations, and is scheduled to open soon as a museum of Cuban-American culture; call for up-to-date information.

South from the marketplace, in Bayfront Park, the **Torch of Friendship** was meant to symbolize the good relations between the US and its southern neighbors. When it was built, there was a pointed space left for the Cuban national emblem among the alphabetically sorted crests of each country. However, the memorial is so neglected now that several missing emblems are noticeable, making Cuba no longer appear the pariah.

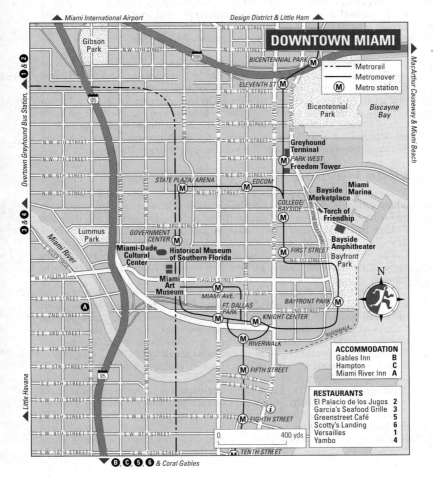

Fifteen minutes' walk south from Flagler Street, the **Miami River** carves downtown in half. The river's southern bank is dominated by Brickell (rhymes with "pickle") Avenue. Named for William Brickell, one of the original Miami landowners, this was *the* address in 1910s Miami. While the early grand homes have largely disappeared, money is still the avenue's most obvious asset: its half-mile parade of **bank buildings** is the largest grouping of international banks in the US. The rise of the banks was matched by new condominiums of breathtaking proportions (and expense) but little architectural merit.

The Design District and Little Haiti

North of downtown, from 36th to 41st streets, and between Biscayne Boulevard and N Miami Avenue, you'll find the groovy but manicured **DESIGN DISTRICT**, filled with interiors showrooms and an increasing number of hip bars and restaurants. Known in the 1940s as Decorators Row, the area had slipped into abandoned disrepair until the mid-1990s, when a developer snapped up swaths of land here and set about recreating its long-lost lustre. Look for the **Living Room** building at 40th Street and N Miami Avenue, with its inside-out entranceway featuring a big pink concrete sofa – it's an irresistible photo opportunity.

Continuing on northeast from the Design District, along NE 2nd Avenue, you'll cruise into **LITTLE HAITI**, an immigrant area filled with Caribbean colors, music, and smells, its trilingual shop signs making sales pitches in English, French, and Creole. In its former incarnation as Lemon City, this neighborhood was the oldest inhabited European settlement in the area, alongside Coconut Grove (see p.648). Today, the best place to soak up the atmosphere is 54th Street, which is lined with stores known as botanicas; these provide supplies for the voodoo-like religion **Santeria**.

Little Havana

The impact on Miami by **Cubans**, unquestionably the largest and most visible ethnic group in the city, has been incalculable. Unlike most Hispanic immigrants to the US, who trade one form of poverty for another, Miami's first Cubans had already tasted success when they arrived during the late Fifties. These non-traditional immigrants – many of the first wave driven out by Castro were doctors, lawyers, and other professionals – were soon enjoying more of the same in Miami, and some now wield considerable clout in the running of the city.

The initial home of Miami Cubans was a few miles west of downtown in what became **LITTLE HAVANA**, whose streets, if the tourist brochures are to be believed, are filled by old men playing dominoes, while puffing on fat, fragrant cigars, and exotic restaurants whose walls vibrate to the pulsating rhythms of the homeland. Naturally, the reality is quite different. Little Havana's parks, memorials, shops, and food stands all reflect the Cuban experience, but the streets are quieter than those of downtown (except during the Little Havana Festival in early March). Today, many successful Cuban-Americans have moved to Coral Gables, or elsewhere in the city, to be replaced by immigrants from parts of Central America, especially Nicaragua.

Make a beeline here for lunch at one of the many small restaurants on SW 8th Street, or Calle Ocho, the neighborhood's main drag. Between 12th and 13th avenues, check out the cluster of memorials that underscores the Cuban-American experience in Miami. Here, the simple stone **Brigade 2506**

7

FLORIDA | Miami

Memorial remembers those who died at the Bay of Pigs on April 17, 1961, during the abortive invasion of Cuba by US-trained Cuban exiles. Veterans of the landing, aging men dressed in combat fatigues, gather here for each anniversary to make all-night-long pledges of patriotism.

Coral Gables

All of Miami's constituent neighborhoods are fast to assert their individuality, though none does it more definitively than **CORAL GABLES**, located southwest of Little Havana. Twelve square miles of broad boulevards, leafy side streets, and Spanish and Italian architecture form a cultured setting for a cultured community.

Coral Gables' creator was a local aesthete, **George Merrick**, who raided street names from a Spanish dictionary to plan the plazas, fountains, and carefully aged stucco-fronted buildings here. Following the first land sale in 1921, $150 million poured in, which Merrick channeled into one of the biggest advertising campaigns ever known. Unfortunately, Coral Gables was taking shape just as the Florida property boom ended. Merrick was wiped out, and died as Miami's postmaster in 1942. But Coral Gables never lost its good looks, and it remains an impressive place to explore. Merrick wanted people to know they'd arrived somewhere special, and as such, eight grand **entrances** were planned on the main approach roads (though only four were completed). Three of these stand along the western end of Calle Ocho as you arrive from Little Havana.

The best way into Coral Gables is along SW 22nd Street, known as the **Miracle Mile**. Long dominated by fusty, no-name ladies'-wear boutiques, it's finally being redeveloped to attract some funkier, livelier tenants (see "Eating," p.649, for some of these). Note the arcades and balconies, and the spirals and peaks of the **Colonnade Building**, nos. 133–169, completed in 1926 to accommodate George Merrick's office. Further west, along Coral Way, the **Merrick House** (by appointment only, Sun & Wed 1–4pm; $2; ☎305/460-5361) was George's boyhood home. In 1899, when he was twelve, his family arrived here from New England to run a 160-acre farm, which was so successful that the house quickly grew from a wooden shack into an elegant dwelling of coral rock and gabled windows (thus inspiring the name of the future city).

While his property-developing contemporaries left ugly scars across the city after digging up the local limestone, Merrick had the foresight to turn his biggest quarry into a sumptuous swimming pool. Opened in 1924, the **Venetian Pool**, 2701 De Soto Blvd (June–Aug Mon–Fri 11am–7.30pm, Sept–Oct & April–May Tues–Fri 11am–5.30pm, Nov–March Tues–Sun 10am–4.30pm, year-round Sat & Sun 10am–4.30pm; $8.50; ☎305/460-5356, ⓦwww.venetianpool.com), is an essential stop on a steamy Miami afternoon. Its pastel stucco walls hide a delightful spring-fed lagoon, with vine-covered loggias, fountains, waterfalls, coral caves, and plenty of room to swim. The café isn't bad, either.

Wrapping its broad wings around the southern end of De Soto Blvd, Merrick's crowning achievement was the fabulous **Biltmore Hotel**, 1200 Anastasia Ave (☎305/445-1926 or 1-800/727-1926, ⓦwww.biltmorehotel .com). With a 26-story tower visible across much of low-lying Miami, everything about the *Biltmore* is over-the-top: 25ft fresco-coated walls, vaulted ceilings, immense fireplaces, custom-loomed rugs, and a massive swimming pool hosting shows by such bathing belles and beaux as Esther Williams and Johnny Weissmuller. Today, it costs upward of $200 a night to stay here, but a fascinating free tour leaves from the lobby every Sunday at 1.30, 2.30, and 3.30pm; meet at the birdcages. There's also a free ghost history tour Thursdays at 7pm.

Coconut Grove

COCONUT GROVE has come a long way since the 1960s, when it was peopled by down-at-the-heel artists and writers: these days, it's trying to rival South Beach, with a glittering cluster of art galleries, fashionable cafés and restaurants, and towering bay-view apartments. Thankfully, though, there's more to "the Grove" – on Biscayne Bay about four miles southwest of downtown – than just cafés and condos.

A century ago, a mix of Bahamian salvagers and New England intellectuals laid the foundations of a fiercely individual community, separated from the fledgling city of Miami by a dense wedge of tropical foliage. In 1914, farm-machinery mogul James Deering blew $15 million on re-creating a sixteenth-century Italian villa within this jungle. A thousand-strong workforce completed his **Villa Vizcaya**, 3251 S Miami Ave (daily 9.30am–4.30pm, gardens open until 5.30pm; $10; ☎305/250-9133, ⓦwww.vizcayamuseum.org), in just two years. Deering's madly eclectic art collection, and his desire that the villa should appear to have been inhabited for four hundred years, result in a thunderous clash of Baroque, Renaissance, Rococo, and Neoclassical fixtures and fittings. The fabulous landscaped **gardens**, with their many fountains and sculptures, are just as excessive. Free **guided tours** (45min) leave from the entrance loggia every 10 minutes and provide solid background, after which you're free to explore at your leisure.

About two miles south along the coast, the 83-acre **Fairchild Tropical Garden**, at 10901 Old Cutler Rd (daily 9.30am–4.30pm; $8, first Wednesday of every month is Contribution Day, when visitors set own entrance fee; ☎305/667-1651, ⓦwww.fairchildgarden.org), is the largest tropical botanical garden in the continental US. The entire range of tropical environments has been reproduced, and there's a good section on native south Florida areas.

Key Biscayne

A compact, immaculately manicured community, **KEY BISCAYNE**, five miles off mainland Miami, is a great place to live – if you can afford it. The moneyed of Miami fill the island's upmarket homes; Richard Nixon had a presidential winter house here. The only way onto Key Biscayne is along the four-mile **Rickenbacker Causeway** ($1 toll), which runs from SW 26th Road just south of downtown. On the way to the island, the causeway soars high above Biscayne Bay, passing over the small, mostly residential Virginia Key, and giving a gasp-inducing view of the Brickell Avenue skyline.

Crandon Park Beach, a mile along Crandon Boulevard (the continuation of the main road from the causeway), is one of the finest landscaped beaches in the city, with crystal-clear waters, barbecue grills, and sports facilities (daily 8am–dusk; $4 per car; ☎305/361-7385). Three miles of yellow-brown beach fringe the park, and give access to a sand bar enabling knee-depth wading far from the shore.

Crandon Boulevard terminates at the entrance to the **Bill Baggs Cape Florida State Recreation Area**, four hundred wooded acres covering the southern extremity of Key Biscayne (daily 8am–dusk; $4 per car; ☎305/361-5811). Hurricane Andrew took a devastating toll here in 1992, but most of the destroyed trees are beginning to grow back thanks to aggressive replanting, and the trails and boardwalks have been repaired. An excellent swimming **beach** lines the Atlantic-facing side of the park, and a boardwalk cuts around the wind-bitten sand dunes toward the 1820s **Cape Florida lighthouse**. Only with the ranger-led tour can you climb up through the 95ft structure; it was attacked by Seminoles in 1836 and incapacitated by Confederate soldiers aiming to disrupt Union shipping during the Civil War.

Eating

Cuban food is what Miami does best, and it's not limited to the traditional haunts in **Little Havana**. The hearty comfort food – notably rice and beans, fried plantains, and shredded pork sandwiches – is found in every neighborhood. Cuban cooking is complemented by sushi bars, American homestyle diners, as well as Haitian, Italian, and Indian restaurants, among a handful of other ethnic cuisines.

Coral Gables is best for upmarket cafés and ethnic Italian and Greek places, while **Coconut Grove** has American, Spanish, New Floridian (sometimes known as Floribbean; a mix of Caribbean spiciness and fruity Florida sauces), and even British. **Seafood** is equally abundant: succulent grouper, yellowfin tuna, and wahoo, a local delicacy, are among five hundred species of fish that thrive offshore. **Stone-crab claws**, served from October to May, are another regional specialty.

A tropical climate provides Florida with a juicy assortment of standard orange and grapefruit citrus, as well as the exotic flavors of the **lychee**, **mango**, **papaya**, **tamarind**, and **star fruits** – many of which are used in sauces and *batidos* (light milkshakes). You'll also want to try Cuban coffee: choose between *café cubano*, strong, sweet, and frothy, drunk like a shot with a glass of water; *café con leche*, with steamed milk, and particularly good at breakfast with *pan cubano* (thin, buttered toast); or *café cortadito*, a smaller version of the *con leche*.

Ayestaran 706 SW 27th Ave, Little Havana ℗ 305/649-4982. This sprawling Cuban restaurant offers hearty daily specials and superb *café con leche* that you can mix to your liking.

Big Pink 157 Collins Ave, South Beach ℗ 305/532-4700. Come to *Big Pink* for large portions of comfort food: mashed potatoes, ribs, macaroni and cheese, and classic "TV dinners," all at near-1950s prices.

David's Café 1058 Collins Ave, South Beach ℗ 305/534-8736. Cuban restaurant with two locations on the beach (the other is at 16th St and Meridian Ave), where suited Cuban businessmen sit alongside surly, trendy teenagers. The food is authentic, and there's eat-in and take-out at both restaurants.

El Palacio de los Jugos 5721 W Flagler Ave, Little Havana ℗ 305/264-1503. A handful of tables at the back of a Cuban produce market, where the pork sandwiches and shellfish soup from the take-out stand are the tastiest for miles.

Front Porch Café 1418 Ocean Drive, South Beach ℗ 305/531-8300. This local hangout is refreshingly low-key, considering its location: the delicious, dinner-plate-sized pancakes will easily take care of both breakfast *and* lunch.

Garcia's Seafood Grille 398 NW N River Drive, downtown ℗ 305/375-0765. Wonderful waterfront café with ramshackle wooden benches and superb, fresh fish dishes for around $11. Breakfast and lunch only.

Greenstreet Café 3468 Main Hwy, Coconut Grove ℗ 305/444-0244. The terrific breakfasts make this café a real scene at weekends. There's a large number of outdoor tables, great for watching the world go by.

Joe's Stone Crabs 11 Washington Ave, South Beach ℗ 305/673-0365. A legendary restaurant, *Joe's* is always packed, thanks to its superb stone crabs – if you're impatient, do as the locals do and head to the take-out window. Crabcakes, fresh fish, and the crispy fried chicken are also good. Open mid-Oct to mid-May.

La Sandwicherie 229 W 14th St, South Beach ℗ 305/532-8934. Don't be put off by the silly name – this place serves serious sandwiches starting at around $6 from its open-air lunch counter. Each giant French loaf doorstop could make two meals, and it's open until 5am.

News Café 800 Ocean Drive, South Beach ℗ 305/538-NEWS. This established, fashionable sidewalk café has front-row seating for the South Beach promenade – although the food's unremarkable. Open 24hr at weekends.

Picnics at Allen's Drug Store 4000 Red Rd, Coral Gables ℗ 305/665-6964. Low-priced home-style cooking – great freshly made burgers – in an old-fashioned drugstore, complete with a jukebox that blasts golden oldies.

Pizza Rustica 863 Washington Ave, South Beach ℗ 305/674-8244. Mouthwateringly fresh gourmet pizza, with slab-like slices costing around $4.

Puerto Sagua 700 Collins Ave, South Beach ℗ 305/673-1115. This Cuban diner serves great, rich black-bean soup, and other filling meals. One of the cheapest eats on the beach.

Rascal House 17190 Collins Ave, Miami Beach ℗ 305/947-4581. Largest, loudest, and most authentic New York–style deli in town. Huge portions are served by waitresses who look like they've worked here since the place's heyday in the 1950s. Highly recommended.

Scotty's Landing 3381 Pan American Drive, Coconut Grove ℗ 305/854-2626. Tasty, inexpensive seafood and fish 'n' chips consumed at marina-side picnic tables. It's tucked away on the water by City Hall, and so can be hard to find – ask if you get lost.

Tap Tap 819 5th St, South Beach ℗ 305/672-2898. Haitian food is at its tastiest and most attractive in one of the best-looking restaurants – the place is hung with local art – on Miami Beach.

Versailles 3555 SW 8th St, Little Havana ℗ 305/444-0240. At this legend in Little Havana, very little English is spoken. Local families, Cuban businessmen, and backpackers congregate here for the wonderfully inexpensive Cuban dishes, served by one of the friendliest staffs in Miami.

Wish inside *The Hotel*, 801 Collins Ave ℗ 305/531-2222. Sumptuous, quirky Floribbean food – think chili-soaked slabs of watermelon – in a lush, fountainside setting. You'll pay for the privilege, but it's worth a splurge.

Yambo 1643 SW 1st St, Little Havana ℗ 305/642-6616. Step out of the USA and into Central America at Yambo, an undiscovered gem serving up good, inexpensive Nicaraguan food.

Nightlife and entertainment

Miami's **nightlife** is still unsurpassed. Drinking tends to take second place to eating and partying; as a result, a number of friendly local bars double as very good **live music** venues. **Reggae** is particularly strong; Miami has a sizable Jamaican population, and local as well as out-of-town acts appear regularly. Miami's **clubs** – especially those specializing in salsa or merengue, and hosted by Spanish-speaking DJs – are among the hippest in the world, with most of the action at South Beach. Door policies are notoriously fierce at current in-spots; the places listed below include laid-back local haunts as well as some of the hotter bars.

Friday's *Miami Herald* carries full weekend entertainment **listings**. The free, weekly *New Times* has reliable information on cafés and clubs, while the free *TWN* (*The Weekly News*) is the key source of **gay and lesbian info**.

If you want to try out the local **sports** scene, the Marlins major league base-ball team and the Dolphins, Miami's pro football team, play at the Pro Player Stadium, sixteen miles northwest of downtown at 2269 Dan Marino Blvd (☏ 305/623-6100, ⓦ www.proplayerstadium.com; take bus #27 from the main bus station).

Bars and live music venues

The Abbey Brewing Company 1115 16th St, South Beach ☏ 305/538-8110. This small, homey spot is South Beach's only microbrewery. Try the creamy Oatmeal Stout – their best and most popular brew. Happy hour Mon–Fri 1–7pm.

Churchill's Hideaway 5501 NE 2nd Ave, Little Haiti ☏ 305/757-1807, ⓦ www.churchillspub.com. A British enclave within Little Haiti, with soccer and rugby matches on TV and UK beers on tap.

Club Deuce Bar & Grill 222 14th St, South Beach ☏ 305/531-6200. This grimy, noisy grunge bar is a remnant from pre-fabulous South Beach. Drinks are cheap, the crowd's indie, and there's a dart-board and pool table.

Grass 28 NE 40th St, Design District ☏ 305/573-3355, ⓦ www.grasslounge.com. This restaurant/bar is currently blazing hot, luring scenesters from South Beach for a drink in its Polynesian-themed open-air eatery. Monday nights are especially popular.

Hoy Como Ayer 2212 SW 8th St, Little Havana ☏ 305/541-2631, ⓦ www.hoycomoayer.net. Despite the city's sizable Cuban population, this dark, smoky joint is about the only place in Miami to hear inventive, high-quality Cuban music. Best-known for its Thursday-night Latin fusion party, *¡Fuácata!*.

Jimbo's inside the park at Virginia Key Beach, Virginia Key ☏ 305/361-7026. Legendary ram-shackle bar where you can help yourself to a beer from a wheelbarrow filled with ice. A good place to chat with the old-timers.

Monty's Bayshore Restaurant 2550 S Bayshore Drive, Coconut Grove ☏ 305/858-1431. Drinkers often outnumber the diners (it's also a restaurant) at this tiki-style bar, drawn here by the gregarious mood and the views across the bay; the loud reg-gae music can be a bit overpowering, though.

Purdy Lounge 1811 Purdy Ave, South Beach ☏ 305/531-4622. An unheralded beachside gem, this large neighborhood bar avoids clogging crowds of out-of-towners by its location on the less-touristed western side of South Beach.

The Raleigh Bar inside the *Raleigh Hotel*, 1775 Collins Ave, South Beach ☏ 305/534-6300. Grab a drink at this recently renovated mid-century gem and make like Audrey Hepburn: this classic hotel bar is a throwback to the heyday of cocktail cul-ture, with its wood panels and master mixologist.

Sky Bar inside the *Shore Club* hotel, 1901 Collins Ave, South Beach ☏ 786/276-6772. Sprawling outdoor bar draped around the hotel pool, with giant overstuffed square seats: dress up and expect a tough door unless you're staying at the hotel. Check out the smaller, attached *Sand Bar*, with its view of the beach and ocean.

Tobacco Road 626 S Miami Ave, downtown ☏ 305/374-1198, ⓦ www.tobacco-road.com This friendly bar – Miami's oldest, from 1912 – is a favorite with locals for its exceptional live blues, jazz, and R&B. Check the website for schedule.

Nightclubs

Cafe Nostalgia 66 SW 6th St, Little Havana ☏ 305/358-1999, ⓦ www.cafenostalgia.com. This legendary Cuban club has finally found a new home on the banks of the Miami River, after an itinerant few years: there's a massive dance floor as well as a landscaped garden and rooftop bar.

Club Tropigala in the *Fontainebleau Hilton*, 4441 Collins Ave, Miami Beach ☏ 305/672-7469. Fabulously camp Vegas-meets-Miami throwback, featuring live acts and an orchestra, with shows Wed–Sat 8.30pm and Sun 8pm. You can either dance, or just soak up the kitsch excess around you. Cover is $20.

Crobar 1445 Washington Ave, South Beach ☏ 305/531-8225, ⓦ www.crobarmiami.com. At this superclub, hardcore dancers and a loved-up crowd get started around 4am.

Mynt Ultra Lounge 1921 Collins Ave, South Beach ☎786/276-6132. Lounge/dance club, washed in green light, with an enormous bar and large, black leather sofas – it's the place to be on Friday, but expect a fierce door any night of the week.

Opium Garden 136 Collins Ave, South Beach ☎305/531-5535. At this giant open-air club, a tent covers the dance floor and multilevel spaces are accessed from the main bar. Not a hotspot anymore, but a fun standby, and handily located for most hotels.

Space 34 34 NE 11th St, downtown ☎305/375-0001 for info, or 786/256-5732 for reservations, ⓦwww.clubspace.com. This downtown pioneer just moved to an even bigger space and switched its name accordingly; most people migrate here when the other venues shut down, for after-hours dancing until dawn – expect a friendly, loved-up, youngish crowd.

The Florida Keys

Folklore, films, and fiction have given **THE FLORIDA KEYS** – a hundred-mile chain of islands that runs to within ninety miles of Cuba – an image of glamorous intrigue they don't really deserve; at least, not now that the go-go days of the cocaine cowboys in the 1980s are long gone. Rather, the Keys are an outdoor-lover's paradise, where fishing, snorkeling, and diving dominate. Terrific untainted natural areas include the **Florida Reef**, a great band of living coral just a few miles off the coast. But for many, the various keys are only stops on the way to **Key West**. Once the richest town in the US, and the final dot of North America before a thousand miles of ocean, Key West has lush, Caribbean-style streets with plenty of convivial bars in which to while away the hours, watching the spectacular **sunsets**.

Wherever you are on the Keys, you'll experience distinctive **cuisine**, served for the most part in funky little shacks where the food is fresh and the atmosphere laid-back. Conch, a rich meaty mollusc, is a specialty, served in chowders and fritters. There's also Key Lime Pie, a delicate, creamy concoction of special Key limes and condensed milk, that bears little resemblance to the lurid green imposter pies served in the rest of the US.

Getting around the Keys could hardly be easier. There's just one route all the way through to Key West: the **Overseas Highway** (US-1). The road is punctuated by **mile markers** (MM), starting with MM127 just south of Miami and finishing with MM0 in Key West, at the corner of Whitehead and Fleming streets. As per Keys convention, addresses are given by the closest mile marker, along with the appellation of either "Oceanside" or "Bayside," depending on whether the place in question faces the Atlantic Ocean or the Florida Bay.

Key Largo

The first and largest of the keys, **KEY LARGO** provides a fine opportunity to visit the Florida Reef, at the **John Pennekamp Coral Reef State Park**, at MM102.5-Oceanside (daily 8am–sunset; $2.50 per car and driver, plus

$2.50 for first passenger, 50¢ for each additional passenger, pedestrians and cyclists $1.50; ☎305/451-1202, ⓦwww.pennekamppark.com). This protected 78-square-mile section of living coral reef is rated as one of the most beautiful in the world. If you can, take the **snorkeling tour** (9am, noon & 3pm; 1hr 30min; $27, plus $6 for equipment; ☎305/451-1621), or the **guided scuba dive** (9.30am & 1.30pm; 1hr 30min; $41; diver's certificate required; ☎305/451-6322). The **glass–bottom boat tour** (9.15am, 12.15pm & 3pm; $20; ☎305/451-1621) is less demanding. On any of these excursions, though, you're virtually certain to spot lobsters, angelfish, eels, and jellyfish along the reef, and shoals of silvery minnows stalked by angry-faced barracuda. The reef itself is a delicate living thing, comprising millions of minute coral polyps extracting calcium from the seawater and growing from one to sixteen feet every thousand years. Sadly, it's far easier to spot signs of death than life: white patches show where a carelessly dropped anchor, or a diver's hand, has scraped away the protective mucous layer and left the coral susceptible to terminal disease.

Key Largo Town and Tavernier

South of Pennekamp, the people of Rock Harbor recognized a good thing when they saw one and changed the name of their community to **KEY LARGO** after the success of the 1948 film in which Humphrey Bogart and Lauren Bacall grappled with Florida's best-known features – crime and hurricanes. The movie's title suggested somewhere exotic, but the film, though set here, was shot almost entirely in Hollywood. Clinging to an image based more in movies than reality, Key Largo and its neighbor **TAVERNIER**, ten miles further on, are really a jumble of filling stations, shopping plazas, and fast-food outlets. There are, however, one or two low-key attractions, but it's the reef and other aquatic activities that are most likely to hold your interest here.

At MM106-Bayside, look for the Colonial-style building that houses the **Key Largo Chamber of Commerce** (daily 9am–6pm; ☎305/451-1414 or 1-800/822-1088); it has piles of brochures, money-saving vouchers, and hotel booking information. Most **motels** offer diving packages: there's the basic but clean *Economy Efficiency* (also known as *Ed & Ellen's*), at MM103.5-Oceanside (☎1-888/333-5536 or 305/451-9949, ⓦwww.ed-ellens-lodgings.com; ❸); beach cottages at the *Seafarer*, MM98-Bayside (☎305/852-5349 or 1-800/599/7112, ⓦwww.keylargoparadise.com; ❸); or the huge chalets and art gallery at the *Kona Kai Resort*, MM97.8-Bayside (☎305/852-4629 or 1-800/365-7829, ⓦwww.konakairesort.com; ❺). For fresh **seafood**, try *Ballyhoo's Grill and Grog*, in the median at MM98 (☎305/852-0822), or *Ganim's Restaurant*, MM99-Bayside (☎305/451-2895).

Islamorada

Once you arrive in **ISLAMORADA** (pronounced "eye-lah-more-RAH-da), some five miles south of Tavernier on Upper Matecumbe Key, make sure to take a trip across to the once-thriving settlement founded by wrecker Jacob Houseman on Indian Key (tours by kayak Thurs–Mon 9am & 1pm depart from Robbie's Marina, MM77.5-Bayside; $15; ☎305/664-9814, ⓦwww.robbies .com); it now boasts a riot of exotic plants and evocative ruins. Otherwise, there's good hiking at **Long Key State Botanical Site**, MM67.5-Oceanside (daily 8am–sunset; cars $3.25 plus 50¢ per person; ☎305/664-4815, ⓦwww.floridastateparks.org), a 965-acre expanse of tropical foliage and mangroves. Long Key has an excellent beach (a rarity in the Keys), and is a great base for deep-sea fishing, too.

This is a much more welcoming place to dawdle than Key Largo: good-value **accommodation** includes the supercheap *Key Lantern/Blue Fin*, MM82-Bayside (☎305/664-4572, ⓦwww.keylantern.com; ❸) – ask for a room at the *Blue Fin*, since these were more recently renovated – and the serene *Drop Anchor*, MM85-Oceanside (☎305/664-4863 or 1-888/664-4863; ❸). As for **eating**, *Hungry Tarpon*, MM77.5-Bayside (☎305/664-0535), serves excellent fresh fish, as does the pricier *Islamorada Fish Company*, MM81.5-Bayside (☎1-800/258-2559). For a change from standard Keys cuisine, try *Manny & Isa's*, MM81.5-Oceanside (☎305/664-5019), a simple Cuban diner where superb Spanish food comes with copious strong, sweet sangría. They also do a delectable Key Lime Pie.

The Middle Keys

Once over Long Key Bridge, you're into **THE MIDDLE KEYS**. At the not-for-profit **Dolphin Research Center**, MM59-Bayside (Wed–Sun 9am–4pm; ☎305/289-1121, ⓦwww.dolphins.org), you can swim with the dolphins for $155 (reservations must be made at least one month in advance).

The largest of several islands in the Middle Keys, **Key Vaca** holds the nucleus of the area's major settlement, **Marathon**. Here you'll find great **fishing** and **watersports** opportunities, as well as a couple of small beaches. **Sombrero Beach**, along Sombrero Beach Road (off the Overseas Highway near MM50-Oceanside), has good swimming waters and shaded picnic tables.

Close by, at MM50.5-Bayside, nestled inside the 64-acre tropical forest of **Crane Point Hammock**, the **Museum of Natural History of the Florida Keys** (Mon–Sat 9am–5pm, Sun noon–5pm; $7.50; ☎305/743-9100, ✉trpcranept@aol.com) provides an excellent introduction to the history and ecology of the area. Follow the quarter-mile **nature trail** past the hammock forest, an area of dense hardwood trees characteristic of the Keys, until you reach the end of the trail. Here, you'll find the reconstructed remnants of a nineteenth-century village established by settlers from the Bahamas.

Marathon has several well-equipped **resorts**, such as the lush, luxurious *Banana Bay*, MM49.5-Bayside (☎1-800/226-2621 or 305/743-3500, ⓦwww.bananabay.com; ❹), and the *Best Western Marathon*, MM48-Bayside (☎305/743-3855, ⓦwww.bestwestern.com; ❹), which has a pool and a bayfront tiki bar. The best **budget option** is the *Sea Dell*, MM50-Bayside (☎305/743-5161 or 1-800/648-3854, ⓦwww.seadellmotel.com; ❷). For **eating**, there's terrific seafood – including succulent beer-steamed shrimp – at the *Castaway* restaurant, 15th Street near MM47.5-Oceanside (☎305/743-6247). The tiny, laid-back *Seven Mile Grill*, by the bridge of the same name at MM47.5-Bayside (☎305/743-4481), serves delicious conch and creamy Key Lime Pie to locals, sea salts, and tourists alike. A cheap option for Cuban food is *Don Pedro Restaurant*, MM53-Oceanside (☎305/743-5247), while *Porky's BBQ*, MM47.5-Bayside (☎305/289-2065), offers cheap, traditional barbecue dishes and burgers, along with conch fritters and other local seafood specialties. Take their free sunset cruise whether you eat there or not.

The Lower Keys

Starkly different from their neighbors to the north, **THE LOWER KEYS** are quiet, heavily wooded, and predominantly residential. Built on a limestone rather than a coral base, these islands have a flora and fauna all their own. It feels very quiet as you head south: seemingly everyone's either gone fishing or is snoozing in a hammock.

The first place of consequence you'll hit after crossing Seven Mile Bridge is one of the Keys' prettiest spots: **Bahia Honda State Park**, at MM37-Oceanside (daily 8am–sunset; car and driver $4, with 50¢ for each additional passenger; pedestrians and cyclists $1; ☎305/872-2353, ⓦwww.bahiahonda-park.com). Its lagoon has an alluring natural beach and pristine, two-tone ocean waters, which can be enjoyed on a leisurely **kayak ride** ($10 per hour).

Divers should head for the **Looe Key Marine Sanctuary**, signposted from the Overseas Highway on **Ramrod Key**: it's a five-square-mile protected reef area, easily the equal of the John Pennekamp Coral Reef State Park (see p.652). The sanctuary office (Mon–Fri 8am–5pm; ☎305/292-0311, ⓦwww.fknms .nos.noaa.gov) can provide free maps, but to visit the reef you'll need the services of a dive shop, like the neighboring Looe Key Dive Center (☎1-800/942-5397, ⓦwww.diveflakeys.com).

Big Pine Key is the main Lower Keys settlement. The town's visitor center is at MM31-Oceanside (Mon–Fri 9am–5pm, Sat 9am–3pm; ☎305/872-2411 or 1-800/872-3722). Of the nearby **motels**, *Looe Key Reef Resort*, MM27.5-Oceanside (☎305/872-2215 or 1-800/942-5397, ⓦwww.divelooekey.com; ❸), is an ideal base for visiting the marine sanctuary. For a real splurge, stay at the idyllic *Little Palm Island*, MM28.5-Oceanside, Little Torch Key (no children; ☎305/872-2524 or 1-800/343-8567, ⓦwww.littlepalmisland.com; ❾), a private islet whose thatched cottages are set in lush gardens a few feet from the beach.

Don't miss the pizza and beer at the dollar-bill-decorated *No Name Pub*, a few miles from the main road at MM30-Bayside (☎305/872-9115, ⓦwww.non-amepub.com). Further on down the Overseas Highway, on Sugarloaf Key at MM20-Bayside, the exceptionally friendly *Mangrove Mama's* (☎305/745-3030; closed Sept) serves stupendous local cuisine in a cheery shack with a tropical garden.

Key West

Closer to Cuba than to mainland Florida, **KEY WEST** often seems rather tenuously bound to the rest of the US. Famed for their tolerant attitudes and laid-back lifestyles, the 30,000 islanders seem adrift in a great expanse of sea and sky, and – despite a million tourists a year – the place resonates with an individual spirit that hits you the instant you arrive. In particular, liberal attitudes have stimulated a large gay influx. Yet as wild as it may at first appear, Key West today is far from being the hippie hangout of a decade ago. Much of the sleaziness has been brushed away through a steady process of restoration, setting the course for the advent of a sizable tourist industry. The town has retained some of its sense of individualism and isolation, though, especially away from the main drag of Duval Street. To best absorb this atmosphere – and the mellow pace of local life – take time to amble the gorgeous, lushly vegetated streets, make meals last for hours, and pause regularly for refreshment in the numerous bars.

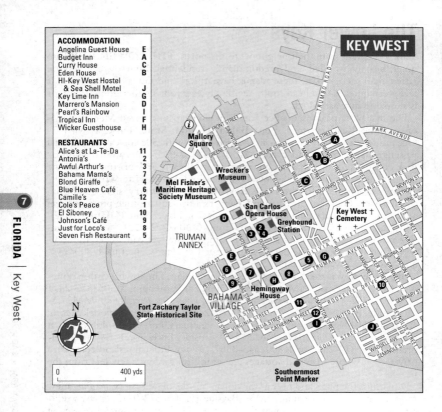

ACCOMMODATION
Angelina Guest House	E
Budget Inn	A
Curry House	C
Eden House	B
HI-Key West Hostel & Sea Shell Motel	J
Key Lime Inn	G
Marrero's Mansion	D
Pearl's Rainbow	I
Tropical Inn	F
Wicker Guesthouse	H

RESTAURANTS
Alice's at La-Te-Da	11
Antonia's	2
Awful Arthur's	3
Bahama Mama's	7
Blond Giraffe	4
Blue Heaven Café	6
Camille's	12
Cole's Peace	1
El Siboney	10
Johnson's Café	9
Just for Loco's	8
Seven Fish Restaurant	5

KEY WEST

Arrival and information

The **airport** (☎305/296-5439) is four miles east of town, with the **Greyhound** station (☎305/296-9072) adjacent to its entrance. There are no shuttle buses into town; a **taxi** costs around $10.

The best place to head for **information** is the Greater Key West Chamber of Commerce, in the center of town next to Mallory Square at 402 Wall St (Mon–Fri 8.30am–6.30pm, Sat & Sun 8.30am–5pm; ☎305/294-2587 or 1-800/527-8539, ⓦ www.keywestchamber.org). The Chamber can give precise dates for Key West's annual **festivals**, the best of which are the Old Island Days (Jan–April), celebrating Key West's history; the Conch Republic Celebration in April; and the Fantasy Fest in late October, which feels like a gay Mardi Gras crossed with Halloween. A good source of **gay information** is the Gay & Lesbian Information Center, 728 Duval St (Mon–Fri 9am–5pm; ☎305/294-4603, ⓦ www.gaykeywestfl.com).

It's best to explore the narrow streets of the mile-square Old Town – which contains virtually everything that you'll want to see – **on foot**. You could do it in little more than a day, though dashing about isn't the way to enjoy the place. The excellent *Sharon Wells' Walking and Biking Guide*, free in local restaurants and bars, details a number of self-guided routes through the Old Town, and lists Wells' own regular walking tours (from $20; ☎305/294-8380,

Ⓦwww.seekeywest.com). **Bikes** can be rented from Adventure Scooter & Bicycle Rentals, with two locations (out of seven around the Old Town) at 1 and 601 Duval St ($8 per day with $150 deposit; Ⓣ305/293-9933, Ⓦkeywest.com/scooter.html). If you're in need of a **taxi** – a bright pink one, no less – call Ⓣ305/296-6666.

Accommodation

During the winter, it's essential to make a **reservation** for accommodation in Key West; you should call ahead to wherever you have in mind as early as possible. In summer, competition for rooms is less fierce, and prices drop by almost fifty percent.

Angelina Guest House 302 Angela St Ⓣ305/294-4480 or 1-888/303-4480, Ⓦwww.angelinaguesthouse.com. This charming guesthouse, tucked away in the backstreets of the Bahamian Village, has a cool, Caribbean feel, and is one of the best deals in town. Room with shared bath ❸, room with private bath ❹.

Budget Inn 1031 Eaton St Ⓣ305/294-3333 or 1-800/403-2866, Ⓦwww.budgetkeywest.com. Found north of the Old Town near the seaport, this is a rare find in Key West, with low prices, pleasant rooms, and a good location. ❸

Curry House 806 Fleming St Ⓣ305/294-6777 or 1-800/633-7439, Ⓔcurrygh@aol.com. Charming gay guesthouse, with just nine large, Colonial-style rooms that are filled with grand antiques; several have private balconies. There's a sumptuous breakfast served poolside each morning. ❹

Eden House 1015 Fleming St Ⓣ305/296-6868 or 1-800/533-5397, Ⓦwww.edenhouse.com. Here, a grotty lobby hides one of the city's best deals – large rooms, free parking, free happy hour every night, and a shaded pool. Room with shared bath $80, room with private bath $95. ❹

HI-Key West Hostel & Sea Shell Motel 718 South St Ⓣ305/296-5719, Ⓦwww.keywesthostel.com. The hostel has cheap dorm beds, a sunny patio, and no curfew, while the *Sea Shell Motel* offers standard rooms at the lowest rates in the neighborhood – the decor's nothing special, but rock-bottom prices more than make up. Hostel $20.50, or $23.50 nonmembers; motel $65. ❶–❸

Key Lime Inn 725 Truman Ave Ⓣ305/294-5229 or 1-800/549-4430, Ⓦwww.keylimeinn.com. The room decor in this cluster of cottages set around a pool is Key West tropical – splurge on one of the bungalows for their seclusion and their verandas. ❹

Marrero's Mansion 410 Fleming St Ⓣ305/294-6977 or 1-800/459-6212, Ⓦwww.marreros.com. According to popular superstition, the former owner of this well-known, supposedly haunted guesthouse – the late Mrs Marrero – rates guests' character by swaying the chandelier in the foyer as they pass through. Ghost-hunters should ask for room 18, as that's where most of the paranormal activity has been reported. Standard room ❹, room 18 ❻

Pearl's Rainbow 525 United St Ⓣ305/292-1450 or 1-800/749-6696, Ⓦwww.pearlsrainbow.com. The lone women-only guesthouse on the island, this attractive former cigar factory serves breakfast and has two pools and two Jacuzzis. ❹

Tropical Inn 812 Duval St Ⓣ305/294-9977, Ⓦwww.tropicalinn.com. The large, airy rooms in this charming restored "conch" house are at the center of the action. Most rooms sleep three, and the more expensive ones have balconies. ❺

Wicker Guesthouse 913 Duval St Ⓣ305/296-2475 or 1-800/880-4275, Ⓦwww.wickerhouse-kw.com. One of the least expensive guesthouses on Key West, the rooms here are impressive, given the price: they're splashily decorated with orange and red bedspreads and (naturally) white wicker furniture. The biggest plus, though, is its chirpy, chatty staff. ❹

The Town

Anyone who visited Key West a decade or so ago would now barely recognize the Old Town's main promenade, the mile-long swath of **Duval Street**. Teetering just on the safe side of seedy for many years, much of the street has been transformed into a tacky tourist strip of boutiques and beachwear shops. For a sense of the locals' town, take time to explore the side streets, where gnarled banyans, tall skinny palms, creepers, and unruly, exotic blooms threaten to overtake the faded wooden houses. Make sure, as well, to visit the

Bahamian Quarter, centered on Thomas and Petronia streets. Originally settled by Cubans and African-Bahamians, this unrestored, untouristed corner of town is an atmospheric patchwork of single-story cigar-makers' cottages, Cuban groceries, and ramshackle old churches, all covered by a rich green foliage.

Numerous **museums** in town concern themselves with "wrecking," or the salvaging of cargo from sunken vessels; it's the industry on which Key West's earliest good times were based. The friendly little **Wrecker's Museum**, 322 Duval St (also known as the Oldest House Museum; daily 10am–4pm; $5; ☎305/294-9502), illuminates the lives of the wreckers, portraying them as brave, uninsured heroes who risked all to save cargoes, ships, and lives. Judging by the choice furniture that fills the house – which was owned by Captain Watlington, the wrecker who lived here from the 1830s – they did pretty well for their pains.

Farther up Duval, at no. 516, the **San Carlos Opera House** (Tues–Sun 11.30am–5pm; $3 donation; ☎305/294-3887) has played a leading role in Cuban exile life since it opened in 1871 as the San Carlos Institute. Financed by a grant from the Cuban government, the present building dates from 1924. Cuban architect Francisco Centurion designed the two-story building in the Cuban Baroque style of that period. Soil from Cuba's six provinces covers the grounds, and a cornerstone was taken from the tomb of Cuban independence campaigner José Martí. There's a passable exhibition on Cuban heritage here, and they also distribute the free Cuban Heritage Trail pamphlet, which details sites of interest around town.

As you approach the southern end of Duval, everything, whether house, motel, gas station, or restaurant, advertises itself as "the Southernmost…" Accurately, the **southernmost point** in Key West, and consequently in the continental US, is at the intersection of Whitehead and South streets. A daft-looking buoy marks the spot. Watch out for people here who'll kindly offer to take your photograph, and then expect tipping for the pleasure.

Back up and just west from the northern end of Duval Street is **Mallory Square**. In the early 1800s, thousands of dollars' worth of salvage was landed at the piers, stored in the warehouses, and flogged at the auction houses here. By day, the square is a souvenir market, with overpriced ice cream, trinkets, and T-shirts. Each night, at the eminently missable tourist-oriented **sunset celebration**, fire-eaters and other entertainers do their stuff for the crowds as the sun goes down. You can escape the cultural wasteland by slipping into the nearby **Customs House** at Greene and Front streets. Long derelict, the Customs House has finally been launched as the **Key West Museum of Art & History** (daily 9am–5pm; $6; ☎305/296-3913, ⓦwww.kwahs.org); it's filled with old newspaper cuttings and portraits of craggy legendary locals.

Nearby, at 200 Greene St, **Mel Fisher's Maritime Heritage Society Museum** (daily 9.30am–5pm; $9; ☎305/294-2633, ⓦwww.melfisher.org) showcases the diamonds, pearls, and daggers, as well as countless vases, an impressive emerald cross, and the obligatory cannon, that Fisher pulled up from two seventeenth-century shipwrecks in 1985. Adding to the romantic tale, Fisher ran a surf shop in California before he arrived in Florida, armed with old Spanish sea charts. The two ships he discovered were the *Nuestra Señora de Atocha* and the *Santa Margarita*, both of which sank forty miles southeast of Key West during a hurricane in 1622. All in all, Fisher's flabbergasting haul is said to be worth millions of dollars. If you're not satisfied with simply lifting a gold bar (chained down, naturally), and fancy some for yourself, the gift shop sells affordable souvenirs alongside expensive salvage relics.

Finally, down Whitehead Street from Greene, you'll find Key West's most popular tourist attraction: the **Ernest Hemingway Home & Museum**, at no. 907 (daily 9am–5pm; $10; ☎305/294-1136, ⒲www.hemingwayhome .com). Sadly, the compulsory half-hour **guided tour** deals more in fantasy than fact: while it's true that Hemingway owned this large, vaguely Moorish house for thirty years, he lived in it for barely ten, and even the authenticity of the furnishings is disputed. That said, some of his most acclaimed novels, including *For Whom the Bell Tolls* and *To Have and Have Not*, were written in the study (the hayloft of a carriage house, which the author entered by way of a rope bridge). Divorced in 1940, Heminway boxed up his manuscripts and moved them to a back room at the original *Sloppy Joe's* (see p.660), before heading off for a house in Cuba with his new wife, journalist Martha Gellhorn. Today, some fifty cats – many of them with six toes, traditionally employed as ship's mascots – pad contentedly around the gardens. Whatever the guides say, Hemingway kept his feline harem while living in Cuba, not Key West, so it's unlikely that the dozens of cats wandering around today are in any way related to Papa's pets.

Eating

In Key West, it's *de rigueur* to sample **conch fritters**; the stand at David Walkowsky and Wall streets (otherwise known as the entrance to Mallory Square) does the best in town, for under two dollars. Also, don't leave without tasting **Cuban food**, as there are several excellent restaurants in town. For the best *café con leche* this side of Miami, try *Sandy's Café* inside the M&M laundromat at Virginia and White streets (☎305/295-0159).

Alice's at La-Te-Da 1125 Duval St ☎305/296-6706. The menu at this upscale eatery is Asian-inflected and seafood-heavy, while the open-air dining room is a lovely place to spend an evening.
Antonia's 615 Duval St ☎305/294-6565. Excellent northern Italian cuisine served in a formal but friendly environment. It's expensive but worth it, especially for the homemade pasta. Dinner only.
Awful Arthur's Seafood Company 628 Duval St ☎305/AWE-SOME. This casual fish shack offers excellent-value nightly specials, such as All You Can Eat Snow Crab for $20.
Bahama Mama's 324 Petronia St ☎305/294-3355. Brightly colored Caribbean café with ample outdoor seating and lilting, jaunty reggae piped around the courtyard.
Blond Giraffe 629 Duval St ☎305/293-6998, ⒲www.blondgiraffe.com. This café won "Best Key Lime Pie" in a town-wide bake-off a couple of years ago; if you want, you can even watch them make it.
Blue Heaven Café corner of Thomas and Petronia sts ☎305/296-0867, ⒲www.blueheavenkw.com. At this excellent bar and restaurant, housed in a colorful shack, rooster chicks peck at your feet as you eat fresh fish, jerk chicken, and fabulous fruit-packed breakfasts.

Camille's 1202 Simonton St ☎305/296-4811. Great, affordable breakfasts and brunches – menu options in the past have included shrimp cakes, blueberry pancakes, or French toast with mango coconut cream sauce.
Cole's Peace 930-A Eaton St ☎305/292-6511, ⒲www.colespeace.com. Tiny, stylish bakery offering crusty bread and unfussy, wholegrain pastries; a healthy place to stop for breakfast.
El Siboney 900 Catherine St ☎305/296-4184. This no-frills family diner serves inexpensive, enormous Cuban dishes, along with good daily specials. Closes at 9pm.
Johnson's Café 801 Thomas St ☎305/292-2286. The motto at this small café is "Bust your belly," and the cheap, enormous sandwiches don't disappoint – they make *Subway* subs look like hors d'oeuvres.
Just for Loco's 517 Truman Ave ☎305/296-1177. Tiny, inexpensive café attached to a laundromat, serving authentic Cuban and Mexican dishes that'll fill you up for around $5.
Seven Fish Restaurant 632 Olivia St ☎305/296-2777. This top-secret restaurant, easy to miss in its tiny white corner building, serves some of the best food in town. There are just over a dozen tables, so it pays to call ahead.

Nightlife and entertainment

The anything-goes nature of Key West is exemplified by the convivial **bars** that make up the bulk of the island's **nightlife**. Gregarious, rough-and-ready affairs, many stay open as late as 4am and feature regular **live music**. The most popular places are grouped around the northern end of Duval Street, no more than a few minutes' stagger from one another. For something a little less macho, keep south of the 500 block of Duval.

Bourbon Street Pub 724 Duval St ☎305/296-1992, ⊛www.bourbonstreetpub.com. This huge video bar is the largest gay-friendly place to drink in the center of town; there's a pleasant garden out back, complete with a large hot tub.

Captain Tony's Saloon 428 Greene St ☎305/294-1838, ⊛www.capttonyssaloon.com. This rustic saloon was the original *Sloppy Joe's*, where Hemingway hung out (see p.659). Today, it's one of the less cheesy choices for live music.

Green Parrot Inn 601 Whitehead St ☎305/294-6133, ⊛www.greenparrot.com. This Key West landmark, open since 1890, draws plenty of locals to its pool tables, dartboard, and pinball machine. There's live music on the weekends.

Hog's Breath Saloon 400 Front St ☎305/292-2032, ⊛www.hogsbreath.com. This bar's one of the best places to catch live music in town, mostly for a nominal cover – just don't be put off by the staggering revelers circling its entrance.

Sloppy Joe's 201 Duval St ☎305/294-5717, ⊛www.sloppyjoes.com. Despite the memorabilia and the crowds, this eminently avoidable bar – with live music nightly – is not the one Hemingway made famous (see *Captain Tony's*, above), nor one that many locals set foot in.

Wax 42 Applerouth Lane ☎305/296-6667, ⊛www.waxkeywest.com. The closest Key West comes to a traditional nightclub, with overstuffed red sofas and bead curtains decorating a chic, dimly lit space. Come only if you want to dance – the music's too loud to talk.

The East Coast

Facing the Atlantic Ocean, Florida's **East Coast** runs for more than three hundred miles north from the northern fringe of Miami. Here, the palm-dotted beaches and warm ocean waves bring to reality the fuzzy sun-soaked playground seen on TV – yet each community has something unique to offer. **Fort Lauderdale**, no longer the party town of popular imagination, is today a sophisticated yachting center and bubbling social scene. To the north, **Boca Raton** and **Palm Beach** are quiet, exclusive communities, their Mediterranean Revival mansions inhabited almost entirely by multimillionaires. Beyond Palm Beach, the coast is still mostly undeveloped; even the **Space Coast**, anchored by the extremely popular **Kennedy Space Center**, is smack in the middle of a nature preserve. Just north, **Daytona Beach** attracts race car- and motorcycle-enthusiasts with its festivals and the Daytona International Speedway. Lastly, enchanting **St Augustine** is the spot where Spanish settlers established North America's first foreign colony.

By car, the scenic route along the coast is **Hwy-A1A**, which sticks to the ocean side of the **Intracoastal Waterway**, formed when the rivers dividing the mainland from the barrier islands were joined and deepened during World War II. When necessary, Hwy-A1A turns inland and links with the much less picturesque **US-1**. The speediest road in the region, **I-95**, runs about ten miles west of the coastline, and is only worthwhile if you're in a hurry.

Fort Lauderdale

A single low-budget Hollywood movie changed **FORT LAUDERDALE** from a mild-mannered little town – that happened to adjoin seven miles of palm-shaded white sands – into a byword for uninhibited beach life. Following the 1960 teen-exploitation movie *Where the Boys Are*, Fort Lauderdale instantly became the number-one Spring Break venue in the US, drawing hundreds of thousands of frenzied students each year. However, having fueled its economic boom on underage drinking and lascivious excess, the city promptly turned its back on the revelers. By the end of the 1980s, it had imposed enough restrictions on boozing and wild behavior to put an end to the bacchanal. Since then, Fort Lauderdale has transformed itself into a thriving pleasure port, catering to individual yacht-owners and major cruise liners alike. It's also one of the fastest-growing residential areas in the country, and has for years been known as one of **gay** America's favorite holiday haunts.

Arrival and information

Both of Fort Lauderdale's public transit terminals are in or close to downtown. Greyhound **buses** pull in at 515 NE 3rd St, while the Amtrak and Tri-Rail **train** station (☎1-800/TRI-RAIL, ⓦwww.tri-rail.com) is two miles west at 200 SW 21st Terrace – take bus #22 into town ($1). The main local **visitor center** is in Port Everglades at 1850 Eller Drive (Mon–Fri 8.30am–5pm; ☎954/765-4466 or 1-800/356-1662, ⓦwww.sunny.org). For their multilingual entertainment/attractions hotline, call ☎954/527-5600.

Local bus #11 runs twice hourly along Las Olas Boulevard between downtown and the beach. You can also use the **water taxi** (daily 10am until midnight; one way $4, all-day pass $5; ☎954/467-6677, ⓦwww.watertaxi.com), which can take you almost anywhere along Fort Lauderdale's many miles of waterfront.

Accommodation

Although Fort Lauderdale is moving inexorably upscale, plenty of **motels** near the beach still offer a reasonable room for around $50 in summer (more like $75 in winter). The tourist office's (see above) free annual *Superior Small Lodgings Guide* has full listings.

Banyan Marina Apartments 111 Isle of Venice ☎1-800/524-4431, ⓦwww.banyanmarina.com. Close to Las Olas Blvd, these apartments, nicely furnished with plush carpets, leather couches, and full kitchens, are on a waterway a short drive from the beach. Apartments from ❺, a few double rooms ❹

Eighteenth Street Inn 712 SE 18th St ☎954/467-7841 or 1-888/828-4466. A real find, with seven creatively decorated rooms and suites bordering a palm-fringed pool. A tasty breakfast is included. ❺

Floyd's International Youth Hostel 445 SE 16th St ☎954/462-0631, ⓦwww.floydshostel.com. In central Port Everglades, this friendly, well-kept private hostel offers, during the daytime, pickups from the Fort Lauderdale airport and the bus and train stations. Dorm beds are $17, private rooms $45. ❶–❷

Pillars at New River Sound 111 N Birch Rd ☎954/467-9639 or 1-800/800-7666. Attractive, spacious resort in the heart of the beach area (though facing the waterway rather than the ocean). Use of a pleasant pool and full breakfast included. ❼

Shell Resort at the Ocean 3030 Bayshore Drive ☎954/463-1723, ⓦwww.shellmotel.com. Motel with colorful, good-sized rooms, just a stone's throw from the beach. ❹

Downtown Fort Lauderdale

Downtown Fort Lauderdale focuses on a few blocks between E Broward and E Las Olas boulevards, which cross US-1 a couple of miles east of I-95. Heavily prettified with parks and promenades, it's a pleasant place for a stroll, especially if you follow the mile-long pedestrian **Riverwalk** along the north shore of the New River. Las Olas Boulevard itself, the main **shopping district**, remains busy day and night, with boutiques, galleries, restaurants, bars, and sidewalk cafés in abundance. It's also home to the stimulating **Museum of Art**, 1 E Las Olas Blvd (Tues–Sat 10am–5pm, Sun noon–5pm; $7; ☎954/525-5500, ⓦwww.museumofart.org). The largely modern collection features several of the twentieth century's biggest names (such as James Rosenquist and Robert Rauschenberg), and also celebrates the work by the CoBrA movement of artists from Copenhagen, Brussels, and Amsterdam. Not far west, the simulators and interactive displays at the **Museum of Discovery & Science**, 401 SW 2nd St (Mon–Sat 10am–5pm, Sun noon–6pm; $14; ☎954/467-6637, ⓦwww.mods.org), should pacify kids pining for Disney. There's also a 3D IMAX theater, a ticket to which is included in admission to the museum; call or visit the website for showtimes.

The beach

Even though downtown's got its charms and attractions, most visitors come to Fort Lauderdale for broad, clean, and undeniably beautiful **beach**. You'll find it by crossing the arching intracoastal waterway bridge, about two miles along Las Olas Boulevard from downtown. At the end of Las Olas, the mood changes appreciably, and beachside Fort Lauderdale begins: airbrush T-shirt, watersports, and beachwear stores are suddenly everywhere. Along the seafront, Fort Lauderdale Beach Boulevard once bore the brunt of Spring Break partying, though only a few beachfront bars suggest the carousing of the past. Today, an attractive new promenade draws an altogether healthier crowd of joggers, in-line skaters, and cyclists.

Eating and drinking

The two main drags for **eating** and **drinking** in Fort Lauderdale are Las Olas and Sunrise boulevards. There are also some fun **bars** near the ocean, as well as a burgeoning restaurant district on West Broward Boulevard, a few blocks west of the Riverwalk.

Casablanca Café intersection of Alhambra and Ocean blvds ☎954/764-3500. An American piano bar in a Moroccan setting, serving a good, eclectic menu, at moderate prices. Expect large portions of Mediterranean specialties, such as paella and Greek salad.

Ernie's BBQ Lounge 1843 S Federal Hwy (US-1) ☎954/523-8636. The scruffy-but-likeable, moderately priced *Ernie's*, south of downtown, is a local legend for its glorious conch chowder.

The Floridian 1410 E Las Olas Blvd ☎954/463-4041. Fort Lauderdale in the 1950s: formica furniture, peeling autographed pictures lining the walls, and outstanding diner food at rock-bottom prices.

La Cantina 2870 E Sunrise Blvd ☎954/565-3839. Enormous, cheap portions of authentic Mexican food – as well as the giant, $9 margaritas – make this a good stop on the beach.

Mangos 904 E Las Olas Blvd ☎954/523-5001. Decent dining, though most people go for the people-watching along Las Olas, and the energetic workout, dancing to roaring live rock/R&B/jazz jams at this singles scene.

Southport Raw Bar 1536 Cordova Rd ☎954/525-2526. South of downtown, near Port Everglades, this boisterous local bar specializes in succulent crustaceans and well-prepared fish dishes.

Taverna Opa 3051 NE 32nd St ☎954/567-1630. A raucous good time can be had at this fun Greek establishment, complete with flowing ouzo and crashing dishes.

Boca Raton

BOCA RATON (literally, "the mouth of the rat"), twenty miles north of Fort Lauderdale, is noteworthy mostly for its abundance of **Mediterranean Revival architecture**. This style, prevalent here since the 1920s, has been kept alive in the downtown area by strict building codes. New structures must incorporate arched entranceways, fake bell towers, and red-tiled roofs whenever possible, ensuring a consistent and distinctive "look."

This all goes back to Addison Mizner, the "Aladdin of architects" (see box, p.664), who swept into Boca Raton on the tide of the Florida property boom in 1925, buying up 1600 acres of farmland. Mizner's vision of gondola-filled canals, luxury hotels, and even a great cathedral never came to fruition, but the few public buildings he completed (along with close to fifty homes) left an indelible mark. His million-dollar *Cloister Inn*, for example, grew into the present **Boca Raton Resort and Club**, 501 E Camino Real, a pink palace of marble columns, sculptured fountains, and carefully aged wood (℡561/447-3000 or 1-888/491-BOCA, ⓦwww.bocaresort.com; ❼). Mizner's spirit is also invoked at **Mizner Park**, off US-1 between Palmetto Park Rd and Glades Rd, a stylish open-air shopping plaza adorned with palm trees and waterfalls. The park is home to the **Boca Raton Museum of Art**, 501 Plaza Real (Tues, Thurs & Fri 10am–5pm, Wed 10am–9pm, Sat & Sun noon–5pm; $8; ⓦ561/392-2500), worth a stop for its drawings by modern European masters – Degas, Matisse, Picasso – and a formidable collection of African art.

A mile north of Hwy-798 (which links downtown Boca Raton with the beach), at 1801 N Ocean Blvd/Hwy-A1A, the **Gumbo Limbo Nature Center** (Mon–Sat 9am–4pm, Sun noon–4pm; $2 donation; ℡561/338-1473, ⓦwww.gumbolimbo.org) covers twenty acres inhabited by osprey, brown pelicans, and sea turtles. Reserve well in advance for the night turtle-watching tours offered between May and July.

A couple miles north of downtown, Boca Raton's most explorable **beachside** area is **Spanish River Park** (daily 8am–dusk; Mon–Fri cars $10, Sat, Sun & holidays $12; pedestrians and cyclists free). Most of these fifty acres of vivid vegetation and high-rise greenery are only penetrable on trails through shady thickets.

Practicalities

Greyhound does not stop in Boca Raton. **Tri-Rail** stops off Yamato Road, west of I-95 at 601 NW 53rd St (℡1-800/TRI-RAIL); there's a connecting shuttle to the town center. The **Chamber of Commerce** is at 1800 N Dixie Hwy (Mon–Thurs 8.30am–5pm, Fri 8.30am–4pm; ℡561/395-4433). The *Townplace Suites*, 5110 NW Eighth Ave (℡561/994-7232; ❸), and *Ocean Lodge*, 531 N Ocean Blvd (℡561/395-7772; ❸), are two great-value **hotels**. *Max's Grill*, 404 Plaza Real (℡561/368-0080), has good, reasonably priced standard American fare, while *Prezzo*, 7820 Glades Rd (℡561/451-2800), serves homemade pastas and oak-oven pizzas. Boca Raton has a rather subdued **nightlife**, but local bar *Flanigan's Guppys*, 45 S Federal Hwy (℡561/395-4324), stays lively most of the week.

Palm Beach

A small island town of palatial homes and gardens, with streets so clean you could eat off them, **PALM BEACH** has been synonymous for nearly a century with the kind of lifestyle only limitless loot can buy. The nation's nobs began wintering here in the 1890s, after Henry Flagler brought his East Coast railroad south from St Augustine, building two luxury hotels on this then-secluded, palm-filled island. Since then, tycoons, sports aces, aristocrats, rock stars, and CIA directors have flocked here, eager to become part of the Palm Beach elite and enjoy its aloofness from mainland, and mainstream, life. Joe Kennedy – father of John, Robert, and Ted – bought the so-called Kennedy Compound here in 1933.

Summer in Palm Beach is very quiet, and the least costly time to stay. The winter months, from November to May, see a whirl of elegant balls, fundraising dinners, and charity galas, as well as the **polo** season – watching a chukker (a playing period of a polo game) or two is the only time Palm Beach denizens show themselves in the less particular environs of West Palm Beach, back on the mainland.

Worth Avenue, close to the southern tip of the island, is filled with designer stores, high-class art galleries, and ultraformal restaurants, and is cruised by Rolls Royces, Mercedes, and Jaguars. Its most appealing aspect is its **architecture**: stucco walls, Romanesque facades, and passageways leading to small courtyards where miniature bridges cross nonexistent canals and spiral staircases climb to the upper levels.

Where Cocoanut Row and Whitehall Way meet, the white Doric columns front Whitehall, also known as the **Flagler Museum** (Tues–Sat 10am–5pm, Sun noon–5pm; $8; ☎561/655-2833, ⓦwww.flagler.org). This, the most overtly ostentatious home on the island, was a $4 million wedding present from Henry Flagler to his third wife, Mary Lily Kenan. As in many of Florida's first luxury homes, the interior design was lifted from the great buildings of Europe: among the fifty-five rooms are an Italian library, a French salon, a billiard room with Swiss fittings, a hallway modeled on St Peter's, and a Louis XV ballroom. All are stuffed with ornamentation, but they lack aesthetic cohesion. Informative 45-minute guided tours depart frequently from the cavernous marble entrance hall, providing a background for Flagler's fascinating rise to success and a glimpse of the Gilded Age in which he flourished.

Built in 1926 in the style of an Italianate palace, **The Breakers** hotel, on South County Road off the main strip (☎561/655-6611 or 1-888/BREAKERS; ❸), operates as the last of Palm Beach's swanky resorts. Its design includes elaborate painted ceilings and huge tapestries. Take the guided tour on Wednesdays at 3pm (free for guests, $15 for the public; call ☎561/655-6611 ext 7691 for information).

Addison Mizner: architect of Palm Beach

A former miner and prizefighter, **Addison Mizner** was an unemployed architect when he arrived in Palm Beach in 1918. Inspired by the medieval buildings he'd seen around the Mediterranean, Mizner built the **Everglades Club**, at 356 Worth Ave – the first public building in Florida in the Mediterranean Revival style. The success of the club, and the house he subsequently built for society bigwig Eva Stotesbury, won Mizner commissions all over Palm Beach as the wintering wealthy decided to swap suites at one of Henry Flagler's hotels for a "million-dollar cottage" of their own.

Brilliant and unorthodox, Mizner designed loggias and U-shaped interiors that made the most of Florida's pleasant winter temperatures, while his twisting staircases to nowhere became legendary. Mizner used untrained workmen to lay crooked roof tiles, sprayed condensed milk onto walls to create an impression of centuries-old grime, and fired shotgun pellets into wood to imitate wormholes. By the mid-1920s, Mizner had created the Palm Beach Style, and he later fashioned much of Boca Raton, as well (see p.663).

Practicalities

In keeping with the upper-crust atmosphere, **public transportation** options around Palm Beach are limited. The West Palm Beach Amtrak (T 1-800/USA-RAIL), Tri-Rail (T 1-800/TRI-RAIL), and Greyhound (T 561/833-8536) stations are all located at 205 S Tamarind Ave in West Palm Beach on the mainland. To get to Palm Beach from there, take any PalmTran bus ($1.25; T 561/841-4BUS) terminating at Quadrille Road, and transfer to the #41, or the #42 (no Sunday service). By car, from I-95 and points west, take Okeechobee Boulevard east into Palm Beach.

The **Convention and Visitors' Bureau** is at 1555 Palm Beach Lakes Blvd (Mon–Fri 9am–5pm; T 561/233-3000). You'll need plenty of money to **stay** here: prices of $200 a night are not uncommon. The elaborate, antique-furnished *Palm Beach Bed & Breakfast*, 365 S County Rd (T 561/832-4009; ❹), offers some of the best rates in town, but you'll need to reserve early. Otherwise, come between May and December, when similarly grand options such as *The Chesterfield*, 363 Cocoanut Row (T 561/659-5800 or 1-800/243-7871; ❺), and *The Plaza Inn*, 215 Brazilian Ave (T 561/832-8666 or 1-800/233-2632; ❺), are at their least expensive. *Charley's Crab*, 456 S Ocean Blvd (T 561/659-1500), is the place to go for reasonably priced **seafood**, while the lunch counter at *Hamburger Heaven*, 314 S County Rd (T 561/655-5277), has been serving its delicious **burgers** since 1945. If money is no object – and you're dressed to kill – make for *Café L'Europe*, 331 S County Rd (T 561/655-4020). Spend less than $50 a head in this super-elegant French restaurant and you'll walk away hungry.

The Space Coast

About two hundred miles north of Palm Beach, the so-called **Space Coast**, the base of the country's space industry, occupies a flat, marshy island bulging into the Atlantic. The **Kennedy Space Center** complex encompasses part of the island and attracts plenty of visitors – many of whom are surprised to find that the rest of the island is the home of a sizable nature preserve, the **Merritt Island National Wildlife Refuge**.

The Kennedy Space Center

The **Kennedy Space Center** is the nucleus of the US space program, and where NASA seizes every opportunity to enthuse young minds with the enduring excitement and adventure of outer space. The center remains a working facility, where space vehicles are developed, tested, and blasted into orbit. **Merritt Island** has been the center of NASA's activity since 1964, when the launch pads at Cape Canaveral US Air Force base, across the water, proved too small to cope with the giant new Saturn V rockets.

To reach the **Visitor Complex** (daily 9am–6pm; Maximum Access Badge $34 adults, $24 children; T 321/452-2121, W www.kennedyspacecenter.com), take exit 212 off I-95 to Hwy-405, and follow the signs; you can also get here by connecting with Hwy-3 off Hwy-A1A. The best **times to visit** are on weekends and in May and September, when crowds are thinner – but at any time, you should still allow an entire day for everything the Space Center has to offer. Check the weather, too, as thunderstorms may force some attractions to close.

Museums and galleries in the main complex include an open-air **Rocket**

Garden of spindly fireworks-like rockets from the 1950s, several interactive displays, and a couple of kid-oriented programs. After you've examined the mission capsules, space suits, and satellites, and clambered through the mock-up Space Shuttle flight deck, you'll want to watch an IMAX movie or join a two-hour guided **bus tour**. The bus passes the 52-story Vehicle Assembly Building and stops at the impressive Apollo/Saturn V Center, where multimedia displays re-create the excitement of the first moon landings and the Apollo 8 launch. For the dates and times of **shuttle launches**, call ☎321/449-4444; you can arrange for $15 viewing passes via the website listed above. However, you get almost as good a view from anywhere within forty miles of the Space Center.

Near the Space Center, at 6225 Vectorspace Blvd in Titusville, the **US Astronaut Hall of Fame** (daily 10am–6pm; $14, or free admission with same-day Maximum Access Badge; see p.665) offers the full space explorer's experience, with G-force, shuttle-landing, and flight simulators.

Practicalities: Cocoa Beach

The closest **motels** to the Kennedy Center are on the mainland along US-1 – or, if you're looking for a bargain rate, in **COCOA BEACH**, a few miles south on a ten-mile strip of shore washed by some of the biggest surfing waves in Florida. Options include the *Luna Sea*, 3185 N Atlantic Ave (☎1-800/586-2732; ❹), *Days Inn*, 5500 N Atlantic Ave (☎321/784-2550; ❸), and *Fawlty Towers*, 100 E Cocoa Beach Causeway (☎321/784-3870; ❸). For great oysters and a super view of the water, head for *Sunset Café Riverfront,* 500 E Cocoa

Beach Causeway (☏321/783-8485) – but go early, as it's frequently mobbed. A great **dinner** option is *The Pier Restaurant*, on the Cocoa Beach Pier (☏321/783-7549), which has a quality, somewhat expensive menu that's especially strong on seafood.

Merritt Island National Wildlife Refuge

NASA doesn't have Merritt Island all to itself: the agency shares it with the **Merritt Island National Wildlife Refuge** (daily dawn–dusk; free). The refuge is promoted, disconcertingly, with the slogan "Where Nature Meets Technology." Alligators, armadillos, raccoons, and bobcats – as well as one of Florida's greatest gatherings of birdlife – live right up against some of the human world's most advanced hardware. Winter is the best time to visit, when the skies are alive with birds migrating from the frozen north and mosquitoes are nowhere to be found. At any other time, especially in summer, the Mosquito Lagoon is worthy of its name: bring repellent.

Eight miles off I-95's exit 220, Hwy-406 leads to the seven-mile **Black Point Wildlife Drive**, which gives a solid introduction to the basics of the island's ecosystem; pick up the free leaflet at the entrance. Be sure to walk in the refuge, too: off the wildlife drive, the five-mile **Cruickshank trail** weaves around the edge of the Indian River. Drive a few miles farther east along Hwy-402 – branching from Hwy-406 just south of the Wildlife Drive and passing the **visitor center** (Mon–Fri 8am–4.30pm, Sat & Sun 9am–5pm; closed Sun April–Sept; ☏321/861-0667) – and then hike the half-mile **Oak Hammock trail** or the two-mile **Palm Hammock trail**, both accessible from the visitor center parking lot.

Daytona Beach

The consummate Florida beach town, with its T-shirt shops, amusement arcades, and wall-to-wall motels, **DAYTONA BEACH** owes its existence to twenty miles of perfect light brown sands. Once a favorite Spring Break destination, when half a million college kids would descend to indulge in underage drinking and wild partying, Daytona Beach now discourages such activity, leaving it free to focus on its true love: motor sports. Life in here now revolves around three major events: the legendary **Daytona 500** stock-car race in February; **Bike Week**, in early March, which sees thousands of leather-clad bikers converge on the city; and the relatively new **Fall Cycle Scene**, in October, which features amateur and pro races, as well as bike demos by Harley-Davidson and Kawasaki.

The origin of Daytona's race-car and motorcycle obsession goes back to the early 1900s, when pioneering auto enthusiasts including Louis Chevrolet, Ransom Olds, and Henry Ford came to Daytona's firm sands to race prototype vehicles beside the ocean. In fact, the world land speed record was smashed here five times by the British millionaire Malcolm Campbell; in 1935, he reached his top speed of 276mph (only to break it shortly thereafter in Utah, at 301mph). As increasing speeds made racing on the sands unsafe, the **Daytona International Speedway**, an ungainly configuration of concrete and steel, was built three miles west of downtown along International Speedway Boulevard (buses #9A and #9B).

Opened in 1959, the massive Speedway holds 168,000 people, and hosts several major race meetings each year, starting in early February with the **Rolex**

24, a 24hr race for GT prototype sports cars, Porsches, and Ferraris. A week or so later, the qualifying trials for the **Daytona 500** begin. If you want to see a race, keep in mind that racing is currently the fastest-growing spectator sport in America, and **tickets** (from $95; call ☎386/253-7223 or visit ⓦwww .daytonainternationalspeedway.com) sell out well in advance. You should also reserve **accommodation** at least six months ahead. Though they can't capture the excitement of a race, **guided van tours** (daily except race days 9.30am–4pm, every half-hour; $7) take you around the racetrack's remarkable curves, whose gradients make this the fastest in the world. Immediately outside the Speedway, the interactive **Daytona USA** (daily 9am–7pm; $16; ☎386/947-6800) gives participants the ability to experience the speed of a Daytona race, and to have a Jeff Gordon stock car fly to pieces before them (both using computer technology, of course).

For all the excitement that racing generates, the best thing about Daytona is the seemingly limitless **beach**: it's 500 feet wide at low tide, and fades dreamily off into the heat haze. Daytona is also one of the few beaches you can drive on – pay $5 at the various entrances and follow the posted procedures. Lined with an all-but-endless procession of enormous but surprisingly low-priced motels, oceanfront Atlantic Avenue holds little to lure you away from the water. At the landward end of Main Street Pier, a $3 ride up the candy-striped **Space Needle** enables you to look down on the surrounding morass of low-rent bars and tattoo parlors. Unfortunately, though, you can't get out to the far end of the pier; Hurricane Floyd knocked out 280 feet of it in 1999.

Practicalities

US-1 (called, in town, Ridgewood Avenue) plows through mainland Daytona Beach, passing the **Greyhound** station at 138 S Ridgewood. **Trolleys** ($1) run the length of the beach until midnight. The **visitor center** is at 126 E Orange Ave (Mon–Fri 9am–5pm; ☎1-800/854-1234, ⓦwww.daytonabeach.com). Any of the Atlantic Avenue **motels** makes a good beach base: there's the *Driftwood Beach Motel*, 657 S Atlantic, slightly north of town in Ormond Beach (☎1-800/490-8935; ❸); the *Del-Aire* at 744 N Atlantic (☎386/252-2562; ❷); or the welcoming, relatively upscale *Plaza Resort & Spa* at 600 N Atlantic (☎1-800/874-7420, ⓦwww.plazaresortandspa.com; ❺).

Good places to **eat** include *Julian's*, 88 S Atlantic Ave, Ormond Beach (☎386/677-6767), a dimly lit, mock-Tahitian lounge with great food, and *Lighthouse Landing* (☎386/761-9271), beside the Ponce Inlet Lighthouse, for fresh fish. Or try the casual *Inlet Harbor*, south of town at 133 Inlet Rd (☎386/767-5590), where you can eat right on the marina, while local bands play their hearts out. The *St Regis Restaurant and Patio Bar*, 509 Seabreeze Blvd (☎386/252-8743), is a local culinary favorite, serving New American fare, the highlight of which is the chicken piccata. For beachside action, the **bars** in and around the *Adam's Mark Daytona Beach Resort*, 100 N Atlantic Ave, and the *Plaza Resort & Spa*, 600 N Atlantic Ave, are good bets, as is *Razzles*, 611 Seabreeze Blvd (☎321/257-6236).

St Augustine

Forty miles north of Daytona Beach, US-1 passes through the heart of charismatic **ST AUGUSTINE**. Few places in Florida are as immediately engaging as this old city, with the size and even some of the looks of a small

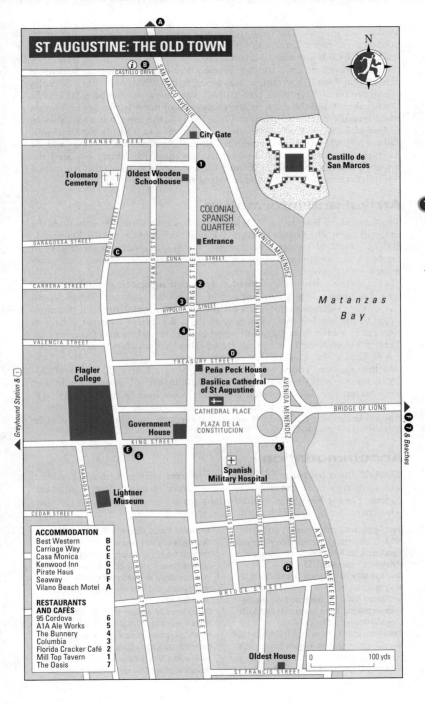

ST AUGUSTINE: THE OLD TOWN

N

CASTILLO DRIVE

ORANGE STREET

City Gate

Castillo de
San Marcos

Tolomato
Cemetery

Oldest Wooden
Schoolhouse

1

COLONIAL
SPANISH
QUARTER

SARAGOSSA STREET

CORDOVA STREET

SPANISH STREET

■ Entrance

CUNA STREET

CARRERA STREET

ST. GEORGE STREET

2

CHARLOTTE STREET

*Matanzas
Bay*

3 HYPOLITA STREET

4

VALENCIA STREET

TREASURY STREET **D**

Peña Peck House

Basilica Cathedral
of St Augustine

✚

CATHEDRAL PLACE

AVENIDA MENENDEZ

BRIDGE OF LIONS

Flagler
College

Government
House

PLAZA DE LA
CONSTITUCION

KING STREET

E **6**

5

Spanish
Military Hospital

Greyhound Station &

GRANADA STREET

Lightner
Museum

CEDAR STREET

AVILES STREET

ST. GEORGE STREET

CHARLOTTE STREET

MARINE STREET

AVENIDA MENENDEZ

G

CORDOVA STREET

BRIDGE STREET

Oldest House

ST FRANCIS STREET

& Beaches

ACCOMMODATION
Best Western   B
Carriage Way   C
Casa Monica   E
Kenwood Inn   G
Pirate Haus   D
Seaway   F
Vilano Beach Motel   A

**RESTAURANTS
AND CAFÉS**
95 Cordova   6
A1A Ale Works   5
The Bunnery   4
Columbia   3
Florida Cracker Café 2
Mill Top Tavern   1
The Oasis   7

0   100 yds

Mediterranean town. The oldest permanent settlement in the US, with much from its early days still intact along its narrow streets, it also offers two alluring lengths of **beach** just across Matanzas Bay.

Though Ponce de León touched ground here in 1513, European settlement didn't begin until half a century later, when Spain's Pedro Menéndez de Avilés put ashore on St Augustine's Day in 1565. Twenty-three years later, Sir Francis Drake's ships razed the town in one of the first of many battles before Florida was eventually ceded to Britain in 1763. By then, the town was a major social and administrative center, soon to be capital of east Florida. Subsequently, Tallahassee (see p.698) became the capital of a unified Florida, and St Augustine's fortunes waned. Since then, expansion has largely bypassed the town – a fact inadvertently facilitating the restoration program that has turned this quiet community into a fine historical showcase.

Arrival and information

The Greyhound **bus** station, 100 Malaga St, is a fifteen-minute walk from the center of town. The **visitor center**, 10 Castillo Drive (daily 8am–5.30pm; ☎1-800/653-2489, ⓦ www.visitoldcity.com), shows a free film on the history of the town, has recommendations for a variety of tours (see below), and information on the numerous local festivals.

St Augustine is best seen **on foot**, though two **sightseeing trains** tour the main landmarks (daily 8.30am–5pm; $14–15; get tickets from 170 San Marco Ave or the visitor center). There's **no public transportation**, so if you want to get to the beaches two miles away and you don't have a car you'll have to either **rent a bike** from the youth hostel (see below), take a **taxi** (Ancient City Cabs; ☎904/824-8161), or use the **Beach Bus** ($5), which stops, among other places, outside the *A1A Ale Works* (see below).

As for organized **tours**, harbor cruises by Scenic Cruise ($12; ☎904/824-1806) leave five or six times a day from the City Yacht Pier, near the foot of King Street. The well-organized and informative Tour St Augustine ($8–10; ☎1-800/797-3778) leads historical and ghost walking tours, while the St Augustine Transfer Co. offers horse-drawn carriage tours both day and night ($20; ☎904/829-2391).

Accommodation

The Old Town has many excellent restored **inns** offering bed-and-breakfast, and there are cheap **motels** outside the center of town along San Marco Avenue. For the best prices, avoid the busy period between May and October, when rates rise by $15–25 a night.

Best Western 6 Castillo Drive ☎1-800/528-1234. Reliable chain's Spanish-style villa provides a pool, a hot tub for nighttime stargazing, and complimentary breakfast. ❹

Carriage Way 70 Cuna St ☎1-800/908-9832, ⓦ www.carriageway.com. One of the Old Town's best-priced B&Bs, in a pretty, centrally located Victorian building. Some rooms offer four-poster beds and fireplaces. ❹

Casa Monica 95 Cordova St ☎1-800/648-1888, ⓦ www.casamonica.com. Elegant Spanish-style hotel established in the heart of the Old Town in 1888, now magnificently restored. ❻

Kenwood Inn 38 Marine St ☎904/824-2116, ⓦ www.oldcity.com/kenwood. Well-situated near the waterfront, this charming, sizable Old Town inn features individually decorated rooms, some with four-poster or canopy beds, as well as a pool, terrace, and complimentary continental breakfast. ❹

Pirate Haus 32 Treasury St ☎904/808-1999, ⓦ www.internationalhaus.com. Near the plaza, the town's only hostel accommodation is popular with backpackers. It has a giant kitchen and a common room stuffed with guidebooks. Beds in air-conditioned dorms are $16; some private rooms ❷

Seaway 481 Hwy-A1A ⓣ 904/471-3466. This small motel is one of several quality family-oriented establishments on busy St Augustine Beach. ❸

Vilano Beach Motel 50 Vilano Rd ⓣ 904/829-2651. This laid-back Art Deco motel is a great base for enjoying the beaches north of town. ❸

The Old Town

Bordered on the west by St George Street, and on the south by Plaza de la Constitucion, St Augustine's **Old Town** holds the well-tended evidence of the town's Spanish period. It may be small, but there's a lot to see: an early start, around 9am, will give you a lead on the tourist crowds, and should allow a good look at almost everything in one day.

Given the fine state of the **Castillo de San Marcos National Monument**, on the northern edge of the Old Town beside the bay (daily 8.45am–4.45pm; $5; ⓦ www.nps.gov/casa), it's difficult to believe that the fortress was started in the late 1600s. Its longevity is due to its design: a diamond-shaped rampart at each corner maximized firepower, and 14ft-thick walls reduced its vulnerability to attack. Inside, there's not a lot to see besides small cases of exhibits in echoing rooms, though venturing along the 35ft ramparts gives good views across the city and the bay.

A hundred yards west of the monument, the eighteenth-century **City Gate** marks the entrance to **St George Street**, once the main thoroughfare and now a tourist-trampled strip. You'll find a bunch of places called "The oldest..." in St Augustine; the **Oldest Wooden Schoolhouse**, set in lush gardens at 14 St George St (daily 9am–5pm; $2.75), is one of the most atmospheric, a restored wooden shack with jerky animatronic dummies portraying nineteenth-century schoolchildren.

Just west from here, on Cordova Street, the evocative, overgrown **Tolomato Cemetery** (9am–6pm) stands on the site of an eighteenth-century Christian Indian village; most graves date from the 1900s. Back on St George, where it meets Cuna Street, a fair-sized plot is taken up by the excellent **Colonial Spanish Quarter** (Sun–Thurs 9am–5.30pm; $6.50). In its seven reconstructed homes and workshops, volunteers dressed as Spanish settlers go about their business at spinning-wheels, anvils, and foot-driven wood lathes.

For a more intimate look at local life during a slightly later period, head south for the **Peña Peck House**, 143 St George St (Mon–Sat 12.30–3.30pm, Sun 10.30–3.30pm; $4.50 suggested donation). Thought to have originally been the Spanish treasury, by the time the British took over in 1763 this was the home of a physician and his gregarious spouse, who turned the place into a high-society rendezvous.

In the sixteenth century, the Spanish king decreed that all colonial towns must be built around a central plaza; thus, St George runs into the **Plaza de la Constitucion**, a marketplace from 1598. On the plaza's north side, the **Basilica Cathedral of St Augustine** (daily 7am–5pm; donation) adds a touch of grandeur, although it's largely a Sixties remake of the late eighteenth-century original. On the plaza's west side, the **Government House Museum**, 48 King St (daily 9am–5pm; $2.50), gives an admirably concise and clear history of the changing demography of the colony.

Tourist numbers lessen as you cross **south of the plaza** into a web of quiet, narrow streets, all just as old as St George. West along King Street, opposite Flagler College, the classy **Lightner Museum** (daily 9am–5pm, last admission 4.30pm; $6; ⓣ 904/824-2874) displays fine and decorative arts in the former *Alcazar Hotel*, one of the most fabulous resorts of the late nineteenth century. More substantial history is available a ten-minute walk away, at 14 St Francis St, in the form of the fascinating **Oldest House** (daily 9am–5pm; $6), which is indeed the oldest house in town, dating from the early 1700s. Its rooms are furnished to show how the house – and people's lives – changed as new eras unfolded.

The beaches

Some fine **beaches** – busiest at weekends – lie just a couple of miles east from the Old Town. Crossing the bay via the Bridge of Lions, and continuing east on Hwy-A1A will bring you to the **Anastasia State Recreation Area**, on Anastasia Island (daily 8am–dusk; cars $3.25, cyclists and pedestrians $1), which offers a thousand protected acres of dunes, marshes, and scrub, linked by nature walks. A few miles further south, **St Augustine Beach** is family terrain, with some good restaurants and a fishing pier. North of Old Town (take May St, off San Marco Ave), the broad, orange **Vilano Beach** pulls a younger crowd.

Eating and drinking

Eating in the Old Town can be expensive, and a number of its cafés and restaurants are closed in the evening. Many people head out to the oceanfront places for dinner, or settle instead for a long night's drinking at one of the nice old bars.

95 Cordova at the *Casa Monica* hotel, 95 Cordova St ☎904/810-6810. This luxurious and elegant restaurant's menu is an eclectic blend of American, Asian, Mediterranean, Caribbean, and Moroccan influences.

A1A Ale Works 1 King St ☎904/829-2977. This convivial, good-looking bar/restaurant is popular with the locals for its excellent, creative New World cuisine and home-brewed beers.

The Bunnery 121 St George St ☎904/829-6166. Tempting homemade sandwiches, quiches, and salads are served in a relaxing courtyard of this old Spanish bakery.

Columbia 98 St George St ☎904/824-3341. Lively New Orleans atmosphere, with a traditional Spanish/Cuban menu. All served up in a sumptuous setting of fountains and candlelit arcades.

Florida Cracker Café 81 St George St ☎904/829-0397. Serves a blend of combo salads, sandwiches, entrees, and homemade desserts. Favorites include hot artichoke and parmesan dip, and conch fritters.

Mill Top Tavern 19 1/2 George St ☎904/829-2329. In a nineteenth-century mill, this historic local bar, with deck seating, boasts a great view of the Castillo and the bay. Excellent live music helps make the place a local favorite.

The Oasis 4000 Ocean Trace Rd ☎904/471-3424. This beach bar is famous for its burgers. Try the "Gonzo Burger," served with three kinds of cheese and piles of extras.

Jacksonville

Situated in the great double loop of the St Johns River, **JACKSONVILLE** struggled for years to throw off its longstanding reputation as an industrial port city of no-nonsense, fun-hating conservatives. Sure enough, during the 1990s, the city began to gain standing as a new service industry center, supplanting the city's dusty lumber-industry origins. Efforts have also been made to enhance Jacksonville's appeal by creating parks and riverside boardwalks, though the sheer size of the city – at 841 square miles, the largest in the US – serves to dilute its easygoing character.

To get an overview of downtown, take the **Skyway monorail** (Mon–Fri 6.30am–11pm, Sat 10am–11pm; 35¢) from the Convention Center to Hemming Park, a ten-minute journey at eye-level with the highrise offices. One noteworthy building, on the north bank of the St Johns River, is the

Florida Theater, 128 E Forsyth St. Here, Elvis Presley arrived in 1957 for his first appearance on an indoor stage, an event noted by *Life* magazine because a juvenile court judge sat through the whole performance to ensure it wasn't too suggestive. Its interior has since been restored with a dazzling gold proscenium arch, and today the theater is used for a variety of performances.

Crossing over to the south bank – try taking the River Taxi ($3 one way; $5 roundtrip) – you'll find the **Museum of Science and History**, 1025 Museum Circle (Mon–Fri 10am–5pm, Sat 10am–6pm, Sun 1–6pm; $7, children $5; ℡904/396-6674, ⓦwww.themosh.org), with its hands-on exhibits and planetarium. For a break from the commerce and industry of the city, visit the **Jacksonville Museum of Modern Art**, 333 N Laura St (Tues, Thurs & Fri 11am–5pm, Wed 11am–9pm, Sat & Sun noon–4pm; $6; ℡904/366-6911, ⓦwww.jmoma.org); its offerings include large Ed Paschke and James Rosenquist canvases. The museum also has a substantial **children's center** where kids can use the concepts of modern art to create their own works.

Just south of the Fuller Warren River bridge (I-95), the **Cummer Museum of Art and Gardens**, 829 Riverside Drive (Tues & Thurs 10am–9pm, Wed, Fri & Sat 10am–5pm, Sun noon–5pm; $6, free Tues after 4pm; ℡904/356-6857, ⓦwww.cummer.org), has comfortable, spacious rooms, with sculpture-lined corridors that contain works by prominent European and American masters. The two acres of lovely Italianate and English gardens that overlook the river are an added bonus.

From all over Jacksonville you can see the 73,000-seat Alltel Stadium, home to the **Jacksonville Jaguars** football franchise (tickets from $20–220; ℡1-877/4JAGS-TIX). It's also the scene of the Florida–Georgia college football clash each fall – an excuse for 48 hours of citywide drinking and partying. Next door is **Metropolitan Park**, a pleasant swath of riverside greenery.

Practicalities

From the Greyhound **bus station** at 10 N Pearl St, it's an easy walk to the **Convention and Visitors Bureau**, 550 Water St, suite 1000 (Mon–Fri 8am–5pm; ℡1-800/733-2668, ⓦwww.visitjacksonville.com). The **train station** is an awkward six miles northwest of downtown at 3570 Clifford Lane. The cheapest **accommodation** can be found at the motels on the city's perimeter, such as the *Comfort Suites*, 1180 Airport Rd (℡904/741-0505; ❸). Downtown, the *Hampton Inn*, 4690 Salisbury Rd (℡904/731-3555; ❹), is a decent option, as is the more scenic *Radisson Riverwalk Hotel*, 1515 Prudential Drive (℡904/396-5100; ❹). For **eating**, the best breakfast and lunch options can be found in and near the Jacksonville Landing Mall, at 2 Independence Drive. Check out *Biscotti's Expresso Café*, 3556 St Johns Ave (℡904/387-2060), or, on the south bank, *The Loop*, 4000 St Johns Ave (℡904/384-7301), which has good-priced pizzas. The *River City Brewing Co.*, 835 Museum Circle (℡904/398-2299), offers classy food, home-brewed beer, and live music.

Jacksonville's beaches

Traveling south from Jacksonville on I-95, then east on Hwy-202, you'll first hit **Ponte Vedra Beach**, whose crowd-free sands and million-dollar homes form one of the most exclusive communities in northeast Florida. A few miles north from here on Hwy-A1A is the much less snooty **Jacksonville Beach**. If you tire of watching the novice surfers, **Adventure Landing**, 1944 Beach Blvd (Feb–May & Sept–Nov Sun–Thurs 10am–11pm, Fri & Sat 10am–1am; ℡904/246-4386), offers an amusement park where each diversion is individually priced, like batting cages ($2), a water park ($22), and go-carts ($6). Two miles north of the old pier, the more commercialized **Neptune Beach** blurs into the identical-looking **Atlantic Beach**; both are more family-oriented, and are best visited for eating and socializing.

Practicalities

For **accommodation** at the Jacksonville Beach try the *Pelican Path B&B By the Sea*, 11 N 19th Ave (℡1-888/749-1177; ❺), which has a pool and bicycles, or the *Best Western Inn*, 305 N 1st St (℡904/249-4949; ❺). Good **eating options** at the beaches are *Harry's*, 1018 N 3rd St, Jacksonville Beach (℡904/247-8855), for its lively New Orleans atmosphere and Cajun recipes; *Ragtime Tap Room*, 207 Atlantic Blvd, Atlantic Beach (℡904/241-7877), where the locals line up every day to pick from the huge seafood menu; and *Sun Dog Diner*, 207 Atlantic Blvd, Neptune Beach (℡904/241-8221), with moderately-priced but ambitious lunches and dinners.

Central Florida

Encompassing a broad and fertile expanse between the east and west coasts, most of **Central Florida** was farming country when vacation-mania first struck the beachside strips. From the 1970s on, this picture of tranquility was shattered: no section of the state has been affected more dramatically by modern tourism. As a result, the most-visited part of Florida can also be one of the ugliest. A clutter of freeway interchanges, motels, and billboards arch around the sprawling city of **Orlando**, where a tourist-dollar chase of Gold Rush magnitude was sparked by **Walt Disney World**, the biggest and cleverest theme-park complex ever created. The rest of central Florida is quiet by comparison.

Orlando and the theme parks

ORLANDO, a quiet farming town in 1970, now welcomes more visitors than any other place in the state. The reason, of course, is **Walt Disney World**, which, along with **Universal Orlando**, **SeaWorld Orlando**, and a host of other attractions, in varying degrees of quality, pulls millions of people a year to a previously featureless plot of scrubland. Few people seek accommodation in Orlando proper, choosing instead to stay in one of the countless motels along **Hwy-192**, fifteen miles south of the city, or **International Drive**, five miles southwest. Despite enormous expansion over the last decade, the city itself remains free of the rabid commercialism that surrounds it.

Arrival and information

The **international airport** is nine miles south of downtown Orlando; you collect brochures and discount coupons at its official **information booth** (daily 7am–9pm). **Shuttle buses** (24hr; best prices offered by Mears

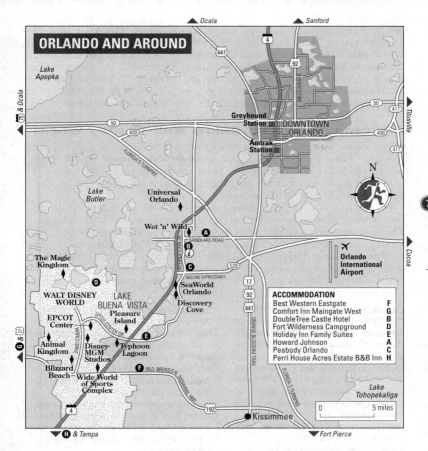

ORLANDO AND AROUND

▲ Ocala   ▲ Sanford

Lake Apopka

441
4
92
75 & Ocala
50
417
Greyhound Station
DOWNTOWN ORLANDO
50
408
408
Trusville
Amtrak Station
417

N

FLORIDA | Orlando and the theme parks

7

Lake Butler
Universal Orlando
Wet 'n' Wild
SANDLAKE ROAD
A
B
i
C
FLORIDA'S TURNPIKE
BEELINE EXPRESSWAY
SeaWorld Orlando
Discovery Cove
528
17
92
441
✈
Orlando International Airport

Cocoa

The Magic Kingdom
D
WALT DISNEY WORLD
LAKE BUENA VISTA
EPCOT Center
Pleasure Island
EPCOT CENTER DR.
WORLD DRIVE
Animal Kingdom
Disney-MGM Studios
Typhoon Lagoon
E
Blizzard Beach
Wide World of Sports Complex
IRLO BRONSON MEMORIAL HWY
F
192
4
G & I
ORANGE BLOSSOM TRAIL
FLORIDA'S TURNPIKE

ACCOMMODATION
Best Western Eastgate   F
Comfort Inn Maingate West   G
DoubleTree Castle Hotel   D
Fort Wilderness Campground   B
Holiday Inn Family Suites   E
Howard Johnson   A
Peabody Orlando   C
Perri House Acres Estate B&B Inn H

Lake Tohopekaliga
0   5 miles

● Kissimmee

▼ H & Tampa   ▼ Fort Pierce

Transportation Group (☎407/423-5566) run to any hotel on International Drive for a flat fee of $14, while a **taxi** to downtown, International Drive, or the motels on Hwy-192 will cost between $30 and $45. **Buses** and **trains** arrive, respectively downtown at the Greyhound terminal, 555 N John Young Parkway (☎407/292-3422), and the Amtrak station, 1400 Sligh Blvd (☎407/843-7611). The efficient **Official Information Center**, 8723 International Drive, suite 101 (daily 8am–7pm; ☎407/363-5872, ⓦwww.orlandoinfo.com), also has brochures and discount coupons.

Getting around the theme parks

You have to be determined to get to the theme parks without a car, but it can be done. Local Lynx **buses** (☎407/841-2279 or 1-800/344-LYNX, ⓦwww .golynx.com) converge at the downtown Orlando terminal between Central and Pine streets. Route #50 heads to Walt Disney World, though it's a somewhat patchy service and takes about an hour, while route #8 goes to International Drive. Along International Drive, between SeaWorld Orlando and Universal Orlando, the **I-Ride trolley service** (☎407/248-9590 or 1-866/243-7483,

@ www.iridetrolley.com) operates every fifteen minutes daily from 8am to 10.30pm, costing 75¢ one way. The pricier Mears Transportation Group runs private **shuttle buses** (T 407/423-5566) between the main accommodation areas, the airport, and Disney World, SeaWorld, and Universal ($10–13 roundtrip). Phone at least a day ahead to be picked up, and confirm a time for your return. **Taxis** are the best way to get around at night – try Yellow Cab (T 407/699-9999); rates begin at $3.75 for the first mile, plus $1.75 for each additional mile.

Accommodation outside Walt Disney World

If you're on a budget, or want to spend time visiting Universal Orlando and the other parks, you'd do best to stay **outside Walt Disney World**. Once you've decided to do so, location is pretty much irrelevant – the parks and attractions are so scattered that wherever you stay you'll spend a lot of time driving back and forth between them.

Competition is fierce, and quoted **rates** can often be negotiated down; independent travelers who show up on spec during the slow periods (Jan, May, and Sept) may well find some bargains. Motels line **Hwy-192** between Disney and Kissimmee (10–20min drive to Disney World). The chain hotels on **International Drive** (about 20min drive from Disney World) are a shade more upmarket, with good restaurants and shops within walking distance. Closest to Disney are the places around **Lake Buena Vista** (5–20min drive).

Best Western Eastgate 5565 W Hwy-192 T 407/396-0707 or 1-800/223-5361. Basic, comfortable, and extremely convenient to Disney, the *Best Western Eastgate* is sheltered from the noise of the highway by a small lake. **②**

Comfort Inn Maingate West 9330 W Hwy-192 T 407/424-8420 or 1-800/440-4473. This hotel's yellow exterior matches the bright, cheerful rooms. A pleasant, economical place to stay, six minutes west of Disney. **②**

DoubleTree Castle Hotel 8629 International Drive T 407/345-1511 or 1-800/952-2785, @ www.doubletreecastle.com. This elaborate theme hotel, complete with Renaissance music and medieval decor, offers all the luxuries, including complimentary chocolate chip cookies. **④**

Holiday Inn Family Suites 14500 Continental Gateway, Lake Buena Vista T 407/387-5437 or 1-877/387-5437, @ www.hifamilysuites.com. The leader in kid-friendly resorts, with bunk bed- and video game-equipped "Kidsuites," free food, and even a spa for the little ones. **⑤**

Howard Johnson 7050 Kirkman Rd T 407/351-2000 or 1-800/327-3808, @ www.howardjohnson-hotelorlando.com. Good-sized rooms, three pools, and free shuttle buses to the major theme parks make this a good base for those without a car. Very reasonable rates, too. **②**

Peabody Orlando 9801 International Drive T 407/352-4000 or 1-800/PEABODY, @ www.peabodyorlando.com. If money's no object, and you like in-room luxuries, access to a fitness center, and floodlit tennis courts, this one's for you. The Peabody Ducks parade through the lobby twice a day. **⑥**

Perri House Acres Estate B&B Inn 10417 Vista Oaks Court, Lake Buena Vista T 407/876-4830 or 1-800/780-4830, @ www.perrihouse.com. The incongruous presence of an eight-room bed-and-breakfast hidden on four wooded acres just a stone's throw from the opulent resorts of Disney is the perfect antidote to all the theme-park frenzy. **⑤**

Accommodation within Walt Disney World

Prices at the fabulously designed **Disney World resorts** (all T 401/939-7429, @ www.disneyworld) scattered around the complex are much higher – sometimes more than $300 per night – than you'll pay elsewhere. However, the benefits (top-notch facilities, free transportation, early access to the parks, brunch with Goofy) can make it worth the extra cash. Though rooms may be available at short notice during the quieter times, you should **book as far ahead** – nine months is not unreasonable – as possible. If you do arrive without reservations, the **Disney Information Center**, exit 350 off I-75, in Ocala (daily 9am–6pm; ☎352/854-0770) can offer discounts on rooms for that night.

A good option if you're **camping**, the *Fort Wilderness Campground* is set on a lovely 700-acre forested site near the Magic Kingdom. Here you can hook up your RV or pitch your tent for $35–82, or rent a six-berth cabin from $229, and still enjoy the privileges of being a Disney guest.

All-Star Resorts Four resorts in the Disney-MGM area near the Blizzard Beach water park, with themes based on sports, music, movies, and twentieth-century pop icons. The most affordable options in Disney, but still perfectly comfortable. **4**

Animal Kingdom Lodge Disney's newest and most spectacular luxury accommodation, where you can wake up to see African wildlife grazing outside your window. **7**

Port Orleans Resort Gaze from your wrought-iron balcony across the mini-New Orleans French Quarter re-created in this resort's courtyard, in Downtown Disney (see p.684). **6**

Wilderness Lodge This convincing re-creation of a backcountry lodge features a frontier log cabin and a wood-burning fire in the lobby. **7**

Walt Disney World

As significant as air-conditioning in making the state what it is today, **WALT DISNEY WORLD** turned a wedge of Florida farmland into one of the world's most lucrative vacation destinations. The immense and astutely planned empire also pushed the state's media profile through the roof: from being a down-at-the-heel mixture of cheap motels, retirement homes, and tacky alligator zoos, Florida suddenly, in 1971, became a showcase of modern international tourism.

Disney World is the pacesetter among theme parks. It goes way beyond Disneyland (see p.1127), which opened in Anaheim, California, in 1955, delivering escapism at its most technologically advanced and psychologically brilliant, across an area twice the size of Manhattan. Its four main theme parks are quite separate entities and, ideally, you should allow a full day for each. The **Magic Kingdom** is the Disney park of popular imagination, where Mickey mingles with the crowds – very much the park for kids, though at its high-tech best capable of thrilling even the most jaded of adults. Known for its giant, golfball-like geosphere, **EPCOT Center** is Disney's celebration of science and technology; this sprawling area involves a lot of walking, and may bore young children. **Disney–MGM Studios** suits almost everyone: its special effects are enjoyable even if you've never seen the movies they're based on. The newest of the four, Disney's **Animal Kingdom**, brings all manner of African and Asian wildlife to the theme-park setting.

Along with the main parks, other forms of entertainment have been created to keep people on Disney property for as long as possible. There are two excellent water parks, **Blizzard Beach** and **Typhoon Lagoon**, a sports complex called **Disney's Wide World of Sports**, and **Pleasure Island**, where you can eat, drink, and dance the night away.

The Magic Kingdom

The **Magic Kingdom** follows the formula established by California's Disneyland, dividing into several themed sections: **Tomorrowland**, **Frontierland**, **Fantasyland**, **Adventureland**, **Liberty Square**, and **Mickey's Toontown Fair**. Fantasyland and Mickey's Toontown Fair are very much for the kids, while the other lands, and in particular Tomorrowland and Frontierland, have the edgier rides. Some attractions are identical to their California forebears, while others are unique or greatly improved. In Tomorrowland, the old favorite **Space Mountain** is in essence an ordinary roller coaster, yet one whose total darkness makes every jump and jolt unexpected. **Splash Mountain** employs water to great effect, culminating in a stunning 52ft death-drop down a waterfall. **Big Thunder Mountain Railroad** puts you on board a runaway train, which hurtles through Gold Rush California in about three minutes. There's also the kid-orientated **The Barnstormer**, a milder attraction perfect for thrillseekers-in-training.

You don't have to be a roller-coaster junkie to enjoy the Magic Kingdom. Many of the best rides in the park rely on "AudioAnimatronic" characters – impressive vocal robots of Disney invention – for their appeal. The most up-to-date are seen in **The ExtraTERRORestrial Alien Encounter**, which will appeal especially to those who are fans of the *Alien* films, though the sensation of being brushed by unseen things in the dark may be too close an encounter for others. A wonderful visual treat is **The Timekeeper**, where you're taken on a trip through time by a zany robot (whose voice is provided by Robin Williams).

Elsewhere, make time for the **Haunted Mansion**, a seriously spooky ghost ride with spectacular holograms, the leisurely **Jungle Cruise**, through waterfalls and cannibal camps in Africa's most "dangerous" territory, and **Pirates of the Caribbean**, the classic boat ride around a pirate-infested Caribbean island.

Fantasyland, the centerpiece of which is **Cinderella's Castle**, a stunning pseudo-Rhineland palace, is very much old-style Disney, with a lot of stuff for kids. For adults, the most endearing ride is the very-1970s **It's a Small World**, a bizarre boat jaunt advocating brotherly love.

EPCOT Center

Even before the Magic Kingdom opened, Walt Disney was developing plans for the **EPCOT** (Experimental Prototype Community of Tomorrow) **Center**,

---

Information, tickets, and how to beat the crowds

For general Disney World **information**, call ☎407/824-4321, or visit ⓦdisney-world.com. **Tickets** cost $53.25 (children aged 3–9 $42.60), and allow unlimited access to all shows and rides in one park only, for that day only. Park Hopper passes gain you entry to all four parks, in any combination, as many times as you like, over any four or five days. Four-day passes cost $211.94 ($169.34 for kids, as above), and five-day passes cost $243.89 ($195.96). A Park Hopper PLUS pass, available for five ($275.86/$221.53), six ($307.81/$247.10), or seven ($339.75/$272.65) days, gives you the same options as the Park Hopper pass, but also includes admission to the water parks, Pleasure Island, or Disney's Wide World of Sports complex, depending on the number of days on your ticket. Unused days and options never expire. If possible, buy tickets well in advance, over the phone, on the Internet, or at a Disney store. If you must buy them at the gate, arrive at least an hour before opening time. The **parking** lots cost $7 a day, but are free if you're staying at a Walt Disney World resort.

Each park is generally **open** daily from 9am to between 6pm and midnight, depending on the time of year; pick up the current schedule when you arrive. Note that Disney's Animal Kingdom closes at 5pm. At its worst, waiting times for the most popular rides can be well over an hour. The best way to **beat the crowds** is to use Disney's FastPass system. Place your admission ticket into a machine at the entrance of the attraction; the machine returns it with another ticket that gives you a time to return to the attraction, usually about two hours later. When that time rolls around, you simply show up, hand your new ticket to the attendant and scoot to the front of the line. Another good tactic upon arrival is to rush to the far end of the park and work backwards, or to head straight for the big rides, getting them out of the way before the mid-afternoon crush.

conceived in 1966 as a real community experimenting with the new ideas and materials of the technologically advancing US. The idea failed to shape up as Disney had envisioned, though: EPCOT didn't open its gates until 1982, when global recession and ecological concerns had put a damper on the belief in the infallibility of science. One drawback of this park is simply its immense size: it's twice as big as the Magic Kingdom, and very sapping on the feet.

The unmissable 180ft geosphere (unlike a semicircular geodesic *dome*, the geosphere is completely round) sits in the heart of **Future World**, which keeps close to EPCOT's original concept of exploring the history and researching the future of agriculture, transport, energy, and communication. Future World is divided into eight pavilions (including the geosphere, with its Spaceship Earth ride), each corporate-sponsored, and featuring own rides, films, interactive computer exhibits, and games. The best of the attractions are **Test Track**, a radical combination of simulator and switchback ride in which you test a high-speed car of the future; **Cranium Command**, where an AudioAnimatronic character is detailed to control the various functions of a 12-year-old boy's brain – a good mix of Disney imagination and humor; and the **3D** cinematic thrill of **Honey, I Shrunk the Audience**. The newest pavilion, **Mission: SPACE**, is an astronaut-like adventure to Mars, and looks set to become one of the park's highlights.

Occupying the largest area in the park is the **World Showcase**, with eleven different "countries" represented by recognizable national landmarks or stereotypical scenes. The **restaurants** here are among the best in Disney World, and it's a great place to watch the spectacular nighttime sound- and light-show, **IllumiNations: Reflections of Earth**.

Disney-MGM Studios

When the Disney corporation began making films and TV shows for adults – most notably *Who Framed Roger Rabbit?* in 1988 – they also set about devising a theme park to entertain adults as much as kids. Buying the rights to the Metro-Goldwyn-Mayer (MGM) oeuvre of films and TV shows, Disney acquired a vast repertoire of instantly familiar images to mold into shows and

The world of Walt Disney

When the brilliant illustrator and animator Walt Disney devised the world's first theme park, California's **Disneyland** (see p.1127), he left himself with no control over the hotels and restaurants that quickly engulfed it, preventing growth and erasing profits Disney felt were rightly his. Determined not to let that happen again, the Disney corporation secretly bought up 27,500 acres of central Florida farmland, acquiring by the late Sixties a site a hundred times bigger than Disneyland. With the promise of a jobs bonanza for Florida, the state legislature gave the corporation the rights of any major municipality – empowering it to lay roads, enact building codes, and enforce the law with its own security force.

Walt Disney World's first "land," the Magic Kingdom, which opened in 1971, was a huge success. Unveiled in 1982, the far more ambitious EPCOT Center represented the first major break from cartoon-based escapism – but its rose-tinted look at the future received a mixed response. Partly due to this, and to some bad management decisions, the Disney empire (Disney himself died in 1966) faced bankruptcy by the mid-1980s. Since then, the corporation has sprung back from the abyss, and it now, under CEO Michael Eisner, steers a tight and competitive business ship. It may trade in fantasy, but where money matters, the Disney Corporation's nose is firmly in the real world.

rides. Opening in 1990, **Disney-MGM Studios** overshadowed the opening of Florida's Universal Studios (see opposite), and at the same time found an extra use for the real film studios based here. On a tour, the people you'll see laboring over storyboards aren't there for show; they really are making films.

Most of the things to do at MGM take the form of rides or shows, and there are fewer exhibit-style attractions when compared with the other Disney parks. Thrill-seekers will be more than happy with the thirteen-story drop in **The Twilight Zone Tower of Terror** – enough to put you off elevators for life – or **Rock 'n' Roller Coaster**, which, with a 2.8-second zero to sixty miles per hour launch, is Disney World's wildest ride.

Don't miss the half-hour **Studios Backlot Tour**, climaxing with the dramatic special effects on the *Catastrophe Canyon* movie set: the interest level fluctuates, but you won't get your money's worth if you miss it. The same applies to **The Magic of Disney Animation**, an enlightening trip through the animation studios, and **Jim Henson's Muppet Vision 3D** show – enormous fun, with some great surprises.

The most popular of the live shows is **Who Wants to be a Millionaire – Play It!**, which recreates the TV show with admirable accuracy, and where the audience plays for a three-day Disney Line cruise to the Bahamas. Also worthwhile, **The Indiana Jones Epic Stunt Spectacular** re-enacts and explains many of the action-packed set pieces from the Steven Spielberg/George Lucas films.

Disney's Animal Kingdom

Disney's Animal Kingdom was opened in 1998 as an animal-conservation theme park with Disney's patented over-the-top twist. The park is divided into six major "lands" – **Africa**, **Camp Minnie-Mickey**, **DinoLand USA**, **Discovery Island**, **Rafiki's Planet Watch**, and **Asia** – each with its own mock-authentic ambiance, largely the result of the versatility of concrete, which is colored, imprinted upon, and formed into an endless variety of shapes.

The best-realized attraction is **Kilimanjaro Safaris**, where a jeep transport takes you through what feels very much like real African wildlands (local oak trees have been trimmed to look like African acacias), viewing giraffes, zebras, elephants, lions, gazelles, and rhinos, as well as taking part in anti-poacher maneuvers. Crossing over to **Asia**, visitors walk through dense vegetation and village ruins to see giant fruit bats, Asian birds, and tigers in the **Maharajah Jungle Trek**, while in **Africa's Pangani Forest Exploration Trail**, a troop of lowland gorillas are definitely worth a look. The park's main thrill ride is in DinoLand USA: **DINOSAUR**, a roller coaster-style vehicle that makes small drops and short stops in the dark as dinosaurs pop out of nowhere and roar.

The remainder of the park requires no more than casual exploration. The *Flights of Wonder* bird show exhibits parrots, hawks, and other unusual birds, while classic Disney characters sign autographs in **Camp Minnie-Mickey**, where you can also catch the *Festival of the Lion King*, a participatory production of upbeat music with some nifty acrobatics, loosely based on its namesake film.

Universal Orlando

For some years, it seemed that TV and film production would move away from California to Florida, which, with its lower taxes and cheaper labor, was more amenable. The opening of Universal Studios in 1990 appeared to confirm that trend. So far, though, for various reasons, Florida has not proved to be a fully realistic alternative. Even so, this hasn't stopped the Universal enclave here, now known as **Universal Orlando**, off I-4, half a mile north of exits 29B or 30A (park opens daily at 9am, closing times vary; one-day pass $53.33, children 3–9 $45.75, under-3s free; two-day pass $103.26/$89.41; three-day pass $119.23/$103.26; parking $8; ☎1-407/363-8000, ⓦwww.uescape.com), from becoming a major player in the Orlando theme-park arena. Though Disney World still commands the lion's share of attention, Universal has siphoned off many visitors with **Universal Studios**' thrilling movie-themed rides, the high-tech, special-effects–laden **Islands of Adventure**, and **CityWalk**, an earthier lure for nightlife dollars than Downtown Disney (see "Nightlife and entertainment," p.684). Furthermore, Universal has achieved full-fledged resort status with its three luxurious on-site **hotels**: *Portofino Bay*, *Hard Rock*, and the *Royal Pacific Resort* (all three ☎1-888/322-5541, ⓦwww.universalorlando.com; ⓻–⓽).

Universal Studios

Like its competitor Disney-MGM, Universal is a working studio, filling more than four hundred acres with the latest in TV and movie production technology. Unlike MGM, there's more emphasis here on movie-related rides than backstage shows. For sheer excitement, nothing in the park matches **Back to the Future The Ride**, a bone-shaking flight-simulator trip from 2015 to the Ice Age. Next best is **Earthquake – The Big One**, which gives you an intensely claustrophobic two minutes of terror as you experience what it's like to be caught on a subway train when an 8.3 Richter-scale quake hits. Along the same lines, **Twister…Ride It Out** is a suffocating but gripping experience in which you stand beside an imitation tornado.

Of the other attractions, **Terminator 2: 3D Battle Across Time** offers second-to-none special effects (for maximum enjoyment, sit in the middle of the auditorium, five or six rows from the front); **Jaws**, a boat trip through shark-infested waters, owes its success to anticipation of horror; and **E.T. Adventure** is an undulating ride on pretend bikes to save E.T.'s home planet – be sure to listen when the little alien says goodbye.

If you want to watch a live show, opt for the two-man *Universal Horror Make-Up Show*, which reveals movie-makeup secrets amidst comic repartee, or *Animal Planet Live!*, featuring amusing tricks by household and exotic animals.

Islands of Adventure

Islands of Adventure is Orlando's leader in state-of-the-art, edge-of-your-seat thrill rides. Though there are plenty of diversions for the less daring, these rides are what brings the crowds, and long lines are typical for many of them (though they do thin out as the evening goes on). Use the **Universal Express** system – akin to Disney's FastPass (see p.678) – to avoid waiting in lines for the most popular rides.

The park is really five superb miniparks – **Marvel Super Hero Island**, **Toon Lagoon**, **Jurassic Park**, **The Lost Continent**, and **Seuss Landing** – all surrounding a lagoon. The very best of the rides is also one of the newest: **The Amazing Adventures of Spider-Man**, which uses every trick imaginable –

The Orlando Flexticket

Universal Orlando, SeaWorld Orlando, and Wet 'n Wild (a water park) have teamed up to create a pass that permits access to each park over a period of fourteen consecutive days. The **Orlando Flexticket** (as it's known) costs $187.39 (ages 3–9 $152.25), or $223.77/$187.56, including Tampa's Busch Gardens (see p.687), with a free shuttle from Orlando to Busch Gardens.

3D, sensory stimuli, motion simulation, and more – to spirit you into another dimension. **Dueling Dragons** may be the next most exciting ride: twin roller coasters ("Fire" and "Ice" – separate lines for each) engineered to provide harrowing near misses with each other. Here, even more so than on other roller coasters, the front seats provide the greatest thrills. Another exciting entry is the **Incredible Hulk Coaster**, with its catapult start, seven full inversions, and two precipitous plunges. **Doctor Doom's Fearfall** provides a panoramic view of the park, but the very short controlled drop, during which you experience a few seconds of weightlessness, is anticlimactic. In a similar vein, **Jurassic Park River Adventure** is a generally tame river-raft trip, where the only thing to shout about is an 85-foot drop.

Offerings for kids include **Dudley Do-Right's Ripsaw Falls** and **Popeye & Bluto's Bilge-Rat Barges**, both good for getting a midday drenching; **Triceratops Discovery Trail**, a petting zoo; **Jurassic Park Discovery Center**, a dinosaur learning center; and the whole of Seuss Landing, where everything is based on Dr Seuss characters. There's one **live performance** offered throughout the day: *The Eighth Voyage of Sindbad* stunt show, where the set, stunts, and pyrotechnics are as good as the jokes are bad.

SeaWorld Orlando and Discovery Cove

SeaWorld Orlando, at Sea Harbor Drive, near the intersection of I-4 and the Bee Line Expressway, is the cream of Florida's sizable crop of marine parks, and should not be missed; allocate a full day to see it all (daily 9am–7pm, longer hours in summer; $55.33, ages 3–9 $45.74; ☎407/351-3600 or 1-800/4-ADVENTURE, ⓦwww.seaworld.com). The big event is the *Shamu Adventure Show* – thirty minutes of tricks performed by a playful killer whale (you'll get drenched if you're sitting in the first fourteen rows of the stadium). Also, try not to miss the sea lion extravaganza, *Clyde and Seamore Take Pirate Island*. The **Wild Arctic** complex, complete with artificial snow and ice, brings you close to beluga whales, walruses, and polar bears, while a simulated ride takes you on a stomach-churning helicopter flight through an Arctic blizzard.

The park's first thrill ride, **Journey to Atlantis**, is part fantasy, part waterslide, part roller coaster, and has a sixty-foot drop (be prepared to get very wet). Much more exhilarating, however, is **Kraken**, a roller coaster that flings you around at speeds of up to 65mph, free-flying and looping-the-loop.

With substantially less razzmatazz, plenty of smaller aquariums and displays offer a wealth of information about the undersea world. Among the highlights, **Penguin Encounter** re-creates Antarctica, with scores of the waddling, flightless birds scampering over an iceberg; the occupants of the **Dolphin Pool** assert their advanced intellect by flapping their fins and soaking passersby; and **Shark Encounter** includes a walk through a glass-walled and -roofed tunnel, offering the closest eye-contact you're ever likely to have with sharks and other scary predators of the deep.

Discovery Cove, next to SeaWorld Orlando on Central Florida Parkway (daily 8am–5.30pm; $137.38 without dolphin swim, $243.88 with dolphin swim; ☎407/370-1280 or 1-877/4-DISCOVERY, ⓦwww.discoverycove .com), is an exclusive venture, limiting visitors to about a thousand a day (reserve well in advance). The main reason for coming here is to swim and play with the dolphins, while other activities include snorkeling up to sharks and barracudas behind a clear partition, wading in a pool full of sting rays (all with their stingers safely removed), and feeding tropical birds. Note that the admission charge includes seven-day access to SeaWorld Orlando.

Orlando's water parks

Of the two Disney-owned **water parks**, **Blizzard Beach**, north of the *All-Star Resorts* (see "Accommodation within Walt Disney World," p.676) on World Drive (daily 10am–5pm; slightly longer hours in summer; $33.02, children 3–9 $26.63; ℡407/560-5408), is the most creative, based on the fantasy that a hapless entrepreneur has opened a ski resort in Florida and the entire thing has started to melt. The star of the show is the **Summit Plummet**, which shoots you down a 120ft vertical drop at more than fifty miles per hour. Gentler rides include toboggan-style slalom courses and raft rides. As well as the slides, **Typhoon Lagoon**, just south of Pleasure Island (daily 10am–5pm; slightly longer hours in summer; $33.02, children 3–9 $26.63; ℡407/560-6296), features geysers, a rainforest, a huge surfing pool, and a shark reef, where you can snorkel among tropical fish. **Wet 'n Wild**, 6200 International Drive (daily 10am–5pm; longer hours in summer; $31.95, children 3–9 $25.95; ℡407/351-9453 or 1-800/992-9453, ⓦwww .wetnwildorlando.com), defends itself admirably in the face of the Disney competition, with a range of excellent slides including the challenging seven-story **Bomb Bay** and the almost vertical **Der Stuka**. Lines are shorter here than at the Disney water parks.

Eating in the Orlando area

Downtown and its environs hold the pick of the locals' **eating** haunts; most visitors, however, head for International Drive's inexpensive all-day buffets and gourmet restaurants. There's a strict embargo on taking food into any of the theme parks, where the best restaurants are in **EPCOT's World Showcase**, particularly the French-, Japanese-, Moroccan-, and Mexican-themed establishments.

Bahama Breeze 8849 International Drive ℡407/248-2499. Decent Caribbean food in an upbeat atmosphere. Dinner only.

Café TuTu Tango 8625 International Drive ℡407/248-2222. Painters and sculptors work as you dine on superb pan-Asian, New World, and Mediterranean food. The walls are decorated with artworks for sale.

The Globe 25 Wall St Plaza ℡407/849-9904. This is a perfect place for inexpensive Nouveau American snacks and light meals. Eat sushi next door at the *Tuk Tuk Room*.

Le Coq au Vin 4800 S Orange Ave ℡407/851-6980. French restaurant with surprisingly low prices for top-notch food. Closed Monday.

Ming Court 9188 International Drive ℡407/351-9988. An exceptional Chinese restaurant, with dim sum and sushi available. Not as costly as you might expect.

Numero Uno 2499 S Orange Ave ℡407/841-3840. Inexpensive downtown Cuban restaurant, serving dishes such as black beans, grouper, and paella. Closed Sunday.

Panera Bread 227 N Eola Drive ℡407/481-1060. One of a national chain, with a wonderful array of baked goods, soups, salads, and sandwiches.

Race Rock 8986 International Drive ℡407 248-9876. A race-car-themed restaurant serving American staples like burgers and milkshakes, all at super-reasonable prices.

Roy's 7760 W Sand Lake Rd ℡407/352-4844. Founded in Hawaii, *Roy's* offers innovative Hawaiian fusion cuisine.

White Wolf Café 1829 N Orange Ave ℡407/895-5590. Down-to-earth café/antique store known for creative sandwiches and generous salads.

Nightlife and entertainment

Though you'll probably be so exhausted from a long day at the parks that boozing and dancing with thousands of others will be the last thing on your mind, the Orlando area is bursting with themed **nightspots** of every persuasion, from medieval banquets to piano bars and country-and-western clubs. It's all relentlessly good, clean fun, sanitized to the hilt.

From around 9pm, each Disney World park holds some kind of closing-time bash, usually involving fireworks and fountains. There's also **Pleasure Island**, exit 26B off I-4 (part of the complex of shops, restaurants, and entertainment venues that comprise **Downtown Disney**; ⓦ www.downtowndisney.com), a remake of an abandoned island, whose pseudo-warehouses are the setting for bars and nightclubs (daily 10am–7pm; free before 7pm, after 7pm $21.25 gains access to all bars and clubs). The most enjoyable are the **Comedy Warehouse** and the **Adventurers' Club**, loosely based on a 1930s gentlemen's club. Take ID (under-18s must be accompanied by a parent or guardian, while some clubs are 21 and up) and a fat wallet.

Not to be outdone by Disney, Universal Orlando has come up with **CityWalk**, Universal Boulevard (ⓣ 407/363-8000, ⓦ www.citywalkorlando .com), thirty acres of restaurants, live music, dance clubs, and shops, wedged between Universal Studios and Islands of Adventure. Hipper than anything Disney has to offer, CityWalk is also much better value ($8.95 for all-night access to every club, plus free parking after 6pm). Head to **Bob Marley – A Tribute to Freedom** for live reggae; **CityJazz** for a cooler, more sophisticated ambiance, with all types of jazz, funk, and soul; the **Latin Quarter** restaurant for Latino beats; and **the groove** for a full-fledged nightclub.

Despite the closure of the complex of bars and restaurants called Church Street Station, **downtown Orlando** continues to be a good alternative for nighttime entertainment, with most of the after-dark action focused along **Orange Avenue**, at clubs like *The Social*, no. 54 (for alt-rock, grunge, and the like), and the chic, South Beach–styled *Sky 60*, no.64.

The West Coast

In the three hundred miles from the state's southern tip to the junction with the Panhandle (see p.697), Florida's **West Coast** embraces all the extremes. Buzzing, youthful towns rise behind placid fishing hamlets; mobbed holiday strips are just minutes from desolate swamplands, and world-class art collections vie with glitzy theme parks. Surprises are plentiful, though the coast's one constant is proximity to the Gulf of Mexico – and sunset views rivaled only by those of the Florida Keys.

The west coast's largest city, **Tampa**, has more to offer than its corporate towers initially suggest – not least the exemplary nightlife scene in the Cuban enclave of **Ybor City**, and the Busch Gardens theme park. For the mass of visitors, though, the Tampa Bay area begins and ends with the **St Petersburg beaches**, whose miles of sea and sand are undiluted vacation territory. South of Tampa, a string of barrier-island beaches run the length of the Gulf, and the mainland towns that provide access to them – such as Sarasota and Fort Myers – have enough to warrant a stop. Inland, the wilderness of the **Everglades** is explorable on simple walking trails, by canoeing, or by spending the night at backcountry campgrounds, with only the gators for company.

Tampa

A small, stimulating city with an infectious, upbeat mood, **TAMPA**, the business hub of the west coast, is well worth a stop. As one of the major beneficiaries of the flood of people and money into Florida, Tampa boasts an impressive cultural infrastructure envied by many larger rivals. In addition to its fine **museums** and **Busch Gardens**, one of the most popular theme parks in the state, the city holds, in the Cuban-influenced **Ybor City**, just northeast of the city center, the west coast's hippest and most culturally eclectic quarter.

Tampa began as a small settlement beside a US Army base that was built in the 1820s to keep an eye on the Seminoles. In the 1880s, the railroad arrived, and the Hillsborough River, on which the city stands, was dredged to allow seagoing vessels to dock. Tampa became a booming port, simultaneously acquiring a major tobacco industry as thousands of Cubans moved north from Key West to the new cigar factories of neighboring Ybor City. The Depression ended the economic surge, but the port remained one of the busiest in the country and tempered Tampa's postwar decline. Today, little seems to stand in the way of Tampa's continued emergence as a forward-thinking and financially secure community.

Arrival and information

Tampa's **airport** (℡813/870-8700, Ⓦwww.tampaairport.com) is five miles northwest of downtown: local HART bus #30 is the least costly connection (Mon–Fri 4.45am–9pm every 30min, weekends less frequent 6.30am–9pm; $1.25). **Taxis** (try United ℡813/253-2424) to downtown or a Busch Boulevard motel cost $15–35; to St Petersburg or the beaches, $35–40. Greyhound **buses** arrive downtown at 610 Polk St (℡813/229-2174); trains at 601 N Nebraska Ave (℡813/221-7600).

The downtown **Visitor Information Center**, 615 Channelside Drive, suite 108A (Mon–Sat 9.30am–5.30pm, Sun 11am–5pm; ℡813/226-0293 or 1-800/44-TAMPA, Ⓦwww.visittampabay.com), and the **Ybor City Visitor Information Center**, 1600 E Eighth Ave, suite B104 (Mon–Sat 10am–6pm, Sun noon–6pm; ℡813/241-8838, Ⓦwww.ybor.org), give out useful leaflets and maps.

Although both downtown Tampa and Ybor City are easily covered on foot, to travel between them without a car you'll need to use the HART **local buses** ($1.25, one-day pass $3, three-day pass $9; ℡813/254-4278, Ⓦwww.hartline.org) or the TECO Line **Streetcar System** ($1.25; ℡813/254-4278, Ⓦwww.tecolinestreetcar.org), a vintage replica streetcar which runs between downtown and Ybor several times an hour daily until 10pm on weekdays, and until 2am on Fridays and Saturdays. Useful HART bus routes are #8 to Ybor City, #5 or #39 to Busch Gardens, #6 to the Museum of Science and Industry, and #30 to the airport.

Accommodation

Tampa is not generously supplied with low-cost **accommodation**; you'll almost certainly save money by staying in St Petersburg (see p.688) or at the beaches (see p.689). There are some good deals, though, at the motels along Busch Boulevard, six miles north of town.

Best Western All Suites 301 University Center Drive, behind Busch Gardens ℡813/971-8930. A reasonable base for seeing the city by car, and so close to Busch Gardens that the parrots escape into their trees. Features a happy hour every afternoon and free breakfast each morning. ❹

Days Inn Busch Gardens/Maingate 2901 E
Busch Blvd ☎813/933-6471. The closest hotel to
Busch Gardens, the *Days Inn* has a 24hr restaurant
and is within walking distance of plenty of others. ❷
Don Vincente de Ybor Historic Inn 1915
Avenida Republica de Cuba ☎813/241-4545 or 1-
866/206-4545, ⓦwww.donvincente.com. A luxurious B&B option in Ybor City. Features sixteen
suites, a fine restaurant, and a cigar and martini
bar that has live entertainment Thursday and
Friday nights. ❺
Gram's Place 3109 N Ola Ave ☎813/221-0596,
ⓦwww.grams-inn-tampa.com. This laid-back inn
offers both private rooms – all themed in different
musical styles – and youth-hostel-style accommodation. $15–25 for a dorm bed; private rooms ❸.
Hilton Garden 1700 E Ninth Ave ☎813/769-
9267, ⓦtampaybborcity.gardeninn.com.
Comfortable digs, even if the decor is a little sterile
to be in the heart of Tampa's most historically rich
neighborhood. ❺
Radisson Riverwalk 200 N Ashley Drive
☎813/223-2222, ⓦwww.radisson.com/tampafl
_riverwalk. Very convenient downtown location,
nicely situated on the banks of the Hillsborough
River. ❹

Downtown Tampa

Of the many futuristic highrise buildings in downtown Tampa, none better
reflects the city's cultural striving than the highly regarded **Tampa Museum
of Art**, on the banks of the Hillsborough River at 600 N Ashley Drive
(Tues–Sat 10am–5pm, third Thurs of every month 10am–8pm, Sun
11am–5pm; $7; ☎813/274-8130, ⓦwww.tampamuseum.com). Specializing in
classical antiques and twentieth-century American art, the museum cleverly
blends selections from the permanent modern collection with prime loaned
specimens of recent US painting, photography, and sculpture.

From the Museum of Art, you'll see the silver minarets and cupolas on the
far side of the river, sprouting from the main building of the University of
Tampa. These architectural ornaments adorn what was formerly the 500-room
Tampa Bay Hotel, financed by steamship and railroad magnate Henry B.
Plant. To reach it, walk across the river on Kennedy Boulevard and descend the
steps into Plant Park.

The structure is as bizarre a sight today as it was when it opened in 1891.
Since the Civil War, Plant had been buying up bankrupt railroads, steadily inching his way into Florida to meet his steamships unloading at Tampa's harbor.
Eventually, he became rich enough to put his fantasies of creating the world's
most luxurious hotel into practice. However, lack of care for the fittings and
Plant's death in 1899 hastened the hotel's transformation from the last word in
comfort to a pile of crumbling plaster. The city bought it in 1905 and leased it
to Tampa University 23 years later. In one wing, the **Henry B. Plant
Museum**, 401 W Kennedy Blvd (Tues–Sat 10am–4pm, Sun noon–4pm; $5;
☎813/254-1891, ⓦwww.plantmuseum.com), holds what's left of the hotel's
original furnishings.

In Tampa's dockland area, a mile or so southeast of the *Tampa Bay Hotel*, the
splendid **Florida Aquarium**, 701 Channelside Drive (daily 9.30am–5pm;
$15; ☎813/273-4000, ⓦwww.flaquarium.org), houses lavish displays of
Florida's fresh- and saltwater habitats, from springs and swamps to beaches and
coral reefs. Animal residents include an impressive variety of fish, birds, otters,
turtles, and alligators.

Ybor City

In 1886, as soon as Henry Plant's ships had ensured a regular supply of Havana
tobacco into Tampa, cigar magnate Don Vincente Martínez Ybor cleared a
patch of scrubland three miles northeast of present-day downtown Tampa and
laid the foundations of **YBOR CITY**. About twenty thousand migrants,
mostly Cuban, settled here and created a Latin American enclave, producing

the top-class, hand-rolled cigars that made Tampa the "**Cigar Capital of the World**." However, mass production, the popularity of cigarettes, and the Depression proved a fatal combination for skilled cigar-makers: as unemployment struck, Ybor City's tight-knit blocks of cobbled streets and redbrick buildings became surrounded by drab, low-rent neighborhoods.

In the midst of a revival, Ybor City buzzes with tourists, and at night the atmosphere reaches carnival proportions, especially on the weekends. The town is trendy and culturally diverse, yet its Cuban roots are immediately apparent, and explanatory background texts adorn many buildings. The **Ybor City State Museum**, 1818 Ninth Ave (daily 9am–5pm; $2; ☎813/247-6323, Ⓦwww.ybormuseum.org), helps you grasp the main points of Ybor City's creation and its multiethnic make-up. The museum also offers cigar-rolling demonstrations (Fri–Sun 10am–1pm) and historic walking tours (Sat 10.30am). The old cigar-rolling factory between 13th and 14th streets and Eighth and Ninth avenues, now called **Ybor Square**, is an office block essentially closed to the public. Standing on the factory's steps in 1893, the Cuban poet and independence fighter José Martí called for money, machetes, and manpower for the country's anti-Spanish struggles. Expatriate cigar workers responded by contributing ten percent of their earnings.

Busch Gardens and the Museum of Science and Industry

Busch Gardens, located two miles east of I-275, or two miles west of I-75, exit 54, at 3000 E Busch Blvd (daily 10am–6pm; $55.58, children $45.95; parking $7; ☎1-888/800-5447, Ⓦwww.buschgardenstampabay.com) is one of Florida's most popular theme parks, offering some of the fastest, largest, most nerve-jangling roller coasters in the country, incongruously set in an interpretation of Colonial-era Africa. A sedate pseudo-steam train or cable car journey allows inspection of a variety of African wildlife, but by far the most popular of the twenty-odd rides are the roller coasters: **Gwazi**, a double wooden coaster that pits the two cars against each other in a race to finish first; **Montu**, where your legs dangle precariously in mid-air; and the devastating and enormous **Kumba**. For those weary of the G-forces, the water rides **Stanley Falls** and **Congo River Rapids** are a refreshing alternative on a hot afternoon, as are the two free cups of Budweiser beer allocated to each adult visitor.

Two miles northeast of Busch Gardens, at 4801 E Fowler Ave, the colossal **Museum of Science and Industry** or MOSI (daily 9am, closing times seasonal; $14.95 including IMAX movie; ☎813/987-6100, Ⓦwww.mosi.org), deals with topics such as health, the environment, and outer space through hands-on activities and a program of shows. Plan your day around the **Challenger Learning Center** (more space adventure where you can defy the laws of gravity), the 75mph **Gulf Coast Hurricane**, and the **IMAX** shows.

Eating

There are plenty of good places to **eat** in Tampa, with a huge concentration of lively restaurants in Ybor City.

Bernini 1702 Seventh Ave, Ybor City ☎813/248-0099. In the lovely old Bank of Ybor City, an Italian joint serving up wood-fired pizza and pasta.
Big City Tavern 1600 E Eighth Ave, Ybor City ☎813/247-3000. Formerly the Centro Español

social club, the *Big City Tavern* offers American cuisine spiced with plenty of ginger and other Asian influences, in an atmospheric dining room.
C'Est La Vie 200 E Madison St ☎813/221-4748. At this good French bakery, there's coffee and

croissants in the morning or quiche and baguettes at lunchtime. Unusually for a downtown eatery, it's open Sundays.

Cephas 1701 E Fourth Ave, Ybor City ☎813/247-9022. A funky Jamaican restaurant offering jerk chicken and curried goat, chicken, and fish.

Columbia 2117 E Seventh Ave, Ybor City ☎813/248-4961, ⓦwww.columbiarestaurant.com. A Tampa – and tourist – institution, the city's oldest restaurant serves fine Spanish and Cuban

food. It also offers flamenco dancing six nights a week. Reservations recommended.

Joffrey's Coffee House 1616 Seventh Ave, Ybor City ☎813/248-5282. The delectable aromas of fruit, coffee, and chocolate are always thick in the air at this reasonably priced coffeehouse.

Shells 11010 N 30th St ☎813/977-8456. Convenient to the hotels near Busch Gardens, this cheap and cheerful seafood restaurant serves consistently good fresh fish.

Nightlife and entertainment

Some recent developments – Channelside, downtown next to the Florida Aquarium, and the International Plaza and Bay Street shopping mall and entertainment complex, near the airport at the junction of West Shore and Boy Scout boulevards – have begun to challenge Ybor City as Tampa's **nightlife** focus. The free *Weekly Planet* (ⓦwww.weeklyplanet.com) has **listings**, as does the Thursday *Tampa Tribune*.

Amphitheater 1609 E Seventh Ave, Ybor City ☎813/248-2331, ⓦwww.amphitheateryborn.com. A vast, elaborate nightclub, playing everything from retro to techno. A good spot for a big night out.

Blue Martini at the International Plaza's Bay Street ☎813/873-2583. Good-looking crowd, slightly older than you'll find in Ybor, at this trendy lounge bar.

Green Iguana 1708 E Seventh Ave, Ybor City ☎813/248-9555. Rock bands play nightly, and DJs keep the young crowd very much in the party mood.

Side Splitters 12938 N Dale Mabry Hwy ☎813/960-1197, ⓦwww.sidesplitterscomedy.com. One of the best comedy clubs in the area.

Skipper's Smokehouse 910 Skipper Rd ☎813/971-0666. Blues and reggae rule at this family-oriented live music venue.

Tampa Theatre 711 Franklin St ☎813/274-8981, ⓦwww.tampatheatre.org. Foreign-language, classic, and cult films shown in an atmospheric 1920s theater. Tickets $8.

St Petersburg

Situated on the eastern edge of the Pinellas Peninsula, a bulky thumb of land poking between Tampa Bay and the Gulf of Mexico, **ST PETERSBURG** is a world away from Tampa, even though the two cities are just twenty miles apart. Declared the healthiest place in the US in 1885, St Petersburg wasted no time in wooing the recuperating and the retired, at one point putting five thousand green benches on its streets to take the weight off elderly legs. Although it remains a mecca for the retired, the city has worked hard to attract young blood, as well. In addition to rejuvenating the pier, which now offers something for all ages, St Petersburg's diverse selection of museums and plethora of art galleries have contributed to its emergence as one of Florida's richest cultural centers. Most remarkable of all, the town has acquired a major collection of works by Salvador Dalí.

The **Salvador Dalí Museum**, 1000 S 3rd St (Mon–Sat 9.30am–5.30pm, Thurs 9.30am–8pm, Sun noon–5.30pm; $12.50, Thurs after 5pm $5; ☎727/823-3767, ⓦwww.salvadordalimuseum.org), stores more than a thousand paintings from the collection of a Cleveland industrialist, A. Reynolds Morse, who struck up a friendship with the artist in the 1940s. **Free tours** (given whenever there are sufficient people) trace a chronological path around the works, from the artist's early experiments with Impressionism and Cubism to the seminal Surrealist canvas *The Disintegration of the Persistence of Memory*.

Once you've done Dalí, the quarter-mile-long **pier**, jutting from the end of 2nd Avenue North, is the town's central focus. The pier often hosts browsable arts-and-crafts exhibitions, and the inverted-pyramid-like building at its head holds five stories of restaurants, shops, and fast-food counters. At the foot of the pier, the **Museum of History**, 335 2nd Ave NE (Mon–Sat 10am–5pm, Sun 1–5pm; $5; ☎727/894-1052, ⊛www.museumofhistoryonline.org), modestly recounts St Petersburg's early twentieth-century heyday as a winter resort. Nearby, the **Museum of Fine Arts**, 255 Beach Drive NE (Tues–Sat 10am–5pm, Sun 1–5pm; $8, including free guided tour on Sunday; ☎727/896-2667, ⊛www.fine-arts.org), holds a superlative collection ranging from pre-Columbian art through Asian and African to the European Old Masters. The **Florida International Museum**, 100 2nd St (during exhibition periods only, Mon–Sat 10am–5pm, Sun noon–5pm, last entry 4pm; $12; ☎727/822-3693, ⊛www.floridamuseum.org), occupies an entire block and, for about a year at a time, displays exhibitions on subjects ranging from Ancient Egypt to John F. Kennedy.

Practicalities

The Greyhound **bus** station is downtown between 18th and 19th avenues, at 180 9th St N (☎727/898-1496). An **Amtrak bus link** from Tampa pulls in some way out of town at the Pinellas Square Mall on 7200 Hwy-19. The **Chamber of Commerce** is at 100 2nd Ave N (Mon–Fri 8am–5pm, Sat 10am–4pm, Sun noon–4pm; ☎727/821-4715, ⊛www.stpete.com). Staying in St Petersburg can be less costly than at the beaches (see below). There is hostel-style **accommodation** at the *Kelly Hotel* in the old *Bay Park Arms* building, 326 1st Ave N (☎727/822-4141), with beds in a four-person dorm room for $20 or private rooms for $25. Of the dozens of cheap motels along 4th Street (Hwy-92), the *Kentucky*, at no. 4246 (☎727/526-7373; ❷), is a good option. The area is also rich in charismatic bed-and-breakfasts, such as *Mansion House*, 105 5th Ave (☎727/821-9391 or 1-800/274-7520, ⊛www.mansionbandb .com; ❺). For sheer luxury, stay at *Renaissance Vinoy Resort*, 501 5th Ave NE (☎727/894-1000 or 1-800/468-3571, ⊛www.renaissancehotels.com/tpasr; ❼). Great, economical Cuban **food** can be had at *Tangelo's Grill*, 226 1st Ave N (☎727/894-1695). Alternatively, try *Moon Under Water*, 332 Beach Drive NE (☎727/896-6160); overlooking the waterfront, this inexpensive British tavern is well known for its cocktails and curries.

The St Petersburg beaches

Framing the Gulf side of the Pinellas Peninsula, a 35-mile chain of barrier islands forms the **St Petersburg Beaches**, one of Florida's busiest coastal strips. When the resorts of Miami Beach lost some of their allure during the 1970s, the St Petersburg beaches grew in popularity with Americans and have since evolved into an established destination for package-holidaying Europeans. The beaches are beautiful, the sea warm, and the sunsets fabulous – yet this is not Florida at its best: the whole area is a little tacky, with large portions lacking in charm and character.

All **buses** ($1.25; ☎727/530-9911, ⊛www.psta.net) to the beaches originate in St Petersburg, at the Williams Park terminal, on 1st Avenue North and 3rd Street North; an **information booth** there has route details. **Route #3** runs daily to Treasure Island Beach on Gulf Boulevard, which links all the St

Petersburg beach communities. At Treasure Island Beach, you can change here for the **Suncoast Trolley**, which connects from Passe-a-Grille in the extreme south to Sand Key in the north.

The southern beaches

In twenty-odd miles of heavily touristed coast, only **Pass-a-Grille**, at the very southern tip of the barrier island chain, has the look and feel of a genuine community – two miles of tidy houses, cared-for lawns, small shops, and a cluster of bars and restaurants. During the week, the town is blissfully quiet, while on weekends informed locals come here to enjoy one of the area's liveliest stretches of sand.

A mile and a half north of Pass-a-Grille, the painfully luxurious **Don Cesar Hotel**, 3400 Gulf Blvd (☎727/360-1881 or 1-800/282-1116, ⓦwww.doncesar.com; ❼), is a grandiose pink castle, filling seven beachside acres. Opened in 1928, and briefly busy with the likes of Scott and Zelda Fitzgerald, it enjoyed a short-lived glamour. During the Great Depression, part of the hotel was used as a warehouse, and later as the spring training base of the New York Yankees baseball team.

Continuing north from the *Don Cesar* on Gulf Boulevard brings you into the main section of **St Pete Beach**, a string of uninspiring hotels, motels, and eating establishments. Further north, **Treasure Island** is even less varied tourist territory. An arching drawbridge leads to **Madeira Beach**, essentially more of the same – although, if you can't make it to Pass-a-Grille, the beach here justifies a weekend fling.

The northern beaches

Much of the northern section of **Sand Key**, the longest barrier island in the St Petersburg chain, and one of the wealthier portions of the coast, is taken up by stylish condos and time-share apartments. The island terminates in the pretty **Sand Key Park**, where tall palm trees frame a scintillating strip of sand. The park occupies one bank of **Clearwater Pass**, across which a belt of sparkling white sands marks the holiday town of **CLEARWATER BEACH**, whose streets still retain an endearing small-town feel. The staff at the well-positioned *Clearwater Beach Hostel*, 606 Bay Esplanade (☎727/443-1211, ⓦwww.clearwaterbeachhostel .com; dorm beds $13, private rooms from $36), will help plan excursions around the area and **rent bikes** for $5 a day. Regular **buses** (#80) provide links to the mainland town of Clearwater – across the two-mile causeway – where you'll find connections to St Petersburg and a Greyhound station.

Beach practicalities

The **motels** that line mile after mile of Gulf Boulevard tend to be cheaper than the **hotels** – typically $80 in winter, and between $50 and $80 in summer. You'll pay $5–10 extra for a room on the beach side of Gulf Boulevard compared with an identical room on the inland side. At the southern beaches, good, cheap accommodation can be found at *Lamara Motel & Apartments*, 520 73rd Ave, St Petersburg Beach (☎727/360-7521 or 1-800/211-5108, ⓦwww.lamara.com; ❷), while the pick of the hotels at the northern beaches is *Sheraton Sand Key*, 1160 Gulf Blvd, Sand Key (☎727/595-1611 or 1-800/325-3535, ⓦwww.sheratonsandkey.com; ❻). It's easy to find a decent place to **eat** around the beaches. *Hurricane Seafood Restaurant*, 807 Gulf Way, Pass-a-Grille (☎727/360-9558), has a well-priced menu of the freshest seafood. *Fetishes*, 6690 Gulf Blvd, St Petersburg Beach (☎727/363-3700), is ideal for a more upscale and intimate dining experience, serving expensive American cuisine. In Clearwater Beach, *Frenchy's Café*, 41 Baymont St (☎727/446-3607), cooks up good grouper sandwiches and seafood gumbo.

Sarasota

Rising on a gentle hillside beside the blue waters of Sarasota Bay, **SARASOTA**, thirty-five miles on from St Petersburg, is one of Florida's better-off and better-looking towns. It's also one of the state's leading cultural centers, home to numerous writers and artists, and the base of several respected performing arts companies. The community is far less stuffy than its wealth might suggest, and downtown Sarasota is fairly lively, with cafés, bars, and eateries complementing the excellent grouping of bookstores for which the place has been known. Don't fail to visit the house and art collections of John Ringling, a multimillionaire who gave Sarasota its ongoing taste for the fine arts, or the barrier island beaches, a couple of miles away across the bay, which are also spectacular.

The Ringling Museum Complex

John Ringling, one of the owners of the fantastically successful Ringling Brothers Circus, which toured the US from the 1890s, acquired during his lifetime a fortune estimated at $200 million (see also p.393). Recognizing Sarasota's investment potential, he built the first causeway to the barrier islands and made this the winter base for his circus. His greatest gift to the town, however, was a Venetian Gothic mansion and an incredible collection of European Baroque paintings, displayed in a purpose-built museum beside the house.

The **Ringling Museum Complex**, which includes the mansion (daily 10am–5.30pm; $15, admission to the art galleries free on Monday; ☎941/351-1660), is at 5401 Bay Shore Rd, three miles north of downtown beside US-41. Begin your exploration by walking through the gardens to the former winter residence of John and Mable Ringling, **Ca' d'Zan** ("House of John," in Venetian dialect), built in 1923 for $1.5 million, and furnished with New York estate sale castoffs for an additional $400,000. A gorgeous piece of work and a triumph of taste and proportion, it's serenely situated beside the bay. On trips to Europe to scout for new circus talent, Ringling became obsessed with Baroque art (which was unfashionable at that time) and acquired more than five hundred Old Masters, a gathering now regarded as one of the finest collections of its kind in the US. To display the paintings, a spacious **museum** was built around a mock fifteenth-century Italian palazzo. As with Ca' d'Zan, the very concept seems absurdly pretentious, but, like the house, it works: the architecture matches the art with great aplomb. Five enormous paintings by Rubens, commissioned in 1625, and the painter's subsequent *Portrait of Archduke Ferdinand*, are highlights, though there's also a wealth of talent from Europe's leading schools of the mid-sixteenth to mid-eighteenth centuries. Free guided **tours** depart regularly from the entrance.

The Sarasota beaches

Increasingly the stamping ground of European package tourists spilling south from the St Petersburg beaches, the white sands of the **Sarasota**

beaches are worth a day of anybody's time. The two islands on which they lie, Lido Key and Siesta Key, are accessible from the mainland, though there is no direct link between them. A third island, Longboat Key, is primarily residential.

The Ringling Causeway crosses the yacht-filled Sarasota Bay from the foot of Sarasota's Main Street to **Lido Key**. The causeway flows into **St Armands Circle**, a roundabout ringed by upmarket shops and restaurants dotted with some of Ringling's replica classical statuary. Continuing south along Benjamin Franklin Drive, you come to the island's most accessible beaches, ending after two miles at the attractive **South Lido Park** (daily 8am–dusk; free).

The bulbous northerly section of tadpole-shaped **Siesta Key**, reached by Siesta Drive off US-41, about five miles south of downtown Sarasota, holds the bulk of the island's residents, with streets that twist around a network of canals. It also holds a belt of dazzlingly bright sand at **Siesta Key Beach** (beside Ocean Beach Boulevard), which has a sugary texture due to its origins as quartz (not the more usual pulverized coral). To escape the crowds, continue south past Crescent Beach and follow Midnight Pass Road for six miles to **Turtle Beach**, a small body of sand that has the island's only **campground**, at 8862 Midnight Pass Rd (from $23 per spot; ☎941/349-3839).

Practicalities

In downtown Sarasota, Greyhound **buses** stop at 575 N Washington Blvd (☎941/955-5735). The **Amtrak bus** from Tampa pulls up at the local bus terminal on Lemon Avenue, between 1st and 2nd streets. Catch the buses here for the Ringling House or the beaches. Call at the **visitor center**, 655 N Tamiami Trail (Mon–Sat 9am–5pm, Sun 11am–3pm; ☎941/957-1877 or 1-800/522-9799, ⓦwww.sarasotafl.org), for discount coupons and leaflets.

On the mainland, **motels** run the length of US-41 (N Tamiami Trail) between the Ringling estate and downtown Sarasota, typically charging around $60 a night. Prices are higher at the beaches. Try the *Flamingo Colony Motel*, 4703 N Tamiami Trail (☎941/355-5135; ❸), or *Lido Vacation Rentals* on Lido Key at 528 S Polk Drive (☎941/388-1004; ❸), which has friendly service and access to an Olympic-sized swimming pool.

Eating options along Main Street include the healthful salads, sandwiches, and smoothies at *Nature's Way*, no. 1572 (☎941/954-3131), as well as the excellent pizza at *Il Panificio*, no. 1703 (☎941/366-5570). *El Habanero*, 417 Burns Court (☎941/362-9562), serves plates piled high with mouth-watering Cuban food.

Fort Myers

Fifty miles south, **FORT MYERS** may lack the elan of Sarasota, but it's nonetheless one of the up-and-coming communities of Florida's southwest coast. Fortunately, most of its recent growth has occurred on the north side of the wide Caloosahatchee River, which the town straddles, allowing the traditional center, along the waterway's south shore, to remain relatively unspoiled.

Once across the river, US-41 strikes **downtown** Fort Myers, picturesquely nestled on the water's edge. Here, the **Fort Myers Historical Museum**, 2300 Peck St (Tues–Sat 9am–4pm; $2.50; ☎239/332-5955), provides thorough insight into the town's past, including the exploits of D Franklin Miles, the local man who developed Alka-Seltzer.

In 1885, six years after inventing the light bulb, **Thomas Edison** collapsed from exhaustion and was instructed by his doctor to find a warm working environment or face an early death. Vacationing in Florida, the 37-year-old Edison bought fourteen acres of land on the banks of the Caloosahatchee and cleared a section of it to spend his remaining winters (which turned out to be many; he lived to be 84). This became the **Edison Winter Estate**, 2350 McGregor Blvd, a mile west of downtown (Mon–Sat 9am–5pm, Sun noon–5pm; guided tours every half-hour; $14, includes entry into the Ford Winter Estate, see below; ☎239/334-3614, ⊛www.edison-ford-estate.com). The tours begin in the gardens, planted with such exotics as African sausage trees and wild orchids. However, the house, which you can glimpse only through the windows, is anticlimactic – its plainness probably due to the fact that Edison spent most of his waking hours inside the **laboratory**, attempting to turn the latex-rich sap of *Solidago edisonii* (a strain of goldenrod weed he developed) into rubber. However, when the tour reaches the engrossing **museum**, the full impact of Edison's achievements becomes apparent: a design for an improved ticker-tape machine provided him with the funds for the experiments that led to the creation of the phonograph in 1877, and financed research that resulted in the incandescent light bulb. Here, too, you'll see some of the ungainly cinema projectors derived from Edison's Kinetoscope – which brought him a million dollars a year in royalties from 1907. Next door, you can also traipse through the plain **Ford Winter Estate**, bought by Edison's close friend Henry Ford in 1915. Much more awe-inspiring is the enormous banyan tree outside the ticket office. At 400 feet around all of its auxiliary trunks, it's the largest tree in the state, and was grown by Edison from a seedling given him by Harvey Firestone in 1925.

The Fort Myers beaches

The **Fort Myers beaches** on **Estero Island**, fifteen miles south of downtown, are appreciably different in character from the west coast's more commercialized beach strips, with a cheerful seaside mood. Accommodation is plentiful on and around Estero Boulevard – reached by San Carlos Boulevard, which runs the seven-mile length of the island. Most activity revolves around the short fishing pier and the **Lynne Hall Memorial Park**, at the island's north end.

Estero Island becomes increasingly residential as you press south, Estero Boulevard eventually swinging over a slender causeway onto the barely developed **San Carlos Island**. A few miles ahead, at the **Lovers Key State Recreation Area** (daily sunrise to sunset; $3.25 per car, $1 for pedestrians and cyclists), a footpath picks a trail over a couple of mangrove-fringed islands and several mullet-filled creeks to **Lovers Key**, a secluded beach. If you don't fancy the walk, a free trolley will transport you between the park entrance and the beach.

Reached only by crossing a causeway (with a $3 toll), the islands of **Sanibel** and **Captiva** are virtually impossible to visit unless you have a car. However, if you have a spare day, these islands offer a wildlife refuge, mangroves, and shell-strewn beaches – for which they are widely renowned. In contrast with the smooth beaches along the gulf side of Sanibel Island, the opposite edge comprises shallow bays and creeks, and a vibrant wildlife habitat under the protection of the **J.N. "Ding" Darling National Wildlife Refuge** (daily except Fri sunrise–sunset; cars $5, cyclists and pedestrians $1; ☎239/472-1100). The main entrance and **information center** are just off the Sanibel–Captiva Road. If you intend to stay here for a night or two, contact the Fort Myers visitor center (see below) beforehand for lodging ideas. By doing so, you'll be treated to a beach experience unlike those in most of Florida – lovely yet with an acute sense of isolation.

Practicalities

Greyhound pulls in at 2275 Cleveland Ave, while daily **Amtrak buses** from Tampa arrive at 6050 Plaza Drive, about six miles east of downtown. The **visitor center** is at 2180 W 1st St, suite 100 (Mon–Fri 8am–5pm; ☎239/338-3500 or 1-800/237-6444, ⓦwww.leeislandcoast.com). Distances within Fort Myers, and from downtown to the beaches, are large, and you'll struggle without a car, though it is possible – just – to reach the beaches on local LeeTran **buses** (☎239/275-8726, ⓦwww.rideleetran.com). LeeTran's **downtown terminal** is at Monroe Avenue and Martin Luther King Jr Boulevard.

Accommodation costs in and around Fort Myers are low between May and mid-December, when 30–60 percent gets lopped off the standard rates. However, in high season, prices skyrocket, and spare rooms are rare. Downtown, look along 1st Street: *Sea Chest*, at no. 2571 (☎239/332-1545; ❷), is among the cheapest. At the beaches, Estero Boulevard is your best bet: the *Beacon*, no. 1240 (☎239/463-5264; ❸), and *Casa Playa*, no. 510 (☎239/765-0510; ❹), are both clean and reliable. Of all the **campgrounds**, only *Red Coconut*, 3001 Estero Blvd (☎239/463-7200), is an easy walk from the beach.

For downtown **food**, try *Bara Bread*, 1520 Broadway (☎239/334-8216), for inexpensive bistro fare and baked goods, or *Oasis Restaurant*, 2260 Dr Martin Luther King Jr Blvd (☎239/334-1556), for large, cheap breakfasts and lunch specials. At the beaches, sample the seafood at *Top O' The Mast*, 1028 Estero Blvd (☎239/463-9424), or the all-you-care-to-eat nightly specials at *The Reef*, 2601 Estero Blvd (☎239/463-4181).

The Everglades

Whatever scenic excitement you might anticipate from one of the country's more celebrated natural areas – whether you arrive west from Miami or south from Fort Myers, seventy miles from either direction along US-41 – there's nothing to herald your arrival in **THE EVERGLADES**. The most dramatic sights are small pockets of trees poking above a completely flat sawgrass plain. Yet, these wide-open spaces resonate with life, forming part of an ever-changing ecosystem, evolved through a unique combination of climate, vegetation, and wildlife.

Though it appears to be flat as a table-top, the limestone on which the Everglades stands actually tilts very slightly towards the southwest. For thousands of years, water from summer storms and the overflow of nearby Lake Okeechobee has moved slowly through the Everglades towards the coast. The water replenishes the sawgrass, which grows on a thin layer of soil formed by decaying vegetation. This gives birth to the algae at the base of a complex food chain that sustains much larger creatures, most importantly **alligators**. After the floodwaters have reached the sea, drained through the bedrock, or simply evaporated, the Everglades are barren except for the water accumulated in ponds – or "gator holes" – created when an alligator senses water and clears the soil covering it with its tail. Besides nourishing the alligator, the pond provides a home for other wildlife until the summer rains return. Sawgrass covers much of the Everglades, but where natural indentations in the limestone fill with soil, fertile tree islands – or "**hammocks**" – appear, just high enough to stand above the floodwaters.

Several **Native American tribes** once lived hunter-gatherer existences in the Everglades. The shell mounds they built can still be seen in sections of the park. In the nineteenth century, the Seminoles, fleeing white settlers from the north, also lived peaceably in the area. By the late 1800s, a few towns had sprung up, peopled by settlers who, unlike the Indians, looked to exploit the land. As Florida's population grew, the damage caused by hunting, road building, and draining for farmland gave rise to a significant **conservation** lobby. In 1947, a section of the Everglades was declared a national park. However, unrestrained commercial use of nearby areas continues to upset the Everglades' natural cycle. The 1500 miles of canals built to divert the flow of water away from the Everglades and toward the state's expanding cities, the poisoning caused by agricultural chemicals from local farmlands, and the broader changes wrought by global warming could yet turn Florida's greatest natural asset into a wasteland.

Everglades National Park

Throughout the last century, the Everglades' boundaries have been steadily pushed back by urban development. Today, **EVERGLADES NATIONAL PARK** bestows federal protection to only a comparatively small section at the tip of the Florida peninsula. In the park, the vital links holding the Everglades together become apparent: the all-important cycle of wet and dry seasons; the ability of alligators to discover water; the tree islands that provide sanctuaries for animals during the floods; and the forces, such as human demands for farmland and fresh water, that threaten to tear them apart.

Arrival and information

There are **three entrances** to the park: Everglades City, at the northwestern corner; Shark Valley, at the northeastern corner; and the one near the Ernest F. Coe Visitor Center, at the southeastern corner. **US-41** skirts the northern edge of the park, providing the only land access between the Everglades City and Shark Valley entrances. There is **no public transportation** along US-41, or to any of the park entrances.

Park entry is free at Everglades City, although from there you can travel only by boat or canoe. At Shark Valley it's $8 per car and $4 for pedestrians and cyclists; near Ernest F. Coe, it's $10 and $5, respectively. Entry tickets are valid for seven days.

The park is **open year-round**, but the most favorable time to visit is **winter**, when the receding floodwaters cause wildlife to congregate around gator holes, ranger-led activities are frequent, and the mosquitoes are bearable. In **summer**, afternoon storms flood the prairies, park activities are substantially reduced, and the mosquitoes are a severe annoyance. Visiting between seasons is also a good bet.

Accommodation

In Everglades City, try the charming and clean *Ivey House B&B*, 107 Camellia St (T 239/695-3299, W www.iveyhouse.com; open Nov–April; reserve ahead; ❸), or the eccentric *The Banks of the Everglades*, 201 W Broadway (T 239/695-3151, W www.banksoftheeverglades.com; ❺), housed in what once was the first bank in Collier County. South of Everglades City, at Chokoloskee (see "Everglades City and around," below), you can rent an **RV** by the night for $40–55, at Outdoor Resorts (T 239/695-2881).

There are well-equipped **campgrounds** (both $14/night) at Flamingo and Long Pine Key, six miles from the Coe entrance. There are also many backcountry spots on the longer walking and canoe trails (permit $14 for up to eight people). Open space for both campgrounds (Flamingo fills quickly) can be checked on the board at the payment station just past the Coe Visitor Center.

The only **hotel** within the park is the *Flamingo Lodge* (☎239/695-3101, ⓦwww.flamingolodge.com; ❹); if you want to stay here during the winter, make reservations months in advance. Ten miles outside the park, in Florida City, *The Everglades International Hostel*, 20 SW 2nd Ave, off Palm Drive (☎1-800/372-3874, ⓦwww.evergladeshostel.com), is the best option for budget-minded travelers who don't want to camp. Beds go for $16 a night and private rooms are available. The hostel runs canoe and bike **tours**, and, for $5, offers roundtrip transport to the park entrance.

Everglades City and around

Purchased and named in the 1920s by an advertising executive dreaming of a subtropical metropolis, **EVERGLADES CITY**, three miles south off US-41 along Route 29, now has a population of just under five hundred. Most who visit are solely intent on diminishing the stocks of sports fish living around the mangrove islands – the aptly titled **Ten Thousand Islands** – arranged like scattered jigsaw-puzzle pieces around the coastline.

For a closer look at the mangroves, which safeguard the Everglades from surge tides, take one of the park-sanctioned **boat trips**. Try either the Everglades National Boat Tours (☎239/695-2591) or Everglades Rentals and Eco Adventures (☎239/695-4666, ⓦwww.evergladesadventures.com), at the *Ivey House B&B* (see above). Trips leave from the dock on **Chokoloskee**, a blob of land – actually a Native American shell mound – marking the southern end of Route 29. The dockside **Gulf Coast visitor center** (daily 8.30am–5pm; ☎239/695-3311) provides details on the cruises, as well as the excellent ranger-led **canoe trips**.

Shark Valley

Driven out of central Florida by white settlers, several hundred Seminoles retreated to the Everglades during the nineteenth century. Their descendants, the **Miccosukees**, still live here – though the coming of US-41 brought a fundamental change in their lifestyle, as tourist dollars became more accessible. For example, the souvenir shop at the **Miccosukee Indian Village** (daily 9am–5pm; $5; ☎305/223-8380) carries both good-quality traditional crafts and items of questionable worth.

A mile east of the village, **Shark Valley** (entrance open daily 9am–5pm) epitomizes the Everglades' "River of Grass" moniker. From here, dotted by hardwood hammocks, the sawgrass plain stretches as far as the eye can see. Aside from a few simple walking trails close to the **visitor center** (daily 8.30am–5.15pm; reduced hours during the summer; ☎305/221-8776), you can see Shark Valley only from a fifteen-mile loop road, ideally covered by renting a **bike** ($5.25 an hour; must be returned by 4pm). Alternatively, a highly informative two-hour **tram tour** (daily; $12, children $8; reservations on ☎305/221-8455) stops frequently to view wildlife, but won't allow you to linger in any particular place, as you'll certainly want to do.

Pine Island and Flamingo

The **Pine Island** section of the park – from the Coe Visitor Center entrance to Flamingo, perched at the end of the park road on Florida's southern tip – holds virtually everything that makes the Everglades tick. Spend a day or two in this southerly portion of the park and you'll quickly grasp the fundamentals of its complex ecology.

Route 9336 (the only road in this section of the park) leads past the Coe Center to the main payment station. A mile further on, the Royal Palm **visitor center** (daily 8am–5pm) is a good place to gather information on the Everglades' various habitats. The large numbers of park visitors who simply want to see an alligator are usually satisfied by walking the half-mile **Anhinga Trail** here: the reptiles are easily seen during the winter, often splayed near the trail, looking like plastic props. They're notoriously lazy, but give them a wide berth, as they can be extremely quick in the right circumstances. All manner of birdlife can also be spotted, from snowy egrets to the bizarre, eponymous anhinga, an elegant black-bodied bird, which, after diving for fish, spends ages drying itself on rocks and tree branches, with its wings fully spread. To beat the crowds, go early to the Anhinga Trail; after that, peruse the adjacent, but very different, **Gumbo Limbo Trail**, a hardwood jungle hammock packed with exotic subtropical growths.

If you're game, continue along Rte-9336 for thirty-seven miles (past many short hiking-trail opportunities) to the tiny coastal settlement of **FLAMINGO**, a former fishing colony now comprising a marina, hotel, and campground. A century ago, the only way to get here was by boat – the place was so remote that it didn't even have a name until the opening of a post office made one necessary. Then, "Flamingo" was chosen, supposedly because of the abundant roseate spoonbills – pink-plumed birds that the locals failed to identify correctly as they killed them for their feathers.

Flamingo now does a brisk trade servicing the needs of sports-fishing enthusiasts. On land, the **visitor center** (Dec–April 9am–5pm; intermittent hours rest of year; ☏239/695-2945) and the marina of the *Flamingo Lodge* (see opposite) are the centers of activity. From the marina, the informative **Backcountry Cruise** ($18; reservations on ☏239/695-3101 ext 322) makes a two-hour foray around the mangrove-enshrouded Whitewater Bay, north of Flamingo. The **Florida Bay Cruise** ($12; same number as above), a must for bird-watchers, is a ninety-minute trip through the marine feeding and nursery grounds of Florida Bay, in between the southern tip of Florida and the Keys.

The Panhandle

Rubbing hard against Alabama in the west and Georgia in the north, the long, narrow **Panhandle** has much more in common with the states of the Deep South than with the rest of Florida. Hard to believe, then, that just a century ago, the Panhandle *was* Florida. At the western edge, **Pensacola** was a busy port when Miami was still a swamp. Fertile soils lured wealthy plantation owners south, helping to establish **Tallahassee** as a high-society gathering place and administrative center – a role which, as the state capital, it retains. But the decline of cotton, the chopping-down of too many trees, and the coming of the East Coast railroad eventually left the Panhandle high and dry. Much of the inland region still seems neglected, and the **Apalachicola National Forest** is perhaps the best place in Florida to disappear into the wilderness. The **coastal Panhandle**, on the other hand, is enjoying better times: despite rows of hotels, much is still untainted, boasting miles of blindingly white sands.

Tallahassee and around

State capital it may be, **TALLAHASSEE** is a provincial city of oak trees and soft hills that won't take more than two days to explore in full. Around its small grid of central streets – where you'll find plenty of reminders of Florida's formative years – briefcase-clutching bureaucrats mingle with some of Florida State University's 25,000 students, who brighten the mood considerably and keep the city awake at night.

Tallahassee was built on the site of an important prehistoric meeting place, and takes its name from the Apalachee Indian: *talwa* meaning "town," and *ahassee* meaning "old." The city's **history** really begins, though, with Florida's incorporation into the US, and Tallahassee's selection as the state's administrative base. When this happened, the local Native Americans, the Tamali tribe, were unceremoniously dispatched to make room for the trio of log cabins in which the first Florida government sat, in 1823. Since then, Tallahassee has been the scene of every major wrangle in Florida politics, including the controversial ballot recount of the 2000 presidential election. The city has also seen its fortunes hindered by the lightning-paced development of south Florida. Today, oddly distanced from most of the people it governs, Tallahassee has a slow tempo and a strong sense of the past, evoked in its historic buildings and museums.

Arrival and information

Tallahassee's Greyhound **bus terminal** is at 112 S Tennessee St (☎850/222-4249), within easy walking distance of downtown, and opposite the local TalTran bus station ($1 per journey; ☎850/891-5200, ⊛www.talgov.com). You can get a free ride into downtown Tallahassee from the bus station on the **Old Town Trolley**, which runs to the Civic Center (near the New Capitol Building) and back (every 10min Mon–Fri 7am–6pm). Otherwise, downtown Tallahassee is best seen on **foot**. For stacks of background information, drop by the **Visitor Information Center**, 106 E Jefferson St (Mon–Fri 8am–5pm, Sat 9am–2pm; ☎850/413-9200 or 1–800/628-2866, ⊛www.seetallahassee.com).

Accommodation

Accommodation in Tallahassee is in short supply only during the sixty-day sitting of the state legislature, from early March, and on fall weekends during home football games of the Florida State Seminoles. **Hotels** and **motels** on N Monroe Street, about three miles from downtown, are far cheaper than those downtown.

Governors Inn 209 S Adams St ☎850/681-6855 or 1-800/342-7717. Every room in this splendid downtown inn is decorated with antique furniture reflecting the period of the governor each is named after. ❻

Super 8 2702 N Monroe St ☎850/386-8818 or 1-800/800-8000. A good option for the budget trav-

eler, this motel offers simple rooms with basic amenities. ❷

University Motel 691 W Tennessee St ☎850/224-8161, ⊛www.universitymotel.com. Given its location on the perimeter of the FSU campus, this place is perfect for visiting parents or homeless students. ❷

The Town

A fifty-million-dollar eyesore dominates the square mile of **downtown Tallahassee**: the vertical vents of the towering **New Capitol Building**, at Apalachee Parkway and Monroe Street (Mon–Fri 8am–5pm; free). Florida's growing army of bureaucrats had previously been crammed into the 1845 **Old Capitol Building** (Mon–Fri 9am–4.30pm, Sat 10am–4.30pm, Sun noon–4.30pm; free), which stands in the shadow of its replacement.

For a more rounded history – easily the fullest account of Florida's past anywhere in the state – visit the **Museum of Florida History**, 500 S Bronough St (Mon–Fri 9am–4.30pm, Sat 10am–4.30pm, Sun noon–4.30pm; free; T850/488-1484, Wdhr.dos.state.fl.us/museum). Detailed accounts of Paleo-Indian settlements, and the significance of their burial and temple mounds, some of which have been found on the edge of Tallahassee, are valuable tools in comprehending Florida's prehistory. The imperialist crusades of the Spanish are outlined with copious finds, though there's little on the nineteenth-century Seminole Wars – one of the bloodier skeletons in Florida's closet. There is plenty on the building of the railroads, however.

The **Black Archives Research Center and Museum**, in the nineteenth-century Union Bank Building, along Apalachee Parkway from the Old Capitol's entrance (Mon–Fri 9am–4pm; free; T850/561-2603), holds one of the largest and most important collections of African-American artifacts in the nation, with oral histories and music stations, as well as some chilling Ku Klux Klan memorabilia.

Eating

With so many politicos and students, there's plenty of good **food** for all budgets in Tallahassee.

Andrew's Capital Grill & Bar/Andrew's 228 228 S Adams St T850/222-3444. This stylish lunch spot has, in the evenings, pricier gourmet meals upstairs, such as tempura-fried oysters and succulent roast lamb.
Barnacle Bill's 1830 N Monroe St T850/385-8734. Inexpensive fresh fish and seafood served in a riotous atmosphere.
Capital Steak House in the *Holiday Inn Select*, 316 W Tennessee St T850/222-9555. Even confirmed white-meat-eaters are giving this steak-house rave reviews for its high-quality Angus beef.
La Fiesta 2329 Apalachee Pkwy T850/656-3392. The very best Mexican food in the city.
Mom and Dad's 4175 Apalachee Pkwy T850/877-4518. Delicious homemade Italian food. Closed Sunday & Monday.
Po' Boys Creole Café 224 E College Ave T850/224-5400, Wwww.poboys.com. A range of Creole delights; also one of Tallahassee's most popular live music venues.

Wakulla Springs State Park

Fifteen miles south of Tallahassee, off SR-61 on SR-267, **Wakulla Springs State Park** (daily 8am–dusk; cars $3.25, pedestrians and cyclists $1.25; T850/224-5950) holds what is believed to be one of the biggest and deepest natural springs in the world. It pumps up half a million gallons of crystal-clear pure water from the bowels of the earth every day – though you'd never guess it from the calm surface.

It's refreshing to **swim** in the cool pool (in a small roped-off area – this is gator territory), but to learn more about the spring, take the thirty-minute **glass-bottom boat tour** ($4.50), and peer down to the swarms of fish hovering around the 180ft cavern through which the water flows. Forty-minute **river cruises** ($4.50) let you glimpse some of the park's inhabitants: deer, turkeys, turtles, herons, egrets, and the inevitable alligators. The lovely wooden *Wakulla Lodge* (T850/224-5950; ❹) is a serene 1930s hotel, with an excellent **restaurant** serving home-cooked country food for breakfast, lunch, and dinner.

The Apalachicola National Forest

With swamps, savannas, and springs dotted liberally about its half-million acres, the **Apalachicola National Forest**, which fans out southwest of Tallahassee, is the inland Panhandle at its natural best. Several roads enable you to drive through a good-sized chunk, with many undemanding spots for a rest and a snack. To see deeper into the forest you'll need to make more of an effort, by following one of the hiking trails, canoeing on the rivers, or simply spending a night under the stars at one of the basic campgrounds. Driving through the forest on Hwy-65, or around it on Hwy-319, you'll eventually pass the large and forbidding **Tate's Hell Swamp**. This is a breeding-ground for the deadly water moccasin snake, and though gung-ho locals sometimes venture in hoping to catch a few to sell to zoos, you're well advised to stay clear.

The main **entrances** to the forest (free) are off Hwy-20 and Hwy-319; three minor roads, routes 267, 375, and 65, form cross-forest links between the two highways. **Accommodation** is limited to camping; apart from Silver Lake and Lost Lake (nine and seven miles west of Tallahassee respectively; $8 per night for both; RV hook-ups, showers, and other facilities available), all the campgrounds are free, with very basic facilities (no running water). For more information, call the **ranger stations** at Apalachicola (☏850/643-2282) or Wakulla (☏850/926-3561).

Panama City Beach

Follow Hwy-98 fifty miles west from Apalachicola and you'll hit the orgy of motels, go-kart tracks, mini-golf courses, and amusement parks that is **PANAMA CITY BEACH**. Entirely without pretension, the area capitalizes blatantly on the appeal of its 27-mile stretch of white sand. The whole place is as commercialized as can be, but with the shops, bars, and restaurants all trying to undercut one another, there are some great bargains to be found. That said, throughout the lively summer (the so-called "100 Magic Days"), accommodation costs are high and reservations essential. In winter, prices drop and visitors are fewer; most are Canadians and – increasingly – Europeans, many of whom have no problem sunbathing and swimming in the cool temperatures.

Getting a tan, running yourself ragged at beach sports, and going all-out on the nightlife are the main concerns in Panama City Beach, one of the country's foremost Spring Break destinations. If you get restless, try go-karting, jet-skiing, or parasailing (all available at many locations along the coastal strip); otherwise, visit one of the amusement parks ($18 for a go-on-everything day-ticket). For scuba-divers, several explorable shipwrecks litter the area; get details from any of the numerous dive shops.

Practicalities

Places to stay, while plentiful, fill with amazing speed, especially at weekends. As a general rule, **motels** at the east end of the beach are smarter and slightly pricier than those in the center. Those at the west end are quiet and family-oriented. The *Sugar Sands Motel*, 20723 Front Beach Rd (☏850/234-8802 or 1-800/367-9221, ⊛www.sugarsands.com; ❷), is an excellent-value oceanfront motel away from the noise. The cheapest places to **eat** are the buffet restaurants on Front Beach Road, which charge $5–10 for all you can manage. Alternatively, try one of the regular lunch or dinner restaurants: *Shuckum's Oyster Pub & Seafood Grill*, 15614 Front Beach Rd (☏850/235-3214); *Mike's*

Diner, 17554 Front Beach Rd (☎850/234-1942), which is also open for breakfast, and until late at night; or *The Treasure Ship*, 3605 Thomas Drive (☎850/234-8881), a seafood restaurant built to resemble a wooden sailing ship.

Pensacola and around

You might be inclined to overlook **PENSACOLA**, tucked away as it is at the western end of the Panhandle. The city, on the northern bank of the broad Pensacola Bay, is five miles inland from the nearest beaches, and its prime features are a naval aviation school and some busy dockyards. Pensacola is, however, worth a visit. The nearby white beaches are relatively untouched, and it boasts a rich history, having been occupied by the Spanish as early as 1559. The town repeatedly changed hands between the Spanish, the French, and the British before becoming the place where Florida was officially ceded by Spain to the US in 1821.

Pensacola was already a booming port by c.1900, when the opening of the Panama Canal was expected to boost its fortunes still further. The many new buildings that appeared in the **Palafox District**, around the southerly section of Palafox Street, in the early 1900s – with their delicate ornamentation and attention to detail – reflect the optimism of the era. Between 1870 and 1930, Pensacola's professional classes took a shine to the area called **North Hill**, just across Wright Street from the Palafox District, commissioning elaborate homes in a plethora of fancy styles. Strewn across the fifty-block area are Neoclassical porches, Tudor Revival cottages, low-slung California bungalows, and the rounded towers of the finest Queen Anne homes.

In earlier times, Native Americans, pioneer settlers, and seafaring traders had gathered to swap, sell, and barter on the waterfront of the **Seville District**, just east of Palafox Street. Those who did well took up permanent residence here, and many of their homes remain in fine states of repair, forming – together with several museums – the **Historic Pensacola Village** ($6; ☎850/595-5985, ⓦ www.historicpensacola.org). Tickets are valid for one week, and allow access to all of the museums and former homes in an easily navigated four-block area. Inside the US naval base on Navy Boulevard, about eight miles southwest of central Pensacola, the **Museum of Naval Aviation** (daily 9am–5pm; free, IMAX movie $6.50; ☎850/453-3604 or 1-800/327-5002, ⓦ www.naval-air.org) exhibits US naval aircraft. They range from the first flimsy seaplane, acquired in 1911, to the Phantoms and Hornets of more recent times.

Santa Rosa Island

On the other (east) side of the bay from the city lie Pensacola's real attraction: the glistening beaches and windswept sand dunes of fifty-mile-long **Santa Rosa Island**. On the island, **Pensacola Beach** in particular has everything you'd want from a Gulf Coast beach: mile after mile of fine white sands, watersports rental outlets, a busy fishing pier, and a sprinkling of motels, beachside bars, and snack stands. A short way west, at the entrance to a part of the **Gulf Islands National Seashore** (a generic name for several parks stretching 150 miles along the coast from here west to Mississippi), on the Fort Pickens Toll Road (7am–10pm; cars $8, pedestrians and cyclists $3), vibrant white sands are walled by a nine-mile-long stretch of high, rugged dunes, and the only reminder of civilization is a foliage-encircled campground.

Practicalities

The Greyhound **bus station** is seven miles north of the city center, at 505 W Burgess Rd (☎850/476-4800); ECAT buses #10A and #10B ($1; ☎850/595-3228 ext 30, ⓦwww.ecat.pensacola.com) link it to Pensacola proper. Pensacola is a stop on Amtrak's "Sunset Limited" service to LA; the **train station** is at 980 E Heinberg St. A good local **taxi** firm is Yellow Cab (☎850/433-3333). ECAT **buses** serve the city, while #21 goes to the beach three times daily; the company's main terminal is at 1515 W Fairfield Drive. At the foot of the city side of the three-mile Pensacola Bay Bridge, the **visitor center**, 401 E Gregory St (daily 8am–5pm; ☎850/434-1234 or 1-800/874-1234, ⓦwww.visitpensacola.com), has the usual worthwhile handouts.

Plenty of budget chain **hotels**, charging $35–55 per night, line North Davis and Pensacola boulevards, the main approach roads from I-10. Central options are *Seville Inn*, 223 E Garden St (☎850/433-8331 or 1-800/277-7275, ⓦwww.sevilleinn.com; ❷), and *Noble Manor*, 110 W Strong St (☎850/434-9544, ⓦwww.noblemanor.com; ❹), a comfortable bed-and-breakfast. At Pensacola Beach, try the airy *Hampton Inn*, 2 Via De Luna Drive (☎850/932-6800 or 1-800/320-8108, ⓦwww.hamptonbeachresort.com; ❹). For **eating** in town, *Hopkins House*, 900 N Spring St (☎850/438-3979), is a local institution, famous for its fried chicken. For beachside dining, *Peg Leg Pete's*, 1010 Fort Pickens Rd (☎850/932-4139), is known for its Cajun food and excellent raw bar.

Louisiana

AL - ALABAMA	IN - INDIANA	MN - MINNESOTA	RI - RHODE ISLAND
AR - ARKANSAS	LA - LOUISIANA	MS - MISSISSIPPI	SC - SOUTH CAROLINA
CT - CONNECTICUT	MA - MASSACHUSETTS	NC - NORTH CAROLINA	VA - VIRGINIA
DE - DELAWARE	MD - MARYLAND	NH - NEW HAMPSHIRE	VT - VERMONT
FL - FLORIDA	ME - MAINE	NJ - NEW JERSEY	WI - WISCONSIN
IL - ILLINOIS	MI - MICHIGAN	PA - PENNSYLVANIA	WV - WEST VIRGINIA

CHAPTER 8

Highlights

* **Swamp tours** Watch out for alligators lurking in the ghostly, Spanish-moss-shaded bayous. **See p.710 & p.743**

* **Sunset over the Mississippi, New Orleans** Settle yourself down on a wooden bench and watch the sky turn violet over one of the world's great rivers. **See p.713**

* **Jackson Square, New Orleans** The heart of the French Quarter, where you can enjoy some of the world's best brass band and jazz music – for free. **See p.714**

* **Uglesich's** Wonderfully delicious seafood, dished up with panache in a tumbledown New Orleans shack. **See p.726**

* **Southwest Louisiana Zydeco Festival, Plaisance** The very best in black Cajun music, food, and arts-and-crafts in the heart of Cajun country. **See p.738**

* **Angola prison rodeo** An unbelievable spectacle, with lifers slugging it out for guts and glory in this notorious maximum-security prison. **See p.746**

8

Louisiana

S wathed in the romance of pirates, voodoo, and Mardi Gras, **LOUISIANA** is undeniably special. Its history is barely on nodding terms with the view that America was the creation of the Pilgrim Fathers; its way of life is proudly set apart. This is the land of the rural, French-speaking **Cajuns** (descended from the Acadians, eighteenth-century French-Canadian refugees), who live in the prairies and swamps in the southwest of the state, and the Creoles of jazzy, sassy **New Orleans**. (The term **Creole** was originally used to define anyone born in the state to French or Spanish colonists – famed in the nineteenth century for their masked balls, family feuds, and duels – as well as native-born, French-speaking slaves, but has since come to define anyone or anything native to Louisiana, and in particular its black population.) Louisiana's distinctive, spicy **cuisine**, regular **festivals**, and, above all, its **music** (**jazz**, **R&B**, **Cajun**, and its bluesy black counterpart, **zydeco**) draw from all these cultures and more. Oddly enough, **northern Louisiana** – Protestant Bible Belt country, where old plantation homes stand decaying in vast cottonfields – feels more "Southern" than the marshy bayous, shaded by ancient cypress trees and laced with wispy trails of Spanish moss, of the Catholic south.

The **French** first settled Louisiana in 1682, braving treacherous swamps and plagues to harvest the abundant cypress. The state was sparsely inhabited before its first permanent settlement, the trading post of **Natchitoches**, was established in 1714, followed by New Orleans in 1718. In 1760, Louis XV secretly handed New Orleans, along with all French territory west of the Mississippi, to his **Spanish** cousin, Charles III, as a safeguard against British expansionism. Louisiana remained Spanish until it was ceded to Napoleon in 1801, under the proviso that it should never change hands again. Just two years later, however, Napoleon, strapped for cash to fund his battles with the British in Europe, struck a bargain with president Thomas Jefferson known as the **Louisiana Purchase**. This sneaky agreement handed over to the US all French lands between Canada and Mexico, from the Mississippi to the Rockies, for a total cost of $15 million. The subsequent "Americanization" of Louisiana was one of the most momentous periods in the state's history, with the port of New Orleans, in its key position near the mouth of the **Mississippi River**, growing to become one of the nation's wealthiest cities. Though the state seceded from the Union to join the Confederacy in 1861, there were important differences between Louisiana and the rest of the slave-driven South. The **Black Code**, drawn up by the French in 1685 to govern Saint-Domingue (today's Haiti) and established in Louisiana in 1724, had given slaves rights unparalleled elsewhere, including permission to marry, meet socially, and take Sundays off. The black population of New Orleans in particular was renowned as exceptionally literate and cosmopolitan.

Though Louisiana was not too badly scarred physically by the Civil War, with

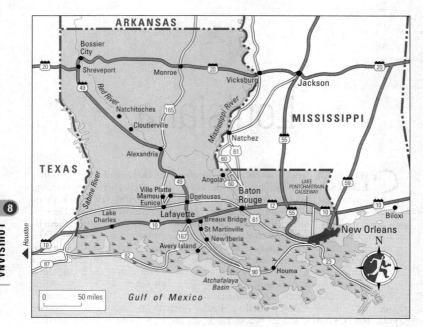

few important battles fought on its soil, its economy was ravaged, and its social structures all but destroyed. The **Reconstruction** era, too, hit particularly hard here, with the once great city of New Orleans suffering a period of unprecedented lawlessness and racial violence. In time, the economy, at least, recovered, benefiting from the key importance of the mighty Mississippi and the discovery of offshore oil in the 1950s – but during the twentieth century Louisiana came to rely more and more heavily upon **tourism**, centered around New Orleans and Cajun country. And it's not hard to see why: whether canoeing along a cypress-clogged bayou, dining in a crumbling Creole cottage on spicy, buttery crawfish, or dancing on a steamy starlit night to the best live music in the world, few visitors fail to fall in love with Louisiana.

Getting around Louisiana

Louisiana is crossed east-west by two major **interstates**, I-20 in the north and I-10 in the south. New Orleans is the hub, traversed by I-10 and served by I-55 and I-59 from Mississippi. I-49 sweeps across southeast to northwest, connecting Cajun country with the north.

The international **airport** is in New Orleans; regional airlines serve the rest of the state and surrounding areas. Amtrak **trains** link New Orleans with New York, Chicago, and Memphis, as well as Los Angeles, via Lafayette. Greyhound **buses** connect the major towns with the rest of the country, and are supplemented by smaller local lines. In addition to the Mississippi's bridges and causeways, **ferries** cross the river at New Orleans, St Francisville in Cajun country, and at various points along the River Road to Baton Rouge.

New Orleans

There's a lot more to **NEW ORLEANS** – the "Big Easy," the "city that care forgot" – than its tourist image as a nonstop party town. At once sordid and sublime, it careers along under an infuriating doublethink. While having enormous amounts of fun, you're liable to be repeatedly struck by the divisions between rich and poor (and, more explicitly, between white and black). Even so, the city's vitality and *joie de vivre* are real, buffeted but not beaten by the vagaries of commercialism and poverty. The melange of cultures and races that built the city still gives it its heart; not "easy," exactly, but quite unlike anywhere else in the States – or the world.

New Orleans began life in 1718 as a **French-Canadian** outpost, an unlikely set of shacks on a disease-ridden marsh. Its prime location near the mouth of the **Mississippi River**, however, led to rapid development, and with the first mass importation of African **slaves**, as early as the 1720s, its unique demography began to take shape. Despite early resistance from its Francophone population, the city benefited greatly from its period as a **Spanish** colony between 1763 and 1800. By the end of the eighteenth century, the **port** was flourishing, the haunt of smugglers, gamblers, prostitutes, and pirates. Newcomers included Anglo-Americans escaping the American Revolution and aristocrats fleeing revolution in France. The city also became a haven for refugees – whites and free blacks, along with their slaves – escaping the slave revolts in Saint-Domingue (Haiti). As in the West Indies, the Spanish, French, and free people of color associated and formed alliances to create a distinctive **Creole** culture with its own traditions and ways of life, its own patois, and a cuisine that drew influences from Africa, Europe, and the colonies. New Orleans was already a many-textured city when it experienced two quick-fire changes of government, passing back into French control in 1801 and then being sold to **America** under the Louisiana Purchase two years later. Unwelcome in the Creole city – today's French Quarter – the Americans who migrated here were forced to settle in the areas now known as the **Central Business District** (or **CBD**) and, later, in the **Garden District**. **Canal Street**, which divided the old city from the expanding suburbs, became known as "the neutral ground" – the name still used when referring to the median strip between main roads in New Orleans.

Though much has been made of the antipathy between Creoles and Anglo-Americans, in truth economic necessity forced them to live and work together. They fought side by side, too, in the 1815 **Battle of New Orleans**, the final battle of the War of 1812, which secured American supremacy in the States. The victorious general, **Andrew Jackson**, became a national hero – and eventually US president; his ragtag volunteer army was made up of Anglo-Americans, slaves, Creoles, free men of color, and Native Americans. They were joined by pirates supplied by the notorious buccaneer **Jean Lafitte**, whose band of privateers made good use of the labyrinth of secluded bayous in the swamp-choked delta of the Mississippi River.

New Orleans' antebellum **golden age** as a major port and finance center for the cotton-producing South was brought to an abrupt end by the Civil War. The economic blow wielded by a lengthy Union occupation – which effectively isolated the city from its markets – was compounded by the social and cultural ravages of **Reconstruction**. This was particularly disastrous for a city

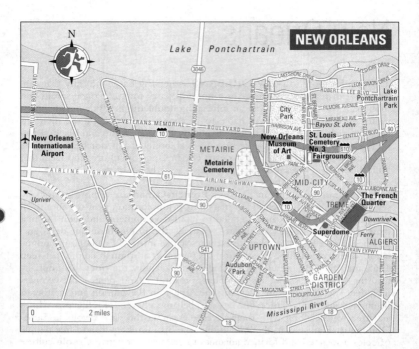

once famed for its large, educated, free black population. As the North industrialized and other Southern cities grew, the fortunes of New Orleans took a
downturn.

Jazz exploded into the bars and the bordellos around 1900, and, along with
the evolution of **Mardi Gras** as a tourist attraction, breathed new life into the
city. And although the Depression hit here as hard as it did the rest of the
nation, it also – spearheaded by a number of local writers and artists – heralded the resurgence of the **French Quarter**, which had disintegrated into a
slum. Even so, it was the less romantic duo of **oil** and **petrochemicals** that
really saved the economy – until the slump of the 1950s pushed New Orleans
well behind other US cities. The oil crash of the early 1980s gave it yet another battering, a gloomy start for near on two decades of high crime rates, crack
deaths, and widespread corruption – but by the end of the century the tide had
begun to turn, and the city now finds itself in relatively stable condition with
a strengthening economy based on **tourism**.

Arrival and information

Louis Armstrong New Orleans International Airport (**MSY**), eighteen
miles northwest of downtown on I-10, has an information booth (8am–9pm)
in its baggage claim area, along with hotel courtesy phones. Flat-rate **taxi** fares
into town are $28 for up to two people, or $12 each for three or more; **shuttles** can also take you to your hotel (every 10min; tickets available 24hr a day

Although the heavily touristed French Quarter is comparatively safe, to wander unwittingly beyond it – even just a couple of blocks – can place your **personal safety** in serious jeopardy. Be careful, and at night always take a cab when traveling any distance outside the Quarter.

in the baggage claim area or from the bus driver; $13 to downtown hotels; ☎504/522-3500). There's also a **public bus** from the airport to Tulane Avenue in the CBD (daily 6am–6.30pm; every 25min; $1.50), but it holds carry-on luggage only. **Greyhound** buses arrive next to **Amtrak** at the Union Passenger Terminal, 1001 Loyola Ave, near the Superdome. This area, in the no-man's-land beneath the elevated Pontchartrain Expressway, is not great; take a **cab** to your lodgings. United Cabs is the best firm (☎504/522-9771).

Before you leave home, it's worth contacting the **New Orleans CVB** (☎1-800/672-6124, ⓦwww.neworleanscvb.com); they mail out stacks of glossy brochures, and the website is full of helpful information. Other good **websites** include ⓦwww.neworleansonline.com, which has downloadable discount coupons and Internet-only accommodation deals, and ⓦwww.nolaalive.com, the online version of the city's daily paper, the *Times Picayune*. (See p.727 for websites related to **entertainment** and music.) Once you've arrived, the best information, including self-guided walking tours, free **maps**, and a variety of discount vouchers can be found at the **Welcome Center**, on Jackson Square at 529 St Ann St in the French Quarter (daily 9am–5pm; ☎504/566-5031).

The main **post office** is at 701 Loyola Ave (Mon–Fri 7am–11pm, Sat 7am–8pm, Sun noon–5pm; zip code 70140); an equivalent service, along with fax, FedEx, photocopying, and phone rental, is offered by the French Quarter Postal Emporium, 1000 Bourbon St (Mon–Fri 9am–6pm, Sat 10am–3pm; ☎504/525-6651), which also has a nice line in postcards.

City transportation

Though New Orleans' most-visited neighborhoods are a dream to **walk** around, getting from one to another is not always easy on foot, and if you're traveling anywhere outside the Quarter after dark you'd be better off calling a **cab** (see above for a number). The Regional Transit Authority (RTA) runs a network of buses ($1.25, exact fare required; 24hr information ☎504/248-3900, ⓦwww.regionaltransit.org). The most useful **routes** include "Magazine" (#11), which runs between Canal Street in the CBD and Audubon Park uptown; and "Esplanade" (#48), from Rampart Street on the edge of the Quarter up to City Park.

You're more likely to use the handsome **St Charles streetcar** (a National Historic Monument, dating back around 100 years) that rumbles a thirteen-mile loop from Carondelet Street at Canal Street, along St Charles Avenue in the Garden District, past Audubon Park to Carrollton uptown ($1.25, exact fare required). The cars trundle along at an average speed of 9mph; it takes about 45 minutes for a full one-way trip. Though the streetcar runs around the clock, service drops off after dark. There's a newer service along the **riverfront**, where trolleys make ten stops between the Convention Center and Esplanade Avenue (Mon–Fri 6am–midnight, Sat & Sun 8am–midnight; every 15min; $1.50, exact fare required). It's a total journey of less than two miles, however, and of most interest for its river views. Plans are well underfoot to resurrect

There is a bewildering variety of **tours** of New Orleans, from whistlestop jaunts in air-conditioned buses to preposterous moonlit ghost-hunts; stop by the welcome center (see "Information," p.709) to see the full range.

Walking tours are especially popular – notwithstanding the possibility of showers and, in summer, debilitating heat and humidity. Those led by **Le Monde Creole**, stopping at French Quarter sites featured in the true-life saga of a Creole family, are superb. They set off from their excellent gift/bookstore at 624 Royal St (Mon–Sat 10.30am & 1.30pm, Sun 10am & 1.30pm; 2hr 30min; $20; ☎504/568-1801; reservations required). The **Bienville Foundation**'s expert French Quarter walking tours emphasize gay and women's history (call for schedule; 2hr to 2hr 30min; $20; ☎504/945-6789; reservations essential), while the **Jean Lafitte National Historic Park Service** offers scholarly and accessible overviews of the Quarter (daily 9.30am; 90min; free; ☎504/589-2636; reservations required; sign up at the NPS visitor center, 419 Decatur St, after 9am on the day). For an insight into the city's rich **black history**, not only of enslaved Africans but also of the many free blacks, join **Eclectic Tours**' walk through the Quarter to St Louis Cemetery No. 1 (daily 8.30am; 2hr; $20; ☎504/467-0758); meet at *Café du Monde* (see p.726).

If the weather's bad, or too hot, you may prefer to take a **bus tour**. New Orleans Tours (☎504/592-0560, ⓦwww.bigeasytours) offer city tours from $39, and a variety of combinations with plantations, swamps, and river cruises.

Many visitors, especially with kids in tow, take a narrated trot through the Quarter in one of the **mule-drawn carriages** that wait behind Jackson Square on Decatur. These can be fun, though you should take the "historic" commentary with a pinch of salt. Rates range from $12 to $15 per person for a trip of between 30 and 45 minutes. Another pleasant way to while away a few hours on a steamy afternoon is on a **river cruise**. The *Natchez* steamboat is by far the best. Leaving from behind the Jackson Brewery mall, it heads seven miles or so downriver before turning back near the Chalmette battlefield, with a running historical commentary from the captain and a live jazz band in the dining room (daily 11.30am & 2.30pm; 2hr; $18, $24.50 with lunch; ☎504/586-8777). The *John James Audubon* riverboat allows you to combine a cruise with a trip to the aquarium (see p.713), the zoo (see p.723), or both. It leaves daily from the aquarium at 10am, noon, 2pm, and 4pm, and from the zoo an hour later (1hr one way; $16.50 roundtrip, $24.50 with aquarium admission, $22.50 with zoo admission, $32.50 with both, children half-price; ☎504/586-8777). The only boat that stops at Chalmette, site of the Battle of New Orleans, is the *Creole Queen* (Wed–Sat 10.30am; 2hr 30min; $19, $25 with lunch; ☎504/529-4567), which leaves from the Riverwalk/Canal Street dock. Tickets for all cruises are sold at booths behind Jackson Brewery and the aquarium.

New Orleans' local **swamps** – many of them protected areas just thirty minutes' drive from downtown – are otherworldly enclaves that provide a wonderful contrast to the city itself. Dr Wagner's Honey Island Swamp Tours, based ten miles north of Lake Pontchartrain, venture onto the delta of the Pearl River, a wilderness occupied by nutrias, black bears, and alligators, as well as ibis, great blue herons, and snowy egrets (daily; 2hr; $25 adults, $15 children, including transport from downtown; ☎985/641-1769, ⓦwww.honeyislandswamp.com).

For details on **ghost**, **voodoo**, and **cemetery tours**, see the box on p.716.

another historic streetcar line, which will run up Canal Street to City Park, uptown; eventually all three tracks will be linked. **VisiTour passes**, available from the welcome center and most major hotels, give unlimited travel on all streetcars and buses ($5 per day, $12 for three consecutive days).

Accommodation

New Orleans has some lovely **places to stay**, from rambling old guesthouses seeping faded grandeur to stylish boutique hotels. **Room rates**, never low (you'll be pushed to find anything half decent for less than $75 a night), increase considerably for Mardi Gras, Jazz Fest, and the Sugar Bowl, when prices can go up by as much as 200 percent and rooms are reserved months in advance. This is not a city in which you want to be stranded without a room, and though it's possible to take a chance on last-minute cancellations and deals, you should ideally make **reservations**. If you do turn up on spec, head immediately for the **welcome center** (see p.709), where you'll find racks of **discount leaflets** offering savings on same-day bookings (generally weekdays only).

Most people choose to stay in the **French Quarter**, in the heart of things. Many accommodations here are in atmospheric **guesthouses**, most of them in old Creole townhouses. In any one place, rooms can vary considerably in size, comfort, and amenities, so be specific if you have certain preferences. Outside the Quarter, the **Lower Garden District** offers budget options near the streetcar line, while the funky **Faubourg Marigny** specializes in bed-and-breakfasts, and the **Garden District** proper has a couple of gorgeous old hotels. The **CBD** is the domain of the city's upmarket chain and boutique hotels, catering mostly to the city's huge numbers of conventioneers. If you want help finding a **B&B room**, contact Bed and Breakfast Inc. (T 504/488-4640 or 1-800/729-4640, W www.historiclodging.com).

In the French Quarter

Chateau Hotel 1001 Chartres St T 504/524-9636, W www.chateauhotel.com. Simple, clean rooms in the quieter part of the Quarter. Some are better than others, so if you feel yours is too small or a bit dark, check to see what else is available. There's an outdoor café-bar by the pool, and rates include continental breakfast (which you can have in your room). ⑤

Cornstalk Hotel 915 Royal St T 504/523-1515, W www.travelguides.com/bb/cornstalk. Casually elegant place in a turreted Queen Anne house, surrounded by a landmark cast-iron fence decorated with fat cornstalks. Appealing, high-ceilinged rooms with lots of period detail, and the location's great. Rates include continental breakfast, which you can eat on the impressive veranda. ④–⑦

A Creole House 1013 St Ann St T 504/524-8076 or 1-800/535-7858, W www.acreolehouse.com. Unfussy guesthouse, bordering on shabby in places, with rooms ranging from cozy nooks with shared bath to suites. Rates include continental breakfast. ③–⑥

Dauphine Orleans 415 Dauphine St T 504/586-1800 or 1-800/521-7111, W www.dauphineorleans .com. Gorgeous upmarket hotel with rooms in restored brick cottages around tranquil, lush courtyards. There's a pool, a snug bar, a library, and a fitness room; rates include breakfast and afternoon tea. ⑤–⑨

Hotel Monteleone 214 Royal St T 504/523-3341, W www.hotelmonteleone.com. This handsome French Quarter landmark is the oldest hotel in the city, owned by the same family since 1886, and hosting a fine array of writers and luminaries since then. At 16 stories, it's something of a giant on Royal St, with an elegant Baroque facade, stunning old marble lobby, very comfy rooms, a revolving bar, and a rooftop pool. ⑦

Olivier House 828 Toulouse St T 504/525-8456, W www.olivierhouse.com. Though a bit dark in places, this atmospheric, rambling Creole house offers good value. The 42 rooms (all with bath) vary, but most have funky antique furniture and shuttered windows; the garden suite has its own interior palms and fountain. There's a tropical courtyard, and a tiny pool. ⑥

Hotel Provincial 1024 Chartres St T 504/581-4995 or 1-800/535-7922, W www.hotelprovincial.com. This sprawling – yet somehow intimate and relaxed – place is set in a quiet part of the Quarter, with rooms opening onto peaceful, gaslit courtyards. Some rooms are filled with antiques, others are more ordinary. There are two nice outdoor pools, a bar, and a fancy restaurant, *Stella*, on site. ⑤

Hotel Villa Convento 616 Ursulines St T 504/522-1793, W www.villaconvento.com. Friendly, family-run guesthouse, often booked with return visitors. Twenty-five no-frills rooms with bath; some have balconies while others open onto a patio. Complimentary continental breakfast served in the buzzing covered courtyard. ⑤

Outside the French Quarter

Columns Hotel 3811 St Charles Ave ☎504/899-9308, ⊛www.thecolumns.com. Wonderfully louche Garden District hotel and bar (see p.728) in an 1883 mansion. Characterful rooms; some come with bath and balcony, but no TVs. Complimentary continental breakfast. Rates increase by 200 percent at Mardi Gras. ❺–❽

The Frenchmen 417 Frenchmen St ☎504/948-2166 or 1-888/365-2775, ⊛www.frenchmenhotel .com. Faubourg Marigny guesthouse with 27 rooms, of variable standards, spread across two 1860 townhouses. There's a patio, a small pool, and a Jacuzzi. Rates include breakfast. ❹–❻

HI-New Orleans Marquette House 2249 Carondelet St ☎504/523-3014, ⊛hometown .aol.com/hineworlns/myhomepage/index.html. Official hostel a block from the streetcar near the Garden District. It's not one of the nicest HI properties, but prices are low. Dorm beds go for $17–21; there are double rooms, a few with kitchens, in a separate building. Day use allowed and no curfew. Reservations recommended. ❶–❸

India House Hostel 124 S Lopez St ☎504/821-1904, ⊛www.indiahousehostel.com. Funky backpackers' hostel well off the beaten track in Mid-City. Owned and run by keen travelers, it's the friendliest, and booziest, of the city's hostels, with regular pool parties and three pet alligators in the yard. Dorm beds $15, plus a few basic rooms with shared bath for a little more than twice the price. The area isn't great at night. ❶–❸

La Salle Hotel 1113 Canal St ☎504/523-5831 or 1-800/521-9450, ⊛www.lasallehotelneworleans .com. Budget option in the CBD near the Quarter. Few frills, just plain rooms – some with bath – free coffee, and daily papers. The area, on the fringes of Tremé, can feel unsafe at night. ❷–❹

Prytania Park 1525 Prytania St ☎504/524-0427 or 1-888/498-7591, ⊛www.prytaniaparkhotel .com. One of the Lower Garden District's more upscale hotels, a spruce, peaceful place with a varied selection of historic and modern rooms. Standard rates aren't that low, but the good-value lofts sleep four or five, and you can often get bargains here by using an online accommodation search engine. ❺

Royal Street Inn 1431 Royal St ☎504/948-7499 or 1-800/449-5535, ⊛www.royalstreetinn.com. Hip Faubourg Marigny lodging above the funky *R-Bar* (see p.728), and run by the same people. The five rooms (all with bath) are decorated on themes ranging from Art Deco to bordello; the four-person suites are good value. It's favored by a young crowd who hang out in the bar; rates include two drinks per night. ❹–❺

St Charles Guest House 1748 Prytania St ☎504/523-6556, ⊛www.stcharlesguesthouse .com. Bohemian Lower Garden District guesthouse offering a variety of rooms, none with phone or TV. Backpackers choose the basic 6ft by 8ft rooms for $45, but for the pricier en-suite doubles you can get better value elsewhere. It's friendly enough, though, with a hostel-like atmosphere, a pool, and free breakfast. They ask for deposits with reservations. No smoking. ❷–❺

St Vincent's Guest House 1507 Magazine St ☎504/523-3411, ⊛www.stvincentsguesthouse .com. Lower Garden District lodging with more than seventy budget rooms in a huge 1861 orphanage. The atmosphere is cheery, if institutional, and there's a small pool – but don't expect luxury. ❸

The City

New Orleans is sometimes called the **Crescent City**, because of the way it nestles between the southern shore of Lake Pontchartrain and a dramatic horseshoe bend in the Mississippi River. This unique location makes the city's layout confusing, with streets curving to follow the river, and shooting off at odd angles to head inland. Compass points are of little use here – locals refer instead to **lakeside** (towards the lake) and **riverside** (towards the river), and, using Canal Street as the dividing line, **uptown** (or upriver) and **downtown** (downriver).

Most visitors spend most time in the battered, charming old **French Quarter** (or *Vieux Carré*), site of the original settlement. On its fringes, the funky **Faubourg Marigny** creeps downriver from Esplanade Avenue, while the Quarter's lakeside boundary, **Rampart Street**, marks the beginning of the historic, run-down African-American neighborhood of **Tremé**. On the other side of the Quarter, across **Canal Street**, the **CBD** (Central Business District), bounded by the river and I-10, spreads upriver to the Pontchartrain Expressway. Dominated by office buildings, hotels, and banks, it also incorporates the **Warehouse District** (currently being revitalized) and, towards the lake, the gargantuan **Superdome**. A ferry ride across the river from the foot of Canal Street takes you to the suburban west bank and the residential district of old **Algiers**.

Back on the east bank, it's an easy journey upriver from the CBD to the rarefied **Garden District**, an area of gorgeous old mansions, some of them in delectable ruin. The **Lower Garden District**, creeping between the expressway and Jackson Avenue, is quite a different creature, its run-down old houses filled with impoverished artists and musicians. The best way to get to either neighborhood is on the streetcar along swanky **St Charles Avenue**, the Garden District's lakeside boundary; you can also approach it from **Magazine Street**, a six-mile stretch of galleries and antique stores that runs parallel to St Charles riverside. Entering the Garden District, you've crossed the official boundary into **uptown**, which spreads upriver to encompass **Audubon Park and Zoo**.

The French Quarter

The heartbreakingly beautiful **French Quarter** is where New Orleans began in 1718. Today, battered and bohemian, decaying and vibrant, it's the spiritual core of the city, its fanciful cast-iron balconies, hidden courtyards, and time-stained stucco buildings exerting a haunting fascination that has long caught the imagination of artists and writers. Official tours are useful for orientation, but it's most fun simply to wander – and you'll need a few days at least to do it justice, absorbing the jumble of sounds, sights, and smells. Early morning, in the dazzling light from the river, is a good time to explore, as sleepy locals wake themselves up with strong coffee in the neighborhood patisseries, shops crank open their shutters, and all-night revelers stumble home.

The Mississippi River

A resonant, romantic, and extraordinary physical presence, the **Mississippi River** is New Orleans' lifeblood and its raison d'être. In the nineteenth century, as the port boomed, the city gradually cut itself off from the river altogether, hemming it in behind a string of warehouses and railroads. But, as the importance of the port has diminished, a couple of downtown parks, plazas, and riverside walks, accessible from the French Quarte, the CBD, and uptown, have focused attention back onto the **waterfront**.

Crossing Decatur Street from Jackson Square brings you to the **Moon Walk**, a paved promenade studded with benches and raised flower boxes, where buskers serenade you as you gaze across the water. Upriver from here, long, thin **Woldenberg Park** makes a good place for passing an hour or so with a picnic, watching the river traffic drift by. At the upriver edge of the park, the **Aquarium of the Americas**, near the Canal Street wharf (Sun–Thurs 9.30am–6pm, Fri & Sat 9.30am–7pm; $14, children $6.50; IMAX $8/$5, aquarium and IMAX $18/$10.50, aquarium and zoo [see p.723], $25/$13.75), features a huge glass tunnel where visitors – rampaging infants, mostly – come face-to-face with rippling rays and ugly sawfish. There's also a swamp complete with a white gator, along with an Amazonian rainforest, petting tank, and IMAX theater.

For details of **river tours**, see p.710. And to read more about the Mississippi River itself, see p.585.

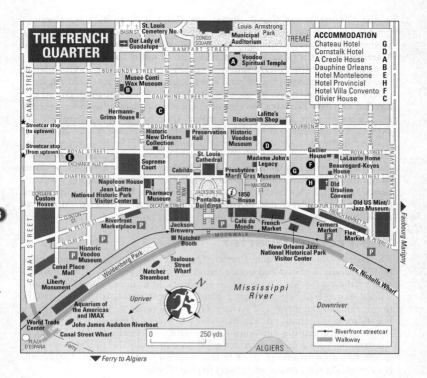

THE FRENCH QUARTER

ACCOMMODATION
Chateau Hotel   G
Cornstalk Hotel   D
A Creole House   A
Dauphine Orleans   B
Hotel Monteleone   E
Hotel Provincial   H
Hotel Villa Convento   F
Olivier House   C

LOUISIANA | New Orleans

The Quarter is laid out in a grid, unchanged since 1721. At just thirteen blocks wide – smaller than you might expect – it's easily walkable, bounded by the Mississippi River, Rampart Street, Canal Street, and Esplanade Avenue, and centering on lively **Jackson Square**. Rather than French, the famed **architecture** is predominantly Spanish Colonial, with a strong Caribbean influence. Most of the buildings date from the late eighteenth century, after much of the old city had been devastated by fires in 1788 and 1794. **Commercial activity** – shops, galleries, restaurants, bars – is concentrated in the blocks between Decatur and Bourbon. Beyond Bourbon, up towards Rampart Street, and in the Lower Quarter, downriver from Jackson Square, things become more peaceful. Here, you'll find quiet, predominantly residential streets where the Quarter's **gay** community lives side by side with elegant dowagers and scruffy artists.

Jackson Square

Ever since its earliest incarnation as the Place d'Armes, a dusty parade ground used for public meetings and executions, **Jackson Square** has been at the heart of the Quarter. Today, with its iron benches, neat lawns, and blaze of flowerbeds, the park at the center of the square manages to stay tranquil despite the streams of photo-snapping tourists, school groups, waiters on their breaks, and the odd crashed-out casualty. Presiding over them all, an **equestrian statue** – the first in the nation, constructed by Clark Mills in 1856 – shows Andrew Jackson in uncharacteristically jaunty mode, waving his hat. It's a sculptural masterpiece, with the horse, rearing on its hind legs, perfectly balanced on the plinth. The hectoring inscription, "The Union Must and Shall be Preserved," was added by Union General "Beast" Butler during the Civil War occupation.

St Peter, Chartres, and St Ann streets are pedestrianized where they border the square. During the day, everyone passes by at some time or another, weaving their way through the tangle of artists, Lucky Dog hot-dog vendors, rainbow-clad palmists, magicians, shambolic brass bands, and blues musicians. A postcard-perfect backdrop for the Jackson statue, **St Louis Cathedral** is the oldest continuously active cathedral in the United States. It's the third church on this spot, built in 1794 after the first two had been destroyed by fire and hurricane. Dominated by three tall slate steeples, the facade, which marries Greek Revival symmetry with copious French arches, is oddly two-dimensional, like some elaborate stage prop for the street drama below. Though the cathedral has always been central to the life of this very Catholic city – Andrew Jackson laid his sword on the altar in thanks for victory at the Battle of New Orleans; voodoo queen Marie Laveau (see overleaf) was baptized and married here – the interior offers little to get excited about.

On the upriver side of the cathedral, the **Cabildo** ($5) was built as the Casa Capitular, seat of the Spanish colonial government. The building – which cuts an impressive dash with its colonnade, fan windows, and wrought-iron balconies – is now part of the **Louisiana State Museum** (see box, below). Inside, the outstanding history museum ably picks its way through the complex tangle of cultures, classes, and races that binds together Louisiana's history, starting with the Native Americans and winding up with the demise of Reconstruction. In keeping with the city's fascination with all matters morbid (see box, p.716), there's a room devoted to disease, death, and mourning, while another displays the viciously racist parade-float designs put out by the Mardi Gras krewes (see p.732) during Reconstruction – Union generals portrayed as vermin and newly liberated blacks as simian fools. Black history is well represented throughout, with as much emphasis on the free people of color as on the city's role as the major slave-trading center of the South. On the second floor you can see the bronze **death mask of Napoleon**, along with the reconstructed **Sala Capitular**, where the Louisiana Purchase was signed in 1803, and where, in 1892, the historic *Plessy vs Ferguson* case, which effectively legalized segregation throughout the South, was first argued.

Forming a matching pair with the Cabildo, the **Presbytère** (part of the Louisiana State Museum; $5), on the downriver side of the cathedral, was designed in 1791 as a rectory. It was never used as such, however, and after completion in 1813 went on to serve as a courthouse. Today, it's an unmissable **Mardi Gras museum**, which covers carnival from every conceivable angle. Full of odd treasures, among them jewel-encrusted costumes, primitive masks, posters, and bizarre dance cards, with videos, interactive themed rooms, music stations, and lots of great captioning, it manages perhaps more than any other museum to give a real sense of what makes this unique city tick. It would take

The Louisiana State Museum

The Cabildo and the Presbytère (see above), along with the 1850 House (p.718), the Old US Mint (p.719), and Madame John's Legacy (p.720), are part of the **Louisiana State Museum**. Each is **open** Tuesday to Sunday from 9am to 5pm; buying a ticket to two or more sites gives a **discount** of 20 percent, good for three consecutive days.

Voodoo

Voodoo, today practiced by around fifteen percent of the city's population, was brought to New Orleans by African slaves via the French colonies of the Caribbean, where tribal beliefs were mixed with Catholicism to create a cult based on spirit worship. French, and later, Spanish authorities tried to suppress the religion (voodoo-worshipers had played an active role in the organization of slave revolts in Haiti), but it continued to flourish among the city's black population. Under American rule, the weekly slave gatherings at **Congo Square** (in what is now Louis Armstrong Park; see p.721), which included ritual ceremonies, turned into a tourist attraction for whites, fueled by sensationalized reports of hypnotized white women dancing naked.

Unlike in the West Indies, where the cult was dominated by male priests, New Orleans had many voodoo priestesses. The most famous was **Marie Laveau**, a hairdresser of African, white, and Native American blood. Using shrewd marketing sense and inside knowledge of the lives of her clients, she was in high demand for her **gris-gris** – pronounced "gree-gree," and meaning spells or potions – which she prepared for wealthy Creoles and Americans, as well as Africans. Laveau died in 1881, after which another Marie, believed to be her daughter, continued to practice under her name. The legend of both Maries lives on, and their **tombs** are popular tourist attractions (see "The Cities of the Dead," below).

Today, voodoo is big business in New Orleans, with a glut of gift shops in the French Quarter selling ersatz gris-gris – pouches or charms carried for good luck – and exotic voodoo dolls; these can be fun, but if you're interested in the reality, head instead to the **Voodoo Spiritual Temple**, 828 N Rampart St (☎504/522-9627, ⓦ www.voodoospiritualtemple.org), which offers open services, tours, and consultations. Visitors are asked to make a donation, and will be encouraged to visit the temple's "cultural center" next door, which sells all sorts of voodoo paraphernalia.

The **Historic Voodoo Museum**, in two locations at 724 Dumaine St and 217 N Peters (daily 10am–8pm; $7 includes both sites), is a ragtag collection of ceremonial objects, paintings, and gris-gris. Its aim, to debunk the myths that surround this misunderstood religion, is undermined somewhat by the self-consciously spooky atmosphere, not to mention its resident 12ft python, crumbling rat heads, and desiccated bats. The gift shop sells gris-gris and voodoo dolls, while the gallery features more expensive folk art. Ask about their readings, rituals, and city tours (☎504/523-7685).

The Cities of the Dead

> There is no architecture in New Orleans, except in the cemeteries . . .
>
> Mark Twain, *Life on the Mississippi*

So much of New Orleans is at, or below, sea level that early settlers who buried their dead – and there were many of them – found that during the frequent flooding great waves of moldy coffins would float to the surface of the sodden earth. Eventually, graves began to be placed, Spanish-style, in above-ground brick and stucco vaults, surrounded by small fences. These **cemeteries** grew to resemble cities, laid out in "streets"; today, as the tombs crumble away amid the overgrown foliage, they have become atmospheric in the extreme. The creepiness isn't totally imaginary, either – though armed muggers, rather than ghosts, are the danger these days. You should **never** venture here alone. Nearly all the city tours (see p.710) include a trip around one of the graveyards; some (see "Tours," opposite) specialize in them.

Lafayette Cemetery No. 1, Washington Ave and Prytania. Built in 1833, by 1852 – when 2000 yellow-fever victims were buried here – the Garden District cemetery was filled to capacity. Today it is an eerie place, with many tombs sinking into the ground, and some of them slowly opening in the shadow of tangled trees. It's no surprise that all this decaying grandeur should capture the imagination of local author Anne Rice, who has used the place in many of her books

– she even staged a mock funeral here, to launch publication of *Memnoch the Devil*; the "corpse" was herself, wearing an antique wedding dress, in an open coffin carried by pallbearers.

St Louis Cemetery No. 1, 400 Basin St between Conti and St Louis. The oldest city of the dead, dating from 1789, this small graveyard is full of crooked mausolea jutting into narrow pathways. On the fringes of the Quarter, it's a regular stop on the tour bus circuit, and you will invariably come across a crowd by the tomb of "voodoo queen" **Marie Laveau**, scratched with brick-dust crosses. They're usually being told how if you knock on the slab and mark a cross, her spirit will grant you any favor. The family who own it have asked that this bogus tradition should stop, not least because people are taking chunks of brick from other tombs to make the crosses. Voodooists – responsible for the candles, plastic flowers, and rum bottles surrounding the plot – deplore the practice, too, regarding it as a desecration that chases Laveau's spirit away.

St Louis Cemetery No. 2, 200 N Claiborne Ave between Iberville and St Louis. Built in 1823, this is one of the most desolate cities of the dead, hemmed in between a Tremé housing project and the interstate. Still, it's a prime example of local cemetery design, with a dead-straight center aisle lined with grandiose Greek Revival mausolea. A second Marie Laveau, thought to be *the* Marie Laveau's daughter, has a tomb here, which is also daubed with red-chalk crosses.

St Louis Cemetery No. 3, 3421 Esplanade Ave, Mid-City. A peaceful burial ground, built in 1856 on the site of a leper colony, St Louis No. 3 is mostly used by religious orders; all the priests of the diocese are buried here, and fragile angels balance on top of the tombs.

A Haunted House

The striking French Empire **LaLaurie Home**, 1140 Royal St at Governor Nicholls St, is New Orleans' most famous **haunted house** (not open to the public). In the nineteenth century, it belonged to the LaLauries, a doctor and his socialite wife Delphine, who, although seen wielding a whip as she chased a slave girl through the house to the roof, was merely fined when the child fell to her death. Whispers about the couple's cruelty were horribly verified when neighbors rushed in after a fire in 1834 – believed to have been started intentionally by the shackled cook – to find seven emaciated slaves locked in the attic. There they saw men, women, and children choked by neck braces, some with broken limbs; one had a worm-filled hole gouged out of his cheek. The doctor's protestation that this torture chamber was, in fact, an "experiment," met with vitriol; the next day the pair escaped the baying mob outside their home, and fled to France. Since then, many claim to have heard ghostly moans from the building at night; some say they have seen a little girl stumble across the curved balcony beneath the roof.

Tours

New Orleans' image as a Gothic, vampire-stalked city has really taken off in recent years, and the choice of **tours** promising **magic**, **voodoo**, **vampires**, and **ghosts** is dizzying. Among the campy, the overpriced, and the just plain silly, there are, nonetheless, a couple worth joining. **Historic New Orleans Walking Tours** has a good "Cemetery/Voodoo" tour covering St Louis Cemetery No. 1, Congo Square, Marie Laveau's home, and the Voodoo Spiritual Temple (Mon–Sat 10am & 1pm, Sun 10am; meet at *Café Beignet*, 334 Royal St) and, after dark, a "Haunted French Quarter" walk, which is slightly more tongue-in-cheek (daily 7.30pm; meet at *O'Flaherty's Bar*, 508 Toulouse St). Both cost $15, last around 2hr, and need no reservations; arrive 15min early. **Save Our Cemeteries** is a nonprofit restoration organization leading fascinating tours of Lafayette No. 1 (Mon, Wed, Fri & Sat 10.30am; 1hr; $6; meet at the Washington Avenue Gate, 1400 block of Washington Ave) and St Louis No. 1 (Sun 10am; 1hr 30min; $12; meet at the *Royal Blend* coffeeshop, 621 Royal St). No reservations are needed for either.

days to see the place in its entirety; if you do have to skim a section or two, make sure to leave time to play dress-up. There's a jumble of satiny clown ensembles by the exit that you're free to try on, and a photo booth where you can pose for a souvenir snap.

The elegant three-story **Pontalba Buildings**, which line St Peter and St Ann streets where they border the square, were commissioned by the formidable Baroness Pontalba, who, having returned from France in 1849 to find her real estate palling in comparison to the American sector across Canal Street, dreamed of replacing the shabby buildings around the Place d'Armes with elegant colonnaded structures resembling those she'd seen in Paris. Planned as both business and residential units, they are still used as such, and remain some of the city's most desirable places to live. These were not, as is commonly claimed, the first apartment buildings in the US, but they were innovative in their use of mass-produced materials and, in particular, of **cast iron** – indeed, it was these very balconies that sparked off the citywide fad for lacy ironwork, which soon came to replace the plainer iron hand-wrought locally by enslaved Africans. Part of the state museum (see p.715), the cordoned-off rooms of the restored **1850 House**, 523 St Ann St ($3), re-create the tastes of the well-to-do Creole families who lived in these fashionable apartments. Unfortunately, though the self-guided tours draw attention to every piece of Vieux Paris china and fine crystal – a treat for decorative arts fans – they leave you with little sense of any real domestic detail.

Decatur Street and Esplanade Avenue

Something of an anomaly among Upper Decatur's brassy T-shirt shops and theme restaurants, the **Jean Lafitte National Historic Park Visitor Center**, 419 Decatur St, is not only a starting point for excellent **walking tours** (see p.710), but also a great introduction to Louisiana's delta region. Listening stations let you eavesdrop on natives expounding, in a variety of accents, on the meaning of all those weird local expressions, while touch-screen monitors feature classic footage of Louis Armstrong, Mahalia Jackson, and Professor Longhair, among others. It's pot luck as to what you'll get during the daily cultural programs, but whatever it is – a walking tour, a talk, a slide show – it'll be good, covering one of a hundred subjects as varied as the modern port, women in New Orleans, or cast- versus wrought-iron.

Downriver along Decatur, the specialty shops of the restored **French Market**, said to be on the site of a Native American trading area and certainly active since the 1720s, sell tourist knick-knacks; for stalls, head towards the old **Farmers' Market**, just off Decatur on N Peters Street, where fresh produce, spices, hot sauce, and the like are sold around the clock. Next door, the flea market is full of bargain oddities, as are the funky thrift and rummage stores opposite on Decatur.

The **New Orleans Jazz National Historical Park Visitor Center** (Wed–Sun 9am–5pm; free; ☎504/589-4841), hidden away in the French Market at 916 N Peters St, is a must for music fans. Though the National Park itself is still a twinkle in its planners' eyes, the center's light, airy room is a superb, informal place to attend the frequent concerts, talks, movies, and workshops, with good acoustics and an intimate scale; afterwards, check out the rare photos, information sheets (including a selection of self-guided jazz walking tours), and the bookstore.

Continuing downriver, you'll come to the outer boundary of the Quarter, **Esplanade Avenue**, an exquisite, oak-shaded boulevard lined with crumbling nineteenth-century Creole mansions. Part of the state museum (see p.715), the

Old US Mint, on the 400 block near the river, houses the fascinating **Jazz Museum**, which traces a detailed history of the music that New Orleans calls its own with a wealth of artifacts including photographs, sheet music, old letters – among them a pencil-written fan letter to pianist Armand Hug from a ten-year-old Harry Connick Jr – and memorabilia. Among the musical instruments, whose battered, well-worn contours are enough to bring tears to the eyes of any jazz buff, are a bugle played by the young **Louis Armstrong** while learning his craft at the Waif's Home, Kid Ory's trombone, Sidney Bechet's soprano sax, and a beautifully engraved horn played by Bix Beiderbecke. The building also features a gallery of decorative arts, and on the ground floor there's an exhibit about the Mint itself, which churned out $300 million worth of currency between 1838 and 1909. Before leaving, stop by the good little museum store, which sells local music, books, and posters.

Across Esplanade from the Quarter, the arty **Faubourg Marigny** is a low-rent area of Creole cottages. Though the Faubourg is gentrifying, and its bars, coffeeshops, and restaurants are expanding further and further beyond the Quarter, it's best **not to wander** too far away from the blocks around Decatur and Frenchmen, the district's main drag. Even Elysian Fields – the street where Stanley and Stella lived in Tennessee Williams' *A Streetcar Named Desire* – can feel distinctly dodgy, despite its heavenly name.

Chartres and Royal streets

A left turn at the 600 block of Esplanade Avenue brings you to the **Old Ursuline Convent** at 1114 Chartres St (tours Tues–Fri 10am, 11am, 1pm, 2pm & 3pm, Sat & Sun 11.15am, 1pm & 2pm; $5). Built in 1745, this is the only intact French Colonial structure in the city, and quite possibly the oldest building in the Mississippi valley. It's one of the many places in the Quarter that are said to be haunted, its corridors roamed by specters of the "casket girls" – white virgins shipped over in the early days of the colony, who were kept here before being sold off as wives in an attempt to stop the increasing number of couplings between French settlers and African or Native American women. Inside the wonderfully peaceful building you can see a mishmash of religious paraphernalia, including the "Doorway to Heaven," a heavy wooden table on which bishops lay in state in St Louis Cathedral. The **Beauregard-Keyes House**, opposite the convent at no. 1113 (tours hourly Mon–Sat 10am–3pm; $5), owes its name to Confederate General Pierre Beauregard – who ordered the first shot of the Civil War at Fort Sumter and rented a room here during Reconstruction – and to popular novelist Frances Parkinson Keyes. She refurbished this "raised cottage" (with the basement at ground level) as her winter home in the 1940s, and her possessions now fill what is essentially a museum of decorative arts. Keyes' novels – including *Madame Castel's Lodger*, a romance about the house's "Beauregard period"– are on sale in the gift shop.

A block north at 1132 Royal St, the handsome **Gallier House**, dating from 1857, is a fascinating little museum (tours every 30min Mon–Sat 10am–3.30pm; $6, or $10 with the Hermann-Grima House, see p.721). James Gallier Jr was a leading architect of the day, and the innovative features he designed for his home, such as the outdoor cistern and cooling system, indoor plumbing, and above-ground storage, soon became essential for anyone wanting to live in comfort in this swampy climate. Meanwhile, the house's filigree cast-iron balconies would have been the last word in chic. Tours, which focus as much on social history as fine furniture, are some of the liveliest in the Quarter.

A rare example of the French Quarter's early West Indies–style architecture, distinctive with its deep wraparound gallery, **Madame John's Legacy**, just off Royal at 628 Dumaine St (part of the Louisiana State Museum, see p.715; $3; buy tickets from the Cabildo), was rebuilt after the fire of 1788 as an exact replica of the 1730 house that had previously stood on the site. It was constructed using the *briquete entre poteaux* technique, in which soft red brick is set between hand-hewn cypress beams, and raised off the ground on stucco-covered pillars. There never was a real Madame John – the name was given to the house by nineteenth-century author George Washington Cable in his tragic short story "'Tite Poulette," and it simply stuck, attracting hundreds of tourists to the city and spawning a nice line in Madame John souvenirs. On the ground floor, an illuminating exhibition details the house's various inhabitants and changes in fortune, and there's also a very good museum of **Southern folk art**. For an account of the **Historic Voodoo Museum**, across Royal at 724 Dumaine, see the box on p.716.

Back on Royal Street, beyond Jackson Square at no. 533, the superb **Historic New Orleans Collection** stands proud among the neighboring antique stores and chi-chi art galleries. Entry to the streetfront gallery (Tues–Sat 10am–4.30pm), which holds excellent temporary exhibitions, is free, but to see the bulk of the collection you'll need to take a guided tour (10am, 11am, 2pm & 3pm; $4). These might cover the galleries upstairs, where fascinating exhibits – including old maps, drawings, and early publicity posters – fill a series of themed rooms, or they might venture into the Williams House, behind the museum beyond a courtyard. The Williamses, prominent citizens in the 1930s, filled their home with unusual, exotic objects – Chinese burial art, samovar lamps, antique maps – and the house is a must for anyone interested in design and decorative arts.

The quirky **Historical Pharmacy Museum**, in an old apothecary a block towards the river at 514 Chartres St (Tues–Sun 10am–5pm; $2), offers a wonderful insight into the history of medicine. On the ground floor, hand-carved rosewood cabinets are cluttered with gris-gris, a fine range of Creole "tonics" used to cure "all the various forms of female weakness," dusty jars of leeches for blood-letting ("to remove irritability"), and various unpleasant-looking drills and corkscrews. Upstairs you can see a nineteenth-century sick room, and a surprisingly intriguing collection of vintage spectacles from around the world.

In 1910, when the Quarter was at its most run-down, an entire block, bounded by Royal, St Louis, Chartres, and Conti, was demolished to make way for a colossal new courthouse. A Beaux Arts behemoth of marble and terracotta, in the 1950s the building was abandoned in favor of more modern premises in the CBD, and eventually fell into disuse. It's currently being restored to house the **Louisiana Supreme Court**, and though the sheer scale of the place is an incongruous sight in the narrow streets of the Quarter, its glossy veined marble facade, gleaming behind huge green palms, makes it an undeniably handsome one.

Bourbon Street

Continuing lakeside up Conti Street brings you to world-renowned **Bourbon Street**. Though you'd never guess it from the hype, there are two faces to this much-mythologized drag. The touristy, booze-drenched stretch spans the seven blocks from Canal to St Ann: a frat-pack cacophony of daiquiri stalls, novelty shops, and dimly lit girlie bars. This enclave is best experienced after dark, when a couple of its **bars** and **clubs** – though by no means all – are worth a look, and the sheer mayhem takes on a bacchanalian life of its own. When the attraction of fighting your way through the crowds of weekending drunks starts to pall, however, it's easy to dip out again into the quieter parallel streets to regain some sort of sanity. If you do manage to make it as far as St Ann, you come to a kind of crossroads, beyond which Bourbon transforms into an appealing, predominantly gay, residential area.

Above Bourbon Street: Rampart Street

Above Bourbon Street, tourists are outnumbered by locals walking their dogs, jogging, or chatting on stoops. Though these quiet streets are fringed by some of the Quarter's finest **vernacular architecture**, "sights" as such are few. Half a block north of Bourbon, at 820 St Louis St, the restored 1831 **Hermann-Grima House** (Mon–Fri tours every 30min 10am–3.30pm; $6, or $10 with the Gallier House, see p.719) illustrates the lifestyle of middle-class Creoles in antebellum New Orleans – with cooking demonstrations in the kitchen every Thursday from October to May – while at the cheesy **Musee Conti Wax Museum** at 917 Conti St (Mon–Sat 10am–5.30pm, Sun noon–5pm; $7) you can enjoy a variety of high-camp tableaux portraying leading figures in the city's history.

Rampart Street, the run-down strip separating the Quarter from **Tremé**, is a boundary rarely crossed by tourists. Though it's home to a couple of popular clubs (*Donna's* and *Funky Butt*; see p.730), both of which are just a short walk from the heart of the Quarter, it can feel hairy at night, and only slightly less so during the day, partly due to the proximity of some of the city's poorest housing projects. However, in the last few years, as the city as a whole has grown more stable and crime rates have begun to fall, Rampart has slowly started to shed its dismal image. Much of this is thanks to the revitalization of **Louis Armstrong Park** as a place to hear music. In general, the park entrance, a huge twinkling arch clearly visible the length of St Ann St, promises more than the park itself delivers, and it's not recommended to wander around alone during the day. It's a different story during the occasional weekend **music festivals**, however, many of which, continuing its long tradition of black music and celebration, are held in **Congo Square**, the small paved area to the left of the entrance arch.

Outside the French Quarter

Tremé, the historic African-American neighborhood where jazz was developed in the bordellos of **Storyville** – long since gone – is named for Claude Tremé, a free black hatmaker who in the nineteenth century owned a plantation on what is now St Claude Street. In the 1800s this was a prosperous area, its shops, businesses, and homes owned and frequented by New Orleans' significant free black population. Nowadays the district is pretty run-down, and it's not recommended to wander around here at night – but it does have two small museums worth a look.

The fascinating **Backstreet Cultural Museum**, in an old funeral parlor at 1116 St Claude St (Tues–Sat 10am–5pm; $3), celebrates local street culture, including jazz funerals and Mardi Gras Indian culture, while the **African-American Museum**, 1418 Governor Nicholls St (Mon–Fri 10am–5pm, Sat 10am–2pm; $5), displays artwork from Africa and the diaspora in three old houses spread across flower-filled courtyards. Directly across the road from the Backstreet Museum, **St Augustine's Church**, 1210 Governor Nicholls, is the earliest mixed-race church in the nation, and has been active since 1842. Though anyone is welcome to attend (Catholic) services, held by the charismatic Father LeDoux, the church is fullest on the occasional Sundays when a local guest musician or singer joins the choir for mass and the pews are packed with tourists. The spruce, light interior is well worth a look, with its stained-glass windows portraying French saints, and its flags printed with affirmations (Unity, Creativity, Self-Determination, Purpose) in English and Swahili.

It's safe enough, using common sense and caution, to venture to these places on foot during the day, but if you're heading for one of Tremé's music clubs (see p.730) you should always take a cab.

The CBD and Warehouse District

Along with the Mint (see p.719, the gray granite **Custom House**, in the Central Business District – or **CBD** – at 423 Canal St, was key in New Orleans' grand antebellum building program. In order to handle the volume of commerce coming through the port, and to celebrate its value to the city, work started in 1848 on what was to be the largest federal building in the nation; rooting such a monster in the city's soggy soil proved difficult, however, and what with the break during the Civil War – when the half-finished building was used by Union General "Beast" Butler as a prison for Confederate soldiers – the Custom House was not completed until 1881. Mark Twain had a point when he dismissed the foreboding Classical interior as "inferior to a gasometer," but fans of Greek Revival architecture should head to the second floor, where a huge **marble hall**, illuminated by a 54ft skylight, poignantly recalls the lofty aspirations and optimism of the city's golden age.

The lakeside edge of the CBD, a tangle of busy gray highways, would be pretty lifeless without the colossal home of the New Orleans Saints football team, the **Superdome**. At 52 acres, with 27 stories and a diameter of 680ft, this is one of the largest buildings in the world. You can't really appreciate the sheer enormity of the place until you venture inside and seat yourself with 76,999 others to see a **game** ($25–50; call ☎504/587-3663 or visit ⊛www.superdome.com for tickets).

Spreading upriver from the foot of Canal Street, the revitalizing **Warehouse District** is being heralded as a thriving arts community. However, though it may be a desirable place to stick a cutting-edge gallery, the attractions are not always immediate for the casual visitor. Most of the sights are concentrated in the **Arts District**, the outcrop of art spaces concentrated around Julia and Camp streets. The hub of the scene is the **Contemporary Arts Center**, 900 Camp St (Tues–Sun 11am–5pm; ground-floor galleries free, changing exhibitions $5, free all day Thurs; ⊛www.cacno.org). It's a beautifully designed space, and there's always something interesting going on, from the temporary shows on the ground floor to major exhibitions upstairs, along with avant-garde performances, classic and art-house movies, lectures, and workshops – plus a free **cybercafé** (Mon–Fri 10am–5pm, Sat & Sun 11am–5pm).

Around the corner, the colossal **National D-Day Museum**, 945 Magazine St (daily 9am–5pm; $10), opened on June 6, 2000, the 56th anniversary of the Allied invasion of Europe. Though its collection concentrates on the events of that devastating day, the museum also does a good job covering other D-Day invasions, in the Pacific. For all but diehard military buffs, the quantity of hardware and uniforms on show may seem a bit much, but luckily there is enough film footage, background material and, especially, oral testimony from both sides of the conflict to make the place thoroughly engaging.

It can be all too easy to forget that easy-living New Orleans has its roots entrenched in the Deep South; anyone who needs reminding should take a look at the **Confederate Museum**, 929 Camp St at Lee Circle (Mon–Sat 10am–4pm; $5). A gloomy Romanesque Revival hulk, designed in 1891 as a place for Confederate veterans to display their mementos, this so-called "Battle Abbey of the South" is a relic from a bygone age. Inside the church-like hall, glass cases are filled with swords, mess-kits, uniforms, and helmets. Though there is little attempt at hindsight or analysis, the sepia photos – of the wealthy, muddy antebellum city, and sad-eyed youths awkward in uniform – are undeniably affecting, and there remains a funereal air about the place, with its bittersweet remembrances of long-lost generals and their forgotten families.

Next door, at 925 Camp St, the **Ogden Museum of Southern Art** (Tues–Sun 9.30am–5.30pm; $10; Ⓦwww.ogdenmuseum.org) is an impressive collection that runs the gamut from rare eighteenth-century watercolors through self-taught art to contemporary sculpture. Currently occupying a swanky four-story gallery (and with a second wing due to open in 2004), it's arranged by theme, with sections including the New Orleans bohemia, the Charleston renaissance, and so on. While many of the artists are lesser known, it's a fascinating place, evoking a strong sense of this distinctive region so preoccupied with notions of the land, of family and religion, poverty and the past, violence and loss. The photography selection is particularly strong, with E.J. Bellocq's direct and humane portraits of Storyville prostitutes, Clarence John Laughlin's haunting 1930s evocations of a devastated, ghost-ridden South, and some fine hyper-realist work from Eudora Welty. Elsewhere, highlights include folk art by Clementine Hunter, the African-American artist whose colorful paintings recall her plantation childhood in northern Louisiana (see p.747), and 1960s jazz portraits by painter Noel Rockmore.

The Garden District and Audubon Park

Pride of uptown New Orleans, the **Garden District**, which drapes itself seductively across a thirteen-block area two miles upriver from the French Quarter, was developed as a residential area in the 1840s by an energetic breed of Anglo-Americans who wished to display their ever-accumulating cotton and trade wealth by building sumptuous mansions in huge gardens. Shaded by jungles of subtropical foliage, the glorious houses – some of them spick-and-span showpieces, others now in ruins – evoke a nostalgic vision of the Deep South in a profusion of porches, columns, and balconies. It's a ravishing spectacle, if somewhat Gothic; you can see it on any number of official or self-guided tours, but the homes are only open to the public during the five-day Spring Fiesta, held around Eastertime (Ⓣ504/581-1367, Ⓦcommunity.nola.com /cc/neworleansspringfiesta).

The historic **St Charles streetcar** is still by far the best way to get to and around the area, affording front-row views of "the avenue," as St Charles Avenue, the Garden District's lakeside boundary, is locally known. From the streetcar, look out for the **Brown House** at no. 4717, and the 1941 replica of **Tara**, the house in *Gone with the Wind*, at no. 5705. You can't miss the **Wedding Cake House** at no. 5809 – an ostentatious Colonial/Greek Revival building, frosted with a layer of balconies, cornices, and columns.

Just before the streetcar takes a sharp turn at the river bend, it stops at peaceful **Audubon Park**, a lovely space shaded by Spanish-moss-swathed trees and looped by cycling and jogging paths. The best thing about **Audubon Zoo**, a ten-minute walk or short shuttle ride from the park's St Charles entrance (summer Mon–Fri 9.30am–5pm, Sat & Sun 9.30am–6pm; rest of year daily 9.30am–5pm; $10, children $5; zoo and aquarium (see p.713) $18, children $9.25), is its beautifully re-created **Louisiana swamp settlement**, complete with Cajun houseboats, wallowing alligators (including a mysterious white, blue-eyed gator with the woefully unmysterious name of "Mr Bingle"), and knobbly cypress knees poking out of the emerald-green water. You can also see white tigers and Komodo dragons, along with re-created habitats including an African savannah, an "Asian domain," and a "jaguar jungle" set among Mayan ruins. If you're in New Orleans in October, make sure to get to the zoo's **Swampfest**, which features live Cajun and zydeco bands, and fabulous local food stalls.

Algiers and Blaine Kern's Mardi Gras World

A free ferry ride from Canal Street brings you within ten minutes or so to the west bank and **Algiers**, a quiet residential neighborhood of pastel stucco Creole architecture and subtropical terraces. The main attraction is **Blaine Kern's Mardi Gras World**, 223 Newton St (daily 9.30am–4.30pm; $13.50), where year-round you can see artists preparing, constructing, and painting the enormous floats used in the Mardi Gras parades. It's a surreal experience wandering these massive warehouses past piles of dusty, grimacing has-beens from parades gone by. In keeping with the carnival spirit, there's plenty of opportunity to dress up, fool around, and take photos – you're free to try on colossal Nixon and Marilyn Monroe papier-mâché heads, velvet cloaks, and towering plumed headdresses. A complimentary minibus picks up and drops off at the ferry landing.

Elsewhere in the city

Towards the lake, in the vast area known as **Mid-City**, New Orleans' 1500-acre **City Park** is crisscrossed with roads, and by no means is as peaceful as Audubon Park. Nonetheless, it's impressively landscaped, streaked with lagoons and shaded by centuries-old live oaks. The chief attraction is the **New Orleans Museum of Art** (Tues–Sun 10am–5pm; $6), which includes works by Degas, Picasso, and Dufy, Rodin sculptures, pre-Columbian pieces, African works, Asian ceramics and paintings, and a fabulous collection of Fabergé jeweled eggs, along with a five-acre sculpture garden among the oaks and magnolias.

The **Chalmette battlefield** (daily 8am–5pm; free), six miles downriver from Canal Street, is where Jackson's ragtag army defeated the British at the Battle of New Orleans in 1815. The battle is commemorated by a 110ft obelisk and an exhibit – a source of delight to war buffs but probably too much of a good thing for casual visitors. Park rangers give short talks, generally coinciding with the arrival of the *Creole Queen* **river cruise** (see box, p.710); if you've come under your own steam, along Hwy-46, you'll have more time to wander around the site (a loop of a mile and a half) and to watch the thirty-minute video which details the events that led up to the War of 1812.

Eating

New Orleans is a gourmand's dream. The **food**, commonly defined as **Creole**, is a spicy, substantial – and usually very fattening – blend of French, Spanish, African, and Caribbean cuisine, mixed up with a host of other influences including Native American, Italian, and German. It tends to be rich and fragrant, using heaps of herbs, peppers, garlic, and onion. Some of the simpler dishes, like red beans and rice, reveal a strong West Indies influence, while others are more French, cooked with long-simmered sauces based on a **roux** (fat and flour heated together) and herby stocks. Many dishes are served **étouffée**, literally "smothered" in a tasty Creole sauce (a roux with tomato, onion, and spices), on a bed of rice. Note that what passes for **Cajun** food in the city is often a modern hybrid, tasty but not authentic; the "blackened" dishes, for example, slathered in butter and spices, made famous by chef Paul Prudhomme in the 1980s. The mainstays of most menus are **gumbo** – a thick soup of seafood, chicken, and vegetables ("gumbo" comes from a West African word for okra, a prime ingredient) – and **jambalaya**, a paella jumbled together from the same ingredients. Other specialties include **po-boys**, French-bread sandwiches crammed with oysters, shrimp, or almost anything else, and **muffulettas**, the round Italian version, stuffed full of aromatic meats and cheese and dripping with garlicky olive dressing. **Seafood** is abundant and can be very cheap. Along with shrimp and soft-shell crabs, you'll get famously good **oysters**; strictly they're in season from September to April, but in many places you'll be able to find them year-round. **Crawfish**, or mudbugs (which resemble langoustines and are best between March and October), are served in everything from omelets to bisques, or simply boiled in a spicy stock. To eat them, tug off the overlarge head, pinch the tail, and suck out the juicy, very delicious flesh.

For an only-in-New-Orleans snack, look out for the absurd, giant hot-dog-shaped **Lucky Dogs** carts set up throughout the Quarter. Featured in John Kennedy Toole's farcical novel *A Confederacy of Dunces*, they've become something of an institution, though in truth the dogs themselves are nothing great.

Finally, European-influenced New Orleans has always been *the* American city for **coffee**; fresh, strong, and aromatic, and often laced with chicory, it's been a big part of life here since long before Seattle got trendy, and locals drink twice the national average.

Gratifyingly, **prices** are not that high compared to other US cities – even at the swankiest places you can get away with $50 per head for a three-course feast with wine. Lunch, in particular, can be a bargain, especially at the more upmarket establishments. And if you're on a really tight budget, don't despair. One of the great pleasures of New Orleans' dining scene is the scores of excellent neighborhood joints serving fantastic food at low prices.

In the French Quarter

Acme Oyster House 724 Iberville St ☏504/522-5973. Noisy, characterful neighborhood restaurant popular with tourists, cops, and businesspeople alike, all of them guzzling inexpensive po-boys, salty fresh crawfish, and plump, briny oysters.
Angeli 1141 Decatur St ☏504/566-0077. This big, dimly lit room is an extension of the groovy Lower Decatur scene outside. The long hours are a welcome rarity in the Quarter, and the Mediterranean salads, sandwiches, and pastas are just the thing after a wild night out.
Croissant d'Or 617 Ursulines St ☏504/524-4663. Peaceful, inexpensive little local place serving delicious French pastries and stuffed croissants, plus quiches, salads, and steaming café au lait, in a pretty tiled building.
Fiorella's 45 French Market Place/1136 Decatur St ☏504/528-9566. This down-home French Market diner has long been a local favorite for its cheap blue-plate specials, crawfish dishes, and amazing fried chicken; nowadays, host to Thursday's essential Bingo! nights (see p.731), it also boasts considerable hipster cred.

Galatoire's 209 Bourbon St ☏504/525-2021. World-class Creole food in landmark mirror-lined dining room. One of the city's oldest restaurants, it's best at lunchtime, on Fri or Sun especially, when you can join the city's old guard (men in seersucker, women in pearls) spending long, convivial hours gorging on turtle soup, oysters en brochette, crabmeat maison, and filet mignon. No reservations, so expect a wait. Jacket and tie required after 5pm and all day Sun.
Girod's 500 Chartres St ☏504/524-9752. Wonderful, romantic restaurant, linked to the *Napoleon House* (see p.728) and hidden away beside its pretty courtyard. Like the bar, the bistro is all cracked plaster, candlelight, and ancient paintings – the perfect setting to linger over robust, creative Creole food with Mediterranean and Caribbean accents. Prices are reasonable and portions are huge. Closed Sun and Mon evenings.
Mr B's 201 Royal St ☏504/523-2078. Buzzy bistro with dark-wood booths, a relaxed, chatty ambiance, and excellent food. The garlic chicken is the city's finest, served drowned in a satiny reduction; the same accolade could go to the signature

barbecue shrimp. It can get pricey, so if you're on a budget, try it for lunch.

Port of Call 838 Esplanade Ave ☎504/523-0120. Strung with tatty nets and lifebuoys, this lively neighborhood bar is *the* place in town for delicious fresh half-pound burgers, served with mushrooms or cheese and a buttery baked potato, and best eaten at the bar.

Tujague's 823 Decatur St ☎504/525-8676. Unpretentious, atmospheric, and with a quintessential New Orleans ambiance, "Two Jacks," 150 years old, is the second-oldest restaurant in the city. The prix fixe menu – shrimp remoulade and beef brisket in secret sauce – has changed little over the years. You can also order a phenomenal chicken Bonne Femme (fried chicken with garlic and parsley) at the old stand-up bar (see p.728).

Outside the French Quarter

Casamento's 4330 Magazine St ☎504/895-9761. Spotless and wonderfully old-fashioned, this uptown oyster bar serves inexpensive ice-fresh oysters and seafood; the overstuffed "loaves," or sandwiches, are especially good. Closed in summer.

Commander's Palace 1403 Washington Ave ☎504/899-8221. You think you've eaten enough good food to last a lifetime and then comes your trip to *Commander's*, the world-famous *grande dame* of the Garden District. The heart-thumpingly rich haute Creole cuisine is pricey (dinner entrees $25–30), but the prix fixe menus prove good value (lunch from $15). Jacket required for dinner and Sun lunch. Reservations essential.

Jacques Imo's 8324 Oak St ☎504/861-0886. Funky uptown restaurant with a colorful patio. The cooking, an inventive Creole–Cajun take on soul food, is astounding and very good value – from the fried oysters and chicken livers to the buttery blackened redfish. It's a great place to fill up before a gig at the *Maple Leaf* a couple of doors away (see p.731), and well worth a trip any time. Dinner only. Reservations advised.

Juan's Flying Burrito 2018 Magazine St ☎504/569-0000. Mainstay of the Lower Garden District boho scene, this Tex-Mex joint serves low-priced tacos, burritos, and overstuffed quesadillas in a convivial neighborhood atmosphere.

Marigny Brasserie 640 Frenchmen St ☎504/945-4472. Casually chic, friendly neighborhood joint in the Faubourg where the top-notch fusion food – mushroom-crusted salmon, seared tuna, Creole crabcakes – means prices, though good value, aren't that low. Dinner and Sunday brunch only.

Old Dog, New Trick 514 Frenchmen St ☎504/943-6368. Bright, veggie restaurant offering imaginative polenta and tempeh concoctions, lots of organic produce, and even a few vegan options. Avoid the bland *udon* noodles and the crumbly burgers, and plump instead for pizzas, marinated tofu dishes, or sandwiches.

Rio Mar 800 S Peters St ☎504/525-3474. New Orleans seafood meets Spanish cuisine in this terrific Warehouse District restaurant. To start, you can't go wrong with the tuna empanadas or daily special ceviches; proceed with paella or fish-packed zarzuela (stew) and you'll be in heaven. Closed Sun.

Uglesich's 1238 Baronne St ☎504/523-8571. The "Yew-gle-sitch-es" draw on Eastern European traditions to create the best food in the city, served in a shabby Lower Garden District seafood joint. Everything is delicious, from the oyster brie soup to the spicy "sizzling shrimp Gail." Feast on raw oysters while you wait for a table (which can be a long time). No credit cards. No reservations. Lunch only, Mon–Fri; closed summer.

Coffee bars and picnic food

Café du Monde 800 Decatur St ☎504/581-2914. Despite the hype, the crowds, and the sugar-sticky table-tops, this landmark café, with a large outdoor patio covered by a distinctive striped awning, is an undeniably atmospheric place to drink steaming café au lait with chicory, and snack on piping hot beignets for a couple of dollars – apart from orange juice and hot chocolate, they serve little else. Daily 24hr.

CC's 941 Royal St ☎504/581-6996. Perch yourself at the counter or linger for hours in plump leather armchairs in this light, airy space. The brews are good and strong, especially the mochasippi, a creamy iced espresso.

Central Grocery 923 Decatur St ☎504/523-1620. Fragrant old Italian deli famed for its muffulettas.

PJs 634 Frenchmen St ☎504/949-2292; other branches around town. Friendly, no-frills Faubourg Marigny place that's a firm favorite with locals for its expertly made coffee (try it iced – it's the best in the city), muffins, bagels, and sandwiches.

Rue de la Course 3128 Magazine St ☎504/899-0242; other branches around town. With their pressed-tin walls, café au lait-colored decor, ceiling fans, and reading lamps, the *Rue* coffee shops have an Old Europe ambiance, buzzing with a mixed local crowd. The coffee is great, as are the biscotti and bagels.

Zotz 2003 Royal St ☎504/943-9689. About as bohemian as it gets, this funky little thrift store of a place features an all-artist staff, lending library, and late-night movies, as well as very good coffees and herbal teas in every flavor imaginable.

Entertainment and nightlife

New Orleans is quite simply one of the best places in the world to hear **live music**. From lonesome street musicians, through the shambling, joyous brass bands, to international names like Dr John and the Neville Brothers, music remains integral to the Crescent City, the thread that stitches the whole place together.

While the French Quarter has its share of atmospheric clubs and bars, there are plenty of good venues elsewhere. And visitors making a beeline for **Bourbon Street**, hoping to find it crammed with cool jazz clubs, will be disappointed. That said, even this tawdriest of streets has a couple of good places to drink and hear live music. In general, it can be hard to separate the drinking scene from the live music scene – most bars feature music at least one night of the week. Those we've listed below under "Bars" tend not to have live music, but many of the places we've reviewed as live music venues (see p.731) are great bars in their own right, too.

To decide where to go, check the **listings papers** (especially the free weekly *Gambit*, and the superb music monthly *Offbeat*; these can be accessed before you set off at ⓦ www.bestofneworleans.com and ⓦ www.offbeat.com, and picked up at restaurants and bars all around town), collect fliers in French Quarter **record stores** such as Magic Bus, 527 Conti St, or Louisiana Music Factory, 210 Decatur St, and keep an ear tuned to the fabulous local **radio station** WWOZ (90.7 FM), which features regular gig information and ticket competitions.

Music in New Orleans often doesn't get going until **late**. However, many venues put on two sets a night, often by different performers, so with a little creative club-hopping you could easily see three outstanding bands in one evening. Another distinctive feature of New Orleans' nightlife is that many shows can be seen – and heard – from the street. If you hear something you like, but don't want to pay the **cover charge** – low or nonexistent in bars, but as much as $20 in some clubs – it's perfectly acceptable to stand outside with a "beer to go" (see below) from another bar, moving on when the fancy takes you.

Bars

As befits its image as a hard-drinking, hard-partying town, New Orleans has dozens of truly great **bars**. However, though **24hr-drinking licenses** are common, don't expect every bar to be open all night; even on Bourbon Street, many bars close whenever they empty, which can be surprisingly early during slow periods. It is also legal to **drink alcohol in the streets** – for some visitors it's practically *de rigueur* – though not from a glass or bottle. Simply ask for a plastic "**to go**" cup in any bar and carry it with you. You'll be expected to finish your drink before entering another bar, however. The **legal drinking age** is 21; you should carry ID, though few bartenders bother asking for it.

In the French Quarter

Lafitte's Blacksmith Shop 941 Bourbon St ☎ 504/523-0066. Ancient, tumbledown bar frequented by artists and writers (how they see by the candlelight remains a mystery), and a few lively tourists. A front for Lafitte's plottings, it's practically unchanged since the 1700s, with beamed ceilings and a blackened brick fireplace. In the evenings, a gloriously cheesy piano player pounds out cocktail-lounge standards – there's a patio for those who want a quieter time.

Molly's at the Market 1107 Decatur St ☎ 504/525-5169. Once famed for being a haunt of politicos and media stars, *Molly's* Irish bar is quintessential French Quarter, pulling a happy crowd of locals, rowdy tourists, waitstaff, and grungy street punks. There's Guinness on tap and Mexican food.

Napoleon House 500 Chartres St ☎ 504/524-9752. Ravishing old bar – all crumbling walls, shadowy corners, and flickering candles – exuding a classic, relaxed New Orleans elegance. On a warm night the courtyard is one of the best places on earth to be. The building was the home of Mayor Girod, who schemed with Jean Lafitte to rescue Napoleon from exile. Closed Sun and Mon evenings.

Port of Call 838 Esplanade Ave ☎ 504/523-0120. Unpretentious drinking hole haunted by a noisy mix of Quarterites, Faubourg denizens, and in-the-know tourists who put the world to rights around the large wooden bar or at the small tables. Great burgers, too (see p.726).

Tujague's 823 Decatur St ☎ 504/525-8676. Wonderful old New Orleans restaurant (see p.726) with an equally atmospheric bar. It's particularly lively at Sunday lunchtime when regulars gather to catch up and gossip.

Elsewhere in the city

Columns Hotel 3811 St Charles Ave ☎ 504/899-9308. Gorgeous Garden District hotel bar seeping faded Southern grandeur; on warm evenings, make for the columned veranda, which overlooks the streetcar line. Happy hour 5–7pm with free food. It's also a local favorite for occasional live jazz, when there's a small cover. For more on the hotel, see p.712.

Ernie K-Doe's Mother-in-Law Lounge 1500 N Claiborne Ave ☎ 504/947-1078. Since the untimely death of local R&B legend Ernie in 2001, his equally eccentric wife Antoinette has kept their Tremé lounge (basically their living room, with the addition of a bar and a small stage) open as something of a shrine to the self-styled "Emperor of the World." Hop in a cab and join the combination of arty hipsters and unimpressed locals that make this place utterly unique.

R-Bar 1431 Royal St ☎ 504/948-7499. Bohemian Faubourg Marigny bar with funky thrift-store decor and a pool table played by some of the coolest sharks in town. It's popular with a youngish set, which includes visitors staying at the guesthouse upstairs (see p.712).

Saturn Bar 3067 St Claude Ave ☎ 504/949-7532. Atmospheric, junk-filled neighborhood dive in the funky Bywater district (beyond the Faubourg), favored by an easy-going mix of artists, service industry workers, and the occasional cool celebrity. The jukebox is phenomenal. Go late, and take a cab there and back.

Jazz

It is generally agreed that **jazz** was born in New Orleans, shaped in the early twentieth century by the twin talents of **Louis Armstrong** and **Joe "King" Oliver** from a diverse heritage of African and Caribbean slave music, Civil War brass bands, plantation spirituals, black church music, and work songs. It suits the city well: hard to define, improvisational, melancholic and jubilant, smooth and downright seedy.

In 1897, in an attempt to control the prostitution that had been rampant in the city since its earliest days, a law was passed that restricted the brothels to a fixed area bounded by Iberville and Lower Basin streets. The area, which soon became known as **Storyville**, after the alderman who pronounced the ordinance, filled with newly arrived ex-plantation workers, seamen and gamblers, and, from the "mood-setting" tunes played in the brothels to bawdy saloon gigs, there was plenty of opportunity for musicians – in particular the solo piano players known as "professors" – to develop personal styles. Children too young to enter the bars set up makeshift "spasm bands" in the streets. Their legacy lives on in the streetwise ragamuffins on every corner, tap dancing, shoe-shining, and playing trumpet.

Jazz was originally looked down upon by the white establishment as the "filthy" music of poor blacks, and, after Storyville was officially closed in 1917 – which coincided with a clampdown on live music played throughout the city – there was a mass exodus of musicians to Chicago and New York. Many more jazz artists left the city or gave up playing altogether during the Depression (King Oliver died an impoverished janitor); but in the 1950s, the city fathers literally changed their tune and began to promote jazz as a tourist attraction. The double-edged nature of the music – indigenous and authentic, and at the same time a commercial construction – persists, but it remains a living, evolving art

△ Intricate French Quarter architecture, New Orleans

form, and you're spoiled for choice of places to see it. The quality ranges from good to exceptional; the best is rarely to be found in the tourist traps.

Local, world-class **musicians**, including the multitalented Marsalis family and trumpeters Terence Blanchard, Irvin Mayfield, and Nicholas Payton all perform regularly. Of the pianists, don't miss Henry Butler, whose superb, superfast modern jazz is matched by his mean R&B and blues repertoire. One of the city's best-loved performers, trumpeter Kermit Ruffins can always be counted on for a good show with his Barbecue Swingers. A fine jazz stylist and true performer, he cut his teeth in local **brass bands**, the ragtag groups who blast out New Orleans' homegrown party music, born from the city's long tradition of street parades. Regulars on the circuit include the ReBirth (Ruffins' old crew), the Lil Rascals and New Birth brass bands, whose ear-splitting spin on traditional tunes is as big a hit in the parades as in the jazz clubs; Soul Rebels and Coolbone, who mix a cacophony of horns with hard funk, hip-hop, party music, and reggae, have a harder "street" sound.

As well as checking out the venues below, it's always worth seeing what's going on at the **Jazz National Historical Park Visitor Center** (see p.718).

Donna's 800 N Rampart St ☎504/596-6914, ⓦwww.donnasbarandgrill.com. Funky barbecue joint on the fringe of the Quarter. Hosting all the best brass bands, it feels like a locals' place but it also attracts a big out-of-town crowd. It's *the* place to be on Monday nights, when a host of local stars drop in to jam with old-timer Bob French, and they dish up free barbecue and beans in the break. Cover varies; one-drink minimum.

Funky Butt 714 N Rampart St ☎504/558-0872, ⓦwww.funkybutt.com. Stylish, intimate club near *Donna's*. The eclectic decor resembles an Art Deco bordello-cum-speakeasy, while the music – cool jazz, piano, and R&B – is great. Cover varies, rising to $15, but you don't have to pay admission if you just want to drink at the bar.

Joe's Cozy Corner 1532 Ursulines St ☎504/561-9216. Few tourists head out to this Tremé bar, where on Sunday nights Kermit Ruffins and the ReBirth play a lively end-of-week set to a mixed group of friends, family, and New Orleanians from all over town. Take a cab there and back.

Palm Court Jazz Café 1204 Decatur St ☎504/525-0200, ⓦwww.palmcourtcafe.com. The aficionados' favorite: top-notch traditional jazz played while you dine in elegant French Quarter surroundings. New Orleans jazz memorabilia adds atmosphere, and they sell collectors' items and records. Reservations recommended for dinner; cover varies, but a seat at the bar costs nothing.

Preservation Hall 726 St Peter St ☎504/522-2841, ⓦwww.preservationhall.com. Shabby old room – with no bar, air-conditioning, or toilets, and just a few seats – long lauded as the best place in New Orleans to hear trad jazz. Though the dereliction is a bit hokey (the hall has only been open since the 1960s), the music can't be beat, and gets better as the night goes on. Sets every 45min 8.30–11.45pm. $5 cover; you can stay as long as you like.

Snug Harbor 626 Frenchmen St ☎504/949-0696, ⓦwww.snugjazz.com. Sophisticated Faubourg Marigny jazz club in a small, two-story space. Shows at 9pm and 11pm, but the restaurant (serving pasta, burgers, and the like) and bar (where you can watch the gigs on closed-circuit TV) stay open late. Regulars include Astral Project, who play cool modern jazz, Charmaine Neville, and Ellis Marsalis. Cover $8–25.

Vaughan's 4229 Dauphine St, in the Bywater ☎504/947-5562. Tiny neighborhood bar that fills on Thursday, Kermit Ruffins' night. The band is crammed up against the audience – a mixed bunch of locals, students, and the players' friends and family; between sets, help yourself to free beans and rice. Take a cab. Cover $12 on Thurs; other nights free.

Other live music

There's far more to New Orleans than jazz alone. Though the "**New Orleans sound**," an exuberant, carnival-tinged hybrid of blues, parade music, and R&B, had its heyday in the early 1960s, many of its greatest stars are still going strong. Check listings papers for gigs by the Neville Brothers, Eddie Bo, Al Johnson, and "soul queen of New Orleans" Irma Thomas.

Blues fans should look out for guitarists Snooks Eaglin and Walter

"Wolfman" Washington, the younger, urban bluesman Kipori "Baby Wolf" Woods, and, for powerful gospel-blues, the formidable Marva Wright. Though many people associate New Orleans with **Cajun** music, it's not indigenous to the city: that said, locals do love to *fais-do-do* (the Cajun two-step) and there are a couple of fantastic places to dance to **zydeco**, its bluesier black relation. The **rock**, **Latin** (**tango** has taken off in a big way), and **funk** scenes are thriving, too. For something unique, scour the listings for **Mardi Gras Indians** (see overleaf) such as the Wild Magnolias, whose rare gigs – you're most likely to catch them around Mardi Gras or Jazz Fest – are the funkiest, most extraordinary performances you're ever likely to see.

Blue Nile 534 Frenchmen St ☎504/948-2583. This battered old music venue has seen a few name changes over the years – but, with its dark corners, starlit ceiling, and largish dance floor, it remains a perennial stalwart on the Frenchmen strip. Currently Latin, swing, and tango.

Café Brasil 2100 Chartres St ☎504/949-0851. Minimalist, arty club at the heart of the Faubourg scene, with eclectic live music (Latin, jazz, klezmer, reggae, world), poetry readings, and a small bar. The crowd often spills onto the street, creating a bohemian block party.

Circle Bar 1032 St Charles Ave ☎504/588-2616. Painfully hip bar in a crumbling old house at Lee Circle. With an inspired, eclectic booking policy, it's renowned for resurrecting jazz and R&B legends from ignominy, and always pulls a gorgeous, hard-partying crowd.

Dragon's Den 435 Esplanade Ave ☎504/949-1750. Opium-den style bar/club above a Thai restaurant in the Faubourg. It's tiny, packed with bright young things lolling on cushions or dancing like demons to R&B, blues, jazz, and brass. Occasional poetry slams, too.

Fiorella's 45 French Market Place/1136 Decatur St ☎504/528-9566. Fried chicken restaurant *Fiorella's* transforms itself on Thursdays with the madcap Bingo! night, hosted by bebop maestro Clint Maedgen and his band. Bingo games, home movies, burlesque craziness, and great live music (jazz, acoustic, rock) – this is New Orleans at its eccentric, arty best.

House of Blues/The Parish 225 Decatur St ☎504/529-2583, ⓦwww.hob.com. Sleek French Quarter venue, part of the national chain. If you can stomach its un-New Orleans attitude and high prices, it's worth checking out for big names; smaller, local acts play at the intimate *Parish* upstairs.

Lounge Lizards 200 Decatur St ☎504/598-1500. Groovy bar/music venue with a friendly, alternative crowd – comfy sofas, costume parties, killer Bloody Marys, and great blues and roots music to boot.

Maple Leaf 8316 Oak St ☎504/866-LEAF. Friendly uptown bar with pressed-tin walls, large dance floor, and a patio. It's a New Orleans favorite for really great blues, R&B, funk, and brass bands; ReBirth's Tuesday-night gigs are legendary. There's chess and pool, too.

Oswalds 504 Esplanade Ave ☎504/569-8361. The decor – pressed tin, red velvet, Spanish kitsch, and a huge circular bar to drape yourself over – is pure New Orleans, as is the oddball crowd. Music varies from flamenco through Europop to trad jazz and brass bands.

Mid-City Lanes Rock 'n' Bowl 4133 S Carrollton Ave ☎504/482-3133, ⓦwww.rockandbowl.com. Eccentric and fun bowling alley-cum-music venue in an unprepossessing Mid-City mall. Though it's especially heaving on Wednesday and Thursday – zydeco nights – they also book great local R&B, blues, and Latin music. Take a taxi.

Tipitina's 501 Napoleon Ave ☎504/895-8477, ⓦwww.tipitinas.com. Legendary uptown venue, named after a Professor Longhair song, with a consistently good funk, R&B, brass, and reggae line-up. The Cajun *fais-do-do* (Sunday from 5–9pm) is fun, too.

8

LOUISIANA | New Orleans

New Orleans' **carnival season** – which starts on Twelfth Night, January 6, and runs for the six weeks or so until Ash Wednesday – is unlike any other in the world. Though the name is used to define the entire season, **Mardi Gras** itself, French for "Fat Tuesday," is simply the culmination of a whirl of parades, parties, street revels, and masked balls, all inextricably tied up with the city's labyrinthine social, racial, and political structures. Mardi Gras was introduced to New Orleans in the 1740s, when **French** colonists brought over the European custom, established since medieval times, of marking the imminence of Lent with masking and feasting. Their slaves, meanwhile, continued to celebrate **African** and **Caribbean** festival traditions, based on musical rituals, masking, and elaborate costumes, and the three eventually fused. From early days carnival was known for cavorting, outrageous costumes, drinking, and general bacchanalia – and little has changed. However, although it is the busiest tourist season, when the city is invaded by millions, Mardi Gras has always been, above all, a party that New Orleanians throw for themselves. Visitors are wooed, welcomed, and showed the time of their lives, but without them carnival would reel on regardless, dressing wildly, drinking and dancing its bizarre way into Lent.

It was in the mid-nineteenth century that **official carnival** took its current form, with the appearance in 1857 of a stately moonlit procession calling itself the Krewe of Comus, Merrie Monarch of Mirth. Initiated by a group of Anglo-Americans, the concept of the "**krewes**," or secret carnival clubs, was taken up enthusiastically by the New Orleans aristocracy, many of them white supremacists who, after the Civil War, used their satirical float designs and the shroud of secrecy to mock and undermine Reconstruction. Nowadays about sixty official krewes equip colorful floats, leading huge processions on different – often mythical – themes. Each is reigned over by a King and Queen (generally an older, politically powerful man and a debutante), who go on to preside over the krewes' closed, masked balls. There are women-only krewes; "super krewes," with members drawn from the city's new wealth (barred from making inroads into the gentlemen's-club network of the old-guard krewes), and important **black** groups. The best known and most important of these is **Zulu**, established in 1909 when a black man mocked Rex, King of Carnival, by dancing behind his float with a tin can on his head; today the Zulu parade on Mardi Gras morning is one of the most popular of the season. There are also many alternative, or **unofficial krewes**, including the anarchic **Krewe du Vieux** (from Vieux Carré, another term for the French Quarter), whose irreverent parade and "ball" (a polite term for a wild party, open to all) is a blast. As in Sydney and Rio, the **gay** community plays a major part in Mardi Gras, particularly in the French Quarter, where the streets teem with strutting drag divas. And then there's the parade of the **Mystic Krewe of Barkus**, made up of dogs, hundreds of whom, during what is surely the campest parade of the season, can be seen trotting proudly through the French Quarter all spiffed up on some spurious theme. Tourists are less likely to witness the **Mardi Gras Indians**, African-American groups who, in their local neighborhoods, organize themselves into "tribes" and, dressed in fabulous beaded and feathered costumes, gather on Mardi Gras morning to compete in chanting and dancing.

One important New Orleans Mardi Gras ritual is the flinging of "**throws**" from the parade floats. Teasing masked krewe members scatter beads, beakers, and doubloons (toy coins) into the crowds, who beg, plead, and scream for them. Souvenirs vary in worth: the bright, cheap strings of beads are least valuable, while the bizarrely garbed coconuts handed out by Zulu are worth their weight in gold. Even outside the parades, tourists embark upon a frantic **bead-bartering** frenzy, which has given rise to the famed "Show Your Tits!" phenomenon – young co-eds pulling up their shirts in exchange for strings of beads and roars of boozy approval from the goggling mobs. Anyone keen to see the show should head for Bourbon Street.

The two weeks leading up to Mardi Gras are filled with processions, parties, and balls, but excitement reaches fever pitch on **Lundi Gras**, the day before Mardi Gras. Some of the city's best musicians play at **Zulu**'s free party in Woldenberg Park, which climaxes at 5pm with the arrival of the king and queen by boat. Following this, you can head to the **Plaza d'España**, where, in a formal ceremony unchanged for over a century, the mayor hands the city to Rex, King of Carnival. The party continues with more live music and fireworks, after which people head off to watch the big **Orpheus** parade, or start a frenzied evening of clubbing. Most clubs are still hopping well into Mardi Gras morning.

The fun starts early on Mardi Gras day, with **walking clubs** striding through uptown accompanied by raucous jazz on their ritualized bar crawls. Zulu, in theory, sets off at 8.30am (but can be as much as two hours late), followed by Rex. Ironically, by the time Rex turns up, many people have had their fill of the official parades. The surreal **St Ann walking parade** gathers in the Bywater, arriving in the Faubourg at around 11am, while the gay costume competition known as the **Bourbon Street awards** gets going at noon. In the afternoon, hipsters head back to the Faubourg, where **Frenchmen Street** is ablaze with bizarrely costumed carousers. The fun continues throughout the Quarter and the Faubourg until **midnight**, when a siren wail heralds the arrival of a cavalcade of mounted police that sweeps through Bourbon Street and declares through megaphones that Mardi Gras is officially over. Like all good Catholic cities, New Orleans takes carnival very seriously. Midnight marks the onset of Lent, and repentance can begin.

Other New Orleans festivals

St Joseph's Day, March 19. Sicilian saint's day, at the mid-point of Lent. Families build massive altars of food in their homes, inviting the public to come and admire them and to share food. The Sunday closest to St Joseph's ("Super Sunday") is the only time outside Mardi Gras that the Mardi Gras Indians (see above) take to the streets.

French Quarter Festival, early April. Free three-day music festival that rivals Jazz Fest for the quality and variety of music on offer. Stages and food stalls, a jazz brunch in Jackson Square, tours of private patios, free evening gigs, parades, and talent contests. ☏504/522-5730, ⓦwww.frenchquarterfestivals.org.

Jazz and Heritage Festival (Jazz Fest), two weekends (Fri–Sun) end April/early May at the Fairgrounds Race Track, Mid-City. Fabulous, enormous festival, with stages hosting jazz, R&B, gospel, African, Caribbean, Cajun, blues, reggae, funk, Mardi Gras Indian, rock, and brass band music, with evening performances in clubs all over town. Also has crafts stalls and phenomenal food stands (don't miss the crawfish bread). ☏504/522-4786, ⓦwww.nojazzfest.com.

Satchmo Fest, end July/early Aug. Free weekend festival, staged at the US Mint (see p.719), to celebrate Louis Armstrong's birthday. Talks and art exhibits focus on Satchmo himself, while the best local jazz and brass bands play live. Also a jazz mass at St Augustine's church in Tremé. ☏504/522-5730, ⓦwww.satchmosummerfest.com.

Southern Decadence, five days around Labor Day weekend. Huge gay extravaganza, bringing nearly 100,000 party animals to the gay bars and clubs of the Quarter and the Faubourg, with an unruly costume parade of thousands on the Sunday afternoon. ⓦwww.southerndecadence.com.

Halloween, Oct 31. Thanks to its long-held obsession with all things morbid, and the local passion for partying and dressing up, New Orleans is a fabulous place to spend Halloween, with haunted houses, costume competitions, ghost tours, and parades all over town.

Cajun country

Cajun country stretches across southern Louisiana from Houma in the east, via **Lafayette**, the hub of the region, into Texas. It's a region best enjoyed away from the larger towns, by visiting the many old-style hamlets that, despite modernization, can still be found cut off from civilization in soupy bayous, coastal marshes, and inland swamps.

Cajuns are descended from the French colonists of Acadia, part of Nova Scotia, which was taken by the British in 1713. The Catholic **Acadians**, who had quietly fished, hunted, and farmed for more than a century, refused to renounce their faith and swear allegiance to the English king, and in 1755 the British expelled them all, separating families and burning towns. About 2500 ended up in French Louisiana, where they were given land to set up small farming communities, enabling them to rebuild the culture they had left behind. Hunting, farming, and trapping, they lived in relative isolation until the 1940s, when major roads were built, immigrants from other states poured in to work in the **oil** business, and **Cajun music**, popularized by local musicians such as accordionist Iry Lejeune, came to national attention. Since then, the history of the Cajuns has continued to be one of struggle. The whole region was hit hard by the oil slump; the erosion of coastal wetlands threatens the existence of towns like Houma and Morgan City; the silting up of the Atchafalaya Basin is having adverse effects on fishing and shrimping; and many coastal towns are in the firing line of the devastating hurricanes that hurtle up from the Gulf of Mexico. After Roosevelt's administration decreed that all American children should speak English in schools, French was practically wiped out in Cajun country, and the local patois of the older inhabitants, with its strong African influences, was kept alive primarily by music. Since the 1980s, CODOFIL (the Council for Development of French in Louisiana) has been devoted to preserving the region's indigenous **language** and culture, and today you will find many signs, brochures, and shopfronts written in French.

The popular image of the Cajuns as partying, fun-loving people is borne out at their many local dances, or **fais-do-dos**, held mostly at weekends. These singing, dancing celebrations, where everyone is welcome to trip a quick two-step, are good places to encounter this unique culture at close hand, and visitors will find plenty of opportunity to join one, whether at a restaurant, a club, or one of the region's many **festivals**. Although **Baton Rouge**, the capital of Louisiana, is not actually in Cajun country, heading out this way from New Orleans, via the **plantations** on the banks of the Mississippi, makes a good approach.

Northwest from New Orleans: plantation country

The fastest roads out from New Orleans toward the west are the major I-10 and US-61; you can also drive along the **River Road**, which hugs both banks of the Mississippi all the way to Baton Rouge, seventy miles upriver. It's not a particularly eventful drive, winding through flat, fertile farmland, but a series of bridges and ferries allows you to crisscross the water, stopping off and touring several restored antebellum **plantation homes** along the way. Before the Civil War, these spectacular homes were the focal points of the vast estates from where wealthy planters – or rather, their slaves – loaded cotton, sugar, or indigo onto steamboats berthed virtually at their front doors. Generally, the superb Laura plantation excepted (see below), **tours**, often led by belles in ballgowns, skimp on details about the estates as a whole, and in particular their often vast slave populations, presenting them instead as showcase museums filled with priceless antiques. The cumulative effect of these evocations of a long-lost "gracious" era can be stultifying, so it's best to pick just one or two. Many of the houses also offer luxurious **B&B** rooms (rates include tours), which as well as being rather wonderful places to sleep, allow you to absorb more of the atmosphere of the plantations than is possible on the walkthroughs.

To get to the River Road from New Orleans, take I-10 west to exit 220, turn onto I-310 and follow it to **Hwy-48**, on the east bank (*above* the river on the map). This shortly becomes **Hwy-44**, or the River Road. For the west bank (*below* the river), cross Destrehan Bridge onto **Hwy-18** rather than branching onto Hwy-48. It's important to note that the levee runs the length of the banks, blocking the river from view, and though you'd never guess it from the tourist brochures, it's the hulking chemical plants that dominate the River Road landscape. There are rural stretches where wide sugarcane fields are interrupted only by moss-covered shacks – the prettiest views are to be found around the small town of **Convent**, on the east bank – but you'll more often find yourself driving through straggling communities of boarded-up lounges and laundromats, scarred by scrap piles and smokestacks.

From **Edgard**, 25 miles along on Hwy-18, you can cross the river to the **San Francisco House** (daily: March–Oct 9.30am–4.40pm; Nov–Feb 9.30am–4pm; $10), two miles upriver of **Reserve** on Hwy-44. Built in a style dubbed "Steamboat Gothic" by novelist Frances Parkinson Keyes, its rails, awnings, and pillars were designed to re-create the ambiance of a Mississippi showboat. The elaborate facade is matched by a gorgeous interior – a riot of pastoral trompe l'oeils, floral motifs, and Italian cherubs. Crossing the river at **Lutcher**, the settlement a few miles beyond San Francisco, brings you to Vacherie and the fascinating **Laura plantation** (daily 9am–4pm; $10). Rather than dwelling lovingly on priceless antiques, the standard tours here, which draw upon a wealth of historical documents – from slave accounts and photographs to private diaries – sketch a vivid picture of day-to-day plantation life in multicultural Louisiana. Uniquely, they also offer very good **slavery tours** (11am & 2.45pm), which concentrate on the institution of slavery under French, Spanish, and American rule.

Nine miles upriver from Laura, **Oak Alley** is the quintessential image of the antebellum plantation home. It's a splendid Greek Revival mansion dating from 1839 – and the magnificent oaks that form a canopy over the driveway are 150 years older (daily: March–Oct 9am–5.30pm; Nov–Feb 9am–5pm; $10). The **restaurant** (8.30–10am & 11am–3pm) serves Cajun food, and you can **stay** in pretty B&B cottages in the grounds (☎225/265-2151, Ⓦwww.oakalley plantation.com; ⑤).

Eighteen miles south of Baton Rouge on the west bank, **Nottoway** is the largest surviving plantation home in the South, a huge white Italianate edifice of 64 rooms, 200 windows, and 165 doors (daily 9am–5pm; $10). The house also has fancy **B&B** rooms (☎225/545-2730, Ⓦwww.nottoway.com; ⑤) and a **restaurant** (daily 11am–2pm & 6–8.30pm).

Baton Rouge

When French explorers first came upon the site of **BATON ROUGE** in 1699, they found poles smeared in animal blood to designate the separate hunting grounds of the Houmas and Bayougoulas Indians. The area on these shallow bluffs therefore appeared on French maps as *Baton Rouge* – "red stick." Now capital of Louisiana and the fifth biggest port in the US, Baton Rouge is an easygoing city for its size. Even the presence of the state's largest **universities**, LSU and Southern, has done surprisingly little to raise the town anywhere much above "sleepy" status.

Surrounded by fifty acres of showpiece gardens, the magnificent Art Deco **Louisiana State Capitol** (daily 8am–4.30pm; free) serves as a monument to **Huey Long**, the "Kingfish," the larger-than-life Democratic state governor who ordered its construction in 1931 and was assassinated in its corridors just four years later. First elected governor in 1928 after a vehemently anti-big-business campaign, Long swiftly concentrated power into his own hands. His massive program of public works included financing charity hospitals by levying heavy taxes on the big oil and gas corporations. Variously labeled a demagogue, a communist, and a fascist, he set himself apart from other Southern populists of the time by refusing to exploit the race issue. Just as his appeal – with slogans like "Every Man a King" – began to reach national proportions, with a bid for the presidency in the offing, he was shot by a local doctor whose exact motives remain unknown.

Other controversial figures to have worked in the building include the segregationist country singer **Jimmie Davis** (Democratic governor 1944–48 and 1960–64), better remembered for writing the song "You Are My Sunshine" and riding his horse up the steps of the capitol than for any political skills; **David Duke**, a former Grand Wizard of the Ku Klux Klan, who was elected as a state representative in 1989, ran unsuccessfully as the Republican candidate for governor in 1991, and was imprisoned in 2003 for conning his supporters out of hundreds of thousands of dollars; and **Eddie Edwards** (Democratic governor 1972–80, 1984–88, and 1992–96) who in 2001 was sentenced to ten years in prison for extorting money from businessmen applying for riverboat casino licenses.

Tours of this stunning building, with its huge murals and sculptures, are enlivened by remnants of Louisiana's maverick political history. Guides point out stray bullets in the marble pillars of the ground-floor corridor and a pencil embedded in the ceiling of the legislative chamber by an exploding bomb. Long decreed that no building in Baton Rouge could be taller than the 450ft capitol (it's the tallest in the nation), so its 27th-floor observation deck (closes 4pm) is the best vantage point to look out over the surrounding Art Deco complexes and lush greenery, the bustling traffic on the sluggish Mississippi, and the tangle of puffing chemical refineries on the horizon.

Mark Twain referred to Baton Rouge's **Old State Capitol** (in use from 1850 to 1932), 100 North Blvd, as "that monstrosity on the Mississippi." A grey, crenellated structure on a mound overlooking the river, it's worth a look for the **Center for Political and Governmental History** (Tues–Sat 10am–4pm, Sun noon–4pm; $4). Movies, interactive exhibits, and some great archive footage of Long's impassioned speeches illuminate Louisiana's scandal-ridden political history.

The splendid **LSU Rural Life Museum**, 4560 Essen Rd, just off I-10 southeast of downtown (daily 8.30am–5pm; $7), re-creates pre-industrial Louisiana life through its carefully restored buildings – among them a plantation house, slave cottages, and a grist mill – spread over 25 acres in a sultry garden setting.

Practicalities

Greyhound **buses**, as well as connecting buses from New Orleans' Amtrak station, come in at 1253 Florida St, fifteen minutes from downtown. Local buses, run by Capital City Transportation (☎225/389-8282), are infrequent; for Yellow Cab, call ☎225/926-3260. The **visitor center** is inside the state capitol (daily 8am–4.30pm; ☎225/342-7317, ⓦwww.visitbatonrouge.com). As for **accommodation**, the *Best Western Chateau Louisianne*, off I-10 at 710 N Lobdell (☎225/927-6700, ⓦwww.bestwestern.com; ❹), has large rooms arranged around a pretty atrium, with a gym and pool on site. Good **B&Bs** include the pretty *Mount Hope Plantation*, 8151 Highland Rd (☎225/761-7000, ⓦwww.mthopeplantation; ❺), housed in a nineteenth-century plantation home.

For **eating**, *Aroyelles on the River*, 333 3rd St (☎225/214-9632), serves blue plate specials and great shrimp po-boys; *Juban's*, 3739 Perkins Rd (☎225/346-8422), has pricey, inventive Creole seafood; and *Petit Marche*, in the Main Street Market, Fifth Street at Main, is where local celebrity chef John Folse dishes up top-quality breakfasts, sandwiches, and lunch specials. Most of the city's **nightlife** centers around the **LSU campus**, along College Drive, Chimes Street, and Highland Road. Try *Swamp Mama's*, 143 3rd St (☎225/344-2583), which has great blues and jazz, and *Tabby's Blues Box*, 244 Lafayette St (☎225/387-9715), a friendly juke joint where veteran bluesman Tabby Thomas and friends play in spartan surroundings.

Lafayette and around

LAFAYETTE, 135 miles northwest of New Orleans on I-10, is geographically central in Cajun country, and is the key city for its oil business. Originally named Vermilionville, after the orangey bayou nearby, it was renamed in 1844 in honor of the Marquis de Lafayette, the aristocratic French hero of the American Revolution. Today it's a quiet place, a city with a small-town feel and no real center. It does, however, offer some lively **Cajun history** and good **restaurants** – and makes a central base for exploring the swamps, bayous, and dance halls of the surrounding region.

Arrival, information, and getting around

Greyhound arrives in Lafayette at 315 Lee St; **Amtrak** pulls in a few blocks north at 133 E Grant St at Jefferson. The **airport**, south of town on Hwy-90, meets daily flights from Houston, Dallas, Memphis, and Atlanta. Pick up essential maps from the Lafayette Parish **visitor center** at 1400 NW Evangeline Thruway at Willow St, exit 103A off I-10 (Mon–Fri 8.30am–5pm, Sat & Sun 9am–5pm; ☎337/232-3737 or 1-800/346-1958, ⓦwww.lafayettetravel.com). To get the best out of the area you'll need a **car**, as the dance halls, restaurants, and hotels are spread out, and the local bus system is of little use to visitors. If you need a **taxi**, try Yellow Checker Cab (☎318/237-5701).

Accommodation in and around Lafayette

Scores of chain **hotels** line Evangeline Thruway just south of I-10, and US-90 and Hwy-182 toward New Iberia. Alternatively, the friendly hamlet of **Breaux Bridge** (see p.742), just eight miles east of Lafayette, makes another appealing base. You can **camp** at KOA Lafayette (☎337/235-2739, ⓦwww.koa.com), five miles west of town, in Scott; they also have 19 cabins, some of them with two rooms (❷–❸).

Cajun festivals

Cajun festivals, held almost weekly it seems, are a wonderful way to experience the food and music of the region. For some of the larger events, it's a good idea to reserve a room in advance; the rest of the world is catching on to the fun. The following is merely a sampler; for full details, check with any tourist office in the area.

Mardi Gras, Feb/March. Cajun Carnival differs from its city cousin; although there are private balls, parties, and formal parades, it is a far more countrified affair. There's plenty of music and street dancing, of course, and country villages like Eunice, Church Point, and Mamou are the scene of the mischievous *Courir de Mardi Gras* (see p.744). ⓦwww.swmardigras.com, ⓦwww.churchpointcourirdemardigras.com.

World Championship Crawfish Étouffée Cookoff, last Sunday in March (the Sunday before, if Easter falls on the last Sunday in March), Eunice. *The* place to taste the very best mudbugs, accompanied by great local music and a fierce spirit of competition among the hundred or so teams. ⓣ337/457-2565.

Festival International de Louisiane, last full week in April. Huge, free five-day festival in Lafayette, with participants from all over the French-speaking world, celebrating a wealth of indigenous music and food. ⓣ337/232-8086, ⓦwww .festivalinternational.com.

Breaux Bridge Crawfish Festival, first full weekend of May (Fri–Sun), Breaux Bridge. Crawfish-eating and -peeling contests, étouffée cookoffs, and mudbug races, along with music, crafts stalls, and dancing. $5 per day, $10 for three days; ⓣ337/332-6655, ⓦwww.bbcrawfest.com. The **African-American Festival**, held on the same days, hosts some great zydeco bands; ⓣ337/332-3819, ⓦwww.kingcrawfish.com.

Southwest Louisiana Zydeco Music Festival, Fri evening & Sat before Labor Day, 457 Zydeco Rd, off Hwy-167, Plaisance, near Opelousas. Top zydeco performers play "black Creole" music; with regional cuisine and African-American arts-and-crafts. $13, $2 for kids; ⓣ337/942-2392, ⓦwww.zydeco.org.

Mamou Cajun Music Festival, the first weekend in Sept (Fri & Sat), Mamou, 10 miles north of Eunice. Traditional live music, food, crafts, and a Cajun Queen beauty contest for the over-65s. $3; ⓣ337/468-3993.

Festivals Acadiens, third weekend in Sept, Lafayette. Huge three-day festival, with Cajun, zydeco, and traditional French bands, as well as indigenous crafts and food. ⓣ337/232-3737 or 1-800/346-1958, ⓦwww.lafayettetravel.com/events/festivals /fest_aca.cfm.

Tri-Parish Fair, four days around the last weekend in Oct, Eunice. Old-fashioned country fair with livestock shows, pie contests, crafts stalls, rodeos, carnival rides, and, of course, music and dancing. ⓣ337/457-7389.

Louisiana Yambilee, last week in Oct. Opelousas goes all out to celebrate the sweet potato, with food stalls, sweet potato auctions, music, and Miss Yambilee and Lil' Miss Yum Yum contests. ⓣ337/948-8848 or 1-800/210-5298, ⓦwww.members .tripod.com/yambilee/yambilee.htm.

Aaah! T'Frere's 1905 Verot School Rd, 6 miles south of I-10, Lafayette ⓣ337/984-9347 or 1-800/984-9347, ⓦwww.tfreres.com. Hospitable B&B in an antique-filled, cypress-built home, offering complimentary "T'juleps" and delicious Cajun/Creole breakfasts. ❺

Bayou Cabins 100 W Mills Ave/Hwy-94, Breaux Bridge ⓣ337/332-6158, ⓦwww.bayoucabins .com. Nine rustic cabins – most of which date from the nineteenth century – on Bayou Teche.

Run by the owners of *Bayou Boudin and Cracklin'* (see p.740); rates include a free taster of their fantastic Cajun food and breakfast served in the café next door. ❸

Bayou Teche B&B 205 Washington St, Breaux Bridge ⓣ337/332-1049, ⓦwww.breauxbridge-live.com/bayoubb. Appealing guesthouse right on the bayou, in an 1812 Creole cottage expanded in the 1880s to become a boarding house. Rates can include a full breakfast at *Café des Amis* (see p.741) or simply coffee and pastries; the exceptionally welcoming host, who knows everything there is to know about the area, leaves you to treat the place like home. ❸–❹

Blue Moon Guest House and Saloon 215 E Convent St, Lafayette ☏ 337/234-2422, ⓦ www.bluemoonhostel.com. Cheerful hostel, in a nineteenth-century house near the university, with five dorms ($15–20; some can be converted to private rooms with notice) and one suite. On-site yoga classes and regular Cajun, zydeco, and bluegrass gigs in the backyard. ❶–❷

Plantation Motor Inn 2810 NE Evangeline Thruway, Lafayette ☏ 337/232-7285. Respectable motel north of town near the interstate, with plain, clean rooms and free continental breakfast. ❸

The Town

In the center, such as it is, of Lafayette stands the Romanesque **Cathedral of St John the Evangelist**, 914 St John St (Mon–Fri 9am–noon & 1–4pm; $1), and the old **cemetery**, where the crumbling raised graves include that of Jean Mouton, the town's Cajun founder. Each of the magnificent branches of the 500-year-old **Cathedral Oak** opposite, spreading over 200ft, weighs seventy tons. Three blocks away, the small **Lafayette Museum**, 1122 Lafayette St (Tues–Sat 9am–4.30pm, Sun 1–4pm; $3), was the "Sunday home" – a townhouse used after Mass, before the family returned to their plantation – of Jean's son Alexandre, Louisiana's first Democratic governor. It's now filled with family memorabilia, Civil War relics, and Cajun Mardi Gras costumes. If you're traveling with kids, the **Lafayette Natural History Museum and Planetarium**, 433 Jefferson St (Tues 9am–9.30pm, Wed–Fri 9am–5pm, Sat 10am–6pm, Sun 1–6pm; $5) is a good bet – its collection includes basketry, musical instruments, pottery, and paintings, as well as the usual bones, fossils, and interactive stations, with some strong temporary exhibits.

South of the town center, the campus of the **University of Louisiana at Lafayette** boasts a swamp – complete with alligators, turtles, water birds, and tattered Spanish moss. Its **art museum** showcases local artists, Southern folk art, and some major French works, along with traveling exhibitions (Tues–Sat 10am–5pm, Sun 1–5pm; $10).

Lafayette has two excellent reconstructions of early Cajun communities. **Vermilionville**, 300 Fisher Rd across from the airport, is the most accessible, and impressive, of the two, extending its scope to explore the culture of the early Creoles as well as the Cajuns (Tues–Sun 10am–4pm; $8). Set in 23 attractive acres on the Bayou Vermilion, it's a living history site, filled with craftspeople using traditional skills. A large replica of an old cotton gin serves as a **theater**, hosting storytellers, plays, and noisy *fais-do-dos*. Cooking demonstrations are staged three times a day, and the **restaurant** serves good Cajun lunches (Tues–Fri 11am–2pm, Sat & Sun 11am–3pm).

Next to Vermilionville, 501 Fisher Rd, the **Acadian Cultural Center**, in the **Jean Lafitte National Historical Park and Preserve** (daily 8am–5pm; free), offers a thorough background on the history and culture of the displaced Cajuns, with a wealth of artifacts and a forty-minute film shown on the hour. Further southwest, ten miles or so from the Lafayette visitor center, Lafayette's other folk-life museum, the smaller **Acadian Village**, 200 Greenleaf Drive (daily 10am–5pm; $7), depicts early nineteenth-century Cajun life along the bayous. Original homes and reproductions of other structures – including a blacksmith's shop and a chapel – line a sluggish bayou set in gardens and woodlands, and are filled with traditional furnishings and crafts.

North of town, off I-49, **Louisiana Heritage and Gifts**, 500 East Gloria Switch Rd (Tues–Sat 10am–5pm) is a wonderful store-cum-gallery that, as well as displaying musical instruments and local folk art, sells a host of good books, CDs, videos, and crafts. They also have good Saturday **jam sessions**.

Cajun music venues

It's easy to "pass a good time" in Cajun country, especially if you're here at the weekend, when the *fais-do-dos* are traditionally held. Though things are quieter during the week, you'll still be able to enjoy authentic local music at many of the restaurants. Cajun music is a jangling, infectious melange of nasal vocals backed by jumping accordion, violin, and triangle, fueled by traces of country, swing, jazz, and blues. Zydeco is similar, but sexier, more blues-based, and more often played by black musicians. Though songs are in French, the patois heard in both bears only a passing resemblance to the language spoken in France. Music is never performed without space for dancing; everyone from the smallest child to most aged grandparent can join in. As well as the popular restaurants *Café des Amis*, *Mulate's*, *Prejean's*, and *Randol's* (reviewed on p.741), plus the *Blue Moon Guest House* (see p.739), venues include dance halls, record stores, river landings, and the streets themselves. Check the music listings in the free weekly *Times of Acadiana* (distributed on Friday) or simply look for signs saying "French dance here tonight."

Atchafalaya Club 1008 Henderson Levee Rd, Henderson, Breaux Bridge ☏337/228-7110. Large dance hall on the levee, linked to *Pat's* seafood restaurant, and hosting Cajun and swamp pop bands.

Bourque's Club 152 Leo Lane, Lewisburg, 10 miles south of Opelousas ☏337/948-8646. One of the last of the old-style country dance halls, with live music Saturday 8pm–midnight and Sunday 5–8pm.

Dragon Café 107 S Main St, Breaux Bridge ☏337/507-3320. Down-home

café hosting fabulous zydeco breakfasts (starting at 8am) on the weekend.

El Sid O's 1523 Martin Luther King Drive, Lafayette ☏337/235-0647. Dancing Friday through Sunday, with great zydeco and blues bands; they also serve Creole food.

Fred's Lounge 420 6th St, Mamou, 10 miles north of Eunice ☏337/468-2300. Extremely welcoming home of the locally famed radio show "Live from Fred's Lounge" (KVPI 1050 AM), with music, dancing, and lots of drinking. You'll want to try Tante Sue's "Hot Damn," which is

Eating in and around Lafayette

They say that a Cajun cooks every part of a pig but its squeal, and it's true that **Cajun dishes** are packed with a jumble of flavors, textures, and, well, pretty much anything that's good and fresh. Though it bears resemblances to the Creole cuisine you'll find in New Orleans – lots of seafood, rice, rich tomatoey sauces and gumbos – this is rustic food, often spicy, and yes, pork features highly on many menus. It's very difficult to eat badly around here, and prices are generally low. At lunchtime, take-out boudin (spicy sausage) is a treat, as are finger-licking specialties like rich pork cracklin' and salty hogshead cheese. Often, eating in Cajun country is inseparable from **dancing** and **music**; evening – or afternoon, or morning – entertainment revolves around restaurants that double as dance halls. Even if you don't feel like two-stepping yourself, it's great fun to watch all the old-timers and young sweethearts whirling around the room while you gorge on a delicious dinner of spicy seafood, washed down with a frosty beer.

Bayou Boudin and Cracklin' 100 Mills Ave, Hwy-94, Breaux Bridge, exit 109 from I-10 ☏337/332-6158. Nineteenth-century Cajun-country cottage on Bayou Teche, serving seafood boudin, hogshead cheese-smothered chicken, and crawfish balls, all prepared on the spot from tradi-

tional recipes. Fabulous for Sunday lunch. Tues–Sat 7am–6pm, Sun 7am–1pm.

Blue Dog Café 1211 W Pinhook Rd, Lafayette ☏337/237-0005. Dine on classy Cajun/Creole food – the crawfish étouffée is great – surrounded by the distinctive blue dog paintings of Cajun artist

warm cinnamon schnapps. Saturday only, 8am–2pm.

Grant Street Dancehall 113 W Grant St, Lafayette ⊕337/237-8513, ⓦwww .grantstreetdancehall.com. Eclectic music venue hosting great hip-hop, swamp pop, and blues, as well as Cajun and zydeco.

Hamilton's 1808 Verot School Rd, Lafayette ⊕337/984-5583. Old zydeco dance hall on the outskirts of town, open Friday and Saturday nights.

La Poussière 1215 Grand Point Ave, Breaux Bridge ⊕337/332-1721. The old folks' favorite, this venerable dance hall hosts *fais-do-dos* on Saturday night & on Sunday from 4–8pm.

Louisiana Heritage and Gifts 500 East Gloria Switch Rd, Lafayette ⊕337/237-9258. No dancing, but a lively jam session on Saturday from 3–5pm at this great music/crafts store (see p.739).

Rendezvous des Cajuns Liberty Center for Performing Arts, S 2nd St and Park Ave, Eunice ⊕337/457-7389, ⓦwww.eunice-la .com/libertyschedule.html. Live Cajun/zydeco radio and TV show, mostly in French, every

Sat 6–7.30pm. Family-oriented and hugely popular.

Richard's 11178 Hwy-190 W, 8 miles west of Opelousas in Lawtell ⊕337/543-6596. Congenial, rustic old place for zydeco bands; regular Saturday-evening dances plus occasional events on Friday and Sunday.

Savoy Music Center 4413 Hwy-190 E, 3 miles east of Eunice ⊕337/457-9563, ⓦsavoymusiccenter.com. Cajun record shop, where accordions are made in the back room. The store is open Tuesday through Friday, but you should aim to be here for the joyous jam sessions on Saturday from 9am–noon.

Slim's Y-Ki-Ki 8393 Hwy-182 N, Opelousas ⊕337/942-6242. Famed old venue for zydeco music and dancing. Friday and Saturday only.

Whiskey River Whiskey River Landing, 1365 Henderson Levee Rd, Henderson, Breaux Bridge ⊕337/228-8567, ⓦwww .angelleswhiskeyriver.com. Live Cajun music and drinking at *Angelle's*, the starting point for a popular swamp tour (see p.743), on Sunday from 4–8pm.

George Rodrigue. Smooth live jazz in the bar Friday and Saturday nights. Closed Sun.

Café des Amis 140 E Bridge St, Breaux Bridge ⊕337/332-5273. Friendly, atmospheric, rustic/arty restaurant serving simply fantastic Cajun/Creole food. Breakfasts, with lots of eggy, crawfish-smothered concoctions, are fabulous – and don't miss the syrup cake. Live zydeco breakfasts Saturday 8–11am, and folk, jazz, and blues on Wednesday evening. Closed Mon.

Dwyer's 323 Jefferson St, Lafayette ⊕337/235-9364. Downtown favorite for huge, inexpensive breakfasts and plate lunches, homecooked burgers, and local specialties. Mon–Fri 4am–4pm, Sat & Sun 5am–2pm.

Mulate's 325 Mills Ave, Breaux Bridge ⊕337/332-4648 and 1-800/634-9880. This is the original Cajun restaurant/dance hall and, though touristy, a favorite with locals, too. Seafood, catfish, and gumbo go for less than $15; dancing nightly at 7pm, and at noon on weekends.

Poche's 3015A Hwy-31, north of Breaux Bridge ⊕337/332-2108. One of the best places to pick up boudin, cracklin', andouille, and old-fashioned pies, as well as tasty home-cooked plate lunches. Mon–Sat 6am–8pm, Sun 6am–6pm.

Poupart's 1902 W Pinhook Rd, Lafayette ⊕337/232-7921. Superb French bakery serving good quiches, continental breakfasts, and sandwiches. Try the exquisite pastries and crawfish pies. Tues–Sat 7am–6.30pm, Sun 7am–4pm. Breakfast and lunch only.

Prejean's 3480 I-49 N, Lafayette ⊕337/896-3247. Huge restaurant offering exquisite Cajun/Creole food, nightly live music, and a small dance floor. Everything is delicious, especially the fish and seafood – don't miss the pepperjack shrimp or any of the oyster dishes. Live music begins at 7pm; watch out for the wonderful Freres Michot, who play on Mondays.

Randol's 2320 Kaliste Saloom Rd, Lafayette ⊕337/981-7080. Locally famed restaurant with a large dance floor. Live Cajun and zydeco nightly and steamed seafood dinners (boiled softshell crabs are a specialty). Dinner only.

Touring Cajun country

You could easily drive through **BREAUX BRIDGE**, eight miles east of Lafayette, and miss it, which would be a big shame. Quite apart from its sweet, old-fashioned main street, its unusual crawfish-emblazoned steel bridge over the Bayou Teche (which announces in French that this is the "crawfish capital of the world"), and its handful of good B&Bs, great restaurants, and music venues, it also makes an appealing base for some of the region's best **swamp tours** (see opposite), and for exploring the wonderful **Lake Martin nature reserve**, three miles south on Hwy-31. There's an end-of-the-earth feel here, where land turns to water, and it's a great experience to drive – or walk the trails – past staggering vistas of tangled cypress flickering with Spanish moss and encroaching greenery creeping onto the narrow road. From February to June tens of thousands of birds nest at the lake, though there's a huge abundance of **birdlife** year-round, including egrets, herons, and spoonbills, not to mention busy nutria splashing through the undergrowth and scores of **alligators** dozing in the sun. If you fancy paddling a **canoe** through this fabulous wilderness, contact Pack and Paddle in Lafayette (☏337/232-5854).

North of Lafayette, the **Cajun Prairie** has been described by folklorist Alan Lomax as the "Cajun cultural heartland." A patchwork of rice and soybean fields scattered with crawfish ponds, the region has a few tiny towns where you'll be greeted with genuine warmth and interest by locals.

GRAND COTEAU, off I-49 ten miles north of Lafayette, is a picture-perfect little town, with whitewashed buildings – including a dazzling white chapel – and prettily winding roads. Since 1866, when a dying woman was miraculously healed by the intercession of a saint in the **Academy of the Sacred Heart**, 1821 Academy Rd, devout Cajun Catholics have made pilgrimages here. You can see the old classrooms of this beautifully columned school, and follow a long path through the ornate gardens, canopied by huge old oaks (Mon–Fri 9am–2pm by appointment; $6; ☏319/662-5275, ⓦwww.ashcoteau.org).

The 1831 **Chretien Point Plantation**, in **SUNSET**, ten miles north of Lafayette on Hwy-93 just off I-10, is one of Louisiana's oldest Greek Revival buildings (daily: April–Sept 11am–5pm; Oct–March 1–5pm; $7). Its main staircase was the model for *Tara's* in *Gone with the Wind*. Mrs Chretien, left to run the plantation after her husband's death in 1832, was very much in the Scarlett O'Hara mode. She scandalized the community by drinking, smoking, gambling, and sitting with the men after dinner, and once shot an intruder, whose ghost is said to roam the corridors. Bullet holes in the front door date from 1863, when Mrs Chretien's son showed a Masonic sign to an attacking Union general, who thereupon directed fire over the roof. The plantation has five luxurious **B&B** rooms (☏337/662-7050 or 1-800/880-7050, ⓦwww.chretien-point.com; ⑥).

Sleepy old **OPELOUSAS**, twenty miles north of Lafayette on I-49, was capital of Louisiana for a short period during the Civil War, and now has five claims to fame. It was the boyhood home of Jim Bowie, Texas Revolutionary hero and inventor of the Bowie knife; the first place in the world to produce an offset newspaper (in 1915); the birthplace of the great zydeco musician **Clifton Chenier** and celebrity Cajun chef **Paul Prudhomme**; and today, even more excitingly, it's the **yam** capital of the universe (see p.738 for a festival celebrating this achievement). You can find out more about the town at the quirky **Opelousas Museum**, 315 N Main St (Mon–Sat 9am–5pm; free), which displays such relics of local history as the barber's stool on which outlaw Clyde Barrow

Swamp tours

Swamp tours are available from many landings in the **Atchafalaya Basin**; you'll pass numerous signs pinned to the old cypress trees along the roadside. The basin is an eerie place: the bulk of its cypress was harvested last century, and now you'll see the twisted silhouettes of their stumps poke out of the sluggish waters. In some places cars cut right across on the enormous concrete I-10 above, and old house-boats lie abandoned, or get used only for weekend retreats. The best tours take you further out, to the backwoods; wherever you go you'll see scores of fishing boats and plenty of wildlife, including sunbathing alligators. The tours below are conduct-ed by Cajuns who see the basin as more than just a tourist attraction and provide fascinating personal commentaries.

Angelle's Atchafalaya Basin Swamp Tours Whiskey River Landing, 1365 Henderson Levee Rd, Henderson, Breaux Bridge ☎337/228-8567, ⓦwww .angelleswhiskeyriver.com. Twenty-five minutes from Lafayette, along I-10 to exit 115, then highways 347 and 332, this quiet landing is also host to a great *fais-do-do* on Sunday from 4–8pm. Swamp tours daily 10am, 1pm & 3pm; 90min; no reser-vations required; $12.

The Atchafalaya Experience 338 N Sterling St, Lafayette ☎337/261-5050, ⓦwww.theatchafalayaexperience.com. The son in this father-son team is a geolo-gist; both guides are lifelong explorers of the swamp, and tours are ecologically sen-sitive. Daily 9.30am & 3pm; 3hr; reservations required; $40.

McGee's Swamp Tours McGee's Landing, 1337 Henderson Levee Rd, Breaux Bridge ☎337/228-2384, ⓦwww.mcgeeslanding.com. Leisurely tours run from Henderson Swamp, a top fishing spot. Daily 10am, 1pm & 3pm; no tours in Jan; 90min; reservations recommended; $12. Café open Tues–Sun.

got his last shave before being shot dead by the FBI in northern Louisiana. Stop by the 1950s *Palace Café*, on the central square at 135 W Landry Ave (☎337/942-2142), for shrimp, crawfish, and gumbo in immaculate **diner** surroundings. If you're tempted to stay the night, head for one of the chain hotels outside town on I-49; both the *Best Western* (☎1-800/942-5540, ⓦwww.bestwestern.com; ❸) – just south of town – and the *Holiday Inn* (☎337/948-3300, ⓦwww.holiday-inn.com; ❹) – just north – are relatively new.

To learn a little about the Cajun prairie, head for friendly **EUNICE**, about twenty miles west of Opelousas. The exemplary **Prairie Acadian Cultural Center** at the **Jean Lafitte National Historical Park**, 250 W Park Ave (Tues–Fri 8am–5pm, Sat 8am–6pm; free), holds far-reaching displays on local life, ranging across family, language, food, and farming, with regular live Cajun music, storytelling, and cookery demonstrations. There's more music at the **Cajun Music Hall of Fame**, 240 S C.C. Duson Drive (Tues–Sat: summer 9am–5pm, winter 8.30am–4.30pm; free), which features accordions, steel gui-tars, fiddles, and triangles among its memorabilia, with a Wall Of Fame honing in on names like Dewey Balfa, Iry LeJeune, and Leroy "Happy Fats" Leblanc. If time is limited, choose these two over the **Eunice Museum**, next to the Hall of Fame at 220 S C.C. Duson Drive (Tues–Sat: summer 9am–5pm, win-ter 8.30am–4.30pm; free) – though this too has its charms; it's an old train depot crammed with a ragbag of toys, musical instruments, farming imple-ments, and Native American artifacts. However long you're in town, don't miss out on Eunice's splendid **food** – *Johnson's Grocery*, 700 E Maple Ave (☎318/457-9314), serves fat, juicy boudin, and spicy hogshead cheese, while *Allison's Hickory Pit*, 501 W Laurel Ave (Thurs–Sun 11am–2pm; ☎318/457-9218), specializes in pork, chicken, steak, and brisket smothered in a tasty, oniony barbecue sauce. At *Ruby's*, 221 W Walnut St (☎318/457-2583), you can eat home-cooked soul food in a wonderful vintage setting. Although there's little else to see in Eunice, the town is central to the region's **music scene**; the regular Savoy Music Center and Liberty Center bashes (see p.741) are supplemented by the riotous annual **Courir du Mardi Gras**, when masked horsemen gallop through the countryside before parading through downtown, where the drinking and dancing continues all day. The **Music Machine**, 235 W Walnut St (daily 9am–7pm), is a good source of local music information, with a fine collection of Cajun, zydeco, and swamp pop; there's a snow-cone stand to boot. *Potier's Prairie Cajun Inn*, at 110 W Park Ave (☎337/457-0440, ☎potiers.net; ❹), next door to the Liberty Center, is a 1920s hospital restored as a friendly **place to stay**.

From here it's twenty miles north to **VILLE PLATTE**, and the fabulous Floyd's Music Store, 434 E Main St (Mon–Sat 8.30am–4.30pm; ⓦwww.floyd-srecords.com), owned by dashing Floyd Soileau, the world's chief distributor of **South Louisiana music**, and stocking everything from zydeco reissues to contemporary swamp pop. If Mr Soileau isn't around, you could well find him listening to the rocking jukebox a couple of doors down at the *Pig Stand*, 318 E Main St (☎337/363-2883), where giant plates of fried chicken, smothered sausage, and ribs come heaped with rice, gravy, black-eyed peas, and potato salad.

South of Lafayette

South of Lafayette, the towns are less immediately welcoming than those in the Prairie, but the surroundings are undeniably atmospheric: this is **bayou country**, a marshy expanse of rivers and lakes dominated by the mighty Atchafalaya swamp, where the soupy green waters creep right up to the edges of the highway. Unsurprisingly, the economy is based on fishing and shrimping, with hunting in the forests and sugar fields, but it's also a semi-industrial landscape, with a web of oil pipelines running beneath the waterways, and refineries and corrugated-iron shacks sharing space with neat white Catholic churches.

Settled in 1765, old **ST MARTINVILLE** on the Bayou Teche, off US-90 and 18 miles south of Lafayette, was a major port of entry for exiled Acadians. Hard to believe now, but in the nineteenth century this country town grew to become known as "le petit Paris," filled with French Royalists fleeing the Revolution and re-creating a glittering city life of soirees and balls. It was later decimated by yellow fever, fire, and hurricane, and is now a peaceful hamlet, kept going by a trickle of tourists. You'll see a lot of references to "Evangeline." To find out why, head for **Evangeline Oak Park**, on Evangeline Boulevard where it meets the bayou. Here stands the **Evangeline Oak**, where real-life Acadian **Emmeline Labiche**, the inspiration for Longfellow's epic poem *Evangeline*, disembarked after her hard journey from Nova Scotia, only to hear that her lover, Gabriel, was engaged to another. From Monday to Saturday, and if the weather is good, you may find a small group of musicians or storytellers around the tree. The park, which has a boardwalk along the bayou, also features the **St Martinville Cultural Heritage Center**, where the **Museum of the Acadian Memorial** (daily 10am–4pm; free) pays tribute to the 3000 refugees displaced from Canada to Louisiana between 1764 and 1788, and the **African-American Museum** (daily 10am–4pm; free) focuses on the arrival of enslaved Africans into southwest Louisiana during the 1700s, the emergence of free people of color, and the violence of Reconstruction. Nearby, the **Acadian Memorial** (daily 10am–4pm; $2) itself has a 30-foot mural marking the Acadians' arrival in Louisiana and a Wall of Names honoring those uprooted during the "Grand Dérangement."

Other sights, such as they are, can be found on or around the town square. The nineeenth-century St Martin de Tours **Catholic church**, at 133 Main St (daily except Fri morning), contains a gold and silver sanctuary light and intricate carved font said to have been gifts from Louis XVI and Marie Antoinette; next door, the off-beat **Petit Paris Museum** exhibits local Mardi Gras costumes (daily 9.30am–4.30pm; $1). Behind the church, the bronze **Evangeline Monument** was donated by the producers of the 1929 movie *The Romance of Evangeline*, and is modeled on Dolores del Rio, its star. On the bayou just north of town on Hwy-31, the **Longfellow–Evangeline State Commemorative Area** (daily 9am–5pm; $2) features a couple of simple **Acadian dwellings** and, in contrast, an 1815 **Creole Plantation House**, made with the *bousillage* mixture (mud, Spanish moss, and animal hair) characteristic of early Louisiana buildings. If St Martinville's sleepy charm wins you over, and you want to stay, try the *Old Castillo*, 220 Evangeline Blvd next to the Evangeline Oak (℡318/394-4010 or 1-800/621-3017; ❸), a comfortable nineteenth-century B&B with huge rooms. Its **restaurant** serves good French Cajun food.

Northern Louisiana

Northern Louisiana is at the heart of the region known as the **Ark-La-Tex**, where the cottonfields and soft vocal drawl of the Deep South Bible-belt merges with the ranches, oil, and country music of Texas, and the forested hills (resplendent in the fall) of Arkansas. Settled by the Scottish and Irish after the Louisiana Purchase, the area is strongly Baptist, with less of a penchant for fun than south Louisiana, though it does share its profusion of **festivals**.

Angola Prison

Isolated at the end of the long and lonely Hwy-60, hemmed in by the Tunica foothills and the Mississippi River some sixty miles northwest of Baton Rouge, **Angola** is the most famous maximum-security prison in the United States, its very name a byword for brutality and desperation. Famous inmates have included blues singer **Leadbelly**, who, as Huddy Ledbetter, served here in the 1930s; today it holds about 5000 prisoners, 77 percent of whom are black. Most of the men – murderers, robbers, rapists – are lifers, and around 100 of them are on Death Row. Outside the main gate, the **Angola Museum** (Mon–Fri 8am–4.30pm, Sat 9am–5pm, Sun 1–5pm; free) offers a fascinating insight into this vexed place. For $3 you can have your photo taken in a replica cell; you are not, however, encouraged to fool with Old Sparky, the electric chair used to execute 87 men and one woman between 1941 and 1991. Fading black-and-white photos and old newspapers reveal appalling prison conditions; the prodding sticks and belts used to beat convicts bring it a little closer to home. You can also see an array of creative prisoner-made weapons – a knife carved from a toothbrush, a blade made from a beef rib – used in the many attempted breakouts and uprisings. Pick up a free copy of the prison magazine, *The Angolite*, an intriguing inmate-run publication filled with uncensored poems, essays, and philosophical musings.

Since 1970, Angola has staged a **prisoner rodeo** every Sunday in October, a harrowing gladiatorial spectacle which draws thousands (there is also a two-day rodeo in April; both events are $10; reservations required; ℡225/655-2030, ⓦangolarodeo.com). These are extraordinary affairs, the crowds baying while lifers are flung, gored, and trampled in their struggle for dignity, glory, and a simple change of scene. Events include bust-outs and bulldogging events, and an unbelievable game of "convict poker" in which players attempt to play cards while being charged by a 2000lb bull.

Natchitoches

Tiny **NATCHITOCHES** (pronounced "Nakitish"), in the sleepy cottonfields of the Cane River, is the oldest European settlement in Louisiana, having begun life as a French trading post in 1714. A Catholic oasis in a Protestant desert, it was swiftly fortified when its Spanish and Native American customers started to combine aggression with commerce.

With its lovingly restored Creole architecture, Natchitoches's exquisite **Front Street**, on the river, bears a passing resemblance to New Orleans' French Quarter, with its lacy iron balconies, spiral staircases, and cobbled courtyards complemented by friendly, old-style stores. The 1717 **Church of the Immaculate Conception**, at Second and Church streets, has many of its original French features, including glass chandeliers and a hand-carved font. Fleurs-de-lis on the nearby **St Denis Walk of Honor** commemorate celebrities with local connections, such as John Wayne, Clementine Hunter (see below), and the cast of the movie *Steel Magnolias*, which was set and filmed here in 1988. **Fort St Jean Baptiste**, on the river at Moreau and Mill streets (daily 9am–5pm; $2), is a five-acre reconstruction of the town's 1716 fort, with rough wooden and adobe buildings enclosed by a tall wooden fence.

The quirky **Bayou Folk Museum** (Mon–Sat 10am–5pm, Sun 1–5pm; $5), in novelist **Kate Chopin**'s old home in nearby **CLOUTIERVILLE** (pronounced "Cloochyville") is filled with all manner of oddities of local interest, along with exhibits relating to Chopin herself, whose nineteenth-century works, in particular her novel *The Awakening*, about a married woman's desire for independence, shocked the nation.

Practicalities

Natchitoches lies 140 miles northeast of Lafayette, on Hwy-6 off I-49. Greyhound comes in on the southeast side of town, on Hwy-1; note that the town has **no public transportation** or taxis. This is **B&B** territory: one of the most luxurious is the *Judge Porter House* at 321 Second St (T318/352-9206, Wwww.judgeporterhouse.com; ⑤), with its romantic porch, gardens, swimming pool, and antique-stuffed rooms. *Chateau d'Terre*, just outside downtown Natchitoches at 109 Jamar Drive (T1-888/798-6566, Wwww.chateaudterre.com; ⑤), offers just two rooms, a tranquil lake view, and an endless supply of cookies.

The **visitor center**, 781 Front St (Mon–Fri 8am–6pm, Sat 9am–5pm, Sun 10am–4pm; T1-800/259-1714, Wwww.historicnatchitoches.com), provides self-guided **walking tours** of the historic downtown. The best place to **eat** is *Lasyone's* (T318/352-3353), around the corner at 622 Second St, which specializes in delicious meat pies (spicy, flaky, and lightly fried), cream pies, red beans and sausage, and fresh, crumbly cornbread.

Cane River National Heritage Area

Just south of Natchitoches, the rural **Cane River roads** are dotted with ramshackle houses and small farms. As you drive past farmers sitting on porches and women hanging out the wash, you'll come across many **plantation homes**, some overgrown and in sad disrepair, others beautifully restored. The **Cane River National Heritage Area**, a collection of restored plantation homes, churches, and forts, stretches for 35 miles south from Natchitoches. Head first for the fascinating **Melrose Plantation**, on Hwy-119 (daily noon–4pm; $7), which was granted in 1794 to Marie Therese Coincoin, a freed slave, by her owner, Thomas Metoyer – the father of ten of her fourteen children. With remarkable resourcefulness Coincoin assembled the original grounds and additional land grants into an 800-acre plantation; she was later able to buy freedom for two of her children and one of her grandchildren. Around 1900, enterprising Melrose owner "Miss Cammie" Henry – a collector and patron of local writing – turned the crumbling Melrose into an arts community, visited by painters and writers such as William Faulkner and John Steinbeck. In the 1940s, a black Melrose cook, **Clementine Hunter**, began to use materials discarded by visiting artists to paint vivid images of life on and around the plantation. She carried on painting until her death at the age of 101, and her works have since become valuable pieces of folk art. Many of them are on show in the 1800 **African House**, which resembles a Congo mud hut and was used as the slave jail, and in the Big House, a typical plantation home, made from brick and *bousillage*.

Texas

CANADA

WASHINGTON

MONTANA

NORTH DAKOTA

MN

WI

MI

ME

VT

NH

NEW YORK

MA

3

14

OREGON

IDAHO

WYOMING

SOUTH DAKOTA

4

MI

RI

CT

2

11

NEBRASKA

IOWA

OHIO

PA

1

NEVADA

UTAH

COLORADO

KANSAS

IL

IN

WV

5

NJ

DE

10

MISSOURI

KENTUCKY

VA

MD

13

CALIFORNIA

12

ARIZONA

NEW MEXICO

OKLAHOMA

AR

TENNESSEE

NC

ATLANTIC OCEAN

AL

6

SC

PACIFIC OCEAN

MS

GEORGIA

9

TEXAS

8

LA

N

MEXICO

15

HAWAII

ALASKA

16

Gulf of Mexico

7

FL

AL - ALABAMA	IN - INDIANA	MN - MINNESOTA	RI - RHODE ISLAND
AR - ARKANSAS	LA - LOUISIANA	MS - MISSISSIPPI	SC - SOUTH CAROLINA
CT - CONNECTICUT	MA - MASSACHUSETTS	NC - NORTH CAROLINA	VA - VIRGINIA
DE - DELAWARE	MD - MARYLAND	NH - NEW HAMPSHIRE	VT - VERMONT
FL - FLORIDA	ME - MAINE	NJ - NEW JERSEY	WI - WISCONSIN
IL - ILLINOIS	MI - MICHIGAN	PA - PENNSYLVANIA	WV - WEST VIRGINIA

CHAPTER 9

Highlights

* **The Menil Collection, Houston** Houston's premier gallery boasts a magnificent collection of ancient and modern artworks, plus the somber Rothko Chapel. **See p.757**

* **Johnson Space Center, Houston** Send your imagination into orbit with a trip to Mission Control, the nerve center for the Apollo moon missions. **See p.760**

* **The River Walk, San Antonio** Texas offers few more romantic experiences than a riverside stroll through the heart of San Antonio. **See p.768**

* **The Sixth Floor Museum, Dallas** Decide for yourself whether Oswald really did shoot JFK, as you overlook Dealey Plaza. **See p.784**

* **The Stockyards, Fort Worth** Watch a cattle drive or tuck into a colossal steak in this cowboy heaven. **See p.790**

* **Rafting the Santa Elena Canyon** The Rio Grande rushes through this narrow gorge in remote Big Bend National Park. **See p.800**

* **Starlight Theater, Terlingua** Enjoy the stars – in the sky and on stage – in this glorious desert bar in a tiny West Texas ghost town. **See p.801**

9

Texas

Still cherishing the memory that it was from 1836 to 1845 an independent nation in its own right, **TEXAS** stands apart from the rest of the United States. While its sheer size – eight hundred miles from east to west and nearly a thousand from top to bottom – gives it a great geographical diversity, it's firmly bound together by a shared history, culture, and ideology. Independence is key to the Texan mentality, from the overriding distrust of government – any government – to the absence of unionized labor. As the old anti-litter campaign put it, "Don't mess with Texas."

Preconceived ideas about what exactly is "Texan" are soon shattered. It's actually one of the most eclectic and cosmopolitan states in the Union and each of the major tourist destinations has its own distinct character. Hispanic **San Antonio**, for example, with its Mexican population and historic importance, has a laid-back feel absent from the big-city neurosis of **Houston** or **Dallas**, while trendy **Austin** revels in a lively music scene and intellectualism found nowhere else in the state.

Regional differences are vast. The swampy, forested **east** is more like Louisiana than the pretty **Hill Country** or the agricultural plains of the **Panhandle**, and the tropical **Gulf Coast** has little in common with the mountainous **deserts** of the west. Changes in **climate** are equally dramatic: snow is common in the Panhandle, whereas the humidity of Houston, in particular, is only made bearable by nonstop high-power air-conditioning.

One thing shared by the whole of Texas is the constant boasting: everything has to be bigger and better than anywhere else. Such chauvinism is tempered both by a delight in self-parody and by the state's melting pot of cultures. The much-cited Texan **friendliness** is not imaginary; to be unwelcoming would simply be unpatriotic. Texas is, after all, named for a Native American word meaning "friend," *tejas*, and a visit here, especially to the Panhandle or the Hill Country, is not for those who want to be alone.

Some history

Early inhabitants of Texas included the Caddo in the east and nomadic Coahuiltecans further south. The **Comanche**, who arrived from the Rockies in the 1600s, soon found themselves at war when the **Spanish** ventured in, looking for gold. In the 1700s, threatened by French hopes of westward expansion from Louisiana, the Spanish began to build **missions** and forts, although these had minimal impact on the indigenous population's nomadic way of life. When Mexico won its independence from Spain in 1821, taking Texas with it it was part of the deal. At first, the Mexicans were keen to open up their land, and offered generous incentives to settlers. Stephen Austin ("the father of

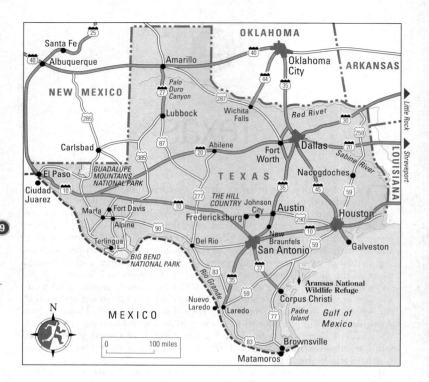

Texas") established Anglo-American colonies in the Brazos and Colorado River valleys. However, the Mexican leader, Santa Anna, soon became alarmed by Anglo aspirations to autonomy, and his increasing restrictions led to the eight-month **Texan Revolution** of 1835–36. The romance of the Revolution draws legions of tourists to **San Antonio**, site of the legendary **Battle of the Alamo**, which, though a military disaster, presaged independence. Today's street names echo the conflict: Crockett, Travis, and Bowie were all heroes at the Alamo, and Houston was the general who finally led the army to victory at San Jacinto.

The short-lived **Republic of Texas**, which included territory now in Oklahoma, New Mexico, Colorado, Kansas, and Wyoming, served to define the state's identity, and in 1845 Texas joined the Union on the understanding that it could secede whenever it so wished. This is still written into its constitution, as is the proviso that it can, at any time, divide itself into five separate states. Not surprisingly, Texans display an unmatched measure of state pride: Texas schoolchildren are as familiar with the heroes of the Alamo as the heroes of the Revolutionary War, and you'll see a ubiquitous state symbol – the **Lone Star** – emblazoned on everything from advertising to architecture.

The influence, especially in the north and east, of settlers from the Southern states and their attendant slave-centered cotton economy resulted in Texas joining the **Confederacy**. No major Civil War battles were fought on Texan soil, however, and it remained relatively unscathed. During Reconstruction, settlers from both the North and the South began to pour in, and the phrase "Gone to Texas" was familiarly applied to anyone fleeing the law, bad debts, or unhappy love affairs. This was also the period of the great cattle drives, when the longhorns roaming free in the south and west of Texas were rounded up and taken to the railroads in Kansas. The Texan – and national – fascination with the romantic myth of the **cowboy** has its roots in this era, and still prevails; today his regalia – Stetson, boots, and bandana – is virtually a state costume, especially in Fort Worth and the west.

Along with ranching and agriculture, **oil** has been crucial. After the first big gusher in 1901, at Spindletop on the Gulf Coast, the focus of the Texan economy – and culture – shifted almost overnight from agriculture toward rapid industrialization. Boom towns flew up as wildcatters chased the wells, and millions of dollars were made as ranchers, who had previously thought their land only fit for cattle, sold out at vast profit. Texas today produces one-third of all the oil in the United States, and the sight of nodding pump jacks is one of the state's most potent images.

Getting around Texas

Texan distances are best negotiated by **car**; in fact, in the larger cities like Dallas or Houston driving is all but essential. **Greyhound** routes are concentrated between the major cities of the east and the central region, though buses also serve the Gulf Coast, the Rio Grande Valley, West Texas, and, to a lesser extent, the Panhandle. Two **Amtrak** trains pass through Texas: *The Texas Eagle* travels between Chicago and San Antonio, stopping in Dallas and Austin; while the *Sunset Limited* stops in Houston, Alpine, and El Paso on its way between Orlando and Los Angeles. An Amtrak Thruway bus links San Antonio with Laredo. **Flying** saves time and can be very cheap; look out for price wars between airlines such as Southwest and smaller local carriers.

Where Texas really falls down is the **public transportation** within the cities themselves; mass transit has proved impractical in a state where long distances – in Houston many people travel at least thirty miles to work – and low gasoline prices make the love affair with the car almost inevitable. **Cycling** only really makes sense within cities like Austin and San Antonio.

Southern Texas and the Gulf Coast

The coastline of **south Texas**, which state residents half-jokingly refer to as the "Third Coast," curves from Port Arthur on the Louisiana border (a shipping and petrochemical town and the birthplace of Janis Joplin) on the much-touristed **Gulf Coast**, down past the urban monster of Houston, to the Rio Grande, the border with Mexico. Giant, cosmopolitan **Houston** dominates everything; its great wealth has led to a thriving arts scene, but ultimately it overpowers, rather than relates to, the rest of the region. Geographically and culturally, this area has two distinct faces. To the east are the seaside resorts of the prairie, rolling away from the hills and forests of East Texas. Much of the coast is feeling the strain of rapid property development, but there are still unspoiled stretches along the **Padre Island National Seashore**. In the south, a Hispanic influence spreads north from the fertile Rio Grande Valley. The border towns here have little charm and are only of interest as points of entry into Mexico for cheap shopping and entertainment. Uniting south Texas is the hot, swampy climate; Houston, especially, is unbearable in the summer, one reason for the mass exodus to the coast.

Houston

HOUSTON is an ungainly beast of a city, confused by overdevelopment during the oil boom and then traumatized by the sudden slump of the early 1980s. It's a suffocating place, choking with traffic and high on humidity, yet for all this, its sheer energy, its relentless Texan pride, and above all its refusal to take itself totally seriously, give it a perverse appeal, while its well-endowed museums and rich nightlife mean there is always something to do. That Howard Hughes came from Houston makes absolute sense: eccentric, domineering, and lurid, the millionaire typified all that makes the city intriguing.

There is no good reason why Houston exists at all; it was founded on a muddy mire in 1837 by two brothers from New York who hoped it would become the capital of the new Republic of Texas. For all their wild claims about its potential as a port, and its (imaginary) urban attractions, the more

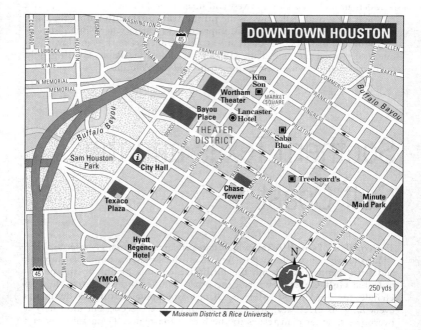

▼ *Museum District & Rice University*

promising site of Austin was made capital in 1839. However, by then Houston had somehow established itself as a commercial center. Oil – discovered in 1901, and, like the city itself, unpredictable and heading for obsolescence – became the foundation, along with cotton and real estate, of vast private fortunes. Among the most famous of the philanthropists responsible for the development of downtown Houston was the unfortunately named Ima Hogg. Her city improvement projects were largely cosmetic, however, and the contradictions of urban life are still writ large here, where abject poverty (not least among the blacks who migrated here from the rural South in the 1960s) coexists with ostentatious wealth.

Arrival and information

Downtown Houston is at the intersection of I-10 (San Antonio–New Orleans) and I-45 (Dallas–Galveston), with most of what you'll want to see encircled by Loop 610, now widened on the west to include the huge Galleria mall. **George Bush Intercontinental Airport** (☎281/230-3000), 23 miles north, is the main hub for Continental Airlines, while the smaller, domestic **William P. Hobby Airport** (☎713/640-3000) is seven miles southeast of downtown, just west of I-45 and a major hub for the budget Southwest Airlines. Both are served by the Airport Express **shuttle** (☎713/523-8888), which drops off at the Galleria and downtown hotels ($19–24 from Intercontinental and Hobby), and Metro **buses** (from Intercontinental on route #101 or #102: Mon–Fri 5.30am–midnight, Sat & Sun 5.20am–12.30am; $1.50; from Hobby on route #101 or #50: daily 5am–midnight; $1.50), which run downtown approximately every half-hour. **Taxis** cost $35 to $45 from Intercontinental, with the downtown fare from Hobby priced at $25 – though the fare to the Galleria from here is $35. Given these prices, renting a **car** can make sense, and all major companies are represented at the airports.

Amtrak arrives at 902 Washington Ave, on the western fringes of downtown. Have your camera ready for a splendid view of the skyline, though the station itself is small, isolated, and barely served by taxis. Try to arrive here, or at the large and modern **Greyhound** terminal, 2121 Main St, during daylight hours, as the immediate surroundings can feel a bit threatening.

The main **tourist office**, a huge space with touch-screen computers and other visual displays, is on the first floor of City Hall, 901 Bagby St (daily 9am–4pm; ☎713/227-3100 or 1-800/365-7575, ⓦwww.houston-spacecityusa.com).

City transportation

There are few options for nondrivers in Houston. The Metro buses are predominantly for commuters; **taxis** (the most reliable firm is Yellow Cabs; ☎713/236-1111) at $4 for the first mile and $1.65 for each additional mile, are expensive; and the humid climate and huge distances make walking unappealing. However, in the face of crippling traffic congestion, efforts are being made to encourage public transportation; a light rail system will begin service sometime in 2004, linking downtown to key tourist destinations. Maps of the city's **bus** routes are available from the Customer Service Center, 813 Dallas Ave (Mon–Fri 7.30am–5.30pm). Local fares are $1 (with free transfers), while the downtown trolleys are free. For more information call ☎713/635-4000 or visit ⓦwww.ridemetro.org.

Gray Line Tours (☎713/670-3254, ⓦwww.grayline.com) and Texas Bus Lines (☎713/523-8888) offer several **sightseeing tours** from $25.

Accommodation

Inexpensive **hotels** are concentrated near the Astrodome and outside the Loop, and motorists should try along I-45 or I-10; alternatively, a few nice **bed-and-breakfasts** and **inns** are scattered about, and can feel quite welcoming in a city as potentially alienating as Houston.

Grant Palm Court Inn 8200 S Main St ☎713/668-8000 or 1-800/255-8904. Reliable motel near the Astrodome, with a small pool but relatively large rooms. ❷

Houston International Hostel 5302 Crawford St ☎713/523-1009, ⓦwww.houstonhostel.com. Near Hermann Park in a pleasant neighborhood; dorm beds $12 for members, $14 for others. ❶

Lancaster Hotel 701 Texas Ave ☎713/228-9500, ⓦwww.lancaster.com/hotel.htm. Small English-flavored hotel in the Theatre District. Expensive, but weekend rates go down to around $160. ❾

Lovett Inn 501 Lovett Blvd ☎713/522-5224 or 1-800/779-5224, ⓦwww.lovettinn.com. Located on a leafy avenue on the edge of the Montrose dis-

trict, this historic house offers first-class service and Southern hospitality. ❹

Magnolia Hotel 1100 Texas Ave ☎713/221-0011 or 1-888/915-1110. Restored 1920s hotel located in downtown with lush, modern ambiance. ❻

Sara's Bed and Breakfast 941 Heights Blvd ☎713/868-1130 or 1-800/593-1130. Less than four miles northwest of downtown, near Memorial Park. A sweet Victorian house with a fine view of downtown Houston, serving continental breakfasts on the porch. ❹

YMCA 1600 Louisiana Ave ☎713/659-8501. Clean downtown rooms with shared bathrooms, a cut above the usual YMCA standards, are available for around $30 plus a $10 key deposit. ❶

The City

It's demoralizing and unwise to try and see too much of Houston in one go; best to concentrate on **downtown** or the **Museum District**, which can be walked around at leisure. Houston's human face is most evident in the **Montrose** area, on the way to yuppification but still home to eccentrics and bohemians.

Downtown Houston

Since the oil crisis in the early 1980s, the frenzy of skyscraper-building has slowed down, but Houston's skyline remains an unforgettable monument to an earlier age of certainty. Observation floors at the **Chase Tower**, 600 Travis St, and the **Texaco Plaza** offer views of the endless plateau over which the city sprawls. Just to the north, the area now covered by the reflecting pool in front of **City Hall** was granted to the city by a colorful rancher on the condition that no one could ever be arrested there for public intoxication, so it attracts a somewhat varied crowd.

Most people escape the Houston heat by staying underground, in the nearly seven miles of air-conditioned **tunnels** entered from the *Hyatt Regency* and the Main Street banks. However, they're a confusing and visually unappealing way to get around, despite the city's pride in their shops and restaurants. One consequence of this bustling subterranean world is a surreal isolation above ground, as few pedestrians emerge into the sunlight long enough to enjoy the various modern sculptures installed along the sidewalks (such as the Mirós outside the Chase Tower).

Nestling below the skyscrapers, **Sam Houston Park** on Bagby Street (Mon–Sat 10am–4pm, Sun 1–5pm; $6) contains restored structures such as a church and shop, while **Market Square** features some of the original buildings at the heart of the early city.

Even if you don't make it to a performance in the **Theater District**, west of Milam Street between Preston and Rusk streets, visit the **Wortham**

Theater Center, 500 Texas St (☎713/237-1439), which houses the city's opera and ballet. The beautifully sculpted interior, perfect acoustics, and secluded private bars take the breath away, as does the knowledge that the whole set-up cost $70 million. The only way to see it, though, is with a ticket to a performance.

Baseball fans won't want to miss **Minute Maid Park** (once embarrassingly named Enron Field), home of the Houston Astros (W www.astros.com). The park, which opened in 2000, features a retractable roof that can withstand hurricane conditions and close in twelve minutes. Tours of the field are available (during the season Mon–Fri 10am, noon, 2pm, 4pm; no 4pm tour on Sat or game days; off-season Mon–Sat 10am, noon, 2pm; $7; ☎713/259-8687).

The Museum District and the Rice University area

Five miles southwest of downtown, the oak-lined, student-thronged boulevards of the **Museum** and **Rice** districts are enjoyable places to explore on foot, full of interesting exhibition spaces and several good bookstores.

A magnificent purpose-built gallery at 1515 Sul Ross St – designed by Renzo Piano, who contributed to the Pompidou Centre in Paris – houses the private **Menil Collection** (Wed–Sun 11am–7pm; free; ☎713/525-9400, W www.menil.org). The superb works, gathered by oil millionaires John and Dominique de Menil, are displayed in spacious rooms, white-walled and naturally lit. Pieces range from paleolithic carvings dating from 15,000 BC, and a female idol from the "Mother Goddess" civilization of Catal Huyuk in Turkey, right up to modern sculptures such as Barnett Newman's 1950 *Here 1*. Artists with rooms to themselves include Max Ernst – look for the bronze *The King Playing with the Queen* – and René Magritte, while there's also a fine array of African art, including woodcarvings from Mali and ivories from Benin. One block east, the minimalist Ecumenical **Rothko Chapel**, 3900 Yupon St at Sul Ross (daily 10am–6pm; ☎713/524-9839, W www.rothkochapel.org), contains fourteen morose paintings commissioned by the Menils from Mark Rothko shortly before his death. The artist, who worked with architect Philip Johnson in designing the chapel, considered these to be his most important works, but many people today deride the building's resemblance to a nuclear bunker. The broken obelisk in the small park outside is dedicated to Dr Martin Luther King Jr. Diagonally opposite, the **Byzantine Fresco Chapel Museum**, 4011 Yupon St (Wed–Sun 11am–6pm; free; ☎713/521-3990, W www.menil.org /byzantine.html), houses a pair of thirteenth-century Cypriot frescoes in a somber contemporary structure.

At the intersection of Bissonet and Main streets, the expansive **Museum of Fine Arts** (Tues–Wed 10am–5pm, Thurs 10am–9pm, Fri & Sat 10am–7pm, Sun 12.15–7pm; $7, free Thurs; ☎713/639-7300, W www.mfah.org) features an eclectic collection from all eras, with Renaissance art especially well represented. Crane your neck upward from the Matisses and Rodins in the pine-shaded **Cullen Sculpture Garden** outside for a view of the downtown skyline.

Hermann Park, three miles south of downtown, is a pleasant green space with its own Japanese meditation garden. Exhibits on natural history at its excellent **Houston Museum of Natural Science** (Mon, Wed–Sat 9am–6pm, Tues 9am–8pm, Sun 11am–6pm; $6, free Tues after 2pm; ☎713/639-4629, W www.hmns.org) include the Cullen Hall of Gems and Minerals, with its fascinating spangly array of diamonds and other jewels. The **Cockrell Butterfly Center** (additional $5) is a giant three-story greenhouse where you can walk among lurid, exotic butterflies as they flutter around a rainforest environment, and even watch them emerge from their cocoons. There's also an IMAX theater (additional $7), a stunning gem collection, and a sundial fountain lapping a map of the Texas coastline. Be aware that the park is best avoided at night.

A short walk away, the **Contemporary Art Museum**, 5216 Montrose Blvd (Tues, Wed, Fri & Sat 10am–5pm, Thurs 10am–9pm, Sun noon–5pm), is worth a look if only for its striking architecture, notably its huge windowless corrugated-steel facade. The **Holocaust Museum Houston**, 5401 Caroline St (Mon–Fri 9am–5pm, Sat & Sun noon–5pm; free; ☏713/942-8000, Ⓦwww.hmh.org), is housed in another eye-catching building, this one with a massive black funnel emerging from a triangular glass wedge. A chilling movie, *Voices*, is on permanent play and the installations focus on concentration camps and local survivors.

The Astrodome, Reliant Stadium, and the Orange Show

Around three miles farther south from the Museum District, down Kirby Drive, Houston's legendary **Astrodome** was the first domed, climatized stadium in the world when it was built in 1965, and lends its name to astroturf, which was first laid down here. It was home to the NFL's Oilers before they relocated to Nashville a few years ago and, with the Astros having played their last baseball season here in 1999, its sparse usage is now restricted to big-wheel truck racing and trade shows. Pro football returned to the area in 2002 with the completion of the 69,500-seat **Reliant Stadium** for the Houston Texans (☏832/667-2000, Ⓦwww.houstontexans.com), though each year the Houston Livestock Show and Rodeo – the world's largest – is held here as well. A few hundred yards beyond the Astrodome, on the far side of the Loop, the big attraction at the **Six Flags AstroWorld** theme park is its many mighty roller coasters, including the suspended-looping "megacoaster" Serial Thriller (opening hours vary; $40; ☏713/799-8404, Ⓦwww.sixflags.com).

Despite the dreams of its creator, **The Orange Show** (March–Dec Sat & Sun noon–5pm, summer also Wed–Fri 9am–1pm; $1; ☏713/926-6368, Ⓦwww.orangeshow.org), five miles east at 2401 Munger Ave, just off I-45 at the Telephone Road exit, is an altogether lower-key affair. Promoted as Houston's most original piece of folk art, it's not really a show, but a suburban house transformed by the monomania of former salesman and would-be inventor Jeff McKissack into a paean to the orange. With one simple purpose – "to get more people to eat more oranges" – McKissack spent twenty years covering his home with celebratory tiles, ironwork, and slogans, with placards displayed by such oddball mannequins as the son of Santa Claus. The fabric of the place is solid ("weak construction would make the orange look weak"), but much of the mosaic work is surprisingly delicate, and it's not quite as garish as it might sound. When he finally opened it to the public in May 1979, McKissack confidently predicted that eight out of every ten Americans would visit. Depressed at the lack of crowds, the author of *How You Can Live 100 Years . . . And Still Be Spry* (in which oranges played a starring role) died in June 1980 aged 77.

The Galleria and around

The ultramodern **Galleria** hypermall lies just west of the Loop, on Westheimer Road. Its three hundred or so smart shops, movie theatres, and restaurants, plus skating rink and health club (with indoor tennis courts), and ornate street lamps and signage, exemplify Houston's love of modern architecture, upmarket style, and Texan tack. Across the way, a waterfall-sized fountain cascades outside the 64-story, black-glass **Williams Tower**, particularly breathtaking when lit at night.

Montrose

Bohemian and fun **Montrose** begins at the junction of Smith and Elgin streets. It's all quirky sleaze, chock-full of tattoo parlors, vintage clothes stores, experimental art galleries, and junk shops selling barbed-wire cacti and other curiosities. While the forces of gentrification are evidently at work, don't think it's all gone the way of the Gap. Though the teenagers who once cruised the streets on Saturday night have been forced elsewhere and the strip joints have closed down, this has long been the base of a very visible **gay** community, and a high concentration of gay bars and clubs remains.

Eating

There's plenty of variety in Houston's **food**: the large immigrant population has left its mark. Look out for Mexican, Vietnamese, and even Indian restaurants, and the many good delis – such as the sixteen outlets of *Antone's Deli* – serving huge salads and sandwiches with an international flavor.

Benjy's 2424 Dunstan Rd, off Kirby Rd ☎713/522-7602. Modern American food with an ethnic bent, plus inventive desserts, served in California-style decor near Rice University.

Black Labrador 4100 Montrose Ave ☎713/529-1199. Open fireplaces and oak beams set the stage for superb English comfort food (bangers, shepherd's pie, and the like) and great black-and-tans and imported Yorkshire bitter.

Goode Company 5109 Kirby Rd ☎713/522-2530. Fabulous barbecue on the road to the Astrodome, with a creative menu, outdoor seating, and C&W atmosphere.

Kim Son 2001 Jefferson St ☎713/222-2461 or 300 Milam St ☎713/222-2790. Massive Vietnamese restaurant with a long menu. Best at lunch for the good-value buffet.

La Strada 5161 San Felipe ☎713/850-9999. Very tasty Italian dishes with a creative and spicy Texan twist, near downtown.

La Tapatia 1749 Richmond Ave ☎713/521-3144. This Mexican diner may look uninviting but its big, low-cost portions are a hit with Montrose residents.

Ruggles Grill 903 Westheimer Rd ☎713/524-3839. One of the best places for a big night out in Montrose, with eclectic regional food at around $18 per entree. Reservations are advisable.

Saba Blue 416 Main St ☎713/228-7222. Fusion-based cuisine (think calamari, *wasabi*, sesame-crusted tuna) served in a hip atmosphere, smack in the middle of the revitalized downtown strip.

This Is It 207 W Gray St ☎713/659-1608. Heaps of soul food at budget prices at this downtown favorite.

Treebeard's 1117 Texas St (at The Cloister) ☎713/229-8248. Cheap and flavorful Cajun food that's good for a downtown lunch (stick to the vegetable plates rather than the lackluster stews). Don't miss the simple, delicious butterbread.

Nightlife and entertainment

There's no shortage of things to do in Houston; just check the listings in the free *Houston Press* (ⓦ www.houstonpress.com). **Cajun** and **zydeco** music have been significant in the city since a wave of migration from rural Louisiana in the early 1960s, and there's a strong **blues** tradition as well, while rootsy Texan **country** is another favorite. The Montrose area supports a very visible **gay** scene, and most of the clubs tend to be very male-dominated. **Miller Outdoor Theater** in Hermann Park, at 2020 Hermann Drive (☎713/284-8354), has free symphony concerts, swing, and opera on summer evenings, a "Juneteenth Blues" festival, and a Shakespeare Festival in August. Downtown's **Theater District** holds considerable options, including the nationally renowned **Alley Theater** at 615 Texas Ave (☎713/228-8421, ⓦ www.alleytheatre.org), which offers last-minute discount seats, and the **Wortham Theater Center**, on the same street (see p.756), home to Houston's opera and ballet companies. **Bayou Place** at Bagby between Texas and Capitol streets, is a relatively new – and ever-expanding – entertainment and restaurant complex that used to be a convention hall; one of its more interesting residents is the **Angelika Film Center** (℡713/225-5232, Ⓦwww.angelika.com), a multiscreen cinema complex that shows many art movies and has a good late-night coffee house. For an even more avant-garde cinematic experience, check out the **Aurora Picture Show** (℡713/868-2101, Ⓦwww.aurorapictureshow.org), an old clapboard church converted into an underground film venue.

Big Easy Social and Pleasure Club 5731 Kirby Drive ℡713/523-9999. The city's best blues, plus occasional zydeco nights in the Rice University area.
Emo's 2700 Albany St ℡713/523-8503. A little hard to find on the edge of Montrose, but this slacker bar gets first-rate alternative bands from the US and around the world. Beer prices are below average, too.
Engine Room 1515 Pease St ℡713/654-7846. Pool tables and an aggressive indie line-up pull in a diverse crowd.
The Last Concert Café 1403 Nance St ℡713/226-8563. East of downtown, in an arty and isolated area, this café has good, cheap Tex-Mex food, and live rock and roots bands in the back garden.

McGonigel's Mucky Duck 2425 Norfolk St ℡713/528-5999. A great folk club featuring national acts, as well as a terrific Irish jam session on Wed.
Rudyard's 2010 Waugh Drive ℡713/521-0521. Solid indie bands and a raucous atmosphere make up for the somewhat surly service.
Sam's Boat and Sam's Place 5720 Richmond Ave ℡713/781-2628. Richmond's top nightlife spot, in all its post-college glory. Yes, it's the bar shaped like a boat.
Spotlight Karaoke 5901 Westheimer Rd ℡713/266-7768. A popular karaoke joint seemingly frozen in 1978, with a great selection of songs and a dedicated crowd.

Around Houston

Houston's double-edged status as having both historical importance and all the trappings of a hyper-modern "space city" is exemplified by two major attractions, both about twenty miles south of the city. The first of these, **San Jacinto Battleground**, 22 miles east of Houston off I-10, was the site of an eighteen-minute fight, two months after the Alamo in 1836, in which the Texans all but wiped out the superbly trained Mexican army. You see little but miles of flat land from the observation deck ($3) of the tallest stone-column **monument** in the world (570ft, topped by a 34ft Lone Star), but the **Museum of History** inside is more interesting, with the stirring 35-minute movie *Texas Forever!* (hourly 9am–5pm; museum daily 9am–6pm; $3.50; ℡281/479-2421, Ⓦwww.sanjacinto-museum.org).

Meanwhile, 25 miles south of the city off I-45 (take bus #246 from downtown), **NASA** has been controlling space flight from the **Johnson Space Center** since the launch of Gemini 4 in 1965 – locals love to point out that the first word ever spoken on the moon was "Houston." As a working facility, it's not fully geared to tourists, but three tram tours will give you a glimpse into different parts of the grounds. Start with an impressive array of hands-on exhibits at the **Space Center Houston** (summer daily 9am–7pm; rest of year Mon–Fri 9am–5pm, Sat & Sun 10am–7pm; $18; ℡281/244-2100, Ⓦwww.spacecenter .org), where you can try on space helmets and inspect moonrocks and remarkably rickety-looking rocket replicas, join astronauts and scientists in the cafeteria, and stock up on gimmicky space-themed merchandising.

The Gulf Coast

You only have to look at the number of condo developments along the **Gulf Coast** to see that this is a major tourist destination. The climate ranges from balmy at **Galveston** to subtropical at the Mexican border, but everywhere it's windy: **Corpus Christi** rivals Chicago as the gustiest city in the States, and a devastating hurricane in 1900 all but leveled the city of Galveston. The fierce tide, progressively gnawing away at the beaches, may pose a threat to tourism, but for now Galveston offers history, shopping, and low-key relief from uptight Houston, while Corpus Christi to the south makes the best base for the beaches of Padre Island National Seashore. **Rockport**, a weathered resort on Hwy-35, is convenient for the **Aransas National Wildlife Refuge**, a haven for endangered whooping cranes, armadillos, and alligators.

Galveston

In 1890 **GALVESTON** – on the northern tip of Galveston Island, the southern terminus of I-45 – was a thriving port, far larger than Houston fifty miles northwest; many newly arrived European immigrants chose to stay here in the so-called "Queen of the Gulf." However, the building of Houston's Ship Canal, after the hurricanes of 1900 killed more than six thousand people and washed away much of the land, left the coastal town to fade slowly away. Thanks to its pretty historic district and its popularity with Houston residents seeking a summer escape, Galveston has undergone a certain revitalization, but the occasionally gritty city still seems to be laboring under the psychic weight of its past calamities.

Arrival, information, and accommodation

Greyhound takes about ninety minutes to cover the fifty miles from Houston, arriving at 714 25th St (around $6 by taxi from downtown). There is no Amtrak service. **Trolleys** (daily 10am–6.30pm; $1; ☏ 409/797-3900, ⓦ www.islandtransit.net) rattle past the historic homes and other sights between the **visitor centers** at 2215 the Strand and 2428 Seawall Blvd (daily 8.30am–5pm; ☏ 1-888/425-4753, ⓦ www.galveston.com).

Hotels in Galveston are pricey in summer and at weekends, but bargains can be found at other times; rates along Seawall Boulevard can drop below $40 per night. Within easy walking distance to the Strand, the town's **East End Historic District** holds some relaxing **B&Bs**.

Commodore on the Beach 3618 Ship's Mechanic Row ☏ 409/763-2375 or 1-800/231-9921, ⓦ www.commodoreonthebeach.com. The adequate, inexpensive rooms overlook the Gulf, and there's a large beachside pool as well. ❹–❻

Gaido's Seaside Inn 3802 Seawall Blvd ☏ 409/762-9625 or 1-800/525-0064. A clean, popular choice, with a good fish restaurant attached. ❹

Garden Inn 1601 Ball St ☏ 409/770-0592 or 1-888/770-7298. Built in 1887, a very pretty Victorian B&B in the historic district featuring well-appointed rooms and a hammock in the backyard. ❺

Hotel Galvez 2024 Seawall Blvd ☏ 409/765-7721. Classy hotel built in 1911, with a beautiful pool and swim-up bar. ❺–❼

Motel 9 1002 Seawall Blvd ☏ 409/763-8561. One of the best values at the lower end of the spectrum. ❸

Queen Anne B&B 1915 Sealy Ave ☏ 409/763-7088 or 1-800/472-0930, ⓦ www.galveston-queenanne.com. Pleasant B&B built in 1905, where all six guestrooms have private baths. ❺

Tremont Hotel 2300 Ship's Mechanic Row ☏ 409/763-0300. Landmark hotel and the grandest place to stay on the island, with tastefully uncluttered Victorian decor in the rooms. ❻–❾

The City

The **Strand** downtown, the nineteenth-century "Wall Street of the Southwest," is the city's epicenter and has been fitted with gaslights, upmarket shops, restaurants, and galleries. The **Texas Seaport Museum** nearby, in amongst a complex of shops and restaurants on Pier 21, just off Water Street (daily 10am–5pm; $6; ☎409/763-1877, ⓦwww.tsm-elissa.org), focuses on the port's role in trade and immigration during the nineteenth century; admission includes boarding the *Elissa*, an 1877 tall ship.

Between the Strand and the beaches to the south, old houses are everywhere, among them the ostentatious **Bishop's Palace**, 1402 Broadway (summer Mon–Sat 10am–5pm, Sun noon–5pm; rest of year daily noon–4pm; $6), with its stained glass, mosaics, and marble; the antebellum **Ashton Villa**, 2328 Broadway (Mon–Sat 10am–4pm, Sun noon–4pm; $5), which shows a film about the 1900 hurricane and has tours starting on the hour; the 1839 **Samuel May Williams Home**, 3601 Ave P (Sat & Sun noon–4pm; $3), a New England residence moved here from Maine; and the city's oldest building, the **Michel B. Menard Home**, 1605 33rd St (Fri–Sun noon–4pm; $6), an imposing wooden structure built in 1838 that now holds a good collection of American antiques. Galveston's old Santa Fe depot, at 25th Street and the Strand, is now the town's **Railroad Museum** (daily 10am–4pm; $5), displaying steam trains, Pullman cars, and endless train-travel-related artifacts in a skillful evocation of a lost era. Look for the eerie white statues standing around the waiting room; you can pick up a telephone and listen to their conversations.

On the west side of town, **Moody Gardens**, at I-45 off the 61st Street exit (daily: summer 10am–9pm; winter Mon–Thurs & Sun 10am–6pm, Fri & Sat 10am–9pm; $10 per attraction, $30-day pass to all attractions; ☎1-800/582-4673, ⓦwww.moodygardens.com), is an environmental research facility where you can happily while away a few hours. The complex is centered on three giant glass pyramids: the Rainforest Pyramid houses exotic plants, birds, and fish from around the world; the Discovery Pyramid is a good-quality science museum with an IMAX cinema; and the impressive Aquarium Pyramid is one of the largest aquariums in the world. Also in the expanding complex are themed outdoor gardens, pleasant walking trails along the shore of scenic **Offatt's Bayou** – where you can take a cruise on a paddlewheeler – and Palm Beach, a popular spot for families where kids can play on a giant yellow submarine. It's worth visiting more than one attraction, especially as the box office (☎409/744-4673 or 1-800/582-4673) offers an array of discounted combo tickets.

The downtown **beaches** of Seawall Boulevard are a constant reminder of Galveston's struggle simply to exist: murky, rocky, and protected behind a ten-mile-long seawall from the ever-encroaching tides and the threat of further hurricanes. **Stewart Beach Park**, the most convenient beach for downtown, is geared toward family fun and gets very crowded; the wide **R.A. Apfell Park**, further east, is marginally quieter during the week, but has live music some weekends and a lively bar. Both of these beaches charge $5 per car.

Eating and drinking

Dining out in Galveston will likely mean settling in at one of the many low-key seafood restaurants along Seawall Boulevard – they're unassuming, but the often delicious fresh fish dishes together with the unapologetically kitschy decor are strangely intoxicating. **Nightlife** in Galveston basically amounts to cover bands, but there are several good noisy bars along Post Office Street between 20th and 23rd streets.

21 2102 Post Office St ☏ 409/762-2101. Elegant, subdued bar with a menu of over twenty varieties of martini.

Casey's 3802 Seawall Blvd ☏ 409/762-9625. Local Gulf seafood at prices lower than most other places like it.

Clary's 8509 Teichman Rd, off I-45 on Offat's Bayou ☏ 409/740-0771. Somewhat pricey, but recommended for the excellent fresh seafood.

Old Quarter Acoustic Café 413 20th St

☏ 409/762-9199. Presents hard-edged folk music; the late Texan singer-songwriter Townes Van Zandt wrote *Rex's Blues* about the café's owner, musician Rex Bell.

Phoenix 220 Tremont St ☏ 409/763-4611. Bakery and popular breakfast spot; don't leave without trying the yummy beignets.

Yaga's Café 2314 the Strand ☏ 409/762-6676. Delicious Caribbean food served in gaudy surroundings to the sounds of reggae and calypso music.

Corpus Christi

The unabashed resort town of **CORPUS CHRISTI** is reached along the coast on Hwy-35 from Houston or Galveston, or on I-37 from San Antonio. Originally a rambunctious trading post, it too was hit by a fierce hurricane, in 1919, but recovered, transforming itself into a center for naval air training, petroleum, and shipping. Much of the population is Hispanic, and the community was devastated in March 1995, when the 23-year-old singer **Selena** was shot dead in a motel parking lot by the former president of her fan club. Selena was on the verge of becoming the first major cross-over star of **Tejano** music, a hybrid of Mexican rhythms, German polka, and reggae-influenced Colombian *cumbia*, and fifty thousand fans turned out for her funeral. In addition to the Selena Auditorium at the Bayfront Convention Center, there's a memorial to the singer just south of Peoples Street on Shoreline Boulevard; the **Selena Museum**, 5410 Leopard St, is stuffed with Selena memorabilia, from her famously extravagant gowns to her Porsche (Mon–Fri 9–11.45am & 1–6pm; $1 suggested donation). The town's visitor center (see below) can supply a free map of Selena-centric stops.

Apart from fishing, sailing, and watersports across the channel on Padre Island (see p.764), there's not a great deal to do in Corpus Christi. The impressive collection of the Philip Johnson–designed **South Texas Institute for the Arts**, 1902 N Shoreline Blvd (Tues–Sat 10am–5pm, Sun 1–5pm, first Thurs of the month until 9pm; $3; ☏361/825-3500, ⓦwww.stia.org), includes pieces by Monet and Picasso. Further along N Shoreline Boulevard, at no. 2710, is the massive **Texas State Aquarium** (summer Mon–Sat 9am–6pm, Sun 10am–6pm; rest of year until 5pm; $12; ☏361/881-1200 or 1-800/477-GULF, ⓦwww.texasstateaquarium.org), which nonetheless feels cramped compared to the sizable aquarium in Galveston. Adjacent is the **USS Lexington** (summer daily 9am–6pm; rest of year until 5pm; $10; ⓦwww.usslexington.com), a World War II aircraft carrier that's impressive to walk around, though the few exhibits on board are weak. The **Corpus Christi Museum of Science and History**, 1900 N Chaparral St (daily: summer 9am–6pm; rest of year 9am–5pm; $10; ☏361/883-2862), specializes in hands-on natural history exhibits on topics ranging from shipwrecks to shells to, curiously, the building of the Selena memorial. Moored in the harbor a short walk from the museum, the **Columbus Fleet** (included in the museum admission) consists of life-sized replicas of Christopher Columbus's *Santa Maria* and *Pinta*.

Practicalities

Greyhound arrives at 702 N Chaparral St downtown. The **visitor center** (☏361/881-1888 or 1-800/678-OCEAN, ⓦwww.corpuschristi-tx-cvb.org) is further along N Chaparral at no. 1823 (daily 9am–5pm; ☏361/561-2000 or 1-800/766-2322). A daytime **trolley** (50¢; ☏361/289-2600) connects the major attractions with area hotels (except Sun); other services include a free downtown "Beach Shuttle" **tram** service (summer only) and a harbor ferry from the South Texas Institute for the Arts to the Texas State Aquarium ($3).

Budget **motels**, inaccessible without a car, line Leopard Street in the northwest. Along N Shoreline Boulevard, the *Bayfront Inn* at no. 601 is a good deal (℡361/883-7271 or 1-800/456-2293; ❸), while the *Omni Bayfront*, at no. 900, offers rooms with a view of the water (℡361/887-1600 or 1-800/843-6664, Ⓦwww.omnihotels.com; ❺). Downtown Corpus's main concentration of **restaurants** is in Water Street Market at 309 N Water St, where the *Water Street Oyster Bar* (℡361/881-9448) serves fresh seafood. For Cajun-style seafood, there's *Landry's*, a floating restaurant moored off the Peoples Street T-Head (℡361/882-6666). Just across the JFK Causeway is *Snoopy's* at 13313 S Padre Island Drive (℡361/949-8815), with ridiculously good fried seafood and crabmeat-stuffed jalapeño peppers.

South toward Mexico

The barrier islands of **Padre Island National Seashore** stretch just offshore for 110 miles south of Corpus Christi, almost down to the Mexican border. The frontier between **Brownsville** and **Matamoros** is not very interesting, however; for a brief taste of Mexico, head almost due west from Corpus one hundred miles to **Laredo**. (US-83 runs along the Rio Grande between Brownsville and Laredo.) Away from the coast, the fertile landscape begins to dry out and citrus groves give way to the brush and mesquite of a region dominated by huge ranches, where Mexican *vaqueros* once held sway.

Padre Island National Seashore and Brownsville

Padre Island National Seashore is not quite as unspoiled these days as its reputation might suggest, with its ranks of condos advancing steadily, but it remains a good destination for bird-watching, beachcombing, and camping. Pick up details at the **visitor center** at 20402 Park Rd 22 (daily: summer 8.30am–6pm; rest of year 8.30am–4.30pm; ℡361/949-8068, Ⓦwww.nps.gov /pais). The park is easily accessed by car, but cab services in Corpus Christi will make the trip for around $30 (Star Taxi ℡361/884-9451). The park itself is open 24 hours, with a $10 admission charge per vehicle, good for one week. Camping on the beach is free, but permits are $5 for the primitive Bird Island Basin and $8 for the semi-primitive *Malaquite Beach Campground*. Note that an impassable canal divides the island, meaning that the pricier and much more touristy **South Padre Island** in the south can only be reached from the mainland – it's a three-hour drive from Corpus Christi.

BROWNSVILLE, just across from South Padre Island, is a scruffy, semitropical resort, populated by retired Texans on winter vacation, where you'll hear more Spanish spoken than English. To cross the border into **Matamoros**, walk across Gateway Bridge at International Boulevard. Wealthier than Brownsville, and considerably larger, the Mexican city is not terribly inspiring, but it has a good market, Mercado Juarez, on calles 9 and 10, and an untouristy main plaza at Calle 5, dominated by the cathedral. If you're intending to stay in Mexico or venture further than twenty miles or so, you must pick up a tourist card from the Mexican Consulate at Twelfth Avenue and Washington Street in Brownsville.

Laredo

The dusty, downtrodden, and rather isolated smuggling center of **LAREDO**, over one hundred miles from the coast, has seen better days even though it's the fastest-growing city in the state. Santa Anna marched his troops through

It's an easy walk across the bridge from San Agustin Plaza in Laredo (see below) to the typical Mexican border town of **NUEVO LAREDO**, so easy, in fact, that this is the most popular crossing along the entire frontier, with most visitors coming simply for evening meals and weekend shopping. There is a lively atmosphere, with all the tourist shops and restaurants concentrated near the international bridge, on "the strip," Avenida Guerrero. Most take American dollars, and bargaining is acceptable at some.

Seven blocks down Avenida Guerrero, the main plaza is the social center of town. **Hotels** include the good-value *Nuevo Romano*, at Doctor Mier 800 (☎871/12-26-94; ❶), with rooms for around US$15, while the *Reforma*, on Avenida Guerrero at Calle Canales (☎871/12-26-50; ❶), is cleaner and better, but you'll still get change from forty bucks. The *El Dorado Bar*, at Avenida Ocampo and Belden (☎871/12-00-15), was the first of the town's **bars and restaurants** to encourage tourism here, serving drinks to Texans escaping Prohibition. It's a bit tacky now; better to head for *El Rancho*, 2124 Av Guerrero (☎871/14-87-53), for *cabrito* (barbecued goat), gua- camole, and cold beer. For a more expensive treat, try *Victoria 3020*, 3020 Victoria St (☎871/13-30-20), which has a wide-ranging Mexican menu and patio seating. As a whole, though, Nuevo Laredo lacks real charm, and can be particularly depress- ing after dark; have a meal but give the nightlife a miss.

As with all border crossings, expect to undergo full immigration procedures when you re-enter the United States.

here in 1836, and in 1840 the city was the center of Zapata's Mexican sepa- ratist protest. The capitol of Zapata's short-lived republic still stands on Zaragoza Street in the historic district, now housing the small **Republic of the Rio Grande Museum** (Tues–Sat 9am–4pm, Sun 1–4pm; $1). San Agustin Plaza, the site of the original Spanish settlement, has been restored with cob- bled streets and Victorian buildings, as has El Mercado, on San Agustin Avenue, the former hub of downtown activity.

Greyhound arrives at 610 Salinas St. The **visitor center** is at 501 San Agustin Ave (Mon–Fri 8am–5pm, Sat 9am–3pm; ☎956/795-2200 or 1–800/361- 3360). **Hotels** include *La Quinta*, 3610 Santa Ursula Ave (☎956/722-0511, ⓦwww.laquinta.com; ❹), a couple of miles north of downtown, with both indoor and outdoor pools, and the more central *La Posada*, 1000 Zaragoza St (☎956/722-1701, ⓦwww.laposadahotel-laredo.com; ❺), just east of the Gateway Bridge, where the dining room offers a big lunch buffet and good steaks. *Toños*, 1202 E Del Mar Blvd (☎956/717-4999), is especially popular at lunch for its Tex-Mex standards, and *Cotulla-Style Pit Bar-B-Q*, 4502 McPherson St (☎956/724-5747), serves spicy regional barbecue as well as other Mexican fare.

9

TEXAS | The Gulf Coast

Central Texas

Central Texas stretches from the prairies of the northeast through the green and fertile Hill Country into the chalky limestone landscape of the west, and includes two of Texas's most pleasant cities: **San Antonio** and **Austin**. Austin in particular, the capital city and home to the progressive University of Texas, helps to give the region an intellectual and political feel uncharacteristic of the rest of the state.

Agriculture has been the mainstay of the economy here ever since the resistant Comanche population was finally packed off to reservations in the 1840s. The slave-driven cotton plantations of the south and east are gone, but the small communities set up by Polish, Czech, Norwegian, and Swedish immigrants in the **Hill Country** maintained, even until very recently, the traditions, architecture, and languages of their homelands. Great cattle drives came trampling through after the Civil War and played a large part in the development of San Antonio.

San Antonio

With neither the modern skyline of an oil town, nor the tumbleweed-strewn landscape of the Wild West, attractive and festive **SAN ANTONIO** looks nothing like the stereotypical image of Texas – despite being pivotal in the state's history. Standing at a geographical crossroads, it encapsulates the complex social and ethnic mixes of all Texas. Although the Germans, among others, have made a strong contribution to its architecture, cuisine, and music, today's San Antonio is predominantly **Hispanic**: abundant Tex-Mex restaurants, the prevalent Catholicism, the Mexican Cultural Institute, and advertising billboards in Spanish all attest to a long history of "Texican" culture.

Founded in 1691 by Spanish missionaries, San Antonio became a military garrison in 1718, and was settled by the Anglos in the 1720s and 1730s under Austin's colonization program. It is most famous for the legendary **Battle of the Alamo** in 1836, when the Mexican General Santa Anna, seeking to curb the aspirations of the Anglo-Americans, wiped out a band of Texan volunteers: hence San Antonio's claim to be the "birthplace of the revolution," borne out by its role during Texas's ten subsequent years of independence. After the Civil War, it became a hard-drinking, hard-fighting "sin city," at the heart of the Texas **cattle** and **oil** empires. Drastic floods in the 1920s wiped out much of the downtown area, but the sensitive WPA program that revitalized two of the city's prettiest sites, **La Villita** and the **River Walk**, laid the foundations for its future as a major tourist destination. San Antonio is now the ninth largest city in the US, but it retains an unhurried, organic feel, thanks to a winning combination of small-town warmth, respect for diversity, and a self-confidence rooted in its own history.

Arrival, information, and getting around

San Antonio International Airport (☎210/207-3450, Ⓦwww.sanantonio.gov/airport) is just north of the I-410 loop that encircles most of the sights. SA Trans Shuttle (☎1-800/868-7707) makes the twenty-minute journey

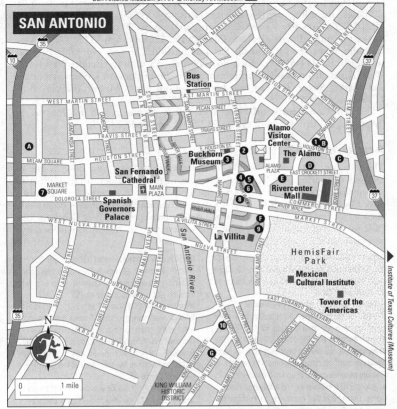

San Antonio Museum of Art & McNay Art Museum ▲

SAN ANTONIO

Bus Station

Alamo Visitor Center

Buckhorn Museum

The Alamo

San Fernando Cathedral

Rivercenter Mall

MARKET SQUARE

Spanish Governors Palace

La Villita

HemisFair Park

Mexican Cultural Institute

Tower of the Americas

KING WILLIAM HISTORIC DISTRICT

0   1 mile

N

9

TEXAS | San Antonio

Institute of Texan Cultures (Museum)

RESTAURANTS, BARS, & CLUBS				ACCOMMODATION			
Bonham Exchange	**1**	Mi Tierra	**7**	A Yellow Rose	**G**	Holiday Inn Crockett	
Boudro's	**6**	Paesano's	**4**	Days Inn	**C**	Hotel	**D**
Casa Rio	**8**	Polly Esther's	**3**	Hampton Inn	**B**	Menger Hotel	**E**
El Mirador	**10**	Swig	**5**	Hilton Palacio		Motel 6	**A**
Jim Cullum's The Landing	**2**	Zuni Grill	**9**	del Rio	**F**		

downtown ($9 one way, $16 roundtrip; every 10–15min 4am–1am), while normal city buses cost only 75¢ but take nearly an hour to make the same trip. Taxis cost about $15 (Yellow Cabs ☎210/226-4242). Amtrak arrives centrally at 350 Hoefgen St, while Greyhound operates from 500 N St Mary's St.

Pick up information on **city transportation** from the **visitor center** at 317 Alamo Plaza, directly across from the Alamo (daily 8.30am–6pm; ☎210/207-6748 or 1-800/447-3372, ⊛www.sanantoniocvb.com), or call the VIA Metropolitan Transit Service (☎210/362-2020, ⊛www.viainfo.net). **Buses** are reliable; journeys within the I-410 loop cost 80¢, and many downtown routes run until 10.30pm. Four downtown **streetcar** routes serve the major attractions for 50¢, from Alamo Plaza. A Day Tripper pass available from the VIA

Downtown Information Center, 112 Soledad St, costs $2 and can be used on all buses, including express services, and trolleys. Gray Line's **bus tours** (☎210/226-1706, ⓦwww.grayline.com) are only really of much use as a way to see the most distant missions (3hr 30min; $22), though VIA's #42 service from the Alamo does stop at the San Jose mission. The very enjoyable $6 **boat tours** (☎210/244-5700), which do a leisurely 35-minute circuit of the River Walk, depart from two locations, just below the bridges on Commerce Street and Market Street. You can rent **bicycles** from Abel's Mobile Bicycle Shop, 1119 Ada St (☎210/533-9927).

The downtown **post office** is next to the Alamo at 615 E Houston St (Mon–Fri 8.30am–5.30pm; ☎210/212-8046; zip code 78205).

Accommodation

The pleasure of a moonlit amble along the river back to your hotel is one of the joys of visiting San Antonio, so it's worth making a determined effort to stay in the center, though you'll pay for the privilege, as downtown is monopolized by **luxury hotels**. To find less expensive lodgings you'll almost certainly need a car; reasonably priced **motels** are clustered just north of Brackenridge Park on Austin Highway, or, more convenient to the airport, on I-35 north toward Austin.

Days Inn (Alamo-River Walk) 902 E Houston St ☎210/227-6233, ⓦwww.daysinn.com. Standard chain motel rooms, two blocks from the Alamo and the River Walk. ❹

Hampton Inn River Walk 414 Bowie St ☎210/225-8500, ⓦwww.hamptoninn.com. Good, clean rooms in a central location. ❺

HI-San Antonio 621 Pierce St ☎210/223-9426, ⓦwww.hiayh.org. Across from Fort Sam Houston, two miles north of downtown (bus #11 or #15). Friendly proprietors make up for the out-of-the-way location, and the pool and kitchen are nice extras. Dorm beds $17 members, $19 others; private rooms $59. Call ahead to reserve in summer.

Hilton Palacio del Rio 200 S Alamo St ☎210/222-1400, ⓦwww.hilton.com. Constructed in sections for the 1968 World's Fair, this luxurious and historic River Walk hotel features a lobby packed with "Texican" art and memorabilia. ❻–❼

Holiday Inn Crockett Hotel 320 Bonham St ☎210/225-6500, ⓦwww.hotelsanantoniotx.com. Historic hotel with modern facilities, in an excellent location just opposite the Alamo. ❻

Menger Hotel 204 Alamo Plaza ☎210/223-4361, ⓦwww.historicmenger.com. Texas's most famous hotel of the great cattle drives; Teddy Roosevelt recruited his "Rough Riders" here in 1898 for the Spanish–American War. Inexplicably, the bar is furnished to re-create the tap-room at the British House of Lords. ❻

Motel 6 San Antonio Downtown 211 N Pecos St ☎210/225-1111, ⓦwww.motel6.com. Clean but slightly worn rooms near Market Square, along with a small pool. ❸

A Yellow Rose 229 Madison St ☎210/229-2903, ⓦwww.ayellowrose.com. A relaxed, welcoming option in the B&B-choked King William Historic District, with beautiful antique-laden rooms. ❺

The Town

Since mission times, the **San Antonio River** has been the key to the city's fortunes. Destructive floods in the 1920s and subsequent oil-drilling reduced its flow, leading to plans to pave the river over. Instead, a careful landscaping scheme, started in 1939 by the WPA, created the Paseo del Rio, or **River Walk**, now the aesthetic and commercial focus of San Antonio. The walk, located below street level, is reached by steps from various spots along the main roads and crossed by humpbacked stone bridges. Cobbled paths, lined with tropical plants and shaded by pine, cypress, oak, and willow, wind for two and a half miles (21 blocks) beside the jade-green water, with much of the city's eating and entertainment concentrated along the way. You can catch a river taxi at a number of places, but strolling is cheaper and just as much fun, for the view of the river slowly changing character between the lively Rivercenter Mall and the quieter, more park-like outskirts. During peak travel seasons, the River walk can turn unpleasantly crowded, with festive vacationers packed three to four rows deep, though a recently opened twelve-mile extension may help ease the foot traffic.

While the **Alamo** (see p.770) is the main attraction in the downtown area, the surreal **Buckhorn Museum**, 318 E Houston St (Sun–Thurs 10am–5pm, Fri & Sat 10am–6pm; $10), is worthwhile for a pleasingly kitsch look at Americana. During San Antonio's heyday as a cowtown, cowboys, trappers, and traders would bring their cattle horns to the original *Buckhorn Saloon* in exchange for a drink. The entire bar has since been transplanted to this downtown location, which boasts an extra floor of exhibition space, thousands of horns on display – mounted as trophies, chandeliers, and chairs – and many stuffed animals, including "Blondie," an unforgettable two-headed lamb.

La Villita ("little town"), on the River Walk opposite Hemisfair Park, was San Antonio's original settlement, occupied in the mid- to late eighteenth century by Mexican "squatters" with no titles to the land. Only when its elevation enabled it to survive fierce floods in 1819 did this rude collection of stone and adobe buildings become suddenly respectable. It is now a National Historic District, turned over to a dubious "arts community" consisting mostly of overpriced craftshops (daily 10am–6pm). It's at its best off-season or at dusk, when the crowds dwindle and the muted colors, smells, and noises are more evocative of earlier times. In contrast, the 25-block **King William Historic District** to the southwest, between the river and S St Mary's Street, contains the elegant late nineteenth-century homes of German merchants. A pleasant incongruity in this Mexican-feeling city, it remains a fashionable residential area and has some stylish B&Bs.

The best of several museums in **HemisFair Park** is the **Institute of Texan Cultures**, 801 S Bowie St (Tues–Sun 9am–5pm; $6.50), which maps the social histories of 26 diverse "Texan" cultures, with especially pertinent African-American and Native American sections, and an intriguing corner devoted to short-lived attempts to introduce the camel to West Texas as a beast of burden. Also worthwhile is the **Mexican Cultural Institute** (daily 10am–5pm; free), which has been expanded into seven gallery spaces and a theatre, while retaining its focus on historic and contemporary Mexican art. The ugly 750ft **Tower of the Americas** east of here is devoid of interest, save for the views from its observation deck (Sun–Thurs 9am–10pm, Fri & Sat 9am–11pm; $3).

West of the river at 115 Main Plaza, the 1731 **San Fernando Cathedral** is the oldest cathedral in the US, though, contrary to the claims of the tourist board, nobody really believes that the Alamo heroes are buried here. Mariachi Masses are held on Saturday at 5.15pm, when crowds overflow onto the plaza. Two blocks west at 105 Plaza de Armas, the beautifully simple, whitewashed **Spanish Governors Palace** (Mon–Sat 9am–5pm, Sun 10am–5pm; $1.50) was once home to Spanish officials during the mission era. Just one story tall, it's hardly a palace, but its flagstone floors, low doorways and beamed ceilings, religious icons and ornate wooden carvings give it a wonderful atmosphere, and it provides an illuminating glimpse of the lifestyles of the civil and religious authorities in this remote outpost. Don't miss the sweet cobbled courtyard, with its fountain, mosaic floor, and lush palms.

Market Square (daily: summer 10am–8pm; rest of year 10am–6pm), a couple of blocks further northwest, dates from 1840. Its outdoor restaurants and bustle are still at the heart of the city's life; fruit and vegetables are on sale early in the morning, while the shops are a compelling mix of color and kitsch. **El**

Mercado, an indoor complex, is meant to resemble a traditional Mexican market, selling tourist-oriented gifts, jewelry, and oddities. A few of the shops are great, even if the air-conditioning and piped music undermine the authenticity of the venture.

It's also worth getting to the beautiful **McNay Art Museum**, 6000 N New Braunfels Ave at Austin Highway (Tues–Sat 10am–5pm, Sun noon–5pm; free). This exquisite Moorish-style villa, complete with tranquil garden, was built in the 1950s to house the art collection of millionaire and folk artist Marion Koogler McNay, which includes modern sculpture, Gothic and medieval works, as well as a sprinkling of major players (Picasso, Monet, and Van Gogh). Buses #11 (Nacogdoches) and #14 (Thousand Oaks) serve the museum from downtown. On the way there, bus #11 passes the **San Antonio Museum of Art**, 200 W Jones Ave (Tues 10am–9pm, Wed–Sat 10am–5pm, Sun noon–5pm; $6, free on Tues 3–9pm), which occupies the old Lone Star Brewery, but it's the added Rockefeller Center for Latin American Art wing that holds most interest, with its particularly fine exhibit on folk art.

Alamo and the other missions

The Alamo (☎210/225-1391, ⓦwww.thealamo.org) is the most famous – for reasons that have nothing to do with its original purpose – of a trail of Catholic missions established by the Spanish along remote stretches of the San Antonio River early in the eighteenth century. San Antonio's most distinctive landmark, it is smack in the center of downtown, but for a real taste of early Spanish influence in Texas, make an effort to get out and see the more distant, less visited missions. Each was laid out like a small fortified town, with the church as aesthetic and cultural focus. The goal was to strengthen Spanish control by "converting" the indigenous Coahuiltecan – in practice, using them as workforce and army. The missions flourished from 1745 to 1775, but couldn't survive the ravages of disease and attack from the Apache and Comanche, and fell into disuse early in the nineteenth century. To get a sense of the history of the Alamo, you could head first for the nearby **Rivercenter Mall**, where the battle is re-enacted on a six-story, Texas-scale IMAX screen (call ☎210/225-4629 for showtimes; $9); fact and sentiment may converge during the 45-minute presentation, but it takes a callous viewer not to be affected by the rousing patriotism of the finale.

The main **visitor center** (daily 9am–5pm; ☎210/932-1001) for the area's string of missions is next to Mission San Jose (see opposite) and contains a movie theater, small museum, and giftshop.

The Alamo

All that is left of the original fort of the **Alamo** – at the meeting of Houston, Crockett, Bonham, and Alamo streets – is the **chapel**, with its large arched facade of delicately carved sandstone, and the **Long Barracks**, now a **museum** (Mon–Sat 9am–5.30pm, Sun 10am–5.30pm; free). The first of the Spanish missions, established as San Antonio de Valero in 1718, it only became known as the Pueblo del Alamo in 1801, after secularization, when it was named for the Mexican home town of a Spanish cavalry unit that used it as a base. The **battle**, immortalized in film and song, occurred on March 6, 1836, when all of the 189 men who had held out for thirteen days against the five-thousand-strong Mexican troops were killed, a massacre dismissed by the Mexican General Santa Anna as "but a small affair." The rebels consisted of a few native Hispanic-Texans, and a majority of volunteers (adventurers like

Davy Crockett and Jim Bowie, and aspiring colonists from other states), dreaming of Texan autonomy and driven by the battle cry of "Victory or Death!"

Though a constant stream of bus tours makes visits crowded and hectic, seeing the Alamo is crucial to understanding Texan pride and stubbornness. The battle memorabilia in the chapel is undeniably emotive, with poignant letters sent home by soldiers preparing to die, and the Long Barracks Museum, hidden away southwest of the shrine's main entrance, presents a twenty-minute video on the history of the missions and the battle. Take time also to sit in peace in the four-acre grounds, a haven from the downtown commotion just outside the walls, amid lush blooms, palms, and cacti, and an irrigation ditch filled with fat fish.

The other missions

The **Mission Trail** runs ten miles south along the river from Alamo Street, down S St Mary's Street and onto Mission Road. Mission Concepción and Mission San José can be reached via Texas Trolley from the Alamo Visitor Center (☎210/212-5395; $28); missions San Juan and Espada require a car. Each of the remaining four missions has been restored to act as an **interpretive center** illustrating some aspect of mission life (daily 9am–5pm; free), while the churches themselves still serve active parishes.

Mission Concepción, 807 Mission Rd, with its distinctive twin towers and cupola, was built between 1731 and 1751. Colorful scraps of original frescoes can still be seen, along with bullet holes from rougher days. Exhibits here concentrate on the religious function of the missions. The 1720 **Mission San José**, 6701 San Jose Drive, which interprets the mission as a social and defense center, is the most complete of all, restored in the 1930s by the WPA. Other notable features include the beautiful carved stone ornamentation, especially the ornate rose window. A Mariachi Mass is held here each Sunday at noon. Of the two smaller and more isolated missions, **Mission San Juan**, 9101 Graf Rd, has displays on agriculture (as well as a unique delicate bell tower), while **Mission San Francisco de la Espada**, 10040 Espada Rd, looks back on ranching at the missions.

Eating

Not surprisingly, San Antonio has good **Tex-Mex** food in all price ranges. Many visitors head straight for the Mexican restaurants on the River Walk, but, charming as it is to eat alfresco beside the river, don't be seduced to such an extent that you never venture above ground. There are many good places downtown and the floor of the **Rivercenter Mall** is packed with assorted fast-food stalls (*Ninfa's Express* is among the best).

Boudro's 421 E Commerce St ☎210/224-8484. One of the best dining spots on the River Walk, with tasty, unusual entrees (ie, quail). Don't miss the prickly-pear margaritas.

Casa Rio 430 E Commerce St ☎210/225-6718. The oldest, most established restaurant on the River Walk, offering cheap but excellent Mexican food: a huge "deluxe dinner" costs around $7.

El Mirador 722 S St Mary's St ☎210/225-9444. Wonderful Mexican breakfasts and lunches for under $5, and pricier Southwestern cuisine in the evening. Specialties include *xocetl* (chicken broth) and *azteca* (spicy tomato) soups. Closed Sun and Aug.

The Guenther House 205 E Guenther St ☎210/227-1061. Delicious cookies and cakes in a cool green flour-mill-cum-museum in the King William Historic District. Good breakfasts and lunches, too.

Mi Tierra 218 Produce Row ☎210/225-1262. Expansive 24-hour joint serving superb, inexpensive Tex-Mex in a bustling old Market Square building.

Paesano's 111 ⓦ Crockett St ☎210/227-2782. Lively Italian restaurant on the River Walk, near the *Hard Rock Café*. Try the excellent shrimp paesano.

Zuni Grill 511 River Walk ☎210/227-0864. Creative Southwestern fare in one of the most stylish River Walk restaurants. Main courses around $14.

Nightlife and entertainment

With its abundance of picturesque settings, San Antonio is a great city for **festivals**. The year's biggest event is April's ten-day **Fiesta San Antonio** (☎210/227-5191, ⓦwww.fiesta-sa.org), marking Texas's victory in the Battle of San Jacinto, with parades, cookouts, and Latin music concerts filling the streets. Also in May is the **Tejano Conjunto Festival** at Rosedale Park and at the Guadalupe Cultural Arts Center on Guadalupe Street (☎210/271-3151, ⓦwww.guadalupeculturalarts.org), west of downtown, which celebrates the German–Mexican country music of south and central Texas. During June's **Texas Folklife Festival** at the Institute of Texan Cultures (see p.769), ten stages showcase the state's huge diversity of music, ranging from gospel to Lebanese. Finally, the **San Antonio Stock Show & Rodeo** (☎210/225-5851, ⓦwww.sarodeo.com) in early February celebrates cowboy and King of the Hill culture over two weeks of rodeo events and country music.

Check the free weekly *Current* (ⓦwww.sacurrent.com) for gigs, films, and events. The live jazz and flamenco in the restaurants along the **River Walk** tend to be rather sanitized, while **N St Mary's Street** (just beyond the bus station toward the art museum) is the main strip for college clubs and bars. The outdoor **Arneson River Theatre**, opposite La Villita, where the river separates the audience from the stage, hosts Mexican folk music and dance during the summer. The outlying areas also hold some great old **country dance halls**, the best of which is Greune Hall.

Bonham Exchange 411 Bonham St ☎210/271-3811. Popular mixed gay club with good house and garage DJs.

Floore Country Store 14464 Old Bandera Rd, downtown Helotes ☎210/695-8827. Old country dance hall, with outdoor dancing.

Gruene Hall 1281 Gruene Rd, Gruene ☎832/629-5077. Dominating this small town (pronounced "green"), 30 miles northeast of downtown San Antonio, is the oldest remaining dance hall in Texas, with top country stars playing here at weekends.

Jim Cullum's The Landing 123 Losoya St, under the *Hyatt Regency* ☎210/325-2495. Traditional jazz every night in a club that's been running for over thirty years.

Polly Esther's 212 College St ☎210/220-1972. It may be a chain, but it's also undeniably fun and enlivened by an ultra-energetic crowd spilling out from the club all over the River Walk.

Swig 111 W Crockett St ☎210/476-0005. The best martinis in the city, with an attractive crowd looking to mingle in a jazzy, classy space.

Tycoon Flats 2926 N St Mary's St ☎210/737-1929. A variety of live music on offer with no cover charge. The patio restaurant serves good vegetarian food for about $5 per plate. Closed Mon.

White Rabbit 2410 N St Mary's St ☎210/737-2221. The main venue for touring indie bands, drawing a raucous young crowd.

Austin

AUSTIN was only a tiny community on the verdant banks of the (Texas) Colorado River when Mirabeau B. Lamar, president of the Republic, suggested in 1839 that it would make a better capital than swampy and disease-ridden Houston. Early building had to be done under armed guard, while angry Comanche watched from the surrounding hills, but despite its perilous location, the city thrived.

These days it wears its status as capital of Texas very lightly; sightseeing rates as a low priority against simply hanging out. Since the 1960s, this laid-back and progressive city has been a haven for artists, musicians, and writers, and today many visitors come specifically for the **music**. Local musicians are renowned for their innovative reworkings of Texas's country, folk, and R&B heritage, often severing their rural roots to use Austin's enthusiastic environment as a

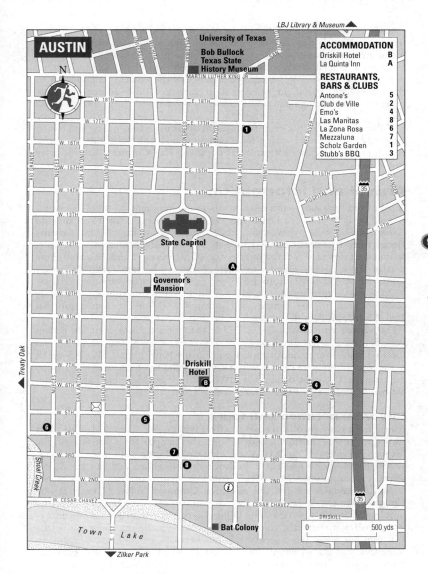

AUSTIN

University of Texas

Bob Bullock
Texas State
History Museum

LBJ Library & Museum

ACCOMMODATION	
Driskill Hotel	B
La Quinta Inn	A

RESTAURANTS, BARS & CLUBS	
Antone's	5
Club de Ville	2
Emo's	4
Las Manitas	8
La Zona Rosa	6
Mezzaluna	7
Scholz Garden	1
Stubb's BBQ	3

State Capitol

Governor's Mansion

Driskill Hotel

Bat Colony

Town Lake

Zilker Park

Treaty Oak

Shoal Creek

0   500 yds

TEXAS | Austin

springboard to national recognition. Janis Joplin had her start here in the early 1960s, and at the end of that decade, Austin was second only to San Francisco in its adherence to the "turn on, tune in, drop out" philosophy, with locals coining the term "headneck" to describe themselves. Musicians hungry for fame still tumble out of buses here from all over Texas to seek their fortunes in the literally hundreds of live venues.

Austin is one of the few cities in the state where **cycling** is a viable alternative to driving. It may not have completely avoided the usual problems of urban growth – thanks to a sizable population leap, ugly suburbs have shot up to threaten its small-town ambiance – but it feels wonderfully safe for visitors, even women traveling alone, and the presence of the vast UT campus adds to the atmosphere, even if almost every shop and streetlamp is adorned with the unsightly burnt-orange and white colors of the college's Longhorns football team.

Within the city limits a great park system offers numerous hiking and biking trails and a wonderful spring-fed swimming pool. Looking further afield, Austin makes a fine base for exploring the green **Hill Country** that rolls away to the west.

Arrival and information

Austin spreads about twenty miles north–south and eighteen miles east–west, severed by I-35 (between Dallas and San Antonio) to the east. The Colorado River runs south of downtown. Flights come in at the tasteful **Austin-Bergstrom International Airport** (☎512/530-2242), located eight miles southeast of downtown at the intersection of highways 71 and 183. From here it takes about twenty minutes to reach downtown by **taxi** (Yellow Checker Cabs; ☎512/452-9999; around $25) or by SuperShuttle vans (☎512/258-3826, ⓦwww.supershuttle.com; $10), while the #100 **bus** runs approximately once an hour to the campus and downtown (Mon–Fri 5am–11pm, Sat 7am–11pm, Sun 8am–10.30pm) for a bargain fare of 50¢.

The **visitor center** is at 201 E 2nd St (Mon–Fri 8.30am–5pm, Sat & Sun 9am–5pm; ☎512/478-0098 or 1-800/926-2282, ⓦwww.austintexas.org) and there's a State Tourist Information Center (daily 9am–5pm; ☎512/305-8400) in the foyer of the state capitol, with changing exhibits of Texacana and a video presentation. The **post office** is at 510 Guadalupe St (Mon–Fri 7am–6.30pm, Sat 8am–3pm; ☎512/494-2210; zip code 78701).

City transporation and tours

Austin has a good **public transportation** system. The Capital METRO **bus** runs downtown, crosstown, and through the campus for a flat fare of 50¢ (express services charge $1), with additional shuttle routes for students, although everybody uses them; look for the Longhorn emblem beside the shuttle's route number (Mon–Fri 5.30am–12.30am, times vary widely on Sat & Sun). Schedules are available from the Customer Service Center at 801 Congress Ave (Mon–Fri 8am–5pm), or you can call the METRO information line at ☎512/474-1200. The Dillo, also run by METRO, is a free downtown **trolley** system that runs along five routes, including three out to the UT campus, every ten to forty minutes between 6.30am and 8.30pm on weekdays, and on a limited schedule on weekends. You can rent **bicycles** from Bicycle Sport Shop, 1426 Toomey Rd (Mon–Fri 10am–7pm, Sat 9am–6pm, Sun 11am–5pm; ☎512/477-3472). Walking is an easy and pleasant way to get around; free guided **walking tours**, organized by Austin's visitor center, leave from the south entrance of the capitol (March–Nov Sat 2pm, Sun 9am; ☎512/478-0098).

Accommodation

I-35 and Congress Avenue are Austin's low-cost **hotel** strips, but **B&Bs** are better options; there are good ones in most areas of the city.

Austin Motel 1220 S Congress Ave ☎512/441-1157, Ⓦwww.austinmotel.com. Basic rooms just south of the Congress Ave Bridge, a favorite with visiting musicians. Opposite Austin's top country music venue, the *Continental Club* (see p.778). ❸

Carrington's Bluff 1900 David St ☎512/479-0638. Very good B&B, central but country-style, a block from Lamar Blvd at Martin Luther King Blvd, with a shady veranda, friendly hosts, and gourmet breakfast. ❹

Driskill Hotel 604 Brazos St ☎512/474-5911, Ⓦwww.driskillhotel.com. Grand historic hotel close to the action along 6th Street, with a glittery clientele. ❽

HI-Austin (Hostelling International) 2200 Lakeshore Blvd ☎512/444-2294 or 1-800/725-2331, Ⓦwww.hiaustin.org. Bargain rates right on the shore of Town Lake. $17 for members, $20 for nonmembers.

La Quinta Inn Austin Capitol 300 E 11th St ☎512/476-1166, Ⓦwww.laquinta.com. Comfortable, central rooms and an outdoor pool within a stone's throw of the capitol. ❹

Hotel San Jose 13165 Congress Ave ☎512/444-7322, Ⓦwww.sanjosehotel.com. Ultra-chic, Zen-like hotel with lovely gardens and a small pool. ❺–❻

Woodburn House 4401 Ave D ☎512/458-4335, Ⓦwww.woodburnhouse.com. Small B&B in the leafy Hyde Park area, within walking distance of the university. Reservation and deposit required. ❺

The City

The Texas **State Capitol**, at 13th Street and Congress Avenue (daily 9am–5pm; public tours every 15min; free), is over 300-feet high, taller than the national capitol in Washington, with a red sunset granite dome that dominates the downtown skyline. The chandeliers, carpets, and even the door hinges of this colossal building are emblazoned with lone stars and other Texan motifs, a theme continued in the added extension, a sleek maze of marble halls. Nearby, the antebellum **Governor's Mansion**, 1010 Colorado St, contains displays on Texan history (free tours Mon–Fri every 20min, 10am–noon). **Congress Avenue**, a stretch of 1950s shops and muted office buildings that slopes south from the capitol down to the river, is worthy of a stroll; at dusk 1.5 million bats – the world's largest urban bat colony – emerge in a large cloud from their hangouts under the bridge. **Sixth Street**, also known as Old Pecan Street, runs west from I-35 to Congress Street, and is the focus of much of the city's nightlife, as well as home to many renovated buildings, galleries, and hip shops. The elegant Romanesque **Driskill Hotel**, on the corner with Brazos Street, has its own self-guided walking tour, with a glossy leaflet recounting the hotel's many links with government since 1886. Between 5th and 6th streets, just west of Lamar Boulevard, the 600-year-old **Treaty Oak** is the last of the Council Oaks, a grove that served as a meeting place for local Native Americans; unfortunately, someone chose to poison the tree in 1989, and only one-third of it remains.

The **Bob Bullock Texas State History Museum** further north, adjacent to the University of Texas (see p.776) at Martin Luther King Jr Boulevard and North Congress Avenue, should satisfy anyone's curiosity for Texas arcana. Among the exhibits are the diary of Stephen F. Austin, generally considered the founder of the state, and a Bible that saved the life of Sam Houston Jr, during the Civil War; a bullet is still lodged in its pages (Mon–Sat 9am–6pm; $5.50). The **Elisabet Ney Museum** at 304 E 44th St is a German-influenced castle-like building in a leafy, historic residential area. It preserves the last studio, with marquettes and finished marbles, of Austin's most celebrated sculptor (Wed–Sat 10am–5pm, Sun noon–5pm; free).

Southwest of the center and across the river from Amtrak, **Zilker Park** is one of the best of Austin's many fine parks, a perfect retreat on sweaty Austin afternoons. One of its main attractions is the spring-fed (and deliciously cold) **Barton Springs Pool**, a 1000-foot turquoise rectangle shaded by pecan trees (daily 5am–10pm; Mon–Fri $2.50, Sat & Sun $2.75). You can paddle in the pebbly creek below the pool free of charge, and take advantage of the hiking and biking trails, the miniature railroad winding beside the river (daily 10am–7pm; $2.75), and, to the west, the wildlife garden of the **Austin Nature and Science Center**, which has hands-on exhibits on the local ecosystem and on conservation in general (Mon–Sat 9am–5pm, Sun noon–5pm; free; ☏512/327-8181). South of the Barton Springs Pool on Robert E. Lee Road, the **Umlauf Sculpture Garden** (Wed–Fri 10am–4.30pm, Sat & Sun 1–4.30pm; $3.50; ☏512/445-5582, ⓦwww.umlaufsculpture.org) is a tranquil, grassy enclave dotted with more than one hundred works in bronze, terracotta, wood, and marble. More outdoor relief can be found farther north on the banks of the Colorado River at **Mayfield Park**, a peaceful idyll complete with water lilies and peacocks. Nearby **Mount Bonnell** also gives great views over the city and surrounding countryside.

The **Austin Museum of Art** is in the process of relocating from its Laguna Gloria location, at 3809 W 35th St, to a permanent facility downtown (check with the museum for the latest details). In the meantime, many exhibits are on view at a separate downtown location, at 823 Congress Ave (Tues–Sat 10am–6pm, Thurs until 8pm, Sun noon–5pm; $3; ☏512/495-9224, ⓦwww.amoa.org).

The University of Texas

Having its own oil well (the drilling rig Santa Rita No. 1 on San Jacinto Blvd) has made the **University of Texas** one of the world's richest universities. Its unparalleled collection of manuscripts by contemporary authors is available to scholars amid tight security in the **Harry Ransom Center**; stories abound of the sums lavished to acquire work from relative unknowns who might someday achieve fame. The Center, in the southwest corner of the campus, also houses an **art gallery** (Mon–Fri 9am–5pm, Sat 9am–noon; free), with a Gutenberg Bible as well as contemporary Latin American and American paintings. Student-guided tours of the main campus building and its tower are offered frequently; call ☏512/475-6633 for details.

The stretch of **Guadalupe Street** running along campus north from Martin Luther King Boulevard to 24th Street is known as "**the Drag**, " fittingly a focus of student activity, and lined with cafés, vintage clothing shops, and bookstores.

The **LBJ Library and Museum** (daily 9am–5pm; free; ☏512/721-0200, ⓦwww.lbjlib.utexas.edu), on the northeast edge of campus at 2313 Red River St, traces the career of the brash and egotistical Lyndon Baines Johnson from his origins in the Hill Country to the House of Representatives, the Senate, and the White House. The curious circumstances surrounding his first senatorial election in 1948 (his primary victory was confirmed only after some "overlooked" votes – all written in the same hand – were found three days after his opponent had apparently won the Democratic nomination) go unmentioned. John Kennedy is said to have made Johnson his vice president to avoid his establishing a rival power base; but in the aftermath of Kennedy's assassination, Johnson's administration (1963–69) was able to push through a far more radical program than Kennedy ever attempted. Johnson's nemesis, Vietnam, is presented here as an awful mess left by Kennedy for him to clear up, at the cost of great personal anguish. There's a replica of the Johnson Oval Office in the White House, as well as gifts presented to the president, including a 1910 Model T from Henry Ford.

Eating

Radical Austin has many more vegetarian and wholefood **restaurants** than is usual in Texas; even chicken-fried steak can be found prepared healthily. There are plenty of good budget restaurants near the university, especially along Guadalupe Street – just look for the crowds. Many of the music venues also serve up decent food.

El Sol y La Luna 1224 S Congress Ave ☎512/444-7770. A fun, family-run Mexican joint on the funky strip of shops and clubs just south of downtown. Especially good for breakfast.

Jovita's 1619 S 1st St ☎512/447-7825. Reliable Tex-Mex food, plus occasional sets by top local country musicians (among them Don Walser) on the porch.

Las Manitas 211 Congress Ave ☎512/472-9357. Authentic, great-value Mexican food and decor right in downtown. Offers breakfast and lunch only – get there early to beat the politicians to a space.

Magnolia Café 2000 S Congress Ave ☎512/445-0000 and 2304 Lake Austin Blvd ☎512/478-8645. A local favorite for breakfast. Open 24hr.

Mezzaluna 310 Colorado St ☎512/472-6770. A moderate to expensive traditional Italian restaurant in the warehouse district between 6th St and the river.

Salt Lick 18300 Farm Rd 1826 ☎512/894-3117. The standard answer for anyone wondering where the city's best BBQ is, even though it's really a few miles' drive into the scenic hill country. Dine on fabulous ribs soaked in a near-perfect BBQ sauce.

Scholz Garden 1607 San Jacinto Blvd ☎512/474-1958. Big portions of German sausage and Tex-Mex food at an Austin legend, which also puts on good live music.

Stubb's BBQ 801 Red River St ☎512/480-8341. Great Texan-style brisket, sausage, and ribs, plus bands of national repute playing the indoor and outdoor stages.

Threadgill's 6416 N Lamar Blvd ☎512/451-5440. An Austin institution since Kenneth Threadgill was given the first license to sell beer in the city after Prohibition. Real home cooking at bargain prices, with free seconds of vegetables like black-eyed peas and okra. Lively atmosphere, with occasional live fiddle music, folk, or country-and-western bands. There's also a downtown branch at 301 W Riverside Drive (☎512/472-9304). Not to be missed.

West Lynn Café 1110 W Lynn ☎512/482-0950. Stylish vegetarian food from around the world at one of the city's most popular restaurants.

Nightlife and entertainment

The only problem you'll have with Austin **nightlife** is being spoiled for choice. On 6th Street in particular, virtually every building houses a club or a bar, and many of these have become rather over-commercialized. It's much better to venture just off 6th where you'll find some of the best clubs, or take a cab to some of the further-flung joints. Three first-rate local newspapers carry listings: the *Daily Texan*, the UT paper (Thurs; Ⓦwww.dailytexanonline.com), the "XLent" supplement to the *Austin American-Statesman* (Thurs; Ⓦwww.austin360.com), and the *Austin Chronicle* (Fri; Ⓦwww.auschron.com).

There's usually something to catch on campus. Big drama and dance names appear in the **Performing Arts Center**, 23rd Street and Robert Dedman Drive (☎512/471-1444, Ⓦwww.utpac.org), and you can see **independent movies** at the Dobie Theater, 2021 Guadalupe and 21st streets. *The Velveeta Room*, 521 E 6th St ($5 cover; ☎512/469-9116), showcases open-mic comedy on Wednesday nights. On the same block is *Esther's Pool*, 525 E 6th St (around $15; ☎512/320-0553, Ⓦwww.esthersfollies.com), home of Esther's Follies, Austin's hippest and funniest cabaret, which combines spoofs of local and national politicians with Texas-style singing and dancing.

Live music

Although Austin's folk revival in the 1960s attracted enough attention to propel Janis Joplin on her way from Port Arthur, Texas, to stardom in California, the city first achieved prominence in its own right as the center of "**outlaw** country" music in the 1970s. **Willie Nelson** and **Waylon Jennings**, disillusioned with Nashville, spearheaded a movement that reworked sentimental country-and-western with an incisive injection of rock 'n' roll. The audiences in Austin, far removed from the hard-drinking honky-tonk crowds of West Texas, provided an environment that encouraged and rewarded risk-taking and experimentation. These days the predominant "**Austin sound**" is a melange of country, folk, blues, psychedelic, and "alternative" influences, though that's not to say the scene is anything but eclectic (with swing particularly popular at the moment); this, after all, is the city that spawned the Butthole Surfers.

The tradition of black Texas bluesmen such as Blind Lemon Jefferson and Blind Willie Johnson, as well as the rocking bar blues of Stevie Ray Vaughan, still lives on here; *Antone's Blues Club* on Guadalupe Street is the place to hear **live blues**, while **folk** music, traditional or with a punk twist, is also thriving, celebrated each year at the **Kerrville Folk Festival** at Rod Kennedy's Quiet Valley Ranch in **Kerrville**, a hundred miles west of Austin on I-10 (☎830/257-3600). The ten-day **South by Southwest Festival**, held in the third week of March, features the best bands from Texas and around the world, along with tons of movies; passes are $475 (in advance) for all film, music, and interactive events; a music-only pass is $325; call ☎512/467-7979 or visit ⓦwww.sxsw.com for information.

Antone's Blues Club 213 W 5th St ☎512/263-4146. Hot, sweaty, and crowded; the best blues club in the city, with big-name national and local acts nightly.

The Backyard 13101 W Hwy 71 ☎512/263-4146, ⓦwww.thebackyard.net. Out-of-the-way club that hosts engaging folk- and country-tinged acts.

The Broken Spoke 3201 S Lamar Blvd ☎512/442-6189. Neighborhood restaurant (good chicken-fried steak) and stomping country-music hall, with all the trappings but well away from the center. The barn-like dance floor regularly attracts the best acts on the Texas circuit. Two-stepping begins at 9pm.

Cactus Café The Texas Union, 24th and Guadalupe sts, University of Texas ☎512/475-6515. One of Austin's favorite venues, putting on consistently good country, rock, and folk music, and regular showcasing new acts.

Club de Ville 900 Red River St ☎512/457-0900. Excellent cocktails and a superb patio setting are the draw at this stylish bar just a few minutes from the 6th Street morass.

Continental Club 1315 S Congress Ave ☎512/441-2444. The premier place to hear hard-edged country sung the Austin way by top-notch artists.

Emo's 603 Red River St ☎512/477-EMOS. Launchpad for Austin's best alternative bands, with a friendly, tattooed, and pierced crowd. Cover varies, patrons under 21 pay extra.

La Zona Rosa 612 W 4th St ☎512/263-4146. Great venue for rootsy bands.

Symphony Square Red River Rd and 11th St ☎512/476-6064. A rough-hewn outdoor amphitheater, below street level on the river, hosting good jazz and classical concerts in summer.

The Hill Country

The rolling hills, lakes, and valleys of the **HILL COUNTRY**, north and west of Austin and San Antonio, were inhabited mostly by Apache and Comanche until after statehood, when German and Scandinavian settlers arrived. Many of the log-cabin farming communities they established are still here, such as **New Braunfels** (famous for its sausages and pastries) and Luckenbach. You may still hear German spoken, and the German influence is also felt in local food and music; *conjunto*, for example, is a blend of Tex-Mex and accordion music. The whole region is a popular retreat and resort area, with some wonderful hill views and lake swimming, and a lot of good places to camp.

New Braunfels

NEW BRAUNFELS, just thirty miles north of San Antonio on I-35, was founded by German immigrants – mostly artisans and artists – in 1845 and it quickly became a trade center. Those days are long gone, and now the community makes its living off tourism. The little town sprung up along two rivers – the Comal and the Guadalupe – both of which are ideal for rafting and tubing. Depending on season and weather, even the least experienced river-goers can easily ride the white water – making the little German town a hugely popular weekend destination.

Although the notion of renting an extra tube or raft for one's beer cooler might horrify white-water purists, hedonistic trips down the Guadalupe are a right of passage for many Texas students. For everybody else, there's the ever-popular **Schlitterbaun** (hours vary; ℡830/625-2351, ⊛www.schlitterbahn .com), which uses cool, refreshing Comal water in its rides. The Schlitterbaum is only open during the summer and hours vary, so check the website. South of town on I-35, the well-signposted **Natural Bridge Caverns** (℡210/651-6101, ⊛www.naturalbridgecaverns.com) is also family friendly, but includes the physically intense Adventure Tour ($125, reservations necessary), which lowers visitors 160 feet by rope into the South Cavern and takes them hiking where there are no trails or lights.

If outdoor activities don't appeal, downtown's historic district has enough antique stores, galleries, and restored buildings to fill a couple of hours. Should you need **to stay**, the *Heidelberg Lodges* (℡830/625-9967, ⊛www.heidelber-glodges.com; ❸) are rustic, but their lovely riverfront location makes them a bargain. For **food**, skip the town's kitschy sausage houses and head for the elegant *Huisache Grill*, 303 W San Antonio St (℡830/620-5033), for sophisticated, reasonably priced cuisine. The **visitors center**, off I-35 exit 187 (℡830/625-2385 or 1-800/572-2626, ⊛www.nbjumpin.com), provides a list of accommodation, as well as information on renting rafts and tubes.

The Lyndon B. Johnson Historical Park

Sixty-five miles west of Austin on US-290, the **Lyndon B. Johnson State and National Historical Park** preserves LBJ's birthplace (1908) and the ranch house where Lady Bird Johnson continued to live long after her husband's death in 1973 (daily 10am–4pm; 1hr 15min tours leave from the visitor center; $3). The Sauer-Beckmann Farmstead, a "living history" farm, depicts German family life in the early 1900s.

The **visitor center** (daily 8.45am–5pm; ℡830/868-7128) and Johnson's boyhood home (daily 9am–4pm; free guided tours every 30min) are at sleepy **Johnson City**, fourteen miles further east; for a good lunch, stop off here at the *Hill Country Cupboard*, at the junction of US-281 and US-290 (℡830/868-4625).

Fredericksburg

FREDERICKSBURG, smack in the middle of the Hill Country, might at first glance look like a pastiche of a German village, overrun by Biergartens and gingerbread storefronts. In fact it's still pretty much the town founded by six hundred enterprising Germans in 1846. They managed to make – and, uniquely, keep – treaties with the local Comanche, and their community, based on hard work and perseverance, survived through epidemics and civil war.

At the weekend, crowds of day-trippers from San Antonio and Austin visit Main Street's galleries, craft shops, antique stores, and numerous fancy tearooms. Several original structures make up the **Pioneer Museum** at 309 W Main St, including a church and a store (Mon–Sat 10am–4pm, Sun 1–5pm; free; for info, contact the Gillespie Country Historical Society ☎830/997-2835, ⓦwww.pioneermuseum.com). The **National Museum of the Pacific War**, 340 E Main St (daily 10am–5pm; $5; ☎830/997-4379, ⓦwww.nimitz-museum.org), incorporates the *Nimitz Steamboat Hotel* – which, with its looming tower really does look like a steamboat – and features a Japanese garden and a historical trail that leads past aircraft, tanks, and heavy artillery.

Practicalities

Like the rest of the Hill Country, Fredericksburg has no Amtrak service, but Greyhound stops at 758 S Washington. The **CVB**, in the Market Square at 106 N Adams St (Mon–Fri 8.30am–5pm, Sat 9am–noon & 1–5pm, Sun 1–5pm; ☎830/997-6523, ⓦwww.fredericksburg-texas.com), has details of the budget **hotels** along E Main Street; of these, the pool-equipped *Sunday House* at no. 501 (☎830/997-4484, ⓦwww.sundayhouseinn.com; ❺) is one of the more luxurious. **Bed-and-breakfast** is big business in historic Fredericksburg; for a list of places, contact B&B of Fredericksburg, 619 W Main St (ⓦwww.bandbf-bg.com; ❷–❻). There's **camping** in the Lady Bird Johnson Municipal Park, three miles southwest on Hwy-16 S, or in the Enchanted Rock State Natural Area, eighteen miles north on Ranch Road 965.

Restaurants and bakeries line Main Street, many of them doing cheap lunch specials. *Dietz Bakery*, at no. 218 (☎830/997-3250), is the oldest in town, good for tasty breads and biscuits. You can eat more substantially at *Friedhelm's Bavarian Inn* at no. 905 (closed Mon; ☎830/997-6300), which specializes in starchy plates of dumplings and sauerkraut.

North and east Texas

Early immigration into **north and east Texas**, during the days of the Republic and following the devastation of the Civil War, was largely from the Southern states. In the 1930s, the northeastern oil fields near **Tyler** (a drab town only redeemed by its beautiful rose gardens) proved to be the richest ever found in the US. In addition to oil, agriculture has become a prime source of commerce, with logging important in the densely forested east. The grand exception is, of course, the **Metroplex** – the area that includes **Dallas** and **Fort Worth**. The main tourist attractions and cultural life of the region are concentrated here, but if you enjoy exploring small-town America, and have a car, the north and east can yield more subtle pleasures. The **national forests** of Angelina, Davy Crockett, Sabine, and Sam Houston in the east offer unsurpassed opportunities for outdoor living: the forest supervisor (☎936/639-8501) in Lufkin, midway between Davy Crockett and Angelina on US-59, has details of free and private **camping** facilities. Fans of the movie will want to check out **Paris**, **Texas**, northeast on US-82.

East Texas

The tall pine forests of **East Texas** bear more relation to Louisiana than to the rest of the state; while undeniably Texan, the locals also identify themselves culturally and geographically with the adjacent corners of Arkansas and Louisiana – the "**Arklatex**" – and you'll find jambalaya and gumbo in restaurants along with standard Texan dishes.

Burial sites and reconstructed dwellings of the sophisticated **Caddo** Indians, an early southeastern mound-building culture, can be seen at the **Caddoan Mounds State Historic Site**, thirty miles west of **Nacogdoches** on Hwy-21. Active between the ninth and fourteenth centuries, the site includes a self-guided walking tour and videos on Caddoan history (Mon & Thurs–Sun 9am–4pm; $2 per person; ☎936/858-3218).

Big Thicket National Preserve

The **Big Thicket National Preserve**, south of the Piney Woods on US-96, is a remarkable composite of natural elements from the southwestern desert, central plains, and Appalachian Mountains, with swamps and bayous to boot. The area once offered ideal refuge for outlaws, runaway slaves, and gamblers; now it just hides a huge variety of plant and animal life, including deer, alligators, armadillos, possums, hogs, and panthers, and over 300 species of birds. Wild flowers, orchids, and towering trees share space with cacti and yucca.

Check in at the visitor center (daily 9am–5pm; ☎409/246-2337, ⓦwww.nps.gov/bith), south of Angelina National Forest off US-69, before entering the site; casual rambling isn't allowed, and hiking or canoeing is best done with the Preserve guides. There is primitive **camping** in designated areas.

Nacogdoches

NACOGDOCHES, north of Angelina National Forest on US-59, claims to be the oldest town in Texas. One of the state's first five Spanish **missions** was established here in 1716, to keep a watchful eye on the French in Louisiana, though a pyramidal **Caddo Indian Mound** on the 500 block of Mound Street testifies to more ancient history. The **Sterne-Hoya House**, 211 S Lanana St, the town's oldest surviving and unreconstructed home, illustrates early pioneer life (Mon–Sat 9am–noon & 2–5pm; free).

The *Clear Springs Café*, 211 Old Tyler Rd (☎936/569-0489), is the best place to **eat** in town, serving superb fried catfish and famously good onion rings in a historic building. If you want to **stay**, the *Jones House*, 141 N Church St (☎936/559-1487; ❹), offers good **bed-and-breakfast** in a cottage close to downtown, while *Mound Street B&B*, 408 N Mound St (☎936/569-2211; ❺), features big rooms in a Victorian home. The venerable downtown **hotel**, the *Fredonia*, 200 N Fredonia St (☎936/564-1234; ❹), is aging but clean. The **Chamber of Commerce** is at 200 E Main St (Mon–Fri 9am–5pm, Sat 10am–4pm, Sun 1–6pm; ☎936/564-7351 or 1-888/564-7351, ⓦwww.visitnacogdoches.org).

Dallas

Contrary to popular belief, there's no oil in glitzy, status-conscious **DALLAS**. Since its foundation as a prairie trading post, by Tennessee lawyer John Neely Bryan and his Arkansan friend Joe Dallas in 1841, successive generations of

entrepreneurs have amassed wealth here through trade and finance, using first cattle and later oil reserves as collateral. One early group of European settlers of the 1850s – a group of French intellectuals and artists known as the La Reunion co-operative – had to pack up and move on after a series of summer droughts and a harsh winter; the few who stayed would include a future mayor of Dallas. The city still prides itself on their legacy of arts and high culture.

The power of **money** in Dallas was demonstrated in the late 1950s, when its financiers threw their weight behind integration. Potentially racist restaurant owners and bus drivers were pressured not to resist the new policies, and Dallas was spared major upheavals. The city's image was, however, catastrophically tarnished by the **assassination** of President Kennedy in 1963, and it took the building of the giant Dallas/Fort Worth International Airport in the 1960s, and the twin successes of the *Dallas* TV show and the Cowboys football team in the 1970s to restore confidence. Then boom turned to crash once more. Unemployment and the demise of the fictional Ewings, not to mention an appalling crime rate, all took their toll, but the indomitable entrepreneurial spirit remains. After great success in the mid-1990s the Cowboys endured a brief slump, but appear to be on the rise again under the leadership of Coach Bill Parcells.

Competitive with Houston, and smug about its cowtown neighbor Fort Worth, Dallas boasts of its "sophistication" and its "old" wealth. For all that, the stuffiness is tempered by a typically Texan delight in self-parody, and there's still fun to be had if you know where to look – especially in the alternative **Deep Ellum** district, with its superb restaurants and nightlife.

Arrival and information

Dallas is served by two major **airports**. **Dallas/Fort Worth** (DFW) (☎972/574-8888, ⓦwww.dfwairport.com), as big as Manhattan and the world's second busiest airport, is exactly midway between the two cities (around 17 miles from each). Telephones in the baggage claim area link up to a variety of different **shuttle buses**, such as Super Shuttle (☎817/329-2000, ⓦwww.supershuttle.com) and Discount Shuttle (☎817/267-5150), all charging around $16 to downtown; **taxis** cost around $40 (Yellow/Checker ☎214/426-6262). The other major airport, **Love Field** (☎214/670-6080), used mostly by Southwest Airlines, lies about nine miles northwest of Dallas, from where **taxis** to downtown cost around $15, shuttles charge $9, or you can take bus #39 to downtown for a total of $1. Greyhound is at 205 S Lamar St downtown, while Amtrak's 1916 Union Station is further west at 400 S Houston St. The Trinity Railway Express (☎817/215-8600, ⓦwww.trinityrailwayexpress.org) service runs commuter service to Fort Worth for $2.25.

The downtown **visitor center** is at the "Old Red" Courthouse, 100 S Houston St, in the thick of the Kennedy-related sights (daily 9am–6pm; ☎214/571-1300, ⓦwww.dallascvb.com). The city also runs a 24-hour Events Hotline (☎214/571-1301). The **post office** is at 1201 Main St (Mon–Fri 6am–4pm, Sat 6am–2pm; ☎214/752-5654; zip code 75202).

City transportation

Dallas proper is circled by Inner Loop 12 (or Northwest Highway) and the Outer Loop I-635 (which becomes LBJ Freeway). A **car** makes sense in a city this size, though the main sights of downtown's Central Business District are easy to tour on foot. **DART**, the Dallas Area Rapid Transit system (☎214/979-1111, ⓦwww.dart.org), operates the city's **buses** ($1.25 local services, $2.25 express buses and trains) and a swish **light rail** network that links downtown

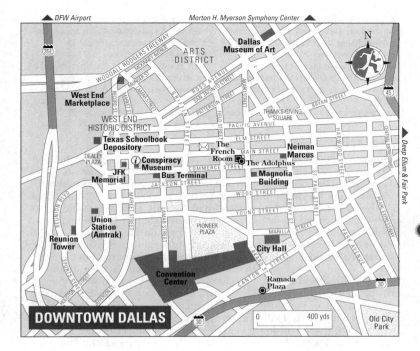

DOWNTOWN DALLAS

0   400 yds

and the Dallas Convention Center with the West End and various sights (fares $1.25 local, $2.25 express, all-day pass $2.50). Both DART buses and trains operate every day from 5am to 12.30am. The **McKinney Trolley** (℡214/855-0006, Ⓦ www.mata.org) runs north from the downtown Dallas Museum of Art to the historic McKinney Avenue area (every 30min daily 10am–10pm; free but volunteer fares accepted).

Accommodation

Room rates in downtown Dallas are firmly geared toward the business traveler, though the swanky hotels offer some reasonable **weekend** deals. Chain **motels** are concentrated a long way out, on the freeways; there's a large group on LBJ Freeway near the Galleria mall, a dozen miles north, for example. **Bed-and-breakfast** can be arranged through B&B Texas Style (℡979/696-9222 or 1–800/899-4538, Ⓦ www.bnbtexasstyle.com; from ❸). There's **camping** in the pretty Lake Park on the Kingfisher Trail, a mile east of I-35 in Lewisville (℡972/219-3550).

The Adolphus 1321 Commerce St ℡214/742-8200, Ⓦ www.hoteladolphus.com. Stunning historic downtown hotel, decorated with antiques. Said to be the most beautiful building west of Venice, Italy, when it was built in 1912, it's still by far Dallas's most glamorous place to stay. ❽
American Dream Bed and Breakfast Marsh

Lane off I-635 exit 24 ℡214/357-6536 or 1-800/373-2690, Ⓦ www.dallas-bed-breakfast .com. A pleasant B&B with ultra-attentive hosts, providing easy access to downtown and DFW airport. ❸
Best Western Market Center 2023 Market Center Blvd ℡214/741-9000 or 1-800/275-7419,

@www.bestwestern.com. Chain motel two miles from downtown, offering complimentary breakfast. ④
La Quinta Dallas North Central 10001 N Central Expressway/Hwy-75 ☎214/361-8200, @www.laquinta.com. Decent-priced rooms, near the ever-popular Galleria mall and the burgeoning Lower Greenville shopping and entertainment district. ④
The Mansion on Turtle Creek 2821 Turtle Creek

Blvd ☎214/559-2100, @www.mansiononturtle-creek.com. First-class hotel offering absolute luxury on a gorgeous landscaped hillside. ⑨
Ramada Plaza 1011 S Akard St ☎214/421-1083, @www.ramada.com. Reliable rooms and a heated pool near the Convention Center. ④
Stoneleigh Hotel 2927 Maple Ave ☎214/871-7111. Classy, comfortable hotel in the Turtle Creek area, three miles north of downtown. ⑦

The City

Downtown Dallas is a paean to commerce. Many of its skyscrapers are landmarks in themselves; at night the red neon Mobil Pegasus on the 1921 Magnolia Building on Akard and Commerce streets appears to gallop over the city, while over two miles of green argon tubing delineate the 72-story Bank of America building. The original **Neiman Marcus** department store, set up in 1907 by sister and brother Carrie Neiman and Herbert Marcus and famed for its glamorous Christmas catalog, is still there on Main Street (Mon–Sat 10am–6pm, Thurs until 8pm). One refuge from the downtown hubbub is the **Center for World Thanksgiving** at **Thanksgiving Square**, at the intersection of Akard, Ervay, and Bryan streets and Pacific Avenue (Mon–Fri 9am–5pm, Sat & Sun 1–5pm), with its meditation garden, fountains, and modern spiraling chapel – though even here pealing bells boom out at regular intervals. South of the square on Ervay Street looms the precarious upside-down pyramid of **City Hall**, possibly familiar as the police station in *Robocop*.

On the north edge of downtown, the **Arts District** boasts the huge and wide-ranging **Dallas Museum of Art**, 1717 N Harwood St (Tues–Sun 11am–5pm, Thurs until 9pm; $6; ☎214/922-1200, @www.dm-art.org), which has plenty of European works downstairs, including a good range of Mondrians, and an especially impressive pre-Columbian collection in the Gallery of the Americas upstairs. Two blocks east, at 2301 Flora St, the magnificent **Morton H. Meyerson Symphony Center**, designed by I.M. Pei, is the home of the symphony orchestra. The vast geometries of glass, onyx, and wood inside cost $80 million, as the tour guides won't let you forget.

West End, Dealey Plaza, and around

Tourists flock to the restored redbrick warehouses of the **West End Historic District**, the site of the original 1841 settlement on Lamar and Munger streets, for the eighty stores and twenty restaurants here. The indoor **marketplace** has become something of an amusement arcade, with a *Planet Hollywood*, tacky gift shops, crazy golf, and fast-food outlets.

A couple of blocks south and west of here lies **Dealey Plaza**, forever associated with the Kennedy assassination (see box, opposite). A small park beside Houston Street's triple underpass, it remains unchanged since the fateful day – in fact, since it was designed by a committee that included LBJ, in the late 1930s – and must be one of the most recognizable urban streetscapes in the world. The **Texas Schoolbook Depository** itself, at 411 Elm St, is now the Dallas County Administration Building, the penultimate floor of which houses **The Sixth Floor Museum** (daily 9am–6pm; $10, or $13 with audio tour; ☎214/747-6660 or 1-888/485-4854, @www.jfk.org). Displays build up a suspenseful narrative, with the infamous blurred 8mm images of Kennedy crumpling into Jackie's arms left until the end, at which point there's likely to be much sobbing from moved visitors, who can exorcize their grief by writing in

The assassination of President Kennedy

It was 12.30pm on **November 22, 1963**, as John F. Kennedy greeted the crowds of Dallas from his ceremonial motorcade, when the shots rang out over Dealey Plaza that killed the president and ended the "Camelot" era.

Within hours, a gunman's nest was discovered in the nearby Texas Schoolbook Depository, and one of its employees, **Lee Harvey Oswald**, was arrested. Two days later, he in turn was shot and killed in a police station by nightclub owner **Jack Ruby**, who said he wanted to spare Kennedy's wife Jackie from having to testify at Oswald's trial. The **Warren Commission**, which investigated the assassination, concluded that Oswald had acted alone, but **conspiracy** theories have flourished ever since. Most accept that Oswald (an ex-Marine who defected to Russia and returned with a Russian wife) fired the shots, but see him as the fall guy in a larger plot, variously attributed to the Mafia, anti-Castroists, Cuba, the KGB, and US government agencies. Claims by witnesses to have heard shots on the famous **Grassy Knoll** on the north side of Elm Street remain unsubstantiated, but visitors can usually be found sniffing around here for clues – along with self-styled guides, ready to engage them in costly conversation. Senate inquiries were finally closed down by the Justice Department in 1988, arguing that there was no "persuasive evidence" of any plot.

the "memory book." The "gunman's nest" has been re-created and, whatever you feel about Oswald's guilt, it is undeniably chilling to look down at the streets below and imagine the mayhem the shooter must have seen that day.

One block west of Dealey Plaza, in the Dallas Historical Plaza on Main and Market streets, an open cenotaph, designed by Philip Johnson and enclosing an 8-foot flat granite block, stands as the **John F. Kennedy Memorial**. Alongside, at 110 S Market St, the **Conspiracy Museum** (daily 10am–6pm; $7) is a dreadful waste of money. It strives to impress with its CD-ROM technology, but in fact displays the usual amateurish hand-drawn diagrams and wild accusations, interpreting virtually every public act in America since the late 1950s as the work of the Professional War Machine.

You can see much of downtown's interest from the 51st-story observation deck in the **Reunion Tower**, 300 Reunion Blvd (daily 10am–10.30pm; $2), on the west side of downtown next to the Amtrak station. The *Dome Lounge*, in the Tower, provides a good place to have a drink.

Pioneer Plaza and Old City Park

The city's main business and administrative district, on the south side of downtown, is focused around City Hall on Marilla Street. **Pioneer Plaza**, at Young and Griffin streets, holds the world's largest bronze sculpture, a monument to the cattle drives that depicts forty longhorn steers under the guidance of three cowboys.

Farther southeast, across I-30, near Harwood Street at 1717 Gano St, Dallas's first park, **Old City Park**, now serves as both recreational area and museum, charting the history of the city from 1840 to 1910 through more than thirty buildings relocated from towns in north Texas, among them a farmhouse, a bank, a train station, a store, a church, and a schoolhouse (hours and tour times vary seasonally, call ahead; $7; ☏214/421-5141, ⓦwww.oldcitypark.org).

Deep Ellum

Dallas's coolest district is **Deep Ellum**, five blocks east of downtown between the railroad tracks and I-30 at Elm and Main streets. Famous in the 1920s for its jazz and blues clubs (and supposedly named by Blind Lemon Jefferson, though it's more likely to stem from the Southern pronunciation of "elm"), the old warehouse district now accommodates avant-garde galleries, theaters, hip clothes stores, and excellent restaurants and clubs. To the despair of its original inhabitants, prices are rocketing as the area drifts toward the mainstream. However, the area's rebellious and nonconformist nature makes a great antidote to the prevalent stuffiness of Dallas.

Fair Park

Not far southeast of Deep Ellum, **Fair Park**, a gargantuan Art Deco plaza bedecked with endless Lone Stars, was built to house the Texas Centennial Exposition in 1936, and hosts the annual State Fair of Texas, the biggest event of its kind in the US. Among its plethora of fine museums are the **Dallas Museum of Natural History** (daily 10am–5pm; ☎214/421-DINO, ⓦwww.dallasdino.org; $6.50), which boasts reconstructions of the 20,000-year-old "Trinity River Mammoth" and a lagoon nature walk; the hands-on **Science Place** (Tues–Fri 9.30am–4.30pm, Sat 9.30am–5.30pm, Sun 11.30am–5.30pm, summer only Mon 9.30am–4.30pm; $7.50; ☎214/428-5555, ⓦwww.scienceplace.org), which sets out to teach kids and adults about physics and dinosaurs and the like using lively temporary exhibits; and the Art Deco **Dallas Aquarium** (daily 9am–4.30pm; $3; ☎214/670-5656, ⓦwww.dallas-zoo.org), known for its salamanders and pupfish exhibits. Three miles south of town on I-35, the same organization that runs the aquarium also runs the top-notch **Dallas Zoo**, where the African habitat is among the highlights (daily 9am–5pm; $7; ☎817/670-5656).

The **Women's Museum** (Tues 10am–9pm, Wed–Sun 10am–5pm; $5; ☎214/915-0860) is the latest addition to Fair Park's museums. Young girls will likely benefit the most from the rah-rah attitude on display, from the Electronic Quilt – a video project highlighting achievements in women's history – to the Wall of Words, featuring inspirational quotes from female leaders. The nearby **African-American Museum** (Tues–Fri noon–5pm, Sat 10am–5pm, Sun 1–5pm; suggested donation $2; ☎214/565-9026) features a superb collection of **folk art** in its permanent collection, complete with detailed biographies of the artists responsible. These include Clementine Hunter, a Louisiana field hand who used materials left over by artists visiting the wealthy plantation where she worked; Charles Williams, known as Artist Chuckie, from Shreveport, Louisiana, who was "discovered" in 1989 when a neighbor's house burned down and he refused to leave his mother's home until his 700 paintings were brought out; and the real stand-out, Bessie Harvey, who died in 1994. She worked with found pieces of wood, spray-painting them and sticking on other materials to produce scenes such as the extraordinary *Jonah and the Whale* and *Two Heads Are Better Than One*. Changing exhibits here focus primarily on African art.

The centerpiece of the park, however, has to be the magnificent **Hall of State Building**, an Art Deco treasure of bronze statues, blue tiles, mosaics, and murals, with rooms decorated to celebrate the different regions of Texas. The park also holds the **Cotton Bowl** stadium (☎214/638-BOWL, ⓦwww.swbellcottonbowl.com), home of the annual college football classic, while for three weeks in October, Fair Park spills over with more than three million revelers enjoying the riotous **State Fair** (☎214/565-9931, ⓦwww.bigtex.com) itself.

Southfork Ranch

The former TV home of the *Dallas* soap's wheeling-and-dealing Ewing clan, **Southfork Ranch** (daily 9am–5pm; $8) lies about 25 miles northeast of

Dallas, beyond I-75 at 3700 Hogge Drive, in Parker. Having lain dormant for two years from 1991, it was purchased by a private firm and has since been kitted out as a convention center-cum-Western mini-theme park, with a **museum** in which you can see the gun that shot JR and Jock Ewing's original 1978 Lincoln Continental. There are also plenty of Stetson-dominated gift shops and *Miss Ellie's Deli*. The **Ranch House** itself is surprisingly small – all the show's interior scenes were shot in California, and the exterior views used a very wide-angled lens. Most recommended for those very serious about their kitsch.

Eating

Many of the less expensive – and least extravagant – of Dallas's five thousand restaurants are concentrated on **Lower Greenville Avenue**, which runs northeast of downtown parallel to I-75, and in the trendier **Deep Ellum**, where even the excellent New American cuisine won't break the bank.

Café Brasil 2815 Elm St ☎214/747-2730. Open 24hr on weekends, with great omelets, crepes, and enchiladas.

El Fenix 1601 McKinney Ave ☎214/747-1121. Don't let its ubiquity within the Metroplex stop you from trying out this very reliable Tex-Mex favorite; don't miss the tortilla soup.

Firehouse 1928 Greenville Ave ☎214/826-2468. An inventive (if a bit pricey) menu – think antelope tenderloin – served smack in the middle of Lower Greenville.

The French Room in *The Adolphus* 1321 Commerce St ☎214/742-8200. Perhaps the best restaurant in the state, with prices to match the top-notch French food and exquisite decor (hand-blown crystal chandeliers, marble floors, and so on).

Gloria's 600 W Davis St ☎214/948-3672. Catfish ceviche, hot banana-leaf tamales, and other low-priced, top-quality El Salvadorean dishes.

Green Room 2715 Elm St ☎214/748-7666. Post-modern decor, with up-to-the-minute American cuisine downstairs, and pizzas on the roof with views across Deep Ellum to downtown.

Mia's 4322 Lemmon Ave ☎214/526-1020. This family-run Mexican restaurant is a favorite with the Dallas Cowboys.

Monica's Aca y Alla 2914 Main St ☎214/748-7140. Wood-grilled nouvelle Mexican food, with dashes of Mediterranean and Asian influences, in a Deep Ellum hot spot jumping with live salsa and mambo on weekends.

Samba Room 4514 Travis Walk ☎214/522-4137. Sexy, Cuban-themed space with fabulous *mojitos* and a beautiful patio.

Sonny Bryan's Smokehouse 2202 Inwood Rd ☎214/357-7120. The original location – it still looks like a shack – of a favorite local barbecue chain, but get there in good time as the meat can be all snapped up by early afternoon.

Entertainment and nightlife

The two **nightlife** destinations in Dallas have to be offbeat **Deep Ellum** – where among the trendy clubs the innovative **Pegasus Theater**, 3916 Main St (☎214/821-6005, ⓦwww.pegasustheatre.org), puts on avant-garde and independent plays – and the ever-so-slightly gritty **Lower Greenville**. Elsewhere nightlife is pretty formal. Mainstream attractions include the **Dallas Symphony Orchestra** at the showpiece Morton H. Meyerson Symphony Center (☎214/670-3600, ⓦwww.dallassymphony.com), and the **Dallas Black Dance Theater** at 2627 Flora St (☎214/871-2376, ⓦwww.dbdt.com). In June and July, free **Shakespeare in the Park** performances are held in Samuell-Grand Park, east of downtown near the intersection of I-30 and Hwy-87 (☎214/559-2778, ⓦwww.shakespearedallas.org).

For a real Wild West night out, head to the **Mesquite Championship Rodeo**, well out of town on I-635 at Military Parkway (April–Oct Fri & Sat 8pm; $10–28; ☎972/285-8777, ⓦwww.mesquiterodeo.com).

Full **listings** can be found in Thursday's *Dallas Observer* (⒲ www.dallasob-server.com), Friday's *Dallas Morning News* (⒲ www.dallasnews.com), or the events information line (☎214/571-1301).

Adair's 2624 E Commerce St ☎214/939-9900. A country-music bar that attracts both old-timers and students with its hard-edged honky-tonk music.

Bar of Soap 3615 Parry Ave ☎214/823-6617. Groovy pub-cum-laundromat on the outskirts of Deep Ellum, opposite Fair Park. Open daily 3pm–2am, no cover.

Club Clearview 2803 Elm St ☎214/939-0077. Deep Ellum warehouse featuring a cool dance club, blacklight room, endless bars, and a great rooftop deck, plus big touring acts.

Club DaDa 2720 Elm St ☎214/744-DADA. Edie Brickell and the New Bohemians began their days at this famed Deep Ellum club, which features open-mic on Sundays, live bands, and club nights.

Muddy Waters 1518 Greenville Ave ☎214/823-1518. Generally acknowledged as the city's best down-home blues bar, with live acts on weekends.

New West 6532 E Northwest Hwy ☎214/361-6083. A welcome break from the sometimes over-busy Deep Ellum scene, with great *Tejano* music and a laid-back but festive crowd.

Sons of Hermann Hall 3414 Elm St ☎214/747-4422. Delightfully old-school country venue where the Texan masters come to play, as well as respectful young outfits channeling the masters.

Trees 2709 Elm St ☎214/748-5009. A Deep Ellum warehouse turned auditorium, popular with up-and-coming indie rock bands.

Fort Worth

Yes, Dallas does have something Fort Worth doesn't have – a real city thirty miles away.

Amon Carter, publisher, *Fort Worthian*, philanthropist

FORT WORTH, often dismissed as some kind of poor relation to Dallas, in fact has a rush and energy largely missing in its more complacent neighbor thirty miles east. Unlike comparably cosmopolitan Dallas, this is one of the most "Western" cities in Texas. In the 1870s it was the last stop on the great cattle drive to Kansas, the **Chisholm Trail**; when the railroads arrived, it became a livestock market in its own right, with its own packing houses, while remaining a haven for cowboys and outlaws. The **cattle** trade is still a major industry, after aviation and defense, but the city can also pride itself on its thriving cultural life. Unlike the more anxious Dallas, Fort Worth doesn't feel the need to brag about its many excellent **museums**. For a place so wealthy (the grand **Western Hills** area claims to have proportionately more millionaires than any other US locale), it's surprisingly laid-back.

Arrival, information, and getting around

The main road between Fort Worth and Dallas, **I-30**, cuts the city north–south; Loop 820 encircles it. An Airporter express **bus** (daily 5am–midnight, every half-hour at peak times; $15; ☎817/334-0092) runs to and from DFW International Airport, seventeen miles northeast (see p.782); a taxi costs around $45. Amtrak pulls in four times per week in either direction just southeast of downtown in the lovely red 1899 Santa Fe Depot, 1501 Jones St (☎817/332-2931). Greyhound operates out of the depot at 901 Commerce St, next to the Convention Center. The city's public transportation system, **The T**, operates **bus service** throughout the city, as well the tourist-oriented **Longhorn Trolley**, which travels between the major attractions and some downtown hotels ($1.25 for the bus, $2.50 for the trolley; ☎817/215-8600, ⒲ www.the-t.com). The Trinity Railway Express (☎817/215-8600, ⒲ www.trinityrailwayexpress.org) service runs commuter service to Dallas for $2.25.

There are three **visitor centers**: in the Stockyards at 130 E Exchange Ave (daily 9am–6pm; walking tours are $6, call for times; ☎817/624-4741, Ⓦ www.stockyardsstation.com), downtown in the CVB at 415 Throckmorton St (Mon–Fri 8.30am–5pm, Sat 10am–4pm; ☎817/336-8791 or 1-800/433-5747), and in the Cultural District at the Will Rogers Memorial Center at 3401 W Lancaster Ave (Mon–Thurs 9am–5pm, Fri & Sat 9am–6pm, Sun noon–4pm; ☎817/882-8588). The downtown Sundance Square and Stockyard areas are well patrolled and safe to walk around after dark; for a **taxi** between the two, call Yellow Cab Co. (☎817/534-5555).

Accommodation

Fort Worth is blessed with plenty of mid-priced **accommodation**, even downtown. The liveliest places to stay are around Sundance Square in downtown, or in the Stockyards; more standard motel rooms can be found along I-35 both to the north and to the south of the city.

Clarion Hotel 600 Commerce St ☎817/332-6900 or 1-800/252-7466. Bright, comfortable rooms in an excellent location, just steps away from Sundance Square and the bus station. ❺

Etta's Place B&B 200 W 3rd St ☎817/255-5760. Ten great rooms right in the heart of the Sundance Square area, offering three-course breakfast, plus several patios and lounges. Named after the schoolteacher girlfriend of the Sundance Kid. ❻

Miss Molly's Bed and Breakfast 109 1/2 W Exchange Ave ☎817/626-1522 or 1-800/996-6559. Quirkily furnished lodging in the heart of the Stockyards, bursting with cowboy kitsch. The friendly hosts serve up a gourmet breakfast. ❺

Park Central Hotel 1010 Houston St ☎817/336-2011, Ⓦ www.parkcentralhotel.com. Centrally located option, convenient for downtown, with a fitness center and pool ❸

Ramada Plaza 1701 Commerce St ☎817/335-7000, Ⓦ www.ramada.com. Geared more to conference trade it's nevertheless a relatively inexpensive option on the edge of downtown. ❻

Stockyards Hotel 109 E Exchange Ave ☎817/625-6427 or 1-800/423-8471. Historic Stockyards hotel, reputedly a favorite haunt of Bonnie and Clyde, with themed rooms like Western, Mountain Man, Indian, and Victorian. The hotel's *Booger Red's Saloon* boasts funky saddle barstools. ❻

The City

Fort Worth's main attractions fall tidily into a triangle anchored by downtown with the Cultural District and the Stockyards two miles away to the west and north respectively. The chief focus of **downtown** Fort Worth is **Sundance Square**, a leafy, redbrick-paved fourteen-block area of shops, restaurants, and bars between First and Sixth streets, ringed by glittering skyscrapers and pervaded with a genuine enthusiasm for the town's rich history. It owes its existence to vast injections of cash from the Bass family; the whole ensemble is dominated by the two gleaming glass skyscrapers of the Bass-owned **City Center Towers**, while the recent addition of the extremely tasteful **Nancy Lee & Perry R. Bass Performance Hall** (☎817/212-4325, Ⓦ www.basshall.com) is evidence of the area's continuing development. Notice the carvings of longhorn skulls everywhere, and the many trompe l'oeil murals – especially the Chisholm Trail mural on Fourth Street between Main and Houston streets. The **Sid Richardson Collection of Western Art**, tucked away at 309 Main St (Tues & Wed 10am–5pm, Thurs & Fri 10am–8pm, Sat 11am–8pm, Sun 1–5pm; free; ☎817/332-6554, Ⓦ www.sidrmuseum.org), has a small but excellent collection of late works by Remington, including some of his best black-and-white illustrations, and early elegiac cowboy scenes by Charles Russell.

Naming the square after the Sundance Kid isn't particularly appropriate; he, and other outlaws such as Bonnie and Clyde, spent their time a few blocks south, just north of I-30 at the city's original settlement. Even into the 1950s **"Hell's Half Acre"** was renowned for bawdy lawlessness; these days it's much less exciting, although the bubbling fountains and pools of its central **Water Gardens** offer refreshing respite.

The Cultural District

The **Cultural District**, two miles west of downtown, is an impressive area of museums and art galleries. The finest collection is at the small **Kimbell Art Museum**, 3333 Camp Bowie Blvd (Tues–Thurs 10am–8pm, Fri noon–8pm, Sat 10am–5pm, Sun noon–5pm; free, around $5 for special exhibits; ☎817/332-8451, ⓦwww.kimbellart.org), a splendid vaulted, naturally lit building designed by Louis Kahn. Downstairs displays concentrate on pre-Columbian and African pieces, with some noteworthy Mayan funerary urns, while upstairs, as well as canvases by Gauguin, Cézanne, Picasso, and Monet, you can admire a seventh-century Khmer figure of a Hindu deity, ancient Chinese bronzes, and a fourteenth-century Japanese polychrome wood statue of ascetic En no Gyoja. The museum café itself is adorned with relief sculptures by Henri Matisse.

American art in the recently renovated and expanded **Amon Carter Museum**, just up the hill at 3501 Camp Bowie Blvd (Tues–Sat 10am–5pm, Sun noon–5pm; free; ☎817/738-1933, ⓦwww.cartermuseum.org), includes great photographs of Western landscapes, as well as a fine assortment of Remingtons and Russells, and works by Winslow Homer and Georgia O'Keeffe. The **Modern Art Museum of Fort Worth**, 1309 Montgomery St (Tues–Fri 10am–5pm, Sat 11am–5pm, Sun noon–5pm; free; ☎817/738-9215, ⓦwww.mamfw.org), which specializes in twentieth-century abstract art, was moved in 2002 to this larger facility, a graceful modern building designed by Tadao Ando. South of here, the wide-ranging **Fort Worth Museum of Science and History** (Mon–Thurs 9am–5.30pm, Fri & Sat 9am–8pm, Sun noon–5.30pm; $13; ☎817/255-9300 or 1-888/255-9300, ⓦwww.fwmsh.org) includes a planetarium and an IMAX theater. Among the museum's most popular exhibits is ExploraZone – a kid-friendly area for investigating topics like magnetism, weather, math, and so on – and DinoDig, where amateur pale-ontologists can dig through an "outdoor discovery zone" for dinosaur bones.

The lively, interactive **Cattle Raiser's Museum** is, for now, slightly farther north at 1301 W Seventh St (Mon–Sat 10am–5pm, Sun 1–5pm; $3; ☎817/332-8551, ⓦwww.cattleraisersmuseum.org) – it's scheduled to be relocated to the Cultural District by 2004. The changing economic face of the cattle trade is traced from the days of the open range, via the great cattle drives, to modern ranching and latter-day cowboys – with displays of spurs, assorted tangles of barbed wire, and some interesting history on the travails of early women pioneers. After the move, the museum will be adjacent to the elaborate and fun **National Cowgirl Museum and Hall of Fame**, 1720 Gendy St ($6; ☎817/336-4475, ⓦwww.cowgirl.net), which honors 163 cowgirls and features exhibits on the history of cowgirls and women in rodeo.

The Stockyards Area

The ten-block **Stockyards Area**, with its wooden sidewalks and old storefronts centered on Exchange Avenue two miles north of downtown, is a glorious evocation of the days when Fort Worth's stockyards made this "the richest little city in the world." It's much more than a cynical creation for cowboy-hungry tourists and even the daily march down East Exchange Avenue of the fifteen or so Texan Longhorn cattle (with six-foot horn spans) is done in good, educational taste. The drives occur, weather permitting, at 11.30am from the corrals behind the Livestock Exchange Building (see below) with the herd arriving back around 4pm; one of the best views of the drive can be had directly in front of the visitor center (see p.789).

Along with the restaurants and bars, the **stores** in Fort Worth will have Western-wear obsessives in heaven. Look out for Fincher's rodeo equipment store and M.L. Leddy's expansive saddle shop; and check out the Maverick Trading Post, which is packed with hip, bright cowgirl regalia and even has a bar serving good cold beers. Though they encourage you to drink first and buy later, this is not a good idea. If all the authenticity is too much to bear, there's a nearby mall with a slightly more tourist-friendly orientation: the shops and restaurants in the Stockyards Station, a brick-floored enclave in the old hog pens, are squeaky clean; one of the best is the Ernest Tubb Record Shop, next to the Stockyards Wedding Chapel. From here the magnificent Tarantula **steam train** puffs along to Eighth Avenue downtown (departs Wed–Sat noon, Sun 3pm; 30min; $10; ☎817/625-RAIL, ⓦwww.tarantulatrain.com).

The Stockyards no longer host live **cattle auctions**; instead, images are beamed by satellite into the huge 1902 **Livestock Exchange Building** at 131 E Exchange Ave, home of the **Stockyards Collections Museum** (Mon–Sat 10am–5pm; free), packed with meaty memorabilia. The mission-style **Cowtown Coliseum** next door, used for rodeos (☎817/625-1025, ⓦwww.cowtowncoliseum.com; ticket prices vary) and concerts, is fronted with a bust of Bill Pickett, the black rodeo star who invented the unsavory but effective practice of "bulldogging" – stunning the bull by biting its lip.

Eating

If you love **steak**, Fort Worth is for you. Meat here is hefty, fresh, and prepared with tender loving care, especially in the Stockyards area, where the many good home-cooking cafés are frequented as much by cattle ranchers as by visitors. Mex and Tex-Mex tastes are well covered, though vegetarians will do less well and should try the upmarket restaurants downtown. The **café** in the Kimbell Art Museum (see opposite) makes for a pleasant place to snack or eat lunch.

Angelo's Barbecue 2533 White Settlement Rd ☎817/332-0357. Venerable westside restaurant open for lunch and dinner, and cited by locals as the best in the city.

Angeluna 215 E 4th St ☎817/334-0080. Tasty Caribbean-Asian-Southern fusion food across the street from Bass Hall.

Cattlemen's Steak House 2458 N Main St ☎817/624-3945. Dim lighting and wall-sized portraits of prize steers set the scene at this Fort Worth institution known for its steaks and margaritas. Dinner around $20.

J&J Oyster Bar 612 N University Drive ☎817/335-2756. Try the fresh crab and oysters at this long-standing favorite near the Cultural District.

Joe T. Garcia's Mexican Dishes 2201 N Commerce St ☎817/626-4356. Nationally famed Mexican restaurant inside the owners' 1930s home, serving hefty set tortilla/fajita dinners (around $10) and frosty margaritas. Outdoor seating is available next to the family swimming pool.

Mi Cocina 509 Main St ☎817/877-3600. A modern, eclectically decorated joint serving up healthy Tex-Mex dishes.

Star Café 111 W Exchange Ave ☎817/624-8701. Neon-lit café serving some of the least expensive steaks – not just in the Stockyards but in the entire city. The chicken-fried steak is a highlight.

Nightlife and entertainment

You'd be hard pushed not to find something to your taste amid Fort Worth's late-night drinking and carousing. This is a truly cosmopolitan city, where roustabouts will happily down a few beers with modern jazz fans. Bar crawling is safe and fun, and there's a great mix of live music venues (though the pick-up joints in the Stockyards are best avoided). Check the *Fort Worth Weekly* (Ⓦwww.fwweekly.com) or the *Fort Worth Star-Telegram* (Ⓦwww.star-telegram.com) for listings. For the performing arts, there's the **Nancy Lee & Perry R. Bass Performance Hall** in downtown (Ⓣ817/212-4280), home of the city's orchestra, opera, theater, and dance companies, and host to visiting spectacles.

In addition to the regular cowboy venues below, the **Chisholm Trail Round-Up** (mid-June) and **Pioneer Days** (Sept) are two hugely enjoyable annual Western-style celebrations in the Stockyards, while Cowtown Coliseum holds a championship **rodeo** (Fri and Sat 8pm; $12.50; Ⓣ817/625-1025, Ⓦwww.cowtowncoliseum.com) and special events throughout the year.

8.0 111 E 3rd St Ⓣ817/336-0880. Highly popular downtown bar in Sundance Square, flamboyantly decorated inside and offering sidewalk seating as well.

Billy Bob's Texas 2520 Rodeo Plaza Ⓣ817/624-7117. The largest honky-tonk in the world, down in the Stockyards, with bull-riding (Fri & Sat 9pm & 10pm), pool tables, bars, restaurants, and stores, and big-name concerts. Live music nightly; open until 2am. Tours Mon–Sat 11am, 2pm & 4pm, Sun 2pm & 4pm. Cover Mon–Thurs & Sun $3–5, Fri & Sat $5–10.

Casa Mañana Theater 3101 Lancaster Ave Ⓣ817/332-6221. Alternative comedy performances and plays in the Cultural District, with a great selection of kid-friendly shows as well.

Flying Saucer 111 E 4th St Ⓣ817/336-7468.

Choose from over 200 beers, often at enticing promotional prices, in a fun Sundance Square setting, where there's live music Tues–Sun.

J&J Blues Bar 937 Woodward Ave Ⓣ817/870-BEER. Westside joint with regional blues acts Thurs–Sat.

J&Js Hideaway 3305 W 7th St Ⓣ817/877-3363. Good neighborhood bar in the Cultural District, and a welcome respite from the more aggressively Western-themed outlets in the city.

White Elephant Saloon 106 E Exchange Ave Ⓣ817/624-1887. Notoriously wild and authentic Stockyards saloon with a cowboy hat hall of fame. Prop yourself up at the long wooden bar and listen to cowboy singer and owner Don Edwards. $4 cover Fri. Open till midnight weekdays, 2am Fri & Sat.

Towards the Panhandle

Routes west from central Texas lead you through the state's "backyard," where farmlands and rough-cut, juniper-covered hills give way to treeless, sandy landscapes. Of the towns, only **Abilene** and **Sweetwater**, both on I-20 toward El Paso, are even marginally interesting to be possible stopovers for long-distance drivers. In theory, this is rich, oil-bearing land, but the cities have taken a battering since the slump.

Abilene and Sweetwater

ABILENE has a certain curiosity value as an oppressively God-fearing Bible city and home to three Christian universities. There's not much reason to stop here, though a downtown stroll reveals a few places along Cypress Street worth a look. At no. 102 the **Grace Museum** (Tues, Wed, Fri & Sat 10am–5pm, Thurs 10am–8.30pm; $5, free after 5.30pm Thurs; Ⓣ915/673-4587, Ⓦwww.thegrace-museum.org) occupies what was once the grandest hotel in this former railroad town and is divided into three distinct sections: regional art, local history, and a children's museum, though you'll be more diverted by the building itself. The **Center for Contemporary Arts** at no. 220 (Tues–Sat 11am–5pm; Ⓣ915/677-8389, Ⓦwww.cca-abilene.org) exhibits work by local artists and is free, while the beautiful **Paramount Theatre** at no. 352 (Ⓣ915/676-9620, Ⓦwww.paramount-abilene.org) is open for self-guided tours of its elaborate

Moorish interior on weekdays between 1pm and 5pm. Evening shows range from theater productions to classic and art films. If you have **to stay**, there are plenty of interstate motels, including the well-kept *Executive Inn*, 1650 I-20 E (☎915/677-2200; ❷), while downtown, *BJ's*, 508 Mulberry St, offers homey, comfortable B&B rooms (☎915/675-5855; ❹). Cypress Street is the place to go for **food**, with the *Cypress Street Station* at no. 158 (☎915/676-3463) offering a more eclectic menu than you would expect from a restaurant in this locale.

Dozy **SWEETWATER**, further west on I-20, began as a general store for buffalo hunters in 1877, and since 1958 has been mildly notable for its **rattlesnake roundup** (Ⓦwww.rattlesnakeroundup.com) on the second full weekend of March, when you can try fried snake (tough but tasty) or buy a transparent toilet seat with a rattler coiled in it. Besides the serious business of the farmers ridding their land of the diamondbacks, there are parades, cookouts, a Miss Snake Charmer Queen contest, and snake-handling demonstrations. Of the **motels** along Georgia Street, one of the nicest is the *Ranch House Motel and Restaurant* (☎915/236-6341; ❷).

The Panhandle

The inhabitants of the **Panhandle**, the southernmost portion of the Great Plains, call it "the real Texas"; it certainly fulfills the fantasy of what Texas should look like. When Coronado's expedition passed this way in the sixteenth century, the gold-seekers drove stakes into the ground across the vast and unchanging vista, despairing of otherwise finding their way home. Hence the name Llano Estacado, or staked plains, which still persists today.

Once the buffalo – and the natives – had been driven away from what was seen as perilous and uninhabitable frontier country, the Panhandle began, around the 1870s, to yield great **natural resources**. Helium, especially in Amarillo, and oil, as well as **agriculture**, have brought wealth to the region, which is also home to some of the world's largest **ranches**.

The Panhandle may hold few actual tourist attractions, but what appeals are its rural charm, its quirkiness, and its distance from the eastern cities. **Music** has particular significance in an area famous for songwriters such as Buddy Holly, Roy Orbison, Waylon Jennings, Mac Davis, Joe Ely, and Natalie Maines from the Dixie Chicks, although most musicians relocate to cosmopolitan centers like Austin. Above all, the exceptionally hospitable people of the Panhandle make it special, along with the starkly romantic landscape strewn with tumbleweeds and mesquite trees.

Lubbock

LUBBOCK, the largest city in the Panhandle, has long been the center of its commerce and transportation, roughly one hundred miles northwest of Abilene and the same distance south of Amarillo. At first this was cattle-grazing land, but the discovery of copious underground water made agriculture profitable.

The prosperity of the city was built on cotton. In recent years, with farmers perpetually plagued by economic struggles, the town's economy has come to rely on manufacturing and retail outlets, but you may still see solitary cotton fields standing defiantly on the outskirts, where farmers have refused to sell out.

With its fields, farms, lumpen bungalows, and faceless block buildings, Lubbock is relentlessly ordinary-looking, its muted downtown area dotted with fading 1950s shopfronts. Which is not to say that it's dull; though Southern Baptism has left its mark, Lubbock has a uniquely Texan sense of fun, clearly evident in its love of music, rodeos, and having a good time.

Arrival, information, and accommodation

Loop 289 circles Lubbock proper, with the **airport** (⊤806/775-2035) a few minutes north; city buses don't come out here, so taxis are the only option to downtown, with fares around $10 (Yellow Taxi ⊤806/765-7474). **Buses** arrive in downtown at 1313 13th St (⊤806/765-6641). The **Citibus** system (⊤806/762-0111, ⊛www.citibus.com) runs commuter routes within the Loop, stopping at around 6.15pm (Mon–Sat only). The **visitor center** is at 1301 Broadway (Mon–Fri 8am–5pm; ⊤806/747-5232 or 1-800/692-4035, ⊛www.lubbocklegends.com).

Prices for **accommodation** are very reasonable in this region, and rooms are plentiful, so there should be no problem finding someplace to stay. Avenue Q has a string of good, reliable chain **hotels**.

Coronado Inn 501 I-27 N ⊤806/763-6441. Northside motel with clean rooms for thirty bucks. ❶

Holiday Inn Lubbock - Hotel & Towers 801 Ave Q ⊤806/763-1200, ⊛www.holiday-inn.com. Popular downtown hotel with an indoor pool, sauna, and whirlpool. ❹

La Quinta Inn-Civic Center 601 Ave Q ⊤806/763-9441, ⊛www.laquinta.com. Decent rooms and free coffee, adjacent to a 24hr restaurant and just across from the Buddy Holly Statue. ❸

Lubbock Inn 3901 19th St ⊤806/792-5181, ⊛www.lubbockinn.com. Newly remodeled motel with basic rooms, a restaurant, and a pool with waterfalls. ❸

Woodrow House B&B 2629 19th St ⊤806/793-3330 or 1-800/687-5235, ⊛www.woodrow-house.com. Eight rooms, each with a Texan theme, in a mansion-style house opposite Texas Tech. ❹

The Town

Downtown Lubbock, and Texas Tech University, are on the northern side of town. Few buildings of interest survive, thanks to the construction boom of the 1950s and a tornado in 1970. However, you can get a stimulating overview of local history at the university's **Ranching Heritage Center**, Fourth Street and Indiana Avenue (Mon–Sat 10am–5pm, Sun 1–5pm; free). Over thirty original ranch buildings, from simple cowboy huts to grand overseers' houses, are set in a harsh landscape spiked with cacti and mesquite. There's an excellent museum on pioneer and cowboy history, and demonstrations on making lye soap, sourdough, and quilts. The adjacent **Texas Tech Museum** (Tues, Wed, Fri & Sat 10am–5pm, Thurs 10am–8.30pm, Sun 1–5pm; free) has further Southwestern displays and Buddy Holly memorabilia.

Buddy Holly

Lubbock's claim to world fame is as the birthplace of Charles Hardin Holley on September 7, 1936. Inspired by the blues and country music of his childhood – and a seminal encounter with the young Elvis Presley, gigging in Lubbock at the *Cotton Club* – **Buddy Holly** was one of Rock 'n' Roll's first singer-songwriters. The Holly sound, characterized by steady strumming guitar, rapid drumming, and his trademark hiccuping vocals, was made famous by hits such as *Peggy Sue, Rave On, Not Fade Away, Oh Boy!*, and *That'll Be the Day*; but Buddy himself was killed at the age of 22 by the Iowa plane crash of February 3, 1959 ("the day the music died") that also claimed the Big Bopper and Ritchie Valens.

In September 1999, the city opened the **Buddy Holly Center** at 19th Street and Avenue G (Tues–Fri 10am–6pm, Sat 11am–6pm; ☎806/767-2686, @www.buddyhollycenter.org), an impressive space that holds Lubbock's collection of Holly memorabilia (contracts, clothes, rare records, autographed items, and yes, those glasses) plus the Texas Music Hall Of Fame and various temporary exhibition galleries. All exhibits are free except for the Holly collection ($3).

An 8-foot bronze **Buddy Holly Statue**, on Eighth Street and Avenue Q, towers over a **Walk of Fame** with plaques to local performers like Roy Orbison and Waylon Jennings (the bassist for Buddy's final concert). **Buddy's birthplace**, at 1911 Sixth St, is now a vacant lot, but there are plenty more substantial things to see.

Other Holly-related sites

J.T. Hutchinson Junior High School 3102 Canton Ave. Buddy and friend Bob Montgomery performed here in the sixth grade.

Lubbock High School 2004 19th St. Buddy and Bob, who graduated in 1955, won the school's "Westerners Round Up" with *Flower of My Heart*. Souvenirs are on sale.

Tabernacle Baptist Church 1911 34th St. A percentage of Buddy's royalties still go to the church that saw his baptism, wedding, and funeral.

Radio Station KRLB 6602 Martin Luther King Jr Blvd. Opened in 1953, this was the first full-time country music station in the US. Buddy and bandmate Jack Neal had their own show.

Fair Park Coliseum 10th St and Ave A. Where Buddy opened shows for Bill Haley and Elvis Presley. His "discovery" here in 1955 led to a contract with Decca.

Buddy's grave in Lubbock's cemetery at the end of 34th St. Take the right fork inside the gate, and the grave, decorated with flowers and guitar picks, is on the left.

Eating

Lubbock has a surprising variety of **eating** places, with good barbecue and Tex-Mex and even some New American restaurants, with a particular concentration along Buddy Holly Avenue (Avenue H). However, many of the most upmarket restaurants close before 10pm.

The town's best Mexican restaurant, *Abuelo's*, 4401 82nd St (☎806/794-1762), has some great fish dishes, punch-packing margaritas, and live music on the patio in summer. *The County Line*, half a mile west of I-27 in Escondido Canyon (☎806/763-6001), serves first-rate barbecue in Lubbock, with all-you-care-to-eat specials for around $15, and outside, ducks and peacocks sauntering around freely. The *Hub City Brewpub*, 1807 Buddy Holly Ave (☎806/747-1535), is a lively and youthful spot, with decent grill food and beers, while the *Pancake House*, 510 Ave Q (☎806/765-8506), is a popular downtown joint for breakfast.

Entertainment and nightlife

The best entertainment that the Panhandle has to offer is at its **annual events**. After having been designated the "Music Crossroads of Texas" by the state legislature in 1999, the city changed the name of the annual Buddy Holly Music Festival to the catchy mouthful of the Music Crossroads of Texas Labor Day Weekend Music Festival – though now it's simply September Fest. Whatever it's called in future years, it'll likely still attract big Texan names like Joe Ely and Tanya Tucker, as well as those playing a straight homage to Mr Holly. **Rodeos** are always rip-roaring fun; Texas Tech holds one each October in Fair Park, and the **ABC Rodeo** is at Lubbock Municipal Coliseum every spring (✆806/793-5800, ⊛www.abcrodeo.com). In the same spirit, there are twirling contests, bull-riding, big-name country performers, and livestock exhibits at the **Panhandle South Plains Fair** (✆806/763-2833, ⊛www.southplains-fair.com) in late September and early October.

Despite its rich musical heritage there isn't a great deal of **nightlife** in Lubbock; most of the local musicians decamp to Austin. Most of the action is in the downtown Historical Depot District, which spreads out for a few blocks from 19th Street and Hwy-27, and has a mix of crass chain bars and sports bars. The oddly named **Lubbock Avalanche-Journal** (⊛www.lubbockonline.com) carries listings. You'd do best to skip the **Cactus Theatre**, 1812 Buddy Holly Ave (✆806/762-3233), which puts on syrupy variety shows with frequent nods to you-know-who.

Amarillo and around

AMARILLO may seem cut off from the rest of Texas, up in the northern Panhandle, but it stands on one of the great American cross-country routes – I-40, once the legendary **Route 66** – roughly 300 miles east of Albuquerque and 250 miles west of Oklahoma City. The name comes from the Spanish for "yellow," the color of the soil characteristic to these parts. An early promoter of the city was so delighted with its potential as a site for lucrative buffalo hunting (for those who braved the Apache and Comanche threat) and as excellent ranching land, that he painted all the buildings bright yellow.

Today, sitting on ninety percent of the world's helium and hosting a world-class cattle market, Amarillo is a prosperous but surprisingly uneventful city. The small "**old town**" consists of a few tree-lined streets and staid old homes; some of the less quaint antique stores along **Sixth Street** (the old Route 66, known locally as "Old San Jacinto") serve equally well as museums of pioneer life. Following I-40 six miles west to exit 60 (Arnot Road) brings you to **Cadillac Ranch** (⊛www.libertysoftware.be/cml/cadillacranch/crmain.htm). An extraordinary vision in the middle of nowhere, ten battered roadsters stand upended in the soil, their tail fins demonstrating the different Cadillac designs from 1949 to 1963. Since the cars were installed in 1974, they have been subject to countless makeovers at the hands of graffiti artists, photographers, and members of the public (encouraged by owner and patron, eccentric helium millionaire Stanley Marsh III, on whose land the cars are planted); occasionally they're shiny blue or red after having been painted for a photo shoot. In 1997 the whole installation was moved two miles west to this present site as the city had begun to encroach and spoil the horizon.

Amarillo is also host to the world's stompingest, snortingest **livestock auction** (☎806/373-7464), in the stockyards at S Manhattan and Third avenues, on the east side of town. The auction proper, held on Tuesday morning, is open to the public, as is the adjacent *Stockyard Café* (☎806/374-6024).

If you enjoy playing cowboys, it's fun to visit one of the many grand old Panhandle **ranches** that have diversified into tourism. Some just open for the day; others provide (usually expensive) accommodation (call Amarillo's CVB for particulars; see below). The ranchers who entertain you are often natural showmen and -women, whose welcome is utterly genuine, though they'd rather be working the animals for real than running a theme park.

Practicalities

Eight local bus lines connect downtown Amarillo with outlying attractions (Mon–Sat 6.30am–6pm; 75¢; ☎806/342-9144), but the city is easier to navigate by car. Greyhound arrives in downtown at 700 S Tyler St (☎806/374-5371). The **CVB** is at 1000 Polk St (Mon–Fri 8am–5pm; ☎806/374-1497 or 1-800/692-1338, ⓦwww.amarillo-cvb.org).

Innumerable budget **hotels** are concentrated along I-40. For a little luxury, *Ambassador Hotel*, 3100 I-40 W, is good value (☎806/358-6161; ❺), while *Auntie's House*, 1712 S Polk St (☎806/371-8054 or 1-888/661-8054, ⓦwww.auntieshouse.com; ❹), is a sweet, welcoming **B&B**. Texana fans will love the tongue-in-cheek Western camp of the *Big Texan Steak House Motel*, 7701 I-40 E at exit 75 (☎806/372-5000 or 1-800/657-7177, ⓦwww.bigtexan.com; ❸). Its restaurant, as well as serving fried rattlesnake and ostrich burgers, offers the 72oz steak challenge: if you can eat it all within an hour, you get it free (losers pony up $54). Other popular Amarillo restaurants include *Arnold Burgers*, 1611 S Washington St (☎806/372-1741), which serves enormous beef patties (up to 24 inches); *Tacos Garcia*, 1412 S Ross St (☎806/371-0411), good for reliable Mexican food in a festive environment; and the self-consciously bohemian *OHMS Gallery Café*, 619 S Tyler St (☎806/373-3233), where the menu is decidedly international – think lasagna, shepherd's pie, and enchiladas.

Canyon

The one "sight" in the former cattle town of **CANYON**, fifteen miles south of Amarillo on I-27, is worth a visit. The **Panhandle-Plains Historical Museum** (daily 9am–6pm, Sun 1–6pm; $4; ☎806/651-2244, ⓦwww.panhandleplains.org) has exhibits on restored pioneer buildings, the history of Texas ranching, natural history displays, a collection of Western art, and even the oldest known assembly line automobile (a 1903 Model A Ford). Even the history of the oil and gas industry is made interesting.

Palo Duro State Canyon Park

Palo Duro Canyon, twelve miles east of Canyon and twenty miles southeast of Amarillo, is one of Texas's best-kept secrets. Plunging 1000 feet from rim to floor, it splits the plains wide open and offers breathtaking views and colors, especially at sunset and in spring, when the whole chasm is scattered with wild flowers. Pillars of sturdy sandstone loom over the flame-colored rocks, which Coronado's explorers named "Spanish Skirts" on account of their resemblance to stripy flounces.

The park itself (ⓦwww.palodurocanyon.com) is located in the most scenic part of the 130-mile canyon (park daily 8am–10pm, visitor center and interpretive center daily 9am–5pm; $3 per person). You can explore the depths on horseback ($12 per hour; reservations ☏806/488-2180), though backpackers and hikers may want to escape the tourist busloads by following the Prairie Dog Town fork into more remote sections of the park. To **camp**, advance reservations are recommended (☏806/488-2227).

You may balk at heart-warming musical extravaganzas, but the outdoor production *TEXAS* has an undeniable pull in an area not exactly throbbing with nightlife, with the dramatic prairie sky as a ceiling, a 600-foot cliff as a backdrop, and genuine thunder and lightning (mid-June to late Aug Thurs–Tues 8.30pm; $8–23; pre-show chuckwagon barbecue 6pm; ☏806/655-2181, ⓦwww.texasmusicaldrama.com).

West Texas

West Texas is the stuff of Wild West fantasy: parched deserts, ghost towns, looming mesas, and above all a sense of utter isolation. Although the area south from the Panhandle down to Del Rio on the Rio Grande is, for convenience, also known as West Texas, the fantasy really begins west of the Pecos River; you can drive for hours without a sign of life to **El Paso**, Texas's shabby western-most city. Most travelers only venture into the desolation to explore **Big Bend National Park**, nearly three hundred miles southeast of El Paso in the curve of the Rio Grande.

Minimal rainfall and harsh land were not the only hindrances to settlement. The **Apache** and **Comanche**, though accustomed in the 1820s to trading with Mexican *comancheros*, were infuriated when hapless white pioneers began to trickle in during the 1830s. With their horsemanship and ability to find scarce water supplies, the Native Americans posed a real threat; upon statehood, a string of cavalry forts were set up with the help of federal money to protect Mexican and Anglo settlers from attack. As trading posts and cattle ranges began to spring up after the Civil War, the paramilitary **Texas Rangers** were sent out on violent vigilante missions. Eventually, as in the Panhandle, a brutal program of buffalo slaughter, supported by the US Army, starved the natives out. Not long afterward, oil was discovered in West Texas and boom towns appeared, with all the attendant lawlessness, gunslinging, and brawling. Those days are long gone, but the area has been capitalizing on its Wild West image ever since.

The Davis Mountains

The temperate climate of the verdant **Davis Mountains**, south of the junction of I-10 and I-20, makes them a popular summer destination for sweltering urban Texans, while the glassy, starry nights facilitate the work of the **McDonald Observatory** about twenty miles north of Fort Davis on Hwy-118 (guided tours of dome and 107-inch telescope daily 11.30am and 2.30pm $7; self-guided tours daily 9am–5pm, free; ☏915/426-3640, ⓦwww.mcdonaldobservatory.org). Nocturnal "star parties" here provide the opportunity to look at the constellations for yourself (Tues, Fri & Sat, time depends on sunset). **Fort Davis National Historic Site** (summer daily 8am–6pm; rest of year daily 9am–8pm; $3 per vehicle; ☎915/426-3224 ext 20, ⓦwww.nps .gov/foda), which starts on the northern edge of the town along Hwy-17, offers good hiking, as well as fishing and swimming at the foot of the canyon in Limpia Creek. Rooms at its romantic *Indian Lodge* are clean and comfortable – and often booked up, so call in advance (☎915/426-3254; ❸).

Fort Davis, a one-street town with less than a thousand residents, at the junction of highways 118 and 17, is a peaceful base for exploring the state park, en route to or from Big Bend. The *Old Texas Inn*, above a wood-fronted drugstore, has clean, colorful **B&B**-style rooms; breakfast is served in the café downstairs, accompanied by country tunes on the jukebox (☎915/426-3118, ⓦwww.oldtexasinn.com; ❸). The more expensive *Hotel Limpia*, opposite (☎915/426-3237 or 1-800/662-5517; ❺), serves home-cooked dinners in its cozy dining room. There's pleasantly little to do in Fort Davis at night, though you can buy "membership" to the hotel's bar for $3. The town's **visitor center** (☎915/426-3015, ⓦwww.fortdavis.com) offers regional information including road maps for the 75-mile scenic loop of the Davis Mountains.

Marfa

MARFA, a small ranching town 21 miles south of Fort Davis on Hwy-17, has a few minor claims to fame. James Dean's last film, the 1956 epic *Giant*, was filmed here; the cast stayed at the historic **Hotel Paisano** on Hwy-17 (☎432/729-3669 or 1-866/729-3669, ⓦwww.hotelpaisano.com; ❹), where the sumptuous, ranch-style lobby, resplendent with dead animal heads and leather furniture, screens *Giant* continuously.

Nowadays, though, the town is probably best-known for the "**Marfa Lights**," mysterious bouncing lights that have been seen in the town's flat fields since the 1880s, attracting conspiracy theorists and alien-hunters. The town's **visitor center**, in the *Hotel Paisano*, can give advice on good vantage points to see the lights.

Just outside of town, follow the signs to the magnificent **Chinati Foundation** (open only for 5hr tours, Wed–Sun 10am; $10; ☎432/729-4362, ⓦwww.chinati.org), home to some of the world's largest permanent art installations. Founded by minimalist Donald Judd, the contemporary pieces include scores of giant aluminum and concrete boxes, both indoors and out.

For **food**, *Jett's*, inside the *Hotel Paisano*, serves good American food that is best enjoyed in the hotel's romantic courtyard. Quicker and cheaper is the *Pizza Foundation* (☎432/729-3377), which offers a relaxed ambiance and creative pizza toppings.

Big Bend National Park

The **Rio Grande**, flowing through 1500-foot gorges, makes a ninety-degree bend south of Marathon to form the southern border of **BIG BEND NATIONAL PARK** – thanks to its isolation one of the least visited of the US national parks, and very much of a kind with the great desert parks of the Southwest.

The Apache, who forced the Chisos Indians out three hundred years ago, told that this hauntingly beautiful wilderness was used by the Great Spirit to dump all the rocks left over from the creation of the world. A breathtaking million-acre expanse of pine-forested mountains and ocotilla-dotted desert, Big Bend has been home to prospectors and smugglers, a last frontier for the true-grit pioneers at the end of the nineteenth century, who took advantage of the rich cinnabar deposits for mercury mining. Today there is camping in specific areas, and some trailer parks, but much of the park remains barely charted territory, the ruins of primitive Mexican and white settlements testament to its power to defeat earlier visitors. Wild animals have fared somewhat better: coyotes, road-runners, and javelinas (an odd-looking bristly black pig-like creature with a pointy snout) all roam free. Violent contrasts in topography and temperature result in dramatic juxtapositions of desert and mountain plant and animal life. Despite the dryness, tangles of pretty wild flowers and blossoming cacti, includ-ing peyote, erupt into color each April.

The most interesting route into Big Bend is from the west. You can't follow the river all the way from El Paso, but Hwy-170 – the **River Road**, reached on Hwy-67 south from Marfa (see p.799) – runs through spectacular desert scenery for around thirty miles west from Ojinaga, climbing stark buttes from where you can peep down to the river below. Before reaching the park bound-ary just beyond Study Butte, you pass through the haunting communities of Lajitas and Terlingua (see opposite).

Once in the park, unless you're prepared to do some strenuous hiking, there are few opportunities to see the river itself; the main road is obliged to run across the desert, north of the outcrop of the Chisos Mountains. A spur road starting west of the headquarters at **Panther Junction** leads south for six miles, up into the alpine meadows of the **Chisos Basin**, ringed by dramatic (though not amazingly high) peaks. The one gap in the rocky wall here is the **Window**, looking out over the deserts and reached by a relatively simple trail. Driving twenty miles south-east of Panther Junction brings you to the riverside **Rio Grande Village** – unless you choose to detour just before, to bathe in some rather dilapidated nat-ural **hot springs** that feed into the river. A footbridge crosses from near the vil-lage to the Mexican hamlet of Boquillas; or you can pay $1 to be rowed across the river, then ride a donkey into nearby Boquillas for a meal and a beer.

At three separate stages within the park boundaries the river runs through gigantic **canyons**. The westernmost, the **Santa Elena**, is the most common **rafting trip**, being accessible from a put-in at Lajitas. Although there is virtu-ally no whitewater, the canyon boasts the technically challenging Rock Slide, and two ethereal Mexican side canyons that can be hiked, as well as stretches where the river swirls between awesome high rock walls, striated at an angle that makes it seem like you're plunging into an abyss. It's possible to drive with-in the park to the eastern end of the canyon, where the towering cliffs sud-denly come to an end and the river meanders through marshy fields; a short hike from here shows the gorge in all its splendor.

The ease of crossing the **international frontier** adds to the thrill of the Big Bend experience, although you can get no further into Mexico than sandbanks populated by browsing burros. This area is so remote that casual traffic across the river is regarded as insignificant; police checks for illegal immigrants take place roughly fifty miles north of Big Bend, on each of the main roads.

Practicalities

The park headquarters at **Panther Junction** (daily 8am–5pm; ☎915/477-2251), where you pay the $15-per-vehicle entrance fee, has orientation exhibits and a daytime gas station. Camping is first-come, first-served. **Rio Grande Village** also has a visitor center, hot shower facilities in the grocery store, a laundry, and a daytime gas station. Camping permits here and at **Chisos Basin** are $10. Further free primitive **campgrounds** are scattered along the 36 marked hiking trails. These have no facilities, and you'll need a wilderness permit from Panther Junction, plus a map, compass, flashlight, and first-aid kit before you can venture onto the trails.

The **Chisos Basin**, which has a visitor center, a store, and a post office, is the site of the park's only roofed accommodation. The motel-style *Chisos Mountains Lodge* (reservations essential; ☏ 915/477-2291, ⓦ www.chisosmountainslodge.com; ❹) offers balcony rooms with gorgeous views; you'll often hear javelinas snuffling for food outside your door. The surprisingly good onsite restaurant, which serves American and Southwestern food, closes at 8pm.

Terlingua and Lajitas

Some of the long-abandoned mercury-mining communities on the fringes of Big Bend are now stuttering back to life as alternative tourist centers. **TERLINGUA** in particular, a strangely appealing little ghost town scattered across the scrubby hills along Hwy-170, is populated by the adventurous types who work for the local rafting companies, along with assorted drifters lured by the solitary desert life. Near its fly-blown cemetery, against a backdrop of evocative ruins, the hugely atmospheric *Starlight Theater, Bar and Restaurant* (☏ 915/371-2326), with its postmodern reinterpretation of Southwestern decor, is the perfect place to enjoy a cold beer and soak up the haunting desert view; it also serves food, and puts on evening shows in summer. A mile or so east along the highway is the only other place to eat in the evening: *La Kiva* (☏ 915/371-2250), attached to the RV-oriented Big Bend Travel Park, is carved into the rock, and attracts a young crowd to its New Age bar, restaurant, and evening gigs. The *Chisos Mining Company Motel* on Hwy-170 (☏ 915/371-2254; ❷) has reasonable **rooms**.

Allow around $125 for a full day's **rafting** along Santa Elena Canyon (see opposite); canyons further out can cost up to $150. Far Flung Adventures, based next door to the *Starlight* in Terlingua, runs all the Big Bend routes, as well as many other Southwestern rivers, and also does memorable multiday music trips with renowned Texan musicians (☏ 915/371-2325 or 1-800/359-4138, ⓦ www.farflung.com).

LAJITAS, west of Terlingua, is the main put-in for rafting trips, but has largely been taken over by the somewhat ersatz *Lajitas on the Rio Grande* resort complex and its five separate hotels (☏ 915/424-3471, ⓦ www.lajitas.com; ❹). However, it attempts to pull in the tourists with its distinguished political figurehead – Clay Henry III, a beer-drinking goat who beat four other candidates, including a wooden Indian and a real person - for the mayoral post. Look for his pen, littered with empty Lone Star Longneck bottles, outside the adobe Lajitas Trading Post.

El Paso

Back when Texas was still Tejas, **EL PASO**, the second oldest settlement in the United States, was the main crossing on the Rio Grande. It still plays that role today, its 600,000 residents joining with another 1.7 million across the river in **Ciudad Juarez**, Mexico, to form the largest binational (and bilingual) megalopolis in North America. At first sight it's not an especially pretty place – massive railyards fill up much of downtown, the belching smelters of copper mills line the riverfront, and the northern reaches are taken up by the giant Fort Bliss military base, where two museums trace the military history of the city from adobe Spanish outpost to largest air defense center in the Western world. Its dramatic setting, however, where the Franklin Mountains meet the Chihuahua desert, gives it a certain bold, rough pioneer edge, bearing more relation to old rather than new Mexico, with little of the pastel softness of the Southwest US. Local legend has it that when Wyatt Earp arrived in sharp-shooting El Paso, he thought it too wild for him, and boarded the first train to Tombstone.

Arrival and information

El Paso's **airport** is about twenty minutes' drive northeast of downtown; Sun Metro **bus** route #33 (☎915/533-3333) will take you downtown for $1 (Mon–Sat until 9pm, Sun until 7pm), while a **taxi** ride will cost $15, although most downtown hotels offer free van rides. Greyhound buses stop at 200 W San Antonio Ave, while Amtrak trains pull in at the Daniel Burnham–designed Union Station at 700 San Francisco St, slightly to the west.

For full **information** on El Paso and its Mexican neighbor, contact the downtown visitor center (daily 8am–5pm; ☎915/534-0601 or 1-800/351-6024, ⓦwww.visitelpaso.com), at 5 Civic Center Plaza in the Convention Center complex.

Accommodation

Prices in El Paso tend to be reasonable and there's a good range of choices, from hostels, functional old downtown hotels, and swanky joints to the usual chain motels along I-10.

Camino Real 101 S El Paso St ☎915/534-3000, ⓦwww.caminoreal.com. El Paso's luxury option. If you can't stay here, at least visit its elegant Southwestern restaurant (see opposite for review) or the wonderfully romantic *Dome Bar*, topped with a colorful Tiffany dome and surrounded by rose and black marble. ❹

Gardner Hotel & Hostel 311 E Franklin St ☎915/532-3661. Atmospheric hotel where John Dillinger bedded down in the 1920s. The hostel costs $13 for members and an extra dollar for others. Rooms vary from dorms to singles with shared bath to clean en suite doubles. ❶–❷

Microtel Inn 2001 Airway Blvd ☎915/772-3650, ⓦwww.microtelinn.com. An inexpensive chain option near the airport, providing a great base for the Mission Trail east of downtown. ❸

Sunset Heights B&B Inn 717 W Yandell Drive ☎915/544-1743. Welcoming Victorian B&B, a few minutes from downtown, serving full breakfasts. ❹

Travelodge City Center 409 E Missouri Ave ☎915/544-3333, ⓦwww.travelodge.com. Large, downtown motel rooms, along with a passable Mexican restaurant on the premises. ❷

The Town

Downtown El Paso holds surprisingly little to see apart from a couple of passable art museums; what character it has continues to be shaped by the **US–Mexico border**. In times past outlaws and exiles from either side of the border would take refuge across the river, and today's traffic remains considerable and not entirely uncontroversial. Manual workers come north to find undocumented jobs, and US companies secretly dump their toxic waste on the south side. The border itself, the Rio Grande, has caused its share of disagreements: the river changed course quite often in the 1800s, and it was not until the 1960s, when it was run through a concrete channel, that it was made permanent. An attractive park, the **Chamizal National Memorial** (daily 8am–5pm; free), on the east side of downtown off Paisano Drive, was built to commemorate the settling of the border dispute and provides a pleasant place to picnic. The **Border Patrol Museum**, 4315 Transmountain Rd at Hwy-54 (Tues–Sun 9am–5pm; free), is a small but engrossing museum explaining the work of the patrollers and highlighting the ingenuity of smugglers. The **Cordova Bridge** heads across the river into Mexico, where there's a larger park and a number of museums; there are no formalities, so long as you have a multiple-entry visa for the US and don't travel more than twenty or so miles south of the border. The El Paso–Juarez "Border Jumper" trolley departs hourly from the visitor center; the $13 roundtrip ticket may be steep, but it does provide a pretty comprehensive tour of the Mexican city's shopping and dining offerings.

Although El Paso is predominantly Hispanic, there is also a substantial population of **Tigua Indians**, a displaced Pueblo tribe, based in a reservation (complete with the almost statutory **casino**) on Socorro Road, southeast of downtown. The reservation's arts-and-crafts center is open to the public, selling pottery and textiles. Adjacent to the reservation, the simple **Ysleta del Sur**, the oldest mission in the United States, marks the beginning of the **Mission Trail** (information office ☎915/534-0677) running alongside scruffy cotton, alfalfa, chili, onion, and pecan fields. Two miles east, the **Socorro mission**, moved from its original seventeenth-century site on the river, shows an unusually heavy Native American influence; the crenelation on either side of the bell tower represents a Tigua rain god. Still an active church, it is relatively unadorned inside, with hand-carved ceiling beams and lattices; major renovation efforts, replacing crumbling concrete, were completed in 2003. Off the beaten track, six miles further along the trail, the cathedral-style **San Elizario** was the chapel for the Spanish military, with whitewashed walls, jewel-colored stained glass, and a decorative tin ceiling. Splendid views of three states and two countries can be seen from the southern rim of the Franklin Mountains, either from Scenic Drive or from the vertigo-inducing Wyler Aerial Tramway (summer Mon & Thurs noon–6pm, Fri–Sun noon–9pm; rest of year Mon, Thurs & Fri noon–6pm, weekends noon–9pm; $7; ☎915/566-6622, ⓦwww.tpwd.state.tx.us/park/tram), which climbs 946 feet to the observation deck and panoramic views.

In **Concordia cemetery**, just northwest of the I-10 and Hwy-54 intersection, a shambling collection of crumbling stones and plain wooden crosses commemorates assorted pioneers and desperados. The grave of **John Wesley Hardin**, the much romanticized gunslinger, is marked by a crooked headstone northwest of the Chinese graveyard, a section walled off since the Chinese built the railroads in the 1880s. El Paso is also the home of Tony Lama, makers of top-quality **cowboy boots**, available at substantial discounts at three outlets across town.

Eating and nightlife

Dining is understandably dominated by Mexican cuisine. After dark, El Paso offers an uninspiring mix of clubs and bars. The *Camino Real* hotel's beautiful *Dome Bar* offers a pleasant drinking atmosphere. Alternatively, head across the border to Ciudad Juarez.

Azulejos Camino Real *Camino Real* hotel, 101 S El Paso St ☎915/534-3020. Without doubt the most pleasant dining space in the city, though the prices of the Tex-Mex and regional fare do reflect the central downtown location.
Cattleman's Steakhouse Indian Cliffs Ranch, Fabens, TX ☎915/544-3200. A regional legend about 25 miles east of El Paso, serving superb food – you can wander around the working ranch, too. To get here take I-10 east to exit 49,

turn right, and drive five miles north.
H&H Coffee Shop & Car Wash 701 E Yandell Drive ☎915/533-1144. These adjacent businesses just off downtown work well together; stop by in the morning for their wicked *huevos rancheros*. Reportedly a favored stop for President Bush and assorted governors.
Puerto Vallarta Grill 1611 Montana Ave ☎915/544-8169. Unassuming local favorite with delicious, seafood-dominated Mexican fare.

Guadalupe Mountains National Park

Roughly one hundred miles east of El Paso, Hwy-62/180 climbs toward Carlsbad Caverns along the southern fringes of the **Guadalupe Mountains**, once a stronghold of the Mescalero Apache. The national park here (free; park headquarters ☏915/828-3251, ⓦ www.nps.gov/gumo) is very much a hiking and camping destination, barely penetrated by roads and without accommodation, food, or even gas. It's possible to hike right to the top of Guadalupe Peak, at 8749ft the highest point in Texas, but most walkers head instead for the painlessly flat trek through **McKittrick Canyon**, passing from bare desert into lush mountain forests beside sheer canyon walls. There are multiple camp sites within the park ($8 per night per tent site, check the rangers station) on a first-come, first-served basis.

The Great Plains

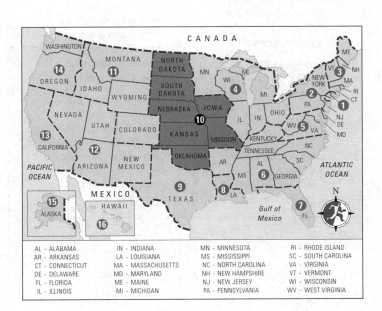

C A N A D A

AL - ALABAMA	IN - INDIANA	MN - MINNESOTA	RI - RHODE ISLAND
AR - ARKANSAS	LA - LOUISIANA	MS - MISSISSIPPI	SC - SOUTH CAROLINA
CT - CONNECTICUT	MA - MASSACHUSETTS	NC - NORTH CAROLINA	VA - VIRGINIA
DE - DELAWARE	MD - MARYLAND	NH - NEW HAMPSHIRE	VT - VERMONT
FL - FLORIDA	ME - MAINE	NJ - NEW JERSEY	WI - WISCONSIN
IL - ILLINOIS	MI - MICHIGAN	PA - PENNSYLVANIA	WV - WEST VIRGINIA

✳ Woolaroc Ranch, Bartlesville, OK Fascinating museum of Western art and history. See p.813

✳ Hannibal, MO This delightful Mississippi River town is still recognizable as the setting for Mark Twain's epic tales of boyhood. See p.820

✳ Live music in Kansas City, MO Choose from a host of venues, from down-home blues joints to slick jazz clubs. See p.832

✳ Dodge City Days and Rodeo, KS A good old time with some good old boys in late July and early August. See p.841

✳ Carhenge, Alliance, NE America's crazy vehicular Stonehenge, planted in a Nebraska wheat field. See p.853

✳ The Badlands, SD This spooky moonscape offers great camping and hiking – and a monument to the Ghost Dancers at Wounded Knee. See p.858

✳ The Black Hills, SD Superb camping, the overblown monuments of Mount Rushmore and Crazy Horse, and wandering bison: the all-American destination. See p.860

10

The Great Plains

THE GREAT PLAINS, stretching west of the Mississippi through **Oklahoma**, **Missouri**, **Kansas**, **Iowa**, **Nebraska**, **South Dakota**, and **North Dakota**, are lumped together in the popular imagination as an unappealing expanse of unvarying flatness and conservative "Middle American" values, a huge national joke to be passed through as fast as possible. Once, however, this was the **West**, a vast empty canvas on which outlaws, fur trappers, buffalo hunters, and cowboys painted their dreams. In the 1870s, the wide open range of the lone prairie, which had originally been known as the **Great American Desert** but was then promoted as a bountiful Garden of Eden, inspired such fascination that General Custer was moved to call it "the fairest and richest portion of the national domain." As well as the main routes west (the Oregon and Santa Fe trails through Missouri, Kansas, and Nebraska), the plains were crisscrossed by the Pony Express, cattle trails, and railroads. Today the massive **Gateway Arch** in St Louis celebrates the traders, explorers, and pioneers who followed their destinies further and further west.

Early maps show the Desert as uninterrupted by towns or roads; even today there are fewer towns, spaced further apart, on the plains than anywhere else in the nation. One sinister note echoes through this openness and emptiness: most of the nation's **nuclear missiles** – marked by unprepossessing concrete blocks fenced into empty fields – sit beneath a land already ravaged by greed.

The Plains, today so apparently uneventful, share a troubled history. The systematic destruction by white settlers of the awesome herds of **bison** presaged the virtual eradication of the **Plains Indians**. Reservations, agencies, and "assigned lands" dwindled as the natural resources of the area attracted white settlement; after 1874, when **gold** was discovered in the Black Hills, the fate of the Native Americans was practically sealed. However, thanks to warriors like **Crazy Horse** and **Sitting Bull**, the struggle for control of the Plains was by no means as easy as the Hollywood Westerns imply. Today the region is ambivalent about this history: many of its museums and monuments to Native Americans seem almost like a veiled celebration of the destruction of their culture.

The Plains are more comfortable playing **cowboys**, glorying in a romantic myth of the Wild West, and flaunting sanitized versions of wicked old cowtowns like **Deadwood** in South Dakota, **Dodge City** (once called the Beautiful, Bibulous Babylon of the Frontier) in Kansas, and **St Joseph**, Missouri, the birthplace of the Pony Express. **Calamity Jane**, **Wild Bill Hickok**, **Billy the Kid**, and **Annie Oakley** all left their marks here when this was the wild frontier, and today, in the sandy scrublands of northern Nebraska and North Dakota, you can still see real cowboy and cattle country.

After Reconstruction, Southern blacks came here in search of an egalitarian future, and black colonies sprang up all around the region. The dreams soon died, though, and there are few black faces to be seen nowadays. There is, however, more evidence of nineteenth-century **Russian** and **German** settlement: many of the oldest families on the Plains are descendants of European Mennonites who escaped religious persecution in the 1870s, bringing with them new farming methods that heralded the region's great agricultural prosperity. The Great Plains still provide the nation with much of its food and export two-thirds of the world's **wheat**, seas of which wave over the flat fields of Iowa, Nebraska, and Kansas. The economy has also long been dependent on **oil**, especially in Oklahoma, and gold in the Dakotas.

Defining the geographical limits of the Plains is difficult, and the term itself is almost a misnomer – there are vast flat expanses and long uninterrupted roads, but there are also canyons, forests, and splashes of unexpected color, as well as two of the nation's mightiest **rivers**: the **Missouri**, which weaves its course southeast from North Dakota, and the **Mississippi**, which it joins at St Louis. Since the 1950s, the siphoning of the underground Ogallala aquifer from Nebraska to Oklahoma has transformed much that was once dusty desert into verdant fields; the consequences of overuse (ensuring the depletion of the reservoir in another fifty-odd years) remain to be seen.

The woods, caves, and springs of the **Ozarks**, the lunar landscapes of South Dakota's **Badlands**, and stately **Mount Rushmore** are the region's most visited areas. Otherwise, there are few immediate attractions, and only St Louis stands out as an urban destination. Drama comes instead in the form of such unpredictable **weather** as freak blizzards, dust storms, lightning storms, and the notorious "twister" tornadoes. Images of the devastating Thirties' dustbowl Depression (when topsoil was whisked as far away as Washington, DC) remain as potent as the fantasy of Dorothy and Toto being swept up from Kansas by a tornado to the land of Oz, while **flooding** is a constant threat – huge swaths of Iowa and Missouri were swamped in 1993.

A **car** is practically obligatory in the Plains, where distances are long, roads straight and seemingly endless, and the population sparse. The main routes (I-94, I-90, I-80, I-70, and I-40) cross from east to west, while north–south travel is often limited to quiet, curving byways. Greyhound **buses** travel the interstates, but often bypass the small towns that provide a real sense of the region. Subsidiary bus lines include Jack Rabbit in South Dakota, and the Jefferson Line, which covers Iowa, Kansas, Missouri, and Oklahoma. True to their image as a crossroads rather than a destination, the Plains are crossed by Amtrak **trains** almost exclusively at night, with South Dakota not covered at all. St Louis, Missouri, has the major **airport**, while Wichita, Kansas, is a regional hub.

Oklahoma

Often ridiculed by the rest of the country as dust-filled and boring, **OKLA-HOMA** has had a traumatic and far from dull history. In the 1830s all this land, held to be useless, was set aside as **Indian Territory**; a convenient dumping ground for the so-called Five Civilized Tribes who blocked white settlement in the southern states. The Choctaw and Chickasaw of Mississippi, the Seminole of Florida, and the Creek of Alabama were each assigned a share, while the rest (though already inhabited by indigenous Indians) was given to the Cherokee from Carolina, Tennessee, and Georgia, who followed in 1838 on the four-month trek notorious as "the Trail of Tears" (see box, p.603). Today the state has a large Native American population – "oklahoma" is the Choctaw word for "red man" – and even the smallest towns tend to have museums of Native American history.

Once white settlers realized that Indian Territory was, in fact, well worth farming, they decided to stay. The Indians were relocated once more, and in a series of manic free-for-all scrambles starting in 1889, entire towns sprang up literally overnight. Those who jumped the gun and claimed land illegally were known as Sooners; hence Oklahoma's nickname, the **Sooner State**. White settlers didn't have an easy life, however; they faced, after great oil prosperity in the 1920s, an era of unthinkable hardship in the 1930s. The desperate migration, when whole communities fled the dust bowl for California, has come to encapsulate the worst horrors of the Depression, most famously in John Steinbeck's novel (and John Ford's film) **The Grapes of Wrath**, but also in Dorothea Lange's haunting photos of itinerant families, hitching and camping on the road, and in the sad yet hopeful songs of Woody Guthrie. After the slump of the early Thirties, improved farming techniques brought life, and people, back to Oklahoma. Today the state is known for its staunch **conservatism**; as a Bible Belt stronghold, bars and liquor stores close early, while tattoo parlors are banned altogether.

Oklahoma is not the flat and unchanging expanse of popular imagination. Most of its places of interest, such as attractive **Tulsa**, lie in the hilly wooded northeast; only the sparse and treeless west is devoid of appeal, on the far side of the central "tornado alley" prairie grassland which holds the state's revitalized capital, **Oklahoma City**. The lakes and parks of the south, which bears more than a passing resemblance to neighboring Arkansas (complete with mountains, pretty foliage, and bluegrass music), have made tourism Oklahoma's second industry after oil.

Getting around Oklahoma

Car travel is the only way to explore Oklahoma. **Amtrak** serves Oklahoma City with one train a day from Fort Worth, Texas, and **Greyhound** buses speed along I-35 and I-40, which converge on Oklahoma City – but public transportation within the towns is minimal. Tulsa and Oklahoma City have **airports**. **Route 66**, which passes through both cities on its way from Missouri to Texas, is no longer a national highway, but if you have plenty of time (and sturdy tires: much of the road is in a bad way), it makes a nostalgic alternative to the interstates. **Travel literature** detailing the small communities and ghost towns along the way is plentiful at roadside **information centers**; or, you can contact the Oklahoma Route 66 Association (☎405/258-0008, ⓦ www.oklahomaroute66.com).

Eastern Oklahoma

Eastern Oklahoma includes the "Green Country" of the northeast, patterned with the foothills of the Ozarks, as well as woods, streams, lakes, and rivers that make it a popular camping destination. Art Deco Tulsa is its cultural center; Tahlequah and Pawhuska are the capitals of the Cherokee and Osage nations respectively.

Tulsa

TULSA is a good-looking city, thanks in part to the striking Art Deco architecture that dates from its Twenties heyday as an immensely wealthy oil town.

Despite – or possibly because of – its pleasant atmosphere, two excellent museums, and thriving art scene, the city tends towards complacency. In addition, fundamentalist Christian attitudes are hard to ignore; Tulsa is known as "the Buckle of the Bible Belt."

Arrival, information, and getting around

Tulsa International Airport lies a few minutes by cab ($20) east of downtown. Hwy-169 from Kansas City skirts the city's east side; I-44, which gives access from the south, is also the main route east–west across town. **Greyhound** comes in downtown at 317 S Detroit Ave. The **CVB**, 616 S Boston Ave (Mon–Fri 8am–5pm; ☎918/585-1201 or 1-800/558-3311, ⓦwww.visittulsa.com), provides information on a self-guided **walking tour** of downtown, as well as local bus schedules; services operate between 5am and 8.30pm, with no Sunday service ($1, transfers 5¢).

Accommodation

Most of Tulsa's budget **hotels** are on the interstates and along W Skelly Drive, forking southwest from I-44. There's camping at the *KOA*, 19605 E Skelly Drive (☎918/266-4227; $22). There are a few **B&Bs** in town, including the *Dream Catcher B&B* (☎918/743-6704; ❸), which often books up nearly a year in advance; check the CVB website (see above) for other listings.

Doubletree Hotel 616 W 7th St ☎918/587-8000. Good downtown location, with tasteful, though chain-like, rooms. ❺
Lexington Hotel Suites 8525 E 41st St ☎918/627-0030. Excellent doubles and suites, some with kitchens. Near the airport. ❹

Trade Winds East Inn 3337 E Skelly Drive ☎918/743-7931. Comfortable but utilitarian rooms at the roadside. ❹
YMCA 515 S Denver Ave ☎918/583-6201. Austere men-only downtown accommodation for $20 per bed. ❶

The City

Downtown Tulsa's most obvious landmark is the ornate **Art Deco Union Depot**, on the First Street and Boston Avenue Overpass, built in the early 1930s and now housing offices. The **320 Boston Building** on Boston Ave, known in the 1920s as the "Oil Bank of America," is worth a look for its huge brass doors, gargoyles, and hand-painted ceilings. Further along the other side of the road, another distinctive Twenties skyscraper, the **Philtower**, 527 S Boston Ave, has a green- and red-tiled sloping roof and crouching gargoyles, a lobby richly decorated in brass and marble, and a small gallery of Tulsa history. **Lyon's Indian Store**, an old trading post a few blocks east at 401 E 11th St, sells authentic goods made by more than thirty Oklahoman tribes, including feather headdresses, bead work, rugs, and jewelry. At 1301 S Boston Ave, the huge and gloriously exuberant Art Deco **Boston Avenue Methodist Church** – at 255ft in height, it's practically cathedral-sized – offers good views of the city from its fourteenth story (free tours Mon–Fri 9am–4pm, Sun 12.15pm).

Black life in Tulsa was traditionally centered around what is now the **Greenwood Historic District**, a small section of narrow streets north of downtown. In 1921, a brutal race riot erupted outside the city courthouse after a black man was accused of assaulting a white woman in a downtown elevator. The commotion spread to Greenwood, where houses, businesses, and churches were burnt to the ground. Other properties fell victim to urban renewal in the mid-1960s, but community leaders managed to save a small grouping of buildings along Greenwood Avenue and Archer Street. The Greenwood Cultural Center, at 322 N Greenwood Ave (Mon–Fri 9am–5pm;

free), houses the **Goodwin–Chappelle Gallery**, a photographic portrait of the neighborhood's history, as well as the **Oklahoma Jazz Hall of Fame**, a fascinating tribute to jazz greats who were either residents of the state (Wardell Gray, Charlie Christian) or passed through on national tours (Cab Calloway, Dizzy Gillespie, Count Basie) to jam with local talent.

Outside downtown, to the south, the 75ft **Creek Council Oak**, 18th St and Cheyenne Ave, marks the spot where the Creek Indians ended their tortuous migration from Alabama in 1836, and founded Tulsa on the Arkansas River. The tree became a tribal meeting site, used ceremonially until 1896. The airy and stylish **Philbrook Museum of Art**, 2727 S Rockford Rd (Tues, Wed, Fri & Sat 10am–5pm, Thurs 10am–8pm, Sun 11am–5pm; tours Thurs, Sat & Sun; $5), in the house of oil man Waite Phillips in the well-heeled suburb of Mapleridge, is a Florentine-style mansion set amid an oasis of fountains and greenery. Though displays include Native American pottery, African sculpture, Chinese jades, and Renaissance paintings, the house itself is every bit as decorative as the art, with ostentatious marble floors, indoor fountains, and sweeping staircases.

Oral Roberts University, 7777 S Lewis Ave, is a must for kitsch obsessives. The campus, which bears a striking resemblance to Disneyland, welcomes visitors with a 60ft-high monument of hands in prayer. The university and television station concept was inspired by visionary Oral Roberts, who back in 1987 announced that God had decided to "call him home" unless he could raise $4.5 million before a certain deadline. Roberts retreated to a lonely vigil at the top of his **Prayer Tower**, a kind of B-movie spaceship, until he got his money, though his credibility was dented when the tower was allegedly struck by lightning at the moment of the deadline. In the base of the tower, you can now see a sycophantic exhibition, to the strains of a heavenly choir, on the great man's life (Mon–Sat 9am–5pm, Sun 1–5pm). In the upper level, the Abundant Life Prayer Group works 24 hours a day to answer phone calls from faith seekers worldwide.

Just northwest of downtown, the **Gilcrease Museum**, 1400 Gilcrease Museum Rd (Mon–Sat 9am–5pm, Sun 11am–5pm; summer Thurs until 8pm; winter closed Mon; free tours daily at 2pm; $3 donation), is set in the gently rolling Osage Hills, with a fine vista from the back and a good view of downtown from the front. Thomas Gilcrease, of Indian heritage, grew very rich after oil was found on his land. His private collection of Western art includes Native American works, as well as excellent Remingtons, Russells, and Morans.

Eating

Tulsa's **restaurants** are diverse and scattered; good options can be found along E 15th Street and S Peoria Avenue in the fashionable **Brookside** district, while downtown holds several down-home diners.

The Bistro at Brookside 3523 S Peoria St ☏918/749-7737. Inventive dishes and an extensive wine list. The Sunday brunches are well worth sampling.
Bourbon Street Café 1542 E 15th St ☏918/583-5555. Extensive Cajun menu, featuring excellent $5 gumbo. Live jazz Fri at 7pm.
Camerelli's 1536 E 15th St ☏918/582-8900. Inexpensive but tasty Italian pasta dishes, with a heavy carnivorous bent.

Casa Bonita 2120 S Sheridan Rd ☏918/836-6464. Strolling mariachis liven up this enormous restaurant, where large spicy dinners are served in rooms featuring a 20ft waterfall and an erupting volcano.
Metro Diner 3001 E 11th St ☏918/592-2616. Fifties-style diner east of downtown, serving good home-baked pies and chicken-fried steaks, as well as great ice-cream sodas.

Nightlife and entertainment

There is even less to do in downtown Tulsa **after dark** than during the day; 15th and Cherry streets just south of downtown, and S Peoria Avenue by the river, are much livelier. If you visit in early September, try to catch the zydeco music and Creole cooking at the **Backdoor Cajun Music Festival**. Newspapers like the *Urban Tulsa Weekly* and *Tulsa World* carry full nightlife **listings**.

Boston's 1738 S Boston Ave ☏918/583-9520. Popular live music venue, with pub food and pool.

Discoveryland! 10 miles west of downtown on W 41st St ☏918/742-5255 or 1-800/245-6552, ⓦwww.discoverylandusa.com. Outdoor venue for performances of Rodgers and Hammerstein's *Oklahoma!*. June–Aug Mon–Sat; $15; pre-show barbecue at 5.30pm for $9.

The Majestic Brady St and Boston Ave ☏918/584-9494. Live music in a converted warehouse; cover charge also gets you into *The Bowery*, a smaller bar one block up at 201 N Main St.

Spotlight Theatre 1381 Riverside Drive ☏918/587-5030. This Art Deco building has been hosting the freakishly popular melodrama *The Drunkard* for the past fifty years – accompanied by pretzels and sandwiches, every Sat at 8.15pm.

Claremore

Thirty miles northeast of Tulsa on Route 66, **CLAREMORE**, the birthplace of **Will Rogers**, populist comedian, journalist, and Twenties film star, is a shrine to a man being slowly forgotten as his films are no longer seen. His career began with a vaudeville show that included lassoing a horse and its rider while giving a witty commentary, and he was renowned for his pithy and good-natured one-liners. Incredibly, when he died in a plane crash in 1935 there was a nationwide thirty-minute silence. One of his most famous declarations, "I never met a man I didn't like," is inscribed on his statue at the **Will Rogers Memorial**, 1720 Will Rogers Blvd (daily 8am–5pm; free), which displays his possessions, such as his "gag book," together with stills and clips from his films. In September, the **Chili Cookoff and Bluegrass Festival** comes to town with its spicy chili competitions, clogging, and bluegrass gigs.

Bartlesville

For forty miles north of Tulsa, the monotony of the plains is relieved only by clumps of spindly scrub oaks. Then comes quiet **BARTLESVILLE**, dominated by the extraordinary **Price Tower** (Tues–Sat 10am–5pm), designed by Frank Lloyd Wright in 1956 – an ugly, cantilevered green oddity at Sixth St and Dewey Ave, resembling a tall tree. The **Frank Phillips Home**, 1107 SE Cherokee Ave (Wed–Sat 10am–5pm, Sun 1–5pm; donation), built in 1908 by the founder of Phillips Oil, displays oil wealth at its gaudiest, with gold faucets, mirrored ceilings, and marble floors. More impressive is his **Woolaroc Ranch**, thirteen miles southwest in the Blackjack Hills, now a wildlife refuge and museum of Western art and history (Tues–Sun 10am–5pm; June–Aug also Mon 10am–5pm; $5; ⓦwww.woolaroc.org), where over sixty thousand artifacts are scattered throughout seven huge rooms. Paintings and decorative art line the walls, from Native American works to the epic Western scenes of Remington and Russell, while artifacts belonging to various tribes, pioneers, and cowboys are gathered in too great an abundance to take in. Look out for the 95-million-year-old dinosaur egg, exquisite Navajo blankets, scalps taken by Native Americans, and Buffalo Bill's weathered saddle.

For **lodging**, choose between the *Travelers Motel*, 3105 SE Frank Phillips Blvd (☏918/333-1900; ❹), and the more upmarket *Hotel Phillips*, 821 S Johnstone Ave (☏918/336-5600 or 1-800/331-0706; ❹).

Tahlequah

A seventy-minute drive southeast from Tulsa on Hwy-51, **TAHLEQUAH** is the capital of the **Cherokee nation**, formed in 1839 when the Trail of Tears finally reached its end. The sophisticated Cherokee had a written constitution, published the first newspaper in Indian Territory (in both Cherokee and English), and set up the Cherokee female seminary, the first higher education school for women west of the Mississippi. The seminary stands today on the campus of **Northeastern State University** on Hwy-82, which has more Native American students than any other academic institution in the US.

Tahlequah itself is uncommercialized, and the **Cherokee Heritage Center**, three and a half miles south off US-62 (Mon–Sat 10am–5pm, Sun 1–5pm; closed Jan; $8.50; ⓦwww.cherokeeheritage.org), presents Native American culture with more dignity than might be expected. The museum is largely interactive, leading the visitor across the Trail of Tears with the use of powerful audiovisual displays. The entrance fee also gets you into a reconstructed seventeenth-century Indian village that offers arts and crafts demonstrations. Summer performances are put on at the Tsa-La-Gi Amphitheater (℡1-888-999-6007), including the gripping Trail of Tears drama.

For a town with such a lovely Main Street, Tahlequah has a pretty poor selection of **hotels**. The best is the *Holiday Inn Express*, 1 Holiday Drive (℡918-456-7800; ❸), which has a pool. The not-so-exciting, but slightly cheaper, *Tahlequah Motor Lodge*, at 2501 S Muskogee Ave (℡918/456-2350; ❸), is another choice. The *Restaurant of the Cherokees*, on US-62 (℡918/456-2070), has an American-food buffet and is located next to the excellent Cherokee Nation Gift Shop.

Muskogee

In the 1830s, the Creek Indians relocated fifty miles southeast of Tulsa to **MUSKOGEE**. After establishing the town as the central meeting place of the Civilized Tribes, in 1905 Native American leaders gathered here to draw up a plan for their own separate state, which was never to be. The arrival of the railroad in the 1870s and the discovery of oil in 1903 both guaranteed that the town would be usurped by white settlers. The **Five Civilized Tribes Museum**, Honor Heights Drive, Agency Hill (Mon–Sat 10am–5pm, Sun 1–5pm; $3), tells the Native Americans' story through costumes, documents, photographs, and jewelry, along with a reconstructed trading post and a printing room. The other unlikely attraction in town is the USS *Batfish*, a World War II–era submarine moored in the Oklahoma grass at 3500 Batfish Rd (Mon & Wed–Sat 9am–5pm, Sun noon–5pm; $4).

Muskogee is an appealing place, with a dozen **motels** within a few blocks along US-69, including a *Days Inn* at 900 S 32nd St (℡918/683-3911; ❸). It also makes a good base for the crystal-clear **Lake Tenkiller**, thirty miles southeast on US-64. Surrounded by woods, cliffs, and quiet beaches, the lake is perfect for fishing, boating, swimming, and scuba-diving. There are camping facilities, but the place is very touristy; call ℡918/457-4403 for full details. The Muskogee Tourism Center, Hwy-69 at Shawnee St (℡918-684-6363 or 1-888/687-6137, ⓦwww.muskogee.org), can provide details about the popular **azalea festival** held in April.

Oklahoma City and beyond

Oklahoma City and Tulsa are separated by one hundred surprisingly green miles along the Will Rogers Turnpike and the famed **Route 66**. Along this historic highway, known as the "mother road," the Blue Whale in Catoosa and the Round Barn in Arcadia are classic American **roadside attractions**. West of the state capital, I-40 carries you across empty agricultural communities, the tedium only broken by the worthwhile **Route 66 Museum** in Clinton. I-44 to Wichita Falls passes near the ruggedly beautiful **Wichita Mountains Wildlife Refuge**; to the north, in the Oklahoma Panhandle, ranches and tiny hamlets are the only signs of life.

Oklahoma City

OKLAHOMA CITY was created in a matter of hours on April 22, 1889, after a single gunshot signaled the opening of the land to white settlement. What was barren prairie at dawn was by nightfall a city of ten thousand. In 1911 the capital was moved here from nearby Guthrie, and in 1928 oil was discovered. Sitting on one of the nation's largest oilfields, the city was brought up short by the slump in the 1980s, though it remains the largest stocker and feeder cattle market in the world. The economy came alive again in the 1990s, aided by tourism development and an inflated sales tax that funded redevelopment in run-down neighborhoods.

The devastating **bombing** of the Alfred P. Murrah Federal Building on April 19, 1995, which killed 168 people, nineteen of them children, literally tore the heart out of the city; the massive community rescue effort has since helped Oklahoma City regain some of its self-confidence, though it will be a while before the city is fully healed. In June 2001, ex-military recluse Timothy McVeigh was executed for the crime; his accomplice, Terry Nichols, is serving a life sentence in jail for his part. A permanent landscaped memorial has been constructed at the former site of the Murrah building, while the Journal Record Building next door has been turned into the Museum and Institute for the Prevention of Terrorism.

Arrival, information, and getting around

Will Rogers World Airport lies southwest of the city and is connected to downtown by an airport shuttle (around $14 one way; ☏405/681-3311). The **CVB** is downtown at 189 W Sheridan Ave (Mon–Fri 8.30am–5pm; ☏405/297-8912 or 1-800/225-5652, ⓦwww.visitokc.com), not far from **Greyhound** at no. 427; there's also a station at the airport. **Amtrak** comes in once a day from Fort Worth at historic Sante Fe Station, on Sante Fe Street.

The **city bus** depot (ⓦwww.gometro.org, ☏405/235-7433) is at 5th Street and N Hudson Avenue in the northwest part of downtown. Buses run daily except Sunday from 6am until 6pm ($1.10). The **Oklahoma Spirit Streetcars** (Mon–Sat 9am–11pm, Sun 10am–6pm; 50¢) run from the hotel strip in the Meridian and the stockyards to downtown, and up to the Cowboy Museum and Lincoln Park. You can rent **bikes** for $10 a day from Miller's Cycling and Fitness Center, 215 W Boyd (☏405/360-3838).

Accommodation

Rooms are very cheap; try along the interstates, especially I-35 S, for chain motels. B&Bs are a good deal, but even the downtown luxury hotels can be affordable. There is a *KOA* campground fifteen miles east of downtown, on I-40 at exit 166 (☏405/391-5000; $15).

▲ Tulsa, Wichita (KS) & Guthrie

OKLAHOMA CITY

▼ E & Norman

North Canadian River

World of Wings Pigeon Center
The Omniplex
National Cowboy & Western Heritage Center
Oklahoma Firefighters Museum
Lincoln Park

MARTIN LUTHER KING AVENUE

63RD STREET
50TH STREET
LINCOLN BOULEVARD
36TH STREET

KELLEY AVENUE

State Capitol
State Museum of History
Harn Homestead Museum

23RD STREET
SANTA FE AVENUE

Henry Overholser Mansion
Oklahoma Heritage Center

10TH STREET

RENO AVENUE

CLASSEN BOULEVARD

WESTERN AVENUE

ACCOMMODATION
Best Western Saddleback Inn ... C
Howard Johnson Lodge Airport ... B
KOA Campground ... D
Plaza Inn ... E
Westin Oklahoma City ... A

RESTAURANTS, BARS, & CLUBS
Bricktown Brewery ... 1
Cattleman's Steakhouse ... 5
Club Rodeo ... 6
Sushi Neko ... 3
Tapwerks Ale House & Cafe ... 2
VCD's Restaurant and Club ... 4

See Inset

Union Station

35

77
235

40 / 270

North Canadian River

CLASSEN BOULEVARD

PENNSYLVANIA AVENUE

3 4

DOWNTOWN OKLAHOMA CITY

BYERS AVE
STILES AVE
RENO AVE

235

PARK AVE
3RD ST
2ND ST

SW Bell Bricktown Ballpark

SHERIDAN AVE
MAIN ST
OKLAHOMA AVE

1 2

Amtrak / Santa Fe Train Depot

Bricktown Canal
2ND ST
COMPRESS

★ Oklahoma Spirit trolley stops

E.K. GAYLORD DR

40

Memorial Center Museum
Public Library
Oklahoma City National Memorial

5TH ST
4TH ST

E.K. GAYLORD DR
BROADWAY AVE
ROBINSON AVE
HARVEY AVE
DEAN A McGEE AVE
PARK AVE

(i)

A

Myriad Convention Center

Myriad Gardens

HUDSON AVE
WALKER AVE

Union Bus Depot

Metro Transit Bus Terminal

ROBERT S. KERR AVE
COLCORD DR
MAIN ST
DEWEY AVE
CALIFORNIA AVE
RENO AVE
LEE AVE
SHERIDAN AVE

SHARTEL AVE

250 yds

Oklahoma State Fair Park

MAY AVENUE

PORTLAND AVENUE

44
3

Stockyards City

5

▼ 6 & Will Rogers World Airport

MERIDIAN AVENUE
MACARTHUR BOULEVARD
10TH STREET
RENO AVENUE

ROCKWELL AVENUE

N

1 mile

40 / 270

COUNCIL ROAD

▲ Amarillo (TX)

▲ D

66
35

Best Western Saddleback Inn 4300 SW 3rd St
☎ 405/947-7000. One block north of I-40, on the
west side of town. Pseudo-Indian decor, with luxurious touches like poolside service. ❹
Howard Johnson Lodge Airport 400 S Meridian
Ave ☎ 405/943-9841. Standard rooms close to the
freeway, with breakfast included. ❸
Plaza Inn I-35 and 29th St ☎ 405/672-2341. No-

frills accommodation to suit a backpacker's
budget. ❷
Ramada Inn Airport South 6800 I-35 S
☎ 405/631-3321. Functional accommodation
directly east of the airport. ❸
Westin Oklahoma City 1 N Broadway
☎ 405/235-2780. Smart rooms with very comfortable beds in the heart of downtown. ❻

The City

Tumbleweeds no longer roll through downtown Oklahoma City, but the city
center remains a quiet affair, with low-key skyscrapers and little in the way of
commercial activity. The hub of activity is around the renovated warehouses of
Bricktown, on Sheridan Ave east of the Santa Fe Railroad, which has developed into a reasonable eating and nightlife center. **Myriad Gardens** on
Sheridan Ave, prettily landscaped with hills, gardens, and waterways, gives great
views across to the brick-towered downtown skyline, and on a sunny day the
Crystal Bridge tropical botanical garden, in a glass tube in the middle of the
park, abounds in garish exotic blooms (daily 9am–6pm; $5).

A few blocks north, at 620 N Harvey Ave, where the Federal Building stood
until the 1995 bombing, throngs of visitors mill somberly about the
Oklahoma City National Memorial (open 24hrs; free). The site, which
dominates the center of the city, includes a field of 168 empty bronze and glass
chairs, and a black reflecting pool flanked by two massive gold barriers marking 9.01–9.03am – the moment of destruction. Nearby, an elm tree that continued to bloom after the blast stands as a lone sentinel. The **Memorial
Center Museum** behind it (Mon–Sat 9am–6pm, Sun 1–6pm; $7) is also
worth a visit, recounting the tragedy in gruesome detail, with TV news coverage from the day, interviews with survivors, and items pulled from the wreckage, such as shredded clothing, cracked coffee mugs, and twisted filing cabinets.
Other sections describe the ensuing FBI investigation and McVeigh trial, and
on the ground floor are tributes to the victims. Outside, the complex is surrounded by a chain-link fence weighed down by tokens and talismans left by
grief-stricken mourners.

Just northeast of downtown, a working oil well pumps crude from underneath the **Capitol Building** (Mon–Fri 8am–4.30pm; free), which sports a
new dome. The Capitol Complex includes the **State Museum of History**
(Mon–Sat 8am–5pm; free), which is located in a new facility across from the
Governor's Mansion. The **Heritage Hills** area nearby, where the cattle barons,
oil millionaires, and bankers used to live, is worth a visit for the luxurious
Victorian **Overholser Mansion**, 405 NW 15th St (Tues–Sat 10am–4pm, Sun
2–4pm; hourly tours $3); nearby, the **Harn Homestead Museum**, 313 NE
16th St (Mon–Fri 10am–4pm; $3), is also worth a wander for its old barn, wag-
ons, and general pioneer spirit.

Sitting atop Persimmon Hill overlooking Route 66, the **National Cowboy
Museum and Heritage Center**, 1700 NE 63rd St (daily: June–Aug
8.30am–6pm; Sept–May 9am–5pm; $8.50; ⓦ www.nationalcowboymuseum.org),
is a real treat, combining "high art" and popular art in one loving collection. In
the works of Remington and Russell the link between Western art and Western
movies is very clear. The paintings look like film stills, and titles such as *Waiting for
Trouble* evoke the cinema's endlessly reworked myths of the West. Large exhibitions focus on contemporary Native American work, much of it colorful, bitter,
and subversive. John Wayne's collection is a delight for the cowboy fetishist, and
the Western Performers Hall of Fame pays homage to movie cowboys and cow-

girls in hilariously reverent oil paintings and memorabilia. The poignant *End of the Trail* sculpture, eighteen feet high, portrays an Indian slumped exhausted – or dead – over his horse. You can also venture into Prosperity Town (a mock-up of a Western town, with details down to hoof marks in the road), the American Rodeo Gallery, and a learning center for little buckaroos. In the garden, dotted with horse graves, corny epigraphs give the much-loved deceased beasts a fitting send-off to "Hoss Heaven."

Lincoln Park, squeezed between Martin Luther King Drive and Hwy-35, contains the **Firefighter's Museum**, the **City Zoo**, and the **Omniplex** (ten acres of futuristic exhibits, with an aquarium and planetarium). At the northern end of the park, the modest **World of Wings Pigeon Center** (Mon–Fri 10am–4pm; free; ⓦ www.pigeoncenter.org) specially breeds homing pigeons for racing. You can inspect the small museum and aviary that houses racing breeds and "fancy" pigeons bred for their looks.

Oklahoma City's **stockyards**, on Agnew Ave and Exchange St, are the busiest in the world, having sold over one hundred million cattle since 1910. They're well worth a visit, though vegetarians and animal-lovers should steer clear. This is the real thing, stomping, snorting, and smelly, with scrawny animals shunted in and out of tiny pens for auction. The roughnecks that spend their lives here, smoking, chatting, even sleeping, take no apparent notice of the quick-fire auctioneer, but nonetheless millions of head of cattle are bought and sold each year, and it can make for addictive entertainment. Morning sales, starting at 8am (Monday and Tuesday only), are the most intense, fizzling out by late afternoon.

Eating

Beef is, of course, good in Oklahoma City, especially around the stockyards. The warehouse restaurants of **Bricktown** are popular with the after-work and singles crowds.

Catfish Cabin 6317 N Meridian Ave ☎ 405/721-7553. This local joint serves up legendary catfish to a loyal crowd.

Cattleman's Steakhouse 1309 S Agnew Ave ☎ 405/236-0416. Cattlemen from the adjacent stockyards eat in this comfortable, pub-like restaurant, which has served great steaks since 1910. The place was allegedly won in a craps game. Lunchtime specials are a good deal.

Sushi Neko 4318 N Western Ave ☎ 405/528-8862. Trendy Japanese restaurant with excellent sushi and outdoor seating.

TapWerks Ale House and Café 121 E Sheridan Ave ☎ 405/319-9599. Very popular Bricktown restaurant with a British-influenced menu and a long list of beers. Open late.

Nightlife and entertainment

If you're into **country music**, Oklahoma City will set you right, with quite a few live music and dance venues. Beyond that, though, there's not much else, other than a few **pubs**, and some progressive **clubs** – especially those in **Bricktown**, which attempt to part Oklahoma City from its cowtown image. For a younger crowd, check out the **Crown Heights** district, north of downtown. Wednesday's *Oklahoma Gazette*, along with lively articles, carries good **listings**.

Bricktown Brewer 1 Oklahoma Ave ☎ 405/232-BREW. Large brewpub, with giant tanks of beer on show in its restaurant. Live jazz most nights.

Club Rodeo 2301 S Meridian Ave ☎ 405/686-1191. Popular dance hall and saloon with nightly live music. Can get a little cheesy some nights, other nights are rollicking fun. Quite a way southwest of downtown, but worth the trip. Hours and cover vary.

Oklahoma Opry 404 W Commerce Ave ☎ 405/632-8322. Popular venue for authentic country music shows, in the style of Nashville's Grand Ole Opry. One show a week, Sat 8pm.

VCD's Restaurant and Club 4200 N Western Ave ☎ 405/524-4203. Cheap and varied food by day, garage rock and the city's few hipsters by night.

Guthrie

GUTHRIE, thirty miles north of downtown Oklahoma City on I-35, was Oklahoma's capital from statehood in 1907 until 1911. Today the 1400-acre **Guthrie Historical District** forms a remarkably complete collection of tastefully restored Victorian architecture. The **State Capitol Publishing Museum**, 301 W Harrison Ave (Tues–Fri 9am–5pm, Sat 10am–4pm, Sun 1–4pm; donation), exhibits printing technology dating back to the earliest newspaper printed in the Oklahoma Territory. The ornate **Doric Scottish Rite Masonic Temple**, 900 E Oklahoma Ave (tours Mon–Fri 10am & 2pm, Sat 10am; $5), is the largest Masonic complex in the world, featuring hundreds of bright stained-glass windows. Guthrie is also home to the **Lazy E Arena**, four miles east of downtown, a huge site which hosts world-champion **rodeos** and **roping competitions**, as well as big-name concerts (☎405/282-3004).

Guthrie's visitor center is at 212 W Oklahoma Ave (Mon–Fri 9am–5pm, Sat 9am–1pm; ☎405/282-1947 or 1-800/299-1889, ⊛www.guthrieok.com). The town has several good **B&Bs**, including the *Haunted Stone Lion Inn*, 1016 W Warner Ave (☎405/282-0012; ❹), a 1907 Victorian mansion with clean rooms and antique claw-foot tubs. The *Harrison House*, 124 W Harrison Ave (☎405/282-1000 or 1-800/375-1001; ❹), is larger than most B&Bs, but still charming; it's housed in Guthrie's first bank building. Cheaper is the *Townhouse Motel*, 223 E Oklahoma Ave (☎405/260-2400; ❷). The *Blue Belle Saloon*, 224 W Harrison, is Oklahoma's oldest **saloon**; the place boasts that Tom Mix tended bar here before going on to Hollywood fame.

Missouri

The state of **MISSOURI**, where the forest meets the prairie and the Mississippi River meets the Missouri River, has just two significant cities. Dominant **St Louis** sits midway down the state's eastern fringe; **Kansas City** is almost directly across on the western border. The pair are linked by I-70, but there's not much in between to warrant stopping off. In contrast, the south features the beautiful hillsides, streams, and ragged lakes of the **Ozark Mountains**, as well as the booming country-and-western town of **Branson**; while in the east, small river towns such as **Hannibal** and serene **Ste Genevieve** brighten the course of the Mississippi. The northwest, home of the Pony Express and outlaw Jesse James, still strikes up images of frontier times.

Although the first French colonists honored the claims of local Native Americans, such as the original Missouri, when the area was sold to the US in 1803 as part of the **Louisiana Purchase**, the Indians were driven west by a great rush of settlers. In the 1840s and 1850s immigrants from Germany and Ireland flooded into eastern Missouri. Outnumbering their pro-slavery predecessors, they swung the balance in favor of staying in the Union during the **Civil War**. However, Confederate guerrilla forces attracted considerable support among slave-owners in the west of the state. Meanwhile, Missouri, and St Louis in particular, was establishing itself as an important **gateway to the**

West. Today, the "Show Me State" (so called because of the supposed skepticism of the typical Missourian) retains a **conservative** air, particularly in its rural areas.

Getting around Missouri

The central corridor between St Louis and Kansas City is well served by **Greyhound**; the journey between the two takes around six hours. Infrequent Greyhound buses run through the southeast, to Springfield and a few Ozark towns, but you'll need a **car** to see the mountains and the river towns in the north. St Louis and Kansas City have major **airports**. Daily Amtrak **trains** from Chicago run to St Louis, from where direct connections can be made to Kansas City, San Antonio, Fort Worth, and Little Rock. For keen **cyclists**, there's the popular Katy Trail, which stretches 230 miles from St Charles to Clinton.

Eastern Missouri

The Mississippi defines Missouri's eastern border, absorbing as major tributaries the Missouri, Ohio, Illinois, and Des Moines rivers. Over the years, innumerable towns have sprung up along the river, their aspirations reflected by such classical names as Alexandria, Antioch, and Athens. **Hannibal**, the boyhood home of **Mark Twain**, is the largest in the northeast, while Gallic **Ste Genevieve** is the prettiest in the south. All have, however, decreased in importance with the growing pre-eminence of **St Louis**. Away from the river, the land rises to the Ozark Plateau, whose deep green valleys are cut by swift, clear streams.

Hannibal

HANNIBAL might well have been just another medium-sized river settlement, had not Samuel Langhorne Clemens, who renamed himself **Mark Twain**, after the cry of pilots on the Mississippi, spent his boyhood here. Although Hannibal does have other industries, downtown is little more than a Twain theme park, with attractions such as museums, period buildings, and wax displays. Just about every business in town is flogging souvenirs featuring Twain's ashen visage, or is named for the scribe, including Huck's Taxi Service, *Injun Joe Campground*, and even the Mark Twain Roofing Company.

Twain wrote surprisingly little about his home town in his extensive nonfiction works; you could say he spoke with his feet when he left for good at 17 to become a journeyman printer, riverboat pilot, journalist, and writer. However, those of his books most specifically set in Hannibal – *The Adventures of Tom Sawyer* and the sequel *The Adventures of Huckleberry Finn* – provide vivid accounts of growing up in the rowdy frontier riverport he renamed St Petersburg for his books.

The Town

Hannibal's riverside location and historical buildings make it almost disturbingly picturesque. Squeezed between two steep bluffs – Tom Sawyer's **"Cardiff Hill"** to the north and **Lover's Leap** to the south – the once-busy community is now quiet except for the occasional creaking of a crane loading cement. You can get an intimate look at the Mississippi aboard the slow-moving **Mark Twain riverboat** (1hr tours 11am, 1.30pm & 4pm, $10; 2hr dinner cruise by reservation 6.30pm, $28; ☎573/221-3222). Twain's youthful stomping-ground was the short, cobbled incline of **Hill Street**, at the north end of town. Adjoining the restored **Mark Twain Boyhood Home**, a simple white-clapboard house where Twain lived between 1844 and 1853, the **Mark Twain Museum** (summer daily 8am–6pm; rest of year times vary; $6; ☎573/221-9010) includes such memorabilia as first editions, letters, photos, original artwork, and one of the author's trademark white coats. Immediately opposite, there's a bookstore in the original home of Laura Hawkins (the model for Tom Sawyer's first love, Becky Thatcher), who visited Twain in Connecticut in 1908 and lived on in Hannibal until 1928. Nearby stands the law office of Twain's father, a justice of the peace who died of pneumonia while the writer was still a boy. Antique, souvenir, and gift stores stretch away from here down **Main Street**, which also holds the **New Mark Twain Museum** (summer daily 9am–6pm; rest of year times vary; same phone as above). Included in the admission price to the original museum and home, the exhibits here re-create scenes from Twain's books, the cave and Huck Finn's raft among them. Upstairs at the gift shop are the fifteen original **Norman Rockwell paintings** commissioned for limited editions of Twain's most popular titles.

About two miles south of town is the **Mark Twain Cave** (summer daily 8am–8pm; times vary rest of the year; $12; ☎573/221-1656) where one-hour tours recall Tom's and Becky's frightening misadventure in the dark. Further south, Hwy-79 towards St Louis offers one of the most **scenic drives** along the Mississippi, continually broken by thin, elongated, thickly wooded islands, and bounded by towering limestone bluffs.

Practicalities

Pick up full details on Hannibal from the **visitor center**, 505 N Third St (April–Oct daily 8am–6pm; Nov–March Mon–Fri 8am–5pm, Sat & Sun limited hours; ☎573/221-2477, ⓦwww.visithannibal.com). **Motel** rates vary wildly according to season. The very central *Best Western Hotel Clemens*, 401 N Third St (☎573/248-1150; ❹), with a pool, is pretty good value, while the *Hannibal Inn*, US-61 at Market St (☎573/221-6610; ❸), on the edge of town, is more basic. *Lula Belle's*, 111 Bird St (☎573/221-6662 or 1-800/882-4890; ❸–❼), has **B&B** rooms of varying degrees of luxury, including some with river views, and serves tasty food. The *Mark Twain Dinette & Family Restaurant*, just up from the Mark Twain Museum at 400 N Third St (☎573/221-5300), serves classic American fare. A mile south of town on Hwy-79, you can **camp** at the shaded *Mark Twain Campground* (☎573/221-1656 or 1-800/527-0304; $17.50 for tents, $21.50 for RVs).

St Louis

Perched just below the confluence of the Mississippi and Missouri rivers, three hundred miles south of Chicago and north of Memphis, cosmopolitan **ST LOUIS** (pronounced, whatever any song might say, "Saint Lewis") owes its vaguely European air to its history and developed cultural infrastructure. Any city capable of producing one of the twentieth century's greatest poets, as well as one of its greatest rock 'n' rollers – namely, **T.S. Eliot** and **Chuck Berry** – probably has a lot going for it.

St Louis was founded in 1764 by the French fur trader Pierre Laclede. However, the American immigration that followed its sale to the US under the **Louisiana Purchase** all but extinguished the refinement it had gained during French and Spanish rule. It subsequently became crucial as the major gateway

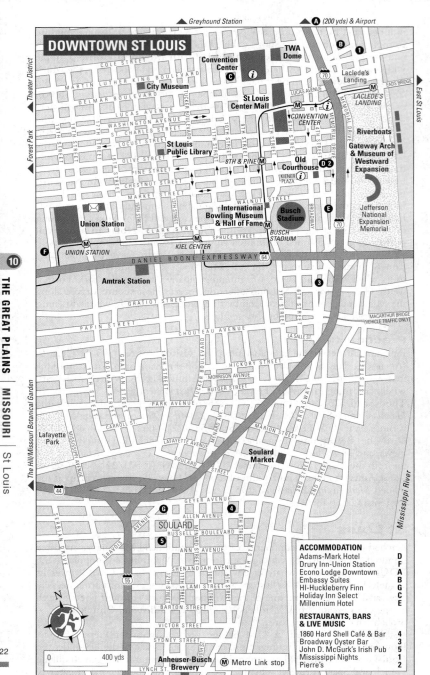

DOWNTOWN ST LOUIS

▲ Greyhound Station
▲ Ⓐ (200 yds) & Airport
Ⓑ
❶

Theater District ◄
Forest Park ◄
The Hill/Missouri Botanical Garden ◄
East St Louis ►

COLE STREET
MARTIN LUTHER KING BOULEVARD
DELMAR BOULEVARD
City Museum
LUCAS AVENUE
WASHINGTON AVENUE
ST CHARLES STREET
LOCUST STREET
OLIVE STREET
PINE STREET
CHESTNUT STREET
MARKET STREET
CLARK STREET
SPRUCE STREET

19TH STREET
18TH STREET
17TH STREET
16TH STREET
15TH STREET
14TH STREET
TUCKER BOULEVARD
12TH STREET
11TH STREET
10TH STREET
9TH STREET
8TH STREET
7TH STREET
6TH STREET

Convention Center Ⓒ
ⓘ
TWA Dome
St Louis Center Mall Ⓜ
CONVENTION CENTER
ⓘ
LUCAS AVENUE
MEMORIAL DRIVE
Laclede's Landing Ⓜ
EADS BRIDGE
LACLEDE'S LANDING
Riverboats

St Louis Public Library
8TH & PINE Ⓜ
Old Courthouse
KIENER PLAZA ⓘ
Ⓓ ❷
Gateway Arch & Museum of Westward Expansion

WALNUT STREET
International Bowling Museum & Hall of Fame
Busch Stadium
Ⓔ
BROADWAY
Jefferson National Expansion Memorial

Union Station
Ⓜ
Ⓜ KIEL CENTER
Ⓕ UNION STATION
DANIEL BOONE EXPRESSWAY 64

Amtrak Station
GRATIOT STREET
PAPIN STREET
CHOUTEAU AVENUE
❸
7TH STREET
LA SALLE ST
MACARTHUR BRIDGE (VEHICLE TRAFFIC ONLY)

HICKORY STREET
MORRISON AVENUE
RUTGER STREET
PARK AVENUE
CARROLL ST
TUCKER BOULEVARD
GRATTAN STREET
DOLMAN STREET
14TH STREET
13TH STREET
MENARD AVE
BROADWAY
MARION STREET
3RD STREET
2ND STREET
1ST STREET

Lafayette Park
LAFAYETTE AVENUE
SOULARD STREET
Soulard Market

Mississippi River ►

44
GEYER AVENUE
ALLEN AVENUE
Ⓖ ❹
SOULARD
RUSSELL BOULEVARD
❺
ANN AVENUE
SHENANDOAH AVENUE
LAMI STREET
BARTON STREET
VICTOR STREET
SYDNEY STREET
55
GRAVOIS AVENUE
SERBIAN DRIVE
MISSISSIPPI AVENUE

N

822

0   400 yds

Anheuser-Busch Brewery
LYNCH ST

Ⓜ Metro Link stop

ACCOMMODATION

Adams-Mark Hotel	D
Drury Inn-Union Station	F
Econo Lodge Downtown	A
Embassy Suites	B
HI-Huckleberry Finn	G
Holiday Inn Select	C
Millennium Hotel	E

RESTAURANTS, BARS & LIVE MUSIC

1860 Hard Shell Café & Bar	4
Broadway Oyster Bar	3
John D. McGurk's Irish Pub	5
Mississippi Nights	1
Pierre's	2

for pioneers on the wagon trails westward. **Transportation** – first steamboats, then trains, and now air haulage – has long been the basis of its considerable industrial strength. However, St Louis has not always had an easy ride. Downtown reached a nadir during the 1970s, but the years since then have seen a remarkable turnaround, with attractions on the revitalized **riverfront** including the magnificent **Gateway Arch** and the restored warehouses of **Laclede's Landing**.

Try not to leave without sampling the **outlying districts**. To the west lie arty **Central West End** and studenty **University** (or "U") **City**, on either side of prodigious **Forest Park**, with its museums and playing fields. The blue-collar **southside** features the markets, antique shops, and jazz pubs of **Soulard** and the Italian shops and cafés of **the Hill**. Directly across the river in Illinois, **East St Louis**, once the stomping ground of jazz stars like Miles Davis and John Coltrane, has very little to offer visitors.

Arrival, information, and getting around

Lambert–St Louis International Airport is a dozen miles northwest of downtown – $27 by taxi or $3 by bus or Metro Link. Some **Greyhound** buses call at the airport, though the main terminal is downtown at 1450 N 13th St. **Amtrak** stops at 550 S 16th St and Market St downtown.

The city has **visitor centers** near the riverfront at 308 Washington Ave (daily 9.30am–4.30pm; ☎314/241-1764), a few blocks back at the America Center in the massive Cervantes Convention Center (Mon–Fri 9am–5pm; ☎1-800/916-0092), and at Kiener Plaza (Mon–Fri 9am–5pm, Sat 9am–2pm; closed Jan & Feb; ☎314/231-0336). For the latest **events**, visit ⊛www.explorestlouis.com.

The Bi-State Transit System (☎314/231-2345) operates the **MetroLink**, a light-rail system serving the airport and most significant tourist sights ($1.25;

T.S. Eliot and Chuck Berry

Thomas Stearns Eliot, who as a naturalized Englishman won the 1948 Nobel Prize for Literature, was born in St Louis on September 26, 1888. His Unitarian aristocrat family traced their ancestry back to the earliest days of settlement in New England; his grandfather, the Rev William Eliot, founded St Louis' Washington University. Eliot lived in the city until he was seventeen, and went to school at Smith Academy on Union Avenue, a period which he later referred to as one of the happiest of his life. The "Prufrock" of his first major poem, "The Love Song of J. Alfred Prufrock," was a St Louis furniture dealer; "the yellow fog that rubs its back upon the window-panes" was the smog drifting across the Mississippi from the city's factories.

Once Eliot had moved to Boston, to attend Harvard University, and then on to Europe, he rarely returned, and he deliberately threw off his drawling St Louis accent. The house in which he was born, at 2635 Locust St, has long since been torn down, and the only memorial to him in the city is the incongruous brass star set into the sidewalk of Delmar Boulevard as part of the St Louis Walk of Fame.

Another honoree of the Walk of Fame, **Chuck Berry**, first saw the light of day on October 18, 1926, at 2520 Goode Ave – an address echoed in his most famous song, "Johnny B. Goode." Berry played his earliest gigs at the *Cosmopolitan Club* at 17th and Bond in East St Louis. Initially seen as a bizarre hybrid, a black hillbilly singing country-and-western, within a few months of his first recording for Chess Records in Chicago ("Maybellene," in 1955), Chuck Berry's blend of razor-sharp lyrics and incisive guitar-playing – not to mention his legendary business acumen – had made him the definitive rock 'n' roll songwriter.

free in downtown Mon–Fri 11am–1.30pm). BSTS buses also go to all of the city's suburbs, though service can be slow and infrequent. Big Shark Bicycle Company, near Forrest Park at 6681 Delmar Blvd ($5/hour or $20/day; ☎314/862-1188), rents **bikes**.

Accommodation

Good-value **lodging** can be found downtown, with appealing weekend rates. For **B&Bs**, contact the Greater St Louis Reservation Service, PO Box 30069, MO 63119 (☎314/961-2252).

Best Western Inn at the Park 4630 Lindell Blvd ☎314/367-7500 or 1-800/373-7501. Good chain motel on the northeast corner of Forrest Park, right by the cafés of Central West End. ❺

Drury Inn – Union Station 201 S 20th St ☎314/231-3900 or 1-800/325-8300. Very tastefully restored accommodation. ❺

Econo Lodge Downtown 1100 N 3rd St ☎314/421-6556. The least expensive downtown option, just a short walk from Laclede's Landing. The area's not pleasant at night, though. ❸

Embassy Suites 901 N 1st St ☎314/241-4200. Comfortable suites in the heart of Laclede's Landing. Buffet breakfast included. ❼

HI-Huckleberry Finn 1904-1908 S 12th St ☎314/241-0076. Dorms (members $18, non-members $21) and single rooms without AC. On the edge of a dodgy area in Soulard, so take bus #73 or #30 from downtown. Office hours 8–10am & 6–10pm. ❶

Holiday Inn Airport Oakland Park 4505 Woodson Rd ☎314/427-4700. Earnest artwork by the deceased owner hangs everywhere at this personable chain. Very close to the airport. ❸

Holiday Inn Select 811 N 9th St ☎314-421-4000. Comfortable rooms and an indoor pool. Next to the Convention Center downtown. ❺

Millennium Hotel 200 S 4th St ☎314/241-9500 or 1-800/325-7353. Ideal downtown setting, with all the facilities you'd expect from a hotel of its size, including a restaurant, fitness center, and business center. ❹–❼

Napoleon's Retreat 1815 Lafayette Ave ☎314/772-6979. Attractive, homey B&B near Lafayette Square, with appealing rates and friendly service. ❹–❺

The riverfront

The one-and-a-half-mile cobbled granite **wharf** along the Mississippi used to lie in the shadow of a dense tangle of warehouses and factories. When river trade decreased, these became an embarrassing eyesore, and most were ripped down. However, some restored structures between the Eads and Martin Luther King bridges now form **Laclede's Landing Historic District**, their cast-iron facades fronting antique stores, office suites, restaurants, and live music venues. In late August, the district hosts the **Big Muddy Blues Festival**, featuring artists of national prominence and a great party atmosphere (information on ☎314/241-5875, ⓦwww.lacledeslanding.org).

On the waterfront itself, where roustabouts once handled cargoes of cotton and ores, assorted permanently moored vessels hold museums, theater shows, a heliport, and casinos. **Cruises** aboard replica paddle-wheelers leave from under the Gateway Arch (April–Nov daily 10am–4.15pm; $9; dinner cruises depart at 7pm, $32.50; ☎314/621-4040 or 1-800/878-7411).

Ten minutes' walk south, more than thirty blocks of derelict buildings were torn down to clear space for the **Jefferson National Expansion Memorial**, dedicated to the US president who negotiated the Louisiana Purchase and thereby opened up the West, and to the pioneers who journeyed along the Oregon and Santa Fe trails. Its highlight, the **Gateway Arch**, designed by Eero Saarinen, was completed in 1965, a 630ft stainless steel parabola of majestic symmetry; in technical terms it's a weighted catenary curve, the outline formed by a heavy cable hanging freely from two points. The arch is at its most striking when its gleaming coat catches a stray reflection – perhaps a rich red sunset or a fireworks display.

So long as you're not claustrophobic, it's fun to take the four-minute **tram ride** up the hollow curving arch. Tiny five-seater capsules carry you to a viewing gallery, repeatedly shifting position as they go so you don't arrive at the top upside down. The views of the Midwestern plains, St Louis, and the mighty Mississippi are spectacular, though looking straight down will make you dizzy. Lengthy lines build up during summer, but you can pick up a numbered ticket earlier in the day and come back at the allotted time. Still, you'll have to wait in another line for the elevator, so expect a 45min roundtrip (daily summer 8.30am–9.20pm; rest of year 9.30am–5.20pm; $7).

In a massive bunker beneath the arch, the **visitor center** (daily: summer 8am–10pm; rest of year 9am–6pm; ☎314/982-1410) shows a riveting **film** about the construction of the monument, and another on the **Lewis and Clark Expedition**, which set off from St Louis in 1804 to explore the Missouri River, as well as potential water passages to the Pacific Ocean ($6 for one film, $10 for two). The expedition returned two years later with details of trade routes, Native American settlements, and observations on animal and plant life. Also in the visitor center complex, the spacious **Museum of Westward Expansion** (free) recounts the Lewis and Clark story, drawing heavily on the pair's very readable journals, while the **Arch Odyssey Theater** shows **IMAX** epics on a four-story screen.

Nearby, engineering buffs will take note of the extraordinary (if not all that attractive) **Eads Bridge**. Completed in 1876, the massive steel structure was St Louis' first bridge across the Mississippi, doing much to facilitate the railroad boom of the gilded age. Pedestrians and cyclists can cross the bridge for excellent views of the city's **skyline**.

Central downtown

One block from the arch along St Louis' main east–west thoroughfare, Market Street, old photographs at the stately **Old Courthouse Museum** (daily 8am–4.30pm; free) record the development of the city and the settling of the West. Two restored courtrooms were the site of the trial of **Dred Scott**, a black slave who argued that having spent time with his owner in non-slave Illinois and Wisconsin, he had the right to be set free. His case was upheld in 1850, but overturned two years later. On appeal, the Supreme Court declared that Scott, born a slave in a slave state, might, like any other chattel, be taken anywhere his master chose to go. The decision, which meant that the US Constitution saw slaves as legitimate personal property, sent shock waves through the corridors of government and hastened the onrush of the **Civil War**. Scott himself, by now a nationally known figure, was voluntarily freed by his new owner, though he died a year later.

The **International Bowling Museum and Hall of Fame**, at 111 Stadium Plaza (summer Mon–Sat 9am–5pm, Sun noon–5pm; rest of year daily 11am–4pm; $6, includes four free frames), is devoted to the favorite sport of such diverse figures as Martin Luther and Homer Simpson, tracing its history from ancient Egypt to the present. It may come as some surprise to learn of bowling's rowdy history: excessive betting on games got it denounced by the Church in fifteenth-century Germany and, three centuries later, the behavior of drunken fans led to all lanes being shut down in London.

See the world's largest pair of underpants and witness the mystic power of the corndog at the whimsical **City Museum**, 701 N 15th St (Wed–Fri 9am–5pm, Sat & Sun 10am–5pm; $7.50; ⓦwww.citymuseum.org). The exhibits, made almost entirely of junk, often border on the bizarre, as one floor is devoted to secret passages and dead-ends. On entering, you will be informed, "Have fun, and don't lose your adult." Over on Market Street at 18th, the focal point of the giant Romanesque **Union Station** is a 230ft clock tower. The station, erected in 1884, was transformed in the early 1980s into a huge complex of shops, cafés, bars, and a hotel. An artificial lake, where you can rent boats, is in the back. The *Hyatt Hotel's* ornate lobby, once the station's main waiting room, is well worth visiting.

West of downtown

Three miles west of downtown, the **theater district**, called **Grand Center**, is staked out with ornate street lamps along Grand Avenue between Lindell and Delmar boulevards. Bright posters advertise the current shows at the **Fabulous Fox Theater**, 527 N Grand Ave (tours Tues, $5; Thurs & Sat, $8, including a special organ performance at 10.30am; ⊤314/534-1111), where you can have a look at the magnificent Siamese-Byzantine interior and massive Wurlitzer organ.

About a mile further west, on the edge of **Forest Park**, trendy shops, wine bars, and c.1900 mansions line the leafy thoroughfares of the **Central West End** district. A few blocks away at 4431 Lindell Blvd, the Romanesque-Byzantine **Cathedral of St Louis**, referred to by locals as the New Cathedral, houses the world's largest collection of mosaic art (daily: May–Sept 7am–7pm; Oct–April 7am–5pm; free).

The decision to put Forest Park four miles directly west of downtown (served by MetroLink every 10 to 30 minutes depending on time of day) aroused much criticism during the 1870s, with opponents claiming that its inaccessibility would make it merely a pleasure ground for the local rich. It's larger than New York's Central Park, and every bit as full of attractions; in summer, the 12,000-seat amphitheater is regularly filled for the Broadway-style **musical theater productions** (⊤314/361-1900, ⓦ www.muny.com).

Standing on **Art Hill** in the central western section of the park, the striking **Beaux Arts St Louis Art Museum** (Tues 1.30–8.30pm, Wed–Sun 10am–5pm; tours at 1.30pm; free), is the only surviving structure from the 1904 World's Fair. Its brief – to cover international art from prehistoric times onwards – may be ambitious, but none of the galleries can be considered as weak points or fillers. It houses one of the world's most extensive collections of **German Expressionism**, devoting an entire gallery to the powerful, spiraling, jagged images of Max Beckmann, and its pre-Columbian artworks cover every significant style, medium, and culture from Mexico to Peru.

In addition to the animals in its "cageless displays," the **St Louis Zoo** (daily 9am–5pm, in summer until 8pm on Tues; free), set in beautiful grounds in the park, boasts a "Living World" exhibit, in which an animatronic robot of Charles Darwin gives synopses of his theories.

The main strengths of the **History Museum**, on the northern fringe of the park (Tues 9.30am–8.30pm, Wed–Sun 9.30am–5pm; free), are its thematic collections of old photos of St Louis, documenting river life, black music in the city, and Charles Lindbergh's 1927 flight in the *Spirit of St Louis* (sponsored by the city's aircraft industry) from New York to Paris. The **St Louis Science Center** (daily: winter 9am–5pm, Fri until 9pm; summer 9am–6pm, Tues until 9pm; free) straddles I-64 and can be entered from either side of the freeway; use one of the radar guns on the covered access bridge to check the speed of cars on the freeway below. General admission is free, but it costs a few dollars to get into the planetarium, the OMNIMAX Theater, and other major exhibits.

Southside

The tens of thousands of Germans who came to St Louis in the mid-eighteenth century settled mostly in the **southside**, which has retained a noticeable

Teutonic influence. These immigrants were skilled brewers; only one of the breweries they opened from the 1850s onwards still stands, but it does happen to be the largest in the world. The one hundred intricate redbrick buildings of the **Anheuser–Busch plant**, 12th and Lynch streets (summer Mon–Sat 9am–5pm, Sun 11.30am–5pm; winter 9am–4pm, Sun 11.30–1pm; free), produce annually a sizeable proportion of the company's 14.3 million barrels of beer, including Budweiser and Michelob. Free **tours** (80min) are mostly company PR, but they're still good fun, and you get two glasses of beer before being shunted into the gift shop.

A few blocks towards downtown, the colorful **Soulard Market**, at Broadway and Lafayette avenues (Wed–Fri 8am–5.30pm, Sat 6am–5.30pm), is a great place to pick up picnic items and fresh fruit, especially on a Saturday. The terraced streets behind it hold the city's best blues and jazz pubs.

Red- white-and-green fire hydrants let you know that you're in the thirty-square-block **Hill district**, a small, neat Italian community three miles east of Soulard. At its heart, **St Ambrose Church** displays a statue of Italian immigrants; all around, the aroma of freshly baked bread drifts out of the small specialty bakeries that share the area with one-room grocery stores and dozens of restaurants.

Just east of the Hill District, at 4344 Shaw Blvd, the 79-acre **Missouri Botanical Garden** (daily 9am–5pm, summer Mon until 8pm; $7; Ⓦ www.mobot.org) is a haven of peace and tranquility, just a few hundred yards from busy I-44. The grounds contain everything from a magnificent Japanese garden through scented rose and English woodland gardens to the Climatron, a huge greenhouse that re-creates a tropical rainforest complete with waterfalls and cliffs.

St Charles

The beautiful little river town of **ST CHARLES**, 25 miles northwest of downtown St Louis and forever threatened by flooding, remains redolent with lazy charm, despite the advent of its first riverboat casino. Three small though distinct **historic districts** are crammed with antique shops, specialty outlets, and good cafés and restaurants, including the *Trailhead Brewery*, 921 S Riverside Drive (Ⓣ636/946-2739), a modern pub housed in an eighteenth-century grist mill. Lewis and Clark set up strategic camp here in 1804, and are remembered in the interesting small **museum**.

St Charles's **CVB**, 230 S Main St (Ⓣ636/946-7776 or 1-800/366-2427, Ⓦ www.historicstcharles.com), has details of downtown's growing range of elegant and amply porched **B&Bs**. The popular **Katy Trail**, which hugs the river along the route of an old railroad before turning west to Clinton, is excellent for hiking or cycling. The Touring Cyclist (Ⓣ636/739-4648) **rents bikes** and provides pick-up and drop-off along the trail. Gambling and showboats are anchored along the riverbanks, while the *St Charles Princess* (Ⓣ636/946-4995) operates sightseeing, lunch, and dinner cruises from Frontier Park.

Eating

Thanks to heavy Italian immigration in the early twentieth century, **Italian food** predominates in St Louis, from humble salami sellers upwards. Otherwise, there are many friendly **Irish pubs**, serving beef sandwiches and stew, while University City's **Delmar Boulevard** offers African, Middle Eastern, Chinese, Indian, and other ethnic places. More expensive cafés are located in **Laclede's Landing**, and the **Central West End** has a scattering of upmarket espresso bars such as the *Coffee Cartel*, 2 Maryland Plaza.

Duff's 392 N Euclid Ave, Central West End ☎314/361-0522. Small, relaxed, and moderately priced, with a French-flavored international menu, as well as homemade desserts and Sunday brunch. Outdoor seating available.

John D. McGurk's Irish Pub 1200 Russell Blvd, at 12th St, Soulard ☎314/776-8309. Freshly baked soda bread, corned beef and cabbage, Irish stew, and imported Guinness on offer. Live Irish music every night.

O'Connell's Pub 4652 Shaw Ave, at Kingshighway Blvd ☎314/773-6600. The best burgers in the city, and the beef sandwiches aren't bad either. Near the Hill district.

Red Sea 6511 Delmar Blvd, U City ☎314/863-0099. Cheap and cheerful Ethiopian restaurant, serving *berbere* sauce with everything. The decor is basic and the service slow, but the food's excellent.

Rigazzi's 4945 Daggett Blvd, the Hill ☎314/772-4900. Popular trattoria, famous for "frozen fish-bowls" of beer. Over thirty different pasta dishes on the menu, from $9, plus pizzas, veal, chicken, and steak.

Saleem's 6501 Delmar Blvd, U City ☎314/721-7947. "Where garlic is king" and St Louisians reckon you get the best ethnic food in the city. Lebanese and Continental menu.

Ted Drewes Frozen Custard 6726 Chippewa Ave ☎314/481-2652; also 4224 S Grand Blvd ☎314/352-7376. A legendary slice of Americana. Try a "concrete" – an ice cream so thick it won't budge if you turn your cup upside down. Open March–Dec.

Nightlife and entertainment

Downtown St Louis' highest concentration of **bars** and **clubs** can be found in **Laclede's Landing**, with nightly jazz, blues, rock, and reggae. Some of the outlying districts are well worth checking out in the evening; these include **the Loop** in U City, whose bars and cafés are not only popular with students, and the slightly more upmarket cafés and wine bars of **Central West End**. Unpretentious **Soulard** is the place to go for good jazz and blues. Every spring, the four-day **Mid-America Jazz Festival** (☎314/241-1888) brings top names together for performances all over St Louis. You should also check out **Grand Center**, centered on North Grand Blvd in midtown, home to stage shows and the **St Louis Symphony Orchestra** (☎314/534-1700). Excellent **listings** can be found in the free weekly *Riverfront Times*.

1860 Hard Shell Café & Bar 1860 S 9th St, Soulard ☎314/231-1860. One of the liveliest bars in Soulard with dancing to blues, R&B, and soul bands. Also serves good Cajun and fish dishes.

Blueberry Hill 6504 Delmar Blvd, U City ☎314/727-0880, ⓦwww.blueberryhill.com. Crammed full of memorabilia, with the downstairs dedicated to Elvis and a jukebox acclaimed by *Cashbox* magazine as the best in the country. The drinks and burgers are good, and live entertainment is offered every weekend (Chuck Berry himself comes in for monthly cameos).

Broadway Oyster Bar 736 S Broadway, downtown ☎314/621-8811. Cramped, crowded, and dark blues club, in an atmospheric old bar.

Mississippi Nights 914 N 1st St, Laclede's Landing ☎314/421-3853. The city's top venue for nonstadium bands.

Pageant 6161 Delmar Blvd, U City ☎314/726-6161. Large bar and live entertainment venue that brings in big-name rock groups.

Pierre's 4th and Chestnut, downtown ☎314/342-4690. Cigar smoking is encouraged in this classy jazz bar in the *Adam's Mark Hotel*. Open Thurs–Sat.

Riddles Penultimate 6307 Delmar Blvd, U City ☎314/725-6985. Very lively bar in the heart of U City, with a young crowd and some sidewalk seating.

Ste Genevieve

Sixty miles south of St Louis, Missouri's oldest community, the tiny, French-and German-heritage **STE GENEVIEVE** retains its eighteenth-century charm through historic cottages, a redbrick square, and summer festivals. A perennial favorite of Mississippi flood waters, the town, with a population of 4500, has recently been sheltered by a $50 million levee, a measure taken to ensure the safety of homes that pre-date the American Revolution. The *St Gemme Beauvais*, 78 N Main St (☎573/883-3562 or 1-877/272-5588; ❸), is a nineteenth-century Greek Revival inn downtown, while Amish variations on catfish, chicken, and seafood are on the menu in the *Anvil Saloon*, 43 S Third St (T573/883-7323).

Western Missouri

As the Mississippi River defines Eastern Missouri, its tributary the Missouri (which gave the state its name) dominates the northwest border. Here along the river, jazz and barbeque flourish in **Kansas City**, while the small town of **Independence** lays on the homespun charm made famous by its favorite son, President Harry S. Truman. Further south, surrounding the hokey family-entertainment center of **Branson**, cool lakes and forested hills provide some breathtaking natural beauty.

Kansas City

KANSAS CITY, 250 miles due west of St Louis, straddles the state line between Kansas and Missouri. Virtually all its main points of interest are on the Missouri side, where the fountains, boulevards, Art Deco and Mediterranean-style buildings, and the encouraging revitalization of downtown, are unusual and welcome features in a Midwestern city. Kansas City, Kansas, on the other hand, is a dull sprawl of suburbs that doesn't have much to attract visitors.

Kansas City was a convenient staging post for 1830s wagon trains heading west. Its consequent prosperity – and rough-and-tumble "sin city" image – was brought to an abrupt end by the **Civil War**. However, its fortunes revived in the 1870s, when the railroads brought the boom in meat packing that was responsible for the development of the huge stockyards, which finally closed down in 1992.

Thanks to political boss **Tom Pendergast**, an outrageous figure with whom the city had a love-hate relationship, Kansas City's many jazz clubs continued to sell alcohol during **Prohibition**. As in Chicago and New Orleans, speakeasies, brothels, and gambling dens went hand in hand with superlative **jazz** – and, to a lesser extent, **blues** – spawning the careers of Count Basie, Duke Ellington, and, in the Fifties, Charlie Parker. KC's resurgent jazz scene, fine restaurants, professional football and baseball teams, and theme parks help make it a popular short-break destination for the people of the western heartland.

Arrival, information, and getting around

From the **airport**, twenty miles northwest of downtown, a convenient forty-minute **shuttle bus** (half-hourly 6am–11.55pm; T816/243-5000) heads to major downtown hotels ($14) and Westport ($15). The equivalent taxi ride costs around $45; call Yellow Cab (T816/471-5000). The isolated **Greyhound** terminal lies well out from downtown in a miserable area at 12th St and Troost Ave. **Amtrak** is in the Union Station at 23rd and Main streets, opposite Crown Center.

The city's main **visitor center** is tucked away on the 25th floor of City Center Square at 1100 Main St (Mon–Fri 8.30am–5pm; T816/221-5242 or 1-800/767-7700, W www.gointokansascity.com); additional information offices are housed in the Country Club Plaza at 4709 W Central St (daily 8am–6pm; T816/691-3800) and in the Grand Hallway of Union Station.

The **Metro Buses** system ($1; T816/221-0660, W www.kcata.org) covers downtown, and has routes out to Independence (see p.832). In addition, seasonal **trolleys** ($7 all-day pass, $10 two-day pass) loop continuously between downtown, Crown Center, Westport, and the Country Club Plaza.

Accommodation

Kansas City's budget **motels** lie along the interstates or out towards Independence, though reasonable central options do exist. The visitor center is the best place to inquire about **B&Bs**. Depending on which direction you are coming from, **camping** choices include the *Trailside Camper's Inn*, I-70 exit 24, 24 miles east of downtown in Grain Valley (☎816/229-2267 or 1-800/748-7729; $24), or the *Cottonwood RV Park*, on Hwy-7 just off 1-70 exit 224, 24 miles west of downtown in Bonner Springs (☎913/422-8038; full RV hook-up $22/night).

Best Western Seville Plaza 4309 Main St ☎816/561-9600. Very central, close to Westport. Completely renovated in 2003. ❹
Historic Suites of America 612 Central St ☎816/842-6544 or 1-800/733-0612. In the heart of the Garment District, beautiful large rooms with fully equipped kitchens. Free breakfast and cocktails. ❻–❽

Holiday Inn Express Westport 801 Westport Rd ☎816/931-1000. Reasonable lodgings on the edge of the trendy Westport district. ❺
Super 8 Independence 4032 S Lynn Court ☎816/833-1888. Clean budget motel, east of the city in Independence. ❷–❹

The City

Kansas City is doing a good job of reinvigorating its **downtown**, and wandering past the restored lofts and small businesses of the **Garment District**, between Sixth and Ninth streets, makes a nice walk to **City Hall**, 414 E 12th St (Mon–Fri 8.30am–4.15pm; free), a fine Art Deco building with an observation deck on its thirtieth floor. Also downtown is the redeveloped **historic district** known variously as **River Market** or **City Market**, on the banks of the Missouri. As well as colorful shops, cafés, and a lively farmers' market at Fifth and Walnut streets, there's a good museum in the complex – **The Treasure of the Steamboat Arabia** – which tells the story behind the 1988 salvaging of a side-wheeler that sank on its way to Council Bluffs in 1856 (Mon–Sat 10am–6pm, Sun noon–5pm; $9.75; ⓦwww.1856.com). Perfectly preserved artifacts – china, guns, gold, and Kentucky bourbon, to name a few – afford unexpected and intriguing insights into frontier life.

The sprawling concrete **Crown Center**, on Grand Ave and Pershing Rd, owned by Hallmark Cards, calls itself "a city within a city," and houses apartments, shops, restaurants, offices, hotels, cinemas, and an ice rink. Interesting displays in its splendidly awful **Hallmark Visitors Center** (Mon–Wed & Sat 10am–6pm, Thurs & Fri 10am–9pm, Sun noon–5pm; free) trace styles of greeting cards alongside political and cultural changes; designs from the 1940s, for example, featured stars and stripes, and Uncle Sam. There are also demonstrations of dyeing and engraving techniques. The nearby **Union Station** is a Kansas City landmark: huge, beautifully renovated, and home to **Science City** (daily 10am–6pm; $9; ⓦwww.sciencecity.com), an incredible arena of futuristic games, movies, and exhibits.

The **18th and Vine Historic Jazz District**, south of I-70 as it sweeps east–west, was the hub of the city's 1930s jazz scene. Formerly an unsafe area of empty lots and boarded-up shops, a huge revitalization project in the 1980s culminated with the opening of the **Negro Leagues Baseball Museum**, 1616 E 18th St (Tues–Sat 9am–6pm, Sun noon–6pm; $6; ⓦwww.nlbm.com). This enthralling collection of photographs, interactive exhibits, and game equipment traces the turbulent history of black baseball in America, which was segregated from the white major leagues for the first half of the twentieth century. In 1920, Kansas City hosted the key meeting that founded the Negro National League – an institution that paved the way for the likes of Jackie Robinson to enter the major leagues. In the same complex is the **American Jazz Museum**

(Tues–Thurs 9am–6pm, Fri & Sat 9am–9pm, Sun noon–6pm; $6), which tells the history of jazz through interactive exhibits, which profile some of its greatest performers, including Kansas City native Charlie Parker and others who cut their teeth in the smoky halls of 18th and Vine. The *Blue Room* functions as a working jazz bar, with Monday-night jam sessions bringing many stars out of the woodwork.

Westport, an attractive district of good restaurants, cafés, and trendy shops between 39th and 45th streets, was the original jumping-off point for the Santa Fe Trail. Stop off for a drink at the city's oldest building, *Kelly's Westport Inn*, 500 Westport St (℡816/753-9193), a shabby but friendly red-brick bar. Five miles south of downtown, beginning at 47th and Main streets, the elegant **Country Club Plaza** dates from the early 1920s. Tree-shaded and upmarket (with branches of Eddie Bauer and Saks), its tiling, mosaics, fountains, and orange trees evoke the streets of Spain; a replica Sevillan tower completes the effect.

Highlights at the extensive **Nelson-Atkins Museum of Art**, a few blocks east at 4525 Oak St (Tues–Thurs 10am–4pm, Fri 10am–9pm, Sat 10am–5pm, Sun noon–5pm; free), include superb Oriental exhibits, with figurines from Tang and Egyptian tombs, plus canvases by Titian, Caravaggio (*St John the Baptist*), and Monet, plus twelve Henry Moore sculptures in a landscaped setting. The pretty **Toy and Miniatures Museum**, further south at 5235 Oak St (Wed–Sat 10am–4pm, Sun 1–4pm; $4), houses an offbeat collection of antique toys, games, and puppets.

During the summer, if the Midwestern humidity gets too much, head for the tropically themed water world **Oceans of**

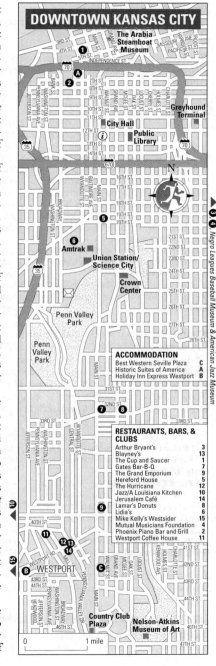

ACCOMMODATION
Best Western Seville Plaza — C
Historic Suites of America — A
Holiday Inn Express Westport — B

RESTAURANTS, BARS, & CLUBS
Arthur Bryant's — 3
Blayney's — 13
The Cup and Saucer — 1
Gates Bar-B-Q — 7
The Grand Emporium — 9
Hereford House — 5
The Hurricane — 12
Jazz/A Louisiana Kitchen — 10
Jerusalem Café — 14
Lamar's Donuts — 6
Lidia's — 8
Mike Kelly's Westsider — 15
Mutual Musicians Foundation — 4
Phoenix Piano Bar and Grill — 2
Westport Coffee House — 11

Fun, or the adjoining **Worlds of Fun**, with its 140–plus rides, out at exit 54 of I–435 (daily late May–early Sept, hours vary; $25 for Oceans, $36 for Worlds).

Eating

Barbecue, once the unfashionable food of the poor, is big news in Kansas City – cheap, cheerful, hickory-smoked, and served with tasty sauces. The **Country Club Plaza** has some great places to sample the spicy cuisine, but they tend to be overpriced and some require formal dress. The restaurants in **Crown Center** and around **Westport** are more casual.

Arthur Bryant's 1727 Brooklyn Ave ☎816/231-1123. *The* place for barbecue, a mile east of downtown in a desolate area. Serving the largest portions you've ever seen of barbecue and beans; the combo plate easily feeds two hefty appetites. This is serious business – don't take too much time deciding, as rookies aren't given any hand-holding.

The Cup and Saucer 412B Deleware St ☎816/474-7375. A unique sandwich and coffee-shop that transforms into a bar by night, where weekend jazz jams are popular.

Gates Bar-B-Q 3205 Main St ☎816/753-0828. Massive portions of BBQ served on platters in a family-style atmosphere.

Hereford House 20th and Main streets ☎816/842-1080. KC's top steakhouse, in a handy downtown spot.

Jerusalem Café 431 Westport Rd ☎816/756-2770. Small Middle Eastern restaurant serving superb falafel and kebabs.

LaMar's Donuts 240 E Linewood Blvd ☎1-800/533-7489. A KC institution, now with branches in several states; this one is the original.

Lidia's 101 W 22nd St ☎816/221-3722. Popular spot housed in an old freight house. Excellent pasta and an extensive wine selection, at affordable prices.

River Market Brewing Company 500 Walnut St ☎816/471-6300. A billiards room and full bar are added attractions to the American-style menu and house brew. Located near City Market.

Stroud's 1015 E 85th St ☎816/333-2132. Classic roadhouse, a long way southeast of downtown, and renowned for its fried chicken.

Nightlife and entertainment

Check out Kansas City's reviving **jazz** and **blues** scene, especially the authentic dives holding wonderful jam sessions into the early hours. The Friday and Sunday editions of the *Kansas City Star* carry **listings**, as does the freebie *Pitch Weekly*. You can also call the **Jazz Hotline** (☎816/753-JASS) or check Ⓦwww.jazzkc.org. **Downtown** is otherwise pretty dead by mid-evening, with most people heading to **Westport** for nightlife from country-and-western to alternative rock.

Blayney's 415 Westport Rd ☎816/561-3747. A good Westport venue with live blues Tues & Wed, and a varied schedule the rest of the week; open nightly until 3am.

The Grand Emporium 3832 Main St ☎816/531-7557. R&B, blues, reggae, and jazz, with superb Cajun and Jamaican food. Twice voted the Best Blues Club in America by the National Blues Foundation.

The Hurricane 4048 Broadway ☎816/783-0884. Trendy dance club in Westport operating until the wee hours.

Jazz/A Louisiana Kitchen 1823 W 39th St ☎816/531-5556. Cajun cuisine and live jazz and blues.

Mike Kelly's Westsider 1515 Westport Rd ☎816/931-9417. American food and live music several nights a week.

Mutual Musicians Foundation 1823 Highland Ave ☎816/471-5212. National Historic Landmark in the 18th and Vine district. Fierce jam sessions begin 1.30am Fri & Sat, with musicians competing in a frenzy for hours. Things can get a bit rough, and the place is not recommended for women alone.

Phoenix Piano Bar and Grill 302 W 8th St at Central Ave ☎816/472-0001. Downtown jazz piano venue featuring popular Sat afternoon sessions.

Independence and Liberty

Bus #24 from Kansas City goes to the small town of **INDEPENDENCE**, twenty minutes east of the city and most famous as the former home of

President Harry S. Truman. The **Truman Presidential Museum and Library**, on US-24 and Delaware St (Mon–Wed & Sat 9am–5pm, Thurs 9am–9pm, Sun noon–5pm; $7), includes a reconstruction of his White House office, and chilling documents pertaining to the development of the atomic bomb. The **Victorian Truman Home**, a mile south at 219 N Delaware St (daily 8.30am–5pm, in winter closed Mon; $3), is decorated as it was when it functioned as the summer White House.

Fifteen miles northeast of Kansas City, on the Old Town Square of **LIBERTY**, Jesse James staged the first-ever daylight bank robbery in 1866 in what's now the **Jesse James Bank Museum** (Mon–Sat 9am–4pm; $4). Among the memorabilia and dusty relics of early banking, you can see the vault and the safe the outlaw raided.

St Joseph

Sixty miles north of Kansas City, **ST JOSEPH** boomed as a supply depot for the California Gold Rush, and today is still a busy manufacturing town. For a brief eighteen months, beginning in 1860, it was the home of the legendary **Pony Express**, which took ten days to deliver mail all the way to Sacramento, California, by continuous horseback relay. The Pony Express was a financial disaster, driven out of business by its inability to compete with the transcontinental telegraph, but riders such as Buffalo Bill Cody went on to become legends. Charlie Miller, the last of the riders, rode from New York to San Francisco in 1931, and died aged 105 in 1955. The full story is told in lively dioramas at the **Pony Express Museum**, 914 Penn St (Mon–Sat 9am–5pm, Sun 1–5pm; $4), which is attractively set in the company's original stables.

It was in St Joseph, on April 3, 1882, that the notorious **Jesse James** was shot in the back by Robert Ford, a 20-year-old member of his own gang who had negotiated a $10,000 reward from the governor. Countless books and films have portrayed Jesse James as a latter-day Robin Hood; in fact, he spent most of the Civil War riding with a band of Confederate guerrillas. The **Jesse James Home Museum** (April–Oct Mon–Sat 10am–5pm, Sun 1–5pm; Nov–March Mon–Sat 10am–4pm, Sun 1–4pm; $2), the one-story frame cottage where James was living incognito while he planned his next bank job, now stands at 12th and Penn streets, having been moved closer to the main highway in the hope of attracting sightseers. A ragged hole in the wall is pointed out as the spot where the bullet supposedly hit, after striking James as he was hanging a picture; you can also see where bloodstained splinters were chiseled from the floor to be sold as souvenirs. As for the assassin, Ford was himself gunned down ten years later, and his killer in turn was also shot.

There are thirteen **museums** in town, most about the Old West, but none really warrant lingering. If you do want to leave the drive to Kansas City or Omaha for another day, you'll find **motels** strung along I-29 as it passes east of downtown, including a *Motel 6* (☎816/232-2311; **❷**) and a *Days Inn* at the intersection with Frederick Blvd (☎816/279-1671; **❸**). The *36th Street Food & Drink Company*, 501 North Belt Hwy (☎816/364-1564; closed Sun), serves great steaks.

Southwest Missouri – Ozark country

There's little to see south of Kansas City before the **Ozark Mountains**. Occupying most of southern Missouri and northern Arkansas (see p.630), the area remained frontier territory until the timber companies moved in at the end of the nineteenth century. When they moved on, the hill-dwellers were left to eke out a living from the denuded terrain; severe droughts forced many to leave for the cities. For those who remain, fishing resorts and tourist attractions supply some work, though the region remains poor and economically backward. None of the Ozark peaks are particularly high, though the roads through them switch, dip, climb, and swerve to provide **stunning views** of steep hillsides thick with oak, elm, hickory, and redbud, all quite resplendent in the fall. **Springfield** is the region's main city, 130 miles south of Kansas City, but the gateway to the Ozarks, the country music town of **Branson**, is more popular by far.

Branson

Nestled among beautiful Ozark lakes, the resort of **BRANSON**, forty miles south of Springfield on US-65, is one of the top tourist destinations in the United States. Over seven million visitors a year are attracted to what's become known as the "Ozark Disneyland" by forty-six music venues (almost all of a country or nostalgia bent), a few theme parks, and lots of good old family fun.

"**The Strip**," until recently merely Hwy-76, looks like it was thrown together with a pitchfork – a hideous agglomeration of theme parks and theaters owned and/or performed in by "big-name" stars. The spectrum ranges from Japanese fiddler Shoji Tabuchi and ancient crooner Andy Williams, to banal mountain humor joints like *Baldknobbers* and *Presleys'* (not *that* Presley). Occasionally, superb acts like Alison Krauss and Union Station will play a series of dates. Lesser lights include Russian comedian Yakov Smirnoff and the show at the Jim Stafford Theatre. **Tickets** for a two-hour show are fairly priced, at around $20, and there's no shortage of takers in summer for most, if not all, of the town's 57,000 seats – a figure said to exceed that of Nashville. Branson shows are firmly geared toward families; you won't find anything remotely edgy or avant-garde, although the *Ripley's Believe It or Not* performance is a step in a new direction.

When you've had it with Branson, escape to nearby **Table Rock Lake**, a beautiful area offering hiking, biking, camping, water-skiing, and world-class fishing.

Practicalities

Greyhound connects Branson with Springfield, Kansas City, and Memphis. Call ahead, or drop in at the local **Chamber of Commerce**, at the intersection of Hwy-65 and Hwy-248 (Mon–Sat 8am–5pm, Sun 10am–4pm; ☎417/334-4136 or 1-800/214-3661, ⓦwww.explorebranson.com), for a copy of their show guide detailing performance schedules of all the theaters. During the high season (May–Oct), **hotel** prices rise, especially on weekends, but you can still find some deals. Branson Vacation Reservations (☎1-800/221-5692) will try to sell you a package deal, but can also book you into a motel, including one of five *Best Western*s (☎1-800/528-1234; ❹). The Ozark Mountain Country B&B, Box 295, Branson, MO 65616 (☎1-800/695-1546), is another reliable **reservation service**, but if you're visiting in the main season call at least a week in advance. Table Rock State Park (☎417/334-4704) has **campsites** for $8. Most places to **eat** are of the family-diner ilk, though it's worth searching out the fat-free menu at *McGuffey's* on the Strip (☎417/336-3600), and the down-home cookin' at *The Farmhouse Restaurant*, downtown (☎417/334-9791).

△ The Gateway Arch, St Louis, Missouri

Kansas

Today's cutesy, gingham-pinafore image of **KANSAS**, associated with *Little House on the Prairie* and *The Wizard of Oz*, is a far cry indeed from the troubled history that made it known as "bleeding Kansas." It took three hundred years after Coronado came in search of gold in 1541 before pioneers established trails across the region, and Kansas's bid for statehood in 1861 is often cited as the catalyst for the Civil War. The 1854 **Kansas-Nebraska Act**, which gave both territories the right to self-determination over slavery, led to fierce clashes between Free Staters and pro-slavery forces. Runaway slaves from the South were given passage through the area, aided by abolitionist John Brown, and Kansas eventually joined the Union as a free state.

After the war, the mighty cattle drives from Texas made towns like Abilene, Wichita, and Dodge City centers of the "**Wild West**." The debauched, male image of the West, spawning such "heroes" as Wyatt Earp and Wild Bill Hickok, is, however, challenged in Kansas, which as well as being the first state to give women the vote in municipal elections, boasts the nation's first female mayor and senator, as well as aviator Amelia Earhart and the battling Prohibitionist Carry Nation.

In 1874, Russian Mennonites brought the grain that was to transform the state into the bountiful "breadbasket" that now harvests most of the nation's wheat. However, only in the west do miles of golden corn sway in Kansas's infamous gusty wind. The green and hilly northeast, patterned with woods and lakes, is home to the unattractive industrial city of Topeka, liberal college town **Lawrence**, and the dull suburbs of Kansas City (though downtown lies across the state line in Missouri). The wild and sparse northwest is pioneer country, while the once-wicked cowtown of **Dodge City** is in the southwest. **Wichita**, the state's largest city, lies in the south-central area.

Getting around Kansas

Greyhound **buses** run to all Kansas's main cities, supplemented by erratic smaller companies; services to the west and southwest are especially poor. Amtrak **trains** head east–west between LA and Chicago through the center of the state, calling, usually in the middle of the night, at Lawrence, Topeka, Emporia, Newton (for Wichita, but without a connecting service), Dodge City, and Garden City. Wichita has the state's biggest **airport**.

East Kansas

Undulating **east Kansas** is laced with lakes, streams, and rivers. The northeast, once crossed by the Oregon, Santa Fe, and Smoky Hill trails, and now home to both Topeka and Lawrence, is more heavily visited than the southeast, where the major attraction is the Little House on the Prairie historical site, located 13 miles southwest of Independence on Hwy-75. The heritage of Kansas's four Indian tribes comes alive in annual powwows, held in major towns as well as the northwestern reservations.

Lawrence

The mellow town of **LAWRENCE** lies on the Kansas River, roughly halfway between Kansas City and Topeka. Tree-lined streets, a welcoming historic downtown, and an aura of old-hippie artsyness make it an appealing destination, with a cultural energy owed in part to the **University of Kansas** (home of the Jayhawk, the mythical bird which is the emblem of its sports teams), and a long liberal and intellectual history. Founded by the New England Emigrant Aid Company in 1854, and a center of Free State activities, Lawrence was the site of a violent Civil War skirmish in 1863, when Missourian Confederate guerrilla Quantrill led about 300 men on the town, killing over 150, wounding hundreds more, and setting the place ablaze. Rebuilding was quick, however, as evidenced by the limestone and brick buildings of today's downtown, centered on Massachusetts Street, and the State University campus, which stands on a steep, tree-covered grassy bank known as Mount Oread.

Arrival, information, and accommodation

Amtrak comes into Lawrence at 413 E 7th St, and **Greyhound** arrives at 2447 W 6th St. The kitsch Fifties-style Lawrence Bus Co. runs **local buses**. The **visitor center** is north of downtown in the renovated Union Pacific Depot, at N 2nd and Locust streets (Mon–Sat 8.30am–5.30pm, Sun 1–5pm; ☎785/865-4499 or 1-888/LAWKANS, ⓦwww.visitlawerence.com).

Adequate but dull budget **rooms** can be found near the bus station at the *Virginia Inn*, 2907 W 6th St (☎785/843-6611; ❸), while the *Super 8* at 515 McDonald Drive (☎785/842-5721; ❸) is a reliable fall-back. If you have a little extra cash, head instead to the lovely all-suite *Eldridge Hotel*, at 7th and Massachusetts streets (☎785/749-5011 or 1-800/527-0909; ❺–❻); twice burned down by pro-slavery forces, it has been restored to an evocative faded elegance, and houses the stylish *Shalor's* restaurant (☎785/749-1005) and the atmospheric *Jayhawker* bar in the lobby. You can camp near downtown at *KOA*, 1473 Hwy-40 (☎785/842-3877; $20 per tent site), or three miles out along W 23rd St at Clinton Lake State Park, where the vehicle fee is $6 and a tent site $7.50 (☎785/842-8562).

The Town

Studded with cafés and eclectic shops, downtown Lawrence is a delight to walk around – and just as busy outside of term time, when day-trippers flock in from less congenial Kansan cities. However, most of the town's formal attractions are congregated on campus. The **University of Kansas Natural History Museum**, on Jayhawk Blvd, at 14th St (Mon–Sat 10am–5pm, Sun noon–5pm; $3 suggested donation), holds a chronological panorama of North American flora and fauna, as well as the now-stuffed horse Comanche, the lone survivor of Custer's cavalry at the Battle of Little Bighorn. Across the road, the **Museum of Anthropology**, in Spooner Hall, presents African and Eskimo artifacts (Mon–Sat 9am–5pm, Sun 1–5pm; free). The **Spencer Museum of Art**, 1301 Mississippi St (Tues, Wed, Fri & Sat 10am–5pm, Thurs 10am–9pm, Sun noon–5pm; free), specializes in world art, with an Oriental gallery, Old Masters, and a pre-Raphaelite masterpiece. Graphic art (shown by appointment) from the Sixties includes some Warhols and exceptional photographs, from Diane Arbus's disturbing portraits to Weegee's documentary exposés of New York City life.

Native American traditions are preserved and packaged for the public each year by the exhibitions of the **Lawrence Indian Arts Show**, held throughout the city from mid-September to the end of October. One venue is the **Haskell Indian Nations University** at 23rd and Massachusetts streets, where the **Hiawatha Visitor Center** and **American Indian Athletic Hall of Fame** are open year-round by appointment (☎785/749-8404).

Eating, drinking, and entertainment

As befits a college town, the **restaurant** scene in Lawrence is dominated by inexpensive eats. **Nightlife**, too, is defined by the students, who can be found in droves along Massachusetts Street. As for the **performing arts**, one of the better places to investigate is Liberty Hall, 642 Massachusetts St (☎785/749-1912). Once a social and political center, this building housed Lawrence's first newspaper until it was burned down by pro-slavery agitators in 1863. Today it puts on art-house films, plays, and concerts.

Buffalo Bob's Smokehouse 719 Massachusetts St ☎785/841-6400. Hickory-smoked barbecue pork, chicken, and ribs for those who can't wait until Kansas City. Tater curl french fries and apple fritters included.

Free State Brewing Co. 636 Massachusetts St ☎785/843-4555. Trendy brewpub serving award-winning amber beer and robust steaks.

Jazzhaus 926 Massachusetts St ☎785/749-3320. As the name suggests, this dimly lit bar hosts weekend jazz gigs.

Paradise Café 728 Massachusetts St ☎785/842-5199. Veggie burgers, soups, salads, fish specials, and breakfast, too.

Teller's 746 Massachusetts St ☎785/843-4111. Excellent nachos and pizza served in a beautifully restored bank building.

Yellow Sub 624 W 12th St ☎785/841-3268. Good sandwiches and lunch specials in a laid-back atmosphere with sweeping views. The campus location keeps it busy during the school year.

West through Kansas

Further west across Kansas, three towns re-create the state's Wild West heritage, although only in the westernmost, **Dodge City**, does the scrubby landscape conform to the cowboy-movie image. **Abilene**, if less famous than Dodge City, has as many outlaw and gunslinger stories, and **Wichita**, about 200 miles southwest of Kansas City, holds an excellent, authentic reconstruction of frontier days in its Old Cowtown Museum.

Abilene

Like all the old cattle-trail cowtowns, **ABILENE**, 115 miles west of Lawrence on I-70, claims to have been the most riproaring of the lot. By the time legendary lawman Wild Bill Hickok became its marshal in 1871, the unruly behavior was already dying down, and little today reminds you of those raucous days. Doing its best, though, is **Old Abilene Town**, at SE Sixth and Kuney streets (May–Sept daily 9am–8pm; free), a replica of the town during its cattle boom. Gunfights and cancan performances are still held when tourists turn up, but the place has seen better days – with most buildings either falling apart or boarded up, it's up for sale and no longer touted by the local tourist office.

These days, Abilene prefers to stress its connections with **Dwight Eisenhower**. The **Eisenhower Center**, 201 SE Fourth St (daily: May–Aug 8am–5.45pm; Sept–April 9am-4.45pm), encompasses his boyhood home, with its original furnishings, the obligatory film, and many photos and papers on display in the spacious museum ($3.50). The former president and his wife are buried in the meditation chapel.

Abilene's **visitor center** is at 201 NW Second St (☎785/263-2231 or 1-800/569-5915). Most of the town's budget **motels** are off I-70 at Hwy-15. The very basic *Diamond*, 1407 NW Third St (☎785/263-2360; ❷), is a decent option, but the best rates are at the *Budget Lodge*, 101 NW 14th St (☎785/263-3600; ❷), a slightly faded but clean motel not far from the I-70 exit.

Wichita

WICHITA, about 165 miles southwest of Lawrence on I-35, is the largest city in Kansas, split by the Arkansas River, which forks just north of downtown into the Big and Little Arkansas rivers (incidentally, Kansans take umbrage if you pronounce it "Arkansaw"; pronounce it here the way it is spelled). Originally settled by the Wichita Indians, who by 1865 had been relocated to Oklahoman Indian Territory, Wichita grew up as a stop on the Chisholm Trail, a Texas-to-Kansas cattle route celebrated in frontier lore and cowboy ballads. Its glory days were to be short-lived, however, as farmers, angry about the damage done by stampeding cattle, erected fences which forced the drives onto different trails further west, creating new cowtowns such as Dodge City. Today three of the world's major aircraft manufacturers (Cessna, Raytheon, and Learjet) are based here, and the city, already sporting a rich arts scene, has been invigorated with a downtown revival.

The City

Downtown Wichita is enlivened mainly by the public art and sculpture that pops up unexpectedly all over the place, in empty lots and even in tree stumps. The exceptional **Wichita-Sedgwick County Historical Museum**, 204 S Main St (Tues–Fri 11am–4pm, Sat & Sun 1–5pm; $2; ⓦ www.wichitahistory.org), is in **Old City Hall**, a heavy stone building decorated with turrets, gargoyles, and arches. The cozy interior is crammed with exhibits on everything from the Wichita Indians through decorative art to Carry Nation, whose initial zeal for singing hymns to errant drunks grew into a campaign against everything from tobacco to corsets. The stately church with vivid stained-glass windows at 601 N Water St houses the **Kansas African American Museum** (Tues–Fri 9am–5pm, Sun 1–5pm; $4), an eclectic antidote to more mainstream views of Great Plains history, with details on Buffalo Soldiers, inventors from across the country, early black Wichitans, and some African art.

Excellent museums in the Riverside stretch of parkland (which also holds walking and bike trails) include the **Indian Center and Museum**, 650 N Seneca Drive (Tues–Sat 10am–5pm, Sun 1–5pm; $3). The 44ft *Keeper of the Plains* statue, facing east at the confluence of the Little and Big Arkansas rivers, was designed in the 1970s by a Kiowa-Comanche artist, Blackbear Bosin, and dedicated by Native Americans and city officials smoking the peace pipe. It's an eerie sight at dusk, reaching into the sky with some unknown offering. The museum itself is small, with changing exhibits of traditional and contemporary Native American art.

Western artist C.M. Russell is the best represented of the veritable who's who of American painters assembled at the **Wichita Art Museum**, 619 Stackman Drive (Tues–Sat 10am–5pm, Sun noon–5pm; $5, Sat free). **Old Cowtown Museum**, 1871 Sim Park Drive (March–Oct Mon–Sat 10am–5pm, Sun noon–5pm; $7), is a seventeen-acre riverside exhibit re-creating the buildings of 1870s Wichita. Looking and feeling like a movie set, the area includes – along with some docile longhorns – the city's first one-room jail, a schoolroom, a store, a smithy, churches, stables, and old homes.

To the north of the city, the surreal geodesic **Bright Spot for Health Center**, 3100 N Hillside Ave (Mon–Thurs 8am–5.30pm; $4), houses the **Garvey Center for the Improvement of Human Functioning**, which aims, by using holistic medicine, to find a cure for cancer. It's all very worthy, but weird: road signs, for example, tell you to "de-stress to 25," and there's a 39ft food guide pyramid. In the southeast of the city, the products of Wichita's airplane industry are on display at the **Kansas Aviation Museum**, in the old Art Deco air terminal at 3350 George Washington Blvd (Tues–Fri 9am–4pm, Sat 1–5pm; $2). A more interesting detour is to **Hutchinson** (on Hwy-50, 45 miles northwest of Wichita), for the **Kansas Cosmosphere and Space Center** (Mon–Sat 9am–9pm, Sun noon–9pm; $11 includes IMAX and planetarium) which features, among other aerospace paraphernalia, the *Apollo 13* command module.

Practicalities

Domestic **flights** arrive at the Mid-Continent Airport, five miles southwest of downtown on Hwy-54 (W Kellogg Drive). **Amtrak** stops at Newton, a small Mennonite town 25 miles north, with a local bus connection to Wichita throughout the day; **Greyhound** comes in to 312 S Broadway Ave, two blocks east of Main Street. **City transportation** consists of **buses** (WMTA; $1 per ride; ☎316/265-7221) and, more appealingly, **trolleys**, which run at lunchtimes and on Saturdays for just 50¢. The resourceful **CVB** is in the heart of downtown at Douglas Avenue and Main Street (Mon–Fri 7.45am–5.15pm; ☎316/265-2800 or 1-800/288-9424, ⓦwww.visitwichita.com). An additional information office is housed in the Wichita Boathouse at 335 W Lewis St (daily 9am–5pm; ☎316/337-9088). City trolley **tours** ($8; Mon–Sat 10am) depart from here, as well.

Inexpensive **lodgings** in Wichita are plentiful, especially near the airport on W Kellogg Drive – try the *Ramada* at no. 6245 (☎316/945-5261; ❸). On the opposite flank of the city is a good *Fairfield Inn*, 333 S Webb Rd (☎316/685-3777; ❸). More upscale, the *Hotel at Oldtown*, at First and Mosley streets (☎316/267-4800; ❺–❼), has a stylish turn-of-the-century flavor and perfect location. Nine miles from town, *Blasi Campground*, 11209 W Hwy-54 (☎316/722-2681), offers tent sites for $18.50.

There are a hoard of **restaurants**, **clubs**, and **bars** around the quaint Old Town Marketplace. Good places to eat include the *River City Brewing Co*, 150 N Mosley St (☎316/263-2739), which has good Kansas steaks, locally brewed beer, and veggie pasta dishes, and the *Old Mill Tasty Shop*, by the railroad tracks at 604 E Douglas Ave (☎316/264-6500), which serves great sandwiches and Southwestern food. Or you can dip into one of the thirteen *Pizza Hut*s around town, including one with a café at 7700 E Kellogg Drive (☎316/263-4044); the chain started here in 1958. *The Brickyard* at 129 N Rock Island St (☎316/263-4044) is an American-style restaurant with a huge patio where rock, jazz, and blues bands perform most nights; the biggest discotheque is *America's Pub*, at 900 E First St (☎316/267-1782).

Dodge City

DODGE CITY, 150 miles west of Wichita, is perhaps the most famous of all America's cowtowns. It has certainly been committed to celluloid more times than any other, especially in 1930s Westerns like *My Darling Clementine* and *Dodge City*. However, this wildest of Wild West cities had a heyday of only a decade, from 1875 until 1886. Established in 1872 along with the Santa Fe Railroad, which transported the hides of millions of Plains buffalo, by 1875 the town of traders, trappers, and hunters had to find a new economic base – the buffalo had been exterminated. The era of the great cattle drives was already under way, and Dodge City became a den of iniquity where gambling, drinking, and general lawlessness were the norm. Such wickedness led to gunfights galore, and the notorious Boot Hill cemetery (where the villains were buried with their boots on) was kept busy by charismatic, morally suspect lawmen such as Bat Masterson and Wyatt Earp.

The Town

Dodge City today is rather more staid, with its old downtown area enveloped by a hinterland of railroad tracks and giant silos. Outside of the two-week **Dodge City Days and Rodeo** (Ⓦ www.dodgecityroundup.com), held near the end of July, the town is content to replay its movie image in the **Boot Hill Museum**, 500 Wyatt Earp Blvd (June–Aug daily 8am–8pm; Sept–May Mon–Sat 9am–5pm, Sun 1–5pm; $7, $8 in summer). The museum centers on the single-sided **Historic Front Street**, which was constructed in 1958 and has been acquiring old buildings from all over the West ever since. There's a bank and a grocer, stagecoach rides, a funeral parlor, a smithy, and even a full-sized railroad station, as well as the *Long Branch Saloon*, scene of a variety show with cancan dancers every night at 7.30pm ($6). Gunfights and showdowns break out with alarming regularity. **Boot Hill cemetery** is higher up the hill, still on museum grounds; there's just a sorry little patch of lawn on one corner of the original site, which was in any case abandoned in 1879 after just six years and thirty-four burials. The bodies were reinterred elsewhere, and as the graves were never marked in the first place, the jokey wooden crosses in the cemetery are more than a little bogus.

Other sights in town include the **Home of Stone**, 112 E Vine St (June–Aug Mon–Sat 9am–5pm, Sun 2–4pm; free), an emotive memorial to pioneer mothers, often forgotten amid the macho Wild West myth-making. The house looks pretty much as it would have when built in 1881, with domestic memorabilia that belonged to early plainswomen. **El Capitan**, at Second St and Wyatt Earp Blvd, is a massive bronze longhorn, facing south towards an identical north-facing statue in Abilene, Texas. Together they mark the beginning and the end of the cattle drives.

Practicalities

Greyhound **buses** from Wichita arrive twice daily at 2405 W Wyatt Earp Blvd. **Amtrak** comes right into downtown, to the historic and renovated Santa Fe Station at Central Ave and Wyatt Earp Blvd. The **CVB** at Third St and Wyatt Earp Blvd (Mon–Fri 8.30am–5pm; ☎ 620/225-8186 or 1-800/OLD-WEST, Ⓦ www.visitdodgecity.org) can offer advice on tourist activities; they also have a **visitor center** at 400 W Wyatt Earp Blvd (summer daily 8.30am–6.30pm; winter Mon–Fri 8.30am–5pm). The Dodge City Trolley runs narrated town **tours** ($5) four times a day from a booth on the Boot Hill parking lot.

Most of Dodge City's **motels** are strung out roughly a mile west of downtown along US-50, still known here as Wyatt Earp Boulevard. The *Budget Host Inn* at no. 2200 (☎ 620/227-8146; ❷) is inexpensive but a little noisy, and offers free rides to the train and bus stations; the *Dodge House* at no. 2408 (☎ 620/225-9900; ❸–❺) has a reliable restaurant; and the *Econo Lodge* at no. 1610 (☎ 620/225-0231; ❷–❸) has an indoor pool and sauna area. **Camping** is an option even for the car-less: the lakeside *Water Sports Campground Recreation*, 500 Cherry St (☎ 620/225-8044; $17 tent sites, no credit cards), lies ten blocks south of Front Street. If you feel like bustin' your own bronco, head for the *Marchel Ranch*, 10873 W Hwy-50 (☎ 620/227-7307 or 1-877/631-6196, Ⓦ www.marchelranch.com), a small ranch offering horse rides, chuck-wagon dinners, and cozy rooms.

As for **food**, *Café at the Plaza*, 100 Military Ave (☎ 620/227-6151), doesn't have much in the way of atmosphere, but the roast beef sandwiches and soups are good and reasonably priced. *Peppercorns*, out near the motels at 1301 W Wyatt Earp Blvd (☎ 620/225-2335), is a conventional highway steakhouse with meals for about $13.

Iowa

Although at times serene, and almost always verdant, nothing about **IOWA** truly stands out: this 55,000-square-mile chunk of the Great Plains doesn't even manage to be completely flat – it just wobbles up and down a little. The state is the very essence of smalltown America, close to the geographical center of the mainland US, and ranking decidedly average in size, population, and level of personal income. Even the cities seem at times to be merely villages grown large.

Iowa's history, too, has been relatively uneventful. It was opened for settlement after the **Black Hawk Treaty** of 1832, a one-sided exercise in negotiation with the Sauk Indians, conducted after many of them had been chased down and slaughtered in neighboring Wisconsin and Illinois. The Northern European immigrants who replaced them made agricultural development their prime concern, turning Iowa into the "Foodbasket of America" – a role it generally achieves with scrupulous efficiency.

Tourist attractions in Iowa are few and far between; the state's most visited destination is the throwback Germanic enclave of the **Amana Colonies**. However, Iowa does also hold a few oddball sites, such as the original locations for the movies *The Bridges of Madison County* (in south-central **Winterset**, birthplace of **John Wayne**) and *Field of Dreams* (near **Dubuque** in the northeast). You can also see, but not enter, the original house that featured in Grant Wood's much-parodied *American Gothic* painting (at Eldon in the southeast, and now owned by the state).

Getting around Iowa

Greyhound buses out of Chicago call at all Iowa's major towns. Daily buses also run from St Louis to Des Moines and Iowa City; these towns are connected less frequently with Minneapolis/St Paul. **Amtrak**'s east–west route misses the cities, stopping instead at assorted small communities in the south. The only sizeable **airport** is in Des Moines.

Somewhat surprisingly, Iowa is a good place for **cycle touring**. Each year the extremely popular cross-state bike ride – the Register's Annual Great Bike Ride Across Iowa, or the **RAGBRAI** – attracts thousands of entrants, any of whom can tell you that the Plains aren't always flat (tour details ☎1-800/474-3342, ⓦwww.ragbrai.org).

Eastern Iowa

Eastern Iowa, in the Mississippi River hinterland, is liberally sprinkled with agribusiness towns that display the continuing influence of their central and northern European pioneers, plus **religious communities** – Amish, Mennonite, and the Amana Colonies. All are easily accessible from **Iowa City**; as home to a huge university it's one of the state's livelier centers. Riverside towns such as northerly **Dubuque** and Burlington, near the Missouri state line, have been enlivened since 1991 by **gambling**, though so far low-stakes poker and roulette games can only be played on board Mississippi paddle-wheelers, decked out in less-than-authentic Mark Twain–era trimmings.

Dubuque

The handsome town of **DUBUQUE**, overlooked by rocky bluffs on the Mississippi around 150 miles west of Chicago, was founded as the first white settlement in Iowa by French-Canadian leadminers in 1788. In the nineteenth century it became a boisterous riverport and logging center. Buildings from this era still stand, but the companies that use them are now in meatpacking and other food industries.

A complex of buildings at Third Street in the old Ice Harbor area, cut off from downtown by Hwy-61, includes an assortment of river-related **museums** (daily 10am–5.30pm; $8.75). Precisely which exhibits are housed in the **Mississippi River Museum**, the **Riverboat Museum**, and the **National Rivers Hall of Fame** (which focuses on "Pathfinders" such as Lewis and Clark, rather than the rivers themselves) seems to vary, but together they tell the story of Mississippi navigation from the days of Robert Fulton's first commercial steamboat in 1807 until the floods of 1993. The fifteen-minute introductory film *River of Dreams* is a good starting point for your explorations. The complex completed a $188 million renovation in 2003 and now features an aquarium, hotel, and entertainment complex, among other attractions.

Once your appetite has been whetted, you can travel along the high-banked Mississippi on a *Spirit of Dubuque* **paddle-wheeler cruise** (May–Sept daily; $12.50 for 90min; ☎319/583-8093 or 1-800/747-8093), or on board one of the more expensive **gambling boats**. Alternatively, what's said to be the world's shortest and steepest **cable-car ride** (April–Nov daily 8am–10pm; 75¢) grinds its way from Fourth Street downtown up a sheer bluff to **Fenelon Place**, a residential street of old money and Victorian architecture. The top offers a sweeping view across the Mississippi to Illinois and Wisconsin. If cable cars don't appeal, then head north to the lovingly maintained, 164-acre **Eagle Point Park** (daily 7am–10pm; $1), set on bluffs high above the river.

Film buffs who enjoyed the 1989 baseball fantasy *Field of Dreams* can meet like-minded souls in surprising numbers at the original movie location, three miles north of Dyersville, which is 25 miles west of Dubuque on US-20. True to the movie's catchphrase – "if you build it, they will come" – crowds still gather on the bleachers to watch phantom games at the edge of the cornfields, and buy souvenirs from two rival family concerns (April–Nov daily 9am–6pm).

Practicalities

The **Iowa Welcome Center** at 300 Main St (daily 9.30am–5.30pm; ☎563/557-9200 or 1-800/798-8844, ⓦwww.traveldubuque.com) is the best place to pick up information on Dubuque. You can **rent a bike** at the Bike Shack, 3250 Dodge St (☎563/582-4381; $15 for four hours, $5 each additional hour). As for places to **stay**, try the *Richards House B&B*, 1492 Locust St (☎563/557-1492; ❹), which is well-managed and veering toward Old World luxury. Bargain hunters might want to stay at the grand redbrick *Julien Inn*, 200 Main St (☎563/556-4200 or 1-800/798-7098; ❶–❸), which was once owned by mobster Al Capone; he used it as his safehouse when trouble was brewing in Chicago. Picturesque **campsites** can be found at Miller Riverview Park, off Greyhound Park Road (☎563/589-4238; $8 per tent site). The *Shot Tower Inn*, at the foot of the cable car at Fourth and Locust streets (☎563/556-1061), serves a standard menu of pizzas and meat dishes.

Cedar Rapids

Seventy miles southwest of Dubuque, **CEDAR RAPIDS**, home of Quaker Oats, is Iowa's industrial leader. In the late 1840s, a meatpacking boom lured thousands of Czechs here. The **Czech Village**, 16th Ave SW and First St (Tues–Sun 9.30am–4pm; $5; ☎319/362-8500), features the excellent *Sykora's* bakery, gift shops, traditional houses, and a new museum of national costumes and immigrant artifacts. The very modern **Museum of Art**, 410 Third Ave SE (Tues, Wed, Fri & Sat 10am–4pm, Thurs 10am–7pm, Sun noon–4pm; $5.50), boasts a comprehensive collection of paintings by Grant Wood, best known for his depictions of 1930s farmlife.

Cedar Rapids' **CVB** is based at 119 First Ave SE (Mon–Fri 8am–5pm; ☎319/398-5009 or 1-800/735-5557, ⓦwww.cedar-rapids.com). For reasonably priced **rooms**, there's the *Best Western Cooper's Mill*, 100 F Ave NW (☎319/366-5323 or 1-800/858-5511; ❸).

The Amana Colonies

The **Amana Colonies** are situated at the intersection of Hwy-151 and Hwy-220, midway between Cedar Rapids and Iowa City. They were founded in 1855 by the **Community of True Inspiration**, pacifist German refugees (not linked to the Amish or Mennonites) who believed that God spoke through prophets – themselves, for example – rather than ordained ministers. Members led a simple, collective lifestyle: each family lived in its own home, but they all ate together and shared profits from the farms. During the Depression, communal ownership became increasingly difficult to maintain, and in 1932 stock was redistributed among all the adults. However, they did keep up their commitment to close family ties, a sense of community, and religious principles. On Sunday mornings, you can still see female church members wearing the traditional black cap, shawl, and apron, with the men dressed in equally sombre attire. Church services for visitors take place at 10am every Sunday in the section known as Middle Amana.

The Amana Colonies today, consisting of seven separate villages set in an immaculate, serene valley, feel like a cross between a ski resort with no mountains and a reservation for Midwestern pioneers. Their prosperity is very evident, though in addition to tasteful clapboard houses standing on well-groomed lawns, and neat plank fences dividing rolling meadows, you'll also come across factories, pizza parlors, and even a golf course. It's geared less for families and more toward Iowan couples on a weekend getaway. The twee streets of the largest village, **Amana**, are lined with restaurants and craft shops, a brewery, several wineries, and a woolen mill – plus a small and somewhat self-congratulatory **Museum of History** (Mon–Sat 10am–5pm, April–Nov also Sun noon–5pm; $5). Picturesque and less commercialized **Homestead**, three miles south of Amana, is enhanced by a 3.5-mile walking trail around a dam on a scenic bend of the Iowa River, built centuries ago by Indians to concentrate fish into one area and thus allow them to be caught more easily.

Practicalities

Conventional addresses are seldom used in the Amana Colonies, but points of interest are well signposted. The **visitor center**, near the junction of Hwy-151 and Hwy-220 (Mon–Sat 9am–5pm, Sun 10am–5pm; ☎319/622-7622 or 1-800/245-5465, ⓦwww.amanacolonies.com), hosts evening theater five nights a week ($22) and has details of **B&Bs** such as *Judy's Guest Haus* (☎319/622-3599; ❸), a restored 1890 colony home in the heart of Amana. Across the road from the visitor center are **tent spaces** at the *Amana Colonies RV Park* (☎319/622-7616; $10 per tent site).

Probably the most compelling reason to visit the colonies is their undeniably excellent old-style **German food**. Apple-cheeked serving staff at the *Amana Barn Restaurant* (☎319/622-3214) in Amana village dish up huge portions of country ham, beef schnitzel, and the like, with pickled baby vegetables; for a lighter snack, call in at *Hahn's Hearth Oven Bakery* in Middle Amana (☎319/622-3439). South Amana's *Market Place Restaurant* (☎319/622-3225) offers sausages galore. As alcohol is not prohibited, some eating establishments, like the *Ronnenberg Restaurant and Bar* (☎319/622-3641), are also popular for locally produced **wine**.

Iowa City and West Branch

IOWA CITY, on I-80 55 miles west of the Mississippi, is refreshingly young at heart. The restored gold-domed **Old Capitol** is a reminder of its days as state capital, before government was transferred to the more central Des Moines. Residents were placated by getting the **University of Iowa** instead. The arty shops and sidewalk cafés of the compact downtown touch the east end of campus, but its red and gray buildings, closeted by tall dark trees, remain aloof from the rest of the town.

About 12 miles east of Iowa City, the tiny Quaker town of **WEST BRANCH** attracts a steady stream of traffic from I-80 for its **Herbert Hoover Library & Museum** (daily 9am–5pm; $3). Informative exhibits and a documentary film cover Hoover's youthful adventures in China, his presidential victory and subsequent disgrace when the nation blamed him for the Great Depression, and his comeback after World War II as the leader of the European humanitarian relief effort. A self-guided **walking tour** begins at the library and includes Hoover's birthplace, a replica of his father's black-smith shop, and the Friends Meetinghouse where he attended Sunday services.

Practicalities

Greyhound stops at 404 E College St, just off downtown. The **CVB** is at 408 First Ave in Coralville, a mile northeast of downtown (☎319/337-6592 or 1-800/283-6592, ⓦwww.icccvb.org). *Iowa House* is a comfortable central **hotel** in the Union building, beside the river on Madison Street (☎319/335-3513; ❸). To the west, inexpensive **motels** in Coralville include the very clean and good-value *Super 8*, 611 First Ave (☎319/337-8388; ❸). The *Coralville Park*, three miles north of I-80 at exit 242 (☎319/338-3543), is a good place to cast a fishing line, has a Devonian-era fossil bed, and offers grassy **tent sites** for $8. Inexpensive **food** is easy to find, be it soup in a sourbread bowl at *Quinton's*, 215 E Washington St (☎319/354-7074); the pastries and espressos served on long comfortable sofas at *Java House*, nearby at 211 E Washington St (☎319/341-0012); or the burgers at *Micky's*, 11 S Dubuque St (☎319/338-6860), a friendly, dimly lit Irish bar.

Central and western Iowa

Pigs outnumber people in **central Iowa**. The only city among the cornfields, state capital **Des Moines** struggles to lift the monotony, and many visitors may prefer the college town of **Ames**. The humdrum west has little to offer.

Des Moines

DES MOINES, near the center of Iowa amid tree-covered hills at the confluence of the sluggish Des Moines and Raccoon rivers, owes its origins to a military fort set up in 1843. The area had already grown into a trading center for farmers by the time the 18-year-old Frederick Hubbell arrived in 1855; within a decade he had founded the Equitable Life and Insurance Corporation to service their need for investment capital. Other companies soon realized the potential of agrarian business, and today the city is the world's third-largest **insurance center**, behind London and Hartford, Connecticut. Illustrious former denizens of Des Moines include President **Ronald Reagan**, who started out as a sportscaster on Radio WHO, and arch-cowboy **John Wayne**, who was born and raised in nearby Winterset.

Arrival, information, and accommodation

Des Moines' **Greyhound** station is just northwest of downtown at 1107 Keosauqua Way. From the very efficient transfer depot at Sixth Ave and Walnut St, **MTA buses** ($1; ☎515/283-8100) run practically everywhere in the city. The **visitor center** is at 405 6th Ave, suite 201 (Mon–Fri 8.30am–5pm; ☎515/286-4960 or 1-800/451-2625, ⊛www.seedesmoines.com).

Accommodation-wise, downtown Des Moines caters mostly for insurance company business, though there are still some fairly inexpensive places to stay. You can **camp** in summer at the *Iowa State Fairgrounds Campgrounds*, E 30th St and Grand Ave (☎515/262-3111; $12). Better still is the Walnut Woods State Park, off Hwy-35 exit 68, where tent sites are $9.

Best Western Starlite Village 929 3rd St ☎515/282-5251. Reasonably priced downtown rooms. ❹

Hotel Fort Des Moines 1000 Walnut Ave at 10th St ☎515/243-1161 or 1-800/532-1466. Exquisite, historical downtown gem with Old World elegance and exemplary service. The indoor swimming pool/spa area has won awards for its tasteful design. Highly recommended. ❹–❻

Motel 6 4817 Fleur Drive ☎515/287-6364. Clean rooms near the airport. ❷

YMCA 101 Locust St at 1st Ave ☎515/288-0131. Slightly faded, men-only downtown rooms for $25; weekly rates available. ID required (passport or social security card only). ❶

YWCA 717 Grand Ave ☎515/244-8961. Clean, dorm-style rooms for women in a safe part of downtown; $10 per bed per night, with discount for weekly stays. ❶

The City

The steel-and-glass skyline of **downtown** Des Moines, most of which shot up during the 1980s, is testimony to the town's ever-growing **insurance trade**. Towering above all is the boxy, 44-story **801 Grand building**, headquarters of the Principal Financial Company. For such a fast-track financial center, the streets are curiously empty; pedestrians instead use the **Skywalk**, a three-mile network of air-conditioned corridors linking twenty blocks of offices, banks, parking lots, restaurants, hotels, and movie theaters.

Most businesses stand on the west bank of the Des Moines River, which cuts downtown in two. In 1857, a group of speculators attempted to shift the commercial hub to the east side by bribing commissioners to site the **state capitol** at E Ninth St and Grand Ave (they apparently offered more than the Westsiders were willing to dish out). Their hopes of huge spin-offs were dashed when the nationwide financial crash later that same year saw property prices collapse. As a result, the five-domed Italian Renaissance–style mass, on the crest of a steep hill, is now detached from the heart of the city (Mon–Fri 8am–4.30pm, Sat & Sun 8am–4pm; free; call for tour times ☎515/281-5591). A short walk downhill, in the futuristic pink-and-brown **State of Iowa**

Historical Building, E Sixth and Locust streets (Tues–Sat 9am–4.30pm, Sun noon–4.30pm; free), displays cover Indian civilization, pioneer times, and the development of Iowan farming, along with plenty of solemn portraits of former governors.

Three miles west, the impressive **Des Moines Art Center**, in a leafy suburb at 4700 Grand Ave (Tues, Wed, Fri & Sat 11am–4pm, Thurs 11am–9pm, Sun noon–4pm; free), is housed in a trio of buildings designed by world-renowned architects Eliel Saarinen, I.M. Pei, and Richard Meier. Works by Matisse, Picasso, and Renoir stand alongside twentieth-century Americans such as Wood, Hopper, and O'Keeffe. The most dynamic exhibits are in the Meier wing, including a gigantic and disturbing Anselm Kiefer canvas.

Eating, drinking, and nightlife

That Iowans eat well is reflected in the quality – and quantity – of food on offer in Des Moines' many **restaurants**. As for **nightlife**, most of it is confined to local watering holes – there's not much at all in the way of dance clubs or live music.

Buzzard Billy's 100 Court Ave ☏ 515/280-6060. Good Cajun cuisine, including alligator dishes; catfish, shrimp, and oyster meals are also a specialty. It's packed on Thursdays for "Crappy Beer Night."
Java Joe's 214 4th St ☏ 515/288-5282. Late-closing coffee bar and sandwich place attached to an artist's gallery, featuring live entertainment at weekends. Internet access available. Open until 11:30pm on weekdays, 1am on weekends.
Papa's Planet 208 3rd St ☏ 515/284-0901. This bar/nightclub is a favorite weekend gathering place for young locals, with guitar bands at low

cover charges and an outdoor street patio.
Spaghetti Works 310 Court Ave ☏ 515/243-2195. Spacious Italian outfit with original interior decor (it has variously served as a glove factory, hat millinery, and fruit market). The all-you-care-to-eat pasta dishes from $5 are great value.
Stella's Blue Sky Diner 3281 100 St ☏ 515/727-4408. Kitsch diner decked out in lurid pink, turquoise, and yellow. Wash down burgers and fries ($4) with divine chocolate, peanut butter, and banana malts. A must for lunch, but be prepared for long lines. Mon–Sat 8am–6pm.

Around Des Moines

Thirty miles north of Des Moines, **Ames** is the home of **Iowa State University**. Smaller and slightly less trendy than Iowa City, it's still a lively little community (by Iowan standards, at least). The **visitor center**, 1601 Golden Aspen Drive, suite 110 (☏515/232-4032 or 1-800/288-7470, ⊛www.acvb .ames.ia.us), can advise on concerts and area attractions. **Room** rates are reasonable out at the *Super 8*, three miles from campus at I-35 and Hwy-30 (☏515/232-6510; ❸); *Godfather's Pizza*, 414 Lincoln Way (☏515/232-9000), is a popular joint.

Ten miles west of downtown Des Moines, at I-80 exit 125, the **Living History Farms** in Urbandale (May–Oct daily 9am–5pm; $10) trace the evolution of agriculture on the Plains. Self-guided **tours** lead from the oval bark homes of an eighteenth-century Iowan settlement, through an 1850s homestead, to a look at the high-tech methods of today. If you want to continue the rural theme, **eat** colossal portions of meat loaf and chops in the *Iowa Machine Shed Restaurant* (☏515/270-6818), or stay in the country-style *Comfort Suites Hotel* (☏515/276-1126; ❹); both are next to the farm entrance.

Winterset

Until Robert Waller's *The Bridges of Madison County* changed everything, sleepy, rundown **WINTERSET**, 25 miles southwest of Des Moines, seemed a long way off the beaten path. The town's one tourist attraction was the modest former

The Bridges of Madison County

The fortunes of Winterset, the county seat of Madison County, have taken an unexpected turn for the better in the years since the publication of Robert Waller's best-selling tearjerker **The Bridges of Madison County**. Fans attracted by the 1995 movie version, which was filmed in and around Winterset and starred Clint Eastwood and Meryl Streep, will be delighted to find everything looking just as it did on screen. *National Geographic* may never have published a feature about the bridges (fictional photographer Robert Kincaid's assignment in the book and film) but there really are six (out of an original nineteen) nineteenth-century **covered bridges** in the immediate neighborhood. None charges for admission or has formal opening hours. For a full list and driving map, drop in at Winterset's visitor center on Courthouse Square.

home of the local pharmacist at 216 S Second St (daily 10am–4.30pm; $2.50), run as a museum in tribute to his son, Marion Robert Morrison. Born in 1907, Morrison grew up to become Hollywood hardman **John Wayne**. His first lead role was in 1930 – but real stardom, as the Ringo Kid in John Ford's *Stagecoach*, didn't come for another nine years. Three decades later, Wayne claimed his only Oscar as Rooster Cogburn, the drunken one-eyed marshal in *True Grit*. Among the photos, personal belongings, and mementos is a glowing personal endorsement of "the Duke" from his buddy Ronald Reagan, who shared his political views, if not perhaps his acting abilities.

These days, Winterset's **visitor center**, on Courthouse Square in the heart of town (Mon–Fri 9am–5pm, Sat 9am–4pm, Sun 11am–4pm; ☏515/462-1185 or 1-800/298-6119, ⓦwww.madisoncounty.com), has become accustomed to handling inquiries from all over the world about the locations for Waller's tale, including hundreds of couples wanting to marry on the bridges themselves. If you don't want to go that far, you can drive out to view the **covered bridges** (see box, above), or at least have a meal in the old-style *Northside Café*, a few doors along from the visitor center, where Clint was made to feel decidedly uncomfortable in the movie. You can also visit the late 1800s homestead that was used in the movie as Francesca Johnson's farm, at 3271 130th St (May–Oct 10am–6pm, or by appointment; $5; ☏515/981-5268). A good time to visit Winterset is the second full weekend of October for the **Bridge Festival**, featuring local bands and artists. **Accommodation** possibilities nearby include the *Village View Motel*, Hwy-92 E (☏515/462-1218 or 1-800/862-1218; ❸). There is a small **campground** at the Winterset City Park on the east end of town (☏515/462-3258; $8).

Nebraska

Hell, I thought I was dead too. Turns out I was just in Nebraska.

Gene Hackman in *Unforgiven*

Though modern transcontinental travelers tend to see **NEBRASKA** in much the same light the early pioneers did, heading west during the Gold Rush – as just another dreary expanse of prairie to get through as fast as possible – this flat and sparsely populated state in fact encompasses quite a few places of interest. However, its most appealing cities, commercial **Omaha** and the livelier state capital, **Lincoln**, are separated by a good three hundred miles of underwhelming, livestock-rearing flatlands from the western Panhandle, where the landscape finally erupts into giant sand hills and valleys, broken by towering rocky columns and hemmed in by sheer-faced buttes.

Western Nebraska was still embroiled in vicious and bloody battles against Native Americans long after the east had been settled; from the first serious uprising in 1854, it was thirty-six years before the US Army could make white control unchallengeable. Close to the South Dakota state line, **Fort Robinson**, where Crazy Horse was murdered, remains one of the West's most evocative historic sites.

Without navigable rivers, Nebraska had to rely on the **railroads** to help populate the land. During the 1870s and 1880s, rail companies, encouraged by grants that allowed them to accumulate one-sixth of the state, laid down such a comprehensive network of tracks that virtually every farmer was within a day's cattle drive of the nearest halt. Thus the buffalo-hunting country of the Sioux and Pawnee was turned into high-yield farmland, which today has few rivals in terms of beef production.

Getting around Nebraska

The Omaha **airport** offers the best domestic links, though planes from other cities in the region also fly to Lincoln. Several Greyhound **buses** traverse I-80 each day on the coast-to-coast marathon, stopping at all the major towns. Amtrak **trains**, traveling through the night, follow a similar route, calling at Omaha, Lincoln, Hastings, Holdredge, and McCook. **Driving** on I-80 can get tedious; if you're not in a rush, Scenic Hwy-2 (see p.853) is a good alternative.

Eastern Nebraska

The silt-laden Missouri River separates Nebraska from Iowa and Missouri to the east. There are few natural ports on this stretch, and **Omaha** remains the only riverfront community of any size. **Lincoln**, 58 miles southwest, is the state's capital and seat of its university.

Omaha

Although **OMAHA**, Nebraska's largest and most easterly city, is visibly a prosperous place, with a great zoo, several museums, and a lively entertainment district, the atmosphere remains sedate and predominantly suburban. As a major terminus on the first transcontinental railroad, Omaha made a logical alternative to distant Chicago as a marketplace for Wyoming and Nebraska ranchers to sell their herds of **cattle**. By the turn of the century, massive stockyards had spread along the southern edge of town, and the city still handles well over one million head of livestock per year.

In downtown Omaha you'll find good bars and cafés along the cobbled streets of the **Old Market district**, plus interesting specialist shops such as the Antiquarian Bookstore, 1215 Harney St (☎402/341-8077), packed with dusty volumes (and local bohemians). Ideal for a picnic, the nearby **Heartland Park of America**, at Eighth and Douglas streets, holds a huge, water-blasting fountain. Train buffs will be impressed with the **Durham Western Heritage Museum**, converted from the Union Pacific railroad station, at 801 S 10th St

(Tues–Sat 10am–5pm; $5), where old train cars and huge model train sets are featured alongside a gallery of Omaha history. Behind its pink-marble Art Deco exterior, the **Joslyn Art Museum**, 2200 Dodge St (Tues–Sat 10am–4pm, Sun noon–4pm; $6, free Sat before noon), contains an eclectic selection of Indian art and twentieth-century American paintings.

The **Great Plains Black Museum**, in the city's predominantly black north side at 2213 Lake St (Tues–Sat 10am–2pm; free), presents the history of African-American people on the prairies. One stimulating section focuses on blacks in the frontier army, where recently freed slaves, who could find no work in the Deep South after the Civil War, were often sent as advance parties into the most hostile and dangerous regions. It was Native American warriors who first called them "buffalo soldiers," because of their tightly curled hair and the color of their skin.

Malcolm X was born in Omaha in May 1925, though his family moved to Michigan immediately thereafter, in the face of Ku Klux Klan death threats to his father, a preacher who followed the back-to-Africa teachings of Marcus Garvey. Omaha tourist authorities don't promote his **birthsite**, at 34th and Evans streets (formerly 3448 Pinkney St), perhaps because the residents of the surrounding neighborhood use it as a dumping ground for old TVs, bent car parts, shredded furniture, and other debris. Years of debate over how to develop the site have yielded a solitary placard, hidden behind some trees, offering a brief biography. By way of contrast, the lavish birthplace of President **Gerald R. Ford**, at 32nd St and Woolworth Ave (Tues–Fri 1–4pm; $2), is open to the public; with his family, he too moved to Michigan as an infant, after his parents separated.

The **Henry Doorly Zoo**, 3701 S 10th St (daily 9.30am–5pm; $9), rightfully considers itself one of the best zoos in America. It started off with two buffalo borrowed from Buffalo Bill; now there's a gigantic free-flying aviary, some rare white Siberian tigers, a magnificent bear canyon, and the large Kingdoms of the Seas aquarium. It's well worth a visit.

Twenty-nine miles southwest of Omaha, at exit 426 on I-80, is a welcome diversion for those seeking relief from pioneer museums. The **Strategic Air and Space Museum** (daily 9am–5pm; $7) is inside two huge hangars containing giant 1950s- and 1960s-era war planes designed and built by the Martin Bomber Company of Omaha. Films, photos, and exhibits concentrate on World War II and the Cold War, the latter highlighted by various weapons including an Atlas-D Intercontinental Ballistic Missile, located outside the museum entrance.

Practicalities

Omaha's **Greyhound** station is at 1601 Jackson St; **Amtrak** trains depart very late at night, and arrive long before the city wakes up, at 1003 S Ninth St. Both depots are well placed for downtown; however, local **public transportation** is poor. The **CVB** is at 6800 Mercy Rd, exit 459 from I-80, near the old racetrack (Mon–Fri 8.30am–4.30pm; ☎402/444-4660 or 1-866/937-6624, Ⓦwww.visitomaha.com). There's also a **welcome center** for Nebraska as a whole, just off I-80 exit 454, across from the zoo at Tenth St and Deer Park Blvd (May–Oct daily 9am–5pm; ☎402/595-3990).

Hotel rates are good, except in mid-June when the college baseball World Series comes to town. Rooms at the circular, almost cute, and certainly pretty unusual *Satellite Motel*, 6006 L St (☎402/733-7373; ❷–❸), come clean and at good prices. The well-kept *Best Western White House Inn*, at 305 N Fort Crook Rd (☎402/293-1600 or 1-800/962-4601; ❸), offers good rates about five miles south of downtown. Located next to the SAC Museum, the Eugene T. Mahoney State Park (☎402/944-2523) has **campsites** ($7), **cabins**, and a **lodge** (❸–❹), in a family-oriented setting. The *Pinecrest Farms B&B*, located 20 miles north, on Country Road A between highways 77 and 79 (☎402/784-6461; ❸), offers an idyllic and romantic setting.

The Old Market district, centered on Tenth and Howard streets, has the liveliest **restaurants** and **bars**. The *Indian Oven*, 1010 Howard St (☎402/342-4856), a superb Asian restaurant, features paneer and vegetable dishes on its extensive menu. *Mo's Pub*, at 422 S 11th St (☎402/342-2550), serves renowned baked casseroles and a long list of salads, while the *Upstream Brewing Company*, 514 S 11th St (☎402/344-0200), has excellent beers and a standard American menu. Whether you fancy terrific desserts or a light meal, the *Garden Café*, 1212 Harney St (☎402/345-9745), won't break the bank. *Mr Toad's*, 1002 Howard St (☎402/345-4488), is a reliable **jazz venue**, with good jam sessions on Sundays.

Lincoln

Tiny Rochester was selected to be state capital in 1867 – on the condition that it change its name to **LINCOLN** in honor of the recently assassinated president. Such was the disappointment in the territorial seat of government, Omaha, that state officials had to smuggle documents, books, and office furniture out of the city in the middle of the night to avoid armed gangs.

Fifty-eight miles southwest of Omaha, the city now serves as an oasis of culture for a large chunk of the Plains. At night, when the students emerge, its compact downtown comes into its own. Of its alphabetical array of broad boulevards, **O Street** (the subject of Allen Ginsberg's poem "Zero Street") is the main drag; 13th and 14th streets are packed with bars and places to eat.

Dwarfing the rest of **downtown**, the central tower of the 1932 Nebraska **state capitol**, 1445 K St (Mon–Fri 9am–4pm, Sat 10am–4pm, Sun 1–4pm; tours every half-hour; free), protrudes 400ft into the sky. Topped by a 20ft statue of a sower on a pedestal of wheat and corn, its remarkably phallic appearance – an adventurous departure from the usual architecture of state capitols – has prompted the nickname "penis of the prairies." For once there's no golden dome, and the superb iridescent murals in the foyer are a welcome alternative to old portraits, flags, and emblems. From the fourteenth-floor observation deck you can survey the flatness of the surrounding farmland.

Twelve thousand years of life on the plains are covered at the **Museum of Nebraska History**, 15th and P streets (Mon–Fri 9am–4.30pm, Sat 9am–5pm, Sun 1.30–5pm; $2 suggested donation), where displays focus on anthropology rather than history. The Elephant Hall, a gallery of towering mammoth, mastodon, and four-tusker skeletons, is the highlight of the **University of Nebraska State Museum** at 14th and U streets (Mon–Sat 9.30am–4.30pm, Sun 1.30–4.30pm; $4). A few blocks away, the **Sheldon Memorial Art Gallery**, 12th and R streets (Tues, Wed & Fri 10am–5pm, Thurs & Sat 10am–5pm & 7–9pm, Sun 2–9pm; free), traces the development of American art, and has a twenty-piece sculpture garden. The 76,000-seater **Memorial Stadium**, at the northern end of campus on Vine Street (tickets ☎402/472-3111 or 1-800/8-BIGRED), is where the brutal "Big Red" Cornhuskers invariably thrash their football opposition.

Practicalities

Lincoln's **Greyhound** station is downtown at 940 P St, while **Amtrak** passes through 201 N 7th St at crazy early-morning hours. Star-Tran (☎402/476-1234) runs good **local buses** (85¢). The **visitor center** is in Lincoln Station, right next to Amtrak (June–Sept Mon–Fri 9am–8pm, Sat 8am–5pm, Sun noon–5pm; rest of year Mon–Fri 9am–6pm, Sat 10am–4pm, Sun noon–5pm; ☏402/434-5348 or 1-800/423-8212, ⓦwww.lincoln.org).

Except on football weekends, it's easy to find inexpensive **accommodation** out by the airport, off I-80 exit 399 – at the *Inn 4 Less* motel (☏402/475-4511; ❷), for example. Downtown, the *Holiday Inn*, 9th and O streets (☏402/475-4011; ❹), is good value, while the *HI-Cornerstone* hostel, 640 N 16th St (☏402/476-0355; ❶), in a church on the edge of campus, offers basic bunks (members $10, nonmembers $13). The Branched Oak State Park, off Raymond Road from Hwy-79, has **tent sites** for $3–7; the more expensive sites have showers.

Restaurants downtown tend to be less than compelling, with grills, pizzerias, and family diners predominating. The *Oven*, 201 N 8th St (☏402/475-6118), offers Indian cuisine with a range of cheap breads and inventive specials, while the Italian menu at cafeteria-style *Valentino's*, 232 N 13th at Q Street (☏402/475-1501), is fast and well-priced. The *Z-Bar*, 136 N 14th St (☏402/435-8754), attracts big-name **jazz** and **blues** acts who drop in en route between Chicago and Kansas City; *Duffy's Tavern*, 1412 O St (☏402/474-3543), pulls in a younger crowd and some good **rock bands**. Across the street at no. 1329, *O'Rourke's Tavern* (☏402/435-8052) is a lively, well-priced hangout. The **Historic Haymarket District**, down by the Amtrak station, holds a further selection of bars and restaurants, including *The Mill*, at 800 P St (☏402/475-5522), which has good coffee and Internet access.

Western Nebraska

After the unerringly flat journey across eastern Nebraska, the far west comes as a refreshing change. In the **Panhandle**, as it's often called, wave upon wave of rumpled sandy hills, thinly coated with prairie grass, back off toward the horizon like a sea in constant turmoil. Early pioneers wrote the area off as unproductive, and it remained barren until massive irrigation work at the start of the twentieth century enabled agricultural settlement. In the **northwest** the sand hills yield to classic John Ford–style Western scenery: pancake-flat valleys, crisscrossed by dry meandering riverbeds and corraled by crusty, contorted bluffs, all under the constant shadow of fast-moving clouds. Emigrants on the **Oregon Trail** used the bizarre outcrops which sprout along the way as "road signs," as a way of knowing that their trek across the Plains was coming to an end.

West along I-80

Interstate 80 is one of the most popular coast-to-coast routes simply because it's the shortest. Scenery is not its strongest suit, and the central swath through 450 miles of Nebraskan farmland is not always a prospect drivers cherish. If time doesn't matter, then it's better to head northwest at dreary Grand Island, 93 miles west of Lincoln, onto **Scenic Hwy-2**, for a lonesome yet exhilarating drive through the Sandhills.

If you stick to I-80, decent pull-off points are few and far between. It's hard to miss the newest attraction at **KEARNEY** – the **Grand Platte River Road Archway Monument** (daily 8am–8pm; $8.50) actually spans the interstate near exit 272. Exhibits inside tell the story of a transient nation and re-creates the hardships of life on the westward trail. The town of Kearney is pleasant enough and offers a strip of inexpensive **restaurants** and studenty **bars**.

Just over halfway across the state at exit 177, **NORTH PLATTE** makes a big deal about its **Buffalo Bill Ranch Historical Park** (daily: April, May, Sept & Oct 9am–5pm; June–Aug 10am–8pm; $2.50 per car), another property of the ubiquitous William "Buffalo Bill" Cody. Today the ranch is run by the state, which places more emphasis on history than tacky folklore. Cody's mansion and various barns can be examined, and an excellent documentary film shows movie clips of his "Wild West Show," which toured America and Europe for thirty years. The park offers **horse rides** ($12 per hour) and **camping** ($3 per night). The *Rambler Motel*, 1420 Rodeo Rd (☎308/532-9290; ❷), has comfortable rooms and an outdoor pool, while the authentic Mexican cantina *La Casita*, at 1911 E Fourth St (☎308/534-8077), boasts an irresistible Elvis room, littered with tacky souvenirs honoring the King.

Thirty miles west, another restaurant sets out to entertain bored drivers, in the one-horse hamlet of **PAXTON**, off exit 145. *Ole's Big Game Lounge & Grill* (☎308/239-4500) serves tasty fried food, with over two hundred wildlife trophies from around the world mounted on its walls, cabinets, and shelves. Fascinating, but not a place for the animal-rights activist.

At **OGALLALA**, twenty miles further along, Old West outlaws were interred at **Boot Hill Cemetery** (10th St and Parkhill Rd; free) in the 1880s. The town sits just nine miles south of "Big Mac" – **Lake McConaughy** reservoir, famous for fishing, watersports, and the sandy beaches along its 105 miles of shoreline. From Ogallala, it's 165 miles to Cheyenne, Wyoming, though Sidney (exit 59) takes you into rugged Oregon Trail country (see p.854).

Scenic Hwy-2 and Alliance

Scenic Hwy-2 meanders and dips for over 330 miles from I-80 to South Dakota's Black Hills. It passes through the **Sandhills** – a mesmerizing landscape carpeted with short-grass prairie and softened by delicate wild flowers and shiny ponds. Apart from a few farmsteads, grain silos, and tiny churches, all you're likely to see on the open road are lazing cattle, a few sluggish rivers, and the occasional mile-and-a-quarter-long freight train weaving its way through the hills. It's a long, desolate, yet incredibly beautiful drive through an anachronistic corner of the US, where small towns are all spick-and-span and everyone could well know each other's name; **Broken Bow**, 77 miles north of I-80, features one of the neatest town squares in the heartland.

The road dawdles for another 200 miles through scattered villages before drifting into **ALLIANCE** – a nice enough little prairie town, which pulls in over 50,000 visitors per year for its one big attraction. **Carhenge**, two and a half miles north on State Hwy-87 (always open; free; ⓦwww.carhenge.com), is a rough copy of Stonehenge – but made with old cars rather than stone. Erected in a cornfield during a family reunion in 1987, this intriguing collection of Chevys, Cadillacs, and Plymouths, painted a brooding battleship grey and tilted at unusual angles, has to be the best picnic site in America's heartland. To some it's an ingenious piece of Pop Art; others view it as great black humor, or an appalling eyesore. After it was built, a few fundamentalist Christians feared it was a Satanic shrine. Certainly, the Nebraska Department of Roads saw nothing amusing about the project. They rapidly declared it a junkyard, and ordered the city of Alliance to remove it, forcing locals to form **Friends of Carhenge**, whose work seems to have secured the monument's future.

Alliance's helpful downtown **CVB** office, 124 W Third St (☎308/762-1520), provides information and sells Carhenge souvenirs. There is no reason to linger in Alliance, but if you arrive late, try the *Days Inn*, 117 Cody Ave, just off Third St (☎308/762-8000; ❸), or the *Super 8*, 1419 W Third St (☎308/762-8300; ❷). For **food**, there's *Ken & Dale's*, 123 E Third St (☎308/762-7252), which serves succulent all-day breakfasts and great pecan pancakes.

The Oregon Trail landmarks

Two of the first landmarks encountered by travelers on the **Oregon Trail**, which in western Nebraska paralleled the route of modern US-26, were the lumpy **Courthouse** and **Jail rocks**, which lie four miles beyond the likeable little town of **Bridgeport**, 36 miles south of Alliance. Fourteen miles west, along Hwy-92, the much-painted and -photographed **Chimney Rock** rises almost 500ft above the North Platte River. Although this phallic outcrop's nineteenth-century stature may have been chipped away by erosion and lightning, it remains one of the most recognizable and memorable landmarks in the West.

The twin towns of **GERING** and **SCOTTSBLUFF**, 25 miles further west, are the commercial center for the farmlands of western Nebraska. Southwest of Gering, the rugged 800ft rampart of **Scotts Bluff National Monument** (daily: summer 8am–7pm; rest of year 8am–5pm; $5 per car) stands like a Nebraskan Gibraltar. Known to the Sioux as Me-a-pa-te ("hill that's hard to get around"), it earned its anglicized name in 1828 after fur trader Hiram Scott was mysteriously found dead at its base. Trips to the top (by foot or free shuttle bus) are rewarded with a magnificent view, and the entrance fee includes the absorbing **Oregon Trail Museum**, which relates the experiences of the early emigrants. Just outside Gering, to the southwest, the spiky **Wildcat Hills** hold some delightful vistas and hiking terrain.

Well-kept **rooms** are available in the *Lamplighter American Inn*, 606 E 27th St, Scottsbluff (☎308/632-7108; ❸); *Woodshed*, 18 E 16th St (☎308/635-3684), is the best spot for family-style **food**, and has a full bar. The towns' **visitor center** can be found at 1517 Broadway, Scottsbluff (daily 8am–5pm; ☎308/436-4340).

Fort Robinson State Park

Some eighty miles north of Scottsbluff, just west of Crawford village, **Fort Robinson State Park**, beside 1000ft crenelated cliffs in the inhospitable White River Valley, preserves the spot where the US Army coordinated its campaign to rid the gold-rich Badlands of the native Sioux. Today, it's a cross between a dude ranch and a living history village; a cosmeticization which makes the memories of the obliteration of an entire way of native life all the more poignant.

Restored fort buildings contain period furnishings, and there are two small museums. A simple stone marks the spot where **Crazy Horse** was killed (see box, below); the **tour train** (three per day; $3) acknowledges it with a mere ten-second halt. Good-value **horseback rides** pass some wondrously weird rock formations, and *Fort Robinson Lodge* (☎308/665-2900; ❹) has nice **rooms** as well as bargain cottages; the *Lodge's* **restaurant** serves cheap buffalo tacos and other beef and bison dishes. There is good **camping** for $8 per person, or you could really rough it at the beautiful but remote Toadstool Geological Park, 25 miles to the north.

The town of **Chadron**, 23 miles east of Fort Robinson, is worth a visit principally for the small **Museum of the Fur Trade**, four miles east on US-20

Crazy Horse

The life of Oglala Sioux leader **Crazy Horse** is shrouded in confusion, misinterpretation, and controversy. So thoroughly did the most enigmatic figure in Plains Indian history avoid contact with whites (outside battle, at least) that no photograph or even sketch of him exists; unlike other Indian chiefs, he refused to visit Washington, DC, or talk to reporters.

Crazy Horse earned his title as a youth, after he single-handedly charged rival Arapahoe and took two scalps. The finest moment in a brilliant military career came in June 1876, when he led a thousand warriors in inflicting a stinging defeat on the superior forces of General George Crook at the Battle of the Rosebud River. Just eight days later Crazy Horse headed the attack at the **Battle of Little Bighorn**, where Custer and his entire company were killed (see p.940).

After Little Bighorn, US Army efforts to round up the Indians were redoubled. In May 1877, Crazy Horse surprised friend and foe alike by leading nine hundred of his people into Fort Robinson. They gave up their weapons, and Crazy Horse, keen to stay in his native land (unlike Sitting Bull, who had retreated to Canada), demanded that the buffalo grounds along the Powder River should remain in Indian hands. Tensions at the army camp rose after a rumor went around the barracks that the Sioux chief had come to murder General Crook. Crazy Horse was arrested on September 5, 1877; during a tussle outside the fort jail, he was bayoneted three times, and died the next morning.

Quite why this undefeated warrior should have surrendered without a fight, and whether he fell victim to a deliberate assassination, remains unclear. What is certain is that his death signaled the closing chapter of the Indian Wars. The Oglala Sioux were forcibly moved to the poor hunting country of Missouri, and settlers immediately swept in their thousands into western Nebraska, South Dakota, Wyoming, and Montana.

Crazy Horse, so one story goes, was buried by his family in an unmarked grave in an out-of-the-way creek called **Wounded Knee** – the very place where thirteen years later three hundred Sioux men, women, and children were slaughtered in the bloody finale to over half a century of barbarism (see p.860).

(summer daily 8am–5pm; $2.50). The museum is a valuable historical archive illustrating the unique barter system that operated between fur traders and local Native Americans.

South Dakota

The wide-open spaces of the Great Plains roll away to infinity on either side of I-90 in **SOUTH DAKOTA**. Though the land is more green and fertile east of the Missouri River, vast numbers of high-season visitors speed straight on through to the spectacular southwest, site of the **Badlands** and the adjacent **Black Hills** – two of the most dramatic, mysterious, and legend-impacted tracts of land in the US. For whites, they encapsulate a wagonload of American notions about heritage and the taming of the West; to Native Americans, they are ancient, spiritually resonant places.

The science-fiction severity of the Badlands resists fitting into easy tourist tastes. The bigger, more user-friendly Black Hills, home of that most patriotic of icons, **Mount Rushmore**, have been subjected to greater exploitation (dozens of physical, historical, and downright commercial attractions, as well as the mining of gold and other metals), but encourage more active exploration, via hiking trails, mountain lakes and streams, and scenic highways.

Time and Hollywood have mythologized the larger-than-life personalities for whom the Dakota Territory served as a stomping-ground: **Custer** and **Crazy Horse** battled here for supremacy over the Plains, while **Wild Bill Hickok** and **Calamity Jane** were denizens of the once-notorious Gold Rush town of **Deadwood**. On a more contemporary note, Kevin Costner's award-winning *Dances with Wolves* (1990), shot in the state, boosted South Dakota's tourism image, though Costner's own ambitious development plans for the Black Hills have meant that he himself has fallen foul of the Sioux.

Sioux tribes dominated the plains from the eighteenth century, having gradually been pushed westwards from the Great Lakes by the encroaching whites. To these nomadic hunters, unlike the gun-toting Christian settlers and federal politicians, the concept of owning the earth was utterly alien. They fought hard to stay free: the Sioux are the only Indian nation to have defeated the United States in war and forced it to sign a treaty (in 1868) favorable to them. Even so, they were compelled, in the face of a gung-ho gold rush, to relinquish the sacred Black Hills, and ultimately the choice lay between death or confinement on reservations. For decades their history and culture were outlawed; until the 1940s it was illegal to teach or even speak their language, Lakota. More Sioux live now on South Dakota's six reservations than dwelled in the whole state during pioneer days, but their prospects are often grim. Nowhere is the legacy of injustice better symbolized than at **Wounded Knee**, on the Oglala Sioux **Pine Ridge Reservation** – scene of the infamous 1890 massacre by the US Army, and also of a prolonged "civil disturbance" by the radical American Indian Movement in 1973.

Today Native American traditions are celebrated by music, dance, and socializing at **powwows**, held in summer on the reservations; the state tourist office can supply dates and locations. Apart from powwows, South Dakota summers are taken up with historical celebrations, volksmarches (a friendly sort of community walking exercise), ethnic festivals, and rodeos. The 200th anniversary of the **Lewis and Clark expedition** began in 2003 and will continue through 2006; check ⓦ www.travelsd.com for event details. The state has 170 parks and recreation areas for hikers and campers. In winter, downhill **skiing** is limited to Terry Peak and Deer Mountain, outside **Lead** in the Black Hills; cross-country skiing and snowmobiling are more prevalent.

Getting around South Dakota

You'll be hard put to see much of South Dakota without a **car**. Amtrak routes bypass the state entirely, though Jefferson (☎ 1-800/444-6287) **bus lines** serve points between Rapid City and Sioux Falls, sites of the two major **airports**. Powder River buses (☎ 1-800/442-3682) serve Black Hills I-90 towns such as Rapid City, Spearfish, and Sturgis, as well as making the two-hour trip to Cheyenne, Wyoming. To see iconic attractions such as Mount Rushmore and the Crazy Horse Memorial, you might hook up with Discovery Tours (☎ 605/722-5788), which runs lively minibus **tours** from Rapid City and Deadwood.

East of the Missouri

For tourists, little in eastern or central South Dakota can be considered essential. **Sioux Falls**, the state's biggest city, is faceless but handy. As one of the country's quietest and smallest capitals, **Pierre** has its charms, while **Mitchell** has a few curiosities, and **Yankton**, comfortably ensconced beside the Missouri across from Nebraska, is a gem-like historic town draped with parks and picket fences, with the excellent Lewis and Clark Recreation Area on its doorstep. The town marks the start of an alternative cross-state route to I-90, trundling through nearby **Vermillion**, home to the exceptional Shrine to Music Museum, plus the Rosebud and Pine Ridge reservations. About sixty miles northwest of Sioux Falls, **De Smet** is known as "Little Town on the Prairie" thanks to the autobiographical books of Laura Ingalls Wilder. You can tour eighteen sites she mentions for smatterings of history, pretty scenery, and homely pride. **Chamberlain**, where I-90 shoots down a steep bluff and over the Missouri River, provides spectacular vistas, and also holds the worthwhile Akta Lakota Museum and Cultural Center.

Mitchell

MITCHELL makes a mildly diverting stop on the seemingly endless drive along I-90. The **Corn Palace** at 604 N Main St (summer daily 8am–9pm; winter Mon–Fri 8am–5pm; free) has been pegged as "the world's largest birdfeeder"; the first Corn Palace was built in 1892 to encourage settlement and to display local agricultural products. Topped with brightly painted onion-shaped domes and minarets, this kitsch Moorish transplant to the Corn Belt is decorated annually (at a cost of about $125,000) with large murals depicting farming and other outdoor scenes. The artists' materials consist exclusively of native corn, grains, and grasses of varying natural colors; further examples of such rural folk art are found inside. Mitchell's **visitor center** is across the street at 601 N Main St (Mon–Fri 9am–5pm; ☎605/996-5567 or 1-800/257-CORN, ⓦwww.cornpalace.com). Other places where you can while away time in Mitchell include a gallery devoted to a Yanktonai Sioux painter; a surprisingly engaging museum of dolls, including a salt-carved Shirley Temple; a pioneer museum; and a prehistoric Native American village.

Both the *Best Western* (☎605/996-5536; ❸) and the *Super 8* (☎605/996-9678; ❸) **motels** lie just off I-90 at exit 332. The *Lake Mitchell Campground*, one mile north of town on Hwy-37 (☎605/995-8457), has grassy tent sites ($13) that overlook the water.

The railroad-themed *Depot*, 210 S Main St (☎605/996-9417), is a fun place to grab a **meal**.

Pierre

Straggling along the east bank of the Missouri River at the center of South Dakota, **PIERRE** is the second smallest and by far the least sophisticated of all the US state capitals. With none of the plush hotels or fancy restaurants catering to power-broking politicos that you find in other capital cities, Pierre is instead a typical South Dakota town, whose 15,000 residents do their best to ignore the fact that it's the seat of state government.

Apart from the black-domed **capitol building** itself, which sits in a pleasant park at the northeast edge of downtown and is open for tours (daily 8am–10pm; free), there's not a lot to detain you here. One exception is the worthwhile **Cultural Heritage Center** (Mon–Fri 9am–4.30pm, Sat & Sun

1–4.30pm; $3), located high on a hill half a mile north of the capitol, and modeled on traditional Plains Indian dwellings. Repository for the usual barrage of pioneer implements and prehistoric artifacts, the museum is one of few such places that does more than pay lip service to the state's significant Native American cultures.

Pierre's **visitor center** is at 108 E Missouri St (☎605/224-7361 or 1-800/962-2034, ⓦ www.pierrechamber.com). *Pier 347*, 347 S Pierre St (☎605/224-2400), offers creative bagels and coffee drinks, while the fast-food chains line up along Sioux Avenue, which also holds the bulk of the town's **motels**, including the clean and comfortable *Governor's Inn*, 700 W Sioux Ave (☎605/224-4200 or 1-800/341-8000; ❸).

The Badlands

The White River **BADLANDS** could be considered a pocket-sized cousin to Arizona's Grand Canyon. Beyond the family resemblance, what's most impressive about the "Badlandscape" is not its scale, as at the Canyon, but rather its sheer strangeness. More than 35 million years ago this area of southwest South Dakota was a saltwater sea; later it became a marsh, into which sank the remains of such prehistoric mammals as sabre-toothed cats and three-toed horses, to be covered with white volcanic ash. Drying as it evolved, the terrain became unable to support the deep-rooted shrubs or trees that might have preserved it, and over the last few million years erosion has slowly eaten away layers of sand, silt, ash, mud, and gravel, to reveal rippling gradations of earth tones and pastel colors. The crumbly earth is carved into all manner of shapes: pinnacles, precipices, pyramids, knobs, cones, ridges, gorges, or, if you're feeling poetic, lunar sandcastles and cathedrals. The Sioux dubbed these incredible contortions of nature *Mako Sica* – literally, "land bad"; early French trappers echoed that with *Mauvaises Terres à Traverser*, or "bad lands to travel across"; they have also been aptly described as "hell with the fires out." Despite this daunting reputation, animals such as bighorn sheep, mule deer, and prairie dogs are at home here, while on average a million visitors pass through each year.

The most spectacular formations can be found within the **Badlands National Park**, particularly its northern sector, while the southern stretches are encompassed by the poverty-stricken Pine Ridge Indian Reservation. Clean-cut **Wall**, just a few miles north of the park boundaries, is the most-visited commercial center in the region.

Badlands National Park

About one-tenth of the Badlands – the most amazing parts – were declared a national park (open year-round) in the 1970s. The two most accessible entrances are off I-90 at exits 131 (northeast entrance) and 109–110 (at the town of Wall), connected by the forty-mile paved loop of Hwy-240, peppered with scenic overlooks; see p.861 for a map of the area. Visitors can backpack or climb just about anywhere; among the best of the marked **hiking trails** are the Door Trail, a half-hour loop that enters the eerie wasteland through a natural "doorway" in the rock pinnacles ten miles south of the northeast entrance, and the even shorter Fossil Exhibit Trail, ten miles further on. The Badlands' rainbow colors are most vibrant at dawn, dusk, and just after rainfall.

Adjoining the Ben Reifel **visitor center**, five miles from the northeast entrance (daily: June–Aug 7am–8pm; rest of year 8am–5pm; $10 per vehicle for seven days; (℡605/433-5361), is the only in-park **accommodation** option. *Cedar Pass Lodge*, which has its own **restaurant** (℡605/433-5460; cabins ❸, cottages ❹; mid-March to Oct), is operated by the Oglala Sioux, who use it as a base for assorted **tours** into the Pine Ridge Reservation (see below), and offer all-inclusive lodging-and-tour **packages**. Another **visitor center**, White River (June–Aug daily 10am–4pm), stands on Hwy-27 in the less-visited and less spectacular southern end of the park. A handful of seasonal **campgrounds** operate both in the park and in Wall (see below). Short scenic **helicopter rides** (from $15; ℡605/433-5322) leave from outside the northeast entrance.

Wall

The town of **WALL**, eight miles north of the Badlands, may look like nothing special, yet thanks to **Wall Drug**, begun modestly in 1931 as a pharmacy and veterinary supplies shop on Main Street, it's known around the world. You'll learn about Wall Drug's presence long before you reach town. Over five hundred billboards along I-90 tout its wares, including the free ice water that was its original sales gimmick. By the time you get to exit 110 (the one with the 85ft Wall Drug dinosaur), you'll be compelled to pull off and see what all the fuss is about.

Behind the hype lies a kitschy emporium that serves up to twenty thousand visitors per day. You can fill up on steaks or cakes in the 520-seat café-cum-Western art gallery, or just enjoy the wall-to-wall collection of photos, memorabilia, animal trophies, and mechanical automata like the Cowboy Orchestra and the Chuckwagon Quartet. The merchandise runs the gamut from quality (an excellent Western bookstore and a complete trail outfitters) to junk (anyone for a rattlesnake mold?). Most compelling, though, is the crackpot cornucopia atmosphere of this ultimate family store, a downmarket, down-home Disneyland wallowing in nostalgia.

Beyond the Wall Drug billboards lie the impressive **Buffalo Gap National Grasslands**, an empty and remote portion of South Dakota so bleak it's almost beautiful. The **National Grasslands Visitor Center**, at 708 Main St (daily 8am–6pm), makes a good jumping-off point and will provide maps.

There's absolutely no reason to spend the night in Wall, but if you're stuck, try the *Best Western Plains Motel*, 712 Glenn St (℡605/279-2145; ❹), or the slightly less expensive *Super 8*, across the road at no. 711 (℡605/279-2688 or 1-800/843-1991; ❹). The *Cactus Café and Lounge* on Main Street (℡605/279-2561) offers a mixed menu of reasonably priced Mexican, Italian, and American **food**.

Pine Ridge Indian Reservation

Pine Ridge, the second largest Indian reservation in the United States (after Arizona's Navajo Nation; see p.1033), overlaps the southern Badlands. It is also located in the nation's poorest county. Its prefab homes and beat-up trucks blend sadly and uneasily with the surrounding dry grasslands, rocky bluffs, and tree-lined creeks.

The largest town, also called **PINE RIDGE**, comprises a collection of shabby, paint-stripped structures. Though the emergence of the profitable Prairie Wind casino in Oglala has improved life here, in many ways the reservation towns are an even more bitter pill to swallow than places like the nearby site of the Wounded Knee massacre: nowhere is America's disparity of wealth and opportunity so evident as in this area, which posts the highest poverty- and alcohol-related death statistics on the continent, and where the average lifespan is just 52 years. Internal strife continues to plague the tribe; in 2000 the entire tribal council was ousted and some members jailed in a money-laundering scandal that put the reservation $5 million in the hole. A group of vigilante elders temporarily took over the tribal HQ, but were later forced out by a court decision.

Red Cloud Indian School, four miles north of Pine Ridge on US-18, is named after a former chief whose fight against the US forced the closure of military forts on Sioux hunting grounds. Each summer, the school holds an Indian art show featuring work by tribes in the US and Canada; it also has a permanent display of star quilts (a Sioux tradition), paintings, and a gift shop (daily 8am–5pm; free). Red Cloud, who later signed a peace treaty with the US and invited Jesuits to teach his tribe "the ways of the white man," is buried in a cemetery on a nearby knoll. The **Oglala Nation Fair**, held over the first weekend in August, features a powwow and rodeo. For details, contact the Oglala Sioux Tribe, Box H, Pine Ridge, SD 57770 (☎605/867-6121). For news and both traditional Lakota Sioux and contemporary American music, tune in to KILI 90.1 FM, "the Voice of the Lakota Nation."

Wounded Knee

No other atrocity against Native Americans remains so potent and poignant as the massacre at **WOUNDED KNEE**. On December 29, 1890, the US Army delivered a coup de grace to the vestiges of Plains Indian resistance, killing several hundred unarmed Sioux men, women, and children. Most were **Ghost Dancers**, followers of a messianic cult who believed that by trance-inducing dancing and singing they could recover their lost way of life. The massacre was triggered by a misunderstanding during a tribal round-up: a deaf Indian, asked to surrender his rifle along with his peers, instead held it above his head, shouting that he'd paid a lot for it. An officer grabbed at the gun, it went off, and the troops started shooting.

A commemorative stone **monument**, surrounded by a chain-link fence, marks the victims' collective gravesite, off Hwy-27 toward the bottom of Pine Ridge Reservation. Somehow it has an intangible feeling of grief and anger, the mass murder here having left an indelible scar on all First Americans. Eighty-three years later, members of the radical **American Indian Movement** (**AIM**) grabbed headlines by occupying Wounded Knee in a dispute over the federal imposition of a tribal government; they were eventually dispersed by armed FBI agents and a paramilitary unit. More peaceably, since the mid-1980s the **Sitanka Wokiksuye** movement has organized an annual pilgrimage to the site, arriving in harsh winter weather by horse and travois, to symbolically release the spirits of their dead ancestors. The tribe has so far refused federal funds to turn the site into a glossy national monument, wanting instead to leave it uncommercialized; a concrete block nearby offers a few souvenirs and local knowledge.

The Black Hills

Our people knew there was yellow metal in little chunks up there, but they did not bother with it, because it was not good for anything.

Black Elk, Oglala Sioux holy man

The timbered, rocky **BLACK HILLS** rise like an island from a sea of rolling hills and flat, grain-growing plains, stretching for a hundred miles between the Belle Fourche River in the north and the Cheyenne to the south, and varying in width from forty to sixty miles. For many generations of Sioux, their value was and still is immeasurable. The Hills are "the heart of everything that is," a kind of spiritual safe, a place of gods and holy mountains where warriors went to speak with Wakan Tanka (the Great Spirit) and await visions. They were dubbed *Paha Sapa*, or Black Hills, even though they are actually mountains (the highest, Harney Peak, rises 7242ft), and the blue spruce and Norway pine trees that cover them only appear to be black from a distance.

Imagining the Hills to be worthless, the United States government drew up a treaty in the mid-nineteenth century that gave them and most of the land west of the Missouri River to the Indians. All such treaties were destined to be broken when the discovery of **gold** turned the Indians' Eden into the white explorers' El Dorado, and fortune-hunters came pouring in. The story has an incomplete postscript: in 1980, the US Supreme Court ordered the federal government to pay the Sioux $105 million in **compensation** for the illegal seizure of the Hills in 1877. After heated debate among Native American representatives, this settlement was rejected and a steering commit-tee subsequently formed to campaign for the return of the Hills themselves to the tribes. The legal battle continues, often hindered by a lack of consensus among the tribes.

The Hills these days are a major tourist destination, albeit attracting more Midwesterners, driven stir-crazy by the endless plains, than international trav-elers for whom forested hills may be less of a novelty. As yet, however, despite the real danger of the entire area becoming an ersatz Western theme park – as evidenced by its T-shirt stores, pseudo-historical wax museums, cowboy supper shows, and water slides – marketing and merchandising aren't so extensive as to rob the Hills of all their beauty or dignity.

The more thickly wooded north is noted more for urban activities, with the casino town of **Deadwood** its busiest spot. No place in the Hills is much more than ninety minutes from the four presidential heads carved into **Mount Rushmore**, but even more remarkable is the **Crazy Horse Memorial**, one of the world's most ambitious works-in-progress. In the shade of these great monuments, the less spoiled southern hills are home to the bison of **Custer State Park** and **Wind Cave National Park**, along with the town of **Hot Springs**.

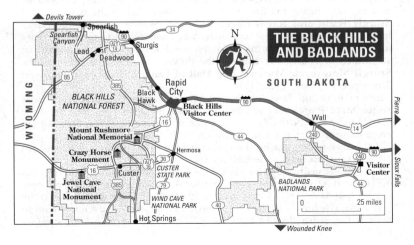

The North Hills

The predominantly privately owned **northern Black Hills** are more commercialized than their southern siblings, with **Rapid City**, the hub, surrounded by more interesting smaller towns, such as **Sturgis**, **Spearfish**, and **Deadwood**. The back roads, especially in the **Spearfish Canyon** area, form a network of prime driving and cycling country. The Black Hills **Information Center**, exit 61 off I-90 (June–Aug daily 8am–8pm; rest of year Mon–Fri 8am–5pm, Sat & Sun 9am–5pm; ☎605/355-3700), is just outside of Rapid City and has an abundance of information on the Black Hills, the Badlands, and Native American points of interest.

Rapid City

South Dakota's second largest town, **RAPID CITY**, is all but swamped with family-fun attractions, though it makes a convenient base for exploring the charms of the Black Hills' lesser communities. In town, the **Journey Museum**, 222 New York St (daily 9am–5pm; $6), leads you through time, beginning with the geologic evolution of the Plains and the era of dinosaurs, right through the life of the Plains Indians to the pioneers who invaded their territory.

    Greyhound pulls into town at 333 Sixth St. The **visitor center** is in the Civic Center, 444 Mount Rushmore Rd N (Mon–Fri 8am–5pm; ☎605/343-1744 or 1-800/487-3223, ⓦwww.rapidcitycvb.com). Rapid City has the cheapest **lodgings** in the Black Hills. The Bavarian wood trimmings and soft Sioux furnishings of the delightful *Hotel Alex Johnson*, 523 Sixth St (☎605/342-1210 or 1-800/888-2539; ❸–❺), provide a great escape from the dull corporate decor prevalent in Rapid City, while the *Best Western Ramkotta Inn*, I-90 exit 59 (☎605/343-8550; ❹), is clean and right off the highway. Both the **food** and **beer** at *Firehouse Brewing Co.*, 610 Main St (☎605/348-1915) – which has plenty of outdoor seating – are worth sampling; while *B&L Bagels*, 512 Main St (☎605/399-1777), is a convenient bakery and deli.

Sturgis

The sleepy town of **STURGIS**, thirty miles north of Rapid City, comes to life in a big way during the first full week of August, when the world-famous **Sturgis Rally and Races** (☎605/347-9158, ⓦwww.sturgismotorcyclerally.com) packs out virtually every motel and campground in the region with motorcycle enthusiasts. For the rest of the year, bikers have to make do with an abundance of Harley souvenirs in the downtown stores, plus the worthy **Sturgis Motorcycle Museum and Hall of Fame**, 1344 Main St (Mon–Fri 9am–6pm, Sat 10am–4pm; $3).

    East of town, off Hwy-34, the volcanic outcrop which dominates **Bear Butte State Park** stands as a lonely sentinel, detached from the rest of the hills. Hundreds of Native Americans come to this site on retreat each year; to avoid disturbing anyone, check with the park's **visitor center** (☎605/347-5240) before setting out on the excellent hike to the summit. Campers can secure a **tent site** within the park for $6.

    The Sturgis **visitor center** (☎605/347-2556, ⓦwww.sturgis-sd.org) lies off I-90 exit 32. Of the wide range of **motels** in Sturgis, the reasonably central *Starlight Motel*, 1802 S Junction Ave (☎605/347-2506; ❸), represents the best value. The lure of breakfast, burgers, and overpriced souvenirs is hard to resist at the garish *Roadkill Café*, 1333 Main St (☎605/347-4502; summer only).

Deadwood

One of the West's wildest Gold Rush towns, **DEADWOOD**, in a deep gulch high in the hills 42 miles northwest of Rapid City, has the rare accolade of being a **National Historic Landmark** in its entirety. Within a year of the discovery of **gold** here in 1876, six thousand gold-diggers had swarmed in to stake their claims; con artists, outlaws, and other dubious frontier types were not far behind. Among them were James Butler, aka **Wild Bill Hickok** – sometime spy, scout, bullwhacker, stagecoach driver, sheriff, and gambler, who spent only a few weeks in Deadwood prior to his murder by a young drifter named Jack McCall – and Martha "**Calamity Jane**" Canary Burke, an illiterate alcoholic whose checkered career included stints as a dishwasher, muleskinner, scout, prostitute, nurse, and Wild West Show performer. She died penniless in 1903, her last wish to be buried beside Hickok in **Mount Moriah Cemetery**, a short but blustery hike from town.

Gambling was outlawed in Deadwood in 1889, the year South Dakota achieved statehood, but betting parlors and brothels flourished well into the twentieth century. Now the old ghosts have been revitalized, since the passing of limited-stakes gambling legislation in 1989. With a residential population of only 2000, Deadwood is now booming again, the old gaming dens and flophouses transformed for the sake of tourism into flash casinos and rustic saloons. Corny but entertaining gunfights, sing-alongs, and community theater are shown sporadically; for details, check with the **CVB**, 735 Main St (℡1-800/999-1876, ⓦwww.deadwood.org).

For an overview of Deadwood past and present, start by visiting the **History and Information Center**, in the heart of town at 3 Siever St (daily: May–Oct 8am–8pm; rest of year 9am–5pm; ℡605/578-2507). Main Street boasts several grand old **hotels**, including the *Bullock* at no. 633 (℡605/578-1745 or 1-800/336-1876; ❹–❻), and the *Franklin Hotel* at no. 700 (℡605/578-2241 or 1-800/688-1876; ❹–❻), which has an elegant Old World dining room. Budget **motels** are found a mile south of town on Hwy-85 towards Lead, including the *Thunder Cove Inn* (℡1-800/209-7361; ❸). The *Penny Motel*, 818 Main St (℡605/578-1842, ⓦwww.pennymotel.com; ❶–❷), offers excellent **hostel** accommodation at $12 for members and $15 for nonmembers, as well as bike rental, shuttle service, and Internet access. *Saloon #10*, 657 Main St (℡605/578-3346), has cold **beer**, sawdust floors, and lots of memorabilia. Above the door is the chair in which Hickok was sitting when he was shot dead, while holding two aces, a pair of eights, and the nine of diamonds – forever after christened the Dead Man's Hand. Several casinos along Main Street aim to lure in the gamblers with cut-price **buffets**, but Deadwood's finest **dining** is at the dinner-only *Jake's*, on the top floor of Kevin Costner's Midnight Star casino, 677 Main St (℡605/578-1555).

Spearfish Canyon area

Aspen, birch, and white spruce spread over the towering limestone cliffs above the nineteen-mile **Spearfish Canyon National Scenic Highway**, which starts on Hwy-14A half an hour's drive west of Deadwood, and threads past sights such as Bridal Veil and Roughlock falls. The route reveals almost as many **gastronomic pleasures** as it does scenic ones. Twenty minutes out of Deadwood, the *Latchstring Restaurant* (℡605/584-3333) serves steaks, pasta, shrimp, and excellent rainbow trout almandine. Marking the southern mouth of the canyon at Hwy-14A and Hwy-85, the *Cheyenne Crossing Country Store* (℡605/584-3510) is a must if you have a hearty appetite; popular menu items include all-day breakfasts with buffalo sausage, enormous Indian tacos, and traditional Indian fry bread.

Marking the canyon's north end, **SPEARFISH** itself reels in the crowds each summer for the popular **Black Hills Passion Play**, a re-enactment of Jesus Christ's death and resurrection (June–Aug Tues, Thurs & Sun 8pm; tickets $10–18; ☎605/642-2646 or 1-800/457-0160). The **visitor center** is at 106 W Kansas St (☎605/642-2626 or 1-800/626-8013, ⓦwww.spearfish.sd.us). Burgers and inventive snacks are served in the **restaurant** at *Lown House B&B*, 745 Fifth St (☎605/642-5663), which also has good-value **rooms** (the loft sleeps six comfortably; ❹–❻). The quiet *Best Western Downtown Spearfish*, 346 W Kansas St (☎605/642-4676 or 1-800/843-6358; ❸), is also recommended. *Sanford's*, 545 Jackson St (☎605/642-3204), is a lively, student-oriented pub and restaurant; for a morning-after coffee, call in at *Common Grounds*, 111 E Hudson St (☎605/642-4292).

From Spearfish, the spectacular **Devils Tower** stands just an hour's drive away across the Wyoming state line (see p.923).

The South Hills

The **southern Black Hills** encompass lower foothills and wooded pasture-land; from a purely physical standpoint they are more attractive than the north, drawing visitors for their scenery and wildlife rather than kitsch or gambling. The two big mountain carvings, **Mount Rushmore** and **Crazy Horse**, mark the northern end of the region; **Custer State Park** and **Wind Cave National Park** account for much of the central zone; while the pleasant town of **Hot Springs** sits on the southern edge.

Mount Rushmore National Memorial

America's two largest stone carvings are a mere seventeen miles apart – no more than spitting distance when you consider the scale on which they're conceived. The better-known **Mount Rushmore National Memorial** (daily: summer 8am–10pm; rest of year 8am–5pm), originally dubbed "The Shrine of Democracy," is the linchpin of the Hills' tourist circuit. It's an easy 24-mile drive southwest of Rapid City, though by far the most impressive approach is to take **Iron Mountain Road** (US-16A) from **Custer State Park** (see p.866), which runs for seventeen miles up and over 5500ft Iron Mountain.

In 1923, state historian Doane Robinson and the sculptor **Gutzon Borglum**, known for carvings such as the leaders of the Confederacy in Stone Mountain, Georgia (see p.554), talked over the possibility of turning the imposing fingers of granite known as the Needles into a dramatic patriotic sculpture. They discussed depictions of such heroic figures of the West as Lewis and Clark, Buffalo Bill Cody, and Jim Bridger. Borglum opted for a nearby mountain named after New York attorney Charles E. Rushmore, upon which he would fashion the faces and heads of four certifiably great American presi-dents: **George Washington**, **Thomas Jefferson**, **Abraham Lincoln**, and Borglum's buddy, **Theodore Roosevelt**.

Borglum talked, dreamed, and worked big. "American art ought to be monu-mental, in keeping with American life," he opined. Sixty when the project began in 1927, he died fourteen years later, $200,000 in debt, just a few months prior to the dedication of the last head – Roosevelt's – in 1939. Inclement weather and uncertain funding had meant that the actual sculpting took about six and a half years, at a total cost of $993,000. Half a million tons of rock were removed to reach the softer, more malleable granite from which the heads were dynamited, drilled, and chiseled into recognizable shape.

The Big Four gaze out impassively, cheek by jowl, arguably a greater engineering feat than an artistic one. Each head is about sixty feet from chin to crown. (By way of comparison, the Statue of Liberty's head is only seventeen feet.) Lincoln, Borglum's favorite, has an eighteen-foot-long nose and the glint in each eleven-foot-wide eye is thirty inches. If he and his fellow presidents had been done full-figure to scale, they'd stand 465ft tall and be able to stride across the Potomac River in Washington, DC, without getting their knees wet.

The best time to view Rushmore is dawn or dusk, when there are fewer people and better lighting. Patriots flock here for a massive **fireworks display** on July 3. Although there is no admission charge, an $8 **parking fee** has been introduced since the construction of a hideous new multilevel parking lot and high-tech **visitor center**; you can, however, park for free at a lot a quarter of a mile away. The **café** here, complete with panoramic windows, as seen in Hitchcock's *North by Northwest*, serves full meals and "Monumental Breakfasts" of hash browns, eggs, country-fried steak with gravy, and a biscuit piled on one plate. With alternative bases such as Rapid City or Custer State Park so close to hand, there's no particular reason to stay in the nearest town, Keystone – a once quiet mining town turned T-shirt hawker's paradise.

Crazy Horse Memorial

In 1939, prompted by the sight of the Rushmore monument, Sioux leader Henry Standing Bear wrote to **Korczak Ziolkowski**, who had just won first prize for sculpture at the New York World's Fair, telling him that Indians "would like the white man to know that the red man has great heroes, too." The chief invited Ziolkowski to take on a similar project – and, less than a decade later, pushing forty and with just $174 to his name, the New Englander moved permanently to the Black Hills to undertake a vastly more ambitious mission than Rushmore – the **Crazy Horse Memorial**, on US-16, five miles north of Custer.

The subject, the revered warrior Crazy Horse on horseback (see p.855), so appealed to Ziolkowski that he set out to make his monument the biggest statue in the world, higher even than the Great Pyramid. The work he began on **Thunderhead Mountain** in 1948 – five Native American survivors of the Battle of Little Bighorn attended the dedication ceremony – didn't stop with his death in 1982; his widow, children, and grandchildren continue to realize his vision. National and international interest has greatly increased as the monument finally starts to take recognizable shape; the breathtaking, 90ft-high face was completed in time for the fiftieth anniversary celebrations in 1998, although it could well be another fifty years before the project is finished. Neither words nor photographs can articulate the enormous scale of the thing. Even in person it's hard to believe that the main viewing terrace at the **visitor center** is nearly a mile from the carving itself, and that the 20ft scale model on show there is 34 times smaller than the end result, which will be 563ft high and 641ft long. All four Rushmore heads could fit in Crazy Horse's head, from which will jut a 44ft stone feather. Nor do the plans stop with the carving: Ziolkowski's descendants hope to build a North American Indian museum, university, and medical training center on the land stretching between the visitor center and the monument.

Ziolkowski himself raised and spent $4 million on the non-profit project. His belief in free enterprise has meant that the undertaking has refused to accept federal or state funds, instead relying entirely on admissions and contributions. He twice turned down $10 million in federal funds, claiming the government had no right to be involved after all the treaties it had broken with the Sioux. The site, open dawn to dusk year-round (and illuminated for an hour each night), is free to Native Americans. **Admission** for all others costs $9. Apart from the monument, the premises include an exhibit of Native American artifacts and crafts, a Native American Cultural Center, the *Laughing Water Restaurant* (May–Oct only), and an extensive gift shop. Coffee and souvenir blast fragments are free. Wonderful **private tours** of the construction site at the top of the mountain are given in exchange for a high-level contribution. On the first weekend in June, the public is invited to hike to the top and see the work close-up.

Custer State Park

The 73,000 sublime, billboard-free acres of **Custer State Park** fill much of the southern-central Black Hills, a perfect antidote to the commercial crassness elsewhere. The **Needles Highway** (Hwy-87; open mid-April to mid-Oct) winds for fourteen miles through pine forests and past the eponymous jagged granite spires in the park's northwestern corner, between Sylvan and Legion lakes. Not far from Sylvan Lake, as you pass close to the summit of Harney Peak (South Dakota's highest point, at 7242ft), look south to spot the **Needle's Eye**, a slender gap in one of the pinnacles that measures three to four feet wide and fifty to sixty feet tall. The eighteen-mile **Wildlife Loop** (separate from the Needles Highway) undulates through the rolling meadows along the park's southern edge. Sunrise and sunset are prime times to spy such critters as elk, bighorn sheep, antelope, deer, burros, and the most plentiful species, bison. Finally, **Iron Mountain Road** (US-16A), to the northeast, makes a dramatic route to Mount Rushmore (see p.864). This is the most likely place to bump into the park's famous "begging burros": tame and disarming four-legged panhandlers who stick their snouts through the windows of passing vehicles in search of handouts.

For a fuller appreciation of the beauty of Custer State Park, forsake your car and set off into the wilderness. Rangers at the park entrances – where you're required to pay **entrance fees** of $3 per person, or $5 per vehicle (the pass remains valid for a week, and admits you to all other South Dakota state parks) – can advise on **hiking** and **biking trails**, while concession firms offer horseback rides, boat rental, and cross-country drives in open-topped jeeps. Good short hikes include the one-hour **Stockade Lake Trail** in the west, which climbs to give distant views across the lake to Harney Peak and the Needles, and the two-hour **Lovers Leap Trail**, which starts from the park's main Peter Norbeck **visitor center**, on Hwy-16A in the east (daily: summer 8am–8pm; rest of year 9am–5pm; ☎605/255-4464).

As long as nightlife isn't high on your agenda, the park's four state-run resorts make it a splendid **place to stay** (for reservations call ☎1-800/658-3530). The finest is the *State Game Lodge* (☎605/255-4541) on Hwy-16A not far from the visitor center, which operates a motel-style lodge and also has some lovely individual cabins (both ❹) at the edge of the woods; the *Pheasant Dining Room* offers hearty, meaty meals. President Coolidge planned to stay for a week when he arrived here in 1927, but found it so much to his liking that he hauled his aides over from DC and ran the country from the lodge for the entire summer. Tucked in the northwest corner on its own artificial lake, the *Sylvan Lake Resort* (☎605/574-2561; ❸–❻) similarly offers 31 comfy cabins, more traditional rooms in its tasteful main building, and the upscale *Lakota Dining Room*. Custer State Park also has eight **campgrounds** (☎1-800/710-2267), which cost $12–16 a night, plus park entrance fees.

The Bison of the Great Plains

In the fifteenth century, the Great Plains were roamed by one hundred million shaggy, short-sighted American **bison** (popularly known as buffalo, a corruption of the French *boeuf*). Apart from eating their flesh, Native Americans used the fur and hide for clothing and shelter, the bones for weapons, utensils, and toys, and the droppings for fuel. Eliminating the bison en masse was a mercilessly effective way to deplete the Indians as well. By 1900 there were fewer than one thousand bison left in North America.

Custer State Park was instrumental in helping to raise that meager number to a head count of 250,000 in the US and Canada. The park's own one thousand bison constitute the country's second largest publicly owned herd, surpassed only by Yellowstone National Park (see p.927). However, over ninety percent of bison in the US are now privately owned – the meat, higher in protein and lower in cholesterol than either chicken or tuna, is becoming something of a cross between a novelty and a delicacy item in restaurants (you can try it in burger form at the *State Game Lodge* in Custer State Park, as well as dozens of other places around South Dakota). The Triple U Ranch, outside Pierre, South Dakota, boasts a herd of 3500 strong, though Ted Turner owns around 20,000, split between his ranches in several western states.

The Custer State Park bison are free to roam where they please until either the last Monday of September or the first Monday in October, when the park stages its annual **roundup**. From selected viewing points, the public is welcome to witness one of the Midwest's more thrilling occasions: helicopters, jeeps, and pickup trucks, as well as riders on horseback, steer the often recalcitrant herd down a six-mile "corridor" and into a series of pens. There the calves are branded and vaccinated, and the whole herd sorted to determine which five hundred will be auctioned off on the third Saturday in November. Proceeds from the sale account for twenty percent of the park's annual revenue.

Don't let the tranquil, easygoing appearance of North America's biggest mammal lull you into a false sense of security. An average bull can stand six feet high at the hump, weigh up to a ton, outrun a horse, turn on a dime, and gore a human most efficiently.

Custer

In little **CUSTER**, five miles west of the park on US-16, the *Bavarian Inn* on the main highway has classic **German dining** and **rooms** (☎605/673-2802 or 1-800/657-4312; ❹), while the *Custer Motel*, 109 Mount Rushmore Rd (☎605/673-2876; ❸), is one of the cheapest places to stay in the Black Hills. Of many garish **campgrounds**, *Flintstones Bedrock City* (☎605/673-4664), with its own small theme park, manages to steal the show. The **visitor center** is at 615 Washington St (☎605/673-2244 or 1-800/992-9818, ⓦwww.custersd.com).

Twelve miles west of Custer is the **Jewel Cave National Monument** (daily 8.30am–6pm; $8–20 for 1–4hr tours; ☎605/673-2288, ⓦwww.nps.gov/jeca), where spelunkers are sure to receive a layer of manganese dust; call ahead for tour details.

Wind Cave National Park

Beneath wide-open rangelands, **Wind Cave National Park**, ten minutes north of Hot Springs (see below), comprises over 100 miles of mapped underground passages etched out of limestone. One of the largest caves in the US, it was discovered in 1881 when a loud whistling noise on the plains led a settler to a hole in the ground – the cave's only natural opening. The wind, caused by differences between atmospheric pressures in the cave and outside, was apparently enough to blow the discoverer's hat off. Nowadays rangers lead a variety of cave **tours** ($6–20 based on length of tour) from the **visitor center** (hours vary seasonally; ☎605/745-4600, ⓦwww.nps.gov/wica/), pointing out delicate features such as frostwork and boxwork along the way. If you come in summer, forget the standard walking tours and opt for the ones that allow you to crawl around in the smaller passages, or explore the caves by candlelight (call ahead).

Even if you lack the time or inclination to delve into the Dakotas' dank bowels, simply **driving** through the park is yet another unmissable Black Hills experience. Its native grass prairieland is home to deer, antelope, elk, coyote, prairie dogs, and a sizeable herd of buffalo.

Hot Springs

The Black Hills' southern anchor, **HOT SPRINGS**, differs from other regional towns in that it hasn't tarted up its downtown to look like a movie set. It doesn't need to. Several dozen utilitarian yet handsome sandstone structures dominate its center, through which flows the sprightly Fall River.

Battles over the town's thermal pools have caused as much grief as the clamor for gold. Before white settlement, the Sioux drove out the Cheyenne, and later landowners, speculators, and settlers dodged and outwitted each other for ownership of the springs. The disputes ceased in 1890 when Fred Evans incorporated numerous small springs and one mammoth hot-water pool into a spa center. Today, **Evans Plunge**, on the north edge of town at 1145 N River St (summer daily 8am–10pm; rest of year times vary; $8; ☎605/745-5165), is a popular family-fun center, where three great slides zoom down into the 87°F waters.

The unique **Mammoth Site** on the Hwy-18 bypass is the only in situ display of mammoth fossils in the US (mid-May through Aug daily 8am–8pm; rest of year times vary; $5.50). In 1974, building on a housing project here came to an abrupt halt when a tractor driver unearthed a seven-foot tusk. Paleontologists soon declared that the workers had discovered the 26,000-year-old grave of Columbian and Woolly mammoths – to date, 52 animals, all male, have been found. Inside the dome, fascinating **tours** explain how these ten-ton mammoths, along with camels, bears, and rodents, were trapped in a steep-sided sinkhole (a pond formed by a collapsed underground cave) and were gradually covered by sediment. Complete skeletons are easy to pick out in the excavation site, which is still being uncovered slowly by groups of summer volunteers.

Seven miles south of Hot Springs, the huge reservoir of the **Angostura Dam State Recreation Area** ($3 per person), set against contorted sandstone bluffs, is a picture-perfect spot for boating and jet-skiing. Equipment can be rented from Breakers Beach Club, a small hut offering beer, snacks, and beach volleyball, at the north entrance.

Information for visitors to Hot Springs is available from the cabin at 630 N River St or from the **CVB**, 801 S Sixth St (May–Sept Mon–Fri 9am–7pm, Sat 9am–6pm, Sun 1–5pm; rest of year Mon–Fri 8am–5pm; ☎605/745-4140 or 1-800/325-6991, ⓦwww.hotsprings-sd.com). **Accommodation** rates are a bit more reasonable than in the hectic northern towns. The *Super 8*, 800 Mammoth St (☎605/745-3888 or 1-800/800-8000; ❹), is unusual in having a bar and restaurant, both of which are recommended; alternatives include the old, faded, riverside *Braun Hotel*, 902 N River St (☎605/745-3187; ❹–❺), and the sumptuous *Villa Teresa B&B*, 801 Almond St (☎605/745-4633; ❹). The *Elkhorn Café*, 310 S Chicago St (☎605/745-6556), serves **sandwiches** and salads on a sunny terrace.

North Dakota

NORTH DAKOTA has no nationally recognizable landmarks, nor is the state's history particularly lurid or glamorous. It seems like somebody's quiet afterthought, a place to pass through. Grain silos loom on the horizon, and the haystacks resemble loaves of bread. In the summer, with the sun baking in a defiantly blue sky and the wind raking strong fingers through tall fields of golden wheat and flax, North Dakota epitomizes all things rural American. Charming, picturesque – and a bit maddening.

The influx of Europeans into the Dakota Territory, spurred by the **Homestead Act of 1862**, precipitated a population and agricultural boom that lasted into the twentieth century. As in South Dakota, the fertile east is more thickly settled than the west, where vast cattle and sheep ranges predominate. It was the east that was hardest hit by the so-called **500-year flood** of 1997, when 1.7 million low-lying acres of farmland were inundated, and the entire state was declared a disaster area. Lately, North Dakotan lawmakers, ashamed of their state's reputation as an arctic wasteland, have proposed that the "North" be dropped from the state's title, leaving just "Dakota," a suggestion most locals vehemently protest.

From **Fargo**, the state's largest city, I-94 passes through the central capital of **Bismarck**, and on to the **Bad Lands** of the west, once cherished by President Theodore Roosevelt. Though the national park bearing his name is a key destination, Roosevelt would surely not be pleased about the continuing disfiguration of much of western North Dakota by strip-mining operations.

Getting around North Dakota

Amtrak runs one **train** per day in each direction between Fargo and Williston in the northwest, via Grand Forks. Greyhound is the major interstate **bus** operator: three or four buses per day make the ten-hour trip from Minneapolis/St Paul to Bismarck, via Grand Forks and Fargo, before heading west along I-94 into Montana.

East of the Missouri River

Far more of North Dakota lies east of the big winding **Missouri River**, the state's uneven dividing line, than west. The **Red River Valley**, the state's furthest eastern strip, is home to two sizeable cities, easygoing **Grand Forks** and the less attractive **Fargo**. Pelicans, geese, swans, prairie chickens, and ring-necked pheasants live off the sloughs and potholes of the rolling, glaciated prairie of south-central North Dakota, while lakes and woodlands dominate the north and the Canadian border. **Spirit Lake Sioux Indian Reservation** at Devils Lake is midway between Grand Forks and the low-slung Turtle Mountains, which are topped by Lake Metigoshe and the **International Peace Garden** (more of a political symbol than a compelling sight).

Grand Forks

GRAND FORKS sits eighty miles north of I-94, right next to Minnesota and a mere 75 miles south of the Canadian border. Even before its foundation a century ago, fur traders had used the area to rest and barter during their travels between Winnipeg and Minneapolis. It's a small, friendly, outdoorsy city, with nineteen parks and several tree-lined avenues of fine homes. Furious construction has rebuilt the downtown area, ravaged in the 1997 floodwaters. But the disaster shook investors' confidence and most of the new buildings lie empty, save for their "for lease" signs posted across the windows.

The most interesting distractions can be found on the redbrick main campus of the **University of North Dakota**. The **North Dakota Museum of Art** (Mon–Fri 9am–5pm, Sat & Sun 1–5pm; donation) offers an eclectic assortment of contemporary art and top touring exhibits. Fascinating tours of the **John D. Odegard School of Aerospace Sciences**, one of the largest civilian pilot-training schools in the world, take in flight simulators, the air-traffic control room, and an altitude chamber.

Grand Forks' **visitor center** is at 4251 Gateway Drive (℡701/746-0444 or 1-800/866-4566, ⓦ www.grandforkscvb.org). **Greyhound** stops at US-81 and Hwy-2, while **Amtrak** pulls in at no. 5555 W Demers Ave. Downtown's *Best Western Town House*, 710 First Ave N (℡701/746-5411; ❸), is Grand Forks' most luxurious **motel**; for about $20 less you can stay in the kitsch splendor of the *Budget Inn West* on US-2 (℡701/775-5341; ❷), and swim in its cowboy-boot-shaped pool. The most serene place to **camp** is 20 miles west on US-2, in the grounds of Turtle River State Park (℡701/594-4445; $11; reservations recommended). For **dining**, the *Roadhouse Café*, 4720 Gateway Drive (℡701/772-1273), serves solid American fare and breakfasts.

Devils Lake

The scruffy town of **DEVILS LAKE**, ninety miles west of Grand Forks on US-2, shares its name with the state's largest natural body of water, which has two state parks and two private campgrounds along more than 300 sprawling, irregular, and growing miles of shoreline. The damming of rivers in the northern part of the state inadvertently caused Devils Lake to rise; so far it has gone up 25 feet and quadrupled in area since 1997. Pastureland has been submerged, dikes built, roads raised, and one town, nearby Churchs Ferry, evacuated. Embarrassed engineers, nervous politicians, and a frustrated public are still at a loss about how to stem the tide – $300 million has already been spent on relief.

Downtown, now saved by a seven-mile-long dike, holds a smattering of nineteenth-century buildings and a few rough-and-ready **bars**. Most of the places to stay, such as the *Super 8* (℡701/662-8656; ❸), are strung along US-2; the *Woodland Resort*, on Creel Bay, about six miles from town (℡701/662-5996, ⓦ www.woodlandresort.com; ❷–❸), rents boats, pontoons, and fishing gear. You can **camp** three miles east of town on Hwy-2 at Shelver's Grove State Park (℡701/766-4015) for $7 per person, $5 per vehicle – but if the lake rises another six inches you'll be swimming in your tent. For more **info**, contact the Devils Lake **CVB**, on Hwy-2E next to the *Great American Inn* (Mon–Fri 9am–5pm; ℡701/265-8188).

Fifteen miles south of town, **Spirit Lake Sioux Indian Reservation** is the site of **Fort Totten Military Post** (daily 8am–5pm; $4), one of the best-preserved frontier military posts in the country. During the last weekend in July, the reservation hosts the thrilling **Spirit Lake Oyate Wacipi Powwow and Rodeo** (daily $5, $10 for a weekend pass). It's an impassioned, alcohol-free, multitribal party at which hundreds of magnificently clothed dancers of all ages compete for cash prizes.

The West

Anyone with a hankering to play cowboy could do worse than follow in the footsteps of **Theodore Roosevelt**, who declared "I never would have been president if it had not been for my experiences in North Dakota." Roosevelt initially came to the state in search of spiritual and physical renewal after the deaths (on the same day) of his mother and first wife. He dubbed what he discovered during his few years in this "grimly picturesque" area, with its clear skies, panoramic views, and weird, colorful landforms, a "perfect freedom." The national park named after him is the choicest destination in the **North Dakota Bad Lands** (distinct from South Dakota's Badlands) that dominate the state's western half.

The **Missouri River** wriggles like a giant raggedy worm out of Montana, down past North Dakota's capital, **Bismarck**, and into South Dakota. En route it is transformed into **Lake Sakakawea**, a virtual inland sea nearly two hundred miles long that's the state's premier water playground. **Scenic state highways 1804 and 1806** follow the routes mapped out by the Lewis and Clark expedition in those respective years.

Bismarck and Mandan

The West seems to begin as soon as you cross the Missouri River from **BISMARCK**, a capital city with a small-town feel, to Mandan. Both were founded in 1872, Bismarck as a military camp to protect railroad crews from hostile Indians and outlaws. Its original name, Edwinton, was changed by the secretary of the Northern Pacific Railroad, both in honor of German Chancellor Otto von Bismarck and in the hope of attracting Teutonic settlers. Though the scheme failed, the name stuck. The city survived an early lawless period (present-day Fourth Street was once dubbed "Murderers' Gulch") and a major fire to become first the territorial and then the state capital.

Contemporary Bismarck is pretty much contained within the oblong between I-94 in the north and Main Avenue to the south. Locals are proud of their nineteen-story limestone **capitol building**, 600 E Boulevard Ave, dating from the mid-1930s and set at the crest of a public park. The interior, a model of spatial economy and marbled Art Deco elegance, is open for free guided **tours** (Mon–Fri 8–11am & 1–4pm, Sat 9–11am & 1–4pm, Sun 1–4pm). Across the street, the superb **North Dakota Heritage Center** (Mon–Fri 8am–5pm, Sat 9am–5pm, Sun 11am–5pm; donation) divides the state's past into six resonant sections, from the dinosaurs onwards. Look out for Sitting Bull's painted robe and the bison "smell box," which offers homesick cowboys and curious tourists a whiff of buffalo dung.

The major reason to venture into **MANDAN** is **Fort Lincoln State Park** ($4), five miles south of downtown via Hwy-1806, where the centerpiece is the **Custer House** (daily: May–Sept 9am–7pm; Oct–April 1–5pm; $4), an admirable reconstruction of the 1874 original designed by the brutally ambitious, indefatigable horseman himself. The guided tour supplies nuggets of quirky information about Custer (he loved to eat raw onions), his wife, and their household prior to his death at Little Big Horn in 1876. Nearer the river, four earthlodge reconstructions stand on the site of the once-vast **On-a-Slant village**, occupied by the Mandan (or River-Dweller) tribe from about 1610 to the late 1700s. After the Mandan abandoned On-a-Slant, they moved upstream and settled on the site that became Fort Mandan, where in 1804 the explorers Lewis and Clark came into contact with the Shoshone woman **Sakakawea** (aka

Sacajawea), who helped guide them west towards the Pacific. The site and adjacent **historical museum** (daily: summer 9am–7pm; Sept 9am–5pm; Oct daily 1–5pm; Nov–Apr by appointment; free with purchase of Custer House ticket) sit below a bluff topped with replicas of the Fort Lincoln infantry post.

Practicalities

Bismarck's **Greyhound** terminal is at 3750 E Rosser Drive; its **visitor center** is at 1600 Burnt Boat Drive (Mon–Fri 7.30am–7pm, Sat 8am–6pm, Sun 10am–5pm; ☎701/222-4308 or 1-800/767-3555, ⓦwww.bismarck-man-dancvb.org). For clean, though small, downtown doubles, try the *Budget Inn Express*, 122 E Thayer Ave (☎701/255-1450; ❷). Great **rooms**, a pool, and breakfast are on offer at *Fairfield Inn*, which has two locations, one near the airport at 135 Ivy Ave (☎701/223-9293; ❹) and the other near the I-94/US-83 interchange at 1120 E Century Ave (☎701/223-9077; ❹). For **camping**, try the excellent Cross Ranch State Park, thirty minutes north of Bismarck on Hwy-1806 (☎701/794-3731; vehicle fee $4, campsites $5–11). Overlapped by a six-thousand-acre nature preserve, the park features sixteen miles of **trails**. Alternatively, you can camp in Fort Lincoln State Park (☎701/667-6340).

    Dining and **nightlife** are plentiful in Bismarck. *Peacock Alley*, 422 E Main St (☎701/255-7917), serves Cajun, Italian, and American cuisine, with lunch specials in the classy adjoining bar. In Mandan, the *Drug Store and Soda Fountain*, 316 W Main St (☎701/663-5900), is a good place to grab a cheap lunch, espresso, or ice cream. There is fine dining at *Meriwether's Restaurant* at the Port of Bismarck (☎701/224-0455), where the *Lewis & Clark* riverboat takes visitors on narrated **historical rides** ($12 daytime, $30 dinner cruise; ☎701/255-4233).

Theodore Roosevelt National Park

The **Theodore Roosevelt National Park**, a huge tract of multihued rock formations, rough grassland, and lazy streams, is split into north and south units approximately seventy miles apart; the area between comprises a checkerboard of federal, state, and privately owned territory. Exploring the park's seventy thousand acres is like entering different rooms, from desert to woods to mountains. Both units (daily dawn–dusk; vehicles $10, pedestrians $5) are at their most subtle at sunrise or sundown, the best times to observe such fauna as elk, antelope, bison, and several fascinating, closely knit prairie dog communities.

    Your first taste of the larger, more popular **southern unit** is likely to be at the breathtaking **Painted Canyon**, seven miles east of the town of Medora off I-94 exit 32. Here and elsewhere in the park, the land is like a sedimentary layer cake that for millions of years has been beaten by hard, infrequent rains, baked by the sun into a kaleidoscope of colors, and cut through to its base by erosive streams and rivers. A mile-long **nature hike** begins at the end of the canyon's boardwalk.

    The southern unit's main **visitor center** in Medora (daily: June to early Sept 8am–8pm; early Sept to May 8am–4.30pm; ☎701/623-4466) counts as park headquarters, and runs tours, nature walks, and lectures by campfire in high season. Out back, the simple cabin was used by the young Roosevelt while a partner in the Maltese Cross Ranch (free guided tours daily until 4.15pm). A highlight of the scenic 36-mile loop road is the sublime view from **Wind Canyon**, ten miles out of Medora. Peaceful Valley Ranch (☎701/623-4496), seven miles from Medora and a mile from the park's first-come, first-served *Cottonwood Campground* ($10 per tent site), arranges horseback tours in summer for $12 per hour.

The smaller **northern unit**, off Hwy-85 near Watford City, receives only a tenth as many visitors, though it's more spectacular than its southern counterpart; the highlight is **Oxbow Overlook**, at the end of a 15-mile scenic drive. The **visitor center** here is open daily (9am–5.30pm; ☎701/842-2333) and closes a half-hour earlier in winter months. Keep in mind that the northern unit is on Central time, while the southern unit is on Mountain time (see p.26).

Medora

MEDORA, the southern gateway to Theodore Roosevelt National Park, languished in obscurity until the early 1960s, but has become one of North Dakota's principal attractions, an inoffensively touristy place with enough to keep you busy, and reasonably interested, for most of a day. The biggest noise in town is the **Medora Musical** (daily 8.30pm; $21–23; ☎1-800/MEDORA-1), a pseudo-Western, super-Americana variety show staged beneath the stars in a vast, modern amphitheater. There is a lot of clogging and yodeling, plenty of accolades to a certain 26th US president, and special guest appearances that range from Chinese chair-stackers to double-jointed Lithuanians. The extravaganza is preceded by a fantastic feed whereby 240 steaks are simultaneously fondued on pitchforks inside giant oil vats (6.30pm; $18).

A better idea is to take to the hills on a mountain **bike** – the **Maah Daah Hey Trail** dips and curves through spectacular country for 120 miles. Rent from Rough Riders Dakota Cyclery in Medora (☎701/623-4808). If the looming influence of Teddy Roosevelt has inspired your inner cowboy, make for the *Dakotah Lodge Guest Ranch* to join an authentic **cattle drive** ($1000; reservations strongly recommended; ☎1-800/508-4897, ⓦwww.dahkotahlodge .com). If a grand seems a bit much to spend, you can take two-day pack trips ($400) or rent horses by the hour ($20). For **accommodation**, you can pitch your own tent for $20, or stay in homey, ranch-style rooms (❸–❹).

The conservative Theodore Roosevelt Medora Foundation owns and operates most of the town and its attractions, including the quaint and central *Rough Rider Hotel* (☎701/623-4444; ❹), as well as the *Medora* (☎701/623-4422; ❸) and *Badlands* (☎701/623-4422; ❹) motels, both of which have outdoor pools. While these hotels only operate from May to September, the *Americinn Motel* (☎701/623-4800 or 1-800/634-3444; ❹) is open year-round. The *Medora Campground* (☎701/623-4435) caters to both tents ($15) and RVs ($21–25). **Eating** options are mostly limited to national chains.

The Rockies

CANADA

WASHINGTON

MONTANA

NORTH DAKOTA

MN

ME

14 OREGON

IDAHO

11 WYOMING

SOUTH DAKOTA

WI

MI

4

MI

NEW YORK

3

VT NH

MA

RI

CT

NEVADA

UTAH

COLORADO

NEBRASKA

IOWA

10

IL

IN

OHIO

PA

1

NJ

DE

WV **5** VA

MD

13 CALIFORNIA

12 ARIZONA

NEW MEXICO

KANSAS

MISSOURI

KENTUCKY

TENNESSEE

NC

PACIFIC OCEAN

OKLAHOMA

AR

AL

SC

GEORGIA

6

ATLANTIC OCEAN

N

MEXICO

15 ALASKA

HAWAII

16

TEXAS

9

8 LA

MS

Gulf of Mexico

7 FL

AL - ALABAMA	IN - INDIANA	MN - MINNESOTA	RI - RHODE ISLAND
AR - ARKANSAS	LA - LOUISIANA	MS - MISSISSIPPI	SC - SOUTH CAROLINA
CT - CONNECTICUT	MA - MASSACHUSETTS	NC - NORTH CAROLINA	VA - VIRGINIA
DE - DELAWARE	MD - MARYLAND	NH - NEW HAMPSHIRE	VT - VERMONT
FL - FLORIDA	ME - MAINE	NJ - NEW JERSEY	WI - WISCONSIN
IL - ILLINOIS	MI - MICHIGAN	PA - PENNSYLVANIA	WV - WEST VIRGINIA

CHAPTER 11

Highlights

✳ **Durango & Silverton Narrow Gauge Railroad, CO** This steam train ride corkscrews through spectacular mountains to the mining town of Silverton. See p.909

✳ **Black Canyon of the Gunnison National Park, CO** Gaze in awe at the primeval black rocks looming over the ferocious Gunnison River. See p.911

✳ **Buffalo Bill Historical Center, WY** Centering on an extraordinary museum, the town of Cody celebrates the life and times of Buffalo Bill. See p.926

✳ **Jackson Hole, WY** Ideal for climbing, biking, or skiing in the Grand Tetons by day, followed by eating, drinking, or stomping in the cowboy bars by night. See p.937

✳ **Going-to-the-Sun road, Glacier National Park, MT** The hairpin turns along this fifty-mile stretch offer staggering mountain views. See p.953

✳ **Dude ranching, MT** Try your hand at horseback riding, roping, and other Western pastimes, with all the comforts of home. See p.949

✳ **Sawtooth Mountains, ID** Of all Idaho's 81 mountain ranges, the Sawtooth summits make for the most awe-inspiring scenic drive. See p.958

The Rockies

E xploring the **Rocky Mountain** states of **Colorado**, **Wyoming**, **Montana**, and **Idaho** could literally take forever. Stretching over one thousand miles from the virgin forests on the Canadian border to the desert of New Mexico, America's rugged spine encompasses an astonishing array of **landscapes** – geyser basins, lava flows, arid valleys, and huge sand dunes – each in its own way as dramatic as the region's magnificent white-topped peaks. The geological grandeur is enhanced by wildlife such as bison, bear, moose, and elk, and the conspicuous legacy of the miners, cowboys, outlaws, and Native Americans who fought over the area's rich resources during the nineteenth century.

Apart from the **Ancestral Puebloan** cliff-dwellers, who lived in southern Colorado until around 1300 AD, most **Native Americans** in this region were nomadic hunters. They inhabited the western extremities of the Great Plains, the richest buffalo-grazing land in the continent. Spaniards, groping through Colorado in the sixteenth century in search of gold, were the first whites to venture into the Rockies. But only after the territory was sold to the US in 1803 as part of the **Louisiana Purchase** was it thoroughly charted, starting with the **Lewis and Clark expedition** that traversed Montana and Idaho in 1805. As a result of the team's reports of abundant game, the fabled "**mountainmen**" had soon trapped the beavers here to the point of virtual extinction. They left as soon as the pelt boom was over, however, and permanent white settlement did not begin until gold was discovered near Denver in 1858. Within a decade, speculators were plundering every accessible gorge and creek in the four states in the search for valuable ores. The construction of transcontinental rail lines and the establishment of vast cattle ranches to feed the mining camps led to the slaughter of millions of buffalo, and conflict with the Native Americans became inevitable. The **Sioux** and **Cheyenne**, led by brilliant strategists like Sitting Bull and Crazy Horse, inflicted decisive victories over the US Army, most notably at Little Bighorn – "**Custer's Last Stand**." However, a massive military operation had cleared the region of all warring tribes by the late 1870s.

Most of those who came after the Native Americans saw the Rockies strictly in terms of profit: they took what they wanted and left. Small communities in this isolated terrain remain exclusively dedicated to coal, oil, or some other single commodity, and all too often the uncertain tightrope walk between boom and bust is evident in their run-down facades.

Each of the four states has its own distinct character. **Colorado**, with fifty peaks over 14,000ft, is the most mountainous and populated, as well as the economic leader of the region. Friendly, sophisticated **Denver** is the only major

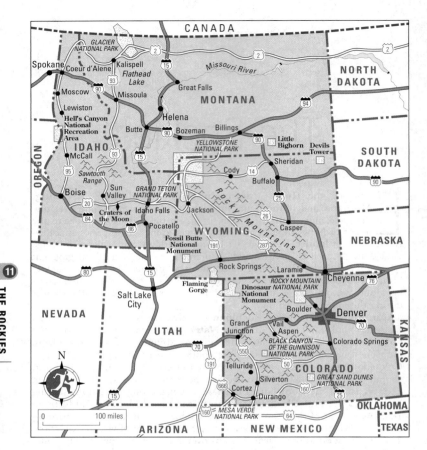

metropolis in the Rockies. It's also the most visited city, in part because it's that much more accessible, and it plays the role of gateway to some of the best ski resorts in the country. Less touched by the tourist circus is vast, brawny **Montana**, where the "Big Sky" looks down on a glorious verdant manuscript scribbled over with gushing streams, lakes, and tiny communities.

Away from gurgling, spitting **Yellowstone**, adjacent **Grand Teton** park and the nearby **Bighorn Mountains**, vast stretches of scrubland fill **Wyoming**, the country's least populous state. Rugged, remote, and desolate **Idaho** holds some of the Rocky Mountains' last unexplored wildernesses, most notably the mighty **Sawtooth** range.

You can expect **temperatures** in the high sixties all the way up to a hundred degrees Fahrenheit, between early June and early September, depending on whether you are in the high desert of Wyoming, the plains of Idaho, or the mountains of Colorado. In the mountains, you should be prepared for wild variations – and, of course, the higher you go the colder it gets. The altitude is high enough to warrant a period of acclimatization, while the intensity of the sun at these elevations can be uncomfortably fierce. In fact, parts of Wyoming and Colorado bask in more hours of sunshine per year than San Diego or Miami Beach. Spring (the "mud season"), when the snow melts, is the least attractive time to visit the Rockies, and while the delicate golds of quaking aspen trees light up the mountainsides in early fall, by October things are generally a bit cold for enjoyable hiking or sports. Most **ski** runs are open by late November and operate well into March – or even June, depending on snow conditions. The coldest month is January, when temperatures below 0°F are common.

Attempting to rush around every national park and major town is a sure way to miss out on one of the Rockies' real delights – coaxing your car along the tight switchback roads that wind up and over precipitous mountain passes, especially through the majestic **Continental Divide**. Remember to check in the rear-view mirror as you go, though – you might be missing that perfect photo for your album. At some point it's worth forsaking motorized transportation, though, to see at least some of the area by **bike**; the Rockies contain some of the most challenging and rewarding cycling terrain on the continent. And of course, you cannot count yourself a visitor to the area without embarking on a hike or two.

Colorado

Geographically diverse **COLORADO** veers from the flat, endless plains of the east to the colossal mountains of the west. In the north, **Native Americans** hunted and trapped in lush mountain valleys in summer, and returned to the prairies for the winter; in the south, the Ancestral Puebloans of Mesa Verde grew corn on their isolated mesas and shared in the great early civilization of the Southwest.

Different parts of what's now Colorado accrued to the US at different times: the east and north were acquired under the **Louisiana Purchase** in 1803, while the south was won 45 years later in the war with **Mexico**. (Land grants issued under Mexican rule were honored by the Americans, which accounts for a still-strong Hispanic influence.) Gold-hungry Spaniards came through in the sixteenth century, and US Army Colonel Zebulon Pike ventured into the mountains on an exploratory expedition in 1806, but the Native American way of life only became seriously threatened with the discovery of **gold** west of Denver in 1858. At that time Colorado was still part of Kansas Territory; it became a territory in its own right in 1861, and a state in 1876. The distractions of the Civil War gave the Native Americans the opportunity to fight back, but they were soon overwhelmed. From then until the end of the century, Colorado boomed; the quantities of gold and silver extracted from the mountains did not really compare with the riches found in California, but they were sufficient to fuel a rip-roaring frontier lifestyle.

For the modern visitor, the obvious first port of call is **Denver**, at the eastern edge of the Rockies and the biggest city for six hundred miles. Outside Denver, the northern half of the state holds the most popular destinations, starting with the dynamic college town of **Boulder** and the spectacular **Rocky Mountain National Park**. The majority of the resorts that have made Colorado the continent's foremost **skiing** destination snuggle into the mountains to the west of Denver: **Summit County** attracts the most visitors, **Vail** is considered best for terrain, and **Aspen** boasts the glitziest apres-ski scene. The far west of the state stretches onto the red-rock deserts of the Colorado Plateau, where the dry climate has preserved the extraordinary natural sculptures of **Colorado National Monument**. **Pikes Peak** towers over the enjoyable city of **Colorado Springs**, but the rest of the state's **southeast** quarter is mostly agricultural plains. To the **southwest**, old mining towns like **Crested Butte** and **Durango** stand revitalized in the mountains, while **Mesa Verde National Park** preserves perhaps the most impressive of all the cliff cities left by the ancient Ancestral Puebloan civilization.

Getting around Colorado

By far the largest **airport** in Colorado is in Denver. Shuttle buses radiate from there to all the main towns and ski resorts – as do commuter-style aircraft. Denver is also a major hub for Greyhound **buses** to all neighboring states. Amtrak **trains** run straight across the middle of Colorado, timed in both directions to pass through magnificent Glenwood Canyon in daylight hours, but are so slow that they're barely more efficient than the hugely enjoyable tourist train, the Durango & Silverton Narrow Gauge Railroad, in the southwest.

Colorado is also one of the best destinations in the world for **cyclists**, hosting numerous on- and off-road championships. For excellent **maps and guides** to cycle routes in the state, contact the State Department of Transportation (☎303/757-9982).

Denver

Its skyscrapers marking the final transition between the Great Plains and the American West, **DENVER** stands at the threshold of the **Rocky Mountains**. Despite being known as the "**Mile High City**," and serving as the obvious point of arrival for travelers heading into the mountains, it is itself uniformly flat. The majestic peaks only begin to rise roughly fifteen miles west of downtown, but are clearly visible, and Denver has, during the last century, had plenty of room to spread out.

Mineral wealth has always been at the heart of the city's prosperity, with all the fluctuations of fortune that this entails. Though local resources have been progressively exhausted, Denver has managed to hang on to its role as the most important commercial and transportation nexus in the state. Its original "foundation" in 1858 was by pure chance; this was the first spot where small quantities of **gold** were discovered in Colorado. There was no significant river, let alone a road, but prospectors came streaming in, regardless of prior claims to the land – least of all those of the **Arapahoe**, who had supposedly been confirmed in their ownership of the area by the Fort Laramie Treaty of 1851.

There was actually very little gold in Denver itself; the infant town swarmed briefly with disgruntled fortune-seekers, who decamped when news came in of the massive gold strike at Central City. Denver survived, however, prospering further with the discovery of **silver** in the mountains. All sorts of shady characters made this their home; Jefferson "Soapy" Smith, for example, acquired his nickname here, selling bars of soap at extortionate prices under

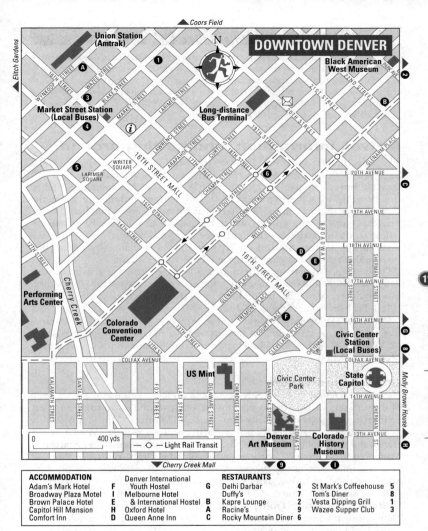

▲ Coors Field

DOWNTOWN DENVER

Union Station
(Amtrak)

Black American
West Museum

Market Street Station
(Local Buses)

Long-distance
Bus Terminal

WRITER
SQUARE

LARIMER
SQUARE

16TH STREET MALL

E. 20TH AVENUE

E. 19TH AVENUE

E. 18TH AVENUE

16TH STREET MALL

E. 17TH AVENUE

Performing
Arts Center

Cherry Creek

E. 16TH AVENUE

Civic Center
Station
(Local Buses)

Colorado
Convention
Center

COLFAX AVENUE

COLFAX AVENUE

US Mint

Civic Center
Park

State
Capitol

E. 14TH AVENUE

E. 13TH AVENUE

Denver
Art Museum

Colorado
History
Museum

0   400 yds

— ○ — Light Rail Transit

▼ Cherry Creek Mall

11

THE ROCKIES | COLORADO | Denver

ACCOMMODATION				RESTAURANTS			
Adam's Mark Hotel	F	Denver International Youth Hostel	G	Delhi Darbar	4	St Mark's Coffeehouse	5
Broadway Plaza Motel	I	Melbourne Hotel		Duffy's	7	Tom's Diner	8
Brown Palace Hotel	E	& International Hostel	B	Kapre Lounge	2	Vesta Dipping Grill	1
Capitol Hill Mansion	H	Oxford Hotel	A	Racine's	9	Wazee Supper Club	3
Comfort Inn	D	Queen Anne Inn	C	Rocky Mountain Diner	6		

the pretence that some contained $100 bills. When the first railroads bypassed Denver – the death knell for so many other communities – the citizens simply banded together and built their own connecting spur.

These days, Denver is a welcoming and enjoyable city, with a fairly liberal outlook. Tourism is based on getting out into the great outdoors rather than on sightseeing in town, but somehow the city's isolation, a good six hundred miles from any conurbation of even vaguely similar size, gives its 2.4-million population a refreshing friendliness; and in a city which is used to providing its own entertainment there always seems to be something going on.

Arrival, information, and getting around

The colossal, ultra-high-tech **Denver International Airport** lies 24 miles northeast of downtown, out on the plains beyond Stapleton. Regular RTD skyRide **buses** can take you downtown ($8 one way, $13 roundtrip) and to Boulder ($10 one way, $16 roundtrip). Buses leave from outside exit 506 in the East terminal and 511 in the West terminal. There are also a number of independent shuttle service options, which can be arranged within the terminal.

Amtrak **trains** arrive on the northwest side of downtown Denver at the beautiful old **Union Station** on Wynkoop Street, and the Greyhound **bus terminal** is every bit as close to the action at 1055 19th St.

The best place to pick up **information** about the city is the **visitor center**, 918 16th St (Mon–Fri 8am–5pm, weekend times vary; ☎303/892-1112, ⊛www.denver.org). The main downtown **post office** is at 951 20th St (Mon–Fri 8am–5pm; zip code 80202).

The Colorado Division of Parks and Recreation (☎303/866-3437) has information and maps for cycling in the city and the mountains, while Gray Line (☎303/289-2841, ⊛www.coloradograyline.com) operates bus tours of Rocky Mountain National Park and the surrounding area (mid-May to mid-Oct).

City transportation

Downtown Denver is fairly easily negotiated on foot, with the occasional help of the very regular **free buses** that run for a mile up and down the 16th Street pedestrian mall at its heart (daily 6am–1am). RTD **buses** (Mon–Fri 6–9am & 4–6pm, $1.25; other times, $1.15), with frequent services to Boulder, sports arenas, and the airport, leave from the underground **Market Street Station** at Market and 16th streets. They are supplemented by a **light rail tram line** that runs five miles through downtown from I-25 and Broadway, across the 16th Street mall and up to Five Points in the northeast (same fares as buses). From June to September, you can also buy a hop-on, hop-off day pass on the **Cultural Connection Trolley** (every 30min 9.30am–10pm; $3), which links Denver's main points of interest. For information and detailed schedules of the entire RTD network, call ☎303/299-6000 or visit ⊛www.rtd-denver.com.

Accommodation

Denver has a good selection of central **accommodation**, ranging from hostels to motels and homey B&Bs, as well as various grand historic downtown hotels. One specialist agency with reasonably priced properties in Denver and throughout Colorado is B&B Colorado, PO Box 6061, Boulder, CO 80306 (☎303/494-4994).

Adam's Mark Hotel 1550 Court Place
☎303/893-3333, ⊛www.adamsmark.com. Giant, luxurious hotel with excellent facilities, adjacent to the 16th Street mall. ❻–❼

Broadway Plaza Motel 1111 Broadway
☎303/893-0303. Within walking distance of downtown, this plain but friendly motel has large and clean rooms (with phones and cable TV),

free parking, and reasonable rates. ❸

Brown Palace Hotel 321 17th St ☎303/297-3111 or 1-800/321-2599, ⓦwww.brownpalace.com. Beautifully maintained downtown landmark dating from 1892, with elegant dining rooms and public areas. Step inside and marvel at the eight-story cast-iron atrium. ❽–❾

Capitol Hill Mansion 1207 Pennsylvania St ☎303/839-5221, ⓦwww.capitolhillmansion.com. Luxurious B&B in an old Victorian mansion. ❺–❼

Comfort Inn Downtown 401 17th St ☎303/296-0400. This very central comfortable chain hotel has good continental breakfast and shares some facilities with the *Brown Palace Hotel* (see above). ❺

Denver International Youth Hostel 630 E 16th Ave ☎303/832-9996, ⓦwww.youthhostels.com /Denver. Dorm beds for $9, four blocks from the capitol, in a not entirely safe area. Office hours are 8–10am & 5–10.30pm. No curfew.

Hampton Inn DIA 6290 Tower Rd, next to the airport ☎303/371-0200, ⓦwww.hamptoninn-suites.com. A comfortable place with continental breakfast and airport shuttle included. ❹

Melbourne Hostel 607 22nd St ☎303/292-6386, ⓦwww.denverhostel.com. A run-down old hostel with no ventilation. An easy – if not all that safe – walk from the center. Dorms from $13–16. No curfew.

Oxford Hotel 1600 17th St ☎303/628-5400 or 1-800/228-5838. Very grand, traditional Western hotel dating from 1891. ❼

Queen Anne Inn 2147 Tremont Place ☎303/296-6666, ⓦwww.queenannebnb.com. Central and very hospitable 1879 B&B near a peaceful park where you can catch carriage rides; each of the 14 rooms is tastefully decorated to an individual theme. ❹–❼

The City

Much of the day-to-day activity **downtown** centers on the shops and restaurants of **16th Street**, which, but for its free buses, is a pedestrian zone; there's also a range of galleries, brewpubs, shops, and lofts in the revitalized district bordered by 14th and 20th, and Wynkoop and Larimer streets, known as **LoDo**, or Lower Downtown.

It was in the **Larimer Square** district, around Market Street between 14th and 15th streets, that William Larimer built Denver's original log cabin. That burned down in a general conflagration within a few years, whereupon a city ordinance decreed that all new construction should be in brick. Restored to its late Victorian appearance, Larimer Square provides another lively focus for shops, bars, and restaurants.

For a quick appreciation of Denver's geographical position, head for the **State Capitol** at Broadway and E Colfax Avenue. The thirteenth of the steps up to the entrance is exactly one mile above sea level; turn back and look west, and you get a commanding view – zealously protected by building regulations – of the Rockies swelling on the horizon. The capitol is a rather predictable copy of the one in Washington, DC, but the free tours (Sept–May Mon–Fri 9.15am-2.30pm; June–Aug 9am–3.30pm) are pleasantly informal, and you can climb its dome for an even better view.

Civic Center Park, right in front of the capitol, is flanked by two of Denver's finest museums. The glass-tile-covered **Denver Art Museum** at 100 W 14th Ave (Tues–Sat 10am–5pm, Sun noon–5pm; $5, free Sat; (☎720/865-5000, ⓦwww.denverartmuseum.org) has a solid collection of paintings from around the world, but is most noteworthy for its superb examples of Native American craftwork, with marvelous beadwork by Plains tribes and some finely detailed Navajo weavings. Some of the pre-Columbian art from Central America – particularly the extraordinary Olmec miniatures – is also spectacular.

The most interesting features of the **Colorado History Museum** at 1300 Broadway (Mon–Sat 10am–4.30pm, Sun noon–4.30pm; $5; ☎303/866-3682, ⓦwww.coloradohistory.org) are to be found in the downstairs galleries. Several dioramas, made under the auspices of the WPA in the 1930s, show historical scenes in fascinating detail, starting with the Ancestral Puebloans of Mesa Verde, following up with trappers meeting with Indians at a "fair in the wilderness" in the early 1800s, and a model of Denver in 1860. An exhaustive archive of **photographs** of the early West showcases the work of W.H. Jackson, who lived from 1843 to 1942.

At the **US Mint**, a short walk northwest at 320 W Colfax Ave (Mon–Fri 8am–3pm), millions of fresh coins gush from the presses in a flurry of flashing metal, but all you'll get to see are the machine-gun turrets on the exterior, mounted in the depths of the Depression.

The **Molly Brown House**, 1340 Pennsylvania Ave (June–Aug Mon–Sat 10am–3.30pm, Sun noon–3.30pm; Sept–May same schedule, closed Mon; $6.50), was home to the "unsinkable" Molly Brown, who is most famous for surviving the sinking of the *Titanic* (she'd already lived through a typhoon in the Pacific) and raising money for the survivors and their families. A poor Irish girl who went West to marry a millionaire, she ended up mixing with high society in Denver; after the *Titanic* brought her notoriety, she went on to become a suffragette and eventually ran for senator. Sadly, the house tours focus more on what the Browns owned and the preservation of the house than on illuminating her extraordinary life.

Denver's black community is most prominent in the old **Five Points** district, northeast of downtown, created to house black railroad workers in the 1870s. The **Black American West Museum** at 3091 California St (summer Mon–Fri 10am–5pm, Sat & Sun noon–5pm; rest of year Wed–Fri 10am–2pm, Sat & Sun noon–5pm; $6; ☎303/292-2566) has intriguing details on black pioneers and outlaws. Perhaps the most interesting section is on cowboys, which debunks a lot of Western myths: one-third of all cowboys are thought to have been black, many of them slaves freed after the Civil War who left the South and found work as cattle hands.

Two or three miles east of downtown en route to the airport, the enormous **City Park** is home to the **Denver Museum of Nature and Science**, 2001 Colorado Blvd (daily 9am–5pm; museum $9, planetarium $8, IMAX $8, all three for $16; ☎303/322-7009, ⓦwww.dmns.org). As with many such museums, its brief extends beyond the (very good) dinosaur exhibits and wildlife displays to include anthropological material on Native Americans, which, though fascinating, does seem rather out of place. There's also a large **zoo** nearby (daily: April–Oct 9am–6pm; rest of year 10am–5pm; summer $11, winter $9, ☎303/376-4800, ⓦwww.denverzoo.org), whose four thousand inmates include a couple of huge lowland gorillas in a large, thickly wooded sanctuary.

Denver's **Six Flags Elitch Gardens** theme park, on the western edge of downtown at 2000 Elitch Circle (summer Thurs–Sun 10am–10pm, Mon–Wed 10am–8pm; rest of year hours vary; $35.99; ☎303/595-4386, ⓦwww.sixflags.com /elitchgardens), is surprisingly close to the city center (accessible by a cycle path along Cherry Creek), and has a state-of-the-art **water park** attached. There are some great white-knuckle rides here, including the Mind Eraser, that catapults you at 60mph through terrifying corkscrew loops; the Tower of Doom, a freefall vertical drop of 70ft; and the Sidewinder, which spins you round an impossibly tight loop and then, sadistically, does it again – backwards.

If you're looking for something a little quieter, the glitzy **Cherry Creek Mall**, a few miles southeast of downtown, is second only to the 16th Street mall as Denver's most popular shopping center. Opposite its main entrance is one of the best **bookstores** in the US, the Tattered Cover Bookstore at 2955 E First Ave (☎303/322-7727), which spreads over four extremely well-stocked floors and has a relaxed American-style restaurant at the top. Even more tranquil is the **Denver Botanical Gardens**, 1005 York St (Oct–April daily 9am–5pm; rest of year Sat–Tues 9am–8pm, Wed–Sun 9am–5pm; $4–8.50; ☎720/865-3500,

ⓦ www.botanicgardens.org), where an excellent array of beautifully displayed plant life thrive, including a rock alpine garden featuring local mountain flora.

Finally, twenty miles west of downtown, high above the Coors Brewery town of Golden, **Buffalo Bill's Memorial Museum and Mountain Parks** on Lookout Mountain (May–Oct daily 9am–5pm; Nov–April Tues–Sun 9am–4pm; $3) is the final resting place of William Cody, famed frontiersman, buffalo-hunter, army scout, and showman, who died in Denver in 1915 (see also p.925). Though now surrounded by huge electricity pylons, the gravesite offers great views in both directions, over the city and out to the mountains. The adjacent museum does a thorough job of outlining Buffalo Bill's past, and one of the more gruesome elements on display is a pistol whose handle has been fashioned from human bone.

Eating

As well as plenty of Western-themed steak and barbecue places, Denver has a cosmopolitan selection of international **restaurants**. Of the several distinct restaurant districts, the **Larimer Square** area is the most easily accessible on foot and has a wide selection. Several of the city's famed **brewpubs** serve good quality meals, too.

Casa Bonita 6715 W Colfax Ave ☎303/232-5115. Absolutely wild Mexican place, seating 1200 diners, a long way out on Colfax. Gunfights, cliff divers, abandoned mines to explore – the only weak link is the food itself, but it's all a lot of fun (especially for kids) and far from expensive.

Cherry Cricket 2641 E 2nd Ave ☎303/322-7666. Excellent burgers and Mexican food served up in a generally dingy sports-bar ambiance make this a great place to nurse a hangover – or even work on getting one (120 different beers on offer) while watching televised sports. Near the Cherry Creek Mall. Open 11am–midnight.

Delhi Darbar 1514 Blake St ☎303/595-0680. Relaxed haunt with decent Indian food and a well-priced lunch buffet.

Duffy's Shamrock 1635 Court Place ☎303/534-4935. Late-night pub/restaurant downtown serving food, including sandwiches, steaks, and seafood, until 1.30am.

Kapre Lounge 2729 Welton St ☎303/295-9207. Exceptionally good Southern-fried chicken in an old, established Five Points soul-food restaurant.

The Palace Arms 321 17th St ☎303/297-3111. This small and classy restaurant tucked in the *Brown Palace Hotel* (see p.883) is the ultimate splurge in town, with a menu of mostly seasonal game specialties, and decorated mostly in antiques from the Napoleonic period – including a pair of Napoleon's dueling pistols.

Racine's 850 Bannock St ☎303/595-0418. Just south of downtown, this large, laid-back place is a Denver institution. Housed in a former auto show-room, the inexpensive restaurant serves excellent egg-based breakfasts, with imaginative pastas, reliably good sandwiches, and spicy Mexican entrees later in the day.

Rocky Mountain Diner 800 18th St ☎303/293-8383. Continental food served up in a festive Western-style atmosphere.

St Mark's Coffeehouse 1416 Market St ☎303/446-2925. The small frontage of this trendy café hides a huge, art-filled room where regulars play chess and hang out day and night – from around 7am to midnight. Brews excellent espresso.

Tom's Diner 601 E Colfax Ave and Pearl St ☎303/861-7493. Wonderfully gritty and authentic 24hr diner, providing cheap deals on big portions of stock diner food at the seedy end of town.

Vesta Dipping Grill 1822 Blake St ☎303/296-1970. Attractive restaurant in a renovated LoDo warehouse serving tasty food in unusual combinations, based around the "art" of dipping meat or veggies in a spectrum of flavors (Mediterranean, Asian, Mexican).

Wazee Supper Club 1600 15th St ☎303/623-9518. Well-established LoDo dining room, serving good cheap burgers, deli sandwiches, and superb pizzas, plus a full range of beers, in an Art Deco atmosphere. One of the few places open really late (2am most nights).

Nightlife and entertainment

Though business still booms for Denver's numerous downtown brewpubs, an onslaught of sports bars in the LoDo district, particularly near Coors Field, have mostly taken over as the city's liveliest nightlife area. And if sports bars don't appeal, there are plenty of other more stylish or relaxing places to drink here, too. Most places close around 1am. For news of **musical** happenings, consult Wednesday's free *Westword*, the hip free monthly *Freestyle*, or the "Weekend" section in the *Denver Post*.

The remarkable **Red Rocks Amphitheater** (℡303/640-2637, Ⓦwww .redrocksonline.com), twelve miles west of downtown Denver, has been the setting for thousands of rock and classical concerts; U2 recorded *Under a Blood Red Sky* here. This 9000-seat venue is squeezed between two 400ft red-sandstone rocks that seem to glow in early morning and late evening. The surrounding Red Rocks Park is open to visitors free of charge during the day (until 11pm on event days).

Denver's pride and joy, the modern **Denver Performing Arts Complex** on 14th and Curtis streets (℡303/893-4100 or 1-800/641-1222, Ⓦwww .denvercenter.org), is home to the Denver Center Theater Company, Colorado Symphony Orchestra, Opera Colorado, and the Colorado Ballet, and hosts performances nightly. Facilities in the complex include eight **theaters**, as well as the **Symphony Hall** (which is in the round, giving it superb acoustics).

In the hunt for **tickets**, both Ticketmaster (℡303/830-8497) and Ticketman (℡303/430-1111) can usually help. You can also try the Ticket Bus, parked on 16th and Curtis streets, in person (daily 10am–6pm), where you'll often find last-minute deals.

Breckenridge Brewery 2220 Blake St ℡303/297-3644. Atmospheric brewpub opposite Coors Field where you can watch the beers being brewed on-site. Serves good pub grub as well.

Brendan's 2009 Larimer St ℡303/308-9933 (closed Sun & Mon). Small basement pub in the LoDo district with regular live blues; big-name acts pop by a few times a month and the cover is rarely more than $10.

El Chapultepec 20th and Market streets ℡303/295-9126. Tiny, popular LoDo venue near Coors Field, with nightly live jazz and occasional big names.

The Church 1160 Lincoln St ℡303/832-3528. A dance club inside a gutted cathedral, combining a downtown nightlife landmark, a wine bar, sushi bar, and three invariably busy dance floors. Plays mostly hard house or garage, though the music and crowd can be eclectic. $5–15 cover.

Comedy Works 1226 15th St ℡303/595-3637. Right off Larimer Square, Denver's major comedy venue is the most likely place to find visiting big-name stand-up acts. Closed Mon.

Cruise Room Bar *The Oxford Hotel*, 1600 17th St ℡303/628-5400. This place is a replica of the Art Deco bar on the *Queen Mary* ocean liner. Worth a stop for the atmosphere alone.

Funky Buddha Lounge 776 Lincoln St ℡303/832-5075. Destination bar with up-to-date tunes on the dance floors, and almost as up-to-date fashions on the clientele.

Grizzly Rose 5450 N Valley Hwy ℡303/295-1330. Celebrated country-and-western venue a 10-minute drive north of downtown on I-25 (exit 215).

The massive venue has bands every night and attracts famous names regularly. Cover $5–10.

Herman's Hideaway 1578 S Broadway ℡303/777-5840. One of Denver's favorite rock clubs, in a homey little bar just south of I-25, with live music Wed–Sat.

Mario's Double Daughters Salotto 1632 Market St ℡303/623-3505. Stylish bar with amusingly named cocktails, and pizzas available from *Two-Fisted Mario's* next door.

Mercury Café 2199 California St ℡303/294-928. When there's not jazz on at *The Merc*, there's swing dancing, poetry readings, or some other form of entertainment. The club is combined with a good-value restaurant, which serves lots of healthy choices, many vegetarian.

Polly Esthers 2301 Blake St ℡303/382-1976. Enormous and consistently popular club with '70s and '80s hits playing on two floors. Cover $5–10.

The Soiled Dove 1949 Market St ℡303/299-0100. Hugely popular bar with an often rowdy rooftop overlooking Market St. Features an eclectic variety of live music almost every night, from local to national names and from jazz to rock.

The Stampede 2430 S Havana St and Park Rd ℡303/337-6909. The massive antique saloon bar is the centerpiece of this country-and-western pick-up joint in suburban Aurora.

Wynkoop Brewing Co 1634 18th St ℡303/297-2700. Good home-brewed beers and bar food in the state's first brewpub, in LoDo opposite Union Station. There's an elegant pool hall upstairs, live entertainment in the comedy lounge.

Northern Colorado

The major attraction for visitors in the Denver area is **Rocky Mountain National Park** to the northwest. Though on the map the distances involved may not look that great, it would be a mistake to attempt to see the whole park on a day-trip from Denver. Segments of the loop drive along the way can be very slow and laborious, and in a single day it's more realistic just to dip a few miles into the park's eastern fringes.

The lively foothill town of **Boulder** can be used as a base, though the smaller mountain towns give you more time in the wilds: **Grand Lake**, near the western entrance, makes a more attractive stopover than overblown **Estes Park** on the east, while **Winter Park** is an affordable, enjoyable ski resort. Further west, midway across the state on either side of the I-70 freeway, you'll find the famous Rocky Mountain ski resorts of **Vail**, **Aspen**, and the rest, and the evocative mining town of **Leadville**. Continuing toward the Utah border, the landscape dips and rises in a patchwork of granite peaks, raging rivers, and red-sandstone canyons, winding up at **Grand Junction** and the memorable scenery of **Colorado National Monument**.

Boulder

BOULDER, just 27 miles northwest of Denver on US-36, is one of the liveliest college towns in the country, filled with a young population that seems to divide its time between phenomenally healthy daytime pursuits and almost equally unhealthy nighttime activities – the town is often referred to as "7 miles surrounded by reality." It was founded in 1858 by a prospecting party who felt that the nearby Flatiron Mountains, the first swell of the Rockies, "looked right for gold"; in fact they found little, but the community grew anyway.

With an easygoing, forward-looking atmosphere and plenty of great places to eat and drink, Boulder makes an excellent place to return each night after a day in the mountains. Downtown centers on the leafy pedestrian mall of **Pearl Street**, lined with all sorts of lively cafés, galleries, and stores – including several places where you can rent **mountain bikes**. The most obvious short excursion is to drive or hike up nearby **Flagstaff Mountain** for views over town and further into the Rockies; any road west joins up with the Peak to Peak Highway, which heads through spectacular montane scenery to Estes Park and Rocky Mountain National Park. For rock climbing, **Eldorado Canyon State Park** offers many opportunities and The Boulder Mountaineer (☎303/442-8355) can answer any questions and, of course, provide gear.

The adventurous **University of Colorado** offers a mixed bag of **events**, including in summer the Colorado Music Festival (☎303/449-1397), held in the Chautauqua Auditorium (☎303/440-7666), and the seven-week Colorado Shakespeare Festival (☎303/492-0554, ⓦwww.coloradoshakes.org). In early March the nearby town of Nederland hosts the offbeat **Frozen Dead Guy Days** (ⓦwww.nederlandchamber.org/FrozenDeadGuyDays), a three-day event with the ostensible purpose of paying tribute to one Bredo Morstøl, a Norwegian who is cryogenically stored in the town. Coffin races and Morstøl look-alike contests are among the featured hijinks.

Practicalities

Local **buses** come into Boulder at the Transit Center, 14th and Walnut streets (☎303/442-1044); there are regular services from Denver and the airport (roughly every hour; $1.15 local fare, $3.50 to Denver, $10 to airport; ☎303/299-

6000). The Boulder Airporter also runs shuttles from Denver International Airport (hourly 6.10am–11.10pm; $19; ☎303/444-0808). Boulder's **local shuttle** bus, the HOP (every 7–20min Mon–Fri 7am–3am, Sat 9am–3am, Sun 10am–6pm; $1.15), links downtown, the university, and the trendy student district known as "the Hill." The hospitable **visitor center** is at 2440 Pearl St (Mon–Thurs 8.30am–5pm, Fri 8.30am–4pm; ☎303/442-2911 or 1-800/444-0447).

Even if you're not **staying** in the historic *Hotel Boulderado*, wonderfully located near Pearl Street at 2115 13th St (☎303/442-4344, ⓦwww.boulderado .com; ❺–❻), it's an atmospheric place to wander into for a drink and to listen to the free evening jazz. Nearby, in another grand old restored building, the *Pearl Street Inn*, 1820 Pearl St (☎303/444-5584, ⓦwww.pearlstreetinn.com; ❻), offers elegant B&B-style accommodations. The *Foot of the Mountain*, 200 W Arapahoe Ave (☎303/442-5688; ❹), is a friendly, log-cabin-style **motel**, nine blocks from downtown beside Boulder Creek. There's also a welcoming **youth hostel** in a Victorian building at 1107 12th St, near the campus (☎303/442-0522, ⓦwww.boulderhostel.com; ❷); dorm beds cost $17, and there are lots of private rooms ($39 single, $45 double).

You won't have any problem finding **bars** and **restaurants** downtown, especially around the Pearl Street area. The local *Boulder Weekly* newspaper is replete with dining and boozing information. *May Wah Cuisine*, 2500 Baseline Rd (☎303/499-8225), is a good-value Chinese restaurant with cheap lunch specials, while *14th St Bar and Grill*, 1400 Pearl St (☎303/444-5854), has a quirky and inventive menu and is adorned with flamboyant artwork. If you feel like splurging, try the *Flagstaff House*, 1138 Flagstaff Rd (☎303/442-4640), where the menu frequently changes but often includes gamey "Rocky Mountain Cuisine," or *Q's Restaurant*, at the *Hotel Boulderado* (see above), with an innovative menu of items like lobster gnocchi and miso-glazed salmon. The *Boulderado* also houses two popular **nighttime** haunts: the *Corner Bar*, with armchair seating, and creative, reasonably priced dishes served until late at night on the patio; and the *Catacombs*, which features nightly live blues, jazz, and acoustic guitar music. It's also one of three bars in Boulder where you're allowed to smoke. The *West End Tavern*, 926 Pearl St (☎303/444-3535), is a great venue for live jazz and comedy, with local microbrews and spectacular Flatiron mountain views from the roof terrace. For getting your groove on, *Round Midnight* at 1005 Pearl St is your best bet; there's a packed dance floor on the weekends (☎303/442-2176).

Rocky Mountain National Park

You don't have to go to **ROCKY MOUNTAIN NATIONAL PARK** to appreciate the full splendor of the Rockies; it is simply one small section of the mighty range, measuring roughly twenty-five by fifteen miles. A tenth of the size of Yellowstone, it attracts around the same number of visitors – around three-and-a-half million per year, and with the bulk of those coming in high summer, the one main road through the mountains can get incredibly congested. However, it is undeniably beautiful, straddling the Continental Divide at elevations often well in excess of ten thousand feet. A full third of the park is above the tree line, and large areas of snow never melt; the name of the **Never Summer Mountains** speaks volumes about the long, empty expanses of arctic-style tundra. Lower down, among the rich forests, are patches of lush greenery; you never know when you may stumble upon a sheltered mountain meadow flecked with flowers. Parallels with the European Alps spring readily to mind – helped, of course, by the heavy-handed Swiss and Bavarian themes of the region's motels and restaurants.

This is not an area that humans have ever made their home, though it lies on the route of old Indian trails, and the Ute would come here to hunt in summer. Early white mining ventures came to nothing, and the region was dedicated as a national park in 1915. The original proposal was for it to be much bigger, extending from Wyoming to Pikes Peak; the existing boundaries were drawn up as a compromise, after long negotiations with Colorado's powerful logging and mining interests.

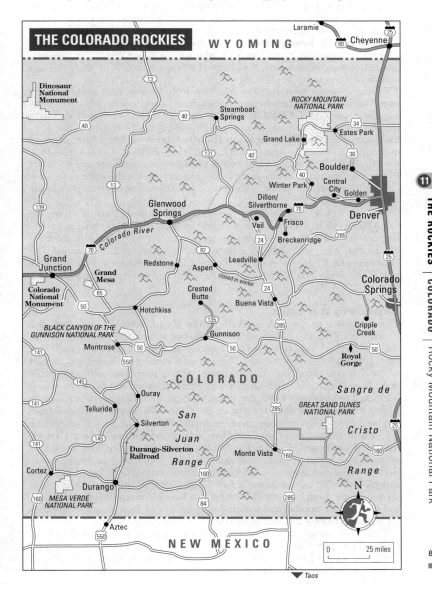

THE COLORADO ROCKIES

Approaching the park

Approaching the park from the **east**, you barely penetrate the foothills of the Rockies before you arrive at the gateway town of **ESTES PARK**, 65 miles northwest of Denver and 90 miles southwest of Cheyenne. At the end of the nineteenth century, Estes Park was the private hunting preserve of the Irish Earl of Dunraven; once he was squeezed out, the town took on the more democratic function it still serves, of providing visitors with food, lodging, and other services. In itself, it's not an attractive place, but its presence does at least ensure that all the necessary evils of mass tourism are confined into one neat valley. The **park headquarters** and main **visitor center** (daily: June–Aug 8am–9pm; Sept–May 8am–5pm; park admission $15 per vehicle, $5 pedestrians and cyclists; information ☏970/586-1206; weather ☏970/586-1333) is a couple of miles north, on US-36.

To reach the **western** entrance, 85 miles from Denver, turn north off I-70 onto US-40, a small detour beyond the junction taking you to the former mining community of **GEORGETOWN**, one of the best-preserved Victorian mining towns in Colorado. The town is, however, mostly known as the starting point of the **Georgetown Loop Railroad**, on Rose Street (summer daily every 85min 10.45am–3pm; $15.50; ☏303/569-2403 or 1-800/691-4386). On the line, 1920s steam trains run a tortuous six-mile roundtrip to Silver Plume, on a route that loops in big arcs – added to enable the engines to overcome the six-percent climb – and includes a trip across a precarious trestle above Clear Creek.

Back on US-40, the highway negotiates **Berthoud Pass** en route to **GRAND LAKE**, a more low-key version of Estes Park. This unlikely **yachting** center, high in the mountains, consists of one main boardwalk-lined street beside the lake with family amusements, lodgings, and restaurants. The **Kawuneeche Visitor Center** of Rocky Mountain National Park is a mile north of town (daily: May–Sept 8am–5pm; Oct–April 8am–4.30pm; ☏970/627-3471).

Exploring the park

The showpiece of the park is **Trail Ridge Road**, between Estes Park and Grand Lake. This 45-mile stretch of US-34, said to be the highest highway in the world, affords a succession of tremendous views, and several short trails start from parking lots along the way. There are no services en route, and rangers advise that you allow three to four hours' driving time. The road is normally open from late May to mid-October. As winter deepens and the snow falls, it is blocked progressively lower down, but you can always expect to get as far as **Many Peaks Curve** from the east or the **Colorado River Trailhead** from the west. Snowfall is typically heaviest during March and April. The definite highlight is the stretch of road on either side of the **Alpine Visitor Center**, halfway along Trail Ridge Road at Fall River Pass (May–Aug 9am–5pm; Sept 10am–4pm); here the peaks and alpine tundra will take your breath away. Between June and September, the visitor center marks the center of the park, and it's really the only requisite stop for any visitor who is happy enough to see the alpine tundra by car. The centre also has **exhibits** relating to the flora and fauna of the tundra (summer only 9am–5pm) and there are good positions for wildlife viewing a little further east along Trail Ridge Road.

While many people do little more than the drive along Trail Ridge Road, the park is best appreciated by getting out of the car and **hiking**. As there are dozens of superb hikes to choose from, think about the kind of experience you're after – photographing a particular animal, for instance, or hiking across the Continental Divide – and plan around this with a ranger's help. Bear in mind that the delicate ecosystem of the wild, wind-blown tundra makes it essential to stay on the paths. Be watchful of your own system at this altitude, too: dehydration and altitude sickness affect some park visitors each year, so plan hikes conservatively and drink plenty of fluids.

You can also drive here in summer along the unpaved **Old Fall River Road**; completed in 1920, the first road to be built in the park. This runs one way only (east–west) along the bed of a valley carved into a U-shape by glaciers. While it doesn't have open mountain vistas, it's much quieter than the Trail Ridge, and there's far more chance of spotting **wildlife**. Roaming the park are moose, coyote, mountain lions, and a total population of perhaps thirty black bears, which, with a plentiful natural food supply, tend to avoid contact with humans. The central and southern tracts of this wilderness are all but impenetrable; only a well-planned hiking expedition can get you into the remoter forests and valleys.

Just inside the park, near the Estes Park entrance, a spur road, open year-round, leads south to two small and pristine alpine lakes. On the way, the **Moraine Park Museum** (summer only daily 9am–5pm) has a well-laid-out set of exhibits on the park's natural history. Beyond here, to ease the traffic in summer, a free and very regular **shuttle bus** from the Glacier Basin parking area runs the last few miles up to **Bear Lake** (every 30min from approximately 5am until 10pm; check at the visitor centers for the day's schedule), which is the park's most definitive viewpoint, with the mountains framed to perfection beyond the cool, still waters. **Sprague Lake**, lower down, has been landscaped to provide access for disabled visitors: a dead-level paved path encircles the shore, and there are special camping facilities for up to twelve people plus six wheelchairs (contact the park HQ for details; see opposite). A shuttle bus from the Glacier Basin parking area runs to Sprague Lake every twenty minutes (7am–7pm).

Park practicalities

Public transportation to Estes Park from Denver International Airport is provided by Estes Park Shuttle ($39 one way; ☏970/586-5151 or 1-800/950-3274). To get around the park if you're not driving, you can either pick up a **tour** from Estes Park, which with admission (not always included in the quoted price) should cost around $70 a day or $35 a half-day, or you can make the trip from Denver, with Gray Line (see p.882).

Five official **campgrounds**, at Moraine Park, Glacier Basin, Aspenglen, Longs Peak, and Timber Creek, provide the only accommodation within the park ($18 per night). All fill early each day; in summer, reservations are essential for Moraine Park and Glacier Basin (☏301/722-1257 or 1-800/365-2267, ⓦreservations.nps.gov), while the others are first-come first-served. Longs Peak imposes a maximum stay of three days, the rest allow one week. For **backcountry camping** you need a permit ($15 fee May–Oct only), valid for up to seven days, and available from park headquarters or the Kawuneeche Visitor Center (see opposite).

Estes Park abounds in lodges, motels, and places to eat; the **Chamber of Commerce**, 500 Big Thompson Ave (May–Sept Mon–Fri 8am–8pm, Sat & Sun 9am–5pm; Oct–April Mon–Fri 8am–5pm, Sat 9am–5pm, Sun 10am–4pm; ☏970/586-4431 or 1-800/443-7837, ⓦwww.estesparkresort.com), has full details. Options include the *Alpine Trail Ridge Inn*, 927 Moraine Ave (☏970/586-4585 or 1-800/233-5023; ❸–❹), *Lazy T Motel*, 1340 Big Thompson Ave (☏970/586-4376 or 1-800/530-8822; ❸–❹), and the glamorous 1909 *Stanley Hotel*, in a fantastic mountainside location at 333 Wonderview Ave (☎970/586-3371 or 1-800/976-1377; ❼). The *Colorado Mountain School*, 341 Moraine Ave (☎970/586-5758; $20 per bed), is the nearest thing to a hostel in town, with dorm beds in cramped rooms and no cooking facilities. The relaxed *Molly B*, 200 Moraine Ave (☎970/586-2766), has an extensive all-day menu, while the excellent dinner buffet at the historic *Baldpate Inn*, 4900 S Hwy-7 (☎970/586-6151; reservations essential), includes hearty soups, freshly baked gourmet breads, and a range of salads, for only $11.

Grand Lake has a highly recommended **youth hostel**: the gorgeous, rambling log-built *Shadowcliff Lodge*, perched high in the woods on Tunnel Road (June–Sept only; ☎970/627-9220; ❷), with dorm rooms for $14–20 and clean and comfortable motel rooms for $40–45. Among a number of moderately priced **motels** is the *Western Riviera Motel & Cabins*, in an attractive spot down by the lake at 419 Garfield St (☎970/627-3580; ❺); note that during summer, some places in Grand Lake insist on a minimum three-night stay. One of the better places to eat is *EG's Garden Grill*, serving quality Mediterranean-style food at moderate prices in a cozy dining room on the boardwalk at 1000 Grand Ave (☎970/627-8404) – you can also sit in the beer garden (happy hour Mon–Sat 5–7pm). Don't miss the fabulous $7.95 breakfast buffet at *Grand Lake Lodge*, 15500 US-34 (☎970/627-3185; open June to mid-Sept).

Winter Park

The former railroad center of **WINTER PARK**, 67 miles northwest of Denver, may not be Colorado's trendiest resort, but its wide, ever-expanding variety of ski and bike terrain, friendly atmosphere, and good-value lodgings draw over one million visitors a year. As the only publicly owned resort in the state, it has great facilities for kids and disabled skiers – and the 200-acre **Discovery Park**, an excellent, economical area for beginners. Experienced skiers, in turn, relish the country's best mogul runs on the awesome **Mary Jane Mountain**, the fluffy snows of the Parsenn Bowl, and the backcountry idyll of **Vasquez Cirque**.

In addition to skiing, you can **snowmobile** the Continental Divide on a one-hour tour with Trailblazers in Fraser ($40; ☎970/726-8452), or around a 25-mile course at Mountain Madness ($35 per hour; ☎970/726-4529), just north of town. **Summer** visitors can enjoy six hundred miles of excellent **mountain-bike** trails, some of the best of which are accessible from the chair lift ($22 for an adult day bike pass), in addition to the super-fun mile-and-a-half-long **Alpine Slide** ($10), and several contemporary music festivals.

Practicalities

Year-round service to Winter Park is provided by Greyhound, stopping downtown outside the **visitor center** at the junction of Hwy-40 and Vasquez Road (daily 8am–5pm; ☎970/726-4118 or 1-800/903-7275, ⓦwww.winterpark-info.com), by Amtrak, five miles north in Fraser, and on Home James shuttles from Denver International Airport ($43; ☎1-800/359-7503). The **Winter Park Ski Train** does roundtrips from Denver every Saturday and Sunday during ski season, leaving at 7.15am and starting back at 4.15pm ($45; 2hr; reservations required; ☎303/296-4754, ⓦwww .skitrain.com). An excellent network of free **shuttle buses** means that a car is not essential in town. Trail maps and general outdoor information are available at the visitor center.

Winter Park offers the best choice of **rooms** among Colorado resorts. As well as **condos** (booked through Winter Park Central Reservations; ☏1-800/979-0332, ⓦwww.winterparkresort.com; ❹ and up), inexpensive **motels** include the downtown *Viking Lodge* (☏970/726-8885 or 1-800/421-4013; ❷–❸). The *YMCA Snow Mountain Ranch*, a few miles north on Hwy-40 (☏970/887-2152; ❸–❹), has good group rates, an indoor pool, library, and guide-led activities. On the face of it, Winter Park's six **ski lodges**, like downtown's *Arapahoe Ski Lodge* (☏970/726-8222 or 1-800/754-0094; ❹–❼), may seem expensive, but these delightful old-style inns offer unmatched comfort, facilities, and value, and are often full board. You also find well-equipped lodging at *Beaver Village Condominiums*, Hwy-40 (☏970/726-8813 or 1-800/824-8438; ❷–❾). Places to **eat and drink** downtown include *Carlos and Maria's* in Cooper Creek Square (☏970/726-9674), good for low-cost margaritas and Mexican food; *Deno's* (☏970/726-5332), with its hundred-plus beers and tasty pasta; and *Hernando's Pizza Pub* (☏970/726-5409), which has fantastic grub, great prices, and a warm, family atmosphere.

Steamboat Springs

Surrounded by wide valleys, **STEAMBOAT SPRINGS**, 65 miles north of Vail, looks like no other Colorado mountain resort. Its roots are in ranching rather than mining, and its downtown area still evokes a pioneer feel – until you spot the upmarket boutiques. In this ski-mad town, rancher-types judge the quality of snowfall by the number of fence wires it covers; they're usually satisfied with a three-wire winter, which corresponds to its average snowfall of 325 inches per year.

The town's top-notch **ski resort** (lift tickets $64 per day), snuggled into Mount Werner four miles south of downtown, is boosted by such activities as dogsled expeditions, hot-air ballooning, and snowmobiling, available in and around town. A favorite year-round activity is to let all the stress seep out at the secluded 105°F **Strawberry Park Hot Springs** ($5–10; Mon–Thurs 10am–10.30pm, Fri–Sun, 10am–midnight), six miles north of town but only accessible by four-wheel-drive vehicles in winter. If you prefer to stay in town, the **Steamboat Springs Health and Recreation Center** offers hot mineral pools ($5; Mon–Fri 5.30am–10pm, Sat & Sun 8am–10pm), as well as workout facilities. In the summertime, opportunities for **mountain biking**, **whitewater rafting**, and **horseback riding** abound. Outfitters throughout the town can assist you with gear and guides.

Practicalities

Most winter visitors fly into **Yampa Valley Airport**, 22 miles out from Steamboat Springs, though it's possible to drive, weather permitting, from Denver over scenic **Rabbit Ears Pass**, or take the Alpine Taxi shuttle direct from Denver International Airport ($70; ☏970/879-2800 or 1-800/343-7433). Visitor information is at 1255 Lincoln Ave, two miles east of downtown (Mon–Sat 9am–6pm, also Sun 9am–6pm during peak times in summer and winter; ☏970/879-0880, ⓦwww.steamboat-chamber.com).

From town, free SST **buses** (☏970/879-3717) run the four miles to the ski resort. Slopeside **lodging**, such as the comfortable *Best Western Ptarmigan Inn* (☏970/879-1730 or 1-800/538-7519; winter ❻, summer ❺), costs more than downtown options like *Rabbit Ears Motel* (☏970/879-1150 or 1-800/828-7702, ⓦwww.rabbitearsmotel.com; winter ❺, summer ❹), or *Nite's Rest Motel* (☏970/879-1212 or 1-800/828-1780, ⓦwww.nitesrest.com; winter ❹–❺, summer ❸). Steamboat Central Reservations (☏1-877/237-2628) can supply information on lodging and packages. You can **camp** at the *Steamboat Springs*

KOA Campground, two miles west of downtown on US-40 (☎970/879-0273; tents $20, hookups $26).

For **food**, *Azteca Taqueria*, 402 Lincoln Ave (☎970/870-9980), has great inexpensive Mexican take-out; for a casual atmosphere and deli-bakery delights try *Winona's*, 617 Lincoln Ave (☎970/879-2483); and for more stylish dining, *Antares*, 57 1/2 8th St (☎970/879-9939), is one of Steamboat's very best, serving an eclectic range of fish and meat dishes. If you've got money to spare, try the delicious dinner at *Hazie's*, up on the mountain (open Tues–Sat for lunch and dinner in ski season, Fri and Sat nights in summer; ☎970/871-5252), which includes a free gondola ride; best of all is their superb $34 summer-only Sunday brunch. Microbrews and decent pub food are available near the ski area at *The Tugboat Grill and Pub* (☎970/879-7070), which also has live music and a dance floor; *The Cellar Lounge*, 703 Lincoln Ave (☎970/871-8917), is a good downtown venue for live bands too.

Summit County

The mix of purpose-built ski resorts, old mining towns, snow-covered peaks, alpine meadows, and crystal lakes that make up **Summit County** lie alongside I-70, around seventy miles west of Denver. Before white settlement, the Ute hunted here every summer: the swanky Keystone Ranch Golf Club now occupies the meadow where they once pitched their tepees. During the late nineteenth century the county witnessed several gold-mining booms; dilapidated **ghost towns** cling to the mountainsides, but one settlement that survived is **BRECKENRIDGE**, whose streets are lined with brightly painted Victorian houses, shops, and cafés. This is the liveliest of Summit County's four towns; **FRISCO**, stretching sedately along a quiet valley, appeals to those looking for a less hectic pace. Both the other towns, **DILLON** and **SILVERTHORNE**, are dull, though the latter contains dozens of cut-price factory outlet stores. The villages at the resorts of **Keystone** and **Copper Mountain** are also unexciting.

Arrival and information

By **car**, Summit County is about two hours from Denver. Greyhound **buses** stop at the Frisco Transit Center ($15 one way) from where free buses radiate to **Copper Mountain**, **Keystone**, and Breckenridge. There are also **shuttles** from Denver International Airport. Resort Express serves **Silverthorne** and Breckenridge ($50; ☎970/468-7600 or 1-800/334-7433), while Supershuttle (☎1-800/258-3826) and Colorado Mountain Express (☎1-800/222-2112) run a more expensive door-to-door service to your hotel in Breckenridge. Summit Stage (6.30am–1.30am; ☎970/668-0999) provides free **local transportation** around the county, and the Breckenridge Downtown Trolley (☎970/453-5000) runs through town and up to the resort. The main **visitor center** (daily 9am–5pm; ☎970/668-2051 or 1-800/424-1554, ⓦwww .townoffrisco.com) is by the lake at the end of Frisco's Main Street, and there's a small welcome center in Breckenridge at 309 N Main St (☎970/453-6018).

Accommodation

Lodgings in Summit County cover all price ranges, with prices doubling in winter. Frisco has the best-priced inns and **motels**, with places like the *Sky-Vue* (☎970/668-3311, ⓦwww.skyvuemotel.com; ❸–❺), *Snowshoe* (☎970/668-3444, ⓦwww.snowshoemotel.com; ❸–❺), as well as the excellent *Frisco Lodge* (see p.895). There are a few downtown **B&Bs** in Breckenridge, where otherwise accommodation usually means a slopeside condo; The Breckenridge Resort

Chamber (Mon–Fri 8am–5pm; ℡970/453-6018 or 1-800/221-1091, Ⓦwww.gobreck.com) can advise on prices and package deals. Resort accommodation at both Copper Mountain (℡1-800/458-8386, Ⓦwww.coppercolorado .com) and Keystone (℡1-800/222-0188, Ⓦwww.keystoneresort.com; ℡0800/898727 in the UK) is first class, but so too are the prices; virtually nothing costs under $100 a night, unless you find an unusual package deal.

Fireside Inn 114 N French St, Breckenridge ℡970/453-6456. Cozy B&B rooms, as well as a few bunk beds costing $30–35 per night in winter, $25 in summer. Winter ❻, summer ❸
Frisco Lodge 321 Main St, Frisco ℡970/668-0195. Simple, motel-style accommodation in an old railroad inn, with kitchenette and access to a hot tub. Winter ❺, summer ❸

HI-Alpen Hütte 471 Rainbow Drive, Silverthorne ℡970/468-6336. Clean bunkrooms in comfortable environs, and there's a midnight curfew. Winter $15–25, summer $12. Private, motel-style rooms are also available. ❹
Ridge Street Inn 212 N Ridge St, Breckenridge ℡970/453-4680. Comfortable, luxurious B&B in the heart of the historic downtown area. Winter ❻, summer ❸–❹

Outdoor activities

Winter is still the busiest time in Summit County. **Breckenridge Ski Area**, the oldest of the four top-class resorts, spans four peaks and offers ideal terrain for all skiers – and snowboarders, with a six-acre park with half-pipe – as does the plush **Keystone Resort**, where the biggest night-ski operation in the US permits skiing until 10pm. The smallest resort in the county, **Arapahoe Basin** (generally known as "A-Basin"; ℡970/468-0718, Ⓦwww.arapahoebasin.com), offers great above-tree-line bowl skiing. All three are owned by the same company and covered by one lift ticket ($42–52 per day), making this one of the best-value deals in the country. The slopes at the other ski area, the ingenious **Copper Mountain** ($41–64 for one day), are divided into three clear sections to keep beginners, intermediates, and experts out of each other's way. You can find out about conditions by calling ℡970/453-6118.

In summer, mountain-bikers and road-racers alike will be happy with the opportunities for **cycling**, particularly the stretch between Frisco and Breckenridge; Racer's Edge at 114 N Main St in Breckenridge (℡970/453-0995) rents out the best bikes. Each resort runs chair lift or **gondola rides** to the top of the mountains, which, as well as stunning views, provide access to great **hiking** and cycling trails. Breckenridge also offers toboggan rides down the dry **Superslide** (summer daily 9am–5pm; $8), mini-golf ($8), and a giant maze ($5).

Eating

With the exception of *Keystone Resort*, Summit County hasn't developed a reputation for fine **dining**, though there's no end of good-value places to eat, especially in Breckenridge.

Alpenglow Stübe Keystone Mountain ℡970/496-4386. The best dining experience in Summit County – take the free gondola ride to the top of 11,444ft North Peak and feast on New American cuisine with a Bavarian edge in beautiful surroundings. It doesn't come cheap though – the six-course meals run around $70.
Blue Moose 540 S Main St, Breckenridge ℡970/453-4859. Inventive café menu, with lots of vegetarian dishes for well under $10. Open for breakfast, when good, inexpensive wheat pan-

cakes are on offer, and for lunch, when sandwiches, soups, and salads take over.
Mi Casa 600 S Park Ave, Breckenridge ℡970/453-2071. The best Mexican food around, including fine chiles rellenos. The tangy fajitas are good value, as is the daily 3–6pm happy hour.
Mountain Java 118 S Ridge St, Breckenridge ℡970/453-1874. Cozy, book-lined coffeehouse serving healthy lunches, low-fat muffins, and gourmet breads along with steaming espresso drinks.

Pika Bagel Bakery & Café 500 S Main St, Breckenridge ☏ 970/453-6246; and 401 Main St, Frisco ☏ 970/668-0902. Friendly outlets for a fruit smoothie and a bagel sandwich.

The Prospector 130 S Main St, Breckenridge ☏ 970/453-6858. Tasty traditional home-cooked breakfasts (try the spicy and excellent *huevos rancheros*) and lunches including roasts and meat-

loaf. Prices are among the lowest in town.

Rasta Pasta 411 S Main St, Breckenridge ☏ 970/453-7467. Good, fairly cheap pasta with a Caribbean twist and served to a soundtrack of reggae music.

Uptown Bistro 304 Main St, Frisco ☏ 970/668-4728. An elegant, upscale restaurant with seafood and Asian specialties.

Drinking

Immediate apres-ski **drinking** is good at the slopeside bars of all four resorts. As the night wears on, Breckenridge offers the most choice, with several late-night music venues, though Frisco too has its moments.

Breckenridge Brewery 600 S Main St, Breckenridge ☏ 970/453-1550. This huge brewpub, one of the first in Colorado and now a landmark at the southern edge of town, serves good-quality microbrews and hearty pub food.

Dillon Dam Brewery 100 Little Dam Rd, Dillon ☏ 970/262-7777. The place for good microbrew ales and inexpensive quality bar food – salads, burgers, and pasta – with entrees from around $8.

Downstairs at Eric's 111 S Main St, Breckenridge ☏ 970/453-1401. Lively basement sports bar, with a good range of microbrews and filling bar food.

Moose Jaw 208 Main St, Frisco ☏ 970/668-3931. Dark wooden bar serving mediocre burgers and a dreary selection of beers until 2am – but a popular local hangout nevertheless.

Leadville

Standing at an elevation of over ten thousand feet, south of I-70 and eighty miles west of Denver, the wonderfully atmospheric old mining town of **LEADVILLE** is the highest incorporated city in the US, with a magnificent view across to broad-shouldered, ice-laden mounts **Elbert** (14,433ft) and **Massive** (14,421ft), Colorado's two highest peaks. As you approach from the south, your first impression is likely to be of giant slag heaps and disused mining sheds, but don't let this put you off: Leadville is rich in character and romance, its old redbrick streets abounding with tales of gunfights, miners dying of exposure, and graveyards being excavated to get at the seams.

For an illuminating romp through the town's grim early history, head for the **Heritage Museum**, 102 E Ninth St (summer daily 10am–6pm; $2.50). Glass cases hold snippets on local fraternal organizations, quack doctors, music-hall stars, and the like, while a host of smoky photographs portray the lawless boomtown that in two years grew from a mining camp of 200 people into Colorado's second largest city.

Of all Leadville's extraordinary tales, perhaps the most compelling is that of **Horace Tabor**, a storekeeper who supplied goods to prospectors in exchange for a share in potential profits, and who hit the jackpot when two prospectors developed a silver mine that produced $20 million inside a year. Tabor collected a one-third share and left his wife to marry local waitress "**Baby Doe**" McCourt in the society wedding of 1883 in Washington, DC, attended by President Chester Arthur. By the time of his death in 1899, Tabor was financially ruined. Baby Doe survived Tabor by 36 years, living a hermit-like existence in the godforsaken wooden outhouses on his only remaining mine – the **Matchless Mine**. The buildings still stand, two miles out on Seventh Street, and in the crude wooden shack in which she died, emaciated and frostbitten, guides recount the story of Baby Doe's bizarre life in full, fascinating detail (daily 9am–4.15pm; $3). Also on Seventh Street is the **Leadville, Colorado & Southern Scenic Railroad** (depot at 326 E 7th St; May–Oct $26.50;

T719/486-3936, Www.leadville-train.com), which takes passengers on a two-and-a-half-hour scenic trip to Fremont Pass.

Back in town, don't miss the **Tabor Opera House**, 308 Harrison Ave (Sun–Fri 9am–5.30pm; $4; T719/486-8409, Www.taboroperahouse.net), where you're free to wander onto the stage, through the ranks of red velvet and gilt seats, and around the eerie, dusty old dressing rooms, while recorded oral histories tell tales of the theater's golden days. They give no details, sadly, of the time in 1882 when Oscar Wilde, garbed in black velvet knee britches and diamonds, addressed a host of dozing miners on the "Practical Application of the Aesthetic Theory to Exterior and Interior House Decoration with Observations on Dress and Personal Ornament."

Outdoor activities

Leadville is an ideal base for some superb **mountain** biking, hiking, and skiing. Bill's Sport Shop, 225 Harrison Ave (T719/486-0739), rents and repairs bikes, while Leadville Ski Country, 116 E Ninth St (T719/486-3836), has a full range of ski gear and snowmobiles, and can organize local ski packages. The resort of **Ski Cooper** (T719/486-2277, Www.skicooper.com), ten miles north, offers good downhill, cross-country, and backcountry skiing, as well as lessons.

Practicalities

Leadville's **visitor center** is at 809 Harrison Ave (summer daily 10am–5pm; T719/486-3900 or 1-800/939-3901). A good **place to stay** is the historic landmark *Delaware Hotel*, 700 Harrison Ave (T719/486-1418 or 1-800/748-2004; ❹–❻), an atmospheric Victorian place where rates include a full breakfast. South of town on US-24 you'll find a string of cheaper motels, among them the dependable *Super 8* (T719/486-3637; ❸). Leadville has a gratifying choice of places to **eat and drink**. *Cloud City Coffee House and Deli*, 711 Harrison Ave (T719/486-1317), serves bagels, buns, and espresso in a grand old hotel lobby, while further along the street at no. 612, *Columbine Café* (T719/486-3599) dishes up imaginative fresh food with lots of vegetarian options, in simple diner surroundings. There's great Mexican and Southwestern food at the spartan *La Cantina*, a mile south on Hwy-24 (T719/486-9021), which also has dancing at the weekends. Among Leadville's fine **bars**, the *Pastime Saloon*, 120 W Second St (T719/486-9434), is a local favorite, with a great mountain view from its patio, and delicious wings and burgers. After his performance at the Opera House (see above), Oscar Wilde drank at the wood-paneled *Silver Dollar Saloon*, 315 Harrison Ave (T719/486-9914); today, it's a welcoming, atmospheric place, filled with Irish memorabilia.

Aspen

Glossy magazines might have you believe that a tollgate outside **ASPEN** only admits film stars and the super-rich. This elite **ski resort**, two hundred miles west of Denver, is indeed home to the likes of Cher, Jack Nicholson, and Goldie Hawn, and while it's not as typically welcoming as the rest of the Rockies, it can be an appealing place to visit in summer – unless you're on an absolute shoestring budget. Visiting in winter requires more cash, though you can save money by commuting to the slopes from Glenwood Springs (see p.902), less than fifty miles away.

From inauspicious beginnings in 1879, this pristine mountain-locked town developed slowly, thanks to its remote location, to become one of the world's

RESTAURANTS, BARS & CLUBS

Boogie's Diner	11
Eric's Bar	7
Explore Booksellers & Bistro	3
J-Bar	1
Jimmy's	4
Little Annie's	8
Main Street Bakery Café	2
Mezzaluna	12
Poppycocks	13
Red Onion	10
Shooters	5
Takah Sushi	6
Wienerstube	9

ACCOMMODATION

Hotel Durant	F
Hotel Jerome	A
Innsbruck Inn	C
L'Auberge D'Aspen	B
Limelight Lodge	E
Mountain Chalet	G
St Moritz Lodge	D

ASPEN

Roaring Fork River

Aspen Center for Environmental Studies

Aspen Art Museum

Rio Grande Park

Aspen Ice Garden

RFTA Rubey Park Transit Center

Silver Queen Gondola

AJAX SKI AREA

Independence Pass & Leadville

0   250 yds

top silver producers. By the time the silver market crashed fourteen years later, it had acquired tasteful residential palaces, grand hotels, and an opera house. In the 1930s, when the population slumped below seven hundred, it was, ironically, the anti-poverty WPA program that gave the struggling community the cash to build its first crude ski lift in 1936. Entrepreneurs seized the opportunity presented by the varied terrain and plentiful snow, and the first chair lift was dedicated on Aspen Mountain (now known as **Ajax**) in 1947. Skiing has since spread to three more mountains – Aspen Highlands, Snowmass, and Buttermilk Mountain, and the jet set arrived in force during the 1960s. **Development** is a burning political issue: tight architectural constraints have been placed on businesses (*McDonald's* is forbidden to have a neon sign), but the last decade has seen yet more Scandinavian-style lodges, condo blocks, and giant houses that remain empty for most of the year.

Arrival and information

In winter, **Independence Pass** on Hwy-82 from Leadville, which provides the quickest access to Aspen, is closed, and the detour through Glenwood Springs, though scenic, adds an extra seventy miles to the trip from Denver. The **airport** is four miles north of town on Hwy-82, served by local buses; if you fly into **Denver**, connecting flights bought in advance only cost another $60 or so. Or you can take a door-to-door shuttle from the airport (be sure to book in advance); companies include Supershuttle (T1-800/258-3826; $10.75). Numerous airlines fly into **Eagle County Airport** near Vail, eighty minutes from Aspen by car or by Colorado Mountain Express ($53).

Once in Aspen, there's no problem **getting around**: the Roaring Fork Transit Agency (T970/925-8484) runs a free skiers' shuttle between the four mountains and serves the airport and outlying areas. The main **Rubey Park transit center** terminal is in the center of town on Durant Avenue.

Aspen's **visitor center** is at 425 Rio Grande Place (Mon–Fri 9am–5pm; T970/925-1940 or 1-800/290-1324, Wwww.aspenchamber.org). The free *Aspen Daily News* ("If you don't want it printed, don't let it happen") is an excellent source of local gossip, news, and food and drink offers.

Accommodation

Stay Aspen Snowmass Central Reservations (T970/925-9000 or 925-4444) runs a superb service, and doesn't balk if you ask for the cheapest available room. It also arranges package deals combining accommodation with lift tickets. Rates vary considerably even in winter; the least expensive times to come are in the "**value seasons**" (last week in Nov, first two weeks of Dec, and first two weeks of April). Between mid-December and January 4, you'll be hard-pressed to find a double for less than $140. If you're traveling in a group, you can save money by renting a **condo**; the Aspen Skiing Company (T970/925-1220 or 1-800/525-6200) is a good source. In summer, **camping** is also an attractive and inexpensive option; the **ranger station**, at 806 W Hallam Rd (Mon–Fri 8am–4.30pm; T970/925-3445), can advise on free wilderness sites and campgrounds. There are several campgrounds on Maroon Creek Road, south of Aspen, and some smaller options out toward Independence Pass. Call the US Forestry Service at T877/444-6777 for reservations and information (Wwww.reserveusa.com).

Durant 122 E Durant St T970/925-8500, Wwww.preferredlodging.com. Small hotel a couple of blocks from the town center and one of Aspen's cheapest deals, with a hot tub, cozy communal lounge area, and continental breakfast. Winter **7**, summer **5**

Jerome 330 E Main St T970/920-1000 or 1-800/331-7213, Wwww.hoteljerome.com. Stately downtown landmark built at the height of the 1880s silver boom. Spacious rooms feature period wallpaper, antique brass, and cast-iron beds, and a gamut of modern amenities. The elegant lobby is worth a look even if you're not staying. **9**

Innsbruck Inn 233 W Main St T970/925-29880, Wwww.preferredlodging.com. Bright basic rooms in an Austrian-style lodge with hand-carved beams, a few blocks from downtown. Continental breakfast is included in rates. Winter **7**, summer **4**

L'Auberge D'Aspen 435 W Main St T970/925-8297, Wwww.preferredlodging.com. Idyllic little cabins, superbly outfitted with kitchens and fireplaces close to downtown. Winter **7**, summer **5**

Limelite Lodge 228 E Cooper Ave T970/925-3025 or 1-800/0832, Wwww.limelite-lodge.com. About the best value in town with two heated pools, continental breakfast, good-sized but snug rooms, and a central location. **4**–**9**

Mountain Chalet 333 E Durant Ave, Snowmass T970/925-7797, Wwww.mtchalet.com. Very friendly, lodge-style accommodation, with large comfortable rooms, pool, hot tub, gym, and fine buffet breakfast. Winter **7**, summer **4**

St Moritz Lodge 334 W Hyman Ave T970/925-3220 or 1-800/817-2069, Wwww.stmoritzlodge.com. Lodge five blocks from downtown housing Aspen's unofficial youth hostel; the private rooms and dorms are some of the best bargains in town and hard to get. Facilities include a small heated pool and a comfortable common room. Continental breakfast included. Winter **6**, summer **3**

The town and the mountains

Despite the virtually limitless recreation opportunities in the surrounding mountains, there's not all that much to do in Aspen itself. Even so, hanging out on the benches around the town's leafy pedestrianized streets, or browsing in the chichi stores and galleries is a pleasant way to spend a couple of hours.

In summer, the Aspen Historical Society Museum, 620 W Bleeker St (☎970/925-3721, ⓦwww.heritageaspen.org), offers **walking tours** of Aspen and nearby ghost towns (guided $10, or self-guided, free). The **Aspen Art Museum** at 590 N Mill St (☎970/925-8050) holds changing exhibits and puts on lectures and special events, while **Aspen Center for Environmental Studies**, 100 S Puppy Smith St (☎970/925-5756), is a wildlife sanctuary that gives guided nature tours of some of the taller peaks in the Elk Mountain Range.

Aspen's four mountains are run by the **Aspen Ski Co** (☎970/925-1220 or 1-800/525-6200, ⓦwww.aspensnowmass.com); call ☎1/888-ASPENSNO for conditions. The mogul-packed monster of **Aspen Mountain**, looming over downtown, is for experienced skiers only. On the other hand, **Buttermilk** is great for beginners, with an excellent ski school that offers a three-day guaranteed "Learn to Snowboard" program, and the wide-open runs of **Snowmass**, though mostly for intermediate skiers, feature some testing routes. **Aspen Highlands** has some new high-speed lifts and offers excellent extreme skiing terrain. Daily **lift tickets** for all mountains cost $68. **Rental** of skis, boots, and poles usually costs around $18 a day – you can also rent snowshoes if you want to trek up and down the mountains. However, the town's best value has to be its fifty miles of groomed **Nordic ski trails** – one of the most extensive free cross-country trail networks in the US. If you don't want to wait for the snow, consider **mountain boarding** – lessons on these snowboards with wheels are offered by the Ski & Snowboard Schools of Aspen (June–Aug; ☎877/282-7736).

Cycling is the main **summer** pursuit; Aspen Velo Bicycles, 465 N Mill St (☎970/925-1495 or 1-888/925-1495), have a plenty of mountain bikes for hire and offer sound guidance on routes and difficulty levels. The **Roaring Fork River**, surging out of the Sawatch range, is excellent for kayaking and rafting, but sections can be dangerous and every summer sees a few fatalities. Blazing Paddles (from $78 for a half-day float trip; ☎970/923-4544, ⓦwww.blazingadventures.com) is not the lowest-priced company, but it does have a good safety record.

If you fancy **walking** in the mountains, the Silver Queen **gondola** climbs from 601 Dean St to the summit of **Ajax** (daily: summer 10am–4pm, $17; winter 9am-4pm, $20), where guided nature walks set off on the hour from 11am to 3pm. Occasional free lunchtime concerts and talks are held up here, and there's a good restaurant as well. Even more alluring is the landscape around the twin purple-gray peaks of the **Maroon Bells**, fifteen miles southwest, soaring above the dark-blue Maroon Lake. The road is closed between 8.30am and 5pm, except for overnight campers with permits, travelers with disabilities, and RFTA buses; the latter leave daily from the Rubey Park transit center (every 30min 9am–4.30pm; $5 roundtrip, or $19 combination ticket with gondola ride). Details on hiking are available from the **ranger station** (see overleaf).

Eating and drinking

Many of Aspen's classy **cafés and restaurants** charge over $25 for a main course, but good budget places exist and competition is keen. New restaurants open and close with alarming regularity; the list below consists of tried and trusted favorites. Note, too, that many of Aspen's bars serve good, reasonably priced food (see opposite).

Boogie's Diner 534 E Cooper Ave ☎970/925-6610. Inexpensive 1950s-style diner occupying an airy second-floor atrium lined with vinyl and chrome. The menu includes great meatloaf and killer shakes, but also a few imaginative tofu veggie options too.

Explore Booksellers and Bistro 221 E Main St ☎970/925-5336. Great bookstore with a shady roof terrace, serving creative, high-quality vegetarian food, good espresso, and pastries.

Little Annie's 517 E Hyman Ave ☎970/925-1098. Lively, popular, and unpretentious saloon-style restaurant serving potato pancakes and hearty stews at lunch, and huge trout, chicken, beef, or rib dinner platters for around $15.

Main Street Bakery Café 201 E Main St ☎970/925-6446. Scrumptious and inventive New American cuisine, plus an excellent wine list, in a casual, chatty setting. Always busy in the morning for its massive, fresh-fruit-packed breakfasts.

Mezzaluna 624 E Cooper Ave ☎970/925-5882. Mid-priced Northern Italian dishes for lunch or dinner, including wood-fired pizzas.

Poppycocks 609 E Cooper Ave ☎970/925-1245. Serving tasty crepes and smoothies from 7am until 2pm.

Takah Sushi 420 E Hyman Ave ☎970/925-8588. Phenomenally good sushi and pan-Asian cuisine, in a buzzing, cheerful atmosphere. Highly recommended but quite expensive.

Wienerstube 633 E Hyman Ave ☎970/925-3357. The best breakfast in Aspen, including eggs Benedict, Austrian sausage, and Viennese pastries, among other things. Great value. Open daily 7am–2.30pm.

Entertainment and nightlife

Going out in Aspen, the capital of **apres–ski**, is fun year-round and need not be expensive. Check the free papers for special offers. In summer, downtown hosts several top-notch festivals. The flagship event is the nine-week-long **Aspen Music Festival**, between late June and late August, when orchestras and operas feature well-known international performers, as well as promising students who come to learn from musical masters (☎970/925-9042). July and early August see the **DanceAspen** festival (☎970/925-7718), which showcases reliably good contemporary shows.

Eric's Bar 315 E Hyman Ave ☎970/920-6707. Everyone in Aspen who's served you that day will be in *Eric's* that night, hanging out in the swanky lounge area, pool room, or the cigar bar.

J-Bar *Hotel Jerome*, 330 E Main St ☎970/920-1000. This grand bar is a good place to soak up the hotel's atmosphere and rub elbows with the well-heeled hotel guests.

Jimmy's 205 S Mill St ☎970/925-6020. A fizzing atmosphere, outstanding food, a top wine list, and occasional salsa dancing make *Jimmy's* a hit with many locals, including the elite ones.

Red Onion Cooper St Mall ☎970/925-9043. Aspen's oldest bar, serving big portions of Mexican food and good burgers. A popular apres-ski spot, especially for its lethal line in jello shots.

Shooters 220 S Galena St ☎970/925-4567. Swinging country-and-western bar that also holds a popular Tuesday-night non-Country disco.

Woody Creek Tavern Upper River Rd, Woody Creek ☎970/923-4585. Unpretentious local bar and a haunt of Hunter S. Thompson, where ranch hands and rock stars shoot pool, guzzle fresh lime-juice margaritas, and eat tasty Tex-Mex. The bar is in tiny Woody Creek – seven miles north of Aspen along Hwy-82, followed by a right on River Road, and then the first left.

Vail

Compared to most other Colorado ski towns, **VAIL**, 122 miles west of Denver off I-70, is a new creation. Only a handful of farmers lived here before the resort – a collection of fake Tyrolean-style chalets and concrete-block condominiums – opened in 1952. During the Ford administration, it served as the Western White House; Gerald Ford and his wife still live here, hosting annual celebrity golf and skiing competitions.

Rated the top **ski** destination in the US by *SKI* magazine, Aspen lures the ultra-rich (more conspicuous here than in Aspen) with the exceptional quality of the snow, the sheer variety of terrain, and the huge number of lifts (expensive at $62 a day, though the ticket also lets you ski Beaver Creek, ten miles west and home to America's top-rated ski school). You can also speed down a

3000ft **bobsled run** for $20 a time, or, in summer, go **mountain biking**: one good option is to use the two available gondolas (mid-June to Aug daily 10am–4.30pm; $12, $19 with bike) to carry your bike, then ride back down the mountain.

Practicalities

From **Denver International Airport**, several companies offer door-to-door shuttle service to Vail and Beaver Creek, including Supershuttle (☎1-800/258-3826) and Colorado Mountain Express (☎1-800/222-2112). **Eagle County Airport**, used by American Airlines among others, lies just 35 miles from the resort. Vail Valley Transportation (☎970/476-8008 or 1-800/882-8872) offers shuttles from the airport to Vail for $32.

Vail spreads for eight miles along the narrow valley floor, with successive adjoining villages from east to west at Vail Village, Lionshead, Cascade Village, and West Vail. Beaver Creek, home of the Fords, lies a further ten miles west. The entire complex is **pedestrianized**; there's no charge for the parking lots in summer, and Vail Buses run free year-round shuttles (☎970/328-8143).

For information on skiing and accommodation, contact Vail Reservations (☎1-800/427-8308; ☎0800/891772 from the UK), or call the **visitor centers** at Vail Village (☎970/479-1394) or Lionshead (☎970/479-1385). Finding an affordable place to **stay** can be a problem. By Vail standards at least, the condos in **Avon**, just below Beaver Creek, are inexpensive. Rates in **Vail Village**, the main social center, are higher; try *Tivoli Lodge* (☎970/476-5615 or 1-800/451-4756; winter ❼, summer ❺), where rates include a continental breakfast and use of an outdoor pool, whirlpool, and sauna; or the sumptuous *Mountain Haus* (☎970/476-2434 or 1-800/237-0922; winter ❼, summer ❻). The *Eagle River Inn*, 145 N Main St (☎970/827-5761 or 1-800/344-1750; winter ❼–❽, summer ❺), is a B&B decked out in tasteful Santa Fe style in the hamlet of **Minturn**, seven miles south of Vail on US-24.

Eating out can also prove expensive. *Jackalope* in West Vail Mall (☎970/476-4314) is a lively saloon and pool hall serving basic food (entrees around $9), and *Vendetta's*, 291 Bridge St in Vail Village (☎970/476-5070), offers fine Italian lunch specials and pasta dinners (around $15).

Nightlife revolves around **The Circuit** on Bridge Street, Vail Village. Most people tour between the bars and discos. The checklist of places to see and be seen includes *The Club* (☎970/479-0556), a basement bar playing loud rock; the *Hong Kong Café*, 227 Wall St (☎970/476-1818), a small venue where crowds spill outside and loud music rules upstairs at *Vendetta's*, the ski patrol hangout; and *Nick's* (☎970/476-5011), below *Russell's Restaurant*, which plays decent dance music.

Glenwood Springs

Bustling, touristy **GLENWOOD SPRINGS** sits at the end of impressive Glenwood Canyon, 160 miles west of Denver and within easy striking distance of Vail and Aspen. Just north of the confluence of the Roaring Fork and Colorado rivers, the town offers endless recreational opportunities. Long used by the Ute as a place of relaxation, the **hot springs** here were the target for unscrupulous speculators who broke treaties and established resort facilities in the 1880s. North from downtown and across the Eagle River is the town's main attraction, the **Glenwood Hot Springs Pool**, 410 N River St (daily: summer 7.30am–10pm; rest of year 9am–10pm; $8; ☎970/945-6571, ⓌWWW .hotspringspool.com), announced by its sulfurous smell. Billed as the "world's largest outdoor mineral hot springs pool," it sports an exhilarating water slide and special "Jacuzzi" seats into which water is jetted. Next door, you can de-stress in the natural subterranean steam baths of the **Yampah Spa Vapor Caves** at 709 E Sixth St (daily 9am–9pm; $ 9.75; ℡970/945-0667, 🌐www.yampahspa .com), where cool marble benches are set deep in ancient caves. The recently reopened **Glenwood Caverns**, 508 Pine St (℡970/945-4CAV or 1-800/530-1635, 🌐www.glenwoodcaverns.com), offer two miles of grottos and labyrinths filled with weird and fascinating crystalline formations. Cave tours last around an hour and cost $15, though if you want the full three-hour crawling-on-your-belly Wild Tour, it costs $50 and must be reserved in advance.

Some of the West's most colorful characters came here in the early days, including Dr John R. **"Doc" Holliday**, a dentist better known as a gambler, gunslinger, and shooter in the gunfight at the OK Corral (see p.1010). A chronic tuberculosis sufferer, Holliday came to the springs for a cure but died just a few months later in November 1887, at the age of 35. He is buried on a bluff overlooking the town in the picturesque Linwood Cemetery. In the pau-pers' section lies the grave of Harvey Logan, alias bank robber Kid Curry, a member of Butch Cassidy's notorious Hole-in-the-Wall gang (see p.920).

Colorado Whitewater Rafting, I-70 exit 114 (℡970/945-8477), arranges good **float trips** and **whitewater rides** along a fairly placid twenty-mile stretch of the Colorado River (half-day from $39). **Hiking** and **mountain biking** trails alongside streams and waterfalls crisscross the White River National Forest surrounding the town, and offer good fishing opportunities. The nearby, family-oriented **Sunlight Mountain Resort** offers some of the least expensive **skiing** in the region, accessible by shuttle from Glenwood Springs ($1; ℡970/945-7491).

Practicalities

Amtrak trains arrive at 413 7th St, at the end of a scenic route through the canyons, gorges, and valleys of central Colorado. Greyhound, traveling along the less inspiring I-70, stops close to downtown at the *Ramada Inn*, 124 W 6th St. The **visitor center**, 1102 Grand Ave (open 24hr; ℡970/945-6589, 🌐www.glenscape.com), stocks the very useful *Glenwood Springs Official Guide*. Regular RFTA **buses** link the town with Aspen (daily 6am–10pm; 1hr; $6; call for schedule ℡970/925-8484).

The enthusiastically run *HI-Glenwood Springs Hostel*, near downtown at 1021 Grand Ave (℡970/945-8545 or 1-800/9-HOSTEL), has spacious dorms (beds $12–14), cheap private rooms (❶), plus kitchen facilities, a giant record collec-tion, and a wealth of local knowledge. They also arrange tours and whitewater trips, and are closed from 10am–4pm. Reasonable **motels** include the *First Choice Inn of Glenwood Springs*, 51359 6th St (℡970/945-8551 or 1-800/332-2233; ❸–❹), at the west end of town, which has striking mountain views, a guest laundry, and a free, good breakfast. The *Daily Bread Café and Bakery*, downtown at 729 Grand Ave (℡970/945-6253), has delicious breakfasts, soups, and salads. *Fiesta Guadalajara*, 503 Pine St (℡970/947-1670), is a decent family-run Mexican place near the hot springs and offers a huge variety of filling options, with its many combination plates priced around $9. A block away in the *Hotel Denver*, the *Glenwood Canyon Brewpub*, 402 7th St (℡970/945-1276), will cer-tainly quench your thirst, with its great hand-crafted microbrews.

Grand Junction

The immediate environs of **GRAND JUNCTION**, 246 miles west of Denver on I-70, abound with outdoor opportunities, and within a fifty-mile stretch you can trace the transition from fertile Alpine valley to full-blown desert.

△ Devils Tower National Monument, Wyoming

Another town that sprang into life in the 1880s with the arrival of the railroads, it now makes its living primarily through the oil and gas industries. Although initial impressions are bound to be unfavorable – an unsightly sprawl of factory units and sales yards lines the I-70 Business Loop – downtown is much nicer, with leafy boulevards encircling a small, tree-lined historic and retail district dotted with sculptures.

Although the Colorado section of Dinosaur National Monument (see p.1066) is ninety miles north of Grand Junction along Hwy-139, the town itself holds the superb **Dinosaur Journey**, 362 Main St (summer daily 9am–5pm; rest of year Tues–Sat 10am–4.30pm; $7; ☎1-888/488-3466, ⓦwww.dinosaurjourney .org), which houses a collection of reconstructed reptiles and giant bones excavated in the region. Occasionally, the museum organizes one- to five-day digs at the Mygatt-Moore quarry, twenty-minutes' drive from here (call for schedule).

The main local attraction around town, however, is the splendid local network of trails, many through parched, rugged, and spectacular desert country. Especially enticing for **hikers** is the remarkable scenery of the **Colorado National Monument**, while **mountain-bikers** flock to the smooth, rolling single-track trails around **Fruita**. Both activities are possible year-round, and are in fact generally more pleasant in the winter months. Trail information and rental bikes (front suspension $28 per day) are to be had from Over the Edge Sports, 202 E Aspen Ave (☎970/858-7220), a block east of the roundabout at the center of Fruita or from several shops in Grand Junction, including Bicycle Outfitters, 248 Ute Ave (☎970/245-2699). Summit Canyon Mountaineering, 549 Main St (☎970/243-2847), can supply you with the necessary information and gear for the prime **rock climbing** in the area, as can Harleys at 2747 Crossroads Blvd (☎970/245-0812).

Grand Junction is also the place to sample Colorado **wine**; contact the visitor center for information on touring the thirteen wineries in the surrounding Grand Valley.

Practicalities

Amtrak stops at Second Street and Pitkin Avenue. Greyhound buses serve Durango, Denver, and Salt Lake City from 230 S Fifth St. The friendly and insightful **visitor center** at 740 Horizon Drive (☎970/244-1480 or 1-800/962-2547, ⓦwww.visitgrandjunction.com) can provide information on daytime excursions and nightlife. Budget **motels** on the interstate – such as the very dependable *Best Western Horizon Inn*, 754 Horizon Drive (☎970/245-1410; ❸), with pool, spa, and continental breakfast – offer great rates; alternatives include the downtown *HI-Grand Junction* in the historic *Hotel Melrose*, 337 Colorado Ave (☎970/242-9636 or 1-800/430-4555), where bunks cost $12 and private rooms start at around $30. *Daniel's Motel*, at 333 North Ave, is basic but cheap and clean, and convenient to downtown (☎970/243-1084; ❷).

You can **eat** casually and inexpensively at the busy *Blue Moon Bar & Grill*, 120 N Seventh St (☎970/242-5406), which serves sandwiches, salads, and bar food, or at the excellent *Rockslide Brew Pub*, 401 Main St (☎970/245-2111), offering filling portions of tasty bar food (Alpine burgers $6.50, Cobb salad $6.50) alongside an impressive array of local beers. Breakfast, meanwhile, is best taken at the *Main St Café*, 504 Main St (☎970/242-7225), an authentic 1950s-style diner.

Colorado National Monument

More than 200 million years of wind and water erosion have gouged out the brightly colored rock spires, domes, arches, pedestals, and balanced rocks along a line of cliffs to form the enthralling **COLORADO NATIONAL**

MONUMENT, just four miles west of Grand Junction. This painted desert of warm reds, stunning purples, burnt oranges, and browns is also home to a high arid vegetation of piñon pine, yucca, sagebrush, and Utah juniper.

The monument has two entrances ($5, valid for seven days) at either end of the twisting, 23-mile **Rim Rock Drive** that passes through it (a 39-mile roundtrip from Grand Junction). The best of many overlooks along the rim drive is the **Book Cliff View**, or the **Parade of the Monoliths**, just off the rim road at the sign for Window Rock Trail. Short hikes include the one-hour **John Otto's Trail**, affording close-up views of several monoliths; longer trails get right down to the canyon floor. One of the best trails is the **Monument Canyon Trail** weaving through a series of scenic spots, while **Unaweep Canyon** is another beautiful area, with excellent **rock climbing.** You can **camp** for $8 in the park's only campground, the basic *Saddlehorn Campground*, or pitch a tent anywhere more than a quarter of a mile off the road for free. For detailed information on trails, call in at the **visitor center** at the north end of the park (June–Aug 8am–7pm; Sept–May 9am–5pm; ☎970/858-3617, ⓦwww.nps.gov/com).

Grand Mesa

The **Grand Mesa**, thirty miles east of Grand Junction on Hwy-65, via I-70, is at 10,000ft the world's largest flat-topped mountain, created over a period of 600 million years by the erosion of the softer rock that surrounded the hard rock of this one-time massive lava flow. Though its full extent can only really be grasped from thirty miles away, visitors who ascend the twisting Hwy-65 to the plateau are rewarded by a tranquil landscape, with over two hundred lakes surrounded by pine and aspen groves. **Lands End Road**, an eleven-mile dirt track, ends at a stunning panorama: lakes, plains, sand hills, and smaller mesas separate thick forest on the left from desert on the right, with the snow-crested San Juan peaks far off in the background.

The helpful **visitor center**, near the Cobbet Lake junction of USFS Rd 121 and Hwy-65 on the southern side of the Mesa, can suggest good places to mountain bike and where to head for on cross-country skis or snowshoes in winter. Pretty campgrounds, open summer only, dot the east side near Alexander Lake (details from the **ranger office** at 764 Horizon Drive in Grand Junction; ☎970/242-8211), as do a motel and some basic cafés. At the bottom of the Mesa, five miles north of **Cedaredge**, the hospitable *Llama's B&B* on Hwy-65 (☎970/856-6836; ❹) offers fantastic breakfasts served on a sun deck, and the chance to meet resident llamas.

Southeast Colorado

The gently undulating plains of **southeast Colorado** come as a surprise to travelers expecting the ski resorts and alpine splendor that characterize the rest of the state. Here instead are hundreds of small farming towns and endless acres of grassland, much of which looks as it did 150 years ago, when traders and early explorers crossed the region along the Santa Fe Trail, following the Arkansas River between Missouri and Mexico.

The southeast's most popular destination is the engaging small city of **Colorado Springs**, which sits at the foot of towering **Pikes Peak**.

Colorado Springs and around

Seventy miles south of Denver on I-25, **COLORADO SPRINGS** was originally developed as a vacation spot in 1871 by railroad tycoon William Jackson Palmer. He attracted so many English gentry to the town that it earned the nickname of "Little London." Despite sprawling for ten miles alongside I-25, modern Colorado Springs, a bastion of conservatism compared to liberal Denver, still retains much of Palmer's vision, thanks to a high military presence (notably the North American Defense Command Headquarters, or NORAD, deep inside Cheyenne Mountain), fundamentalist religious organizations, the exclusive Colorado College, and a well-to-do Anglo-American community.

At the **Pro Rodeo Hall of Fame**, 101 Pro Rodeo Drive, off I-25 exit 147 (daily 9am–5pm; $6; ⓦwww.prorodeo.com), videos and displays explain the sport's various disciplines (calf roping, barrel racing, and the like). Other local exhibits of note are housed at the **Colorado Springs Fine Arts Center**, 30 W Dale St (Tues–Fri 9am–5pm, Sat 10am–5pm, Sun 1–5pm; free; ⓦwww.csfineartscenter.org), ranging from Native American art to Post-Modern pieces; the displays and demonstrations of specialized mining equipment at the **Western Museum of Mining and Industry**, east of I-25 exit 156A (Mon–Sat 9am–4pm, Sun noon–4pm; $7); and the town's history museum, the **Colorado Springs Pioneer Museum**, 215 S Tejon St (Tues–Sat 10am–5pm, Sun 1–5pm; free), part of which is a restored courtroom, location for a number of Perry Mason episodes.

Motorists whisk through the incredible **Garden of the Gods**, on the west edge of town off US-24 W, without bothering to get out of their vehicles. This gnarled and warped red sandstone rockery was lifted up at the same time as the nearby mountains (around 65 million years ago), but has since been eroded into finely balanced overhangs, jagged pinnacles, massive pedestals, and mushroom formations. The **visitor center**, at the park's eastern border (daily 9am–5pm; ☎719/634-6666, ⓦwww.gardenofgods.com), has details on hiking and mountain-biking **trails**.

Further south, about 45 miles from downtown, is the **Royal Gorge** (south on Hwy-115, then west on US-50; open year-round 10am to around 5pm; $19; ☎1-888/333-5597, ⓦwww.royalgorgebridge.com), a vertiginous 1053ft crack, spanned by the world's highest (and rather rickety) wooden suspension bridge. The gorge is the focus of several other attractions, which though quite commercialized, can still scare the living daylights out of you, including an aerial tram, incline railway, and the Skycoaster – a tower providing bungee-style drops over the roaring Arkansas River (open daily in summer, weekends seasonally; separate $15 fee).

Practicalities

From **Denver International Airport** there are a number of inexpensive **flights**, or you can book the Colorado Springs Shuttle (☎719/578-5232; $27). Greyhound **buses** stop at 120 S Weber St downtown. Colorado Springs' **visitor center** is at 104 Cascade St (daily: summer 9am–5pm; rest of year 10am–4pm; ☎719/635-7506 or 1-800/368-4748). For **accommodation**, there's the elegant, rustically themed *Old Town Guesthouse*, 115 S 26th St (☎719/632-9194 or 1-888/375-4210, ⓦwww.oldtownguesthouse.com), where hors d'oeuvres at check-in and a turn-down service are among the many personal touches. In summer, the neat and busy *Garden of the Gods Campground*, 3704 W Colorado Ave (☎719/475-9450; ❶), has $40 cabins for two, and a $28 campground.

Appealing places to **eat** downtown include the excellent *Olive Branch*, 23 S Tejon Ave (☎719/475-1199), for good vegetarian food. The *Phantom Canyon Brewing Co*, 2 E Pikes Peak Ave (☎719/635-2800), is a great place for microbrews and authentic pub food. Out in Old Colorado City, the family-owned *Henri's Mexican*, 2427 W Colorado Ave (℡719/634-9031), pulls in the crowds with home-style food and superb margaritas. Nearby is one of the area's best **bars**, *Meadow Muffins*, 2432 W Colorado Ave (℡719/633-0583), festooned with movie memorabilia, and serving good burgers, sandwiches, and salads. It also hosts live music and stays open late (until 2am Fri & Sat).

Pikes Peak

Though there are thirty taller mountains in Colorado alone, **Pikes Peak**, just west of Colorado Springs, is probably the best known – largely because the view from its summit inspired Katherine Lee Bates to write the words to *America The Beautiful*. The 14,110ft peak was first mapped by Zebulon Pike in 1806, who never climbed it himself. By the end of the century gondola trails had been built to carry rich tourists like Ms Bates to the top. In 1929 it took Bill Williams, a Texan, twenty days and 170 changes of trousers to scale the mountain, pushing a peanut with his nose.

You can reach the top by a long **hike**, or by a difficult **toll road** (summer 7am–7pm; rest of year 9am–3pm; $10 per person or $35 per car; ℡719/385-7325 or 1-800/318-9505, ⊛www.pikespeakcolorado.com). The thrilling **Pikes Peak Cog Railway** grinds its way up an average of 847ft per mile on its ninety-minute journey to the summit; from 11,500ft onward it crosses a barren expanse of tundra, scarred by giant scree flows. From the bleak and windswept top, it's possible to see Denver seventy miles north, and the endless prairie to the east, while to the west mile upon mile of giant snowcapped peaks rise into the distance. The train leaves from 515 Ruxton Ave in **Manitou Springs**, six miles west of Colorado Springs (mid-May to Nov; $26.50, reservations advised; ℡719/685-5401, ⊛www.cograilway.com).

Great Sand Dunes National Park

Fifty square miles of silky shifting sand, the **Great Sand Dunes National Park** huddle against the craggy Sangre de Cristo Mountains, around 170 miles southeast of Colorado Springs along I-25 and Hwy 160. Over millions of years, fine glacial sands have been blown east from the San Juan Mountains and deposited at the base of the Sangre de Cristos.

Winds blow here every day, so footprints aren't left for long, but the dampness of the sand only a foot below the surface means that the general shape of the dunes has remained unchanged for centuries. A strange, eerie, yet beautiful place, the dunes harbor a number of small, endemic creatures, including the giant sand-treader camel cricket and the small kangaroo rat. Most visitors go little further than the "beach" beside Medano Creek, which runs along the eastern and southern side of the dune mass; but the climb up the dunes themselves, though incredibly tiring, is not to be missed – for the fun **slide** down (bring your own dune board) as much as for the views of the amazing desolate scenery. A walk along sandy trails, squeezed between the dunes and the mountains, and a night spent out at one of the underused backcountry campsites are also worthwhile.

The **visitor center** is three miles beyond the park entrance ($4 per vehicle; ℡719/378-6300, ⊛www.nps.gov/grsa), behind which lies the **Mosca picnic area** – the main gateway for exploring the dunes. The most unforgettable way to stay overnight hereabouts, and one that will leave sand in your gear for weeks, is to pitch on the dune mass itself. For this you'll need to pick up a free **backcountry permit** at the visitor center; the permit is also required for the park's seven primitive backcountry sites ($10). Most campers, however, stay at the large *Pinyon Flats Campground* ($10), the only site in the park accessible by car and usually crowded with RVs; it's run on a first-come, first-served basis and is often full in July and August. The *Great Sand Dunes Oasis Store* (☎719/378-2222) just before the monument entrance offers showers, laundry, and arid tent sites ($10), as well as a small number of basic **cabins** (❸). Behind the store at 7900 Hwy-150 N (☎719/378-2900, ⓦwww.gsdlodge.com; ❹), the *Great Sand Dunes Lodge* has pleasant rooms with dunes views, an indoor pool, and a **restaurant** that closes at 7pm. Otherwise, the closest restaurant is thirty miles away in Alamosa, where the *East West Grill*, 408 4th St (☎307/589-4600), serves fine pasta salads and Asian noodles.

Southwest Colorado

The high mountain passes of **southwest Colorado** are classic mining territory; dotted through the valleys you'll find all sorts of well-preserved late-Victorian frontier towns. As the pioneers moved in, first illegally and then backed by the federal government, they drove the Ute away into the poorer land of the far southwest.

From **Durango**, the main town of southwest Colorado, the dramatic **San Juan Skyway** completes a loop of over two hundred miles through the mountains, north along US-550 and then back via Hwy-145 and US-160. The stretch of road north of Durango, negotiating its way over stunning high passes, is known as the **Million Dollar Highway** for the gold-laden gravel that was used in its construction. Remote **Crested Butte**, to the north of the San Juan Mountains, is a gorgeous nineteenth-century mining village turned ski resort and one of Colorado's major attractions.

Durango

DURANGO is the largest town in southwest Colorado and the best hub for exploring the Four Corners region. It was founded in 1880 as a refining town and rail junction for Silverton, 45 miles north, and steam trains continue to run along the spectacular old mining route through the Animas Valley, though nowadays tourists, not sacks of gold, are the money-making cargo. **The Durango & Silverton Narrow Gauge Railroad** runs up to four roundtrips daily between May and October, from a depot at 479 Main Ave at the south end of town (all leave in early morning; three and a half hours one way; $60 roundtrip; reserve tickets at least two weeks in advance; ☎970/247-2733, ⓦwww.durangotrain.com). The views from the train as it chugs through huddles of lush aspen are spectacular, framed by the clear Animas River below and rocky outcrops looming above. (The trains are slow, however, so if you want to save time you can take a bus one way to Silverton on the Million Dollar Highway).

Durango has also become one of the West's latest boomtowns, attracting a large influx of long-distance computerized teleworkers. Combine them with the local population of students from **Fort Lewis College** and outdoors enthusiasts who come to ride and hike the area's superb trails, and you end up with a town that has a youthful, energetic buzz.

Greyhound services between Denver and Albuquerque call in at 275 E 8th Ave. Durango's **visitor center**, near the train station (summer Mon–Fri 8am–7pm, Sat 10am–6pm, Sun 11am–5pm; rest of year Mon–Fri 8am–6pm, Sat 8am–5pm, Sun 10am–4pm; ☎970/247-0312 or 1-800/525-8855,

@www.durango.com), has full lists of **accommodation**, topped by the land-mark *Strater Hotel* at 699 Main Ave (@970/247-4431 or 1-800/247-4431, @www.strater.com; summer ❻–❼, winter ❹). The innumerable **motels** north of town along Main Avenue increase their rates in summer; try the good-value *Siesta* at 3475 Main Ave (@970/247-0741; ❷–❸), on the north-ern fringes of town, or the small, comfortable *End O' Day Motel*, 350 E 8th Ave (@970/247-1722; ❸), only a ten-minute walk southeast from downtown. The *Scrubby Oaks*, three miles east at 1901 Florida Rd (@970/247-2176; ❹), is a good-value mountain-view **B&B**. There are plenty of places to **eat and drink**: *Carver's Bakery & Brewpub*, 1022 Main Ave (@970/259-2545), opens at 6.30am for breakfast, serves Southwestern lunches and dinners, and keeps buzzing later on in its brewpub role. *Steamworks Brewing Co*, 801 E 2nd Ave (@970/259-9200), is another good choice for sampling local brews and also has a varied menu.

Silverton

Journey's end for the narrow-gauge railroad from Durango comes at **SILVERTON** ("silver by the ton," allegedly), spread across a small flat valley surrounded by high mountains. It's one of Colorado's most atmospheric mountain towns, with wide, dirt-paved streets leading off toward the hills to either side of its one main road. Silverton's zinc- and copper-mining days only came to an end in 1991, and while the population has dropped since then, those that remain have so far resisted suggestions that its future lies in gambling to draw in the tourists. They are, however, extremely reliant on the seasonal tourist train; so while the false-fronted stores along "Notorious Blair Street" are a reminder of the days when **Wyatt Earp** dealt cards in the *Arlington* saloon, the town is defined by the restaurants and gift shops that fill up between 11am and 2pm when tourists are deposited in town.

Although tourism makes Silverton tick, it's pretty quiet here in the evenings as most visitors make it a day-trip on the train. Bargain **accommodation** is to be had at the *Triangle Motel*, 848 Greene St (@970/387-5780; ❸), at the south end of town, which also offers good-value two-room suites and jeep rental, though the old-style, central *Grand Imperial Hotel*, 1219 Greene St (@970/387-5527 or 1-800/341-3340; ❹–❺), with its forty creaky, antique-furnished rooms, is not much more expensive. The tin-walled *Silverton Hostel*, 1025 Blair St (check-in daily 8–10am & 4–10pm; @970/387-0115; ❶), has $11 dorm beds. For **food**, there's *Romero's*, 1151 Greene St (@970/387-0123), an enjoyable Mexican cantina with a menu of tasty, authentic food, plus fan-tastic salsa.

Ouray

The equally attractive mining community of **OURAY** lies 23 miles north of Silverton, on the far side of the 11,018ft **Red Mountain Pass**, where the bare rock beneath the snow really is red, thanks to mineral deposits. The Million Dollar Highway twists and turns here, passing abandoned mine workings and rusting machinery in the most unlikely and inaccessible spots; back roads into the moun-tains offer rich pickings, for hikers or drivers with four-wheel-drive vehicles.

Ouray itself squeezes into a narrow but verdant valley, with the commercial-ly run **Ouray Hot Springs** beside the Uncompahgre River at the north end of town. A mile or so south, a one-way-loop dirt road leads to Box Canyon Falls Park (daily 8am–7pm; $2), where a straightforward 500ft trail, partly along a swaying wooden parapet, leads into the dark, narrow Box Canyon. At the far end, the falls thunder through a tiny cleft in the mountain.

The local **visitor center** is on the northern edge of town beside the hot springs (daily 8am–6pm; ☎970/325-4746 or 1-800/228-1876). At *Box Canyon Lodge*, an old-style timber **motel** at 45 Third Ave below the park (☎970/325-4981 or 1-800/327-5080; ❹), you can bathe in natural hot tubs. The luxurious B&B *St Elmo Hotel*, 426 Main St (☎970/325-4951; ❺), holds a good **restaurant**, and the *Ouray Coffee House*, next to the springs at 960 Main St (☎970/325-0401), has an appealing patio for light lunches.

Telluride

Lying at the flat base of a bowl of vast steep-sided mountains, **TELLURIDE**, 120 miles northwest of Durango on Hwy-145, is located in one of the most picturesque valleys in the Rockies. Another former mining village, in the 1880s the town was briefly home to the young Butch Cassidy, who robbed his first bank here in 1889. These days Telluride (or "to hell you ride," as it was known during its boisterous past) is better known as the home of a top-class **ski resort** that rivals Aspen as the prime winter destination for the stars. It has, however, achieved its trendy status without losing its character, exemplified by the low-slung buildings on the wide main street, beautifully preserved as a National Historic District. Healthy young bohemians with few visible means of support but top-notch ski or snowboarding equipment seem to form the bulk of the 1200 inhabitants, while most of the glitzy visitors tend to hang out two miles above the town in **Mountain Village**; the two places are connected by a free year-round gondola service. In summer, the **hiking** opportunities are excellent; one three-mile roundtrip walk leads from the head of the valley, where the highway ends at Pioneer Mill, up to the 365ft **Bridal Veil Falls**, the largest in Colorado. Come winter, nearly half the ski trails in Telluride are geared for experts, and the new Prospect Bowl nearly doubles the size of the skiing terrain.

Accommodation is much less expensive in summer than during ski season, though prices do go up for the Bluegrass Festival in June, the Jazz Festival at the beginning of August, and the Film Festival at the start of September. As well as being the town's official **information service**, Telluride Central Reservations, 666 W Colorado Ave (summer daily 9am–7pm; rest of year Mon–Fri 9am–5pm; ☎970/728-4431 or 1-800/525-3455, ⓦwww.telluridemm.com), coordinates **lodging** and package deals, with free lift tickets for the first month of the season for guests in certain lodges. Skiing comes half-price if you stay in any of seven neighboring towns. Of specific places, the 1895 *New Sheridan Hotel*, 231 W Colorado Ave (☎970/728-4351 or 1-800/200-1891; winter ❻, summer ❹), offers surprisingly good rates, a cozy library, and a rooftop hot tub, as well as its own bar and chop house (with vegetarian options). The *Victoria Inn*, 401 W Pacific Ave (☎970/728-6601 or 1-800/611-9893; ❺), has clean, motel-style doubles.

Eddie's, a sports bar at 300 W Colorado Ave (☎970/728-5335), serves good Italian **food** and home-brewed ales, while *Smugglers Brewpub and Grille*, at San Juan Avenue and Pine Street (☎970/728-0919), is a lively evening hangout with a wide-ranging menu and some good local brews.

Black Canyon of the Gunnison National Park

The **Black Canyon of the Gunnison National Park** (250 miles southwest of Denver, reachable from US-50 to the south or Hwy-92 from the north), more than lives up to its bleak-sounding name. The view down into the fearsome, black-rock canyon to the foaming Gunnison River below is about as macabre as mountain scenery gets. Over two million years the river eroded a deep, narrow gorge, leaving exposed cliffs and jagged spires of crystalline rock more than 1.7 billion years old. The aspen-lined road leading to the top of the canyon winds uphill until the trees abruptly come to an end, the road levels out, and the scenery takes a dramatic turn – stark black cliffs, with the odd pine clinging to a tiny ledge in desperation. Falcons nest around the **Painted Wall** – the highest cliff in Colorado – standing 2250ft above the thundering Gunnison River. From twelve marked viewpoints along the six-mile rim drive you can see several places where the Black Canyon is obviously far deeper than it is wide. Snowshoeing and cross-country skiing are possibilities here in winter, while in summer there are good opportunities for fishing, hiking, and advanced-level climbing and kayaking.

The **visitor center** (open year-round 8.30am–4pm; ☎970/641-2337, ⓦwww.nps.gov/blca) on the south rim has details on the two first-come, first-served campgrounds, one on each side of the canyon, as well as information on the nearby **Curecanti National Recreation Area** (good for windsurfing on the Bay of Chickens) and **Gunnison Gorge National Conservation Area** (a choice spot for hunting and fishing).

Crested Butte

The beautiful Victorian mining village of **CRESTED BUTTE**, 150 miles northeast of Telluride and 230 miles southwest of Denver, almost died off in the late 1950s when its coal deposits were exhausted. However, the development of 11,875ft **Mount Crested Butte** into a world-class **ski resort** in the 1960s, and a **mountain-bikers'** paradise two decades later, means that today it can claim to be the best year-round resort in Colorado. The old town is resplendent with gaily painted clapboard homes and businesses, and zoning laws ensure that condos and chalets are confined to the resort area, tucked behind the foothills three miles up the road. The rapid transition from near-ghost town to sporting heaven has lured young people here from throughout the West, producing an addictive laid-back atmosphere.

Arrival and information

Crested Butte is not an easy place to get to, especially in winter and spring when **roads** can be cut off by snow and avalanches. Most skiers **fly** in: ten flights per day from Denver, and at least one per week from Atlanta, Dallas, and Houston, touch down at **Gunnison Airport**. From here, Alpine Express ($40 roundtrip; ☎970/641-5074) will drive you the 28 miles to your accommodation. Once in Crested Butte there's no need for a car: free **buses** ply the three-mile route between the town and resort every fifteen minutes. The **visitor center** is at Elk Avenue and Sixth Street (daily 9am–5pm; ☎970/349-6438 or 1-800/545-4505, ⓦwww.cbinterative.com).

Accommodation

The choice in Crested Butte lies between staying up at the ski area or in downtown; you're likely to flit between the two areas every day, so it's only worth staying at the mostly more expensive mountainside lodgings if you're obsessed with getting first tracks. Crested Butte Vacations (☎970/349-2222 or 1-800/544-8448; ☎0800/894085 from the UK) can book accommodation and advise on money-saving package deals. In any case, be sure to reserve a room in advance during winter.

Among the **B&B** options, the historic log home of the *Claim Jumper B&B* 704 Whiterock Ave (☎970/349-6471; ❺), with its six variously themed rooms amid a jumble of Americana, make it one of the most enjoyable in Colorado. The 1881 *Forest Queen Hotel & Restaurant*, 127 Elk Ave (☎970/349-5336; ❸), offers seven clean and basic rooms in the center of Crested Butte, and the large and friendly *Crested Butte International Hostel*, 615 Teocalli Ave (☎970/349-0588 or 1-888/389-0588; ❶), has dorm beds at $17 in summer, and $24 – assuming you manage to get one – in winter.

The Town and mountain

Despite the presence of a pretty and well-preserved Victorian downtown core, people come to Crested Butte only to head out again into the surrounding mountains where the skiing and mountain biking in particular are world-class.

In skiing and snowboarding circles the Butte is best known for its extreme terrain, with lifts serving out-of-the-way bowls and faces that would only be accessible by helicopter at other resorts. It's no surprise then that the resort hosts both the US extreme skiing and snowboarding championships. That said, there are plenty of long intermediate runs mixed in over the mountain's thousand skiable acres, keeping the slopes accessible to all. Fourteen chair lifts (adult day lift passes $55) link 86 runs, which are usually uncrowded thanks to the resort's isolated location. Cross-country, especially telemark, skiing attracts thousands, while snowmobiling is a great way to rest your legs. For something a little different, try a **horseback ride** through the snow with Fantasy Ranch ($85; ☎970/349-5425).

In summer, **mountain bikes** all but outnumber cars around the town, especially during **Fat Tire Week** in July, one of the oldest festivals in the young sport and one that, according to local legend, evolved from a race over the rocky 21-mile **Pearl Pass** to Aspen on newspaper bicycles in the 1970s. You can still ride this route – 190 miles shorter than the road – but some of the most exciting trails are much nearer the town and include the gorgeous 401 trail with its wide-open vistas; the thickly wooded Dyke Trail; and the long, varied, and occasionally challenging Deadman's Gulch. The visitor center (see opposite) can help out with a basic map and route description for main trails, and local bike shops like The Alpineer, 419 6th St (☎970/349-5210, ⓦwww.alpineer.com), are well-equipped with route maps and rental bikes.

Eating and drinking

Crested Butte lays claim to a surprising number of gourmet **restaurants**, which charge much less than their equivalents in the more glitzy resorts. Good, reasonably priced food is also easy to find; even around the ski lifts, a filling lunch can be had for $5. At the other end of the scale, the pricey *Le Bosquet*, 6th Street and Bellevue Avenue, in the Majestic Plaza (☎970/349-5808), offers excellent and imaginative French cuisine. For a bit of atmosphere, try the *Powerhouse*, 130 Elk Ave (☎970/349-5494); while the Mexican food here is comparable to nearby *Donita's Cantina* at no. 330, this restaurant's setting – a fondly restored 1880s generating station with a huge wooden bar and 65 varieties of tequila – gives *Powerhouse* the edge.

The early **apres-ski** center is *Rafters*, right by the lifts. By early evening most visitors have found their way to downtown, for no-nonsense local bars such as *Kochevars* and *The Talk of the Town*. For a definitive, cavernous Colorado microbrewery, head for *Idlespur Brewpub*, 226 Elk Ave (☎970/349-5026), which has a roaring fire in winter and hearty, inexpensive bar food.

Cortez

The town of **CORTEZ**, in the far southwest corner of Colorado, consists basically of one long curve of highway (US-160), roughly 25 miles up from the **Four Corners Monument** that marks the meeting place of Colorado, New Mexico, Arizona, and Utah. Its primary function is as an overnight stop for visitors to Mesa Verde National Park, heading to or from the canyonlands of northern Arizona. Nothing in town commands much attention, though the giant **Sleeping Ute Mountain** to the southwest, visible from all over, makes a dramatic backdrop, looking uncannily like a warrior god asleep with his arms folded across his chest.

The **visitor center** at 928 E Main St (daily 8am–6pm; ☎970/565-4048 or 1-800/253-1616) has information on the entire state. **Motels** include the clean and basic *Aneth Lodge*, 645 E Main St (☎970/565-3453 or 1-877/263-8454; ❸), and the bland but reliable *Budget Host Inn*, 2040 E Main St (☎970/565-3738; ❸). *Dry Dock Restaurant*, 200 W Main St (☎970/564-9404), dishes up great seafood in its pleasant garden, while *Main Street Brewery*, 21 E Main St (☎970/564-9112), serves bar fare. *Francisca's*, 125 E Main St (☎970/565-4093), is the best place in town for authentic Mexican food, and is often packed.

Mesa Verde National Park

MESA VERDE NATIONAL PARK, the only national park in the US devoted exclusively to archeological remains, is set high in the plateaus of southwest Colorado, off US-160 halfway between Cortez and Mancos. It's an astonishing place, so far off the beaten track that its extensive **Ancestral Puebloan ruins** were not fully explored until 1888, when a local rancher discovered them on his land.

Between the time of Christ and 1300 AD, Ancestral Puebloan civilization expanded to cover much of the area known as the "**Four Corners**." Their earliest dwellings were simple pits in the ground, but before they vanished from history they had developed the architectural sophistication needed to build the extraordinary complexes of Mesa Verde. Most of the best-preserved Ancestral Puebloan relics are in modern New Mexico, Arizona, and Utah; see p.979 for more background information and a list of other sites.

Mesa Verde is a densely wooded plateau, cut at its southern edge by sheer canyons that divide the land into narrow fingers. The Ancestral Puebloans are thought to have been the only inhabitants the region has ever had: no one has lived here since the thirteenth century, and neither have any traces been found of a human presence before 500 AD. The people who built the first pit-houses here in the sixth century were already skilled potters leading a stable agricultural life; they owned domesticated turkeys and grew corn. After several hundred years, they moved off the mesa tops and began to construct spectacular multistory apartments and entire communities, nestling in rocky alcoves high above the canyons. Why they did so is not clear, though recent evidence suggests that Ancestral Puebloan culture was not quite as peaceful as previously imagined; in any case the soil at Mesa Verde ultimately appears to have been depleted, and they are thought to have migrated into what's now New Mexico to establish the pueblos where their descendants still live.

Touring the park

The access road to Mesa Verde climbs south from US-160 ten miles east of Cortez. Once past the entrance station ($10 fee per vehicle), the road climbs and twists for fifteen miles to the **Far View visitor center** (late April to late Oct daily 8am–5pm; ☎970/529-4461). Exhibits inside cover Navajo, Hopi, and Pueblo crafts and jewelry. Immediately beyond, the road forks south to the two main constellations of remains: **Chapin Mesa** to the south, and **Wetherill Mesa** to the west. To tour any of the major ruins you must buy **tickets** at the visitor center: $1.75 for each attraction, valid for one specific time only. On Chapin Mesa, Cliff Palace is usually open between 9am and 5pm daily from late April until early November, and Balcony House for the same hours between late April and mid-October; at busy times, you can't tour both on the same day. On Wetherill Mesa, generally accessible between late May and early September, tours of Long House operate between 9am and 4pm daily.

Six miles toward Chapin Mesa from the visitor center, the **Archeological Museum** holds the park's best displays on the Ancestral Puebloans, and also sells tour tickets for the remainder of the season after the visitor center closes in late fall (daily: summer 8am–6.30pm; rest of year 8am–5pm). It's also the starting point for the short, steep hike down to **Spruce Tree House**, the only ruin that can be seen in winter – a neat little village of three-story structures, snugly molded into the recesses of a rocky alcove and fronted by open plazas.

Beyond the museum, Ruins Road (April to early Nov daily 8am–dusk) consists of two one-way, six-mile loops. If you're pressed for time, follow the eastern one only, to reach **Cliff Palace**, the largest Ancestral Puebloan cliff dwelling to survive anywhere. Tucked a hundred feet below an overhanging ledge of pale rock, its 217 rooms once housed over 200 people. Even if you don't have a tour ticket (see above), you can get a great view from the promontory where tour groups gather, below the parking lot. Entering the ruin itself, especially on a quieter day, provides a haunting evocation of a lost and little-known world, as you walk through the empty plazas, and peer down into the mysterious *kivas* (circular, stone-lined ceremonial pits or buildings). Fading murals can still be discerned inside some of the structures.

Balcony House, a little further on, is one of the few Mesa Verde complexes that was clearly geared towards defense; access is very difficult, and it's not visible from above. Guided tours involve scrambling up three hair-raising ladders and crawling through a narrow tunnel, teetering all the while above a steep drop into Soda Canyon. Park authorities present it as more "fun" than the other ruins, but unless you share the fearless Ancestral Puebloan attitude to heights, you might prefer to give it a miss.

From the end of the tortuous twelve-mile drive onto **Wetherill Mesa** (daily late May to early Sept 8am–4.30pm; excluding cycles and large vehicles like RVs), a free miniature train loops around the tip of the mesa to reach the **Long House**, the park's second largest ruin, set in its largest cave. Hour-long tours descend sixty or so steps to reach its central plaza, then scramble around its 150 rooms and 21 *kivas*.

Park practicalities

Mesa Verde gets very crowded in high summer; the best months to visit are May, September, and October. The park remains open all year, though most of the sights are inaccessible in winter, as detailed above, and concessions such as gas, food, and lodging only operate between late April and mid-October.

Most visitors stay in nearby towns; the only **rooms** in the park itself are at the summer-only *Far View Motor Lodge*, near the visitor center (Box 277, Mancos, CO 81328; ☎970/529-4421 or 1-800/449-2288, ☎970/533-7731 in winter, ⓦwww.visitmesaverde.com; ❺), where the balconies have superb views and the lack of phones and TVs make for a tranquil stay. The lodge's *Metate Room* restaurant provides fabulous **meals** featuring buffalo and elk, with ingredients like beans, flat bread, and roasted corn. Food is also available year-round at *Spruce Tree Terrace* near the Chapin Mesa museum. You can **camp** at the pleasant and very large *Morefield Campground*, four miles up from the entrance (late April to mid-Oct; ☎970/529-4421; $10), and there are also several commercial campgrounds nearby.

Ute Mountain Tribal Park

Abutting Mesa Verde National Park to the south is the Ute Mountain Indian Reservation, in which Ancestral Puebloan **cliff dwellings** spread over the out-of-the-way but utterly enthralling **Ute Mountain Tribal Park**, including the eighty-room **Lion House** and the precarious **Eagle's Nest Cliff** perched in a cavernous natural alcove. The only way to visit the dwellings is by joining a Ute-led tour, arranged at the tribe's **visitor center** (no fixed hours; ☎970/565-3751 ext 282 or 1-800/847-5485), housed in a former gas station at the intersection of US-160 and US-666. Full-day tours (8.30am–4.30pm) cost $30 and involve walking three miles and climbing five tall ladders; easier half-day trips, on which you see petroglyphs but no cliff dwellings, are $20. Bring water and food as there's none for sale in the park. You're welcome to drive your own (sturdy) vehicle on the tours, but paying $5 extra entitles you to ride in the guide's jeep.

Wyoming

Pronghorn antelope all but outnumber people in wide-open **WYOMING**, the ninth largest but least populous state in the union, with just 460,000 residents. Above all, this is classic **cowboy country** – the inspiration behind *Shane*, *The Virginian*, and countless other Western novels – where the days of the open range are evoked by rodeos, country-and-western dance halls, and ranchwear stores. The state emblem, seen everywhere, is a hat-waving cowboy astride a bucking bronco.

Northern Wyoming is the prime tourist goal, with well over three million per year heading for the simmering geothermal landscape of **Yellowstone National Park**, and the craggy mountain vistas of the adjacent, and equally outstanding, **Grand Teton National Park**. Wedged in between Yellowstone and South Dakota to the east are the helter-skelter **Bighorn Mountains**, likeable Old West towns such as **Cody** and **Buffalo**, and the otherworldly outcrop of **Devils Tower**.

The meager supply of buffalo in early Wyoming caused fierce intertribal wars over hunting grounds and kept the **Native American** population down to around 10,000. However, Sioux, Cheyenne, and Blackfoot combined to inflict notable defeats on the US Army before it could clear the way for pioneer settlement in the 1870s. The cattle ranchers and sheep-farming homesteaders who followed engaged in violent **range wars** over grazing rights to the wiry grasslands.

Unlikely as it may seem, this rowdy, heavily male-dominated state was the first to grant women the vote in 1869 – a full half-century before the rest of the country, on the grounds that the enfranchisement of women would attract settlers and increase the population, thereby hastening statehood. A year later Wyoming appointed the country's first women jurors, and the "Equality State" elected the first female US governor in 1924.

The absence of rivers to irrigate farmland has effectively put a lid on agricultural and population growth. These days, any weather-beaten, denim-clad stranger is more likely to be an oil roustabout than a genuine cowboy, fuel and mineral extraction having replaced livestock as the mainstay of the economy in the early part of the twentieth century.

Getting around Wyoming

Greyhound **buses** operate along I-80 through the south. The rest of the state is covered only patchily by regional bus companies; it takes considerable time and planning to get where you want to go, so having your own car is definitely the best option. Jackson has the state's largest **airport**, though flights also go to Casper and Cheyenne. **Cycling** across northern Wyoming can be great fun, although if you're crossing the Bighorns you'll need to pick your routes carefully, as roads here have incredibly steep gradients.

South and central Wyoming

State capital **Cheyenne** is the only town of real note in the lower two-thirds of Wyoming. Set in the heart of rich prairie – a surprise after the scrubland, mountain, and desert of most of the region – it has closer economic ties with Omaha or Denver than with the rest of Wyoming, a point the more northerly oil city of **Casper** stressed in its unsuccessful bids to become the seat of government. West of Cheyenne, smaller **Laramie** possesses an agreeable frontier feel, while the spectacular wilderness of the **Wind River Range**, accessible from **Pinedale** and **Lander**, accounts for most of the west-central portion of the state.

Cheyenne

The approach into **CHEYENNE**, dropping into a wide dip in the plains, leaves enduring memories for most travelers. With the snow-crested Rockies looming in the distance and short, sun-bleached grass encircling the town, the sky suddenly appears gargantuan, dwarfing the city's leafy suburbs and everything else below it. A quick walk around reveals a diverse community, shaped by railroads, state politics, and even nuclear arms. When the Union Pacific Railroad reached this site in 1867, soldiers had to drive out the "**Hell on Wheels**" brigade of gamblers, moonshiners, and hard-drinking gunmen who stayed one step ahead of the railroads, claiming land and then selling it for huge profit before moving on to the next proposed terminal.

Union Pacific's sprawling yards and fine old terminus now mark the eastern edge of downtown, while to the west the city's longstanding military installation was expanded in 1957 to house the first US intercontinental ballistic missile base. Cowboy culture is big here, too, as the ranchwear stores and honky-tonks dotted around town attest. Along with the world's largest outdoor rodeo, the nine-day **Cheyenne Frontier Days** festival (T 307/778-7222 or 1-800/227-6336, W www.cfdrodeo.com) in late July attracts thousands of people to its concerts with top country stars, parades, chuckwagon races, air shows, and free pancake breakfasts. The rest of the year, it's pretty quiet; would-be cowboys have to make do with the **Old Cheyenne Gunfight**, at Cheyenne Depot Plaza in front of the Union Pacific Depot building (mid-June to Aug 1 Mon–Fri 6pm, Sat "high noon" and 6pm; free), in which gunslingers act out incidents from the town's turbulent first decade.

Sixteenth Street, or Lincolnway, is the retail and entertainment heart of Cheyenne. Five minutes' walk north up leafy Capitol Avenue near the unspec-tacular State Capitol, the **Wyoming State Museum**, at no. 2320, takes a sober look at Wild West history (June–Aug Mon–Fri 8.30am–5pm, Sat 9am–4pm, Sun noon–4pm; Sept–May Mon–Fri 8.30am–5pm, Sat noon–4pm; free). The **Cheyenne Frontier Days Old West Museum**, five minutes' drive from downtown at 4501 N Carey Ave (Mon–Fri 9am–5pm, Sat & Sun 10am–5pm; $3), is more lighthearted, telling how the railroad came to town, with some great old engines and well-presented temporary exhibits. Much of the place is devoted to the Frontier Days celebrations, with photos, costumes, and videos evoking the annual frenzy.

Practicalities

Greyhound **buses** (☎307/634-7744 or 1-800/231-2222) run east and west along I-80 and south to Denver, while Powder River buses (☎307/635-1327) travel through eastern Wyoming to Colorado, Montana, and South Dakota. Both companies share the depot at 222 Deming Drive, beside Central Avenue several blocks south of downtown. The **visitor center**, at One Depot Square, 121 W 15th St, suite 202 (Oct 1–April 30 Mon–Fri 8am–5pm; May 1–Sept 30 Mon–Fri 10am–6pm, Sat 9am–6pm, Sun 10am–4pm; ☎307/778-3133 or 1-800/426-5009, ⊛www.cheyenne.org), has a free detailed map of the city, and operates a two-hour **trolley tour** of Cheyenne in summer ($8 for adults, $4 for children) as well as **ghost tours** during Halloween season. For informa-tion on the state in general, stop by the **Wyoming Travel Information Center**, perched at the windy highway junction of I-25 and College Drive (daily 8am–5pm, closed holidays; ☎307/777-2883 or 1-800/225-5996).

Although places to **stay** are normally inexpensive, prices double during the Frontier Days festival. Budget motels line up along West Lincolnway, like the *Atlas Motel* at no. 1524 (☎307/632-9214; ❶–❸), and there are inexpensive rooms downtown in the historic *Plains Hotel*, 1600 Central Ave (☎307/638-3311; ❹). Best of the upmarket options is the *Nagle Warren Mansion*, 222 E 17th St (☎307/637-3333 or 1-800/811-2610, ⊛www.naglewarrenmansion.com; ❺–❻), which offers superb bed-and-breakfast in opulent surroundings. **Campers** should head for *AB Camping* at 1503 W College Drive (April 1 to Oct 15; ☎307/634-7035; $13).

Cheyenne has no shortage of **diners** serving cowboy-sized breakfasts, lunches, and Mexican food; try *Los Amigos*, 620 Central Ave (☎307/638-8591). *Sanford's*, 115 E 17th St (☎307/634-3381), is a big, lively **brewpub** with great food and a mixed crowd, and comedy and live music downstairs. The *Terry Bison Ranch*, some ten miles out of town, serves steaks, burgers, and hearty Western meals amid its fields of buffalo (☎307/634-4171; May–Oct).

Laramie and around

LARAMIE lies fifty miles west of Cheyenne on I-80, or slightly further via the spectacular Happy Jack Road (Hwy-210), which slices through plains stud-ded with bizarrely shaped boulders and outcrops. At first Laramie seems typi-cal of rural Wyoming, but behind downtown's quaint Victorian facades lurk hard-rocking record stores, day spas, vegetarian cafés, and secondhand book-stores – unusual for rodeo land, and due to the **University of Wyoming**, whose campus spreads east from the town center.

The centerpiece of the ambitious **Wyoming Territorial Park**, west of town at 975 Snowy Range Rd (mid-May to Sept daily 10am–6pm; $5; ℡1-800/845-2287, Ⓦwww.wyoprisonpark.org), is the old territorial **prison**. A touch over-restored, it holds informative displays on the Old West and women in Wyoming, and huge mugshots of ex-convicts, among them Butch Cassidy, who was incarcerated here for eighteen months in 1896, for – as was the crime of most of the inmates – cattle-rustling.

The **Wyoming Children's Museum and Nature Center** at 968 N 9th St (Tues–Thurs 9am–noon, 3pm–5pm; Sat 9am–1pm; $2 for adults, $3 for children 3yrs and over; ℡307/745-6332) is a great hands-on experience, with gold panning, a crawl-through beaver lodge, and some live reptiles. The **University of Wyoming visitor center**, 1408 E Ivinson Ave (Mon–Fri 8am–5pm; ℡307/766-4075), can direct you to several free museums and sights of interest on campus, including the Anthropology Museum, the Museum of Geology, the University Art Museum, and the Rocky Mountain Herbarium.

Practicalities

Greyhound pulls in at Tumbleweed Express gas station in Bluebird Lane, 2.5 miles east of downtown beside Grand Avenue. The **visitor center** is at 210 Custer St (Mon–Fri 8am–5pm; ℡307/745-4195 or 1-800/445-5303, Ⓦwww.laramie-tourism.org). **Room** rates are good at the downtown *Travel Inn*, 262 N 3rd St (℡307/745-4853 or 1-800/227-5430; ❷–❸), while the *Motel 6* at 621 Plaza Lane (℡307/742-2307; ❷) is cheaper still, and clean and pleasant to boot. *Corona Village*, 421 Boswell Drive (℡307/721-0167), serves authentic and inexpensive Mexican **food**. *Jeffrey's Bistro*, 123 Ivinson Ave (℡307/742-7046), has plenty of good vegetarian options including lasagna, and salad and sandwich combos (entrees $6–10), while buzzing *Lovejoy's Bar and Grill*, at 101 Grand Ave (℡307/745-0141), is a friendly student hangout that serves good espresso, bagels, muffins, and lunch specials. Students, yuppies, and bikers pack out the frontier-style *Buckhorn Bar*, 114 Ivinson Ave (℡307/742-3554), for live rock bands; the friendly *Cowboy Saloon*, 108 S 2nd St (℡307/721-3165), is a fun place to hear country music.

The Medicine Bow Mountains

Just outside Laramie, **Hwy-130** dips into the huge wind-gouged bowl of **Big Hollow**, passes through rustic **Centennial**, and starts the steep climb up the **Medicine Bow Mountains**, one of Wyoming's most picturesque drives. Overlooks at the top of the 10,847ft Snowy Range Pass (closed in winter) present picturesque alpine lakes and meadows, tight against steep mountain faces, and at lower levels there are plenty of good places to stop – pack a picnic and sit by **Marie Lake**, where the snowcapped peaks are reflected in the dark glassy waters.

Some 21 miles west of Laramie, in the shadow of the Snowy Mountain range at 2091 Hwy-130, the superb **Vee-Bar Guest Ranch** (℡307/745-7036 or 1-800/483-3227) is one of the best in the country, offering week-long summer packages for would-be cowhands of all ages. Accommodation is in luxurious log cabins by a rushing stream, and rates include all meals, your own horse, a camp-out, mountain tours, river tubing, and fishing – or you're free simply to sit on your deck and take in the views. In winter they offer wonderful bed-and-breakfast (❻). For cheaper lodging, try the *Old Corral Hotel*, 2750 Scenic

Hwy-130, ☎307/745-5918; ❸–❹). Laden with silly Wild West paraphernalia, it offers themed rooms, a little outdoor hot tub, and a restaurant serving tumbleweed (fried onions) but no alcohol.

Forty-nine miles out from Centennial, sleepy **SARATOGA** is hemmed in by the Snowy and Sierra Madre ranges. The **Hobo Hot Springs** on Walnut Avenue is a free outdoor pool fed by natural 114°F springs. Easily the best place to **stay** is the antique-furnished *Wolf Hotel*, 101 E Bridge Ave (☎307/326-5525; ❸), which has a good restaurant and bar, and you can get subs, salads, and low-priced lunch specials at *Stumpy's*, 218 N First St (☎307/326-8132).

Southwest Wyoming

The long and monotonous drive across southern Wyoming on I-80 – the route also followed by the old train track – holds little to delight the eye, though

Butch Cassidy and the Sundance Kid

Without doubt the two most engaging characters to roam the Rocky Mountains of northern Colorado and southern Wyoming, **Butch Cassidy and the Sundance Kid** remain legends not only of the Old West but of a romantic outlaw existence in which breaking the law became an expression of personal freedom. Thanks in large part to the 1969 Hollywood film *Butch Cassidy and the Sundance Kid* (which starred Paul Newman and Robert Redford), these two former thieves and cattle rustlers continue to cast a long shadow across the Rockies.

Butch Cassidy was born **George LeRoy Parker** in the town of Beaver, Utah, on 6 April, 1866. Taught the art of cattle-rustling by ranch-hand Mike Cassidy, Parker borrowed his mentor's last name, then picked up the handle "Butch" while working as a butcher in Rock Springs, Wyoming. He pulled his first bank job in Telluride, Colorado, in 1889, and soon found himself in the company of a like-minded group of outlaws known as the **Wild Bunch**. Among them was one **Harry Longabaugh** – the Sundance Kid – who picked up his nickname following a jail stint in Sundance, Wyoming. The Wild Bunch were eclectic in their criminal pursuits, and the gang's résumé would include horse-rustling as well as the robbing of trains, banks, and mine payrolls; between them they gave away a fortune in gold to friends and even strangers in need, hence their reputation as latter-day Robin Hoods.

The image of a dashing, philanthropic band of outlaws did not sit well with authorities, who mustered teams of lawmen – and gunmen – to go after them. The gang took to laying low through the winter months in **Brown's Hole**, a broad river valley in remote northwest Colorado, and they were also known to visit the southern Wyoming towns of Baggs, Rock Springs, and Green River. Their saloon excesses were tolerated, though, because at the end of a spree they would meticulously account for every broken chair and bullet hole, making generous restitution in gold. The gang, however, was eventually undone by their own vanity and love of a good time. During a visit to Fort Worth, Texas, five of the men posed for a photo in smart suits and derby hats, looking so dapper that the photographer proudly placed the photo in his shop window where it was seen the following day by a detective from the famous Pinkerton's agency.

Wearying of life on the run, Butch and Sundance sailed for **South America** in 1902, and were soon trying their hand at gold-mining, while robbing the occasional bank or train. The Hollywood version was true enough to this point, but Butch Cassidy did not die in a hail of bullets at the hands of Bolivian soldiers in 1909 as depicted in the film – although it seems that Harry Longabaugh did. The last say belongs to Josie Morris, an old girlfriend from Butch's Brown's Hole days, who insisted that he came to see her on his return from South America, and claimed furthermore that he died an old man in Johnny, Nevada, some time during the 1940s.

geologists and fossil enthusiasts will be in their element, and it may provide some travelers with their first glimpse of the red-rock scenery of the West.

Rawlins

There would be little reason to stop at the tiny prairie town of **RAWLINS**, a hundred miles west of Laramie, but for one extraordinary sight: the unmissable **Wyoming Frontier Prison**, at Fifth and Walnut streets (hourly tours 8.30am–5.30pm June–Aug, by reservation only the rest of the year; $4.25; ☎307/324-4422). In service until 1981, this huge, creepy jail with dark, neglected cells, peeling walls, and echoing corridors can make for a troubling experience – not least due to the fascinating life stories and anecdotes told with aplomb by the exceptional guides – and the darkest moment comes as the gas chamber (in use from 1937 until 1965) is revealed.

Just to the west, the Continental Divide briefly splits into two in the **Great Divide Basin**. In theory, rain that falls here should remain here, unable to flow toward either ocean – unfortunately virtually all of it evaporates, and the brick-red hell of the **Red Desert** stretches implacably away to the horizon.

Fossil Butte National Monument

Remote **Fossil Butte National Monument**, about fifty miles north of I-80, preserves a fossilized cross-section of the fish population of a lake that existed here fifty million years ago. From a distance, you can clearly see the corresponding pale limestone strata on the flat-topped Butte itself, but the various trails turn out to show you less than the displays at the **visitor center** (daily: June–Aug 8am–7pm; Sept–May 8am–5pm; free; ☎307/877-4455).

Casper

Dreary **CASPER**, halfway up Wyoming on I-25, may not seem an obvious place to visit, but at a good 150 miles from anywhere of similar size it makes a likely pit stop. Originally at the spot where the Oregon Trail crossed the North Platte River – you can visit a reconstruction of the 1860s **Fort Caspar** that gave it its (misspelled) name – Casper has been the center of Wyoming's oil region since 1890, and though its population (and appearance) fluctuates between periods of high and low demand, the town still hasn't completely shaken off the signs of harder times.

Casper's biggest bright spot is the **Nicolaysen Art Museum**, 400 E Collins Drive (summer Tues–Sat 10am–5pm, Sun noon–4pm; rest of year Tues–Fri 10am–7pm, Sat 10am–5pm, Sun noon–4pm; free; ☎307/235-5247), which displays old and new art by Wyoming artists. For a portrayal of life at an Oregon Trail Outpost, visit the **National Historic Trails Interpretive Center**, 1501 N Poplar St (☎307/261-7700).

Powder River **buses**, serving Cheyenne, Denver, Cody, Billings, and Rapid City, have a base at the *Parkway Plaza Hotel*, I-25 and Center St (☎307/266-1904 or 1-800/442-3682), and south of the **visitor center** at 500 N Center St (☎307/234-5362, ☻www.casperwyoming.org). Bargain **motels** include the *National 9 Showboat Motel*, 100 W F St (☎307/235-2711; ❷). For **food**, try *Casper's Good Cooking*, 581 N Poplar St (☎307/237-3033), a cheerful, 24-hour place just off the interstate.

The Wind River range

Roads to Grand Teton and Yellowstone national parks from southern Wyoming skirt the **Wind River Mountains**, the state's longest and highest range, with some of the Rockies' most beautiful and challenging backpacking terrain. No roads cross the mountains; you can either see them from the **east**, by driving through the Wind River Indian Reservation on US-26/287, or from the less accessible **west**, by taking US-191 up from I-80 at Rock Springs.

Wind River Indian Reservation

The **Wind River Indian Reservation** occupies a large (and largely forgotten) swath of west central Wyoming, overshadowed by the high snow-capped peaks to the west and south. It is the only Indian reservation in Wyoming, and extends roughly seventy miles from the natural spa of **Thermopolis** in the east, through arid grasslands and desiccated uranium-rich badlands, to **Dubois** in the west, with the rich fishing grounds of the cottonwood-lined Wind River at its heart. The reservation was created in 1863 as a permanent home for the Eastern Shoshone, but due to US government imposition, it soon came to accommodate the Northern Arapaho as well; these days the Arapaho account for more than double the Shoshone population. Near **Fort Washakie** – named for the centenarian Chief Washakie, who held the Shoshone together throughout the period of white expansion – is the likely grave of **Sacagawea**, the guide of Lewis and Clark's expedition. **Powwows** – gatherings that have both spiritual and social significance to Native Americans – are held mainly in summer, and are open to the public. Contact the Shoshone Tribal Cultural Center (Mon–Fri 8am–5pm; ☎307/332-9106) for details on how to join in.

The friendly one-horse town of **LANDER**, southwest on US-287, makes an appealing base, with a string of cheap motels along Main Street and an excellent **B&B** at the Art Nouveau–style *Blue Spruce Inn*, 677 S Third St (☎307/332-8253 or 1-888/503-3311; ④). Good places to **eat** include the locals' favorite *Gannett Grill*, 126 Main St (☎307/332-8228), for a great burger or a few beers at the bar next-door; the *Ranch*, 148 Main St (☎307/332-7388), for family-style dining and local microbrews; and *Amoretti's*, 202 Main St (☎307/335-8500), which offers upscale Italian food. The funky *Magpie Coffee House*, 159 N Second St (☎307/332-5565), is the place for espresso, light breakfasts, lunches, and, most vitally, dessert.

In nearby **Sinks Canyon State Park**, the Popo Agie River plunges underground, only to re-emerge half a mile later in a huge spring (trail information from the ranger office at 333 S Hwy-789 in Lander).

Dubois

The former logging town of **DUBOIS** ("dew-boys"), squeezed into the northern tip of the Wind River valley, and an oasis among the badlands, turned to tourism after its final sawmill closed in 1987. Given a head start by being just fifty miles southeast of Grand Teton National Park (via the dramatic **Togwotee Pass**), Dubois is home to the biggest herd of bighorn sheep in the lower 48 states, and celebrates that fact with its **National Bighorn Sheep Center**, a half-mile northwest of town on US-26/287 (daily: summer 9am–8pm; rest of year 9am–5pm; closed for part of winter; $2; ☎307/455-3429).

Dubois is a bargain alternative to Jackson (see p.937), thanks to **motels** such as the log-built *Branding Iron*, 401 W Ramshorn St (☎307/455-2893 or 1-888/651-9378, ⓔbrandingiron@wyoming.com; ❷–❸), with its kitchenettes, and the beautifully restored historic **B&B** *Twin Pines Lodge and Cabins*, 218 Ramshorn St (☎307/455-2600 or 1-800/550-6332, ⓔtwinpines@wyoming .com; ❸–❹). The evening pastime is listening to country crooners in classic

⑪

Western **bars** like the *Rustic Pine*, 121 E Ramshorn St (☎307/455-2772), which also serves steaks. *The Hang-Out*, 151 Bald Mountain Rd (☎307/455-3800), is good for sandwiches, soups, and coffee.

Pinedale

On the western side of the Wind River range, tiny well-to-do **PINEDALE** on US-191 offers unrivaled access to the mountains. Once a major logging center, it now attracts second-homeowners and hikers. The excellent **Museum of the Mountain Man**, 700 E Hennick Rd (May–Sept daily 10am–5pm; rest of the year by appointment only; $4; ☎307/367-4101), commemorates the town's role as a rendezvous for fur trappers in the 1830s.

A sixteen-mile road winds east from Pinedale past Fremont Lake to **Elkhart Park**, from where trails lead past beautiful **Seneca Lake** and along rugged Indian Pass to the glaciers and 13,000ft peaks; the Pinedale Ranger Station office at 29 Fremont Lake Rd (June–Aug Mon–Sat 8am–5pm; rest of year Mon–Fri 8am–5pm; ☎307/367-4326) has information on good hiking routes.

Motels are easily found on the main drag, Pine Street, including the appealing and central *Lodge at Pinedale*, no. 1054 W (☎307/367-8800, ⓦwww.pinedalelodge.com; ❸–❺), with continental breakfast, swimming pool, and hot tub. *McGregor's Pub*, 21 N Franklin Ave (☎307/367-4443), offers **food** and a good pint.

Northwest and north central Wyoming

Northern Wyoming has more to offer than just a handy route between the Black Hills and Yellowstone, though the surreal volcanic monument of **Devils Tower**, the abrupt **Bighorn Mountains**, and the desertscape of the **Bighorn Basin** are notable natural attractions in a land steeped in the history of Native American wars, outlaw activity, and pioneer hardships. The small town of **Cody**, developed by Buffalo Bill himself, is one of the more commercialised settlements around here, and a worthwhile stopover.

Devils Tower National Monument

Though Congress designated **DEVILS TOWER**, in far northeastern Wyoming, as the country's first national monument in 1906, it took Steven Spielberg's inspired use of it as the alien landing spot in *Close Encounters of the Third Kind* to make this eerie 867ft volcanic outcrop a true national icon. Plonked on top of a thickly forested hill, itself a full six hundred feet above the peaceful Belle Fourche River, it resembles a giant wizened tree stump; but, painted ever-changing hues by the sun and moon, it can be hauntingly beautiful. Sioux legend says the tower was formed after three young girls jumped onto a boulder to escape a vicious bear. They were rescued when the great god, seeing their plight, made the rock rise higher and higher; the bear's desperate efforts to climb up scored the sides of the column.

Four short trails loop the tower, beginning from the **visitor center** (mid-June to mid-Sept daily 8am–7.45pm; mid-Sept to mid-June weather dependent; ☎307/467-5283) at its base, three miles from the main gate. There will invariably be a few foolhardy souls attempting to scale the tower, despite objections from local Native American communities for whom this is a sacred place. The **entrance fee** per car (good for seven days) is $8, and until October you can **camp** for $12 a night – arrive early or you'll end up paying more than twice that at one of the nearby commercial campgrounds. For a bite to **eat**, try the *KOA Kampground Longhorn Café* (summer 7am–9pm; late spring and early fall 9am–3pm; ☎307/467-5395) at the main gate, which has good buffalo burgers.

Buffalo

Snuggled among the southeastern foothills of the Bighorn Mountains, quiet, attractive **BUFFALO** remains largely unaffected by the bustle of the nearby I-90/I-25 intersection. Although **Main Street**, now lined with frontier-style stores, used to be an old buffalo trail, the place was actually named after Buffalo, New York. The **Jim Gatchell Museum**, 100 Fort St, stacked full of Old West curiosities pertaining to soldiers, ranchers, and Native Americans, is well worth a visit (June–Aug daily 8am–8pm; May, Sept & Oct Mon–Fri 8am–5pm; $2).

Pick up information from the **visitor center**, 55 N Main St (Mon–Fri 8am–5pm; ☎307/684-5544). Should you need to stay, the historic *Mansion House Motel*, 313 N Main St (☎307/684-2218 or 1-888/455-9202; ❸), offers impressive **rooms** at bargain rates that include continental breakfast. *Tom's Diner*, 41 N Main St (☎307/684-7444), is an excellent spot for breakfast or lunch, and in the evening you can **dine** at the *Winchester Steakhouse*, 117 E Hwy-16 (☎307/684-8636), then stop for a drink in the lovingly restored, late nineteenth century *Occidental Hotel*, 10 N Main St.

Through the Bighorn Mountains

Of the three scenic highways through the **Bighorn Mountains**, US-14A from **Burgess Junction**, fifty miles west of Victorian **Sheridan**, is the most spectacular. The massive and heavily wooded Bighorns soar abruptly from the plains to over 9000ft; the loftiest peaks, protruding above the timberline, seem bald beside their dark-coated neighbors. The road edges its way up **Medicine Mountain**, on whose windswept western peak the mysterious **Medicine Wheel** – the largest such monument still intact – stands protected behind a wire fence. Local Native American legends offer no clues as to the original purpose of these flat stones, arranged in a circular "wheel" shape with 28 spokes and a circumference of 245ft – though the pattern suggests sun-worship or early astronomy. To get there, you'll have to drive along a precipitous dirt track (past an incongruous radar dome) to within a mile of the site and hike the rest of the way. Even if US-14A isn't closed by snow (usually Nov–May), or even if the Medicine Wheel isn't being used by local Native Americans for religious ceremonies, you might still find the dirt track impassable due to bad weather.

The route down the west side, with gradients of ten to twenty percent and three awesome runaway truck ramps, is said to have cost more to build per mile than any other road in America. Tight hairpin bends will keep drivers' eyes off the magnificent overlooks, but the best view comes near the bottom, when the road lets you out into the **Bighorn Basin**. This ultra-flat, sparsely vegetated valley, walled in by mighty mountains on three sides and ragged foothills to the north, can strike you as a land that time forgot.

Bighorn Canyon National Recreation Area

Before US-14A gets to Lovell, Hwy-37 turns north to the **Bighorn Canyon National Recreation Area**, an unexpected red-rock wilderness straddling the border between Wyoming and Montana. No road runs the full length of the canyon which, since being flooded by the 525ft Yellowtail Dam (only accessible from Montana), has become primarily the preserve of watersports enthusiasts. In summer, **boat tours** leave from **Horseshoe Bend**, where the marina (℡307/548-7230) rents out assorted equipment, and a shadeless beach of red sand offers swimming in the most bizarre of settings. The **Devil's Canyon overlook**, just off Hwy-37 three miles over the border into Montana, affords landlubbers an opportunity to gauge the knee-knocking 1000ft-plus drop into the abyss.

A **visitor center** just east of Lovell on US-14A (daily 8.30am–5pm; ℡307/548-2251) supplies information on local activities and has maps of the Medicine Wheel area.

Cody

Supremely entertaining (if cheesy and pricey), the Wild West town of **CODY**, 79 miles east along US-14 and the North Fork of the Shoshone River from Yellowstone, was the brainchild of investors who, in 1896, persuaded "Buffalo Bill" Cody to get involved in their development company, knowing his approval would attract homesteaders and visitors alike. During summer, tourism is big business, but underneath all the Buffalo Bill–linked attractions

Buffalo Bill

The much-mythologized exploits of **William Frederick "Buffalo Bill" Cody**, born in Iowa in 1846, began at the age of just eleven, when the murder of his father forced him to take a job as an army dispatch rider. An early escape from ambush brought Cody fame as the "Youngest Indian Slayer of the Plains"; four years later, he became the youngest rider on the legendary **Pony Express**. After a stint fighting for the Union, Cody found work – and a lifelong nickname – supplying buffalo meat to workers laying the transcontinental railroad. He killed over 4200 animals in just eighteen months, before rejoining the army in 1868 as its chief scout. In the next decade, when the Plains Indian Wars were at their peak, he earned a Congressional Medal of Honor and a remarkable record of never losing any troops in ambushes. Among battles in which he took part was the 1877 encounter with Sioux forces in which he killed – and scalped – Chief Yellow Hand.

By the late 1870s, exaggerated accounts of Cody's adventures were appearing back east in the "dime novels" of Ned Buntline, and with the Indian Wars all but over he took to guiding Yankee and European gentry on buffalo hunts. He referred to the vacationers as "dudes," and called his camps "dude ranches." The theatrical productions he laid on for his rich guests developed into the world-famous **Wild West Show**. First staged in 1883, these spectacular outdoor carnivals usually consisted of a re-enactment of an Indian battle such as Custer's Last Stand, featuring Sioux who had been present at Little Bighorn, trick riders, buffalo, clowns, and exhibition shooting and riding by the man himself. The show spent ten of its thirty years in Europe, and made Buffalo Bill "the most famous and recognized man in the world." Dressed in the finest silks and sporting a well-groomed goatee, Cody stayed in the grandest hotels and dined with heads of state; Queen Victoria was so enthusiastic in her admiration that rumors circulated of an affair between them.

In later life, a mellowing Cody played down his past activities, to the point of urging the government to respect all Native American treaties and put an end to the wanton slaughter of buffalo and game. Although the Wild West Show was reckoned to have brought in as much as one million dollars per year, his many investments failed badly, and, in January 1915, a penniless 69-year-old Buffalo Bill died at his sister's home in Denver. His grave can be found atop Lookout Mountain, outside Golden, Colorado (see p.885).

and paraphernalia, Cody manages to retain the feel of a rural Western settlement. It's certainly not a place where you'd expect avant-garde painter **Jackson Pollock** to have been born and raised.

The wide, dusty main thoroughfare, **Sheridan Avenue**, holds an array of souvenir and ranchwear shops, and is the scene of parades and rodeos during the annual **Cody Stampede**, held on the weekend of July 4. Between June and August there's a **rodeo** every night at Stampede Park, the open-air stadium on the road to Yellowstone, at 421 W Yellowstone Ave (8.30pm; $13; ⊕307/587-5155).

On the western side of town is **Old Trail Town**, 1831 DeMaris Drive, (May–Sept 8am–8pm; $5; ⊕307/587-5302), a collection of buildings dating from between 1879 and 1901 and salvaged from the surrounding region; among them are cabins and saloons frequented by Butch Cassidy and the Sundance Kid, and Curly, the Crow scout of George Custer. The remains of famed mountain man **Jeremiah Liver Eatin' Johnston** are also buried here.

Cody is also home to some of the premier **Western stores** in the US, which make for a fascinating visit whether you're shopping or just browsing. Finely crafted belts and buckles are available at Seidel's, 1200 Sheridan Ave (⊕307/587-1200) – choose from trophy- or ranger-style **buckles** in sterling silver or bronze and have your name engraved on it. For **cowboy boots**, head for Wayne's, 1250 Sheridan Ave (⊕307/587-5234), where stylish offerings include lizard-skin.

Buffalo Bill Historical Center

The nation's most comprehensive collection of Western Americana, Cody's giant **Buffalo Bill Historical Center** at 720 Sheridan Ave comprises several distinct museums (April daily 10am–5pm; May daily 8am–8pm; June to mid-Sept daily 7am–8pm; mid-Sept to Oct daily 8am–5pm; Nov–March Tues–Sat 10am–3pm; $15 ticket is valid for two consecutive days; ⊕307/587-4771, Ⓦwww.bbhc.org).

At the **Buffalo Bill Museum** artifacts from William Cody's various careers, such as guns, gifts from European heads of state, billboards, clothes, and dime novels, trace the years of the Pony Express, Civil War, Indian Wars, and Wild West shows. The lives of western Native Americans are celebrated in the **Plains Indian Museum**: many of the ceremonial garments are in stunning condition. A superb bear-claw necklace is a standout, and there's also a poignant display of Ghost Dance shirts, worn for the ritual song and dance that would hasten the day when all whites would be buried by a heaven-sent fall of soil. The US Army condemned Ghost Dances as unacceptable shows of resistance, and mobilized troops to disrupt ceremonies.

In the beautifully laid-out **Whitney Gallery of Western Art**, the contrasting styles of Frederic Remington and Charles M. Russell command the most attention. The propagandist Remington dwells on conflict, depicting the Indian as a savage in the path of progress, while Russell's work shows a consistent respect for the Native American way of life.

The largest known collection of American-made firearms in the world is housed in the **Cody Firearms Museum**, alongside interactive computer displays on mechanisms and gun safety.

Practicalities

For information and accommodation reservations, contact Cody's **visitor center** at 836 Sheridan Ave (summer Mon–Sat 8am–7pm, Sun 10am–3pm; rest of year Mon–Fri 8am–5pm; ⊕307/587-2777, Ⓦwww.codychamber.org).

Cody is the site of the **Yellowstone Regional Airport**. Powder River Coaches arrive at Daylight Donuts, 1452 Sheridan Ave (T 1-800/442-3682), and also offer one-day Yellowstone tours; **float trips** on the Shoshone are available from, among others, Wyoming River Trips (T 307/587-6661 or 1-800/586-6661).

Cody's showpiece Western **hotel**, the *Irma* at 1192 Sheridan Ave (T 307/587-4221 or 1-800/745-4762, W www.irmahotel.com; ❹–❺), was named for Buffalo Bill's daughter in 1902, and retains a superb original cherrywood bar, a gift to Buffalo Bill from Queen Victoria. Among good-value motels, the friendly *Skyline Motor Inn*, high above town on the main through highway at 1919 17th St (T 307/587-4201 or 1-800/843-8809; ❷–❹), stands out.

Sheridan Avenue is the place for an evening's **eating** and **entertainment**: after a steak at the always-packed restaurant at the *Irma* hotel (see above), call in for a drink at the *Proud Cut Saloon*, at no. 1227. You may need a cowboy hat to really feel comfortable at *Cassie's*, 214 Yellowstone Ave, where entertainment ranges from line-dancing classes to country-rock bands, and you can settle in for a full evening including dinner, although the menu is surprisingly expensive. *Peter's Café Bakery*, at 1191 Sheridan Ave, is the morning place for coffee or a full breakfast.

Wapiti Valley

The drive west from Cody to Yellowstone is a superb preparation for the splendors of the park itself, skirting the artificial lake created by the Buffalo Bill Dam before running alongside the Shoshone River through the open, high **Wapiti Valley**, the heart of Wyoming's "beef country," and finally climbing through the rugged mountains to Sylvan Pass. Lodges and campgrounds appear at intervals without spoiling the magnificent landscape of the surrounding Shoshone National Forest. The *Elephant Head Lodge*, along US-14/16/20 (T 307/587-3980, W www.elephantheadlodge.com; ❺), is one such option, should you need a place to stay.

Yellowstone National Park

Millions of visitors each year come to **YELLOWSTONE NATIONAL PARK**, America's oldest national park and the largest in the lower 48 states, to glory in its magnificent mountain scenery and abundant wildlife, and above all to witness hydrothermal phenomena on a unique scale. Measuring roughly sixty by fifty miles, and overlapping slightly from Wyoming's northwestern corner into Idaho and Montana, the park centers on a 7500ft-high plateau, the caldera of a vast volcanic eruption that occurred a mere 600,000 years ago. Into it are crammed more than half the world's **geysers**, in which the rain and snow that seep through the bedrock escape the pressure-cooker conditions under the surface in intermittent spectacular blasts, plus thousands of **fumaroles** jetting plumes of steam, **mud pots** gurgling with acid-dissolved muds and clays, and **hot springs**.

For many visitors, Yellowstone amounts to an extraordinary experience, combining the **colors** of the Grand Canyon of the Yellowstone, limpid Yellowstone Lake, the wild flower meadows and the rainbow-hued geyser pools; the **sounds** of subterranean rumblings, belching mud pools, and steam hissing from the mountainsides; and the constant **smells** of drifting sulfurous fumes, with the presence of browsing bull moose, shambling bears, heavy-bearded bison, herds of elk, and ubiquitous scurrying **marmots**. It is, however, very popular; if you

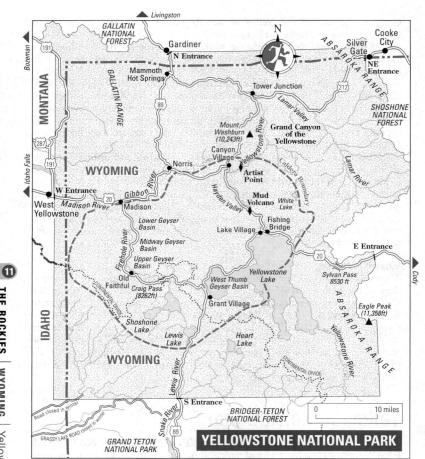

let yourself get frustrated by the inevitable crowds and expense, you risk missing something very special. The key to appreciating the park is to take your time, and to plan carefully; above all, try to allow for a stay of at least three days.

Arrival and information

Two of the five main **entrances** to Yellowstone are in Wyoming, via **Cody** in the east and **Grand Teton National Park** to the south. The others are in Montana: **West Yellowstone** (west), **Gardiner** (north), and **Cooke City** (northeast). Most roads are open from late May to October only (see box, opposite). **Admission** ($20 per car, $10 for pedestrians or cyclists) is good for seven days, and includes entry to the Grand Teton park.

The **park headquarters** are at **Mammoth Hot Springs**, near the north entrance (daily: June–Sept daily 8am–7pm; Oct–May 9am–5pm; ☎307/344-2263). Tune into 1610 AM for weather information, and consult the free newspaper *Yellowstone Today* for activities and current regulations. Other, summer-only **visitor centers** are located approximately every twenty miles along the main **Loop Road**. Each issues backcountry hiking permits, and has an exhibit on a different aspect of the park – natural and human history (Mammoth Hot Springs), geothermal activity (Old Faithful and Norris), the National Park Service (Norris), wilderness areas and the 1988 fires (Grant Village), wildlife (Fishing Bridge), and bison (Canyon). Excellent National Park Service leaflets (50¢ each), which can be found at major sights as well as visitor centers, cover the important landmarks, marking trails and points of interest.

To get to Yellowstone by **bus**, take Karst Stage (☎406/586-8567) from Bozeman, via West Yellowstone or Gardiner; Powder River Coach (☎1-800/442-3682), which runs tours and day-trips from Cody; or Amfac/TW Services (☎307/344-7311) from West Yellowstone, Gardiner, or Billings, which also runs day-tours inside the park in summer. Similar services are offered by 4X4 (☎1-800/517-8243) from Gardiner, Cooke City, West Yellowstone, and Bozeman; Buffalo Bus Co. (☎406/646-9353 or 1-800/426-7669) from West Yellowstone; Greyhound runs as far as Bozeman and West Yellowstone (for details call ☎402/330-8552 or 1-800/229-9424).

Accommodation in the park

All accommodation within the park is run by Amfac Parks and Resorts (PO Box 165, Yellowstone National Park, WY 82190; ☎307/344-7311, ⓦwww.travelyellowstone.com). **Reservations**, strongly recommended from June through September, are essential over public-holiday weekends. Prices beyond the park boundaries are a little lower, but staying inside can be wonderfully relaxing; none of the rooms has a TV, and only a few apres-hike revelers stay up past midnight. Every location has a lodge building offering dining facilities (closing at 9.30pm) and sometimes a laundromat, grocery store, gift shop, and gas station.

Canyon Lodge and Cabins Simple frame cabins, all en suite, half a mile from the Grand Canyon of the Yellowstone. ❸–❹

Grant Village Spartan en suite rooms on the southwest shore of Yellowstone Lake, and the southernmost accommodation in the park. ❹

Winter in Yellowstone

Blanketed in four feet of snow between November and April, Yellowstone takes on a whole new appearance in winter: a silent and bizarre world where waterfalls freeze in mid-plunge, geysers blast towering plumes of steam and water into the cold, crisp air, and buffalo, beards matted with ice, stand around in huddles. Only the road from Gardiner to Cooke City via Mammoth Hot Springs is kept open (the Beartooth Highway is closed), and you can only stay at the *Mammoth Hot Springs Hotel* or the *Old Faithful Snow Lodge* (accessible by snowmobile).

Winter vacationing in Yellowstone took off in a big way in the 1960s. Amfac/TW Services (☎307/344-7311, ⓦwww.travelyellowstone.com) runs **snowcoach** tours of the park from West Yellowstone, Flagg Ranch at the southern entrance, Old Faithful and Mammoth Hot Springs ($80–135). Yellowstone Alpen Guides (☎406/646-9591 or 1-800/858-3502) runs slightly cheaper excursions out of West Yellowstone ($100). **Snowmobile** rental, generally cheapest in West Yellowstone, costs around $120 a day (note that only a limited number of snowmobiles is allowed in the park at any one time, so reserve ahead). Much less expensive is **cross-country skiing**; several miles of groomed trails explore the park's west side. Call ☎307/344-7311 for full details.

Lake Yellowstone Hotel and Cabins Grand Colonial-style hotel rooms, and dark, dingy en suite cabins. The "Sun Room," looking over the lake, is a great place for an evening drink. ④–⑤

Mammoth Hot Springs Hotel & Cabins 1930s lodging right at the north end of the park offering very basic cabins, without shower or toilet, en suite cabins, and hotel rooms with or without bath. Especially popular in winter. ③–④

Old Faithful Inn and Lodge The most beautiful lodge in the US and consequently very popular.

The amazing 1903 inn – said to be the world's largest log building – has assorted rooms plus budget and en suite cabins. You can watch Old Faithful erupt from the terrace bar. ③–⑥

Old Faithful Snow Lodge and Cabins Along with *Mammoth Hot Springs Hotel*, this is the only accommodation open in the winter. Built in 1998, the lodge has a modern hotel feel about it, while the en suite cabins are pretty basic but well sealed against the cold. Open May to mid-Oct & mid-Dec to early March. ⑤

Accommodation in gateway towns

In addition to **Jackson** (see p.937) and **Cody** (p.925) in Wyoming, the small towns just outside the park's western and two northern gates offer alternative and somewhat cheaper lodging, as well as more nightlife. **West Yellowstone**, the largest town, at the west entrance, is disfigured by gift stores and fast-food joints, but the surrounding national forest lands are well worth exploring. **Gardiner** lies next to the northwest entrance, just five miles from Mammoth Hot Springs; prices here tend to be a little higher than elsewhere. More developed **Cooke City** is ten miles from the northeast entrance on US-212.

High Country Motel US-212, Cooke City ☎ 406/838-2271. Good value, if basic, motel rooms, some with kitchens for an extra $10. ②

Hillcrest Cottages 200 Scott St, Gardiner ☎ 406/848-7353. Comfortable cottages with kitchenettes. Good value, especially the larger ones which will accommodate up to six people. ④

Hoosier's Motel US-212, Cooke City ☎ 406/838-2241. Comfortable modern motel with its own popular bar. Mid-May through October. ③

Round Up Motel and Dude Motor Inn 3 Madison Ave, West Yellowstone ☎ 406/646-7301 or 1-800/833-7669, ⓔ roundup@wyellowstone .com. Located in one of the quieter parts of town but only a block from all the action, the rooms here are clean and well maintained, and some have two bedrooms and kitchenettes. ④

Sleepy Hollow Lodge 124 Electric St, West Yellowstone ☎ 406/646-7707, ⓔ sleepyhollow @wyellowstone.com. Attractive log cabins with fully equipped kitchens and a free continental breakfast, plus a fly-tying bench for anglers. Good value. ④

Stage Coach Inn 209 Madison Ave, West Yellowstone ☎ 406/646-7381 or 1-800/842-2882, ⓔ sci@wyellowstone.com. One of the town's oldest and most historic buildings, with comfortable rooms, an attractive lobby and reading area, a hot tub and sauna, and a good restaurant. Open year-round and there are some great off-season deals, with rooms for under $40. ⑤

West Yellowstone International Hostel at Madison Hotel 139 Yellowstone Ave ☎ 406/746-7745 or 1-800/838-7745. A real boon for budget travelers, this is one of the very few hostels in Montana. The attractive log-hewn building dates back to 1912 and has rooms with bunks for up to four people ($20 each) and private rooms for around $50. Open late May–early Oct. ①–②

Yellowstone Village Inn corner Main and 2nd streets, Gardiner ☎ 406/848-7417 or 1-800/228-8158, ⓦ www.yellowstoneVinn.com. Forty basic but clean and comfortable rooms, with kitchen suites. There's also an indoor pool, and horseback riding, fishing, and rafting can be organized for you. ③–④

Camping

Xanterra operate five of the twelve campgrounds in Yellowstone, including one for RVs only. The other seven operate on a first-come, first-served basis; you have to arrive early in the day to get a site during June, July, and August, as most are full by 11am. It might be worth booking your first night at one of the four reservation-only sites just to make sure there's a place for you on the day you arrive. The remaining five campgrounds – Bridge Bay, Canyon, Grant Village, Madison, and Fishing Bridge – accept **reservations** (☎307/344-7311, same-day reservations ☎307/344-7901, ⓦwww.travelyellowstone.com). **Fees** range from $10–15 per night for tent camping, and upwards of $27 for RVs, and campgrounds operate from mid-May or early June through to September, October, or November. Though all campgrounds have toilet facilities, not all have showers. RV owners should note that generators are not allowed at the following campgrounds: Indian Creek, Pebble Creek, Slough Creek, and Tower Fall.

To camp in the **backcountry**, you'll need a permit – free from visitor centers, information stations, and ranger stations; these can be collected no earlier than 48 hours in advance of your camping trip. You can also camp at commercial grounds in the gateway towns and in neighboring national forests such as Gallatin (☎307/344-7381) to the northwest and Shoshone (☎307/527-6241) to the east.

Eating in the park

Snack bars and **restaurants** inside the park aren't cheap, but given where you are they're not hideously expensive either. Buying food at the general stores can get pricey, though. There's not a lot of menu variation among the **restaurants**, which are located at *Old Faithful Inn, Old Faithful Snow Lodge, Roosevelt Lodge, Lake Yellowstone Hotel, Mammoth Hot Springs Hotel, Canyon Lodge,* and *Grant Village*; however, *Old Faithful Inn* and *Lake Yellowstone Hotel* are the clear standouts for location, mood, and ambiance. Entrees ($14–22) run from salmon and steak to roast dinners and lighter choices such as burgers or Caesar salads ($8), with desserts ($4–5) and a basic range of beers and wines available too. Note that **dinner reservations** are required during summer at *Old Faithful Inn* (☎307/545-4999), *Lake Yellowstone Hotel* (☎307/242-3899), and *Grant Village* (☎307/242-3499); you won't get a table without one. The restaurants are also open for **breakfast** and **lunch**; they usually offer a breakfast buffet that includes fresh fruit, cereals, pastries, and standard cooked breakfast items, all for around $7.

Eating in gateway towns

The gateway towns hold few culinary delights, but do offer cheaper prices and more variety. In **West Yellowstone**, *Nancy P's*, 29 Canyon St (☎406/646-9737), is good for breakfast, and *Rustlers's Roost*, 234 Firehole Ave (☎406/646-7622), offers local wild game, including elk and bison, with tasty dinners starting around $15. The lively and friendly *Town Café* (☎406/848-7322) on Park Street in **Gardiner** serves good filling breakfasts, and the stylish *Beartooth Café* in **Cooke City** is probably the best place for breakfast, burgers, and inexpensive dinners in any of the peripheral towns.

Touring the park

All of Yellowstone's major sights are labeled and signposted within a few hundred yards of the 142-mile **Loop Road**, a figure-of-eight circuit fed by roads from the five entrances. Although the **speed limit** is a radar-enforced 45mph (important given the number of bison and other massive beasts likely to run in front of your car), the traffic makes journey times hard to predict. To get the most out of a visit, even if you're short of time, choose one or two areas to explore thoroughly. Only in the early morning is **cycling** bearable or safe; there are no mountain-bike trails. Though you can expect to **walk** considerable distances along the canyon and geyser trails, it's worth leaving the backcountry hiking for the more scenically rewarding Grand Teton National Park (see p.934).

A brief human history of Yellowstone

Although Native Americans had long hunted in what is now **Yellowstone National Park**, they were decimated by disease (and, in their absence, the wildlife thrived) by the time the first white man arrived in 1807 – **John Colter**, a veteran of the Lewis and Clark expedition (see also p.944). His account of the exploding geysers and seething cauldrons of "Colter's Hell" was widely ridiculed. However, as ever more trappers, scouts, and prospectors hit upon Yellowstone, the government eventually sent out survey teams in 1870. Just two years later, Yellowstone was set aside as the first **national park**, in part to ensure that its assets were not entirely stripped by hunters, miners, and lumber companies.

At first, management of the park was beset by problems; Congress devoted enthusiasm but little funding toward its protection. Irresponsible tourists stuck soap down the geysers, ruining the intricate plumbing; bandits preyed on stagecoaches carrying rich excursionists; and the Nez Percé even killed two tourists as they raced through the park (see p.961). Congress took the park out of civilian hands in 1886, and put the army in charge. By the time they handed it over to the newly created National Park Service in 1917, the ascendancy of the automobile in Yellowstone had begun.

The conflict between tourism and wilderness **preservation** has raged ever since. The elimination of predators such as mountain lions and wolves allowed the elk herd to grow unsupportably large; the former policy of permitting bears to feed from tourist scraps resulted in maulings. Most of these issues have since been addressed, but ecologists now warn that the park cannot stand alone as some pristine paradise, and must be seen as part of a much larger "Greater Yellowstone Ecosystem"; this notional ecosystem encompasses Yellowstone, the Tetons, the Snake River Valley south of Jackson to just over the Idaho border, and the northern Wind River Mountains. In 1995, amid vociferous complaints from local ranchers fearing a subsequent loss of livestock, several packs of **wolves** were reintroduced to the park. They've since made an emphatic comeback, and from the original fourteen animals released, there are now more than 150 wolves comprising fifteen packs roaming the Greater Yellowstone area.

The **fires** that razed 36 percent of the park in 1988 also brought Yellowstone's environmental policies into focus. Despite President Reagan's dismay, park authorities insisted that the burn was a natural part of the forest's eco-cycle, clearing out 200-year-old trees to make way for new growth. The scarred mountainsides are slowly but surely recovering, as evidenced by forests of young saplings. While the summer of 2003 saw the most fires in the park since 1988, they left nowhere near as much destruction in their wake.

The following account runs clockwise around the Loop Road, from Old Faithful to the Yellowstone Lake area, both of which lie in the southern reaches of the park.

Geyser country: from Old Faithful to Mammoth Hot Springs

For well over a century, the dependable **Old Faithful** has been the most popular geyser in the park, erupting more frequently than any of its higher or larger rivals. As a result, a half-moon of concentric benches, backed by visitor facilities including the gigantic log-built *Old Faithful Inn*, now surround it at a respectful distance on the side away from the Firehole River. On average, it "performs" for the expectant crowds every 78 minutes, with a minimum gap of half an hour and a maximum of two hours; approximate schedules are displayed in the nearby visitor center and in the lobby of the inn. The first sign of activity is a soft hissing as water splashes repeatedly over the rim. After several minutes, a column of water shoots to a height of 100 to 180ft, the geyser spurting out a total of 11,000 gallons.

Two miles of boardwalks lead from Old Faithful to dozens of other geysers in the Upper Basin. If possible, try to arrive when **Grand Geyser** is due to explode. This colossus blows its top on average just twice a day, for twelve to twenty minutes, in a series of four powerful bursts that climb to 200ft. Other highlights along the banks of the Firehole River, usually lined with browsing buffalo, include the fluorescent intensity of the **Grand Prismatic Spring** at **Midway Geyser basin**, especially breathtaking in the early evening when human figures and bison herds are silhouetted against plumes of mineral spray.

Thirty miles north of Old Faithful, in the less crowded **Norris Geyser Basin**, two separate trails explore a pallid landscape of whistling vents and fumaroles. **Steamboat** is the world's tallest geyser, capable of forcing near-boiling water over 300ft into the air; full eruptions are entirely unpredictable (two of the most recent were on May 2, 2000, and October 2, 1991), but it usually delivers lesser bursts of ten to forty feet a couple of times a day. The **Echinus Geyser** is the largest acid-water geyser known; every 35 to 75 minutes it spews crowd-pleasing, vinegary eruptions of forty to sixty feet. The **Emerald Spring** is a 27-foot-deep pool where the vivid blue water combines with the yellow of the crater to create a stunning, jewel-like hue.

At **Mammoth Hot Springs**, at the northern tip of the Loop Road, terraces of barnacle-like deposits cascade down a vapor-shrouded mountainside. Tinted a marvelous array of grays, greens, yellows, browns, and oranges by algae, they are composed of travertine, a form of limestone which, having been dissolved and carried to the surface by boiling water, is deposited as tier upon tier of steaming stone.

Tower and Roosevelt areas

The main landmark of Yellowstone's **Tower** and **Roosevelt** areas, east of Mammoth Hot Springs, is **Mount Washburn**, one of the park's highest peaks, whose lookout tower can be reached by an enjoyable all-day hike or a grueling cycle ride. A more manageable trail leads down to the spray-drenched base of **Tower Fall**. From Tower Junction, US-212 wanders away east through the meadows of serene **Lamar Valley**, where moose and buffalo graze, toward the ice-packed peaks of the **Beartooth Mountains**.

The Grand Canyon of the Yellowstone

The Yellowstone River roars and tumbles for 24 miles between the sheer golden-hued cliffs of the 1540ft **Grand Canyon of the Yellowstone**, its course punctuated by two narrow but striking **waterfalls**: the 109ft **Upper Falls** and the thunderous **Lower Falls**, plummeting 308ft. Both rims of the canyon offer superb vistas, short trails, and intense scenery, but the north side is the more popular, as sightseeing can be combined with a visit to the nearby stores and snack bars. To try to see some bears, stake out a roadside spot just south of Tower Junction at dawn or dusk.

On the south rim, **Artist Point** looks down 700ft to the river, which swirls between mineral-stained walls. Nearby, **Uncle Tom's Trail** descends steeply into the canyon, to a spray-covered platform gently vibrating in the face of the pounding Lower Falls. A few miles south, the river widens to meander over tranquil, marshy **Hayden Valley**. Buffalo, elk, and deer congregate here, so it's an unsuitable place to go on foot.

Yellowstone Lake

North America's largest alpine lake, the deep and (usually) deceptively calm **Yellowstone Lake** fills the eastern half of the Yellowstone caldera. At 7733ft above sea level it's high enough to be frozen for half the year, but in summer it's filled with tourists out on cruises (one hour; $7.30), rowboats ($6 per hour), motor launches ($30 per hour), and fishing expeditions ($55 for two hours). Boat tours leave from the Bridge Bay Marina near Lake Village.

At the **West Thumb Geyser** basin, north of Grant Village, hot pools empty into the tranquil waters and fizz away into nothing, and it's easy to see why early tourists would have made use of the so-called **Fishing Cone** by cooking fresh-caught fish in its boiling waters.

The ominous rumblings and sulfurous stench of the **Mud Volcano** area, north of the lake, make it the moodiest and ugliest of the park's thermal regions. A one-mile boardwalk winds through gurgling pools of sickly brown and yellow mud, past trees that have been steamed to death, to the bleak, barren shores of **Sour Lake**: an unnerving sight at the best of times, at dusk it makes a chemical waste dump look appealing. Joining a free ranger-led tour here gives you the chance to get off the boardwalk and head into the backcountry, where the **Big Gumper**, which blew into existence in the 1970s, bubbles with big gray globs of smelly mud.

Grand Teton National Park and Jackson Hole

The classic triangular peaks of **GRAND TETON NATIONAL PARK**, which stretches for fifty miles between Yellowstone and Jackson, are every bit as dramatic as the mountains of its congested neighbor, and a visit should be more than an afterthought on the route south. Though not especially high or extensive by Rocky Mountain standards, these sheer-faced cliffs make a magnificent spectacle, rising abruptly to tower 7000ft above the valley floor. A string of gemlike lakes is set tight at the foot of the mountains; beyond them lies the broad, sagebrush-covered **Jackson Hole** river basin (a "hole" was the pioneers' term for a flat, mountain-ringed valley), broken by the winding Snake River.

The Shoshone people knew the mountains as the *Teewinot* ("many pinnacles"), but their present name, meaning "large breast," was bestowed by over-imaginative French-Canadian trappers in the 1830s. After Congress set the mountains aside as a national park in 1929, it took another 21 years of legal wrangling for Grand Teton to reach its current size – local ranchers protested that the economy of Jackson Hole would be ruined if further land was surrendered to tourism. Meanwhile, John D. Rockefeller Jr bought up a large swath of Jackson Hole and presented it to the government for free (on the condition that the Grand Teton Lodge Company, which he then owned, would be the exclusive operator of park concessions).

Seeing the park

No road crosses the Tetons, but those that run along their eastern flank were designed with an eye to the mountains, affording stunning views at every turn. Two excellent side-trips are the **Jenny Lake Scenic Loop**, leading to a face-to-face encounter with towering, partly hunchbacked **Grand Teton Mountain**, and the narrow track up **Signal Mountain**, which gives a fine view of the five main Teton pinnacles and Jackson Hole.

Hiking trails, too, have been laid out so that no time is wasted in getting to the highlights. One easy and popular walk is along the sandy beaches of **Leigh**

Falls River

Grassy Lake Reservoir

YELLOWSTONE NATIONAL PARK

Lake of the Woods

JOHN D. ROCKEFELLER JR. MEMORIAL PARKWAY

Flagg Ranch

TARGHEE NATIONAL FOREST

Snake River

89

GRAND TETON NATIONAL PARK

TETON NATIONAL FOREST

Moose Creek

Jackson Lake

Colter Bay Visitor Center

Two Ocean Lake

Emma Matilda Lake

Jackson Lake Lodge

Jackson Lake Junction

PACIFIC CREEK RD

Moran Junction

Moran Canyon

Signal Mountain (7593ft)

Moran Entrance Station

TARGHEE NATIONAL FOREST

Leigh Canyon

Leigh Lake

TETON PARK ROAD

Snake River

Cascade Canyon

Jenny Lake

Grand Targhee Resort

Grand Teton (13,770ft)

Jenny Lake Visitor Center

Middle Teton (12,804ft)

Garnet

South Teton (12,514ft)

Bradley Lake

Avalanche Canyon

Taggart Lake

191

TETON NATIONAL FOREST

Death Canyon

Moose Visitor Center

Moose Entrance Station

Phelps Lake

Moose Junction

GROS VENTRE ROAD

Open Canyon

Granite Canyon

Jackson Hole Airport

Gros Ventre River

Lower Slide Lake

Teton Village

Gros Ventre Junction

Jackson Hole Ski Area

MOOSE WILSON RD

NATIONAL ELK REFUGE

TETON NATIONAL FOREST

Teton Pass (8429ft)

Wilson

22

National Museum of Wildlife Art

191

N

GRAND TETON NATIONAL PARK

0   5 miles

Jackson

11

THE ROCKIES | WYOMING | Grand Teton National Park

935

Lake, where the imposing 12,605ft **Mount Moran** bursts out dramatically from the lake shores. Also very accessible are the cascading **Hidden Falls**, reachable by a two-mile walk along the south shore of Jenny Lake; it's also fun to take the shuttle boat ($5 roundtrip) across the lake and walk the remaining 800 yards. More adventurous is the rocky nine-mile trail from Hidden Falls through U-shaped **Cascade Canyon**, which leads to aptly named **Lake Solitude**. Another strenuous hike, and an excellent way to reach the tree line in a short distance, is the five-mile trail from **Lupine Meadows**, just south of Jenny Lake, which skirts small glacial pools like Amphitheater and Surprise lakes.

On the flat roads of the Hole, **cycling** is a joy; rent a bike down in Jackson ($25–30). To admire the Tetons from **water**, take a float trip along the Snake River (see p.938) or rent a rowing boat from Colter Bay or Signal Mountain marinas ($25). In winter, all hiking trails are open to cross-country **skiers**, and **snowmobiles** can be rented from various outlets in Jackson. Excellent **rock climbing** opportunities exist within the park as well. Contact the Jenny Lake Visitors Center (T307/739-3343) for climbing details. **Climber's Ranch**, within the park on **Teton Park Road**, has basic dorm accommodation for climbers only (June–Sept only; T307/733-7271; $9).

Practicalities

Shuttle buses to the park run from Jackson and Yellowstone. The **visitor centers** are just off the main road in **Moose** (daily: Memorial Day to Labor Day 8am–7pm, rest of the year 8am–5pm; T307/739-3399) to the south, and at **Colter Bay** (mid-May to end Sept daily 8am–8pm; T307/739-3594), halfway up, on the east shore of Jackson Lake. There are smaller centers at **Jenny Lake** (June–Sept daily 8am–7pm; T307/739-3343) and **Flagg Ranch** (June–Sept daily 9am–6pm; T1-800/443-2311). The **Indian Arts Museum** (daily: summer 8am–8pm; spring & fall 8am–5pm; T307/739-3594; free) at Colter Bay has an extensive collection of Plains Native American craftwork.

The free *Teewinot* newspaper gives details of trails, facilities, and ranger-led activities. The **entrance fee** of $20 per car ($10 for pedestrians and cyclists) also covers Yellowstone.

Most **rooms**, services, and activities within the park are managed by the Grand Teton Lodge Co. (T307/543-2811 or 1-800/628-9988, Wwww.gtlc.com) and reservations are essential in summer. Prices for the comfortable rooms in *Jackson Lake Lodge* (❼–❽) depend on whether or not you want a mountain view; *Colter Bay Village Cabins* (❷) are more utilitarian, and in high summer they also have $32 "tent cabins" – canvas cabins each with four bunk beds (bed linen available for hire), a wood-burning stove, and an outdoor barbecue grill. There's good accommodation at *Signal Mountain Lodge* (T307/733-5470, Wwww.signalmtnlodge.com; ❹–❼), which has bland motel-style units with two double beds, bathroom, and fridge, or much nicer rustic log cabins with two doubles plus private bath. All of the five summer-only park **campgrounds** work on a first-come, first-served basis ($12 per site). Visitor centers or entrance stations can advise on availability, or you can call (T307/739-3603) for recorded information. Individual campgrounds tend to fill in July and August in roughly the following order: Jenny Lake (8am; 49 sites, tents only), Signal Mountain (10am; 86 sites), Colter Bay (noon; 306 sites), Lizard Creek (2pm; 60 sites), and Gros Ventre (evening; 360 sites); Gros Ventre is the only campground suitable for large RVs. For backcountry camping, you need a **permit**, available free from the Moose and Colter Bay visitor centers and the Jenny Lake Ranger Station, near the Jenny Lake Visitor Center. The park **restaurants and snack bars**, especially at Colter Bay, are good but a little pricey. *Dornan's Original Moose Chuckwagon* (T307/733-

2415), however, just outside the southern entrance in Moose, serves all-you-care-to-eat pancake breakfasts and rib dinners for a song. For the ultimate in relaxation, have an early-evening **drink** in *Jackson Lake Lodge's Blue Heron Lounge*, where you can recline in comfortable chairs and watch the ever-changing blues, grays, purples, and warm pinks of Mount Moran through huge picture windows.

Jackson

The overgrown but thoroughly enjoyable community of **JACKSON** is tucked in at the end of **Jackson Hole**, ten miles from Teton national park's southern gate. Hunched around a tree-shaded square, marked by an arch of tangled elk antlers at each corner, the Old West–style boardwalks of **downtown** front designer boutiques, craft shops, and over thirty galleries. Every summer evening, except Sundays, an amateurish shoot-out is staged in the town square (6.15pm). In winter, time is better spent visiting the **National Elk Refuge** on the north edge of town, where you can take a horse-drawn sleigh ride among a 10,000-strong herd of elk (late Dec to late March daily 10am–4pm; $12 for adults, $8 for kids); rides leave from the National Museum of Wildlife Art, and a combined museum-and-sleigh-ride ticket is good value at $15 for adults, $11 for children.

Jackson is home base for two of Wyoming's best ski areas: **Snow King** (☎307/733-5200 or 1-800/522-5464, ⓦwww.snowking.com) is Jackson's family-friendly hill, also lit for night-skiing, while **Jackson Hole Mountain Resort** (☎307/733-2292 or 1-888/333-7766, ⓦwww.jacksonhole.com) is a massive mountain with a huge vertical drop and terrain best suited to upper intermediate-to-extreme downhillers. Summer visitors can enjoy **chair lift** rides – up 7751ft Snow King Mountain from Snow King Avenue, six blocks from the town square (daily in season 9am–6pm, mid-summer 9am–8pm; $8) – and come down by hiking, cycling, or taking the thrilling 2500ft **Alpine Slide** ($6 a turn), a summer toboggan run. Out at **Teton Village**, home of **Jackson Hole Mountain Resort** (☎307/733-2292), aerial **trams** swoosh their way 10,536ft to the top of Rendezvous Mountain, where there's a spectacular panorama of the valley and mountain ranges (daily: June–Aug 9am–7pm; May & Sept 9am–5pm; $17).

Arrival, information, and activities

Jackson's **airport** is actually within the national park, eight miles north; it's linked to town by the All Star Transportation van service (☎307/733-2888; $8 one way), while the regular **taxi** fare is around $20. Jackson Hole Express (☎307/733-1719 or 1-800/652-9510) operates two direct **shuttle services** daily between the international airport in **Salt Lake City** and Jackson (around 5hr; $47 one way); pick-up and drop-off in Jackson is at the MiniMart on West Broadway.

Jackson's excellent **Wyoming Information Center**, 532 N Cache St (daily: summer 8am–7.30pm; rest of year 9am–5pm; ☎307/733-3316, ⓦwww.jacksonholechamber.com), has detailed statewide information. Nearby, the **Bridger-Teton National Forest Headquarters**, 340 N Cache St (Mon–Fri 8am–4.30pm; ☎307/739-5500), has details of hiking and back-country camping.

Transport around Jackson Hole is provided by START **buses** (☎307/733-4521, ⓦwww.startbus.com), which also run to Teton Village, twelve miles northwest. The **visitor center** has racks of leaflets detailing **bus tours** of Jackson and the parks: Gray Line, 330 N Glenwood St (☎307/733-4325 or 1-800/443-6133), will pick you up at your hotel and take you through either Teton or Yellowstone park on a brisk one-day drive for $60. Guided **bike** tours in the area are run by Teton Mountain Bike Tours (T 307/733-0712 or 1-800/733-0788), and cost $55 for a half-day tour including equipment.

Dozens of companies in Jackson offer **float trips** and whitewater **rafting** on the Snake River (half-day around $40, full-day $60). Try Dave Hansen Whitewater, 455 N Cache St (T 307/733-6295 or 1-800/732-6295, W www.davehansenwhitewater.com), or Jackson Hole Whitewater, 650 W Broadway (T 307/733-1007 or 1-800/700-7238). Leisure Sports, 1075 Hwy-89 S (T 307/733-3040), offers reasonable rental rates for rafts, kayaks, tubes, and bikes.

Accommodation

Accommodation in Jackson is fairly expensive in summer; rates in winter drop by around 25 percent and potentially good value for a ski vacation. **Camping** is at *Wagon Wheel Campground*, 525 N Cache St, behind the *Wagon Wheel Motel* (T 307/733-4588; $15 tents, $45 RVs).

The Alpine House 285 N Glenwood St
T 307/739-1570 or 1-800/753-1421,
W www.alpinehouse.com. B&B accommodation in a bright, cheerful 21-room house. Winter packages, including ski passes or cross-country expeditions, are good value. Summer ❻, winter ❺
Antler Inn 43 W Pearl St T 307/733-2535. Very central, but reasonably quiet, with sauna and hot tub. Some rooms have log fires. ❸–❹
Best Western Lodge at Jackson Hole 80 S Scott Lane, Teton Village T 307/739-9703 or 1-800/458-3866. Some rooms have log fires, kitchenettes, and hot tubs. Rates include an excellent continental breakfast, and there's a pool and Jacuzzi. Look out for the whimsical carved bears climbing all over the log-built exterior. ❻
Bunkhouse in the Anvil Motel 215 N Cache St
T 307/733-3668. Mid-range motel a block from the town square that also has beds in a large, dreary dorm (no kitchen facilities to speak of). Summer ❹, winter ❸, dorm $22.

Hostel X Teton Village T 307/733-3415,
W www.hostelx.com. Excellent slopeside hostel where amenities include a lounge fireplace, TV and games room, ski lockers and storage, microwave oven, free tea and coffee, but no kitchen. Summer dorm bed $19. Rooms for one or two people $52; for three or four $65. ❷
Virginian Lodge 750 W Broadway T 307/733-2792 or 1-800/262-4999. The 170 rooms are pretty basic but complemented by a big outdoor pool and a hot tub that sits in the middle of a grass-covered courtyard. There's a family-style restaurant on-site, as well as a saloon, liquor store, and guest laundry. Summer ❸, winter ❹
The Wort Hotel 50 N Glenwood St T 307/733-2190 or 1-800/322-2727, W www.worthotel.com. Jackson's most venerable high-end property, combining Old World style with modern facilities that include two large hot tubs, a grill-bistro, and an attractive bar, *The Silver Dollar*. Summer ❾, winter ❼–❽

Eating and nightlife

The year-round tourist trade makes Jackson Wyoming's liveliest nighttime community, with an ever-changing roster of **restaurants** and **nightspots**.

Anthony's 62 S Glenwood St T 307/733-3717. Imaginative Italian food at fair prices by Jackson standards (entrees $15–20).
Bubba's Bar-B-Que Grill 515 W Broadway
T 307/733-2288. Inexpensive dinners offering baby back ribs, sandwiches, steaks, and such – it's also the premier breakfast spot for locals, and a double stack of the plate-sized blueberry pancakes is a top choice.
The Bunnery 130 N Cache St T 307/733-5474. This bakery-cum-café offers great breakfasts, as well as baked goodies, espressos, stuffed omelets, and sandwiches.
Cadillac Grill 55 N Cache St T 307/733-3279.

Fancy Art Deco restaurant on the main square, serving up huge burgers, as well as buffalo, wild boar, caribou, antelope, and seafood entrees for $15–22. Reservations recommended.
Harvest Natural Foods Café 130 W Broadway
T 307/733-5418. Earnest health-food store with a veggie food counter: burgers, tofu, baked goods, and fruit smoothies – to eat in or take out.
Mangy Moose Teton Village T 307/733-4913. Jackson Hole's legendary ski-bum hangout, the *Moose* is famed for its apres-ski sessions that segue into rowdy evenings of live rock or reggae (cover charge for live bands $5–10). The bustling upstairs dining room serves decent basic fare like

burgers, chicken, and pasta; the *Moose's Belly* downstairs dishes up a pretty ordinary $7 skiers' breakfast buffet.

Million Dollar Cowboy Bar 25 N Cache St ℡ 307/733-2207. Hugely touristy Western-themed bar, with saddles for seats, a large dance floor, karaoke, and big steaks. Cover $3.

Mountain High Pizza Pie 120 W Broadway ℡ 307/733-3646. Offers casual, low-priced, and healthy pizza, calzones, and salads.

Old Yellowstone Garage 175 Center St ℡ 307/734-6161. One of Jackson's finest restaurants, offering flawless service and an Italian-themed menu that changes daily. Sunday night features all-you-care-to-eat pizza for just $10. Reservations essential.

Pearl Street Bagels 145 W Pearl Ave ℡ 307/739-1218. It's all in the name: a plethora of fresh and tasty bagels, from tomato-herb to cinnamon-raisin. Daily 6.30am–6pm.

The Rancher 20 E Broadway ℡ 307/733-3886. Dollar drinks are on offer every Tuesday night at this local pool-hall hangout.

The Silver Dollar Bar 50 N Glenwood St ℡ 307/733-2190. The closest thing to an upscale bar in town, but still pretty relaxed and casual; hosts singers and piano players of variable quality. The silver dollars embedded in the bar-top number 2032. No cover.

Snake River Brewery 265 S Millward St ℡ 307/739-BEER. Popular for its $6 lunch deals and has plenty of seasonal beers on tap.

Thai Me Up 75 E Pearl St ℡ 307/733-0005. Red, green, and yellow curries featured alongside interesting seafood variations and noodle dishes (entrees $12–16) at Jackson's only Thai restaurant.

Montana

MONTANA is Big Sky country. The nickname is no empty cliche: the entire state is blessed with a huge blue roof that both dwarfs the beautiful countryside and complements it perfectly. The US Rocky Mountains find their northernmost limits in the western portion of the state, a region of snowcapped summits, turbulent rivers, spectacular glacial valleys, heavily wooded forests, and sparkling blue lakes, at their most dramatic in **Glacier National Park**. By contrast, the **eastern** two-thirds is high prairie: sun-parched in summer and wracked by icy blizzards each winter. Grizzlies, elk, and Rocky Mountain bighorn sheep are also present in greater numbers than just about anywhere else in North America.

Preconceptions of a desolate land populated by cowpokes are soon shattered: each of Montana's small cities has its own proud identity. The university and sawmill community of **Missoula**, for example, possesses a high-culture feel absent from the heavily Irish, copper-mining town and union stronghold of **Butte**, while elegant state capital **Helena** still harks back to its prosperous gold-mining years, and **Bozeman**, just to the south, is one of the hippest mountain towns in the US.

The fur trappers and gold miners who were the first whites to brave this inhospitable terrain soon moved on, but as white settlers invaded Native American hunting grounds, conflict was inevitable. A key plank of army strategy was to starve the Native Americans into submission: "For the sake of a lasting peace let them [professional hunters] kill, skin, and sell until the buffalo are exterminated. Then your prairies can be covered by the speckled cow and the festive cowboy," declared General Philip Sheridan. By the late 1870s the buffalo were almost gone, and most of Montana had been cleared for settlement.

The speckled cow and festive cowboy were not in for an easy time. The horrendous winter of 1886 wiped out many herds, and the "sodbusters" who planted wheat in the wake of bankrupt ranchers often fared little better.

Plagues of grasshoppers, droughts, falling wheat prices, and erosion of the top-soil caused farms to fail everywhere in the 1920s, during which time Montana was the only state to record a population decline.

Wheat has since made a revival, and now, with lumbering and coal mining, forms the base of Montana's economy. Tourism is currently the state's second biggest earner, though, apart from skiing, the harsh climate generally restricts the season to the months between June and September.

Getting around Montana

Considering Montana's size and sparse population, transportation connections are not bad. Greyhound and regional **bus** companies like Intermountain (north from Butte and Missoula to Glacier) and Rimrock serve towns on I-90 and I-15. Delta and Northwest offer the most **flights** to Montana, landing in seven towns. Amtrak **trains** cross the north, stopping east and west of Glacier National Park without making it easier to see the park itself. Western Montana, in particular, is great **cycling** territory; the Adventure Cycling organization, whose national headquarters are in Missoula (see p.948), can provide special maps. However, the best way to get around this huge state is clearly by **car**, with practically every interstate exit in the west leading to areas of mountain solitude, interesting landmarks, or small communities.

Eastern Montana

Before ranchers and farmers settled the flat prairie of **eastern Montana**, it was prime **buffalo** territory: one early traveler waited three nights while a massive herd crossed his path. Native Americans fought hard to hold onto their land; the crushing defeats they inflicted on the US Army include the legendary victory at **Little Bighorn**.

The eastern Montana plains are intermittently broken by mountains, of which the most impressive are the icy **Beartooth Range**, crammed between the town of Red Lodge and Yellowstone. Don't expect much from the region's towns; most are sleepy farm-supply centers, and **Billings**, Montana's largest city with a population of over 90,000, doesn't have a great deal to offer.

Little Bighorn Battlefield National Monument

In June 1876, massive US Army detachments were sent to southeastern Montana to subjugate the Sioux and Cheyenne. A key unit in the campaign was the crack **Seventh Cavalry**; at its head was the flamboyant **Lt Col George Armstrong Custer**.

Few if any US soldiers have achieved the fame or opprobrium of Custer. During an erratic career, he graduated last in his class at West Point in 1861; was the US Army's youngest-ever major general; was suspended for ordering the execution of deserters from a forced march he led through Kansas primarily to see his wife; and became notorious for allowing the murder in 1868 of almost one hundred Cheyenne women and children.

On June 25, 1876, Custer's was the first unit to arrive in the **Little Bighorn Valley**. Disdaining to await reinforcements, he set out to raze a tepee village along the Little Bighorn River – which turned out to be the largest-ever gathering of Plains Indians. As a party of his men pursued fleeing women and children, they were encircled by two thousand Sioux and Cheyenne warriors emerging from either side of a ravine. The soldiers dismounted to attempt to shoot their way out, but were soon overwhelmed; simultaneously, Custer's command post on a nearby hill was wiped out. Archeologists have discounted the idea of **Custer's Last Stand** as a heroic defiance in which Custer was the last cavalryman left standing; the battle lasted less than an hour, with the white soldiers being systematically and effortlessly picked off. The most decisive Native American victory in the West – led by Sitting Bull – was also their final great show of resistance. An incensed President Grant piled maximum resources into a military campaign that brought about the effective defeat of all Plains Indians by the end of the decade.

The **monument** is 56 miles southeast of Billings, with the entrance one mile east of I-90 on US-212. You can trace the course of the battle on a five-mile self-guided driving tour through the grasslands (daily: 8am–dusk; $10 per car), following the high ridge overlooking the valley, or on a narrated bus tour (spring–fall; $10). White-marble tablets mark where individual soldiers fell, and a sandstone obelisk stands above their mass grave on "Last Stand Hill" (Custer himself lies in West Point Military Academy). Dioramas in the **visitor center and museum** (mid-April to May 8am–6pm; June–Aug 8am–8pm; rest of year 8am–4.30pm; $10 per vehicle; ☎406/638-2621) outline the battle, while the US military **cemetery** nearby holds soldiers from all of America's wars (admission to the cemetery is free; explain at the gate that you're only going there and not to the battlefield).

Hardin

Little Bighorn is the focus of the Crow Indian Reservation. Little **HARDIN**, thirteen miles northwest, makes its living from tourists seeking authentic Native American artifacts and other Western mementos. Each year, on the weekend closest to the battle's June 25 anniversary, the **Little Bighorn Days** festival centers on re-enactments of the battle at a site eight miles west of the town (*not* at the original battlefield). Other activities include Native American dancing, downtown parades, dinner dances, and a rodeo.

The least expensive place to **stay** is the *Western Motel*, off Hwy-313 at 831 W Third St (☎406/665-2296; ❸–❹). *The Purple Cow*, Hwy-47 N (☎406/665-3601), is a cheerful family **diner** serving home-cooked feasts.

Billings

By Montana standards, **BILLINGS** is a big city. Its dramatic setting, bounded on its north and east sides by the 400ft crumpled sandstone cliffs of the **Rimrock**, certainly makes it something more than a pockmark on the prairie. The town has made an attempt to spruce itself up with the development of an attractive and quite lively row of galleries, bars, and restaurants along Montana Avenue. However, scarring the west side of downtown are the tracks and warehouses of the Northern Pacific Railroad, whose president, Frederick Billings, gave the city its name.

Just north of Montana Avenue you'll find a massive selection of cowboy paraphernalia at Lou Taubert, 123 N Broadway (☎406/245-2248), which specializes in all things Western. An enormous selection of hats, boots, shirts, jeans, and jackets will make dressing up like John Wayne never look more appealing.

A couple of blocks northeast, the **Yellowstone Art Museum**, 401 N 27th St (Tues, Wed, Fri & Sat 10am–5pm, Thurs 10am–8pm, Sun noon–5pm; $5; ☎406/256-6817, ⓦyellowstone.artmuseum.org), partly housed in the town's 1910 jail, specializes in regional and Western exhibits, including an absorbing display of book illustrations, paintings, and posters by cowboy illustrator Will James.

Billings' **bus station**, served by Greyhound along I-90 and I-15, and Powder River, heading north from Wyoming, is at 2501 First Ave N (℡406/245-5116). Accommodation options include *The Dude Rancher*, 415 N 29th St (℡406/259-5561 or 1-800/221-3302, ⓦwww.duderancherlodge.com; ❸), a reasonably priced, bright and cheerful **motel** with a good restaurant and coffee shop attached. Cheaper alternatives line I-90, off exit 446, including a *Super 8* at 5400 Southgate Drive (℡406/248-8842; ❸). *Billings KOA* is half a mile south of I-90 in an attractive spot beside the Yellowstone River, with good shady tent sites for $20. This was America's first *KOA* and the facilities include a store, outdoor pool, laundry, and mini-golf course.

Downtown, hearty **meals** can be found at *The Beanery Bar and Grill*, 2314 Montana Ave (℡406/896-9200), tucked inside the restored old Northern Pacific Depot. *Casey's Golden Pheasant*, 109 N Broadway (℡406/256-5200), is a lively jazz and blues **bar** with good Cajun food. For coffee and something sweet, try *Café Jones* at 2712 Second Ave (℡406/259-7676).

Red Lodge and the Beartooth Scenic Highway

The atmospheric mountain town of **RED LODGE**, sixty miles south of Billings at the foot of the awesome Beartooth Mountains, makes an altogether pleasant stop. During winter, it acts as a base for skiers using the popular **Red Lodge Mountain**, six miles west on US-212 (℡406/446-2610, lodging reservation service ℡1-800/444-8977, ⓦwww.redlodgemountain.com), where ski-lift passes cost $39 a day.

Originally founded to dig coal for the transcontinental railroads, Red Lodge faced extinction in 1924, when its largest coal mine closed, but its future was secured by the construction of the 65-mile **Beartooth Scenic Highway** to Cooke City at the northeastern entrance to Yellowstone National Park (see p.928). Other roads in the Rockies may be higher, but none gives quite such a top-of-the-world feeling as this succession of tight switchbacks, steep grades, and exciting overlooks. Even in summer the springy tundra turf of the 10,940ft **Beartooth Pass** is covered with snow that (due to algae) turns pink when crushed. All around are gem-like corries, deeply gouged granite walls, stretches of scree, and huge blocks of roadside ice.

Though Red Lodge boasts plenty of reasonable **motels** grouped south of town – the *Yodeler*, 601 S Broadway (℡406/446-1435, ⓦwww.yodelermotel.com; ❷), is friendly, clean, and central. By far, the nicest place to stay is the lovely *Pollard Hotel*, 2 N Broadway (℡406/446-000 or 1-800/POLLARD; ❹–❾), an 1893 brick building with a pool, sauna, comfortable old library, and superb restaurant (see below); Western heroes Buffalo Bill, Calamity Jane, and others have stayed here. One of the best **B&Bs** in town, *Bear Bordeaux*, 302 S Broadway (℡406/446-4408; ❹), is a well-decorated downtown home with colorful rooms and great mountain views. There is a hot tub, as well as filling breakfasts and an enormous video library (each room has a VCR). **Camping** at the *KOA* (℡406/446-2364; June–Sept), four miles north, costs $20, or you can rent a cabin for around $40.

Some of the best **food** in town, if not in the entire Rocky Mountain region, is served at the *Pollard*, where *Arthur's Grill* (℡406/446-0001) features sublime, simple dishes in a wonderfully serene, wood-lined dining room. Also on Broadway, *Bogart's* at no. 11 S (℡406/446-1784) is popular for its Mexican and Californian cuisine, and the nearby *Red Lodge Pizza Company*, no. 123 S (℡406/446-3933), is a lively combination pizza joint and brewhouse with one of the largest ranges of beers in town. The friendly *Bridge Creek Restaurant*, at no. 116 S (☎406/446-9900), serves sensational clam chowder alongside beef, seafood, burgers, quesadillas, and the like. Red Lodge has a cheerful **nightlife** scene, especially in winter – get a real feel for the town at the *Snow Creek Saloon*, 124 S Broadway, an always-busy bar popular with locals and visitors alike.

Western Montana

The **western** third of Montana sees the state at its best – from Big Timber westwards, I-90 squeezes between dramatic mountain ranges, making an exhilarating approach to Yellowstone country. Here the awe-inspiring big skies must be seen to be believed – you'll spot entirely different types of weather from one horizon to the next. The region is replete with outdoor opportunities and bustling communities, though the only mining camps to grow into substantial permanent settlements were state capital **Helena** and craggy **Butte**, which made its money from copper. Between them they conjure up more of a feel for the rambunctious times, the lust for profit, and the post-bust hardships of the era than all the hyped-up ghost towns in the Rockies combined.

Bozeman

Pretty, tree-lined **BOZEMAN** lies at the north end of the lush Gallatin Valley, 142 miles west of Billings and a mere ninety miles north of Yellowstone. Founded by farmers in 1863, it's the only sizeable town in Montana not to owe its roots to mining, railroading, or lumbering. The smart-looking storefronts along the busy Main Street just beg to be window-shopped, and you may just bump into one of the Hollywood celebrities who have set up home or business in this increasingly trendy town.

South of downtown, as **Montana State University** peters out into a beautiful wilderness in the shadow of the mountains, the huge **Museum of the Rockies** at S Seventh Avenue and Kagy Boulevard (summer daily 8am–8pm; rest of year Mon–Sat 9am–5pm, Sun 12.30–5pm; $8; ☎406-994/DINO, ⓦwww.montana.edu/wwwmor) looms into view. Besides Native American weapons and a fine selection of Western landscape paintings, the collection includes impressive dinosaur finds and a **planetarium** as well. Though far smaller in scale, the **Pioneer Museum**, 317 W Main St (June–Sept Mon–Fri 10am–4.30pm, Sat 1–4pm; Oct–May Mon–Fri 11am–4pm, Sat 1–4pm; free), is also very good, with an intriguing, well-presented selection of locally gathered historic objects, including cartoons drawn by local boy Gary Cooper in his pre-movie-star days. The excellent photo collection features some great old images of early tourism at Yellowstone. Striking a modern note, the **Compuseum**, Bridger Park Mall, 2304 N 7th Ave, suite B (June–Aug daily 9am–5pm; Sept–May Tues, Wed, Fri & Sat noon–4pm, Thurs 4pm–8pm; $4; ☎406/582-1288, ⓦwww.compuseum.org), follows the evolution of computers, from their bulky, awkward beginnings to the compact incarnations of today; also on display are some well-intentioned inventions that never quite hit mainstream America.

Bozeman is well placed for those seeking **outdoor activities**, particularly in rugged Hyalite Canyon just south of town, which has top-notch hiking and mountain biking in summer and excellent ice climbing in winter, or at the challenging ski area, Bridger Bowl (lift tickets $36; ☎406/587-2111, ⓦwww.bridgerbowl.com). An hour's drive south down the beautiful Gallatin

Valley is the popular Big Sky Resort (lift tickets $59; ☎1-800/548-4486, Ⓦwww.bigskyresort.com), where there's plenty of top-quality powder and steep slopes on 11,166ft Lone Mountain to satisfy skiers at all levels.

For more details on outdoor activities, check with the ranger office, 3710 Fallon St (Mon–Fri 8am–5pm; ☎406/587-6920; 24hr recreation recording ☎406/587-9784), which also provides information on local walking trails. Chalet Sports at 108 W Main St (☎406/587-4595) rents out mountain bikes and ski equipment.

Practicalities

Greyhound and Rimrock cruise the interstates from 625 N Seventh St (☎406/587-3110), while Amfac/TW Services runs a bus a day to Yellowstone (see p.929); and from the same spot you can also take the Karst Stages bus service (☎406/586-8567) each morning and evening in summer to Big Sky and West Yellowstone. The Downtown Bozeman Association **Visitor Center** at 224 E Main St (☎406/586-4008, Ⓦwww.historicbozeman.com) has loads of maps and information plus limited free **Internet** access, which is also available at the **public library** at 220 E Lamme St. Central **motels** lining Seventh Avenue include the *Rainbow* at no. 510 N (☎406/587-4201; ❷–❸). Main Street also has a few worthy options: the rambling *Lewis and Clark*, no. 824 W (☎406/586-3341 or 1-800/332-7666; ❸), though gaudy, is very good value and centrally located, with a pool, sauna, gym, and hot tub. The friendly *International Backpackers Hostel*, 405 W Olive St (☎406/586-4659; ❶), has bunk beds for $12 and a fully equipped kitchen. More upmarket is the lovely *Voss Inn*, 319 S Willson Ave (☎406/587-0982, Ⓦwww.bozeman-vossinn.com; ❺), a lovely Victorian home with period furniture in each room.

Bozeman boasts plenty of good **places to eat**. The health-conscious *Community Co-op* on Ninth Avenue and Main Street (☎406/587-4039) serves terrific vegetarian dishes and mouth-watering desserts. Local favorites include the *McKenzie River Pizza Co.*, 232 E Main St (☎406/587-0055), which offers fresh and somewhat unusual toppings, and *John Bozeman's Bistro*, 125 W Main St (☎406/587-4100), with its Jamaican jerk pork-loin sandwiches and steak Napoleon with stuffed lobster tail. For gourmet coffee and pastries, try *The Leaf and Bean* at 35 W Main St.

Places to **drink** include *Montana Aleworks*, 611 E Main St (☎406/587-7700), where over forty microbrews are on tap, and *Molly Brown's* and the *Haufbrau*, both good rowdy bars at Eighth Avenue and Main Street. For **live music**, the raucous *Zebra Cocktail Lounge* at 321 E Main St offers an eclectic mix. Check the *Tributary* and *BoZone* for local entertainment listings.

Missouri Headwaters State Park

Officially, the Missouri River begins its circuitous journey to the Mississippi, and eventually the Gulf of Mexico, at the confluence of the Jefferson, Madison, and Gallatin rivers. Three miles north of I-90, halfway between Bozeman and Butte, and maintained as the **Missouri Headwaters State Park** ($3 per vehicle; camping $5), these marshy grasslands beneath a shallow bluff were identified by Lewis and Clark in July 1805. Three years later, **John Colter**, a veteran of that expedition who was the first to describe Yellowstone (see box, p.932), was captured here by a party of Blackfoot, who, after killing his companion, stripped him and made him run for his life. Colter killed the one pursuer who kept up with him, hid under a snag on the river, and reached safety on the Bighorn River eleven days later. Fur trappers who followed in the wake of Lewis and Clark included Kit Carson; traces remain of the nineteenth-century town they created.

Butte

Eighty miles west of Bozeman, copper-mining **BUTTE** (pronounced "beaut" as in "beauty") is bunched on a steep, almost treeless hillside where massive black headframes of long-abandoned pits soar up among paint-bare homes, stark gray business premises, and a ring of surface workings and dirty-yellow slag heaps. It's an oddly compelling landscape, best appreciated at dusk, when the golden pink light casts a glow on the mine-scoured hillsides, and the old neon signs illuminate uptown's historic brick buildings.

Exploration of this friendly, atmospheric town soon reveals a community rich in ethnic and trade-union culture. Among immigrants to leave their mark were the **Irish** – Butte still hosts the biggest St Patrick's Day celebrations in the Rockies, with an estimated 40,000 customers passing through the famous old *M&M Bar* every March 17 – and miners from **Cornwall**; the traditional meat-and-potato pasty (*PAST-ee*) is still served in most cafés.

From its early days, Butte stood out as a "Gibraltar of Unionism" in the anti-union West. Miners used their collective strength to obtain a minimum wage and an eight-hour day, and it became impossible to get work without a union card. Such confidence bred radicalism, and Butte sent the largest delegation to the founding convention of the IWW (the "Wobblies") in 1906. The eventual consolidation of mining operations under the huge Anaconda Company led to inter-union rivalries and rioting, and in 1983 the last mine closed. Today conflicts rage between the clean-up lobby (the town's largest disused mine, the Berkeley Pit, is slowly filling with heavily poisoned groundwater) and the traditionalists, keen to develop new methods to exploit the mineral-rich seams that once made Butte the "richest hill on earth." To take a look at the ecological disaster that is the 1800-foot-deep, 5600-foot-wide, and 7000-foot-long **Berkeley Pit**, head for Continental Drive. Here, a viewing platform surveys the whole horrifying mess, the most toxic stretch of water in the United States (summer daily 8am–9pm; free).

Uptown lies Butte's extensive **historic district**. On W Park Street, the excellent, although rather grandly named, **World Museum of Mining** (daily 9am–6pm April–Oct; $5; ☎406/723-7211, ⓦwww.miningmuseum.org) is packed with fascinating memorabilia from the local boom years. Outside, beyond the scattered collection of rusting machinery – baffling to all but experts – the museum's 35-building **Hell Roarin' Gulch** re-creates a cobbled-street mining camp, complete with saloon, bordello, church, schoolhouse, and Chinese laundry. Above it all looms the blackened headframe of the 3200-foot-deep Orphan Girl mineshaft.

In an old noodle parlor at 17 W Mercury St, the tiny **Mai Wah Museum** (June–Aug Tues–Sat 11am–3pm; free) focuses on the history of Butte's Chinese community with its small, intriguing collection of photos, cooking implements, kites, fireworks, menus, and books. At the end of the nineteenth century the narrow strip between Galena and Mercury streets was known as China Alley, the bustling heart of a 600-strong community; by the 1940s widespread racism had reduced the number to just a few families. At the other end of the cultural spectrum is the **Dumas Brothel Museum**, 45 E Mercury St (May–Sept daily 9am–5pm; tours $3.50; ☎406/782-3808). The Dumas was built as a brothel in 1890 and stayed in business until 1982. It's the only surviving building in what was once a thriving red-light district, and the guided tour gives you a good insight into what life was like for the occupants and their clients during Butte's heyday. The tour takes in the building's underground "bedrooms," accessible through tunnels that connected with the uptown business district.

At night the 90ft **Our Lady of the Rockies** statue is illuminated by flood-lights. Built entirely by voluntary labor – there had just been a major layoff at one of the mines – it was set in place on top of the Continental Divide, some 3500ft above Butte, by helicopter.

Practicalities

Greyhound and Intermountain Transit **buses** drop off downtown at 101 E Front St. From June to September, ninety-minute **trolley tours** of town (11am, 1.30pm, 3.30pm; $6) leave from the **Chamber of Commerce**, 1000 George St (May–Aug daily 8am–8pm; Sept & Oct daily 8am–5pm; Oct–May Mon–Fri 9am–5pm; ☎406/723-3177 or 1-800/735-6814). The chain **motels** line the interstate, out on the "Flat." The efficient *Best Western Butte Plaza*, 2900 Harrison Ave (☎406/494-3500 or 1-800/543-5814; ➍), has good rooms, an excellent pool, steam room and gym, and generous continental breakfast; while uptown, the historic *Finlen Hotel*, 100 E Broadway (☎406/723-5461; ➋), has rooms in the original 1920s building and a more modern annex. The *Scott Inn*, 15 W Copper St (☎406/723-7030; ➍–➎), is a charming B&B in a historic old manor.

Butte has plenty of good places to **eat and drink**, most of them uptown. The funky, friendly *Blue Venus* coffee house, 124 Main St, serves good espresso, light breakfasts, and lunches, while *Metals Banque*, 8 W Park St (☎406/723-6160), offers tasty Tex-Mex in an old bank vault complete with enormous metal safe. More upscale, though still relatively informal, the *Uptown Café*, 47 E Broadway (☎406/723-4735), serves fixed five-course gourmet meals, particu-larly strong on Mediterranean-style seafood. *The Copper King Saloon,* at 1000 S Montana St (☎406/723-9283), is a lively bar in which to spend an evening.

Helena and around

In 1864 a party of disheartened prospectors working over the present site of **HELENA**, more or less halfway between Yellowstone and Glacier, decided to have one final dig along a likely-looking ravine – and struck lucky on what is now **Last Chance Gulch**, the town's attractive main street. More than $20 million of gold was extracted, but Helena retained an orderly appearance, set neatly at the foot of two rounded mountains with a fine view over the golden-brown **Prickly Pear Valley**. Over fifty successful prospectors remained here as millionaires, and their palatial residences still enhance the west side of town. Hollywood star Gary Cooper was born and raised in this quintessentially Western town; actress Myrna Loy also lived here as a child, and is commemorated by the **Myrna Loy Center for the Performing Arts** at 15 N Ewing St (☎406/443-0287).

Inside the massive Neoclassical **state capitol**, atop a small hill surrounded by lawns at Sixth and Montana avenues (daily 8am–6pm; free), huge murals by "cowboy artist" C.M. Russell depict scenes from Montana's history. You can see more of his work at the excellent **Montana Historical Society Museum**, 225 N Roberts St (June–Aug Mon–Fri 8am–6pm, Sat & Sun 9am–5pm; rest of year Mon–Fri 8am–5pm, Sat 9am–5pm; free), as well as early photographs of pioneer life. The majestic red-tiled spires of the **Cathedral of St Helena** rise 230ft at 530 N Ewing St, while elaborate Bavarian stained glass, white-marble altars, and gold leaf decorate the interior. Also worth a visit is the **Holter Museum of Art**, 12 E Lawrence St (June–Sept Mon–Sat 10am–5pm, Sun noon–5pm; Oct–May Tues–Fri 11.30am–5pm, Sat & Sun noon–5pm; free), which exhibits painting, sculpture, photography, and ceramics. West of downtown, the **Archie Bray Foundation**, 2915 Country Club Ave (Mon–Sat 10am–5pm; ☎406/443-3502), hosts world-renowned ceramic artists who hone their craft while you watch.

Practicalities

Between them, Intermountain and Rimrock (which links with Greyhound), offer connections throughout Montana from Helena's **bus station** at 3122 Prospect Ave (☎406/442-5860). Between mid-May and September the Historical Society runs **tours** in an imitation steam train three times a day from the corner of Sixth Avenue and Roberts Street ($5; 1hr; ☎406/442-1023 or 1-888/423-1023). There's a **visitor center** at 225 Cruse Ave (Mon 9am–5pm, Tues–Fri 8am–5pm; ☎406/442-4120), where you can pick up a free visitor's map; a good source of local listings is the free *Lively Times*. Information and maps on local hiking trails and camping are available from **Helena National Forest Ranger Station**, 2001 Poplar St (☎406/449-5490).

The northernmost blocks of Last Chance Gulch form a low-key **pedestrianized mall**, decorated with mining-themed sculptures and fountains, and enlivened by bars, sidewalk coffee shops, and restaurants. The *Budget Inn Express*, 524 Last Chance Gulch (☎406/442-0600 or 1-800/862-1334; ❷), offers comfortable **rooms** in a good-value downtown location, while for something more traditional and stylish try *The Barrister Bed & Breakfast*, 416 N Ewing St (☎406/443-7330 or 1-800/823-1148; ❹), a lovely Victorian mansion situated beside the cathedral and originally used as priest's quarters. Campers should head for *Helena Campground and RV Park*, 5820 N Montana Ave (☎406/458-4714, ⒻF458-6001), situated about 3.5 miles north of town, where sites are $22.

Places to **eat** include *The Bagel Co*, 735 N Last Chance Gulch (☎406/449-6000), which is open for breakfast bagels and coffee from 6am (Sun 7am). *Bert and Ernie's*, at 361 Last Chance Gulch (☎406/443-5680), serves classy lunches and has a popular saloon bar, while the *Windbag Saloon* at no. 19 (☎406/443-9669) is a big old barn of a place that serves a reasonable pint of Guinness, and good burgers and steaks. A little more upscale, *On Broadway*, 106 Broadway (☎406/443-1929), offers excellent Italian food and wine.

Gates of the Mountains

Sixteen miles north of Helena off I-15, you can take a two-hour **boat tour** through the **Gates of the Mountains** (daily June–Sept; $9.50; ☎406/458-5241, Ⓦwww.gatesofthemountains.com). This dramatic stretch of the Missouri River, which enters a gorge between sheer 1200ft cliffs that rise abruptly from the northern shores of a tranquil lake, was named by Meriwether Lewis (of the Lewis and Clark expedition). The area offers excellent hiking and backpacking opportunities. The **Helena National Forest Office** (☎406/449-5201) can provide maps and local **camping** information.

Missoula

Blue-collar and academic cultures converge in **MISSOULA** (pronounced "Mizoula"), framed by the striking Bitterroot and Sapphire mountains, to produce one of the most vibrant and friendly small towns in the country. It's a town of contrasting faces – truck sales yards and bookstores, continental cafés and gun shops – where nearly everyone seems to be connected to either the city's huge sawmills or the 10,000-student University of Montana.

The **visitor center**, across the river from the campus, at 825 E Front St (☎406/543-6623), can provide details on **trails** such as the grueling one leading from its office up **Mount Sentinel**, embellished by a huge concrete letter "M." The top gives a great view of the area, especially the rugged Hellgate River Canyon. Other worthwhile trails traverse the **Rattlesnake Wilderness**,

Missoula has enjoyed close ties with **cycling** since 1896, when it became home to the 25th Infantry Bicycle Corps, founded to test the military potential of bikes as a means of transporting troops in mountainous regions. Its tasks included a 1900-mile ride to St Louis, where the army decided against the use of cycles and the soldiers came home by train.

Today Missoula is one of the best cities in the country for cycling, offering dozens of great road- and dirt-bike routes. The council even employs a bicycling coordinator (☎406/523-4626), but the best source of **information and trail maps** is the Adventure Cycling Association, 150 E Pine St (☎406/721-1776; see also p.940). The Bicycle Hangar, 1801 Brooks Ave (☎406/728-9537), rents out good-quality cycles.

which, despite its name, is serpent-free. The most developed of the city's two small **ski** areas is **Montana Snowbowl**, twelve miles northwest, which has a good range of slopes for all abilities and boasts a summer **chair lift** (Fri, Sat & Sun noon–5pm; $6, $2 for bikes; ☎406/549-9777). **Marshall Mountain**, seven miles east of Missoula (☎406/258-6000), is geared toward the novice.

Tours of the Forest Service **Smokejumper Center**, ten miles out of town on US-93, look at the methods used to train smokejumpers, highly skilled firefighters who parachute into forested areas to stop the spread of wildfires. A small visitor center explains their work (Memorial Day to Labor Day 10am–5pm; free; ☎406/329-4934).

Missoula is home to a number of **authors**, among them Norman *A River Runs Through It* MacLean, crime writers James Lee Burke and James Crumley, and several good bookstores, including Fact & Fiction, 220 N Higgins St (☎406/721-2881).

Practicalities

Greyhound, Rimrock, and Intermountain share the **bus depot** at 1660 W Broadway (☎406/549-2339). **Motels** along East Broadway, between downtown and campus, include the *Campus Inn* at no. 744 (☎406/549-5134 or 1-800/232-8013; ❹), and, for more luxury, the spacious *Holiday Inn Express Riverside* at no. 1021 (☎406/549-7600; ❹). *Goldsmith's B&B*, 809 E Front St (☎406/721-6732; ❹–❺), beside the river across from the campus, offers comfortable rooms and award-winning food in its Italian restaurant (dinner only). For **camping** in Missoula try the *Missoula KOA*, 3695 Tina Ave (exit 101 off I-90) – just follow the signs from W Broadway. Sites are $25.

Morning espressos and gooey pastries are the specialty at *Break Espresso*, 432 N Higgins St (☎406/728-7300); you can pick up the best picnic lunch in town over the road at *Wordens* deli, Higgins and Spruce streets (☎406/549-1293). For tasty Italian **food**, join the inevitable line at *Zimorino's Red Pies Over Montana*, 424 N Higgins St (☎406/721-7757); try the white pizza or any of the specialty sauces. The *Mustard Seed*, 419 W Front St (☎406/728-7825), is popular for its tasty pan-Asian food, including a passable sushi – no mean feat in Montana, and *The Raven*, 130 E Broadway (☎406/829-8188), with top coffee, three pool tables, and a great jukebox, makes for one of the best hangouts in town.

When Milo Milodragonovitch, the heavy-drinking, coke-snorting private eye in James Crumley's *Dancing Bear*, was left battered and bleeding miles from Missoula, he was consoled by the knowledge that he would soon be back in what he considered to be "the town with the best bars in a state of great bars." It's hard to argue with either claim. The **bar** Milodragonovitch uses as an impromptu office is based on *Charley B's*, 428 N Higgins St – a dark but lively no-frills local place now known as the *Dinosaur Café* (☎406/549-2940). Also worth checking out are *The Oxford Saloon,* 337 N Higgins St (☎406/549-0117), a Montana institution and a friendly joint with as varied a clientele as any bar in Montana, and the *Rhinoceros*, 158 Ryman St (☎406/721-6061), which pours over fifty beers from around the world. *The Blue Heron Club*, 140 W Pine St (☎406/543-2525), is Missoula's coolest **live music** venue, usually featuring the best of the local and regional rock scene. Pick up a copy of the weekly *Independent* or Friday's *Missoulian* for local happenings and live music listings.

The Flathead Valley

The sheer splendor of the remote 28-mile-long **Flathead Lake** – the largest freshwater lake west of the Mississippi – provides a welcome diversion on the long route north toward Glacier National Park, reached by following US-93 north from I-90 to the Flathead Indian Reservation. Before reaching the lake, stop off and view the bison herds at the **National Bison Range** (mid-May to late Oct daily 8am–8pm; late Oct to mid-May 8am–5pm; $4 entrance fee; no trailers; ☎406/644-2211). The main entrance is at the small town of Moiese, twenty miles west of St Ignatius off Hwy-212.

Between Polson in the south and Somers in the north, US-93 follows the lake's western shore, while the smaller Hwy-36 runs up the east, scrunched beneath the Mission Mountains. Both offer superb views of the deep alpine waters; US-93's curve around Elmo in the west, where conical **Wild Horse Island** rises starkly from the crystal-blue depths, is especially memorable.

Flathead Lake is a major destination for **watersports** enthusiasts, with the prime spot for launching fishing and pleasure boats being **Bigfork** in the northeast. In summer, organized cruises are offered aboard the *Far West* (☎406/857-3203) from Somers, and the *Port Polson Princess* ($10–16; ☎406/883-2448) from *Best Western KwaTaqNuk Resort* at Polson. General **information** on the Flathead Valley is available by calling the visitor center at ☎1-800/543-3105. The lake's biggest town, **Polson**, has quite an extensive range of facilities. Here, the Flathead tribe owns the *Best Western KwaTaqNuk Resort*, which has a pool and its own marina with boat rentals, at 303 US-93 E (☎406/883-3636 or 1-800/882-6363; ❹–❺); the *Port Polson Inn*, also overlooking the lake from US-93 E (☎406/883-5385 or 1-800/654-0682; ❸–❹), is slightly less expensive. If you have time to linger, *Averill's Flathead Lake Lodge* in Bigfork (☎406/837-4391, ⓦwww.averills .com; ❾), is a comfortable dude ranch where seven- and fourteen-day stays include horseback riding along scenic trails, water-skiing, fishing, and sailing, as well as steer roping and barn dancing. For information on other dude ranches in Montana, contact the **Dude Ranchers' Association** (☎307/587-2339, ⓦwww.duderanch.org).

If you're just passing through, it's worth pausing at *Watusi*, 318 Main St (☎406/883-6200), for its delicious, healthy **lunches**.

Kalispell

Thirty miles southwest of Glacier, and fifteen miles north of Flathead Lake, good-sized **KALISPELL** corners a significant portion of the tourist trade en route to Glacier. There's not much to do here, but in high season it may be the closest you'll get to staying near the park.

A stylish **accommodation** option is the venerable *Kalispell Grand Hotel*, 100 Main St (☎406/755-8100 or 1-800/858-7422; ❹); the *Hilltop Inn*, 801

E Idaho St (☎406/755-4455; ❸), has clean, comfortable, good-value rooms with queen beds; and *Cavanaugh's West Coast Kalispell Center Hotel,* 20 N Main St (☎406/752-6660 or 1-800/843-4667; ❹), is one of the best-appointed hotels in town with a restaurant, indoor pool, sauna, and hot tub.

For excellent **food**, try the Chinese dishes at the *Alley Connection* in the *Kalispell Hotel* or the game and seafood options at *Café Max*, 121 Main St (☎406/755-7687). *Montana Coffee Traders*, 328 W Center St (☎406/756-2326), also has tasty wraps, salads, pasta, and burritos. If you're looking for a lively night out, the *Hellroaring Saloon & Eatery* on Big Mountain above Whitefish is the place to be – especially during ski season.

Whitefish

The resort and lumber village of **WHITEFISH**, seventeen miles north of Kalispell, has a lively vibe summer or winter. Hacked out of thick forests, it lies on the south shore of beautiful **Whitefish Lake** in the shade of the *Big Mountain Ski Resort* (lift tickets $49; ☎406/862-1900). The narrow roads around the lake and foothills deserve to be **cycled** – bikes can be rented from Glacier Cyclery, 326 E 2nd St (from $25 a day; ☎406/862-6446) – and the surrounding mountains provide great outdoor action year-round. Big Mountain is the second biggest ski hill in the state, and is also open in summer for great lift-accessed hiking and mountain biking ($12).

Amtrak drops off downtown on Central Avenue, en route to and from Glacier National Park, and there's a useful **tourist information counter** in the depot building. Intermountain **buses** call in at Your C-stop gas station at 403 2nd St on their way between Missoula and Glacier during summer.

Whitefish has two **hostels**, a rare commodity in Montana. The *Bunkhouse Travelers Inn & Hostel*, 217 Railway St (☎406/862-3377), has bunk accommodation ($13) or private rooms ($30), and the smaller *Non-Hostile Hostel*, 300 W 2nd St (☎406/862-7447), has bunks for four people ($15 each).

Of the inexpensive **motels** lining US-93, *Allen's Motel*, no. 6540 (☎406/862-3995; ❷–❸), is a decent choice a mile south of downtown. **B&Bs** in the area include the friendly little *Duck Inn*, 1305 Columbia Ave by the river (☎406/862-3825 or 1-800/344-2377; ❺), and the rural *Crenshaw House*, three miles south of town at 5465 US-93 (☎406/862-3496 or 1-800/453-2863; ❹–❼).

For **dining**, the *Great Northern Bar and Grill*, 27 Central Ave (☎406/862-2816), is a busy, friendly spot with pool tables, deli food, and live music, while *Truby's* at 115 Central Ave (☎406/862-4979) is an excellent choice for pizza and pasta. *Whitefish Times*, 344 Central Ave (☎406/862-2444), is a great place to relax with coffee, cakes, and a wide range of complimentary magazines and newspapers.

Glacier National Park

Two thousand lakes and a thousand miles of rivers, threading between thick forests and glorious meadows, weave a blue-and-green carpet below the tightly packed peaks of **GLACIER NATIONAL PARK** – a haven for bighorn sheep, mountain goats, black bears and threatened grizzlies, wolves, and mountain lions. Though the park still holds fifty small glaciers, it takes its name from the huge flows of ice that carved these immense valleys millennia ago. Crisp air, freezing waterfalls, and year-round snow combine to give the impression of being very close to the Arctic Circle; in fact, the latitude here is lower than that of London.

△ Going-to-the-Sun Road over Logan Pass, Montana

Arrival and information

There are **visitor centers** just inside the park's **western** entrance at **Apgar**, on the shores of gorgeous McDonald Lake, twenty miles east of Whitefish and just 35 miles south of the Canadian border (May–Oct; hours vary, but at least 9am–4.30pm daily and until 8pm in summer) and at the main **east** gate at **St Mary**, seventy miles west of **Shelby** (daily: late May to late June, early Sept to mid-Oct 8am–5pm; late June to early July 8am–9pm; early July to early Sept 7am–9pm). Another visitor center (early June to mid-Oct; hours vary, but always open at least 10am–5pm daily) stands at the top of **Logan Pass** on the Going-to-the-Sun road – the one through-road between the two entrances, usually only passable between early June and mid-October. The park itself is open year-round, however, and it's well worth entering as far as Lake McDonald or St Mary's Lake even when the road is blocked and the visitor center is closed. The **entrance fee** of $10 per vehicle is good for seven days; for **park information** call ℡ 406/888-7800 or go to ⓦ www.nps.gov/glac.

Glacier combines with the adjacent, much smaller Waterton Lakes National Park (℡ 403/859-2224) in Canada to form the **Waterton-Glacier International Peace Park**, though Going-to-the-Sun road does not pass that way. Both parks operate their own fees and regulations, and to get to Waterton's separate entrance, north of St Mary, you have to pass customs and pay a $4 entrance fee.

The southern border of the park is skirted by the low-lying US-2, which remains open all year and constitutes an attractive alternative drive. Amtrak **trains** follow the same route, stopping at West Glacier, a short walk from the west gate, and in the south at East Glacier (thirty miles south of St Mary) and Essex Park.

Intermountain (℡ 406/563-5246) operates a fairly frequent summer bus service from Missoula, Kalispell, Whitefish, and, to the east, Great Falls. Travelers arriving by public transportation are faced with the problem of how to see the actual park: bright red vintage "jammer" buses (so called because of the need to jam the gears into place) run throughout the park on narrated **sightseeing tours** from the main lodges (May–Oct; ℡ 406/888-9817). They also offer shuttles from the Amtrak station at West Glacier to the *Village Inn* and *Lake McDonald Lodge*, hikers' shuttles from *Many Glacier Hotel* to the various trailheads including Logan Pass, The Loop, and Siyeh Bend, and a number of one-way tours and connections. Sun Tours (℡ 406/226-9220 or 1-800/786-9220) offers guided tours led by members of the Blackfoot Indian tribe, providing a historical perspective to the park's beauty.

Accommodation within the park

Accommodation options within the park, along with the *Glacier Park Lodge* in East Glacier, are run by Glacier Park Inc. (May–Sept: East Glacier Park, MT 59434 ℡ 406/226-5551; rest of year: Viad Corporate Center, Phoenix, AZ 85077 ℡ 602/207-6000). Most rooms cost over $80, though you can stay more cheaply at the *Swiftcurrent Motor Inn* at Many Glacier on the upper east side (June–Sept; ❹, basic cabins ❷); the lakeside *Rising Sun Motor Inn* (June–Sept; ❹–❺), seven miles in from the east gate at St Mary; and the *Village Inn* (mid-May to Sept; ❺–❻) in Apgar, which fronts onto Lake McDonald and has stunning views. Nearby, the lovely *Lake McDonald Lodge* has a few affordable motel rooms (June–Sept; ❺–❻), but these, like the better rooms, are in the lodge itself and need to be reserved well in advance. More upscale are the *Prince of Wales Hotel* in Waterton (❽–❾; May–Sept) and the *Many Glacier Hotel* (❻–❼; June to mid-Sept).

The park's thirteen **campgrounds** – all first-come, first-served, ranging from $12 to $17 – fill up by late morning during July and August; ask at any visitor center for locations and availability or call ℡ 406/888-7800. For advanced reservations, call ☎1-800/365-CAMP. Most are open from late May to mid-September, though Apgar, Bowman Lake, Kintla Creek, Logging Creek, Many Glacier, Quartz Creek, St Mary, and Two Medicine are open for very basic camping in winter ($6), when facilities are absolutely minimal and may not include water. For overnight backpacking, get a permit from any visitor center.

Accommodation outside the park

Another Glacier Park Inc. operation, the massive log-built *Glacier Park Lodge* (mid-May to Sept; ➅–➇), off US-2 at the **eastern edge** of the park, is a terrific place to stay, with simple rooms, a cozy lobby lined with enormous Douglas-fir pillars, a veranda with mountain views, a swimming pool, and a very good restaurant. Though very near the lovely Two Medicine Lake area, it's a long drive from the park entrances at St Mary and Many Glacier. Two miles outside the **western entrance**, the beautifully refurbished 1910 *Belton Chalet* (➅) offers tastefully appointed rooms with period furniture and with no phones or TV to disturb your stay. On the southern boundary at **Essex**, the *Izaak Walton Inn* (☎406/888-5700; ➄), halfway between the east and west gates, is an atmospheric 1939 building, originally used to house railroad workers charged with keeping the lines clear in winter – to this day, Amtrak stops at the front door. In the village of East Glacier Park, near the Amtrak station, the simple *Backpacker Inn* hostel (☎406/226-9392; ➊), behind *Serrano's Mexican Restaurant*, offers shared dorm space for $10–12. Up in **Polebridge**, the *Northfork Hostel* (☎406/888-5241) is extremely cozy, with no electricity. Beds cost $15 dollars and cabins start at $30; tepees are $10.

Information on other **lodging** in the immediate vicinity is available from Glacier Country (☎1-800/338-5072), while popular alternative bases to the west of the park include **Whitefish** and **Kalispell** (see pp.950 & 949).

Exploring the park

Driving the fifty-mile **Going-to-the-Sun road** from west to east (which can take several hours, even when summer restrictions on vehicle size – aimed primarily at banning RVs – are in force) creates the illusion that you'll be climbing forever. After a stealthy ascent of the foothills, when the road appears to be heading straight into the huge bare mountain that fills the entire windscreen, each successive hairpin confronts you with a new colossus. At the east end of ten-mile **Lake McDonald**, the road starts to climb in earnest. Snowmelt from waterfalls gushes across the road, spilling over the sheer drops on the other side. The winding route nudges over the **Continental Divide** at **Logan Pass** (6680ft) – a bewildering area where the peaks that looked so unscaleable from the valley floor are now mere hillocks of ice. Four miles on, there's an overlook at **Jackson Glacier**, one of the few glaciers visible from the roadside. Once you get down to the east gate, continue about five miles southeast on US-89 for a stunning view of the start of the Great Plains, which stretch 1600 miles east to Chicago.

Glacier National Park is a hiker's paradise, with exceptionally beautiful views at every turn. Good short **trails** start from **Avalanche Creek** on the west flank of the Divide. The mile-long **Trail of the Cedars** loop leads through dark forest to a wall of contoured vivid red sandstone, from where a four-mile path continues gently uphill, past several waterfalls, to glacier-fed **Avalanche Lake**. The most popular trail in the park – it can be teeming at weekends and holidays – begins at Logan Pass, following a boardwalk for a mile and a half across beautiful wild flower alpine meadows framed by extraordinary craggy peaks en route to serene **Hidden Lake**.

At **Swiftcurrent Lake**, north of the east entrance and reached by the minor Many Glacier entrance, an easy two-mile loop trail runs along the lakeshore, and an exciting nine-mile trail heads to **Iceberg Lake**, so called for the blocks of ice that float on its surface even in midsummer.

From **St Mary Lake**, you can weave a mile and a half up through fir forest to the crashing, frothing **St Mary Falls** and on to the taller **Virginia Falls**; combined with an early-morning boat trip from the Rising Sun launch to the trailhead (see below), this can be an experience verging on the sublime.

Down in the quiet southeastern end of the park, the two-mile **Aster Park** trail gives access to some of Glacier's most astounding scenery. Starting at Two Medicine Lake, framed by the ever-receding massifs, it leads through spruce forest into flower-filled meadows, passing a couple of beaver ponds before ascending steeply through the forest to a small outcrop. From here there are fantastic views of the mighty Sinopah and Rising Wolf mountains, and the calm lakes below.

Tour boats explore all of the large lakes, charging $8–10 for one-hour trips, including sunset cruises on Lake McDonald and St Mary Lake. You can also rent canoes, rowboats, and outboards. The lakes, teeming with cutthroat trout, are excellent for **fishing**; regulations are outlined in a free pamphlet available from visitor centers.

Both Glacier Raft Co. (☎406/888-5454 or 1-800/235-6781, ⓦwww.glacier-raftco.com) and Wild River Adventures (☎1-800/700-7056), based outside the west gate, offer half-day (around $40) and full-day (around $70) **float trips** down the middle fork of the Flathead River, which runs along the park boundary.

Eating and drinking

Food in the park, served in the various hotel dining rooms, is nothing special. The best place to head in the immediate vicinity – outside the lodges – is East Glacier Park, where *Serrano's*, 29 Dawson Ave (mid-April to mid-Oct; ☎406/226-9392), serves delicious Mexican food and microbrews. On the east side of Hwy-49, next to *Brownie's*, is the cozy *Whistlestop Café*, which has a great menu featuring terrific huckleberry pie. On the northeast side of Glacier the funky *Two Sisters Café* on Hwy-89 in Babb (☎406/732-5535) is obvious from the "Aliens Welcome" sign on the roof, and the food is top notch.

Idaho

IDAHO, sandwiched in between Washington, Oregon, and Montana, was the last of the states to be penetrated by white settlers, and rivals Alaska in the sheer scale of its barely explored **wilderness** areas. Though much of its scenery amply deserves national-park status, its citizens have long been suspicious of encroachment by federal government and tourism alike, and only now is its potential for adventurous travel being appreciated.

With a marked absence of urban centers (the pleasant state capital **Boise**, in the south, being the only real exception), Idaho is very much a destination for the outdoors enthusiast. Natural wonders in its five-hundred-mile stretch include **Hell's Canyon**, America's deepest river gorge, the dramatic **Sawtooth National**

Recreation Area, and the black, barren **Craters of the Moon**. Beyond these, **hikers** and **backpackers** have the choice of no fewer than 81 mountain ranges, interspersed with virgin forest and lava plateaus, while the mighty **Snake** and **Salmon rivers** offer endless scope for **fishing** and **whitewater rafting**.

In 1805, **Lewis and Clark** declared central Idaho's bewildering labyrinth of razor-edge peaks and wild waterways to be the most difficult leg of their mammoth journey from St Louis to the Pacific. Only their Shoshone guides enabled them to get through; to this day, there is no east–west road across the heart of the state. Reports of game animals tripping over each other in their profusion attracted the usual legions of itinerant trappers, but the Gold Rush of the 1860s and white pressure for land hastened the violent end of traditional life: four hundred Shoshone men, women, and children were killed along the Bear River in 1863, the Nez Percé were driven out (see box, p.961), and by the end of the 1870s the "Indian problem" had been eradicated. The name "Idaho," incidentally, was invented by a mining lobbyist, who felt it sounded Indian; it was originally proposed for what is now Colorado.

The central wilderness still divides the state into two distinct halves. The heavily forested **north**, interspersed with glacial lakes now fronted by resorts like **Sandpoint** and **Coeur d'Alene**, has always had strong trading links with Spokane in Washington; in the **south**, irrigation programs begun in the 1880s – partly instigated by Mormons – have transformed the scrubland to either side of the Snake River into the fertile fields responsible for the state's license-plate tag of "Famous Potatoes." Idaho's isolation, and small (1 million) population, have kept it largely out of the mainstream of recent US history. Indeed, the state's remoteness has attracted assorted unwelcome guests – neo-Nazi survivalists awaiting the Second Coming and/or nuclear holocaust.

Getting around Idaho

Bus services between northern and southern Idaho are very poor, and a **car** is essential for extensive travel. Only one **Amtrak** route crosses the state, ultimately linking Seattle with Chicago, and stopping only at Sandpoint in northern Idaho, though Spokane is not far across the border. Boise also has an **airport**, though Spokane and Salt Lake City can be more convenient for northern and southern Idaho respectively.

Southern Idaho

To drivers on the interstates, **southern Idaho** appears to consist of little more than miles of vegetable fields and a few rocky or sandy desert stretches; only state capital **Boise** provides any urban interest. A trip into the interior along US-20, however, brings you to the spectacular ragged outcrops of the **Sawtooth Mountains**. During summer, the much-hyped **Sun Valley** ski resort is a good base for mountain bikers, rafters, and hikers, and has the best bars and restaurants in this remote zone – in winter it has the most glitzy ski scene in the northern Rockies.

Idaho Falls

Of the two largest towns in southeast Idaho, **IDAHO FALLS** makes a better overnight stop than down-at-heel Pocatello, being approximately 100 miles from Craters of the Moon to the west and Yellowstone and Grand Teton to the northeast. The first sign you see of this likeable but quiet community, as you approach along I-15, sixty miles north of Pocatello, is its seven-tier wedding-cake Mormon temple, rising from the flat Snake River Valley. The **falls** for which the town was named are now entirely tamed, by a long, low concrete dam running diagonally across the river very near downtown – but they form a pleasant focus for the greenbelt of parkland that lines both banks of this agricultural town.

Much of the country en route to Yellowstone is every bit as spectacular as in the national parks, and far less crowded; the magnificent **Mesa Falls**, for example, are a worthwhile brief detour along Hwy-47, roughly forty miles short of West Yellowstone.

Practicalities

The **visitor center** at 630 W Broadway (year-round Mon–Fri 8am–5pm, also Sat 10am–4pm in summer; ☎208/523-1010 or 1-800/634-3246) has information on the whole area, including a large relief model of the entire valley. **Hotels** and **restaurants** are congregated on the west bank of the river, near the interstate, while the old downtown area on the east side retains a fair number of shops. The bizarre, towering *Holiday Inn-West Bank* at 475 River Parkway (☎208/523-8000 or 1-800/465-4329; ❺) has some of the most expensive rooms in town. The easily accessible *Best Western Cotton Tree Inn*, 900 Lindsay Blvd (☎208/523-6000 or 1-800/662-6886; ❺), has large, comfortable rooms with Internet connection in some, a pool, hot tub, and a fitness center, while the large *Days Inn Stardust* nearby at no. 700 (☎208/523-8900; ❸–❺) offers cheaper accommodation. Good restaurant choices include *Jaker's Steak, Ribs & Fish House*, 851 Lindsey Blvd (☎208/524-5240), and the *Brownstone Restaurant & Brewpub*, on River Parkway (☎208/535-0310), which also brews its own tasty Idaho Pilsner and has a more sophisticated feel than many of its neighbors.

Craters of the Moon National Monument

The eerie **Craters of the Moon National Monument** is around ninety miles west of Idaho Falls, less than twenty miles beyond Arco. At first sight, its 83 square miles look like a sooty-black wasteland, but closer inspection reveals a surreal cornucopia of lava cones, lava tubes, buttes, craters, caves, and splatter cones. Here and there, sagebrush clings to the bleak soil, and trees have been battered by the fierce winds into bonsai-like contortions. All these features were formed without the aid of a volcano as such; instead, at roughly two-thousand-year intervals over the last thirteen thousand years, successive waves of lava have oozed from gaping wounds in the earth's crust. The next wave is thought to be due any time now.

The park **visitor center** is on US-20 (daily: summer 8am–6pm; rest of year 8am–4.30pm; ☎208/527-3257); entrance is $5 per car, $3 per bicycle, and spaces at the *Lava Flow* **campground** cost $10 (May–Oct). A seven-mile **loop road**, open late April to mid-November, takes you around lava fields, where hiking trails of varying difficulty lead past assorted cones and monoliths – don't stray from the trails, as the rocks are razor-sharp and can reach temperatures of 200°F. In winter, the road is open for **cross-country skiing**; for a conditions report, call ☎208/527-3257. "**Caves**" formed by molten lava tubes can be explored, alone or on frequent ranger-led tours.

Halfway between the park and Idaho Falls on US-20, the unassuming red-brick Experimental Breeder Reactor No. 1 (**EBR-1**) – in lay terms, the **world's first nuclear power station** – stands just south of the 890-square-mile Idaho National Engineering Laboratory. Even the first prototype nuclear submarine was built and tested here. Now decommissioned, it's a free museum (☎208/526-000).

Sun Valley

Although these days **Sun Valley** is the common label for the entire Wood River Valley area – in the center of southern Idaho, 150 miles west of Idaho Falls and east of Boise – technically it is just the name of a **ski resort**. This was the 1930s brainchild of Union Pacific Railroad chairman Averell Harriman, who, on discovering his railroad was obliged to maintain a passenger service, decided an alpine ski center would be an ideal stimulus for tourism. His scout, Austrian ski champion Count Schaffgotsch, set out to find dry powder snow on open treeless slopes, sheltered by higher mountains. Having turned down Aspen for being too high up, the Count decided on **Dollar** and **Bald mountains**, here in the relatively gentle foothills of the Sawtooths near the old sheep-ranching village of **KETCHUM**. The Sun Valley name was chosen because the snow remained even in the brightest winter sun; early brochures showed skiers stripped to the waist. The world's first chair lift was built here in 1936, and the resort was an instant success.

Sun Valley's season runs from late November through to April; as well as downhill skiing (daily lift pass $66 at Bald Mountain, $26 at Dollar Mountain), you can also set off cross-country. Ketchum itself is a lively little town with plenty of accommodation, and an oasis of nightlife in this otherwise thinly populated zone. Up to a point, it resembles the Colorado ski towns, though summer trade is not quite as busy.

Among summer outdoor activities are **cycling** along thirty miles of excellent trails – including the former railroad tracks, long since paved over – as well as **mountain biking** on the superb lift-accessed trails on Bald Mountain, and **rafting** on the rivers to the north (see overleaf). The **Sports Complex** (T208/622-4111) on Sun Valley Road, south of Dollar Road, offers a Nordic ski center, tennis, ice skating, winter sleigh rides, and guided horseback rides.

Ernest Hemingway completed *For Whom the Bell Tolls* as a celebrity guest in the resort in 1939, and lived in Ketchum for the last two years of his life, before his suicide; his very plain grave can be found in the town cemetery.

Practicalities

There's a free in-town shuttle service between 7.30am and midnight. Ketchum's **visitor center**, on the corner of 4th and Main streets, runs a free reservation service for **accommodation** (daily 9am–5pm; T208/726-3423 or 1-800/634-3347, Wvisitsunvalley.com). Room rates everywhere are highest in the heavy summer and winter seasons. You can save a bundle by staying in nearby Hailey, twelve miles south of Ketchum.

The luxurious 600-room *Sun Valley Lodge* resort is very expensive in season, though worth every cent in spring and fall (T208/622-4111 or 1-800/786-8259; winter & summer ❼–❽, spring & fall ❹); also run by the resort is the *Sun Valley Inn* (winter & summer ❺–❼). A cheaper option in Ketchum is the comfortable, welcoming *Lift Tower Lodge*, 703 S Main St (T208/726-5163 or 1-800/462-8646; ❺), while the more upmarket, opulently furnished *River Street Inn*, 100 River St (T208/726-3611), is also a good choice for its cozy, intimate rooms, hot tub, and excellent breakfasts. The reasonably luxurious *Best Western Tyrolean Lodge* (T208/726-5336 or 1-800/333-7912; ❺) is also a fine, good-value choice.

The *Dining Room* at the *Sun Valley Lodge* (T208/622-2150) serves some of the best and most elegant **meals** in Idaho, while in Ketchum, the welcoming *Ketchum Grill*, 520 East Ave (T208/726-4460 or 726-7434), has plenty of delicious vegetarian options. Well-to-do *Cristina's*, 520 Second St E (T208/726-4499), is a culinary highlight, especially at lunchtimes, when delicious deli meats and Asian salads are served on its back patio. The village also has a number of decent **drinking** spots; *Whiskey Jacques* at 206 N Main St (☎208/726-3200) is a good local watering hole, as is the busy *Grumpy's* at 860 Warm Springs Rd, a popular burger and beer joint.

Sawtooth National Recreation Area

North of Ketchum and Sun Valley, Hwy-75 climbs through ever-larger mountains and forests to top out after twenty miles at **Galena Summit**, one of the most spectacular panoramic viewpoints in all the Rockies. Spreading out far below, the meadows of the Sawtooth Valley stretch northward, bearing minimal traces of the long-abandoned gold-mining settlements. The simple road meanders beside the young **Salmon River**, whose headwaters rise in the forbidding icy peaks to the south, and the serrated ridge of the **Sawtooth Mountains** forms an impenetrable barrier along the western horizon.

Backpackers are guaranteed solitude in these high fastnesses, dotted with around five hundred remote Alpine lakes – pick up details of primitive **camping** sites and hiking trails at the **Sawtooth National Recreation Area headquarters** (☎208/726-7672 or 1-800/260-5970), eight miles out of Ketchum. Fly-fishing for brown trout and salmon is a popular local pastime here as well.

At tiny **STANLEY**, a few miles north, dirt roads radiating from the junction of Hwy-75 and Hwy-21 have assorted **motels** such as the rustic *Valley Creek Motel* (☎208/774-3606; ❹–❺), and the large, cozy, and well-situated *Mountain Village Lodge* (☎208/774-3661 or 1-800/843-5475; ❸), which has sixty comfortably furnished rooms and a natural hot springs spa – and copies of *The Roadkill Cookbook* for sale by the front desk. The *Rod and Gun Club Saloon*, on Ace of Diamonds Avenue, is a lively local **bar** that also serves decent pub grub. Out of season Stanley virtually closes up; in summer its main activity is organizing **rafting trips** (check in advance; weather conditions – such as heavy snowmelt – can make conditions too dangerous). Operators include The River Company (☎208/774-2244), which charges $67–87.

Boise

Anywhere in the US, the verdant community of **BOISE** (pronounced *Boy-zee*) would come across as a bustling and likeable small city; located in arid southwestern Idaho, it's all the more appealing. The town straddles I-84, just 350 miles from Salt Lake City to the southeast and a trifling 490 miles from Seattle in the northwest.

The town grew up under the protective wing of Fort Boise, established in 1862 for the benefit of pioneers using the Oregon Trail. After adapting (or misspelling) the name originally given to the area by French trappers – *les bois*, the woods – the earliest residents boosted the town's appearance by planting hundreds more trees.

The City

To explore Boise's compact, friendly **downtown**, start at the central **State Capitol** at Jefferson Street and Capitol Boulevard. This squat replica of the national capitol exhibits gemstones such as the star garnet, found only in Indo-China and Idaho. **Old Boise Historic District**, nearby, is an elegant area of brick houses, shops, and restaurants that has undergone major restoration. The unusual **Idaho Basque Museum and Cultural Center** at 607–611 Grove St (Tues–Fri 10am–4pm, Sat 11am–3pm; $1),) is located in a former boarding house that was for many years home to Basque immigrants fresh from the western Pyrenees, who came to central Idaho, with its equally mountainous terrain, to employ their shepherding skills. The museum traces the Basque cultural heritage and hosts regular traditional dance nights.

It's impossible not to be impressed by the contrast between the urban greenery and the humpy desert hills all around. The city is rightly proud of the **Greenbelt**, some nineteen miles of paths that crisscross the tranquil **Boise River** to link nine separate parks. In **Julia Davis Park**, the **Idaho Historical Museum** (Mon–Sat 9am–5pm, Sun 1–5pm; donation) chronicles Native American and Basque history, as well as the experience of the Chinese miners of the 1870s and 1880s, who picked over mines long since abandoned by whites. The state legislature, controlled by unreconstructed Confederates who had fled the South after the Civil War, did nothing to stamp out racial violence, and forced the Chinese to pay $4 a month, a considerable amount at the time, just to live in the Territory.

The **Old Idaho Penitentiary** nestles beneath desert hills at 2445 Old Penitentiary Rd, off Warm Springs Avenue (daily: summer 10am–6pm; rest of year noon–5pm; $5; ☎208/334-2844). This imposing sandstone-walled citadel feels like a desolate outpost, despite being just a mile from downtown. Constructed in 1870 to hold robbers, rustlers, and other desperadoes, it remained open until 1974. Self-guided tours take you through the cramped solitary-confinement unit, and the gallows room where the last hanging in Idaho was carried out in 1957. Restoration work has sensibly avoided trying to make this brutal prison look more palatable. A small museum displays confiscated weapons and mugshots of former inmates, including one Harry Orchard, who blew up the state governor in 1905 and served out his sentence here, dying in 1954 at the age of 88. Oddly situated beside the penitentiary, the **Idaho Botanical Gardens** (mid-April to mid-Oct Mon–Fri 10am–3pm, Sat & Sun 10am–5pm) has nine themed gardens.

Practicalities

Greyhound **buses** and the Boise–Winnemucca/Northwestern Stage Lines stop at 1212 W Bannock St. The city's Boise Urban Services (BUS) (☎208/336-1010) run a fairly extensive local bus service – fares are 75¢ adults, 50¢ youths (6–18 yrs), 35¢ flat fare on Saturday. The **visitor center** (April–Sept Mon–Fri 10am–6pm; Oct–March Mon–Fri 10am–3.30pm; ☎208/344-5338, ⓦ www.boise.org) is in the Boise Center next to The Grove plaza. Downtown's best **places to stay** are *The Grove Hotel*, 245 S Capitol Blvd (☎208/333-8000 or 1-800/426-0670; ❻), which has luxury accommodation in large, well-appointed rooms, many with great views over the city and mountains beyond, and the *Owyhee Plaza Hotel*, 1109 Main St (☎208/343-4611 or 1-800/233-4611; ❺), a renovated, older hotel in the heart of downtown with an outdoor pool and free airport shuttle. If you're on a tight budget try *Sands Motel*, 111 W State St (☎208/343-2533; ❷), within easy walking distance of downtown, although the rooms are a bit tatty and it can be noisy. The nicest **B&B** is the *Idaho Heritage Inn B&B*, 109 W Idaho St (☎208/342-8066, ⓦ www.idheritageinn.com; ❹), a lovely Victorian building that was once the residence of Governor Chase A. Clark and later Senator Frank Church. If you're **camping**, head a couple of miles northwest of downtown to *On The River RV Park*, 6000 N Glenwood St (☎208/375-7432 or 1-800/375-7432), which has shady tent sites for $20 beside the Greenbelt and Boise River.

You're spoiled for choice when it comes to **eating** in Boise. *Milford's Fish House* in the Eighth Street Marketplace, 405 S 8th St (☎208/342-8382), serves good fresh fish and has a wide selection of beers; popular among locals is *Goldy's*, 108 S Capitol Blvd (☎208/345-4100), where you can create your own breakfast combos. Of the city's many good ethnic restaurants, try *Aladdin*, 111 Broadway (☎208/368-0880), for Egyptian food and belly dancing on Fridays and Saturdays, or *Bar Gernika*, 202 Capitol Blvd (☎208/344-2175), for Basque specialties – particularly good are the range of tapas. Other fine downtown **bars** and restaurants include the bustling *Bittercreek Alehouse*, 246 N 8th St (☎208/345-1813), with its huge selection of beers; the *Grape Escape Wine Bar*, 800 W Idaho St (☎208/368-0200), serving good-value Latin dishes; and *Bardenay Restaurant & Distillery*, 610 Grove St (☎208/426-0538), which meticulously distills its own gin, rum, and vodka in America's first legal distillery/pub, and features an excellent menu. After dining, check out *The Big Easy*, 416 9th St (☎208/367-1212), one of Idaho's top rock venues.

Northern Idaho

The wilderness peaks and pinnacles of the Sawtooth, Salmon River, and Clearwater mountains make traveling through the heart of Idaho impossible. There are only two routes from south to north: up the eastern fringe from Idaho Falls, or, more enjoyably, along US-95 via Hwy-55 out of Boise. At first barren and infertile, not until just before Lewiston does the scenery unfold into superb pastoral farmland. The **Nez Percé** hunted buffalo, gathered berries, and fished here for hundreds of years, until gold was discovered and they were forced to beat a bloody retreat.

The heavily forested far north of the Idaho Panhandle is broken by hundreds of deep glacial lakes, the largest of which have resort towns such as **Coeur d'Alene** and **Sandpoint**. While not major destinations, they can make good one- or two-day stops.

Hell's Canyon Region

From the busy but not over-commercialized little watersports and ski resort of **McCALL**, 110 miles north of Boise, Hwy-55 climbs steadily to merge with US-95 and follow the turbulent **Little Salmon River**. Just south of the hamlet of Riggins, thirty miles on, comes the only good opportunity to see **Hell's Canyon** from Idaho. With an average depth of 5500ft this is the deepest river gorge in the US, though its low-relief formation, hemmed in by a series of gradually ascending false peaks, means that it lacks the impact of the steep-walled Grand Canyon. Nevertheless, it is impressive, with Oregon's Wallowa and Eagle Cap ranges rising behind it and the river glimmering far down below. Hwy-241 leads toward the overlooks; the final few miles of dirt road require a four-wheel-drive vehicle and permission from the Riggins forest ranger office on Hwy-95 (Mon–Fri 8am–5pm; ☎208/628-3916). The canyon is also accessible by road from Oregon (see p.1294) and by boat from Lewiston.

RIGGINS itself reclines in a steeply rising T-shaped canyon. This is prime **white-water-rafting** country, and outfitters, spread along a one-mile stretch of the one-street village, outnumber cafés and shops. The **Chamber of Commerce** (☎208/628-3441) has details. From Riggins, US-95 heads north along the Salmon River Valley for thirty miles to the rumpled terrain around **White Bird**, the start of Nez Percé country.

The Nez Percé

The first whites to encounter the **Nez Percé** were the weak, hungry, and disease-ridden Lewis and Clark expedition in 1805. Though the Native Americans had the explorers at their mercy, they gave them food and shelter, and cared for their animals until the party was ready to carry on westward.

Relations between the Nez Percé (so called by French-Canadian trappers because of their shell-pierced noses) and whites remained excellent for over half a century – until the discovery of gold, and white pressure for space, led the government to persuade some renegade Nez Percé to sign a treaty in 1863, taking away three-quarters of tribal land. As settlers started to move into the hunting grounds of the Wallowa Valley in the early 1870s, the majority of the Nez Percé, under the leadership of **Chief Joseph**, refused to recognize the agreement. In 1877, after much vacillation, the government decided to enact its terms and gave the tribe thirty days to leave. The Nez Percé asked for more time to round up their livestock and avoid crossing the Snake River at a dangerous time; the general in charge refused.

The ensuing tensions resulted in skirmishes that caused the deaths of a handful of settlers – the first whites ever to be attacked by Nez Percé – and a large army force began to gather to round up the Nez Percé. Chief Joseph then embarked upon the famous **Retreat of the Nez Percé**. Around 250 warriors (protecting twice as many women, children, and old people) outmaneuvered army columns many times their size, launching frequent guerrilla attacks in a series of hair-breadth escapes. After four months and 1700 miles, the Nez Percé were cornered just thirty miles from the relative safety of the Canadian border. Chief Joseph then (reportedly) made his much-quoted speech of surrender:

Hear me my chiefs! I am tired. My heart is sick and sad.
From where the sun now stands I will fight no more forever.

The Native Americans had been told that they would be put on a reservation in Idaho; instead, they were taken to Oklahoma, where the marshy land caused a malaria epidemic. Chief Joseph died in 1904 on the Colville reservation in Washington, but decades later the Nez Percé were allowed to return to the Northwest, where today some 1500 live in a reservation between Lewiston and Grangeville – a minute fraction of their original territory.

The **Nez Percé National Historic Park**, containing 24 separate sites, is spread over 12,000 square miles of north central Idaho. At the visitor center in **Spalding**, ten miles east of Lewiston (☎208/843-2261), the **Museum of Nez Percé Culture** (daily: summer 8am–5.30pm; rest of year 8am–4.30pm; free) is good on arts and crafts but weak on history; the heavily ravined **White Bird Battlefield**, seventy miles further south on US-95, was where the Native Americans inflicted 34 deaths on the US Army at no cost to themselves, in the first major battle of the Retreat. Further exhibits on Nez Percé history can be found in the Wallowa County Museum in Joseph, Oregon (see p.1293).

There are few compelling reasons to visit industrial **LEWISTON**, 110 miles north of Riggins (which was Territorial capital for one year before Boise took over). One is to drive down the old road into town from the top of Lewiston Hill, just north – what seems like an intricate network of roads crisscrossing a series of mounds is, in fact, a single tarmac ribbon, which twists and turns for several miles down the steep hillside. Another is the **Lewiston Round-up**, a massive rodeo held on the second weekend of September (☎208/746-6324, ⓦwww.lewistonroundup.org).

For the rest of the year, the main reason to subject yourself to the nasty smells emanating from the local paper mills is for the fantastic journey through Hell's

Canyon on the Salmon River. Boats sail past abandoned mine shafts and Native American caves, with mountain goats, bobcats, snakes, and birds of prey adding further interest. Of the various outfitters, Snake River Adventures, 227 Snake River Ave (℡1-800/262-8874), offers the best value: an all-day, wet-and-wild trip to Granite Creek costs around $120 including lunch. Contact the **visitor center** on the north side of the Clearwater River at 313 N 2nd St (May–Sept Mon–Fri 9am–5pm; ℡208/746-5172) for details on other options.

Moscow

The thirty miles of US-95 between Lewiston and **MOSCOW** wind through the beautiful rolling hillsides of the fertile Palouse Valley – a patchwork of green lentils, bright yellow rape, soft white wheat, and (100-foot-thick) black topsoil. Roadside red barns and farmhouses complete a marvelous rural picture.

With ten thousand year-round residents and a similar number of **University of Idaho** students, Moscow is a friendly, culturally rich town that makes a good overnight stop. Bookstores, galleries, bars, and sidewalk cafés line up along the tree-shaded and partly pedestrianized **Main Street**, the only shopping thoroughfare. Theater, music, and avant-garde cinema are on offer throughout the year, while summer sees a sprinkling of big-budget arts festivals.

The town's name might raise a few eyebrows, but it's pretty ordinary compared to the first settlers' choice of Hog Heaven. A proposal to rename it Paradise was seen as a trifle over the top; the present name comes from one early resident's hometown in Pennsylvania.

Practicalities

Moscow's **visitor center** is at 411 S Main St (℡208/882-1800 or 1-800/380-1801); Northwest Trailways (a Greyhound affiliate) stops at the basic *Royal Motor Inn*, 120 W Sixth St (℡208/882-2581; ❷). For a bit more comfort, try the *Mark IV Motor Inn*, 414 N Main St (℡208/882-7557 or 1-800/833-4240; ❸), which has a nice pool and hot tub. On weekends when college football games are in town, rooms can be hard to find, and rates can be higher. Among places to **eat**, the *Best Western University Inn Pantry*, 1516 Pullman Rd (℡208/882-0550), is open from 6am to 10pm and serves burgers, pasta, steak, and the like.

Coeur d'Alene

When US Army Chief of Staff William Tecumseh Sherman set up camp in 1877 on the present site of **COEUR D'ALENE**, fifty miles north of Moscow on US-95, he found the sparkling blue lake, surrounded by wild flower borders and lush forest, so appealing that he ordered a fort to be built here. Another large structure now stands on the beautiful shoreline of long, narrow Lake Coeur d'Alene; looking not unlike an office block, the phenomenally expensive **Coeur d'Alene Resort**, which boasts the world's only floating golf green, completely dominates downtown (℡208/765-4000 or 1-800/688-5253; ❻–❾). Not surprisingly, it's a bitter local debating point.

Downtown is unremarkable despite its reasonably appealing sidewalk cafés and rather pricey shops. Directly east of the resort, a small public beach backs onto a balmy park area. Scenic **lake cruises** leave from the nearby City Dock (three daily in summer; $15.75; ℡208/765-4000). You can also see the lake on a twenty-minute **sea plane flight** from here, for $40 with Brooks Seaplane (℡208/664-2842).

Greyhound **buses** stop at 157 Spruce St (☎208/664-3343), situated a couple of miles north of downtown, especially inconvenient as there's no public transport within the town. The **Coeur d'Alene Visitor and Convention Services**, at 3rd and Spruce streets (Mon–Fri 8:30am–5pm; ☎1-877/782-9232, ⓦwww.coeurdalene.org), has a good range of free helpful publications. Along Sherman Avenue, the *Flamingo Motel* at no. 718 (☎208/664-2159 or 1-800/955-2159; ❹) is close to downtown, while one of the best **B&Bs** is *Amor's Highwood House*, 1206 Highwood Lane (☎208/667-4735; ❹), located in a quiet residential area near the lake and also within walking distance of downtown. For **eating** out, *Las Palmitas*, 201 N 3rd St (☎208/664-0581), is a lively, moderately priced Mexican restaurant and bar set in the town's old railroad depot. Somewhat more upmarket is *Beverly's*, a top choice for seafood and meat in the *Coeur d'Alene Resort* (☎208/765-4000).

East from Coeur d'Alene on I-90

Traveling east on I-90 toward Missoula, Montana (see p.947), you pass the surprisingly good ski hill of Silver Mountain (☎208/783-1111 or 1-800/204-6428, ⓦwww.silvermt.com) at Kellogg, some forty miles from Coeur d'Alene. It has the world's longest single-stage gondola (3.1 miles), which is open year-round for fine skiing in winter ($38), and some good mountain biking ($20) and hiking ($13.95) in summer.

A further ten miles east on I-90 are the authentic Western-style streets of friendly **WALLACE**, where most of the town's buildings are listed on the National Register of Historic Buildings, and evoke strong images of its silver-mining days. See them on the 75-minute **Sierra Silver Mine Tour** that leaves from 420 N Fifth St every half-hour and is a fun trolley-car trip that takes you to the mine via the town's streets; at the mine you descend a thousand feet underground on a guided tour (summer daily 9am–4pm; $7). In town, check out the unusual *Oasis Rooms Bordello Museum*, 605 Cedar St (May–Oct daily 10am–5pm; Nov & Dec Wed–Sun noon–4.30pm; $5; ☎208/753-0801), a former brothel that has been left exactly as it was when it was raided and closed down by the FBI in 1987. **Dining** options include *The Jameson Hotel*, 304 Sixth St (☎208/556-1554), where you can enjoy lunch or dinner surrounded by vintage furnishing and decor.

Sandpoint

Forty-four miles north of Coeur d'Alene in the shadows of the spiky Selkirk Mountains, **SANDPOINT**, a buzzing little town and northern Idaho's most attractive resort, is at the northwestern end of Lake Pend Oreille (pronounced "Pon-duh-ray"). Smaller and less commercialized than Coeur d'Alene, Sandpoint's lazy downtown is brightened by **Cedar Street Bridge Public Market**, a covered mall of stalls, shops, and cafés overlooking placid Sandy Creek. At the south end of the lake, **Farragut State Park**, 13400 Ranger Rd (cars $3; ☎208/683-2425), a former naval training base, is a popular spot for hiking, camping, and the like.

Amtrak **trains** pass through early in the morning in both directions. **Accommodation** possibilities include the comfortable *Lakeside Inn*, beside the lovely white sandy beach at 106 Bridge St (☎208/263-3717 or 1-800/543-8126; ❹–❺); the *K2 Inn at Sandpoint* downtown, 501 N Fourth Ave (☎208/263-3441; ❹), with very cheap rates – if you stay six nights the seventh is free; and *Coit House*, 502 N Fourth Ave (☎208/265-4035; ❹), a tastefully restored Victorian B&B within walking distance of downtown and the lake.

The Southwest

CANADA

WASHINGTON

MONTANA · NORTH DAKOTA · MN · MI

OREGON ⑭ · ⑪ · SOUTH DAKOTA · WI · ④ · MI · VT · NH ③ · ME · NEW YORK · MA

IDAHO · WYOMING · NEBRASKA · IOWA · ② · PA · RI · CT ①

NEVADA · UTAH · COLORADO · KANSAS · IL · IN · OHIO · WV ⑤ · VA · NJ · DE · MD

⑬ CALIFORNIA · ⑫ · MISSOURI · KENTUCKY · NC

PACIFIC OCEAN · ARIZONA · NEW MEXICO · OKLAHOMA · TENNESSEE · SC · ATLANTIC OCEAN

AR · AL · ⑥ · GEORGIA

MS

MEXICO · TEXAS · ⑨ · ⑧ LA

⑮ ALASKA · HAWAII · ⑯ · Gulf of Mexico · ⑦ FL · N

AL - ALABAMA	IN - INDIANA	MN - MINNESOTA	RI - RHODE ISLAND
AR - ARKANSAS	LA - LOUISIANA	MS - MISSISSIPPI	SC - SOUTH CAROLINA
CT - CONNECTICUT	MA - MASSACHUSETTS	NC - NORTH CAROLINA	VA - VIRGINIA
DE - DELAWARE	MD - MARYLAND	NH - NEW HAMPSHIRE	VT - VERMONT
FL - FLORIDA	ME - MAINE	NJ - NEW JERSEY	WI - WISCONSIN
IL - ILLINOIS	MI - MICHIGAN	PA - PENNSYLVANIA	WV - WEST VIRGINIA

* **Santa Fe, NM** Great museums, fascinating history, atmospheric hotels – New Mexico's capital is a must on any Southwest itinerary. **See p.972**

* **The Havasupai Reservation, AZ** This little-known offshoot of the Grand Canyon remains home to its original Native American inhabitants and stunning turquoise waterfalls. **See p.1030**

* **Monument Valley, AZ** Though the eerie sandstone monoliths of Monument Valley are familiar the world over, they still take every visitor's breath away. **See p.1035**

* **Canyon de Chelly, AZ** Ruined Ancestral Puebloan "cliff dwellings" pepper every twist and turn of this stupendous sheer-walled canyon. **See p.1035**

* **Scenic Hwy-12, UT** Crossing the heart of Utah's red-rock wilderness, Hwy-12 is perhaps the most exhilarating drive in the US. **See p.1048**

* **Bellagio, Las Vegas, NV** Las Vegas's most opulent hotel must be seen to be believed, and its sumptuous buffet is the best in town. **See p.1074**

The Southwest

The four sparsely populated Southwestern desert states of **New Mexico**, **Arizona**, **Utah**, and **Nevada** are extraordinary, unforgettable, and unique. They stretch from Texas to California across an elemental landscape ranging from towering monoliths of stark red sandstone to snow-capped mountains, on a high desert plateau that repeatedly splits open to reveal yawning canyons. The raw power of the scenery, uninterrupted from horizon to horizon, is overwhelming, and is complemented by the emphatic presence of numerous Native American cultures and the palpable legacy of America's Wild West frontier.

Among the earliest inhabitants were the **Ancestral Puebloans** (the former name for them, "**Anasazi**," has now fallen into disrepute; see p.979). The remains of their cliff palaces and cities, abandoned around seven hundred years ago, are scattered throughout the region, but their direct descendants, the **Pueblo** peoples of New Mexico and the **Hopi** in Arizona, still lead much the same lifestyle, in the same general vicinity.

Less sedentary tribes, such as the **Navajo** and the **Apache**, are thought to have migrated into the Southwest from the fourteenth century onwards. They adopted local agricultural and craft techniques and appropriated vast tracts of territory, which they in turn soon had to defend against bands of European immigrants. The first such, in 1540, was a party of **Spanish** explorers led by Coronado, who spent two years searching for mythical El Dorado–style cities of gold. Sixty years later, Hispanic colonists founded the province of **New Mexico**, an ill-defined region that covered not only all of the Southwest but much of modern California and Colorado; many of the Catholic missions they established remain intact. Not until 1848 – by which time New Mexico had spent thirty years as a neglected backwater of the newly independent nation of Mexico – was the region forcibly taken over by the **United States**. Almost immediately, large numbers of outsiders began to pass through on their way to Gold Rush California.

Thereafter, increasingly violent confrontations took place between the US government and the Native Americans. The entire **Navajo** population was rounded up and forcibly removed to the barren plains of eastern New Mexico in 1864 (though they were soon allowed to return to northeastern Arizona), and the **Apache**, under warrior chiefs Cochise and Geronimo, fought extended battles with the US cavalry. Though the nominal intention was to open up Indian lands to newly American settlers, few ever succeeded in extracting a living from this harsh terrain.

One exception were the **Mormons** (or the Church of Jesus Christ of Latter-Day Saints), whose flight from religious persecution brought them by the late

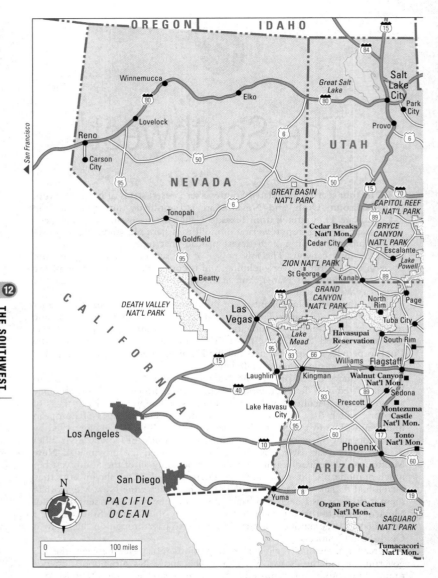

1840s to the alkaline basin of Utah's **Great Salt Lake**. Through sheer hard work, and the cooperative management of limited water resources, they established what amounted to an independent country, with outlying communities all over the Southwest. Even here they met with resistance, and until the Civil War intervened, there was a real possibility that the US might declare war on them. They still constitute seventy percent of Utah's population and maintain virtual control of the state's government.

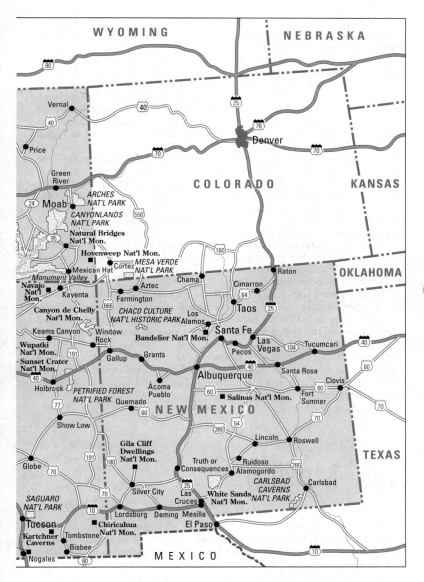

Despite their common heritage, each of the four Southwestern states remains quite distinct. New Mexico bears the most obvious traces of long-term settlement, the Native American pueblos of the north coexisting alongside towns such as Santa Fe, Albuquerque, and Taos, which clearly retain their Spanish Colonial identity. In Arizona, the history of the Wild West is more conspicuous, in towns such as **Tombstone**, site of the legendary shoot-out at the OK Corral. Over a third of the state belongs to Native American tribes, such as the

Apache, Hopi, and Navajo, most of whom live in the red-rock lands of the northeast corner, notably amid the splendor typified by the **Canyon de Chelly** and **Monument Valley**.

The canyon country of northern Arizona – even the immense **Grand Canyon** – won't prepare you for the uninhabited but compelling landscape of southern Utah, where **Zion** and **Bryce canyons** are just the best known of a string of national parks and monuments. **Moab**, poised in the east between majestic **Canyonlands** and the surreal **Arches**, has become a top destination for youthful outdoors enthusiasts. Nevada, on the other hand, is nothing short of desolate; gamblers are lured in the millions by the bright lights of **Las Vegas**, but away from the casinos there's little to see or do.

You can count on warm sunshine anywhere in the Southwest for nine months of the year, with incredible sunsets most evenings. Summer is the peak tourist season, for no good reason – air temperatures topping 100°F can make outdoor life unbearable, while in late summer awesome thunderstorms sweep in without warning, causing flash floods and forest fires. By October, perhaps the best time to come, the crowds are gone and in the mountains and canyons the leaves turn red and gold. Winter brings snow to higher elevations – there's excellent skiing in **northern Utah** and in the **Sangre de Cristo Mountains** of New Mexico – while spring sees wild flowers bloom in otherwise barren desert. Note that the climate varies sharply according to elevation, with mountains often 30°F cooler than the plains.

More than almost anywhere in the US, the backcountry wildernesses of the Southwest are ideal for (well-planned) **camping** and backpacking expeditions. It's vital to be prepared for the harshness of the desert: always carry water, and if you venture off the beaten track let someone know where you're going and when you'll return.

Unless you have your own vehicle, many of the most fascinating corners of the region are utterly inaccessible. Scheduled public **transportation** runs almost exclusively between the big cities – which are not at all where you should aim to spend your time.

New Mexico

Settled in turn by Native Americans, Spaniards, Mexicans, and Yankees, **NEW MEXICO** is among the most ethnically and culturally diverse of all the states in the US. Each successive group has built upon the legacy of its predecessors; their histories and achievements are intertwined, and in some ways the late-coming white Americans from the north and east have had comparatively little impact. Signs of the region's rich heritage are everywhere, from ancient pictographs and cliff dwellings to the design of the state's license plates, taken from a **Zia** symbol for the sun – the one near-constant fact of life in this arid land.

New Mexico's indigenous peoples – especially the **Pueblo Indians**, clear descendants of the **Ancestral Puebloans**, as the name suggests – provide a sense of cultural continuity. After the **Pueblo Revolt** of 1680 had forced a temporary Spanish withdrawal into Mexico, the missionary endeavor here was less brutal than elsewhere. The proselytizing padres co-opted the natives without destroying their traditional ways of life, as local deities and celebrations were incorporated into Catholic practice. Somewhat bizarrely to outsiders, grand churches still dominate many Pueblo settlements, often adjacent to the underground ceremonial chambers known as *kivas*, and almost always built in the local adobe style.

The Americans who took over from the Mexicans in 1848 saw New Mexico as a useless wasteland. But for a few mining booms and range wars – such as the Lincoln County War, which brought **Billy the Kid** to fame (see p.998) – New Mexico was left relatively undisturbed until it finally became a state in 1912. During World War II, it was the base of operations for the top-secret **Manhattan Project**, which built and detonated the first atomic bomb, and since then it has been home to America's premier weapons research outposts. By and large, people here work close to the land – mining, farming, and ranching – with tourism increasingly underpinning the economy.

Northern New Mexico centers on the magnificent landscapes of the **Rio Grande Valley**, which contains its two finest cities: **Santa Fe**, the adobe-fronted capital, and the artists' colony and winter resort of **Taos**, with its nearby pueblo. More than a dozen **Pueblo** villages can be found in the mountainous area between the two, while to the west lie the ancient ruins at **Bandelier** and **Puyé**. The broad swath of **central New Mexico** along I-40 – the interstate that succeeded the old **Route 66** – pivots around the state's biggest city, **Albuquerque**, with the extraordinary mesa-top Pueblo village of **Ácoma** ("Sky City") an hour's drive west. In wild, wide-open **southern New Mexico**, the deep **Carlsbad Caverns** are the main attraction, while you can still stumble upon old mining and cattle-ranching towns that have somehow hung on since the end of the Wild West.

For many visitors, the defining feature of New Mexico is its **adobe architecture**, as seen on homes, churches, and even shopping malls and motels. Adobe bricks are a sun-baked mixture of earth, sand, charcoal, and chopped grass or straw, set with a mortar of similar composition, and then plastered over with mud and straw. The color of the soil used dictates that of the final building, and thus subtle variations are seen all across the state. However, adobe is a far from convenient material: it needs replastering every few years and turns to mud when water seeps up from the ground, so many buildings have to be sporadically raised and bolstered by the insertion of rocks at their base. These days, most of what looks like adobe is actually painted cement or concrete, but even this looks attractive enough in its own semi-kitsch way, and hunting out such superb genuine adobes as the remote **Santuario de Chimayó** on the "**High Road**" between Taos and Santa Fe, the formidable church of **San Francisco de Asis** in Ranchos de Taos, or the multi-tiered dwellings of **Taos Pueblo**, can provide the focus of an enjoyable New Mexico tour.

You'll also become familiar with another New Mexico trademark, the bright-red *ristras*, or strings of dried **chili peppers**, that adorn doorways throughout the state; festooned on restaurant entrances, they serve as warnings of the fiery delights that await within.

Getting around New Mexico

Public transportation is rare in New Mexico; Santa Fe, for example, does not have a rail service. Amtrak **trains** do, however, pass through Albuquerque, pit stop for transcontinental Greyhound **buses** and site of the only major **airport** – linked by shuttle services with the rest of the state. Texas's **El Paso** (see p.801) is a more convenient transportation hub for Carlsbad. A few companies offer guided **coach tours** in the Santa Fe and Taos area, but as usual it's best to get around by **car**.

Northern New Mexico

The mountainous north is the New Mexico of popular imagination, with its pastel colors, vivid desert landscape, and adobe architecture. Even **Santa Fe**, the one real city, is hardly metropolitan in scale, holding well under 100,000 residents, and the narrow streets of its small, historic center, though thronged with tourists, retain the feel of bygone days. Ranging along the headwaters of the Rio Grande 75 miles northeast, the amiable frontier town of **Taos** – immortalized by Georgia O'Keeffe and D.H. Lawrence – is remarkable chiefly for the stacked dwellings of neighboring **Taos Pueblo**.

An hour's drive west from Taos or Santa Fe brings you to **Bandelier National Monument**, where ancient cliff dwellings were carved out of the same forested volcanic plateau that now holds the eerie **Los Alamos National Weapons Laboratory**. Alternatively, the hills to the east of the Rio Grande hold a succession of characterful Hispanic hamlets, strung along a scenic mountain highway known as the **High Road**.

Santa Fe

For the last twenty or so years, **SANTA FE** has ranked among the chic-est destinations in the US, repeatedly voted the country's most popular city by upmarket travelers. That appeal rests on a very solid basis: it's one of America's oldest and most beautiful cities, founded by Spanish missionaries a decade before the Pilgrims reached Plymouth Rock. Spread across a high plateau at the foot of the stunning Sangre de Cristo Mountains, New Mexico's capital still glories in the adobe houses and Baroque churches of its original architects, while its newer museums and galleries attract art-lovers from all over the world.

As upward of a million and a half tourists every year descend upon a town of just sixty thousand inhabitants, Santa Fe has inevitably grown somewhat overblown; long-term residents bemoan what's been lost, while first-time visitors are inclined to wonder what all the fuss is about. The urban sprawl as you approach from the interstate makes for a lousy introduction, while the rigorous insistence that every downtown building should look like a seventeenth-century Spanish Colonial palace takes a bit of getting used to. This is the only city in the world where what at first glance appears to be a perfectly preserved ancient adobe turns out to be a highrise parking lot, and where it would be illegal to build a gas station that didn't resemble an Indian prayer chamber.

There's still a lot to like about Santa Fe, however, with its compact, peaceful downtown and walkable streets. Though Santa Fe style may have become something of a cliché, that cliché is changing: the pastel-painted, wooden coyotes that were the obligatory souvenir a dozen years ago have, for example, been replaced by cast-iron sculptures of Kokopelli, the hunch-backed Ancestral Puebloan flute-player. In a town where the *Yellow Pages* list over 250 art galleries, you'll get plenty of opportunities to buy one.

Arrival, information, and getting around

Despite its fame, Santa Fe is well off the beaten track. Most out-of-state visitors fly into Albuquerque, and either rent a vehicle at the airport for the hour's drive up to Santa Fe, or catch a shuttle van for around $25 with either Santa Fe Shuttle (☏505/243-2300 or 1-888/833-2300, ⓦwww.santafeshuttle.com) or Twin Hearts Express (☏505/751-1201 or 1-800/654-9456, ⓦwww.twin-heartsexpress.com). **Buses** from all over the Southwest to the Greyhound

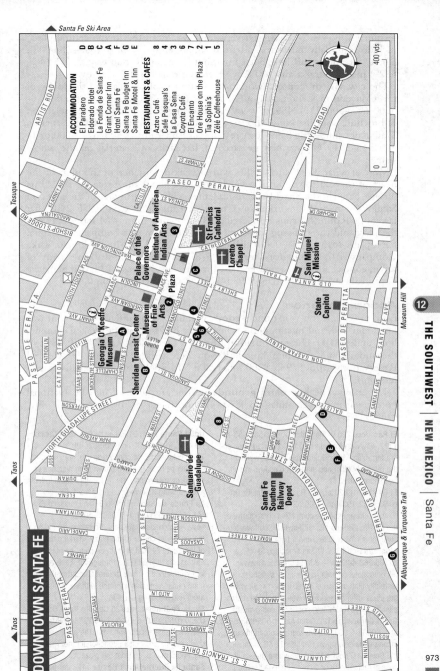

DOWNTOWN SANTA FE

▲ Santa Fe Ski Area

▲ Tesuque

▲ Taos

▲ Taos

▲ Museum Hill

▲ Albuquerque & Turquoise Trail

N

400 yds

ACCOMMODATION
El Paradero   D
Eldorado Hotel   B
La Fonda de Santa Fe C
Grant Corner Inn   A
Hotel Santa Fe   F
Santa Fe Budget Inn G
Santa Fe Motel & Inn E

RESTAURANTS & CAFÉS
Aztec Café   8
Café Pasqual's   4
La Casa Sena   3
Coyote Café   6
El Encanto   7
Ore House on the Plaza 2
Tia Sophia's   1
Zélé Coffeehouse   5

Georgia O'Keeffe Museum

Sheridan Transit Center

Museum of Fine Arts

Palace of the Governors

Institute of American Indian Arts

Plaza

St Francis Cathedral

Loretto Chapel

San Miguel Mission

State Capitol

Santuario de Guadalupe

Santa Fe Southern Railway Depot

terminal at 858 St Michael's Drive, a long way from the town's central plaza, include four daily buses to and from Albuquerque ($13; ☎505/471-0008). There's no direct **rail** link, but Lamy Shuttle vans ($10 one way; ☎505/982-8829) meet Amtrak trains to Lamy, seventeen miles to the southeast.

The city **visitor center**, two blocks northwest of the plaza in the lobby of the Convention Center, 201 W Marcy St (Mon–Fri 8am–5pm; ☎505/955-6200 or 1-800/777-2489, ⊛www.santafe.org), stocks a very limited selection of brochures, but the New Mexico Department of Tourism, 491 Old Santa Fe Trail (daily: June–Aug 8am–7pm; rest of year 8am–5pm; ☎505/827-4000 or 1-800/545-2040, ⊛www.newmexico.org), has racks of material on the whole state.

Most of what there is to see lies within walking distance of the plaza at the heart of the old town, but it's worth knowing about the Santa Fe Trails **bus** service, based at the Sheridan Transit Center, a block northwest of the plaza on Sandoval Street (Mon–Fri 6am–11pm, Sat 8am–8pm; ☎505/955-2001; flat fare 50¢). Route #2 runs up Cerrillos Road, while route #M loops between the plaza and the outlying museums. Santa Fe's only **taxi** company is Capital City Cabs (☎505/438-0000); **bikes** can be rented at Sun Mountain Bike Company, 107 Washington Ave (☎505/820-2902). For a **walking tour** of town, contact Afoot in Santa Fe, based in the *Inn at Loretto*, 211 Old Santa Fe Trail (daily 9.30am; $10; ☎505/983-3701, Ⓔxoporter@earthlink.net).

Accommodation

Even in winter, you won't find a **room** within walking distance of downtown for under $60, and in summer – when every bed is frequently taken – there's little under $100. The main road in from I-25, Cerrillos Road, holds most of the motels and the one hostel. If you get stuck, call Santa Fe Central Reservations (☎505/983-8200 or 1-800/776-7669, ⊛www.santafecentral-res.com).

The most appealing **campgrounds** nearby are in the Santa Fe National Forest, starting seven miles up Hwy-475, northeast of town (summer only; ☎505/753-7331).

El Paradero 220 W Manhattan Ave ☎505/988-1177, ⊛www.elparadero.com. Converted Spanish-era farmhouse near Guadalupe Street. Twelve of the relatively plain and simple rooms are en suite, two share baths. ❹

El Rey Inn 1862 Cerrillos Rd at St Michael's Drive ☎505/982-1931 or 1-800/521-1349, ⊛www.elreyinnsantafe.com. Most characterful of the Cerrillos Rd motels, with stylish Southwestern-style rooms, nice suites, and a pool. ❹

Eldorado Hotel 309 W San Francisco St ☎505/988-4455 or 1-800/955-4455, ⊛www.eldoradohotel.com. Consummately stylish, tastefully tiled upmarket hotel, a short walk west of the plaza, offering spacious well-appointed rooms, plus a rooftop swimming pool, spa, and gym. ❾

Grant Corner Inn 122 Grant Ave ☎505/983-6678 or 1-800/964-9003, ⊛www.grantcornerinn.com. Incongruous downtown clapboard B&B, alongside the Georgia O'Keeffe Museum, where guests enjoy considerable luxury and lavish breakfasts. Not all rooms are en suite. ❻

Hotel Santa Fe 1501 Paseo de Peralta at Cerrillos Rd ☎505/982-1200 or 1-800/825-9876, ⊛www.hotelsantafe.com. Attractive, very comfortable adobe hotel (just) within walking distance of the plaza, owned and run by Picuris Pueblo Indians and featuring its own good restaurant. ❻

La Fonda de Santa Fe 100 E San Francisco St ☎505/982-5511 or 1-800/523-5002, ⊛www.lafondasantafe.com. Gorgeous old inn on the southeast corner of the plaza. Marking the end of the Santa Fe Trail, it features hand-painted murals and stained glass throughout. Each opulently furnished room is different, and there's a good restaurant, plus a lounge with live entertainment and a rooftop bar. ❾

Santa Fe Budget Inn 725 Cerrillos Rd at Don Diego ☎505/982-5952 or 1-800/288-7600, ⊛www.santafebudgetinn.com. The most central chain motel; large, clean, functional if not inspiring, and a mile or so from the plaza. ❹

Santa Fe International Hostel 1412 Cerrillos Rd at Alta Vista ☎505/988-1153. Antiquated HI-AYH hostel, housed in a ramshackle motel a couple of miles out of the city, which can be damp and cold in winter. Dorm beds for $16, private rooms for $35 single, $45 double. ❶/❷

Santa Fe Motel & Inn 510 Cerrillos Rd at Paseo de Peralta ☎505/982-1039 or 1-800/930-5002, ⊛www.santafemotelinn.com. Small, quiet, pleas-

ant adobe motel near downtown. No connection to the *Hotel Santa Fe* next door. ❺

Silver Saddle 2810 Cerrillos Rd at Siler ☎505/471-7663, ⊛www.motelsantafe.com. Busy, down-to-earth, but surprisingly characterful motel, well out from downtown. ❸

Downtown Santa Fe: around the plaza

Santa Fe's old central **plaza** is still the focus of town life, especially during the annual **Indian Market** on the weekend after the third Thursday in August, when buyers and craftspeople come from all over the world, and during the Labor Day weekend for the **Fiestas de Santa Fe**. Apart from an influx of art galleries and stylish restaurants, the web of narrow streets around the plaza has changed little through the centuries. When the Yankees took over in 1848, they neglected the adobes and chose instead to build in wood, but many of the finer adobe houses have survived. Since a preservation campaign in the 1930s, almost every non-adobe structure within sight of the plaza has been designed or redecorated to suit the city-mandated Pueblo Revival mode, with rounded, mud-colored plaster walls supporting roof beams made of thick pine logs. Santa Fe today, in fact – at least at its core – looks much more like its original Spanish self than it did a hundred years ago.

The **Palace of the Governors** fills the entire northern side of the plaza. Part of the Museum of New Mexico (see box, overleaf), this low-slung and initially unprepossessing structure is actually the oldest public building in the US. Originally sod-roofed, it was constructed in 1610 as the headquarters of Spanish Colonial administration; the name may now seem misleadingly grand, but the building was once much larger. Until 1913, the palace itself looked like a typical, formal, territorial building, with a square tower at each corner; its subsequent adobe "reconstruction" was based on pure conjecture. The well-preserved interior, organized around an open-air courtyard, holds excellent displays on the history of Hispanic New Mexico, as well as a sensational collection of art of Ancient America, and a well-stocked bookstore. The arcaded adobe veranda along its front, offering protection from both sun and wind, serves as a market for local Native American crafts-sellers.

Just west of the palace, the **Museum of Fine Arts** is housed in a particularly attractive adobe, with ornamental beams and a cool central courtyard, and focuses on changing exhibits of contemporary painting and sculpture by mostly local artists. Of greater appeal to most visitors is the showpiece **Georgia O'Keeffe Museum**, a block northwest at 217 Johnson St (July–Oct Mon–Thurs, Sat & Sun 10am–5pm, Fri 10am–8pm; Nov–March closed Wed; $8, free Fri 5–8pm; under-16 free; ☎505/946-1000, ⊛www.okeeffemuseum.org). This boasts the largest collection of O'Keeffes in the world, including many of the desert landscapes she painted near **Abiquiu**, forty miles northwest of Santa Fe, where she lived from 1946 until her death in 1986. In its permanent collection, housed in its first two galleries, some less familiar New York cityscapes make a surprising contrast to the sun-bleached skulls and iconic flowers, as sold in print galleries throughout the Southwest. However, most of the museum is given over to touring exhibitions devoted to differing aspects of O'Keeffe's work, typically on show for three to four months, so there's little guarantee as to which precise pieces may be displayed at any one time.

Across the tiny Santa Fe River to the southwest, three blocks along Guadalupe Street, you'll find a less celebrated but equally attractive little district, centered around the small **Santuario de Guadalupe** (May–Oct

The Museum of New Mexico

A **combination ticket**, costing $15 and valid for four days, grants admission to the four leading Santa Fe museums that jointly constitute the **Museum of New Mexico** – the Palace of the Governors, the Museum of Fine Arts, the Museum of Indian Arts and Culture, and the Museum of International Folk Art. All otherwise charge $7 admission, and are open daily except Mondays between 10am and 5pm, and also between 5pm and 8pm on Fridays, when admission is free. At publication time, the ticket also covered the new Museum of Spanish Colonial Art, but that introductory offer was expected to expire at some point in the near future. The Georgia O'Keeffe Museum, however, is not included. For more information, contact ☎505/476-5100 or check ⓦ www.museumofnewmexico.org.

Mon–Sat 9am–4pm; Nov–April Mon–Fri 9am–4pm; donation). Complete with a fine Baroque reredos (altarpiece), the shrine was built at the end of the eighteenth century to mark the end of the **Camino Real** highway from Mexico City. Old warehouses and small factory premises nearby, such as the **Sanbusco Centre** on Montezuma Avenue, have been converted to house boutiques, art galleries, and restaurants.

Follow the river upstream, or walk two blocks east from the plaza, and you approach **St Francis Cathedral**, looming at the top of San Francisco Street. The first church west of the Mississippi to be designated a cathedral, it was commissioned in 1869 in the formal – and, frankly, dreary – Romanesque style popular in France by **Archbishop Lamy**, the French-educated title figure in Willa Cather's novel *Death Comes for the Archbishop*. The nearby **Loretto Chapel**, a block away at the start of the Old Santa Fe Trail, is known for its so-called "Miraculous Staircase," an elegant spiral built without nails or obvious means of support (winter Mon–Sat 9am–5pm, Sun 10.30am–5pm; summer Mon–Sat 9am–6pm, Sun 10.30am–5pm; $2.50, under-7 free). During construction, the church's designer is said to have been killed by Lamy's cousin, so that for years there was no way up to the choir loft. According to legend, an unknown carpenter arrived in answer to the nuns' prayers, built the stairs, and then disappeared.

Two blocks south, across the river along the Old Santa Fe Trail, is the ancient **San Miguel Mission** (Mon–Sat 9am–5pm, Sun 1.30–4pm; $1). Only a few of the massive adobe internal walls survive from the original 1610 building, most of which was destroyed in the 1680 Pueblo Revolt. The chapel is the heart of the old **Barrio de Analco** workers' district, whose many two-hundred-year-old houses now form one of Santa Fe's most appealing residential neighborhoods.

Not far away to the east, gallery-lined **Canyon Road** – which stakes a claim to being the oldest street in the US, dating from Pueblo days – climbs a steady but shallow incline along the riverbed and is lined by dozens of fine adobes.

The outlying museums

On a slightly raised plateau two miles southeast of the town center, with extensive views of the hills and mountains that almost entirely surround the city, stands Santa Fe's other concentration of museums, reachable by Santa Fe Trails bus #10. The delightful **Museum of International Folk Art**, part of the Museum of New Mexico, focuses on a huge collection of clay figurines and models from around the world, arranged in colorful dioramas that include a Pueblo Feast Day with dancing *kachinas* and camera-clicking tourists. The Hispanic Heritage Wing is an engaging reminder of just how close New

Mexico's ties have always been with Mexico itself, while the museum's gift shop sells some unusual ethnic souvenirs. The **Museum of Indian Arts and Culture**, across the attractively landscaped plaza and also part of the Museum of New Mexico, holds a superb array of Native American pottery, ranging from **Ancestral Puebloan** pieces right up to the works of twentieth-century revivalists, and covers contemporary Southwestern cultures in fascinating detail.

In the same complex, the **Museum of Spanish Colonial Art** opened in 2002 to display traditional Hispanic religious artworks, such as the *santos* (naïve painted images) and *bultos* (carved wooden statues of saints) that are so pervasive in the iconography of Santa Fe (daily except Mon 10am–5pm; $6, under-16 free; ☏505/982-2226, Ⓦ www.spanishcolonial.org). Although the museum makes a valiant attempt toward placing Colonial art in a global context, as yet it adds little to the stronger displays in the neighboring folk art museum.

Fifteen miles southwest of the city, three miles from exit 276 off I-25, the **Rancho de las Golondrinas** (June–Sept Wed–Sun 10am–4pm; guided tours available by reservation, also in April, May & Oct; $5; ☏505/471-2261, Ⓦ www.golondrinas.org) preserves the eighteenth-century "Ranch of the Swallows." As well as the main adobe farmstead, once a fortified outpost on the Camino Real, this living-history complex includes a water mill, a Penitente chapel, and several other early Hispanic structures – and it's also a lovely spot in its own right.

Eating

Santa Fe has been renowned as a culinary hot spot since the 1980s, when a stupendous feat of marketing managed to make dishes such as banana-crusted sea bass seem quintessentially Southwestern, and is now said to have more quality **restaurants** per head than any other US city. Even if you don't pay the wallet-busting prices of the big-name attractions, there's some memorable dining to be had, and the sheer inventiveness of the city's menus makes up for its lack of interesting ethnic alternatives.

Aztec Café 317 Aztec St ☏505/820-0025.
Counterculture hangout off Galisteo Street, offering a travelers' notice board and a nice patio, plus coffees, pastries, light meals, and live music.

Café Pasqual's 121 Don Gaspar Ave ☏505/983-9340. Lovely, very lively Old/New Mexican restaurant, serving top-quality food (including breakfast) in an attractive tiled dining room a block south of the plaza. Entrees include chicken *mole enchiladas* ($19) and black mussels steamed with lemongrass ($24); as an appetizer, try the delicious Pigs and Figs salad, made with bacon, figs, and mozzarella ($13).

Coyote Café 132 W Water St ☏505/983-1615.
Celebrity chef Mark Miller's showcase restaurant, just off the plaza. The *à la carte* prices can be ferocious, with entrees like fried red-banana-crusted sea bass or cumin-roasted duck breast at $25–32, but at times they also serve a *prix-fixe* set dinner for around $40. For a cheaper taste, try the rooftop café.

El Encanto 416 Agua Fria ☏505/988-5991.
Stylish Mexican restaurant offering both casual and fine dining in the former convent of the Santuario de Guadalupe. The main specialty is *botanas*, the Mexican equivalent of *tapas*, while $13–20 entrees include a delicious foil-wrapped tuna steak with olives and capers. Closed Sun.

La Casa Sena 125 E Palace Ave ☏505/988-9232. Charming courtyard restaurant, a block from the plaza; zestful Southwestern lunches, with entrees around $10, are the best deal, though the $42 set dinners are consistently good. *La Cantina*, adjoining, is a little cheaper and its staff perform Broadway show songs as they work.

La Plazuela *La Fonda de Santa Fe*, 100 E San Francisco St ☏505/982-5511. Delightful, beautifully decorated Mexican restaurant in the heart of *La Fonda* inn, open daily for all meals, and with an open-air feel despite the glass ceiling. All the usual Mexican dishes are on offer at reasonable prices, and the cooking is well above average.

Mu du noodles 1494 Cerrillos Rd ☎505/983-1411. Largely but not exclusively vegetarian place, near the hostel. Its pan-Asian menu may not always be authentic, but it's still tasty. Dinner only, closed Sun.
Ore House on the Plaza 50 Lincoln Ave ☎505/983-8687. "Nueva Latina" restaurant, where the menu ranges from $5 green-chili stews to elaborate $28 dinner entrees, and the location on the plaza, complete with *ristra*-garlanded balcony, is unbeatable.

Tia Sophia's 210 W San Francisco St ☎505/983-9880. Spicy, very inexpensive Mexican diner west of the plaza that's a huge hit with lunching locals. Daily except Mon 7am–2pm.
Zélé Coffeehouse 201 Galisteo St ☎505/982-7835 Roomy downtown coffeehouse serving pastries, omelets, sandwiches, and killer granola, plus great juices and smoothies, with some sidewalk seating as well.

Nightlife and entertainment

Santa Fe has the range of **nightlife** you'd expect in a small city rather than a major metropolis, though its cultural scene livens up in summer. For full listings of what's going on, check the free weekly *Reporter* or the "Pasatiempo" section of Friday's *New Mexican*. Year-round, musical and theatrical performances – by touring artists as well as local groups – are hosted in downtown Santa Fe at the **Lensic Performing Arts Center**, a strikingly converted former movie theater at 211 W San Francisco St (☎505/988-7050). The much-anticipated Santa Fe Opera season runs from late June through August in a magnificent renovated amphitheater seven miles north of town (☎505/986-5900 or 1-800/280-4654, ⓦwww.santafeopera.org).

Some of the most atmospheric places to **drink** in town are in the old hotels – the downstairs lounge and rooftop bar of *La Fonda* on the plaza spring to mind (see p.974) – but otherwise conventional bars are surprisingly few and far between.

Catamount Bar 125 E Water St ☎505/988-7222. Downtown bar with plenty of microbrews on tap, and live rock or blues most nights.
Cowgirl Hall of Fame 319 S Guadalupe St ☎505/982-2565. Very busy country-and-western-themed restaurant and bar, with regular live music.
The Dragon Room *Pink Adobe*, 406 Old Santa Fe Trail ☎505/983-7712. Classy, atmospheric bar inside a romantic 300-year-old adobe restaurant facing the San Miguel Mission, with eccentric decor and an eclectic mix of regulars.

El Farol 808 Canyon Rd ☎505/983-9912. Historic bar-cum-restaurant that serves Spanish *tapas* to musical accompaniment from blues to flamenco.
Evangelo's 200 W San Francisco St ☎505/982-9014. The only good bare-bones bar in easy walking range of the plaza, with a pool table, a jukebox, and occasional live music.
The Paramount and Bar B 331 Sandoval St ☎505/982-8999. Cool, glamorous former restaurant that's become Santa Fe's premier venue for clubbing and alternative live music; the smaller *Bar B* programs its own specialized events.

Bandelier National Monument

Cut into the forested mesas of the Pajarito Plateau, 35 miles northwest of Santa Fe, the cliff dwellings and Ancestral Puebloan ruins of **Bandelier National Monument** ($10 per vehicle) are spread across fifty square miles of pine woods and deep stream-cut gorges. Named after archeologist Adolph Bandelier, who publicized the place in the 1880s, the ruins date from around 1300 AD, at the very end of the Ancestral Puebloan period (see box, opposite). Various itinerant groups, seeking sanctuary from drought and invasion, gathered here to build a community that amalgamated their assorted cultures. At the end of the narrow switchbacking road down from Hwy-4, the **visitor center** provides an excellent overview of the site (daily: summer 8am–6pm; rest of year 8am–4.30pm; ☎505/672-3861, ⓦwww.nps.gov/band).

The first stop along the paved 1.5-mile trail beyond, looping through **Frijoles Canyon**, is **Tyuonyi**, a circular, multistory village of which only the

The Ancestral Puebloans

Few visitors to the Southwest are prepared for the awesome scale and beauty of the desert cities and cliff palaces left by the **Ancestral Puebloans**, as seen all over the high plateaus of the "**Four Corners**" district, where Colorado, New Mexico, Arizona, and Utah now meet.

The earliest humans reached the Southwest around 10,000 BC, but the Ancestral Puebloans first appeared as the **Basketmakers**, near the San Juan River, more like two thousand years ago. Named for their woven sandals and bowls, they lived in pits in the earth, roofed with logs and mud. Over time, the Ancestral Puebloans adopted an increasingly settled lifestyle, becoming expert farmers and potters. Their first freestanding houses on the plains were followed by multistoried **pueblos**, in which hundreds of families lived in complexes of contiguous "apartments." The astonishing **cliff dwellings**, perched on precarious ledges high above remote canyons, which they began to build around 1100 AD, were the first Ancestral Puebloan settlements to show signs of defensive fortifications. Competition for scarce resources became even fiercer toward the end of the thirteenth century, and recent research suggests that warfare and even cannibalism played a role in their ultimate dispersal. Moving eastward, they joined forces with other displaced groups in a coming-together that eventually produced the modern **Pueblo Indians**. Hence the recent change of name, away from "Anasazi," a Navajo word meaning "ancient enemies," in favor of "Ancestral Puebloan."

Among the most significant **Ancestral Puebloan sites** are:

Mesa Verde Magnificent cliff palaces, high in the canyons of Colorado; see p.914.

Bandelier National Monument Large riverside pueblos, and cave-like homes hollowed from volcanic rock; see opposite.

Chaco Canyon The largest and most sophisticated freestanding pueblos, far out in the desert; see p.994.

Wupatki Several small pueblo communities, built by assorted tribal groups; see p.1020.

Walnut Canyon Numerous canyon-wall houses above lush Walnut Creek; see p.1020.

Betatakin Canyon-side community set in a vast rocky alcove in the Navajo National Monument; see p.1034.

Canyon de Chelly Superbly dramatic cliff dwellings in glowing sandstone canyon; now owned and farmed by the Navajo; see p.1035.

Hovenweep Enigmatic towers poised above a canyon; see p.1059.

---

ground floor and foundations survive. A side path leads up to dozens of **cave dwellings**, their rounded chambers scooped out of the soft volcanic rock; you can scramble up to, and even enter, some of them, to peer out across the valley. The main trail continues to the **Long House**, an 800-foot series of two- and three-story houses built side by side against the canyon wall. Though most of the upper stories have collapsed, you can still see the holes that held the roof beams, and the rows of petroglyphs carved above them. Half a mile beyond that, protected by a rock overhang 150ft above the canyon floor, a reconstructed *kiva* sits in **Ceremonial Cave**. To reach it you have to climb a succession of rickety ladders and steep stairs cut into the crumbly rock.

Los Alamos

If you approach Bandelier from the east, you'll pass **Los Alamos National Laboratory**, the main US center for the research and development of **nuclear**

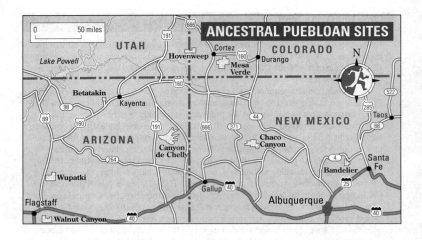

weapons (as well as neurobiology, computer science, and solar and geothermal energy). Virtually all the work at this, one of the foremost scientific research establishments in the world, is military-based, and consequently most of the complex is off limits – the small and over-simplified **Bradbury Science Museum** (Tues–Fri 9am–5pm, Sat–Mon 1–5pm; free) is the only part you can visit. What's both remarkable and unnerving about the place is that the people who work here seem oblivious to the fact that not everybody has learned to love the Bomb. The local radio station is called KBOM, and museum guides glow with excitement as they describe their weapons' devastating power.

From Santa Fe to Taos: the pueblos

The quickest route between Santa Fe and Taos follows US-84 as far as the Rio Grande, then continues northeast along the river on Hwy-68 – not that the switch from one to the other, at **Española**, is discernible to the naked eye. US-84 passes through the heartland of the **northern pueblos**, a cluster of tiny Tewa-speaking communities that have survived for over five centuries.

To reach the most beautifully sited village, leave US-84 at **Pojoaque**, twelve miles north of Santa Fe, and head east, uphill, for five miles. Apart from a large *kiva*, not much remains in **NAMBE PUEBLO**'s old plaza area, but the triple-decker **Nambe Falls**, another four miles on, are well worth seeing (daily: March, Sept & Oct 7am–7pm; April & May 7am–8pm; June–Aug 6am–8pm; $5, plus $10 camera permit). There's riverside **camping** below the falls (March–Sept only; $20).

The main reason to visit **SANTA CLARA PUEBLO** – five miles north of Pojoaque and the same distance west of the largest town along US-84, Española – is to see the ancestral home of its people: the dramatic **Puyé Cliff Dwellings** in Santa Clara Canyon, an eleven-mile drive on paved roads west of the pueblo. Be sure to **call ahead** on ☎505/753-7330 before you plan to visit, however, as the site was closed indefinitely, following recent forest fires, as this book went to press.

Like the similar ruins at Bandelier (see p.978), the ancient community of **Puyé** was set against the south-facing cliffs at the edge of the Pajarito Plateau and was occupied between 1250 and 1550. Two tiers of "apartments" were

The first Spaniards to explore what's now New Mexico were greeted by a settled population of around a hundred thousand people, living in perhaps a hundred villages and towns. However, the people the Spaniards named the **Pueblo Indians** (*pueblo* is Spanish for "village") soon grew to resent the imposition of Catholicism and the virtual enslavement of Pueblo laborers. In the **Pueblo Revolt** of 1680, the various tribes banded together and ousted the entire Colonial regime, killing scores of priests and soldiers and sending hundreds more south to Mexico. After the Spanish returned in 1693, the Pueblos showed little further resistance, and they have coexisted surprisingly amicably ever since, accepting aspects of Catholicism – most pueblos have a large adobe church at their core – without giving up their traditional beliefs and practices.

New Mexico is now home to around forty thousand Pueblo Indians, with each of its nineteen autonomous pueblos having its own laws and system of government. All have been modernized to some extent, and the recent explosion of Native American gaming has seen many open their own **casinos**, at sites usually located along the major highways well away from the residential areas. However, all also proudly retain the "Old Ways." Saints' days, major Catholic holidays such as Easter and the Epiphany, and even the Fourth of July, are celebrated with a combination of Native American traditions and Catholic rituals, featuring elaborately costumed dances and massive communal feasts.

Most pueblos are not the tourist attractions they're often touted to be. The best known, **Taos** and **Ácoma**, retain their ancient defensive architecture, but the rest tend to be dusty adobe hamlets scattered around a windblown plaza. Unless you arrive on a feast day, or are a knowledgeable shopper in search of Pueblo crafts (most pueblos have their own specialties), visits are liable to prove disappointing. In addition, you'll certainly be made to feel unwelcome if you fail to behave respectfully – don't go "exploring" places that are off limits to outsiders, such as shrines, *kivas*, or private homes.

Fifteen of the pueblos are concentrated along the Rio Grande north of Albuquerque, with a longstanding division between the seven **southern pueblos**, south of Santa Fe, most of which speak Keresan, and the group to the north, which mostly speak Tewa (pronounced *tay-wah*) and jointly promote themselves as the **Eight Northern Indian Pueblos** (☏505/852-4265 or 1-800/793-4955, ⊛www.8northern.org). Visitors to each are required to register at a visitor center; some charge an admission fee of $3 to $10, and all charge additional fees of up to $25 for still photography, $15–50 for video cameras, and up to $100 for sketching. There's no extra charge for feast days or dances, but photography is often forbidden on special occasions.

hollowed into the upper canyon wall, while a large freestanding pueblo occupied the mesa-top just above. The trail up from the visitor center is easy at first, but eventually involves climbing at least one steep ladder, plus some deeply worn "staircases" in the rock. What seem like cozy little cave dwellings were originally interior rooms in larger complexes; each was fronted by several adobe-walled rooms, as the countless holes that once supported roof-beams now testify.

The High Road

The satisfying if circuitous drive along the "**High Road**" enables you to combine a tour of the Pueblo region with the trip from Santa Fe to Taos. Leaving US-68/84 a dozen miles north of Santa Fe, near Nambe Pueblo, it leads high into the pines and aspens of the **Sangre de Cristo Mountains**, passing a number of pueblos as well as several timeless Hispanic villages. Dotted with isolated tin-roofed shacks and barns, these hills are said to be the heartland of the secretive **Penitentes**, fanatical Catholics who, in the nineteenth century, were renowned for forming Lenten processions along the ridges, flagellating themselves with yucca whips while chanting prayers.

Chimayó

The quaint mountain village of **CHIMAYÓ**, 25 miles north of Santa Fe at the junction of Hwy-503 and Hwy-76, is the site of New Mexico's most famous Spanish Colonial church, the 1816 **Santuario de Chimayó** (daily: May–Sept 9am–6pm; Oct–April 9am–4pm). Known as the "Lourdes of America" for the devotion of its many pilgrims, this round-shouldered, twin-towered adobe beauty squats behind an enclosed courtyard; a pit in the floor of a small room to one side holds the "holy dirt" for which the site is venerated. A smaller and more ramshackle chapel nearby contains a diminutive statue of Santo Niño, the Lost Child – more of a doll, if truth be told – to whom expectant mothers bring gifts such as tiny pairs of shoes.

Two properties make Chimayó an appealing overnight destination. The *Rancho de Chimayó*, Hwy-503 (closed Mon Nov–April; ℡505/351-4444), must be the best traditional New Mexican **restaurant** in the state, serving superb *flautas* and a mouthwatering sopaipilla, stuffed with meat and chiles, on a lovely sun-drenched outdoor patio. On the edge of town, *Casa Escondida* (PO Box 142, Chimayó, NM 87522; ℡505/351-4805 or 1-800/643-7201, Ⓦ www.casaescondida.com; ❹) is a very tasteful **B&B**, where each of the eight comfortable rooms has its own private bathroom.

Taos

Still home to one of the longest-established Native American populations in the United States, though transformed by becoming first a Spanish Colonial outpost, and more recently a hangout for bohemian artists and New Age dropouts, **TAOS** (which rhymes with "mouse") has become famous out of all proportion to its size. Just six thousand people live in its three component parts: **Taos** itself, around the plaza; sprawling **Ranchos de Taos**, three miles to the south; and the Native American community of **Taos Pueblo**, two miles north.

Beyond the usual unsightly highway sprawl, Taos is a delight to visit. As well as museums, galleries, and stores to match Santa Fe, it still offers an unhurried pace and charm, and the sense of a meeting place between Pueblo, Hispanic, and American cultures. Its reputation as an **arts colony** began at the end of the nineteenth century, with the arrival of painter Joseph Henry Sharp. He was soon joined by two young New Yorkers, Bert Phillips and Ernest L. Blumenschein; legend has it that their wagon lost a wheel outside Taos as they headed for Mexico in 1898, and they liked it so much they never got around to leaving. The three men formed the nucleus of the **Taos Society of Artists**, established in 1915. Soon afterward, society heiress and arts patron Mabel Dodge arrived, and married an Indian from the Pueblo to become Mabel Dodge Luhan. She in turn wrote a fan letter to English novelist **D.H. Lawrence**, who visited three times in the early 1920s; his widow Frieda made her home in Taos after his death. New generations of artists and writers have "discovered" Taos ever since, but the most famous of all was **Georgia O'Keeffe**, who stayed for a few years at the end of the 1920s. Her renditions of the church at Ranchos de Taos, in particular, were a major influence on contemporary Southwestern art.

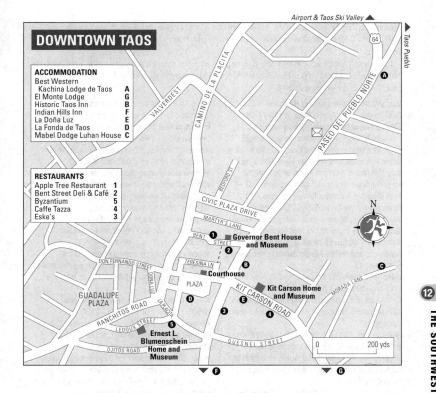

DOWNTOWN TAOS

ACCOMMODATION
Best Western
  Kachina Lodge de Taos **A**
El Monte Lodge **G**
Historic Taos Inn **B**
Indian Hills Inn **F**
La Doña Luz **E**
La Fonda de Taos **D**
Mabel Dodge Luhan House **C**

RESTAURANTS
Apple Tree Restaurant **1**
Bent Street Deli & Café **2**
Byzantium **5**
Caffe Tazza **4**
Eske's **3**

Governor Bent House and Museum

Courthouse

Kit Carson Home and Museum

Ernest L. Blumenschein Home and Museum

N

0   200 yds

Arrival, information, and getting around

Two daily Greyhound and TNM&O **buses** from Albuquerque ($25) and Santa
Fe ($17) arrive at **Taos Bus Center** (℡505/758-1144), opposite the well-
equipped local **visitor center**, two miles south of the plaza at the intersection
of Hwy-68 and US-64 (daily 9am–5pm; ℡505/758-3873 or 1-800/732-8267,
ⓦwww.taoschamber.com). Twin Hearts Express (℡505/751-1201 or 1-
800/654-9456, ⓦwww.twinheartsexpress.com) also connects Taos with Santa
Fe ($25) and the Albuquerque airport (one way $40, roundtrip $75).

   Walking is the best way to get around the compact center, while hourly Red
Chile **buses** (50¢ one way, $1 for an all-day pass; ℡505/751-4459) cover a
twelve-mile route along the highway, and **trolley tours** visit the main attractions (Historic Taos Trolley Tours; May–Oct twice daily from visitor center and
plaza; $33; ℡505/751-0366, ⓦwww.taostrolleytours.com). Another option is
to rent a **bike** from Gearing Up, 129 Paseo del Pueblo Sur (℡505/751-0365).

Accommodation

Taos has **accommodation** to meet all needs, at prices well below those of
Santa Fe (though thanks to the local ski resort midwinter rates are no lower
than midsummer). There are no budget options near the plaza, but the
Snowmansion hostel, near the Ski Valley to the north, offers bare-bones bunks
or simple rooms. Otherwise, chain motels line Hwy-68 south of town, while
three or four adobe-styled motels on Kit Carson Road just east of the plaza

provide quieter alternatives. Taos Central Reservations (☎505/758-9767 or 1-800/821-2437, ⓦwww.taoswebb.com/plan/tcr) can reserve lodging in advance.

The best places to **camp** are the nine summer-only campgrounds in **Carson National Forest** (☎505/758-8851), reached by following Kit Carson Road east until it becomes US-64.

Abominable Snowmansion Hostel/HI-Taos
Taos Ski Valley Rd, Arroyo Seco ☎505/776-8298, ⓦwww.taoswebb.com/hotel/snowmansion. Pleasant, friendly, independent hostel-cum-ski lodge, at a tight curve in the road up to Taos Ski Valley, five miles north of downtown. Office hours daily 8–11am & 4–10pm. Dorm beds $17–22; bargain private rooms and camping space. ❶–❷

Best Western Kachina Lodge de Taos 413 Paseo del Pueblo Norte ☎505/758-2275 or 1-800/522-4462, ⓦwww.kachinalodge.com. Large, tasteful, family motel at the Taos Pueblo turnoff, with lots of Southwestern art, a good restaurant, live music, and nightly Pueblo dance performances in summer. ❹

El Monte Lodge 317 Kit Carson Rd ☎505/758-3171 or 1-800/828-8267. Rural 1930s motel half a mile east of the plaza, offering comfortable en suite accommodation in a complex of adobe cottages. ❸

La Doña Luz 114 Kit Carson Rd ☎505/758-4874 or 1-800/758-9187, ⓦwww.ladonaluz.com. Hispanic-flavored rooms of differing standards in this peaceful adobe B&B, a very short walk east of the plaza. ❹–❺

La Fonda de Taos 108 South Plaza ☎505/758-2211 or 1-800/833-2211, ⓦwww.hotellafonda

.com. This 1930s hotel on the plaza, long a Taos landmark, has been totally re-vamped and modernized to hold 24 luxurious suites, with Southwestern furnishings and tiled bathrooms. ❻

Historic Taos Inn 125 Paseo del Pueblo Norte ☎505/758-2233 or 1-888/458-8267, ⓦwww.taosinn.com. Rambling, ravishing – and very Southwestern – central hotel. Each of its 37 rooms plays a variation on the Pueblo theme, while both *Doc Martin's* restaurant (see p.986) and the *Adobe Bar* are packed nightly. ❸–❽

Indian Hills Inn 233 Paseo del Pueblo Sur ☎505/758-4293 or 1-800/444-2346, ⓦwww.taosnet.com/indianhillsinn. The only cheapish highway motel within walking distance of the plaza; be sure to get a room away from the street. ❸

Mabel Dodge Luhan House 240 Morada Lane ☎505/751-9686 or 1-800/846-2235, ⓦwww.mabeldodgeluhan.com. Gorgeous 200-year-old adobe B&B complex, not far northeast of the plaza off Kit Carson Lane, where the lovely guest rooms are named for creative former guests such as Willa Cather and Ansel Adams. Two rooms, including the light-filled solarium, share a bathroom painted by D.H.Lawrence, while there's also a cheaper lodge annex with more modern fittings. ❹

Taos plaza and the museums

The old Spanish **plaza**, still at the heart of Taos, is now ringed by jewelry stores, art galleries, and restaurants; all conform to the predominant Pueblo motif of rounded brown adobe. Specific sights are few – a small **museum** off the lobby of the *La Fonda de Taos* hotel has a collection of sexy but amateurish paintings by D.H. Lawrence, and the tree-filled square itself is often animated by guitar-toting buskers – but the surrounding streets are perfect for an aimless stroll, and it's easy to spend half a day just mooching around. Some of the best places to eat or drink, as well as a number of top-notch art and crafts galleries, are on **Bent Street**, a block north of the plaza. The street takes its name from the first American governor of New Mexico, Charles Bent; his house here, in which he was murdered in 1847, has been preserved as a ramshackle little **museum of frontier Taoseño life** (daily: April–Oct 9.30am–5pm; Nov–March 10am–4pm; $2).

Just east of the plaza, across the highway at the end of Taos's sole surviving stretch of wooden boardwalk, is the dusty but evocative adobe dwelling that was home to mountain man, mason, and part-time US cavalry officer **Kit Carson** (see p.1033) for 25 years in the mid-1800s. It too is now a **museum**, filled with saddles, rifles, and Wild West paraphernalia (daily: April–Oct 9am–5pm; Nov–March 10am–4pm; $5). A single $20 ticket, valid for a year, grants admission to both this and six other Taos museums, including the three large enough to be described below.

Two blocks south of the plaza at 222 Ledoux St, the much-restored 1790 **house** of artist and collector **Ernest L. Blumenschein**, co-founder of the town's 1920s arts colony, displays paintings and furniture (daily: April–Oct 9am–5pm; Nov–March 11am–4pm; $5).

Two miles north of the Taos Pueblo turning, reached by a dirt road that angles into a tricky five-way intersection, the **Millicent Rogers Museum** (April–Oct daily 10am–5pm; Nov–March daily except Mon 10am–5pm; $6) shows off a superb collection of craft works. Objects range from Ancestral Puebloan and Mimbres pottery to the contemporary black-on-black ceramics of San Ildefonso Pueblo potter Maria Martinez, plus Hopi *kachinas* (see p.1039), and beautiful Navajo blankets. Affecting exhibits trace the development of Spanish Colonial religious art in the New World; the highlight is a "Death Cart," in which a skeleton holding a bow and arrow rides in a rickety wooden carriage.

Ranchos de Taos

South of the central plaza area, to either side of Hwy-68, **Ranchos de Taos** was originally a separate community, composed of the farms that fed the town of Taos. Each *rancho* had its own main house, or *hacienda*; one has been restored as a **museum** of Colonial life. The **Hacienda Martínez** (daily: April–Oct 9am–5pm; Nov–March 10am–4pm; $5), two miles southwest of the plaza on Ranchitos Road, was built in 1804 by Don Antonio Martínez, an early mayor of Taos. Within its thick, windowless, adobe walls – sealed like a fortress against what were then still-prevalent Indian raids – two dozen rooms are wrapped around two patios, holding animal pens and a well. Trade goods of the kind Don Antonio once carried south along the Rio Grande are displayed alongside tools, looms, and simple furnishings.

In Ranchos' small unpaved plaza, the mission church of **San Francisco de Asis** faces its broad shoulders, or more accurately its massive adobe buttresses, to the passing traffic on Hwy-68. Built around 1776, it's one of Colonial New Mexico's most splendid architectural achievements, with subtly rounded walls and corners disguising its underlying structural strength. Though the ever-changing interplay of light and shade across its golden exterior has fascinated painters from Georgia O'Keeffe onward, the interior is equally intriguing, with a magnificently ornate green-and-red reredos (altarpiece) framing several naïve paintings.

Taos Pueblo

Continuously inhabited for approaching one thousand years, the two multi-story adobes at **Taos Pueblo**, two miles north of Taos plaza and half a mile east of Hwy-68, jointly constitute the most impressive Native American dwelling place still in use. Hlauuma, the north house, and Hlaukwima, the south house, are separated by the Rio Pueblo de Taos, which flows down the hills from the sacred Blue Lake, inaccessible to outsiders. Those residents that still remain here have made few concessions to the modern world, living without toilets, running water, or electricity.

The pueblo is generally open to visitors from 8am until 5pm from Monday to Saturday, and between 8.30am and 5pm on Sunday, but it often closes for tribal events such as festivals or funerals, and remains closed between mid-February and early April; contact Taos Pueblo Tourism (☎505/758-1028, ⓦwww.taospueblo.com) before you visit. Assuming the pueblo is open, park your vehicle at the edge of the plaza, and pay an **entrance fee** ($10 per person, plus $5 per still camera, $20 per video camera), that entitles you to join one of the guided **walking tours**, led by Pueblo residents, which leave at regular intervals. These may help overcome any awkwardness you might feel, but they won't take you beyond the limited public areas through which you're free to wander alone.

For most of the year, Pueblo life continues with scant regard for the intrusion of tourists, but feast days and dances, held throughout the summer, can be spectacular. The biggest parties are the **Corn Dances** in June and July, and the **Feast of San Gerónimo** at the end of September, when outsiders flock to join the general revelry.

Taos Ski Valley

Fifteen miles north of Taos lie the challenging slopes of **Taos Ski Valley**, reached via an attractive road that winds up through a narrow gap in the mountains from the village of Arroyo Seco. Located on the north flank of **Wheeler Peak**, the highest point in New Mexico at 13,161ft, the demanding runs are usually open to skiers – snowboarding, incredibly, continues to be banned on the slopes – between late November and early April (daily lift tickets late Nov to mid-Dec $33, mid-Dec to late March $49, late March to early April $40; information ☏505/776-2291 or 1-800/347-7414, reservations ☏1-800/776-1111, ⓦwww.skitaos.org).

Eating, drinking, and nightlife

Taos is too small to offer much **nightlife**, but it does have a fine selection of **restaurants** in all price ranges, and several coffeehouses. If your main priority is to **drink**, the *Adobe Bar* in the *Taos Inn* (see p.984) is the coziest spot in town, while *Eske's*, a short way south at 106 Des Georges Lane (☏505/758-1517), is a lively brewpub.

Apple Tree Restaurant 123 Bent St ☏505/758-1900. Café-style restaurant in an old adobe north of the plaza, where most of the predominantly New Mexican entrees, such as barbecue duck fajitas or mango chicken enchiladas, cost $12–16. The courtyard seating is ideal for summer evenings.

Bent Street Deli & Café 120 Bent St ☏505/758-5787. Airy, partly outdoor place, just north of the plaza with good-value breakfasts, sandwich lunches, and tasty dinners for under $20. Closed Sun.

Byzantium 112 La Placita at Ledoux St ☏505/751-0805. Romantic and classy courtyard restaurant southwest of the plaza, where lunch consists of flavorful salads and sandwiches. Much of the dinner menu has a contemporary pan-Asian feel, with Asian seafood cakes ($11) or duck green curry ($23) alongside herb-crusted pork tenderloin or vegetable potpie. Closed Tues & Wed.

Caffè Tazza 122 Kit Carson Rd ☏505/758-8706. Trendy, central café with nice sunlit terrace, selling

coffees and light veggie meals to students and assorted crazies.

Doc Martin's *Taos Inn*, 125 Paseo del Pueblo Norte ☏505/758-1977. Delicious, inventive New Mexican food in a romantic adobe inn, on the main road just east of the plaza. Most dinner entrees, such as *piñon*-crusted salmon or smoked lamb sirloin, are $16–23, except on Friday and Saturday when a three-course *prix-fixe* dinner menu costs around $20.

Island Coffees and Hawaiian Grill 1032 Paseo del Pueblo Sur ☏505/758-7777. Friendly, very inexpensive Hawaiian-themed café near the visitor center, serving Kona coffee plus noodle dishes, curries, and sandwiches, and offering cut-rate Internet access.

Taos Pizza Outback 712 Paseo del Pueblo Norte ☏505/748-3112. Hard-to-find pizzeria, a mile north of town, with a welcoming, youthful ambiance and huge portions of great food – the $9 calzones are amazing.

Chama

Eighty-five miles northwest of Taos on US-64 – which crosses the dramatic Rio Grande Gorge Bridge – beyond Abiquiu and the red rocks around Ghost

Ranch, tiny **CHAMA** is the base for trips on the **Cumbres and Toltec Scenic Railroad** (late May to late Oct; ☏505/756-2151 or 1-888/286-2737, Ⓦ www.cumbrestoltec.com), an exhilarating high-mountain ride, following the course of the Los Piños Gorge. Daily excursions run from Chama through the High Brazos Mountains on the border with Colorado; you can either take a motor coach to Antonito, Colorado, and return by train (depart 8.30am; $60), go by train and return by coach (depart 10am; $60), or take a roundtrip for the day by train to a point halfway along (depart 10am; $45).

Modern timber **lodges** like the comfortable *Vista del Rio*, 2595 US-84/64 (☏505/756-2138 or 1-800/939-9943, Ⓦ www.vistadelriolodge.com; ❸), line the river south of town, while the *Gandy Dancer* is a three-bedroom **B&B** in a purple-clapboard mansion, near the station at 299 Maple St (☏505/756-2191 or 1-800/424-6702, Ⓦ www.gandydancerbb.com; ❹).

From Santa Fe to Albuquerque

Driving from **Santa Fe to Albuquerque**, you have three options. One route loops through the mountains to the west via **Bandelier** (see p.978) and the appealing village of Jemez Springs, while another follows the slumbering **Turquoise Trail** through the ghost towns further east. Even the direct sixty-mile sprint down **I-25** has its moments, with views of Sandia Crest to the east and the sprawling Rio Grande to the west.

The Turquoise Trail

The "**Turquoise Trail**," less glamorously known as Hwy-14, is a detour off I-25 that leads between the Sandia and Ortiz mountains, and a couple of the long-abandoned mining camps along the way still just about rank as towns in their own right.

Archeologists estimate that ninety percent of the **turquoise** treasures seized by the Spanish from the Aztec capital of Tenochtitlan was originally mined from the dusty rolling hills that surround the northernmost town, **CERRILLOS**. Prehistoric Indians scooped hundreds of tons of rock from the hillsides; after the **Pueblo Revolt** many shafts were buried to hide them from the Spanish, and tales of fabulous "lost mines" still abound.

With its unpaved roads and old wooden buildings, Cerrillos is an atmospheric spot, and still holds a bit of life; as late as 1983 robbers made off with $500,000 worth of gold from the nearby Ortiz Mines. Tourists, however, have to content themselves with the **Casa Grande Trading Post, Turquoise Mining Museum, and Petting Zoo**, an endearing shop-cum-museum that offers a random assortment of old bills and letters, porcupine quills, rattlesnake skins, and petrified wood.

A dozen miles further on, the New Agey village of **MADRID** consists of a straggle of wooden cottages on either side of the narrow highway. Several hold interesting crafts and antiques stores; if you're close enough to home to carry furniture, there are some real bargains to be had. One attractive old mining home, *Java Junction* (☏505/438-2772, Ⓦ www.java-junction.com; ❸), houses a **coffee shop** downstairs and a **B&B** apartment upstairs, with kitchen and bathroom. Behind the lively *Mine Shaft Tavern* (☏505/473-0743), there's an accessible mine shaft.

Coronado State Monument

If you do drive the I-25 route, be sure to stop off along the way at **Coronado State Monument**, just off the freeway on the far side of the Rio Grande, eighteen miles north of Albuquerque (daily: 8.30am–5pm; April–Oct $4, Nov–March $2). Named for the Spanish explorer who wintered here in 1540 (and who, in frustration at not finding any of the vast riches he was searching for, tortured and brutally murdered a number of local Indians), the monument consists of a large **adobe pueblo** beside the Rio Grande. You can enter its restored *kiva* to see reproductions of its multi-hued murals. The originals, preserved in the **visitor center**, include scenes of a rabbit hunt – the animals are still abundant in the undergrowth by the river.

The small town of **ALGODONES**, five miles north on the east bank of the river, holds one of New Mexico's most relaxing rural **B&Bs**, *Hacienda Vargas*, set in a lovely, restored adobe trading post at 1431 El Camino Real (☎505/867-9115 or 1-800/261-0006, ⓦwww.haciendavargas.com; ❹).

Albuquerque and central New Mexico

Although to most travelers **central New Mexico** is an area to be raced through as quickly as possible, it does hold isolated pockets of interest, with the scenery, at least in the west, the main attraction. Dozens of small towns hang on to the last remnants of **Route 66**, the winding old "Chicago-to-LA" transcontinental highway long since superseded by I-40.

Albuquerque – New Mexico's largest city, with a third of the state's population – sits dead center, at the intersection of I-40 and I-25. It's also a main stop for Amtrak and Greyhound, and holds New Mexico's only major **airport**. Though the area **east of Albuquerque**, stretching toward Texas, is among the most desolate parts of the Southwest, one or two towns merit a quick detour off the interstate, thanks to **Wild West** heroes like Kit Carson and Billy the Kid. The mountainous region **west of Albuquerque** has more to see – above all **Ácoma Pueblo**, the mesa-top community known as "Sky City."

East of Albuquerque: Tucumcari and Fort Sumner

The long line of truck stops, diners, and motels at **TUCUMCARI**, the biggest town between Albuquerque and Amarillo, Texas (see p.976), has made it a favorite I-40 pit stop, punctuated with neon signs. During the day you can while away an hour at the mind-boggling **Tucumcari Historical Museum** at 416 S Adams St (June–Aug Mon–Sat 9am–6pm; Sept–May Tues–Sat 9am–6pm; $2.11), which boasts one of the world's greatest collections of barbed wire. If you need **to stay**, literally hundreds of inexpensive rooms lie along this stretch of old Route 66; the *Best Western Pow Wow Inn*, 801 W Tucumcari Blvd (☎505/461-0500 or 1-800/527-6996; ❸), is a cut above the many cheaper dives. For **food**, there's the *Big Dipper*, 101 Second St at Main St (☎505/461-4430), an appealingly old-fashioned downtown diner.

FORT SUMNER, south of I-40 some way short of Tucumcari, means different things to different people. To the Navajo, it's where frontiersman and US Army colonel **Kit Carson** dragged them in 1864 after destroying their orchards and burning their villages in Arizona (see p.1033). What little is left of the reservation is now the **Fort Sumner State Monument**, seven miles east of the modern town (daily 8.30am–5pm; $1). To Wild West fanatics, Fort Sumner is a pilgrimage spot because legendary outlaw **Billy the Kid** was gunned down here by Pat Garrett in 1881. His grave stands behind the jumbled **Old Fort Sumner Museum** (daily 9am–5pm; $3), his tombstone shielded from memento-seekers by a steel cage.

Albuquerque

Sprawling at the heart of New Mexico, where the main east–west road and rail routes cross both the Rio Grande and the old road south to Mexico, **ALBU-QUERQUE** is, with half a million people, the state's only major metropolis. Though many tourists dash straight from the airport up to Santa Fe, without a thought for Albuquerque, the "**Duke City**" has a good deal going for it. Like Phoenix, it's grown a bit too fast for comfort in the last fifty years, but the original Hispanic settlement is still discernible at its core, and its diverse, cosmopolitan population gives it a rare cultural vibrancy. Even if its architecture is often uninspired, the setting is magnificent, sandwiched between the Rio Grande – lined by stately cottonwoods – and the dramatic, glowing **Sandia Mountains**. Specific highlights for visitors include the intact **Spanish plaza**, the neon-lit **Route 66** frontage of Central Avenue, and the excellent **Indian Pueblo Cultural Center**; while every October Albuquerque hosts the nation's largest **hot-air balloon** rally, attracting upward of 100,000 people to its mass ascensions.

Arrival and information

Albuquerque's **International Sunport** is four miles southeast of downtown. All the major **car rental** chains have outlets here, while a **taxi** into town with Yellow Cab (℡505/247-4888) costs around $10, and Checker Airport Express (℡505/765-1234) runs door-to-door shuttles at similar rates.

Both Amtrak and Greyhound are located in an otherwise deserted area, five easy minutes' walk south of downtown. The modern Greyhound **bus terminal**, 300 Second St SW (℡505/243-4435), is used by long-distance east–west services, as well as four daily buses up to Santa Fe ($12) and Taos ($22), and has good-sized left-luggage lockers. Two daily Amtrak **trains** – one heading west to Los Angeles, the other east to Chicago – arrive immediately behind Greyhound, at 214 First St.

Free listings magazines and brochures are available from the **visitor center**, downtown in the Albuquerque Convention Center, 401 Second St (Mon–Fri 9am–5pm; ℡505/842-9918 or 1-800/284-2282, ⓦwww.itsatrip.org). Further **information kiosks** can be found in Old Town, in the Plaza Don Luis on Romero NW (daily: April–Oct 9am–5pm; Nov–March 9.30am–4.30pm), and at the airport (daily 9.30am–8pm).

Accommodation

The twenty-mile length of **Central Avenue**, the old Route 66, is lined with the flashing neon signs of dozens of $30-a-night **motels**. If you want to escape your car for a while, you'll have to pay a little extra to stay in the heart of Old Town – which holds few accommodation options – or downtown. Larger convention hotels are congregated along the interstates, and out near the airport.

Aztec Motel 3821 Central Ave NE ℡505/254-1742. Albuquerque's oldest Route 66 motel, featuring a great restored neon sign and festooned with folk art. Most of its guests are permanent residents, but it's still a safe and atmospheric (if plain) option for tourists. ❶
Barcelona Suites Hotel 900 Louisiana Blvd NE ℡505/255-5566 or 1-877/227-7848,

ⓦwww.barsuites.com. Spacious suite-only hotel, three miles east of downtown and two blocks south of I-40. All the units have kitchens, and there are indoor and outdoor pools. ❹
Casas de Sueños 310 Rio Grande Blvd SW ℡505/247-4560, ⓦwww.casasdesuenos.com. Beautifully furnished, exotic, and friendly B&B, very close to Old Town, with themed cottages and

smaller rooms. One of New Mexico's most appealing places to stay. ❹–❽

Comfort Inn – Airport 2300 Yale Blvd SE ☎505/243-2244 or 1-800/221-2222. Good-value motel, served by free shuttles from the airport across the road, and with complimentary breakfasts. ❸

El Vado Motel 2500 Central Ave SW ☎505/243-4594. Vintage adobe Route 66 motel, within easy reach of Old Town. ❷

La Posada de Albuquerque 125 Second St NW ☎505/242-9090 or 1-800/777-5732, ⓦwww.laposada-abq.com. Historic hotel in convenient downtown location, built in Mexican style by Conrad Hilton in 1939. Large, very classy, renovated rooms with antique wooden furnishings, a beautiful wood-paneled lobby, a superb restaurant, and a spacious, atmospheric bar. ❹

Monterey Nonsmokers Motel 2402 Central Ave SW ☎505/243-3554 or 1-877/666-8379, ⓦwww.nonsmokersmotel.com. Clean, fifteen-room motel, two blocks west of Old Town, with pool, laundry, and a strict nonsmoking policy. ❸

Route 66 Hostel 1012 Central Ave SW ☎505/247-1813, ✉ctaylor939@aol.com. Albuquerque's only hostel, a friendly place on the outskirts of Old Town and a mile west of downtown, offers dorm beds for $15, kitchen facilities, and very plain but bargain-priced private doubles. Office hours daily 7.30–10.30am & 4–11pm. ❶

Old Town

Once you've cruised up and down **Central Avenue**, looking at the flashing neon and 1940s architecture of this twenty-mile stretch of Route 66 (Sun Tran buses do it all day for 75¢), most of what's interesting about Albuquerque is concentrated in **Old Town**, the recently tidied-up old Spanish heart of the city. As the billboards on the interstate nearby rightly proclaim, "it's darned old and historic." The tree-filled **main plaza** is overlooked by the twin-towered adobe facade of **San Felipe de Neri church**, and circled by horse-drawn carriages that you can hop on for a short tour ($5). It's a very pleasant place to wander or have a meal, even if there's not a whole lot otherwise to do. One of the more bizarre of the many knick-knack shops is the **Rattlesnake Museum** southeast of the plaza at 202 San Felipe St NW (Mon–Fri noon–6pm, Sat 10am–6pm, Sun 1–5pm; $2), which has live rattlers on display. Nearby, Gus's Trading Post, 2026 Central Ave NW, is one of the best-value shops in the Southwest for buying the perfect bolo tie or other pieces of Indian **jewelry**.

Still on Central Avenue, in the Old Town Shopping Center half a block west of the plaza, the intriguing little **Turquoise Museum** (Mon–Sat 9.30am–6pm; $2) may look like just another mall store, but turns out to be more of a fortified bank vault, filled with rare and beautiful turquoise nuggets.

The **New Mexico Museum of Natural History**, four blocks northeast of the plaza at 1801 Mountain Rd NW (daily 9am–5pm; closed Mon in Jan & Sept; $5), has full-scale, animated models of dinosaurs, a simulated volcanic eruption, and a replica of an Ice Age snow cave, as well as an engaging, touchable collection of fossils and dinosaur bones. Nearby, the **National Atomic Museum**, with its "impressive array of American fission weapons," has moved to new premises at 1905 Mountain Rd NW from its previous location within Kirtland Air Force Base, due to heightened security concerns (daily 9am–5pm; $2; ☎505/245-2137 ext 105, ⓦwww.atomicmuseum.org). Displays trace the history of nuclear science and weapons from the early discoveries of Madame Curie up to modern robotic devices such as the "truck-killing standoff weapon" Fireant.

The riverfront

The Rio Grande has shifted its course in the last three hundred years, so there's an unexpectedly low-key gap west of Old Town, much of it left undeveloped in deference to the unruly river. Along the wooded eastern riverbank, the **Bio Park** holds two attractions that focus on the natural world. Not for the squeamish, the **Albuquerque Aquarium** (June–Aug Mon–Fri 9am–5pm, Sat

& Sun 9am–6pm; Sept–May daily 9am–5pm; $8) offers such diverse experiences as eating in a restaurant beside a glass-walled tank filled with live sharks and walking through a tunnel surrounded on all sides by fierce-eyed moray eels. Across the way, the **Rio Grande Botanic Garden** (same hours; same ticket) consists of two large conservatories – one holding rare plants from the Sonoran and Chihuahua deserts, the other more temperate Mediterranean species – plus a series of walled gardens.

At the lower-key **Rio Grande Nature Center** (daily 8am–5pm; $1), two miles north of Old Town on Rio Grande Boulevard, informative displays describe Albuquerque's wildlife, and two short but enjoyable nature trails along the riverside will have you feeling far removed from the city.

Indian Pueblo Cultural Center

The **Indian Pueblo Cultural Center**, at 2401 12th St NW, one block north of I-40, is a stunning museum (daily 9am–4.30pm; $4; ☎505/843-7270, ⓦ www.indianpueblo.org) and crafts market (daily 9am–5.30pm; free), owned and run as a cooperative venture by the diverse Pueblo Indians of New Mexico. Its horseshoe-shaped design deliberately echoes the architecture of the Ancestral Puebloan city of Pueblo Bonito, in Chaco Canyon (see p.994), and the central courtyard is the venue for free Pueblo dances, every Saturday and Sunday at 11am and 2pm.

This is New Mexico's one major museum about Native Americans curated by Native Americans, and the displays downstairs have a clear and distinct point of view. The shared Ancestral Puebloan heritage at the root of Pueblo culture is explained in detail, as is the impact of the Spanish conquistadors. Describing the **Pueblo Revolt** of 1680 as the "first civil war," it states that by allowing the defeated Spaniards to leave unharmed, the Pueblo peoples "showed them more mercy than they showed us." There's also as good an explanation as you're ever likely to get of a topic Pueblo Indians rarely discuss with outsiders: how indigenous Pueblo religion has managed to coexist with imported Catholicism. Videos illustrate modern Pueblo life, and the stores upstairs sell outstanding pottery and jewelry, while a good-quality **café** serves assorted Pueblo specialties.

Sandia Crest

The forested 10,500-foot peaks of the **Sandia Crest** tower over Albuquerque to the east, affording particularly beautiful views from the top at and after sunset, when the city lights sparkle below. In summer it's a good 25°F cooler up here than in the valley, and in winter you can go downhill or cross-country **skiing** (mid-Dec to mid-March; lift tickets $35 per day; ☎505/242-9052, ⓦ www.sandiapeak.com). If you don't want to drive the scenic but twisting twenty-mile route from Albuquerque, take the **Sandia Peak Tramway** (summer daily 9am–9pm; winter Mon, Tues, Thurs–Sun 9am–8pm, Wed noon–8pm during ski season, 5–8pm otherwise; $15), the world's longest single-span tramway at 2.7 miles; it leaves from the end of Tramway Road at the city's northeast edge.

Eating

The chefs of Santa Fe may be trying to redefine Southwestern cuisine, but Albuquerque still knows what it likes – mountainous Mexican meals. This is the place to get to grips with what real New Mexican food is all about, with family diners all over the city competing to create the spiciest chiles rellenos and enchiladas.

Artichoke Café 424 Central Ave SE ☎ 505/243-0200. Simple but classy restaurant in the heart of downtown, with indoor and outdoor seating, serving a good, varied menu of California-influenced modern American cuisine; most entrees well under $20. Closed Sun.

Conrad's *La Posada de Albuquerque*, 125 2nd St NW ☎ 505/242-9090. Classic 1930s Art Deco hotel diner, modernized and serving expensive but excellent Hispanic-influenced dishes, including tasty salads and *tapas*, plus the signature dish – a superb seafood paella, complete with lobster and saffron rice. Open daily for all meals.

Flying Star 3416 Central Ave SE ☎ 505/255-6633. Lively, crowded University District café serving eclectic international cuisine to a largely student clientele. The vast menu ranges through breakfast specialties, salads, and blue-plate specials such as Vietnamese noodles or pasta pomodoro for $8. Open daily from 6am until late.

Frontier 2400 Central Ave SE ☎ 505/266-0550. Legendary 24-hour diner across from the university, where an unceasing parade of characters chow down on burgers, burritos, and great vegetarian enchiladas.

High Finance 40 Tramway Rd NE ☎ 505/243-9742. Pricey seafood and steak place in an unparalleled location, at the top of the Sandia Peak Tramway – see overleaf – with eagle's-eye sunset views.

Kanome 3128 Central Ave SE ☎ 505/265-7773. Bright, colourful, and modern pan-Asian diner near the university, where few of the Thai, Chinese, or Japanese entrees cost over $10. Open daily for dinner only.

Drinking and nightlife

Downtown Albuquerque has been revitalized in recent years by the emergence of a host of **bars** and **nightclubs**, many of which double as small theaters or music venues. Free magazines such as the weekly *Alibi* can tell you all you need to know about what's coming up or going down.

Assets Grille & Southwest Brewing Company 6910 Montgomery Blvd NE ☎ 505/889-6400. Lively microbrewery with indoor and outdoor seating, plus Italian food. Closed Sun.

Caravan East 7605 Central Ave NE ☎ 505/265-7877. Enormous honky-tonk, where tenderfeet can do the two-step with throngs of urban cowboys.

Club Rhythm and Blues 3523 Central Ave NE ☎ 505/256-0849, ⊛ www.clubrb.com. University District bar that plays host to Latin, swing, and jazz bands as well as blues. Closed Sun.

El Rey Theatre 620 Central Ave SW ☎ 505/243-7546. Live music from salsa to country and all points in between; the adjoining *Golden West Saloon* is the venue of choice for Albuquerque's metal maniacs.

KiMo Theater 423 Central Ave NW ☎ 505/848-1370. Gorgeous, city-owned "Pueblo Deco" theater, dating from the late 1920s, which puts on an eclectic program of opera, dance, and theater performances, kids' movie shows, and also regular live bands.

The Launchpad 618 Central Ave SW ☎ 505/764-8887, ⊛ www.launchpadrocks.com. Dance and live music space that showcases touring indie, reggae, and blues bands, and also has a cluster of pool tables.

West of Albuquerque: I-40 to Arizona

Driving between Albuquerque and Arizona, you could easily be so put off by the parade of billboards and hoardings offering cut-price cigarettes and Indian jewelry that you'd miss out on some of central New Mexico's most interesting places, such as **Ácoma Pueblo** and **Chaco Canyon**, which lie south and north of I-40 respectively.

Ácoma Pueblo

The amazing **Ácoma Pueblo**, south of I-40 fifty miles west of Albuquerque, encapsulates a thousand years of Native American history. Its focus is the ancient village known as "**Sky City**," perched atop a magnificent isolated mesa, 367ft high and 7000ft above sea level. Probably occupied by Chacoan migrants between 1100 and 1200 AD, when the great pueblos of Chaco Canyon were still in use, Ácoma has adapted to repeated waves of invaders ever since, while retaining its own strong identity. As the Ácomans have long been happy to take the tourist dollar – they run a large casino beside the interstate, and have hosted the Miss America Pageant – visitors seldom feel the awkwardness possible at other pueblo communities. Nonetheless, Ácoma is the real thing, and its sense of unbroken tradition can reduce even the least culturally sensitive traveler to awestruck silence.

To see Sky City, you have to join one of the hour-long guided **bus tours** (daily: April–Oct 8am–7pm; Nov–March 8am–4pm; admission $10, plus $10 for photo permit, no video tripods; ☏505/470-0181 or 1-800/747-0181, ⓦwww.skycity-tourism.com), which leave regularly from the small visitor center at the base of the mesa. The main stop is at the **San Esteban del Rey** mission, a thick-walled adobe church completed in 1640. Its earthen-floored nave is capped by a roof made of pine logs, which are said to have been carried here from the top of Mount Taylor, twenty miles away, without once touching the ground. Catholicism did eventually take root among the Pueblo people, but tales of the early mission days often speak of the Spanish priests as harsh and unfeeling taskmasters, many of whom came to rather sticky ends. The sheer visual impact of the building is undeniable – due in part to its sheer incongruity – and it's striking that the Ácomans obviously never felt inclined to follow its architectural example. Instead they went on constructing the multistory stone and adobe houses around which the tour then proceeds. Only thirteen families live permanently on the mesa; most Ácomans prefer to reside down below, where they can get electricity, running water, and jobs. Villagers do, however, come up here during the day to sell pottery and fry-bread, and maintain their family homes for occasional use.

Instead of taking the bus back down, you can walk along the old path, scrambling over boulders and through narrow clefts. Away to the east, legend has it that the forbidding **Enchanted Mesa** once held its own Pueblo community; the only access to the top was via a system of ropes strung between the mesa itself and an adjoining rock pillar. When that pillar collapsed one day while the men were away from the village, the women and children were left stranded, their cries for help fading as they starved away.

Grants

The old Route 66 town of **GRANTS**, fifteen miles west of Ácoma, holds half a dozen budget motels, including a good *Super 8*, 1604 E Santa Fe Ave (☏505/287-8811; ❷). In the heart of town, the *Mission at Riverwalk*, 422 W Santa Fe Ave (☏505/285-4632), is an appealing converted church that now doubles as a community theater and healthy café, serving sandwiches, smoothies, and coffee. The local **visitor center** doubles as the comprehensive and enjoyable **New Mexico Museum of Mining** at 100 N Iron Ave (May–Sept Mon–Sat 9am–5pm, Sun 9am–4pm; Oct–April Mon–Sat 9am–4pm; $3; ☏505/287-4802, ⓦwww.grants.org), offering a chance to make a virtual descent into a mock-up of one of the region's many **uranium mines**.

El Morro National Monument

Hidden away on Hwy-53 south of the Zuni Mountains, 42 miles west of Grants, **El Morro National Monument** feels as far off the beaten track as it's possible to be in the modern US. Incredibly, however, this pale-pink sandstone cliff was a regular rest stop for international travelers before the Pilgrims landed at Plymouth Rock, thanks to a cool, perennial pool of water that collects at the base of a tumbling waterfall. This spot was first recorded by Spanish explorers in 1583 – *el morro* means "the headland" – and in 1605, Don Juan de Oñate, the founder of New Mexico, carved the first of many messages that earned it the American name of **Inscription Rock**.

Translations and explanations of El Morro's graffiti are displayed in the **visitor center** (daily: summer 9am–7pm; winter 9am–5pm; admission $4 per vehicle, or $3 per person; ☎505/783-4226, ⊛www.nps.gov/elmo). You can see the real thing on a half-mile trail, which stays open until an hour before the visitor center closes. Not far beyond some **Ancestral Puebloan petroglyphs**, scraped into the desert varnish, Don Juan's chiseled signature celebrates "the discovery of the South Sea"; he was returning from an expedition that had taken him all the way to the mouth of the Colorado River.

Chaco Canyon

For casual visitors, the long, bumpy ride to the Ancestral Puebloan ruins of **Chaco Canyon**, north of I-40 between Grant and Gallup, may seem more bother than it's worth. True, the site protected as the **Chaco Culture National Historical Park** is the largest pre-Columbian city in North America; for beauty and drama, however, it can't compete with lesser settlements such as Canyon de Chelly (see p.1035). The low-walled canyon is a mere scratch in the scrubby high-desert plains, and the Chaco Wash that runs through it is often completely dry.

Once you accept that you won't have amazing photos to show the folks back home, however, there's still plenty about Chaco to take your breath away. Over 3600 separate sites have been logged in the canyon, of which the thirteen principal ones are open to visitors. Six, arrayed along the canyon's north wall, are what are known as "Great Houses" – self-contained pueblos, three or four stories high, whose fortress-like walls concealed up to eight hundred rooms.

Both the routes to Chaco Canyon entail driving twenty miles over rough but passable dirt roads. Open all year, these should not be attempted during or within a day of a rainstorm. Whether you approach from the south, by following Hwy-57 up from **Seven Lakes**, eighteen miles northeast of **Crownpoint**, or from the north or east, by turning off Hwy-44 at **Nageezi**, 36 miles south of **Bloomfield,** you enter the park at its southeast corner, close to the **visitor center** (daily: summer 8am–6pm; winter 8am–5pm; ☎505/786-7014, ⊛www.nps.gov/chcu). The basic first-come, first-served *Gallo* **campground** ($10), a short way east, is the only visitor facility in the park; from April to October it's usually full by 3pm.

The gates of the canyon's eight-mile one-way **loop road** are immediately north of the visitor center, and open the same hours. The major stop is at the far end, where **Pueblo Bonito** ("beautiful town" in Spanish) – said to have been the biggest single building in America until structural steel was developed in 1898 – can be explored on an easy half-mile trail. Work on this four-story D-shaped structure, which is almost perfectly aligned east–west, started in 850 AD and continued for three hundred years. Entering the ruin via its lowest levels, the path reaches its central plaza, which held at least three **Great Kivas** – ceremonial chambers thought to have been used by entire communities rather than individual clans or families. From there, you can walk through the passageways and chambers of the pueblo proper, where the rows of neatly finished doorways, each framed by the next, are Chaco's most photographed feature.

Gallup

Just half an hour from the Arizona border, 65 miles west of Grants, the famous Route 66 town of **GALLUP** is a handy but uninteresting I-40 pit stop. A five-mile line of the old Route 66 frontage contains some of the least expensive **motels** in the US, ranging from the *Colonial*, 1007 W Coal Ave (☎505/863-6821; ❶), and the *Blue Spruce Lodge*, 1119 E Hwy-66 (☎505/863-5211; ❶), to the pricier national chains. Unless you're falling asleep at the wheel, the only place really worth stopping for in Gallup is the lovely *El Rancho Hotel*, 1000 E 66 Ave ((℡505/863-9311 or 1-800/543-6351, ⓦwww.elranchohotel.com; ❸/❹), built in 1937 by the brother of movie director D.W. Griffith as a home away from home for the many Hollywood stars filming nearby. Nowadays you can ogle their signed photos in the spacious Spanish Revival lobby, grab a bite in its decorative restaurant, or spend the night in the Ronald Reagan Room, the Marx Brothers Room, or the Mae West Room. Some guestrooms are in the original ranchhouse, the rest in a two-story motel building alongside.

The Navajo and other local Native Americans come together in **Red Rock State Park**, four miles east of Gallup, on the second weekend in August for the **Inter-Tribal Indian Ceremonial**, the largest such gathering anywhere. Four days of dances and craft shows have as their highlight a Saturday morning parade through the town.

Southern New Mexico

Most of the travelers who come to **southern New Mexico** are here to visit **Carlsbad Caverns National Park**. Crassly commercialized it may be, but, like the Grand Canyon, it's too amazing a geological spectacle to miss. Northwest of Carlsbad, the **Sacramento** and **Jicarilla mountains** are home to the **Mescalero Apache** reservation as well as some rough-and-ready resorts rising from the desert plains once roamed by Billy the Kid and other Wild West outlaws. The desolate dunes of the **White Sands** – half national park, half missile and bombing range – spread west of the mountains with the rolling hills of the **Rio Grande Valley** beyond. The little-visited southwest corner is among the most attractive reaches of the Southwest, with more ghost towns and fine scenery, plus the pre-Columbian remains of the **Gila Cliff Dwellings National Monument**.

Carlsbad Caverns National Park

CARLSBAD CAVERNS NATIONAL PARK consists of a tract of the Guadalupe Mountains that's so riddled with underground caves and tunnels as to be virtually hollow. Tamed in classic park-service style with concrete trails and electric lighting, this subterranean wonderland is now a walk-in gallery, where tourists come in droves to marvel at its intricate limestone tracery. Though the summer crowds can get pretty intense, in a strange way that's part of the fun – coming to Carlsbad feels like a real throwback to the great 1950s boom in mass tourism. Before you decide to join in, however, be sure to grasp that the park is a *long* way from anywhere else – three hundred miles southeast of Albuquerque and 150 miles northeast of El Paso, Texas.

To reach the park, follow the narrow, twisting seven-mile road that leaves US-62/180 at **White's City**, twenty miles southwest of the town of **CARLS-BAD**. This ends at the **visitor center** – part of a complex that includes a restaurant, a gift shop, a day-care center, and even a kennel – where you can pay entrance fees and pick up details of the day's schedule of tours (daily: June to mid-Aug 8am–7pm; mid-Aug to May 8am–5pm; ℡505/785-2232, ⓦwww.nps.gov/cave).

Almost all park visitors confine their attention to the main cave, **Carlsbad Cavern** itself, and the standard park fee of $6 per person for three days covers access to this cave only; note that Golden Eagle passes (see p.51) are not accept-

△ View from Inspiration Point, Bryce Canyon National Park, Utah

ed. Direct elevators drop to the Cavern's centerpiece, the **Big Room**, 750 vertical feet below the visitor center (summer first down 8.30am, last up 6.30pm; rest of year first down 8.30am, last up 4.55pm), but you can choose instead to walk down via the **Natural Entrance Route** (last entry summer 3.30pm; rest of year 2pm). This steep, paved footpath switchbacks into the guano-encrusted maw of the cave, taking fifteen minutes to reach the first of the formations and another fifteen to reach the Big Room. All visitors are obliged to ride the elevator back out.

Measuring up to 1800ft long and 250ft high, the Big Room is festooned with stalactites, stalagmites, and countless unnameable shapes of swirling liquid rock. All are a uniform stone gray; the rare touches of color are provided by slight red or brown mineral-rich tinges, improved here and there with gentle pastel lighting. Most visitors take an hour or so to complete the reasonably level trail around the Room's perimeter. Whatever the weather up top – summer highs exceed 100°F – the temperature down here is always a cool 56°F, so dress warmly.

Adjoining the Big Room, the **Underground Lunchroom** is a vast formation-free side cave paved over in the 1950s to create a diner-cum-souvenir-shop that sells indigestible lunches in polystyrene containers, plus Eisenhower-era souvenirs like giant pencils and Viewmaster reels. To modern eyes, this strange installation seems absurd, but moves to close it down have been stymied by its place in popular affections.

The main appeal of walking down used to be that the trail meandered through beautiful side caves such as the **King's Palace**, filled with translucent "draperies" of limestone, but these are now open to guided tours only, which start from the Big Room (daily summer 9am, 11am, 1pm & 3pm; winter 10am & 2pm; $8). Additional tours, scheduled in the visitor center, can take you along the **Left Hand Tunnel** route down from the visitor center ($7), or on a much more demanding descent into either **Spider Cave** or the **Hall of the White Giant** (both $20). It's also possible to take a two-hour tour of **Slaughter Canyon Cave**, 25 miles southwest of the visitor center (typically summer daily 8am & 11am, spring and fall Sat & Sun 8am & 11am, winter Sat & Sun 10am; call ☎505/785-2232 for exact schedule; $15). To get there, drive five miles south of White's City on US-62/180, then eleven miles west on Hwy-418, and finally hike the steep half-mile up to the cave entrance.

The recesses of Carlsbad Caverns are the summer home of around a million Mexican free-tailed **bats**. Each evening, at dusk or a little later, having slept all day suspended from the ceiling of the imaginatively titled Bat Cave, they emerge in cloud-like spirals, and disperse across the desert in search of delectable insects. There's no public access to the cave, and park visitors watch the spectacle from the amphitheater seating that faces the cave mouth, while rangers give a free and informative "Bats aren't as bad as you think" presentation.

Practicalities

No matter how you get to Carlsbad Caverns, you have to cross seemingly endless miles of the **Llano Estacado**, the deathly flat rangeland that covers southeast New Mexico and the Texas Panhandle. The route from El Paso, Texas, has the advantage of passing through **Guadalupe Mountains National Park**, a beautiful though little-visited complement to Carlsbad, which offers superb camping (see p.804).

WHITE'S CITY is not a town but a privately owned tourist complex, which as well as featuring a little water park provides the closest **accommodation** and **camping** to the national park, including the mock-adobe *Best*

Western Cavern Inn (☎505/785-2291 or 1-800/228-3767, ⓦwww.whitescity .nm; ❹); the *White's City RV Park* (same number), which has tent camping space; and the *Velvet Garter Restaurant* (same number). The town of **CARLS-BAD** itself, 25 miles north of White's City, holds little of interest outside its many motels, such as the central *Holiday Inn*, 601 S Canal St (☎505/885-8500 or 1-800/742-9586, ⓔholidayinn1@pccnm.com; ❹), and the clean, comfort-able *Super 8*, 3817 National Parks Hwy (☎505/887-8888; ❸). The *Firehouse Grill & Club*, 222 W Fox St (☎505/234-1546), has a wide-ranging menu, cov-ering seafood and pasta as well as steaks.

Roswell

Seventy-five miles north of Carlsbad, the small ranching town of **ROSWELL** is renowned because an alien spaceship supposedly crash-landed nearby on July 4, 1947. The commander of the local air force base authorized a press statement announcing that they had retrieved the wreckage of a flying saucer, and despite a follow-up denial within a day – claiming that it was in fact a weather balloon – the story has kept running. In 1997, as 100,000 *X-Files* fanatics descended upon Roswell for a six-day festival to mark the "Incident's" fiftieth anniversary, the US government revealed that the errant weather balloon had crashed while monitoring the atmosphere for evidence of Soviet nuclear tests. Nonetheless, their imaginations further stimulated by TV series like *Roswell* and *Taken*, UFO theorists remain unconvinced.

Despite its best intentions, and the wishful thinking of the truly weird clien-tele who drift in from the plains, the central **International UFO Museum**, 114 N Main St (daily 9am–5pm; free; ☎505/625-9495, ⓦwww.iufomrc.org), inadvertently exposes the whole tawdry business as transparent nonsense. Its showpiece is a model of the notorious "alien autopsy"; built for the movie *Roswell*, you can't help suspecting it was also featured in the grainy "documen-tary" autopsy footage that created a brief international sensation in 1995.

By way of contrast, the longstanding **Roswell Museum**, 100 W 11th St (Mon–Sat 9am–5pm, Sun 1–5pm; free), boasts an excellent, multifaceted col-lection with nary an alien corpse to be seen. Its most sensational section cele-brates pioneer rocket scientist Robert Goddard (1882–1945), while historical artifacts elsewhere range from armor and pikes brought by Spanish conquista-dors to astronaut Harrison Schmitt's spacesuit. A huge gallery also displays Southwestern landscapes by Henriette Wyeth and Peter Hurd, and a solitary Georgia O'Keeffe, *Ram's Skull With Brown Leaves*.

Roswell's **visitor center** is at 426 N Main St (Mon–Sat 9am–5pm; ☎505/624-0889, ⓦwww.roswell-nm.com). The finest **motel** in town, the *Best Western Sally Port Inn*, 2000 N Main St (☎505/622-6430 or 1-800/548-5221, ⓦwww.bestwestern.com; ❹), also has a good **restaurant**; the *Super 8*, 3575 N Main St (☎505/622-8886 or 1-800/800-8000; ❸), and the *Frontier Motel*, 3010 N Main St (☎505/622-1400 or 1-800/678-1401, ⓦwww.frontiermotelroswell .com; ❷), are cheaper and serviceable.

Lincoln

One of the most enduring of New Mexico's many legendary Wild West fig-ures was a Brooklyn-born, one-time bus boy named William Bonney, better known as **Billy the Kid**. Many towns lay claim to him, but he first came to fame as an 18-year-old in the **Lincoln County War**, which erupted in 1878 in the frontier town of **LINCOLN** – on Hwy-380 halfway between Carlsbad and Albuquerque – when rival groups of ranchers and merchants fought to gain control of the town and the hundreds of square miles of grazing lands sur-rounding it. Since those days, no new buildings have joined the venerable false-fronted structures that line Main Street, and the entire town is now the **Lincoln State Monument**. Visitors can stroll its length at any time, while the cheapest way to visit its various historical sites is via a joint admission ticket, sold at the sites (daily 8.30am–5pm, though not all remain open throughout the winter; $6, or $3.50 for each individual site; ☎505/653-4372).

Displays in the modern **Lincoln County Historical Center**, at the east end of town, cover Hispanics, cowboys, "Buffalo Soldiers" – the black cavalrymen stationed at nearby Fort Stanton – and Apaches, as well as the Lincoln County War. Billy the Kid's most famous jailbreak is commemorated at the **Lincoln County Courthouse**, at the other end of the street; waiting here under sen-tence of death, he shot his way out and fled to Fort Sumner, where Sheriff Pat Garrett eventually caught up with him (see p.998). On the first weekend of August, the town fills up, and its streets echo with gunfire once again, during the three-day **Old Lincoln Days** festival.

Near the courthouse, the *Wortley Pat Garrett Hotel* – once owned by Sheriff Pat Garrett – offers eight plain but appealing **hotel** rooms (open late April to mid-Oct only; PO Box 96, Lincoln, NM 88338; ☎505/653-4300 or 1-8777/WORTLEY; ❸), and its **dining room** serves simple stews and sand-wiches at lunchtime only. If you like a bit more comfort, head to the nearby *Casa de Patrón* **B&B** (PO Box 27, Lincoln, NM 88338; ☎505/653-4676 or 1-800/524-5202, ⓦwww.casapatron.com; ❹), where the more expensive rooms are in a separate but less atmospheric modern annex.

Ruidoso

The **Sacramento**, **Capitan**, and **Jicarilla mountains**, which rise at the west-ern edge of the Llano Estacado, 85 miles northwest of Carlsbad, form a rare respite from the scrubby flatness. Spread out along winding roads that cut through dense groves of pine, fir, and aspen, the main town here, **RUIDOSO** – named for the Ruidoso ("noisy") River – is the fastest-growing resort in the Southwest.

The **Ruidoso Downs** racetrack, just east of town, plays host to a 77-day rac-ing season that culminates on Labor Day with the **All-American Futurity**, one of the world's richest horse races. Alongside, the **Hubbard Museum of the American West** (daily 9am–5.00pm; $5; ☎505/378-4142, ⓦwww.zianet.com/museum) holds displays on the natural and human-related history of horses, with a selection of memorabilia from around the world such as horse-drawn Russian sleighs, English road coaches, and Wild West stage-coaches.

In winter, attention turns to the 12,000-foot slopes of **Ski Apache** (☎505/336-4356, ⓦwww.skiapache.com), a downhill ski area northwest of town on Hwy-532 where lift tickets cost around $45 per day. Though operated by the Mescalero Apache, it's not on tribal land – they bought it as a going con-cern.

Brochures from Ruidoso's **visitor center**, 720 Sudderth Ave (Mon–Sat 9am–5pm, Sun 1–4pm; ☎505/257-7395 or 1-800/253-2255, ⓦwww.ruidoso.net), list dozens of **motels**, such as the inexpensive *Apache*, 344 Sudderth Ave (☎505/257-2986 or 1-800/426-0616, ⓦwww.ruidoso.net/apache; ❷), and the *Super 8*, beside US-70 at 100 Cliff Drive (☎505/378-8180 or 1-800/800-8000; ❷), but supply still fails to meet demand on big race days. **Dining** pos-sibilities range from the classy French cuisine of *La Lorraine*, 2523 Sudderth

Drive (lunch Wed–Sat, dinner Mon–Sat, closed Sun; ☎505/257-2954), to the sandwiches and coffee at the nearby *Books and Beans*, 2501 Sudderth Drive (lunch only, closed Sun; ☎505/630-2326).

White Sands National Monument

Filling a broad valley west of Ruidoso and the Sacramento Mountains, the **White Sands** are 250 square miles of glistening, three-story-high dunes, not of sand, but of finely ground gypsum eroded from the nearby peaks. Unfortunately, most of the desert valley is under the control of the US military, who use it as a missile range and training ground for pilots, and as a landing site for the **space shuttle**; only the southern half of the dunes is protected within **White Sands National Monument** (and even that is often closed for an hour or two at a time while missile tests are under way). The best place to start is at the **visitor center**, just off US-70, which illuminates the unique plants and animals that dwell here (daily: summer 8am–7pm; winter 8am–5pm; ☎505/479-6124, ⓦwww.nps.gov/whsa). An eight-mile paved road ($3) stretches into the heart of the dunes, where you can scramble and slide in the sheer white landscape.

ALAMOGORDO, which sits at the base of the Sacramento Mountains, sixteen miles east of the Monument along US-54, holds the nearest food and lodging.

Las Cruces and Mesilla

From White Sands, US-70 heads southwest across the Tularosa Valley to **LAS CRUCES** – "the Crosses" – a large, modern farming community on the Rio Grande at the junction of I-10 and I-25. The town takes its name from the dozens of white crosses set up in the sands to mark the graves of early travelers killed by the Apache, but any real sense of its history is pretty well buried by motels and fast-food franchises.

The little-changed Hispanic Colonial village of **MESILLA**, just south of I-10 two miles west, was until the 1870s one of the Southwest's largest towns, with upward of eight thousand inhabitants. During the Civil War, it even served briefly as the Confederate capital of New Mexico and Arizona, but it went into swift decline when the railroad bypassed it in favor of Las Cruces in 1881. Mesilla's delightful Old West **plaza** has a real frontier feel to it, even though most of the old adobes that surround it – including the former courthouse where Billy the Kid was tried and sentenced to death in 1881 – now house art galleries and souvenir shops. **Restaurants** include the steak-oriented *Double Eagle* (☎505/523-6700) and *La Posta*, a Mexican cantina (closed Mon; ☎505/524-3524), while the *Mesón de Mesilla*, 1803 Av de Mesilla (☎505/525-2380 or 1-800/732-6025, ⓦwww.mesondemesilla.com; ❸), a gorgeous "boutique resort" **hotel** five minutes' walk east, has a top-class dining room, plus fifteen guest rooms offering widely varying facilities.

The southwest corner

I-10 heads west from Las Cruces across the wide-open rangeland that fills out the southwest corner of New Mexico, also known as the "**Bootheel**" for the way it steps down toward Mexico. It's so sparsely inhabited that there are roughly three square miles per person. Towns are few and far between: **DEMING**, sixty miles west of Las Cruces, has a few motels and cafés and is one of two stops for Amtrak trains. Even if you're racing through on the interstate, make time for the very good displays at **Deming Luna Mimbres Museum**, 301 S Silver Ave (Mon–Sat 9am–4pm, Sun 1.30–4pm; free), which relates the region's Native American and Wild West past, and has a great show of minerals and gemstones. **LORDSBURG**, too, on I-10 twenty miles short of Arizona, has a string of gas stations, cafés, and motels, but little else.

Silver City

Rarely visited and almost entirely wilderness, the semi-arid, forested, volcanic **Mogollon** and **Mimbres mountains** soar above the high desert plain of southwest New Mexico to over ten thousand feet. But for a number of copper mines, the area is protected within the **Gila National Forest**. The mountains are some of the most remote in the US, little altered since Apache warrior **Geronimo** was born here at the headwaters of the Gila River.

Halfway up the mountains, the biggest settlement, **SILVER CITY**, lies 45 miles north of I-10 at the junction of US-180 from Deming and Hwy-90 from Lordsburg. The Spanish came here in 1804, sold the Mimbreño Indians into slavery, and opened the **Santa Rita copper mine**, just east of town below the Kneeling Nun monolith. The town was re-established in 1870 as a rough-and-tumble silver camp – **Billy the Kid** spent most of his childhood here. A fine selection of ornate old buildings is scattered along elm-lined avenues and across the surrounding hills. The excellent **Silver City Museum** at 312 W Broadway (Tues–Fri 9am–4.30pm, Sat & Sun 10am–4pm; free) tells the boom-and-bust tales, and holds fine specimens of **Casas Grandes pottery**, beautiful Navajo rugs, and basketry from all the major Southwest tribes. Three blocks east, the original Main Street was washed away in a great flood and has become the cottonwood-shaded **Big Gulch Park**.

In downtown Silver City, the *Palace Hotel*, 106 W Broadway (☎505/388-1811, ⓦwww.zianet.com/palacehotel; ❷), is a small, nicely restored nineteenth-century hotel, kitted out with historic rather than contemporary fittings, where the ambiance – and the rates – are great. Just outside town, *Bear Mountain Guest Ranch* (☎505/538-2538 or 1-877/620-2327, ⓦwww.bearmountainlodge.com; ❹) is a large 1920s ranch, now run as a B&B by the Nature Conservancy, that makes a great base for bird-watching, cycling, mountain biking, or cross-country skiing. Bullard Street in the heart of town holds atmospheric **saloons and cafés** like the *Jalisco Café* at no. 100 (☎505/388-2060).

Gila Cliff Dwellings National Monument

Beautiful, twisting Hwy-15 threads north from Silver City into the mountains, passing the picturesque old mining camp of Pinos Altos during its fifty-mile, two-hour climb to the **Gila Cliff Dwellings National Monument**. A mile beyond the monument's **visitor center**, a further mile-long trail (daily: summer 8am–5pm; winter 8am–4.30pm; ☎505/536-9461, ⓦwww.nps.gov/gicl) sets off beside a year-round stream.

Only once you've followed the stream for half a mile do you get your first glimpse of the ancient pueblo, abandoned seven centuries ago by the **Mogollon** peoples. What look from below like three separate caves turn out, when you climb the hillside, to be a single deep alcove with three entrances. Each entrance was sealed with stones and mortar, even though behind them lay around forty interconnected rooms, sharing a communal plaza at the rear. While they may not be as architecturally impressive as those of Mesa Verde (see p.914), exploring them alone – you can wander freely through the chambers now that the entrances have been re-opened – allows you to imagine yourself as one of the original occupants.

The monument maintains four small, free **campgrounds** in the immediate vicinity, including the *Forks* beside the Gila River, which is equipped with running water in summer only.

Arizona

The tourism industry in **ARIZONA** has, literally, one colossal advantage – the **Grand Canyon** of the Colorado River. It's the single most awe-inspiring spectacle in a land of unforgettable geology, and one of the few places in the world that you absolutely have to see at least once in your life. However, the Grand Canyon is by no means the most interesting or memorable destination in the state. Indeed, in comparison to its inhuman scale, other parts of Arizona have a more abiding emotional impact, precisely because of the sheer drama of human involvement in this forbidding but deeply resonant desert landscape.

Over a third of the state still belongs to the **Native Americans** who have lived here for centuries, and who outside the cities form the majority of the population. In the so-called **Indian Country** of northeastern Arizona, the reservation lands of the **Navajo Nation** hold the stupendous **Canyon de Chelly** and dozens of other marvelously sited **Ancestral Puebloan ruins**, as well as the stark rocks of **Monument Valley**. The Navajo surround the homeland of one of the most stoutly traditional of all Native American peoples, the **Hopi**, who live in remote **mesa-top villages**. The third main tribal group is the **Apache**, in the harshly beautiful southeastern mountains – the last Native Americans to give in to the overwhelming power of the white American invaders.

Away from the reservations, **Wild West** towns like **Tombstone**, site of the famed gunfight at the OK Corral, give a clear sense of Arizona's characteristically rough-and-ready, pioneer mentality; this was the last of the lower 48 states to join the Union, in 1912. The **cities**, however, are not nearly so much fun. In **Phoenix**, the capital, well over a million souls are scattered over a 500-square-mile morass of shopping malls and tract-house suburbs; **Tucson** is rather more appealing, but is still liable to wear thin after a couple of days.

Though the open spaces of southern Arizona can be harsh and violent – most of the southwestern quarter, along the parallel I-8 and I-10 highways, is used as a bombing range – the bleakness is balanced somewhat by the many nature reserves that protect its amazing flora and fauna, such as **Saguaro National Park**, just outside Tucson, with its giant cactuses, real-life roadrunners, and rare Gila monsters.

Getting around Arizona

Arizona is better served by public transportation than much of the Southwest, but it's still hard to get around without a car. Greyhound **buses** stop at the major cities and most towns along the interstates, while Amtrak **trains** cross the state on two transcontinental routes (via Tucson in the south, or Flagstaff further north). Seeing the backcountry, however – and especially the reservations – is all but impossible without a car. The largest airport is at Phoenix, and assorted good-value, short-hop **flights** cover the principal destinations.

Tucson, Phoenix, and southern Arizona

Most of Arizona's compelling natural attractions are in its northern reaches, but the **southern** half of the state holds ninety percent of its people, all its significant cities, and several important historic sites. Apart from a couple of Spanish missions, the bulk of what there is to see is frontier Americana, especially in **Tombstone**, in the southeast corner. **Phoenix**, the state capital, is huge, sprawling, and dull; **Tucson** makes a better base for visiting this part of the US and for trips south of the border into Mexico.

Tucson and around

After serving as a Colonial outpost under the Spanish and Mexicans, and then as territorial capital for both the US and Confederate governments, **TUCSON** (pronounced *Too-sonn*) – a mere sixty miles north of Mexico on the cross-country I-10 – has grown into a modern mini-metropolis of around 750,000 people without entirely sacrificing its historic quarters. Now equal parts college town and retirement community, it's one of the more attractive big cities of the Southwest – which admittedly isn't saying much. Although it suffers from the same Sunbelt sprawl as Albuquerque and Phoenix, it does have a compact center, some enjoyable restaurants, and pretty good nightlife, energized by the 35,000 students at the University of Arizona. The city is also redeemed by having so much superb landscape within easy reach, from the forested flanks of **Mount Lemmon** to the rolling foothills of **Saguaro National Park**.

Arrival and information

Tucson International Airport, eight miles south of downtown (☎520/573-8000), receives far fewer long-distance flights than Phoenix. It's connected to central Tucson by the slow Sun Tran **bus** #11 or #6 ($1), and the $15 shuttle vans of Arizona Stagecoach (☎520/889-1000, ⓦwww.azstagecoach.com). For **taxi** service, call Allstate Cab (☎520/798-1111). The Amtrak station, downtown at 400 E Toole Ave, is served by three **trains** weekly in each direction between Los Angeles and points east, with connecting buses running north to Phoenix. Greyhound **buses** also stop very centrally, at 2 S Fourth Ave.

Tucson's downtown **visitor center**, at 100 S Church Ave (Mon–Fri 8am–5pm, Sat & Sun 9am–4pm; ☎520/624-1817 or 1-800/638-8350, ⓦwww.visittucson.org), has free maps and information. Old Pueblo Tours (☎520/795-7448, ⓦwww.oldpueblotours.com) offer two-hour guided **city tours** for $25, while Great Western Tours (☎520/572-1660, ⓦwww.gwtours.net) can take you further afield, including to San Xavier Mission ($30), or Tombstone and Bisbee ($95).

Accommodation

Tucson offers a broad range of **accommodation**, with reasonably priced hotels and motels in the central area, as well as some atmospheric **B&Bs** both in the historic center and out in the surrounding desert. It also has its fair share of **resorts** and **dude ranches**. Rates drop when the mercury rises, and some places are open only in the peak winter and spring seasons.

Catalina Park Inn 309 E First St ☎520/792-4541 or 1-800/792-4885, ⓦwww.catalina-parkinn.com. A beautiful but not overly fussy historic B&B across from a quiet park but within walking distance of the university and happening Fourth Avenue. Summer ❹, winter ❺

Clarion Santa Rita Hotel & Suites 88 E Broadway Blvd ☎520/622-4000 or 1-800/252-7466. Large and very central hotel that's an unexpected downtown bargain. With its tiles and stucco it's all pretty stylish, and it also features the good Mexican *Café Poca Cosa* (see p.1007) downstairs. Summer ❸, winter ❹

Flamingo Hotel & Suites 1300 N Stone Ave ☎520/770-1910 or 1-800/300-3533, ⓦwww.flamingohoteltucson.com. Attractively renovated motel, barely a mile north of downtown. ❸

Ghost Ranch Lodge 801 W Miracle Mile ☎520/791-7565 or 1-800/456-7565, ⓦwww.ghostranchlodge.com. Charming, old-fashioned motel/resort, roughly ten miles north of downtown, with south-of-the-border stylings, a cactus-filled garden, and amazingly low rates. Summer ❷, winter ❹

Hotel Congress 311 E Congress St ☎520/622-8848 or 1-800/722-8848, ⓦwww.hotcong.com. Bohemian downtown hotel, an easy walk from Amtrak, with vintage Art Deco furnishings, $18

hostel beds for HI-AYH members (no reservations), and simple private rooms. There's a small café and a lively bar downstairs, and at night it's one of the hottest music venues in town. Dorms ❶, private rooms summer ❶, winter ❸

Tanque Verde Ranch 14301 E Speedway Blvd ☎520/296-6275 or 1-800/234-3833, ⓦwww.tanqueverderanch.com. Arizona's most authentic dude ranch, an irresistibly romantic 400-acre spread adjoining Saguaro National Park twenty miles east of downtown, with luxury accommodation in individual *casitas* and a stable of over a hundred horses. Rates include all meals and a full program of rides. ❾

Westward Look Resort 245 E Ina Rd ☎520/297-1151 or 1-800/722-2500, ⓦwww.westwardlook.com. Updated historic resort on attractive landscaped grounds in the northern section of the city, offering extra-large rooms and suites. Summer ❹, winter ❽

The Town

Tucson has two main historic centers: the **downtown core** along the (usually bone-dry) Santa Cruz River, bisected by Congress Street, and the quarter around the **University of Arizona** campus, a mile to the east. The city was founded in the late 1700s by Catholic missionaries who came from Mexico, then a Spanish colony, to convert the Pima Indians. Nothing very substantial remains from this era, but hundreds of artifacts are now displayed inside the many historic adobe homes in and around the **El Presidio** district of cafés, art galleries, and B&Bs, two blocks north of Broadway. Access to much of El Presidio is controlled by the **Tucson Museum of Art**, 140 N Main Ave (June–Aug Tues–Sat 10am–4pm, Sun noon–4pm; Sept–May Mon–Sat 10am–4pm, Sun noon–4pm; $5, free Sun; ☎520/624-2333, ⓦwww.tucsonarts.com). The main building displays changing exhibitions of modern paintings and sculpture, while an adjoining adobe holds an excellent collection of folk art and pre-Columbian artifacts. The district's oldest house, La Casa Cordova, showcases the city's Mexican heritage.

Three blocks south, engulfed by the Tucson Convention Center complex, the adobe **Sosa-Carrillo-Frémont House**, 151 S Granada Ave (Wed–Sat 10am–4pm; free), is the sole survivor of a neighborhood torn down during the 1960s. Built for merchant Leopoldo Carrillo in 1858, it was briefly rented by former explorer John C. Frémont when he was Governor of Arizona in 1878. Though much restored, it offers a vivid sense of the more civilized side of frontier life.

Tucson's other main area of interest, around the University of Arizona, spreads between Sixth Street and Speedway Boulevard, a mile east of downtown. Its highlights are the on-campus **Arizona State Museum** (Mon–Sat 10am–5pm, Sun noon–5pm; free; ☎520/621-6302, ⓦwww.statemuseum .arizona.edu), where an exceptionally comprehensive assembly of Native American artifacts from the very earliest days traces the evolution of the various Southwest tribes, and the **Center for Creative Photography** (Mon–Fri 9am–5pm, Sat & Sun noon–5pm; $2; ☎520/621-7968, ⓦwww.creativephotography.org), featuring work by Ansel Adams, among other modern masters.

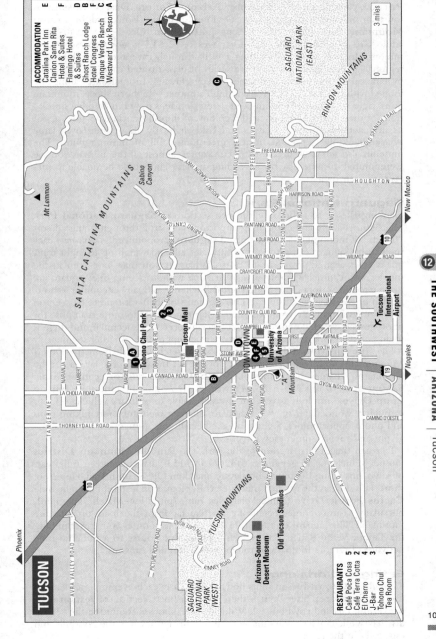

TUCSON

ACCOMMODATION
Catalina Park Inn	E
Clarion Santa Rita Hotel & Suites	F
Flamingo Hotel & Suites	D
Ghost Ranch Lodge	B
Hotel Congress	F
Tanque Verde Ranch	C
Westward Look Resort	A

RESTAURANTS
Café Poca Cosa	5
Café Terra Cotta	2
El Charro	4
J-Bar	3
Tohono Chul Tea Room	1

Arizona-Sonora Desert Museum

Part zoo, part garden, the top-quality **Arizona-Sonora Desert Museum** is fourteen miles west of the university along Speedway Boulevard, in **Tucson Mountain Park** (daily: March–Sept 7.30am–5pm; Oct–Feb 8.30am–5pm; adults $10 Nov–April, $9 May–Oct, ages 6–12 $1.75; ⓦwww.desertmuseum.org). Indoor displays, including a walk-through cave and mine, highlight regional geology and history, and a series of glass-fronted cages are occupied by tarantulas, rattlesnakes, and other creepy-crawlies. In enclosures along the looped path beyond – a hot walk in high summer – bighorn sheep, mountain lions, jaguars, and other seldom-seen desert denizens prowl in credible simulations of their natural habitats, and a colony of impish prairie dogs goes about its impenetrable business. Hawks and bald eagles fly about their own large aviary, thankfully separated from a greenhouse full of hummingbirds. The museum also serves as an animal rescue center: almost all the animals you see were injured in some way before ending up here, and would be unable to survive on their own.

Saguaro National Park

Flanking Tucson to either side, the two sections of **Saguaro National Park** offer visitors a rare and enthralling opportunity to stroll through strange desert "forests" of monumental, multi-limbed **saguaro** (pronounced *sa-wah-row*) cactuses. Each saguaro can grow up to fifty feet tall and weigh up to eight tons, but it takes around 150 years to do so. Whatever you may have seen in the movies, you can drive a long way in Arizona without seeing one; saguaro are unique to the Sonora Desert, and the thrill when you finally encounter a thousand at once is deeply satisfying. Both segments of the park tend to be seen on short forays from the city: in summer, it's far too hot to do more than pose for photographs, dwarfed beneath some especially eccentric specimen, and there is in any case no lodging, or even permanent campground, in either segment.

The **Tucson Mountain District**, which stretches north from the Desert Museum around fifteen miles west of downtown Tucson, on the far side of the mountains, charges no admission fee. Beyond the **visitor center** (daily 8.30am–5pm; ☎520/733-5158, ⓦwww.nps.gov/sagu), the nine-mile **Bajada Loop Drive** – not fully paved, but always passable to ordinary vehicles – loops through a wonderland of weird saguaro, offering plentiful short hiking trails and photo opportunities. Signal Hill is especially recommended, for its petroglyphs and superb sunset views.

To reach the eastern section of the park, the **Rincon Mountain District** ($6 per vehicle, or $3 per hiker; ☎520/733-5153), drive seventeen miles east of town, first along Broadway Boulevard and then Old Spanish Trail. Here, too, short trails such as the quarter-mile Desert Ecology Trail lead off the eight-mile **Cactus Forest Drive** (daily: April–Oct 7am–7pm; Nov–March 7am–5pm), but many visitors come specifically to hike far from the road, up into the mountains. The saguaro cactuses thin out almost as soon as you start climbing the Tanque Verde Ridge Trail, which leads in due course to a hundred-mile network of remote footpaths through thickly forested canyons.

Eating and drinking

Though downtown Tucson shuts down pretty early each evening – it's hard to find anything open after 9pm – the city has a fine selection of **restaurants**. Mexican joints and cowboy-style Wild West steakhouses abound in the central districts, while fancier restaurants congregate further north in the Foothills, and especially in the resort hotels.

Café Poca Cosa 88 E Broadway Blvd ☎520/622-6400. Stylish downtown café, with secluded outdoor seating, that serves tasty but inexpensive Mexican cuisine with plenty of contemporary Southwestern flair. Entrees under $10 at lunch, around $17 at dinner. Closed Sun.

Café Terra Cotta 3500 Sunrise Drive ☎520/577-8100. Inventive Southwestern cuisine, way north of downtown in the Foothills. The menu ranges from gourmet pizzas cooked in a wood-burning oven to meats grilled with chiles, all at under $20.

Cup Café *Hotel Congress*, 311 E Congress St ☎520/798-1618. Jazzy downtown café, straight out of the 1930s but updated to include an espresso bar, and serving a bewilderingly broad menu from 7am until after midnight daily.

El Charro 311 N Court Ave ☎520/622-1922. Housed in the same El Presidio building since 1922, this place claims to be the oldest Mexican restaurant in the US, and now has its own lively bar next door. The moderately priced food is good, though not especially fiery; specialties include fine *chimichangas*.

J-Bar *Westin La Paloma Resort*, 3770 E Sunrise Blvd ☎520/615-6000. Terrific Southwest-Mex cuisine by Tucson's nationally acclaimed chef Janos Wilder at half the price of his upscale restaurant, *Janos*, next door. That and the view make it work the trip north to the Foothills. Closed Mon.

Tohono Chul Tea Room Tohono Chul Park, 7366 N Paseo del Norte ☎520/797-1222. Attractive adobe café in a small desert park on the northern fringes of town. Open daily 8am–5pm; ideal for breakfast, a light lunch, or a scones-and-jam afternoon tea.

Nightlife

Most of the arty **cafés** and **nightclubs** on Congress Street downtown double as bars and restaurants, while several student-oriented places can be found in the university area. There are half a dozen country-and-western saloons on the outskirts of town as well. For a full rundown, check the listings in the free *Tucson Weekly*.

Choice options include *Club Congress*, inside *Hotel Congress* at 311 E Congress St (☎520/622-8848), a hectic, trendy, late-opening bar with live music a couple of nights each week. For microbrews and simple food, head for *Gentle Ben's Brewing Co*, 865 E University Blvd (☎520/624-4177), which is regularly packed out with students. A bit out from the center and brimming with Stetsons is *The Maverick, King of Clubs*, 4702 E 22nd St (☎520/748-0456), an old-fashioned country-music honky-tonk with live music nightly except Monday. There's also *The Rialto Theatre*, 318 E Congress St (☎520/740-0126, ⓦwww.rialtotheater.com), a 1920s vaudeville theater that's reopened as Tucson's hottest venue for touring bands.

Biosphere 2

The giant Plexiglass bubble known as **Biosphere 2** looms out of the desert thirty miles north of Tucson, at mile marker 96.5 on Hwy-77 near Oracle. Completed in 1991, it contains five separate "biomes," or self-contained ecosystems – rainforest, marsh, savannah, desert, and a 25-foot-deep ocean. Designed as a working model of Biosphere 1, planet Earth itself, it was stocked like a real-life Noah's Ark with four thousand plant and animal species.

Eight "Biospherians" were sealed into Biosphere 2 in September 1991, their "mission" being to survive in isolation for two full years. They more or less succeeded, but much of what transpired was replete with irony; hungry Biospherians planted bananas and papayas in what was supposed to be the inviolate rainforest, and destroyed parts of the desert to boost oxygen, while the ocean proved impossible to keep clean. After a second, even more farcical, mission had to be abandoned after six months, Biosphere 2 was taken over by Columbia University.

In its brief heyday, Biosphere 2 ranked among Arizona's most popular tourist destinations. Now that no one is locked inside, the crowds have dwindled, but the two-and-a-half-hour guided tours are still worth taking (tours daily 10am–4pm; $13; ☎520/838-6100, ⓦwww.bio2.edu). Most of that time is spent peering into the greenhouses hoping to spot any sign of life larger than an ant, but visitors are also allowed into the futuristic living quarters, tacked onto the back of the main block. For an extra $10, you can join a "World of Discovery" tour, which takes you right inside the greenhouses, and offers close-up views of the massive "lung" that enables the whole thing to breathe.

The all-day *Cañada del Oro* café serves good **meals** on an appealing terrace, while there's also good-value **lodging** at the on-site *Biosphere 2 Hotel* (☎520/838-6139 or 1-800/828-2462; ❹).

South to the border: the Mission Trail

South from Tucson, I-19 heads straight for the Mexican border, 65 miles away, passing some tangible reminders of the region's Spanish and Mexican heritage. The first of these, the **Mission San Xavier del Bac** – the best-preserved mission church in the United States – lies just west of the freeway, nine miles south of downtown Tucson on the fringe of the vast arid plain of San Xavier Indian Reservation (daily 9am–6pm; donation). It was built for the Franciscans between 1783 and 1797, and even today its white-plastered walls and towers seem like a dazzling desert mirage; how much more dramatic they must have been two centuries ago, when to Christian missionaries and Apache warriors alike they symbolized the Spanish quest to subdue and convert the native peoples of the Southwest. No one knows the name of the architect responsible for its Spanish Baroque, even Moorish lines – it consists almost entirely of domes and arches, making only minimal use of timber – let alone the identities of the O'odham craftsmen who embellished its every feature. The ideal time to come is on Sunday morning, when four separate Masses draw large congregations from the reservation.

Fifty miles further south, barely twenty miles north of the border, stands the evocative ruin of another eighteenth-century mission church, preserved as **Tumacácori National Historical Park** (daily 8am–5pm; $3 per person). Topped by a restored whitewashed dome, the mission is home only to the birds that fly down from the Patagonia Mountains. Behind its red-tinged, weather-beaten facade, the plaster has crumbled from the interior walls to reveal bare adobe bricks. A few traces of a mural can still be discerned in the raised sanctuary, but little remains of the priests' living quarters alongside. A very informative museum is housed in the small **visitor center** at the entrance.

Nogales, Arizona, and Nogales, Mexico

Twenty miles south of Tumacácori, an hour from Tucson, sits the largest of the Arizona–Mexico border towns, **NOGALES** – in effect two towns, one in the US and one across the border in Mexico, which are known jointly as *Ambos Nogales* (both Nogales). There's nothing in particular to see on either side of the border, though the contrast between the orderly streets of the American town and the jumbled white-washed houses clinging to the slopes in Mexico hits you as soon as you come in sight. Nogales, Arizona is a dreary little community, while Nogales, Mexico, is basically a lively, large-scale street market.

Crossing the border is straightforward, as Mexican visas are only required by travelers heading more than 21km south of the border. US citizens should, however, carry their passports or birth certificates, while foreign visitors should check that their visa status entitles them to re-enter the US; if you're on or eligible for the Visa Waiver Scheme (see p.16), you're fine. If driving, leave your car on the US side; you'll see lots of cheap lots as you approach the border. There's no need to change money: US dollars are accepted by stores and businesses across the border.

None of the Arizona-side **motels** stands within a mile of the border; the closest is the *Best Western Siesta Motel*, 673 N Grand Ave (☎520/287-4671 or 1-888/215-4783; ❷). Most visitors prefer to **eat** in Mexico, where abundant cafés and diners line the busy central streets. Classier dining is offered by *La Roca*, hollowed into the rocky hillside just east of the railroad, a couple of blocks from the border at calle Elias 91, where a full seafood meal costs under $20.

The southeast corner

Among thousands of acres of unspoiled and magnificent wilderness, southeast Arizona contains numerous well-preserved and highly atmospheric **ghost towns**. I-10 buzzes across the region toward the New Mexico border, but for a grand tour of the region you can detour south instead along the more scenic US-80.

Kartchner Caverns State Park

Arizona's newest state park – **Kartchner Caverns**, seven miles south of Benson – centers on caves in the Whetstone Mountains that were discovered in 1974. Unlike Carlsbad Caverns, they're unusual in being "live," or still growing, but they're not really worth traveling across the country to see, and with a visit for a family of four costing $50 in admission fees alone, they're also wildly overpriced.

Admission to the park costs $10 per vehicle, but visitors can only see the caves on **guided tours**, which cost a further $14 per adult, $6 per child aged 7–13. Most of these are fully booked, so **reservations** must be made as far in advance as possible (by phone only; Mon–Fri 8am–5pm; ☎520/586-2283). You have to pay the full fee by credit card when you book; the fees are not refundable, though you can change precise timings. It's not possible to make same-day reservations by phone, but a recorded message indicates whether space is likely to be available if you turn up without a reservation. If you fail to get in, you'll have to content yourself with the displays in the large **Discovery Center** instead (daily 7.30am–6pm; park information ☎520/586-4110 or ⓦwww.pr.state.az.us).

Tours start every twenty minutes, from 8.40am until 4.40pm daily, and spend 45 minutes threading through the caverns' two upper "rooms," the **Throne Room** and the **Rotunda Room**. The most spectacular feature is the striated **coloring** of the cavern walls, created by eons of unseen flooding and illuminated by a dramatic sound-and-light show. All of which you'll have to commit to memory, as no photography or filming is permitted.

Tombstone

Perhaps the most famous town in the Wild West, **TOMBSTONE** lies 22 miles south of I-10 on US-80, 67 miles southeast of Tucson. More than a century has passed since its mining days came to an end, but "The Town Too Tough to Die" clings to an afterlife as a tourist theme park. With its dusty streets, wooden sidewalks, and swinging saloon doors, it's surprisingly unchanged. Most adults, however, have seen too many inauthentic replicas and movie re-creations for even the real thing to retain much appeal, and so Tombstone is reduced to trying to divert kids with tacky dioramas and daily shoot-outs. The best time to visit is during **Helldorado Days** in late October, when the air is cooler and the sun less harsh, but the streets are full of gun-toting strangers acting out gun battles and stagecoach robberies.

Tombstone only began life as a silver-boomtown in 1877, and by the end of the 1880s it was all but deserted again. However, on the day that gave it the notoriety that's kept it alive, its population stood at more than ten thousand. It was 2pm on October 26, 1881, when **Doc Holliday**, along with **Wyatt Earp** and his brothers Virgil and Morgan (who all served as local sheriffs), confronted a band of suspected cattle rustlers, the Clantons, in the legendary **Gunfight at the OK Corral**. Within a few minutes, three of the suspects were dead. The Earps were accused of murder, but charges were eventually dropped.

Although the gunfight in fact took place on Fremont Street, the **OK Corral** itself remains the major attraction for visitors (daily 8.30am–5pm; $2.50, or $4.50 if you're there for the 2pm gunfight; ☎520/457-3456, ⓦwww.ok-corral .com), despite the fact that it holds little more than crude dummies that show the supposed locations of the Earps and the Clantons, in complete contradiction to contemporary reports of the fight.

A couple of blocks along Allen Street, the **Bird Cage Theater** (daily 8am–6pm; $5) was once Tombstone's leading venue for entertainment of all kinds. Seven "bird cages," much like theater boxes but curtained off and said to have been used by prostitutes, hang from either side of the main hall. The dusty, cluttered theater now holds a motley collection of curiosities, including a revolting foot-long "merman" from China, while downstairs you can see the old gaming tables and bordello rooms. The exhibits are real enough, but there's little historical accuracy to many of the makeshift signs. You might want to skip it entirely in favor of **Tombstone Courthouse State Historic Park** on Toughnut and Third streets, just off the main drag (daily 8am–5pm; $2.50). This one-time seat of Cochise County features the little-changed courtroom where several well-known trials of the time took place. Excellent exhibits include two detailed alternative versions of what might have actually happened at the OK Corral.

Central **motels** include the *Tombstone Motel*, 502 E Fremont St (☎520/457-3478 or 1-888/455-3478, ⓦwww.tombstonemotel.com; ❸), while the classier mountain-view *Best Western Lookout Lodge* is a mile north on US-80 W (☎520/457-2223 or 1-877/652-6772, ⓦwww.tombstone1880.com/bwlook-outlodge; ❹), just across from the Boot Hill Graveyard. Among old-style **saloons** serving burgers and beer in a raucous atmosphere are the *Crystal Palace* at Fifth and Allen streets, and *Big Nose Kate's* at 417 E Allen St, where you can still join an ongoing card game.

Bisbee

Crammed into a narrow gorge 25 miles south of Tombstone, the town of **BISBEE** is rivaled only by Jerome, near Sedona, as Arizona's most atmospheric Victorian relic. Like Jerome, its fortunes were built on a century of mining mundane copper from the surrounding mountains, rather than a few ephemeral years of gold and silver. Its solid brick buildings still stand as an enduring testament to the days when Bisbee's population of twenty thousand outstripped both Phoenix and Tucson to make it the largest city between New Orleans and San Francisco. Phelps Dodge finally closed down its Bisbee operations in 1975, having extracted more than six billion dollars' worth of metals. As the miners moved away, however, artists and retirees moved in, preserving Bisbee's original architecture while turning it into a thriving, friendly little community that caters to tourists without being overwhelmed by them.

Walking Bisbee's narrow central streets, lined with galleries and antiques stores, is a pleasure in itself, but if you'd like to know more of the background it's well worth calling in at the **Bisbee Mining and Historical Museum**, 5 Copper Queen Plaza (daily 10am–4pm; adults $4, under-18s free).

The best **place to stay** is the venerable *Copper Queen Hotel*, 11 Howell Ave (☎520/432-2216 or 1-800/247-5829 in Arizona, ⓦwww.copperqueen.com; ❹), with a plush bar and a good **restaurant** with terrace seating.

Southwest Arizona: Yuma

There's virtually nothing in the vast desert plain of southwest Arizona to tempt you off the twin freeways that sprint to California. The US Army stages tank battles in its Yuma Proving Grounds between I-10 and I-8, while the air force drops bombs and tests Stealth technology in the more mountainous region bordering Mexico. The largest town hereabouts, **YUMA**, is little more than an oversized pit stop for freight trains and cross-country truckers. **Yuma Territorial Prison**, now a state park (daily 8am–5pm; $3) beside the Colorado River, was known a century ago as the "Hell Hole of Arizona," holding over a hundred of the Wild West's most violent criminals. Its first inmates were forced to build the adobe walls that later contained them; you can wander around the grounds and cell blocks at will, and visit the small museum.

Neon-lit budget **motels** along the main drag include the good-value *Yuma Cabana*, 2151 S Fourth Ave (☎928/783-8311 or 1-800/874-0811, ⓦwww.yumacabana.com; ❷), while the **River City Grill**, downtown at 600 W Third St (☎928/782-7488), is a bright "international" restaurant that has rapidly established itself as Yuma's most fashionable hangout.

Phoenix

The state capital and largest city in Arizona, **PHOENIX** holds only minimal appeal for tourists. When it began life in the 1860s, it must have seemed like a good idea. The sweltering little farming town stood in the heart of the large Salt River Valley, with a ready-made irrigation system left by ancient Indians (the name Phoenix honors the fact that the city rose from the ashes of a long-vanished **Hohokam** community). Within a century, however, Phoenix had turned into what writer Edward Abbey called "the blob that is eating Arizona," acquiring as it did so the money and political clout to defy the self-evident absurdity of building a huge city in a virtually waterless desert. Now the sixth largest city in the US, it has filled the entire valley, engulfing the neighboring towns of **Scottsdale**, **Mesa**, and **Tempe** in the process, and encompassing over a million people within the city boundaries and more than two million in the metropolitan area. Arizona's financial and industrial epicenter may just be getting into its stride; boosters claim the megalopolis will one day stretch 150 miles, from Wickenburg to Tucson.

The city's phenomenal rise was originally fueled by its image as a healthy oasis, where the desert had been tamed and transformed into a suburban idyll. While retirees still flock to enclaves such as **Sun City**, Phoenix now has a deserved reputation as the most unpleasant city in the Southwest – Las Vegas with no casinos, or LA with no beach. Above all, it's **hot**; between June and August daytime highs average over 100°F, making it the hottest city outside the Middle East.

In winter, when temperatures rarely drop below 65°F, tourists from colder climes arrive in large numbers. They pay vast sums to warm their bones in the luxury resorts and spas, concentrated especially in Scottsdale, that are the modern equivalent of the 1930s dude ranches. Unlike golf, tennis, and shopping, sightseeing rarely ranks high on the agenda – which is just as well, since there's a good deal of truth in the charge laid by Phoenix's older arch-rival, Tucson, that the city is sorely lacking in culture and history. Apart from the **Heard Museum**'s excellent Native American displays, the cactuses at the **Desert Botanical Garden**, and Frank Lloyd Wright's architecture studio at **Taliesin West**, Phoenix is short of must-see attractions. In fact, if you're on a touring vacation, you'd miss little if you bypassed it altogether.

Arrival, information, and getting around

Sky Harbor International Airport is three miles east of downtown (☎602/273-3300, ⓦwww.phxskyharbor.com). Red Line **buses** on the Valley Metro system (☎602/253-5000) connect the airport with downtown (Mon–Sat), plus Tempe and Mesa (Mon–Fri), but it's easier to take a door-to-door **shuttle bus**, at $10–12 for downtown destinations and $20 for Scottsdale, with SuperShuttle (☎602/244-9000 or 1-800/BLUE VAN, ⓦwww.supershuttle.com). Arizona Shuttle Services (☎928/795-6671 or 1-800/888-2749, ⓦwww.arizonashuttle.com) runs an hourly service south to Tucson, costing $24.

There's no Amtrak **train** service to Phoenix, but Greyhound **buses** arrive at 2115 E Buckeye Rd (☎602/389-4200), close to the airport. Getting around without a car is not ideal – it can take hours to cross town – but it's not impossible. Valley Metro's commuter routes charge $1.25 per ride; pick up a schedule at Central Station, downtown at 302 N Central Ave at Van Buren St. Tourists are more likely to use the purple DASH buses (Mon–Fri 6.30am–5.30pm; 30¢), which run between the Arizona Center and the Capitol downtown. For a **cab**, call Checker Cab (☎602/257-1818).

Phoenix's main **visitor center** is at Adams and Second streets downtown (Mon–Fri 8am–5pm; ☎602/254-6500 or 1-877/225-5749, ⓦwww.phoenix-cvb.com); there's also an office at 24th Street and Camelback Road, at the northeast corner of the Biltmore Fashion Park (Mon–Sat 10am–9pm, Sun noon–6pm). Scottsdale has its own visitor center at 7343 Scottsdale Mall (Mon–Fri 8.30am–6pm, Sat 10am–4pm, Sun 11am–4pm; ☎480/945-8481 or 1-800/877-1117, ⓦwww.scottsdalecvb.com). The main **post office** is at 4949 E Van Buren St, though the branch at 522 N Central Ave is more convenient for downtown.

Accommodation

Metropolitan Phoenix is so huge that it's worth paying a bit extra to ensure that your **accommodation** is near the places you want to visit. Oddly enough, downtown Phoenix is not one of the more expensive areas, with cheap motels lining the somewhat run-down W Van Buren Street a few blocks north of the center. The summer room rates, given below, rise significantly in winter, when snowbirds from all over the US fill the upscale resorts of Scottsdale in particular.

Arizona Biltmore Resort & Spa 24th St and Missouri Ave ☎602/955-6600 or 1-800/950-0086, ⓦwww.arizonabiltmore.com. Extraordinarily lavish 500-room resort, designed by Frank Lloyd Wright in the 1930s, and renovated while retaining its Art Deco trimmings. ❾

Budget Lodge Motel 402 W Van Buren St ☎602/254-7247. Reasonably attractive rooms at very attractive rates – not far from downtown, but you'll feel safer if you drive rather than walk. ❷

Days Inn Scottsdale Fashion Square Resort 4710 N Scottsdale Rd, Scottsdale ☎480/947-5411 or 1-800/325-2525, ⓦwww.scottsdale-daysinn.com. Though not all that prepossessing, this two-story motel, across the street from Fashion Square Mall, has perfectly acceptable rooms plus an outdoor pool, and can be a real bargain. Summer ❸, winter ❹

Econo Lodge Scottsdale Inn Resort 6935 Fifth Ave, Scottsdale ☎480/994-9461 or 1-800/528-7396, ⓦwww.econolodge.com. Good-value motel with pool, a short walk from Scottsdale's shopping district. ❸

Fiesta Inn 2100 S Priest Drive, Tempe ☎480/967-1441 or 1-800/528-6481, ⓦwww.fiestainnresort.com. Old-style resort, not as plush as its Scottsdale counterparts, but not as

expensive either, offering large rooms plus restaurant, pool, tennis courts, and spa. Summer ❹, winter ❻

Metcalf House Hostel 1026 N Ninth St above Roosevelt St ☎602/254-9803. A 15min walk north of the Arizona Center downtown, with no curfew and cheap bike rental. No phone reservations taken, but space is usually available. Dorm beds at $12 for HI-AYH members, $15 others. ❶

San Carlos Hotel 202 N Central Ave ☎602/253-4121 or 1-866/253-4121, ⓦwww.hotelsancarlos.com. Atmospheric, very central Twenties' hotel, with tasteful good-value rooms, a nice café, and a rooftop swimming pool. Summer ❹, winter ❻

Tempe Mission Palms Hotel 60 E Fifth St, Tempe ☎480/894-1400 or 1-800/547-8705, ⓦwww.missionpalms.com. Very comfortable Southwestern-themed hotel in Tempe's revitalized Mill Avenue district, with a rooftop swimming pool. Summer ❸, winter ❻

Tempe Super 8 Motel 1020 E Apache Blvd, Tempe ☎480/967-8891 or 1-800/800-8000. Chain motel, within half a mile of the university and five miles of the airport. Summer ❷, winter ❸

YMCA 350 N First Ave ☎602/253-6181. Grungy but central single rooms for men and women, with shared bathrooms. Very low weekly rates. No reservations taken. ❶

Central Phoenix

Downtown Phoenix – defined as the few blocks east and west of Central Avenue, and north and south of Washington Street – is too hot, too run-down, and too spread out to walk around in any comfort. The only time it's buzzing is when the World Series–winning Arizona Diamondbacks are playing at the Bank One Ballpark. At other times, life tends to revolve around the modern **Arizona Center** mall, on Van Buren Street between Third and Fifth streets, which is nonetheless a pale imitation of the mega-malls further north.

What little remains of Phoenix's nineteenth-century architecture now constitutes **Heritage Square**, a couple of blocks southeast of the Arizona Center at 115 N Sixth St. Rather than original adobe ranch houses, however, it preserves a quaint assortment of Victorian homes, converted into tearooms and toy museums. You can get a better impression of the early days at the **Phoenix Museum of History**, across the street at 105 N Fifth St (Mon–Sat 10am–5pm, Sun noon–5pm; $5), which features the city's first jail – a rock with a chain attached. Twenty sun-baked blocks west, the sparkling copper dome of the disused **Arizona State Capitol** dominates the low-level sprawl. Documents in the dull, dry museum within do little to bring the state's political history to life (Jan–May Mon–Fri 8am–5pm, Sat 10am–3pm; June–Dec Mon–Fri 8am–5pm; free).

Two more significant attractions lie a mile or so north of downtown. Thanks to extensive remodeling, the **Phoenix Art Museum**, 1625 N Central Ave (Tues, Wed & Fri–Sun 10am–5pm, Thurs 10am–9pm; $7, free Thurs 5–9pm; ☎602/257-1222, Ⓦwww.phxart.org), has plenty of space to display its permanent collection, which includes paintings by Georgia O'Keeffe and Rufino Tamayo, as well as *de rigueur* Western art by Russell and Remington and some middleweight Old Masters, and features stimulating temporary exhibitions as well. Three blocks north and a block east, the **Heard Museum**, 22 E Monte Vista Rd (daily 9.30am–5pm; $7; ☎602/252-8848, Ⓦwww.heard.org), has also been greatly enlarged, while still showcasing the lovely old buildings in which it was founded. It provides a fascinating introduction to the Native Americans of the Southwest, and their arts and crafts in particular. There's a special emphasis on the Hohokam, with plenty of artifacts from the large town, now known as "La Ciudad," which occupied the site of modern Phoenix during the twelfth century. Elsewhere, the superb pottery collection ranges from stunning Mimbres bowls to modern Hopi ceramics, but the real highlight is a refrigerated room filled with **kachina dolls** arranged according to the Hopi sacred calendar.

In **Papago Park** at the south end of Scottsdale, the fascinating **Desert Botanical Garden** (daily: Oct–April 8am–8pm; May–Sept 7am–8pm; $7.50) is filled with an amazing array of cactuses and desert flora from around the world. Prime specimens include spineless "totem pole" cactuses from the Galápagos Islands, and "living stone" plants from South Africa. Separate enclaves are devoted to **butterflies** – at their best in August and September – and **hummingbirds**, of which Arizona boasts fifteen indigenous species.

Finally, if Phoenix gets too hot to bear, the coolest place to beat the heat is on the east side of town at the Big Surf **water park**, 1500 N McClintock Ave (May–Sept only, Mon–Sat 10am–6pm, Sun 11am–7pm; $17.50), where you can ride 5-foot waves or careen down waterslides into a giant freshwater lagoon.

Taliesin West and the Cosanti Foundation

Whatever its general appearance may suggest, Phoenix has managed to attract some visionary designers. Notable among them is **Frank Lloyd Wright**, who came to the city to work on the *Biltmore Hotel*, and stayed for most of the 25 years before his death in 1959. His winter studio, **Taliesin West** – located at 114th Street and Frank Lloyd Wright Boulevard, at Scottsdale's northeastern edge – is now an architecture school and a working design studio, with regular multimedia exhibits of the man's life and work (Oct–May daily 10am–4pm; June & Sept daily 9am–4pm; July & Aug Mon & Thurs–Sun 9am–4pm; ☏480/860-2700, Ⓦwww.franklloydwright.org). The site can only be seen on **guided tours**; you can join either an hour-long "Panorama Tour" ($17.50) or a ninety-minute "Insight Tour" ($22), which are offered at very regular intervals, rising to more than one every half-hour between February and mid-April.

Less well known, but in many ways more compelling, is the **Cosanti Foundation**, four miles west of Taliesin at 6433 Doubletree Rd (Mon–Sat 9am–5pm, Sun 11am–5pm; $1 donation; ☏1-800/752-3187, Ⓦwww.cosanti.com). The buildings, designed by **Paolo Soleri**, an Italian-born ex-student of Wright, and constructed out of rammed earth and concrete, have a much more organic feel than Taliesin. Crafts workshops make bells and cast bronzes, and a small museum shows drawings and models of Soleri's life's work: **Arcosanti**, a space-age, environmentally sensitive project designed to be (someday) an entirely self-sufficient community of five thousand people, which emerges from the desert just an hour's drive north, a mile east of I-17 at Cordes Junction. Hour-long guided tours are given throughout the day (daily 10am–4pm; $8 donation; ☏520/632-7135, Ⓦwww.arcosanti.org), and an airy and spacious café serves healthy and tasty meals.

Eating

Most of the **restaurants** in greater Phoenix have retreated to the malls in recent years, so unless you're prepared to pay resort prices, it's hard to find a good restaurant with very much atmosphere. The mall places aren't at all bad, however, and there's plenty of variety. Apart from a block or two in central Scottsdale, no area of the metropolis is small enough to walk around while you look for a place to eat, but if you're happy to drive, neighborhood diners – especially Mexican – can still be found.

Alice Cooper'stown 101 E Jackson St ☏602/253-7337. Barbecue restaurant-cum-sports bar, owned by the rock star and alongside downtown's America West Arena. The food's better than you'd expect, and the atmosphere is fun, with waiters in full Alice make-up. Lunch and dinner daily.

Ed Debevic's Short Orders Deluxe 2102 E Highland Ave ☏602/956-2760. Burgers and fries, malts and cokes, served amid frenetic retro-Americana that includes a mini-jukebox on every table.

House of Tricks 114 E Seventh St, Tempe ☏480/968-1114. Tiny, romantic modern-American place in the university district, with lots of vegetarian options. Closed Sun.

Malee's on Main 7131 E Main St, Scottsdale ☏480/947-6042. Very popular and dependably good Thai place in downtown Scottsdale, serving all the usual items – pad Thai noodles, chicken green curry – at reasonable prices.

Monti's La Casa Vieja 3 W First St, Tempe ☏480/967-7594. Tempe's oldest adobe house,

built in 1873, is now an atmospheric Western-themed diner serving a conventional steak-and-chicken menu at extraordinarily low prices. Lunch and dinner daily.

Pizzeria Bianco Heritage Square, 623 E Adams St ☏602/258-8300. Good-quality pizzas in a very convenient downtown location. Closed Mon.

Roxsand Biltmore Fashion Park, 2594 E Camelback Rd ☏602/381-0444. Eclectic, futuristic restaurant in an upmarket uptown mall. Dinner entrees drawn from the major world cuisines – especially Asian, with plenty of spicy Thai and Chinese sauces – start at around $20, but lunch can be a bargain.

Roy's 7001 N Scottsdale Rd, Scottsdale ☏480/905-1155. Ravishing Pacific Rim restaurant in a very chic dining district. Meaty entrees, mostly at $20–25, include Szechuan barbecued pork ribs or rack of lamb, while specials usually include Hawaiian fish dishes. Dinner only.

Sam's Café Arizona Center, 455 N Third St ☏602/252-3545. Hectic downtown mall joint, with

patio seating, that's nonetheless a great place to try out modern Southwestern cuisine at old-fashioned prices.
Todai Seafood Buffet Biltmore Fashion Park, 2502 E Camelback Rd ☎602/381-0444 or 957-

9123. Superb all-you-care-to-eat Japanese buffet, where the spread includes sushi and sashimi as well as noodles and barbecue. Lunch $13–15, dinner $22–24.

Nightlife, entertainment, and sports

For a rundown of what's on musically in Phoenix, pick up the free weekly *New Times* in local record or book stores, or check out the bars and clubs listed below. Both the **Phoenix Symphony Hall**, 225 E Adams St (☎602/262-7272), and the **Scottsdale Center for the Arts**, 7380 E Second St (☎480/994-2787, ⓦ www.scottsdalearts.org), put on classical music, theater, and ballet. The **Arizona Diamondbacks** play major league baseball beneath the retractable roof of the Bank One Ballpark (☎602/514-8500 or 1-888/777-4664, ⓦ www.azdiamondbacks.com), while the **Phoenix Suns** play NBA basketball at the America West Arena, 201 E Jefferson St (☎602/379-7867, ⓦ www.suns.com), and football's **Arizona Cardinals** are based at the university's Sun Devil Stadium (☎602/379-0102, ⓦ www.azcardinals.com).

Bash on Ash 230 W Fifth St, Tempe ☎480/966-8200, ⓦ www.bashonash.com. Live music in the heart of Tempe, featuring reggae, rock, soul, or salsa nightly except Mon.
Char's Has The Blues 4631 N Seventh Ave ☎602/230-0205, ⓦ www.charshastheblues.com. Phoenix's longest-standing, best-loved blues venue, attracting big-name touring stars.
Coyote Springs Brewing Company Town & Country Shopping Center, 4883 N 20th St

☎602/256-6645. Mall microbrewery that puts on R&B several nights of the week.
Mr Lucky's 3660 NW Grand Ave ☎602/246-0686. Massive country-music honky-tonk, featuring real-life bull-riding at weekends.
Phoenix Live! Arizona Center, 455 N Third Ave ☎602/252-2502. Anodyne but very central alliance of three separate clubs under a single roof, with a single cover charge.

East of Phoenix: the Superstition Mountains

Relief from the tedious Phoenix sprawl is provided by the **Superstition Mountains** that rise to the east. The main route through the angular mountains, Hwy-88 (popularly known as the **Apache Trail**), is full of cars on summer weekends; the road cuts off northeast from US-60 about ten miles east of downtown Phoenix. Despite the many dams along the Salt River, it makes for a pleasant drive, with lots of picnic spots and campgrounds along the way. The road turns to gravel just beyond the funky hamlet of **Tortilla Flat**, before reaching the cliff dwellings of **Tonto National Monument** (daily 8am–5pm; $3 per person), where the remains of a large pueblo built in the mid-fourteenth century by Salado Indians are preserved in the mouths of three distinct caves.

Highway 88 rejoins US-60 at the nondescript mining town of **Globe**, on the western edge of the two-million-acre San Carlos Apache Indian Reservation, roughly sixty miles south of the awesome **Salt River Canyon**.

Central Arizona

The I-40 interstate crosses the center of Arizona, skirting the **Navajo Reservation** that fills the northeastern corner of the state. Though the narrow strip of land to either side can be extraordinarily beautiful, with double rainbows reaching across the desert plain and fiery dawns blazing along the horizon, it holds few specific places worth stopping for until you come to the **Flagstaff** area. Itself a pleasant town, Flagstaff makes a base for several interesting excursions – to ancient **Native American sites** and the New Age center of **Sedona**, but above all to the **Grand Canyon**. Beyond Flagstaff to the west, there is once again little of interest.

East of Flagstaff

The widely touted **Meteor Crater** (daily: mid-May to mid-Sept 6am–6pm; mid-Sept to mid-May 8am–5pm; $10, under-18s $5; Ⓦwww.meteorcrater .com), six miles south of the interstate on a well-marked road nearly forty miles east of Flagstaff, might have been interesting 22,000 years ago, when a meteorite blasted a huge hole, nearly a mile across and over five hundred feet deep, into the scrubby plateau. These days, however, it's a privately run tourist operation, managed in mock–Park Service style and absurdly overpriced. Visitors cannot hike into the actual crater.

Two old Route 66 towns, **WINSLOW** and **HOLBROOK**, are kept alive by transcontinental truckers. Each town consists of little more than a strip of motels, such as the *Best Western Adobe Inn* in Winslow at 1701 N Park Drive (Ⓣ928/289-4638; ❸), and the concrete teepees of the *Wigwam Motel* at 811 W Hopi Drive in Holbrook (Ⓣ928/524-3048 or 1-800/414-3021, Ⓦwww .galerie-kokopelli.com/wigwam; ❷). In addition, Winslow is now graced once more by the restored splendor of the 1929 *La Posada Hotel*, at 303 E Second St (Ⓣ928/289-4366, Ⓦwww.laposada.org; ❹).

Petrified Forest National Park

At **Petrified Forest National Park**, which straddles I-40 a dozen miles east of Holbrook, a fossilized prehistoric forest of gigantic trees has been unearthed by erosion. The original cells of the wood have been replaced by multicolored crystals of quartz. Cross-sections, cut through with diamond saws and polished, look stunning, and can be seen in the two **visitor centers**, thirty miles apart at the north and south entrances. On the ground, however, the trees are not all that exciting: segmented, crumbling, and very dark. Here and there rough concrete walkways have been laid over the terrain – and often over the tree trunks themselves. The **Long Logs Walk** near the southern entrance is probably the best section, but they're still just a bunch of logs lying in the sand, even if they are stone logs.

The northern section of the national park – site of the main visitor center and **entrance station** (daily: summer 7am–7pm; winter 8am–5pm; $10 per vehicle; Ⓣ928/524-6228, Ⓦwww.nps.gov/pefo) – is renowned for its views of the **Painted Desert**, an undulating expanse of solidified sand dunes, which at different times of day take on different colors (predominantly bluish shades of gray and reddish shades of brown).

Flagstaff

Northern Arizona's liveliest and most attractive town, **FLAGSTAFF** occupies a superbly dramatic location beneath the San Francisco Peaks, halfway between New Mexico and California. Straddling the I-40 and I-17 interstates, it's both a way station for tourists en route to the Grand Canyon, just eighty miles northwest, and a worthwhile destination in its own right.

Downtown, where barely a building rises more than three stories, oozes Wild West charm. Its main thoroughfare, Santa Fe Avenue, used to be **Route 66**, while before that it was the pioneer trail west. A stroll around its central few blocks is gloriously evocative of the past, while just to add to the atmosphere, the tracks of the Santa Fe Railroad still cut downtown in two, so life in Flagstaff remains punctuated both day and night by the mournful wail of passing trains.

Flagstaff's first settlers arrived in 1876, lured from Boston by tales of mineral wealth and fertile land. They soon moved on, disappointed, toward Prescott, but stayed long enough to celebrate the centenary of American independence by flying the Stars and Stripes from a towering pine tree. This flagpole became a familiar landmark on the route west, and as the town grew it inevitably became known as Flagstaff. It was a cosmopolitan place, with a strong black and Hispanic population working in the (originally Mormon-owned) lumber mills and in the cattle industry, and Navajo and Hopi heading in from the nearby reservations to trade.

Modern Flagstaff, with a population of a little over fifty thousand, makes an ideal base for travelers. As well as the abundant hotels, restaurants, bars, and shops within easy walking distance of downtown, outlets of the national food and lodging chains line the interstates, while hostels and student diners cater for budget travelers.

Arrival and information

Daily Amtrak **trains** heading both east and west pull in at the station in the very center of town, part of which doubles as a very helpful **visitor center** (Mon–Sat 7am–6pm, Sun 7am–5pm; ☏928/774-9541 or 1-800/842-7293, ⓦwww.flagstaffarizona.org).

Open Road Tours and Transportation (☏928/226-8060 or 1-800/766-7117, ⓦwww.openroadtours.com), based at the station, runs twice-daily **bus services** via Williams to the Grand Canyon ($69 for adults, $35 for under-12s). The first leaves Flagstaff at 8.30am, the second at 3pm. Greyhound, based a few blocks south of downtown at 399 S Malpais Lane (☏928/774-4573 or 1-800/231-2222), runs four daily buses to Phoenix, and also heads west to Las Vegas, Los Angeles, San Diego, and San Francisco, and east toward Albuquerque. Two local hostels – the *DuBeau* and the *Grand Canyon*, listed below – arrange inexpensive **excursions for backpackers**.

The least expensive **car rental** is Budget Rent-a-Car, 175 W Aspen Ave (☏928/813-0156); Avis, Hertz, Enterprise, and National also have outlets. Absolute Bikes, 18 N San Francisco St (Mon–Sat 9am–6pm; ☏928/779-5969, ⓦwww.absolutebikes.net), rents out **mountain bikes**.

Accommodation

Flagstaff's dozens of **motels** and **B&Bs** provide reasonable value, while budget travelers can benefit from a couple of high-quality **hostels**. Most of the chain motels are congregated well to the east, along Butler Avenue and Lucky Lane, but staying nearer downtown is usually much more fun.

DuBeau International Hostel 19 W Phoenix Ave ☏928/774-6731 or 1-800/398-7112, ⓦwww.dubeau.com. Welcoming independent hostel just south of the tracks, whose converted en suite motel rooms serve as four-person dorms at $16 per bed in summer, $14 in winter, or private doubles at $35. It also runs $18 one-way shuttle rides to the Grand Canyon (full-day tours $43). ❶

Econolodge West 2355 S Beulah Blvd ☏928/774-2225 or 1-800/490-6562, ⓦwww.travelsouthwest.com. Relatively appealing chain motel, in white-clapboard style with large

rooms and suites, south of downtown near the interstate. ❸

Grand Canyon International Hostel 19 S San Francisco St ☏928/779-9421 or 1-888/442-2696, ⓦwww.grandcanyonhostel.com. Independent hostel, under the same friendly management as the similar *DuBeau* nearby, and offering the same tours, plus dorm beds at $16 in summer, $12 in winter, and private rooms at $25. ❶

The Inn at Four Ten 410 N Leroux St ☏928/774-0088 or 1-800/774-2008, ⓦwww.inn410.com. This bright ranch home, now an antique-furnished B&B, has nine en suite rooms. ❹

Monte Vista 100 N San Francisco St ☏ 928/779-6971 or 1-800/545-3068, ⓦ www.hotelmonte-vista.com. Atmospheric little 1920s hotel in the heart of downtown, where the assorted restored rooms, with and without attached bathrooms, are named for celebrity guests from Bob Hope to Michael Stipe. Rates rise by up to $20 at weekends. ❸–❹

Super 8 West 602 W Route 66 ☏ 928/774-4581 or 1-888/324-9131. Smart, good-value chain motel, arranged around an enclosed swimming pool, alongside a Barnes & Noble bookstore less than a mile southwest of downtown. ❸

The Town

Flagstaff's appealing **downtown** stretches for a few redbrick blocks north of the railroad. Filled with cafés, bars, and stores selling Route 66 souvenirs and Indian crafts, as well as outfitters specializing in tents, clothing, and all sorts of contraptions for outdoor adventures, it's a fun place to stroll around, even if it holds no significant tourist attractions or historic buildings. Your most lasting impression is likely to be of the magnificent San Francisco Peaks, rising smoothly from the plains on the northern horizon, and topped by a jagged ridge.

The exceptional **Museum of Northern Arizona**, however, three miles northwest of downtown on US-180, rivals Phoenix's Heard Museum as the best museum in the state (daily 9am–5pm; $5, under-18s $2; ☏ 928/774-5213, ⓦ www.musnaz.org). Its main emphasis is on documenting Native American life, with an excellent run-through of the Ancestral Puebloan past and contemporary Navajo, Havasupai, and Hopi cultures, but it also actively encourages the development of traditional and even new skills among Native American craftworkers. The exquisite inlaid silver jewelry now made by the Hopi, for example, is the result of a museum-backed program to find work for Hopi servicemen returning from World War II. At all times, marvelous pots, rugs, and *kachina* dolls are on display – a pleasant surprise after the low standards often seen elsewhere – but the time to come is for one of the Indian Craftsmen Exhibitions each summer. During its annual **Native American Marketplaces**, every item is for sale. The Hopi show takes place on the weekend closest to July 4, the Navajo one at the start of August, the Zuni one at the start of September, and the Pai event later in September.

Eating and nightlife

There's enough money around in Flagstaff to support several upscale **restaurants**, while the area around San Francisco Street, both north and south of the tracks, must be the liveliest **nightspot** between Las Vegas and Santa Fe, filled with vegetarian cafés, espresso bars, and pubs.

Alpine Pizza 7 N Leroux St ☏ 928/779-4109. Raucous student hangout downtown, with decent pizza and lots of beer.

Beaver Street Brewery & Whistle Stop Café 11 S Beaver St ☏ 928/779-0079. Inventive sandwiches and salads, wood-fired pizza, and outdoor barbecue in the beer garden in summer.

Black Barts 2760 E Butler Ave ☏ 928/779-3142. Enjoyable Western-themed steakhouse on the east edge of town, with a delicious smell of burning wood, and wait staff who sing and dance on stage in between serving up barbecued steaks, ribs, and chicken ($16–23).

Dara Thai 14 S San Francisco St ☏ 928/774-0047. Large Thai place just south of the tracks, where the service is great and a plate of delicious pad Thai noodles costs just $6 for lunch, $8 for dinner.

Downtown Diner 7 E Aspen Ave ☏ 928/774-3492. Classic Route 66 diner a block north of the main drag, featuring leatherette booths and hefty burgers and sandwiches.

Flagstaff Brewing Company 16 E Route 66 ☏ 928/773-1442. Popular downtown pub, with outdoor seating, big windows, and live music Wed–Sat.

Macy's European Coffee House & Bakery 14 S Beaver St ☏ 928/774-2243. Not merely superb coffee, but heavenly pastries to go with it, plus more substantial vegetarian dishes such as black bean pizza, and even couscous for breakfast.

The Museum Club 3404 E Route 66 ☎ 928/526-9434. A real oddity; this log-cabin taxidermy museum somehow transmogrified into a classic

Route 66 roadhouse, saloon, and country-music venue, now a second home to hordes of dancing cowboys.

Around Flagstaff

The area around Flagstaff is extraordinarily rich in natural and archeological wonders, with three national monuments – **Sunset Crater**, **Wupatki**, and **Walnut Canyon** – within 25 miles. Of these, only Sunset Crater has even a campground, and none has indoor lodgings. There's no scheduled public transportation, so if you don't have your own vehicle you'll have to take a guided tour.

Sunset Crater and Wupatki national monuments

North of Flagstaff, the **San Francisco Volcanic Field** of around four hundred volcanoes is prominent on the western horizon from the Hopi Mesas, and its peaks are said to be the home of their powerful *kachina* spirits. Several hiking trails lead into the San Francisco Peaks, and a chairlift operates in summer (mid-May to mid-Sept daily 10am–4pm; mid-Sept to mid-Oct Fri–Sun 10am–4pm; $9) from the **Arizona Snowbowl** almost to the summit of Mount Agassiz (12,350ft), though you can't hike any further from there. For a brief period each winter this becomes a mildly hectic ski area.

Some of the volcanoes are still active, though the most recent eruption was that of **Sunset Crater** (twelve miles from Flagstaff on US-89) in around 1066 AD. The crater was named by John Wesley Powell for the many colors of its cone, which swells from a black base through reds and oranges to a yellow-tinged crest. It's too unstable for walkers to be allowed onto the rim, but a trail passes through lava tubes around its base. The national monument's **visitor center** is nearby (daily 8am–5pm; ☎ 928/526-0502, ⓦ www.nps.gov/sucr; $3 per person), opposite the *Bonito* **campground** (☎ 928/527-0866; $10; late May to mid-Oct).

A dozen miles further north, the ancient ruins at **Wupatki National Monument** appear to show different tribal groups living side by side in harmony (daily: summer 8am–7pm; winter 8am–5pm; admission $3 per person, including Sunset Crater; ☎ 928/679-2365, ⓦ www.nps.gov/wupa). The **Sinagua** were joined here by many others, including the **Ancestral Puebloans**, when the Sunset Crater explosion deposited a rich new layer of topsoil. The specific site known as Wupatki (meaning "tall" or "big house"), standing proud on its natural foundations of red sandstone, is just the largest of innumerable sites.

Walnut Canyon National Monument

Between 1100 and 1250AD, **Walnut Canyon**, ten miles east of Flagstaff just south of I-40, was home to a thriving Sinagua community. Literally hundreds of their **cliff dwellings** can still be seen nestling beneath overhangs in the sides of the canyon. They simply walled off alcoves where the softer levels of the striated rock had eroded away, and then put up partitions to make separate rooms.

A large scenic window in the **visitor center** (daily: June–Aug 8am–6pm; March–May & Sept–Nov 8am–5pm; Dec–Feb 9am–5pm; $3 per person; ☎ 928/526-3367, ⓦ www.nps.gov/waca) gives an excellent overall view. Beyond it, a short trail of steep steps leads across a narrow causeway to an isthmus of rock high above a gooseneck of Walnut Creek. Along the path, you can go inside several Sinagua homes; note the T-shaped doorways that could only be entered headfirst and the ceilings blackened by the smoke of generations of fires. No accommodation, and only minimal snack food, is available.

Sedona and Red Rock Country

US-89A threads its way south from Flagstaff down the spectacular **Oak Creek Canyon** to emerge after 28 miles at **Sedona**, on the threshold of the extraordinary **Red Rock Country**. Up from the valley rise giant mesas and buttes of stark red sandstone, where Zane Grey set a number of his Wild West adventures. The boom-and-bust mining town of **Jerome** looks down from a mountainside to the south, while back beside I-17 toward Phoenix are further haunting Sinagua ruins.

Sedona

Though local boosters make much of its setting, amid some definitive Southwestern canyon scenery, the New Age resort of **SEDONA** adds nothing to the beauty of its surroundings. Architecturally, it's a real mess, with several miles of ugly redbrick sprawl interrupted by the occasional mock-historical mall monstrosity. To the artists, healers, walking wounded, and wealthy retirees who have flocked here in the last two decades, however, Sedona is "the next Santa Fe." Whether you love it or hate it will probably depend on whether you share their wide-eyed awe for angels, crystals, and all matters mystical – and whether you're prepared to pay over-the-odds prices for the privilege of joining them.

Established in 1902 by one Theodore Schnebly, and named after his wife, Sedona remained for most of the twentieth century a small farming settlement, unmarked on most maps. German surrealist painter Max Ernst moved here in the 1940s – the bizarre backdrops of his later canvases seem less surreal once you've seen where they were painted – and Hollywood movie-makers filmed in the area from the 1950s onward. However, Sedona's big break came in 1981, when Page Bryant, author and psychic, "channeled" the information that Sedona is in fact "the heart *chakra* of the planet." Since she pinpointed her first **vortex** – a point at which, it is claimed, psychic and electromagnetic energies can be channeled for personal and planetary harmony – the town has achieved its own personal growth, and blossomed as a focus for **New Age** practitioners of all kinds.

If you don't have much time to spend exploring, a cruise along US-89A enables you to see most of the sights, albeit from a distance; the best parts are south along Hwy-179 within Coconino National Forest. The closest **vortex** to town is on **Airport Mesa**; turn left up Airport Road from US-89A as you head south, about a mile past the downtown junction known as the **"Y"**. The vortex is at the junction of the second and third peaks, just after the cattle grid. Further up, beyond the precariously sited airport, the **Shrine of the Red Rocks** looks out across the entire valley.

Sedona's **visitor center**, just north of the "Y," has full listings of lodgings and tour operators (Mon–Sat 8.30am–5pm, Sun 9am–3pm; ☎928/282-7722 or 1-800/288-7336, ⓦwww.visitsedona.com or www.sedonachamber.com). The town is an expensive place to **stay**; what pass for budget **motels** include the *Sedona Motel*, close to the "Y" at 218 Hwy-179 (☎928/282-7187; ❹), and the renovated *Los Abrogados Lodge*, a little further north at 270 N US-89A (☎928/282-7125 or 1-800/521-3131, ⓦwww.ilxresorts.com; ❸). The luxurious *Enchantment Resort*, 525 Boynton Canyon Rd (☎928/282-2900 or 1-800/826-4180, ⓦwww.enchantmentresort.com; ❾), has taken over ravishing Boynton Canyon eight miles west.

Fournos, 3000 W Hwy-89A (reservations required; ☎928/282-3331), is a lovely little Greek **restaurant**, open for dinner at 6pm and 8pm from Thursday

Vortex Tours of Red Rock Country

As few of the side roads around Sedona are paved – in part because the town's ardent libertarians would not pay the necessary taxes – there's a booming business in **off-road tours**, and especially those that visit the region's so-called **"vortexes"** (see overleaf). These are run by companies such as Earth Wisdom Tours ($45 and up; ☎928/282-4714 or 1-800/482-4714, ⓦwww.earthwisdomtours.com), who teach their clients "the ancestral secrets of the Medicine Wheel," and the garish Pink Jeep Tours ($35–90; ☎928/282-5000 or 1-800/873-3662, ⓦwww.pinkjeep.com). Nonetheless, a lot of the best scenery is visible from the highway, and many of the jeep roads are perfectly passable in ordinary vehicles. So long as you're happy to remain in ignorance as to which rocks are really electromagnetic tuning forks vibrating in harmony with Alpha Centauri, there's no great need to take a commercial tour. If you *really* want to get off-road, you can also head for Legends of Sedona Ranch (☎928/282-6826 or 1-800/848-7728), where "horses are free . . . but rides ain't," an hour on **horseback** costing around $40.

to Saturday, and for brunch on Sunday at noon; the *Coffee Pot Restaurant*, 2050 W Hwy-89A (☎928/282-6626), is a large old-style diner, serving all the burgers, Mexican dishes, and fried specials you could hope for; and *Savannah*, just north of the "Y" at 350 Jordan Rd (☎928/282-7959), is a chic upscale Continental place.

Jerome

The former mining town of **JEROME**, high above the Verde Valley on US-89A about thirty miles south of Sedona, is conspicuous from quite a distance: an enormous letter "J" is etched deep into the hillside above it, and a large chunk of that hillside is missing altogether, having been blown apart for **opencast copper mining**. This land abounds in mineral wealth – thick veins of copper are interspersed with gold and silver, and an endless supply of limestone is still extracted for cement – but serious exploitation only started in 1876. The **United Verde** mine was partly financed by New Yorker Eugene Jerome (a cousin of Winston Churchill's mother, Jennie Jerome), who insisted that the new town bear his name. Until the current tortuous road was built, the only way up to Jerome was the precipitous rail line connecting the mine with the world's largest copper smelter at Clarkdale.

From the early 1950s, when the mines closed down, until as recently as the 1970s, Jerome was a **ghost town** in which it was possible to turn up and move into an empty house. Many who did so are still here, making a living from arts and crafts, and the town itself has made a dramatic recovery. It's a bit of a tourist trap, but is nonetheless fascinating to explore. The hillside is so steep that the stone houses (it was far too expensive to haul timber up here) tend to have two stories at the front and four or five at the back. Under the repeated concussion of more than two hundred miles of tunnels being blasted into the mountainside, the whole town used to slip downhill at the rate of five inches per year, and the **Sliding Jail** on Hull Avenue came to rest 225ft from where it was built.

The old-style *Inn at Jerome*, 309 N Main St (☎928/634-5094 or 1-800/634-5094, ⓦwww.innatjerome.com; ❸), has five themed B&B **rooms**, with and without private bathrooms, as well as a **bar**, and operates a **café**, the *Jerome Grille*. The *English Kitchen* (☎928/634-2132) has been at 119 Jerome Ave since 1899. Under Chinese ownership, it was an opium den; later the Wobblies held their meetings downstairs. Now it's open for breakfast and lunch every day except Monday, and its terrace offers a commanding view of the valley. Many of the **shops** stock only souvenirs, but interesting crafts showrooms around town include the Knapp Gallery at 408 Lower Main St, and Made in Jerome Pottery, higher up opposite the post office.

Montezuma Castle National Monument

In an idyllic setting just above Beaver Creek and just east of I-17, around 25 miles from Sedona, **Montezuma Castle National Monument** focuses on a superbly preserved Sinagua **cliff dwelling** (daily: summer 8am–7pm; winter 8am–5pm; $3; ☎928/567-3322, ⓦwww.nps.gov/moca). Filling an alcove in the hillside with a wall of pink adobe, its five stories taper up to fit the contours of the rock. Apparently, the fingerprints of the masons are still visible on the bricks, and the sycamore beams remain firmly in place, but visitors are not permitted to climb up. The ruins of an even larger dwelling "next door," which was burned out around 1400, can be examined more closely. This once had 45 rooms, as well as little "cupboards" recessed into the walls.

West of Flagstaff: I-40 to California

Everything along I-40 west of Flagstaff is dominated by the road's function as the main route between Las Vegas and the Grand Canyon. The first town you reach, **WILLIAMS**, seems to exist solely to capture the passing tourist trade, with a historic **railroad** running north to the Canyon (see p.1062 for more details). Things here, though, do liven up come winter, when the slopes of Mount Williams and the rest of the surrounding **Kaibab National Forest** offer good skiing, particularly for cross-country aficionados. Forty-five miles further west at the town of **SELIGMAN**, one of the longest surviving stretches of the old Route 66 heads off on a northern loop through the **Hualapai Indian Reservation** and a dozen quickly fading towns, **PEACH SPRINGS** in particular, that look like they're straight out of *The Grapes of Wrath*. This makes a great detour on what is otherwise a very dull drive; it also provides the best access to the less visited western reaches of the Grand Canyon, around **Havasu Canyon** (see p.1031).

Unless you need to fill your tank, or fill up on fast food, there's little reason to stop at **KINGMAN**, the largest town in western Arizona, from where US-93 branches north to Las Vegas and I-40 continues to Los Angeles.

Lake Havasu City

Forty miles southwest of Kingman, ten miles from the California border, a detour south brings you to one of the more bizarre sights of the American desert – the old gray stone of **London Bridge**, reaching out to an artificial island across the stagnant waters of the dammed Colorado River at **LAKE HAVASU CITY**. The resort's developer, Robert P. McCulloch, bought the bridge (under the impression it was Tower Bridge – or so the story goes) for $2.4 million in the late 1960s, and painstakingly shipped it across the Atlantic chunk by chunk before reassembling it over a channel dug to divert water from Lake Havasu, creating an island on the other side of the bridge known as Pittsburgh Point. That said, it's not often you see anything quite as boring in Arizona as London Bridge. Lake Havasu City is one of those places with an undeniable attraction for the parched urbanites of Phoenix, who flock to fish on the lake or race on jet-skis, but it holds minimal appeal for travelers from further afield. Moreover, between March and June, it's permanently filled with students on **spring break**, drinking and partying around the clock.

Motels abound, ranging from the perfectly adequate *Havasu Motel*, 2035 Acoma Blvd (☎928/855-2311; ❶/❷), to the extravagant riverfront *London Bridge Resort*, 1477 Queen's Bay Rd (☎928/855-0888 or 1-800/624-7939; ❹–❻), where the lobby is all but filled by a gilt replica stagecoach. Among several good-value **restaurants** is *Shugrue's*, in the Island Fashion Mall at the end of London Bridge (☎928/453-1400), which serves fresh fish, salads, and pasta.

The Grand Canyon

Although almost five million people visit **GRAND CANYON NATIONAL PARK** every year, the canyon itself remains beyond the grasp of the human imagination. No photograph, no set of statistics, can prepare you for such vastness. At more than one mile deep, it's an inconceivable abyss; varying between four and eighteen miles wide, it's an endless expanse of bewildering shapes and colors, glaring desert brightness and impenetrable shadow, stark promontories and soaring, never-to-be-climbed sandstone pinnacles. Somehow it's so impassive, so remote – you could never call it a disappointment, but at the same time many visitors are left feeling peculiarly flat. In a sense, none of the available activities can quite live up to that first stunning sight of the chasm. The **overlooks** along the rim all offer views that shift and change unceasingly from dawn to sunset; you can **hike** down into the depths on foot or by mule, hover above in a **helicopter**, or raft through the **whitewater rapids** of the river itself; you can spend a night at **Phantom Ranch** on the canyon floor, or swim in the waterfalls of the idyllic **Havasupai Reservation**. And yet that distance always remains – the Grand Canyon stands apart.

Until the 1920s, the average **visitor** would stay for two or three weeks. These days it's more like two or three hours – of which forty minutes are spent actually looking at the canyon. The vast majority come to the **South Rim** – it's much easier to get to, there are far more facilities (mainly at **Grand Canyon Village**), and it's open all year round. There is another lodge and campground at the **North Rim**, which by virtue of its isolation can be a lot more evocative, but at one thousand feet higher it is usually closed by snow from mid-October until May. Few people visit both rims; to get from one to the other demands either a two-day hike down one side of the canyon and up the other, or a 215-mile drive by road.

Finally, there's a definite risk that on the day you come the Grand Canyon will be invisible beneath a layer of **fog**, thanks to the 250 tons of sulfurous emissions pumped out every day by the Navajo Generating Station, seventy miles upriver at Page.

Admission to the park, valid for seven days on either rim, is $20 per vehicle or $10 for pedestrians and cyclists.

The South Rim

When someone casually mentions visiting the "Grand Canyon," it's almost certainly the **South Rim** that they're referring to. To be more precise, it's the thirty-mile stretch of the South Rim that's served by a paved road; and most specifically of all, it's **Grand Canyon Village**, the small canyon-edge community, sandwiched between the pine forest and the rim, that holds the park's **lodges**, **restaurants**, and **visitor center**. The reason nine out of every ten visitors come here is not, however, because this is a uniquely wonderful spot from

THE GRAND CANYON

Geology and history of the canyon

Layer upon layer of different rocks, readily distinguished by color, and each with its own fossil record, recede down into the Grand Canyon and back through time, until the strata at the river bed are among the oldest exposed rocks on earth. And yet how the canyon was **formed** is a mystery. Satellite photos show that the Colorado actually runs through the heart of an enormous hill (which Native Americans called the Kaibab, "the mountain with no peak"); experts cannot agree on how this could happen. Studies show that the canyon still deepens, at the slow rate of 50ft per million years. Its fantastic sandstone and limestone formations were not literally carved by the river, however; they're the result of erosion by wind and extreme cycles of heat and cold. These features were named – **Brahma Temple**, **Vishnu Temple**, and so on – by Clarence Dutton, a student of comparative religion who wrote the first Geological Survey report on the canyon in 1881.

While it may look forbidding, the Grand Canyon is not a dead place. All sorts of desert **wildlife** survive here – sheep and rabbits, eagles and vultures, mountain lions, and, of course, spiders, scorpions, and snakes. The **human** presence has never been on any great scale, but signs have been found of habitation as early as 2000 BC, and the **Ancestral Puebloans** were certainly here later on. A party of **Spaniards** passed through in 1540 – less than twenty years after Cortés conquered the Aztecs – searching for cities of gold, and a Father Garcés spent some time with the Havasupai in 1776. **John Wesley Powell**'s expeditions along the fearsome and uncharted waters of the Colorado in 1869 and 1871–72 were what really brought the canyon to public attention. A few abortive attempts were made to mine different areas, but facilities for tourism were swiftly realized to be a far more lucrative investment. With the exception of the Indian reservations, the Grand Canyon is now run exclusively for the benefit of visitors, although even as recently as 1963 there were proposals to dam the Colorado and flood 150 miles of the Canyon, and the Glen Canyon dam has seriously affected the ecology downstream.

which to see the canyon, but simply because the canyon's tourist facilities just happen to have been concentrated here ever since the arrival of the railroad a century ago.

However, it's as good a place to start as any. The canyon can be admired from countless vantage points, not only within the village but also along the eight-mile **Hermit Road** to the west and the 23-mile **Desert View Drive** to the east, while the village itself is more attractive than you might imagine, and once the day-trippers have gone seldom feels as crowded as the horror stories might suggest.

Getting to the South Rim

Nearly all visitors make their way to the South Rim by heading north of I-17 from either **Williams** (58 miles south) or **Flagstaff** (81 miles southeast). Most of the route is through thick ponderosa pine forests, so the route followed by the restored **steam trains** of the Grand Canyon Railway up from Williams is not especially scenic, even if it does make a fun ride (departs Williams daily 10am; from $55 roundtrip; ☎928/773-1976 or 1-800/843-8724, ⓦwww .thetrain.com). For details of buses from Flagstaff, see p.1018.

The small **airport** at Tusayan – six miles from the South Rim, and used primarily by "flight-seeing" tour companies (see p.1029) – also welcomes scheduled services, especially from Las Vegas, with operators such as Scenic Airlines (from $60 one way; ☎702/638-3300 or 1-800/634-6801, ⓦwww.scenic .com).

Arrival and information

A proposed new transportation scheme to ease traffic congestion in the national park has been only minimally implemented and it's looking as if it never will be. Under the scheme, private vehicles would be banned from the canyon area, with visitors ferried around instead on a **light rail** network, but all that's happened so far is the construction of the large **Canyon View Information Plaza**, located well short of the village center near Mather Point, which was originally intended as the hub for the railroad but has instead become the main information point for visitors. Its well-illustrated open-air displays and trail guides are complemented by a good bookstore and a visitor center staffed by helpful rangers (daily: May to mid-Oct 8am–6pm; mid-Oct to April 8am–5pm; ☎928/638-7888, ⓦwww.nps.gov/grca). Although it looks great, ludicrously no parking is available, so it's done nothing to relieve the traffic problem.

For the foreseeable future, **Grand Canyon Village** remains accessible to private vehicles, as is the road east from the village to Desert View. Both the road west from the village to **Hermit's Rest**, however, and the short access road to **Yaki Point** – the first overlook east of Mather Point, and the trailhead for the popular **South Kaibab Trail** – are only open to private vehicles during December, January, and February. Free **shuttle buses** run on three routes: the ponderous **Village Route**, which loops laboriously between Grand Canyon Village and the information plaza; the **Kaibab Trail Route** between the plaza and Yaki Point; and the eight-mile **Hermit's Rest Route**, which heads west to eight canyon overlooks.

South Rim accommodation

All the "lodges" in Grand Canyon Village are operated by the park concessionaire, Amfac, and charge similar prices. In terms of seeing the canyon, it makes little difference where in the village you stay. Even in the "rim-edge" places – the magnificent 1905 *El Tovar Hotel* (❺) and the *Bright Angel* (rooms ❸, rim-side cabins ❹), *Thunderbird*, and *Kachina* lodges (both ❹) – few rooms offer much of a view, and in any case it's always dark by 8pm. Further back are *Maswik Lodge* (cabins ❸, rooms ❺), and the two-part *Yavapai Lodge* not far from the information plaza (❹). For details on making reservations at all of these options, see the box overleaf.

Camping facilities (and a laundry) are available at the *Mather* campground and RV park, near the information plaza, at least one section of which is open year-round. Sites for up to two vehicles and six people cost $15 per night between April and November, when reservations, which are strongly recommended, can be made up to five months in advance through Spherics (same-day ☎928/638-2611; advance ☎1-800/365-2267 or from outside the US ☎301/722-1257), or online at ⓦwww.reservations.nps.gov. No reservations are accepted between December and March, when sites are first-come, first-served, and the fee drops to $10 per night. The summer-only *Desert View* campground, 26 miles east, is first-come, first-served, costs $10, and has no hookups. It's also possible to camp inside the canyon itself, if you first obtain a permit from the **Backcountry Reservations Office** near *Maswik Lodge* (daily 8am–noon & 1–5pm; call ☎928/638-7875 Mon–Fri 1–5pm only); each permit costs $10, plus $5 per person per night.

If all the park accommodation is full, the nearest alternative is the underwhelming service village of **Tusayan**. *Seven Mile Lodge* (☎928/638-2291; ❸) offers the least expensive rooms; while the newer *Grand Hotel* (☎928/638-3333, ⓦwww.gcanyon.com; ❹) is more stylish. Much the most popular of the commercial **campgrounds** outside the park – with families, at least – is *Flintstone's Bedrock City* (mid-March to Oct; $12 tents, $16 RV hook-ups; ☏928/635-2600), 22 miles south at the junction of Hwy-64 and Hwy-180, which has its own little prehistoric theme park.

South Rim eating

Due to the canyon's remoteness and lack of water, **food prices** tend to be well above average; if you're on a tight budget, bring your own food. Both *Yavapai* and *Maswik* lodges have reasonable basic cafeterias, open until 9pm and 10pm respectively. *Bright Angel Lodge* has its own **restaurant**, as well as the *Arizona Steakhouse*; both are open until 10pm and offer entrees costing $15–25. At *El Tovar*, where the dining room looks right out over the canyon, the sumptuous menu is enormously expensive. Breakfast is the most affordable meal; lunch and dinner can easily cost upwards of $40. Most of the hotels in **Tusayan** have their own dining rooms.

Exploring the South Rim

The fact that these days most visits to the South Rim start at the Canyon View Information Plaza, at **Mather Point**, rather than in Grand Canyon Village, doesn't mean you're missing out. In fact the canyon panorama that spreads out below Mather Point is more comprehensive than any obtainable from the village. The views to the east in particular are consistently stupendous; it's hard to imagine a more perfect position from which to watch the **sunrise** over the canyon.

The Colorado is visible from various vantage points along the rim-edge footpath near Mather Point. In addition, if you walk west for around ten minutes – that is, turn left along the rim from the information plaza – you'll come to **Yavapai Point**. From here, you can see two separate tiny segments of the river, one of which happens to include both the suspension footbridge across the Colorado and Phantom Ranch (see p.1030). Nearby, if you can tear your eyes away from its panoramic bay windows, the **Yavapai Observation Station** (daily: hours vary from 8am–8pm in summer down to 8am–5pm in winter; free) has illuminating displays on how the canyon may have been formed.

The **West** and **East Rim drives** extend along the South Rim for several miles in either direction from the information plaza and Grand Canyon Village, paralleled to the west by the **Rim Trail** on the very lip of the canyon. No one overlook can be said to be the "best," but there are far too many to stop at them all. Obvious short walks include an excursion to see the **sunset**, which is particularly magical at Hopi Point, to the west.

Driving or taking a shuttle bus along the East Rim Drive opens up further dramatic views. **Desert View**, 23 miles out from the village, is, at 7500ft, the highest point on the South Rim. Visible to the east are the vast flatlands of the **Navajo Nation**; to the northeast, **Vermillion** and **Echo Cliffs**, and the gray bulk of **Navajo Mountain** ninety miles away; to the west, the gigantic peaks of **Vishnu** and **Buddha temples**, while through the plains comes the narrow gorge of the **Little Colorado**. The odd-looking construction on the very lip of the canyon is **Desert View Watchtower**, built by Fred Harvey in 1932 in a conglomeration of Native American styles and decorated with Hopi pictographs. It contains a **gift shop**, as does the general store a few yards away.

Into the canyon

Hiking any of the trails that descend **into the Grand Canyon** offers something more than just another view of the same thing. Instead you pass through a sequence of utterly different landscapes, each with its own distinct climate, wildlife, and topography. However, while the canyon can offer a wonderful wilderness experience, it's essential to remember that it can be a hostile and very unforgiving environment, grueling even for expert hikers.

The South Rim is 7000ft above sea level, an altitude that for most people is fatiguing in itself. Furthermore, all hikes start with a long, steep descent – which can come as a shock to the knees – and unless you camp overnight you'll have to climb all the way back up again when you're hotter and wearier.

If you're day-hiking, the golden rule is to keep track of how much time you spend hiking down, and allow twice that much to get back up again. Average summer temperatures inside the canyon exceed 100°F; to hike for eight hours in that sort of heat, you have to drink an incredible thirty pints of water. Always carry at least a quart per person, and much more if there are no water sources along your chosen trail. You must have food as well, as drinking large quantities without also eating can cause water intoxication.

There's only space here to detail the most popular trail, the **Bright Angel**. Many of the others, such as the **Hermit**, date from the days prior to 1928, when the obstreperous Ralph Cameron controlled access to the Bright Angel and many other rim-edge sites by means of spurious mining claims, and the Park Service had to find other ways to get visitors down to the Colorado. These other trails tend to be overgrown now, or partially blocked by landslides; check before setting out.

Bright Angel Trail

The **Bright Angel Trail**, followed on foot or mule by thousands of visitors each year, starts from the wooden shack in the village that was once the Kolb photographic studio. The trail switchbacks for 9.6 miles down to **Phantom Ranch** beside the river, but park rangers have a simple message for all would-be hikers: don't try to hike down and back in a single day. It might not look far on the map, but it's harder than running a marathon. Instead, the longest feasible day-hike is to go as far as **Plateau Point** on the edge of the arid Tonto Plateau, an overlook above the Inner Gorge from which it is not possible to descend any further – a twelve-mile roundtrip that will probably take you at least eight hours. In summer, water can be obtained along the way.

The first section of the trail was laid out by miners a century ago, along an old Havasupai route, and has two short tunnels in its first mile. After another mile, the **wildlife** starts to increase (deer, rodents, and the ubiquitous ravens), and there are a few **pictographs** that have been all but obscured by graffiti.

At the lush **Indian Gardens** almost five miles down, where you'll find a ranger station and campground with water, the trails split to Plateau Point or down to the river via the **Devil's Corkscrew**. The latter route leads through sand dunes scattered with cactuses and down beside **Garden Creek** to the Colorado, which you then follow for more than a mile to get to Phantom Ranch.

Phantom Ranch

It's a real thrill to spend a night at the very bottom of the canyon, at the 1922 **Phantom Ranch**. The **cabins** are reserved exclusively for the use of excursionists on two-day mule trips ($338 per person for one night, $461 for the winter-only two-night trips), booked through Xanterra (see overleaf). Beds in the four ten-bunk **dorms** ($28) are usually reserved way in advance, also through Xanterra, but it's worth checking for cancellations at the Bright Angel transportation desk as soon as you reach the South Rim. Do not hike down without a reservation, and even if you do have one, reconfirm it the day before you set off. All supplies reach Phantom Ranch the same way you do (an all-day hike on foot or mule), so **meals** are expensive, a minimum of $17 for breakfast and $21 for dinner.

The **suspension bridge** here was set in place in 1928 (hanging from twin cables carried down on the shoulders of 42 Havasupai). The delta of **Bright Angel Creek**, named by Powell to contrast with the muddy **Dirty Devil** upriver in Utah, is several hundred feet wide here, and strewn with boulders. All the water used on the South Rim now comes by pipeline from the North Rim, and crosses the river on the 1960s Silver Bridge nearby.

The Havasupai Reservation

The **Havasupai Reservation** really is another world. Things have changed a little since a 1930s anthropologist called it "the only spot in the United States where native culture has remained in anything like its pristine condition," but the sheer magic of its turquoise waterfalls and canyon scenery makes this a very special place. Traditionally, the Havasupai would spend summer on the canyon floor and winter on the plateau above. However, when the reservation was created in 1882, they were only granted land at the bottom of the canyon, and not until 1975 did the concession of another 251,000 acres up above make it possible for them to resume their ancient lifestyle.

Havasu Canyon is a side canyon of the Grand Canyon, about 35 miles as the raven flies from Grand Canyon Village, but almost two hundred miles by road. Turn off the interstate at Seligman or Kingman, onto AZ-66 (which curves north between the two), stock up with food, water, and gas, and then turn on to Arrowhead Hwy-18. Plans to build a road – or even a tramway – down into Havasu Canyon have always been rejected, in part because much of the income of the five or six hundred Havasupai comes from guiding visitors on foot, mule, or horseback. Instead, the road ends at **Hualapai Hilltop**, from where an eight-mile trail zigzags down a bluff and leads through the stunning waterless Hualapai Canyon to the village of **SUPAI**. Riding down costs $70 one way, $120 roundtrip, while hiking is free; all visitors, however, pay a $20 entry fee on arrival at Supai.

Beyond Supai the trail becomes more difficult, but leads to a succession of spectacular waterfalls, including **Havasu Falls**, one of the best for swimming, and **Mooney Falls**, which was named after an unfortunate prospector who dangled here for three days in the 1890s, at the end of a snagged rope, before falling to his death.

A **campground** ($10; ☎928/448-2141) stretches between Havasu and Mooney Falls, and Supai itself holds the **motel**-like *Havasupai Lodge* (☎928/448-2111; ➍), along with a **café**, a **general store**, and the only **post office** in the US still to receive its mail by pack train. From time to time Supai is hit by freak floods, which can result in the temporary closure of the campground and lodge.

To the North Rim

The 215-mile route by road from Grand Canyon Village to the **North Rim** follows AZ-64 along the East Rim Drive to Desert View, then passes an overlook into the gorge of the Little Colorado, before joining US-89 fifty miles later at **CAMERON**. The Cameron Trading Post has the best selection of Native American crafts in the Grand Canyon area, and remains a trading center for the Navajo Nation. It also has a good-quality **motel** and **restaurant** (☎928/679-2231 or 1-800/338-7385, ⓦwww.camerontradingpost.com; ➍).

Fifteen miles north of Cameron is the junction with US-160, which heads northeast via Tuba City toward Monument Valley and Colorado. Continuing north, after another forty miles of barren wasteland, US-89 branches off to climb the mesa to the right, heading for Page and Glen Canyon Dam (see p.1060).

Lees Ferry

The direct route to the North Rim, now US-89A, crosses the Colorado at last over the single arch of **Navajo Bridge**, almost five hundred feet above the river. There are in fact two Navajo Bridges, the 1929 original, now reserved for pedestrians, having been supplanted by a wider facsimile in 1995. Until the first was built, a ferry service operated six miles north at **LEES FERRY**. Established in 1872, at the instigation of the Mormon Church, by John D. Lee, it was the only spot within hundreds of miles to offer easy access to the banks of the river on both sides. The Colorado, however, could still be a raging torrent, and the crossing was carried out in both directions by casting out and struggling across while being swept downstream. Lee himself was on the run after the **Mountain Meadows Massacre** in Utah in 1857, in which he led an armed white band clumsily disguised as Indians in their slaughter of a wagon train of would-be settlers.

Lees Ferry is the sole launching point for **whitewater rafting** trips into the Grand Canyon – the first point where boats can get out again is at Diamond Creek, twelve days away by muscle power. The ferry site still holds the atmospheric remains of Lee's Lonely Dell ranch, as well as a basic **campground** (☎928/355-2334; $10), while back on US-89A beneath the red of the **Vermillion Cliffs** you'll find a succession of **motels** – *Marble Canyon Lodge* (☎928/355-2225 or 1-800/726-1789; ❸), *Cliff Dweller's Lodge* (☎928/355-2228; ❸), and the beautifully located, rustic *Lees Ferry Lodge* (☎928/355-2231 or 1-800/451-2231, ⓦwww.leesferrylodge.com; ❸). All have **restaurants**.

The turning south to get to the North Rim, off US-89A onto AZ-67, comes at **JACOB LAKE**, home to the *Jacob Lake Inn* (☎928/643-7232, ⓦwww.jacoblake.com; ❹) and a **campground**, but not much else. From here – along a road that's closed in winter – it's 27 miles to *Kaibab Lodge* (mid-May to mid-Oct only; ☎928/638-2389 in summer, ☎928/526-0924 in winter, or 1-800/525-0924, ⓦwww.canyoneers.com; ❸). Beyond here it's another fourteen miles to the canyon itself.

The North Rim

Higher, more exposed to the elements, and far less accessible than the South Rim, the **NORTH RIM** of the Grand Canyon receives less than a tenth as many visitors. While that doesn't mean you'll have the place to yourself, it can still make you feel as though you're venturing into unexplored wilderness. The basic principle, however, is the same as at the South Rim, with a cluster of venerable Park Service buildings where the main highway reaches the canyon, and a handful of rim-edge roads where drivers can take their pick from additional lookouts. Only one hiking trail sees much use, the **North Kaibab Trail**, which follows Bright Angel Creek down to Phantom Ranch.

Tourist facilities on the North Rim, concentrated at **Bright Angel Point**, open for the season on May 15 and close on October 15. **Accommodation** at *Grand Canyon Lodge* (❺) is in cabins that spread back along the ridge from the lodge entrance, very few of which have canyon views. Advance reservations are essential, and are handled, as for the South Rim, by Xanterra (same-day ☎928/638-2611, advance ☎303/297-2757 or 1-888/297-2757, ⓦwww.grandcanyonnorthrim.com). Just over a mile north is the *North Rim Campground*, where $15 spaces can be reserved – though backpackers won't need to book – through Spherics (same-day ☎928/638-2611, advance ☎1-800/365-2267 or from outside the US ☎301/722-1257, ⓦwww.reservations.nps.gov). The *Lodge* also holds a good **restaurant**, plus a saloon, and an espresso bar; ask at the information desk for details of **mule rides** (1hr $20, half-day $45, full-day canyon expeditions $95; ☎435/679-8665, ⓦwww.onpages.com/canyonrides).

The park itself remains open for day-use only after October 15, but no food, lodging, or gas is available, and visitors must be prepared to leave at a moment's notice. It's shut down altogether by the first major snowfall of winter, which in recent years has started to come as late as December.

⑫

Northeastern Arizona: Indian Country

The deserts of northeastern Arizona, popularly known as **INDIAN COUN-TRY**, hold some of the most fascinating **pre-Columbian ruins** in North America, in the most striking settings imaginable. The cliff palaces of **Canyon de Chelly**, and **Betatakin** and **Keet Seel** in the Navajo National Monument, are among the greatest architectural achievements of the **Ancestral Puebloans**, made that much more special by the fact that the lands on which they stand are still lived on and worked by their heirs, the Hopi and Navajo.

The **NAVAJO NATION**, the largest Native American reservation in the US, fills most of the region, extending into western New Mexico and stretching to include the majestic sandstone pillars of Monument Valley in southernmost Utah. Although the migrant Navajo have embraced the American Way – driving pickup trucks and wearing baseball caps – you get a very real sense that you're traveling through a foreign country here. Everyone can speak English, but Navajo, a language so complex that it was used as a secret military code during World War II, is still the lingua franca. Supermarkets mark their prices in Navajo, and the reservation follows its own rules over Daylight Savings; in frontier-style towns like Tuba City, the time on the clock can vary according to whether you're in an American or a Navajo district.

When white immigrants began to arrive in force during the early nineteenth century, the Navajo – who call themselves *Dineh*, "The People" – had lived in Arizona for hundreds of years; within a generation, they lost almost everything. When the Yankees took over from the Mexicans, things just got worse, hitting bottom in 1864 when Kit Carson rounded up every Navajo he could find and forced them all to move to Fort Sumner in the desolate plain of eastern New Mexico (see p.988). A few years later, the Navajo were allowed to return, the US government granting them most of the vast acreage they hold today (law-suits arising from territorial disputes with the **Hopi**, their neighbors and predecessors, have dragged on ever since). Most of the 250,000-plus Navajo today work the land as shepherds and farmers on widely scattered smallhold-ings, though many craftspeople also live by selling their wares from small stands set up along highways and in tourist stops.

Visiting this region can be fascinating and rewarding, but it's important to respect the people and places you encounter. The Ancestral Puebloans, the region's first occupants, have long since vanished, but many of the relics they left behind are on land that is still of spiritual significance to their modern counterparts – Native Americans come here from all over the Southwest and beyond to take pride in their heritage. Similarly, it is offensive to photograph or otherwise intrude upon people's lives without permission; one reason why the Hopi, for example, banned photography was because it was such an inter-fering nuisance.

On a practical note, don't expect extensive **tourist facilities**. Most towns exist solely as bureaucratic outposts that only come alive during the annual tribal fairs and rodeos, and have little to offer visitors beyond a handful of places to eat and even fewer hotels and motels. For more information, contact the **Navajo Nation Tourism Office** (☏928/871-6436, ⓦwww.discovernava-jo.com).

Navajo National Monument

Navajo National Monument, in the northwest quarter of the reservation, pro-tects two of Arizona's biggest and most beautifully sited cliff dwellings. From

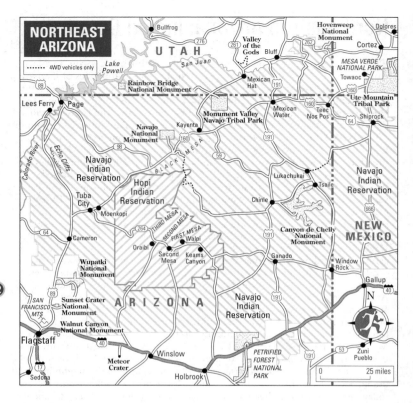

behind the useful **visitor center** (daily: summer 8am–6pm; rest of year 8am–5pm; monument admission free; ☎928/672-2700, ⓦwww.nps.gov/nava) at the end of paved Hwy-564, ten miles north of US-160, a ten-minute trail crosses the plateau to a viewpoint overlooking **Betatakin**, an exceptionally well-preserved 135-room masonry structure tucked away in a large natural alcove halfway up the 700-foot-high, brilliant-red sandstone on the far side of a canyon. It's only possible to hike down to Betatakin – which feels as though it was abandoned seven years, not seven centuries ago – by joining one of the unforgettable six-hour ranger-guided hikes (May–Sept daily 8.15am), which rendezvous roughly a mile from the visitor center. Numbers are limited, and no advance bookings are taken, so get to the visitor center as early as possible on the day – or stay the previous night at the very attractive free **campground** in the forest alongside.

In summer, you can also visit the even larger Ancestral Puebloan site of **Keet Seel**. However, the seventeen-mile roundtrip hike from the visitor center is too grueling to attempt in a single day, so you'll have to stay overnight in the small **campground** near the site, having obtained a permit from the visitor center at least a day in advance.

Most people pass through this area on their way somewhere else, so there aren't many **places to stay**. However, **TUBA CITY**, west of the monument, has the large, modern *Quality Inn Tuba Trading Post* (☎928/283-4545 or 1-800/644-8383; ❹), while the coal and uranium mining town of **KAYENTA**,

22 miles northeast of the monument at the junction of US-160 and US-163, holds the similarly anonymous but adequate *Best Western Wetherill Inn* (☎928/697-3231, ⓦwww.gouldings.com; ❹) and *Holiday Inn* (☎928/697-3221, ⓦwww.sixcontinentshotels.com; ❹), which has a distinctive and good-value **restaurant**.

Monument Valley

The classic Wild West landscape of stark sandstone buttes and forbidding pinnacles of rock, poking from an endless expanse of drifting red sands, has become an archetypal image. Only when you arrive at **MONUMENT VALLEY** – which straddles the Arizona–Utah state line, 24 miles north of Kayenta and 25 miles southwest of Mexican Hat – do you realize how much your perception of the West has in fact been shaped by this one spot. Such scenery does exist elsewhere, of course, but nowhere is it so perfectly distilled. While moviemakers have flocked here since the early days of Hollywood – this was where John Ford made John Wayne a star – the sheer majesty of the place still takes your breath away. Add the fact that it remains a stronghold of **Navajo** culture, little affected by tourism, and Monument Valley can be the absolute highlight of a trip to the Southwest.

The biggest and most impressive of the monoliths are a pair called **The Mittens**, one East and one West, each of which has a distinct thumb splintering off from its central bulk. The taller of the two rises a thousand feet above the valley floor, with sand dunes lapping at its base. Over a dozen other spires are spread around nearby, along with **rock art panels** and an assortment of minor but nicely sited **Ancestral Puebloan ruins**.

You can see the buttes for free, towering alongside US-163, but the four-mile detour to enter **Monument Valley Tribal Park** is rewarded with much closer views (daily: May–Sept 7am–7pm; Oct–April 8am–5pm; $5; ☎435/727-3353). A rough, unpaved road drops from behind the visitor center to run through Monument Valley itself. The 17-mile **self-drive route** makes a bumpy but bearable ride in an ordinary vehicle, and takes something over an hour to complete (daily: summer 8am–6pm; rest of year 8am–4.30pm). You're allowed to stop en route to stretch your legs, but not to hike for any distance. However, the Navajo-led **jeep** or **horseback tours** into the backcountry are very much recommended; a two-hour jeep trip costs from around $25 per person if arranged at the visitor center, slightly more if organized through *Goulding's Lodge* (see below). As well as stopping at such movie locations as the **Totem Pole** (atop which Clint Eastwood had some perilous moments in *The Eiger Sanction*), these tours pause so you can watch weavers at work in a Navajo *hogan* (traditional eight-sided dwelling).

The *Haskeneini* (☎928/727-3312) is a reasonable **restaurant** at the visitor center, not far from the very exposed *Mitten View* **campground** (first-come, first-served; water available in summer only; summer $10, winter $5). The only **accommodation** in the immediate vicinity is six miles west, in Utah at *Goulding's Lodge* (☎435/727-3231, ⓦwww.gouldings.com; ❻), a 1920s trading post that now offers pricey motel rooms with magnificent views, a fairly good restaurant, a general store and gas station, a small movie museum, and its own campground (summer $24, winter $15; same phone).

Canyon de Chelly National Monument

A short distance east of **CHINLE**, sixty miles southwest of Kayenta and seventy miles north of I-40, twin sandstone walls emerge abruptly from the desert floor, climbing at a phenomenal rate to become the awesome thousand-foot cliffs of **CANYON DE CHELLY NATIONAL MONUMENT**. Between these sheer sides, the meandering course of the Chinle Wash can be discerned by its fringe of cottonwoods as it winds through grasslands and planted fields. Here and there a Navajo *hogan* stands in a grove of fruit trees, a straggle of sheep is penned in by a crude wooden fence, or ponies drink at the water's edge. And everywhere, perched above the valley on ledges in the canyon walls and dwarfed by the towering cliffs, are the long-abandoned adobe and stone dwellings of the **Ancestral Puebloans**.

There are two main canyons, which branch apart a few miles upstream: **Canyon de Chelly** (pronounced *de shay*) to the south and **Canyon del Muerto** to the north. Each twists and turns in all directions, scattered with vast rock monoliths, while several smaller canyons break away. The whole labyrinth threads its way northward for thirty miles into the Chuska Mountains.

Canyon de Chelly is a magnificent place, easily on a par with the best of the Southwest's national parks. Its relative lack of fame owes much to the continuing presence of the **Navajo**, for whom the canyon retains enormous symbolic significance (although they did not build its cliff dwellings). Casual visitors are restricted to peering into the canyon from above, from overlooks along the two "rim drives." There's no road in, and, apart from one short trail, you can only enter the canyons with a Navajo guide.

Some history

The first known inhabitants of the canyon were **Ancestral Puebloan Basketmakers**, who dwelled here from around 300 AD. During the next thousand years, they advanced from living in pit houses dug into the soil to building elegant cliff dwellings, and developed fine pottery and weaving. For some centuries after the Ancestral Puebloans left the area (see p.979), the **Hopi** came here to farm each summer, returning for the winter to the mesas to the east, but as time went by, **Navajo** migrants from the north and west eventually displaced the Hopi altogether.

From 1583 onward, the Navajo were locked with the Spanish in a bloody cycle of armed clashes and slave raids. The US Army in turn failed repeatedly to dislodge the Navajo, but none of the various truces and treaties they agreed to could restrain the rapacious hunger for land by New Mexican settlers. The end appeared to have come with the brutal round-up and deportation (the "**Long Walk**") of the entire Navajo people, completed by Kit Carson in 1864 when he starved the last of them down from Navajo Rock and destroyed their homes and livestock. So barbaric was the Navajo's imprisonment at Fort Sumner, however, that Congress soon allowed them to return. To this day, 25 Navajo families still farm the Canyon de Chelly in summer, the matrilineal descendants of the women among whom it was reapportioned in the 1870s.

The view from above: the rim drives

Each of the two "rim drives" from the visitor center offers a succession of spectacular overlooks; allow two to three hours for each of the forty-mile roundtrips. Thefts from cars have been a major problem, so it's wise to heed the prominent warnings.

The first significant stopping point along the South Rim Drive is **Junction Overlook**, after four miles, far above the point where the two main canyons branch their separate ways; as you scramble across the bare rocks you can see Canyon de Chelly narrowing away, with a *hogan* immediately below. Two miles further along, by which time the canyon is 550ft deep, **White House**

Into the canyons

Tours of the canyon floor, organized by *Thunderbird Lodge* (see below), zigzag along the washes, which vary from two- or three-feet deep during the spring thaw to completely dry in summer. For most of the year, the bone-shaking tours are in open-top flatbed trucks that lurch over the rutted earth, and the heat can be incredible; in winter they carry on in glass-roofed army vehicles with caterpillar tracks. To reach as far as Spider Rock (see below), you have to take the full-day tour ($63.50), but the half-day trip at $39 still enables you to see a wide variety of sites and terrain, including the White House Ruins.

The visitor center also arranges highly recommended 4.5-mile, four-hour **group hikes**, which cost $15 per person. The precise schedule varies, but usually includes a morning trip via the White House Trail and an afternoon hike in the Canyon del Muerto; separate **night hikes** last just two hours but cost slightly more. Justin's Horse Rentals (☎928/674-5678) and Tsotsonii Ranch (☎928/674-8425) organize horseback trips for $10 per person per hour, plus $15 an hour for a guide.

Overlook looks down on the highly photogenic **White House Ruins**. This is the only point from which unguided hikers can descend to the canyon floor, taking perhaps 30 to 45 minutes to get down and a good hour to get back up. The beautiful if precarious trail, at times running along ledges chiseled into the slick rock, culminates with a close-up view of the ruins; the most dramatic dwellings, squeezed into a tiny alcove sixty feet up a majestic cliff, were once reached via the rooftops of now-vanished structures. Visitors are forbidden to walk for more than a hundred yards in either direction beyond the site. Back up on the South Rim Drive, twelve miles along, the view from **Sliding House Overlook** reveals more Ancestral Puebloan ruins seemingly slipping down the canyon walls toward the ploughed Navajo fields below, while eight miles further on the road ends above the astonishing **Spider Rock**, where twin 800-foot pinnacles of rock come to within 200ft of the canyon rim.

The **North Rim Drive** runs twenty miles up Canyon del Muerto to **Massacre Cave**, where the Spanish expedition of 1805, led by Lieutenant Narbona, killed around one hundred Navajo women, children, and old men. The "cave" is just a pitifully exposed ledge, upon which the huddled group were easily picked off by the Spanish, using ricochets off the overhang above. Visible from the nearby **Mummy Cave Overlook** is the **House Under The Rock**, with its central tower in the Mesa Verde style – the single most striking ruin in the monument. Of the two viewpoints at **Antelope House Overlook**, one is opposite Navajo Fortress, an isolated eminence atop which the Navajo were besieged for three months in 1863, while the other looks down on the twin ruined square towers of Antelope House. The **Tomb of the Weaver** across the wash is where the embalmed body of an old man was found wrapped in golden eagle feathers.

Practicalities

The Canyon de Chelly **visitor center**, on the road from Chinle (daily May–Sept 8am–6pm; Oct–April 8am–5pm; ☎928/674-5500, ⓦwww.nps .gov/cach), has informative displays, and provides guides for unorthodox hiking or motorized expeditions. Facilities nearby are overstretched, so it's essential to book your **accommodation** well in advance. The most appealing options are the *Thunderbird Lodge* (☎928/674-5841 or 1-800/679-2473, ⓦwww.tbirdlodge.com; ❺), very near the canyon entrance, which arranges the standard sightseeing tours and has an adequate cafeteria, and the *Chinle Holiday Inn* (☎928/674-5000, Ⓔholidayinncdc@cybertrails.com; ❹), slightly further back toward Chinle, where the food is a lot better. The free, minimally equipped *Cottonwood* **campground** has pleasant sites among the trees alongside *Thunderbird Lodge*. Chinle itself is a brief nondescript straggle on the highway, with service stations, *Taco Bell*, *Kentucky Fried Chicken*, a post office, and a laundry.

Window Rock

The seat of the Navajo Tribal Council, the reservation's governing body, is on its eastern edge, along the New Mexico border. It was based for fifty years at Fort Defiance, a US cavalry outpost, until in the 1930s **WINDOW ROCK** was established as a new capital. Named for the natural stone arch on its northern side, it's not a great place to get a grasp of Navajo culture, but it does at least have gas stations, shops, and a **motel**, the showpiece *Navajo Nation Inn* at 48 W Hwy-264 (℡928/871-4108 or 1-800/662-6189; ❸). The adjacent **Navajo Tribal Museum** (summer Mon–Fri 8am–8pm & Sat 10am–4pm; rest of year Mon–Fri 8am–5pm; donation) gives the background on tribal history and displays high-quality crafts.

The Hopi Mesas

Almost uniquely in the United States, the **Hopi** people have lived continuously in the same place for over eight hundred years. Some invaders have come and gone in that time, others have stayed; but the villages on **First**, **Second**, and **Third mesas** have endured, if not exactly undisturbed then at least unmoved.

To outsiders, it's not obvious why, with the whole Southwest to pick from, the Hopi should have chosen to live on three barren and unprepossessing fingers of rock poking from the southern flanks of **Black Mesa** in the depths of northeast Arizona. There are two simple answers. The first lies within the mesa itself: although it has no perennial streams, its subterranean rocks are tilted at just the correct angle to deliver a tiny but dependable trickle of water, while the "black" in its name comes from the coal that gives the Hopi limitless reserves of fuel. The second is that the Hopi used to farm and hunt across a much wider area, and have only been restricted to their mesa-top villages by the encroachment of their Navajo neighbors. While the Hopi are celebrated for their skill at "**dry farming**," managing to preserve enough precious liquid to grow corn, beans, and squash on hand-tilled terraces, this precarious and difficult way of life has nonetheless been forced upon them.

By their very survival, and the persistence of their ancient beliefs and ceremonies, the Hopi have long fascinated outsiders. While visitors are welcome, the Hopi have no desire – or need, as the tribe has finally begun to earn considerable amounts from mineral leases – to turn themselves into a tourist attraction. Although stores and galleries on the reservation provide plenty of opportunity to buy crafts such as pottery, basketwork, silver overlay jewelry, and hand-carved *kachina* dolls, tourists who arrive in the hope of extensive sightseeing – let alone spiritual revelations – are likely to leave disappointed, and quite possibly dismayed by what they perceive as conspicuous poverty.

Visiting the Hopi Mesas

The essential first stop for visitors is the modern, mock-Pueblo **Hopi Cultural Center** below Second Mesa, which holds a **museum** (summer Mon–Sat 8am–5pm, Sun 9am–4pm; winter Mon–Fri 8am–5pm; $3; ℡928/734-6650), as well as a **cafeteria** and **motel** (℡928/734-2401,

Hopi ceremonies

The Hopi feel neither the urge nor the obligation to divulge details of their **religious beliefs and practices** to outsiders. To that end, they have resisted attempts to make Hopi a written language, or to expose it to scrutiny by teaching it in schools. As a result, Hopi spirituality has been repeatedly misrepresented to the world, whether as barbarous devil-worship or New Age guff. There is in any case no single unified Hopi religion; ceremonials vary from clan to clan and village to village. The most basic common element is the role of the *kachinas* – "spirit messengers" that may represent the spirits of the dead and live in the San Francisco peaks north of Flagstaff.

There are over three hundred different *kachinas*. At one time, they visited the mesas in person; now they come in the form of masked dancers. Not every village follows the same ceremonial calendar, but in general the *kachinas* arrive each year in early February for the Powamuya ceremony, or **Bean Dance**. They continue to visit throughout the growing season, before returning home after the Niman ceremony, or **Home Dance**, in July.

The Hopi do not worship the *kachinas*; their main significance is as examples and allegories for the children. All Hopi babies receive *tihus* – what outsiders know as *kachina* dolls, which have become very popular crafts objects – at their first Niman ceremony, and the girls receive further dolls at each Powamuya and Niman ceremony thereafter.

For much of the twentieth century, Hopi **ceremonies** were promoted as tourist attractions. Even after cameras were banned in 1916, occasions such as the **Snake Dance**, when members of the Snake clan dance with live snakes between their teeth, attracted as many as 2500 outsiders. In recent years, however, the Hopi have moved toward the exclusion of non-Native Americans. By 1989, Second Mesa had closed all its ceremonies to outsiders, and it was joined by all the First Mesa villages in 1992 after the publication of a Marvel comic that characterized the *kachinas* as violent avengers.

While spectators are now very unlikely to be allowed at any *kachina* dances, some **social dances**, however, held between August and January when the *kachinas* are away from the mesas, may still be "open." Held in the village plazas, these usually take place at the weekends, so that Hopi who live off the reservation can attend. Specific timings tend not to be announced until a few days in advance; for information, contact the Cultural Center (see opposite). If you do get the chance to attend, wear clothing that fully covers your body, keep your distance, and do not photograph, sketch, or question either dancers or audience.

Ⓦ www.hopionline.com; ❹). In summer, its unexotic but adequate rooms are usually booked solid a week or more in advance.

Unless your visit coincides with a social event that's open to tourists (see box, above), the only way to see the mesa-top villages is to take a **guided tour** of the most impressive one, **WALPI** (summer Mon–Fri 9am–6pm; winter Mon–Fri 9.30am–4pm; $5; ☏928/737-2262). By Hopi standards, Walpi is not in fact that old; it was hastily thrown together in the immediate aftermath of the Pueblo Revolt of 1680, when the people of First Mesa decided to move to a more secure site in the face of possible Spanish or Navajo attack. The spot they chose is absolutely stunning, standing alone at the narrow southernmost tip of the mesa, and connected to the other First Mesa villages by the merest slender neck of stone, with a drop of three hundred feet to either side. It's now home to around 35 people, who do without electricity or running water.

To see Walpi, take Hwy-264 to modern **POLACCA**, at the foot of First Mesa, then drive a mile up the twisting paved road until it ends in

SICHOMOVI. The tours assemble in Sichomovi's small community center, setting off at regular intervals for a half-hour walk to and around Walpi. Depending on the time of year, you'll either be in a group of twenty or so, or on your own, but either way there's plenty of opportunity to ask questions, and to buy pottery, *kachina* dolls, and fresh-baked *piiki*, a flatbread made with blue cornflour.

Utah

With the biggest, most beautiful, and most pristine landscapes in North America, **UTAH** has something for everyone: from brilliantly colored canyons, across endless desert plains, to thickly wooded and snow-covered mountains. This unmatched range of terrain, almost all of which is public land, makes Utah *the* place to come for **outdoor pursuits**, whether your tastes run to hiking, off-track mountain biking, whitewater rafting, or skiing.

Southern Utah has more **national parks** than anywhere else in the US; in fact it has often been suggested that the entire area should become one vast national park. The most accessible parts – such as **Zion** and **Bryce Canyon** – are by far the most visited, but lesser-known parks like **Arches** and **Canyonlands** are every bit as dramatic. Huge tracts of this empty desert, in which fascinating pre-Columbian pictographs and Ancestral Puebloan ruins lie hidden, are all but unexplored; seeing them in safety requires a good degree of advance planning and self-sufficiency.

In the **northeast** of the state, the **Uinta Mountains** remain uncrossed by road and form one of the most extensive US wilderness areas outside Alaska, while **Flaming Gorge** and **Dinosaur** preserve more desert splendor. Though the **northwest** is predominantly flat and dry, the granite mountains of the **Wasatch Front** tower over state capital **Salt Lake City** – a surprisingly attractive and enjoyable stopover – while Alta, Snowbird, and the resorts around Park City offer some of the best **skiing** in North America.

Led by Brigham Young, Utah's earliest Anglo settlers – the **Mormons** – arrived in the Salt Lake area in 1847, and set about the massive irrigation projects that made their agrarian way of life possible. At first they provoked great suspicion and hostility back East; Congress turned down their first petition for statehood in 1850, in part because of the religious significance of the proposed name, **Deseret**, a Mormon word meaning "honeybee" (the state symbol is still a beehive, to denote industry). The Republican Convention of 1856 railed against slavery and polygamy in equal measure; had the Civil War not intervened, a war against the Mormons was a real possibility. Relations eased when the Mormon Church realized in 1890 that it had better drop polygamy on its own terms before being forced to do so. Statehood followed in 1896, and a century on, seventy percent of Utah's two-million-strong population are Mormons. The Mormon influence is responsible for the layout of Utah's towns, where residential streets are as wide as interstates, and all are numbered block-by-block according to the same logical if ponderous system.

Despite Brigham Young's early opposition to the search for mineral wealth, Mormon businessmen became renowned as fiercely pro-mining and anti-conservation. Only since the early 1980s – once the uranium bonanza was definitely over – has tourism been appreciated as a major industry, and former mining towns such as **Moab** developed facilities for wide-eyed travelers smitten by the allure of the desert. Increased tourism has also led to a relaxation of Utah's notoriously arcane **drinking laws**. In most towns, at least one restaurant will be licensed to sell beer, wine, and mixed drinks to diners, and it may also be licensed to sell beer in its bar or lounge. Beer is also sold in a few other locations, but to drink stronger liquor you'll have to become a member of a "**private club**"; most sell temporary membership for a token fee. Take-out bottled drinks, including beer, can only be purchased in State Liquor Stores.

Getting around Utah

It's nearly impossible to get anywhere in Utah without your own **car**. Amtrak and Greyhound serve Salt Lake City and a few provincial towns, but practically nowhere else. However, a couple of firms offer **bus tours** of the national parks, and if you're feeling adventurous, southern Utah also has an unbeatable range of mountain biking and river rafting: see p.1057 for a list of companies.

Southern Utah: the national parks

Southern Utah is a peculiar combination of the mind-boggling and the mundane. Its **scenery** is stupendous, a stunning geological freakshow where the earth is ripped bare to expose cliffs and canyons of every imaginable color, unseen rivers gouge mighty furrows into endless desert plateaus, and strange sandstone towers thrust from the sagebrush. By contrast, however, the tiny **Mormon towns** scattered across this epic landscape are, almost without exception, boring in the extreme, so most visitors spend as much time as possible **outdoors**.

While Southern Utah's five national parks are complemented by many lesser-known but equally dramatic wildernesses, they make the most obvious targets for travelers. In the southwest, **Zion National Park** centers on an awe-inspiring canyon, backed by barren highlands of white sandstone, while **Bryce Canyon** is a blaze of orange pinnacles. To the east, **Arches** holds an eroded desertscape of graceful red-rock fins and spurs, all on a more manageable scale than the astonishing hundred-mile vistas of neighboring **Canyonlands**. Both lie within easy reach of **Moab**, a disheveled former mining town turned Utah's hippest destination. The fifth park, **Capitol Reef**, stretches through the middle of the state, pierced by slender, ravishing canyons.

The defining topographical feature of southwest Utah is the **Grand Staircase**. Named by pioneer river-runner John Wesley Powell, it consists of a series of plateaus, stacked tier upon tier, that climb from the North Rim of the Grand Canyon. The **Chocolate Cliffs**, near the border with Arizona, are followed by the dazzling **Vermillion Cliffs**, then the **White Cliffs** – a 2000-foot wall of Navajo sandstone, best seen at Zion – the **Grey Cliffs**, and finally the **Pink Cliffs** of Bryce. Although it took a billion years of sedimentation for these rocks to form, the staircase itself has only been created in the last dozen million years by the general upthrust of the **Colorado Plateau**, which stretches away to the east.

This is a tough land, and a rough one for travelers: as there are fewer roads than anywhere else in the US, almost nobody gets far into the deep backcountry. Even within the parks, overground access is more often than not limited to heavy-duty, high-clearance **four-wheel-drive vehicles**, **hikers**, and, increasingly, to **mountain bikes**. The best way of all to experience the region is as the first explorers did: by **water**, along such rivers as the Colorado and the Green. Dozens of companies offer river-rafting trips, floating downstream and camping out under the clear night sky surrounded by the sights, sounds, and smells of the desert.

St George and Cedar City

Southern Utah's two biggest towns, **St George** and **Cedar City**, lie fifty miles apart on I-15 en route between Las Vegas and Salt Lake City. Both make reasonably pleasant and serviceable bases, if not ones that are likely to detain you for very long.

St George

ST GEORGE was the winter home of Brigham Young and other early Mormon leaders, who basked in the comparatively mild climate of "Utah's Dixie." Set at the foot of a broad, reddish-brown sandstone cliff, it's a pretty enough town, centering around the fine 1877 **LDS Temple** at 440 South 300 East, the oldest still in use anywhere. The rest of the town holds quaint pioneer homes, including Brigham Young's much-restored **adobe house** on 200 North First West (daily 9am–9pm; free).

Travelers driving up I-15 can call in at the **Utah Visitor Center**, just inside the state line (daily: summer 8am–9pm; winter 8am–5pm; ☎435/673-4542, ⓦwww.utah.com). Virtually all St George's commercial life takes place along the main drag, St George Boulevard, where the twenty or so **motels** include the popular *Dixie Palm* at no.185 E (☎435/673-3531; ➋). Among various good **restaurants** in the Ancestor Square development is the *Pizza Factory*, 1 W St George Blvd (closed Sun; ☎435/628-1234). The St George Shuttle bus (☎435/628-8320 or 1-800/933-8320) connects with Las Vegas and Salt Lake City on request.

Cedar City

CEDAR CITY, 53 miles north of St George and approximately half its size, is no more worthy of a stop. Founded as an iron-mining town in the late 1850s, it's now kept alive by the Southern Utah State College on its western fringe, and by the flood of theatergoers who come to watch the enthusiastic productions of the **Utah Shakespeare Festival**, held on campus every summer (☎435/586-7878, ⓦwww.bard.org).

The large local **visitor center** stands at 581 N Main St (summer Mon–Fri 8am–7pm, Sat 9am–1pm; winter Mon–Fri 8am–5pm; ☎435/586-5124 or 1-800/354-4849, ⓦwww.scenicsouthernutah.com or www.cedarcity.org). **Main Street** is handy for food and lodging; motels with pools include two *Best Westerns*, the *El Rey Inn* at no. 80 S (☎435/586-6518, ⓦwww.bwelrey.com; ➌–➎), and the smart *Town and Country Inn* at no. 200 N (☎435/586-9900, ⓦwww.utahbestwestern.com; ➍). *Godfathers Pizza* at no. 241 N (☎435/586-1111) offers Italian specialties in a lively atmosphere, while *Sullivan's* at no. 301 S (☎435/586-6761) is part steakhouse, part coffee shop.

Zion National Park

With its soaring cliffs, riverine forests, and cascading waterfalls, **ZION NATIONAL PARK** is the most conventionally beautiful of Utah's parks. On

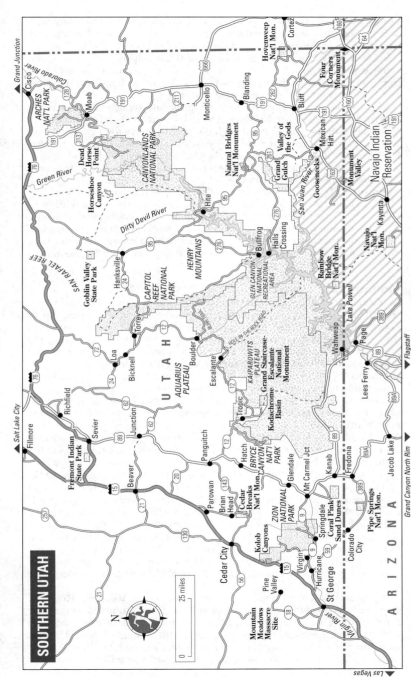

SOUTHERN UTAH

first glance, it's also the least "Southwestern"; its centerpiece, **Zion Canyon**, is a lush oasis that feels far removed from the otherworldly desolation of Canyonlands or the downright weirdness of Bryce. Like California's Yosemite Canyon, it's a spectacular gorge, squeezed between mighty walls of rock and echoing with the sound of running water; also like Yosemite, it can get claustrophobic in summer with its approach roads clogged with traffic and its limited facilities crammed with sweltering tourists.

Too many visitors see Zion Canyon as a quick half-day detour off the interstate, as they race between Las Vegas (158 miles southwest) and Salt Lake City (320 miles northeast). Beautiful though the **Scenic Drive** through the canyon may be, Zion deserves much more of your time than that. Even the shortest hiking trail within the canyon can help you escape the crowds, while a day-hike will take you away from the deceptive verdure of the valley and up onto the high-desert tablelands beyond.

Summer is by far the busiest season. That's despite temperatures in excess of 100°F, and violent thunderstorms concentrated in August and a week or so to either side. If you can, come in April or May, to see the spring flowers bloom – though the mosquitoes are also at their peak – or in September and October, to enjoy the fall colors along the river. The **admission charge** for Zion, valid in all sections of the park for seven days, is $20 per vehicle, or $10 for motor-cyclists, cyclists, and pedestrians.

⑫

Visiting Zion Canyon

In **Zion Canyon**, mighty walls of Navajo sandstone rise nearly half a mile above the groves of box elders and cottonwoods that line the loping North Fork of the **Virgin River**. The awe of the early Mormon settlers who called this "Zion" is reflected in the names of the stupendous slabs of rock along the paved six-mile **Scenic Drive** from the park entrance – the **Court of the Patriarchs**, the **Great White Throne**, and **Angel's Landing**.

Although Hwy-9 remains open to through traffic all year, the Scenic Drive is accessible to private vehicles during the winter only. Between April and October, all visitors, other than guests staying at *Zion Lodge* (see p.1046), are obliged to leave their vehicles either in Springdale (see p.1046) or at the large new **visitor center** just inside the park (daily: April–Oct 8am–7pm; Nov–March 8am–5pm; ☎435/772-3256, ⓦ www.nps.gov/zion). Free **shuttle buses** run on two separate loops in summer – one between Springdale and the visitor center, with nine stops en route, and the other between the visitor center and the end of the Scenic Drive, also with nine stops including *Zion Lodge*.

The Scenic Drive ends at the foot of the **Temple of Sinawava**, beyond which the easy but delightful **Riverside Walk** trail continues on another half a mile up the canyon, to the point where the river fills the entire floor (a very welcome bathing spot in drier seasons). The current is too dangerous for traveling upstream from this point, but at certain times of the year (check with the visitor center), hikers determined to experience **The Narrows** – where the canyon is only 20ft across and the walls tower some 800ft straight up – can wade for eight miles downstream through the chilly river from a remote spot thirty miles north.

Less ambitious walkers might prefer to wander up to **Weeping Rock**, an easy half-hour roundtrip from the road to a gorgeous spring-fed garden that dangles from a rocky alcove. From the same trailhead, a mile beyond *Zion Lodge*, a more strenuous and exciting route cuts through narrow **Hidden Canyon**, whose mouth turns into a waterfall after a good rain. Directly across from the lodge a short (two-mile roundtrip) and fairly flat trail winds up at the

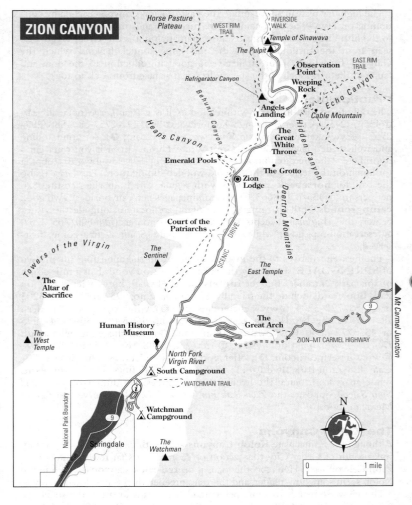

Emerald Pools, a series of three clearwater pools, the best (and furthest) of which has a small sandy beach at the foot of a gigantic cliff; at certain times of the year a broad waterfall sprinkles down over the trail.

The single best half-day **hike** climbs up to **Angel's Landing**, a narrow ledge of whitish sandstone protruding some 1750ft above the canyon floor. Starting on the same route as for the Emerald Pools, the Angel's Landing trail switchbacks sharply up through the delightful coolness of **Refrigerator Canyon** before emerging on the canyon's west rim; near the end you have to cross a heart-stopping five-foot neck of rock with sheer drops to either side (there's a steel cable to grab hold of). That roundtrip takes a good four hours, but backpackers can continue another twenty miles to the gorgeous Kolob Canyons district (see overleaf).

The high dry plateau above and to the **east** of Zion Canyon, reached by continuing on Hwy-9 at the Scenic Drive turnoff, stands in a complete contrast to the lush Virgin River gorge. Its most dramatic sight is the **Great Arch**, best seen from the turnouts before the mile-long tunnel, beyond which the **Canyon Overlook** nature trail gives a good introduction to the flora and fauna of the park, such as the speedy lizards that race from rock to rock.

Practicalities

The only **food and lodging** within Zion itself is at *Zion Lodge* (open all year; ☎435/772-3213, reserve through Xanterra at ☎303/297-2757 or 1-888/297-2757, Ⓦwww.xanterra.com or Ⓦwww.zionlodge.com; ❺), set amid rolling and well-shaded lawns near the Great White Throne. Even if you can't get a room here – they're often booked up by tour groups – it's well worth stopping for lunch on the terrace of the fine old wooden dining room. The *Lodge* is also the base for **horseback** excursions, with regular one-hour rides costing $20 per person (☎435/679-8665, Ⓦwww.onlinepages.net/canyonrides). Two good **campgrounds**, both charging $14 per night, are located alongside the visitor center; the *Watchman* accepts reservations in summer (☎1-800/365-2267, Ⓦreservations.nps.gov), while the summer-only *South* is first-come, first-served.

The best alternatives to the in-park lodge are in the appealing small town of **SPRINGDALE**, set among the riverbank cottonwoods half a mile south of the park entrance. Budget **motels** along Hwy-9, known here as Zion Park Boulevard, include the friendly *El Rio Lodge*, no. 995 (☎435/772-3205 or 1-888/772-3205, Ⓦwww.elriolodge.com; ❷), while two pricier modern alternatives, the *Best Western Zion Park Inn* at no. 1215 (☎1-800/934-7275 or 435/772-3200, Ⓦwww.zionparkinn.com; ❹), and the extremely stylish *Desert Pearl Inn*, no. 707 (☎435/772-8888 or 1-888/828-0898, Ⓦwww.desertpearl.com; ❺), offer good views and pools. The *Spotted Dog Café*, 428 Zion Park Blvd (☎435/772-3244), is the finest local **restaurant**, while apart from being the liveliest **bar** for miles, the dinner-only *Bit and Spur Saloon*, opposite the *Zion Park Inn* (☎435/772-3498), serves very good Mexican food.

The Kolob Canyons

Although the immaculate **Kolob Canyons** are just three miles off I-15, twenty miles south of Cedar City, this section of Zion receives far fewer visitors than Zion Canyon itself. Here, too, the focus is on **red-rock canyons**, which in the Kolob seem somehow redder, and the trees greener, than those down below.

The view from the five-mile paved road that heads up from the small but worthwhile **visitor center** (daily: May–Sept 8am–7pm; Oct–April 8am–6pm; ☎435/586-9548) is amazing, but hiking along either of two main trails will give you a sense of what makes this place so special. The first and shorter of the two starts two miles from the visitor center and follows Taylor Creek on a five-mile roundtrip to **Double Arch Alcove**, a spectacular natural amphitheater roofed by twin sandstone arches; there's also a small waterfall a quarter of a mile further along. The other trail starts from the north side of the parking area at Lee Pass, four miles beyond the visitor center, and follows a well-marked route for seven miles past LaVerkin Falls to **Kolob Arch**, which at over 300ft across rivals Landscape Arch in Arches (see p.1054) as the world's longest natural rock span. There are no permanent campgrounds in the Kolob Canyons, but two dozen backcountry sites are allotted by rangers each day; check at the visitor center.

Cedar Breaks National Monument

The shortest drive between Zion and Bryce, along the Virgin River and then north on US-89 across the high plain of Long Valley, is spectacular enough, but the longer route through the maple and aspen groves of the **Dixie National Forest** is even more dramatic. Halfway between Cedar City and US-89, Hwy-148 cuts sharply north through the eerie fringes of **Cedar Breaks National Monument**, where the soft sandstone has crumbled away from the edge of a high wooded plateau to create a natural amphitheater of bizarre and brilliantly colored formations.

Cedar Breaks is in a sense just a pocket version of Bryce Canyon to the east, but that's no reason not to come. Most of the plateau is over 10,000ft high, so it's usually quite cold; in fact the roads through are often blocked by snow until June. **Point Supreme**, which has a small summer-only **visitor center** (May–Sept daily 8am–6pm; fee $3 per person; ☎435/586-9451, ⓦwww.nps.gov/cebr), **snack bar**, and **campground** ($12), is a mile into the park from the south, and has the best view.

East of Cedar Breaks, Hwy-143 passes through pine forests and across lava flows, then drops past Panguitch Lake to reach the broad Sevier River valley at the squeaky-clean Mormon farming town of **PANGUITCH**. Here you'll find eight gas stations, twenty-odd **motels**, such as the *Marianna Inn*, 699 N Main St (☎435/676-8844 or 1-800/331-7407, ⓦwww.mariannainn.com; ❹), and not much else.

Bryce Canyon National Park

The surface of the earth can hold few weirder-looking spots than **BRYCE CANYON**. Named for Mormon settler Ebenezer Bryce, who memorably declared that it was "a helluva place to lose a cow," it is not in fact a canyon at all. Along a twenty-mile shelf on the eastern edge of the thickly forested **Paunsaugunt Plateau**, 8000ft above sea level, successive strata of dazzlingly colored rock – yellows, reds, whites, and flaming oranges – have slipped and slid and washed away to leave a menagerie of multihued and contorted **stone shapes**.

Like Cedar Breaks, the formations here have been eroded out of the muddy sandstone by a combination of icy winters (the temperature drops below freezing 200 nights out of the year) and summer rainstorms. The racks of top-heavy pinnacles known as "**hoodoos**" were formed when the harder upper layers of rock stayed firm as the lower levels were worn away beneath them. These hoodoos – **Thor's Hammer**, visible from Sunset Point, is the most alarmingly precarious – look down into technicolor ravines, all far more vivid than the Grand Canyon and much more human in scale. The whole place is at its most inspiring in winter, when the figures stand out from a blanket of snow.

The park approach road runs south from Hwy-12 about twenty miles east of Panguitch; the **entrance fee** is $20 per vehicle, per week. Although the park introduced a **free shuttle bus** system in 2000, visitors can still drive to all the scenic overlooks year round. The buses only run between mid-June and mid-August, on one route, which is completely optional. That connects the *Ruby's Inn* complex, at the intersection of Hwy-12 and Hwy-63, with the overlooks in Bryce Amphitheater. If that's as far as you want to go – and for most people, even keen hikers, it's entirely sufficient – then there's no reason to use your own car. If you want to get as far south as Rainbow Point, however, there's no bus service.

Of the succession of scenic overlooks into **Bryce Amphitheater**, at the heart of the park, the two most popular are on either side of *Bryce Canyon Lodge* (see below): the more northerly, **Sunrise Point**, is 350 yards from the parking lot and so is slightly less crowded than **Sunset Point**, where most of the bus tours stop. A network of **hiking trails** also drop abruptly from the rim down into the amphitheater – bear in mind that you'll have to walk back up the same distance that you go down. One good three-mile trek switch-backs steeply from Sunset Point through the cool 200-foot canyons of **Wall Street**, where a pair of 800-year-old fir trees stretch to reach daylight. It then cuts across the surreal landscape into the basin known as the **Queen's Garden**, where the stout and remarkable likeness of Queen Victoria sits in majestic condescension – pointed out by a brass plaque – before climbing back up to the rim at Sunrise Point. A dozen trails crisscross the amphitheater, but it's surprisingly easy to get lost, so don't stray from the marked routes.

Sunrise and Sunset points notwithstanding, the best view at both sunset and dawn (which is the best time for taking pictures) is from **Bryce Point**, at the southern end of the amphitheater. From here, you can look down not only at the Bryce Canyon formations but also take in the grand sweep of the whole region, east to the **Henry Mountains** and north to the Escalante range. The park road then climbs another twenty miles south, by way of the intensely colored **Natural Bridge**, an 85-foot rock arch spanning a steep gully, en route to its dead end at **Rainbow Point**.

Practicalities

The park's **visitor center**, just past the entrance, is a valuable source of information on current weather and hiking conditions (daily: mid-June to mid-Sept 8am–8pm; May to mid-June and mid-Sept to Oct 8am–6pm; Nov–April 8am–4.30pm; ℡435/834-5322, ⓦwww.nps.gov/brca). Much the best place to **stay** is the venerable *Bryce Canyon Lodge*, one hundred yards from the rim between Sunrise and Sunset points (April–Oct only; same-day reservations ℡435/834-5361, otherwise reserve through Xanterra ℡303/297-2757, ⓦwww.brycecanyonlodge.com; ❺), where rustic cabins cost a few dollars more than basic doubles. It also has a **dining room**, a grocery store, a laundry, and public showers.

The northern approaches to the park, just off Hwy-12, are guarded (not to say disfigured) by two **motels**, both owned by the same company and open year-round; the large *Best Western Ruby's Inn* (℡435/834-5341 or 1-800/468-8660, ⓦwww.rubysinn.com; summer ❹, winter ❷), which has a dreadful restaurant, and the cheaper, newer (and misleadingly named) *Bryce View Lodge* (℡435/834-5180 or 1-888/279-2304, ⓦwww.bryceviewlodge.com; ❸). *Ruby's Inn* has its own **campground** ($15.50), and there are also two first-come, first-served campgrounds within the park, which charge $10 per night; *Sunset Campground*, close to Sunset Point, and *North Campground*, near the visitor center. Backpackers can choose from dozens of sites below the rim, all south of Bryce Point; pick up the required permit at the visitor center, and take lots of water.

Bryce Canyon to Capitol Reef: Highway 12

Turning its back on the grand amphitheater of Bryce Canyon, the tiny hamlet of **TROPIC**, which straggles along Hwy-12 eight miles east of the park entrance, seems almost embarrassed about the flamboyant geological phenomena ranged along the ridge above it. The practical-minded people of this

Mormon farming community (population 380) don't especially concern themselves with tourists, but they have restored Ebenezer Bryce's log cabin, which stands next to the **Bryce Pioneer Village** motel-cum-restaurant (T435/679-8546 or 1-800/222-0381, Wwww.bpvillage.com; ❷–❸). An unmarked road heads west from the cabin two miles to the park boundary, from where it's a two-mile hike up to the main formations.

Back on Hwy-12, the road curves along the edge of the Table Cliff Plateau before dropping down into the remote canyons of the **Escalante River**, the last river system to be discovered within the continental US and site of some of the finest **backpacking** routes in the Southwest. As soon as you walk even a hundred yards off the main highway, you're in a wilderness that few travelers ever see.

ESCALANTE, 33 miles east of Cannonville, was just another roadside town until it was given a new lease on life in 1996 by the surprise Presidential proclamation that created the vast **Grand Staircase–Escalante National Monument** (free). The interagency **visitor center** at the west end of town (mid-March to Oct daily 7.30am–5.30pm; Nov to mid-March Mon–Fri 8am–4.30pm; T435/826-5499, Wwww.ut.blm.gov/monument), is a mine of up-to-date information on all the public lands in the vicinity, and can suggest **hiking** or **mountain-biking** trips into the backcountry. The most accessible local highlight is **Calf Creek**, sixteen miles east of Escalante, where a well-marked trail leads just under three miles upstream to a gorgeous shaded dell replete with a 125-foot waterfall, and a nice undeveloped **campground** ($7) as well. More ambitious trips start from trailheads along the dusty but usually passable **Hole-in-the-Rock Road**, which turns south from Hwy-12 five miles east of town. A trio of slender, storm-gouged **slot canyons**, including the delicate, graceful Peek-a-Boo Canyon and the downright intimidating Spooky Canyon, can be reached by a mile-long hike from the end of Dry Fork Road, 26 miles along, while from **Hurricane Wash**, 34 miles along, you can hike five miles to reach Coyote Gulch, and then a further five miles, passing sandstone bridges and arches, to the Escalante River. Under normal conditions, two-wheel-drive vehicles should go no further than **Dance Hall Rock**, 36 miles down the road, a superb natural amphitheater sculpted out of the slickrock hills. The pick of Escalante's **motels** is unquestionably the *Prospector Inn*, 380 W Main St (T435/826-4653, Wwww.prospectorinn.com; ❸), which adjoins the friendly, high-quality *Prospector Restaurant*, 400 W Main St (T435/826-4658).

Until the mid-1980s, when it was paved through to Capitol Reef, Hwy-12 ended at **BOULDER**, thirty miles beyond Escalante. **Anasazi State Park** (daily: mid-May to mid-Sept 8am–6pm; mid-Sept to mid-May 9am–5pm; $5 per vehicle or $3 per person), which holds the excavated and partially reconstructed remains of a small Ancestral Puebloan village, is set on a shallow knoll overlooking Boulder Creek.

Due **east** from Boulder, all except twenty miles of the old dirt **Burr Trail** has (controversially) been paved, providing easy access to the southern reaches of **Capitol Reef National Park** and down to **Lake Powell**. At the junction of Hwy-12 and the Burr Trail, the modern *Boulder Mountain Lodge* (T435/335-7460 or 1-800/556-3446, Wwww.boulder-utah.com; ❹) has twenty comfortable rooms and a reasonable restaurant. The best place to **eat** lies a few yards further east, in the spotless form of the *Boulder Mesa Restaurant*, 155 E Burr Trail Rd (T435/335-7447), which is open daily for all meals.

North of Boulder, Hwy-12 makes a gorgeous drive up onto the Aquarius Plateau, with marvelous vistas to the east across waves of gold and red sandstone outcrops; there's a lovely **campground** (T435/425-3702; $9) at Oak Creek, fifteen miles along.

Capitol Reef National Park

CAPITOL REEF might sound like something you'd find off the coast of Australia, but its towering ochre-, white-, and red-**rock walls** and deep **river canyons** are of a piece with the rest of the Utah desert. The outstanding feature is a multilayered, 1000-foot-high reef-like wall of uplifted sedimentary rock, a section of which reminded an early traveler of the grand dome of the US Capitol. Stretching for over a hundred miles north to south, but only a few miles across, the seemingly impenetrable barrier of the **Waterpocket Fold** was warped upward by the same process that lifted the Colorado Plateau, and the sharply defined sedimentary layers on display here trace over two hundred million years of geological activity. The Waterpocket Fold is sliced through in a number of places by deeply incised river canyons – some only twenty feet wide, but hundreds of feet deep – often accessible only by foot.

The one paved road through the park, Hwy-24, cuts across the northern half of the Fold, following the deep canyon of the **Fremont River**; motorists who stick to this road do not incur an entrance fee. Beneath the enormous and very prominent rock outcrop known as the **Castle**, the **visitor center** (daily: June–Sept 8am–7pm; Oct–May 8am–4.30pm; ☎435/425-3791, ⓦwww.nps .gove/care) has explanatory exhibits and an irresistible campground ($10), set amid the cherry, apple, and peach orchards of the abandoned Mormon community of **FRUITA**; in season, you can pick all the fruit you can gobble down. To the west, the **Goosenecks Overlook** gazes down 500ft into the entrenched canyons cut by Sulphur Creek. Further east, beyond Fruita's former schoolhouse, are some extraordinary **Fremont petroglyphs**, figures of bighorn sheep and stylized space-people chipped into the varnished rock a thousand years ago; a five-minute radio broadcast (AM 1540) describes their makers. Another four and a half miles along, one of Capitol Reef's best **day-hikes** heads up along the gravelly riverbed through **Grand Wash** – a beautiful (and usually quite cool) canyon where, it's said, Butch Cassidy and his gang used to hide out.

Few other paved routes run through the park, so to reach the spectacular backcountry canyons you may have to put up with many miles of dusty and spine-rattling roads – renting a mountain bike from Pedal Pusher, at 151 W Main St, Torrey (☎435/425-3378 or 1-800/896-5773), is a good idea. The paved, popular **Scenic Drive** ($5 per vehicle) heads twelve miles south from the visitor center, past the top of Grand Wash to **Capitol Gorge** and back. A more adventurous sixty-mile loop trip explores **Cathedral Valley** in the north, while a 125-mile southern route starts at the foot of the volcanic **Henry Mountains**, then follows the Burr Trail through **Muley Twist Canyon**, and continues west to Boulder (see p.1049).

The nearest **food and lodging** to Capitol Reef is eleven miles west, in and near the rapidly growing town of **TORREY**, which all but closes down in winter. The *Sand Creek Hostel & Bunkhouse*, 540 W Main St (closed mid-Oct to March; ☎435/425-3577; ❶), is a thriving little complex that offers camping for $9, dorm beds for $10, and a couple of inexpensive private cabins for $28, while the *Best Western Capitol Reef Resort*, east of town at 2600 E Hwy-24 (☎435/425-3761 or 1-888/610-9600; ❸), is a well-equipped modern motel, with great views and a good pool. If you want to escape the run-of-the mill motel eateries, *Café Diablo*, 599 W Main St (☎435/425-3070) is a surprisingly inventive dinner-only restaurant.

Goblin Valley

Fifty fairly desolate miles east of Capitol Reef along Hwy-24, you reach the tiny crossroads of **Hanksville**. Twenty miles north on Hwy-24, a right turn takes you onto a 32-mile dirt road to a real anthropological and artistic wonder – the rock paintings of **Horseshoe Canyon**, a remote subsection of Canyonlands National Park (see below).

Half a mile further north on Hwy-24, a side road to the east veers off to **Goblin Valley State Park** (open 24hr; $5), where thousands of gnome-like figures loom out of the soft Entrada sandstone. The **Carmel Canyon** trail loops for over a mile through a throng of misshapen rock pillars, many of which seem to have eyes and other human features; in the 2000 movie spoof *Galaxy Quest*, the entire valley comes to life. Stay at the well-equipped **campground** (☎1-800/322-3770; $10) if you want to see the place by moonlight, when it looks especially spooky.

Green River

The uneventful riverside town of **GREEN RIVER**, just east of the Hwy-24 junction on I-70, is the largest community on a 200-mile stretch of interstate. One good reason to visit is the **John Wesley Powell River History Museum**, 885 E Main St (daily: summer 8am–8pm; rest of year 8am–5pm; $2), which features the anything-but-dry personal accounts of the men who first successfully navigated the Colorado River from near its source all the way through the Grand Canyon. In summer, **raft trips** from the museum – which also doubles as the local **visitor center** – float downriver to the **Crystal Geyser**, a 100-foot cold-water gusher, and every Memorial Day hundreds of boats set out on weekend-long convoy trips that cruise down the Green River to its confluence with the Colorado, then head upriver to Moab.

Green River holds several bargain-rate **motels**, and one slightly classier option: the *Best Western River Terrace*, 880 E Main St (☎435/564-3401 or 1-800/528-1234, Ⓦwww.bestwestern.com; ❹), which has a pool, river views, and a decent restaurant.

Canyonlands National Park

CANYONLANDS NATIONAL PARK, the largest and most magnificent of Utah's national parks, is as hard to define as it is to map. Its closest equivalent, the Grand Canyon, is by comparison simply an almighty crack in an otherwise relatively flat plain; the Canyonlands area is a bewildering tangle of canyons, plateaus, fissures, and faults, scattered with buttes and monoliths, pierced by arches and caverns, and penetrated only by a paltry handful of dead-end roads.

The 527 square miles of the park are just the core of a much larger wilderness that stretches to the horizon in every direction. To nineteenth-century explorers, this was the epitome of useless desolation; only since uranium prospectors blazed crude trails across the trackless wastes in the 1950s has it become at all widely known. Even after the park was created in 1964, it took a couple of decades before tourists arrived in appreciable numbers.

Canyonlands focuses on the Y-shaped confluence of the **Green** and **Colorado rivers**, buried deep in the desert forty miles southwest of Moab. There's only one spot from which you can see the rivers meet, however, and that's a five-mile hike from the nearest road. With no road down to the rivers, let alone across them, the park therefore splits into three major sections. The **Needles**, east of the Colorado, is a red-rock wonderland of sandstone pinnacles and hidden meadows that's a favorite with hardy hikers and four-wheel-drive enthusiasts, while the **Maze**, west of both the Colorado and the Green, is a virtually inaccessible labyrinth of tortuous, waterless canyons. In the wedge of the "Y" between the two, the high, dry mesa of the **Island In The Sky**

Canyonlands National Park charges an **entry fee** of $10 per vehicle, $5 for cyclists or hikers, valid for seven days in all sections of the park. Only limited numbers of visitors are allowed to spend a night or more in the backcountry. **Backpacking** permits, covering a maximum party of seven persons in the Needles and Island In The Sky districts, or five persons in the Maze, cost $10. Permits for **four-wheel-drive** or **mountain-biking** expeditions that involve backcountry camping, issued for groups of up to three vehicles with a total of fifteen people in the Island In The Sky, ten in the Needles, or nine in the Maze, are $30. **Reservations** are essential for the most popular areas, especially in the peak seasons of spring and fall. Permits must be purchased at least two weeks in advance, and must be picked up in person, as well – with every member of the group present – from the appropriate park visitor center, at least one hour before it closes.

For application forms, and full details of the park's complex regulations, visit or write to the **National Park Service Reservations Office**, 2282 S West Resource Blvd, Moab UT 84532-8000; call ☏435/259-4351 (Mon–Fri 8am–4pm), or contact a park visitor center. The park's website is at ⊛www.nps.gov/cany.

commands astonishing views across the whole park and beyond, with several overlooks that can easily be toured by car. Getting from any one of these sections to the others involves a drive of at least a hundred miles.

Canyonlands is not a place that lends itself to a short visit. With no lodging, and little camping, inside the park, and no loop road to whisk you through it, it takes a full day to have even a cursory look at a single segment. If you're among the many visitors who find the conditions too grueling to spend much time out of your car – summer temperatures regularly exceed 100°F, and most trails have no water and little shade – then the Island In The Sky is the most immediately rewarding option. On the other hand, if you fancy a long day-hike you'd better to set off into the Needles (see opposite).

Island In The Sky and Dead Horse Point State Park

Reached by a good road that climbs steadily up from US-191, 21 miles south of I-70, the **Island In The Sky** district looks out over hundreds of miles of flat-topped mesas that drop in 2000-foot steps to the river. Four miles along from its **visitor center** (daily: summer 8am–6pm; winter 8am–4.30pm; ☏435/259-4712), the **Mesa Arch Trail** is the area's best short hike, looping for a mile around the mesa-top hillocks to the edge of the abyss, where long, shallow Mesa Arch frames an extraordinary view of the **La Sal Mountains**, 35 miles northeast. The definitive vantage point, however, is **Grand View Point Overlook**, another five miles on at the southern end of the road. An agoraphobic's nightmare, it commands a hundred-mile prospect of layer upon layer of bare sandstone, here stacked thousands of feet high, there fractured into bottomless canyons. The Island In The Sky's only developed **campground**, the first-come, first-served and waterless *Willow Flat* ($5), is just back from the **Green River Overlook**, reached by taking the right fork shortly after the Mesa Arch trailhead.

On the way in to Island In The Sky, a turnoff long before the visitor center cuts across south to the smaller but equally breathtaking **Dead Horse Point**, located at the tip of a narrow mesa, which looks straight down 2000ft to the twisting Colorado River. Cowboys used the mesa as a natural corral, herding up wild horses then blocking them in behind a piñon pine fence that still marks its 90-foot neck. One band of horses was left here too long and died –

hence the name. As a Utah state park, Dead Horse Point charges its own $5 admission fee, and national-park passes cannot be used. The **visitor center** (daily: summer 8am–6pm; winter 8am–5pm; ☎435/259-2614) stands two miles short of the point itself, and there's also a **campground** ($11; reservations mid-March to mid-Oct only, costing $5 extra, on ☎1-800/322-3770).

The Needles and Newspaper Rock

Taking its name from the thousands of colorful sandstone pillars, knobs, and hoodoos that punctuate its many lush canyons and basins, the **Needles** district allows a more intimate look at the Canyonlands environment than does Island In The Sky. Here you're not always gazing thousands of feet downward or scanning the distant horizon; instead you can wander through seemingly endless acres of stone figures.

The road ends with a great collection of mushroom-shaped hoodoos at the **Big Spring Canyon Overlook**. A memorable and demanding eleven-mile roundtrip hike from here remains the only way to get to the **Confluence Overlook**, 1000ft above the point where the Green River joins the muddy waters of the Colorado, to flow together, parallel but separate, toward fearsome **Cataract Canyon**. Various short walks head off the road at selected viewpoints; one of the best is **Pothole Point**, a mile before **Big Spring Canyon**. A longer day-trip, or a good overnight hike, leaves from near the *Squaw Flat* **campground** ($10) to the green meadow of **Chesler Park**, cutting through the narrow cleft of the Joint Trail. Check in at the **visitor center** (daily: summer 8am–6pm; winter 8am–4.30pm; ☎435/259-4711) near the park boundary to get up-to-date information, as well as backcountry permits if you plan to camp out. The only way to **reach the river** from within the park is by taking the hot and dry trail down through Lower Red Canyon to **Spanish Bottom**; this is the start of the Cataract Canyon rapids, so don't try to swim across.

The 35-mile drive in to the Needles from US-191 is among the prettiest in the state, winding along Indian Creek through deep red-rock canyons lined by pines and cottonwoods. **Newspaper Rock**, twelve miles in, is the best of many similarly named sites; here hundreds of tiny **petroglyphs**, many of which show deer, antelope, bear claws, and helmeted human figures, have been etched in the jet-black desert varnish of a red-sandstone boulder by centuries of passing hunters and travelers. There's a lovely (free) streamside **campground** just across the road.

The Maze and Horseshoe Canyon

Only about one in a hundred of the half-million visitors who come to Canyonlands every year makes it into the harsh backcountry of the remote **Maze** district. Filling up the western third of the park, on the far side of the Colorado and Green rivers, the Maze is noted for its ancient rock-art panels and for its many-fingered box canyons, accessible only by jeep or by long, dry hiking trails. If you're tempted, call into the Hans Flat **ranger station**, 46 miles east of Hwy-24 (daily 8am–4.30pm; ☎435/259-2652).

Pretty, tree-lined **Horseshoe Canyon**, reached halfway down a long, long dirt road that loops south from Green River itself to join Hwy-24 just south of Goblin Valley (see p.1050), contains the greatest concentration of **ancient rock art** in the Southwest. Allowing at least an hour's driving from the highway both before and after, plus five hours for the six-mile roundtrip hike down into the canyon itself, you'll need to set aside a full day, but it's well worth the effort, both for the joy of the walk and for the sight of the "**Great Gallery**" at the far end. Hundreds of mysterious, haunting pictographs – mostly life-sized human figures, albeit weirdly elongated, or draped in robes and adorned with strange, staring eyes – were painted onto these red-sandstone walls, probably between 500 BC and 500 AD. Rangers from Hans Flat (see above) lead guided hikes into Horseshoe Canyon on summer weekends (April–Oct Sat & Sun 9am).

Arches National Park

The writer Edward Abbey, who spent a year as a ranger at **ARCHES NATIONAL PARK** in the 1950s, wrote in *Desert Solitaire* that its arid landscape was as "naked, monolithic, austere, and unadorned as the sculpture of the moon." It certainly is one of the least terrestrial places on this planet. Massive fins of red and golden sandstone stand to attention out of the bare desert plain, and over 1800 natural arches of various shapes and sizes have been cut into the rock by eons of erosion. Apart from the single ribbon of black asphalt that snakes through the park, there's nothing even vaguely human about it. The narrow, hunching ridges are more like dinosaurs' backbones than solid rock, and under a full moon, at twilight, or during the lightning strikes of a distant thunderstorm, you can't help but imagine that the landscape has a life of its own.

While you could race through in a couple of hours, to do Arches justice you should plan to spend a whole day here at the very least. A twenty-mile road cuts uphill sharply from US-191 and the park **visitor center** (daily: mid-April to early Oct 7.30am–6.30pm; mid-March to mid-April and middle two weeks in Oct 7.30am–5.30pm; late Oct to mid-March 8am–4.30pm; $10 per vehicle or $5 for motorcyclists, cyclists, and pedestrians; ☎435/719-2299, ⓦ www.nps .gov/arch). Exhibits here explain how the arches are formed and point out some of the more photogenic examples. The first possible stop is the south trailhead for **Park Avenue**, an easy trail leading one mile down a scoured, rock-bottomed wash. If you stay on the road, the **La Sal Mountains Viewpoint** provides a grandstand look at the distant peaks rising over 12,000ft above the surrounding desert, as well as the huge red chunk of **Courthouse Towers** closer at hand. Beyond the Towers, the road follows the foot of the salmon-hued sandstone of the **Great Wall**.

From **Balanced Rock** – a 50-foot boulder atop a slender 75-foot pedestal – a turning to the right winds for two miles through the **Windows** section, where a half-mile trail loops through a dense concentration of massive arches, some over 100ft high and 150ft across. A second trail, fifty yards beyond, leads to **Double Arch**, a staunch pair of arches that together support another arch overhead.

Beyond Balanced Rock, the main road drops downhill for two miles past Panorama Point and the turnoff to **Wolfe Ranch**, where a century-old log cabin now serves as the trailhead for the exposed three-mile roundtrip hike up to **Delicate Arch**, which, as a freestanding crescent of rock perched at the brink of a deep canyon, is by far the most impressive arch in the park. Three miles beyond the Wolfe Ranch turnoff, the deep, sharp-sided mini-canyons of the **Fiery Furnace** section form a (usually quite cool) labyrinth through which rangers lead regular hikes in spring, summer, and fall ($8; reserve in advance at the visitor center).

The road continues on to the **Devil's Garden** trailhead, from which an easy one-mile walk leads to a view of the astonishing 306-foot span of **Landscape Arch**, now too perilously slender to approach more closely. Several other arches lie along short spur trails off the route; seeing them all, and returning from **Double O Arch** via the longer primitive trail, requires a total hike of

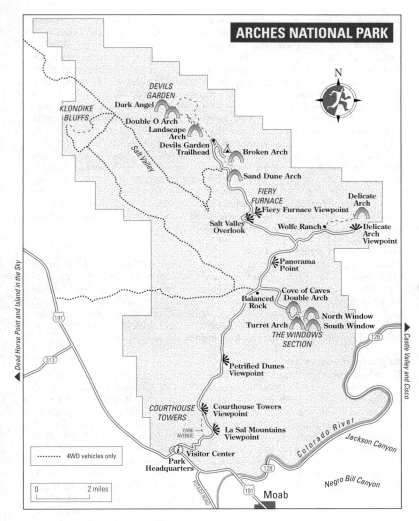

N

Dead Horse Point and Island in the Sky ►

191

313

DEVILS GARDEN

KLONDIKE BLUFFS

Dark Angel

Double O Arch

Landscape Arch

Devils Garden Trailhead

Broken Arch

Sand Dune Arch

Salt Valley

FIERY FURNACE

Fiery Furnace Viewpoint

Delicate Arch

Salt Valley Overlook

Wolfe Ranch

Delicate Arch Viewpoint

Panorama Point

Cove of Caves Double Arch

Balanced Rock

North Window

Turret Arch

South Window

THE WINDOWS SECTION

128

◄ *Castle Valley and Cisco*

Petrified Dunes Viewpoint

COURTHOUSE TOWERS

Courthouse Towers Viewpoint

PARK AVENUE

La Sal Mountains Viewpoint

ℹ Visitor Center

Park Headquarters

Colorado River

Jackson Canyon

POTASH ROAD

128

191

Moab

Negro Bill Canyon

---------- 4WD vehicles only

0   2 miles

just over seven miles. Arches' only **campground** ($10; water only available mid-March to Oct) is across from the trailhead; all of its first-come, first-served sites tend to be occupied by early morning in season. Permits for **backcountry camping**, allowed anywhere that's a mile from the road and half a mile from any trail, are issued at the visitor center.

Moab

Founded in the late 1800s, **MOAB** was hardly a speck until the 1950s, when prospector Charlie Steen discovered uranium in the nearby hills. When the ensuing mining boom finally waned, the conservative hold of Moab's mine-owners and businessmen over the land waned with it, and the town threw in its lot with tourism. Over the last twenty years, it has transformed itself into the Southwest's number one adventure-vacation destination.

Moab still isn't a large town, though – the population has yet to reach ten thousand – and neither is it an attractive one. The setting is what matters. With two national parks on its doorstep, plus millions more acres of public land, Moab is an ideal base for outdoors enthusiasts. At first, it was a haven for **mountain bikers** lured by the legendary **Slickrock Bike Trail** (see box, opposite). Then the **jeep** drivers began to turn up, and the **whitewater-rafting** companies moved in, too. These days it's almost literally bursting, all year, with legions of Lycra-clad vacationers from all over the world.

Perhaps the main reason Moab has grown so fast is that out-of-state visitors tend to find Utah's other rural communities so irredeemably boring. As soon as Moab emerged from the pack, it became a beacon in the desert, attracting tourists ecstatic to find a town that stayed up after dark. Moab amounts to little more than a few miles of motels, restaurants, and bars, but that's enough to make it the only southern-Utah town where you can stay for a week and still feel that you haven't seen everything, and everyone, a dozen times.

Arrival and information

Moab's superb **visitor center**, in the heart of town at Center and Main streets (daily: summer 8am–9pm; winter 9am–noon & 1–5pm; ☎435/259-8825 or 1-800/635-6622, ⓦwww.discovermoab.com), carries stacks of information on Moab itself, plus brochures and maps for the nearby parks and public lands. ARK Bighorn Express (☎801/328-9920 or 1-888/655-7433, ⓦwww.goark.com) run daily shuttle **buses** between Salt Lake City and Moab, continuing on to Monticello, while the nearest Amtrak station is at Green River.

Accommodation

If you've already been in Utah for a while when you reach Moab, its glittering neon **motel** signs will come as a big surprise. At last count, there were 28 motels and a dozen B&Bs in town, but every one of the thousand-plus rooms is taken on many nights between mid-March and October – when you'd be lucky to find anything below $60 – so reservations are strongly recommended. Agencies such as Moab/Canyonlands Central Reservations (☎435/259-5125 or 1-800/505-5343, ⓦwww.moab.net/reservations) can help.

Commercial **campgrounds** nearby include the well-shaded *Slickrock Campground*, 1301 N Hwy-191 (☎435/259-7660 or 1-800/448-8873, ⓦwww.slickrockcampground.com; $16), a mile north of town; if you're happy to put up with far more primitive facilities to escape the crowds, head instead for the Bureau of Land Management's **Sand Flats Recreation Area**, along the top of the mesa to the east of town, near the Slickrock Bike Trail, at 1924 S Roadrunner Hill (☎435/259-6111; $8).

Aarchway Inn 1551 N Hwy-191 ☎435/259-2599 or 1-800/341-9359, ⓦwww.moab-utah.com /aarchway/inn.html. Well-equipped motel with a nice pool, not far from the Colorado River at the north end of town. ❹
Best Western Greenwell Inn 105 S Main St ☎435/259-6151 or 1-800/528-1234, ⓦwww.quinstar.com/greenwell. Central, modern hotel that offers spacious good-value rooms with tasteful furnishings and fittings. ❹

Gonzo Inn 100 W 200 South ☎435/259-2515 or 1-800/464-6696, ⓦwww.gonzoinn.com. Luxurious if rather self-consciously hip inn, complete with kitsch-retro furnishings, quirky artworks, and an in-house espresso bar. ❺
Inca Inn Motel 570 N Main St ☎435/259-7261, ⓦwww.moab-utah.com/inca/inn.html. Clean, minimally equipped but adequate budget motel. ❷
Lazy Lizard International Hostel 1213 S Hwy-191 ☎435/259-6057, ⓦwww.gj.net/~lazylzrd.

Amiable, very laid-back independent hostel, well south of the center, with $8 beds in six-person dorms, $6 camping, and private cabins for $22, plus hot tub, kitchen, and Internet access.

Moab Valley Inn 711 S Main St ☎435/259-4419 or 1-800/831-6622, ⊛www.moabvalleyinn.com. Modern, large, and well-equipped motel at the south end of town, with pool, hot tub, and on-site car and four-wheel-drive rental. ❹

Adventure-travel outfitters in southeast Utah

Moab is the main center for companies running **adventure trips** through the back-country and along the raging waters of southwest Utah. Varying from half-day jaunts to week-long expeditions, such trips not only get you to places you'd never otherwise reach, but also provide a sense of the region's natural splendor that can't be had by car or on foot.

River trips

Among Moab's dozen licensed operators offering **motorized** one-day trips along the Colorado River for around $45 and up are Western River Expeditions (☎801/942-6669 or 1-800/453-7450, ⊛www.westernriver.com), Adrift Adventures (☎435/259-8594 or 1-800/874-4483, ⊛www.adrift.net), and Tag-a-Long Expeditions (☎435/259-8946 or 1-800/453-3292, ⊛www.tagalong.com). The trips start northwest of Moab, near the butte known as Fisher Towers, and arrive near town in the afternoon; many companies give passengers the chance to float quieter stretches in two-person kayaks. The same operators run **oar-powered** trips that are slower but much quieter, and less expensive than motorboat trips. Longer (2- to 7-day) trips head through Cataract Canyon and other wild Canyonlands spots.

Mountain biking

While the Moab area is ideally suited to mountain-bike touring, only experienced riders should attempt its most challenging route, the famous **Slickrock Bike Trail**. This ten-mile, half-day loop starts atop the mesa about three miles east of Moab, threading its way among the sandstone knobs with views of the La Sal Mountains and the Colorado River; wear a **helmet**, take lots of **water**, and keep an eye and an ear out for motorcyclists, who are also allowed on the trail. A more relaxing alternative is to explore the dirt roads leading through the red-rock country of Kane Creek, west of town.

  Bike shops offering daily rental and guided tours include Rim Tours (☎435/259-5223 or 1-800/626-7335, ⊛www.rimtours.com), Kaibab Adventure Outfitters (☎435/259-7423 or 1-800/451-1133, ⊛www.kaibabtours.com), and Poison Spider (☎435/259-7882 or 1-800/635-1792, ⊛www.poisonspiderbicycles.com).

Jeep tours

Most of the thousands of miles of **jeep trails** around Moab were built years ago by miners and haven't been maintained since. The visitor center has a free map and guide to some of the more popular ones, and you can rent a four-wheel-drive jeep or pickup truck for around $100 per day from Slickrock 4x4 Rentals at 284 N Main St (☎435/259-5678 or 1-888/238-5337). **Guided jeep tours** (around $100 per person per day) are offered by Nichols Expeditions (☎435/259-3999 or 1-800/648-8488, ⊛www.nicholsexpeditions.com) and Tag-a-Long Expeditions (see above).

Scenic flights

From a small airfield twenty miles north of Moab on US-91, Redtail Aviation (☎435/259-7421 or 1-800/842-9251) and Slickrock Air Guides (☎435/259-6216, ⊛www.slickrockairguides.com) run unforgettable **flights** over the Canyonlands area and beyond: a perfect opportunity to appreciate the labyrinthine complexity of the Maze, to see the confluence of the two great rivers, and even to pick out inaccessible Ancestral Puebloan ruins – and well worth the $100 per-person rate for a one-hour reconnaissance.

Eating and drinking

Moab offers by far the greatest range of **restaurants** in southern Utah, and for once most places make the effort to cater for vegetarians. With two pubs and a winery, there's also no problem getting a **drink**, while **coffee bars** are springing up everywhere. Note that many local restaurants, tired of low-tipping foreign customers, have taken to including a fifteen-percent service charge on all checks.

Buck's Grill House 1393 N Hwy-191 ☎435/259-5201. Belying its stockade-like exterior, this "American Western Food" joint is actually a sophisticated affair, serving rich, classy Southwestern food, such as game hen or pork ribs, at very reasonable prices. Open for dinner nightly.

Center Café 60 North 100 West ☎435/259-4295. Expensive but exquisite restaurant, offering gourmet dining with a Pacific twist. Entrees ($20–30) range from Asian barbecue salmon to rack of lamb. Open for dinner nightly; closed Dec–Feb.

Eddie McStiff's 57 S Main St ☎435/259-2337. Central pub, next to the visitor center, which serves some interesting beers, including raspberry and blueberry varieties, and also a diverse and inexpensive menu of salads, pizzas, and pasta.

Jailhouse Café 101 N Main St ☎435/259-3900. Very popular central café, open for breakfast only, until noon on weekdays and 1pm at weekends. There's indoor and outdoor seating year-round, and great specials like ginger pancakes and eggs Benedict.

Mondo Café 59 S Main St ☎435/259-5911. Groovy all-day hangout next to *Eddie McStiff's* (see above), serving espresso coffees and the odd pastry or sandwich.

Sunset Grill 900 N Hwy-191 ☎435/259-7146. Charlie Steen's luxury hilltop home is now a fine restaurant, with meat and seafood entrees for $13–21, great desserts, and stunning views. The tortuous if short approach road from the north end of town means it's no place to drink and drive. Dinner only, closed Sun.

Natural Bridges National Monument

One of the prettiest and least traveled highways in southern Utah, **Hwy-95** runs for over a hundred miles southeast from Capitol Reef, through dozens of red-rock canyons, and across the Dirt Devil and Colorado rivers before topping out on the sagebrush plains of San Juan County. En route it gives access to the marvelous collection of sandstone spans at **Natural Bridges National Monument**, forty miles west of US-191. Three canyons come together here, and at each junction the streams that carved them have also formed sandstone bridges. The largest, **Sipapu Bridge**, is 268ft across at its base and over 200ft high, and can be seen from the nine-mile paved road that loops through the monument; hike less than a mile down into the canyon for a closer look. **Kachina Bridge**, the next along the road, is nearly as high but twice as thick, and has Ancestral Puebloan pictographs at its base. The oldest, slimmest, and most fragile bridge – **Owachomo**, a mile and a half up Armstrong Canyon – spans 180ft but is only nine feet thick at its thinnest point. A strenuous eight-mile trail along the canyon bottom leads past all three bridges.

Admission to the monument is $6 per vehicle. The **visitor center** (daily: March–Oct 8am–5pm; Nov–Feb 9am–4.30pm; ☎435/692-1234, ⓦwww.nps .gov/nabr), four miles off Hwy-95, has free trail guides and a slide show explaining how the bridges were formed, as well as a brief introduction to the Ancestral Puebloan sites. Camping is allowed only in the small **campground** ($10) near the visitor center, which also has the only drinkable water in the monument.

Monticello

The small town of **MONTICELLO** stands 56 miles south of Moab on US-191, sixteen miles beyond the turnoff for the Needles section of Canyonlands (see p.1053). Its strip of budget **motels** includes *Canyonlands Motor Inn*, 197 N Main St (℡435/587-2266 or 1-800/952-6212; ❷), and a *Super 8*, 649 N Main St (℡435/587-2489 or 1-877/246-9378; ❸). Good, large, standard **meals** can be had at the *MD Ranch Cookhouse*, 380 S Main St (℡435/587-3299). Information on the town, and on the parks and public lands in the vicinity, can be picked up from the **visitor center**, in the courthouse at 117 S Main St (April–Oct Mon–Fri 8am–5pm, Sat & Sun 10am–5pm; Nov–March Mon–Fri 8am–5pm; ℡435/587-3235 or 1-800/574-4386, ⓦwww.southeastutah.org).

The San Juan River, Mexican Hat, and Bluff

From Natural Bridges, Hwy-261 runs south for some 25 miles before coming to what looks like a dead end at the edge of Cedar Mesa. From here, high above the eerie sandstone towers of the **Valley of the Gods** (where much of *Thelma and Louise* was filmed), the road turns to gravel before dropping over a thousand feet in little over two twisting, hairpin-turning miles down the "**Moki Dugway**." Six miles from the foot of the switchbacks, the barely marked Hwy-316 shoots across what seems like a flat valley floor to yet another overlook, this time high above the **San Juan River** at the extraordinary and aptly named **Goosenecks State Reserve** (open 24hr; free). A textbook example of what geologists call an entrenched meander, the river, a thousand feet below, snakes around in such convoluted twists and turns that it flows six miles in total for every one mile west.

Back on Hwy-261 and just south, sleepy **MEXICAN HAT**, briefly a frenzied gold-mining camp, takes its name from a riverside **sandstone hoodoo**, just north of town, that looks more than a little like a south-of-the-border sombrero. More of a cluster of buildings on the banks of the river than a town, it's good fun and makes a convenient base for visiting Monument Valley, twenty miles south (see p.1035). The best **place to stay** is the *San Juan Inn* (℡435/683-2220 or 1-800/447-2022; ❸), right on the river, which has its own grocery store and trading post, as well as the amiable *Olde Bridge Bar and Grill*, which offers cold beers and Navajo tacos. Just up the road, *Mexican Hat Lodge* (℡435/683-2222, ⓔmueller@sanjuan.net; ❸) has an atmospheric steakhouse.

The rafts you may see emerging from the water at Mexican Hat went in at **BLUFF**, twenty miles upstream. The road between the towns, US-163, doesn't follow the river very closely but is still an enthralling drive, and when you get there the town itself has a number of **Mormon pioneer houses** along its backstreets. Places to **eat** in Bluff include the *Twin Rocks Café* (℡435/672-2341) and the *Cottonwood Steakhouse* (℡435/672-2282), while an excellent new motel at the south end of town, the *Desert Rose Inn*, 701 W Hwy-191 (℡435/672-2303 or 1-888/475-7673, ⓦwww.desertroseinn.com; ❸), holds thirty attractively decorated rooms.

Hovenweep National Monument

Hidden in the no-man's-land that straddles the Utah–Colorado border, the remote **Ancestral Puebloan ruins** at **Hovenweep National Monument** offer a haunting sense of timeless isolation. Located 25 miles east of US-191 along Hwy-262, which branches off halfway between Bluff and Blanding, and 35 miles west of Cortez, Colorado (see p.914), Hovenweep preserves six distinct conglomerations of ruins sprouting from the rims of shallow desert canyons and dwarfed by the distant mountains, but easy access is restricted to **Little Ruin Canyon**, behind the smart new **visitor center** (daily: March–Oct 8am–6pm; Nov–Feb 8am–5pm; $6 per vehicle or $3 per person; ☎970/562-4282, ⓦwww.nps.gov/hove). A mile-long loop trail offers good views of the largest ruins, including the grandly named **Hovenweep Castle**, constructed around 1200 AD.

No accommodation, gasoline, or food is available at or anywhere near Hovenweep, but a 31-site **campground** beside the ranger station remains open all year ($10; no reservations).

Lake Powell and Glen Canyon Dam

The mighty rivers and canyons of southern Utah come to an abrupt and ignoble end at the Arizona border, where the **Glen Canyon Dam** stops them dead in the stagnant waters of **Lake Powell**. Ironically, the lake is named for John Wesley Powell, the first white man to explore the canyonlands in depth, and the first person to run the Colorado River through the Grand Canyon. The roaring torrents with which he battled are now lost beneath these placid blue waters, and the blocked-up Colorado, Green, Dirty Devil, San Juan, and Escalante rivers are now a playground for houseboaters and water-skiers. The construction of the dam in the early 1960s outraged **environmentalists** (Edward Abbey's *Monkey Wrench Gang* made their first big splash here, sabotaging bulldozers and simulating huge cracks in the dam at the opening ceremonies) and **anthropologists** (innumerable Ancestral Puebloan pictographs are submerged hundreds of feet below the surface). The dam has created one of the most peculiar – and utterly unnatural – landscapes imaginable, the deep and tranquil lake a surreal contrast with the surrounding dry slickrock and sandstone buttes.

Lake Powell has 1960 miles of shoreline, which is more than the entire Pacific coast of the US, and 96 water-filled side canyons. The water level fluctuates considerably, so for much of the time the rocks to all sides are bleached for many feet above the current waterline, with a dirty-bath tidemark sullying the golden sandstone. Most of the many summer visitors bring their own boats, or rent a vessel from one of the four marinas that fringe the lake.

If you're passing through, by far the most accessible stop is **Wahweap Marina**, just off US-89 on the way between Zion and the Grand Canyon, where *Wahweap Lodge* (☎928/645-2433 or 1-800/528-6154, ⓦwww.visit-lakepowell.com; ❻) has comfortable lakeside rooms and some of the best food within a day's drive. The same company arranges **houseboat rental** from Wahweap or other Lake Powell marinas; boats sleep four or more people and cost from $650 for three nights in winter, $1100 in summer. There's **camping** on the lakeshore at each of the marinas. The nearest **budget accommodation** is across the Arizona border in **PAGE**, home of the usual assortment of chain motels and diners, including a *Motel 6*, 637 S Lake Powell Blvd (☎928/645-3919 or 1-800/466-8356, ⓦwww.motel6.com; ❷).

GLEN CANYON DAM itself, in between Page and Wahweap, can be seen from the **Carl Hayden Visitor Center** (daily: Oct–April 8am–5pm; May–Sept 7am–7pm; ☎928/608-6404, ⓦwww.nps.gov/glca) on the west bank. Security concerns have meant that **free tours** of the dam have been suspended since September 11, 2001; check with the visitor center for the latest details.

The cheapest way to get out on the waters of Lake Powell is to take the **ferry** ($12 per car) between **Halls Crossing** and **Bullfrog** marinas, two-thirds of the way up the lake; from here the Burr Trail heads west toward Capitol Reef (see p.1050), while Hwy-276 runs northeast to Natural Bridges (see p.1058).

The spectacular and extremely remote **Rainbow Bridge National Monument**, the world's largest natural bridge, can be visited on **guided boat tours** from Wahweap and Bullfrog marinas ($109 full-day, $83 half-day; ☎928/645-2433 or 1-800/528-6154, ⓦwww.visitlakepowell.com). It lies roughly fifty miles by water from either direction, including a final mile or two down the narrow, winding side channel of Forbidding Canyon. From the unappealing jetty where the boats moor, bobbing in a morass of pond scum, a ten-minute walk leads to the astonishing giant sandstone gateway, springing up nearly 300ft from just above the waterline, with Navajo Mountain visible through its magnificent smooth curve. Its upper section is composed of Navajo sandstone, while the base belongs to the harder Kayenta formation, which is not as easily cut by flowing water. Despite the increase in tourism since the lake's creation, the monument remains an inspiring sight, and a place of special importance to the Navajo.

Northern Utah

Compared to the scenic splendor of the southern half of the state, northern Utah holds little to interest the tourist, although **Salt Lake City**, the capital, is by far the state's largest and most cosmopolitan urban center. The dramatic Wasatch Mountains that line Salt Lake's eastern horizon do however come into their own in winter, as they constitute one of the nation's premier **ski destinations**. The **northeast corner** has coal mines, old railroad towns and, along the Wyoming border, the **Uinta Mountains**, uncrossed by road and showing hardly a sign of civilization. From the **northwest**, the harshly alkaline **Great Basin** plain stretches uneventfully west across Nevada to California.

Salt Lake City

Disarmingly pleasant and easygoing, **SALT LAKE CITY** is well worth a stopover of a couple of days. It's not a particularly thrilling destination in itself, but its setting is superb, towered over by the **Wasatch Front**, which marks the dividing line between the comparatively lush eastern and the bone-dry western halves of northern Utah. The area offers great hiking and cycling in summer and fall and, in winter, some of the world's best skiing. Salt Lake City's bid to raise its international profile by hosting the **2002 Winter Olympics** resulted in a major building program both in the city itself and in the surrounding ski valleys, along with a degree of notoriety following the taint of corruption that surrounded its selection. Nonetheless, though people elsewhere in the US still tend to imagine Salt Lake City as decidedly short on spontaneous public fun, so long as you're willing to switch gears and slow down, its unhurried pace, and the positive energy and lack of pretence of its people, can make for a surprisingly enjoyable experience.

Arrival, information, and getting around

Salt Lake City International Airport (☎801/575-2400) is a mere four miles west of downtown. A **taxi** into town costs around $15; cheaper **shuttle vans** to downtown destinations are run by Xpress Shuttles (☎801/596-1600 or 1-800/397-0773; reserve 24hrs in advance), while Canyon Transportation (☎801/255-1841) serves the ski areas. Long-distance Greyhound-Trailways buses arrive downtown, at 160 W South Temple Blvd (☏801/355-9579), as do Amtrak **trains**, at 320 S Rio Grande Ave. Local buses, and also TRAX trams, are operated by the Utah Transit Authority (☏801/743-3882, ⓦwww.rideuta.com); journeys within the immediate downtown area are free.

Gray Line (☏801/521-7060) offers **bus tours** ranging from city jaunts to multiday trips to the national parks. To reach the best parts of the surrounding mountains, however, you'll need a **car** – all the rental companies are represented at the airport – or a cycle and strong legs. **Bikes** can be rented from Utah Ski & Golf, 134 W 600 South St (☏801/355-9088).

Visitor centers supplying information on the city itself can be found downtown at 90 S West Temple Blvd in the Salt Palace Convention Center (summer Mon–Fri 8am–6pm, Sat & Sun 9am–5pm; winter Mon–Fri 8am–5pm, Sat & Sun 9am–5pm; ☏801/521-2822 or 1-800/541-4955, ⓦwww.visitsaltlake .com), or in Terminal 2 of the airport (daily except Sat 9am–9pm). For details on the rest of Utah, stop by the Utah Travel Council, which occupies the imposing Council Hall across from the capitol at 300 N State St (Mon–Fri 9am–6pm; ☏801/538-1030). The downtown **post office** is at 230 W 200 South St (Mon–Fri 8am–5.30pm, Sat 8am–1.30pm; ☏801/978-3001; zip code 84101).

Accommodation

Salt Lake City is well equipped with **accommodation**, with downtown options that range from budget motels and B&B inns to rather more luxurious hotels, and the usual mid-range places near the airport and along the interstates. There's so much capacity for business travelers that weekend rates can be real bargains.

Brigham Street Inn 1135 E South Temple Blvd ☏801/364-4461 or 1-800/417-4461. Luxurious, peaceful – and inconspicuous – B&B a few blocks east of downtown toward the mountains. ❺

Holiday Inn Airport 1659 W North Temple Blvd ☏801/533-9000 or 1-800/HOLIDAY, ⓦwww.bristolhotels.com. Well-equipped, well-priced hotel, served by free airport shuttles and not too far from downtown. ❸

Hotel Monaco 15 W 200 South ☏801/595-0000 or 1-800/805-1801, ⓦwww.monaco-saltlakecity .com. Extremely hip, very upscale downtown hotel, housed in a former bank. ❻

International Ute Hostel 21 E Kelsey Ave ☏801/595-1645, ⓦwww.infobytes.com /utehostel. Much the better of Salt Lake City's two hostels, this small private establishment, a few miles south of downtown, offers $15 dorm beds

and a couple of private rooms ($35), plus bike rental, a hot tub, and free airport pickup. ❶–❷

Motel 6 176 W 600 South St ☏801/531-1252. Reliable budget motel in downtown, handy for Amtrak. ❸

Peery Hotel 110 W 300 South St ☏801/521-4300 or 1-800/331-0073, ⓦwww.peeryhotel .com. 1910 downtown landmark, entirely renovated in 1999, offering very tasteful, comfortable rooms. ❺

Salt Lake City Marriott Downtown 75 S West Temple Blvd ☏801/531-0800 or 1-800/228-9290. Very central, characterful, and attractively furnished hotel, facing the visitor center and equipped with a good pool. ❻

Travelodge – Temple Square 144 W North Temple Blvd ☏801/533-8200. Most central and least expensive of three local *Travelodges*. ❸

Temple Square

The geographical – and spiritual – heart of Salt Lake City is **Temple Square**, the world headquarters of the **Mormon Church** (or the Church of Jesus Christ of Latter-Day Saints – LDS). Its focus, the monumental **Temple** itself, was completed in 1893 after forty years of intensive labor. The multi-spired granite edifice rises to 210ft above the city – it's not the tallest building on the mainly flat skyline but, thanks to its crisply angular silhouette, it's just about the only interesting one. Only confirmed Mormons may enter the Temple, and even they do so only for the most sacred LDS rituals – marriage, baptisms, and "sealing," the joining of a family unit for eternity.

SALT LAKE CITY

N

89

TRAX

State Capitol

The Tabernacle

Family History Library

Mormon Temple

Beehive House

Temple Square

ZCMI Center

Delta Center

Salt Palace

Crossroads Plaza

Amtrak Station

ACCOMMODATION

Marriott Downtown	B
Hotel Monaco	C
Motel 6	E
Peery Hotel	D
Travelodge-Temple Square	A

RESTAURANTS & CAFÉS

Lamb's Restaurant	2
Market Street Grill	6
Martine's	1
Oasis Café	3
Orbit Café	4
Rio Grande Café	5

0   400 yds

Wander through the gates of Temple Square, however, and you'll swiftly be snapped up by one of the many waiting Mormons, and shepherded to join a free 45-minute **tour** of the various sites within. As well as monuments to Mormon pioneers, you'll be ushered into the odd oblong shell of the **Mormon Tabernacle**. No images of any kind adorn its interior, which is home to the world-renowned Mormon Tabernacle Choir; a helper at the lectern laconically displays its remarkable acoustic properties by tearing up a newspaper and dropping a nail. There's free admission to the choir's 9.30am Sunday broadcast, and its rehearsals on Thursday evenings at 8pm.

The primary aim of the tours is to awaken your interest in the Mormon faith; differences from Christianity are played down in favor of a soft-focus video of Old Testament scenes. The tour ends in the northern of the square's two **visitor centers**, where an array of touch-screen computers provide woolly answers to questions like "What is the purpose of life?" and "Who was Joseph Smith?" In the southern visitor center, a surprisingly good free movie tells the story of the arrival of Salt Lake City's first Mormon settlers.

Downtown Salt Lake City

A block east of Temple Square along South Temple Boulevard, the **Beehive House** (summer Mon–Sat 9.30am–6.30pm, Sun 10am–1pm; winter Mon–Sat 9.30am–4.30pm, Sun 10am–1pm; free) is a plain white New England–style house, with wraparound verandas and green shutters. Erected in 1854 by church leader **Brigham Young**, it's now a small museum of Young's life, restored to the style of the period. Free twenty-minute tours, which you have to join to see much of the house, are given at least every half-hour.

The **Family History Library**, across West Temple Boulevard from Temple Square (Mon 7.30am–5pm, Tues–Sat 7.30am–10pm; free; ☏801/240-2331 or 1-800/453-3860 ext 22331, Ⓦwww.familysearch.org), is intended to enable Mormons to trace their ancestors and then baptize them into the faith by proxy, but it's open to everyone. The world's most exhaustive genealogical library is surprisingly user-friendly, giving immediate access, through CD-ROMs and banks of computers, to birth and death records from over sixty countries, some dating back as much as five hundred years. All you need is a person's place of birth, a few approximate dates, and you're away; volunteers provide help if you need it, but leave you alone until you ask. Next door to the library, the **Museum of Church History and Art** (Mon–Fri 9am–9pm, Sat & Sun 10am–7pm; free) charts the rise of the Mormon faith in art and artifact.

The area southwest of Temple Square, now the site of the massive **Salt Palace** convention center and sports arena (home of the Utah Jazz basketball team), has undergone a rapid transformation. The surrounding district of brick warehouses around the Union Pacific railroad tracks is quickly filling up with designer shops and art galleries, signs that even Mormons can be yuppies.

Capitol Hill

Quite why the Mormons chose not to put their Temple on the gentle hill that stands above today's Temple Square is anyone's guess. As a result, when Utah was granted statehood in 1896, it was free to become the site of the imposing, domed **Utah State Capitol** (summer Mon–Sat 8am–8pm; rest of year Mon–Sat 8am–6pm; free). Along with the plaques and monuments you might expect, the corridors of power are packed full of earnest and rather diverting exhibits of great Utah moments.

Now called **Capitol Hill**, the neighborhood around the capitol holds some of Salt Lake City's grandest c.1900 homes, with dozens of ornate Victorian houses lining Main Street and Quince Street to the northwest; **walking tour maps** of the district are available from the Utah Heritage Foundation, 355 Quince St.

Eating

Though Salt Lake City has a perfectly good selection of **restaurants**, it lacks an atmospheric – let alone hip – dining district. If you like to compare menus, the only downtown area with much potential is the block or two to either side of West Temple Street, south and east of the Salt Palace.

Bambara *Hotel Monaco*, 15 W 200 South ☏801/363-5454. Chic, post-Deco, and pricey downtown restaurant, with a fabulous menu ranging from buffalo carpaccio to crab cakes and lamb sirloin on puy lentils.

Lamb's Restaurant 169 S Main St ☏801/364-7166. Great breakfasts, best eaten at the long shiny counter, and excellent-value set meals throughout the day. Closed Sun.

Market Street Grill 48 Market St ☏801/322-4668. As close as Salt Lake City comes to a New York City bar and grill, with fresh seafood, especially oysters, plus steaks in all shapes and sizes. $9 lunch specials, full dinners $15–30.

Martine's 22 E 100 South ☏801/363-9328. Formal, dimly lit, and upmarket Southwestern restaurant, in a central location facing the ZCMI mall. Most menu items can be served as "tapa" (appetizer) or entree. Closed Sun.

Oasis Café 151 S 500 East ☎ 801/322-0404.
Classy but inexpensive café serving very good food
(dinner entrees $16–22) with plenty of appealing
vegetarian options. Live acoustic music or jazz in
the evening.

Orbit Café 540 W 200 South ☎ 801/322-2808.
Large, postmodern diner, which serves tasty
sandwiches and ethnic specials for lunch, and
then fancier late-night meals (until 4am Fri &
Sat).

Rio Grande Café 270 S Rio Grande ☎ 801/364-

3302. Spirited and stylish Mexican cantina in the
old Denver and Rio Grande railroad station, still
used by Amtrak, three blocks west of downtown.

Ruth's Diner 2100 Emigration Canyon Rd
☎ 801/582-5807. Good-value indoor and patio
dining, often accompanied by live music, set in
and around old railroad carriages in a narrow
canyon just three miles east of town. There's a
wide selection of fresh dishes, great salads, and
Utah's best breakfasts. For more sophisticated and
expensive fare, try *Ruth's* sister restaurant, the
Santa Fe, next door.

Drinking and nightlife

Salt Lake City doesn't roll up the sidewalks when the sun goes down. Many
drinking venues are technically private clubs, in which a nominal membership fee entitles the cardholder and up to five guests to two weeks' use of the
facilities, but there are also a handful of **brewpubs** for which membership is
not required. Good options for an evening out include the *Dead Goat Saloon*,
165 S West Temple Blvd (☎ 801/328-4628), a raucous, semi-subterranean
saloon, with live loud music most nights. The casual, friendly *Squatters Pub*, 147
West Broadway (☎ 801/363-2739), offers a range of beers available until 1am
every day, plus a simple menu. Salt Lake's premier live music venue, the *Zephyr
Club*, 301 S West Temple Blvd (☎ 801/355-2582), hosts semi-famous jazz,
blues, country, or rock names most nights to an upmarket clientele (cover
$5–15).

To find out about the broad range of **fringe** art, music, and clubland happenings, pick up free papers such as *City Weekly*, or tune to radio station KRCL
91FM.

Park City

Despite Brigham Young's strictures against prospecting for precious metals – he
feared a Gentile "Gold Rush" – the first mining camp at **PARK CITY**, just
thirty miles east of downtown Salt Lake City along I-80 through the mountains, was established in the late 1860s. In 1872 George Hearst laid the foundations of the Hearst media empire by paying $27,000 for a claim that became
the Ontario Silver Mine, worth $50 million. These days, the **Park City
Mountain Resort** (☎ 435/649-8111, ⓦ www.parkcitymountain.com), and
the nearby **The Canyons** (☎ 435/649-5400, ⓦ www.thecanyons.com) and
(skiers-only) **Deer Valley** (☎ 435/649-1000 or 1-800/424-3337, ⓦ www
.deervalley.com) resorts constitute Utah's largest **ski area**, with the season usually running from mid-November to mid-April. Daily lift passes for each resort
cost around $60; equipment rental outlets include Park City Sport (☎ 1-
800/523-3922) and Gart Brothers (☎ 1-800/284-4754). In addition, Park City
hosts the prestigious **Sundance Film Festival**, held during the second half of
January each year (☎ 801/328-3456, ⓦ www.sundance.org).

Park City has for many years been engulfed by an ever-growing sprawl of
new condos, factory outlets, and other developments, and has become completely unrecognizable since being overhauled for the 2002 Winter Olympics.
Its restored **Main Street** now makes only token gestures toward mimicking
the mountain mining community it used to be, its shops and restaurants striving instead to emulate the chic resorts of Colorado.

Practicalities

Park City's **visitor center**, 528 Main St (May & Oct daily 11am–5pm; rest of year Mon–Fri 10am–7pm, Sat & Sun noon–6pm; ☎435/649-6100 or 1-800/453-1360, ⊛www.parkcityinfo.com), doubles as an enjoyable museum of town history, and stands above the town's original jailhouse. Lewis Bros Stages (☎435/649-2256 or 1-877/491-8111, ⊛www.lewisbrothers.com) runs scheduled **shuttles** from downtown Salt Lake City ($26) and the airport (up to $50), and mountain **bikes** can be rented from White Pine Touring, 201 Heber Ave (daily 10am–7pm; ☎801/649-8710).

Accommodation rates double in the ski season; the visitor center can provide full listings of resorts and other lodgings. The *Old Miners' Lodge*, right next to the ski lift at 615 Woodside Ave (☎435/645-8068 or 1-800/648-8068; ❹), is an 1893 lodge restored as a comfortable B&B. The unassuming *Chateau Apres-Ski*, 1299 Norfolk Ave (☎435/649-9372 or 1-800/357-3556; ❶–❹), is a cheap, cozy alternative with some $28 dorm beds, while the *Park City International Hostel*, 268 Main St (☎435/655-7244, ⊛www.parkcityhostel .com; ❶), is a smart, deluxe hostel where dorm beds cost $30. *Morning Ray Café*, also at 268 Main St (☎435/649-5686), serves good breakfasts and has a wide-ranging lunch menu, while the dinner-only *Chimayo*, 368 Main St (☎435/649-6222), offers cutting-edge contemporary Southwestern cuisine. The *Wasatch Brew Pub*, nearby at 250 Main St (☎435/649-0900), is open until midnight daily and serves good food as well as microbrewed beer.

Northeast Utah

Most of Utah's **northeastern corner** – due east of Salt Lake City, where Wyoming takes a bite out of its otherwise perfect rectangle – is taken up by the forbidding **Uinta Mountains**, very much of a piece with the rest of the Rockies. However, to the east of the mountains the terrain reverts to the classic Southwestern desert plains, with the small town of **Vernal** serving as the base for explorations of the wildernesses of **Flaming Gorge** and **Dinosaur**.

Dinosaur National Monument

Dinosaur National Monument straddles the border between Utah and Colorado in a remote area only conceivably visitable in your own vehicle. Divided into two separate sections, the monument was created to preserve a rock stratum in its Utah half, seven miles north of Jensen on Hwy-149, east of Vernal, which has over the years provided brontosaurus skeletons and other astonishing remains to museums around the world. Uniquely, in the **Dinosaur Quarry** building, a tilted layer of sandstone has been painstakingly exposed to display an incredible jigsaw of fossilized dinosaur bones, which imaginative visitors might piece together.

The other half of the monument is a 25-mile drive north of the flyblown and unattractive little town of Dinosaur, Colorado, the site of the main **visitor center** (daily: summer 8am–7pm; winter 8am–4.30pm; $10 per vehicle; ☎435/781-7700, ⊛www.nps.gov/dino). At the end of the road **Harpers Corner** provides a phenomenal view of the goosenecks of the Green and Yampa rivers as they approach their confluence at imposing **Steamboat Rock**.

Flaming Gorge

It took a major controversy in the 1950s to spare the Green and Yampa confluence from submergence by a new dam. **Flaming Gorge**, starting around 25 miles north of Vernal, was not so lucky; the damming of the Red Canyon of the Green

River in 1964 has turned it into a National Recreation Area, another "splendid recreational playground" for watersports enthusiasts, anglers, and hikers.

Ambivalence about its creation can't obscure its continuing beauty, however, which can be appreciated from various points on the loop drive that circles the canyon, calling at Green River, Wyoming, at its northern end. The **Gorge** itself is an incandescent wall of red rock named by John Wesley Powell and best seen from the **Antelope Flat** marina-cum-campground on the eastern side. **Red Canyon visitor center** (summer daily 9.30am–5pm) to the west is another good stop, with a dramatic overlook and the attractive nearby *Red Canyon Lodge*, a complex of new and restored cabins offering varying degrees of luxury (☎435/889-3759, ⓦwww.redcanyonlodge.com; ❹). The actual dam is not all that exciting.

Vernal

Although **VERNAL**, thirty miles west of the Colorado border on US-40 as it heads to Salt Lake City, is the largest community in northeast Utah, and holds a mildly diverting dinosaur museum, for most visitors it's only significant as an overnight stop. Budget **motels** lining Main Street include the *Sage* at no. 54 W (☎435/789-1442 or 1-800/760-1442, ⓦwww.vernalmotels.com; ❷), which has its own adjacent **restaurant**, and the *Best Western Antlers Motel* at no. 423 W (☎435/789-1202; ❷).

Nevada

NEVADA is without doubt the most desolate state in the US, consisting largely of endless tracts of bleak, empty desert. Its flat sagebrush plains are cut intermittently by angular mountain ranges, and the lack of rainfall or fertile soil has ensured its maintenance as untouched wilderness. Apart from the huge acreages given over to mining and to grazing cattle and sheep, much of Nevada is under the control of the **military**, who use it to test aircraft and weapons systems, including Stealth fighters and atomic bombs. Dozens of intriguing small communities are scattered around the state, some showing signs of strong Basque influence. Many more are decrepit roadside ghost towns, often little more than a gas-station-cum-general-store, flanked by a saloon and perhaps a brothel – Nevada is the only US state not to have outlawed **prostitution**, though it is illegal in Las Vegas.

Though millions of people pass through on their way to and from California, there's only one real reason why anyone ever *visits* Nevada, and that is to **gamble**: as soon as you cross the state border, you'll be attacked by a 24-hour onslaught of neon signs and gimmicky architecture, each advertising the best odds and biggest jackpots, nowhere more than in the surreal oasis of **Las Vegas**. Even the smaller and more down-to-earth settlements of **Reno** and state capital **Carson City** revolve around the casino trade. At least the casinos' energetic pursuit of passing trade keeps rooms and especially food inexpensive, so the towns make good places to break a long journey – and, with Nevada's relaxed marriage and divorce laws, make or break a relationship.

Getting around Nevada

As there's almost nothing in Nevada outside of Las Vegas and Reno, it's hardly surprising that getting around the state's vast empty spaces is nearly impossible without a car. Las Vegas is no longer served by Amtrak, but Reno still welcomes daily trains between San Francisco and Salt Lake City; both Las Vegas and Reno have **airports**.

Las Vegas

Shimmering from the desert haze of Nevada like a latter-day El Dorado, **LAS VEGAS** is the most dynamic, spectacular city on earth. At the start of the twentieth century, it didn't even exist; now it's home to over one million people, and boasts fourteen of the world's fifteen largest hotels, whose flamboyant, no-expense-spared **casinos** lure in thirty-seven million tourists each year.

Las Vegas has been stockpiling superlatives since the 1950s, but never rests on its laurels for a moment. First-time visitors tend to expect the city to be a repository of kitsch, but the casino owners are far too canny to be sentimental about the old days. Yes, there are a few Elvis impersonators around, but what characterizes the city far more is its endless quest for **novelty**. Long before they lose their sparkle, yesterday's showpieces are blasted into rubble, to make way for ever more extravagant replacements. A few years ago, when the fashion was for fantasy, Arthurian castles and Egyptian pyramids mushroomed along the legendary Strip; now Vegas demands nothing less than entire cities, and boasts pocket versions of New York, Paris, Monte Carlo, and Venice.

While the city has certainly cleaned up its act since the early days of Mob domination, there's little truth in the notion that it's become a **family** destination. In fact, for kids, it's not a patch on Orlando. Several casinos have added theme parks or fun rides to fill those odd non-gambling moments, but only five percent of visitors bring children, and the crowds that cluster around the exploding volcanoes and pirate battles along the Strip remain almost exclusively adult. Neither is Vegas as consistently **cheap** as it used to be. It's still possible to find good, inexpensive rooms, and the all-you-care-to-eat buffets offer unbeatable value, but the casino owners have finally discovered that high-rollers happy to lose hundreds of dollars per night don't mind paying premium prices to eat at top-quality restaurants and stay in plush hotels.

Although Las Vegas is an unmissable destination, it's one that palls for most visitors after a couple of (hectic) days. If you've come solely to gamble, there's not much to say beyond the fact that all the casinos are free, and open 24 hours per day, with acres of floor space packed with ways to lose money: million-dollar slots, video poker, blackjack, craps, roulette wheels, and much, much more.

A history of Las Vegas

The name Las Vegas – Spanish for "the meadows" – was originally applied to a group of natural springs that from 1829 onward served as a way-station for travelers on the Old Spanish Trail. In 1900, the valley had a population of just thirty people. Things changed in 1905, with the completion of the now-defunct rail link between Salt Lake City and Los Angeles.

Though Nevada was the first state to outlaw gambling, in 1909, it was made legal once more in 1931, and the workers who built the nearby **Hoover Dam** flocked to Vegas to bet away their pay packets. Providing abundant cheap elec-

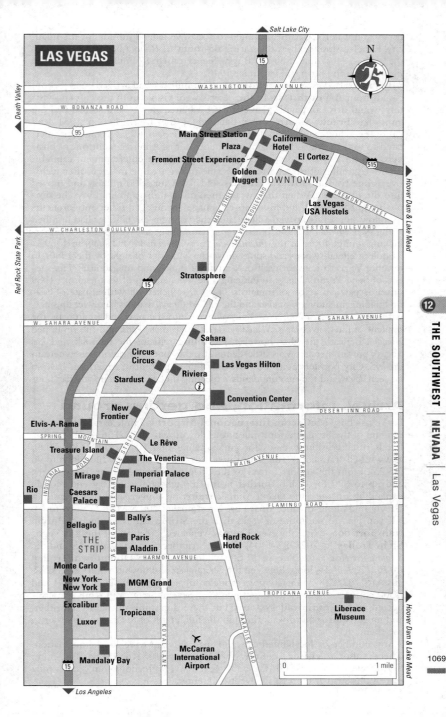

tricity and water, the dam amounted to a massive federal subsidy for the infant city. Hotel-casinos such as the daring 65-room *El Rancho* began to appear in the early 1940s, and mobster Bugsy Siegel raised $7 million to open the *Flamingo* on the Strip in December 1946.

By the 1950s, Las Vegas was booming. The military had arrived – mushroom clouds from **A-bomb tests** in the deserts were visible from the city, and visitors would drive out with picnics to get a better view – and so too had big guns like **Frank Sinatra**, who debuted at the *Desert Inn* in 1951, and **Liberace**, who received $50,000 to open the *Riviera* in 1955. As the stars gravitated toward the Vegas honeypot, nightclubs across America went out of business, and the city became the nation's undisputed live-entertainment capital.

The beginning of the end for Mob rule in Vegas came in 1966, after reclusive airline tycoon **Howard Hughes** sold TWA for $500 million and moved into the *Desert Inn*. When the owners tired of his non-gambling ways, he simply bought the hotel, and his clean-cut image encouraged other entrepreneurs to follow suit. **Elvis** arrived a little later; the young rock 'n' roller had bombed at the *New Frontier* in 1956, but started a triumphant five-year stint as a karate-kicking lounge lizard at the *International* (now the *Las Vegas Hilton*) in 1969.

Endless federal swoops and stings drove the Mob out of sight by the 1980s, in time for Vegas to reinvent itself on a surge of junk-bond megadollars. The success of Steve Wynn's *Mirage* in enticing a new generation of visitors, from 1989 onward, spawned a host of imitators. The 1990s kicked off with a spate of casino building, including *Excalibur* and the *MGM Grand*, that has barely let up since, with *Luxor* and *New York–New York* followed into the new millennium by the opulent quintet of *Bellagio*, *Mandalay Bay*, the *Venetian*, *Paris*, and the revamped *Aladdin*. Beneath the glitz, however, **gambling** remains the bedrock, and Las Vegas's pre-eminence seems little dented by the spread of casinos elsewhere in the US. City boosters point out that only fifteen percent of Americans have so far seen Vegas, and they're confidently expecting the rest to turn up any day now.

Arrival, information, and getting around

Las Vegas's busy **McCarran International Airport** is a mile east of the southern end of the Strip, and four miles from downtown (☎702/261-5211). Some hotels run free shuttle buses for guests, while Bell Trans (☎702/380-7990, ⓦwww.bell-trans.com) run **minibuses** to the Strip ($4) and downtown ($5.25). From the airport, a **taxi** to the Strip costs from $10 for the southern end up to $20 for casinos further north, though fares can vary enormously depending on the time taken. Amtrak **trains** no longer serve Las Vegas, but Greyhound's long-distance **buses** use a terminal at 200 S Main St downtown.

If you plan to see more of Vegas than the Strip, a **car** is invaluable. **Public transport** does exist, however. The oak-veneered streetcars of the **Las Vegas Strip Trolley** (☎702/382-1404) ply the Strip between *Mandalay Bay* and the *Stratosphere*, for a flat fare of $1.50, while the similar **Downtown Trolley** (☎702/229-0624) loops between the *Stratosphere* and downtown for 50¢. CAT buses (☎702/228-7433, ⓦwww.catride.com) serve the whole city; #301 and #302 connect the Strip to downtown ($2). Several Strip casinos are also connected by free **monorail systems**, but these don't link up with each other, and most require you to walk through the full length of the casinos in order to use them.

Any number of local freesheets and magazines provide local information. There's also a **visitor center** at 3150 Paradise Rd (daily 8am–5pm; ☎702/892-7575 or 1-800/332-5333, ⓦwww.vegasfreedom.com), half a mile east of the Strip at the vast Convention Center.

Getting married in Las Vegas

Second only to making your fortune as a reason to visit Las Vegas is the prospect of **getting married**. Over a hundred thousand weddings are performed here each year, many so informal that bride and groom just wind down the window of their car during the ceremony, and a Vegas wedding has become a byword for tongue-in-cheek chic.

You don't have to be a local resident or take a blood test to get wed here. Assuming you're both at least eighteen years old and carrying picture ID – and not already married – simply turn up at the Clark County Marriage License Bureau, downtown at 200 S Third St (Mon–Thurs 8am–midnight, and continuously from 8am on Fri to midnight on Sun; ☎702/455-4415, ⊛www.co.clark.nv.us), and buy a marriage license for $50 cash.

Wedding chapels claim to charge as little as $50 for basic ceremonies, but at that sort of rate even the minister is an "extra" costing an additional $40. Reckon on paying at least $100 for the bare minimum, which is liable to be as romantic a process as checking in at a hotel, and to take about as long. The full deluxe service ranges up to around $600. Novelty options include plighting your troth amid the pirates aboard HMS *Britannia* outside *Treasure Island* (☎702/894-7700); on the deck of the USS *Enterprise* at the *Hilton* (☎702/697-8750); floating on a gondola in the *Venetian*'s Grand Canal (☎702/414-4253); or cavorting in medieval costume at *Excalibur* (☎702/597-7278).

Candlelight Wedding Chapel 2855 Las Vegas Blvd S ☎702/735-4179 or 1-800/962-1818, ⊛www.candlelightchapel.com. Busy little chapel across from *Circus Circus*, where you get a carnation bouquet with the $179 wedding package, or a garter with the $499 option.

Graceland Wedding Chapel 619 S Las Vegas Blvd ☎702/474-6655 or 1-800/824-5732, ⊛www.gracelandchapel.com. Home of the King – an Elvis impersonator will act as best man, give the bride away, or serenade you, but unfortunately he can't perform the service.

Little Church of the West 4617 Las Vegas Blvd S ☎702/739-7971 or 1-800/821-2452. This fifty-year-old chapel is on the National Register of Historic Places, and has moved progressively down the Strip to its current site south of *Mandalay Bay*. Among the more peaceful and quiet places to exchange your Vegas vows – if that's really what you want.

Little White Chapel 1301 S Las Vegas Blvd ☎702/382-5943 or 1-800/545-8111, ⊛www.alittlewhitechapel.com. Where Bruce Willis and Demi Moore married each other, and Michael Jordan and Joan Collins married other people. Open all day every day, with ceremonies in the roofed-over driveway (or "Tunnel of Love") for those in a major hurry.

Accommodation

Although Las Vegas has well over 125,000 motel and hotel rooms, it's best to book **accommodation** ahead if you're on a tight budget, or arriving on Friday or Saturday; upward of 200,000 people descend upon the city every weekend. Whatever you may have heard, Las Vegas hotels no longer offer incredibly cheap deals at the drop of a hat. It is true that serious gamblers can get their accommodation free, but to count as "serious" you'd have to commit yourself to gambling several thousand dollars.

Precise **room rates** are entirely dictated by supply and demand. Even if you stay in the same room for several consecutive days, you'll be charged a different rate for each day, depending on the day of the week, and what's going on in town. The only sure-fire way to get a cut-price room, however, is to **visit**

during the week rather than on the weekend. Rates rise enormously on Friday or Saturday, by perhaps $30 to $50 extra in a lower-end property, $100 in the big-name casinos. On top of that, many hotels won't accept Saturday arrivals. The **Las Vegas Convention & Visitors Authority** offers an availability and reservations service at ☎1-800/332-5334.

Aladdin 3667 Las Vegas Blvd S ☎702/785-5555 or 1-877/333-9474, ⓦ www.aladdincasino.com. Much more manageable than most of its giant neighbors, with each of its 2600 spacious rooms within easy reach of an elevator, and first-class dining and shopping. Mon–Thurs & Sun ❹ , Fri & Sat ❻

Bellagio 3600 Las Vegas Blvd S ☎702/693-7111 or 1-888/987-6667, ⓦ www.bellagiolasvegas.com. Extremely luxurious rooms, with plush European furnishings and marble bathrooms, an amazing pool complex, and some of the best restaurants in town. Sun–Thurs ❼ , Fri & Sat ❽

Caesars Palace 3570 Las Vegas Blvd S ☎702/731-7110 or 1-800/634-6661, ⓦ www .caesars.com. Right in the heart of the Strip, the epitome of 1960s luxury continues to offer the last word in pseudo-Roman splendor, with top-class restaurants and shops. Sun–Thurs ❹ , Fri & Sat ❼

California Hotel 12 Ogden Ave at First St ☎702/385-1222 or 1-800/634-6255, ⓦ www.the-cal.com. Almost all the guests in this mid-range downtown casino are Hawaiian, and Hawaiian food and drink dominate the bars and restaurants. The actual rooms are plain but adequate. Sun–Thurs ❷ , Fri & Sat ❸

Circus Circus 2880 Las Vegas Blvd S ☎702/734-0410 or 1-800/444-2472, ⓦ www.circuscircus .com. Venerable Strip hotel popular with budget tour groups. Kids love the theme park and (almost) nonstop circus acts, while adults love the low room rates. Sun–Thurs ❷ , Fri & Sat ❹

Las Vegas USA Hostels 1322 E Fremont St ☎702/385-1150 or 1-800/550-8958, ⓦ www.usahostels.com. Well-kept independent hostel in a grim neighborhood ten blocks east of downtown, offering dorm beds for $13 and private double rooms for $38, plus use of a good pool,

Internet access, and shuttle buses. The friendly staff arrange city and national-park tours, including a weekly clubbing night. No curfew. ❶/❷

Luxor Las Vegas 3900 Las Vegas Blvd S ☎702/262-4000 or 1-800/288-1000, ⓦ www.luxor.com. A night in this vast smoked-glass pyramid is one of the great Las Vegas experiences. All the 2000 enjoyably Egyptian-themed rooms in the pyramid itself face outward and have tremendous views. Sun–Thurs ❸ , Fri & Sat ❺

MGM Grand 3799 Las Vegas Blvd S ☎702/891-7777 or 1-800/929-1111, ⓦ www.mgmgrand .com. Waiting for any kind of service, especially check-in, at the world's largest hotel can be horrendous, but you get a good standard of accommodation for the price, and it holds several of Las Vegas's finest restaurants. Sun–Thurs ❹ , Fri & Sat ❺

New York–New York 3790 Las Vegas Blvd S ☎702/740-6050 or 1-800/693-6763, ⓦ www.nynyhotelcasino.com. Rooms at the most exuberantly fun Strip casino are very nice, if a bit small, and filled with Art Deco furnishings and flourishes. Sun–Thurs ❹ , Fri & Sat ❻

Paris–Las Vegas 3655 Las Vegas Blvd S ☎702/946-7000 or 1-888/266-5687, ⓦ www.parislasvegas.com. Flamboyant French-themed casino, where the rooms and services are pitched slightly below those of Las Vegas's most upscale joints, but the location, views, and general ambiance are superb. Sun–Thurs ❺ , Fri & Sat ❼

The Venetian 3355 Las Vegas Blvd S ☎702/414-1000 or 1-888/283-6423, ⓦ www.venetian.com. Even the standard rooms at this upscale Strip behemoth are split-level suites, with antique-style canopied beds atop raised platforms, plus spacious living rooms. Sun–Thurs ❼ , Fri & Sat ❽

The City

Though the Las Vegas sprawl measures fifteen miles wide by fifteen miles long, most tourists stick to the six-mile stretch of **Las Vegas Boulevard** that includes the downtown area, slightly southeast of the intersection of I-15 and US-95, and the Strip, home to the major casinos. In between lie two somewhat seedy miles of gas stations, fast-food drive-ins, and wedding chapels, while the rest of town is largely residential, and need barely concern you.

The Strip

For its razor-edge finesse in harnessing sheer, magnificent excess to the deadly serious business of making money, there's no place like the **Las Vegas Strip**.

It's hard to imagine that Las Vegas was once an ordinary city, and Las Vegas Boulevard a dusty thoroughfare scattered with the usual edge-of-town motels. After six decades of capitalism run riot, with every new casino–hotel setting out to surpass anything its neighbors ever dreamed of, the Strip seems to be locked into a hyperactive craving for thrills and glamour, forever discarding its latest toy in its frenzied pursuit of the next jackpot.

Each casino is a self-contained fantasyland of high camp and genuine excitement. Huge moving walkways sweep you in from the sidewalk, almost against your will; once inside, it can be almost impossible to find your way out. The action keeps going day and night, and in this sealed and windowless environment you rapidly lose track of which is which. Even if you do manage to get back onto the streets during the day, the scorching heat is liable to drive you straight back in again; night is the best time to venture out, when the neon's blazing at its brightest.

Mandalay Bay

As the Strip pushes deeper into the desert, the newest casinos tend to rise at its southern end, not far west of the airport. The procession kicks off with the glowing gilded tower of **Mandalay Bay**, which boasts a vaguely Burmese theme. Financed through the profits from its neighbors, *Luxor* and *Excalibur*, and built in 1999, *Mandalay Bay* is more upmarket than either, and its excellent restaurants, as well as the *House of Blues* music venue, keep it lively at night. During the day, all it has to offer the casual sightseer is the **Shark Reef** aquarium, right at the back of the property (daily 10am–11pm; $15, under-12s $10), which you're meant to explore as a steamy, half-submerged temple complex, encountering crocodiles, jellyfish, and, of course, sharks. It's expensive considering how long it takes to see, and all the so-called "coral" on offer is actually a multicolored mix 'n' match plastic kit.

Luxor

A block north of *Mandalay Bay* stands the 36-story pyramid of **Luxor**. From the palm-fringed avenue of sphinxes guarding the entrance, to the reconstruction of Tutankhamun's tomb inside, the whole building plays endless variations upon the theme of Egyptian archeology, and it ranks as a real must-see. In Las Vegas's closest approximation to Disneyland, three separate simulator rides and 3D movies combine to relate a confusing saga of derring-do that's overpriced at $24. Meanwhile, the most powerful artificial light-beam ever created shines up from the pyramid's apex.

Excalibur

Luxor's architect, Veldon Simpson, had previously designed the less sophisticated **Excalibur**, immediately north. A mock-up of a medieval castle, complete with drawbridge, crenellated towers, and a basement stuffed with fairground-style sideshows for the kids, it's usually packed out with low-budget tour groups. Its brief reign as the world's largest hotel, from 1990 to 1993, ended when the five-thousand-room **MGM Grand** – another Simpson creation – opened across the street. Turnover in the casino is so phenomenal that when the crowds at the June 1997 Holyfield–Tyson debacle mistook the popping of champagne corks for gunfire and panicked, forcing the gaming tables to close for two hours, the loss was estimated in millions of dollars. Its main attraction, the **Lion Habitat**, is a walk-through wooded zoo near the front entrance, where real lions lounge around a ruined temple beneath a naturally lit dome. Admission is free (daily 11am–11pm), while for $20 you can have your photo taken with a cute little lion cub (11am–5pm; closed Tues).

New York–New York

Excalibur and the *MGM Grand* are not the only giants facing off across the intersection of Las Vegas Boulevard and Tropicana Avenue, said to be the busiest traffic junction in the US. The northwest corner, diagonally opposite the veteran *Tropicana*, is occupied by an exuberantly meticulous re-creation of the Big Apple, **New York–New York**. This miniature Manhattan – created, like the original, in response to space limitations – boasts a skyline featuring twelve separate skyscrapers and is fronted, naturally, by the Statue of Liberty. Unusually, the interior is every bit as carefully realized, with a lovely rendition of Central Park at dusk (not perhaps somewhere you'd choose to be in real life). In one respect, it even surpasses New York itself: for $10 you can swoop around the whole thing at 65mph on the hair-raising Manhattan Express **roller coaster**.

Aladdin

North of the *MGM Grand*, the $1.4-billion **Aladdin** opened in August 2000 as Las Vegas's first megacasino of the new millennium, but it really represented the last gasp of the 1990s construction boom. Beset by funding difficulties from the word go, the resort was tipped into bankruptcy by the terrorist attacks of September 2001. Nonetheless, it remains open, and ironically the factors that held it back financially mean that it's actually quite a nice place, as you can explore its gigantic **Desert Passage** shopping mall, go to concerts at its 7000-seat auditorium, and get to and from your hotel room without ever crossing the casino floor.

Paris

Next door to the *Aladdin*, **Paris** was the 1999 handiwork of the same designers as *New York–New York*. With a half-size Eiffel Tower straddling the Arc de Triomphe and the Opera, it all feels a little compressed, but once again the attention to detail is a joy. There's also a fine assortment of top-notch French restaurants. Elevators soar through the roof of the casino and up to the summit of the Eiffel Tower, for stunning views of the city, at their best after dark (daily 10am–midnight; $9).

Bellagio

The Eiffel Tower was cheekily positioned to enjoy a perfect prospect of **Bellagio**, opposite, *Mirage*-owner Steve Wynn's 1998 attempt to build the best hotel in world history. *Bellagio* is undeniably a breathtaking achievement, but Wynn set himself a pointless and self-defeating task (he sold his stake in the place after just two years). Traditionally, casino theming has always been playful – you're not supposed to think that being in *Luxor* is like being in ancient Egypt, just that it's fun to pretend. No longer, however, is it enough to create an illusion: *Bellagio* wants to be somehow more authentic than the original. The trouble is that *Bellagio* is not in Europe; it's in Las Vegas and stuffed full of slot machines (inlaid with jewel-like precision into marble counters, perhaps, but still slot machines). The main hotel block, a stately curve of blue and cream pastels, stands aloof from the Strip behind an eight-acre artificial lake in which hundreds of submerged fountains erupt every half-hour in Busby Berkeley water-ballets, choreographed with booming music and colored lights.

Otherwise, *Bellagio*'s proudest boasts are the **Via Bellagio**, a covered mall of impossibly glamorous designer boutiques, and its opulent **Conservatory**, where a network of flowerbeds beneath a Belle Epoque canopy of copper-framed glass is replanted every few weeks with ornate seasonal displays.

Caesars Palace

Across Flamingo Road from *Bellagio* – this is the intersection where rapper Tupac Shakur was gunned down in 1996 – the long-established **Caesars Palace** still encapsulates Las Vegas at its best. Here, the walkway delivers you past grand marble staircases that lead nowhere, and full-size replicas of Michelangelo's *David*, into a vast labyrinth of slots and green baize, peopled by strutting half-naked Roman centurions and Cleopatra-cropped waitresses. Above the stores and restaurants of the extraordinary **Forum**, the blue-domed ceiling dims and glows as it endlessly cycles from dawn to dusk and back again, while the animatronic statues that top its ornate fountains come to life at regular intervals. There's a fancier version on offer in the 3D Imax simulator ride at the far end, **Race for Atlantis** (Mon–Thurs & Sun 10am–11pm, Fri & Sat 10am–midnight; $10). What you pay is expensive for what you get – you're shaken to smithereens in front of a four-minute sci-fi B-feature – but few kids seem to leave disappointed.

Mirage

Nighttime crowds jostle for space on the sidewalk outside the glittering **Mirage**, beyond *Caesars*, to watch the somewhat half-hearted volcano that erupts every fifteen minutes, spewing water and fire into the lagoon below. Inside, a couple of Siegfried and Roy's white tigers lounge dopily in a glass-fronted enclosure, and you can also pay to see more of them in the **Secret Garden & Dolphin Habitat** in the garden (Mon, Tues, Thurs & Fri 11am–5pm, Sat & Sun 10am–5pm; dolphins Mon–Fri 11am–7pm, Sat & Sun 10am–7pm; $10, under-10s free, or $5 on Wed when only the dolphin area is open). Next door, a pirate galleon and a British frigate, crewed by actors, do noisy battle outside **Treasure Island** (every 90min after dark; free). Around the back, behind the Fashion Show Mall at 3401 Industrial Rd, you can admire (if not step on) the King's very own blue suede shoes at **Elvis-A-Rama** (Mon–Sat 10am–6pm, Sun 10am–5pm; $10). As well as displaying a stunning array of Elvis memorabilia, the museum puts on hourly impersonator shows, included in the admission price.

Venetian

Across the Strip, the facade of another newcomer, the 1999 **Venetian**, includes loving facsimiles of six major Venice buildings, as well as the Rialto Bridge and the Bridge of Sighs. The main emphasis in the casino itself is on the **Grand Canal Shoppes**, reached via a stairwell topped by vivid frescoes copied from yet more Venice originals. The ludicrous re-creation of the **Grand Canal** at the top, complete with gondolas and singing gondoliers ($12.50 a ride), is quintessential Las Vegas, and as such utterly irresistible – it's *upstairs*, for God's sake.

In fall 2001, the *Venetian* opened not just one but two distinct Guggenheim **art museums**, designed in an ultra-modern style by Dutch architect Rem Koolhaas. The large **Guggenheim Las Vegas**, a dramatic and versatile space that played host to temporary exhibitions, has already closed, and will doubtless be replaced by something even more exciting in the near future. The **Guggenheim Hermitage** is still there, providing much-needed funds for St Petersburg's legendary State Hermitage Museum in return for displaying its finest treasures on a six-monthly changing rotation (daily 9am–8.30pm; $15, under-13s $7). Exhibitions so far have tended to focus on Impressionism and Cubism, with Monet, Picasso, and Van Gogh well represented.

The *Venetian* also holds the first US outpost of **Madame Tussaud's** renowned waxwork museum, which calls itself the **Celebrity Encounter** (Mon–Thurs & Sun 11am–7pm, Fri & Sat 11am–10pm; $15, under-13s $10), so named because visitors can pose with, touch, caress, and mock the effigies of Siegfried and Roy, Liberace, Tom Jones, and Frank Sinatra, among others. The whole experience is ridiculously expensive, its token animatronic show-pieces not a patch on the free shows at *Caesars*.

Circus Circus and around

The family-oriented **Circus Circus**, another mile north, uses live circus acts to pull in the punters – a trapeze artist here, a fire-eater there – and also has an indoor theme park, the **Adventuredome** (Mon–Thurs 11am–6pm, Fri 11am–midnight, Sat & Sun 10am–midnight), where you can pay separately for each roller coaster or river-ride, or buy an all-day pass costing $19 for anyone over 4ft, $14 for those under. If you really want to cool off, you'd do better to head on to the flumes and chutes of Vegas's one purpose-built water park, **Wet 'n' Wild**, 2601 S Las Vegas Blvd (summer daily 10am–8pm; $27).

Half a mile east of *Circus Circus* at 3000 Paradise Rd, the **Las Vegas Hilton** is home to the **Star Trek Experience** (daily 11am–11pm; $25). In a museum-like atmosphere, glossy display panels recount a wordy *Star Trek* chronology that takes in World War III in 2053 and the birth of Spock in 2230, while diminutive Ferengi stroll among you. The whole thing culminates when you're sent on a mildly vomit-inducing motion-simulator ride through deep space to emerge in a shopping area that you could have reached without paying, where memorabilia prices boldly go to well over $2000 for a leather jacket.

Traditionally *Circus Circus* has marked the northern limit of the Strip, though the 1996 opening of the **Stratosphere**, half a mile toward downtown, tried to change that. At 1149ft, the *Stratosphere* is the tallest building west of the Mississippi, and the outdoor deck and indoor viewing chamber in the sphere near the summit offer amazing panoramas across the city ($5). Two utterly demented thrill rides can take you even closer to heaven; the world's highest roller coaster ($5) swirls around the outside of the sphere, while the ludicrous Big Shot ($8) shunts you to the very top of an additional 160-foot spire, from which you free-fall back down again.

Downtown and the Liberace Museum

As the Strip has gone from strength to strength, **downtown** Las Vegas, the city's original core, has by comparison been neglected. Long known as "Glitter Gulch," and consisting of a few compact blocks of lower-key casinos, its current revival centers on the roofing-over of five entire blocks of its principal thoroughfare, Fremont Street, between Main Street and Las Vegas Boulevard. In the **Fremont Street Experience**, this "Celestial Vault" is studded with over two million colored light bulbs, choreographed by computer in dazzling nightly displays (hourly 8pm–midnight; free).

Almost all Las Vegas's handful of museums are eminently missable, with one unarguable exception: the **Liberace Museum**, two miles east of the Strip at 1775 E Tropicana Ave (Mon–Sat 10am–5pm, Sun 1–5pm; ☎702/798-5595, ⓦwww.liberace.org; $7). Popularly remembered as a beaming buffoon who knocked out torpid toe-tappers, Liberace, who died in 1987, started out playing piano in the rough bars of Milwaukee during the 1940s. A decade later, he was being mobbed by screaming adolescents and ruthlessly hounded by the scandal-hungry press. All this is recalled by a yellowing collection of cuttings and family photos, along with an electric candelabra, bejeweled quail eggs with inlaid pianos, rhinestone-covered fur coats, glittering cars, and more. The music, even piped into the scented toilets, may not have improved with age, but the museum is a satisfying attempt to answer the seminal question, "How does a great performer top himself on stage?"

Eating

Little more than a decade ago, the **restaurant** scene in Las Vegas was governed by the notion that visitors were not prepared to pay for gourmet food, and the only quality restaurants were upscale Italian places well away from the Strip. Now, however, the situation has reversed, as the major casinos compete to attract culinary superstars from all over the country to open Vegas outlets. Many tourists now come to the city in order to eat at the best restaurants in the United States, without having to reserve a table months in advance or pay sky-high prices. The restaurants reviewed below form only a tiny proportion of the total. The choice on the Strip in particular is overwhelming, and you'll almost certainly find a good restaurant to suit your tastes and budget in your own hotel. For that reason, the places reviewed here tend toward the higher end of the spectrum; they're the exceptional ones that are worth making a special effort to reach.

Buffets

Almost every casino still features an all-you-care-to-eat **buffet**. At its best, the traditional buffet experience is like being granted unrestricted access to the food court in an upmarket mall: you'll get good fast food, but not great cooking. The best such buffets tend to be in casinos away from both the Strip and downtown that depend on locals as well as tourists. By contrast, those at the largest Strip casinos, like *Excalibur* and the *MGM Grand,* are often poor. A new development, however, has been for high-end casinos like *Bellagio* and *Paris* to raise buffet prices to a level that makes it possible to provide true gourmet feasts.

The Buffet *Bellagio*, 3600 Las Vegas Blvd S ☎702/791-7111. Far and away Las Vegas's best buffet. With other buffets, you may rave about what good value they are; with this one, you'll rave about what good food it is. Breakfast is $13; lunch is $16, and can include sushi, sashimi, and dim sum; and dinner, with choices like lobster claws, fresh oysters, and venison, is $25.

Carnival World Buffet *Rio*, 3700 W Flamingo Rd ☎702/252-7777. Excellent value, half a mile west of the Strip. The variety is immense, including Thai, Chinese, Mexican, and Japanese stations as well as the usual pasta and barbecue, and even a fish 'n' chip stand. $10 for breakfast, $12 for lunch, and $17 for dinner.

Garden Court Buffet *Main Street Station*, 200 N Main St ☎702/387-1896. Downtown's best-value buffet, ranging from fried chicken and corn at the "South to Southwest" station, to tortillas at "Ole," and pork chow mein and oyster tofu at "Pacific Rim." Breakfast is $5, lunch $7.50, while dinner is usually $11, but rises to $15 for Friday's seafood spread.

Le Village Buffet *Paris*, 3655 Las Vegas Blvd S ☎702/967-7000. Superb French cuisine, with great seafood, succulent roast chicken, and super-fresh vegetables. The setting is a little cramped, squeezed into a very Disney-esque French village, but the food is *magnifique*. Breakfast is $12, lunch $19, and dinner $22.

Todai Seafood Buffet Desert Passage mall, *Aladdin*, 3663 Las Vegas Blvd S ☎702/892-0021. Not to be confused with the *Aladdin*'s own (adequate but not exceptional) buffet, *Todai* specializes in magnificent all-you-care-to-eat Japanese spreads. It's seafood heaven, with unlimited sushi and sashimi plus hot entrees, noodles, and barbecued and teriyaki meats. Lunch Mon–Fri $15, Sat & Sun $17; dinner Sun–Thurs $26, Fri & Sat $28.

Restaurants

America *New York–New York*, 3790 Las Vegas Blvd S ☎702/740-6451. Cavernous 24-hour diner, with a vast 3D "map" of the United States curling from the ceiling, and a staggeringly eclectic menu. At any hour of the day or night, there really is something for everyone, and it's all surprisingly good.

Binion's Horseshoe Coffee Shop *Binion's Horseshoe*, 128 E Fremont St ☎702/382-1600. The 24-hour Las Vegas coffee shop of your dreams, in the basement of a veteran downtown casino. Between 10pm and 5am, a steak dinner costs just $5. Breakfast is better value than most buffets: the $4.99 "Benny Binion's Natural," served 2am–2pm, consists of two eggs, bacon, sausage, or ham, toast, tea or coffee, and magnificent home fries.

Commander's Palace *Aladdin*, 3667 Las Vegas Blvd S ☎702/892-8272. The first-ever outpost of New Orleans' finest (and most expensive restaurant) abuts the Strip at the front of the Desert Passage mall. The decor is formal but redolent of Louisiana atmosphere, and the food is sumptuous. Open daily for lunch and dinner.

Il Fornaio *New York–New York*, 3790 Las Vegas Blvd S ☎702/650-6500. The nicest place to enjoy the atmosphere of the casino, this rural-Italian restaurant is a real joy. Choose from pizzas for around $12, or full meals like mixed antipasto ($9.50), followed by seafood linguini ($19) or rotisserie chicken ($16). The delicious olive breads, pastries, and espresso coffees are also sold in a separate deli nearby.

Mon Ami Gabi *Paris*, 3655 Las Vegas Blvd S ☎702/944-4224. The only major casino restaurant to offer open-air seating on the Strip, with the feel of a proper French sidewalk bistro. At lunch, try the gloriously authentic onion soup ($6.50), mussels ($11) as an appetizer or entrée ($20), or thin-cut *steak frites* ($19–21). Dinner features more expensive steak cuts and fish entrees.

Mr Lucky's 24/7 *Hard Rock Hotel*, 4455 Paradise Rd ☎702/693-5000. Stylish 24-hour coffee shop, with an open kitchen, faux-fur-clad booths, and a subdued tan-and-cream paint job, where the food is well above average.

Olives *Bellagio*, 3600 Las Vegas Blvd S ☎702/693-8181. *Bellagio*'s finest restaurant may be the kind of place that calls a $10 pizza an "individual oven-baked flatbread," and your food is more likely to be arranged vertically than horizontally, but the largely Mediterranean menu is uniformly fresh and superb. Great for lunch, at under $20; dinner is pricier.

Zefferino Grand Canal Shoppes, *The Venetian*, 3355 Las Vegas Blvd S ☎702/414-3500. Very romantic, and yet utterly playful Italian restaurant, with its ornate balconies overlooking the Grand Canal. Dinner entrees can be pricey, with basic ravioli at $25 and fish soup at $45, but the $20 three-course set lunch, served daily except Sun, is exceptional value.

Bars and clubs

Alcohol is very easy to come by in Las Vegas. All the casinos have plenty of bars, but if you want a drink, there's no need to look for one; instead, a tray-toting waitress will come and find you. The old-fashioned **Las Vegas lounge** has returned in force, both knowingly retro-styled for twenty-something rockers and lovingly re-created for older visitors looking to recapture the quieter flavor of the Rat Pack era. In addition, Las Vegas has finally come of age as an international **clubbing** capital. No longer are clubbers considered a breed apart from tourists; instead, the success of nightclubs at hipper casinos like the *Hard Rock* and *Mandalay Bay* has prompted all their major rivals to follow suit, often with spectacular results. If you fancy sampling a few, **Club-A-Go-Go** run escorted tours of three top-name Las Vegas clubs, including party bus and instant VIP admission (Wed, Thurs & Fri; $40; ☎1-800/258-2218 or ⓦwww .clubagogo.com).

Gipsy 4605 Paradise Rd ☎702/731-1919. High-profile gay dance club, whose success has spurred the emergence of the surrounding gay business district. There's normally some form of live entertainment, and there are beer busts most nights too. Daily except Mon.

House of Blues *Mandalay Bay*, 3950 Las Vegas Blvd S ☎702/632-7600. The Strip's premier live music venue, the voodoo-tinged, folk-art-decorated *House of Blues* has a definite but not exclusive emphasis on blues, R&B, and black music in general. Prices range up to $75 for big-name stars.

Ra *Luxor*, 3900 Las Vegas Blvd S ☎702/262-4400. Despite the splendidly camp Egyptian motifs, *Ra* feels like a real city nightclub, booking big-name DJs to cater to a ferociously hip and very glamorous crowd. Cage dancers watch over a changing schedule of special nights. Closed Mon & Tues.

Rain In The Desert *The Palms*, 4321 W Flamingo Rd ☎702/940-7246. Vast, no-expense-spared 1200-capacity club in the city's newest casino, kitted out with all manner of special effects – not just waterfalls and its own river, but also roving fog – and fire-dispensing "trusses." Thurs–Sat only.

THE SOUTHWEST | NEVADA | Las Vegas

rumjungle *Mandalay Bay*, 3950 Las Vegas Blvd S ☎702/632-7408. You have to run a gauntlet of go-go dancers and volcanic gas jets just to get into this bar-restaurant-nightclub. Inside, the leopard-skin-clad staff serve well-priced cocktails, plus a vast menu of rums, and it's too loud to do anything more than watch, or join, the dance floor action.

Venus Lounge *The Venetian*, 3265 Las Vegas Blvd S ☎702/414-4870. Gloriously kitsch retro-lounge, right by the Strip. The main room offers plush couches, live music at weekends, and go-go dancers in giant Martini glasses; the adjoining *Taboo Cove* is a lovingly re-created, dimly lit tiki bar. Closed Mon & Tues.

Entertainment

There was a time when Las Vegas represented the pinnacle of any showbusiness career. In the early 1960s, when Frank Sinatra's Rat Pack were shooting hit movies like the original *Ocean's 11* during the day then singing the night away at the *Sands*, the city could claim to be the capital of the international entertainment industry. It was even hip. Now, however, although the money is still there, the world has moved on. As the great names of the past fade from view, few of the individual performers popular with traditional Vegas visitors are considered capable of carrying an extended-run show. The tendency instead is to rely on lavish stunts and special effects, or to bring in big-name rock and pop stars for short seasons. A fair number of old-style Vegas revues are still soldiering on, but there are more stimulating contemporary productions than you might imagine.

Blue Man Group *Luxor*, 3900 Las Vegas Blvd S ☎702/262-4400. Enter a strange and unfamiliar world, in which three bald blue performance artists sell out a 1250-seat theater inside a giant pyramid every night of the week. Don't expect stars, or a plot, or even words; instead you get synchronized eating of breakfast cereal, plus deafening, exhilarating drumming from the Men themselves, and some stunning special effects. Sun, Mon, Wed–Fri 7pm & 10pm, Tues 7pm, Sat 4pm, 7pm & 10pm. $79–90.

Celine Dion in A New Day *Caesars Palace*, 3570 Las Vegas Blvd S ☎702/731-7865. Celine serves up Las Vegas entertainment on an epic scale in *Caesars*' vast new purpose-built Colosseum. Unless you're a big fan, however – in which case you'll love the amazing sound – what's been dubbed the "Cirque de Celine" may well leave you cold. Celine herself is dwarfed on the gigantic stage, while the Cirque du Soleil trimmings seem at odds with the lightweight songs. Wed–Sun 8.30pm, $87.50–200.

Lance Burton *Monte Carlo*, 3770 Las Vegas Blvd S ☎702/730-7160. The best family show in Las Vegas, featuring master magician Lance Burton. Most of it consists of traditional but very impressive stunts with playing cards, handkerchiefs, and doves, but large-scale illusions include the disap-

pearance of an entire airplane and a narrow escape from hanging. Tues–Sat 7pm & 10pm. $55 and $60.

Legends in Concert *Imperial Palace*, 3535 Las Vegas Blvd S ☎702/794-3261. Enjoyable celebrity-tribute show, with a changing roster of stars that ranges from the Righteous Brothers to Shania Twain. Daily except Sun 7.30pm & 10.30pm. $40, including 2 drinks, ages 12 and under $25.

Mystère *Treasure Island*, 3300 Las Vegas Blvd S ☎702/796-9999. Fabulous Cirque du Soleil showcase, with tumblers, acrobats, trapeze artists, pole climbers, clowns, and strongmen, but no animals apart from fantastic costumed apparitions. Wed–Sun 7.30pm & 10.30pm. $88, ages 12 and under $35.

O *Bellagio*, 3600 Las Vegas Blvd S ☎702/693-7722. Las Vegas's most expensive show is a remarkable testament to how much is possible when the budget is barely an issue. Any part of the stage at any time may be submerged to any depth. One moment a performer can walk across a particular spot, the next someone may dive head-first into it from the high wire. From the synchronized swimmers onward, the Cirque du Soleil display their magnificent skills to maximum advantage. Mon, Tues, Fri–Sun 7.30pm & 10.30pm. $93.50 and $121.

Lake Mead and the Hoover Dam

Almost as many people visit Las Vegas as they do **Lake Mead**, the vast reservoir thirty miles southeast of the city that was created by the construction of the Hoover Dam. As with the similarly incongruous Lake Powell (see p.1059), it makes a bizarre spectacle, the blue waters a vivid counterpoint to the surrounding desert, but it gets excruciatingly crowded all year round.

Though the Lake Mead National Recreation Area straddles the border between Nevada and Arizona, the best views come from the Nevada side. Even if you don't need details on how to sail, scuba-dive, water-ski, or fish from the marinas along the five-hundred-mile shoreline, call in at the Alan Bible **visitor center** (daily 8.30am–4.30pm; ☎702/293-8990, ⓦ www.nps.gov/lame), four miles northeast of Boulder City on US-93, to enjoy a sweeping prospect of the whole thing.

Eight miles on, beyond the rocky ridges of the Black Mountains, US-93 reaches the **Hoover Dam** itself. Designed to block the Colorado River and provide low-cost electricity for the cities of the Southwest, it's among the tallest dams ever built (760ft high), and used enough concrete to build a two-lane highway from the West Coast to New York. It was completed in 1935, as the first step of the Bureau of Reclamation program that culminated with the Glen Canyon Dam (see p.1060). Because of the events of September 11, 2001, the dam no longer offers extensive behind-the-scenes tours, but you can still ride an elevator to the turbine room at the bottom. Regular half-hour guided tours leave from the **Hoover Dam Visitor Center** on the Nevada side of the river (daily 8.30am–5.45pm; $10, plus $5 parking; ☎702/293-1824).

Crossing Nevada

The bulk of Nevada – the largest but least populated state in the Southwest – is made up of dry, flat plains sliced by knife-edge volcanic mountain ranges. Called the **Great Basin** because its rivers and streams have no outlet to the ocean, the land has a certain eerie, even hypnotic, beauty. Its attractions are hard to pinpoint, but there's an indefinable, very American sense of the endless frontier, of wide-open space.

The main route across Nevada, **I-80**, shoots from Salt Lake City to Reno, skirting dozens of bizarrely named small towns – Winnemucca, Elko, Battle Mountain – packed with casinos, bars, brothels, motels, and little else. The other main route, **US-50**, has a reputation as the loneliest highway in America, with the least traffic and roadside life. Older and slower than I-80, it follows much the same route as did the riders of the Pony Express in the 1860s, though many of the towns along it have faded away, and some have been entirely abandoned. US-50 passes by Nevada's sole national park, **Great Basin National Park** in the eastern mountains, before it links up with I-80 at Reno and then cuts off to the southwest to circle magnificent **Lake Tahoe**. One last main route, **US-95**, links Reno and Las Vegas, passing near Death Valley (see p.1144), as well as Nevada's most famous and most evocative ghost town, **Goldfield**.

Great Basin National Park

Just across the border from Utah, **Great Basin National Park** was created in 1986 by the amalgamation of the Lehman Caves National Monument and the Wheeler Peak Scenic Area. It's a distillation of the range of scenery the Nevada desert offers, from angular peaks to high mountain meadows cut by fast-flowing streams. The **Lehman Caves** are some of the most extensive and fascinating limestone caves in the country, not as big as Carlsbad Caverns, but if anything more densely packed with intriguing formations. Guided tours leave regularly throughout the day, costing $2 for 30min, $6 for 1hr, or $8 for

90min, from the **visitor center** near the mouth of the caves (daily: summer 8am–5pm; winter 8am–4.30pm; ☎775/234-7331, ⓦwww.nps.gov/grba), five miles west of the hamlet of **Baker**.

From the Lehman Caves, a twelve-mile road climbs the east flank of the bald and usually snowcapped **Wheeler Peak**, and trails lead past alpine lakes and through a grove of gnarled, ancient bristlecone pines to the 13,063ft summit. Few people ever come here, but in winter the mountains and meadows make for excellent off-track cross-country skiing. The nearest real town, **ELY**, an hour's drive away, has two worthwhile museums – the entertaining **Nevada Northern Railway Museum** (daily except Mon 11am–1pm; $3; ⓦnevadanorthernrailway.net), which offers $18 rides on a restored steam train, and the **County Museum** (daily 9am–4pm; free) – as well as a dozen **motels** (try *Motel 6*, 770 Avenue O; ☎775/289-6671; ❷) and a handful of casinos and restaurants.

Elko

One of the few Nevada towns worth aiming for, if you're here at the right time of year, is **ELKO**, a straggling highway town a hundred miles from the Utah border. The self-proclaimed last real cowtown in the West is the center of one of the largest open-range cattle-ranching regions in the US, and the fitting home of the annual **Cowboy Poetry Gathering**, held here every January. People get together in a sort of celebration of folk culture, telling stories around campfires, singing about the lonesome life on the range, and keeping alive the dying traditions and tales of the Wild West.

During the 72-hour party of the **National Basque Festival**, each Fourth of July weekend, hulking men throw huge logs at each other amid a whole lot of carousing and downing of platefuls of Basque food. The food is available year-round in restaurants like the *Star Hotel*, two blocks south of the main drag at 246 Silver St (☎775/738-9925). Greyhound and Amtrak both stop in Elko, and there are dozens of budget motels, such as the *Centre Motel*, 475 Third St (☎775/738-7226; ❷). Elko's **visitor center** is at 700 Moren Way (Mon–Fri 9am–5pm; ☎775/738-4091 or 1-800/248-ELKO, ⓦwww.elkocva.com).

Reno and around

If you don't make it to Las Vegas, you can get a feel for the nonstop, neon-lit gambler's lifestyle by stopping in **RENO**, on I-80, very near the California border. "The biggest little city in the world," as it likes to call itself, is a somewhat downmarket version of the glitz and glamour of Vegas, with miles of gleaming slot machines and poker tables, along with tacky wedding chapels and quickie divorce courts. While the town itself may not be much to look at, its setting – at the foot of the snowcapped **Sierra Nevada**, with the Truckee River winding through the center – is superb.

There are three things to do in Reno: gamble, get married, and get divorced. The **casinos** are concentrated in the downtown area, along Virginia Street on either side of the railroad tracks. To get **married**, the requirements are the same as in Las Vegas (see p.1071), though here you obtain your **marriage license** at the **Washoe County Court**, Virginia and Court streets (daily 8am–midnight; $50; ☎775/328-3260). Wedding chapels all around the city will help you tie the knot, including Heart of Reno Wedding Chapel, 243 S Sierra St (☎775/786-6882).

Practicalities

Reno's **Cannon International Airport** is a couple of miles southeast of downtown, a twenty-minute ride on local bus #24. Greyhound **buses** use the terminal at 155 Stevenson St; daily Amtrak **trains** call at 135 E Commercial Row downtown, six hours out of San Francisco en route for Salt Lake City.

The downtown **visitor center**, in the National Bowling Stadium at 300 N Center St (daily 8am–6pm; ☎1-888/HIT-RENO, ⓦwww.renolaketahoe .com), should be able to help you find an inexpensive **place to stay**, though rates tend to double at weekends. All the big casinos offer accommodation – the pick of them are the *Atlantis*, 3800 S Virginia St (☎775/825-4700 or 1-800/723-6500, ⓦwww.atlantiscasino.com; ❸); *Silver Legacy*, 407 N Virginia St (☎775/325-7401 or 1-800/687-7733, ⓦwww.silverlegacyreno.com; ❸); and *Circus Circus*, 500 N Sierra St (☎775/329-0711 or 1-888/682-0147, ⓦwww .circusreno.com; ❸). Reno's best **buffet** is at the *Eldorado*, 345 N Virginia St (☎775/786-5700 or 1-800/648-5966, ⓦwww.eldoradoreno.com; ❸).

Carson City

US-395 heads south from Reno along the jagged spires of the **High Sierra**, past **Mono Lake**, **Mount Whitney**, and **Death Valley**. Just thirty miles south of Reno, **CARSON CITY**, state capital of Nevada, is small by comparison but has a number of elegant buildings, some excellent historical museums, and a handful of world-weary casinos.

Carson City was named after frontier explorer Kit Carson in 1858, and is still redolent with Wild West history. A good introduction to the region is the **Nevada State Museum** at 600 N Carson St (daily 8.30am–4.30pm; $4). Housed in the former Carson Mint, it covers the geology and natural history of the Great Basin desert, from prehistoric times up through the heyday of the 1860s, when the silver mines of the nearby Comstock Lode were at their peak. Amid the many guns and artifacts is the reconstructed **Ghost Town**, from which a tunnel allows entry down into a full-scale model of an **underground mine**.

Greyhound **buses** between Reno and Los Angeles stop once a day in each direction, at 111 E Telegraph Ave. Among budget **motels** are the *Super 8* at 2829 S Carson St (☎775/883-7800; ❷), and the *Park Inn Hardman House* at 917 N Carson St (☎775/882-7744; ❹). The **visitor center**, on the south side of town at 1900 S Carson St (Mon–Fri 8am–5pm, Sat & Sun 10am–3pm; ☎775/687-7410, ⓦwww.carson-city.org), can help with practical details and provide maps for self-guided architectural walking and driving **tours** of the town, taking in the State Capitol, the museums, and many of the fine 1870s Victorian wooden houses and churches on the west side.

Virginia City

Much of the wealth on which Carson City – and indeed San Francisco – was built came from the silver mines of the **Comstock Lode**, a solid seam of pure silver discovered underneath Mount Hamilton, fourteen miles east of Carson City off US-50, in 1859. Raucous **VIRGINIA CITY** grew up on the steep slopes above the mines, and a young writer named Samuel Clemens made his way here from the east with his older brother, the acting Secretary to the Governor of the Nevada Territory, to see what all the fuss was about. His descriptions of the wild life of the mining camp, and of the desperately hard work that men put in to get at the valuable ore, were published years later under his pseudonym, **Mark Twain**. Though Twain also spent some time in the Gold Rush towns of California's Mother Lode, on the other side of the Sierra – which by then were all but abandoned – his tales of Virginia City life, collected in *Roughing It*, form a hilarious eyewitness account of the hard-drinking life of the frontier miners. There's not much to Virginia City nowadays, since all the old storefronts have been taken over by hot-dog vendors and tacky souvenir stands, but the surrounding landscape of arid mountains still feels remote and undisturbed.

California

AL - ALABAMA	IN - INDIANA	MN - MINNESOTA	RI - RHODE ISLAND
AR - ARKANSAS	LA - LOUISIANA	MS - MISSISSIPPI	SC - SOUTH CAROLINA
CT - CONNECTICUT	MA - MASSACHUSETTS	NC - NORTH CAROLINA	VA - VIRGINIA
DE - DELAWARE	MD - MARYLAND	NH - NEW HAMPSHIRE	VT - VERMONT
FL - FLORIDA	ME - MAINE	NJ - NEW JERSEY	WI - WISCONSIN
IL - ILLINOIS	MI - MICHIGAN	PA - PENNSYLVANIA	WV - WEST VIRGINIA

CHAPTER 13

Highlights

* **San Diego Zoo** About as humane and "natural" as a zoo can get, with a vast collection of rare species. **See p.1096**

* **Getty Center** A striking modernist monument to a high culture–hoarding oil magnate. **See p.1123**

* **Mono Lake** A strange and remote sight that's well worth the trip – prime bird-watching territory amid blue waters and gnarled tufa columns. **See p.1149**

* **Joshua Tree National Park** The eerily twisted "arms" of Joshua trees beckon visitors to explore this long-abandoned mining country. **See p.1142**

* **Highway 1** A thrilling, circuitous drive along the US's West Coast, with pounding Pacific surf and dramatic cliffside vistas. **See p.1155**

* **Yosemite National Park** Giant sequoias, towering waterfalls, the sheer face of Half Dome – your eyes will hardly get a rest. **See p.1169**

* **Alcatraz** Eerie, legendary one-time maximum-security prison stuck out on "the Rock" in San Francisco Bay. **See p.1185**

California

Publicized and idealized all over the world, **CALIFORNIA** has quite the formidable reputation – a terrestrial paradise of sun, sand, and surf, with high mountain ranges, fast-paced glitzy cities, primeval old-growth forests, and vast stretches of deserts. Imbued with history, the landscape ranges from rock carvings left by indigenous peoples to the eerie ghost towns of the Gold Rush pioneers.

All this, however, lies under the constant threat of the Big One – a massive **earthquake** of unimaginable destruction – along with the floods, fires, and other assorted disasters that gave the state a fearsome reputation in the 1990s. Its politics have also undergone a seismic shift. Although formerly the power base for such right-wing stalwarts as Ronald Reagan and Richard Nixon, it has also been the source of some of the country's most progressive **political movements**. The fierce protests of the Sixties may have died down, but California remains the heart of liberal America, at the forefront of environmental awareness, gay pride, and social experimentation, and a firm bulwark of the Democratic Party – despite the removal of its much-despised governor in a 2003 recall election. **Economically**, too, the region is crucial, whether in the film industry, the music business, the financial markets, or the all-consuming sector of real estate.

California is too large to be fully explored in a single trip, but in an area so varied it's hard to pick out specific highlights, and much will depend on the kind of vacation you're looking for. **Los Angeles** is far and away the biggest and most stimulating city: a maddening collection of freeways, beaches, suburbs, elite enclaves, and extreme lifestyles. To the south, the growing metropolis of **San Diego** has broad, welcoming beaches and easy access to Mexico, while further inland, the **desert areas**, most notably **Death Valley**, comprise a barren and inhospitable landscape of volcanic craters and salt pans that in summer becomes the hottest place on Earth.

Most people, though, follow the shoreline north up the **central coast**: a gorgeous run that takes in lively small towns such as **Santa Barbara** and **Santa Cruz**. California's second city, **San Francisco**, is about as different from LA as it's possible to get: the most European-styled major city in the West, set on a series of steep hills, its wooden houses tumbling down to water on three sides. It is also well placed for the national parks to the east, such as **Yosemite**, where waterfalls cascade into a sheer glacial valley, and **Sequoia/Kings Canyon** with its gigantic trees, as well as the ghost towns of the **Gold Country**. North of San Francisco the countryside becomes wilder, wetter, and greener, approaching Oregon through spectacular and almost deserted volcanic tablelands and the increasing slope of the verdant Klamath Mountains.

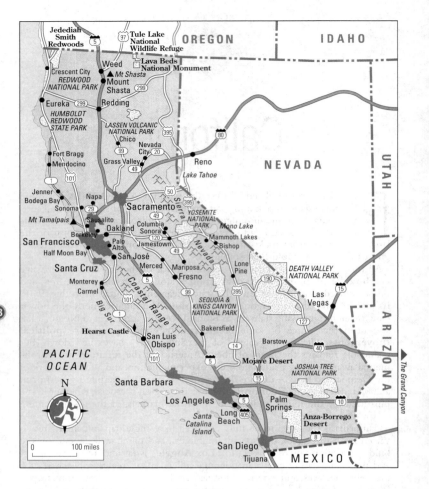

The Grand Canyon ▶

The **climate** in **southern California** features seemingly endless days of sunshine and warm, dry nights, with occasional bouts of torrential flooding in the winter. LA's notorious smog is at its worst when the temperatures are highest, from July through September. All along the **coast** mornings can be hazily overcast, especially in May and June; in the Bay Area around San Francisco it can be chilly all year, and fog rolls in to spoil many a sunny day. Much more so than in the south, winter in **northern California** can bring rain for weeks on end, causing massive mudslides that wipe out roads and hillside homes. Most hiking trails in the **mountains** are blocked between October and June by the snow that keeps California's ski slopes among the busiest in the nation.

Some history

Around half a million people – almost half the population of what has become the US – were living in tribal villages along the West Coast when the Spaniard

Juan Cabrillo first sighted San Diego harbor in 1542, and named **California** after an imaginary island (inhabited by Amazons) from a Spanish novel. **Sir Francis Drake** landed near Point Reyes, north of San Francisco, in 1579, where the "white bancks and cliffes" reminded him of Dover. In 1602 **Sebastián Vizcáino** bestowed most of the place-names that still survive; his exaggerated description of **Monterey** as a perfect harbor led later colonizers to make it the region's military and administrative center. The Spanish occupation began in earnest in 1769, combining military expediency with missionary zeal. Father **Junípero Serra** first established a small mission and *presidio* (fort) at San Diego, before arriving in June 1770 at Monterey. By 1804 a chain of 21 missions, each a long day's walk from the next along the dirt path of *El Camino Real* (The Royal Road), ran from San Diego to San Francisco. Native Americans were either forcibly converted into Catholicism or killed; though not all gave up without a fight, disease ensured that they were soon wiped out.

When Mexico gained its independence in 1821, in theory it also acquired control of California. However, **Americans** were already starting to arrive, despite the immense difficulty of getting to California – three months by sea (either around Cape Horn or by portage across the isthmus of Panama), or four months overland in a covered wagon. Though the non-native population was a mere ten thousand in 1846, the growing belief that it was the **Manifest Destiny** of the United States to cover the continent from coast to coast, evident in the imperialist policies of President James K. Polk, soon led to the **Mexican–American War**. Virtually all the fighting took place in Texas; Monterey was captured by the US Navy without a shot fired, and by January 1847 the Americans controlled the entire West Coast.

By chance, a mere nine days before the signing of the treaty that ended the war, flakes of **gold** were discovered in the Sierra Nevada. Prospectors flooded in from all parts of the world in the most madcap migration in history, ultimately leading to California's 1850 entry into the US as the **31st state**. It took just fifteen years to pick the land clean of visible gold, but a few industrialists – the likes of Charles Crocker, Leland Stanford, and Collis Huntington – achieved jaw-dropping fortunes. Through the advocacy of these magnates (who largely built their fortunes from selling goods and services for mining – not from mining itself), along with federal subsidies, the **transcontinental railroad** was completed in 1869. Built using mostly Chinese laborers, the railway was an engineering feat and a major social and cultural turning point. The crossing from New York now took just five days, and a railroad rate war brought fares down to as little as $1 for a one-way ticket, which attracted hordes of newcomers from the Great Plains to Southern California and helped make Los Angeles the state's biggest city.

Thanks to this migration, along with periodic real-estate booms and the rise of the **film industry**, California became the nation's fastest-growing state. During the **Great Depression** of the Thirties, for example, entire families of "**Okies**" from the Dust Bowl packed up everything they owned and set off for the farms of the Central Valley, though they often found bleak terrain and a hostile attitude to newcomers. Heavy industry followed during **World War II**, in the form of shipyards and airplane factories, and many workers – both white and African-American – and military personnel stayed on afterwards.

As home to the **Beats** in the Fifties and the **hippies** in the Sixties, California was at the cutting edge of cultural change. However, the illusions of the Flower Power days were shattered by the violence of the 1969 rock concert at Northern California's Altamont Speedway, and when the Vietnam-era protests ended with the abolition of the draft, much of the state's creative ferment did, too – most evident in the segue from the rebellious psychedelic scene of the 1960s to the indulgent, cocaine-fueled "Me Generation" of the 1970s. The economic counterpart of this shift also developed when **Proposition 13**, in 1978, augured a national trend to dramatically cut taxes at the cost of government solvency. The 1980s saw further right-wing gains, with a string of laissez-faire Republican governors, the associated decline of public-sector financing for health-care and education, and a prison-building boom and "tough on crime" attitude that saw police chiefs like LA's Daryl Gates using military tanks and SWAT teams with little or no public over-sight. These policies had a predictable outcome in the Nineties, which crash-landed in a tangled mess of economic scandal, a depressed real-estate market, rising unemployment, gang violence, race riots in LA, and a head-spinning cycle of high-tech boom-and-bust in San Francisco – compounded by **earthquakes**, **drought**, and **flooding**.

At first, the turn of a new century brought some relief from the previous decades' calamities, but this was quickly subverted with a **power crisis** in 2001 and an ongoing meltdown in state finances. For this, Governor **Gray Davis** was recalled by voters, and replaced (after a carnivalesque recall election) with action-movie star **Arnold Schwarzenegger**. In most states this action would be both unlikely and absurd, but in the Golden State it seems like just another twist in its strange and curious history.

Recently, more-conservative Californians have been fleeing for more hos-pitable climes in Colorado and Arizona, though the state continues to attract countless **new migrants** from the rest of the US and the world. With much of the influx coming from Latin America, Spanish is now the lingua franca in many communities, and **Hispanics** increasingly provide much of the eco-nomic growth and cultural vitality of this dynamic, ever-changing place.

Getting around California

If you want to explore California to the fullest, you'll doubtless need a **car**. A city such as Los Angeles couldn't exist without the automobile, and in any case to drive down the coastal freeways invites irresistible mental images of muscle-car cruising. Car **rental** in California is among the cheapest in the country, and the savings made by easy access to campgrounds and chain motels can easily offset the initial cost.

Amtrak **trains** connect **San Diego** and **LA**, with a stop at Fullerton for buses to Disneyland. One daily service runs up the coast from LA, stopping at **Oakland** and **Emeryville**, the nearest stations to San Francisco; this contin-ues on via Sacramento to Seattle. Another line from Oakland runs along the Central Valley, but only connects with LA by bus. Greyhound **buses** also link all the main cities.

For quick hops between the major cities – especially LA and San Francisco – you can't beat **flying**, though airline-industry woes have eliminated routes, forced cutbacks in many services, and hiked costs. Even so, you can still find competitive rates if your plans are flexible enough to take advantage of off-peak deals. Regular scheduled fares, not surprisingly, are high.

If you plan to do any **long-distance cycling**, traveling from north to south can make all the difference – the wind blows this way in the summer, and the ocean side of the road offers the best views. Be careful if you cycle along the coast on Hwy-1: despite the stunning views, the highway has heavy traffic, tight curves, and is prone to fog.

San Diego

Relatively free from smog and byzantine freeway systems, **SAN DIEGO**, set around a gracefully curving bay, represents the more conservative side of southern California. The second most-populous city in California may be affluent and libertarian, but it's also easygoing and far from smug. Although it was the site of the first mission in California, the city only really took off with the arrival of the Santa Fe Railroad in the 1880s, and in terms of trade and significance it has long been in the shadow of Los Angeles. However, during World War II the US Navy made San Diego its Pacific Command Center, and the military continues to dominate the local economy, alongside tourism.

Arrival, information, and getting around

Both **trains** and **buses** leave you in the heart of downtown San Diego: Greyhound at Broadway and First Avenue is more central than Amtrak's Santa Fe Depot, at the west end of Broadway. **Lindbergh Field Airport** is only two miles out, on bus #2 (daily 6am–midnight; $2.25).

The **International Visitors Information Center** is downtown at 11 Horton Plaza, F Street at First Avenue (daily 9am–5pm; ℡619/236-1212, Ⓦwww.sandiego.org). The general delivery **post office** is at 2535 Midway Drive, between downtown and Mission Beach (Mon 7am–5pm, Tues–Fri 8am–5pm, Sat 8am–4pm; ℡1-800/275-8777; zip code 92138), while the main downtown post office is at 815 E St (Mon–Fri 8.30am–5pm; ℡619/232-8612).

Getting around without a car, by day at least, is comparatively easy. Three major companies operate **buses** in the area (complete system information can be found at Ⓦwww.sdcommute.com), the main one being San Diego Transit Corporation, or SDTC (fares $1.75–2.50; ℡619/233-3004 or 1-800/266-6883, Ⓦwww.sandiegotransit.com); service is frequent and reliable, transfers are free, and the exact fare is required (dollar bills accepted). The other operators are North County Transit District ($1.50; ℡1-800/COMMUTE, Ⓦwww.gonctd.com) and County Transit System ($2; ℡619/874-4001, Ⓦwww.sdcounty.ca.gov/dpw/transit). The **Transit Store**, 102 Broadway (Mon–Sat 8.30am–5.30pm; ℡619/234-1060), has detailed timetables and sells a **Day Tripper Transit Pass** for one- to four-day visits ($5, $9, $12, and $15, respectively). The passes apply also to the tram-like **San Diego Trolley**, which runs throughout the area (tickets $1.25–3) and covers the sixteen miles from the Santa Fe Depot to the Mexican border-crossing at San Ysidro. It's a 45-minute journey ($4.50 roundtrip; every 15min from 5am to midnight), and the last trolley back leaves at 1am on Saturday night. **Bicycle** rental shops include Rent-a-Bike, 523 Island St (℡619/232-4700), and Hamel's Action Sport Center, 704 Ventura Place, Mission Beach (℡619/488-5050).

Accommodation

Accommodation is plentiful throughout San Diego, with budget travelers especially well served. The best-placed, though mall-like, **campground** is

Campland on the Bay, 2211 Pacific Beach Drive (☎1-800/4BAY-FUN, ⓦwww.campland.com), linked to downtown by bus #30, where a basic site starts at $40 (summer rate $53) and more elaborate "Super Sites" can run $90–173 (summer $160–277). For a more serene camping option, there's **San Elijo Beach State Park**, Rte-21 south of Cardiff-by-the-Sea (☎1-800/444-7275; $17–25).

Hotels, motels, and B&Bs

Bahia Resort 998 West Mission Bay Drive, Mission Bay ☎1-888/576-4229 or 858/488-0551, ⓦwww.bahiahotel.com. Prime beachside accommodation with expansive ocean views, watersport rentals, pool, and Jacuzzi. Rooms range from cozy but pleasant rooms in a palm-garden setting to pricier bayside suites. ❼

Balboa Park Inn 3402 Park Blvd, Hillcrest ☎619/298-0823, ⓦwww.balboaparkinn.com. Elegant, gay-oriented B&B, within walking distance of Balboa Park and museums. All are romantic one- and two-bedroom themed suites (with Parisian, Impressionist, and Tarzan motifs, to name a few) with coffeemakers and mini-fridges. ❺

Beach Haven Inn 4740 Mission Blvd, Pacific Beach ☎858/272-3812 or 1-800/831-6323, ⓦwww.beachhaveninn.com. Nice rooms around a pool and spa; continental breakfast included. With air-conditioning, kitchenettes, and cable TV, it's one of the better values at the beach. ❻

Crystal Pier Hotel and Cottages 4500 Ocean Blvd, Pacific Beach ☎858/483-6983 or 1-800/748-5894, ⓦwww.crystalpier.com. Beautiful, deluxe cottages situated right on Pacific Beach pier. All units are suites with private deck, and most have kitchenettes. ❽

Heritage Park B&B 2470 Heritage Park Row, Old Town ☎619/299-6832 or 1-800/995-2470, ⓦwww.heritageparkinn.com. Restored Queen Anne mansion chock-full of Victorian trappings. Breakfast and afternoon tea are included, and classic movies are shown nightly. ❻

Horton Grand 311 Island Ave at 3rd Ave, downtown ☎619/544-1886 or 1-800/542-1886, ⓦwww.hortongrand.com. Classy, modernized amalgam of two century-old hotels, with fireplaces in most of the 108 rooms and friendly staff clad in Victorian attire. ❻

Hotel del Coronado 1500 Orange Ave, Coronado ☎619/522-8000 or 1-800/468-3533, ⓦwww.hoteldel.com. The luxurious place that put Coronado on the map and is still the area's major tourist sight (see p.1094) – especially after a recent $55 million restoration. ❽

J Street Inn 222 J St, downtown ☎619/696-6922. Near the Gaslamp District, Greyhound station, and waterfront, this little-known bargain has units with microwaves, refrigerators, and cable TV. ❹

Ocean Beach Motel 5080 Newport Ave, Ocean Beach ☎619/223-7191. Not too pretty, but right across the street from the sand, with ocean views and kitchenettes available. ❸

Surf & Sand Motel 4666 Mission Blvd, Pacific Beach ☎858/483-7420. Clean, comfortable motel close to the beach; offers pool, cable TV, and mini-fridges or kitchenettes. ❻

US Grant Hotel 326 Broadway, downtown ☎619/232-3121 or 1-800/237-5029, ⓦwww.usgranthotel.com. Across from Horton Plaza, an elite favorite from 1910 onward, with Neoclassical styling, countless chandeliers, marble floors, and cozy but elegant rooms. ❼

Wyndham Emerald Plaza 400 Broadway, downtown ☎619/239-4500, ⓦwww.wyndham.com/EmeraldPlaza. Upscale, highrise lodging with spacious rooms oriented toward business travelers, with pool, spa, and exercise facilities. ❽

Hostels

Banana Bungalow 707 Reed Ave, Pacific Beach ☎858/273-3060 or 1-800/5-HOSTEL, ⓦwww.bananabungalow.com/sub/bbsd.html. Friendly place, with slightly scruffy rooms, but the proximity to the beach – along with the free breakfasts, keg nights, barbecues, bonfires, among other things – draws a party-all-night, sleep-all-day crowd. There is no better value in San Diego if you want to be right on the beach. Dorm beds for $20, private rooms $49. Take bus #34. ❶–❷

HI-San Diego Downtown 521 Market St at 5th Ave, downtown ☎619/525-1531 or 1-800/909-4776, ⓦsandiegohostels.org/downtown.htm. Handy for the Gaslamp District and Horton Plaza. HI members $18, others $25, and private doubles $44–55. Free coffee and bagels. No curfew. ❶–❷

HI-San Diego Pt Loma/Elliott 3790 Udall St, Ocean Beach ☎619/223-4778 or 1-800/909-4776, ⓦsandiegohostels.org/pointloma.htm. A couple of miles back from the beach and minus the relentless party atmosphere prevailing in other hostels, offering a large kitchen, patio, and common room with TV. Well-run and friendly, with dorms for $15–18 and private rooms for three people or more at $20–25 per person. Take bus #35 from downtown. ❶

USA Hostels – San Diego 726 5th Ave, downtown ☎619/232-3100 or 1-800/438-8622, ⓦwww.usahostels.com/sandiego/s-index.html. Well-placed hostel on the edge of the Gaslamp District. Converted from an 1890s hotel, with 6 to 8 beds per room, sheets, and continental breakfast, for $19. Doubles $46. Offers free bike use, organized tours to Tijuana, Sea World, and the Zoo, and a handy shuttle to LA. ❶–❷

The City

With its mix of laid-back libertarians and staunch conservatives, San Diego embodies a work-hard, play-hard ethic, although it leans more towards the second part of the equation. Featuring an easily navigable central area, scenic bay, 42 miles of beaches, and plentiful parks and museums, the city is hard not to like from the moment you arrive.

Downtown San Diego

The vibrant and active core of **downtown** San Diego is the best place to start exploring. Since the late 1970s, several blocks of 1920s architecture have been stylishly renovated, with the sleek modern buildings symbolizing the city's growing economic importance on the Pacific Rim. Downtown is safe by day, but can be unwelcoming at night when the financial zone shuts down. After dark, you're better off heading to the restaurants and clubs of the comparatively well-lit and well-policed Gaslamp District.

The tall Moorish archways of the **Santa Fe Railroad Depot**, at the western end of Broadway, built in 1915 for the Panama-California Exposition, still evoke a sense of grandeur. Nearby, the postmodern contours of the **American Plaza**, an array of highrise offices and glass-roofed public areas, contain the main terminal of the San Diego Trolley and the **Museum of Contemporary Art**, or MCA San Diego, 1001 Kettner Blvd (Thurs–Tues 11am–5pm; free; ☎619/234-1001, ⓦwww.mcasandiego.org), which stages compelling temporary shows and has a permanent collection focusing on American minimalism, Pop Art, and Latino art. American Plaza marks the western end of **Broadway**, which slices through the middle of downtown, at its most hectic between Fourth and Fifth avenues. Shoppers, sailors, yuppies, and slackers linger around the fountains outside **Horton Plaza** (Mon–Sat 10am–9pm, Sun 11am–7pm, hours vary by season), a giant mall of 137 stores and San Diego's de facto city center. Head for the open-air eating places on its top level; though the standard fast-food grub is pricey, it can be fun to linger over a coffee and watch the parade of tourists go by. Take time on your way out to look at the 21ft-tall **Jessop Clock** on level one, made for the California State Fair of 1907.

South of Broadway, a few blocks from Horton Plaza, lies the sixteen-block **Gaslamp District**, once the seedy heart of frontier San Diego but now filled with smart streets lined with classy cafés, antique stores, art galleries, and, of course, "gas lamps" – powered by electricity. A tad artificial it may be, but its late nineteenth-century buildings are intriguing to explore, especially on the two-hour **walking tour** (Sat 11am; $8; ☎619/233-4692) that begins from the small cobbled square at Fourth and Island avenues. Also worth a peek is the **Horton Grand**, 311 Island Ave, a reconstruction of two nineteenth-century hotels, with Old World decor and staff in Victorian costumes (see "Accommodation," opposite).

West of downtown, the Embarcadero pathway follows the curve of the bay and leads to the **Maritime Museum**, 1306 N Harbor Drive (daily 9am–8pm,

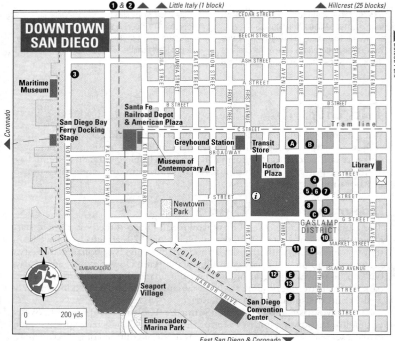

① & **②** ▲ ▲ Little Italy (1 block)   ▲ Hillcrest (25 blocks)

DOWNTOWN SAN DIEGO

Coronado ◄

▲ *Coronado*

Maritime Museum

③

San Diego Bay Ferry Docking Stage

Santa Fe Railroad Depot & American Plaza

Greyhound Station

Museum of Contemporary Art

Newtown Park

Transit Store

Horton Plaza

Library

Gaslamp District

Seaport Village

Embarcadero Marina Park

San Diego Convention Center

▼ *East San Diego & Coronado*

Balboa Park ▶

N

0   200 yds

ACCOMMODATION		RESTAURANTS, BARS, & CLUBS		Café Seville	11
HI-San Diego Downtown	D	Anthony's Star of the Sea	3	Candelas	13
Horton Grand	E	Bella Luna	9	The Casbah	2
J Street Inn	F	Blue Tattoo	4	Croce's Restaurant and Jazz Bar	7
US Grant	A	Buffalo Joe's	10	Filippi's Pizza Grotto	1
USA Hostels – San Diego	C	Café 222	12	Fio's Cucina Italiana	6
Wyndham Emerald Plaza	B	Café Lulu	5	Sammy's	8

summer closes 9pm; $7), where the most interesting of three vintage sailing craft is the *Star of India*, built in 1863 and now the world's oldest merchant ship still afloat.

Coronado

Across San Diego Bay from downtown, the isthmus of **Coronado** is a well-scrubbed resort community with a major naval station occupying its western end. It's reached by the majestically modern **Coronado Bay Bridge**, a curving 11,000-foot span that's one of the area's signature images ($1 toll for southbound travelers without passengers), its struts decorated with enormous murals depicting scenes of daily Hispanic life, best seen from the community park beneath the bridge in the district of Barrio Logan. The town of Coronado grew up around the **Hotel del Coronado** (see "Accommodation," p.1092), a Victorian whirl of turrets and towers erected as a health resort in 1888. The "Del" is where Edward VIII (then Prince of Wales) first met Coronado housewife Wallis Warfield Simpson here in 1920, and where *Some Like It Hot* was filmed in 1958, posing as a Miami Beach hotel. A guided, hour-long **historical** tour (Mon–Sat 11am & 1pm, Sun 3pm; $15) wends its way around the hotel, beginning in the lobby. The simplest and most scenic way to get to Coronado is on the **San Diego Bay ferry** ($2 each way; ☎619/234-4111), which leaves Broadway Pier daily on the hour between 9am and 9pm (Fri & Sat 10pm). Tickets are available at San Diego Harbor Excursion, 1050 N Harbor Drive (☎619/234-4111, ⓦww.sdhe.com).

Balboa Park

Sumptuous **Balboa Park** contains one of the largest groups of **museums** in the US, as well as charming landscaping, traffic-free promenades, and Spanish Colonial–style buildings. Within easy reach of downtown by **buses** #7, #16, and #25, the park is large but fairly easy to get around **on foot** – if you get tired, there's always the free tram. The $30 **Balboa Park Passport**, which allows one-time admission to all thirteen of the park's museums and its Japanese garden (plus the San Diego Zoo, for an extra $25), is available from the **visitor information center** (daily 9am–4pm; ☎619/239-0512, ⓦwww.balboapark.org), inside the on-site House of Hospitality. Most of the museums are closed on Mondays, and free on varying Tuesdays.

Most of the major museums flank El Prado, the pedestrian-oriented road that bisects the park. Minor works by Rembrandt and El Greco and a stirring collection of Russian icons make the stifling formality of the **Timkin Museum of Art** (Tues–Sat 10am–4.30pm, Sun 1.30–4.30pm; closed Sept; free; ☎619/239-5548, ⓦgort.ucsd.edu/sj/timken) worth enduring. The **San Diego Museum of Art** (Tues–Sun 10am–6pm, Thurs closes 9pm; $8, children $3; ☎619/232-7931, ⓦwww.sdmart.org) has few individually striking items in its permanent collection, save for a small selection of seventeenth-century works by Hals and Rembrandt, but it's the main venue for touring shows and boasts some exquisitely crafted pieces from China and Japan as well. While outside, don't miss the **Sculpture Court and Garden**, with its formidable works by Henry Moore and Alexander Calder. Straddling El Prado, the **Museum of Man** (daily 10am–4.30pm; $6; ☎619/239-2001, ⓦwww.museumofman.org) veers from the banal to the engaging to the bizarre, including demonstrations of tortilla-making and Mexican loom-weaving, replicas of huge Mayan stones, interesting Native American artifacts, and various Egyptian relics.

Close to the Park Boulevard end of El Prado, the child-oriented **Reuben H. Fleet Science Center** (Mon, Tues & Thurs 9.30am–5pm, Wed & Sat 9.30am–8pm, Fri 9.30am–9.30pm, Sat 9.30am–6pm; science center $6.75, with theater or simulator $11.75, all three $15; ☎619/238-1233, ⓦwww.rhfleet.org) is notable mainly for its Space Theater's huge IMAX screen and virtual-reality simulator, which takes you on stomach-churning trips into outer and inner space. Across Plaza de Balboa, the **Natural History Museum** (daily 10am–5pm; $8, children $5; ☎619/255-0216, ⓦwww.sdnhm.org) has a great collection of fossils, hands-on displays of minerals, and entertaining exhibits on dinosaurs and crocodiles. Just behind, in the **Spanish Village Art Center** (daily 11am–4pm; free; ⓦwww.spanishvillageart.com), craftspeople in 37 studios and galleries practice their skills at painting, sculpture, pottery, and glassworking. At the southern end of Pan American Plaza, the **Aerospace Museum** (daily 10am–4.30pm, summer closes 5.30pm; $8, children $3; ☎619/234-8291, ⓦwww.aerospacemuseum.org) recounts the history of aviation, loaded with close to seventy planes including the *Spitfire*, *Hellcat*, and the mysterious spy plane *Blackbird*. Next door at the **Automotive Museum** (daily 10am–4pm; $7, children $3; ☎619/231-2886, ⓦwww.sdautomuseum.org) car enthusiasts will enjoy lingering over motorcycles and classic cars of all kinds, such as a 1948 Tucker Torpedo – one of only fifty left.

San Diego Zoo

The enormous **San Diego Zoo** (daily mid-June to early Sept 7am–10pm; early Sept to mid-June 9am–4pm; last entry one hour before closing; T619/234-3153, W www.sandiegozoo.org), immediately north of the main museums, is one of the world's most renowned, with more than four thousand animals from eight hundred different species, among them very rare Chinese pheasants, Mhorr gazelles, and a freakish two-headed corn snake. Its wide selection of animals are restrained in "psychological cages," which lack bars. Basic admission, including the children's zoo, is $19.50 (children 3–11 $11.75); a Deluxe Tour ticket ($32, children $19.75) includes a bus tour and a roundtrip ride on the Skyfari overhead tramway. If you want to take in the zoo's **Wild Animal Park**, near Escondido, a combined ticket will set you back $52.65, or $35.35 for kids.

Old Town San Diego and Presidio Hill

In 1769, Spanish settlers chose **Presidio Hill** as the site of the first of California's missions. They soon began to build homes at the foot of the hill, which was dominated in turn by Mexican officials and then by early arrivals from the eastern US. **Old Town San Diego**, reachable from downtown via the Trolley, is now a state historical park and the site of several original adobe dwellings – and the inevitable souvenir shops. Most of the stores and restaurants stay open from 10am until at least 10pm, but the best time to visit is during the afternoon when the daily **free walking tour** (2pm) lets you inside the more interesting of the adobes. Tours leave from the **Seeley Stables**, just off the central plaza, where you'll find many well-preserved horse-drawn carriages and wagons from the nineteenth century. Details are available from the **visitor center**, 4002 Wallace St (daily 10am–5pm; T619/220-5422).

The Spanish-style building now atop Presidio Hill is only a rough approximation of the original mission – moved in 1774 – but its **Serra Museum** (Fri–Sun 10am–4.30pm; $5) offers an intriguing examination of Junípero Serra, the padre who led the Spanish colonization and Catholic conversion of California. The **Mission San Diego de Alcalá** itself was relocated six miles north to 10818 San Diego Mission Rd (daily 9am–4.45pm; $3 donation), to be near a water source and fertile soils – and to be safer from attack. The present building (take bus #43 from downtown) is still a working parish church, with a small **museum**; among the craft objects and artifacts from the mission is the crucifix held by Serra at his death in 1834. Despite controversy over his legacy, and allegations of mission-related violence against Native peoples, Serra was beatified in 1998 in a Vatican ceremony.

East San Diego and Hillcrest

Scruffy **East San Diego** is largely suburban sprawl, only really of interest if you want to venture into its western fringes as far as 1925 K St, the site of **Villa Montezuma** (Fri–Sun 10am–4.30pm; also open Thurs in Dec; $5; T619/239-2211), a florid show of Victoriana, with a rich variety of onion domes and all manner of loopy eccentricities. Known to some as the "haunted house," a nickname that seems entirely reasonable, it was built for Jesse Shepard – English-born but noted in the US as a composer, pianist, author, and all-round aesthete. The glorious stock of furniture remains, as do many ornaments and oddments and the dramatic stained-glass windows. To get to the villa without a car, take bus #3, #5, or #16, each stopping within about five blocks of the villa, or use the trolley, transferring to the Euclid Avenue line and getting off near 20th Street.

North of downtown and on the northwest edge of Balboa Park, **Hillcrest** is a lively and artsy area at the center of the city's **gay community**, and is about as close as San Diego gets to having a bohemian air. Go there either for something to eat – there's a selection of interesting cafés and restaurants around University and Fifth streets – or simply to stroll around the fine gathering of Victorian homes.

Ocean Beach and Point Loma

Ocean Beach, six miles northwest of downtown and reached by bus #35, rivals Pacific Beach in its surfing and party atmosphere, although Ocean Beach has a more down-to-earth feel, and is replete with excellent secondhand music shops. Once a notorious Hell's Angels hangout, this has since become one of the most sought-after San Diego addresses, with **Newport Street** the prime spot where most young backpackers spend their time, among rows of cheap snack bars, surf and skate shops, and T-shirt stalls.

At the southern end of the hilly green peninsula of **Point Loma**, stretching south from Ocean Beach, **Cabrillo National Monument** (daily 9am–5.15pm; 7-day pass $5 per car, pedestrians and cyclists $2; Ⓦ www.nps .gov/cabr) marks the spot where Juan Cabrillo and crew became the first Europeans to land in California, albeit briefly, in 1542. The startling views from this high spot, across San Diego Bay to downtown and down the coast to Mexico, easily repay a trip here. A platform atop the western cliffs of the park makes it easy to view the November-to-March **winter whale migration**, when scores of gray whales pass by en route to their breeding grounds off Baja California, Mexico. The nearby visitor center (daily 9am–5.15pm; free) contains information on the history and wildlife of the point, and lies near the **Old Point Loma Lighthouse** (daily 9am–5pm; free), which offers tours that lead past replica Victorian furnishings and equipment from the 1880s.

Mission Bay, Mission Beach, and Pacific Beach

North of Ocean Beach, **Mission Bay** is the site of San Diego's most popular tourist attraction: **SeaWorld** (daily: mid-June to Aug 9am–dusk; rest of year 10am–dusk; $45, children $35, parking $7; Ⓣ 619/226-3901, Ⓦ www.seaworld .com), best known for its "performances" by killer whales and dolphins. Other spectacles include moray eels protruding from the hollow rocks of the Forbidden Reef, sharks circling menacingly in the Shark House, and polar bears and walruses loping about the mock North Pole of the Wild Arctic. However, nerve-jangling thrill rides like the Haunted Lighthouse and Shipwreck Rapids remind you that the place is really more of an old-fashioned theme park than a real aquarium.

Anyone of a nervous disposition, or with a scrawny physique, might find nearby **Mission Beach** – the peninsula that separates Mission Bay from the Pacific Ocean – and its seamless northern extension, **Pacific Beach**, an intimidating spot, populated as they are by scads of scantily clad babes and surf-board-clutching dudes. Despite first impressions, however, the city authorities are trying to limit its anarchic character by clamping down on drug- and alcohol-fueled mayhem, to the chagrin of old-time hedonists. **Ocean Front Walk**, the concrete boardwalk running the length of both beaches, is the fastest way to get about – on rollerblades or by bicycle – when summer traffic is bumper-to-bumper on Mission Boulevard.

La Jolla

A more pretentious air prevails in **La Jolla** (pronounced "La Hoya"), an elegant beach community just to the north that mystery writer Raymond Chandler once described as "a nice place – for old people and their parents." Stroll its immaculate, gallery-filled streets, fuel up on some California cuisine at one of the many sidewalk cafés, or visit the La Jolla site of the **Museum of Contemporary Art**, 700 Prospect St (daily 11am–5pm, closes Thurs 7pm; $6, students $2; Ⓦ www.mcasandiego.org), which has a huge, regularly changing stock of paintings and sculptures from 1955 onwards, highlighted by California pop and minimalism. On the seaward side of the museum lies the small and tasteful **Ellen Scripps Browning Park**, named for the philanthropist whose Irving Gill–designed home now houses the museum. Where the park meets the coast is the popular **La Jolla Cove**, much of it an ecological reserve whose clear waters make it perfect for snorkeling (if you can ever find a parking space).

Just up the road, architecture fans won't want to miss a chance to tour one of the premier sites for high modernism in the US, the **Salk Institute for Biological Studies**, 10010 N Torrey Pines Rd (daily 8.30am–5pm; tours daily 11am & noon; information at ☏ 858/453-4100 ext 1200, Ⓦ www.salk.edu), not only a respected institution for molecular biology and physics, but also a considerably influential design by architect Louis I. Kahn. A collection of austere geometric concrete blocks and walls, featuring stark vistas that look out over the Pacific Ocean and possessing a strange, almost Neoclassical serenity.

Eating

Wherever you are in San Diego, you'll have few problems finding some place good to **eat** at reasonable prices. Everything from crusty coffee shops to stylish ethnic restaurants is in copious supply here, with seafood at its best around Mission Beach and the Gaslamp District, and the latter also home to the greatest concentration of restaurants, aimed at both tourists and locals.

Anthony's Star of the Sea 1360 N Harbor Drive, downtown ☏ /232-7408. Pricey Franco-California-style preparations of seafood, justly famed for its freshness and variety, served on a terrace on the waterfront.

Bella Luna 748 5th Ave, downtown ☏ 619/239-3222. Romantic, moon-themed restaurant serving up wonderful Italian favorites – including hefty servings of pasta and succulent *calamari* – to a relaxed, artsy crowd.

Berta's 3928 Twiggs St, Old Town ☏ 619/295-2343. One of the best-kept secrets in town, offering low-priced, authentic cooking from all over Latin America, with a range of hot and spicy concoctions to make you pound the table for more.

Café 222 222 Island Ave at 2nd Ave, downtown ☏ 619/236-9902. Industrially decorated café serving some of the city's best breakfasts and lunches – mainly fresh twists on staples like sandwiches, burgers, and salads – and at reasonable prices. Open daily 7am–1.45pm.

Candelas 416 3rd Ave, downtown ☏ 619/702-4455. Gaslamp District restaurant offering swank, pricey Mexican fare with inventive combinations of seafood and meat dishes – the California cuisine influence is deliciously apparent.

Casa de Bandini 2600 Calhoun St, Old Town ☏ 619/297-8211. The crowds come in thick, ravenous packs to sample the delicious combo plates, potent margaritas, and appealing (or annoying) mariachi musicians. Chow down on the festive patio, and you're in the catbird seat.

Chilango's Mexican Grill 142 University Ave, Hillcrest ☏ 619/294-8646. Gourmet food for under $10, with solid emphasis on Mexican vegetarian cooking, is served in this tiny storefront locale, which is packed to the rafters in the evenings.

Crest Café 425 Robinson Ave, Hillcrest ☏ 619/295-2510. Don't let the dumpy exterior fool you – this place offers solid, tasty American fare on the cheap, including a fair selection of homemade desserts.

Croce's Restaurant and Jazz Bar 802 5th Ave, downtown ☎619/233-4355. Pricey but excellent range of pasta and salads; the Sunday jazz brunch is popular.

Filippi's Pizza Grotto 1747 India St at Date St, downtown ☎619/232-5094. Great pizzas and a handful of scrumptious pasta dishes served in a small room at the back of an Italian grocery.

Fio's Cucina Italiana 801 5th Ave at F St, downtown ☎619/234-3467. Stylish, high-priced Italian place serving the likes of lobster ravioli and *osso buco*, and ideal for special occasions.

Ichiban 1449 University Ave, Hillcrest ☎619/299-7203. This unpretentious and popular restaurant is a good choice for quality, reasonably priced Japanese cuisine. The combo platters are especially well priced.

Kono's 704 Garnet Ave, Pacific Beach ☎858/483-1669. Crowded, touristy place for breakfast or lunch on the boardwalk, with hefty and inexpensive portions of eggs, sandwiches, hamburgers, and other American favorites.

Living Room Coffeehouse 1010 Prospect St, La Jolla ☎858/459-1187. One in a chain of local coffee shops, with great sandwiches, soups, quiches, and pastries in a living room–like setting.

Mexican Village 120 Orange Ave, Coronado ☎935/435-1822. Longstanding Mexican diner of ballroom dimensions, good for cheap, south-of-the-border staples and renowned for authentic music and mind-numbing margaritas.

Mission Café and Coffeehouse 3795 Mission Blvd, Mission Beach ☎858/488-9060. A wide range of eclectic choices, from French toast and tamales with eggs to tortillas with spicy seasonings to "roll-ups" stuffed with meat and pasta. Beer, specialty coffees, shakes, and smoothies all on tap. Open late.

Point Loma Seafoods 2805 Emerson St, Ocean Beach ☎619/223-1109. Fast, inexpensive counter serving San Diego's freshest fish and chips, along with a mean crabcake sandwich that makes the locals cheer. Often crowded, especially on weekends.

Sammy's 770 4th Ave, downtown (just outside of Horton Plaza) ☎619/230-8888. Affordable California cuisine in a Mediterranean atmosphere. Pizza, pasta, salads, seafood, and chicken are the staples, while the rich, messy sundaes are a highlight.

Taste of Thai 527 University Ave, Hillcrest ☎619/291-7525. Terrific Thai at reasonable prices in the center of Hillcrest; expect a wait on weekends.

Nightlife

Although San Diego's money is lavished on **classical music**, **opera**, and **theater** (half-priced tickets and information at the **Arts Tix** booth at 28 Horton Plaza, Tues–Thurs 11am–6pm, Fri & Sat 10am–6pm, Sun 10am–5pm; ☎619/497-5000), the crowds flock to beachside **discos** and boozy **music venues**. For full listings, pick up the free *San Diego Reader* from shops, bars, and cafés around town.

Blind Melons 710 Garnet Ave, Pacific Beach ☎858/483-7844. College-oriented spot with live rock, blues, and reggae bands nightly.

Blue Tattoo 835 5th Ave, downtown ☎619/238-7191. Stylish dance club featuring bouncy tunes, "foam parties," and a strict door policy – so make sure to come clad in your hippest clubwear.

Buffalo Joe's 600 5th Ave, Gaslamp District ☎619/236-1616. Very popular, almost unavoidable nightspot loaded with tourists and some locals, with a broad selection of live tune, from aggressive rockers to snappy funk to tribal dance-beats to horn-rimmed nerd pop.

Café Crema 1001 Garnet Ave, Pacific Beach ☎858/273-3558. Wake yourself up here before going to the bars, or sober up afterwards, with one of their large coffees. Features sidewalk seating, late hours (till 4am on weekends), and on-site Internet access.

Café Lulu 419 F St, downtown ☎619/238-0114. Hipster joint with eye-catching, mildly freakish decor, as well as a good selection of coffees and late-night food orders until 2am.

Café Sevilla 555 4th Ave, downtown ☎619/233-5979. Traditional Spanish cuisine upstairs, hip Latin American–flavored club downstairs, with flamenco, house, and funk grooves to whet your musical appetite. Draws a trendy European crowd.

Casbah 2501 Kettner Blvd, downtown ☎619/232-4355. Grungy joint that nevertheless hosts a solid, varying roster of blues, funk, reggae, rock, and indie bands.

The Flame 3780 Park Blvd, Hillcrest ☎619/295-4163. The city's premier lesbian club, with pool tables and dancing, and live musical acts from early evening to early morning. Tuesday is "Boys' Night."

Humphrey's by the Bay 2241 Shelter Island Drive, Point Loma ☎619/523-1010. Live funk, soul, and R&B, along with weekly disco nights and live jazz on Sundays, make this restaurant a local favorite for music, as well as seafood.

Kensington Club 4079 Adams Ave, north of Hillcrest ☎619/284-2848. Great joint for beer, wine, and cocktails, but also for wide-ranging live music selections, from thumping-dance DJs to head-banging rockers to more sedate ambient groovers. High on the hip-and-cool meter.

Live Wire 2103 El Cajon Blvd, just east of Hillcrest ☎619/291-7450. With a wide selection of imported beers, pinball, pool, and quasi-bohemian decor, a fine choice for music and boozing, especially with occasional DJ nights and power-chord performances from local rockers.

Rich's 1051 University Ave, Hillcrest ☎619/295-2195. Originally a mainly gay club, but now attracts numerous straights for the heavy dance grooves on weekends and "Hedonism" night on Thursday, when the hatcheck even accepts T-shirts and jeans.

Thrusters Lounge 4633 Mission Blvd, Pacific Beach ☎858/483-6334. Cozy bar and club where the dance beats come hard and heavy on weekends, and jazz and rock make occasional appearances the rest of the week.

Winston's Beach Club 1921 Bacon St, Ocean Beach ☎619/222-6822. A former bowling alley, this local club has rock bands most nights, with occasional reggae and 1960s-style acts as well. Close to the pier.

Out from San Diego: the Anza-Borrego Desert

Most of eastern San Diego County, which otherwise consists largely of sleepy suburban communities, is taken up by the 937-square-mile **Anza-Borrego Desert** (free; $5 per vehicle), much of it comprising the largest desert state park in the US. Some of it can be covered by car, although four-wheel-drive vehicles are necessary for the more obscure – and most interesting – routes. The best **time to come** is winter, when daytime temperatures stay around 85°F. In the fiercely hot summer, it's best left to the lizards, but when the desert blooms, between March and May, scarlet ocotillo, orange poppies, white lilies, purple verbena, and other wildflowers paint a memorable, and fragrant, picture. To find out more information, and begin your trip at a good jumping-off point, stop by the **park visitor center**, near park headquarters at 200 Palm Canyon Drive (daily 9am–5pm, weekends only in summer; ☎760/767-4205).

Historical reminders in the desert span Native American tribes, early white explorers, and Gold Rush fortune-hunters. Approaching from the west, Hwy-78 descends to Scissors Crossing, the junction with Hwy-S2, which follows the **Butterfield Stage Route**, which began service in 1857 as the first regular line of communication between the East and the newly settled West. Further on, the old adobe rest stop of **Vallecito** (pronounced "vy-ay-SEE-toe") **Stage Station** (Sept–May only 9am–sunset; $2) gives a good indication of the privations of early desert travel. To the south, **Agua Caliente Regional Park** (Sept–May daily 9.30am–5pm; $5) features a few naturally fed pools, one kept at its natural 96°F, while around Imperial Valley in the least-visited portion of Anza-Borrego, there's a vivid and spectacular clash as gray rock rises from the edges of the red desert floor.

The only substantial settlement in the desert is **BORREGO SPRINGS**, at the northern end of Hwy-S3 along Hwy-S22, which is a good base for the area's canyon walks, some with free but waterless **campgrounds** (campsites $7–19). Camping is also available at the *Borrego Palm Canyon* campground ($10–16), near the Anza-Borrego park visitor center. From here, a 1.5-mile trail

Tijuana: a taste of Mexico

You could hardly find a more eye-opening day-trip out from San Diego than the Mexican border town of **Tijuana**. While far from the most culturally rich place in Mexico, every year some twenty million people cross here from the US. Most of them are Californians on shopping expeditions, seeking somewhere cheap and colorful to spend money on blankets, pottery, cigarettes, tequila, dentistry, and car repair, or junkets of seniors on the hunt for affordable **pharmaceutical drugs** – available through many of the town's cut-rate pharmacies and usually without a prescription. Keep in mind, though, that while everything is lower-priced in Tijuana than in the US, the quality and safety of the merchandise are sometimes questionable.

Although the vast economic gulf separating the two countries is more than obvious – you're immediately confronted by shabbily dressed trinket vendors and children selling woven bracelets and gum – Tijuana is, in fact, one of Mexico's wealthier cities, and somewhat safer than it was a decade ago. The main streets and shopping areas are a few blocks from the border in downtown, where the major thoroughfare is **Avenida Revolución**. Stroll around for a while to get in the mood and then retire to one of the many bars and watch the tourist throngs lubricate themselves with stiff margaritas. At night, the action mostly consists of North American youths drinking themselves stupid in flashy discos, grungy strip joints, and rowdy Rock 'n' Roll **bars**. One of the best examples of the latter is *Rodeo Santa Fe*, on Avenida Paseo Tijuana in Pueblo Amigo Plaza, Zona Rio (☎011526/682-4967), a wild "rodeo" staged indoors with Tex-Mex and Latino music, a mechanical bull, lots of cowboy gear, and, if you need a break from the cowpoke scene, a frenetic upstairs disco. For **food**, safe choices include *Café La Especial*, Avenida Revolución 718 (☎011526/685-6654), offering rich, satisfying Mexican staples at cheap prices, and *La Fonda Roberto*, 2800 Cuauhtemoc Blvd (☎011526/686-4687), a longstanding favorite for its exotic combinations of ingredients and inventive menu including cactus salad and pumpkin quesadillas – and also for inexpensive prices.

Heavy traffic, and insurance limitations, make crossing into Mexico **by car** a risky business; from San Diego you can take either the Trolley (see p.1091) or bus #932 from the Santa Fe Railroad Depot (both $4.50 roundtrip). However, if you do decide to drive into Mexico, invest in **auto insurance**, which can be had for as little as $10–15 per day in San Ysidro, just before the border crossing. Dollars are accepted as readily as pesos, so there's no need to **change money**, though prices are better if you do. **Border formalities** are minimal; if you're planning to go further than 75 miles into the country or stay for more than three days, pick up a Mexican Tourist Card from consulates in the US – the one in San Diego is downtown at 1549 India St (Mon–Fri 8am–1pm; ☎619/231-8414) – or at the Mexican Customs office just inside the Tijuana side of the border. When returning to the US, however, even within a single day, immigration procedures are stringent – joking about smuggling weapons or illegal drugs can bring a humiliating interrogation, so be wary of saying or doing anything foolish. It's also a good idea to have your **passport** in tow if you want to expedite the process with minimal hassles. **Hotels** are cheap, with many low-cost lodgings close to the center. Recommended choices include *La Villa de Zaragoza*, Avenida Madero 1120 (☎011526/685-1837; ❸), whose clean rooms have air-conditioning and cable TV; and *Camino Real*, Paseo de los Heroes 10305 (☎011526/633-4001 or 1-800/7-CAMINO, ⓦwww.tjcamino.com; ❺), which has plush rooms and two restaurants and bars.

takes you to a small oasis with palms and a waterfall. **Hotels** in town are fairly pricey; only the *Oasis*, 366 W Palm Drive (☎760/767-5409; ❹), and *Hacienda del Sol*, 610 Palm Drive (☎760/767-5442; ❹), are even close to affordable, with some rooms in each equipped with kitchenettes. Decent **restaurants** include *Pablito's* (☎760/767-5753), in the commercial development The Center, for its

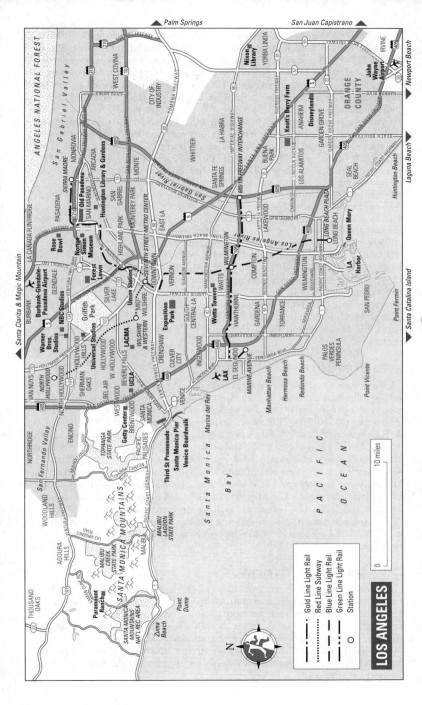

LOS ANGELES

Gold Line Light Rail
Red Line Subway
Blue Line Light Rail
Green Line Light Rail
Station

10 miles

0

Shuttle (☎1-800/545-7745, ⓦwww.laxchequer.com), SuperShuttle (☎310/782-6600 or 1-800/554-3146, ⓦwww.supershuttle.com), and Coast Shuttle (☎310/417-3988) run all over town, delivering you to your door. Fares depend on your destination but are generally around $25–30 (plus tip), with a journey time of between 30 and 45 minutes. **Taxis** from the airport are always expensive: at least $25 to downtown and West LA, $30 to Hollywood, and $90 to Disneyland.

If you're arriving from elsewhere in the US, or from Mexico, you might just land at one of the **other airports** in the LA area – at Burbank, Long Beach, Ontario, or Orange County's John Wayne Airport in Costa Mesa. MTA buses (☎213/626-4455 or 1-800/COMMUTE, outside LA ☎1-800/2-LARIDE, ⓦwww.mta.net) serve them all – phone on arrival and tell them where you are and where you want to go.

The main **Greyhound** bus terminal, at 1716 E Seventh St (☎213/629-8401, ⓦwww.greyhound.com), is in a seedy section of downtown, but access is restricted to ticket-holders, so it's safe enough inside. LA's other Greyhound stations handle fewer services: in Hollywood, 1715 N Cahuenga Blvd (☎323/466-6384); Pasadena, 645 E Walnut St (☎626/792-5116); North Hollywood, 11239 Magnolia Blvd (☎818/761-5119); Long Beach, 1498 Long Beach Blvd (☎562/218-3011); and Anaheim, 100 W Winston Rd (☎714/999-1256). Only the downtown terminal is open around the clock; all have toilets and luggage lockers.

Arriving in LA by **train** you'll be greeted with the Mission Revival architecture of Union Station, 800 N Alameda St (☎213/624-0171), on the north side of downtown, from which you can also access the city's MTA bus lines.

Information

LA has a number of **visitor centers**. The downtown one is at 685 S Figueroa St (Mon–Fri 8am–5pm, Sat 8.30am–5pm; ☎213/689-8822, ⓦwww.lacvb.com); others, all open normal weekday working hours, are in Santa Monica, 1400 Ocean Ave (☎310/393-7593, ⓦwww.santamonica.com); near Disneyland, 800 W Katella Ave (☎714/999-8999, ⓦwww.anaheimoc.org); Beverly Hills, 239 S Beverly Drive (☎310/248-1015, ⓦwww.beverlyhillscvb.com); Hollywood, at Janes House, 6541 Hollywood Blvd (☎1-800/228-2452); and Long Beach, 1 World Trade Center, suite 300 (☎562/436-3645, ⓦwww.visitlongbeach.com). All supply free local **maps**, but you'd do better to pick up Gousha Publications' fully indexed *Los Angeles CityMap* ($3), or for a pocket-sized, laminated map, try *Streetwise Los Angeles* ($5) – both are available in many bookstores.

For poste restante, or general delivery, use the main downtown **post office** at 760 N Main St (Mon–Fri 8am–7pm, Sat 8am–4pm, pick up letters Mon–Fri 8am–3pm; zip code 90012).

City transportation

The sheer scale of LA – its detractors call it "nineteen suburbs in search of a city" – means that it really is difficult to get around without a car, unless you're confining your visit to more centralized spots like Santa Monica, Pasadena, or downtown LA. Even though the traffic is often bumper-to-bumper, the freeways are the only way to cover long distances quickly. If you're driving yourself, avoid traveling at rush hours and phone ahead for directions whenever possible. Otherwise, try to relax on the fastest alternative, **express buses**.

Guided tours

Some of your best bets for touring downtown and other spots are the 2.5hr **walking tours** offered by the LA Conservancy (Sat 10am; $8–10; ☎213/623-CITY, ⓦlaconservancy.org), which concentrate on various aspects of the city's architecture, history, and culture. Innumerable **bus tours** introduce the city as well, though only the specialists below show you anything you couldn't see more cheaply yourself. Costs are $30 minimum; most will collect you from your hotel. The **mainstream** bus tours whiz you past the main sights and the **homes of the stars** (though you often won't see much more than the ivy-covered gates of the rich and famous), padding out the experience with views of palm trees and wide boulevards. Operators include **Casablanca Tours**, at the *Hollywood Roosevelt* hotel, 6362 Hollywood Blvd (☎323/461-0156, ⓦwww.casablancatours.com), which focuses on the golden age of cinema; and **Hollywood Fantasy Tours**, 6671 Hollywood Blvd (☎323/469-8184), which shows off Beverly Hills and Hollywood only.

Specialist tours

Black LA Tours ☎323/750-9267. Black historical and entertainment tours of once-famed Central Avenue and key African-American history museums and cultural attractions. Prices vary.

Googie Tours ☎323/980-3480. Pilgrimages to Southern California's remaining space-age glass and formica diners, quirky cocktail lounges, classic fast-food joints, and other jewels of pop architecture. $40.

LA Bike Tours 6729 Hollywood Blvd, Hollywood ☎323/466-5890 or 1-888/775-BIKE, ⓦwww.labiketours.com. Two-wheeled sightseeing tours of major city attractions like the Getty Center and the Golden Triangle in Beverly Hills, lasting from 90min to a full day. Bike and helmet included, plus lunch. $50–95.

Neon Cruises 501 W Olympic Blvd, downtown ☎213/489-9918, ⓦwww.neon-mona.org/cruise.html. Three-hour-long, eye-popping evening tours of LA's best remaining neon art, once a month on Saturdays, sponsored by the Museum of Neon Art. Very popular, so reserve well ahead. $45.

Public transportation

LA's **Metrorail** train system was envisioned to cover the whole of Los Angeles County, but is currently made up of only four limited lines, each distinguished by color: the **Red Line** stretches from Union Station through Hollywood to North Hollywood in the San Fernando Valley; the **Green Line** goes from Hawthorne to Norwalk along the Century Freeway (but stops short of LAX); the **Blue Line** connects downtown through Watts to the Pacific Transit Mall in Long Beach; and the new **Gold Line** links the Blue Line to the San Gabriel Valley through Old Pasadena. Tickets cost $1.35 one way, or 75¢ at night from 9pm–5am, and trains run every five to fifteen minutes (more infrequently at night). By contrast, **Metrolink** commuter trains ($3–10 one way; ☎1-800/371-LINK, ⓦwww.metrolinktrains.com) operate primarily inter-suburban to downtown routes on weekdays, though they can be useful if you find yourself in far-flung cities in Orange, Ventura, Riverside, and San Bernardino counties.

Car-less Angelenos are still most well served, however, by **buses**, most of which are run by the LA County Metropolitan Transit Authority (MTA or "Metro; ☎213/626-4455 or 1-800/COMMUTE, ⓦwww.mta.net). Information can also be obtained in person at three locations: 515 S Flower St, level C of Arco Plaza, downtown (Mon–Fri 7.30am–3.30pm); 5301 Wilshire Blvd, Mid-Wilshire (Mon–Fri 9am–5pm), or 6249 Hollywood Blvd,

Hollywood (Mon–Fri 10am–6pm). Buses on the major arteries between downtown and the coast run roughly every fifteen minutes between 5am and 2am; other routes, and the **all-night services** along the major thoroughfares, are less frequent. At night, be careful not to get stranded alone downtown waiting for a connection.

The standard **one-way fare** is $1.35; **transfers** cost 25¢ more, but must be made within an hour; **express buses**, and any others using the freeway, are $1.85 up to $3.35. If you're staying a while, you can save some money with a **weekly** or **monthly pass**, which cost $11 and $42, respectively. There are also the mini **DASH** buses, which operate through the LA Department of Transportation, or LADOT (☎808-2273 for area codes 213, 310, 323, and 818, ⓦwww.ladottransit.com), with a flat fare of 25¢. Six routes run through downtown every five to ten minutes between 6.30am and 6pm on weekdays, and every fifteen to twenty minutes between 10am and 5pm on Saturdays and Sundays. Other DASH routes travel widely throughout the metropolis.

You'll be hard pressed to find an available **taxi** cruising the streets, so call ahead; among the more reliable companies are the Independent Cab Co. (☎1-800/521-8294), LA Taxi (☎1-800/200-1085), and United Independent Taxi (☎1-800/411-0303). Fares include a base charge of around $2; add $1.60 per mile, and tack on another $2.50 if you're getting picked up from LAX.

Major LA bus routes

To and from LAX:
Downtown #42, #439
Getty Center/San Fernando Valley #561
Hollywood #220 (then transfer to #4 at Santa Monica Blvd)
Long Beach #232
San Pedro #225
West Hollywood #220

To and from downtown:
Burbank Studios #96
Exposition Park #38, #81
Forest Lawn Cemetery, Glendale #90, #91
Huntington Library, San Marino #79, #379
LAX #42, #439 (also #439 for South Bay)
Long Beach #60
Orange County, Knott's Berry Farm, Disneyland #460 (express)
Pasadena #401, #402
San Fernando Valley #424, #425
San Pedro #445, #446, #447 (all express), transfer to DASH #142 for Catalina terminal
Santa Monica #20, #22, #320, #322, #434 (express)
Venice #33, #333, #436 (express)

Major city routes:
Along Hollywood Blvd #1
Along Melrose Ave #10, #11
Along Santa Monica Blvd #4, #304
Along Sunset Blvd #2, #3, #302
Along Wilshire Blvd #20, #21, #22, #320 (limited stops, but faster than #20)

Cycling

Cycling in LA may sound perverse, but in some areas it can be one of the better ways of getting around. There are beachside bike paths between Santa Monica and Redondo Beach, and from Long Beach to Newport Beach, and many equally enjoyable inland routes, notably around Griffith Park and Pasadena (the LA River route, however, is justifiably notorious, loaded with broken glass and bands of budding criminals). Contact AAA, 2601 S Figueroa St (Mon–Fri 9am–5pm; ☎213/741-3686, ⊛www.aaa-calif.com), or the LA Department of Transportation, known as CalTrans, 120 S Spring St (Mon–Fri 8am–5pm; ☎213/897-3656, ⊛www.dot.ca.gov), for maps and information. The best place to **rent a bike** for the beaches is on Washington Street around Venice Pier, where outlets include Spokes 'n' Stuff, 4175 Admiralty Way (☎310/306-3332) and 1700 Ocean Ave (☎310/395-4748); in summer bike-rental stands line the beach. Prices range from $10 a day for a clunker to $20 a day or more for a mountain bike.

Accommodation

Finding a **place to stay** in LA is easy; finding somewhere inexpensive and well located is difficult. Downtown has both upscale and budget hotels, Hollywood has a wide range of cheap motels, and the Westside and Malibu are mid- to upper-range territory. If you're not driving, choose your base carefully to avoid lengthy cross-town journeys between these areas, or divide your stay between them. The nearest **campgrounds** to LA are along the Orange County coast, such as *Bolsa Chica* in Huntington Beach (☎1-800/444-7275), and in the mountains and beaches around Malibu, notably Malibu Creek State Park (☎1-800/706-8809) and Leo Carrillo State Beach (☎1-818/706-1310). Campsites run $14–25.

Hotels, motels, and B&Bs

Since LA has few **booking agencies**, and visitor centers don't make reservations (though they do offer information and advice), you can only reserve a **room** through a travel agent or reservations website, or by contacting the hotel directly. Ask if there are special weekend or midweek rates. Especially at the lower end of the price scale, hotels are less expensive if reserved by the week than by the night.

Downtown and around

Biltmore 506 S Grand Ave ☎213/624-1011 or 1-800/222-8888, ⊛www.thebiltmore.com. Neoclassical 1923 architecture combined with modern luxury to make your head swim, including a health club modeled on a Roman bathhouse, cherub and angel decor, and a view overlooking Pershing Square. Significantly cheaper rates on weekends. **❾**

City Center Motel 1135 W 7th St ☎213/628-7141. Budget option with small rooms and tacky 1960s decor, but free continental breakfast and airport shuttle bus. **❷**

Downtown LA Standard 550 S Flower St ☎213/892-8080, ⊛www.standardhotel.com.

Located in a former oil-company building, the latest branch of LA's self-consciously trendy chain features sleek, modern furnishings and quirky decor, but is best for its rooftop bar. Although billed as a "business hotel," the party scene is pretty much constant. **❼**

Figueroa 939 S Figueroa St ☎213/627-8971 or 1-800/421-9092, ⊛www.figueroahotel.com. Well-placed mid-range hotel with pleasant rooms, 24hr coffee shop, pool, and Jacuzzi. **❺**

Miyako Inn 328 E 1st St ☎213/617-2000, ⊛www.miyakoinn.com. Despite the grim concrete-box exterior, this is a pleasant hotel featuring clean rooms with fridges, spa, and karaoke bar. **❻**

Orchid 819 S Flower St ☎ 213/624-5855 or 1-800/874-5855. The best deal in the heart of downtown, near the Seventh and Flower Red Line subway station. Comfortable and safe, even if the rooms are a bit plain. Weekly rates. ❷

Park Plaza 607 S Park View St ☎ 213/384-5281. Facing dicey MacArthur Park, a 1920s hotel with a sumptuous lobby and marble floor, and a tasteful mix of Neoclassical and modern decor. Ongoing renovation promises to make the ordinary rooms more appealing. ❻

Westin Bonaventure 404 S Figueroa St ☎ 213/624-1000 or 1-800/228-3000, ⓦ www.westin.com. Modernist luxury hotel with five glass towers that resemble cocktail shakers, a six-story atrium with a "lake," and elegantly remodeled, conic-shaped rooms. A breathtaking exterior elevator ride ascends to the rotating *Bona Vista* cocktail lounge. Suites upwards of $2000. ❽–❾

Hollywood

Chateau Marmont 8221 Sunset Blvd ☎ 323/656-1010, ⓦ www.chateaumarmont.com. Exclusive Norman Revival hotel, which resembles a dark castle or Hollywood fortress and has hosted all manner of celebrities. Largely suites and bungalows. ❾

Dunes Sunset 5625 Sunset Blvd ☎ 323/467-5171. An acceptable, no-frills motel along a grim stretch on the east side of Hollywood. Good for reaching downtown. ❸

Hollywood Metropolitan 5825 Sunset Blvd ☎ 323/962-5800 or 1-800/962-5800, ⓦ www.metropolitanhotel.com. A sleek highrise with good rooms, decent views, and disabled access. The best option in its price range. ❺

Hollywood Roosevelt 7000 Hollywood Blvd ☎ 323/466-7000, ⓦ www.hollywoodroosevelt .com. The first hotel built for the movie greats in 1927, now in the *Clarion* chain. The rooms are unremarkable, but the place reeks of atmosphere, with a "History of Hollywood" exhibit on the second floor. Also offers a Jacuzzi, fitness room, and swimming pool. ❻

Orchid Suites 1753 Orchid Ave ☎ 323/874-9678 or 1-800/537-3052, ⓦ www.orchidsuites.com. Roomy, if spartan, suites with cable TV, kitchenettes, and heated pool. Very close to the most popular parts of Hollywood – adjacent to the massive Hollywood & Highland mall. ❹

Renaissance Hollywood 1755 N Highland Blvd ☎ 323/856-1200, ⓦ www.renaissancehollywood .com. The hotel centerpiece of the Hollywood & Highland mall complex, with upscale rooms and suites, and a prime location in the heart of Tinseltown. ❼

West LA

Bel Air 701 Stone Canyon Rd ☎ 310/472-1211 or 1-800/648-1097, ⓦ www.hotelbelair.com. The nicest hotel in LA bar none – and the only one in Bel Air – in a lushly overgrown canyon above Beverly Hills. If you can't afford the rooms, which can reach $500 a night, go for a beautiful brunch by Swan Lake. ❾

Claremont 1044 Tiverton Ave ☎ 310/208-5957. An amazingly good deal for the area, this cheerful and inexpensive little hotel sits very close to UCLA and Westwood Village. Rooms are fairly basic, but the main difficulty is the lack of parking. ❸

Culver Hotel 9400 Culver Blvd ☎ 310/838-7963 or 1-800/888-3-CULVER, ⓦ www.culverhotel.com. A lovely, restored historic landmark featuring red-and-black decor, old-fashioned iron railings in the lobby, and cozy rooms with good views of Culver City, just south of West LA. ❺

Grafton 8462 Sunset Blvd ☎ 323/654-6470, ⓦ www.graftononsunset.com. A recently redesigned mid-level boutique hotel, with attractive furnishings, in-room stereos and VCRs in rooms, plus a pool, fitness center, and complimentary shuttle to nearby malls and businesses. ❻

Le Montrose 900 Hammond St ☎ 310/855-1115, ⓦ www.lemontrose.com. Elegant West Hollywood hotel with Art Nouveau stylings, featuring rooftop tennis courts, pool, and Jacuzzi. Most rooms are suites with full amenities. ❽

Santa Monica, Venice, and Malibu

Cadillac 8 Dudley Ave, Venice ☎ 310/399-8876, ⓦ www.thecadillachotel.com. Restored Art Deco hotel and hostel right on the Venice Boardwalk. Bright, airy atmosphere and friendly staff. Dorms ❶, hotel rooms ❺

Channel Road Inn 219 W Channel Rd, Pacific Palisades ☎ 310/459-1920, ⓦ www.channelroad-inn.com. Romantic getaway nestled in lower Santa Monica Canyon, with ocean views, hot tub, and free bike rental. Rooms priced according to view, size, and amenities. ❼–❾

Inn at Venice Beach 327 Washington Blvd, Venice ☎ 310/821-2557 or 1-800/828-0688, ⓦ www.innatvenicebeach.com. Located near Venice Beach and the canals, with simple, tasteful rooms featuring balconies and fridges. ❻

Malibu Surfer 22541 Pacific Coast Hwy, Malibu ☎ 310/456-6169, ⓦ www.malibusurfmo.qpg.com. King-sized beds, refrigerators, and TVs make this roadside motel an excellent budget stop, despite the unappealing retro-kitsch decor. ❹

Shangri-La 1301 Ocean Ave, Santa Monica ☎ 310/394-2791, ⓦ www.shangrila-hotel.com.

Wonderfully restored Art Deco treasure overlooking Palisades Park and the Santa Monica beach, with clean and sleek, if basic, rooms. ❽

Near LAX

Days Inn 901 W Manchester Blvd ☎310/649-0800 or 1-800/231-2508, 🌐www.the.daysinn.com. Modern hotel with clean rooms and an outdoor pool in a grubby neighborhood by the 405 freeway. Offers free parking and free LAX shuttle. ❹

Quality Inn 5249 W Century Blvd ☎310/645-2200 or 1-800/228-5151, 🌐www.qualityinn.com. Good-value motel, with ten floors of comfortable, fully equipped rooms, plus restaurant and bar. Free shuttle buses to LAX every 15min. ❸

The South Bay and LA Harbor

Barnabey's 3501 N Sepulveda Blvd, Manhattan Beach ☎310/545-8466, 🌐www.barnabeyshotel.com. Quaint Victorian inn decorated with Belle Epoque touches, offering rooms with plush beds and old-time fixtures and detailing, as well as a pool and Jacuzzi. ❻

Hotel Hermosa 2515 PCH, Hermosa Beach ☎310/318-6000, 🌐www.hotelhermosa.com. In a busy part of town, between Hermosa and Manhattan beaches, a sumptuous hotel with rooms starting at moderate prices (though rising up to $350 suites) and a short walk to the beach. ❹–❾

Seahorse Inn 233 N Sepulveda Blvd, Manhattan Beach ☎310/376-7951 or 1-800/233-8050. Typical roadside motel, but clean and comfortable, and a few blocks from the sands. ❸

Westin Long Beach 333 E Ocean Blvd, Long Beach ☎562/436-3000, 🌐www.westin.com. A solid bet for bayside luxury at affordable prices (cheaper when booked online), right by the convention center, with a spa, fitness center, and pool. ❻

Around Disneyland

Desert Palm Inn and Suites 631 W Katella Ave, Anaheim ☎1-800/635-5423, 🌐www.anaheimdesertpalm.com. Large, comfortable rooms with refrigerators, microwaves, VCRs, and continental breakfast. ❺

Disneyland Hotel 1150 W Cerritos Ave, Anaheim ☎714/956-6400, 🌐disneyland.disney.go.com/disneylandresort. Cookie-cutter rooms without much charm but still, an irresistible stop for many. The Disneyland monorail does stop outside (theme park admission is separate). ❾

Disneyland Pacific Pier 1717 S Disneyland Drive, Anaheim ☎714/956-6425, 🌐disneyland.disney.go.com/disneylandresort/ResortHotels. Renovated concrete complex turned into overflow accommodation for park visitors; farther from the main theme park than its counterpart on Cerritos Ave, but shuttles are available and rooms are slightly cheaper, with the same amenities. ❼

Park Place Inn 1544 S Harbor Blvd, Anaheim ☎714/776-4800, 🌐www.stovallshotels.com/park_place. *Best Western* chain hotel across from Disneyland, with the customary clean rooms and no-frills amenities. ❹

The San Gabriel and San Fernando valleys

Artists Inn 1038 Magnolia St, South Pasadena ☎1-800/799-5668, 🌐www.artistsinns.com. Themed B&B with ten rooms and suites (some with spas) honoring famous painters and styles. Best of all is the Italian Suite, with an antique tub and sun porch. ❼

Ritz-Carlton Huntington 1401 S Knoll Ave, Pasadena ☎626/568-3900, 🌐www.ritzcarlton.com. Landmark hotel, c.1900, luxuriously designed and discreetly tucked away in residential Pasadena. Suites start at $500, with more basic rooms for less than half the price. ❽

Safari Inn 1911 W Olive St, Burbank ☎818/845-8586, 🌐www.anabelle-safari.com. Classic mid-century motel, renovated but still loaded with pop-architecture touches. Features a pool, fitness room, Burbank airport shuttle, and in-room fridges, with some suites also available. ❺

Sportsmen's Lodge 12825 Ventura Blvd, Studio City ☎818/769-4700, 🌐www.slhotel.com. Retro multi-story motel built around a pool, offering 177 basic rooms featuring tacky decor and thirteen suites, as well as a Jacuzzi, exercise room, and restaurant. ❻

Hostels

Hostels are dotted all over the city, though some limit stays to a few nights. Colleges and fraternity houses let out space during summer; for details call UCLA's Interfraternity Council (☎310/825-7878) and USC's off-campus housing office (☎1-800/USC-4632, 🌐housing.usc.edu).

Banana Bungalow 2775 Cahuenga Blvd W, in Cahuenga Pass ☎323/851-1129 or 1-800/446-

7835, 🌐www.bananabungalow.com. Huge hostel in the Hollywood Hills near Hwy-101, with a party atmosphere, free shuttle buses to Venice Beach, Universal Studios, and Magic Mountain, and as much beer as you can drink for $3 every second night. Dorms $18–20; singles or doubles $61 and up. **❶–❷**

HI-Anaheim/Fullerton 1700 N Harbor Blvd, Fullerton ☏714/738-3721, ⓦwww.hostelweb .com/losangeles/fullerton.htm. Spacious and comfortable lodging, five miles north of Disneyland. Summer check-in 5–11pm; rest of year 4–11pm. Mornings open 7.10am–noon. Orange County Transit Authority bus #43 stops outside. Members $15, others $18. **❶**

HI-LA/Santa Monica 1436 2nd St, Santa Monica ☏310/393-9913, ⓦwww.hostelweb.com/losan-geles/los_angeles.htm. Huge hostel in a well-restored old building, a few strides from the Santa Monica sands. Members $25, others $28, private rooms $66. Open 24hr. **❶**

HI-LA/South Bay 3601 S Gaffey St, #613 ☏310/831-8109, ⓦwww.hostelweb.com/losange-les/south_bay.htm. Located in the LA Harbor area, overlooking the ocean. MTA bus #446 passes close by, but it's a 2hr journey from downtown. You can also take SuperShuttle from LAX. There's a pool, and free trip to the local aquarium. Open 7am–midnight. Members $15, others $18; private rooms $37. **❶**

Hollywood International 6820 Hollywood Blvd, Hollywood ☏323/463-0797 or 1-800/750-6561, ⓦwww.hollywoodhostels.com. One of three good-value locations in the area, with free tea and coffee, game room, gymnasium, patio garden, kitchen, and laundry. Offers tours of Hollywood, theme parks, Las Vegas, and Tijuana. Shared rooms start at $17, private rooms $40. **❶–❷**

Hostel California 2221 Lincoln Blvd, Venice ☏310/305-0250. Built for the 1984 Olympics, with six-bed dorms, free shuttle bus to LAX, big-screen TV, and cable. Dorms $17, private rooms $34. **❶**

Huntington Beach Colonial Inn 421 8th St, Huntington Beach ☏714/536-3315, ⓦwww.hunt-ingtonbeachhostel.com. Four blocks from the beach; mostly double rooms. Open 8am–11pm. Key rental after 1pm ($1, plus $20 deposit). Dorms $18, private rooms $20 per person. **❶**

Orange Drive Manor 1764 N Orange Drive, Hollywood ☏323/850-0350, ⓦorangedrivehos-tel.com. Centrally located hostel (right behind the Chinese Theatre), offering tours to film studios, theme parks, and homes of the stars. Members $16, others $18, private rooms $36. **❶**

Orbit Hotel 7950 Melrose Ave, West Hollywood ☏323/655-1510 or 1-877/ORBIT-US, ⓦwww .orbithotel.com. Retro-1960s hotel and hostel with sleek Day-Glo furnishings and ultra-hip modern decor, offering complimentary breakfast, movie screening room, patio, café, private baths in all rooms, shuttle tours, and $20-per-day car rental. Dorms $18–20, private rooms $49–55. **❶–❷**

Venice Beach Cotel 25 Windward Ave, Venice ☏310/399-7649, ⓦwww.venicebeachcotel.com. Located in a historic beachside building, this colonnaded hostel (or "cotel") has dorm rooms for around $15–18, and private rooms $35–49. **❶–❷**

The City

With only limited space between the desert, mountains, and ocean, LA has long since filled in the gaps between what were once small and isolated towns. As a result, today it's a massive conglomeration of interconnected, amorphous districts, often with little in common.

If LA has a heart, it's **downtown**, in the center of the basin, which offers a taste of almost everything you'll find elsewhere around the city, from upscale art along Bunker Hill to the abject dereliction of Skid Row, compressed into an area of small, easily walkable blocks. The area **around downtown** contains some decaying Victorian suburbs, 1920s Art Deco buildings, and the center of LA's enormous and growing Latino population.

West from downtown, **Hollywood** has streets imbued with movie myths and legends – even if the genuine glamour is long gone. Adjoining **West LA** is home to the city's newest money, shown off in Beverly Hills and along the Sunset Strip. **Santa Monica** and **Venice** further to the west are the quintes-sential seafront LA of palm trees, white sands, and laid-back living, while the coastline itself stretches another twenty miles northwest to glamorous **Malibu**, home to the movieland elite.

Suburban **Orange County**, to the southeast, holds little of interest apart from **Disneyland**, a few museums, and a handful of libertine beach towns. On the far side of the northern hills lie the **San Gabriel and San Fernando valleys**, or simply "the Valley," seen by mainstream Los Angeles as nothing more than endless tract homes and strip malls, but in reality quite interesting.

Downtown LA

Downtown LA embraces the city's every social, economic, and ethnic division. Only in the last few decades has a handful of sizeable office towers appeared on its formerly low-slung skyline, over which LA City Hall – built in 1928 – loomed as the tallest structure until 1960. In the boom years following World War II, as businesses spread out across the basin, downtown seemed to be heading for permanent decay, but corporate revitalization and piles of urban-renewal dollars have given it a new lease on life, at least economically.

The whole area can easily be seen in a day on foot, aided by the odd 25¢ ride on a DASH **bus** (T213/808-2273, W www.ladottransit.com). LA's original settlement at **The Plaza** is the obvious first stop, before crossing into the municipal confines of the **Civic Center** and the corporate zone of **Bunker Hill**, and continuing through the chaos along **Broadway**.

The Plaza District

Within the **El Pueblo de Los Angeles Historic Park**, 845 N Alameda St (free; T213/628-2381, W www.ci.la.ca.us/ELP), the square known as **the Plaza** is roughly the site of the city's original late eighteenth-century townsite, and a few evocative early buildings remain in situ. The plaza church **La Placita**, the city's oldest, serves as a sanctuary for illegal Central American refugees and the site of some enjoyable Sunday "Mariachi Masses" (11.30am & 4.30pm). **Olvera Street**, which runs north from the plaza, contrived in part as a pseudo-Mexican village market, offers a cheery collection of food and craft stalls and the historic **Avila Adobe** (daily 9am–5pm; free), technically the city's oldest building, though it's been completely rebuilt in the last thirty years. Other worthwhile sights include the **Sepulveda House** (Mon–Sat 10am–3pm; free), an 1887 Eastlake Victorian structure that has rooms highlighting different periods in Mexican-American history, and the **Garnier Building**, recently reopened as the **Chinese American Museum** (T213/626-5240, W www.camla.org), which details the local history of Chinese settlement, society, and culture.

Across Alameda Street from the Plaza, the magnificent Mission Revival **Union Station** is chiefly used as a Metrorail and Amtrak terminal, although it was once the site of **Chinatown**, which now sits a few blocks to the north and is mainly of interest for a host of fine restaurants.

Civic Center

South from the Plaza, across the Santa Ana Freeway, the **Civic Center**'s plodding office buildings surround the lifeless plaza of the Music Center, home to several of LA's high-culture institutions. The unmistakable visual highlight is the curving, titanium-paneled **Disney Hall** (W wdch.laphil.com), a Frank Gehry–designed concert space that serves as the home of the LA Philharmonic. A block away, the **Our Lady of the Angels** Catholic church (tours Mon–Fri 1 & 3pm, Sat 11.30am & 2pm, Sun 11.30am & 2.30pm; free; W www.olacathedral.org) resembles a concrete fortress on the outside – but features exquisite decor inside, such as a grand marble altar and ultra-thin alabaster screens for diffusing light. The Civic Center's other main attraction, just to the east, is the Art Deco **City Hall**, which has a 360° observation deck on the 28th floor (free daily tours 10am & 11am; ☎213/485-4423), while on the south side of the plaza, free tours of the **Los Angeles Times** building (Mon–Fri 11.15am; ☎213/237-5757, Ⓦwww.latimes.com) show how the West Coast's biggest newspaper is put together.

Bunker Hill

Until a century ago the area south of the Civic Center, **Bunker Hill**, was LA's most elegant neighborhood, its elaborate Victorian mansions and houses connected by funicular railroad to the growing business district down below. But after a half-century of decay, a wrecking-ball approach to 1960s urban renewal transformed it into the amorphous **Financial District**, sprouting colossal new towers. Amid the fancy offices and luxury condos of the California Plaza on Grand Avenue, the **Museum of Contemporary Art** (**MOCA**; Tues–Sun 11am–5pm, Thurs 11am–8pm; $8, students $5, free Thurs 5–8pm; ☎213/626-6222, Ⓦwww.moca.org) was designed by showman architect Arata Isozaki as

ACCOMMODATION

Biltmore	E
City Center Motel	G
Downtown LA	
Standard	F
Figueroa Hotel	I
Kawada	B
Miyako Inn	A
Orchid	H
Park Plaza	D
Westin Bonaventure	C

RESTAURANTS

Clifton's Cafeteria	6
La Luz del Dia	3
Langer's Deli	4
Ocean Seafood	1
Original Pantry	7
Pacific Dining Car	5
Philippe the Original French Dip	2

Metrorail Stations

0   500 yds

DOWNTOWN LA

South Central LA

a "small village in the valley of the skyscrapers," and offers a playful array of reddish geometric blocks. In addition to work by Franz Kline, Mark Rothko, Robert Rauschenberg, and Claes Oldenburg, and the impressive multimedia memorials of Antoni Tàpies, it houses a compelling collection of paintings and sculpture by the rising stars you're likely to come across in trendy city galleries. A ticket also entitles you to same-day entry into **The Geffen Contemporary** (same hours as above), further east at 152 N Central Ave, a former police garage now used for MOCA's edgier temporary shows. Across from the Geffen, **Little Tokyo** is an appealing collection of historic sites, restaurants, and galleries, highlighted by the comprehensive **Japanese American National Museum** (Tues–Sun 10am–5pm; $6), covering all aspects of local Japanese history and culture.

Back atop Bunker Hill, catercorner to MOCA, the superficial but amusing **Wells Fargo Museum** (Mon–Fri 9am–5pm; free), at the base of the shiny red towers of the Wells Fargo Center, tells the story of the bank of Gold Rush California. A few blocks southwest rise the sparkling glass tubes of the **Westin Bonaventure Hotel** (see "Accommodation," p.1108), whose lobby is an Escher-style labyrinth of spiraling ramps and balconies that are best negotiated with a color-coded map. But brace yourself and step inside for a ride in the glass-walled elevators that run up and down the outside of the building (famously showcased in the Clint Eastwood flick, *In the Line of Fire*), giving splendid views over much of the downtown and beyond.

Broadway

Although it's hard to picture now, **Broadway** was once LA's most fashionable shopping and entertainment district. Today it's largely taken over by the hustle and bustle of Hispanic clothing and trinket stores, all to a soundtrack of blaring salsa music. You can sample a vivid taste of the area at the broadly ethnic **Grand Central Market**, between Third and Fourth streets, where you'll find everything from pickled pigs' feet to sheep's brains. Right alongside, the whimsical terracotta facade of the 1918 **Million Dollar Theater** mixes buffalo heads with bald eagles, and was seen in the film *Blade Runner*, as was the neighboring 1893 **Bradbury Building**, no. 304, highlighted by a magnificent sunlit atrium surrounded by stylish wrought-iron balconies and open-cage elevators. While the moviehouse has since become a church, the **Los Angeles Theater**, 615 S Broadway, still shows movies during the annual "Last Remaining Seats" film festival in June (details at ⓦwww .laconservancy.org), and is even more extravagant, built in ninety days for the world premiere of Charlie Chaplin's *City Lights* in 1931. The best old moviehouse still in regular use, though, is the **Orpheum**, at no. 630, a neo–French Renaissance marvel of grand staircases and chandeliers. A few blocks south and west, don't miss the **Museum of Neon Art**, 501 W Olympic Blvd (Wed–Sat 11am–5pm, Sun noon–5pm; $5), featuring classic theater signs, more modern neon creations, and a range of strange kinetic art. Apart from the museum, the other major attraction in the area is the welter of commercial activity in the **Garment District**, bounded by Los Angeles and San Pedro streets and Seventh and Ninth avenues, where you can pick up decent fabric for as little as $2 per yard.

Around downtown

The LA sprawl begins as soon as you leave downtown, diverse environs cut through by freeways and with large distances separating their few points of interest. As such, it makes little sense to see them consecutively.

MacArthur Park and around

Reachable on the Red Line subway, the dilapidated patches of green and the large lake of dicey **MacArthur Park** are the nearest open spaces to the sidewalks of downtown, and teem with street vendors hawking their wares in front of busy swap meets, overlooked by the looming sign of the departed *Westlake Theatre*. Nearby, the **Grier-Musser Museum**, 403 S Bonnie Brae St (Wed–Sat noon–4pm; $6), offers a glimpse of the days when this now-decrepit neighborhood was a pleasant middle-class suburb of downtown, and the local Victorian houses boasted neo-Gothic turrets, Italianate windows, and gingerbread detailing. Surprisingly enough, some homes in the neighborhood still do. Just don't jump out of your car to investigate; the crime rate is among the city's highest. Half a mile west in a safer zone, the seminal **Bullocks Wilshire** department store, 3050 Wilshire Blvd, is the epitome of late 1920s Art Deco in LA, with a colossal copper tower, and has been reincarnated as the law library of adjacent **Southwestern University** (tour information ☏213/738-8240, ⓦwww.swlaw.edu/bullockswilshire).

Inside the **Ambassador Hotel**, 3400 Wilshire Blvd, the *Cocoanut Grove* club flourished from the early 1920s to the late 1940s, and the large ballroom featured in the 1937 and 1954 versions of *A Star Is Born*. The hotel's most notorious event occurred on June 5, 1968, when **Bobby Kennedy** was fatally shot in the hotel kitchen after his victory in the California Democratic Primary. Converted into a filmmaking location, nowadays the *Ambassador* is closed to public view and under threat of demolition (check out ⓦwww.theambassadorhotel.com for the latest).

Wilshire Boulevard continues west from the *Ambassador* into West LA (see p.1120). South of Wilshire, along Olympic Boulevard between Vermont and Western avenues, **Koreatown** is five times larger than the more touristy areas of Chinatown and Little Tokyo, and is home to the largest concentration of Koreans outside Korea. Beyond good authentic restaurants, though, there's not much for visitors to see here.

Exposition Park

South of downtown, across Exposition Boulevard from the fortress-like USC campus, **Exposition Park** is one of the most appreciated parks in LA. The **California Science Center** here, off Figueroa Street at 700 State Drive (daily 10am–5pm; $6; ☏323/724-3623, ⓦwww.casciencectr.org), contains enough enjoyable working models and thousands of gadgets to keep kids absorbed. Just outside, an **IMAX Theater** ($7.50, children $4.50; $1 extra for 3D shows) attracts youthful patrons of nature documentaries, while closer to Exposition Boulevard, but still part of the Science Center, the recently renovated **Air and Space Gallery** is marked by a sleek jet stuck to its facade and offers a series of satellites, telescopes, airplanes, and rockets, as well as the menacing presence of an LAPD helicopter "air ship" – to complement their constant drone in the skies above. To the south, the **California African American Museum**, 600 State Drive (Tues–Sun 10am–5pm; free; ⓦwww.caam.ca.gov), has stimulating exhibits on the history, art, and culture of America's black communities.

The **Natural History Museum of Los Angeles County**, 900 Exposition Blvd (Mon–Fri 9.30am–5pm, Sat & Sun 10am–5pm; $9; ☏213/763-3466, ⓦwww.nhm.org), is the nicest building in the park, with its echoey domes and travertine columns. Foremost among the exhibits is a tremendous stock of dinosaur skeletons that includes the skull of a Tyrannosaurus rex, and the frame of a Diatryma – a huge flightless bird. Other fascinating displays include Mayan pyramid murals and the reconstructed contents of a Mexican tomb. The last major sights in the park are the **LA Coliseum**, familiar as the site of the 1932 and 1984 Olympics and for its towering headless statues, and the **Rose Garden** (daily 10am–5pm; free), whose flowers are at their most fragrant in April and May, when the bulk of the 45,000 annual visitors come by to admire the 16,000 rose bushes.

South Central LA

South Central LA hardly ranks on the tourist circuit, but does have a few isolated points of interest. The population has historically been mostly black, but is increasingly Hispanic and Asian. It doesn't look so run-down at first sight, as it's mostly made up of detached bungalows with palm-shaded lawns, but just about all its residents get an abysmal deal in schooling and employment, and have little chance of climbing the social ladder and escaping. Testament to this bleak reality is the number of burned-out, vacant lots still undeveloped more than a decade after the 1992 **riots** that engulfed the area.

A crumbling reminder of the old days of black LA can be found along **Central Avenue** running south from downtown, where hot jazz clubs and fine hotels and restaurants once thrived. Only a few spots enliven the gloom now, including the wildly Streamline Moderne **Coca-Cola Bottling Plant**, 1334 S Central Ave, which resembles a giant white ocean liner, and the **African-American Firefighters Museum**, 1401 S Central Ave (Tues–Thurs 10am–2pm; donation), housed in LA's first all-black fire station, which operated from 1913 to 1980 and now displays historic equipment and memorabilia from the era. Several miles south, the **Dunbar Hotel**, 4225 S Central Ave, was the first US hotel built specifically for blacks and patronized by almost every prominent African-American from the 1930s to the 1950s. Although you can only see its restored lobby and facade – the structure is now used for elderly housing – the hotel is the site for the swinging Central Avenue Jazz Festival in August (details at ☎213/847-3169).

The district of **Watts**, on the southernmost fringe of downtown, achieved notoriety as the site of the six-day **Watts Riot** of August 1965 and the gun battle that killed Patti Hearst's Symbionese Liberation Army (SLA) kidnappers in 1975. Its only real attractions to casual visitors are the stunning, Gaudíesque **Watts Towers**, 1765 E 107th St, striking pieces of folk art constructed from iron, stainless steel, old bedframes, and cement, and decorated with fragments of bottles and around 70,000 crushed seashells. The towers are usually open on Saturdays, but the schedule can be erratic; call the adjacent Watts Towers Arts Center, 1727 E 107th St (Tues–Sat 10am–4pm, Sun noon–4pm; free; ☎323/847-4646, ⓦwww.artscenecal.com/WattsTowers.html), for more details.

Hollywood

If a single place-name encapsulates the LA dream of glamour, money, and overnight success, it's **Hollywood**. Millions of tourists arrive on pilgrimages; millions more flock here in pursuit of riches and glory. Those who do strike it rich here get out as soon as they can, just as they always have; the big film companies, too, long ago relocated, leaving Hollywood a blend of prostitutes, petty criminals, visiting tourists, and slumming hipsters – all under the shadow of grand old movie palaces and dive hotels. Recent attempts at renovation have tried to change this reality, at least superficially, but the district will doubtless never attain the mythical status it continues to hold in the minds of some of its more star-struck visitors.

HOLLYWOOD

Downtown ▲ ● ❶ ⓖ ⓗ & Los Feliz ▲

▲ Griffith Park

ACCOMMODATION
Banana Bungalow .... A
Dunes Sunset .... G
Hollywood International ...... F
Hollywood Metropolitan ..... H
Hollywood Roosevelt .... E
Orange Drive Manor .... D
Orchid Suites C
Renaissance Hollywood ...... B

RESTAURANTS, BARS, & CLUBS
Arena 15
Beauty Bar 7
Boardner's 6
Cat 'n' Fiddle 13
Club Lingerie 10
The Derby 1
Dragonfly 16
Florentine Gardens 12
Hampton's 14
The Knitting Factory 4
Lava Lounge 9
Musso & Frank Grill 3
Opium Den 8
The Palace 2
Roscoe's Chicken
and Waffles 11
The Ruby 5

John Anson Ford Theater

Hollywood Bowl

Hollywood Bowl Museum

Hollywood Heritage Museum

Kodak Theatre

Hollywood Entertainment Museum

Chinese Theatre

Movie star Sculpture

Hollywood & Highland Mall

El Capitan Theater

Hollywood History Museum

Egyptian Theater

Frederick's of Hollywood

Janes House

Stages Theater Center

Capitol Records Tower

Pantages Theater

Hollywood Palladium

Cinerama Dome

GOWER GULCH

HOLLYWOOD HILLS

WHITLEY HEIGHTS

Runyon Canyon Park

Wattles Park

N

500 yds

▲ Sunset Strip & West Hollywood

Melrose Avenue ▲

Mid-Wilshire ▲

Hollywood Forever Cemetery ▶ Paramount Studios ▶

A brief history of Hollywood

Once the home of the country's largest Presbyterian church, Hollywood started life as a **temperance colony** in 1887, intended to provide a sober, God-fearing alternative to raunchy downtown LA, eight miles away by rough country road. The film industry, of course, was drawn here from the East Coast not by puritanical morality, but by the predictable sunshine, low taxes, cheap labor, and diverse shooting locations – and as a way of dodging Thomas Edison's restrictive motion-picture patents. Nearby **Silver Lake** was the first (temporary) site of the movie business, but the first permanent studio opened in Hollywood in 1911, and within three years the place was packed with filmmakers such as **Cecil B. DeMille**, who shared his barn-converted office space with a horse and other budding magnates like Samuel Goldwyn, Adolph Zukor, and Jesse Lasky. The space has since reopened as the **Hollywood Heritage Museum**, 2100 N Highland Ave (Sat & Sun 10am–3.30pm; free; ☎323/974-4005, ⊛www.hollywoodheritage.org), exhibiting interesting antiques and treasures from the silent era.

The industry expanded fast, and eager new arrivals soon swamped the original small-scaled community. Once movie-making had proved itself to be a financially secure business – with the success of D.W. Griffith's racist epic **The Birth of a Nation** in 1914 – film production became a conglomerated, mechanical, and specialized system. Small companies either went bust or were incorporated into the big studios, which had by the 1930s almost all relocated to more distant LA digs in Culver City, Burbank, and West LA – of the big names, only Paramount remained.

The **demise of the studio system** came in the 1950s, through government antitrust actions, the postwar revival of the international film industry, and, of course, television. A few lean decades followed. In the 1970s and 1980s, though, directors like Steven Spielberg and George Lucas re-engineered American movies around the concept of the **blockbuster** – high-priced, special-effects-laden epics that would appeal to as a wide range of audiences as possible. Thanks to this trend, and the ongoing financial consolidation of American media enterprises, Hollywood continues to be a symbol for the enduring success of American movies – slick, entertaining fare with gorgeous actors and happy endings – and a mechanized dream factory of international proportions.

Central Hollywood

The myths, magic, and mystery of **Central Hollywood** create a pervasive sense of nostalgia that makes the area deeply appealing in a way no measure of commercialism can ever diminish. Although you're much more likely to find a porno theater than spot a real star, new investments and redevelopment projects have taken root in places, most prominently the **Hollywood Highland** theater and retail complex at the eponymous intersection. Nevertheless, this district can still get hairy after dark, so keep one eye on your pocketbook.

The obvious place to begin exploring Hollywood Boulevard is the junction of **Hollywood and Vine** – the legendary location for budding stars to be "spotted" by big-shot directors and whisked off to fame and fortune, though you'll find little more than a subway stop and low-rent businesses here these days. At 6608 Hollywood Blvd, the purple and pink **Frederick's of Hollywood** has been (under-) dressing Hollywood's sex goddesses since 1947, as well as mortal bodies all over the world via mail order. Inside, the **Celebrity Lingerie Hall of Fame** (Mon–Fri 10am–9pm, Sat 10am–7pm, Sun 11am–6pm; free) displays some of the company's most famous corsets, bras, and panties, donated by glitterati ranging from Lana Turner to Cher.

A little further on, the **Egyptian Theater**, at no. 6712, was financed by impresario Sid Grauman in a modest attempt to re-create the Temple of Thebes. The very first Hollywood premiere (*Robin Hood*) took place here in 1922. Now owned by the city, this great old building has been restored by American Cinematheque, a film preservation group that plays an assortment of revival and art-house films, as well as a promotional documentary chronicling the rise of Hollywood as America's movie capital (hour-long shows Sat & Sun 2pm & 3.30pm; $7; Ⓦwww.americancinematheque.com). No visitor should miss the mundane yet magical handprints and footprints in the concrete concourse of the **Chinese Theatre**, across Highland Avenue at 6925 Hollywood Blvd. Actress Norma Talmadge (supposedly by accident) trod in wet cement while visiting the construction site, and the practice has continued ever since, from Mary Pickford and Douglas Fairbanks Sr, at the 1927 opening of *King of Kings*, to modern ceremonies for the likes of Anthony Hopkins. For many decades, this has been *the* spot for movie premieres, an odd version of a classical Chinese temple, replete with quasi-Chinese motifs and upturned dragon tails. Unfortunately, the theater has recently been swallowed by the colossal **Hollywood Highland** complex, an uninspired mall offering the pricey chain merchants, though its **Kodak Theatre** is notable as the site of the annual Academy Awards.

The **Hollywood Roosevelt**, opposite at 7000 Hollywood Blvd, was movieland's first luxury hotel, its *Cinegrill* restaurant hosting the likes of W.C. Fields and F. Scott Fitzgerald, not to mention legions of hangers-on. Across the street, the **Hollywood Entertainment Museum**, 7021 Hollywood Blvd (Tues–Sun 11am–6pm; $8.75, students $4.50; Ⓣ323/465-7900, Ⓦwww.hollywoodmuseum.com), houses a collection of movie- and TV-related knick-knacks that is mainly worth a look for the full set of the TV show *Cheers* and the bridge of the *Enterprise* from *Star Trek*. Some of the museum's most intriguing items – namely the Max Factor make-up and beauty collection – have been relocated to the **Hollywood History Museum**, just southeast at 1660 N Highland Ave (daily 10am–6pm; $7; Ⓣ323/464-7770), which exhibits on four levels the fashion, sets, make-up, special effects, and art design of the Golden Age of movies.

Further south, near Santa Monica Boulevard and Gower Street, **Hollywood Forever Cemetery** (daily 8am–5pm; free) is the district's most famous graveyard, and features all manner of buried celebrities. A mausoleum contains the resting place of **Rudolph Valentino**, the celebrated screen lover who died aged just 31 in 1926, and to this day on each anniversary of his passing (August 23), at least one "Lady in Black" – as his posthumous devotees are known – will likely be found mourning. The ostentatious memorial to **Douglas Fairbanks Sr**, who with his wife Mary Pickford did much to introduce social snobbery among Tinseltown types, is just outside. South of the cemetery, **Paramount Studios**, 5555 Melrose Ave, no longer offers tours, though you can still glimpse the studio's famed **gate**. However, the original studio entrance – which Gloria Swanson rode through in *Sunset Boulevard* – is now inaccessible.

Griffith Park

The greenery and mountain slopes that make up vast **Griffith Park** northeast of Hollywood (daily 5.30am–10.30pm, mountain roads close at dusk; free) offer a welcome respite from the often mind-numbing chaos of LA, offering lush fern and azalea gardens, a bird sanctuary, and many miles of fine trails – though its **LA Zoo**, 5333 Zoo Drive (daily 10am–5pm; $8.25, children $3.25; Ⓣ323/644-6400, Ⓦwww.lazoo.org), pales in comparison to its San Diego counterpart (see

△ Outside Mann's Chinese Theatre, Hollywood

p.1096). The landmark **Griffith Observatory**, 2800 E Observatory Rd (closed for renovation until 2005), has been used as a backdrop in innumerable Hollywood films, most famously *Rebel Without a Cause*, and the surrounding acres add up to the largest municipal park in the country. Above the landscaped flat sections, the hillsides are rough and wild, marked by foot and bridle paths that lead into desolate but appealingly unspoiled terrain with great views over the LA basin and out to the ocean (provided the city smog isn't too thick). One way to explore is on a rented **bike** from Spokes 'n' Stuff, near the park ranger station, at 4400 Crystal Springs Rd (weekends during daylight hours; $6 per hour; T323/662-6573). Definitely worth a look is the **Gene Autry Museum of Western Heritage**, 4700 Western Heritage Way, which is devoted to true Wild West history and its Hollywood interpretation (Tues–Sun 10am–5pm, Thurs closes at 8pm; $7.50, children $3; T323/667-2000, Wwww.autry-museum .org). The park is safe by day, but has a reputation for violence after dark.

The Hollywood Hills

The views from the **Hollywood Hills** take in a bizarre assortment of opulent properties, perhaps most famously the **Chemosphere** at 776 Torreyson Drive, a UFO-like house balanced on a huge pedestal. Around these canyons and slopes, which run from Hollywood itself into Benedict Canyon above Beverly Hills, mansions are so commonplace that only the half-dozen fully blown castles really stand out. On Mulholland Drive are Rudolph Valentino's extravagant **Falcon Lair** (1436 Bella Drive) and Errol Flynn's **Mulholland House** (7740 Mulholland Drive). Guided tours (see box, p.1105) can point out which is which, but for the most part you can't get close to the most elaborate dwellings anyway, and none is open to the public. For an up-close look at some of the area's landmark architecture, take in a concert at the **Hollywood Bowl**, 2301 N Highland Ave (T323/850-2000, Wwww.hollywoodbowl.org), the massive concrete bandshell that's been built and reconstructed three times in the last eighty years. Although the summer music offerings are rarely highbrow, it's as good a spot as any to hear the roar of the *1812 Overture*.

Throughout Hollywood, you can see the **Hollywood Sign**, erected as a property advertisement in 1923 (when it spelled "Hollywoodland," until 1949) and illuminated with four thousand light bulbs. The sign is also famous as a suicide spot, though few have followed the 1932 example of would-be movie star Peg Entwhistle, who started out at Beachwood Drive (a route that affords a fine view of the sign) and picked a path up through the thick bush to leap to her death from the 50ft "H." Nowadays, infrared cameras and radar-activated zoom lenses have been installed to catch graffiti writers. Curious tourists who can't resist a close look are liable for a steep fine.

West LA

LA's Westside begins immediately beyond Hollywood in **West LA**, bordered by the foothills of the Santa Monica Mountains to the north and the Santa Monica Freeway to the south. West LA is the place where the city's nouveau riche flaunt their fortunes most conspicuously, from the trendy confines of West Hollywood and shadowy wealth of Bel Air to the high-priced shopping strips of Beverly Hills.

The Museum Mile

From downtown to West LA, the area around Wilshire Boulevard is known rather amorphously as **Mid-Wilshire**. Toward the western side of this strip, the **Miracle Mile**, between La Brea and Fairfax avenues, was the premier property development of the 1930s. Many of the area's department stores have since moved out, but recent development has created a "**Museum Mile**" in their place, the city's designated arts center. The museums begin at the **La Brea Tar Pits**, where an astonishing assortment of prehistoric bones has been recovered. For thousands of years, animals who tried to drink from the thin layer of water covering this smelly pool of tar became stuck fast and preserved for posterity; it's now surrounded by life-sized replicas of such victims as mastodons and saber-toothed tigers, some of them reconstructed and on display next door at the impressive **George C. Page Museum**, 5801 Wilshire Blvd (Mon–Fri 9.30am–5pm, weekends opens at 10am; $6, students $3.50; ℡323/934-7243, Ⓦwww.tarpits.org).

On the west side of the La Brea Tar Pits, the enormous **LA County Museum of Art (LACMA)**, 5905 Wilshire Blvd (Mon, Tues & Thurs noon–8pm, Fri noon–9pm, Sat & Sun 11am–8pm; $9, students $5, children free; ℡323/857-6000, Ⓦwww.lacma.org), comprises a set of drab blocks (due to be replaced in a few years by a bizarre Rem Koolhaas design), but its collections are among the best in the world. The **Fearing Collection** of funereal masks and sculpted guardian figures from pre-Columbian Mexico is highly impressive, but where the museum really excels is in its specializations: **German Expressionist** prints and drawings, scrolls and ceramics in the **Pavilion for Japanese Art**, and entire rooms devoted to Auguste Rodin, 17th-century Dutch masters, rare jewelry and porcelain, and Hollywood fashion designers. LACMA continues on to the western end of the Museum Mile to Fairfax Avenue, where blockbuster shows and children's art are the highlights of **LACMA West** (same hours and ticket), occupying a former department store building that has been compared to an oversized perfume bottle.

Further west, the **Petersen Automotive Museum**, 6060 Wilshire Blvd (Tues–Sun 10am–6pm, Fri until 9pm; $10, parking $6; ℡323/930-2277, Ⓦwww.petersen.org), pays homage to motorized vehicles of all kinds on three floors, with special exhibits such as the Golden Age of custom cars, Hollywood prop cars, and "million-dollar" vehicles.

West Hollywood

North along Fairfax Avenue from the Museum Mile, **West Hollywood** was for many years notorious for after-hours vice clubs and general debauchery. Since its 1984 incorporation as a city, however, it's become much more upmarket, home to Los Angeles's prominent – and affluent – gay community, as well as elderly residents and Russian immigrants. **Melrose Avenue**, LA's trendiest shopping street and one of the unmistakable symbols of Southern California, runs parallel to the less eventful main drag of **Santa Monica Boulevard**, where neon and Art Deco abound among a fluorescent rash of designer and secondhand boutiques, exotic antique shops, and avant-garde galleries. **La Brea Avenue**, a less-heralded shopping strip, runs perpendicular to the east side of the Melrose district, offering more space, fewer tourists, and chic clothing stores, upscale restaurants. and even trendier galleries.

North of West Hollywood, on either side of La Cienega Boulevard, is the two-mile-odd conglomeration of restaurants, hotels, billboards, and nightclubs on Sunset Boulevard known as the **Sunset Strip**, one of LA's best areas for nightlife. Its clubs first appeared in the early 1920s, along what was then a dusty dirt road linking the Hollywood movie studios with West LA. With the rise of TV the Strip declined, only reviving in the 1960s when a scene developed around the landmark *Whisky-a-Go-Go* club, no. 8901, which featured seminal psychedelic rock bands such as The Doors, Love, and Buffalo Springfield, and later in the 1970s around the *Sunset Hyatt* hotel, no. 8401, the infamous "Riot House" where Led Zeppelin raced motorcycles in the hallways and rock stars committed countless acts of debauchery. Greta Garbo was one of many stars to appreciate the quirky, if gloomy, Norman castle of the **Chateau Marmont Hotel**, towering over the east end of the Sunset Strip at no. 8221 (see "Accommodation," p.1108). Howard Hughes used to rent the entire penthouse so he could keep an eye on the bathing beauties around the pool below, and comedian John Belushi died of a heroin overdose in the bungalow he used as his LA home.

Beverly Hills and around

Beverly Hills is one of the world's wealthiest residential areas, patrolled by more cops per capita than anywhere else in the US. Glorified by immaculate shops (such as those on **Rodeo Drive**), squeaky-clean streets, and ostentatious displays – notably the faux-European shopping alley **Rodeo Two** – the city is undoubtedly the height of LA pretension. Still, there are a number of worthwhile and unassuming spots for visitors interested in things other than commodities. The **Museum of Television and Radio** (Wed–Sun noon–5pm; $6; ☎310/786-1025, ⓦwww.mtr.org) is one such place, chronicling fifty years of the boob tube, while the **Beverly Hills Trolley** (summer & Dec daily noon–5pm; rest of year Sat noon–4pm; $5) offers tourists a forty-minute glimpse of the city's highlights, departing hourly from the corner of Dayton Way and Rodeo Drive. For a view of the city's assorted art and architecture, a fifty-minute trolley tour takes you to a number of less familiar, though still compelling, sights (Sat 11am; $5). By contrast, one of the city's most prominent icons, the pink **Beverly Hills Hotel**, at Sunset Boulevard and Rodeo Drive, has been entertaining local bigwigs and Hollywood royalty in its stately rooms and *Polo Lounge* bar for more than ninety years.

In the verdant canyons and foothills above Sunset Boulevard, palatial estates lie hidden behind landscaped security gates. **Benedict Canyon Drive** climbs past many of them, including, at 1740 Green Acres Drive, Harold Lloyd's **Green Acres**. With its secret passageways and large screening room, the home survives intact, though much of the spacious grounds, which contained a waterfall and nine-hole golf course, have been broken up into smaller lots.

Just outside Beverly Hills, **Century City** is a charmless expanse of concrete and steel that was once the studio lot for 20th Century-Fox, which now stands off-limits at 10201 Pico Blvd. A bit further east, the **Museum of Tolerance**, 9786 W Pico Blvd (April–Oct Mon–Thurs 11.30am–6pm, Fri 11.30am–5pm, Sun 11am–7.30pm; Nov–March closes at 3pm on Fri; $10, students $7; ☎310/553-8403, ⓦwww.wiesenthal.com/mot), uses videotaped interviews to provide LA's frankest examination of the 1992 riots, and looks at international hate and intolerance in general, tracing the rise of Nazism to a harrowing conclusion in a replica gas chamber.

Westwood

West of Beverly Hills and north of Wilshire Boulevard, **Westwood** is one of LA's more user-friendly neighborhoods, a grouping of low-slung redbrick buildings that went up in the late 1920s around Broxton Avenue, along with the nearby campus of the nascent **University of California at Los Angeles (UCLA)**. Known then as "Westwood Village," it's an area that is easily explored on foot, and one very much shaped by the proximity of the campus, the lifeblood of the area. Once LA's prime movie-going district, Westwood Village has lost some of its cinematic eminence due to a lack of parking, but remains the most densely packed movie-theater district in the country, and its 1931 **Westwood Village Theater**, 961 Broxton Ave, is still often used for premieres or special "sneak previews" to gauge audience reactions.

South of Westwood, Wilshire Boulevard exploded in the 1970s with oil-rich highrise developments and condominium towers. Inside one such building, on the corner with Westwood Boulevard, is the **UCLA Hammer Museum** (Tues, Sat & Sat noon–7pm, Wed–Fri noon–9pm; $5, parking $2.75; ☏310/443-7000, ⓦwww.hammer.ucla.edu), amassed over seven decades by Armand Hammer, flamboyant boss of Occidental Petroleum, and now administered by UCLA. The works by Rembrandt and Rubens aren't so stunning, but Van Gogh's intense and radiant *Hospital at Saint Rémy* is a jewel and compelling temporary exhibits provide another draw. Outside the museum, Hammer's marble tomb in **Westwood Memorial Park**, 1218 Glendon Ave, stands near the lipstick-covered plaque that marks the final resting place of Marilyn Monroe.

The Getty Center

Towering over the surrounding area, the **Getty Center**, near the Sepulveda Pass north of Wilshire Blvd (daily 10am–6pm, Sat & Sun closes 9pm; free, parking $5; ☏310/440-7300, ⓦwww.getty.edu), was designed by Richard Meier at a cost of $1 billion. A towering modernist temple clad in acres of travertine, this is LA's biggest attempt to make a mark on the international art scene, its various buildings devoted to conservation, acquisition, and other philanthropic tasks, and its surrounding gardens arranged with rigid geometric precision. Parking reservations are required for peak hours such as weekends and holidays; otherwise, take MTA bus #561, which stops on Sepulveda Boulevard.

Two years after the original Getty museum opened in Malibu in 1974 (see p.1125), oil magnate John Paul Getty died, leaving it $1.3 billion. Obliged by law to spend a percentage of its now $5 billion endowment every year, it can outbid anyone to get what it wants, which is usually anything except contemporary art – a real deficiency in the museum's collections.

Still, the quality of the **exhibits** is extraordinary, especially in the rooms devoted to decorative arts, where you can see a formidable array of ornate French furniture from the reign of Louis XIV, with clocks, chandeliers, tapestries, and gilt-edged commodes filling several overwhelmingly opulent chambers. Although Getty himself was much less interested in painting, a sizeable collection has been amassed since his death, featuring all the major names from the thirteenth century on, including Van Gogh's *Irises* and several Rembrandt portraits. Elsewhere in the museum, photography is well represented with works by Man Ray, Moholy-Nagy and other notables, and there's also a rich assortment of classical, Renaissance, and Baroque sculpture – highlighted by Bernini's *Boy with a Dragon*, depicting a plump, possibly angelic toddler bending back the jaw of a dragon with surprising ease.

Venice, Santa Monica, and Malibu

Set along an unbroken twenty-mile stretch of white-sand beaches, the small, self-contained communities that line **Santa Monica Bay** feature some of the best vistas LA has to offer, with none of the smog or searing heat that can make the rest of the metropolis unbearable. The entire area is well served by public transportation, near enough to the airport, and a wide choice of accommodation makes it a good base for seeing the rest of the city.

Venice

Venice was laid out in marshlands in 1905 by developer Abbot Kinney as a romantic replica of a northern Italian city, complete with a twenty-mile network of canals. The original plan to create a West Coast art-and-culture zone failed, followed by a more successful turn as an amusement park; however, the coming of the automobile industry finished it off altogether. Most of the canals were filled in, and the area fell into disrepair and was later taken over by grim oil wells (Orson Welles's 1958 film *Touch of Evil* starred the then-derelict Venice as a seedy Mexican border town). Kinney was, however, ahead of his time, and the pseudo-European atmosphere has made Venice one of the coast's trendier spots. Chic cafés and restaurants abound near the beach, where an alternative art scene centers on the **Beyond Baroque Literary Arts Center**, 681 Venice Blvd (Tues–Fri 10am–5pm, Sat noon–5pm; ☎ 310/822-3006, ⊛ www.beyond-baroque.org), and the easy, laid-back vibe attracts countless slackers and hipsters.

The town's main artery, **Windward Avenue**, runs from the beach into what was the Grand Circle of the canal system. Its original Neoclassical **arcade**, around the intersection with Pacific Avenue, is alive with health-food shops, secondhand record stores, and roller-skate rental stands, although less and less of it remains with each passing year. Nearby, the few remaining **canals** display renovated white bridges and pedestrian-friendly footpaths (best accessed northbound on Dell Avenue from Washington Boulevard), along with a bevy of the latest modern and postmodern housing designs.

Southerly **Venice Beach** itself is the reason most people come here. Nowhere else does LA parade itself quite so openly as along the wide pathway of **Venice Boardwalk**, packed year-round at weekends and every day in summer with jugglers, fire-eaters, roller-skating guitar players, and people-watchers. South of Windward is **Muscle Beach**, a legendary outdoor weightlifting center where serious-looking dudes pump serious iron, and high-flying gymnasts swing on the rings and bars. If you'd like to check the place out yourself, contact the Venice Beach Recreation Center, 1800 Ocean Front Walk (☎ 310/399-2775), for more information. Near the pier, outlets such as Spokes 'n' Stuff (☎ 310/395-4748), rent out **bikes** and **rollerblades**.

At night Venice Beach is a dangerous place taken over by street gangs and drug dealers, and walking on the beach after dark is illegal.

Santa Monica

Immediately north of Venice, **Santa Monica** is the oldest and biggest of LA's resorts, perched on palm-tree-shaded bluffs, or "the palisades," above the blue Pacific. Once a wild beachfront playground, it's now a self-consciously healthy and liberal community with a large expatriate British and Irish contingent.

The Santa Monica beachfront grew into a giant funfair city when it was linked to downtown LA by the suburban streetcar system. It was the location for many of the underworld stories of Raymond Chandler, most memorably as "Bay City" in *Farewell My Lovely*, but today Chandler wouldn't recognize the place. The gambling ships and bathing clubs have gone, and Santa Monica is now well known for its tight rent-control policy and stringent planning and development regulations.

Santa Monica reaches nearly three miles inland, but most spots of interest are within a few blocks of the beach. Make your first stop the **visitor center** (daily 10am–4pm; ☎ 310/393-7593, ⊛ www.santamonica.com), in a kiosk just south of Santa Monica Boulevard in **Palisades Park**, the enjoyable, cypress-tree-lined strip along the top of the bluffs which makes for striking views of the surf below. Two blocks east of Ocean Avenue, the **Third Street Promenade**, a pedestrianized stretch with street vendors, buskers, and itinerant evangelists, is the closest LA comes to having an urban energy, though colorless chain stores are crowding out many of the quirky boutiques and oddball shops, especially north of Arizona Avenue. Still, the rest of the Promenade remains by far the best place to come for alfresco dining, beer-drinking, and people-watching.

The real focal point of Santa Monica is down below, on the **beach**, which is better for sunbathing than swimming, and around the refurbished **Santa Monica pier**, which boasts a well-restored 1922 wooden **carousel** (daily 9am–6pm; 50¢) that was featured in the 1973 movie *The Sting*. Although the familiar thrill rides of **Pacific Park** (summer daily 11am–11pm, Sat & Sun closes at 12.30am; $20, kids $11; ☎310/260-8744, ⓦwww.pacpark.com) may catch your eye, save your money for the **Santa Monica Pier Aquarium** (summer Mon–Fri 2–6pm, Sat & Sun 12.30–6.30pm; $3; ☎310/393-6149, ⓦwww.healthebay.org/smpa), just below the pier at 1600 Ocean Front Walk, where you can find out about marine biology and get your fingers wet touching sea anemones and starfish.

Five miles north along the curving **Pacific Coast Highway (PCH)**, the opulent **Getty Villa**, 17985 PCH (☎310/440-7300, ⓦwww.getty.edu/museum/villa.html), is the site of the original Getty Museum. Poised above the ocean, the complex is closed until 2005, when it will re-emerge as a showcase for antiquities.

Malibu

Twenty miles north of Santa Monica at the top of the bay, **Malibu** is a whole other world, its beach-colony houses owned by those famous enough to need isolation and rich enough to afford it. It's not all that impressive on arrival, however, with ramshackle surf shops and fast-food stands scattered along PCH around the graceful **Malibu Pier**. **Surfrider Beach** here was the surfing capital of the world in the 1950s and early 1960s, as seen in the *Beach Blanket Bingo* movies of Annette Funicello and Frankie Avalon (the surf is best in late summer; check the surfing report at ⓦwww.surfrider.org). Just beyond is **Malibu Lagoon State Park** (daily 9am–7pm; parking $7), a nature reserve and bird refuge, and nearby is the **Adamson House** (grounds 8am–sunset, house Wed–Sat 11am–3pm; $3; ☎310/456-8432, ⓦwww.adamsonhouse.org), a stunning Spanish Colonial–style home featuring opulent decor and colorful tilework.

Most Malibu homes are tucked away in the narrow canyons on the fringes of town. There's very little to see, despite tourists' futile attempts to peek into the exclusive **Malibu Colony** celebrity retreat, located along an unmarked stretch near PCH. You'd do better to visit **Malibu Creek State Park**, on Las Virgenes Road to the north near Mulholland Drive, where 20th Century-Fox filmed many Tarzan pictures, as well as the TV show *M★A★S★H*. The 4000-acre park includes a large lake, some waterfalls, and nearly fifteen miles of hiking trails. Further west, the **Paramount Ranch**, 2813 Cornell Rd, is another studio backlot with a phony rail crossing, cemetery, and Western movie set used for, among other things, the TV drama *Dr. Quinn Medicine Woman*.

Five miles along the coast from Malibu Pier, **Zuma Beach** is the largest and most crowded of the Los Angeles County beaches. Adjacent **Point Dume State Beach**, below the imposing promontory of Point Dume, is a lot more relaxed, and the rocks at its southern tip, **Pirate's Cove**, are a good place to view seals and migrating gray whales in winter. At the northwestern edge of LA County, **Leo Carrillo** ("ca-REE-oh") **State Beach Park**, 35000 PCH, sits at the end of MTA bus route #434. The mile-long sandy beach is divided by Sequit Point, a bluff with underwater caves and a tunnel you can pass through at low tide, and is also one of LA's best campgrounds (see p.1107).

The South Bay and LA Harbor

South from LA along PCH, beyond the runways of LAX and the oil refineries of squalid El Segundo, is an eight-mile coastal strip of the quieter and less pretentious South Bay beach towns: **Manhattan Beach**, **Hermosa Beach**, and **Redondo Beach**. Each has a beckoning strip of white sand – much more open to the public than those around Malibu – and Manhattan and Hermosa are especially well equipped for surfing and beach sports. They're also well connected by the regular #439 bus to downtown LA. To the south are **Long Beach** – site of the LA Harbor – and **Catalina Island**.

Long Beach

Thanks to a billion-dollar clean-up, downtown **Long Beach** is no longer the seedy stomping grounds of off-duty sailors that it was decades ago. These days, **Pine Avenue** is an enjoyable stretch of restored architecture and antique stores (linked by the Blue Line light rail to downtown LA; see p.1105), but the main reason most tourists come here, to the far side of LA's massive harbor, is to see the **Queen Mary** (daily 10am–6pm; $25 self-guided tours; ☎562/435-3511, ⓦwww.queenmary.com). The Cunard flagship from the 1930s until the 1960s, the boat is now a luxury hotel, and the guided tours ($5 extra) present a sentimentalized version of its days of elegance and refinement. Across the bay along Thoreline Drive, the **Aquarium of the Pacific** (daily 9am–6pm; $19, children $10; ☎562/590-3100, ⓦwww.aquariumofpacific.org) is a terrific exploration of aquatic flora and fauna from geographic and climatic zones around the world, while further west, the **Long Beach Museum of Art**, 2300 E Ocean Blvd (Tues–Sun 11am–5pm; $5; ☎562/439-2119, ⓦwww.lbma.org), is the home of some of LA's more experimental modern artworks.

Santa Catalina Island

The enticing island of **Santa Catalina**, twenty miles offshore from Long Beach, has been in private hands since 1811, when the resident Tongva natives were forced to resettle on the mainland. Most of it remains a wilderness, devoted to the conservation of unique species such as the **Catalina shrew** (so rare it's only been sighted twice), and tourism has been held largely at bay. Hotels are unobtrusive among the whimsical architecture, and cars are largely forbidden; consequently, the two thousand islanders walk, ride bikes, or drive golf carts. **Ferry** trips to Catalina ($30–42) run several times daily from Long Beach. Operators include Catalina Cruises (☎1-800/228-2546), Catalina Express (☎1-800/481-3470, ⓦwww.catalinaexpress.com), and, from Newport Beach, Catalina Passenger Service (☎949/673-5245).

The island's one town, **AVALON**, can be fully explored on foot in an hour, with maps issued by the Chamber of Commerce at the foot of the ferry pier (☎310/510-1520, ⓦwww.visitcatalina.org). Begin at the sumptuous Art Deco **Avalon Casino**, 1 Casino Way, a 1920s structure that still shows movies featuring mermaid murals, gold-leaf ceiling motifs, an Art Deco ballroom, and a small **museum** (daily 10.30am–4pm, Jan–March closed Thurs; $2) displaying Native American artifacts from Catalina's past. On the slopes above, the **Zane Grey Pueblo Hotel**, 199 Chimes Tower Rd (☎310/510-0966, ⓦwww.zanegreyhotel.com; ❺), is the former home of the Western author, who visited Catalina to film *The Vanishing American* and liked the place so much he never left. The hotel's seventeen rooms are themed after his books, and the pool is shaped like an arrowhead.

Accommodation in Avalon is pricey – the least expensive hotel is usually the *Atwater*, 125 Sumner Ave (☎1-800/626-1496; ❸), and the most is the sumptuous, six-room *Inn on Mount Ada* (☎310/510-2030, ⓦwww.catalina .com/mtada; ❾), with sweeping ocean views. Budget options are the one mountainside and three seaside **campgrounds** (☎310/510-8368, ⓦwww .scico.com/camping; $12 per person, children $6), though most of them are fairly primitive and isolated.

Anaheim: Disneyland and around

In the early 1950s, illustrator and filmmaker Walt Disney conceived a theme park where his hugely popular characters – Mickey Mouse, Donald Duck, Goofy, and the rest – would come to life, animated quite literally, and his fab-ulously successful company would rake in even more money from them. He chose the **Orange County** burg of Anaheim as the location for **Disneyland** on the hunch that these acres of orange groves, thirty miles southeast of down-town LA, would become Southern California's next major focus of population growth – which they did. Besides Disneyland, the area has a couple of other attractions, notably the smaller **Knott's Berry Farm** theme park and the **Richard Nixon Museum and Library** in Yorba Linda.

Disneyland

To make the most of **Disneyland**, 1313 Harbor Blvd (summer daily 8am–1am; rest of year Mon–Fri 10am–6pm, Sat 9am–midnight, Sun 9am–10pm; $47 adults, $37 kids, parking $8; ☎714/781-4565, ⓦdisneyland .com), just throw yourself right into it. Don't think twice about anything (including the high admission price) and go on every ride you can. As for **accommodation**, you're better off visiting the park just for the day and spending the night elsewhere, as most of the **hotels** and **motels** nearby cost well in excess of $75 per night (see "Accommodation," p.1109). Both Disneyland and the California Adventure are 45 minutes by **car** from down-town using the Santa Ana Freeway. Arrive early, as traffic and ride lines quick-ly become nightmarish, especially in the summer; and keep in mind that you're not permitted to bring your own **food** to either park.

Among Disneyland's best **rides** are three in **Adventureland**: the Indiana Jones Adventure, an interactive archeological dig and 1930s-style newsreel show leading up to a giddy journey along 2500ft of skull-encrusted corridors with fireballs, falling rubble, venomous snakes, and, inevitably, a rolling boulder finale; the Pirates of the Caribbean, a boat trip through underground caverns, giving you the chance to sing along with animatronic pirates; and the Haunted Mansion, a riotous "doom buggy" tour in the company of the house spooks. By contrast, **Frontierland** has mainly lower-end Wild West–themed carnival attractions, **Fantasyland** low-tech fairy-tale rides, and **Toontown**, a cartoon-ish zone aimed at the kindergarten set. It's more worthwhile to zip right through these areas and head straight for **Tomorrowland**, Disney's vision of the future, where the Space Mountain roller coaster plunges through the pitch-blackness of outer space, the Star Tours ride simulates a journey into the world of George Lucas, and Innoventions offers a fun opportunity to look at, and play with, the latest special effects.

The latest adjunct to Disneyland is the **California Adventure**, technically a separate park, but connected in architecture, style, and spirit – though a lot less fun. Aside from its more exciting roller coasters and slightly better food, the Adventure is really just another "land" to visit on your Disney trek, albeit a much bigger and more expensive one: you cannot get access to both parks with a single-day admission ticket. Instead, you either have to shell out another $47 or spend $99 for a two-day pass that covers both.

Knott's Berry Farm

If you're a bit fazed by the excesses of Disneyland, you might prefer the more down-to-earth **Knott's Berry Farm**, four miles northwest, off the Santa Ana Freeway at 8039 Beach Blvd (summer Sun–Thurs 9am–11pm, Fri & Sat 9am–midnight; rest of year Mon–Fri 10am–6pm, Sat 10am–10pm, Sun 10am–7pm; $43, children $33; ☎714/220-5200, ⓦwww.knotts.com), whose roller coasters are far more exciting than anything at its rival. Although there are ostensibly six themed lands here, you should spend most or all of your time in just two areas: **Fiesta Village**, home to the Jaguar, a high-flying coaster that spins you around the park concourse; and the **Boardwalk**, which is all about heart-thumping thrill rides. Knott's has recently added its own adjacent water park, **Soak City USA** (May–Sept only, hours vary but generally 10am–8pm; $24, children $17, $13 for entry after 3pm), offering twenty-one rides of various heights and speeds.

Richard Nixon Library and Birthplace

Mickey Mouse may be its most famous resident, but conservative Orange County's favorite son is former president **Richard Milhous Nixon**, born in 1913 in what's now freeway-caged **Yorba Linda**, eight miles northeast of Disneyland. His birthplace and final resting place at 18001 Yorba Linda Blvd (Mon–Sat 10am–5pm, Sun 11am–5pm; $6, kids $2; ☎714/993-5075, ⓦwww.nixonfoundation.org) is an unrelentingly hagiographic library and museum that features oversized gifts from world leaders, amusing campaign memorabilia, a 12ft high, 600lb chunk of the Berlin Wall, and a collection of obsequious letters written by and to Nixon.

Throughout the museum, Nixon's face leers down in Orwellian fashion from almost every wall, but only in the **Presidential Auditorium** do you get the chance to ask him a question, although the choice is limited to those programmed into a computer, as are the stock answers – which do not include "I am not a crook."

Orange County Coast

A string of towns stretching from the edge of the LA Harbor to the border of San Diego County 35 miles south, the **Orange County Coast** is chic suburbia with a shoreline: swanky beachside houses line the sands, and the general ambiance is easygoing, libertarian, and affluent. As the names of the main towns suggest – **Huntington Beach**, **Newport Beach**, and **Laguna Beach** – most of the good reasons to come here involve sea and sand, though a handful of museums and festivals can also make for an interesting excursion as well. Check out the **International Surfing Museum**, 411 Olive Ave, Huntington Beach (Wed–Sun noon–5pm, summer open daily; $3; ☎714/960-3483, ⓦwww.surfingmuseum.org), and Laguna Beach's **Pageant of the Masters** (select August days 8.30pm; $15–65; ☎949/494-1145 or 1-800/487-3378, ⓦwww.foapom.com), a strange spectacle in which participants dress up as characters from famous paintings. To the far south, **San Juan Capistrano** merits a stop as the site of the best-kept of all the Californian **missions**, Ortega Highway and Camino Capistrano (daily 8.30am–5pm; $6; ☎949/234-1300, ⓦwww.missionsjc.com).

The San Gabriel and San Fernando valleys

The northern limit of LA is defined by two long valleys lying over the hills from the central basin, starting close to one another a few miles north of downtown and spanning outwardly in opposite directions – east to the deserts around Palm Springs, west to Ventura on the Central Coast. Although derided by Angelenos, the valleys do feature a few worthwhile points of interest.

The San Gabriel Valley

East of Pasadena, ten miles north of downtown LA, the **San Gabriel Valley** was settled by farmers and ranchers on the lands of the eighteenth-century Mission San Gabriel – still tourable at 428 S Mission Drive (daily 9am–4.30pm; $5; ☎626/457-3035, ⓦsangabrielmission.org), in the heart of the small town of **San Gabriel**. The Valley's main appeal, though, is **Pasadena**, which started as a luxury resort in the 1880s, then became a residential area and underwent a major renovation in the 1980s, with modern shopping centers slipping in behind 1920s facades, and the blocks around the historic shopping precinct of **Old Pasadena** along Colorado Boulevard, now fashionable for their restaurants, cinemas, and bookstores (and accessible on the Gold Line light rail route).

Aside from its famous **Rose Parade** in January and **Rose Bowl** stadium west of town, Pasadena's two best offerings are the splendid collection of the **Norton Simon Museum**, 411 W Colorado Blvd (Wed–Mon noon–6pm, Fri closes at 9pm; $6, students $4; ☎626/449-6840, ⓦwww.nortonsimon.org), one of LA's greatest and least-heralded institutions, with a prime selection of Old Masters and modern works (Rubens, Rembrandt, Hals, Monet, Klee, Picasso), and the **Gamble House**, 4 Westmoreland Place (hour-long tours Thurs–Sun noon–3pm; $8, students $3; ☎626/793-3334, ⓦgamblehouse.usc .edu), a Craftsman mansion with Arts and Crafts decor and Japanese-inspired design elements – one of the more intriguing wooden lodges in the country. Maps and booklets on Pasadena, available at the **Convention and Visitors Bureau**, 171 S Los Robles Ave (Mon–Fri 8am–5pm, Sat 10am–4pm; ☎626/795-9311, ⓦwww.pasadenavisitor.org), detail worthwhile self-guided tours of the city's architecture, history, and museums.

South of Pasadena, in the dull, upper-crust little suburb of **San Marino**, the **Huntington Museum and Library**, off Huntington Drive at 1151 Oxford Rd (Tues–Fri noon–4.30pm, Sat & Sun 10.30am–4.30pm; $12.50, students $10.50, ☎626/405-2100, ⓦwww.huntington.org), contains numerous manuscripts and rare books, such as a Gutenberg Bible and the Ellesmere Chaucer – the latter an illuminated manuscript of *The Canterbury Tales* dating from around 1410. Paintings include Gainsborough's *Blue Boy* and Reynolds' *Mrs Siddons as the Tragic Muse*, and the whole complex is set off by acres of beautiful themed **gardens**.

The San Fernando Valley

The **San Fernando Valley**, spreading west, is "the Valley" to most Angelenos: a sprawl of tract homes, mini-malls, and fast-food diners. It has more of a middle-American feel than anywhere else in LA. In the gateway town of **GLENDALE**, eight miles north of downtown LA, **Forest Lawn Cemetery**, 1712 S Glendale Ave (daily 9am–5pm; free), was immortalized with biting satire by Evelyn Waugh in *The Loved One*. Those buried here include Errol Flynn, Walt Disney, Clara Bow, Nat King Cole, Chico Marx, Clark Gable, and Jean Harlow, the latter entombed in a marble-lined room paid for by her fiancé William Powell.

Beyond the San Fernando Valley, an hour north of central LA, the three-hundred-acre theme park of **Magic Mountain**, Magic Mountain Parkway at I-5 (summer daily 10am–10pm; rest of year Sat & Sun only 10am–8pm; $45, kids $30, $7 parking; ☎661/255-4100, ⓦ www.sixflags.com), holds the region's wildest roller coasters (sixteen and counting), with a new fright-ride unleashed nearly every summer.

Burbank and the studios

Hollywood may be synonymous with the movies, but the studios themselves moved out of Tinseltown long ago; the nitty-gritty business of actually making films goes on over the hills in otherwise boring **BURBANK**. Available studio tours include a peek inside **NBC**, 3000 W Alameda St (Mon–Fri 9am–4pm; $7; ☎818/840-3537), and a technically minded trek into **Warner Bros Studios**, 4000 Warner Blvd (May–Sept Mon–Fri 9am–3pm; Oct–April Mon–Fri 9am–4pm; $33; reservations only at ☎818/846-1403, ⓦ www.wbstudiotour .com). Disney's animation building, at 500 S Buena Vista St, is closed to the public, however.

The largest of the backlots belongs to **Universal Studios**, whose four-hour tours (daily: summer 8am–10pm; rest of year 9am–7pm; $47; ☎818/508-9600, ⓦ www.universalstudioshollywood.com) are more like a trip around an amusement park, with high-tech rides and "evening spectaculars" based on current movies. The shows are without exception cheesy, but for fans of explosions and pratfalls, they're an absolute must.

Eating

LA **eating** covers every extreme: whatever you want to eat and however much you want to spend, you're spoiled for choice. Try to take at least a few meals in the higher-end restaurants, many of which serve superb food in consciously cultivated surroundings. At the cheaper end of the scale, the options are almost endless, and include terrific burger stands where you can scarf down mountains of fries, and free food available for the price of a drink at **happy hours**. LA is also littered with **celebrity-owned** outfits – *Dive!*, *Planet Hollywood*, and the like – though you're better off going to a swank Westside eatery if you want to spot any actual stars.

Downtown

Clifton's Cafeteria 648 S Broadway ☎213/627-1673. Classic 1930s cafeteria with plenty of bizarre decor: redwood trees, a waterfall, even a mini-chapel. The food is less daring – traditional meat-and-potatoes American – though it is cheap.
Dong Il Jang 3455 W 8th St ☎213/383-5757. Cozy little Korean restaurant where the meat is cooked at your table and the food is consistently good, especially the grilled chicken and beef. Tempura dishes and a sushi bar are an added draw.
El Cholo 1121 S Western Ave ☎323/734-2773. One of LA's first big Mexican restaurants and still one of the best, offering a solid array of staples like enchiladas and tamales – despite the frequent presence of drunken fratboys from USC.

La Luz del Dia 107 Paseo de la Plaza ☎213/628-7495. Authentic Mexican eatery on Olvera Street, worth seeking out for the fiery burritos, enchiladas, and stews, all served in sizeable portions.
Langer's Deli 704 S Alvarado ☎213/483-8050. One of LA's finest delis, with an excellent selection of take-out meats and baked goods. Offers twenty ways of eating what is LA's best pastrami sandwich. Open daylight hours only; curbside pick-up available.
Ocean Seafood 750 N Hill ☎213/687-3088. Cavernous and often crowded Chinese restaurant serving low-priced, excellent food – try the abalone, crab, shrimp, or duck.
Original Pantry 877 S Figueroa St ☎213/972-9279. Former mayor Richard Riordan owns this

classic old diner, which serves huge pork chops and American breakfasts 24hrs a day.

Pacific Dining Car 1310 W 6th St ☏213/483-6000. Starched linen and very expensive steaks in a former railroad carriage styled after an English supper club. Good-value breakfasts available. Open until 2am.

Philippe the Original French Dip 1001 N Alameda St, Chinatown ☏213/628-3781. Renowned sawdust café with long communal tables, a decor unchanged since 1908, and juicy, artery-clogging French dips loaded with turkey, pork, beef, or lamb.

Hollywood

Casa Carnitas 4067 Beverly Blvd ☏323/667-9953. On the southeast edge of Hollywood, tasty, cheap Mexican food from the Yucatan, with dishes inspired by Cuban and Caribbean cooking. Lots of seafood, too.

Fred 62 1854 N Vermont Ave, Los Feliz ☏323/667-0062. Classic retro-diner fare with a soda fountain, streamlined booths, and 24hr operation. Offers stylish twists on staples like salads, burgers, and fries, and a tempting array of pancakes and omelets.

French Quarter 7985 Santa Monica Blvd ☏323/654-0898. Inside the French Market Place, a gay-run, New Orleans–themed Cajun restaurant with food that's more tasty than it is authentic.

Hampton's 1342 N Highland Ave ☏323/469-1090. Longstanding comfort-food favorite, with hefty hamburgers served with a choice of over fifty toppings, plus an excellent salad bar.

Mexico City 2121 Hillhurst Ave ☏323/661-7227. Spinach enchiladas and other Californian versions of Mexican standards served in red booths, with a great view of the street from the wall-length window.

Pink's Hot Dogs 709 N La Brea Ave ☏323/931-4223. The quintessence of chili dogs, featuring items like a cheese-chili-hot dog combo wrapped up in a gooey tortilla package. Open until 2am, or 3am weekends.

Roscoe's Chicken and Waffles 1514 N Gower St ☏323/466-7453. An unlikely spot for Hollywood's elite, this LA dining institution attracts all sorts for its fried chicken, greens, goopy gravy, and thick waffles.

Shibucho 3114 Beverly Blvd ☏323/387-8498. Excellent sushi here in the heart of Little Tokyo; go with someone who knows what to order, as the waiters don't speak English.

Yukon Mining Company 7328 Santa Monica Blvd ☏323/851-8833. Colorful 24hr coffee shop where you're likely to see local drag queens, newly arrived Russians, and neighborhood pensioners.

West LA

Apple Pan 10801 W Pico Blvd ☏310/475-3585. Grab a spot at the counter and enjoy freshly baked pies and juicy hamburgers. Adjacent to the Westside Pavilion mall.

Ca' Brea 346 S La Brea Ave ☏323/938-2863. One of LA's best choices for Californian and also Italian cuisine, and especially good for *osso buco* and risotto. Getting in is difficult, so reserve ahead and expect to pay a bundle.

Campanile 624 S La Brea Ave ☏323/938-1447. Expensive Northern Italian restaurant with an indoor fountain and delicious pastries from *La Brea Bakery* next door.

Canter's Deli 419 N Fairfax Ave ☏323/651-2030. Waitresses in pink uniforms and running shoes serve kosher soup and sandwiches in a kitsch, white-vinyl setting, with its own bizarre cabaret.

Chung King 11538 W Pico Blvd ☏310/477-4917. The best neighborhood Chinese restaurant in LA, serving spicy Szechuan food: don't miss out on the *bum-bum* chicken.

Cobras and Matadors 7615 Beverly Blvd ☏323/932-6178. A fine *tapas* restaurant where you can sample all of your Castilian favorites in a hushed, dramatic setting.

El Coyote 7312 Beverly Blvd ☏323/939-2255. An eatery known to practically every Westsider, for better or worse. Labyrinthine restaurant serving heaps of heavy Mexican food in a gloomy atmosphere. The cheap and lethal margaritas are the real draw, though.

Gumbo Pot 6333 W 3rd St, in the Farmers Market ☏323/933-0358. Delicious and dirt-cheap Cajun cooking in a bustling setting; try the *gumbo yaya* of chicken, shrimp, and sausage or the fruit-and-potato salad.

Mishima 8474 W 3rd St ☏323/782-0181. Chic, popular eatery serving bowls of delicious *udon* and *soba* noodles at low prices.

Tail o' the Pup 329 N San Vicente Blvd ☏310/652-4517. A pop architecture treat, shaped like a hot dog wrapped in a massive cement bun. Munch on savory red hots before shopping at the nearby Beverly Center mall.

Tommy Tang's 7313 Melrose Ave ☏323/937-5733. Excellent Thai food in a very popular restaurant; also the incongruous setting for biweekly drag nights that include glammed-up waiters.

Santa Monica, Venice, and Malibu

Bagel Nosh 1629 Wilshire Blvd, Santa Monica ☏310/451-8771. A neighborhood favorite for its sizeable breakfasts of omelets and bagel sandwiches, picked up from an old-fashioned short-order counter.

Café 50s 838 Lincoln Blvd, Venice ℡ 310/399-1955. No doubts about this place: Ritchie Valens on the jukebox and burgers on the tables.

Chaya 110 Navy St, Venice ℡ 310/396-1179. Coolly elegant culinary crossroads serving Japanese and Mediterranean foods to a smart clientele. Try the huge California-roll platter for two.

Chinois on Main 2709 Main St, Santa Monica ℡ 310/392-9025. One of LA's most renowned, and most expensive, restaurants, run by chef Wolfgang Puck, and serving *nouvelle* Chinese dishes.

Inn of the Seventh Ray 128 Old Topanga Canyon Rd, just off Topanga Canyon ℡ 310/455-1311. The ultimate New Age restaurant, serving vegetarian and wholefood dishes in a relatively secluded environment. Excellent desserts, too.

Lighthouse Buffet 201 Arizona Ave, Santa Monica ℡ 310/451-2076. All-you-care-to-eat sushi; indulge to your heart's content for $10 at lunchtime or $20 in the evening.

Marix Tex-Mex Playa 118 Entrada Drive, Pacific Palisades ℡ 310/459-8596. Flavorful fajitas and big margaritas in this rowdy beachfront cantina. Another free-spirited branch at 1108 N Flores St, West Hollywood ℡ 323/656-8800.

Norm's 1601 Lincoln Blvd, Santa Monica ℡ 310/450-0074. The prototypical LA diner, with colorful 1950s architecture and ample $4 breakfasts.

Valentino 3115 Pico Blvd ℡ 310/829-4313. Some call it the finest Italian restaurant in the US – traditional Northern Italian dishes, with an infusion of California Cuisine dash and experiment. Expect to max out your credit card.

South Bay and LA Harbor

Alegria Cocina Latina 115 Pine Ave, Long Beach ℡ 562/436-3388. *Tapas*, gazpacho, and a variety of *platos principales* served with sangría on the patio, and to the beat of live flamenco at weekends. Good location near the harbor in downtown Long Beach.

Johnny Reb's 4663 N Long Beach Blvd, Long Beach ℡ 562/423-7327. Delicious and inexpensive Southern food served in huge helpings – try the catfish, ribs, and hushpuppies.

The Spot 110 Second St, Hermosa Beach ℡ 310/376-2355. A staggering array of vegetarian dishes, based on Mexican and other international cuisines and free of refined sugar or any animal products.

Disneyland and around

Angelo's 511 S State College Blvd, Anaheim ℡ 714/533-1401. Straight out of TV's *Happy Days*, a drive-in complete with roller-skating car-hops and juicy burgers. Open until 2am at weekends.

Knott's Chicken Dinner Restaurant 8039 Beach Blvd, located just outside Knott's Berry Farm ℡ 714/220-5080. Famous for fried chicken long before Disneyland was around – serving cheap and tasty meals for 70-odd years. Park admission not required.

Ruby's 1 Balboa Pier, Newport Beach ℡ 949/675-RUBY. A solid spot for burgers and fries – the only eatery on this popular pier and one of the few cheap spots in this upscale burg.

The San Gabriel and San Fernando valleys

Dr Hogly-Wogly's Tyler Texas Bar-B-Q 8136 Sepulveda Blvd, Van Nuys ℡ 818/780-6701. Queue up for the chicken, sausages, ribs, and beans – some of the best in LA.

Fair Oaks Pharmacy and Soda Fountain 1526 Mission St, South Pasadena ℡ 626/799-1414. Serving good fountain drinks and diner food since the hallowed days of Route 66. Preserved with plenty of period detail.

Genmai Sushi 4454 Van Nuys Blvd, Van Nuys ℡ 626/986-7060. Japanese-style vegetarian restaurant with brown rice, sushi, and seasonal macrobiotic dishes.

Merida 20 E Colorado Blvd, Pasadena ℡ 626/792-7371. Mexican restaurant with dishes from the Yucatan; try the spicy pork wrapped and steamed in banana leaves.

Sea Star 2000 W Main St, Alhambra ℡ 626/282-8833. Affordable dim sum at its best: pork, *baos*, potstickers and dumplings, and sweets.

Wolfe Burger 46 N Lake St, Pasadena ℡ 626/792-7292. A great place for chili, tamales, burgers, and *huevos rancheros.*

Nightlife and entertainment

Exploring the jungle of LA **nightlife** can be great fun. Even the quietest venue offers a chance to eavesdrop on a bit of vapid dialogue; the most raucous ones will take your breath away. In all the bars, clubs, and discos, you'll need to be 21 and will be asked for ID. The best sources of **listings** are *LA Weekly* and the "Calendar" section in the *LA Times* on Friday.

Bars and coffeehouses

LA's **bars** are rarely the scruffy boozing places found elsewhere in the US, due in part to the generally high degree of health consciousness – not to mention the very early (dawn) starting time of the movie business working day. Nonetheless, there's a wide range of choices, from the funky dive bars of Hollywood to the chic enclaves of West LA and Santa Monica. As elsewhere along the West Coast, **coffeehouses** are established all over the city as popular meeting places.

Anastasia's Asylum 1028 Wilshire Blvd, Santa Monica ℡ 310/394-7113. Comfortable place with quirky decor and customers, and strong coffee and tea. Also with nightly entertainment of varying quality.

Barney's Beanery 8447 Santa Monica Blvd, West Hollywood ℡ 310/654-2287. Well-worn pool-hall bar, popular with graying rebels and sullen youth. Stocks more than two hundred beers and serves food of marginal quality.

Beauty Bar 1638 N Cahuenga Blvd, Hollywood ℡ 323/464-7676. Drinking spot devoted to nails, hair, and cosmetics, with a welter of 1950s-style salon gadgets and retro-decor, and a similarly themed cocktail list.

Boardner's 1652 N Cherokee Ave, Hollywood ℡ 323/462-9621. A likeably unkempt neighborhood bar with a mix of salty old-timers and hip newbies.

The Dresden Room 1760 N Vermont Ave, Hollywood ℡ 323/665-4298. Wed night is open-mic, otherwise the resident husband-and-wife lounge act takes requests from the crowd.

El Adobe 5536 Melrose Ave, Mid-Wilshire ℡ 323/462-9421. An old favorite for potent margaritas, this Mexican restaurant has a laid-back So-Cal vibe, though the food is only adequate.

Gotham Hall 1431 Third St Promenade, Santa Monica ℡ 310/394-8865. Purple-felt pool tables and mind-numbing cocktails are the main draw for the youthful clientele here.

Insomnia 7286 Beverly Blvd, West LA ℡ 323/931-4943. A chic spot for chugging cappuccinos while sitting in comfortable sofas and admiring the vivid amateur art on the walls.

King's Road Espresso House 8361 Beverly Blvd, Hollywood ℡ 323/655-9044. Sidewalk café in the center of a busy shopping strip. Popular with the trendy crowd as well as a few interloping tourists.

Lava Lounge 1533 N La Brea, Hollywood ℡ 323/876-6612. Cheesy, retro decor, glowing cocktails, and plenty of rock and surf music, along with Brubeck jazz and lounge favorites.

Mr T's Bowl 5621 N Figueroa Ave, Highland Park ℡ 323/960-5693. Former bowling alley, just northeast of downtown, now a quirky bar with a regular crowd of hipsters and locals. On weekends, there's live music, with a strong punk-surfer bent.

Novel Café 212 Pier Ave, Santa Monica ℡ 310/396-8566. Stacks of used books and high-backed wooden chairs set the tone; good coffees, teas, and pastries, with funky old sofas on the mezzanine to curl up in.

Tiki-Ti 4427 W Sunset Blvd, Hollywood ℡ 323/669-9381. Tiny grass-skirted cocktail bar straight out of *Hawaii Five-0*, packed with kitschy pseudo-Polynesian decor, on the edge of Hollywood.

Ye Olde Kings Head 116 Santa Monica Blvd, Santa Monica ℡ 310/451-1402. Prime LA spot for swigging British brews and munching on steak-and-kidney pie.

Clubs and discos

LA's **clubs** are among the wildest in the country, ranging from faddish hangouts to industrial noise cellars. The trendier side of the club scene is, as always, hard to pin down, with some venues changing names and clientele every six months or so; check the *LA Weekly* before setting out.

Club Lingerie 6507 Sunset Blvd 323/466-8557. Long-established, though recently remodeled dance club with intimate bar and hip-hop, dance, and R&B music.

The Derby 4500 Los Feliz Blvd, Hollywood ℡ 323/663-8979. Swing, rockabilly, and bebop, with dance lessons to get you up to speed. Drinks are pricey, but the circular bar and domed wooden ceiling are hard to resist.

Dragonfly 6510 Santa Monica Blvd, Hollywood ℡ 323/466-6111. Disco and house music, with the odd bit of rock at this established hipster hangout featuring two large dance floors and a so-called "eye-contact" bar.

Mayan 1038 S Hill St, downtown ℡ 213/746-4287. Get past the doorman and you're in with LA's coolest, to shake a leg to Latin, a fusion of dance beats, and salsa in a gorgeous former

Although proportionately not as big as that of San Francisco, the **gay scene** in LA is no less prominent. West Hollywood is synonymous with the (affluent white) gay lifestyle, while the other major gay community is Silver Lake, most evidently along Hyperion Boulevard, home to working-class blacks, whites, and Hispanics; other places like Venice, Los Feliz, Studio City, and even Laguna Beach in Orange County are comfortable gay and lesbian locales.

The city's best known gay and lesbian bookshop is **A Different Light**, 8853 Santa Monica Blvd, West Hollywood (☎310/854-6601, ⓦwww.adlbooks.com), with monthly art shows, readings, and musical events. **The Gay Community Yellow Pages** (☎323/469-4454) is a comprehensive annual directory of gay businesses, publications, services, and gathering places; it also publishes a gay restaurant guide. The **Gay and Lesbian Community Services Center**, 1625 N Schrader Blvd, Hollywood (☎323/993-7400), is the community's prime resource for counseling, health testing, and information.

Gay and lesbian bars and clubs

7969 7969 Santa Monica Blvd, West Hollywood ☎323/654-0280. Legendary club back in business after closing due to fire, and offering high-energy dance tunes on weekend and Tuesday nights.

Arena 6655 Santa Monica Blvd, Hollywood ☎323/462-0714. Many clubs under one huge roof, large dance floors throbbing to funk, Latin, and hi-NRG grooves. At the same address, *Circus* presents more electronica dance clubs and eye-opening weekend drag shows.

Jewel's Catch One 4067 W Pico Blvd, Mid-Wilshire ☎323/734-8849. Sweaty dance barn covering two floors, with gay men on Wednesdays, lesbians on Thursdays.

Mother Lode 8944 Santa Monica Blvd ☎310/659-9700. Strong drinks, wild dancing to house and hi-NRG music, and periodic drag antics make this one of the more colorful and frenetic of West Hollywood's clubs.

The Palms 8572 Santa Monica Blvd ☎310/652-6188. Mostly house and pop music dance nights at West Hollywood's most established lesbian bar, which increasingly caters to a mixed crowd.

Queen Mary 12449 Ventura Blvd, Studio City, in the San Fernando Valley ☎818/506-5619. A regular gay crowd at the back and straight visitors at the front at this well-established drag club. Features midweek karaoke.

Rage 8911 Santa Monica Blvd, West Hollywood ☎310/652-7055. Very flashy gay men's club playing the latest hi-NRG hits. Also with drag comedy. Drinks are fairly cheap.

Revolver 8851 Santa Monica Blvd, West Hollywood ☎310/659-8851. Sleek bar, intimate lounge, and regular karaoke and drag shows. Oriented toward gay men.

movie palace done up in pre-Columbian style. Fri and Sat only; no sneakers.
The Palace 1735 N Vine St ☎323/462-3000. One of LA's better clubs, with a solid range of rock and alternative acts during the week, turning into a dance club on weekend nights.

The Ruby 7070 Hollywood Blvd ☎323/467-7070. A wide selection of feverish dance clubs nightly, except Mondays and Tuesdays, with everything from retro-kitsch to grinding industrial to perky house.
Sugar 814 Broadway, Santa Monica ☎310/899-1989. Electronic beats, from house to hip-hop, served up in a sleek glass-and-steel interior.

Live music

LA has an overwhelming choice of venues for **live music**: ever since the 1960s, the local **rock** scene has been excellent, with up-and-comers traditionally getting their first break in clubs on the Sunset Strip; **country** is also fairly

CALIFORNIA | Los Angeles

⑬

prevalent, at least away from trendy Hollywood; **jazz** is played in a few authentic downbeat dives, though **reggae** is much less common; finally, **salsa** is immensely popular, and not just among LA's Hispanics. In many clubs, **cover charges** can vary widely, depending on the prominence of the headliner and the night of the week, so call ahead.

Babe and Ricky's Inn 4339 Leimert Blvd, South Central ☎ 323/295-9112. One of LA's top spots for blues, attracting plenty of quality, nationally known acts.

Baked Potato 3787 Cahuenga Blvd West, North Hollywood ☎ 818/980-1615. A small, near-legendary contemporary jazz spot, where many reputations have been forged. Don't come looking for bland lounge jazz/muzak – instead, expect to be surprised.

Conga Room 5364 Wilshire Blvd, Mid-Wilshire ☎ 323/938-1696. Live Cuban, salsa, and South American music throughout the week at this hip, lively club on the Miracle Mile.

Doug Weston's Troubadour 9081 Santa Monica Blvd, West Hollywood ☎ 310/276-6168. A 1960s mainstay that used to be known for heavy riffs and shaggy manes, but now hosts more alternative and acoustic line-ups.

El Rey Theater 5515 Wilshire Blvd, Mid-Wilshire ☎ 323/936-4790. Although not as famous as its Sunset Strip counterparts, this rock and alternative venue is possibly the best spot to see explosive new bands and still-engaging oldsters. Also offers a variety of dance club nights.

Foothill Club 1922 Cherry Ave, Signal Hill ☎ 562 /984-8349. Located near Long Beach, a glorious country venue from the days when hillbilly was cool. Punk, surf, and roots-rock Thursday to Saturday, with the occasional garage band and dance music.

Gabah 4658 Melrose Ave, Mid-Wilshire ☎ 323/664-8913. This eclectic spot mixes reggae, dub, funk, and rock – fun despite being in a dicey neighborhood.

Golden Sails Hotel 6285 E Pacific Coast Hwy, Long Beach ☎ 562/596-1631. Some of the best reggae bands from LA and beyond perform on Fridays and Saturdays in an anonymous hotel setting.

Knitting Factory 7021 Hollywood Blvd, Hollywood ☎ 323/463-0204. West Coast branch of landmark New York club (see p.120), featuring a wide range of eclectic interpretation, much of it avant-garde.

Largo 432 N Fairfax Ave, Mid-Wilshire ☎ 323/852-1073. Intimate cabaret venue with interesting jazz, rock, and pop acts.

Luminarias 3500 Ramona Blvd, Monterey Park, East LA ☎ 323/268-4177. A hilltop Mexican restaurant where the live salsa is as good as the spicy food. Fri and Sat shows.

McCabe's 3103 W Pico Blvd, Santa Monica ☎ 310/828-4497. The back room of LA's premier acoustic guitar shop; long the scene of excellent and unusual folk and country shows.

Opium Den 1605 1/2 N Ivar Ave, Hollywood ☎ 323/466-7800. A strip club-turned-nightclub where an array of upcoming rock and punk acts take turns on the overly small stage.

The Roxy 9009 Sunset Blvd, West Hollywood ☎ 310/276-2222. The showcase of the rock industry's new signings, intimate and with a great sound system.

Rusty's Surf Ranch 256 Santa Monica Pier ☎ 310/393-7437. Offers not only surf music but live folk and country as well, along with karaoke. A popular spot for tourists, near the end of the pier.

Spaceland 1717 Silver Lake Blvd, Hollywood ☎ 213/833-2843. Excellent place to catch up-and-coming local and national rockers and other acts.

Viper Room 8852 Sunset Blvd, West Hollywood ☎ 310/358-1881. Stellar live acts playing house, swing, disco, jazz, and more.

Whisky-a-Go-Go 8901 Sunset Blvd, West Hollywood ☎ 310/652-4202. For many years LA's most famous rock 'n' roll club, nowadays featuring mainly hard rock.

Classical music, opera, and dance

Despite its size, LA has few outlets for **classical music**. The Los Angeles Philharmonic (☎ 213/850-2000, ⓦ www.laphil.org), the city's only big name, performs regularly during the year, and the Los Angeles Chamber Orchestra (☎ 213/622-7001, ⓦ www.laco.org) performs at assorted venues.

As for **opera**, LA Opera (☎ 213/972-8001, ⓦ www.laopera.org) stages productions between September and June, from heavy *opera seria* to lighter operettas, as does Orange County's Opera Pacific in Costa Mesa (☎ 1-800/34-OPERA, ⓦ www.operapacific.org). Perhaps the city's most exciting company is the Long Beach Opera (☎ 562/439-2580, ⓦ www.lbopera.com), which is anything but provincial, putting on challenging but well-regarded performances of modern and lesser-known operas. **Dance** in Los Angeles has its annual big event with UCLA's Dance Kaleidoscope (☎323/343-5120, ⓦwww.performingarts.ucla.edu), held over two weeks in July.

Disney Hall First St at Grand Ave, downtown ⓦwdch.laphil.com. Newly opened for the 2003–2004 season of the LA Philharmonic, a striking Frank Gehry design (see p.1111) hosting a range of music and arts groups. A high-profile gambit to draw the tourists back to downtown LA.
Dorothy Chandler Pavilion in the Music Center, 135 N Grand Ave, downtown ☎213/972-7211, ⓦwww.musiccenter.org. Former home of the LA Philharmonic, now mainly used by the LA Opera.
Hollywood Bowl 2301 N Highland Ave, Hollywood ☎323/850-2000, ⓦwww.hollywoodbowl.org. The LA Philharmonic gives open-air summer concerts (July–Sept Tues–Sat evenings), leaning toward familiar pops offerings.
John Anson Ford Theater 2850 Cahuenga Blvd, Hollywood ☎323/461-3673, ⓦwww.lacountyarts.org/ford.html. As well as UCLA's summer "Dance Kaleidoscope," this open-air venue also has eclectic productions by local groups.
Orange County Performing Arts Center 600 Town Center Drive, Costa Mesa ☎714/556-ARTS,

ⓦwww.ocpac.org. Home of the county's own Pacific Symphony Orchestra and Opera Pacific, as well as touring big names in pop and jazz.
Pacific Amphitheater 100 Fair Drive, Costa Mesa ☎949/740-2000. A big open-air venue drawing mainstream crowds, Orange County's answer to the Hollywood Bowl.
Pasadena Dance Theater 1985 Locust Ave, Pasadena ☎626/683-3459, ⓦwww.pasadenadance.org. A prominent San Gabriel Valley dance venue, hosting diverse groups throughout the year.
Shrine Auditorium 665 W Jefferson Blvd ☎213/749-5123, box office at 655 S Hill St. A striking white Islamic-domed complex hosting regular performances by choral gospel groups and touring pop acts.
UCLA Center for the Performing Arts ☎310/825-4401, ⓦwww.performingarts.ucla.edu. Coordinates a wide range of touring companies, and also runs the experimentally inclined "Art of Dance" series between September and June.

Comedy

The **comedy** scene in LA has long been a national proving ground for aspiring jokesters, and it's also a good place to catch live performances by established television names like Jay Leno and Drew Carey.

Acme Comedy Theater 135 N La Brea Ave, West Hollywood ☎323/525-0202. A broad range of sketch and improv comedy, hosting the odd big name, as well as variety shows.
Comedy & Magic Club 1018 Hermosa Ave, Hermosa Beach ☎310/372-1193. Strange couplings of magic acts and comedians, highlighted by Jay Leno occasionally testing material here.
Comedy Store 8433 W Sunset Blvd, West Hollywood ☎323/656-6225. Popular comedy showcase spread over three rooms; you can usually get in, even on weekends.

Groundlings Theater 7307 Melrose Ave, Hollywood ☎323/934-9700. Only the gifted survive at this pioneering improvisation venue, where Pee Wee Herman got his start.
The Improvisation 8162 Melrose Ave, West Hollywood ☎323/651-2583. Prime destination for out-of-town comedy-lovers and known for hosting some of the best acts in the area – so book ahead.
Laugh Factory 8001 Sunset Blvd, West Hollywood ☎323/656-1336. Nightly stand-ups of varying standards and reputations, with the occasional big name. Features a variable open-mic night.

Theater

Not surprisingly, LA has a very active **theater** scene; ticket services like Theatre LA (☎213/614-0556, ⓦwww.theatrela.org) provide full-price and half-price tickets and take reservations. The *LA Weekly* and the *LA Times* "Calendar" section both have full listings and reviews.

Alex Theater 216 N Brand Blvd, Glendale ☎1-800/872-8997. Gloriously restored movie palace, with a great neon spike and quasi-Egyptian forecourt, hosting a fine range of musical theater, comedy, film, and one-person shows.

The Complex 6476 Santa Monica Blvd, Hollywood ☎323/469-9338. An association of six small theaters putting on innovative works you may not see anywhere else.
Mark Taper Forum 135 N Grand Ave, downtown

213/972-0700. Theater in the three-quarter round, mostly known for its conservatism and adherence to the established repertoire.
Pantages Theater 6233 Hollywood Blvd, Hollywood ☎ 323/468-1770. Quite the stunner: an exquisite, atmospheric Art Deco theater, in the heart of historic Hollywood, hosting major touring Broadway productions.
Stages Theater Center 1540 N McCadden Place, Hollywood ☎ 323/465-1010. With three stages offering twenty to one hundred seats, an excellent place to catch a wide range of comedies and dramas.

Film

Major feature films are often released in LA months (or years) before they play anywhere else in the world. You can catch **mainstream releases** in any mall-based multiplex like the Beverly Center Cineplex, 8500 Beverly Blvd, West LA (☎ 310/652-7760), AMC Century 14, 10250 Santa Monica Blvd, Century City (☎ 310/553-8900), or the Universal City 18, at Universal Studios CityWalk, San Fernando Valley (☎ 818/508-0588). Short runs of **foreign films** are screened at the eight Laemmle Theaters (ⓦ www.laemmle.com), but if you're after a golden-age-of-film **atmosphere**, head for one of the historic downtown movie palaces along Broadway, where the delirious furnishings may hold your attention longer than the all-action double bills.

Bing at the LA County Art Museum, 5905 Wilshire Blvd, Mid-Wilshire ☎ 323/857-6010. Afternoon screenings of many Hollywood classics from the Warner Bros archives. Matinees cost just $3, evening shows $8.50.
Chinese 6925 Hollywood Blvd, Hollywood ☎ 323/464-8111. Landmark cinema showing mainstream fare with a large main screen, six-track stereo sound, and wild chinoiserie interior.
Egyptian 6712 Hollywood Blvd, Hollywood ☎ 323/466-FILM. Renovated showcase for classic and foreign films, in the middle of historic Hollwood.
El Capitan 6834 Hollywood Blvd, Hollywood ☎ 323/467-7674. Legendary Hollywood venue restored to full glory and renovated a second time. Expect to see plenty of animated and live-action Disney fare.

Nuart 11272 Santa Monica Blvd, West LA ☎ 310/478-6379. Rarely seen classics, foreign films, documentaries, and sometimes Oscar contenders in December.
Orpheum 842 S Broadway, downtown ☎ 213/239-0939. The grandest of the remaining downtown movie palaces regularly open to the public, screening mainly Hollywood blockbusters.
Silent Movie 611 N Fairfax Ave, West LA ☎ 323/655-2510. As its name suggests, showings of silent Chaplin, Laurel and Hardy, Ramon Navarro thrillers, and so on. Every show is accompanied by an organist.
Village 961 Broxton Ave, Westwood ☎ 310/208-5576. One of the best places to watch a movie in LA, equipped with a giant screen, fine seats, and modern sound system, and a frequent spot for Hollywood premieres.

Shopping

Not surprisingly for a city identified with mass consumerism and colossal shopping centers, you can buy virtually anything in LA. The big **department stores** or exclusive **Rodeo Drive** are the first options for many tourists, along with the city's massive **malls**. The **CityWalk** mall at Universal Studios (☎ 818/508-9600) is a bland but popular choice, while West Hollywood's **Beverly Center**, at Beverly and La Cienega boulevards (☎ 310/854-0070), has designer stores and fourteen cinemas; both the **Century City Mall**, 10250 Santa Monica Blvd (☎ 310/553-5300), and West LA's new **Grove**, 6301 W 3rd St (☎ 323/571-8830), are aimed at middle-class and upscale shoppers. Many of the city's trendier boutiques line **Melrose Avenue** between La Brea and Fairfax avenues.

Baseball: the **LA Dodgers** (☎323/2241-HIT, ⓦwww.dodgers.com) play at Dodger Stadium near downtown, seats $6–21; the **Anaheim Angels** (☎1-888/796-4256, ⓦwww.angelsbaseball.com) at Anaheim Stadium in Orange County, seats $7–30.

Basketball: the **LA Lakers** (☎213/480-3232, ⓦwww.lakers.com) and **LA Clippers** (☎213/742-7430, ⓦwww.clippers.com) both play at the Staples Center south of downtown. The crummy Clippers are a cheap date ($10–120), while the world-beating Lakers will cost you plenty ($25–195).

Football: Pasadena's 102,000-seat **Rose Bowl** (☎626/577-3100, ⓦwww.rosebowlstadium.com) is the site of the annual New Year's Rose Bowl football game, but if you're after pro football, you're out of luck: LA hasn't had a franchise in nearly a decade.

Hockey: the **LA Kings** are based at Staples Center (☎1-888/KINGS-LA, ⓦwww.lakings.com), seats $20–200; the **Mighty Ducks** represent Orange County and play at Arrowhead Pond (☎714/704-2500, ⓦwww.mightyducks.com) in Anaheim, seats $25–175.

Soccer: the **LA Galaxy** (☎1-877/3-GALAXY, ⓦwww.lagalaxy.com) play at the Home Depot Center in the South Bay, seats $12–35.

Books

Acres of Books 240 Long Beach Blvd, Long Beach ☎562/437-6980. Worth a trip down the Blue Line to wallow in LA's largest, and most disorganized, secondhand collection. You may not be able to find the title you're looking for, but chances are you'll still see something good.

Book Soup 8818 Sunset Blvd, West Hollywood ☎323/659-3110. Right on the Sunset Strip and packed to the gills with an eclectic selection, this shop is as good for spotting celebrities as it is for browsing.

Dutton's 11975 San Vicente Blvd, Brentwood ☎310/476-6263. One of LA's best general bookstores, if a bit cluttered. Other branches in the San Fernando Valley, 5146 Laurel Canyon Blvd (☎818/769-3866), and Burbank, 3806 W Magnolia Blvd (☎818/840-8003).

Larry Edmunds Book Shop 6644 Hollywood Blvd, Hollywood ☎323/463-3273. Stacks of books on every aspect of film and theater, plus movie stills and posters.

Midnight Special 1318 Third St Promenade, Santa Monica ☎310/393-2923. Excellent for lefty politics, social sciences, and general fiction and literature. Open late.

Samuel French Theatre & Film Bookshop 7623 Sunset Blvd, Hollywood ☎323/876-0570. Famed for its performing arts selection, the best in town, with a prime selection of cinema books as well.

Sisterhood Bookstore 1351 Westwood Blvd ☎310/477-7300. Westside landmark selling music, cards, jewelry, and books, pertaining to all aspects of the women's movement.

Taschen 354 N Beverly Drive, Beverly Hills. Fun, weird, and edifying titles that focus on everything from Renaissance art to kitsch Americana to fetish photography.

Music

Amoeba Music 6400 W Sunset Blvd, Hollywood ☎323/245-6400. Popular record store highlighted by a vast selection of titles – supposedly numbering around half a million – on CD, tape, and vinyl, which you can freely hear at listening carrels throughout the store.

Destroy All Music 3818 Sunset Blvd, Silver Lake ☎323/663-9300. Stocks all your punk-rock heroes, new and old, from Southern California to Europe. Located next door to the *You've Got Bad Taste* music store and punk-rock museum (☎213/669-1718).

Penny Lane 12 W Colorado Blvd, Pasadena ☎626/564-0161. New and used records at reasonable prices. Always crowded, this local chain features listening stations from which you can sample up to a hundred discs.

Record Surplus 11609 W Pico Blvd, West LA ☎310/478-4217. The best spot for used music in LA (or anywhere for that matter), loaded with ancient LPs, out-of-print CDs, new releases, and all manner of assorted junk you have to see to believe.

Rhino Records 1720 Westwood Blvd, West LA ☎310/474-8685. The biggest selection of international independent releases, not to mention the full selection of Rhino's eclectic music catalog.

⑬

CALIFORNIA | Los Angeles

The Deserts

The **deserts** of Southern California occupy a quarter of the state. Untouched but for the three million acres used for military bases, this hot and often inhospitable wilderness exerts a powerful fascination for venturesome travelers. The two distinct regions are the **Low Desert** in the south, the most easily reached from LA, containing the opulent artificial oasis of **Palm Springs** and the primeval expanse of **Joshua Tree**; and the **Mojave** or **High Desert**, dominated by **Death Valley** and stretching along Hwy-395 to the sparsely populated **Owens Valley**, infamous as the place from which LA stole its water.

It is impossible to do justice to this area without a car. Palm Springs can be reached on public transit, but only the periphery of Joshua Tree is accessible and it's a long hot walk to anywhere worth seeing. You can get as far as dreary Barstow on Greyhound and Amtrak, but no transportation traverses Death Valley, leaving only the Owens Valley with daily Greyhound service between LA and Reno.

The Low Desert

Most visitors to the **Low Desert** head straight for its irrefutable capital, that bastion of right-wing politics and sun-scorched refuge of the Hollywood elite, **Palm Springs**. In these few square miles, some quip that the average age and average temperature are about the same – a steady 88. Still, it has a gorgeous setting and you'll find it hard to avoid: it's the first major town east from LA on I-10, at the center of the **Coachella Valley**, part of the most intensively productive agricultural area in the world, which grows dates and citrus fruits in vast quantities.

The sublime landscape of **Joshua Tree National Park**, one of the most spectacular of California's national parks, lies one hour's drive east of Palm Springs, three and a half from LA.

Palm Springs

Amid lush farmland replete with countless golf courses, condos, and millionaires, **PALM SPRINGS** embodies a strange mix of Spanish Colonial and mid-twentieth-century styling. The massive bulk of Mount San Jacinto looms over its low-slung buildings, casting a welcome shadow over the town in the late afternoon heat. Ever since Hollywood stars first came here in the 1930s, laying claim to ranch estates and holing up in elite hotels, the clean dry air and sunshine, just 120 miles east of LA, have made Palm Springs irresistible to the masses. For years, high-school kids arrived in droves for the drunken revelry of Spring Break, until civic zeal ran them out of town, while others have come specifically to sober up: the **Betty Ford Center** in nearby Rancho Mirage draws a star-studded patient list to its booze- and drug-free environment, attempting to undo a lifetime's worth of hedonism in 28 days. In recent years, the city has also become a major **gay** resort.

Long ago, Palm Springs was the domain of the **Cahuillan** tribe, who were allocated this land in the 1890s, though exact zoning wasn't settled until the 1940s, by which time the development of hotels and leisure complexes was well under way. Under an odd checkerboard system, every other square mile forms part of the **Agua Caliente** (Spanish for "hot water") **Indian Reservation**, and the high rents – and an in-town casino – have made this the second-richest tribe in America, worth more than $2 billion.

Arrival, information, and getting around

Arriving by car, you drive into town on N Palm Canyon Drive, passing the **visitor center** at no. 2781 (daily 9am–5pm; T 1-800/347-7746, W www.palm-springs.org). Greyhound **buses** (10 daily from LA; 3–4hr) pull in at 311 N Indian Canyon Drive, while Amtrak **trains** from LA (3 weekly) stop just south of I-10 at N Indian Avenue, about ten minutes from downtown. The local operator SunBus (6am–8pm; T 760/347-9628, W www.sunline.org) circulates in all the local resort towns, charging $1 per trip and $3 for a day pass. One enjoyable option outside the blistering summer months is to rent a **bike** from Bighorn Bicycles, 302 N Palm Canyon Drive (T 760/325-3367), who charge $25–35 for a half- to a full-day, depending on the model.

Companies such as Palm Springs Celebrity Tours, 4751 E Palm Canyon Drive (T 760/770-2700), offer **tours** of celebrity homes and enclaves from $17 for a basic, hour-long trip to $23 for more involved treks. You can also do it yourself, with a map of the stars' homes ($6) from the visitor center. Guided tours of Palm Springs' stash of notable **modernist architecture**, among them designs by R.M. Schindler and Richard Neutra, are organized by PS Modern Tours (90min to several hours; T 760/318-6118, E psmoderntours@aol.com).

Accommodation

Luxury **hotels** outnumber the cheaper variety in Palm Springs, but prices drop by as much as seventy percent as temperatures soar in the summer. The north end of town, along Hwy-111, holds many of the lower-priced places, including countless motels, virtually all of which have pools and air-conditioning. The prices below are **summer rates**; expect to pay $75–100 more per night at other times.

Ballantines 1420 N Indian Canyon Drive T 760/320-1178, W ballantineshotels.com. Remodeled motel with modern luxuries and sporting "vintage 1950s kitsch" in its themed rooms (bachelor pads, Hollywood glamour, etc). Worth it for a fun splurge. **6**

Casa Cody 175 S Cahuilla Rd T 760/320-9346 or 1-800/231-2639, W www.casacody.com. Built in the 1920s, this historic Southwestern-style B&B offers attractive rooms and a shady garden. **6**

Hampton Inn 2000 N Palm Canyon Drive T 760/320-0555. Features a beautiful outdoor pool – a must-have in the desert, plus free continental breakfast and comfortable rooms. **4**

Ingleside Inn 200 W Ramon Rd T 760/325-0046 or 1-800/772-6655, W www.inglesideinn.com. Historic but expensive downtown option, where the guest list has included Dalí, Garbo, and Brando. Many rooms have antiques, fireplaces, whirlpool tubs, and patios. **6**

Villa Royale 1620 S Indian Trail T 760/327-2314, W www.villaroyale.com. Elegant inn with nicely furnished rooms and suites, as well as in-room Jacuzzis and a good restaurant. **6**

The Willows 412 W Tahquitz Canyon T 760/320-0771, W www.thewillowspalmsprings.com. The reason celebrities were first attracted to Palm Springs in the 1930s: a stunning hangout for the Hollywood elite that provides great views and opulent rooms. **9**

Downtown Palm Springs

Downtown Palm Springs stretches for half a mile along **Palm Canyon Drive**, a wide, bright, and modern strip of chain stores that has engulfed the town's quaint Spanish Colonial–style buildings. Shops run the gamut from upscale boutiques to tacky T-shirt emporia and bookstores devoted exclusively to dead celebrities.

The luxuriously housed **Palm Springs Desert Museum**, 101 Museum Drive (Tues–Sat 10am–5pm, Sun noon–5pm; end July to end Sept Fri–Sun only, 10am–5pm; $7.50, children $3.50; ☎760/325-7186, ⓦwww.psmuseum.org), is strong on Native American and Southwestern art, though its only permanent display is a collection of Asian and African works. Some interesting natural-science exhibits focus on the animal and plant life of the desert, demonstrating that it's not all sandstorms and rattlesnakes. There is a modern art gallery and some lovely sculpture courts on the grounds, and the museum hosts performances of music, theater, comedy, and dance in the 450-seat **Annenberg Theater** (tickets ☎760/325-4490). The major cultural center in the desert is the **McCallum Theater**, 73000 Fred Waring Drive, Palm Desert (☎760/340-2787, ⓦwww.palmsprings.com/mccallumtheatre), with films, music, opera, ballet, and plays.

Not to be missed is the **Tramway Gas Station**, 2901 N Palm Canyon Drive, a classic example of pop architecture with an upswept roof and boomerang design, slated to be the new home of the city's visitor center in 2004. There's also an anarchic piece of landscape gardening at **Moorten Botanical Gardens**, 1701 S Palm Canyon Drive (Mon, Tues, Thurs–Sat 9am–4.30pm, Sun 10am–4pm; $3; ☎707/327-6555, ⓦwww.moplants.com /moorten), a strange cornucopia of every desert plant and cactus, in settings designed to simulate their natural environments, but lumped together in no particular order. Finally, near the airport, the **Palm Springs Air Museum**, 745 N Gene Autry Trail (daily: summer 9am–3pm; rest of year 10am–5pm; $8; ☎760/778-6262 ext 222, ⓦwww.palmspringsairmuseum.org), contains an impressive collection of World War II fighters and bombers, including Spitfires, Tomcats, and a B-17 Flying Fortress.

Around Palm Springs

Most visitors to Palm Springs never leave the poolside, but desert enthusiasts still visit to hike and ride in the **Indian Canyons** (daily 8am–5pm, summer schedule varies; $6; ☎760/325-5673), three miles southeast of downtown along S Palm Canyon Drive. Centuries ago, ancestors of the Cahuilla developed extensive communities here, growing melons, squash, beans, and corn. The canyons are about fifteen miles long, and can be toured by car, although it's worth walking at least a few miles; the easiest trails lead past the waterfalls, rocky gorges, and palm trees of **Palm Canyon** (3 miles) and **Andreas Canyon** (1 mile). Some areas are set aside for **trailblazing** in jeeps and four-wheel-drive vehicles: you can rent one from Off-Road Rentals, four miles north of town at 59755 Hwy-111 (Sept–June only; $35 per hour; ☎760/325-0376, ⓦwww.offroadrentals.com), or take a guided jeep adventure around the Santa Rosa Mountains with Desert Adventures, 67555 E Palm Canyon Drive, Cathedral City (2–4hr; $80–120; ☎760/324-JEEP, ⓦwww.red-jeep .com/jeep_tours.html).

If the desert heat becomes too much to bear, large cable cars grind and sway over eight thousand feet up the **Palm Springs Aerial Tramway**, Tramway Road, just off Hwy-111 north of Palm Springs (daily 10am–9.45pm, weekends open at 8am; $20.80, children $13.80; ☎760/325-1391, ⓦwww.pstramway .com), passing through five climatic zones on the way to the 10,815ft summit of Mount San Jacinto, where there's a **bar** and **restaurant** at the Mountain Station. In the opposite direction from downtown Palm Springs, a few miles east of town, the **Living Desert**, a combination garden and zoo at 47900 Portola Ave, Palm Desert (daily: summer 8.30am–1pm; rest of year 9am–5pm; $10; ☎760/346-5694, ⓦwww.livingdesert.org), represents different desert regions around the world, with cactus and palm gardens, and throws in an incongruous section devoted to African desert animals, such as giraffes, zebras, cheetahs, and warthogs.

Eating and drinking

Although most of the better **restaurants** in Palm Springs are ultra-expensive, more reasonable options can be found with a little effort; alternatively, head to gay-friendly **Cathedral City** ("Cat City"), five miles east along Hwy-111. All listings are in Palm Springs unless otherwise stated.

Agua Bar & Grill 110 N Indian Canyon Drive ☎760/778-1515. Elegant setting with fine eclectic menu and swank piano bar. Located at downtown's *Spa Resort Casino*.

El Gallito 68820 Grove St, Cathedral City ☎760/328-7794. Just east of downtown Palm Springs, a busy Mexican cantina that has the best food for miles and often a wait to match – get there around 6pm to avoid the crowds.

Las Casuelas 368 N Palm Canyon Drive ☎760/325-3213. Local Mexican favorite that's been around since 1958, and remains popular for its hefty portions and laid-back atmosphere. The best bet in a local chain.

Le Vallauris 385 W Tahquitz Canyon Way, next to the Desert Museum ☎760/325-5059. Excellent contemporary California-Mediterranean cuisine in a gorgeous setting. Expect to pay more than $80

per person. Reservations only.

Native Foods 1775 E Palm Canyon Drive ☎760/416-0070. One of the town's better and cheaper choices for vegetarian cuisine, located in a shopping mall.

Peabody's Café 134 S Palm Canyon Drive ☎760/322-1877. Live jazz, cool poetry, and tasty coffee are on offer at this friendly java joint.

Shame on the Moon 69950 Frank Sinatra Drive, Rancho Mirage ☎760/324-5515. Moderately priced California cuisine and excellent service are the draw here, attracting a loyal gay clientele. Located five miles east of downtown Palm Springs.

Thai Smile 651 N Palm Canyon Drive ☎760/320-5503. Uninspiring decor but great, authentic Thai curry and noodle dishes, at all very reasonable prices.

Joshua Tree National Park

Where the low Colorado Desert meets the high Mojave northeast of Palm Springs, **JOSHUA TREE NATIONAL PARK** protects 1250 square miles of grotesquely gnarled and ragged plants, which aren't technically trees at all, but a type of **yucca**, an agave. Named by Mormons in the 1850s, who saw in their craggy branches the arms of Joshua pointing to the promised land, Joshua trees can rise up to forty feet tall, but have to contend with extreme aridity and rocky soil. All around lie great heaps of boulders, pushed up by the Pinto Mountain fault, their edges rounded and smoothed by flash floods and harsh winds.

This unearthly landscape is ethereal at sunrise or sunset, when the desert floor is bathed in red light; at noon it can be a threatening furnace, with temperatures sometimes topping 125°F in summer, and rising even higher in the Low Desert section of the park below 3000ft. Still, the park attracts campers, day-trippers, and rock-climbers for its unspoiled beauty, gold-mine ruins, ancient petroglyphs, and incredible rock formations.

Be selective in your explorations. As with any desert, the heat can be punishing and an ambitious schedule is impossible most of the year. Brief yourself at the visitor centers, and never venture anywhere without a map. On unmarked roads restricted to four-wheel-drive use, don't think about taking a normal car – you'll soon grind to a halt, and it could be quite a few panic-stricken hours before anybody finds you. When hiking, stick to the trails: Joshua Tree is full of abandoned gold mines, so watch for loose gravel around openings, stay away from the edges, never trust the safety of ladders or timber, and bear in mind that the rangers rarely check mines for casualties. Even on the simpler trails, allow around an hour per mile.

One of the easiest hikes (3 miles long) starts one-and-a-half miles from Canyon Road, six miles from the visitor center at Twentynine Palms, at **Fortynine Palms Oasis**; it's accessible only on foot. West of the oasis, quartz boulders tower around the *Indian Cove* campground; a trail from the eastern branch of the campground road heads to **Rattlesnake Canyon**, where, after rainfall, the streams and waterfalls break an otherwise eerie silence among the monoliths.

Moving south into the main body of the park, the **Wonderland of Rocks** features rounded granite boulders that draw rock-climbers from around the world. Well-signposted nature trails lead one mile to **Hidden Valley**, where cattle-rustlers used to hide out, and to the rain-fed **Barker Dam**, one mile to the east. The latter is Joshua Tree's crucial water supply, built by cattlemen around the turn of the twentieth century. One negotiable trail climbs four miles past abandoned mines, where some buildings and equipment are still intact, to **Lost Horse Mine**, 450ft up – which once produced around $20,000 in gold a week, and now consists of antiquated foundations and equipment.

You can find a brilliant desert panorama of badlands and mountains at the 5185ft **Keys View** nearby, from where Geology Tour Road leads down to the east through the best of Joshua Tree's **rock formations** and, further on, to the **Cholla Cactus Garden**.

Practicalities

Less than an hour's drive northeast from Palm Springs, Joshua Tree National Park (always open; $10 per vehicle for 7 days, $5 per cyclist or hiker) is best approached along Hwy-62, which branches off I-10. You can enter the park via the west entrance, at the town of **Joshua Tree**, or the north entrance at Twentynine Palms, where you'll also find the **Oasis Visitor Center**, 74485 National Park Drive (daily 8am–5pm; ☎760/367-5525, ⊛www.joshuatree .org). Alternatively, if you're coming from the south, there's another entrance and the **Cottonwood Visitor Center** (daily 8am–4pm; ☎760/367-5500), seven miles north of I-10. It's worth stopping at one of the visitor centers to collect free maps and guidebooks.

The park has nine established **campgrounds**, all in the northwest except for one at Cottonwood. Only two have water – *Black Rock Canyon* ($12) and *Cottonwood* ($10) – and except for *Indian Cove* ($10), all the others are free. You can reserve sites at *Black Rock* and *Indian Cove* by calling the National Park Service Reservation Center (☎1-800/365-2267, related info at ⊛www.joshua .tree.national-park.com/camping.htm). The rest are operated on a first-come, first-served basis. Come prepared – gathering firewood is not allowed, and you should stock up on water. There are good **motels** and decent restaurants in **TWENTYNINE PALMS**, a small desert town two minutes' drive from the park. The best place to stay is the pleasantly historic *Twentynine Palms Inn*, 73950 Inn Ave (☎760/367-3505, ⊛www.29palmsinn.com; ❺), with its wooden cabins and adobe bungalows, although the *El Rancho Dolores*, nearby at no. 73352 (☎760/367-3528; ❷), provides cheaper, no-frills accommodation; rates quoted are for September through June. The best choice for food is the *Twentynine Palms Inn*, with its homemade bread and vegetables picked fresh from an onsite garden, though you can also grab a snack at *Finicky Coyote*, 73511 Twentynine Palms Hwy (☎760/367-2429), or basic Mexican fare at *Ramona's*, nearby at no. 72115 (☎760/367-1929). Morongo Basin Transit Authority **buses** (☎760/367-7433 or 1-800/794-6282, ⊛www.mbtabus .com) run twice daily between Palm Springs and Twentynine Palms (1 hr 15min; $10 one way, $15 roundtrip), but not into the park itself.

The High Desert

The stretches of the **Mojave Desert** that most people see from the road are predictably arid and desolate. Consequently few visitors are inspired to explore further, but this **High Desert** – sited above 2000ft – offers some of the most dramatic scenery in Southern California, rolling with lush grasses, startling volcanic formations, large stands of Joshua trees, and even, in some spots, piñon pines.

Death Valley National Park

DEATH VALLEY is the hottest place on earth and almost entirely devoid of shade, much less water – carry plenty for both car and body. Its sculpted rock layers form deeply shadowed, eroded crevices at the foot of sharply silhouetted hills, their exotic mineral content turning ancient mudflats into rainbows of sunlit iridescence. The valley was named by a party of white settlers who stumbled through in 1849, looking for a short cut to the Gold Rush towns; they survived despite running out of food and water. Throughout the summer, the **temperature** in Death Valley averages 112°F, and the ground can reach near boiling point. Better to come during the spring, when wildflowers are in bloom; outside the summer, it's generally mild and dry.

The central north–south valley contains two main outposts, **Stovepipe Wells** and **Furnace Creek**, where the **visitor center** (daily 8am–6pm; seven-day pass $10 per vehicle, $5 per pedestrian or cyclist; ☎760/786-2331, ⓦwww.nps.gov/deva) is located. The entrance fee is payable at the park entrance **ranger stations**, which provide free maps and information.

Many of the most unusual sights are located south of Furnace Creek. A good first stop, seven miles along Hwy-178/Badwater Road, is the **Artist's Palette**, an eroded hillside covered in an intensely colored mosaic of reds, golds, blacks, and greens. A few miles further south, a dirt road heading west leads to **Devil's Golf Course**, a field of salt pinnacles and hummocks protruding a couple of feet from the desert floor. Another four miles on, **Badwater** is an unpalatable but nonpoisonous 30ft-wide pool of water, loaded with chloride and sulphates, which is the only home of the soft-bodied Death Valley snail. From the pool, a pair of four-mile hikes crossing the hot valley floor drop a further two feet down to the **lowest point in the western hemisphere**, 282ft below sea level.

The badlands around **Zabriskie Point**, overlooking Badwater and the Artist's Palette off Hwy-190, four miles south of Furnace Creek, were the inspiration for Antonioni's eponymous 1970 movie. More visually appealing is **Dante's View**, twenty-one miles south on 190 and ten miles along a very steep access road; its best vista of the wide, parched desert floor is during the early morning, when the pink-and-gold Panamint Mountains are highlighted by the rising sun.

Near Stovepipe Wells, some thirty miles northwest of Furnace Creek, spread fifteen rippled and contoured square miles of ever-changing **sand dunes**.

Hordes of overheated tourists wait patiently to wander through the surreal luxury of **Scotty's Castle** (tours daily on the hour 9am–5pm; $8; reservations ☎760/786-2392), forty miles north of Stovepipe Wells. Built in the 1920s as the $2-million desert retreat of Chicago insurance broker Albert Johnson, it was named after "Death Valley" Scotty, a cowboy and prospector who managed the construction and claimed the house was his own and financed by a hidden gold mine. Fifty-minute **tours** of the opulently furnished house take in the

△ The Napa Valley Wine Train, Napa Valley

decorative wooden ceilings, indoor waterfalls, and a remote-controlled player piano. The house remains as it was when Johnson died in 1948. Scotty himself lived here until 1954, and is buried just behind the house.

Eight miles west gapes the half-mile-wide **Ubehebe Crater**, the rust-tinged result of a massive volcanic explosion some three thousand years ago; half a mile south sits its thousand-year-old younger brother, **Little Hebe**. Beyond the craters the road continues south for another twenty dusty miles to **Racetrack Valley**, a two-and-a-half-mile mudflat across which giant boulders seem slowly to be racing, leaving faint trails in their wake.

Practicalities

Being out in the middle of nowhere, Death Valley has no scheduled public transportation. If you plan to **stay**, you must reserve ahead. AMFAC (☎760/786-2345 or 1-800/236-7916, ⓦwww.furnacecreekresort.com) operates two hotels on natural oases at Furnace Creek – the gorgeous 1920s adobe *Furnace Creek Inn* (➐–➒), and the ordinary (if still pricey) *Furnace Creek Ranch* (➎–➏), about half a mile north, which has two **restaurants** and a nice bar. Far more reasonable is *Stovepipe Wells Village* (☎760/786-2387, ⓦwww .stovepipewells.com; ➌) on Hwy-190 about thirty miles northwest of Furnace Creek, offering its own mineral-water pool and restaurant. **Camping** in one of the many National Park Service campgrounds costs $10–16 depending on facilities and location, or is free if you don't mind being up in the Panamint Range, far from the valley's sights: the only campground that takes reservations is *Furnace Creek* (☎1-800/365-2267), just north of town.

The High Sierra and the Owens Valley

The towering **eastern** peaks of the **HIGH SIERRA** drop abruptly to the empty landscape of the **OWENS VALLEY**, sixty miles west of Death Valley. Almost the entire range is wilderness: well-maintained roads lead to trailheads at over ten thousand feet, providing access to the stark terrain of spires, glaciers, and clear mountain lakes. US-395 is the lifeline of the area connecting several small towns, all with plenty of budget motels. As there is virtually **no public transporation** in this area (except for CREST; see p.1148), you'll really need a **car** to get around.

Mount Whitney and Lone Pine

Rising out of the northern Mojave Desert, the mountainous backbone of the Sierra Nevada announces itself with a bang two hundred miles north of Los Angeles at 14,494ft **Mount Whitney**, the highest point in the lower 48 states. A silver-gray ridge of pinnacles forms a nearly sheer wall of granite, dominating the small roadside town of **LONE PINE** eleven thousand feet below. **Motels** here include the *Dow Villa Motel/Historic Dow Hotel* at 310 S Main St (☎760/876-5521 or 1-800/824-9317, ⓦwww.dowvillamotel.com; ➌), where John Wayne always stayed when filming in the area, and the *Best Western Frontier Motel*, 1008 S Main St (☎760/876-5571 or 1-800/528-1234; ➌). Those headed north might want to push on sixteen miles to Independence, where the slightly run-down but atmospheric *Winnedumah Hotel* bed-and-breakfast inn, 211 N Edwards St (☎760/878-2040; ➌), also operates as an HI-**hostel** with $21 beds (with membership, and without breakfast). You can **camp** at *Tuttle Creek* campground (free; no water) on Horseshoe Meadow Road some four miles west of Lone Pine beyond the Alabama Hills (see below). The *Pizza Factory*, 301 S Main St (℡760/876-4707), and the diner-style *Mt Whitney Restaurant*, 227 S Main St (℡760/876-5751), are decent places to **eat**. The **Eastern Sierra Interagency Visitor Center**, a mile south of town on US-395 at the junction of Hwy-136 (daily 8am–4.50pm; ℡760/876-6222), is a great source of information about the Owens Valley.

Many early Westerns, and the epic *Gunga Din*, were filmed in the **Alabama Hills** to the west, a rugged expanse of bizarrely eroded sedimentary rock. Some of the oddest formations are linked by the **Picture Rocks Circle**, a paved road that loops around from Whitney Portal Road, passing rocks shaped like bullfrogs, walruses, and baboons.

Two thousand eager souls make the strenuous 22-mile roundtrip **hike** (12–16hr; 6100ft ascent) to the summit of Mount Whitney each summer. Permits are needed and are awarded by lottery: ensure your application (available at ⓦwww.fs.fed.us/r5/inyo) is postmarked or fax-dated no sooner than February 1; the lottery begins on February 15, so it's best to mail or fax your application as close to that date as possible. Send your application to the Wilderness Permit Office, Inyo National Forest, 351 Pacu Lane, suite 200, Bishop, CA 93514 (℡760/873-2483), or fax it to ℡760/873-2484. All hikers pay a $15 fee.

One-day ascents start at dawn from either the *Whitney Portal* **campground** (mid-May to mid-Oct; ℡1-877/444-6777; $30), or the one-night-only first-come, first-served *Whitney Trailhead* site ($6) at the end of twisting Whitney Portal Road, reachable via trailhead shuttle (℡760/878-2119). The trail cuts up to boulder-strewn Trail Crest Pass, the southern end of the 220-mile John Muir Trail to Yosemite, then climbs along the top of vertical cliffs. At the rounded summit, a stone cabin serves as an emergency shelter – though not one you'd choose to be in during a lightning storm.

Big Pine and the White Mountains

Nearly fifty miles north, hikes lead from the end of Glacier Lodge Road, ten miles west of nondescript **BIG PINE**, up to the **Palisades Glacier**, the southernmost glacier in the northern hemisphere. Along the opposite wall of the five-mile-wide Owens Valley, the ancient, bald, and dry **White Mountains** are home to the gnarled **bristlecone pines**, the oldest living things on earth. Occupying a narrow band at around ten thousand feet, and often covered in snow until mid-June, some of these gnarled trees have been alive for over four thousand years. Battered and beaten by the harsh environment into contorted but beautiful shapes, even when dead they hang on without decaying for upwards of another thousand years, slowly being eroded by wind-driven ice and sand.

The most accessible collection of these magnificent trees is **Schulman Grove** ($3 per person, or $5 per vehicle), named after dendrochronologist Dr Edmund Schulman, who revealed the extreme longevity of the trees in the mid-1950s. Located 24 twisting but paved miles from Big Pine off Hwy-168, the grove centers on the **visitor center** (open late May–Oct; recorded info on ℡760/873-2500). Two trails radiate out from here: the mile-long **Discovery Trail**, which passes some photogenic examples; and a longer loop which passes but intentionally fails to identify the oldest tree, the 4700-year-old Methuselah. **Patriarch Grove**, twelve miles further, along a dusty dirt road that gives spectacular views of the Sierra Nevada and the Great Basin ranges, contains the largest and comparably ancient bristlecone.

In the White Mountains there's the free, waterless *Grandview* **campground**, or you can retreat to the **motels** along US-395 in Big Pine – the *Big Pine Motel*, 370 S Main St (℡760/938-2282; ❸), and the *Starlight Motel*, 511 S Main St (℡760/938-2011; ❸).

Bishop

BISHOP, to a Californian, means outdoor pursuits. The largest town (population 3500) in the Owens Valley, it's an excellent base for cross-country skiing, fly-fishing, and especially rock-climbing. **Motels**, such as the *El Rancho*, 274 W Lagoon St (℡760/872-9251 or 1-888/872-9251; ❸), the *Thunderbird*, 190 W Pine St (℡760/873-4215; ❸), and bargain restaurants can be found within a block of US-395. The **visitor center** at 690 N Main St (Mon–Fri 9am–5pm, Sat & Sun 10am–4pm; ℡760/873-8405, ⓦwww.bishopvisitor.com) can provide details of the many **adventure travel specialists** based in town. For **hiking** and **camping** information, the White Mountain Ranger Station, 798 N Main St (May–Oct daily; rest of year Mon–Fri; call for hours; ℡760/873-2500), will be of more use.

Mammoth Lakes

Forty miles north along US-395 from Bishop, then five miles west on Hwy-203, the resort town of **MAMMOTH LAKES** offers the state's premier ski slopes outside the Lake Tahoe basin, and in summer hosts on- and off-road bike races. The setting is stunning, but the town is pricey and prone to testosterone overload. To ski **Mammoth Mountain** (℡1-800/MAMMOTH, ⓦwww.mammothmountain.com), which looms up behind the resort, pick up **lift tickets** ($57 Mon–Fri, $62 Sat, Sun & holidays) from the Main Lodge on Minaret Road, where you can also rent **equipment** ($27 for basic skis, boots, and poles), and book three-hour **lessons** ($55). In summer, fifty miles of snow-free slopes transform themselves into the 3500-acre **Mammoth Mountain Bike Park** ($15 a day for unlimited trail access and rides on the bike shuttle and gondola; add $17 for bike rental).

One appealing summer-only destination is the **Devil's Postpile National Monument**, seven miles southwest of Mammoth Mountain ($7, includes shuttle bus). A collection of slender, blue-gray basaltic columns, some scaling sixty feet, the Postpile was formed as lava from a volcanic eruption cooled and fractured into multi-sided forms. From here, a two-mile hike along the San Joaquin River leads to **Rainbow Falls**, which refract the midday sun perfectly.

Practicalities

Year-round Carson Ridgecrest Eastern Sierra Transit (CREST) **buses** (℡760/872-1901 or ℡1-800/922-1930) stop in the *McDonald's* parking lot on Hwy-203. During the ski season, get around on the five-line Mammoth Shuttle (℡760/934-3030). For information, go to the combined US Forest Service **ranger station** and Mammoth Lakes **visitor center**, on the main highway half a mile east of the town center (daily 8am–5pm; ℡760/924-5500, ⓦwww.visitmammoth.com).

Mammoth's plentiful **accommodation**, which includes two hostels, are costliest in winter. *Mammoth Mountain Inn* on Mammoth Mountain (℡760/934-2581 or 1-800/626-6684; ❻–❼), is a touch sterile but it's at the heart of all the ski and bike action, while the *Cinnamon Bear Inn*, 113 Center St (℡760/934-2873 or 1-800/845-2873; ❹–❺), is a 22-room B&B that's reasonably priced and close to downtown. *Davison St. Guesthouse*, 19 Davison St

(T760/924-2188; **①**–**③**), offers mountain views from its four-bed rooms ($58–67) and dorms ($27–31). There are **campgrounds** ($12) close to Devil's Postpile National Monument, and free waterless sites in the Inyo National Forest off US-395 around eleven miles north.

Restaurants tend to be expensive but casual: *Giovanni's*, in the Minaret Village Mall on Old Mammoth Road (T760/934-7563), is popular for pasta and pizza, with great lunchtime deals; while *The Lakefront Restaurant*, at Tamarack Lodge (T760/934-3534), offers superb lake views and good French-Californian cuisine – for a price. *Whiskey Creek*, at Main and Minaret (T760/934-2555), is a lively **bar** and restaurant, with its own good micro-brews.

Mono Lake, Lee Vining, and Bodie Ghost Town

The blue expanse of **Mono Lake** sits in the midst of a volcanic desert table-land at the north end of the valley. It looks like a science-fiction landscape, with two large islands, one light-colored, the other black, surrounded by salty, alka-line water. Strange sandcastle-like formations of **tufa** (calcium deposited from springs) have been exposed over the fifty years since the City of Los Angeles extended an aqueduct into the Mono Basin through an eleven-mile tunnel, dropping the **water level** by over forty feet and creating the biggest environ-mental controversy in California. Mono Lake is the primary nesting ground for the state's **California gull** population – twenty percent of the world total – and a prime stopover point for thousands of grebes and phalaropes. As the water levels dropped, the islands in the middle of the lake, where the seagulls lay their eggs, became peninsulas, and the colonies fell prey to coyotes and other mainland predators. The landlocked water became increasingly alkaline, threatening the unique ecosystem. Though the California Supreme Court ruled in 1983 that Mono Lake must be saved, it wasn't until 1991 that emer-gency action was taken.

For more details about Mono Lake and the fight for its survival, stop by the **Mono Lake Committee Information Center**, in the small town of **LEE VINING** on US-395 (daily: July & Aug 9am–10pm; rest of year 9am–5pm; T760/647-6595, @www.leevining.com), or a mile north at the excellent **Mono Basin Scenic Area Visitor Center** (May–Oct daily 9am–5.30pm; Nov–April generally weekends only 9am–4pm; T760/647-3044). **Motels** along US-395 include *El Mono Motel* (T760/647-6310; **③**) and *Murphey's* (T760/647-6316 or 1-800/334-6316; **④**). Also on US-395, the diner-style *Nicely's Restaurant* (T760/647-6477) is a Fifties vinyl palace that opens at 6am, while five miles north, the more upscale, south-of-the-border-leaning *Mono Inn Restaurant* (T760/647-6581) is owned by Ansel Adams' granddaughter.

Northeast of Lee Vining, in a remote, high desert valley, stands a well-preserved and evocative relic of the gold-mining 1870s. The **Bodie State Park** (open all year but often inaccessible by car in winter; $1 per person; T760/647-6445, @ceres.ca.gov/sierradsp/bodie) is perhaps the best **ghost town** in the US, with many of its structures still intact but not gussied up for tourists. With thirty saloons and dance halls and a population of ten thousand, it was once the raunchiest and most lawless mining camp in the west; over 150 wooden buildings survive in a state of arrested decay around the intact town center, littered with old bottles, bits of machinery, and old stagecoaches. The ruins of the mines themselves, in the hills east of town, are off limits to visitors except on the frequent tours.

The Central Coast

Between the hustle of LA and San Francisco, the four hundred miles of the **Central Coast** come as a welcome respite, sparsely populated outside a few medium-sized cities and lined by clean sandy beaches. The topography is at its most dramatic along **Big Sur**, one of the most rugged and beautiful stretches of coastline in the world, where the brooding Santa Lucia Mountains rise steeply out of the thundering Pacific surf. To the south, **Santa Barbara** is a wealthy resort full of old and new money, while **Santa Cruz** in the north is a coastal town redolent of the Sixties. In between, languorous **San Luis Obispo** makes a good base for visiting **Hearst Castle**, the hilltop palace of publishing magnate William Randolph Hearst, and the inspiration for the Xanadu pleasure palace in the film *Citizen Kane*.

Almost all of the towns grew up around the original Spanish Catholic **missions**, each a long day's walk from the next, and once enclosed within thick walls to prevent Native American attack. Still featuring attractive nineteenth-century architecture, **Monterey**, a hundred miles south of San Francisco, was California's capital under Spain and Mexico, and briefly the state capital in 1850.

Amtrak's *Coast Starlight* **train** runs along the coast up to San Luis Obispo before cutting inland north to San Francisco and up to Seattle; Greyhound **buses** stop at most of the towns, especially along the main highway, US-101.

Santa Barbara

The six-lane coastal freeway that races past oil wells and winding hills slows to a leisurely pace a hundred miles north of Los Angeles at **SANTA BARBARA**. Beautifully sited on gently sloping hills above the Pacific, the town's low-slung Spanish Revival buildings feature ubiquitous red-tiled roofs and white stucco walls, while its golden beaches are wide and clean, lined by palm trees along a curving bay. Although a large portion of downtown has been replaced by a vast, upscale shopping mall, Santa Barbara has managed to retain its quaintly upscale yet relaxed character.

The mission-era feel of Santa Barbara is no accident. After a devastating earthquake in 1925, the entire town was rebuilt in the image of an apocryphal Spanish Colonial village, with numerous arcades linking shops, cafés, and restaurants, and a pedestrian-friendly layout that serves visitors well. **State Street**, the main drag, is home to an appealing assortment of diners, bookshops, coffee bars, and nightclubs. The few remaining genuine mission structures are preserved as **El Presidio de Santa Barbara** (daily 10.30am–4.30pm; $4; ☎805/965-0093, ⊛www.sbthp.org), at the center of which are the barracks of the old fortress **El Cuartel**, standing two blocks east of State Street at 123 Canon Perdido. The second-oldest building in California, it now houses historical exhibits and a scale model of the small Spanish colony. Nearby, the **Santa Barbara Historical Museum**, 136 E de la Guerra St (Tues–Sat 10am–5pm, Sun noon–5pm; donation; ☎805/966-1601, ⊛www.santabarbara-museum.com), presents other aspects of the city's past, from Ice Age geology to artifacts from Native settlements to photographs of more recent times. Three blocks north of El Presidio, the still-functional **County Courthouse**, 1100

Anacapa St (Mon–Fri 8am–5pm, Sat & Sun 10am–5pm; free), is a first-rate piece of Spanish Revival architecture, an idiosyncratic variation on the mission theme that's widely known as one of the finest public buildings in the US. Take a break in the sunken gardens, explore the quirky staircases, or climb the seventy-foot-high **clock tower** for a nice view out over the town.

State Street leads half a mile down from the town center to **Stearns Wharf**, the oldest wooden pier in the state, built in 1872 but nearly destroyed in November 1998, when a third of the pier was engulfed in flames. Restoration efforts have now made it home to shopping stalls and food vendors, with magnificent **beaches** stretching in either direction.

In the hills above the town is the engaging **Museum of Natural History**, 2559 Puesta del Sol Rd (daily 10am–5pm; $7; ☎805/682-4711, ⓦwww.sbnature.org), which has informative displays on the plants and animals of Southern California. The museum entrance itself is constructed out of the skeleton of a blue whale. Nearby, **Mission Santa Barbara** (daily 9am–5pm; $4; ⓦwww.sbmission.org) is the so-called "Queen of the Missions," though it was one of the later ones constructed in California, in 1820. Its colorful twin-towered facade – facing out over a perfectly manicured garden towards the sea – combines Romanesque and Spanish Mission styles, giving it a heavy, imposing character lacking in some of the prettier missions in the chain. A small **museum** here displays historical artifacts from the mission archives. Other notable missions in the area are the Franciscan **Santa Inés**, just outside the town of Solvang, heading north on US-101, and **La Purísima**, about twenty miles northwest of Solvang on Hwy-1, the most completely restructured of all the missions.

Arrival, information, and accommodation

Greyhound **buses** from LA and San Francisco stop every few hours downtown at 34 W Carrillo St; Amtrak **trains** arrive at the old Southern Pacific station at 209 State St, a block west of US-101. The **visitor center** is at 1 Santa Barbara St, East Beach (Mon–Sat 9am–5pm, Sun 10am–5pm; ☎805/965-3021, ⓦwww.santabarbara.com). You can walk to most places, although a frequent **shuttle bus** (25¢) loops around Santa Barbara during the day, with Santa Barbara Metropolitan Transit District buses ($1.25; ☎805/683-3702, ⓦwww.sbmtd.gov) covering the outlying areas into the evening.

Although there are a few reasonable places to **stay** in town, most hotels are either expensive or hard to find. Enlist help from **Hot Spots**, a 24-hour hotel reservation center and espresso bar at 36 State St (☎805/564-1637 or 1-800/793-7666, ⓦwww.hotspotsusa.com), which offers information and specials on lodging. The nearest useful **camping** spots are ten miles south of Santa Barbara at Carpinteria State Beach (☎805/684-2811 or 1-800/444-7275; $18), and El Capitan State Beach to the north (☎805/968-1033 or 1-800/444-7275; $18).

Banana Bungalow Hostel 210 E Ortega St ☎805/963-0154 or 1-800/3-HOSTEL, ⓦwww.bananabungalow.com. Dorm beds here are cheap and comfortable ($18), if you don't mind a nonstop party atmosphere. ❶

Bayberry Inn 111 W Valerio St ☎805/569-3398, ⓦwww.bayberryinnsantabarbara.com. Lovely little spot offering eight comfortable B&B rooms themed around various berries, and with canopy beds and Victorian furnishings. ❼

Cheshire Cat 36 W Valerio St ☎805/569-1610, ⓦwww.cheshirecat.com. Upscale, tastefully decorated B&B with hot tub, bikes for guests' use, and an Alice in Wonderland theme. Complimentary wine on arrival, and breakfast under a palm tree. ❽

Harbor View Inn 28 W Cabrillo Blvd ☎805/963-0780 or 1-800/755-0222, ⓦwww.harborviewinnsb.com. Casually luxurious option with on-site restaurant and bar, pool and Jacuzzis, and elegant rooms with oceanfront views and refrigerators. ❽

Montecito del Mar 316 W Montecito St ☎1-888/464-1690, ⓦwww.santabarbarahotel316 .com. One of the city's best deals, a Spanish Revival inn with a wide range of rooms, offering pleasant decor, three spas, complimentary breakfast, and an excellent location three blocks from the sands. ❺

State Street 121 State St ☎805/966-6586. An old Mission-style establishment located near the beach and offering complimentary breakfast. ❷

Eating, drinking, and nightlife

Although Santa Barbara, as a college town, has plenty of places for munching on comfort food and swilling beer, the unquestioned center for local and tourist activity is **State Street**, which is lined with a number of good **restaurants**, **bars**, and **clubs**.

Chad's 625 Chapala St ☎805/568-1876. Modern American cuisine served in the intimate atmosphere of a historic Victorian home.

Citronelle 901 Cabrillo Blvd ☎805/963-4717. Stylish big-name restaurant you've read about in all the food-fashion mags, with delicious entrees like lamb shank and porcupine shrimp, sweeping coastal views, and, not surprisingly, exorbitant prices.

Coffee Bean & Tea Leaf 811-A State St ☎805/966-2442. A solid café and a great place to watch the evening clubgoers parade by.

El Paseo 10 El Paseo ☎805/962-6050. Upscale Mexican restaurant sited in a historic home with a colorful fountain courtyard.

Hot Spots Espresso Bar 36 State St ☎805/963-4233. A block from the beach, a cozy 24hr spot for java, pastries, and other snacks. It also offers one of the city's better hotel-reservation services (see overleaf).

Madhouse 434 State St ☎805/962-5516. Mellow spot cashing in on the retro-cocktail craze, with easygoing style and modern decor.

Mousse Odile 18 E Cota St ☎805/962-5393. French cuisine with a California flair, focusing on pasta, steak, and seafood. Swank but cozy.

Natural Café 508 State St ☎805/962-9494. Offers scrumptious veggie meals and prime vistas for people-watching.

Pascucci 729 State St ☎805/963-8123. Somewhat snooty but worth it for cheap and delicious pasta, gourmet pizzas, and panini.

Sushi-Teri 1013 Bath St ☎805/963-1250. One in a local chain of sushi joints, with cheap prices and hefty chicken bowls, mouth-watering rolls, and a nice selection of fish platters.

Zelo 630 State St ☎805/966-5792. Fashionable bar and restaurant that evolves into a dance club as the night wears on, offering dance, Latin, retro, and other eclectic fare throughout the week.

San Luis Obispo

SAN LUIS OBISPO, 160 miles north of Santa Barbara and halfway between LA and San Francisco, is a few miles inland, but makes the best base for exploring the surrounding coastal regions. Still primarily an agricultural center, it holds more nineteenth-century architecture than any other California city (especially around Buchon Street), as well as good restaurants, a couple of pubs, and – outside summer holiday weekends – plenty of accommodation.

The compact core of San Luis is eminently walkable, centered on the late eighteenth century **Mission San Luis Obispo de Tolosa** (daily 9–4pm, May–Sept closes 5pm; $2; ☎805/781-8220, ⓦwww.missionsanluisobispo .org), a dark and unremarkable church that was the prototype for the now ubiquitous red-tiled roof, developed to replace the original, flammable thatch in response to Native American arson attacks. Between the mission and the visitor center, **Mission Plaza**'s terraces step down along San Luis creek, along which footpaths meander, crisscrossed by bridges every hundred feet, and overlooked by shops and outdoor restaurants on the south bank. **Higuera Street**, a block south of Mission Plaza, is the main drag, and springs to life on Thursday afternoons for the **Farmers' Market**, when the street is closed to cars and filled with vegetable stalls, barbecues, and street-corner musicians. The highlight of the area, though, is the historic **Fremont Theater**, 1035 Monterey St, an Art Deco marvel that becomes a riot of splashy neon at night and still plays movies. A few blocks southeast of the theater, the **Dallidet Adobe and Gardens**, 1185 Pacific St (summer Sun 1–4pm, otherwise by appointment; donation; ☎805/543-6762), is a handsome 1860s residence and one of the area's oldest buildings, with a pleasant garden sitting in the shadow of a pair of huge redwood trees.

Arrival, information, and accommodation

The Greyhound **bus** depot is at 150 South St, half a mile from the center of town, while Amtrak **trains** stop at the end of Santa Rosa Street, half a mile south of the business district. The **Chamber of Commerce**, 1039 Chorro St (☎805/781-2777, ⓦwww.slochamber.org), provides brochures for **self-guided walking tours** of notable sights. The local transit company, San Luis Obispo Regional Rideshare (☎805/541-2277, ⓦwww.rideshare.org), has information on various transit options in the region, including shuttles and taxis. Available from several different operators, **bus** rides in town cost 75¢.

Monterey Street was the site of the world's first (now long gone) **motel** – the *Motel Inn*. Rates for its modern counterparts are generally low, though if you want a nice view of the ocean, you're better off taking a short drive south to **Pismo Beach**, a beach town that makes a pleasant stopover.

Apple Farm 2015 Monterey St ☎805/544-2040, ⓦwww.applefarm.com. Charming Victorian inn with a range of appealing rooms, with canopy beds, complimentary breakfast, and attractive surroundings. **❼**

Best Western Shorecliff Lodge 2555 Price St, Pismo Beach ☎805/773-4671, ⓦwww.shorecliff.com. Reliable chain motel with a dramatically sited swimming pool and a cliff-hugging gazebo over the Pacific. **❻**

Economy Motel 652 Morro St ☎805/543-7024. A particularly good-value, clean, and cozy budget option, with the usual amenities. **❷**

Edgewater 280 Wadsworth Ave, Pismo Beach ☎805/773-4811, ⓦwww.edgewater-inn.com. Right on the beach, offering hot tubs, a heated pool, and kitchenettes in some rooms. **❹**

Hostel Obispo 1617 Santa Rosa St ☎805/544-4678, ⓦwww.hostelobispo.com. At $20 a night, this hostel is the best value around, offering a convenient central location, cheap bike rentals, and complimentary pancake breakfasts. Private rooms $55. **❶–❸**

San Luis Inn 404 Santa Rosa St ☎805/544-0881, ⓦwww.sanluisinn.com. Clean rooms, complimentary breakfast, and a heated pool. **❸**

Eating and drinking

Higuera Street is the prime place to **eat**, especially during the Farmers' Market on Thursday, with a nice range of unassuming restaurants and **bars**. Other good dining choices can also be found throughout town, along with a few microbreweries.

Buona Tavola 1037 Monterey St ☎805/545-8000. Serviceable bistro featuring a good selection of Northern Italian food and wine.

Oasis 675 Higuera St ☎805/543-1155. Delicious Middle Eastern cuisine – the set lunches are especially good value.

Splash Café 197 Pomeroy Ave, Pismo Beach ☎805/773-4653. Wide-ranging, seafood-oriented menu, featuring a fine clam chowder.

Taj Palace 795 Foothill Blvd ☎805/543-0722. The city's top choice for Indian cuisine, though a bit pricier than other ethnic diners.

Z Pie 1060 Osos St ☎805/544-9743. Unusual and delectable takes on the old-fashioned pot-pie, stuffed with the likes of steak and cabernet, shrimp and roasted garlic, or caramel pippin apple – a gut-busting gourmet treat for only $5.

Hearst Castle

Forty-five miles northwest of San Luis Obispo, the hilltop **Hearst Castle** is one of the most extravagant estates in the world. The former holiday home where publisher **William Randolph Hearst** held court for such guests as Winston Churchill, Charlie Chaplin, George Bernard Shaw, and Charles Lindbergh brings in more than a million visitors a year. Its interior is a garish hodgepodge of walls, floors, and ceilings ripped from European churches and castles and mixed with Gothic fireplaces and Moorish tiles, while nearly every room bursts with Greek vases and medieval tapestries. Ironically, the same financial power and lust for collecting that allowed Hearst to hoard these artifacts for himself have made them viewable to far more people than they otherwise would have been in their respective lands.

Work on Hearst's nearly four-hundred-square-mile ranch began in 1919, managed by architect Julia Morgan, who designed each room and building in the spirit of the works destined to be housed inside. The castle was never truly completed: rooms were torn out as soon as they were finished to accommodate yet more acquired treasure. The main facade, a twin-towered copy of a Mudejar cathedral, stands atop steps curving up from the world's most photographed swimming pool, which is filled with spring water and lined by a Greek colonnade and marble statues – the height of aesthetic glory, or irredeemably vulgar, depending on your taste.

The most dramatic time to visit is in the morning, when coastal fog often enshrouds the hill slopes below the castle, making it resemble *Citizen Kane's* eerily evocative Xanadu, which was modeled on the estate. Five different, two-hour guided **tours** (summer daily 8am–4pm; rest of year 8.20am–3.20pm; $12 unless specified; ☎1-800/444-4445, ⓦwww.hearst-castle.org) leave from the visitor center just off Hwy-1. A tour is essential, as are reservations; new visitors

The real Citizen Kane

Often portrayed as a power-hungry monster – most memorably by Orson Welles in his thinly veiled *Citizen Kane* – **William Randolph Hearst** was born in 1863 as the only son of a multimillionaire mining engineer, and learned the newspaper trade in New York under Joseph Pulitzer, the inventor of "Yellow Journalism," of which Hearst became its greatest practitioner. When he published his own *Morning Journal*, Hearst fanned the flames of American imperialism to ignite the Spanish–American War of 1898. As he told his correspondents in Cuba: "You provide the pictures, and I'll provide the war." Hearst eventually controlled an empire which during the 1930s sold twenty-five percent of the nation's newspapers – and sixty percent of those sold in California.

Despite his war-mongering nationalism, Hearst was otherwise politically moderate, a lifelong Democrat who served two terms in the House of Representatives but failed to be elected mayor of New York, let alone president. Besides his many newspapers, Hearst owned eleven radio stations and two movie studios, which he used to make his longtime mistress, Marion Davies, a star. Both were aboard Hearst's yacht when in 1924 the famed silent-movie producer Thomas Ince – a party guest – died amid suspicious circumstances. Hearst was never prosecuted, but the charge of murder, combined with the more familiar ones of jingoism and corporate monopoly, only helped reinforce the man's dark legend. When the Depression hit, he was forced to sell off most of his holdings, but he continued to exert power and influence – including an attempt to suppress Welles's film and launch a campaign against it – until his death in 1951, aged 88.

are directed to the Experience Tour ($18), which gives an overview of the castle and its treasures, while the Garden Tour offers a peek at the castle's blooms, as well as the guest house and wine cellar. From April to October, docents in period dress take visitors on evening tours of the castle ($24), speaking of Hearst in the present tense.

The Big Sur Coast

Starting just north of Hearst Castle, the ninety wild and undeveloped miles of rocky cliffs along the **Big Sur Coast** form a sublime landscape where redwood groves line river canyons and the Santa Lucia Mountains rise out of the blue-green Pacific. Running through this striking terrain is the circuitous, exhilarating route of **Hwy-1**, carved out of bedrock cliffs 500ft above the ocean, and **public transportation** is limited to the Monterey-Salinas Transit (MST) bus (℡831/899-2555, Ⓦwww.mst.org), which runs south from Monterey to Nepenthe twice daily during the summer (Rte-22; $3.50 one way). The roads and campgrounds get packed on summer weekends, and hardly anyone braves the turbulent winters, when violent storms can erode cliffsides and toss sections of the highway into the sea. The southern coastline of Big Sur is comparatively gentle, with sandy beaches hiding below crumbling ochre cliffs. To find out more, contact the regional **Chamber of Commerce** (℡831/667-2100, Ⓦwww.bigsurcalifornia.org).

Roughly midway along the Big Sur Coast, **ESALEN** is named for the long-gone native tribes who once enjoyed its natural **hot spring**, situated on a clifftop high above the raging Pacific surf. Since the 1960s, when people came to Big Sur to smoke pot and get back to nature, Esalen has been at the forefront of the New Age movement, and the spring is now owned and operated by the Esalen Institute (by reservation only; ℡831/667-3005, Ⓦwww.esalen.org), which aims to instruct neophytes on the "potentialities and values of human existence," although most yuppies simply come for the yoga and massage treatments.

Three miles north on Hwy-1, **Julia Pfeiffer Burns State Park** (daily dawn–dusk; $6 parking; ℡831/667-2315) offers some of the best day-hikes in the Big Sur area, including a ten-minute walk along the cliffs to an overlook of McWay Falls, which crash onto a beach below. A less-traveled path leads down from Hwy-1 two miles north of the waterfall through a two-hundred-foot-long tunnel to the remains of a small wharf at **Partington Cove**, one of the few places in Big Sur where you can get to the sea. As with other Big Sur parks, Pfeiffer Burns provides camping sites for $12–16 per night (reserve at ℡831/667-2315, Ⓦwww.reserveamerica.com), while private operations like nearby *Ventana Campground* (℡831/667-2712; $25–35) offer campsites with bath houses equipped with hot water and electricity. Seven miles north of Pfeiffer Burns, lovely old *Deetjen's Big Sur Inn* (℡831/667-2377; ❺) has ski-lodge-style log cabins with rooms hand-crafted from thick redwood planks and in-room fireplaces, plus fine breakfasts and fish and veggie meals in its dining room.

Further north at **NEPENTHE**, the rooftop *Nepenthe* restaurant, just off Hwy-1 (℡831/667-2345), offers pricey steaks and seafood, though you can find similarly impressive views, and more affordable prices, at *Café Kevah* (℡831/667-2344), which serves organic breakfasts and lunches on its terrace. Across the highway, the **Henry Miller Library** (Wed–Mon 11am–6pm; donation: ℡831/667-2574, Ⓦwww.henrymiller.org), displays and sells books by the author, who lived elsewhere in the area intermittently until the 1960s. Two miles north along Hwy-1, unmarked Sycamore Canyon Road leads a mile west to Big Sur's best strip of coast, **Pfeiffer Beach** (daily dawn–dusk), a white sand stretch dominated by a large rock whose color varies from brown to red to orange in the changing light. The beach has been closed for renovations, with no scheduled reopening date – call ☎831/667-2315 for up-to-date information.

Big Sur River Valley

Immediately north of the Pfeiffer Beach turnoff, Hwy-1 drops into the valley of the Big Sur River, where the majority of the accommodation and restaurants are dotted sporadically along six miles of the highway. Your first stop should be at the US Forest Service **ranger station** (daily 8am–6pm; ☎831/667-2315), which issues the camping permits required for the Ventana Wilderness in the mountains above, and can provide information on staying at the other parks in the area.

One of these parks, sheltered **Pfeiffer Big Sur State Park**, features deep, clear swimming holes that form in the steepwalled river gorge during late spring and summer, and a hiking trail that leads half a mile up a canyon shaded by redwoods to the sixty-foot **Pfeiffer Falls**. The **campgrounds** here charge $12–18 and are often full on summer weekends (☎831/667-2315 or 1-800/444-7275, ⓦwww.reserveamerica.com).

Just north of Pfeiffer Big Sur, the cluster of shops, lodgings, and restaurants known as **The Village** is the most feasible base for seeing the area. **Accommodation** fills up in summer, but if you can afford it, it's worth spending a night in one of the rustic riverside rooms at the *Big Sur River Inn Resort* (☎831/667-2700 or 1-800/548-3610, ⓦwww.bigsurriverinn.com; ❹–❽), which has an upscale **restaurant** with seafood standards and solid American cuisine, which you can enjoy in a riverside garden setting or on a sunny terrace. There are also good-sized cabins in the *Big Sur Lodge* (☎831/667-3100 or 1-800/424-4787, ⓦwww.bigsurlodge.com; ❺–❽), where the plush rooms have porches and large showers, but no phones or TVs. Alternatively try the more basic cabins at *Big Sur Campgrounds and Cabins*, a mile north of Pfeiffer Big Sur State Park (☎831/667-2322; ❸).

The Monterey Peninsula

At the northern edge of the Big Sur coast, a hundred miles south of San Francisco, are the rocky headlands of the **Monterey Peninsula**, where gnarled cypress trees mark the collision between the cliffs and the sea. The lively harbor town of **Monterey** was the capital of California under the Spanish and briefly under the Mexicans and Americans, and retains many old adobe houses and places of genuine historic appeal alongside the requisite tourist traps. **Carmel**, on the other hand, three miles to the south, is a self-consciously quaint village of million-dollar holiday homes and art galleries, famous for once having elected Clint Eastwood as its mayor.

Arrival, information, and getting around

Northbound Greyhound **buses** stop at the Exxon station on the Monterey waterfront, 1042 Del Monte Ave, while **Amtrak** requires you to change in the sprawling agricultural town of **Salinas** inland, and take a further 55-minute

⑬

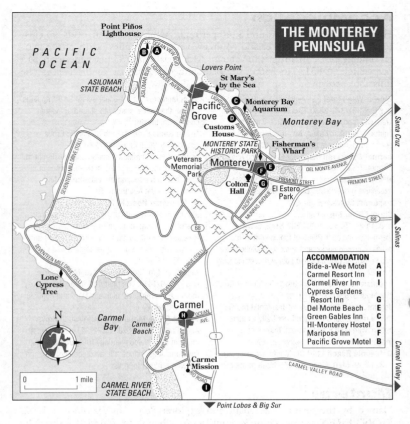

THE MONTEREY PENINSULA

PACIFIC OCEAN

Point Piños Lighthouse

ASILOMAR STATE BEACH

Lovers Point

St Mary's by the Sea

Pacific Grove

Monterey Bay Aquarium

Customs House

Monterey Bay

MONTEREY STATE HISTORIC PARK

Fisherman's Wharf

Veterans Memorial Park

Monterey

Colton Hall

El Estero Park

DEL MONTE AVENUE

FREMONT STREET

FREMONT STREET

Lone Cypress Tree

Carmel

Carmel Bay

Carmel Beach

CARMEL VALLEY ROAD

N

Carmel Mission

CARMEL RIVER STATE BEACH

0   1 mile

Point Lobos & Big Sur

Santa Cruz

Salinas

Carmel Valley

ACCOMMODATION

Bide-a-Wee Motel	A
Carmel Resort Inn	H
Carmel River Inn	I
Cypress Gardens Resort Inn	G
Del Monte Beach	E
Green Gables Inn	C
HI-Monterey Hostel	D
Mariposa Inn	F
Pacific Grove Motel	B

13

CALIFORNIA | The Monterey Peninsula

trip on the hourly local bus #21 into Monterey.

Pick up information at the Monterey **visitor center**, 401 Camino El Estero at Franklin St (daily Mon–Sat 9am–6pm, winter closes at 5pm; Sun 9am–5pm, winter 10am–4pm; ☎831/649-1770); the **Chamber of Commerce**, 380 Alvarado St (Mon–Fri 8.30am–5pm; ☎831/648-5360, ⓦwww.mpcc.com); or, in Carmel, the **Monterey County Visitor Center**, 137 Crossroads Blvd (daily 9.30am–6pm; ☎1-888/221-1010, ⓦwww.montereyinfo.org), which can also help with hotel reservations.

Getting around the peninsula and points beyond is surprisingly easy on Monterey Salinas Transit buses (☎831/899-2555, ⓦwww.mst.org). The most useful routes from Monterey are #4 and #5 to Carmel, #21 to Salinas, #1 to Pacific Grove, and #22 along the Big Sur Coast to Nepenthe (twice daily, summer only). The base charge is $1.75 for travel on the peninsula, though this can double or triple the further you go (eg, Watsonville to Nepenthe). There's also a free shuttle bus, the WAVE, from downtown to the Aquarium on Cannery Row.

Another option is to **rent a bike**: try Adventures by the Sea, 201 Alvarado Mall ($6 per hour, $24 for two days; ☎831/372-1807, ⓦwww.adventuresbythesea .com), or Bay Bikes, outside the Maritime Museum at 640 Wave St ($10–15 per hour, $20–30 per day; ☎831/659-5824, ⓦwww.montereybaybikes.com).

Accommodation

Hotels and **B&Bs** cost around $140 per night, while cheaper **motels** are clustered along Fremont Street and Munras Avenue, two miles north of the center. The nearest **camping** is in Veterans Memorial Park ($3 per pedestrian, $15 per vehicle; ☎831/646-3865), site of Steinbeck's fictional *Tortilla Flat*, in the hills above town.

Bide-a-Wee Motel 221 Asilomar Ave, Pacific Grove ☎831/372-2330. Excellent value for the area, with spruced-up rooms, some with kitchenettes and microwaves. Two-minutes' walk to the ocean. Prices double at weekends. ❸

Carmel Resort Inn Carpenter St and 2nd Ave, Carmel ☎831/624-3113 or 1-800/454-3700, ⓦ www.carmelresortinn.com. One of the least expensive properties in Carmel; cottage rooms come with fireplaces. ❹–❻

Carmel River Inn Rio Rd at Hwy-1, Carmel ☎831/624-1575 or 1-800/882-8142, ⓦ www .carmelriverinn.com. Pleasant rooms come with patios or private decks, and some with kitchenettes and fireplaces, plus a heated pool and riverside location. ❺

Cypress Gardens Resort Inn 1150 Munras Ave, Monterey ☎831/373-2761, ⓦ www.cypressgardensinn.com. More like an old-fashioned motel than a resort, but still a good, centrally located option, with a pool and Jacuzzi. Rooms have fridges, microwaves, and balconies. ❹

Del Monte Beach 1110 Del Monte Ave, Monterey ☎831/649-4410. A bargain B&B close to the center of Monterey. All the usual quaint B&B trappings for half the typical cost, with shared baths and continental breakfast. ❸

Green Gables Inn 104 5th St, Pacific Grove ☎831/375-2095 or 1-800/722-1774, ⓦ www.foursisters.com/inns/greengablesinn.html. Plush doubles in one of the prettiest homes in a town of fine houses, on the waterfront a few blocks from the Aquarium. ❻

HI-Monterey Hostel 778 Hawthorne St, Monterey ☎831/649-0375, ⓦ www.montereyhostel.org. Located downtown near Cannery Row, a standard hostel with dorms for $23 and private rooms for $54. Three-night maximum stay. ❶–❸

Mariposa Inn 1386 Munras Ave, Monterey ☎831/649-1414. The best deal in Monterey. Cozy rooms with fireplaces, plus a hot tub and continental breakfast. ❺

Pacific Grove Motel Lighthouse Ave at Grove Acre, Pacific Grove ☎831/372-3218. Nice, small motel in a marvelous setting, 100 yards from the sea. Amenities include a heated pool, hot tub, and in-room refrigerators. ❹

Monterey

Named by the Spanish merchant and explorer Sebastian Vizcaíno in 1602, **MONTEREY** was not colonized until 1770, when it was founded as the military and administrative center of a territory that extended east to the Rockies and north to Canada. By the time the US took possession of it in the mid-nineteenth century, Monterey had become something of a backwater, though in 1849 it was the site of the negotiating and writing of the state constitution, and soon became the first capital of the state of California, before being superseded by Sacramento.

The compact town center features some of the best vernacular **buildings** of California's Spanish and Mexican Colonial past, most of which stand unassumingly within a few blocks of the tourist-thronged waterfront. A loosely organized **Path of History** connects the 37 sites of the **Monterey State Historic Park**, though most can't be entered unless you're part of a ninety-minute guided historic **walking tour** (daily 10am & 2pm, also Fri–Sun 11am; $5) that leaves hourly from the park's Stanton Center.

The best place to get a feel for life in old Monterey is the **Larkin House**, on Jefferson Street, a block south of Franklin (entry only on walking tour), home of the first and only American Consul to California. The New England–born Thomas Larkin, who was influential in persuading the Californians to turn towards the US and away from Mexico, is credited with developing the now-common Monterey style of architecture, mixing adobe walls, balconies of Greek Revival Southern plantations, and a Yankee taste for ornament. The house, the first two-story adobe in California, is filled with millions of dollars' worth of antiques and memorabilia, and is surrounded by gorgeous gardens. Larkin also helped organize the would-be state's **constitutional convention**, which took place just around the corner at **Colton Hall** (daily 10am–noon & 1–5pm, winter closes 4pm; free), whose museum is furnished as it was during the event, with old-fashioned quill pens on the tables and an early map of the West Coast on display – used by the delegates to form the boundaries of the 31st state.

The **Stevenson House**, four blocks east at 530 Houston St (entry only on walking tour; closed for renovation), is filled with memorabilia belonging to Robert Louis Stevenson, who passed through in 1879 and foresaw that Monterey's Mexican-influenced lifestyle was no match for the "Yankee craft" of the "millionaire vulgarians of the Big Bonanza." Six blocks north, tacky **Fisherman's Wharf** is something of a tourist trap loaded with disused wharves and canneries, some of them converted into boutiques and diners. At the foot of the wharf, the **Customs House** (daily 10am–4pm; free) is the oldest governmental building on the West Coast, with portions built by Spain in 1814, Mexico in 1827, and the US in 1846 – though it hasn't collected duties for 135 years. Two blocks south, the **Pacific House** (daily 10am–5pm; $2) has been a courthouse, boarding house, and dance hall since its construction in 1847, and is now the best of the local **museums**, with displays on Monterey history and a decent collection of Native American artifacts.

Heading north from the wharf, a **bike path** runs two miles to Pacific Grove along **Cannery Row** – named after John Steinbeck's literary portrait of the rough-and-ready workers of its fish canneries. During World War II some 200,000 tons of sardines were caught and canned here each year, but with overfishing the stocks were exhausted by 1945. The abandoned canneries reopened in the 1970s as malls and restaurants, and now teem with tourists instead of fish. Along the route, the engaging **Monterey Bay Aquarium**, 886 Cannery Row (daily 10am–6pm, summer opens 9.30am; $17.95, children 3–12 $8.95; ☎831/648-4888 or 1-800/756-3737, ⓦwww.montereybayaquarium.org), has one of the world's largest, most spectacular displays of sealife in the world. Book tickets well in advance and allow a day for your visit, which should include stops at the huge Kelp Forest tank, the touch pool (where you can pet bat rays), the two-story exhibit devoted to sea otters, and the dark and evocative Jellies: Living Art exhibition, a set of rooms with glowing, multicolored jellyfish dipping and swirling before your eyes.

Pacific Grove

A few miles north of Monterey along the peninsula, **PACIFIC GROVE** – or "Butterfly Town USA," as it likes to call itself – began as a campground and Methodist retreat in 1875, where Christian revivalists prohibited booze, bare skin, and reading the Sunday newspapers, and which still holds ornate wooden **cottages** from those long-forgotten days. One of the few other reminders of that pious period is the deep-red wooden Gothic church **St Mary's by the Sea**, Central Aveue at 12th Street, with a simple interior of polished redwood beams and an authentic signed Tiffany stained-glass window, nearest the altar on the left.

Ocean View Boulevard circles the coast around the town, passing the headland of **Lovers Point** – originally called Lovers of Jesus Point – where preachers used to hold sunrise services. Surrounded in early summer by the red-and-purple blooming ice plant, it's one of the peninsula's best **beaches**. Every year, from November through early March, hundreds of thousands of golden

Monarch **butterflies** come to Pacific Grove to escape the winter chill, forming orange and black blankets on the **Butterfly Trees**, on Ridge Road, a block west of Lighthouse Avenue. At the end of the avenue, near the tip of Monterey Peninsula, stands the 150-year-old **Point Piños** lighthouse (Thurs–Sun 1–4pm, summer daily 10am–6pm; $2), the oldest continuously operating lighthouse on the California coast and, perhaps contrary to grander expectation, is basically a quaint farmhouse with a revolving light poking out from its roof.

If you have time, consider taking the **Seventeen Mile Drive** (daily dawn–dusk; $8 per car), a privately owned, scenic toll road that loops along the coast south to Carmel and provides beautiful vistas of rugged headlands and the glistening shoreline. One particular highlight along the way is the **Lone Cypress Tree**, whose solitary silhouette has been the subject of many a postcard in these parts.

Carmel

Set on gently rising bluffs above a sculpted rocky shore, **CARMEL** is well known for its ridiculously inflated real-estate prices, neat rows of quaint shops and miniature homes along Ocean Avenue, and a largely untouched coastline. Unfortunately, the town also has a thick air of stultifying pretension, peppered with tacky middlebrow galleries and mock-Tudor tearooms, and lacking any authentic sense of small-town culture. Don't expect to see street addresses, mail delivery, or franchise businesses in town either: they're all banned by the local laws. Despite the town's cramped atmosphere, **Carmel Mission Basilica**, 3080 Rio Rd (Mon–Sat 9.30–5.30pm, Sun 10.30am–5pm; $2; ☎831/624-1271, ⓦwww.carmelmission.org), provides a rare hint of genuine interest as the second of the California Spanish missions, built in 1771 and claimed to be the most romantic of them all. Three small museums in the mission compound trace its history with antiques and memorabilia, while the darker side of the dainty building becomes apparent via the graves of more than three thousand local Native Americans in the adjacent **cemetery**.

The town's best feature, however, is the largely untouched nearby coastline. **Carmel Beach**, west of town, is a tranquil cove of blue water bordered by soft white sand and cypress-covered cliffs, though the tides are deceptively strong and dangerous, so be careful if you chance a swim. **Point Lobos State Reserve**, two miles south of the Carmel Mission on Hwy-1 (daily summer 9am–7pm, winter 9am–5pm; $4 per vehicle; ☎831/624-4909, ⓦwww.parks.ca.gov), has plenty of natural justification to support its claim of being "the greatest meeting of land and water in the world." Spread over two square miles, the park has more than 250 bird and animal species along its hiking trails, and the sea here is one of the richest underwater habitats in California. Gray whales are often seen offshore, migrating south in January and returning with young calves in April and early May. Because the point juts so far out into the ocean, chances are good of seeing them from as little as a hundred yards away.

Eating

There are many excellent places to **eat** on the peninsula. However, if you're on anything like a tight budget, the best cheap eats are on the north side of Monterey, along Fremont Street and just south of Cannery Row on and around Lighthouse Avenue.

Bookworks 667 Lighthouse Ave, Monterey ☎831/372-2242. Unpretentious café serving light lunch fare at reasonable prices, sometimes accompanied by live music.

Fishwife 1996 Sunset Drive at Asilomar Blvd, Pacific Grove ☎T831/375-7107. Longstanding local favorite, serving great seafood dishes at reasonable prices ($10–15 a plate); try the lip-smack-ing king prawns sautéed in red peppers and lime juice.

La Boheme Dolores and 7th sts, Carmel ☎831/624-7500. Cozy French-inspired bistro offering fixed-price, multi-course dinners for $25–30 per person.

Old Monterey Café 489 Alvarado St, Monterey ☎831/646-1021. Reasonable more-than-you-can-eat breakfasts with hefty pancakes and omelets, plus tasty sandwiches. Breakfast and lunch only. Closed Mon.

Paolina's San Carlos St between Ocean & 7th sts, Carmel ☎831/624-5599. Fresh homemade pasta in a casual courtyard setting, at half the price of other Carmel restaurants.

Papa Chano's 462 Alvarado St, Monterey ☎831/646-9587. Delicious, cheap Mexican food, featuring burritos and a rich *chorizo*. The chicken rotisserie branch, two doors down, also offers inexpensive fare.

Pasta Mia Trattoria 481 Lighthouse Ave, Pacific Grove ☎831/375-7709. Tasty homemade pasta, grilled seafood, and veal (starting at $10–15), served up in a rustic, homey setting.

Pepper's Mexicali Café 170 Forest Ave, Pacific Grove ☎831/373-6892. Gourmet Mexican seafood done in a California style, with heaping servings and at reasonable prices.

Robata Grill & Sake Bar 3658 The Barnyard, Carmel ☎831/624-2643. One of the few good local choices for sushi and tempura, though it can be pricey.

Sardine Factory 701 Wave St, Monterey ☎831/373-3775. Despite the industrial-sounding name, this is California seafood cuisine served in French château splendor at less-than-expected prices, with entrees starting at $20.

Schooners in the *Monterey Plaza Hotel*, 400 Cannery Row, Monterey ☎831/372-2628. Colorful California bistro in a historic hotel with views over the bay.

Drinking and nightlife

Since Pacific Grove and Carmel offer few decent **nightlife** options, all listings below are for Monterey, though it's hardly regarded as a hub of hip after-dark entertainment. Still, mid-September's **Monterey Jazz Festival** (☎1-800/307-3378, ⓦwww.montereyjazzfestival.org) is the oldest of its kind in the world. Check out the widely available *Go!* or *Coast Weekly* for current **listings**.

Crown and Anchor 150 W Franklin St ☎831/649-6496. All your English favorites, from fish 'n' chips to bangers 'n' mash, at this unpretentious local pub, best known for its wide selection of brews.

Lallapalooza 474 Alvarado St ☎831/645-9036. Swank martini bar for relaxed social-climbing, with well-mixed drinks at high prices.

Lighthouse Bar & Grill 281 Lighthouse Ave ☎831/373-4488. Friendly, if a bit dilapidated, gay pub where the locals hang out, with a pool table and Sunday "beer bust."

Mucky Duck 479 Alvarado St ☎831/655-3031. Tudor-style bar offering British food with a California flair. Occasional live music; DJ dancing on the back patio.

Planet Gemini 625 Cannery Row ☎831/373-1449. Comedy and music (rock, rap, and dance) venue with a $3–10 cover. Closed Mon.

Santa Cruz

The unassuming community of **SANTA CRUZ**, 75 miles south of San Francisco, is in many ways the quintessential California beach town, sited at the foot of thickly wooded mountains beside a clean sandy beach, and having grown considerably in the last few years, after the destruction of the 1989 earthquake. In the 1960s, Ken Kesey's band of Merry Pranksters turned the local youth on to LSD long before it defined a generation, and the area is still among the most politically and socially progressive in California. It's also surprisingly untouristy: no hotels spoil the miles of coastline, most of the land is agricultural, and roadside stands are more likely to sell apples or sprouts than postcards and trinkets.

The **Santa Cruz Boardwalk**, 400 Beach St (May–Aug daily 11am–10pm; rest of year hours vary; $1.80–3.60 per ride, unlimited rides $24.95; ⓦwww.beachboardwalk.com), is one of the last surviving beachfront amusement parks on the West Coast, and the main attraction for visitors. Although it can get packed on weekends with teenagers on the prowl, most of the time it's a friendly funfair, where barefoot hippies mix with mushroom farmers and tourists. The highlight is the eighty-year-old **Giant Dipper**, a wild and rickety wooden roller coaster on the National Register of Historic Places, which often doubles in the movies as a Coney Island ride.

The **beach** next to the boardwalk is popular, but can get rowdy and dirty. For more peace and quiet, follow the coast out of town to one of the smaller beaches such as Capitola or New Brighton. From **West Cliff Drive**, you'll see some of the biggest waves in California, not least at **Steamer Lane**, beyond the Municipal Pier. **Cowell Beach**, just north of the Municipal Pier, is the best place to give surfing a try; Club Ed (☏831/459-9283, ⓦwww.club-ed.com), in the parking lot, rents boards ($7 per hour, $20 per day) and assists with lessons. The ghosts of surfers past are animated at the **Surfing Museum**, in the old Abbott Memorial lighthouse on the point (Thurs–Mon noon–4pm; donation), where the boards on display range from early 12ft redwood planks to modern high-tech multifinned cutters. A clifftop cycle path runs two miles out from here to **Natural Bridges State Beach** (daily 8am–dusk; $6 per car), where waves once cut holes through the coastal cliffs and formed delicate stone arches – though only one of them remains.

In the hills above Santa Cruz, the local branch of the **University of California** (reachable on Metro bus #1) famously has as its mascot the **banana slug**, and is renowned as a progressive bastion whose students regard their liberal Berkeley counterparts as more than a bit too career-minded. The campus is verdant and pleasant enough, though one of its few highlights for visitors is the **Arboretum** (daily 9am–5pm; free; ☏831/427-2998, ⓦwww2.ucsc.edu/arboretum), world famous for its experimental techniques of cultivation and stocked with numerous plants from around the world.

Arrival, information, and accommodation

Greyhound **buses** (☏831/423-1800) from San Francisco, Oakland, and San Jose stop five times a day at 425 Front St, in the center of town. Santa Cruz has an excellent public transit system known as the **Metro**, on which the basic fare is $1.50 and an all-day pass $4.50 (☏831/425-8600, ⓦwww.scmtd.com). Electric Sierra Cycles, 302 Pacific Ave (☏831/425-1593), rents **bikes** for around $25 per day. The **visitor center** is at 1211 Ocean St (Mon–Sat 9am–5pm, Sun 10am–4pm; ☏831/425-1234 or 1-800/833-3494, ⓦwww.santacruz.org).

Off season, Santa Cruz has plenty of inexpensive places to **stay**, though rates can be much higher on weekends. Of the many good **campgrounds** in the area, the best is at *New Brighton State Beach* (☏831/464-6330 or 1-800/444-7275, ⓦwww.reserveamerica.com; $12–14), three miles south at 1500 Park Ave, near the beachfront village of Capitola.

Capitola Venetian 1500 Wharf Rd, Capitola ☏831/476-6471, ⓦwww.capitolavenetian.com. Beach hotel with one- to three-bed rooms, some with stoves, fridges, fireplaces, and ocean views. Rates vary wildly, from $60 on a winter weekday to $250 on a summer weekend. ❸–❾

Capri Motel 337 Riverside Ave, Santa Cruz ☏831/426-4611. The cheapest of the dozen motels near the boardwalk, with basic but clean rooms. ❷

Cliff Crest B&B Inn 407 Cliff St, Santa Cruz ☏831/427-2609, ⓦwww.cliffcrestinn.com. An 1887 refurbished Queen Anne with five elegant guest rooms, set in lovely gardens at the top of Beach Hill, with breakfast served in a conservatory. Winter ❼, summer ❾

HI-Santa Cruz 321 Main St, Santa Cruz ☏831/423-8304, ⓦwww.hi-santacruz.org. Well-situated hostel offering dorm beds from $20. Often booked up in advance. ❶

Pleasure Point Inn 2-3665 E Cliff Drive, Santa Cruz ☎ 408/291-0299, ⒲ www.pleasurepointinn .com. Stylishly modern B&B boasting clifftop views, a roof sundeck, and hot tub; rooms have stereos and Jacuzzis. ❽

Eating, drinking, and nightlife

The main drag of **Pacific Avenue** is peppered with many relaxed **restaurants** and **bars**, while the town itself has the Central Coast's rowdiest **nightlife**, ranging from coffeehouses to nightclubs where the music varies from surf-thrash and reggae to Sixties-styled rock – sometimes all on the same dance floor. Consult the free *Good Times* magazine for what's on.

Blue Lagoon 923 Pacific Ave ☎ 831/423-7117. A major gay hangout that draws a mixed crowd for techno and hip-hop DJs on weekends.

The Catalyst 1011 Pacific Ave ☎ 831/423-1336. Medium-sized club with nightly entertainment and one of the best bets for catching big-name touring artists and up-and-coming locals.

The Crepe Place 1134 Soquel Ave ☎ 831/429-6994. Serves up affordable stuffed crepes with a tasty assortment of both savory and sweet fillings.

Gabriella Café 910 Cedar St ☎ 831/457-1677. Elegant Californian cuisine in a comfortable rustic setting. Operates a good wine shop a block away that serves tasty panini.

Kuumbwa Jazz Center 320 Cedar St ☎ 831/427-2227. Friendly and intimate spot showcasing both traditional and modern jazz. Mondays draw the big names. Cover anywhere from $1 to 15.

Miramar 45 Municipal Wharf ☎ 831/423-4441. One of several good seafront restaurants on the wharf, with stunning oceanside views. Maine lobster on Thursdays for $10.

Rio Theatre 1205 Soquel Ave ☎ 831/423-8209, ⒲ www.riotheatre.com. Historic theater that presents a mix of cult films and eclectic music concerts.

Zoccoli's Deli 1534 Pacific Ave ☎ 831/423-1711. Italian deli with rich and hearty fare, including a delicious minestrone soup and other staples. Owners also run the excellent *Pasta House* at 431 Front Ave (☎ 831/423-1717), where the portions are generous.

The coast north to San Francisco

Twenty-five miles north along the coast from Santa Cruz, the beginning of the San Francisco Peninsula is marked by **Pigeon Point Lighthouse**, 210 Pigeon Point Rd, an 1872 structure that took its name from the clipper ship *Carrier Pigeon*, which broke up on the rocks off the point, one of many shipwrecks that led to the construction of the lighthouse in the late nineteenth century. At the time of publication, the lighthouse was closed for renovation; but you can still spend the night in the old lighthouse-keeper's quarters (☎ 650/879-0633, ⒲ www.norcalhostels.org; ❶–❷) and soak your bones in a hot tub ($6 per 30min), cantilevered out over the rocks. Dorm beds cost $20 each and there are also four private doubles for an extra charge.

Just before Pigeon Point, beautiful **Big Basin Redwoods State Park** ($6 parking; ☎ 831/338-8860) offers 25 square miles of wilderness with 300ft-tall redwoods and a compelling ten-mile **trail** leading from the fog-shrouded hills to the sparkling ocean. Closer down towards the shore, giant blubbery North Elephant Seals can be found mating every December and January in the **Año Nuevo State Reserve**, off New Year's Creek Rd (daily 8am–dusk; $6 parking; ☎ 650/879-0227), a ritual in which the males of the species – fifteen-foot-long, three-ton brutes – collide on the rocks and sand dunes to fight for a mate. It's a bizarre spectacle, and one you shouldn't miss if you're in the area during the winter.

The Central Valley

The vast **interior** of California is split down the middle by the **Sierra Nevada** (Spanish for "snowy range"), or High Sierra, a sawtooth range of snow-capped peaks that stands high above the semi-desert of the Owens Valley (see p.1146). The wide **Central Valley** (also known as the San Joaquin Valley) in the west was made super-fertile by irrigation projects during the 1940s, and is now almost totally agricultural. Even if the nightlife begins and ends with the local ice-cream parlor, after the big cities of the coast it can all be quite refreshing. However, the real reason to come here is to reach the **national parks** of **Sequoia** and **Kings Canyon** – whose huge trees form the centerpiece of a rich natural landscape – and **Yosemite**, where waterfalls cascade down towering walls of silvery granite. Few roads penetrate the hundred miles of wilderness to the east, but the entire region is crisscrossed by hiking trails leading up into the pristine alpine backcountry.

The arrow-straight I-5 barrels straight up from LA to San Francisco. Four daily **trains** and frequent Greyhound **buses** run through the valley, calling at the towns along Hwy-99, in particular Merced, which has bus connections to Yosemite but otherwise doesn't merit a look-in.

Bakersfield

The first town you come to across the rocky peaks north of Los Angeles, an unappealing vision behind a forest of oil derricks, is the flat and featureless **BAKERSFIELD**. This is the unlikely home of one of the liveliest **country music** scenes in the nation, stemming from the arrival during the Depression of Midwestern farmers, with their hillbilly instruments and campfire songs. In the mid-1960s, the gutsy honky-tonk style of Bakersfield artists such as Merle Haggard and Buck Owens challenged the slick commercial output of Nashville, but hopes of luring the major country-music record labels to "Nashville West" foundered with the emergence of rivals like Austin, Texas.

Nevertheless, the numerous honky-tonks of Bakersfield are still jumping every Friday and Saturday night. There's seldom a cover charge, and live sets usually entail one band playing for four or five hours from around 8pm, with a fifteen-minute break every hour. Stetson hats and rhinestone Nudie shirts are the sartorial order of the day, and audiences span generations. Most venues are hotel lounges or restaurant backrooms; don't miss the country bar *Trouts*, 805 N Chester Ave (☏661/399-6700), for a down-to-earth honky-tonk experience. Closer to town, you might also try the *Buck Owens Crystal Palace*, 2800 Buck Owens Blvd (☏661/328-7560), where the $6 cover includes a show (Buck himself plays on Friday and Saturday nights), and a museum of Buck Owens memorabilia; or the clubbier *Rockin' Rodeo*, 3745 Rosedale Hwy (☏661/323-6617), with a New Country or rock DJ every night.

Practicalities

You have to come to Bakersfield from LA by Amtrak Thruway bus to catch the train through the valley to San Francisco and northern California. Several Greyhound **bus** routes require changes here too, calling at 1820 18th St. The handiest **visitor center** is at 1725 Eye St (Mon 9am–5pm, Tues–Fri 8am–5pm;

☎661/327-4421). Bargain overnight stays include the *EZ-8*, 2604 Buck Owen Blvd (☎661/322-1901; ❶), and the adjacent *La Quinta*, 3232 Riverside Drive (☎661/325-7400 or 1-800/531-5900; ❹), both pool-equipped and a short stagger from *Buck Owens Crystal Palace* (see above). For **food**, *Zingo's* at 3201 Buck Owen Blvd (☎661/321-0627) is a 24-hour truckstop where frilly-aproned waitresses deliver plates of diner staples; *24th Street Café*, 1415 24th St (☎661/323-8801), does top-rate breakfasts; *Joseph's*, hidden back off the road at 3013 F St (☎661/322-7710), serves huge calzone and other Italian dishes; and the *Noriega Hotel*, 525 Sumner St (☎661/322-8419), offers excellent all-you-care-to-eat Basque meals at long communal tables.

Sequoia and Kings Canyon

The southernmost of the Sierra Nevada national parks, preserving ancient forests of giant sequoia trees, are Sequoia and Kings Canyon. As you might expect, **Sequoia National Park** contains the thickest concentration – and the biggest specimens – of sequoias to be found anywhere, tending (literally) to overshadow its assortment of meadows, peaks, canyons, and caves. **Kings Canyon National Park** has few big trees but compensates with a gaping canyon gored out of the rock by the Kings River as it cascades down from the High Sierra. The few established sights of both parks are near the main roads, leaving the vast majority of the landscape untrammeled and unspoiled, but well within reach for willing hikers.

Arrival and information

No **public transportation** of any kind serves the parks, but they're easily reached by **car**: the closest large town is **Visalia**, just under fifty miles away on Hwy-198, or a slightly longer, but faster, drive uses Hwy-180 from Fresno: note that there is **no gas** in the parks. The **entrance fee** ($10 per car, $5 per pedestrian or cyclist: valid seven days) entitles you to a detailed map of the paired parks, and a copy of the free *Sequoia Bark* newsletter, which details accommodation, guided hikes, and other activities. The two parks are separate but jointly run; for **information** call ☎559/565-3341 or visit ⓦwww.nps.gov/seki.

Accommodation and eating

The least expensive **rooms** are in the motels near the park entrances: *Sierra Inn Motel* (☎559/338-0678, ⓕ338-0789; ❸), fourteen miles west of the southern entrance on Hwy-180 and, near the southern entrance on Hwy-198, *Gateway Lodge* (☎559/561-4133, ⓕ561-3656; ❺). Inside the parks, all facilities are managed by Kings Canyon Park Services (KCPS; ☎559/335-5500 or 1-866/522-6966, ⓦwww.sequoia-kingscanyon.com; ❺–❻) who operate cabins and hotel units at Stony Creek, Grant Grove, and Cedar Grove; and Delaware North Parks Services (DPNS; ☎559/253-2199 or 1-888/252-5757, ⓦwww.visitsequoia.com; ❻–❼) who run the upmarket *Wuksachi* in Sequoia. Space is at a premium during the high season (May to mid-Oct), but you can usually pick up cancellations on the day. Summer prices range from $50 for basic cabins without bath to $160 for stylish modern hotel rooms. In winter the cheaper cabins are too cold; and only those at Grant Grove drop their prices below $50.

Recorded **camping** information for both parks is at ☎559/565-3341. Campgrounds are dotted all over both parks, charging an average of $14 a pitch,

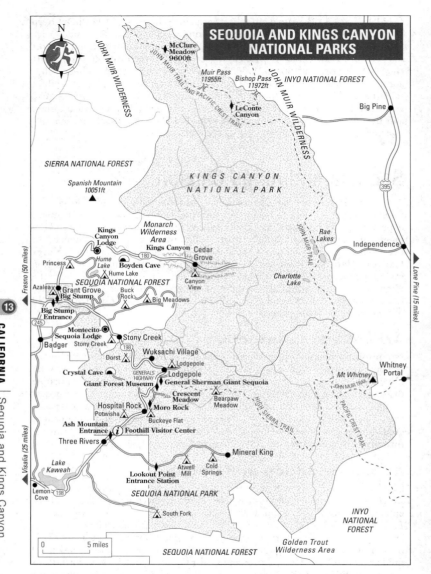

SEQUOIA AND KINGS CANYON NATIONAL PARKS

N

JOHN MUIR WILDERNESS

McClure
Meadow
9600ft

JOHN MUIR TRAIL AND PACIFIC CREST TRAIL

Muir Pass
11955ft

Bishop Pass
11972ft

JOHN MUIR WILDERNESS

INYO NATIONAL FOREST

Big Pine

LeConte
Canyon

395

SIERRA NATIONAL FOREST

Spanish Mountain
10051ft

KINGS CANYON
NATIONAL PARK

Rae
Lakes

Independence

Monarch
Wilderness
Area

Kings Canyon

Cedar
Grove

180

JOHN MUIR TRAIL

Kings
Canyon
Lodge

Boyden Cave

Hume
Lake

Charlotte
Lake

Princess

Hume Lake

Canyon
View

Azalea

SEQUOIA NATIONAL FOREST

Grant Grove
Big Stump

Buck
Rock

Big Meadows

Big Stump
Entrance

245

Montecito
Sequoia Lodge

Badger

Stony Creek

Stony Creek

198

Dorst

Wuksachi Village

Whitney
Portal

Crystal Cave

GENERALS
HIGHWAY

Lodgepole

Lodgepole

Mt Whitney

Giant Forest Museum

General Sherman Giant Sequoia

JOHN MUIR TRAIL

Hospital Rock

Crescent
Meadow

Bearpaw
Meadow

HIGH SIERRA TRAIL

Potwisha

Moro Rock

PACIFIC CREST TRAIL

Ash Mountain
Entrance

Buckeye Flat

Foothill Visitor Center

Three Rivers

Mineral King

Lake
Kaweah

Atwell
Mill

Cold
Springs

Lookout Point
Entrance Station

SEQUOIA NATIONAL PARK

Lemon
Cove

198

INYO
NATIONAL
FOREST

South Fork

0   5 miles

Golden Trout
Wilderness Area

SEQUOIA NATIONAL FOREST

though there are a couple of free, waterless sites in the national forest between the two. In **Sequoia**, the busiest campground is *Lodgepole*, which you can reserve up to five months in advance through the National Park Reservation System (☎1-800/365-2267, ⓦwww.reservations.nps.gov). In **Kings Canyon**, the bulk of the sites are around Grant Grove, with another at Cedar Grove – all cost around $18. For **backcountry** camping, pick up a free permit from a visitor center or ranger station. And remember this is **bear country**: in established campgrounds use the bearproof food boxes, in the backcountry rent bear canisters from the stores in Cedar Grove, Grant Grove, and Lodgepole.

There are pricey **food** markets and cafeterias in the various villages, and a couple of restaurants, notably bargain buffets at the *Montecito-Sequoia Lodge* in the national forest between the two parks. Three Rivers, on the southern approach to Sequoia, has the best range of places to eat nearby.

Sequoia National Park

While trees are seldom scarce in **SEQUOIA NATIONAL PARK** – patches where the giant sequoias can't grow are thickly swathed with pine and fir – the scenery varies. Paths lead through forests and meadows; longer treks rise above the tree line to the barren peaks of the High Sierra. Soon after entering the park from the south, Hwy-198 becomes the **Generals Highway** and climbs swiftly into the dense woods of the aptly labeled **Giant Forest**, where displays in the new **Giant Forest Museum** explain the lifecycle of the giant sequoias and what's being done to protect the remaining groves. From here you can explore along Crescent Meadow Road, which spurs east past the **Auto Log** – a fallen sequoia chiseled flat for motorists to drive onto. Just beyond, a loop road leads to the granite monolith of **Moro Rock** (a three-mile marked trail leads from Giant Forest), which streaks wildly upward from the green hillside. Views from its remarkably level top can stretch 150 miles. A hewn staircase makes it easy to climb the rock in fifteen minutes, although the altitude can be a strain.

Continuing east along Crescent Meadow Road, you pass under the **Tunnel Log**, which fell across the road in 1937 and had a vehicle-sized hole cut through it. At the end of the route, **Crescent Meadow** is, like other grassy fields in the area, more accurately a marsh, too wet for the sequoias that form an impressive boundary around. A perimeter trail leads to **Tharp's Log**, a cabin hollowed out of a fallen sequoia by Hale Tharp who, while searching for a summer grazing ground for his sheep, was led here by Native Americans in 1856. He was not only the first white man to see the giant sequoias but the first to live in one. Just north of Giant Forest, back on the Generals Highway, is the biggest sequoia of them all, the 2200-year-old, 275ft **General Sherman Tree**. While it's certainly a thrill to see what is held to be the largest living thing on the planet, its extraordinary dimensions are hard to grasp alongside the almost equally monstrous sequoias around.

Whatever your plans, you should stop at **Lodgepole Village**, three miles north of the Sherman Tree, for the geological displays and film shows at the **visitor center** (June to Aug daily 8am–6pm; May & Sept daily 9am–5pm; Oct–April Fri–Mon 9am–4.30pm). You can explore the glacial canyon on the **Tokopah Valley Trail** (2hr), which leads to the base of Tokopah Falls, beneath the 1600ft **Watchtower** cliff. The top of the Watchtower is accessible by the fatiguing but straightforward six-mile **Lakes Trail**.

Kings Canyon National Park

Kings Canyon National Park is wilder and less visited than Sequoia, with a maze-like collection of canyons and a sprinkling of isolated lakes – the perfect environment for careful self-guided exploration. To reach the canyon proper, you have to pass through the hamlet of **Grant Grove**, where there's a useful **visitor center** (daily: mid-May to Aug 8am–6pm; rest of year 8am–5pm) and the 2.5-mile **Big Stump Trail** shows off the remains of the logging that took place in the 1880s. Several massive trees from these parts were sliced up and sent to the Atlantic seaboard to convince cynical easterners that such enormous trees really existed. A mile west of Grant Grove, a large stand of sequoias contains the **General Grant** and **Robert E. Lee** trees, which rival the General Sherman in size.

Kings Canyon Highway (Hwy-180; May–Oct only) descends from Grant Grove into the steep-sided Kings Canyon, cut by the furious gushings of various forks of the Kings River. Whether or not this is the deepest canyon in the US, as some would have it, its wall sections of granite and gleaming blue marble, and the yellow pockmarks of blooming yucca plants (May and early June, in particular), are magnificent. A word of warning: don't be tempted by the clear waters of the river; people have been swept away even when paddling close to the bank in a seemingly placid section.

Once into the national park proper, the canyon sheds its V-shape and gains a floor. **Cedar Grove Village** here is named for its proliferation of incense cedars. There's a **ranger station** across the river (June–Aug daily 9am–5pm; May, Sept & Oct hours reduced). Apart from the scenery, you should look out for the **flowers** – leopard lilies, shooting stars, violets, lupins, and others – and **birdlife**, too. The longer hikes beside the creeks, many seven or eight miles long, are fairly strenuous. An easy alternative is to wander around the green **Zumwalt Meadow**, four miles from Cedar Grove Village and a short walk from the road, which spreads beneath the forbidding gray walls of Grand Sentinel and North Dome.

Just a mile further on, Kings Canyon Road comes to an end at **Copper Creek**. Thirty years ago vehicles were prohibited from penetrating further, and instead the multitude of canyons and peaks that constitute the Kings River Sierra are networked by **hiking paths**, almost all best enjoyed armed with a tent, provisions, and a wilderness permit from the trailhead ranger station.

The Sierra National Forest

The entire gaping tract of land between Kings Canyon and Yosemite is taken up by the less-visited **Sierra National Forest**. If you want to hike and camp in complete solitude, this is the place to do it. But don't try lone exploration without thorough planning – public transportation is nonexistent here, and roads and trails are often closed due to bad weather. The best-placed source of information is the **Pineridge Ranger Station** (daily 8am–4.30pm; ☏559/855-5360), located along Hwy-168 at Prather, five miles west of the forest entrance.

Of the forest's two main regions, the **Pineridge district**, forty miles east from Fresno using Hwy-168, is the best to explore. The popular Shaver Lake and Huntington Lake, rich in campgrounds (reserve in summer on ☏1-877/444-6777), soon give way to the isolated alpine landscapes beyond the 9200ft Kaiser Pass. The sheer challenge posed by the rugged, unspoiled terrain of the adjoining **John Muir Wilderness** can make the national parks look like holiday camps. You can bathe outdoors at the nearby **Mono Hot Springs**, or for the full hot springs experience, head for the *Mono Hot Springs Resort* here (mid-May to Oct; ☏559/325-1710, ⓦwww.monohotsprings.com; ❷–❹), which has indoor mineral baths along with self-catering cabins. The road narrows and twists on to Edison Lake and the *Vermillion Valley Resort* (☏559/259-4000, ⓦwww.edisonlake.com; ❸–❹), from where you can catch a small ferry across the lake to the trailheads. Ranger stations at Huntington Lake (Thurs–Mon 8am–4.30pm, closed winter) on Hwy-168, and another fifteen miles east at Kaiser Pass (Wed–Mon 8am–4.30pm, closed winter) issue free backcountry permits and also have camping and wilderness information.

Yosemite National Park

More gushing adjectives have been thrown at **YOSEMITE NATIONAL PARK** than at any other part of California. However excessive the hyperbole may seem, the instant you turn the corner that reveals **Yosemite Valley**, you realize it's actually an understatement – this is one of the world's most dramatic

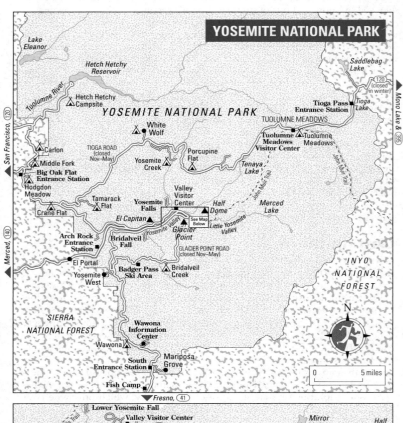

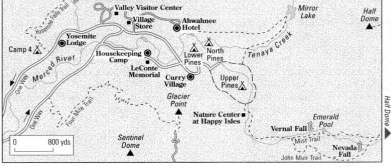

geological spectacles. Just seven miles long and at most one mile across, it is walled by near-vertical three-thousand-foot cliffs, streaked by tumbling waterfalls and topped by domes and pinnacles that form a jagged silhouette against the sky. At ground level, grassy meadows are framed by oak, cedar, and fir trees; deer, coyotes, and even black bears are not uncommon. Tourists are even commoner, but the park is big enough to absorb the crowds: you can visit at any time of year, even in winter when the waterfalls ice up and the trails are blocked by snow, and out of summer the valley itself is rarely overcrowded.

Yosemite Valley was made by glaciers gouging through the canyon of the Merced River: the ice scraped away the softer granite but only scarred the harder sections, which became the existing cliffs. The lake that formed when the glaciers melted eventually silted up to create the present valley floor. Native Americans lived here in comparative peace until the mid-nineteenth century, when the threatening approach of Gold Rush settlers led them to launch raiding parties. In 1851 Major James Savage's Mariposa Battalion trailed the Native Americans into the foothills and beyond, becoming the first whites to set foot in Yosemite Valley, and the native community were soon forced out to make way for farmers, foresters, and tourists. In 1864 Yosemite became the country's first national park, thanks in great part to the campaigning work of naturalist **John Muir**. A Scottish immigrant who traveled the entire area on foot, Muir spearheaded the conservation movement that led to the founding of the Sierra Club, with the express aim of preserving Yosemite. In 1913, the construction of a dam in the Hetch Hetchy Valley just north, to provide water for San Francisco, was a setback; but the publicity actually aided the formation of the present National Park Service in 1916, which promised – and has since provided – greater protection.

Getting there

Getting to Yosemite by car is straightforward, though the only road in from the east, Hwy-120 from Lee Vining, is closed from early November to around the beginning of June. **Gas** is pricey in the park and unavailable in Yosemite Valley. **Public transportation** into the park centers on the Amtrak-accessible Central Valley town of Merced, from where YARTS **buses** (℡209/388-9589 or 1-877/989-2787, ⓦwww.yarts.com) make the two-hour run to Yosemite Valley four or five times a day, charging $10 each way. All services call at the Merced Transport Center, 710 W 16th St, for Greyhound connections, and at the Amtrak station, 324 W 24th St at K Street, where two of the services connect with trains from San Francisco. YARTS also runs a once-daily summer-only service over the Tioga Pass road from Mammoth Lakes and Lee Vining ($20 roundtrip). Bus fares are inclusive of **park entry**, which otherwise costs $20 per vehicle, $10 per pedestrian or cyclist, and is valid for seven days.

If you need somewhere to stay overnight before heading to Yosemite, consider the *HI-Merced Home Hostel* (℡209/725-0407; members $15, others $18), where the staff pick you up from the train or bus and drop you off at the appropriate station the following morning. If you'd rather be closer to the park, try the lively *Yosemite Bug Hostel & Lodge*, 6979 Hwy-140 (℡209/966-6666 or 966-6667, ⓦwww.YosemiteBug.com; rooms ❸, bunks $16), at **Midpines**, on the YARTS bus route, where there's an excellent bar and café.

For recorded **information** on the park, roads, and weather, call ℡209/372-0200. The park also has a website: ⓦwww.nps.gov/yose.

Yosemite Valley

The three roads from the Central Valley end up at **Yosemite Valley**, roughly in the center of the park's 1200 square miles, and home to its most dramatic scenery. This is the busiest part of Yosemite, with **Yosemite Village** holding the main shops and the useful **visitor center** (daily: June–Sept 8am–6pm; mid-Oct to May 9am–4.30pm; ☎209/372-0299).

There's little in the village of any great interest; the reason to come here is to explore the valley itself. One of the most popular trails is the **Mist Trail** (3 miles roundtrip; 2–3hr; 1000ft ascent), which winds up so close to the sensual **Vernal Fall** that during the spring snowmelt period (mid-April to mid-June) hikers are drenched by the spitting water, but rewarded by vivid rainbows cast by the water. Vernal Fall seldom completely dries up, but like all those in the valley, it is best seen in spring; by August falls can be reduced to a trickle, and others disappear altogether.

The more strenuous trail to **Upper Yosemite Fall** (7 miles roundtrip; 4–7hr; 2700ft ascent) leads up along a steep switchback path from behind the *Camp 4* campground, near *Yosemite Lodge*. This almost continuous ascent is very sapping on the leg muscles, but you get fine views over the valley on the way up, and after about two miles, a chance to appreciate the power (and volume) of the water as it crashes almost 1500ft in a single cascade. A mile and a half further on the same trail, you reach the top of the fall, more spectacular views, and riverside spots for a much deserved picnic.

Of the two major cliffs visible from the valley, the 3600-foot **El Capitan** is one of the world's biggest pieces of exposed granite, so large that rock-climbers on its face are virtually invisible to the naked eye. **Half Dome**, the sheerest cliff in North America, is only seven percent off the vertical. Once past Vernal Fall, it's a strenuous ascent, the final section aided by way of a steel staircase hooked on to its curving back (late May to mid-Oct only); if you plan a one-day assault, you'll need to start at the crack of dawn.

The most spectacular views of Yosemite Valley are from **Glacier Point**, the top of a 3200ft almost-sheer cliff, 32 miles by road from the valley. It's possible to get there on foot using the vertiginous **Four-Mile Trail** (4.8 miles one way; 3–4hr; 3200ft ascent) though the lazy prefer to take the bus up (details on overleaf) and the trail down. The valley floor lies directly beneath the viewing point, and there are tremendous views across to Half Dome and the distant snowcapped summits of the High Sierra.

Practicalities

Prices within Yosemite are uniformly higher than outside the park, but not unaffordable. Of the **hotels** in the valley, try *Yosemite Lodge* (❺) or *Curry Village*, a mile from Yosemite Village, which has similarly priced rooms, plus fixed tent cabins (❸) and cabins (❹–❺); it also offers showers for nonguests ($2). For hotel information and reservations, call ☎559/252-4848 or visit Ⓦ www.yosemitepark.com.

Camping in the valley is only permitted in campgrounds, such as *Camp 4 Walk-in* ($5 per person), just west of *Yosemite Lodge*, which is popular with rock-climbers and has a bohemian reputation; it lacks showers and can only be reserved on the day at the kiosk on-site. Other valley campgrounds cost $18 per site, and you can reserve up to five months ahead in summer (☎1-800/436-7275; from outside the US or Canada ☎301/722-1257): reserve as far in advance as you can, though there are occasionally cancellations.

As for **food**, there are expensive and generally poor stores, diners, and snack bars in Yosemite Village, the best of which is *Degnan's Deli*, where massive sandwiches cost around $6. The *Food Court* at *Yosemite Lodge* offers filling and inexpensive meals, and the *Curry Pavilion* at *Curry Village* has an all-you-care-to-eat buffet for $12. The baronial-style *Ahwahnee Dining Room* (☎209/372-1489) has the best (and most expensive) food in Yosemite and a great $32 Sunday brunch; a jacket is required for dinner. There's also a great deck at *Curry Village* where you can order pizza and margaritas.

Once in Yosemite Valley, **getting around** is easy, but cars spoil everybody's fun. If you drive in for the day, park at *Yosemite Village* and ride the frequent, free **shuttle buses** that loop around the valley in summer (daily 7am–10pm), calling at all points of interest. A number of bicycle paths cross the valley floor but **bike rental** is limited to outlets at *Yosemite Lodge* and *Curry Village* ($21 a day). There are also **guided tours** (☎209/372-1240), hikes, and horseback trips. Pick up a copy of *Yosemite Today* or browse ⓦwww.yosemitepark.com for details.

Outside the valley

The **Mariposa Grove**, close to the park's southern entrance, is the biggest and best of Yosemite's groves of **giant sequoia** trees. To get to the towering growths, walk the 2.5-mile loop trail from the parking lot at the end of the road, which is also served by a free bus from the park entrance. The most renowned of the grouping, well marked along the route, is the **Grizzly Giant**, thought to be over 2700 years old.

On the eastern edge of the park, **Tuolumne** (June–Oct only) has an atmosphere quite different from the valley; here, at 8600 feet, you almost seem to be level with the tops of the surrounding snow-covered mountains. The air always has a fresh, crisp bite, and early summer reveals a plethora of colorful wildflowers. It's a better starting point than the valley for backcountry hiking into the High Sierra, where eight hundred miles of trails, both long and short, crisscross their way along the Sierra Nevada ridges. To spend a night in the backcountry, you must get a free **wilderness permit**, available up to 24 weeks in advance from the Wilderness Center, Box 545, Yosemite, CA 95389 (☎209/372-0740, ⓦwww.nps .gov/yose/wilderness), or no more than 24 hours in advance from the nearest visitor center. There are tent cabins at *Tuolumne Meadows Lodge* (☎559/252-4848, ⓦwww.yosemitepark.com; ❸) and camping at the *Tuolumne Meadows* campground for $18 per site if you have a vehicle, $5 per person if you're hiking.

San Francisco

SAN FRANCISCO proper occupies just 48 hilly square miles at the tip of a slender peninsula, almost perfectly centered along the California coast. Arguably the most beautiful, certainly the most liberal city in the US, it remains true to itself: a funky, individualistic, surprisingly small city whose people pride themselves on being the cultured counterparts to their cousins in LA – the last bastion of civilization on the lunatic fringe of America. It's a compact and approachable place, where downtown streets rise on impossible gradients to reveal stunning views of the city, the bay, and beyond, and blanket fogs roll in unexpectedly to envelop the city in mist. This is not the California of monotonous blue skies and slothful warmth – the temperatures rarely exceed 70°F, and even during summer can drop much lower.

The original inhabitants of this area, the **Ohlone Indians**, were all but wiped out within a few years of the establishment in 1776 of the **Mission Dolores**, the sixth in the chain of Spanish Catholic missions that ran the length of California. Two years after the Americans replaced the Mexicans in 1846, the discovery of gold in the Sierra foothills precipitated the rip-roaring **Gold Rush**. Within a year fifty thousand pioneers had traveled west, and east from China, turning San Francisco from a muddy village and wasteland of sand dunes into a thriving supply center and transit town. By the time the **transcontinental railroad** was completed in 1869, San Francisco was a lawless, rowdy boomtown of bordellos and drinking dens, something the moneyed elite – who hit it big on the much more dependable silver Comstock Load – worked hard to mend, constructing wide boulevards, parks, a cable car system, and elaborate Victorian redwood mansions.

In the midst of the city's golden age, however, a massive **earthquake**, followed by three days of fire, wiped out most of the town in 1906. Rebuilding began immediately, resulting in a city more magnificent than before; in the decades that followed, writers like Dashiell Hammett and Jack London lived and worked here. Many of the city's landmarks, including Coit Tower and both the Golden Gate and Bay bridges, were built in the 1920s and 1930s. By World War II San Francisco had been eclipsed by Los Angeles as the main West Coast city, but it achieved a new cultural eminence with the emergence of the Beats in the 1950s and the hippies in the 1960s, when the fusion of music, protest, rebellion, and of course, drugs that characterized 1967's "Summer of Love" took over the Haight-Ashbury district.

In a conservative America, San Francisco's reputation as a liberal oasis continues to grow, attracting waves of resettlers from all over the US. It is estimated that over half the city's population originates from somewhere else. It is a city in a constant state of evolution, fast gentrifying itself into one of the most high-end towns on earth – thanks, in part, to the disposable incomes pumped into its coffers from its sizeable singles and gay contingents. Gay capital of the world, San Francisco has also been the scene of the dot.com revolution's rise and fall. The resultant wealth at one time made housing prices skyrocket – often at the expense of the city's middle and lower classes – but the closure of hundreds of start-up IT companies has brought real-estate prices back down to (almost) reasonable levels. Despite the city's current economic ebbs and flows, your impression of the city likely won't be altered – it remains one of the most proudly distinct places to be found anywhere.

Arrival and information

All international and most domestic flights arrive at **San Francisco International Airport** (SFO), inconveniently located about fifteen miles south of the city. San Mateo County Transit (SamTrans) **buses** (☎1-800/660-4287) leave every half-hour from the lower level of the airport; the #KX express ($3) takes around thirty minutes to reach the Transbay Terminal in downtown, while the slower #292 ($1.10) stops everywhere and takes nearly an hour. On the #KX, you're allowed only one carry-on bag; on the #292, you can bring as much as you want provided you can carry it onto the bus yourself. The SFO Airporter bus ($10) picks up outside each baggage claim area every fifteen minutes and travels to Union Square and the Financial District. The SuperShuttle, American Airporter Shuttle, and Bay Shuttle

minibuses depart every five minutes from the lower level of the circular road and take passengers to any city-center destination for around $12 a head. Be ruthless – competition for these and the several other companies running shuttle service is fierce and queues nonexistent. **Taxis** from the airport cost $25–30 (plus tip) for any downtown location, more for the East Bay and Marin County – definitely worth it if there is more than one of you. If you're planning to drive, the usual **car rental** agencies operate free shuttle buses to their depots, leaving every fifteen minutes from the upper level, but you have to load and unload your bags yourself. The opening of a BART (Bay Area Rapid Transit) station at the airport now provides a direct link to downtown; the thirty-minute journey costs $4.70 (☎415/817-1717, ⓦ www.bart.gov).

Several domestic airlines (Jet Blue and Southwest are two) and United fly into **Oakland International Airport** (OAK; see p.1202 for details), across the bay. This is actually closer to downtown San Francisco than SFO, and is efficiently connected with the city by the $2 (exact change only) AirBART shuttle bus, which drops you at the Coliseum BART station. From there, hop onto a Daly City BART tain and you'll be in downtown San Francisco in around fifteen minutes ($2.75).

By bus and train

All of San Francisco's **Greyhound** services use the **Transbay Terminal** at 425 Mission St, south of Market Street, near the Embarcadero BART station (☎1-800/231-2222, ⓦ www.greyhound.com). **Green Tortoise** (☎1-800/867-8647) buses pull in behind the Transbay Terminal at First and Natoma streets. **Amtrak** trains stop across the bay in **Richmond** and continue to **Oakland**, from where free shuttle buses run across the Bay Bridge to the Transbay Terminal, or you can take BART. A more efficient route is to get off the train at Richmond, where a transfer to the nearby BART can get you into San Francisco more quickly. Although Emeryville, the stop before Oakland, is technically closer to San Francisco, don't get off there as consistent public transportation to the city is nonexistent.

Information

The **San Francisco Visitor Information Center**, on the lower level of Hallidie Plaza at the end of the cable car line on Market Street (Mon–Fri 9am–5pm, Sat & Sun 9am–3pm; ☎415/391-2000, ⓦ www.sfvisitor.org), has free maps of the city and the Bay Area, and can help with lodging and travel plans. Its free *San Francisco Book* provides detailed, if a little selective, information about accommodation, entertainment, exhibitions, and stores.

San Francisco's two main **post offices**, with telephone and general delivery facilities, are at Sutter Street Station, 150 Sutter St at Montgomery Street, in the Financial District (Mon–Fri 8.30am–5pm), and Rincon Finance Station, 180 Steuart St at Mission Street, SoMa (Mon–Fri 7am–6pm, Sat 9am–2pm).

City transportation

San Francisco is the rare American city where you don't need a car to see everything. In fact, given the chronic shortage of parking downtown, horrible traffic, and zealous meter maids, going carless makes sense. The public transportation system, **MUNI**, though much maligned by locals for its unpredictable schedule,

Useful bus routes

#5 From the Transbay Terminal, west alongside Haight-Ashbury and Golden Gate Park to the ocean.

#7 From the Ferry Terminal (Market St) to the end of Haight Street and to Golden Gate Park.

#15 From Third Street (SoMa) to Pier 39, Fisherman's Wharf, via the Financial District and North Beach.

#20 (Golden Gate Transit) From corner of Mission and First streets to the Golden Gate Bridge ($1.75).

#22 From the Marina up Pacific Heights and north on Fillmore.

#28 and **#29** From the Marina through the Presidio, north through Golden Gate Park, the Richmond, and the Sunset.

#30 From the Caltrain depot on Third Street, north to Ghirardelli Square, via Chinatown and North Beach, and out to Chestnut Street in the Marina district.

#38 From Geary Street via Civic Center, west to the ocean along Geary Boulevard through Japantown and the Richmond, ending at Cliff House.

MUNI train lines

MUNI F-Market line Restored vintage trolleys from other cities run downtown from the Transbay Terminal and Fisherman's Wharf, up Market Street, and into the heart of the Castro.

MUNI J-Church line From downtown to the edge of the Castro and on to the Mission and Noe Valley.

MUNI K-Ingleside line From downtown through the Castro to Balboa Park.

MUNI L-Taraval line From downtown west through the Sunset to the zoo and Ocean Beach.

MUNI M-Ocean View From downtown west by the Stonestown Galleria shopping center and San Francisco State University.

MUNI N-Judah line From downtown west through the Inner Sunset and to Ocean Beach, via the outer Haight.

From the MUNI N-Judah line or #5 and #38 bus routes, you can connect to **bus #44**, which goes by the **De Young Museum, Japanese Tea Garden, California Academy of Sciences**, and **Steinhart Aquarium** in Golden Gate Park. A MUNI transfer will get you **discounts** at these places.

covers every neighborhood inexpensively. Bikes are a good option, as marked bike routes – with lanes – direct riders to all major points of interest. Walking the compact metropolis is the best bet, with each turn revealing surprises like stunning homes and bustling marketplaces, though factor in the killer hills, some of them angled at a steep 30 degrees – in other words, wear comfortable shoes at all times.

MUNI

The city's public transportation is run by the **San Francisco Municipal Railway**, or MUNI (℡ 415/673-6864, Ⓦ www.sfMUNI.com). A comprehensive network of buses, trolleybuses, and cable cars runs up and over the city's hills, while the underground trains become streetcars when they emerge from the downtown metro system to split off and serve the suburbs. On buses and trains the flat **fare** is $1.25 (correct change only); with each ticket you buy, ask for a **free transfer** – good for another two rides on a train or bus, and a fifty-percent reduction on cable cars if used within ninety minutes. Cable cars cost $3 one way (no transfers). Most of the streetcar lines (J, K, L, M, and N) require proof of payment (meaning they can check your ticket), so hold on to a valid ticket, pass, or transfer or you may be subject to a steep fine.

If you're staying a few days, the MUNI **Passport** is available in one-day, three-day, and seven-day denominations ($9, $15, $20) and is valid for unlimited travel on MUNI and also the Bay Area Rapid Transit (BART) system (see p.1202) within the city limits. A **Fast Pass** costs $45 for a full calendar month. MUNI trains run **throughout the night** on a limited service, except those on the M-Ocean View line, which stop around 1am. **Buses** run all night, but services are greatly reduced after midnight. For **more information**, pick up the handy MUNI map from the Visitor Information Center or bookstores.

Bikes are allowed on MUNI buses equipped with bicycle racks (on the front of the bus) and on BART, except during peak commute hours.

Other transportation services

Various other public transportation networks serve San Francisco and the Bay Area. Along Market Street in downtown, MUNI shares the station concourses with BART, which runs to the East Bay – including downtown Oakland and Berkeley – and the outer suburbs. The **Caltrain** commuter railway (depot at Fourth and King streets, in the South of Market, or SoMa, district) links San Francisco along the peninsula south to San Jose. **Golden Gate Ferry** boats (☎415/923-2000, ⓦwww.goldengate.org) leave from the Ferry Building at the Embarcadero, crossing the bay past Alcatraz to Sausalito and Larkspur in Marin County. **Blue & Gold Fleet** (☎415/705-5555, ⓦwww.blueandgoldfleet.com) runs to Sausalito and Tiburon from Pier 41 at Fisherman's Wharf. The **Alameda–Oakland ferry** (☎510/522-3300, ⓦwww.transitinfo.org /AlaOakFerry) operates between Oakland's Jack London Square, the Ferry Building, Fisherman's Wharf (Pier 39), and Pac Bell Park ($5 one way) and, in summer, to Angel Island ($12 roundtrip; daily late May–Oct).

Taxis ply the streets, and you can flag one down (especially downtown), but finding one can be a pain. If you're phoning ahead, try Veterans (☎415/552-1300) or Yellow Cab (☎415/626-2345). Fares within the city are roughly $1.70 for the first mile and $1.80 per mile thereafter, plus the customary fifteen-percent tip.

If you fancy **cycling**, the handiest option is Blazing Saddles (☎ 415/202-8888, ⓦwww.blazingsaddlessanfrancisco.com), which has several locations around the city – two of the most convenient are at 1095 Columbus Ave at Francisco Street, in North Beach, and Pier 41 at Fisherman's Wharf. Rates for a standard bike are $7 per hour, $28 per day (tandem $11 per hour and $48 per day). Another option is Bay City Bikes, 2661 Taylor St at Beach Street, at Fisherman's Wharf, with rates beginning at $25 per day (☎415/346-2453, ⓦwww.baycitybike.com).

Organized tours

One way to orient yourself is an **organized tour**. Gray Line Tours ($37; ☎415/558-9400, ⓦwww.graylinesanfrancisco.com), for example, trundles round the city in four fairly tedious hours. Considerably more thrilling are the one-hour **bay cruises** operated by the Blue & Gold Fleet ($20; ☎415/773-1128, ⓦwww.blueandgoldfleet.com) from piers 39 and 41 – though be warned that everything may be shrouded in fog. If you're feeling flush, the expensive **aerial tours** of the city and Bay Area in light aircraft or helicopters are unbeatable – try

San Francisco Helicopter Tours (☎1-800/400-2404, ⓦwww.sfhelicoptertours.com), which offers spectacular flights starting at $120 per passenger.

The best of the **walking tours** include City Guides, sponsored daily by the San Francisco Public Library (free; ☎415/557-4266, ⓦwww.sfcityguides.org); Cruisin' the Castro ($40; ☎415/550-8110, ⓦwww.webcastro.com/castrotour), an absorbing and witty tour of the gay community; the Victorian Home Walk, which swings past the pick of the city's posh old homes ($20; ☎415/252-9485, ⓦwww.victorianwalk.com); and the self-guided Barbary Coast tour, marked by bronze medallions set in the sidewalk, which highlights the oldest parts of the city (ⓦwww.sfhistory.org). Three Babes and a Bus ($35, which includes all cover charges; ☎1-800/414-0158, ⓦwww.threebabes.com) takes a luxury coachload of people looking for a good time to different nightclubs around the city – and is less cringe-inducing than it might sound. There are also special mural tours of the Mission by Precita Eyes that take in the district's distinctive street art (see p.1188 for details).

Accommodation

Annual visitors far outnumber San Francisco's 800,000 people, and the city isn't short on lodging, but be sure to reserve in advance, sometimes several months in advance for visits in the summer and fall. Some thirty thousand beds are available in the city but expect to pay around $100 per room in any decent hotel or motel in season; if you want to snag one of the smart bargains or hostel beds we've listed below, make sure to reserve in advance in high season. You'll also normally find significantly better rates in rooms that share baths.

For **B&Bs**, the city's fastest-growing source of accommodation, consult the list below and following, or contact a specialist agency such as Bed and Breakfast California (12711 McCartysville, Saratoga, CA 95070; ☎408/781-3774 or 1-800/872-4500, ⓦwww.bbintl.com) or Bed and Breakfast San Francisco (Mon–Fri 9.30am–5pm; ☎1-800/452-8249, ⓦwww.bbsf.com). British visitors can reserve rooms through **Colby International** (ⓦwww.colbyintl.com), while once you're in the city, San Francisco Reservations (Mon–Fri 6am–11pm, Sat & Sun 8am–11pm; ☎1-800/677-1500, ⓦwww.hotelres.com) will find you a room starting from around $100 a double. If all else fails and you've got a car, **motels** are legion along the highways and bigger roads throughout the Bay Area, at a standard rate of $40–50 a night. In all cases, bear in mind that all quoted room rates are subject to a **fourteen-percent room tax**.

Camping isn't an option in San Francisco itself, though throwing down a bag in Golden Gate Park or the Presidio may seem tempting. Camping is illegal within the city, and can be dangerous as well.

Hotels, motels, and B&Bs

Adagio Hotel 550 Geary St at Jones, Theater District ☎415/775-5000, ⓦwww.jdvhospitality.com. The decor at this hotel echoes its ornate Spanish Revival facade with deep reds and ochres. Rooms are large and, even better, there's free Internet access and printing onsite. ❺

Allison 417 Stockton St at Sutter, Chinatown ☎415/986-8737 or 1-800/628-6456. Shockingly good-value prime location hotel and one of the best options for budget travel anywhere in the city, with rooms that are big, bright, and spotless. ❷ shared bath, ❸ private bath.

Archbishop's Mansion 1000 Fulton St at Steiner, Fillmore ☎ 415/563-7872 or 1-800/543-5820, ⓦwww.thearchbishopsmansion.com. The last word in camp elegance, this B&B is crammed with $1 million worth of antiques, including the very chandelier that featured in the ballroom of *Gone With the Wind*. ❻

Beck's Motor Lodge 2222 Market St at Sanchez, Castro ☎ 415/621-8212 or 1-800/227-4360. The clientele's more mixed than you'd expect from its Castro location, and the soft, bluish rooms are plusher than the gaudy yellow motel exterior might suggest. ❹

Bel Aire Travelodge 3201 Steiner St at Greenwich, Cow Hollow ☎415/921-5162 or 1-800/280-3242. Rooms are recently refurbished, if a little dark, but the friendly owners make up for it. ❸

Best Western Carriage Inn 140 Seventh St at Mission, SoMa ☎ 415/552-8600. Enormous, elegant rooms with sofas and working fireplaces, free room-service breakfast each morning, and a shuttle to Union Square – the only downside is its slightly sketchy location. ❺

Boheme 444 Columbus Ave at Vallejo, North Beach ☎ 415/433-9111, ⓦ www.hotelboheme .com. Smack in the middle of Beat heartland, this small, 15-room hotel has tiny but dramatic rooms, with canopied beds. Columbus Avenue can be noisy, so if you're a light sleeper, ask for a room at the back. ❼

The Carl 198 Carl St at Stanyan, Haight-Ashbury ☎ 415/661-5679 or 1-888/661-5679, ⓦ carlhotel .citysearch.com. A bargain for its Golden Gate Park location. The small but florally pretty rooms come with microwaves and fridges. ❹ private, ❸ both shared

Clift 495 Geary St at Taylor, Theater District ☎415/775-4700 or 1-800/658-5492, ⓦ www .ianschragerhotels.com. The rooms are vaguely oriental with quirky touches like the Louis XIV–style chairs with mirrors on the seat and back, and sleigh beds – pity the bathrooms are so small. ❼

Commodore International 825 Sutter St at Jones, Theater District ☎ 415/923-6800 or 1-800/338-6848, ⓦ www.thecommodorehotel.com. Rooms are decorated in warm, earthy colors offset by shiny steel Deco-style fixtures. If you're traveling in a group of four or more, ask about the funky, airy suite where rates start at only $200. ❸

Del Sol 3100 Webster St at Lombard, Cow Hollow ☎ 415/921-5520 or 1-877/433-5765, ⓦ www.jdvhospitality.com. Funky updated motor lodge with a tropical theme, plus a swimming pool: the best place for budget cool in the city. ❺

Hotel Astoria 510 Bush St at Grant, Chinatown ☎415/434-8889 or 1-800/666-6696, ⓦ www .hotelastoria-sf.com. The decor here is friskier than that of many other budget hotels, with TV and full in-room amenities; continental breakfast is included in the rate and there's discounted parking nearby ($20/24hr). ❸

Monaco 501 Geary St at Taylor, Union Square ☎415/292-0100 or 1-800/214-4220, ⓦ www .monaco-sf.com. One of the newer, quirky bou-

tique hotels in town, housed in a historic Beaux Arts building with canopied beds in each room and complimentary goldfish to keep you company. ❽

The Mosser 54 Fourth St at Market, SoMa ☎415/986-4400, ⓦ www.themosser.com. This hotel is a recent funky conversion fusing Victorian touches like ornamental molding with mod leather sofas. The chocolate and olive rooms may be tiny, but each is artfully crammed with amenities including multi-disc CD players. ❺

Ocean Park Motel 2690 46th Ave at Wawona, Ocean Beach ☎415/566-7020, ⓦ www.ocean-parkmotel.citysearch.com. A fair way from downtown (25min by MUNI), this is nonetheless a great Art Deco motel that's convenient for the beach and the zoo, and has an on-site kids' play area. ❹

The Phoenix 601 Eddy St at Larkin, Tenderloin ☎415/776-1380 or 1-800/248-9466, ⓦ www .thephoenixhotel.com. This raucous retro motel is a favorite with up-and-coming bands when they're in town; there's a small pool, and the rooms are eclectically decorated in tropical colors and have changing local artwork on the walls. ❺

Queen Anne 1590 Sutter St at Octavia, Fillmore ☎415/441-2828 or 1-800/227-3970, ⓦ www .queenanne.com. Gloriously excessive restored Victorian. Each room is stuffed with gold-accented Rococo furniture and bunches of silk flowers: the parlor (where afternoon sherry is served) is overfilled with museum-quality period furniture. ❻

The Red Victorian Bed, Breakfast and Art 1665 Haight St at Cole, Haight-Ashbury ☎415/864-1978, ⓦ www.redvic.com. Quirky B&B owned by Sami Sunchild and decorated with her ethnic arts. Rooms vary from simple to opulent: the best feature is the shared bathrooms, including a goldfish-filled toilet cistern. ❹

San Remo 2237 Mason St at Chestnut, North Beach ☎415/776-8688 or 1-800/352-7366, ⓦ www.sanremohotel.com. Quirky option close to Fisherman's Wharf. Rooms in this warren-like converted house are cosy and chintzy: all share spotless bathrooms and a few have sinks. ❸

Sir Francis Drake 450 Powell St at Sutter, Union Square ☎415/392-7755 or 1-800/227-5480, ⓦ www.sirfrancisdrake.com. The lobby is a hallucinogenic evocation of all things heraldic, crammed with faux British memorabilia – the rooms are calmer, with a gentle apple-green color scheme and full facilities. ❻

Stanyan Park Hotel 750 Stanyan St at Waller, Haight-Ashbury ☎415/751-1000, ⓦ www .stanyanpark.com. Overlooking Golden Gate Park, this small hotel has 35 sumptuous rooms busily decorated in country florals, heavy drapes, and junior four-poster beds. ❻

Surf Motel 2265 Lombard St at Pierce, Cow Hollow ℡415/922-1950. This old-school motel has two tiers of bright, simple rooms that are sparklingly clean. ❸

Van Ness Motel 2850 Van Ness Ave at Chestnut, Civic Center ℡415/776-3220 or 1-800/422-0372, ⓦvannessmotel.citysearch.com. Standard, bland motel, notable more for its location than the hotel itself. Within walking distance of Fort Mason. ❸

Westin St Francis 335 Powell St at Sutter, Union Square ℡415/397-7000 or 1-800/WESTIN-1, ⓦwww.westin.com. This completely renovated landmark hotel has a sumptuous lobby, four restaurants and lounges, a fitness center, and a spa; be prepared for surprisingly plain rooms. ❽

Hostels and YMCAs

The Globe Hostel 10 Hallam Place, SoMa ℡415/431-0540, ⓦwww.globe-hostel.com. Lively South of Market hostel with a young clientele and 33 rooms, split between dorms and private rooms. There's free coffee and, best of all, no curfew. Dorm beds $19.

Green Tortoise 494 Broadway at Montgomery, North Beach ℡415/834-1000 or 1-800/867-8647, ⓦwww.greentortoise.com/san.francisco .hostel.2.html. This laid-back hostel is the best place to stay if money's tight: there's room for 130 people in dorm beds and double rooms (with shared bath). Both options include free Internet access, use of the small on-site sauna, and complimentary breakfast. No curfew. Dorm beds $19–22.

HI-San Francisco City Center 685 Ellis St at Larkin, Tenderloin ℡415/474-5721, ⓦwww .norcalhostels.org. Recent conversion from the old *Atherton Hotel*, this is a spiffy new hostel; its 272 beds are divided into four-person dorms, each with en suite bath. There's no curfew and overall, it's friendly, funky, and oozes California cool. Dorms $22 members, $25 others; private rooms $66 members, $69 others.

HI-San Francisco Fort Mason Building 240, Fort Mason ℡415/771-7277, ⓦwww.hiayh.org or www.norcalhostels.org. On the waterfront between the Golden Gate Bridge and Fisherman's Wharf, this is a choice option for an outdoorsy traveler, a standard hostel housed in a historic former Civil War barracks. Be aware that although public transport connects the hostel with the main sights, it's a little out of the way on the federal complex at Fort Mason. $22.50.

HI-San Francisco Union Square 312 Mason St at Geary, Union Square ℡415/788-5604. With almost 300 beds, this downtown hostel still fills up quickly in peak season: four-person dorms are

spotless, sharing bathroom facilities between eight people. The private rooms are pricier and sleep two people. Dorms $22 members, $25 others; Private rooms $60 members, $66 others.

Pacific Tradewinds Guesthouse 680 Sacramento St at Kearny, Chinatown ℡415/433-7970 or May–Oct only ℡1-800/486-7975, ⓦwww.san-francisco-hostel.com. The best budget accommodation in the center of town, this small hostel offers free, high-speed Internet access, a clean kitchen, plus a large, communal dining table that's an easy way to get to know fellow travelers. Dorm beds $18.

YMCA Central Branch 220 Golden Gate Ave at Leavenworth, Tenderloin ℡415/885-0460, ⓦwww.centralymcasf.org. Rooms may be simple, but this is a great deal in the city center: $12 overnight parking, free breakfast, free use of YMCA fitness center, Internet access at a nominal fee, and on-site laundry. It's a shame it's in a gritty part of the Tenderloin. Dorm beds $24 a night, private bath $62 a night.

Gay and lesbian accommodation

24 Henry 24 Henry St at Sanchez, Castro ℡415/864-5686 or 1-800/900-5686, ⓦwww .24henry.com. This small blue and white home tucked away on a leafy residential street north of Market is predominantly a gay male guesthouse with 5 simple rooms, one with private bath. ❹

Inn on Castro 321 Castro St at Market, Castro ℡415/861-0321, ⓦwww.innoncastro2.com. This luxurious B&B is spread across two nearby houses: it has eight rooms and three apartments available, all of which are brightly decorated in individual styles and have private baths and phones. ❺

Noe's Nest 3973 23rd St at Noe, Noe Valley ℡415/821-0751, ⓦwww.noesnest.com. Seven-room B&B (six with private bath) on a quiet street in Noe Valley. Lavish breakfasts are served each morning, and there's a hot tub too. ❹

The Parker House 520 Church St at 18th, Castro ℡415/621-3222 or 1-888/520-7275, ⓦwww.parkerguesthouse.com. This converted Edwardian mansion is set in beautiful gardens and has a friendly vibe, thanks to its ample, large common areas: there's a sunny breakfast room and on-site sauna. ❻, ❺ without bath

The Renoir 45 McAllister St, at Seventh, Civic Center ℡415/626-5200 or 1-800/576-3388, ⓦwww.renoirhotel.com. This wedge-shaped building is a historic landmark with 135 rooms that have recently been unexcitingly, if florally, refurbished. Especially popular during Gay Pride for its Market Street views along the parade route. ❺

The City

San Francisco is a city of hills and distinct neighborhoods. As a general rule, geographical elevation means wealth – the higher up you are, the better off you are. Commercial square-footage is surprisingly small and mostly confined to the downtown area, and the rest of the city is made up of primarily residential neighborhoods with street-level shopping districts, easily explored on foot. Armed with a good map and strong legs, you could plough through much of the city in a day, but the best way to get to know San Francisco is to dawdle.

Union Square

The city's heart can be found around **Union Square**, located north of Market Street and bordered by Powell and Stockton streets, which was recently spruced up with the addition of shady trees and benches. Cable cars clank past bustling shoppers and theater-goers who gravitate to the district's many upscale hotels, department stores, and boutiques. The statue in the center commemorates Admiral Dewey's success in the Spanish–American War, though the square takes its name from its role as gathering place for stumping speechmakers during the US Civil War. (The woman who posed for the monument, Alma de Bretteville, became a local celebrity, marrying into the wealthy Spreckels family and donating her collection of Rodin sculptures to found the California Palace of the Legion of Honor – see p.1192.) The square witnessed the attempted assassination of President Gerald Ford outside the (now *Westin*) **St Francis Hotel** in 1975, and was also the location of Francis Ford Coppola's film *The Conversation*, where Gene Hackman spied on strolling lovers. Many of **Dashiell Hammett**'s detective stories, such as *The Maltese Falcon*, are set partly in the *St Francis*; in fact, during the 1920s, he worked there as a Pinkerton detective.

Cable cars

It was the invention of the **cable car** that put the high in San Francisco's high society as it made life on the hills both possible and practical. Since 1873, these little trolleys have been an integral part of life in the city, supposedly thanks to Scots-born Andrew Hallidie's concern for horses. Having watched a team struggle and fall, breaking their legs on a steep San Franciscan street, Hallidie designed a pulley system around the thick wire rope his father had patented for use in the California mines (the Gold Rush was slowing, and so the Hallidies needed a new market for their product). Despite locals' initial doubts, a transportation revolution followed. At their peak, just before the 1906 earthquake, over six hundred cable cars traveled 110 miles of track throughout the city at a maximum 9.5mph; over the years, usage dwindled and, in 1964, nostalgic citizens voted to preserve the last seventeen miles (now just ten) as a moving historic landmark.

Today there are three lines. Two of them, the Powell & Mason and the Powell & Hyde lines run from Hallidie Plaza off Union Square at Powell and Market streets to Fisherman's Wharf. The Powell & Hyde is the steepest, reaching a hair-raising 21-degree grade between Lombard and Chestnut streets. The oldest route, the California line, climbs Nob Hill along California Street from the Embarcadero, rattling past the fanciest hotels in the city. The cars fasten onto a moving two-inch cable, which runs beneath the streets, gripping on the ascent then releasing at the top and gliding down the other side. You can see the huge motors that still power these cables in the **Cable Car Museum and Powerhouse**, 1201 Mason St at Washington Street (daily: April–Sept 10am–6pm; Oct–March 10am–5pm; free; ℗ www.cablecar-museum.com).

DOWNTOWN SAN FRANCISCO

Pier 39

Maritime Museum

FISHERMAN'S WHARF

S F Art Institute

NORTH BEACH

TELEGRAPH HILL

Coit Tower

RUSSIAN HILL

CHINATOWN

City Lights Bookstore

Transamerica Pyramid

JACKSON SQUARE HISTORICAL DISTRICT

Cable Car Museum

Columbus Tower

Ferry Building

NOB HILL

Embarcadero Center

Grace Cathedral

Wells Fargo Museum

Embarcadero (MUNI/BART)

Burritt Alley

FINANCIAL DISTRICT

Transbay Terminal

Montgomery Street (MUNI/BART)

Union Square

Macy's

Museum of Modern Art

SOUTH OF MARKET

Powell Street (MUNI/BART)

TENDERLOIN

Metreon Shopping Center

Yerba Buena Center for the Arts

CIVIC CENTER

United Nations Plaza

City Hall

Civic Center (MUNI/BART)

Opera House

Caltrain Depot

East Bay & Sausalito

Pac Bell Park

N

0   500 yds

ACCOMMODATION				RESTAURANTS	
24 Henry	ee	The Mosser	W	Asia de Cuba	15
Allison	P	Noe's Nest	gg	Café Jacqueline	1
Hotel Astoria	O	Ocean Park Motel	dd	Caffe Trieste	4
Archbishop's Mansion	J	Pacific Tradewinds Guesthouse	N	Cosmopolitan Café	11
Beck's Motor Lodge	cc	The Parker House	hh	Farallon	14
Bel Aire Travelodge	C	The Phoenix	Y	House of Nanking	6
Best Western Carriage Inn	bb	Queen Anne	H	Kokkari Estiatorio	7
Boheme	E	Red Victorian	I	Plouf	12
The Carl	L	The Renoir	aa	Sam Woh	9
Clift	U	Sam Wong Hotel	G	Sears Fine Food	13
Commodore International	R	San Remo	D	Tadich Grill	10
Del Sol	A	Sir Francis Drake	Q	The Helman	3
The Globe Hostel	ii	Stanyan Park Hotel	K	Trattoria Contadina	2
Green Tortoise	F	Surf Motel	B	Yank Sing	8
HI-San Francisco City Center	X	Van Ness Hotel	M	Yuet Lee	5
HI-San Francisco Union Square	T	Westin St Francis	S		
Inn on Castro	ff	YMCA Central Branch	Z		
Monaco	V				

On Geary Street, on the south side of the square, the **Theater District** is a pint-sized Broadway of restaurants, tourist hotels, and serious and "adult" theaters. On the eastern side of the square, **Maiden Lane** is a chic urban walkway that before the 1906 earthquake and fire was one of the city's roughest areas, where homicides averaged around ten a month. Nowadays, aside from some prohibitively expensive boutiques, its main feature is San Francisco's only **Frank Lloyd Wright building** (now occupied by the Xanadu Tribal Art Gallery), an intriguing circular space at no.140 that was a prototype for the Guggenheim Museum in New York – if it's open, feel free to wander inside, but just don't expect a warm welcome from the tourist-weary staff.

The Financial District

North of the city's main artery, Market Street, the glass-and-steel skyscrapers of the **Financial District** have sprung up in the last twenty years to form its only real highrise area. Sharp-suited workers clog the streets and coffee kiosks during business hours, but after 6pm, the area pretty much shuts down. Stop at the corner of Kearny and Market streets to admire **Lotta's Fountain**, one of San Francisco's most treasured artifacts, named after Lotta Crabtree, one of the first children brought to the city by pioneering families. It was around here that people gathered to hear news following the 1906 earthquake and fire, and also where famed soprano Luisa Tetrazzini gave a free concert on Christmas Eve, 1910.

Once cut off from the rest of San Francisco by the double-decker Embarcadero Freeway – damaged in the 1989 earthquake and finally torn down two years later – the **Ferry Building**, at the foot of Market Street, was modeled on the cathedral tower in Seville, Spain. Before the bridges were built in the 1930s it was the arrival point for fifty thousand cross-bay commuters daily. A few ferries still dock here (see p.1176), but after years of playing home to colorless offices, it's finally undergoing a massive renovation that's seen shops and cafés start to line its halls. The first new tenant is the **Ferry Plaza Farmers Market**, which has moved indoors from its old site in front of the building – it's an excellent place to sample the sumptuous local produce (Sat 8am–2pm, Tues 10am–2pm, Thurs 3–7pm; ☎415/353-5650, ⓦwww.ferryplazafarmersmarket.com).

Since the freeway was pulled down, the area around it, known as **The Embarcadero**, has experienced a dramatic renaissance – from an area of charmless office blocks into a swanky waterfront district with some of the city's finest restaurants and hotels springing up to make the most of the views of the bay.

From the vast and unimaginative **Embarcadero Center** shopping mall and the square concrete tubing of the fountains in **Justin Herman Plaza** at the foot of Market, it's a few blocks down to **Montgomery Street**, where the grand pillared entrances and banking halls of the post-1906 earthquake buildings era jostle for attention with a mixed bag of modern towers. The best known is undoubtedly the **Bank of America** monolith, 555 California St, at Kearney, where the state's largest financial institution has its headquarters; this enormous building was initially unpopular when finished in 1971, though affection has grown over the years for the broad-shouldered hulk. The **Wells Fargo History Museum**, 420 Montgomery St (Mon–Fri 9am–5pm; free; ☎ 415/396-2619, ⓦwww.wellsfargo.com), traces the far-from-slick origins of San Francisco's big money, right from the days of the Gold Rush, with mining equipment, gold nuggets, photographs, and a genuine retired stagecoach.

Jackson Square and the Barbary Coast

A century or so ago, the eastern flank of the Financial District formed part of the **Barbary Coast**. This area of landfill appeared thanks to the hundreds of ships that lay abandoned by sailors heading for the Gold Rush; enterprising San Franciscans used the dry ships as hotels, bars, and stores. At the time, the district was a rough-and-tumble place that gave San Francisco an unsavory reputation as **Baghdad by the Bay**, packed as it was with saloons and brothels where hapless young males were given Mickey Finns and forcibly taken aboard merchant ships and pressed into involuntary servitude. William Randolph Hearst's *Examiner* newspaper lobbied frantically to shut down the quarter, resulting in a 1917 California law prohibiting prostitution. Remains of the cradle of San Francisco can be seen in the **Jackson Square Historic District**, not an actual square but an area bordered by Washington, Columbus, Sansome, and Pacific streets; these were the only buildings downtown to escaped the catastrophic 1906 fire unharmed, and Jackson Street in particular provides a hint of what early San Francisco looked like. A detour down the redbrick-lined Hotaling Place, with its hitching posts and antique lamps, is similarly revealing.

The landmark **Transamerica Pyramid** (T 415/983-4100, W www.tapyramid .com), at the foot of diagonal Columbus Avenue and Washington, is San Francisco's tallest building. The 48-story structure, capped by a colossal 212ft hollow spire, arose in 1972 amid a city-planning furor that earned it the name of "Pereira's Prick," after its LA-based architect William Pereira, and since then it's been indisputably the signature of San Francisco's skyline. Though it survived the 1989 earthquake undamaged, for security reasons there's no longer access to the 27th-floor viewing deck. The block on which the Transamerica Pyramid stands is a historic one: Rudyard Kipling, Robert Louis Stevenson, Mark Twain, and William Randolph Hearst all rented office space in the building that originally stood on this site, and regularly hung around the notorious *Bank Exchange* bar within. Legend has it that Dr Sun Yat-sen – whose statue is in Chinatown, three blocks away – wrote the Chinese constitution and orchestrated the successful overthrow of the Manchu Dynasty from his second-floor office here. Next door is the pleasant **Transamerica Redwood Park** with fountains perfect for an outdoor lunch. Heading west on Jackson or Pacific streets from the area leads you back to Columbus and the green-copper siding of the **Columbus Tower**, 906 Kearny St, the de facto beginning of North Beach. Director and San Francisco native Francis Ford Coppola owns the building, and his *Niebaum-Coppola Café* on the ground floor serves sandwiches, pasta, and wine from his Napa Valley winery.

Chinatown

Chinatown's 24 square blocks smack in the middle of San Francisco make up the second-largest Chinese community outside Asia (after New York City). It has its roots in the migration of Chinese laborers to the city after the completion of the transcontinental railroad, and the arrival of Chinese sailors keen to benefit from the Gold Rush. The city didn't extend much of a welcome: they were met by a tide of vicious racial attacks and the 1882 Chinese Exclusion Act, the only law in American history aimed at a single racial group that prevented Chinese naturalization. Many visitors assume that the neighborhood remains autonomous, with its own schools, banks, and newspapers, but nowadays, the Chinese population has been joined by Vietnamese, Koreans, Thais, and Laotians: by day the area seethes with activity, while by night it's a blaze of neon. Overcrowding is compounded by a brisk tourist trade – sadly, however, Chinatown boasts some of the tackiest stores and facades in the city, making it more akin to shopping in a bad part of Hong Kong than in Beijing. Indeed, Chinese tourists are often disappointed in the neighborhood's disorder – for a truer sense of everyday Chinese life in San Francisco, you're better off heading to the Richmond district in the city's northwestern corner.

Gold-ornamented portals and brightly painted balconies sit above the souvenir shops and restaurants of narrow **Grant Avenue**, the tourist thoroughfare; pass under the entrance arch at Bush Street and you'll be met by an assault of plastic Buddhas, cloisonné "health balls," noisemakers, and chirping mechanical crickets in every doorway. **Old St Mary's Church**, 660 California St at Grant Street (☎415/288-3800), was one of the few San Francisco buildings to survive the 1906 earthquake and fire, and there's a good photo display of the damage to the city in the entranceway.

Parallel to Grant Avenue, **Stockton Street** is crammed with exotic fish and produce markets, bakeries, and herbalists, and is the local main drag. Inside the **Ellison Herb Shop**, 805 Stockton St at Sacramento Street, Chinatown's best-stocked herbal pharmacy, you'll find clerks filling orders the ancient Chinese way – using hand-held scales and abacuses – from cabinets filled with dried bark, roots, sharks' fins, cicadas, ginseng, and other staples. Here, between Grant and Stockton, jumbled alleys hold the most worthwhile stops in the area. The best of these is **Waverly Place,** a two-block corridor of brightly painted balconies that was lined with brothels before the 1906 catastrophe and now home to three opulent but skillfully hidden **temples:** Norras at no. 109, Jen Sen on the second floor of no.146, and Tien Hou on the fourth floor of no. 125. The latter is the most impressive, with its ornate interior splashed with gold and vermilion. All three temples are still in use and open to visitors (daily 10am–5pm). Although the temples don't charge admission, it's respectful to leave a donation and not use cameras or camcorders inside.

Some of the hundred-plus **restaurants** in Chinatown (see p.1192 for recommendations) are historical landmarks in themselves. *Sam Wo*, 813 Washington St at Grant Avenue, is a cheap and churlish ex-haunt of the Beats, where Gary Snyder taught Jack Kerouac to eat with chopsticks and had them both thrown out with his loud and passionate interpretation of Zen poetry.

North Beach

Resting in the hollow between Russian and Telegraph hills, and bisected by throbbing Columbus Avenue, **North Beach** has always been a gateway for immigrants, especially the Italians who flocked here during the Gold Rush. It became the center of an alternative scene in 1953, after the opening of the **City Lights Bookstore,** 261 Columbus Ave at Broadway (☎ 415/362-8193, ⓦwww.city-lights.com); the first paperback bookstore in the US stands amid the flashing neon and sleazy clubs at this intersection, open until midnight seven days a week, and still owned by poet and novelist Lawrence Ferlinghetti. The **Beat Generation** briefly made the store (and the city) the literary capital of America, achieving overnight notoriety when charges of obscenity were leveled at Allen Ginsberg's poem *Howl* in 1957, which he first performed in a gallery in Cow Hollow. It was the hedonistic antics of the Beats, as much as their literary merits that struck a chord, and North Beach came to symbolize a wild and subversive lifestyle. The roadtrips and riotous partying, the drug-taking, and the embrace of Eastern religions were emulated nationwide, while tourists poured into North Beach for "Beatnik Tours." Then, when the Beat movement imploded, the younger hipsters – whom Kerouac & Co. had derided as juniors, or "hippies," for their dovish views – gathered in Haight-Ashbury, thus beginning the psychedelic Sixties (see p.1190).

Next to the bookstore, **Vesuvio's**, an old North Beach bar where the likes of Dylan Thomas and Kerouac would get loaded, remains a haven for the lesser-knowns to pontificate on the state of the arts. At the crossroads of Columbus and Broadway, poetry meets porn in a raucous assembly of strip joints, coffeehouses, and drag clubs. The most famous of these is the *Condor Club*, 300 Columbus Ave (now reincarnated as the *Condor Sports Bar*), where Carol "44 inches" Doda slipped out of her top one night and kickstarted the concept of topless waitresses in 1964. The landmark site still preserves photos and clippings from the original club's heyday.

As you continue north on Columbus Avenue, you enter the heart of the old **Italian neighborhood**, an enclave of narrow streets and leafy enclosures. Explorations lead to small landmarks like the **Café Trieste**, 609 Vallejo St at Kearny (℡415/982-2605), where the jukebox blasts out opera classics to a heavy-duty art crowd sipping cappuccinos and browsing slim volumes; legend has it that Francis Ford Coppola wrote the screenplay for *The Godfather* here. Dawdle in the grassy plaza known as **Washington Square Park** that plays host to dozens of local Chinese each morning practising *t'ai chi*, then head up the very steep steps on Filbert Street to reach Telegraph Hill and the **Coit Tower**, which affords grand views of the city and beyond (daily 10am–5pm; $3; ℡415/362-0808, ⓦwww.coittower.org).

Alcatraz

Before the rocky islet of **Alcatraz** became America's most dreaded **high-security prison**, in 1934, it had already served as a fortress and military jail. Surrounded by the freezing, impassable water of San Francisco Bay, it made an ideal place to hold the nation's most wanted criminals – men such as Al Capone and Machine Gun Kelly. The conditions were inhumane: inmates were kept in solitary confinement, in cells no larger than nine by five feet, most without light. They were not allowed to eat together, read newspapers, play cards, or even talk; relatives could visit for only two hours each month. Escape really was impossible. Nine men managed to get off the rock but none gained his freedom – the only two to make it to land (who had used a jacket stuffed with inflated surgical rings as a raft) were soon apprehended.

Due to its massive running costs, the prison finally closed in 1963. The island remained abandoned until 1969, when a group of Native Americans staged an occupation as part of a peaceful attempt to claim the island for their people, citing treaties that designated all federal land not in use as automatically reverting to their ownership. Using all the bureaucratic trickery it could muster, the government finally ousted them in 1971, claiming the operative lighthouse qualified it as active.

At least 750,000 tourists each year take the excellent hour-long, self-guided audio **tours** of the abandoned prison, which include some sharp anecdotal commentary as well as campy re-enactments of prison life featuring improvised voices of the likes of Capone and Kelly. Note that the island's name is a corruption of the Spanish for pelicans (*alcatraces*), although the only reason the current islet is known as Alcatraz is thanks to a muddle-headed English mapmaker and captain. He confused the names of several outcrops in the bay in 1826 – what we know as Yerba Buena Island was in fact the original Alcatraz.

Boats to Alcatraz leave from Pier 41 ($13.25 including audio tour, $9.25 without; frequent departures from 9.30am, last boat leaves Alcatraz at 4.30pm off season, 6.30pm high season); allow around two hours for a visit. Advance reservations are essential – in peak season, it's impossible to snag a ticket for same-day travel, so be warned (allow two weeks; ℡415/705-5555, ⓦwww.nps.gov/alcatraz and ⓦwww.blueandgoldfleet .com). Night tours are also available May through Sept from Thursday to Sunday departing at 6.20pm and 7.05pm and returning at 8.45pm and 9.30pm ($23.50).

To the west of Columbus, **Russian Hill** was named for six unknown Russian sailors who died here on an expedition in the early 1800s. In the summer, there's always a long line of cars waiting to drive down the tight curves of **Lombard Street**. Surrounded by palatial dwellings and herbaceous borders, Lombard is an especially thrilling drive at night, when the tourists leave and the city lights twinkle below. Even if you're without a car, the journey up here is worth it for a visit to the **San Francisco Art Institute**, 800 Chestnut St (daily 8am–9pm; free; ☎415/771-7020, ⓦwww.sanfranciscoart.edu), where the Diego Rivera Gallery has an outstanding mural created by the painter in 1931. Walking south from the Institute for four blocks on Jones Street, you'll find **Macondray Lane**, a pedestrian-only "street" thought to be one of the inspirations for Armistead Maupin's rollicking saga, *Tales of the City* (see p.1406).

Fisherman's Wharf

San Francisco rarely tries to pass off pure, unabashed commercialism as a worthy tourist attraction, but with **Fisherman's Wharf** and the nearby waterfront district, it makes an exception. Eminently skippable, it's the one place in town guaranteed to produce shudders of embarrassment from most locals.

An inventive use of statistics allows the area to proclaim itself the most-visited tourist attraction in the entire country; in fact, this crowded and hideous ensemble of waterfront kitsch and fast-food stands makes a sad and rather misleading introduction to the city. It may be hard to believe, but this was once a genuine fishing port; the few fishing vessels that can still afford the exorbitant mooring charges are usually finished by early morning and get out before the tourists arrive. The shops and bars here are among the most overpriced in the city, and crowd-weary families do little to add to the ambiance.

If you wish to get out on the water, sixty-minute **bay cruises** depart several times a day from piers 39 and 41 (see p.1176). Better instead to head west to the museums of **Fort Mason** and on to the expanse of green parkland along the **Marina district**, which affords excellent views of the Golden Gate Bridge.

Nob Hill

The posh hotels and Masonic institutions of **Nob Hill** exemplify San Francisco's old wealth, which arrived in the late 1800s with the robber-baron industrialists who moved here to build the Central Pacific Railroad. These financiers – who gave Nob Hill its name, after either "nabob," a Moghul prince, or "snob" – all built opulent mansions on the hill, only to see every one of them burn down in the fire caused by the earthquake of 1906. Today, aside from astounding views over the city and beyond, there are very few real sights to reward the stiff climb (or cable car ride) up the hill.

Begun soon after the fire, lumbering **Grace Cathedral** (☎415/749-6300, ⓦwww.gracecathedral.org), perched on top of the hill, is one of the biggest hunks of sham-Gothic architecture in the US. It took more than sixty years to finish this structure – and it suffers from a hodgepodge of styles as a result: the ugly reinforced concrete from the 1960s is particularly off-putting. For no reason other than the fact they were available, the entrance is adorned with faithful replicas of the fifteenth-century Ghiberti doors of the Florence Baptistry; the one place worth detouring inside here is the AIDS Interfaith Chapel, adorned with Keith Haring's vibrant cast bronze altar. A block east, be sure to go inside the **Fairmont Hotel**, 950 Mason St at Sacramento, to get a sense of the opulence that once ruled the hill: take its elevators up for a great view of the city. Across from the *Fairmont*, the brownstone of the **Pacific Union Club** was the only original Nob Hill structure left standing after the fire.

The Tenderloin, Civic Center, and SoMa

While parts of San Francisco can almost seem to be an urban utopia, the adjoining districts of **the Tenderloin** and **Civic Center** reveal harsher realities and are a gritty reminder that not everybody has it so easy. **SoMa**, the urban district *S*outh of *Ma*rket Street, meanwhile, was transformed by the dot-com boom – from an industrial wasteland to a hive of loft offices and granite-walled eateries, centered on the lovely Yerba Buena Gardens; of course, the Internet crash ended much of its economic upswing, though the area's slowly reviving again.

The majestic federal and municipal buildings of **Civic Center**, squashed between the Tenderloin and SoMa, can't help but look strangely out of sync, both with their immediate neighbors and with San Francisco as a whole. Their grand Beaux Arts style is at odds with the quirky wooden architecture of the rest of the city: little wonder, as they're the sole remnant of a grand architectural plan to transform the city's downtown into a boulevard-dotted, Parisian-inspired place after the buildings there were levelled in the 1906 earthquake. It was at the huge, green-domed **City Hall**, on the northern edge of the dismal **United Nations Plaza**, that Mayor George Moscone and gay Supervisor Harvey Milk were assassinated in 1978 (see p.1189). The recently restored gold plate dome is an impressive relic of Gold Rush–era largesse – if you want to take one of the free, fascinating tours round its interior, sign up at the Docent Tour kiosk on the Van Ness Avenue side of the building (tours Mon–Fri 10am, noon & 2pm, Sat & Sun 12.30pm; ☎415/554-4799, ⓦwww.ci.sf.ca.us/cityhall).

Formerly one of San Francisco's least desirable neighborhoods, SoMa enjoyed a rebirth during the 1990s that converted many of its warehouses to offices for the fledgling Internet industry, but the district has taken a tumble since the dot-crom crash and most of those office spaces now stand empty. The area's anchor attraction, though, is the **SF Museum of Modern Art**, 151 Third St at Mission (Fri–Tues 11am–6pm, Thurs 11am–9pm; $10, $5 Thurs 6–9pm, free first Tues of every month; ☎415/357-4000, ⓦwww.sfmoma.org), which opened here in January 1995. Major works include paintings by Jackson Pollock, Frida Kahlo, and Diego Rivera, though the temporary exhibitions are the museum's strongest suit thanks to newly acquired financial muscle. However, the allegation that the building, designed by Swiss architect Mario Botta, is far more beautiful than anything inside, is pretty hard to dispute – it's flooded with natural light from a striking cylindrical skylight while the upper galleries are connected by a vertigo-inducing metal catwalk.

Opposite the museum is the other totem of civic pride, the **Yerba Buena Center for the Arts**, 701 Mission St at Third (Tues, Wed, Sat & Sun 11am–6pm, Thurs & Fri 11am–8pm; $6, free first Tues of month; ☎415/978-2787, ⓦwww.yerbabuenaarts.org). This spectacular $44 million project features performance and gallery spaces used by both national and international touring exhibitions – though frankly the big draw here is the stunning five and a half acres of gardens in which it sits. The 50ft Sierra granite waterfall memorial to Martin Luther King Jr is especially moving, inscribed with excerpts from his speeches, Next to the gardens stands the **SONY Metreon** mall (☎415/369-6000, ⓦwww.metreon.com), an enormous 3D advertisement for the electronics giant that is only worth stopping by for its cinema, the most convenient multiscreen to downtown.

Sights in this massive area thin out considerably as you head south into a warehouse-lined former wasteland – though at night, this is the nexus of San Francisco's club culture. There are dozens of dance clubs here (see listings p.1198 for details) as well as the legendary **Folsom Street**, once synonymous with S&M. Though Folsom has calmed down from its chaps-and-whips hey-day in the 1970s, it's still home to bars which cater to the city's leather community and can be quite a scene, especially at weekends.

In the far southern reaches of SoMa stands **Pac Bell Park**, overlooking the waters at Third and King streets. Home to baseball's San Francisco Giants, the stadium is a remarkable addition to the city's waterfront. The faux old-brick building offers superb views of the bay beyond the outfield fences, some of the finest food to ever grace a ballpark, as well as the chance to see the odd home run splash into the bay. If the team's not playing while you're in town, check out the park on one of the twice-hourly tours (non-game days only, 10am–2pm; $10; ☎415/972-2000, ⓦwww.sfgiants.com).

The Mission

Vibrant, hip, and ethnically mixed, **the Mission** is easily San Francisco's most interesting neighborhood. A mile or so south of downtown, nestled in a basin, it's also the warmest and the summer fogs that dog the rest of the city leave this area alone. The traditional first stop for immigrants, the Mission was initially predominantly Scandinavian, then Irish before becoming a sizeable Latin American settlement. Though hipster Anglos have in recent years swarmed to its old buildings and cheap rents, it's still a joyously Hispanic place and one of the unmissable sights of the city.

The area takes its name from the old **Mission Dolores**, 3321 16th St at Dolores (daily 9am–4pm; $1 suggested donation; ☎415/621-8203, ⓦwww.graphicmode.com/missiondolores), the oldest building to survive the 1906 earthquake and fire. Founded in 1776, it was the sixth in a series of missions built along the Pacific coast as Spain staked its claim to California; the graves of the Native Americans it tried to "civilize" can be seen in the cemetery next door, along with those of white pioneers. Go early in the morning to avoid the tour buses.

The Hispanic heart of the Mission lies east of Mission Street between 16th and 24th streets. Here you'll absorb the district's original Latin flavor among the Nicaraguan, Salvadoran, Costa Rican, and Mexican stores and restaurants, as well as markets selling tropical fruits and *panaderias* baking traditional pastries. Meanwhile, to catch the Anglo pulse of the area, head along to the same stretch along Valencia Street, one block west: the profusion of independent bookstores and thrift stores around here makes for heavenly browsing, and the vicinity of 22nd Street has become a new gourmet-dining scene. Though tours of the **Levi Strauss & Co. factory**, 250 Valencia St at 14th Street, have been discontinued, it's worth stopping by to take a snap of the huge yellow building, constructed after the original factories were destroyed in the 1906 earthquake.

What really sets the Mission apart from the city's other neighborhoods are its **murals** – there are over two hundred in all, though many are more heartfelt than skilled or beautiful. The densest concentration is along **Balmy Alley**, between Folsom and Harrison off 24th Street, which is especially known for its politically charged paintings depicting the agonies of many Central American countries. For a more detailed recap of the murals' history and meaning, join one of the **tours** run by the mural organization, Precita Eyes, 2981 24th St at Harrison (tours Sat & Sun 1.30pm; $12; ☎415/285-2287, ⓦwww.precitaeyes.org).

The Castro

Progressive and celebratory, but also increasingly comfortable and wealthy, **the Castro** is the city's gay capital, providing a barometer for the state of the grown-up and sobered gay scene. Some people insist that this is still the wildest place in town, while others reckon it's a shadow of its former self; all agree that things are not the same as ten or even five years ago, when a walk down the Castro would have had you gawping at the revelry. Most of the same bars and hangouts still stand, but these days they're host to an altogether different and more conservative breed. Cute shops and restaurants lend a young professional feel to the place. A visit to the district is a must if you're to get any idea of just what San Francisco is all about, though in terms of visible street life, the few blocks around Castro and Market streets contain about all there is to see – the liveliest time to stroll around is on Sunday afternoons, when the streetside cafés are packed with well-groomed Castro residents.

Harvey Milk Plaza, by the Castro MUNI station, is dedicated to the assassinated gay supervisor, who owned a camera store in the Castro. The man who shot Milk and Mayor George Moscone, Dan White, was a disgruntled ex-colleague who resigned in protest at their liberal policies; at the trial, his plea of temporary insanity caused by harmful additives in his fast food – the so-called "Twinkie defense" – won him a sentence of five years' imprisonment for manslaughter and the derision of the local gay community. Reactions were angry enough to spark the "White Night" riots, which were among the most violent San Francisco has ever witnessed, as protesters marched into City Hall, burning police cars as they went. As for White, he was released from prison in 1985 and, unable to find a job, committed suicide soon afterwards.

Gay and lesbian San Francisco

San Francisco is still the indisputable **gay capital of the world** – but today the local gay community is much less outrageous and activist than it was in the past. For most of the year, though, the scene still has its raucous and raunchy moments – notably in June, with the Gay and Lesbian Film Festival, Gay Pride Week, and the Gay Freedom Day Parade. October is also good, when the street fairs are in full swing and Halloween transforms the Castro into a costumed wonderland. Recently, though, city officials have tried to move the celebration to Civic Center, where there's better crowd control and safety; this has somewhat dampened the holiday's anything-goes atmosphere.

It's worth noting that San Francisco is definitely **gay male-centric**. Though the 1980s saw the flowering of a **lesbian** culture to rival the male 1970s upsurge, now those bars for women have all but closed down (the exception being the Mission's *Lexington Club*, see p.1197), and the nightlife revolves around a handful of women's club nights. Frankly, the place to seek out lesbian culture is in the bookstores.

Good **listings periodicals** include *Gloss*, *Frontiers*, *The Bay Area Reporter*, and *Bay Times*; these can be found in many Castro bars and cafés. Other useful publications include *Betty and Pansy's Severe Queer Review of San Francisco* ($10.95), available in gay bookstores, and *The Lavender Pages*, a free telephone-cum-resource book. The new LGBT Community Center, 1800 Market St at Octavia (☏415/865-5555, ⓦwww.sfcenter.org), has a walk-in information desk on its first floor, and also regularly hosts performances by comedy and theater groups on-site – check the website or call for details. You'll find gay **accommodation** and **bars** listed on pp.1197 and 1196, respectively.

Before heading down Castro Street into the heart of the neighborhood, take a short walk to the former location of the **Names Project** at 2363A Market St, which sponsored the creation of "**The Quilt**" – a gargantuan blanket in which each panel measures six feet by three feet (the size of a grave site) and bears the name of a person lost to AIDS. Made by lovers, friends, and families, the panels are stitched together and regularly tour the country and the world; it has been spread on the Mall in Washington, DC, several times to dramatize the epidemic. The 54-ton Quilt and Names Project Foundation moved to a permanent home in Atlanta in 2001.

The junction of **Castro and 18th Street**, known as the "gayest four corners of the earth," marks the Castro's center, cluttered with bookstores, clothing stores, cafés, and bars. The side streets offer a slightly more exclusive fare of exotic delicatessens, fine wines, and fancy florists amid manicured and leafy residential roads.

Haight-Ashbury

The fame of **Haight–Ashbury**, two miles west of downtown San Francisco, far outstrips its size and its appeal. No more than eight blocks in length, centered on the junction of Haight and Ashbury streets, "The Haight" was a run–down Victorian neighborhood until it was transformed into the hub of counterculture cool during the 1960s. Since then the area has become gentrified, but it retains a collection of radical bookstores, laid–back cafés, record stores, and secondhand clothing emporia, not to mention a ragged collection of hangers-on.

All there is to do in the Haight today is to stroll around the **shops**, and pick your way past the dozens of beggars. The one place worth spending serious cash is at the eastern end of Haight Street, around Fillmore Street, which is known as the **Lower Haight**. For decades a primarily African-American

The hippies

The first **hippies** were an offshoot of the Beats, many of whom had moved out of their increasingly expensive North Beach homes to take advantage of the low rents and large spaces in the Victorian houses of the Haight. The post-Beat bohemia that subsequently began to develop here in the early 1960s was initially a small affair, involving drug use and the embrace of Eastern religion and philosophy, together with a marked anti-American political stance and a desire for world peace. Where Beat philosophy had emphasized self-indulgence, the hippies, on the face of it at least, stressed such concepts as "universal truth" and "cosmic awareness." Characters like Ken Kesey and his Merry Pranksters set a precedent of wild living and challenging authority. The use of drugs was seen as an integral – and positive – part of the movement. **LSD**, especially, which was not then illegal, was claimed as an avant-garde art form, pumped out in private laboratories and distributed by Timothy Leary and his supporters with a prescription – "Turn on, tune in, drop out" – that galvanized a generation into inactivity. Life in the Haight took on a theatrical quality: Pop Art found mass appeal, light shows became legion, and dress flamboyant. The psychedelic music scene, spearheaded by the Grateful Dead, Jefferson Airplane, and Janis Joplin, became a genuine force nationwide, and it wasn't long before kids from all over America started turning up in Haight-Ashbury for the free food, free drugs, and free love. Money became a dirty word, the hip became "heads," and the rest of the world were "straights."

During the heady days of the massive "be-in" in Golden Gate Park in 1966 and the so-called "Summer of Love" the following year, no fewer than 75,000 pilgrims turned the busy little intersection of Haight-Ashbury into the center of alternative culture.

neighborhood, it has been transformed over the past decade by youthful immigrants from Britain into a stomping ground for the city's rave culture. Refreshingly free of aging hippies, it's packed with DJ-directed record shops and a boisterous population of club kids.

Golden Gate Park

In a city with an abundance of green space, **Golden Gate Park** stands out as not just the largest, but also the most beautiful, and safest, of its parks. Spreading three miles or so west from the Haight as far as the Pacific, it was constructed on what was then an area of wild sand dunes buffeted by the spray from the ocean. Despite the throngs of joggers, polo players, roller-skaters, cyclists, and strollers, it never seems to get overcrowded and you can always find a spot to be alone.

Of the park's several museums, the best, sadly, is under long-term reconstruction. The **M.H. de Young Museum** (☎415/863-3330, ⓦ www.thinker.org), with its large and diverse range of paintings and sculpture, is not due to reopen until 2005: when it does, its twisted, copper-capped new building will offer double the exhibition space. In the meantime, its holdings have been transferred to the California Palace of the Legion of Honor (see overleaf). Opposite the museum, the **California Academy of Sciences** (daily: Memorial Day to Labor Day 9am–6pm; rest of year 10am–5pm, first Wed of month open until 8.45pm; $8.50, $2.50 discount with MUNI transfers; ☎415/750-7145, ⓦ www.calacademy.org), is a good place to amuse restless children, with its 30ft dinosaur skeleton, life-sized replicas of elephant seals and other California wildlife, and live colony of black-footed penguins. Over six thousand specimens of aquatic life can be viewed in its **Steinhart Aquarium** (daily 10am–5pm; admission included in museum ticket), the best being the alligators and other reptiles lurking in a simulated swamp. Slightly to the west, the **Japanese Tea Garden** (daily 9am–6pm; ☎415/751-1171) is dominated by a massive bronze Buddha, while carp-filled ponds and bonsai and cherry trees lend a tranquil feel, as long as you can ignore the busloads of tourists that pour in regularly throughout the day. The best way to enjoy the garden is to get there around 9am and have a breakfast of tea and fortune cookies in the tea house ($3.50 any time).

The Golden Gate Bridge and beyond

The orange towers of the **Golden Gate Bridge**, perhaps the best-loved symbol of San Francisco, are visible from almost every high point in the city. The bridge, which spans 4200ft, had taken only 52 months to design and build when it was opened in 1937: note that the ruddy color was originally intended as a temporary undercoat before the gray topcoat was applied, but locals liked it so much, the bridge has stayed orange ever since. Driving on it is a real thrill since you race along under the towers, while the half-hour walk across allows you to take in its enormous size and absorb the views of the Northern California headlands, as well as the city itself. The view is especially beautiful at sunset, when the glow of the waning day paints the white city a delicate pink.

The **Fort Point National Historic Site** beneath the bridge gives a good sense of the place as the westernmost outpost of the nation. This brick fortress, built in the 1850s, has a dramatic site, reachable via Marine Drive in the Presidio, where the surf pounds away beneath the great span of the bridge high above – a view made famous by Kim Novak's suicide attempt in Alfred

Hitchcock's *Vertigo*. The other attraction in the shadow of the bridge is the beaches at the tip of the peninsula, though dangerous riptides and excruciatingly cold water make it impossible to swim with any confidence.

Make sure to head inland to **Lincoln Park**, at 34th Avenue and Clement Street, which offers striking views of the Marin headlands and is home to the stately **California Palace of the Legion of Honor** (Tues–Sun 9.30am–5pm; $8, free every Tues, surcharge for special exhibitions; ☎415/863-3330, ⓦwww.thinker.org), one of the best museums in the city. Its isolated, windswept location, high on a bluff overlooking the ocean, is unsurpassably romantic, and deters the hordes that swarm the MoMA and the museums in Golden Gate Park. The bronze cast of Rodin's *The Thinker* on a pedestal in the center of the front courtyard offers a foretaste of the museum's expansive holdings by the French sculptor, including *The Athlete*, *Fugit Amor*, and a small cast of *The Kiss*. Sadly, the magnificent museum is somewhat let down by its lackluster collection of Old Masters – many of the artworks, including those by Giambologna, Cellini, and Cranach, are "attributed to" or "the workshop of," rather than bona fide masterpieces. The Impressionist and Post-Impressionist galleries are stronger, though, and contain works by Courbet, Manet, and Monet among others – look for the lively oil sketches by Degas and Seurat's characteristically trippy view of the Eiffel Tower.

Eating

With well over three thousand restaurants crammed onto the small peninsula, and scores of bars and cafés open all day, **eating** in San Francisco is never difficult, and while the hype around the city is relentless, it's in its restaurants where that hype is unquestionably deserved. Be warned: San Francisco closes early, and you'll be struggling to find places that will serve you after 10 or 11pm. **Mexican** food is big in the Mission, **Italian** places abound in North Beach, and, of course, Chinatown naturally has plenty of **Chinese** restaurants, while the **Japan Center** – the heart of Japantown, located at Post Street between Geary, Laguna, and Fillmore, a mile west of Union Square – boasts a few fine Japanese places. In health-conscious San Francisco you'll find **vegetarian** entrees on every menu and quite a few entirely vegetarian restaurants. With the vineyards of Napa and Sonoma Valley on the city's doorstep, quality **wines** have a high profile in most San Francisco restaurants. State law prohibits **smoking** in all restaurants, cafés, and bars, as evidenced by the crowds of people puffing on the pavements.

Downtown and Chinatown

Asia de Cuba *Clift Hotel*, 495 Geary St at Taylor, Theater District ☎415/923-2300. Cuban food served family-style in huge portions in an extremely trendy setting – even so, it's a delicious experience, enhanced by the opium-den-like ambiance.

Cosmopolitan Café 121 Spear St Unit B-8, in the Rincon Center, Financial District ☎415/543-4001. This modern American bistro is an appealing choice for dinner in a deserted area. The standard modern American food (entrees $18–22) is spruced up with great condiments like sweet,

chunky house-made ketchup, not to mention friendly, efficient service.

Farallon 450 Post St at Powell, Union Square ☎415/956-6969. Sumptuously styled as an undersea grotto, serving highly creative seafood dishes in small portions. Definitely worth a splurge if you're into elegant dining experiences.

House of Nanking 919 Kearny at Jackson, Chinatown ☎415/421-1429. One of the city's most popular Chinese restaurants, despite the lack of decor and elbow room. You wait ages for a table, but the inexpensive food doesn't disappoint.

Kokkari Estiatorio 200 Jackson St at Front, Financial District ☎415/981-0983. By far, the best

Greek restaurant in town, offering staples such as lamb and eggplant that are served both separately and cooked together as moussaka.

Plouf 40 Belden Lane at Bush, Chinatown ☏415/986-6491. Convivial South-of-France seafood bistro, with sidewalk seating in good weather. The garlicky mussels – the house specialty – are the best in the city.

Sam Woh 813 Washington St at Grant, Chinatown ☏415/982-0596. The space is unpleasantly cramped, the food is mediocre, and the service downright unpleasant. So why bother? It's open late and back in the Fifties this was the spot Jack, Allen, and the rest of the Beats used to come when they were too wired to go to bed.

Sears Fine Food 439 Powell St at Post, Union Square ☏415/986-1160. A classic breakfast joint with a hearty old-fashioned ambiance: try the plate of eighteen tiny Swedish pancakes, or for groups of six or more, the Ranch Breakfast of pancakes, eggs, bacon, and the works.

Tadich Grill 240 California St at Battery, Financial District ☏415/391-1849. Half diner, half gentleman's club, staffed by white-jacketed waiters and serving hearty steaks and salads.

Yank Sing 427 Battery St at Clay, Financial District ☏415/781-1111. A cavernous spot that regularly tops locals' lists for the best dim sum in the city. Despite being routinely packed during lunch hours, the waitstaff can almost always find a spot for you in the seemingly endless warren of dining rooms.

Yuet Lee 1300 Stockton St at Broadway, Chinatown ☏415/982-6020. Cheap and cheerful Chinese restaurant with a good seafood menu. Surprisingly good food served as late as 3am. Closed Tuesdays.

North Beach, the Embarcadero, Fisherman's Wharf, and the Marina

Baker Street Bistro 2953 Baker St at Lombard, Cow Hollow ☏415/931-1475. Cramped but charming café with a few outdoor tables. The slightly older, neighborhood crowd enjoys simple food served by French staff. Wines are well priced and the $14.50 *prix fixe* dinner is a bargain.

Bistro Yoffi 2231 Chestnut St at Pierce, Marina ☏415/885-5133. Eclectic modern American cuisine served in an attractive bistro that's refreshingly quirky given its location, packed with potted ferns and mismatched chairs. There's a great garden out back.

Café Francisco 2161 Powell St at North Point, Fisherman's Wharf ☏415/397-2602. Cheap neighborhood café that's great for a lazy breakfast

lounging with the newspapers or a quiet lunchtime sandwich only blocks from the wharf.

Café Jacqueline 1454 Grant Ave at Green, North Beach ☏415/981-5565. A romantic, candlelit gourmet experience, this restaurant serves only chef-owner Jacqueline Margulis's signature soufflés, both savory and sweet (crab and chocolate are top picks).

Caffè Trieste 601 Vallejo St at Grant, North Beach ☏415/392-6739. Small, crowded, and authentic Italian coffeehouse – stop by on Saturday afternoons for the amateur opera hour when local ladies warble for tips.

Greens Fort Mason Center, Building A, Marina ☏415/771-6222. The queen of San Francisco's vegetarian restaurants, with a gorgeous view of the bay. Book ahead.

The Helmand 430 Broadway at Kearny, North Beach ☏415/362-0641. The decor here is simple and unassuming – unlike the food, which is unforgettable. The menu features tangy and spicy Afghani staples like *kaddo borwani* (caramelized pumpkin).

Mama's 1701 Stockton St at Washington Square, North Beach ☏415/362-6421. Cheery bright yellow tablecloths and sunny staff give this homey diner a lift: try the crab Benedict or one of the gooey, cake-like French toast specials. Expect lines at the weekend, whatever the time, so bring a book.

Trattoria Contadina 1800 Mason St at Union, North Beach ☏415/982-5728. This tiny, family-owned trattoria still caters primarily to the local Italian community, serving outstanding renditions of traditional dishes, like rigatoni with eggplant and smoked mozzarella.

Civic Center, Tenderloin, SoMa, and The Mission

Asia SF 201 9th St at Howard, SoMa ☏415/255-2742. More of an experience than a restaurant, this only-in-San Francisco spot features "gender illusionist" staff who put on a campy nightly revue. Though the show's the real draw, the sushi and cocktails are good.

Betty's Café 167 11th St at Howard, SoMa ☏415/431-2525. Known for its hearty $2.65 breakfast specials, including choice of meat, eggs, hash browns, and toast. No frills, but who'd expect them at prices like these.

Boogaloo's 3296 22nd St at Valencia, Mission ☏415/824-3211. Open 8am–3.30pm. Breakfast is the big draw here: black beans and *chorizo* (spicy sausage) feature heavily among the Latinized versions of American diner classics, costing $5–7 per dish. The decor's basic, but perked up with bright orange and yellow tables.

Late-night eating

For that midnight snack or early-morning binge, check out the following **24-hour** dependables:

Bagdad Café 2295 Market St at 16th St, Castro ☎415/621-4434. The best-price 24-hour option in the neighborhood.

Caffè Greco 423 Columbus Ave at Vallejo, North Beach ☎415/397-6261. The best place to come for a dark, pungent, pick-me-up espresso – you can also graze on pastries.

El Farolito 2779 Mission St at 24th, Mission ☎415/824-7877. Twenty-four-hour *taqueria*.

Mario's Bohemian Cigar Store 566 Columbus Ave at Union, North Beach ☎415/362-0536. The cigars are long gone, but it's definitely still a boho hangout – they're likely here for the huge, doorstopping panini.

Yuet Lee 1300 Stockton St at Broadway, Chinatown ☎415/982-6020. Terrific Chinese seafood until 3am; daily except Tuesday.

Café Flore 2298 Noe St at Market, Castro ☎415/621-8579. Wedged into the triangle at the corner of Market and Noe streets, this café has a sunny, plant-filled courtyard that's a great place to grab a coffee and a gooey cake; be aware that it can be very cruisey, especially during the early evening.

El Farolito 2779 Mission St at 24th, Mission ☎415/824-7877. A scruffy local institution, this 24-hour *taqueria* is basic, with rows of long formica tables, but the food is outstanding and cheap – try a *quesadilla suiza* (tortilla with creamy Swiss and chicken).

Fringale 570 4th St at Brannan, SoMa ☎415/543-0573. Delightful, low-key charmer on a quiet SoMa block offering service that's as exceptional as the food, which is predominantly French, but with Basque touches like serrano ham.

Lulu 816 Folsom St at 4th, SoMa ☎415/495-5775. Famed Californian restaurant with a rustic, rather cramped dining room serving family-style, Italian-inspired dishes. The wine list is spectacular.

Luna Park 694 Valencia St at 18th, Mission ☎415/553-8584. Groovy local favorite, decked out like a lush bordello with deep red walls and ornamental chandeliers. Most of the entrees, like a tuna salad *niçoise* or *moules frites*, hover around $14.

Saigon Sandwiches 560 Larkin St at Ellis, Tenderloin ☎415/474-5698. Hole-in-the-wall store selling superb, made-to-order Vietnamese sandwiches for $2 each: choose from barbecued chicken or pork, and meatballs.

Shalimar 532 Jones St at Geary, Tenderloin ☎415/928-0333. A happy find in the downtrodden Tenderloin, this divey spot serves delicious, cheap Pakistani food, all of it made to order before your eyes.

Swan Oyster Depot 1517 Polk at California, Polk Gulch ☎415/673-1101. No frills – and officially, no full meals – at this cheap seafood counter. Grab a stool and hang onto it (it gets crowded and competitive in here) and suck down some cheap shellfish and seafood.

Ti Couz 3108 16th St at Valencia, Mission ☎415/252-7373. This friendly but hip *crêperie* was one of the pioneers of the newly groovy Mission scene on Valencia Street. It still holds its place as one of the best of the cheaper restaurants around, serving buckwheat savory pancakes for $6 or so.

Truly Mediterranean 3109 16th St at Valencia, Mission ☎415/252-7482. Fast threatening to overtake the beloved burrito as the locals' favorite portable dinner item, this hole-in-the-wall's version of the falafel comes wrapped in thin, crispy bread. A second location can be found at 1724 Haight St at Cole, Haight-Ashbury.

Tu Lan 8 6th St at Market, SoMa/Tenderloin ☎415/626-0927. A legend ever since Julia Child first sampled the Vietnamese cooking in this cramped, dingy space on one of the seediest blocks in town. The food's consistently fresh, flavorful, and cheap.

The Castro, Haight-Ashbury, and Japantown

Brother-in-Laws Bar-B-Q 705 Divisadero St at Grove, Western Addition ☎415/931-7427. The service and atmosphere here are dreadful, but it still packs people in thanks to delicious, crunchy short-end ribs and smokey brisket.

Chow 215 Church St at Market, Castro ☎415/552-2469. Unfussy comfort food, like pasta and wood-fired pizza, some with an Asian twist. Spaghetti and meatballs is great value for $6 and most dishes cost no more than $10.

EOS 901 Cole St at Carl, Cole Valley ℡415/566-3063. The best place to sip a glass of wine and enjoy Euro-Asian inspired cuisine. The restaurant is very pricey, so stick to the wine bar next door for a similar experience at a lower price.

Frjtz 579 Hayes St at Laguna, Hayes Valley ℡415/864-7654. Trendy little *friterie*, serving cones of crunchy Belgian-style fries with dips like tabasco-chive ketchup and spicy yogurt peanut.

Home 2100 Market St at Church, Castro ℡415/503-0333. The menu at this mixed-gay diner is designed to offer the things that a chef cooks at home for his friends – primarily comfort food like *moules frites* (around $10–12 per entree). There's an enjoyable patio bar with DJs at the weekend.

Maki Japan Center, 1825 Post St at Webster, Japantown ℡415/921-5125. One of the many tasty, tiny places in the Japan Center, this restaurant specializes in *wappan meshi*, a wood steamer filled with vegetables, meat, and rice.

Rosamunde Sausage Grille 545 Haight St at Fillmore, Lower Haight ℡415/437-6851. Small storefront grill with a few stools at the bar, serving just-grilled sausages on a sesame roll. Choose from a cherry-laced chicken sausage to the light flavors of a shrimp, scallop, and snapper sausage.

Stelline 330 Gough St at Hayes, Hayes Valley ℡415/626-4292. Red-checkered tablecloths, a handwritten and photocopied menu, plus affable, chatty staff make this a cheap, relaxed place to grab lunch.

Suppenküche 601 Hayes St at Laguna, Hayes Valley ℡415/252-9289. Satisfying and delicious German cooking near Civic Center in a loud, lively bar/restaurant decked out like a traditional Bavarian pub. Don't miss the potato pancakes appetizer – it's enough alone for a light supper.

Thep Phanom 400 Waller St at Fillmore, Lower Haight ℡415/431-2526. Delicate decor and beautifully prepared Thai dishes in the Lower Haight. Only $8 for a main course, but expect to wait for a table.

The Sunset and the Richmond

Chapeau! 1408 Clement St at 15th, Richmond ℡415/750-9787. Downtown-quality French food at foggy Richmond prices, and crowded with locals enjoying a relaxed provincial atmosphere

Fountain Court 354 Clement St at 5th Ave, Richmond ℡415/668-1100. Unusual Chinese restaurant serving authentic Shanghai food – less familiar than Cantonese staples, perhaps, but just as delicious. Try the Shanghai dumplings or lion's-head soup.

Pizzetta 211 23rd Ave at California, Richmond ℡415/379-9880. Inventive and unusual pizzas are featured on a different menu each week, offering whatever's fresh and seasonal as a topping (although you'll usually find eggs on at least one option).

PJ's Oyster Bed 737 Irving St at Ninth, Sunset ℡415/566-7775. From Tuesday through Thursday this rowdy, unpretentious restaurant offers spicy, tangy Cajun dishes like blackened catfish and alligator fillets. Watch out for the free Jello vodka shots the owner periodically passes around.

Wing Lee Bakery 503 Clement St at 6th Ave, Richmond ℡415/668-9481. No-nonsense Chinese dim sum store, one of several on this strip. There's little English spoken, so it's something of a lucky dip snack, but the fillings are more authentic than what you'll find downtown.

Nightlife and entertainment

Compared to many US cities, where you need money and attitude in equal measure, San Francisco's **nightlife** scene demands little of either. It is not unusual for restaurants to provide live music, and you can often eat and be entertained for no extra cost. This is no 24-hour city, however, and the approach to socializing is often surprisingly low-key, with little of the pandering to fads and fashions that goes on elsewhere. The casualness is contagious, and manifests in a club scene that, far as it is from the cutting edge of hip, is encouragingly inexpensive compared to those in other cities. For $30–40 you can get a decent night out, including cover charge and a few drinks. Always have your ID with you, otherwise you cannot get past the bouncers at all clubs and music venues. Smoking is illegal in bars and clubs, though locals routinely flout the law at the risk of incurring a ticket.

The Sunday *Chronicle*'s "Pink Pages" supplement, along with the free weekly *Bay Guardian* and the *San Francisco Weekly*, are the best sources of **listings**. Ticketmaster (☎ 415/421-8497, ⊛ www.ticketmaster.com) is the major **ticket** agency, with outlets in Tower Records and Rite Aid stores. Tickets.com (☎ 415/776-1999, ⊛ www.tickets.com) is also worth a try.

Bars

San Francisco, while famous for its restaurants, has a huge number of **drinking establishments**, ranging from comfortably scruffy jukebox joints to chic watering holes.

Bambuddha *The Phoenix Hotel*, 601 Eddy St at Larkin, Tenderloin ☎ 415/885-5088. Sleek, South Pacific–inspired cocktail lounge with terrific DJs and strong drinks.

Bigfoot Lodge 1750 Polk St at Washington, Polk Gulch ☎ 415/440-2355. Bar themed as a 1950s ski lodge: expect plenty of faux wood and hunting trophies, as well as an enormous papier mâché statue of Bigfoot himself.

Blondie's Bar & No Grill 540 Valencia St at 16th, Mission ☎ 415/864-2419. Always packed, this fun bar with a good-sized patio serves huge cocktails and often hosts live music. As a bonus, the newly opened *Wetspot* back room is also smoker-friendly.

Edinburgh Castle 950 Geary St at Polk, Tenderloin ☎ 415/885-4074. Just your average Scottish bar run by Koreans; it's filled with heraldic Highland memorabilia and offers a mean version of fish and chips.

Gordon Biersch Brewery 2 Harrison St at Embarcadero, SoMa ☎ 415/243-8246. Bayfront microbrewery in a converted coffee warehouse, with a great selection of beers that pulls in a downtown twenty-something crowd.

Li Po's Bar 916 Grant Ave at Jackson, Chinatown ☎ 415/982-0072. Named after the Chinese poet, *Li Po's* is a little grotty, although that's part of its charm: it's one of the few places to drink in Chinatown.

Mad Dog in the Fog 530 Haight St at Fillmore, Lower Haight ☎ 415/626-7279. Aptly named by the two lads from Birmingham, England, who own the joint, this is one of the Lower Haight's most loyally patronized bars, with darts and English beer.

Persian Aub Zam Zam 1663 Haight St at Clayton, Haight-Ashbury ☎ 415/861-2545. A Casbah-style cocktail lounge featuring a retro jazz jukebox; the famed and ornery owner may be dead, but his regulars clubbed together and bought the bar to preserve its vibe. Try a signature gin martini.

Red Room *Commodore International Hotel*, 827 Sutter St at Jones, Theater District ☎ 415/346-7666. This trendy, sexy bar is – as its name implies – completely red: walls, furniture, glasses, and even many of the drinks.

The Redwood Room *Clift Hotel*, 495 Geary St at Taylor, Theater District ☎ 415/775-4700. This club-by, landmark bar was recently given a hip makeover, with lightboxes on the wall displaying paintings that phase and fade between portraits. It's great fun – just don't choke on the drinks prices.

Tonga Room *Fairmont Hotel*, 950 Mason St at California, Nob Hill ☎ 415/772-5278. This base-ment bar is styled like a Polynesian village, com-plete with a pond and simulated rainstorms, and a grass-skirted band playing terrible jazz and pop covers from a floating raft. The cocktails are out-rageously overpriced, but the kitschy setting is worth every cent. Cover $3 after 8pm.

Tunnel Top 601 Bush St at Stockton, Union Square ☎ 415/986-8900 This funky, industrial bar is hidden behind a seedy storefront on top of the Stockton Street tunnel. One of the few tobacco-friendly places downtown.

Gay and lesbian bars

San Francisco's **gay and lesbian bars** are many and varied, ranging from cozy cocktail lounges to no-holds-barred leather-and-chain hangouts. The scene may no longer be quite as wild as its reputation would have you believe, but at its best it can still be hard to beat.

Badlands 4131 18th St at Castro, Castro ☎ 415/626-9320, ⊛ www.sfbadlands.com. Recently reno-vated, this video bar attracts a pretty, thirty-some-thing crowd and is usually packed at weekends.

Cat Club 1190 Folsom St at 8th, SoMa ☎ 415/431-3332. This dark, loud club is one of the city's lesbian hotspots, mixing dancing and live performances. It's livelier the later you arrive. Cover $5–10.

The Eagle Tavern 398 12th St at Harrison, SoMa ℡ 415/626-0880. A good old-fashioned leather bar, particularly popular on Sundays when it holds a late-afternoon "beer bust" for charity.

Esta Noche 3079 16th St at Valencia, Mission ℡ 415/861-5757. This gay Latin drag bar hosts nightly shows that are great fun and attract a young, racially mixed clientele.

Lexington Club 3464 19th St at Lexington, Mission ℡ 415/863-2052, ⓦ www.lexingtonclub .com. The only place in the city where the girls outnumber the boys (men must be accompanied by a woman to enter), this bustling lesbian bar attracts all sorts with its no-nonsense decor, friendly atmosphere, and excellent jukebox.

Liquid 2925 16th St at Capp, Mission ℡ 415/ 431-8889 Though you could walk right on by without noticing it, this tiny, fun club is one of the city's best places to dance with a friendly, mixed gay-lesbian-straight crowd. Cover $2–10.

Martuni's 4 Valencia St at Market, Mission ℡ 415/ 241-0205, ⓦ martunis.citysearch.com. This piano bar attracts a well-heeled, middle-aged crowd, all keen to sing along to classics from Judy, Liza, and Edith.

Midnight Sun 4067 18th St at Castro, Castro ℡ 415/861-4186, ⓦ www.midnightsunsf.com. Long, narrow video bar, always busy with well-dressed white boys checking out the movies shown on the monitors, as well as each other.

Pilsner Inn 225 Church St at Market, Castro ℡ 415/621-7058. The best neighborhood gay bar in the Castro, filled with a diverse, slightly older crowd playing pool and darts. There's a large, smoker-friendly patio out back.

Powerhouse 1347 Folsom St at Doré Alley, SoMa ℡ 415/861-1790. One of the prime pick-up joints in the city, this very cruisey old-school leather bar has plenty of convenient dark corners.

The Stud 399 Folsom St at 9th, SoMa ℡ 415/252-7883. Legendary gay club that's still as popular as ever, attracting a diverse, energetic, and uninhibited crowd. Check out the fabulously freaky drag-queen cabaret at "Trannyshac" (Tues). Cover $5–8.

Live music: rock, jazz, and folk

San Francisco's **music scene** reflects the character of the city: laid-back, eclectic, and not a little nostalgic. The options for catching live music are wide and the scene is definitely on the up and up, with the city regularly spawning good young bands. San Francisco has never recaptured its crucial Sixties role, though in recent years the city has helped launch acid jazz (beat-heavy jazz that's become *de rigueur* dinner-party music across the country), a classic swing revival, and the East Bay pop-punk sound. Check the *San Francisco Bay Guardian* and *SF Weekly* free weeklies, and the *San Francisco Chronicle*, for listings.

Bimbo's 365 Club 1025 Columbus St at Chestnut, North Beach ℡ 415/474-0365, ⓦ www.bimbos365.com. Classy lounge with table-side drink service (2 minimum) and a varied high-quality roster of music styles from jazz to ska. Cover $20 and up.

Biscuits and Blues 401 Mason St at Geary, Union Square ℡ 415/292-2583, ⓦ biscuitandblue.city-search.com. Lively blues supper club with inexpensive Southern cuisine and hot blues acts nightly. Reservations recommended for dinner shows. Cover $5–15.

Boom Boom Room 1601 Fillmore St at Geary, Japantown ℡ 415/673-8000, ⓦ www.boom-boomblues.com. Once owned by the late blues legend John Lee Hooker, this small, intimate bar delivers straight-ahead jazz or classic blues acts nightly. Cover $5–12.

Bottom of the Hill 1233 17th St at Missouri, Potrero Hill ℡ 415/621-4455, ⓦ www.botto-mofthehill.com. Hangout for rock and country music, live seven nights a week, drawing a late-twenty- to thirty-something crowd. There's an outdoor all-you-care-to-eat barbecue on the patio Sun. Cover $5–10.

Bruno's 2389 Mission St at 20th, Mission ℡ 415/648-7701, ⓦ www.brunoslive.com. Like something from a Scorsese movie, this retro-1960s restaurant has an intimate live venue attached where there's usually jazz or nu-school R&B. Cover $5–7 (no cover for diners).

Café du Nord 2170 Market St at Sanchez, Castro ℡ 415/861-5016, ⓦ www.cafedunord.com. Primarily a jazz club, this popular bar is also a great place to enjoy live swing, Latin, and blues over good food, or just have a beer and shoot some pool. Cover $3–8.

Elbo Room 647 Valencia St at 17th, Mission ℡ 415/552-7788, ⓦ www.elbo.com. The birth-place of acid jazz, often home to world music performers. Cover $4–7.

The Fillmore Auditorium 1805 Geary St at Fillmore, Japantown ℡ 415/346-6000, ⓦ www.thefillmore.com. A local landmark, *The*

Fillmore was at the heart of the 1960s counter-culture, masterminded by the legendary Bill Graham. It reopened in 1994 after several years' hiatus and is home now to rock and alt-rock touring acts. Cover varies.

The Great American Music Hall 859 O'Farrell St at Polk, Tenderloin ☎ 415/885-0750, ⊛ www.musichallsf.com. Historic former bordello and saloon that has been converted into a popular venue for rock, blues, and world music acts. Cover $10–20.

The Ramp 855 China Basin at Illinois, China Basin ☎ 415/621-2378. A bayside restaurant serving up live salsa on summer Sunday afternoons.

Tongue & Groove 2513 Van Ness Ave at Union, Cow Hollow ☎ 415/928-0404, ⊛ www.tongueandgroovesf.com. Local bands ranging from rock and funk to Seventies retro and alternative – one of the most inventive and reliable options in the city. Cover $8–10.

The Up & Down Club 1151 Folsom St at 7th, SoMa ☎ 415/626-2388. A mix of live and DJ-spun danceable grooves – there's usually jazz downstairs. Cover $5.

Clubbing

Still trading on a reputation for hedonism earned decades ago, San Francisco's **nightclubs** in fact trail light years behind those of other large American cities. That said, the compensations are manifold – it is rare to encounter high cover charges, ridiculously priced drinks, feverish posing, or long lines, though a few of the cavernous dance clubs in SoMa do have lines on weekends. The greatest concentration of clubs is in **SoMa** and, recently, the **Mission**. You must bring your ID to get in to all clubs; most require you to be at least twenty-one. Unlike most other cities, where the action never gets going until after midnight, many San Francisco clubs have to close at 2am during the week, so you can usually be sure of finding things well under way by 11.30pm.

1015 Folsom 1015 Folsom St at 6th, SoMa ☎ 415/431-1200. Multi-level superclub, popular across-the-board for late-night dancing: the music's largely house and garage, and expect marquee names like Sasha and Digweed on the main floor. $10–15.

DNA Lounge 375 11th St at Harrison, SoMa ☎ 415/626-1409, ⊛ www.dnalounge.com. Changes its music style nightly, but draws the same young hipsters, a mixed gay-straight crowd. $15–20.

The EndUp 401 6th St at Harrison, SoMa ☎ 415/357-0827, ⊛ www.theendup.com. Open all night (though you can only drink until 2am), and attracting hardcore gay and straight clubbers for after-hours dancing on its cramped dance floor. If you want a break from the beats, there's an outdoor patio with plenty of seating.

Hush Hush 496 14th St at Guerrero, Mission ☎ 415/241-9944. A great place to hang out or dance, this hidden bar has no sign outside; inside, there's a slightly older crowd, playing pool or dancing to housey disco and classic 1970s funk, Wednesday to Saturday.

Justice League 628 Divisadero St at Hayes, Western Addition ☎ 415/289-2038, ⊛ www.justiceleaguelive.com. This club attracts big-name DJs, primarily for hip-hop and electronica nights. It's a groovy place to dance, thanks to the graffiti artists' murals on the walls. $12–15.

The Make-Out Room 3225 22nd at Mission, Mission ☎ 415/647-2888, ⊛ www.makeoutroom.com. This small, dark space is primarily a place to drink at the enormous mahogany bar, but there are regular performances by local indie bands on Sunday and Monday. $6–10.

Sno-drift 1830 3rd St at 16th, China Basin ☎ 415/431-4766. Alpine ski lodge-themed club where almost everything is igloo-white, including an enormous padded vinyl bar. Music varies, but is mainly house. $15.

Space 550 550 Barneveld Ave at Oakdale, Hunter's Point ☎ 415/289-2001. This enormous warehouse club is known for its trancey, industrial dance programming. Although it's a long way out, in an iffy part of town, serious clubbers will think it's worth the trek. $5–15.

Classical music, opera, and dance

Though the San Francisco arts scene has a reputation for provincialism, this is the only city on the West Coast to boast its own professional **symphony**, **ballet**, and **opera** companies. These companies rely entirely on private contributions for their survival and low-priced tickets are rare, if not non-existent. Look out in summer for the free concerts in Stern Grove (at 19th Ave and Sloat Blvd), where the symphony, opera, and ballet give open-air performances for ten successive Sundays (starting in June). Last-minute standing-room tickets are another option for those on a budget.

The **San Francisco Opera Association** (tickets and info ℡ 415/864-3330, ⒲ www.sfopera.org) has been performing in the opulent War Memorial Opera House, 301 Van Ness Ave at Grove, in the Civic Center since the building opened in 1932, pulling in big names like Placido Domingo and Kiri Te Kanawa on a regular basis. Its main season runs from the end of September for thirteen weeks, and its opening night is one of the principal social events on the West Coast. Also housed here is the **San Francisco Ballet** (℡ 415/864-3330, ⒲ www.sfballet.org), whose regular season starts in February, while performances of *The Nutcracker* occur during the Christmas season.

Next door, the **Louise M. Davies Symphony Hall**, at 201 Van Ness Ave at Hayes (℡ 415/864-6000, ⒲ www.sfsymphony.org), is the permanent home of the San Francisco Symphony, hosting a year-round season of classical music and sometimes performances by other, often offbeat musical and touring groups.

Theater

The majority of the **theaters** in downtown's Theater District are not especially innovative, but tickets are reasonably inexpensive – up to $20 a seat – and there's usually good availability. For last-minute bargains try the **Tix Bay Area** booth inside the Union Square garage, between Stockton and Powell streets (Tues–Thurs 11am–6pm, Fri & Sat 11am–7pm; recorded info ℡ 415/433-7827). It's also an outlet for Ticketmaster.

American Conservatory Theater (ACT) Geary Theater, 415 Geary St at Taylor, Theater District ℡ 415/742-2228, ⒲ www.act-sfbay.org. San Francisco's flagship theater company, the Tony Award–winning ACT puts on eight major plays each season.

Beach Blanket Babylon *Club Fugazi*, 678 Green St at Powell, North Beach ℡ 415/421-4222. This legendary musical revue, filled with celebrity impersonations and towering hats, has been running since 1974. Highly recommended, but remember to book in advance. Tickets from $25.

Golden Gate Theater 1 Taylor St at Golden Gate Ave and Market, Tenderloin ℡ 415/551-2000, ⒲ www.bestofbroadway-sf.com. San Francisco's most elegant theater (in its least elegant neighborhood), with marble flooring, Rococo ceilings, and gilt trimmings. It's a pity the program doesn't live up to the surroundings – generally a mainstream diet of touring musicals.

Lorraine Hansberry Theater 620 Sutter St at Mason, Theater District ℡ 415/474-8800. The mainstay of African-American theater in San Francisco. Traditional theater as well as contemporary political pieces and jazz/blues musical revues.

Magic Theatre Fort Mason Center, Building D, Fort Mason ℡ 415/441-8822, ⒲ www.magictheatre.org. Specializes in contemporary American playwrights and emerging new talent; Sam Shepard traditionally premieres his work here.

New Conservatory Theater Center 25 Van Ness Ave at Market, Civic Center ℡ 415/861-8972, ⒲ www.nctscf.org. This mid-sized theater is known for its performances of musicals in concert. Tickets start at $20.

Theater Artaud 450 Florida St at Mariposa, Mission ℡ 415/621-7797, ⒲ www.artaud.org/theater/TheaterHome.html. Modern theater in a converted warehouse offering dance and theater performances, many less obscure than the theater's artsy name might imply.

Theater on the Square 450 Post St at Powell, Union Square ℡ 415/433-9500. Converted Gothic theater hosting drama, musicals, comedy, and mainstream theater pieces. San Francisco's main fringe venue.

Theater Rhinoceros 2926 16th St at S Van Ness, Mission ℡ 415/861-5079, ⒲ www.therhino.org. San Francisco's leading gay theater space, performing everything from light, humorous productions to those that confront gay issues.

Shopping

While boasting the large-scale facilities and international names you'd expect in a major city, San Francisco's **shopping scene** is low-key and unpretentious. This means prices are slightly lower, and shopping here is a pleasant, relatively stress-free activity.

If you want to run the gauntlet of designer labels, or just watch the style brigade consume, **Union Square** is the place to be. The heart of the city's shopping territory, it has a good selection of big-name and chic stores worth a few hours if you're into serious dollar-dropping.

Books

Abandoned Planet Bookstore 518 Valencia at 16th, Mission ☎415/861-4695. Encouraging its customers to "Break the TV habit!" this eccentric and utterly left-wing San Francisco bookstore crams its shelves with left-wing and anarchist volumes.

Borders Books and Music 400 Post St at Powell, Union Square ☎415/399-1633. Massive, emporium-style bookstore with some 160,000 books to chose from, as well as CDs, videos, and software on four floors. Convenient if unexciting.

City Lights Bookstore 261 Columbus Ave at Broadway, North Beach ☎415/362-8193. America's first paperback bookstore, and still San Francisco's best. The range of titles includes house publications.

A Clean, Well Lighted Place for Books Opera Plaza, 601 Van Ness Ave at Golden Gate, Civic Center ☎415/441-6670. The stock here is now more mainstream and less impressively exhaustive than it once was, but it's worth checking out for the regular readings by authors.

A Different Light 489 Castro St at 18th, Castro ☎415/431-0891, ⊛www.adlbooks.com. Well-stocked and diverse gay bookstore.

Forever After Books 1475 Haight St at Ashbury, Haight-Ashbury ☎415/431-8299. The windows of this store are blocked by the piles of accumulated paperbacks – it's worth rifling your way through the mountains given the cheap prices.

Get Lost 1825 Market St at Valencia, Hayes Valley/Mission ☎415/437-0529. Tiny travel bookstore, crammed with unusual titles alongside the standard guidebooks.

The Great Overland Bookstore Company 2848 Webster St at Union, Cow Hollow ☎415/351-1538. Cluttered with piles of books, this is a first-rate, old-fashioned store with mint-condition first editions as well as cheap paperbacks.

Green Apple 506 Clement St at 6th Ave, Richmond ☎415/387-2272. In the heart of the Richmond district, this relaxed and welcoming store features new and used books (rare out-of-print volumes as well as standards), plus a well-priced selection of CDs and vinyl recordings.

Kayo 814 Post St at Leavenworth, Theater District ☎415/749-0554. Glorious vintage paperback store, crammed with bargain classics.

Modern Times 888 Valencia St at 20th, Mission ☎415/282-9246. Progressive community bookstore with a good selection of Latin American literature and publications on women's issues and contemporary cultural studies.

Music

Amoeba Records 1855 Haight St at Stanyan, Haight-Ashbury ☎415/831-1200. A massive, independent record and CD store with one of the largest and best used collections you'll ever find (over one million new and used). They also host live in-store performances.

Aquarius Records 1055 Valencia St at 21st, Mission ☎415/647-2272. Small neighborhood store with friendly, knowledgeable staff and a good range of indie rock, jazz, and things experimental and obscure.

BPM 573 Hayes St at Laguna, Hayes Valley ☎415/487-8680. One of the top DJ record stores in the city, with the latest UK imports from top-name British DJs and masses of flyers for upcoming events.

CD & Record Rack 3987 18th St at Castro, Castro ☎415/552-4990. Castro emporium with a superb selection of dance music, including a few 1970s twelve-inch singles.

Compound Records 597 Haight St at Steiner, Lower Haight ☎415/864-8309. Throbbing, chic DJ-aimed store, known for its cutting-edge selection of dance music imported from the UK.

Groove Merchant Records 687 Haight St at Pierce, Lower Haight ☎415/252-5766. Come here for secondhand soul, funk, and jazz: the owner is passionate and knowledgeable, so don't be afraid to ask questions.

Jack's Record Cellar 254 Scott St at Haight, Lower Haight ☎415/431-3047. The city's best source for American roots music – R&B, jazz, country, and Rock 'n' Roll – especially on LP. Closed Sun–Tues.

Sports in San Francisco

San Francisco's dedication to its **professional sports** teams can verge on the obsessive. Tickets for the big events can sell out, but it's usually possible to show up on the day, and it needn't cost all that much: an outfield seat to watch baseball from the "bleachers" goes for around $5, while promotional specials like Wednesday Dollar Days, run by the Oakland team, can reduce prices of seats and hotdogs to only $1. Advance tickets for all Bay Area sports events are available through Ticketmaster's charge-by-phone ticket service (☎415/421-TIXS, ⓦwww.ticketmaster.com), or through the teams' headquarters.

Baseball: The **Oakland A's** play at the usually sunny Coliseum (ⓦwww.oaklandathletics.com), which has a BART stop in front. The **San Francisco Giants** play at Pac Bell Park, where home runs sometimes land in the bay (☎415/972-2000, ⓦwww.sfgiants.com). There are five hundred bleacher-seat tickets made available two-and-a-half hours before game time and long lines form early and often. Walk up to the ticket booths at 24 Willie Mays Plaza, near Third and King streets, to get them.

Football: The **San Francisco 49ers**, many-time Super Bowl champions, also play at 3Com Park, where you may have to pay as much as $100 per seat (☎415/656-4900, ⓦwww.sf49ers.com), and the **Oakland Raiders**, blue-collar heroes and runners-up in the 2003 Superbowl, bash heads at the Oakland Coliseum (ⓦwww.raiders.com).

Basketball: The reliably awful **Golden State Warriors** play at the newly renovated Oakland Arena (☎510/986-2200, ⓦwww.nba.com/warriors).

Ice hockey: The **San Jose Sharks** (☎408/287-7070, ⓦwww.sj-sharks.com) play at their own arena in San Jose.

Soccer: The **San Jose Earthquakes** (☎408/985-4625, ⓦwww.sjearthquakes.com), major-league soccer champs in 2001, draw large crowds at San Jose State's Spartan Stadium.

Mikado 1737 Post St, Japantown ☎415/922-9450. Enormous Japanese record store sprawled across three units of the Japan Center, with an exhaustive selection of Asian music.
Mission Music Center 2653 Mission St at 22nd, Mission ☎415/648-1788. Music from all over the continent, but especially South America.

Record Finder 258 Noe St at Market, Castro ☎415/431-4443. One of the best independents, with a range as broad as it's absorbing.
Virgin Megastore 2 Stockton St at Market, Union Square ☎415/397-4525. Three floors packed with books, videos, and music, plus a café overlooking Market Street.

The Bay Area

Of the six million people who make their home in the vicinity of San Francisco, only a lucky one in eight lives in the city itself. Everyone else is spread around the **Bay Area**, a sharply contrasting patchwork of very rich and very poor towns dotted down the peninsula or across one of the two impressive bridges that span the chilly waters of the exquisite natural harbor. In the **East Bay** are industrial Oakland and intellectual Berkeley, while south of the city, the **Peninsula** holds the gloating wealth of Silicon Valley, which gained its nickname from the multibillion-dollar technology industry. To the north across the Golden Gate Bridge is the woody, leafy landscape and rugged coastline of **Marin County**, an elitest pleasure zone of conspicuous luxury and abundant natural beauty.

The East Bay

The largest and most-traveled bridge in the US, the **Bay Bridge** connects downtown San Francisco to the East Bay, part graceful suspension bridge and part heavy-duty steel truss. Now recovered from its partial collapse during the 1989 earthquake, the Bay Bridge works a lot harder for a lot less respect than the more famous (and better-loved) Golden Gate: a hundred million vehicles cross it each year. The heart of the East Bay is **Oakland**, a resolutely blue-collar city that spreads north to the progressive university town of Berkeley; the two communities all but merge into one city, and the hills above them are topped by a twenty-mile string of forested **regional parks**.

Arrival, information, and getting around

Flights direct to the East Bay touch down at **Oakland Airport**, just outside town (☎510/577-4015 or 1-800/992-7433 for automated flight info, ⓦwww.oaklandairport.com). The AirBART shuttle van (every 15min; $2; ☎510/577-4294) runs to the Coliseum BART station from where you can hop on BART (see below) to Berkeley, Oakland, or San Francisco. There are numerous door-to-door **shuttle buses** from the airport, such as Bridge Airporter Express (☎510/481-1050 or 1-800/300-1661) – expect to pay around $16 to downtown Oakland, $30 to San Francisco. Note that the **Greyhound** station is in a dodgy part of northern Oakland on San Pablo Avenue at 21st Street. **Amtrak** terminates at Second Street near Jack London Square in West Oakland, where you can catch a free shuttle bus to downtown San Francisco (a smoother alternative is to get off at Richmond and change onto the nearby BART trains).

There are two main **visitor centers**: Oakland CVB is on the ground floor of a huge modern block at 475 14th St (Mon–Fri 8.30am–5pm; ☎510/839-9000, ⓦwww.oaklandcvb.com), while Berkeley's office is at 2015 Center St (Mon–Fri 9am–5pm; ☎510/549-7040, ⓦwww.visitberkeley.com).

The underground **BART** system links the East Bay with San Francisco (Mon–Fri 4am–midnight, Sat 6am–midnight, Sun 8am–midnight; $1.10–4.70; ☎510/465-BART, ⓦwww.bart.gov). **AC Transit** (☎510/891-4777, ⓦwww.actransit.org) buses cover the entire East Bay area, with a more limited service running to Oakland and Berkeley from the Transbay Terminal in San Francisco; they're the only option for crossing the Bay when BART shuts down for the night.

East Bay accommodation

The East Bay's **motels** and **hotels**, which cost between $60 and $90 a night, are barely better value for money than their San Francisco counterparts. However, they give visitors the chance to stay just outside of the city's hubbub whilst affording easy access to it.

Bancroft Hotel 2680 Bancroft Way, Berkeley ☎510/549-1000 or 1-800/549-1002, ⓦwww.bancrofthotel.com. Small hotel – just 22 rooms – with good location and service. Breakfast included. ❺

The Claremont Resort & Spa 41 Tunnel Rd, Berkeley ☎510/843-3000 or 1-800/551-7266, ⓦwww.claremontresort.com. The lap of luxury among Berkeley hotels in a 1915 building. Even the basic rooms are a treat, but you'll pay for the privilege. Spa sessions start at $95/hour for facials or massages. ❾

Dean's Bed and Breakfast 480 Pedestrian Way, Rockridge ☎510/652-5024, ⓦwww.bbonline.com /ca/deans. A hidden gem with swimming pool and Japanese garden, close to the Rockridge BART stop. Single or double ❹

Downtown Berkeley YMCA 2001 Allston Way at Milvia St, Berkeley ☎510/848-9622, ⓦwww.baymca.org. Berkeley's best bargain accommodation, just one block from the Berkeley BART stop. Rates, starting at around $39 for a single, $50 for a double, include use of gym and pool. ❷–❸

Hotel Durant 2600 Durant Ave, Berkeley
☎510/845-8981 or 1-800/238-7268,
ⓦwww.hoteldurant.com. Upscale hotel at the
heart of UC Berkeley, featuring large, airy rooms –
worth splashing out if budgets allow. ❼
Hotel Shattuck Plaza 2086 Allston Way,
Berkeley ☎510/845-7300, ⓦwww.hotelshattuck-
plaza.com. Comfortable, central rooms in a well-
restored older hotel. ❹

Jack London Inn 444 Embarcadero West,
Oakland ☎510/444-2032, ⓦwww.jacklon-
doninn.com. Kitschy 1950s-style motor lodge
located next to Jack London Square. ❺
Waterfront Plaza Hotel 10 Washington St,
Oakland ☎510/836-3800 or 1-800/729-3638,
ⓦwww.waterfrontplaza.com. Plush, modern hotel
moored on the best stretch of the Oakland waterfront. ❼

Oakland

OAKLAND, the workhorse of the Bay Area, is one of the largest ports on the
West Coast. It has also been the breeding ground of revolutionary **political
movements**. In the Sixties, the city's fifty-percent black population found a
voice through the militant Black Panthers, and in the Seventies the
Symbionese Liberation Army, kidnappers of heiress Patty Hearst, obtained a
ransom of free food for the city's poor. It's not all hard graft, though: the climate is often sunny and mild when San Francisco is cold and dreary, and there's
great hiking in the redwood- and eucalyptus-covered hills above the city.

Despite this, there's not all that much to see within the city, the major concession to the tourist trade being the waterfront Jack London Square, an asep-
tic cluster of national chains that have nothing to do with the writer. At the
far eastern end of the promenade, however, you will find **Heinhold's First
and Last Chance Saloon**, a slanting tiny bar built in 1883 from the hull of
a whaling ship. Jack London really did drink here, and the collection of yel-
lowed portraits of him on the wall are the only genuine thing about the writer
you'll find on the square. A half-mile north up Broadway from the waterfront,
Oakland's restored downtown is anchored by chain stores and the gargantuan
open-air **City Center** complex of offices and fast-food outlets. Beside it, at
Broadway and 14th Street, the massive greenspace of **Frank Ogawa Plaza** is
a pleasant place to eat lunch outdoors, while further east on Tenth and Oak
streets, the **Oakland Museum of California** (Wed–Sat 10am–5pm, Sun
noon–5pm; $6, free every second Sunday of month; ☎510/238-2200,
ⓦwww.museumca.org) has a good exhibit of California history, including the
Beat Generation.

Though many drum on about London or the Beats, it's worth noting that
another local writer, **Gertrude Stein**, who was born in Oakland at around the
same time as the macho and adventurous London, is barely commemorated
anywhere. Perhaps it's because it was Stein who wrote "what was the use of me
having come from Oakland, it was not natural for me to have come from there
yes write about it if I like or anything if I like but not there, *there is no there there*"
– a quote that has haunted the city ever since. Nonetheless, the majority of
Oakland residents are proud of their city, and would argue that there is indeed
a *there* there, notably in the small, trendy community of **Rockridge** and the
lively neighborhoods around Piedmont and Grand avenues.

Joaquin Miller Park, the most easily accessible of Oakland's hilltop parks,
stands above East Oakland (take AC Transit bus #64 from downtown). It was
once home to the "Poet of the Sierras," Joaquin Miller, who made his name
playing the eccentric frontier American in the salons of 1870s London. His
poems weren't exactly acclaimed (his greatest poetic achievement was rhyming
"teeth" with "Goethe"), but his prose account of the time he spent with the
Modoc Indians near Mount Shasta (see p.1225) remains invaluable. His house,
a small white cabin called **The Abbey**, still survives here, as do the thousands
of trees he planted.

Berkeley

BERKELEY (named for the English philosopher–theologian George Berkeley) is dominated by the **University of California**, one of America's most famous – and infamous – universities. Its grand buildings and thirty thousand students give off an energy that spills south down raucous **Telegraph Avenue**, where aging hippies peddle rainbow bracelets in front of vegetarian restaurants, music stores, and pizza joints. The very name of Berkeley conjures up images of dissent. **Sproul Plaza**, in front of the school's entranceway, Sather Gate, is where the Free Speech Movement began, and, as some historians would argue, the experience known as the Sixties. Among the sites of the almost-daily pitched battles of the Sixties and early Seventies, part of the broad campus revolt against the Vietnam War, was the now-seedy **People's Park**. Things have calmed down considerably, and now the campus prides itself on its high academic rankings and Nobel-laureate-laden faculty. Today's students yell profanities and shout down Bible-thumpers on Sproul Plaza, unaware of the irony of it all; feel free to stroll around the campus's tree-shaded pathways and contemplate the dissent of years long gone. Free student-led **tours** leave from the visitor services office, 101 University Hall (Mon–Sat 10am, Sun 1pm; ☎ 510/642-5215).

Telegraph Avenue holds most of the student hangouts, and several excellent bookstores. Older students congregate in **Northside**, popping down from their woodsy hillside homes to partake of goodies from "Gourmet Ghetto" – the restaurants, delis, and bakeries on Shattuck Avenue like the renowned *Chez Panisse* (see below). North of here, on the hills, **Tilden Regional Park** has good trails and a fine rose garden. Along the bay itself, at the **Berkeley Marina**, you can rent windsurfing boards and sailboats, or just watch the sun set behind the Golden Gate.

Eating

As befits the birthplace of California cuisine, the East Bay offers a choice of good **restaurants**. Berkeley is both an upmarket diner's paradise and a student town where you can eat cheaply and well, especially on and around Telegraph Avenue.

Breads of India 2448 Sacramento St, Berkeley ☎510/848-7684. A consistently craved and cramped Indian spot, particularly big at lunchtime. Leave lots of room for the breads, the restaurant's specialty.

Café Intermezzo 2442 Telegraph Ave near Haste, Berkeley ☎510/849-4592. Huge sandwiches on homemade bread, even bigger salads, and great coffee.

Café Rouge 1782 4th St, Berkeley ☎510/525-1440. Southern French and Northern Italian restaurant specializing in delicately prepared organic meats and equipped with its own butcher shop. Dinner entrees hover around $18; lunch is cheaper ($9–12).

Cha-Am 1543 Shattuck Ave, North Berkeley ☎510/848-9664. Climb the stairs up to this unlikely, always crowded small restaurant for deliciously spicy Thai food at bargain prices.

Cheeseboard Pizza 1512 Shattuck Ave, North Berkeley ☎510/549-3055. Incredibly good gourmet pizza at an incredible $2.50 a slice. Irregular hours, but usually open for lunch and dinner Tues–Sun.

Chez Panisse 1517 Shattuck Ave, North Berkeley ☎510/548-5525. First and still the best of the California cuisine restaurants, overseen by legendary chef Alice Waters. Dinner is served at two sittings, 6pm and 8.30pm; the *prix fixe* menu costs $50 on Mondays, $65 Tuesday through Thursday, and $75 Friday and Saturday. The *Café* upstairs is comparatively inexpensive. Reservations recommended for the *Café*, essential for the main restaurant.

Fenton's Creamery 4226 Piedmont Ave, Oakland ☎510/658-7000. The ultimate old-style ice-cream parlor in which to indulge sweet cravings. Sandwiches, fries, and other snacks are available to offset the sundae buzz. Open until 11pm on weeknights, midnight at weekends.

Homemade Café 2454 Sacramento St, Berkeley ☎510/845-1940. Nontraditional Californian-style

Jewish and Mexican food served for breakfast and lunch – at shared tables when it's crowded. Next to *Breads of India*, opposite.

Juan's Place 941 Carleton St, West Berkeley ℡510/845-6904. The original Berkeley Mexican restaurant, with great food (tons of it) and an interesting mix of people.

La Mediterranee 2936 College Ave, Berkeley ℡510/540-7773. Great Middle Eastern food in a relaxed atmosphere.

La Note 2377 Shattuck Ave, Berkeley ℡510/843-1535. The appropriately sunny, light cuisine of Provence isn't the only flavor you'll find in this petite dining room: students and teachers from the jazz school next door routinely stop in for casual jam sessions.

Tropix Backyard Café 3814 Piedmont Ave, Oakland ℡510/653-2444. Large portions of fruity Caribbean delicacies at reasonable prices, with authentic jerk sauce and thirst-quenching mango juice. Outside seating on the patio.

Zachary's Chicago Pizza 5801 College Ave, Oakland ℡510/655-6385. Locals flock to this campus standby for stuffed pizzas (available with whole-wheat crust). Come early as it gets very busy. Open for lunch, dinner, and take-out.

Cafés and bars

The many bohemian **cafés** in Berkeley are full from dawn to near midnight with earnest characters wearing their intellects on their sleeves; if you're not after a caffeine fix, you can generally get a glass of beer or wine. For serious drinking you're better off in one of the many **bars**, particularly in rough-hewn Oakland. Grittier versions of what you'd find in San Francisco, they're mostly blue-collar, convivial, and almost always less expensive.

The Alley 3325 Grand Ave, Oakland ℡510/444-8505. Ramshackle old-timers' piano bar where locals come specifically to sing. Music starts at 9pm. Closed Mon.

Bison Brewing Company 2598 Telegraph Ave, Berkeley ℡510/841-7734. Eat and drink at great prices on the terrace, where some of the best Bay Area beers are brewed. Noisy bands perform on weekends.

Caffè Mediterraneum 2475 Telegraph Ave, Berkeley ℡510/841-5634. Berkeley's oldest café, straight out of the Beat Generation archives: beards and berets optional, books de rigueur.

Coffee Mill 3363 Grand Ave, Oakland ℡510/465-4224. This café doubles as an art gallery and often hosts poetry readings, too.

Heinhold's First and Last Chance Saloon 56 Jack London Square, Oakland ℡510/839-6761. Authentic waterfront bar that's hardly changed since around 1900, when Jack London himself drank here. They've never even bothered to fix the slanted floor that was caused by the 1906 earthquake.

Jupiter 2181 Shattuck Ave, Berkeley ℡510/843-8277. Many, many beers to select from at this local favorite, which offers live jazz on weekends and an outdoor beer garden.

Pyramid Brewery 901 Gilman St, Berkeley ℡510/528-9880. Great microbrewed beers in a popular pub, with industrial-chic decor and outdoor movie screenings on summer weekends.

Starry Plough 3101 Shattuck Ave, Berkeley ℡510/841-2082, ⓦwww.starryploughpub.com. Lively Irish bar that features bargain-price live rock and country many nights of the week.

The White Horse 6551 Telegraph Ave at 66th St, North Oakland ℡510/652-3820. Oakland's oldest gay bar – a small, friendly place with mixed dancing for men and women nightly.

Live music and entertainment

Nightlife is where the East Bay really comes into its own. Though traditional **clubs** are virtually nonexistent, there are plenty of **live music venues**, from smoky jazz cafés to sweaty R&B dives. Live dance music thrives here; there's also plenty of holdovers still jangling along in poppy, punky guitar bands that echo Green Day and Nirvana.

The range of **films** screened here is top-notch. Berkeley's **Pacific Film Archives** at 2575 Bancroft Ave ($8; ℡510/642-5249 for tickets, ⓦwww.bampfa.berkeley.edu), one of the finest film libraries in California, puts on contemporary international films, plus old favorites. The free *East Bay Express* has the most comprehensive listings of what's on.

Ashkenaz 1317 San Pablo Ave, Berkeley ℡510/525-5054, ⓦwww.ashkenaz.com. World music and dance café hosting acts from modern Afro-beat to the best of the Balkans. Kids and under-21s welcome. Cover $5–10.

Freight and Salvage 1111 Addison St, West Berkeley ☎510/548-1761, ⓦwww.thefreight.org. Singer-songwriters perform in a coffeehouse setting. Cover $5–20.

Gilman Street Project 924 Gilman St, West Berkeley ☎510/525-9926. On the outer edge of the hardcore punk, indie, and experimental scene, this institution helped launch Green Day and Sleater-Kinney. No alcohol, all ages. Weekends only; cover $5–10.

Kimball's East 5800 Shellmound St, in the Emerybay Public Market, Emeryville ☎510/658-2555, ⓦwww.kimballs.com. The prime jazz and

blues venue in the Bay Area, with big-name players in an intimate setting. Cover $10–25.

Stork Club 2330 Telegraph Ave, Oakland ☎510/444-6174, ⓦwww.storkcluboakland.com. Presently a favorite with DJs and indie bands, this historic club features a jukebox that specializes in country tunes. Closed Mon; cover $5.

Yoshi's World Class Jazz House 510 Embarcadero W, Oakland ☎510/238-9200, ⓦwww.yoshis.com. The centerpiece of Oakland's revived Jack London Square, this combination jazz club and sushi bar routinely attracts the biggest names in jazz. Cover $5–40.

The Peninsula

The city of San Francisco sits at the tip of a five-mile-wide neck of land commonly referred to as the **Peninsula**. Home of old money and new technology, the Peninsula stretches for fifty miles of relentless suburbia south from San Francisco along the Bay, winding up in the futuristic roadside landscape of the "Silicon Valley" near **San Jose**.

There was a time when the region was largely agricultural, but the continuing computer boom – spurred by Stanford University in **Palo Alto** – has replaced the orange groves and fig trees of yesteryear with office complexes and parking lots. Surprisingly, however, most of the land along the **coast** – separated from the bayfront sprawl by a ridge of redwood-covered peaks – remains rural and undeveloped; it also contains some of the best **beaches** in the Bay Area, all well worth a day-trip from San Francisco.

Palo Alto

In recent years, **Palo Alto**, home of preppy, conservative **Stanford University** (☎650/723-2300, ⓦwww.stanford.edu), has become somewhat of a social center for Silicon Valley's nouveau riche, as evidenced by the trendy cafés and chic new restaurants that have popped up along its main drag, **University Avenue**. The town doesn't offer a lot in terms of sights other than Spanish Colonial homes, but it's a great place for a lazy stroll and a gourmet meal. Wash down a California-style Greek dish from *Evvia*, 420 Emerson St (☎650/326-0983), or a heaping plate of Cajun-influenced food from *Nola*, 535 Ramona St (☎650/328-2722), with a microbrewed beer from the *Gordon Biersch Brewery*, 640 Emerson St (☎650/323-7723), or a latte from *Caffè Verona*, 236 Hamilton Ave (☎650/326-9942). The old-style malt and burger joint, *The Peninsula Creamery*, 566 Emerson St (☎650/323-3131), serves massive portions at inexpensive prices, while *MacArthur Park*, 27 University Ave (☎650/321-9990), is a great barbecue restaurant with more than two hundred wines on offer. Surprisingly affordable **rooms** are available at the *Cardinal Hotel*, 235 Hamilton Ave, in the heart of downtown (☎650/323-5101, ⓦwww.cardinalhotel.com; shared bath ❷, private bath ❹).

San Jose

Burt Bacharach could easily find **SAN JOSE** today by heading south from San Francisco and following the heat and smog that collects below the Bay. Although one of the fastest-growing cities in California, it is not strong on identity – though in area and population it's close to twice the size of San

Francisco. Sitting at the southern end of the peninsula, San Jose has in the past 25 years emerged as the civic heart of Silicon Valley, surrounded by miles of faceless high-tech industrial parks where the next generations of computers are designed and built. Ironically, it's also acknowledged as the first city in California, though the only sign of this is the unremarkable eighteenth-century **Mission Santa Clara de Asis**, on the pleasant campus of the Jesuit-run Santa Clara University.

The area's most famous landmark is the **Winchester Mystery House**, 525 S Winchester Blvd, just off I-280 near Hwy-17 (mid-Oct to April daily 9am–5pm; May to early June & Sept to mid-Oct Sun–Thurs 9am–5pm, Fri & Sat 9am–7pm; mid-June to Aug daily 9am–7pm; $15–25 depending on the tour; ☎408/247-2000, ⊛www.winchestermysteryhouse.com). Sarah Winchester, heiress to the Winchester rifle fortune, was convinced upon her husband's death in 1884 that he had been taken by the spirits of men killed with Winchester rifles, and believed that unless a room was built for each of the spirits, the same fate would befall her. The sound of hammers never ceased as work on the mansion went on 24 hours a day for the next thirty years – stairs lead nowhere, windows open on to solid brick. Today it's a relentlessly hyped commercial cash cow, but is still worth a detour. The **Rosicrucian Museum**, 1342 Naglee Ave (Tues–Fri 10am–5pm, Sat & Sun 11am–6pm; $9; ☎ 408/947-3636, ⊛www.rosicrucian.org), houses a brilliant collection of Assyrian and Babylonian artifacts, while the revamped **Tech Museum of Innovation** (daily 10am–5pm; $9; ☎408/294-TECH, ⊛www.thetech.org), downtown at 201 S Market St, contains hands-on displays of high-tech engineering as well as the inevitable IMAX theater.

San Jose's **visitor center** is at 125 S Market St (Mon–Fri 8am–5pm, Sat & Sun 11am–5pm; ☎408/295-9600 or 1-800/SAN-JOSE, ⊛www.sanjose.org), and also has a branch in the convention center across the street (same hours; ☎408/977-0900). Downtown **accommodation** is grossly overpriced, serving as it does high-tech executives and conventioneers. Options include the *Valley Inn*, 2155 The Alameda (☎408/241-8500, ⊛www.valleyinnsanjose.com; ❹), and the *Executive Inn*, 1215 S First St (☎408/280-5300 or 1-800/509-7666; ❹). Good old-fashioned American **food** is dished up at *Original Joe's*, 301 S First St (☎408/292-7030). Grab a stool at the counter or settle into one of the comfy booths and enjoy a burger or a plate of pasta at this San Jose institution, where $10 goes a long way (open 11am–1am). For fresh coffee and pastries, head to *Café Matisse*, 371 S First St (☎408/298-7788).

The coast

The **coastline** of the Peninsula south from San Francisco is a world away from the valley of the inland: mostly undeveloped, with a few small towns, and countless beaches that run 75 miles down to the mellow cities of Santa Cruz and **Capitola**. Past Daly City just south of San Francisco, Hwy-1 hugs the precipitous cliffs of Devil's Slide to the clothing-optional sands of **Gray Whale Cove State Beach** (daily 8am–sunset; ☎650/728-5336, ⊛www.parks.ca.gov). Despite the name, it's not an especially great place to look for migrating gray whales, but there is a stairway from the bus stop down to a fine strand of sand. Two miles further on Hwy-1, the red-roofed buildings of the 1875 **Point Montara Lighthouse**, set among the windswept Monterey pine trees at the top of a steep cliff, have been converted into a **youth hostel** (☎650/728-7177, ⊛www.norcalhostels.org/pointmontara-lighthouse.html; ❶). Just beyond the hostel, down California Street, the **Fitzgerald Marine Reserve** (☎650/728-3584; free) has three miles of diverse oceanic habitat, peaceful trails, and, at low tide, the best tidal pools. But continue a tiny bit further for the historic **Moss Beach Distillery** (☎650/728-5595, Ⓦwww.mossbeachdistillery.com), a great place to grab a snack and a beer on its windswept patio – they provide enormous blankets to help brave the fog. Continuing a few miles south on Hwy-1, the hamlet of **El Grenada** has other good roadside lunch stops like the *Highway One Diner* (☎650/726-4991), and its beaches are always clogged with surfers and crowds of spectators watching them. There's a long breakwater here you can walk out on as well. The next town, growing **Half Moon Bay**, allows camping on a first-come, first-served basis on some of its beaches (☎650/726-8820; $12). Gas up here; fuel stations are rare for the next fifty miles to Santa Cruz.

Marin County

Across the Golden Gate from San Francisco, **Marin County** is an unabashed introduction to Californian self-indulgence: a pleasure zone of conspicuous luxury and abundant natural beauty, with sunshine, sandy beaches, high mountains, and thick redwood forests. Often ranked as the wealthiest county in the US, Marin has attracted a sizeable population of wealthy young professionals to its swanky waterside towns, though in the past the region served as logging headquarters.

The modern **ferries** that travel across the bay from San Francisco can make a great start to a day out. Boats to the chic bayside settlement of **Sausalito** leave from the Ferry Building on the Embarcadero, run by Golden Gate Ferry (7.40am–8pm, half-hourly during rush hour, less often during the rest of the day, and every two or so hours on weekends; $5.60 each way; ☎415/923-2000 or 455-2000, Ⓦwww.goldengate.org) or Pier 41 at Fisherman's Wharf, run by Blue & Gold Fleet ferries (6–7 trips daily; $7.25 each way; ☎415/705-8200). **Biking** over here makes for a beautiful ride over the Golden Gate Bridge (unless there's fog) and allows you to explore the headlands freely. Bikes are allowed on the ferry back to San Francisco.

Across the Golden Gate: the Marin Headlands

The largely undeveloped **Marin Headlands**, across the Golden Gate Bridge from San Francisco, afford some of the most impressive views of the bridge and the city behind. The coastline here is much more rugged than it is on the San Francisco side, and it makes a great place for an isolated clifftop scramble among the concrete remains of old forts and gun emplacements. Heading west on Bunker Hill Road takes you up to the brink of the headlands before the road snakes down to Fort Barry and wide, sandy **Rodeo Beach**, from which numerous hiking trails branch out. Check in at the Marin Headlands Visitor Center (daily 9.30am–4.30pm; ☎415/331-1540) above Rodeo Lagoon for free maps. The largest of the fort's old buildings has been converted into the spacious but homey *HI-Marin Headlands* **hostel** (☎415/331-2777 or 1-800/979-4776 ext 168, ⓌheadlandshosTel.homesTead.com; ❶), an excellent base for more extended explorations of the inland ridges and valleys.

Sausalito

Pretty, smug little **SAUSALITO**, along the Bay below US-101, was once a gritty community of fishermen and sea traders, full of bars and bordellos. Now exclusive restaurants and pricey boutiques line its picturesque waterfront promenade, and expensive, quirky houses climb the overgrown cliffs above

Bridgeway Avenue, the main road and bus route through town. Ferries from San Francisco arrive next to the Sausalito Yacht Club in the town center. If you have sailing experience, split the daily rental fee of a four- to six-person sailboat at Cass's Marina, 1702 Bridgeway Ave (rates from $157/day; ☎415/332-6789, ⓦ www.cassmarina.com).

Aside from walking, shopping, and sucking in the sea air, Sausalito has a one-of-a-kind exhibit in the **Bay Model Visitor Center**, 2100 Bridgeway (Tues–Sat 9am–4pm; donation; ☎415/332-3870), where elevated walkways in a huge building lead you around a scale model of the entire bay, surrounding deltas, and its aquatic inhabitants, offering insight on the enormity and diversity of this area.

If you decide **to stay**, *Casa Madrona* at 801 Bridgeway Ave (☎415/332-0502 or 1-800/567-9524, ⓦ www.casamadrona.com; ➐) is a deluxe **hotel** hideaway in the hills above the bay that also houses *Mikayla*, a delectable seafood **restaurant** (☎415/331-5888). For less expensive food, head across to *California Kitchen*, 400 Caledonia St (☎415/331-0220), which serves simple sandwiches and fresh pastries, or try terrific, low-cost Indian dishes at *Sartaj*, 43 Caledonia St (☎415/332-7103). The *No Name Bar*, 757 Bridgeway Ave (☎415/332-1392), is a smoky ex-haunt of the Beats hosting frequent live jazz.

Mount Tamalpais and Muir Woods

Mount Tamalpais dominates the skyline of the Marin peninsula, looming over the cool canyons of the rest of the county and dividing it into two distinct parts: the wild western slopes above the Pacific Coast and the increasingly suburban communities along the calmer bay frontage. The Panoramic Highway branches off from Hwy-1 along the crest above Mill Valley, taking ten miles to reach the center of **Mount Tamalpais State Park** (☎415/388-2070, ⓦ cal-parks.ca.gov), which has some thirty miles of hiking trails and many campgrounds. While most of the redwood trees that once covered its slopes have long since been chopped down to build San Francisco's Victorian houses, one towering grove remains, protected as the **Muir Woods National Monument** (daily 8am–sunset; $3; ☎415/388-2595). It's a tranquil and majestic spot, with sunlight filtering three hundred feet down from the treetops to the laurel- and fern-covered canyon below. Being so close to San Francisco, Muir Woods is a popular target, and the paved trails nearest the car park are often packed with coach-tour hordes; more secluded hiking paths include the Matt Davis Trail, leading south to Stinson Beach and north to Mount Tamalpais.

Mill Valley

From the east peak of Mount Tamalpais, a quick two-mile downhill hike follows the Temelpa Trail through velvety shrubs of chaparral to the town of **MILL VALLEY**, the oldest and most enticing of the inland towns of Marin County. Originally a logging center, it was from here that the destruction of the surrounding redwoods was organized, but for many years the town has made a healthy living out of tourism and October's annual **Mill Valley Film Festival**, a world-class event that draws Bay Area stars and up-and-coming directors alike.

The restored town centers today around the redwood-shaded square of the *Depot Bookstore and Café* (Mon–Sat 7am–10pm, Sun 8am–10pm; ☎415/383-2665), a popular bookstore, café, and meeting place at 87 Throckmorton Ave. The **Chamber of Commerce** is next door at 85 Throckmorton Ave (Mon–Fri 10am–noon and 1–4pm; ☎415/388-9700, ⓦ www.millvalley.org).

Far and away the best place to **stay**, if you can afford it, is the *Mill Valley Inn*, 165 Throckmorton Ave (☎415/389-6608 or 1-800/595-2100, ⓦwww.mill-valleyinn.com; ❼–❾), a gorgeous European-style inn with elegant rooms and two private cottages. There's a branch along the waterfront: the sumptuous *Acqua Hotel*, 555 Redwood Hwy (☎415/380-0400 or 1-888/662-9555, ⓦwww.acquahotel.com; ❼–❽), on Richardson Bay. *Piazza D'Angelo*, at 22 Miller Ave (☎415/388-2000), has delicious pizzas and pastas, while the *Sunnyside Café*, 31 Sunnyside Ave (☎415/388-5260), claims "the customers are rarely right" but serves large, affordable breakfasts and lunches nonetheless. *Sweetwater*, at 153 Throckmorton Ave (☎415/388-2820, ⓦwww.sweetwater-saloon.com), is a comfortable saloon that doubles as Marin's prime **live music** venue, with gigs ranging from jazz and blues all-stars to Jefferson Airplane survivors.

Point Reyes National Seashore

The westernmost tip of Marin County comes at the end of the **Point Reyes National Seashore**, a near-island of wilderness bordered on three sides by over fifty miles of isolated coastline – pine forests and sunny meadows hemmed in by rocky cliffs and sandy, windswept beaches. This wing-shaped landmass is a rogue piece of the earth's crust that has been drifting steadily northward along the San Andreas Fault, having started out some six million years ago as a suburb of Los Angeles. When the great earthquake of 1906 shattered San Francisco, the land here, at the epicenter, shifted over sixteen feet in an instant, though damage was confined to a few skewed cattle fences.

The **Bear Valley visitor center** (Mon–Fri 9am–5pm, Sat, Sun & holidays 8am–5pm; ☎415/464-5100, ⓦwww.nps.gov/pore), two miles southwest of Point Reyes Station in Olema, has engaging displays on local geology and natural history, plus details of hiking trails. Just to the north, Limantour Road heads six miles west to the *HI-Point Reyes* **hostel** (closed 10am–4.30pm; ☎415/663-8811, ⓦwww.norcalhostels.org; ❶) in an old ranch house. Nearby **Limantour Beach** is good (and cold) for swimming.

Eight miles west of the hamlet of Inverness, a small road leads down to **Drake's Beach**, the presumed landing spot of Sir Francis Drake in 1579. Appropriately, the coastline resembles the southern coast of England – cold, wet, and windy, with chalk-white cliffs rising above the wide sandy beach. The road continues southwest another four miles to the very tip of Point Reyes, where a precarious-looking **lighthouse** (Thurs–Mon 10am–4.30pm; tours first and third Sat of each month; free; ☎415/669-1534, ⓦwww.nps.gov/pore) stands firm against the crashing surf. The bluffs here are excellent for watching sea lions and, from mid-March to April and late December to early February, migrating gray whales.

The Gold Country

More than 150 years before techies from all over the world rushed to California in search of Silicon gold, rough-and-ready forty-niners invaded the

GOLD COUNTRY of the Sierra Nevada, about 150 miles east of San Francisco, in search of the real thing. The area ranges from the foothills near Yosemite to the deep gorge of the Yuba River two hundred miles north, with **Sacramento** as its largest city. Many of the mining camps that sprung up around the Gold Country vanished as quickly as they appeared, but about half still survive. Some are bustling resorts, standing on the banks of whitewater rivers in the midst of thick pine forests; others are just eerie ghost towns, all but abandoned on the grassy rolling hills. Most of the mountainous forests along the Sierra crest are preserved as near-pristine wilderness, with excellent hiking, camping, and backpacking. There's also great skiing in winter, around the mountainous rim of **Lake Tahoe** on the border between California and Nevada, aglow under the bright lights of the nightclubs and casinos that line its southeastern shore.

Sacramento

California's state capital, **SACRAMENTO**, in the flatlands of the Central Valley, was founded in 1839 by the Swiss John Sutter. He worked hard for ten years to build a busy trading center and cattle ranch, only to be thwarted by the discovery of gold at a nearby sawmill in 1848. His workers quit their jobs to go prospecting, and thousands more flocked to the goldfields of the Central Mother Lode, without any respect for Sutter's claims to the land. Sacramento became the main supply point for the miners, and remained important as the western headquarters of the transcontinental railroad. Flashy office towers and hotel complexes have now sprung from its rather suburban streetscape, enlivening the flat grid of leafy, tree-lined blocks, and going some way toward resurrecting the rowdy, free-for-all spirit of the city's Gold Rush past.

Sacramento is not especially prominent on most travelers' itineraries. There's not a great deal to see, though the wharves, warehouses, saloons, and stores of the historic core along the **riverfront** have been restored and converted into the touristy shops and restaurants of **Old Sacramento**. On the northern edge of the old town, the **California State Railroad Museum** (daily 10am–5pm; $3) brings together a range of lavishly restored 1860s locomotives, with "cow-catcher" front grilles and bulbous smokestacks. The old passenger station and freight depot, a block south on Front Street, now serve as the summer depot for a refurbished **Central Pacific Railroad steam train** (summer weekends 11am–5pm; $6), which makes a seven-mile, 45-minute roundtrip along the river.

Further east, and isolated from downtown, the dome of the **state capitol** stands proudly in a spacious green park two blocks south of K Street Mall. Recently restored to its original elegance, and still the seat of state government, the luxurious building brims over with finely crafted details. Although you're free to walk around, you'll see a lot more if you take one of the free hourly **tours** (daily 9am–5pm).

Sutter's Fort State Historic Park (daily 10am–5pm; $3), on the east side of town at 27th and L streets, is a re-creation of Sacramento's original settlement. An adobe house displays relics from the Gold Rush, and on summer weekends volunteers dress up and act out scenes from the 1850s.

Practicalities

Most tourists arrive in Sacramento by car, taking a logical break from driving on Rte-80. **Trains** come in at Fifth and I streets, near Old Sacramento, while an almost continuous stream of Greyhound **buses** arrives at Seventh and L streets. The **airport** is twelve miles northwest of the city: SuperShuttle Sacramento vans ($12; ☎1-800/BLUE-VAN) take you directly to your downtown destination.

Sacramento's most accessible **visitor information center** is at 1101 Second St (daily 10am–5pm; ☎916/442-7644). Besides the central *HI-Sacramento Hostel*, 900 H St (☎916/443-1691; ❶), there are plenty of **places to stay** within walking distance of the city center – the best value being the *Econo Lodge*, 711 16th St (☎916/443-6631 or 1-800/553-2666; ❷–❹). Further away, the *Vizcaya Mansion*, 2019 21st St (☎916/455-5243 or 1-800/456-2019, ⓦwww.sterlinghotels.com; ❻–❼), offers historic luxury in a quiet residential area; *Savoyard Bed & Breakfast*, 3322 H St (☎916/442-6709 or 1-800/772-8692, ⓦwww.savoyard.com; ❺–❻), is a sumptuous night's stay across from the city's Rose Garden; and *On the Bluffs*, 9735 Mira Del Rio (☎916/363-9933, ⓦwww.onthebluffs.com; ❺–❻), has rooms with river views. *Paesano's*, at 1806 Capitol Ave (☎916/447-8646), is a deservedly popular pizza **restaurant**; *Tapa the World*, at 2115 J St (☎916/442-4353), serves delicious *tapas* until midnight, often accompanied by live flamenco guitar; and *Centro Cocina Mexicana*, 454 28th St near J Street (☎916/442-2552), offers innovative Californian–Mexican fusion cuisine. For alternative **live music** try *Old Ironsides*, 1901 Tenth St (☎916/443-9751). Pick up the free weekly *Sacramento News & Review* for more entertainment details.

The Mines

In the romantically rugged landscape of the Gold Country, overshadowed by the 10,000ft granite peaks of the Sierra Nevada, fast-flowing rivers cascade through steeply walled canyons. During the fall, the flaming reds and golds of poplars and sugar maples on the slopes stand out against an evergreen background of pine and fir. The camps of the **southern mines** of the Gold Country were the liveliest and most uproarious of all the Gold Rush settlements, and inspired most of the popular images of the era: Wild West towns full of gambling halls, saloons, and gunfights in the streets. Freebooting prospectors in these "placer" mines sometimes panned for nuggets of gold in the streams and rivers; further **north**, the diggings were far richer and more successful, but the gold was (and still is) buried deep underground, and had to be pounded out of hardrock ore.

Sonora, Columbia, Jamestown, and Mariposa

The center of the southern mining district is **SONORA**, set on steep ravines roughly a hundred miles east of San Francisco. This friendly and animated logging town boasts numerous Victorian houses and false-fronted buildings on its main Washington Street. The Tuolumne County Visitors Bureau, 542 West Stockton Rd off Hwy-49 (☎209/533-4420 or 1-800/446-1333, ⓦwww.thegreatunfenced.com), is the best source of information.

Sonora's onetime arch-rival, **COLUMBIA**, three miles north on Parrots Ferry Road, is now a ghost town (and a state historic park), with a carefully restored Main Street that gives an excellent – if slightly contrived – idea of what Gold Rush life might have been like. In 1854 it was California's second largest city, and it missed becoming the state capital by two votes – just as well, since by 1870 the gold had run out and the town was abandoned.

The **Railtown 1897 State Historic Park**, on the corner of Fifth and Reservoir streets along the way to Sonora, in **JAMESTOWN**, holds an impressive collection of old steam trains including the one used in *High Noon* (daily 9.30am–4.30pm). Further south, after a breathtaking drive over the Don Pedro Lake and Merced River, is **MARIPOSA**, gateway to Yosemite and one of the last Gold Rush towns on Hwy-49. Its **California State Mining and Mineral Museum**, a mile or so south of the historic downtown (daily: May–Sept 10am–6pm; Oct–April 10am–4pm; $1), has a working 1860s stamp mill model and hundreds of mineral samples.

Practicalities

In downtown Columbia, the best **place to stay** is right on the historic Main Street in the balconied *City Hotel* (℡209/532-1479 or 1-800/532-1479, ⓦwww.cityhotel.com; ❺); in Sonora, *Sterling Gardens* is a comfortable B&B with four guestrooms among ten acres at 18047 Lime Kiln Rd (℡209/533-9300, ⓦwww.sterlinggardens.com; ❺), while the well-placed *Gunn House Hotel* (℡209/532-3421; ❹) is right in town at 286 S Washington St; motels on Hwy-49 between Sonora and Jamestown include the good-value *Miner's Motel* (℡209/532-7850 or 1-800/451-4176; ❸). Jamestown's Main Street is lined by old Gold Rush hotels such as the fantastic *Jamestown Hotel* (℡209/984-3902 or 1-800/205-4901, ⓦwww.jamestownhotel.com; ❹–❻), which boasts an impressive restaurant while being close to other good options, including *Morelia Mexican*, across the street. Sonora has a wide variety of **places to eat** along Washington Street: *Alfredo's* at no. 123 is a local favorite for Mexican food, and *The Old Stan*, at no. 177, has *tapas* and Mediterranean dishes.

Grass Valley, Nevada City, and Downieville

The compact communities of **GRASS VALLEY** and **NEVADA CITY**, four miles apart in the Sierra Nevada Mountains, were the most prosperous and substantial of the gold-mining towns. Since the 1960s, artists and craftspeople have settled in the elaborate Victorian homes of the surrounding hills and gorges. In Grass Valley, the **North Star Mining Museum** (May–Oct daily 10am–5pm; donation) at the south end of Mill Street is housed in what used to be the power station for the North Star Mine. Its giant water-driven **Pelton wheel**, fitted with a hundred or so iron buckets, once powered the drills and hoists of the mine. Dioramas show the day-to-day working life of the miners, three-quarters of whom had emigrated here from the depressed tin mines of Cornwall (bringing the Cornish pasty with them).

The last mine in California to shut down was its richest, the **Empire Mine** (May–Aug 9am–6pm; Sept–April 10am–5pm; $2), now preserved as a state park in the pine forests a mile southeast of Grass Valley. It closed in 1956, after more than six million ounces of gold had been recovered, when the cost of getting the gold out of the ground exceeded $35 an ounce, which was the government-controlled price at the time. Machinery sold off when the mine closed has been replaced from other disused workings and now augments the excellent and very informative **museum** at the entrance.

The excellent Grass Valley **visitor center** at 248 Mill St (Mon–Fri 9.30am–5pm, Sat 10am–3pm; ℡530/273-4667 or 1-800/655-4667) is housed in a replica of the original home of Lola Montez, an Irish entertainer and former mistress of Ludwig of Bavaria, who retired here after touring America with her provocative "Spider Dance" and kept a grizzly bear in her front yard.

Towns don't get much quainter than **Nevada City**. Amid all the shops and restaurants in the city center, the lacy-balconied and bell-towered **Old Firehouse** at 214 Main St houses a small **museum** of social history of the region (May–Oct daily 11am–4pm; Nov–April Thurs–Sun 11.30am–4pm; donation).

Both towns are very compact and connected every thirty minutes by the Gold Country Stage **minibus** (Mon–Fri 8am–5pm, Sat 9.15am–5.30pm; $1, $2 for a day pass; ☎530/477-0103). The five daily Amtrak Thruway **buses** from Sacramento and Auburn stop on Sacramento Street in Nevada City and on West Main Street in Grass Valley.

North on Hwy-49, an hour's drive from Nevada City, you'll head into the most rugged and beautiful part of the Gold Country, where waterfalls tumble over black rocks bordered by pines and maples. **DOWNIEVILLE** is in the midst of an idyllic setting and particularly popular with mountain bikers; it abuts an extensive trail system with moderate to extreme bike trails. Oddly, as the only mining camp to have ever hanged a woman, the town has restored a gallows to commemorate that grisly passage of its history.

Accommodation

Accommodation in the revamped old Gold Rush **hotels** doesn't come cheap, but if you can afford to splash out on a B&B, Nevada City has some excellent options.

Holbrooke Hotel 212 W Main St, Grass Valley ☎530/273-1353 or 1-800/933-7077. Historic hotel, once visited by Mark Twain, and right in the center of town. Breakfast included. ❸–❺
Holiday Lodge 1221 E Main St, Grass Valley ☎530/273-4406 or 1-800/742-7125. Comfortable, basic accommodation with perks such as a swimming pool, free breakfast, and free local calls. ❸–❹
Outside Inn 575 E Broad St, Nevada City ☎530/265-2233, ⓦwww.outsideinn.com. Quiet,

1940s motel with swimming pool, and only a 10min walk from the center of town. ❸–❺
The Parsonage 427 Broad St, Nevada City ☎530/265-9478. Century-old Victorian B&B with great breakfasts and helpful hosts. Close to the town center. ❹–❻
Swan-Levine House 328 S Church St, Grass Valley ☎530/272-1873. Attractively decorated, sunny rooms in an old Victorian hospital run by two artists. ❹–❺

Eating and drinking

Both Grass Valley and Nevada City have good places to eat, as well as many bars and saloons, where you'll often be treated to free live music.

Broad Street Books & Espresso 426 Broad St, Nevada City ☎530/265-4204. Pastries, light fare, and espresso with wonderful tree-shaded outdoor seating.
Café Mekka 237 Commercial St, Nevada City ☎530/478-1517. Relaxed coffee shop, popular with arty locals.

Posh Nosh 318 Broad St, Nevada City ☎530/265-6064. Casual lunch and dinner dining, with lovely indoor patio and good vegetarian options.
Tofanelli's 302 W Main St, Grass Valley ☎530/272-1468. Stylish restaurant with a deliciously eclectic menu.

Lake Tahoe

One of the highest, largest, deepest, cleanest, and coldest lakes in the world, **Lake Tahoe** is perched high above the Gold Country in an alpine bowl of forested granite peaks. Longer than the English Channel is wide, and more than a thousand feet deep, it's so cold that perfectly preserved cowboys who drowned over a century ago have been recovered from its depths. The lake lures weekenders from the Bay Area and beyond with sunny beaches in the summer, snow-covered slopes in the winter, and bustling casinos year-round.

Arrival, information, and getting around

Daily Greyhound buses from San Francisco and Sacramento stop at *Harrah's* casino in **Stateline**, Nevada. From there, local STAGE **buses** serve the communities of Tahoe City and South Lake Tahoe. Amtrak Thruway **buses** arrive several times daily from Sacramento, heading for Carson City. You can rent **bicycles** from numerous outlets, including the Mountain Sports Center (☎530/542-6584, ⊛www.camprichardson.com) in South Lake Tahoe's *Camp Richardson Resort*, and from Olympic Bike Shop (☎530/581-2500) in Tahoe City. There are four official **visitor centers** around the lake: in California at 1156 Ski Run Blvd, South Lake Tahoe (☎530/544-5050 or 1-800/288-2463), and 245 North Lake Blvd, Tahoe City (☎530/581-6900); and in Nevada at 969 Tahoe Blvd, Incline Village (☎775/832-1606), and on Hwy-50 in Round Hill, just across the state line (☎775/588-4591, ⊛www.tahoechamber.org). For accommodation and event information, the Tahoe Central Reservation Service can be reached at ☎1-800/288-2463 or ⊛www.virtualtahoe.com.

Accommodation

There are dozens of bargain **motels** along the Southshore, though weekday rates from $50 can easily double at weekends and in summer. In Tahoe City, there are fewer budget choices, but as prices skyrocket around the lake, you'll rarely find a great deal in any direction. The South Lake Tahoe Visitors Authority (☎1-800/288-2463) runs a free **room reservation service**, which can also help you with Northshore and Reno reservations.

Doug's Mellow Mountain Retreat 3787 Forest Ave, South Lake Tahoe ☎530/544-8065. Basic hostel-style accommodation in essentially Doug's home, with cooking facilities and cheap bike rental. ❶

Forest Inn Suites 1 Lake Parkway, South Lake Tahoe ☎530/541-6655 or 1-800/822-5950, ⊛www.forestinn.com. Reasonably priced guest rooms and suites, along with a fitness center and hot tub on-site. A cut above the motels on the strip and quieter, too, and they often offer special package deals. ❺–❼

Inn at Heavenly 1261 Ski Run Blvd ☎530/544-4244 or 1-800/692-2246, ⊛www.innatheavenly.com. Friendly inn with cozy wood-paneled rooms and cabins. Continental breakfast and use of spa included in rates. ❹–❻

River Ranch Hwy-89 and Alpine Meadows Rd, Tahoe City ☎530/583-4264 or 1-800/535-9900,

⊛www.riverranchlodge.com. Historic lodge on the Truckee River with a casual atmosphere and one of the lake's best restaurants. ❹–❻

Stardust Lodge 4061 Lake Tahoe Blvd, South Lake Tahoe ☎530/544-5211 or 1-800/262-5077, ⊛www.stardust-tahoe.com. Simple suites and guestrooms with kitchenettes, and an easy walk to the casinos and the lake. ❹–❻

Tahoe City Inn 790 North Lake Blvd, Tahoe City ☎530/581-3333 or 1-800/800-8246, ⊛www.tahoecityinn.com. The basic, centrally located rooms can cost as little as $49 midweek in the low season. ❷–❹

Tamarack Lodge 2311 North Lake Blvd, Tahoe City ☎530/583-3350 or 1-888/824-6323, ⊛www.tamarackattahoe.com. One of the best deals anywhere on the lake, with comfortable and clean cabins and rooms. ❷–❻

South Lake Tahoe and around

In **South Lake Tahoe**, the lakeside's largest community, ranks of restaurants, modest motels, and pine-bound cottages stand cheek by jowl with the high-rise gambling dens of Stateline, just across the border in Nevada. If you happen to lose your money at the tables and slot machines, you can always explore the beautiful hiking trails, parks, and beaches in the surrounding area.

The **Heavenly Gondola**, well-situated in the heart of town, takes vistors to an elevation of 9136ft (winter Mon–Fri 9am–4pm, Sat & Sun 8.30am–4pm; rest of year call ☏775/586-7000 for opening hours; $20, kids $12). From there, enjoy breathtaking views from East Peak Lake, East Peak Lookout, or Sky Meadows. Hikes are graded from easy to strenuous. Closer to the water, the prettiest part of the lake is found along the southwest shore, at **Emerald Bay State Park**, ten miles from South Lake Tahoe, which has a number of good shoreline **campgrounds**. A mile from the parking lot, **Vikingsholm** is a reproduction of a Viking castle, built as a summer home in 1929 and open for hourly tours (summer daily 10am–4pm; $3). In **Sugar Pine Point State Park**, two miles north, the huge **Ehrman Mansion** (daily 11am–4pm; $3) is decorated in Thirties-era furnishings; the extensive lakefront grounds were used as a location in *The Godfather II*.

The rest of the 75-mile **drive** is lovely enough, though certainly not the "most beautiful drive in America," as one locally produced brochure touts; a better way to see it is to take a paddlewheel **boat cruise** on the *MS Dixie II*, from Zephyr Cove (three departures daily in summer, one in winter, call for times; $25–51; ☏775/589-4906, ⊛www.laketahoecruises.com), reached on a free shuttle from South Lake Tahoe, or sign up for other boat tours through one of the larger casinos.

Tahoe City

Tahoe City, the hub on the lake's northwestern shore, does not escape the tourists, but nevertheless manages to retain a more relaxed small-town attitude than South Lake Tahoe. Hwy-89 meets Hwy-28 at Lake Tahoe's only outlet, the **Truckee River**. At the mouth of the river, the **Gatekeeper's Cabin Museum** (May to mid-June Wed–Sun 11am–5pm; mid-June to mid-Oct daily 11am–5pm; $2), contains a well-presented hodgepodge of artifacts from the nineteenth century, and a good collection of native basketware. **Rafting** down the Truckee is a common activity in summer, with raft rental companies clustered at the bottom of the river at the junction of highways 28 and 89.

A couple of miles south along Hwy-89, 500 yards past the Kaspian picnic grounds, hike ten minutes up the unmarked trail to the top of **Eagle Rock** for amazing panoramic views of the royal-blue lake. Several miles further along the highway is **Chamber's Beach**, which in summer is as popular for sunning and swimming as it is for socializing.

Squaw Valley, the site of the 1960 Winter Olympics, is situated five miles west of Tahoe City off of Hwy-89, although the original facilities (except the flame and the Olympic rings) are now swamped by the rampant development that has made this California's largest ski resort (see box, below).

Eating and drinking

Fast food and casino all-you-care-to-eat buffets are standard in Southshore, while Tahoe City has a better range of moderately priced restaurants and a couple of good bars, all within a few minutes of each other.

Lakehouse Pizza 120 Grove St, Tahoe City ☏530/583-2222. Tahoe's best place for pizza is also a popular spot for cocktails on the lake at sundown. **Pierce Street Annex** in the back of the Safeway complex, Tahoe City ☏530/583-5800. The place for drinking and dancing on the Northshore, but with sometimes-cheesy music. Popular with the younger Tahoe City crowd. **Red Hut Waffle Shop** 2749 Lake Tahoe Blvd, South Lake Tahoe ☏530/541-9024. Ever-popular coffee shop, justifiably crowded on early winter mornings with carbo-loading skiers.

Lake Tahoe skiing

Lake Tahoe has some of the best **downhill skiing** in North America, and its larger resorts rival their Rocky Mountain counterparts. Although skiing is certainly not cheap – the largest ski areas charge at least $50 for the privilege of using their mountain for a single day – many resorts offer decent-value rental/lift ticket/lesson packages or multiday discounts. **Snowboarding** has caught on in a big way, and the same resorts that once scoffed at the sport have now installed massive snow parks with radical half-pipes and jumps. **Cross-country skiing** is also popular. Most resorts **rent** skis for about $30 and snowboards for $35.

Downhill skiing

Heavenly reachable by shuttle from Southshore, two miles from the casinos, or via the gondola right on Hwy-50, next to the state line (☎775/586-7000 or 1-800/243-2836, ⓦwww.skiheavenly.com). Prime location and sheer scale (85 runs and 29 lifts) make this one of the lake's most frequented resorts, and it also offers the highest vertical skiing served by a lift. Non-skiers can take a scenic gondola ride ($20) for the view in winter or summer. Lift tickets are $57.

Homewood five miles south of Tahoe City on Hwy-89 (☎530/525-2992 or 1-877/525-7669, ⓦwww.skihomewood.com). Smaller and more relaxed than its massive resort neighbors, Homewood boasts some surprisingly good skiing with unbeatable views of the lake and reasonable prices. Lift tickets go for $45, and drop as low as $25 mid-week.

Kirkwood Ski Resort 35 miles south of South Lake Tahoe on Hwy-88 (☎209/258-6000, ⓦwww.kirkwood.com). A bit out of the way if you're in Tahoe but worth the trip as a destination in itself for numerous recreational possibilities, including excellent hiking and biking trails. Lift tickets are $60.

Squaw Valley USA Squaw Valley Rd, halfway between Truckee and Tahoe City (☎530/583-6955 or 1-888/766-9321, ⓦwww.squaw.com). Thirty-three lifts service over four thousand acres of unbeatable terrain at the site of the 1960 Winter Olympics. Non-skiers can take the cable lift ($17) and use the ice-skating/swimming pool complex for the day. Lift tickets are $58.

Cross-country skiing

Royal Gorge in Soda Springs, ten miles west of Truckee (☎530/426-3871 or 1-800/666-3871, ⓦwww.royalgorge.com). The largest and best of Tahoe's cross-country resorts has 204 miles of groomed trails. Trail fee $26, rental fee $18, and lessons (group $20, private $30).

Spooner Lake in Nevada at the intersection of Hwy-50 and Hwy-28 (☎775/749-5349, ⓦwww.spoonerlake.com). The closest cross-country resort to South Lake Tahoe has lake views and 63 miles of groomed trails. Trail fee $19, rental fee $18, and lessons $39.

River Ranch Hwy-89 and Alpine Meadows Rd, Tahoe City ☎530/583-4264 or 1-800/535-9900. Historic lodge on the Truckee River serving quality New American cuisine in a relaxed atmosphere.

Rosie's Café 571 North Lake Blvd, Tahoe City ☎530/583-8504. Cozy restaurant with a vaulted ceiling and fireplace featuring delicious grilled meats, sandwiches, and filling breakfasts.

Sprouts 3123 Lake Tahoe Blvd near Alameda Ave, South Lake Tahoe ☎530/541-6969. Almost, but not completely, vegetarian, with good organic sandwiches, burritos, and smoothies.

Sunnyside Restaurant and Lodge 1850 West Lake Blvd, near Tahoe City ☎530/583-7200. One of the most popular places to have cocktails at sunset on the deck overlooking the lake.

Tahoe House Bakery Hwy-89, half a mile south of Hwy-28, Tahoe City ☎530/583-1377. Family-style bakery and deli, popular with locals.

Taj Mahal 3838 Lake Tahoe Blvd, in the *Quality Inn*, South Lake Tahoe ☎530/541-6495. Basic Indian fare with a good eleven-course lunch buffet.

Tep's Villa Roma 3450 Hwy-50, South Lake Tahoe ☎530/541-8227. Longstanding Southshore institution that serves large portions of hearty Italian food.

Donner Lake

Twenty-five miles north of Lake Tahoe, **Donner Lake**, surrounded by alpine cliffs of silver-gray granite, was the site of a gruesome tragedy in 1846, when the **Donner Party**, heading for the Gold Rush, found their route blocked by early snowfall. They stopped and built crude shelters, hoping that the snow would melt; it didn't. Fifteen of their number braved the mountains in search of help from Sutter's Fort in Sacramento; only two men and five women made it, surviving by eating the bodies of the men who died. A rescue party set off immediately, only to find more of the same: thirty or so half-crazed survivors, living off the meat of their fellow travelers. The horrific tale is recounted in the small **Emigrant Trail Museum** (daily 10am–4pm; $1), just off Donner Pass Road in Donner State Park.

Northern California

The massive and eerily silent volcanic lands of **northern California** have more in common with Oregon and Washington than with the rest of the state. Its small settlements live by logging, fishing, and farming, though locals have been joined in recent years by New Agers, ex-hippies, and an ever-growing contingent of tourists. Once you're past the atypically lush valleys of the **Wine Country**, the coast stretches for four hundred miles of rugged bluffs and forests. Aside from the beautiful deserted beaches that stripe the coast, trees are the big attraction, thousands of years old and hundreds of feet high, dominating a landscape swathed in swirling mists. The **Redwood National Park** teems with campers and hikers in summer, but out of season it can be idyllic. The remote wildernesses of the interior can be enchanting, especially around the **Shasta Cascade** and **Lassen Volcanic National Park**.

  Public transportation is, not surprisingly, scarce, though Greyhound buses run from San Francisco and Sacramento up and down I-5 and US-101.

The Wine Country

The warm and sunny hills of **Napa** and **Sonoma valleys**, an hour north of San Francisco, are by reputation, if not statistically, at the center of the American wine industry. In truth, less than five percent of California's wine comes from the region, but what it does produce is America's best. In summer, cars jam Hwy-29 through its heart, as visitors embark on a day's free drinking, thinly disguised as an avid interest in wine.

The Napa Valley

A thirty-mile strip of gently landscaped hillsides, the **Napa Valley** looks more like southern France than a near-neighbor of the Pacific Ocean. The one anomaly is the town of **Napa** itself, a sprawling, ungainly city of 60,000 best avoided in favor of the wineries and small towns north on Hwy-29. Nine miles north, first up is **YOUNTVILLE**, named in honor of the valley's pioneer, George C. Yount. Today the town is anchored by **Vintage 1870**, 6525 Washington St (daily 10.30am–5.30pm), a shopping and wine complex in a converted winery that also houses Napa Valley Aloft (☎1-800/944-4408, Ⓦwww.nvaloft.com), who specialize in sunrise tours of the valley.

Of the large wineries at the valley's southern end, **Robert Mondavi**, at 7801 St Helena Hwy in Oakville (daily 10am–5pm; $10; ☎1-888/766-6328, Ⓦwww.mondavi.com) offers the most informative and least sales-driven tours and tastings

A little further up the valley past the pretty village of **ST HELENA**, **Beringer Vineyards**, at 2000 Main St (daily 10am–5pm; $5; ☎707/963-7115, Ⓦwww.beringer.com), is modeled on a German Gothic mansion and has graced the cover of many a wine magazine. Spacious lawns and a grand tasting room, heavy on the dark wood, make for quite a regal experience.

Homey **CALISTOGA**, at the very tip of the valley, is well known for its mud baths, whirlpools, and mineral water, though its wineries are just as appealing. South of town, **Clos Pegase**, 1060 Dunaweal Lane (daily 10.30am–5pm; ☎707/942-4981, Ⓦwww.clospegase.com), is a flamboyant, high-profile winery that draws a link between fine wine and fine art, with an excellent sculpture garden around buildings designed by postmodern architect Michael Graves. Tastings are $5, and there are tours at 11am and 2pm. The **Chateau Montelena**, 1429 Tubbs Lane (☎707/942-5105, Ⓦwww.montelena.com), just north of town, is one of the valley's oldest and smallest wineries, with an impressive medieval facade and a reputation for first-class Chardonnays. A mile further up the road, evidence of Calistoga's lively underground activity can be seen at the **Old Faithful Geyser** (daily 9am–6pm; $8; ☎707/942-6463), which spurts boiling water sixty feet into the air at forty-minute intervals. The water source was discovered during oil drilling here in the 1920s, when search equipment struck a force estimated to be up to a thousand pounds per square foot. In time, landowners turned it into a high-yield tourist attraction, using the same name as the famous spouter in Yellowstone National Park.

Practicalities

From San Francisco there are daily Gray Line **bus tours** ($55; ☎415/558-9400 or 1-888/428-6937) to the Wine Country; otherwise take the Blue & Gold Fleet tour that leaves daily from Fisherman's Wharf for a bus trip through Napa and Sonoma valleys with stops at three wineries ($60; ☎415/705-5555). Napa itself doesn't offer much in the way of budget lodging; you're better off in Sonoma, where at least the cost of a room is offset by pleasant surroundings.

In **St Helena**, *Hotel St Helena*, 1309 Main St (☎707/963-4388; ❼–❾), provides cozy rooms right in the center of town, while *Sunny Acres Bed & Breakfast*, a working vineyard set on twenty acres, 397 Main St (☎707/963-2826; ❽), offers three sumptuous rooms. St Helena's **restaurants** range from the California fusion cooking of *Pinot Blanc*, 641 Main St (☎707/963-6191), to the haute cuisine and four-hundred-plus wine list at the gigantic *Wine Spectator Greystone Restaurant*, 2555 Main St (☎707/967-1010).

In **Calistoga**, *Dr Wilkinson's Hot Springs*, 1507 Lincoln Ave (☎707/942-4102, Ⓦwww.drwilkinson.com; ❺–❼), is a legendary health spa and hotel, while less expensive lodgings (and spa facilities) lining the main drag, Lincoln Avenue, include the quiet, modern *Comfort Inn* at no. 1865 (☎707/942-9400; ❹–❺ weekdays, ❻–❼ weekends). Downtown's most enticing hotel can be found at 1457 Lincoln Ave in the historic *Mount View Hotel and Spa* (☎707/942-6877 or 1-800/816-6877, Ⓦwww.mountviewhotel.com; ❻–❼ double, ❽–❾ cottage with patio and Jacuzzi). Creative cuisine, featuring unheard-of combinations such as *chile rellenos* with walnut pomegranate sauce, makes **dining** at the *Wappo Bar Bistro*, 1226 Washington St (Ⓣ707/942-4712), a delicious adventure. The *Calistoga Inn*, 1250 Lincoln Ave (Ⓣ707/942-4101), serves great seafood appetizers, including wheat-ale steamed clams and mussels, plus a wide range of wines, microbrewed beers, and excellent desserts. *Brannan's Grill*, 1374 Lincoln Ave (Ⓣ707/942-2233), serves fresh oysters, salmon, and roasted Sonoma chicken in an airy wood-interior bistro.

Sonoma Valley

On looks alone, the crescent-shaped **Sonoma Valley** beats Napa hands down. This altogether more rustic valley curves between oak-covered mountain ranges from the Spanish Colonial town of **SONOMA** to Glen Ellen, a few miles north along Hwy-12. It's far smaller than Napa, and many of its wineries are informal, family-run businesses, where a charge for tasting is still frowned upon and visitors are few.

The restored **Mission San Francisco Solano de Sonoma** (daily 10am–5pm; $2), just east of the spacious plaza in Sonoma, was the last and northernmost of the California missions, and the only one established in northern California by the nervous Mexican rulers, who were fearful of expansionist Russian fur-traders. The plaza was also the sight of the Bear Flag Revolt, the 1846 action that propelled California into independence from Mexico, and then statehood. Sonoma's wineries are concentrated a mile east, within walking distance, and include the grand old **Buena Vista Winery**, 18000 Old Winery Rd (free tasting daily 10am–5pm; historical tours daily 2pm; Ⓣ1-800/678-8504, Ⓦwww.buenavistawinery.com), which has champagne cellars, tunnels of oak caskets, and a high-ceilinged tasting room. A ten-minute drive further north, in charming Glen Ellen, is the **Benziger Family Winery**, 1883 London Ranch Rd (daily 10am–5pm; $10 for four tastings; Ⓣ1-888/490-2739, Ⓦwww.benziger.com). A self-guided tour explains how wine grapes are cultivated and flavored, and four times daily a tram tour takes you around the vineyard along the side of Mount Sonoma. A half-mile up London Ranch Road, **Jack London State Park** (daily 9.30am–5pm, until 7pm in summer; $3 per car) sits on the 140 acres of ranchland owned by the famed author of *The Call of the Wild*. Here you'll find the author's final resting place, along with a decent museum that houses a collection of souvenirs that he picked up while traveling the globe.

Practicalities

The only **public transportation** between the valleys is the Greyhound buses heading to and from San Francisco, which stop at Sonoma City Hall and Napa's Pearl Street (Ⓣ1-800/229-9424). **Accommodation** is pricey, though the *Sonoma Hotel*, 110 W Spain St (Ⓣ707/996-2996, Ⓦwww.sonomahotel .com; ❺–❼), has French country–style doubles and a great bar, and the *Swiss Hotel*, 18 W Spain St (Ⓣ707/938-2884; ❻–❼), is in a landmark building on the plaza with four-poster beds in each room. Good shopping and cafés abound on the square; *La Casa*, 121 E Spain St (Ⓣ707/996-3406), is a friendly, festive, and inexpensive Mexican **restaurant** across from the Sonoma Mission, while hidden away on 315 Second St E, the *Vella Cheese Company* (Mon–Sat 9am–6pm; Ⓣ1-800/848-0505) attracts cheese aficionados from far and wide with their hand-made Monterey Jack, sharp Cheddar, and Asiago.

The northern coast

The fog-bound towns and windswept, craggy beaches of the **northern coast** couldn't be farther removed from Southern California's sandy, sunny strip of ocean. Stretching north of San Francisco to the Oregon border, the area is better suited for hiking and camping than sunbathing, with a climate of cool temperatures year-round and a huge network of national, state, and regional parks preserving magnificent **redwood** trees. Throw on your hiking boots and get out onto the trails that sweep past lolling seals, migrating whales, and some of the oldest, tallest trees on earth.

The Sonoma Coast and Russian River Valley

Despite the weekend influx from San Francisco, the villages of the **Sonoma Coast** and **Russian River Valley** seem all but asleep for most of the year. Tucked along the slow, snaking Hwy-1, towns include **BODEGA BAY**, where Hitchcock filmed *The Birds*. From here, a great thirteen-mile hike leads along the rugged cliffs to busy **Goat Rock Beach**, where the Russian River joins the ocean. A prime seal- and whale-watching spot, the beach is less than a mile from equally pleasing **JENNER**, which is a good place for clam chowder and ocean-staring.

About ten miles inland on Hwy-116, toward the warm and pastoral Russian River Valley, **GUERNEVILLE** is a well-established gay resort. It offers plenty of **places to stay** – though many are expensive. *The Willows*, 15905 River Rd (☎707/869-2824 or 1-800/953-2828, ⓦwww.willowsrussianriver.com; ④–⑥), provides luxurious rooms alongside the river, while the **campground** at *Johnson's Resort* on First Street also has cabins (☎707/869-2022, ⓦwww .johnsonsbeach.com; ①). The popular *Russian River Resort* ("*Triple R*"), 16390 Fourth St (☎707/869-0691 or 1-800/4-1RESORT, ⓦwww.russianriverresort .com; ④–⑥), serves alcohol and food, and has comedy and karaoke nights, while *Main St Station*, 16280 Main St (☎707/869-0501), is a great pizzeria with nightly live jazz. The **Armstrong Redwoods State Reserve** ($2 per car, pedestrians free), two miles north, contains 750 very dense acres of enormous redwoods interspersed by trails – one of the best ways to see it is on horseback. Guided expeditions run by the Armstrong Woods Pack Station (☎707/887-2939, ⓦwww.redwoodhorses.com) vary in length from half a day ($60 and up) to three-day pack trips ($675).

MONTE RIO, three miles back down the river toward the coast, is a lovely old resort town, at the entrance to the 2500-acre **Bohemian Grove**, where the richest and most powerful men in the country traditionally gather in privacy each July for two weeks of (supposedly male-only) high jinks.

The Mendocino coast

The coast of **Mendocino County**, 150 miles north of San Francisco, is a dramatic extension of the Sonoma coastline – the headlands a bit sharper, the surf a bit rougher, but otherwise more of the same. **MENDOCINO** itself looks like a transplanted New England fishing village: weathered and charming, with plenty of art galleries and boutiques. Just south of town, hiking and cycling trails weave through the unusual **Van Damme State Park**, on Hwy-1 ($2–3; ☎707/937-5804), where the ancient trees of the Pygmy Forest are stunted to waist height because of poor drainage and soil chemicals. Two-hour sea cave tours through the park are available through Lost Coast Kayaking (three times daily; $45; ☎707/937-2434).

The best of the affordable **accommodations** in the center of town is the *Sea Gull Inn*, 44960 Albion St (☎707/937-5204 or 1-888/937-5204, Ⓦwww.mcn.org/a/seagull; ❷–❻), though the antique-filled rooms at *The Mendocino Hotel and Garden Suites*, 45080 Main St (☎707/937-0511 or 1-800/548-0513, Ⓦwww.mendocinohotel.com; ❹–❾), are more luxurious. The town's oldest **bar** is *Dick's Place* on Main Street, the closest thing you'll find to a local hangout. Of Mendocino's **restaurants**, the most famous is *Café Beaujolais*, 961 Ukiah St (☎707/937-5614), which specializes in organic California cuisine. *955 Ukiah Street* (☎707/937-1955) serves some of the best food in town: entrees are considered a steal for $15–25 a plate (daily from 6pm; closed Tues). For slightly cheaper fare with a great view, try the *Bay View Café*, 45040 Main St (☎707/937-4197), which serves tasty standards from salads to fish and chips daily. *Tote Féte Bakery*, behind the deli of the same name at 10450 Lansing St (daily until 4pm; ☎707/937-3140), produces delicious breads, pastries, and muffins, which you can eat outside on the tree-shaded deck.

The Humboldt coast

Humboldt is by far the most beautiful of the coastal counties: almost entirely forestland, overwhelmingly peaceful in places, in others plain eerie. The impassable cliffs of **Kings Range** prevent even the sinuous Hwy-1 from reaching the "Lost Coast" of its southern reaches. To get there you have to travel US-101 through the deepest redwood territory as far as **GARBERVILLE**, a one-street town with a few good bars that is the center of the "Emerald Triangle," which produces the majority of California's largest cash crop, marijuana. Every August, the town hosts the enormous **Reggae on the River** festival (information on ☎707/923-4583, Ⓦwww.reggaeontheriver.com).

Redwood country begins in earnest a few miles north, at the **Humboldt Redwoods State Park**, California's largest redwood park. The serpentine **Avenue of the Giants** weaves for 33 miles through trees that block all but a few strands of sunlight, but you can exit at numerous points to get back on US-101. This is the habitat of *Sequoia sempervirens*, the coastal redwood, with ancestors dating back to the days of the dinosaurs, and some are over 350ft tall. Three campgrounds fill up quickly in summertime (reserve through PARKNET at ☎1-800/444-7275 or call ☎707/946-2409 for information, Ⓦwww.humboldtredwoods.org; $12).

Tiny **SAMOA**, a few minutes by car over the bay from Eureka, holds the last remaining cookhouse in the West. Lumbermen came to the *Samoa Cookhouse* (☎707/442-1659) to eat gargantuan meals after a day of felling redwoods; the oilskin tablecloths and burly workers have gone, but the lumber-camp style remains, with long tables and colossal portions of red meat.

ARCATA, twelve miles north of Eureka, a small college town with an earthy, mellow pace, has a grassy central plaza surrounded by good restaurants, and some excellent white-sand, windswept beaches to the north. The *Fairwinds Motel*, 1674 G St (☎707/822-4824; ❷–❸), is probably the best deal in town. More upscale, the *Hotel Arcata*, 708 Ninth St (☎707/826-0217 or 1-800/344-1221, Ⓦwww.hotelarcata.com; ❸–❻), is central and offers standard rooms and nicer suites. The working *Humboldt Brewery*, 856 Tenth St, maker of the not uncontroversial Humboldt Hemp Ale, has its own bar and low-priced restaurant.

Willow Creek, forty miles east of Arcata, is the self-proclaimed gateway to "**Bigfoot Country**." Reports of giant 350- to 800-pound humanoids wandering the forests of northwestern California have circulated since the late nineteenth century, fueled by long-established Indian legends, but weren't taken seriously until 1958, when a road maintenance crew found giant footprints. Thanks to their photos, the Bigfoot story went worldwide. However, in 2002, the bereaved family of Ray L. Wallace claimed he made the 1958 footprints, a hoax they had promised to keep secret until after his death. But the number and variety of prints (over forty, since 1958) still points to a Bigfoot mystery, and the small **visitor center** in Willow Creek has details of Bigfoot's alleged activities. Information on the adjacent **Hoopa Valley Indian Reservation** can be found here and at the **Hoopa Museum** in Hoopa, north of Willow Creek on Highway 96. The site of several violent confrontations between Native Americans and whites over fishing territory, the reservation was finally declared a sovereign territory in 1988, and is currently working on restoration of the Trinity River and its depleted fish stocks.

Redwood National Park

Thirty miles north of Arcata, the small town of **ORICK** marks the southern limit, and busiest section, of the **Redwood National Park**. **Tall Trees Grove** here is home to one of the world's tallest trees – a mighty 367-footer. Many visitors hike to it on the 8.5-mile trail from Bald Hill Road near Orick, but make sure to visit the **information center** (daily 9am–5pm; ☎707/464-6101), from which you can obtain the needed free permit to drive and camp the back roads leading to the tree.

Of the three state parks within the Redwood National Park area, **Prairie Creek** is the most varied and popular, and while bear and elk roam in plain sight, you can also be taken around here by the rangers for a **tour** of the wild and damp profusion. Highlights include the meadows of **Elk Prairie** in front of the **ranger station** (daily: summer 9am–6pm; rest of year 9am–5pm; ☎707/464-6101), where herds of Roosevelt Elk – massive beasts weighing up to twelve hundred pounds – wander freely, protected from poachers.

Spectacular coastal views can be had from trails in the Klamath area, especially the **Klamath Overlook**, on Requa Road about three-quarters of a mile down to the sea. You can jump over, lumber under, or glide through all the naturally contorted and sculpted **Trees of Mystery** (daily: summer 8am–8pm; winter 9am–5pm; $12), except the impressive **Cathedral Tree**, where nine trees have grown from one root structure to form a spooky circle. The *HI-Redwood National Park* **hostel** (☎707/482-8265, 🕸www.norcalhostels.org; ❶) on US-101 has dorm beds from $16 to $19.

The park headquarters are in **CRESCENT CITY** at 1111 Second St (daily 9am–5pm; ☎707/464-6101), but you can pick up information all over the park. There are **campgrounds** everywhere; three that have showers and water are *Prairie Creek* on US-101, *Mill Creek*, five miles south of Crescent City, and *Jedediah Smith*, eight miles north of Crescent City on the Smith River. If you must come in summer, make reservations through PARKNET (☎1-800/444-7275), and if things get really desperate, head up US-101 and look for **motels** around Crescent City.

The northern interior

The remote **northern interior** of California, cut off from the coast by the **Shasta Cascade** range and dominated by forests, lakes, and mountains, is largely uninhabited and infrequently visited. Interstate 5 leads through the heart of this near-wilderness, forging straight through the unspectacular farmland of **Sacramento Valley** to **Redding** – the region's only buses follow this route. Redding isn't much of a place in itself, but it's a good base for the **Whiskeytown-Shasta-Trinity area** and the more demanding **Lassen National Volcanic Park**. Mountaineers and the spiritually-minded flock to **Mount Shasta**, which is close enough to the volcanic **Lava Beds** at the very northeastern tip of the state for them to be a long but feasible day's car trip.

Chico

Charming little **CHICO**, about midway between Sacramento and Redding, some twenty miles east of I-5, is a good stopoff if you don't want to attempt to cover the whole valley from top to bottom in one day, or if you're here to visit Lassen Volcanic National Park (see opposite) and need somewhere to stay. Home to **Chico State University**, the laid-back town is loved by mountain bikers for its many trails. Cheap rooms downtown can be found at the *Holiday Inn*, 685 Manzanita Court (T530/345-2491 or 1-800/310-2491; ❸–❹), and there are several good restaurants, notably *La Hacienda Inn*, 2635 Esplanade (T530/893-8270), a Mexican spot famed for its special pink sauce, known as "Heroin Sauce" for its addictive sweet flavor.

Redding and Shasta

A sprawling expanse of chain stores with a shopping mall at its heart and a poured-concrete convention center at its gate, **REDDING** appears to be an anomaly amidst the natural splendor of the northern interior. The region's largest city, with 70,000 people, it has acted as a northern nexus since the late nineteenth century, when the Central Pacific Railroad came through. Today it remains a crossroads, bulging with cookie-cutter motels and diners. If you have a car and need **to stay**, try the *Best Western Hilltop Inn*, 2300 Hilltop Drive (T530/221-6100 or 1-800/336-4880; ❹–❻); the *Deluxe Inn*, 1135 Market St (T530/243-5141; ❷–❸), is slightly less luxurious but close to the Greyhound station.

SHASTA, six miles west of Redding and not to be confused with Mount Shasta, is more appealing, though barely. The row of half-ruined brick buildings here was once a booming gold-mining town, literally at the end of the road from San Francisco and on the very edge of the wilderness. The **Courthouse** has been turned into a museum (Wed–Sun 10am–5pm; $2), full of historical California artwork and mining paraphernalia, while the gallows and prison cells are a grim reminder of the daily executions that went on here.

From Shasta, precipitous Hwy-299 climbs into the **Whiskeytown-Shasta-Trinity National Recreation Area**, which has artificial beaches, forests, and camping facilities at three lakes – Trinity, Whiskeytown, and Shasta. Sadly, during summer it's completely congested, as windsurfers, motorboats, jet skis, and recreational vehicles block the narrow routes that serve the lakes. An extensive system of tunnels, dams, and aqueducts directs the plentiful waters of the Sacramento River in to California's Central Valley to irrigate cash crops. The lakes are pretty enough, but residents complain they're not a patch on the wild waters that used to flow from the mountains before the Central Valley Project came along in the 1960s.

Lassen Volcanic National Park

About fifty miles over gently-sloping plains east from Red Bluff on Hwy-36, or forty miles east from Redding on Hwy-44, the 106,000 acres that make up the pine forests, crystal-green lakes, and boiling thermal pools of the **LASSEN VOLCANIC NATIONAL PARK** are one of the most unearthly parts of northern California's forbidding climate, which brings up to fifty feet of snow-fall each year, keeping the area pretty much uninhabited outside the brief summer season. **Mount Lassen** itself last erupted in 1915, when the peak blew an enormous mushroom cloud some seven miles skyward, tearing the summit into chunks that landed as far away as Reno; scientists predict that it is the likeliest of all the West Coast volcanoes to blow again.

The thirty-mile tour of the park along Hwy-89 from **Manzanita Lake** in the north should take no more than a few hours. There is a $10 access fee per vehicle to the park. The Mount Lassen explosion denuded the devastated area, ripping out every tree and patch of grass. Slowly the earth is recovering a green blanket, but the most vivid impression is one of complete destruction. Marking the halfway point, **Summit Lake** is a busy camping area set around a beautiful icy lake, close to which are the park's most manageable hiking trails. From a parking area to the south (8000ft up), the steep, five-mile ascent to Lassen Peak begins. Experienced hikers can do it in four hours, but wilderness seekers will have a better time pushing east to the steep trails of the **Juniper Lake** area.

Continuing south along Hwy-89, Lassen's indisputable show-stealers are **Bumpass Hell** and **Emerald Lake**, the former (named for a man who lost a leg trying to cross it) a steaming valley of active pools and vents that bubble away at a low rumble all around. The trails are sturdy and easy to manage, but you should never venture off them. The crusts over the thermal features are often brittle, and breaking through could plunge you into very hot water. Before leaving the park at **Mineral**, make an effort to stop at **Sulphur Works**, an acrid cauldron of steam vents. A magnificent but grueling trail leads for a mile around the site to the avalanche-prone summit at **Diamond Peak**, which affords great views over the entire park and forestland beyond.

The Park Service has its **headquarters** in Mineral (Mon–Fri 8am–4.30pm; PO Box 100, Mineral, CA 96063; ☎530/595-4444, ⊛www.nps.gov/lavo), where you can get free maps and information (there's a box outside when it's closed, and they'll leave your backcountry permits here if you arrive late), including the *Lassen Park Guide*. Another **visitor center** (summer daily 9am–5pm; ☎530/595-4444 ext 5180) is at Manzanita Lake, just inside the northern entrance, and includes the Loomis Museum, which documents the park's eruption cycle.

Mount Shasta City and Mount Shasta

Roughly sixty miles north of Redding, a scenic road branches off I-5 to the tiny town that describes itself as "the best kept secret in California": **MOUNT SHASTA CITY**, hard under the enormous bulk of the 14,162ft **Mount Shasta**. Still considered active despite not having erupted for two hundred years, this lone peak dominates the landscape for a hundred miles around, and its "energies" attract New Agers by the score. If you want to climb to the summit (10hr; crampons and ice axe needed most of the year), or simply to explore the flanks of the mountain along the many trails, you must obtain a free permit from the **ranger district office**, 204 W Alma St (April–Oct Mon–Sat 8am–4.30pm; rest of year Mon–Fri 8am–4.30pm; ☎530/926-4511), or you can self-issue one at the main trailheads.

Greyhound **buses** on the Redding–Oregon run stop on N Mount Shasta Boulevard, a couple of blocks from the **Chamber of Commerce**, 300 Pine St (daily: summer 9am–5.30pm, winter 10am–4pm; ☎530/926-3696 or 1-800/926-4865, ⓦwww.mtshastachamber.com). There's budget **accommodation** at the excellent *Alpenrose Cottage Guest House*, 204 E Hinkley St (☎530/926-6724, ⓦwww.snowcrest.net/alpenrose; ❶–❸), and the *Best Western Tree House Motor Inn*, 111 Morgan Way (☎1-800/545-7164 or 530/926-3101; ❹–❺). Nicer still, the *McCloud Hotel Bed & Breakfast*, 408 Main St, McCloud (☎530/964-2822 or 1-800/964-2823, ⓦwww.mchotel.com), has rooms with Jacuzzis (❻–❼) and without (❹–❺). *Lake Siskiyou Campground* (☎530/926-2618) is four miles west of town and the most picturesque in the area.

Some of the town's best **meals** can be found at *Lily's*, 1013 S Mount Shasta Blvd (☎530/926-3372), which serves Mexican fare, prime rib, and, surprisingly, a wide range of vegetarian dishes and big Sunday brunches. For Italian cuisine and cocktails, head for *Mike and Tony's*, 501 S Mount Shasta Blvd (☎530/926-4792). Breakfast, or bagels any time, can be found at the *Bagel Café and Bakery*, a favorite with Mount Shasta's spiritual community at 315 N Mount Shasta Blvd (☎530/926-1414).

Lava Beds National Monument

Lava Beds National Monument ($10 per vehicle for seven days), in the far northeastern corner of the state, is one of the most remote and beautiful of California's parks, and also one of its most interesting. The history of these volcanic caves and huge black lava flows is as violent as the natural forces that created them. Before the Gold Rush the area was home to the **Modoc** Indians, but repeated and bloody confrontations with miners led the government to order them into a reservation shared with the Klamath, their traditional enemy. After only a few months the Modocs drifted back to the isolation of the lava beds, and in 1872 the army was sent in. Fifty-five Modoc warriors, under the leadership of "Captain Jack," held back an army ten times the size of theirs for five months from a natural fortress of passageways now known as **Captain Jack's Stronghold**, at the park's northern tip. You can retrace the conflict and read scathing editorials from national papers condemning the US Army over its mission, through well-detailed self-guided trails in the park and informative exhibits at the **visitor center** (daily: summer 8am–6pm; rest of year 8am–5pm; ☎530/667-2282, ⓦwww.nps.gov/labe).

The bulk of the lava tube caves are close to the visitor center from where you can take the free ranger-led tours (daily 2pm) or, with some nerve and a good light source (free loaner flashlights from the visitor center), explore the caves alone. You can camp near the visitor center, but there are no shops nearby, so bring everything you need with you. Nearby is the **Modoc Ranger Station** (Mon–Fri 8am–5pm; ☎530/233-5811), which has general information on the Modoc National Forest. North and west of the Lava Beds region, the **Klamath Basin National Wildlife Refuge** ($3 permit needed; self-issuing boxes on premises) hosts millions of birds migrating along the Pacific Flyway. The **visitor center** (Mon–Fri 8am–4.30pm, Sat & Sun 10am–4pm; ☎530/667-2231) is off Hill Road near the northwest entrance for the Lava Beds. Surprisingly, the best way of spotting the wildlife is by driving along designated routes; getting out of the car and walking scares the birds off.

The Pacific Northwest

AL - ALABAMA	IN - INDIANA	MN - MINNESOTA	RI - RHODE ISLAND
AR - ARKANSAS	LA - LOUISIANA	MS - MISSISSIPPI	SC - SOUTH CAROLINA
CT - CONNECTICUT	MA - MASSACHUSETTS	NC - NORTH CAROLINA	VA - VIRGINIA
DE - DELAWARE	MD - MARYLAND	NH - NEW HAMPSHIRE	VT - VERMONT
FL - FLORIDA	ME - MAINE	NJ - NEW JERSEY	WI - WISCONSIN
IL - ILLINOIS	MI - MICHIGAN	PA - PENNSYLVANIA	WV - WEST VIRGINIA

CHAPTER 14

Highlights

* **Pike Place Market, Seattle, WA** Seattle's lively urban market holds an array of fine restaurants, seafood and produce vendors, and street entertainers. See p.1236

* **Port Townsend, WA** A charming Victorian town on the Olympic Peninsula, whose gingerbread homes and waterside vistas make for lovely picture postcards. See p.1252

* **Quinault Rainforest, WA** Sublime hiking trails meander through this dense lakeside forest in Olympic National Park. See p.1258

* **Mount St Helens, WA** Still a haunting sight two decades after it blew its top, the most renowned volcano in the continental US. See p.1262

* **Sandcastle competition, OR** An annual summertime eruption of seaside sculpture and local color, held in the always-popular burg of Cannon Beach. See p.1285

* **Crater Lake, OR** Cradled in what's left of a hollowed-out volcano, this sheer blue lake makes a stunning year-round destination. See p.1289

* **Hells Canyon, OR** Even deeper than the Grand Canyon, this remote gorge boasts excellent white-water rafting on the Snake River. See p.1293

The Pacific Northwest

The **PACIFIC NORTHWEST** states of **Washington** and **Oregon**, while similar in climate, topography, and liberal politics, are quite different in their attitudes toward growth and expansion. Washington's sprawling development, bustling military bases, and notorious freeway gridlock contrast dramatically with Oregon's lower-scaled design and more easygoing temperament, thanks in no small measure to its stringent land-use laws and "urban-growth boundaries" around its larger cities.

Significantly cooler than California to the south, both are split by the great north–south spine of the **Cascade Mountains**, with their western sides more appealing by far. Throughout this hilly western terrain, regular rainfall and a moist climate have created a verdant landscape, thick with woodlands that on the **Olympic Peninsula** have become small rainforests. Not surprisingly, this fertile land is where the region's population is most heavily concentrated, yet much of it remains remarkably pristine – especially in Oregon – scattered with remote, rugged beaches. Both **Seattle** and **Portland** lie roughly fifty miles from the Pacific Ocean along the I-5 freeway, running from Canada to California. Seattle, the commercial and cultural capital of the Northwest, is a major port perched on the edge of the beautiful, island-strewn **Puget Sound**, with numerous ferries darting among the container traffic. Portland lies adjacent to the rich farmlands of the Willamette Valley, long the historic heartland of Oregon.

Across the Cascades, the land to the **east** is far drier and less hospitable, peppered with desert and scrubland, much of which is prone to drought and periodic wildfires, which have become increasingly common in recent years. Of the towns, only **Spokane** in Washington is of any appreciable size, though Oregon's booming resort town of **Bend** is a far more appealing destination, as its Cascade-straddling location makes it a useful base for sampling the mountains, desert, and especially the beautiful **Columbia River Gorge** to the north. Of outstanding interest also is the scarred territory between Seattle and Portland around **Mount St Helens**, which erupted with devastating effect in 1980.

Some history

The **first inhabitants** of the Pacific Northwest may have reached the continent across a land bridge over what is now the Bering Strait between Siberia and Alaska, from 12,000 to 20,000 years ago near the end of the last Ice Age.

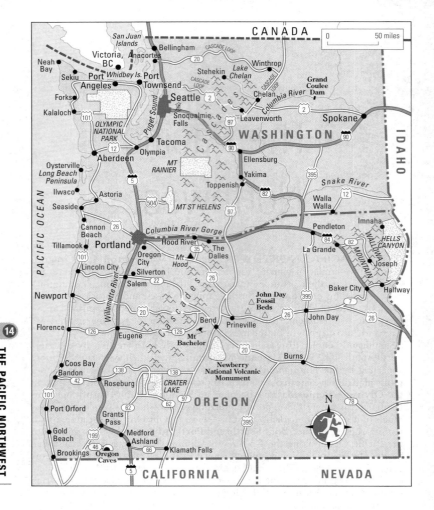

It wasn't until the early nineteenth century that was there a significant white presence in the region, though the newcomers were initially very much confined to trading and exploration along the coast rather than to making permanent settlements.

By that time, Russian trappers had begun to make their way down from the north, and Canadians from the northeast, while European sea captains such as James Cook and George Vancouver came in search of the fabled **Northwest Passage**, an ice-free route between the Atlantic and the Pacific. A brief period of hectic competition, in which entrepreneurs of many nationalities vied for fur-trading profits, came to an end only when the whole coast was all but "trapped out." Explorers Meriwether Lewis and William Clark, who reached the Oregon coast near present-day Astoria in 1804, were the first whites to cross the interior of the continent, and within forty years American settlers were streaming in along the **Oregon Trail**. This legendary period of immigration gave de facto control of the region to the United States, and official title followed in 1846 with the signing of a land pact with Britain that established a territorial boundary for the US and Canada at the 49th Parallel. In 1859 Oregon became the second **American state** west of the Great Plains (after California), while thirty more years passed before Washington entered the Union.

Around that time, railroads stretching westward reached Portland and Seattle, and Chief Joseph of the Nez Percé made his last bid on behalf of displaced native tribes (see p.961). Oregon and Washington began their economic ascent, aided by timber sales and, in the case of Seattle, the booming trade supplying prospectors on their way to Alaska's Klondike Gold Rush. Later decades would see the rise and fall of the lumber market and the aerospace industry, and, most recently, the near-collapse of the **high-tech sector**, from which the region still hasn't recovered. As of 2003, the Pacific Northwest remains the most economically depressed part of the US, with the nation's highest unemployment rate.

Washington

Although **Seattle** is one of America's most likeable and vibrant cities, well worth a few days of your time, perhaps its greatest asset is its proximity to the glorious scenery of **Puget Sound**, the deep-water channel around which much of the population of **western Washington** lives. Some of the islands here serve as stepping stones to the **Olympic Peninsula** to the west, whose mountains are home to rare elk and lush vegetation that merges into rainforest, and whose rustic beaches have remained pristine for centuries. Dazzling **Olympic National Park** occupies the bulk of the peninsula, and a hike along one of its clearly laid-out trails is a definite highlight of any trip. Wet, often stormy **weather** is almost sure to set the backdrop for many an outdoor pursuit in western Washington, but its hold on the area is not complete – warm temperatures and blue skies reign during the summer.

Not quite as rainy as the mountains to the northeast, the **southern coast** is flatter and more accessible but not as appealing, littered with workaday towns and would-be resorts. The nearest real attraction lies a few hours east, where you can marvel at the eye-opening volcanic scenery of **Mount St Helens**.

Dry and desolate, the sprawling prairie-plateau that makes up most of **eastern Washington** is a long, slow grind with little of interest, though if a cross-country trek takes you through **Spokane**, the **Grand Coulee Dam** is worth a detour. Otherwise you're only likely to come out here if you're traveling the Cascade loop, a memorable four-hundred-mile roundtrip drive through the stunning **Cascade Mountains**.

Getting around Washington

Seattle is well served by both **trains** and **buses**. Amtrak runs its *Coast Starlight* train once daily south to Portland and LA, while its *Cascades* line runs four times per day south to Eugene, Oregon, and north to Vancouver in British

Columbia. Amtrak's daily *Empire Builder* route heads east (to Chicago), just as Greyhound provides bus service east across the Cascades to **Spokane** and beyond, with other routes to Wenatchee (for Chelan), Ellensburg, Yakima, and Walla Walla. Areas not covered by Greyhound are usually accessible on local buses, though this can be time-consuming and inconvenient.

Getting to and along the coast is more difficult and requires some planning. **Ferries** from Seattle shuttle across to Winslow on **Bainbridge Island**, from where Kitsap Transit services (☏360/373-2877 or 1-800/501-RIDE, ⓦwww.kitsaptransit.org) link with Jefferson Transit for bus access to Port Angeles, Port Townsend, and Olympic National Park. In the Seattle and Puget Sound area, ferries (mostly run by Washington State Ferries; Washington ☏206/464-6400 or 1-800/84-FERRY, British Columbia ☏250/381-1551, ⓦwww.wsdot.wa.gov/ferries) are a reliable and enjoyable method of getting to such places as **Whidbey Island** and the **San Juan Islands**. There are also long-distance services to Canada from Seattle, Anacortes, and Port Angeles, and to Alaska from **Bellingham**; see p.1251.

Seattle

Located on the shore of sparkling Elliott Bay, with attractive Lake Washington behind and the snowy peak of Mount Rainier in the distance, **SEATTLE** has a magnificent setting, its modern skyline of glass skyscrapers gleaming across the bay as an emblem of three decades of aggressive urban renewal. The most prominent city in the Pacific Northwest – or anywhere north of San Francisco and west of Denver for that matter – it's more than just an isolated outpost on the edge of the US, but rather an appealing destination in its own right, loaded with friendly charm and a slew of funky coffeehouses, good restaurants, and engaging clubs.

Seattle's beginnings were inauspiciously muddy. Flooded out of its first location on Alki Point in what is now the suburb of West Seattle, in the 1850s the town shifted to the present location of Pioneer Square, renaming itself after the Native American Chief Sealth, who helped reduce violent tensions between whites and local indigenous peoples. As the surrounding forest was gradually felled and the lumber shipped out, Seattle grew slowly until the Klondike Gold Rush of 1897 put it firmly on the national map. World War I boosted shipbuilding, and the city was soon a large industrial center. Trade unions, based around shipworkers, grew strong, and the Industrial Workers of the World, or "Wobblies," coordinated the US's first general strike here on February 6, 1919.

Since the beginning of the twentieth century, the **Boeing** corporation has been crucial to the city's economic strength, booming during World War II and employing one in five of Seattle's workforce by the 1960s. The prosperity that Boeing and more recent success stories such as **Microsoft** and Internet shopping giant **Amazon.com** brought the city was obvious, reflected in an explosion of upscale restaurants, glossy museums, and well-funded cultural institutions – to the point where Seattle attracted scads of fresh arrivals and experienced both exponential growth and increasingly nightmarish traffic jams. Still, just as the violent 1999 WTO protests and a February 2001 **earthquake** shook Seattle's foundations, so too did the concomitant demise of the frenzied local high-tech scene, with countless upstart firms going **bankrupt** and much downtown office space emptying out. Within just a few years, the city had gone from a national marvel of new-economy vigor to a depressed symbol of the failures of the bubble economy.

Despite Seattle's rollercoaster economy, its more established neighborhoods remain distinctive, and it has a pleasantly down-to-earth ambiance. Moreover, with the continuing struggles of local businesses, visitors are apt to find many good deals in accommodation, dining, and package sightseeing tours.

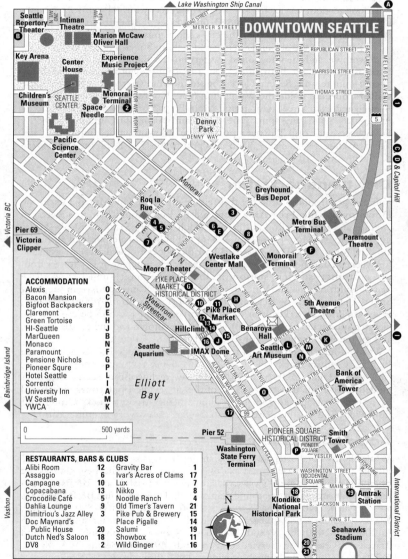

Lake Washington Ship Canal

DOWNTOWN SEATTLE

Seattle Repertory Theater

Intiman Theatre

Marion McCaw Oliver Hall

Key Arena

Center House

Experience Music Project

Children's Museum

SEATTLE CENTER

Space Needle

Monorail Terminal

Pacific Science Center

Denny Park

Roq la Rue

Greyhound Bus Depot

Metro Bus Terminal

Paramount Theatre

Monorail

Pier 69

Victoria Clipper

Moore Theater

Westlake Center Mall

Monorail Terminal

PIKE PLACE MARKET HISTORICAL DISTRICT

Waterfront Streetcar

Pike Place Market

5th Avenue Theatre

Hillclimb

Benaroya Hall

Seattle Aquarium

IMAX Dome

Seattle Art Museum

Bank of America Tower

Elliott Bay

Pier 52

Washington State Ferry Terminal

PIONEER SQUARE HISTORICAL DISTRICT

Smith Tower

Klondike National Historical Park

Amtrak Station

Seahawks Stadium

ACCOMMODATION

Alexis	O
Bacon Mansion	C
Bigfoot Backpackers	D
Claremont	E
Green Tortoise	H
HI-Seattle	J
MarQueen	B
Monaco	N
Paramount	F
Pensione Nichols	G
Pioneer Squre	P
Hotel Seattle	L
Sorrento	I
University Inn	A
W Seattle	M
YWCA	K

RESTAURANTS, BARS & CLUBS

Alibi Room	12	Gravity Bar	1
Assaggio	6	Ivar's Acres of Clams	17
Campagne	10	Lux	7
Copacabana	13	Nikko	8
Crocodile Café	5	Noodle Ranch	4
Dahlia Lounge	9	Old Timer's Tavern	21
Dimitriou's Jazz Alley	3	Pike Pub & Brewery	15
Doc Maynard's		Place Pigalle	14
Public House	20	Salumi	19
Dutch Ned's Saloon	18	Showbox	11
DV8	2	Wild Ginger	16

0   500 yards

N

Safeco Field & Museum of Flight & Airport

Arrival and information

Flights land at **Sea-Tac Airport** (☎1-800/544-1965, ⊛www.portseattle
.org/seatac), fourteen miles south of downtown Seattle. Outside, the Gray Line
Airport Express bus (5.20am–11.20pm every 30min; $8.50 one way, $15
roundtrip; ☎206/626-6088, ⊛www.graylineofseattle.com) provides a 25-
minute journey to downtown hotels. ShuttleExpress (daily 4am–midnight;
☎206/622-1424 or 1-800/487-RIDE, ⊛www.shuttleexpress.com) offers one-
way, door-to-door service for $21. Metro express city bus #194 ($1.25, $2 dur-
ing peak hours Mon–Fri 6–9am & 3–6pm) takes 35 minutes to reach downtown's Transit Tunnel. A **taxi** to the city center costs $30–35.

   The Amtrak station at Third Avenue and Jackson Street, a dozen blocks south
of downtown, and the Greyhound bus terminal, at Eighth Avenue and Stewart
Street to the east, are both an easy bus ride from downtown, or a fifteen-to-
twenty-minute walk. Several blocks towards downtown from Greyhound is the
visitors bureau, inside the Washington State Convention Center at Seventh
Avenue and Pike Street (year-round Mon–Fri 8.30am–5pm, additional hours
April–Oct Sat 10am–4pm, June–Aug Sun 10am–4pm; ☎206/461-8304,
⊛www.seeseattle.org). The main **post office** is downtown at Union Street and
Third Avenue (Mon–Fri 7.30am–5.30pm; ☎206/748-5417 or 1-800/275-
8777; zip code 98101).

City transportation

You can get around Seattle for **free** either on foot or by **Metro bus** in the
Downtown Ride Free Area, bordered by Jackson and Battery streets, 6th
Avenue, and the waterfront. Otherwise, adult fares are $1.25, or $1.50–2 during peak hours (Mon–Fri 6–9am & 3–6pm); kids' fares are 50¢, and all tickets
are valid for an hour. **Day-passes** ($2.50; bought from the driver) are available
for weekend and holiday travel; during the week, purchase passes for $5 from
the **customer service station** in the Metro Transit Tunnel at Westlake
Station, Fifth Avenue and Vine Street (Mon–Fri 9.30am–5pm), or in the King
Street Center, 201 S Jackson St (Mon–Fri 8am–5pm; ☎206/553-3000,
⊛www.metrokc.gov/kcdot or transit.metrokc.gov). Passes can be used on the
elevated monorail ($3, kids $1.50) between downtown and the Seattle Center,
and on the waterfront streetcar ($1.25 off-peak, $1.50 peak).

   Washington State **ferries** run to Vashon and Bainbridge islands; tickets from
Pier 52, Colman Dock ($5–10; ☎206/464-6400, ⊛www.wsdot.wa.gov/fer-
ries). Gray Line (☎206/626-5208, ⊛www.graylineofseattle.com) organizes
guided three-hour **bus tours** ($29) of the city, while **boat tours** are offered
by several local operators, the best choice being Argosy's Locks Cruise tour
from Pier 57 (2 1/2 hrs; $30; ☎206/623-4252, ⊛www.argosycruises.com).

Accommodation

While there's no shortage of **hotels** in Seattle, it can be difficult to find the
middle ground between smart places and seedy dives. The best choices are
often downtown. Also of good value are the city's **hostels** and **B&Bs**, the latter of which are abundant around Capitol Hill. Three specialist **B&B agencies**
are A Pacific Reservation Service (☎206/439-7677 or 1-800/684-2932,
⊛www.seattlebedandbreakfast.com), Seattle Bed and Breakfast Association
(☎206/547-1020 or 1-800/348-5630, ⊛www.seattlebandbs.com), and
Travelers' Reservation Service (14716 26th Ave NE, Seattle, WA 98155;
☎206/364-5900), all of which provide lodging throughout the state.

Hotels, motels, and B&Bs

Alexis 1007 1st Ave, downtown ☏ 206/624-4844 or 1-800/426-7033, ⓦ www.alexishotel.com. Renovated old hotel between Pike Place Market and Pioneer Square. Has hot tubs and fireplaces, an Aveda spa, fitness center, and cigar bar. Nearly half the rooms are suites. ❽

Bacon Mansion 959 Broadway E, Capitol Hill ☏ 206/329-1864 or 1-800/240-1864, ⓦ www.baconmansion.com. Eleven elegant rooms and spacious suites, just north of Broadway's main drag. The least expensive rooms are fairly cheap for the area, although the price doubles at the high end. Two-night minimum stay on weekends. ❹

Claremont 2000 4th Ave, Belltown ☏ 206/448-8600 or 1-800/448-8601, ⓦ www.claremonthotel.com. An intimate, European-style hotel in downtown Seattle, with weekend rates for basic rooms significantly lower than weekday rates for suites. Complimentary continental breakfast included. ❻

Hotel Seattle 315 Seneca St, downtown ☏ 206/623-5110. Basic, clean rooms in a central location near the Seattle Art Museum, with modern, but not antiseptic, ambiance. ❹

MarQueen 600 Queen Ave N, Seattle Center ☏ 206/282-7407 or 1-800/445-3076, ⓦ www.marqueen.com. Refurbished 1918 building with 56 rooms and suites, period antiques, and amenities like hardwood floors, kitchenettes, microwaves, and fridges, as well as an onsite spa. ❻

Monaco 1101 4th Ave, downtown ☏ 206/621-1770 or 1-800/715-6513, ⓦ www.monaco-seattle.com. Luxurious boutique hotel with bland exterior, but a striking lobby, fitness center, and elegant suites with CD players and fax machines – some with Jacuzzis as well. ❽

Paramount 724 Pine St, downtown ☏ 206/292-9500, ⓦ www.westcoasthotels.com/paramount. Luxury chain hotel with impressive European-styled exterior, though somewhat unexciting rooms, given the steep rates. Some suites have hot tubs, though. ❽

Pensione Nichols 1923 1st Ave, Belltown ☏ 206/441-7125, ⓦ www.seattle-bed-breakfast.com. Classy little B&B that's a great deal for the area, with small but clean rooms, shared baths, and simple, tasteful decor in a classic 1904 building. Suites with kitchenettes add about $75 to the total, but they can be shared by four people. ❺

Pioneer Square 77 Yesler Way, Pioneer Square ☏ 206/340-1234, ⓦ www.pioneersquare.com. Restored 1914 brick hotel built by Seattle pioneer Henry Yesler, and one of the few good mid-price establishments with adequate comfort. Saloon and juice bar on the lobby floor. ❻

Sorrento 900 Madison St, First Hill ☏ 206/622-4400 or 1-800/426-1265, ⓦ www.hotelsorrento.com. Modernized, 76-room edifice with a European flair, stylish decor, and posh onsite restaurant, on the east side of I-5 from downtown. The regal exterior surrounds a circular courtyard with palm trees. ❾

University Inn 4140 Roosevelt Way NE, University District ☏ 206/632-5055 or 1-800/733-3855, ⓦ www.universityinnseattle.com. Business-oriented hotel off University Way. Some rooms have kitchens, all have complimentary breakfast; there's also an onsite pool and spa. ❺

W Seattle 1112 4th Ave, downtown ☏ 206/264-6000, ⓦ www.whotels.com. Stylish modern tower with a staff of beautiful people and smart, cozy rooms. An even better draw is the ambiance: there's a chic lobby bar with often-packed "cocktail couches" downstairs. ❾

Hostels

Bigfoot Backpackers 126 Broadway Ave E, Capitol Hill ☏ 206/720-2965 or 1-800/600-2965. Reached via an alley near the busiest corner in the area, with 45 beds, including dorms ($17) and a few private rooms ($35 single, $45 double). No curfew and lots of extras: free breakfast, downtown pickup, Internet access, and parking. ❶–❷

Green Tortoise 1525 2nd Ave, between Pike and Pine, downtown ☏ 206/340-1222 or 1-888/424-6783, ⓦ www.greentortoise.net. Old-style hotel digs now functioning as a hostel, with four-to-a-room dorms ($21) and some private doubles ($42). Free breakfast, Internet access, and pickups at Amtrak, Greyhound, or ferries. ❶–❷

HI-Seattle 84 Union St, behind Pike Place Market, downtown ☏ 206/622-5443 or 1-888/662-5443, ⓦ www.hiseattle.org. Modern and well-equipped hostel popular with families. Dorm rooms start at $25, while hotel-styled private rooms cost up to $100. Open 24hr. Reservations strongly advised in summer. ❶–❹

YWCA 1118 5th Ave, downtown ☏ 206/461-4888, ⓦ www.ywcaworks.org. Functional accommodation open to women only; a safe and clean choice for visitors on a budget, for $35–60. The higher-priced rooms include a private bath. ❷–❸

The City

Nicely located as the hub of the metropolis, downtown Seattle sits alongside the curve of Elliott Bay just off the I-5 freeway. Crowded with plenty of hotels, restaurants, and attractions, it's the obvious starting point on any trip around the city. The favorite downtown draw for many locals and tourists alike is **Pike Place Market** and its lively array of stalls and cafés, while further south, the nineteenth-century center of **Pioneer Square** is lined with popular bars and clubs. A bit to the west, a stroll along the somewhat touristy **waterfront** rewards you with fabulous views of the bay, while at the **Seattle Center** in the north, the **Space Needle** presides over cultural institutions and carnival rides, as well as the ever-popular **Experience Music Project**. Several outlying districts are often livelier than downtown: **Capitol Hill**'s cafés and bars are the heart of the city's hipster and gay scene, and the **University District** is a student area with inexpensive cafés and uptempo nightlife.

Pike Place Market and the Seattle Art Museum

Centrally located at Pike Street and First Avenue, **Pike Place Market** (daily Mon–Sat 9am–6pm, Sun 11am–5pm; ☎206/682-7453, ⓦwww.pikeplacemarket.org) is the oldest continuous working public market in the US. Farmers first brought their produce here in 1907, lowering food prices by selling straight from the barrow. The market prospered during the Depression, but by the 1960s it was shabby and neglected, and the authorities decided to flatten it altogether. After vigorous protests, Seattlites voted overwhelmingly to preserve its original character, while also making it the affordable domain of the elderly and poor. The restoration has been highly successful: the whole place, stretched over several city blocks, bustles with energy, and a real attempt has been made to keep it true to its roots. There's plenty to enjoy, with street entertainers playing to busy crowds, the aroma of organic coffee drifting from cafés, and stalls offering piles of lobsters, crabs, salmon, vegetables, fruit, and flowers. Further inside, handmade jewelry, woodcarvings, and silk-screen prints are on sale, while small shops close by stock a massive range of ethnic foods.

Just down the road, the **Seattle Art Museum**, 100 University St and First Ave (Tues–Sun 10am–5pm, Thurs open until 9pm; $10, ticket includes entry to the Seattle Asian Art Museum; free first Thurs of month; ⓦwww.seattleartmuseum.org), occupies a Robert Venturi–designed building – noteworthy for its giant engraved letters – and features international touring exhibitions and eclectic collections of African, Pacific, and Native American work, with a more limited selection of modern art. Outside the main entrance is the 48ft "**Hammering Man**," a kinetic sculpture by Jonathan Borofsky, which has become the museum's enigmatic emblem.

The Business District

Between Second and Seventh avenues, most of downtown is given over to the steel-and-glass office towers of Seattle's **Business District**. A handful of sights provide interesting diversions to those with a little time on their hands; foremost among them – at least for tourists – is **Westlake Center**, 400 Pine St (daily 10am–9pm), a giant, multi-story enclosed mall that is most notable as the southern terminus of the 1.3-mile **monorail** (Mon–Fri 7.30am–11pm, Sat & Sun 9am–11pm; one-way fare $3, kids $1.50; ⓦwww.seattlemonorail.com), a holdover from the 1962 Seattle World's Fair that still connects to the Seattle Center and provides the city with one of its prime emblems. Further south, the darkly looming **Bank of America Tower** (nicknamed "the BOAT"), 701

Fifth Ave, has three concave walls that give the structure an oddly curving silhouette. At nearly a thousand feet high, it's the biggest building west of the Mississippi River by number of stories (76), though not the tallest overall (LA's Library Tower owns that distinction). Head to the 73rd-floor **observation deck** (Mon–Fri 8.30am–4.30pm; $5, kids $3) for a predictably good panoramic view of the surrounding area.

The waterfront
Continuing west from Pike Place Market, stairs in the complex lead down to the steep staircase of the **Hillclimb**, in turn conveying foot traffic to the **waterfront** below. Almost opposite the stairway, **Pier 59**, an old wooden jetty that once served tall ships, now houses the underwater viewing dome of the **Seattle Aquarium** (daily June–Aug 10am–7pm, rest of year 10am–5pm; $11, kids $7; Ⓦwww.seattleaquarium.org), with around four hundred species of fish, birds, plants, and marine mammals, and boasting a reasonably spacious and easily navigable layout, part of which is actually outdoors near the shoreline. A combined ticket admits you to the 3-D **IMAX Dome** next door (daily starting at 10am; $7, $2 for each additional movie; ℡206/622-1868, Ⓦwww .seattleimaxdome.com), where 70mm films on the huge curved screen include the always-popular *Eruption of Mount St Helens*. On Pier 54 to the south, the most famous of the waterfront's fish-and-chip stands, **Ivar's Acres of Clams** (℡206/624-6852, Ⓦwww.ivars.net), has its own special stop ("Clam Central Station") on the restored vintage **waterfront streetcar** (daily 6.30am–7pm; $1.25, $1.50 peak, seniors 25¢, kids 50¢), which links Pioneer Square and the train station with Pier 70, mostly following the waterline. Along the way, **Colman Dock** at Pier 52 is the terminal for Washington State Ferries (see p.1234).

Pioneer Square and around
A few blocks inland from the ferry terminal, **Pioneer Square** is Seattle's oldest district, though it was nearly destroyed in the 1960s; it has since been renovated with appealing bookshops and galleries, adding a bit of sophistication to the old red-brick and wrought-iron buildings. Things get more raucous at night, when rock and jazz boom out from the taverns and panhandlers become more aggressive.

By far the most interesting way to find out about the city's seamy past is on a 90-minute **Underground Tour** from *Doc Maynard's* tavern, 610 First Ave (daily on the hour 11am–4pm or 6pm; $9, kids $5; ℡206/682-4646, Ⓦwww.undergroundtour.com), which details how, after a disastrous 1889 fire, this area was rebuilt with the street level raised by one story, so what used to be storefronts are now underground, linked by subterranean passageways. One block east, on the edge of Pioneer Square, the 1914 white-terracotta **Smith Tower**, 506 Second Ave, was the city's first skyscraper, as well as its longtime visual icon – until the Space Needle appeared in the 1960s to become the city's main postcard symbol. These days, it's best for the prime views from its 35th-floor **observation deck** (Sat & Sun 11am–4pm; $5).

A couple blocks south at 117 S Main St, **Klondike Gold Rush National Historical Park** (daily 9am–5pm; free; Ⓦwww.nps.gov/klse) houses a small museum celebrating the days when, thanks to a formidable campaign to promote Seattle as the gateway to Alaskan gold, prospectors streamed in and traders – and con artists – made their fortunes. The dog population fared less well as many a hapless mutt was harnessed to a sledge so that gold-seekers could practice "mushing" up and down Seattle's streets before facing Alaskan snow. Just as interesting, the nearby cobblestoned square of **Occidental Park**, between Main and Washington streets at Occidental, holds four totem poles carved with mythical creatures from Northwest native legends.

A few blocks south of Pioneer Square, professional football fans can check out a Seahawks game at **Seahawks Stadium**, 800 Occidental Ave S (☎1-888/635-4295, ⓦwww.seahawks.com), while major league baseball enthusiasts can visit **Safeco Field**, further south at First Avenue and Atlantic Street, to watch the Mariners (☎206/346-4001, ⓦwww.mariners.mlb.com).

Belltown

Just to the north of Pike Street Market and extending one mile towards the Seattle Center, the chic **Belltown** area (also referred to as the Denny Regrade) has left its alternative legacy behind and is now choked with yuppie-friendly cafés, vintage clothing stores, and assorted galleries, centered around the five-block area of Second Avenue between Lenora and Battery. Although the godfather of the early-1990s grunge scene, **Sub Pop Records**, began its operations in Belltown (and still occupies an office at 2514 4th Ave), these days the bohemian musicians, artists, and hipsters are much less in evidence, replaced by tourists, social climbers, and a smattering of homeless people. A hint of the old scene can be found at clubs like the **Crocodile Café**, 2200 Second Ave (☎206/441-5611, ⓦwww.thecrocodile.com), and in funky galleries like **Roq La Rue**, 2316 Second Ave (Tues–Fri 2–6pm, Sat noon–4pm; free; ☎206/374-8977, ⓦwww.roqlarue.com).

The Seattle Center

Continuing north from Belltown, the **Seattle Center** (ⓦwww.seattlecenter.com) dates from the 1962 Seattle World's Fair – the "Century 21 Exposition" – and since then the 74-acre complex has become the city's cultural hub, the site of museums, sporting events, concerts, and festivals, as well as ancient-looking carnival rides aimed at the pre-teen set. The Center is best reached by the **monorail**, which runs from the third floor of Westlake Center, Fifth Avenue and Pine Street downtown (see p.1236), and drops you close to the **Space Needle**, the Space Age-modernist city icon, which is most appealing at night when it's lit up. The panoramic view from the observation deck, where there's a bar, is unmatched (daily 9am–11pm, Sat & Sun closes at midnight; $12, two trips in 24hr $18; ⓦwww.spaceneedle.com).

Southwest of the Needle, the **Pacific Science Center** (Sept–May 10am–5pm, Sat & Sun closes at 6pm; summer daily 10am–6pm; $9, kids $6.50; ⓦwww.pacsci.org) is recognizable by its modernist white arches and shallow, stagnant "lake." The hands-on adventure park is full of science-related exhibits for children, and includes a planetarium and IMAX theater. Also good for the kids is the **Children's Museum**, in the Center House complex (Mon–Fri 10am–5pm, Sat & Sun 10am–6pm; $6; ⓦwww.thechildrensmuseum.org), which offers plenty of tot-friendly activities and attractions like the **artificial mountain forest**, which lets kids crawl through logs or simulate a rock climb.

The most recent highlight of the Seattle Center, though, is the Frank Gehry–designed **Experience Music Project** (daily 10am–5pm, Sat & Sun closes at 9pm; $20, kids $15; ⓦwww.emplive.com), a giant burst of colored metal made of sweeping aluminum curves – into which the monorail passes – that houses an 80,000-piece collection of rock memorabilia divided up into exhibits on different phases of popular music history, along with a gallery-shrine to the original Seattle guitar-god, Jimi Hendrix. As much an interior amusement park as a bona fide museum (check out the Sound Lab, where you can bang on drums and keyboards to your heart's delight), the "EMP" never loses the sense of freewheeling pleasure associated with 1960s rock and pop.

Capitol Hill

A fifteen-minute bus ride east of downtown takes you to **Capitol Hill**, the city's alternative center since gays, hippies, and assorted radicals moved in during the 1960s and 1970s, and which today remains a good choice for eating, buying music, and clubbing. The shops and cafés around **Broadway** are abuzz with bohemian activity and are littered throughout with storefront coffee vendors and espresso carts. East of Broadway from Twelfth to Ninth avenues, the **Pike/Pine Corridor** is filled with all-night coffeehouses, live music venues, and trendy bars. A block south, the **Center on Contemporary Art**, or **CoCA**, 1420 11th Ave (Tues–Thurs 2–8pm, Fri–Sun noon–5pm; $5 donation; ☎206/728-1980, ⊛www.cocaseattle.org), has a small space given over to constantly rotating exhibits of work that's far more risqué than what you'll see in the Seattle Art Museum's contemporary galleries.

By contrast, the northern end of the district features striking mansions, like the **Shafer–Baillie Mansion**, 907 14th Ave E, which sit near **Volunteer Park** 1247 15th Ave (daily 6am–11pm), named after Spanish–American War veterans. Here you'll find the 1912 **Conservatory**'s hothouses, home to flowers, shrubs, and orchids from jungle, desert, and rainforest habitats (daily 10am–4pm, summer closes at 7pm; free), as well as the old **Water Tower** that provides a free, sweeping view of Seattle, albeit through wire mesh. In the same park, the **Seattle Asian Art Museum**, 1400 E Prospect St (Tues–Sun 10am–5pm, Thurs closes at 9pm; $3; ⊛www.seattleartmuseum.org), boasts a seven-thousand-piece collection of ceramics, jade, and snuff bottles from Japan, China, Korea, and Southeast Asia.

Ten blocks east, on the other side of Capitol Hill, **Washington Park Arboretum** (daily 7am–dusk; free; ⊛depts.washington.edu/wpa) is a lush showcase for indigenous Puget Sound vegetation, with plenty of charming footpaths and a variety of regional tree species. At the south end of the park, the immaculately landscaped **Japanese Gardens** flash banks of pink flowers beside neat little pools with exotically colored carp (March–Nov daily 10am–dusk; $3; ⊛www.seattlejapanesegarden.org).

The University District

Across Union Bay from Washington Park, the **University District**, or the "U" District, is a busy hodgepodge of coffeehouses, cinemas, and clothing, book, and record stores catering to the University of Washington's 35,000 students. The area centers on University Way, known as "**The Ave**," and is lined with inexpensive ethnic restaurants and the cavernous **University Bookstore**, 4326 University Way NE (☎206/634-3400, ⊛www.bookstore.washington.edu). Although the sidewalks are always bustling, the area doesn't have quite so many late-opening clubs and music venues as does nearby Capitol Hill.

On campus, the **Henry Art Gallery**, 15th Ave NE and NE 41st St (Tues–Sun 11am–5pm, Thurs closes at 8pm; $6, free Thurs 5–8pm and for any student with ID; ⊛www.henryart.org), presents the most imaginative exhibits to be found in any of Seattle's art museums, and houses American and European paintings and photography from the last two centuries. The **Burke Memorial Museum**, 17th Ave NE and NE 45th St (daily 10am–5pm, Thurs closes at 8pm; $6.50; ⊛www.washington.edu/burkemuseum), holds the US's largest collection of Native American art and artifacts west of the Mississippi – namely masks, totem poles, and baskets – and presents exhibits on the natural and cultural history of the Pacific Rim, displaying selections from its huge collection of 2.75 million fossils and Ice Age skeletons, including the remains of a 12,000-year-old sloth.

Along the Lake Washington Ship Canal

As with the "U" District, Seattle's northern neighborhoods are sliced off from the rest of town by the **Lake Washington Ship Canal**, which connects Lake Union with Elliott Bay to the west and Lake Washington to the east. On the north shore of Lake Union, **Gas Works Park**, 2101 N Northlake Way (daily 4.30am–11.30pm, parking lot open 6am–9pm; free), provides an unexpected delight. A former gas plant turned postmodern park, children now play on grassy hills that were once slag heaps and decaying, graffiti-covered machines offer surreal evidence of the site's previous industrial incarnation. Further west, near the mouth of the canal, a procession of boats passes through the **Hiram M. Chittenden Locks** (daily 7am–9pm), reachable by bus #17 from downtown, where migrating salmon and trout negotiate a **fish ladder** laid out with viewing windows, through which you can see enormous fish leaping up (late summer for salmon, fall and early winter for trout).

Beyond the locks is Salmon Bay, with **Fisherman's Terminal** on its south side, 3919 18th Ave W (daily 7am–4.30pm; ⓦ www.portseattle.org/harbor), crowded with Seattle's fishing fleet and stalls selling freshly caught fish. On the northern side of Salmon Bay, blue-collar **Ballard** (reached by several buses from downtown) is undergoing gentrification, and its historic **Ballard Avenue**, between 17th and 22nd avenues NW, is now home to new galleries, bars, and restaurants behind the stately facades of hundred-year-old buildings. The heritage of the Scandinavian fishermen who settled in Ballard in the late nineteenth century is celebrated at the **Nordic Heritage Museum**, 3014 NW 67th St (Tues–Sat 10am–4pm, Sun noon–4pm; $5; ⓦ www.nordicmuseum.com), offering memorabilia and folk art associated with their long journey from the Old World through Ellis Island and eventually to the West Coast.

Fremont and the Woodland Park Zoo

North of downtown Seattle across the ship canal, **Fremont** is a consciously hip area with a spate of used bookshops and artsy cafés. The focus is the stretch of Fremont Avenue N that runs from N 34th to N 37th streets; just off N 34th Street, the **Fremont Sunday Market** (April–Nov 10am–5pm; free) hosts vendors of used jewelry, furniture, clothing, trinkets, music, and other curiosities. One long block west, on the side of a warehouse at N 35th St and N Phinney Ave, the **Fremont Outdoor Cinema** ($5 donation; ☎206/781-4230, ⓦ www.outdoorcinema.com), runs a colorful variety of Hollywood blockbusters, cult films, and sing-a-long musicals every Saturday night at dusk during July and August. Fremont's other main attractions are its quirky **public artworks** scattered around the district, most notably the **Fremont Troll** lurking under the Aurora Bridge, 36th St and Aurora Ave, emerging from the gloom with an actual VW Bug in its clutches.

A bit further north, Aurora Avenue leads out of Fremont toward the **Woodland Park Zoo**, N 55th St and Phinney Ave N (daily 9.30am–4pm, summer closes at 6pm; $10, kids $7.50; ⓦ www.zoo.org), one of Seattle's top attractions, where more than 250 species reside in a sleek facility with a spacious layout, humane enclosures, and exhibits thematically arranged to reflect different climates and terrains – Northern Trail, Tropical Asia, Tropical Forest, Temperate Forest, and so on.

The Museum of Flight

The biggest of Seattle's museums, the **Museum of Flight**, a twenty-minute bus ride (#174) south of downtown at 9404 E Marginal Way (daily 10am–5pm, until 9pm on Thurs; $11, kids $6.50; ⓦ www.museumofflight.org), is partly housed in the magnificently restored 1909 **"Red Barn"** that was the original Boeing manufacturing plant, and which now displays relics from the early days of flight, including the nearly decrepit 1914 *Caproni Ca 20*, the world's first fighter plane. Elsewhere, in the **Great Gallery**, displays of more than fifty full-sized airplanes lead from ancient prototypes to the Wright Brothers, from the growth of Boeing to a replica of John Glenn's 1962 Mercury space capsule. One unmistakable highlight is the chance to sit in the cockpit of an SR-71 Blackbird, the type of spy plane once used to fly 80,000 feet above the jungles of Vietnam. The museum has built a new wing to house its acquisition of the **Champlin Collection**, with around 25 classic fighters from both world wars.

Eating

Seattle has many excellent choices for **restaurants**, from the funky diners of Capitol Hill and ethnic restaurants of the University District to the seafood of Pike Place Market – where the options include salmon, crab, trout, mussels, and classic clam chowder. Moreover, local **coffeehouses** host an engaging cultural scene, and are inexpensive choices for whiling away the time (though if you plan to do a bit of Internet browsing, keep in mind that rates average 10¢ per minute). Corporate giant *Starbucks* started here in the early 1970s (in an extant location in the Pike Place Market), though you're better off sampling a local brew that you can't find in your hometown minimall. Better yet, check out one of the 200-plus **espresso carts** scattered about town, each colorfully styled and uniquely designed.

Restaurants and cafés

Assaggio 2010 4th Ave, Belltown ☎ 206/441-1399. A fine, mid-priced Italian joint, with a friendly ambiance and a menu sprinkled with some surprises – like fusilli in cream sauce with currants and pinenuts – among the expected pizzas, pasta, and veal.

Café Flora 2901 E Madison St, Capitol Hill ☎ 206/325-9100. Tasty, filling vegetarian restaurant strong on desserts like coconut-ginger rice cakes, and creative entrees like mashed potato tacos and wild mushroom curry.

Café Septieme 214 Broadway E, Capitol Hill ☎ 206/860-8858. A trendy, bustling European-style bistro offering sophisticated and imaginative homemade food such as vegetable fritattas and eggplant steaks, at moderate prices. Great desserts, too.

Campagne 1600 Post Alley, downtown ☎ 206/728-2800. Superb French provincial cooking near the Pike Place Market, with delicious foie gras and excellent desserts. A less expensive branch, *Café Campagne*, can be found downstairs, and is often packed with gourmands.

Copacabana 1520 Pike Place, downtown ☎ 206/622-6359. Inside the market, the fine South American dining here is highlighted by shrimp soup and corn pie. The always-popular balcony seating offers a good view of the hordes.

Crocodile Café 2200 2nd Ave, Belltown ☎ 206/448-2114. Best known as Belltown's prime nightlife haunt for alternative music, it's also a diner by day, serving big, cheap breakfasts under stuffed animals, papier-mâché sculptures, and cheesy thrift-store album sleeves.

Dahlia Lounge 1904 4th Ave, Belltown ☎ 206/682-4142. Beautifully presented, Asian-influenced seafood dishes, and the prices to match – dinner will cost around $50 per person.

Gravity Bar 415 Broadway E, Capitol Hill ☎ 206/325-7186. Industrial-chic eatery home to postmodern vegetarian cuisine, with delicious rice-and-veggie dishes, meatless pizza, and novel juice drinks – highlighted by the pepper/garlic/citrus concoction called the "Liver Flush."

Nikko 1900 5th Ave, downtown ☎ 206/322-4641. Sushi and barbequed dishes are the main attractions at this solid Japanese restaurant, where you can save a few bucks by eating from the lunch buffets.

Noodle Ranch 2228 2nd Ave, Belltown ⏀206/728-0463. Affordable pan-Asian cuisine starting at $10, which lures in hungry souls for the fine noodle dishes and scrumptious satays.

Piroshki on Broadway 124 Broadway E, Capitol Hill ⏀206/322-2820. Closet-sized eatery serving up some of the town's best "piroshki": delicious Russian pastries stuffed with all kinds of meat and veggies, and handmade by the owner.

Place Pigalle 81 Pike St, on the staircase behind the market ⏀206/624-1756. Great seafood offerings – mussels, crab, sturgeon – with fine French cuisine make this small spot an excellent choice, despite the high prices. Patio open in warm weather.

Saigon Deli 4142 Brooklyn Ave NE, University District ⏀206/634-2866. Tiny diner with fine Vietnamese fare, most of it for under $6. A good option for take-out.

Salumi 309 Third Ave S, Pioneer Square ⏀206/621-8772. Sausages made the old-fashioned way, served on delicious sandwiches with homemade bread, and issued piping hot. Succulent ingredients include the likes of oxtail, prosciutto, lamb, and numerous kinds of hog parts.

Wild Ginger 1400 Western Ave, downtown ⏀206/623-4450. An extremely popular, well-designed, upscale restaurant with an extensive menu of fiery dishes from Southeast Asia, India, and China. Try the tuna manada – yellowfin tuna fried in spicy Indonesian sauce.

Coffeehouses

Allegro Espresso Bar 4214 University Way ⏀206/633-3030. One of the better spots to taste local brews around the University, with Internet access in an adjoining room, for customers only.

Bauhaus Books & Coffee 301 E Pine St, Capitol Hill ⏀206/625-1600. A hangout for the dressed-in-black crowd with large tables, a used-book section – focusing on art and architecture volumes – and good coffee.

Lux 2226 First Ave, Belltown ⏀206/443-0962. Dark, moody coffeehouse with curious art and antiques – falling somewhere between high art and a thrift shop – and coffee drinks that are tasty and well prepared.

Online Coffee Company 1720 E Olive Way, Capitol Hill ⏀206/328-3731. Offers large black monitors and stylish wooden desks for serious Web-surfing. First 30 minutes free with a coffee purchase – otherwise $6 per hour.

Still Life in Fremont 709 N 35th St, Fremont ⏀206/547-9850. One of the area's best hangouts, offering breakfast specials, sandwiches, quiches, and offbeat dishes like corn tortilla pie. Quirky art and free live music also make this a unique, appealing spot.

Vivace Espresso 901 E Denny Way, Capitol Hill ⏀206/860-5869. A large haunt for serious java-drinkers and run by self-proclaimed "espresso roasting and preparation specialists"; their sidewalk café at 321 Broadway E is the prime people-watching perch in the area.

Drinking and nightlife

Seattle's **nightlife** revolves around its engaging **bars** and **live music** venues, even if the local club scene is rather paltry compared to that of Los Angeles or New York City. Like other West Coast cities, though, Seattle boasts an excellent selection of microbrewed beers. The tavern scene is most accessible, and touristy, in **Pioneer Square**, where the "joint cover night" plan (Sat & Sun $10, Mon–Fri $5) allows you entrance into eight different live music venues. Although its grunge heyday is long gone, **Belltown** still hosts well-known bands at the old, atmospheric **Moore Theater**, 1932 Second Ave (⏀206/443-1744, ⓦwww.themoore.com), and at alternative joints like the *Crocodile Café* (see opposite).

Bars and clubs

Alibi Room 85 Pike St ⏀206/623-3180. Swank martini bar tucked in a dramatic alley behind the Pike Street Market. Excellent food in café-type rooms upstairs, DJs spinning tunes on the dance floor downstairs, and a good selection of film scripts in the library.

Comet Tavern 922 E Pike St, Capitol Hill ⏀206/323-9853. The oldest bar on Capitol Hill and a grunge institution – not surprisingly a smoky dive and a bit of a rocker's hangout, with pool tables.

Doc Maynard's Public House 610 1st Ave S, Pioneer Square ⏀206/682-4649. Fun, restored 1890s saloon popular with tourists and featuring pile-driving rock bands.

Dutch Ned's Saloon 201 1st Ave S, Pioneer Square ⏀206/340-8859. Friendly bar hosting Seattle Slam poetry night (Wed 9pm; $3), and 32 brews on tap.

Kells Irish Pub 1916 Post Alley, Pike Place Market ⏀206/728-1916. Free-spirited Irish bar and restaurant in a central location, with patio seating and nightly performances by Irish-oriented folk and rock groups.

Linda's Tavern 707 E Pine St, Capitol Hill ☎206/325-1220. Popular with musicians for its jukebox stocked with classics and current indie rock acts. DJs spin two or three nights a week (usually Tues–Thurs and weekends).

Old Timer's Tavern 620 1st Ave S, Pioneer Square ☎206/623-9800. Crowded tavern featuring blues and R&B music (Tues & Wed), karaoke (Sun & Mon), and frenetic live salsa on the weekends.

Pike Pub & Brewery 1415 1st Ave, downtown ☎206/622-6044. Small craft brewery serving its own beers, as well as numerous bottled brands; has a large wine list and an extensive fish- and pizza-heavy menu to boot.

Pyramid Alehouse 1201 1st Ave S ☎206/682-3377. Across the street from Safeco Field, an excellent regional brewery with a warehouse-like space that serves a dozen Pyramid brands, including some fruit-flavored varieties and an extra-special bitter (ESB).

Music venues

Baltic Room 1207 Pine St E, Capitol Hill ☎206/625-4444. Stylish alternative music venue – playing everything from industrial and electronica DJs to rock and jazz bands – comprising three different sections, and selling beer, wine, and cigars.

Crocodile Café 2200 2nd Ave, Belltown ☎206/441-5611. A hip alternative joint promoting everything from rock to avant-garde jazz and spoken word. Also a good diner (see p.1241).

Dimitriou's Jazz Alley 2033 6th Ave, downtown ☎206/441-9729. Best big-name jazz spot in town, showcasing international jazz acts, as well as up-and-coming brilliants. Tickets start around $20.

DV8 131 Taylor N ☎206/448-0888. A few blocks east of the Seattle Center, a converted roller rink that plays host to a nice range of beats – house, garage, hip-hop, jungle – and periodically offers live shows by rock and dance bands.

Paramount Theatre 911 Pine St, downtown ☎206/682-1414. Large 1928 movie palace, seating around three thousand and often hosting well-known rock 'n' roll bands. Tickets around $30.

Showbox 1426 1st Ave, downtown ☎206/628-3151. A good alternative choice for regional rock acts, and quite affordable compared to the bigger-name venues. Grab a drink in the venue's adjacent *Green Room* bar before the show. Across from Pike Place Market.

Tractor Tavern 5213 Ballard Ave NW, Ballard ☎206/789-3599. A popular joint in Ballard with great character, especially good microbrewed beers, and roots music of all kinds – zydeco, Irish, blues, bluegrass.

Performing arts and festivals

Seattle offers a handful of compelling venues for the **performing arts**, many based around Seattle Center. The most prominent opening in recent months is that of Marion Oliver McCaw Hall, a sleek, modern facility that hosts the **Seattle Opera** (☎206/389-7676, ⓦwww.seattleopera.org). In the same complex, **Pacific Northwest Ballet** (☎206/441-2424, ⓦwww.pnb.org) puts on around seven programs from September to June and has an active repertoire of seventy works. Away from Seattle Center, **Seattle Symphony Orchestra** performs in the glass-walled **Benaroya Concert Hall**, 3rd and Union streets (☎206/215-4747, ⓦwww.seattlesymphony.org). Tickets tend to sell out in advance, but there are sometimes half-price tickets on the day of the performance for students and seniors.

For **theater**, Seattle's longest-established small company is the **Seattle Repertory Company** (☎206/443-2222, ⓦwww.seattlerep.org) at the Seattle Center, while next door, the **Intiman Theater** (☎206/269-1900, ⓦwww.intiman.org) performs classics and premieres of innovative new works. A bit to the north at 100 W Roy St, **On the Boards** presents contemporary performances (☎206/217-9888, ⓦwww.ontheboards.org), and big-name musicals open at the **Fifth Avenue Theatre**, 1308 5th Ave (☎206/625-1418, ⓦwww.5thavenuetheatre.org) or the **Paramount**, 911 Pine St (☎206/682-1414, ⓦwww.theparamount.com), both downtown.

Seattle's major **events** include **Bumbershoot**, hosting five hundred artists on twenty stages around town on Labor Day weekend (☎206/281-7788, ⓦwww.bumbershoot.org), and the **Northwest Folklife Festival**

(☎206/684-7300, ⓦwww.nwfolklife.org), a Memorial Day event drawing folk musicians from around the world. In late May, the **Seattle International Film Festival** (☎206/464-5830, ⓦwww.seattlefilm.com) centers on such classic moviehouses as the **Egyptian**, 801 E Pine St (☎206/323-4978), and the **Harvard Exit**, 807 E Roy near Broadway (☎206/323-8986), both in Capitol Hill. **Seafair**, held from late July to early August (☎206/728-0123 ext 108, ⓦwww.seafair.com), is a colorful celebration with airplane spectacles, hydroplane events, and milk-carton races.

For **listings**, *Seattle Weekly* is free from boxes on the streets and many cafés and stores, and is good for reviews of theater, cinema, and the arts, as is the Friday edition of the *Seattle Post Intelligencer* newspaper. Free papers *The Stranger* and *The Rocket* provide solid coverage of the regional music scene.

Out from Seattle: Bainbridge and Vashon islands

For a brief escape from Seattle, the half-hour ferry ride across Elliott Bay to **Bainbridge Island** provides a relaxing, scenic experience. Washington State Ferries leave from Pier 52 (hourly 5.30am–1.35am; foot passengers $5.10 round-trip, vehicle and driver $9 roundtrip, $11.25 peak season; ☎206/464-6400 or 1-800/84-FERRY, ⓦwww.wsdot.wa.gov/ferries) for the 35-minute trip to the island, a green and rural spot occupying less than fifty square miles, which is mostly private land. The island's only conventional attraction, the **Bloedel Reserve**, 7571 NE Dolphin Drive, off the Agatewood Road exit of Hwy-305 (Wed–Sun 10am–4pm; $6; by reservation only at ☎206/842-7631, ⓦwww.bloedelreserve.org), is a natural conservatory containing nearly 150 acres of gardens, ponds, meadows, and wildlife habitats. If you want to pitch a tent on the island, there's **camping** at the far end in Fay Bainbridge State Park ($15–21; ☎206/842-3931, ⓦwww.parks.wa.gov). Otherwise, accommodation is limited to **B&Bs**, details of which can be obtained from the **visitor center** in the town of Winslow, 590 Winslow Way E (☎206/842-3700, ⓦwww.bainbridgechamber .com). A decent choice for cheap **eating** is *Harbour Public House*, 231 Parfitt Way SW, Winslow (☎206/842-0969), a renovated 1881 house now used for serving up the usual range of seafood, salads, burgers, and beer.

Eight daily Washington State Ferries from Seattle and West Seattle also make the short trip to easygoing, bicycle-friendly **Vashon Island**. Ferries from

Onward to Canada and Alaska

Victoria on Canada's Vancouver Island is just two to three hours away by the high-speed, passenger-only *Victoria Clipper* from Seattle's Pier 69 (summer four daily, winter one daily; $59–79 one way, $99–142 roundtrip; ☎206/448-5000, ⓦwww.vic-toriaclipper.com). Other services to Vancouver Island from Washington State run out of Anacortes (see p.1248), Port Angeles (see p.1254), and Bellingham (see p.1251). Kenmore Air schedules five flights daily from downtown Seattle on Lake Union to Victoria (☎1-800/543-9595; $116 one way, $177–198 roundtrip; ⓦwww.kenmoreair .com), as well as six flights to the San Juan Islands ($98 one way, $163–194 roundtrip).

The much more expensive **Alaska Marine Highway** (☎360/676-0212 recorded schedule information, ☎360/676-8445 administrative office, ⓦwww.akmhs.com; winter $270, summer $296) is a three-day ferry ride that winds between islands and a fjord-lined coast from **Bellingham**, ninety miles north of Seattle, to Skagway, Alaska (see p.1312).

downtown Seattle's Pier 50 are passenger-only (Mon–Fri 6.10am–8.35pm; 25min trip; $7.10 roundtrip), while West Seattle trips are also for vehicles (daily 5.30am–2am; 15min; foot passengers $3.30 roundtrip, vehicle and driver $11.75 roundtrip, $14.75 peak season). A few pleasant beaches lie along the coast of this island, where the community of **VASHON** is little more than a simple hamlet. The *AYH Ranch Hostel*, 12119 SW Cove Rd (☎206/463-2592, ⓦwww.vashonhostel.com; ❶–❷), six miles from the Seattle–Vashon ferry dock at the north end of the island, offers log-cabin dorm beds and tepees for $16, or private rooms for $55. Phone ahead to make a reservation and arrange a free pickup at the jetty. There are also a number of good **B&Bs**, among them *Artist's Studio Loft,* 16592 91st Ave SW (☎206/463-2583, ⓦwww.asl-bnb.com; ❺), and the *Swallow's Nest Guest Cottages*, 6030 SW 248th St (☎206/463-2646, ⓦwww.vashonislandcottages.com; ❺). Good **places to eat** are *Casa Bonita*, 17623 100th Ave SW (☎206/463-6452), offering reliable Mexican fare, and *Rock Island Pizza*, 17322 Vashon Hwy SW (☎206/463-6814), which has gourmet pizzas and microbrews.

Puget Sound

Broad and deep **Puget Sound** hooks far into western Washington, an array of tiny islands and ragged peninsulas teeming with yachts, oceangoing ships, fishing trawlers, and even nuclear submarines. At first, the dense forest in these parts deterred homesteaders, but soon small logging communities sprang up, and the Sound became a vital waterway. As more settlers arrived, the demand for land grew, and in the 1850s treaties confining Native Americans to reservations were put before tribal leaders. Some signed, including Chief Sealth of the Duwamish-Suquamish peoples, but others refused and accusations of forgery were rampant. Even today, the courts still struggle with these issues.

The southern end of the Sound is increasingly urban, littered with far-flung bedroom communities of the Seattle metropolis. Places like formerly industrial **Tacoma** and the small state capital of **Olympia** are slowly becoming known for more than pollution and politicians, respectively, while beyond this are countless appealing mountains, forests, and lakes. Popular weekend escapes include rural **Whidbey Island** and the beautiful **San Juan Islands** further north.

Tacoma

Unavoidable on the main Seattle–Portland route of I-5, **TACOMA** has fought one of the worst reputations in the Pacific Northwest, a military-oriented industrial town with pervasive pollution and a toxic brew of chemicals lingering in Commencement Bay. In recent years, though, the massive **Tacoma Dome** has become a major concert venue (ⓦwww.tacomadome.org), and the downtown historical district has experienced a resurgence, with a slew of new museums, theaters, and restaurants to attract tourists without a sense of regional prejudice.

Among the smattering of galleries and theaters in the city center is the two-block-long **Antique Row**, Broadway between S 7th and S 9th streets, a popular strip where fifteen dealers in historic collectibles, old-fashioned curiosities, and worn-out junk have set up shop in some great Victorian buildings. Nearby, the **Broadway Center for the Performing Arts**, 901 Broadway (☎253/591-5894, ⓦwww.broadwaycenter.org), comprises two stunning old moviehouses, the Pantages and the Rialto, landmarks with terracotta facades and copious historic-revival decor. Further south, the **Tacoma Art Museum**, 1701 Pacific Ave (Tues–Sun 10am–5pm, Thurs open until 8pm; $5; ⓦwww.tacomaartmuseum .org), hosts decent touring exhibitions and shows off the colorful works of local glassblower Dale Chihuly. Adjacent is the copper-domed **Union Station** (Mon–Fri 10am–4pm), built in 1911, which has been impressively restored as a courthouse. The arty pedestrian overpass **Bridge of Glass** connects the station to the new **Museum of Glass** (Tues–Sat 10am–5pm, Sun noon–5pm; $10, kids $4; ⓦwww.museumofglass.org), a Chihuly spectacle that presents his work and that of other glassblowers, along with a hodgepodge of modern art. In the same area, the huge **Washington State History Museum**, 1911 Pacific Ave (Mon–Sat 10am–5pm, Thurs open until 8pm, Sun noon–5pm; $7, free Thurs 5–8pm; ⓦwww.wshs.org/wshm), has fine exhibits on native tribes, frontier towns, railroads, logging, and other regional history.

If you have time, head four miles north of downtown to picturesque **Point Defiance Park**, at Pearl Street off Ruston Way, which at seven hundred acres is one of the largest urban parks in the USA. Its **Five-Mile-Drive** loop has fine vistas of Puget Sound and various points from which you can lose yourself on the many appealing trails.

Practicalities

Hotels in Tacoma are usually less expensive than their counterparts in Seattle. The downtown *Sheraton Tacoma*, 1320 Broadway (☎253/572-3200 or 1-800/325-3535, ⓦwww.sheratontacoma.com; ❼), has the best chain-hotel rooms in town, though the **B&B** rooms at *The Villa*, about a mile northeast of downtown at 705 N 5th St (☎253/572-1157, ⓦwww.villabb.com; ❼), are more appealing for about the same price. This Renaissance Revival mansion is surrounded by luxurious gardens, and some of the rooms have private verandas with views of Commencement Bay and the Olympic Mountains. The usual **motel** chains line the freeways, and you can **camp** in **Dash Point State Park**, 5700 SW Dash Point Rd, Federal Way ($15–21; ⓦwww.parks.wa.gov), five miles northeast of Tacoma, which has wide beaches and some decent hiking trails. For a bite to **eat**, the *Antique Sandwich Company*, 5102 N Pearl St (☎253/752-4069), is an authentic luncheonette filled with locals and occasional live music; *Engine House no. 9*, 611 N Pine St (☎253/272-3435), is a friendly tavern good for beer and pizza; and *Spar Tavern*, 2121 N 30th St (☎253/627-8215), is a classic brick diner and watering hole serving up burgers, seafood, and beer, plus blues on Sunday nights.

Olympia

Just a muddy little logging town when picked as Washington's territorial capital in 1853, **OLYMPIA** has never really become the metropolis its founders had hoped, instead continuing to remain something of a backwater despite government efforts to spruce it up. Its downtown area is small, with a few blocks of stores and restaurants presided over by the **Old Capitol**, Washington St at 7th Ave (Mon–Fri 8am–5pm; free), an 1892 jewel with gothic turrets and arched windows. Nevertheless, Olympia is quite a busy little place, with state employees knocking around during the day and students from Evergreen State College, a popular liberal-arts school, pepping up the nightlife. There's also the well-established **Olympia Farmers Market**, 700 N Capitol Way (April–Oct Thurs–Sun 10am–3pm; Nov–Dec Sat & Sun only; ⓦwww.farmers-market.org), with a nice selection of fruits, vegetables, herbs, and baked goods, and handcrafted items like soaps and puzzles.

The state offices are arranged around neat lawns on the **Capitol Campus**, just south of downtown. The grand Neoclassical **Legislative Building** was completed in 1928 after more than three decades of work, and is a close replica of the Capitol building in Washington, DC. These days the building has been shuttered for earthquake repairs, but is due to reopen November 2004 (☏360/586-3460, ⊛www.ga.wa.gov/visitor). On the northern side of the campus, the **Capitol Conservatory and Gardens**, 11th Ave at Water St (Mon–Fri 8am–3pm; free; ☏360/586-TOUR), is worth a look for its eclectic selection of plants from tropical to northern regions, many of which are grown and used to decorate other gardens on the campus. Eight blocks south, the small **State Capitol Museum**, 211 W 21st Ave (Tues–Fri 10am–4pm, Sat noon–4pm; $2; ⊛www.wshs.org/wscm), juxtaposes a restored dining room with displays of Native American basketwork and natural history.

Practicalities

The **Greyhound** station is at 107 Seventh Ave at Capitol Way (☏360/357-5541, ⊛www.greyhound.com), five blocks north of the Capitol Campus in Olympia; the **Amtrak** station is about eight miles southeast and not on the bus route. Intercity Transit (IT; ☏360/786-1881, ⊛www.intercitytransit.com) runs **local buses**, providing a free service between downtown and the Capitol Campus (otherwise 75¢, one-day pass $1.50).

Olympia's **visitor center** (Mon–Fri 8am–5pm; ☏360/586-3460) is on the Capitol Campus, 14th Avenue and Capitol Way. In-town **accommodation** is geared towards business travelers; *Best Western Aladdin Motor Inn*, 900 Capitol Way (☏360/352-7200 or 1-800/367-7771, ⊛www.bestwestern.com; ❹), is a predictably clean motor lodge with an outdoor pool, while the *Harbinger Inn*, 1136 E Bay Drive (☏360/754-0389, ⊛www.harbingerinn.com; ❹), is a pleasant 1910 **B&B** in a renovated mansion, offering five rooms with period furnishings a mile from downtown. The *Phoenix Inn*, 415 Capitol Way (☏360/570-0555, ⊛www.phoenixinnsuites.com; ❻), is the best choice of the higher-priced establishments, with fridges and microwaves in each room, plus onsite pool, Jacuzzi, and gym. There's also **camping** at forested **Millersylvania State Park**, 12245 Tilley Rd ($15–21; ☏360/753-1519), south of Olympia, two miles east of I-5, exit 99.

Of places to **eat**, the *Urban Onion*, 116 Legion Way (☏360/943-9242), has delicious burgers for the vegetarian and carnivore alike, while a few blocks away, *Spar Café*, 114 Fourth Ave E (☏360/357-6444), is a diner which has catered to Olympia's working class since 1935.

Whidbey Island

With its sheer cliffs and craggy outcrops, rocky beaches and prairie countryside, **WHIDBEY ISLAND** is a favorite vacation retreat for urbanites, as well as the largest island in the continental US – nearly fifty miles in length from north to south. A naval base occupies its northern end, but in the southern and central parts, narrow country roads wind through farmland and small villages.

Although it's possible to reach the island by road – Hwy 20 off I-5 drops into the north end of Whidbey, some 85 miles north of Seattle – the **ferry** is usually a better option. The quickest route from Seattle is to head thirty miles north to Mukilteo and catch the ferry to **Clinton** on Whidbey's southern tip (weekdays 5am–9pm every half-hour, 9pm–1am hourly; weekends 6am–8am hourly, 8am–9pm every half-hour, 9pm–1am hourly; 20min trip; foot passengers $3.10 roundtrip, vehicle and driver $7 roundtrip, $5.50 peak season). From Port Townsend on the Olympic Peninsula (see p.1253) an hourly ferry goes to **Keystone**, in the middle of the island just south of the town of Coupeville

(6.30am–8.30pm; 30min; foot passengers $2 roundtrip, vehicle and driver $7 roundtrip, $8.75 peak season; ⓦwww.wsdot.wa.gov/ferries). Whidbey's **bus** system, Island Transit (daily except Sun; ⓣ360/321-6688, ⓦwww.islandtransit.org), runs eleven routes along the length of the island for free.

One of the better spots to linger on the island is **Langley**, just a few miles away from where the ferry docks in Clinton, with its Old West main street of wooden storefronts set on a picturesque bluff overlooking the water. The **visitor center** is at 208 Anthes St (daily 9am–5pm; ⓣ360/221-6765, ⓦwww.langley-wa.com). A good **place** to stay is *Country Cottage of Langley*, 215 6th St (ⓣ360/221-8709 or 1-800/718-3860, ⓦwww.acountrycottage.com; ❼), which has five rooms in a restored 1920s farmhouse, all with CD players and fridges, and the more expensive suites have Jacuzzi tubs and fireplaces. Among the limited **food** options in town, *Langley Village Bakery*, 221 2nd St #1 (ⓣ360/221-3525), has great baked goods, pizza, and soups.

The middle part of the island contains **Ebey's Landing National Historic Reserve** (ⓦwww.nps.gov/ebla), compelling for its World War II–era military garrisons **Fort Casey** and **Fort Ebey**, which have since been converted into evocative state parks. Fort Ebey is also a good spot to **camp** ($15–21; ⓣ360/678-4636), with a number of hiking trails. Nearby, charming little **Coupeville** features preserved Victorian mansions and other historic structures, visible on a walking tour from the **Island County Historical Museum**, at Alexander and Front streets (daily 10am–4pm, summer closes at 5pm; donation; tours June–Sept weekends 11am; $2; ⓦwww.islandhistory.org). By contrast, **Oak Harbor**, despite being Whidbey's largest town, is drab and uneventful. To the north, at **Deception Pass State Park** (daily 8am–dusk; ⓣ360/675-2417), a steel bridge arches gracefully over the narrow gorge between Whidbey and Fidalgo Island, connecting point for the San Juan Islands beyond.

On the edge of Coupeville, you'll find **accommodation** at the appealing *Captain Whidbey Inn*, 2072 W Captain Whidbey Inn Rd, two miles west of town at Penn Cove (ⓣ360/678-4097, ⓦwww.captainwhidbey.com; ❺), a nautical-themed **hotel** serving superb food. The *Anchorage Inn*, 807 N Main St (ⓣ360/678-5581, ⓦwww.anchorage-inn.com; ❺), however, is in a more central location. The local **Chamber of Commerce**, 107 S Main St (ⓣ360/678-5434, ⓦwww.centralwhidbeychamber.com), has lists of **B&Bs** and other places to stay. For **eating**, try *Knead & Feed*, 4 Front St (ⓣ360/678-5431), offering homemade breads, pies, and cinnamon rolls at its bakery, and serviceable lunches, dinners, and weekend breakfasts.

The San Juan Islands

North and west of Whidbey Island, midway between Seattle and Vancouver, the beautiful **SAN JUAN ISLANDS** are scattered across the northern reaches of Puget Sound, though only a few have facilities for visitors. Every summer brings more visitors than the islands can easily accommodate, especially on the largest ones, San Juan and Orcas, so you'll need to book in advance.

Arrival and getting around

Washington State Ferries runs a dozen boats per day – or up to fifteen in summer – to the islands from the harbor a few miles west of **Anacortes**, a gritty port 75 miles north of Seattle at the end of Hwy-20. The ferry stops at four of the 172 islands (Lopez, Shaw, Orcas, and San Juan; ⓣ1-888/808-7977, ⓦwww.wsdot.wa.gov/ferries), and the slow cruise through the archipelago is a visual delight. Motorists should get to the port early, as there's often an hour's wait or more to get vehicles onto a summer crossing; pedestrians and cyclists have less of a hassle. Roundtrip **fares** to the islands – $8–9.60 for foot passengers and $26–36 for a car and driver, with fares varying by the destination and season – are collected only on the westbound journey, and there is no charge for foot passengers on inter-island trips (bringing a bike is an additional $4, though). One ferry a day (two in summer) goes on to Sidney in British Columbia. A passenger-only service to Orcas and San Juan islands runs from Bellingham (see p.1251) during the summer months.

Kenmore Air (☎1-800/543-9595, ⓦwww.kenmoreair.com) runs **seaplane flights** from Seattle to five harbors in the San Juans for $98 (one way) and $163–194 (roundtrip). West Isle Air (☎360/293-4691 or 1-800/874-4434, ⓦwww.westisleair.com) flies between Anacortes and San Juan or Orcas island for $35 each way, or from Bellingham to the islands for $45.

If you want to catch an early ferry (the first one leaves before 6am) from Anacortes, you may as well stay the night. Commercial Avenue is lined with numerous budget **hotels**, the least generic of which is the *Islands Inn*, no. 3401 (☎360/293-4644, ⓦwww.islandsinn.com; ❸), offering bayside views and fireplaces, while the *Majestic Hotel*, no. 419 (☎360/293-3355; ❹), is a nicely renovated option, with old-fashioned decor and a good onsite restaurant and bar.

Lopez Island

Modest and unassuming **LOPEZ ISLAND** is a quiet spot whose rolling hills make it a supremely enjoyable place to ride a **bicycle** (which you can rent for $5 per hour, or $25 per day, from Lopez Bicycle Works; ☎360/468-2847, ⓦwww.lopezbicycleworks.com), although there are scant few other things to do if you're an intrepid sightseer. The main destination is **Shark Reef Park** (☎360/378-8420), at the island's southwest tip on Shark Reef Road, where a ten- to fifteen-minute walk through dense forest is rewarded by beautiful vistas at the water's edge, from where you can spot the occasional sea lion past the tidepools. For **accommodation**, on the edge of little **Lopez Village**, about four miles from the ferry dock, *Lopez Islander* (☎360/468-2233 or 1-800/736-3434, ⓦwww.lopezislander.com; ❻) is a delightful and spacious resort hotel, and not far from the excellent *Bay Café* (☎360/468-3700). For a change of pace, and a quiet respite in the woods, *Blue Fjord Cabins* (☎1-888/633-0401, ⓦwww.interisland.net/bluefjord; ❹) offers two cozy, secluded cabins.

Orcas Island

The most alluring destination in the San Juans for striking scenery, horseshoe-shaped **ORCAS ISLAND** teems with rugged hills and leafy timber that tower over its leisurely roads, craggy beaches, and abundant wildlife. The ferry lands in the tiny burg of **Orcas**, mainly interesting for its grand Victorian *Orcas Hotel* (☎360/376-4300, ⓦwww.orcashotel.com; ❺), whose plushest rooms have Jacuzzis, balconies, and harbor views. You can rent **bicycles** and **mopeds** (around $25 and $50 per day, respectively) around the ferry dock to cycle inland through the island's fetching farm country.

Most visitors head ten miles north to the drab main town of **Eastsound**, where the **Chamber of Commerce**, on North Beach Rd, just past Eastsound Square (☎360/376-2273, ⓦwww.orcasisland.org), provides maps and information. Places to **eat** include *Bilbo's Festivo*, North Beach Rd and A St (☎360/376-4728), for its reasonably good Mexican food, and *Portofino Pizzeria*, along A St (☎360/376-2085), for tasty, handcrafted pizzas and calzones. Nestled at the end of West Beach Road, the *Beach Haven Resort*

(☎360/376-2288, ⓦwww.beach-haven.com; ❺) is one of the island's several holiday resorts tucked away in distant corners and a great place to **stay**. Its beachfront log cabins line a densely wooded, sunset-facing cove; in summer they are only available by the week.

The island's real highlight is **Moran State Park**, off Horseshoe Hwy southeast of Eastsound (☎1-800/452-5687, ⓦwww.orcasisle.com/~elc), where more than thirty miles of hiking trails wind through dense forest and open fields to freshwater lakes, and to the summit of the 2409ft **Mount Constitution** – the San Juans' highest point – where there are great views to be had from a rugged stone observation tower. The park's four **campgrounds** ($15–21) fill up early in summer, so book ahead. Further along, the lovely *Doe Bay Village & Resort*, Star Rte-86, 18 miles east of Eastsound on Horseshoe Hwy (☎360/376-2291, ⓦwww.doebay.com; ❶–❺), is tucked into a secluded bay and offers everything from primitive campsites to modern cabins. In tiny nearby **Olga**, *Café Olga* (☎360/376-5098) serves tasty **meals** and fruit pies, but is often swamped by people visiting the adjoining art gallery.

San Juan Island

SAN JUAN ISLAND, the ferry's last stop before Canada, is the only place where the ferry drops you in something resembling a town. The lone incorporated spot on the archipelago, **Friday Harbor**'s wharfside blocks seem more commercially active than the rest of the islands put together. San Juan Shuttle circles between twelve communities and points of interest on the island, running from downtown Friday Harbor to Roche Harbor and passing the Lakedale Campground and English Camp parksite along the way ($4 one way, $7 round-trip, $10 day-pass, $17 two-day pass, or $18 for 25-min guided bus tour; ☎360/378-8887 or 1-800/887-8387, ⓦwww.sanjuantransit.com). **Bikes** ($30 a day) and **scooters** ($50 a day) can be rented at Island Bicycles, 380 Argyle St (Thurs–Sat only; ☎360/378-4941, ⓦwww.islandbicycles.com), while **mopeds** are available from Susie's Mopeds, First and A streets ($17 per hour or $51 per day; ☎360/378-5244 or 1-800/532-0087, ⓦwww.susiesmopeds.com). **Maps**, essential on such twisting and badly marked roads, are available at the **visitors center**, in the Cannery Building next to the terminal at 91 Front St (Mon–Fri 9am–4.30pm; ☎360/378-8887). Further information is available from the main office of the San Juan Island Historical Park, First and Spring streets (daily summer 8am–5pm; rest of year 8.30am–4.30pm; ☎360/378-2240, ⓦwww.nps.gov/sajh).

Friday Harbor's cafés, shops, and waterfront make for pleasant wandering, and the small **Whale Museum**, 62 First St N (daily summer 10am–5pm, rest of year noon–5pm; $5; ⓦwww.whalemuseum.org), offers an interesting look at the sights and sounds of local cetaceans. To see the real thing, head past the coves and bays on the island's west side to **Lime Kiln Point State Park**, 6158 Lighthouse Rd, named after the site's former lime quarry. Orca ("killer") whales come here in summer to feed on migrating salmon, and there's usually at least one sighting a day. San Juan Tours (☎360/378-1323 or 1-800/450-6858, ⓦwww.sanjuansafaris.com) is one of several companies offering three-hour **whale-watching cruises** (May–Sept only; $49).

Elsewhere on the island, at the northwest tip is **Roche Harbor**, established in the 1880s around the limestone trade, and highlighted by the gracious white *Hotel de Haro*, 248 Reuben Memorial Drive (☎360/378-2155 or 1-800/451-8910, ⓦwww.rocheharbor.com; ❺), built over the harbor in 1886 to house visiting lime-buyers and still appealing for its upscale suites, more standard rooms, and quaint cottages. On the other side of the island at the southern tip,

American Camp (dawn–11pm; free; ☎360/378-2902, ⓦwww.nps.gov/sajh) is a national park whose territory once played a role in the infamous "Pig War," an 1859 border conflict between the US and Britain. More appealing is **English Camp**, to the west (same information as American Camp), where forests overlook pleasant green fields and maple trees near the shore, and four buildings from the 1860s and a small formal garden have been restored.

In addition to the *Hotel de Haro*, choices to **stay** include places in Friday Harbor like *Friday's*, 35 First St (☎360/378-5848 or 1-800/352-2632, ⓦwww.friday-harbor.com/lodging; ❺), a cozy central inn, or one of two cabins on a former sailboat parked in Slip K-13 in the port, now converted into the charming *Wharfside* B&B (☎360/378-5661, ⓦwww.slowseason.com; ❻). *Blair House*, 345 Blair Ave (☎360/378-5907 or 1-800/899-3030, ⓦwww.fridayharborlodging.com; ❺), offers three units nicely enclosed by trees, and a big front porch and hot tub. The Bed & Breakfast Association of San Juan Island (PO Box 3016, Friday Harbor, WA 98250; ☎360/378-3030, ⓦwww.san-juan-island.net) can also hook you up with a room, though most start at around $100 in high season, when it's essential to reserve ahead, especially during late July's popular **San Juan Island Jazz Festival** (☎360/378-5509). There's a pleasant, cyclist-only **campground** called *Pedal Inn*, 1300 False Bay Drive ($5; ☎360/378-3049), while *Lakedale Campground* ($21; ☎1-800/617-2267, ⓦwww.lakedale.com), six miles from the ferry on Roche Harbor Rd (accessible by bus), has everything from simple campsites to elegant lodge rooms and log cabins (❻–❾).

Of Friday Harbor's plentiful places to **eat**, *Bella Luna*, 175 First St (☎360/378-4118), is good for Italian fare; *Cannery House*, 174 First St (☎360/378-2500), has fresh seafood, soups, sandwiches, and homemade breads; and *San Juan Donut Shop*, 209 Spring St (☎360/378-5059), provides hefty breakfasts from 6am. For Roche Harbor, try *Roche Harbor Restaurant*, 248 Reuben Memorial Drive (☎360/378-5757), one of the town's few decent spots to eat, with steak and seafood entrees and pleasing waterside vistas.

Bellingham

A successful blend of industry, Victorian architecture, and college-town liveliness, **BELLINGHAM** runs ten miles along a broad curve of Bellingham Bay, 85 miles north of Seattle and just 18 miles south of the Canadian border. Serving as the southern terminus of the **Alaska Marine Highway** (see box, p.1244), ferries sail from the Cruise Terminal on the edge of the brick-and-sandstone **Fairhaven** district – three miles south of downtown (I-5 exit 250) – which, with its hip bookstores, cafés, and clothing stores, is easily the town's most appealing area. By contrast, **downtown** itself is fairly mundane, but likeable enough, and has a few good restaurants.

Bellingham's chief attraction is its access to a wide range of excellent parks – set among the bluffs and forests surrounding the city, with myriad hiking trails – and, further east, the foothills of **Mount Baker**, 56 scenic miles along Hwy-542, best known for its skiing, with a seven-month season from early November until late May (☎360/734-6771, ⓦwww.mtbaker.us; daily lift tickets $36 on weekends, $28 midweek).

Practicalities

Greyhound **buses** and Amtrak **trains** pull in at the **Bellingham Cruise Terminal** in the Fairhaven district. Victoria-San Juan Cruises (☎360/738-8099 or 1-800/443-4552, ⓦwww.whales.com) operates a passenger-only summer service to San Juan Island and Victoria in British Columbia ($69 one way, $79 roundtrip), though it's primarily aimed at whale-watchers. Local Whatcom Transit **buses** (☎360/676-RIDE, ⓦwww.ridewta.com) ply thirty routes for a fare of 50¢, with the **transit center** at E Magnolia and Railroad Ave. The **visitor center** is at 904 Potter St, off I-5 exit 253 (☎360/671-3990 or 1-800/487-2032, ⓦwww.bellingham.org).

The best **rooms** in Bellingham are the eight quaint units at the gabled Victorian *North Garden Inn*, 1014 N Garden St (☎360/671-7828 or 1-800/922-6414, ⓦwww.northgardeninn.com; ❹), a beautiful B&B near downtown and just off I-5, with first-class breakfasts and a great view of the bay. Also off I-5 (exit 253) is the reliable *Best Western Lakeway Inn*, 714 Lakeway Drive (☎360/671-1011, ⓦwww.bellingham-hotel.com; ❹). At the *HI-Bellingham Hostel* in Fairhaven Park, 107 Chuckanut Drive (☎360/671-1750), you can get a dorm-room bed for $16. The best place to **camp** is **Larrabee State Park**, seven miles south of Bellingham on Hwy-11 ($15–21), though there are other campgrounds along the road to Mount Baker as well.

Downtown has several decent places to **eat** and **drink**, including *Dirty Dan Harris*, 1211 11th St (☎360/676-1011), for solid prime rib and steaks, and *Dos Padres*, 1111 Harris Ave (☎360/733-9900), for cheap Mexican staples. In **Fairhaven**, *Tony's*, 1101 Harris Ave (☎360/733-6319), is a hip coffee shop, sometimes hosting live music, while inside Village Books, 1208 11th St, the *Colophon Café* (☎360/647-0092) is open until 9 or 10pm and serves good soups and salads and great desserts.

The Olympic Peninsula

West of Puget Sound lies the great mass of the **Olympic Peninsula**, much of it now protected land. Small towns are sprinkled sparingly along US-101, which loops around the peninsula's coast, while at the core the Olympic Mountains catch rain clouds as they drift in from the Pacific and drench the surrounding area. In the western river valleys, the dense vegetation thickens into rainforest, which, along with the forests – primarily Sitka spruce, western hemlock, Douglas fir, alder, and maple – and unspoiled Pacific beaches, provide habitat for a huge variety of wildlife and seabirds.

Although large areas of national forest surround the rugged and verdant preserve of **Olympic National Park**, the legacy of timber clear-cutting provides an all-too-visible scar on the landscape, especially if you venture off the main roads into an ecological dead zone riddled with ugly stumps and eroded hillsides. The lumber trade brought the first Western settlers here in the nineteenth century, and while almost every town has a sawmill, the industry teeters in crisis, despite the ongoing efforts of federal bureaucrats to open up more land for timber corporations.

Port Townsend

With its brightly painted Victorian mansions, convivial cafés, and healthy cultural scene, **PORT TOWNSEND** has always had aspirations beyond its small-time logging roots. Gothic mansions sprang up above the flourishing port in the 1890s, when confident predictions of a railroad terminus lured in rich buyers. Unfortunately for the investors, the trains never arrived, and the town was left with a glut of stylish residences and a very small business district.

Perched on the peninsula's northeastern tip across from Keystone on

Whidbey Island, Port Townsend's physical split – half on a bluff, half at sea level – reflects nineteenth-century social divisions, when wealthy merchants built their houses uptown, far above the rowdy clamor and working-class color of the port below. The downtown area rests at the base of the hill, its shops and pleasant cafés centering on **Water Street**, which sports an attractive medley of 1890s brick and stone buildings. In recent times the old mansions have been restored, and the town has mellowed into an artsy community with hippie undertones and a fair amount of charm. For a more detailed look at the area's rich history, check out the museum of the **Jefferson County Historical Society**, 540 Water St (daily 11am–4pm, Sun opens at 1pm; $2; Ⓦwww.jchsmuseum.org), which has an eclectic assortment of items including a photographer's chair draped with bear and buffalo skins, unusual late nine-teenth- and early twentieth-century two-necked harp guitars, and in the base-ment, prison cells that were used as the city jail. Also eye-catching is the grand **Jefferson County Courthouse**, Walker and Jefferson streets (Mon–Fri 9am–5pm; Ⓦwww.co.jefferson.wa.us), a towering red Romanesque Revival edifice with a clock tower that looks like a medieval version of Big Ben.

Though fairly bustling year-round, the town is busiest during its string of **sum-mer festivals** – principally American Fiddle Tunes in early July, Jazz Port Townsend in late July, and the Wooden Boat Festival in September. Some of these take place at the state park at **Fort Worden** (☏360/344-4400, Ⓦwww.olympus.net/ftworden), the remains of a military encampment two miles north of town.

Practicalities

Although Port Townsend is easily accessed by road, you can also get there by **ferry** from Keystone (foot passengers $2 roundtrip, vehicle and driver $7 roundtrip, $8.75 peak season). Get maps and information at the helpful **visitor center**, 2437 E Sims Way (Mon–Fri 9am–5pm; ☏360/385-2722 or 1-888/365-6978, Ⓦwww.ptguide.com), twelve blocks south of the Ferry Terminal on Hwy-20.

There's a good choice of **places to stay**, but prices are fairly high – with the exception of the *HI-Olympic Hostel*, 272 Battery Way (☏360/385-0655 or 1-800/909-4776; $17 dorms, $25 private rooms), in Fort Worden State Park – and vacancies rare in the height of summer. The town's specialty is its **B&Bs**, the best of which occupy grand Victorian mansions uptown, such as the *Ann Starrett Mansion*, 744 Clay St (☏360/385-3205 or 1-800/321-0644, Ⓦwww.starrettmansion.com; ❻), an 1889 Queen Anne with elegant ceiling frescoes, a splendid spiral staircase, and antique furnishings, and the delightful 1888 *Quimper Inn*, 1306 Franklin St (☏360/385-1060 or 1-800/557-1060, Ⓦwww.olympus.net/quimper; ❺), with five rooms furnished with period decor. There are also several fine, nineteenth-century downtown **hotels**, the best being *Manresa Castle*, Seventh and Sheridan streets (☏360/385-5750 or 1-800/732-1281, Ⓦwww.manresacastle.com; ❺–❼), a quasi-French castle from 1892 that has thirty rooms ranging from cozy single units to swanky suites in the tower.

Port Townsend has many fine places to **eat** and **drink**, among them *Fountain Café*, 920 Washington St (☏360/379-9343), with seafood and pasta specialties like oyster stew and wild mushroom risotto, and the *Silverwater Café*, 237 Taylor St (☏360/385-6448), with good fresh seafood such as Northwest floribunda and ahi tuna with lavender pepper. Also excellent is *Sweet Laurette Patisserie*, 1029 Lawrence St (☏360/385-4886), the best French-style bakery in town, featuring elaborate (and expensive) cakes that resemble artworks, and cheaper scones, pies, and pastries with fresh local ingredients.

Port Angeles

Originally named "Puerto de Nuestra Señora de los Angeles" by the Spanish in 1791, **PORT ANGELES** is the peninsula's main town and the most popular point of entry into Olympic National Park, a few miles to the south. Like many other similarly sized towns in the Pacific Northwest, the community is an odd mix of timber-industry grittiness and picturesque beauty, its working-class harbor streaked with industrial chimneys and backdropped by striking mountains. There are few reasons to linger, but the town is a good jumping-point to more compelling destinations.

Although it's preferable to stay inside the park, Port Angeles has a number of inexpensive chain **motels** near its uninspiring one-way main drags, First Street and Front Street. These include the *Best Western Olympic Lodge*, 140 Del Guzzi Drive (T1-800/600-2993, Wwww.portangeleshotelmotel.com; **❹**), and *Traveler's Motel*, 1133 E First St (T360/452-2303, Wwww.travelersmotel.net; **❷**), but for more upscale accommodation, try *Domaine Madeleine*, 146 Wildflower Lane (T360/457-4174, Wwww.domainemadeleine.com; **❻**–**❽**), an elegant B&B with art-themed rooms and a lovely five-acre garden. If you are staying inside the park, at any of the sixteen excellent **campgrounds** ($8–16; T360/565-3130, Wwww.nps.gov/olym), you'll need your own vehicle. Try *Heart o' the Hills*, six miles south of Port Angeles, along Hurricane Ridge Road, or further west, *Elwah* and *Altaire* (closed in winter) are equally good with access to the numerous hiking trails; these three campgrounds are all $10 per night.

For **breakfast** or **lunch**, head for the tiny *First Street Haven*, 107 E First St and Laurel (T360/457-0352), for its seafood, sandwiches, and pasta; for **dinner**, the upscale *Bella Italia*, 118 E First St (T360/457-5442), has decent seafood and traditional Italian cuisine, while *Thai Peppers*, 222 N Lincoln St (T360/452-4995), is surprisingly good for Thai meals.

Port Angeles has the peninsula's best **transportation** connections, which make moving on an easy prospect. Olympic Bus Lines (T360/452-3858, Wwww.olympicbuslines.com) offers daily trips to Seattle ($29) and Sea-Tac Airport ($43), while Clallam Transit buses (75¢–$1.50; T360/452-4511 or 1-800/858-3747, Wwww.clallamtransit.com) go west from Port Angeles around the peninsula to Lake Crescent, Neah Bay, and Forks, and east to Sequim – from there connecting with Jefferson Transit (50¢–$1; T360/385-4777, Wwww.jeffersontransit.com) buses to Port Townsend. Black Ball Transport (T360/457-4491, Wwww.cohoferry.com) runs **ferries** to Victoria in Canada (2–4 daily except Feb) for $9 walk-on one-way fare and $33.50 for a car, while Victoria Express (T360/452-8088 or 1-800/633-1589, Wwww.victoriaexpress.com) operates a faster passenger-only service (2–3 daily) for $25 roundtrip. The **visitor center**, 121 E Railroad St, beside the ferry terminal (summer daily 7am–6pm; rest of year Mon–Fri 10am–4pm; T360/452-2363, Wwww.portangeles.org), has information on the entire peninsula and can put you in touch with local river-rafting and sea-kayaking operators.

Neah Bay and Cape Flattery

Whereas US-101 takes a turn inland from Port Angeles to skirt Olympic National Park, Hwy-112 clambers along the coast for seventy miles to **NEAH BAY**, the tiny fishing village that is home to the **Makah** tribe, seagoing Native Americans almost wiped out by a smallpox epidemic in 1850. The name, given to the tribe by its neighbors, means "generous with food," though in recent years their name has also been synonymous with controversy, regarding an

△ The Space Needle, Seattle, Washington

ongoing series of court battles between the tribe and environmentalists over the resumption of tribal **whale hunting** on the high seas.

In 1970, tidal erosion near Cape Alava uncovered an ancient Makah site that had been buried by a mudslide five hundred years ago. The first witnesses found bizarre scenes of green alder leaves, lying where they had fallen centuries ago, shriveling as soon as they were exposed. The **Ozette Dig**, one of the most significant archeological finds in North America, uncovered thousands of artifacts: harpoons, intricately-carved seal clubs, watertight boxes made without metal, bowls, toys – all from an era before trade with Europeans. The site was reburied in 1981, but the finds are displayed at Neah Bay's **Makah Cultural and Research Center**, Hwy-112 at Bayview Ave (daily summer 10am–5pm, rest of year Wed–Sun only; $4; ⓦ www.makah.com/museum), a well-curated museum displaying marine dioramas, dugout cedar canoes, fishing gear, and a life-sized replica of a fifteenth-century Makah longhouse.

At the northern corner of the Makah Reservation is **CAPE FLATTERY**, the continental US's northwesternmost point, a remote headland accessible on an unpaved road from Neah Bay. A half-mile hike from the road through the rainforest leads to the cape that once "flattered" Captain Cook with the hope of finding a harbor. Below the cape, the waves have worn caves into the sheer rock of the cliff face, while opposite, on **Tatoosh Island**, the Coast Guard runs a remote lighthouse (closed to public view).

You can get to Neah Bay on Clallam Transit (see p.1254), though there are few good options for **accommodation**. Given the area's drab motels, to find anything special you'll have to head seventeen miles east to **Sekiu**, a sports fishing town, to reach *Van Riper's Resort*, 280 Front St (ⓣ360/963-2334, ⓦ www.vanripersresort.com; ❸–❻), which has a range of simple motel rooms and campsites, and more elaborate lodge units and waterfront suites, along with beach access and boat rentals.

Olympic National Park

Stunning **Olympic National Park** covers much of the peninsula's mountainous interior and a detached 57-mile strip of the Pacific coast. Created in 1938 by Franklin D. Roosevelt, partly to ensure the survival of the rare Roosevelt elk, it now has the largest remaining herd in the US. More than two hundred miles of wild rivers wind through the park, while the valleys of the Quinault, Queets, and Hoh rivers contain sizeable tracts of **temperate rainforest** – one of the world's rarest types of climatic forest, seen elsewhere only in Patagonia and New Zealand.

The main **visitor center**, in Port Angeles at 600 E Park Ave (daily 9am–4pm, summer closes 8pm; ⓣ360/452-0330 or 565-3100, ⓦ www.nps.gov/olym), has useful brochures and trail maps, while the **Wilderness Information Center**, 3002 Mount Angeles Rd (April & May daily 8am–4.30pm; May & June daily 7.30am–6pm; July Sun–Thurs 7.30am–6pm, Fri & Sat 7.30am–8pm), supplies information on trail conditions in the area; smaller visitor centers are located at **Hurricane Ridge** and **Hoh Rainforest**. The **entrance fee** is $5 for individuals or $10 per car; both fees are good for seven days of park access. The **weather** is consistently erratic and often rainy – there's even a fair amount of snow as late as June. No roads cross the park, but many run into it, so you'll probably end up making several forays into different sections around the peninsula's western rim.

Hurricane Ridge and Lake Crescent

The main visitor center marks the start of a winding, precipitous road that climbs seventeen miles to daunting **Hurricane Ridge**, where the jagged peaks and sparkling glaciers of the Olympic Mountains spread majestically before you. A **day lodge** on the ridge (May–Oct) has tourist facilities and information. From here, **Hurricane Hill Trail** (3-mile round-trip) is a moderate hike, climbing through wildflower meadows to the peak where, on a clear day, Cape Flattery, the Straits of Juan de Fuca, Vancouver Island, and the Cascade Mountains are all in view. In winter, Clallam Transit **buses** (☎360/452-4511, ⓦwww.clallamtransit.com) climb up to the ridge for cross-country skiing access.

Ten miles west of Port Angeles, glacially carved **Lake Crescent** is popular for trout fishing and hiking on shoreline trails. *Lake Crescent Lodge* (☎360/928-3211, ⓦwww.lakecrescentlodge.com; ❹–❼; May–Oct) is well placed among dense forest on the lake's south shore, offering simple rooms to elegant cottages. Another good place to stay, *Sol Duc Hot Springs Resort* (☎360/327-3583, ⓦwww.northolympic.com/solduc; ❺; March–Oct), is set deep in the park twelve miles off US-101, providing free guest access to **Sol Duc Hot Springs** (otherwise $10) – three pools with mineral-rich waters bubbling out of the ground at 100 to 108F°.

Forks

Beyond the Sol Duc turnoff, US-101 cuts across Olympic National Forest to dreary **FORKS**, a logging burg nestled between the Olympic Mountains and coastal sections of the park. Other than its neighboring temperate rainforests and world-class river fishing, there's little reason to visit the town, except as a base for touring the mountains. Decent **accommodation** is available at *Miller Tree Inn*, 654 E Division St (☎360/374-6806, ⓦwww.millertreeinn.com; ❹–❻), with Victorian-styled suites and pleasant guest rooms, and at *Olympic Suites*, 800 Olympic Drive (☎360/374-5400 or 1-800/262-3433, ⓦwww.olympicsuitesinn.com; ❸), with spacious one- and two-bedroom units. The town's **visitor center** is at 1411 S Forks Ave (Mon–Fri 10am–4pm; ☎360/374-2531 or 1-800/44-FORKS, ⓦwww.forkswa.com).

Hoh Rainforest

One of the park's most popular areas, the **Hoh Rainforest** sits nineteen miles along Upper Hoh River Road, which branches off from US-101 twelve miles south of Forks. From the visitor center (see below), there are two short **trails** to explore: the Hall of Mosses Trail, and the slightly longer Spruce Trail, following along the glacier-fed Hoh River. More energetic hikers can undertake the 36-mile Hoh River Trail up to the base of 8000ft Mount Olympus. Climbing the ice-covered peak is a major undertaking; if you want to **camp** along the route, check in with the rangers and get a wilderness permit ($5, with $2 overnight fee), good for fourteen days of travel for any one of ninety sites. Cougars, black bears, eagles, beavers, and other wildlife are very much present in the park, and in winter Roosevelt elk from higher elevations gather here. For more information, nineteen miles inland from US-101, is the **visitor center** (daily 9am–4pm, summer closes 6.30pm; ☎360/374-6925).

South to Kalaloch and the ocean beaches

Beyond the Hoh turnoff, US-101 dips down to the wild **beaches** of the Pacific coast, where black rocks jut out of the tumultuous sea, and the strong undertow, floating tree trunks, and dramatic tides make the waters striking to watch, if rather unsafe for swimming. The hiking can be magnificent, though, and a series of short, appealing trails head down to and along the seashore – **Ruby Beach**, named for its red-and-black-pebbled sand, is the unmistakable highlight. Near the end of the park's coastal stretch, **KALALOCH** has a few **campgrounds** ($12–16; reserve at ☎1-800/365-CAMP), and the impressive *Kalaloch Lodge* (☎360/962-2271, ⓦwww.visitkalaloch.com), which has basic lodge rooms (**④–⑥**) and more upscale cabins (**⑤–⑦**), as well as a good onsite restaurant. The **ranger station** here also provides information and suggestions for hiking trips (☎360/962-2283).

Queets River Rainforest

South of Kalaloch, US-101 turns inland to circumvent the wilderness of the Quinault Indian Reservation before reaching the 25-mile dirt road that branches northeast to the **Queets River Rainforest**, the least visited of the three main rainforest areas, but worthwhile for its rustic, accessible trails, and especially for the luxuriant flora and fauna along the well-marked trail at the end of the turnoff. Here you can also get a glimpse of the **world's tallest Douglas fir tree** – 220ft tall and 45ft around.

Lake Quinault and the Quinault Rainforest

The most accessible of all the rainforests is the **Quinault Rainforest**, around the shores of glacier-carved **Lake Quinault**, just off US-101. The lake itself was already a popular resort area when Teddy Roosevelt visited in the 1900s and proclaimed it part of an expanded Olympic National Park. Thick and impressive groves fan off from the road, explored by a series of hiking trails: one of the best is the half-mile **Maple Glade Trail** on the north shore, leading through rainforest vegetation. Longer and more difficult trails, such as the dark, four-mile **Quinault Loop Trail**, through looming stands of old-growth trees, take hikers up the forested river valley and into the Olympic Mountains.

The best of Lake Quinault's three **hotels** is the charming 1926 *Quinault Lodge* (☎360/288-2900 or 1-800/562-6672, ⓦwww.visitlakequinault.com; **⑥**), on the shores of Lake Quinault, offering rooms with fireplaces or lakeside views, and a pool and sauna. There are also five lakeside **campgrounds** ($11–16), information for which is available at the **ranger station** (Mon–Fri 8am–4.30pm, Sat & Sun 9am–4pm; ☎360/288-2525, ⓦwww.olympus.net /onf), at 353 S Shore Rd.

Aberdeen and the southwest coast

Heading south on US-101 from Lake Quinault, leaving the national park, it's about forty hilly miles through clear-cut timber land to industrial **ABERDEEN**. Once a major seaport, the place has little claim to fame nowadays, except as Kurt Cobain's hometown – from which he escaped as soon as he could.

At Aberdeen there's a choice of routes: US-12/Hwy-8 lead east towards Olympia (see p.1246), while Hwy-101 pushes south over the hills, threading along the shore of muddy Willapa Bay and the **southwest coast** of Washington. Here, the **Long Beach Peninsula** is something of a low-rent resort area, offering little more than chain motels and a smattering of tourists, who come to browse in the kite shops, gnaw on saltwater taffy, and pick up tacky souvenirs. Worth a trip to the northern tip, however, is **OYSTERVILLE**, a forested collection of rusting old buildings that's the home of **Oysterville Sea Farms** (☎360/665-6585), recognizable by its bayside piles of discarded shells and renowned for its freshly packaged oysters ($5 per pound). Also good for the palate is the **Pacific Coast Cranberry Museum**, 2907 Pioneer Rd in the town of Long Beach (☎360/642-5553, ⓦwww.cranberrymuseum.com), which gives you the opportunity to wander through a cranberry bog and pick up berry-flavored treats.

Down at the far southwestern tip of Washington, near the mouth of the Columbia River, the last points of interest are within scenic **Fort Canby State Park** (daily summer 6.30am–10pm, rest of year closes 4pm; Ⓦwww.parks.wa.gov). The evocative **North Head Lighthouse** (summer daily 11am–3pm; $1), now over a century old, still stands watch, while the informative historical displays of the **Lewis and Clark Interpretive Center** (daily 10am–5pm; $2) tell all about the historical hazards of navigating the Columbia River. Fortunately, you'll be spared any such difficulty as you travel south on Hwy-101 over the 1966 span of the **Astoria Bridge**, crossing the state boundary into Oregon (see p.1284).

The Cascade Mountains

The idyllic beauty of the snowcapped **Cascade Mountains** actually conceals awesome volcanic power – as demonstrated by the 1980 explosion of **Mount St Helens**. The Cascades offer mile upon mile of dense forested wilderness, stretching from Canada to Oregon, traversed by a skein of beautiful trails – which, for all but a few summer months, you'll need snowshoes to hike. The most popular access point is **Mount Rainier**, set in its own national park some ninety miles southeast of Seattle, while the haunting scenery around Mount St Helens compels visitors from near and far. Further north, the **North Cascades National Park** demands more time; Hwy-20, the high mountain road that crosses the Cascades, is by far the most spectacular route to eastern Washington.

The North Cascades and the Cascade Loop

When Hwy-20 opened up the rugged **North Cascades** in 1972, the towns of the eastern foothills created the **Cascade Loop**, a four-hundred-mile roundtrip that channeled tourist traffic along highways 20, 153, 97, and 2 (☏509/662-3888, Ⓦwww.cascadeloop.com). The complete trip is only feasible during the summer, since at other times snow closes the mountain passes, and can be rather exhausting if driven all at once. Unless you have at least three days to explore the territory in full, you're better off taking a few selected treks through the gorgeous environs, and making brief stops at the small, sometimes quirky, towns along the way. Hwy-20 begins its long journey inland at **Anacortes** (see p.1248), from where it crosses the coastal flatlands – passing the **North Cascades National Park Information Center** (Mon–Fri 8am–4.30pm, open daily in summer; ☏360/856-5700, Ⓦwww.nps.gov/noca), 2105 Hwy-20 near Sedro Woolley, where you can learn about the geology, climate, and wildlife of the area.

Winthrop

From the information center, the highway threads through high mountain passes to tiny **WINTHROP**, an old mining town decked out in a Wild West get-up, and the original setting for Owen Wister's *The Virginian*. While the effect is more than a bit cheesy, the false-fronted "saloons" and "dance halls" do make for some good snapshots. If you'd like to **stay**, try either the *Hotel Rio Vista*, 285 Riverside Ave (☏509/996-3535 or 1-800/398-0911, Ⓦwww.hotelriovista .com; ❸–❻, varies by season), whose facade resembles something out of an old-time Hollywood Western, but offers nice suites with hot tubs, kitchenettes, and

DVD players; or the more basic lodging at the *Best Western Cascade Inn*, 960 Hwy-20 (℡509-996-3100 or 1-800/468-6754, ⓦwww.winthropwa.com; ❹).

As for **eating** and **drinking** options, *Winthrop Brewing Co*, 155 Riverside Ave (℡509/996-3183), dispenses solid microbrews like the excellent Outlaw Pale Ale, and the Duck Brand Cantina, 248 Riverside Ave (℡509/996-2192, ⓦwww.methownet.com/duck), serves up cheap and tasty Mexican fare, and has six simple, Western-themed rooms in its onsite B&B (❸). The nearby **visitor center**, 202 Riverside Ave (℡509/996-2125, ⓦwww.winthropwashington .com), has a good range of tourist information and backcountry permits.

Chelan and Stehekin

The well-kept resort of **CHELAN**, sixty miles south of Winthrop, nestles at the foot of Lake Chelan, whose spectacularly deep waters fill a glacially-carved trough nestled in the mountains. Of several good **lodging** options, *Campbell's Resort*, 104 W Woodin Ave (℡509/682-2561 or 1-800/553-8225, ⓦwww.campbellsresort.com; ❹–❻), is the most appealing for its range of lakeside rooms and suites – some of which come with fireplaces, kitchenettes, and balconies – though rates vary widely by season. Cheaper digs are available at the *Apple Inn Motel*, 1002 E Woodin Ave (℡509/682-4044; ❸). Spots to **eat** include *Peter B's Bar & Grill*, 116 E Woodin Ave (℡509/682-1031), and *Deepwater Brewing & Public House*, 225 Hwy-20 (℡509/682-2720), which has burgers, salads, and steaks, as well as its own microbrews. The **ranger station** at 428 W Woodin Ave (daily 7.30am–4.30pm; ℡509/682-2576) can ply you with hiking maps when you're ready to hit the trails.

The Lake Chelan Boat Company, 1418 W Woodin Ave (℡509/682-2224 info, ℡509/682-4584 reservations, ⓦwww.ladyofthelake.com), runs a passenger ferry service to the head of Lake Chelan, with scheduled stops at Field's Point, Lucerne, and Stehekin. Leaving from the jetty a mile west of town on Woodin Avenue, the *Lady of the Lake II* takes four hours to cruise the 55 miles of the nation's deepest gorge, leaving daily (May–Oct) at 8.30am and returning at 6pm ($16.50 one way, $26 roundtrip). There's also the year-round *Lady Express* (May–Oct $28.50 one way, $45 roundtrip; Nov–April $26 roundtrip), which reaches Lake Chelan's mountainous western tip in half the time, and the *Lady Cat*, a high-speed catamaran that takes you on a thrilling 75min jaunt (June–Sept only; $57 one way, $90 roundtrip). These cruises feature 60- to 90-minute layovers at **STEHEKIN**, a tiny, isolated village otherwise accessible only by a Chelan Airways **seaplane** ($80 one way, $120 roundtrip; ℡509/682-5555, ⓦwww.chelanairways.com), which is also available for airborne **tours** of the region ($80–169). At Stehekin there are **campsites** and trailheads leading to some of the best hiking and backpacking in the North Cascades. Bikes and canoes are available from the *North Cascades Stehekin Lodge* (reserve at ℡509/682-4494, ⓦwww.stehekin.com; ❹–❻), where the lakeside rooms are a bit pricier than standard units. For camping and hiking information (and, for some of the trails, a free wilderness permit), visit the **Golden West Visitor Center** near the Stehekin jetty (April–Oct daily 8am–5pm; ℡360/856-5700, ⓦwww.nps.gov/noca).

Leavenworth

A few miles south of Chelan, the Cascade Loop turns west along US-2 at **Wenatchee**, the workaday town that grows nearly half the country's supply of apples. From there, the loop heads for pocket-sized **LEAVENWORTH**, a Bavarian theme town where even the *Safeway* and *McDonald's* are decked out in high gables and half-timbered woodwork. It only takes about an hour to explore the place, but there are plenty of outdoor activities to be had in the spectacular mountain setting. The **ranger station**, just off US-2 at 600 Sherbourne St (daily 7.45am–4.30pm; ☎509/782-1413), provides trail guides and hiking information, and **bikes**, **canoes**, and **kayaks** can be rented from several outlets, including Leavenworth Mountain Sports, 940 Hwy-2 at Icicle Rd (☎509/548-7864). The nearby **visitor center**, 894 Hwy-2 (☎509/548-5807, ⓦwww.leavenworth.org), has copious listings of places to **stay** and **eat**. Downtown options include the cozy rooms and suites of the *Hotel Pension Anna*, 926 Commercial St (☎509/548-6273, ⓦwww.pensionanna.com; ❹–❻), decked out in cheerful Teutonic kitsch; and the comparable *Enzian Motor Inn*, 590 Hwy-2 (☎509/548-5269 or 1-800/223-8511, ⓦwww.enzianinn.com; ❺), where the rooms are a bit more tasteful. The *Andreas Keller*, 829 Front St (☎509/548-6000), doles out hefty helpings of gut-busting German cuisine, as does *King Ludwig's*, 921 Front St (☎509/548-6625), which also features lively Bavarian dancing, hearty pork schnitzel, and beer-bearing barmaids – bring your Tyrolean hat.

West of Leavenworth, US-2 crosses the mountains over Stevens Pass, but the principal east–west highway, I-90, lies further to the south, connecting Seattle with the Yakima Valley. Near I-90 is the 268ft **Snoqualmie Falls** (☎425/831-5784, ⓦwww.snoqualmiefalls.com), featuring evocative nature walks overrun by tourists, and the luxurious *Salish Lodge*, 6501 Railroad Ave SE (☎425/888-2556 or 1-800/826-6124, ⓦwww.salishlodge.com; ❾), where much of the David Lynch TV series *Twin Peaks* was filmed.

Mount Rainier National Park

Set in its own national park, glacier-clad **MOUNT RAINIER** is the highest (14,410ft) and most accessible peak in the Cascades, and a major Washington landmark. Recurrent puns characterize its name as a description of its weather: often very wet, with heavy snowfalls during the long winter season (except if joking, pronounce the name as "ray-NEER"). Not until midsummer does the snowpack melt enough to unblock roads, and then the deer, mountain goats, and marmots reappear, the alpine meadows become ablaze with dazzling wildflowers, and Mount Rainier makes for some perfect hiking.

If you only have a day to explore the park, consider traversing the south and east sides from the Nisqually entrance to **Paradise**, with a side trip to **Sunrise**. The stunning eighty-mile drive winds through river valleys and lowland forests with glaciated peaks and magnificent vistas. There are numerous **trails** radiating from Paradise, such as the 1.2-mile Nisqually Vista Trail loop and the five-mile Skyline Trail to Glacier Overlook, the perfect spot to ponder the awesome Nisqually Glacier. In all, more than three hundred miles of trails criss-cross Mount Rainier National Park, ranging from short, simple interpretive walks, to the Pacific Crest Trail that cuts through the park's eastern edge, and the 93-mile Wonderland Trail that encircles Mount Rainier itself.

Climbing Mount Rainier itself is hazardous and should only be undertaken by experienced climbers who are physically fit and properly equipped for the ensuing rigors. The long-established guide service, Rainier Mountaineering, in Paradise (☎360/569-2227 or 253/627-6242 in winter, ⓦwww.rmiguides.com), offers a one-day climbing course followed by a two-day guided climb to the summit for $771.

The Paradise **visitor center** (May to mid-Oct daily 9am–7pm; winter Sat & Sun 10am–5pm; ☎360/569-2211 ext 2328) has films and exhibits on natural history and a circular observation room for viewing the mountain.

Practicalities

Admission to the park is $10 per vehicle, $5 per person, for a one-week pass. The park has four **entrances**: **Nisqually** in the southwest corner, **Stephen's Canyon** in the southeast, **White River** in the northeast, and **Carbon River** in the northwest. Only the Nisqually entrance is open year-round (for cross-country skiing; the others open June–Sept). For map and trail conditions, stop by the **visitor centers** at Longmire, Ohanapecosh, Paradise, and White River (details at ⓦwww.nps.gov/mora). During the summer, you can drive the 240 miles of roads that almost encircle Mount Rainier National Park to the various entrances. The Nisqually entrance is the only part serviced by public **transportation** – either on a ten-hour day-trip with Gray Line from Seattle (May–Sept; $54; ⓣ360/624-5077 or 1-800/426-7505, ⓦwww.graylineseattle.com), or from Sea-Tac Airport to Paradise via Rainier Shuttle (May–Oct; $46 one way; ⓣ360/569-2331, ⓦwww.rainiershuttle.com), or on a shuttle from the Ashford Mountain Center (June–Sept; rates vary; ⓣ360/569-2604, ⓦwww.ashfordmountaincenter.com). There is no public transportation within the park.

Two national park lodges provide **accommodation**: *National Park Inn* (ⓣ360/569-2275, ⓦwww.guestservices.com/rainier; ❹), nestled in a forest at Longmire, is a classic rustic lodge open year-round, with 25 guestrooms and a restaurant, while further up the mountain, *Paradise Inn* (mid-May to early Oct; ⓣ360/569-2275; ❹), is a massive 1917 wooden lodge, where the striking views, not the functional rooms, are the main draw. Make reservations well in advance. Outside the park, in the town of Ashford, *Whittaker's Bunkhouse*, 30205 SR 706 E (ⓣ360/569-2439; ❶–❹), is a favorite among local climbers and hikers, an old loggers' bunkhouse with both dorm beds and double rooms, with private baths. The park's six serviceable **campgrounds** require **permits** (ⓣ360/569-2211 or ⓦreservations.nps.gov) and reservations (free; ⓣ1-800/365-CAMP), which you can obtain up to 24 hours in advance from any hiking center in the park. For overnight **backpacking**, pick up a required wilderness permit, free from Longmire, White River, or Paradise ranger stations (ⓣ360/569-2211).

Mount St Helens

The Klickitat tribe that called **MOUNT ST HELENS** *Tahonelatclah* ("Fire Mountain") knew what they were talking about: the volcano erupted on May 18, 1980, leaving a scorched area of near-total destruction. Its blast wave flattened the surrounding forests, heavy clouds of ash settled as far away as Portland, and a massive mudflow sent an avalanche of debris down the Toutle River Valley. Since then, the forests have begun their regrowth, and many animal species have made a surprisingly quick recovery, though the scarred landscape still testifies to the awesome force of nature. All this has led to Mount St Helens justifiably becoming a major tourist attraction.

Located in a remote pocket of Gifford Pinchot National Forest, the area around the mountain has three entry routes. Most visitors arrive along Hwy-504, off I-5 roughly halfway between Olympia and Portland. The road snakes through dark green forests until bald, spiky trees give way to thousands of lifeless gray trees lying in combed-down rows, knocked flat as the blast waves bounced off the hillsides. At the end is the **Johnson Ridge Observatory** (May–Sept daily 10am–6pm; ⓣ360/274-2140), offering breathtaking views of the still-steaming lava dome and crater, plus mildly interesting displays, a film of the eruption of Mount St Helens, and testimonials by blast survivors. On bright summer days, **views** of the mountain can be both unexpectedly

The eruption of Mount St Helens

From its first rumblings in March 1980, **Mount St Helens** drew the nation's attention as one of the (recent) rare examples of volcanic activity in the continental US. Residents and loggers were evacuated and roads were closed, but by April the entrances to the restricted zone around the steaming peak were jammed with reporters and sightseers. But the mountain didn't seem to be doing much, and impatient residents demanded to be allowed back to their homes. Harry Truman, operator of the *Lodge at Spirit Lake*, famously refused to move out and became a national celebrity – lauded for his "common sense" by Washington's governor.

A convoy of homeowners was waiting at the barriers, about to go and collect their possessions, when the **explosion** finally came on May 18 – powered by subsurface water heated to boiling by geothermal activity, and causing a chain reaction that blew apart the peak not upwards but sideways, ripping a great chunk out of the northwest side of the mountain. An avalanche of debris slid into Spirit Lake, raising it by two hundred feet and turning it into a steaming cauldron of mud, as dark clouds of ash buried Truman and suffocated loggers on a nearby slope. Altogether, 57 people died on the mountain: a few were there doing their official duties, but most, like Harry Truman, had ignored the warnings. The wildlife population was harder hit: about a million and a half animals – deer, elk, mountain goats, cougar, and bears – were killed, and thousands of fish were boiled alive in sediment-filled rivers. There were dire economic effects, too, as falling ash devastated the land, and millions of feet of timber were lost. These days, the volcanic result is still visible, and not just up-close on the mountain roads – looking north from Portland, you can't help but notice the unmistakable silhouette of a ruined gray mound looming over the northern horizon, the remains of what was once a lively and romantic winter playground.

picturesque and starkly ominous. The only real disadvantage with the Hwy-504 approach to Mount St Helens is its popularity – you can expect long caravans of SUVs and RVs on any fair-weather day, and exponentially huge numbers of tourists at the observatory.

One alternative is to take Hwy-503 from Portland (or I-5) to **Cougar**, on the mountain's southern side – a surprisingly moist and verdant terrain, which last saw a major eruption two thousand years ago – from where the summer-only forest roads USFS-90, -25, and -99 wind along its flanks to **Windy Ridge** on the northeast side of the mountain. Attracting only a fraction of the tourists swarming on Johnson Ridge, this is the best place to view the volcanic apocalypse up close: entire slopes denuded of foliage, colossal tree husks scattered like twigs, and huge dead zones where anything alive was simply vaporized. Windy Ridge can also be accessed from the north from **Randle** along USFS-25 and -99, which provides access to what remains of Spirit Lake and passes through lava flows with numerous viewpoints en route.

Practicalities

Mount St Helens National Monument charges a $6 **Monument Pass** that allows visitors access to all the areas around it, while the $3 **Site Day Pass** is good only for the Coldwater Ridge and Mount St Helens visitor centers, and the Johnston Ridge Observatory. En route to Windy Ridge from Hwy-503 is the **Mount St Helens Volcanic Monument Headquarters** (daily 8am–5pm; ☎360/247-3900, @www.fs.fed.us/gpnf/mshnvm) in Amboy, which has maps and information. Just off the I-5 near Castle Rock is the **Mount St Helens Visitor Center** (daily 9am–5pm; ☎360/274-2103), complete with informative exhibits, while the **Coldwater Ridge Visitor Center**, 3029 Spirit Lake Hwy (daily 10am–6pm, winter 9am–4pm; ☎360/274-2131), focuses on the ways plants and animals have successfully recolonized the blast zones.

Although there aren't any **campgrounds** within the national monument, there are several dotted along the approach roads, including at **Seaquest State Park** (daily summer entry 8am–8pm, rest of year 8am–5pm; campsites $15–21; ☎1-800/452-5687), which abuts Silver Lake about five miles east of I-5 on Hwy-504; other options are the **private campgrounds** in the vicinity of Cougar (June–Aug only; $15; ☎503/813-6666).

Eastern Washington

The big, dry, and hot expanse of **eastern Washington** has little in common with its green, western counterpart: faded olive-colored sagebrush covers many acres, and massive red rocks loom over the prairies, while huge bare patches of basalt and torn-away groundcover (from centuries of Ice Age floods) give the area the unattractive geological moniker of the "**channeled scablands.**" To the south lies the lower Yakima Valley, a vast agricultural belt with miles of orchards and farms flanking the Yakima River. With more than three hundred sunny days a year, the region is the largest producer of apples in the world, though that claim is increasingly threatened by cheap fruit imports from China. In the last twenty years, this has also become one of the Northwest's major wine regions. The area towns are agricultural and commercial centers, but only **Spokane** has any degree of cultural life. Nevertheless, some are decent bases for winery tours or outdoor activities such as rafting, fishing, hiking, and skiing.

Ellensburg

If you're traveling east of the mountains along I-90, the first notable stop will be **ELLENSBURG**, a dusty little town with fetching nineteenth-century red-brick architecture, a regional university, and not much else – except for the **Ellensburg Rodeo** (tickets start at $10; ☎509/962-7831 or 1-800/637-2444, ⓦwww.ellensburgrodeo.com), held over Labor Day weekend and featuring Stetson-wearing cowhands roping steers, riding bulls, and braving bucking broncos.

Greyhound stops at 1512 Hwy-97. The **visitor center**, 609 N Main St (Mon–Fri 8am–6pm, Sat 10am–4pm, Sun 10am–2pm; ☎509/925-3137, ⓦwww.ellensburg-chamber.com), provides maps and **hotel** options; one safe choice is the basic *Ellensburg Inn*, 1700 Canyon Rd (☎509/925-9801; ❹). The Art Deco *Valley Café*, 103 W Third Ave (☎509/925-3050), is a good place to **dine** on eclectic American fare.

Yakima and Toppenish

To the south on I-82, the agricultural hub of **YAKIMA** has very few attractions, but is an excellent base to visit the tasting rooms of the award-winning vintners scattered throughout the Yakima Valley (for information call the Yakima Valley Wine Growers Association ☎1-800/258-7270, ⓦwww.yakimavalleywine.com). The only appealing part of downtown is among the brightly painted railroad cars of **Track 29**, Yakima Ave at N First St (☎509/542-4879), a mall that houses a serviceable collection of shops and food vendors.

Wine-tour maps, as well as lodging and dining information, can be found at the **visitor center**, 10 N Eighth St (Mon–Fri 8.30am–5pm, also summer weekends 9am–4pm; ☎509/575-3010 or 1-800/221-0751, ⓦwww.visityaki-ma.com). Greyhound stops nearby at 602 E Yakima Ave. Standard-issue **motels** and **diners** abound along N First Street; also on the block is *Gasparetti's*, no. 1013 (☎509/248-0628), providing agreeable Italian fare, while at Track 29, *Grant's Brewery Pub*, 32 N Front St (☎509/575-2922), serves hand-crafted ales and tasty pub food. *Santiago's*, 111 E Yakima Ave (☎509/453-1644), has the usual range of Mexican staples. There's **camping** across the Yakima River on Hwy-24 at **Sportsman State Park** ($15–21; ☎509/575-2774 or 1-800/562-0990).

Twenty miles south of Yakima, **TOPPENISH**, the main town on the Yakima Indian Reservation, has a Wild West feel enlivened by buildings with historic Western murals. The **Chamber of Commerce** (☎509/865-3262) provides brochures on the murals and information on **accommodation**. The modern and comfortable *Best Western Lincoln Inn*, 515 S Elm St (☎509/865-7444 or 1-800/222-3161; ❸), is the best choice, and there are also a few good **restaurants** in the area, notably *Snipes Mountain Brewery & Restaurant*, 905 Yakima Valley Hwy in nearby Sunnyside (☎509/837-BREW), which serves great regional food, microbrews, and wine.

Walla Walla

About 120 miles east of Yakima along I-82 and US-12, **WALLA WALLA** is an uneventful college and agricultural town best known for its sweet onions – eaten raw like apples. There's little to see here, but this was the place where the missionary **Dr Marcus Whitman** arrived from the East Coast in 1836, first trying to convert the local Cayuse, then turning his attention to white settlers. After a series of conflicts with the Cayuse, and accusations of fatally poisoning the tribe with measles, in November 1847 a band of natives murdered Whitman, his wife, and eleven others. Fifty more, mostly children, were taken captive, and although they were later released, angry settlers raised vigilante bands against the tribe. When the story hit the newspapers back East, it generated such fear about native uprisings that the government finally declared the Oregon land (then including Washington) a US territory, which meant the army could be sent in to protect the settlers – and deal harshly with Native Americans.

The site where the **Whitman Mission** was burned down (daily 8am–4.30pm, summer until 6pm; $3; ☎509/522-6360, ⓦwww.nps.gov /whmi), in a lovely little dell seven miles west of town off US-12, has simple marks on the ground to illustrate its layout; a **visitor center** shows a film on Whitman and exhibits the weapon thought to have polished him off. Of more pseudo-historical value, the **Fort Walla Walla Museum**, 755 Myra Rd (April–Oct daily 10am–5pm; ⓦwww.fortwallawallamuseum.org; $6), is a curious mock-up of a pioneer village, with sixteen shacks loaded with antiques and Old West dioramas.

Greyhound stops at 315 N Second St, a few blocks from Walla Walla's **visitor center**, 29 E Sumach (Mon–Fri 8.30am–5pm, Sat & Sun 9am–5pm; ☎509/WW-VISIT, ⓦwww.wwchamber.com). The *Walla Walla Suites*, 7 E Oak St (☎509/525-4700; ❹), provides good basic **accommodation**, while the *Green Gables Inn*, 922 Bonsella St (☎1-888/525-5501, ⓦwww.greengablesinn .com; ❺), is a comfortable B&B in an old mansion, with private baths, fridges, and VCRs in the rooms. There are a few good **eateries**, mostly downtown: *Merchants Ltd French Bakery*, 21 E Main St (☎509/525-0900), is a nice spot for espresso and pastries.

Spokane

The wide-open spaces and drab little burgs of eastern Washington don't prepare you for **SPOKANE** ("spo-CAN"), the region's only real city of any size. A few miles from the Idaho border, its scattering of grandiose late nineteenth-century buildings – built on the spoils of Idaho silver mines – sport some unexpectedly elegant touches. But its heyday is long gone, and shades of the dreary freight town it became still haunt the city today. It's not a place to linger long, but its pleasant parks and striking architecture can nicely fill a half-day. The town's hub is hundred-acre **Riverfront Park** (ⓦwww.spokaneriverfrontpark.com), sprawling over two islands in the middle of the Spokane River. Bisecting the park, the river tumbles down a series of rocky shelves known as the **Spokane Falls**, once a fishing site for native peoples and later the home of the first pioneers. Attractions include an ice-skating rink, the charming hand-carved **Looff Carousel** (April–July daily 11am–6pm; $2), and the **Gondola Skyride** cable cars (closed until fall 2004), which normally run above the falls from the west end of the park. **Day passes** to all attractions are $15.

Most of the relics of Spokane's early grandeur can be found several blocks southwest on West Riverside Avenue, where Neoclassical facades cluster around Jefferson Street. The city's other architectural highlights include the newly renovated 1914 **Davenport Hotel**, 10 S Post St (ⓣ1-800/899-1482 or 509/455-8888, ⓦwww.thedavenporthotel.com; ❼), with its wildly ornate lobby and spacious, well-designed suites; the **Clark Mansion**, 2208 W Second Ave (ⓣ509/838-8300), an 1897 marvel that's now home to *Patsy Clark's*, a swank international-cuisine restaurant; and the Tudor Revival **Campbell House**, 2316 W First Ave. The latter is tourable as a part of the **Northwest Museum of Art and Culture**, at the same site (Tues–Sun 11am–5pm; $7; ⓦwww.northwestmuseum.org), a newly redesigned museum focusing on historic and modern artworks, popular culture, regional heritage, and international art from as far away as nineteenth-century Japan and seventeenth-century Holland.

Practicalities

Amtrak, Greyhound, Northwestern Trailways (ⓣ1-800/366-3830, ⓦuser.nwadv.com/northw), and local bus lines share the **transit center** at 221 W First St. The **visitor center** is at 201 W Main St (Mon–Fri 8.30am–5pm; ⓣ509/747-3230 or 1-800/776-5263, ⓦwww.visitspokane.com). Apart from the stylish *Davenport* (above), affordable **accommodations** include the basic *Towne Center Motel*, 901 W First Ave (ⓣ509/747-1041; ❸), the *Travelodge*, 33 W Spokane Falls Blvd (ⓣ509/623-9727, ⓦwww.spokanetravelodge.com; ❹), and the *West Coast Ridpath*, 515 W Sprague Ave (ⓣ509/838-2711, ⓦwww.westcoasthotels.com; ❺), a 350-room hotel with good views over the city. More generic motels line I-90, and there's **camping** in Riverside State Park ($15–21; ⓣ509/456-3964), six miles northwest off Hwy-291. For **eating**, *Luna*, 5620 S Perry St (ⓣ509/448-2383), serves up delicious, pricey Northwest Cuisine and cheaper gourmet pizzas, while innovative vegetarian cuisine is available at *Mizuna*, 214 N Howard St (ⓣ509/747-2004), including a mean orange-pepper tofu.

The Grand Coulee Dam and around

Eighty miles west of Spokane, amid parched, dusty land scoured by Ice Age–era floods, the vast **Grand Coulee Dam** holds the honor of being the largest concrete structure in the world – at least until China's Yangtze River Dam dwarfs it upon completion. When work began in 1933, it was as much a political icon as an engineering feat. Perhaps the most ambitious scheme of Roosevelt's New Deal, this massive dam provided jobs for hundreds of workers from all over the country, including folk singer **Woody Guthrie**, who also worked on the Bonneville Dam in the Columbia Gorge (see p.1278) and was commissioned to write twenty songs about the project.

The dam's unquestioned heyday was during World War II, when its water-power was harnessed into making the aluminum that became essential to the production of war materiel. Now the world's third-biggest producer of **hydro-electricity**, the dam has certainly controlled flooding lower down the Columbia. Unfortunately, power-guzzling agricultural and industrial demands have made this dam, like others along the Columbia, a potent symbol of the decline of native salmon, whose migration routes have largely disappeared in recent decades, thanks to the looming turbines and concrete walls in their way.

The earlier, more heroic story of power production is detailed in the **visitor center**, on Hwy-155 on the west side of the dam (daily 9am–5pm; free; ☎509/633-9265, ⓦwww.grandcouleedam.org), which also runs free tours of the dam and its four massive generating plants (daily every half-hour 10am–5pm). The **dam** itself is initially something of an anticlimax; because of its horizontal layout, it just doesn't look that big – a trick of the hugely scaled scenery that surrounds it. On summer nights (June–Sept) it's lit up by a **laser show** that takes place from 8.30pm to 10pm, depending on the month.

The neighboring towns of **Coulee Dam**, **Grand Coulee**, and **Electric City** have a few generic **motels** and fairly dire **restaurants**. More appealingly, more than thirty **campgrounds** are scattered around the long, spindly reservoir of **Lake Roosevelt**, which becomes more woody and secluded as you get further north. The more noteworthy spots include *Spring Canyon Campground*, located on the lake itself ($10 May–Sept, rest of year $5; ☎509/633-9188, ⓦwww.nps.gov/laro), and *Steamboat Rock State Park*, twelve miles south of Grand Coulee ($15–21; ☎509/633-1304).

Oregon

For nineteenth-century pioneers, riding in covered wagons over the mountains and deserts of the arduous Oregon Trail, the rich and fertile **Willamette Valley** was the promised land, and an obvious choice for Oregon's first settlements. Today, the valley is still the heart of the state's social, political, and cultural existence. **Portland**, the biggest city, has a cozy European feel; **Salem**, the state capital, maintains a small-town air; and **Eugene**, at the southern foot of the valley, is a likeable college community.

East of Portland, waterfalls cascade down mossy cliffs along the **Columbia River Gorge**, south of which looms the imposing presence of **Mount Hood**. Central Oregon, and its popular recreation hub of **Bend**, is located on a high chaparral desert, with close access to the southern Cascades, as well as numerous lakes and rivers dropping into striking canyons. Further south, around **Grants Pass** the major rivers carve steep gorges and make for some excellent whitewater rafting, while the liberal hamlet of **Ashland** offers a splash of culture with its annual Shakespeare Festival.

Several highways link the Willamette Valley to the coast, whose most northerly town, **Astoria**, enjoys a magnificent setting strewn with imposing Victorian homes, looking across to the coast of southwest Washington (see p.1246). South along the **Oregon coast**, wide and protected expanses of sand are broken by jagged black monoliths, pale lighthouses look out from stark headlands, and rough cliffs conceal small, sheltered coves. With its sand dunes, dense forests, and sheer variety, the coast is every bit as appealing as its Californian counterpart, and though colder, is also more accessible.

The rugged deserts and lava fields of **Eastern Oregon** are more remote and were only settled once the prime land in the west had already been taken. The colonization involved not only ferocious "Indian campaigns" but also bitterly violent range wars between sheep-farmers and terrorist "sheep-shooters" (associations of cattle ranchers). Sheep and cows now graze in peace, and some small towns still celebrate their cowboy roots with annual rodeos.

Wherever you go, make an effort to pronounce the state's name as "OR-uh-gun"; calling it "ORY-gone" will immediately mark you as an outsider, and is sure to invite a curt correction.

Getting around Oregon

Portland is well connected by **train** and **bus** along the I-5 freeway to Seattle in the north and California to the south. Amtrak runs its *Coast Starlight* train once daily north to Seattle or south to LA, its *Cascades* line four times daily between Eugene and Vancouver, BC, and a special unnamed service to Astoria several times a week. Bus routes radiate from Portland out to Spokane in Washington, across southern and central Oregon and to the coast. There's also a twice-daily service from Portland to San Francisco along US-101, and another following the line of I-84 east from Portland as far as Pendleton, and then south towards Boise in Idaho. Finally, Pacific Trails (☎503/692-4437) runs buses from Portland to the Oregon Coast; once there (and formidable wind gusts aside), **cycling** along the coast is a rewarding endeavor.

Having your own vehicle can facilitate access to many of the state's more remote spots, especially if you're planning to sample the great hiking and camping options on hand (see Ⓦwww.oregonstateparks.org for the range of choices).

Portland

Having been spared Seattle's aggressive, remorseless development, **PORT-LAND** retains a pleasant, small-city feel, both for its well-preserved Beaux Arts architecture and walkable urban core, as well as its easygoing atmosphere. That said, there's not a lot to keep intrepid explorers here for more than a day, with most of the city's handful of major attractions located within close walking distance of each other on the short city blocks – half the size of most American cities. On the other hand, while Portland's unpretentious bohemian flavor may be lost on more gung-ho travelers, the city remains an excellent spot for casual visitors to slack around for weeks at a time, with a wealth of good diners, microbreweries, clubs, bookstores, and coffeehouses.

The city was named after Portland, Maine, following a coin toss between its two East Coast founders in 1845 ("Boston" was the other option). Its location on a deep part of the **Willamette River**, just 78 miles from the Pacific and surrounded by fertile valleys, made it a perfect trading port, and it grew quickly, replacing its clapboard houses with ornate facades and Gothic gables. Nevertheless, throughout the nineteenth century it remained a raunchy, bawdy place, notorious for gambling, prostitution, and opium dens. The situation was dire enough that Simon Benson, one of the area's magnates in the timber trade – an industry that largely defined the city's wealth until the later twentieth century – even paid for the creation of numerous "**Benson Bubblers**" around town to encourage local laborers to guzzle a liquid other than alcohol. Whether this plan had any effect is doubtful, but these constantly flowing, four-headed drinking fountains are still one of the prime fixtures on downtown streets – just lean over for a gulp.

The lumber industry gradually started to decline, and by the 1970s, Portland's historic buildings had decayed or were sacrificed to parking lots and expressways. In the last few decades, however, much effort has been made to salvage what was left of its past, replacing concrete with red brick, and introducing folksy statues and murals. Although the city's rehabilitation, along with its "urban growth boundary" to limit unrestrained development, has done much for its reputation nationwide, it's also achieved an unfortunate reputation as financial ground zero, facing the nation's worst unemployment rates, school-funding crises, and dismal economic conditions. Unlike most other cities, though, local residents haven't been moving out in droves, which makes for a rather strange situation: a colorful, vibrant city largely running on fumes.

Arrival and information

Portland International Airport (PDX) is a thirty-minute drive from downtown, by either the Gray Line Airport Express bus (every 45min 5am–midnight; $15 one way, $22 roundtrip; ☏1-888/684-3322, ⓦwww.grayline.com), which drops off at major hotels, or the MAX "Red Line" light rail (3–5 hourly, 4am–11pm; $1.60), which connects to the airport near Terminal C and takes about forty minutes to reach Pioneer Square downtown. A **cab** from the airport into town costs $25–30. Greyhound, 550 NW 6th Ave, and Amtrak, close by at 800 NW 6th Ave, are both in the Pearl District and conveniently located within easy walking distance of the center; if you arrive at night, take a cab – this part of town is deserted and dicey after dark.

The **visitor center**, in Pioneer Square at 701 SW 6th Ave (Mon–Fri 8.30am–5.30pm, Sat 10am–4pm, Sun 10am–2pm; ☏503/275-8355 or 1-877/678-5263, ⓦwww.pova.org), has plenty of maps and information on both the city and the state. Portland's main **post office** is at 715 NW Hoyt St (☏503/294-2124; zip code 97205). Unlike most US states, Oregon has **no sales tax** – a major reason for its budgetary woes – so buying goods here can be somewhat cheaper than in neighboring states.

City transportation

Although you can see much of the compact city center on **foot**, or along the city's impressive, extensive network of **cycling** paths and trails (ⓦwww .trans.ci.portland.or.us/bicycles for maps and information), Portland also has an excellent public transit network. Its **light rail** system, Metropolitan Area Express (MAX), channels tourists around central downtown and Old Town, connects to the western and eastern suburbs, and tunnels under Washington Park and the zoo. Tri-Met **buses** are based at the downtown **transit mall** along Fifth Avenue (southbound) and Sixth Avenue (northbound). Each bus shelter is labeled with a

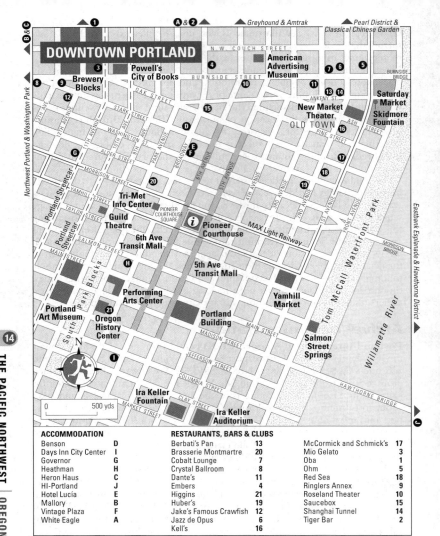

ACCOMMODATION

Benson	D
Days Inn City Center	I
Governor	G
Heathman	H
Heron Haus	C
HI-Portland	J
Hotel Lucia	E
Mallory	B
Vintage Plaza	F
White Eagle	A

RESTAURANTS, BARS & CLUBS

Berbati's Pan	13		McCormick and Schmick's	17
Brasserie Montmartre	20		Mio Gelato	3
Cobalt Lounge	7		Oba	1
Crystal Ballroom	8		Ohm	5
Dante's	11		Red Sea	18
Embers	4		Ringlers Annex	9
Higgins	21		Roseland Theater	10
Huber's	19		Saucebox	15
Jake's Famous Crawfish	12		Shanghai Tunnel	14
Jazz de Opus	6		Tiger Bar	2
Kell's	16			

color which serves as a code for a block of bus routes in a particular area of the city. Although excellent for transportation, the mall is not a place to linger: it's well-known as a drug-dealing zone. The **Tri-Met Customer Assistance Office** in Pioneer Square (Mon–Fri 8.30am–5.30pm; ☎503/238-7433, for disabled customers ☎503/238-4952, ⊛www.trimet.org) offers free transit maps and sells all-zone day tickets ($4), "Quik Tik" six-hour passes ($3), books of ten tickets ($12.50), and monthly passes ($47) with special disabled rates ($34).

The brightly colored cars of the **Portland Streetcar** line ply a tourist-oriented route between Portland State University, the Pearl District, and

Northwest Portland, covering most downtown sights on NW and SW 10th and 11th streets. Fares are free inside Fareless Square, otherwise $1.30 (Ⓦwww.portlandstreetcar.org). Portland's **taxis** don't stop in the street; you'll have to either get one at a hotel or call Broadway Cab (☏503/227-1234) or Portland Taxi Co. (☏503/256-5400).

Accommodation

Scads of flavorless **motels** line the interstates and Sandy Boulevard northeast of the city center, but for a few dollars more you're far better staying downtown, where you'll find **hostels**, **B&Bs**, and a good range of **hotels**, the pick of which occupy grand and elegantly restored old buildings.

Hotels, motels, and B&Bs

Benson 309 SW Broadway ☏503/228-2000 or 1-888/523-6766, Ⓦwww.bensonhotel.com. The typical spot for visiting dignitaries and celebs, this classy hotel has a superb walnut-paneled 1912 lobby, swank bedrooms with modern appointments, and a range of rooms, suites, and even penthouses. ❽

Days Inn City Center 1414 SW 6th Ave ☏503/221-1611, Ⓦwww.daysinn.com. Great location with smart, well-tended motel rooms. Excellent value for the area. ❸

Edgefield 2126 SW Halsey St ☏503/669-8610 or 1-800/669-8610, Ⓦwww.mcmenamins.com/edge. Fifteen minutes east of the airport in the drab suburb of Troutdale, this unique brewery-resort features restaurants, bars, winery and tasting room, distillery, movie theater, gardens, and an 18-hole British golf course. Also with its own hostel, at $20 per dorm bed. Rooms ❹

Governor 611 SW 10th Ave ☏1-800/554-3456 or 503-224-3400, Ⓦwww.govhotel.com. What some claim to be Portland's best hotel, with elegant rooms and suites with fireplaces, spas, sofas, and stylish decor, plus an onsite pool and fitness center. Centrally located a block from MAX and streetcar lines. ❼

Heathman 1001 SW Broadway at Salmon St ☏503/241-4100 or 1-800/551-0011, Ⓦwww.heathmanhotel.com. Occupies a finely restored Neoclassical building, with an elegant, teak-paneled interior and much marble and brass. Splendid rooms and suites, excellent restaurant, and popular lobby-lounge where you can swill among the swells. ❼–❾

Heron Haus 2545 NW Westover Rd ☏503/274-1846, Ⓦwww.heronhaus.com. Stylish 1904 Tudor B&B, with some large suites featuring fireplaces, spas, and cozy sitting areas. Excellent continental breakfast and close hiking access to Portland's expansive Forest Park. ❻

Hotel Lucía 400 SW Broadway ☏503/225-1717, Ⓦwww.hotellucia.com. Minimalist, Asian-influenced lobby, arty B&W photos in the hallways and

chic decor throughout make this one of the city's more prominent boutique hotels – though the rooms can be quite cramped. ❻

Inn at Northrup Station 2025 NW Northrup St ☏503/224-0543, Ⓦwww.northrupstation.com. Poised on the streetcar line (thus the name) in Northwest Portland and offering a range of colorful suites with splashy retro designs, some with kitchens, patios, and wet bars. ❺

Kennedy School 5736 NE 33rd Ave ☏503/249-3983 or 1-888/249-3983, Ⓦwww.mcmenamins.com/kennedy. Thirty-five B&B rooms, in a refurbished schoolhouse with chalkboards and cloakrooms, plus modern conveniences. Excellent breakfast, multiple brewpubs, movie theater, outdoor bathing pool, and "detention bar." ❺

Mallory 729 SW 15th Ave ☏503/223-6311 or 1-800/228-6857, Ⓦwww.malloryhotel.com. Stylish lobby, but rather plain – though affordable – rooms in this old Portland favorite. Well placed along the MAX tracks, though west of the downtown action across I-405. ❺

Vintage Plaza 422 SW Broadway ☏503/228-1212 or 1-800/263-2305, Ⓦwww.vintageplaza.com. An intimate boutique hotel with oversized rooms and a calm, relaxed atmosphere. Wine is offered in the afternoons in the lobby. One of the city's few dog-friendly hotels. ❻

White Eagle 836 N Russell St ☏503/282-6810, Ⓦwww.mcmenamins.com/eagle. Hands-down Portland's best bargain, a refurbished old hotel converted into a hip brewpub in an industrial-bohemian neighborhood. Rooms are clean and simple, and surprisingly cheap, with shared baths. Live music nightly. ❷

Hostels

HI-Portland Hawthorne 3031 SE Hawthorne Blvd ☏503/236-3380 or 1-866/447-3031, Ⓦwww.portlandhostel.com. Cheery Victorian house, well located in the heart of the Hawthorne District, offering Internet access, van tours of local sights, barbeques, and occasional live music

performances. $19 dorms, $48 private rooms.
❶–❷
HI-Portland Northwest 1818 NW Glisan
T 503/241-2783, W www.2oregonhostels.com.
Located in a nineteenth-century home in

Northwest Portland, near the popular *Mission Theatre & Brewpub* and just east of the main action on 21st and 23rd streets. Contains espresso bar and family rooms. $21 dorms, doubles with private bathrooms $52. **❶**

The City

The **Willamette** (pronounced "wuh-LAM-it") River bisects Portland into its east and west sides, with **Burnside Street** delineating the north from the south; each street address describes its relation to these dividers – NE, SE, NW, and SW. The downtown core lies between the river's west bank and the I-405 freeway, in the city's southwest quadrant; the northwest and Eastside are mostly residential.

Downtown

Named after the adjacent **Pioneer Courthouse**, a squat 1868 structure that still maintains its judicial function, **Pioneer Courthouse Square** is the indisputable center of Portland. Surrounded by **downtown**'s historic terracotta buildings, the square's curving brick terraces are perennially filled with music and people. Within close distance are some of Portland's leading attractions along SW Broadway and the Park Blocks – a melange of old and new, where fading plasterwork and ceramic reliefs face concrete and glass, punctuated by small grassy parks. From the square, you can take a two-and-a-half hour **walking tour** of the city's highlights (Fri–Sun 10.30am; $15; W www.portlandwalkingtours.com).

Broadway epitomizes Portland's mix of early grandeur and new wealth, with prestigious hotels sharing space with cultural institutions, such as the grand old Paramount movie theater, restored as part of the impressive **Portland Center for the Performing Arts**, 1111 SW Broadway (W www.pcpa.com). One block west, the **Portland Art Museum**, 1219 SW Park Ave (Tues, Wed & Sat 10am–5pm, Thurs & Fri 10am–8pm, Sun noon–5pm; $10; W www.pam.org), has a wide-ranging collection of Northwest Native American masks, Mexican statues, and ancient Chinese figures, and hosts annual blockbuster exhibitions of historic art drawn from various countries – Russia, Japan, and France, among others. Nearby, decorated with huge *trompe l'oeil* pioneer murals, the newly renovated **Oregon History Center**, 1200 SW Park Ave (Tues–Sat 10am–5pm, Sun noon–5pm; $6; W www.ohs.org), is primarily a research facility, but has some imaginative exhibits exploring different facets of the state's history. Between the museum and the history center run the **South Park Blocks**, a twelve-block green belt and favorite Portland hangout, where retirees commingle with teen slackers and the homeless – all under the shadow of statues of Teddy Roosevelt riding on to victory at San Juan Hill and Abe Lincoln standing rigidly with a long, dark expression. Twice a week, the park hosts a very popular **farmers' market** (May–Oct Wed 10am–2pm, May–Nov Sat 8.30am–2pm; W www.portlandfarmersmarket.org) that draws fruit and vegetable growers from around the region, and other local vendors of bread, pastries, beeswax candles, and other handicrafts. Around lunchtime on Saturdays, there are also free **cooking demonstrations** held by some of the city's more notable chefs.

A five-minute walk away, at the junction of Madison and Fifth avenues, is one of Portland's few notable pieces of modern architecture – Michael Graves' **Portland Building**, a monumental concrete box with "ironic" blue ribbons, though not worth more than a glance unless you're a design student. Several blocks east, Portland's riverfront has been rescued from a century of burial beneath wharves, warehouses, and an express highway. The area is now lined by a favorite urban oasis, the two-mile-long **Tom McCall Waterfront Park** (created by demolishing the highway in the 1970s), where flocks of Canadian geese abound on the grass, and young and old alike dash through the fountains of **Salmon Street Springs**. As a cheap and fun way to get wet, the springs are second only in popularity to the user-friendly **Ira Keller Fountain**, SW 3rd and Clay, a huge concrete water sculpture just west of the riverfront, where you can clamber around and get drenched on huge blocks and pillars. Further north, the small **Yamhill Historic District** is lined with 1890s buildings, and the **Yamhill Marketplace** (built in 1982), SW 2nd at Yamhill, has a few produce stalls and cafés, though most of its interior has been turned into a gym.

Old Town and Chinatown

Old Town, the area around and just south of the **Burnside Bridge**, is where Portland was founded in 1843. The site tended to flood, however, and when the railroad came in 1883 the town center soon shifted away; its big, ornate buildings became warehouses and it plummeted down the social scale. These days, missions for the homeless coexist with galleries, brewpubs, boutiques, and, especially, clubs – the area is unavoidable if you're in town to dance to DJs or live music. The **Saturday Market** (March–Dec Sat 10am–5pm, Sun 11am–4.30pm; ⓦ www.portlandsaturdaymarket.com) packs the area south of, and under, the Burnside Bridge with arts and crafts stalls, eclectic street musicians, spicy foods, and lively crowds, all crammed cheek-to-jowl by the MAX tracks. At First and Ankeny stands the **Skidmore Fountain**, a bronze basin raised by caryatids above a granite pool, designed to provide European elegance for the citizens and water for hard-working nineteenth-century horses. Across the fountain's angular plaza, an ornamental colonnade stretches from the side of the **New Market Theater**, a restored theater-cum-vegetable-market that is now full of cafés.

Nearby along west Burnside, the ornamental gate at Fourth Avenue marks **Chinatown**, once the second-largest Chinese community in the US until the 1880s, when racist attacks forced most Chinese workers to leave. There's still enough of a community here to support a range of cheap ethnic restaurants and dive bars; otherwise, the main attractions are the **American Advertising Museum**, 211 NW 5th Ave (Wed–Sun noon–5pm; $5; ⓦ www.admuseum .org), which gives a fascinating account of the rise of advertising, from posters to tapes of old radio and TV ads, and the enticing **Classical Chinese Garden**, NW 3rd Ave at Everett (daily: April–Oct 9am–6pm; Nov–March 10am–5pm; $7; ⓦ www.portlandchinesegarden.org), a Suzhou-styled garden with traditional vegetation, ponds, and walkways.

Pearl District and Northwest Portland

North of Burnside lies the chic **Pearl District**, an old industrial zone now gentrified with upscale lofts, galleries, restaurants, and boutiques, at its swankiest between NW 10th and 12th avenues, and Glisan and Lovejoy streets. A bit further south, the biggest recent redevelopment is the **Brewery Blocks**, NW 11th to 13th avenues between Burnside and Davis streets, a monumental renovation of the former Blitz-Weinhard brewery into high-end restaurants, retail shops, and condos. Across the street is the famous **Powell's City of Books**, 1005 W Burnside St (daily 9am–11pm; ⓦ www.powells.com). With more than a million new, used, and rare books on four floors, Powell's occupies an entire block, as well as separate annexes around town, and provides free color-coded maps so customers don't get lost.

Further west, what's known in brochures as Nob Hill is called **Northwest Portland** by locals. Stretching from W Burnside Street along a dozen blocks of NW 23rd and NW 21st avenues, the neighborhood is choked with fine restaurants and boutiques, and the assortment of multicolored Victorian piles adds a San Franciscan tinge.

Forest Park and Washington Park

A few miles west of Northwest Portland, the wooded bluffs of the West Hills – with their winding streets, historic estates, and burgeoning McMansions – contain the massive **Forest Park** (ⓦ www.friendsofforestpark.org), the country's largest urban greenspace, interlaced with countless hiking trails, including the thirty-mile loop of the **Wildwood Trail**. This trail can be accessed around NW 31st Avenue and Upshur Street; otherwise, follow NW Thurman until it dead-ends and follow **Leif Erickson Drive** (closed to traffic) into the hills.

South of the bulk of Forest Park, the elegant houses of the wealthy include the ever-popular **Pittock Mansion**, 3229 NW Pittock Drive (daily noon–4pm, summer 11am–4pm, closed Jan; $5.50; ⓦ www.pittockmansion .com), a 1914 Renaissance Revival creation whose most attractive attribute is its stunning – and free – view of the city from the front lawn. Beyond the mansion, the forested, 130-acre **Washington Park** is home to a number of Portland's most popular attractions. These include the expansive city views from the **International Rose Test Garden** (daily 7am–9pm; free), featuring a wide array of bright summertime blooms; the tranquil **Japanese Garden** (daily: April–Sept 10am–7pm; Oct–March 10am–4pm; $6.50; ⓦ www .japanesegarden.com), actually a collection of five traditional gardens with ponds, bridges, foliage, and sand designs; and the **Oregon Zoo** (daily: April–Sept 9am–6pm; Oct–March 9am–4pm; $8; ⓦ www.zooregon.org), whose most unusual feature is its Elephant Museum, detailing the biological and cultural history of pachyderms – and decorated with a giant mastodon skeleton. Close by, the rather staid **World Forestry Center** (daily 10am–5pm; $4.50; ⓦ www.worldforestry.org) is largely an ode to the timber industry, but the **Hoyt Arboretum**, 4000 Fairview Blvd (daily 6am–10pm; free; ⓦ www.hoytarboretum.org), is well worth a leisurely walk for its collection of ten thousand trees and plants from throughout the region and the world.

Most Washington Park attractions have convenient access to a MAX light-rail ($1.60 from downtown), whose station is buried deep underground and accessible only by elevator. Once you get here, you can hop on a summertime **shuttle** (every 15min June–Sept 10am–7pm; $1.25) and access all the park's major sights on a cheap day-pass ticket.

The Eastside

While the west shore of the Willamette River provided a deep port, the east side was too shallow for shipping, and so the area remained undeveloped for the first fifty years of Portland's life. The Morrison Bridge crept across at the end of the nineteenth century; since then, most of the city's population has lived in the **Eastside**, in various neighborhoods that are mostly residential. Perhaps the best reason to venture in this direction is to walk or bike the three-mile loop of the **Eastbank Esplanade**, a $30-million concourse that connects from the Hawthorne to the Steel bridge on floating walkways and cantilevered footpaths, offering striking views of downtown and close-up perspectives on the city's industrial zone and the roar of I-5. Near the south end of the esplanade, the splashy exhibits of the **Oregon Museum of Science and Industry**, 1945 SE Water Ave (June–Aug daily 9.30am–7pm, rest of year

Tues–Sun 9.30am–5.30pm; $8.50; ⓦ www.omsi.edu), are primarily geared toward children, with hundreds of interactive booths, toys, and kiosks aimed at those with only a sketchy knowledge of science.

More appealing, two miles further east, the **Hawthorne District** is Portland's best alternative culture zone. With Hawthorne Boulevard as its axis between 34th and 45th streets, and dominated by the sparkly, quasi-Moorish 1927 *Bagdad Theater & Pub* at no. 3702 (☎ 503/236-9234), the area teems with bookstores, hip cafés, dive bars, cheap ethnic restaurants, and as yet only a handful of corporate chain stores. Six blocks north, **Belmont Avenue** is a historic corridor thick with boutiques, novelty shops, and ethnic restaurants, centered around the neon lights of the Avalon Theatre, no. 3451, while a mile southwest around 26th Avenue, **Clinton Street** is home to several good diners, funky bars, and vintage clothiers (the best being Xtabay, at no. 2515).

Only sports fans and conventioneers should bother to visit the overly hyped **Rose Quarter**, west of I-5 between the Steel and Broadway bridges (ⓦ www.rosequarter.com), where a green-spired convention center and basketball stadium are the only points of interest amid a clutch of overpriced restaurants and dreary chain motels. Much better in this section of Northeast Portland is the stretch of **NE Broadway** between NE 12th and 20th streets, an up-and-coming strip notable for its range of ethnic and Northwest Cuisine restaurants.

Eating

As in Seattle, Portland's **Northwest Cuisine** is a mix of international cooking and fresh regional produce, and the city offers many excellent **dining** options for all palates and pocketbooks. Downtown, the Pearl District and Northwest Portland have swank cocktail bars, sedate bistros, brewpubs, and Pacific-fusion and vegetarian restaurants, while Hawthorne Boulevard has the best cheap grub and ethnic diners. Downtown also has numerous **food carts** that dole out Mexican food, Italian panini, Indian cuisine, and rice-bowl bentos – concentrated in parking lots at SW 5th and Oak, and SW 9th and Alder.

Bangkok Kitchen 2534 SE Belmont Ave ☎ 503/236-7349. Forget the higher-priced joints downtown (1.5 miles west): this dreary-looking spot has Portland's best – and cheapest – Thai food. And if you can't stomach the ugly red-vinyl booths or kitschy decor, just order take-out.

Bombay Cricket Club 1925 Hawthorne Blvd ☎ 503/231-0740. Excellent restaurant a mile west of the main Hawthorne scene with arguably the town's best Indian food, and its most aggravating service. Try to ignore the snooty attitudes and dive into the delicious *vindaloos* and tandooris.

Brasserie Montmartre 626 SW Park Ave ☎ 503/224-5552. The city's most popular French bistro, with tasty pasta and free live jazz on most evenings. The favorite lunching spot for shoppers at nearby Nordstrom.

Dot's Café 2521 SE Clinton St ☎ 503/235-0203. In the center of the small-but-hip Clinton district, a cheap, if grungy, late-night spot decked out in garage-sale decor, offering the classic bacon cheeseburger, vegan burritos, and the best grilled-cheese sandwich in Portland.

Higgins 1239 SW Broadway ☎ 503/222-9070. Nationally recognized Northwest Cuisine restaurant, where fresh local ingredients and scrumptious desserts are served in cozy quarters just south of the city's main attractions.

Jake's Famous Crawfish 401 SW 12th Ave ☎ 503/226-1419. A landmark restaurant for more than a hundred years, with a staggering choice of fresh seafood like "Columbia River Sturgeon," "Depot Bay Dungeness Crab," and spicy crawfish cakes. The innocuous-sounding "Bag of Chocolate" is a famously delicious, belt-breaking dessert.

McCormick and Schmick's 235 SW 1st Ave at Oak St ☎ 503/224-7522. The first location of what's become a national chain of fine seafood restaurants, with fresh nightly specials and a lively oyster bar with a happening singles scene. Entrees around $15.

Mio Gelato 25 NW 11th Ave ☎ 503/226-8002. Easily the best *gelato* (Italian ice cream) in the Pacific Northwest, located in one of the Brewery Blocks. Fruit flavors like lime, grapefruit, and kiwi are enough to make your taste buds tremble with delight.

Oba 555 NW 12th Ave ☎503/228-6161. Flashy, Nuevo Latino eatery in the Pearl District that fuses flavors from all over Latin America to create food you won't find anywhere else in town – most inviting during happy hour in the bar, when the tasty entrees are $3–4.

Papa Haydn 701 NW 23rd Ave, Northwest Portland ☎503/223-7317. Expect at least a half-hour wait for a table at this upscale eatery on weekend nights – worth it for a taste of the fifty-odd desserts on the menu.

Pix Patisserie 3402 SE Division ☎503/232-4407. Popular hot-spot with a colorful range of inventive French desserts prepared by a Parisian-trained chef known as the "Pixie." The restaurant's bright red walls are unmistakable on an otherwise bleak stretch of the Eastside.

Toney Bento 1423 SE 37th Ave ☎503/234-4441. A lively Hawthorne spot with giant bowls of tasty, inexpensive noodle concoctions, and delicious sushi – made by a master first-generation chef.

Wildwood 1221 NW 21st Ave ☎503/248-9663. Trendy Northwest Portland restaurant with a warm interior, friendly staff, and imaginative food. Fresh local ingredients – the likes of morel mushrooms, Pacific salmon, and Painted Hills beef – are the rule.

Nightlife

Portland's smart cocktail lounges and dive bars easily rival those of Seattle. The city is a beer-drinker's haven, with more than thirty local **microbreweries**, including *Rogue Ales Public House*, 1339 NW Flanders St (☎503/222-5910), and *Bridgeport Brewing*, 1313 NW Marshall St (☎503/241-3621). The McMenamins "concept" brewpubs sell their own locally brewed ales in unique settings, such as former schoolhouses and renovated hotels (Ⓦ www.mcmenamins.com). The **coffee**-swilling scene looms large, but without Seattle's ubiquitous coffee carts – naturally, though, *Starbucks* is everywhere. For **music**, Portland maintains a small but vital presence on the national map, with countless alternative and punk bands relocating here in the last few years. To get a sense of the scene, the coolest venues are located around east and west Burnside.

Bars, brewpubs, and coffeehouses

Cobalt Lounge 32 NW 3rd Ave ☎503/225-1003. A fun club in Old Town with stiff drinks and a party crowd, where DJs mix new house sounds with retro-1970s and -80s favorites on rotating evenings.

Goose Hollow Inn and Tavern 1927 SW Jefferson St ☎503/228-7010. Great microbrews, the city's best Reuben sandwich, and a convenient location near the MAX tracks, a mile west of downtown. Watch for colorful owner Bud Clark, the city mayor in the 1980s.

Huber's 411 SW 3rd Ave ☎503/228-5686. Portland's oldest bar is an elegant spot with arched stained-glass skylight, mahogany paneling, and terrazzo floor. Famous for roast turkey sandwiches and flaming Spanish coffees.

Kell's 112 SW 2nd Ave ☎503/227-4057. Longstanding favorite Irish bar, with fine authentic cuisine (Irish stews, soda bread, and the like) and a range of microbrews, imported beers, and of course, Irish (and Scotch) whiskey.

Lucky Labrador 915 SE Hawthorne Blvd ☎503/236-3555. Just across the river from downtown, this unpretentious brewpub occupies a large warehouse space with an outdoor patio. Fresh ales, great sandwiches, BBQ specials, and a delicious peanut-curry bento.

Nocturnal 1800 E Broadway ☎503/239-5900. Increasingly popular and crowded nightspot, with a subterranean bar attracting young adults who look like teenagers, and a ground-level, all-ages concert space attracting the real thing.

Pied Cow 3244 SE Belmont Ave ☎503/230-4866. Longstanding favorite for coffee, tea, and dessert in a stately Victorian house, with late-night hours, lush garden seating, and the chance to puff fruit-flavored tobacco from a hookah pipe.

Produce Row 204 SE Oak St ☎503/232-8355. Be one of the rare tourists at this local favorite, stuck in an unglamorous location by the railroad tracks, across the river in an industrial zone, but boasting thirty brews on tap and a nice range of live music from country to rock.

Rimsky-Korsakoffee House 707 SE 12th Ave ☎503/232-2640. Despite having an awful pun of a name and possibly the city's worst service, an excellent place to linger for hours on end over dessert and coffee. Immensely popular with bohemians and slackers.

Ringlers Annex 1223 SW Stark St ☎503/525-0520. Great people-watching in the sizeable basement of the ornate wedge-shaped 1917 Flatiron

Building. Companion bar, *Ringlers*, is two blocks away at 1332 W Burnside St (☎ 503/225-0627).

Shanghai Tunnel 211 SW Ankeny St ☎ 503/220-4001. Located just off Burnside Street, a subterranean bar popular with hipsters and offering Asian-style soul food.

Stumptown Roasters 3356 SE Belmont Ave ☎ 503/232-8889. Widely acknowledged as the city's best coffee, made from a blend of seven different types of java. The most engaging of a local chain of three coffeehouses, with hip customers but only functional decor.

Tao of Tea 3430 SE Belmont St ☎ 503/736-0119. More than 120 different kinds of teas are served in an exquisite room with Zen-like decor and a somewhat pretentious air. Elegant meals of affordable vegan and Indian food.

Tiger Bar 317 NW Broadway T503/222-7297. Über-hip, swank lounge with a tiger-striped bar and long banquettes. Dark, sultry, and smoke-friendly, with late-night food.

Live music and clubs

Berbati's Pan 10 SW 3rd Ave ☎ 503/248-4579. Features a reconstructed nineteenth-century European bar in back and nightly selection of eclectic bands – local to international – usually for less than $10 cover.

Crystal Ballroom 1332 W Burnside St ☎ 503/778-5625. Just above the *Ringlers* bar, a nineteenth-century dance hall with a "floating" floor on springs. Bands range from hippie to hip-hop and feature the best of Portland's indie rock and good DJs in "Lola's Room" upstairs.

Dante's 1 SW 3rd Ave ☎ 503/226-6630. Perhaps the city's hippest nightspot. Cabaret acts and live music mix with the club's signature "Sinferno" Sunday strip shows, "Karaoke from Hell" Mondays,

and the disturbing lounge-punk stylings of "Storm and the Balls" Wednesdays.

Embers 11 NW Broadway ☎ 503/222-3082. An often-crowded club with drag shows in the gay-oriented front room and high-energy dancing in the straight-leaning room in back. Cool fish-tank bar top.

Goodfoot 2845 SE Stark St ☎ 503/239-9292. Frenetic underground live-music joint and dance club decorated in mildly retro-70s decor, and always sweaty, smoky, and packed on weekends – but still worth it to hear top-notch DJs spinning and scratching the lights out.

Jazz de Opus 33 NW 2nd Ave ☎ 503/222-6077. Cozy, low-key atmosphere with excellent live jazz and grilled food. No cover most nights.

Ohm 31 NW 1st Ave ☎ 503/223-9919. Located near the Saturday Market by the light rail tracks, a top spot for electronica and hip-hop music, with both live acts and DJs. Weekends are packed and stuffy, so come during midweek for a more relaxed environment.

Red Sea 318 SW 3rd Ave ☎ 503/241-5450. Dine on African/Middle Eastern cuisine while you groove to reggae and African tunes on weekends. Also offers the occasional belly dancer.

Roseland Theater 8 NW 6th Ave ☎ 503/224-2038. Located in one of the city's dicier corners, but a top spot for rock and alternative acts – often the last affordable venue for fans before the groups start touring the bigger concert halls with higher-priced tickets.

Saucebox 214 SW Broadway ☎ 503/241-3393. Easily missable spot – identified by a sign with an ice cube – features great pan-Asian cuisine, colorful cocktails, and eclectic nightly music that attracts black-clad poseurs and serious hipsters.

Performing arts and film

The **performing arts** scene in Portland revolves around the **Portland Center for the Performing Arts**, 1111 SW Broadway (☎ 503/248-4335 or 224-4000, ⓦ www.pcpa.com), a complex comprising two main buildings – the **Arlene Schnitzer Concert Hall** and the **New Theater Building**, containing the Dolores Winningstad Theater and Newmark Theater. The "Schnitz" is a sumptuously restored 1928 vaudeville and movie house that presents big musical extravaganzas, dance, and theater, hosting performances by the **Oregon Symphony Orchestra** (☎ 503/228-1353, ⓦ www.orsymphony.org) and **Oregon Ballet Theater** (☎ 503/222-5538, ⓦ www.obt.org), among others. Several blocks east at SW 3rd Ave, between Market and Clay, the **Ira Keller Auditorium** (☎ 503/274-6560) is home to traveling musicals and the classics-oriented **Portland Opera** (☎ 503/241-1407, ⓦ www.portlandopera.org).

If you're interested in catching a **film**, the monolithic Regal chain owns most of the town's theaters, but decent alternatives include Cinema 21, 616 NW 21st Ave (☎ 503/223-4515, ⓦ www.cinema21.com), for foreign and independent movies; the Guild, 879 SW 9th Ave (℡503/221-1156), for classics and retrospectives; and the historic Hollywood Theatre, 4122 NE Sandy Blvd (℡503/281-4215, ⓦwww.hollywoodtheatre.org), for all of the above.

During the summer, **free concerts** are held at Pioneer Courthouse Square, Tom McCall Waterfront Park, the zoo, and the amphitheater at the International Rose Test Garden. The free *Willamette Week* (ⓦwww .wweek.com), available on any street corner, carries **listings** of what's on and where, as does the other, smaller alternative paper, the *Portland Mercury* (ⓦwww.portlandmercury.com), and the Friday edition of the main local newspaper, *The Oregonian* (ⓦwww.oregonian.com). *Just Out* is the chief gay/lesbian publication (ⓦwww.justout.com).

Around Portland: the Columbia River Gorge and Mount Hood

Due east of Portland along the I-84 interstate, the **Columbia River Gorge** is a striking, almost forbidding setting with gusty winds, craggy rocks, and incredible views resembling the heroic landscapes of Albert Bierstadt. Scoured into a deep, wide U-shape by huge Ice Age–era floods that also carved up Eastern Washington, the gorge is a nationally protected scenic area, where striking waterfalls tumble down sheer cliffs, and fir and maple trees turn fabulous shades of gold and red in the fall. Much more rugged in the nineteenth century before the arrival of modern dams, this was the ominous final leg of the Oregon Trail, where many pioneers met a dark end negotiating perilous rapids on flimsy wooden rafts.

The most dramatic part of the gorge, between Troutdale and the town of **Hood River**, is just north of the snowy peak of Mount Hood, where the serpentine highway offers scenes of a starkly romantic, mist-shrouded river landscape in the spring, giving way to colorful windsurfers in the summer bounding over the whitecapped waves. The ideal way to explore the area is by driving along the narrow, winding **Historic Columbia River Highway** (accessible at exits 22 or 35 off I-84), which boasts several excellent vantage points, particularly at **Crown Point**, where the aptly-named **Vista House** – a marvelous WPA structure perched high above the gorge about ten miles east of Troutdale – is currently being restored to its original rustic grandeur (see ⓦwww.vistahouse.com for details). Further east, some highway sections are now closed to automotive traffic due to the road's difficulty in handling modern traffic loads, and are designed more for hikers and cyclists.

Back on I-84 below, the most spectacular of the waterfalls en route is **Multnomah Falls** (accessed by an unexpected left-lane exit; daily 8am–9pm; free), whose waters plunge 530ft down a rock face, collect in a pool, and then drop another seventy feet. Be warned: this is the state's second most popular attraction (after a Native American casino) and the crowds can get quite thick on the trails and viewing bridges. Further east, **Bonneville Dam** (daily 9am–5pm; free; ℡541/374-8820) is Oregon's counterpart to Washington's Grand Coulee, a huge New Deal project that generates regional electricity and offers a chamber where you can see salmon making their way upstream – although the numbers dwindle each year.

Mount Hood

To the south along Highway 35, **Mount Hood** is a dormant volcano rising about eleven thousand feet, the tallest peak in the Oregon Cascades. The **Mount Hood Loop** – a combination of highways 35 and 26 – takes in both the mountain and the gorge, and one of the joys of the area is to explore the mountain by foot along some of the trails radiating out from its slopes; contact the Mount Hood Information Center (see below) for more information. The highest point on the loop at some 4000ft, **Barlow Pass** is named after Sam Barlow, a wagon-train leader who blazed the first "road" around the mountain, which became the unpleasant alternative to the even more dangerous Columbia River route on the Oregon Trail. Much of the Barlow Road is still followed by the loop, including the steep ridges where wagons frequently skidded out of control and plummeted downhill. You can still see deep gashes on some of the trees where ropes were fastened to check the wagons' descent. Note that the section of US-26 just south of the mountain is one of the state's most dangerous stretches, where blinding late-afternoon sunshine causes several fatal wrecks every year.

Near the intersection of highways 35 and 26, a turn-off leads to the rough-hewn stone of *Timberline Lodge* (☎503/272-3311 or 1-800/547-1406, ⊛www.timberlinelodge.com; ❺), a colossal New Deal structure that is part of the year-round *Timberline* **ski resort** (☎503/219-3192; lift tickets $39), and the exterior setting for Stanley Kubrick's *The Shining* (though without that film's hedge maze). Two other downhill ski areas – Mount Hood Meadows (⊛www.skihood.com; $44) and Mount Hood SkiBowl (⊛www.skibowl.com; $39) – offer nighttime **skiing** from November to April (around $20). There are also many miles of cross-country skiing trails throughout the **Mount Hood National Forest**. For more information on mountain activities, contact the Mount Hood Information Center (☎503/622-4822 or 1-888/622-4822, ⊛www.mthood.info).

Hood River

Adjacent to the Columbia River, north of Mount Hood, charming little **HOOD RIVER** is a gusty center for river windsurfing and mountain biking – with outfitters' shops lining the hillside streets and a riverfront park to take in the local sporting scene – and offers a good base for exploring the gorge. One of the most exquisite **places to stay** in the entire region is the *Columbia Gorge Hotel*, just off I-84 at the far west end of town, at 3000 Westcliff Drive (☎541/386-5566 or 1-800/345-1921, ⊛www.columbiagorgehotel.com; ❽), where hacienda-style buildings perch on a clifftop right above the gorge. The hotel's exquisite gardens even have their own waterfalls, the rooms are lavish and relaxing, and the highly regarded Sunday tea service ($22 per person) is a pricey, but savory, indulgence. More central, and less expensive, options include the *Hood River Hotel*, 102 Oak Ave (☎541/386-1900 or 1-800/386-1859, ⊛www.hoodriverhotel.com; ❹), built in 1913 and featuring tasteful rooms and more elaborate suites plus a good Italian restaurant, and the basic but clean *Love's Riverview Lodge*, 1505 Oak St (☎541/386-8719 or 1-800/789-9568, ⊛www.riverviewforyou.com; ❸). The *Full Sail Brewing Co*, 506 Columbia St (☎541/386-2247), is a popular evening spot to regale tall tales of the day's activities, and there are several inexpensive places to **eat**, the best bets being the burgers at the *6th Street Bistro*, 6th and Cascade (☎541/386-5737), and the marionberry milkshakes at *Mike's Ice Cream*, 504 Oak St (☎541/386-6260). The town's **visitor center**, by the river in Port Marina Park (☎1-800/366-3530, ⊛www.hoodriver.org), can provide information on all the area's attractions, including the engaging summertime **fruit loop** (⊛www.hoodriverfruitloop.com), a driving concourse around the county that connects to growers of cheap and delicious apples, pears, cherries, and peaches.

The Willamette Valley

South of Portland, the **WILLAMETTE VALLEY** has a diverse agricultural scene, but is best known for its grapes. Hwy-99 W, the scenic route through wine country, accesses more than two dozen acclaimed **wineries**, most of which pour superb Pinot noirs, Chardonnays, and Rieslings. Pick up a wine-country tour map from any local visitor center (or from ⓦ www.oregonwine.org), and expect the odd traffic delay in little burgs like **Dundee**, now a well-known draw for vino. The Valley also has some of the best examples of **covered bridges**, with thirty-four in the state spanning creeks near Scio, Albany, and Cottage Grove (check out the directory at ⓦ coveredbridges.stateoforegon.com), and is the site of the renowned *Joel Palmer House*, 600 Ferry St, Dayton (℡ 503/864-2995, ⓦ www.joelpalmerhouse.com), to which Portland urbanites make special trips for its delicious, if expensive, Northwest Cuisine.

From Portland, I-5 courses through the Willamette Valley on its way to California, but bypasses historic **Oregon City**, the first state capital, at the end of the Oregon Trail. Today, the split-level, working-class town comprises a short main street, connected by steps, steep streets, and a cliff-face elevator to an uptown area of old wooden houses set on a bluff. The highlight is unquestionably the **John McLoughlin House**, 713 Center St (Wed–Sat 10am–4pm, Sun 1–4pm; $4; ⓦ www.mcloughlinhouse.org), the 1846 dwelling of an Oregon Trail pioneer that's loaded with many artifacts and details on local history.

Salem and around

The main reason to visit **SALEM** is to see the modern, white Vermont-marble **State Capitol**, 900 Court St NE (Mon–Fri 7.30am–5.30pm; free), whose cupola is topped by a large gold-leaf pioneer, axe in hand, eyes to the West. At the entrance, there's a marble carving of explorers Lewis and Clark processing regally towards the Willamette Valley. There are also hourly historical **tours** of the building and its tower for groups of ten or more (reserve at ℡ 503/986-1388). Across the street, tree-lined **Willamette University** merits a stroll as the oldest university in the West, while **Mission Mill Village**, 1313 Mill St SE (Mon–Sat 10am–5pm; $7; ⓦ www.missionmill.org), is worth seeing for its historic pioneer buildings and preserved nineteenth-century woolen mill.

Greyhound is conveniently located at 450 Church St NE, as well as Amtrak at 13th and Oak. The **visitor center** (℡ 503/581-4325 or 1-800/874-7012, ⓦ www.scva.org) is in Mission Mill Village. There are plenty of decent **motels**, among them the *Phoenix Inn Suites*, 4370 Commercial St SE (℡ 503/588-9220, ⓦ www.phoenixinn.com; ❹), while the *Marquee House*, 333 Wyatt Court NE (℡ 503/391-0837 or 1-800/949-0837, ⓦ www.marqueehouse.com; ❹), is a stately **B&B** close to downtown. If you're **camping**, head for the huge waterfalls and lush forests of **Silver Falls State Park** (℡ 503/873-8681; $18–21), 26 miles east of Salem via highways 22 and 214, justifiably the state's most popular park – which means you'll have to reserve many weeks in advance.

For **food**, you're best off downtown, where the *Dairy Lunch Café*, 347 Court St (℡ 503/363-6433), is a classic 1960s diner with primo burgers; *Jonathan's Oyster Bar*, 445 State St (℡ 503/362-7219), serves fresh seafood, Cajun and Southwestern cuisine; and the pleasant *Arbor Café*, 345 High St NE (℡ 503/588-2353), has a nice range of pasta, sandwiches, and salads.

Finally, fans of modern architecture won't want to miss the **Oregon Garden**, further east in **SILVERTON** at 879 W Main St (daily 9am–3pm, summer closes 6pm; $7; ⓦ www.oregongarden.org), where, beyond the predictable array of local foliage, the main attraction is Frank Lloyd Wright's elegant **Gordon House** (daily 10am–2pm, summer closes 5pm; extra $2), which was moved here after being saved from demolition. Although intended as mass housing for the middle class, today such "Usonian" homes – with their cantilevered roofs, horizontal layouts, and narrow windows – are curious artifacts from a time when high-class design wasn't solely the province of the elite behind high, guarded walls.

Eugene

A lively mix of students, hippies, and blue collars, **EUGENE** is a liberal enclave where the late Ken Kesey and some of his Merry Pranksters came to live after their retreat from California. On a slightly different note, the town was also the filming location for much of the movie *Animal House*.

Although short on sights, it's an energetic cultural center, to which the **University of Oregon** in the city's southeast corner lends a youthful bohemian feel, especially along 13th Avenue just west of campus. For pursuits far removed from the National Lampoon variety, the glassy, modern **Hult Center**, Sixth Ave and Willamette St (☏541/682-5746, ⓦ www.hultcenter.org), is home to several arts organizations, including the local opera, symphony, ballet, and renowned Oregon Bach Festival. The other major attraction is the **Saturday Market**, Eighth Ave and Oak St (April–Dec 10am–5pm; ⓦ www.eugenesaturdaymarket .org), a thirty-year institution and something of a neo-hippie carnival, with live folk music and street performers. Tie-dye and wholefoods set the tone, but rastas, skateboarders, and students join in, too.

Eugene is also a prime spot for **sports**, with most of its fame deriving from the university's stellar track program, which gave rise to the likes of legendary runner Steve Prefontaine and Nike co-founder (and track coach) Bill Bowerman. Trails and paths abound for walkers and cyclists in the city center, along the river banks, and up imposing **Spencer's Butte**, south of town. You can rent bikes from Pedal Power, 535 High St ($5 per hour, $20 per day; ☏541/687-1775).

Practicalities

Greyhound stops at 987 Pearl St at Tenth Ave, and Amtrak at Fourth Ave and Willamette St. Eugene has a terrific bus system, the LTD ($1.25; ☏541/687-5555, ⓦ www.ltd.org), offering day passes for $2.50, and 25¢ rides on the "Breeze" shuttle linking downtown, the university, and local malls. The **visitor center** is at 115 W 8th Ave (Mon–Fri 8.30am–5pm, Sat 10am–4pm; ☏541/484-5307 or 1-800/547-5445, ⓦ www.visitlanecounty.org).

The best **places to stay** include the prominent *Eugene Hilton*, 66 E 6th Ave (☏541/342-2000 or 1-800/937-6660, ⓦ www.eugene.hilton.com; ❻), close to the Hult Center, and *Campbell House*, 252 Pearl St (☏541/343-1119 or 1-800/264-2519, ⓦ www.campbellhouse.com; ❺), an elegant 1892 Victorian with eighteen rooms. *Franklin Inn*, 1857 Franklin Blvd (☏541/342-4804; ❸), has affordable rooms near the university, while the *Eugene International Hostel*, 2352 Willamette St (☏541/349-0589; $19), offers twenty clean and comfortable dorm beds.

With thousands of students to feed, Eugene has plenty of places to **eat**. *Café Zenon*, 898 Pearl St (☏541/343-3005), has an eclectic menu filled with international dishes; *Chanterelle*, 207 E 5th Ave (☏541/484-4065), is an intimate French bistro; the *Oregon Electric Station*, 27 E 5th Ave (☏541/485-4444), serves top-notch prime rib and seafood in renovated railway cars; and the amazingly delicious truffles of *Euphoria Chocolate*, 6 W 17th Ave (☎541/343-9223, ⓦwww .euphoriachocolate.com), provide reason alone to visit Eugene.

Live **music** is also big in town. *Jo Federigo's*, 259 E 5th Ave (☎541/343-8488, ⓦwww.jofeds.com), has nightly jazz and serves solid Italian cuisine, while funky, downscale *WOW Hall*, 291 W 8th Ave (☎541/687-2746, ⓦwww .wowhall.org), showcases up-and-coming rockers. For a taste of the music scene near the university, stroll along **13th Avenue**. Ten miles west of Eugene on US-126, little **Veneta** hosts the **Oregon Country Fair** (☎541/343-4298, ⓦwww.oregoncountryfair.org) in mid-July, a hippie-flavored festival of music, art, food, and dancing. Traffic can be heavy, and even if you have a car it's easier to go by bus – the LTD operates special services.

South to California

South of Eugene along I-5, not too far from the California border, unenticing **Grants Pass** depends on the vigorous Rogue River for its living. Half a day of **whitewater rafting** costs around $50, a full day $70 – the **visitor center**, just off I-5 at 1995 NW Vine St (☎1-800/547-5927 or 541/476-7717, ⓦwww .visitgrantspass.org), provides brochures from more than two dozen licensed river guides. Beyond Grants Pass, I-5 dips southeast through **Ashland**, taking a mountainous inland route to California, while US-199 heads southwest to the California (and south Oregon) coast, passing near the **Oregon Caves**.

Oregon Caves National Monument

Thirty miles southwest of Grants Pass along US-199, at the dull burg of **Cave Junction**, Hwy-46 veers east twenty miles to the **Oregon Caves National Monument** (tours daily March–Nov: hours vary, often 9am–5pm; 75min; $7.50; ☎541/592-2100, ⓦwww.nps.gov/orca). Tucked in a wooded canyon at the end of a narrow, twisting road and kept at a constant temperature of 41°F, it's actually one enormous cave, with smaller branching passages, where the dripping marble walls are covered with elaborate stalactites, stalagmites, and flowstone.

Close to the cave entrance, surrounded by forest, is the appealing *Oregon Caves Chateau*, 2000 Caves Hwy (mid-May to Sept; ☎541/592-3400; ⑤), an elegant 1930s lodge with grand public rooms; reservations are advised. Alternatively, there are drab lodgings in Cave Junction – try the *Holiday Motel*, 24810 Redwood Hwy (☎541/592-3003; ❸) – or several **campgrounds** along Hwy-46, with *Grayback* and *Cave Creek* being the closest to the monument (☎541/592-2166 for reservations).

Ashland and the Shakespeare Festival

Throughout Oregon, the progressive hamlet of **ASHLAND**, forty miles southeast of Grants Pass, is identified with William Shakespeare – a real anomaly among the timber and dairy-farming towns that blanket the state. Since 1945, the **Oregon Shakespeare Festival** has been held here between February and October, packing audiences into the half-timbered **Elizabethan Theatre**, and cycling through the Bard's complete oeuvre every few years. The town's setting, between the Cascade and the Siskiyou mountains, is magnificent, with good skiing in the winter and river-rafting in summer. There's also some excellent fringe theater – not to mention pleasant cafés, galleries, and a friendly atmosphere throughout.

The **Angus Bowmer Theatre**, adjacent to the Elizabethan Theatre, stages both Shakespearean and more recent works, while the austere **New Theatre** has a mostly modern repertoire. The three theaters share the same box office,

15 S Pioneer St (ⓣ541/482-4331, ⓦwww.orshakes.org), and tickets average around $35 (with standing room at the Elizabethan Theatre for $10), and summer prices are $10–15 more expensive. For a dose of musical comedy to relieve the drama, try the **Oregon Cabaret Theater**, in a renovated pink church at First and Hargadine ($18–24; ⓣ541/488-2902, ⓦwww.oregoncabaret.com).

The **visitor center** is at 110 E Main St (Mon–Fri 9am–5pm; ⓣ541/482-3486, ⓦwww.ashlandchamber.com), and there's a seasonal information kiosk – with longer hours – at the entrance to Lithia Park off Main Street. Greyhound **buses** drop passengers on the edge of town near the I-5 freeway exit. Ashland has more than sixty **B&Bs** (❹–❽), most of which are in charming Victorian homes; the Ashland B&B Network (ⓣ1-800/944-0329, ⓦwww.abbnet.com) or Southern Oregon Reservation Center (ⓣ1-800/547-8052, ⓦwww.sorc.com) can get you a room at one of them (and theater tickets). Perhaps the finest B&B overall is the *Mount Ashland Inn*, five miles south at 550 Mt Ashland Ski Rd (ⓣ541/482-8707, ⓦwww.mtashlandinn.com; ❼), offering five suites in a scenic wooden lodge, with fireplaces and hot tubs. In town, the best **hotel** is the prominent *Ashland Springs*, 212 E Main St (ⓣ541/488-1700, ⓦwww.ashlandspringshotel.com; ❺), with its charming two-story lobby, day spa, afternoon tea, and nicely appointed rooms. Budget options include the friendly, clean, and well-placed *Ashland Hostel*, 150 N Main St (ⓣ541/482-9217, ⓦwww.ashlandhostel.com; $20), and *The Palm*, 1065 Siskiyou Blvd (ⓣ541/482-2636, ⓦwww.palmmotel.com; ❷–❹), one of the better **motels** on this stretch of road.

The main choices for **eating** and **drinking** can be found along **Main Street**, near the entrance to Lithia Park. The choices vary widely, from the eclectic entrees of *The Firefly*, 23 N Main St (ⓣ541/488-3212), to the upscale French *Chateaulin*, 50 E Main St (ⓣ503/482-2264). Overall, your best bet is *Greenleaf*, 49 N Main St (ⓣ541/482-2808), an inexpensive but excellent eatery with tasty staples like pasta, burgers, salads, and seafood nicely crafted with fresh local ingredients.

The Oregon Coast

The **Oregon coast** is as beautiful as any stretch of coastline in America. While the California sun draws off the tan-seeking masses (Oregon summers are generally mild), Oregonians are left to hike and clam-dig along their own secluded four hundred miles, almost all of it public land. State parks and campgrounds abound, and extensive and often isolated beaches offer numerous free activities, from beachcombing to shell-fishing and whale-watching. Although the state's shoreline hasn't escaped commercialism (only lucky travelers find budget rooms without booking ahead in July and August), and it has its occasional eyesores of development, the Oregon coast could well be considered the least exploited in the entire US.

A number of coastal state parks offer novel accommodation in the form of seaside **cabins** and **yurts** – Mongolian-style domed circular tents with wooden floors, electricity, and lockable doors, as well as bunk beds and a futon (yurts $27 per night, cabins $35; ⓣ1-800/452-5687, ⓦwww.oregonstateparks.org). Alternatively, you can **camp** for $15–20 at various sites on the coast.

For the most scenic transportation along the waves, **cycling** is always a good option, whether within the state parks, along US-101 (following the coastline to the California border), or on the many smaller "scenic loop" roads. Pick up the *Coast Bike Route Map* from any major visitor center.

Astoria

Set near the mouth of the Columbia River, the port of **ASTORIA** was founded in 1811 as a base for exporting furs to Asia by the millionaire John Jacob Astor. "Fort Astoria" survived only a painful year and a half, beset by natural disasters and internal feuds, before it was sold to the British (Washington Irving made the best of the saga in his novel *Astoria*). A small replica of the old fort stands at 15th and Exchange streets, but nowadays many of Astoria's canneries and port facilities have vanished, as the city tries to reinvent itself for tourists interested in nautical history and working-class Northwest color.

From the east, the main road into Astoria, **Marine Drive**, runs parallel to the waterfront, once crammed with saloons and brothels in the nineteenth century, many equipped with built-in trap doors for "shanghaiing" drunken customers, who might wake up halfway across the Pacific. Things are tamer now, but exhibits from Astoria's seafaring past are on display at the **Columbia River Maritime Museum**, 1792 Marine Drive (daily 9.30am–5pm; $8; ⓦ www.crmm.org), which also features impressive displays of scrimshaw, native artifacts, and reconstructed ships.

From Marine Drive, numbered streets climb up towards fancy Victorian mansions, many now renovated B&Bs. Beyond, painted emblems on the street direct you to the top of Coxcomb Hill, where the **Astoria Column** is decorated with a winding mural depicting pioneer history, and offers stunning views for anyone willing to climb its 164 gloomy spiral stairs. Back in town, further west, the **Flavel House**, 441 8th St (daily 10am–5pm, summer 11am–4pm; $5; ⓦ www.clatsophistoricalsociety.org), is one of the grandest of the city's mansions, the 1886 Queen Anne home of sea captain George Flavel. While the main rooms are set up as dioramas featuring period furniture and decor, more interesting is the ungainly display of local castoffs like bank-teller windows, farm tools, and horse carriages hiding in the basement.

A few miles southwest of town is **Fort Clatsop** (daily 8am–5pm, summer closes 6pm; $3; ⓦ www.nps.gov/focl), a reconstruction of the stockade and winter quarters Lewis and Clark built here in 1805. In the summer, docents in pioneer costumes give exhibitions on shooting flintlock muskets, pouring molten bullets, and making beef-tallow candles. Further west, also off US-101, **Fort Stevens State Park** (ⓣ503/861-1671) offers good trails and camping and miles of beaches, on which you can find the rusting hulk of the **Peter Iredale**, a 1906 shipwreck slowly sinking into the sand, but still enough of a marvel to clamber over at low tide. Although Fort Stevens was developed as a Union post in the Civil War, **Battery Russell** is its most significant military relic. The fort was shelled during World War II by a passing Japanese submarine, which makes it, incredibly, the only military installation on the mainland US to have been fired on by a foreign government since 1812.

Practicalities

Pacific Trails (ⓣ503/692-4437) operates a once-daily **bus** service from Portland to Astoria (and Seaside), while Amtrak provides summer service only (Fri–Mon 7.30am; 4hr; $40). The Greyhound station is at 95 W Marine Drive, and the **visitor center** is nearby at no. 111 (summer daily 8am–6pm; winter Mon–Fri 9am–5pm, Sat & Sun 10am–2pm; ⓣ503/325-6311, ⓦ www.oldoregon.com), near the base of the US-101 bridge over the Columbia, which leads into southwest Washington. To make a leisurely trip along the waterfront, hop aboard the **Astoria Trolley** (summer Mon–Thurs 3–9pm, Fri–Sun noon–9pm; rest of year Sat & Sun noon–6pm; $2), historic rail cars that ply a tourist-oriented route. You can **camp** at Fort Stevens State Park ($18–20; ⓣ1-

800/452-5687), or stay in one of the mundane **motels** along Marine Drive, but the town's most distinctive offerings are its **B&Bs**, many of them in Victorian mansions. Among the best are *Franklin St Station*, 1140 Franklin St (☏503/325-4314 or 1-800/448-1098, ⊛www.franklin-st-station-bb.com; ⑤), having seven rooms with balconies overlooking town, and the *Rosebriar*, 636 14th St (☏503/325-7427 or 1-800/487-0224, ⊛astoria-usa.com/rosebriar; ④), a renovated 1902 convent with great river views.

Several good places to **eat** are sprinkled throughout downtown. *Columbian Café*, 1114 Marine Drive (☏503/325-2233), has gourmet seafood and vegetarian meals, and offers evening jams by regional musicians in its *Voodoo Room* (Thurs–Sun; $5); and the *Home Spirit Baking Company*, 1585 Exchange (☏503/325-6846), serves homemade sourdough bread and ice cream in a lovely Victorian home. If all else fails, make like the locals and head to *Pig 'n Pancake*, unavoidable at 146 W Bond St (☏503/325-3144, ⊛www.pignpancake.com), where you can get your fill of delightfully greasy, stupor-inducing breakfasts.

Seaside and Cannon Beach

Seventeen miles south of Astoria, **SEASIDE** is a rather seedy resort, the one spot on the Oregon coast nature-lovers try assiduously to avoid – a mix of crude carnival rides and depressing chain motels, where an endless parade of pimply teenagers and middle-aged burnouts patrol the town's central concrete walkway, **the Prom**. If you have to stay here, try the ten comely Victorian rooms of the 1893 *Gilbert Inn*, 341 Beach Drive (☏503/738-9770, ⊛www.gilbertinn.com; ⑤), or the *HI-Seaside Hostel*, 930 N Holladay Drive (☏503/738-7911, ⊛2oregonhostels.com; dorms $20, private rooms $39), also the site of Greyhound arrivals. A colorless array of places to **shop** and **eat** are concentrated along Broadway, and the **visitor center** is at 7 N Roosevelt Drive (☏503/738-6391 or 1-800/444-6740, ⊛www.seasidechamber.com).

Nine miles south from Seaside, the more upmarket and pleasant **CANNON BEACH** manages, unlike Seaside, to retain its small-town air despite decades of relentless commercialism. The place is at its liveliest during the annual **Sandcastle Competition** (⊛www.cannon-beach.net/cbsandcastle), a one-day event held around Memorial Day and starting when the tide permits, drawing artistic sand-crafters and hapless sand-shovelers from around the region. You're apt to see anything from dinosaurs and sphinxes to mermaids and monkeys carved out of sand, with Jesus and Elvis also putting in frequent appearances. Cannon Beach's best natural draw is its 240ft **Haystack Rock**, a black monolith crowned with nesting seagulls – accessible at low tide, though definitely not climbable. To escape the town's inevitable crush of tourists, head four miles north to **Ecola State Park**, where dense conifer forests decorate the basaltic cliffs of Tillamook Head, or south to **Oswald West State Park**, named after the pioneering governor who helped preserve most of the state's beaches, where there's a beautiful beach, rocky headland, and coastal rainforest. *Oswald West* (☏1-800/551-6949; $10), a tent-only campground popular with surfers, provides wheelbarrows to transport your gear to the site.

Accommodation is tight, especially at competition time. *Cannon Beach Hotel*, 1116 S Hemlock St (☏503/436-1392, ⊛www.cannonbeachhotel.com; ④), is a cozy boutique hotel, while the *Waves Motel*, 188 W Second St (☏503/436-2205 or 1-800/822-2468, ⊛www.thewavesmotel.com; ④–⑧), has studios and suites on the seafront. For **food**, *Midtown Café*, 1235 S Hemlock St (☏503/436-1016), has the best breakfast in town, and the *Bistro*, 263 N Hemlock St (☏503/436-2661), doles out a fine range of fresh seafood.

⑭

THE PACIFIC NORTHWEST | OREGON | The Oregon Coast

Tillamook and Lincoln City

South of Cannon Beach, the next major stop, **TILLAMOOK,** provides two good reasons to drop in: the main one being the **Tillamook Cheese Factory** (daily 8am–6pm; free; ⓦ www.tillamookcheese.com), just north of town on US-101, where you can watch cheese being made on a self-guided tour, providing glimpses of hair-netted workers beside conveyor belts and bent over large, milky vats. You can also devour a cone from one of the factory's two ice-cream counters, where the company's oversized scoops are devoured by equally oversized customers. However, tastier cheese can be had just to the south at the **Blue Heron** (daily 9am–5pm; free; ⓦ www.blueheronoregon.com), where you can sample the pepper-encrusted brie before heading out back to have a close encounter with a goat or rooster in a quasi-petting zoo.

Further south, there's no avoiding **LINCOLN CITY**: the ugliest town on the Oregon coast, sprawling along the highway for seven congested, dreadful miles – the legacy of consolidating five beach towns in the 1960s. In the unlikely event you decide to stay here, there's plenty of cheap and dreary **accommodation** to choose from – the **visitor center**, on US-101 (☏ 541/996-2152, ⓦ www.lincolncity.org), has the full list. For somewhere to **eat**, you're better off heading on to Newport.

Newport

Thirty miles south of Lincoln City, **NEWPORT** is both an active port and something of a resort. While the **Historic Bayfront** along Bay Boulevard is the obvious first stop for many – with its souvenir shops, seafood diners, and hordes of sea lions wallowing on the wharves – the town's real highlight is uncrowded **Nye Beach**, a quiet oceanside gem further to the west. Here, there are few official sights other than a deserted, modern **Vietnam War Memorial** (24hr; free), a gnarled and twisted spire on a bluff, but the beach makes for an excellent stroll, and the seaside development is a bit more restrained than elsewhere in town. To the south, across the bridge at 2820 SE Ferry Slip Rd, the impressive **Oregon Coast Aquarium** (daily summer 9am–6pm; rest of year 10am–5pm; $10.75; ⓦ www.aquarium.org) is home to sea otters, seals, and tufted puffins, as well as Passages of the Deep, a shark-oriented underwater tunnel. Just north of town, Newport's other top attraction is **Yaquina Head** (daily dawn–dusk; $5), an officially decreed "Outstanding Scenic Area" with a marine biology center, cape lighthouse, and manmade tidepools constructed in a former quarry.

Practicalities

The Greyhound station is at 956 SW 10th St, and the **chamber of commerce** is at 555 SW Coast Hwy (☏ 541/265-8801 or 1-800/262-7844, ⓦ www.newportchamber.org). The most prominent place to **stay** is the *Sylvia Beach Hotel*, on Nye Beach at 267 NW Cliff St (☏ 541/265-5428, ⓦ www.sylviabeachhotel.com; ❹–❻), whose twenty rooms bear the name of a famous writer (it also has dorm beds; ❶). Every evening, mulled wine is served in the upstairs library, where you can look studious with other guests posing as intellectuals. Less pretentious is the neighboring *Nye Beach Hotel* (☏ 541/265-3334, ⓦ www.nyebeach.com; ❺), with six great oceanfront rooms featuring stove heating, balconies, and hot tubs. Newport also has a handful of fine **B&Bs** (which you can review at ⓦ www.moriah.com/npbba), the best of which is the *Beach House*, 107 SW Coast S (☏ 866/215-6486 or 541/265-9141, ⓦ www.beachhousebb.com), with its three spacious, well-furnished units. For drab, low-end lodging, countless **motels** line US-101.

There's a cluster of first-rate **cafés** and **restaurants** on Bay Boulevard at the bayfront. The *Whale's Tale*, 452 SW Bay Blvd (℡541/265-8660), has good seafood and isn't quite as crowded as *Mo's Original* (℡541/265-2979) or *Mo's Annex* (℡541/265-7512), both in the 600 block, two decent chain seafood restaurants that are always thick with tourists. *Rogue Ales House* (℡541/265-3188), no. 748, is the liveliest spot for food and beer, and on Nye Beach, *April's*, 749 NW 3rd St (℡541/265-6855), offers fine Continental cuisine – the town's best restaurant by default.

Bandon

At the mouth of the Coquille River along US-101, easygoing **BANDON** combines old-town restoration with a strong New Age, arts-and-crafts presence. Originally a Native American settlement, when white townsfolk dynamited Tupper Rock, a sacred tribal site, to build the sea wall, the town was cursed to burn down three times: it's happened twice so far, in 1914 and 1936, and the superstitious are still waiting for the final conflagration.

Bandon's main attraction is its rugged **beach**, strewn with unusual rock formations and magnificent in stormy weather, when giant tree stumps are tossed up out of the ocean like matchsticks. In calmer conditions, clam-diggers head off to the river's mudflats, crabbers gather at the town dock, and the whole scene makes for a delightful stroll. The **visitor center** is centrally located at 300 SE 2nd St (℡541/347-9616, ⓦwww.bandon.com), and there's oceanfront **accommodation** just south of town at the outstanding *Sunset Motel*, 1865 Beach Loop Drive (℡541/347-2453 or 1-800/842-2407, ⓦwww.sunsetmotel.com; ❸–❼), which comprises motel rooms, condos, and, best of all, seafront cabins. In town, the place to stay is the *Sea Star Guest House*, 370 1st St (℡541/347-9632, ⓦseastarbandon.com; ❸), boasting very affordable rooms and suites, part of which is given over to the *HI-Sea Star Hostel* (dorm beds $19). You can also **camp** just north of town at **Bullards Beach State Park** (℡541/347-2209), where the disused Coquille River Lighthouse casts a romantic silhouette over miles of windswept sands.

West of town, there's good **seafood** at *Bandon Boatworks*, 275 Lincoln Ave SW (℡541/347-2111), and at various eateries along 1st and 2nd streets in the center of town. Pick up a tasty block of cheese at the *Bandon Cheese Factory*, 680 E 2nd St (℡541/347-2456), or famously tangy treats at *Cranberry Sweets*, 1st St at Chicago SE (℡541/347-9475).

South to California

Towns are fewer and farther apart going south on US-101 from Bandon, with the coastline at its prettiest beyond **Port Orford** – known principally for its unusual **dry dock**, on which a crane hoists boats aloft – where forested mountains sweep smoothly down to the sea. These mountains mark the western limit of the **Siskiyou National Forest**, a vast slab of remote wilderness best explored by boat along the turbulent Rogue River from workaday **Gold Beach**. Here, the Greyhound station is at 29770 Colvin St, while the **visitor center**, on the main road at 29279 S Ellensburg (℡541/247-7526 or 1-800/525-2334, ⓦwww.goldbeachchamber.com), has details of rafting and powerboat excursions plus prices for the town's basic motels and hotels. Finally, at the state's far southwestern corner, **Brookings** has a warmer climate, and is best used as a base for exploring northern California's **Redwood National Park** (see p.1223). Contact the local **visitor center** (Mon–Fri 9am–5pm; ℡541/469-3181, ⓦwww.brookingsor.com) for more details.

Central Oregon

East of the Cascades, Oregon grows warmer, drier, and wilder; green valleys give way to the high desert with sagebrush, juniper trees, craggy hills, and stark rock formations broken up by the occasional tract of pine forest. **Central Oregon's** volcanic landscape – much of it laid down in massive basaltic flows some sixteen million years ago – features cracked lava beds, towering cone-like hills, and deep craters such as beautiful **Crater Lake** in the south.

Bend and around

BEND is the most useful and appealing base for visiting central Oregon, giving access both to mountain grandeur and an eerie volcanic landscape, and packed with restaurants, microbreweries, and outdoor-gear shops. Greyhound buses from Portland and Eugene arrive at 1315 NE 3rd St, the **visitor center** is at 63085 N Hwy-97 (☎541/382-8048 or 1-877/245-8484, ⓦwww .visitbend.org), and the **Central Oregon Welcome Center**, 572 SW Bluff Drive (☎541/389-8799 or 1-800/800-8334, ⓦwww.covisitors.com), has brochures and accommodation listings. Beyond recreation, the area's main attraction is undoubtedly the **High Desert Museum**, 59800 US-97 (daily 9am–5pm; $8.50; ⓦwww.highdesert.org), a fascinating collection of artifacts from Native American and pioneer history, along with displays of regional flora and fauna, and a reconstructed pioneer homestead and sawmill out back.

Aside from the anonymous budget **motels** strung out along US-97, the compact town center is the best place to find accommodation, especially several smart **B&Bs** in stately, early twentieth-century residences, such as the *Lara House*, 640 NW Congress St (☎541/388-4064, ⓦwww.larahouse.com; ❺), and the *Sather House*, 7 NW Tumalo Ave (☎541/388-1065 or 1-888/388-1065, ⓦwww.satherhouse.com; ❹). The *Bend Cascade Hostel*, 19 SW Century Drive (☎541/389-3813; $28), has dorm beds for $15, only a short walk from the free ski shuttle to Mount Bachelor. Camp in **Tumalo State Park** (☎541/388-6055), a wooded dell by the Deschutes River five miles northwest along US-20, which offers **yurts** as well as large canvas-covered **tepees** (both $27).

For **eating** and **drinking**, there are cafés with an easy-going feel, Western-style diners, brewpubs, chic restaurants, and everything in between. *Pine Tavern*, 967 NW Brooks St (☎541/382-5581), and *Bend Brewing*, 1019 NW Brooks St (☎541/383-1599), both serve microbrewed ales and stouts and sturdy American cuisine, while the *Deschutes Brewery and Public House*, 1044 Bond St (☎541/385-8606), brews and serves one of the Northwest's most prominent beers, Black Butter Porter, among others. *West Side Café & Bakery*, 1005 NW Galveston Ave (☎541/382-3426), has filling breakfasts and *Cup of Magic*, 1304 NW Galveston (☎541/330-5539), has great coffee and baked goods.

Mount Bachelor and the Cascades Lake Highway

The Northwest's largest ski resort, **Mount Bachelor** (☎541/382-2442 or 1-800/829-2442, ⓦwww.mtbachelor.com; lift tickets $44), caters to downhill and cross-country skiers, and snowboarders alike, 22 miles southwest of Bend. Its Olympic-standard facilities are open from mid-November to late May, snowfall permitting. Mount Bachelor is also the first stop on the **Cascade Lakes Highway**, known as "Century Drive" – a hundred-mile mountain loop road giving access to trailheads into the **Three Sisters** – a trio of spiky peaks visible throughout central Oregon – or, further south, the **Diamond Peak** wilderness area and a sprinkling of campgrounds (see ⓦ www.oregonstateparks.org for information). Get details from **Deschutes National Forest Ranger Station**, just outside of Bend at 1645 NE Hwy-20 (☎541/388-2715), or in Bend at 1230 NE 3rd St (☎541/388-5664).

Newberry National Volcanic Monument

The so-called **Lava Lands** cover a huge area of central Oregon, with the greatest concentration of sizeable lava formations – conical buttes, craggy caves, and the rocky molds of tree trunks – in the Bend area located at **Newberry National Volcanic Monument** (dawn–dusk; five-day parking passes $5). Dating back seven thousand years to the eruption of Mount Newberry, the monument is actually a huge, gently sloping crater laced with hiking paths, nature trails, campgrounds, and prime fishing spots. Some of the rugged highlights (most free with monument admission) include the chilly, mile-long **Lava River Cave** (summer daily 9am–5pm; $3, plus $2 for a lamp), an eerie but walkable subterranean passage made from a hollow lava tube; the **Lava Cast Forest**, a surreal walk near the circular, basalt casts of tree trunks burnt by lava before they could fall; and the surreal landscape of the **Big Obsidian Flow**, huge hills of volcanic black glass that native tribes throughout the Northwest once used to make arrowheads. As the rock is still quite sharp and brittle – and especially rare – you're strongly advised not to take home any geological souvenirs. The **Lava Lands visitor center** (April–Oct daily 9am–5pm; ☎541/593-2421; $5), eleven miles south of Bend on US-97, is an excellent source of maps and information on hiking trails, and provides access to the monument's other major sight, **Lava Butte**, a massive 500ft cinder cone, whose narrow rim you can reach by car and traverse in a twenty-minute walk.

Crater Lake National Park

Despite its stunning natural beauty, Oregon has only one national park, located just over a hundred miles south of Bend. The blown-out shell of Mount Mazama holds the deep, blue, resoundingly beautiful **CRATER LAKE** (seven-day access fee $10; ⓦ www.nps.gov/crla), formed after an explosion 42 times greater than that of Mount St Helens (see p.1263). The biggest island on the lake, **Wizard Island**, is actually the tip of a still-rising cinder cone. In its snowy isolation, the lake, at a depth of nearly two thousand feet, is awe-inspiring; in summer, too, it's spectacular, when wildflowers bloom along its high rim. The most popular, though still strenuous, hike is up **Garfield Peak**, an 8054ft mountain that offers a tremendous view of the lake and is particularly striking – and harder to reach – during winter. More intrepid hikers can explore the marginally better views offered by the park's tallest outcrop, **Mount Scott**, rising to almost nine thousand feet.

You'll need a **car** to get to the park, though only the southern roads (US-62 from Medford or US-97 from Klamath Falls) are open year-round. The northern access road (via Hwy-138) is closed from mid-October to June, as is the spectacular, 33-mile "Rim Drive" around the crater's edge. Regular **boats** cruise the lake (late June to mid-Sept daily 10am–4pm; 1hr 45min; $19.25), reached via the sheer, mile-long **Cleetwood Cove trail**, which provides the only access to the lakeshore. The trail is on the north shore, but visitor facilities are clustered on the south at tiny **Rim Village**, where the **visitor center** (June–Sept 9.30am–5pm) is a few steps from *Crater Lake Lodge* (☎541/830-8700, ⓦ www.craterlakelodges.com; ⑥; mid-May to mid-Oct), a grand old lodge built in 1915; ask for a room overlooking the lake – the lodge perches on the rim of the caldera. Operated by the same company, *Mazama Village Motor Inn* (early June to mid-Oct; ⑤) is seven miles from the crater, but has an adjoining **campground** ($10) in a quiet wooded setting. There are also two campgrounds, the large *Mazama* ($10) and the much smaller *Lost Creek* ($14.75), both inside the park boundary. The **park headquarters** are at the Steel Visitors Center (May–Oct 9am–5pm; rest of year 10am–4pm; ☎541/594-3100, ⓦ www.crater.lake.national-park.com), a year-round facility a few miles south of the rim on the main access road.

Klamath Falls

Sixty miles southeast of Crater Lake, the burg of **KLAMATH FALLS** isn't particularly pretty (only appearing in the national news as the site of angry water-shortage protests by local farmers), but it does boast the **Favell Museum**, 125 W Main St (Wed–Sat 9.30am–5.30pm; $5; ⓦ www.favellmuseum.com), which hosts a fine collection of native artifacts and a large assortment of Wild West paintings and sculptures.

Klamath Falls sits in the middle of **Klamath Basin**, whose low-lying lakes and marshes once formed a vast wetland stretching far beyond the California border. Much of the basin has been drained for cattle grazing, but six sections are now protected as **national wildlife refuges**, with the resident bird population increasing to upwards of a million during spring and fall migrations. The town's **visitor center**, 507 Main St (daily 9am–4.30pm; ☎541/445-6728, ⓦ klamathcounty.net), issues detailed maps of the basin and its bird sanctuaries.

Eastern Oregon

Eastern Oregon, though seldom drawing in visitors like the rest of the state, can be surprisingly beautiful. The **John Day Fossil Beds** along US-26, the remote, snowcapped **Wallowa Mountains**, and the deep slash of **Hells Canyon** are all overwhelmingly dramatic landscapes, and not to be missed if you have the time to explore the outback, preferably in a four-wheel-drive vehicle. Eastbound on Hwy-126/26 from Redmond, you'll emerge from a brief passage through the **Ochoco National Forest** – itself worth a look for its wooded slopes, craggy canyons, and rocky pillars – into a bare, sun-scorched landscape of ochre and beige, the topography of Oregon's former Wild West country.

John Day Fossil Beds and around

Many eastern Oregon features are named, rather inexplicably, after **John Day**, an employee of fur trapper John Jacob Astor, best known for being attacked and stripped naked by natives and enduring fits of dementia. As regional writer Ralph Friedman remarks, places in the state bearing his name are "probably the only ones in Oregon honoring a man acknowledged to have been violently insane." The most significant of his namesakes are the **John Day Fossil Beds**, which hold some of the most revealing fossil formations in the US, preserved in a layer of volcanic ash while the Cascades formed, just after the extinction of the dinosaurs 65 million years ago. There are three fossil-bed sites, the most westerly being the **Painted Hills** unit, six miles off US-26 down a paved side road. Striped in shades of beige, rust, and brown, the surfaces of these evocative, sandcastle-like hills are quilted with rivulets worn by draining water.

Back on US-26, thirty miles east, is the **Sheep Rock** unit, just north of the junction with Hwy-19. Here, the **visitor center** (Mon–Fri 9am–5pm; free; ☎541/987-2333, ⊛www.nps.gov/joda) is in an old rancher's homestead and has a modest selection of fossils, but will be moved to the larger and more elaborate **Condon Paleontology Center** when it opens in 2004. A mile further north is the **Blue Basin**, a natural amphitheater where a mile-long trail leads past various fossil replicas, like that of a saber-toothed cat and a tortoise that hurtled to its death millions of years ago.

Beyond the fossil beds, the largest town along US-26 between Baker City and Prineville is little **John Day**, the home of one of Oregon's key historical sights. The fascinating **Kam Wah Chung & Co. Museum**, just off US-26 (May–Oct Mon–Thurs 9am–noon & 1–5pm, Sat & Sun 1–5pm; $3), was once the residence, opium den, and general store of famed Chinese herbalist **Ing Hay**, whose apothecary wares – five hundred herbs, dried lizard, bear claw, bottle of rattlesnakes – have been preserved and are still on display, providing an authentic, unexpected glimpse into Oregon's pioneer history.

Baker City

In the forested hills east of John Day, US-26 turns southeast for the long run down to Idaho. More enjoyable is the far shorter drive on Hwy-7 through the

The Oregon Trail

Between the 1840s and 1870s, more than a quarter-million Americans journeyed by wagon train from the Midwest to Oregon in search of a new start. Ever since Lewis and Clark completed their successful survey of the Oregon Country in 1806, the idea of "manifest destiny" had both politicians and prospective settlers keen to see their country expand from coast to coast, regardless of who or what might be in the way. The first migrants were further inspired by the missionaries who went west to try to Christianize Native Americans in the 1830s, and who sent back glowing reports of the region's temperate climate, fertile soil, dense forests, fish-rich rivers, and absence of malaria.

With the promise of generous land grants, in spring 1843 more than a thousand would-be migrants gathered at Independence and Westport on the banks of the Missouri, preparing for the **"Great Migration."** The pioneers were a remarkably homogenous bunch, nearly all experienced farmers, using ox-pulled wagons with flimsy canvas roofs to transport supplies and often walking alongside their vehicles, instead of riding and adding extra weight to them.

Traversing almost two thousand miles of what are now Missouri, Nebraska, Wyoming, and Idaho, the migrants forced their wagons across pristine rivers, forests, and mountains, pausing at the occasional army fort or missionary station to recuperate. They also bartered supplies with various tribes in return for rafts and knowledge of the outback. After three months on the trail, they arrived at what is now the town of The Dalles. From there the group faced an uneasy choice before reaching the lush Willamette Valley just beyond: build rafts and risk the treacherous currents and whirlpools of the Columbia River or take the equally perilous Barlow Road around Mount Hood (see p.1278), notorious for its swiftly changing weather and steep hillsides.

Over the next thirty years, fifty thousand more settlers arrived in the Willamette Valley, with others moving into Washington and California. Along with helping Oregon to become a state in 1859, the migration spawned a cottage industry of specialist suppliers and wagon-builders, and traffic on the trail was such that the route was miles wide in parts. Inevitably, there are few surviving signs of the passing of the migrants, but they are commemorated by several museums, the best of which is near Baker City (see p.1292).

southern reaches of the **Wallowa-Whitman National Forest** to the Gold Rush boomtown of **BAKER CITY**, now the commercial center for Eastern Oregon. The **Oregon Trail Interpretative Center**, five well-signposted miles east of town at Flagstaff Hill (daily: April–Oct 9am–6pm; Nov–Mar 9am–4pm; $5; ☎541/523-1843, ⊛oregontrail.blm.gov), has audiovisual displays and four miles of trails revealing well-preserved wagon ruts and other points of interest from that historic route (see box, overleaf). Back in town, the **Oregon Trail Regional Museum**, 2480 Grove St (April–Oct daily 9am–4pm; $3.50), show-cases artifacts from pioneer days, but is most notable for its fine collection of rocks, petrified wood, and fluorescent geodes glowing under ultraviolet light.

Baker City's Main Street has many handsome early twentieth-century, red-brick buildings, but most of the **accommodation** is on the town periphery in routine motels along Tenth or Campbell streets. You're better off sampling one of the town's interesting **B&Bs** in old-time residences, such as *Baer House*, 2333 Main St (☎541/523-1055 or 1-800/709-7637, ⊛www.baerhouse.com; ❹), a fetching 1882 Victorian home with rooms awash in period antiques. Otherwise, try the opulent historic setting of the *Geiser Grand*, 1996 Main St (☎541/523-1889, ⊛www.geisergrand.com; ❺), a classic 1889 hotel decked out with a stained-glass ceiling and mahogany fixtures. The vast Wallowa–Whitman National Forest, stretching east and west of town, has many **campgrounds**; get details from the **visitor center**, 490 Campbell St, beside exit 304 on I-84 (☎541/523-3356 or 1-800/523-1235, ⊛www.visitbaker.com). Good **restaurants** include the cheap *Front Street Café*, 1840 Main St (☎541/523-0223), and the dependable pub fare at *Barley Brown's Brewpub*, 2190 Main St (☎541/523-4266). Greyhound **buses** connect to Portland from 515 Campbell St.

La Grande and Pendleton

The large, flat **Grande Ronde Valley**, north of Baker City on I-84, is now mostly used for agriculture, but was once marshland, fatally boggy to pioneer wagons, which forced the Oregon Trail to keep to the higher but tougher ground around the hills as it headed northwest to the Blue Mountains. The valley's hub is the dusty burg of **LA GRANDE**, where information is available at the **chamber of commerce**, 1912 4th St (☎541/963-8588 or 1-800/848-9969, ⊛www.visitlagrande.com), but for local color and history you're better off pushing northwest on I-84, following the route of the Oregon Trail, to **PENDLETON**, where Stetsons and pick-up trucks abound. This town is best known as the home of the immensely popular, annual four-day **Pendleton Round-Up** in mid-September, combining traditional rodeo with extravagant pageantry; get tickets from the Round-Up Association, PO Box 609, Pendleton, OR 97801 ($11–17 per rodeo session; ☎541/276-2553 or 1-800/45-RODEO, ⊛www.pendletonroundup.com). The **Round-Up Hall of Fame**, 1205 SW Court Ave (June–Aug Mon–Sat 10am–5pm; free), is stuffed with associated memorabilia. The famed **Pendleton Woolen Mills**, 1307 SE Court Place (tours Mon–Fri 9am, 11am, 1.30pm & 3pm; 20min; free; ⊛www.pendleton-usa.com), will mainly appeal to those interested in textiles, although you can always pick up a sweater while there, while the fascinating **Pendleton Underground**, 37 SW Emigrant at 1st St (Mar–Oct Mon–Sat 9.30am–3pm, rest of year varies; 90min; $10; ⊛www.pendletonundergroundtours.org), lets you tour the town's extensive network of subterranean passageways, used during Prohibition as saloons, card rooms, and brothels – and as a refuge for the area's much-abused Chinese population.

The **chamber of commerce**, 501 S Main St (Mon–Fri 9am–5pm; ☎541/276-7411 or 1-800/547-8911, ⊛www.pendleton-oregon.org), is a short walk from the Greyhound station. **Accommodation** options include the five Victorian rooms of the *Parker House B&B*, 311 N Main St (℡541/276-8581, ⓦwww.parkerhousebnb.com; ❹), and the functional *Oxford Suites*, 2400 SW Court Place (℡1-877/545-7848, ⓦwww.oxfordsuites.com; ❸). Be sure to book early at Round-Up time. Most **restaurants** dole out hefty portions of all-American fare like burgers and fries, although *Raphael's*, 233 SE 4th Ave (℡541/276-8500), offers a touch of upscale, nouveau Northwest cuisine.

The Wallowa Mountains

The **Wallowa Mountains**, reached by leaving I-84 at La Grande and heading east on Hwy-82, are one of Eastern Oregon's loveliest and least-known areas. At the northern tip of the glacially-carved **Wallowa Lake**, the tiny town of **JOSEPH** is a perfect spot to spend the night. **Motels** such as the *Indian Lodge*, 201 S Main St (℡541/432-2651, ⓦwww.eoni.com/~gingerdaggett; ❷), are inexpensive, and there are quite a few **B&Bs** of varying quality, the best of which is probably the *Bronze Antler*, 309 S Main St (℡541/432-0230, ⓦwww.bronzeantler.com; ❸–❺ by season), with its rustic, Arts and Crafts design and antique European furniture. Also on Main Street are many antique and craft stores and the small **Wallowa County Museum**, 110 S Main St (summer daily 10am–5pm; donation; ⓦwww.co.wallowa.or.us/museum), where the story of the Nez Percé (see p.961) is presented along with a limited collection of pioneer artifacts.

A mile or so south of Joseph, **Wallowa Lake** is inhabited by the Native American legend of the Wallowa Lake Monster, a great horned beast known to some as "Wally." At its far end, the state park has **camping** ($18; ⓦwww.wallowalake.net), and the **Wallowa Lake Tramway**, 59919 Wallowa Lake Hwy (daily: June–Aug 10am–5pm; May & Sept 10am–4pm; $19 roundtrip; ⓦwww.wallowalaketramway.com), which whisks visitors to the top of 4000ft **Mount Howard**, where short trails lead to magnificent overlooks. Much of the mountain scenery behind Joseph makes up the **Eagle Cap Wilderness** ($5 passes; ⓦwww.fs.fed.us/r6/w-w/ecwild), whose lakes, streams, and peaks are accessible only via hiking trails. Backcountry camping and hiking around here are strikingly remote – contact the **Wallowa Mountains Visitor Center**, 88401 Hwy-82 (Mon–Fri 8am–5pm; ℡541/426-5546, ⓦwww.wallowacounty.org), for details of the Eagle Cap, as well as Hells Canyon.

Hells Canyon

East of Joseph, marking the Idaho border, the **Snake River** has cut the deepest chasm on the continent – **Hells Canyon**, a 130-mile gorge edged by a series of gradually ascending false peaks, a thousand feet deeper than the Grand Canyon. With the **Seven Devils** mountains rising above it and the river glimmering in its depths, the canyon is arrestingly awe-inspiring, yet still best known as the site of the ill-fated 1974 motorcycle jump by daredevil Evel Knievel.

The area is preserved as the **Hells Canyon National Recreation Area** (day-pass $5; ⓦwww.fs.fed.us/hellscanyon), where deer, otters, mink, black bears, mountain lions, and elk live, along with rattlesnakes and black-widow spiders. Mechanical vehicles are banned above water-level in much of the canyon, so you can only explore on foot or horseback. The forest roads that skirt the area are rough and slippery, and many are closed by snow much of the year. If you intend to use them, check with the **rangers** in Enterprise, 88401 Hwy-82 (℡541/426-5546), or Baker City, 1550 Dewey Ave (℡541/523-6391), before you go – bear in mind that summer temperatures here regularly reach 100°F or more.

Of the two routes approaching the canyon from Oregon, the more difficult begins in Joseph. From here, Little Sheep Creek Highway leads to **Imnaha** where a narrow and vertiginous graveled Forest Service road leads to the ultimate view from **Hat Point**, site of a campground and lookout tower. Beyond Hat Point, the road fades into a trail that leads to the bottom of the canyon, but to undertake this trek you must be very fit and well-equipped. The easier approach is at the south end of the canyon, along Hwy-86 east from Baker City. On the way, tiny **Halfway** makes a good stopoff, with **accommodation** at *Halfway Motel*, 170 S Main St (☎541/742-5722, ⓦwww.halfwayor .com/motel-rvpark; ❷), and the three cabins and five rooms available at the rustic farmhouse of the *Clear Creek Farm B&B*, 48212 Clear Creek Rd (call for directions; ☎541/742-2238, ⓦwww.neoregon.com/ccgg; ❺).

The other approach heading into the canyon, from Halfway on Hwy-86, meets the Snake River at Oxbow Dam, where a rough Forest Service road leads to **Hells Canyon Dam**, the launching-point for exhilarating jet-boat and rafting trips through the canyon. *Hells Canyon Adventures* (☎541/785-3352 or 1-800/422-3568, reservations required; ⓦwww.hellscanyonadventures.com) and other companies run sightseeing **tours** in summer (2–3hr; $30–40 per person). Skimming over the rapids, the boats take you between deceptively low, bare hills to an old pioneer homestead, as well as operating a "drop-off" service, taking you to hiking trails along the canyon and picking you up the same day or later in the week ($30 per person).

Alaska

AL - ALABAMA	IN - INDIANA	MN - MINNESOTA	RI - RHODE ISLAND
AR - ARKANSAS	LA - LOUISIANA	MS - MISSISSIPPI	SC - SOUTH CAROLINA
CT - CONNECTICUT	MA - MASSACHUSETTS	NC - NORTH CAROLINA	VA - VIRGINIA
DE - DELAWARE	MD - MARYLAND	NH - NEW HAMPSHIRE	VT - VERMONT
FL - FLORIDA	ME - MAINE	NJ - NEW JERSEY	WI - WISCONSIN
IL - ILLINOIS	MI - MICHIGAN	PA - PENNSYLVANIA	WV - WEST VIRGINIA

CHAPTER 15

Highlights

* **Sitka** Russian influence blended with Native heritage and fabulous coastal scenery, making this one of Alaska's most diverting towns. See p.1304

* **The Chilkoot Trail** Follow in the (frozen) footsteps of the Klondike prospectors on this demanding 33-mile trail near Skagway. See p.1314

* **Talkeetna** Every Alaska visitor's favorite small town is the base for superb flightseeing trips around Mount McKinley. See p.1329

* **Denali National Park** Alaska's finest park offers superb mountain scenery and incomparable wildlife-spotting around the highest peak in North America. See p.1330

* **Aurora borealis** The spectacular after-dark displays of the Northern Lights are at their best around Fairbanks from mid-September to mid-March. See p.1336

* **Dalton Highway** This lonely and grueling 500-mile road leads north from Fairbanks to the Arctic Ocean. See p.1336

⑮

Alaska

N o other region in North America fires the imagination like **ALASKA** – a derivation of *Alayeska*, an Athabascan word meaning "great land of the west." Few who see this land of gargantuan ice fields, sweeping tundra, glacially excavated valleys, lush rainforests, deep fjords, and occasionally smoking volcanoes leave unimpressed. **Wildlife** may be under threat elsewhere, but here it is abundant, with Kodiak bears standing twelve feet tall, moose stopping traffic in downtown Anchorage, wolves prowling national parks, bald eagles circling over the trees, and rivers solid with fifty-plus-pound salmon.

More than twice the size of Texas, Alaska's sheer size is hard to comprehend. If superimposed onto the Lower 48 (the rest of the continental United States) it would stretch from the Atlantic to the Pacific, and its coastline is longer than the rest of the US combined. All but three of the nation's twenty highest peaks are found within its boundaries and one glacier alone is twice the size of Wales. And not only does it contain America's **northernmost** and **westernmost** points, but, because the Aleutian Islands stretch across the 180th meridian, it contains the **easternmost** point as well.

A mere 600,000 people live in this huge state – over forty percent of them in **Anchorage** – of whom only one-fifth were born in the state: as a rule of thumb, the more winters you have endured, the more Alaskan you are. Often referred to as the **"Last Frontier,"** Alaska in many ways mirrors the American West of the nineteenth century: an endless, undeveloped space in which to stake one's claim and set up a life without interference – or at least that's how Alaskans would like it to be. Throughout this century, tens of thousands have been lured by the promise of wealth, first by gold and then by fishing, logging, and, most recently, oil. However, Alaska's 86,000 **Native peoples**, who don't have the option of returning to the Lower 48 if things don't work out, have been greatly marginalized, though Native corporations set up as a result of pre-oil boom land deals have increasing economic clout.

Traveling around Alaska still demands a spirit of adventure, and to make the most of the state you need to have an enthusiasm for striking out on your own and roughing it a bit. Binoculars are an absolute must, as is bug spray; the **mosquito** is referred to as the "Alaska state bird" and it takes industrial-strength repellent to keep it away. On top of that, there's the **climate**, though Alaska is far from the popular misconception of being one big icebox. While winter temperatures of -40°F are commonplace in Fairbanks, the most touristed areas – the southeast and the Kenai Peninsula – enjoy a maritime climate (45–65°F in summer) similar to that of the Pacific Northwest, meaning much more rain (in some towns 180-plus inches per year) than snow. Remarkably, the summer temperature in the Interior often reaches 80°F.

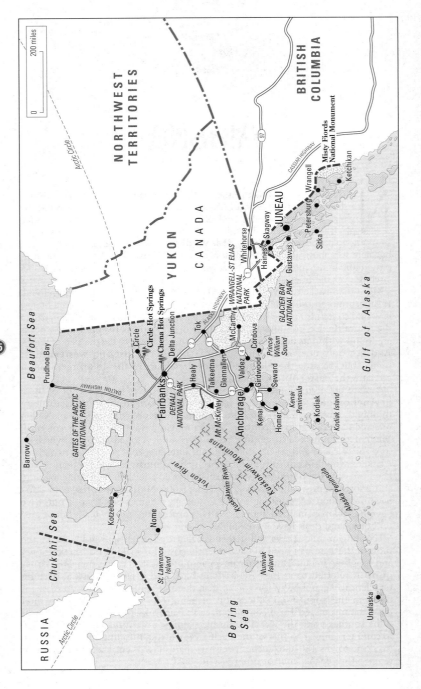

RUSSIA

Arctic Circle

Chukchi Sea

Beaufort Sea

NORTHWEST TERRITORIES

Arctic Circle

0   200 miles

Barrow

Kotzebue

Nome

St. Lawrence Island

Bering Sea

Nunivak Island

Prudhoe Bay

DALTON HIGHWAY

GATES OF THE ARCTIC NATIONAL PARK

Yukon River

Circle
Circle Hot Springs
Chena Hot Springs
Delta Junction

ALASKA HIGHWAY

Fairbanks

DENALI NATIONAL PARK

Mt McKinley

Healy

Talkeetna

Kuskokwim River

Kuskokwim Mountains

Anchorage

Kenai

Homer

Kenai Peninsula

Girdwood

Seward

Kodiak

Kodiak Island

Alaska Peninsula

Unalaska

YUKON

CANADA

Tok

WRANGELL-ST ELIAS NATIONAL PARK

McCarthy

Glennallen

Valdez

Prince William Sound

Cordova

Gulf of Alaska

Whitehorse

97

Haines
Skagway

JUNEAU

Gustavus

GLACIER BAY NATIONAL PARK

Sitka

Petersburg Wrangell

CASSIAR HIGHWAY

Misty Fjords National Monument

Ketchikan

BRITISH COLUMBIA

Alaska is far more expensive than most other states: apart from two dozen hostels and myriad campgrounds there's little budget accommodation, and **eating** and **drinking** will set you back at least twenty percent more than in the Lower 48 (perhaps fifty percent in more remote regions). Still, experiencing Alaska on a **low budget** is possible, though it requires planning and off-peak travel. From June to August room prices are crazy; May and September, when tariffs are relaxed and the weather only slightly chillier, are just as good times to go, and in April or October you'll have the place to yourself, albeit with a smaller range of places to stay and eat. Ground **transportation**, despite the long distances, is reasonable, with backpacker shuttles ferrying budget travelers between major centers. **Winter**, when hotels drop their prices by as much as half, is becoming an increasingly popular time to visit, particularly for the dazzling **aurora borealis** (see box, p.1336).

Some history

It is thought that Alaska has been inhabited for longer than anywhere else in the Americas; it was here, across the broad plains of the "land bridge" now submerged below the Bering Straits, that humans first reached the "New World" **from** eastern Russia, most likely around 14,000 years ago.

These first settlers can be classified into four groups, which lived within well-defined regions until Europeans arrived. The **Aleut**, in the inhospitable Aleutian Islands, built underground homes and hunted sea mammals such as walrus for food and clothing, while the nomadic **Athabascan** herded caribou in the Interior. The warrior **Tlingit** lived in the warmer coastal regions of the southeast, where food was plentiful, in contrast to the **Eskimos** (or, more correctly, the Yup'ik and Iñupiat), who inhabited the northwestern coast, living off fish and larger marine life. Descendants of all these groups can be found in Alaska today, and a few live in much the same way as their ancestors. Most, however, have been integrated into the modern American way through conquest, rape, marriage, and religion.

In 1741, Danish explorer **Vitus Bering**, working for the Tsar of Russia, became the first Caucasian to set foot on Alaskan soil and found huge numbers of fur seals and **sea otters** – whose treasured pelts were made into hats. Russians, and later British and Spaniards, joined in the ensuing slaughter, both of the otters and the Aleut, who were enslaved and forced to hunt on behalf of the fur traders. By the end of the century, the Russians had established their Alaskan capital at present-day **Sitka**, pushed down the coast as far as Northern California and, in the process, decimated the sea otter colonies.

During the 1860s, limited returns and domestic economic problems forced Russia to sell its lands to America. On October 18, 1867, Secretary of State William Seward purchased what was disparagingly known as "**Seward's Folly**" or "Seward's Icebox" for $7.2 million – less than 2¢ per acre. Alaska soon turned out to be a literal **gold mine** with major discoveries at Juneau (1880), Nome (1898), and Fairbanks (1902). With logging companies and commercial fishing operations soon descending upon Alaska, the government began to take a more active interest in its affairs, and in 1959 Alaska became the **49th state**.

Alaska's next boom followed the discovery of oil at Prudhoe Bay on the Arctic Ocean, and fortune-seekers headed to Alaska in the mid-1970s to build the **trans-Alaska pipeline** from Prudhoe Bay to the ice-free port of Valdez. Today, Alaska still derives about eighty percent of its wealth from oil and gas; indeed, each resident receives an annual dividend check which in 2000 reached $1963, though in 2003 it was only $1107. The state is still in economic transition and continues to be prone to extreme boom-and-bust cycles. Once lucra-

15

ALASKA

tive fishing and lumber industries are fast giving way to tourism as a source of income, and the ethical question of how best to use Alaskan lands in the future has led to bitter controversy. Nowhere is this more apparent than in the case of the Arctic National Wildlife Refuge, a vast tract of tundra in Alaska's northeast that has some degree of protection, but is constantly under threat from the oil men and Alaska's Republican governor, senators, and congressman.

Getting to Alaska

Alaska is a long way from the rest of the United States, and whichever way you get there is going to be **expensive**. Once you accept that, however, there is no question as to which is the most **enjoyable** method – the memorable ferry trip on the Alaska Marine Highway.

By air

Anchorage is no longer the major air crossroads it once was, but it's still easy to **fly** to Alaska. Most, but not all, flights from the Lower 48 are routed through Seattle. The most frequent service from the west coast is operated by Alaska Airlines (☎1-800/252-7522, ⊛www.alaskaair.com), whose moneysaving package enables you to fly to towns like Juneau, Sitka, Cordova, and Fairbanks at little extra cost. Roundtrip fares from Seattle to Anchorage are around $400 if bought two weeks in advance, and $600 or more on short notice, though there are occasional Web specials. Better still, foreigners traveling from outside North America can make use of the "Best of the West" air pass (see opposite).

By sea

The **ferries** of the state-run **Alaska Marine Highway System** (☎1-800/642-0066, ⊛www.alaska.gov/ferry) cover many areas unreachable by car, currently operating in two separate regions with an occasional "Cross-Gulf" trip linking them. The popular **southeast** route runs a thousand miles from Bellingham, just north of Seattle, through a wonderland of pristine waters, narrow fjords, and untouched forests to Skagway, at the northern end of the **Inside Passage**, stopping at Ketchikan, Wrangell, Sitka, Juneau, and Haines. The whole trip takes three days and costs $306 for walk-on passengers, $658 for a small car, $47 for bicycles, and $71 for kayaks. It is possible to sleep – and even to pitch a tent – on the "solarium," a covered, heated upper deck, while a two-berth cabin costs from $216. The **southwest** ferry system connects the Kenai Peninsula and Prince William Sound to the Aleutians, and the Kennicott ferry now links the two systems by running between Juneau and Seward once or twice a month in summer. Throughout the system, section passenger fares depend on distance traveled: $201 from Bellingham to Ketchikan; $70 from Ketchikan to Sitka; $37 from Sitka to Juneau; and $186 from Juneau to Seward. While the ferry is a bargain for foot passengers prepared to rough it, an extended voyage with vehicle and an overnight cabin (both of which should be reserved in advance) becomes expensive. If you're driving up from the Lower 48, consider boarding a ferry at Prince Rupert in British Columbia, two days' drive north of Seattle. This saves the cost of one day at sea from Bellingham without missing much of the natural spectacle.

By road

For many people, the drive up to Alaska through Canada is one of the major highlights of a visit to the state. The only road is the 1500-mile **Alaska Highway** from Dawson Creek in British Columbia to Fairbanks, which was originally built by the military in just eight months. It comes with a fearsome reputation, but is now fully paved and equipped with gas stations, campgrounds, and hotels along the way. It remains as beautiful as ever, and still demands a spirit of adventure from drivers who attempt it.

No direct **buses** run to Alaska, though for around $155 ($89 7-day advance purchase) you can hop on a Greyhound in Seattle and, after a few transfers over two grueling days, reach Whitehorse in the Yukon, from where Alaska Direct (☎1–800/770-6652) make the run to Anchorage ($165) or Fairbanks ($140).

Getting around Alaska

Getting around Alaska on the cheap can be tough; **public transportation** is limited, and many areas are only accessible by boat or plane, which is quick and convenient but invariably pricey. With little traffic, **hitching** is hard work, but is more acceptable, and generally safer, than elsewhere.

With the exception of the ferry system (see overleaf), **Anchorage** is very much the hub of Alaska, with several **bus** companies running to major destinations: Seward with Seward Bus Line (☎907/224-3608, ⓦwww.sewardbuslines.com; $40); Homer with Homer Stage Line (☎907/235-2252, ⓦwww.homerstageline .com; $45); Denali ($59) and Fairbanks ($79) with Alaska Trails & Tours (☎1-888/600-6001, ⓦwww.alaskashuttle.com); and Glennallen ($42), Tok ($70), and Whitehorse ($165) with Alaska Direct (☎1-800/770-6652, ⓦokalaska.com /dirctbus).

The expensive **Alaska Railroad** runs nearly five hundred miles from Seward north through Anchorage to Fairbanks, with a spur to Whittier for ferries to Valdez. One-way **fares** from Anchorage are: Denali $125, Fairbanks $175, and Seward $59.

Driving around Alaska in summer requires no special skills, though the less-traveled routes often have a gravel surface and caution is required. Wildlife, especially moose, can be a danger any time, even on city streets. In spring and fall you should be prepared for snow, and it is wise to carry a **survival kit**, particularly in winter, as traffic can be sparse even on major routes. Conditions on the roads can change rapidly – call ☎907/835-4242 for south-central Alaska, ☎907/456-7623 for the Interior, or look under Traveler Info / Road Conditions at ⓦwww.dot.state.ak.us.

Travel by **plane** is not always more expensive than other methods, especially if you can map out your itinerary in advance with the state's largest operator, Alaska Airlines (see opposite), which flies to most major communities and uses subcontractors such as ERA Aviation (☎1-800/866-8394, ⓦwww.flyera .com) and PenAir (☎1-800/448-4226, ⓦwww.penair.com) to get to smaller towns. If you are traveling from outside North America, consider pre-purchasing an Alaska Airlines "Best of the West" **air pass** that allows you to reserve up to ten one-way flights either within Alaska ($109 each leg), or from outside the state (essentially Seattle or LA to Anchorage; $169), or any combination of these. **Chartering a plane** might sound extravagant but can be an inexpensive alternative for groups of four or more, and may be the crowning glory of an Alaskan vacation. To arrange this, contact any operator of small planes (every town has at least one). ERA Aviation and PenAir are good places to start, though they may refer you to another company.

Southeast Alaska

Southeast Alaska – also known as the panhandle – is archetypal Alaska: an awesome six-hundred-mile-long tableau of fjords, mountains, glaciers, a thousand islands, and thick conifer forests lining the **Inside Passage**. All of its communities have their economic base in lumber, fishing, and tourism and are set amid magnificent scenery. The state's southernmost town, **Ketchikan**, rich in Native heritage, makes a pretty introduction, tiny **Wrangell** emits a pioneer air, while **Sitka** retains a Russian influence. Further north are swanky **Juneau**, the capital; **Haines**, with its mix of old-timers and arty newcomers; and **Skagway**, thoroughly redolent of the old gold-mining days. You could spend months exploring here, but most are content to focus on the highlights, particularly the towns of Sitka and Skagway, and **Glacier Bay National Park**, an expensive side-trip from Juneau that penetrates one of Alaska's most stunning regions.

The area's first settlers were the **Tlingit** (*Hlin-get*), and it was not until the end of the eighteenth century that Russian expansionists burst into the region. Their appearance sharply altered the indigenous way of life; soon a steady stream of freelance profiteers, keen on tapping the region's gold, fur, fish, and lumber appeared. Today, southeast Alaska's small communities resound with tales of endurance, folly, and cruelty.

With no roads connecting towns, by far the best way to travel is by **ferry**, though at some stage make sure you take a **floatplane** ride. For a true outdoor adventure, you can rent a **cabin** in the huge Tongass National Forest – which encompasses most of southeast Alaska – for around $35 per night; details from the visitor centers in Juneau (see p.1307) and Ketchikan (see opposite), or through the NRRS reservation service (ⓦwww.reserveusa.com).

Ketchikan and around

KETCHIKAN, five hundred miles north of Seattle, is Alaska's "first city," being the first port of call for many cruise ships. Consequently, its historic downtown, wedged between water and forested mountains, becomes saturated in summer with elderly tourists. Beyond the souvenir shopping, it can be a delight, built into steep hills and partly propped on wooden pilings, dotted with boardwalks, wooden staircases, and totem poles.

By 1886, white settlers had opened the first of dozens of canneries in what was soon to be the "salmon capital of the world." Forests of cedar, hemlock, and spruce, which had provided timber for Tlingit homes and totems, also fed the town's sawmills. The timber and fishing industries have declined, and, since the closure of the antiquated pulp mill in 1997, Ketchikan has increasingly looked to tourism as its savior, with the nearby **Misty Fiords National Monument** as the prime draw.

The state's fourth largest city is a strong contender for the nation's wettest; annual precipitation averages 165 inches. The tourist board shrugs it off as "liquid sunshine" and, indeed, Ketchikan's perennial drizzle and sporadic showers won't spoil your visit.

Arrival and information

Ferries dock two miles north of downtown on Tongass Highway; city **buses** stop here every 30 minutes until 9.30pm (Sun 3.30pm). Alaska Airlines serves the **airport**, which is on an island and is linked to town by half-hourly ferries ($4 roundtrip). The **visitor center** stands downtown at 131 Front St (daily 6am–6pm; ☏907/225-6166 or 1-800/770-3300, ⓦwww.visit-ketchikan.com), and for information about the surrounding Tongass forests visit the **Southeast Alaska Discovery Center**, 50 Main St (daily 8am–5pm; ☏907/228-6220, ⓦwww.fs.fed.us/r10/tongass), a striking cedar-framed building which houses absorbing displays ($5) of the region's natural habitats and native culture.

Scores of companies run **sightseeing excursions**, among them Rainbird Deluxe Tours (☏1-888/505-8810) who does a tour through the sights of town and visit Saxman (2hr; $30). Northern Tours of Alaska (☏907/247-6457, ⓦwww.northerntoursofalaska.com) does a similar tour and sometimes has an extended tour (3hr; $40) which also visits Totem Bight. Promech Air (☏907/225-3845 or 1-800/860-3845, ⓦwww.promechair.com) and Taquan Air (☏907/225-8800 or 1-800/770-8800, ⓦwww.taquanair.com) offer **float-plane** trips from just $65, while Southeast Sea Kayaks (☏907/225-1258 or 1-800/287-1607, ⓦwww.kayakketchikan.com) will take you **sea kayaking** along the fjords; a four-and-a-half-hour trip costs around $70 with day rental for experienced paddlers from $30.

Accommodation

Hotels in Ketchikan vary widely, and the closest **campgrounds** to town ($10) are in the attractive Ward Lake Recreation Area, five miles northwest of the ferry terminal.

Captain's Quarters B&B 325 Lund St ☏907/225-4912, ⓦwww.ptialaska.net/~captbnb. Three spacious rooms separate from the owner's house, all with queen-sized beds and cable TV, and one with a kitchen, in a nautically themed hillside house with some great views over the town. Continental breakfast included. ❹

Eagle View Hostel 2305 5th Ave ☏907/225-5461, ⓦwww.eagleviewhostel.com. Suburban house shared with the owner and with great views of the Narrows. Single sex dorm beds (as well as one double room) cost $28 including bed linen, towel, and use of the kitchen, barbecue, and sauna. No lockout or curfew. Follow Jefferson off Tongass Highway then turn right onto 5th. Open April–Oct and by reservation. ❶

HI-Ketchikan in the United Methodist Church, 400 Main St ☏907/225-3319, ✉ktnyh@eagle.ptialaska.net. Very basic youth hostel with beds for $12 (nonmembers $15), June–Aug only. ❶

The New York Hotel 207 Stedman St ☏907/225-0246, ⓦwww.thenewyorkhotel.com. Nicely refurbished hotel by the small boat harbor with cozy but tastefully decorated rooms and a good café. ❺

The town

The bulk of Ketchikan's historic buildings lie on **Creek Street**, a rickety-looking boardwalk along Ketchikan Creek. This was a red-light district until 1954; now all the former houses of ill-repute are given over to gift shops and galleries. **Dolly's House**, 24 Creek St, once the home and workplace of Dolly Arthur, the town's most famous madam, is now a small museum stuffed with saucy memorabilia (generally daily 8am–5pm; $4).

Most of the totem poles you see around town are authentic replicas, but the **Totem Heritage Center**, 601 Deermount St (daily 8am–5pm; $5), exhibits the largest collection of original totem poles in the US: 33 mostly nineteenth-century examples recovered from abandoned Native villages. The Tlingit-run **Saxman Totem Park**, two miles south of town, displays the world's largest standing collection of poles and an authentic tribal house. Admission, including a chance to see sculptors at work, is free, but two-hour **guided tours** (several daily; $35) will help to decipher the images. Fourteen of the best replica totem poles and a rebuilt tribal house stand in **Totem Bight State Park**, breathtakingly set on a forested strip of coast overlooking the Narrows, ten miles north of town on the Tongass Highway. On the way back, take some time out to do the easy but enjoyable boardwalk trail up to **Perseverance Lake**, starting on Ward Lake Road, four miles north of town.

Eating and drinking

Inexpensive **food** in Ketchikan tends to be rather good, a rare combination in Alaska. The place is also renowned for its hard **drinking**. Steer clear of the *First City Tavern*, a favorite with commercial fishers and cannery workers eager to forget the sight and smell of raw fish.

Arctic Bar 509 Water St. Basic, dark boozing bar with a great view over the water once the cruise ships have left.

Diaz Café 335 Stedman St ☎907/225-2257. Great inexpensive diner food with some tasty Filipino dishes.

The New York Café 207 Stedman St ☎907/225-0246. Perch on bentwood chairs as harbor light streams in through the big windows; the menu is loaded with excellent soups, burgers, wraps, and salads (mostly $8–11) plus some sumptuous desserts, and espresso coffee. It is licensed too,

but only open daytime except for weekend dinners.

Pizza Mill 808 Water St ☎907/225-6646. Ketchikan's oldest pizza joint is a great low-key place for gourmet pizzas (known here as Yuppie Pies; from $11 for a 12-inch), subs, burgers ($7–9), burritos ($6–7), salads, and draft beer.

Steamers 76 Front St ☎907/225-1600. Large, bustling restaurant opposite the cruise-ship dock with great views and seafood to match – not to mention a well-stocked bar with a plethora of beers on tap and occasional live music.

Misty Fiords National Monument

Twenty-two miles east of Ketchikan on the mainland, the awe-inspiring **MISTY FIORDS NATIONAL MONUMENT** consists of 2.3 million acres of deep fjords flanked by sheer 3000ft glacially scoured walls topped by dense rainforest. As befits its name, the monument is at its most atmospheric when swathed in low-lying mists. No roads lead here, but the kayak and floatplane operators listed on p.1303 do. Four-hour cruise-in/fly-out tours are run by Alaska Cruises (☎907/225-6044 or 1-800/225-1905, ⓦwww.goldbelttours .com; $240). Fourteen rustic cabins (mostly $35) are rented out by the Forest Service (☎1-877/444-6777).

Wrangell

With a population of just 2600, **WRANGELL**, the second stop on the ferry system, is altogether quieter than Ketchikan and has a distinctly old-fashioned feel. Right in the busy harbor, accessible by a short boardwalk, **Chief Shakes Island** holds an excellent collection of totem poles and a replica tribal house filled with Tlingit blankets. The ancient rock carvings at **Petroglyph Beach**, half a mile or so north of town along Evergreen Avenue, date back as far as 7500 years and are only obscured during high tide.

Ferries dock right in town but seldom stop over long enough to allow explorations of the sights, so you may want to stay: try the **campground** at *City Park* (one night max; free), less than two miles south on Zimovia Highway, or the clean and central *Wrangell Hostel*, 220 Church St (☎907/874-3534, ⓔpresby@aptalaska.net; ➊), a Presbyterian church where $18 gets you a mattress on the floor. The **airport**, with daily connections to other Southeastern towns, is a mile and a half north of town, and by 2004 the **visitor center** (Mon–Fri 10am–4pm; ☎907/874-3901) should have moved to a permanent new home in the new Nolan Museum & Civic Center on Outer Drive.

One of the highlights of an Inland Passage ferry ride is negotiating the 46 tight turns of the 22-mile-long **Wrangell Narrows** between Wrangell and the "Norwegian" fishing town of Petersburg on the route north. At times it feels like you can reach out and touch the steep-walled shore, and at night the ferry has to negotiate a slalom course of navigation lights.

Sitka

Perched on the seaward edge of the Inside Passage and eleven hours from Petersburg, **SITKA** ranks as one of Alaska's prettiest and most historic towns. Fuji-like **Mount Edgecumbe** volcano rises menacingly across Sitka Sound from the spot where Russian colonists established a fort in 1799. Three years later, Tlingit warriors massacred the imperialist troops and their Aleut slaves, but were themselves cannoned into submission in 1804. Under Russian occupation the town was rebuilt and christened **Novo Arkhangel'sk** (New Archangel), the capital of Russian America – a role it retained beyond the 1867 transfer of ownership to the US, until federal powers passed control to Juneau in 1906. Sitka today earns its keep mostly from fishing and tourism; it's all too keen to flog tacky "Russiocana" – you'll find more nesting dolls here than the rest of the US put together – but the town also has a wealth of great outdoor opportunities and a fine reputation for its festivals, especially the chamber-oriented **Summer Music Festival** each June and the **Alaska Day Festival** (celebrating the Russia–US transfer) on the days leading up to October 18.

Arrival, information, and accommodation

Traditional **ferries** and a new fast catamaran jointly visit Sitka around five times per week, mooring seven miles northwest of town on Halibut Point Road (☎907/747-8737), from where Sitka Tours **shuttles** (☎907/747-8443; $7 roundtrip) run downtown; they also do three-hour tours of town ($12). Alaska Airlines runs a daily service on the Seattle–Juneau–Anchorage route from the airport on Japonski Island, a pleasant half-hour walk from downtown or $5 ride with Sitka Tours. **Mountain bikes** can be rented from Yellow Jersey Cycles, 329 Harbor Drive (☎907/747-6317), and Sitka Sound Ocean Adventures (☎907/747-6375, ⓦwww.ssoceanadventures.com), who work out of a bus parked by Centennial Hall, rents **kayaks** ($30 a half-day, double $40) as well as organizing day-long guided trips on the Sound ($125). The **CVB** office is in the Centennial Building, 330 Harbor Drive (☎907/747-3220, ⓦwww.sitka.org), and is usually only staffed when a cruise ship is in town, but has loads of handy leaflets.

Sitka has a good range of **accommodation**: the spartan *HI-Sitka* hostel, 303 Kimshan St (☎907/747-8661; ❶; closed Sept–May), in a Methodist church a mile from downtown, has beds for $13 (nonmembers $16); the historic *Sitka Hotel*, 118 Lincoln St (☎907/747-3288, ⓦwww.sitkahotel.com; ❹), offers a touch of old-fashioned style and good-value rooms that come with and without bathrooms; *Finn Alley Inn B&B*, 711 Lincoln St (☎907/747-3655, ⓦwww.ptialaska.net/~seakdist/finn; ❺), is well located and its large half-basement apartment has private entrance, full kitchen, and a continental breakfast delivered to the room; and the *Westmark Shee Atiká*, 330 Seward St (☎907/747-6241 or 1-800/544-0970, ⓦwww.westmarkhotels.com; ❻), owns the flashest rooms in town. **Campers** should head a mile north of the ferry dock to the *Starrigavan* campground (☎1-877/444-6777; $12) or seven miles east of Sitka to the free but basic *Sawmill Creek* site.

The Town

The best place to get a grasp of Sitka's Russian past and the lay of the land is from the rocky vantage point of **Castle Hill**, where Alaska was officially transferred to the US on October 18, 1867; an informative plaque marks the spot. A two-minute stroll to the heart of downtown leads to **St Michael's Cathedral** on Lincoln Street. A fine piece of rural Russian church architecture, completed in 1848 and rebuilt after a disastrous fire in 1966, it displays priceless original icons (daily 9am–4pm when cruise ships are in town; $2). Guided tours take in the restored chapel, schoolroom, and living quarters of the large mustard-colored 1842 **Russian Bishop's House**, by the harbor – a log structure that is the oldest standing building in Alaska (summer daily 9am–5pm; rest of year by appointment; ☎907/747-0110; $3).

Four blocks further along at 104 College Drive, the **Sheldon Jackson Museum** (summer daily 9am–5pm; rest of year Tues–Sat 10am–4pm; $4) houses a compact but extensive accumulation of Native artifacts. All of the tools, utensils, and craft objects from Aleut, Athabascan, Tlingit, and especially Aleut peoples were collected by the Reverend Doctor Sheldon Jackson on his wide-ranging travels throughout Alaska as a missionary and the territory's first General Agent for Education.

At the end of Lincoln Street, in a verdant copse between ocean and creek, **Sitka National Historic Park** embraces both the town's Tlingit heritage and its days of Russian rule. When Tsarist troops attacked a Tlingit fort on this site in 1804, the Natives withstood bombardment for six days, but after running out of gunpowder, decided to abandon the fort silently at night. The next day Russians stormed the stockades only to find them empty except for a few dead children, whom they alleged were murdered to accomplish the retreat in complete silence. Nothing remains of the fort except a grassy clearing, but the evocative air is enhanced by several vividly painted **totem poles** alongside the footpaths, all replicas of nineteenth-century classic designs. A **visitor center** (summer daily 8am–5pm; $3) features good interpretative displays on what is commonly called the "Battle of Sitka," as well as hosting Native craft workshops.

Sitka's **trail system** ranges from shoreside strolls to harder climbs up Gavan Hill and steep Mount Verstovia: for more information visit the **Forest Service office**, 204 Siganaka Way (☎907/747-6671).

Eating

Sitka's **restaurants** aren't exactly going to set gourmet tongues wagging, though there are several decent places to dine out. The best bargain in town is the *Sheldon Jackson College Dining Room*, David Sweetland Hall, a simple cafeteria-style place with all-you-care-to-eat breakfast (6.30–8am; $5), lunch (11.30am–1pm; $7), and dinner (4.45–6pm; $10): follow the road opposite the entrance to the Sheldon Jackson Museum. For great coffee, tasty sandwiches, pastries, and light lunches duck through Old Harbor Books at 201 Lincoln St to *The Backdoor* (☎907/747-8856). The *Bayview Restaurant*, upstairs at 407 Lincoln St (☎907/747-5440), offers great sea views and well-prepared dishes on its standard Alaskan menu, but for something outstanding (if pricey) reserve for dinner at *Ludvig's Bistro*, 256 Katlian St (☎907/966-3663), an excellent Mediterranean place where a broad range of Spanish-, Portuguese-, Italian-, and Moroccan-influenced dishes are done to perfection. For evening **drinks**, join the crowds in the *Westmark Shee Atiká*'s bar, or the down-to-earth *Pioneer Bar* on colorful Katlian Street.

Juneau and around

The sophisticated and vibrant city of **JUNEAU** is unlike any other state capital in the nation. Accessible only by sea or air, it is exceptionally picturesque, hard against the **Gastineau Channel**, with steep, narrow roads clawing up into the rainforested hills behind. Gold features heavily in its history. In 1880, two prospectors – one of them Joe Juneau – made **Alaska's first gold strike** in the rainforest along the banks of the Gastineau Channel. Named Gold Creek, the camp grew rapidly. Until the last mine was shut down in 1944, this was the world's largest producer of low-grade ore – all the flat land in Juneau, stretching from downtown to the airport, is landfill from mine tailings. Today, state government provides much of the employment, and tourism plays its part with the drive-to **Mendenhall Glacier** and the watery charms of **Tracy Arm Fjord** as temptation.

Arrival, information, and getting around

The **ferry terminal** is fourteen miles northwest of downtown at Auke Bay; ferries often arrive at unearthly hours, so getting into town can be a problem. Apart from taking a $30 taxi ride, the only transport is the city's Capital Transit **bus service** (Mon–Sat hourly 7am–10.30pm, Sun 9.30am–6pm; ☎907/789-6901; $1.50), which stops a mile and a half south outside DeHarts grocery. The ferry dock is not to be confused with the **cruise-ship terminal**, right downtown. Buses also pick up from close to the airport (actually on Mallard Street, behind the Nugget Mall), nine miles north of downtown, which sees daily Alaska Airlines flights. The Juneau Visitors Information Desk, at the airport on the ground floor, is usually open for all arrivals.

The main **visitor center**, Centennial Hall, 101 Egan Drive (summer Mon–Fri 8.30am–5pm, Sat & Sun 9am–5pm; rest of the year Mon–Fri 9am–5pm; ☎907/586-2201 or 1-888/581-2201, ⓦwww.traveljuneau.com), contains an AMHS ferry booking office and an unstaffed desk devoted to brochures about the Tongass National Forest, including material on Glacier Bay, Tracy Arm Fjord, and the trails and cabins in Juneau's wooded surroundings. For more details call at the Tongass National Forest district ranger office, 8465 Old Dairy Rd (Mon–Fri 8am–5pm; ☎907/586-8800, ⓦwww.fs.fed .us/r10/tongass).

Popular **hikes** from Juneau include the undemanding Perseverance Trail and, over the bridge on Douglas Island, the Treadwell Mine Historic Trail. *Driftwood Lodge* (see below), rents out **mountain bikes** for $25 a day, and Juneau Outdoor Center (☎907/586-8220, ⓦwww.juneaukayak.com) rents out top-quality kayaks (single $45 a day, double $60).

Accommodation

Juneau has the widest range of accommodation in Southeast Alaska, and some fine **camping** either at the *Mendenhall Lake Campground* ($10), spectacularly situated near the glacier and accessible by buses #3 or #4 and a short hike, or at the basic *Thane Road Tent Camping* ($5), just a mile south of downtown. All of the places listed below are handy for downtown.

Alaskan Hotel and Bar 167 S Franklin St ☎907/586-1000 or 1-800/327-9374, ⓦwww.alaskanhotel-juneau.com. Pleasant old hotel with a salacious past and a fine bar in the heart of downtown. Twelve doubles with shared or private bath. ❸–❹

Cashen Quarters B&B 303 Gold St ☎907/586-9863, ⓦwww.cashenquarters.com. Central B&B with five rooms and continental breakfast brought to you. ❹

Driftwood Lodge 435 Willoughby Ave ☎907/586-2280 or 1-800/544-2239, ⓦwww.driftwoodlodge.com. Motel one block from the waterfront, with large rooms including kitchenettes. Offers courtesy bus to airport and ferry. ❺

Juneau Hostel 614 Harris St ☎907/586-9559, ⓦwww.juneauhostel.com. Clean, comfortable, and relaxed hostel, in an old home near downtown, with dorm beds for just $10, but an inconvenient daytime lock-out (9am–5pm) and an 11pm curfew. ❶

Historic Silverbow Inn 120 2nd St ☎907/586-4146 or 1-800/586-4146, ⓦwww.silverbowinn.com. Attractive small hotel linked to the restaurant and bakery of the same name, with smallish but nicely furnished and tastefully decorated rooms, each with TV and phone, and with a good continental breakfast included. ❻

The Town

From the kiosk in Marine Park, it takes an hour and a half to follow the self-guided Juneau **walking tour**. Many original buildings stand in the **South Franklin Street Historic District** – Juneau managed to avoid the fires that destroyed many other gold towns in Alaska. The onion-domed **St Nicholas Russian Orthodox Church**, on Fifth and Gold (Mon–Sat 9am–6pm; $2 donation), contains icons and religious treasures, while the well-presented **Alaska State Museum**, 395 Whittier St (daily 8.30am–5.30pm; $5), covers Native culture, Russian heritage, and the first gold strikes. Its pride and joy is the logbook in which Bering reported his first sighting of Alaska. The smaller **City Museum**, at Main and Fourth streets (summer Mon–Fri 9am–5pm, Sat & Sun 10am–5pm; rest of year Fri & Sat noon–4pm; $3), displays relics from the mining era.

The best views of town are from the top of the **Mount Roberts Tramway** (summer daily 9am–9pm; $22), which careers up from the cruise-ship dock 1800 feet up Mount Roberts, where there's a nature center and some easy trails.

Eating and drinking

Downtown has a reasonable selection of places to **eat and drink**, but most fill up very quickly when cruise ships are in town.

Alaskan Hotel Bar 167 S Franklin St ☎907/586-1000. Great old bar, with live music most nights, especially towards the weekend.

Bacar's 230 Seward St ☎907/463-5091. Quirky little restaurant worth seeking out for its sumptuous breakfasts ($6–9), and clam chowder and burger lunches ($8–11). Open daily 6am–3pm.

Hangar on the Wharf Merchants Wharf ☎907/586-5018. Renovated, historic floatplane hangar right on the wharf with a tremendous view of the waterfront and over twenty beers on tap,

plus pool tables on the mezzanine, and a lively atmosphere, especially at weekends when there is live rock or jazz. Food extends from wraps and burgers at lunch to items like jambalaya and halibut tacos ($9–12) later on.

Heritage Café Emporium Mall, 174 S Franklin St ☎907/586-1087. About the best café in Juneau, with good espresso, lunch specials, soups, and sandwiches.

Olivia's de Mexico 222 Seward St ☎907/586-6870. Juneau's most authentic Mexican, tucked away in a basement but producing excellent *mole* and fajitas along with expected staples. Closed Sun.

Silverbow Bakery and Restaurant 120 2nd St ☎907/586-4146. Wonderful bakery and coffee bar with big windows that catch the morning sun (if you're lucky enough to see any). Traditionally boiled and baked bagels and superb pastries bolster a menu of homemade breads used to make hot and cold deli sandwiches ($5–11). On Saturday nights there's a great restaurant serving varied and imaginative dishes, from salads and

soups ($6–9) to kielbasa and pierogies ($11), Indonesian peanut noodles with either tofu or chicken ($12), and pesto and red pepper burgers ($9); and some evenings you can even stick around for the movie.

Uncle Sam's Cafeteria 2nd floor, 709 W 9th St ☎907/586-3430. Low-cost dining with a view, inside the Federal Building. Open for breakfast ($4) from 7am, then lunches including daily specials ($6) such as taco salad or chicken-fried steak. Closes 4pm.

Mendenhall Glacier and Tracy Arm Fjord

There are certainly bigger and more spectacular glaciers in Alaska, but the twelve-mile-long, one-and-a-half-mile-wide **Mendenhall Glacier**, thirteen miles from downtown, is easily the most accessible. Should your knowledge of cirques and striations be a little rusty, the **visitor center** (built on a point occupied by the glacier as recently as 1940) has all you need to know (summer daily 8am–6.30pm; rest of year Sat & Sun 9am–4pm; $3; ☎907/789-0097). Hiking trails include the West Glacier Trail, on which, with extreme caution and without official approval, you can explore the ice caves.

Capital Transit buses leave for Mendenhall hourly from downtown; get off at Glacier Spur Road for the visitor center, or Montana Creek Road for the West Glacier trail. MGT (☎907/789-5460, ⓦwww.mightygreattrips.com) charges $5 each way from town as part of their Glacier Express tour.

Alaska Travel Adventures runs three-hour **float trips** on the Mendenhall River (☎907/789-0052 or 1-800/478-0052; $95), while Temsco (☎907/789-9501, ⓦwww.temscoair.com; $190) offers one-hour **helicopter trips** with 25 minutes on the glacier itself.

One of the best day-trips out of Juneau is up the narrow, twisting **Tracy Arm Fjord**, with waterfall-fringed cliffs and common sightings of whales and seals. Day-long **cruises** with Goldbelt's stable twin-hulls (☎907/586-8687 or 1-800/820-2628, ⓦwww.goldbelttours.com; $119) or with Adventure Bound Alaska (☎907/463-2905 or 1-800/228-3875; $105) are both worthwhile.

Glacier Bay National Park

When Captain George Vancouver sailed through Icy Strait in 1794, **GLACIER BAY** didn't exist. Since then, the Grand Pacific Glacier has receded 65 miles, to reveal a tranquil world of deep fjords lined by rock walls and fed by fifteen other receding tidewater glaciers. The flora of the bay ranges from mature spruce forests to delicate plant life, while brown and black bear, moose, mountain goats, sea otters, humpback whales, porpoise, seals, and a colorful array of birds have made the area their home. Most, if not all of them can be seen on a **day-cruise** through Glacier Bay (the only way to access the area). The most spectacular moment comes when the boat, having negotiated its way through three miles of icebergs, comes face to face with the massive wall of the Grand Pacific Glacier.

AMHS ferries don't go to **Gustavus**, the nearest town to the park, so the cheapest way to get there is with Alaska Airlines, who fly in once each afternoon in summer from Juneau for around $60 each way if reserved well in advance. Smaller operators such as LAB (☎907/766-2222 or 1-800/426-0543, ⓦwww.labflying.com) have more flights but charge around $65 from Juneau and connect Gustavus directly with Haines. You might want to fly out and cruise back to Juneau on the **Gustavus Ferry** (3hr; ☎1–800/820–2628, ⓦwww.goldbelttours.com; $69 each way, bikes $10, kayaks $40).

The ferry and flights are met by a bus ($12) which takes you ten miles to Bartlett Cove, site of the **park headquarters** and the dock for the eight-hour Glacier Bay **day-cruise** ($159) – the principal way of experiencing the park's wonders short of paddling. Also here, the park's only **hotel**, *Glacier Bay Lodge* (☎1–800/820–2628, ⓦwww.goldbelttours.com; ❼), features tasteful rooms. The only budget alternative at Bartlett Cove is the first-come, first-served campground (free) beside the fjord.

Further accommodation can be found in Gustavus in the form of *Bear's Nest B&B* (☎907/679–2440, ⓦwww.gustavus/bearsnest; ❹), a completely self-contained and fully furnished cabin with a double bed upstairs and a single futon down, plus a more basic A-frame. Breakfast ingredients are provided, though you'll have to bring everything else from Juneau, or wander next door to the *Bear's Nest Café*.

Haines

The small community of **HAINES** sits on a peninsula between the Chilkat and the Chilkoot inlets at the northern end of the longest and deepest fjord in the US, Lynn Canal. The town tends to be overshadowed by its brasher neighbor, Skagway, but it remains a real Alaskan experience nonetheless. When the weather is clear, it is nothing short of spectacular, with snow-covered **Mount Ripinsky** rising up behind, the **Chilkoot and Chilkat mountains** hemming it in on either side, and glaciers spilling out into the deep fjord. The community itself is an interesting mix of locals and urban escapees from the Lower 48.

The Tlingit fished and traded here for years before 1881, when the first missionaries arrived and renamed the settlement for a prominent Presbyterian, Mrs F. Haines. Today, the town survives on fishing and tourism, and though cruise ships tend to press on to Skagway, it remains a popular spot, which in mid-August hosts the cookouts, crafts, and log-rolling of the **Southeast Alaska Fair**. The fairgrounds also hold **Dalton City**, a free pioneer theme park notable only in that its buildings came from the movie sets of Jack London's *White Fang*, which was filmed in the Haines area in 1989.

Arrival and information

Haines's AMHS **ferry** terminal is five miles north of town, with a daily service to and from Juneau and Skagway. Local **taxis** meet all ferry arrivals; downtown costs $8. To get between Skagway and Haines you'll find it quicker and more flexible to travel with Chilkat Cruises & Tours (☎907/766–2100 or 1–888/766–2103, ⓦwww.chilkatcruises.com), who run a passenger-only fast ferry (3 daily; $24 one way, $39 roundtrip), to the shuttle dock near Fort Seward.

From town, the Haines Highway runs 151 miles to the Alaska Highway in Canada; Alaska Direct buses (☎1–800/770–6652, ⓔalaskadirect@msn.com) run to Haines three days a week from Tok ($100), Anchorage ($195), and Fairbanks ($185).

The **visitor center**, 122 Second St (summer Mon–Fri 8am–7pm, Sat & Sun 9am–6pm; rest of year Mon–Fri 8am–5pm; ☎907/766–2234 or 1–800/458–3579, ⓦwww.haines.ak.us), has all kinds of maps and information.

Accommodation

As well as the usual mid-range **accommodation**, Haines has half a dozen handy **campgrounds**. The best two are the tent-only *Portage Cove*, on a great beach less than a mile from Fort Seward on S Front Street (no vehicles; $5), and the peaceful *Port Chilkoot Camper Park*, Mud Bay Road beside Fort Seward (T 907/766-2000 or 1-800/542-6363; $8), with pay-showers and a laundromat on site.

Bear Creek Cabins and Hostel Small Tract Rd T 907/766-2259, W kcd.com/hostel. Good hostel over a mile south of Fort Seward with coin-op laundry, free bikes, no lock-out or curfew, and $3 rides from the ferry terminal. Campers ($14 for two) can use hostel facilities. Dorms $16, cabins ❷
Hotel Hälsingland 13 Fort Seward Drive T 907/766-2000 or 1-800/542-6363, W www.hotelhalsingland.com. The town's grandest hotel, recently renovated and still retaining original features in some rooms: ask to look at a few before choosing. Rooms ❺, shared bath ❹

Mountain View Motel 57 Mud Bay Rd T 907/766-2900 or 1-800/478-2902, E budget@mtnview.com. Nine comfortable rooms with cable TV, free coffee, and most with functional kitchenettes. ❹
The Summer Inn B&B 117 Second Ave T 907/766-2970, W www.summerinn.wytbear .com. Immaculately kept downtown B&B with shared-bath rooms, some with good sea views and a good cooked breakfast. It's all light and airy, and amenities include clawfoot baths, quilts, and fresh flowers. ❹

The Town

In the center of town, the **Sheldon Museum & Cultural Center**, 11 Main St (summer Mon–Fri 11am–6pm, Sat & Sun 2–6pm; rest of year daily except Sat 1–4pm; W www.sheldonmuseum.org; $3), does a great job of showing how Haines fits into its Chilkat environment and the wider Tlingit world, and exhibits fine examples of woodwork, clothing, and the distinctive yellow and black Chilkat blanket in wolf, raven, and killer whale designs.

Half a mile away, grassy **Fort William H. Seward** was established in 1903 to contain general Gold Rush lawlessness, and territorial disputes with Canada. It is now the site of **Alaska Indian Arts** (mid-May to mid-Sept Mon–Fri 9am–5pm; free), with a gallery for locally produced sculpture, photos, and carving, and a back room where you can watch and chat to carvers as they work on huge totem poles.

Nearby, the stuffed birds of the **American Bald Eagle Foundation**, 113 Haines Hwy at Second Avenue (summer Mon–Fri 10am–5pm, Sat 1–5pm; $3), make a poor substitute for seeing the world's largest gathering of **bald eagles**, which flock to the banks of the Chilkat River each fall. An upwelling of groundwater keeps the river from freezing, allowing an unusually late run of chum salmon, which the eagles come to feed on. By November over three thousand of these once-endangered rare birds – as many as two dozen to a tree – are gathered along a five-mile sand bar at the **Chilkat Bald Eagle Preserve**, nine miles north of town on the Haines Highway.

Two great, wild **state parks** – Chilkoot Lake and Chilkat – are just a half-hour cycle ride to the north and south of town respectively. Chilkat in particular has some good trails and vistas, while well-tramped treks lead from town to the summits of Mount Riley and the much more difficult Mount Ripinsky. Haines is also a popular starting point for **rafting trips**: Chilkat Guides on Beach Road (T 907/766-2491, W www.raftalaska.com) is one of many operators to offer four-hour **float trips** ($79) down the Chilkat River, ideal for viewing eagles and other wildlife.

Eating and drinking

Haines's most exciting **bars** and **restaurants** can be found in the Fort Seward area. In the evening visitors converge on the friendly bar at the *Hotel Hälsingland*, while some locals stick to the more raucous joints downtown.

Bamboo Room 11 2nd St near Main T 907/766-2800. Standard diner popular for its well-prepared meals (especially the locally caught halibut and

chip dinner), and fresh-baked pies.
Bear-Rittos 12 Main St T 907/766-2117. *Chimichangas*, burritos, and enchiladas with a

choice of vegetable, chicken, beef, salmon, and halibut for $5–11 to eat-in at booths, or to take out.
Fireweed Bakery and Café Building 37, Blacksmith Road ☎907/766-3838. Coffee, pastries, breakfasts, sandwiches, and great pizza

served inside or out. Closed Sun.
Mountain Market 312 3rd Ave at Haines Hwy ☎907/766-3340. Combined natural-food grocery and espresso bar that's one of the best morning spots in town, thanks to a $5.50 bagel breakfast, $7 tortilla wraps or just a muffin with your mocha.

Skagway and around

SKAGWAY, the northernmost ferry stop on the southeast route, sprang up overnight in 1897 as a trading post serving **Klondike Gold Rush** pioneers about to set off on the five-hundred-mile ordeal. It was also the last stop before the harrowing White Pass Trail, also known as the "Dead Horse Trail," on which over three thousand horses perished during the winter of 1897–98 from severe weather, rugged ground, and exhaustion. Having grown from one cabin to a town of twenty thousand in three months, Skagway, rife with disease and desperado violence, was reported to be "hell on earth." It boasted over seventy bars and hundreds of prostitutes, and was controlled by organized criminals, including **Jefferson "Soapy" Smith**, notorious for cheating hapless prospectors out of their gold. One of his scams was to operate a bogus telegraph office through which he concocted false messages from loved ones in the Lower 48 urgently demanding money, which Soapy, of course, took responsibility for sending. He met a nasty end in 1898 after a shoot-out with Frank Reid, head of a vigilante group.

By 1899, the Gold Rush was over, but the completion in 1900 of the White Pass and Yukon Route railway from Skagway to Whitehorse, the Yukon capital, ensured Skagway's survival. Today, the town's 800 residents have gone to great lengths to maintain (or re-create) the original appearance of their home, much of which lies in the **Klondike Gold Rush National Historic Park**, and in summer as many as five cruise ships a day call in to appreciate the effort.

Arrival, information, and getting around

AMHS ferries and an independent operator (see p.1310) arrive daily from Haines at the foot of the main thoroughfare, Broadway, and just a block from the **train station** from where two to five trains a day run over the White Pass to Fraser, British Columbia. Here you can connect with buses to Whitehorse, Yukon. Yukon Alaska Tourist Tours (☎907/983-2115) charge $40 and run twice daily to Whitehorse: buy tickets from Sgt. Preston's Trading Post, 2nd Ave between Broadway and Spring, close to where the bus leaves. From there Alaska Direct **buses** (☎1-800/780-6652) run to Anchorage and Fairbanks three times a week.

Skagway is very compact, and most of the sights can easily be seen on foot. The Klondike Gold Rush National Historic Park **visitor center**, Broadway at 2nd Avenue (May–Sept daily 8am–6pm; ☎907/983-2921, Ⓦwww.nps.gov/klgo), holds talks, leads walking tours, and has historical displays and an impressive movie about the Gold Rush, as well as maps and information on the Chilkoot Trail. Skagway's **visitor center** (summer daily 8am–6pm; ☎907/983-2854 or 1-888/762-1898, Ⓦwww.skagway.org) is on Broadway between Second and Third avenues in the Arctic Brotherhood Hall building.

Accommodation

In such a touristy little town, prices run slightly higher, and places are often reserved up far in advance. For camping, there's the pleasantly secluded *Mountain View RV Park*, Broadway at 12th (☎907/983-3333 or 1-888/778-

7700, Ⓦwww.alaskarv.com; $14), a large RV-dominated site with all the expected facilities, full RV hook-up ($25), and dry RV sites ($18).

Alaskan Sojourn Main St at 8th Ave Ⓣ907/983-2030, Ⓦwww.alaskansojourn.com. Well-set-up hostel with a good kitchen, cozy lounge area, sunroom, free Internet access, and spacious, single-sex, eight-bunk dorms ($20), each with its own bathroom. There's no daytime lock-out or curfew, and there's one private room. ❸

At the White House 475 8th Ave at Main St Ⓣ907/983-9000, Ⓦwww.atthewhitehouse.com. High-standard B&B in one of Skagway's original homes; restored and modernized rooms with super-comfy beds, cable TV, and ceiling fans. A continental breakfast buffet is served and there's always tea, coffee, and home-baked cookies on hand. ❺

Chilkoot Trail Outpost Dyea Ⓣ907/983-3799, Ⓦwww.chilkoottrailoutpost.com. Comfortable modern log cabins in the woods at this welcoming B&B located almost 9 miles from Skagway and a quarter mile from the start of the Chilkoot Trail. Hikers' cabins come with a double-plus-single bunk, private bathroom, satellite TV/VCR, and buffet breakfast, but you'll need a sleeping bag. The larger cabins sleep up to four and come with bedding, microwave, and coffee maker. Large cabins ❻, hikers ❹

Cindy's Place Mile 0.2 Dyea Rd Ⓣ907/983-2674 or 1-800/831-8095, Ⓦwww.alaska.net/~croland. Three cabins in the woods two miles from downtown Skagway, one budget, two more luxurious log-built affairs with private bathrooms (one with a wood-burning stove), phone, and cooking equipment. All guests have free use of the hot tub and mountain bikes, and there are thoughtful touches like a dozen varieties of tea and coffee in the cabins, and homemade jams and jellies for breakfast. Deluxe ❺, budget ❷

Gold Rush Lodge 6th Ave at Alaska St Ⓣ907/983-2831, Ⓦwww.goldrushlodge.com. Immaculately kept and tastefully decorated motel where the smallness of the rooms is compensated by appointments like cable TV with VCR, phone, fridge, microwave, and coffee pot. ❹

Skagway Home Hostel 3rd Ave and Main St Ⓣ907/983-2131, Ⓦwww.skagwayhostel.com. In-with-the-family hostel in a century-old building with bunks in single-sex dorms ($15) and one private room (❷). There's a communal feel, ample supplies for cooking (honesty box), and an 11pm curfew. ❶

The Town

Strolling up Broadway you can't miss the eye-catching facade of the 1899 **Arctic Brotherhood Hall**, decorated with over ten thousand pieces of driftwood and housing the Skagway Visitor Center. Many of the other buildings hereabouts form part of the **Klondike Gold Rush National Historic Park**, notably the former **Mascot Saloon** on Broadway (daily 8am–6pm; free), and **Moore House**, Fifth Avenue at Spring Street (May–Sept daily 10am–noon & 1–5pm; free), a museum **devoted to** Skagway's original resident that features stories and photos of the Gold Rush. There's further detail in the recently refurbished **City of Skagway Museum** (summer daily 9am–5pm; $2), which contains Soapy's Derringer pistol and good Tlingit artifacts.

About a mile and a half north of town, the **Gold Rush Cemetery** is the final resting place of many of the stampeders. Among them are Soapy Smith and Frank Reid, who, according to his gravestone, "gave his life for the honor of Skagway"; a local prostitute, on the other hand, is remembered for "giving her honor for the life of Skagway."

If you've had enough of Soapy and his cronies, you may feel like **hiking**; one of the best short trails leads from the cemetery to the 300ft high Reid Falls. The useful *Skagway Trail Map*, available from the visitor center, details other walks in the area, including those in the Dewey Lakes system, which pass pretty subalpine lakes and tumbling waterfalls, and the more difficult scramble uphill to Denver Glacier. Sockeye Cycles, Fifth Avenue and Broadway (Ⓣ907/983-2851, Ⓦwww.cyclealaska.com), rents out well-maintained **mountain bikes** for $20 a half-day, and the neighboring Mountain Shop (Ⓣ907/983-2544) rents and sells backpacking supplies.

A lazier way to take in the scenery is on the **White Pass and Yukon Route** railway (early May to late Sept; 2–3 departures daily; Ⓣ907/983-2217

or 1–800/343–7373, Ⓦ www.whitepassrailroad.com), which follows the gushing Skagway River upstream past waterfalls and ice-packed gorges and over a
1000ft-high wooden trestle bridge, stopping at the Canadian border ($89
roundtrip) before occasionally continuing to Lake Bennett, British Columbia
(steam-hauled; $160). There's no shortage of riders, so get there early and grab
a seat on the left-hand side going up. The company also offers a through bus
service to Whitehorse after a train ride to Fraser, British Columbia ($95 one
way).

Eating and drinking

Most of Skagway's **bars** and **restaurants** line the touristy part of Broadway. A
few blocks along, at the corner of Sixth Avenue and Broadway, the *Days of 98
Show* is an entertaining, if somewhat cheesy, historical musical about Soapy
Smith ($16).

Corner Café State St at 4th Ave ☎ 907/983-2155.
Daytime diner much favored by Skagway's outdoor
set, serving stuffed croissants with salad or soup
for $8, or halibut burger for $9.
The Haven State St at 9th Ave ☎ 907/983-3553.
Relaxed coffee shop with sofas and stacks of
magazines, serving good espresso, egg or granola
breakfasts, mouthwatering panini and fresh salads
– Santa Fe, Greek, Caesar – all available with
added chicken ($7–9).
Red Onion Saloon Broadway at 2nd Ave
☎ 907/983-2222. An 1898 bar and former bordello
with heaps of character, draft beers, and excellent
pizza.

Sabrosa Broadway at 6th Ave ☎ 907/983-2469.
Daytime café and bakery tucked in behind the gift
shops that's great for breakfast (from $4) and
lunches of burritos ($7), vegetarian chili (cup $3,
bowl $6), and tarragon, pecan, and chicken salad
($8). Shaded outdoor seating for those hot days.
Stowaway Café 205 Congress Way ☎ 907/982-
3463. Stop by during the day for top-quality lunches of halibut sandwich ($11) or blackened-chicken
Caesar ($9), and again in the evening for the likes
of coconut prawns ($20), sweet and sour vegeta-
bles ($15), and pecan pie ($6), all served in a congenial atmosphere with views of the small boat
harbor.

The Chilkoot Trail

Alaska's most famous trail, the 33-mile **CHILKOOT TRAIL**, is a hike
through one huge wilderness museum following the footsteps of the original
Klondike prospectors. Starting in **Dyea**, nine miles from Skagway, and ending
in **Bennett** in Canada, the trail climbs through rainforest to tundra often
strewn with haunting reminders of the past, including ancient boilers that once
drove aerial tramways, and several collapsed huts.

The three- to five-day hike can be strenuous, especially the final ascent up
from Sheep Camp (1000ft) to Chilkoot Pass (3550ft). You must be self-sufficient for food, fuel, and shelter, and be prepared for foul weather. Campgrounds
line the trail, as well as emergency shelters with stoves and firewood. There are
also ranger stations at Dyea, Sheep Camp, and Lindeman City. Dyea is accessible by road, and the White Pass and Yukon Railway runs a service for hikers
returning to Skagway for $65.

The main hiking season runs from July to early September, when there is a
quota system: for details call Parks Canada (☎ 867/667-3910 or 1–800/661-
0486) or consult Ⓦ www.nps.gov/klgo/chilkoot. Whether you have a reservation or not, you must first visit the Skagway **Trail Center**, Broadway at 1st
Avenue (early June to early Sept daily 8.30am–4.30pm), where rangers make
sure you understand the challenges and dangers, and can advise on weather
conditions and current bus and train schedules for the trip back to Skagway.
While here, you must also pay out a rather extravagant Can$50 for a Canadian
permit.

Anchorage

Wedged between the two arms of Cook Inlet and the imposing Chugach Mountains, **ANCHORAGE** is home to over forty percent of Alaska's population and serves as the transportation center for the whole state. A sprawling city on the edge of one of the world's great wildernesses, it often gets a bad press from those who live elsewhere in the state and deride it as being "just half an hour from Alaska." However, it has its attractions and, with its beautiful setting, can make a pleasant one- or two-day stopover.

By the time Captain James Cook came up what is now Cook Inlet in 1778, in search of a Northwest Passage to the Atlantic, Russian fur trappers had already started to settle the area, trading copper and iron for fish and furs with the Native Americans. Though Cook was sure that the inlet was not the Passage, he sent boats out in a southeasterly direction to investigate. When they were forced to turn back by the severe tides, Cook named this gloriously scenic stretch **Turnagain Arm**.

Anchorage itself began life in 1915 as a tent city for construction workers on the Alaska Railroad. During the 1930s, hopefuls fleeing the Depression came pouring in from the Lower 48, and World War II – and the construction of the Alaska Highway – further boosted the city's size and importance. The opening of the airport established Anchorage – equidistant between New York and Tokyo – as the "Crossroads of the World," and statehood in 1959 brought in yet more optimistic adventurers.

Arrival and information

Anchorage Airport, five miles southwest of town, is served by bus #7, part of the citywide **People Mover** (Mon–Fri 7am–11pm, Sat 9am–9pm, Sun 10am–7pm; $1.25 flat fare or $2.50 day-pass from the driver). Downtown Connection (☎907/344-6667, ✉info@akdowntownconnnection.com) has on-demand transportation from the airport to downtown hotels and train station for $6 per person, and a taxi for around $18. The **train station** is downtown at 411 W 1st Ave (☎907/265-2494 or 1-800/544-0552), and the major sights are easily reached on foot.

The **Log Cabin Visitor Center**, downtown at 4th and F (daily: May & Sept 8am–6pm; June–Aug 7.30am–7pm; Oct–April 9am–4pm; ☎907/274-3531, Ⓦwww.anchorage.net), has all the brochures you could need and details of an easy self-guided downtown walking tour. Across the street, the **Alaska Public Lands Information Center** (June–Aug daily 9am–5pm; rest of year Mon–Fri 10am–5pm; ☎907/271-2737, Ⓦwww.nps.gov/aplic) has an excellent natural history display plus maps and more brochures. It can help plan trips into the Interior, and make reservations both for accommodation and the shuttle bus to Denali National Park – important in summer.

Accommodation

Inexpensive **accommodation** in Anchorage can be hard to find, especially in summer, and many places are reserved months in advance. **Campers** should head for the central *Ship Creek Landings RV Park*, 150 N Ingra (☎907/227-0877, Ⓦwww.alaskarv.com; $14), or the more woodsy *Centennial Campground* (☎907/343-6986; $15), five miles north on Glenn Highway.

Alaskan Samovar Inn 720 Gambell St ☎907/277-1511 or 1-800/478-1511. No-nonsense motel close to downtown with cable TV and spa baths. ❹

Anchorage Guesthouse 2001 Hillcrest Drive ☎907/274-0408, Ⓦwww.akhouse.com. Upscale backpacker-style hostel, just over a mile from downtown and handy for midtown and the Coastal Trail (bikes available for $10 a half-day). Other perks include sheets, towels, breakfast, use of kitchen, free gear storage, free local calls, and reasonably priced Internet access. Dorm beds cost $28 and there are private doubles and kings. ➌

Earth B&B 1001 W 12th Ave ☏ 907/279-9907, Ⓦ www.alaskaone.com/earthbb. A B&B unlike any other, enthusiastically and liberally run by multilingual Dutch émigré, Margriet, who makes the place hospitable for Denali-bound climbers during the season and a broad cross-section of folk for the rest of the year. Bus #6, #36, or #60 from downtown. ➍

HI-Anchorage 700 H St ☏ 907/276-3635, Ⓦ www.alaska.net/~hianch. Functional and very central hostel with luggage storage, Internet access, and laundry along with a daytime lock-out and evening curfew. Dorm beds $20 (nonmembers $23). Reserve well ahead in summer. ➊

Oscar Gill House 1344 W 10th Ave ☏ 907/279-1344, Ⓦ www.oscargill.com. Lovely B&B in a 1913 house, comprehensively restored while maintaining character and an understated elegance. Two rooms share a bath while the largest has its own,

and there's also an apartment for longer stays, all tastefully done and looked after by very welcoming hosts, Mark and Susan Lutz. Private bath ➎, shared ➍

Qupqugiac Inn 640 W 36th Ave, midtown ☏ 907/562-5681, Ⓦ www.qupq.com. Great budget hotel with clean, simple rooms, each with phone and satellite TV, and a communal lounge area with self-catering facilities. Bus #9 from downtown passes within a block, along Arctic Blvd. Rooms with bath ➍, without ➌

Spenard Hostel International 2845 W 42nd Place ☏ 907/248-5036, Ⓦ www.alaskahostel.org. Well-organized and friendly hostel in a residential suburb with nearby mall just a mile and a half from the airport (bus #6). $10 bike rental, no curfew or lock-out, and dorm beds for $16. ➊

Voyager Hotel 501 K St at 5th Ave ☏ 907/277-9501 or 1-800/247-9070, Ⓦ www.voyagerhotel .com. The best of the mid- to upper-range hotels featuring spacious rooms (with a kitchenette) and most of the facilities of the large business hotels at much lower cost. Reserve well in advance in summer. ➐

The City

Travelers eager to rush off into the "real" Alaska tend to overlook cosmopolitan Anchorage – a blend of old and new, urban blight and rural parks – but there is plenty to see, and it's worth spending some time here experiencing big-city Alaska. The city is laid out on a grid; numbered avenues run east–west, lettered streets north–south.

Your first stop should be the **Anchorage Museum of History and Art**, 121 W Seventh Ave (summer daily 9am–6pm and to 9pm on Thurs; rest of year Tues–Sat 10am–6pm, Sun 1–5pm; $6.50), an excellent overview of the state and its history told through intricate dioramas, alongside beautiful examples of carved ivory and basketware. The art gallery which is part of the museum is notable for the works by Alaska's best-known painter, Sydney Laurence, particularly his monumental oil painting of Mount McKinley.

The rest of the downtown sites are more modest: the **Imaginarium**, 737 W Fifth Ave (Mon–Sat 10am–6pm, Sun noon–5pm; $5), has hands-on displays telling you all about glaciers, the Northern Lights, polar bears, and the private life of the dopey-looking moose; the period-furnished 1915 **Oscar Anderson House Museum**, 420 M St (June to mid-Sept Mon–Fri noon–5pm; $3), illustrates early Anchorage life; and the **Alaska Experience Center**, Sixth Avenue and G Street (summer daily 9am–10pm; $12), presents forty minutes of Alaska's best scenery, shot from choppers and beamed onto a 180° wraparound screen, and the admission price includes a film of the devastating 1964 Good Friday **earthquake** that leveled much of downtown – 8.6 on the Richter Scale and North America's strongest-ever quake.

Seven miles to the east on the outskirts of town lies the **Alaska Native Heritage Center**, Muldoon Road exit from Glenn Highway (summer daily 9am–6pm; $21). It is expensive and still finding its feet, but provides an excellent introduction to the state's five main ethnic groups. Each is represented by a typical house where Native guides interpret their culture. Throughout the

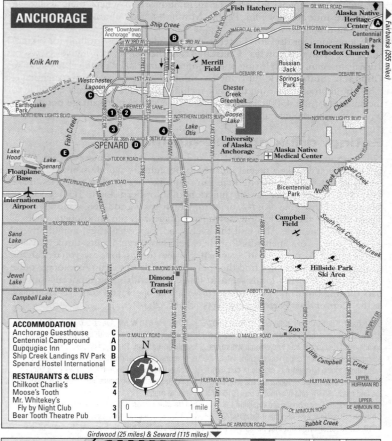

ANCHORAGE

Fish Hatchery

Alaska Native Heritage Center **Ⓐ**

St Innocent Russian Orthodox Church

Knik Arm

Ship Creek

Centennial Park

Fairbanks (355 miles)

See "Downtown Anchorage" map

Merrill Field

Russian Jack Springs Park

Chester Creek Greenbelt

Westchester Lagoon **Ⓒ**

Earthquake Park

Goose Lake

Lake Otis

University of Alaska Anchorage

Alaska Native Medical Center

SPENARD **Ⓓ**

Lake Hood

Lake Spenard

Floatplane Base

International Airport

Sand Lake

Jewel Lake

Bicentennial Park

Campbell Field

Hillside Park Ski Area

Dimond Transit Center

Campbell Lake

Zoo

ACCOMMODATION
Anchorage Guesthouse	C
Centennial Campground	A
Qupqugiac Inn	D
Ship Creek Landings RV Park	B
Spenard Hostel International	E

RESTAURANTS & CLUBS
Chilkoot Charlie's	2
Moose's Tooth	4
Mr. Whitekey's Fly by Night Club	3
Bear Tooth Theatre Pub	1

N

0   1 mile

ALASKA | Anchorage

15

Girdwood (25 miles) & Seward (115 miles) ▼

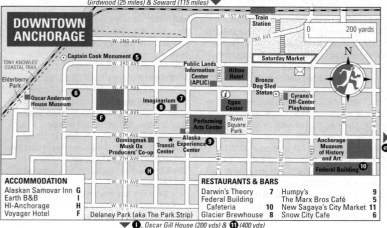

DOWNTOWN ANCHORAGE

Train Station

TONY KNOWLES' COASTAL TRAIL

Captain Cook Monument **5**

Elderberry Park

Oscar Anderson House Museum **6**

Saturday Market

Public Lands Information Center (APLIC)

Hilton Hotel

Bronze Dog Sled Statue

Imaginarium **8** **7**

Egan Center

Cyrano's Off-Center Playhouse

Performing Arts Center

Town Square Park

Oomingmak Musk Ox Producers' Co-op

Transit Center

Alaska Experience Center **9**

Anchorage Museum of History and Art

Federal Building **10**

0   200 yards

N

ACCOMMODATION
Alaskan Samovar Inn	G
Earth B&B	I
HI-Anchorage	H
Voyager Hotel	F

RESTAURANTS & BARS
Darwin's Theory	7	Humpy's	9
Federal Building Cafeteria	10	The Marx Bros Café	5
		New Sagaya's City Market	11
Glacier Brewhouse	8	Snow City Cafe	6

Delaney Park (aka The Park Strip) ▼

Ⓘ, Oscar Gill House (200 yds) & **11** (400 yds)

1317

day, cultural groups perform in the main auditorium where there is also an instructive introductory film. People Mover #4 takes almost an hour to get here from downtown.

On long summer days it is better to stay outside, perhaps strolling (or biking) along the **Tony Knowles Coastal Trail** that offers restorative views of Turnagain Arm, or exploring the mountains and lakes of the 495,000-acre **Chugach State Park**, just fifteen minutes' drive east from Anchorage. Challenging trails traversing the park include an often treacherous scramble to the summit of the 4500ft Flattop Mountain, a spectacular vantage point from which to view the city and Cook Inlet.

Eating, drinking, and nightlife

Nowhere in Alaska will you find a more diverse range of places to eat. That's not to say you'd make a special journey for its culinary wonders, but after a few weeks in the wilds, the scene here can seem like heaven. For groceries, make for Carr's supermarket at the junction of Northern Light Boulevard and Minnesota Drive (bus #3, #4, or #36), which has a good deli section.

Good **bars** abound in downtown Anchorage, and the atmosphere varies as much as the clientele. Also visit the lively (and somewhat edgy) neighborhood of **Spenard** – on Spenard Road between Northern Lights Boulevard and International Airport Road – which can be fun as long as you're careful. Women travelers may not find the "bohemian" side of macho Anchorage quite as endearing as many locals seem to think it is, with some innocent-looking bars turning out to be strip joints. Shows, plays, opera, and concerts take place at the **Center for Performing Arts** (☎907/263-2787).

Bear Tooth Theatre Pub 1230 W 27th Ave ☎907/276-4200, ⓦwww.beartooththeatre.net. Top-notch combination restaurant, bar, and cinema where, for $3 on top of your meal price, you can dine while watching a movie (second-run, classic or cult; $3). Menu has a wide range – Caesar salads ($6), burritos and tacos ($5–8), and gourmet pizzas ($15 for a 16-inch), and the microbrews are excellent.

Chilkoot Charlie's 2435 Spenard Rd ☎907/272-1010. Sawdust-strewn barn that packs them in nightly for pricey drinks, pool, foosball, two floors of DJ-led dance, and live music from 9.30pm.

Darwin's Theory 426 G St at 4th Ave ☎907/277-5322. Straightforward local bar good for moderately priced boozing and neighborly encounters with colorful local characters.

The Federal Building Cafeteria 222 W 7th at C St ☎907/277-6736. Breakfast and lunch cafeteria that's about the best budget value downtown, certainly a cut above the fast-food joints and more filling. Steaming clam chowder or one of their entrees costs around $5.

Glacier Brewhouse 737 W 5th St ☎907/274-2739. Hugely popular restaurant, bar, and microbrewery serving wonderful food and drink. At least half a dozen toothsome house-brewed beers accompany alder-wood-baked gourmet pizza ($11), spit-grilled three-peppercorn prime rib ($23), or steamed Alaskan King crabs ($30).

Humpy's 610 W 6th Ave ☎907/276-2337. Popular watering hole with live music and a strong college-bar feel. The likes of charbroiled salmon, burgers, soups, and salads (mostly under $10) are helped down with local microbrews plus English and Belgian bottled beers, and over thirty top-shelf single malts.

The Marx Bros. Café 627 W 3rd Ave ☎907/278-2133. The best all-round fine dining downtown served up in a historic house with views of the water. Start on the likes of Kachemak Bay oysters with pepper vodka and ginger sorbet ($12) or Neapolitan seafood mousse ($12), and follow it up with yellow-fin tuna in a black-bean ginger *beurre blanc* with stir-fried baby bok choy ($26). Dinner only.

Mr Whitekey's Fly By Night Club 3300 Spenard Rd at 32nd Ave ☎907/279-7726. Zany cabaret and live music venue which, throughout summer, hosts *The Whale Fat Follies* (June to mid-Sept Tues–Sat 8pm; $13-20; 16 and over only), a satirical and occasionally bawdy slant on Alaska.

Moose's Tooth 3300 Old Seward Hwy at 33rd Ave ☎907/258-2537. A perennial favorite, always alive with diners tucking into some of the town's best gourmet pizza.

New Sagaya's City Market 900 W 13th Ave at I St ☎907/274-6173. Trendy and expensive grocery store, deli, and café with a great selection that

ranges from organic vegetables and great cheeses to pizza, wraps, Thai dishes, and good coffee. The nearest groceries to downtown.
Snow City Café 1034 W 4th Ave ☎907/272-6338. Probably the city's best breakfast spot – eggs Florentine for $9, fruit & granola for $5 – and great for relaxing over a pot of Earl Grey and a

slice of cake. Soups and salads pad out a lunchtime menu which might include pesto chicken pasta ($9) or tofu stir-fry ($9). They're not open for dinner except for soup and sandwiches on Wednesday when there's an Irish music session, and Sunday when it's open mic.

Kenai Peninsula and Kodiak Island

South of Anchorage, the Seward Highway hugs the shore of **Turnagain Arm** past **Girdwood** and the ski resort of **Alyeska**. Just beyond, a side road cuts to the ever-popular **Portage Glacier**, and continues through a new tunnel to **Whittier**, little more than a ferry dock for accessing Prince William Sound (see p.1325).

Beyond Portage, the Seward Highway enters the **Kenai Peninsula**, "Anchorage's playground," which at over nine thousand square miles is larger than some states. The peninsula offers an endless diversity of activities and scenery, mostly concentrated around major communities such as **Seward**, the base for cruises into the inspirational **Kenai Fjords National Park**, and artsy **Homer**, where the waters and shorelines of the glorious **Kachemak Bay State Park** are the main destination.

Most Alaskans come to the Kenai Peninsula to **fish**: the Kenai, Russian, and Kasilof rivers host "combat fishing," with thousands of anglers standing elbow to elbow using strength and know-how to pull in thirty-pound-plus king salmon. **Campgrounds** along the rivers fill up fast, especially in July and August.

A hundred miles beyond Homer in the Gulf of Alaska, the "Emerald Isle" of **Kodiak Island** offers some of Alaska's most uncommon and pleasing landscapes, and is home to the **Kodiak bear**, an overgrown subspecies of the grizzly.

Girdwood and Portage Glacier

Outdoorsy **GIRDWOOD**, 37 miles south of Anchorage, lies two miles inland in the shade of the **Alyeska Resort**, Alaska's largest winter sports complex and the lowest-elevation ski resort in the world – Mount Alyeska's 3939ft summit rises from just 270 feet above sea level. Downhill runs and an extensive night-skiing operation run from November to mid-April (tows $46 a day), and in summer you can ride the Alyeska Tramway ($16) up to stunning views and some good hiking territory. Girdwood Ski and Cyclery, Mile 1.5 Alyeska Highway (☎907/783-2453; closed Mon & Tues), rent city **bikes** ($25 a day) to explore the immediate surroundings, and Class V Whitewater (☎907/783-2004, ⓦwww.alaskanrafting.com) run a range of **rafting** trips from gentle scenic float trips on the Portage River (3hr; $50) to serious Class III–V whitewater on the Six-Mile River ($75–135).

The resort's *Alyeska Prince Hotel* (☎907/754-1111 or 1-800/880-3880, ⓦwww.alyeskaresort.com; ❽) is a grand ski lodge with half a dozen good restaurants and service to match. Alternatively, try the Austrian-run *Alyeska View B&B*, Vail Drive (☎907/783-2747, ⓦwww.alyeskaview.com; ❹), or *Alyeska Home Hostel* (☎907/783-2099; ❶), with $12.50 bunks. There's tasty, inexpensive **food** at *The Bake Shop* (☎907/783-2831) on Olympic Circle at the base of the ski tows, and at the unmissable *Double Musky Inn* on Crow Creek Road (☎907/783-2822): budget on $30 a head and a meal to remember.

Eleven miles south of Girdwood, a road leads to Whittier, past **Portage Glacier**, an unbearably popular day-tour from Anchorage. Frustratingly, you can't see the glacier from the parking lot; instead you must pay Gray Line $25 for a cruise around the lake's corner to the glacier's snout. Two USFS **campgrounds** ($9–12) can be found two or three miles back down the road.

Seward and the Kenai Fjords National Park

SEWARD, ringed by glaciers and mountains 127 miles south of Anchorage, sprang to life in 1903 after engineers declared this ice-free port the ideal starting point for railroad tracks to the Interior. Since then it has been a key freight terminal, but tourism – particularly cruises into Kenai Fjords National Park – is now its most conspicuous business.

Seward's main activities are enjoying the scenery and visiting the wonders at the waterfront **SeaLife Center** (daily: summer 8am–8pm; rest of year 9am–6pm; $12.50), a successful marriage of marine research and visitor education partly funded by the Exxon Valdez oil spill settlement. The center offers the chance to watch ongoing cold-water research in action and marvel at the underwater antics of stellar sea lions, harbor seals, and adorable puffins. After a visit to the center, another good local option is the four-hour hike up nearby **Mount Marathon** for some glorious views. The trail here is also the scene of an annual Fourth of July race thanks to the antics of two pioneers who, in 1909, bet each other to run up and down the 3022-foot mountain – the current race record is 43 minutes 23 seconds.

Most visitors also drive thirteen miles out to **Exit Glacier** ($5 parking), one of the few in the state you can approach on land. From the ranger station at the end of the road, a short stroll leads to the still-active glacier, though signs warn you back from the ice wall and its inviting blue clefts. Exit Glacier is part of the **KENAI FJORDS NATIONAL PARK**, a magnificent 580,000-acre region of peaks, glaciers, and craggy coastline. Its towering mountains are mantled by the prodigious three-hundred-square-mile Harding Icefield, feeding the three dozen retreating glaciers, that have exposed the dramatic fjords after which the park is named.

Eight of these tidewater glaciers "calve" icebergs into the sea with thunderous booms, and the fjords also hold a wealth of **marine wildlife** – sea otters, porpoises, seals, stellar sea lions, plus orca, gray, humpback, and minke whales – as well as the seabird rookeries on the cliffs of the Chiswell Islands. The best of the **cruises** from Seward are conducted aboard the large boats of Kenai Fjords Tours (☎1-800/468-8068; $54–139); pay out for the longer day-tours that go right up to the calving tidewater glaciers.

The park's **visitor center**, 1212 Fourth Ave in Seward's small boat harbor (summer daily 9am–6pm; rest of year Mon–Fri 8am–5pm; ☎907/224-3175), provides maps, film shows, and details on regional hikes.

Practicalities

Trains from Anchorage arrive and depart daily (☎1-800/544-0552; $55 one way, $90 roundtrip) at the depot next to the dock for **ferries** from Valdez and Kodiak. Seward Bus Line (☎907/224-3608) charges $35 for a one-way ride from Anchorage. Seward's two hubs of activity, the small boat harbor and downtown, are joined by the mile-long Fourth Avenue; if you don't feel like walking, hop on **Seward's Trolley** (daily 10am–7pm every 30min; $2, day-pass $5).

ALASKA | Seward • Kenai Fjords National Park

The main **visitor center** is at Mile 2 Seward Hwy (summer daily 8am–6pm; rest of year Mon–Fri 8am–5pm; ℡907/224-8051, ⓦwww.sewardak.org).

For budget **accommodation** downtown, go for the *Moby Dick Hostel*, 432 Third Ave (℡907/224-7072, ⓦwww.mobydickhostel.com; ❶–❸), with bunks ($18), limited kitchen facilities, and private rooms (some with kitchenettes), or move upscale to *Murphy's Motel*, 911 Fourth Ave (℡907/224-8090 or 1-800/886-8191, ⓦwww.murphysmotel.com; ❺), close to the small boat harbor. Alternatively, head out of town either to the rural hostel-style *Kate's Roadhouse*, Mile 5.5 Seward Hwy (℡907/224-5888, ⓦwww.ak-biz.com/katesroadhouse; ❶), or lovely log *Alaska's Treehouse B&B*, off Timber Street at Mile 7 Seward Hwy (℡907/224-3867, ⓦwww.seward.net/treehouse; ❹), which offers a hot tub and sauna, and great breakfasts. There's also the excellent and central *Waterfront* **campground** (℡907/224-4055; $8), off Ballaine Boulevard on the shores of Resurrection Bay.

Eating in Seward is fairly reasonably priced: for a coffee or light meal make for *Resurrect Art*, 320 Third Ave, a coffee house and gallery in a former church. More substantial eating is best done at the eclectic *Christo's Place*, 113 Fourth Ave (℡907/224-5255), where most mains are $15–20, or the upscale *Ray's Waterfront Bar and Grill*, by the harbor (summer only; ℡907/224-3012), which has nice views and big steak and seafood dinners for around $25.

Homer and around

HOMER, 226 miles south from Anchorage, is the Kenai Peninsula's southernmost road-accessible town. It commands a truly magnificent setting, spread beneath gently sloping verdant bluffs with a four-mile finger of land – The Spit – slinking out into the dark waters of Kachemak Bay, into which flow crystal-blue glaciers, framed by dense black forest. With abundant activities, a lively nightlife, and a varied, youthful population that supports a thriving arts community, it's so appealing you'll probably want to linger a few days extra.

Russians, drawn by the abundance of coal, were the first whites to reach the area, and by the mid-1800s several American companies had followed suit. In 1896, **Homer Pennock**, a gold-seeker from Michigan, set up the community that still bears his name. Every summer in recent years, young people from the Lower 48 have arrived here in droves to work on the halibut boats, many living in an impromptu tent city on the beach.

Arrival, information, and getting around

Ferries arrive at the end of The Spit from Seldovia, Kodiak, and Seward. Homer Stage Lines (℡907/235-2252) runs a daily **bus** service between Anchorage and Homer for $40 each way.

Most hotels, restaurants, and shops are in town, while almost all of the fishing charter and tour operators can be found along the twee boardwalks of The Spit. There is no public transport between the town and The Spit so you may want to rent a bike from Homer Saw & Cycle, 1532 Ocean Drive (℡907/235-8406; $25 a day), or just grab a cab.

The main **visitor center** is at 201 Sterling Hwy (summer Mon–Fri 9am–8pm, Sat & Sun 10am–6pm; ℡907/235-7740, ⓦhomeralaska.org), and almost next door there's the brand new **Islands and Ocean Visitor Center**, 95 Sterling Hwy (summer daily 9am–6pm; ℡907/235-6961, ⓦwww.islandsandocean.org), designed to showcase various facets of the Alaska Maritime National Wildlife Refuge through interactive exhibits, replica seabird cliffs, and sections on the work of biologists in remote locations.

Accommodation

Homer's good-value **hotels** and **B&Bs** are often fully booked in midsummer; the visitor center, though, can help if you arrive without reservations. There's **camping** on The Spit beach for $6 and at the wooded *Karen Hornaday Hillside Campground*, Campground Road (☎907/235-1583; $6).

Driftwood Inn 135 W Bunnel Ave ☎907/235-8019 or 1-800/478-8019, ⓦwww.thedriftwood-inn.com. Rambling older hotel with an extensive and varied range of rooms, RV parking, and a communal TV lounge with video library. Breakfast is not included, though there is free tea and coffee and breakfast is available. Private bath ❹–❺, shared bath ❹
Homer Hostel 304 W Pioneer Ave ☎907/235-1463, ⓦwww.homerhostel.com. Centrally located hostel in a converted home where you sleep in made-up beds and bunks ($22), in 4- to 6-bed dorms, and relax in a big lounge with TV/VCR and a great view of the mountains. There's no curfew or lock-out, bikes and fishing rods can be rented for $10 and $5 a day respectively. Rooms ❷
Kiana B&B Mile 5 East End Rd ☎907/235-8824, ⓦwww.akms.com/kiana. Very hospitable B&B

occupying the upper floor of a modern house with great views from the guest lounge and some rooms. There's also a great little cabin out the back, a hot tub under the stars, and full continental breakfast is served. ❺
Old Town B&B 106 W Bunnell Ave ☎907/235-7558, ⓦwww.xyz.net/~oldtown. Beautiful B&B located in a 1936 building, with wooden-floor rooms, all with a restrained antique decor and tremendous sea views. Breakfast is served in the *Two Sisters* bakery down the street. ❹
Seaside Farm Hostel Mile 5 East End Rd ☎907/235-7850, ⓦwww.xyz.net/~seaside. Excellent if inconveniently sited hostel on a small farm with a large outdoor cooking and lounge area, camping ($6 per site but no use of hostel facilities), bunks ($15), and some great cabins (❷). Closed Oct to April. ❶–❷

The Town and around

The downtown **Pratt Museum**, 3779 Bartlett St (daily 10am–6pm; $6), features high-quality works by local craftspeople, as well as Inuit and other Native artifacts, aquariums, and historic Homer oddities. Many of Homer's most popular activities, however, revolve around The Spit. To Alaskan anglers, Homer is "**Halibut Central**": a full day's fishing excursion with any of the charter companies begins at around $150. If you don't mind joining the crowds, it's cheaper and simpler to visit the **Fishing Hole**, a tiny bight on The Spit, which is stocked with salmon and offers good fishing from mid-May to mid-September.

The prime tourist attraction in the Homer area is exploring the 250,000 acres of forested mountains, glaciers, pristine fjords, and inlets that comprise **Kachemak Bay State Park**, directly across the bay from Homer. Bird species here include puffin, auklets, kittiwakes, and storm petrels, and marine creatures such as seals, sea otters, and whales are also plentiful. Rainbow Tours on Cannery Row (☎907/235-7272, ⓦwww.rainbowtours.net) operates two-hour sightseeing cruises ($20) to **Gull Island** – a 15,000-strong rookery. The most popular destination is the gorgeous hamlet of **Halibut Cove**, where boardwalks link art galleries and *The Saltry* restaurant: the *Danny J* **ferry** (☎907/235-7847) makes two daily trips to Halibut Cove, on the south shore of the bay, via Gull Island rookery, for $45 roundtrip, $22 if you book in for an evening meal.

The area's best trails, most of them manageable in a day, are those in the Kachemak Bay State Park on the south side of Kachemak Bay: pick up the park's hiking trails leaflet ($2.50) and other information from the visitor center. The most-traveled route, up to **Grewingk Glacier**, is an easy three-and-a-half-mile trek above the spruce and cottonwood forest to the foot of the glacier, from where you get splendid views of the bay.

Eating and drinking

Not surprisingly, Homer's culinary scene focuses most on fresh fish. For **nightlife**, head out to a colorful bar or to the relaxed **Pier One Theater** (May–Sept; ☎907/235-7333), next to the fishing hole on the Spit.

Café Cups 162 Pioneer Ave ☎907/235-8330. Relaxing yet vibrant café serving some of the best coffee and great sandwiches and salads.

Fat Olive's 276 Olsen Lane ☎907/235-3448. Chic modern restaurant with strong Italian leanings, a convivial atmosphere and a good selection of microbrews. They also do excellent take-out pizza under the name Fat Rack Pizza.

The Homestead Mile 8.2 East Rd ☎907/235-8723. Open for dinner nightly for crab-and-shrimp cakes ($13) followed by Mediterranean pasta ($20), half a pound of King crab ($23), or sautéed scallops ($21).

Lands End Resort at the end of The Spit ☎907/235-0400 or 1-800/478-0400. Plush and not-too-pricey restaurant offering an absolutely wonderful view of the bay as well as a fairly standard but tasty Alaskan menu. Breakfast is a must.

Salty Dawg The Spit. No self-respecting drinker should pass up a few jars in the *Dawg* with its dark interior, life preservers pinned to the wall, and what is reliably claimed to be the only surveyors' benchmark located in a bar in the US.

Two Sisters Espresso/Bakery 233 E Bunnell Ave ☎907/235-2280. Great little spot for that morning coffee either in the bakery or at tables out on the deck. Good too for pizza, soups, and quiches at moderate prices.

Kodiak

A nine-hour ferry ride connects Homer with **KODIAK ISLAND**, at a hundred miles long and sixty wide, the largest island in the US. In the north it is thick with spruce forests, but the interior is carpeted by wild grasses studded with marshes, lumpy knolls, and reeded lakes. This is prime territory for the renowned **Kodiak bear**, a subspecies of the grizzly, which weighs up to 1500 pounds. Streams chock-full of spawning salmon allow these monsters to thrive in the **Kodiak National Wildlife Refuge**, covering the southwestern two-thirds of the island. Roughly ten bears inhabit each square mile around Red and Fraser lakes, and bear-watching trips are big business. In addition to *Ursus*, the Emerald Isle provides a favorable habitat for **bald eagles**, and as many as two million seabirds nest along the fjords, bights, and bays. Accommodation in the nine **wilderness cabins** ($35 a night) dotted throughout the island is drawn by lottery each year; for details, contact Kodiak National Wildlife Refuge Visitor Center (see p.1324).

The warm **Japanese Current** that flows around the island supports a mild maritime climate along with plenty of rain and fog, creating poor flying conditions and the distinct possibility that your stay could be extended by a day or two. If you want to avoid peak-season prices, note that May and June are notoriously wet, but September weather is usually fairly reliable.

All but two thousand of the island's 12,000 inhabitants live in and around its only major town, the likeable and busy fishing port of **KODIAK** on the northeastern tip. Before Russian explorers established a community here in 1792, Aleut and Alutiiq had fished the area for millennia. After Alaska was transferred to the US, Kodiak survived as a center for trappers, whale-hunters, and salmon-fishers, and in 1939 was just another sleepy Alaskan village when a massive military base was established here and the population rocketed to around 50,000. However, most of Kodiak's wealth comes from fishing the rich waters of the Gulf, and the town maintains a fleet of over 2700 fishing vessels. Tourism definitely plays second fiddle; few cruise ships stop, but this bustling little town has a splendid range of activities, good B&Bs, and a lively nightlife.

Arrival, information, and getting around

AMHS ferries from Homer dock downtown three times a week in summer. Alaska Airlines and ERA Aviation jointly dispatch seven one-hour flights a day from Anchorage at around $250 roundtrip. The local bus ($2) is very infrequent so you may want to catch a cab the five miles into town ($10). The most practical way to explore the island is to **fly**; Island Air Service (☎486-6196, ⓦ kodiakislandair.com) will give you close-up views of bears for around $400.

The helpful **visitor center** is by the ferry dock at 100 Marine Way (June–Aug Mon–Fri 8am–5pm, Sat & Sun dependant on ferry arrivals; Sept–May Mon–Fri 8am–5pm; ☎907/486-4782, ⓦwww.kodiak.org) and the **Kodiak National Wildlife Refuge Visitor Center**, 1390 Buskin River Rd, close to the airport, four miles south of town (April–Sept Mon–Fri 8am–7pm, Sat noon–4pm; ☎907/487-2600, ⓦwww.r7.fws.gov/nwr/kodiak), stocks a wealth of information on bears and the backcountry.

Accommodation

Most **lodging** in Kodiak is expensive, but the hotels and B&Bs are generally very good. The best place to **camp** is in *Fort Abercrombie State Historical Park*, four miles north of town ($8). There's no hostel, so the cheapest rooms are at the *Shelikof Lodge*, 211 Thorsheim Ave (☎907/486-4141, ⓦwww .shelikoflodge.com; ❹), though you may prefer the well-located *Harborview B&B*, 312 W Rezanof Drive (☎907/486-2464 or 1-888/283-2464, ⓦwww .kodiakonnection.com; ❺), with home-cooked breakfast, cable TV, and one room with a wonderful view of the harbor. For comfortable hotel rooms try the *Best Western Kodiak Inn*, 236 W Rezanof Drive (☎907/486-5712 or 1-888/563-4254, ⓦwww.kodiakinn.com; ❻), with all the expected amenities.

The Town and around

Downtown Kodiak is usually lively, with plenty of comings and goings in the small boat harbor and adjacent bars and cafés on Marine Way. The small **Baranov Museum** (summer Mon–Sat 10am–4pm, Sun noon–4pm; rest of year Tues–Sat 10am–3pm; $2), in an old Russian house opposite the dock, holds Aleut, Russian, and American pioneer artifacts, including an impressive collection of whalebones. Nearby, the small but beautifully formed **Alutiiq Museum**, 218 Mission Rd (June–Aug Mon–Fri 9am-5pm, Sat 10am–5pm; Sept–May Tues–Fri 9am–5pm, Sat 10.30am–4.30pm; $2), centers on the life and culture of the island's native people.

Etched out of lush rainforest, less than four miles north, **Fort Abercrombie State Historical Park** is a great place to do some seabird- and **whale-watching**, camp or take a shoreline hike: a meadow at the north end provides a dazzling blaze of color in summer. Other moderately easy **hiking trails** originating near town go to the top of Pillar Mountain and Termination Point. However, most trails are not maintained and can be confusing; get precise details from the visitor center or the rangers at Fort Abercrombie. The undulating and unpaved **Chiniak Highway** runs for 48 miles to Cape Greville and the *Road's End Café*, sweeping through tightly bunched spruce and passing many abandoned World War II defenses, plus prime vistas of Chiniak Bay.

Eating and drinking

Food in Kodiak is generally good. *Harborside Coffee & Goods*, 216 Shelikof St (☎907/486-5862), offers coffee, pastries, soups, and muffins; *El Chicano*, 103 Center Ave (☎907/486-6116), presents fairly authentic Mexican dishes at reasonable prices; and *The Chart Room*, inside the *Best Western* at 236 W Rezanof Drive (☎907/486-5712), has Kodiak's most formal dining, serving king crab legs ($30) or halibut steaks ($17) with good harbor views. *Henry's Great Alaskan*

Restaurant, 512 Marine Way (☎907/486-3313), is the downtown entertainment hub, open from 11am until the fun runs out.

Prince William Sound

Prince William Sound, a largely unspoiled wilderness of steep fjords and mountains, glaciers and rainforest, rests calmly at the head of the Gulf of Alaska. Sheltered by the Chugach Mountains in the north and east, and the Kenai Peninsula in the west, and with its sparkling blue waters full of whales, porpoise, sea otters, and seals, the Sound has a relatively low-key tourist industry. The only significant settlements, spectacular **Valdez**, at the end of the trans-Alaska pipeline, and to a lesser extent **Cordova**, a fishing community only accessible by sea or air, are the respective bases from which to see the **Columbia** and **Childs glaciers**.

The region's first settlers, the Chugach Eskimos, were edged out by the more aggressive Tlingit, who in turn were displaced first by Russian trappers in search of sea otter pelts, and then by American gold prospectors and fishers. The whole glorious show was very nearly spoiled forever on Good Friday 1989, when the **Exxon Valdez** spilled 11 million gallons of its cargo of crude oil. Although the long-term effects have yet to be fully determined, the spill fortunately affected just a fifth of the Sound and today no surface pollution is visible.

Valdez

VALDEZ, 304 road miles from Anchorage and the northernmost ice-free port in the Western Hemisphere, lies at the head of a fjord that reaches inland twelve miles from Prince William Sound. Sometimes hyped as "Little Switzerland" for its stunning backdrop of steep mountains, glaciers, and waterfalls, and a record annual snowfall of over forty feet, Valdez (pronounced *val-Deez*) offers great hiking, rafting, sea kayaking, wildlife-viewing, and, of course, fishing.

The 1890s **Gold Rush** transformed Valdez from a remote whaling station into a flourishing settlement, when thousands of prospectors arrived to head over the deadly Valdez and Klutina glaciers on the Valdez Trail to the mines in the Yukon. Only three hundred of the 3500 miners who set out made it to the goldfield – those that did not perish from frostbite and starvation gave up. Valdez came to depend on fish canneries, logging, and occasional military use for its economic survival, until Good Friday 1964: the epicenter of North America's largest **earthquake** (see p.1316) was just 45 miles away. Shockwaves turned the ground to quivering jelly, snapping roads, toppling buildings, and killing 33 residents. However, the citizens of Valdez refused to be intimidated, and moved sixty-odd buildings to the more stable present site four miles away.

The town's fortunes rose again during the 1970s, when oil was found beneath Prudhoe Bay, and Valdez became the southern terminus of the 800-mile **trans-Alaska pipeline**, which carries up to two million barrels of oil per day. Although winds and tides ensured that no oil from the *Exxon Valdez* made it into the port of Valdez, ironically the spill triggered an economic boom for the city as it was the most accessible site from which to direct the massive **cleanup.** The operation, which lasted into 1991, cost Exxon and the government over one hundred billion dollars, and called on eleven thousand workers in over one thousand boats and three hundred planes to scour the beaches. All seems pristine now, though many species have still not fully recovered their former numbers.

Arrival and information

One of the most exciting things about Valdez is getting here; both car and ferry rides are unforgettable. The **Richardson Highway** holds epic scenery: restful alpine meadows, angry-looking waterfalls, mountain glaciers, the icy summit of **Thompson Pass**, and the waterfall-fringed **Keystone Canyon**. Alaska Trails & Tours (T 1-888/600-6001) run along this route from Fairbanks, Delta Junction, and Glennallen, but only when numbers make the journey viable.

Ferries from Cordova, Whittier, or Seward dock at the end of Hazelet Avenue (T 907/834-4800). If the weather is clear, the ride offers superb views of the Columbia Glacier. ERA Aviation (T 1-800/866-8394) flies three times daily to Anchorage ($100–125 each way) from the **airport** five miles north. From there, **taxis** (T 907/835-2500) run downtown for around $10.

The central **visitor center** (summer Mon–Fri 8am–7pm, Sat 9am–6pm, Sun 10am–5pm; T 907/835-4636 or 1-800/770-5954, W www.valdezalaska.org) is at 200 Fairbanks St.

Accommodation

Valdez's **accommodation** gets snapped up pretty quickly and there's no hostel, but a free phone (summer only) outside the visitor center connects with some of the fifty-plus **B&Bs**. **Campers** can choose between the central but busy *Bear Paw Camper Park* (T 907/835-2530; $19), and the inconvenient *Valdez Glacier Campground* ($10), seven miles from town past the airport. The cheapest rooms are at *L&L's B&B*, 533 W Hanagita St (T 907/835-4447, W www.lnlalaska.com; ❸), with five comfortable shared-bath rooms ten minutes' walk from the center, but with a couple of free bikes to get around and a good self-serve breakfast. Other good candidates are the renovated *Keystone Hotel*, 401 Egan Drive (T 907/835-3851 or 1-888/835-0665, W www.alaskan.com/keystonehotel; ❺), which has comfortable rooms (some with bath) and a light continental breakfast; the motel-style *Downtown B&B*, 113 Galena Drive (T 907/835-2791 or 1-800/478-2791, W www.alaskaone.com/downinn; ❹); and *Blueberry Mary's*, 810 Salmonberry Way (T 907/835-5015, W www.alaska.net/~bmary; ❹), a secluded B&B a mile from town with stupendous views of Valdez Arm, comfortable rooms, a sauna, and breakfast pancakes with blueberries from the local hillside.

The Town and around

The **Valdez Museum**, 217 Egan Drive (summer Mon–Sat 9am–6pm, Sun 8am–5pm; $3), carries just the right amount of detail on the Gold Rush, glaciation, the oil pipeline that supports the town's economy, and a display on the oil spill. Its **annex**, at 436 Hazelet St (summer daily 9am–4pm; $1.50), covers the 1964 earthquake at length. For security reasons, you can no longer tour the pipeline terminal, but if you feel cheated get along to the **Video Tour of Alaska's Petroleum Industry & Pipeline Exhibit** (summer daily 9.30am, 11.30am & 1.30pm; $5) at the Community College.

You'll need transport to get to the **Maxine & Jesse Whitney Museum**, at the airport (summer daily 9am–8pm; $5), with its astounding collection of carved ivory and an assortment of dead beasts, including a couple of moose hides with Alaskan scenes burned into them by an early pioneer. If you fancy something more active, Keystone Raft and Kayak Adventures, at Mile 17 on the Richardson Highway (T 907/835-2606 or 1-800/328-8460, W www.alaskawhitewater .com), can take you **rafting** ($35) along the Lowe River as it surges through Keystone Canyon. Anadyr Adventures (T 907/835-2814 or 1-800/865-2925, W www.anadyradventures.com) rents **mountain bikes** for $8 an hour and offers **sea kayaking** along the fjord with hopes of whale encounters from $75.

While here, you should take a cruise out into Prince William Sound, principally to see the spectacular **Columbia Glacier**, nearly four miles wide at its face and towering three hundred feet above the sea. Unfortunately it is receding rapidly and the fjord is now so choked with ice that you can't get close to the face. You can see it at long range from the AMHS **ferries** running between Valdez and Whittier, but for a closer look at this calving giant go with Stan Stephens Glacier & Wildlife Cruises (℡907/835-4731 or 1-866/867-1297, Ⓦwww.stanstephenscruises.com), who pick their way through a floating icefield and point out such sights as Bligh Reef, where the *Exxon Valdez* ran aground. Choose between a six-hour cruise at $85 and the nine-hour cruise that also visits the Meares Glacier ($119).

Eating

Don't schedule a gourmet night out while in Valdez, but the **dining** selection will satisfy for the night or two you're here. Budget halibut sandwiches and salmon wedges are good from the *Halibut House*, 208 Meals Ave (℡907/835-2788), but the best all-round dining is at *Mike's Palace*, 201 N Harbor Drive (℡907/835-2365), which dishes up Italian-oriented fare along with burgers and Mexican dishes. Oil-boom survivor *The Pipeline Club*, 136 Egan Drive (℡907/835-4332), is also worth a try for top-quality steak and seafood, as well as for its lively dark bar.

Cordova and the Copper River Delta

Far quieter than Valdez, and only accessible by sea or air, **CORDOVA** is an unpretentious fishing community set in forests and mountains on the southeastern edge of the Sound. In 1906, the Irish engineer **Michael J. Heney** chose Cordova as the port from which to ship the copper mined in Kennicott (see p.1332), a hundred miles northeast, and gambled on cutting a path between two active glaciers for his proposed Copper River and Northwestern Railroad – the CR&NW – ridiculed at the time as the "Can't Run & Never Will." Nonetheless, in 1911 he spanned the Copper River with the elaborate "**Million Dollar Bridge**" and the railroad was completed. Despite the effort, the mines were exhausted just 27 years later and Cordova shifted its dependency to fishing, which itself was dealt a potentially fatal blow in 1989 with the grounding of the *Exxon Valdez*. For the next two seasons, the community reeled from the effects of the **oil spill**; since then fortunes have slowly improved.

Today the "Million Dollar Bridge," heavily battered by the 1964 earthquake, cuts a lonely figure at the end of the Copper River Highway, a 48-mile gravel road that traverses the wondrous wetlands of the **Copper River Delta**, a major breeding ground for America's migratory birds backed by the Chugach Mountains. It is a tranquil spot for fishing, bird-watching, or **hiking** along many of the excellent trails, such as the easy Saddlebag Glacier Trail which ends by Saddlebag Lake. The road ends right next to the bridge and beside the incredibly active **Childs Glacier**.

By far the best way to experience the bridge is in your own vehicle rented (for around $70 a day, unlimited mileage) from either Copper Coast Car Rentals (℡907/424-5356) or Cordova Car Rentals (℡907/424-5982, Ⓦwww.ptialaska.net/~cars) at the airport. Alternatively, Copper River and Northwest Tours (℡907/424-5356) runs a five-hour tour to the bridge for $45 including lunch (though currently only on Wednesdays).

Cordova itself has few sights; the **small boat harbor** is the core of the town's activity, particularly when the fleet is in, from May until September.

The **Cordova Historical Museum**, 620 First St (summer Mon–Sat 10am–6pm, Sun 2–4pm; rest of year Tues–Sat 1–5pm; $1 donation), has quirky exhibits on local history, including the evolution of the little **ice worm** that lives in the glaciers, and the funky festival that celebrates its existence each mid-February.

Practicalities

There is no road access to Cordova; daily **flights** from Anchorage and Juneau land at the airport twelve miles down the Copper River Highway. A **bus** runs from the airport for $12. Thrice-weekly **ferries** dock a mile north of town, though in 2005 these should be replaced by a daily **fast ferry** to Valdez and Whittier. The tiny **Chamber of Commerce** is at 404 First St (summer only Tues–Fri 10am–5am, Mon & Sat 10am–2pm; ☎907/424-7260, ⓦ www.cordovachamber.com).

Cordova has no **hostel** and the only tent **camping** close to town is at the scruffy *Odiak Camper Park* on Whitshed Road, half a mile south of town (☎907/424-6200; $18), so you might want to rent a car and camp out along the Copper River Delta.

The cheapest option in town is the very basic *Alaskan Hotel*, 600 First St (☎907/424-3299; ❷), though you may prefer the *Northern Nights Inn*, 501 Third St (☎907/424-5356; ❸–❹), or the cosy modern *Cordova Lighthouse Inn*, Nicholoff Way (☎907/424-7080; ❹), overlooking the small boat harbor.

For **food**, check out the popular *Killer Whale Café*, 507 First St (☎907/424-7733), above the Orca Bookshop, or the excellent breakfasts and gourmet pizzas at the *Cordova Lighthouse Café* below the *Cordova Lighthouse Inn*. Wash it all down afterwards with a drink at the *Alaskan Hotel*'s **bar**.

Interior and northern Alaska

Interior and northern Alaska cannot fail to live up to expectations of the "great land." For the most part it's a rolling plateau divided by the Alaska and Brooks ranges, crisscrossed by river valleys, punctuated by glaciers, and with views of imposing peaks, including ever-present Mount McKinley, the nation's highest. Even in high summer, when RVs clog the George Parks Highway, people are still hugely outnumbered by game: moose, Dall sheep, grizzly bears, and herds of caribou sweep over seemingly endless swathes of taiga (sparse birch woodland) and tundra.

Heading north from Anchorage the first essential stop is the tiny town of **Talkeetna**, which has great views of Mount McKinley and the opportunity to fly around it. The mountain is at the heart of **Denali National Park**, the jewel of the Interior. If you prefer your wilderness with fewer people and regulations, head east for the vast and untrammeled world of **Wrangell–St Elias National Park**.

Fairbanks, Alaska's second city, is diverting in its own right and serves as the hub of the North, with roads fanning out to **hot springs** and the **Dalton Highway**, threading five hundred miles to the Arctic Ocean at **Prudhoe Bay**.

Weather in the region can vary enormously from day to day, with even greater seasonal variations: in winter temperatures can drop to -50°F for days at a time, while summer days reach a sweltering 90°F. However, the major problem during the warmer months is huge mosquitoes; don't forget to bring insect repellent.

Talkeetna

A hundred miles north of Anchorage, **TALKEETNA** has a palpable small-town Alaska feel: rumor has it that this eclectic hamlet was the model for Cicely in TV's *Northern Exposure*, but to its credit Talkeetna doesn't use this as tour-bus bait. The town is lent an international flavor by the world's mountaineers, who come here to scale the 20,320-foot **Mount McKinley**, which in Alaska is usually referred to by its original Athabascan name of **Denali**, "the Great One." Whatever you choose to call it, North America's highest mountain rises from 2000ft lowlands, making it the world's tallest from base to peak (Everest et al rise from high terrain).

Though central to Denali National Park (see p.1330), the mountain is best seen from Talkeetna, where the **overlook** just south of town reveals the peak's transcendent white glow, in sharp contrast to the warm colors all around.

From mid-April to mid-July Denali climbers amass in Talkeetna to be flown to the mountain: only half of the 1200 attempting the climb each year succeed, due to extreme weather conditions. Air-taxi companies also run **flightseeing** trips ranging from a spectacular one-hour ($120) flight to the full ninety-minute grand tour ($175) completely encircling the mountain. K2 Aviation (☎907/733-2291 or 1-800/764-2291, ⓦwww.flyk2.com), the choice of most climbing expeditions, offers the widest range of options, including glacier landings (extra $50) in planes fitted with skis.

Talkeetna's famed **Moose Dropping Festival** falls on the second weekend of July; little brown balls can be purchased (with a sanitary coat of varnish) for use as earrings, necklaces, and so on, throughout the town. In addition to these highly desirable lumps of Alaskana, the festival features dancing, drinking, and a moose-dropping throwing competition and some more drinking.

Practicalities

Talkeetna is at the end of a fourteen-mile spur off the George Parks Highway, which can usually be hitched. Bus services avoid Talkeetna except for The Park Connection (daily from Anchorage; $41; ☎1-800/266-8625); Anchorage to Denali **trains** stop half a mile south of the center of Talkeetna once a day. Information is widely available from shops around town and from the **Talkeetna Ranger Station**, on B Street (summer daily 8am–6pm; ☎907/733-2231).

For a town of just three hundred, Talkeetna teems with good **accommodation**, the cheapest being central *Talkeetna Hostel International* on I Street (☎907/733-4678, ⓦwww.talkeetnahostel.com; bunks $25, rooms ❹). Dating back to 1917, the central *Talkeetna Roadhouse* (☎907/733-1351, ⓦwww.talkeetnaroadhouse.com; ❶–❹), also has bunks ($21) and bolsters its old-style atmosphere with some great home cooking and rooms with shared bathrooms. Easily the fanciest hotel hereabouts is the *Talkeetna Alaskan Lodge* (☎907/733-9500 or 1-888/959-9590, ⓦwww.talkeetnalodge.com; ❽), on the hill to the south of town. **Campers** can stay at the *Talkeetna River Park* ($12), at the western end of Main Street, but many stroll a hundred yards further west from the latter and (unofficially) pitch on the river flats.

Good places to **eat** include the bakery/diner at the *Talkeetna Roadhouse* (see above), and the *West Rib Pub & Grill*, Main Street (☎907/733-3354), which has good burgers and sandwiches. And make sure you stop for a **drink** in the wonderfully ancient *Fairview Inn* on Main Street.

Denali National Park

The six-million-acre **DENALI NATIONAL PARK**, 240 miles north of Anchorage, is named after the Athabascan word for its most famous denizen, **Mount McKinley**, which is often shrouded in cloud, and only around one-quarter of visitors actually get to see the snow-covered massif. The mountain is far from being the park's only attraction, however. A ride through Denali on a shuttle bus offers a glimpse of a vast world of tundra and taiga, glaciers, huge mountains, and abundant wildlife – the Park Service reports that 95 percent of visitors see **bears**, **caribou**, and **Dall sheep**, 82 percent moose, and over one-fifth **wolves**, along with porcupine, snowshoe hare, red foxes, and over 160 bird species.

Visiting Alaska without trying to see Denali is unthinkable for most travelers, and therein lies the park's problem. In the height of summer, the visitor center and the service hotels out on the Parks Highway are a stream of RVs, tour buses, and the like. Things pick up in the park itself, and backcountry hiking, undertaken by only a tiny fraction of visitors, remains a wonderfully solitary experience.

In **winter**, Denali is transformed into a ghostly, snow-covered world. Motorized vehicles are banned and transportation, even for park personnel, is by snowshoe, skis, or dogsled as temperatures dive and northern lights glitter over the snows.

Getting to the park

Driving to Denali Park takes about five hours from Anchorage, three from Fairbanks, and **hitching** is quite easy with twenty hours of summer daylight. A couple of **bus** companies run services from Anchorage to Fairbanks via Denali: Alaska Trails & Tours (☎1-888/600-6001, ⓦwww.alaskashuttle.com) charges $59 from Anchorage and $39 from Fairbanks. One Denali-bound **train** a day leaves Anchorage (8.15am; $125) and Fairbanks (8.15am; $50), depositing you at 4pm and noon respectively at the train station a mile and a half inside the park entrance. **Park entry** costs $5 per person and is valid for a week.

Sightseeing, hiking, and other activities

To preserve flora and fauna, the only vehicles allowed on Denali's narrow, unpaved ninety-mile road are a few tour buses and green **shuttle buses**, for which you should reserve well in advance (☎907/622-7275 or 1-800/622-7275). You can try for a seat up to two days in advance from the **visitor access center** (May–Sept daily 7am–8pm; ☎907/683-1266), just inside the park entrance, where you can pick up a free copy of the *Denali Alpenglow* paper and a wide range of literature, and join ranger-led activities including short hikes and the popular, and free, dogsled demonstration held daily at 10am, 2pm, and 4pm.

Shuttle buses run to either the **Eielson Visitor Center** at Mile 66 ($23), where rangers lead one-hour tundra tours each day at 1.30pm, or to the aptly named **Wonder Lake** at Mile 84 ($31); roundtrips take about eight and ten hours respectively. The shuttle drivers don't give guided tours, but with forty pairs of watchful eyes on board, you're almost guaranteed to see the big mammals. You can also hop off at any point for a day-hike (no permits required) and return to the road to flag down the next bus back, if it has room. Buses run 6 to 8 times daily, and there are also buses used mainly by campers that will pick up stragglers at the end of the day.

Overnight backcountry camping is the best way to appreciate Denali's scenery and its inhabitants. Don't expect it to be easy though, as there are no formal trails, and with thick spongy tundra and frequent river crossings even hardy hikers find themselves limited to five miles a day. The park is divided into 43 units and only a designated number of hikers is allowed into each section at a time. Free permits are available, one day in advance, from the visitor center's **Backcountry Desk** (daily 7am–8pm), though high demand means you should be prepared to hike in the less popular areas. The Backcountry Desk will also teach you about avoiding run-ins with bears and issue you with bear-resistant containers for food storage. Special camper buses reserved for those with campground or backcountry permits cost $22.50. It's not a bad idea to reconnoitre the park on a full-day bus trip in order to choose where you might like to hike on subsequent days. If there's room, buses also carry bikes; cyclists can be dropped off wherever they like, but are obliged to keep to the road.

An alternative to going it alone is to join a **narrated tour** (T 1-800/276-7234) along the park road: either the three-hour Natural History Tour ($41) or the full-day Tundra Wildlife Tour ($76), which penetrates as far as Mile 53, stopping frequently to observe wildlife.

Just outside the park entrance, several **rafting** companies offer two-hour trips down the Nenana River: all offer a gentle "scenic float" and an eleven-mile "Canyon Run" through Class III and IV rapids – they cost around $60 individually and $85 for a joint run. Denali Outdoor Center (T 907/683-1925 or 1-888/303-1925, W www.denalioutdoorcenter.com) charges a couple of dollars more than some of the others, but offers a quality experience.

Practicalities

With the exception of several exclusive lodges deep in the heart of the park, there are no hotels in Denali, so your choice is between camping, the $130-a-night gaggle of summer-only hotels a mile north of the park entrance, or the cheaper offerings either ten miles further north in the little coal-mining town of **HEALY**, or spots a few miles south along the George Parks Highway. The cheapest place by the park entrance is the primitive *McKinley Denali Cabins*, Mile 238.5 (T 907/683-2733; ❷–❺), effectively tents with a mattress but no heat or electricity – charged at $32 for one, up to $48 for four, plus some more salubrious cabins. Next up is *Denali Sourdough Cabins* (T 907/683-2773; ❺), whose comfy cabins are surrounded by spruce trees.

The only real hostel hereabouts is the excellent *Denali Mountain Morning Hostel and Lodge*, Mile 224, thirteen miles south (T 907/683-7503, W www.hostelalaska.com; cabins ❹, rooms ❸, bunks ❶), set in wooded seclusion and with a bargain shuttle service ($3 a day) to the park. Accommodation is in spacious dorms ($23) or separate cabins, there's an efficient kitchen, all manner of games, and the hosts will do everything to facilitate your Denali visit. In Healy there's the high-quality *Motel Nord Haven*, Mile 249.5 Parks Hwy (T 907/683-4500 or 1-800/683-4501, W www.motelnordhaven.com; ❻), and the lovely *Earth Song Lodge*, Mile 4, Stampede Rd (T 907/683-2863, W www.earthsonglodge.com; ❺), has a cluster of cabins with great mountain views and a café on site.

Camping is the best way to experience Denali up close, with most of the park's six campgrounds open from mid-May to mid-September. The best sites are at **Wonder Lake** ($16) with a stunning view of McKinley; failing that, **Igloo Creek** ($9) is good for spotting Dall sheep, while **Riley Creek** ($12–18) near the entrance is open year-round. All sites are bookable at the main visitor center or on T 1-800/622-7275. If you don't do this you may have to wait a day or two to get a spot. The best alternative is *Denali Grizzly Bear Cabins & Campground*, Mile 231.1, seven miles south of Denali (T 907/683-2696, W www.denalligrizzlybear.com; ❶–❻), set in the trees close to the Nenana River with a wide variety of attractive cabins all around.

Eating is expensive hereabouts, with only a limited range of grocery stores for those preparing their own meals, and a small selection of fairly pricey restaurants close to the park entrance, such as the *Black Bear Coffee House* (☎907/683-1656), serving light meals; and *Lynx Creek Pizza and Pub* (☎907/683-2548), where the menu includes pasta dishes and Mexican specialties, as well as pizza and draft microbrews.

Wrangell-St Elias National Park

As Denali becomes more crowded, people are increasingly making the trip to more out-of-the-way **WRANGELL-ST ELIAS NATIONAL PARK** in the extreme southeast corner of the Interior. Here, four of the continent's great mountain ranges – the Wrangell, St Elias, Chugach, and Alaska – cramp up against each other, and even the usually reserved National Park Service literature breaks ranks by saying, "Incredible. You have to see Wrangell-St Elias . . . to believe it – and even then you won't be so sure." Everything is writ large: glacier after enormous glacier, canyon after dizzying canyon, and nine of the sixteen highest peaks in the US, all laced together by braided rivers and idyllic lakes where mountain goats, Dall sheep, bears, moose, and caribou roam.

The first whites in the area came in search of gold but instead hit upon one of the continent's richest copper deposits. The mines closed in 1938, after 27 frantic years of production, and today **Kennicott**, with over thirty creaking, disused buildings, is a virtual ghost town. You can visit the mill complex on fascinating two-hour **walking tours** run by St Elias Alpine Guides ($25; ☎1-888/933-5427, ⓦwww.steliasguides.com), which is based in nearby **McCarthy**, the main social hub. They also run a number of hikes, ice-climbing trips, mountain-bike rides, raft trips, and even glacier skiing out into what is essentially a trailless park.

Practicalities

Half the fun is getting to McCarthy along 58 rugged miles of the McCarthy Road, which follows the trackbed of the long abandoned railroad that once linked the Kennicott mill to the port at Cordova. Take it slow and stop often to admire the scenery and abandoned trestle bridges. At the end of the road you cross the Kennicott River on a footbridge and continue half a mile to McCarthy on foot, from where a shuttle bus runs along the rough five-mile dirt road to Kennicott. Hitching along the McCarthy Road can be a hit-or-miss affair; if you haven't got a vehicle you can go with Backcountry Connections (summer Mon–Sat; ☎907/822-5292 or 1-866/582-5292, ⓦwww.alaska-backcountry-tours.com), who charge $115 roundtrip from Glennallen.

Accommodation around McCarthy and Kennicott isn't cheap, though you can **camp** for a modest fee at a new Park Service site on the edge of McCarthy close to the base of the glacier. There are two hostels: *Kennicott River Lodge and Hostel* (☎907/554-4441, ⓦwww.ptialaska.net/~grosswlr; ❸), near the road end, has four-bunk cabins ($28 per person) and nice common areas; *Lancaster's Backpacking Hotel*, in McCarthy (☎907/554-4402, ⓦwww.mccarthylodge .com; ❸) has simple shared-bath rooms costing $40 for one, $60 for two. Showers are an extra $6. The associated *Ma Johnson Hotel/McCarthy Lodge* (☎907/554-4402; ❻) is very pleasant and atmospheric, and in Kennicott there's the upscale *Kennicott Glacier Lodge* (☎907/554-4477, ⓦwww.kennicottlodge .com; ❼), which also has the town's one restaurant (reserve for dinner). The park's **visitor center** is just south of Glennallen at Mile 107 on the Richardson Highway (summer daily 8am–6pm; ☎907/822-7440, ⓦwww.nps.gov/wrst).

Fairbanks

FAIRBANKS, 358 miles north of Anchorage, is at the end of the Alaska Highway from Canada and definitely at the end of the road for most tourists. Though flat and somewhat bland, its central location makes a great base for exploring a hinterland of gold mines and hot springs, and a staging point for both the tiny villages scattered around the surrounding wilderness, and for journeys along the **Dalton Highway** (aka the "Haul Road") to the Arctic Ocean oil community of **Prudhoe Bay**.

Alaska's second most populous town was founded accidentally, in 1901, when a steamship carrying E.T. Barnette, a merchant with all his wares on board, ran aground in the shallows of the Chena River. Unable to transport the supplies he was carrying, Barnette set up shop in the wilderness and catered to the few trappers and prospectors trying their luck in the area. The following year, with the beginnings of the **Gold Rush**, a tent city sprang up on the site, and Barnette made a mint. In 1908, at the height of the gold stampede, Fairbanks had a population of 18,500, but by 1920 the population had dwindled to only 1100. To thwart possible Japanese attacks during World War II, several huge **military bases** were built and the population rebounded, getting a further boost in the mid-1970s when it became the transportation center for the **trans–Alaska pipeline** project: construction and other oil-related activities brought a rush of workers seeking wages of up to $1500 per week and the population reached an all-time high. The city's economy dropped dramatically with the oil crash, and unemployment hit twenty percent before government spending put the city back on track.

The spectacular **aurora borealis** is a major winter attraction, as is the **Ice Festival** in mid-March, with its ice-sculpting competition and open-sled dog race on the frozen downtown streets. Summer visitors should try to catch the three-day **World Eskimo–Indian Olympics** in mid-July, when contestants from around the state compete in the standard dance, art, and sports competitions, as well as some unusual ones like ear-pulling, knuckle hop, high kick, and the blanket toss, where age and wisdom often defeat youth and strength.

Fairbanks suffers remarkable extremes of climate, with winter temperatures dropping to -70°F and summer highs topping 90°F. Proximity to the Arctic Circle means over 21 hours of sunlight in midsummer, when midnight baseball games take place under natural light, and 2am bar evacuees are confronted by bright sunshine.

Arrival, information, and getting around

Alaska Airlines fly frequently from Anchorage to **Fairbanks Airport**, four miles southwest of downtown; the MACS **bus** Yellow Line (Mon–Sat; $1.50) runs downtown, but the long wait between services means you'll probably want to grab a **taxi** (around $15). The airport is also a gateway for flights into the bush; Frontier Flying Service (℡907/474-0011 or 1-800/478-6779, ⓦwww.frontierflying.com) operates a reliable service. From 2004 the daily **trains** from Anchorage will stop beside the Johanen Expressway inconveniently distant from downtown, though there will hopefully be some bus or shuttle service. It is far cheaper to get here by bus with Alaska Trails & Tours (℡1-888/600-6001, ⓦwww.alaskashuttle.com), who drop off at the visitor center and major hostels and hotels.

The best way to get around is by car, but the five **bus lines**, run by MACS (℡907/459-1011), provide a reasonable service; call for information or collect

15

ALASKA | Fairbanks

a schedule from the visitor center (see below). Among the companies that can whisk you off into the surrounding bush and fly you to the **Arctic Circle**, the widest choice is with the Northern Alaska Tour Company (℡907/474-8600, ⓦwww.northernalaska.com).

The **visitor center**, at 550 First Ave (summer daily 8am–8pm; rest of year Mon–Fri 8am–5pm; ℡907/456-5774 or 1-800/327-5774, ⓦwww.explore-fairbanks.com), carries a vast amount of information on lodging and activities. For information on the area's parks, including Denali, stop by the useful **Alaska Public Land Information Center** (APLIC) at 250 N Cushman St (summer daily 9am–6pm; rest of year Tues–Sat 10am–6pm; ℡907/456-0527, ⓦwww.nps.gov/aplic).

Accommodation

The motels and hotels in downtown Fairbanks tend to be either quite pricey or pretty dodgy. **B&B**s are plentiful, with rooms from $75 a night; the visitor center offers free phone calls and all the brochures. Thankfully there are a couple of good hostels, and for campers there's the tranquil and convenient *Tanana Valley Campground*, 1800 College Rd at Aurora Drive (mid-May to mid-Sept; ℡907/456-7956; $9), on the MACS bus Red line and with free bikes for guests to use.

Ah, Rose Marie 302 Cowles St at 3rd Ave ℡907/456-2040, ⓦwww.akpub.com/akbbrv/ahrose. Small but well-run and justly popular B&B where a hearty breakfast is served on the glassed-in veranda. ❹

Billie's Backpackers 2895 Mack Rd ℡907/479-2034, ⓦwww.alaskahostel.com. Welcoming though somewhat cramped hostel, in a nice area and handily placed on the bus route between downtown and the university. Bikes and Internet access available. Bunks $22, camping $10. ❶

Fairbanks Hotel 517 3rd Ave ℡907/456-6411, ⓦwww.fbxhotl.com. Good-value downtown hotel done in ersatz Miami Beach Deco style, with cheerily decorated rooms each with cable TV and a washstand. Shared bath ❹, private bath ❺

Golden North Motel 4888 Old Airport Way ℡1-800/447-1910, ⓦwww.goldennorthmotel.com. Spotlessly clean motel near the airport with cable TV and continental breakfast. Courtesy pickups are available, but inconveniently located unless you have your own wheels. ❹

GoNorth Base Camp 3500 Davis Rd ℡907/479-7272, ⓦwww.paratours.net. A kind of outdoors hostel in a forested area with accommodation in large fixed tents with five beds ($20; bring a sleeping bag). Just one communal area means it can be a little noisy. Bikes available for $20 a day.

Midge's Birch Lane B&B 4335 Birch Lane ℡907/388-8084 or 1-800/479-4895, ⓦwww.alaskaone.com/midgebb. Relaxed, welcoming, and spacious house in the quiet University district. Rooms with and without private bathrooms. ❹

Minnie Street B&B Inn 345 Minnie St ℡907/456-1802 or 1-888/456-1849, ⓦwww.minniestreetbandb.com. Top-line B&B with every luxury taken to the nth degree, plus in-room phones with dataports, a spacious deck and a barbecue area. One room has a Jacuzzi and there's a full breakfast. Room with Jacuzzi ❼, private bath ❻, shared bath ❺

The Town

Besides the visitor centers, the main point of interest **downtown** is the small **Fairbanks Community Museum**, 450 Cushman St at 5th Avenue (summer Mon–Sat 10am–6pm, Sun noon–4pm; donation appreciated), containing locally donated trapping, mining, and dogsled racing equipment. The museum also acts as the public face of the **Yukon Quest** dogsled race – a grueling thousand-mile marathon between Fairbanks and Whitehorse – selling related books, videos, and T-shirts. A similarly wintry theme is pursued at the **Ice Museum**, 500 2nd Ave at Lacey Street (summer daily 10am–6pm; $8), a year-round chance to get a taste of the annual Ice Sculpting competition by way of a slide show and walk-in refrigerators housing some small ice carvings.

A couple of miles west on the banks of the Chena River, the **Pioneerland** complex celebrates Alaskan history in a very touristy, but not unpleasant way; admission is free, though different attractions charge small fees. Two reasonable **museums** cover the early pioneering days, and a miniature railway encircles the entire park; there's plenty here for the kids to do.

From the downtown area, College Road heads west past **Creamer's Field**, thick with sandhill cranes and Canada geese, especially in spring and fall. Further out, the **University of Alaska Fairbanks (UAF) Museum** (summer daily 9am–7pm; rest of year closing times vary; $5; ☎907/474-7505) occupies a corner of the attractive campus on the northeastern edge of town and houses some of the state's best examples of Native Alaskan artifacts and pioneer relics, as well as natural and human history displays. Currently being expanded, it should soon be even better.

Unashamedly touristy but fun and very popular is a four-hour **cruise** down the Chena River on the "Riverboat Discovery" ($45; ☎907/479-6673), which includes a visit to a mock Native village.

Eating and nightlife

Fairbanks' **eating** options are varied, with good Thai particularly prevalent. They're also well scattered, with downtown and College Road, toward the university, having the greatest concentrations. Nowhere downtown sells groceries: the closest is Fred Meyer at the eastern end of College Road. Fairbanks has its decent **nightspots**, though none lie in hard-drinking downtown.

Alaska Coffee Roasting Co. West Valley Plaza, 4001 Geist Rd ☎907/457-5282. Fairbanks' best coffee, roasted daily on the premises served in a cozy café hung with carpets and woodcarvings from the owner's native Ethiopia. There's a good selection of wraps, cakes, and muffins, too.

Blue Loon Mile 353.5 Parks Hwy ☎907/457-5666, ⓦwww.theblueloon.com. Late-closing hotspot five miles west of Fairbanks that's always good for a convivial drink. Hosts local and touring bands (sometimes a DJ) several nights a week, and screens cult and art-house movies. Closed Mon.

The Diner 244 Illinois St ☎907/451-0613. Reliable joint serving diner fare cooked to perfection at good prices.

Gambardella's Pasta Bella 706 2nd Ave, downtown ☎907/456-3417. Fairbanks' best Italian and not wildly expensive, with a pleasant outdoor area for those endless summer evenings.

Gulliver's Books Café 3525 College Rd ☎907/474-9574. Pleasant spot above a bookstore, serving chicken tarragon wraps, pesto turkey melts, bagels, biscotti, and coffee all at reasonable prices, and offering free Internet access to boot.

Hot Tamale 112 N Turner Rd ☎907/457-8350. Authentic downtown Mexican decorated in a kind of "cantina kitsch" style with a full Mexican menu

though particularly noted for their all-you-care-to-eat $10 buffet lunch and dinner.

Howling Dog Saloon Mile 11 Old Steese Hwy, Fox ☎907/457-8780. An inconvenient eleven miles north of town, but perhaps the best bar in the north – unassuming, unpretentious, and fun. Live rock and R&B bands perform and it's the ideal place to play volleyball under the midnight sun.

The Marlin 3412 College Rd ☎907/479-4646. Poky wood-paneled cellar bar that defines the cutting edge of Fairbanks' music scene with live bands – blues, jazz, and rock – playing most evenings from around 9pm and only a small cover charge, if any.

Pump House Mile 1.3 Chena Pump Rd ☎907/479-8452. A local favorite in a historic pumphouse, stuffed with gold-mining paraphernalia and set by the Chena River with a deck to watch river life go by. Great for steak, seafood, and burgers, and also pulls in a substantial drinking crowd.

Thai House 526 5th Ave, downtown ☎907/452-6123. A small but ever-popular restaurant serving the usual range of Thai dishes, but all done to perfection and at very modest prices for around $9. The green and red curries with zucchini, peas, and peppers are especially good. Closed Sun.

Around Fairbanks: two hot springs

Chena Hot Springs, the most accessible and developed resort in the area, stands in a clearing sixty miles east of Fairbanks amid a wonderfully bucolic swath of

The Northern Lights

The **aurora borealis**, or "Northern Lights," an ethereal display of light in the upper-most atmosphere, give their brightest and most colorful displays in the sky above Fairbanks. For up to one hundred winter nights, the sky appears to shimmer with dancing curtains of color ranging from luminescent greens to fantastic veils that run the full spectrum. Named after the Roman goddess of dawn, the aurora are caused by an interaction between the earth's magnetic field and the **solar wind**, an invisible stream of charged electrons and protons continually blown out into space by the innate violence of the sun. The earth deflects the solar wind like a rock in a stream, with the energy released at the magnetic poles – much like a neon sign.

The Northern Lights are at their most dazzling from December to March, when nights are longest and the sky darkest, but late September can be good for summer visitors. They are pretty much visible everywhere, but the further north is better, especially around Fairbanks.

muskeg (grassy swampland) and forest traversed by good hiking trails and teeming with moose. Nonguests can use the hot pools and large outdoor "rock pool" for $10 a day, or stay at the fully equipped resort (℡907/452-7867 or 1-800/478-4681, Ⓦ www.chenahotsprings.com; ❹–❻), where camping costs $20. The resort also rents out canoes and mountain bikes, as well as offering rafting float trips.

The traditional favorite for folks from Fairbanks has been the more rustic **Arctic Circle Hot Springs**, 130 miles northeast of the city along scenic Steese Highway. Though closed in 2003 they hope to reopen in 2004. Call first as it is a long drive through pristine scenery beside the Chatanika River to the tiny mining village of **Central**, then eight miles to the resort (℡907/520-5113; ❶–❹), where you can camp, take a dorm bed, or stay in deluxe rooms.

The Dalton Highway

Built in the 1970s to service the **trans–Alaska pipeline**, the mostly gravel-surfaced **Dalton Highway**, or Haul Road, runs from Fairbanks five hundred miles to the oil facility of Prudhoe Bay on Alaska's north coast, some three hundred miles beyond the Arctic Circle. It is a long, bumpy, and demanding drive, so be prepared with spare tires, gas, provisions, and, ideally, a sturdy four-wheel-drive vehicle: most regular rentals aren't permitted up here. Just beyond the Fairbanks city limits you start to get glimpses of the pipeline snaking up hills and in and out of the ground. At 188 miles, a sign announces that you've just crossed the **Arctic Circle**. The **Northern Alaska Tour Company** (℡907/474 8600 or 1-800/474-1986, Ⓦ www.northernalaska.com) will drive you up in a minibus and fly you back down to Fairbanks for around $250 (you can save over $100 by taking the minibus back, but it makes for a long day and you miss out on the flight).

Most people are happy to return south at this point, but the highway plugs on through increasingly barren territory, finally dispensing with trees as you climb through the still largely unmapped and unexplored **Brooks Range**, a 9000ft chain mostly held within the **Gates of the Arctic** National Park. From the crest at Atigun Pass you descend through two hundred miles of grand glaciated valleys and blasted arctic plains to the end of the road at dead-boring **Deadhorse**. You can't stroll by the ocean or camp here, so your choices are confined to staying in one of the $120-per-night hotels and taking a $37 tour past the adjacent – and off-limits – **Prudhoe Bay** oil facility to the Arctic Ocean where you can dip your toe or go for the full body immersion.

By far the best way to do it is with Northern Alaska, which runs a three-day fly/drive tour to Prudhoe Bay for around $750.

Hawaii

AL - ALABAMA	IN - INDIANA	MN - MINNESOTA	RI - RHODE ISLAND
AR - ARKANSAS	LA - LOUISIANA	MS - MISSISSIPPI	SC - SOUTH CAROLINA
CT - CONNECTICUT	MA - MASSACHUSETTS	NC - NORTH CAROLINA	VA - VIRGINIA
DE - DELAWARE	MD - MARYLAND	NH - NEW HAMPSHIRE	VT - VERMONT
FL - FLORIDA	ME - MAINE	NJ - NEW JERSEY	WI - WISCONSIN
IL - ILLINOIS	MI - MICHIGAN	PA - PENNSYLVANIA	WV - WEST VIRGINIA

* **Waikiki Beach, Oahu**
Learn to surf, or just sip
a cocktail, on the world's
most famous beach. See
p.1346

* **Pearl Harbor, Oahu**
Relive December 7, 1941
– the "day that will live in
infamy" – by visiting the
sunken USS *Arizona*.
See p.1347

* **Kilauea Eruption, Big
Island** The Big Island
gets bigger day by day,
thanks to the spectacu-
lar eruption of its
youngest volcano,
Kilauea. See p.1359

* **Downhill biking, Maui**
Freewheel forty miles

down the slopes of
Maui's mighty Haleakala
volcano. See p.1361

* **Lahaina, Maui** This former whaling port ranks
among the most charac-
terful historic towns in
Hawaii. See p.1362

* **Lumahai Beach, Kauai**
This superb, if danger-
ous, beach has featured
in countless movies. See
p.1368

* **Kalalau Trail, Kauai** The
magnificent Na Pali
coastline of Kauai can
be admired from one of
the world's greatest hik-
ing trails. See p.1368

16

Hawaii

With their fiery volcanoes, palm-fringed beaches, verdant valleys, glorious rainbows, and awesome cliffs, the islands of **HAWAII** boast some of the most spectacularly beautiful scenery on earth. However, despite their isolation, two thousand miles out in the Pacific, they belong very definitely to the United States. If you expect your South Seas idyll to be completely unspoiled, forget it; the fantasy of a dream holiday in Paradise remains firmly rooted in the creature comforts of home. Pulling in up to seven million tourists per year, including honeymooners from all over the world, frequent fliers cashing in their mileage, and almost two million Japanese, the islands can seem at times like a gigantic theme park.

Honolulu, on **Oahu**, is by far the largest city of the fiftieth state; the island's resort annex of Wikiki is also the main tourist center. The biggest island, **Hawaii** itself, is known as the **Big Island** in a vain attempt to avoid confusion. **Maui** and **Kauai** also attract mass tourism, while smaller **Molokai** remains far quieter. All the islands share a similar topography and **climate**. Ocean winds shed their rain on the northeast, **windward** coast, keeping it wet and green; the southwest, **leeward** (or "Kona") coasts can be almost barren, and so make ideal locations for big resorts. While temperatures remain consistent throughout the year at between 70°F and 85°F, rainfall is heaviest from December to March. That is nonetheless the most popular time to visit, enabling mid- to upper-range hotels to add a premium of at least $30 per night to their standard room rates. A visit to Hawaii doesn't have to cost a fortune, however; there are plenty of **budget** facilities if you know where to look. The one major expense you really can't avoid, except possibly on Oahu, is car rental – rates are very reasonable, but gas is pricey.

Some history

Each of the Hawaiian islands was forced up like a vast mass of candle drippings by submarine volcanic action, all fueled by the same "hot spot," which has remained stationary as the Pacific plate drifted above. The process continues at Kilauea on the Big Island, where lava explodes into the sea to add new land day by day, while the oldest islands are now mere atolls way to the northwest. Until two thousand years ago, these unknown specks were populated only by what few organisms had been carried here by wind or wave. The first known human inhabitants were the **Polynesians**, who arrived in two principal migrations: one from the Marquesas in the eighth century, and another from Tahiti four or five hundred years later.

No Western ship chanced upon Hawaii until **Captain Cook** arrived at Kauai in 1778. He was amazed to find a civilization sharing a culture – and

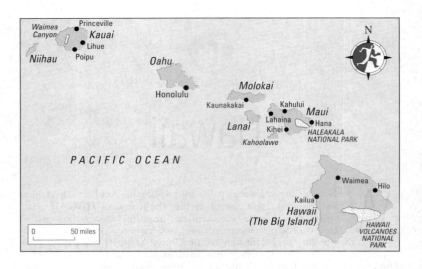

language – with the peoples of the South Pacific. The Hawaiians, too, were amazed, having long since lost contact with the outside world. Although they killed Cook himself in Hawaii in 1779 (see p.1357), he had started an irreversible process of change. The first Polynesians had brought the plants and animals necessary to create a self-sufficient way of life. Westerners took things further, and in reshaping the islands to suit their needs decimated most of the indigenous flora and fauna – as well as the Hawaiians themselves. Cook's men estimated that there were a million islanders; the population today is roughly the same, but perhaps eight thousand **pure-blood Hawaiians** are left.

As well as bringing venereal and other diseases, Cook's voyage opened the fur trade between the Pacific Northwest and China. Passing ships traded arms to the Hawaiians, and within a few years, **Kamehameha** became the first king to unite all the islands. The sudden advent of capitalism was devastating. When the fur traders realized that Hawaiian **sandalwood** fetched enormous prices in China, the mass of the population abandoned taro-farming and fishing to capitalize on the sandalwood trade.

With the dislocation of traditional ways, Hawaiian **religion** fell apart. After the death of Kamehameha in 1819, the female regent Kaahumanu set out to break the **kapu** (taboo) system that held society together. Her public defiance of the injunctions forbidding women to eat alongside men, or to eat bananas or pork, threw the islands into moral anarchy – just as the first Puritan **missionaries** arrived from New England in 1820. Their wholehearted capitalism and harsh strictures on the easygoing Hawaiian lifestyle might have been calculated to compound the chaos. White advisers and ministers soon dominated the government, and the children of the missionaries became Hawaii's wealthiest and most powerful class.

Although the Civil War severely disrupted **whaling** – which with the sandalwood forests denuded had become the island's main source of revenue – it triggered a Hawaiian **sugar** boom that replaced Confederate sugar in the markets of the north. From then on, the machinations of the sugar industry moved Hawaii inexorably towards **annexation** by the US. In 1887 an all-white group of "concerned businessmen" forced King David Kalakaua to surrender power to an assembly elected by property-owners (of any nationality) rather than citizens. When, after his death, his sister Liliuokalani announced her desire to proclaim a new constitution, the businessmen called in the US warship *Boston* and declared a provisional government. US President Cleveland (a Democrat) responded that "Hawaii was taken possession of by the United States forces without the consent or wish of the government of the islands . . . (It) was wholly without justification . . . not merely a wrong but a disgrace." The provisional government found defenders in the Republican US Congress, however, and declared itself a republic on July 4, 1894.

On August 12, 1898, Hawaii was formally **annexed** as a territory of the United States. At this point there was no question of Hawaii becoming a state; the whites were outnumbered ten to one, and had no desire to afford the natives the protection of US labor laws, let alone to give them the vote. Consequently, Hawaii was, for the first half of the twentieth century, the virtual fiefdom of the **Big Five**, conglomerations started by the missionary families and rooted in their massive landholdings. By controlling agriculture, they also dominated transportation, banks, utilities, insurance – and government. The inevitable integration of Hawaii into the American mainstream was hastened by its crucial role in the war against Japan, and the expansion of tourism thereafter. The islands finally became the fiftieth of the United States in 1959, after a plebiscite showed a seventeen-to-one majority in favor. The only group to oppose statehood were the few remaining native Hawaiians.

Support has been growing over the last couple of decades for the concept of **Hawaiian sovereignty**, on the basis that those of Hawaiian descent should gain at least the rights already held by Native American nations on the mainland. In 1993, the US Congress and President Clinton issued a formal apology to native Hawaiians "on the occasion of the 100th anniversary of the illegal overthrow of the Kingdom of Hawaii"; debate rages as to what form restitution might take, with some campaigners arguing for a complete restoration of **independence**.

Modern Hawaii

Roughly sixty percent of the million-plus modern Hawaiians were born here. Around one-third are Caucasian (many of them US military personnel), one-third Japanese, and one-sixth Filipino, with 200,000 claiming at least some Hawaiian ancestry. The traditional reliance on agriculture seems to be in terminal decline, with sugar and pineapple plantations closing one after the other, and the need to import virtually all the basics of life resulting in an extraordinarily high **cost of living**.

Visitors in search of **ancient Hawaii** will find that few vestiges remain. What is presented as "historic" usually postdates the missionary impact. Although the ruins of temples (*heiaus*) to the old gods still stand in some places – notably on the Big Island – and committed campaigners work to revive traditional philosophies, the "old towns" are pure nineteenth-century Americana, with false-front stores and raised wooden boardwalks. The two biggest **festivals** are the Big Island's week-long **Merrie Monarch Festival**, honoring King David Kalakaua (mid-April), and the statewide **King Kamehameha** events (around June 11). Authentic **hula** dancing is a powerful art form, but you're most likely to encounter it bastardized in a **luau**. Primarily tourist money-spinners, these "traditional feasts" provide an opportunity to sample Hawaiian **foods** such as *kalua* pig, baked underground, and local fish such as *ono*, *ahi*, *mahi mahi*, and *lomi-lomi* (raw salmon). *Poi* – a paste made from mashed taro root – remains a staple of the diet, much as it was when one of Captain Cook's men described it as "a disagreeable mess."

The Hawaiian **language** endures primarily in place names and music. At first glance it looks unpronounceable – especially as it is written using a mere twelve letters (the five vowels, plus *h, k, l, m, n, p*, and *w*) – but usually, each letter is enunciated individually, and long words often break down into repeated sounds, such as "*meha-meha*" in "Kamehameha." Hawaii itself is more correctly written (and pronounced) *Hawai'i*, but for visual clarity we've omitted the glottal stops in this book.

Getting to and around Hawaii

Honolulu, just under six hours by plane from the US West Coast, is one of the world's busiest centers for air traffic; return fares from **LA**, **San Francisco**, and **Seattle** start at around $350. There are also direct flights from the mainland to Maui, the Big Island, and Kauai. Many flights to the US from **Australia** – such as those on Continental – include free stopovers in Hawaii. **European** travelers should buy all-inclusive tickets from Europe.

The principal **inter-island carriers** are Hawaiian Airlines (℡808/835-3700 or 1-800/367-5320, ⓦwww.hawaiianair.com) and Aloha Air (℡808/484-1111 or 1-877/879-2564, ⓦwww.alohaairlines.com), together with its subsidiary Island Air (℡808/484-2222 or 1-800/323-3345). They connect all the major islands several times per day, with standard one-way fares of around $85. Discount travel agents, and virtually all resorts, hotels, B&B agencies, and even hostels in Hawaii can arrange discounts on inter-island flights.

All the airports have car rental outlets; with the exception of Oahu, however, **bus** services on the islands barely exist.

Oahu

Three quarters of Hawaii's population live on **OAHU**, which has monopolized the islands' trade and tourism since the first European sailors realized that **Honolulu** offered the safest in-shore anchorage for thousands of miles of ocean. Over eighty percent of visitors to Hawaii still arrive in Honolulu – albeit by air now, rather than by sea – and most remain for their entire vacation. Oahu effectively confines tourists to the tower-block enclave of **Waikiki**, just east of downtown Honolulu; there are few rooms anywhere else. In much the same way, the **military** are closeted away in relatively inconspicuous camps. On any given day, the numbers of military personnel and tourists on Oahu are roughly the same.

Overcrowding and rampant development mean Oahu can't be recommended over the **Neighbor Islands** (as the other Hawaiian islands are known), but it can still give a real flavor of Hawaii. Oahu has some excellent **beaches**, with those on the north shore a haven for **surfers** and campers, and the **cliffs** of the windward side are awesome.

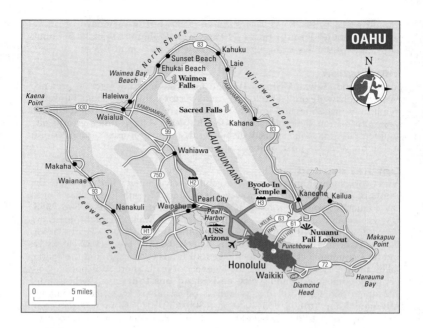

Honolulu

Until the Europeans came, **HONOLULU** was insignificant; soon so many foreign ships were frequenting its waters that it had become Kamehameha's capital, and it remains the economic center of the archipelago. While the city covers a long (if narrow) strip of southern Oahu, **downtown** is a manageable size, and a lot quieter than its glamorous image might suggest. The tourist hotels, and most of Honolulu's hustle, are concentrated among the skyscrapers of very distinct **Waikiki**, a couple of miles east.

The setting is beautiful, right on the Pacific and backed by dramatic cliffs and the extinct volcanoes of **Punchbowl** (a military cemetery) and **Diamond Head**; but then beauty is not so rare a commodity on Hawaii, and you can see this sort of scenery in plenty of other places without a city in the middle of it. What attracts most visitors to stay in Honolulu, and especially Waikiki, is the sheer **hedonism** of shopping, eating, and generally hanging out in the sun. It's also the center of an exemplary **public transportation** system that facilitates exploration of the whole island.

Arrival, information, and getting around

The runways of Honolulu's **International Airport**, just west of downtown, extend out to sea on a coral reef. **Car rental** outlets abound on the island, but a car is not especially desirable in Honolulu, what with city traffic and hefty parking fees in Waikiki. The nine-mile (not at all scenic) drive to Waikiki takes anything from 25 to 75 minutes; the Airport-Waikiki Shuttle (one way $7, roundtrip $12; ☎808/839-0911) is one of many **shuttle services** that run to any Waikiki hotel. Regular **buses #19** and **#20** also head to Waikiki, but don't allow large bags, cases, or backpacks. A **taxi** will cost around $25.

Information

Although the **Hawaii Visitors Bureau** maintains a strong Internet presence (ⓦ www.gohawaii.com), it no longer runs a visitor center in Waikiki. However, free listings magazines and leaflets are everywhere you turn, and all the hotels have information desks. Kiosks around Kalakaua Avenue offer greatly discounted rates for island tours, helicopter rides, dinner cruises, surfing lessons, and so on. Waikiki's **post office** is at 330 Saratoga Rd.

Getting around

A network of over sixty **bus** routes, collectively named TheBus, covers the whole of Oahu. All journeys, however long, cost $2, with free transfers onto any connecting route if you ask as you board (information ☎808/848-5555, ⓦ www.thebus.org). The most popular routes with Waikiki-based tourists are **#2** to downtown, **#8** to Ala Moana Shopping Center, **#20** to Pearl Harbor, **#22** to Hanauma Bay, and the bargain "**Circle Island**" buses (#52 clockwise and **#55** counterclockwise), which take four hours to loop around the central valley and the east coast, passing the legendary North Shore surf spots.

Among companies running **city and island bus tours**, for anything from $22 up to $65 for a full day, as well as off-island packages, are Polynesian Adventure Tours (☎808/833-3000 or 1-800/622-3011, ⓦ www.polyad.com) and Roberts (☎808/539-9400 or 1-800/831-5541, ⓦ www.roberts-hawaii.com).

Accommodation

All the accommodation listed below is in or near **Waikiki**; very little is available in central Honolulu. Waikiki accommodation covers a wide range, and the highest rates will bring absolute luxury, but it's possible to find comfortable lodging for much less. It's also such a tiny place that there's little point paying the $50-plus premium on top of usual rates to get an ocean view.

Aloha Punawai 305 Saratoga Rd ☎808/923-5211 or 1-866/713-9694, ⓦ www.alternative-hawaii.com/alohapunawai/. Miniature hotel, opposite the post office, offering clean air-conditioned apartments and studios, all with kitchenettes. ❹

The Breakers 250 Beach Walk ☎808/923-3181 or 1-800/426-0494, ⓦ www.breakers-hawaii.com. Small, intimate hotel on the western edge of central Waikiki; all rooms have kitchenettes and TV, and there's a bar and grill beside the pool. ❹

Hale Pua Nui 228 Beach Walk ☎808/923-9693. Small, ageing but clean hotel that's among central Waikiki's best deals. Offers simple studio apartments with two beds, kitchenettes, and free local calls. Reserve well ahead. ❸

Hawaiiana Hotel 260 Beach Walk ☎808/923-9693. Pleasant little family hotel, abounding in tiki images, where the rooms are ranged around two pools; all have kitchenettes, some have balconies. ❹

New Otani Kaimana Beach Hotel 2863 Kalakaua Ave ☎808/923-1555 or 1-800/356-8264, ⓦ www.kaimana.com. Intimate, Japanese-toned beachfront hotel half a mile east of central Waikiki. ❻

Outrigger and **Ohana** linked hotel chains with numerous locations around Waikiki, mostly high-rises (reservations *Outrigger* ☎1-800/688-7444, ⓦ www.outrigger.com; *Ohana* ☎1-800/462-6262, ⓦ www.ohanahotels.com). Choices include the *Ohana Maile Sky Court*, 2058 Kuhio Ave (❺), or the slightly more luxurious *Ohana Waikiki Surf*, 2200 Kuhio Ave (❻); most of the other *Ohana*s have rooms for around $125, while the *Outrigger*s, such as the *Reef on the Beach*, 2169 Kalia Rd (❽), are more expensive. ❺–❾

Polynesian Beach Club Hostel 2584 Lemon Rd ☎808/922-1340, ⓦ www.hawaiihostels.com. Clean, efficiently run hostel, a block from the sea. Some rooms hold four $19 bunk beds, some serve as good-value private doubles, and there are also private suites. Free snorkels and boogie boards are available; there's cheap Internet access; and meals are served in the communal area some nights. **①**–**②**

The Royal Hawaiian 2259 Kalakaua Ave ☎808/923-7311 or 1-800/325-3535, ⓦwww.sheraton.com. This 1920s "Pink Palace," commanding the beach, is one of Waikiki's best-loved landmarks. The original building looks out across terrace gardens to the sea, but is now flanked by a less atmospheric tower block, which holds the most expensive suites. **⑨**

Waikiki Beachside Hostel 2556 Lemon Rd ☎808/923-9566, ⓦwww.hokondo.com. Small hotel block near the park in eastern Waikiki that has been converted into a popular, lively private hostel, with dorm beds for $18, plus pricier double rooms. **①**–**③**

The City

Downtown Honolulu is surprisingly small, set back a little from the sea and focused around a spacious plaza on King Street that includes **Iolani Palace** and the **state capitol**. The palace was built for King David Kalakaua in 1882, but, apart from its *koa*-hardwood floors, contains little that is distinctively Hawaiian, or that justifies the high tour price (Tues–Sat 9am–2.15pm; $20). Across the road is a flower-bedecked, gilt statue of Kamehameha the Great.

To reach the nearby ocean, pedestrians have to negotiate fearsome traffic. Although the sea may be turquoise, the shorefront is concrete, not beach, and you can't wander along it for any distance. The **Aloha Tower** on Pier 9 used to be the city's tallest building; the area around its base has been converted into a mall, fronting onto the city docks and better for dining than it is for shopping. The view from the top of the tower is little short of ugly, but is good for getting your bearings (daily 9am–5pm; free). The **Hawaii Maritime Center** (daily 8.30am–5pm; $7.50), just east of Aloha Tower, documents Hawaii's seafaring past in superb detail, from ancient migrations through to white contact, nineteenth-century trade, and tourism in the twentieth century. A stunning film from 1922 (with Clara Bow in a bit part) shows the true-life drama of whaling, and there's a wall of gigantic historic surfboards as well. In the adjacent dock are the fully rigged four-master *Falls of Clyde* and the replica Polynesian canoe *Hokulea*, whose voyages to Tahiti and New Zealand over the last two decades have inspired tremendous interest in traditional methods of navigation.

Though few tourists seem to know about it, Honolulu residents take great pride in the stunning fine art on display at the **Academy of Arts**, half a mile east of the capitol at 900 S Beretania St (Tues–Sat 10am–4.30pm, Sun 1–5pm; $7; ☎808/532-8700, ⓦwww.honoluluacademy.org). Highlights of the superb collection of paintings include Van Gogh's *Wheat Field*, Gauguin's *Two Nudes on a Tahitian Beach*, and one of Monet's *Water Lilies*. The Academy also holds some fascinating depictions of Hawaii by visiting artists, including a pencil sketch of Waikiki drawn in 1838, and vivid, stylized studies of Maui's Iao Valley and Hana coast by Georgia O'Keeffe, plus magnificent ancient **Chinese** ceramics and bronzes.

Chinatown

TheBus #2 from Waikiki drops you at Hotel and Bishop streets, in front of the gleaming high-tech Executive Center in downtown Honolulu. Just five minutes' walk away down Hotel Street, the faded green-clapboard storefronts of **Chinatown** seem like another world. Traditionally the city's red-light district, the narrow streets leading down to the Nuuanu Stream are still characterized by pool halls, massage parlors, and heavy-duty bars.

It's well worth delving into a few of Chinatown's inconspicuous alleyways. Some of its old walled courtyards are now modern malls, but the businesses remain much the same as ever, and you can still find herbalists weighing out dried leaves in front of vast arrays of bottles. Pig snouts and salmon heads are among the food specialties at **Oahu Market**, on N King and Kekaulike streets.

Bishop Museum

The anthropological collection at the **Bishop Museum** at 1525 Bernice St (daily 9am–5pm; $15; ☎808/847-3511, ⓦwww.bishopmuseum.org) – well away from both the ocean and downtown, near the foot of the Likelike Highway – showcases real Polynesian culture, as opposed to the fakery of Waikiki. Three floors of one of Hawaii's oldest houses display ancient carved stone and wooden images of gods, magnificent feather *leis* and cloaks, and a full-sized *hale* (traditional hut) brought here from Kauai, in addition to Japanese samurai armor and a full-sized sperm whale hanging in the central well. There are also excellent special exhibitions for kids, and a planetarium. TheBus #2 from Waikiki stops two blocks away on Kapalama Street.

Punchbowl

High above Honolulu, lush lawns growing in the caldera of an extinct volcano are the emotive setting for the **National Memorial Cemetery of the Pacific** (daily: March–Sept 8am–6.30pm; Oct–Feb 8am–5.30pm), in which are buried casualties from all US Pacific wars, Vietnam, as well as Hawaiian shuttle astronaut Ellison Onizuka. This spot is said to have held an ancient sacrificial temple, and is on TheBus route #15 from town.

Waikiki

Built on a reclaimed swamp, **Waikiki** is very nearly an island, all but separated from Honolulu between the sea and the Ala Wai canal (which provides the drainage to make its incredible highrise profusion possible). Once home to Kamehameha the Great, the site may be venerable, but these days its *raison d'être* is rampant commercialism. You could, just about, survive here with very little money, buying snacks from the omnipresent ABC convenience stores, but there would be no point – there's nothing to see here, and the only thing to do apart from surf and sunbathe is to stroll along the seafront **Kalakaua Avenue** and shop.

The most striking thing about the parallel **Waikiki Beach** is how narrow it is, a thin but nonetheless attractive strip of shipped-in sand. Compared to many other Hawaiian beaches, it's overcrowded and small, but it's still a wonderful place to spend a lazy day, and the fact that it's lined by a pedestrian walkway, with several pleasant gardens en route, makes it a refuge from the resort frenzy nearby.

Two possible diversions on the eastern fringes of Waikiki are **Honolulu Zoo** (daily 9am–4.30pm; $6; ☎808/971-7171, ⓦwww.honoluluzoo.org), where you can walk through a mock African savannah set against the magnificent backdrop of Diamond Head, and the more expensive oceanfront **Waikiki Aquarium** (daily 9am–5pm; $7; ☎808/923-9741, ⓦwaquarium.otted .hawaii.edu) which, as well as holding sharks and monkfish seals, has a tank devoted to the many-hued reef fish of Hanauma Bay (see opposite).

Diamond Head

Waikiki's most famous landmark is the pinnacle of **Diamond Head**, another extinct volcano just to the east. The lawns of the crater interior are oddly bland, but a straightforward hiking trail leads up a mile or so to the summit, and a panorama of the whole coast, passing through a network of tunnels built during World War II. TheBus #22 and #58 stop on the road nearby.

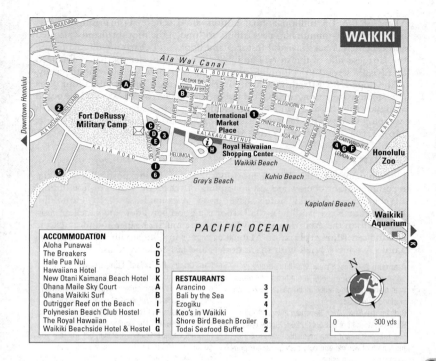

WAIKIKI

Ala Wai Canal

ALA WAI BOULEVARD

KAPIOLANI BOULEVARD

Downtown Honolulu

Fort DeRussy
Military Camp

KALIA ROAD

International
Market
Place

Royal Hawaiian
Shopping Center

Waikiki Beach

Gray's Beach

Kuhio Beach

Kapiolani Beach

Honolulu
Zoo

Waikiki
Aquarium

PACIFIC OCEAN

ACCOMMODATION

Aloha Punawai	C
The Breakers	D
Hale Pua Nui	E
Hawaiiana Hotel	D
New Otani Kaimana Beach Hotel	K
Ohana Maile Sky Court	A
Ohana Waikiki Surf	B
Outrigger Reef on the Beach	I
Polynesian Beach Club Hostel	F
The Royal Hawaiian	H
Waikiki Beachside Hotel & Hostel	G

RESTAURANTS

Arancino	3
Bali by the Sea	5
Ezogiku	4
Keo's in Waikiki	1
Shore Bird Beach Broiler	6
Todai Seafood Buffet	2

0   300 yds

Hanauma Bay

A few miles to the east, the magnificent crescent-shaped **Hanauma Bay**, formed when the wall of a crater collapsed and let in the sea, is renowned as Oahu's best place to **snorkel** (daily except Tues 6am–6pm; $5). Thanks to recent conservation measures, which include a strict limit on visitor numbers and a ban on feeding the fish, it has recovered well from years of overuse, and the sea once more abounds in brightly colored fish. Access is controlled via a visitor center, which shows educational videos about the bay's fragile ecology. Hourly buses run by the bay from Waikiki.

Pearl Harbor

Almost the whole of **Pearl Harbor**, the principal base for the US Pacific fleet (just over one hour west of Waikiki, beyond the airport, on TheBus #20), is off-limits to visitors. However, the surprise Japanese attack of December 7, 1941, which an official US inquiry called "the greatest military and naval disaster in our nation's history," is commemorated by a simple white memorial set above the wreck of the battleship **USS Arizona**, still discernible in the clear blue waters. More than 1100 of its crew – who had earned the right to sleep in late that Sunday morning by coming second in a military band competition – are entombed there.

Free tours of the memorial operate between 8am and 3pm each day, but it can be two or three hours after you pick up your numbered ticket at the **Pearl Harbor visitor center** (daily 7.30am–5pm, last program starts 3pm; ☎808/422-0561) before you're called to board the ferry that takes you there.

Many of the 1.5 million annual visitors are Japanese; a surprisingly even-handed twenty-minute film pays tribute to "one of the most brilliantly planned and executed attacks in naval history," and books and charts are on sale telling the Japanese side of the story. The USS *Arizona* memorial was partly financed by Elvis Presley's 1961 Honolulu concert, his first show after leaving the army.

The huge **USS Missouri**, which survived the attack and was used four years later for the ceremony in Tokyo Harbor that ended World War II, is moored alongside the *Arizona*. Guided visits include the actual surrender site as well as sweeping views of the harbor from the *Missouri*'s bridge (daily 9am–5pm; tours $16–25; ℡1-877/MIGHTYMO, Ⓦwww.ussmissouri.com).

Eating

Honolulu and Waikiki offer an enormous range of **dining** possibilities, and the recommendations below are just a sampling of what's on offer. For fine dining, all the larger Waikiki hotels have good restaurants, and, in Honolulu, **Restaurant Row mall** near the harbor is a good bet. There are excellent fast-food malls in the **Ala Moana Center**, and the much cheaper and more exotic **Maunakea Marketplace** on Maunakea Street in Chinatown, while Waikiki's Kuhio Avenue is lined with snack outlets and fast-food franchises.

Arancino 255 Beach Walk, Waikiki ℡808/923-5557. Good Italian trattoria in the heart of Waikiki, with plenty of moderately priced pasta, pizza, and seafood specialties.

Bali by the Sea *Hilton Hawaiian Village*, 2005 Kalia Rd, Waikiki ℡808/941-2254. Highly refined gourmet restaurant, with irresistible views of the full length of Waikiki and very tasteful (and expensive) Pacific Rim cuisine.

Ezogiku 2546 Lemon Rd, Waikiki ℡808/923-2013. Plain and very inexpensive Japanese diner, with three branches in Waikiki – the others are at 2420 Koa Ave and 2146 Kalakaua Ave. Ramen soups plus rice and curry dishes, all at $6–8, to eat in or take out.

Kakaako Kitchen Ward Center, 1200 Ala Moana Blvd ℡808/596-7488. Mall diner that dishes up high-quality Hawaiian-style fast food; pretty much everything, from the hamburger stew to the signature dish chicken linguine, costs $7–10, and there's a menu of daily $8 specials like meat loaf or pot roast.

Keo's in Waikiki 2028 Kuhio Ave, Waikiki ℡808/951-9355. Hawaii's best Thai restaurant, and though its menu isn't exceptional, everything, from the specialty "Evil Jungle Prince" curries onwards, tastes great, and all entrees cost under $15. Breakfast is both American and Asian; lunch and dinner are entirely Thai.

Sam Choy's Breakfast, Lunch, and Crab 580 N Nimitz Hwy ℡808/545-7979. Copious quantities of modern Hawaiian cuisine, plus a microbrewery, located a mile or two west of downtown Honolulu.

Sansei Restaurant Row, 500 Ala Moana Blvd ℡808/536-6286. The central Honolulu setting may not be particularly attractive, but whether you go for the full Pacific Rim menu or stick to the sushi bar, the food is excellent and well worth the prices (entrees $17–29).

Shore Bird Beach Broiler *Outrigger Reef on the Beach*, 2169 Kalia Rd, Waikiki ℡808/922-2887. Open-air oceanfront restaurant serving a $9 breakfast buffet, and dinner with an open salad bar for $13–20, depending on choice of entree. Guests cook their own meat or fish on a communal grill.

Todai Seafood Buffet 1910 Ala Moana Blvd, Waikiki ℡808/947-1000. Stylish all-you-care-to-eat Japanese buffet in western Waikiki. Lunch costs $15 and dinner $27, but the range and quality of the food, including sushi, shrimp, crab, and lobster, makes it a real bargain.

Yakiniku Canellia 2494 S Beretania St ℡808/946-7595. Korean buffet restaurant a mile north of Waikiki, where you select slices of marinated beef, chicken, or pork and grill it yourself at the gas-fired burners set into each table. Open daily for lunch ($12) and dinner ($18).

Nightlife

Most of Honolulu's **nightlife** is concentrated in Waikiki, where fun-seeking tourists set the tone. On the whole, the available entertainment is on the bland side. Hawaii tends to be off the circuit for touring musicians, so if you enjoy

The nation that invented **surfing** – long before the whites came – remains its greatest arena. The sport was popularized early in the twentieth century by Olympic swimmer Duke Kahanamoku, using a 20ft board; these days most are around six feet. Smaller **boogie boards** make an exhilarating initiation. **Windsurfing**, too, is rapidly growing, often using the same favorite beaches, usually on the north shore of each island. **Snorkeling** and **diving** are top-quality, although Hawaii's **coral** has fewer brilliant hues than those seen in warmer equatorial waters.

Bear in mind, however, that **drownings** in Hawaii are all too common. Waves can sweep in from two thousand miles of open ocean onto beaches that are unprotected by any reef. Not all beaches have lifeguards and warning flags, and unattended beaches are not necessarily safe. Watch the sea carefully before going in, and never take your eyes off it thereafter. Fierce **rogue waves** can appear from the blue to drag waders – or even those walking along the shore – far out to sea in seconds, and powerful **undertows** may not be detectable until too late. If you do get swept out, don't fight the big waves; wait for the current to die down before trying to swim back to shore.

Sea creatures to avoid include black spiky **sea urchins**, Portuguese man-of-war **jellyfish**, and **coral** in general, which can give painful infected cuts. **Shark attacks** are much rarer than popular imagination suggests; those that do occur are usually due to "misunderstandings," such as surfers idling on their boards looking a bit too much like turtles from below.

live music you'll probably have to settle for little-known local performers (even rising stars of contemporary Hawaiian music tend to prefer to keep their credibility by not playing in Waikiki too often). Look out also for special events at downtown's beautifully restored Hawaii Theater, 1130 Bethel St (☏808/528-0506).

Chai's Island Bistro Aloha Tower Marketplace, 101 Ala Moana Blvd ☏808/585-0011. Sumptuous and very expensive Thai restaurant, where the very finest Hawaiian musicians perform for diners nightly 7–8.30pm.

Duke's Canoe Club *Outrigger Waikiki on the Beach*, 2335 Kalakaua Ave ☏808/923-0711. Smooth Hawaiian sounds wash over this oceanfront Waikiki cocktail bar nightly from 4pm to 6pm and 10pm to midnight – including big-name "Concerts on the Beach" Fri–Sun 4–6pm. No cover charge.

Hula's Bar and Lei Stand *Waikiki Grand Hotel*, 134 Kapahulu Ave ☏808/923-0669. Waikiki's most popular gay venue occupies a suite of oceanview rooms across from the Honolulu Zoo. As well as a state-of-the-art dance floor equipped with giant video screens, there's also a more casual lounge area. Daily 10am–2am.

Ocean Club Restaurant Row, 500 Ala Moana Blvd ☏808/526-9888. Flamboyant, frenetic downtown bar-cum-restaurant that serves inexpensive food in the early evening and turns into a wild dance club as the night wears on. Over-22s only; no T-shirts.

Wave Waikiki 1877 Kalakaua Ave ☏808/941-0424. In so far as Waikiki has an alternative rock scene, this is it, with a bar upstairs and dance floor down below, and DJs rather than live bands most nights. Daily 9pm–4am.

Windward Oahu

The most spectacular moment on a tour of Oahu comes as you cross the Koolau Mountains on the **Pali Highway** (Hwy-61) to see the sheer green cliffs of the windward side of the island veiled by swirling mists. The highest spot, just four miles out of Honolulu heading northeast, is the **Nuuanu Pali Lookout**. Kamehameha the Great finalized his conquest of Oahu here in

1795, forcing hundreds of enemy warriors over the edge of the cliffs; Mark Twain saw the battlefield seventy years later, littered with skulls.

The best way to get a close-up view of the inaccessible inland cliffs is on the attractive hiking trails in **Kahana Valley State Park** (open 24hr; free), a dozen miles short of the island's northernmost tip.

Oahu's leading paying attraction, with one million annual visitors, is the **Polynesian Cultural Center**, slightly further north at Laie (Mon–Sat noon–9pm; $40–105; ☎1-800/367-7060, ⓦwww.polynesia.com). This haphazard mixture of real and bogus Polynesia – in which the history is firmly on the latter – is owned by the Mormons, and staffed by students from the adjacent Brigham Young University, who perform tired music and dance routines. TheBus #52 takes roughly two hours to get this far.

North Shore Oahu

The **surfing beaches** of northern Oahu are famous the world over, but they're minimally equipped for tourists. **Waimea**, **Sunset**, and **Ehukai** beach parks (the latter is home of the Banzai Pipeline, perhaps the most famous surfing spot in the world) are all laid-back roadside stretches of sand, where you can usually find a quiet spot to yourself. In summer, the tame waves may leave you wondering what all the fuss is about; see them at full tilt in the winter, and you'll have no doubts.

HALEIWA is the main surfers' hangout, combining alternative shops and cafés with upfront tourist traps. Most of the **food** around is vegetarian; at the back of the Celestial Natural Foods store, 66-443 Kamehameha Hwy, the *Paradise Found Café* (☎808/637-4640) serves breakfast and lunch, both for about $6, while *Cholo's Homestyle Mexican*, in the North Shore Marketplace across the street (☎808/637-3059), is a busy, plain but very lively Mexican joint.

For **accommodation**, you'll have to head five miles northeast to the *Backpacker's Vacation Inn*, at 59-788 Kamehameha Hwy by Waimea Bay (☎808/638-7838, ⓦwww.backpackers-hawaii.com; ❶–❺), which has dorm beds for $15–18 a night, as well as some great-value ocean-view private rooms and studios.

The Big Island

The **Big Island of Hawaii** is well named – it could hold all the other islands put together with room to spare. The entire island has the population of a medium-sized town, with 150,000 people (half what it was in Captain Cook's day) and a low level of tourism compared to Oahu or Maui; despite its fair share of restaurants, bars, and so on, this is basically a rural community. Development may put an end to that some day, but for the moment there are sleepy old towns all over the island that have remained unchanged for a century. The few resorts are built on the barren lava flows of the **Kona** coast to catch maximum sunshine, and though the beaches here are great, these are otherwise the least beautiful areas on the island.

The Big Island is still growing, its southern shore inching ever further out to sea, thanks to the **Kilauea** volcano, which has destroyed roads and even towns, and spews out pristine beaches of jet-black sand. **Hawaii Volcanoes National Park**, which includes **Mauna Loa** as well as Kilauea (though not **Mauna Kea**, further to the north and higher than either at 13,796ft), is absolutely compelling; you can explore steaming craters and cinder cones, venture into the rainforest, and at times approach within feet of the eruption itself. The summits of Mauna Loa and Mauna Kea have the clearest air on earth – and astronomical observatories to take advantage of it – but down below, when the tradewinds drop, the island is prone to a choking sulphurous haze known as "**vog**."

As befits the birthplace and base of **King Kamehameha**, more of the ancient Hawaii survives on the Big Island than anywhere else in the islands. **Puuhonua O Honaunau National Historical Park** preserves a "place of refuge" for *kapu*-breakers and defeated warriors, and there are further temples north along the Kohala coast, while **Waipio Valley**, where Kamehameha spent his youth, remains as lush and green as ever.

Flights to the Big Island arrive at both **Hilo** on the rainy east coast, or the resort town of **Kailua** (often referred to as Kona) on the west. If you don't rent a **car**, you may not get to the interesting sites; one bus daily links Hilo and Kailua, and organized bus tours go to specific attractions, but public transportation is all but nonexistent.

Windward Hawaii

Almost all the rain that falls on the slopes of Mauna Kea flows down to the sea on the eastern side of the Big Island. As a result, myriad streams and waterfalls nourish dense jungle-like vegetation, ensuring that the main road north along the coast from Hilo – the only sizeable base for travelers – is alive with flowering trees and orchids.

Hilo

Although it's the Big Island's capital and largest town, just 45,000 people live in **HILO**, which remains endearing and unpressured. Mass tourism has never taken off here, mainly because it rains too much. However, the rain falls mostly at night, and America's wettest city blazes with tropical blooms against a backdrop of rainbows.

Hilo has always been at the mercy of fire and water. Cataclysmic tsunami killed 96 people in April 1946, and a further 61 in May 1960. Countless lava flows have also threatened to engulf it; in 1881 Princess Ruth (see p.1355) summoned up all her spiritual power to halt one on the edge of town, while in 1984 another flow stopped just eight miles short.

Arrival, information, and getting around
Downtown Hilo is compact and very walkable. However, the urban area extends for several miles, and the **airport** at **General Lyman Field** (☎808/935-4782), on the eastern outskirts, is well beyond walking distance. If you're not renting a car at the airport, a taxi into town is your only alternative, costing around $8.

The **Hawaii Visitors Bureau** is at 250 Keawe St (Mon–Fri 8am–noon & 1–4.30pm; ☎808/961-5797, ⓦwww.bigisland.org). From the Mooheau Bus Terminal on Kamehameha Avenue, Hilo's Hele-On **bus** (☎808/961-8744) operates a small-scale local service, plus one daily bus each to Kailua (Mon–Sat) and down to Hawaii Volcanoes National Park (Mon–Fri).

Accommodation

Hilo, and the whole east coast, has fewer major resort hotels than usual in Hawaii, but there are several **accommodation** options; the less expensive ones tend to be in town rather than around the loop of **Banyan Drive** on the seafront near the airport.

Arnott's Lodge and Hostel 98 Apapane Rd ☎808/969-7097, ⓦwww.arnottslodge.com. Laid-back accommodation in a two-story lodge, tucked away in the woods two miles southeast of down-town. Call from the airport for free pickup. Twelve-bed dorms ($19 a bed) and private rooms available, plus organized island tours and lava hikes. ❶–❸
Dolphin Bay Hotel 333 Iliahi St ☎808/935-1466, ⓦwww.dolphinbayhilo.com. Very nice, very friend-ly little hotel, just across the river from downtown, offering spotlessly clean one- and two-bedroom suites with kitchens. ❸

Shipman House B&B Inn 131 Kaiulani St ☎808/934-8002 or 1-800/627-8447, ⓦwww.hilo-hawaii.com. Magnificent Victorian mansion, converted into a plush B&B, with three grand antique-furnished en suite rooms in the main house, plus two more in a guest cottage. ❼
Uncle Billy's Hilo Bay Hotel 87 Banyan Drive ☎808/961-5818, 1-800/442-5841 (within Hawaii) or 1-800/367-5102 (within the US), ⓦwww.unclebilly.com. Family-run hotel, the oldest on Banyan Drive, with pleasantly ubiquitous Polynesian decor and a budget restaurant. ❹

Downtown Hilo

There is a simple and tragic reason why **downtown Hilo** looks so appealingly low-key, with its modest streets and wooden stores: all the buildings that stood on the seaward side of Kamehameha Avenue were destroyed by the two tsuna-mi of 1946 and 1960. After 1960, no attempt was made to rebuild "Little Tokyo," which had housed Hilo's predominantly Japanese population, and the seafront is now occupied by a succession of pleasant gardens. The story is told in the high-tech **Pacific Tsunami Museum**, on Kamehameha Avenue at Kalakuaua Street (Mon–Sat 9am–4pm; $7; ☎808/935-0926, ⓦwww.tsunami.org). A scale model shows how the city looked before the 1946 disaster; contemporary footage and personal letters bring home the full impact of the tragedy. The section devoted to the wave of 1960 is even more poignant. Locals had several hours' warning that it was on its way, but many flocked to the seafront to watch it come in; pho-tos show them waiting excitedly for the cataclysm that was about to engulf them.

The focus of the two-part **Lyman Museum** at 276 Haili St (Mon–Sat 9.30am–4.30pm; $7; ☎808/935-5021, ⓦwww.lymanmuseum.org) is the origi-nal 1830s **Mission House**, furnished in dark *koa* wood, which belonged to Calvinist missionaries David and Sarah Lyman. The museum next door starts with a fascinating display of ancient weapons and then documents Hawaii's vari-ous ethnic groups, including the Portuguese brought here in 1878 from the overpopulated but similarly volcanic Azores, whose *braginha* became the ukelele.

A couple of miles up Waianuenue Avenue, at **Rainbow Falls**, just to the right of the road, a spectacular wide waterfall plummets 100ft across the mouth of a huge cavern. Continue another two miles to reach the bubbling, foaming pools known as the **Boiling Pots**.

Eating and nightlife

Most of Hilo's (eminently missable) **nightlife** is in the Banyan Drive hotels, though there are a few shows at downtown's restored Palace Theater. As well as its **restaurants**, early risers will enjoy the daily 7am **Suisan Fish Auction**, at Banyan Drive and Lihiwai Street, where you can buy from the night's catch of marlin and other big fish.

Bears Coffee 110 Keawe St ☏808/935-0708. Hilo's most bohemian breakfast hangout, one block back from the ocean in the heart of downtown.

Café Pesto 130 Kamehameha Ave ☏808/969-6640. Large, Pacific-influenced Italian restaurant, facing the ocean from downtown Hilo, serving tasty calzones and pizzas.

The Seaside Restaurant 1790 Kalanianaole Ave ☏808/935-8825. Located just over two miles southeast of town, this superb, if plain, fish restaurant presides over thirty-acre fishponds brimming with trout, mullet, and catfish. A full fish supper costs around $20.

Tsunami 250 Keawe St ☏808/961-6789. Sushi, noodles, and other Asian specialties at amazingly low prices, near the Hawaii Visitors Bureau.

North from Hilo

The **Belt Road** (Hwy-19) follows the **Hamakua coast** north of Hilo, clinging to the hillsides and crossing ravines on slender bridges. At first the fields are crammed into narrow rain-carved "gulches," but further north the land spreads out. For a glimpse into the interior, head into the mountains after fifteen miles to the 450ft **Akaka Falls**. A short loop trail through the forest, festooned with wild orchids, offers views of Akaka and other jungle-like tropical waterfalls.

Waipio Valley

Highway 240, which turns north off the Belt Road at **HONOKAA**, comes to an abrupt end after nine miles at the edge of **Waipio Valley**. As the southernmost of six successive sheer-walled valleys, this is the only one accessible by land – and it's as close as Hawaii comes to the classic South Seas image of an isolated and self-sufficient valley, dense with fruit trees and laced by footpaths leading down to the sea. Spectacular waterfalls cascade down the valley's flanks, but recurrent tidal waves have ensured that only a few taro farmers now live here.

It's perfectly possible to walk down the steep, mile-long track into Waipio, but most visitors take tours, either in the four-wheel-drive vehicles of the Waipio Valley Shuttle (Mon–Sat 9am, 11am, 1pm & 3pm; ☏808/775-7121, ⓦwww.waipiovalleytour.com; $40), at the Waipio Valley Art Works in Kukuihaele, a mile from the end of the road; in horse-drawn wagons (☏808/775-9518; $45); or on horseback (☏808/775-0419; $75).

North Kohala

On the green slopes of **Kohala Mountain**, at the northern tip of the Big Island, traditional plantation towns such as **HAWI** survive virtually unchanged – run-down in an appealing sort of way, the all-purpose stores still floored with creaking planks. Call in at the spacious *Bamboo Restaurant and Bar* (☏808/889-5555; closed Mon) to enjoy one of the friendliest and most Hawaiian restaurants in the state.

Polulu Valley, where North Kohala's main artery, Hwy-270, comes to a dead end, is the last of the chain of inaccessible valleys, and for the moment is every bit as pristine as Waipio. The fear of tsunami, which led the Hawaiians to abandon these once densely populated valleys, is probably their best defense against the rapacity of the developers.

Waimea and the interior

The **interior** of the Big Island comes as a surprise: pastoral meadows roll over gentle hills where once stood forests of sandalwood. This is cattle-ranching country, most of it – ten percent of the island – owned by the United States's largest private ranch, the **Parker Ranch**.

WAIMEA (also known as **Kamuela**) is not the company town it once was – the Parker Ranch now employs just one hundred of its eight thousand inhabitants – but more of a sophisticated country-town resort that retains traces of its cowboy past. Though you can no longer tour the ranch itself, there's an interesting **visitor center** (Mon–Sat 9am–5pm; $6.50; ☎ 808/885-7655, ⓦ www.parkerranch.com) in town; the nearby **Kamuela Museum** is enjoyably eclectic and eccentric, with an extensive range of ancient Hawaiian artifacts (daily 8am–5pm; $5).

Waimea practicalities

B&Bs are booming in Waimea, with the best being the very appealing *Waimea Gardens Cottage* (☎ 808/985-7488; ❻). The main alternative, the refurbished *Kamuela Inn* (☎ 808/885-4243; ❸), is part inn, part luxury hotel. *Merriman's* in Opelo Plaza (☎ 808/885-6822) wins awards for its innovative **cuisine**, but if paying over $20 for an entree puts you off, cross the street and walk a few yards to the *Waimea Coffee Co.* in Parker Square (☎ 808/885-4472), which offers good coffees and vegetarian specials.

The Saddle Road

The fifty-mile **Saddle Road** cuts across the Big Island from Hilo to Kona, between Mauna Kea and Mauna Loa. Even locals consider it dangerous, especially at night, as there are no facilities and it's a winding, foggy drive. Rental-car companies forbid their clients from driving on it, but if you choose to chance it, do so in the daytime. Expect some great views of the volcanoes – and a good deal of mist even then.

The Kona coast

Hawaii's leeward **Kona coast** divides into two distinct areas. To the north of its only sizeable community, **Kailua**, barren lava trails down to the sea from the third highest of the Big Island's volcanoes, Hualalai. Thanks to the relentless sun on its superb beaches, luxury hotels dot the shoreline as incongruous green patches in the wasteland. To the south, the hillsides are more fertile, and although the condos are spreading, you can still get a real feel for the old Hawaii in the land where Captain Cook met his end.

North Kona and the resorts

The best of the spectacular sandy beaches along the Kona coast – safe for summer swimming, though with tempestuous winter surf – lie to the north of Kailua. **Hapuna Beach**, almost forty miles up the coast, is deservedly the most famous, despite being overshadowed by the giant *Hapuna Beach Prince Hotel* (☎ 808/880-1111 or 1-888/774-6236, ⓦ www.hapunabeachhotel; ❾); it's still possible to rent $20 beachside cabins in the adjoining state park (☎ 808/974-6200). For idyllic seclusion, head instead for **Kona Coast State Park** (daily except Wed 9am–8pm; free), reached via a bumpy dirt road just a couple of miles north of Keahole Airport (see below).

Several extraordinary **resort hotels** lie in the district of South Kohala, thirty miles north of Kailua (see below). Three separate enclaves – Waikoloa, Mauna Kea, and Mauna Lani – have been landscaped out of this inhospitable lava desert, each one a self-contained oasis holding two or three hotels, a beach or two, and nothing else. Although **Waikoloa** is the least exclusive of the three, it's home to the ludicrously ostentatious, mile-long *Hilton Waikoloa* (℡808/886-1234 or 1-800/445-8667, ⓦwww.hiltonwaikoloavillage.com; ⑨), said to consume seven percent of all the island's energy. Guests travel the distance to and from their rooms by electric boats or monorail.

Kailua (Kona)

Although the Big Island's main resort is officially called **KAILUA**, and its postal address is "Kailua-Kona," you're likely to hear it referred to as **Kona** as often as not. It's quite an attractive little town that has played a major part in Hawaiian history, but it's also more affected by tourism than any other Big Island community, and its seafront row of fast-food restaurants and souvenir shops could be those of almost anywhere.

Arrival

The largely open-air **Keahole Airport**, situated on a field of black lava nine miles north of Kailua, has the usual car rental places; otherwise Speedishuttle **buses** into town cost around $20 per person (℡808/329-5433 or 1-800/977-2605, ⓦwww.speedishuttle.com). In Kailua, a regular **shuttle bus** runs the six-mile length of Alii Drive every ninety minutes (Mon–Sat 8.30am–7.30pm; $2; ℡808/775-7121). One daily Hele-On bus (see p.1352) follows Hwy-11 around the north of the island to Hilo, leaving Kailua just before 6am and returning in the evening.

Accommodation

Alii Drive is lined for about five miles south from Kailua with **hotels and condos**, but none offers much in the way of budget accommodation. The listings below therefore include a couple of places a bit further along the coast.

King Kamehameha's Kona Beach Hotel 75-5660 Palani Rd ℡808/329-2911 or 1-800/367-6060, ⓦwww.konabeachhotel.com. Established landmark hotel at the northern end of oceanfront Kailua, set around a picturesque little beach and facing the Ahuena Heiau (see p.1356). ⑥

Kona Seaside Hotel 75-5646 Palani Rd ℡808/329-2455 or 1-800/560-5558, ⓦwww.sand-seaside.com. Six floors of reasonable air-conditioned rooms, with and without kitchens. Discounted car rental also available. ⑤

Kona Tiki Hotel 75-5968 Alii Drive ℡808/329-1425. This simple three-story motel, right beside the ocean and a mile south of central Kailua, is very popular with bargain hunters. No phones or TVs, but some rooms have kitchenettes. ③

Patey's Place 75-195 Ala Ona Ona ℡808/326-7018, ⓦwww.hawaiian-hostels.com. Renovated budget hostel that's a popular choice with backpackers and surfers. Offers beds in 4-person dorms ($19.50), plus some private rooms with shared bath. ①–②

The Town

Hulihee Palace (daily 9am–4pm, Sat & Sun 10am–4pm; $6) faces out to sea from the center of Kailua. Built as the governor's residence in 1838, it's not all that imposing from the outside, but within it's notable for massive *koa*-wood furnishings, made to fit the considerable girth of the various members of the Hawaiian royal family who later lived here, such as the redoubtable four-hundred-pound Princess Ruth. The 1836 **Mokuaikaua Church**

directly opposite – Hawaii's first church – holds a museum on the early days of Hawaiian Christianity. A peculiar "sausage-tree" from Mozambique, named after the elongated fruit that dangles from its branches, grows in the grounds. Nearby, the *King Kamehameha* hotel (see p.1355) dominates the northern end of the bay. King Kamehameha's funeral rites were performed in the ancient temple of **Ahuena Heiau**, which juts into the sea in front of the hotel's beach.

Some of the world's best fishing, snorkeling, and scuba spots are approached by sea from Kailua. Expensive two-hour tours on Atlantis Submarines ($84, under-12s $42; ☎808/543-8359, ⓦwww.atlantissubmarines.org) descend one hundred feet to a coral reef, accompanied by the *Star Wars* theme, to see a frenzy of feeding fish and the occasional lurking shark. The catamaran *Fair Wind* (daily: 9am departure $87, shorter 2pm departure $55; ☎808/322-2788, ⓦwww.fair-wind.com) goes to Kealakekua Bay, for snorkeling and a bit of scuba. To charter a boat to **fish** for the big ones, contact the Charter Desk (☎808/329-5735, ⓦwww.charterdesk.com); rates start at $70 for a half-day.

Eating and drinking

Competition ensures that the **restaurants** and **bars** of central Kailua – especially those along the seafront – are well priced, though the relentless vacation atmosphere means the place can seem a bit unreal.

Huggo's 76-6828 Kuhakai St ☎808/329-1493. Lunch and dinner served on a large terrace with ocean views. The menu includes burgers, salads, and sandwiches, as well as Pacific Rim specialties, and there's often live evening entertainment.
Ocean View Inn 75-5683 Alii Drive ☎808/329-9998. Very inexpensive Hawaiian and Asian diner overlooking the sea, with roast beef dinners, traditional fish dishes, and even Chinese cuisine. Closed Mon.

Oodles of Noodles Crossroads Shopping Center, 75-1027 Henry St ☎808/329-2222. Pan-Asian noodle joint, a mile up from the ocean near the highway, serving great dinners from around $15.
Sibu Café Banyan Court Mall, 75-5695 W Alii Drive ☎808/329-1112. Popular, informal Indonesian restaurant, with no views but some atmospheric outdoor seating. Serves $11–14 entrees, including a tasty shrimp *sate*.

Kealakekua Bay

Kealakekua Bay, a dozen miles south of Kailua, was where Captain Cook was killed on his second voyage to Hawaii (see box, opposite). One of ancient Hawaii's major population centers, it's now barely inhabited, and the white **obelisk** on the death site – legally a small piece of England – is all but inaccessible. You can only get to within a mile of the bay by car, at **Napoopoo Beach**, though you'll get a glimpse of it from the road on the way down. The bay itself is the best place on the Big Island for **snorkeling**, even if there are sharks further out. It's also possible to hike down to the monument, but it's a grueling four-hour roundtrip, for which you need to carry all your water and supplies. The trail starts just before the town of **CAPTAIN COOK**, which is also home to the bargain *Manago Hotel* (☎808/323-2642, ⓦwww.managohotel.com; ❶–❷), offering comfortable ocean-view rooms amid flowering Japanese gardens.

This region, South Kona, is the prime source of **Kona coffee**, which sells here for around $20 a pound (including shipping). A mile south of Captain Cook, the *Coffee Shack* (daily 7am–5pm; ☎808/328-9555) serves wonderfully fresh coffee and smoothies on a terrace that enjoys staggering views all the way down to Kealakekua Bay.

When **Captain James Cook** sailed into Kealakekua Bay on January 17, 1779, he was on his second visit to Hawaii, after a year spent searching for the fabled Northwest Passage. When he anchored his ship, the *Resolution*, in this sheltered harbor, as many as ten thousand Hawaiians gathered to greet him. For three weeks, he was fed and feted by Chief Kalaniopuu, attending temple ceremonies and wrestling matches, and replenishing his supplies.

The departure of the *Resolution*, amid declarations of friendship, might have been the end of things, had the ship not been forced to return just a week later, following a storm that left it in tatters. This time the islanders were not so hospitable, and far from keen to part with further scarce resources. On February 14, Cook led a landing party of nine men in a bid to kidnap Kalaniopuu and force the islanders to return a stolen small boat. In an undignified scuffle, in which he was surrounded by thousands of hostile warriors including the future Kamehameha the Great, Cook was stabbed and died at the water's edge. His body was treated as befit a dead chief: the skull and leg bones were kept, and the rest cremated.

Although the legend soon grew that the Hawaiians had taken Cook to be the great god *Lono*, Hawaiian commentators now argue that such tales say more about European attitudes to Cook than about Polynesian perceptions. To the European mentality of the time, it was self-evident that a noble figure of the Enlightenment such as Captain Cook must appear god-like to superstitious "natives."

The major anomaly in the legend is quite why the Hawaiians would have killed this "god." Some proponents say it was a sacrifice, even though it happened in battle, while others argue that the man who struck the final blow "didn't know" that Cook was a "god." The usual explanation, that it was simply an accident, serves both to perpetuate the idea of Hawaiians as "innocent" savages, and to absolve Cook himself of any responsibility for his fate. What seems more likely is that his actions in peremptorily dismantling a temple at Napoopoo for use as firewood antagonized the priests, and when he infuriated the chiefs as well by seizing Kalaniopuu, deference gave way to defiance.

Puuhonua O Honaunau – "The City of Refuge"

Puuhonua O Honaunau National Historical Park (daily 7.30am–5.30pm; $5 per vehicle), four miles on from Kealakekua, is the single most evocative historical site in all of the Hawaiian islands, jutting into the Pacific on a small peninsula of jagged black lava. The grounds include a palace, complete with fishpond and private canoe landing, and three *heiaus* (places of worship), guarded by large carved effigies of gods – reproductions, but still eerie in their original setting. An ancient "**place of refuge**" lies firmly protected behind the mortarless masonry of the sixteenth-century **Great Wall**. Those who broke ancient Hawaii's intricate system of *kapu* (taboo) – perhaps by treading on the shadow of a chief or fishing in the wrong season – could expect summary execution unless they fled to the sanctuary of such a place. As chiefs lived on the surrounding land, transgressors had to swim through the shark-infested seas. If successful, they would be absolved and released overnight.

△ Ancient carvings on the Big Island

Hawaii Volcanoes National Park

The Big Island's southernmost volcanoes, **Mauna Loa** and **Kilauea**, jointly constitute **HAWAII VOLCANOES NATIONAL PARK**, thirty miles from Hilo and eighty from Kailua. It's possibly the most dramatic of all the US national parks, which besides having two active volcanoes, includes desert, arctic tundra, and rainforest.

Evidence is everywhere of the awesome power of the volcanoes to create and destroy; no map can keep up with the latest whims of the lava flow. Whole towns have been engulfed, and what were once prized beachfront properties lie buried hundreds of yards back from the sea.

Kilauea Caldera

The main focus of the park is **Kilauea Caldera**. Close to the rim, on the eleven-mile **Crater Rim Drive**, both the **visitor center** (daily 7.45am–5pm; $10 per vehicle; ☎808/967-7311, ⊛www.nps.gov/havo) and the fascinating **Jaggar Museum** of geology (daily 8.30am–5pm; free) offer basic orientation. Kilauea is said to be the home of the volcano goddess **Pele**, who has followed the "hot spot" from island to island. In 1824 Queen Kapiolani, a recent convert to Christianity, defied her by descending into the crater, reading aloud from her Bible, eating the *tabu* red *ohelo* berries, and throwing stones into the pit. When Mark Twain came here in 1866, he observed a dazzling lake of liquid fire; since a huge explosion in 1924 it's been shallower and quieter, a black dusty expanse dotted with hissing steam vents. Enthusiastic hikers should set time aside to follow the long trails that explore the caldera floor. Both the **Halemaumau Trail**, a seven-mile roundtrip, and the **Kilauea Iki Trail**, a total of five miles, involve picking your way from cairn to cairn across an eerie landscape of cracked and jagged lava.

Among shorter routes, the mile-long **Devastation Trail** is a boardwalk laid across the scene of a 1959 eruption; scientists are monitoring how long vegetation takes to re-establish itself. Most of what you see is new growth – fresh lava is full of nutrients, and rainwater and seeds soon collect in the recesses – but a few older trees survived partial submersion in ash by growing "aerial roots" some way up their trunks.

Chain of Craters Road

Chain of Craters Road winds down to the sea from Crater Rim Drive, sweeping around a succession of cones and vents in an empty landscape where the occasional dead white tree trunk or flowering shrub pokes up. Fresh sheets of lava constantly ooze down the slopes to cover the road. When a new road is built on top of the flow, more lava covers it. Along the coast, the scale of the damage since 1983 has been too great to repair – over seven miles have been lost – so now the road is a dead end, and getting shorter year by year. One by one the landmarks along its seafront stretch have been destroyed, and before long it may not follow the shoreline at all.

Check current conditions at the **visitor center** when you arrive, and make sure you have enough gas. The end of the road is a fifty-mile roundtrip from the park entrance, and there are no facilities of any kind along the way. For the last few years, depending on where current volcanic activity is concentrated, it has been possible at times to walk across the congealed lava blocking Chain of Craters Road to see molten rock gush from the earth – sometimes directly into the sea. The park's **Volcano Update line** (☎808/985-6000) has the latest details; for information on ranger-led tours, call the visitor center.

Practicalities

The national park operates two free **campgrounds** on a first-come, first-served basis, while the famous *Volcano House*, on the very edge of the crater within the park (☎808/967-7321, ⓦwww.volcanohousehotel.com; cabins ❷, rooms ❹), has spectacular views, and good food in the evening, although the prices for its simple motel-style rooms are rather high. Otherwise, the small and inconspicuous town of **VOLCANO**, just before the park entrance on the Hilo side, provides the best places to **stay** in the vicinity, with B&Bs such as *Hale Ohia* (☎808/967-7986, ⓦwww.haleohia.com; ❹), south of the highway across from the village. *Kilauea Lodge*, on the leafy main street (☎808/967-7366, ⓦwww.kilauealodge.com; ❻), is a comfortable inn with a very good **restaurant**.

Maui

The island of **MAUI**, the second largest in the Hawaiian chain, is Oahu's fastest-growing rival, attracting roughly a third of all visitors to the state. Some would say that things have gone too far, with formerly remote, unspoiled beaches, around **Kaanapali** and **Kihei** for example, having been swamped by sprawling resorts. On the other hand, the crowds come to Maui for the good reason that it's still beautiful. This is probably the best equipped of all the islands for **activity** holidays – whale-watching, windsurfing, diving, sailing, snorkeling, and cycling. Temperatures along the coast can be searing, especially at historic **Lahaina**, but it's always possible to escape to somewhere cooler. **Upcountry Maui**, on the slopes of the mighty **Haleakala** volcano, is a delight, well away from the bustle, while the waterfalls and ravines along the tortuous road out west to **Hana** outclass anything on Oahu.

Kahului and Wailuku

Almost half of Maui's 120,000 inhabitants – the workers who keep this fantasy island going – live in the twin towns of **KAHULUI** and **WAILUKU**, to the north of the "neck" connecting its two mountainous sections. The land here can be so flat you fear the waves will wash right over it. Kahului is the main commercial center; Wailuku, if not aesthetically pleasing, is one of the few towns on Maui that feels like a genuine community, and the presence of budget accommodation and restaurants – and the stunning **Iao Needle** nearby – make it a good central base.

Arrival and information

Virtually all visitors to Maui arrive at **Kahului Airport**, which is well placed for all the island's major destinations and has an information booth. Speedishuttle **buses** (☎808/661-6667 or 1-800/977-2605, ⓦwww.speedishuttle.com) connect the airport regularly with resorts around the island.

From the moment you arrive on Maui, promotional handouts and free newspapers will bombard you with details on the island's wide range of **activities**. Operators in all the tourist areas, especially along Front Street in Lahaina (see p.1362), including Barefoot's Hawaii at no. 834 (☏1-888/222-3601, ⓦwww.tombarefoot.com), offer cut-rate deals.

Snorkeling and diving

Maui's best-known **snorkeling** and **diving** spot is the tiny crescent of **Molokini**, poking above the sea – all that's left of a once-great volcano. There's no beach or landfall of any kind, but you do see a lot of fish, including deep-water species. Countless cruises leave early each morning (to avoid the worst of the heat) from Maalea Harbor; snorkelers can pay anything from $45 to $100 for a morning trip, and from $30 for a shorter afternoon jaunt. Vessels range from the forty-passenger *Blue Dolphin* (☏808/622-0075) up to the 150-seater *Prince Kuhio* (☏808/242-8777).

Downhill cycle rides

One of Maui's more unusual opportunities is to be taken by van to the top of **Haleakala**, watch the sun rise, and then ride a bicycle 39 miles down to Paia by the sea – without pedaling once. Serious cyclists may find the slow pace of the trip frustrating; complete novices or the unfit shouldn't try; the in-betweens will think it's great. Companies running trips for around $80 (including pickups) include Haleakala Bike Co. (☏808/575-9575 or 1-888/922-2453, ⓦwww.bikemaui.com) and Maui Downhill (☏808/871-2155 or 1-800/535-2453, ⓦwww.mauidownhill.com).

The offices of the **Maui Visitors Bureau** are hard to find, tucked away at 1727 Wili Pa Loop in Wailuku (Mon–Fri 8am–4.30pm; ☏808/244-3530 or 1-800/525-6284, ⓦwww.visitmaui.com), and it's easier simply to pick up information in major hotels.

Accommodation

Wailuku is nowhere near Maui's main resort areas, and lacks any hotels, but thanks to its two hostels and convenient restaurants, it's the island's most popular destination for budget travelers.

Banana Bungalow 310 N Market St, Wailuku ☏808/244-5090 or 1-800/846-7835, ⓦwww.mauihostel.com. Friendly, lively hostel that offers $20 dorm beds as well as some bare, basic doubles. Some organized trips and cut-price car rental. ❶–❷

Northwind Hostel 2080 Vineyard St, Wailuku ☏808/242-1448, ⓦwww.northwind-hostel.com. Ramshackle hostel with much the same communal feel as *Banana Bungalow*, along with $18 dorm beds and some plain private rooms. ❶–❷

Exploring Kahului and Wailuku

There's no sightseeing to speak of in either Kahului or Wailuku, though you may well become familiar with both while shopping for food and other necessities, which are better value here than elsewhere on the island. **Market Street** in Wailuku also contains several interesting curio and souvenir shops, and commands a view across to Haleakala.

Wailuku's Main Street heads straight into the **West Maui Mountains**, stopping three miles in at **Iao Needle**, a stunning 1200ft pinnacle of green-clad lava. It stands, head usually in the clouds, at the intersection of two lush valleys; you can't climb the needle itself, but hiking trails lead off in all directions, and as few visitors follow them for any distance, you can soon be alone in the wilderness. Kamehameha won control of Maui here in 1790, in a battle determined by a cannonade directed by two European gunners.

Eating

While both Kahului and Wailuku hold a handful of good-value **restaurants**, neither has anything that could be considered fine dining.

Maui Bake Shop & Deli 2092 Vineyard St, Wailuku ☏ 808/244-7117. Great deli, where you can pick up inexpensive breakfasts and lunches or simply buy superb fresh bread.

Maui Coffee Roasters 444 Hana Hwy, Kahului ☏ 808/877-2877. Relaxed espresso bar serving good breakfasts, lunch specials, and, of course, coffees.

Saeng's 2119 Vineyard St, Wailuku ☏ 808/244-1567. Pleasant, plant-filled restaurant, serving top-quality Thai food at bargain prices (entrees come in well under $20).

West Maui

Despite the guaranteed sunshine that draws the vacationers, you can feel somewhat cut off if you choose to stay on Maui's **west coast**, where the prices are higher than elsewhere on the island, and the long drive to get there is worsened by heavy traffic. The hotels and shopping centers are concentrated in the two main resorts, **Lahaina** and **Kaanapali**, although development has sensibly been restricted to the *makai* (oceanward) side of the Honoapiilani Highway, leaving the inland hills and valleys untouched except by drifting rainbows.

Lahaina

LAHAINA, West Maui's only real town, is one of the prettiest communities in all Hawaii. During the early nineteenth century it served as capital of the entire Kingdom of Hawaii, but it has barely grown since then, and still resembles the peaceful tropical village it used to be. Its main oceanfront street is lined with timber-frame buildings; coconut palms sway to either side of the mighty central banyan tree; surfers swirl into the thin fringe of beach to the south; and the mountains of West Maui dominate the skyline.

The view out to sea from Lahaina, towards the island of **Lanai**, is superb. If you have the time, consider taking a ferry there for the day; there's little to see on the island, but the main beach, at Hulopoe Bay, is a delight. Expeditions provides five sailings daily, from Lahaina Harbor ($25 each way; ☏ 808/661-3756, ⓦ www.go-lanai.com).

Accommodation

If you have the money to spend on resort-style **accommodation**, Lahaina and the coast to the north have some good options, but there's very little available for under $100 per night.

Best Western Pioneer Inn 658 Wharf St ☏ 808/661-3636 or 1-800/4575457, ⓦ www.pioneerinnmaui.com. Characterful and very lively old hotel, right in the thick of things. Tastefully furnished rooms come with private bath and air-conditioning. ❺

Ohana Maui Islander 660 Wainee St ☏ 808/667-9766 or 1-800/462-6262, ⓦ www.ohanahotels.com. Very central, low-key but attractively refurbished, mid-range accommodation. ❺

Old Lahaina House PO Box 10355, Lahaina, HI 96761 ☏ 808/667-4663 or 1-800/847-0761, ⓦ www.oldlahaina.com. Good-quality en suite B&B rooms in a friendly private home, complete with pool. ❹

Whale-hunting and whale-watching

The first **whaling ships** arrived in Hawaii in 1820, the same year as the missionaries – and had an equally dramatic impact. With the ports of Japan closed to outsiders, Hawaii swiftly became the center of the industry. Any Pacific port of call must have seemed a godsend to the whalers, who were away from New England for three years at a time, and paid so badly that most were either fugitives from justice or just plain mad (see p.237). Hawaii was such a paradise that up to fifty percent of each crew would desert, to be replaced by native Hawaiians, born seafarers eager to see the world. Soon King Kamehameha IV had established his own whaling fleet, and the economy adapted to meet the sailors' needs.

Until the 1840s, Honolulu, which permitted drinking, was the whalers' favorite port. Then potatoes and prostitution lured them to **Lahaina** as well, which by 1857 stretched for several miles. The sea here was calm enough for ships to dock beside the open road and stock up on provisions at a grassy marketplace beside a central canal.

At the peak of the trade, almost six hundred whaling vessels docked in Honolulu in a single year. Decline came with the Civil War – when many whaling ships were bought up and deliberately sunk to blockade Confederate ports – and an 1871 disaster, when 31 vessels lingered in the Arctic too long, became frozen in, and had to be abandoned.

Ironically, the waters just off western Maui now rate among the world's best areas for whale-watching and whale research. Between January and March each year, and for up to a month either side of that, **humpback whales** use the ocean channels here as both sanctuary and playground. The whales are often clearly visible from the shore, but specific whale-watching trips can take you much closer (with money-back guarantees if you don't see one). Operators include the nonprofit Pacific Whale Foundation ($20; ☎808/249-8811 or 1-800/942-5311, ⒲www.pacificwhale.org).

Food and nightlife

Lahaina's harborside malls contain a tremendous selection of **restaurants**, national and local chain outlets, and take-out places, not all of them good by any means, but covering a wider spectrum than the hotels.

David Paul's Lahaina Grill *Lahaina Inn*, 127 Lahainaluna Rd ☎808/667-5117. Upmarket dinner-only restaurant serving Maui's finest Pacific Rim cooking; it's slightly cramped, but the food is great.

The Feast at Lele 505 Front St ☎808/667-5353. An inspired cross between a *luau* and a gourmet restaurant. Each of the five Polynesian courses consists of at least two dishes – a colossal amount of food, but it's excellent and unusual, and the beachfront setting is superb. The $90 charge, though steep, includes unlimited cocktails and

other beverages. Reservations are essential. April–Sept Tues–Sat 6pm, Oct–March Tues–Sat 5.30pm.

Pacific 'O 505 Front St ☎808/667-4341. Pacific Rim cuisine served in an attractive oceanfront mall restaurant; try the amazing $30 Shrimp Nui.

Sunrise Café 693A Front St at Market St ☎808/661-8558. Small, laid-back, and very central café, with outdoor seating beside its own tiny patch of beach. Espressos, smoothies, salads, sandwiches, and daily specials are all on offer, with prices starting at around $6.

Kaanapali

KAANAPALI, just a few miles north of Lahaina but reliably cooler, was never a town; fields of sugar cane here were replaced in the 1960s by highrise hotels and condos, each no doubt comfortable enough but soulless en masse. Besides several perfect family **beaches** – swimming and snorkeling are best at **Black Rock**, in front of the *Sheraton* – the other main attraction is the **whaling museum** in the Whalers Village mall (daily 9.30am–10pm; free). Grisly but fascinating exhibits include a cast-iron "try pot," used for reducing whale blubber at sea; such pots gave rise to the stereotyped, but not entirely untrue, image of cannibals cooking missionaries in big black cauldrons.

A free shuttle bus connects Kaanapali with Lahaina, and a trolley operates within the resort. The warnings of the car rental companies concerning the sinuous **Kahekili Highway**, which on the map looks like a good route to continue on around northwest Maui and back to Wailuku, should be taken seriously; it's an exceptionally dangerous drive. Two of Maui's most famous **surfing** spots, at Mokuleia Bay and Honolua Bay, are a few miles along it, however, before the road gets too hair-raising.

Kihei and Wailea

Maui's other main resort area is south of Kahului, across the isthmus. The long strip of hotels, malls, and condos begins at **KIHEI**, with the road heavily built up on both sides, but thins out beyond the manicured lawns of **WAILEA**, near some superb beaches. **Paluea Beach** is ideal for families, while **Little Beach**, reached by a trail from cactus-lined **Makena (Big) Beach**, is famous for (illegal) nudism. Beyond that, the main road deterioriates to become a rough one-lane track with minimal visibility, and which peters out altogether just before **La Pérouse Bay**. Once a significant population center, the beach here is good for snorkeling, and **dolphins** regularly come to play with swimmers, though you're forbidden to encourage them.

Few of the **accommodation** options are geared towards budget travelers, though the pretty little *Sunseeker Resort*, 551 S Kihei Rd (☎808/879-1261 or 1-800/532-6284, Ⓦwww.maui.net/~sunseekr; ❸), which looks like an old-fashioned motel, has great-value ocean-view rooms, and the *Wailana Inn*, 14 Wailana Place (☎808/874-3131 or 1-800/399-3885, Ⓦwww.wailanabeach.com; ❺), is a slightly more expensive and comfortable version. For **food**, *Sansei*, at the Kihei Town Center (☎808/879-0004), offers great-value sushi and Pacific Rim concoctions.

Upcountry Maui

Hawaii is not always a land tarnished by civilization. **Central Maui**, in the nineteenth century "a dreary expanse of sand and shifting sandhills, with a dismal growth . . . of thornless thistles," is now a pastoral idyll, thanks to an ingenious system of irrigation channels.

The highway to the top of **Haleakala** climbs higher, at a faster rate, than any road on earth. Starting in rich meadows, it climbs past purple-blossoming jacaranda, firs, and eucalyptus to reach open ranching land, and then ascends in huge curves to the volcanic desert and the crater itself.

Haleakala

Though **HALEAKALA** – "the House of the Sun" – is the world's largest dormant volcano, you may not appreciate its full ten-thousand-foot majesty until you're at the top. Shield volcanoes are not as dramatic as the classic cones, as lava oozes from fissures along broad flanks to create a long, low profile, and the summit is often obscured by clouds. That it hasn't erupted for two hundred years doesn't necessarily mean it won't ever again – in 1979, for example, Haleakala was thought more likely to explode than Mount St Helens (see p.1262).

The higher reaches of the mountain are a **national park**, which never closes (admission $10 per vehicle). Manhattan would fit comfortably into the awe-inspiring **crater**, almost eight miles across, which was for the ancient Hawaiians a site of deep spiritual power. The most popular time to come is for the **sunrise**; the **visitor center** at the top operates from just before dawn until 3pm (☎808/572-4400, ⊛www.nps.gov/hale). Hiking trails of varying difficulty cross the crater floor, where **camping** is permitted in three remote cabins that are awarded by lottery two months in advance. They require a hike of four to ten miles and a $40 fee per night. In addition, fifteen to twenty-five free tent sites outside the crater are available every day (first-come, first-served).

Makawao and Paia

Coming down from Haleakala, Hwy-365 leads north to two laid-back little country towns populated mainly by old Californian hippies: **MAKAWAO**, five miles up from the ocean, and **PAIA**, Maui's first plantation town, near the great windsurfing beach of **Hookipa**. Neither offers any accommodation, but in the center of Makawao, the friendly Italian restaurant *Casanova's*, 1188 Makawao Ave (☎808/572-0220), puts on live music at night, courtesy of the local community of rock exiles. Fresh fish is the specialty at the oceanfront *Mama's*, a mile east of Paia at 799 Poho Place (☎808/579-8488), while vegetarians will be glad of the top-quality food at *Fresh Mint*, 115 Baldwin Ave, in Paia (☎808/579-9144).

The road to Hana

The rains that fall on Haleakala cascade down Maui's long windward flank, covering it in thick, jungle-like vegetation. Convicts in the 1920s hacked out a road along the coast that has become a major tourist attraction, twisting in and out of gorges, past innumerable waterfalls and over more than fifty tiny one-lane bridges. All year round, and especially in June, the route is ablaze with color from orchids, rainbow eucalyptus, and orange-blossomed African tulip trees. The usual day's excursion is roughly fifty miles (three hours) each way from Paia, to **Oheo Gulch** just past Hana.

Hana

The former sugar town of **HANA** itself might seem a disappointment at the end of the road; it's a pleasant enough little community that isn't especially interested in attracting tourists. **Hasegawa's General Store** is a friendly place to pick up supplies, and a delightful **red-sand beach** can be reached by a precarious trail from the end of Uakea Road. Rooms at the deluxe *Hotel Hana-Maui* (☎808/248-8211 or 1-800/3215-4262, ⊛www.hotelhanamaui.com; ❾) *start* at around $400; *Joe's Place* on Uakea Road is a basic but affordable alternative (☎808/248-7033, ⊛www.joesrentals.com; ❸). There's also **camping** beside the black-sand beach at lovely Waianapanapa State Park, four miles short of Hana (☎808/984-8109; $5).

Beyond Hana

Ten miles out of Hana is the gorgeous **Oheo Gulch** – a far-flung outpost of Haleakala National Park (admission free), where waterfalls tumble down the hillside to oceanfront meadows. If you hike a mile or two into the hills, you'll soon escape the crowds and reach cool rock pools that are ideal for swimming. If you're averse to going back the same way you came, in normal conditions (but *not* rain) it is possible to follow the road right around southern Maui, though bear in mind that its unpaved stretches invalidate rental-car insurance. Eventually, after a thirty-mile climb up bleak lava fields, it rounds the corner to give spectacular views out to the island of **Kahoolawe** (a naval bombing range until 1990, which has now been returned for restoration to the Hawaiians). You're now back in upcountry Maui, and soon come to the **Tedeschi Winery** (daily 9am–5pm; free), Hawaii's only vineyard, which produces white, red, and rosé wines, as well as Maui Brut sparkling wine.

Kauai

Although no point on the tiny island of **KAUAI** is as much as a dozen miles from the sea, the variety of its landscapes is quite incredible. This is the oldest of the major islands, and the forces of erosion have had more than six million years to sculpt it into fantastic shapes. The mist-shrouded extinct volcano **Mount Waialeale** at its heart is the world's wettest spot, draining into a high landlocked swamp, and full of unique plants and animals. Nearby is the chasm of **Waimea Canyon**, while the north shore holds the vertiginous green cliffs of the awe-inspiring **Na Pali** coast, familiar to millions from films such as *Jurassic Park* and *South Pacific*, but the sole preserve of adventurous **hikers**. Kauai is a place to be active, on sea and land; and if you only take one **helicopter** flight in your life, this is the place to do it.

Lihue

Flights to Kauai arrive at the capital, **LIHUE**, which stands slightly inland of little Nawiliwili Harbor. It's roughly at the midpoint of the one main road that encircles the island (prevented from completing a loop by the Na Pali cliffs), but as a base it's pretty undistinguished. The population is just five thousand, and downtown consists of a few tired plantation-town streets set well back from the sea and surrounded by anonymous malls.

The small **Kauai Museum** at 4428 Rice St (Mon–Fri 9am–4pm, Sat 10am–4pm; $5) traces the island's history from the mythical *menehune* (the most ancient Hawaiian people) through Captain Cook's 1778 landfall and on to its sugar-growing heyday. Kauai was the one island not conquered by Kamehameha the Great; he spent six years amassing a fleet that never sailed, and settled in the end for accepting economic tribute.

Practicalities

Lihue's **airport** is only two miles from downtown ($8 by **taxi**; Wailua or Kapaa cost closer to $20). Along with the usual **car** rental outlets, it also has

helicopters – Safari Helicopter Tours (☎808/246-0136 or 1-800/326-3356, ⓦwww.safariair.com) is typical, offering basic tours from $120. The **Hawaii Visitors Bureau** is in town at 4334 Rice St (Mon–Fri 8am–4.30pm; ☎808/245-3971 or 1-800/262-1400, ⓦwww.kauaivisitorsbureau.org).

There's no great point staying in Lihue rather than along the coast. However, the *Garden Island Inn*, near the harbor at 3445 Wilcox Rd (☎808/245-7227 or 1-800/648-0154, ⓦwww.gardenislandinn.com; ❹), is a lovely, refurbished three-story motel, dripping with purple bougainvillea. For a quick meal in the heart of town, call in at *Hamura's Saimin*, 2956 Kress St (☎808/245-3271), a family-run communal Japanese food counter, which is open very late and specializes in bowls of *saimin* (noodles) for $3.50. A mile or two east, the *Hanamaulu Restaurant and Tea House* (☎808/245-2511) is a delightful old place, complete with fishponds, that serves both Chinese and Japanese food.

East Kauai

Most Kauaians live between Lihue and the overlapping communities of **WAILUA**, **WAIPOULI**, and **KAPAA**, whose malls, condos, and hotels blend into each other a few miles north of the capital. All the way along there's an exposed thin strip of beach; only Wailua is especially aesthetic, and you have to go further north for snorkeling.

Accommodation

Most East Shore **hotels** are in the luxury bracket, but there are several possibilities on a more affordable scale.

Hotel Coral Reef 1516 Kuhio Hwy, Kapaa ☎808/822-4481 or 1-800/843-4659, ⓦwww.hotelcoralreef.com. Simple little hotel facing the beach that offers some of Kauai's best rates. ❸

Kauai International Hostel 4532 Lehua St, Kapaa ☎808/823-6142, ⓦwww.kauaihostel.net. Kauai's only hostel, across from Kapaa Beach and open to everyone except Hawaiian residents, with a maximum one-week stay. $20 dorm beds and a few private rooms are available. ❶–❸

Lae Nani 410 Papaloa Rd, Wailua ☎808/822-4938 or 1-800/367-7052, ⓦwww.outrigger.com. Irresistible complex of luxurious oceanfront apartments and condos, with lovely swimming alongside. ❼

Eating

Kapaa is the only town in East Kauai with anything like a center; you can windowshop for **restaurants** along its street of wooden stores, which are fronted by a beach park.

Caffè Coco 4-1639 Kuhio Hwy, Wailua ☎808/822-7990. Attractively ramshackle café, serving cheap and wholesome, if not entirely vegetarian, breakfasts and lunches for under $10, plus changing dinner specials. Closed Mon.

Korean Bar-B-Q Restaurant 4-3561 Kuhio Hwy, Wailua ☎808/823-6744. Unassuming barbecue diner serving excellent grilled meats and chicken; the best bet for a bargain meal, with large combos for under $10.

Mema 4-361 Kuhio Hwy, Wailua ☎808/823-0899. Large, attractive Thai/Chinese restaurant offering great curries with fresh spices for around $10.

A Pacific Café 4-831 Kuhio Hwy, Kapaa ☎808/822-0013. Very popular for its exotic and utterly wonderful Pacific cuisine, though entrees are expensive ($20–28). Dinner only.

North Kauai

That part of northern Kauai that is unique and unspoiled seems to be diminishing all the time. The astonishing valleys of the **Na Pali coast**, however, are likely to remain inviolate – though accessible enough by canoe to sustain large Hawaiian populations, their awesome walls shield them from any attempt to build roads.

Long, golden **Secret Beach**, hidden away from the road up from Kapaa, is among Kauai's best-looking beaches, though swimming here is usually unsafe. An unofficial center for campers and nudists, local landowners have been cracking down on long-term stays. To get there, drive up Hwy-56 from the south, pass **Kilauea**, and then turn right at Kalihiwai. Take the second right onto a dirt track leading to a parking area, and the beach is a ten-minute walk down through the woods. At the far end, a waterfall of beautiful fresh mountain water cascades down the cliffs, and there are often spinner dolphins just offshore, especially around the picturesque 1913 Kilauea **lighthouse**. The cliffs above are a bird sanctuary.

Hanalei

For the moment, major development stops beyond the resort of **Princeville**, mainly because the road then crosses seven successive one-lane bridges. The first is over the Hanalei River, where the valley stretching away inland is a National Wildlife Refuge. Here endangered Hawaiian ducks, coots, and stilts are protected by the preservation of their major habitats – natural wetlands and taro ponds. As a result, this is a rare chance to see a Hawaiian landscape relatively unchanged since ancient times.

The small town of **HANALEI**, set around a magnificent bay, has some low-key apartments for rent, but otherwise little formal accommodation. Of local **restaurants**, the busy *Hanalei Gourmet* in the Hanalei Center mall (☎808/826-2524) makes an ideal stop for breakfast or a sandwich lunch, and also has live music every night.

Gorgeous **Lumahai Beach**, at the western edge of Hanalei Bay, has starred in countless movies, among them *South Pacific*, but is too treacherous for swimming. All the roadside beaches from here on, however, are good for snorkeling. Just two miles from the start of the Na Pali coast (see below), the *Hanalei Colony Resort* (☎808/826-6235 or 1-800/628-3004, ⓦwww.hcr.com; ❼) is Kauai's most dramatic waterfront property, within a few feet of the pounding surf; its units all have two bedrooms. The road finally comes to an end at **Kee Beach**, perhaps the loveliest spot of all.

The Na Pali coast

The lush valleys of the **Na Pali coast**, separated by knife-edge ridges of rock often thousands of feet high but just a few feet thick, make Kauai one of the world's great hiking destinations. Although many of the best views (other than from a helicopter) are from the trails in Kokee State Park (see opposite) or boat trips out to sea from Hanalei, the **Kalalau Trail** along the shore is unforgettable. The full eleven miles to Kalalau Valley is arduous and gets progressively more dangerous; in places you have to scramble along a precipitous (and shadeless) wall of crumbly red rock.

However, the first two miles of the trail, to **Hanakapiai Beach**, are probably the most beautiful. They're steep but straightforward, passing through patches of dense vegetation where you clamber over the gnarled root systems of the splay-footed *hala* (pandanus) tree. Creepers and vines hang down, and it's all exposed to the sun. From the beach, a further hour's arduous hike (off the main trail) leads inland to the natural amphitheater of the towering **Hanakapiai Falls**. It takes at least four and a half hours to get to the falls and back from the trailhead at Kee Beach, opposite the ten-mile marker at the end of the road. Hikers and campers doing anything more than a day-hike must obtain **permits**, costing $10 per person per night, from the State Parks Office (3060 Eiwa St, Lihue, HI 96766; Mon–Fri 8am–3.30pm; ☎808/274-3444). Accidents and drownings are not uncommon, and the staff need a record of who may be missing.

South Kauai

POIPU, Kauai's principal beach resort, lies on the south coast roughly ten miles west of Lihue, where sunshine is more consistent and there's great surfing and snorkeling. Its finest **hotel** is the sumptuous *Hyatt Regency*, 1571 Poipu Rd (☎808/742-1234 or 1-800/554-9288, ⓦwww.kauai-hyatt.com; ⓭), while *Grantham Resorts* (☎808/742-7220 or 1-800/325-5701, ⓦwww.grantham-resorts.com; ⓹–⓽) quotes much lower prices for local condos than you'll be offered by individual properties. The best restaurants are two upmarket Pacific Rim options: *Casa di Amici*, 2301 Nalo Rd (☎808/742-1555), and *Roy's Poipu Bar & Grill* (☎808/742-5000), in the Poipu Shopping Village mall.

West Kauai

Two of the major scenic attractions in all Hawaii – the gorge of **Waimea Canyon** and **Kokee State Park** (with its views of the Na Pali cliffs to one side and the sodden Alakai Swamp to the other) – can only be reached from the **west coast** of Kauai. The coast itself, however, is nondescript. **WAIMEA**, the largest town here, is just one short street at the foot of the poorly marked road up to the canyon. The statue of **Captain Cook**, which commemorates his "discovery" of Hawaii here on January 20, 1778, is an exact replica of one in Cook's home town of Whitby, England. Western Kauai's only **accommodation** option is *Waimea Plantation Cottages* (☎808/338-1625 or 1-800/992-4632, ⓦwww.waimea-plantation.com; ⓺), set in an attractive coconut grove, and with a good restaurant and brewpub in the main plantation house.

Waimea Canyon and Kokee State Park

It's not unreasonable to call **Waimea Canyon** the "Grand Canyon of the Pacific." At three thousand feet, it may not be quite as deep as its Arizona rival, but the colors – all shades of green against the bare red earth – are absolutely breathtaking. Erosion by torrential rains created this landscape, but the process began when a massive geological fault almost split Kauai in two. The road from Waimea climbs beside the widening gorge, until after eight miles the mile-wide canyon can be seen in all its splendor. Each of the roadside lookouts is definitely worth stopping for.

Explore **Kokee State Park**, higher up, as early in the day as possible; by late morning the valleys may be filled with mist and clouds. Hiking trails lead off from both sides of the highway, and although the ranger station at **KOKEE**, the park headquarters, is often unstaffed, you can pick up trail information from the small but informative **Kokee Natural History Museum** nearby (daily 10am–4pm; $1 donation), where displays center on the area's indigenous wildlife. Kauai is the only island where mongooses have not killed off most native **birds**, and at this height mosquitoes are no threat either, so some of the world's rarest species (such as the *o'o a'a*) survive here and nowhere else.

  Kokee Lodge Housekeeping Cabins, next to the park headquarters, are rented by the day (PO Box 819, Waimea, Kauai, HI 96796; ☎808/335-6061; ❷), and there's free **camping**, available with a permit from the parks office in Lihue (see p.1367). For **food**, *Kokee Lodge* has lunch specials for around $8.

Awaawapuhi Trail

The **Awaawapuhi Trail** drops steeply from the road beyond Kokee, passing through three miles of dense forest before emerging abruptly onto a staggering view of a valley open only to the ocean, tucked between the Na Pali cliffs – their sheer razorback ridges almost vertical, though somehow covered with clinging vegetation.

Kalalau Lookout and Pihea Trail

A few miles further up, **Kalalau Lookout** stands over the valley where the Kalalau Trail ends – though to attempt a descent would be certain suicide. The **Pihea Trail** follows the course of a lunatic attempt to extend the road beyond its current end. At times it narrows to a few feet, with precipitous drops to either side, and visibility can drop to nothing as the clouds siphon across the ridges. Inland lies the **Alakai Swamp**, where the heaviest rainfall on earth collects in the volcanic rock; the few humans who manage to penetrate the mists are assailed on all sides by the shrills, whistles, and buzzes of a jungle without mammals or snakes. The trail running through the swamp consists of a boardwalk for almost its entire six-mile length, though in places the planks just rest on cloying black mud. Giant ferns dangle above the trail, and orchids gleam from the undergrowth. If you make it all the way to the end, you're rewarded with a stupendous panorama of Hanalei Bay.

Contexts

Contexts

A brief history of the USA

There is much more to the history of America than the history of the United States alone. In these few pages, however, there's little room to do more than briefly survey the peopling and political development of the disparate regions that now form the USA. That said, many of the events and issues discussed below are covered in more detail in the relevant chapters, while the books listed on pp.1396–1407 are invaluable resources for serious students.

First peoples

The first definitely dated trace of human beings in the Americas stems from just 14,000 years ago, when the true pioneers of North America, nomadic hunter-gatherers from Siberia, reached what's now **Alaska**. Thanks to the last ice age, when sea levels were three hundred feet lower than in the modern Bering Strait, a "**land-bridge**" – actually a vast plain, measuring six hundred miles north to south – connected Eurasia to America.

At that time, Alaska effectively formed part of Asia rather than North America, being separated by impenetrable glacier fields from what is now Canada and points south. Much like an air lock, the region has "opened" in different directions at different times; migrants reaching it from the west, oblivious to the fact that they were leaving Asia, would at first have found their way blocked to the east. Several generations might have passed, and the connection back towards Asia been severed, before an eastward passage appeared. When thawing ice did clear a route into North America, it was not along the Pacific coast but via a corridor that led east of the Rockies and out onto the Great Plains.

This migration was almost certainly spurred not by the urge to explore what must have seemed unpromising territory, but the pursuit of large mammal species, and especially **mammoth**, that had already been harried to extinction throughout almost all of Eurasia. A huge bonanza awaited the hunters when they finally encountered America's own indigenous "**megafauna**," such as mammoths, mastodons, giant ground sloths and enormous long-horned bison, all of which had evolved without fear of, or protection against, human predation.

Within a thousand years, both North and South America were filled with a total of ten million people. Although that sounds like a phenomenal rate of spread, only a small group of original human settlers need have been responsible. To achieve that impact, it would have taken a band of just one hundred individuals to enter the continent, and then advance a mere eight miles per year, with a population growth of 1.1 percent each year. The mass **extinction** of the American megafauna coincides so exactly with the advent of humans that humans must surely have been responsible, eliminating the giant beasts in each locality in one fell swoop, before pressing on in search of the next kill.

Quite apart from its ecological impact, the consequences of the elimination of large land mammals were legion. It precluded future American civilizations from domesticating any of the major animal species that were crucial to Old

World economies. Without cattle, horses, sheep, or goats, or significant equivalents, they lacked the resources used elsewhere to supply food and clothing to large settlements, provide draught power to haul ploughs or wheeled vehicles, or increase mobility and the potential for conquest. What's more, most of the human diseases later introduced from the rest of the world evolved in association with domesticated animals; the first Americans developed neither immunity to such diseases, nor any indigenous diseases of their own that might have attacked the invaders.

At least three distinct waves of **migrants** arrived via Alaska, each of whom went on to settle in, and adapt to, a more marginal environment than its predecessors. The second, five thousand years on, were the "**Nadene**" or Athapascans – the ancestors of the Haida of the Northwest, and also the Navajo and Apache of the Southwest – while the third, another two thousand years later, found their niche in the frozen Arctic north and became the **Aleuts** and the **Inuits**.

Within the modern United States, the earliest known settlement site, dating back 12,000 years, has been uncovered at Meadowcroft in southwest Pennsylvania. Five hundred years later, the Southwest was dominated by what archeologists call the **Clovis** culture, whose distinctive arrowheads were first identified at Clovis, New Mexico. Subsequent subgroups ranged from the Algonquin farmers of what's now New England to peoples such as the Chumash and Macah, who lived by catching fish, otters, and even whales along the coasts of the Pacific Northwest.

Nowhere did a civilization emerge that could rival the wealth and sophistication of the great cities of ancient Mexico, such as Teotihuacan or Tenochtitlan. However, the influence of these far-off cultures did filter north; the cultivation of crops such as beans, squash, and maize made the development of large communities possible, and northern religious cults, including those that performed human sacrifice, are thought to owe much to Central American beliefs. The so-called **Moundbuilders** of the **Ohio** and **Mississippi** valleys developed sites such as the Great Serpent Mound in modern Ohio and Poverty Point in Louisiana. The most prominent of these early societies, now known as the **Hopewell** culture, flourished between around 1 and 400 AD. Later on, **Cahokia**, just outside present-day St Louis, became the largest pre-Columbian city in North America, centered on a huge mound topped by some form of temple, and reaching its peak between 1050 and 1250 AD.

In the deserts of the **Southwest**, the Hohokam settlement of Snaketown, near what's now Phoenix in Arizona, set about grappling with the same problems of water management that plague the region today. Nearby, the **Ancestral Puebloan** "Basketmakers" developed pottery around 200 AD, and began to gather into the walled villages later known as pueblos, possibly for protection against the threat of Athapascan invaders, such as the Apache, who were arriving from the north. Ancestral Puebloan "cities," such as Pueblo Bonito in New Mexico's Chaco Canyon – a center for the turquoise trade with the mighty Aztec – and the "Cliff Palace" at Mesa Verde in Colorado, are the most impressive monuments to survive from ancient America. Although the Ancestral Puebloans are no longer identifiable as a group after the twelfth century – they probably dispersed after a devastating drought – many of the settlements created by their immediate descendants have remained in use ever since. Through centuries of migration, war, and changes of government, the desert farmers of the **Hopi Mesas** in Arizona (see p.1038), and the pueblos of **Taos** and **Ácoma** in New Mexico, have never been dispossessed of their homes.

Estimates of the total indigenous population held by the Americas before the arrival of the Europeans vary widely. Although serious suggestions for North

America range between two and twelve million, an acceptable median figure would be around fifty million people in the Americas as a whole, with five million of those in North America, speaking around four hundred different languages.

European contacts

The greatest seafarers of early medieval Europe, the **Vikings**, established a colony in Greenland around 982 AD. Under the energetic leadership of Eirik the Red, this became a base for voyages along the mysterious coastline to the west. **Leif Eiriksson** – also known as Leif the Lucky – spent the winter of 1001–02 at a site that has been identified with L'Anse aux Meadows in northern Newfoundland. Climatic conditions may well have been much better than they are today, though it remains unclear what were the "grapes" that led him to call it **Vinland**. Subsequent expeditions returned over the next dozen years, and may have ventured as far south as Maine. However, repeated clashes with the people the Vikings knew as **Skraelings** or "wretches" – probably Inuit, also newcomers to the area around this time – led them to abandon plans for permanent settlement.

A further five centuries passed before the crucial moment of contact with the rest of the world came on October 12, 1492, when **Christopher Columbus**, sailing on behalf of the Spanish, reached San Salvador in the Bahamas. A mere four years later the English navigator John Cabot officially "discovered" Newfoundland, and soon British fishermen in particular were setting up makeshift encampments in what became known as **New England**, to spend the winter curing their catch.

Over the next few years various expeditions mapped the eastern seaboard. In 1524, for example, the Italian **Giovanni Verrazano** sailed past Maine, which he characterized as the "Land of Bad People" thanks to the inhospitable and contemptuous behavior of its natives, and reached the mouth of what would become the Hudson River. The great hope initially was to find a sea route in the Northeast that would lead to China – the fabled **Northwest Passage**. To the French **Jacques Cartier**, the St Lawrence Seaway seemed a distinct possibility, and successive expeditions explored and attempted (unsuccessfully) to settle the northern areas of the Great Lakes region from the 1530s onwards. Intrepid trappers and traders began to venture ever further west.

To the south, the Spaniards had started to nose their way up from the Caribbean in 1513, when **Ponce de Leon**'s expedition in search of the Fountain of Youth landed at what is now Palm Beach, and named the region of **Florida**. Spanish attentions for the next few years focused on the lucrative conquest of Mexico, but in 1528 they returned under Panfilo de Narvaez, whose voyage ended in shipwreck somewhere in the Gulf. One of his junior officers, **Cabeza de Vaca**, managed to survive, and together with three shipmates spent the next six years on an extraordinary odyssey across Texas into the Southwest. Sometimes held as slaves, sometimes revered as seers, they finally managed to get back to Mexico in 1534, bringing tales of golden cities deep in the desert, known as the **Seven Cities of Cibola**.

One of Cabeza de Vaca's companions was a black African slave called **Estevanico the Moor**, a giant of a man who had amazed the native peoples they encountered. Rather than return to a life of slavery, he volunteered to map the route for a new expedition; racing alone into the interior, with two colossal greyhounds at his side, he was killed in Zuni Pueblo in 1539. The following year, **Francisco Vázquez de Coronado**'s full party managed to prove to everyone's intense dissatisfaction that the Seven Cities of Cibola did not exist. They reached as far as the Grand Canyon, encountering the Hopi and other pueblo peoples along the way. Hernán Cortés, the conqueror of the Aztec, had meanwhile traced the outline of the peninsula of Baja California, and in 1542 Juan Cabrillo sailed right up the coast of California, failing to spot San Francisco Bay in the usual mists.

Although no treasures were found in North America to match the vast riches plundered from the Aztec and Inca empires, a steady stream of less spectacular discoveries – whether new foodstuffs such as potatoes, or access to the cod fisheries of the northern Atlantic – began to boost economies throughout Europe. It was the Spanish who established the first permanent settlement in the present United States, when they founded **St Augustine** on the coast of Florida in 1565 – permanent, at least, until it was burned to the ground by Sir Francis Drake in 1586. In 1598 the Spanish also succeeded in subjugating the pueblo peoples, and founded the colony of New Mexico along the Rio Grande. This was more of a missionary rather than military enterprise, and its survival always precarious due to the vast tracts of empty desert that separated the colony from the rest of Mexico. Nonetheless, the construction of a new capital, **Santa Fe**, began in 1609 (see p.972).

The growth of the colonies

The great rivalry between the English and the Spanish in the late sixteenth century extended right around the world. Freebooting English adventurers-cum-pirates contested Spanish hegemony along both coasts of North America. Sir Francis Drake staked a claim to California in 1579, five years before **Sir Walter Raleigh** claimed **Virginia** in the east, in the name of his Virgin Queen, Elizabeth I. The party of colonists he sent out in 1585 established the short-lived settlement of **Roanoke**, now remembered as the mysterious "Lost Colony" (see p.516).

The Native Americans encountered by the earliest settlers were seldom hostile at the outset. To some extent the European newcomers were obliged to make friends with the locals; most had crossed the Atlantic to find religious freedom or to make their fortunes, and lacked the experience or even the inclination to make a success of the mundane business of subsistence farming. Virginia's first enduring colony, **Jamestown**, was founded by Captain John Smith on May 24, 1607. He bemoaned "though there be Fish in the Sea, and Foules in the ayre, and Beasts in the woods, their bounds are so large, they are so wilde, and we so weake and ignorant, we cannot much trouble them"; not surprisingly, six out of every seven colonists died within a year of their arrival in the New World.

Gradually, however, the settlers learned the techniques necessary to cultivate the strange crops that grew in this unfamiliar terrain. As far as the English government was concerned, the colonies were strictly commercial ventures, intended to produce crops that could not be grown at home, and it was inconceivable to them that the colonists might have goals of their own. After early failures with sugar and rice, Virginia finally found its feet with its first **tobacco** harvest in 1615 (the man responsible, John Rolfe, is now better known as the husband of Pocahontas). A successful tobacco plantation requires two things in abundance: land, which intensified the pressure to dispossess the Indians, and labor. No self-respecting Englishman came to America to work for others; when the first **slave** ship called in at Jamestown in 1619, the captain found an eager market for his cargo of twenty African slaves. By that time there were already a million slaves in South America.

The 102 **Puritans** known to history as the "**Pilgrim Fathers**" were deposited on Cape Cod by the *Mayflower* in late 1620, and soon moved on to set up their own colony at Plymouth (see p.224). Fifty of them died during that winter, and the whole party might well have perished but for their fortuitous encounter with the extraordinary **Squanto**. This Native American had twice been kidnapped and taken to Europe and succeeded in making his way home; during his wanderings he had spent four years working as a merchant in the City of London, and had also lived in Spain. Having recently come home to find his entire tribe exterminated by smallpox, he decided to throw in his lot with the English. With his guidance, they finally managed to reap their first harvest, celebrated with the mighty feast of **Thanksgiving** that is still commemorated today.

Of greater significance to the history of New England was the founding in 1630 of a new colony, further up the coast at Naumkeag (which became Salem), by the Massachusetts Bay Company. Its governor, **John Winthrop**, soon moved to establish a new capital on the Shawmut peninsula – the city of **Boston**, complete with its own university of Harvard. His vision of a Utopian "City on a Hill" did not extend to sharing Paradise with the Indians; he argued that they had not "subdued" the land, and it was therefore a "vacuum" for the Puritans to use as they saw fit. While their faith helped individual colonists to endure the early hardships, the colony as a whole failed to maintain a strong religious identity (the Salem witch trials of 1692 did much to discredit the notion that the New World had any moral superiority to the Old), and breakaway groups soon left to create the rival settlements of Providence and Connecticut.

Between 1620 and 1642, sixty thousand migrants – which amounted to 1.5 percent of the population – left England for America. Those who came in pursuit of economic opportunities tended to join the longer-established colonies, where in effect they diluted the religious zeal of the Puritans. Groups hoping to find spiritual freedom were more inclined to start afresh; thus **Maryland** was created as a haven for Catholics in 1632, and fifty years later **Pennsylvania** was founded by the Quakers.

The English were not alone, however. After Sir Henry Hudson rediscovered Manhattan in 1609, it was "bought" by the **Dutch** in 1624 – though the Indians who took their money were passing nomads with no claim to it either. The Dutch colony of New Amsterdam, founded in 1625, lasted less than forty years before it was captured by the English and renamed **New York**; by that time, there was a strong Dutch presence on the lower reaches of the Hudson River.

From their foothold in the Great Lakes region, meanwhile, the **French** sent the explorers Joliet and Marquette to map the course of the Mississippi in 1673. They turned back once they had established that the river did indeed flow into the Gulf of Mexico, but their trip cleared the way for the foundation of the huge and ill-defined colony of **Louisiana** in 1699. The city of **New Orleans**, at the mouth of the Mississippi, was created in 1718.

While the Spanish remained firmly ensconced in Florida, things were not going so smoothly in the Southwest. In the bloody **Pueblo Revolt** of 1680, the pueblo peoples managed to drive the Spanish out of New Mexico altogether, only to have them return in force a dozen years later. Thereafter, a curious synthesis of traditional and Hispanic religion and culture began to evolve, and, but for hostile raids from the north, the Spanish presence was not seriously challenged.

With the arrival of the foreigners, things were also changing in the unknown hinterland. The frontier in the east was pushing steadily forward, as colonists seized Indian land, with or without the excuse of an "uprising" or "rebellion" to provoke them into bloodshed. The major killer of the indigenous peoples, however, was **smallpox**, which worked its way deep into the interior of the continent long before the Europeans. (Scientists speculate that the Native Americans may have had no equivalent "new" diseases to inflict on the newcomers because of the long period their ancestors had spent crossing the Arctic in subzero temperatures.) As populations were decimated, great migrations took place. In addition, around this time the **horse** arrived on the Great Plains. The original inhabitants of the region were sedentary farmers, who also hunted buffalo by driving them over rocky bluffs. The bow and arrow was discovered around the fifth century, but the acquisition of horses (probably captured from the Spanish, and known at first as "mystery dogs") made possible the emergence of an entirely new, nomadic lifestyle. Groups such as the Cheyenne and the Apache swept their rivals aside to dominate vast territories, and eagerly seized the potential offered by firearms when they were introduced in due course. This created a very dynamic, but fundamentally unstable culture, as they became dependent on trade with Europeans for the necessities of life.

The American Revolution

The American colonies prospered during the **eighteenth century**, with the cities of Boston, New York, and **Philadelphia** in particular becoming home to a wealthy, highly educated, and highly articulate middle class. Frustration began to mount at the inequities of the colonies' relationship with Britain. While they were allowed to trade among themselves, the Americans could otherwise only sell their produce to the British, and all transatlantic commerce had to be undertaken in British ships.

Although full-scale independence was not an explicit goal until late in the century, the main factor making it possible was the economic impact of the pan-European conflict known as the **Seven Years' War**. Officially, the war in Europe lasted from 1756 to 1763, but fighting among the English, French, and Spanish in North America broke out a little earlier. Beginning in 1755 with the mass expulsion of French settlers from Acadia in Nova Scotia (triggering their epic migration to Louisiana, where as the **Cajuns** they remain to this day), the British went on to conquer all of Canada. In forcing the **surrender of Québec** in 1759, General Wolfe brought the war to a close; the French ceded Louisiana to the Spanish rather than let it fall to the British, while Florida passed into British control for a year before reverting to the Spanish. All the European monarchs were left hamstrung by debts, and it became apparent to the British that colonialism in America was not as profitable a business as in those parts of the world where the native populations could be coerced into working for their overseas masters.

There was one other major player on the scene – the **Iroquois Confederacy**. Evidence of Iroquois culture, characterized by military expansionism and even human sacrifice, has been found in the Great Lakes region dating from around 1000 AD onwards. Forever in competition with the Algonquin and the Huron, the southern Iroquois had by the eighteenth century resolved themselves into a League of Five Nations – the Seneca, Cayuga, Onondaga, Oneida, and Mohawk, all in what's now upstate New York. Wooed by both French and British, the Iroquois for most of the century charted an independent course between the two. During negotiations with the colonists in 1744, an Onondaga chief, unimpressed by the squabbling representatives of Pennsylvania, Virginia, and Maryland, had recommended "by your observing the same methods our wise forefathers have taken, you will acquire fresh strength and power." Benjamin Franklin, who was present, wrote in 1751 that "It would be a very strange thing if . . . ignorant savages should be capable of forming a scheme for such a union . . . that has subsisted ages and appears indissoluble; and yet that a like union should be impracticable for ten or a dozen English colonies."

Shortly after the Seven Years' War, an unsuccessful insurrection by the Ottawa tribe in 1763, led by their chief **Pontiac**, led the cash-strapped British to conclude that, while America needed its own standing army, it was not unreasonable to expect the colonists to pay for it.

In 1765, the British introduced the **Stamp Act**, which required duty on all legal transactions and printed matter in the colonies to be paid to the British Crown. Firm in the belief that there should be "no taxation without representation," delegates from nine of the colonies met in the Stamp Act Congress in October 1765. By that time, however, the British prime minister responsible for the Act had already been dismissed by King George III. Only briefly, in Georgia, were the offending stamps ever distributed, and the Act was repealed in 1766.

However, in 1767, Chancellor Townshend made political capital at home by proclaiming "I dare tax America," as he introduced a program of legislation that included the broadly similar Revenue Act. That led the merchants of Massachusetts, inspired by **Samuel Adams**, to vote to boycott English goods; they were subsequently joined by all the other colonies except New Hampshire. Townshend's Acts were repealed in turn by a new prime minister, Lord North, on March 5, 1770. By chance, on that same day a stone-throwing mob surrounded the Customs House in Boston; shots from the guards killed five people in what became known as the **Boston Massacre**. Even so, most of the colonies resumed trading with Britain, and the crisis was postponed for a few more years.

In May 1773, Lord North's **Tea Act** relieved the debt-ridden East India Company of the need to pay duties on exports to America, while still requiring the Americans to pay duty on tea. Massachusetts called for the colonies to unite in action, and its citizens took the lead on December 16 in the **Boston Tea Party**, when three tea ships were boarded and 342 chests thrown into the sea. As John Adams put it, "to let it be landed would be giving up the principle of taxation by Parliamentary authority."

The infuriated British Parliament thereupon began to pass a body of legislation collectively known as both the "Coercive" and the "Intolerable" Acts, which included closing the port of Boston and disbanding the government of Massachusetts. Thomas Jefferson argued that the acts amounted to "a deliberate and systematical plan of reducing us to slavery." To discuss a response, the first **Continental Congress** was held in Philadelphia on May 5, 1774, and attended by representatives of all the colonies except Georgia.

War finally broke out on April 18, 1775, when General Gage, the newly imposed governor of Massachusetts, dispatched four hundred British soldiers to destroy the arms depot at **Concord**, in order to prevent weapons from falling into rebel hands. Silversmith **Paul Revere** was dispatched by the citizens of Boston on his legendary ride to warn the rebels, and the British were confronted en route at Lexington by 77 American "Minutemen," and the resulting skirmish led to the "shot heard round the world."

Congress set about forming an army at Boston, and decided for the sake of unity to appoint a Southern commander, **George Washington**. One by one, as the war raged, the colonies set up their own governments and declared themselves to be states, and the politicians set about defining the society they wished to create. The writings of pamphleteer Thomas Paine – especially *Common Sense* – were, together with the Confederacy of the Iroquois, a great influence on the **Declaration of Independence**. Drafted by Thomas Jefferson, this was adopted by the Continental Congress in Philadelphia on July 4, 1776. The anti-slavery clauses originally included by Jefferson – himself a slave-owner – were omitted to spare the feelings of the Southern states, though the section that denounced the King's dealings with "merciless Indian Savages" was left in.

At first, the Revolutionary War went well for the British. General Howe crossed the Atlantic with around twenty thousand men, took New York and New Jersey, and ensconced himself in Philadelphia for the winter of 1777–78.

The Constitution

As signed in 1787 and ratified in 1788, the **Constitution** stipulated the following form of government:

All **legislative** powers were granted to the **Congress of the United States**. The lower of its two distinct houses, the **House of Representatives**, was to be elected every two years, with its members in proportion to the number of each state's "free Persons" plus "three fifths of all other persons" (meaning slaves). The upper house, the **Senate**, would hold two Senators from each state, chosen by state legislatures rather than by direct elections. Each Senator was to serve for six years, with a third of them to be elected every two years.

Executive power was vested in the **President**, who was also Commander in Chief of the Army and Navy. He would be chosen every four years, by as many "**Electors**" from each individual state as it had Senators and Representatives. Each state could decide how to appoint those Electors; almost all chose to have direct popular elections. Nonetheless, the distinction has remained ever since between the number of "popular votes," across the whole country, received by a presidential candidate, and the number of state-by-state "electoral votes," which determines the actual result. Originally, whoever came second in the voting automatically became **Vice President**.

The President could **veto** acts of Congress, but that veto could be overruled by a two-thirds vote in both houses. The House of Representatives could **impeach** the President for treason, bribery, or "other high crimes and misdemeanors," in which instance the Senate could remove him from office with a two-thirds majority.

Judicial power was invested in a **Supreme Court**, and as many "inferior Courts"as Congress should decide.

The Constitution has so far been altered by 27 **Amendments**. Those that have introduced significant governmental changes include **14** and **15**, which extended the vote to black males in 1868 and 1870; **17**, which made senators subject to election by direct popular vote, in 1913; **18**, introducing women's suffrage, in 1920; **22**, restricting the president to two terms, in 1951; **24**, which stopped states using poll taxes to disenfranchise black voters; and **26**, which reduced the minimum voting age to 18, in 1971.

Washington's army was encamped not far away at Valley Forge, freezing cold and all but starving to death. It soon became clear, however, that the longer the Americans could avoid losing an all-out battle, the more likely it was that the British would over-extend their lines as they advanced through the vast and unfamiliar continent. Thus, General Burgoyne's expedition, which set out from Canada to march on New England, was so harried by rebel guerrillas that he found himself obliged to surrender at Saratoga in October 1777. As the logistical difficulty of maintaining the British war effort became ever more apparent, other European powers took delight in coming to the aid of the Americans. Benjamin Franklin led a wildly successful delegation to France to request support, and soon the nascent American fleet was being assisted in its bid to cut British naval communications by both the French and the Spanish. The end came when Cornwallis, who had replaced Howe, was instructed to dig in at Yorktown and wait for the Royal Navy to come to his aid, only for the French to seal off Chesapeake Bay and prevent reinforcement. Cornwallis surrendered to Washington on October 17, 1781, just fifteen miles from the site of the first English settlement at Jamestown.

The ensuing **Treaty of Paris** granted the Americans their independence on generous terms – the British completely abandoned their Native American allies, including the Iroquois, to the vengeance of the victors – and Washington entered New York as the British left in November 1783. The Spanish were confirmed in their possession of Florida.

The victorious US Congress met for the first time in 1789, and the tradition of awarding political power to the nation's most successful generals was instigated by the election of George Washington as the first president. He was further honored when his name was given to the new capital city of **Washington, DC**, deliberately sited between the North and the South.

The nineteenth century

In its first century, the territories and population of the new **United States of America** expanded at a phenomenal rate. The white population of North America in 1800 stood at around five million, and there were another one million African slaves (of whom thirty thousand were in the North). Of that total, 86 percent lived within fifty miles of the Atlantic, but no US city could rival Mexico City, whose population approached 100,000 inhabitants. (Both New York and Philadelphia reached that figure within twenty years, however, and New York had passed a million fifty years later.)

It had suited the British to discourage settlers from venturing west of the Appalachians, where they would be far beyond the reach of British power and therefore inclined to carry on independent existences. For George Washington, however, any agreement to follow such a policy had been a "temporary expedient to quieten the minds of the Indians." Adventurers such as **Daniel Boone** started to cross the mountains into Tennessee and Kentucky during the 1770s. Soon makeshift rafts, made from the planks that would later be assembled to make log cabins, were careering west along the Ohio River (the only westward-flowing river on the continent).

In 1801, the Spanish handed Louisiana back to the French, on the express undertaking that the French would keep it for ever. However, Napoleon swiftly realized that any attempt to hang on to his American possessions would

THE GROWTH OF THE UNITED STATES

Louisiana Purchase 1803
Ceded by Spain 1819
Texas annexed 1845
Oregon Territory established 1846
Ceded by Mexico 1848
Bought from Mexico 1854
Bought from Russia 1867
Annexed 1898

The date of statehood is given for each state.

involve spreading his armies too thinly. He chose instead to make the best of things by selling them to the United States for $15 million, in the **Louisiana Purchase** of 1803. The new territories extended far beyond the boundaries of present-day Louisiana (see map opposite), and for President Thomas Jefferson it was a matter of urgency to send the explorers **Lewis and Clark** to map them out. With the help of Sacagawea, their female Shoshone guide, they followed the Missouri and Columbia rivers all the way to the Pacific; in their wake, trappers and "mountain men" came to hunt in the wilderness of the Rockies. The **Russians** had already reached the Pacific Northwest by this time and established a network of fortified outposts to trade in the pelts of beaver and otter.

British attempts to blockade the Atlantic, primarily intended as a move against Napoleon, gave the new nation its first chance to flex its military muscles. Although British raiders succeeded in capturing Washington, DC, and burned the White House to the ground, the **War of 1812** most significantly provided the US with a cover for aggression against the Native American allies of the British. Thus **Tecumseh** of the Shawnee was defeated near Detroit, and **Andrew Jackson** moved against the Creek of the southern Mississippi. Jackson's campaign against the Seminole in Florida enabled the US to gain possession of the state from the Spanish; he was rewarded first with the governorship of the new state, and later by his election to the presidency. During his period in office, in the 1830s, Jackson went even further, and set about clearing all states east of the Mississippi of their native populations. The barren region that later became Oklahoma was designated as "Indian Territory," home to the "Five Civilized Tribes." The Creek and the Seminole, and the Choctaw and Chickasaw of Mississippi were eventually joined by the Cherokee of the lower Appalachians there, after four appalling months on the forced march known as the "**Trail of Tears**."

For the citizens of the young republic, it took only a small step from realizing that their country might be capable of spreading across the whole continent to supposing that it had a quasi-religious duty – a "**Manifest Destiny**" – to do so. At its most basic, that doctrine amounted to little more than a belief that might must be right, but the idea that they were fulfilling the will of God inspired countless pioneers to set off across the plains in search of a new life.

Mexico had by now gained its independence from Spain. The Spanish territories of the Southwest had never attracted enough migrants to turn into full-fledged colonies, and the American settlers who arrived in ever-increasing numbers began to dominate their Hispanic counterparts. The Anglos of **Texas** rebelled in 1833, under the leadership of General Sam Houston. Shortly after the legendary setback at the **Alamo** (see p.770), in 1836, they defeated the Mexican army of Santa Anna, and Texas became an independent republic in its own right.

The ensuing **Mexican War** was a bare-faced exercise in American aggression, in which most of the future leading figures of the Civil War received their first experience fighting on the same side. The conflict resulted in the acquisition not only of Texas, but also of Arizona, Utah, Colorado, Nevada, New Mexico, and finally California, in 1848. A token US payment of $15 million to the Mexican government was designed to match the Louisiana Purchase. Controversy over whether slavery would be legal in the new states was rendered academic when it turned out that, on virtually the same day the war ended, gold had been discovered in the Sierra Nevada of California. The resultant **Gold Rush** created California's first significant city, San Francisco, and brought a massive influx of free white settlers to a land that was in any case utterly unsuitable for a plantation-based economy.

Proponents of Manifest Destiny seem never to have given much thought to the **Pacific Northwest**, which remained nominally under the control of British Canada. However, once the Oregon Trail started to operate in 1841 (see p.1291), American settlers there swiftly outnumbered the British. In 1846, a surprisingly amicable treaty fixed the border along the 49th parallel, just as it already did across eastern Canada, and left the whole of Vancouver Island to the British.

The Civil War

From the moment of its inception, the unity of the United States had been based on shaky foundations. Great care had gone into devising a **Constitution** that balanced the need for a strong federal government with the aspirations for autonomy of its component states. That was achieved by giving Congress two separate chambers – the **House of Representatives**, in which the number of representatives from each state depended upon its population, and the **Senate**, in which each state, regardless of size, had two members. Thus, although in theory the Constitution remained silent on the issue of **slavery**, it allayed the fears of the less populated Southern states (where although the slaves lacked the vote, each was counted as three-fifths of a person when it came to determining the number of representatives elected per state) that the voters of the North might destroy their economy by forcing them to abandon their "peculiar institution." However, it gradually became apparent that the system only worked so long as there were equal numbers of "Free" and slave-owning states. The only practicable way to keep the balance was to ensure that each time a new state was admitted to the Union, a matching state taking the opposite stance on slavery was also admitted. Thus the admission of every new state became subject to endless intrigue. The 1820 **Missouri Compromise**, under which Missouri joined as a slave-owning state and Maine as a Free one, was straightforward in comparison to the prevaricating and chest-beating that surrounded the admission of Texas, while the Mexican War was widely seen in the North as a naked land grab for new slave states.

Abolitionist sentiment in the North was not all that great before the middle of the nineteenth century. At best, after the importation of slaves from Africa ended in 1808, Northerners had vague hopes that slavery was an anachronism that might simply wither away. As it turned out, the profitability of the Southern plantations was dramatically boosted by the development of the cotton gin, and the increased demand for manufactured cotton goods triggered by the **Industrial Revolution**. What ultimately changed the situation was the rapid growth of the nation as a whole, making it ever more difficult to maintain a political balance between North and South.

Matters came to a head in 1854, when the **Kansas–Nebraska Act** sparked guerrilla raids and mini-wars between rival settlers by allowing both prospective states self-determination on the issue. That same year, the **Republican Party** was founded, on the platform of resisting the further expansion of slavery. Escaped former slaves such as Frederick Douglass were by now inspiring Northern audiences to moral outrage, and Harriet Beecher Stowe's *Uncle Tom's Cabin* found unprecedented readership.

In October 1859, **John Brown** – a white-bearded, wild-eyed veteran of some of Kansas's bloodiest infighting – led a dramatic raid on the US Armory at Harpers Ferry, West Virginia, intending to secure arms for a slave insurrection (see p.472). Swiftly captured by forces under the command of Robert E. Lee, he was hanged within a few weeks, proclaiming that "I am now quite certain that the crimes of this guilty land will never be purged away but with blood."

The Republican candidate for the presidency in 1860 was the little-known **Abraham Lincoln** from Kentucky; he won no Southern states, but with the Democrats split into Northern and Southern factions he was elected with 39 percent of the popular vote. Within weeks, on December 20, South Carolina became the first state to secede from the Union; the **Confederacy** was declared on February 4, 1861, when it was joined by Mississippi, Florida, Alabama, Georgia, Louisiana, and Texas. Its first (and only) president was **Jefferson Davis**, also from Kentucky; at their inauguration, his new vice-president remarked that their government was "the first in the history of the world based upon the great physical and moral truth that the negro is not equal to the white man." Lincoln was inaugurated in turn in March 1861, proclaiming that "I have no purpose, directly or indirectly, to interfere with the institution of slavery in the States where it exists. I believe I have no lawful right to do so, and I have no inclination to do so." He was completely inflexible, however, on one paramount issue: the survival of the Union.

The **Civil War** began just a few weeks later. The first shots were fired on April 12, when a much-postponed federal attempt to resupply Fort Sumter, in the harbor at Charleston, South Carolina, was greeted by a Confederate bombardment that forced its surrender. Lincoln's immediate call to raise an army against the South was greeted by the further secession of Virginia, Arkansas, Tennessee, and North Carolina. Within a year, both armies had amassed 600,000 men; Robert E. Lee had been offered command of both and opted for the Confederacy, while George McLellan became the first leader of the Union forces. Although the rival capitals of Washington, DC, and Richmond, Virginia, were a mere one hundred miles apart, over the next four years operations of war reached almost everywhere south of Washington and east of the Mississippi.

Tracing the ebb and flow of the military campaigns – from the Confederate victories of the early years, via Grant's successful siege of Vicksburg in 1863 and Sherman's devastating March to the Sea in 1864, to Lee's eventual surrender at Appomattox in April 1865 – it's easy to lose sight of the fact that it was not so much generalship as sheer economic (and man) power that won the war. The war pitted the **Union** of 23 Northern states, holding over 22 million people, against the **Confederacy** of 11 Southern states, with 9 million people. As for potential combatants, the North initially drew upon 3.5 million white males aged between 18 and 45 – and later recruited blacks as well – whereas the South had more like one million. In the end, around 2.1 million men fought for the Union, and 900,000 for the Confederacy. Of the 620,000 soldiers who died during the conflict, a disproportionate 258,000 came from the South – representing one quarter of its white men of military age. Meanwhile, not only was the North able to continue trading with the rest of the world as it maintained its industrial and agricultural output, but it also stifled the Confederacy with a devastating **naval blockade**. The Southern war effort was primarily financed by printing $1.5 billion of paper currency, which with neither reserves nor income to support it was so eroded by inflation that it became worthless.

Even so, the Confederacy came much closer to victory than is usually appreciated. The repeated out-maneuvering of federal forces by General **Robert E. Lee**, and his incursions into Union territory, meant that in each of three successive years, from 1862 to 1864, there was a genuine possibility that Northern morale would collapse, allowing opponents of the war to be elected to power and agree to peace. After all, the Revolutionary War had shown how such a war could be won: for the Union to triumph, it had to invade and occupy the South, and destroy its armies, but for the South to win it only had to survive until the North wearied of the struggle.

The dashing tactics of Confederate generals Lee and Jackson, forever counter-attacking and carrying the fight to the enemy, may have been in the finest romantic traditions of the Old South, but they arguably contributed to the Southern defeat. The grim, relentless total-war campaigning of Grant and Sherman eventually ground the South down. There's a particular irony in the fact that had the Confederacy sued for peace before Lee gave it fresh hope, a negotiated settlement might not have included the abolition of slavery. In the event, as the war went on, with Southern slaves flocking to the Union flag and black soldiers fighting on the front line, emancipation did indeed become inevitable. Lincoln took the political decision to match his moral conviction by issuing his **Emancipation Proclamation** in 1862, though the **Thirteenth Amendment** outlawing slavery only took effect in 1865.

Lincoln himself was assassinated within a few days of the end of the war, a mark of the deep bitterness that would almost certainly have rendered successful **Reconstruction** impossible even if he had lived. There was a brief period, after black men were granted the vote in 1870, when Southern states elected black political representatives, but without a sustained effort to enable former slaves to acquire land, racial relations in the South swiftly deteriorated. Thanks to white supremacist organizations such as the Ku Klux Klan, nominally clandestine but brazenly public, Southern blacks were soon effectively disenfranchised once more. Anyone working to transform the South came under attack either as a carpetbagger (a Northern opportunist who headed South for personal profit) or a treacherous scalawag (a Southern collaborator).

The aftermath of the Civil War can almost be said to have lasted for a hundred years. While the South condemned itself to a century as a backwater, the rest of the re-United States embarked on a period of expansionism and prosperity.

The Indian Wars

With the completion of the transcontinental railroad in 1867, Manifest Destiny became an undeniable reality. Among the first to head west were the troops of the federal army, with Union and Confederate veterans alike marching under the same flag to do battle with the remaining Native Americans. Treaty after treaty was signed, only to be broken as it became expedient to do so (usually upon the discovery of gold or precious metals). When the whites overreached themselves, or when driven to desperation, the Indians were capable of fighting back. The defeat of **General George Custer** at Little Bighorn in 1876, by **Sitting Bull** and his Sioux and Cheyenne warriors (see p.940), provoked the full wrath of the government. Within a few years, leaders such as **Crazy Horse** of the Oglala Sioux and **Geronimo** of the Apache had been forced to surrender, and their people were confined to reservations. One final act of resistance came in the form of the visionary, messianic cult of the **Ghost Dance**, whose practitioners hoped that by correct ritual observance they could win back their lost way of life, in a land miraculously free of white intruders. Such aspirations were regarded as hostile, and military harassment of the movement culminated in the massacre at **Wounded Knee** in South Dakota in 1890.

A major tactic in the campaign against the Plains Indians was to starve them into submission, by eliminating the vast herds of bison that were their primary source of food. As General Philip Sheridan put it, "For the sake of a lasting peace . . . kill, skin and sell until the buffalo are exterminated. Then your prairies can be covered by the speckled cow and the festive cowboy." More significant than the activities of the much-mythologized cowboys, however, was the back-breaking toil of the miners up in the mountains, and the home-steading families out on the plains.

Industry and immigration

The late nineteenth century was an era of massive **immigration** to North America from the rest of the world, with influxes from Europe to the East Coast paralleled by those from Asia to the West. As in Colonial times, national groups tended to form enclaves in specific areas – examples range from the Scandinavian farmers of Minnesota and the northern Plains, to the Basque shepherds of Idaho, and the Cornish miners of Colorado. In the Southwest, where individual hard work counted for less than shared communal effort, the **Mormons** of Utah had fled persecution eastward across the United States to become the first white settlers to eke a living from the unforgiving desert.

The fastest growth of all was in the nation's greatest **cities**, especially New York, Chicago, and Boston. Their industrial and commercial strength enabled them to attract and absorb migrants not only from throughout Europe but also from the Old South – particularly ex-slaves, who could now at least vote with their feet.

Now that it stretched "from sea to shining sea," the territorial boundaries of the US had reached almost their current form. In 1867, however, Secretary of State William Seward agreed to buy **Alaska** from the crisis-torn Russian government for $7.2 million. The purchase was at first derided as "Seward's Folly," but it was not long before the familiar Midas touch of the Americans was revealed by the discovery of gold there as well.

The various US presidents of the day, from the victorious General Grant (a man palpably out of his depth) onwards, now seem anonymous figures compared to the industrialists and financiers who manipulated the national economy. These "**robber barons**" included such men as John D. Rockefeller, who controlled seventy percent of the world's oil almost before anyone else had realized it was worth controlling; Andrew Carnegie, who made his fortune introducing the Bessemer process of steel manufacture; and J.P. Morgan, who went for the most basic commodity of all – money. Their success was predicated on the willingness of the government to cooperate in resisting the development of a strong labor movement. A succession of widely publicized strikes – such as those on the railroads in 1877, in the mines of Tennessee in 1891, and in the steel mills of Pittsburgh in 1892 – were forcibly crushed.

The nineteenth century had also seen the development of a distinctive American voice in **literature**, which rendered increasingly superfluous the efforts of passing English visitors – such as Charles Dickens, and the Trollopes, mother and son – to "explain" the United States. From the 1830s onwards, a wide range of writers set out to find new ways to describe their new world, with results as varied as the introspective essays of Henry Thoreau, the morbid visions of Edgar Allan Poe, the all-embracing novels of Herman Melville, and the irrepressible poetry of Walt Whitman, whose endlessly revised *Leaves of Grass* was an exultant hymn to the young republic. Virtually every leading participant in the Civil War wrote at least one highly readable volume of memoirs, while public figures as disparate as Buffalo Bill Cody and the showman P. T. Barnum also produced lively autobiographies. The boundless national self-confidence found its greatest expression in the vigorous vernacular style of **Mark Twain**, whose depictions of frontier life, whether in the journalistic *Roughing It* and *Life on the Mississippi*, or fictionalized in novels like *Huckleberry Finn*, gave the rest of the world perhaps its most abiding impression of the American character.

Many Americans saw the official "closure" of the Western frontier, announced by the Census Bureau in 1890, as tantamount to depriving the country of the Manifest Destiny that was its *raison d'être*, and were prompted to search for new frontiers further afield. Such **imperialist ventures** reached a crescendo in 1898, with the annexation of the Kingdom of **Hawaii** – which even then-President Cleveland condemned as "wholly without justification . . . not merely wrong but a disgrace" – and the double seizure of Cuba and the Philippines in the **Spanish–American War**, which catapulted **Theodore Roosevelt** to the Presidency. Though he took the African proverb "speak softly and carry a big stick" as his motto – and was hardly, if truth be told, noted for being soft-spoken – Roosevelt in office did much to heal the divisions within the nation. While new legislation reigned in the worst excesses of the Robber Barons, and of rampant capitalism in general, it alleviated popular discontent without substantially threatening the business community, or empowering the labor movement. A decade into the twentieth century, the United States had advanced to the point that it knew, even if the rest of the world wasn't yet altogether sure, that it was the strongest, wealthiest country on earth.

The twentieth century

It may not have been apparent to everyone at the time, but the first few years of the twentieth century witnessed the emergence of many of the features that came to characterize modern America. In 1903 alone, Wilbur and Orville Wright achieved the first successful powered **flight**, and Henry Ford established his Ford Motor Company. Ford's enthusiastic adoption of the latest technology in mass production – the assembly line – gave Detroit a head start in the new **automobile** industry, which swiftly became the most important business in America. Both **jazz** and **blues** music came to the attention of a national audience for the first time during that same period, while Hollywood acquired its first **movie** studio in 1911, and its first major hit in 1915 with D. W. Griffith's unabashed glorification of the Ku Klux Klan in *Birth of a Nation*.

This was also a time of growing **radicalism**. Both the NAACP (National Association for the Advancement of Colored People) and the socialist International Workers of the World ("the Wobblies") were founded in the early 1900s, while the campaign for women's suffrage also came to the forefront. Writers such as Upton Sinclair, whose *The Jungle* exposed conditions in Chicago's stockyards, and Jack London proselytized to the masses; contemporary improvements in the educational system suggest this may well have been the most literate period in US history.

President Wilson managed to keep the US out of the **Great War** for several years but, when the time came, American intervention was decisive. With the Russian Revolution illustrating the dangers of anarchy, the US also took charge of supervising the peace. However, although Wilson presided over the postwar negotiations that resulted in the Treaty of Versailles in 1919, isolationist sentiment at home kept the US from joining his pet scheme to preserve future world peace, the League of Nations.

Back home, the 18th Amendment to the Constitution, in 1920, forbade the sale and distribution of alcohol, while the 19th finally gave all American women the vote. Quite how **Prohibition** ever became the law of the land is something of a mystery; certainly, in the buzzing metropolises of the Roaring Twenties, it enjoyed little conspicuous support. There was no noticeable elevation in the moral tone of the country, and Chicago in particular became renowned for the street wars between bootlegging gangsters such as Al Capone and his rivals.

The two Republican presidents who followed Wilson did little more than sit back and watch the Roaring Twenties unfold. At least until his premature death, **Warren Harding** enjoyed considerable public affection, but he's now remembered as probably the worst of all US presidents, thanks to the cronyism and corruption of his associates. It's hard to say quite whether **Calvin Coolidge** did anything at all; his laissez-faire attitude extended to working a typical four-hour day, and announcing shortly after his inauguration that "four-fifths of our troubles would disappear if we would sit down and keep still."

The Depression and the New Deal

By the middle of the 1920s, the US was enough of an industrial powerhouse to be responsible for more than half the world's output of manufactured goods. After leading the way into a new era of prosperity, however, it suddenly found itself dragging the rest of the world down into economic collapse. It's hard to say exactly what triggered the **Great Depression**; the consequences were out of all proportion to any one specific cause. Possible factors include American overinvestment in the floundering economy of postwar Europe, combined with high tariffs on imports that effectively precluded European recovery. Conservative commentators at the time chose to interpret the calamitous **Wall Street Crash** of October 1929 as a symptom of impending depression rather than a contributory cause, but the quasi-superstitious faith in the stock market that preceded it showed all the characteristics of such classic speculative booms as Britain's eighteenth-century South Sea Bubble. On "Black Tuesday" alone, enough stocks were sold to produce a total loss of ten thousand million dollars – more than twice the total amount of money in circulation in the US. Within the next three years, industrial production was cut by half, the national income dropped by 38 percent, and, above all, unemployment rose from 1.5 million to 13 million.

National self-confidence, however shaky its foundations, has always played a crucial role in US history, and President Hoover was not the man to restore it. Matters only began to improve in 1932, when the patrician figure of **Franklin Delano Roosevelt** accepted the Democratic nomination for president with the words "I pledge myself to a new deal for America," and went on to win a landslide victory. At the time of his inauguration, early in 1933, the banking system had all but closed down; it took Roosevelt the now-proverbial "Hundred Days" of vigorous legislation to turn around the mood of the country.

Taking advantage of the new medium of radio, he used his "Fireside Chats" to cajole America out of crisis; among his earliest observations was that it was a good time for a beer, and that therefore the experiment of Prohibition was over. The **New Deal** took many forms and worked through many newly created agencies, but was marked throughout by a massive growth in the power of the federal government, which only now seems to be under threat. Among its accomplishments were the National Recovery Administration, which created two million jobs; the Social Security Act, of which Roosevelt declared "no damn politician can ever scrap my social security program"; the Public Works Administration, which built dams and highways the length and breadth of the country; the Tennessee Valley Authority, which by generating electricity under public ownership for the common good was probably the closest the US has ever come to institutionalized socialism; and measures to legitimize the role of the unions and revitalize the "Dust Bowl" farmers out on the plains.

Roosevelt originally saw himself as a populist who could draw support from every sector of society. By 1936, however, business leaders – and the Supreme Court – were making it clear that as far as they were concerned he had done more than enough already to kick-start the economy. From then on, as he secured an unprecedented four consecutive terms as president, he was firmly cast as the champion of the little man.

After the work-creation programs of the New Deal had put America back on its feet, the deadly pressure to achieve victory in **World War II** spurred industrial production and know-how to new heights. Once again the US stayed out of the war at first, until it was finally forced in by the high-stakes gamble of the Japanese, who launched a pre-emptive strike on Hawaii's Pearl Harbor in December 1941. In both the Pacific and in Europe, American manpower and economic muscle eventually carried all before it. Roosevelt died early in 1945, after laying the foundations for the postwar carve-up with Stalin and Churchill at Yalta, and thus was spared the fateful decision, made by his successor Harry Truman, to use the newly developed atomic bomb on Hiroshima and Nagasaki.

The coming of the Cold War

With the war won, Americans were in no mood to revert back to the isolationism of the 1930s. Amid much hopeful rhetoric, Truman enthusiastically participated in the creation of the **United Nations**, and set up the **Marshall Plan** to speed the recovery of Europe – a task in which it was far more successful than any of the corresponding attempts made 25 years earlier. However, as Winston Churchill announced in Missouri in 1946, an "**Iron Curtain**" had descended upon Europe, and Joseph Stalin was transformed from ally to enemy almost overnight.

The ensuing **Cold War** lasted for more than four decades, at times fought in ferocious combat (albeit often by proxy) in scattered corners of the globe, and during the intervals diverting colossal economic resources towards the stockpiling of ever more destructive arsenals. Some of its ugliest moments came in its earliest years; Truman was still in office in 1950 when war broke out in **Korea**. A dispute over the arbitrary division of the Korean peninsula into two separate nations, North and South, soon turned into a stand-off between the US and China (with Russia, in theory at any rate, lurking in the shadows). Two years of a bloody stalemate ended, with little to show for it, except that Truman had by now been replaced by the genial **Dwight D. Eisenhower**, the latest war hero to turn president.

The Eisenhower years are often seen as an era characterized by bland complacency. Once Senator **Joseph McCarthy**, the "witch-hunting" anti-Communist scourge of the State Department and Hollywood, had finally discredited himself by attacking the army as well, middle-class America seemed to lapse into a wilful suburban stupor. Great social changes were starting to take shape, however. World War II had introduced vast numbers of women and members of ethnic minorities to the rewards of factory work, and it had shown many Americans from less prosperous regions the lifestyle that was attainable in other parts of their own country. The development of a **national highway system**, and a huge increase in automobile ownership, encouraged people to pursue the American Dream wherever they chose. Combined with increasing mechanization on the cotton plantations of the South, this led to another **mass exodus** of blacks from the rural South to the cities of the North, and to a lesser extent the West. The cities of **California** entered a period of rapid growth, with the aeronautical industries of Los Angeles in particular attracting thousands of prospective workers.

It was also during the 1950s that **television** reached every home in the country. Together with the LP record, it created an entertainment industry that seemed designed to promote mass conformity, but which swiftly showed itself capable of addressing the needs of consumers who had previously been barely identified. **Youth culture** burst into public prominence from 1954 onwards, with Elvis Presley's recording of "*That's Alright Mama*" appearing within a few months of Marlon Brando's moody starring role in *On the Waterfront* and James Dean's in *Rebel Without a Cause*.

The civil rights years

Racial segregation of public facilities, which had remained the norm in the South ever since Reconstruction, was in 1954 finally declared illegal by the Supreme Court ruling on *Brown* v. *Topeka Board of Education*. Just as a century before, however, the Southern states saw the issue more in terms of states' rights than of human rights, and attempting to implement the law, or even to challenge the failure to implement it, required immense courage. The action of Rosa Parks in refusing to give up her seat to a white man on a bus in Montgomery, Alabama, in December 1955 triggered a successful mass boycott (see p.610), and pushed the 27-year-old **Rev Dr Martin Luther King Jr** to the forefront of the civil rights campaign. Further confrontation took place at the Central High School in Little Rock, Arkansas, in 1957 (see p.627), when the reluctant Eisenhower found himself forced to call in federal troops to counter the state's unwillingness to integrate its education system.

The election of **John F. Kennedy** to the presidency in 1960, by the narrowest of margins, marked a sea-change in American politics, even if in retrospect his policies do not seem exactly radical. At 43 the youngest man ever to be elected president, and the first Catholic, he was prepared literally to reach for the moon, urging the US to victory in the Space Race in which it had thus far lagged humiliatingly behind the Soviet Union. The two decades that lay ahead, however, were to be characterized by disillusion, defeat, and despair. If the Eisenhower years had been dull, the 1960s in particular were far too interesting for almost everybody's liking.

Kennedy's sheer glamour made him a popular president during his lifetime, while his assassination suffused his administration with the romantic glow of "Camelot." His one undisputed success, however, came with the **Cuban missile crisis** of 1962, when the US military fortunately spotted Russian bases in Cuba before any actual missiles were ready to use, and Kennedy faced down premier Khrushchev to insist they be withdrawn. On the other hand, he'd had rather less success the previous year, in launching the abortive **Bay of Pigs** invasion of Cuba, and he also managed to embroil America deeper in the ongoing war against Communism in Vietnam, by sending more "advisers," including Green Berets, to Saigon.

Although a much-publicized call to the wife of Rev Martin Luther King Jr, during one of King's many sojourns in Southern jails, was a factor in Kennedy's election success, he was rarely keen to identify himself with the **civil rights** movement. The campaign nonetheless made headway, given added momentum by the global television coverage of such horrific confrontations as the onslaught by Birmingham police on peaceful demonstrators in 1963. The movement's defining moment came when Rev King delivered his electrifying "I Have a Dream" speech during the March on Washington later that summer. King was subsequently awarded the Nobel Peace Prize for his unwavering espousal of Gandhian principles of nonviolence. Perhaps an equally powerful factor in middle America's recognition that the time had come to address racial inequalities, however, was the not-so-implicit threat in the rhetoric of **Malcolm X**, who argued that black people had the right to defend themselves against aggression.

After Kennedy's assassination in November 1963, his successor **Lyndon B. Johnson** pushed through legislation that enacted most of the civil rights campaigners' key demands. Even then, violent white resistance in the South continued, and only the long, painstaking and dangerous work of registering Southern black voters en masse eventually forced Southern politicians to mend their ways.

Johnson won election by a landslide in 1964, but his vision of a "**Great Society**" soon foundered. Instead, he was brought low by the war in **Vietnam**, where US involvement escalated beyond all reason or apparent control. Broad-based popular opposition to the conflict grew in proportion to the American death toll, and the threat of the draft heightened the mood of youthful rebellion. San Francisco in particular responded to psychedelic prophet Timothy Leary's call to "turn on, tune in, drop out"; 1967's "Summer of Love" saw the lone beatniks of the 1950s transmogrify into an entire generation of hippies.

From the earliest days of the civil rights struggle, Dr King had argued that social justice could only be achieved through economic equality. That message was given a new urgency by riots in the ghettos of Los Angeles in 1965 and Detroit in 1967, and the emergence of the Black Panthers, an armed defense force in the tradition of the now-dead Malcolm X. King also began to denounce the Vietnam War; meanwhile, after refusing the draft with the words "No Vietcong ever called me nigger," Muhammad Ali was stripped of his title as world heavyweight boxing champion.

In 1968, the very social fabric of the US reached the brink of collapse. Shortly after Johnson's plummeting popularity forced the president to withdraw from the year-end elections, Martin Luther King was gunned down in a Memphis motel. Next, JFK's brother **Robert Kennedy**, now redefined as spokesman for the nation's dispossessed, was fatally shot just as he emerged as Democratic front-runner. It didn't take a conspiracy theorist to see that the spate of deaths reflected a malaise in the soul of America.

Richard Nixon to Jimmy Carter

Somehow – perhaps because the brutally suppressed riots at the Chicago Democratic Convention raised the specter of anarchy – the misery of 1968 resulted in the election of Republican **Richard Nixon** as president. Eisenhower's vice-president while still in his thirties, Nixon had famously told the press after his failed bid for the governor of California in 1962 that "you won't have Nixon to kick around any more." Now he was back, and it soon became apparent that he had scores to settle with his countless perceived enemies, above all in the media. Nixon's impeccable conservative credentials enabled him to bring the US to a rapport with China, but the war in Vietnam dragged on, to claim a total of 57,000 American lives. Attempts to win it included the secret and illegal bombing of Cambodia, which raised opposition at home to a new peak, but ultimately it was simpler to abandon the original goals in the name of "peace with honor." The end came either in 1972 – when Henry Kissinger and Le Duc Tho were awarded the Nobel Peace Prize for negotiating a treaty, and Tho at least had the grace to decline the award – or in 1975, when the Americans finally withdrew from Saigon.

During Nixon's first term, many of the disparate individuals politicized by the events and undercurrents of the 1960s coalesced into **activist groupings**. Feminists united to campaign for abortion rights and an Equal Rights Amendment; gay men in New York's *Stonewall* bar fought back after one police raid too many; Native Americans formed the American Indian Movement; and even prisoners attempted to organize themselves, resulting in such bloody debacles as the storming of Attica prison in 1971. Nixon directed various federal agencies to monitor the new radicalism, but his real bugbear was the anti-war protesters. Increasingly ludicrous covert operations against real and potential opponents culminated in a botched attempt to burgle Democratic National Headquarters in the **Watergate** complex in 1972. It took two years of investigation for Nixon's role in the subsequent cover-up to be proved, but in 1974 he **resigned**, one step ahead of impeachment by the Senate, to be succeeded by **Gerald Ford**, his own unelected appointee as Vice President.

With the Republicans momentarily discredited, former Georgia governor **Jimmy Carter** was elected president as a clean-handed outsider in the bicentennial year of 1976. His victory showed how far the US had come in a decade, let alone two centuries; a crucial constituency for this new-style Southern Democrat was the recently enfranchised black population of the South. However, Carter's enthusiastic attempts to put his Baptist principles into practice on such issues as global human rights were soon perceived as naive, if not un-American. Misfortune followed misfortune. He had to break the news that the nation was facing an **energy crisis**, following the formation of the OPEC cartel of oil producers. Worse still, the Shah of Iran was overthrown, and staff at the US embassy in Tehran were taken hostage by Islamic revolutionaries. Carter's failed attempts to arrange their release was seized upon by the Republicans as a sign of his weak leadership, and all but destroyed his hopes of winning re-election in 1980. Instead he was replaced by a very different figure, the former Hollywood movie actor **Ronald Reagan**.

The Reagan–Bush years

Reagan was a new kind of president. Unlike his workaholic predecessor, Jimmy Carter, he made a virtue of his hands-off approach to the job, joking that "they say hard work never killed anybody, but I figured why take the risk?" That laissez-faire attitude was especially apparent in his domestic economic policies, under which the rich were left to get as rich as they could. The common perception that Reagan was barely aware of what went on around him allowed his popularity to remain undented by a succession of scandals, including the labyrinthine **Iran-Contra** affair, under which illegal arms sales to Iran were used to fund support for the Contra rebels in Nicaragua. When Reagan was finally confronted with proof that he had been wrong in his insistence that "I did not trade arms for hostages," he produced an extraordinary apology: "My heart and my best intentions still tell me that's true, but the facts and the evidence tell me it is not."

Reagan's most enduring achievement came during his second term, when, with his credentials as a Cold Warrior beyond question, the electorate allowed him greater leeway than a Democrat might have received to negotiate **arms-control** agreements with **Mikhail Gorbachev**, the new leader of what he had previously called the "Evil Empire." On the down side, his successors were left to cope with the explosion in the **national debt** that followed the combination of extensive **tax cuts** alongside the deregulation of the financial markets, the collapse of the savings and loan system, and above all, the enormous increases in defense spending that funded such pet projects as the Strategic Defense Initiative ("**Star Wars**").

In 1988, **George Bush** became the first Vice President in 150 years to be immediately elected to the presidency. Despite his unusually broad experience in foreign policy (which included a spell as director of the CIA), Bush did little more than sit back and watch in amazement as the domino theory suddenly went into reverse. One after another, the Communist regimes of eastern Europe collapsed, until finally even the Soviet Union crumbled away. Bush was also president when **Operation Desert Storm** drove the Iraqis out of Kuwait in February 1991, an undertaking that lasted 100 hours and in which virtually no American lives were lost. At the moment of triumph in Kuwait, Bush's soaring popularity seemed certain to guarantee his re-election.

And yet the much-anticipated "**peace dividend**" – the dramatic injection of cash into the economy that voters expected to follow the end of the arms race – never materialized. As one Democrat contender for the 1992 presidential nomination, Paul Tsongas, succinctly put it, "the Cold War is over and Japan won." Between 1980 and 1990, the US had gone from being the world's largest creditor to being the world's largest debtor. The national debt had trebled from $908 billion to $2.9 trillion, and much of the borrowing came from Japan, spared from incurring military expenditures on anything like the same scale. With the 1992 campaign focussing on domestic affairs rather than what was happening overseas, twelve years of Republican government were ended by the election of Arkansas Governor **Bill Clinton**.

Clinton and the end of the century

Clinton's first two years were characterized by his failure to deliver on specific promises – most obviously, to reform the health-care system. That enabled the Republicans to sweep to power in Congress in 1994, and resulted in two years of legislative gridlock. Displaying a better grasp of the popular mood, Clinton managed to assign most of the blame for the government's ineffectiveness to the Republicans and was elected to a second term with surprising ease. However, the "Comeback Kid" found holding on to office more of a challenge, when his adulterous affair with White House intern Monica Lewinsky was exposed in 1998. Special Prosecutor Kenneth Starr's exhaustive probing led to the disgrace of **impeachment**, but the Senate ultimately failed to convict, sensing perhaps that the American people did not feel Clinton's indiscretions were serious enough to merit removal. Clinton had lost his moral if not his actual authority, however, and the nation limped into the twenty-first century devoid of effective leadership.

The new millennium

As Clinton left the presidency, the economy was **booming**, coming to the end of a record ten-year burst of sustained growth that had seen the budget deficit eradicated far ahead of even the most optimistic schedule, and the Dow Jones rise by over 260 percent since the day Clinton came to office. His former Vice President, however, **Al Gore**, seemed too ashamed of his boss's character failings to bring himself to campaign on his economic record, and contrived to throw away the 2000 presidential election. Clinton is generally agreed to have won the 1996 election via "**triangulation**," adopting elements of his opponents' agenda to scoop up middle-ground voters; arguably, both Gore and his Republican opponent, **George W. Bush**, followed Clinton's example so well, and so precisely targeted the center of the political spectrum, that the result was inevitable: a **tie**. With the final conclusion depending on a mandatory re-counting of votes in Florida, where various irregularities and mistakes complicated the issue, the impasse was ultimately decided by the conservative **Supreme Court**, and Bush won the presidency. At the time, the charge that he had "stolen" the election was expected to seriously impair his presidency, while the authority of the Supreme Court was also threatened by the perception of its ruling as partisan.

A **recession** was probably due whoever was in the White House, as the bursting of the dot-com bubble drove hundreds of high-tech companies into bankruptcy. However, during his first months in office Bush showed little sign of halting the slide, and also seemed alarmingly indifferent to the concerns of America's friends and neighbors abroad. As well as cutting taxes and federal spending, he alienated environmentalists by rejecting US compliance with the 1997 Kyoto Agreement on global warming, and announcing that he hoped to open the Arctic National Wildlife Refuge (ANWR) to oil and gas development.

Then the atrocity of **September 11th, 2001**, abruptly made matters infinitely worse, inflicting a devastating blow to both the nation's economy and its pride. Over three thousand people were killed in the worst **terrorist attack** in US history, when two hijacked planes were flown into the **World Trade Center** in New York City, and one into the **Pentagon**. (A fourth crashed in Pennsylvania after its passengers and crew attempted to regain control.) The attacks were quickly linked to the al-Qaida network of Saudi Arabian terrorist **Osama bin Laden**, and within weeks President Bush declared an open-ended war against terrorism.

Bush found himself confronting a new, changed world where the costs of maintaining vigilance and military preparedness seem incalculable, and yet the costs of not doing so might prove even higher. Far from balking at the challenge, he has re-written the traditional rule-book of diplomacy and international law, declaring in June 2002 that the US has a right to launch **pre-emptive attacks**: "If we wait for threats to fully materialize, we will have waited too long . . . We must take the battle to the enemy, disrupt his plans, and confront the worst threats before they emerge." By the end of 2003, US-led invasions had taken control of both **Afghanistan** in 2001, and **Iraq** in 2003. While bin Laden was still nowhere to be seen, Iraqi dictator **Saddam Hussein** was apprehended in December 2003 – yet a clear sense of where the **war on terror** would be directed next remains elusive. We live in dangerous times.

Books

I t would be futile to attempt to provide a comprehensive overview of American literature in the limited space available. The following bibliography is, therefore, an idiosyncratic selection of books intended as a starting point for interested readers. Books tagged with the ★ symbol are particularly recommended.

History and society

Stephen E. Ambrose and Douglas Brinkley *Rise to Globalism*. A compelling account of US foreign policy from 1938 to the present day that never pulls its punches, and always seems to have something new to say.

★ **James Baldwin** *No Name on the Street, The Fire Next Time, Evidence of Things Not Seen*, and many others. The most brilliant prose stylist of twentieth-century America. Stunningly incisive accounts of the black experience in the cities of the USA, although Baldwin was such a powerful polemicist that he was occasionally swept away by his own rhetoric.

John Berendt *Midnight in the Garden of Good and Evil*. Voodoo, transvestism, and murder; best-selling true-life tales of life and death in contemporary Savannah – see p.561.

Dee Brown *Bury My Heart at Wounded Knee*. Thirty years on from its first publication, this remains the best narrative of the impact of white settlement and expansion on Native Americans across the continent.

Bill Bryson *Made in America*. A compulsively readable history of the American language, packed with bizarre snippets, which does much to illuminate the history of the nation.

★ **Mike Davis** *City of Quartz*. City politics, neighborhood gangs, unions, film noir, and religion are drawn together in this award-winning, leftist, hyperbolic history of Los Angeles.

John Demos *The Unredeemed Captive*. This story of the aftermath of a combined French and Indian attack on Deerfield, Massachusetts, in 1704 illuminates frontier life in the eighteenth century.

★ **W.E.B. DuBois** *The Souls of Black Folk*. Seminal collection of largely autobiographical essays examining the separation of the races in American society at the start of the twentieth century.

Joseph J. Ellis *Founding Brothers*. Enjoyable and informative essays on the "revolutionary generation" that bring the characters of Washington, Jefferson, et al to life.

Brian Fagan *Ancient North America*. Archeological history of America's native peoples, from the first hunters to cross the Bering Strait up to European contact.

Frances Fitzgerald *Cities on a Hill*. Intelligent, sympathetic exploration of four of the odder corners of American culture, including San Francisco's gay Castro district and the Rajneeshi community in eastern Oregon.

Tim Flannery *The Eternal Frontier*. "Ecological" history of North America that reveals how the continent's physical environment has shaped the destinies of all its inhabitants, from horses to humans.

Shelby Foote *The Civil War: a Narrative*. Epic, three-volume account containing anything you could possibly want to know about the "War Between the States."

John Kenneth Galbraith *The Great Crash 1929*. An elegant and authoritative interpretation of the Wall Street Crash and its implications.

David Halberstam *The Fifties*. A delightfully readable yet satisfyingly comprehensive overview of the Eisenhower years.

Tony Horwitz *Confederates in the Attic: Dispatches from the Unfinished Civil War*. Strange meld of past and present, as journalist Horwitz explores the places in the South where die-hards keep the Civil War very much alive.

Frederick Hoxie (ed) *Indians in American History*. Eye-opening collection of essays focusing on the role of Native Americans in US history, presenting them as active and aware (if hopelessly outgunned) players rather than passive victims. Filled with illustrations and extensive quotes from journals and contemporary accounts.

J.B. Jackson *American Space*. Engagingly written work that traces the transition of America from a rural to an urban and industrialized nation in the crucial decade immediately after the Civil War.

Roger G. Kennedy *Rediscovering America*. Collected essays by one of America's most readable historians, appointed by Clinton to run the National Park Service. Kennedy looks behind the gloss of conventional tellings to reveal something of the real story of how America came to be.

Joe Klein *The Natural*. Klein's overview of the Clinton presidency is not quite as gripping as *Primary Colors*, his originally anonymous fictionalization of the 1992 campaign, but he still offers compelling insights into the enigma.

Meriwether Lewis and William Clark *The Original Journals of the Lewis and Clark Expedition, 1804–1806*. Eight volumes of meticulous jottings by the Northwest's first inland explorers, scrupulously following President Jefferson's orders to record every detail of flora, fauna, and native inhabitant.

Magnus Magnusson and Herman Pálsson (trans) *The Vinland Sagas*. If you imagine stories that the Vikings reached America to be no more than myths, here's the day-to-day minutiae to convince you otherwise.

James M. McPherson *Battle Cry of Freedom*. Extremely readable history of the Civil War, which integrates and explains the complex social, economic, political, and military factors in one concise volume.

Clyde A. Milner II, Carol A. O'Connor, and Martha A. Sandweiss *The Oxford History of the American West*. Fascinating collection of essays on Western history, covering topics ranging from myths and movies to art and religion.

James Mooney *The Ghost Dance Religion and The Sioux Outbreak of 1890*. An extraordinary Bureau of Ethnology report, first published in 1890 but still available in paperback. Mooney persuaded his Washington superiors to allow him to roam the West in search of first-hand evidence, and even interviewed Wovoka, the Ghost Dance prophet, in person.

Samuel Eliot Morison *The European Discovery of America*. An excellent resource for anyone interested in the early navigators who explored the Americas, divided into two fat volumes – *The Northern Voyages* and *The Southern Voyages* – and written by a former admiral who meticulously retraced many of the routes himself.

Roderick Frazier Nash *Wilderness and the American Mind*. Classic study of the American take on environmental and conservation issues over the past couple of hundred years. Especially good sections on John Muir and his battles to preserve Yosemite.

Stephen Plog *Ancient Peoples of the Southwest*. Much the best single-volume history of the pre-Hispanic Southwest, packed with diagrams and color photographs.

Marc Reisner *Cadillac Desert*. Concise, engaging account of the environmental and political impact on the West of the twentieth-century mania for dam-building and large-scale irrigation projects.

★ **Alan Taylor** *American Colonies*. Perhaps the best book on any single era of American history – a superb account of every aspect of the peopling of the continent, from remote antiquity until the Declaration of Independence.

Stephen Trimble *The People*. Excellent introduction to all the Native American groups of the Southwest, bringing the history up to date with contemporary interviews.

★ **Mark Twain** *Roughing It, Life on the Mississippi*, and many others. Mark Twain was by far the funniest and most vivid chronicler of nineteenth-century America. *Roughing It*, which covers his early wanderings across the continent, all the way to Hawaii, is absolutely compelling.

Geoffrey C. Ward, with Ric and Ken Burns *The Civil War*. Illustrated history of the Civil War, designed to accompany the TV series and using hundreds of the same photographs.

Allen Weinstein and David Rubel *The Story of America*. This glossy volume is so beautifully illustrated you might not expect the text to be first-rate too. In fact, it provides fascinating detail and analysis on the one representative topic it chooses to cover from each of 26 eras.

Richard White *It's Your Misfortune and None of My Own*. Dense, authoritative and all-embracing history of the American West, which debunks the notion of the rugged pioneer by stressing the role of the federal government.

Juan Williams *Eyes on the Prize*. Informative and detailed account of the Civil Rights years from the early 1950s up to 1966, with lots of rare, and some very familiar, photos.

Edmund Wilson *Patriotic Gore*. Fascinating eight-hundred-page survey of the literature of the Civil War, which serves in its own right as an immensely readable narrative of the conflict.

Biography and oral history

Muhammad Ali *The Greatest*. Powerful and entertaining autobiography of the Louisville boy who grew up to become world heavyweight boxing champion. The most memorable parts deal with his fight against the Vietnam draft and the subsequent stripping away of his world championship title.

Maya Angelou *I Know Why the Caged Bird Sings*. First of a five-volume autobiography that provides an ultimately uplifting account of how a black girl transcended her traumatic childhood in 1930s Arkansas.

Paul Auster (ed) *True Tales of American Life* (UK)/*I Thought My Father Was God* (US). Anthology of true-life stories sent to Auster for a National Public Radio project. Arranged by subject, it's best dipped into at random; among the mawkish and the mundane are just enough quirky, touching, and plain crazy tales to make it worth the while.

Donald A. Barclay, James H. Maguire, and Peter Wild (eds) *Into the Wilderness Dream*. Gripping collection of Western exploration narratives written between 1500 and 1800; thanks to any number of little-known gems, the best of many such anthologies.

William F. Cody *The Life of Hon. William F. Cody, Known as Buffalo Bill*. Larger-than-life autobiography of one of the great characters of the Wild West. Particularly treasurable for the moment when he refers to himself more formally as "Bison William."

Frederick Douglass, et al *The Classic Slave Narratives*. Compilation of ex-slaves' autobiographies, ranging from Olaudah Equiano's kidnapping in Africa and global wanderings to Frederick Douglass's eloquent denunciation of slavery. Includes Harriet Jacobs' story of her escape from Edenton, North Carolina – see p.513.

Jill Ker Conway (ed) *Written by Herself*. Splendid anthology of women's autobiographies from the mid-1800s to the present, including sections on African-Americans, scientists, artists, and pioneers.

U.S. Grant *Personal Memoirs*. Encouraged by Mark Twain, the Union general and subsequent president wrote his autobiography just before his death, in a (successful) bid to recoup his horrendous debts. At first the book feels oddly downbeat, but the man's down-to-earth modesty grows on you.

Henry Hampton and Steve Fayer *Voices of Freedom*. Hugely impressive oral history of the Civil Rights movement.

Joyce Johnson *Minor Characters*. Johnson, Jack Kerouac's girlfriend and "muse," tells her own story and those of the other women in the 1950s East Village scene, revealing the stiflingly reactionary male elitism of the Beats.

Florence King *Confessions of a Failed Southern Lady*. Hilarious autobiography of a girl who grows up with her faded Southern belle grandmother and foul-talking, heavy-smoking mother, only to effect the greatest rebellion of all by falling in love with a woman.

Malcolm X, with Alex Haley *The Autobiography of Malcolm X*. Searingly honest and moving account of Malcolm's progress from street hoodlum to political leadership. Written on the hoof over a period of years, it traces the development of Malcolm X's thinking before, during, and after his split from the Nation of Islam. The conclusion, when he talks about his impending assassination, is painful in the extreme.

Edmund Morris *Theodore Rex*. Thoroughly engaging and superbly researched biography of Theodore Roosevelt, tracing the energetic and controversial president's far-reaching achievements between 1901 and 1909.

Tony Parker *A Place Called Bird*. Fascinating oral history based on interviews with the inhabitants of a tiny town in the very center of Kansas, the heartland of the Midwest.

Quinta Scott and Susan Croce Kelly *Route 66*. Moving oral histories and monochrome photographs trace the life of the 2000-mile highway immortalized in film, novels, and song.

Joanna L. Stratton *Pioneer Women.* Original memoirs of women – mothers, teachers, homesteaders, and circuit riders – who ventured across the Plains from 1854 to 1890. Lively, superbly detailed accounts, with chapters on journeys, homebuilding, daily domestic life, the church, the cowtown, temperance, and suffrage.

Studs Terkel *American Dreams Lost and Found.* Interviews with ordinary American citizens. As illuminating a guide to US life as you could hope for.

Geoffrey C. Ward, Dayton Duncan, and Ken Burns *Mark Twain: an Illustrated Biography.* Tied in with the superb TV series, this classy and readable volume is filled with essays from various authors interspersed with Twain's own words – taken from published works, personal diaries, and letters – and many rare photographs of the subject.

★ **Frank Waters** *Book of the Hopi.* Extraordinary insight into the traditions and beliefs of the Hopi, prepared through years of interviews and approved by tribal elders.

Entertainment and culture

Kenneth Anger *Hollywood Babylon.* A vicious yet high-spirited romp through Tinseltown's greatest scandals, amply illustrated with gory and repulsive photographs, and always inclined to bend the facts for the sake of a good story. A shoddily researched second volume covers more recent times.

Joshua Berrett (ed) *The Louis Armstrong Companion: Eight Decades of Commentary.* Broad selection of essays, interviews, letters, reviews, and autobiography, revealing the world's most influential musician in all his complexity. A fine introduction to the subject, featuring lots of previously unpublished material: standouts include Armstrong's own lament about defeatism and negativity in his fellow black men.

Charlotte Greig *Will You Still Love Me Tomorrow?* Enthusiastic feminist appraisal of (predominantly American) girl groups from the 1950s (the Chantels and the Crystals) through to 1980s rap stars like Salt'n'Pepa. Though inevitably somewhat dated now, its many photos and personal recollections still make it a great read.

★ **Peter Guralnick** *Lost Highways, Feel Like Going Home* and *Sweet Soul Music.* Thoroughly researched personal histories of black popular music, packed with obsessive detail on all the great names. His more recent Elvis biographies, *Last Train to Memphis* and *Careless Love*, trace the rise and fall of the iconic star in an unsensational but nonetheless gripping documentary manner, while also performing the rare trick of evaluating him seriously as a musician.

Gerri Hershey *Nowhere to Run: the History of Soul Music.* Definitive rundown on the evolution of soul music from the gospel heyday of the 1940s through the Memphis, Motown, and Philly scenes to the sounds of the early 1980s. Strong on social commentary and political background and studded with anecdotes and interviews.

Greil Marcus *Dead Elvis.* Vastly entertaining overview of the many Elvis myths, if a little hastily put together from previously published articles. Marcus's *Mystery Train* is an intelligent and absorbing overview of American popular music, from Robert Johnson to Elvis Presley and Randy Newman.

Michael Ondaatje *Coming through Slaughter.* Extraordinary, dream-like fictionalization of the life of doomed New Orleans cornet player Buddy Bolden, written in a lyrical style that evokes the rhythms and pace of jazz improvisation.

Robert Palmer *Deep Blues.* Readable history of the development and personalities of the Delta Blues.

⭐ **Geoffrey C. Ward, Ken Burns, et al** *Jazz: a History of America's Music.* While the story peters out somewhat after bebop, this highly readable volume (linked to the TV series) boasts hundreds of illustrations and rare photographs, first-hand accounts and lively essays to provide a beautifully drawn picture of America's home-grown music and its icons.

Travel writing

Edward Abbey *The Journey Home.* Hilarious accounts of whitewater rafting and desert hiking trips alternate with essays by the man who inspired the radical environmentalist movement Earth First! All of Abbey's many books, especially *Desert Solitaire*, a journal of time spent as a ranger in Arches National Park, make great traveling companions.

James Agee and Walker Evans *Let Us Now Praise Famous Men.* A deeply personal but also richly evocative journal of travels through the rural lands of the Depression-era Deep South, complemented by Evans' powerful photographs.

Stephen Brook *New York Days, New York Nights.* An Englishman's drily witty impressions of the Big Apple in the 1990s, with chapters on every aspect of the place, from flotation chambers to Jewish restaurants. Brook's *Honky Tonk Gelato* treats Texas in a similar, if sometimes patronizing vein.

Bill Bryson *The Lost Continent.* Using his boyhood home of Des Moines in Iowa as a benchmark, the author travels the length and breadth of America to find the perfect small town. Hilarious, if occasionally a bit smug. *A Walk in the Woods* applies his trademark irony to the Appalachian Trail from Georgia to Maine, but suffers from too much nature and too few quirky characters.

J. Hector St-John de Crèvecoeur *Letters from an American Farmer and Sketches of Eighteenth-Century America.* A remarkable account of the complexities of Revolutionary America, first published in 1782.

Robert Frank *The Americans.* The Swiss photographer's brilliantly evocative portrait of mid-century American life from coast to coast, with striking images contextualized by an introductory essay from Jack Kerouac.

⭐ **Ian Frazier** *Great Plains.* An immaculately researched and well-written travelogue containing a wealth of information on the people of the American prairielands from Native Americans to the soldiers who staff the region's many nuclear installations.

Jack Kerouac *On the Road.* Definitive account of transcontinental Beatnik wanderings, which now reads as a curiously dated period piece. Not as incoherent as you might expect.

James A. MacMahon (ed) *Audubon Society Nature Guides.* Attractively produced, fully illustrated and easy-to-use guides to the flora and fauna of seven different US regional ecosystems, covering the entire country from coast to coast and from grasslands to glaciers.

Virginia and Lee McAlester *A Field Guide to American Houses*. Well-illustrated and engaging guide to America's rich variety of domestic architecture, from pre-Colonial to postmodern.

John McPhee *Encounters with the Arch Druid*. In three interlinked narratives, the late environmental activist and Friends of the Earth founder David Brower confronts developers, miners, and dam-builders, while trying to protect three different American wilderness areas – the Atlantic shoreline, the Grand Canyon, and the Cascades of the Pacific Northwest.

William Least Heat-Moon *Blue Highways*. Account of a mammoth loop tour of the US by back roads, in which the author interviews ordinary people in ordinary places. A good overview of rural America, with lots of interesting details on Native Americans. His next book, *Prairyerth*, opted for the microcosmic approach, taking six hundred loving pages over the story of Chase County, Kansas.

Jonathan Raban *Old Glory*. A somewhat pompous though always interesting account of Raban's journey on a small craft down the Mississippi River from the headwaters in Minnesota to the bayous of Louisiana.

Bernard A. Weisberger (ed) *The WPA Guide to America*. Prepared during the New Deal as part of a make-work program for writers, these guides paint a fairly comprehensive portrait of 1930s and earlier America. Also available are state-by-state guides, most of them out of print but easily found in US libraries and secondhand bookshops.

Edmund White *States of Desire: Travels in Gay America*. A revealing account of life in gay communities across the country, focusing heavily on San Francisco and New York.

Fiction

General Americana

★ **Raymond Carver** *Will You Please Be Quiet Please?* Stories of the American working class, written in a distinctive sparse, almost deadpan style that perhaps owes something to Hemingway and certainly influenced untold numbers of contemporary American writers. The stories served as the basis for Robert Altman's film *Short Cuts*.

Don DeLillo *White Noise; Underworld*. The former is his best, a funny and penetrating pop culture exploration, while the latter is one of those typically flawed attempts to pack the twentieth-century American experience into a great big novel. Worthwhile, though.

★ **John Dos Passos** *USA*. Hugely ambitious novel (originally a trilogy) that grapples with the US in the early decades of the twentieth century from every possible angle. Gripping human stories with a strong political and historical point of view.

Dennis Johnson *Jesus' Son*. Junkies and thieves and all the usual trappings of a Beat-era collection of stories, but from 1990s urban America.

William Kennedy *Ironweed*. Terse, affecting tale of a couple of down-on-their-luck drunks haunted by ghosts from a checkered past; excellent evocation of 1930s America, specifically working-class Albany, New York.

⭐ **Herman Melville** *Moby-Dick*. Compendious and compelling account of nineteenth-century whaling, packed with details on American life from New England to the Pacific.

New York City

Paul Auster *New York Trilogy*. Three Borgesian investigations into the mystery and madness of contemporary New York. Using the conventions of the detective novel, Auster unfolds a disturbed and disturbing picture of the city.

Truman Capote *Breakfast at Tiffany's* and *In Cold Blood*. The first story is about a fictional social climber in New York called Holly Go-Lightly; the second concerns the true-life stories of two serial killers in the heartland. The subject matter of these two stories could hardly be more different, but the degree of insight drawn from two uniquely American stories is equally high in both accounts.

Michael Chabon *The Amazing Adventures of Kavalier & Clay*. Pulitzer Prize–winning novel charting the rise and fall of comic book-writing cousins in New York City – one a refugee from World War II Prague, the other a closeted Brooklynite.

Jonathan Franzen *The Corrections*. While it never quite lived up to the hype – what could? – this ambitious saga, about a classically dysfunctional American family, manages to capture all that late twentieth-century navel

E. Annie Proulx *Accordion Crimes*. Proulx's masterly book comes as close to being the fabled "Great American Novel" as anyone could reasonably ask, tracing a fascinating history of immigrants in all parts of North America through the fortunes of a battered old Sicilian accordion.

searching in a nutshell. And it's very funny in places, too.

⭐ **Chester Himes** *Cotton Comes to Harlem*, *Blind Man with a Pistol*, and many others. Action-packed and uproariously violent novels set in New York's Harlem, starring the much-feared detectives Coffin Ed Johnson and Grave Digger Jones.

Jonathan Lethem *Motherless Brooklyn*. A hilarious crime caper starring Lionel Essrog, a Prince-loving private detective with Tourette's syndrome, on the trail of a killer in Brooklyn's characterful neighborhoods.

Grace Paley *Collected Stories*. Shrewd love–hate stories written over a lifetime by the daughter of Russian-Jewish immigrants, who published dead-on accounts of New York life in three installments: her first book of stories came out in the 1950s, her second in the early 1970s and her third in the late 1980s.

J.D. Salinger *The Catcher in the Rye*. Classic novel of adolescence, tracing Holden Caulfield's sardonic journey through the streets of New York.

New England

John Irving *The Cider House Rules*. One of Irving's more successful sprawling novels, weaving themes of love, suffering, and the many facets of the abortion debate against a

Maine backdrop.

Dennis Lehane *Mystic River*. An ambiguous but powerful meditation on loss and loyalty, rendered as a suspense novel set in a blue-collar Boston neighborhood.

H.P. Lovecraft *The Best of H.P. Lovecraft: Bloodcurdling Tales of Horror and the Macabre*. Creepy New England stories from the author Stephen King called "the twentieth century's greatest practitioner of the classic horror tale."

Florida and the South

William Faulkner *The Reivers*. The last and most humorous work of this celebrated Southern author. *The Sound and the Fury*, a fascinating study of prejudice, set like most of his books in the fictional Yoknatapawpha County in Mississippi, is a much more difficult read.

Carl Hiaasen *Basket Case*, and many others. Hiaasen is the funniest crime writer on the scene – and a razor-sharp chronicler of Florida's weirder, wilder side. This one sees dead rock stars, a grumpy investigative reporter, and a giant frozen lizard caught up in a fast-moving caper plot.

Zora Neale Hurston *Spunk*. Short stories celebrating black culture and experience from around the country, by a writer from Florida who became one of the bright stars of the Harlem cultural renaissance in the 1920s.

Harper Lee *To Kill a Mockingbird*. Classic tale of racial conflict and society's view of an outsider, Boo Radley, as seen through the eyes of children.

Cormac McCarthy *Suttree*. McCarthy is better known for his "modern Western" works like *Blood Meridian* and *All the Pretty Horses*, but this beautifully written tale, of a Knoxville, Tennessee, scion opting for a hard-scrabble life among a band of vagrants on the Tennessee River, is his best.

Carson McCullers *The Heart is a Lonely Hunter*. McCullers is unrivaled in her sensitive treatment of misfits, in this case the attitude of a small Southern community to a deaf-mute.

Margaret Mitchell *Gone With the Wind*. Worth a read even if you know the lines of Scarlett and Rhett by heart.

★ **Toni Morrison** *Beloved*. Exquisitely written ghost story by the Nobel Prize–winning novelist, which recounts the painful lives of a group of freed slaves after Reconstruction, and the obsession a mother develops after murdering her baby daughter to spare her a life of slavery.

Flannery O'Connor *A Good Man is Hard to Find*. Short stories, featuring strong, obsessed characters, that explore religious tensions and racial conflicts in the Deep South.

Alice Walker *In Love and Trouble*. Moving and powerful stories of black women in the South, from the author of the much-acclaimed *The Color Purple*.

Eudora Welty *The Ponder Heart*. Quirky, humorous evocation of life in a backwater Mississippi town. Her most critically acclaimed work, *The Optimist's Daughter*, explores the tensions between a judge's daughter and her stepmother.

Bailey White *Mama Makes up Her Mind* and *Sleeping at the Starlight Motel*. Witty, touching tales of Georgian life. The eponymous, eccentric mother is the delightful central character of the former, while the fond portrayal of White's small home-town in the second is spot-on.

Louisiana

James Lee Burke *Black Cherry Blues*. Perhaps the best in Burke's series featuring Cajun cop Dave Robicheaux. Here Robicheaux sets out to expose alliances between government and organized crime in Louisiana and Montana.

George Washington Cable *The Grandissimes*. Romantic saga of Creole family feuds, written c.1900 but set during the Louisiana Purchase. Superb evocation of steamy Louisiana elite, the Creole lifestyle, and the resistance of New Orleans to its Americanization. Apparently shocking at the time for its sympathetic portrayal of blacks.

★ **Kate Chopin** *The Awakening*. Subversive story of a bourgeois married woman whose fight for independence ends in tragedy. The swampy Louisiana of a century ago is portrayed as both a sensual hotbed for her sexual awakening and as her eventual nemesis.

★ **John Kennedy Toole** *A Confederacy of Dunces*. Anarchic black tragicomedy in which the pompous and repulsive anti-hero Ignatius J. Reilly wreaks havoc through an insalubrious and surreal New Orleans.

The Great Lakes and the Great Plains

★ **Willa Cather** *My Ántonia*. Stunning book set in Nebraska that provides a great sense of the pioneer hardships on the Plains.

Louise Erdrich *The Beet Queen*. Offbeat tale of passion and obsession among poor white North Dakota folk – particularly women – against the backdrop of an economy and culture changing with the introduction of sugar beet as a crop in the 1940s. Erdrich's other novels play through the tensions between tradition and "progress" in Native American communities.

Garrison Keillor *Lake Wobegon Days*. Wry, witty tales about a mythical Minnesota small town, poking gentle fun at the rural Midwest.

Elmore Leonard *Freaky Deaky*. One of the funniest of Leonard's many tough, brutal thrillers. Set in Detroit, it follows two former Sixties radicals who turn to crime.

Mari Sandoz *Old Jules*. Written in 1935, this fictionalized biography gives a wonderful insight into the life of the author's pioneer Swiss father on the Nebraskan plains. Sandoz's other major work, *Crazy Horse*, contains great historical overviews but is spoiled somewhat by her insistence on narrating it through Sioux eyes.

Richard Wright *Native Son*. The harrowing story of Bigger Thomas, a black chauffeur who accidentally kills his employer's daughter. The story develops his relationship with his lawyer, the closest he has ever come to being on an equal footing with a white.

The Rockies and the Southwest

James Crumley *The Wrong Case*. The lack of an intricate plot is more than compensated for by accounts of Montana scenery and the hapless detective Milo Milodragonovic, a man with a drinking problem and a knack for doing things the hard way. An enjoyable, easy read.

A.B. Guthrie Jr *Big Sky*. When first published in the Thirties it shattered the image of the mythical West peddled by Hollywood. Realistic historical fiction at its very best, following desperate mountain man and fugitive Boone Caudill, whose idyllic life in Montana was ended by the arrival of white settlers.

Tony Hillerman *The Dark Wind*, and many others. The adventures of Jim Chee of the Navajo Tribal Police on the reservations of northern Arizona, forever dabbling in dark and mysterious forces churned up from the Ancestral Puebloan past.

Barbara Kingsolver *Pigs in Heaven*. A magnificent evocation of tensions and realities in the contemporary Southwest, by a Tucson-based writer who ranks among America's finest prose stylists.

Norman MacLean *A River Runs Through It*. Unputdownable – the best ever novel about fly-fishing, set in beautiful Montana lake country.

Annick Smith *Homestead*. Beautifully written episodes of a Montana life, a host of characters, and personal and cultural insights, all offset by Smith's tangible passion for that huge, awesome landscape.

California

Raymond Chandler *The Big Sleep* and *Farewell My Lovely*. The original incarnations of archetypal tough guy and iconic private eye Philip Marlowe are far more complex and beautifully written than the related movies would lead you to expect. Pulp fiction at its finest – written by an American raised in London.

Armistead Maupin *Tales of the City*. Long-running saga comprising sympathetic and entertaining tales of life in San Francisco, that also work surprisingly well as suspenseful stand-alone novels. That many of its key characters are gay meant that over the years the series became a chronicle of the impact of AIDS on the city. Maupin's *Maybe the Moon* is the poignant true-life story of his friend, the short person who played ET in the movie but was never allowed to reveal her true identity.

Thomas Pynchon *The Crying of Lot 49*. Shorter, funnier, and more accessible than *Gravity's Rainbow*, this novel of techno-freaks and potheads in Sixties California reveals, among other things, the sexy side of stamp collecting.

John Steinbeck *The Grapes of Wrath*. The classic account of a migrant family forsaking the Midwest for the Promised Land. Steinbeck's lighthearted but crisply observed novella *Cannery Row* captures daily life on the prewar Monterey waterfront. The epic *East of Eden* updates and resets the Bible in the Salinas Valley and details three generations of familial feuding.

Nathanael West *The Day of the Locust*. West wrote dark novels wholly vested in the American experience; this one, set in LA, is an apocalyptic story of fringe characters at the edge of the film industry.

The Pacific Northwest

David Guterson *Snow Falling on Cedars*. Gripping, atmospheric mystery novel, evocatively capturing interracial tensions in the postwar Pacific Northwest.

Tobias Wolff *This Boy's Life*. A memoir that reads more like a novel, this mournful book – leavened by self-deprecating humor – recounts Wolff's tough upbringing in a small Washington State town.

Alaska

Tom Bodett *The End of the Road*. First novel by the broadcaster from Homer, Alaska, who shot to fame as the voice on *Motel 6* radio commercials. Funny, witty, and certainly better than his often shallow collections of essays (*As Far as You Can Go without a Passport*), but for the best value invest in some of his taped books.

Jack London *The Call of the Wild and Other Stories*. London's classic tale, of a family pet discovering the ways of the wilderness while forced to pull sleds across Alaska's Gold Rush trails, still makes essential reading before a trip to the far north.

Film

T he list below focuses on key films in certain genres that have helped define the American experience for domestic and foreign audiences alike, cementing cultural stereotypes such as the gangster, cowboy, and blonde chorus girl, as well as national iconography such as expansive prairies, open highways, big-city skyscrapers, and suburban dream homes. Films tagged with the ✳ symbol are particularly recommended.

Music/musicals

8 Mile (Curtis Hanson, 2002). Eminem makes an impressive screen debut in the thinly fictionalized saga of Rabbit, a wannabe rapper in the mean streets of Detroit.

Gimme Shelter (Albert and David Maysles, 1969). Excellent documentary about the ill-fated Rolling Stones concert at Altamont. Its searing look at homegrown American violence and Vietnam-era chaos at the end of the 1960s also includes an on-camera stabbing.

Gold Diggers of 1933 (Mervyn LeRoy/Busby Berkeley, 1933). The most entertaining in a famous trio of 1933 films (including *42nd Street* and *Footlight Parade*), in which choreographer Berkeley pioneered stunning overhead-crane shots of precision dance numbers featuring lines of glamorous chorines.

Meet Me in St Louis (Vincente Minnelli, 1944). Most famous for its Judy Garland number "The Trolley Song," this charming piece of nostalgia celebrates turn-of-the-century America through the ups and downs

of a St Louis family during the 1903 World's Fair.

On the Town (Stanley Donen/Gene Kelly, 1949). An exuberant musical tour of New York City, led by director Kelly and Frank Sinatra, who play sailors on shore leave.

★ **Singin' in the Rain** (Stanley Donen/Gene Kelly, 1952). Beloved musical comedy about Hollywood at the dawn of the sound era, featuring memorable tunes like "Make 'Em Laugh" and the title song, along with energetic performances by star Kelly, sidekick Donald O'Connor, and a pixie-ish Debbie Reynolds.

Woodstock (Michael Wadleigh, 1969). *Gimme Shelter*'s upbeat counterpart, documenting the musical pinnacle of the hippie era, showing a half-million flower children peacefully grooving to Jimi Hendrix, The Who, and Sly and the Family Stone while getting stoned, muddy, and wild on an upstate New York farm.

Silent era

Birth of a Nation (D.W. Griffith, 1915). Possibly the most influential film in American history, both for its pioneering film technique (close-ups, cross-cutting, and so on) and

appalling racist propaganda, which led to a revival of the KKK and a resurgence in lynchings across the country.

C

CONTEXTS | Film

The General (Buster Keaton, 1926). A fine introduction to Keaton's acrobatic brand of slapstick and his inventive cinematic approach, in which the Great Stone Face chases down a stolen locomotive during the Civil War.

The Gold Rush (Charlie Chaplin, 1925). Chaplin's finest film: the Little Tramp gets trapped in a cabin during an Alaska blizzard in an affecting story that mixes sentiment and high comedy in near-perfect balance.

Greed (Erich von Stroheim, 1923). An audacious scene-by-scene adaptation of Frank Norris's novel *McTeague*, a tragic tale of love and revenge in San Francisco at the end of the nineteenth century. Slashed from ten to two-and-a-half hours by MGM, the film remains a cinematic triumph for its striking composi-tions, epic drama, and truly bleak ending.

Intolerance (D.W. Griffith, 1916). The greatest debacle of the silent era, a colossal bomb that helped destroy Griffith's career, but still fascinates for its multiple storylines, arch melodrama, and stunning Babylonian set (a replica was built as part of a shopping mall in Hollywood).

Sunrise (F.W. Murnau, 1927). Among the most beautiful Hollywood productions of any era. *Sunrise*'s German émigré director employed striking lighting effects, complex traveling shots, and emotionally compelling performances in a tale of a country boy led astray by a big-city femme fatale.

Westerns

Man of the West (Anthony Mann, 1958). Reformed outlaw Gary Cooper returns to his former gang, led by psycho Lee J. Cobb, in this disturbing masterpiece by one of the genre's great directors.

McCabe and Mrs. Miller (Robert Altman, 1971). Entrepreneur Warren Beatty brings prostitution to a Washington State town and tries to reinvent himself as a gunslinger, in what's often referred to as an anti-Western because of its stark, snowy landscapes, soft-focus images, and unromantic outlook.

Once upon a Time in the West (Sergio Leone, 1968). The quintessential spaghetti Western, actually filmed in Spain by an Italian director, steeped in mythic American themes of manifest destiny and rugged individualism.

Red River (Howard Hawks, 1948). Upstart Montgomery Clift battles beef-baron John Wayne on a momentous cattle drive through the Midwest. Prototypical Hawks tale of clashing tough-guy egos and no-nonsense professionals on the range.

The Searchers (John Ford, 1956). Perhaps the most iconic of Ford's many Westerns; a highly influential production with vivid cinematography and epic scale, in which John Wayne relentlessly hunts down the Indian chief who massacred his friends and family.

The Wild Bunch (Sam Peckinpah, 1969). A movie that says as much about the chaotic end of the 1960s as it does about the West, featuring a band of killers who hunt for women and treasure and wind up in a bloodbath unprecedented in film history.

Americana

Citizen Kane (Orson Welles, 1941). Arguably the greatest American movie ever, inverting the rags-to-riches saga: a poor country boy finds nothing but misery when he inherits a fortune.

E.T. The Extra-Terrestrial (Steven Spielberg, 1982). Reagan-era blockbuster as well as a sentimental variation on 1950s monster flicks, courtesy of the director's ongoing interest in absentee fathers, suburban fantasies, and otherworldly saviors. A fine example of American cinema's never-ending search for lost innocence.

Mr. Smith Goes to Washington (Frank Capra, 1939). Tub-thumping populist film that still resonates for its rosy belief in the goodness of the common man, dark view of political elites, and earnest hope for America's future. Though less familiar, the director's *Meet John Doe* offers a grimmer variation on the tale.

Nashville (Robert Altman, 1975). A long, woolly epic, typical of Altman's style, about 24 characters adrift in the nation's capital of country music, who come together at a political rally and witness an unexpected assassination.

North by Northwest (Alfred Hitchcock, 1959). Not only an exciting chase film, in which international criminal James Mason hunts down ad-man Cary Grant, but also a fun travelogue that starts on New York's Madison Avenue and ends on the cliff-face of Mount Rushmore in South Dakota.

Rebel Without a Cause (Nicholas Ray, 1955). The apotheosis of adolescent angst, with James Dean lamenting the hypocrisies of family life and engaging in all manner of fisticuffs, deadly drag races, and nighttime battles with the cops.

The Wizard of Oz (Victor Fleming, 1939). A cinematic institution and Technicolor extravaganza that shows Hollywood at its zenith, romanticizing small-town life in the Midwest and offering up eye-popping fantasies of good and evil witches, dancing dwarves, flying monkeys, and Judy Garland sporting ruby shoes on a yellow-brick road.

Road movies

Badlands (Terrence Malick, 1973). Midwest loner-loser Martin Sheen and girlfriend Sissy Spacek take a spellbinding tour of the heartland while on a random murder spree. A dark view of life on the road as a synonym for existential futility.

Easy Rider (Dennis Hopper, 1969). Peter Fonda and director Hopper head out in search of America while riding on a groovy set of wheels, pick up nerdy Jack Nicholson on the way, get high in a New Orleans cemetery, and get killed by gun-toting rednecks. A road movie as a metaphor for political and cultural conflict.

Lost in America (Albert Brooks, 1985). Hilarious take on the unbearable lightness of yuppiedom, in which a couple trades everything in for a motor home, the open road, and a date with destiny in Las Vegas.

Thelma and Louise (Ridley Scott, 1991). The road movie as feminist manifesto, in which two friends (Susan Sarandon and Geena Davis) wind up on the run after one of them kills a would-be rapist. Plenty of striking images of the American Southwest.

Two-Lane Blacktop (Monte Hellman, 1971). A slow, hypnotic narrative starring musicians James Taylor and Dennis Wilson as two burnouts who live to drag race, but couldn't care less for the nubile girl in their car or goofball racer Warren Oates.

Film noir and gangster films

Bonnie and Clyde (Arthur Penn, 1967). Warren Beatty and Faye Dunaway play Depression-era gangsters in a film that did much to destroy Hollywood's censorship code by ushering in an era of open sexuality and unmitigated blood and violence.

Chinatown (Roman Polanski, 1974). Jack Nicholson plays Jake Gittes, a morally aloof private eye whose dogged investigations reveal municipal corruption, racism, and incest in LA. A dark twist on film noir, in which the hero causes as many problems as he solves.

★ **Double Indemnity** (Billy Wilder, 1944). In many ways the quintessential film noir: insurance salesman Fred MacMurray is corrupted by femme fatale Barbara Stanwyck, with stylishly dark photography and memorably fatalistic ending.

Gangs of New York (Martin Scorsese, 2002). Scorsese's stunning evocation of the gang-ridden world of New York, just before the Civil War, features an unforgettable performance by Daniel Day-Lewis as "The Butcher."

★ **The Godfather** (Francis Ford Coppola, 1972). The film that revived the gangster genre for modern times, avoiding the cartoonish mobsters and no-nonsense G-men of its predecessors and focusing instead on the family hierarchy of organized crime and its deep connections to all levels of American society.

Kiss Me Deadly (Robert Aldrich, 1955). Outlandish portrait of vicious antihero Mike Hammer, a private eye searching LA for the great "whatsit," tormenting elfin vixens and half-witted thugs along the way, and winding up in a beachside nuclear fireball.

Maltese Falcon (John Huston, 1941). A forerunner of a spate of film noir pictures made later in the 1940s, in which Bogart plays his trademark role of Philip Marlowe, the cool and calculating detective who runs up against sexy schemer Mary Astor, low-life Peter Lorre, and evil flesh-pile Sydney Greenstreet.

Scarlet Street (Fritz Lang, 1945). A lesser-known noir that ranks among the genre's finest, in which Edward G. Robinson plays a frustrated painter sucked into a moral abyss with a crass hooker (Joan Bennett) and her violent pimp (Dan Duryea); the ending is merciless.

White Heat (Raoul Walsh, 1949). Gangster/noir hybrid featuring James Cagney as a mother-fixated criminal who's repeatedly conned by ostensible good-guy Edmond O'Brien and ends up atop a burning industrial plant, screaming, "Look at me, Ma! Top o' the world!"

Independent and cult movies

Blue Velvet (David Lynch, 1986). A young man (Kyle Maclachlan) peers under the cheery facade of apple-pie America and finds a sinister nether-world of tortured lounge singers, vicious sex games, and nitrous-inhaling perverts.

Bowling for Columbine (Michael Moore, 2002). Maverick director Moore bagged an Oscar for this eye-opening documentary into US gun culture.

Fargo (Joel Coen, 1996). Set amid the snowy landscapes of northern Minnesota and North Dakota, a quirky tale of a scheming car sales-man whose plan to kidnap his own wife and keep the ransom money goes terribly wrong. Widely regarded as the Coen Brothers' best film

On location

Although many memorable sights are off limits to the public or exist only on the backlot tours of movie-studio theme parks, there are still countless filmmaking loca-tions that widely advertise their Tinseltown appearances or make quiet efforts to accommodate visitors. This list provides an overview of notable films; you could conceivably make an entire vacation out of traveling from spot to spot.

2001: A Space Odyssey (Stanley Kubrick, 1968). Monument Valley, Arizona, p.1035.

Back to the Future (Robert Zemeckis, 1985). Gamble House, Pasadena, p.1129.

Badlands (Terrence Malick, 1973). Badlands National Park, South Dakota, p.858.

Being There (Hal Ashby, 1979). Biltmore Estate, Asheville, North Carolina, p.532.

The Birds (Alfred Hitchcock, 1963). Bodega Bay, California, p.1221.

Blade Runner (Ridley Scott, 1982). Los Angeles: Union Station, p.1111, Bradbury Building, p.1113.

The Bridges of Madison County (Clint Eastwood, 1995). Winterset, Iowa, p.848.

Chinatown (Roman Polanski, 1974). Los Angeles: Santa Catalina island, p.1126, *Biltmore Hotel*, p.1107.

Citizen Kane (Orson Welles, 1941). Hearst Castle, California, p.1154 – inspiration for film's "Xanadu."

Close Encounters of the Third Kind (Steven Spielberg, 1978). Devils Tower, Wyoming, p.923.

Easy Rider (Dennis Hopper, 1969). New Orleans cemeteries pp.716–717; Sunset Crater, Arizona, p.1020.

Five Easy Pieces (Bob Rafelson, 1970). San Juan Islands, Washington, p.1248.

Galaxy Quest (Dean Parisot, 1999). Goblin Valley, Utah, p.1050.

Grapes of Wrath (John Ford, 1940). Petrified Forest, Arizona, p.1017.

Greed (Erich von Stroheim, 1923). Death Valley, California, p.1144.

High Plains Drifter (Clint Eastwood, 1972). Mono Lake, California, p.1149.

Intolerance (D.W. Griffith, 1916). "Babylon" set, Hollywood, California, p.1115.

Jaws (Steven Spielberg, 1975). Martha's Vineyard, Massachusetts, p.233.

Little Big Man (Arthur Penn, 1970). Custer State Park, South Dakota, p.866.

Manhattan (Woody Allen, 1978). Central Park, p.96), Brooklyn Bridge, p.83.

Midnight in the Garden of Good and Evil (Clint Eastwood, 1998). Savannah, Georgia, p.561.

Mr. Smith Goes to Washington (Frank Capra, 1939). Lincoln Memorial, p.427.

Mystery Train (Jim Jarmusch, 1989). *Arcade*, Memphis, Tennessee, p.588.

Nashville (Robert Altman, 1975). Parthenon, p.595, Grand Ole Opry, p.594.

(Ethan Coen co-wrote and produced).

Pulp Fiction (Quentin Tarantino, 1994). A touchstone for American independent cinema, composed of three interlocking vignettes and directed with stylish verve and audacity.

Shadows (John Cassavetes, 1967). An early example of a principled auteur working outside the Hollywood system. The semi-improvised film, featuring a fine cast of lesser-known actors, tells a powerful tale of racism's scabrous effect on a sibling relationship.

Slacker (Richard Linklater, 1990). Emblematic of Generation X ennui in the 1990s, this indie great also manages to highlight 96 characters with episodic monologues over the course of 24 hours in Austin, Texas. Memorable alone for its collection of paranoid conspiracy rants.

Taxi Driver (Martin Scorsese, 1976). Robert De Niro does a memorable turn as Travis Bickle, a psychotic loner and would-be assassin whose infatuation with a teen prostitute (Jodie Foster) inspired a real-life assassination attempt on Ronald Reagan five years later.

A Rough Guide to Rough Guides

In the summer of 1981, Mark Ellingham, a recent graduate from Bristol University, was traveling around Greece and couldn't find a guidebook that really met his needs. On the one hand there were the student guides, insistent on saving every last cent, and on the other the heavyweight cultural tomes, whose authors seemed to have spent more time in a research library than lounging away the afternoon at a taverna or on the beach.

In a bid to avoid getting a job, Mark and a small group of writers set about creating their own guidebook. It was a guide to Greece that aimed to combine a journalistic approach to description with a thoroughly practical approach to travelers' needs – a guide that would incorporate culture, history, and contemporary insights with a critical edge, together with up-to-date, value-for-money listings. Back in London, Mark and the team finished their Rough Guide, as they called it, and talked Routledge into publishing the book.

That first *Rough Guide to Greece*, published in 1982, was a student scheme that became a publishing phenomenon. The immediate success of the book – with numerous reprints and a Thomas Cook Prize shortlisting – spawned a series that rapidly covered dozens of destinations. Rough Guides had a ready market among low-budget backpackers, but soon also acquired a much broader and older readership that relished Rough Guides' wit and inquisitiveness as much as their enthusiastic, critical approach. Everyone wants value for money, but not at any price.

Rough Guides soon began supplementing the "rougher" information about hostels and low-budget listings with the kind of detail on restaurants and quality hotels that independent-minded visitors on any budget might expect, whether on business in New York or trekking in Thailand.

These days the guides – distributed worldwide by the Penguin Group – offer recommendations from shoestring to luxury and cover more than 200 destinations around the globe, including almost every country in the Americas and Europe, more than half of Africa, and most of Asia and Australasia. Our ever-growing team of authors and photographers is spread all over the world, particularly in Europe, the USA, and Australia.

In 1994, we published *The Rough Guide to World Music* and *The Rough Guide to Classical Music*, and a year later *The Rough Guide to the Internet*. All three books have become benchmark titles in their fields – which encouraged us to expand into other areas of publishing, mainly around popular culture. Rough Guides now publish:

- Travel guides to more than 200 worldwide destinations
- Dictionary phrasebooks to 22 major languages
- History guides ranging from Ireland to Islam
- Maps printed on rip-proof and waterproof Polyart™ paper
- Music guides running the gamut from Opera to Elvis
- Restaurant guides to London, New York, and San Francisco
- Reference books on topics as diverse as the Weather and Shakespeare
- Sports guides from Formula 1 to Man Utd
- Pop culture books from *Lord of the Rings* to Cult TV
- World Music CDs in association with World Music Network

Visit ⓦ **www.roughguides.com** to see our latest publications.

SMALL PRINT

Rough Guide credits

Text editor: Hunter Slaton
Layout: Dan May, Michelle Bhatia
Cartography: Stratigraphics, the Delhi team, Miles Irving, Ed Wright
Proofreader: Diane margolis
Editorial: London Martin Dunford, Kate Berens, Helena Smith, Claire Saunders, Geoff Howard, Ruth Blackmore, Gavin Thomas, Polly Thomas, Richard Lim, Lucy Ratcliffe, Clifton Wilkinson, Alison Murchie, Fran Sandham, Sally Schafer, Alexander Mark Rogers, Karoline Densley, Andy Turner, Ella O'Donnell, Keith Drew, Andrew Lockett, Joe Staines, Duncan Clark, Peter Buckley, Matthew Milton; **New York** Andrew Rosenberg, Richard Koss, Yuki Takagaki, Hunter Slaton, Chris Barsanti, Thomas Kohnstamm, Steven Horak
Design & Layout: London Dan May, Diana Jarvis; **Delhi** Madhulita Mohapatra, Umesh Aggarwal, Ajay Verma

Production: Julia Bovis, John McKay, Sophie Hewat
Cartography: London Maxine Repath, Ed Wright, Katie Lloyd-Jones, Miles Irving; **Delhi** Manish Chandra, Rajesh Chhibber, Jai Prakash Mishra, Ashutosh Bharti, Rajesh Mishra, Animesh Pathak
Cover art direction: Louise Boulton
Picture research: Mark Thomas, Jj Luck
Online: New York Jennifer Gold, Cree Lawson, Suzanne Welles; **Delhi** Manik Chauhan, Amarjyoti Dutta, Narender Kumar
Marketing & Publicity: London Richard Trillo, Niki Smith, David Wearn, Chloë Roberts, Demelza Dallow, Kristina Pentland; **New York** Geoff Colquitt, David Wechsler, Megan Kennedy
Finance: Gary Singh
Manager India: Punita Singh
Series editor: Mark Ellingham
PA to Managing Director: Julie Sanderson
Managing Director: Kevin Fitzgerald

Publishing information

This seventh edition published April 2004 by
Rough Guides Ltd,
80 Strand, London WC2R 0RL
345 Hudson St, 4th Floor,
New York, NY 10014, USA
Distributed by the Penguin Group
Penguin Books Ltd,
80 Strand, London WC2R 0RL
Penguin Putnam, Inc,
375 Hudson Street, NY 10014, USA
Penguin Books Australia Ltd,
487 Maroondah Highway, PO Box 257,
Ringwood, Victoria 3134, Australia
Penguin Books Canada Ltd,
10 Alcorn Avenue, Toronto, Ontario
M4V 1E4 Canada
Penguin Books (NZ) Ltd,
182–190 Wairau Road, Auckland 10,
New Zealand
Typeset in Bembo and Helvetica to an original design by Henry Iles.
Printed in Italy by LegoPrint S.p.A.

1440pp includes index
A catalogue record for this book is available from the British Library.

ISBN 1-84353-262-X

1 3 5 7 9 8 6 4 2

Help us update

We've gone to a lot of effort to ensure that the seventh edition of **The Rough Guide to the USA** is accurate and up-to-date. However, things change – places get "discovered", opening hours are notoriously fickle, restaurants and rooms raise prices or lower standards. If you feel we've got it wrong or left something out, we'd like to know, and if you can remember the address, the price, the time, the phone number, so much the better.

We'll credit all contributions, and send a copy of the next edition (or any other Rough Guide if you prefer) for the best letters. Everyone who writes to us and isn't already a subscriber will receive a copy of our full-color thrice-yearly newsletter. Please mark letters: **"Rough Guide USA Update"** and send to: Rough Guides, 80 Strand, London WC2R 0RL, or Rough Guides, 345 Hudson St, 4th Floor, New York, NY 10014. Or send an email to ⓔ**mail@roughguides.com**

Have your questions answered and tell others about your trip at
ⓦ**www.roughguides.atinfopop.com**

Acknowledgments

Sam: At Rough Guides, a big thank you to Hunter Slaton and Greg Ward, both of them a real pleasure to work with; of the many people who helped in the USA, I am particularly grateful to Bruce Morgan, Wendy Morgan, Kelly Strenge, Mary-Lynn Chauffe, Bob Harris, Beverley Gianna, and Christine de Cuir.

Greg: Thanks as ever to Sam, a boon companion and friend through all seven editions and a whole lot more besides; to Hunter for a great job in the hot seat; and, for help on the road, to Edie Jarolim, David Nicholson, Steve Lewis, Jean McKnight, Mona Mesereau, Alex Turner, Rebecca Howerton Finlay, and Roger and Elaine Thomas.

The editor: Thanks aplenty to my authors (especially Sam and Greg) and contributors, all of whom did an excellent job; to Dan May, for his tireless typesetting; Yuki Takagaki, without whose editing backup I couldn't have completed the book; Steven Horak; Richard Koss; Katie Lloyd-Jones, Maxine Repath, Ed Wright, Miles Irving and the Delhi cartography team for great maps; Jj Luck for her fine picture research; Diane Margolis for her eagle-eyed proofreading; Todd Obolsky for the index; Tania Johnson, Sarfraz Idrees, and everyone else at accounts payable; and, as always, Andrew Rosenberg for his steady editorial guidance.

The authors and contributors would like to thank the visitor centers, state tourism offices, and others who were so generous with their help, especially Bruce Morgan, Wendy Morgan, Kelly Strenge, Bob Harris, Beverley Gianna, Christine de Cuir, Ruth Sykes, Mary-Lynn Chauffe, Victoria Artigliere, Alexandra Turner, Greer Beaty, Jane Begarnie, Julia Berg, Nancy Nicholls, Patricia Griffin, Andrea Thornton, Carol S. Lohr, Wendi Streeto, Erica Backus, Jackie Bunyan, Vanessa Alexander, Mollie Murphy, Brandy Humphries, Margo Buege, Sharon Goodrich, George Hayward, Candy Aluli, Pam Brodine, Bruce Brossman, Lynn Holt, Donna Kreutz, Jerry Thull, Sandy Zanella, Cindy Malin, Kathy Harper, Jay Humphreys, Renny Loisel, Tanya Pampalone and Laurie Armstrong at the San Francisco CVB, Rob Delameter, Tom Walton, Wendy Downing, Lisa Treister, Erica Freshman, Tara Solomon, Jacquelynn D. Powers, the Washington, DC, National Park Rangers, Smita Pathak, Kathleen Dunphy, Coreen Cousins, Rob Dewall, Wes Penderson, Lukas H. Hoch, Peter Nurczynski, Sasha Weleber, Dave Dejong, Angela Arnold Dejong, Nick Bell, the Beck family in Sacramento, Bill Tweed at Kings Canyon National Park, Debra Schweizer at Yosemite National Park, Brian Averill, Barbara Bowman and everyone at the Grand Junction Visitor and Convention Bureau, Deborah Dix, Tom King, Tracey Kirk, Daniel Lerner, Ruth and David Mattison, Pat McKinney, Bob Morris, Tariro Mundawarara, Gary Sharp, Mark Stone, Shona Thind, Sol Zwerdling, Nancy Vargo, Heather Weber, Steve Piatt, Bill Buchanan, Nancy and Danny Whittle, Mary Weidman, Robin Bernstein, Nicole Kief, Susan Freedman, and Michael and Steve Pareles.

Readers' letters

Thanks to all the readers who have taken the time and trouble to write in with comments and suggestions. Listed below are those who were especially helpful: apologies for any errors, omissions, or misspellings.

Carolyn & Panos Alevizakis, John P. Athanasourelis, Jon N. Austin, Nicholas Bacon, Jason Bailey, Stephanie K. Bailey, Rob Beach, Nick E. Bingos, Jeannette and Kevin Binns, Alan Bird, Travis Bjorklund, Sue Blansett, Brian Catlos, Riccardo Cocchi, Angela Colliss, Margaret Cronin, Paul Davis, Andrew Dupuy, Angela Dutton, Nichola and Andrew Eberlin, Andy and Ann-Marie Fitzsimmons, Helen Forman, Victoria Forsyth, DeEtta S. Frampton, Betty Gardiner, Diana Graizbord, Pyrs Gruffudd, Ms C. Gwilliam, Christopher Hallam, Robert Harvey, Gerry Hill, Amy Hinsley, Colin Hitchings, Deborah Hodgson, Michael Holdsworth, Mark Holmström, Pennie Hutchins, Emily Killoren, Victoria Kitchener, David K.M. Klaus, DeWayne Knight, Rebekah Kohn, Dan Kriwitsky, Claudia Krüger, David Lacey, A. Lane, David Lewis, Steve Lindblom, Jeff Linwood, Chris Lyons, Birgit Mader, Martina Maier, Bill Martin & Sandra Mason, Sally Martin, Tobias Mathia, J. McGartland, Mark Meadows, Chris Merrow, Nick Mistretta, Julie Mize, H.N. Mok, Tasmim Noor, Carlos Salazar, Joseph Onek, Richard Osborne, Amit Parmar, Steve Parrino, Lu Ann Pelle, Elizabeth Porter, Andy Pusey, Karen Quayle,

Sean Ramplee, Wolfgang Regel, Jan Willem Reitsma, Dr Chris Reynolds, Lee Robinson, Robert P. Rosetta, Diane Rourke, Felicity Saldana, Daniel Sarasino, Clayton Sauer, Andreas Schumann, Andrew Searle, Stacey Sebastian, Geoff Sharpe, Robin Louis Shepherd, Gene Simon, The Reverend and Mrs. Alan Smith, Fiona Softley, Ineke van 't Spijker, Julie Stagg, Chris Starr, Ross Summers, Emma Thomas & Tom Eagleton, Siân Thomas, Stacey Thompson, John Townsend, P.A. Twombley, Jon Vaden, Ellen Villeneuve, Gary Walker, Gwyn Williams, Sarah Williams, Jennifer Winder, Aileen and David Winstanley, Steve Winwood, Jenny Woodley, Mark Yolles, Andrew Young, and David Yuro

Photo credits

Cover
Main China Lake, California © Getty
small front top picture Battle Lake, Minnesota © Getty
small front lower picture Capitol © Getty
back top picture Mount Rushmore © Getty
back lower picture New York © Getty

Color introduction
Dallas Skyline with fireworks © Jeremy Woodhouse/Masterfile
Freeways in Los Angeles © Robert Harding Picture Library
House and flag © Noel Hendrickson /Masterfile
Las Vegas, Nevada © Robert Harding Picture Library
Raft on the Colorado River, Gran Canyon, AZ © John Russell/Network Aspen
Jukebox © Cooperphoto/CORBIS
Jefferson Memorial across the Tidal Basin, Washington, DC © Melinda Berge/Network Aspen
Bison herd, Custer State National Park, SD © Geoffrey Clifford/Network Aspen
Road sign © David Paler
Crawfish © Philip Gould/CORBIS

Things Not to Miss
1. Bridalveil Falls © Phil Schermeister/Network Aspen
2. White House Ruin © Donald Young
3. Highway 1 near Bixby Bridge © Robert Holmes
4. View from South Rim © Richard Reynolds/TDOC
5. Chicago skyline © Illinois Tourism
6. South Beach Art Deco © Paul Chesley/Network Aspen
7. Saguaro cactus, Saguaro National Park © John Warden/Network Aspen
8. Lincoln Memorial, Washington Monument and the Capitol © Alan Becker/Network Aspen
9. Graceland, Elvis Presley's grave © Roger Garwood & Trish Ainslie/CORBIS
10. Birthplace of Dr Martin Luther King Jr ©
Georgia Department of Tourism
11. Sign at Wrigley Field © Rich McHugh
12. Glacier National Park © John Warden/Network Aspen
13. Las Vegas strip © Norman Godwin/Network Aspen
14. Florida alligator © Donald Young
15. Grand Prismatic Hot Spring, Yellowstone National Park © David Hiser/Network Aspen
16. Central Park © Geereint Tellem/Travel Ink
17. Savannah mansion © Georgia Department of Tourism
18. Mickey Mouse shaking hands with his former, black and white, self. © Roman Soumar/CORBIS
19. South Philly cheesesteak © Terry Way
20. Mount St Helens © Kirkendall/Spring
21. Rodeo grounds © Jeffery Aaronson/Network Aspen
22. Sixth street © Austin Convention and Visitors Bureau
23. Aurora borealis © Johnny Johnson/AlaskaStock.com
24. Crabs © Doug Berry
25. Airborne in The Canyons © Dan Campbell
26. Country Music Hall of Fame, Gibson Guitar on display, circa 1951 © Kevin Fleming/CORBIS
27. Lava flowing into sea © Kirk Lee Aeder
28. Fall foliage in Massachusetts © Alan Becker/Network Aspen
29. Kentucky Derby © EPA European Press Agency
30. Mardi Gras © Kevin Fleming/CORBIS
31. Niagara Falls © Bill Bachmann
32. Monticello © Virginia Tourism Corporation
33. Alamo Square San Francisco, California © Bill Brooks/Masterfile
34. Fish vendor, Pike Place Market © Norman Godwin/Network Aspen
35. Mount Rushmore © Paul Chesley/Network Aspen
36. Louisiana sternwheeler © Alan Becker/Network Aspen
37. The open road © Dawn Kish

SMALL PRINT

SMALL PRINT

Index

Map entries are in color

A

B

O
INDEX

Rough Guide favorites

Americana

College towns

Ann Arbor, MI	p.339
Athens, GA	p.557
Berkeley, CA	p.1204
Boulder, CO	p.887
Burlington, VT	p.280
Chapel Hill, NC	p.526
Flagstaff, AZ	p.1017
Madison, WI	p.391
Missoula, MT	p.947

Rough Guide favorites

Sports

Angola Prison Rodeo, LA	p.746
Cheyenne Frontier Days, WY	p.917
Daytona Beach, FL	p.667
Fenway Park, Boston, MA	p.220
Indianapolis Speedway, IN	p.354
Kentucky Derby, Louisville, KY	p.574
Rose Bowl, Pasadena, CA	p.1129
Wrigley Field, Chicago, IL	p.370

E

INDEX

I (tab marker)

INDEX

INDEX

I
INDEX

INDEX

Rough Guide favorites

Movie locations
Alice's Restaurant p.241
The Birds p.1221
The Bridges of Madison County p.848
Close Encounters of the Third Kind p.923
The Eiger Sanction p.1035
Field of Dreams p.843
Giant p.799
Mystery Train p.588
Mystic Pizza p.254
Rocky p.167
The Shining p.1279
Thelma and Louise p.1059
Witness p.171

Rough Guide favorites

Historic sites

Map symbols

Maps are listed in the full index using colored text

-------	International border		♀	Museum
--·--·--	State border		🏛	Monument
---	Chapter boundary		⚲	Ski area
80	Interstate		■	Restaurant
30	US Highway		◉	Accommodation
1	State highway		Å	Campsite
=====	Tunnel		P	Parking
-----	Path/trail		★	Bus stop
======	Railroad		⊞	Hospital/medical center
— —	Ferry route		ⓘ	Information center
———	River		⊠	Post office
⌓	Cave		⊙	Statue
⩕	Mountain range		⛲	Fountain/gardens
▲	Mountain peak		▃▃▃	Wall
⚶	Waterfall		⌒	Arch
ⳗ	Spring		⸙	Church (regional maps)
⩊	Marshland/swamp		▬	Building
⸮	Gorge		⊞	Church (town maps)
⤬	Battlefield		⬭	Stadium
♦	Point of interest		⊞⊞	Cemetery
✈	Airport		▦	Park
✗	Airfield		▦	Forest
⬇	Viewpoint/lookout		▦	Beach
⚑	Lighthouse		▧	Indian reservation